Schroeder's
ANTIQUES
Price Guide

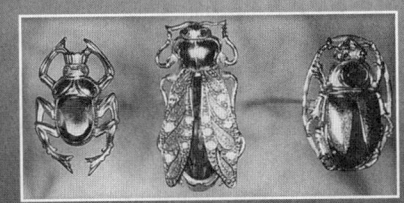

Edited by
Sharon & Bob
Huxford

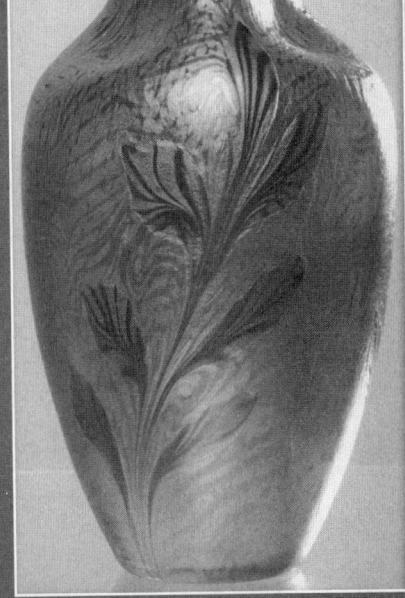

cb

COLLECTOR BOOKS
A Division of Schroeder Publishing Co., Inc.

COLLECTOR BOOKS
P.O. Box 3009
Paducah, Kentucky 42002-3009
www.collectorbooks.com

Copyright © Schroeder Publishing Co., Inc., 2004

The current values in this book should be used only as a guide. They are not intended to set prices, which vary from one section of the country to another. Auction prices as well as dealer prices vary greatly and are affected by condition as well as demand. Neither the editors nor the publisher assumes responsibility for any losses that might be incurred as a result of consulting this guide.

Searching For A Publisher?

We are always looking for people knowledgeable within their fields. If you feel that there is a real need for a book on your collectible subject and have a large comprehensive collection, contact Collector Books.

Introduction

As the editors and staff of *Schroeder's*, our goal is to compile the most useful, comprehensive, and accurate background and pricing information possible. Our guide encompasses nearly 500 categories, many of which you will not find in other price guides. Our sources are varied; we use auction results and dealer lists, and we consult with national collectors' clubs, recognized authorities, researchers, and appraisers. We have by far the largest Advisory Board of any similar publication on the market. Each year we add several new advisors and now have over 425 who cover almost all our categories. They go over our computer print-outs line by line, deleting listings that are misleading or too vague to be of merit; they often send background information and photos. We appreciate their assistance very much. Only through their expertise and experience in their special fields are we able to offer with confidence what we feel are useful, accurate evaluations that provide a sound understanding of the dealings in the marketplace today. Correspondence with so large an advisory panel adds months of extra work to an already monumental task, but we feel that to a very large extent this is the foundation that makes *Schroeder's* the success that it has become.

Our Directory, which you will find in the back of the book, lists each contributor by state. These are people who have allowed us to photograph various examples of merchandise from their show booths, sent us pricing information, or in any way have contributed to this year's book. If you happen to be traveling, consult the Directory for shops along your way. We also list clubs who have worked with us and auction houses who have agreed to permit us the use of photographs from their catalogs.

Our Advisory Board lists only names and home states, so check the Directory for addresses and telephone numbers should you want to correspond with one of our experts. Remember, when you do, **always** enclose a self-addressed, stamped envelope (SASE). Thousands of people buy our guide, and hundreds contact our advisors. The only agreement we have with our advisors is that they edit their categories. They are in no way obligated to answer mail. Some are dealers who do many shows a month. The time they spend at home may be very limited, and they may not be open to contacts. There's no doubt that the reason behind the success of our book is their assistance. We regret seeing them becoming more and more burdened by phone and mail inquiries. We have lost some of our good advisors for this reason, and when we do, the book suffers and consequently, so do our readers. Many of our listed reference sources report that they constantly receive long distance calls (at all hours) that are really valuation requests. If they are registered appraisers, they make their living providing such information and expect a fee for their service and expertise.

If you find you need more information than *Schroeder's* provides, there are other sources available to you. Go to your local library; check their section on reference books. Museums are public facilities that are willing and able help you establish the origin and possibly even the value of your particular treasure. In today's world of e-commerce, there are many websites you may visit that are full of pertinent, up-to-date information. Check the yellow pages of your phone book. Other cities' phone books are available from either your library or from the telephone company office. Look under the heading *Antique Dealers*. Those who are qualified appraisers will mention this credit in their advertisement. But remember that if you sell to a dealer, he will expect to buy your merchandise at a price low enough that he will be able to make an appreciable profit when he sells it. Once you decide to contact one of these appraisers, unless you intend to see them directly, you'll need to take photographs. Don't send photos that are under- or overexposed, out of focus, or shot against a background that detracts from important details you want to emphasize. It is almost impossible for them to give you a value judgement on items they've not seen when your photos are of poor quality. Shoot the front, top, and the bottom; describe any marks and numbers (or send a pencil rubbing), explain how and when you acquired the article, and give accurate measurements and any further background information that may be helpful.

The auction houses listed in the Directory nearly all have a staff of appraisal experts. If the item you're attempting to research is of the caliber of material they deal with, they can offer extremely accurate evaluations. Of course, most have a fee. Be sure to send them only professional-quality photographs. Tell them if you expect to consign your item to their auction. If you disagree with the value they suggest, you are under no obligation to do so.

Nearly 500 categories are included in our book. We have organized our topics alphabetically, following the most simple logic, usually either by manufacturer or by type of product. If you have difficulty in locating your subject, consult the index. Our guide is unique in that much more space has been allotted to background information than in any other publication of this type. Our readers tell us that this is a feature they enjoy. To be able to do this, we have adopted a format of one line listings wherein we describe the items to the fullest extent possible by using several common-sense abbreviations; they will be easy to read and understand if you will first take the time to quickly scan through them.

The Editors

Editorial Staff

Editors
Sharon and Bob Huxford

Research and Editorial Assistants
Loretta Suiters, Michael Drollinger, Donna Newnum

Layout
Terri Hunter

Scanning
Donna Ballard

Cover Design
Beth Summers

On the front cover: Hubley cast-iron still bank, Santa With Tree, 6", EX, $650.00 (photo courtesy Dunbar Gallery); Loetz vase, inlaid floral design, signed Loetz Austria, rare, 7½", M, $11,000.00; Steiner "Backward in Time" doll, 8", $1,500.00 (photo courtesy McMasters Doll Auctions); Bug hatpins (considered good luck in Victorian times), $450.00 – 600.00 each (from the collection of Virginia Woodbury, president of the American Hatpin Society); Vaseline glass cigar lighter, Hobnail, cast-iron base, counter-top style, 8" diameter, $2,000.00 (photo courtesy of Jackson's Auctioneers & Appraisers); Roycroft tabouret with square overhanging top on four-sided plank base with keyhole cutouts, refinished, carved orb and cross mark, 20½x15", $6,000.00; Benedict lamp, hammered copper and mica six-sided shade on six-sided base, 26", shade 20" diameter, EX, $4,000.00 (photo courtesy Treadway Galleries); Weller duck garden ornament, attribution, unsigned, 18", minor restoration, $7,000.00 (photo courtesy Treadway Galleries); Japanese tin Dreamboat Hot Rod Racer, battery-operated, 7", $250.00 (photo courtesy Dunbar's Gallery).

On the back cover: Newcomb College art pottery high-glaze vase, waterlilies on blue body, base marked with Newcomb cypher, registration mark "BK9," "W," and Leona Nicholson's decorator's mark, 1906, $23,000.00.

Listing of Standard Abbreviations

The following is a list of abbreviations that have been used throughout this book in order to provide you with the most detailed descriptions possible in the limited space available. No periods are used after initials or abbreviations. When two dimensions are given, height is noted first. If only one dimension is listed, it will be height, except in the case of bowls, dishes, plates, or platters, when it will be diameter. The standard two-letter state abbreviations apply.

For glassware, if no color is noted, the glass is clear. Hyphenated colors, for example blue-green, olive-amber, etc., describe a single color tone; colors divided by a slash mark indicate two or more colors, i.e. blue/white. Teapots, sugar bowls, and butter dishes are assumed to be 'with cover.' Condition is extremely important in determining market value. Common sense suggests that art pottery, china, and glassware values would be given for examples in pristine, mint condition, while suggested prices for utility wares such as Redware, Mocha, and Blue and White Stoneware, for example, reflect the probability that since such items were subjected to everyday use in the home they may show minor wear (which is acceptable) but no notable damage. Values for other categories reflect the best average condition in which the particular collectible is apt to be offered for sale without the dealer feeling it necessary to mention wear or damage. For instance, advertising items are assumed to be in excellent condition since mint items are scarce enough that when one is offered for sale the dealer will most likely make mention of that fact. The same holds true for toys, banks, coin-operated machines, and the like. A basic rule of thumb is that an item listed as VG (very good) will bring 40% to 60% of its mint price — a first-hand, personal evaluation will enable you to make the final judgement; EX (excellent) is a condition midway between mint and very good, and values would correspond.

AD	after dinner	dtd	dated	ldgl	leaded glass	re	regarding
Am	American	dvtl	dovetail	litho	lithograph	rfn	refinished
appl	applied	emb	embossed, embossing	lt	light	rnd	round
att	attributed to	embr	embroidered	M	mint	rpl	replaced
bbl	barrel	Emp	Empire	mahog	mahogany	rpr	repaired
bk	back	eng	engraved, engraving	mc	multicolor	rpt	repainted
bl	blue	EPNS	electroplated nickel silver	MIB	mint in box	rstr	restored
blk	black	EX	excellent	MIG	Made in Germany	rtcl	reticulated
brn	brown	Fed	Federal	MIP	mint in package	rvpt	reverse painted
bulb	bulbous	fr	frame, framed	mk	mark	s&p	salt and pepper
bsk	bisque	Fr	French	MOC	mint on card	sgn	signed
b3m	blown 3-mold	ft, ftd	foot, feet, footed	MOP	mother-of-pearl	SP	silverplated
C	century	G	good	mt, mtd	mount, mounted	sq	square
c	copyright	gr	green	NE	New England	std	standard
ca	circa	grad	graduated	NM	near mint	str	straight
cb	cardboard	grpt	grain painted	NRFB	never removed from box	sz	size
Chpndl	Chippendale	H	high, height	NP	nickel plated	trn	turned, turning
CI	cast iron	Hplwht	Hepplewhite	opal	opalescent	turq	turquoise
compo	composition	hdl, hdld	handle, handled	orig	original	uphl	upholstered
cr/sug	creamer and sugar	HP	hand painted	o/l	overlay	VG	very good
c/s	cup and saucer	illus	illustration, illustrated by	o/w	otherwise	Vict	Victorian
cvd	carved	imp	impressed	Pat	patented	W	width
cvg	carving	ind	individual	pc	piece	wht	white
dbl	double	int	interior	ped	pedestal	w/	with
decor	decoration	Invt T'print	Inverted Thumbprint	pk	pink	w/o	without
demi	demitasse	irid	iridescent	pnt	paint	X, Xd	cross, crossed
dk	dark	L	length, long	porc	porcelain	yel	yellow
Dmn Quilt	Diamond Quilted	lav	lavender	prof	professional	(+)	has been reproduced
drw	drawer			QA	Queen Anne		

A B C Plates

Children's plates featuring the alphabet as part of the design were popular from as early as 1820 until after the turn of the century. The earliest English creamware plates were decorated with embossed letters and prim moralistic verses, but the later Staffordshire products were conducive to a more relaxed mealtime atmosphere, often depicting playful animals and riddles or scenes of pleasant leisure-time activities. They were made around the turn of the century by American potters as well. All featured transfer prints, but color was sometimes brushed on by hand to add interest to the design.

Be sure to inspect these plates carefully for damage, since condition is a key price-assessing factor, and aside from obvious chips and hairlines, even wear can substantially reduce their values. Another problem for collectors is the fact that there are current reproductions of glass and tin plates, particularly the glass plate referred to as Emma (child's face in center) and a tin plate showing children with hoops. These plates are so common as to be worthless as a collectible.

For further information we recommend *A B C Plates & Mugs, Identification and Value Guide*, by Irene and Ralph Lindsay (Collector Books); and *ABCs of ABC Ware* by Davida and Irving Shipkowitz (Schiffer Books). Our advisor for this category is Dr. Joan George; she is listed in the Directory under New Jersey.

Ceramic

Abraham Lincoln transfer, 7½", $600.00.

A Firm Faith Is the..., red transfer, unmk, 7¼" 145.00
Aesop's Fable, cock & fox, mc transfer, ABC rim, unmk, 5½" ...135.00
Aesop's Fable, man & boy riding donkey, brn transfer, unmk, 7".135.00
April, figure between roses, mc transfer, unmk, 6¾" 160.00
B, Boat, Bat, Ball, mc transfer, 5" 225.00
Birds of paradise, mc transfer, Edge Malkin & Co, 6" 150.00
Blood Relations, puppies in basket, brn transfer, unmk, 7" 140.00
Boys playing marbles, mc transfer, unmk, 5½" 165.00
Buck jumping hunter, mc transfer, Elsmore & Son, 8" 165.00
Cats (3) pulling tablecloth, brn transfer, unmk, 7¼" 175.00
Children under umbrella w/doll, red transfer, unmk, 7½" 140.00
Children w/rabbit, red transfer, unmk, 7½".................................125.00
Cows beside & sheep in pond, mc transfer, unmk, 6¾" 180.00
Crusoe Making a Boat, bl transfer, BP Co, England, 6".............175.00
Dog pulling cart w/2 children, bl transfer, unmk, 6¾".................140.00
Family on picnic, bl transfer, unmk, 6¾".....................................135.00
Family on picnic, mc transfer, unmk, 5"......................................140.00
Federal Generals, mc transfer, unmk, 7"......................................400.00
Flowers That Never Fade, Meekness, mc transfer, unmk, 7¼" 250.00
Franklin's Proverbs, Employ Time Well..., mc transfer, unmk, 7½"..165.00
Franklin's Proverbs, Importance of..., brn transfer, Adams, 8".....140.00
Girls w/umbrellas, red transfer, Staffordshire, 7" 165.00
Going to Market, mc transfer, Elsmore & Son, 8" 150.00
Guardian, dog & sleeping boy, mc transfer, Elsmore & Foster, 7" .225.00
Horse, brn transfer w/mc details, Adams, 7¼" 180.00

Kestrel, mc transfer, unmk, 7"...140.00
Kittens in basket, In a Soft Place, brn transfer, 7" 125.00
Man w/Alpine horn & dog, monochrome, unmk, 6"....................140.00
Nursery Tales, Old Mother Hubbard, mc transfer, 7¼" 230.00
Our Donkey & Foal, mc transfer, unmk, 6"..................................145.00
Pray Tell Us Ladies, dk transfer, unmk, 6" 140.00
Queen Victoria, coronation portrait, from $800 to 1,000.00
Queen Victoria, in garden...450.00
Rider rents horse, center dmn panel, bl transfer, CA & Sons, 7½" .155.00
Sioux Indian chief, brn transfer, CA & Sons, 7" 140.00
Tulip & the Butterfly..., mc transfer, Meakin, 6".........................165.00
Village blacksmith, mc transfer, unmk, 5¼"..................................150.00
Walk, The; figure on horse, mc transfer, unmk, 7" 145.00

Glass

ABCs emb/enameled on rim, milk glass, unmk, 7" 60.00
Christmas Eve, unmk, 6", from $175 to.......................................150.00
Diamond center (resembles snowflake), unmk, 6¼", from $50 to.60.00
Ducks, deep yel, unmk, 6", from $60 to...70.00
Emma (child's face), vaseline, bl or orange, unmk, 8", ea.............30.00
Fan center, scalloped rim, unmk, 6", from $65 to..........................75.00
Months, days, clock face & scalloped ABC rim, unmk, 7"............60.00
Numbers around center, ABC rim, carnival glass, unmk, 7½" 120.00
President Garfield, smooth rim, 6" 150.00
Rooster, smooth rim, unmk, 6", from $65 to 75.00

Tin

ABCs emb around rim, unmk, 4½" 85.00
ABCs emb around rim, unmk, 6¼", from $60 to 95.00
ABCs in sq, unmk, 8"...90.00
Girl & boy w/hoop, unmk, 3" 150.00
Her Majesty Queen Victoria, unmk, 8" 250.00
Hi Diddle Diddle..., unmk, 8¾", from $80 to..............................100.00
Horse profile, unmk, 5½", from $160 to......................................175.00
Jumbo, emb elephant, unmk, 5½", from $100 to.........................160.00
Mary Had a Little Lamb, unmk, 7¾", from $130 to 160.00
Victoria & Albert portraits, unmk, 4¼" 250.00
Washington bust portrait & emb stars, unmk, 6" 185.00
Who Killed Cock Robin?, unmk, 7¾"...125.00

Abingdon

From 1934 until 1950, the Abingdon Pottery Co. of Abingdon, Illinois, made a line of art pottery with a white vitrified body decorated with various types of glazes in many lovely colors. Novelties, cookie jars, utility ware, and lamps were made in addition to several lines of simple yet striking art ware. Fern Leaf, introduced in 1937, featured molded vertical feathering. La Fleur, in 1939, consisted of flowerpots and flower-arranger bowls with rows of vertical ribbing. Classic, 1939 – 1940, was a line of vases, many with evidence of Chinese influence. Several marks were used, most of which employed the company name. In 1950 the company reverted to the manufacture of sanitary ware that had been their mainstay before the art ware division was formed.

Highly decorated examples and those with black, bronze, or red glaze usually command at least 25% higher prices.

For further information we recommend *Abingdon Pottery Artware 1934 – 1950, Stepchild of the Great Depression*, by Joe Paradis (Schiffer).

#30, vase, Chang, bronze...225.00
#99, Goose, leaning, 1948-50, 2½"..30.00
#102, vase, Beta, 1938-39, 10"..25.00

#103, vase, Gamma, 10" 36.00
#109, vase, Alpha, 1938-41, 6" 15.00
#111, vase, Gamma, 1938-39, 6" 22.50
#112, vase, Delta, 6" 25.00
#113, water jug...95.00
#115, vase, Classic, 1939-49, 10" 25.00
#119, vase, Classic, 10" 30.00
#125, bowl, Classic, 6½x11" 30.00
#125, candle holder, Classic, single, 1940-41, 2x3½", pr..............42.50
#130, vase, Classic, 1940, 8" 25.00
#143, vase, Classic, 1940-41, 5½" 20.00
#149, flowerpot, Le Fleur, 3" 15.00
#151, flowerpot, La Fleur, 1947-50, 5" 12.00
#152, vase, yel, 8¾" 22.00
#155, vase, Classic, 9" 20.00
#170, vase, Classic, 7" 20.00
#172, vase, Classic, 1941, 7" 18.00
#258, lamp base, fluted shaft, 23" 75.00
#302, vase, Lung, 1934-38, 11" 225.00
#303, cornucopia, 1934-36, 7½" 40.00
#305, bookends, Sea Gull, 6", pr..................................85.00
#309, vase, Neo Classic, 12½" 120.00
#315, vase, Athenian, 1947, 9" 35.00
#317, ashtray, rnd, 1934-37 ....15.00
#327, vase, Modern #2, 6" 70.00
#336, bowl, sq, 1935-41, 9" 35.00
#348, cigarette box, Trix, 3¾x4¾" 40.00
#349, chalice, 1935-37, 5½" 78.00
#366, flowerpot, Egg & Dart, 1936-37, 5¼" 15.00
#375, wall pocket, Morning Glory, dbl, 1936-40, 6½"...........40.00
#377, wall pocket, Morning Glory, ivory, 9x6¼" 40.00
#384, candle holders, Daisy, 1936-38, 4½", pr 25.00
#390, vase, Morning Glory, 1936-39, 10" 47.50
#411, vase, Volute, 10½" 75.00
#421, vase, Fern Leaf, 8¾" 50.00
#432, fruit boat, Fern Leaf, 6½x15" 50.00
#442, vase, Laurel, 5½" 45.00
#446, vase, Laced Cuff, 1938-39, 10" 40.00
#449, cornucopia, Shell, 4½" 35.00
#452, bowl, Asters, 1938-40, 15x9" 40.00
#454, bowl, Asters, 6½" 40.00
#456, ashtray, New Mode, 5¾" 40.00
#458, vase, Lattice, 1939, 5½" 42.50
#463, vase, Star, 7½", from $20 to 25.00
#474, cornucopia, 1939-50, 5" 15.00

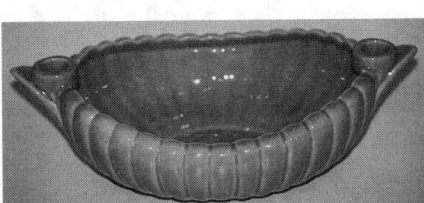

#473, bowl/candle holder, Combination, 7x12", $100.00.

#475, window box, 1939-40, 7" L 20.00
#483, vase, Petite Bud, 8"...30.00
#491, vase, flower arranger, 1940-50, 5" 25.00
#493, wall pocket, dbl; horn shaped, 8½".......................75.00
#505, candle holders, Shell, dbl, 1940-49, pr 40.00
#511, vase, Ionic, 8" 35.00
#514, vase, Swirl, chartreuse, 11", from $25 to 35.00
#521, vase, Bali, 1940-41, 9" 50.00
#529, bowl, Ti Leaf, 5x16"...40.00

#531, bowl, Fleur de Lis, 1941, 14x9" 25.00
#536, bowl, Regency, gr, 7x9x5" 35.00
#543, bowl, Bulb, 5½" 12.50
#548, bowl, Round, 14"" 25.00
#550, vase, Fluted, 1941-50, 11" 28.00
#555, ashtray, 8" dia 18.00
#556, vase, 1941-46, 12½" 50.00
#558, cache pot, 1947, 4¾", from $15 to 18.00
#560, cache pot, 6½" 15.00
#568, mint compote, pk, ftd, 1942-47, 6" dia 25.00
#569, cornucopia, low, 1947-48, 8" L 12.50
#573, figurine, Penguin, decor, 5½" 30.00
#576, window box, 1947-50, 12¼" 22.50
#577, vase, pillow form, 1947-50, 7" 22.50
#580D, box, Butterfly, 1947, 4¾" dia 80.00
#581, vase, dbl cornucopia; bl, 8½" 40.00
#589, wall bracket, Acanthus, 1947, 7" 62.50
#594, vase, Hour Glass, 9" 32.00
#597, vase, Trumpet, 9" 40.00
#600, vase, Laurel, 12", from $45 to 50.00
#601D, wall pocket, Butterfly, 1947-49, 8½" 100.00
#629, vase, Poppy, 6½" 30.00
#632, vase, Anchor, 1948-49, 7½" 40.00
#641, bowl, Whirl, 1948, 6½"...32.50
#647, urn, 13½" 50.00
#667, planter, Gourd, 1949-50, 5½" 15.00
#670, planter, Pooch, 4" 35.00
#676D, wall vase, Book, 1949, 6½" 90.00
#683, teapot, Daisy, 6¼" 50.00
#691D, tea set, Daisy, 1949-50, 3-pc................................120.00
#698, vase, Chinese Terrace, 6" 40.00
#705, vase, Modern, 8" 35.00
#710, planter, Drape, 7" 25.00
Cookie jar, #471, Old Lady, decor, minimum value 300.00
Cookie jar, #495, Fat Boy..250.00
Cookie jar, #549, Hippo, decor, 1942 ....250.00
Cookie jar, #588, Money Bag...75.00
Cookie jar, #602, Hobby Horse..185.00
Cookie jar, #611, Jack-in-Box..275.00
Cookie jar, #622, Miss Muffet 205.00
Cookie jar, #651, Choo Choo (Locomotive) 150.00
Cookie jar, #653, Clock, 1949 ....100.00
Cookie jar, #663, Humpty Dumpty, decor 250.00
Cookie jar, #664, Pineapple 95.00
Cookie jar, #665, Wigwam 250.00
Cookie jar, #674, Pumpkin, 1949, minimum value 325.00
Cookie jar, #677, Daisy, 1949..50.00
Cookie jar, #678, Windmill, from $200 to 225.00
Cookie jar, #693, Little Girl, from $60 to........................75.00
Cookie jar, #694, Bo Peep, from $250 to 275.00
Cookie jar, #695, Mother Goose, from $295 to 295.00
Cookie jar, #696, Three Bears, from $90 to 100.00

Adams, Matthew

In the 1950s a trading post in Alaska contacted Sascha Brastoff to design a line of porcelain with scenes of Eskimos, Alaskan motifs, and animals indigenous to that part of the country. These items were to be sold in Alaska to the tourist trade.

Brastoff selected Matthew Adams, born in April 1915, to design the Alaska series. Pieces from the line he produced have the Sascha B mark on the front; some have a pattern number on the reverse. They did not have the rooster backstamp. (See the Sascha Brastoff category for information on this mark.)

After the Alaska series was introduced and proved to be successful, Matthew Adams left the employment of Sascha Brastoff (working three years there in all) and opened his own studio. Pieces made in his studio are signed Matthew Adams in script and may have the word Alaska on the front. Mr. Adams's studio is now located in Los Angeles, but at this time, due to his age, he has ceased production. Our advisor for this category is Marty Webster; he is listed in the Directory under Michigan. Feel free to contact Mr. Webster if you have any further information.

Ashtray, Eskimo face, hollow star shape, 13".................................75.00
Ashtray, Eskimo family, 8½".................................40.00
Ashtray, grizzly bear on brn, free-form, 6½" L.................................45.00
Ashtray, husky dog, 13x10".................................65.00
Ashtray, walrus, star shape, 10x12".................................95.00
Ashtray, walrus on gr, boomerang shape, 6x11".................................65.00
Bowl, console; glacier on bl, 12x20".................................165.00
Bowl, Eskimo girl w/igloo, #150, 11½".................................130.00
Bowl, grizzly bear on brn, free-form, 6½" L.................................45.00
Bowl, husky dog, 6".................................40.00
Bowl, igloo & dog, boat shape, #138, 9½".................................50.00
Bowl, polar bear on gr, free-form, 7½" L.................................50.00
Bowl, ram on gr, free-form, 7".................................55.00
Bowl, salad; ram & mtn top, 13¼x15", +6 sm bowls.................................155.00
Bowl, seal, oval, 9".................................50.00
Bowl, seal on blk, free-form, w/lid, #145, 7½" L.................................75.00
Bowl, walrus, yel, w/lid, 7".................................75.00
Bowl, walrus & glacier on brn, free-form, 8".................................65.00
Bowl, walrus on blk, free-form, #104, 6½" L.................................50.00
Box, glacier on bl, w/lid, 12".................................95.00
Box, seal, wht, 2¼x6".................................50.00
Charger, caribou on dk bl, 18".................................150.00
Charger, Eskimo w/harpoon, 16".................................135.00
Charger, walrus on dk bl, 17".................................150.00
Coffeepot, ram on gr, 11½", +6¼" mugs.................................180.00
Compote, grizzly bear on brn, tall, 8½" dia.................................70.00
Cookie jar, cabin, elliptical shape, #023, 7x5".................................100.00
Cookie jar, Eskimo mother & child on brn, 7".................................75.00
Cookie jar, mother & child on brn, 8".................................75.00
Creamer, polar bear on blk, 4¾".................................30.00
Creamer, seal, #144, 5x5¼".................................20.00
Cup & saucer, sled on bl.................................25.00
Dish, Eskimo, #187, 1¾x7¼x8¼".................................20.00
Dish, Eskimo lady on gr, elbow shape, 12".................................40.00
Dish, log cabin, w/lid, #145, 4x7½x5".................................20.00
Ginger jar, seal on brn/wht, #095, 6½".................................45.00
Humidor, seal on gr, #025, 5¾".................................45.00

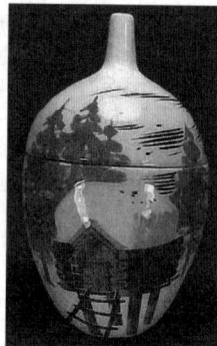

Jar, cabin, 7", $75.00.

Jar, Eskimo lady on brn, w/lid, 7½".................................50.00
Jar, Eskimo on ice bl, 6".................................30.00

Jar, polar bear on gr, w/lid, 7½".................................65.00
Jar, walrus on lt bl, w/lid, #1492, 7½".................................50.00
Lighter, cabin on stilts, 5x5".................................50.00
Lighter, glacier, 6".................................30.00
Lighter, walrus, #183, 6".................................25.00
Mug, husky dog, #112A, 4½x4¾".................................45.00
Pitcher, Eskimo, 13".................................90.00
Pitcher, Eskimo mother & child, 13", +6 5½" mugs.................................195.00
Pitcher, grizzly bear, 11", +6 4" tumblers.................................200.00
Pitcher, husky dog, wht on teal, bulbous, 5".................................65.00
Plate, Eskimo girl, #162, 7½".................................50.00
Plate, igloo & Northern Lights, #162, 7½".................................36.00
Platter, house, 12".................................45.00
Pot, walrus, w/lid, 12".................................55.00
Shakers, rams on gr, 4", pr.................................50.00
Tankard, man on brn, 19", +6 mugs.................................250.00
Tankard, polar bear on blk, w/lid, 13".................................200.00
Teapot, walrus on ice bl, 6½".................................75.00
Tile, Eskimo mother & child, 12¾x10½".................................125.00
Tile, mtns & glacier on blk, 10x8½".................................75.00
Tile, walrus on bl, 10x8½".................................75.00
Tray, polar bear & iceberg, #910, 13x9¾".................................75.00
Tumbler, cabin.................................20.00
Vase, glacier on gray, #143, 5½".................................50.00
Vase, house on yel, 11½".................................100.00
Vase, iceberg on gray, 7".................................50.00
Vase, mother & child on teal, cylindrical, 17".................................165.00
Vase, mtn & glacier on blk, #114, 12".................................80.00
Vase, polar bear on gr, 10".................................100.00
Vase, reindeer, 4½".................................45.00
Vase, sea lion & seaweed, oval, #128, 8".................................95.00
Vase, seal & glacier on brn, free-form, #911, 11".................................125.00
Vase, walrus on ice on bl, 10".................................110.00
Water set, walrus, 11½" pitcher+6 4½" mugs.................................255.00

Adams Rose, Early and Late

In the second quarter of the nineteenth century, the Adams and Son Pottery produced a line of hand-painted dinnerware decorated in large, red brush-stroke roses with green leaves on whiteware, which collectors call Adams Rose. Later, G. Jones and Son (and possibly others) made a similar ware with less brilliant colors on a gray-white surface.

Note: Early English dinnerware values have softened considerably due to the influence of the Internet which makes good examples that once were hard to find much more accessible. Unless otherwise noted, our values are for items in mint condition or nearly so; be sure to discount prices for damage.

Tea bowl and saucer, early, $330.00; Bowl, early, marked Adams, 4¼x9½", $800.00; Sauce dish, early, marked Adams, 4½", $75.00.

Bowl, late, 3x6¼".................................70.00
Coffepot, late, 8".................................875.00
Creamer, late, 4½".................................135.00

Pitcher, early, scalloped hdl & rim, rpr, 9", VG 235.00
Pitcher, water; late, 3-color, emb at spout/hdl, 7½" 300.00
Plate, early, scalloped edge w/beading, EX color, 9" 165.00
Plate, early, scalloped rim, ca 1825, 9"...........................150.00
Plate, early, scalloped rim, 10¾", VG.............................45.00
Plate, stick spatter, mk England, lion/unicorn crest, 7"........65.00
Plate, toddy; mk Adams, 5"..350.00
Sugar bowl, late, w/lid, 6"...350.00
Wash bowl & pitcher, early, prof rstr, 12", 4½x13½" 2,100.00
Waste bowl, early, unmk, 3¼x6½", EX 85.00

Advertising

The advertising world has always been a fiercely competitive field. In an effort to present their product to the customer, every imaginable gimmick was put into play. Colorful and artfully decorated signs and posters, thermometers, tape measures, fans, hand mirrors, and attractive tin containers (all with catchy slogans, familiar logos, and often-bogus claims) are only a few of the many examples of early advertising memorabilia that are of interest to today's collectors.

Porcelain signs were made as early as 1890 and are highly prized for their artistic portrayal of life as it was then . . . often allowing amusing insights into the tastes, humor, and way of life of a bygone era. As a general rule, older signs are made from a heavier gauge metal. Those with three or more fired-on colors are especially desirable.

Tin containers were used to package consumer goods ranging from crackers and coffee to tobacco and talcum. After 1880 can companies began to decorate their containers by the method of lithography. Though colors were still subdued, intricate designs were used to attract the eye of the consumer. False labeling and unfounded claims were curtailed by the Pure Food and Drug Administration in 1906, and the name of the manufacturer as well as the brand name of the product had to be printed on the label. By 1910 color was rampant with more than a dozen hues printed on the tin or on paper labels. The tins themselves were often designed with a second use in mind, such as canisters, lunch boxes, even toy trains. As a general rule, tobacco-related tins are the most desirable, though personal preference may direct the interest of the collector to peanut butter pails with illustrations of children, or talcum tins with irresistible babies or beautiful ladies. Coffee tins are popular, as are those made to contain a particularly successful or well-known product.

Perhaps the most visual of the early advertising gimmicks were the character logos, the Fairbank Company's Gold Dust Twins, the goose trademark of the Red Goose Shoe Company, Nabisco's ZuZu Clown and Uneeda Kid, the Campbell Kids, the RCA dog Nipper, and Mr. Peanut, to name only a few. Many early examples of these bring high prices on the market today.

Our listings are alphabetized by product name or, in lieu of that information, by word content or other pertinent description. When no condition is indicated, the items listed below are assumed to be in excellent condition, except glass and ceramic items, which are assumed mint. Remember that condition greatly affects value (especially true for tin items). For instance, a sign in excellent or mint condition may bring twice as much as the same one in only very good condition, sometimes even more. On today's market, items in good to very good condition are slow to sell, unless they are extremely rare. Mint (or near-mint) examples are high.

We have several advertising advisors; see specific subheadings. For further information we recommend *General Store Collectibles, Vols. I and II*, by David L. Wilson; *Advertising Thermometers* by Curtis Merritt; *Antique & Contemporary Advertising Memorabilia* by B.J. Summers; *Encyclopedia of Advertising Tins, Vol. II*, by David Zimmerman; and *Advertising Paperweights*, by Richard Holiner and Stuart Kammerman. *Garage Sale and Flea Market Annual* by Sharon and Bob Huxford is another good

reference. All of these books are available at your local bookstore or from Collector Books.

See also Advertising Dolls; Advertising Cards; Automobilia; Coca-Cola; Banks; Calendars; Cookbooks; Paperweights; Posters; Sewing Items.

Key:
cb — cardboard
dc — diecut
fs — flange sign
ps — porcelain sign
sf — self-framed
tc — tin container
ts — tin sign

AG Spalding & Bros Outfitters, ps, 2-sided, wht/gr on gr, 8x18", VG..2,100.00
Alka-Seltzer, sign, dc cb stand-up, Speedy w/wand & glass, 40", EX.125.00
Alka-Seltzer, themometer, dial, metal/glass, 12" dia, EX+...........130.00
American Ace Coffee, tc, keywind, pilot w/cup, red on bl, 1-lb, EX+.125.00
American-Maid Bread, pan scraper, dc litho tin bread loaf, EX+.220.00
Ammon & Person Baby Brand Butterine, pocket mirror, girl, 3x2", EX.375.00
Anamosa Ice Cream, sign, dc cb, Uncle Sam/cone, 1930s, 27x12", EX+.130.00
Anheuser-Busch, sign, cb, Custer's Last Fight, 1930s, fr, 36x47", VG+.850.00
Anna Held Cigar 5 Cents, sign, 2-sided cb diagonal hanger, 12x12", EX..350.00
Apache Trail Cigars, tc, slip lid, scarce, 5½x6x4", NM............1,700.00
Arden Ice Cream, ps, wht lettering on red oval, 1959, 36x48", M .400.00
Arden Ice Cream, ps, 2-sided dc step emblem, 1933, 32x28", NM .1,200.00
Armstrong's Linoleum, dc cb stand-up, baby/highchair, 1920s, 35", EX..500.00
Artie Cigar, ts, sf stand-up, man seated on tower on red, 10x6", EX+ .1,200.00
Baby Ruth Peppermint Gum, cb box w/contents, 1920s, 5x6x4", EX .2,600.00
Bagley's Burley Boy, pocket tin, boy boxer, 4", EX+ 2,800.00
Baker's Nursery Talcum Powder, tc, bl w/graphics, 6", EX...........300.00
Bergner & Engel Brewery, sign, cb, 1880s bar patron w/mug, 16x13", G.115.00
Big Smith Work Clothes, clock/sign, light-up, electric, 22x20", EX .135.00
Billings-Chapin Paints, match holder, tin litho, 5½", EX+.........600.00
Bissell Sweeper, dc cb stand-up of girl w/real sweeper, 1920, 36", EX .465.00
Bixby Best Blacking, box, wood w/paper labels, 3x9x9", VG+ 35.00
Blue Jay 5¢ Cigars, pocket tin, vertical, 5", EX+ 850.00
Bohemian Plug Mixture, tc, sq w/rnd slip lid, graphics/text, 6x5", EX.1,600.00
Borden's, night light, Elsie head, rubber-type compo, 9", NM.....180.00
Borden's Ice Cream, clock, light-up, Elsie logo, Universal, 15" sq, EX.300.00
Borden's Malted Milk, tip tray, young lady w/product, 5" dia, EX+..350.00
Bowey's Hot Choclate, dispenser, aluminum/enameled graphics, 9", EX..150.00
Bowey's Hot Choclate, tc, yel can w/blk graphics, 10x7x7", EX ...50.00
Boyertown Casket Co, paperweight, cast metal casket, 5", EX+ .350.00
BP Clark & Co, candy scoop, emb glass, 7", VG 175.00
Brickmore's Gall Cure, sign, dc cb trifold w/3 scenes, 33x50", VG+.520.00
Brownie Crackers & Cookies, trolley sign, cb, 3 images, 11x21", NM+.160.00
BT Babbit, sign, girl/chickens, metal strips, 1892, 28x14", EX+ .950.00
Buckingham Tobacco, door push bar, porc, Smoke...Throat Easy, 32", EX.200.00
Budweiser, ts, ...In Bottles, disc w/logo, gold trim, 10" dia, EX....325.00
Buffalo's Best/Beck's Bottle Beer, tip tray, eagle logo, 4" dia, NM..325.00
Bull Dog Cut Plug De Luxe, pocket tin, bl, 4½", EX+ 825.00
Bull Durham, ts, scene on convex disc in ornate fr, 36" sq, VG ..3,565.00

Buster Brown

Buster Brown was the creation of cartoonist Richard Felton; his comic strip first appeared in the *New York Herald* on May 4, 1902. Since then Buster and his dog Tige (short for Tiger) have adorned sundry commercial products but are probably best known as the trademark for the Brown Shoe Company established early in this century. Today hundreds of Buster Brown premiums, store articles, and advertising items bring substantial prices from many serious collectors.

Bank, molded plastic, BB & Tige busts atop ball, 1960s, 4" dia, EX .35.00
Clicker, tin shoe-sole form, bl (Blue Ribbon) lettering on yel, VG.20.00
Clicker, tin w/head image of BB & Tige, VG.................................20.00

Comic book, 1959, EX 25.00
Container, BB Mustard, cb w/tin top & bottom, red, 2-oz, EX+ .100.00
Kite, paper, BB Shoes for Boys/graphics, 34", VG 15.00
Pocket mirror, BB Shoes for Boys & Girls/BB & Tige on wht, rnd, EX .85.00
Rug, BB & Tige on yel w/bl border, Mowhawk, 54" dia, VG 300.00
Sign, cb hanger, BB Bread, BB writing on chalkboard, 11x8", EX ..200.00

Sign corner, diecut metal litho, double-sided, 14x24", EX, $4,000.00.

Sign, flange, Fountain/Drink..., yel/red/wht, 1961, 15x22", NM .750.00
Sign, mortarboard w/easel bk, Authorized.../BB & Tige, 14x15", VG ..110.00
Sign, porc, Drink..., red oval/gold V emblem on wht, 8x22", EX+ .175.00
Watch fob, BB Shoes, cello, 1930s, NM 125.00

Calox Oxygen Tooth Powder, display case, metal & glass, 13x8x4", EX ..375.00
Camel Cigarettes, sign, dc cb stand-up, Navy girl, 1943, 31", EX .125.00
Campbell's Soups, ts, ...Ready in a Jiffy, kid/soup list, 12x18", EX+ .150.00
Capital City Carriage Co, sign, graphics on wood, 12x16", EX+ .1,200.00
Cardinal Cut Plug, pocket tin, scarce, 4½", VG+ 925.00
Carhartt's Overalls & Gloves, poster, cloth bk, worker, 58x40", VG ..650.00
Case, sign, porc/neon, 2-sided, eagle on globe logo, 40x72x17", VG .1,600.00
Castle Hall Twins Cigars, stork figure w/sign, chalk, 22", VG 550.00
Cherry Smash, bottle topper, dc cb, colonial boy w/glass, 12", NM+ ..50.00
Chesterfield Cigarettes, poster, WWI sailor on bl, 44x28", VG .575.00
Chief Watta Pop, display of chief's head w/suckers, plaster, NM .735.00
Clabber Baking Powder, banner, cloth, logo girl, 1901, 18x37", EX ..625.00
Cleo Cola, ts, emb, Genuine...12 for 5, Egyptian graphics, 13x27", EX ..325.00
Clicquot Club, clock, light-up, Telechron, 1940s, 15" dia, NM ..450.00
Clover Brand Shoes, tip tray, Blk boy w/watermelon, oval, EX+ .200.00
Columbia Batteries, ts, devil/battery image on blk, 14x20", EX+ .450.00
Columbia Cut Plug Smoking Tobacco/Sears, tc, red/wht/bl, 6", VG+ .220.00
Columbia Grafonola, ts, Don't Get Up..., graphics on yel, 18x24", EX+ .700.00
Comfort Powder, tc, nurse/baby, 4x2½" dia, EX 500.00
Continental Fire Insurance Co, ps, soldier/bl text on wht, 18x12", EX .200.00
Country Club Ice Cream, ps, 2-sided, The Cream of Quality, 28x20", EX+ .300.00
Cream Dove Shortening/Peanut Butter, pocket mirror, boy w/can, rnd, EX .300.00
Cunningham's Ice Cream, tray, factory scene, oval, VG+ 175.00
De Laval Cream Separators, broom holder, litho tin, 3½" dia, M .650.00
Devilish Good Cigar, ts, emb/chain hanger, open box/lt bl, 10x14", EX .150.00
Double Cola, fs, Drink... on ornate oval, 2-sided, dtd 1947, 18", NM .825.00
Doxie Cigars, cigar can, paper label w/horse head, slip lid, 5" T, VG+ .375.00

Dr. Pepper

A young pharmacist, Charles C. Alderton, was hired by W.B. Morrison, owner of Morrison's Old Corner Drug Store in Waco, Texas, around 1884. Alderton, an observant sort, noticed that the drugstore's patrons could never quite make up their minds as to which flavor of extract to order. He concocted a formula that combined many flavors, and Dr. Pepper was born. The name was chosen by Morrison in honor of a beautiful young girl with whom he had once been in love. The girl's father, a Virginia doctor by the name of Pepper, had discouraged the relationship due to their youth, but Morrison had never forgotten her. On December 1, 1885, a U.S. patent was issued to the creators of Dr. Pepper. Our advisor for Dr. Pepper is Craig Stifter; he is listed in the Directory under Illinois. See also Soda Fountain Collectibles.

Bottle opener/spoon, The Friendly Pepper Upper, EX+ 385.00
Bottle topper, Cindy Garner, EX+ 165.00
Bottle topper, Virginia Kavanaugh, NM....................................220.00
Clock, metal/glass diagonal light-up, 10-2-4/dots, Pam, 15" sq, VG .60.00
Clock, octagonal, neon, rvpt glass, EX+ 1,200.00
Decal, Please Pay When Served, 1930s-40s, 8x9", EX+ 200.00
Fan, cb w/wooden hdl, pretty girl, Earl Morgan art, EX.................75.00
Fan pull, cb, beach girl w/umbrella, G 80.00
Hot beverage heater, ceramic insulator w/ads, 7", NM+ 85.00
Menu board, tin chalkboard, bottle/clock/grid logo on yel, 23x17", VG ..175.00
Mirror, boy/girl kissing in oval, wood fr, not old, 29x20", VG.......40.00
Poster, 2 sea nymphs, logo upper left, 1970s-80s, 20x14", NM+ ...30.00
Sign, cb, Join Me!, girl in car, 1940s, 32x40", NM 575.00
Sign, cb, 10-2-4 wood fr, girl/bottle/clock/grid logo, 29x34", VG+ .200.00
Sign, flange, Fountain/Drink DP, panel atop oval, 1961, 15x22", NM .750.00
Sign, porc, 10-2-4/Drink DP, red-on-wht circle, 10" dia, NM 150.00
Sign, tin, sf, 10-2-4 clock/lg bottle/grid logo on gold, 54x18", G+ .150.00
Thermometer, dial, Hot or Cold, Pam, 1950s-60s, 12" dia, NM .125.00

Thermometer, red and white, 12" diameter, NM, $125.00.
(Photo courtesy Autopia)

Thermometer, tin, Hot or Cold, red & wht, 26x7", NM.............150.00
Tray, You'll Like It To!, w/graphics, 1930s-40s, VG+ 280.00

Eagle Lye, crumb scraper & tray, Shonk litho, VG+ 130.00
Eskimo Pie, ps, bl lettering on wht, 7x36", EX............................200.00
Ever Ready Lighters, art plate, litho tin, Arab man/woman, 10", VG+ .300.00
Feen-a-mint, ps, The Chewing Laxative..., red/wht/bl, 8x30", EX ..625.00
Ferry's Seeds, counter display, metal/wood step box, 17x27x12", EX .200.00
Florida Gum, display box, cb, w/contents, 1920s, 5x6x4", EX .2,900.00
Gillette, ts, man w/pipe on beach, foreign text, 14x10", EX 650.00
Goelitz Butter Sweets, candy scoop, emb litho tin, mini, VG+ ..150.00
Good Will Soap, wagon, wood w/stenciling, spoke wheels, 33", EX .1,000.00
Gran'pa Graf's Root Beer, sign, dc wood, head/bottle, 1940s, 30", EX+ .325.00
Gulf No-Nox Motor Fuel, poster, car/attendant/plane, 1920s, 33x27", EX .1,750.00
Hance Bros & White, sign, dc cb, 10¢ Remedy, frog/banjo, 13x20", EX .2,900.00
Hand Bag Cut Plug, lunch box, leather-look bag shape, 6x7x4", EX ..150.00
Harrison's St Nicholas Mace, tc, red w/graphics, ½-oz, 3", EX+ .350.00
Hazzard Smokeless Gun Powder, tc, brn on gold, 1890s, 6x4x1½", EX+ .675.00
HD Lee Co, display case/4 Buddy Lee dolls, wood/glass, 1923, 15x20" .1,700.00
Heinz Preserved Peaches, crock, paper label/imprinted logo, 5x6", EX+ .1,050.00
Heinz's Plum Butter, bucket, wooden firkin w/paper label, 10", EX .1,650.00
Helmar Turkish Cigarettes, sign, paperboard, logo girl, fr, 26x18", EX .650.00
Hicks Capudine Liquid, tray, cherub graphics, 10" dia, EX+ 850.00
High Grade Smoking Tobacco, pocket tin, oval vertical, gr, 4", VG+ .950.00

Hills Bros Coffee, sign, dc cb stand-up, man/girl, 61", EX+ **1,600.00**
Hills Bros Tea & Coffee, thermometer, porc, curved top, 21", VG+ .**425.00**
Hindoo Granulated Plug Smoking Tobacco, pocket tin, 3½", EX+ .**825.00**

Hires

Charles E. Hires, a drugstore owner in Philadelphia, became interested in natural teas. He began experimenting with roots and herbs and soon developed his own special formula. Hires introduced his product to his own patrons and began selling concentrated syrup to other soda fountains and grocery stores. Samples of his 'root beer' were offered for the public's approval at the 1876 Philadelphia Centennial. Today's collectors are often able to date their advertising items by observing the Hires boy on the logo. From 1891 to 1906, he wore a dress. From 1906 until 1914, he was shown in a bathrobe; and from 1915 until 1926, he was depicted in a dinner jacket. The apostrophe may or may not appear in the Hires name; this seems to have no bearing on dating an item. Our advisor for Hires is Craig Stifter; he is listed in the Directory under Illinois.

See also Soda Fountain Collectibles.

Bottle carrier, cb box, Drink Moxie, EX **25.00**
Bottle carrier, wood, Quarter Case, VG+ **30.00**
Bottle topper/bottle, dc cb, 10¢ Off/Try a Real Black Cow, EX.....**15.00**
Clock, plastic, Since 1884/Old Fashion Moxie, gold fr, 16" sq, EX ..**200.00**
Dispenser, hourglass shape, w/spigot & pump, 13", EX.............**1,550.00**
Dispenser, metal box w/flat lid, 1940s, 22x12x16", VG+ **300.00**
Fan, rocking horse/Moxie man, 1922, EX **100.00**
Mug, ceramic hourglass shape, Hires boy, 4", EX **175.00**
Recipe folder, boy looking at Hires sign, VG **20.00**
Sign, cb, For Finer Flavor, lady w/food tray, 12" dia, NM...........**160.00**
Sign, cb stand-up, Hires to You!, party scene, 16x12", NM........**225.00**
Sign, emb ...For Pleasure & Thirst, lg bottle, lt bl, 18x56", NM.**425.00**
Sign, flange, Made w/..., check-mk logo, red/wht/bl, 12x14", EX.**325.00**
Sign, paper, Thirsts Gently Suffocated..., Josh w/mug, 1914, 7x11", EX.**400.00**
Sign, tin, '20s lady w/glass on yel, wood fr, 16x22", VG+.............**200.00**
Sign, tin, bull's-eye logo, emb, 24" dia, EX..................................**225.00**
Sign, tin, R-J logo on disc, lt bl border, 12" dia, NM+...................**75.00**
Thermometer, dial, Drink... on woodgrain, 12" dia, EX+ **80.00**
Thermometer, tin, It's Always a Pleasure, 1950s, 25", EX **350.00**
Thermometer, tin bottle shape, Since 1876 label, 29", NM........**275.00**

Holsum Bread, match holder, red/wht/bl litho tin, rectangular, EX .**750.00**
Horton Washing Machines, sign, cb, wringer washer, 28x21", VG.**40.00**
Howel's Orange Julep 5¢, sign, rvpt glass w/chain hanger, 6x10", EX..**4,000.00**
Imperial Shaving Stick, tc, man shaving, 2-pc, 3½x1½" dia, EX+ .**400.00**
Indian Motorcycles, match safe, emb metal w/circle logo, 2½", EX.**220.00**
International Ice Cream Co, thermometer, porc, wht, 1910-20s, 27", EX+..**300.00**
Iroquois Beer, bubble clock, glass/metal, Indian profile, 16" dia, VG..**475.00**
Iroquois Brewery, ps, emb dc Indian chief's head in profile, 20", EX..**4,400.00**
Ivory Soap, soap dispenser, metal w/glass container, Pat 1923, 7", EX.**85.00**
Jacobsen's Brown Beauty 5¢ Cigar, sign, paper, lady in tree, 20", VG.**475.00**
Jersey Coffee, store bin, red-pnt wood w/stencling, 100-lb, VG+.**875.00**
John Adams Havana Cigar, sf ts, oval image of Adams, 14x11", EX+.**600.00**
John Deere, clock, light-up, metal & glass, logo on wht, 15" dia, VG.**375.00**
John Deere Grain Binder, brochure, ca 1930, 24 pgs, 9", EX, A ...**35.00**
Kendall's Spavin Cure, sign, paper, Victorian lady w/horse, 35x29", EX.**800.00**
Kenny's Coffees-Teas, tip tray, lady in center, 4" dia, EX.............**150.00**
Kenny's Maid Coffee, pail, slip lid, bail hdl, 4-lb, 8", EX+ **325.00**
Kickapoo Joy Juice, menu chalkboard, emb tin, Speshuls, '65, 30", NM.**300.00**
Kickapoo Joy Juice, sign, cb, Explosives Permit!..., 11x9", NM...**100.00**
Knox Gelatin, display, 3-D dc cb, cow's head/2 girls on box, 16", EX..**1,400.00**
Kodak, ps, 2-sided hanger, Developing & Printing/film box, 14x20", EX.**600.00**

Kroger, delivery scooter, wood w/stenciled lettering, 36x32x14", EX..**300.00**
Lee, ps, ...Union-Alls=Overalls/Whizits, yel w/red trim, 36x60", VG+.**450.00**
Levi's, banner, pnt denim, cowboy/moon, 28x74", VG...............**500.00**
Life Savers, display rack, litho tin, 3-tier, brn, 17x10x10", EX+ .**300.00**

Log Cabin Syrup

Log Cabin syrup tins have been made since the 1890s in variations of design that can be attributed to specific years of production. Until about 1914, they were made with paper labels. These are quite rare and highly prized by today's collectors. Tins with colored lithographed designs were made after 1914. When General Foods purchased the Towle Company in 1927, the letters 'GF' were added.

A cartoon series, illustrated with a mother flipping pancakes in the cabin window and various children and animals declaring their appreciation of the syrup in voice balloons, was introduced in the 1930s. A frontier village series followed in the late 1940s. A schoolhouse, jail, trading post, doctor's office, blacksmith shop, inn, and private homes were also available. Examples of either series today often command prices of $125.00 to $200.00 and up.

Pull toy, Towle's...Syrup, log cabin display, wood, 14x18x12", VG...**950.00**
Pull Toy, Towle's...Syrup, Log Cabin Express, tin, 6", EX **900.00**
Sign, Towle's...Syrup, cb stand-up, The Syrup Camp, 23x28", EX+ ..**875.00**
Sign, Towle's...Syrup, sign, dc 3-D cb, cabin scene, 10x16x28", EX ..**725.00**

Tin container, Towle's Log Cabin Syrup, boy in doorway, 1930s, table size, no cap, VG+, from $100.00 to $150.00. (Photo courtesy Buffalo Bay Auction Co.)

Tin container, Towle's Wigwam Syrup, red/bl/yel, 1920s, 4x4x3", EX..**750.00**
Tin container, Towle's...Ready Spread, snap lid, 5x4" dia, VG+ ...**75.00**
Tin container, Towle's...Syrup, Express Office, 5", NM **265.00**
Tin container, Towle's...Syrup, Frontier Jail, 6½", EX+ **150.00**
Tin container, Towle's...Syrup, gr paper label, 1897, 1-gal, VG...**850.00**
Tin container, Towle's...Syrup, paper label, 1914, 6-oz, 3", VG+..**450.00**
Tin container, Towle's...Syrup, Trading Post, 6½", EX................**150.00**

Log Cabin Brownies (Nabisco), cb box, cabin graphics, 2.75-oz, VG+.**160.00**
Lowell & Covel Co, pail, litho tin, Peter Cottontail graphics, 3", EX.**525.00**
Lowell Fertilizer Co, J Ottman litho of farm scene, fr, 11x13", EX.**225.00**
Lowney's Cocoa, string holder, litho tin, 1908, 24x16", NM ...**5,200.00**
Lucky Strike Roll Cut Tobacco, pocket tin, wht, flip lid, 4½", EX ..**650.00**
Lucky Tiger for Hair & Scalp, sign, cb stand-up, graphics, 34x22", EX+.**500.00**
Luden's Cough Drops, tip tray, Give Instant Relief, 3½" dia, VG.**185.00**
Manila Girl 5¢ Cigar, sign, cb hanger, gold on blk, oval, 11x9", VG+.**400.00**
Mansfield's Pepsin Gum, dispenser, metal/glass, 12x5x5", NM+ .**3,000.00**
Mason's Challenge Blacking, box, wood w/paper labels, 2½x8x11", VG+.**60.00**
Matoaka Blue Ribbon Smoking Tobacco, pocket tin, 4½", EX.**3,200.00**
Mayo's Tobacco, roly poly, Satisfied Customer, VG+ **465.00**
Miller High Life, mirror sign, applied bl surface w/graphics, 4x8", EX.**275.00**
Monarch Finer Foods, clock, light-up, Telechon, 15" dia, EX+ ..**300.00**
Morton Salt, display, cb, half of a salt box, 1939, 20", EX..........**160.00**

Moxie

The Moxie Company was organized in 1884 by George Archer of Boston, Massachusetts. It was at first touted as a 'nerve food' to improve the appetite, promote restful sleep, and in general to make one 'feel better'! Emphasis was soon shifted, however, to the good taste of the brew, and extensive advertising campaigns rivaling those of such giant competitors as Coca-Cola and Hires resulted in successful marketing through the 1930s. Today the term Moxie has become synonymous with courage and audacity, traits displayed by the company who dared compete with such well-established rivals. Our advisor for Moxie is Craig Stifter; he is listed in the Directory under Illinois.

Clock, figure-8, Baird, rstr, 31" 1,500.00
Lozenges product box, red, 2-pc, very rare, 3x2x1", VG+ 130.00
Match holder, bottle shape, litho tin, 7x2½", EX+ 625.00
Sign, cb standup, It's a Hit Says Ted Williams, 9x13", NM.........450.00
Sign, tin, sf, billboard & car, Drink..., 1930s, 13x19", VG+........600.00
Sign, ts, dc Frank Archer seated on box pointing finger, 6x3", EX ..100.00
Toy, auto w/horse & rider, litho tin, red or bl, 8" or 9", EX+, ea...2,475.00
Umbrella/parasol, red/blk on wht, rare, EX 350.00

Munsing Union Suits, dc ts on ped w/3 extended clothes rods, 45", EX..2,050.00
Nabisco, ps, dc emblem, red name on wht oval w/red trim, 33x48", EX+.350.00
National Beer, tip tray, deep rim, Am Art Works, 4½" dia, EX+.485.00
National Biscuit Co, clock, pressed oak/pendulum, 1980s promo, 36", EX.200.00
Nature's Remedy, clock, pendulum, Gilbert, 31x16", VG 700.00
Nehi, fs, bottle w/dc top on yel panel, Drink...Ice Cold, 14x18", NM+..550.00
Nesbitt's, thermometer, tin, bottle cap/professor on yel, 27", NM.250.00
Nevins Candy, display case, metal & glass, octagonal, 70x24x25", EX.700.00
Niagara Punch, ts, Drink.../bottle on yel, 9x20", EX+ 225.00
North Pole Cut Plug, tc, sq w/rnd slip lid, polar scene, 6x6x4", EX+ .725.00
North Pole Smoking Tobacco, lunch box, gr/North Pole graphics, 6", EX .975.00
Northrup King Sterling Seeds, poster, woman w/corn, 1912, 30x21", EX+.475.00
NuGrape Soda, fs, 2-sided dc tin oval w/hand-held bottle, 14x20", EX.600.00
OFC Whiskey, ts, river scene w/stag, ornate fr, 37x29", G+........700.00
Old Abe Bright Chewing tobacco, tc, Lincoln graphics, 2x6" dia, VG+.675.00
Old Chum Tobacco, ps, wht lettering on bl, yel/bl trim, 18x30", EX.450.00
Old Honesty Plug Tobacco, banner, oilcloth, Chew.../dog, 50x18", VG+.350.00
Old Senica Stogies, tc, rnd, slip lid, Indian head on yel, 6", EX+ .300.00

Old Crow

Old Crow whiskey items have become popular with collectors primarily because of the dapper crow dressed in a tuxedo, top hat, etc., that was used by the company for promotional purposes during the 1940s through the 1960s. However, there is a vast variety of Old Crow collectibles, some of which carry only the whiskey's name. In the 1970s ceramic decanters shaped like chess pieces were available; these carried nothing more than a paper label and a presentation box to identify them. In 1985, the 150th anniversary of Old Crow, the realistic crow that had been extensively used prior to 1950 re-emerged.

Very little Old Crow memorabilia has been issued since National Distillers Products Corporations, the parent company since 1933, was purchased by Jim Beam Brands in 1987. No reproductions have surfaced, although a few fantasy items have been found where the character crow was borrowed for private use. Note that with the increased popularity of Old Crow memorabilia, many items have surfaced, especially the more common ones, thus their values have decreased. Our advisors for Old Crow collectibles are Judith and Robert Walthall; they are listed in the Directory under Alabama.

Ashtray, Bakelite, 3½" dia, NM..25.00
Ashtray, ceramic, blk w/'Old Crow,' etc, 5" dia..........................35.00
Back-bar display, ceramic, 'Broken Leg' mug holds bottle, 5¼", NM..200.00
Bank, wooden bbl, 1985, 6", EX...15.00
Bingo card, 100 proof, late 1940s, 7½x8¼"................................45.00
Bottle display, glass cylinder w/gold plastic crow.........................50.00
Bottle opener, metal bottle shape, 2⅝", NM...............................25.00
Bottle pourer, plastic figure, sm...5.00
Chess set (32 decanters), ltd ed, empty w/orig boxes & rug........200.00
Cocktail glass, crow stem, safety edge, Libbey, 1970s, from $10 to.15.00
Decanter, figural, Old Crow Distillery Co of Frankfort KY, 13½".50.00
Decanter, figural, orange vest, Royal Doulton, w/box, 12½".......125.00
Dice, I Buy, You Buy, crow on 1, ½" set of 2 ....45.00
Dice cup, Bakelite, blk w/yel lettering, felt-lined, NM...............100.00
Doorstop, cut-out 2-D wood crow, 21", EX...............................125.00
Figure, brass, on rnd ftd base, 11"..85.00
Figure, compo, name emb on base, 1940s, 27½", VG.................450.00

Figure, painted composition, 11½x3½", EX, from $75.00 to $125.00. (Photo courtesy B.J. Summers)

Figure, plastic, Advertising Novelty & Sign Co, 32", EX............200.00
Figure, plastic, in birdcage, 9"..125.00
Jigger, blk lettering on clear glass, no crow, NM 5.00
Key chain, 2-D figural Old Crow, from $3 to 5.00
Label, paper, gold, shows Hermitage Distillery bbls, ca 1903, 4+x4+".25.00
Lighter, 14k gold-plated, Florentine, from $25 to 30.00
Lipstick tissue booklet, Cub Products, 1⅞x3", M, from $15 to 20.00
Money clip, chromed metal, emb disc w/crow on 2" clip, EX........35.00
Phone dialer, hard plastic crow figure, 'Call For' emb on bk, EX.....5.00
Pitcher, ceramic, 'Broken Leg' decor, NM................................100.00
Pitcher, ceramic, olive gr w/emb crow in reserve, McCoy, 7"........30.00
Pitcher, glass w/metal ring & hdl, 5"...25.00
Plaque, ceramic plate w/applied 4¾" crow, 8", NM...................125.00
Pocketknife, pearlized hdls, 2 blades..30.00
Roly-poly, plastic, 9"...95.00
Shot glass, Old Crow & crow fired on in blk 20.00
Stirrer, plastic, full-figure crow on end, from $1 to.......................3.00
Thermometer, rnd dial, 1950s, 9x13", EX 150.00
Thermometer, Taste of Greatness, 1960, 5¾x13½", from $75 to.100.00

Orange Crush, menu board, glass case w/menu slots, NM+ 500.00
OTC Medical Supports, display, plaster plaque of pharmacist, 25", VG.115.00
Pal Ade, thermometer, tin, yel, 1950, 24", NM 400.00
Parrot Brand Crackers, dc cb parrot in ring holding cracker, 13", EX+.1,550.00
Paw-Nee Olde Style Oats, cb container, yel w/red, 2-lb 10-oz, EX.120.00
Penny's Select Beer, tip tray, lady/bottle, Nordhem litho, 4" dia, EX..360.00

Pepsi-Cola

Pepsi-Cola was first served in the early 1890s to customers of Caleb D. Bradham, a young pharmacist who touted his concoction to be medicinal as well as delicious. It was first called 'Brad's Drink' but was renamed Pepsi-Cola in 1898. Various logos have been registered over the years. The familiar oval was first used in the early 1940s. At about the same time, the two 'dots' (indicated in our listings by '=') between the words Pepsi and Cola became one, though more recent items may carry the double-dot logo as well, especially when they're designed to be reminiscent of the old ones. The bottle cap logo came along in 1943 and with variations was used through the early 1960s. Our advisor for Pepsi is Craig Stifter; he is listed in the Directory under Illinois. See also Soda Fountain Collectibles.

Bottle carrier, cb, P=C Bigger/Better, 6 12-oz/25¢, NM+ 30.00
Bottle carrier, wood, 6-pack, triangular w/cut-out hdl, 1930s, EX+..150.00
Bottle carrier, 6-pk, metal w/P-C oval on bl stripes, 8x8x5", VG..50.00
Bottle topper, Pepsi & Pete, I Make Sure..., 1930s, 14x12", EX+.625.00
Calendar, 1943, Famous American Paintings, complete, 23", VG .50.00
Can, cone top, P=C bottle cap/2 Full Glasses, 1940s, VG+........425.00
Clock, molded plastic, light-up, Drink.../cap above clock, 19x14", VG..100.00
Clock, P=C red/wht/bl rnd logo, light-up, Telechron, 15" dia, EX+ .325.00
Clock, Say Pepsi Please/bottle cap, dbl-bubble light-up, 15" dia, EX..550.00
Menu board, plastic light-up, modern logo/menu slots, 21x54x8", G.25.00
Menu board, sf tin chalkboard, modern logo, med bl trim, 1976, 27", G.30.00
Radio, plastic bottle form, P=C oval logo, 23", EX.....................400.00
Radio, plastic dispenser w/leather strap, Say Pepsi Please, EX.....175.00
Sign, bottle, dc emb tin, P=C oval logo, 30", EX 225.00
Sign, bottle cap, dc emb tin, P=C logo, red/wht/bl, 14", EX+.....350.00
Sign, paper, Listen to Country-Spy..., 8x19", NM+ 85.00
Sign, porc, Enjoy a Pepsi on wht light beam/cap on yel, 12x29", VG..230.00
Sign, tin, Enjoy...Five Cents flank cap on med bl, 1940s, 10x26", EX+..400.00
Thermometer, tin, modern logo above/below on wht, lg numbers, 28", VG.30.00
Toy dispenser, plastic P-C logo on wht, 10", EXIB.........................85.00
Tray, Enjoy P=C/Hits the Spot, 10x14", EX 90.00

Perfection Cigarettes, sign, stone litho, bust of lady, fr, 31x24", VG.700.00
Peter Pan Fresh Bread, broom holder, stenciled tin, EX+............350.00
Phillip Morris, fs, Buy 'Em Here!/Call For.../Johnny w/pk, 12x14", NM.330.00
Pickwick Coffee, mask, cb, Mr Pickwick face, 1930s, NM+..........65.00
Pinocchio Chewing Gum, cb box, graphics on bl, 1940, 2x6x8", VG+ .325.00

Planters Peanuts

The Planters Peanut Co. was founded in 1906. Mr. Peanut, the dashing peanut man with top hat, spats, monocle, and cane, has represented Planters since 1916. He took on his modern-day appearance after the company was purchased by Standard Brands in November 1960. He remains perhaps the most highly recognized logo of any company in the world. Mr. Peanut has promoted the company's products by appearing in ads; on product packaging; on or as store displays, novelties, and premiums; and even in character at promotional events (thanks to a special Mr. Peanut costume).

Among the favorite items of collectors today are the glass display jars which were sent to retailers nationwide to stimulate 'point-of-sale' trade. They come in a variety of shapes and styles. The first, distributed in the early 1920s, was a large universal candy jar (round covered bowl on a pedestal) with only a narrow paper label affixed at the neck to identify it as 'Planters.' In 1924 an octagonal jar was produced, all eight sides embossed, with Mr. Peanut on the narrow corner panels. On a second octagon jar, only seven sides were embossed, leaving one of the large panels blank to accommodate a paper label.

In late 1929 a fishbowl jar was introduced, and in 1932 a beautiful jar with a blown-out peanut on each of the four corners was issued. The football shape was also made in the 1930s, as were the square jar, the large barrel jar, and the hexagon jar with yellow fired-on designs alternating on each of the six sides. All of these early jars had glass lids which after 1930 had peanut finials.

In 1937 jars with lithographed tin lids were introduced. The first of these was the slant-front streamline jar, which is also found with screened yellow lettering. Next was a squat version, the clipper jar, then the upright rectangular 1940 leap year jar, and last, another upright rectangular jar with a screened, fired-on design similar to the red, white, and blue design on the cellophane 5¢ bags of peanuts of the period. This last jar was issued again after WWII with a plain red tin lid.

In 1959 Planters first used a stock Anchor Hocking one-gallon round jar with a 'customer-special' decoration in red. As the design was not plainly evident when the jar was full, the decoration was modified with a white under-panel. The two jars we've just described are perhaps the rarest of them all due to their limited production. After Standard Brands purchased Planters, they changed the red-on-white panel to show their more modern Mr. Peanut and in 1963 introduced this most plentiful, thus very common, Planters jar. In 1966 the last counter display jar was distributed: the Anchor Hocking jar with a fired-on large four-color design such as that which appeared on peanut bags of the period. Prior to this, a plain jar with a transfer decal in an almost identical but smaller design was used.

Some Planters jars have been reproduced: the octagon jar (with only six of the sides embossed), a small version of the barrel jar, and the four peanut corner jar. Some of the first were made in clear glass with 'Made in Italy' embossed on the bottom, but most have been made in Asia, many in various colors of glass (a dead giveaway) as well as clear, and carrying only small paper stickers, easily removed, identifying the country of origin. At least two reproductions of the Anchor Hocking jar with a four-color design have been made, one circa 1978, the other in 1989. Both, using the stock jar, are difficult to detect, but there are small differences between them and the original that will enable you to make an accurate identification. With the exception of several of the earliest and the Anchor Hocking, all authentic Planters jars have 'Made in USA' embossed on the bottom, and all, without exception, are clear glass. Unfortunately, several paper labels have also been reproduced, no doubt due to the fact that an original label or decal will greatly increase the value of an original jar. Jar prices continue to remain stable in today's market.

In the late 1920s, the first premiums were introduced in the form of story and paint books. Late in the 1930s, the tin nut set (which was still available into the 1960s) was distributed. A wood-jointed doll was available from Planters Peanuts stores at that time. Many post-WWII items were made of plastic: banks, salt and pepper shakers, cups, cookie cutters, small cars and trucks, charms, whistles, various pens and mechanical pencils, and almost any other item imaginable. Since 1981 the company, as a division of Nabisco (NGH) has continued to distribute a wide variety of novelties. In late 2000 NGH was sold to Philip Morris Cos. and Nabisco was combined with its Kraft Foods unit. With the increased popularity of Mr. Peanut memorabilia, more items surface, and the value of common items decrease.

Note that there are many unauthorized Planters/Mr. Peanut items. Although several are reproductions or 'copycats,' most are fantasy items and fakes. Our advisors for Planters Planters are Judith and Robert Walthall; they are in the Directory under Alabama.

Key:
al — aluminum	pfl — peanut finial lid
cc — common colors	pl — plastic
(green, light blue, red, tan)	pm — papier-mache
MrP — Mr. Peanut	pnut — peanut
okl — octagon knob lid	shp — shipping

Box, cb, ...The Peanut Store, MrP graphics, 3-lb, 10x6x6", EX+ ..50.00
Cookie cutter, red pl MrP figure bowing or tipping hat, EX 20.00

Costume, plastic, white embossed letters on black hat (two needing restoration), cane included, 47x18" diameter, EX, $300.00.

Display, dc cb, lady seated holding 5¢ Salted Peanuts pack, 26", NM..900.00
Display box, cb, 24 5¢ Bags, 1950s, 3x6x5", M 60.00
Doll, MrP, jtd wood w/pnt features, 8½", VG+ 150.00
Doll, stuffed cloth, Chase Bag Co, 1967, 21", EX 30.00
Doll, stuffed cloth, Chase Bag Co, 1970, 18", NM 25.00
Jar, Barrel, pfl, paper label, 1935, 12¼", EX................................250.00
Jar, Fishbowl, okl, no label, 1929, 12½", EX 75.00
Jar, Fishbowl, okl, Planters on base, orig label, 12½", VG, $150 to .175.00
Jar, Football, pfl, 1931, 8½", EX 225.00
Jar, Four Peanut Corner, pfl, 1932, 14" (+) 225.00
Jar, Hexagon, Planters/MrP in yel on 3 panels, 8" dia, VG 100.00
Jar, Octagon, 6 sides emb, pfl, clear & colors, repro.....................35.00
Jar, Octagon, 7 sides emb, okl, no label, 12", EX 85.00
Jar, Octagon, 8 sides emb, okl, 1924, 12", EX 250.00
Pedal car, pl, yel w/bl ad stripe, Kingsbury Toys, 41", VG.............75.00
Salad fork & spoon set, wood w/ceramic figural hdls, MIB 135.00
Shakers, MrP, bent knee, pk pl, 1960s, 3", MIP 18.00
Shakers, MrP, str legs, gr pl, 1950s, 4", NMIB..............................35.00
Whistle, pl MrP figure, common, 2½", EX 5.00

Popsicle, ts, Everybody Likes...Refreshing-Easy To Eat, 12x36", NM..525.00
Portner Brewing Co, match holder, bottle form, litho tin, 7", VG+ .550.00
Post Toasties, display box, hearth scene, ca 1907, 20x14x5", EX+..360.00
Post Toasties, sign, cb, Sweet Memories, fr, c 1909, 24x17", G...425.00
Pulver's Chocolate/Cocoa/Gum One Cent, dispenser, tin/glass, 24", EX ..12,500.00
Pulver's Kola Pepsin Chewing Gum 5¢, gum tc, 2-pc, 1x3x½", VG+..450.00
Quaker Maid Milk, ps, dc emblem w/graphics, bl/wht on red, 24x41", EX+..575.00

RCA Victor

Nipper, the RCA Victor trademark, was the creation of Francis Barraud, an English artist. His pet's intense fascination with the music of the phonograph seemed to him a worthy subject for his canvas. Although he failed to find a publishing house who would buy his work, the Gramophone Co. in England saw its potential and adopted Nipper to advertise their product. The painting was later acquired and trademarked in the United States by the Victor Talking Machine Co., which was purchased by RCA in 1929. The trademark is owned today by EMI in England and by General Electric in the U.S. Nipper's image appeared on packages, accessories, ads, brochures, and in three-dimensional form. You may find a life-size statue of him, but all are not old. They have been manufactured for the owner throughout RCA history and are marketed currently by licensees, BMG Inc. and Thomson Consumer Electronics (dba RCA). Except for the years between 1968 and 1976, Nipper has seen active duty, and with his image spruced up only a bit for the present day, the ageless symbol for RCA still listens intently to 'His Master's Voice.' Many of the items have been reproduced in recent years. Exercise care before you buy.

The recent phenomenon of Internet auctions has played havoc with prices paid for Victor and RCA Victor collectibles. Often prices paid for online sales bear little resemblance to the true value of the item. Reproductions are often sold as old on the Internet and bring prices accordingly. It is common knowledge that auction prices, more often than not, are inflated over sales made through traditional sales outlets. The Internet has exacerbated the situation by focusing a very large number of buyers and sellers through the narrow portal of a modem. The prices here are intended to reflect what one might expect to pay through traditional sales.

Items marked (+) are often reproduced and care should be taken to ascertain age or provenance. Our advisor for RCA Victor is Roger R. Scott; he is listed in the Directory under Oklahoma.

Bank, flocked metal, 9" 125.00
Buckle, His Master's Voice, brass, Nash Tiffany London...............25.00
Chair, NP pipe fr w/armrest, plastic bk/seat, logo on bk, M 100.00
Chair, RCA dealer's, vinyl & chrome 125.00
Clock, PAM, RCA Records, w/Nipper...500.00
Clock, RCA Victor, Spinner..500.00
Curtains, RCA 40.00
Figure, Nipper, chalkware, Victor, 4"..40.00
Figure, Nipper, chalkware, 8", EX..60.00
Figure, Nipper, crystal, Fenton, 4"..50.00
Figure, Nipper, papier-mache, rpt, 32".......................................525.00
Figure, Nipper, papier-mache, 11"..50.00
Figure, Nipper, papier-mache, 18"..350.00
Figure, Nipper, papier-mache, 36"..600.00
Figure, Nipper, plaster, Visco..100.00
Figure, Nipper, plaster, 14½x7½x5", VG (+)...............................200.00
Figure, Nipper, plastic, 36", EX...235.00
Figure, Radio Man, jtd wood, Maxfield Parrish, M.......................900.00
Pin dish, German...50.00
Pin dish, Nippon 125.00
Pin-bk button, Little Nipper 40.00
Plate, Nipper, collector's edition 50.00
Pocket watch, old...400.00
Puzzle record, Victor, MIP...100.00
Record brush, leather bk 40.00
Record display, dog & phonograph, chalkware (+)........................150.00
Shakers, dog & RCA phonograph, plastic, pr 45.00
Sign, canvas, His Master's Voice, 26x19" 1,500.00
Sign, neon, letters on metal fr, 14x40" 125.00
Sign, plastic/metal, ...Radio, light-up, 1940s, 15x37", EX............180.00
Sign, porc, record shape w/trademk image on red label, 24", VG..300.00
Smoker's set, Nipper, old...500.00
Snow globe..50.00
Stick pin, Victor, celluloid 125.00
Watch fob, EX...30.00
Water glass, etched Nipper, set of 6..100.00

Rainbo Bread, door push bar, steel oval on T-bar, 9x27", NM+ ..200.00
Rawleigh's Talcum & Baby Powder, tc, hexagonal, wht, 5", EX..240.00
Red Crown Gasoline/Polarine, thermometer, porc, red/wht/blk, 73", VG..1,500.00

Red Goose Shoes

Realizing that his last name was difficult to pronounce, Herman Giesecke, a shoe company owner resolved to give the public a modified, shortened version that would be better suited to the business world. The results suggested the use of the goose trademark with the last two letters, 'ke,' represented by the key that this early goose held in his mouth. Upon observing an employee casually coloring in the goose trademark with a red pencil, Giesecke saw new advertising potential and renamed the company Red Goose Shoes. Although the company has changed hands down through the years, the Red Goose emblem has remained. Collectors of this desirable fowl increase in number yearly, as do prices. Beware of reproductions; new chalkware figures are prevalent.

Clock, light-up, glass/metal, Pam, 1954, 15" dia, NM+ 550.00
Display figure, plaster, red, 12x9", EX...275.00
Glider, red paper goose, 9", NM..10.00
Pull toy, elephant, wood, 4x3½", VG...100.00
Sign, cb stand-up, goose, 10x6", NM..20.00

Sign, neon, 24", EX, $1,320.00. (Photo courtesy Buffalo Bay Auction Co.)

Sign, neon goose on wht oval, 1930s-40s, 24x12", NM+.........1,900.00
Sign, porc, Red Goose Shoes on chest of goose, yel ground, 17x12", VG.165.00
Sign, tin, ...For Boys & Girls, yel/red, 13x19", EX 125.00

Red Indian Cut Plug Tobacco, lunch pail, blk on red, 4x8x5", VG+.1,150.00
Regalia Cigars, ts, full box on table, period gold fr, 16x12", EX ..175.00
Remington/Du Pont/Time Cutlery, clock, emb tin over wood, 24x18", EX.80.00
Richard Mansfield Cigars, tc, oval portrait on woodgrain, 6" dia, EX+ ..75.00
Rienzi Beer/Bartholomay Brewery, tip tray, horse/rider, 4" dia, EX+.300.00
Schrafft's Candy, tin pail, Old Woman in Shoe graphics, 4x4" dia, EX+ .925.00
Schrafft's Chocolates, display shelf, dc lady w/sign, rstr, 30" 700.00
Schrafft's Kiddyland Candys, tc, mc graphics, 1920s, 5x3" dia, EX+.625.00

Seven-Up

The Howdy Company of St. Louis, Missouri, was founded in 1920 by Charles L. Grigg. His first creation was an orange drink called Howdy. In the late 1920s Howdy's popularity began to wane, so in 1929 Grigg invented a lemon-lime soda called Seven-Up as an alternative to colas. Grigg's Seven-Up became a widely accepted favorite. Our advisor for this category is Craig Stifter; he is listed in the Directory under Illinois.

See also Soda Fountain Collectibles.

Bill hook, celluloid button, I'd Hang for a Chilled 7-Up, EX+ 35.00
Broom stand, 2-legged rack w/sign, 1940s, 28x20", EX+ 700.00
Clock, light-up, plastic w/wood fr, You Like It..., 15" sq, NM 100.00
Lamp, 28-oz bottle on trn wood base, sq logos on shade, 23", EX .100.00

Money clip, enameled dollar symbol w/logo, M 30.00
Sign, cb, We're a Fresh Up Family!, w/graphics, 1948, 11x21", NM.65.00
Sign, cb hanger, Season's Greetings, 3-D, w/bottle, 2-sided, EX+ .50.00
Sign, flange, tin, sq logo on, 2-sided, dtd 9-47, 10x13", EX+ 225.00
Sign, porc, Fresh Up w/7-Up, rnd corners, 20x28", NM.............475.00
Sign, tin, Fresh Up/bottle/All Family Drink on wht, gr trim, 17x6", NM .200.00
Sign, tin, Fresh Up/logo on gr/wht vertical stripes, 1958, 11x23", VG..200.00
Sign, tin, Fresh Up/sq logo on gr/wht panel, dtd 10-60, 13x7", NM.75.00
Sign, tin, sq logo/First Against Thirst on wht, gr trim, 20x28", G .40.00
Sign, tin bottle form, emb, dtd 7-62, NM+ 375.00
Thermometer, dial, Fresh Clean Taste, gr/wht stripes, 10" dia, EX+ .150.00
Thermometer, dial, 7-Up Likes You rnd logo, 10" dia, NM.........230.00
Thermometer, porc, curved ends, Bubble Girl bottle on wht, 15x6", EX.150.00
Thermometer, porc, curved ends, Fresh Up/bottle on wht, 15x6", M.180.00

Sex-ine Pills, match holder, litho tin, 2 men, early 1900s, 9x5", EX.800.00
Sharples, match holder, tin, The Pet of the Dairy, 7x2", NM+ ...750.00
Sharples Separator Co, ts, milkmaid & girl, woodgrain sf, 39x28", VG+.2,250.00
Skookum Syrup, tc, teepee form, 12-oz, VG+ 450.00
Snow Boy Washing Powder, poster, boy/sled, Knapp, 1898, 40x27", EX.3,300.00
Solace Tobacco, sign, litho on paper, lady on ladder, ca 1884, 29", EX.750.00
Soul Kiss Toilet Requisites, cb gift box w/4 containers, 3x3x1", EX.675.00
Sparrow Choclates, tip tray, girl standing on chair, EX 400.00
Spic-N-Span, tc, wht/wht/bl w/dog graphics, pry lid, 5", EX.......200.00
Squirrel Brand Peanut Bars, cb box, graphics on yel, 2-pc, 3x6x10", EX.350.00
Squirt, clock, light-up, boy/bottle, Telechron, 1946, 15" dia, NM.625.00
Squirt, clock, light-up, Switch to..., Pam, 15" dia, EX+ 375.00
Squirt, fs, Drink...It's Tart Sweet, flag on yel, dtd 1941, 14x18", EX .350.00
Squirt, menu board, tin chalkboard, Switch to..logo, 1950, 28", EX.150.00
St Bruno/Imperial Tobacco, 3-D cb stand-up, Blk field workers, fr, EX.700.00
Star Soap, sign, litho on paper, baby graphics, wood fr, 15x22", EX.520.00
Stephenson Union Suits, pocket mirror, trapeze act on yel, oval, EX.400.00
Stollwerck Gold Brand Chocolate ..., ts, dc stand-up, 1907, 96", EX.1,375.00
Studebaker Buggies, poster, buggy/options, 1912, 25x19", EX 220.00
Stuyler's Pepsin Gum, tc w/paper label, heart shape, sample, VG+ .25.00
Sunbeam Bread, door push bar, dc tin load on bl bar, 9x27", EX+ .350.00
Sunbeam Bread, sign, dc cb stand-up, Miss Sunbeam w/real loaf, 50", EX..200.00
Sunbeam Bread, ts, Reach for...Energy-Packed Bread/girl, 1953, 55", NM..1,200.00
Superba Shoe Polish, wisk broom holder, litho tin, cat graphics, VG+.575.00
Surbrugs Tobacco, pocket mirror, nude in tobacco leaves, 3x2", EX.825.00
Sure Shot Tobacco, store bin, rectangular w/Indian graphics, EX.1,300.00
Swansdown Coffee, tc, yel w/red lettering, oval graphics, 2-lb, VG+ .300.00
Sweet Briar Graham Flour, cb canister w/paper label, 7x4" dia, VG+.250.00
Sweet Loma Fine Cut, store bin, rnd w/sq slip lid, red, 10x9" dia, EX.2,100.00
Sweet-Orr Pants/Shirts/Overalls, ps, tug-of-war logo, 29x73", VG .450.00
Taka-Kola, tip tray, girl/clock face, 4" dia, EX..............................245.00
Tanlac Tonic, display, cb, 3-panel, multiple scenes, 33x51", VG .450.00
Taxi Crimp Cut Tobacco, pocket tin, vertical, flip lid, EX+ 4,800.00
Temple Bar Reddy Rubbed Tobacco, pocket tin, dbl concave, 4", VG+ ..600.00
Texaco, banner, Texaco Presents, Eddie Cantor..., 35x56", G+ 60.00
Three Feathers Plug Cut, pocket tin, vertical, VG+ 200.00
Tucketts Cigars, display case, metal w/glass slant front, 21", VG...160.00
Turkish Dyes, cabinet, wood/cb front, stenciled marquee, 28", EX.360.00
Uncle Sam Smoking Tobacco, pocket tin, red/wht/bl on bl, vertical, VG+.3,400.00
United States Tires, watch fob/pocket mirror, tire form, VG+ 500.00
Vaseline, ledger marker, litho tin, blk on red, 12½x3", VG+ 225.00
Velvet Pipe Tobacco, ps, pocket tin/wht lettering on bl, 12x39", EX .685.00
Venus Drawing Pencils, display case w/marquee, wood, 1920s, 10x10", EX.550.00
Vess Billion Bubble Beverages, clock, metal & glass, 16" dia, EX ...425.00
Wamphum Coffee, tc, bl w/Indian maiden graphics, 3-lb, VG+ .250.00
Ward's Cakes, display case, litho tin, 1920s, 21x17x13", VG+ .2,500.00
Waterman's Ideal Fountain Pen, festoon, dc cb, Xmas wreath/2 swags, VG.160.00

Westinghouse Mazda Lamps, sign, dc cb stand-up, reminder ad, 16", EX ..100.00
Whistle Soda, ts, emb, elf w/bottle on push cart, 30x26", EX (NOS) ..400.00
White Rock Sparkling Beverages, fs, fairy on wht oval, 17x20", EX .100.00
Wilson's Certified Brand Peanut Butter, tin pail, pry lid, 11-oz, EX+ .425.00
Wm Haslage & Co Grocery & Tea Dealers, salt-glaze crock, 1890, 17", EX..750.00
Wonder Mocha & Java, ts, girl, Kaufmann & Strauss, 1890, rstr, 7x14"..325.00
Wrigley's Chewing Gum 5¢, dispenser, metal, 28x4x5", EX 175.00
Wrigley's PK Chewing Sweet, decal sign, Wrigley's kid, 1920s, 11", EX.450.00
Wrigley's Spearmint, sign, dc cb, boy/girl in swing, 14x11", EX ..950.00
Yucatan Gum, display tc, hinged lid, yel w/HD Beach litho, sq, EX.280.00
Yuengling's Beer, tip tray, girl in bonnet, Shonk litho, 4" dia, EX.350.00
Zimmerman Mfg Co True Blue Vehicles, pocket mirror, rnd, EX.450.00

Advertising Cards

Advertising trade cards enjoyed great popularity during the last quarter of the nineteenth century when the chromolithography printing process was refined and put into common use. The purpose of the trade card was to acquaint the public with a business, product, service, or event. Most trade cards range in size from 2" x 3" to 4" x 6"; however, many are found in both smaller and larger sizes.

There are two classifications of trade cards: 'private design' and 'stock.' Private design cards were used by a single company or individual; the images on the cards were designed for only that company. Stock cards were generics that any individual or company could purchase from a printer's inventory. These cards usually had a blank space on the front for the company to overprint with their own name and product information.

Four categories of particular interest to collectors are:

Mechanical — a card which achieves movement through the use of a pull tab, fold-out side, or movable part.

Hold-to-light — a card that reveals its design only when viewed before a strong light.

Diecut — a card in the form of something like a box, a piece of clothing, etc.

Metamorphic — a card that by folding down a flap shows a transformed image, such as a white beard turning black after use of a product.

For a more thorough study of the subject, we recommend *Reflections 1* and *Reflections 2* by Kit Barry; his address can be found in the Directory under Vermont. *Victorian Trade Cards* by Dave Cheadle (Collector Books) is another fine reference. Values are given for cards in near-mint condition.

A No 1 Chocolate Tablets, girl drinking product 35.00
Adams' Gum, hands w/playing cards, Which Wins? 40.00
AMC cereals, woman ordering product over telephone 20.00
American Ball Blue, circus man on ball, man w/whip, clown 25.00
American Rubber Co, Danbury Fair 1890, girl on box 35.00

Ayer's Cherry Pectoral, two small children hug large bottle of product, J. C. Ayer & Co., Lowell, MA, 4½x2¼", EX+, $40.00. (Photo courtesy Early American History Auctions)

Beeman's Pepsin gum, girl 'Playing Grandma' knitting on box 25.00
Bissell Sweeper, Christmas 1890 model, product in center...........25.00
Bixby's Best Blacking, man in suit, boy shining shoes, dog..........35.00
Bixby's Best Blacking, 2 boys shining king's shoes 35.00
Bixby's French Blueing, 2 women doing laundry..........................15.00
Bixby's Royal Polish, mother sending children to school.............35.00
Cat nursing kittens, food bowl, yarn ball, broom 10.00
Charter Oak Lawn Mower, 1 woman mowing, 1 in chair.............40.00
Chase & Sanborn, woman reading tea leaves, 2 girls watching.....40.00
Chesebrough Co, Egyptian Obelisk in Central Park, NY 6.00
Comstock's Worm Medicine, race horse & jockey, Maud...........25.00
Comstock's Worm Medicine, race horse & jockey, Sleepy Tom 25.00
Conkey's Poultry Remedies, chicken w/bandage 35.00
Cottolene, person wearing cap & gown, product, books..............25.00
Crown Sewing Machines, women in kitchen, children, croquet ...20.00
Dog w/puppies, 3 dogs standing, farm scene 8.00
Dr Buckland's Scotch Oats Essence, girl in grain field.................12.00
Eagle Condensed Milk, US cruiser ship Vesuvius 20.00
Eclectric Oil, cat in product box holding bottle...........................7.00
Edison Phonograph, boy w/product & hatchet............................70.00
Flagg's Animal Food, Chinese flag, boy feeding chicken 15.00
Garland Stoves, pinwheel toy 40.00
Gem Ice Cream Freezer, girl feeding product to doll....................35.00
Granite Ironware, 2 women w/product 25.00
Haas' Veterinary Medicine, children playing w/grandpa..............35.00
Heinz, girl carrying products, wearing paper hat 40.00
Highland Evaporated Cream, children w/doll, The Little Doctor.35.00
Hodges' Bleachery, cherubs cleaning hats in machine 35.00
Imperial Granum Infant Food, children, crest in center..............40.00
Indian Queen Perfume, Am Indian woman w/flowers 25.00
Ivorine Cleaner, monkeys cleaning elephant, Egypt 25.00
Judson's Pills, soldiers in armour w/shield, arrows 35.00
Kermott's Mandrake Pills, 2 men in boat, lg letter K 35.00
Kickapoo Indian Medicine, Am Indian children on horses...........40.00
Kickapoo Indian Medicine, 2 Am Indian women 40.00
Knockabout Club Books, camping scenes...................................25.00
Loyal Soap, Columbia holding product, eagle, boxes 25.00
M&L Adamant Varnishes, 4 boys w/products & brush.................50.00
Maddock & Sons Dinnerware, 2 examples of product 55.00
Magnolia Balm, 5 women, 1 man holding product, on ship 40.00
Mathes & Co, blk cat w/bow-tie diecut.......................................25.00
Midland Coffee, girl holding product & petting dog 35.00
Mrs Dinsmore Cough Cure, image of woman on front & bk.........15.00
New Process Soap, woman w/fan & book....................................8.00
Nicholson's Liquid Bread, nun serving crusader 40.00
Parker's Tonic, 2 men at table, 1 healthy w/product, 1 sick 8.00
Patent Steam Dish Washer, woman w/fan in kitchen...................75.00
Peninsular Stove, mechanical, images of products on stage 135.00
Prickly Ash Bitters, girl sitting on tree branch 20.00
Punch & Judy Mechanical Bank, image of product 485.00
Puzzle card, Dr Bosanko's medicine, man in boat.......................25.00
Quaker Oats, Quaker w/product box and 'Pure' scroll 45.00
Quaker Oats, woman w/box standing on rocks in water..............30.00
Rice's Seeds, couple in bed, plant growing into window...............25.00
Ridge's Food, baby drinking from bottle w/product name............15.00
Runkel Bros Cocoa, girl in flower w/product, Morning Glories 35.00
Sanford's Ginger, Black children w/watermelons 30.00
Scott Adie Ltd Tailors, image of store, plaid bkground................40.00
Shoninger Organ Co, man playing organ, 1 woman, cherubs 30.00
Spanish Blueing, children playing on street 12.00
Spanish Blueing, girl knocking over dinner table 12.00
Spanish Blueing, man w/product, boy on street 12.00
Sparks' Medicine, free sample bottle, image of Mr Sparks............40.00
Speaking Dog Mechanical Bank, image of product 300.00

Splendid Tobacco, US weather signal flags 40.00
Swift & Co Lard, schoolroom w/pigs as teacher & pupils..............40.00
Taylor's Cherokee Remedy, girl w/box, plant, dog & umbrella 50.00
Vanity Fair Tobacco, 5 scenes w/anthropomorphic frogs 65.00
Walter Baker Drinking Chocolate, woman serving product........165.00
Yosemite Valley scene, Jay Smith druggist 35.00

Advertising Dolls and Figures

Whether your interest in ad dolls is fueled by nostalgia or strictly because of their amusing, often clever advertising impact, there are several points that should be considered before making your purchases. Condition is of utmost importance; never pay book price for dolls in poor condition, whether they are cloth or of another material. Restoring fabric dolls is usually unsatisfactory and involves a good deal of work. Seams must be opened, stuffing removed, the doll washed and dried, and then reassembled. Washing old fabrics may prove to be disastrous. Colors may fade or run, and most stains are totally resistant to washing. It's usually best to leave the fabric doll as it is.

Watch for new dolls as they become available. Save related advertising literature, extra coupons, etc., and keep these along with the doll to further enhance your collection. Old dolls with no marks are sometimes challenging to identify. While some products may use the same familiar trademark figures for a number of years (the Jolly Green Giant, Pillsbury's Poppin' Fresh, and the Keebler Elf, for example) others appear on the market for a short time only and may be difficult to trace. Most libraries have reference books with trademarks and logos that might provide a clue in tracking down your doll's identity. Children see advertising figures on Saturday morning cartoons that are often unfamiliar to adults, or other ad doll collectors may have the information you seek.

Some advertising dolls are still easy to find and relatively inexpensive, ranging in cost from $1.00 to $100.00. The hard plastic and early composition dolls are bringing the higher prices. Advertising dolls are popular with children as well as adults. For a more thorough study of the subject, we recommend *Advertising Dolls With Values* by Myra Yellin Outwater (Schiffer). When no condition is noted, values apply to dolls in excellent condition; so to evaluate your doll, you may have to adjust your prices up or down. Just be sure to discount prices for soil, missing parts, wear, or damage of any type.

American Airline Stewardess, Am Character, Am Airlines, 1967, 12" .10.00
Andy Capp, foam rubber, Concorde Confections, ca 1972, 6½"...10.00
Aunt Sarah, printed stuffed cloth, Aunt Sarah's Pancake House, 1973 ..8.00
Benjamin Franklin, printed stuffed cloth, B Franklin Savings & Loan..7.00
Betty Crocker, cloth w/suede hair/yarn ponytails, General Mills, 13".25.00
Billy, litho stuffed cloth, McIntosh Country Apples, 1969, 16½" ...8.00
Bonnie Breck, vinyl, Hong Kong, Breck Co, 1972, 9" 12.00
Buster Brown, litho cloth, Buster Brown Shoes, 13" 75.00
Campbell Kid, compo, Horsman, Campbell Soup Co, 1947, 12½"..175.00
Cap'n Crunch, litho stuffed cloth, Quaker Oats, 1978, 15½" 8.00
Caravelle Candy Bar, plastic, poseable limbs, Peter-Paul, 10" 7.00
Chester Cheeta, Cheetos, 18", NM 20.00
Chore Girl, litho stuffed cloth, Chore Girl, 1970s, 16" 10.00
Cozy Glo Kid, compo, nude w/towel, Westinghouse, 12½".........200.00
Drooper, litho stuffed cloth, Kellogg's, 1969, 12" 6.00
Fisk Boy, bsk, 2-pc sewn-on pajamas, missing tire & candle, 4" ..150.00
Fluffy Lamb, plush, Del Monte, 1984 ....20.00
Fresca Dog, plush, Coca-Cola, ca 1970, 18" 10.00
George Washington, litho stuffed cloth, Gillette, 1974, 15" 6.00
Great Root Bear, brn fabric/orange jacket, A&W Root Beer, 13" ...5.00
Icee Bear, bank, vinyl figure, 1970s, 8", VG 20.00
Jumbo Elephant, stuffed print cloth, Jumbo Peanut Butter, 16", EX+.525.00
La Belle Chocolatier, china pincushion type, Baker's Chocolate .300.00

Little Oscar, inflatable vinyl, Oscar Mayer, 29" 4.00
Lushie Peach, plush, Del Monte, 1982 ....20.00
Maisy, stuffed cloth, removable jumper, Georgia-Pacific, 1966, 18"..10.00
Marky Maypo, vinyl, Maypo Cereal, 1980, 10" 12.00
Merry, litho on cloth, uncut, Birds Eye Frozen Foods, 1953, 11"..15.00
Miss Curity, vinyl, Ideal, Kendall Corp, 1949, 14" 75.00
Miss Revlon, vinyl, Ideal, Revlon Inc, 1956, 18" 50.00
Mr Bib, plastic, hands on hips/chest banner, Michelin, 1981, 12", NM....65.00
Mr Clean, wht-pnt vinyl, Proctor & Gamble, 1961, 8" 85.00
Mr Kool Penguin, plastic, electric, Kool Cigarettes, 9" 325.00
Munchkin, inflatable vinyl, Dunkin Donuts, 1976, 24" 10.00
Play Doh Boy, litho stuffed cloth, Play Doh, 1969 ....10.00
Poppin' Fresh, rubber, Pillsbury, 1971, 7", NM..........................20.00
Radio Man, jtd wood/compo majorette figure, GE, 1930s, 19", EX+ ...920.00
Reddie Tomato, plush, Del Monte, 1982 ....20.00
Scotsman, compo, traditional costume, Highland Mist Whiskey, 28" ...125.00
Shake Hans, vinyl, poseable limbs, Jack-in-the-Box 3.00
Shakey Chef, litho stuffed cloth, Shakey's Pizza Restaurant, 18".....8.00
Smokey Bear, vinyl, Dakin, Aim Toothpaste, 8" 15.00

South African Boy, printed cloth bag, Sea Island Sugar, Gobo, copyright 1935, 15x9¾", $150.00.
(Photo courtesy P.J. Gibbs)

Speedy, vinyl, red/wht/bl, Alka Seltzer, 5½" 110.00
Tastykake Baker, litho stuffed cloth, Tastykake Bakeries, 1974, 13"...8.00
Tropic-Ana, litho stuffed cloth, Tropicana, 1977, 17", NM..........25.00
Uncle Mose, litho on cloth, uncut, Aunt Jemima Mills Co, 15"...50.00

Agata

Agata is New England peachblow (the factory called it 'Wild Rose') with an applied metallic stain which produces gold tracery and dark blue mottling. The stain is subject to wear, and the amount of remaining stain greatly affects the value. It is especially valuable (and rare) on satin-finish items when found on peachblow of intense color. Caution! Be sure to use only gentle cleaning methods.

Currently rare types of art glass have been realizing erratic prices at auction; until they stabilize, we can only suggest an average range of values. In the listings that follow, examples are glossy unless noted otherwise. A condition rating of 'EX' indicates that the stain shows a moderate amount of wear. Our advisors for this category are Betty and Clarence Maier; they are listed in the Directory under Pennsylvania.

See also Green Opaque.

Bowl, sauce; G color & mottling 350.00
Cruet, some wear to stain, 6" 865.00
Finger bowl, EX stain & color, ruffled, 5¼" 460.00
Pitcher, reeded hdl, water sz 2,500.00
Punch cup, EX bl & amber stain, pk hdl, 2½", from $400 to......650.00
Tumbler, lemonade; M staining, 5"...2,000.00
Tumbler, lemonade: EX stain 1,750.00
Vase, lily; EX mottling, 7¾"...850.00
Vase, lily; wear to stain, 9" 435.00
Vase, satin, EX stain, waisted neck, 3½" 2,185.00

Agate Ware

Clays of various natural or artificially dyed colors combined to produce agate ware, a procedure similar to the methods used by Niloak in potting their Mission Ware. It was made by many Staffordshire potteries from about 1740 until about 1825.

Bowl, cream, brown, and rust, scalloped rim, mid-eighteenth century, 5¾", NM, $1,600.00; Mug, rust and cream, ca 1750, 3", $1,100.00; Spoon tray, shaped rim with flared sides, ca 1750, minor restoration, 5½", $635.00.

Fork, steel tines, Staffordshire, 1760s, rpr, 7" 230.00
Teapot, bl & brn to cream, 1760s, 3¾", NM 925.00
Teapot, brn & rust to cream, globular, mid-1700s, rstr, 4¾"........500.00
Teapot, globular, 3-paw ft, arched hdl, stick spout, 4⅝x6¾", VG...220.00
Vase, scroll hdls w/goat masks at shoulders, festoons, 18th C, 15" ...1,375.00

Akro Agate

The Akro Agate Company operated in West Virginia from 1914 until 1951, and in addition to their famous marbles they made children's dishes, powder jars with Scottie dogs on top, candlesticks, and ashtrays, for instance — in many colors and patterns. Though some of their glassware was made in solid colors, their most popular products were made of the same swirled colors as their marbles. Though many pieces are not marked, you will find some that are marked with their distinctive logo: a crow flying through the letter 'A' holding an Aggie in its beak and one in each claw. Some novelty items may instead carry one of these trademarks: 'J.V. Co., Inc.,' 'Braun & Corwin,' 'N.Y.C. Vogue Merc Co. U.S.A.,' 'Hamilton Match Co.,' and 'Mexicali Pickwick Cosmetic Corp.'

Color is a very important worth-assessing factor. Some pieces may be common in one color but rare in others. Occasionally an item will have exceptionally good colors, and this would make it more valuable than an example with only average color. When buying either marbles or juvenile tea sets in original boxes, be sure the box contains its original contents.

Note: Recently unearthed original written information has discounted the generally accepted attribution of the Chiquita and J.P. patterns to the Akro company, proving instead that they were made by the Alley Agate Company.

For more information we recommend *The Complete Line of the Akro Agate Co.* by our advisors, Roger and Claudia Hardy (available from them); they are listed in the Directory under West Virginia. Our advisor for miscellaneous Akro Agate is Albert Morin, who is in the Directory under Massachusetts.

Concentric Rib

Creamer, yel or med bl, 1⁵⁄₁₆", ea 12.00
Cup, lt bl, 1⁵⁄₁₆" 12.00
Pitcher, dk gr, 2⅞" 28.00
Saucer, wht, 2¾" 3.00
Sugar bowl, dk gr or wht, 1⁵⁄₁₆" 12.00
Teapot, pk or dk ivory, 2⅜" 24.00
Tumbler, dk gr or canary yel, 2" 7.00

Concentric Ring

Cereal, lg, lt or med bl, 3⅜"...28.00
Creamer, sm, med/royal bl, 1⅜"...16.00
Cup, lg, orange, 1¾"..32.00
Cup, lg, purple, 1¾"...80.00
Pitcher, lg, med royal bl, 2⅞"..100.00
Plate, lg, apple/dk gr, 4¼"...20.00
Saucer, lg, apple/dk gr, 2¾"...10.00
Set, lg, bl/ivory marbleized, 21-pc 1,600.00
Set, sm, bl transparent, 16-pc...550.00
Sugar bowl, lg, bl/wht marbleized, 1¾"................................100.00
Sugar lid, lg, wht, 2⅜"...16.00
Teapot, lg, bl transparent, no lid, 2¾"..................................160.00
Tumbler, lg, ivory/wht, 2"...80.00

Interior Panel

Cereal, lg, canary yel or med bl lustre, 3⅜", ea 32.00
Cereal, lg, dk gr, 3⅜"...24.00
Cereal, lg, gr/wht marbleized, 3⅜" 28.00
Creamer, sm, pk lustre, 1⁵⁄₁₆"..76.00
Creamer, sm, topaz transparent, 1⁵⁄₁₆"................................60.00
Cup, lg, lemon & oxblood, 1½"..72.00
Cup, lg, orange, 1½"...24.00
Pitcher, sm, gr transparent, 2⅞"...36.00
Plate, sm, dk gr lustre, 3⁵⁄₁₆"..8.00
Saucer, lg, pk lustre, 3¼"...12.00
Set, lg, med bl or canary yel, 21-pc......................................650.00
Set, lg, topaz transparent, 21-pc..400.00
Set, sm, canary yel, 16-pc..448.00
Set, sm, gr/wht marbleized, 8-pc...172.50
Sugar bowl, lg, topaz transparent, 1½"...................................44.00
Sugar bowl, sm, canary yel, 1⁵⁄₁₆"...56.00
Sugar bowl, sm, gr/wht marbleized, 1⁵⁄₁₆"..............................32.00
Sugar lid, lg, ivory...12.00
Teapot, lg, dk gr, 2¾"...80.00
Teapot, lg, Royal Blue, no lid, 2¾".......................................65.00
Teapot, sm, pk or med bl lustre, no lid, 2½", ea......................40.00
Tumbler, lg/sm, gr or topaz transparent, ea 14.50

Miss America

Creamer, red transparent, 1¾" 160.00
Plate, red onyx, 4½"...60.00
Saucer, wht, 3⅝"..19.00
Set, gr transparent, 17-pc (serves 4)..................................1,185.00
Set, gr transparent, 8-pc...448.00
Set, wht, 8-pc...230.00
Set, wht w/decal, 11-pc (serves 2).......................................500.00
Sugar bowl, gr transparent, 1¾"..100.00
Sugar lid, red transparent, 2⅝"...105.00
Sugar lid, wht, 2⅝"..50.00
Teapot, wht w/decal, no lid, 2½"..80.00
Teapot lid, gr transparent, 2⅞"...120.00

Octagonal

Cereal, lg, dk gr, 3⅜" 14.50
Cereal, lg, orange, 3⅜"...100.00
Creamer, lg, med or dk bl, open hdl, 1½"...............................32.00
Creamer, lg, wht/ivory, 1½"..16.00
Creamer, sm, pale bl, open hdl, 1¼".......................................24.00
Cup, lg, turq or lt bl, closed hdl, 1½".....................................32.00

Cup, sm, canary yel, open hdl, 1¼" 32.00
Pitcher, sm, pale bl, open hdl, 3" 44.00
Plate, sm, apple gr, 3⅜" 12.00
Saucer, sm, wht/ivory, 2¼" 12.00
Set, lg, turq & wht, 17-pc (serves 4) 315.00
Set, sm, gr/orange/canary yel/pale bl, 16-pc 310.00
Sugar bowl, lg, canary yel, open hdls, 1½" 20.00
Sugar bowl, lg, pale bl, open hdls, 1½" 36.00
Teapot, lg, Lemonade & Oxblood, open hdl, 3⅝" 140.00
Teapot, lg, med or dk bl, open hdl, no lid, 3⅝" 52.00
Teapot lid, sm, ivory, open hdl, 2" 12.00
Tumbler, sm, apple gr, 2" 16.00
Water set, pale bl pitcher+2 ea: apple gr/canary yel/orange tumblers..155.00

Raised Daisy

Creamer, sm, lt or dk yel, 1⁵⁄₁₆" 32.00
Cup, sm, dk gr, 1⁵⁄₁₆" 32.00
Pitcher/teapot, sm, dk turq or dk bl, emb daisies, 2⅜" ...36.00
Plate, sm, dk turq or dk bl, 3" 22.50
Sugar bowl, sm, dk ivory, 1⁵⁄₁₆" 100.00
Teapot, sm, dk gr, no lid, 2⅜" 40.00
Tumbler, sm, dk ivory or yel (dk or lt), plain, scarce, 2" 60.00
Water set, emb daisies, turq pitcher+6 yel tumblers..........155.00

Stacked Disc

Creamer, sm, wht or canary yel, 1⁵⁄₁₆" 12.00
Cup, sm, lt bl, 1⁵⁄₁₆" 12.00
Cup, sm, pk or dk ivory, 1⁵⁄₁₆" 80.00
Plate, sm, canary yel, 3¼" 72.00
Plate, sm, med or dk bl, 3¼" 7.00
Saucer, sm, med or dk bl, 2¾" 10.00
Saucer, sm, wht, 2¾" 3.00
Sugar bowl, sm, lt bl, 1⁵⁄₁₆" 16.00
Teapot, sm, med or lt bl or dk gr, no lid, 2⅜" 14.50
Teapot lid, sm, dk gr, 2⁵⁄₁₆" 4.00
Tumbler, sm, canary yel, pk or dk ivory, 2" 8.00

Stacked Disc and Interior Panel

Cereal, lg, wht or yel, 3⅜" 52.00
Creamer, lg, med or Royal Blue, 1¾" 32.00
Creamer, sm, gr transparent, 1⅜" 40.00
Cup, lg, gr transparent, 1¾" 32.00
Cup, sm, bl/wht marbleized, 1⅜" 60.00
Cup, sm, canary yel, 1⅜" 80.00
Plate, lg, dk gr, 4¼" 24.00
Plate, sm, canary yel, 3⁵⁄₁₆" 20.00
Plate, sm, gr transparent, 3⁵⁄₁₆" 22.50
Sugar bowl, lg, bl/wht marbleized, 1¾" 100.00
Sugar bowl, sm, bl transparent, 1⅛" 52.00
Sugar lid, lg, ivory, 2¾" 16.00
Teapot, lg, gr transparent, 2¾" 120.00
Teapot, lid, lg, ivory, 2¹¹⁄₁₆" 12.00
Teapot, sm, med or Royal Blue, 2⅜" 52.00
Teapot lid, sm, bl or gr transparent, 2⅜" 16.00
Tumbler, sm, gr transparent, 2" 14.50
Tumbler, sm, ivory or wht, 2" 80.00

Stippled Band

Cereal, lg, gr transparent, rare, 3⅜" 100.00
Creamer, lg, Azure Blue transparent, 1½" 40.00

Creamer, sm, topaq or gr transparent, 1¼" 68.00
Cup, sm, topaz transparent, 1¼" 12.00
Pitcher, sm, gr transparent, 2⅞" 32.00
Plate, lg, topaz or gr transparent, 4¼" 8.00
Sugar bowl, lg, Azure Blue transparent, 1½" 64.00
Teapot, lg, gr transparent, 2⅝" 60.00
Teapot, sm, gr transparent, 2⅜" 25.00
Teapot lid, sm, topaz or gr transparent, 2⅜" 20.00

Miscellaneous

Ashtray, blk, sq 45.00
Ashtray, coaster type, 4¼" 60.00
Ashtray, emb star w/AA mk 500.00
Ashtray, leaf form, 4⅛", from $5 to 15.00
Ashtray, marbleized, 5" sq, from $60 to 90.00
Ashtray, Mexicali Hat, from $25 to 30.00

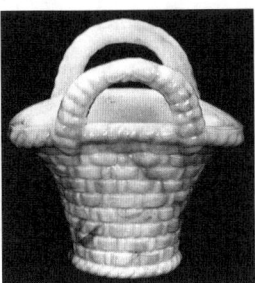

Basket, green and white marbleized, 4", $25.00.

Basket, 1-hdl, red marbleized 500.00
Candlestick, Inkwell, Type I, gr 25.00
Candlestick, Inkwell, Type II, marbleized......................20.00
Flowerpot, #1311, 4" 195.00
Flowerpot, Banded Dart, #302, 5½", from $65 to 85.00
Flowerpot, Ribbed Top (Thumb Pot), #290, blk, 1¼" 50.00
Flowerpot, Ribs & Flutes, #297 (Type I & II), 3", ea from $9 to...13.00
Jardiniere, #306CF, solid color, 5" 35.00
Jardiniere, bell shaped, solid colors, 4¾", from $60 to 80.00
Planter, Japanese, #650, solid color other than blk, 11¼", $400 to.......450.00
Planter, Lilly, ivory, 5¼", from $35 to 40.00
Planter, Oval Scalloped Top Graduated Dart, #651, any color, 8½".......45.00
Puff box, Apple, orange...250.00
Puff box, Colonial Lady, dk gr..................................450.00
Puff box, Colonial Lady, lt gr....................................200.00
Puff box, Scottie dog, lt or dk pk 95.00
Puff box, Scottie dog, wht 80.00
Puff jar, Sawtooth, solid orange, from $300 to 350.00
Smoker's set, oxblood, MIB......................................145.00
Vase, Cornucopia, crystal, plain ft, 3¼" 150.00
Vase, Graduated Dart, #316, Type I (smooth top), 6¼" 200.00
Vase, Grecian Urn, blk or crystal, 6-sided ft, 3¼"...........200.00
Vase, Ribs & Flutes, #311, solid color, 8", from $150 to.....175.00
Vivaudou, mortar & pestle, pk 30.00
Vivaudou, mortar & pestle, 2-tone 100.00
Vivaudou, shaving mug, blk 35.00

Alamo Pottery

Alamo art pottery (1945 – 1951) was a division of the Alamo Pottery of San Antonio, Texas, which was primarily a maker of sanitary ware (bathroom fixtures). The art pottery division was founded by Jake Rowe, Richard Potter, and Bruce Blunt and produced vitreous china items which have survived the decades without crazing and with the high gloss glazes still gleaming as if new. (Mrs. Potter was a valuable resource in compiling information about Alamo history.)

Rowe, Potter, and Blunt developed glazes, processes, and mold shapes from which came styles and colors that ran the gamut from elegant, classically styled vases to whimsical figurals, and from pale translucent aquas and yellows to bold crayon greens, blues, and yellows. The vast majority of the pieces are monochromatic, and the rare sponge- or spatter-ware pieces are at a premium.

Alamo is usually marked with a mold number (from 701 to 908, and P-2, P-3, and presumably P-1). Many also have an oval Alamo Pottery ink stamp in either black or blue. Bottoms are generally unglazed, although a few pitchers with glazed bottoms exist. Flea bites in the glaze are fairly common and unless excessive are tolerated by most collectors. Crazing and staining are nonexistent, and virtually all interiors are fully glazed. These items were originally intended for the floral trade, and most sold for less than $3.00.

The art pottery division of Alamo closed in 1951 due to high costs of storing and shipping. Rowe, Potter, and Blunt moved to Gilmer, Texas, and founded Gilmer Pottery (see Gilmer listing), which produced many items often mistaken for Alamo.

Bowl, #245, 3x6" 9.00
Bowl, pet feeding; #730, duck, bear & bunny on sides, 7" dia 33.00
Figurine, swan, #725, 5½x5" 30.00
Flowerpot, #829-5, diagonal waves, 5" 12.00
Flowerpot, #829-9, diagonal waves, 8½" 30.00
Pitcher, #757, 4¼" 20.00
Vase, #718, wht, faceted sides, 8½x3" 25.00
Vase, #722, ruffled, 7¼" 15.00
Vase, #829-6, 5x6" dia 16.50
Vase, 15" 110.00

Alexandrite

Alexandrite is a type of art glass introduced around the turn of the century by Thomas Webb and Sons of England. It is recognized by its characteristic shading, pale yellow to rose and blue at the edge of the item. Although other companies (Moser, for example) produced glass they called alexandrite, only examples made by Webb possess all the described characteristics and command premium prices. Amount and intensity of blue determines value. Our prices are for items with good average intensity, unless otherwise noted. Our advisors for this category are Betty and Clarence Maier; they are listed in the Directory under Pennsylvania.

Bowl, ruffled, 2½x5" 900.00
Finger bowl, Honeycomb, crimped/ruffled, 3¾", +underplate .2,200.00
Vase, floriform; 8 optic ribs, scalloped/flared rim, ftd, 6½" 1,345.00
Vase, mushroom shape w/wide flange, EX color, 2½x4½" 1,600.00
Vase, Raindrop, pinched/ruffled top, 4¼" 700.00
Wine, 4¼" 1,500.00

Almanacs

The earliest evidence indicates that almanacs were used as long ago as ancient Egypt. Throughout the Dark Ages they were circulated in great volume and were referred to by more people than any other book except the Bible. *The Old Farmer's Almanac* first appeared in 1793 and has been issued annually since that time. Usually more of a pamphlet than a book (only a few have hard covers), the almanac provided planting and harvesting information to farmers, weather forecasts for seamen,

medical advice, household hints, mathematical tutoring, postal rates, railroad schedules, weights and measures, 'receipts,' and jokes. Before 1800 the information was unscientific and based entirely on astrology and folklore. The first almanac in America was printed in 1639 by William Pierce Mariner; it contained data of this nature. One of the best-known editions, Ben Franklin's *Poor Richard's Almanac*, was introduced in 1732 and continued to be printed for twenty-five years.

By the nineteenth century, merchants saw the advertising potential in a publication so widely distributed, and the advertising almanac evolved. These were distributed free of charge by drug stores and mercantiles and were usually somewhat lacking in information, containing simply a calendar, a few jokes, and a variety of ads for quick remedies and quack cures.

Today their concept and informative, often amusing text make almanacs popular collectibles that may usually be had at reasonable prices. Because they were printed in such large numbers and often saved from year to year, their prices are still low. Most fall within a range of $4.00 to $15.00. Very common examples may be virtually worthless; those printed before 1860 are especially collectible. Quite rare and highly prized are the Kate Greenaway 'Almanacks,' printed in London from 1883 to 1897. These are illustrated with her drawings of children, one for each calendar month.

Unless otherwise noted, our values are for examples in very good condition. See also Kate Greenaway.

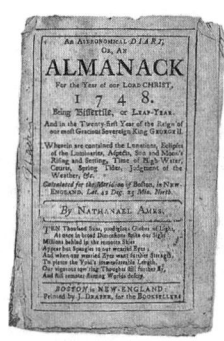

1748, An Astronomical Diary Or an Almanack..., Nathaniel Ames, Boston: J Draper, 14-page, 6x4", VG, from $150.00 to $200.00.

1780, Nathaniel Low, printed by N Willis, Court St, 22-pg 95.00
1788, Astronomical Almanack, Nathaniel Low, Boston 50.00
1845, Boston, SN Dickeson, 168-pg, EX 38.00
1848, Old Rough & Ready 1849 Almanac, Zachary Taylor campaign....200.00
1860, Tribune Almanac & Political Register, Horace Greeley & Co 40.00
1861, Leavitt's Farmer's Almanac, complete, 4½x6½" 50.00
1870, Dr Jane's Medical Almanac, 49-pg..40.00
1876, Hoofland's Almanac & Family Receipt Book, 39-pg, 6¼x8¾" 35.00
1876, Hostetter's Illustrated, 20-pg 25.00
1884, Collins Brothers, St Louis MO, medical cures, 32-pg 215.00
1884, Moore's Indian Root Pill Almanac, EX 40.00
1888, Ayer's American Almanac, Dr JC Ayer & Co, Lowell MA ...12.00
1888, Diamond Dye Almanac & Household Guide, 32-pg, 6x8¼", EX.....40.00
1895, Frederick MD...12.00
1895, Hazeltine's Pocket Book Almanac, 30+-pg, 1⅜x2", EX.......35.00
1899, Montgomery Ward Almanac & Year Book, 96-pg, 6x8", EX 40.00
1902, Studebaker Farmers, 52-pg 45.00
1904, Moore's, Sydney Australia, softcover 30.00
1904, Old Farmer's Almanac, part of cover missing......................12.00
1910, Dr AW Chase, Almanac for Home, Factory, Farm & Office 15.00
1910, International Harvester, 80-pg, 5x8", EX 75.00
1910, Raleigh's, cookbook & medical guide, 64-pg......................17.00
1913, Marshall's Illustrated Almanac & Pocket Compendium......17.50
1922, Agricultural Almanac, John Baer's Sons, Lancaster PA.......20.00
1922, MacDonald's Farmers Almanac, Binghamton NY...............10.00

1925, World Almanac Book of Facts, 128-pg **40.00**
1937, Dr JH McLean's Medicine Co, St Louis **10.00**
1938, Herbalist, herbal remedies, 64-pg **20.00**
1940, Healthway Products, EX..............................**15.00**
1940, Miles Laboratories, Elkhart IN..............................**15.00**
1941, Miles New Weather Almanac, Miles Nervine Products **15.00**
1941, Raleigh's Good Health Guide Almanac & Cookbook, 32-pg .**20.00**
1946, Cricket's..............................**85.00**
1946, Farm Woman's Almanac, Garden Seed Co, Lancaster PA ..**12.00**
1947, WLS Family & Almanac, 55-pg **20.00**
1949, Bell Telephone System **15.00**
1949, Raleigh's Good Health Guide, 60th Anniversary, 31-pg......**17.00**
1950, Trail Blazers Almanac & Pioneer Guide, 5x8" **10.00**
1955, Ford Farm-Ranch-Home, Ford Motor Comp, 208-pg **10.00**

Aluminum

Aluminum, though being the most abundant metal in the earth's crust, always occurs in combination with other elements. Before a practical method for its refinement was developed in the late nineteenth century, articles made of aluminum were very expensive. After the process for commercial smelting was perfected in 1916, it became profitable to adapt the ductile, nontarnishing material to many uses.

By the late '30s, novelties, trays, pitchers, and many other tableware items were being produced. They were often handcrafted with elaborate decoration. Russel Wright designed a line of lovely pieces such as lamps, vases, and desk accessories that are becoming very collectible. Many who crafted the ware marked it with their company logo, and these signed pieces are attracting the most interest. Wendell August Forge (Grove City, Pennsylvania) is a mark to watch for; this firm was the first to produce hammered aluminum (it is still made there today), and some of their examples are particularly nice. Upwardly mobile market values reflect their popularity with today's collectors. In general, 'spun' aluminum is from the '30s or early '40s, and 'hammered' aluminum is from the '30s to the '60s.

For further information, refer to *Collectible Aluminum, An Identification and Value Guide* by Everett Grist, listed in the Directory under Tennessee; *Vintage Bar Ware* by Stephen Visakay; and *Collector's Encyclopedia of Russel Wright* by Ann Kerr. Another excellent reference is *Hammered Aluminum, Hand Wrought Collectibles*, by our advisor, Dannie Woodard, see the Directory for Texas.

Ashtray, bamboo, Everlast, ¾x5" **15.00**
Ashtray, sailboat on water, 4 rests, Wendell August Forge, 4½" sq ...**20.00**
Basket, fruit & flowers, twisted hdl, Cromwell, 9x10" dia **10.00**
Basket, wild roses, serrated edge, hammered hdl, Continental, 4x6" ...**20.00**
Beverage server, 2 sets of concentric circles, Kromex, 11x5" **25.00**
Bowl, bittersweet, notched rim, DePonceau, 2x11" **25.00**
Bowl, spun (no decor), flared rim, Kensington, 11" **10.00**
Cake stand, band of shields, serrated edge, ftd, 8x12" **15.00**
Candlesticks, hdld saucer w/removable sockets, unmk, pr **20.00**
Candy dish, fruit & flowers, dbl-bowl w/center hdl, Cromwell, 13" W.**10.00**
Casserole, flower band & finial, hammered base w/D hdls, Everlast.**5.00**
Casserole holder, sailing ships armada, clip-type hdls, Forman, 3x9" .**5.00**
Coaster, flying goose, unmk..............................**10.00**
Coaster, pine cone & needles, unmk **6.00**
Coaster, Scottie dog, unmk..............................**8.00**
Crumber & tray, leaves, Everlast..............................**10.00**
Cup, hammered effect, rolled lip, ear hdls, copper colored, 3x3" **1.00**
Ice bucket, hammered int, beaded lip, twisted hdl, Buenilum, 6x5" .**15.00**
Ice bucket, medieval helmet shape, Made in Hong Kong, 16x10" .**20.00**
Key chain, teddy bear, DeMarsh Forge **12.00**
Lazy Susan, fruit & flowers, serrated edge, Cromwell, 16" dia **5.00**
Mint dish, dogwood, glass insert, Wendell August Forge, 12" dia ..**45.00**

Napkin holder, thistles, crimped edge, unmk, 4x6x2" **10.00**
Pitcher, acorns & leaves, ice lip, coiled hdl, Continental, 8x6" **20.00**
Pitcher, hammered effect, ice lip, flared cylinder, tall hdl, 8x6" **5.00**
Plaque, hobbyist; laurel wreath design, hammered/fluted rim, unmk, 14"..**2.00**
Silent butler, wheat, Kraftware, 6½" dia..............................**10.00**
Tray, bar; flying geese, self-hdld, Wendell August Forge, 17x9" **35.00**
Tray, bread; berry vines, unmk, 13x7" **5.00**
Tray, bread; floral spray, rectangular, unmk, 127" **5.00**
Tray, cheese & cracker; acorns & leaves, Continental, 15" dia **15.00**
Tray, palms, 2-tier, scalloped/serrated edges, 9x12"..............**5.00**
Tray, pine cones & dogwood, 3-tier, marble finial, 12x13" dia **5.00**
Tray, sandwich; scenic pines, appl hdls, A Armour, 13x9"..............**40.00**
Tray, sandwich; stylized cactus, Kensington, 12" dia **10.00**
Tray, serving; bamboo, appl bamboo-shaped hdls, Everlast, 14x9" .**30.00**
Tray, serving; morning glories, floral china insert, Cromwell, 11".**35.00**
Tray, serving; poinsettias, wire loop hdls, unmk, 18x11"..............**5.00**
Tray, serving; roses, appl hdls w/leaves, Continental, 17" dia **10.00**
Tray, serving; tropical fish, appl hdl, World Hand Forged, 15x10" .**25.00**
Tray, snack; fruit, lipped, self-hdld, unmk, 10x6"..............**2.00**
Tray, snack; sailboat scene, Wendell August Forge, 5x8" **20.00**
Tray, tidbit; fruit & flowers, 4-section, center hdl, Cromwell, 9" sq .**5.00**
Trivet, grapevines, Everlast, 10" dia..............................**10.00**
Umbrella stand, larkspur, Wendell August Forge, 22" **285.00**
Vase, chrysanthemums, cylindrical, Continental, 10x5"..............**85.00**

AMACO, American Art Clay Co.

AMACO is the logo of the American Art Clay Co. Inc., founded in Indianapolis, Indiana, in 1919, by Ted O. Philpot. They produced a line of art pottery from 1931 through 1938. The company is still in business but now produces only supplies, implements, and tools for the ceramic trade.

Values for AMACO have risen sharply, especially those for figurals, items with Art Deco styling, and pieces with uncommon shapes. Our advisors for this category are Dave Rago and Suzanne Perrault; they are listed in the Directory under New Jersey.

Bookends, horses, gr crystalline, 5" **175.00**
Bowl, turq bl, crescent moon hdl, #118, 5x5½"..............................**110.00**
Bust, Deco lady, head & neck on sq base, bright bl gloss, 7x3", pr..**325.00**

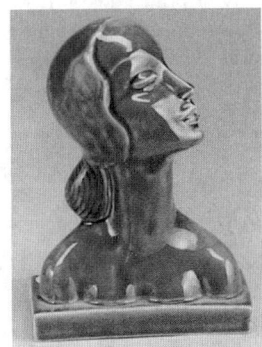

Bust of a woman, bright blue glossy glaze, stamped mark, 8½x5¾", $275.00.
(Photo courtesy Dave Rago)

Ginger jar, bright bl glossy glaze, w/lid, 9½" **225.00**
Vase, dk gr, gourd shape w/rim to-width hdls, 4-buttress platform base, #19, 12½" ..**350.00**

Amberina

Amberina, one of the earliest types of art glass, was developed in 1883 by Joseph Locke of the New England Glass Company. The trademark was registered by W.L. Libbey, who often signed his name in script within the pontil.

Amberina was made by adding gold powder to the batch, which produced glass in the basic amber hue. Part of the item, usually the top, was simply reheated to develop the characteristic deep red or fuchsia shading. Early amberina was mold-blown, but cut and pressed amberina was also produced. The rarest type is plated amberina, made by New England for a short time after 1886. It has been estimated that less than 2,000 pieces were ever produced. Other companies, among them Hobbs and Brockunier, Mt. Washington Glass Company, and Sowerby's Ellison Glassworks of England, made their own versions, being careful to change the name of their product to avoid infringing on Libbey's patent. Prices realized at auction seem to be erratic, to say the least, and dealers appear to be 'testing the waters' with prices that start out very high only to be reduced later if the item does not sell at the original asking price. A lot of amberina glassware is of a more recent vintage — look for evidence of an early production, since the later wares are worth much less than glass-ware that can be attributed to the older makers. Generic amberina with hand-painted flowers will bring lower prices as well. Our values are taken from auction results and dealer lists, omitting the extremely high and low ends of the range. See also Libbey.

Key: NE — New England Glass Company

Bowl, Dmn Quilt, fuchsia to amber, 5".........................225.00
Bowl, fuchsia to amber, slight ribbing, 8"......................290.00
Bowl, Int Rib, 12-crimp rim, 2½x4½".............................375.00
Bowl, Invt T'print, shaped 8-lobe rim, 8"......................130.00
Celery vase, Invt T'print, sq petaled top, NE, 6¼"............575.00
Celery vase, Venetian Dmn, crimped/everted rim, NE, 4¾x3¼".230.00
Condiment set, Baby Invt T'print cylinder shakers & mustard jar in fr.1,325.00
Creamer, sq mouth, amber hdl, NE, 4½x4"........................290.00
Cruet, Swirl, squat bulb base, faceted amber stopper, EX color, 5¾".575.00
Cup, punch; Dmn Optic, ribbed hdl, NE..........................185.00
Decanter, Dmn Quilt, faceted amber stopper, 12½"...............260.00
Fishbowl, optic ribs, spherical w/short everted rim, Mt WA, 5x8".1,200.00
Mug, Baby T'print, bbl shape, ribbed hdl, 2½".................230.00
Mustard pot, Invt T'print, bbl shape, SP lid/bail/spoon, Mt WA, 4¼".575.00
Mustard pot, Venetian Dmn, bbl form, SP lid/bail/spoon, NE, 4x1⅞".1,000.00
Pitcher, Daisy & Button, very heavy, Hobbs & Brockunier, 5"...425.00
Pitcher, Invt T'print, appl hdl, 7¼"...........................150.00
Pitcher, Invt T'print, sq mouth, EX color, NE, 7x6"..........1,035.00
Pitcher, Invt T'print, sq mouth, outstanding color, NE, 5¾"...690.00
Pitcher, tankard; Venetian Dmn, NE, rare sz, 7x4".............750.00
Pitcher, water; Dmn Quilt, reverse color, amber hdl, bulbous....145.00

Punch bowl, paneled sides, 7¼x15", with 17" underplate, $2,500.00.

Punch cup, reverse Coin Spot, reeded hdl, 2½"...............100.00
Toothpick holder, optic design, tricon rim, 2¼".............385.00
Tumbler, Dmn Quilt, EX amber to fuchsia, NE, 3½", set of 4....200.00
Tumbler, juice; ribbed, concave sides, 4"...................175.00
Vase, amber rigaree collar, ribbed w/sq top, lt bl rim, 3½".....600.00
Vase, amber rigaree neck band, gourd form, dimpled sides, 9"...980.00

Vase, Dmn Quilt, cylindrical w/tightly crimped flaring rim, NE, 4"....900.00
Vase, Dmn Quilt, rigaree at waisted neck, scalloped rim, 5½"....575.00
Vase, gold florals, ruffled amber top, petal ft, 11½"...........350.00
Vase, Invt T'print, crimped/incurvate rim, NE, EX color, 6¼"...750.00
Vase, Jack-in-pulpit, Invt T'print, fuchsia to amber, amber ft, 13"..300.00
Vase, lily; att Mt WA, 10x4"...................................485.00
Vase, Stork & Cattail (pressed pattern), sqd w/4 rim arches, NE, 5"..2,600.00
Vase, trumpet form, tri-fold top, NE, 9".......................350.00

Plated Amberina

Bowl, 5 inverted lobes, Aurora/NE Glass Works label, 7½"....3,500.00
Cup, punch; 12-rib, 2⅜"......................................3,750.00
Lemonade, amber hdl..1,800.00
Tumbler, 3¾", from $2,000 to.................................2,300.00
Vase, lily form, 6¼"...2,800.00
Vase, 12-rib, 6¼"..5,750.00

American Bisque

The American Bisque Pottery operated in Williamstown, West Virginia, from 1919 to 1982. The company was begun by Mr. B.E. Allen and remained an Allen-family business until its sale in 1982. Figural pottery was produced from approximately 1937 until about the time the pottery closed.

American Bisque pottery is often identified by the 'wedges' or dry-footed cleats on the bottom of the ware. Many designs are unique to the American Bisque Company, such as cookie jars with blackboards and magnets, others with lids that doubled as serving trays, and some with 'action pieces' which show movement. American Bisque pieces are very collectible and are available in a broad variety of color schemes; some items are decorated with 22 – 24k gold. Many items are modeled after highly popular copyrighted characters.

Bank, pig wearing bl jeans w/suspenders, 6".................110.00
Cookie jar, Bear, CJ-701......................................50.00
Cookie jar, Chest, CJ-562, from $150 to......................175.00
Cookie jar, Chick, CJ-702, from $100 to......................125.00
Cookie jar, Churn, CJ-765.....................................35.00
Cookie jar, Floral, CJ-561....................................30.00
Cookie jar, French Poodle, CJ-751, from $100 to..............125.00
Cookie jar, Grandma, CJ-752, from $100 to....................125.00
Cookie jar, Jack in the Box, CJ-753, from $125 to............175.00
Cookie jar, Lady Pig, CJ-755..................................70.00
Cookie jar, Pig, CJ-703.......................................70.00
Cookie jar, Puppy, CJ-754.....................................60.00
Cookie jar, Recipes, CJ-563..................................100.00
Pitcher, pig figural w/clover blossom & leaves on bk, 7½".....45.00
Planter, donkey pulling cart, 7x5"............................18.00
Planter, Kewpie doll sitting by open stump, pk, 5¾"...........15.00
Planter, kitten, crying, arms extended, bunny by his side.....30.00
Planter, squirrel sitting upright holding lg acorn, 5x5"......14.00
Shakers, pig figural, clover bud on skirt, 4", pr............22.00

American Encaustic Tiling Co.

A.E. Tile was organized in 1879 in Zanesville, Ohio, for the production of dust-pressed encaustic floor tile. After several important flooring commissions, such as the New York State Capitol in Albany, the company diversified to the production of decorative embossed tiles covered in glossy glazes. The German sculptor Herman Mueller would prove to be their finest modeler, working with glaze chemist Karl Langenbeck. By the late 1920s, A.E. had become one of the largest tile manufacturers in the world, employing over one thousand workers in plants in Ohio, New Jersey, and California. The operation was reorganized by the Schweiker brothers after World War II and would eventually become the American Olean Tile Company. It is now known as Dal-Tile. Our advisors for this category are Suzanne Perrault and Dave Rago; they are listed in the Directory under New Jersey .

Key: cs — cuerda seca

Mark 1 — THE AMERICAN ENCAUSTIC TILE CO. LIMITED (stamped)
Mark 2 — AETCO L.A. (stamped)
Mark 3 — Large circular mark

Frieze (2-tile), stylized flower, cs, bl/gr/wht/amber, mk 2, fr, 12x6" .325.00
Panel, emb Colonial man, burgundy gloss, mk 3, 18x6", EX.......325.00
Panels, emb Bacchanalian scenes, mc gloss, mk 3, 18x6", EX, pr.575.00

Panel, relief-molded lady in Renaissance dress, emerald green gloss, large circular mark, 18x6", EX, $375.00.
(Photo courtesy Dave Rago Auctions)

Tile, Dedication AE Tile Works...1892, lady's profile, bl gloss, 4", NM.125.00
Tile, emb floral, red/ivory glossy mottle, mk 3, 6" 40.00
Tile, emb lady in bonnet profile, lt bl (rare), A&C oak fr, mk 1, 8" .225.00
Tile, stove; emb child's head, burgundy gloss, emb mk, 3" dia, NM .125.00
Tile, water mill (photographic), emb/cvd, caramel gloss, stamped, 6" ..225.00
Tiles, portrait of man (lady), olive gloss, stamped mk, 6", pr.......275.00
Vase, bust of Deco lady, umber/lt gr crystalline, 2" rim line, 12".400.00

American Indian Art

That time when the American Indian was free to practice the crafts and culture that was his heritage has always held a fascination for many. They were a people who appreciated beauty of design and colorful decoration in their furnishings and clothing; and because instruction in their crafts was a routine part of their rearing, they were well accomplished. Several tribes developed areas in which they excelled. The Navajo were weavers and silversmiths, the Zuni, lapidaries. Examples of their craftsmanship are very valuable. Today even the work of contemporary Indian artists — weavers, silversmiths, carvers, and others — is highly collectible. Unless otherwise noted, values are for items with no obvious damage or excessive wear (EX/NM). For a more thorough study we recommend *Arrowheads and Projectile Points, Indian Axes, Indian Artifacts of the Midwest,* and *Indian Trade Relics.* All have been written by our advisor, Lar Hothem; you will find his address in the Directory under Ohio.

Key:
bw — beadwork	p-h — prehistoric
dmn — diamond	s-s — sinew sewn

Apparel and Accessories

Before the white traders brought the Indian women cloth from which to sew their garments and beads to use for decorating them, clothing was made from skins sewn together with sinew, usually made of animal tendon. Porcupine quills were dyed bright colors and woven into bags and armbands and used to decorate clothing and moccasins. Examples of early quillwork are scarce today and highly collectible.

Early in the nineteenth century, beads were being transported via pony pack trains. These 'pony' beads were irregular shapes of opaque glass imported from Venice. Nearly always blue or white, they were twice as large as the later 'seed' beads. By 1870 translucent beads in many sizes and colors had been made available, and Indian beadwork had become commercialized. Each tribe developed its own distinctive methods and preferred decorations, making it possible for collectors today to determine the origin of many items. Soon after the turn of the century, the craft of beadworking began to diminish.

Arm bands, Shoshone, full dmn & circle bw on canvas, 1920s, 2x10¼" .100.00
Belt, Crow lady's, floral bw, ca 1950, 38x4"..................................200.00
Breech clout, Cheyenne, trade cloth w/ribbonwork/bw panels, 1930s, 47"..60.00
Dress, Blackfeet, shell & bw yoke on red wool, 1890s, 35x46" .2,000.00
Dress, Cheyenne, s-s, ochred buckskin, elk teeth/bw, 19th C, 35x52".4,750.00
Dress, Navajo Teec Nos Pos, woven, fringe & silver decor, 1920s, 45"..475.00
Dress, Yakima, red trade cloth w/bw yoke, shells & tradebeads, 1960s..70.00
Garters, Chippewa, loomed, mc bw w/drops, 1890s, 9x3", pr......200.00
Gauntlets, Plateau, floral bw & fringe, 1930s, 12x6½".................250.00
Gauntlets, wht buckskins, silk embr floral, fringe, high-top, 1930s..200.00
Jacket, Cree, tanned buckskin, silk embr floral, 1960s, 68", M ...180.00
Jacket, Plateau lady's, smoked buckskin w/bw trim, 1950s...........225.00
Leggings, Blackfoot, hide w/geometric bw, +matching breech clout, 1910..250.00
Leggings, Cheyenne, s-s bw on tanned ochred antelope hide, 1870s, 18".1,100.00
Leggings, Nez Perce, trade cloth panel & bw panels, ca 1900, 31x11".180.00
Leggings, Shoshone lady's, geometric bw, 3x25" 120.00
Leggings, Ute, buckskin, wide & narrow bw strip ea side, 1930, 30" 475.00
Mittens, Athabascan, hide w/fur trim, floral bw, 1920s, 15x8"....200.00
Mittens, Athabascan, leather w/floral beadwork & fur trim, 1970s, 17" 80.00
Moccasins, Apache, s-s hide w/circle & geometric bw, 1890s, 9½" 1,700.00
Moccasins, Assiniboine, s-s full bw buckskin slippers, 1920s, 7" .150.00
Moccasins, Cheyenne, mc bw, yel ochre on tongue/cuffs, 10½".1,485.00
Moccasins, Cree, buckskin, mc floral bw toes, high vamp, 1920s, 10".160.00
Moccasins, Crow, full bw high-top buckskin w/striped toes, 1950, 7".110.00
Moccasins, Crow, full geometric bw on wht, 1910, 10" 800.00
Moccasins, Crow, lady's, full bw, hard soles 375.00
Moccasins, Crow, s-s buffalo hide w/ornate geometric bw, 1900s, 10"..250.00
Moccasins, Crow child's, full bw high-tops w/striped toes, 6½" ..110.00
Moccasins, Iroquois child's, puckered toes, sm bw, velvet flaps, 1880.90.00
Moccasins, Plains Cree, s-s buckskin w/bw insert/toe strips, 1890, 10"..225.00
Moccasins, Potowatami, buckskin, bw on flaps & toe strips, 1890s, 10".250.00
Moccasins, red ochre & bw florals, puckered soles, 1900s, 11" ...130.00
Moccasins, Santee Sioux, quilled hide w/mc floral bw toes, 1890s, 10".1,100.00
Moccasins, Sioux, s-s, full bw, rawhide soles, 1920s, 9½" 400.00
Moccasins, Sioux, s-s, striking overall geometric bw, 1900s, 5".1,300.00
Robe, Plains, pnt on buffalo hide (faint), 19th C, 36x31"...........400.00
Sash, floral bw, long red wool fringe, ca 1910, 5x33"..................650.00
Sash, Hopi, traditional style w/fringe & embr, 1950s, 8x36"......275.00
Sash, Ojibway, loomed, bw geometrics, fringe, 1900s, 3x38".......325.00
Sash, Potowatami, full bw w/twisted wool yarn fringe, 1950s, 17x1¾" .70.00
Shirt, war; Yurok/Hupa, bw strips on arms, ca 1860, 54x28"....8,500.00
Vest, Cree, wht buckskin w/silk embr floral & horses, 1960s, M.175.00
Vest, Kootenai, velvet panels, buckskin bk, dmn designs, 1920s.100.00
Vest, Sioux, s-s buffalo hide w/full bw, ca 1880, man's sz..........6,000.00

Bags and Cases

The Indians used bags for many purposes, and most display excellent form and workmanship. Of the types listed below, many collectors consider the pipe bag to be the most desirable form. Pipe bags were long, narrow, leather and bead or quillwork creations made to hold tobacco in a compartment at the bottom and the pipe, with the bowl removed from the stem, in the top. Long buckskin fringe was used as trim and complemented the quilled and beaded design to make the bag a masterpiece of Indian art.

Apache, throw-over style w/shells & tin dangles, 1890s, 36x8½" .1,700.00
Arapaho, leather dispatch w/bw dmns on wht, bugle beads/fringe, 1880s..1,900.00
Cheyenne, tepee, s-s buffalo hide w/quilled lines, bw, cones, 1890s.1,300.00
Cheyenne, tepee, s-s quill & bw on buffalo hide, 1880s, 9x14", EX.7,000.00
Crow, parfleche, mc geometric pnt decor, 1920, mini, 7½x11"...225.00
Crow, parfleche, old mineral pnt, 20th C, 11x19" 700.00
Great Lakes, bandolier, trade cloth w/contour floral bw, 1880s, 35" .1,600.00
Mandan, pipe, ochred s-s buffalo hide, plaited quillwork, 1860, 16" .225.00
N Plains, knife, ornate bw, quills, tin cones, fringe, 20th C, 19".850.00
Nez Perce, arm, old snap, full floral/geometric bw, 1920s, 10x9".375.00
Nez Perce, full bw w/horse figure on buckskin, fringed, 1940s, 12x12" .1,500.00
Nez Perce, twined cornhusk w/woven geometrics, 1930s, 18x14" .900.00
Plateau, rectangular, full bw w/flowers & bird, 1930s, 10½x6½".300.00

Baskets

In the following listings, examples are basket form and coiled unless noted otherwise.

Achomawi, twined, reddish stair-step design, 1910, 4x5"............425.00
Apache, bowl, geometrics, finely coiled, 1890s, 4x16".............2,500.00
Apache, butterflies & crosses, finely coiled, 1920, 3x10"............800.00
Apache, canteen, pitch sealing, ca 1900, 9x3½" 550.00
Apache, water tus & cup, pitch covered, braided horsehair hdls, 1950s .150.00
Chemehuevi, eagles & swastikas all around, 1920s, 4x6½".........600.00
Cherokee, plaited river cane, diagonal design, hdl, 1920s, 11x16" .450.00
Cherokee, storage, plaited, Agnes Welch (documentation), 1972, 13½".225.00
Hupa/Yurok, head wear, parallelograms & geometrics, 1940s, 7x3½" ..375.00
Klamath, gambling tray, ca 1900, 13", w/4 bone game pcs.......1,800.00
Klamath, gambling tray, w/4 incised game pcs, ca 1900, 13"....1,800.00
Klickitat, berry, hard shell, imbricated design traces, 1890s, 8x9x8"..200.00
Navajo, wedding basket, fine weave, ca 1960, 1x4¾" 120.00
Nootka/Makah, bottle, mc whaling scene, w/lid, 1950, 4½x1¾" .120.00
Nootka/Makah, floral designs, w/lid, ca 1910, 6x9½".................950.00
Nootka/Makah, mat, mc rows & 4 story figures, 1940s, 9x7" 250.00
Panamint, bowl, red & blk geometrics, 1930, 3¼x6", NM 1,300.00
Panamint, earthworm, fine weave, 1940s, 3x7" 1,200.00
Papago, bowl, radiating lines, 1970, 3¾x13½" 140.00
Papago, bowl, str sides, geometrics, EX patina, ca 1945, 7x8" 120.00
Papago, bowl, wheat stitch patterned coils, 1970, 9½x6¼" 150.00
Pima, bowl, checkerboard design, oval, 1930s, mini, 2x3x2" 130.00
Pima, bowl, fret & cross design, 1930s, 4½x15"..........................650.00
Pima, bowl, hourglass designs, 1935, 2x11"................................250.00
Pima, bowl, old style w/radiating Z designs, 1930s, 4½x9"..........150.00
Pima, bowl, swastika & fret design, ca 1910, 4½x14"..................650.00
Pima, bowl, traditional geometrics, flat bottom, str sides, 3x7x4½"..90.00
Pima, friendship, horsehair, Adalene Jose, 1970s, mini, 2⅛" 100.00
Pima, mat, Man in Maze, 1940s,½x10" dia....................................375.00
Pima, overall geometrics, 1930s, 11x13" 600.00
Pima, V designs in brn & blk, ca 1935, 1x2" 300.00
Pit River, twined, reddish stair-step design, 1910s, 6x4" 425.00
Pomo, bottle, traditional design, 1920, 12x4" 325.00
Pomo, burden, traditional conical form, 1870s, 18x21" 1,400.00
Popago, storage, Gila monster design, ca 1974, 16x19"............1,000.00
Quinault, gathering, banded design, ca 1900, 6x9"......................150.00
Salish, trunk, imbricated geometrics, 1880s, 30x22x18".............550.00

Salish, trunk, woven imbricated star and cross design, with lid and handles, ca 1900, 13x21x12", EX, $500.00. (Photo courtesy Allard Auctions Inc.)

Tlingit, bowl, str sides/4-color, 3-row banded decor, 1940s, 6x5¾".350.00
Tlingit, twined, mc geometrics, sm rpr, ca 1910, 3x4" 160.00
Ute, tray, butterfly decor, Mary Clark, 1980, 19" 425.00
Washo, jar, rattlesnake designs, hdl, ca 1935, 4½x4½" 350.00
Yavapai, tray, tight weave, mc design, 1920s, 3x10" 900.00
Yavapai Apache, olla, deer/butterflies/cactus/geometrics, 1935, 13x13"..1,300.00
Yurok, bowl, blk parallelograms, 1920s, 5½x4" 700.00
2nd Mesa Hopi, bowl, kachina faces & ears of corn, 1940s, 5½x7¾".400.00
2nd Mesa Hopi, plaque, red/blk/yel radiating designs, 1940s, 16".275.00
3rd Mesa Hopi, plaque, dbl-sided, geometrics, 1930s, 13" 275.00

Blades and Points

Relics of this type usually display characteristics of a general area, time period, or a particular location. With study, those made by the Plains Indians are easily discerned from those of the west coast. Because modern man has imitated the art of the Indian by reproducing these artifacts through modern means, use caution before investing your money in 'too good to be authentic' specimens. For a more thorough study we recommend *Arrowheads of the Central Great Plains* by Daniel J. Fox, *Field Guide to Flint Arrowheads and Knives of the North American Indian* by Lawrence N. Tully, and *Flint Blades and Projectile Points* by Lawrence N. Tully.

Bifurcated/stemmed, wht flint, serrated, Early Archaic, MO, 2¾" .75.00
Diagonal-notch, tan chert, Archaic, MO, 4¾"...........................225.00
Dovetail/St Charles, pk-tan flint, hip-roof base corners, Archaic, 4" ..400.00
Etley, Burlington flint, Late Archaic, 4⅜x1⅜"...........................150.00
Gibson, Burlington chert, Middle Woodland, MO, 2⅞x1½"........60.00
Graham Cave, Burlington chert, Early Archaic, MO, 4x1¼" 250.00
Hardin, cream & gray flint, Early Archaic, IN, 4½"...................285.00
Hardin, tan-cream stone, barbed, Early Archaic, MO, 5½" 250.00
Hemphill, wht & yel fossiliferous chert, Archaic, MO, 3⅛x1¼" .125.00
Lanceolate, bl Upper Mercer w/fossils, late Paleo, OH, 2⅝" 25.00
Lost Lake, chalcedony, serrated edges, Early Archaic, KY, 3½". 1,000.00
Mason, lt mottled flint, Woodland or Red Ochre, MO, 4⅛" 150.00
Mason, mottled flint or chert, Woodland/Red Ochre, IL, 2¾x1⅛".75.00
Meadowood, striated jasper, Late Archaic, 3¼"..........................750.00
Mehlville, creamy flint, resharpened/shortened, Archaic, OH, 1¾".55.00
Rectangular, striated gray flint, Paleo, KY, 2x3½" 150.00
Smith, bl & wht flint, well made, Late Archaic, MO, 4x3½".....350.00
Stemmed, reddish tan chert, Archaic, MO, 4¾x2¼" 175.00
Thebes, wht Burlington chert, resharpened, Archaic, 2⅜x1¾" ..100.00
Triangular, brn chert, Archaic, IL, 4¼" 35.00
Turkey tail, hornstone, Early Woodland, KY, 3¾" 200.00

Ceremonial Items

Bonnet, Nez Perce, ermine on wool felt, buffalo horns, s-s, 1910s .**4,000.00**
Dish, feast; NW Coast, cvd/pnt bird & animal form, 22x8x10"..**325.00**
Drum, Blackfoot, hide covered, red ochre & brass tacks, 1950s, 4x20".**435.00**
Drum, Kwakiutl, hand type w/HP sun, Mojars, 1987..................**140.00**
Drum, Pueblo, hide-covered hollow log, ca 1920, 10x15", from $250 to .**300.00**
Drum, Pueblo, rawhide-covered log w/beads & red pnt, 1950s, 17x9".**120.00**
Headdress, Crow, deer & porcupine roach, ca 1940, 13x3", +stand ..**425.00**
Horn bonnet, Blackfoot, buffalo cape w/tail drop, bw headband, 1920s.**400.00**
Mask, Iroquois, False Face, woven cornhusk, 19th C, 11x8".......**550.00**
Mask, Kwakiutl, cvd moon, Alert Bay BC, 20th C, 23" dia........**400.00**
Mask, Lalooska, cvd/pnt, wolf frontlet, ca 1970, 14x8x7"...........**400.00**
Mask, Lalooska, cvd/pnt dbl transformation: man/eagle, 1975, 21".**2,000.00**
Mask, NY Coast style, cvd/pnt cedar, 1970, 9½x7"....................**180.00**
Mask, Tlingit, cvd/pnt cedar, ca 1920, 10x9"..............................**400.00**
Rattle, Blackfoot, buffalo scrotum w/red ochre, bw hdl, 11½x2½" ..**300.00**
Rattle, Kwakiutl, cvd/inlaid deer hoof, ca 1910, 15½x5" **375.00**
Rattle, Plains, buffalo scrotum w/tail terminal & charm, 20th C, 18"..**850.00**
Soul catcher, cvd & inlaid, ca 1970, 8¼x1½" **275.00**
Spoon, Blackfoot, mtn goat horn w/bw hdl, 19th C, 8x2½".......**100.00**

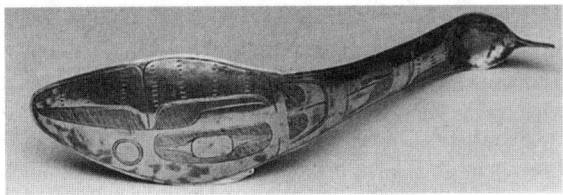

Spoon, Haida (attributed to Charles Edenshaw), engraved silver with totemic devices, 5½", $715.00.

Wand, horn w/bw hdl, horsehair suspensions, 20th C, 36x7" **225.00**
War shirt, Blackfoot, hide w/geometric bw, bibs & fringe, 1880s, 56" .**8,000.00**
War shirt, Yurok/Hupa, basketry, bw strips on arms, 1860s, 54x28".**8,500.00**

Dolls

Hopi, Kachina, Badger (Honan), Angie Larco, 11"....................**165.00**
Hopi, Kachina, Chiwavi, sgn Colletata, ca 1985, 17½x13" **1,300.00**
Hopi, Kachina, Eagle Dancer, sgn Keith Mike, 1980, 25x19"..**1,400.00**
Hopi, Kachina, Eagle Dancer Kawahu, Naknaatiya/83, fur wings, 16".**165.00**
Hopi, Kachina, Hana Clown w/watermelon, Cal Yestewa, 1960s, 11x6".**160.00**
Hopi, Kachina, Hemis w/lg headdress, Loretta Multine, ca 1980, 12x5".**100.00**
Hopi, Kachina, Honan Hanna, 1-pc, sgn R Lanza Sr, 1985, 11½x6"..**110.00**
Hopi, Kachina, leather skirt & trim, ca 1920, 10x4" **600.00**
Hopi, Kachina, Maiden, 1-pc, ca 1940, 10x5" **100.00**
Hopi, Kachina, Mtn Sheep, Phillip N Toymewa, 1985, 10x13"..**375.00**
Hopi, Kachina, Pong (mtn sheep), Bill Sewemanenewa, 15"......**250.00**
Hopi, Kachina, White Buffalo Dancer, C Cleveland, 1970, 13x4".**70.00**
Hopi, Kachina, White Buffalo dancer of Kocha Mosairv, Earl Yowytewa, 10"..**240.00**
N Plains, traditional dancer, complete costume, Angier, 1994, 18" .**100.00**

Domestics

Blanket, Chimayo, geometric design, mc wool, 1940s, 80x51", EX .**70.00**
Blanket, Navajo, Crystal pattern w/many feathers, 1910s, 52x81" .**2,750.00**
Blanket, Navajo transitional, lines & parallelograms, 1920s, 48x33".**150.00**
Blanket, wearing; Chimayo, geometrics on turq, 1940s, 46x70" .**200.00**
Blanket, wearing; Navajo lady's, stripes, ca 1890, rare, 48x65" ...**325.00**
Box, bark w/porcupine quill designs ea side, 1860s, 2¾x3½"......**250.00**
Box, pill; Navajo, silver w/turq stone on lid, ca 1970, 1½x¾" **110.00**

Cradle, Apache, bentwood & yel cloth, traditional design, 1980s, 28".**100.00**
Cradle, Apache, cloth, made for & w/orig doll, 1940s, 20½x9x11" ..**275.00**
Cradle, Paiute, hooded basketry w/yarn laces, geometric design, 1970 .**100.00**
Cradle cover, Central Plains, orange/red quill work, fringed, 27", VG .**4,300.00**
Game, Cheyenne, pin & bone, ca 1930, 11x½" **200.00**
Scoop, burl, made from 1 pc, att, 1830s, 7x20x12" **1,000.00**
Tepee, Crow, sun/moon/hands design, full liner, ca 1900, 25x15'..**1,500.00**
Toy, Crow, leather horse w/bw saddle blanket & hooves, 1920s, 11x13"..**180.00**

Jewelry and Adornments

As early as 500 A.D., Indians in the southwest drilled turquoise nuggets and strung them on cords made of sinew or braided hair. The Spanish introduced them to coral, and it became a popular item of jewelry; abalone and clam shells were favored by the Coastal Indians. Not until the last half of the nineteenth century did the Indians learn to work with silver. Each tribe developed its own distinctive style and preferred design, which until about 1920 made it possible to determine tribal origin with some degree of accuracy. Since that time, because of modern means of communication and travel, motifs have become less distinct.

Quality Indian silver jewelry may be antique or contemporary. Age, though certainly to be considered, is not as important a factor as fine workmanship and good stones. Pre-1910 silver will show evidence of hammer marks, and designs are usually simple. Beads have sometimes been shaped from coins. Stones tend to be small; when silver wire was used, it is usually square. To insure your investment, choose a reputable dealer.

Bandolier, shoulder; hairpipe bone w/buffalo hide spacers, 1890s, 37" .**250.00**
Belt, Zuni inlay, Life Scenes conchos, sgn B Bicenti, 1970s, 43½" ..**1,500.00**
Bolo, Zuni, Devil Dancer inlay, sgn VTL, ca 1970, 27".............**130.00**
Bracelet, Navajo, silver w/11 Castle Dome turq+11 red corals, 1970.**170.00**
Bracelet, Navajo, silver w/5 lg natural Castle Dome turq, 1970s..**110.00**
Bracelet, Zuni, cuff, hummingbird inlay, Edaaki, 1960s, 2½" W .**900.00**
Bracelet, Zuni, stone-to-stone Rainbow God, turq/shell/jet, 1930s, 3".**375.00**
Breastplate, hairpipe/bone/trade bead w/mc ribbons, 1920s, 31x7½".**275.00**
Breastplate, 4½" bone hair pipes/pony beads/etc, 1940s, restrung ..**160.00**
Buckle, Navajo, silver w/natural Kingman turq, sgn LLL, 1950s, 3x4" .**110.00**
Buckle, Zuni, turq, jet & shell inlay, 1940, 1½".........................**350.00**
Cuff links, Navajo, coral & silver, 1950, 1½", pr.......................**180.00**
Earrings, Zuni, coral needlepoint drops, 1970s, 2½" **140.00**
Earrings, Zuni, silver & Blue Gem turq petit-point, 3", pr...........**40.00**
Earrings, Zuni, silver w/turq/jet/MOP/coral inlay, 1940, 1¼x1" ...**90.00**
Jackla, Navajo, natural turq w/corns, ca 1950, 11".....................**80.00**
Necklace, Santo Domingo, turq nuggets on heshi w/pr jacklas, 1950, 31".**120.00**
Necklace, Santo Domingo, 6-strand, turq/pipestone heshi, 1960, 28" .**325.00**
Necklace, Santo Domingo, 6-strand turq heshi+shell pendant, 1960, 28".**350.00**
Necklace, Santo Dominto, turq nugget on heshi w/pr jacklas, 1950s...**120.00**
Necklace, Zuni, silver & jet inlay bear w/silver feather drops, 1970.**400.00**
Necklace, Zuni, 10-strand shell bird fetish on shell heshi, 1975, 29".**110.00**
Pin, Navajo, silver & turq, figure-8 shape, 1940s, 4¼x1½"...........**50.00**
Pin, Zuni, solid silver inlay deer, old sq style, ca 1950, 2x1½" **225.00**
Ring, Navajo, silver w/natural Landers bl turq stone, 1½x1" **110.00**
Ring, Navajo, silver w/natural turq stone, 1950, 1¼x¾" **60.00**
Ring, Navajo, 14k gold w/triangular turq stone, ca 1970.............**170.00**
Ring, Navajo man's, heavy silver w/lg turq stone, 1950, ¾x1¼"..**100.00**
Ring, Zuni, silver w/channel-inlay turq, ca 1940, 2x2¼".............**90.00**
Ring, Zuni, turq needlepoint cluster, 1960s, EX quality **100.00**
Squash blossom, Zuni, turq & silver cluster, 1940s, 31½x1½" **750.00**
Watch band, Zuni, turq/jet/spiny oyster shell inlay, 1930s, 2¾" W.**140.00**

Pipes

Pipe bowls were usually carved from soft stone, such as catlinite or red pipestone, an argilaceous sedimentary rock composed mainly of hardened clay. Steatite was also used. Some ceremonial pipes were simply styled, while others were intricately designed naturalistic figurals, sometimes in bird or frog forms called effigies. Their stems, made of wood and often covered with leather, were sometimes nearly a yard in length.

Catlinite, L-shaped pregnant woman effigy, Plains, 1840s-50s, 4½x4"..**1,800.00**
Catlinite, war bundle platform type, Pawnee, 1860-70, 4".......**1,300.00**
Cvd stone, extended animal-shaped bowl, ca 1900, 8x2¾"..........**60.00**
Hardstone, 8-sided bowl & stem, late p-h, 1⅝"............................**125.00**
Pipestone (tan), tubular w/flared mouthpc, Adena, OH, 5¾".**3,200.00**
Pottery, bear head effigy, EX molding, Iroquois, 1600-1750, 5" stem..**1,000.00**
Pottery, elbow w/expanded bowl & stem openings, Mississippian, 4½".**150.00**
Pottery, trumpet, ring bowl, Iroquois, ca 1670, 5¼"....................**450.00**
Sandstone (close-grained), tubular, late Archaic, TN, from $250 to ..**350.00**
Untempered clay, human head effigy, Mississippian, 2½".............**75.00**

Pottery

Indian pottery is nearly always decorated in such a manner as to indicate the tribe that produced it or the pueblo in which it was made. For instance, the designs of Cochiti potters were usually scattered forms from nature or sacred symbols. The Zuni preferred an ornate repetitive decoration of a closer configuration. They often used stylized deer and bird forms, sometimes in dimensional applications.

Santo Domingo, olla, ivory slip and black on red clay, brick painted base, 14½", $3,650.00.

Acoma, bowl, geometrics, blk on wht slip, Lucy Lewis, 1¾x2"...**165.00**
Acoma, jar, geometric avian design on creamy slip, 4½x7½", EX.**110.00**
Acoma, seed jar, lizards, V Garcia, ca 1970, 8x8½"....................**200.00**
Anasazi, pitcher, blk on wht, geometric decor, p-h, 7½x6".........**375.00**
Casas Grandes, pitcher, bees design, Ava Trillo, 1995, 5½x3½"..**110.00**
Chaco, dipper, blk on wht, p-h, minimal rstr, 5x10¾"................**300.00**
Dipper, Anasazi, blk on wht, 4x7"..**250.00**
Ho Ho Kam, jar, circles & zippers, red on buff, p-h, 5½x6".........**100.00**
Hopi, ashtray, mc, Frog Woman Joy Navasie, 1950, 2x5"............**120.00**
Hopi, bowl, redware w/blk traditional int design, 1946, 2x6" **100.00**
Hopi, jar, mc geometrics on lt buff, Frog Woman symbol, 7x5"..**580.00**
Hopi, jar, swirled geometrics, brn/red on buff, Fannie Nampeyo, 4x5".**770.00**
Hopi, seed vessel, lizards/geometric, brn/tan, Feather Woman, 3x5½".**660.00**
Jemez, bowl, serpent cvd on delineated shoulder, red/buff, Daubs, 6"..**195.00**
Laguna, bowl, mc geometric design, 1890s, 6x10½"....................**900.00**
Pueblo, olla, mc decor, 1940s, 9x10½"......................................**225.00**
Santa Clara, bowl, blkware, feathers, polished, 2¾x3"................**110.00**
Santa Clara, bowl, blkware, geometrics, Betty & Lee Tafoya, 3½x4"..**250.00**
Santa Clara, bowl, blkware, polished, M Tafoya, 1940, 2½x7½" .**700.00**
Santa Clara, bowl, blkware, serpent, Teresita Naranyo, 3½".......**360.00**
Santa Clara, bowl, deeply cvd, Legoria & Celes, 1950s, 4½x6½" .**225.00**
Santa Clara, bowl, deer heads, Ernest & Marian Rose, 1988, ½x1¾"..**140.00**
Santa Clara, jar, blkware, serpent, sgn M Naranjo, 1950, 4½x5".**225.00**
Santa Clara, jar, buff color, twisted form, Reyes Madalena, 1960, 5x5"..**80.00**
Santa Clara, seed jar, blkware, sun face, sgn Corn Moquino, 3x4" .**300.00**

Santa Clara, seed jar, brn w/poinsettia design, L Neito, 1985, 3¾" .**60.00**
Santa Clara, seed jar, buff redware w/cvd rabbits, Medicine Flower, 2"..**715.00**
Santa Clara, turtle caricature, sgn Margaret & Luther, 1970s, 3½"..**160.00**
Santa Clara, vase, blkware, serpent, ca 1950, 6x7½"..................**120.00**
Santa Clara, wedding jar, blkware, serpent, Margaret/Luther, '60s, 10".**3,000.00**
Santo Domingo, dough bowl, blk & cream traditional design on red, 1950.**275.00**
Santo Domingo, dough bowl, geometrics, 1930s, 6x16½"..........**350.00**
Santo Domingo, olla, blkware, sgn R Aguilar, ca 1995, 14x14"..**250.00**
Tonto, olla, mc geometrics, p-h, 5x7"......................................**225.00**
Zia, Zia bird, brn/wht on redware, Lucy Lucero, 2⅝x5¼"...........**110.00**
Zuni, jar, frog & heartline deer designs, sq neck, 1930s, 6¼"......**425.00**

Pottery, San Ildefonso

The pottery of the San Ildefonso pueblo is especially sought after by collectors today. Under the leadership of Maria Martinez and her husband Julian, experiments began about 1918 which led to the development of the 'black-on-black' design achieved through exacting methods of firing the ware. They discovered that by smothering the fire at a specified temperature, the carbon in the smoke that ensued caused the pottery to blacken. Maria signed her work (often 'Marie') from the late teens to the 1960s; she died in 1980. Today examples with her signature may bring prices in the $500.00 to $4,500.00 range.

Bowl, blkware, geometric band, Alice Rueben Martinez, 1970s, 4x5" .**120.00**
Bowl, blkware, incurvate rim, Julian, 1960, 2¾x4½", NM...........**60.00**
Bowl, geometrics, wht on polished redware, JC Vigil/73, 3x4½"..**140.00**
Jar, blkware, feathers, Blue Corn, 4 4¾"....................................**700.00**
Jar, blkware, feathers, flared shoulder, Marie & Julian, 2¾"........**935.00**
Jar, blkware, feathers, Santana & Adam, 1960s, 4¾x4¾"...........**850.00**
Jar, blkware, geometric band, Marie & Julian, ca 1940, 9x10".**6,000.00**
Plate, blkware, feathers, Marie & Santana, lt wear, 14½"........**4,950.00**
Plate, gunmetal finish, Marie Poveka, 1960s, 5½"......................**700.00**

Rugs, Navajo

Big Rock area, tight weave, stepped geometrics & Xs, 1960, 55x36"..**450.00**
Coal Mine Mesa, butterfly & parallelograms, 1980s, 47x31" **225.00**
Crystal, fishook designs, 1930s, 72x52" **750.00**
Crystal, pictorial w/2 stepped dmns, side w/feathers/Nahokas, 38x61".**875.00**
Crystal area, hand carded, gray/tan/wht geometric medallions, 92x42".**965.00**
Ganado, dbl central lozenge, ca 1930, 82x47" **750.00**
Ganado, fret/geometric devices, 3-color w/dbl red X, early, 65x50" .**685.00**
Ganado, hand-loomed, museum quality, 1930s, 40x66" **1,800.00**
Ganado Red, central & water bug designs, 1935, 62x98" **2,250.00**
Klagetoh, red & wht geometrics, ca 1935, 70x35"....................**2,500.00**
Klagetoh, red/blk/wht/gray geometrics, 1930s, 57x34"..............**450.00**
Klagetoh pictoral w/sunrise dmn, sacred corn/bow & arrow, 36x72".**550.00**
Pictorial, Christmas Tree, ca 1980, 30x24" **500.00**
Pictorial w/mc feather designs, ca 1935, 65x43" **1,700.00**
Pine Springs, vegetal dyed geometrics, 1945, 58x33" **400.00**
Saddle, dbl, striped, Betty James, 1980, 57x28" **110.00**
Saddle, stripes, mc w/red & orange, butterflies in corners, 30x30"..**135.00**
Serrated dmns & Valero Stars & feathers, 1930s, 80x44" **3,000.00**
Teec Nos Pos, red/blk/wht geometrics, 1940s, 68x42" **850.00**
Transitional, all natural wool, striped, 1930s, 57x54" **225.00**
Tuba City, Storm pattern, Sunie Begay, ca 1980, 71x58" **475.00**
US flag design w/48 stars, 1940, 45x27" **475.00**
Western Reservation, red/blk/gray geometrics, ca 1935, 76x54" .**850.00**
Wide Ruins, hand loomed, vegetal dyes, 1960, 32x50" **250.00**
Yei, 3 females/cornstalks/Rainbow God, mc on gray & wht, 34x56".**1,200.00**
Yei figures (2) & 3 cornstalks, natural/aniline, 1940, 45x30"......**200.00**
2 Gray Hills, central lozenge, Betsy Begay, ca 1980, 40x29" **375.00**
2 Gray Hills, central lozenge, Georgia Cohoe, 1980s, 46x26" .**1,100.00**

2 Gray Hills, central lozenge, 1970, 49x31" 170.00
2 Gray Hills, elongated sunrise, blk/wht/gray, A James, 55x34" ..275.00
2 Gray Hills, hand spun, all natural, 1960s, 49x34" 700.00
2 Gray Hills, stepped devices w/stylized butterfly, early, 68x38", VG.220.00
2 Gray Hills, tapestry, tan/gray w/blk in dmn geometric, '70s, 29x19"..465.00

Shaped Stone Artifacts

Bannerstone, banded glacial slate, ball type, Archaic, MO, 1½x2" .500.00
Bannerstone, banded glacial slate, curved pick type, Archaic, 5¾" .700.00
Bannerstone, gr banded slate, crescent type, Archaic, IN, 4⅞".1,000.00
Bannerstone, gray hardstone, winged, drilled, Archaic, 4" 200.00
Bannerstone, quartzite, bottle subtype, Archaic, IL, 2⅞x3⅛" .3,800.00
Bannerstone, speckled hardstone, saddlebk type, Archaic, IN, 2⅜".700.00
Bar amulet, banded slate, drilled hole ea end, Woodland, ¾x5"..1,100.00
Birdstone, popeye hardstone type, late Archaic, 1 eye missing, IN, 3"..1,100.00
Boatstone, speckled hardstone, Woodland, OK, ⅞x1⅝x3⅛"......300.00
Discoidal, dk hardstone, Cahokia type, Mississippian, MO, 1¼x3" .325.00
Discoidal, dk porphyry, bifacially cupped, Mississippian, 1¾x4¾" .1,000.00
Gorget, banded slate, Keel type, Archaic (?), IN, 3x1¾" 900.00
Gorget, banded slate, quadriconcave type, early Woodland, 1⅝x3⅞" ...425.00
Gorget, banded slate, spinebk type, Archaic, 1¼x4x⅝" 750.00
Gorget, banded slate, 2-hole, Adena/early Woodland, OH, 3x4⅝" .1,500.00
Gorget, elliptical, banded slate, Adena/early Woodland, IN, 5⅛" ..285.00
Pendant, bell shape, dk banded slate, Adena/early Woodland, 4⅛"..200.00
Pendant, dk hardstone, spud shape, Mississippian, IA, 4½x2¼".750.00
Pendant, gr hardstone, Woodland, 1½x3⅞", minimum value.....750.00
Pendant, keyhole type, banded slate, Adena, IN, 4½" 300.00
Plummet, dk hematite, grooved top, teardrop form, Archaic, 2½" .275.00

Tools

Adz, full groove, wide & deep, OH 165.00
Adz, knobbed, polished & formed lower bit, PA, 7x1" 250.00
Adz, speckled hardstone, Adena, OH, 4½x1¾"...........................55.00
Adz, wht Burlington chert, Archaic, IL, 5x2" 100.00
Axe, blk diorite, full groove, polished 1 side, AZ, 2x3½" 40.00
Axe, brn granite, ¾-groove, EX lines, IA, 2¾x6¼" 800.00
Axe, brn jasper-like stone, full groove, long poll, WI, 2¼x4x4½"..225.00
Axe, fine-grain gr granite, barbed, full groove, TN, 5x7x2¼".....650.00
Axe, gr hardstone, ¾-groove, NOH, 7⅜x4½"..........................875.00
Axe, gray & blk conglomerate hardstone, ¾-groove, Archaic, MO, 6".985.00
Axe, gray-gr hardstone, full groove, OH, 4½x6½x2¼"..............400.00
Axe, mottled granite, ¾-groove, OH, 2⅛x4¾"..........................150.00
Axe, speckled granite, ¾-groove, PA, 4x13"................................125.00
Axe, speckled hardstone, fluted, ¾-groove, WI, scarce type.......700.00
Axe, trophy; orange/brn/blk gneiss, MI, 2⅜x5", from $2,500 to..4,500.00

Axe head, dark hardstone, nicely polished, 4", $600.00. (Photo courtesy Jacksons Auctioneers & Appraisers)

Celt, flint, EX polish, IN, 2½x1½"..85.00
Celt, greenstone, AL, 7¼x2x⅝"...400.00
Celt, hematite, IA, 1⅝x2⅞x½"..150.00

Chisel, slate, IN, 7¼x1¾", from $95 to 125.00
Drill, chalky wht flint or chert, Archaic, IL, 4x1½"....................175.00
Drill, dk bl Upper Mercer flint, Archaic, OH, 2¼" 95.00
Drill, gray & wht flint, Archaic, IN, 2¼" 8.00
Drill, Gray IN chert, Archaic, IN, 2½x⅜".....................................15.00
Drill, lt gray IN flint, made from Archaic blade, notched base, 2⅛".15.00
Drill, mixed chert, Archaic, IL 2x⅝"...30.00
Gouge, greenstone, IL, 5⅜x2¼' 15.00
Hammerstone, central pit (may be on ea end), from $5 to............10.00
Hammerstone, dk brn hardstone, polished, Archaic, KY, 4x4½" ..20.00
Hoe, cream flint w/lg brn swirl, Mississippian, IL, 7¾" 800.00
Knife, brn-tan flint, Paleo, MO, 5x1⅜"..95.00
Knife, E Woodlands, crooked, wire wrap, wood hdl, 1900, 10x1" .90.00
Knife, wht chert or flint, Paleo, OH, 4x1¼" 25.00
Maul, quartzite conglomerate, full groove, Archaic, IN, 3½x5¼" .395.00
Pestle, brn hardstone, hoof type, Archaic, KY, 3x4½" 25.00
Pestle, polished hardstone, basal damage, Archaic, OH, 5½x2¾"..150.00
Plummet, gray hematite, polished, grooved top, Archaic, IL 300.00
Scraper, L-shape, forged steel blade, rawhide wrap, 1930, 12x2".140.00
Spade, tan flint, Mississippian, IL, 12x4⅝" 300.00
Spatulate, dk flint, highly polished, TN, 7x3" 650.00
Spud, hardstone, secondary shaping for lacing, OH, 7x3" 350.00
Tomahawk, Woodlands, wrought-iron spontoon head, pnt hardwood shaft.325.00

Weapons

Bow, S Plains, Bois de Arc fighting, sharp ends, 19th C, 60" 225.00
Club, Crow, rstr rawhide wrap & bw hdl, ca 1890, 24" 190.00
Club, Plains, fixed stone head, s-s, hide-covered shaft, 1870s, 40" .160.00
Club, rawhide cover, ca 1880s, 15x2¾", G 120.00
Tomahawk, spike-bk, belt type, 19th C, 10x6¼" 200.00

Miscellaneous

Model tepee, Blackfoot, pnt hide w/bw, tin cones, 1900s, 28x16" ..500.00
Peace medal, John Adams, bronze colored, 1797, 3" 160.00
Peace medal, King George, brass colored, 1757, 1¾" 150.00
Peace medal, President John Q Adams, copper colored, 1825, 3" .130.00
Totem pole, NW Coast, cvd/pnt wood, 3-figure, 1880s, 21x2½" .325.00

American Painted Porcelain

The American china-painting movement can be traced back to an extracurricular class attended by art students at the McMicken School of Design in Cincinnati. These students, who were the wives and daughters of the city's financial elite, managed to successfully paint numerous porcelains for display in the Woman's Pavilion of the 1876 United States Centennial Exposition held in Philadelphia — an amazing feat considering the high technical skill required for proficiency, as well as the length of time and multiple firings necessary to finish the ware. From then until 1917 when the United States entered World War I, china painting was a profession as well as a popular amateur pursuit for many people, particularly women. In fact, over 25,000 people were involved in this art form at the turn of the last century.

Collectors and antique dealers have discovered American hand-painted porcelain, and they have become aware of its history, beauty, and potential value. For more information on this subject, *American Painted Porcelain: Collector's Identification & Value Guide*, *Antique Trader's Comprehensive Guide to American Painted Porcelain*, and *Painted Porcelain Jewelry and Buttons: Collector's Identification & Value Guide* by Dorothy Kamm are the culmination of a decade of research; we recommend them highly for further study.

Though American pieces are of high quality and commensurate with their European counterparts, they are much less costly today. Generally, you will pay as little as $20.00 for a 6" plate and less than $75.00 for many other items. Values are based on aesthetic appeal, quality of the workmanship, size, rarity of the piece and of the subject matter, and condition. Age is the least important factor, because most American painted porcelains are not dated. (Factory backstamps are helpful in establishing the approximate time period an item was decorated, but they aren't totally reliable.)

Our advisor for this category is Dorothy Kamm; she is listed in the Directory under Florida.

Bar pin, brass-plated bezel, 1½" W, from $25 to	45.00
Belt buckle brooch, oval, 1¾x2⅛", from $90 to	175.00
Bonbon bowl (depending on size), from $18 to	85.00
Bowl, fruit; from $60 to	80.00
Box, 4¾ dia, from $50 to	75.00
Brooch, brass-plated bezel, oval, 2x1½", from $55 to	75.00
Brooch, gold-plated bezel, 1½" dia, from $35 to	55.00
Brooch/pendant, heart shape, gold-plated bezel, 2x1¾", from $50 to	85.00
Cake plate, from $35 to	75.00
Candlestick, from $45 to	125.00
Celery tray, from $35 to	75.00
Condiment set, poppy, tray/shakers/toothpick, 1891-1914, from $45 to	55.00
Cruet, from $60 to	80.00
Cuff pin, rectangular, brass-pated bezel, ¼x1⅛", from $12 to	18.00
Cup & saucer	45.00
Cup & saucer, bouillon; from $35 to	55.00
Ewer (depending on size), from $100 to	175.00
Gravy boat, from $55 to	75.00
Handy pin, brass-plated bezel, 1½", from $30 to	40.00
Hatpin holder, from $88 to	125.00
Jam jar, from $30 to	75.00
Jardiniere (depending on size), from $65 to	375.00
Mug, from $40 to	75.00
Napkin ring, from $10 to	25.00
Pendant, gold-plated bezel, 1" dia, from $50 to	200.00
Pin tray, from $30 to	50.00
Pitcher, lemonade; from $175 to	225.00
Plate, 6", from $10 to	35.00
Plate, 8", from $45 to	75.00

Plate, overglaze paints, burnished gold rim, ca 1875 – 1935, 8¼", from $25.00 to $50.00. (Photo courtesy Dorothy Kamm)

Salt cellar, from $20 to	40.00
Scarf pin, medallion, brass-plated bezel & shank, 1¼" dia, $35 to	65.00
Shakers, pr, from $25 to	40.00
Shirtwaist button, 1" dia, from $20 to	40.00
Shirtwaist set, brooch, brass-plated mts, 1¾"+ cuff links, $150 to	350.00
Stein, from $75 to	150.00
Tea or coffee set, ea set, from $175 to	300.00
Whiskey set, ears of corn, sgn, Surquist, 1903-17, 8-pc, $300 to	400.00

Amphora

The Amphora Porcelain Works in the Teplitz-Turn area of Bohemia produced Art Nouveau-styled vases and figurines during the latter part of the 1800s through the first few decades of the twentieth century. They marked their wares with various stamps, some incorporating the name and location of the pottery with a crown or a shield. Because Bohemia was part of the Austro-Hungarian empire prior to WWI, some examples are marked Austria; items marked with the Czechoslovakia designation were made after the war. All decoration described in the listings that follow is hand painted unless otherwise indicated.

Our advisor for this category is John Cobabe; he is listed in the Directory under California.

Bowl, mc birds, ftd, 5x8"	100.00
Candlestick, bl & gr organic form, hdl, 11"	1,000.00
Ewer, fern leaves, sgn, mk #3430, 7½"	150.00
Pitcher, flower medallion on bl, glossy cobalt hdl, 7½"	85.00
Planter, flowers & vines in relief, brn matt, hdls, 5x7"	225.00
Vase, dragon & crab in relief, ivory/brn/bl/gr/gold, 22¼"	5,750.00
Vase, dragon figure, yel/tan/gold on mauve mottle, #4548 50, 20"	5,750.00
Vase, flowers, cobalt w/gold on wht, curved lines, 8¼"	300.00
Vase, flowers, mc on bl to gr, rim-to-hip hdls, 10⅝"	350.00
Vase, gourd form w/full-length 3-D lady clinging to side, 19"	700.00
Vase, hawk on tree/floral spray, hdls, #'d, 13⅛"	275.00
Vase, insects, mc w/gold, 8½"	600.00
Vase, lg gr enamel leaves/bl buds on brn matt, gourd form, 7½"	280.00
Vase, metallic w/appl faux cabochons & froth, #5086-56 (?), 17"	3,820.00
Vase, profile of lady, gold outlines, 7"	850.00
Vase, profile of maid in forest, sepia w/purple & gr vine accents, 15"	2,800.00
Vase, roses & fired-on gold, buttressed hdls, 7", NM	225.00
Vase, sculpted floral band on spider web ground, 18½"	950.00
Vase, trees w/apples & leaves, 12"	425.00
Vase, 2 lg appl roses among sm buds & leaves, twig hdls, #3647, 10x10"	365.00

Animal Dishes With Covers

Covered animal dishes have been produced for nearly two centuries and are as varied as their manufacturers. They were made in many types of glass (slag, colored, clear, and milk glass) as well as china and pottery. On bases of nests and baskets, you will find animals and birds of every sort. The most common was the hen.

Some of the smaller versions made by McKee, Indiana Tumbler and Goblet Company, and Westmoreland Specialty Glass of Pittsburgh, Pennsylvania, were sold to food-processing companies who filled them with prepared mustard, baking powder, etc. Occasionally one will be found with the paper label identifying the product and processing company still intact.

Many of the glass versions produced during the latter part of the nineteenth century have been recently reproduced. In the 1960s, the Kemple Glass Company made the rooster, fox, lion, cat, lamb, hen, horse, turkey, duck, dove, and rabbit on split-ribbed or basketweave bases. They were made in amethyst, blue, amber, and milk glass, as well as a variegated slag. Kanawha, L.G. Wright, and Imperial made several as well. It is sometimes necessary to compare items in question to verified examples of older glass in order to recognize reproductions. Reproduction is continued today.

For more information, we recommend *Covered Animal Dishes* by Everett Grist, whose address is in the Directory under Tennessee; *Collector's Encyclopedia of Milk Glass* by Betty and Bill Newbound; *Westmoreland Glass* by Charles West Wilson; and *American Slag Glass* by Ruth Grizel. In the listings below, when only one dimension is given, it is the greater one, usually length. See also Greentown and other specific companies.

Bird, milk glass, rnd basketweave vase, Vallerysthal, 6½".............**95.00**
Cat, milk glass, lacy base, glass eyes, WG on base 150.00
Cat, milk glass, wide-rib base, unmk, 5½" **50.00**
Chick on eggs, bl frost w/HP decor, basket base..........................100.00
Dog, amber, wide-rib base, Westmoreland..................................**65.00**
Dog, milk glass w/bl head, wide-rib base, Westmoreland, 5¼" **85.00**
Duck, Atterbury; slag (any color), Wright or Imperial repro 70.00
Duck, milk glass, split-rib base, unmk McKee, 5½" 185.00
Duck, milk glass, wavy base, Challinor Taylor, 8" 125.00
Duck, Pintail; bl opaque, split-rib base, Kemple, 5½".................125.00
Fox, Ribbed; milk glass, lacy Atterbury base, no date, 6¼" 100.00
Frog, milk glass, condiment container, unmk McKee, 5½" **550.00**
Hand & Dove, milk glass, lacy base, WG on base 110.00
Hen, Little; milk glass, mk Hazel Atlas 15.00
Hen, milk glass, Fenton, 8" 150.00
Hen, milk glass w/bl head, dmn basketweave base, Westmoreland, 5¼" .**85.00**
Hen, Straight Headed; clear, Indiana Glass, lg 15.00
Hen w/chicks, milk glass, condiment container, unmk McKee, 5½".**165.00**
Lamb, milk glass, picket base, Westmoreland Specialty **95.00**
Lion, milk glass, scroll base, unmk, 5½" **95.00**
Pekinese dog, milk glass, att Sandwich, 4¾" 500.00
Puppy Love, boy & dog on lid of dbl tub, milk glass, att Dermay.**200.00**
Rabbit, clear, basketweave base, US Glass, 8" **95.00**
Rabbit, milk glass, condiment container, unmk McKee, 5½" 175.00
Rooster, milk glass, basketweave base, Westmoreland repro........110.00
Rooster, milk glass, wide-rib base, Westmoreland Specialty, 5¼"..**35.00**
Rooster, milk glass w/HP details, glass eyes, Challinor Taylor, 7" .135.00
Swan, Closed Neck; milk glass, Westmoreland Specialty **75.00**
Swan, milk glass, condiment container, unmk McKee, 5½" 220.00
Turkey, milk glass, condiment container, base mk McKee, 5½"..**220.00**

Appliances, Electric

Antique electric appliances represent a diverse field and are always being sought after by collectors. There were over one hundred different companies manufacturing electric appliances in the first half of the twentieth century; some were making over ten different models under several different names at any given time in all fields: coffeepots, toasters, waffle irons, etc., while others were making only one or two models for extended periods of time. Today collectors and decorators alike are seeking those items to add to a collection or to use as accent pieces in a period kitchen. Refer to *Toasters and Small Kitchen Appliances* published by L-W Book Sales for more information. If you're especially interested in vintage fans, we recommend *The Collector's Guide to Electric Fans* by John Witt (Collector Books).

Always check the cord before using and make sure the appliance is in good condition, free of rust and pitting. Unless noted otherwise, values are for appliances in excellent condition. Prices may vary around the country.

Bread maker, Climax #04, Landers Frary & Clark, 10x12", EX.....**45.00**
Bread maker, Universal #4, Landers Frary & Clark, crank hdl, EX..**25.00**
Bread maker, Universal #8, Landers Frary & Clark, ca 1909, 12x14" ..**30.00**
Broiler, Manning-Bowman Smokeless, chrome, 1940s, NM..........**25.00**
Broiler, Sunbeam, carousel rotisserie, dome window, 1950s style, M.**70.00**
Can opener, Rival Can-O-Mat, yel, wall mt, MIB.........................**40.00**
Coffee maker, Associated Dry Goods NY NY #F71, Deco chrome, rnd dome ...**35.00**
Coffee maker, Farberware, chrome, 30-cup, EX..............................**35.00**
Coffee maker, Farberware, chrome w/blk Bakelite hdl, cloth cord, 1930s .**40.00**
Coffee maker, Sunbeam Coffeemaster, ca 1940s, NM....................**40.00**
Coffee maker, Sunbeam C30, chrome w/blk hdl, ca 1956, NM.....**35.00**
Coffee urn, Anchorware Chromium Plated, cloth cord, 14", NM.**60.00**
Dough mixer, Hobart #219175, 3-speed, w/bowl & paddle, EX ..**115.00**
Egg cooker, Hankscraft, ceramic & chrome, 1930s, 7x7", EX........**25.00**

Egg cooker, Sunbeam E2, cloth cord, 1940s, 8"............................**35.00**
Expresso maker, chrome atomic shape, Made in Italy, 1950s, M.**265.00**
Fan, Emerson #7166FG, French Gray (chips), 6 12" blades, ca 1930s, EX..**265.00**
Fan, Emerson #79648-AX, 4-blade, blk w/bl & silver badge, 1941, EX..**60.00**
Fan, General Electric #42X548, 10" blades, 1936, EX **25.00**
Fan, General Electric #75423 Star Oscillator, 12" blades, 1918, VG .**150.00**
Fan, Westinghouse #165D3, 4 16" blades, ca 1955, NM **38.00**
Fan, Westinghouse Whirlwind, S wire guard, ca 1919, EX............**25.00**
Heater, Arvin, Noblitt-Sparks...Model 203A, 1320 watts, 12x6"..**25.00**
Heater, Samson #185, Deco chrome w/cast metal base, 18x14" **30.00**
Hot plate, Simplex, SP, 4 settings, wht hdl, 5x7½"......................**30.00**
Kettle, General Electric, chrome dome shape w/blk hdl, 7½" **17.50**
Kettle, Manning-Bowman, lacquered copper, porc knob, late 1930s, EX .**25.00**
Mixer, General Electric, turq, hand held, 1950s, NM...................**35.00**
Mixer, General Electric, wht, 3-beater, 12-speed, EX w/bowl........**55.00**
Mixer, General Electric #149M8, 115 volt, milk glass bowls, EX.**42.50**
Mixer, Hamilton Beach Solid State Deluxe, stainless steel, EX.**42.50**
Mixer, Hobart KitchenAid K5A, cream color, EX w/13 accessories.**155.00**
Mixer, Kenmore, cream colored w/glass bottom mk Glasbake, EX .**35.00**
Mixer, KitchenAid K-4B, wht, 115 volts, w/bowl, EX **70.00**
Mixer, KitchenAid 3-C, 10-speed, w/bowl, EX **42.50**
Mixer, Maynard Deluxe Master Mixer #88, pk hdls & center, hand held.**30.00**
Mixer, Miracle Electric Food, 75 watts, wht, tilts up, EX **30.00**
Mixer, Sunbeam Mixmaster, jade-ite bowls, porc juicer, EX........**115.00**
Percolator, General Electric Automatic, chrome w/blk hdl, 1960s, MIB.**45.00**
Percolator, Hotpoint, chrome, 3-ftd, cloth cord, 9-cup, M...........**27.50**
Percolator, Proctor Silex, gr w/clear glass, 12-cup **25.00**
Percolator, Royal Rochester, bird & flower front, missing cord, 14".**55.00**
Percolator, Universal, chrome w/blk Bakelite hdl, 10½", EX **30.00**
Popcorn popper, aluminum w/3 gr wooden hdls, switch in cord, 1930s .**35.00**
Popcorn popper, Jolly Time, Mirro-Matic, 3-qt, NM w/instructions..........**40.00**
Popcorn popper, Kwikway, red wood hdl, blk wood legs, 8¾x8½".**25.00**
Popcorn popper, Mirro Aluminum, blk ft & hdls, NM................**15.00**
Popcorn popper, Popper Chef #1702, Dominion, w/4 colored bowls, MIB.**32.50**
Popcorn popper, Sears Kenmore, aluminum w/blk hdl & ft, NM..**22.50**
Popcorn popper, Sunbeam Great Am Popcorn Machine, ca 1976, MIB.**25.00**
Popcorn popper, West Bend, aluminum w/glass lid, 1950s, EX......**15.00**

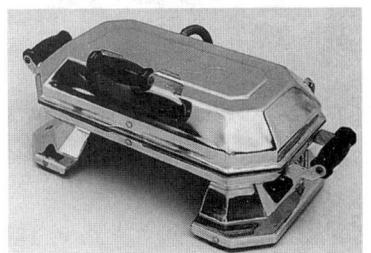

Sandwich grill, Waage Mfg. Co., Chicago, Illinois, chrome with embossed top, Bakelite handles and wafer feet, 1930s, 4½x13½x6½", EX, $55.00.

Skillet, pk enamel on aluminum, ca 1960, EX **15.00**
Skillet, Presto Electric Fry Pan/skillet, ca 1956, M **37.50**
Skillet, Sunbeam, w/brn crockery insert, MIB (G box) **35.00**
Toaster, Gold Seal, nickel w/blk wood hdls, 1920s, 6⅞"...............**95.00**
Toaster, Hotpoint, chrome & Bakelite, heat control in cord, 1930s, 7".**30.00**
Toaster, Lasco Automatic Pop-Up, chrome w/blk hdls, 1940s, 7½".**125.00**
Toaster, Royal Rochester, NP steel, 1910-15, 6⅝"........................**125.00**
Toaster, Son-Chief Speed Master, chrome w/walnut hdls, 1930s, 7¼".**35.00**
Toaster, Sunbeam Toastwich, chrome, 1930s, 4⅝x10¾x7¼".......**165.00**
Toaster, Toastwell, chrome w/blk Bakelite hdls, 2-slot, 1940s, 6¾".**65.00**
Toaster, White Cross, chrome, brn hdls & base, 1940s, 7½".........**40.00**
Toaster oven/broiler, Toastmaster #5236, chrome, M....................**30.00**
Vacuum cleaner, AirWay, tall canister, brn hose, EX **65.00**
Vacuum cleaner, Electrolux #1205, ca 1968, EX complete **95.00**
Vacuum cleaner, Electrolux Automatic E canister, cordwinder, EX.**40.00**

Vacuum cleaner, General Electric Roll-Easy R1, late 1950s, EX.**285.00**
Vacuum cleaner, Kirby Classic III, red plaid bag, 1950-50s, NM...**90.00**
Vacuum cleaner, Regina Pneumatic Cleaner, solid oak base, EX ..**70.00**
Waffle iron, General Electric, dbl, eng tulip ea lid, EX.................**60.00**
Waffle iron, Manning-Bowman Twin-O-Matic, metal & plastic, EX.**65.00**
Waffle iron, Universal, chrome w/blk hdls, cloth cord, NM..........**40.00**

Arc-En-Ciel

Named after the French word for 'rainbow,' the Arc-En-Ciel Pottery Company was short-lived, operating only from 1903 until 1905. It occupied the old Radford Pottery in Zanesville, Ohio, for the exclusive purpose of producing art wares. Mostly covered in lustered glazes, these were exhibited at the St. Louis Purchase Exhibition of 1904, but to little commercial avail. The lack of demand caused production to be changed to a more utilitarian type of ware. The new Brighton line gave its name to yet another incarnation for the pottery.

One of the original members of the Arc-En-Ciel team, John Lessell, would become art director at the Weller Pottery and introduce his own versions of lustred artware in his LaSa and Lamar lines in the early 1920s. When marked, pieces are stamped with a rainbow-shaped logo containing the name Arc-En-Ciel. Our advisors for this category are Suzanne Perrault and Dave Rago; they are listed in the Dirctory under New Jersey.

Vase, gold-tone with raised figures, no mark, 7", $150.00.
(Photo courtesy Dave Rago Auctions)

Vase, bl-gray gloss, classic form w/hdls, mk, 9"..............................**175.00**
Vase, gold-tone w/bust of Lincoln & eagle, mk, 6¾", EX............**150.00**
Vase, mottled/textured/dripping gray gloss, bulbous, mk, 10x6"..**540.00**

Arequipa

The Arequipa Pottery operated from 1911 until 1918 at a sanitorium near Fairfax, California. Its purpose was two-fold: therapy for the patients and financial support for the institution. Frederick H. Rhead was the originator and director. The ware, made from local clays, was often hand thrown, simply styled and decorated. Marks were varied but always incorporated the name of the pottery and the state. A circular arrangement encompassing the negative image of a vase beside a tree is most common.

Examples are evaluated according to quality of artwork; size and shape are less important. Those done by Rhead himself are most desirable.

Key:
A — Arequipa   CA — California

Vase, gunmetal blk w/abstract cvg, A/CA/AP, 4¾x3¾", NM..**3,740.00**
Vase, olive gr matt, gourd shape, pnt A/CA/1012 in bl on wht, 6x5".**750.00**

Vase, purple w/squeezebag yel/orange/gr irises, pnt 670/A/CA, 10x5".**74,750.00**
Vase, seafoam gr matt, cvd to brn clay w/eucalyptus, A/#d, BL, 5x4"..**4,300.00**
Vase, sheer gr/turq gloss w/cvd arabesques, 1916, OC/A, 14x6", $3,500 to **4,500.00**
Vase, speckled lt bl matt cvd w/floral, A/905/16, FHW?, 6x5½" .**2,530.00**

Argy-Rousseau, G.

Gabriel Argy-Rousseau produced both fine art glass and quality commercial ware in Paris, France, in 1918. He favored Art Nouveau as well as Art Deco and in the '20s produced a line of vases in the Egyptian manner, made popular by the discovery of King Tut's tomb. One of the most important types of glass he made was pate-de-verre. Most of his work is signed. Items listed below are pate-de-verre unless noted otherwise.

Bowl, rasberry vines, clear/purple frost, 4" **2,100.00**
Box, flower & foliage, mc on gray w/purple/pk slashes, 5" dia .**4,300.00**
Pendant, rose/branch, rose/brn/frost, 2¼" dia **690.00**
Plaque, 2 tigers amid rayed panels, 7x6" **5,750.00**
Tray, berries & leaves, brick red/purple/gray, 1½x3½".............**1,000.00**
Vase, fruit on vines, lt aqua/gr/gray/orange brn, ovoid, 5⅜".....**1,575.00**

Art Deco

To the uninformed observer, Art Deco evokes images of chrome and glass, streamlined curves and aerodynamic shapes, mirrored prints of pink flamingos, and statues of slender nudes and greyhound dogs. Though the Deco movement began in 1925 at the Paris International Exposition and lasted to some extent into the 1950s, within that period of time the evolution of fashion and taste continued as it always has, resulting in subtle variations.

The French Deco look was one of opulence — exotic inlaid woods, rich material, lush fur, and leather. Lines tended toward symmetrical curves. American designers adapted the concept to cover every aspect of fashion and home furnishings from small inexpensive picture frames, cigarette lighters, and costume jewelry to high-fashion designer clothing and exquisite massive furniture with squared or circular lines. Vinyl was a popular covering, and chrome-plated brass was used for chairs, cocktail shakers, lamps, and tables. Dinnerware, glassware, theaters, and train stations were designed to reflect the new 'Modernism.'

The Deco movement made itself apparent into the '50s in wrought iron lamps with stepped pink plastic shades and Venetian blinds. The sheer volume of production during those twenty-five years provides collectors today with fine examples of the period that can be bought for as little as $10.00 or $20.00 up to the thousands. Chrome items signed 'Chase' are prized by collectors, and blue glass radios and tables with blue glass tops are high on the list of desirability in many areas.

Those interested in learning more about this subject will want to read *Collector's Guide to Art Deco* by Mary Frank Gaston (published by Collector Books).

See also Bronzes; Chase; Frankart; Jewelry; Lalique; Radios; etc.

Armoire, mahog vnr, fitted center section, Fr, 1930s, 71x71"..**1,950.00**
Ashtray, chrome open sphere, 1 rest, Manning-Bowman **45.00**
Ashtray, flamingo at side, pewter, EX patina, 4½" L.....................**12.50**
Ashtray, rose-tone marble, 3 rests, 2x6"..**25.00**
Ashtray, silver-tone metal, stepped hdl, glass insert, Seville, 33"..**200.00**
Ashtray, yel mirrored metal, 4 rests, ½x4¾" dia **37.50**
Barometer, dk brn & butterscotch Catalin, Taylor, from $35 to....**45.00**
Beverage set, chrome/Bakelite, Manning-Bowman, pitcher+6 glasses+tray.**575.00**
Box, cigarette; seated wht-metal nude supports glass Ridgeley box.**225.00**
Box, dresser; pk glass w/gilt metal lid, ballerina finial, 6½" L **250.00**
Box, jewel, nickel silver, velvet-lined casket form, 2½x6½" **40.00**

Box, powder; creamic, draped dancing nude atop lid, Germany .**100.00**
Box, wooden, stylized mc triptych landscape w/gesso outlines, 4x12x10".**230.00**
Candle holders, brass split leaves on rnd base, Sweden, 4¾", pr ...**95.00**
Canisters, tin w/blk dmn hdls, Deco lettering, 2 8½"+2 4½".........**55.00**
Carafe, gr enamel, Am Thermos Bottle Co, from $40 to..............**60.00**
Carafe, polished chrome, Manning-Bowman, from $30 to **40.00**
Card holder, chromed nude dancer supports glass holder, 1930s, 10"..**198.00**
Ceiling fixture, wht glass, linear design, 10x12"............................**85.00**
China cabinet, 2 glass doors form lg circle, burl walnut fr/posts, 53" .**3,000.00**
Cigarette holder, blk & orange plastic, 12", from $50 to **60.00**
Clock, Westclock Moonbeam, yel celluloid, flash alarm, 5½x6½"..**85.00**
Doop panel, scrolling/foliate wrought iron, 1928, 82x24", 4 for .**5,875.00**
Figure, ape parent & child, lav matt, Ceramique de Bruxelles, 9" .**515.00**
Figure, draped nude, bronzed wht metal, marble base, Fayral, 21"..**2,000.00**
Figure, lady dancer w/fan, porc, metal base, att Herwig & Co, 12" ..**300.00**
Figure, panther on base, recumbent, bronze, Barye, 4¼x7½" **385.00**
Figure, Spanish lady, pnt pot metal & ivorine, marble base, 10".**300.00**
Flower frog, nude holds drape wide, Coronet/MIG, 13½" **140.00**
Goblets, silver, long slim stems, 7¼x3 14", 8 for **545.00**
Incense burner, cast metal Egyptian kneeling figure, Vantiens....**400.00**
Jewelry cabinet, mahog, half-cylinder door, Ruhlmann, 19x21", 23" legs.**235.00**

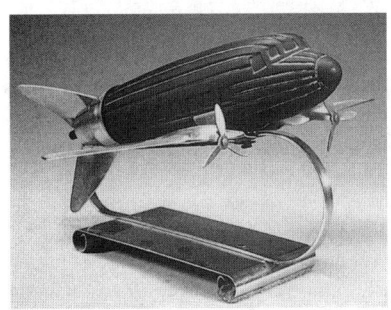

Lamp, cobalt frosted glass airplane with chrome wings, propellers, and tail, on chrome base, EX, $575.00.

Lamp, horizontal rib 11" pk satin glass rosebud-top shade, Vlieghe/Fr..**515.00**
Lamp, molded glass lady w/draped arms extended, oval base w/light, 11"..**400.00**
Lamp, table; gr frosted glass, in form of Saturn, ca 1939, 11½"...**375.00**
Lamp base, nudes/grapevines, etch brass silver-wash ovoid, 1925, 21".**500.00**
Light cover, wht frosted glass w/gray geometric design, 13½" sq ...**35.00**
Magazine rack, nude & greyhound, bronze & silver finish, 15½x11".**800.00**
Mirror, scroll fr-work ea side/below w/coat hooks, Fr, 3x40" **2,940.00**
Mirror, trapezoidal w/lower half fr w/wrought iron, 30x24"......**1,175.00**
Mirror, vanity; on faux marble base w/pot-metal dancing nude ..**250.00**
Night light, chrome airplane w/frosted bl glass center................**175.00**
Nightstands, walnut/cherry veneer, stepped/curvilinear, 27x28", pr.**690.00**
Note pad holder, blk Bakelite Scottie shape, 8¼" L **75.00**
Paperweight, elephant figural, butterscotch onyx, 5¼x4¼" **55.00**
Pen holder, lady figural, glossy blk on red clay, 5¾".......................**30.00**
Pencil sharpener, maroon & chrome, from $35 to **50.00**
Place setting, stainless w/red Bakelite hdls, 4-pc **35.00**
Planter, wrought iron, 2 serpents entwine reeded stem, petal bowl, 40" .**5,875.00**
Sconce, NP brass w/curved arm, frosted geometric-emb glass shade, 7" .**70.00**
Sconce, pnt metal w/frosted glass pk rvpt shade, Am, $45 to........**55.00**
Table, salon; macassar ebony w/26x17" rpl mirror top, glass shelf, VG..**900.00**
Tray, serving; chrome, center hdl, Kromex, 1940s, 7½x8½" **17.50**
Vase, chrome w/ribbed body, flared ft, unmk, 9", pr.....................**55.00**
Wall sconces, etched clear fans on metal V-shaped mts, Fr, 12", pr.**1,150.00**

Art Glass Baskets

Popular novelty and gift items during the Victorian era, these one-of-a-kind works of art were produced in just about any type of art glass in use at that time. They were never marked. Many were not true production pieces but 'whimsies' made by glassworkers to relieve the tedium of the long work day. Some were made as special gifts. The more decorative and imaginative the design, the more valuable the basket. For more information, we recommend *Collector's Encyclopedia of American Art Glass*, by John A. Shuman, III (Collector Books).

Note: Prices on art glass baskets have softened due to the influence of the Internet which has made them much more accessible.

Amberina irid ribbed swirl, shaped rim, clear hdl & ft, 9" **300.00**
Amberina w/amber thorn hdl & ruffle, 7¼x5" **335.00**
Bluerina, clear twisted thorn hdl, 7½" **550.00**
Cranberry threading on crystal, appl flowers, 11½" **700.00**
Cranberry to wht opal w/silver mica, crystal rigaree rim, 8x11"..**375.00**
Custard w/appl amber hdl & flowers, 7", from $200 to...............**225.00**
Dmn Quilt, frosted chartreuse to clear, frosted hdl, 4¼x5" **100.00**
Dmn Quilt, pk opal, appl vaseline leaves & hdl, 6½x5" **165.00**
Hobnail, chartreuse, 5x3¼" **100.00**
Lime gr opal, clear ruffled rim & hdl, 6½x5¾" **160.00**
Lime opal w/appl lime flower & ft, thorny twist hdl, crimped, 11"..**100.00**
Peachblow, appl amber ft, amber thorn hdl, 6" **175.00**
Persimmon cased w/ochre & clear, thorn hdl, crimped, 5¾", $300 to...**350.00**
Pk o/l, clear braided hdl, 5½x5½" **100.00**
Spangle, bl/red/yel w/gold mica, pk int, amber hdl, 11x10".........**300.00**
Spangle, bl/wht/crystal w/mica, ruffled rim, thorn hdl, 8½" **295.00**
Spangle, yel-gold spatter w/mica, reeded/pointed hdl, 7x7" **100.00**
Spatter, bl/yel/red/cream w/wht int, crystal casing, thorn hdl, 8".**165.00**
Tomato w/yel ext, 15 rib, 4-lobe rim, twist hdl, 9x6"..................**250.00**
Venetian pk stripes w/gold flecks, clear hdl **85.00**
Wht opal, crimped rim, clear petal-like ft, 4¼", from $125 to....**175.00**
Wht opal w/clear twisted hdl, rim folded 2 sides, 4¾", $85 to **125.00**
Wht opal w/pk thorn hdl, 5½", from $120 to **130.00**
Wht opal w/tan & mica flecks, crimped/ruffled, clear hdl, 7¼" ..**325.00**
Wht opaque, appl amber-stemmed pk flowers, amber hdl w/twist, 7".**80.00**
Yel & pk stripes, wht int, ruffled rim, clear twisted thorn hdl, 8".**135.00**

Art Nouveau

From the famous 'L'Art Nouveau' shop in the Rue de Provence in Paris, 'New Art' spread across the continent and belatedly arrived in America in time to add its curvilinear elements and asymmetrical ornamentations to the ostentatious remains of the Rococo revival of the 1800s. Nouveau manifested itself in every facet of decorative art. In glassware Tiffany turned the concept into a commercial success that lasted well into the second decade of this century and created a style that inspired other American glassmakers for decades. Furniture, lamps, bronzes, jewelry, and automobiles were designed within the realm of its dictates. Today's market abounds with lovely examples of Art Nouveau, allowing the collector to choose one or several areas that hold a special interest. Our advisor for this category is Steven Whysel; he is listed in the Directory under Florida. See also Bronzes; Galle; Jewelry; Loetz; Tiffany; Silver; specific manufacturers.

Box, pill; brass, emb cherub, ½x1¾" dia **62.00**
Bust, lady, bronzed-colored metal, sgn Boulede Neige, 6½x3½x2" .**210.00**
Casket, jewelry; copper-colored wht metal, sgn JB, ca 1915, 3x8x3".**150.00**
Frame, gilt brass, lady's head w/flowers, 6x4", EX......................**100.00**
Lamp, bronzed metal lady upright in 'waves' holds nautilus shell, 18" .**300.00**
Lamp, patinated metal organic std w/nautilus shell shade, 17"..**1,765.00**
Lamp, spelter C-form organic std w/petaled MOP shade, 13", pr.**2,645.00**
Letter holder, brass, lady playing mandolin, 4½x4¾x2¼".............**95.00**
Mirror, bronze oval fr w/rtcl leaves & floral stem, P/#332, 1900, 19" .**1,645.00**
Newell lamp, bronzed, Egyptian goddess on marble base, Elias, 27".**950.00**

Plaques, ladies with flowing gowns and flowers, recently regilded, mother-of-pearl inlaid frames, ca 1895, 20x10", $1,980.00 for the pair.

Screen, 3-panel, stick/ball spindles above/below art prints, 49x66" .3,350.00
Sculpture, bronzed metal, Founatine aux Fauvettes, Moreau, 25" .1,450.00
Torchere, bronze, detailed maiden post, 3-D griffin base, 74" ..9,500.00
Vase, bronzed metal, 3-D maid sits on hdld shoulder, Moreau, 18", pr..1,680.00
Vase, bud; bronze w/curvilinear pierced hdls, stick neck, unmk, 10" 260.00
Vase, gilt nude w/glass blossom by clear vase, Geschutzt 5468, 7⅝".450.00
Vase, pewter, hexagonal rim, floral relief, Orivit, ca 1905, 13¾"..650.00
Wallpaper, stylized iris & floral, Bramley 5501 TSC, 6 rolls........765.00

Arts and Crafts

The Arts and Crafts Movement began in England during the last quarter of the nineteenth century, and its influence was soon felt in this country. Among its proponents in America were Elbert Hubbard (see Roycroft) and Gustav Stickley (see Stickley). They rebelled against the mechanized mass production of the Industrial Revolution and against the cumulative influence of hundreds of years of man's changing taste. They subscribed to a theory of purification of style: that designs be geared strictly to necessity. At the same time they sought to elevate these basic ideals to the level of accepted 'art.' Simplicity was their virtue; to their critics it was a fault.

The type of furniture they promoted was squarely built, usually of heavy oak, and so simple was its appearance that as a result many began to copy the style which became known as 'Mission.' Soon factories had geared production toward making cheap copies of their designs. In 1915 Stickley's own operation failed, a victim of changing styles and tastes. Hubbard lost his life that same year on the ill-fated *Lusitania*. By the end of the decade the style had lost its popularity.

Metalware was produced by numerous crafts people, from experts such as Dirk van Erp and Albert Berry to unknown novices. Metal items or hardware should not be scrubbed or scoured; to do so could remove or damage the rich, dark patina typical of this period. Collectors have become increasingly fussy, rejecting outright pieces with damage or alteration to their original condition (such as refinishing, patina loss, repairs, and replacements). As is true for other categories of antiques and collectibles, premium prices have been paid for objects in mint original and untouched condition. Our advisor for this category is Bruce Austin; he is listed in the Directory under New York. See also Heintz; Limbert; Roycroft; Silver; Stickley; van Erp; specific manufacturers.

Note: When no condition is noted within the description lines, assume that values are given for examples in excellent condition. That is, metal items retain their original patina and wooden items are still in their original finish. Values for examples in conditions other than excellent will be indicated in the descriptions with appropriate condition codes.

Key: h/cp — hammered copper

Armchair, JM Young, #493, 5-slat bk, rstr spring cushion, 39x28" .1,100.00
Armchair, Prairie School, molded design, orig leatherette bk/seat, 39" .750.00
Bench, window; Am, 4 sq post legs, thru tenons, low stretcher, 27", VG.700.00
Bookcase, Harden, 2 sliding do w/brass hdl, 2-shelf, thru tenons, 56"..600.00
Bookcase, oak, 2-door, ldgl panels top ea, 4 int shelves, 58x42", VG .460.00
Bookends, Craftsman Studios (att), h/cp, tooled floral, 6", pr ..240.00
Bookstand, Am, shaped sides, slanted top shelf, 2 lower, 41x17x8"...200.00
Bookstand, Barber Bros, V-trough top, 2 shelves, slab sides, 28x28x9"..260.00
Bowl, h/silver, 5-lobed, 5-petal rim, 9" 200.00
Bowl, KopperKraft, h/cp, incurvate, 6" 550.00
Box, h/cp, straps at ea edge/nailheads, 11x7½" 850.00
Box, Jarvie, bronze w/relief Prairie design, dtd 1912, 4½" L........750.00
Box, repousse metalwork w/sunflowers, bronze/copper patina, 12x9"..925.00
Candlestick, Jarvie, brass, egg-shaped cup, slim, disk base, 11".435.00
Candlesticks, Hurley, bronze, base w/5 sea horses, 12", pr........4,000.00
Candlesticks, Jarvie, bronze, orig patina, 11", pr.........................425.00
Candlesticks, Liberty, #0222, pewter, 4-legged cup/sq base, 4", pr.1,600.00
Carpet, geometrics, bl/brn/cream/orange/red, 122x116", VG 460.00
Chair, cube; oak, 7 wide/narrow slats form bk, 3-slat arms, 36x28x22" .900.00
Chair, host; oak w/metal & wood peacock inlay, cutout in apron, 43".435.00
Chair, Morris; Lifetime #583, flat arms, 4-slat bk, rstr cushions, 25".2,500.00
Chair, Morris; Paine, flat arms, thru tenons, spring cushion, 38½".2,750.00
Chair, Morris; 4 curved horizontal bk slats/open arms/leather uphl, VG..900.00
Chair, oak, 8 spindles in bk, dbl side stretchers, pegged, 40", pr .230.00
Chair, side; England, bk panel w/floral inlay, rush seat, 1910s, 38".750.00
Chair, side; oak, str crest rail/3 vertical bk slats/shaped seat, 44" .175.00
Chair, side; 8-spindle bk, leather seat w/orig tacks, 41½"...........765.00
Chair, Spratling, studded leather sling seat, fish cutout, arms, 33"..1,700.00
Chamberstick, Germany, wrought iron, strap hdl, hammered decor, 8"..100.00
Chest, McHugh (style of), #510, 2 short drw/5 long, brass hdw, 59x32"..1,000.00
China cabinet, Lifetime, Puritan, 2 6-pane & 2 panel doors, 67x38"..1,100.00
Desk, drop-front, drw, low shelf, side stretchers, 43x39x16"........400.00
Dish, Am, copper w/silver o/l nasturtiums, 6¾"...........................230.00
Dresser, Compac Furniture, tall mirror amid ½ drws, long drw, 70x48".950.00
Fainting couch, slanted headrest over slatted sides, orig leather, 75" ..750.00
Floor lamp/bookcase, att Shop o/t Crafters, 3 shelves w/24" ldgl shade.1,725.00
Footstool, Lakeside Craftshop, narrow, rstr leather top, rfn, 15x15x8".1,100.00
Footstool, sq posts w/H stretcher, leather uphl, 15x17x12" 265.00
Frame, Carence Crafters, h/cp w/tooled foliage, 5½x4"..............850.00
Frame, Orvit, pewter w/sun, snail & flower on whiplash stems, 10x9"..1,500.00
Frame, silver on h/brass, appl copper foliage/bird, triangular, 12".290.00
Hall tree, pole on X base, long corbel above ea ft, 64", VG........150.00
Hat rack, brass w/emb oak leaves & acorns, 3 iron dbl hooks, 21" dia.250.00
Inkwell, Liberty & Co, pewter w/enameled inclusions, 4"...........600.00
Jar, Benedict, h/c, EX patina, 7" 190.00
Jardiniere, h/c, corset shape w/hdls, EX patina, 12x18" 400.00
Lamp, NY, h/cp & mica, dome shade w/strapwork, med patina, unmk, 17"..1,725.00
Lamp, table; Riviere Studios (att), 18" slag shade w/metal o/l, 27"..2,300.00
Lamp, Trautmann, 21" ldgl brickwork shade in h/cp fr, copper std, 24"..10,000.00
Letter opener, ET Hurley, bronze, totem pole w/turq eyes, 8¾" ..700.00
Magazine stand, 3-shelf, slab sides, rfn, 37x27x13" 100.00
Mirror, h/cp fr w/rivets in corners, 13x21½" 700.00
Nightstand, Michigan Chair Co, 1-door, lower shelf, 30x25x14", VG ..345.00
Rocker, arm; 3-slat bk, wide open arms, spring seat, rpl uphl, 35".1,115.00
Rocker, Lifetime, #688½, 2 wide slats under ea arm, corbels, 31"..2,700.00
Rocker, Plail Furniture, bbl form, narrow slats, rstr leather, 31"..2,100.00
Rug, drugget; asymmetrical pattern, mc on oatmeal & brn, 83x51"..350.00
Sconce, Harry Dixon, h/cp, 11" 400.00
Server, oak, bksplash on 34x21" top over drw & lower shelf, 36" .1,265.00
Settle, Am, even-arm, 20 bk slats, sq legs, slat seat, rfn, 98"....1,150.00
Settle, oak, arched crest rail, 15 slats, D arms w/5 slats, 70" 1,380.00
Settle, oak, even-arm, crest rail over 9 wide vertical slats, 65", VG.2,200.00
Settle, Plail Furniture, curved bk/narrow slats, rstr seat, rfn, 46" W.2,900.00
Settle, Prairie School, even-arm, leatherette bk/seat, 33x81" ..1,200.00

Settle, 13-slat bk, joined by sq posts, rpl seat, 36x77½x27" **650.00**
Settle, 18 vertical slats, arms, rectangular seat rail, rfn, 78" L..**1,000.00**
Sideboard, oak, mirror bksplash w/shelf & corbel supports, 53x52"..**345.00**
Sideboard, Paine, shelf over mirrored bk, 3 short center drws, 54x54"..**1,265.00**
Smoke set, Benedict, h/cp w/appl cameo, 5-pc **200.00**
Smoking cabinet, Lakeside Craftshop, 13" sq top, 2 doors, label, 32" ..**325.00**
Spoon, silver bowl flows into wooden hdl, 7" **160.00**
Stand, European, brass/bronze metal, hammered/cutouts, 31x13x6½"..**800.00**
Table, Am, paneled sides w/Moorish-style cutouts, 18x13" sq.....**230.00**
Table, Am, 8-sided top w/corbels, cut-out sides, ca 1912, 24x17"..**975.00**
Table, England, rnd, deep apron w/heart cutout, shelf, 28x25" .**1,150.00**
Table, library; HP Robertson, oak, oval 48" top & shelves ea side drw..**920.00**
Table, library; 26x24" top, 4-leg, lower shelf, very simple, VG ...**800.00**
Table, lunch; post legs, thru tenons, X stretchers, 30x48x30" **825.00**
Table, oak, 15" dia top, 3 legs, lower shelf w/incurvate sides, 18".**750.00**
Table, oak, 4 sides w/tree & star cutouts, rpl 15" sq top, 20" **200.00**
Table, Prairie School, oak, cut corners, median shelf, 34x14" sq.**485.00**
Table, rnd top w/sq post legs, median shelf, ca 1912, 30x17" dia..**460.00**
Table, Standard Table Co, oak, rnd 48" top/octagon ped, +4 leaves..**345.00**
Table, trestle; Michigan Chair Co, shelf, key tenons, 29x48x29".**800.00**
Tray, h/emb copper w/2 sq tile inserts, hdls, rectangular, 20" L ...**500.00**
Vase, h/cp, grapes/vines at incurvate rim, organic hdls, 15x10"..**950.00**
Vase, Hairnian, h/cp, heavy gauge, 6" **550.00**
Vase, Jauchens Olde Copper Shop, h/cp w/gr & brn patina, 4x6½"..**850.00**
Vase, Kipp, h/cp, heavy gauge, radial hammering, long hdl, 7½"..**2,000.00**
Vase, Liberty, pewter, 3-hdl, decor around body, 7½" **700.00**
Vase, Nonconnah, roses emb/HP on dk gr, bulbous, rare, 6½".**1,600.00**
Vase, Pearson, h/cp w/lg emb ducks, 9½x11"............................**2,800.00**
Waste basket, golden oak slats linked w/leather thongs, 13x13"..**175.00**
Watering can, h/cp, 4" **60.00**
Woodblock print, April Fall, snow scene, sgn Lack, 8x6" **300.00**
Woodblock print, city harbor scene, H Rivere, oak fr, 21x33" **600.00**
Woodblock print, desert scene, B Whitehead, fr, 18½x14½" **600.00**
Woodblock print, Haystack Rock, N Basset Hall, 3½x4½"+mat.**950.00**
Woodblock print, horse & rainbow landscape, H Rivere, oak fr, 10x14".**550.00**
Woodblock print, houses/shoreline, AW Dow, in oak fr, 6x4" **2,100.00**
Woodblock print, On the Hill, Eva Maria Marcus, 9x11½"+mat & fr..**450.00**
Woodblock print, Oriental child w/butterflies, H Hyde, 7½x3"+fr.**260.00**
Woodblock print, Oriental girl w/flowers, H Hyde, oak fr, 7½x2½" .**325.00**
Woodblock print, sailboats, bls & wht, Richert (att), 4x5" +oak fr.**325.00**
Woodblock print, Twins, trees, gr/tan/blk, AT Thompson, fr, 10x8"...**400.00**
Woodblock print, Winter Nights, Oscar Erickson, #d, matted & fr.**425.00**

Austrian Glass

Many examples of fine art glass were produced in Austria during the times of Loetz and Moser that cannot be attributed to any glasshouse in particular, though much of it bears striking similarities to the products of both artists.

Bottle, scent; gr w/mc neck band, paper label, 20th C, 4½" **230.00**
Bowl, amber/rose w/overall irid gold threading, 2½x8" **70.00**
Bowl, gr w/random ruby threading, 1910, 6" **175.00**
Compote, gr irid, threaded, 8-pinch rim, swollen stem, wide emb ft, 9".**175.00**
Pokal, lt gr w/HP knight on horsebk & scrolled acanthus, 18" ..**400.00**
Vase, amber to rust w/oil spots, cup rim/bun base, unmk, 8"....**1,175.00**
Vase, appl trees w/pine cones, P Daschel, 11", NM **550.00**
Vase, bl irid w/gold & silver oil spots, 10½"................................**145.00**
Vase, clear crackle flattened fan form w/brn tab hdls, 13" L........**765.00**
Vase, floriform; cherry red to gr irid w/purple highlights, 10x7"..**345.00**
Vase, gr irid, stick neck w/4-pinch rim, 8" **50.00**
Vase, gray w/gr irid oil spots, drapery mold, sq rim, 6" **200.00**
Vase, red irid w/cranberry & wht opal allover swirls, 10½" **300.00**

Vase, tan irid w/HP orange poppies, gourd form, 8½" **560.00**
Vase, threaded amtheyst, upright open beak-like rim, Pallme-Konig, 15"..**355.00**

Austrian Ware

From the late 1800s until the beginning of WWI, several companies were located in the area known at the turn of the century as Bohemia. They produced hard-paste porcelain dinnerware and decorative items primarily for the American trade. Today examples bearing the marks of these firms are usually referred to by collectors as Austrian ware, indicating simply the country of their origin. Of those various companies, these marks are best known: M.Z. Austria; Victoria, Carlsbad, Austria (Schmidt and Company); and O. & E.G. (Royal) Austria. Of these three companies, Victoria, Carlsbad, Austria, is the most highly valued.

Though most of the decorations were transfer designs which were sometimes signed by the original artist, pieces marked Royal Austria were often hand painted and so indicated alongside the backstamp.

Collectors should note that in our listings transfer decorations showing 'signatures' (sgn), such as 'Wagner,' 'Kauffmann,' 'LeBrun,' etc., were not actually painted by those artists but were merely based on their original paintings. Our advisor for this category is Mary Frank Gaston.

Dessert set, floral w/gold, Carlsbad, 12-pc **200.00**
Ewer, floral on smooth gray, textured gold top/base sections, 11".**200.00**

Plate, cherubs on yellow with gold trim, small handles, 11¼", $70.00.

Vase, amphora style w/incised leaves & color 'jewels' w/gold, 6½"..**115.00**
Vase, pierced organic formations on bulbous base, gr/purple irid, 6"..**315.00**
Vase, sm flowers emb, lav on ochre, 4 integral waist hdls, 10" **230.00**

Autographs

Autograph collecting, also known as 'philography' or 'love of writing,' used to be a hobby shared by a few thousand dedicated collectors. But in recent years, autograph collecting has become a serious pursuit for more than 2,000,000 collectors worldwide. And in the past decade, more investors are adding rare and valuable autograph portfolios to their traditional investments. One reason for this sudden interest in autograph investing relates to the simple economic law of supply and demand. Rare autographs have a 'fixed' supply, meaning that unlike diamonds, gold, silver, stock certificates, etc., no more are being produced. There are only so many Abraham Lincoln, Marilyn Monroe, and Charles Lindbergh autographs available. In the meantime, it's estimated that more than 20,000 new collectors enter the market each year, thus creating an ever-increasing demand. Hence, the rare autographs generally rise steadily in value each year. Because of this scarcity, a serious collector will pay over $10,000.00 for a photograph signed by both Wilbur and Orville Wright, or as much as $25,000.00, perhaps more, for a handwritten letter of George Washington.

But by far, the majority of autograph collectors in the country do it for the love of the hobby. A polite letter and self-addressed, stamped envelope sent to a famous person will often bring the desired result. And occasionally one receives not only an autograph but a nice handwritten letter thanking the fan as well!

In terms of value, there are five general types of autographs: 1) mere signatures on an album page or card; 2) signed photographs; 3) signed documents; 4) typed letters signed; and 5) handwritten letters. The signatures are the least valuable, and handwritten letters the most valuable. The reasoning here is simple: with a handwritten letter, not only do you get an autograph but the handwritten message of the person as well. And this content can sometimes increase the value many times over. A handwritten letter of Babe Ruth's thanking a fan for a gift might fetch a few thousand dollars. But if the letter were to mention Ruth's feelings on the day he retired, it could easily sell for $10,000.00 or more.

Today the Internet has become a popular way to buy and sell autographs. A word of warning: be very careful when buying over the internet. It is an easy way for unscrupulous forgers to sell their fakes and disappear. Teenagers need to be especially aware that many of the 'signed' photos on the Internet of Sarah Michelle Gellar, Brad Pitt, Katie Holmes, Leonardo DeCaprio, Kate Winslett, and many others are either signed by secretaries or are outright forgeries. Make sure the Internet dealer offers a full money-back guarantee of authenticity and belongs to one of the major autograph organizations. Ask how long the dealer has been in business and for personal references if possible. Remember the old Latin warning, 'caveat emptor,' let the buyer beware.

There are several major autograph collector organizations where members can exchange celebrity addresses or buy, sell, and trade their autographed wares. Philography can be a fun and rewarding hobby. And who knows! In ten or twenty years, those autographs you got for free could be worth a small fortune!

Our advisor for autographs is Tim Anderson; he is listed in the Directory under Utah.

Key:
ALS — handwritten letter signed
ANS — handwritten note signed
AQS — autograph quotation signed
DS — document signed
ins — inscription
ISP — inscribed signed photo
LH — letterhead
LS — signed letter, typed or written by someone else
sig — signature
SP — signed photo

Adams, John Quincy; DS, certificate of recommendation, 1810.1,725.00
Aldrin, 'Buzz'; sig on 1959 Life cover, complete magazine...........200.00
Armstrong, Neil; sgn US Astronaut Hall of Fame program, 6-pg..460.00
Arnold, Benedict; LS, re 2 deserters, as colonel, 1775 ....6,000.00
Baker, Phil; SP, blk & wht, 8½x11"...60.00
Barnum, PT; ALS, Waldemore Bridgeport CT LH, 1887...........410.00
Barton, Clara; LS, to friend, 1866, 4 8x5" pgs, EX.....................515.00
Biddle, Nicholas; DS, as President of Bank of US, 1839 ....150.00
Blythe, Betty; SP, blk & wht, 1929, 8x10" 175.00
Booth, Edwin; ALS, traveling plans, no date, 8x5" 250.00
Bow, Clara; sgn manuscript Nocturnal Visitor, 4-pg, EX 960.00
Brynner, Yul; SP, blk & wht, 8x10" 135.00
Calhoun, Alice; ISP, sepia, ca 1920s, 7½x9½"..........................80.00
Cantor, Eddie, sig on 2x3½" card...50.00
Carey, MacDonald; ISP, blk & wht, 8x10" 35.00
Chevalier, Maurice; sig on 3x5" card..45.00
Cleveland Preston, Frances F; sig on card 75.00
Cobb, Ty; SP, blk & wht, 8x10, EX 960.00
Collyer, June; SP, sepia, 1928, 5x7"...80.00
Coolidge, Calvin; LS, as president, White House LH, 1924 ....500.00
Davis, Jefferson; LS, short reply, bold sig, 1875, 8x5".............1,350.00

De Wolfe, Billy; inscr sig on album pg..40.00
Dinehart, Alan; ISP, sepia, 8x10"...90.00
Douglas, Melvin; sig on 3x5" card..42.00
Dunbar, Dixie; ISP, sepia, 1936, 8x10"......................................45.00
Eisenhower, Dwight D; DS, appointing ambassador, 1957 ....715.00
Eisenhower, Dwight D; sig on penciled doodle pg, 1959, 2¾x5½" .260.00
Evans, Dale; sig on album pg...44.00
Fairbanks, Douglas Jr; sig on album pg.......................................44.00
Fisher, Gail; sig on 3x5" card..40.00
Flynn, Errol; sgn check to Southern California Telephone Co, EX..225.00
Gable, Clark; SP, WWII vintage, in military uniform by plane..1,000.00
Gehrig, Lou; cut sig, w/MLB photo, fr & matted, EX.................520.00
Gish, Lillian; sig on album pg...45.00
Gobel, George; sig on lg wht card...35.00
Guinness, Sir Alec; SP, blk & wht, 1950s, 3½x5" 75.00
Hall, Jon; sig on wht index card..48.00
Halloway, Stanley; SP, blk & wht, 3½x5".....................................35.00
Hancock, John; ALS, as Govoner of Massachusetts, 1784.......6,000.00
Harrison, Rex; sig on 3x5" card...50.00
Hayes, Helen; sig on lg album pg..30.00
Hendrix, Jimi; 'Are You Experienced' album, Love Always, EX.1,050.00
Hendrix, Jimi; sgn autograph book, EX 910.00
Hoover, Herbert; sig on Waldorf-Astoria stationery 125.00
Howe, Julia Ward; ALS, mourning stationery, illegible date, 6x5" .325.00
Hussey, Ruth; ISP, sepia, 1942, 5x7" 45.00
Jackson, Andrew; DS, grant of acreage, 1832 ....925.00
Jackson, Andrew; LS, as general, military business, 1820, 2-pg ..2,250.00
Jewell, Isabel; SP, sepia, 8x10" 145.00
Kennedy, John & Jacqueline; SP, shown in open car, 1960, 10x13" .5,175.00
Kiley, Richard; sig on 3x5" card...35.00
King, Martin Luther Jr; cut sig, fr w/picture, 25x21" 1,375.00
Kingsford, Walter; ISP, sepia, 1945, 5x7"..................................45.00
Lamour, Dorothy; SP, sepia, 1937, 5½x7"..................................55.00
Lee, Ching Wah; SP, sepia, movie scene, 3½x5" 40.00
Lennon, John; cut sig, w/Beatles photo, fr & matted, EX...........680.00
Lillie, Beatrice; sig on 3x5" card 40.00

Lindbergh, Charles; signed card framed with contemporary photo portrait, card dated from Paris May 1927, $700.00.

Love, Bessie; SP, blk & wht, 8x10" 45.00
Lytell, Bert; sig on album pg..55.00
Mantle, Mickey; sig on album pg..225.00
McDowall, Roddy; sig on 3x5" card..40.00
McKinley, Wm; DS, appointment, as President, 1900.................460.00
Mifflin, Thomas; DS, as Gov of PA, on vellum, 1794 ....635.00
Monroe, Marilyn; cut sgn, w/photo, prof matting, 4x2" sgn.....1,000.00
Montgomery, Douglas; ISP, sepia, ca 1930s, 8x10".....................50.00
Morris, Chester; sig on 3x5" card..45.00
Newman, Paul; sig on 3x5" card, 1968 ....75.00
Nixon, Richard; sig on 3x5" card, 1968.....................................125.00

Oakley, Annie; DS & dated 2/19/02, 3½x2½" **5,000.00**
Olivier, Sir Laurence; SP, blk & wht, movie scene, 3½x5" **50.00**
Pasternak, Joe; LS on MGM stationery, 1959 .... **65.00**
Peppard, George; sig on 3x5" card **35.00**
Polk, Sarah Childress; LS, regrets, 1888, 7½x5" **415.00**
Presley, Elvis; sig on card, 3x3½" **360.00**
Ralston, Marcia; SP, sepia, 5x7" **45.00**
Rich, Irene; ISP, sepia, 1920s, 6½x8½" **50.00**
Rockefeller, Nelson; sig on 3x5" card **55.00**
Rogers, Will; ISP, blk & wht, 13¼x10½"+fr **415.00**
Roland, Gilbert; ISP, blk & wht, 1970, 8x10" **45.00**
Romero, Cesar; sig on 3x6" card **40.00**
Roosevelt, Franklin D; LS on State House LH, as Govenor of NY .. **410.00**
Roosevelt, Theodore; in fr w/photo, poem & flag drawing **275.00**
Savalas, Telly; sig on 3x5" card **40.00**
Sherman, William T; ANS, Union general, 2x3½" card **440.00**
Sills, Milton; SP, sepia, 1920s, 5x7" **60.00**
Skelton, Red; sig on 3x5" card **40.00**
St Clair, Arthur; DS, as Governor of NW Territory, 1799 .... **435.00**
Stanley, Forrest; SP, sepia, 8x10" **55.00**
Stone, Fred; sig on 3x5" paper **40.00**
Sullivan, Billie; ISP, sepia, 8x10" **95.00**
Taylor, Zachary; DS, requisition of medicine, as colonel, 1832 ... **750.00**
Thalberg, Irving; LS, on MGM stationery, 1927 .... **250.00**
Theby, Rosemary; SP, sepia, 5x7" **75.00**
Truman, Harry S; sgn 4x6" card dtd 8/3/67 .... **130.00**
Tunney, Gene; sig on textured paper **125.00**
Villechaize, Herve; ins on bk of 3½x8" postcard **40.00**
Wayne, John; sgn & dtd June 7, 1941, 3x4", EX **450.00**
Whalen, Michael; ISP, sepia, 1936, 5x7" **55.00**
Wilson, Marie; ISP, sepia, 8x10" **85.00**
Wood, Natalie; SP, To Cindy Best Wishes Natalie Wood, 8x10" . **550.00**
Wright, Orville; sig on check, boldly sgn, 1931, EX **300.00**
York, Alvin C; sig on business card (his personal business) **385.00**

Automobilia

While some automobilia buffs are primarily concerned with restoring vintage cars, others concentrate on only one area of collecting. For instance, hood ornaments were often quite spectacular. Made of chrome or nickel plate on brass or bronze, they were designed to represent the 'winged maiden' Victory, flying bats, sleek greyhounds, soaring eagles, and a host of other creatures. Today they often bring prices in the $75.00 to $200.00 range. R. Lalique glass ornaments go much higher!

Horns, radios, clocks, gear shift knobs, and key chains with company emblems are other areas of interest. Generally, items pertaining to the classics of the '30s are most in demand. Paper advertising material, manuals, and catalogs in excellent condition are also collectible.

License plate collectors search for the early porcelain-on-cast-iron examples. First year plates (e.g., Massachusetts, 1903; Wisconsin, 1905; Indiana, 1913) are especially valuable. The last of the states to issue regulation plates were South Carolina and Texas in 1917, and Florida in 1918. While many northeastern states had registered hundreds of thousands of vehicles by the 1920s making these plates relatively common, those from the southern and western states of that period are considered rare. Naturally, condition is important. While a pair in mint condition might sell for as much as $100.00 to $125.00, a pair with chipped or otherwise damaged porcelain may sometimes be had for as little as $25.00 to $30.00.

Our advisor for this category is Leonard Needham; he is listed in the Directory under California. See also Gas Globes and Panels.

Book, Austin-Healey 3000 MKS I & II Driver's Handbook, 1960s, 68-pg . **30.00**
Book, Cadillac & LaSalle Preliminary Service Information, 1932, VG .. **120.00**
Book, My Life & Work, Henry Ford w/S Crowther, 1922, 1st ed, VG .. **125.00**
Book, 75 Years of Chevrolet, Dammann, Chestline Publishing, 1986, G . **30.00**
Booklet, dealer's; Cadillac, Gentle Art of Motoring, 1948, 12-pg, EX . **12.00**
Booklet, Keep on Rolling, Am Automobile Assoc, 1943, 40-pg, EX . **12.00**
Brochure, Cadillac El Dorado, 1953, unfolds to 21¾x24" poster .. **65.00**
Brochure, dealer's; Buick, 1964, 64 internal pgs, 10½x14", VG **30.00**
Brochure, dealer's; Chevrolet Station Wagon, 1963, G **8.00**
Brochure, dealer's; Dodge Luxury Liner, 1940, 24-pg, 11x9", EX .. **40.00**
Brochure, dealer's; Dodge Sportsman Wagon, 1966, 8-pg, 8½x11", VG .. **15.00**
Brochure, dealer's; Golden Anniversary Packard Custom, 1949, 12-pg, NM .. **140.00**
Brochure, sales; Cadillac Type 53, ca 1916, 32-pg, G **120.00**
Catalog, Chevrolet Showroom, 1946, 11¼x9", VG **275.00**
Catalog, Chevrolet Shworoom, pnt chips/upholstery samples, 1952, EX . **225.00**
Catalog, parts; Model T Ford, 1925, cover missing, G- **8.00**

Clock, Cadillac Service, logo in center, yellow case with glass lens, $165.00. (Photo courtesy B.J. Summers and Wayne Priddy)

Emblem, body; Buick, enamel & chrome, 1940s, 1¾x7½", VG ... **80.00**
Emblem, body; Crosley, chrome w/red lettering, 5x5⅛" **80.00**
Emblem, body; Oldsmobile, oval, 1930s, 1¼x5", VG **120.00**
Emblem, body; Studebaker, rectangular, ¾x1½", VG **60.00**
Emblem, body; Thunderbird; enamel on chrome, 1½x9¼", VG ... **80.00**
Emblem, fender; Thunderbird, 1959 (?), 1⅝" dia, EX **90.00**
Emblem, hood; Buick, elk's head & shield, mc enamel, 1940s-50s, 2¼" . **60.00**
Emblem, hood; Ford, V8, late 1830s (?), 3¼x2¼", VG **40.00**
Emblem, hood; Frazer, mc enamel & Fr motto, 1940s, 5½x3⅜", VG .. **90.00**
Emblem, hood; Plymouth, enamel on chrome, 1930s (?), 4⅞x1⅞", VG .. **40.00**
Emblem, radiator; Buick, bl enamel & chrome, possible rpt, 1⅞" dia . **140.00**
Emblem, radiator; Buick, bl enamel & chrome, 2¼x1⅞", VG **110.00**
Emblem, radiator; Cadillac, ca 1920s, 2⅛" dia, EX **150.00**
Emblem, radiator; Chevrolet, bl enamel, 1⅜x4", VG **120.00**
Emblem, radiator; Durant, enamel & chrome, 1920s, 2¼x1½", VG .. **80.00**
Emblem, radiator; Erskine, bl enamel, 2" dia, G **60.00**
Emblem, radiator; Essex Super Six, minor pnt loss, 1⅝" dia, G **80.00**
Emblem, radiator; Ford, bl enamel on oval, 1928-30, G **60.00**
Emblem, radiator; Ford, oval, 1931, VG **60.00**
Emblem, radiator; Ford 60, unknown year, EX **80.00**
Emblem, radiator; Hudson Super Six, red & wht triangle, 2½", EX .. **120.00**
Emblem, radiator; Hudson 8, worn enamel, 2½" **40.00**
Emblem, radiator; Hupmobil 8, mc enamel, rectangular, 1930s, G . **120.00**
Emblem, radiator; Nash, ca 1930s (?), 1⅞x2¼", EX **80.00**
Emblem, radiator; Oldsmobile, bl & wht enamel on chrome, 1918, EX . **140.00**
Emblem, radiator; Studebaker, wht enamel, 2⅛" dia, G **40.00**
Guage, tire pressure; US Gauge Co, measures up to 50 psi, VG in pouch .. **20.00**
Handbook, mechanic's; Ford, 1949, 36-pg, EX **40.00**
Hood latch, Ford, 1930s, VG **40.00**
Hood ornament, Cadillac, 1960s, 4x3¼", EX **40.00**
Hood ornament, Thunderbird, 2x4½", NM **90.00**
Hubcap, Chandler, screw-on, 1920s (?), G **20.00**
Lamp, side; Cadillac, Gray & Davis, 1914, VG **250.00**
Lamps, side; Nash, ca late 1920-early '30s, 5" dia, pr, G **60.00**
License plate, 1918 CA Dealer, orig bell tab, EX **40.00**

Light, Reelite's Auto Service, plugs into lighter socket, 1930s, MIB ..**20.00**
Magazine, Antique Automobile, 1926 Franklin cover, 1967, VG ...**3.00**
Manual, accessories; Buick, red/wht/bl cover, 1962, 24-pg, EX **12.00**
Manual, Chevrolet Steering Gear Service, 1949, EX....................**15.00**
Manual, owner's; Buick, for 6-cylinder models, 1920, 64-pg, G **40.00**
Manual, owner's; Buick, 1917, VG **60.00**
Manual, owner's; Cadillac V-16, 1932, VG.................................**350.00**
Manual, owner's; Chevrolet Four Ninety & Superior Models, 1923, EX.**85.00**
Manual, owner's; Chrysler 58, 1926, EX **80.00**
Manual, owner's; CT Electric truck, 1921, EX **60.00**
Manual, owner's; DeSoto Airstream, 1936, 48-pg, 6x9", G **10.00**
Manual, owner's; Erskine, ca 1928, G...**40.00**
Manual, owner's; Essex, 5th edition, 1920s, 68-pg, 5¾x9", EX **60.00**
Manual, owner's; Falcon-Knight, 1928, 72-pg, 6x9", VG **60.00**
Manual, owner's; Hudson Wasp, 1956, 32-pg, 4½x8", EX **40.00**
Manual, owner's; Kaiser, 1947, 1st edition, G **20.00**
Manual, owner's; Model T Ford, 1914, VG **60.00**
Manual, owner's; Nash Ambassador, 1952, 48-pg, 4½x8", VG **26.00**
Manual, owner's; Rambler, 1956, EX **20.00**
Manual, owner's; Studebaker Commander, 1940, VG **40.00**
Manual, repair; Chevrolet, 1927, 224-pg, G...............................**60.00**
Manual, shop; Chevrolet, 1941, 292-pg, 8¼x10¾" **40.00**
Manual, shop; Chevrolet, 1942, 318-pg, 8¼x10¾", VG **40.00**
Name tag, Remy Magneto, brass, ¾x2⅛", EX..............................**30.00**
Parts list, DeSoto Passenger Car, 1941, 184-pg, 8¼x10¾" **40.00**
Parts list, Ford, 1913, G...**90.00**
Photo, Autocar Diesel factory, DC-10064/logging trailer, 1946, 8x10".**24.00**
Photo, Packard 400 Touring Sedan, factory made, 1951, 8x10", NM..**24.00**
Pin-bk button, Chevrolet, New Chevrolet Six, 1929, NM............**65.00**
Pin-bk button, Chevrolet, Watch the Leader, 1950s, ¾", EX........**20.00**
Postcard, Buick factory photo, 1950 postmark, EX.......................**7.00**
Postcard, Salon de L'Automobile 1913-14, Fr auto show, EX **12.00**
Promotional car, Edsel 2-door hardtop, friction drive, 1958, EX.**150.00**
Promotional car, Ford Thunderbird, 1965, VG **115.00**
Promotional truck, Chevrolet Pickup, 1972, 8¼", NM **150.00**

Sign, light up; Carbureter Repairs, 11x29x5", NM, from $550.00 to $600.00. (Photo courtesy Dunbar Gallery)

Slide rule, Watson Motor Truck Performaster, HS Watson, 1950s, 9¼".**80.00**
Song book, Chevrolet, Sing of the USA, 1964, 24-pg, 8½x11", G.............**20.00**
Speedometer, Stewart Warner, 3¼" dia, G **9.00**
Token, General Motors Motorama, emb metal, 1954, EX **22.00**
Wrench, Ford 5-Z-289, ca 1925, 8⅜" **20.00**
Wrench, hub cap; Hudson, 13", G...**15.00**
Wrench, hup cap; Chevrolet, lt rust, G..**10.00**
Wrench, open end; Cadillac, ⅝x¹¹⁄₁₆", 6" L..................................**80.00**
Wrench, open end; Ford T-1917, 5¼", G.....................................**10.00**

Autumn Leaf

In 1933 the Hall China Company designed a line of dinnerware for the Jewel Tea Company, who offered it to their customers as premiums.

Although you may hear the ware referred to as 'Jewel Tea,' it was officially named 'Autumn Leaf' in the 1940s. In addition to the dinnerware, frosted Libbey glass tumblers, stemware, and a melmac service with the orange and gold bittersweet pod were available over the years, as were tablecloths, plastic covers for bowls and mixers, and metal items such as cake safes, hot pads, coasters, wastebaskets, and canisters. Even shelf paper and playing cards were made to coordinate. In 1958 the International Silver Company designed silverplated flatware in a pattern called 'Autumn' which was to be used with dishes in the Autumn Leaf pattern. A year later, a line of stainless flatware was introduced. These accessory lines are prized by collectors today.

One of the most fascinating aspects of collecting the Autumn Leaf pattern has been the wonderful discoveries of previously unlisted pieces. Among these items are two different bud-ray lid one-pound butter dishes; most recently a one-pound butter dish in the 'Zephyr' or 'Bingo' style; a miniature set of the 'Casper' salt and pepper shakers; coffee, tea, and sugar canisters; a pair of candlesticks; an experimental condiment jar; and a covered candy dish. All of these china pieces are attributed to the Hall China Company. Other unusual items have turned up in the accessory lines as well and include a Libbey frosted tumbler in a pilsner shape, a wooden serving bowl, and an apron made from the oilcloth (plastic) material that was used in the 1950s tablecloth. These latter items appear to be professionally done, and we can only speculate as to their origin. Collectors believe that the Hall items were sample pieces that were never meant to be distributed.

Hall discontinued the Autumn Leaf line in 1978. At that time the date was added to the backstamp to mark ware still in stock in the Hall warehouse. A special promotion by Jewel saw the reintroduction of basic dinnerware and serving pieces with the 1978 backstamp. These pieces have made their way into many collections. Additionally, in 1979 Jewel released a line of enamel-clad cookware and a Vellux blanket made by Martex which were decorated with the Autumn Leaf pattern. They continued to offer these items for a few years only, then all distribution of Autumn Leaf items was discontinued.

It should be noted that the Hall China Company has produced several limited edition items for the National Autumn Leaf Collectors Club (NALCC): a New York-style teapot (1984); an Edgewater vase (1987, different than the original shape); candlesticks (1988); a Philadelphia-style teapot, creamer, and sugar set (1990); a tea-for-two set and a Solo tea set (1991), a donut jug, and a large oval casserole. Later came the small ball jug, one-cup French teapot, and a set of four chocolate mugs. Other special items over the past few years made for them by Hall China include a sugar packet holder, a chamberstick, and an oyster cocktail. Additional items are scheduled for production. All of these are plainly marked as having been made for the NALCC and are appropriately dated. A few other pieces have been made by Hall as limited editions for an Ohio company, but these are easily identified: the Airflow teapot and the Norris refrigerator pitcher (neither of which was previously decorated with the Autumn Leaf decal), a square-handled beverage mug, and the new-style Irish mug. A production problem with the square-handled mugs halted their production. Additional items available now are a covered onion soup, tall bud vase, china kitchen memo board, and egg drop-style salt and pepper shakers with a mustard pot. They have also issued a deck of playing cards and Libbey tumblers. See *Garage Sale & Flea Market Annual* (Collector Books) for suggested values for club pieces. Our advisor for this category is Gwynne Harrison; she is listed in the Directory under California. For more information we recommend *Collector's Encyclopedia of Hall China*, *Third Edition*, by Margaret and Kenn Whitmyer.

Apron, oilcloth, from $600 to **1,000.00**
Baker, French, 2-pt...**175.00**
Baker, French, 3-pt...**25.00**
Baker, souffle; 4½"...**60.00**

Baker/souffle, 4⅛" 12.00
Bean pot, 1-hdl..1,000.00
Blanket, Autumn Leaf color, Vellux, full sz.........175.00
Blanket, Autumn Leaf color, Vellux, twin sz, from $100 to........175.00
Blanket, Vellux, bl, king sz...............................200.00
Book, Mary Dunbar Cookbook 30.00
Bottle, Jim Beam, w/stand.................................130.00
Bowl, cereal; 6", from $8 to................................12.00
Bowl, flat soup; 8½"..20.00
Bowl, fruit; 5½"...6.00
Bowl, mixing; New Metal, 3-pc set.....................325.00
Bowl, salad; 9""..20.00
Bowl, soup; Melmac...20.00
Bowl, vegetable; oval...25.00
Bowl, vegetable; oval, Melmac, from $40 to..........50.00
Bowl, vegetable; oval, w/lid, from $50 to...............70.00
Bowl, vegetable; rnd, 9"....................................175.00
Bowl, vegetable; Royal Glasbake, milk wht, divided...............150.00
Bowls, refrigerator; plastic lids, 3-pc set, from $250 to........325.00
Bread box, metal, from $400 to 800.00
Butter dish, 1-lb, bud 'rayed' knob, rare 3,000.00
Butter dish, ¼-lb, regular, ruffled top, from $175 to 250.00
Butter dish, ¼-lb, wings top 1,500.00
Cake safe, metal, motif on top or sides, 5", ea..........50.00
Calendar, 1920s to 1930s, from $100 to 200.00
Candle holder, Chamber, club gift, 1991...............125.00
Candlesticks, metal, Douglas, pr, from $70 to.........100.00
Candy dish, metal base, from $500 to 600.00
Canisters, metal, rnd, w/coppertone lid, set of 4, from $600 to .1,200.00
Canisters, sq, 4-pc set, from $295 to.....................350.00
Case, carrying; Jewel salesman, from $150 to..........300.00
Casserole, Heatflow, w/lid, rnd, 2-qt.....................85.00
Casserole, rnd, Heatflow, clear, w/lid, Dunbar, 1½-qt, from $50 to .75.00
Casserole, rnd, w/lid, 2-qt, from $30 to..................45.00
Catalog, Jewel, hard-bound cover, from $20 to 50.00
Cleanser can, from $750 to.............................1,500.00
Clock, electric...550.00
Clock, salesman's award 250.00
Coaster, metal, 3⅛"..8.00
Coffee dispenser, from $200 to............................400.00
Coffee percolator, electric, all china, 4-pc..............400.00
Coffeepot, all china, 4-pc, from $275 to.................350.00
Coffeepot, Rayed, 8-cup 45.00
Coffeepot, Rayed, 9-cup 45.00
Cooker, waterless; metal, Mary Dunbar, from $50 to 75.00
Cookie jar, Big Ear, Zeisel, from $250 to................350.00
Cookie jar, Tootsie, 'Rayed'................................310.00
Cover, plastic, for mixer, Mary Dunbar, from $35 to..........50.00
Creamer & sugar bowl, Rayed, 1930s style 80.00
Creamer & sugar bowl, Ruffled-D, 1940s style, from $40 to..........65.00
Cup, custard; Radiance, from $6 to........................10.00
Cup & saucer, regular, Ruffled-D 9.00
Dripper, metal, for 8- or 9-cup coffeepot 35.00
Flatware, silverplate, serving pc, ea, from $135 to 175.00
Flatware, stainless steel, serving pc, ea, from $90 to 130.00
Fondue set, complete, form $200 to.......................300.00
Fry pan, Mary Dunbar, top stoveware glass 175.00
Hot pad, metal, oval, 10¾", from $12 to.................15.00
Hot pad, rnd, metal bk, 7¼", from $15 to................25.00
Hurricane lamps, Douglas, w/metal base, pr, minimum value......500.00
Jug, ball form, #3..40.00
Jug, batter; Sundial (bowl), rare 5,500.00
Jug, utility; Rayed, 2½-pt, 6".................................25.00
Marmalade, 3-pc, from $100 to...........................125.00

Mug, conic style (must be) marked Approved by Mary Dunbar, 1966 – 1976, $60.00.

Mug, chocolate; club pc, 1,500 made, 1992, 4-pc set...................100.00
Mustard, 3-pc, from $100 to................................120.00
Napkin, ecru muslin, 16" sq.................................50.00
Pie plate, Heatflow, clear glass, Mary Dunbar, from $45 to 60.00
Pie plate, 9½" 35.00
Plate, 6", from $5 to..8.00
Plate, 7¼", from $5 to...10.00
Plate, 8", hard to find..18.00
Platter, oval, 13½"..28.00
Saucepan, warmer base, Douglas..........................500.00
Saucepan, wood hdl, w/lid, 1½-qt, from $150 to.........200.00
Saucer, regular, Ruffled D 2.50
Saucer, St Denis, from $6 to..................................8.00
Shakers, Casper, ruffled, regular, pr......................30.00
Shakers, range; left & right hdls, pr, from $20 to.........45.00
Tablecloth, cotton sailcloth w/gold stripe, 54x72" 140.00
Teakettle, metal, porc, from $200 to......................300.00
Teapot, Aladdin, from $50 to................................80.00
Teapot, Newport, 1933, from $200 to....................275.00
Teapot, Rayed, long spout, 1935 ....95.00
Teapot, Rayed, long spout, 1978, rare, from $800 to...............1,600.00
Teapot, Solo, club pc, 1,400 made, 1991 ....100.00
Toaster cover, plastic, Mary Dunbar.......................50.00
Towel, tea; cotton, 16x33" 60.00
Toy, Circus Train, from $900 to........................1,200.00
Toy, Jewel Truck, gr, from $350 to........................425.00
Toy, Jewel Truck, orange & wht, from $200 to..........225.00
Toy, Jewel Van, brn, Buddy L, from $400 to.............650.00
Tray, metal, oval 100.00
Tumbler, Brockway, 9-oz, 13-oz or 16-oz, ea............45.00
Tumbler, Libbey, frosted, 14-oz, 5½".......................20.00
Tumbler, Libbey, frosted, 9-oz, 3¾".........................32.00
Tumbler, Libbey, gold & frost on clear, 10-oz............75.00
Tumbler, Libbey, gold frost etched, flat or ftd, 10-oz, ea 65.00
Tumbler, Libbey, gold frost etched, flat or ftd, 15-oz, ea 65.00
Vase, Edgewater, club pc, #d (626 made), 1987 ....450.00
Warmer, oval, from $150 to.................................225.00

Aviation

Aviation buffs are interested in any phase of flying, from early developments with gliders, balloons, airships, and flying machines to more modern innovations. Books, catalogs, photos, patents, lithographs, ad cards, and posters are among the paper ephemera they treasure alongside models of unlikely flying contraptions, propellers and rudders, insignia and equipment from WWI and WWII, and memorabilia from the flights of the Wright Brothers, Lindbergh, Earhart, and the Zeppelins. See also Militaria. Our advisor for this category is John R. Joiner; he is listed in the Directory under Georgia.

Ashtray, TWA, red metal w/wht letters, concave dome shape, 5" dia .20.00
Bank, 23 different airlines on base, Ohio Art D-174, 7¼" 18.00
Booklet, Capitol Airlines Viscount by Rolls Royce, 10-pg, EX 35.00
Brochure, South America, Fly There by BOAC, 17½x15" 20.00
Calendar, Northwest Airlines, 1955, 24x17", NM+ 40.00
Champagne flute, Western Airlines, 60 Years, red on clear, 8" 35.00
Coffee mug, Eastern, bl logo (both sides) on wht, EX 50.00
Coffeepot, American Airlines, logo & eagle eng, w/lid, 1951, 10" .85.00
Coffeepot, Eastern Airlines, marked Oneida USA, w/lid, 8½", EX .40.00
Cordial, British Overseas Airline, BOAC etched on clear, 1940s, 3" ..25.00
Cup, Aleghenny Airlines, red & bl on wht, Federal, 3", EX...........30.00
Cup, Eastern Airlines, Great Silver Fleet, red & bl on wht...........55.00
Flight bag, United Air Lines Hawaii, red/orange/blk print, 1970s.45.00
Flight log, Trans-Australia Airlines, 1952, 4½x7" 20.00
Flight manual, Eastern/Mohawk Martin 404, 1962, in binder, EX..110.00
Gift set, Texas International Airlines, wallet & buckle, NMIB.....70.00
Golf umbrella, Mohawk Airlines, nylon, 1970s, 58½" dia.............60.00
Luggage label, Pan American, passengers boarding float plane, 1930s.45.00
Manual, DC-3 Operating Instructions, 1944-45, VG 35.00
Menu, inflight; Singapore Airlines, 1974, 4-pg, EX 30.00
Model, Canadian Pacific DC-8, Empress of Vancouver, 16x18" wingspan..180.00
Model, Eastern L1011, N301EA Whisperliner, 21x18¾" wingspan ..310.00
Model, Eastern N5 1012 Constellation, metal w/plastic base, 8x8" .160.00
Paperweight, Eastern Airlines, 50 Years of Service, medallion, 1978.30.00
Pennant, Welcome Lindbergh, wht on bl, 10x14¾", EX.............225.00
Photo, Douglas DC-3, Western Airlines, blk & wht, 1937, 8x10" .30.00
Pin, Eastern Airlines, hat in ring, marked 10k, w/tie tack...........230.00
Pin, Eastern Airlines, SS airplane, 1x1" 50.00
Pin, merit; TWA, propeller shaped w/dmn in center, mk 10k,½" .60.00
Playing cards, Air Pacific, MIP (sealed) 17.50
Playing cards, Chicago Southern Airlines, 2 decks w/boxes, VG+ .130.00
Playing cards, Mohawk Vista Prop Jet, dbl-deck in plastic case, EX..45.00
Pocket diary, Singapore Airlines, 1978, EX 45.00
Propeller, wood, rfn, 108" 200.00
Safety card, National Airlines, Boeing 727, quad-fold, 1972, EX..50.00

Souvenir button and plane pin, Spirit of St. Louis, Lindbergh portrait center, red, white, and blue ribbon, metal plane, from $200.00 to $300.00. (Early American Historical Auctions Inc.)

Teapot, United Airlines, wht w/silver print & trim, Rego, 5" 60.00
Timetable, Air Wisconsin, October 26/1969, NM+ 55.00
Timetable, American Airlines, 11/1/34, NM.................................60.00
Timetable, American Airways, 30-pg, 1932, EX 50.00
Timetable, East Africa Airlines, 27-pg, 11/1/71, EX 35.00
Timetable, Eastern Airlines, 8-pg, 7/1/35, EX 45.00
Timetable, Souvenir Air Map, American Airlines, 1931, EX........45.00
Timetable, United Airlines, 12-pg, 1936, NM+ 55.00
Timetable, United Airlines, 1943, M...40.00
Travel bag, Capitol Airlines, wht on bl, nylon, NM+ 65.00
Tumbler, Delta Airlines, SS w/logo, mk #3759, 3¾" 60.00
Tumbler, Japan Airlines, emb lines at top, JAL etched, ftd, 2⅞" ..17.50
Wings, American Airlines, 3¼"...165.00

Wings, American Airlines Pilot, 10k gold filled, 1940s, 2½" 365.00
Wings, Continental Airlines, 1950s, 3".....................................200.00

Baccarat

The Baccarat Glass Company was founded in 1765 near Luneville, France, and continues to this day to produce quality crystal tableware, vases, perfume bottles, and figurines. The firm became famous for the high-quality millefiori and caned paperweights produced there from 1845 until about 1860. Examples of these range from $300.00 to as much as several thousand. Since 1953 they have resumed the production of paperweights on a limited edition basis. Our advisors for this category are Randall Monsen and Rod Baer; their address is listed in the Directory under Virginia.

See also Bottles, Commercial Perfume; Paperweights.

Bowl, Swirl, Rose Tiente, rolled-over rim, 3x9" 80.00
Busts, Madonna & Christ, ca 1870 – 90, EX, pr 360.00
Candlestick, Swirl, Rose Tiente, 7⅛" 190.00
Champagne flutes, Vienne, gold rimmed (top & bottom), set of 6, MIB .260.00
Crystal ball, Sirius, 5⅞", w/4x4" holding dish 570.00
Decanter, Capri, 13½" 260.00
Decanter, dmn-cut design, sq, w/stopper, 10" 215.00
Decanter, Massena, w/stopper, MIB...280.00
Decanter, Nancy, w/stopper, MIB 365.00
Decanter, Oceanie, w/stopper, MIB 360.00
Decanter, Remy Martin Louis XIII, w/stopper, 11" 200.00
Egg, cobalt w/gold floral, 2¾x2" 100.00
Figurine, antelope, reclining, 5x6", MIB 180.00
Figurine, Black Labrador Retriever, blk, 4½x7½" 290.00
Figurine, bunny, sitting up, blk, 3⅛x2½x2" 100.00
Figurine, Chinese Zodiac Dragon, 3¼x4½", MIB 155.00
Figurine, Christmas Angel, 6", MIB 115.00
Figurine, elephant, trunk up, 4¼x5¼" 195.00
Figurine, elephant, 4¾x8", MIB 340.00
Figurine, galloping horse, 5½", MIB 200.00
Figurine, golfer, putting, 8⅝", MIB 160.00
Figurine, gorilla, 6x6¼", MIB 320.00
Figurine, horse, rearing, 8", MIB 200.00
Figurine, horse head, blk, 6½x6x2", MIB.................................210.00
Figurine, horse head, 9x9½x4¼" 165.00
Figurine, Madonna w/child, 9¼"...100.00
Figurine, snowy Christmas tree, MIB.......................................160.00
Figurine, whale, bl, 8¾" L, MIB 155.00
Glass, highball; Harmonie, set of 6, 5¾", MIB 390.00
Glass, highball; Massena..65.00
Goblet, Asservillers, 6¼"...40.00
Goblet, Rohan, stemmed, 4" 40.00
Goblet, sherry; Lorraine (Cassino), 4¼" 40.00
Goblet, water; Lorraine (Cassino), 5⅝" 40.00
Goblet, wine; Brummel, stemmed...80.00
Goblet, wine; Saint Remy, stemmed, 10-oz, 8⅜" 55.00
Goblet, wine; Vega, colored bowl w/stacked-ball stem, MIB.........80.00
Lamp, banquet; cherubs milk glass base, dbl burner, electrified, 23" .1,150.00
Perfume bottle, King Ramses, w/stopper, both mk #66, 6" 925.00
Perfume bottle, Velivole, w/stopper, eng gilt, 3" 780.00
Tray, Swirl, Rose Tiente, rectangular, 9x13" L 75.00
Tumbler, Swirl, Rose Tiente, 4¾" 40.00
Tumbler, whiskey; Harmonie, set of 6, 12-oz, 4", MIB................380.00
Vase, etched roses, 8½x8" 265.00
Vase, gr to clear w/cut ovals, flared rim, shouldered, 7" 300.00
Vase, Harmonie, 11¾", MIB...200.00
Vase, horse trophy; NYRA horse logo, 9¾" 255.00

Badges

The breast badge came into general usage in this country about 1840. Since most are not marked and styles have changed very little to the present day, they are often difficult to date. The most reliable clue is the pin and catch. One of the earliest types, used primarily before the turn of the century, involved a 't-pin' and a 'shell' catch. In a second style, the pin was hinged with a small square of sheet metal, and the clasp was cylindrical. From the late 1800s until about 1940, the pin and clasp were made from one continuous piece of thin metal wire. The same type, with the addition of a flat back plate, was used a little later. There are exceptions to these findings, and other types of clasps were also used. Hallmarks and inscriptions may also help pinpoint an approximate age.

Badges have been made from a variety of materials, usually brass or nickel silver; but even solid silver and gold were used for special orders. They are found in many basic shapes and variations — stars with five to seven points, shields, disks, ovals, and octagonals being most often encountered. Of prime importance to collectors, however, is that the title and/or location appear on the badge. Those with designations of positions no longer existing (City Constable, for example) and names of early western states and towns are most valuable.

Badges are among the most commonly reproduced (and faked) types of antiques on the market. At any flea market, ten fakes can be found for every authentic example. Genuine law badges start at $30.00 to $40.00 for recent examples (1950 – 1970); earlier pieces (1910 – 1930) usually bring $50.00 to $90.00. Pre-1900 badges often sell for more than $100.00. Authentic gold badges are usually priced at a minimum of scrap value (karat, weight, spot price for gold); fine gold badges from before 1900 can sell for $400.00 to $800.00, and a few will bring even more. A fire badge is usually valued at about half the price of a law badge from the same time and material. Our advisor for this category is Gene Matzke; he is listed in the Directory under Wisconsin.

Special Deputy Sheriff, nickel-plated shield, custom-engraved officer's name, $75.00.

Chessie Railroad Police, Special Agent, cat logo center seal, 2x2"..**140.00**
Chicago Police, State Society Prevention of Cruelty, 6-point star..**100.00**
Chicago Police Lieutenant Retired, 5-point star shape, 1920s **100.00**
Columbus Police, scales of justice cut-out, sterling, 2½" dia.......**250.00**
Dept of Corrections, Attica Prison Guard, 1970s **60.00**
Deputy Sheriff, Monterey Co Calif, SP nickel w/leather bk, 1930s..**100.00**
Detroit Detective, silver w/blk enamel, pre-1970s **150.00**
Fort Scott Police, scrolling around name **150.00**
Galveston Seawall, Section Texas, 1909, brass w/gold gilt **75.00**
German Navy Sea Pilot, WWI, wreath w/crown & bow, gilded .**775.00**
German Panzer Tank, wreath w/tank & eagle, WWII era **160.00**
Indian Police, Wind River Wyoming, 6-point star w/bear in center.**85.00**
Indian Refining Company (Texaco), Patrolman, nickel, IL seal.**165.00**
Louisiana Registered Chauffeur, pelican feeding young, 1922 .....**785.00**
Metropolitan Police, Pre-Consolidation of New York, 2¾x2¼"..**2,500.00**
Military Police, Kelly Field, shield w/eagle atop **190.00**
New York Fire Dept #154, 20 Years, 1916, star shape, 1⅞x2".....**100.00**

Norfolk & Western Railway, State of Virginia, Lieutenant, gold-tone.**175.00**
Omaha Metropolitan Police, shield w/eagle atop, nickel w/steel pin..**135.00**
Passaic City Police, Chicago Police, Chief's Staff, star shape......**200.00**
Sheriff's Posse Comitatus, star in circle **55.00**
Union Pacific Police, spring pin & Burgess clasp, 3x2¼"...........**155.00**
US Apache Police, brass, shield w/eng **70.00**
Utica Police, Detective (banner over shield), 1920s **100.00**

Banks

In general, bank values are established on the auction block and sales between collectors and dealers, and the driving force that determines the final price is condition. The spread between the price of a bank in excellent condition and the identical model in only good condition continues to widen. In order to be a seasoned collector in the pursuit of wise investments, one must learn to carefully determine overall condition by assessing the amount and strength (depth) of the paint, and by checking for breaks, repairs, and replaced parts; all bear heavily on value. Paint and casting variations are other considerations the collector should become familiar with.

Banks continue to maintain their value. Mechanicals often bring astronomical prices, making it imperative that collectors understand the market. Let's take a look at the price variations possible on an Uncle Sam mechanical bank. If you find one with considerable paint missing but with some good color showing, the price would be around $1,000.00. If it has repairs or restoration, the value could drop to somewhere near $800.00 or less. Still another example with two thirds of its original paint and no repairs would probably bring $1,800.00. If it had only minor nicks, it could go as high as $3,500.00. Should you find one in 95% paint with no repairs, $5,000.00 or more would not be out of line. After considering all of these factors, remember: the final price is always determined by what a willing buyer and seller agree on for a specific bank.

Mechanical banks are the 'crème de le crème' in the arena of cast-iron toy collecting. They are among the most outstanding products of the Industrial Revolution and are recognized as some of the most successful of the mass-produced products of the nineteenth century. The earliest mechanicals were made of wood or lead. In 1869 John Hall introduced Hall's Excelsior, made of cast iron. It was an immediate success. J. & E. Stevens produced the bank for Hall and as a result soon began to make their own designs. Several companies followed suit, most of which were already in the hardware business. They used newly developed iron-casting techniques to produce these novelty savings devices for the emerging toy market. The social mores and customs of the times, political attitudes, racial and ethnic biases, the excitement of the circus, and humorous everyday events all served as inspiration for the creation of hundreds of banks. Designers made the most of simple mechanics to produce models with captivating actions that served not only to amuse but promote the concept of thrift to the children. The quality and detail of the castings were truly remarkable. The majority of collectible banks were made from 1870 to 1910; however, they continued to be manufactured until the onset of WWII. J. & E. Stevens, Shepard Hardware, and Kyser and Rex were some of the most prolific manufacturers of mechanicals. They made still banks as well.

Still banks are widely collected. Various materials were used in their construction, and each material represents a subfield in still bank collections. No one knows exactly how many different banks were made, but upwards of three thousand have been identified in the various books published on the subject. Cast-iron examples still dominate the market, but lead banks from Europe are growing in value. Tin and early pottery banks are drawing more interest as well. American pottery banks which were primarily collected by Americana collectors are becoming more important in the still bank field.

To increase your knowledge of banks, attend shows and auctions. Direct contact with collectors and knowledgeable dealers is a very good way to develop a feel for prices and quality. It will also help you in gaining the ability to judge condition, and you'll learn to recognize the more desirable banks as well.

Both mechanical and still banks have been reproduced. One way to detect a reproduction is by measuring. The dimensions of a reproduced bank will always be fractionally smaller, since the original bank was cast from a pattern while the reproduction was made from a casting of the original bank. As both values and interest continue to increase, it becomes even more important to educate ourselves to the fullest extent possible. We recommend these books for your library: *The Bank Book* by Norman, *The Dictionary of Still Banks* by Long and Pitman, *The Penny Bank Book* by Moore, *Penny Banks Around the World* by Don Duer, and *Penny Lane* by Davidson, which is considered the most complete reference available. It contains a cross-reference listing of numbers from all other publications on mechanical banks. Another book to consider is *Collector's Guide to Glass Banks* by Charles V. Reynolds.

All banks are assumed to be complete and original unless noted otherwise in the description. A number of banks are commonly found with a particular repair. When this repair is reflected in our pricing, it will be so indicated. When traps (typically key lock, as in Uncle Sam) are an integral part of the body of the bank, lack of such results in a severe reduction in the value of the bank. When the trap is underneath the bank (typically a twist trap, as in Eagle and Eaglets), reduction in value is minimal.

To most accurately represent current market values, we have used condition codes in our listings that correspond with guidelines developed by today's bank collectors.

Our advisor for mechanical and still banks is Clive Devenish, who is listed in the Directory under California.

NM — 98% paint   VG — 80% paint
PR (pristine) — 95% paint G — 70% paint
EX — 90% paint

Key:
AL — aluminum   NP — nickel-plated
CI — cast iron   RM — Robert McCumber Book:
M — Andy Moore Book: *Registering Banks*
   The Penny Bank Book   WM — white metal
N — Bill Norman Book:
   The Bank Book

Advertising

Decker's Iowana (pig), M-603, CI, 2¼", EX.................................150.00
Eureka gas stove, M-1350, pnt tin, 5¼", EX...............................60.00
GE refrigerator, M-1331, pnt CI, 4¼", EX 100.00
Kelvinator refrigerator on Legs, M-1338 variant, CI, 4⅜", VG....150.00
Mellow furnace, M-1363, pnt CI, 3¾", NM...............................80.00
Roper stove, M-1341, CI/tin, worn pnt, 3¾" 140.00
Singer electric sewing machine, M-1369, tin/CI, 5⅛", EX..........400.00
Zenith radio, M-823, WM, 3¾", EX..45.00

Book of Knowledge Banks

Book of Knowledge banks were produced by John Wright (Pennsylvania) from circa 1950 until 1975. Of the thirty models they made during those years, a few continued to be made in very limited numbers until the late 1980s; these they referred to as the 'Medallion' series. (Today the Medallion banks command the same prices as the earlier Book of Knowledge series.) Each bank was a handcrafted, hand-painted duplicate of an original as was found in the collection of

The Book of Knowledge, the first children's encyclopedia in this country. Because the antique banks are often priced out of the range of many of today's collectors, these banks are being sought out as affordable substitutes for their very expensive counterparts. It should also be noted that China has reproduced banks with the Book of Knowledge inscription on them. These copies are flooding the market, causing original Book of Knowledge banks to decline in value. Buyers should take extra caution when investing in Book of Knowledge banks and purchase them through a reputable dealer who offers a satisfaction guarantee as well as a guarantee that the bank is authentic. Our advisor for Book of Knowledge banks is Dan Iannotti; he is listed in the Directory under Michigan.

World's Fair, NM, $225.00; Cat and Mouse, NM, $225.00; Eagle and Eaglets, NM, 245.00.

Always Did 'Spise a Mule (Boy on Bench), M...........................250.00
Always Did 'Spise a Mule (Jockey), NM.....................................195.00
Boy on Trapeze, NM...275.00
Bulldog, M..195.00
Creedmore, M..250.00
Jonah & Whale, M..225.00
Magician, NM 225.00
Paddy & Pig, M...250.00
Punch & Judy, M...250.00
Uncle Sam, M..225.00

Mechanical

Always Dis 'Spise a Mule (jockey), N-2950, CI, PR 3,800.00
Atlas, N-1080, CI, EX 5,500.00
Bank of Education, N-1170, CI, VG 700.00
Bear & Tree Stump, N-1210, CI, VG..800.00
Boy on Trapeze, N-1350, CI, VG 2,500.00
Boy Scout (rpl flag), N-1370, CI, VG......................................2,800.00
Bulldog Standing, N-1450, CI, EX 800.00
Butting Ram, N-1590, CI, VG 6,000.00
Calumet (lg, cb), N-1650, EX..175.00
Calumet (sm, tin), N-1660, EX..250.00
Camera, N-1670, CI, VG 6,500.00
Chocolate Menier (vending), N-1800, tin, EX 750.00
Circus Ticket Collector, N-1830, CI, VG................................2,500.00
Clown on Globe, N-1930, CI, VG...2,750.00
Darktown Battery, N-2080, CI, EX 6,000.00
Elephant Pull Tail, N-2300, CI, EX 375.00
Elephant Swings Trunk (lg), N-2310, CI, VG 150.00
Elephant Swings Trunk (sm), N-2330, CI, VG...........................75.00
Elephant Three Stars, N-2340, CI, VG......................................475.00
Football Bank (English - Soccer), N-2430, CI, G 1,900.00
Frog on Round Base, N-2530, CI, VG 950.00
Hen & Chick (rpl chick), N-2790, CI, VG.............................2,800.00
Indian Shooting Bear (orig feathers), N-2980, CI, EX............4,000.00
Jolly N (all orig), many variations, EX, ea from $200 to.........1,000.00

Jonah & the Whale, N-3490, CI, EX................................5,500.00
Kiltie, N-3550, CI, VG..1,600.00
Little Joe, N-3690, CI, EX...425.00

Magician, N-3760, CI, J. & E. Stevens, EX, $3,600.00.

Mammy & Child (rpl spoon), N-3790, CI, VG 4,800.00
Mosque Bank, N-4010, CI, EX...2,200.00
New Creedmoor, N-4220, CI, EX 1,100.00
Organ Bank, Boy & Girl; N-4310, CI, VG...........................1,250.00
Organ Bank, Cat & Dog; N-4320, CI, VG..............................900.00
Organ Grinder & Performing Bear, N-4350, CI, VG 4,600.00
Owl Turns Head, N-4380, CI, VG..800.00
Paddy & the Pig (rpl ft), N-4400, CI, G................................1,850.00
Panorama, N-4410, CI, PR...19,000.00
Pelican (man thumbs nose), N-4520, CI, VG 2,000.00
Popeye Knockout Bank, N-4620, tin, EX.................................600.00
Santa Claus, N-5010, CI, EX...3,900.00
Stump Speaker, N-5370, CI, PR..6,800.00
Tabby Bank, N-5410, CI, EX..1,750.00
Tammany, N-5420, CI, EX...950.00
Thrifty Tom's Jigger Bank, N-5510, tin, PR..........................2,200.00
Toad on Stump, N-5570, CI, VG 650.00
Trick Pony, N-5640, CI, G..1,000.00
Two Frogs, N-2540, CI, EX..4,800.00
Watchdog Safe Bank, N-5890, CI, EX....................................900.00
Weeden's Plantation, N-5910, tin, VG.................................2,600.00
William Tell, N-5940, CI, PR...2,400.00

Registering

Bean Pot, M-951, CI, 3", EX...250.00
Beehive Registering Savings Bank, CI/NP, 5⅜", EX.................275.00
Bestmaid, tin, 4¾", EX..75.00
Buddy (L) Savings & Recording Bank, sheet metal, 6⁵⁄₁₆", EX ..125.00
Chein Thrifty Elf 'Dime a Day' Register, RM Pg 127, tin, EX.......85.00
Clown & Monkey Daily Dime Bank, RM Pg 225, tin, EX 75.00
Dandy Self Registering Savings Bank, tin, 4¾", NM 360.00
Donald Duck Clock Vault, tin, Spanish sayings on drum, EX.....140.00
Elves Rolling Coins To Bank Dime Register, RM Pg 126, tin, EX..125.00
Gem Registering, RM Pg 18, CI, 6¹⁄₁₆" L, EX 1,800.00
Keene Savings Bank, tin, EX..350.00
Keep 'Em Smiling Dime Register, RM Pg 124, tin, EX..............250.00
New York World's Fair Dime Register, RM Pg 129, tin, EX 75.00
Penny Saver, CI, 5⅛", VG..80.00
Popeye Dime Register (pocket), M-1573, silver pnt on tin, 2½", EX..........75.00
Prince Valiant Dime Bank, RM Pg 127, tin, EX 85.00
Prudential Registering Savings Bank (10¢), CI/NP, 7¼", EX 350.00
Snow White Dime Register (pocket), M-1567, tin, 2½" sq, EX..........150.00
Uncle Sam, M-1290, sheet steel w/blk & gold, 6¼", EX.............80.00

Still

$100,000 Money Bag, M-1262, CI, 3⅝", EX..............................400.00
Amherst Buffalo, M-556, CI, 5¼", EX 475.00
Arcade Steamboat, M-1460, CI, 2⅜" H, EX..............................460.00
Baby in Egg (Black), M-261, lead, 7¼", EX.............................450.00
Baseball Player, M-18, CI, 5¾", VG.......................................160.00
Baseball Player, M-19, CI, 5¾", NM....................................1,025.00
Battleship Maine, M-1439, CI, 6", EX..................................4,500.00
Bear Stealing Pig, M-693, CI, rpl screw, 5½", G.....................550.00
Billy Bounce (Give Billy a Penny), M-15, CI, 4¾", VG.............350.00
Blackpool Tower, M-984, CI, partial rpt, rpl screw, 7⅜"............100.00
Buffalo, M-560, CI w/gold pnt, 3⅛", EX..................................130.00
Bugs Bunny by the Tree, M-278, CI, 5½", EX 125.00
Building w/Eagle Finial, M-1134, CI, 9¾", EX.........................850.00
Bulldog (seated), M-396, CI, 3⅞", NM....................................400.00
Bulldog w/Sailor Cap, M-363, lead, 4⅜", EX............................400.00
Buster Brown & Tige, M-241, CI, gold & red pnt, 5½", VG .160.00
Buster Brown & Tige, M-242 variant, CI, 5½", NM 850.00
Cadet, M-8, CI, crack at slot, 5¾", VG 150.00
Camel (kneeling), M-770, CI, 2½", EX....................................750.00
Camel (sm), M-768, CI, sm, 4¾", EX......................................225.00
Campbell Kids, M-163, CI, gold pnt, 3¾", EX...........................300.00
Captain Kidd, M-38, CI, 5⅝", G...130.00
Cat on Tub, M-358, CI, gold pnt, 4⅛", EX...............................160.00
Charles Russell, M-247, wht metal, gold pnt, 6¼", EX.................50.00
Charlie McCarthy on Trunk, M-207, compo, 5¼", M..................430.00
City Bank w/Chimney, M-1101, CI, old rpt, 6¾".....................1,450.00
City Bank w/Teller, M-1097, CI, 5½", NM................................570.00
Colonial House, M-992, CI, 4", EX...125.00
Columbia Bank, M-1070, CI, 5¾", EX.....................................560.00
Columbia Tower, M-1118, CI, rpl turnpin, 6⅞", VG 675.00
County Bank, M-1110, CI, 4¼", G..160.00
Crosly Radio, M-819, CI, 5⅛", EX..675.00
Crown Building, M-1225, CI, 5", NM 3,000.00
Cupola, M-1146, CI, 4⅛", EX..340.00
Dime Bank, M-1183, CI, 4¾", EX...125.00
Dog by Ball, M-390, lead/tin, 2⅛", VG...................................230.00
Dolphin, M-33, CI, gold pnt, 4½", EX.....................................800.00
Donkey w/Saddle & Reins, M-497 variant, lead, 4", EX.............110.00
Double Decker Bus, M-1490, CI, bl pnt, 2¼", NM..................1,025.00
Duck, M-624, CI, 4¾", EX 300.00
Duck on Tub, M-616, CI, 5⅜", EX..200.00
Dutch Girl w/Flowers, M-181, CI, 5¼", EX...............................110.00
Elephant on Wheels, M-446, CI, 4⅛", EX................................330.00
Eureka Trust & Savings Safe, CI, 5¾", EX...............................425.00
Feed My Sheep (lamb), M-596, lead, gold pnt, 2¾", VG............140.00
Fido, M-417, CI, 5", EX...125.00
Fido on a Pillow, M-443, CI, 7⅜", EX.....................................350.00
Flat Iron Building, M-1159, CI, 8¼", EX...............................2,400.00
Flat Iron Building, M-1160, CI, no trap, 5¾", EX 370.00
Football Player, M-11, CI, 5⅞", EX...400.00
Forlorn Dog, M-408, wht metal, 4¾", G....................................75.00
Fortune Ship, M-1457, CI, 4⅛", NM.....................................1,600.00
Foxy Grandpa, M-320, CI, 5½", EX..340.00
Foxy Grandpa, M-320, CI, 5½", G..195.00
Frowning Face, M-12, CI, 5⅝", EX......................................1,650.00
General Butler, M-54, CI, 6½", EX.......................................3,600.00
General Grant, M-115 variant, CI, Harper, 5⅝", EX................3,400.00
Globe, M-812, CI, 5", VG 250.00
Globe on Arc, M-789, CI, red pnt, 5¼", EX..............................380.00
Globe on Arc, M-789, CI, 5¼", G...125.00
Globe Savings Fund, M-1199, CI, 7⅛", EX............................3,000.00
Golliwog, M-85, CI, 6¼", EX...500.00

Good-Luck Horseshoe (Buster Brown), M-508, CI, 4¼", EX ...300.00
Graf Zeppelin, M-1428, CI, 1¾" H, EX 220.00
Grizzly Bear, M-703, lead, pnt worn in bk, 2¾" 100.00
Hansel & Gretel, M-1016, tin, 2¼", EX 125.00
Harper Stork Safe, M-651, CI, hdl missing, 5½", EX 850.00
High Rise, M-1217, CI w/japanning, 5½", EX...................300.00
High Rise, M-1219, CI, 4⅝", EX 390.00
High Rise Tiered, M-1215, CI, 5¾", EX 350.00
Home Savings, M-1126, CI, 5⅞", EX............................290.00
Horse on Tub (decorated), M-509, CI, 5¼", VG...............155.00
Horse on Wheels, M-512, CI, 5", EX 425.00
Horseshoe Wire Mesh, M-524, CI/tin, G- Arcade label, 3¼", VG..95.00
I Made Chicago Famous (pig), M-629, CI, Harper, 2⅛", EX 220.00
I Made St Louis Famous (mule), M-489, CI, Harper, 4¾", EX ..1,950.00
Independence Hall, M-1244, CI, 8⅞", EX.......................600.00
Iron Master's Cabin, M-1027, CI, 4¼", EX....................3,300.00
Jimmy Durante, M-259, WM, 6¾", EX 200.00
Labrador Retriever, M-412, CI, 4½", EX........................270.00
Lindy Bank, M-124, AL, 6½", EX 180.00
Lion, M-765, CI, sm, 4", EX 100.00
Lion on Tub, M-747, CI, 4⅛", EX................................150.00
Lion on Wheels, M-760, CI, 4½", EX 300.00
Litchfield Cathedral, M-968, CI, 6⅝", EX......................450.00
Main Street Trolley (no people), M-1469, CI, gold pnt, 3", EX..300.00
Maine (battleship), M-1439, CI, 6" H, NM 4,000.00
Mammy w/Hands on Hips, M-176, CI, 5¼", EX 150.00
Mammy w/Spoon, M-168, CI, 5⅞", EX 225.00
Man on Bale of Cotton, M-37, CI, 4⅞", EX...................3,600.00
Mary & Lamb, M-164, CI, 4¾", VG 700.00
Mary & Lamb, M-164, CI, 4⅜" (ex Moore collection), NM 3,800.00
Metropolitan Safe, CI, 5⅞", NM..............................2,200.00
Mickey Mouse Post Office, tin, cylindrical, 6", NM 140.00
Middy, M-36, CI, w/clapper, 5¼", G............................135.00
Model T (2nd version), M-1483, CI, 4", NM.................1,050.00
Monkey w/Removable Hat, M-740, brass, 3⅞", EX...................900.00
Mulligan, M-177, CI, 5¾", EX 160.00
Mutt & Jeff, M-157, CI, gold pnt, 4¼", EX 150.00
Newfoundland (dog), M-440, CI, 3⅝", EX 300.00
Ocean Liner, M-1444, lead, 2¾" H, VG 140.00
Oregon (battleship), M-1450, CI, rpl guns, 3⅞", G 230.00
Oregon (battleship), M-1452, CI, rpl turnpin, VG..................400.00
Oriental Camel, M-769, CI, 3¾", G 325.00
Pass Round the Hat (Derby), M-1381, CI, 1⅝", EX................200.00
Peaceful Bill/Harper Smiling Jim, M-109, CI, 4", EX.............2,400.00
Pearl Street Building, M-1096, worn gold overpnt, 4¼" 380.00
Pet Safe, M-866, CI, 4½", EX..................................225.00
Pig (standing), M-478, CI, 3", EX 240.00
Policeman, M-182, CI, Arcade, 5½", EX......................1,100.00
Polish Rooster, M-541, CI, 5½", EX 1,250.00
Porky Pig, M-264, CI, 6", EX+ 400.00
Porky Pig, M-264, CI, 6", VG..................................175.00
Professor Pug Frog, M-311, CI, 3¼", EX.......................330.00
Puppo, M-416, CI, 4⅞", VG 155.00
Quilted Lion, M-758, CI, 3¾", EX.............................300.00
Reindeer, M-376, CI, 6¼", NM................................280.00
Retriever w/a Pack, M-436, CI, 4¹¹⁄₁₆", EX....................150.00
Rhino, M-721, CI, 2⅝", NM..................................1,050.00
Roller Safe, M-880, CI, 3¹¹⁄₁₆", EX............................225.00
Roof Bank Building, M-1122, CI, 5¼", G.......................300.00
Rooster, M-548, CI, 4¾", EX..................................130.00
Rumplestiltskin, M-27, CI, 6", VG.............................200.00
Sailor, M-27, CI, 5¼", G......................................85.00
Sailor, M-28, CI, 5½", G.....................................125.00
Sailor, M-29, CI, 5⅝", NM 800.00

Santa Claus, Ive's, M-56, CI, 7¼", EX 700.00
Save & Smile, M-1641, CI, 4¼", EX 375.00
Scottie (standing), M-435, CI, 3¾", VG 140.00
Seal on Rock, M-732, CI, 3½", EX.............................600.00
Skyscraper, M-1238, CI, 3¾", EX..............................100.00
Skyscraper, M-1239, CI, 4⅜", EX..............................135.00
Skyscraper (6 posts), M-1241, CI, 6½", EX 300.00
Songbird on Stump, M-664, CI, 4¾", EX.......................650.00
Squirrel w/Nut, M-660, CI, 4⅛", VG...........................470.00
State Bank, M-1078, CI, w/key, 8", NM 1,350.00
State Bank, M-1083, CI, 4⅛", EX..............................250.00
State Bank, M-1085, CI, 3", EX................................300.00
Stop Sign, M-1479, CI, 4½", G.................................220.00
Tally Ho, M-535, CI, 4½", EX.................................275.00
Tank, M-1436, lead, 3", VG....................................725.00
Temple Bar Building, M-1163, CI, 4", EX 600.00
Tower Bank, M-1208, CI, 9¼", EX.............................400.00
Transvaal Money Box, M-1, CI, recast pipe, 6¼", VG............3,200.00
Triangular Building w/Clock, M-1235, CI, 6", EX 650.00
Trust Bank, The; M-154, CI, 7¼", EX 4,500.00
Turkey (lg), M-585, CI, 4¼", EX...............................450.00
Turkey (sm), M-587, CI, 3⅜", EX 150.00
Two-Faced Black Boy (lg), M-83, CI, EX........................300.00
Two-Faced Black Boy (sm), M-84, CI, 3⅛", EX 200.00
Two-Faced Devil, M-31, CI, 4¼", EX...........................700.00
US Army/Navy Safe, electroplated CI, 6⅛", EX................1,200.00
US Mail, M-838, CI, sm, 3⅝", EX..............................75.00
USA Mail Mailbox w/Eagle, M-851, CI, 4⅛", EX 75.00
Watch Me Grow, M-279 variant, tin, 5¾", EX....................70.00
Westminster Abbey, M-973, CI, old gold pnt, 6¼" 250.00
White City Barrel #1, M-908, NP, EX...........................150.00
White City Barrel on Cart, M-907, CI, 4", EX 525.00
Woolworth Building (lg), M-1041, CI, 7⅞", EX..................300.00
Woolworth Building (sm), M-1042, CI, 5¾", EX.................175.00
World Time Bank, M-1539, CI, orig paper, 4⅛", EX.............500.00
Yellow Cab, M-1493, CI, 4¼", VG............................1,200.00
1882 Villa, M-959, CI, 5⅞", VG...............................800.00
1890 Tower Bank, M-1198, CI, 6⅞", EX.......................1,200.00
1893 World's Fair Administration Building, M-1072, CI, 6", EX ..650.00

Barber Shop Collectibles

Even for the stranger in town, the local barber shop was easy to find, its location vividly marked with the traditional red and white striped barber pole that for centuries identified such establishments. As far back as the twelfth century, the barber has had a place in recorded history. At one time he not only groomed the beards and cut the hair of his gentlemen clients but was known as the 'blood-letter' as well, hence the red stripe for blood and the white for the bandages. Many early barbers even pulled teeth! Later, laws were enacted that divided the practices of barbering and surgery.

The Victorian barber shop reflected the charm of that era with fancy barber chairs upholstered in rich wine-colored velvet; rows of bottles made from colored art glass held hair tonics and shaving lotion. Backbars of richly carved oak with beveled mirrors lined the wall behind the barber's station. During the late nineteenth century, the barber pole with a blue stripe added to the standard red and white as a patriotic gesture came into vogue.

Today the barber shop has all but disappeared from the American scene, replaced by modern unisex salons. Collectors search for the barber poles, the fancy chairs, and the tonic bottles of an era gone but not forgotten. See also Bottles; Razors; Shaving Mugs.

Bowl, dk sapphire bl glass w/emb ribs, mc floral w/gold, 4⅝".**375.00**
Brush, soap; wood hdl & golden badger hair, 6", EX......................**23.00**
Cabinet, sterilizer; blond varnish, blk shiny top, Deco style, 28" L.**100.00**

Chair, Koken, cast iron and porcelain with restored burgundy and gold paint, reupholstered black tucked leather, 53", M, $1,150.00. (Photo courtesy James Julia)

Clothes brush, wooden w/natural fibers, 8", EX **18.00**
Jar, satin glass, 12-sided, metal lid w/hollow knob (1-pc), 9".........**50.00**
Pole, mc pnt tin tube w/red sheet metal flag & cutouts, 1890s, 59x23".**925.00**
Pole, Paidar #1391, red/wht/bl stripes, CI mt, ca 1930s, rstr, 36".**1,500.00**
Pole, red/wht/bl weathered pnt on wood, pnt wooden caps, ca 1900, 40".**600.00**
Pole, trn wood, early red & wht pnt, ball finial, early, 47".........**675.00**
Pole, trn wood, old red/wht/bl/gold pnt, missing finial, worn, 39".**225.00**
Pole, trn wood cylinder, mc rpt w/gold ball finials, ca 1850, 85", VG.**460.00**
Pole, trn wood w/red & wht spirals, on base, 60x9x9"................**200.00**
Pole, trn/gilt/pnt wood, ½-rnd wall mt, 1890s, 53x12", EX **1,950.00**
Poles, pnt wood, gilt acorn finials, Am, 19th C, 79", pr, EX....**2,200.00**
Sign, Barber Shop, porc w/red/wht/bl enamel, 9x18", EX..............**20.00**
Strap, honing; leather, Imported...WL Buck Co..., 1930s, 24", EX..**100.00**
Strop, leather strip & 8½" wooden block, blk wood hdl, brass collar .**30.00**
Tin container, Olive-Tone Hair Trainer Wax, red/wht, rnd, NM..**35.00**
Trimmer, mustache; Durham Duplex, etched blade, ca 1940s-50s, EX..**15.00**
Vase, shaving paper; blk purple amethyst w/overall hobnails, 7".**200.00**
Vase, shaving paper; emerald gr w/Mary Gregory decor, 9⅛"....**700.00**
Vase, shaving paper; med gr w/emb ribs & mc florals, 7¼" **500.00**
Wall pocket, tin emb Comb–Brush on front, 8"............................**20.00**

Barometers

Barometers are instruments designed to measure the weight or pressure of the atmosphere in order to anticipate approaching weather changes. They have a glorious history. Some of the foremost thinkers of the seventeenth century developed the mercury barometer, as the discovery of the natural laws of the universe progressed. Working in 1644 from experiments by Galileo, Evangelista Torrecelli used a glass tube and a jar of mercury to create a vacuum and therefore prove that air has weight. Four years later, Rene Descartes added a paper scale to the top of Torrecelli's mercury tube and created the basic barometer. Blaise Pascal, working with Descartes, used it to determine the heights of mountains; only later was the correlation between changes in air pressure and changes in the weather observed and the term 'weather-glass' applied. Robert Boyle introduced it to England, and Robert Hook modified the form and designed the wheel barometer.

The most common type of barometer is the wheel or banjo, followed by the stick type. Modifications of the plain stick are the marine gimballed type and the laboratory, Kew, or Fortin type. Another style is the Admiral Fitzroy of which there are twelve or more variations. The above all have mercury contained either in glass tubing or wood-box cisterns.

The aneroid is a variety of barometer that works on atmospheric pressure changes. These come in all sizes ranging from 1" in diameter to 12" or larger. They may be in metal or wood cases. There is also a barograph which records on a graph that rotates around a drum powered by a seven-day clock mechanism. Pocket barometers (altimeters) vary in sizes from 1" in diameter up to 6". One final type of barometer is the symphisometer, a modification of the stick barometer; these were used for a limited time as they were not as accurate as the conventional marine barometer. Our advisor for this category is Bob Elsner; he is listed in the Directory under Florida.

Prices are subject to condition of wood, tube, etc.; number of functions; and whether or not they are signed.

American Stick Barometers

Chas Wilder, Peterboro, NH	1,250.00
DE Lent, Rochester, NY	1,250.00
EO Spooner Storm King, Boston, MA	1,450.00
FD McKay Jr, Elmira, NY	3,100.00
Simmons & Sons, Fulton, NY	1,250.00

English Barometers

Note: The 10" mahogany wheel listed below is marked 'Royal Exchange London Optician to King George IV Prince of Wales.' It may be referenced in Goodison, page 85.

Admiral Fitzory, various kinds, ea from $500 to	3,000.00
Fortin type (Kew or Laboratory) metal on brd w/milk glass, $750 to	950.00
Marine gimballed, sgn Walker, London	4,000.00
Right angle, sgn John Whitehurst, ca 1790	15,000.00
Stick, mahog bow-front w/urn-shaped cistern, S Mason, Dublin, 1824-30	5,000.00
Stick, rosewood, sgn L Casella, London	1,650.00
Stick, rosewood w/ivory scale, sgn Adie, dbl vernier, ca 1840	3,200.00
Symphisometer, sgn Adie	3,950.00
Wheel, 6", sgn Stanley, Peterborough	1,500.00
Wheel, 8", sgn F Molten, Norwich	1,450.00
Wheel, 10", mahog, J Smith Royal Exchange...Optician...Prince of Wales	1,950.00
Wheel, 10", MOP, sgn Spelzini, London	1,950.00

Other Types

Aneroid, 4-6" dia in brass case w/½-rnd thermometer, $150 to	250.00
Mahog barograph (recording type), sgn Negretti & Zambra	950.00
Pocket barometer (altimeter), w/case, from $200 to	300.00

Barware

Back in the thirties when social soirees were very elegant affairs thanks to the influence of Hollywood in all its glamour and mystique, cocktails were often served up in shakers styled as miniature airplanes, zeppelins, skyscrapers, lady's legs, penguins, roosters, bowling pins, etc. Some were by top designers such as Norman Bel Geddes and Russel Wright. They were made of silverplate, glass, and chrome, often trimmed with colorful Bakelite handles. Today these are hot collectibles, and even the more common Deco-styled chrome cylinders are often priced at $25.00 and up. Ice buckets, trays, and other bar accessories are also included in this area of collecting.

For further information we recommend *Vintage Bar Ware* by Stephen Visakay, our advisor for this category; he is listed in the Directory under New Jersey.

See also Bottle Openers.

Bar, traveling; chrome-plated airplane, Germany, 1928, 12" wingspan...**8,500.00**
Cocktail glass, amber w/pierced chrome holder, Cambridge, 3½"...**30.00**
Cocktail glass, pastel glass w/silver band, ftd, 4½x2¾" **18.00**
Cocktail picks, Dominos, plastic compo, 4½", 8 in domino stand..**140.00**
Cuff links, gold & SP mini shakers on spring, 1930s, from $125 to...**135.00**
Ice bucket, aluminum, curl hdls, Kraftware Trademk, EX.............**45.00**
Ice bucket, aluminum & Bakelite, knob finial, Kromes, 10", EX ..**42.50**
Ice bucket, aluminum w/copper-tone lid & hdl, unmk, 8"............**40.00**
Ice bucket, chrome w/Bakelite trim, porc liner, Keystone Ware, 10½"...**150.00**
Jigger, chrome plated, sq plastic hdl, 7" **10.00**
Jigger, Gorham Stoplight, gr/yel/red 'signs' on side, NM **165.00**
Martini picks, swirled Bakelite bar w/shaped picks (6), EX.........**225.00**
Martini picks, 5" shaker holds 6 olive picks, RHV & Co, BN **175.00**
Martini spike, Gorham Sterling 429, Pat Pend, 6¼", MIB..........**125.00**
Napkin, rooster bartender on wht, Fabrès, from $8 to **10.00**
Roly poly, glass, sailboats on cobalt, Hazel Atlas, 2½x2¼" **12.00**
Server, hot/cold, Penguin, aluminum w/blk Bakelite hdls, West Bend..**38.00**
Set, ruby w/silver o/l stripes, 1930s, shaker+ice bowl+6 ftd cocktails....**535.00**
Shaker, bl frost w/chrome top, 11½", +4 bl frosted 4½" martinis.**215.00**
Shaker, brass w/pewter hdl, 12", EX...**65.00**
Shaker, brushed aluminum, Skyscraper, brass finial, Kensington, 13".**165.00**
Shaker, chrome, 'Recipe,' blk Bakelite hdl, Forman, 1930s, EX.**165.00**
Shaker, chrome, brn swirl Bakelite detail, Farber Bros KromeKraft, 12".**80.00**
Shaker, chrome, Empire, w/red Catalin trim, Revere, 11⅜" ...**1,400.00**
Shaker, chrome, w/curved blk hdl, Farber Bros, 1940s, 2½-qt, 15".**185.00**
Shaker, chrome, w/Deco hdl, Farber Bros, 1940s, 11", M **65.00**
Shaker, glass, barbell, ruby w/gold stripes, 1930s, +4 ftd martinis .**435.00**
Shaker, glass, clear w/etch rooster, SP rim/spout, Hawkes, 9"......**150.00**
Shaker, glass, clear w/rooster-head stopper, Heisey, 13¾"............**175.00**
Shaker, glass, clear w/sterling floral o/l, chrome lid, 11" **85.00**
Shaker, glass, clear/emb, dial in plastic lid shows recipes, 12" **35.00**
Shaker, glass, cobalt, chrome lid w/Bakelite cap, +6 ftd martinis.**485.00**
Shaker, glass, cobalt w/wht flags, Hazel Atlas, 1930s, 11" **135.00**
Shaker, glass, cobalt w/wht pyro recipes, stepped chrome lid, 10½" ..**180.00**
Shaker, glass, cobalt w/windmills, 1930s, 10", +2 roly polys+ice pail..**145.00**
Shaker, glass, Hour Glass, clear w/mc stripes, chrome lid, 11" .**85.00**
Shaker, glass, lady's leg, ruby w/chrome, mk Derby Shelton, 1937, EX.**1,450.00**
Shaker, glass, mc rings on clear, chrome lid, Depression era, 11½"...**32.50**
Shaker, glass, ruby w/silver rings, chrome lid, 11" **235.00**
Shaker, glass, ruby w/sterling o/l tavern scene, 9½" **185.00**
Shaker, glass, Skyscraper, cobalt w/chrome top, 1930s, +6 tumblers..**565.00**
Shaker, glass, Skyscraper, pebbled frost w/concentric gold rings, 14" ..**225.00**

Shaker, Krome Kraft, Farber Bros., 1930s, party size, from $65.00 to $85.00.
(Photo courtesy Stephen Visakay)

Shaker, silver, twist-to-pour top, Sterling 1 Pt, w/monogram, 8½"...**325.00**
Shaker, SP, Cone, w/red bands, Napier, 1934, 9x3¾"..................**375.00**
Shaker, SP, Derby Gold Bag, sm rpr, ca 1925...........................**1,875.00**
Shaker, SP, Penguin, Napier, ca 1936, 12", NM **1,750.00**

Shaker, SP, Rooster, hammered, Wallace Bros, ca 1928, 14½"...**4,000.00**
Swizzle sticks, playing card motif, plastic, 1940s, 6½", 4 for..........**45.00**
Swizzle sticks, tuxedoed men, glass, 1930s, 7¼", 4 for **65.00**
Take a Shot, bullet form holds 4 shot cups, Japan, 1930s, 3".........**55.00**
Tray, chromium on brass, 5 O'Clock #813, Bel Geddes, 6¾x4⅝"..**22.00**
Tray, glass, cut/etched olives, Lucite hdls, 12x18" **95.00**
Tray, glass w/NP fr, rvpt flying ducks, 1928, 11x19" **95.00**
Tray, glass w/wood fr & metal hdls, rvpt, Pat...1926, 12x17¾" **195.00**
Tray, metal, rooster on weather vane on gr, 1940s-50s, 9x14" **40.00**
Tray, SP, Lurelle Guild, 10½", from $650 to................................**850.00**
Tumbler, cobalt glass, West Virginia Specialty, from $18 to **22.00**
Tumbler, Spun, clear or pastel glass, Imperial, 3" **16.00**

Basalt

Basalt is a type of unglazed black pottery developed by Josiah Wedgwood and copied by many other companies during the late eighteenth and early nineteenth centuries. It is also called 'Egyptian Black.' See also Wedgwood.

Potpourri vase, spiral fluted, rtcl shoulder & insert, w/lid, 9", EX ..**1,100.00**
Teapot, classical reliefs between columns w/festoons, rstr, 9¾" L ..**350.00**
Teapot, red/blk foliage, Sybil finial, no mk, 1880s, 5" **2,350.00**

Baskets

Basket weaving is a craft as old as ancient history. Baskets have been used to harvest crops, for domestic chores, and to contain the catch of fishermen. Materials at hand were utilized, and baskets from a specific region are often distinguishable simply by analyzing the natural fibers used in their construction. Early Indian baskets were made of corn husks or woven grasses. Willow splint, straw, rope, and paper were also used. Until the invention of the veneering machine in the late 1800s, splint was made by water-soaking a split log until the fibers were softened and flexible. Long strips were pulled out by hand and, while still wet and pliable, woven into baskets in either a cross-hatch or hexagonal weave.

Most handcrafted baskets on the market today were made between 1860 and the early 1900s. Factory baskets with a thick, wide splint cut by machine are of little interest to collectors. The more popular baskets are those designed for a specific purpose, rather than the more commonly found utility baskets that had multiple uses. Among the most costly forms are the Nantucket Lighthouse baskets, which were basically copied from those made there for centuries by aboriginal Indians. They were designed in the style of whale-oil barrels and named for the South Shoal Nantucket Lightship where many were made during the last half of the nineteenth century. Cheese baskets (used to separate curds from whey), herb-gathering baskets, and finely woven Shaker miniatures are other highly-prized examples of the basket-weaver's art.

In the listings that follow, assume that each has a center bentwood handle (unless handles of another type are noted) that is not included in the height. Unless another type of material is indicated, assume that each is made of splint. Prices are subjective and hinge on several factors: construction, age, color, and general appearance.

See also American Indian; Eskimo; Sewing; Shaker.

Buttocks, blk w/red & bl splotches, 26-rib, 10½" H **385.00**
Buttocks, EX color, minor damage, 9½x13" **225.00**
Buttocks, EX color, 17x19" **275.00**
Buttocks, gr pnt, 19th C, 13½" **1,400.00**
Buttocks, rich color, minor damage, 7x8½" **175.00**
Buttocks, 12-rib, eye-of-God hdl, minor damage, 8¼" H **125.00**
Buttocks, 20-rib, lt natural patina, tightly woven, 6¼x7" **165.00**
Buttocks, 24 wide ribs+wide center band w/over weaving, 9x15"..**210.00**

Buttocks, 30-rib, multicolor floral decoration, minor damage, 5x10x10½", $440.00; 30-rib, multicolor painted decoration, applied foot, 6¼x10x11", $210.00.

Buttocks, 32-rib, fine weave, lt stains, 5⅜x5½x5½" 440.00
Buttocks, 34-rib, hickory splint, EX patina, 8½x14" 300.00
Covered, dbl hdl, 12x19x11" 175.00
Eel, 19th C, stationary splint hdl, 14x10" 450.00
Egg, oak splint, Lookout Mt cvd in hdl, 23-rib, 1900s, 8x9x8½" .265.00
Egg, oak splint, 29-rib, wrapped rim, ca 1880, 9½x9½x9½" 325.00
Gathering, lt brn stain, tapered sides, 15½x15" 125.00
Gathering, mortise & tenon fr w/corner posts, 8x22x10" 120.00
Gathering, rnd w/2 bentwood hdls, 10x24½" 220.00
Gathering, 86-rib, cut nails attach hdl, PA, 1860s, 10x10x10½" .295.00
Goose feather, twisted rings on bottom, ovoid, 2-hdl, 23½" H ..185.00
Half, rich dark color, minor breaks, 7½x8" 350.00
Hanging, 3 tiered compartments & stepped bk panel, mc decor, 41x26" .250.00
Melon, 18-rib, Eye-of-God hdl, EX color, 15" H.........................300.00
Melon, 20-rib, natural brn, dry gr pnt int, 13x14", VG 110.00
Mini, oak splint, wrapped rim, late 1800s, 5" 235.00
Mini, sweetgrass, 19th C, 1½x2½" 435.00
Nantucket, cvd hdl, trn/scribed wooden base, 19th C, 6x5" 1,200.00
Nantucket, cvd swing hdl, wood base, F Sylvar, 5¼x8¾x6½" .1,500.00
Nantucket, swing hdl, trn wood base, early 20th C, minor breaks, 11x9" .1,200.00
Nantucket, wood disk base, brass tabs/plaque on bentwood hdl, 6x3½" .1,870.00
Nantucket, 3 dk cane bands, swing hdl, inscribed, Sylvaro/44, 14x11".2,000.00
Pnt, med gr, rnd, minor wear, 8½x13½" dia 1,700.00
Pnt, red w/bl & wht lashing, wht HP hdl decor, 1800s, 11x15" dia, EX .400.00
Rye straw, top coil w/red wool remnants, single loop hdl, 4x12x8" ..175.00
Shenandoah Valley (att), EX patina, 9¼x9" dia 95.00
Staved, vertical bentwood slats fixed w/wire, wear, 17x13" dia ...245.00
Utility, cvd wood hdls, 19th C, 11x29" 600.00
Willow w/pnt decor, EX color & patina, 1900s, 6½x14½x11½" ..85.00

Battersea

Battersea is a term that refers to enameling on copper or other metal. Though originally produced at Battersea, England, in the mid-eighteenth century, the craft was later practiced throughout the Staffordshire district. Boxes are the most common examples. Some are figurals, and many bear an inscription. Values are given for examples with only minimal damage, which is normal. Our advisor for this category is John Harrigan; he is listed in the Directory under Minnesota.

Box, birds, mc in wht reserves on yel, rpr bk, 1⅞" 135.00
Box, Love & Live Happy+birds, mc on wht, mirror, base damage, 1½"..330.00
Box, portraits (month before/month after marriage) invert, 1¾", EX.550.00
Box, scrolls/roses, gold/mc on wht, lobed shape, loose lid, 2" 165.00
Box, Token of Esteem+lovebirds on plinth on cobalt, base rpr, 1½".135.00

Box, Trifle From...+flowers & bird on wht w/pk base, mirror, 1¾" .350.00
Box, Trifles.../bird's nest on aqua w/wht beaded edge, 1¾" L, VG ..165.00
Box, wht rose in cobalt dmn reserve on pk w/blk 'moss', oval, 2", EX..195.00
Knob, Dancing Girl (plays triangle), mc, Bilston, 1⅞", pr (1 VG) ..275.00
Knob, Gen WA portrait, brn on wht, Bilston, sm chips, 2", pr ..2,000.00
Knob, lady & eagle, mc, Bilston, 2", pr 575.00
Knob, Sacred to Friendship, lady at tomb, mc, Bilston, 1½", pr...275.00
Knob, swordsman on rearing horse, mc, Bilston, 1¾", pr.........1,150.00

Bauer

The Bauer Pottery Company is one of the best known of the California pottery companies, noted for both its artware and its dinnerware. In the past ten years, Bauer has become particularly collectible, and prices have risen accordingly. The pottery actually started in Kentucky in 1885. It moved to Los Angeles in 1910 where it remained in operation until 1962. The company produced several successful dinnerware lines, including La Linda, Monterey, and Brusche Al Fresco. Most popular and most significant was the Ringware line introduced in 1932 which preceded Fiesta as a popular solid-color everyday dinnerware. The earliest pieces are unmarked, although to collectors they are unmistakable, partly due to their distinctive glazes which have an almost primitive charm due to their drips, misses, and color variations.

Another dinnerware line favored by collectors is Speckleware, its name derived from the 1950s-era speckled glaze Bauer used on various products, including vases, flowerpots, and kitchenware items as well as the dinnerware. Though not as popular as Ringware, Speckleware holds its value and is usually available at much lower prices than Ring. Keep an eye out for other flowerpots and mixing bowls as well.

Artware by Bauer is not so easy to find now, but it is worth seeking out because of the high values. So-called oil jars sell for upwards of $1,500.00, and Rebekah vases routinely fetch $400.00 or more. Matt Carlton is one of the designers of the most desirable handmade ware.

After WWII a flood of foreign imports and loss of key employees drastically curtailed their sales, and the pottery began a steady decline that ended in failure in 1962. Prices listed below reflect the California market. For more information we recommend *Collector's Encyclopedia of Bauer Pottery* and *Collector's Encyclopedia of California Pottery, Second Edition*, both by Jack Chipman (Collector Books).

In the lines of Ring and Plain Ware, pricing depends to some extent on color. Use the low end of our range of values for light brown, Chinese Yellow, orange-red, jade green, red-brown, olive green, light blue, turquoise, and gray; the high-end colors are Delph Blue, ivory, dusty burgundy, cobalt, chartreuse, papaya, and burgundy. Black is 50% higher than the high end; to evaluate white, double the high side. Use the low end of the range to evaluate Monterey items in all colors but Monterey Blue, burgundy, and white — those are high-end colors. You'll need to double the high end for black in this line as well as Monterey Moderne. An in-depth study of colors may be found in the books referenced above.

Our advisor for this category is Michele Miele; she is listed in the Directory under Montana.

Art Pottery, #200 Hi-Fire and Matt Carlton

Vase, #10 stock, chartreuse, Hi-Fire...125.00
Vase, carnation; Jade Green, Matt Carlton, 10" 350.00
Vase, Chinese Yellow, signature style, Matt Carlton, 12", minimum..1,500.00
Vase, fan; Matt Carlton, 3¾", from $75 to...................................150.00
Vase, garden; Fred Johnson, Hi-Fire, 18", minimum value 750.00
Vase, Rebekah; Matt Carlton, 12", from $900 to.....................1,500.00
Vase, Ring cylinder, Hi-Fire, 10", from $125 to 175.00

Brusche Al Fresco and Contempo

Al Fresco, bowl, fruit; speckled or solid, 5", from $10 to **12.00**
Al Fresco, creamer & sugar bowl, speckled or solid **25.00**
Al Fresco, mug, solid colors, hdld, 8-oz **10.00**
Al Fresco, plate, dinner; speckled or solid, 10", from $12 to **15.00**
Contempo, cup & saucer, Spice Green...**12.00**
Contempo, mug, Gloss Pumpkin, Kitchenware, 8-oz....................**15.00**
Contempo, teapot, beige **65.00**

Cal-Art and Garden Pottery

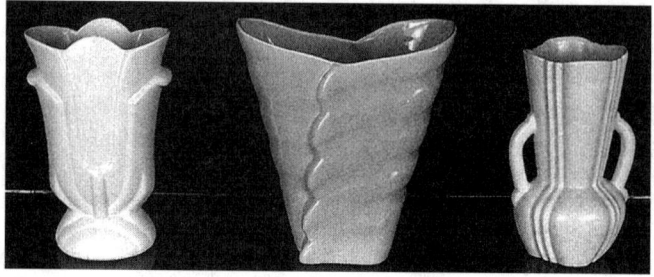

Cal-Art vases: White matt, 7½", $80.00; Yellow (late color), 8", $75.00; White matt, handles, 8", $75.00. (Photo courtesy Jack Chipman)

Flowerpot, Cal-Art Swirl #3, glossy, 3", from $20 to......................**25.00**
Jardiniere, Cal-Art Swirl #6, glossy, 6", from $50 to **60.00**
Jardiniere, Cal-Art Swirl #12, speckled pk, 12" **125.00**
Spanish pot, #4, speckled colors, 4", from $18 to...........................**25.00**
Spanish pot, Hi-Fire #5, gloss wht, 5"...**35.00**
Swan, Cal-Art, matt wht, med, 9" **65.00**
Vase, Cal-Art, burgundy, Robot midget, 4" **35.00**

Gloss Pastel Kitchenware (aka GPK)

Bowl, mixing; #24, all colors, from $30 to......................................**40.00**
Cookie jar (aka Beehive), all colors, from $95 to **150.00**
Pitcher, all colors, w/ice lip, 2-qt, from $75 to **90.00**
Teapot, Aladdin style, all colors, 8-cup, from $160 to **200.00**

Plain Ware

Bean pot, ind, from $135 to **185.00**
Bowl, mixing; #3, colors other than yel, 2-gal, minimum value..**350.00**
Bowl, mixing; #3, yel, 2-gal...**175.00**
Creamer, yel, ind, handmade by Matt Carlton...............................**95.00**
Ramekin, from $15 to...**25.00**

Ring Ware

Bowl, mixing; #18, Jade Green, dbl ring **130.00**
Bowl, mixing; #24, cobalt bl, dbl ring..**90.00**
Bowl, salad; lt bl, low, 9" **60.00**
Bowl, salad; orange-red, low, 9"...**75.00**
Carafe, orange-red w/copper raffia-wrapped hdl............................**120.00**
Casserole, Jade Green, ind, rare, 5½"..**250.00**
Cookie jar, Delph Blue, no lid **110.00**
Cookie jar, Delph Blue, w/lid...**350.00**
Cup & saucer, cobalt bl..**50.00**
Cup & saucer, Delph Blue...**45.00**
Plate, dessert; Chinese Yellow, 6½"..**15.00**
Plate, dinner; Jade Green, 9½" **35.00**

Plate, dinner; orange-red, 9½" **30.00**
Plate, salad; cobalt, 7½" **30.00**
Shakers, Jade Green, squat style, pr **45.00**
Tumbler, cobalt, no hdl, 12-oz..**50.00**
Tumbler set, Chinese Yellow, w/hdls, set of 6, 12-oz, minimum value..**180.00**

Speckled Kitchenware

Buffet server, speckled wht, no fr **40.00**
Casserole, speckled pk, w/fr, 1½-qt..**40.00**
Casserole, speckled pk, w/fr, 2-qt **60.00**
Mug, Kitchenware, speckled gr, 8-oz **15.00**
Pitcher, pelican; speckled bl, 20-oz...**45.00**
Pitcher, pelican; speckled yel, 20-oz **35.00**
Teapot, speckled gr, Monterey Moderne style **45.00**

Miscellaneous

Baker, tuna; burgundy, Chicken of the Sea, w/orig stand...............**45.00**
Bowls, mixing; Hi-Fire, various colors, 4-pc set, from $150 to **200.00**
Cookie jar, fish; speckled gr, Cemar turned Bauer.........................**75.00**
Jar, oil; Jade Green, 16", minimum value **850.00**
Vase, stock; speckled wht, #677, Tracy Irwin design, 12½".........**175.00**

Bavaria

Bavaria, Germany, was long the center of that country's pottery industry; in the 1800s, many firms operated in and around the area. Chinaware vases, novelties, and table accessories were decorated with transfer prints as well as by hand by artists who sometimes signed their work. The examples listed here are marked with 'Bavaria' and the logos of some of the various companies which were located there.

Bottle scent; Pierro w/urn, flower stopper, glass dauber, 5" **165.00**
Bowl, chrysanthemums & roses w/gold, emb scrolls, 3x10½"........**45.00**
Bowl, mc flowers w/gold, ZS & Co, lg **85.00**
Cake plate, mc roses in yel center, wide rose-colored rim, RC mk .**70.00**
Figurine, sheep & shepherd, pastels, Gerold Porzellan, 6½x7" ...**110.00**
Pickle dish, mc floral w/gold on elongated leaf form, 11x4½".......**32.00**
Plate, daisies, gilt, Osborne, 6¾", set of 6.......................................**40.00**
Plate, roses, mc on pastel w/gold, ZS&Co, 12⅜" **70.00**
Plate, stag portrait, scalloped rim, mk Punch Bavaria, 9½" **65.00**
Tankard, strawberries w/gold, 11" **165.00**
Teapot, alternating panels w/gold, +6 c/s **225.00**
Vase, Noemi portrait, HP, gold reserve, ruffled, TG/beehive, 10".**515.00**

Beer Cans

In the early 1930s one of America's largest can-manufacturing companies approached an East Coast brewery with a novel concept — beer in cans. The brewery decided to take a chance on the idea, and in January, 1935, the beer can was born.

The 'church key' style can opener was invented at the same time, and early flat top cans actually had instructions on how to use it to open a can.

Canned beer soared in popularity, and breweries scrambled to meet the canning challenge. Since many companies did not have a machine to fill a flat-top can, the cone top was invented. Brewery executives believed its shape would be more acceptable to consumers used to buying bottled beer, and it easily passed through existing bottling machinery. The more compact flat-top can dominated sales, and by the 1950s cone tops were obsolete.

About values: Condition is critical when determining the value of a beer can. Prices quoted are for like-new condition cans, free of rust, dents, scratches, and other damage. Like any collectible, value drops in direct proportion to condition, and off-grade cans are often worth no more than one-half of retail value. Information in our descriptions is given in this specific order: 1) name of brew; 2) company — may be simply repetitive; and 3) city/state or state.

All cone tops with original caps, ca 1930s: Fort Pitt Special, NM, $65.00; Kaier's Special Beer, M, $80.00; Edelweiss Light Beer, M, $185.00.

$1,000 Beer, Gettelman, Milwaukee WI, 1950s, G 9.00
Atlas Prager, Atlas, Chicago IL, flat top, 1950s, VG......................3.00
Atles Beer, Atles, Detroit MI, crowntainer, 1940s, VG 65.00
Ballantine Ale, Ballantine, Newark NJ, 1960s, gal, NM 175.00
Ballantine Beer, Ballantine, Newark NJ, gal, NM.........................67.00
Berghoff Beer, Berghoff, Ft Wayne IN, cone top, 1940s, VG+ 25.00
Black Pride Beer, West Bend Lithia, West Bend WI, pull top, 1970s, EX .7.50
Blackhawk Beer, Blackhawk, Cleveland OH, flat top, 1950s, VG .20.00
Blatz Old Heidelberg Beer, Blatz, Milwaukee WI, cone top, 1930s, EX .90.00
Boston Stock Ale, Boston Beer, Boston MA, cone top, 1940s, qt, G.65.00
Budweiser, Anheuser-Busch, St Louis MO, pull tab, 1970s, 16-oz...5.00
Burgemeister Beer, Burgermeister, San Francisco CA, flat top, 1950s, G ..12.50
Carling Blk Label, Brewing Co of Am, Cleveland OH, cone top, 1940s, EX.32.50
Chief Oshkosh Beer, Oskosh, Oshkosh WI, cone top, 1950s, EX..138.00
Clipper Pale Beer, Grace Bros, Santa Rosa CA, flat top, 1940s, VG.130.00
Coors Beer, Coors, Golden CO, flat top, 1950s, EX........................3.00
Country Club Beer, Goetz, St Joseph MO, cone top, 1950s, EX ...36.00
Diehl Beer, Diehl, Defiance OH, cone top, G+ 30.00
Drewry's Beer, Drewy's Ltd, South Bend IN, flat top, 1950s, VG ..22.50
E&B Special Beer, E&B Brewing, Detroit MI, cone top, 1940s, NM.55.00
Fehr's XL Beer, Fehr, Louisville KY, crowntainer, 1940s, VG 20.00
Fehr's XL Beer, Ortlieb, Philadelphia, crowntop, 1940s, VG.........20.00
Fitzgerald's Pale Ale, Fitzgerald Bros, Troy NY, flat top, 1950s, VG ..22.50
Fox Head 400, Fox Head, Wakesha WI, flat top, 1950s, VG 18.00
Frankenmuth Ale, Frankenmuth, Frankenmuth MI, cone top, 1940s, VG.45.00
Gibbons Beer, The Lion, Wilkes-Barre PA, cone top, VG 28.00
Grain Belt Beer, Minneapolis, Minneapolis MN, cone top, 1940s, EX.35.00
Great Lakes Beer, Schen Edelweiss, Chicago IL, flat top, VG.......20.00
Home Beer, Associated, Chicago IL, pull tab, 1960s, NM.............22.00
Hull's Export Beer, Hull, New Haven CT, flat top, G....................15.00
Iroquois Draft Ale, Iroquois, Buffalo NY, pull tab, 1970s, EX..........7.00
Jax Beer, Jackson, New Orleans LA, flat top, 1950s, EX................10.00
Keeley Beer, Best, Chicago IL, flat top, 1950s, VG......................15.00
Knickerbocker Bock, Ruppert, New York NY, flat top, 1950s, EX..13.00
Lebanon Valley Beer, Lebanon Valley, Lebanon PA, cone top, 1940s, EX.85.00
Menominee Beer, Menominee Marinette, Menominee MI, cone top, 1940s, G..25.00
Mug Ale, Burkhardt, Akron OH, flat top, 1950s, G 55.00
Namar Beer, Cooper, Philadelphia PA, cone top, G 48.00

Oconto Beer, Oconto, Oconto WI, flat top, 1950s, VG 10.00
Old St Louis Beer, Lami, St Louis MO, flat top, 1950s, VG..........22.00
Old Style Lager, Heileman, Lacrosse WI, flat top, 1950s, EX........27.50
Ortlieb's Export Beer, Ortlieb Brewing, Philadelphia PA, 1940s, VG..42.50
Peerles Beer, Lacross, Lacrosse WI, cone top, 1950s, EX 72.50
Pfeiffer's Beer, Pfeiffer, Detroit MI, flat top, 1950s, EX 15.00
Rahr's Beer, Rahr-Green Bay, Green Bay WI, cone top, 1950s, VG .75.00
Rahr's Beer, Rahr-Green Bay, Green Bay WI, flat top, 1950s, EX.12.00
Reingold Beer, US Brewing, Chicago IL, flat top, 1950s, VG 20.00
Royal Pilsner, Koller, Chicago Il, J-spout cone top, G+ 85.00
Schmidt's Ale, Schmidt's, Philadelphia PA, cone top, 1950s, qt, G..30.00
Sierra Beer, Reno, Reno NV, cone top, 1940s, VG 60.00
Sterling Draught Beer, Sterling, Evansville IN, 1960s, EX 47.50
Stock Ale, Croft, Boston MA, cone top, 1940s, G.........................30.00
Tempo Beer, Blatz, Milwaukee WI, flat top, VG..........................50.00
Tudor Beer, Best, Chicago IL, flat top, 1950s, EX 15.00
Valley Brew Pale, El Dorado, Stockton CA, flat top, 1930s, VG..15.00

Bellaire, Marc

Marc Bellaire, originally Donald Edmund Fleischman, was born in Toledo, Ohio, in 1925. He studied at the Toledo Museum of Art under Ernest Spring while employed as a designer for the Libbey Glass Company. During World War II while serving in the Navy, he travelled extensively throughout the Pacific. As a result of this experience, he developed an even broader and enriched sense of design and color.

Marc settled in California in the 1950s where his work attracted the attention of national buyers and agencies who persuaded him to create ceramic lines of his own, employing hand-decorating techniques throughout. He built a studio in Culver City, and there he produced high-quality ceramics, often decorated with ultramodern figures or geometric patterns and executed with a distinctive flair. His most famous line was Mardi Gras, decorated with slim dancers in spattered and striped colors of black, blue, pink, and white. Other major patterns were Jamaica, Balinese, Beachcomber, Friendly Island, Cave Painting, Hawaiian, Bird Isle, Oriental, Jungle Dancer, and Kashmir. Kashmir usually has the name Ingle on the front and Bellaire on the reverse.

It is to be noted that Marc was employed by Sascha Brastoff during the 1950s. Many believe that he was hired for his creative imagination and style.

During the period from 1951 to 1956, Marc was named one of the top ten artware designers by *Giftwares Magazine*. After 1956 he taught and lectured on art, design, and ceramic decorating techniques from coast to coast. Many of his pieces were one of a kind, commissioned throughout the United States.

During the 1970s he set up a studio in Marin County, California, and eventually moved to Palm Springs where he opened his final studio/gallery. There he produced large pieces with a Southwestern style. Mr. Bellaire died in 1994. Our advisor for this category is Marty Webster; he is listed in the Directory under Michigan.

Ashtray, Beachcomber, free-form, 11" 45.00
Ashtray, Bird Isle, blk birds on cream, 8" 85.00
Ashtray, Clown, mc on cream, 7" 65.00
Ashtray, Jamaica, musicians on brn, 10x14"....................................85.00
Ashtray, Mardi Gras, figures on blk, rolled rim, 9" 100.00
Ashtray, Mardi Gras, figures on blk, 14x14"..................................125.00
Ashtray, Mardi Gras, figures on blk, 4x8½".....................................35.00
Ashtray, Still Life, matt fruits & leaves, 10x15".............................100.00
Bowl, Beachcomber, low teardrop shape, 12" L............................100.00
Bowl, Cortillian, lady w/bl bird, 13x9" 125.00
Bowl, Fruit, 3 pears, yel & gr... 45.00
Bowl, Jungle Dancer, 11½x5½"...150.00

Box, African figures on lid, 6" **95.00**
Box, Jamaica, man w/guitar, free-form, B46, 8" **115.00**
Box, Mardi Gras, 10" dia **150.00**
Box, 3 geisha girls, wht & gray, 6" **35.00**
Candlestick, Jamaica man, 10½" **125.00**
Charger, fisherman w/net, 16" **150.00**
Charger, Polynesian King & Queen, 15" **200.00**
Charger, stylized bird on branch, 15" **165.00**
Compote, Cave Painting, 4-ftd, 6x12" **100.00**
Compote, Cotillian, 4-ftd, 8x17" **200.00**
Cookie jar, Stick People, wooden lid, 10" **150.00**
Dish, Leaf, gr/wht on gray, free-form, 9x15" **55.00**
Ewer, Mardi Gras, figures on blk, 18" **400.00**
Figuirne, Mardi Gras, female seated, 5½" **150.00**
Figurine, Bali, dancer (fancy) w/headdress, 24" **1,200.00**
Figurine, bird w/long neck, 17" **250.00**
Figurine, buffalo, brn & cream, 10x10" **260.00**
Figurine, bull, 9" **345.00**
Figurine, horse, gray/gr/brn, 8x7½" **140.00**
Figurine, Jamaica, man playing guitar..........................**300.00**
Figurine, Mardi Gras, man reclining, very slim, 18" **500.00**
Figurine, Mardi Gras, man standing, very slim, 24" **700.00**
Figurine, Mardi Gras, man standing, 11½" **235.00**
Figurine, Polynesian man standing, 12"........................**500.00**
Lamp, Mardi Gras, long-neck vase on wood base, 28"......**450.00**
Pitcher, water; walrus, 11½", +6 4½" mugs..................**255.00**
Platter, fisherman w/net, 16" dia..................................**150.00**
Platter, Friendly Island, 10" **135.00**
Platter, Hawaiian, 3 figures on orange, 13x7"..............**55.00**
Platter, Mardi Gras, figures on blk, 12x18"..................**250.00**
Platter, Polynesian dancer, egg shape, 15x11" **250.00**
Platter, underwater design in sea gr, 16" **100.00**
Shakers, rams on gr, 4", pr..**50.00**
Switch plate, dancer on blk, B-26, 4¾x3" **150.00**
Tankard, man on brn, 19", +6 mugs..............................**250.00**
Tankard, polar bear on blk, w/lid, 13" **200.00**
Teapot, walrus on ice bl, 6½"..**75.00**
Tile, Eskimo mother & child, 12¾x10½"......................**125.00**
Tile, mtns & glacier on blk, 10x8½" **75.00**
Tile, walrus on bl, 10x8½" **75.00**
Tray, Black man dancing, triangular, 17x8½" **75.00**
Tray, Hawaiian figures, peach & blk, 14x10" **145.00**
Tray, Jungle Dancer, figure on blk/gr, 12" dia **145.00**

Tray, Mardi Gras, figures on black, 9x10", $125.00.

Tray, polar bear & iceberg, #910, 13x9¾" **75.00**
Tumbler, cabin **20.00**
Vase, Balinese women, hourglass shape, 8"..................**100.00**
Vase, Black Cats, hourglass shape, 8" **100.00**
Vase, glacier on gray, #143, 5½" **50.00**
Vase, house on yel, 11½" **100.00**

Vase, iceberg on gray, 7" **50.00**
Vase, Indian on horsebk, mk Bellaire 89, 10"..............**150.00**
Vase, Mardi Gras, figures on blk, 18" **250.00**
Vase, Mardi Gras, hourglass shape on 3 ft, 11" **125.00**
Vase, mother & child on teal, cylindrical, 17"..............**165.00**
Vase, mtn & glacier on blk, #114, 12" **80.00**
Vase, polar bear on gr, 10" **100.00**
Vase, Polynesian woman, 9"..**100.00**
Vase, reindeer, 4½" **45.00**
Vase, sea lion & seaweed, oval, #128, 8" **95.00**
Vase, seal & glacier on brn, free-form, #911, 11" **125.00**
Vase, Stick People, irregular beak-like opening, 12"....**250.00**
Vase, walrus on ice bl, 10"..**110.00**

Belleek, American

From 1883 until 1930, several American potteries located in New Jersey and Ohio manufactured a type of china similar to the famous Irish Belleek soft-paste porcelain. The American manufacturers identified their porcelain by using 'Belleek' or 'Beleek' in their marks. American Belleek is considered the highest achievement of the American porcelain industry. Production centered around artistic cabinet pieces and luxury tablewares. Many examples emulated Irish shapes and decor with marine themes and other naturalistic styles. While all are highly collectible, some companies' products are rarer than others. The best-known manufacturers are Ott and Brewer, Willets, The Ceramic Art Company (CAC), and Lenox. You will find more detailed information in those specific categories. Our advisor for this category is Mary Frank Gaston.

Key:
AAC — American Art China
CAP — Columbian Art Pottery

Bowl, florals, pk on wht w/in & w/out, AAC, 2½x5" **400.00**
Cream soup, Bouquet, Coxon, w/underplate **275.00**
Cup, demitasse; Orient pattern, Morgan **225.00**
Cup & saucer, demitasse; Tridacna, gold trim, CAP....................**225.00**
Cup & saucer, demitasse; wht w/pk int & saucer, gold trim, CAP..**225.00**
Plate, Boulevard, Coxon, 10½" **275.00**
Plate, floral border w/in wide yel rim, Coxon, 10½"....................**275.00**
Plate, peacocks & mixed florals w/gold, Gordon, 7" **120.00**
Salt cellar, sponged gold, scalloped, pk int, AAC, 2½" **145.00**
Teapot, dragon figural, gold-paste leaves, CAP, 7½x9" **1,600.00**
Tumbler, Souvenir David's Society...1899, 4¼"..........................**325.00**
Vase, floral on wht, gold emb hdls, AAC, 12" **1,200.00**

Belleek, Irish

Belleek is a very thin translucent porcelain that takes its name from the village in Ireland where it originated in 1859. The glaze is a creamy ivory color with a pearl-like lustre. The tablewares, baskets, figurines, and vases that have always been made there are being crafted yet today. Shamrock, Tridacna, Echinus, and Thorn are but a few of the many patterns of tableware which have been made during some periods of the pottery's history. Throughout the years, their most popular pattern has been Shamrock.

It is possible to date an example to within twenty to thirty years of crafting by the mark. Pieces with an early stamp often bring prices nearly triple that of a similar but current item. With some variation, the marks have always incorporated the Irish wolfhound, Celtic round tower, harp, and shamrocks. The first three marks (usually in black) were used from 1863 to 1946. A series of green marks identified the pottery's offerings from 1946 until the seventh mark (in gold/brown) was introduced in 1980 (it was discontinued in 1992). The eighth mark was blue and closely resembled the gold mark. It was used from 1993 to 1996. The ninth, tenth, and eleventh marks went back to the simplicity of the first mark with only the registry mark (an R encased in a circle) to distinguish them from the original. The ninth mark, which was used from 1997 to 1999, was blue. A special black version of that mark was introduced for the year 2000 and a Millennium 2000 banner was added. The tenth or Millennium mark was retired at the end of 2000, and the current green mark was introduced as the eleventh mark. Belleek Collector's International Society limited edition pieces are designated with a special mark in red. In the listings below, numbers designated with the prefix 'D' relate to the book *Belleek, The Complete Collector's Guide and Illustrated Reference, Second Edition*, by Richard K. Degenhardt (published by Wallace-Homestead Book Company, One Chilton Way, Radnor, PA 19098-0230). The numbers designated with the prefix 'B' are current production numbers used by the pottery.

Our advisor for this category is Liz Stillwell; she is listed in the Directory under California.

Key:
A — plain (glazed only)
B — cob lustre
C — hand tinted
D — hand painted
E — hand-painted shamrocks
F — hand gilted
G — hand tinted and gilted
H — hand-painted shamrocks and gilted
J — mother-of-pearl
K — hand painted and gilted
L — bisque and plain
M — decalcomania
N — special hand-painted decoration
T — transfer design

I — 1863 – 1890
II — 1891 – 1926
III — 1926 – 1946
IV — 1946 – 1955
V — 1955 – 1965
VI — 1965 – 3/31/1980
VII — 4/1/1980 – 1992
VIII — 1/4/1993 – 1996
IX — 1997 – 1999
X — 2000 only
XI — 2001 – current

Further information concerning Periods of Crafting (Baskets):
1 — 1865 – 1890, BELLEEK (three strand)
2 — 1865– 1890, BELLEEK CO. FERMANAGH (three strand)
3 — 1891 – 1920, BELLEEK CO. FERMANAGH IRELAND (three strand)
4 — 1921 – 1954, BELLEEK CO. FERMANAGH IRELAND (four strand)
5 — 1955 – 1979, BELLEEK ® CO. FERMANAGH IRELAND (four strand)
6 — 1980 – 1985, BELLEEK ® IRELAND (four strand)
7 — 1985 – 1989, BELLEEK ® IRELAND 'ID NUMBER' (four strand)
8 – 12 — 1990 to present (Refer to *Belleek, The Complete Collector's Guide and Illustrated Reference, 2nd Edition*, Chapter 5)

Aberdeen Vase, M/S, D58-IV, A	550.00
Belgian Hawker Female, D15-VII, D	225.00
Belleek Flowered Pot, S/S, D47-II, B	275.00
Birds Nest Basket, D123-5	400.00
Blarney Cup & Saucer, D567-II, C	500.00
Book, Complete Collection Guide, R Degenhardt	135.00
Cardium on Shell, D260-II, G	150.00
Cherry Blossom Plate Flowered, D1685, C	725.00
Cone Cream & Sugar, D434 & 435-II, C	360.00
Cone Flower Pot, D223-VI, B	40.00
Cottage Butter Dish, D2079-V, B	225.00
Crinkled Flower Pot, D228-III, B	185.00
Dragon Fly Vase, L/S, D1915-VII, D	95.00
Earthenware Bread Tray, Give Us This Day...Bread, D2081-I, A	750.00
Enchanted Holly Dinner Plate, D1928-VII, D	75.00
Enchanted Holly Salad Plate, D1929-VII, D	45.00

Erne Basket, D1688-4, D	575.00
Fan Cup & Saucer, D694-II, G	575.00
Feather Vase, S/S, D155-III, A	175.00
Fermanagh Vase, D139-V, B	110.00
Forget-Me-Not Trinket Box, D111-II, A	650.00
Grass Moustache Cup & Saucer, D739-I, D	700.00
Harp Shamrock Butter Dish, D1356-V, E	90.00
Hexagon Kettle, D409-II, L/S, C	725.00
Hexagon Salt, D291-II, C	125.00
Indian Corn Spill, D190-I, B	500.00
Iris Harp w/Applied Shamrock, D1640-II, E	700.00
Irish Pot Cream & Sugar, D232-III, A	150.00
Ivy Cream & Sugar, D241-II, B	210.00
Lifford Creamer, D301-VII, B	75.00
Lotus Creamer, pk tint hdl, D244-II, D	125.00
Mask Milk Jug, D1485-VI, A	125.00
Melon Vine Wall Bracket, D1804-II, A	1,800.00
Moore Vase, D87-VI, B	70.00
Neptune Cup & Saucer, D414-II, C	225.00
Owl Vase, D1774-VI, B	60.00
Pig, L/S, D231-III, B	200.00
Ribbon Cream & Sugar, D243-V, B	95.00
Shamrock Basket, D109-2, S/S, D	900.00
Shamrock Biscuit Barrel, D531-VII, E	110.00
Shamrock Breakfast Cup & Saucer, D373-II, E	350.00
Shamrock Butter Tub, D1565-IV, E	60.00
Shamrock Covered Muffin Dish, D388-III, E	400.00
Shamrock Egg Cup, D389-II, E	185.00

Shamrock Honey Pot on Stand, D530-II E, $750.00.

Shamrock Trinket Box, D112-III, E	500.00
Shamrock Trunk Stump Spill, D1224-VII, E	50.00
Sheerin Vase, D1781-VII, K	75.00
Single Root Spill, D151-II, D	575.00
Spoons Coral & Spade, D296-NM	105.00
Straw Basket, D79-II, J	700.00
Sunflower Vase, D188-III, A	225.00
Swan, S/S, D255-V, B	110.00
Telegraph insulator, D1055-NM, A	60.00
Thorn Ashtray, N/A-V	20.00
Toy Shamrock Cream & Sugar, D234-III, E	150.00
Toy Shell Creamer, D250-II, S/S, D	350.00
Tridacna Hostess Set, D1352-VI, B	90.00
Triple Shell Menu Holder, D535-III, E	320.00
Typha Jug Spill, D94-VII, E	40.00
Undine Creamer, D305-VI, B	95.00
US Bicentennial Plate '1976,' D1894-VI, C	125.00
US Bicentennial Plate Flowered, D1695-5, K	5,500.00
Victoria Shell, D128-V, B	450.00
Wall Plaque, Praise Ye the Lord, D1808-I, D	950.00

Bells

Some areas of interest represented in the study of bells are history, religion, and geography. Since Biblical times, bells have announced morning church services, vespers, deaths, christenings, school hours, fires, and community events. Countries have used them en masse to peal out the good news of Christmas, New Year's, and the endings of World Wars I and II. They've been rung in times of great sorrow, such as the death of Abraham Lincoln.

For further information, we recommend *World of Bells* by Dorothy Malone Anthony (a series of ten books). All have over two hundred colored pictures covering many bell categories. See also Nodders; Schoolhouse Collectibles.

Brass, 1878 Sagneileur cow bell, reproduction, 5", $45.00 (originated in Switzerland in 1878 but has been made and sold in U.S. since 1900).

Brass, counter top, English, 1930s-40s, EX 140.00
Brass, figural, lady holding baby, 4¼" 340.00
Brass, figural, lady holding bird, 3x2" 185.00
Brass, figural, turtle shape, wind-up, German, 1850-1900 ....250.00
Brass, ship's, Empire Louth eng, ca 1920, 10x8"...........................110.00
Brass, USN eng, heavy, 9x9½", w/clapper & bracket 575.00
Bronze, temple, Hindu, standing lion atop ornate base, 11"..........80.00
CI, brass-colored wash on ornate 4-ftd base, 3x3" 125.00
CI, dinner, mk CS Bell Co 1886, No 3 Yoke, orig clapper, 11"...160.00
Glass, cranberry swirl w/opal edge, ribbed swirl crystal hdl, 12½" .115.00
Metal, scrollwork in bl enamel, mk China, ca 1920s, 4½" 80.00
Oak, dinner, gong, fruit & scroll cvgs, massive, 41".....................780.00
Porcelain, figural, lady, pnt, mk #18255, German, 4x2¼" 85.00
Sleigh, brass, 15 graduated bells on leather strap, 55" L, VG 200.00
SP, figural, lady, clapper ft, 3⅛x2" 100.00

Bennett, John

Bringing with him the knowledge and experience he had gained at the Doulton (Lambeth) Pottery in England, John Bennett opened a studio in New York City around 1877, where he continued his methods of decorating faience under the glaze. Early wares utilized imported English biscuit, though subsequently local clays (both white and cream-colored) were also used. His first kiln was on Lexington Avenue; he built another on East Twenty-Fourth Street. Pieces are usually signed 'J. Bennett, N.Y.,' often with the street address and date. Later examples may be marked 'West Orange, N.J.,' where he retired. The pottery was in operation approximately six years in New York. Pieces signed with other initials are usually worth less. Our advisor for this category is Robert Tuggle; he is listed in the Directory under New York.

Plate, azalea branches/butterfly, wht/gr/gold on dk bl, 15" 4,750.00
Plate, 5 heart reserves w/daisies & poppies, tan/wht/red on dk bl, 15" ..4,000.00

Bennington

Although the term has become a generic one for the mottled brown ware produced there, Bennington is not a type of pottery, but rather a town in Vermont where two important potteries were located. The Norton Company, founded in 1793, produced mainly redware and salt-glazed stoneware; only during a brief partnership with Fenton (1845 – 47) was any Rockingham attempted. The Norton Company endured until 1894, operated by succeeding generations of the Norton family. Fenton organized his own pottery in 1847. There he manufactured not only redware and stoneware, but more artistic types as well — graniteware, scroddled ware, flint enamel, a fine parian, and vast amounts of their famous Rockingham. Though from an esthetic standpoint his work rated highly among the country's finest ceramic achievements, he was economically unsuccessful. His pottery closed in 1858.

It is estimated that only one in five Fenton pieces were marked; and although it has become a common practice to link any fine piece of Rockingham to this area, careful study is vital in order to be able to distinguish Bennington's from the similar wares of many other American and Staffordshire potteries. Although the practice was without the permission of the proprietor, it was nevertheless a common occurrence for a potter to take his molds with him when moving from one pottery to the next, so particularly well-received designs were often reproduced at several locations. Of eight known Fenton marks, four are variations of the '1849' impressed stamp: 'Lyman Fenton Co., Fenton's Enamel Patented 1849, Bennington, Vermont.' These are generally found on examples of Rockingham and flint enamel. A raised, rectangular scroll with 'Fenton's Works, Bennington, Vermont,' was used on early examples of porcelain. From 1852 to 1858, the company operated under the title of the United States Pottery Company. Three marks — the ribbon mark with the initials USP, the oval with a scrollwork border and the name in full, and the plain oval with the name in full — were used during that period.

Among the more sought-after examples are the bird and animal figurines, novelty pitchers, figural bottles, and all of the more finely modeled items. Recumbent deer, cows, standing lions with one forepaw on a ball, and opposing pairs of poodles with baskets in their mouths and 'coleslaw' fur were made in Rockingham, flint enamel, and occasionally in parian. Numbers in the listings below refer to the book *Bennington Pottery and Porcelain* by Barret. Our advisors for Bennington (except for parian and stoneware) are Barbara and Charles Adams; they are listed in the Directory under Massachusetts.

Baker, Rockingham, flared sides, 2⅛x14⅛x10¾" 400.00
Bank, flint enamel, ftd ball form w/tail finial, 1850-60 mk, 6½" ..750.00
Book flask, Bennington Battle, flint enamel, rstr, 11" 2,500.00
Book flask, Bennington Battle, flint enamel w/brn & bl, 7¾" .1,500.00
Book flask, Bennington Companion G, 1849-58 mk, 8".........1,500.00
Book flask, Ladies' Companion, flint enamel, 1849-58 mk, 5½" .1,200.00
Book flask, Life of Kossuth, flint enamel, sm line, 5¾" 625.00
Bottle, Coachman, Rockingham, Lyman Fenton..., 10⅜", EX 800.00
Bottle, Toby, flint enamel, brn/orange on tan, 1849 mk, 10¾" .1,000.00
Candlestick, flint enamel, brn w/gr traces, 9⅜x4¾" 600.00
Candlestick, flint enamel, flanged base, flaw, 7¾" 500.00
Cuspidor, flint enamel, brn w/dk gr & bl, emb seashells, 10½" dia .140.00
Cuspidor, flint enamel, 1849 mk..400.00
Figure, spaniel on base, Rockingham, att, ca 1850, 12" 375.00
Inkwell, sleeping youth figural, Rockingham, 4x5½" 300.00
Jar, Toby, flint enamel, 1849 mk, rstr, 4¼" 675.00
Jar, Toby, lt gr sponging, brn-amber int, 1849 mk, 4½", EX........650.00
Jug, Little Brown Jug scribed on Albany glaze, att, ca 1876, 3"...135.00
Pie plate, Rockingham, 1849 mk, 11¼", NM 650.00
Pitcher, Cascade, parian, waterfall body, branch hdl, mk, 9½" ...550.00
Pitcher, flint enamel, sm heart at tip of ea rib, Lyman Fenton, 10".900.00

Pitcher, milk; Rockingham, floral panels, hexagonal, rpr, 6¾" ...**150.00**
Pitcher, Toby, Rockingham, 6" **250.00**
Vase, Tulip, flint enamel, mk DD, 9", NM **800.00**
Wash bowl & pitcher, flint enamel, Scalloped Rib, prof rprs...**1,100.00**

Stoneware

Key: c/s — cobalt on salt glaze

Churn, #3/flower, c/s, E&LP Norton, rstr, ca 1880, 9" **1,300.00**
Cream pot, #3/sunburst floral, J&E Norton, ca 1855, 12", EX **600.00**
Crock, #2/accents, c/s, L Norton, stone ping on bk, 11" **225.00**
Crock, #2/flower (simple), c/s, Julius Norton, stain, 10½" **250.00**
Crock, #2/flower basket, c/s, J&E Norton, line, 9½" **1,500.00**
Crock, #3/bird on plume, E&LP Norton, rstr, ca 1870, 10½" **500.00**
Crock, #3/floral (EX art), c/s, J Norton & Co, ca 1861, 10½", EX .**550.00**
Crock, #5/chicken pecking corn, c/s, J Norton & Co, line/rstr, 13" ..**1,300.00**
Crock, cake; #11/2/thistle, c/s, J&E Norton, ca 1855, 7½" **715.00**
Crock, leaf (lg/fancy), c/s, E&LP, 8½x10" **300.00**
Inkwell, lion's head, mid-1800s, att, 2x2⅜", EX **250.00**
Jar, #3/thistle, c/s, J&E Norton, flakes/spider, ca 1855, 13" **635.00**
Jar, #4/peacocks in tree, c/s, J&E Norton, ca 1855, 14" **5,500.00**
Jar, preserve; #11/2/floral, c/s, E&LP Norton, ping, ca 1880, 10½".**275.00**
Jug, #1/bird on branch, c/s, J Norton, 11", NM........................**880.00**
Jug, #1/bird on log, c/s, J&E Norton, ca 1855, 11" **650.00**
Jug, #1/flower (dbl), c/s, Julius Norton, 1840s, stain, 11" **450.00**
Jug, #2/floral, c/s, J&E Norton, ca 1855, 14" **1,000.00**
Jug, #2/floral spray, c/s, J&E Norton, ca 1855, 13" **685.00**
Jug, #2/flower (triple), c/s, Norton & Fenton, rpr, ca 1845, 12½" .**385.00**
Jug, #2/plume, c/s, E&LP Norton, ca 1880, 11½" **250.00**
Jug, #3/bird on plume, c/s, J Norton & Co, prof rstr, 16" **400.00**
Jug, #3/floral, c/s, E&LP Norton, spidering, ca 1880, 15" **275.00**
Jug, #3/floral spray (stylized), c/s, E&LP Norton, 1870s, 14"......**325.00**
Jug, #3/flower, c/s, J&E Norton, stain, ca 1859, 15"...................**385.00**
Jug, #3/peacock on stump, c/s, J&E Norton, ca 1859, 15"........**2,975.00**

Beswick

In the early 1890s, James Wright Beswick operated a pottery in Longston, England, where he produced fine dinnerware as well as ornamental ceramics. Today's collectors are most interested in the figurines made since 1936 by a later generation Beswick firm, John Beswick, Ltd. They specialize in reproducing accurately detailed bone-china models of authentic breeds of animals. Their Fireside Series includes dogs, cats, elephants, horses, the Huntsman, and an Indian figure, which measure up to 14" in height. The Connoisseur line is modeled after the likenesses of famous racing horses. Beatrix Potter's characters and some of Walt Disney's are charmingly recreated and appeal to children and adults alike. Other items, such as character Tobys, have also been produced. The Beswick name is stamped on each piece. The firm was absorbed by the Doulton group in 1973.

Beatrix Potter, Amiable Guinea Pig, B3.....................................**300.00**
Beatrix Potter, And This Pig Had None, B6..................................**85.00**
Beatrix Potter, Anna Maria, B3a...**450.00**
Beatrix Potter, Apply Dappley, bottle out **250.00**
Beatrix Potter, Aunt Petitoes, B6...**75.00**
Beatrix Potter, Babbity Bumble, B6..**250.00**
Beatrix Potter, Benjamin Ate Lettuce Leaf, B6a...........................**50.00**
Beatrix Potter, Benjamin Bunny, ears out, 3B.............................**195.00**
Beatrix Potter, Benjamin Bunny, 3B...**55.00**
Beatrix Potter, Bommy Brock, lg eye patch, B3............................**65.00**
Beatrix Potter, Cecily Parsley, B3...**95.00**
Beatrix Potter, Cottontail, B6..**45.00**

Beatrix Potter, Diggory Diggory Delvet, B3.................................**75.00**
Beatrix Potter, Foxy Whiskered Gentleman, B3 ....**75.00**
Beatrix Potter, Goody & Timmy Tiptoes, C3...........................**275.00**
Beatrix Potter, Hunca Munca Sweeping, B3 ....**75.00**
Beatrix Potter, Jemima Puddleduck, B10...................................**50.00**
Beatrix Potter, Jemima Puddleduck, B3.....................................**55.00**
Beatrix Potter, Johnny Townmouse, B3......................................**55.00**
Beatrix Potter, Lady Mouse, B2...**185.00**
Beatrix Potter, Little Pig Robinson Spying, B6...........................**150.00**
Beatrix Potter, Mother Ladybird, B6..**115.00**
Beatrix Potter, Mr Drake Puddleduck, B6...................................**75.00**
Beatrix Potter, Mr Jackson, B6..**65.00**
Beatrix Potter, Mrs Flopsy Bunny, B3..**65.00**
Beatrix Potter, Mrs Rabbit & Bunnies, 3B...................................**85.00**
Beatrix Potter, Mrs Tiggy Winkle Washing, B8A **200.00**
Beatrix Potter, No More Twists, B6..**55.00**
Beatrix Potter, Old Woman in Shoe, B3......................................**45.00**
Beatrix Potter, Old Woman in Shoe Knitting, B3..........................**95.00**
Beatrix Potter, Peter & the Red Handkerchief, B6........................**65.00**
Beatrix Potter, Pigling Eats Porridge, B6..................................**195.00**
Beatrix Potter, Poorly Peter Rabbit, B6......................................**65.00**

Beatrix Potter, Ribby and the Patty Pan, BS 6a, 3¼", from $40.00 to $45.00.

Beatrix Potter, Samuel Whiskers, B3 ....**45.00**
Beatrix Potter, Tabitha Twitchit & Miss Moppet, B3 ....**150.00**
Beatrix Potter, Tom Kitten, B4 ....**75.00**
Beatrix Potter, Tom Thumb, B6...**85.00**
Bird, American Robin, #2187, 4⅜x5" **165.00**
Bird, Cedar Waxwing, #2184, 4½" **165.00**
Bird, Cuckoo, #2315, 5"...**150.00**
Bird, Gamecock, mc gloss, #2059, 9½"....................................**325.00**
Bird, Green Woodpecker, #1218B, 1967-89, 9"........................**220.00**
Bird, Green Woodpecker, #1344, 5"..**110.00**
Bird, Greenfinch, 1st version, #2105A, 3" **48.00**
Bird, Pochard Duck, #1520, 5½"..**125.00**
Bird, Ring-Neck Pheasant, no flowers on base, #1225B, 1967-77, NM.**185.00**
Bird, Sea Gull, wings side, #658, 14" L.......................................**95.00**
Bird, Swan, head down, #1685, 2"..**65.00**
Cat, Cheshire, tabby, #2480, 11½" **635.00**
Cat, Kitten, seated, gray matt, #1436, 3¼" **35.00**
Cat, Persian, seated, face up, ginger, #1867, 8½" **70.00**
Cat, Zodiac, seated, facing right, #1560, 11"............................**160.00**
Cow, Hereford Bull, wooden plinth, #A2542, 7½"....................**185.00**
Cow, Hereford Calf, roan, #854, 4½"..**135.00**
Cow, Red Friesian, #1362B, 4½"..**300.00**
Disney, Cheshire Cat, #3480, 1973-82, 1½" **300.00**
Disney, Eeyore, Owl or Piglet, ea...**100.00**
Disney, Fish Footman, Alice series **285.00**
Disney, Mock Turtle, #2478, 1973-83.......................................**175.00**

Dog, Basset Hound, #2045B, 1970-89, 6".............................130.00
Dog, Bull Terrier Romany Rhinestone, wht, #970, 6½" 70.00
Dog, Corgi, golden brn matt, #1736, 2¾" 20.00
Dog, Foxhound, 1st version (thick legs & tail), #941, 2¾" 45.00
Dog, Selyham plaque, bow at neck, #301, 7½" 135.00
Dog, Terrier, walking, #1062, 4" 135.00
Dog, Yorkshire Terrier, recumbent, #1944, 3½" 110.00
Farm animal, Ayrshire calf, brn & wht glossy, #1249, 2¾" 100.00
Farm animal, Friesian cow, brn & wht matt, #1362, 4½" L 285.00
Farm animal, Hereford cow, brn & wht, #948, 5x8½" 400.00
Fish, Perch, #1975, 1963-71, 6¼" 200.00
Fish, Trout, ash bowl, #1599, 5" 165.00
Horse, Exmoor Pony Heatherman, bay, #1645, 6½" 190.00
Horse, Foal (comical), gray, #728, 5" 90.00
Horse, Hackney, blk matt, #1361, 7¾" 165.00
Horse, Highland Pony, dun color, #1544, 1961-69 ....145.00
Horse, Huntsman, standing, gray gloss, 8¼" 285.00
Horse, Mare & Foal on Base, brn gloss, 2nd version, #953, 7¾".....135.00
Horse, Quarter Horse, wht matt, #2186, 8¼" 170.00
Horse, Shire mare, recumbent, brn, #2459, 5x8" 300.00
Horse, Stocky Jogging Mare, wht matt, 3rd version, #855, 6" 140.00
Huntsman Series, lady on standing gray horse, #1730 ....215.00
Huntsman Series, man on standing brn horse, #1501, 8¼".........175.00
Wild animal, Bear, standing, #1313, 2½" 110.00
Wild animal, Bush Baby, w/candlestick, #1380, 2" 95.00
Wild animal, Giraffe, #1597, 4¼"..................................110.00
Wild animal, Leopard, seated, #841, 6¼x9½" 300.00
Wild animal, Reindeer, #1688, 3¾"..................................80.00
Wild animal, Stag, #2629, 13½".....................................235.00
Wild animal, Zebra, tan & blk, #845A, 7¼".........................235.00

Bicycles

The time frame of collecting cycling items extends from the days of ancient manumotive transport to the present. The eras most interesting to collectors are (simplistically) the 1860s, with the Velocipede; 1875 – 89, famous for the high wheel; 1890 – 1900, when the safety bicycle was developed; 1920 – 1955, for the balloon tire. Virtually every aspect of collecting is encompassed — everything from late eighteenth century prints to jerseys worn in last year's Tour de France. The collector can break the field down to a particular category, medium, or history. One can make special collections of cycling photographs, the bikes themselves, porcelains, lithographs, related toys, etc. There are over fifteen different circa 1819 hobby horse plates which in themselves would make a most wonderful and challenging collection. Cycliana encompasses virtually every aspect of art, antiques, and collectibles. Any one of these fields could relate to social, sport, financial, or mechanical history. Below is a select group of items from a few of these categories.

Our advisor for this category is Lorne Shields; he is listed in the Directory under Canada. (Mr. Shields is interested in the acquisition of early cycliana and offers to help evaluate early bicycle-related items.) Unless noted otherwise, our values are for items in excellent condition.

Key:
A — as found   Ht — hard tires
Bt — balloon tires   Ld — lever driven
C — complete   Pt — pneumatic tires
Fw — front wheel   Rw — rear wheels

Adult's Vehicles

Bike, ladies', shaft-drive, distressed Pt/wheels, Spalding, 28", G .550.00
Bike, ladies', wht wall, w/light, 26", Roadmaster/AMF, 1950, orig/VG.75.00

Bike, men's, Black Phantom, Bt, 26", Schwinn, 1955, NM orig .750.00
Bike, men's, Pt, Indian/Hendee Mfrg, Chicopee Falls MA, 1915, C/A ..2,000.00
Hi-Wheeler/Penny Farthing, 50" Fw, C&J Chicago, 1887, brakes/saddle,EX .2,800.00
Hobby horse/draisienne, 31" Fw, ft-to-ground propelled, 1819, A/orig.12,500.00
Motorcycle bicycle, men's, Pt, Columbia, 1925, A 400.00
Safety bike, men's, Pt, Victor, 1896, C/orig/A............................700.00
Safety bike, narrow Ht 28" Fw/30" Rw, hammock saddle/bell, 1889, VG..1,500.00
Tricycle, Columbia 2-Track, 1885, unrstr/A 15,000.00
Tricycle, Sociable for 2, side-by-side, Ht, Starley, 1882, rstr/EX..25,000.00
Velocipede/boneshaker, 39" Fw/35" buggy-type Rw, 1869, maker ?, rstr/G..2,000.00

Children's Vehicles

Bike, scooter style, propels through up/down motion, Ingo, 1935, VG .350.00
Fairy-style trike, steel 12 Fw/20" Rw, Ld w/tiller, bkrest, 1900, EX .400.00
Tricycle, pedals, 14" Fw, wood fr/metal parts, 1885, VG orig pnt/G-.350.00
Youth bicycle, Ht, hammock saddle, orig parts, 1887, C/A.......2,000.00

Miscellaneous

Ad litho, hi-wheel bike race, Chicago, NH Van Siklen, 1891, fr, 40x26".2,500.00
Ad litho, White (Bicycle) Central Park NY, Thulstrup, 1895, fr, 30x17"..1,000.00
Bell, bronze cast w/claw clamp for narrow handlebars, 1885, 3½", VG .350.00
Bell, CI, dbl-clip clamp, rampant lion logo, 1900-20, EX..............30.00
Blotter, Monark of Chicago ad, EX graphics w/factory image, 1900, 8x3"..25.00
Book, Canterbury Pilgrimage, J Pennell, softbk, 1885, Am couple in England.100.00
Books, Wheelmen & Outing, Vol 1-5, Oct 1882-Mar 1885, bound, M, 5 for.500.00
Bottle, Electric Cycle Lamp Oil, dmn facets, paper label, Am, 1900, 5" .50.00
Brooch, sterling & gold w/hearts & 3-D bike, hallmk 1897 England..150.00
Button, clothing; metal w/Penny Farthing cycle, 1885, Am, ⅝", M .10.00
Calendar, Victor Bicycles/Overman, metal fr w/365 flip pgs, 6x3", VG .85.00
Camera, Cycle POCO Rochester #1-7, folding bed plate, bulb, 1900, $100 to.150.00
Catalog, Columbia Bicycle Co, Westfield MA, 1884, NM..........150.00
Catalog, Racycle, Miami Cycle & Mfrg of Middletown OH, 1902, VG.50.00
Cheroot cigar cutter, 3-D Penny Farthing, hand held, 1890, 2", NM.150.00
Chocolate mold, rabbit on bike, 2-pc, 11" 125.00
Clock, man on bike in Plus 4s, gilt bronze, British United, 1893, 7", VG .500.00

Clock, Victorian automata of a man holding his Penny Farthing; includes barometer and thermometer; wheels revolve on the hour; bronze, ca 1890; EX, all original and working; 16", $10,000.00. (Photo courtesy Lorne Shields)

Cup, collapsible, w/couple on tandem bike, dtd 1897, 19th C, common.15.00
Cyclometer, for hi-wheel bike, Lakins, 1886, Am, VG 1,500.00
Cyclometer, for safety bike, Seth Thomas, Am, 1896, MIB 150.00
Fairing, velocipede w/rider, English, 1869, 3¼" 75.00
Figurine, lady on bike, porc, Fr bsk, 1900, 7", NM 125.00
Figurines, man/lady on bike, bsk porc, Heubach, 1897, 15", pr..1,800.00
Game, Bicycle Race, brd type, McLoughlin Bros, 1895, C, in box, VG .350.00
Game, Cycling Tour, brd type, Spear Works Bavaria, 1896, in box, G..175.00
Hatpin holder, lady velocipedest, porc, Fr, 1869, 5" 350.00

Humidor, Penny Farthing/tricyclists, wood fr/bronze top, Holland, 1885.**1,500.00**
Ice cream mold, pewter, male or female, hinged, 1910, 4½" **100.00**
Lamp, carbide; P&H, 1930, cracked front lens, C **40.00**
Lamp, oil; Penny Farthing, hangs in bike's hub, Columbia ID, 1882, C.**1,500.00**
Lamp, oil; safety bike, front bracket mt, 20th C, Am, 1899........**450.00**
Medal, LAW Club Outing, bronze, Boston, 1896, VG **45.00**
Medal, 1st Place, hand-engr gold/enamel/garnet, Am, 1887, 5" L.**750.00**
Paperweight, Col AA Pope Columbia Bicycle Co, ca 1884-96, Am, NM, ea .**45.00**
Photograph, albumen, cabinet sz, lady cyclist on mid-1890s safety, M..**25.00**
Photograph, carte de visite, Penny Farthing cyclist, English, 1880, NM .**40.00**
Photograph, tintype, 8th plate, interior w/unusual Ht bike, 1888.**65.00**
Pin-bk, advertising many brands & images, Whitehead & Hoag, 1886, $5 to.**60.00**
Pipe, meerschaum, lady on hi-wheel bike, amber stem, EX patina, +case..**750.00**
Pitcher, glass, lady on safety bike, Am, 1900, 10", M **1,000.00**
Plate, boy w/cap, majolica, 1900, lt crazing, 7" **65.00**
Plate, velocipede lady, comic blk transfer, English/Fr issues, 1869 VG .**150.00**
Playing cards, bike design, Am Playing Card, 52+Joker, +box, $10 to.**35.00**
Pocketknife, aluminum sides ea w/bike scene, Germany, 1900, 5½", VG.**75.00**
Poster, Bearings Magazine, Chas A Fox, litho, Am/1896, 13x18", M.**150.00**
Poster, Crescent Cycles, Nouveau lady, Fr ed for USA, linen mt, 63x42".**4,500.00**
Poster, Harper's Magazine, male cyclist, Penfield, 1900, 17x12" .**750.00**
Print, Century Run, J Hambridge, cycle scene, fr, 1897, 14x18", M..**250.00**
Sheet music, United States Wheel March, Chicago printing, 1897, VG .**30.00**
Sheet music, Velocipede Gallop, Henry Atkins of Cincinnati, 1870 .**175.00**
Sign, Iver Johnson Cycles, litho tin, company fr, 1898, 22x14", VG..**350.00**
Statue, spelter, race winner/detailed 3-D cycle, Germany/1925, 18" .**750.00**
Stein, All Heil, w/cycles, pewter thumblift, Germany/1900, ½-L, NM.**125.00**
Stein, hi-wheel cycle scene, pewter thumblift, Mettlach, 1888, 1-L, M..**850.00**
Thermometer, 3-D Penny Farthing, celluloid, celsius, Fr, 2" W ..**125.00**
Trade card, men's/ladies' bike ad litho, 1890-1900, various, ea, $5 to.**25.00**
Trade card, W Duke-Sons, risque lady hi-wheeler does tricks, 1 of 25, M.**40.00**
Trade stimulator, 5¢, mechanical bike w/#d wheels, glass case, 1890s..**3,500.00**
Trophy, 3-D Penny Farthing cyclist at top, Meriden SP Co, 13", VG..**500.00**
Watch, hi-wheeler, silveroid open face, wear/non-working, 1885, VG..**350.00**
Watch, racing bikes 1 side, silver hunter case, stem wind, works, VG .**250.00**

Big Little Books

The first Big Little Book was published in 1933 and copyrighted in 1932 by the Whitman Publishing Company of Racine, Wisconsin. Its hero was Dick Tracy. The concept was so well accepted that others soon followed Whitman's example; and though the 'Big Little Book' phrase became a trademark of the Whitman Company, the formats of his competitors (Saalfield, Goldsmith, Van Wiseman, Lynn, and World Syndicate) were exact copies. Today's Big Little Book buffs collect them all.

These hand-sized sagas of adventure were illustrated with full-page cartoons on the right-hand page and the story narration on the left. Colorful cardboard covers contained hundreds of pages, usually totaling over an inch in thickness. Big Little Books originally sold for 10¢ at the dime store; as late as the mid-1950s when the popularity of comic books caused sales to decline, signaling an end to production, their price had risen to a mere 20¢. Their appeal was directed toward the pre-teens who bought, traded, and hoarded Big Little Books. Because so many were stored in attics and closets, many have survived. Among the super heroes are G-Men, Flash Gordon, Tarzan, the Lone Ranger, and Red Ryder; in a lighter vein, you'll find such lovable characters as Blondie and Dagwood, Mickey Mouse, Little Orphan Annie, and Felix the Cat.

In the early to mid-'30s, Whitman published several Big Little Books as advertising premiums for the Coco Malt Company, who packed them in boxes of their cereal. These are highly prized by today's collectors, as are Disney stories and super-hero adventures.

For more information we recommend *Collector's Guide to Children's Books, Volumes 1, 2,* and *3,* by Diane McClure Jones and Rosemary Jones (Collector Books). Our advisor for this category is Ron Donnelly; he is listed in the Directory under Alabama.

Note: At the present time, the market for these books is fairly stable — values for common examples are actually dropping. Only the rare, character-related titles are increasing somewhat.

Ace Drummond, Whitman #1177, 1935, EX **18.00**
Adventures of Huckleberry Finn, Whitman #1422, EX.................**25.00**
Andy Panda & the City of Ice, Whitman #1441, NM **40.00**
Arizona Kid, On the Bandit Trail, Whitman #1192, EX **15.00**
Bambi's Children, Whitman #1497, NM..**70.00**
Big Chief Wahoo & the Magic Lamp, Whitman #1483, NM **35.00**
Blondie & Bouncing Baby Dumpling, Whitman #1476, NM........**40.00**
Brenda Star & the Masked Imposter, Whitman #1427, NM.........**35.00**
Buck Jones in the Fighting Rangers, Whitman #1188, EX **35.00**
Buck Jones in the Roaring West, Whitman #1174, VG **25.00**
Bugs Bunny All Pictures Comic, Whitman #1435, 1944, EX........**35.00**
Bugs Bunny in Risky Business, Whitman #1440, VG **25.00**
Captain Midnight & Sheik Joman Khan, Whitman #1402, EX....**60.00**
Clyde Beatty Daredevil Lion & Tiger Tamer, Whitman #1410, 1939, NM.**45.00**
David Copperfield, Whitman #1148, VG **35.00**
Dick Tracy & the Mad Killer, Whitman #1436, 1947, NM...........**55.00**

Dick Tracy and the Spider Gang, Whitman #1446, VG, $60.00.

Dick Tracy in Chains of Crime, Whitman #1185, NM **75.00**
Don Winslow Navy Intelligence Ace, Whitman #1418, 1942, EX .**35.00**
Donald Duck Gets Fed Up, Whitman #1462, EX **40.00**
Ellery Queen, The Master Detective, Whitman #1472, 1942, NM.**45.00**
Fighting Hero's Battle of Freedom, Whitman #1401, 1943, NM...**30.00**
Flash Gordon & the Red Sword Invaders, Wnitman #1479, NM.**75.00**
Flash Gordon & the Witch Queen of Mongo, Whitman #1190, NM.**90.00**
G-Man & the Gun Runners, Whitman #1469, NM......................**40.00**
G-Man Breaking the Gambling Ring, Whitman #1493, 1938, NM.**45.00**
G-Man vs the Red X, Whitman #1147, VG **35.00**
Gene Autry & the Land Grab Mystery, Whitman #1430, 1948, NM.**40.00**
George O'Brien in Gun Law, Whitman #1418, EX **30.00**
Hairbreath Harry in Dept QT, Whitman #1101, EX **25.00**
Jack Armstrong & the Ivory Treasure, Whitman #1435, NM **35.00**
Jungle Jim & the Vampire Woman, Whitman #1139, NM **65.00**
Little Annie Roonie & the Orphan House, Whitman #1117, VG..**30.00**
Little Orphan Annie & the Mysterious Shoemaker, Whitman #1449, NM.**50.00**
Lone Ranger & the Red Renegades, Whitman #1489, EX **40.00**
Lone Ranger & the Vanishing Herd, Whitman #1196, NM **65.00**
Mickey Mouse & the Magic Lamp, Whitman #1429, NM...........**70.00**
Mutt & Jeff, Whitman #1113, NM..**75.00**
Peggy Brown & the Mystery Basket, Whitman #1411, NM.........**35.00**
Perry Winkle & the Rinkeydinks Get a Horse, Whitman #1487, NM.**45.00**
Popeye & Castor Oil the Detective, Whitman #1497, EX **40.00**
Porky Pig & His Gang, Whitman #1404, VG................................**45.00**

Roy Rogers & the Deadly Treasure, Whitman #1437, VG **40.00**
Shadow & the Living Death, Whitman #1430, 1940, NM **165.00**
Smilin' Jack & the Escape From Death Rock, Whitman #1445, NM .**45.00**
Tailspin Tommy in the Famous Payroll Mystery, Whitman #747, NM .**60.00**
Tarzan & the Golden Lion, Whitman #1448, NM **65.00**
Tarzan & the Land of the Giant Apes, Whitman #1467, 1949, EX ..**45.00**
Tom Mix & the Stranger From the South, Whitman #1183, EX ..**40.00**
Tom Mix & Tony Jr on Terror Trail, Whitman #762, 1934, NM ..**65.00**
Uncle Don's Strange Adventures, Whitman #1114, VG **20.00**
Zip Sauders King of the Speedway, Whitman #1465, EX **25.00**

Bing and Grondahl

In 1853 brothers M.H. and J.H. Bing formed a partnership with Frederick Vilhelm Grondahl in Copenhagen, Denmark. Their early wares were porcelain plaques and figurines designed by the noted sculptor Thorvaldsen of Denmark. Dinnerware production began in 1863, and by 1889 their underglaze color 'Copenhagen Blue' had earned them worldwide acclaim. They are perhaps most famous today for their Christmas plates, the first of which was made in 1895.

See also Limited Edition Plates.

Bonbon, Sea Gull, #222, 6" **50.00**
Bowl, center; sea horse hdl, wht octagon w/gold trim **36.00**
Bowl, coupe soup; NPM2 ....**30.00**
Bowl, fruit/dessert; Sea Gull **42.00**
Bowl, rim soup; Blue Traditional, 7½" **58.00**
Bowl, rim soup; Sea Gull, #23, 8½" **40.00**
Bowl, vegetable; Sea Gull, oval, 9½" **125.00**
Cake plate, Sea Gull, ftd **110.00**
Cake plate, Sea Gull, triangular, #40, 9" **90.00**
Candlestick, Sea Gull, #501 ....**50.00**
Coffeepot, NPM2 ....**95.00**
Coffeepot, Sea Gull, #91A **180.00**
Compote, Sea Gull, lg **100.00**
Creamer, Blue Traditional, #303 ....**78.00**
Creamer, Sea Gull **60.00**
Cup, farmer's; Sea Gull, #104 ....**70.00**
Cup & saucer, Blue Traditional, #102, 2½" **65.00**
Cup & saucer, coffee; Sea Gull, #103 ....**45.00**
Cup & saucer, NPM2 ....**30.00**
Cup & saucer, Sea Gull, flat **45.00**
Cup & saucer, tea; Sea Gull, #108 ....**45.00**
Egg cup, Blue Traditional, 2⅜" **22.00**
Figurine, angel, kneeling, arms extended, #BSB5, 1980 ....**145.00**
Figurine, angel boy, wht, #203-42, 1986-87 ....**85.00**
Figurine, angel boy praying on knees, #610, 1955 ....**140.00**
Figurine, Avocet, European; #100, 1979 ....**465.00**
Figurine, baby sparrow, #1852 ....**60.00**
Figurine, ballerina, #2325 ....**110.00**
Figurine, ballerina, Don Quixote, #SP9, 1980 ....**210.00**
Figurine, ballerina, Giselle, #SP28, 1980 ....**210.00**
Figurine, ballerina, Romeo, #807C, 1983 ....**195.00**
Figurine, bird on branch, #2311 ....**60.00**
Figurine, blackbird, #2405 ....**100.00**
Figurine, bobolink, #475, 1964-71 ....**795.00**
Figurine, boy w/cup, #1713 ....**175.00**
Figurine, boy w/earache, #2209 ....**65.00**
Figurine, boy w/pot, #2251 ....**150.00**
Figurine, calf, reclining, #2168, 2x3", from $80 to **100.00**
Figurine, cat, #2517, mini **30.00**
Figurine, centaur, bronze, #LB3, 1985, from $2,200 to **2,300.00**
Figurine, children playing, #1568 ....**170.00**

Figurine, children reading, #1567 ....**165.00**
Figurine, clown, #2353, 9½", from $100 to **130.00**
Figurine, cockatoo, #2178, 5½" **85.00**
Figurine, duck, #1537 ....**70.00**

Figurine, Fisherman's Wife, #1702, 11", $185.00.

Figurine, gazelle, #1693 ....**210.00**
Figurine, German shepherd, recumbent, #2197 ....**150.00**
Figurine, girl w/doll, #1526, 3½x4¼" **150.00**
Figurine, goat, #1700 ....**110.00**
Figurine, gull, laughing, #1727 ....**130.00**
Figurine, kingfisher, #1619, 4½" **90.00**
Figurine, kingfisher, #1885 ....**90.00**
Figurine, lady w/geese, #2254 ....**210.00**
Figurine, Little Hairdresser, #2367 ....**145.00**
Figurine, Love Refused, #1614, 7", from $175 to **200.00**
Figurine, man w/accordion, #1661 ....**175.00**
Figurine, man w/trident & nude lady, #30 ....**265.00**
Figurine, nude on steps, #2302 ....**175.00**
Figurine, perch, #1645 ....**145.00**
Figurine, Sandman, #2055 ....**150.00**
Figurine, seal pup, #2468 ....**70.00**
Figurine, Selyham terrier, #2071 ....**75.00**
Figurine, shepherdess w/sheep, #2010 ....**285.00**
Figurine, titmouse, tail down, #1635 ....**75.00**
Figurine, Youthful Boldness, #2162, kissing pr, 7½" **200.00**
Gravy boat, Sea Gull, attached underplate **145.00**
Nut dish, Sea Gull, star shape, #42A, 5" **35.00**
Pitcher, Sea Gull, #187, 16-oz **100.00**
Plate, bread & butter; Blue Traditional, #27, 6¼" **28.00**
Plate, bread & butter; Sea Gull **18.00**
Plate, dessert; Sea Gull, 6⅞" **22.00**
Plate, luncheon; Sea Gull, #4, 9½" **60.00**
Plate, luncheon; Sea Gull, 8¾" **35.00**
Plate, salad; Sea Gull, 7½" **32.00**
Platter, Blue Traditional, #16, 16" **245.00**
Platter, Sea Gull, #18, 10" **85.00**
Shakers, Blue Traditional, pr **65.00**
Shakers, Sea Gull, pr **58.00**
Shell dish, Sea Gull, 3⅜" **25.00**
Sugar bowl, Sea Gull, #185, 3¾" **85.00**
Sugar bowl, Sea Gull, #94, w/lid **85.00**
Teapot, NPM2 ....**95.00**
Teapot, Sea Gull, #654, 4-cup **185.00**
Vase, red/brn/gr matt (copper-look), bulbous body, 6¼" **300.00**

Binoculars

There are several types of binoculars, and the terminology used to refer to them is not consistent or precise. Generally, 'field glasses' refers to simple Galilean optics, where the lens next to the eye (the ocular) is concave and dished away from the eye. By looking through the large lens (the objective), it is easy to see that the light goes straight through the two lenses. These are lower power, have a very small field of view, and do not work nearly as well as prism binoculars. In a smaller size, they are opera glasses, and their price increases if they are covered with mother-of-pearl (fairly common but very attractive), abalone shell (more colorful), ivory (quite scarce), or other exotic materials. Field glasses are not valuable unless very unusual or by the best makers, such as Zeiss or Leitz. Prism binoculars have the objective lens offset from the eyepiece and give a much better view. This is the standard binocular form, called Porro prisms, and dates from around 1900. Another type of prism binocular is the roof prism, which at first resembles the straight-through field glasses, with two simple cylinders or cones, here containing very small prisms. These can be distinguished by the high quality views they give and by a thin diagonal line that can be seen when looking backwards through the objective. In general, German binoculars are the most desirable, followed by American, English, and finally French, which can be of good quality but are very common unless of unusual configuration. Japanese optics of WWII or before are often of very high quality. 'Made in Occupied Japan' binoculars are very common, but collectors prize those by Nippon Kogaku (Nikon). Some binoculars are center focus (CF), with one central wheel that focuses both sides at once. These are much easier to use but more difficult to seal against dirt and moisture. Individual focus (IF) binoculars are adjusted by rotating each eyepiece and tend to be cleaner inside in older optics. Each type is preferred by different collectors. Very large binoculars are always of great interest. All binoculars are numbered according to their magnifying power and the diameter of the objective in millimeters; 6 x 30 optics magnify six times and have 30 millimeter objectives.

Prisms are easily knocked out of alignment, requiring an expensive and difficult repair. If severe, this misalignment is immediately noticeable on use by the double-image scene. Minor damage can be seen by focusing on a small object and slowly moving the binoculars away from the eye, which will cause the images to appear to separate. Overall cleanliness should be checked by looking backwards (through the objective) at a light or the sky, when any film or dirt on the lenses or prisms can easily be seen. Pristine binoculars are worth far more than when dirty or misaligned, and broken or cracked optics lower the value far more. Cases help keep binoculars clean but do not add materially to the value.

As of 2003, any significant changes in value are due to Internet sales. Some of the prices listed here are lower than would be reached at an online auction. Revisions of these values would be inappropriate at this point for these reasons: First, values are fluctuating wildly on the Internet; 'auction fever' is extreme. Second, some common instruments can fetch a high price at an Internet sale, and it is clear that the price will not be supported as more of them are placed at auction. In fact, an overlooked collectible like the binocular will be subject to a great increase in supply as they are retrieved from closets in response to the values people see at an online auction. Third, sellers who have access to these Internet auctions can use them for price guides if they wish, but the values in this listing have to reflect what can be obtained at an average large antique show. The following listings assume a very good overall condition, with generally clean and aligned optics.

Our advisor for this category is Peter Abrahams, who studies and collects binoculars and other optics. Please contact, especially to exchange reference material (SASE required with written questions). Mr. Abrahams is listed in the Directory under Oregon.

Field Glasses

Fernglas 08, German WWI, 6x39, military gr, many makers	50.00
Folding, modern, hinged flat case, oculars outside	10.00
Folding or telescoping, no bbls, old	125.00
Ivory covered, various sm szs & makers	200.00
LeMaire, bl leather/brass, various szs, other Fr same	25.00
Metal, emb hunting scene, various sm szs & makers	45.00
Pearl covered, various sm szs & makers	90.00
Porc covered, delicate painting, various sm szs & makers	200.00
US Naval Gun Factory Optical Shop 6x30	75.00
Zeiss 'Galan' 2.5x34, modern design look, early 1920s	120.00

Prism Binoculars (Porro)

Barr & Stroud, 7x50, Porro II prisms, IF, WWII	120.00
Bausch & Lomb, 6x30, IF, WWI, Signal Corps	50.00
Bausch & Lomb, 7x50, IF, WWII, other makers same	90.00
Bausch & Lomb Zephyr, 7x35 & other, CF	140.00
Bausch & Lomb/Zeiss, 8x17, CF, Pat 1897	140.00
Crown Optical, 6x30, IF, WWI, filters	50.00
France, various makers & szs, if not unusual	30.00
German WWII 10x80, eyepcs at 45 degrees	500.00
German WWII 6x30, 3-letter code for various makers	60.00
Goertz Trieder Binocle, various szs, unusual adjustment	85.00
Huet, Paris 7x22, other sm szs, unusual shapes	80.00
Leitz 6x30 Dienstglas, IF, good optics	75.00
Leitz 8x30 Binuxit, CF, outstanding optics	150.00
M19, US military 7x50, ca 1980	150.00
Nikon 9x35, 7x35, CF, 1950s	100.00
Nippon Kogaku, 7x50, IF, Made in Occupied Japan	150.00
Ross Stepnada, 7x30, CF, wide angle, 1930s	250.00
Ross 6x30, standard British WWI issue	50.00
Sard, 6x42, IF, very wide angle, WWII	900.00
Toko (Tokyo Opt Co) 7x50, IF, Made in Occupied Japan	45.00
Universal Camera 6x30, IF, WWII, other makers same	50.00
US Naval Gun Factory Optical Shop 6x30, IF, filters, WWI	70.00
US Naval Gun Factory Optical 10x45, IF, WWI	200.00
US Navy, 20x120, various makers, WWII & later	2,200.00
Warner & Swasey (important maker) 8x20, CF, 1902	200.00
Wollensak 6x30, ca 1940	50.00
Zeiss Deltrintem 8x30, CF, 1930s	95.00
Zeiss DF 95, 6x18, sq shoulder, very early	160.00
Zeiss Starmorbi 12/24/42x60, turret eyepcs, 1920s	2,500.00
Zeiss Teleater 3x13, CF, bl leather	120.00
Zeiss 15x60, CF or IF, various models	700.00
Zeiss 8x40 Delactis, CF or IF, 1930s	230.00

Roof Prism Binoculars

Hensoldt Dialyt, various szs, 1930s-80s	140.00
Hensoldt Universal Dialyt, 6x26, 3.5x26, 1920s	120.00
Leitz Trinovid, 7x42 & other, CF, 1960s-80s, EX	500.00
Zeiss Dialyt, 8x30, CF, 1960s	400.00

Birdcages

Birdcages can be found in various architectural styles and in a range of materials such as wood, wicker, brass, and gilt metal with ormolu mounts. Those that once belonged to the wealthy are sometimes inlaid with silver or jewels. In the 1800s, it became fashionable to keep birds, and some of the most beautiful examples found today date back to that era. Musical cages that contained automated bird figures became popular; today these command prices of several thousand dollars. In the latter 1800s, wicker styles came into vogue. Collectors still appreciate their graceful lines and find they adapt easily to modern homes.

Oriental-cvd wood w/cranes, stepped ft, ivory spacers, cast hook, 25" .110.00
Wire, Victorian style w/cupola, scalloped wire trim, flags, 33x16".700.00
Wire octagon w/laced wicker at roof, pale gr pnt, 1900s, 29x18" .220.00
Wooden fr, mc pnt/wire screening, dbl arched doors, 20th C, 31x20x17" .200.00

Bisque

Bisque is a term referring to unglazed earthenware or porcelain that has been fired only once. During the Victorian era, bisque figurines became very popular. Most were highly decorated in pastels and gilt and demonstrated a fine degree of workmanship in the quality of their modeling. Few were marked. See also Heubach; Nodders; Dolls; Piano Babies.

Black man playing accordion, 4" 125.00
Candleabrum, 1 cup above & 1 to ea side of figural lady stem, 22" .320.00
Couple under umbrella, pastels, 6" 135.00
Gent (& lady), ea w/child on shoulder, standing by tree trunk, 23", pr.440.00
Lady skater fallen, legs in air & pantaloons showing, rpr, 4" 50.00
Man w/flower basket stands before 2 vases, pastels, Fr, 8x5" 135.00

Plaque, mother and child, pastel with lustre trim, French, 1880s, 10½x8½", in 21½x19½" glass-encased gold frame, $525.00.

Three Graces, Continental, 12½" 110.00
Two maids support shell, 9½" 135.00

Black Americana

Black memorabilia is without a doubt a field that encompasses the most widely exploited ethnic group in our history. But within this field there are many levels of interest: arts and achievements such as folk music and literature, caricatures in advertising, souvenirs, toys, fine art, and legitimate research into the days of their enslavement and enduring struggle for equality. The list is endless.

In the listings below are some with a derogatory connotation. Thankfully, these are from a bygone era and represent the mores of a culture that existed nearly a century ago. They are included only to convey the fact that they are a part of this growing area of collecting interest. Black Americana catalogs featuring a wide variety of items for sale are available; see the Directory under Clubs, Newsletters, and Catalogs for more information. We also recommend *Black Collectibles* by P.J. Gibbs (Collector Books).

See also Cookie Jars; Postcards; Posters; Sheet Music.

Ad page, Aunt Jemima Pancakes, McCall's March 1962, 13¼x9¾", EX..18.00
Ad page, Wonderful Wife...Got, Aunt Jemima...Pancakes, 1956, full pg..19.00
Ashtray, native lady's head beside, smoking mouth, ceramic, 5½" .65.00
Bank, boy beside orange, pnt ceramic, FL souvenir, 1940s, 5¼" ...75.00
Bank, boy on orange pig, pnt ceramic, FL souvenir, 1940s-50s, 6½".75.00
Bank, boy on pig, pnt plastic, 1940s, 6¾" 95.00
Bank, boy on watermelon slice, pnt ceramic, 1940s, rare, 6".........95.00
Bank, boy sitting by ball, pnt ceramic, 1940s, 4½" 175.00
Bank, Lucky Joe, clear glass w/tin lid, 1940s-50s, 4½" 55.00
Bank, Mammy, pnt pottery, brn skin, wht dress w/bl, 1940s, 6½" .105.00
Bank, man & woman heads, pnt compo, hanging, Mexico, 1940s, 6¼", pr..95.00
Bib, barbecue, chef grilling, printed silk, 1930s, 18x13" 65.00
Book, Little Alexander, Besse Schiff, hardbk, 1955, 8x10¾", EX .89.00
Book, Little Black Sambo, Kellogg's Story Book of Games, 1931, VG .60.00
Book, Little Black Sambo, Picture Parade, cb cover, 1942, 8x10", EX.125.00
Book, Little Black Sambo Storybook, paper cover, 1940s, 16-pg, EX.90.00
Book, Little Professor of Piney Woods, B Day, 1st ed, 1955, w/jacket..59.00
Book, Little Washington's Holidays, LE Roy, 1st ed, 1925, 144-pg, EX..49.00
Book, Presents Past & Present, golliwog, F Loeser Co Inc, 1920s, 12-pg.75.00
Book, Sambo's Restaurant Family Funbook, 1978, 11-pg...............32.00
Book, song; Count Basie's Piano Styles, 1940s, 32-pg, EX............39.00
Book, song; Duke Ellington's Streamlined Piano Solos, 1940s, 32-pg..38.00
Book, song; Hazel Scott Boogie-Woogie, 1943, 48-pg, EX 35.00
Book, Story of Little Black Sambo, 1963 (15th printing), 58-pg, EX.45.00
Book, Treasury of Steven Foster, hardbk, 1st ed, Random House, 1946.55.00
Book, Well Done Noddy (golliwogs), E Blyton, hardbk, 5½x7½", EX.29.00
Book, Your Funny Little Noddy (golliwog), Blyton, hardbound, 1950, EX..29.00
Book, 10 Little Niggers, Mother Goose Rhymes, Donohue, 1800s, 7x8¼".125.00
Book, 2 Blk Crows in the AEF, CE Mack, hardbk, 1st edition, 1928, EX.65.00
Bottle, scent; golliwog stopper, Made in France, 1930s, 2½" 125.00
Brush, Mammy figural, pnt wood w/bristle skirt, 1940s, 4½".........75.00
Cabinet card, sm girl sits on bucket w/shovel in hand, 5½x3½"...22.50
Christmas card, Wishing You..., caricature, Tuck, 1870s, 4¾" sq, EX.39.00
Cookbook, Cream of Wheat Diamond Cook Book, chef cover, early, VG..60.00
Cookbook, Pancakes Unlimited, Aunt Jemima cover, 1958, 31-pg, EX.49.00
Cookie jar, Aunt Jemima, plastic, F&F 650.00
Cookie jar, Chef, blk face, bl pants, Japan, 1930s, 10½", EX 495.00
Cookie jar, Mammy, blk face, decor apron, Japan, 1930s, 10", NM .795.00
Doll, cloth, embr face, orig clothes, 1940s-50s, 15", EX 135.00
Doll, compo, orig diaper, rpl dress, unmk, 1930s, 8½", EX..........110.00
Doll, compo baby, HP eyes & mouth, jtd shoulders & hips, 1930s, 8½".110.00
Figurine, boy at outhouse door, Next at base.................................45.00
Figurine, boy w/head at alligator's open mouth, Japan, 5" 125.00
Figurine, comic girl w/fan, boy behind, pnt bsk, 1980s, 8x 5¾x4" .45.00
Figurine, Jungle Imp, pnt ceramic, Irene Nye, 1930s, 4¾" 75.00
Figurine, minstrel w/cane, chenille, wood base, Japan, 1950s, 3¾"...........18.00
Figurine, native boy w/lg eyes sits w/watermelon, pnt chalk, 5" 95.00
Figurine, native standing, c Irene Nye #206, 4¾" 75.00
Figurine, native w/ear to ground, c Irene Nye #203, 4" L 75.00
Film, Our Gang in Mickey's Pals, Styme cover, 8mm, 1950s, EX..29.00
Game, Tops & Tails, 48 cards make 24 pictures, caricatures, EXIB....75.00
Greeting card, New Year angel, 1880s, 4¾x3⅜", EX.....................30.00
Grocery reminder, I Hasta Have, Mammy pnt on wood w/list, 12" 85.00
Match safe, Mammy figural, blk skin, lt clothes, Japan, 6"..........250.00
Measuring cup, Aunt Jemima Pancake Mix, plastic, 1980s, ¼-cup.......35.00
Memo pad, Mammy figural, apron is pad, 11", VG........................75.00
Muffler, Sambo's Restaurant, knit, 54"+fringe, EX.........................49.00
Mug, exaggerated features on brn ceramic, cold pnt, USA, 3½"..........39.00
Noisemaker, minstrel, tin litho, US Metal Toy Co, 5⅜x3" 35.00
Paper dolls, Oh Susanna, 5 caricatures, 1950, 12-pg book, NM....65.00
Paper plate, Aunt Jemima Days, 9¼", EX 30.00
Pitcher, syrup; Aunt Jemima, F&F, 5½" 70.00
Place mat, Story of Aunt Jemima, paper, 1950s, 14x9¾", EX 35.00
Plaque, boy & girl w/watermelon slice, pnt chalkware, 5", VG.....45.00

Plaque, boy eating watermelon, chalkware, mc, 5" **60.00**
Postcard, Darky's Prayer, Curt Teich & Co, ca 1951, 3½x5", EX..**16.00**
Postcard, Tea Cup's Fortune Telling, Mammy, Harry Roseland, EX.**30.00**
Print, Ef I Wuz a Millionaire, Mose, Outcault, 1901, 10½x14¾" .**75.00**
Print, Pore Lil Mose, Outcault, 1901, 10½x14¾" **75.00**
Program, Coretta Scott King Speaks in Detroit, 1965, 20-pg, VG..**135.00**
Program, souvenir; Louis Armstrong, 1960s, 22-pg, 12¼x9¼" **48.00**
Record, Blue Tail Fly, caricature picture sleeve, 78rpm, 1953, EX..**40.00**
Record, Brave Little Sambo, picture story sleeve, 78rpm, 1950s, EX.**95.00**
Record album, Uncle Remus Stories, 78rpm, 1940s, EX................**49.00**
Sack, Aunt Jemima Corn Meal, paper, mc graphics, 1960s-70s, 11½"..**22.00**
Shaker, nude lady sits w/watermelon slice, nodder, Japan, 2-pc, 3½"..**200.00**
Shakers, Aunt Jemima & Uncle Mose, plastic, F&F, 3½", pr, EX.**55.00**
Shakers, Aunt Jemima & Uncle Mose, plastic, F&F, 5", pr, EX **75.00**
Shakers, boy & girl w/watermelon, pnt chalkware, souvenir, pr, VG.**50.00**
Shakers, chef's head, blk skin, pnt ceramic, Japan, 3½", pr...........**75.00**
Shakers, comic graduates, HP ceramic, Japan, 1950s, 3½", pr **145.00**
Shakers, Mammy & Chef, lt brn faces, waving, Japan, 1940s, 2½", pr.**38.00**
Shakers, native busts, she w/bone in hair, ceramic, Japan, 2¾", pr.**45.00**
Sheet music, Bandana Land, lady's portrait, EX **30.00**
Sheet music, Gold Dust Twins Rag, 2 children at piano cover, EX .**60.00**
Sheet music, I'll Dance...Dixieland, marching band cover, 1909, EX.**29.00**
Sheet music, Rag-A-Tag Rag, minstrel face, 1910, 3-pg, 14x10¾", EX..**35.00**
Sheet music, When You Sang Hush-A-Bye Baby to Me, Mammy & child, EX.**25.00**
Table card, Aunt Jemima Restaurant, diecut, 1953, 3x4¾"...........**45.00**
Trade card, Operator in Wool, Atkinson House..., 1880s, 4½x2⅞"..**26.00**
Trade card, Revival, Ehrich Bros, 1882, 2¾x4½", EX **29.00**
Wall pocket, Mammy's face, Occupied Japan, 7" **150.00**

Black Cats

Made in Japan during the '50s, these novelty cats may be found bearing the labels of several different importers, all with their own particular characteristics. The best known and most collectible of these cats are from the Shafford line. Even when unmarked, they are easily identified by their red bows, green eyes, and white whiskers, eyeliners, and eyebrows. Relco/Royal Sealy cats are tall and slender, and their bow ties are gold with red dots. Wales is a wonderful line with yellow eyes and gold detailing; Enesco cats have blue eyes, and there are other lines as well. When evaluating your black cats, be sure to inspect their paint and judge them accordingly. Fifty percent paint should relate to 50% of our suggested values, which are given for cats in mint (or nearly mint) paint. Enthusiastic bidding on Internet auctions have resulted in much higher prices on the more hard-to-find items as reflected in our listings. For more information we recommend *Collectible Cats, Book II*, by Marbena "Jean" Fyke.

Our advisor for this category is Sammie Berry; she is listed in the Directory under Florida.

Ashtray, flat face, Shafford, hard-to-find sz, 3¾"...........................**50.00**
Ashtray, flat face, Shafford, 4¾", from $18 to **25.00**
Ashtray, head shape, not Shafford, several variants, ea, from $15 to..**25.00**
Ashtray, head shape, Shafford, 3", from $25 to **30.00**
Bank, seated, coin slot in top of head, Shafford, from $225 to....**275.00**
Bank, upright cat, Shafford features, mk Tommy, 2-part, minimum value.**175.00**
Cigarette lighter, Shafford, 5½", from $175 to.............................**190.00**
Cigarette lighter, sm cat stands on book by table lamp.................**45.00**
Condiment set, upright cats, yel eyes, 2 bottles/pr shakers in wire fr.**95.00**
Condiment set, 2 joined heads, J&M bows, spoons, Shafford, 4", $125 to.**135.00**
Cookie jar, cat's head, Shafford, from $80 to **100.00**
Creamer, Shafford, from $20 to..**30.00**
Creamer, yel eyes, gold trim, upraised left paw is spout, 6½x6"....**40.00**
Creamer & sugar bowl, head lids are shakers, yel eyes, 5⅜" **50.00**
Cruets, upright cats, she w/V eyes, he w/O eyes, Shafford, pr, $60 to.**75.00**

Decanter, long cat w/red fish in mouth as stopper..........................**75.00**
Decanter, upright cat holds bottle w/cork stopper, Shafford, $50 to..**65.00**
Demitasse pot, tail handle, bow finial, Shafford, 7½", from $175 to .**200.00**
Egg cup, cat face on bowl, ped ft, Shafford, from $50 to...............**75.00**
Grease jar, sm head, Shafford, from $150 to................................**175.00**
Ice bucket, cylindrical w/emb yel-eyed cat face, 2 szs, ea..............**75.00**
Measuring cups, 4 szs on wood wall rack w/pnt cat face, Shafford, rare.**450.00**
Mug, cat's head above rim, Shafford, 3½" **50.00**
Mug, cat's head below rim, Shafford, scarce, 3½" **225.00**
Mug, Shafford, hard to find, 4", from $65 to **75.00**
Pitcher, milk; upright cat, Shafford, 6" or 6½", ea, from $120 to .**140.00**
Pitcher, squatting cat, pour through mouth, Shafford, rare, 5" **90.00**
Pitcher, squatting cat, pour through mouth, Shafford, scarce, 4½".**75.00**
Pitcher, squatting cat, pour through mouth, Shafford, very rare, 5½".**250.00**
Planter, Shafford, from $35 to...**45.00**
Pot holder caddy, 'teapot' cat, 3 hooks, Shafford, minimum value..**200.00**

Shakers, range size, Shafford, 5", $35.00; Long and crouching, shaker each end, Shafford, 10", from $75.00 to $100.00.

Shakers, round-bodied 'teapot' cats, Shafford, pr **75.00**
Shakers, upright cats, Shafford, 3¾" (or slightly smaller), pr **22.00**
Spice set, triangle, 3 rnd tiers (8 in all), in wood wall mt, rare ...**750.00**
Spice set, 4 cat shakers hook onto wireware cat-face rack, Shafford..**600.00**
Spice set, 6 sq shakers in wood fr, Shafford, minimum value **175.00**
Spice set, 9 pcs in wood fr, yel eyes, Wales, from $85 to **110.00**
Sugar bowl, Shafford, from $20 to **30.00**
Teapot, ball-shaped body, head lid, Shafford, med szs, ea, from $30 to .**40.00**
Teapot, ball-shaped body, head lid, Shafford, sm, 4-4½", ea..........**25.00**
Teapot, ball-shaped body, head lid, Shafford, 7", from $50 to **60.00**
Teapot, cat face w/dbl spout, Shafford, scarce, 5", minimum value.**250.00**
Teapot, upright cat w/lift-off head, Shafford, rare, 8", minimum value.**350.00**
Tray, flat face, wicker hdl, Shafford, scarce, from $75 to **100.00**
Utensil rack, flat-bk cat w/3 slots for utensils, cat only, Shafford .**100.00**
Utensil: strainer, dipper or funnel, wood hdl, Shafford, ea **100.00**
Wall pocket, 'teapot' cat, Shafford, minimum value....................**185.00**
Wine, emb face, gr eyes, Shafford, sm...**50.00**

Black Glass

Black glass is a type of colored glass that when held to strong light usually appears deep purple, though since each glasshouse had its own formula, tones may vary. It was sometimes etched or given a satin finish; and occasionally it was decorated with silver, gold, enamel, coralene, or any of these in combination. The decoration was done either by the glasshouse or by firms that specialized in decorating glassware. Crystal, jade, colored glass, or milk glass was sometimes used with the black as an accent. Black glass has been made by many companies since the seventeenth century. Contemporary glasshouses produced black glass during the Depression, seldom signing their product. It is still being made today.

To learn more about the subject, we recommend *A Collector's Guide to Black Glass, Books I and II*, written by our advisor, Marlena Toohey; she is listed in the Directory under Colorado. Look for her newly updated value guide. See also Tiffin, L.E. Smith, and other specific manufacturers.

Ashtray, elephant in center, Greensburg, #2, ca 1930s-30s, 4"	**35.00**
Ashtray, hat shape w/Dobbs emb on rim, 1930-50, 2½" H	**30.00**
Bonbon, clear swan neck & head hdl, Viking, #974-1S, 5¼"	**35.00**
Bottle, shoe form, screw cap, unmk, 1880-1910, 3½x5¼"	**60.00**
Bowl, console; Autumn, McKee, 1934, 5½x12"	**60.00**
Bowl, console; Satin Ribbon etch, ftd, US Glass, #8098, 1930s	**80.00**
Bowl, console; wide flat rim, 1930s, 11"	**25.00**
Bowl, Doric, Westmoreland, 1980s, 12"	**68.00**
Bowl, emb flower, scalloped oval w/uptrn hdls, ca 1930s, 4¾x8"	**50.00**
Bowl, flared rim, ca 1920s, 10½"	**25.00**
Bowl, flowerlite; cupped, clear frog w/candle hole, Viking, 4½"	**50.00**
Bowl, rolled rim, ca 1920-30s, 11"	**50.00**
Box, stork wading among grasses in wht, brass ft, 6½" dia	**385.00**
Candlestick, overall molded 'crackle' design, ca 1930s, 7"	**15.00**
Candlestick, 2-light, spear-shape center section, 1930s, 6½"	**65.00**
Candy dish, 3-compartment, ornate metal fr, ca 1925-35	**40.00**
Celery vase, clear swan hdl, Viking, 1940-60s	**80.00**
Comport, scalloped edge, floral decor, McKee, #157	**40.00**
Drawer pull	**15.00**
Jug, emb tavern scene, European, ca 1900, 5"	**55.00**
Mayonnaise ladle, ca 1920s	**40.00**
Plate, grill; 3-compartment, 9"	**30.00**
Plate, plain, smooth rim, after 1923, 8"	**15.00**
Plate, 2 sides rolled up, hdls, 7"	**25.00**

Powder box with ornamental lid, Mary Gregory-style stork painting, 7¾", $30.00.

Salver, 3-ftd, US Glass, ca 1920s, 6½	**50.00**
Sugar bowl, 6 rings form body, angular hdls, ftd	**25.00**
Sugar bowl & creamer, Greensburg, #5029-2, ca 1925-30	**40.00**
Tray, center hdl, flat rim, LE Smith, 8½"	**52.50**
Tray, rectangular, hdls, ca 1925-40, 10½" L	**25.00**
Tray, scalloped, 3-ftd, Lancaster, #1831/7, 10"	**30.00**
Tumbler, clear bowl, blk ft, ca 1929-35, 12-oz	**15.00**
Tumbler, str sides, flat, 1930s or later, 16-oz	**23.00**
Vase, bud; gold decor, HC Fry, #804, ca 1929-33	**30.00**
Vase, waisted, scalloped top, Greensburg, #1018, ca 1925-35, 6"	**20.00**
Window box, Snake Dance, LE Smith, #404, ca 1930s	**30.00**

Blown Glass

Blown glass is rather difficult to date; eighteenth and nineteenth century examples vary little as to technique or style. It ranges from the primitive to the sophisticated, but the metallic content of very early glass caused tiny imperfections that are obvious upon examination, and these are often indicative of age.

In America, Stiegel introduced the English technique of using a patterned, part-size mold, a practice which was generally followed by many glasshouses after the Revolution. From 1820 to about 1850, glass was blown into full-size three-part molds. In the listings below, glass is assumed clear unless color is mentioned. Numbers refer to a standard reference book, *American Glass*, by Helen and George McKearin. See also Bottles and specific manufacturers. Our advisor for this category is Mark Vuono; he is listed in the Directory under Connecticut. See also Bottles.

Bowl, apple gr, rolled rim, pontil, sm chip, 5½x9¾"	**850.00**
Bowl, brilliant amethyst, 16-rib, flared rim, folded lip, ftd, 3x4"	**550.00**
Bowl, cobalt, flared rim, appl scroll hdls, rough pontil, 19th C, 6" H	**400.00**
Bowl, dk cobalt, rolled rim, pontil scar, 1850-80, 5¼" H	**170.00**
Bowl, dk olive gr, rolled lip, pontil, 4⅝x9½"	**750.00**
Bowl, dk violet, 16-rib, ground pontil, 3½x4¾"	**985.00**
Bowl, Pillar Mold, bright canary yel, sheared rim, att Pittsburgh, 7"	**700.00**
Canister, clear w/appl cobalt rings & finial wafer, 10x5" dia	**660.00**
Canister, clear w/2 dk sapphire rings, 1 on lid, wafer finial, 14x7"	**770.00**
Compote, ruby bowl, clear ft, 1870, 5¾x8"	**350.00**
Creamer, brilliant cobalt, 20-dmn, appl ft/hdl, 3⅞"	**550.00**
Creamer, brilliant cobalt, 21-slightly swirled ribs, ovoid, 4"	**440.00**
Creamer, brilliant peacock bl, hdl w/flourish at terminal, ftd, 4¾"	**440.00**
Creamer, cobalt, 10-Dmn Quilt, 4¾"	**245.00**
Creamer, cobalt, 24 right-swirled ribs, cobalt ball lid, 3"	**275.00**
Fishbowl, aquamarine, inward rolled rim, ped ft, 8x9"	**350.00**
Flask, chestnut; cobalt, 18 swirled ribs, sheared/polished lip, 3"	**400.00**
Flask, dk amber, 24 vertical ribs, wear/pot stones, 6¾"	**1,265.00**
Fly trap, dk cobalt, 3 appl ft, tooled open base, 1900s, 6"	**190.00**
Fly trap, med apple gr, 3 applied ft, ca 1900, 7½"	**90.00**
Goblet, presentation w/shield, cannon & anchor, monogram, 6⅜"	**235.00**
Hat whimsey, amber, some sickness, 4x6"	**110.00**
Jar, bl aqua, pontil scar, 3¾x3¼"	**170.00**
Jar, utility; bright yel amber, sheared mouth, pontil, 11"	**900.00**
Milk pan, lt gr, thick folded rim, open blister, 4x10½"	**965.00**
Mug, brilliant cobalt, appl hdl w/flourish at terminal, 4"	**1,155.00**
Pan, dk amber, folded rim w/tooled pour spout, pontil, 3⅜x9⅝"	**550.00**
Patty pan, folded rim, paneled base, 2x5½"	**175.00**
Pitcher, aquamarine, appl lily pad decor at base, pontil, 7½"	**6,000.00**
Pitcher, aquamarine, appl theading, bulbous, reeded hdl, 6¼"	**850.00**
Rolling pin, cobalt, tooled 1 end, open lip at other, 28"	**120.00**
Salt cellar, cobalt, 14-dmn pattern, appl ft, rough rim, 2⅝"	**190.00**
Salt cellar, dk cobalt, Dmn Quilt, 2½x3"	**245.00**
Smoke bell, bulb form w/appl ring & folded rim, lt scratches, 11½"	**175.00**
Smoke shade, appl ring, folded rim, 10½" dia	**30.00**
Sugar bowl, brilliant dk cobalt, Dmn Quilt, folded 14-rib ft, 6", EX	**825.00**
Sugar bowl, dk cobalt, Dmn Quilt, appl ft, cone-shape finial, 6½"	**1,925.00**
Vase, bright gr, elongated trumpet form, rnd base, 20"	**1,115.00**
Vase, hyacinth; med amethyst, tooled rim, pontil, 7⅝"	**300.00**
Vase, med forest gr, flared mouth, pontil scar, New England, 6⅛"	**1,200.00**
Vase, peacock bl, 12-flute, turn-over rim, 7½"	**9,400.00**
Vase, smoke bl, flared rim, knob stem, 7½x6¾", NM	**275.00**
Vase, trumpet form on rnd ft, ca 1950, 17"	**295.00**
Wine, amethystine, baluster stem, swag bowl w/flared rim, 5½"	**110.00**
Wine, dk purple amethyst, tooled rim, bubbles, pontiled ft, 3⅝"	**130.00**
Wine, eng bird & flowers, twist stem, flat ft, pontil, 6"	**210.00**

Blown Three-Mold Glass

A popular collectible in the 1920s, 1930s, and 1940s, blown three-mold glass has again gained the attention of many. Produced from approximately 1815 to 1840 in various New York, New England, and Midwestern glasshouses, it was a cheaper alternative to the expensive imported Irish cut glass.

Distinguishing features of blown three-mold glass are the three distinct mold marks and the concave-convex appearance of the glass. For every indentation on the inner surface of the ware, there will be a corresponding protuberance on the outside. Blown three-mold glass is most often clear with the exception of inkwells and a few known decanters. Any colored three-mold glass commands a premium price.

The numbers in the listings that follow refer to the book *American Glass* by George and Helen McKearin. Our advisor for this category is Mark Vuono; he is listed in the Directory under Connecticut.

Decanter, GII-16, yel olive, sheared mouth, pontil, Keene, pt....**700.00**
Decanter, GII-19, yel olive, pontil, Keene, qt, EX **600.00**
Dish, GIII-6, flared sides, folded rim, 1½x6" **220.00**
Flip, GI-6, etched flourishes at rim, 6⅛" **360.00**
Flip, GI-6, etched rim w/X-hatched ovals, 6⅛" **330.00**
Flip, GII-19, amethystine, pot stones, 5¾" **330.00**
Flip, GIII-22, 4¾x3¾" **300.00**
Inkwell, GIII-29, olive gr, 1½x2¼" **250.00**
Pitcher, GII-18, bulbous, reeded hdl, att Sandwich, 6½", NM ...**475.00**
Pitcher, GIV-7, tooled rim w/pour spout, Sandwich, 7¼" **600.00**
Sugar bowl, GII-18, bbl w/appl ft, domed lid, 1820-40, 5½x5¼"..**4,000.00**

Blue and White Stoneware

Salt glaze or molded stoneware was most commonly produced in a blue and white coloration, much of which was also decorated with numerous 'in-mold' designs (some 150 plus patterns). It was made by practically every American pottery from the turn of the century until the mid-1930s. Crocks, pitchers, wash sets, rolling pins, and other household wares are only a few of the items that may be found in this type of 'country' pottery, now one of today's popular collectibles.

Logan, Brush-McCoy, Uhl Co., and Burley Winter were among those who produced it; but very few pieces were ever signed. Naturally, condition must be a prime consideration, especially if one is buying for resale; pieces with good, strong color and fully molded patterns bring premium prices. Normal wear and signs of age are to be expected, since this was utility ware and received heavy use in busy households.

In the listings that follow, crocks, salts, and butter holders are assumed to be without lids unless noted otherwise. Items are in near-mint condition unless noted otherwise. Though common pieces seem to have softened to some degree, scarce items and those in outstanding mint condition are stronger than ever. For further information we recommend *Blue and White Stoneware* by Kathryn McNerny.

See also specific manufacturers.

Bank w/Money Bank stencil, coin slot, break to open, 4x3"....**1,200.00**
Bean pot, Boston Baked Beans, Swirl, heavy diffused pattern, w/lid..**425.00**
Bowl, Apricot, 9½" **125.00**
Bowl, Daisy on Lattice, 10¾" **140.00**
Bowl, milk; Flying Bird shoulder, 3¾x9½".............................**525.00**
Bowl, milk; Flying Bird shoulder, 3¾x9½", w/matching lid.....**1,200.00**
Bowl, mixing; Flying Bird, 4x7½".......................................**475.00**
Bowl, Reverse Pyramids w/Reverse Picket Fence, 2½x4½" **65.00**
Bowl, Wedding Ring, 6 szs, $150 ea, or set of 6 for **1,000.00**
Bowl, Wildflower (stenciled), 4½x7" **125.00**
Bowl (milk crock), Apricot, w/hdl..**225.00**
Box, powder; Wildflower & Fishscale, w/lid, rare **375.00**
Butter crock, Apricot, appl wood & wire hdl, w/lid, 4x7" **275.00**
Butter crock, Basketweave & Morning Glory, w/lid, 4x7½" **500.00**
Butter crock, Butterfly, orig lid & bail, 6½" **225.00**

Butter crock, Cows, appl wood & wire hdl, w/lid, 4½x7¼" **450.00**
Butter crock, Daisy & Trellis, orig lid & bail, 4½" **175.00**
Butter crock, Daisy & Waffle, 4x8", NM................................**175.00**
Butter crock, Dragon Fly & Flower, no lid, 4½x7" **125.00**
Butter crock, Draped Windows, 4½x8" **235.00**
Butter crock, Eagle, orig lid & bail, M **1,000.00**

Butter crock, Elk, 4¾x7¼", $475.00.

Butter crock, Grapes & Leaves, dbl ring around rim, 3x6½" **175.00**
Butter crock, Lovebirds, w/lid, 5½x6", M................................**500.00**
Butter crock, Peacock, w/lid, 6x6" **600.00**
Butter crock, Wild Flower (stenciled), w/lid, 6½x7¼" **175.00**
Butter jar, Wildflower, appl wood & wire hdl, 5x7" **275.00**
Canister, Basketweave, Cloves, orig lid, 4½" **200.00**
Canister, Basketweave, Coffee, orig lid, 7½" **350.00**
Canister, Basketweave, Pepper, orig lid, 4½" **200.00**
Canister, Basketweave, Put Your Fist In, orig lid, 7½" **750.00**
Canister, Basketweave, Salt, orig lid, 7½" **350.00**
Canister, Basketweave, Sugar, orig lid, 7½" **350.00**
Canister, Basketweave, Tobacco, orig lid, 7½" **750.00**
Canister, Snowflake (stenciled), rpl lid, 6½x5¾" **150.00**
Canister set, Basketweave, 9-pc...**5,000.00**
Chamberpot, Fishscale & Wild Rose, no lid, 5½x9¼" **250.00**
Chamberpot, Peacock, 9¾" **1,250.00**
Chamberpot, Wildflower, stenciled pattern, 6x11" **135.00**
Chamberpot, Wildflower & Fishscale, w/lid..............................**400.00**
Coffeepot, Bull's Eye, rim chips, 9¾x3¾" (base)....................**2,550.00**
Coffeepot, Oval, Diffused Blue, bl-tipped knob, str sides, 11x4"..**2,500.00**
Coffeepot, Peacock, patterned sloped sides, 7x10", M............**4,500.00**
Coffeepot, Swirl, w/lid and metal base plate **900.00**
Cookie jar, Brickers, flat button finial, 8x8"............................**725.00**
Cooler, iced tea;, Blue Band, flat lid, complete, 13x11" **295.00**
Cooler, water; Apple Blossom, brass spigot, 17x15" **2,500.00**
Cooler, water; Blue Band, orig lid..**250.00**
Cooler, water; Cupid, brass spigot, patterned lid, 15x12" **700.00**
Cooler, water; Polar Bear, brass spigot, rare, 1-gal, 17x15"..**3,100.00**
Cooler, water; Polar Bear, Ice Water, w/lid, hairlines, 6-gal, 15¼"..**900.00**
Cup, Wildflower w/emb Ribbon & Bow, 4½x2½" **85.00**
Cuspidor, Basketweave & Morning Glory, 5x7½" **150.00**
Cuspidor, Butterfly & Shield, 6x7½"......................................**150.00**
Cuspidor, Flower Panels & Arches, 7x7½" **225.00**
Custard cup, Fishscale, 5x2½" **135.00**
Egg storage crock, Barrel Staves, bail hdl, 5½x6" **200.00**
Grease jar, Flying Bird, orig lid, 4x4½" **1,100.00**
Ice crock, Barrel Staves, rope/tongs/ice block emb, 4½x6" **225.00**
Jardiniere, Flowers, hairline, 7x⅞" (complete w/stand & crock)..**800.00**
Meat tenderizer, Wildflower...**650.00**
Mug, Basketweave & Flower, 5x3" **150.00**
Mug, beer; advertising, Diffused Blue, sqd hdl **150.00**
Mug, Flying Bird, 5x3" **175.00**
Mug, plain..**65.00**
Mug, Windy City (Fannie Flagg), Robinson Clay Products **200.00**

Pie plate, Blue Walled Brick-Edge star emb base, 10½" 225.00
Pitcher, Acorns, stenciled, 8x6½" 175.00
Pitcher, American Beauty Rose, 10"..450.00
Pitcher, Apricot, 8" 250.00
Pitcher, Barrel, +6 mugs 395.00
Pitcher, Basketweave & Morning Glory, 9" 325.00
Pitcher, Blue Band, plain 200.00
Pitcher, Blue Band Scroll, emb design.......................................300.00
Pitcher, Bluebird, 9x7"...450.00
Pitcher, Butterfly, 9x7"...500.00
Pitcher, Castle & Fishscale, 8"..195.00
Pitcher, Cattails, stenciled design, bulbous, 7" 225.00
Pitcher, Cattails, w/advertising, 9½" 433.00
Pitcher, Cattails, 10"...300.00
Pitcher, Cherry Band, w/adv date 1914, 9½" 1,425.00
Pitcher, Cherry Cluster, 7½"..650.00
Pitcher, Cherry Cluster & Basketweave, 10"..............................375.00
Pitcher, Columns & Arches, 8¾x5"...425.00
Pitcher, Daisy Cluster, rare, 7x7" 800.00
Pitcher, Doe & Fawn, bl, 8½"...185.00
Pitcher, Dutch Boy & Girl by Windmill, 9"................................200.00
Pitcher, Dutch Landscape, stenciled, Diffused Blue, tall.............225.00
Pitcher, Eagle w/Shield & Arrows, rare, 8" 875.00
Pitcher, Fishscale & Wild Rose (part of wash set), 10"...............130.00
Pitcher, Flying Bird, 9"..625.00
Pitcher, Garden Rose, 9"..500.00
Pitcher, Garden Rose Sponge, 9"..800.00
Pitcher, Girl & Dog, regular bl, 9"...800.00
Pitcher, Girl & Dog, sponge, 7"...1,000.00
Pitcher, Grape & Shield, 8½x5"..150.00
Pitcher, Grape w/Rickrack, any sz...250.00
Pitcher, Grazing Cows, bl, 7½"...400.00
Pitcher, Grazing Cows, bl, 8"...250.00
Pitcher, Grazing Cows, 6½"...500.00
Pitcher, hot water; Wildflower & Fishscale, sm 150.00
Pitcher, Indian Boy & Girl (Capt John Smith & Pocahontas), 6".300.00
Pitcher, Indian Good Luck (Swastika), 8½"................................200.00
Pitcher, Iris, 9"..375.00
Pitcher, Leaping Deer, sponge, 8"...1,500.00
Pitcher, Leaping Deer, 8½"..375.00
Pitcher, Leaping Deer in 1 oval, Swan in other (mfg error), 8".1,500.00
Pitcher, Lincoln, allover deep bl, 4¾x4¾"..................................250.00
Pitcher, Lincoln, allover deep bl, 6x4".......................................300.00
Pitcher, Lincoln, allover deep bl, 7x5".......................................500.00
Pitcher, Lincoln, allover deep bl, 8x6"....................................1,000.00
Pitcher, Lovebird, arc bands, deep color, 8½", EX 500.00
Pitcher, Lovebird, pale color, 8½" 300.00
Pitcher, Monk, dk cobalt..350.00
Pitcher, Peacock..1,700.00
Pitcher, Pine Cone, sponge, rare, 9½".....................................2,000.00
Pitcher, Pine Cone, 9½"..1,500.00
Pitcher, Poinsettia, 6½"...275.00
Pitcher, Rose on Trellis, 8x5½"..225.00
Pitcher, Scroll & Leaf, advertising, 8".......................................450.00
Pitcher, Shield, prof rpr, 8"...200.00
Pitcher, Stag & Pine Trees, 9"...425.00
Pitcher, Swan, in oval, deep color, 8½", EX...............................400.00
Pitcher, Tulip, 8x4"...325.00
Pitcher, Wild Rose, solid bl, 9x6"..450.00
Pitcher, Wild Rose, sponged bands, 9" 500.00
Pitcher, Wildflower/Cosmos, w/advertising.............................2,100.00
Pitcher, Windmill & Bush, 9"...175.00
Pitcher, Windmills, 7¼", EX..195.00
Pitcher, Windy City (Fannie Flagg), Robinson Clay, 8½"...........450.00

Roaster, Diffused Blue, appl hdls, flat finial, 9x19" 225.00
Roaster, Wildflower, domed lid, 8½x12" 225.00
Rolling pin, Blue Band, advertising, Andka, Nebr, 14x4" 900.00
Rolling pin, Blue Band, no advertising, 14x4".............................375.00
Rolling pin, Swirl, baker's sz, 16"..1,500.00
Rolling pin, Swirl, orig wooden hdls, 13" 1,500.00
Rolling pin, Wildflower, advertising, Analomink PA, dtd 1905.1,100.00
Rolling pin, Wildflower, plain..375.00
Rolling pin, Wildflower, w/center decor, 15x4½" 650.00
Salt crock, Apricot, no lid...130.00
Salt crock, Butterfly, orig lid 350.00
Salt crock, Eagle, w/lid...800.00
Salt crock, Grapevine on Fence, pale bl, orig lid, 6½x6¾".........300.00
Salt crock, Peacock, w/lid...1,000.00
Scuttle mug (shaving), rare 1,025.00
Soap dish, Beaded Rose..135.00
Soap dish, cat's head (heavily reproduced, be careful)................175.00
Soap dish, Indian in War Bonnet 250.00
Soap dish, Wildflower & Fishscale 150.00
Spice set, Basketweave, 6-pc, w/lids, all M 2,000.00
Teapot, Swirl, dbl wire bail hdl, ball shape, 9x6½" 1,200.00
Toothbrush holder, Bow Tie, stenciled flower 50.00
Toothbrush holder, Wildflower & Fishscale 325.00
Vinegar cruet, rare, 4½x3" 375.00
Wash bowl & pitcher, Rose on Trellis..300.00
Wash bowl & pitcher, Wildflower & Fishscale 500.00
Wash set, Wildflower & Fishscale, complete, 7-pc 2,500.00
Washboard, sponge..400.00
Water bottle, Diffused Blue Swirl, stopper w/cork, 10x5½" 800.00
Whipped cream jar, 4¾x6¾"...550.00

Blue Ridge

Blue Ridge dinnerware was produced by Southern Potteries of Erwin, Tennessee, from the late 1930s until 1956 in twelve basic styles and two thousand different patterns, all of which were hand decorated under the glaze. Vivid colors lit up floral arrangements of seemingly endless variation, fruit of every sort from simple clusters to lush assortments, barnyard fowl, peasant figures, and unpretentious textured patterns. Although it is these dinnerware lines for which they are best known, collectors prize the artist-signed plates from the '40s and the limited line of character jugs made during the '50s most highly. Examples of the French Peasant pattern are valued at double the prices listed below; very simple patterns will bring 25% to 50% less.

Our advisors, Betty and Bill Newbound, have compiled four lovely books, *Blue Ridge Dinnerware, Revised Third Edition; The Collector's Encyclopedia of Blue Ridge, Volumes I* and *II;* and *Best of Blue Ridge,* all with beautiful color illustrations and current market values. They are listed in the Directory under North Carolina. For information concerning the National Blue Ridge Newsletter, see the Clubs, Newsletters, and Catalogs section of the Directory.

Ashtray, rnd, advertising, from $60 to 70.00
Basket, aluminum edge, 7", from $25 to 30.00
Bonbon, Charm House, china, from $175 to 225.00
Bonbon, divided, center hdl, china, from $95 to 125.00
Bowl, Square Dancers, 11½", from $175 to.................................200.00
Bowl, vegetable; rnd, 8", from $20 to 30.00
Box, Dancing Nudes, china, from $600 to 750.00
Box, powder; rnd, from $100 to 150.00
Box, Sherman Lily, from $700 to...900.00
Butter pat/coaster, from $30 to 35.00
Carafe, w/lid, from $100 to 150.00

Character jug, Paul Revere, from $600 to 700.00
Child's feeding dish, divided, from $175 to 200.00
Child's plate, from $125 to 175.00
Chocolate pot, from $200 to 225.00
Counter sign, from $500 to 575.00
Creamer, demi; earthenware, from $45 to 50.00
Creamer, ped ft, china, from $50 to 65.00
Creamer, Waffle shape, from $15 to 20.00
Cup & saucer, Jumbo, from $75 to 100.00
Demitasse pot, china, from $250 to 300.00
Demitasse pot, earthenware, from $125 to 175.00
Deviled egg dish, from $60 to 75.00
Gravy tray, from $60 to 70.00
Lazy Susan, complete, from $550 to 650.00
Leftover, w/lid, sm, from $50 to 65.00
Pie baker, from $35 to 45.00
Pitcher, Alice, china, 6", from $175 to................225.00
Pitcher, Betsy, china, from $200 to 250.00
Pitcher, Martha, earthenware, from $70 to 75.00
Pitcher, Spiral, Premium, 7", from $150 to.............175.00
Plate, advertising, lg, from $300 to..................325.00
Plate, Christmas Doorway, from $85 to 95.00
Plate, dinner; 9¼", from $20 to 24.00
Plate, dinner; 10½", from $20 to 25.00
Plate, Quail, artist sgn, from $400 to................425.00
Plate, sq, 7", from $12 to 15.00
Plate, Square Dance, 14", from $350 to................400.00
Plate, Still Life, 8½", from $25 to....................30.00
Platter, 12½-13", from $25 to 30.00

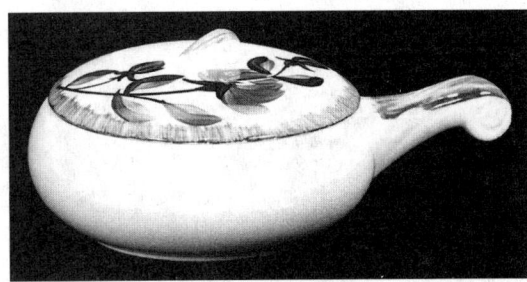

Ramekin, stick handle, small, $30.00.

Relish, loop hdl, china, from $70 to 75.00
Relish, T-hdl, from $65 to 70.00
Shakers, Apple, 2¼", pr, from $55 to 60.00
Shakers, Blossom Top, pr, from $75 to 85.00
Shakers, Chickens, pr, from $150 to 175.00
Shakers, Skyline, pr, from $35 to 40.00
Shakers, tall ft, china, pr, from $75 to..............100.00
Sugar bowl, regular shape, w/lid, from $18 to..........25.00
Sugar bowl, Waffle, w/lid, from $15 to 20.00
Tea tile, rnd or sq, 3", from $85 to..................100.00
Teapot, Fine Panel, china, from $175 to 225.00
Teapot, Mini Ball, china, from $200 to 250.00
Teapot, Palisades, from $125 to 150.00
Teapot, Piecrust, from $175 to 200.00
Teapot, Snub Nose, china, from $200 to 250.00
Teapot, sq rnd, 6", from $90 to 100.00
Teapot, Woodcrest, from $175 to.......................200.00
Tidbit, 2-tier, from $30 to...........................40.00
Toast, French Peasant, w/lid, from $275 to 300.00
Tray, demi; Colonial, French Peasant, from $210 to....225.00

Tray, demi; Colonial, 5½x7", from $150 to..............175.00
Tray, for waffle set, 9½x13½", from $100 to............125.00
Tray, snack; Martha, from $150 to.....................175.00
Vase, boot form, 8", from $85 to......................95.00
Vase, bud; from $225 to...............................250.00
Vase, hdls, china, from $95 to........................100.00

Blue Willow

Blue Willow, inspired no doubt by the numerous patterns of the blue and white Nanking imports, has been popular since the late eighteenth century and has been made in as many variations as there were manufacturers. English transfer wares by such notable firms as Allerton and Ridgway are the most sought after and the most expensive. Japanese potters have been producing Willow-patterned dinnerware since the late 1800s, and American manufacturers have followed suit. Although blue is the color most commonly used, mauve and black lines have also been made. For further study we recommend the book *Blue Willow*, with full-color photos and current prices, by Mary Frank Gaston, our advisor for this category. In the following listings, if no manufacturer is noted, the ware is unmarked. See also Buffalo.

Baking dish, oven proof, mk Japan, 2½x5" 40.00
Biscuit jar, metal hdl, unmk Japan, 6", from $150 to 175.00
Bone dish, kidney shape, Bourne & Leigh, 6¼", from $45 to 55.00
Bowl, chestnut; rtcl lattice sides, hdls, English, no mk, 10" 1,000.00
Bowl, cream soup; Homer Laughlin, from $25 to...............30.00
Bowl, flat soup; Eagle, 8" 12.50
Bowl, Maestricht, 2¾x9⅞" 120.00
Bowl, ped ft, John Tams Ltd, 5x9¼", from $150 to 175.00
Bowl, soup/cereal; scalloped, flow bl, Doulton, 7½", from $100 to .120.00
Bowl, vegetable; hdls, w/lid, Japan, 9", from $75 to.........100.00
Bowl, vegetable; oval, Japan................................35.00
Bowl, vegetable; variant center pattern, pictorial border, 10" 25.00
Bowl, vegetable; woods Ware, 10" 40.00
Breakfast set, ind; Spode/Copeland, toast rack+c/s+cr/sug, 5-pc .225.00
Butter dish, Royal China, ¼-lb, from $150 to................35.00
Candle holders, sq, Doulton, 7½", pr, from $400 to 500.00
Casserole, Empress, w/lid, Homer Laughlin, from $70 to...........75.00
Cheese dish, sq plate w/canted corners, sq lid, Biltshaw & Robinson.250.00
Clock, Traditional pattern/pictorial border, 8-day, German works, tin.165.00
Coffeepot, Booths, gold trim, mk Real Old Willos, 8½" 210.00
Condiment shaker, pierced silver lid, Taylor Tunnicliffe & Co, 2".55.00
Creamer, Japan...10.00
Creamer, red, Royal China..................................15.00
Creamer & sugar bowl, w/lid, Steventon & Sons, 3", 4", from $70 to.80.00
Cup, chili; Japan, 3½x4" 50.00
Cup, demitasse; red, restaurant ware.......................10.00
Cup & saucer, Meakin for Nieman-Marcus, 1970s 30.00
Cup & saucer, Royal China..................................6.00
Egg cup, dbl, 3½" or 4¼", ea...............................30.00
Gravy boat, Ridgway's, 8" L, from $70 to 80.00
Gravy boat, Wood & Sons, 7" L..............................65.00
Jug, batter; frosted glass, Hazel Atlas, 10"...............100.00
Ladle, unmk, 7" L, from $140 to 160.00
Measuring cups, Japan (label), 4 on wall-mt 'dipper' rack, 8" L..165.00
Mustard pot, bbl shape, unmk, 2½", from $65 to..............75.00
Pitcher, Burleigh pattern, cylindrical, Burgess & Leigh, 7" 350.00
Pitcher, Chicago Jug, Doulton, 1907, 3-pt 500.00
Pitcher, milk; Homer Laughlin, 5".........................45.00
Pitcher, Traditional center, Wedgwood, 1929+ mk, 11¼"...........150.00
Pitcher, w/lid, Japan, 11"................................125.00
Plate, Booth's Variant center, gold trim, 8-sided, Booth's, 8¾" 60.00

Plate, bread & butter; Royal China 3.00
Plate, chop; unmk Royal China, 12" 35.00
Plate, dinner; Imperial, 9¾" 27.00
Plate, dinner; Linder & Carter, 9½" 24.00
Plate, dinner; Moriyama, 9¼" 12.00
Plate, grill; heavy, Japan 18.00
Plate, Royal China, 9¾", from $12 to 15.00
Plate, salad; red, Wallace China....................................8.00
Plate, soup; Royal China, 8¼", from $12 to....................15.00
Plate, Traditional center, rtcl rim, unmk English, 7¼" 165.00
Platter, Homer Laughlin, 13" 25.00
Platter, Two Temples II (simplified), floral border, unmk Am, 12x9".45.00
Relish, Booth's center pattern, Bow-Knot border, Wood & Sons, 9" .30.00
Relish tray, Booths center pattern, Bow-Knot border, Wood & Sons, 9" ..30.00
Salt box, wall mt, wood lid, unmk Japan, 5" 110.00
Shakers, Royal China, pr..25.00
Shakers, wood bottoms, Japan, 3¾", pr.........................12.00
Spoon rest, dbl (2 rests), Japan, 9", from $40 to..............50.00
Sugar bowl, rope & anchor finial, unmk, 6", from $45 to............55.00
Sugar bowl, w/lid, Japan 15.00
Tea bowl, Pountney & Co, 3½" dia.................................85.00
Tea set, child's; Occupied Japan, 6¾" plates/c&s, 22-pc.............200.00
Teapot, Allerton's, 6", NM..225.00
Toast rack, Grimwades, 6", from $80 to........................100.00
Tumbler, glass, Hazel Atlas, 5" 20.00
Tumbler, water; glass, Jeannette, 5½" 12.00
Tureen, w/lid & ladle, unidentified English mk, 15x11", from $800 to.1,000.00
Waste bowl, Doulton mk, 3½x6½", from $125 to 150.00

Bluebird China

The earliest examples of the pudgy little bluebird in the apple blossoms decal appear in the late 1890s. The craze apparently peaked during the early to mid-1920s and had all but died out by 1930. More than fifty manufacturers, most of whom were located in East Liverpool, Ohio, produced bluebird dinnerware. There are variations on the decal, and several are now accepted as 'bluebird china.' The larger china companies like Homer Laughlin and KT&K experimented with them all. One of the variations depicts larger, more slender bluebirds in flight. The latter variety was made by Knowles, Taylor, and Knowles, W.S. George (Derwood), French Co., Sterling Colonial, and Pope Gosser. The dinnerware was never expensive, and shapes varied from one manufacturer to another. Today, the line produced by Homer Laughlin is valued most highly; it is also the most available. Besides the companies we've already mentioned, you'll find the trademarks of Cleveland; Carrolton; Limoges China of Sebring, Ohio; Salem; Taylor Smith Taylor; and there are others.

Our advisor for this category is Kenna Rosen; she is listed in the Directory under Texas. Watch for her new book on this subject.

Bone dish, Empress, Homer Laughlin 100.00
Bowl, berry; Cleveland, ind...12.50
Bowl, deep, Derwood, WS George, 4¾", from $50 to............75.00
Bowl, deep, Homer Laughlin, 5½"................................50.00
Bowl, gravy; Hopewell China, w/saucer 100.00
Bowl, sauce; SP Co, 4½" 12.50
Bowl, soup; PMC Co, 8" 30.00
Bowl, vegetable; Cleveland, 9¾" 65.00
Butter dish, Buffalo Mfg, 5" dia....................................150.00
Butter dish, Carrollton, 6¼" sq.....................................150.00
Butter dish, Empress, Homer Laughlin 250.00
Butter dish, Salem China...250.00
Butter dish, Steubenville, 4½" holder w/in 7" dish................175.00
Butter dish, Victory, Knowles Taylor Knowles 200.00

Butter pat (all unmk) 25.00
Calendar plate, 1921 advertising pc, DE McNicol.............95.00
Canister set, rnd, unmk, 6½x5", 6 for 300.00
Casserole, Buffalo Mfg, w/lid.......................................175.00
Casserole, CP Co, child's, 8x3" 75.00
Casserole, Homer Laughlin Empress, rnd, w/lid, 8½"..............150.00
Casserole, Ostro China, mk Princess Anne, 10½" dia..............95.00
Casserole, Pope Gosser, w/lid, 10½x10½"....................100.00
Casserole, Royal China International, 7x11½".................125.00
Casserole, SPI Clinchfield China, w/lid 150.00
Casserole, Taylor Smith & Taylor, w/lid, 11x7½".............150.00
Casserole, The Potters Cooperative, E Liverpool, rnd, 8½" 125.00
Chamber pot, w/lid, unmk, late 1890s...........................250.00
Chocolate cup, ftd, no mk, 3½"....................................85.00
Coffeepot, Sterling Colonial 150.00
Covered platter/food warmer, Buffalo Mfg, 19x13".............125.00
Cream & sugar bowl, SP Co, w/lid 85.00
Creameer & sugar bowl, HR Wyllie, w/lid......................150.00
Creamer, Derwood, WS George....................................30.00
Creamer, no mk, 4¼" 25.00
Creamer & sugar bowl, Homer Laughlin, w/lid.................180.00
Creamer & sugar bowl, Knowles Taylor Knowles...............75.00
Creamer & sugar bowl, TA McNichol, w/lid......................75.00
Creamer & sugar bowl, w/lid, HR Wyllie 150.00
Cup, tea; unmk 15.00
Cup & saucer, Buffalo Mfg 50.00
Cup & saucer, from $40 to 80.00
Cup & saucer, Owen China, St Louis..............................25.00
Custard cup, Knowles Taylor Knowles, 3½" 35.00
Dish, oval, Hudson, Homer Laughlin, 1x5¼x4" 45.00
Egg cup, Buffalo Mfg, very rare, 2½" 75.00

Egg cup, 3½", $85.00; Creamer, unmarked, 4", $75.00.

Gravy w/attached underplate, Homer Laughlin, 4x9¾" 200.00
Ladle, sauce; gold scrolling...40.00
Mug, baby's; Cleveland China 100.00
Mug, coffee; Homer Laughlin.......................................80.00
Mug, coffee; unmk, 3½"..80.00
Pitcher, wash; Bennett China 500.00
Pitcher, water; Buffalo Mfg, 7" 175.00
Pitcher, water; Cable, Homer Laughlin 280.00
Pitcher, water; Carrollton Pottery..................................180.00
Pitcher, water; Crown Pottery Co..................................390.00
Pitcher, water; DE McNicol..150.00
Pitcher, water; Empress, Homer Laughlin.......................250.00
Pitcher, water; Harker Pottery Co, ca 1890, 8x9" 200.00
Pitcher, water; Knowles Taylor Knowles, w/lid.................275.00
Pitcher, water; National China 250.00
Plate, baby; ELP Co China, 7½x7½" 150.00
Plate, bread; hdls, gold trim, unmk, 10" 150.00

Plate, dessert; Limoges, 6" 8.00
Plate, dinner; Cleveland, 9" 25.00
Plate, dinner; Knowles Taylor Knowles, 9¾" 40.00
Plate, dinner; Wilmer Ware, 20" 20.00
Plate, Homer Laughlin, 8½" 40.00
Plate, National China, 8" 40.00
Plate, rtcl, sq, unmk, 9" 40.00
Plate, scalloped, Homer Laughlin, 7¼" 50.00
Plate, Steubenville, 9" 40.00
Platter, Carollton, sqd oval, 17¾x12¾" 95.00
Platter, Edwin M Knowles, 14½x11" 75.00
Platter, Hopewell China, 13x10" 75.00
Platter, Hopewell China, 17½x13" 100.00
Platter, Pope Gosser, 17x13" 125.00
Platter, Thompson Glenwood, 13x10" 75.00
Platter, unmk, 9x7" 45.00
Platter, West End Pottery Co, 15½x11" 100.00
Platter, 10 bluebirds, gold trim at rim, DE McNichol, 15¼x11¼" .75.00
Saucer, Homer Laughlin 15.00
Soap dish, WS George 130.00
Sugar bowl, Illinois China Co, w/lid, 7x6" 50.00
Syrup, Homer Laughlin, 6½" 175.00
Syrup, unmk, 4" 35.00
Tea set, child's, Summit China Co 1,025.00
Tea set, CPCo, child sz, 21-pc 400.00
Teapot, Carollton 250.00
Teapot, ELP Co, 8½x8½" 250.00
Teapot, Homer Laughlin, from $750 to 1,200.00
Teapot, KT&K mk, 3½x7¼" 250.00

Boch Freres

Founded in the early 1840s in La Louviere, Boch Freres Keramis became the foremost producer of art pottery in Belgium. Though primarily they served a localized market, in 1844 they earned worldwide recognition for some of their sculptural works on display at the International Exposition in Paris.

In 1907 Charles Catteau of France was appointed head of the art department. Before that time, the firm had concentrated on developing glazes and perfecting elegant forms. The style they pursued was traditional, favoring the re-creation of established eighteenth century ceramics. Catteau brought with him to Boch Freres the New Wave (or Art Nouveau) influence in form and decoration. His designs won him international acclaim at the Exhibition d'Art Decoratif in Paris in 1925, and it is for his work that Boch Freres is so highly regarded today. He occasionally signed his work as well as that of others who under his direct supervision carried out his preconceived designs. He was associated with the company until 1950 and lived the remainder of his life in Nice, France, where he died in 1966. The Boch Freres Keramis factory continues to operate today, producing bathroom fixtures and other utilitarian wares. A variety of marks have been used, most incorporating some combination of 'Boch Freres,' 'Keramis,' 'BFK,' or 'Ch Catteau.' A shield topped by a crown and flanked by a 'B' and an 'F' was used as well.

Bowl, geometrics, bl/cobalt on wht crackle, #10L9/#1187, 10" ...435.00
Box, floral/berries, sq w/indented corners, #14/58, 3x5" 200.00
Box, solid/floral rays, blk/gr/mc, 3x5" dia 300.00
Ginger jar, allover chintz floral, red/wht, gilt finial, 15" 325.00
Lamp base, geometrics, 6-sided, mk, 12½" 200.00
Vase, birds, 3-color on wht crackle, Keramis, 2x6" 900.00
Vase, bright bl crackle, mk, 9½x6" 65.00
Vase, bundled stems w/3 flowers, gr/gold on turq gloss, #708, 11", pr .920.00
Vase, concentric circles, yel/brn/brn, bulbous, rpr, 9" 80.00

Vase, Art Deco floral on pillow form, #1291/#2333, ink stamp, 9", $375.00.

Vase, floral, cream & brn on blk band on brn mottle, 10½" 490.00
Vase, floral, mc on gray crackle, #d, 7" 300.00
Vase, flower clusters, mc on crackled ivory, D2366/267, 9¾" 400.00
Vase, ribbons w/fruit & leaves, mc on gray & wht, #683, 17¾" ..825.00
Vase, seed pods/stems, tan/gr/brn on med bl, 13x6" 385.00
Vase, wide/scalloped floral top on vertical stripes, 11" 450.00

Boehm

Boehm sculptures were the creation of Edward Marshall Boehm, a ceramic artist who coupled his love of the art with his love of nature to produce figurines of birds, animals, and flowers in lovely background settings accurate to the smallest detail. Sculptures of historical figures and those representing the fine arts were also made and along with many of the bird figurines, have established secondary-market values many times their original prices. His first pieces were made in the very early 1950s in Trenton, New Jersey, under the name of Osso Ceramics. Mr. Boehm died in 1969, and the firm has since been managed by his wife. Today known as Edward Marshall Boehm, Inc., the private family-held corporation produces not only porcelain sculptures but collector plates as well. Both limited and non-limited editions of their works have been issued. Examples are marked with various backstamps, all of which have incorporated the Boehm name since 1951. 'Osso Ceramics' in upper case lettering was used in 1950 and 1951. Our advisor for this category is Leon Reimert; he is listed in the Directory under Pennsylvania.

Alec's Red Rose, #30039, 1980-81 ....975.00
American Goldfinch, #400-39, 1976-80 ....400.00
Black-Capped Chickadee, #438, 1957-72 ....395.00
Black-Headed Grosbeak, #400-03, 1969 ....850.00
Bob-White Quail, #40210, 1982-87 ....1,950.00
Bunting, indigo, on base, #429, 1957-75 ....350.00
Camellia, Betty Sheffield, #2002, 1972-81 ....250.00
Camellia, Pat Nixon, #2002, 1972-80 ....295.00
Canada Geese, #408, 1953, from $500 to 600.00
Cat Bird w/Hyacinth, #483, 1965-73 ....1,200.00
Christ Child, #BSB1, 1979 ....100.00
Cygnet, sitting, eyes open, #400-46, 1975 ....280.00
Deer Mouse, #400-89D, 1979-81 ....155.00
Dolphins, #10083, 1989 ....775.00
Eagle, Young America Presidential Edition, #498A, 1973 ....695.00
Elephant, African calf, #200-44, 1977 ....795.00
Fallow Stag, #50012, 1978-87 ....3,250.00
Fledgling Blackburnian Warbler, #478, 1964-72 ....185.00
Fledgling Blue Jay, #436, 1957 ....225.00
Fledgling Bluebird, #442, 1958, from $195 to 225.00
Fledgling Chickadee, #461, 1962 ....225.00
Fledgling Grouse, #400-68, 1978-81 ....250.00
Fledgling Western Bluebirds, #494, 1968 ....375.00

Fox, #40108, 1979 ....175.00
Gardenia, #F250, 1989, from $200 to........................250.00
Great Horned Owl, #20074, 1980-87 ....150.00
Jennifer w/Looking Glass, #AL-4, 1986-87 ....500.00
Koala, #400-36, 1976, lg 600.00
Lesser Prairie Chickens, #464, 1962-64 ....1,800.00
Madonna, #613, 1958, 4½" 150.00
Madonna la Pieta, #601, 1952 ....350.00
Magnolia Grandiflora, #F101, 1979-80 ....275.00
Mockingbird w/Nasturtium, #400-52, 1978-80.......2,000.00
Mourning Doves, #443, 1958-73 ....1,400.00
Mourning Doves, #40189, 1981-84.........................1,900.00
Northern Water Thrush, #490, 1967.........................900.00
Nyala, #5001, 1973-76..1,900.00
Ocelot Baby, #400-40, 1976-77................................595.00
Owl bookends, #453D, 1960-69, pr 400.00
Panda, reclining cub, #400-74, 1974 ....595.00
Peace Rose, #2008, 1972-81, 8" 200.00
Pelican, #40161, 1980-82 ....1,475.00
Penguin, #20116, 1984-90 ....155.00
Polar Bear w/Cubs, #20114, 1983 ....750.00
Pope John XXIII, #621, 1960....................................550.00
Prothonotary Warbler, #445, 1958-73 ....425.00
Rabbit, standing, #40227, 1983-90............................110.00
Rhino calf, blk, #200-62, 1979 ....795.00
Ruby-Crowned Kinglets, #434, 1957-62....................525.00
Screech Owl, #40132, 1980...................................1,750.00
Seal Pup, #40127, 1979-87, from $95 to....................125.00
Snow Buntings, #40021, 1972-80.........................1,200.00
Snowy Owl, #40122, 1980..175.00
Squirrel, #400-94, 1979..195.00
St Maria Goretti, #603, 1952.....................................350.00
Swordfish, #40314, 1987...495.00
Tree Sparrow, #468, 1963..375.00

Tropical Fish with Staghorn Coral, #35, 1983, 14½x12x8½", $800.00. (Photo courtesy Neal Auction Company)

Tufted Titmice, #482, 1965-72 ....1,200.00
Verdins, #400-02, 1969-79 ....875.00
Waterlilies, bl & wht w/gr leaves, #F272 ....440.00
White-Tailed Fawn, #20119, 1984-87 ....300.00
Woodcock, #413, 1954-66...800.00
Yellow-Shafted Flicker, #400-16, 1971-80...............1,750.00

Bohemian Glass

The term 'Bohemian glass' has come to refer to a type of glass developed in Bohemia in the late sixteenth century at the Imperial Court of Rudolf II, the Hapsburg Emperor. The popular artistic pursuit of the day was stone carving, and it naturally followed to transfer familiar procedures to the glassmaking industry. During the next century, a formula was discovered that produced a glass with a fine crystal appearance which lent itself well to deep, intricate engraving, and the art was further advanced.

Although many other kinds of art glass were made there, we are using the term 'Bohemian glass' to indicate glass overlaid or stained with color through which a design is cut or etched. (Unless otherwise described, the items in the listing that follows are of this type.) Red or yellow on clear glass is common, but other colors may also be found. Another type of Bohemian glass involves cutting through and exposing two layers of color in patterns that are often very intricate. Items such as these are sometimes further decorated with enamel and/or gilt work.

Bottle, dresser; rose, floral panels, w/gilt, 20th C, 8¼" 85.00
Bowl, gr, geometric cuttings, ftd, 20th C, 3¾x9½" 85.00
Bowl, ruby, flower & panel cuttings, 20th C, 4¼x10" 90.00
Candy dish, red, geometric cuttings, ftd, w/lid, ca 1900, 11x3¼".200.00
Celery vase, ruby, deer/trees/etc in 18 panels, ca 1900, 9"...........200.00
Compote, ruby, floral cuttings, clear stem/ft, 20th C, 9x7½" 75.00
Decanter, gr, geometric cuttings, slim, 1920s, 16" 125.00
Decanter, ruby, vintage, 20th C, 10"...70.00
Dessert bowl, yel, deer/birds/cartouch, 1900s, +6" underplate, 12 for .575.00
Goblet, amber, German buildings, ca 1880, 6½" 250.00
Goblet, ruby, deer & trees in landscape, ca 1890, 6½" 175.00
Goblet, ruby, flowers & vines, 1890s, 5" 80.00
Pitcher, ruby, stars & flourishes, heavy, 9¾x5¾" 105.00
Pokal, ruby, stag/forest, dome lid w/spire finial, late 19th C, 16"..600.00
Rose bowl, cobalt, stylized floral, 4½" H...................................125.00
Tumbler, red, eng harvesters, German inscription, ca 1860, 6¼".400.00
Vase, cobalt, stick form w/silver o/l, 1900s, 8¼"........................295.00

Bookends

Though a few were produced before 1880, bookends became a necessary library accessory and a popular commodity after the printing industry was revolutionized by Mergenthaler's invention, the linotype. Books became abundantly available at such affordable prices that almost every home suddenly had need for bookends. They were carved from wood; cast in iron, bronze, or brass; or cut from stone. Chalkware and glass were used as well. Today's collectors may find such designs as ships, animals, flowers, and children. Patriotic themes, art reproductions, and those with Art Nouveau and Art Deco styling provide a basis for a diverse and interesting collection.

Currently, figural cast-iron pieces are in demand, especially examples with good original polychrome paint. This has driven the value of painted cast-iron bookends up considerably.

For further information we recommend *Collector's Guide to Bookends, Identification and Values,* by Louis Kuritzky, our advisor for this category; he is listed in the Directory under Florida. See also Arts and Crafts.

Angelus Call to Prayer, in relief, CI, Connecticut Foundry, 5½" ..55.00
Bishop's Cathedral, pnt CI, ca 1929, 5½" 45.00
Cherub Reading, bronze clad, att Armor Bronze, ca 1925, 6" 150.00
Christian Science Building, brass, NY World's Fair, 1939, 4¼".....95.00
Church, in relief, CI, ca 1925, 9"...75.00
Country Cottage, in relief, pnt CI, Hubley, 1924, 5½".................70.00
Covered Wagon, in relief, CI, WH Howell, shopmark #14, ca 1926, 4½".65.00
Crane, gray metal, Dodge, ca 1946, 6¾" 75.00
Crusaders, in relief, CI, Hubley #300, 5½"....................................75.00
Dante & Beatrice, gray metal, mc, Ronson, ca 1923, 6".............175.00
Dutch boy & girl, kneeling, gray metal, mc pnt, Ronson, 5½" ...175.00

Egyptian Face, bronze, 1930, 6" **175.00**
End of the Trail, in relief, iron, Connecticut Foundry, 1928, 5" **50.00**
Flying Geese, in relief, pnt CI, Judd #9688, ca 1928, 5½" **165.00**
Grand Pegasus, pnt gray metal, stone base, ca 1925, 7¾" **275.00**
Horse on Arc, gray metal, Dodge, ca 1947, 5½" **60.00**
Ibex Couple, CI, gr patina, Hubley #4017, 5" **175.00**
Indian Maiden's Bowl, copper clad, ca 1930, 5" **125.00**
John Harvard, seated, gray metal, mk Daniel C French #2654, 7"..**450.00**
Library Monk, gray metal, mc pnt, Ronson, LV Aronson, 1920..**125.00**
Lincoln's Monument, bronze, WB, shopmark, ca 1930, 5½" **150.00**
Little Red Riding Hood, gray metal, Ronson, LV Aronson, 1925, 6".**350.00**
Madonna & Child, in relief, iron, EX patina, Verona, ca 1925, 6¾"..**150.00**
Masonic Emblem, in relief, pnt CI, Judd, ca 1928, 5¼" **100.00**
Minstrel Clown, pnt gray metal on marble base, K&O, ca 1929, 5¼".**175.00**
Oak Leaf, pnt gray metal, PM Craftsman, ca 1965, 6½" **45.00**
One Feather, Indian in relief, CI, ca 1928, #44, 6¼" **125.00**
Panther Pair, gray metal on marbleized metal base, Ronson, 1925, 10".**250.00**
Peacock Splendor, bronze, ca 1930, 5¾" **175.00**
Penguin Family, gray metal, ca 1925, 4¾" **225.00**
Pharaoh, seated figure, bronze clad, Armor Bronze, ca 1926, 7" .**175.00**
Pink lady, chalk on polished stone base, Hrisch, 1943, 5½".......**125.00**
Pirate Stands Alone, CI, shiny finish, Littco, ca 1928, 7" **110.00**
Pontiac, emblem, aluminum, Bruce Fox, 1983 ....**50.00**
Retro Scottie, looking bk, gray metal, Frankart, ca 1930, 4½"....**125.00**
Ride the Waves, sailing ship, bras, AM Greenblatt Studios, 5½"..**120.00**
Rough Rider, CI, gr patina, ca 1925, 5½" **100.00**
Ruling Couple, Egyptian, mc, Bellinni, Italy, ca 1980, 7"..........**110.00**
Scottie on Fence, bronze, ca 1928, 6"..............................**175.00**
Soldier w/Sabre, gray metal/celluloid, stone base, att Hirsch, 8¼"..**275.00**
Thinker, in relief, gray metal, Ronson, ca 1930, 5½" **95.00**
Those Who Go Down to Sea in Ships, att Phila Metal Craftsman, ca 1980.**125.00**
Trout, leaping, gray metal, ca 1934, 6½" **125.00**
Turbanned Scholar, pnt gray metal, LV Aronson, 1923, 3¼"......**110.00**
We're Home Dad, elephants, gray metal/celluloid, stone base, 6"..**175.00**
Whistler's Mother, gray metal/celluloid, marble base, Hirsch, 6½".**175.00**
Wirehaired Fox Terrier, brass, English registry mk, ca 1925, 5".....**95.00**
Ye Olde Inn, in relief, Syroco Wood, ca 1940, 6¼" **45.00**
10 Commandments, gray metal, Ronson, LV Aronson, 1922, 3¾".**175.00**

Bootjacks and Bootscrapers

Bootjacks were made from metal or wood. Some were fancy figural shapes, others strictly business. Their purpose was to facilitate the otherwise awkward process of removing one's boots. Bootscrapers were handy gadgets that provided an effective way to clean the soles of mud and such. Our advisor for this category is Louis Picek; he is listed in the Directory under Iowa.

Bootjacks

Pistol form, cast iron, folding, American Bull (?), ca 1890s, EX, $175.00.

Am Bull Dog, pistol shape, CI, blk pnt, 8", from $75 to..............**90.00**
Beetle, pnt CI, 11"..**85.00**
Cricket, CI, mk Harbester Bros & Co, Reading PA, 11x4¼"......**110.00**
Dog, holds U-shaped bone in mouth, CI..............................**25.00**
Heart figural, scalloped sides, CI, 13" L............................**225.00**
Labrador Retriever, CI, 3x10x4¾"..................................**15.00**
Longhorn Steer, brass, 10"..**15.00**
Mermaid, hands outstretched above head, CI, 10" **15.00**
Moose, CI, 11x8"...**15.00**
Mule head, CI, 11x5"..**100.00**
Naughty Nellie, lady on bk, CI......................................**18.00**
Pistol, CI, emb boars ea side, folding, 9" **275.00**
Pistol, CI, 3x11¼"..**15.00**
Wooden, carved floral design, tooled-leather look, Acme, 10" **12.00**

Bootscrapers

Black shoeshine boy atop, CI, oval base, 13", VG **140.00**
Cat, long tail sticks up, CI, 10x15"................................**35.00**
Dachshund, blk CI, 5x5x13"..**50.00**
Duck, full body, CI, 14½" L..**350.00**
Elephant, trunk in air, CI mtd on wooden base, 9x11"................**30.00**
Lyre, in pie-pan shaped base, CI, mk VMG 1901 ....**25.00**
Scottie dog, CI, orig pnt, EX..**185.00**
Scottie dogs (2), sits between wall (scraper), brass, 4x10½"..........**85.00**

Borsato, Antonio

Borsato was a remarkable artist/sculptor who produced some of the most intricately modeled and executed figurines ever made. He was born in Italy and at an early age enjoyed modeling wildlife from clay he dug from the river banks near his home. At age eleven, he became an apprentice of Guido Cacciapuotti of Milan, who helped him develop his skills. During the late '20s and '30s, he continued to concentrate on wildlife studies. Because of his resistance to the fascist government, he was interred at Sardinia from 1940 until the end of the war, after which he returned to Milan where he focused his attention on religious subjects. He entered the export market in 1948 and began to design pieces featuring children and more romantic themes. By the 1960s his work had become very popular in this country. His talent for creating lifelike figures has seldom been rivaled. He contributed much of his success to the fact that each of his figures, though built from the same molded pieces, had its own personality, due to the unique way he would tilt a head or position an arm. All had eyelashes, fingernails, and defined musculature; and each piece was painted by hand with antiquated colors and signed 'A. Borsato.' He made over six hundred different models, with some of his groups requiring more than one hundred and sixty components and several months of work to reach completion.

Borsato died in 1982. Today, some of his work is displayed in the Vatican Museum as well private collections.

Prices vary according to size and the amount of work involved. Single figures often fetch $1,200.00. Larger pieces, for instance, 'Gypsy Camp' or 'Revelry,' may go from $15,000.00 to as high as $20,000.00. 'Play Gypsy Play' was originally made in the early '30s; a second version followed in the late '40s, and a limited edition was created to mark the thirtieth anniversary of the date he began his work. Though he planned to make thirty of these limited edition groupings, he died after only thirteen had been completed. This version was larger than the first two and has sold on the secondary market for more than $50,000.00. Various pieces were made in two mediums, gres and porcelain, with porcelain being double the cost of gres. In the listings that follow, our suggested values should be regarded as conservative.

Our advisor for this category is Elizabeth Langtree, she is listed in the Directory under California.

Boulevaldier, man seated on rustic bench, 6¼x5½" **1,350.00**
Canine Casualty, man applies first aid to dog, 9x9" **2,560.00**
Child's Prayer, child on lady's lap w/hands folded, 8x6x9½" **1,925.00**
Cobbler's Dilemna, man & boy at bench, 10½x7½x8½" **2,900.00**
Coffee Counter, 3 figures surrounding coffee urn, 10x9" **4,000.00**
Comfort & Love, courting couple, lady & dog in interior, 12x22" .**13,600.00**
Dog Trainer, man working w/upright poodle, 6x9½" **1,600.00**
Elders' Delight, aged couple w/basket of snails, 11x8" **3,240.00**
Elegant Harmony, man at piano, 2nd w/violin, lady beside, 13x15" .**9,600.00**

Excursion, 12x18x8", $6,500.00. (Photo courtesy Elizabeth Langtree)

Fagoters, man w/bundle on bk w/goat & dog, 11½x8½" **2,100.00**
Farmer's Twilight, man offers produce to lady, 7x10" **3,475.00**
Fiddler's Revelry, man seated/playing fiddle, 6x10" **2,140.00**
Grandma's Well, lady/child/goose at well, 10x12" **5,125.00**
Lover's Lane, figures in horse-drawn carriage on base, 11x24" .**8,775.00**
Nomads, 2 figures w/loaded pack horse & sheep on rocky base, 13x22" ..**11,240.00**
Psyche & Eros, classical couple on base, 7¾x8" **1,575.00**
Siesta's Price, fruit card, peddler asleep while cash drw is robbed..**3,200.00**
St George, man on rearing stallion facing dragon, 17¼x11¾"..**6,625.00**

Bossons Artware

Bossons closed operations December 1996. The late William Henry Bossons founded the company (formerly located in Congleton, England) in 1944; his son, W. Ray Bossons (deceased 1999) was manager from 1951 until his retirement in 1994. The company was always owned and managed by the Bossons family, who have stored the only remaining molds (many have been destroyed) and at the present time have no intention of selling them or the Bossons's name.

With the company's closing in 1996, all Bossons are now categorized as discontinued; as stock holdings are depleted, some are appreciating at a very fast rate, especially those that are new in original boxes. (See line items for examples.) Many of the heads that sold in the US for under $5.00 are now in the range of $100.00 to $300.00. The Character Studies or 'Masks' (Dickens and all the Seafarers) have always been most popular. Now even the Wildlife Collections and many of the descriptive High Relief plaques have become extremely popular as well (i.e., Floral Plaques and depictions of English life and historical monuments), as have table lamps and nightlights (porcelain products of limited production). The lifelike studies of dogs and cats are coveted by animal enthusiasts.

Bossons were exported to nearly forty countries, so collector interest is widespread. Canada and the U.S. were the most important importers, but Australia, New Zealand, and South Africa, to mention a few, have become primary havens for collectors wanting to find the rarest specimens.

Major points to remember: 1) Not all will have the name incised under the collar (e.g., Syrian, Smuggler, Tibetan, and Tyrolean, see *Schroeder's* seventeenth Ed. for pictures).

2) Many character studies in gypsum plaster are produced in England that are not Bossons; to be specific, Legends, Naturecraft, and those incised with only 'Made in England.' Fraser-Art products are Bossons, so are products marked Briar Rose. Osborne Ivorex is not Bossons. Though all rights to Osborne products were purchased by Bossons in 1971, the appearance and coloring were changed and then issued under the Bossons name. (For pictures and technical details about plaster faces that are *not* Bossons, typical trademarks, Bossons Ivorex and Bossons Briar Rose Products, link on the net directly to www.donsbossons.com.)

3) Except in very rare cases, all carry the incised copyright: 'Bossons, Congleton, England, World copyright reserved' on the back *and* in most cases under the collars, along with that particular Bossons's specific name. The Fraser-Art Division (named for Mrs. Ruth Fraser Bossons) is becoming one of the most popular areas of collecting. Invented by Ray Bossons, Fraser-Art was high quality ware with bold design and fine detail. It was made of hard PVC/Stonite® and colorfully hand painted. *Important:* The copyright date is most often a mold date and can help determine value. (An exception is the 'blue hat' Sardinian, which though copyrighted 1959 wasn't released or introduced to the public until 1962; it was discontinued in 1969. It has a filled-in back and an incised 1961(c) under the collar. However, the 'blue hat' model was also released with an exterior wire hanger, but with a hollow back. Though it has a 1961(c) incision, there is no 1959(c) on the back. In 1989 Bossons released a version of Sardinian with a green hat. Further confusing the issue of copyrights, several models of the 'green hat' were released with the original 1961(c) incision. Under advisement from Bossons collectors, the company agreed to include an additional 1988 copyright on the back, the year of introduction.) Though the blue version with the filled-in back is older, the 1988 version was made for only four years, so fewer were made, and it is now the higher priced of the two. This is only one of several examples where the Bossons copyright serves to confuse rather than help determine values.

Though they can be used for authentication, painted initials on the underside are not a critical consideration when determining value. Incised initials, e.g. FW (Fred Wright), AB (Alica Brindley), and WRB (W. Ray Bossons) are sculptors/modelers and are extremely important in authenticating Bossons and in some cases for determining value. Mold makers' incised initials on the backs of Bossons are extremely important when authenticating Bossons. A few examples include K (Ken Potts), P (George Proudlove), and D (Damen Smith).

Suggestions for evaluating Bossons based on rarity and condition:

A. Attempt to determine the copyright (release) date from under the collar and/or on the back.

B. Length of production helps determine rarity. With few exceptions, the earlier Character Heads (1958 – 63) and latest (1986 – 98) are found in fewer numbers. Production dates can be found in *Imagical World of Bossons, Vol. 1, 1946 – 82*, and *Vol. II, 1982 – 94*, by Dr. Robert E. Davis. (See advisors' Directory listing for information on this publication.) The final productions from 1994 to 1996 can be viewed in Bossons's yearly brochures or by contacting our advisor. Examples in rare color combinations may be valued at 200% to 300% of retail.

C. Condition is a major factor. If in 'new' condition and in original colors, a Bossons is worth 100% of its retail value. On the other hand, a Bosson worth $165.00 in mint condition might only be worth from $15.00 to $25.00 in poor condition. A professional restoration could maintain value, just be sure the item warrants restoration. Premium prices are obtained for only pristine, perfect Bossons, either in factory new condition and in their original boxes or perfectly returned to their original structural and coloring beauty by a professional restoration artist recommended by Bossons.

Beware of fakes and look-alikes; above all, know your dealer. Internet auctions are flooded with plaster 'faces' and figures claiming to be Bossons in mint condition which are neither mint nor Bossons. A frequently copied fake Bossons is Harry Wheatcroft, the famous English rose grower who developed the Peace Rose in his Nottingham gardens. This past year, fraudulent examples of Bossons's six military masks have been sold on eBay. Also five copies of the rare Caspian Woman (with no veil) were sold. The IBSC has also become aware of a serious copyright violation being made by a company in Pakistan, who are copying, repainting, and releasing many of the original Wildlife Series and Dogs and Cats of Distinction. (Our advisor welcomes questions concerning authenticity and identification.)

See Clubs, Newsletters, and Catalogs in the Directory for International Bossons Collectors' Society (IBCS). Our advisor for this category is Dr. Don Hardisty; since 1984 he has been recommended by Bossons to restore their products. He is listed in the Directory under New Mexico. For restoration and purchasing questions, the dos and don'ts of Bossons repairing, visit his website at www.donsbossons.com.

Barbarossa, 1944, (issue: $65), MIB, from $185 to.......................250.00
Blackbeard, 1992, (issue: $45), MIB, from $185 to.....................225.00
Cossack, 1996, (issue: $65), Autumn 1996 Collection, MIB, from $185 to .325.00
Dickens Character (9 in the series), MIB, ea, from $85 to..........125.00
Dickens Character (9 in the series), w/imperfections, ea, from $25 to....35.00
Evzon, 1996, (issue: $65), Autumn 1996 Collection, MIB, from $185 to..325.00
Nuvolar, 1996 (issue: $65), Autumn Collection, MIB, from $185 to .325.00
Old Salt, MIB...125.00
Old Salt, w/imperfections, from $15 to...25.00

Plaster wall figure, Donald Duck playing string bass, from the Stars of Disneyland series which includes Mickey and Minnie Mouse and Goofy, modeler Fred Wright, marked c 1958 Bossons England copyright reserved/No 7, released for one year only (1961 – 62), very rare, 9", from $2,500.00 to $3,000.00.

(Photo courtesy Dr. Don Hardisty)

Sardinian, bl hat, 1959, filled-in bk, c 1961, M, from $85 to......125.00
Sardinian, gr hat, 1988, produced 4 yrs only, M, from $185 to ...225.00
Seafarer, Clipper Captain, 1993 (issue: $45), MIB, from $275 to.350.00
Sindbad, 1996, (issue: $65), Autumn 1996 Collection, MIB, from $185 to .325.00

Bottle Openers

At the beginning of the nineteenth century, manufacturers began to seal bottles with a metal cap that required a new type of bottle opener. Now the screw cap and the flip top have made bottle openers nearly obsolete. There are many variations, some in combination with other tools. Many openers were used as means of advertising a product. Various materials were used, including silver and brass.

A figural bottle opener is defined as a figure designed for the sole purpose of lifting a bottle cap. The actual opener must be an integral part of the figure itself. A base-plate opener is one where the lifter is a separate metal piece attached to the underside of the figure. The major producers of iron figurals were Wilton Products, John Wright Inc., Gadzik Sales, and L & L Favors. Openers may be free standing and three dimensional, wall hung or flat. They can be made of cast iron (often painted), brass, bronze, or aluminum.

Numbers within the listings refer to a reference book printed by the FBOC (Figural Bottle Opener Collectors) organization. Those seeking additional information are encouraged to contact FBOC, whose address can be found in the Directory under Clubs, Newsletters, and Catalogs. The items below are all in excellent original condition unless noted otherwise.

Bear Head, F-426, brn w/red & blk pnt, lt rust, wall mt..............135.00
Big-Eyed Owl, copperized metal, gold eye/gr eye, 3½"................55.00
Billy Goat, F-73, CI, EX old patina, 4⅜" 82.50
Billy Goat, F-74, CI, wht pnt, John Wright, 1940s, 2¾".............115.00
Black boy & crocodile, pnt CI, souvenir of Aberdeen MO, 3¼x4½".250.00
Black Crow, golf cap & cigarette, w/corkscrew, Dansk..............70.00
Canada Goose, F-105, pnt CI, 3¾" L.......................................85.00
Chipmunk, CI, possible rpt, John Wright, ca 1950, 2x2⅞"..........82.50
Cowboy, F-26, mc pnt on CI..300.00
Dodo Bird, F-122, CI, worn pnt, 3¼"..185.00
Dog, eyes move, vinyl/plastic, 1950s, 7" 35.00
Dolphin, chromed metal, screw-top opener in belly, cap type in tail .35.00
Donkey, F-60, CI, orig blk/brn/beige pnt, chips, 4x3½"................60.00
Double-Eye, F-414, orig pnt on CI, lt rust 65.00
Elephant, F-48, brass-colored metal, 3½" 45.00
False Teeth, pnt CI, F-420, 3½x2½" 85.00
Fish, wooden scales w/metal rivets, MOP eyes, 1970s, 7½x6".......22.50
Hockey Player, Molson Ice advertising, open mouth opener, 16x18x13" .225.00
Lady's Leg, metal, flat, Toast the House in many languages, 10" ...32.50
Lobster, F-268, mk Iron Art MJ268, EX red pnt, 3½" L 10.00
Lucifer, human-goat figure w/cloven ft, metal, 1900s....................75.00
Man Butler, pnt resin, w/corkscrew, old....................................60.00
Maori Chief, solid brass, Kiwiana, pre-1950s...............................50.00
Mermaid, holding ball over her head, metal, 6½"..........................80.00
Military Hat, pnt metal, Loyal Prod NYC..., 1¼x3" 80.00
Moose, F-75, frontal view, brass-colored metal, Alaska, 4½x2".......25.00
Mr Dry, F-416, orig pnt, rust/chips..120.00
Native Woman, blk pnt on brass, gr glass eyes, 4½" 45.00
Nude, w/arms up, F-173 (similar, no base at ft), shiny brass, 6¾" .60.00
Nude Lady, brass, holds banner: Certified Paint, 4¼"....................35.00
Parrot, F-112, CI w/copper accents, 3½" 55.00
Parrot, F-116, gold-tone metal, 5x1½" 55.00
Parrot, Lg; F-108, CI, EX mc pnt, John Wright, ca 1910-20, 5½", VG..60.00
Parrot, Lg; F-109, CI, mc pnt, 5¼" 35.00
Parrot, Lg; F-110, bronze, 4¾x3½" 50.00
Parrot on Perch, F-114, pnt CI, 4½" 175.00
Pelican, F-130, pnt CI..125.00
Pig, wht metal, screw tail, 5 12"..100.00
Rooster, F-97, pnt CI, Wilton, 1947, 3⅛x2⅝" 60.00
Sailing Ship, brass, flat, 4½" 45.00
Sea Gull, F-123, pnt CI..45.00
Ship's Wheel, from New Zealand vessel: MV Rangitoto, ca 1950s..50.00
Springer Spaniel, pnt CI, Scott Prod Inc, 3¾" 120.00
Swordfish, anodized & NP metal, Kiwiana, 1950s, 4½" 30.00
Woman's Shoe, F-209, aluminum, 1982 club pc, M 180.00
3 Wise Monkeys, vinyl/plastic, 1950s, 7"....................................30.00
4-Eyed Man, pnt CI, F-414, blk hair...55.00

Bottles and Flasks

As far back as the first century B.C., the Romans preferred blown glass containers for their pills and potions. Though you're not apt to find many of those, you will find bottles of every size, shape, and color made to hold perfume, ink, medicine, soda, spirits, vinegar, and many other liquids. American business firms preferred glass bottles in which to package their commercial products and used them extensively from the late eighteenth century on. Bitters bottles contained 'medicine' (actually herb-flavored alcohol), and judging from the number of these found today, their contents found favor with many! Because of a heavy tax imposed on the sale of liquor in seventeenth century England by King George, who hoped to curtail alcohol abuse among his subjects, bottlers simply added 'curative' herbs to their brew and thus avoided taxation. Since gin was taxed in America as well, the practice continued in this country. Scores of brands were sold; among the most popular were Dr. H.S. Flint & Co. Quaker Bitters, Dr. Kaufman's Anti-Cholera Bitters, and Dr. J. Hostetter's Stomach Bitters. Most bitters bottles were made in shades of amber, brown, and aquamarine. Clear glass was used to a lesser extent, as were green tones. Blue, amethyst, red-brown, and milk glass examples are rare. (Please note that color is a strong factor when pricing bottles. For example, an amber Hostetter's bitters sells for $25.00 or less, but a green variant can bring hundreds of dollars. An aqua scroll flask may bring $50.00, but a cobalt blue variation will command over $1,000.00.)

Perfume or scent bottles were produced abroad by companies all over Europe from the late sixteenth century on. Perfume making became such a prolific trade that as a result beautifully decorated bottles were fashionable. In America they were produced in great quantities by Stiegel in 1770 and by Boston and Sandwich in the early nineteenth century. Cologne bottles were first made in about 1830 and toilet-water bottles in the 1880s. Rene Lalique produced fine scent bottles from as early as the turn of the century. The first were one-of-a-kind creations done in the cire perdue method. He later designed bottles for the Coty Perfume Company with a different style for each Coty fragrance.

Spirit flasks from the nineteenth century were blown in specially designed molds with varied motifs including political subjects, railroad trains, and symbolic devices. The most commonly used colors were amber, dark brown, and green.

Pitkin flasks were the creation of the Pitkin Glass Works which operated in East Manchester, Connecticut, from 1783 to 1830. However, other glasshouses in New England and the Midwest copied the Pitkin flask style. All are known as Pitkins.

From the twentieth century, early pop and beer bottles are very collectible as is nearly every extinct commercial container. Dairy bottles are a relatively new area of interest; look for round bottles in good condition with both city and state as well as a nice graphic relating to the farm or the dairy.

Bottles may be dated by the methods used in their production. For instance, a rough pontil indicates a date before 1845. After the bottle was blown, a pontil rod was attached to the bottom, a glob of molten glass acting as the 'glue.' This allowed the glassblower to continue to manipulate the extremely hot bottle until it was finished. From about 1845 until approximately 1860, the molten glass 'glue' was omitted. The rod was simply heated to a temperature high enough to cause it to afix itself to the bottle. When the rod was snapped off, a metallic residue was left on the base of the bottle; this is called an 'iron pontil.' (The presence of a pontil scar thus indicates early manufacture and increases the value of a bottle.) A seam that reaches from base to lip marks a machine-made bottle from after 1903, while an applied or hand-finished lip points to an early mold-blown bottle. The Industrial Revolution saw keen competition between manufacturers, and as a result, scores of patents were issued. Many concentrated on various types of closures; the crown bottle cap, for instance, was patented in 1892. If a manufacturer's name is present, consulting a book on marks may help you date your bottle. For more information we recommend *Bottle Pricing Guide, 3rd Edition,* by Hugh Cleveland.

Among our advisors for this category are Madeleine France (see the Directory under Florida), Mark Vuono (Connecticut), and Monsen and

Baer (Virginia). Examples in the following listings (most of which have been sold through cataloged auctions) are assumed to be in clear glass unless color is indicated. See also Advertising, various companies; Blown Glass; Blown Three-Mold Glass; California Perfume Company; Czechoslovakia; De Vilbiss; Fire Fighting; Lalique; Steuben; Zanesville Glass.

Key:
am — applied mouth	grd — ground pontil
bbl — barrel	GW — Glass Works
bt — blob top	ip — iron pontil
b3m — blown 3-mold	ps — pontil scar
cm — collared mouth	rm — rolled mouth
fl — filigree	sb — smooth base
fm — flared mouth	sl — sloping
gm — ground mouth	sm — sheared mouth
gp — graphite pontil	tm — tooled mouth

Barber Bottles

Clear frost & amethyst Lutz-style art glass, sb, 7⅜" 375.00
Clear w/ruby red stringing, sb, 7¾" 400.00
Cobalt, emb ribs, wht & gold floral, low body, rm, ps, 7⅝".........475.00
Cranberry opal spatter, stepped design, tm, ps, 8⅜" 300.00
Dk purple amethyst, ribbed bell w/mc enameling, tm, ps, 6⅞" ...300.00
Dk purple amethyst w/wht & gold Nouveau flowers, rm, ps, 8⅛" .230.00
Emerald gr, Brilliantine, emb ribs & mc florals, tm, ps, 4" 400.00
Lime gr frost, Coin Spot & HP Nouveau decor, rm, ps, 8"..........325.00

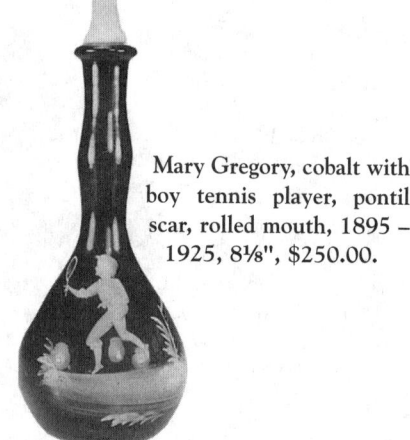

Mary Gregory, cobalt with boy tennis player, pontil scar, rolled mouth, 1895 – 1925, 8⅛", $250.00.

Milk glass, Bay Rum & HP florals, ps, 9¼" 250.00
Milk glass, HP cherubs on dog-faced cloud, tm, ps, 7½" 250.00
Milk glass, HP cherubs w/grapes, tm, ps, 7⅝" 200.00
Milk glass, HP cherubs w/pigeon cage, ps, tm, 7¾" 200.00
Milk glass cased in yel frosted dmns, tm, sb, 20th C, 7⅛"..........185.00
Milk glass w/HP cherubs & sheaf of grain, tm, ps, 7¾" 350.00
Pk frost cased in clear, overall Hobnail, rm, ps, 6¾" 500.00
Pk-orange Lutz type, Brilliantine, sb, 4" 475.00
Turq w/emb ribs, mc florals, tm, ps, 7¾" 230.00
Turq w/emb ribs & floral silver o/l, tm, ps, 9" 550.00
Yel amber, Coin Spot, tm, ps, 7¼" 350.00
Yel-gr, ribbed & corseted w/wht & red floral, ps, 7½" 100.00
Yel neck w/clear ball body, Hobnail, 7⅛" 550.00

Bitters Bottles

Bourbon Whiskey, med strawberry puce, bbl, sb, am, 9⅜" 950.00
Bourbon Whiskey..., dk strawberry puce, bbl, sb, am, 9⅜" 575.00

Brown's Celebrated Indian Herb...1868, amber, Indian Queen, 12"..**425.00**
Brown's Celebrated Indian Herb...1868, dk amber, Indian Queen, 12"..**750.00**
Brown's Celebrated Indian Herb...1868, yel amber, Indian Queen, 12"..**1,000.00**
Brown's Celebrated Indian Herb...1869, yel amber, Indian Queen, 12"..**900.00**
Bryant's Stomach..., olive gr, lady's leg, 8-sided body, sb, 12"...**5,250.00**
Dr AW Coleman's Anti Dyspeptic..., dk yel olive, arched shoulder, 10"..**2,100.00**
Dr AW Coleman's Anti Dyspeptic..., med bl gr, sl cm, ip, 9"..**3,200.00**
Dr Bishop's Wa-Hoo...Conn, red amber, semi-cabin, sb, am, 10".**900.00**
Dr Campbell's Scotch..., med orange amber, strapside flask, tm, sb, 6".**200.00**
Dr CW Roback's Stomach..., dk yel w/amber & olive tones, bbl, sb, 10".**950.00**
Dr Hostetter's Stomach, med yel w/amber tones, McC&Co on sb, 9"..**125.00**
Dr XX Lovegood's Family, med amber, semi-cabin, sb, 10", EX.**1,200.00**
Dr XX Lovegood's Family..., dk amber, cabin, bubbles, sb, 10½".**3,000.00**
Drake's 1860 Plant'n X Pat 1862, yel amber, 6-log, sb, 9¾"........**185.00**
Excelsior Aromatic...NY, reddish amber, semi-cabin, sb, 10½".**1,500.00**
Fish WH Ware Pat 1866, clear, fish, sb, tm, 11½" **1,200.00**
Fish WH Ware Pat 1866, med yel olive, fish, am, sb, 11⅝".....**3,000.00**
Fish..., yel w/amber tone, fish figural, cm, sb, 11½" **550.00**
Greeley's Bourbon, smoky topaz puce, bbl, sb, am, 9¼", NM......**475.00**
Greeleys' Bourbon, smoky olive gr, bbl, sb, am, 9¼" **3,000.00**
Hall's..., golden amber, bbl form, sq cm, sb, 9¼"...........................**150.00**
HP Herb Wild Cherry..., med yel amber, cabin, sb, am, 10⅛"...**450.00**
JFL Capitol (on base), med amber, pineapple, dbl cm, ip, 9¼"..**1,800.00**
Kelly's Old Cabin...Pat 1863, med amber to yel amber, log cabin, 9"..**1,700.00**
Kimball's Jaundice...NH, yel amber, sl cm, ip, 7"......................**1,550.00**
Lediard's Celebrated Stomach..., med bl gr, dbl cm, ip, 10⅛".....**375.00**
Lediard's Morning Call, med yel olive, cylinder, sl cm, sb, 10" ...**350.00**
Lediard's OK Plant'n...1840, med amber, semi-cabin, sb, 10"..**1,200.00**
National Tonic..., lt yel amber, sq w/arched shoulders, sb, 9¼".**8,500.00**
National..., dk strawberry puce, ear of corn, Pat 1867 on sb, 12½".**1,600.00**
National..., golden amber, ear of corn form, sb, 12⅜" **350.00**
National..., yel wmber, ear of corn form, sl cm w/ring, sb, 12⅜".**500.00**
Old Abe's Ague & Stomach..., aquamarine, sq cm, sb, 7¼"........**275.00**
Old Home...Laughlin's & Bushfield, med amber, semi-cabin, sb, 9¾".**1,800.00**
Old Home...Wheeling W Va, golden amber, modified cabin, sb, 9¾".**2,500.00**
Old Sachem...Wigwam Tonic, dk amber, bbl, sb, am, 9½"..........**325.00**
Old Sachem...Wigwam Tonic, ginger ale, bbl, sb, sq cm, bubbles, 10".**4,250.00**
Old Sachem...Wigwam Tonic, med topaz puce, bbl, sb, am, crude, 9⅜".**800.00**
Schroeder's...Louisville KY, yel tobacco amber, crude, 8¾".........**450.00**
ST Drake's 1860 Plant'n X Pat 1862, copper puce, 6-log, sb, 10".**220.00**
ST Drake's 1860 Plant'n X Pat 1862, dk cherry puce, 6-log, sb, 10"..**200.00**
ST Drake's 1860 Plant'n X Pat 1862, yel olive, 4-log, sb, 10"..**3,000.00**
ST Drake's 1860 Plant'n X Pat 1862, yel w/olive tone, 6-log, sb, 10"..**2,300.00**
Wheeler's Berlin...Baltimore, dk olive gr, 6-sided, sb, 9¾".......**8,000.00**

Black Glass Bottles

Many early European and American bottles are deep, dark green, or amber in color. Collectors refer to such coloring as black glass. Before held to light, the glass is so dark it appears to be black.

Kidney, deep olive green with amber tone, pontil scar, applied string lip, Dutch, ca 1760 – 90, 6¾", $700.00.

Demijohn, dk olive gr, sl cm, ps, nice whittle, 18".......................**85.00**
Globular, dk olive amber w/mc pnt scene & Anys, sm, ps, 10¼".**1,700.00**
Globular, dk olive amber w/mc pnt scene & Creme de Noyeaux, 11½".**1,700.00**
Seal: EG 1769 in emb heart, med yel olive gr, ps kick-up, 9⅛".**1,300.00**
Seal: HM 183, Patent on shoulder, dk olive amber, ps, 12½" **230.00**
Seal: John Tabor 1767, dk olive amber, am, ps kick-up, 10⅛".**2,400.00**
Seal: Middle Temple, dk olive gr, b3m, am, ps, 11¼" **190.00**
Seal: RI Olborne 1735, dk olive amber mallet, am, ps, chip, 7" ..**3,000.00**

Blown Glass Bottles and Flasks

Chestnut flask, med amber w/olive tone, ps, New England, 8⅛".**500.00**
Chestnut flask, yel gr, 15 left-swirl ribs, am, ps, 5¼" **4,250.00**
Club, cornflower bl, 24 right-swirl ribs, beehive form, ps, 8" **900.00**
Globular, aquamarine, 24 left-swirl ribs, ps, Midwest, 7¾"..........**750.00**
Globular, citron, 24 left-swirl ribs, rm, ps, Midwest, 8¼" **325.00**
Globular, golden amber, 24 left-swirl ribs, ps, Midwest, 8½".......**650.00**
Globular, golden amber, 24 vertical ribs, ps, Midwest, 7⅝" **2,750.00**
Pitkin flask, bright yel gr, 16 right-swirl ribs, ps, Midwest, 7"......**850.00**
Pitkin flask, golden amber, 36 left-swirl ribs, sm, ps, Midwest, 6".**1,100.00**
Pitkin flask, med to deep sea gr, 32 right-swirl ribs, ps, 7¾"........**800.00**
Pitkin flask, sea gr, 32 left-swirl ribs, sm, ps, Midwest, 6½".........**500.00**
Pitkin flask, sea gr, 36 left-swirl ribs, ps, Midwest, 6⅞" **325.00**
Pocket flask, bright amethyst, 20 vertical ribs, ps, Midwest, 6½".**2,100.00**
Pocket flask, bright olive yel, 24 vertical ribs, ps, Midwest, 4¾".**1,300.00**
Pocket flask, bright yel, 20 vertical ribs, sm, ps, Midwest, 6½" ...**800.00**
Pocket flask, bright yel gr, 14 left-swirl ribs, Midwest, 4"........**3,750.00**
Pocket flask, dk amber, 24 left-swirl ribs, ps, Midwest, 4¾" **750.00**
Utility, bright forest gr, tm, ps, New England, 7⅞" **400.00**

Cologne, Perfume, and Toilet Water Bottles

Amethyst, emb sunburst, tm, ps, shallow chip, 1¾" **325.00**
Blk amethyst, scallop form, tm, ps, 2½" **300.00**
Bright teal bl gr, corseted & paneled, att Sandwich, 4⅝"............**500.00**
Cobalt, emb sunburst, 18 beads ea side, tm, ps, 2¾"....................**525.00**
Cobalt, emb sunburst, 30 beads ea side, tm, ps, 2⅞"....................**500.00**
Cobalt, scallop from, rough sm, sb, 2¼" **140.00**
Dk gr, corset waist, tm, sb, orig glass stopper, 6"...........................**75.00**
Med amethyst, 16 left-swirl ribs, bulbous, fm, att Pittsburgh, 5⅜".**1,300.00**
Milk glass, Jess Perfume...Paris label, 10-sided, sb, metal cap, 2"...**90.00**
Olive amber, tombstone w/emb sunflower, rm, Mt Vernon, 4"..**3,750.00**
Sapphire bl, scallop form, tm, sb, 1¾" **275.00**
Star & Punty, apple gr, hexagonal tapered stopper, Sandwich, 7", EX.**825.00**
Star & Punty, canary, Sandwich, 6", EX, pr **585.00**
Teal gr, 20 vertical ribs, flattened ovoid, sm, ps, 1820-40, 3" **750.00**
Yel gr, 20 vertical ribs, flattened ovoid, sm, ps, 1820-40s, 3" **700.00**

Commercial Perfume Bottles

One of the most popular and growing areas of perfume bottle collecting is what are called 'commercial' perfume bottles. They are called commercial because they were sold with perfume in them — in a sense one pays for the perfume and the bottle is free. Collectors especially value bottles that retain their original label and box, called a perfume presentation. If the bottle is unopened, so much the better. Rare fragrances and those from the 1920s are highly prized. 'Tis a sweet, sweet hobby. Our advisors are Randy Monsen and Rod Baer; they are listed in the Directory under Virginia.

Avon, Quaintance, clear w/red rose cap, 2½", MIB (presentation).**55.00**
Caron, Muguet de Bonheur, std shape replica w/sm label, 3½", MIB.**66.00**
Corday, Femme du Jour, blk flask w/gold decor, empty, ca 1925, 4".**495.00**
D'Orsay, Muguet, clear w/gold label, faceted ball top, 4½", MIB .**600.00**

Darnèe, Colleen Moor, gr opaque, gold labels, empty, 5¾".........300.00
E Arden, Cyclamen, wht fan w/gold, orig bow, M in triangle box .3,575.00
E Arden, Memoire Cherie, frosted female shape, empty, 4½".....285.00
Estèe Lauder, Cinnabar, Foo dog figural, empty, 1¾", EX.......275.00
Gabilla, Fleur de Jour, gold label, sealed, 3", MIB (pk)................440.00
H Rubenstein, Apple Blossom, clear mini w/pk cap, empty, 1½", EXIB..75.00
H Rubenstein, Heaven Scent, Harlequin holder, 2¾", MIB 35.00
Jardin, Vrai Narcisse, clear decanter, metallic label, 5½" 120.00

Jovoy, Severem, camel and rider, clear with frosted rider stopper, missing label, copyright Lordonnais 1922 France, 3½", $880.00. (Photo courtesy Monsen and Baer)

L Lelong, Opening Night, clear, 2¼", M in stage presentation box .150.00
L Vanderbilt, Concentrated Extract, bl w/butterfly, 2¼", M in bag .200.00
Lenthèric, clear w/bow, molded ribbon, 3¼", MIB 65.00
Lionceau, Parfum pour Blondes, gr w/beige wash, M in tasseled box.935.00
Lubin, Epidor, clear horseshoe w/button stopper, empty, 3¼", NMIB.385.00
Matchabelli, Added Attraction, red & gold crown, 1½", MIB (red).200.00
Moiret, Circè, blk w/frosted woman & dog frieze, empty, 3½".....200.00
Revlon, Moon Drop, Raja's Elephant on chain, solid, 2⅜", MIB.135.00
Richard Hudnut, Le Debut Noir, blk glass octagon, 1¾", EX........88.00
Schiaparelli, Shocking, metal heart w/rhinestones, 1½", MIB....255.00
Vigny, Le Golliwogg, frosted w/blk stopper, 3" to top of hair, empty .300.00
Vivadoux, Mai d'Or, vial shape, red/gold label, empty, 3¼", EXIB.75.00
Weill, Bamboo, clear pagoda w/red stopper, label, 3½" 275.00

Dairy Bottles

Chapman's Dairy, Warren OH, blk pyro, rnd ½-pt, EX 38.00
Clover Farms...Reading PA, gr pyro, rnd qt....................................60.00
Garden Farm Dairy, Denver CO, 2-color pyro, ½-pt 45.00
Gold Spot Dairy, Enid OK, bl pyro, rnd qt.....................................38.00
Kroger Dairy emb script, K emblem on bk, cream top, ½-pt 32.00
Martin Dairy, Hillsboro NH, brn pyro, rnd qt...............................27.50
Ozark Dairy, St Louis MO, baby w/bottle, red pyro, rnd qt 35.00
Roberts Dairy, Stop & Think..., policeman, red pyro, rnd ½-gal ..40.00
Scharf & Sons...New Albany IN emb, pnt......................................87.50
Seminole Maid...Seminole OK, red pyro, qt...................................62.50
Shiveley's Milk No Manchester IN, red pyro, cream top, qt...........55.00
Slate Belt Dairy, baby drinking, 2-color pyro, rnd qt 25.00
Sutton Farms, ME seal, Good Morning..., blk & orange pyro, rnd qt..50.00
Tolleston Dairy, Pure...Gary, Ind emb, ½-pt....................................28.00
Use City Creamery Milk Phone 382, red pyro, rnd qt 24.00
Waukesha Dairy Co...WI emb, cream top, ½-pt 22.50

Figural Bottles

Bear, dense blk, sm, sb, appl face, att Russia, 11⅜" 220.00
Bear, dk aquamarine w/appl face, A&T 1890 on side of base, tm, 9¼".350.00
Bear, ice bl w/appl face, tm, sb, 10⅜" 175.00
Black waiter, clear w/partial orig pnt, blk glass head, 14⅜".........175.00
Duck swallowing bottle neck, milk glass w/red loops, Atterbury, 12".1,600.00
Lovebirds (2) & cherub faces ea side, bl opaque, emb Salve, 9¾".200.00
Monkey on bbl pulls hat over ears, milk glass, Geschutz on sb, 9½".1,400.00

Santa, clear w/EX mc pnt, FE-Co 0351 emb near sb, 7½" 130.00
Strawberry, frosted ruby red, gm, sb, 6"......................................450.00
Water bird, clear, am, label: Imp & Roy Creme d' Abricots..., 12¾".100.00

Flasks

Adams/Jefferson, GI-114, lt yel olive, sm, tubular ps, ½-pt.........550.00
Anchor/Phoenix, GXIII-53, dk Prussian Blue, am, sb, pt.........9,500.00
Anchor/Phoenix, GXIII-53, dk strawberry puce, sl cm, pt.......4,500.00
Benjamin Franklin/TW Dyott MD, GI-96, aquamarine, sm, ps, qt..475.00
Corn for the World/Monument, GVI-6, aqua, sm, ps, pt 200.00
Cornucopia/Urn, GII-17, emerald gr, sm, ps, crude, pt...............600.00
Cornucopia/Urn, GIII-7, dk yel olive gr, open bubble, ½-pt.......100.00
Eagle/(plain), GII-143, 7-Up Green, sl cm, ip, chip, calabash 160.00
Eagle/Clasped Hands, GXII-21, med amber, am, sb, pt 200.00
Eagle/Clasped Hands, GXII-25, aquamarine, am, sb, pt................90.00
Eagle/Clasped Hands, GXII-33, med amber, am, sb, ½-pt...........180.00
Eagle/Clasped Hands, GXII-43, bright yel gr, dbl cm, ps, flake, qt..750.00
Eagle/Clasped Hands, GXII-43, brn amber, dbl cm, ip, calabash, qt..450.00
Eagle/Cornucopia, GII-58, lt yel olive, sm, ps, ½-pt, NM........9,000.00
Eagle/Eagle, GII-101, lime gr, am, sb, crude, qt, EX......................70.00
Eagle/Eagle, GII-24, cobalt, tm, open pontil, 6⅝".....................4,000.00
Eagle/Eagle, GII-26, lt gr, sm, ip, chip, qt..................................550.00
Eagle/Eagle, GII-29, bright aquamarine, sm, ps, chip, pt 425.00
Eagle/Eagle, GII-31, aquamarine, dbl cm, ps, qt..........................325.00
Eagle/Franklin Frigate, GII-42, aquamarine, sm, ps, haze, pt.......120.00
Eagle/General Washington, GI-5, gr-aquamarine, ps, stain, pt, rare..2,000.00
Eagle/Louisville KY..., GII-33, dk golden amber, cm, sb, ½-pt.1,100.00
Eagle/Lowell RR, GV-10, lt to med yel olive, sm, ps, ½-pt 275.00
Eagle/Masonic Arch, GIV-16, brilliant aquamarine, sm, ps, pt .2,400.00
Eagle/Masonic Arch, GIV-24, med olive amber, sm, ps, ½-pt...275.00
Eagle/Prospector, GXI-34, lt apple gr, am, sb, qt........................160.00
Eagle/Success to RR, GV-8, yel olive, sm, ps, pt 400.00
Eagle/Tree, GII-60, yel amber, tm, ps, ½-pt 2,200.00
Eagle/Willington, GII-62, dk olive gr, sl cm, sb, pt......................275.00
Fisherman/Hunter, GXIII-6, lt gr aqua, am, ps, calabash, NM 140.00
Flora Temple/Horse, GXIII-23, teal, cm, sb, pt 400.00
Gen Taylor/Capt Bragg, GX-4, yel olive gr, tm, ps, pt, EX.....1,300.00
Gen Taylor/Monument, GI-73, lt amethystine, sm, ps, qt..........750.00
Hunter/Fisher, GXIII-4, deep wine, am, calabash 800.00
Hunter/Fisherman, GXIII-4, apricot w/copper overtones, ip, calabash.425.00
Jenny Lind/Factory, GI-104, cornflower bl, cm, ps, sm stain, calabash .700.00
Jenny Lind/Glass Factory, GI-99, bright bl-gr, sl cm w/ring, ps, qt .2,100.00
Lafayette/Masonic Arch, GK-89, dk olive gr, tm, ps, ½-pt 1,500.00
Louis Kossuth/US Steam Frigate..., GI-112, gr aquamarine, calabash.300.00
Scroll, GIX-10, cobalt, tm, open pontil, pt.................................3,100.00
Scroll, GIX-10, golden yel amber, sm, open pontil, flake, pt.......500.00
Scroll, GIX-11, amber, sm, open pontil, flake, pt 375.00
Scroll, GIX-11, lt to med yel gr, sm, open pontil, pt....................200.00
Scroll, GIX-14, lt smoky bl gr, sm, open pontil, pt 110.00
Scroll, GIX-45, aqua, sm, ps, lt stain, pt......................................800.00
Scroll, GIX-45, bl aqua, sm, ps, haze, pt......................................400.00
Scroll, GIX-46, dk bl aqua, sm, ps, shallow flake, qt....................750.00
Scroll, GIX-5, yel gr, am, ip, crude, qt...950.00
Sheaf of Wheat/Farm Tools, GXIII-35, red amber, sm, crude, qt..230.00
Sheaf of Wheat/Star, GXIII-43, yel gr, sl cm, ps, calabash 325.00
Sheaf of Wheat/Tree, GXIII-46, bright bl-gr, dbl cm, ps, calabash, qt..600.00
Spring Garden GW/Log Cabin, GXIII-58, aqua, am, sb, pt 130.00
Star & Arm/Seeing Eye, GIV-43, brilliant amber, sm, ps, pt.......475.00
Success to RR/Horse Pulling Cart, GV-5, dk emerald, sm, pt..1,100.00
Success to RR/Horse Pulling Cart, GV-5, yel amber, tm, ps, pt ..425.00
Success to RR/Locomotive, GV-1, bl aqua, tm, open pontil, pt..500.00
Summer/Winter, GXIV-46, bl aqua, dbl rm, ps, calabash, NM ...140.00
Sunburst, GVIII-1, yel olive gr to striated olive, ps, pt 12,500.00

Sunburst, GVIII-2, apple gr, tm, ps, pt 500.00
Sunburst, GVIII-3 variant, med to dk yel olive, sm, ps, crude, pt..750.00
Sunburst, yel olive, sm, ps, Keene, ½-pt............................550.00
Taylor/Taylor, GI-73, lt smoky amethyst, tm, ps, chip, pt............700.00
Taylor/Taylor, GI-73, med moss gr, tm, ps, flake, pt................3,750.00
Washington/Eagle, GI-11, bl aquamarine, sm, ps, pt................1,700.00
Washington/Jackson, GI-31, yel amber w/olive tone, sm, ps, Keene, pt..450.00
Washington/Jackson, GI-32, med yel amber, tm, ps, pt 220.00
Washington/Jackson, GI-34, med yel amber, tm, ps, ½-pt 325.00
Washington/plain, GI-48, bright yel olive, tm, open pontil, pt..4,500.00
Washington/plain, GI-48, med to lt emerald, sq cm, pontil, pt..2,400.00
Washington/Sheaf of Wheat, GI-59, dk cobalt, sm, ps, ½-pt..18,500.00
Washington/Taylor, GI-41, bl aqua, am, sb, ½-pt 85.00
Washington/Taylor, GI-54, dk grape amethyst, tm, ps, qt 3,750.00
Washington/Tree, GI-36, aquamarine, dbl cm, ps, calabash, qt ..190.00

Food Bottles and Jars

Pepper sauce, aquamarine cathedral, sl cm, ps, 11" 140.00
Pepper sauce, WH Clay's Richmond..., aquamarine, cylindrical, sb, 10" ..210.00
Pickle, bl aquamarine, cathedral panels, rm, sb, 11⅜" 275.00
Pickle, cathedral, med teal w/gr tone, rm, sb, 11⅞" 550.00
Pickle, Shaker Society Home Made..., yel olive, tm, sb, label, 7"..400.00
Picle, bl aquamarine, cylindrical w/5 flutes, 2-pc mold, 10½" 130.00
Sanborn Parker...Boston Pickles, yel w/olive tone, sb, 8¼" 240.00
Utility, med emerald gr, appl disk/m, lg open pontil, 7¼" 100.00
Utility, med yel olive, fm, open pontil, crude/bubbles, 5" 150.00

Ink Bottles

Cathedral, dk cobalt, 6-sided, Carter's on sb, 9¾" 100.00
Cobalt, E Maurin, shoe form w/emb laces, sm, sb, 2⅜x4¼" 300.00
Cone, dk sapphire bl, rm, ps, 2⅜x2¼" 200.00
Cone, med bl gr, rm, open pontil, 1⅞" 325.00
Cylinder, emerald gr, 22 vertical ribs, gm, rim cut down/roughness, 2"..765.00
Cylinder, olive gr, 5 stacking rings form, lt wear, 1½" 2,585.00
Dmn Diaper, olive gr, appl rim disk, Coventry, 1⅞x2¼", EX......265.00

Gross and Robinson's American
Writing Fluid, brilliant aquamarine, flared mouth, pontil scar,
1840 – 60, 4", $500.00.

Igloo, J&IEM, yel amber, tm, sb, 1¾"...325.00
Igloo, lt to med bl gr, gm, sb, 1⅝"..150.00
Master, dk olive amber, am, label: Brickett & Thayer..., ps, 9¾"..140.00
Sq w/chamfered corners, olive gr, 36 left-swirl ribs, att Pitkin .1,400.00
Teakettle, amethyst, paneled octagonal form w/brass cap, 2x2x3½"..470.00
Teakettle, blk purple amethyst, gm, sb, orig neck band & lid, 2¼"..200.00
Teakettle, blk w/gold staves, bbl form, sb, 2⅛" 375.00
Teakettle, clear dog figural, sb, 1⅞"...450.00
Teakettle, dk cobalt bbl, gm, sb, orig neck band & lid, 2¼" 825.00
Teakettle, emerald gr, paneled octagon, brass cap, chip, 2x3½"..585.00
Umbrella, aquamarine, Blake NY, crude ps, 3x2¾" 325.00
Umbrella, dk yel amber, 8-sided, rm, open pontil, 2½" 130.00
Umbrella, golden amber, 16 sides, sm, ps, New England, 2⅛x2⅛"..600.00

Medicine Bottles

Note: Warner's bottles listed below are not American versions, and
some are valued higher than those from Rochester, New York.

A Mosher, deep teal, oval, sl cm, ip, 1845-60, 8¾" 3,000.00
Alexander's Silameau, sapphire bl, flattened bell from, ps, haze, 6".475.00
Brant's Purifying Extract...NY, aquamarine, dbl cm, ps, lt haze, 10"..275.00
Brewster Dentist, clear, tm, ps, orig stopper, 3¾"..........................210.00
By AA Cooley Hartford..., dk olive gr, oval, tm, open pontil, 4⅜".350.00
C Heimstreet...NY, sapphire bl, octagonal, dbl cm, sb, full label, 7"..375.00
Dr Graves' Hygeian Alternative..., aquamarine, dbl cm, ps, chip, 10" .475.00
Genuine Swaim's Panacea..., bright aquamarine, cm, ps, 7¾" 550.00
Gun Wa's Chinese Remedy..., golden yel amber, dbl cm, sb, 8" ..475.00
GW Merchant Lockport NY, bright citron, am, sb, 5⅛" 275.00
Henshaw & Edmands...Boston, med emerald gr, cm w/stopper, ip, 11⅜"..1,000.00
HT Hembold Genuine...Phila, milk glass, tm, sb, EX label, 6¼"...525.00
Jacob's Pharmacy Atlanta, med amber, tm, WT&CO USA on sb, 4⅞".150.00
LQC Wishart's Pine Tree...1859, bl gr, sl cm, sb, 7⅞" 230.00
MB Robert's Vegetable Embrocation, bl gr, sl cm, open pontil, 5½" .450.00
Moore's Revealed MRR..., med yel amber, am, strap sides, sb, 8⅞" .180.00
Mrs SA Allen's World's Hair Restorer..., amethyst, tm, sb, 7".....220.00
Peruvian Syrup, bluish aqua, cylinder, sb, am, 9½" 90.00
Primley's Iron & Wahoo Tonic..., straw yel w/amber tone, sb, 9½".230.00
Reed's London Cordial Gin, aquamarine, rectangle, sl cm, ip, 10".250.00
S Brechbill's Worm..., bluish aqua, rm, ps, 4"................................170.00
Swaim's Panacea Philada, aquamarine, paneled cylinder, ps, 8"..650.00
Swaim's Panacea Philada, bright yel gr, paneled cylinder, ps, 8".800.00
Swaim's Panacea Philada, dk olive gr, dbl cm, ps, 7⅞" 600.00
Swaim's Panacea Philada, lt bl gr, paneled cylinder, sb, 7⅞".......100.00
Swaim's Panacea Philada, med yel olive, paneled cylinder, ps, 7⅝".550.00
Swift's Syphilitic Specific, bright sapphire bl, sq cm, sb, 9", NM..500.00
T Morris Perot...Philada, sapphire-steel bl, emb panel, sb, 9¾" .1,200.00
Warner's Safe Cure, dk yel olive, heavy cm, sb, 7⅛" 80.00
Warner's Safe Cure...USA, dk red amber, dbl cm, sb, 9⅝"..........130.00

Mineral Water and Soda Bottles

Artesian Spring Co...Water, bright yel olive gr, dbl cm, sb, pt....100.00
Caladonia Sporing Wheelock VT, golden yel to yel amber, sb, qt, NM..450.00
Congress & Empire Spring Co..., dk olive gr, dbl cm, sb, flake, qt .65.00
Congress & Empire Spring Co...Water, dk bl gr, sl cm, sb, crude, qt..75.00
Congress & Empire Spring..., yel olive w/amber tone, dbl cm, sb, qt..425.00
Congress & Empire...Hotchkiss' Sons..., emerald gr, dbl cm, sb, qt.100.00
Congress & Empire...Hotchkiss' Sons..., yel olive, sl cm, sb, pt ..550.00
Excelsior Spring Saratoga NY, dk red amber, sl cm, sb, bruise, pt.95.00
F Schrader Scranton PA, med emerald gr, bt, sb, 7" 100.00
GW Hubbard...CT, lt bl gr, cylinder, heavy cm, ip, ½-pt.............500.00
GW Weston...NY, dk forest gr, cylinder, sl cm w/ring, ps, pt.......400.00
H Knebel New York, dk bl gr, bt, ip, shallow chips, 7" 65.00
H Knebel's...NY, cobalt, 8-sided, bt, ip, haze, 7½" 325.00
Highrock Congress Spring..., dk teal bl, sl dbl cm, sb, pt 230.00
Highrock Congress Spring...NY, dk teal, sl cm w/ring, sb, stain, pt..650.00
J Jenckes, med emerald gr, bt, ip, 7⅛"...200.00
J&JW Harvey...Conn, bl gr, cylinder, heavy cm, ip, ½-pt 140.00
KR S Water S Smith...1865, med cobalt, 10-sided, bt, ip, 7⅜"...375.00
L Gahre Bridgeton NJ G, yel gr, dbl cm, sb, 6¾".............................80.00
Luke Beard, dk bl gr, 10-pin, sl cm, ip, 7" 500.00
MT Crawford Hartford CT Brown Stout, dk teal bl, bt, ip, 7⅛"..220.00
P Conway Bottler...Filbert, med cobalt, sl dbl cm, ip, 7" 250.00
Saratoga (star) Spring, dk olive gr, sl cm, sb, bubbles, pt............150.00
Saratoga (star) Spring, tobacco amber, sl cm, sb, pt......................125.00
Saratoga Red Spring, bl gr, sl cm, sb, pt 110.00
Star Spring Co (star)..., amber w/red tone, sl cm, sb, bubbles, pt .120.00

Superior Soda... (eagle/shield/flags), med cobalt, sl cm, ip, 7¾".**1,100.00**
Vermont Spring Saxe & Co..., med emerald gr, sl cm, sb, qt.........**75.00**

Poison Bottles

Poison, clear, triangular, tm, sb, 3", EX..**150.00**
Poison, cobalt, tm, sb, 2¾"..**90.00**
Poison, med amber, rectangular, tm, S&D on sb, NM label, 4¾"..**210.00**
Poison, med amber, tm, JTMCO on sb, 5" **475.00**
Poison Bowman's Drug..., cobalt, irregular hexagon, tm, sb, 6¼".**850.00**
Poison Not To Be Taken..., med yel amber, dmn shape, tm, sb, 8¾".**100.00**
Poison The Owl Drug Co, cobalt, triangular, tm, sb, 9¾" **500.00**
Santonin (skull & X-bones)..., dk amber w/2-color pyro letters, 5⅝".**750.00**
Strychnia Poison, clear, oval, outward rm, sb, 2⅜".....................**110.00**
TODC Trademark (owl on mortar & pestle), cobalt, sq, tm, sb, 6¼".**125.00**

Sarsaparilla Bottles

Dr Townsend's Comp..., aquamarine, sq w/beveled corners, ip, 9½".**2,000.00**
Dr Townsend's...Albany NY, olive gr, sl cm, ps, base flake, 9½".**275.00**
Dr Townsend's...NY, bright yel olive, sq w/beveled corners, 9¼".**375.00**
Dr Townsend's...NY, dk amber (blk), sq w/beveled corners, ip, 9⅝"..**900.00**
Dr Townsend's...NY, dk yel olive, sq w/beveled corners, ps, 9½".**240.00**
Dr Townsend's...NY, teal, sq w/beveled corners, sb, 9¼" **180.00**
Old Dr J Townsend's..., dk emerald gr, sq w/beveled corners, ip, 9"..**800.00**
Old Dr J Townsend's..., ice bl, sq w/beveled corners, ip, 9⅝"...**1,300.00**

Spirits Bottles

AM Bininger, golden amber, cannon bbl form, sb, 12½", EX **325.00**
Aromatic Schnapps..., med olive gr, sl cm, sb, 9" **100.00**
Bininger's Golden Apple Cordial..., yel olive gr, sl cm, sb, 9¾".**3,250.00**
Bininger's Nightcap No 19..., golden amber, oval flask, chip, 8¼"..**240.00**
Bininger's Peep-o-Day..., golden amber, dbl cm, sb, 7⅝" **700.00**
Chestnut Grove, golden amber Bininger-form jug, am, ps, 9" **180.00**
Chestnut Grove..., yel golden amber, flattened Bininger type, 8⅞".**230.00**
Griffith Hyatt & Co..., golden amber, globular, sq cm, ps, 7½".**700.00**
HA Graef's Son Canteen NY, dk yel olive, canteen, 6½"...........**200.00**
L Lyons...Ohio..Brandy..., golden amber, am w/ring, sb, haze, 13¾".**475.00**
RB Cutters Pure Burbon, smoky pk puce, pear form, sl cm, ip, 9".**750.00**
That's the Stuff, bright yel golden amber, bbl form, ps, 10" **2,100.00**

Boxes

Boxes have been used by civilized man since ancient Egypt and Rome. Down through the centuries, specifically designed containers have been made from every conceivable material. Precious metals, papier-mache, Battersea, Oriental lacquer, and wood have held riches from the treasuries of kings, snuff for the fashionable set of the last century, China tea, and countless other commodities. In the following descriptions, when only one dimension is given, it is length. See also Toleware; specific manufacturers.

Ash burl w/EX figure, rectangular, 2½x9¼x5¼" **350.00**
Bentwood, bl pnt, 1-finger lid, base w/overlapped seams, 8" L....**495.00**
Bentwood, dk over lt gr, 1-finger lid/base, iron tacks, 5¼" dia..**2,420.00**
Bentwood, relief-cvd pinwheel lid, thin gr wash, iron tacks, 11" dia.**935.00**
Bentwood, 1-finger lid & base (opposing), gr rpt, att Hersey, 5¾" L.**465.00**
Bible, poplar book shape, 3-color pnt w/brn vinegar decor, 16" L...**275.00**
Bible, walnut w/cvd vines & floral panel, wire nails, 6x17x12" **85.00**
Bird's eye maple/mahog/satinwood vnr, lid w/dmn motif, 1800s, 3x8x5".**500.00**
Bride's, bentwood, mc floral/1854 on bl, oval, 15" L, EX **990.00**
Bride's, bentwood w/German verse & floral decor, laced seames, 12".**715.00**

Bride's, bentwood w/laced seams, PA Dutch decor/verse, 7x12x18".**770.00**
Burl, EX figure, scrubbed w/red shellac int, trn ft, 3x8" dia.........**330.00**
Candle, blk walnut w/poplar base, dvtl, slide lid, 5x5x18" **110.00**
Candle, hanging, tin cylinder w/hanging rings in crest, tooled, 12" L .**85.00**
Candle, pine w/thin red, slide lid, dvtl, chamfered lid, 10" **350.00**
Candle, poplar, slide-lid, pnt decor, dvtl, 15" L...........................**325.00**
Cedar w/star inlay on front, appl scrolled ft, dvtl, 8½x13½" ...**1,100.00**
Chip-cvd hardwood w/cherry finish, rosettes/edging, wire nails, 6x6x7".**185.00**
Document, pnt pine w/stenciled fruit, 1800s, 4¾x12x8"...........**590.00**
Dome top, poplar w/gr pnt & reserve w/feathery trees, 1800s, 7x12x6"..**2,875.00**
Exotic wood w/shell inlay panel w/star & geometrics, 1800s, 4x9x12"..**300.00**
Grpt pine w/stenciled stars, hinged lid, sgn/1800s, 6x9x12"........**350.00**
Knife, flame mahog vnr, bow front, scalloped corners w/inlay, 16".**550.00**
Leather, gr w/brn corners, brass tacks, sq nails, 4x6x11", VG......**275.00**

Letter box, tortoise shell and quillwork, ivory crest on lid, England, 4x10x5", **$880.00.** (Photo courtesy Neal Auction Company)

PA decor: cvd compass stars, red/wht on bl, dome top, orig hdw, 5x4x6".**11,500.00**
Pine, orig pnt w/dk gray-gr decor, New England, 1830-40, 19x23x24".**1,035.00**
Pine, slide lid, chamfered edges, dvtl case, 10x23x11".................**220.00**
Pine w/gr pnt, dome top, wire end hdls, staple hinges, 10" L......**385.00**
Pine w/leather hinges, gr pnt w/mc border, Am, 19th C, 5x14x9½".**975.00**
Pine/poplar w/red pnt, appl lid molding, slotted for divider, 12" L..**300.00**
Pipe, pine, worn blk pnt, chamfered edges/dvtl drw/canted sides, 17x7".**440.00**
Pipe, pine w/wht pnt traces, pierced bk, 19th C, 20x7x5"...........**500.00**
Pipe, pine/red stain, fancy scroll crest w/heart cutout, 1813, 17".**1,300.00**
Pnt decor appl later, polka-dot tulips/hearts, 5-color on gray, 21".**1,870.00**
Pnt pine, 2-color tulips on mustard, blk stripes, wear/warped, 12".**770.00**
Pnt w/compass rose, fans at corners, wallpaper lined, 1800s, 3x9x6".**765.00**
Pnt/decor wht pine, dome top, New England, 1830s, 19x29x17", EX..**975.00**
Poplar (thick) w/gr pnt, sq nails, 3-part int, arch crest, 14" **550.00**
Poplar w/orange & gr pnt, wire nails, appl molding, 13" L..........**385.00**
Smoke decor, chamfered sliding lid, 1830s, 6x8x6½" **765.00**
Storage, poplar w/old brn pnt, sm brass butt hinges, sm lock, 8x17".**50.00**
Tobacco, Dutch copper eng 3 wise men/manger, brass lid/base, 7" L.**440.00**
Valuables, inlaid burl walnut, dvtl w/line inlay, PA, 5x9x5" **525.00**
Wall, brn mustard pnt, 2-compartments, slant top, 19th C, 28x14x7".**5,465.00**
Wall, red-pnt pine, pierced rnd bk on rectangle, 12x9x5" **1,850.00**
Wallpaper covered, lighthouse & ships, faded/sewn rprs, 10x15x12".**1,400.00**
Woven splint w/gr & blk rpt, German verse on lid, 11x22x12"..**220.00**
Writing, burled olivewood vnr on mahog, brass bound, 6x9x12", EX.**250.00**
Writing, mahog Georgian w/brass hdls, side drw, rstr, 6x22" **575.00**
Writing, mahog/pine, dvtl, inlay brass hdls, velvet insert, 7x11x17" .**400.00**

Bradley and Hubbard

The Bradley and Hubbard Mfg. Company was a firm which produced metal accessories for the home. They operated from about 1860 until the early part of this century, and their products reflected both the Arts and Crafts and Art Nouveau influence. Their logo was a device with a triangular arrangement of the company name containing a smaller triangle and an Aladdin lamp. See also Bookends. Our advisor is Bruce Austin; he is listed in the Directory under New York.

Lamps

Frog, CI figural w/mechanical mouth, glass eyes & servents bell, 13"....**900.00**
Hanging, 22" 6-panel shade w/½-panel metal o/l of lg flower..**1,600.00**
Hanging, 24" shade w/6 bent panels & crown, heavy leaf/flower o/l....**950.00**
Parlor, amber globe shade, orig burner, enamel base, brass hdls, 20"..**375.00**
Piano, brass w/10½x11" ball shade, 59" **800.00**
Table, 14" o/l 6-panel shade & 4-panel base w/veined leaves, 22" .**1,600.00**
Table, 15" o/l 6-panel shade w/potted plant border; coppery base .**800.00**
Table, 15" o/l 6-panel shade w/trefoil border; #234 std.............**1,000.00**
Table, 16" HP 6-panel pyramidal shade; brass std, 2-socket, 1910, 23" .**1,850.00**
Table, 20" Coin Dot wht opal globe shade, electrified, 22" **450.00**
Table, 20" gr/wht slag 6-panel shade; brass-color base **390.00**
Table, 20" ldgl tilework shade w/wide grapevine apron; std adjusts .**2,300.00**
Table, 20" rvpt shade, 8 ridged bent panels w/stylized flower rim, 24" .**3,235.00**
Table, 22" ldgl grapes/vines shaped shade; base w/4-arm support, EX.**1,950.00**
Table, 24" bent-panel o/l shade w/exotic birds; ornate base w/cherubs..**4,150.00**

Miscellaneous

Andirons, CI w/appl dmns & simulated hammering, 21", pr **495.00**
Ashtray, CI, emb man smoking pipe, 3-ftd, 7⅝" L........................**90.00**
Candlestick, brass, orig patina, 7¼"..**70.00**
Candlesticks, brass w/gr patina, sq ped form, #201, 9¾", pr........**115.00**
Candlesticks, cast brass, Art Nouveau style, 8⅝x3⅞", pr............**275.00**
Desk set, cast brass, note clip+calendar stand+inkwell+letter holder .**300.00**

Fireplace set, wrought iron, four-piece tool set, andirons, and large fire fender, unmarked, $1,400.00.

Inkstand, CI w/glass well, Art Nouveau lady design, #3166, 7½" L.**165.00**
Letter holder, brass-colored CI, stag & dog, 1840s, 6½x9"..........**300.00**
Letter holder, SP brass w/emb cherubs, ornate, 7x9½" **250.00**
Plaques, Nouveau ladies' portraits, #1810/#1811, 8½", pr...........**450.00**
Smoke stand, 3 intertwined sea serpents, old pnt, 28x14" dia.....**550.00**
Thermometer, wht metal w/brass coating, Cupid head on base, 11"..**435.00**

Brass

    Brass is an alloy consisting essentially of copper and zinc in variable proportions. It is a medium that has been used for both utilitarian items and objects of artistic merit. Today, with the inflated price of copper and the popular use of plastics, almost anything made of brass is collectible, though right now, at least, there is little interest in items made after 1950. Our advisor, Mary Frank Gaston, has compiled a lovely book, *Antique Brass and Copper*, with full-color photos.
    See also Candlesticks.

Ashtray, tortoise shell trim, 4 rests, 3½", from $60 to..................**70.00**
Basket, woven wire, tightly woven ft, rope-twist hdl, 12½x13¼" .**55.00**
Bowl, hand-tooled, ftd, Dutch Colonial, 18th C, 5½x9⅞" **285.00**
Box, engr scene on lid & front, wooden bottom, velvet lined, 3x11"..**80.00**
Box, slipper; emb tavern scene, mtd on casters, 14x17x11" **185.00**
Candelabra, hollow domed stem w/stepped base, 7-socket, 20", pr.**200.00**
Candelabra, 3-light, English, mid-1800s, 20x16", pr, from $1,000 to .**1,200.00**
Candelabrum, 3-arm, detailed scrolls, EX patina, 1900s, 12" **125.00**
Candle holder, 8-sided base, English, mid-1800s, 7x2½", $350 to ..**400.00**
Ceiling fixture, single light, chain pull, 1930s, 4" **98.00**
Chamberstick, heart shape, English, 7¼" L, from $250 to **275.00**
Coal hod, copper liner, punched designs, English, mid-1800s, 22" .**650.00**
Coal scuttle, invt helmet shape on rnd base, swing hdl, English, 13" .**100.00**
Coffeepot, dragon-eye spout, eng names, ca 1900, from $125 to .**150.00**
Curtain tie-bk, pineapple design, sm, pr, from $35 to **45.00**
Dipper, 7½" copper bowl, 26" brass hdl, late 1800s, from $175 to.**200.00**
Door hdl, w/keyhole opening, simple style, early 20th C, $60 to ..**75.00**
Doorknob, simple rnd style, early 20th C, from $15 to..................**20.00**
Egg cutter, Hofritz Germany, pre-WWII era, 5" **95.00**
Ewer, HP flower garden, late 19th C, 15½" **335.00**
Fire dog, simple styling w/stepped base, European, 7x8½", pr.....**350.00**
Footman, cut-out top, 4-leg, mid-1800s, 14½x13" **1,000.00**
Footman, 4 brass corner finials, solid top w/freize, 19th C **1,450.00**
Grease gun, unmk, 14" **125.00**
Jardiniere, emb grapes, ftd, mid-20th C, 8x7¼", from $80 to......**100.00**
Jardiniere, eng birds & trees in panels, from $500 to...................**600.00**
Jardiniere, 2 lion's head ring hdls, 11x9" **350.00**
Kettle, forged hdl w/rattail ends, 13x19⅝".................................**185.00**
Kettle, str sides, brass bail, 11x9½", from $200 to **250.00**
Kettle, toddy; 4 bun ft, wood hdl, Victorian, VG+ **110.00**
Kettle stand, cabriole legs/clover ft, rtcl top/sides, 13x13x18" **400.00**
Lamp, desk; goose neck, electric, simple brass dome shade, $225 to..**275.00**
Lamp, peg; enameled glass base, Fr, mid-1800s, pr, from $800 to.**1,000.00**
Mail box, envelope style, lion's head opener, mid-20th C, from $65 to .**75.00**
Mitten warmer, eng sailing ship, England, 7⅜"............................**65.00**
Mitten warmer, Falstaff figure emb on lid, wood hdl, England, 9".**110.00**
Mortar, 3¼x5½", +7" pestle, from $120 to **140.00**
Pail, spun, mk Iiram Hayden...Conn Pat Mar 18 1851, 9"+hdl.....**170.00**
Pan, candy making; rounded bottom, hdls, 16" dia, from $225 to.**250.00**
Planter, 2 lion heads w/ring hdls, ring-trn base, Kinney Mfg, 14x12".**330.00**
Plaque, emb rampant lions support shield & crown, 1830-50, 31"..**650.00**
Potpourri holder, advertising, 19th C, ca 1865 ....**125.00**
Punch bowl, silver lined, enamel flowers, ca 1930s, 12", +12 cups .**600.00**
Sconce, floral openwork w/2 dolphins, mirror bk, 2-arm, 23x8" .**110.00**
Sconce, Medusa head in relief, oval, English, 1830s, 16x18"....**2,000.00**
Sconce, 2 arms w/center (match holder) cup, early 20th C, 11½" .**165.00**
Sconce, 6 arms, crystal prisms, electric, 26x21" **400.00**
Shovel, ember; English, ca 1710, 15¾" **295.00**
Skimmer, rtcl shell shape w/ornate hdl, 23" **150.00**
Spittoon, minor pits & dents, ca 1800, 8½" **400.00**
Spittoon, 2-pc, Farris Mfg...Illinois, 3¼x7¼", from $60 to...........**75.00**
Statue, Space Shuttle, solid, 10x5½" **165.00**
Stool, chased design on seat, 3-leg, 14x12" dia, from $200 to.....**225.00**
Tea caddy, copper label, 8", from $200 to....................................**225.00**
Teapot, w/stand & burner, mk SAS in circle, 1800s, from $600 to.**700.00**
Teapot, 4-ftd, gr glass hdl, 9x8"...**290.00**
Token, Chicken Ranch, LaGrange TX, EX.....................................**200.00**
Tray, armorial design, mk England, late 1800s, 12x9", from $160 to .**175.00**
Tray, 3 emb kittens form tray, #1640, 7x5"..................................**165.00**
Vase, carriage, emb floral decor, conical, 10", pr, from $300 to...**350.00**
Vase, hammered ft, unmk, ca 1890-1900, 9¾"..............................**125.00**
Warming pan, pierced/chased lid, grpt trn hdl, 34" **285.00**
Watering can, hinged lid, European, 8x11", from $120 to...........**135.00**
Wine cooler, ped ft, ring hdls w/lion's heads, mid-20th C, 10x8".**125.00**

Brastoff, Sascha

The son of immigrant parents, Sascha Brastoff was encouraged to develop his artistic talents to the fullest, encouragement that was well taken, as his achievements aptly attest. Though at various times he was a dancer, sculptor, Hollywood costume designer, jeweler, and painter, it is his ceramics that are today becoming highly regarded collectibles.

Sascha began his career in the United States in the late 1940s. In a beautiful studio built for him by his friend and mentor, Winthrop Rockefeller, he designed innovative wares that even then were among the most expensive on the market. All designing was done personally by Brastoff; he also supervised the staff which at the height of production numbered approximately 150. Wares signed with his full signature (not merely backstamped 'Sascha Brastoff') were personally crafted by him and are valued much more highly than those signed 'Sascha B.,' indicating work done under his supervision. Until his death in 1993, he continued his work in Los Angeles, in his latter years producing 'Sascha Holograms,' which were distributed by the Hummelwerk Company.

Though the resin animals signed 'Sascha B.' were neither made nor designed by Brastoff, collectors of these pieces value them highly. After he left the factory in the 1960s, the company retained the use of the name to be used on reissues of earlier pieces or merchandise purchased at trade shows.

In the listings that follow, items are ceramic and signed 'Sascha B.' unless 'full signature' or another medium is indicated. For further information we recommend *The Collector's Encyclopedia of California Pottery, Second Edition*, by Jack Chipman, available from Collector Books or your local bookstore.

Our advisor for this category is Lonnie Wells; she is listed in the Directory under California.

Ashtray, copper w/enameled bl & wht flowers,¾x5½" **35.00**
Ashtray, peacock, 3 cigarette rests, 6¾" dia **28.00**
Ashtray, red w/copper bubbles, enameled copper, 8" dia **40.00**
Ashtray, 20-Mule Team Borax, 13½x5" **130.00**
Ashtray, 5 partridges, gray/brn/silver w/gold birds on wht, 5¾" sq..**30.00**
Bowl, fish decor, mc, 3x13½x9½" **110.00**
Charger, Star Steed, 15" dia **60.00**
Covered box, Star Steed, mc on gr bkground, 7¾x5x2½" **140.00**
Creamer & sugar bowl, blk w/gold decor, gold lid on sugar **65.00**
Dish, fish shape, bl blocks w/gold accents, mk L9, 13¾x4½" **45.00**
Figurine, Hindsight bear, translucent bl resin, 4½x7" **210.00**
Figurine, rooster, gold on speckled gold, 17x11" **165.00**
Figurine, seal, orange resin, 2 blk beaded eyes, 7x9½" **300.00**
Necklace, gold-plated w/lion's head pendant, 2⅛" dia on 24" chain..**95.00**
Pitcher, fruit on rust-brn, 7¼x6" **250.00**
Pitcher, turq w/blk & bl decor, #68, 10¾" **80.00**
Plaque, blues & gold, #418T, 17¾" dia **115.00**
Plate, Atomic Fruit, scalloped edge, ca 1947, 11½" dia.............**165.00**
Plate, Chi Chi Bird, 8½" dia.................**200.00**
Plate, Roof Tops, eng copper pnt moss gr, mk #411, 11" dia **55.00**
Vase, Aztec Horse, #066, bulbous, 5½x8½" **130.00**
Vase, Chi Chi Birds, mother/chicks on 1 side, chicks on other, 9½".**200.00**
Vase, Roof Tops, on wht, #047, 8½" **120.00**
Vase, Roof Tops, 5½x4" **50.00**
Vase, Star Steed, bulbous, mk F24, 10½" **130.00**
Vase, Star Steed on bl, #047 ....**130.00**
Vase, turq w/bl & blk decor, egg shape, 8x4¼" **50.00**
Vase, wht w/gold, bl & bl/gr bands, #L16, 8¼" **65.00**

Brayton Laguna

A few short years after Durlin Brayton married Ellen Webster Grieve, his small pottery, which he had opened in 1927, became highly

successful. Extensive lines were created and all of them flourished. Hand-turned pieces were done in the early years; today these are the most difficult to find. Durlin Brayton hand incised ashtrays, vases, and dinnerware (plates in assorted sizes, pitchers, cups and saucers, and creamers and sugar bowls). These early items were marked 'Laguna Pottery,' incised on unglazed bases.

Brayton's childrens' series is highly collected today as is the Walt Disney line. Also popular are the Circus line, Calasia (art pottery decorated with stylized feathers and circles), Webton ware, the Blackamoor series, and the Gay Nineties line. Each seemed to prove more profitable than the lines before it. Both white and pink clays were utilized in production. At its peak, the pottery employed more than 150 people. After World War II when imports began to flood the market, Brayton Laguna was one of the companies that managed to hold their own. By 1968, however, it was necessary to cease production.

For more information on this as well as many other potteries in the state, we recommend *The Collector's Encyclopedia of California Pottery, Second Edition*, by Jack Chipman; he is listed in the Directory under California.

Bowl, eggplant w/turq int, dripping blk rim, handmade, 3¾x7" .**225.00**
Candle holders, Blackamoor w/legs crossed, 4¾", pr, from $140 to..**170.00**
Chess pc, King, blk, 14" **55.00**
Chess pc, Queen, blk, 12" **45.00**
Cookie jar, pretzels decor **275.00**
Figurine, Bedtime, man & woman in bedclothes, Gay 90s series, 8¾".**160.00**

Figurine, bird, red and black, 17", $125.00.

(Photo courtesy Lee Garmon)

Figurine, Black Choir Boy, wht outfit, holding song book, 5" **90.00**
Figurine, Black dice player w/gr gloves & pk hat **90.00**
Figurine, blk bird, stylized, twisted head & neck, mk #H-49, 9½"..**160.00**
Figurine, bull, brn, head held high, 4¼" **35.00**
Figurine, Butch, children's series, 8" **80.00**
Figurine, cow, brn, seated, 4" **35.00**
Figurine, donkey (6x4") & cart (10"), ceramic & wood, set **130.00**
Figurine, Dutch girl, bl dress w/wht apron & hat, 7" **35.00**
Figurine, Ellen, children's series, 7" **175.00**
Figurine, Figaro, on hind legs, 3½" **110.00**
Figurine, lady in lav dress w/basket & hat in hands, 8½" **90.00**
Figurine, pelican, wht w/gr beak, mk #4143, 7½x3½" **40.00**
Figurine, Pluto, looking up, Disney.................**130.00**
Figurine, Pluto, sniffing the ground, Disney **100.00**
Figurine, red fox, seated, 4x4" **65.00**
Figurine, Sally, children's series, 7" **40.00**
Figurine, Sambo, bibs/hat, children's series, 7¾", $150 to..........**185.00**
Figurine, skunk, blk & wht, 3¾".................**35.00**
Figurine, swan, dk & lt bl, preening bk, 1940 ....**25.00**
Figurine, swan, turq w/orange beak & feet, 1940 ....**25.00**

Figurine/planter, Blackamoor, kneeling 130.00
Figurine/planter, Frances, 8" 60.00
Figurine/planter, peasant woman holding basket....................55.00
Figurines, Chinese Foo Dogs, gr & tan w/gold, rocky bases, 8", pr..225.00
Figurines, Oriental couple, blk w/gold shell at ear, #S34, 19", pr..55.00
Figurines, Victorian couple, man seated beside lady 120.00
Figurines, Zizi & Fifi, maroon & gr, pr...................................500.00
Flower holder, wht elephant in bl shorts, bowl on head, 5¼" 65.00
Pitcher, African mask shape, blk, 8x7" 90.00
Plate, bl, handmade, 9¾" 70.00
Shakers, Black Chef & Mammy, 4½", pr...................................45.00
Shakers, Black Chef & Mammy, 6½", pr.................................185.00
Shakers, Black couple, brn w/yel flowers, mk K-26, 5½", pr..........35.00
Shakers, peasant couple, yel attire, 5½", pr.............................75.00
Tile, Mexican man sleeping by tree & cacti, HP, 6x6" 545.00
Vase, sea horse, wht w/turq trim, pk pocket behind, 8½"...........115.00

Bread Plates and Trays

Bread plates and trays have been produced not only in many types of glass but in metal and pottery as well. Those considered most collectible were made during the last quarter of the nineteenth century from pressed glass with well-detailed embossed designs, many of them portraying a particularly significant historical event. A great number of these plates were sold at the 1876 Philadelphia Centennial Exposition by various glass manufacturers who exhibited their wares on the grounds. Among the themes depicted are the Declaration of Independence, the Constitution, McKinley's memorial 'It Is God's Way,' Remembrance of Three Presidents, the Purchase of Alaska, and various presidential campaigns, to mention only a few.

'L' numbers correspond with a reference book by Lindsey; 'S' refers to a book by Stuart. Our advisor for this category is Darlene Yohe; she is listed in the Directory under Arkansas.

Actress, Give Us This Day Our Daily Bread, oval, $90.00.

American Flag, 38 stars, L-51, 11x8" 235.00
Banner Baking Powder 85.00
Barley (Cable Edge & Stippled)...65.00
Bible 50.00
Black Builders of Bicentennial, 1776-1976.................................35.00
Cleopatra, Spinx's head in bkground, clear, 13x8½".................60.00
Cleveland/Thurman, clear/frosted, L-325, 9½x8½" 215.00
Constitution..60.00
Continental (Memorial H all), hand & bar hdls, 12¾"..............60.00
Cupid & Venus, 10½" dia 55.00
Currier & Ives, balking mule...60.00
Eagle, Constitution, motto, oval...60.00
Fleur-de-lis w/Pan Am (Buffalo) Exposition center 17.50

Frosted Lion, Give Us This Day, 12½x9"...................................175.00
Garden of Eden...45.00
Garfield Drape, We Mourn, L-303, 11½"....................................80.00
Gladstone, 9" 45.00
Grant, Let Us Have Peace...65.00
Grant, Let Us Have Peace, amber...85.00
In Remembrance, 3 Presidents, frosted.......................................60.00
Independence Hall...125.00
It Is Pleasant To Labor, grapes & leaf center, 12¾" dia.............55.00
Knights of Labor, amber, oval, L-512, 12" 145.00
Let Us Have Peace, amber 65.00
Memorial Hall..65.00
Merry Christmas, bells in center, shallow bowl shape...............75.00
Mormon Tabernacle, stippled border, rare...............................425.00
Moses Montifiore, L-239 ....75.00
Nelly Bly, L-136, 12" 200.00
Niagara Falls, L-489..95.00
Old State House, L-32..55.00
Pope Leo XIII, L-240, 10" 35.00
Preparedness, L-481..300.00
Prescott Stark..60.00
Ruth the Gleaner, Gillinder..145.00
Sheaf of Wheat, Give Us This Day, 11" dia.................................40.00
Transcontinental Railroad, 9x12"...95.00
Volunteer, emerald gr, L-101..575.00
Warrior...80.00
Washington Centennial, frosted center.....................................145.00
101, farm implement center 65.00

Bretby

Bretby art pottery was made by Tooth & Co., at Woodville, near Burton-on-Trent, Derbyshire, from as early in 1884 until well into the twentieth century. Marks containing the 'Made in England' designation indicate twentieth century examples.

Bookends, lion, wht, 6" on 3½x3¼" base, pr 55.00
Cat dish, Pussy in gr on wht stoneware, 2¾x7¼" 35.00
Figurine, antelope, lying down, 5" L 45.00
Flower frog, mc parrot (7½") on underbowl, 10" dia 360.00
Jug, milk; blk w/floral decor, #2503...60.00
Loving cup, cobalt, 3 top-to-bottom hdls, 5¼" 130.00
Mug, King George VI's head, plays For He's a Jolly Good Fellow, 9".300.00
Novelty, vintage car, red w/blk roof & gilt accessories, 4x5" 30.00
Vase, bl/gr/ivory/red drip, hdls, sm rpr, 5" 200.00
Vase, brn w/gray center band w/pk floral decor, 8"....................45.00
Vase, copper-like w/appl jewels, invt cone w/integral hdls, 9".....375.00
Vase, gr w/brn & wht mottle, 1920s, w/hdls, 4½" 100.00
Vase, mottled yel/gr/tan/gr, #1688, 2¾x3½" 50.00
Vase, orange w/thick gr veins, bulbous w/long neck, 6⅞".............70.00
Vase, sailing ship & man in rowboat, mc on lt yel, 1886, 7¼x4" .195.00

Bride's Baskets and Bowls

Victorian brides were showered with gifts, as brides have always been; one of the most popular gift items was the bride's basket. Art glass inserts from both European and American glasshouses, some in lovely transparent hues with dainty enameled florals, others of Peachblow, Vasa Murrhina, satin, or cased glass, were cradled in complementary silverplated holders. While many of these holders were simply engraved or delicately embossed, others (such as those from Pairpoint and Wilcox) were wonderfully ornate, often with figurals of cherubs or animals or birds. The bride's basket was no longer in fashion after the turn of the century.

Watch for 'marriages' of bowls and frames. To warrant the best price, the two pieces should be the original pairing. If you can't be certain of this, at least check to see that the bowl fits snugly into the frame. Beware of later-made bowls (such as Fenton's) in Victorian holders and new frames being produced in Taiwan. In the listings that follow, if no frame is described, the price is for a bowl only.

Our advisors for this category are Barbara and Steve Aaronson; they are listed in the Directory under California.

Alabaster w/HP floral, int: peachblow, 11"; Meriden fr w/Cupid reserve .1,100.00
Apricot satin Herringbone w/gr int, HP flowers/butterfly, ruffled .2,300.00
Apricot satin w/HP bird on branch; SP Tufts fr, 7x18½" 1,500.00
Apricot to wht satin w/HP; rstr Middletown #658 fr w/Indian & rabbit..3,200.00
Bl Dmn Quilt MOP, pleated rim; rstr Tufts #1952 fr, 13" 1,250.00

Blue Herringbone mother-of-pearl with crimped top and applied ribbon edge, silver-plated Reed and Barton frame, 11" to top of handle, $1,500.00.
(Photo courtesy John A Shuman III)

Bl Invt T'print w/HP floral; rstr Wilcox #2622 fr w/Grecian lady, 20".3,000.00
Bl Invt T'print w/HP florals, 9"; rstr Wilcox #2622 19¾" fr 3,000.00
Bl satin w/HP floral, gold rim, 3½x7½"; SP Rogers #1070 fr 750.00
Cranberry, Invt T'print; rstr Pairpoint #2180 fr w/enamel berries, 9" .1,500.00
Cranberry spatter w/HP floral, 5x8"; rstr Pelton Bros fr, 14½".1,500.00
Cranberry w/floral, simple form; Wm Rogers fr w/side ornaments, 10"..690.00
Cranberry w/HP floral 3x8¾"; rstr Pairpoint #2180 9" fr 1,500.00
Custard w/HP decor; rstr Meriden #01532 7" fr w/filigree & cherub hdl..850.00
Custard w/HP floral; rstr cherub Meriden #01532 fr, 7" 850.00
Oyster irid w/HP floral, ruffled, 12"; Reed & Barton figural stem (EX).575.00
Pk, ruffled; rstr SP fr w/figural cherub support, #221, 8½"...........650.00
Pk & yel spatter, ruffled; rstr Hartford #1707 fr w/Greenaway girl, 7"..950.00
Pk cased w/crenulated rim, 8½"; Pairpoint fr w/cherries, 10½"...360.00
Pk cased w/HP floral, 4¼x8½"; rstr Tufts #231 fr w/cherries, 9".895.00
Pk cased w/HP floral & butterfly; SP Pairpoint fr, 11x10"..........650.00
Pk satin w/HP decor; rstr Aurora #721 5¾" fr 750.00
Pk w/HP floral w/gold, ruffled, 10¾"; SP Aurora fr, 13" 250.00
Spangle, yel/wht swirl w/bl daisies, crimped/folded heart rim, 11"..90.00
Vaseline Hobnail, int: cranberry, ruffled, 4½x11" 550.00
Vaseline to pk w/yel & gr flowers, crimped/ruffled, 12"; Benedict fr..400.00
Wht opaline w/allover decor, pk int, 12"; Middletown fr w/fruit hdls.515.00

Bristol Glass

Bristol is a type of semi-opaque opaline glass whose name was derived from the area in England where it was first produced. Similar glass was made in France, Germany, and Italy. In this country, it was made by the New England Glass Company and to a lesser extent by its contemporaries. During the eighteenth and nineteenth centuries, Bristol glass was imported in large amounts and sold cheaply, thereby contributing to the demise of the earlier glasshouses here in America. It is very difficult to distinguish the English Bristol from other opaline types. Style,

design, and decoration serve as clues to its origin; but often only those well versed in the field can spot these subtle variations.

Bottle, barber; fox hunt scene, w/gold, ca 1890s, 7¾" 290.00
Bottle, scent; bl opaque w/HP floral, tulip stopper, 10½", pr 175.00
Box, patch; pk, floral & fans, w/gold, 1x2" dia 150.00
Box, wht, children building snowman, 2⅜x4½" 145.00
Cracker jar, bl, daisies & foliage, SP mts, 6½x4¾" 175.00
Ewer vase, pk, intricate gold pattern/neck ring/hdl, 6½" 125.00
Jar, pk w/mc floral & wht dots, w/lid, 8⅜" 145.00
Lamp, blk, scenic, 31" 175.00
Rose bowl, wht, duck on snowy bank, 4" 150.00
Sweatmeat, bl w/floral, SP mts, 5½" 145.00
Teapot, cream w/birds/scenes, appl spout, 5¼x4½" 275.00
Tumble-up, lt yel, violets, sgn V Gherke, 5x2½" 75.00
Vase, caramel w/mc floral, red flashing at rim, 8¾x4¼" 45.00
Vase, jack-in-pulpit; gray-gr w/lt bl int, floral, 8½" 58.00
Vase, pale custard, water scene, stick neck, 14¼" 150.00
Vase, pk, mc floral spray, bulbous, 6" 45.00
Vase, pk, 2 prs of birds in flowering tree, bk: floral, w/gilt, 31"..800.00
Vase, ruby w/mc floral, blown baluster, scalloped rim, 12x6" 125.00
Vase, wht opal w/mc floral & gold, 8⅞" 65.00
Vase, wht w/bl int, floral w/bird on branch, ruffled, ftd, 10¾" 70.00
Vase, yel w/mc floral, tapered cylinder, 13" 85.00

British Royalty Commemoratives

Royalty commemoratives have been issued for royal events since Edward VI's 1547 coronation through modern-day occasions, so it's possible to start collecting at any period of history. Many collectors begin with Queen Victoria's reign, collecting examples for each succeeding monarch and continuing through modern events.

Some collectors identify with a particular royal personage and limit their collecting to that era, ie., Queen Elizabeth's life and reign. Other collectors look to the future, expanding their collection to include the heir apparents Prince Charles and his first-born son, Prince William.

Royalty commemorative collecting is often further refined around a particular type of collectible. Nearly any item with room for a portrait and a description has been manufactured as a souvenir. Thus royalty commemoratives are available in glass, ceramic, metal, fabric, plastic, and paper. This wide variety of material lends itself to any pocketbook. The range covers expensive limited edition ceramics to inexpensive souvenir key chains, puzzles, matchbooks, etc.

Many recent royalty headline events have been commemorated in a variety of souvenirs. Buying some of these modern commemoratives at the moderate issue prices could be a good investment. After all, today's events are tomorrow's history.

For further study we recommend *British Royal Commemoratives* by our advisor for this category, Audrey Zeder; she is listed in the Directory under Washington.

Key:
A/S — Andrew/Sarah	invest — investiture
ann — anniversary	jub — jubilee
BD — birthday	K/Q — King Queen
C/D — Charles/Diana	LE — limited edition
chr — christening	mem — memorial
Chs — Charles	Pr — Prince
com — commemorative	Prs — Princess
cor — coronation	QM — Queen Mother
EPNS — electro-plated nickel silver	wed — wedding
ILN — Illustrated London News	Wm — William
inscr — inscribed	vis — visit

Album, Royal Family by Panini, completely filled, 1984...............**50.00**
Bank, C/D 1981 wed portrait, bl, Adams, rnd, 3"...........**50.00**
Beaker, George V jub, sepia portrait, mc official design, 4"...........**55.00**
Beaker, wed; C/D, glass, mc portrait, 4⅝"...........**25.00**
Book, Royal Souvenirs, by Geoffrey Warren, hardbk, 1977...............**45.00**
Book, The Queen & Prs Anna, Lisa Sheridan, 1959, hardbk........**25.00**
Booklet, Earl Harewood wed, Pitkins, 1949...........**20.00**
Booklet, Prs Margaret's Wed Day, Pitkins, 1960...........**15.00**
Bookmark, Pr Edward wed, wht leather w/gold decor, 9x1½".......**15.00**
Cards, tribute; Diana, boxed set, 1997, 3½x2½"...........**20.00**
Coin, Prs Diana, 1999 5-pound, special pack, Royal Mint...........**30.00**
Compact, Elizabeth II cor, mc portrait, 3¾"...........**60.00**
Dish, mem; Prs Diana, irid glass, 3½"...........**30.00**
Doll, Elizabeth II, state robes, vinyl, Nisbit, ca 1950, 8½"...........**150.00**
Egg cup, Edward VIII, mc portrait/decor, gold rim, ftd, 1937........**55.00**
Egg cup, Elizabeth II 2002 jub, blk silhouette, ftd...........**15.00**
Ephemera, Elizabeth II 1977 jub pub beer mat, cb, 4x4"...........**6.00**
Figure, Prs Diana, HP, dk bl drsss, 1997, 11¾"...........**85.00**
Magazine, Daily Mail, Prs Diana mem, 9-6-97...........**30.00**
Magazine, Observer, Elizabeth II 1983 visit to California, 3-13-83.**30.00**
Magazine, Sphere, Prs Margaret wed, 5-14-60...........**35.00**
Miniature, George V cor jug, mk K/Q decor, T&K, 3"...........**75.00**
Miniature, photo album of 1982 Royal family, 1¼x2"...........**35.00**
Mug, C/D engagement, lion/unicorn/announcement, Mays........**150.00**
Mug, C/D wed, milk glass, mc portrait/decor...........**25.00**
Mug, Elizabeth II 2002 jub, queen's mc portrait on maroon...........**20.00**
Mug, George VI cor, mc portrait/decor Art Deco style, 3"...........**35.00**
Mug, Pr Henry 1984 BD, mc decor, miniature, 1½"...........**35.00**
Mug, Prs Beatrice 1988 BD, wht w/gold decor, Wedgwood, 3"...**100.00**
Mug, Prs Diana 5th ann of death, LE 50, Chown...........**70.00**
Newspaper, Di Badly Injured, News of the World, 8-31-97...........**60.00**
Newspaper, Edward VII funeral, The Queen, 5-21-1910...............**30.00**
Newspaper, Prs Diana mem, The Sun, 9-1-97...........**20.00**
Novelty, Eliabeth II cor pocketknife, mc decor, 5x2½"...........**45.00**
Photograph, Prs Diana 1987 at London gala, blk & wht, 6x8"......**50.00**
Photograph, Prs Elizabeth & Margaret, blk & wht, 7½x6"...........**50.00**
Pin-bk button, George VI 1949 New Zealand visit, mc decor, 1½".**35.00**
Plate, C/D wed, mc portrait, emb design on rim, 9½"...........**65.00**
Plate, Elizabeth II 1959 Canada visit, mc decor, Paragon, 10½".**125.00**

Plate, King George and Queen Elizabeth 1939 Canada Visit, Royal Winton, 10½", $55.00.

Plate, Prs Anne 1973 wed, bl jasper, Wedgwood, 4½"...........**60.00**
Plate, Prs Diana 1987, 3 portraits, Royal Doulton, 10½"...........**250.00**
Plate, Queen Elizabeth cor, #1609, 9"...........**40.00**
Postcard, Elizabeth II 2002 jug, queen's portrait+5 previous monarchs..**5.00**
Postcard, George V at front WWI, mc, Daily Mail, unused...........**15.00**
Postcard, Prs Margaret 2002 mem, mc portrait w/doves & rose.......**5.00**
Poster, Prs Diana 1998, Dresses for Humanity, mc, 21x34"...........**45.00**
Pressed glass, Pr Wm 10th BD, portrait, amber, 3½"...........**35.00**
Print, Prs Diana mem, artist sgn Heiner, 11x16"...........**50.00**
Puzzle, Prs Diana mem, The English Rose, 5 pc, MIB...........**50.00**

Spoon, King George VI, relief portrait/decor, 4¼"...........**30.00**
Spoon, loving; C/D wed, brass, relief decor, 9½"...........**45.00**
Spoon, mc portrait w/tiara, SP, ca 1982...........**25.00**
Teapot, Elizabeth II 2002 jub, head shape, gold crown, 8"...........**95.00**
Thimble, Elizabeth II 2002 jub, young queen's portrait, mc decor...**6.00**
Tin, Eliabeth II cor, mc portrait, octagonal, 5x4x1"...........**35.00**
Tin, George VI cor, mc portrait & decor, octagonal, 5x4"...........**40.00**
Tin, Queen Elizabeth cor, full-face portrait, 7"...........**25.00**
Towel, Elizabeth II 2002 jub, queen's portrait, mc guards decor....**10.00**
Trinket box, C/D wed, heart shape, 2¼x1¾"...........**30.00**
Trinket box, George VI Canada visit, ftd, w/lid, Adams...........**75.00**

Broadsides

Webster defines a broadside as simply a large sheet of paper printed on one side. During the 1880s, they were the most practical means of mass-communication. By the middle of the century, they had become elaborate and lengthy with information, illustrations, portraits, and fancy border designs. Those printed on coated stock are usually worth more.

$25 Reward...Samuel Minot..., 1853, folded, 11x10"...........**200.00**
A Solid South, appeal to vote against Tilden, 1876, 16x22".......**325.00**
Cattle auction, PA, 1893, cattle images/herd described, 18¼x12"..**285.00**
Don't Give Up the Ship, War of 1812, 11x18"...........**310.00**
Eastern & Western Mail Stages..., July 1835, 19¾x13¼"........**1,380.00**
Fare $2 & Bound for Albany..., printed, ca 1835, 12¼x7¼".......**750.00**
Great Nat'l Moral & Political Exhibition, PT Barnum, 1856, 13x10½".**400.00**
Hon WF Cody Buffalo Bill...US Army, chromolitho, 1880, 33½x25".**11,500.00**
Labor Day Excursion, Grand Trunk & Canadian RR, 1939, 7x16".**55.00**
Marshal's Sale...1861 at 12 o'clock..., laid down, 10½x8¼"........**430.00**
Mr Fillmore's Speech Delivered at Albany, 1856, EX...........**650.00**
Mt Desert & Machias Inslide Line, steamer scene, 1872, 19x12".**1,150.00**
NE Rum Crystal Spring Distillery...MA, chromolitho, 1880, 18x24"..**2,875.00**
New Eastern & Western Route...Central Railroads, 1857, 39x22".**515.00**
Now Is the Time To Serve..., MA, 1861-62, 18½x23¼"...........**750.00**
OH Monument Fund, Lincoln memorial contributions, 1865, 8¾x7½"..**400.00**
People's Ticket, Thurman, Clinton & Tayler, 1820, 11x18"........**135.00**
Phoenix Hall, Tableaux Vivants & Canocert, MO Soldier Benefit, 6x12".**1,750.00**
Photography work available, services/prices, NH, 1866, 9½x6"..**125.00**
Pie Plant Extraordinary, Canadian Steamship & Express RR travel, 9x12"..**215.00**
Raise Mules & Get Rich...Vermont, chromolitho on paper, 1890s, 20x15".**700.00**
Shall the Union Be Preserved..., Civil War era, 18x12"...........**1,725.00**
Shiloh! Campaign of 1862, condemns Grant for defeat, 17½x11½".**800.00**
Side-wheeler boat excursion, 4 stops to Richmond, 1760s, 14x11"..**200.00**
Splendid Amusement, Startling Feats of Legerdemain, 1855, 18x8".**55.00**
Steam Packet General Lincoln departure notice, 1833, 12x10", EX .**920.00**
Theatrical, John Wilkes Booth will appear..., Jan 1863, 12½x4½".**975.00**
4th of July Celebration, Niagara Falls, 1862, 13x4½"...........**65.00**

Bronzes

Thomas Ball, George Bessell, and Leonard Volk were some of the earliest American sculptors who produced figures in bronze for home decor during the 1840s. Pieces of historical significance were the most popular, but by the 1880s a more fanciful type of artwork took hold. Some of the fine sculptors of the day were Daniel Chester French, Augustus St. Gaudens, and John Quincy Adams Ward. Bronzes reached the height of their popularity at the turn of the century. The American West was portrayed to its fullest by Remington, Russell, James Frazier, Hermon MacNeil, and Solon Borglum. Animals of every species were modeled by A.P. Proctor, Paul Bartlett, and Albert Laellele, to name but a few.

Art Nouveau and Art Deco influenced the medium during the '20s, evidenced by the works of Allen Clark, Harriet Frismuth, E.F. Sanford, and Bessie P. Vonnoh.

Be aware that recasts abound. While often esthetically satisfactory, they are not original and should be priced accordingly. In much the same manner as prints are evaluated, the original castings made under the direction of the artist are the most valuable. Later castings from the original mold are worth less. A recast is not made from the original mold. Instead, a rubber-like substance is applied to the bronze, peeled away, and filled with wax. Then, using the same 'lost wax' procedure as the artist uses on completion of his original wax model, a clay-like substance is formed around the wax figure and the whole fired to vitrify the clay. The wax, of course, melts away, hence the term 'lost wax.' Recast bronzes lose detail and are somewhat smaller than the original due to the shrinkage of the clay mold.

American School, Wine Goddess, cast, gr patina, mk IWP, 1940s, 14"..**230.00**
Austrian, lamp: Middle Eastern lady's boudoir scene, cold-pnt, 14"..**2,115.00**
Berndorf, dancer in puff-sleeve gathered bodice, tall boots, 18"..**1,100.00**
Bourgouin, Eugene; Cupid, silvered, Susse Freres ed, 12" L.........**800.00**
Bulio, woman w/grapes, putto beside her, marble base, 25"......**3,360.00**
Cartier, 2 dogs, 1 seated, 1 standing/peering, marble base, 13x20"..**1,065.00**
Chapu, H; woman reaching up face of stone wall, Barbenienne, 29"..**2,185.00**
Charpentier, Felix Maurice; Improvisateur, flute player/dog, 31"..**1,725.00**
Chiparus, dancing pr, mc/gilt elaborate attire, ivory faces/arms, 25"..**28,000.00**
Clemenien, nude dancing on 1 ft, holding baton above head, 25"..**1,550.00**
Coriolan, Emile; bust of Turkish infantryman, chainmail helmet, 34"..**8,800.00**
Coudray, winged Victory, sword resting in right hand, gears at ft, 36"..**3,360.00**
De Raniere, A; First Cigarette, ¾-figure of boy, 22"..............**1,120.00**
Debut, standing Norseman, hands crossed over axe, 22"..........**1,765.00**
Descomps, E Joe; seated female nude looking bk to right, 16x24"..**1,600.00**
Drouot, E; Curious, classical woman w/2 doves at her ft, 24"..**3,920.00**
Drouot, E; Victory, winged figure, w/gilt/brn patina, 40"..........**3,450.00**
Droust, E; musing inventor, seated, w/compass & vice, 23"......**1,790.00**
Dubricand, A; kingfisher, fish in mouth, in marshy base, 1870, 7"..**670.00**
Dumage, H; lady in draped robe, breast exposed, w/sword & shield, 38"..**5,300.00**
Dumage, H; 4 putti frolick w/goat, EX detail/color, 23" W......**6,700.00**
Falconet, nude, standing, drape across left leg, 23"..................**1,950.00**

Fremiet, Joan of Arc, EX patina, $7,840.00. (Photo courtesy Jackson's Auctioneers & Appraisers)

Gardet, Georges; Tiger Attacking Tortoise, dk gr-brn, #535L, 18" L.**1,035.00**
Gaudez, A; David, standing w/slingshot, revolving base, Tiffany, 32"..**5,000.00**
Gaudez, A; Etoile du Matin, draped lady, right arm raised, 27"..**2,240.00**
Gauguie, H; seminude male hunter steps over crouching lion, 1885, 20"..**1,950.00**
Gruber, bust of lady, elaborate floral bonnet, gilt/red patina, 12x13"..**770.00**
Hebert, Emile; seminude leaning against sq pillar smelling flower, 25"..**2,000.00**
Kunst, 2-figure fountain: nude & creature (boy-serpent), 32"..**5,300.00**

Ledieu, Signoret; Diana seated on a rock, fish below, marble base, 34".**5,000.00**
Legrand, August Ernest; Ready for Battle, warrior, 20"................**285.00**
Lemoyne, seminude female warrior w/flag, Aux Armes lettered base, 30".**2,800.00**
Levasseur, A; Diane, right arm raised, bow behind her, 28".....**3,000.00**
Lorenzl, Josef; dancer on 1 leg, on onyx base, 1925, Paris, 12"..**1,175.00**
Louchet, Peyre; Nouveau woman w/flowing hair, 2-color, Paris, 13"..**1,175.00**
MacMonnies, Frederick; Pan of Rohallion, holds 2 flutes to mouth, 29"..**16,000.00**
Madrassi, Diana seated, looking w/hand over eyes, dog at ft, 28"..**4,480.00**
Marin, J; winged Victory standing over seated male, marble base, 32"..**2,745.00**
Marioton, Eug; Patrie, seminude warrior, left arm extended, 37"..**2,800.00**
Marjoulle, A; seminude warrior repairs armor, holds hammer, 31"..**3,470.00**
Meurice, Froment; seminude being tempted by devil, gold doré, 36"..**11,000.00**
Monsi, pheasant on cvd onyx base, 13"..**785.00**
Moreau, M; Colombe, admiring bird perched on raised right arm, 26"..**3,195.00**
Moreau, M; dancing lady, putto ea side, marble base, 1885, 20"..**3,360.00**
Moreau, M; draped nymph dancing w/harp, 1900, Concour, 29"..**5,290.00**
Moreau, M; seminude w/bird & grapes, 2-color, 35"...............**3,000.00**
Moreau, M; woman at water well, swivel marble base, 26"......**3,900.00**
Moreau, M; 2 draped maidens dancing w/Pan, 23"...................**3,360.00**
Morise, Marie Louis; Napoleon on horse, gilt w/red accents, 26".**5,200.00**
Nelson, AB; Mutine, bust of lady, 18"..**560.00**
Pautrot, Ferdinand; Startled Finch on a Perch, gold-gr patina, 5"..**260.00**
Philippe, P; nude female on brn onyx base, ca 1930, 12½"......**1,150.00**
Philippe, P; standing maid, gilt/patina/ivory, 1920s, 83V, 13"..**3,525.00**
Picault, E; Honor Patria, seminude warrior w/sword, 3-color, 31".**5,300.00**
Picault, E; Memoria, draped lady sits before memorial marker, 31"..**4,700.00**
Picault, E; Pax et labor, man gazing down, hammer in right hand, 29"..**3,000.00**
Picault, E; seated nude at well, wall behind, marble base, 27"..**4,425.00**
Picault, E; 2 classical women on globe, 2-color, mc marble base, 30"..**5,600.00**
Plagnet, 2 leaping antelope, blk marble base, 11x23"...............**600.00**
Pollet, Nouveau semi-nude, winged putti at her ft, 20"...............**900.00**
Rioton, A; Le Travail, blacksmith w/anvil, 1885, 31"...............**3,350.00**
Roman Bronze Works NY, President & Mrs B Harrison, 26", pr.**4,000.00**
Roulleau, J; winged Victory & blacksmith on marble base, 54"..**17,360.00**
Salmson, Jean-Jules; Pandore, silvered, on marble base, 18"....**4,300.00**
Schork, Dutch peasant girl, 2-tone verde gr patina, #82/CA, 34".**4,750.00**
Scudder, Janet; Young Pan, playing pipes, dk brn patina, Gorham, 14"..**8,625.00**
SE/93, charging stag, 13x10"..**1,680.00**
Unsgn, bust of Diana, EX detail & color, 24"...........................**2,500.00**
Unsgn, man walking 2 lions, blk marble base, 28" L...............**1,960.00**
Unsgn, plant stand, seminude w/extended hoof ft supports onyx top, 33".**4,300.00**
Unsgn, 2 nude wrestlers, After the Antique, Barbedienne Fonderu, 15"..**4,700.00**
Vaerenbergh, VG; bust of girl; head/socle of ivory, 22"...........**3,720.00**
Vanderstrader, bust of Lady, gold dore w/ivory face, marble ped, 9".**750.00**
Vermare, Andre Cedar; Joan of Arc, gilt-bonze, 11/11/09, 15"...**920.00**
Villanis, Emmanuele; Esmerelda, fortune teller, Garanti Paris, 29".**2,950.00**
Villanis, Emmanuele; Sapho, playing harp, Paris, ca 1900, 29"..**4,115.00**
Waagen, North African musician, cold-pnt, 1900, 22"...........**1,410.00**

Brouwer

Theophilis A. Brouwer operated a one-man studio on Middle Lane in East Hampton, Long Island, from 1894 until 1903, when he relocated to West Hampton. He threw rather thin vesssels of light, porous white clay which he fired at a relatively low temperature. He then glazed them and fired them in an open-flame kiln, where he manipulated them with a technique he later patented as 'flame painting.' This resulted in lustered glazes, mostly in the orange and amber family, with organic, free-form patterns. Because of the type of clay he used and the low firing, the wares are brittle and often found with damage. This deficiency has kept them undervalued in the art pottery market. Brouwer turned to sculpture around 1911. His pottery often carries the whalebone mark, M-shaped for the Middle Lane Pottery, and reminiscent of the genuine whalebones

Brouwer purportedly found on his property. Other pieces are marked 'Flame' or 'Brouwer.' Our advisors for this category are Suzanne Perrault and Dave Rago; they are listed in the Directory under New Jersey.

Key: fp — fire-painted

Bud vase, fp yel/brn lustre, flared w/squat base, 7x4", EX, $400 to..**600.00**
Vase, appl leaves, fp gr/orange/yel, flared/ruffled, spherical, 5", EX.**2,100.00**
Vase, fp amber/gr/yel, flat shoulder, 3½x4" **1,035.00**
Vase, fp amber/orange/yel/brn, closed-in rim, 5x5½", NM..........**920.00**
Vase, fp amber/yel/bright brn, 5x6", rstr base o/w EX, from $350 to..**450.00**
Vase, fp amber/yel/orange, ribbed, factory drilled, label, 13x9", NM.**5,750.00**
Vase, fp bright yel/orange/brn, 6x6", 2 drill holes o/w EX **975.00**
Vase, fp purple/amber/yel, flat shoulder, 6x4", NM..................**1,090.00**
Vase, fp yel/orange/purple, 4x5", VG/EX, from $300 to..............**400.00**
Vase, thick bronze dripping over fp, partial label, 12x7", EX-..**8,625.00**

Brownies by Palmer Cox

Created by Palmer Cox in 1883, the Brownies charmed children through the pages of books and magazines, as dolls, on their dinnerware, in advertising material, and on souvenirs. Each had his own personality, among them The Bellhop, The London Bobby, The Chairman, and Uncle Sam. But the oversized, triangular face with the startled expression, the protruding tummy, and the spindle legs were characteristics of them all. They were inspired by the Scottish legends related to Cox as a child by his parents, who were of English descent. His introduction of the Brownies to the world was accomplished by a poem called *The Brownies Ride*. Books followed in rapid succession, thirteen in the series, all written as well as illustrated by Palmer Cox.

By the late 1890s, the Brownies were active in advertising. They promoted such products as games, coffee, toys, patent medicines, and rubber boots. 'Greenies' were the Brownies' first cousins, created by Cox to charm and to woo through the pages of the advertising almanacs of the G.G. Green Company of New Jersey. Perhaps the best-known endorsement in the Brownies' career was for the Kodak Brownie, which became so popular and sold in such volume that their name became synonymous with this type of camera.

Since the late 1970s a biography on Palmer Cox has been written, a major rock band had their concert T-shirts adorned with his brownies, and a reproduction of the Uncle Sam candlestick is known to exist. Bacause of the resurging interest in Cox's brownies beware of other possible reproductions. Our advisor for this category is Anne Kier; she is listed in the Directory under Ohio.

Ad, Brownie Rubber Stamps & the Greatest Show on Earth, 10x7", EX.**15.00**
Advertising card, Brownies watching ball game, Lud Havener, EX...**80.00**
Ashtray, Brownie scene, RS Germany, 1913 ....**95.00**
Basket, SP, Brownies w/chocolate advertising, Tufts **265.00**
Book, A Fox Grows Old, 1946, EX..**15.00**
Book, Adventures of a Brownie, Miss Mulock, 1898, EX **80.00**
Book, Another Brownie Book, NY, 1890, 1st ed, w/dust jacket, VG..**250.00**
Book, Another Brownie Book, 144 pgs, 1967, 9½x6¾", EX **15.00**
Book, Brownie Clown of Brownie Town, 1908 ....**235.00**
Book, Brownies & Goblins, Grosset Dunlap, no date, VG...........**45.00**
Book, Brownies & Other Stories, ca 1900, VG.........................**55.00**
Book, Brownies & Other Stories, 1918, EX **40.00**
Book, Brownies & Prince Florimel, Century, 1918, VG **95.00**
Book, Brownies & the Farmer, 1902, 8¾x6¾", VG+ **40.00**
Book, Brownies at Home, w/dust cover, 1942, VG **35.00**
Book, Brownies at Home, 144 pgs, Century Co, 1893, VG...........**85.00**
Book, Brownies in Fairyland, Century Co **45.00**
Book, Comic Yarns in Verse, Prose & Picture, 1898, 7½x5", VG.**18.00**

Book, Funny Animals, 1 color image, many blk/wht, 1903, 10x7½", VG..**18.00**
Book, Funny Stories About Funny People, 1905, EX.....................**35.00**
Book, Little Goody Two Shoes, 1903, EX **40.00**
Book, Queerie Queers, color plates, EX................................**145.00**
Book, The Brownies, Their Book, 1897, EX **185.00**
Book, Wit & Wisdom, 32 pgs, 1890, 7x4½", VG **15.00**
Bottle, soda; emb Brownies, M...**30.00**
Brownie Portrait Cubes, McLoughlin Bros, c Cox 1892, VG......**300.00**
Calendar, Brownies, color litho, 1898, EX **225.00**
Camera, Eastman-Kodak Brownie 2A, in orig box...................**145.00**
Candlestick, Bobby, majolica, 7½" **300.00**
Candy dish, 15 Brownies, ball ft, Tufts SP, 7x5½"...................**265.00**
Cigar box, wood w/Our Brownies emb inner lid label, EX+........**185.00**
Cigar holder/ashtray, full-figure Brownie, Pairpoint SP..........**425.00**
Comic book, The Brownies, Dell Four-Color, #398, 1952, VG.....**20.00**
Creamer, Little Boy Blue verse & 4 Brownies, gold trim, china....**95.00**
Creamer, Scottsman head, majolica, 3¼" **100.00**
Cup, SP w/9 enameled Brownies, Middletown Plate Co, 3"........**235.00**
Cup & saucer, demi; comical action Brownies, Ceramic Art Co..**110.00**
Figure, Chinaman, papier-mache head, 9", EX **450.00**
Figures, papier-mache w/stick legs, jtd arms, 1900s, 5", EX, 4 for .**1,500.00**
Fruit crate label, harvesting orange juice, 1930s, 10x11", EX........**25.00**

Game, Nine Pins, litho-on-wood bowling set, McLoughlin, complete with original wood stands and balls, EX (in original box), $2,000.00.

Humidor, Bobby head figural, majolica, 6" **250.00**
Ice cream bag, Cox illus, 5¢ orig value, 1930s, M......................**40.00**
Magazine page, Ladies' Home Journal, Cox illus, ca 1890 ....**15.00**
Match holder, Brownie on striker, majolica **235.00**
Needle book, Brownies, 1892 World's Fair, rare **75.00**
Nodder, Brownies (3) on donkey, bsk, German, 1890s, 6½x6¼"..**1,950.00**
Paper doll, Indian Brownie, Lion Coffee, EX **40.00**
Paperweight, Brownie figural, SP...**145.00**
Pencil box, rolling pin shape, 15 Brownies in boat **95.00**
Picture, on bank of river, bl ink, fr, 7x5¾", EX.........................**70.00**
Pin box, Brownies running across lid, SP, EX..........................**150.00**
Pitcher, china, Brownies playing golf on tan, 6" **185.00**
Pitcher, china, 2 Brownies on front, 3 on bk, 4½" **110.00**
Plate, porc, mk La Francaise, 7"...**85.00**
Plate, SP, Brownies on rim, 8½" **95.00**
Print, Brownies fishing, matted, 1895, 13½x15½".......................**55.00**
Print, Brownies toboggan ride, matted, 1895, 13½x15½" **55.00**
Rubber stamp, set of 12, NM **100.00**
Sheet music, Dance of the Brownies......................................**30.00**
Sign, emb Brownies on tin, Howell's Root Beer, EX..................**185.00**
Sign, orange crate; serving & drinking juice, Brownies Brand, 11x10".**35.00**
Stationery, Ten Little Brownies, envelopes/note paper/box, 1930s, G.**25.00**
Table set, brass, emb Brownies, 3-pc (knife/fork/spoon), no box...**85.00**
Table set, brass, emb Brownies, 6", in orig box **95.00**
Toy, Movie Top, litho tin w/3 windows, ca 1927, 1⅞x4¾" dia ...**150.00**
Trade card, Estey Organ Co, playing instruments, 3x5" **15.00**

Trade card, Mitchell, Lewis & Stave Co, 3x5", VG......................30.00
Trade card, Sheriff's Sale Segars, Brownies & product, 5x3" 25.00
Tray, china, 2 fencing Brownies, self hdls, 6¼x4½"....................110.00
Tray, tin, Brownies w/giant dish of ice cream, 13¼x10½", EX....185.00

Brush-McCoy

George Brush began his career in the pottery industry in 1901 working for the J.B. Owens Pottery Co. in Zanesville, Ohio. He left the company in 1907 to go into business for himself, only to have fire completely destroy his pottery less than one year after it was founded. In 1909 he became associated with J.W. McCoy, who had operated a pottery of his own in Roseville, Ohio, since 1899. The two men formed the Brush-McCoy Pottery in 1911, locating their headquarters in Zanesville. After the merger, the company expanded and produced not only staple commercial wares but also fine artware. Lines of the highest quality such as Navarre, Venetian, Oriental, and Sylvan were equal to that of their larger competitors. Because very little of the ware was marked, it is often mistaken for Weller, Roseville, or Peters and Reed.

In 1918 after a fire in Zanesville had destroyed the manufacturing portion of that plant, all production was contained in their Roseville (Ohio) plant #2. A stoneware type of clay was used there, and as a result the artware lines of Jewel, Zuniart, King Tut, Florastone, Jetwood, Krakle-Kraft, and Panelart are so distinctive that they are more easily recognizable. Examples of these lines are unique and very beautiful, also quite rare and highly prized!

After McCoy died, the family withdrew their interests, and in 1925 the name of the firm was changed to The Brush Pottery. The era of hand-decorated art pottery production had passed for the most part, having been almost completely replaced by commercial lines. The Brush-Barnett family retained their interest in the pottery until 1981 when it was purchased by the Dearborn Company.

For more information we recommend *The Collector's Encyclopedia of Brush-McCoy Pottery* by Sharon and Bob Huxford, and *Sanford's Guide to Brush-McCoy Pottery, Books I and II*, written by Martha and Steve Sanford, our advisors for this category, and edited by David P. Sanford. They are listed in the Directory under California.

Of all the wares bearing the later Brush script mark, their figural cookie jars are the most collectible, and several have been reproduced. Information on Brush cookie jars (as well as confusing reproductions) can be found in *Collector's Encyclopedia of Cookie Jars* by Joyce and Fred Roerig; they are listed in the Directory under South Carolina. Beware! Cookie jars marked Brush-McCoy are not authentic.

Cookie Jars

Antique Touring Car..700.00
Boy w/Balloons..800.00
Chick in Nest (+)..400.00
Cinderella Pumpkin, #W32...250.00
Circus Horse, gr (+)..950.00
Clown, yel pants...200.00
Clown Bust, #W49...300.00
Cookie House, #W31..125.00
Covered Wagon, dog finial, #W30, minimum value (+)............550.00
Cow w/Cat on Bk, brn, #W10 (+)................................125.00
Cow w/Cat on Bk, purple, minimum value (+)......................1,000.00
Davy Crockett, no gold, mk USA (+).............................300.00
Dog & Basket...250.00
Donkey Cart, ears down, gray, #W33 ....400.00
Donkey Cart, ears up, #W33, minimum value 800.00
Elephant w/Ice Cream Cone (+) 500.00
Elephant w/Monkey on Bk, minimum value....................5,000.00

Fish, #W52 (+)..500.00
Formal Pig, gold trim, #W7 Brush USA (+)..................475.00
Formal Pig, no gold, gr hat & coat (+)..........................300.00
Gas Lamp, #K1 ....75.00
Granny, pk apron, bl dots on skirt................................325.00
Granny, plain skirt, minimum value (+)........................400.00
Happy Bunny, wht, #W25...225.00
Hen on Basket, unmk...125.00
Hillbilly Frog, minimum value (+)..............................4,500.00
Humpty Dumpty, w/beany & bow tie (+)......................275.00

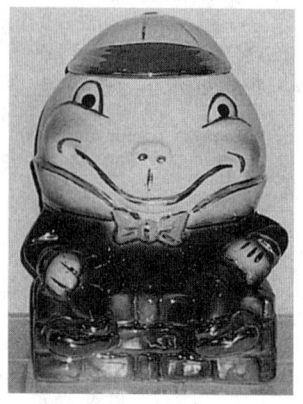

Humpty Dumpty with beanie and bow tie, gold trim (has been reproduced), from $400.00 to $500.00. (Photo courtesy Joyce and Fred Roerig)

Humpty Dumpty, w/peaked hat & shoes 225.00
Laughing Hippo, #W27 (+)..750.00
Little Angel (+)...800.00
Little Boy Blue, gold trim, #K25, sm............................700.00
Little Boy Blue, no gold, #K24 Brush USA, lg (+)..........800.00
Little Girl, #017 (+)...550.00
Little Red Riding Hood, gold trim, mk lg, minimum value (+) ..850.00
Little Red Riding Hood, no gold, #K24 USA, sm 550.00
Night Owl...125.00
Old Clock, #W10...150.00
Old Shoe, #W23 (+)...125.00
Panda, #W21 (+)..250.00
Peter, Peter Pumpkin Eater, #W24 ....300.00
Peter Pan, gold trim, lg (+)..800.00
Peter Pan, no gold, sm...550.00
Puppy Police (+)..585.00
Raggedy Ann, #W16..475.00
Sitting Pig (+) 400.00
Smiling Bear, #W46 (+)..350.00
Squirrel on Log, #W26..100.00
Squirrel w/Top Hat, blk coat & hat...............................275.00
Squirrel w/Top Hat, gr coat...250.00
Stylized Owl..350.00
Stylized Siamese, #W41..450.00
Teddy Bear, ft apart...250.00
Teddy Bear, ft together...200.00
Treasure Chest, #W28...170.00

Miscellaneous

Basket, Floradora, hanging, #457, 1929, 8", from $75 to............110.00
Bowl, Jetwood, Type I, #01, 5" opening, from $450 to 550.00
Bowl, Matt Green, #195, 6", from $45 to.....................................70.00
Bowl, Zuniart, incurvate rim, #01, 4", from $350 to...................400.00
Candlestick, Brown Onyx, #032, 10", from $125 to 150.00
Candlesticks, Majolica, brn, #025, 3", pr, from $90 to.................110.00
Creamer, Corn, #59, 4", from $150 to 175.00

Cuspidor, Blue Onyx, #01, 7", from $150 to **175.00**
Cuspidor, Decorated Ivory, from $250 to.......................................**300.00**
Cuspidor, Willow, bl, #014, 1915, from $75 to.............................**150.00**
Flower block, Florastone, #05, 3½", from $200 to **225.00**
Jar, porch; Blue Drip, #0150, 30", from $1,800 to....................**3,200.00**
Jar, sand; Athenian, #444, w/sand tray, from $1,200 to............**1,600.00**
Jardiniere, Decorated Sylvan, 1916, 7½", from $600 to **900.00**
Jardiniere, Lotus, #235, 1917, 6", from $175 to.........................**225.00**
Jardiniere, Moderne Kolorkraft, #260, 1929, 10", from $175 to..**200.00**
Jardiniere, Scenic Egyptian, brn, 1912, 10½", from $400 to **500.00**
Jardiniere, Sylvan II, #280, 1935, 9½", from $75 to **100.00**
Jardiniere, Venetian, #218, 1913, from $350 to **400.00**
Jardiniere & pedestal, Blended, #2360, from $700 to **800.00**
Jug, Dutch Kids, #53, 1912, 4-pt, from $125 to **175.00**
Jug, Green Onyx, #130, 10", from $175 to..................................**200.00**
Lamp, oil; Olympia, early 1900s, from $200 to **250.00**
Lamp, Vestal Duo-Tone, #729, 1933, 11", from $450 to.............**600.00**
Planter, Swan, #631, 1948, 6x9½", from $50 to...........................**60.00**
Tankard, Loy-Nel-Art, late, 11", from $250 to.............................**300.00**
Vase, Aegean Inlaid, cylindrical, #97, 11", from $200 to.............**250.00**
Vase, Berries & Leaves (aka Bittersweet), #750, 1945, 6", $40 to .**50.00**

Vase, Blue Onyx, #112, 9½", from $125.00 to $200.00.

Vase, Brown Onyx, #049, 7", from $60 to **80.00**
Vase, Cleo, shouldered, #040, 1914, 12", from $700 to **900.00**
Vase, Ivotint, #0192, 1929, 7½", from $125 to **150.00**
Vase, Jewel, slim, flared ft, #041, 10", from $500 to....................**650.00**
Vase, King Tut, Egyptian Scarab, #046, 12" **1,800.00**
Vase, Moderne Kolorkraft, #0155, 1929, 5", from $75 to **100.00**
Vase, New Art Vellum, Nymph, #427, 1932, 9", from $50 to **60.00**
Vase, Panelart, #071, 9", from $1,500 to **2,000.00**
Vase, Rosewood, 1904, 9", from $150 to **175.00**
Vase, Southern Belle, #218, from $60 to **75.00**

Buffalo Pottery

The founding of the Buffalo Pottery in Buffalo, New York, in 1901, was a direct result of the success achieved by John Larkin through his innovative methods of marketing 'Sweet Home Soap.' Choosing to omit 'middle-man' profits, Larkin preferred to deal directly with the consumer and offered premiums as an enticement for sales. The pottery soon proved a success in its own right and began producing advertising and commemorative items for other companies, as well as commercial tableware. In 1905 they introduced their Blue Willow line after extensive experimentation resulted in the development of the first successful underglaze cobalt achieved by an American company. Between 1905 and 1909, a line of pitchers and jugs were hand decorated in historical, literary, floral, and outdoor themes. Twenty-nine styles are known to have been made.

Their most famous line was Deldare Ware, the bulk of which was made from 1908 to 1909. It was hand decorated after illustrations by Cecil Aldin. Views of English life were portrayed in detail through unusual use of color against the natural olive green cast of the body. Today the 'Fallowfield Hunt' scenes are more difficult to locate than 'Scenes of Village Life in Ye Olden Days.' A Deldare calendar plate was made in 1910. These are very rare and are highly valued by collectors. The line was revived in 1923 and dropped again in 1925. Every piece was marked 'Made at Ye Buffalo Pottery, Deldare Ware Underglaze.' Most are dated, though date has no bearing on the value. Emerald Deldare was made on the same olive body and on standard Deldare Ware shapes, featured historical scenes and Art Nouveau decorations. Most pieces are found with a 1911 date stamp. Production was very limited due to the intricate, time-consuming detail. Needless to say, it is very rare and extremely desirable.

Abino Ware, most of which was made in 1912, also used standard Deldare shapes, but its colors were earthy and the decorations more delicately applied. Sailboats, windmills, and country scenes were favored motifs. These designs were achieved by overpainting transfer prints and were often signed by the artist. The ware is marked 'Abino' in hand-printed block letters. Production was limited; and as a result, examples of this line are scarce today.

Commercial or institutional ware was another of Buffalo Pottery's crowning achievements. In 1917 vitrified china production began, and the firm produced for accounts worldwide. After 1956 all of their wares bore the name Buffalo China. Buffalo China (commercial and institutional ware) is being produced today by Oneida Silver Company.

Our advisor for this category is Lila Shrader; she is listed in the Directory under California.

See also Bluebird China.

Key:
BS — bottom stamped   SL — side logo
C — commercial ware marked   TM — top marked

Abino

Cup & saucer, windmill & canal scene **395.00**
Plate, windmill scene, 10" **510.00**
Toothpick holder, seascape, lighthouse in distance, 2½" **425.00**
Vase, sailing scene w/distant shoreline, 8" **985.00**
Vase, windmill scene, cylindrical, 6½" **880.00**

Commercial Ware

Ashtray/matchbox holder, Biltmore/Los Angeles, 5¾" dia............**45.00**
Butter pat, 'Finer's' in blk script on ivory, 2½" **34.00**
Butter pat, clipper ship decor, 1927 ....**26.00**
Butter pat, lion logo for Harry M Stevens Inc................................**19.00**
Butter pat, Sea Cave, Multifleure, 2½" **48.00**
Butter pat, The Tacoma, TM in shades of gray & gr......................**28.00**
Butter pat, USSB, Granite State pattern, 2¾" **12.00**
Children's ware, Mother Goose plate for Statler Hotel, 7" **35.00**
Creamer, Blue Willow, hdl, ind, 3¼" **39.00**
Creamer, Blue Willow, no hdl, dtd 1927, ind..................................**29.00**
Creamer, Chatham Bars Inn, sea gull decor, no hdl, ind, 2¾" **26.00**
Creamer, Hotel Clark, no hdl, ind..**17.00**
Creamer, Mandalay, no hdl, ind, 2¾" **29.00**
Creamer, Salvation Army, no hdl, ind, 2¼" **38.00**
Creamer, USBF w/fisheries' flag, hdl, 1927, ind, 2¾" **88.00**
Cup & saucer, demitasse; Palace Hotel (San Francisco), BS **33.00**
Cup & saucer, Fallen Leaf Lodge, BS, 1927 ....**48.00**
Cup & saucer, LAAC (Los Angeles Athletic Club), 1926............**59.00**
Cup & saucer, Tahoe Tavern...**47.00**

Gravy boat, Kenmore, various colors, 1920-30s, ea from $9 to **15.00**
Jam/jelly container, gr checkered border, w/lid, 1923, 3¾"............**26.00**
Jam/jelly container, tan w/brn or blk band, w/lid, 3½" **14.00**
Mug, coffee; Kenmore, various colors, 1980s-2000s, from $3 to **6.00**
Mug, coffee; tan w/color band, 1980s/2000s, from $2 to **4.00**
Mug, Roycroft (Oneida), 4" **23.00**
Mug, Sea Cave, Multifleure, 4½"..**55.00**
Mug, US Army Medical Department, 1980s-2000s, 3½", from $8 to..**12.00**
Mustard, Masonic emblem, Wilmington, slotted lid, 1923, 2½" ...**22.00**
Mustard, WCCC w/crossed golf clubs, slotted lid, 1927, 2½" **32.00**
Pitcher, Salvation Army, 1927, 7"...**160.00**
Plate, Blue Willow, Oneida, 8¼"..**7.00**
Plate, dinner; Pat's Café/Fine Beer & Wine, 8¼" **28.00**
Plate, dinner; Roycroft, 1926, 9¾"...**97.00**
Plate, grill; Blue Willow, Buffalo China, very early......................**45.00**
Plate, salad; Jonesey' Jolly... w/blk-face musical notes, 1925, 8½" .**126.00**
Platter, Ahwahnee Hotel (for Yosemite Nat'l Park), 1929, 9x6"..**46.00**
Platter, Lenhardt superimposed over lg detailed tree, 1923, 8x6"..**22.00**
Platter, Palace Hotel, San Francisco, 1917, 9½x6½"....................**18.00**
Platter, USFS, 1927, 9x6" **98.00**
Relish dish, delicate floral design w/fluted edge, 1920, 9¼x4" **12.00**
Relish dish, US Navy, Captain's Mess w/pennant, 7x4" **26.00**
Shakers, Roycroft Inn, cylindrical, 1995, 3", pr, from $26 to........**35.00**
Shakers, Roycroft Inn, 1925, 3¼", pr **575.00**
Shaving mug, dbl; Wildroot, detachable metal hdl......................**135.00**
Spittoon, 'Finer's' in blk script on ivory, 1923, 9" dia................**110.00**
Tray, pin; Biltmore Hotel (Los Angeles), BS, 5x3½"....................**34.00**
Tumbler, Roycroft, BS & SL, 1926, 4x3"..**305.00**
Vase, Multifleure, pear shape, 8"...**248.00**
Vase, Roycroft, Oneida, 5" **24.00**

Deldare

Plaque, An Evening at Ye Lion Inn, signed Delaney, dated 1907, 13½", NM, $550.00.

Ashtray/matchbox holder, Fallowfield Hunt, 6" dia **1,250.00**
Basket, sgn RS (Ralph Stuart), 14" to top of hdl....................**3,575.00**
Bowl, cereal; Ye Olden Days, 6½" **128.00**
Bowl, Emerald, Dr Syntax Reading His Tour..., 9" **995.00**
Bowl, fruit; Ye Village Tavern, 3¼x9", from $288 to **410.00**
Bowl, nut; Ye Lion Inn, 3x8" **412.00**
Bowl, rim soup; Fallowfield Hunt, Breaking Cover, 9", from $235 to.**369.00**
Candle holder, Emerald, buttefly decor, shield-bk w/hdl on bk side..**1,250.00**
Candle holder, Ye Lion Inn, shield-bk w/hdl on bkside, 1925.....**665.00**
Chamberstick, city scenes, finger ring, w/match holder, 5½" dia .**550.00**
Chamberstick, city scenes, finger ring, 1½x5½" dia **395.00**
Creamer, Fallowfield Hunt scene (uncaptioned) **190.00**
Cup, Ye Olden Times..**62.00**
Cup & saucer, bouillon; Fallowfield Hunt, hdls **738.00**
Cup & saucer, chocolate; Fallowfield Hunt scene (untitled) **565.00**
Cup & saucer, chocolate; Ye Village Street, from $300 to...........**425.00**
Hair receiver, Ye Village Street, w/lid, 5" dia **675.00**

Humidor, Emerald, There Was an Old Sailor..., 8", from $495 to.**1,300.00**
Humidor, Ye Lion Inn, octagonal, 7"..**500.00**
Mug, Fallowfield Hunt, Breaking Cover, 3½", from $298 to.......**335.00**
Mug, Fallowfield Hunt, untitled, 2½", from $550 to **775.00**
Mug, Scenes of Village Life, 2½", from $380 to..........................**480.00**
Mug, Ye Lion Inn, 4¼"..**165.00**
Mustard, Scenes of Village Life..., scroll hdl, slotted lid, 3¾" ..**2,090.00**
Pitcher, Emerald, Dr Syntax Stopt by Highwaymen, 6"..............**640.00**
Pitcher, Fallowfield Hunt, 8"...**410.00**
Pitcher, Their Manner of Telling Stories..., 6" **385.00**
Plaque, wall; Emerald, Lost, sgn Stuart, 13½" dia....................**3,575.00**
Plate, bread & butter; Fallowfield Hunt, 7½"..............................**105.00**
Plate, calendar for 1910, 9½", from $1,150 to **1,900.00**
Plate, chop; An Evening at Ye Lion Inn, 14" dia..........................**284.00**
Plate, dinner; Emerald, Dr Syntax Making a Discovery, 10" **1,125.00**
Plate, dinner; Fallowfield series, Breaking Cover, 10"................**195.00**
Plate, dinner; Ye Village Gossips, decor, unglazed, 10" **82.00**
Plate, luncheon; Emerald, Dr Syntax Disputing His Bill, 9½".**2,310.00**
Plate, luncheon; Ye Olden Times, 9½", from $77 to **100.00**
Relish dish, Fallowfield Hunt, The Dash, 12x6" **780.00**
Relish dish, Ye Olden Times, 9x6"...**410.00**
Saucer, Ye Olden Times, 6"...**56.00**
Stein, Fallowfield theme, pewter lid mk Seattle Hotel, 4¾" **425.00**
Tankard, Fallowfield Hunt, Hunt Supper, 12" **1,155.00**
Tile, tea; Traveling in Ye Olden Days, pewter rim, 6"..................**225.00**
Tiles, Fallowfield Hunt, 6 8" tiles forming top for oak coffee table.**3,650.00**
Toothpick holder, Emerald, Art Nouveau floral, 2¼" **600.00**
Tray, card; Ye Lion Inn, tab hdls, 7"..**225.00**
Tray, dresser; Emerald Ware, Dr Syntax Rural Sports..., 12x9"..**1,780.00**
Tray, pin; Emerald, Dr Syntax, 6½x3½"......................................**628.00**
Tray, pin; Ye Olden Days, 6¼x3½"...**240.00**
Tray, tea; Heirlooms, 12x10½", from $455 to **550.00**
Vase, Emerald, Art Nouveau by Wm Forster, pear shape, 8½"..**1,320.00**
Vase, Emerald, Kingfisher, 8"..**2,820.00**
Vase, Ye Village Parson/Ye Village Schoolmaster, 8½"................**890.00**
Vase, 3 Ladies, 8¼" **990.00**

Miscellaneous

Bowl, fruit; rose decor w/rich gold, RS Prussia-like, 11" **135.00**
Bowl, vegetable; Bonrea, Vienna, oval, 6x7½", ea, from $45 to....**75.00**
Butter dish, Beverly, Vienna, Bluebird, w/ice ring, 8" dia, $65 to.**120.00**
Butter dish, Blue Willow, w/ice ring, 1917, 8" dia **162.00**
Butter dish, Blue Willow, 1917, 8" dia...**95.00**
Butter pat, Blue Willow, from $15 to...**45.00**
Butter pat, Bluebird **29.00**
Butter pat, Empress, teal gr floral border w/rich gold trim **25.00**
Butter pat, Gaudy Willow, 2⅞"..**168.00**
Butter tub, floral w/gold, tab hdls, ice ring, 5¼" **88.00**
Canister, Rice (tea, sugar, etc), bl & wht w/blk letters, 6½" **125.00**
Canister, Salt (Pepper, Nutmeg, etc), wht w/gold, blk letters, 3"..**45.00**
Canister, Sugar (Flour, Coffee, etc), wht w/gold, blk letters, 6½" .**85.00**
Chamber pot, Blue Willow, hdl, 1911 ....**235.00**
Chamber pot, Chrysanthemum, gr on ivory, w/hdl & lid, 9½" dia.**100.00**
Chamber pot, yel w/pk roses, 5½x9"...**51.00**
Charger, Blue Willow, emb Goettmann's on front, 13".................**56.00**
Children's dishes, Violets, 8 pcs: 2 c/s+2 plates+sug+lid..............**66.00**
Children's ware, feeding dish, Campbell Kids w/alphabet, 7½".....**85.00**
Chocolate pot, Vienna, 8" **175.00**
Cup & saucer, Bluebird, from $25 to...**36.00**
Cup & saucer, Bonrea, gr w/rich gold **16.00**
Cup & saucer, Bonrea, Vienna, bl w/rich gold, from $18 to..........**28.00**
Egg cup, dbl; Bluebird, 3¼"...**56.00**
Jug, Blue Willow, lid w/recessed hdl, 6"......................................**135.00**

Jug, Buffalo Hunt, scene adapted from Remington's 'Her Calf,' 6" .395.00
Jug, Cinderella, mc w/rich gold, 6", from $525 to 685.00
Jug, Geranium, cobalt, 6½", from $285 to 390.00
Jug, Geranium, mc, 3½", from $120 to..200.00
Jug, Holland, children seated in circle, 6", from $465 to............550.00
Jug, Hounds & Stag, polychrome, 6½" 590.00
Jug, Landing of Roger Williams, 6¼" 415.00
Jug, Orchid Spray, w/lid, 5¾" 325.00
Jug, Robin Hood, mc, 8¼", from $400 to....................................510.00
Jug, Triumph, bl w/rich gold, 7" 490.00
Jug, Whirl of the Town, rich gold, 6½", from $700 to.................825.00
Mug, novelty w/titles: Vacation, Expectation, etc, 4½" 65.00
Pitcher, Art Nouveau, cobalt w/rich gold, 8" 945.00
Pitcher, Blue Willow, rich gold, 8", from $245 to 285.00
Pitcher, Chrysanthemum, brn on ivory, 11¼", from $155 to 265.00
Pitcher, Pilgrim w/Miles Standish on 1 side, Priscilla on other, 9" .1,055.00
Pitcher, Roosevelt Bears, mini, 4", from $165 to 325.00
Plate, Bangor w/rich cobalt & Indian Red, 10½"..........................85.00
Plate, Christmas; Christmas Carol scene, mc, 1958, 9" 19.00
Plate, Christmas; Scrooge, mc, 1953, 9" 32.00
Plate, commemorative; Gen James Wolfe, Quebec, 7½" 48.00
Plate, commemorative; New Bedford Fifty years Ago, bl & wht, 10".110.00
Plate, commemorative; St Mary Magdalen Church, 7½" 16.00
Plate, dessert/salad; Blue Willow, scalloped, 8¼" 16.00
Plate, Dr Syntax Disputing His Bull, cobalt, 9" 245.00
Plate, fraternal; Modern Woodsman, 1911, 7½" 89.00
Plate, Gaudy Willow, 6", from $77 to 98.00
Plate, Geranium, cobalt, 9¾"...188.00
Plate, Japan pattern, mc, 1907, 10¼" 38.00
Plate, Maple Leaf, various szs, ea from $6 to 26.00
Plate, moose from Deer set based on RK Beck painting, 9"...........42.00
Plate, pk roses, gold border, varied patterns & szs, ea from $6 to ..22.00
Plate, Sesquicentennial, 1832-1982, bl on ivory, 9½".....................22.00
Plate, Sesquicentennial, 1832-1982, mc, ltd ed, 11¾"....................41.00
Plate, Vienna, rich gold, various szs, ea from $12 to 26.00
Platter, Blue Willow, 12x9½", from $110 to 175.00
Platter, from Fish set based on RK Beck painting, mc, 15x11"......89.00
Platter, Roycroft, TM, 8¼x6½" 357.00
Saucer, Roosevelt Bears, 'We're Here To Learn...,' 5" 135.00
Sugar bowl, Bonrea w/rich gold, w/hdls & lid 24.00
Tankard, Fallowfield decor, yel/brn/gr on ivory body, 12¼" 1,650.00
Teapot, Argyle, vitreous china, 'tea ball' infuser 158.00
Teapot, Blue Willow, 6" 165.00
Teapot, platinum decor on vitreous china, 'tea ball' infuser 127.00
Toilet set, Chrysanthemum, bl/gr pitcher+bowl+pot+soap dish+2 pcs..235.00
Tureen, Blue Willow, hdls, notched lid, 10 "dia.........................320.00
Tureen, Blue Willow, hdls, w/lid, 4½x9½" 285.00
Vase, Geranium, cobalt & wht, bulbous, 3¾" 225.00

Buggy Steps

History is very interesting concerning the development of the cart. The first recorded mention is from 2500 B.C. in Mesopotamia (now Iraq). In America, the Pilgrims were first to use carts in 1621. George Washington ordered three carriages from England, but shipment was delayed, and after three months at sea, they arrived warped and unusable. Two new carriages were ordered from Philadelphia — thus the building of carriages began in America. The American Carriage Manufactures Association turned the American carriage business into the finest in the world. While the heyday of the buggy is considered to be from 1865 to 1910, this estimation may actually be expanded. There were many types; they ranged from the Conestoga wagon, prairie schooner, and cart to the elegant carriages of the day. Buggy steps played their part in the egress and digress of

travelers, from president to child alike. Many different steps were manufactured, registered, and their patents secured. Early manufacturers proudly displayed their names upon each step. Some iron steps were handcrafted by the local blacksmith. These bear no mark of origin and are highly collectible. Today with the refurbishing and full restoration of old buggies, collectors require correct buggy step replacement. The following is a list of a few of the most sought after buggy steps. Prices quoted below are only a general guideline. Type and condition must be considered. Our advisor for this category is John Waddell; he is listed in the Directory under Texas.

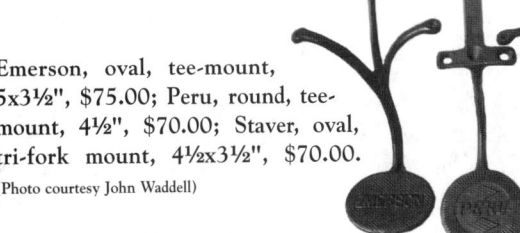

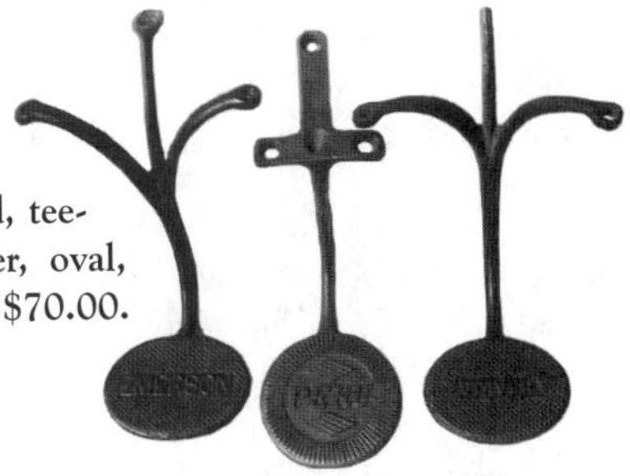

Emerson, oval, tee-mount, 5x3½", $75.00; Peru, round, tee-mount, 4½", $70.00; Staver, oval, tri-fork mount, 4½x3½", $70.00.
(Photo courtesy John Waddell)

AB Co 55.00
Abbott Buggy Co..55.00
Beebe Cart 55.00
C&W Co 55.00
Cadillac 70.00
Cole 55.00
Columbia 70.00
Creamer Scott Co...65.00
Dean & Co 75.00
Deere 85.00
Easy 65.00
Eckhart...60.00
Ferguson...55.00
Freeport..60.00
Harper 65.00
Henney Buggy Co 80.00
L Burg Mfg Co 55.00
M&T Co, w/elephant 85.00
Moon Bros..80.00
Ney, Canton, Ohio 80.00
Parsons & Goodfellow 55.00
Peerless 55.00
Racine W&C Co..65.00
Rambler..70.00
Rockford...70.00
S Frazier & Co 65.00
Sattley, Racine 70.00
Scott Cart 60.00
Selle Co...55.00
Spaulding 75.00
Stoughton 55.00
Studebaker 85.00
Thompson...60.00
Tiger 75.00
WO Hesse & Son..70.00
WS Frazier & Co 65.00

Burmese

Burmese glass was patented in 1885 by the Mount Washington Glass Co. It is typically shaded from canary yellow to a rosy salmon color. The yellow is produced by the addition of uranium oxide to the mix. The salmon color comes from the addition of gold salts and is achieved by reheating the object (partially) in the furnace. It is thus called 'heat sensitive' glass. Thomas Webb of England was licensed to produce Burmese and often added more gold, giving an almost fuchsia tinge to the salmon in some cases. They called their glass 'Queen's Burmese,' and this is sometimes etched on the base of the object. This is not to be confused with Mount Washington's 'Queen's Design,' which refers to the design painted on the object. Both companies added decoration to many pieces. Mount Washington-Pairpoint produced some Burmese in the late 1920s and Gundersen and Bryden in the '50s and '70s, but the color and shapes are different.

Our advisors for this category are Dolli and Wilfred Cohen; they are listed in the Directory under California. In the listings that follow, examples are assumed to have the satin finish unless noted 'shiny.' See also Lamps, Fairy.

Bowl, Gundersen, int flower decor, ped ft, 2½x6" 175.00
Bowl, jack-in-pulpit; Mt WA, crimped rim, 5¾" dia 395.00
Bowl, Mt WA, Dmn Quilt, 2 folded-in sides, appl rim decor, 6½" L.600.00
Bowl, Mt WA, rectangular rim, 5¼" 250.00
Bowl, Mt WA, tricornered, low, 5" 250.00
Bowl, oak leaves/blueberries, flaring rim 2¾x3½" 375.00
Bowl, Webb, ruffled, Queen's, 2¼x5" 250.00
Candy dish, Dmn Quilt, pinched/rolled-over rim, 3x1x4" 275.00
Condiment set, Mt WA, ribbed/cylinder shakers+cruet in Pairpoint fr .1,495.00
Cup, punch; Mt WA, yel rim/hdl, thin walls, 2¾" 295.00
Epergne, Webb, 3 fairy lamps+3 bud vases+ruffled 5" vase at top, 10"..2,295.00
Epergne, Webb, 4 pyramid shades above 2 tiers of crimped bowls, 17x10" .2,750.00
Mustard pot, Mt WA, ribbed ovoid, SP mts w/Pairpoint spoon, 4½".395.00
Plate, shiny, 6", set of 6 ....420.00
Rose bowl, Webb, floral, amethyst w/gr & brn foliage, 2¼x2¼", pr.690.00
Rose bowl, Webb, floral, hexagonal top, 3¼" H 395.00
Rose bowl, Webb, floral/leaf stem in amethyst/gr, incurvate, 3½".395.00
Rose bowl, Webb, grapevines, hexagonal top, 3¼" H 395.00
Shade, gaslight; Mt WA, shiny, flaring/lobed rim, 5½" dia 385.00
Toothpick holder, Mt WA, Dmn Quilt, shiny, sq top, 2½" 350.00
Toothpick holder, Mt WA, emb/HP ferns, flowers & scrolls, lobe sides ..750.00
Toothpick holder, Mt WA, lt optic Dmn Quilt, tumbler form w/pinch rim .385.00
Tumbler, Mt WA, shiny, thin walls..295.00
Tumbler, Mt WA, thin walls 250.00
Tumbler, Webb, ivy tendrils, 3¾" 500.00
Vase, flared/ruffled rim, 4", pr 395.00
Vase, Jack-in-pulpit; Mt WA, ruffled, 7" 490.00
Vase, lily; Mt WA, 10" 385.00
Vase, lily; Mt WA, 8½", pr 695.00
Vase, lily; Webb, sepia vines/leaves, yel berries/red rose, thin, 7".685.00
Vase, Mt WA, Deco flowers, bulbous w/stick neck, 10¼" 1,035.00
Vase, Mt WA, egg shape on 3 yel ft, 2¾" 345.00
Vase, Mt WA, floral (pointillism), berries, elongated teardrop, 10".1,035.00
Vase, Mt WA, gourd form, 12"...900.00

Vase, Mt. Washington, rose bud, 9", $2,500.00.

Vase, Mt WA, scalloped rim, long can neck, squat body, 4⅝" 465.00
Vase, Mt WA, scalloped top, long can neck, squat body, 6½".....500.00
Vase, Mt WA, trailing Persian floral, rnd w/stick neck, 11½"..1,450.00
Vase, Webb, berries/vines, ruffled 5-pointed rim, 3" 450.00
Vase, Webb, bulbous w/crimped top, circle mk, 3", pr................350.00
Vase, Webb, ivy vines, bulbous w/flaring ruffled rim, Queen's, 3¼".375.00
Vase, Webb, ruffled top, short ped ft w/ruffled rim, 4½"..............190.00
Vase, Webb, tiny bl/coral floral sprigs, bulbous w/trumpet neck, 12".935.00

Butter Molds and Stamps

The art of decorating butter began in Europe during the reign of Charles II. This practice was continued in America by the farmer's wife who sold her homemade butter at the weekly market to earn extra money during hard times. A mold or stamp with a special design, hand carved either by her husband or a local craftsman, not only made her product more attractive but also helped identify it as hers. The pattern became the trademark of Mrs. Smith, and all who saw it knew that this was her butter. It was usually the rule that no two farms used the same mold within a certain area, thus the many variations and patterns available to the collector today. The most valuable are those which have animals, birds, or odd shapes. The most sought-after motifs are the eagle, cow, fish, and rooster. These works of early folk art are quickly disappearing from the market.

Molds

Acorn & leaf, rope twist border, dk patina, 4⅝" 135.00
Acorns (2) & leaves divided by twisted rope, 6x4½" 145.00
Anchor, rectangular, 5x4" 200.00
Beaver, simple cvg, minor damage/stains, 3⅜" 400.00
Cow, Pat Aug 8 1871 on top, 6½x4¾" 180.00
Cow, standing at fence, rope twist border, scrubbed, 4¼"............225.00
Cow (dbl), dvtl corners, 1800s, 6x3" w/7" plunger 350.00
Cow (stylized), rope twist border, dk patina, 4⅞" 220.00
Flower, EX details, minor damage, 1½" dia 200.00
Flower, maple wood w/pattern on hdl, 5½x3¾" dia 150.00
Flower (dbl) w/leaves, 6x4⅛" dia..140.00
Flower w/leaf (stylized), EX cvg, 3½x4½"+hdl...........................160.00
Flower w/leaves & stem (stylized), 6x4⅝"..................................125.00
Olive branch, scrubbed, 4⅞"..100.00
Pineapple in sq, 1⅞"...200.00
Pineapples (2), wooden body (6x3") & plunger..........................135.00
Pomegranate, case mk Patd Apr 17, 1866, 3¾" 110.00
Sheaf of wheat, dtd April 17, 1866, 6½x5" dia...........................110.00
Sheaf of wheat, 3x2½" 145.00
Sheaves of wheat (2), dvtl corners, 5x6½x4" +hdl......................150.00
Sheep, rope twist border, rfn/2 filled-in cracks, 2¾" 300.00
Sheep, scrubbed, age crack, ca 1860s, 3⅞" 215.00
Strawberry, scrubbed, 1¾"...200.00
Swan, wings out, EX detail, mini, 1¾" dia 330.00
Swan (stylized), 3½" dia...150.00
Thistle, rope twist border, edge damage, 4⅞"..............................100.00
Thistle, wear/minor chips, 3¼"..135.00
War bonnet w/feathers, vine border, hdl cracked/edge damage, 2".110.00
4-leaf clover, 1-lb sz 70.00
8 sqs: leaves/acorns/etc, dvtl fr w/brass tacks, on 2 ft, 3½x12x5"..120.00

Stamps

Acorn & thistle, screw-in hdl, 3⅞" 135.00
Acorns/leaves, short age crack, 3⅝" 110.00
Bird, deeply cvd, wheat sheaves top & bottom, 2½" dia 150.00

Birds (2) on heart, crack in wood, 3" dia......................45.00
Cow (deep cvg), scrubbed, age cracks, 4⅜"......................165.00
Cow (simple cvg), screw-in hdl, 4⅜"......................110.00
Cow/rabbit, 2-sided, 2½x2¼" dia......................175.00
Crested bird on flowering branch, trn inset hdl, 1¾x2⅜"......................245.00
Eagle, w/wheat & star, 3½x5"......................400.00
Eagle on laurel branch w/star overhead, scrubbed, 1-pc, 4½" dia.385.00
Eagle w/rayed starbursts, dk patina, lg 1-pc hdl, wear, 4⅜"......................330.00
Eagle w/shield, circle rim, dry surface, 4"......................150.00
Eagle w/shield & laurel leaves (stylized), EX patina, 3"......................275.00
Eagle w/star, 1-pc hdl, EX patina, 4⅛"......................385.00
Heart/leaves, chip-cvd stars, lollipop hdl, hanging hole, 6½"..1,375.00
Heron in nest, EX details, stamped initials, inset hdl, 3⅜"......................550.00
Pineapple, deeply cvd edging, 2½" dia......................200.00
Pomegranate w/concentric circle, 1-pc, EX patina, 4¼"......................150.00
Prince of Wales feather crest, varnished, screw-in hdl, 3¼"......................110.00
Radiating leaves, chip-cvd edge, lollipop hdl, age crack in bk, 9".330.00
Rooster w/leafy foliage, 1-pc hdl, 3" dia......................350.00
Sheaf of wheat, threaded inset hdl, 3⅝" dia......................275.00
Sunflower, 3¾x2½"......................335.00
Swan, EX detail, old rfn, worm holes, 4" dia......................300.00
Swirl, lollipop hdl, 8x3¾" dia......................165.00
Thistle, cvd sides w/EX patina, remainder varnished, 4½"......................110.00
Tulip, PA, age cracks, 5"......................600.00
Tulip (stylized), rayed edge, hdl missing, 4½"......................135.00
Tulips/buds, EX cvg, PA, age cracks/hdl missing, early, 4⅝"....1,000.00

Buttonhooks

The earliest known written reference to buttonhooks (shoe hooks, glove hooks, or collar buttoners) is dated 1611. They became a necessary implement in the 1850s when tight-fitting high-button shoes became fashionable. Later in the nineteenth century, ladies' button gloves and men's button-on collars and cuffs dictated specific types of buttoners, some with a closed wire loop instead of a hook end. Both shoes and gloves used as many as twenty-four buttons each. Usage began to wane in the late 1920s following a fashion change to low-cut laced shoes and the invention of the zipper. There was a brief resurgence of use following the 1948 movie *High Button Shoes*. For a simple, needed utilitarian device, buttonhook handles were made from a surprising variety of materials: natural wood, bone, ivory, agate, and mother-of-pearl to plain steel, celluloid, aluminum, iron, lead and pewter, artistic copper, brass, silver, gold, and many other materials, in lengths that varied from under 2" to over 20". Many designs folded or retracted, and buttonhooks were often combined with shoehorns and other useful implements. Stamped steel buttonhooks often came free with the purchase of shoes, gloves, or collars. Material, design, workmanship, condition, and relative scarcity are the primary market value factors. Prices range from $1.00 to over $500.00, with most being in the $10.00 to $100.00 range. Buttonhooks are fairly easy to find, and they are interesting to display.

Our advisor for this category is Richard Mathes; he is listed in the Directory under Ohio. See also The Buttonhook Society listing in the Directory under Clubs, Newsletters, and Catalogs.

Buttonhook/penknife, ivory side plates, man's......................50.00
Collar buttoner, stamped steel, advertising, closed end, 3"......................20.00
Glove hook, gold-plated, retractable, 3"......................90.00
Glove hook, loop end, agate hdl, 2½"......................60.00
Shoe hook, colored celluloid hdl, 8"......................15.00
Shoe hook, lathe-trn hardwood hdl, dk finish, 8"......................15.00
Shoe hook, SP w/blade, repousse hdl, Pat Jan 5 1892, 5"......................40.00
Shoe hook, stamped steel, advertising, 5"......................8.00
Shoe hook, sterling, floral & geometrics, 8"......................55.00

Shoe hook, sterling, Nouveau lady's face, 6½"......................75.00
Shoe hook, sterling, W w/arrow, hammered Florentine decor, mk.55.00
Shoe hook/shoehorn, combination, steel & celluloid, 9"......................35.00

Bybee

The Bybee Pottery was founded in 1845 in the small town of Bybee, Kentucky, by the Cornelison family. Their earliest wares were primarily stoneware churns and jars. Today the work is carried on by sixth-generation Cornelison potters who still use the same facilities and production methods to make a more diversified line of pottery. From a fine white clay mined only a few miles from the potting shed itself, the shop produces vases, jugs, dinnerware, and banks in a variety of colors, some of which are shipped to the larger cities to be sold in department stores and specialty shops. The bulk of their wares, however, is sold to the thousands of tourists who are attracted to the pottery each year.

Bowl, mixing; mauve w/tan accents, 4¾x10½"......................30.00
Candlesticks, bl, dished bottom, hdld, mk, 5x4", pr......................65.00
Cookie jar, bl, w/lid, 8"......................50.00
Creamer & sugar bowl, wht & gr spongeware, 4"......................20.00
Pitcher, figural, chick, bl, 5"......................25.00
Pitcher, maroon w/HP floral, mk BB......................30.00
Pitcher, powder bl w/brn-wash top, #550, 6½"......................60.00
Planter, gr w/brn-wash top, 2 hdls, 4¼x4½"......................50.00
Plate, pie; ruffled rim, 11"......................30.00
Plate, wht w/Christmas wreath decor, mk BB, 8"......................35.00
Vase, bulbous bottom w/ringed neck, #543, 5"......................75.00

Vase, green variation feldspathic glaze, marked Genuine Bybee, 1930s, 8½", $350.00. (Photo courtesy Southern Folk Pottery Collectors Society)

Vase, robin-egg bl, str sides, hand thrown, 8"......................80.00

Cabat

From beginning experimentation with pottery in New York City around 1940, through several different types of clay, designs, and glazes, and relocation to Arizona, the Rose Cabat 'Feelie,' so named because 'it feels so good,' evolved into present forms and glazes in the late 1950s. Rose was aided and encouraged through the years by her late husband Erni. Their small 'weed pots' are readily recognizable by their light weight, tiny thin necks, and soft glazes. Pieces are marked with a hand-incised 'Cabat' on the bottom.

Vase, aqua bl w/mustard streaks to blk enamel at base, #35A, 3x2½"..275.00
Vase, aqua to dk mustard w/ochre speckles, ovoid, 6½x4"......................1,750.00
Vase, blk drip on bright aqua w/cream frost at neck, 2¾x2⅛"....275.00
Vase, cinnamon streaks/speckled brn on lt yel tan, ovoid, 3x2¼"..250.00
Vase, Cloudburst, bl drip on vivid wht w/gray streaks, onion, 2¾"..300.00

Vase, cream drip on khaki gr, brn & ochre patches, onion, 2¾x2¼"..250.00
Vase, emerald drip over royal bl, bottle, 4x1½" 300.00
Vase, gr & bl crystalline matt, 3"...200.00
Vase, gr/aqua/lime w/brn specks, mushroom, 2x2⅛"...............275.00
Vase, gray w/lav bl streaks, bottle neck, 3½x1½"...................275.00
Vase, mocha brn matt w/tan & blk speckles, 3½x2"....................220.00

Calendar Plates

Calendar plates were advertising giveaways most popular from about 1906 until the late 1920s. They were decorated with colorful underglaze decals of lovely ladies, flowers, animals, birds and, of course, the twelve months of the year of their issue. During the 1950s they came into vogue again but never to the extent they were originally. Those with exceptional detailing or those with scenes of a particular activity are most desirable, so are any from before 1906.

1920, Victory, The Great World War, 8¼", $65.00.

1904, Happy New Year, Cupid & bell, 8" 50.00
1907, 4 ladies in vintage clothing, Pownall Hardware, 10" 105.00
1908, pk rose border 30.00
1908, red rose w/leaves, MC Kittle, Belle Vernon PA, 9"..............40.00
1909, cherries & strawberry blossoms, Imperial, 7½"...................60.00
1909, Gibson-type girl transfer, Theis Shoe Co, worn gold rim, 9¼".80.00
1909, monks drinking wine, 9" 55.00
1909, P Cummings Confectionary & Ice Cream, 8" 55.00
1909, red rose, Comp Zimmerman, Blackduck MN, 9" 70.00
1909, tabby cat, Comp AE Palmer, Dresden China, 8⅜" 35.00
1910, holly berries on 3 sides w/Hauri Bros Grocery ad, 7¼" 45.00
1910, Indian chief, months on headdress's feathers, 7½"..............75.00
1910, lady center w/seasonal flowers between ea 3 months, 9" 55.00
1910, magnolias w/holly leaves & berries, Am China Co, 8½" 60.00
1910, man w/kreel stream fishing, 7¼" 40.00
1910, months on pgs of open book, gr ivy & forget-me-nots, 6¾" .40.00
1910, Washington's Old Home at Mt Vernon, 9⅛".......................50.00
1911, Abe Lincoln center, 9"...150.00
1911, deer scene in center w/wildlife at rim, Trandle China, 9¾"..40.00
1911, girl w/buggy walks w/boy tooting horn, 8¾"........................70.00
1911, poppies, Comp Andrews Jewelry, Dresden, gold rim 35.00
1911, Pt Arena Lighthouse w/cherubs & roses, Carnation McNicol, 9¼".45.00
1911, sea & shoreline w/sm boat on beach, 7⅝"...........................50.00
1911-12, dbl-year, pk ribbons & roses, 8½" 80.00
1912, airplane/scenic view, fruit/flower border, 8½", EX...............65.00
1912, Lincoln, Garfield & McKinley, Am flag, 9¼" 70.00
1913, lady & cherub at creek's bank w/lady & man reflection 50.00
1913, Rainbow Falls, Yosemite Valley, 9⅜"..................................95.00
1914, deer at stream, 7" 35.00
1914, Washington Capitol, gold scalloped rim, 9⅛"......................65.00
1917, silver vase w/pk roses, 7" 60.00
1918, American flag, Theodore Goodman Furniture/Carpets..., 8"..35.00

1919, WWI airplane/battleships/flags, Peace w/Honor, 8½", EX...70.00
1920, US Flag in center w/Allied country symbols at edge...........65.00
1921, WWI theme w/bluebirds & flowers, scalloped rim, 8¼"...120.00
1922, grapes & leaves, Pioneer Flour Mills, Texas, 8¼"...............75.00
1932, windmill scene, mk Woods Burlem England, 8½" 110.00
1956, windmill w/gold floral, squarish, 10¼"..............................15.00
1957, Community Grade School, Madison City IL Centinnial, 10".45.00
1967, Fox Terrier head, Walter's Auction Gallery, 9" 27.00
1970, zodiac signs, red transferware, Alfred Meakin, 9"..............50.00
1973, Bountiful Butterfly theme, Wedgwood 55.00

Calendars

Calendars are collected for their colorful prints, often attributed to a well-recognized artist of the period. Advertising calendars from the turn of the century often have a double appeal when representing a company whose tins, signs, store displays, etc., are also collectible.

See also Parrish, Maxfield.

1889, Hood's Sarsaparilla, girl in bl w/bonnet, 10" 160.00
1890, Star Wind Mill, yard long, windmill/horses, brn tones, 35", VG .235.00
1900, Hood's Sarsaparilla, diecut, 2 girls, 1 in pk, 1 in bl, 7" 130.00
1903, Prudential Insurance, lovely lady in oval of flowers, 13"...100.00
1903, Wellsbach Lamps, The Light of the Home, girl by lamp, 15", EX.325.00
1904, Christian Herald, 4 girl faces w/butterfly wings, 30"..........180.00
1905, Sleep Eye Milling Co, village scene, 7", EX 350.00
1906, Hood's Sarsaparilla, Sweet Content, complete, 12", VG-....30.00
1906, New Wrisley Sample Room, chrome litho w/boy in wht, 27"..150.00
1906, Pabst Extract, Indian Calendar (yard long), 37"............1,000.00
1907, EP Hadley's Grocery Store, 2 baby chicks & toadstool, 14"..75.00
1908, Grand Union Tea, girl playing tea w/doll & cat, 29".........280.00
1910, AA Lifebevre Dry Goods, diecut, girl/apple tree, 19", EX+.175.00
1910, Zett's Bavarian Beer, bar scene, unused in orig tube 265.00
1912, women in fancy dresses, Charles Dana Gibson, 6 pgs, 15".110.00
1913, Megargee Bros, Indian maiden, Hayes litho, 30" 410.00
1914, Springfield Breweries, C Ward Traver illus of lady, 31", VG .575.00
1916, De Laval, Do You Like Butter?, complete, 24", EX............550.00
1920, Chevrolet Motor Cars, man w/box, 2 dogs jumping, 32"...175.00
1923, Mount Airy Tire & Battery Co, 5 Miles, incomplete, 19", EX..130.00
1926, Miller, York's...Shoe House, diecut, 5 girls dancing, 16"....135.00
1926, Socony Gasoline/Motor Oils, Socony Land, 25", VG+ 80.00
1927, Sherwood Williams Paints, Indian maiden, 18".................105.00
1928, Martin Bros, Livestock...Union Stockyards, Chicago, 19".125.00
1929, De Laval, child & pup on steps, incomplete, 25", VG.........90.00
1930, 2 ladies picking grapes, Mucha, 22x13½" 1,125.00
1931, Rosemary, Zula Kenyon sgn, 5½x4" print w/artist bio, 12x8".125.00
1933, Calotabs, lady in profile, incomplete, 34", EX...................35.00
1934, Wrigley's Spearmint, Myrt & Marge (radio), incomplete, 15", VG.90.00
1937, Orange-Crush, blacksmith & boy sit drinking, 33½" (in fr).415.00
1941, Myers Pumps, lady/products/factory, complete, 50", EX........55.00
1942, Morrel Hams, Disney's 3 Little Pigs, complete, 30", NM ..375.00
1944, Goodyear Shoe Products, military man w/boy, 37x20" 90.00
1948, Dr Pepper, Miss North, South, East & West, 4 pgs, 22" 90.00
1948, Dr Pepper, Sweethearts 110.00
1950, New Breeds, 12 new aircrafts, Chas Hubell illus, 26" 130.00
1951, Goebel Beer, 1863 Civil War baseball game, incomplete, 27", EX+ ..50.00
1952, Blue Ridge Lines, bus/bridge/coach in sky, 26", VG+ 30.00
1952, Chesapeake & Ohio RR, Chessie cat & man on train, 20".95.00
1952, Great Northern RR, Indian chief in red............................95.00
1953, Goebel Beer, 1887 baseball image, incomplete, 27", EX+.100.00
1953, Pennsylvania RR, train yard scene, 29" 95.00
1955, Harold's Club, Reno NV, Queen of Hearts, 15" 165.00
1956, Horlacher Brewing Co, Elvgren pinup art, complete, 34", EX+ .100.00

1957, Simon's Pure Beer/Ale, dogs playing poker, complete, 28", EX+ 30.00
1958, Playboy Playmates, 13"...165.00
1966, Dr Pepper, Donna Loren pictured, 24" 100.00
1968, Hires, raise acetate sheet & de-clothe lady, 16" 135.00
1968, Horlacher Brewing Co, pinup surfer, complete, 33", EX......50.00
1970, Harold's Club, pinup girls, art by Fritz Willis, 26"..............105.00

California Faience

California Faience was founded in 1915 by Chauncey R. Williams and William V. Bragdon in Berkeley, California. Although the product line was always marked 'California Faience,' the firm was known as 'The Tile Shop' until 1914. Production was reduced after 1933, but the firm stayed in business as a studio and factory until 1959. The product line consisted of hand-pressed tiles and slip-cast vases, bowls, flower frogs, and occasional figures. Items produced before 1934 were made of dark brown or reddish brown clay. After that, tan clay was used. The firm made many of the tiles used at Hearst Castle, San Simeon, California. In the late 1920s, a line was produced in white porcelain marked 'California Porcelain.'

The multicolored art tiles are especially popular with collectors. Generally speaking, matt glazes were in use before 1921; examples are rare. The company's most common forms are glazed in glossy 'Persian Blue.' Almost all known pieces are marked on the bottom. Occasional unmarked pieces are seen in a pale creamy clay, probably made from discarded molds after the firm closed. Unmarked tiles are presently being made from original molds by Deer Creek Pottery, Grass Valley, California. They can be distinguished from the old tiles as they are thinner and there is a repetition of the raised designs on their backs. Our advisor for this category is Dr. Kirby William Brown; he is listed in the Directory under California.

See also Tiles.

Bowl, blk matt & bl gloss, low, rnd, 9" 160.00
Bowl, gr variegated, ribbed-lobed sides, porc, 13½".....................410.00
Bowl, Persian Blue gloss, scalloped, 6"..75.00
Bowl, plum & bl gloss, low, rnd, 11½" 165.00
Candle holder, blk matt & bl gloss, 7¼" 85.00
Figure, bear seated, brn matt, 6" L...2,300.00
Flower frog, bl matt, rnd w/11 holes, 3½" dia 30.00

Head vase, glossy white, 9", $400.00.
(Photo courtesy Dr. Kirby William Brown)

Jar, bl matt, squat, w/lid, 5½"..610.00
Jar, yel gloss w/mc band, w/lid, 4"...1,500.00
Lamp base, bl-gr gloss, spherical, porc, 6"....................................400.00
Pitcher, variegated green, porc, 6¾"..240.00
Pot, strawberry; yel gloss, 5¼" 110.00
Tile, Ave Maria w/shield, mc, sq, 4" 130.00

Tile, border; mc tendrils, curved, 4x1⅝" 65.00
Tile, border; mc waves, str, 6¼x1 3¾" 45.00
Trivet, mc peacock, 5½" dia 465.00
Vase, bl (shaded) gloss, Oriental shape, 7½".................................160.00
Vase, bl gloss, broad trumpet shape, 10" dia..............................250.00
Vase, bl matt, squat, rnd sides, 3¾"..305.00
Vase, bl matt w/incised butterflies, squat/tapered, 5"................2,650.00
Vase, brick red matt, Pueblo Indian form, 5" 805.00
Vase, brn matt w/cuenca band near top, tapered, 8¼"..............2,530.00
Vase, cream gloss, globular, porc, 5"...65.00
Vase, elongated leaves on gr matt, 4¾".......................................1,610.00
Vase, gr matt, apple shape, 3¼" 430.00
Vase, peach gloss, Oriental shape, porc, 8½" 250.00
Vase, Persian Blue gloss, cylindrical, 4⅜"....................................130.00
Vase, yel satin, Oriental shape, 6½" 90.00
Wall shelf, leaves intertwined, yel & gr gloss, 11" W 390.00

California Perfume Company

D.H. McConnell, Sr., founded the California Perfume Company (C.P. Company; C.P.C.) in 1886 in New York City. He had previously been a salesman for a book company, which he later purchased. His door-to-door sales usually involved the lady of the house, to whom he presented a complimentary bottle of inexpensive perfume. Upon determining his perfume to be more popular than his books, he decided that the manufacture of perfume might be more lucrative. He bottled toiletries under the name 'California Perfume Company' and a line of household products called 'Perfection.' In 1928 the name 'Avon' appeared on the label, and in 1939 the C.P.C. name was entirely removed from the product. The success of the company is attributed to the door-to-door sales approach and 'money back' guarantee offered by his first 'depot agent,' Mrs. P.F.E. Albee, known today as the 'Avon Lady.'

The company's containers are quite collectible today, especially the older, hard-to-find items. Advanced collectors seek 'go with' items labeled Goetting & Co., New York; Goetting's; or Savoi Et Cie, Paris. Such examples date from 1871 to 1896. The Goetting Company was purchased by D.H. McConnell; Savoi Et Cie was a line which they imported to sell through department stores. Also of special interest are packaging and advertising with the Ambrosia or Hinze Ambrosia Company label. This was a subsidiary company whose objective seems to have been to produce a line of face creams, etc., for sale through drugstores and other such commercial outlets. They operated in New York from about 1875 until 1954. Because very little is known about these companies and since only a few examples of their product containers and advertising material have been found, market values for such items have not yet been established. Other items sought by the collector include products marked Gertrude Recordon, Marvel Electric Silver Cleaner, Easy Day Automatic Clothes Washer, pre-1915 catalogs, California Perfume Company 1909 and 1910 calendars, and 1916 Calopad Sanitary Napkins.

There are hundreds of local Avon Collector Clubs throughout the world that also have C.P.C. collectors in their membership. If you are interested in joining, locating, or starting a new club, contact the National Association of Avon Collectors, Inc., listed in the Directory under Clubs, Newsletters, and Catalogs. Those wanting a National Newsletter Club or price guides may contact Avon Times, listed in the same section. Inquiries concerning California Perfume Company items and the companies or items mentioned in the previous paragraphs should be directed toward our advisor, Dick Pardini, whose address is given under California. (Please send a large SASE and be sure to request clearly the information you are seeking; not interested in Avons, 'Perfection' marked C.P.C.s, or Anniversary Keepsakes.) For more information we recommend *Bud Hastin's New 16th Edition Avon Collector's Encyclopedia.*

Note: Our values are for items in mint condition. A very rare item might go for 10% more. Damage, wear, missing parts, etc., must be considered; items judged to be in only good to very good condition should be priced at up to 50% of listed values, with fair to good at 25% and excellent at 75%. Parts (labels, stoppers, caps, etc.) might be evaluated at 10% of these prices.

American Ideal Box 'C' Set, perfume+powder sachet, 1911, M..310.00
Army & Navy Kit, 6 grooming items, 1918, MIB........................215.00
Atomizer Set, atomizer+3 perfumes, ca 1900, M.......................385.00
Baby Set, oil+powder+soap+boric acid, 1925, M in yel box 310.00
Baking Powder 'California,' 16-oz, 1-lb or 5-lb szs, M, ea 80.00
Bay Rum, came in 4-, 8- & 16-oz, 1890s, M, ea...........................150.00
Daphne Set, 1-oz perfume, face powder, rouge, 1918, M 205.00
Easy Day/Simplex Automatic Clothes Washer, 1918, MIB.........100.00
Flavoring Extract Set, 20 1-oz bottles in blk case, 1912, M 1,130.00
Gentleman's Shaving Set, 7 items, 1923, MIB............................320.00
Gertrude Recordon's Facial Treatment Set, 4-pc, 1929, MIB......257.50
Gift Box Set #1, ½-oz perfume+powder sachet, 1915, MIB........180.00
Holly Set, pr ½-oz perfumes, 1912, M in holly-pattern box........265.00
Little Folks Set, 4 sm perfumes, 1915, MIB................................300.00
Manicure Set, holds 8 different items, 1912, M 255.00
Marvel Electric Silver Cleaner, 1918, MIB 100.00
Memories That Linger Set, 3 different perfumes, 1913, M..........335.00
Mission Garden Perfume, Bavarian glass, 1½-oz, MIB 200.00
Natoma Rose Talcum, triangular tin container, 1914, 4-oz, M....165.00
Shoe White, 5-oz sack of powder, 1915, MIB..............................77.50
Supreme Huile D'Olive Oil, 1-pt or 1-qt can, 1923, M, ea 53.00
Trailing Arbutus Gift Box 'T,' 3-pc, 1915, M in mc box.............310.00
Vernafleur Threesome Gift Set, 3-pc, 1928, MIB 210.00
Violet Gift Set 'H,' 1-oz perfume+talc+sachet+atomizer, M 355.00

Calling Cards, Cases, and Receivers

The practice of announcing one's arrival with a calling card borne by the maid to the mistress of the house was a social grace of the Victorian era. Different messages (condolences, a personal visit, or a good-by) were related by turning down one corner or another. The custom was forgotten by WWI. Fashionable ladies and gents carried their personally engraved cards in elaborate cases made of such materials as embossed silver, mother-of-pearl with intricate inlay, tortoise shell, and ivory. Card receivers held cards left by visitors who called while the mistress was out or 'not receiving.' Calling cards with fringe, die-cut flaps that cover the name, or an unusual decoration are worth about $3.00 to $4.00, while plain cards usually sell for around $1.00.

Receiver, silver plate, bird perched at side, Pairpoint, 9", $265.00.

Case, ivory/MOP, silk-lined int, ca 1910, 2¾x4¼x⅝", EX............85.00
Case, silver, emb foliage/monument, N Mills, Birmingham 1851, 4x3" ..550.00
Case, sterling, man w/mandolin+mother/daughter etc relief, bk: peacock.250.00
Receiver, SP, bird by glass vase, Simpson Hall & Miller #116.....650.00

Receiver, SP, bird perched at rim, #91, rstr 495.00
Receiver, SP, center etched glass vase, butterfly ea side, 12½" L.850.00
Receiver, SP, dog & cat emb, Hartford #0937, rstr 375.00
Receiver, SP, emb bird, boy stands at base, Meriden Britannia #141.425.00
Receiver, SP, Greenaway girl & dog under umbrella, Tufts #3104.750.00
Receiver, SP, scrolling decor, upright, Meriden #2049.................140.00
Receiver, SP, 2 etched glass vases at sides, Meriden B #108, 10x11" .750.00

Camark

The Camden Art and Tile Company (commonly known as Camark) of Camden, Arkansas, was organized in the fall of 1926 by Samuel J. 'Jack' Carnes. Using clays from Arkansas, John Lessell, who had been hired as art director by Carnes, produced the initial lustre and iridescent Lessell wares for Camark ('CAM'den, 'ARK'ansas) before his death in December 1926. Before the plant opened in the spring of 1927, Carnes brought John's wife, Jeanne, and stepdaughter Billie to oversee the art department's manufacture of Le-Camark. Production by the Lessell family included variations of J.B. Owens' Soudanese and Opalesce and Weller's Marengo and Lamar. Camark's version of Marengo was called Old English. They also made wares identical to Weller's LaSa. Pieces made by John Lessell back in Ohio were signed 'Lessell,' while those made by Jeanne and Billie in Arkansas during 1927 were signed 'Le-Camark.' By 1928 Camark's production centered on traditional glazes. Drip glazes similar to Muncie Pottery were produced, in particular the green drip over pink. In the 1930s commercial castware with simple glossy and matt finishes became the primary focus and would continue so until Camark closed in the early 1960s. Between the 1960s and 1980s the company operated mainly as a retail store selling existing inventory, but some limited production occurred. In 1986 the company was purchased by the Ashcraft family of Camden, but no pottery has yet been made at the factory.

For further information we recommend *Collector's Encyclopedia of Camark Pottery, Book II*, by David Edwin Gifford. Our advisor for this category is Tony Freyaldenhoven; he is listed in the Directory under Arkansas.

Bank, seated pig w/bow tie, wht, w/accents, 6¾" 160.00
Bowl, yel to bl matt, 2x6¼" 250.00
Candlestick, bl & wht stipple, Arkansas die stamp, 1¼"...............50.00
Candlesticks, Ivory, flower form, unmk, 1x3" dia, pr 30.00
Candlesticks, Lechner's Bas Relief Iris, HP, yel, #269 USA, 5¼", pr..70.00
Candlesticks, pineapple form, brn & gr, USA R-51, 3½", pr 40.00
Corn bottle, yel & gr, cork stopper, 1st block letter, 7¾" 100.00
Creamer, Lechner's Festoon of Roses, HP, w/lid, #653 USA, 5½".80.00
Dealer sign, blk lettering on yel, unmk, 6" 300.00
Figurine, cat, blk, tail up, unmk, 12½" 200.00
Figurine, cat, climbing, wht, 15" L..70.00
Figurine, horse, ivory, mk Harry Lee Gibson, ink stamp, 9x8¼".250.00
Fishbowl, Wistful Kitten, Emerald Green, unmk, 8¾" 80.00
Fishbowl cat, cinnamon...40.00
Flower frog, 2 birds, yel w/gold, Nor-So I, 10¼" 50.00
Flower vase, rose w/gr overflow, 1st block letter, 4½" 80.00
Humidor, bl & wht stipple, w/lid, 1st block letter, 5¾" 100.00
Jug, ball; yel w/blk specks, orig cork in cap, 7½" 48.00
Pitcher, batter; gray & bl mottle, parrot hdl, mk, #200, 6¼" 120.00
Pitcher, bl & gr drip, slim neck, trifold top, 9½" 215.00
Pitcher, Lechner's Festoon of Roses, HP on rose pk, unmk, 6½"...60.00
Pitcher, lemonade; lemons & leaves on cream, 7¾" 55.00
Pitcher, waffle batter; gray & bl mottle, parrot hdl, mk #200, 6¼".110.00
Planter, gray & bl mottle, ruffled rim, unmk, 4¾" 100.00
Shakers, S&P shapes, burgundy, unmk, 2¾", pr...........................25.00
Shelf sitter, Humpty Dumpty, HP details, unmk, 5½" 160.00
Sugar jar, Autumn (brn), 1st block letter, 8".................................80.00

Vase, Azurite Blue, shouldered, unmk, 4¼" 25.00
Vase, bl & wht stipple, 1st block letter, 5¼" 35.00
Vase, bud; gr to bl matt, long trumpet neck, #424, 9½" 250.00
Vase, burgundy, emb flower, integral hdls, USA #571, 7½" 45.00
Vase, Celestial Blue w/blk overflow, cylindrical, 10¾" 275.00
Vase, Delphinium Blue, Deco, low hdls, 1st block letter, 6" 60.00
Vase, dk orange w/tall pine tree scene in blk, mk LaCamark, 10¼"..1,000.00
Vase, frosted gr, bulbous, 4¼", from $30 to 40.00
Vase, gr coraline, mk, 8", from $800 to 1,000.00
Vase, gr overflow on orange, rim-to-hip hdls, 4½", from $60 to....80.00
Vase, Mirror Black, 1st block letter, 4¼" 50.00
Vase, olive gr w/lt overflow, Deco octagon, #404, 6" 160.00
Vase, orange crackle, gold stamp, 8¼", from $300 to 400.00

Vase, Orange Green Overflow, mark #420, 10", from $400.00 to $500.00. (Photo courtesy David Edwin Gifford)

Vase, oxblood w/blk palm tree scene, silver lustre, LeCamark, 8½" ..1,000.00
Vase, Royal Blue, twisted form, flared rim, sticker, 8¾" 50.00
Vase, Sea Green, unmk, 4½" 35.00
Vase, Sea Gull, gr gloss, early circular mk, #418, 9½" 500.00
Vase, wht crackle, pinched sides, unmk, 9½", from $400 to 500.00
Vase, yel top w/drips over bl, ring hdls, unmk, 5¾" 300.00
Vase, yel w/bl overflow, gold stamp, 7¾" 275.00
Wall pocket, Iris (HP/bas-relief), Lechner, 9", from $300 to 400.00

Cambridge Art Pottery

The Cambridge Art Pottery (not to be confused with the Cambridge Art Tile Works of Covington, Kentucky) was founded in 1901 in Cambridge, Ohio. Charles Upjohn, formerly from the Weller Pottery, was hired as designer and modeler. Cambridge would be known mostly for three artware lines: Terrhea, their variation of Rookwood's Standard Glaze line, underglaze painted with polychrome slips and covered in an amber overglaze; Oakwood, a flambé glaze mix of autumnal colors; and Acorn, a smooth and satiny matt green finish in the Arts and Crafts style. They also produced a commercially successful utilitarian line, Guernsey, named after the county for which Cambridge was the seat. After 1908 only that last line remained, and in 1909 the pottery name was changed to Guernsey Earthenware. Cambridge pieces are usually stamped with a CAP mark ('AP' within a larger 'C') with the name of the line above or below. Our advisors for this category are Suzanne Perrault and Dave Rago; they are listed in the Directory under New Jersey.

Coffeepot, Terrhea, blkbirds on glossy terra cotta, mk, 8½x6" 125.00
Ewer, Oakwood, amber/gr flambe, squat base, Oakwood/208, 7½" .125.00
Vase, Terrhea, Am Indian portrait, Arthur Williams, rstr at neck, 24" .6,500.00
Vessel, Acorn, matt gr w/lustre, acorn stamp, squat, 3¼x6¾" 425.00
Vessel, Terrhea, roses, ftd, 7", EX 150.00

Cambridge Art Tile Works

The Cambridge Art Tile Works (not to be confused with the Cambridge Art Pottery of Cambridge, Ohio) initially managed in Cincinnati, Ohio, in 1887. In 1889 they moved to the site where their goods were being manufactured, the Mount Casino Art Tile Company, of Covington, Kentucky. These two companies merged, taking on the title of the Cambridge Tile Manufacturing Company. They employed as modelers Clement Barnhorn and Ferdinand Mersman, both of whom had worked at the Rookwood Pottery. The tiles they produced were in the same style as others made throughout the Ohio Valley at the time: dust-pressed with classical subjects or floral displays and covered in single-color majolica glazes.

The company expanded several times over the following years, manufacturing mantels, floor tiles, and mosaics. In 1927 it took over the Wheatley Pottery of Cincinnati and organized the Cambridge-Wheatley Corporation to sell tiles made in both locations. During the decades that followed, it would alter and refine its production regularly to compete with domestic and foreign tile manufacturers. The company closed its doors in 1986. Cambridge tiles are usually embossed with the company's name on white clay.

Our advisors for this category are Suzanne Perrault and Dave Rago; they are listed in the Directory under New Jersey.

Frieze: berries/spider/web, raspberry gloss, mk, 6", 6+2 corners, NM..375.00
Pr of portraits: boy & girl, gr gloss, mk, 6", from $150 to 250.00
3-tile panel: dog/dying deer, brn majolica, mk, ea 6", NM 475.00
3: nude, 1 as day/1 as night, red gloss, unmk, fr, ea 18x6", $1,500 to..2,000.00

Cambridge Glass

The Cambridge Glass Company began operations in 1901 in Cambridge, Ohio. Primarily they made crystal dinnerware and well-designed accessory pieces until the 1920s when they introduced the concept of color that was to become so popular on the American dinnerware market. Always maintaining high standards of quality and elegance, they produced many lines that became bestsellers; through the '20s and '30s they were recognized as the largest manufacturer of this type of glassware in the world.

Of the various marks the company used, the 'C in triangle' is the most familiar. Production stopped in 1958. For a more thorough study of the subject, we recommend *Colors in Cambridge Glass* by the National Cambridge Collectors, Inc.; their address may be found in the Directory under Clubs. *Glass Animals and Figural Flower Frogs of the Depression Era* by Lee Garmon and Dick Spencer is a wonderful source for an in-depth view of their particular aspect of glass collecting. They are both listed in the Directory under Illinois. See also Carnival Glass; Glass Animals.

Apple Blossom, amber, ashtray, heavy, 6" 125.00
Apple Blossom, amber, bowl, relish; 4-part, 12" 70.00
Apple Blossom, amber, cheese & cracker (11½" plate) 75.00
Apple Blossom, amber, stem, sherbet; tall, #3130, 6-oz 30.00
Apple Blossom, crystal, bowl, pickle; 9" 30.00
Apple Blossom, crystal, butter dish, 5½" 195.00
Apple Blossom, crystal, ice bucket 95.00
Apple Blossom, crystal, pitcher, #3130, 64-oz 215.00
Apple Blossom, crystal, plate, dinner; 9½" 55.00
Apple Blossom, pk or gr, bowl, bonbon; 5½" 40.00
Apple Blossom, pk or gr, comport, tall, 7" 95.00
Apple Blossom, pk or gr, cup..35.00
Apple Blossom, pk or gr, plate, grill; 10" 65.00
Apple Blossom, pk or gr, tumbler, ftd, #3135, 10-oz......................45.00
Candlelight, bonbon, hdls, #3900/130, 7" 40.00

Candlelight, bowl, flared, 4-toed, #3900/62, 12"..................90.00
Candlelight, bowl, hdls, #3900/34, 11"..................90.00
Candlelight, candlestick, #646, 5"..................65.00
Candlelight, mayonnaise, 3-pc, #3900/129..................75.00
Candlelight, plate, 4-toed, #3900/26, 12"..................75.00
Candlelight, stem, cordial, #3776, 1-oz..................85.00
Caprice, bl or pk, bonbon, ftd, #133, 6" sq..................50.00
Caprice, bl or pk, bowl, crimped, 4-ftd, #53, 10½"..................85.00
Caprice, bl or pk, cake plate, ftd, #36, 13"..................395.00
Caprice, bl or pk, creamer, #38, mid..................22.00
Caprice, bl or pk, plate, lemon; hdld, #152, 6½"..................30.00
Caprice, bl or pk, stem, water; blown, #300, 9-oz..................50.00
Caprice, bl or pk, tumbler, water; ftd, #300, 10-oz..................40.00
Caprice, bl or pk, vase, crimped top, #340, 9½"..................425.00
Caprice, crystal, ashtray, #215, 4"..................8.00
Caprice, crystal, bowl, relish; 4-part, oval, #126, 12"..................90.00
Caprice, crystal, candlestick, keyhole, 3-light, #638..................25.00
Caprice, crystal, coaster, #13, 3½"..................15.00
Caprice, crystal, plate, cabaret; 4-ftd, #33, 14"..................40.00
Caprice, crystal, stem, claret; blown, #301, 4½"..................40.00
Chantilly, bowl, relish/pickle; 7"..................32.00
Chantilly, butter dish, rnd..................235.00
Chantilly, cocktail icer, 3-pc..................65.00
Chantilly, marmalade & lid..................60.00
Chantilly, pitcher, upright..................250.00
Chantilly, shakers, hdld, pr..................40.00
Chantilly, stem, claret; #3625, 4½-oz..................45.00
Chantilly, stem, oyster cocktail; low, #3779, 4½-oz..................18.00
Chantilly, tumbler, 13-oz..................26.00
Cleo, amber, cup & saucer, bouillon; hdls, Decagon..................55.00
Cleo, amber, pitcher, w/lid, 22-oz..................250.00
Cleo, amber, sugar bowl, ftd..................22.00
Cleo, bl, bowl, vegetable; oval, Decagon, 9½"..................145.00
Cleo, bl, ice pail..................250.00
Cleo, bl, plate, hdls, Decagon, 11"..................120.00
Cleo, bl, tumbler, ftd, #3022, 12-oz..................95.00
Cleo, pk or gr, basket, 2 hdls, uptrn sides, Decagon, 7"..................30.00
Cleo, pk or gr, candlestick, 1-light, 2 styles, ea..................30.00
Cleo, pk or gr, stem, wine; #3077, 3½-oz..................70.00
Daffodil, basket, hdls, low ft, #55, 6"..................40.00
Daffodil, cake plate, #1495, 11½"..................75.00
Daffodil, candlestick, arch, 2-light, #3900/72..................65.00
Daffodil, creamer, #253, ind..................30.00
Daffodil, mayonnaise, ftd, w/ladle & liner plate, #533..................95.00
Daffodil, shakers, squat, #360, pr..................65.00
Daffodil, stem, cockail; #3779, 3-oz..................35.00
Daffodil, tumbler, ftd, #1937, 5-oz..................22.00
Decagon, bl, bowl, almond; ftd, 6"..................50.00
Decagon, bl, bowl, cranberry; flat rim, 3¾"..................32.00
Decagon, bl, comport, low ft, 6½"..................35.00
Decagon, bl, ice tub..................65.00
Decagon, bl, plate, dinner; 9½"..................70.00
Decagon, bl, server, center hdl..................45.00
Decagon, bl, tray, celery; 11"..................50.00
Decagon, bl, tumbler, ftd, 12-oz..................38.00
Decagon, pastel colors, bowl, bouillon; w/liner..................25.00
Decagon, pastel colors, bowl, vegetable; rnd, 9"..................30.00
Decagon, pastel colors, creamer, ftd, tall, lg..................10.00
Decagon, pastel colors, ice tub..................45.00
Decagon, pastel colors, plate, bread & butter; 6¼"..................5.00
Decagon, pastel colors, salt cellar, ftd, 1½"..................25.00
Decagon, pastel colors, stem, water; 9-oz..................20.00
Decagon, pastel colors, tray, service; oval, 11"..................30.00
Diane, bottle, bitters..................175.00

Diane, bowl, bonbon; hdls, 5¼"..................25.00
Diane, bowl, pickle; 9½"..................40.00
Diane, butter dish, rnd..................165.00
Diane, candlestick, 3-light, 6"..................45.00
Diane, cup..................20.00
Diane, mayonnaise, w/liner & ladle..................50.00
Diane, plate, salad; 8"..................14.00
Diane, platter, 13½"..................95.00
Diane, stem, water; #1066, 11-oz..................35.00
Diane, tumbler, ftd, #3135, 10-oz..................22.00
Diane, tumbler, 13-oz..................35.00
Elaine, bowl, nut; 4-ftd, ind, 3"..................60.00
Elaine, bowl, tab hdls, 11"..................95.00
Elaine, candlestick, 2-light, 6"..................45.00

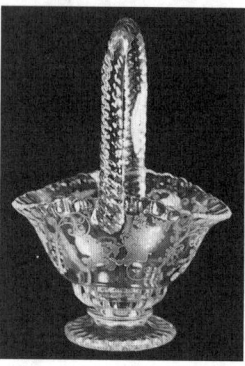

Elaine, favor basket, rare, 6½", from $200.00 to $225.00.

Elaine, hurricane lamp, candlestick base..................190.00
Elaine, pitcher, Doulton..................350.00
Elaine, shakers, flat, pr..................50.00
Elaine, stem, goblet; #1402..................35.00
Elaine, stem, wine; #3500, 2½-oz..................45.00
Elaine, vase, ftd, 8"..................100.00
Gloria, crystal, bowl, fruit; 5" sq..................22.00
Gloria, crystal, bowl, relish; 2-part, hdls, 8"..................35.00
Gloria, crystal, comport, fruit cocktail; 4"..................18.00
Gloria, crystal, cup, rnd or sq..................20.00
Gloria, crystal, plate, dinner; sq..................70.00
Gloria, crystal, shakers, metal tops, ftd, pr..................60.00
Gloria, crystal, stem, sherbet; tall, #3130, 6-oz..................20.00
Gloria, crystal, tumbler, ftd, #3115, 12-oz..................30.00
Gloria, gr, pk or yel, bowl, bonbon; crimped, ftd, 5"..................50.00
Gloria, gr, pk or yel, bowl, cereal; 6"..................55.00
Gloria, gr, pk or yel, bowl, cream soup; w/sq saucer..................85.00
Gloria, gr, pk or yel, bowl, salad; tab hdls, 9"..................100.00
Gloria, gr, pk or yel, butter dish, hdls..................395.00
Gloria, gr, pk or yel, comport, low, 7"..................100.00
Gloria, gr, pk or yel, oil, ftd, hdld, tall, w/stopper..................250.00
Gloria, gr, pk or yel, shakers, short, pr..................125.00
Gloria, gr, pk or yel, stem, cocktail; #3035, 3-oz..................35.00
Gloria, gr, pk or yel, tray, sandwich; center hdl, 11"..................75.00
Gloria, gr, pk or yel, tumbler, ftd, #3115, 10-oz..................45.00
Imperial Hunt Scene, colors, bowl, 8"..................90.00
Imperial Hunt Scene, colors, cup..................65.00
Imperial Hunt Scene, colors, ice bucket..................195.00
Imperial Hunt Scene, colors, plate, 8"..................22.50
Imperial Hunt Scene, colors, stem, cordial; #3085, 1-oz..................195.00
Imperial Hunt Scene, colors, tumbler, ftd, #3085, 5-oz, 3⅞"..................45.00
Imperial Hunt Scene, crystal, creamer, flat..................15.00
Imperial Hunt Scene, crystal, ice bucket..................100.00
Imperial Hunt Scene, crystal, plate, 8"..................20.00

Imperial Hunt Scene, crystal, shakers, pr 100.00
Imperial Hunt Scene, crystal, stem, sherbet; #1402, 7½" 45.00
Imperial Hunt Scene, crystal, tumbler, flat, #1407, 7-oz............20.00
Marjorie, comport, #4011...45.00
Marjorie, cut stopper, #17, 28-oz...................................195.00
Marjorie, jug, w/lid, #106, 30-oz....................................225.00
Marjorie, nappy, #4111, 4"...20.00
Marjorie, stem, cafe parfait; #7606, 5½-oz..........................45.00
Marjorie, stem, cordial; #3750, 1-oz................................110.00
Marjorie, sugar bowl, str sides, flat, #1917/18......................75.00
Marjorie, tumbler, ftd, #3750, 12-oz.................................25.00
Mt Vernon, bottle, bitters; #62, 2½-oz...............................65.00
Mt Vernon, bowl, cereal; #32, 6"......................................12.50
Mt Vernon, bowl, crimped, rolled rim, #117, 12".....................32.50
Mt Vernon, bowl, oval, 4-ftd, #136, 11"..............................27.50
Mt Vernon, box, ftd, #15, 4½"..37.50
Mt Vernon, candlestick, 2-light, #110, 5".............................25.00
Mt Vernon, coaster, ribbed or plain, 3"................................5.00
Mt Vernon, comport, #81, 8"...25.00
Mt Vernon, hurricane lamp, #1607, 9".................................85.00
Mt Vernon, plate, salad; #5, 8½"......................................7.00
Mt Vernon, salt cellar, oval, hdls, #102.............................12.00
Mt Vernon, shakers, short, #88, pr....................................20.00
Mt Vernon, stem, claret; #25, 4½-oz..................................13.50
Mt Vernon, tumbler, bbl shape, #13, 12-oz............................15.00
Mt Vernon, vase, ftd, #46, 10"...60.00
No 520 Byzantine, Peach Blo or gr, bowl, bouillon; hdls, #934.....22.50
No 520 Byzantine, Peach Blo or gr, bowl, finger; #3060.............25.00
No 520 Byzantine, Peach Blo or gr, gravy or sauce boat 95.00
No 520 Byzantine, Peach Blo or gr, plate, dinner; #810, 9½" 60.00
No 520 Byzantine, Peach Blo or gr, stem, wine; #3060, 2½-oz......22.50
No 520 Byzantine, Peach Blo or gr, sugar bowl, rim ft, #138.........20.00
No 704 Windows Border, colors, bowl, fruit; 5¼"......................16.00
No 704 Windows Border, colors, bowl, oval, w/lid, #915, 12".....125.00
No 704 Windows Border, colors, butter dish, #920....................125.00
No 704 Windows Border, colors, candlestick, #437, 9½" 45.00
No 704 Windows Border, colors, ice bucket, short, bail hdl, #970 .95.00
No 704 Windows Border, colors, pickle tray, #907, 9" 30.00
No 704 Windows Border, colors, plate, service; 10½" 75.00
No 704 Windows Border, colors, stem, parfait; #3060, 5-oz..........40.00
No 704 Windows Border, colors, sugar bowl, flat, #137................20.00
No 704 Windows Border, colors, tumbler, ftd, #3075, 8-oz............20.00
Nude stem, amethyst, claret, 4½-oz...................................425.00
Nude stem, blk/crystal, wine, 6½" 200.00

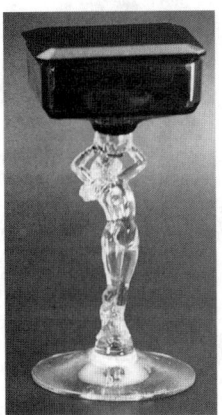

Nude stem, box, amethyst and crystal, $295.00.

Nude stem, Carmen/crystal, claret, 4½-oz..........................435.00
Nude stem, Carmen/frost, wine 290.00
Nude stem, crystal, compote, shell-shaped bowl, 5½x5¼".........275.00

Nude stem, crystal/frost, cocktail, 5⅝" 40.00
Nude stem, emerald gr/frost, wine 230.00
Nude stem, Gold Crystal/frost, wine 230.00
Nude stem, Heatherbloom, claret, 4½-oz...........................485.00
Nude stem, mocha/crystal, cocktail, 6½" 200.00
Nude stem, royal bl/frost, wine 295.00
Nude stem, Royal Blue, claret, 4½-oz...............................440.00
Portia, basket, uptrn sides, 2 hdls.....................................30.00
Portia, bowl, bonbon; hdls, 5¼" 30.00
Portia, bowl, pickle/relish; 7" 40.00
Portia, cake plate, hdls, 13½"..65.00
Portia, cocktail shaker, w/stopper....................................195.00
Portia, creamer, ftd...22.00
Portia, pitcher, ball form 275.00
Portia, stem, cocktail; #3130, 3-oz....................................20.00
Portia, stem, goblet; #3121, 10-oz.....................................30.00
Portia, stem, water; ftd, #3121, 10-oz.................................25.00
Portia, vase, flower; 13"..150.00
Rosalie, amber or crystal, bowl, cream soup 20.00
Rosalie, amber or crystal, bowl, Decagon, 12".......................85.00
Rosalie, amber or crystal, bowl, 3-part, w/lid, 8½".................65.00
Rosalie, amber or crystal, celery, 11".................................25.00
Rosalie, amber or crystal, creamer, ftd...............................15.00
Rosalie, amber or crystal, pitcher, #955, 62-oz.....................195.00
Rosalie, amber or crystal, platter, 15"...............................100.00
Rosalie, amber or crystal, relish, 2-part, 11".........................30.00
Rosalie, amber or crystal, tumbler, ftd, #3077, 8-oz.................16.00
Rosalie, bl, pk or gr, bottle, Fr dressing..............................195.00
Rosalie, bl, pk or gr, bowl, basket; hdls, 11".........................75.00
Rosalie, bl, pk or gr, bowl, fruit; 5½".................................22.00
Rosalie, bl, pk or gr, cheese & cracker...............................75.00
Rosalie, bl, pk or gr, comport, 6¾"...................................55.00
Rosalie, bl, pk or gr, plate, salad; 7½"...............................15.00
Rosalie, bl, pk or gr, relish, 2-part, 9"...............................45.00
Rosalie, bl, pk or gr, stem, water goblet; #3077, 9-oz...............28.00
Rosalie, bl, pk or gr, tumbler, ftd, #3077, 12-oz....................40.00
Rose Point, ashtray, #3500/126, 4"...................................42.50
Rose Point, basket, wide, #3500/56, 7"...............................65.00
Rose Point, bowl, nappy, hdls, #3400/1179, 5½" 42.50
Rose Point, bowl, oblong, ftd, #3500/118, 12".......................190.00
Rose Point, bowl, ram's head, squared, #3500/27, 8"................495.00
Rose Point, candelabrum, 2-light, w/bobeches & prisms, #1268.225.00
Rose Point, candy box, w/lid, #1066 stem, 5⅜".....................210.00
Rose Point, cup, AD: #3400/69 ....300.00
Rose Point, decanter, ball form, w/stopper, #3400/119, 12-oz 350.00
Rose Point, hat, #1704, 5" 495.00
Rose Point, ice bucket, #1402/52.....................................235.00
Rose Point, mayonnaise, sherbet type, w/ladle, #19.................85.00
Rose Point, pickle dish, #3400/59, 9"................................70.00
Rose Point, pitcher, Doulton, #3400/141, 80-oz 400.00
Rose Point, plate, breakfast; #3400/62, 8½"........................25.00
Rose Point, plate, torte; #3400/65, 14"..............................155.00
Rose Point, shakers, chrome tops, ftd, #3400/77, pr.................60.00
Rose Point, stem, cocktail; #3104, 3½-oz............................295.00
Rose Point, stem, water goblet; #3106, 10-oz 40.00
Rose Point, tumbler, iced tea; ftd, #7801, 12-oz.....................85.00
Rose Point, tumbler, str dsides, #498, 10-oz.........................50.00
Rose Point, vase, keyhole, ftd, #1234, 12"...........................165.00
Tally Ho, amber or crystal, ashtray, 4"................................12.50
Tally Ho, amber or crystal, bowl, belled, 10½".......................35.00
Tally Ho, amber or crystal, bowl, nappy, hdls, 6" 17.50
Tally Ho, amber or crystal, cheese & cracker, 13½" 65.00
Tally Ho, amber or crystal, creamer, ftd..............................12.50
Tally Ho, amber or crystal, mug, hdld stein, 12-oz...................25.00

Tally Ho, amber or crystal, plate, buffet lunch; 18".................45.00
Tally Ho, amber or crystal, stem, sherbet, high, 7½" 18.00
Tally Ho, Carmen or Royal, ash well, center hdl, 2-pc 35.00
Tally Ho, Carmen or Royal, bowl, low ft, 10½" 85.00
Tally Ho, Carmen or Royal, bowl, 3-compartment, 8½" 70.00
Tally Ho, Carmen or Royal, candlestick, 5" 40.00
Tally Ho, Carmen or Royal, comport, 4½" H 27.50
Tally Ho, Carmen or Royal, cup, punch; flat.........................20.00
Tally Ho, Carmen or Royal, plate, salad; 7½" 20.00
Tally Ho, Carmen or Royal, relish, 4-compartment, 10" 40.00
Tally Ho, Carmen or Royal, tumbler, short, 10-oz....................42.00
Tally Ho, Forest Green, bowl, flat rim, 12½" 50.00
Tally Ho, Forest Green, bowl, nappy, hdls, 6" 25.00
Tally Ho, Forest Green, coaster, 4" 15.00
Tally Ho, Forest Green, cup, whiskey; hdld, 2½-oz...................20.00
Tally Ho, Forest Green, goblet, cocktail 16.00
Tally Ho, Forest Green, plate, chop; 14" 50.00
Tally Ho, Forest Green, shaker, glass top 35.00
Tally Ho, Forest Green, sugar bowl, ftd 35.00
Valencia, basket, ftd, hdls, #3500/55, 6" 30.00
Valencia, bowl, salad dressing; divided, #1402/95 ....45.00
Valencia, comport, #3500/36, 6" 30.00
Valencia, mayonnaise, 3-pc, #3500-59................................45.00
Valencia, relish, 3-compartment, #3500/69, 6½" 35.00
Valencia, shakers, #3400/18, pr.....................................65.00
Valencia, stem, cordial; #3500 ....75.00
Valencia, sugar bowl, #3500/14......................................15.00
Valencia, tumbler, #3500, 16-oz.....................................30.00
Wildflower, bowl, bonbon, ftd, hdls, 6".............................35.00
Wildflower, bowl, relish; 3-hdl, 3-part, #3400/91, 8"...............37.50
Wildflower, butter dish, #3900/52, ¼-lb.............................225.00
Wildflower, comport, blown, #3121, 5⅜"..............................65.00
Wildflower, pitcher, ball form, #3400/38, 80-oz.....................350.00
Wildflower, plate, dinner; #3900/24, 10½"...........................95.00
Wildflower, stem, cordial; #3121, 1-oz..............................70.00
Wildflower, sugar bowl, #3900/41....................................20.00
Wildflower, tumbler, water; #3121, 10-oz............................30.00
Wildflower, vase, flower; ftd, #6004, 8"............................70.00

Cameo

The technique of glass carving was perfected 2,000 years ago in ancient Rome and Greece. The most famous ancient example of cameo glass is the Portland Vase, made in Rome around 100 A.D. After glass blowing was developed, glassmakers devised a method of casing several layers of colored glass together, often with a light color over a darker base, to enhance the design. Skilled carvers meticulously worked the fragile glass to produce incredibly detailed classic scenes. In the eighteenth and nineteenth centuries Oriental and Near-Eastern artisans used the technique more extensively. European glassmakers revived the art during the last quarter of the nineteenth century. In France, Galle and Daum produced some of the finest examples of modern times, using as many as five layers of glass to develop their designs, usually scenics or subjects from nature. Hand carving was supplemented by the use of a copper engraving wheel, and acid was used to cut away the layers more quickly.

In England, Thomas Webb and Sons used modern machinery and technology to eliminate many of the problems that plagued early glass carvers. One of Webb's best-known carvers, George Woodall, is credited with producing over four hundred pieces. Woodall was trained in the art by John Northwood, famous for reproducing the Portland Vase in 1876. Cameo glass became very popular during the late 1800s, resulting in a market that demanded more than could be produced, due to the tedious procedures involved. In an effort to produce greater volume, less elabo-

rate pieces with simple floral or geometric designs were made, often entirely acid etched with little or no hand carving. While very little cameo glass was made in this country, a few pieces were produced by James Gillinder, Tiffany, and the Libbey Glass Company. Though some continued to be made on a limited scale into the 1900s (and until about 1920 in France), for the most part, inferior products caused a marked reduction in its manufacture by the turn of the century. Beware of new 'French' cameo glass from Romania and Taiwan. Some of it is very good and may be signed with 'old' signatures. Know your dealer! Our advisor for this category is Don Williams; he is listed in the Directory under Missouri. See also specific manufactures.

English

Bottle, scent; floral/lilies/leaves, wht on bl, 6½"......................1,900.00
Bowl, finger; floral, wht on rose, 5", w/underplate...................2,200.00
Bowl, tassled rope lattice, amber/orange/wht, frost ft, 3½x4½".1,100.00
Plaque, flowers, wht on citron, 5½x3½" 1,200.00
Purse bottle, duck head, wht feathers, citron bill, RD1109, 9"..7,000.00
Purse bottle, roses/buds/butterfly, wht on bl, Gorham cap, 8½" .3,000.00
Vase, blossoms on convoluted stems, wht on gr, 8" 4,300.00
Vase, flower/buds/leaves, cattails beyond, wht on raisin, 5" 2,000.00
Vase, flowers/buds, wht on magenta, 6" 1,235.00
Vase, flowers/butterfly, wht on bl, 2x2½"............................2,500.00
Vase, foliage, wht on turq, 1½", pr.................................1,265.00
Vase, honeysuckle vine/flowers, wht on pk, can neck, 5".........1,100.00
Vase, morning glories, wht on gr, stick neck, 2"...................1,050.00
Vase, morning glories/vines, wht on red, 10" 2,200.00
Vase, morning glory/butterfly, wht on bl, unmk, gourd form, 5¾", NM..1,600.00
Vase, poppies/butterflies/rose branches, wht on bl, ftd, 8½" 2,800.00

French

Bottle, floral branches, cranberry/textured, att St Louis, 5".........150.00
Bottle, trailing wild roses, yel/clear, cylindrical, 1900s, 6½"........175.00
Vase, birch trees/country stream, sq rim, Lamartine, 6¼" 1,200.00
Vase, birds in flight, rose on frost, squatty, Delatte, 4x4½" 700.00
Vase, bud; red thistles on needlepoint texture, att St Louis, 7"...325.00
Vase, Egyptian scene w/figures, brn on frost, Arsall, 8x8"............885.00

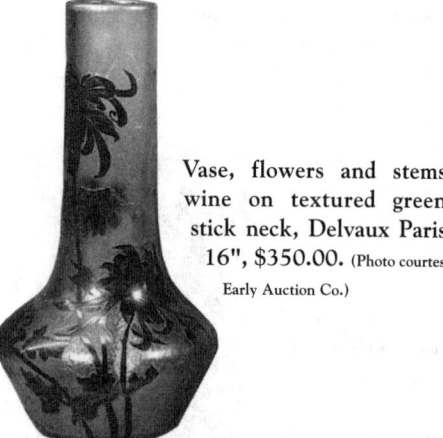

Vase, flowers and stems, wine on textured green, stick neck, Delvaux Paris, 16", $350.00. (Photo courtesy Early Auction Co.)

Vase, grapes, lt purple on yel/red/brn, Degue, 8½".....................325.00
Vase, hyacinths on leafy stems, gr/bl on gray, slim/ftd, 16".......2,415.00
Vase, lilies, gray/dk bl/chartreuse, Verrie de...Mabut, 9" 900.00
Vase, scenic w/lg trees, gr/brn on frost, Lamartine, 6½x5" 980.00
Vase, tall stems on trumpet body, scroll lower border, Richard, 12".435.00
Vase, thistles, ruby on lt rose frost, shouldered, 3¼"...................260.00

Vase, village & lake, pillow shape, Michel, 8" 850.00
Vase, violets, lav on frost, sphere w/quatralobe rim, Pantin, 5"...500.00
Vase, wild flowers, aqua/irid, Cristallerie de Pantin, 9" 1,265.00

Canary Ware

Canary ware was produced from the late 1700s until about the mid-nineteenth century in the Staffordshire district of England. It was potted of yellow clay and the overglaze was yellow as well. More often than not, copper or silver lustre trim was added. Decorations were usually black-printed transfers, though occasionally hand-painted polychrome designs were also used.

Creamer, flowers, red/gr w/pk lustre accents & rim, 2¾" 880.00
Jug, Bonaparte Dethron'd, red transfer cartoon, ca 1814, wear, 5" .1,175.00
Jug, Independencia ou Morte, blk transfer, att Hartley Greens & Co, 7".880.00
Mug, bird on branch/trim lines in pk lustre, wear, 2½" 500.00
Mug, strawberries & leaves, sm rpr, child's, 2½" 575.00
Mug, Trifle for Edward in octagon panel w/oak leaves, 2", EX...575.00
Plate, red transfer: dancing villagers, emb palmette border, 10"..650.00
Teapot, lady playing piano, 2 children w/sm instruments, 5", EX.500.00
Tureen, battle scenes in red transfer, Fr, 1820, w/lid, 11", VG.1,200.00

Candle Holders

The earliest type of candlestick, called a pricket, was constructed with a sharp point on which the candle was impaled. The socket type, first used in the sixteenth century, consisted of the socket and a short stem with a wide drip pan and base. These were made from sheets of silver or other metal; not until late in the seventeenth century were candlesticks made by casting. By the 1700s, styles began to vary from the traditional fluted column or baluster form and became more elaborate. A Rococo style with scrolls, shellwork, and naturalistic leaves and flowers came into vogue that afforded the individual silversmith the opportunity to exhibit his skill and artistry. The last half of the eighteenth century brought a return to fluted columns with neoclassic motifs. Because they were made of thin sheet silver, weighted bases were used to add stability. The Rococo styles of the Regency period were heavily encrusted with applied figures and flowers. Candelabra with six to nine branches became popular. By the Victorian era when lamps came into general use, there was less innovation and more adaptation of the earlier styles. For more information, we recommend *Glass Candlesticks of the Depression Era*, by Gene Florence and *The Glass Candlestick Book, Vol. 1* and *Vol. 2*, by Tom Felt and Elaine & Rich Stoer (Collector Books). See also Silver; Tinware; specific manufacturers.

Brass, petal bases, conforming bobeches, push-up knob in shafts, England, eighteenth century, 8¼", $1,380.00 for the pair.

Black Forest, cvd mtn goat in front of tree trunk holder, 17", VG..175.00
Brass, baluster column w/mid-drip pan, dome base, crown/E mk, 8", VG..745.00
Brass, baluster shaft, triangle base, Spain, 17th C, 9" 460.00
Brass, baluster trn w/pushups, 1850s, 11", pr 175.00
Brass, capstan, inscr linear decor, 16th C, dents, 5¾x5", pr.........1,850.00
Brass, capstan style, trn decor, vertical extracting holes, 5".........200.00
Brass, capstan w/trn decor on socket, drip pan, Dutch, 17th C, 5"....600.00
Brass, column w/raised rings, side pushup, saucer base, early, 7", pr.220.00
Brass, English Rococo, scroll base/foliate shaft/leaf bobeche, 7", pr..145.00
Brass, Fed, beaded detail, side pushup, threaded base, 7", pr, G ..250.00
Brass, Fed, sq base, pushups, 4½", pr...75.00
Brass, QA, octagon base w/raised ring, 3 rings on threaded std, 5½".165.00
Brass, QA, scalloped base, pushup, burnished, 7⅝", pr...............770.00
Brass, QA, scalloped base, well-formed stem, polished, 8", pr 300.00
Brass, ring-trn columns w/rosettes at center, mk Good Luck, 12", pr..275.00
Brass, sq base w/invected corners, wafer stem, pricket, 7¼" 275.00
Brass, str tapered column on sq base, pushups, 9½", pr 440.00
Brass, trn shaft w/cupped drip, stepped dome base, mid-17th C, 8x4"..750.00
Candelabra, gilt/patinated bronze, 5-arm, Chas X, 1830s, 25", pr.2,000.00
Hogscraper, brass wedding ring, lt pitting, 7½" 220.00
Iron w/brass band on candle cup, 1800s, jointed arm adjusts to 22".590.00
Pewter, baluster trn shafts, trn & stepped base, England, 9"........700.00
Pine, blk pnt, trn pricket, tin saucer-shaped cups, Am, 1800s, 26", pr.925.00
Rush light, wrought iron, twist stem, counterweight, tripod, 16".330.00
SP, Cupid stems, fluted/leafage dome base, Spanish, 20th C, 8", pr.300.00
SP, emb/chased vintage bobeches/wafers/scalloped bases, mk TW, 9", pr.135.00
Tin plate, octagonal drip pan, Eastern US, early 1800s, 6¾" dia, pr..445.00
Wrought iron, spiral stem w/finger loop, conical wooden base, 10".160.00

Candlewick

Candlewick crystal was made by the Imperial Glass Corporation, a division of Lenox Inc., Bellaire, Ohio. It was introduced in 1936, and though never marked except for paper labels, it is easily recognized by the beaded crystal rims, stems, and handles inspired by the tufted needlework called candlewicking, practiced by our pioneer women. During its production, more than 741 items were designed and produced. In September 1982 when Imperial closed its doors, thirty-four pieces were still being made.

Identification numbers and mold numbers used by the company help collectors recognize the various styles and shapes. Most of the pieces are from the #400 series, though other series numbers were also used. Stemware was made in eight styles — five from the #400 series made from 1941 to 1962, one from #3400 series made in 1937, another from #3800 series made in 1941, and the eighth style from the #4000 series made in 1947. In the listings that follow, some #400 items lack the mold number because that information was not found in the company files.

A few pieces have been made in color or with a gold wash. At least two lines, Valley Lily and Floral, utilized Candlewick with floral patterns cut into the crystal. These are scarce today. Other rare items include gifts such as the desk calendar made by the company for its employees and customers; the dresser set comprised of a mirror, clock, puff jar, and cologne; and the chip and dip set.

Ashtray, #400/64, ind 8.00
Ashtray, eagle, #1776/1, 6½" 55.00
Ashtray set, nesting, sq, #400/650, 3-pc 130.00
Bell, #400/108, 5" 95.00
Bowl, #400/92B, 12" 45.00
Bowl, celery boat, oval, #400/46, 11" 65.00
Bowl, cupped edge, #400/75F, 10" 45.00
Bowl, fruit; #400/3F, 6" 12.00
Bowl, heart w/hand, #400/49H, 5"...22.00

Bowl, jelly; w/lid, #400/59, 5½" 75.00
Bowl, lily; 4-ftd, #400/74J, 7" 75.00
Bowl, relish; 2-part, #400/84, 6½" 25.00
Bowl, relish; 4-part, #400/55, 8½" 22.00
Bowl, relish; 5-part, #400/209, 13½" 82.50
Bowl, salad; #400/75B, 10½" 40.00
Bowl, 3-ftd, #400/182, 8½" 135.00
Cake stand, low ft, #400/67D, 10" 60.00
Candle holder, rolled edge, #400/79R, 3½" 17.50
Candle holder, 3-light, beaded center, #400/147 ....40.00
Candy box, #400/59, 5½" dia 50.00
Cigarette box, w/lid, #400/134 ....35.00
Clock, 4" dia 295.00
Compote, #400/63B, 4½" 40.00
Compote, beaded stem, #400/48F, 8" 100.00
Creamer, flat, bead hdl, #400/126 ....32.50
Fork & spoon set, #400/75 ....40.00
Hurricane lamp, candle base, #400/79, 2-pc 135.00
Ice tub, hdls, #400/168, 7" 250.00
Jar tower, 3-section, #400/655 ....495.00
Ladle, mayonnaise; #400/135, 6¼" 12.00
Marmalade set, tall jar, domed bead ft, w/lid & spoon, 3-pc ...100.00
Mayonnaise set, plate+divided bowl+2 ladles, #400-84, 4-pc ...45.00
Oil, bead base, #400/164, 4-oz 55.00
Oil, bulbous bottom, hdld, #400/278, 4-oz 75.00
Pitcher, #400/24, 80-oz 165.00
Pitcher, Manhattan, #400/18, 40-oz 250.00
Pitcher, plain, #400/416, 20-oz 40.00
Pitcher, short, rnd, #400/330, 14-oz 210.00
Plate, bread & butter; #400/1D, 6" 8.00
Plate, crescent salad; #400/120, 8¼" 65.00
Plate, crimped, hdls, #400/72C, 10" 42.00
Plate, salad; #400/5D, 8½" 12.00
Plate, salad; #4003D, 7" 9.00
Plate, service; #400/13D, 12" 35.00
Plate, torte; #400/17D, 14" 50.00
Punch ladle, #400/91 ....30.00
Sauce boat, #400/169 ....50.00
Shakers, bead ft, str sides, chrome lid, #400/247, pr 20.00
Shakers, bulbous w/bead stem, plastic lids, #400/16, pr 110.00

Shakers, #400/190, bead base, footed, $47.50 for the pair.

Stem, brandy; #3800 ....60.00
Stem, parfait; #3400, 6-oz 58.00
Stem, sherbet; #400/190, 6-oz 16.00
Stem, tea; #4000, 12-oz 35.00
Stem, water goblet; #3800, 9-oz 40.00
Sugar bowl, domed ft, #400/18 ....135.00
Sugar bowl, plain ft, #400/31 ....7.00
Tidbit server, 2-tier, cupped, #400/2701 ....60.00
Tray, fruit; center hdl, #400/68F, 10½" 150.00

Tray, relish; 5-compartment, #400/102, 13" 77.50
Tray, uptrn hdls, #400/42E, 5½" 25.00
Tumbler, #400/19, 10-oz 14.00
Tumbler, ftd, #3400, 9-oz 20.00
Tumbler, sherbet; #400/18, 6-oz 60.00
Tumbler, water; #400/18, 9-oz 75.00
Vase, bud; bead ft, #40028C, 8½" 110.00
Vase, fan; #400/287F, 6" 40.00
Vase, rose bowl; ftd, #400/132, 7½" 450.00
Vase, sm neck, ball w/bead ft, #400/25, 4" 65.00

Candy Containers

Figural glass candy containers were first created in 1876 when ingenious candy manufacturers began to use them to package their products. Two of the first containers, the Liberty Bell and Independence Hall, were distributed for our country's centennial celebration. Children found these toys appealing, and an industry was launched that lasted into the mid-1960s.

Figural candy containers include animals, comic characters, guns, telephones, transportation vehicles, household appliances, and many other intriguing designs. The oldest (those made prior to 1920) were usually hand painted and often contained extra metal parts in addition to the metal strip or screw closures. During the 1950s these metal parts were replaced with plastic, a practice that continued until candy containers met their demise in the 1960s. While predominately clear, they are found in nearly all colors of glass including milk glass, green, amber, pink, emerald, cobalt, ruby flashed, and light blue. Usually the color was intentional, but leftover glass was used as well and resulted in unplanned colors. Various examples are found in light or ice blue, and new finds are always being discovered. Production of the glass portion of candy containers was centered around the western Pennsylvania city of Jeannette. Major producers include Westmoreland Glass, West Bros., Victory Glass, J.H. Millstein, J.C. Crosetti, L.E. Smith, Jack Stough, and T.H. Stough. While 90% of all glass candies were made in the Jeannette area, other companies such as Eagle Glass, Play Toy, and Geo. Borgfeldt Co. have a few to their credit as well.

Buyer beware! Many candy containers have been reproduced. Some, including the Camera and the Rabbit Pushing Wheelbarrow, come already painted from distributors. Others may have a slick or oily feel to the touch. The following list may also alert you to possible reproductions:

Amber Pistol, L #144 (first sold full in the 1970s, not listed in E&A)

Auto, D&P #173/E&A #33/L #377

Auto, D&P #163/E&A #60/L #356

Black and White Taxi, D&P #182/L #353 (silk-screened metal roofs are being reproduced. They are different from originals in that the white section is more silvery in color than the original cream. These closures are put on original bases and often priced for hundreds of dollars. If the top is not original, the value of these candy containers is reduced by 80%.)

Camera, D&P #419/E&A #121/L #238 (original says 'Pat Apld For' on bottom, reproduction says 'B. Shakman' or is ground off)

Carpet Sweeper, D&P 296/E&A #133/L #243 (currently being sold with no metal parts)

Carpet Sweeper, E&A #132/L #242 (currently being sold with no metal parts)

Charlie Chaplin, D&P 195/E&A #137/L #83 (original has 'Geo. Borgfeldt' on base; reproduction comes in pink and blue)

Chicken on Nest, D&P #10/E&A #149/L #12

Display Case, D&P #422/E&A #177/L #246 (original should be painted silver and brown)

Dog, D&P #21/E&A #180/L #24 (clear and cobalt)

Drum Mug, D&P #431/E&A #543/L #255

Happifats on Drum, D&P #199/E&A #208/L #89 (no notches on repro for closure to hook into)

Fire Engine, D&P 258/E&A #213/L #386 (repros in green and blue glass)

Independence Hall, D&P #130/E&A #342/L #76 (original is rectangular; repro has offset base with red felt-lined closure)

Jackie Coogan, D&P #202/E&A #345/L #90 (marked inside 'B')

Kewpie, D&P #204/E&A #349/L #91 (must have Geo. Borgfeldt on base to be original)

Mailbox, D&P #216/E&A #521/L #254 (repro marked Taiwan)

Mantel Clock, D&P #483/E&A #162/L #114 (originally in ruby flashed, milk glass, clear, and frosted only)

Mule and Waterwagon, D&P #51/E&A #539/L #38 (original marked Jeannette, PA)

Naked Child, E&A 546/L #94

Owl, D&P #52/E&A #566/L #37 (original in clear only, often painted. Repro found in clear, blue, green, and pink with a higher threaded base and less detail.)

Peter Rabbit, D&P #60/E&A #618/L #55

Piano, D&P #460/E&A #577/L #289 (original in only clear and milk glass, both painted)

Rabbit Pushing Wheelbarrow, D&P #72/E&A #601/L #47 (eggs are speckled on the repro; solid on the original)

Rocking Horse, D&P #46/E&A #651/L #58 (original in clear only, repro marked 'Rocky')

Safe, D&P #311/E&A #661/L #268 (original in clear, ruby flashed, and milk glass only)

Santa, D&P 284/E&A #674/L #103 (original has plastic head; repro [1970s] is all glass and opens at bottom)

Santa's Boot, D&P #273/E&A #111/L #233

Scottie Dog, D&P #35/E&A #184/L #17 (repro has a ice-like color and is often slick and oily)

Station Wagon, D&P #178/E&A #56/L #378

Stough Rabbit, D&P #53/E&A #617/L #54

Uncle Sam's Hat, D&P #428/E&A #303/L #168

Wagon, U.S. Express D&P #530 (Glass is being reproduced without any metal parts.)

Other reproductions are possible. If in doubt, do not buy without a guarantee from the dealer and return privilege in writing.

Our advisor for glass containers is Jeff Bradfield; he is listed in the Directory under Virginia. You may contact him with questions, if you will include an SASE. See Clubs, Newsletters, and Catalogs for the address of the Candy Container Collectors of America. A bimonthly newsletter offers insight into new finds, reproductions, updates, and articles from over four hundred collectors and members, including all authors of books on candy containers. Dues are $25.00 yearly. The club holds an annual convention in June in Lancaster, Pennsylvania, for collectors of candy containers.

'L' numbers used in this guide refer to a standard reference series, *An Album of Candy Containers*, Vols. 1 and 2, by Jennie Long. 'E&A' numbers correlate with *The Compleat American Glass Candy Containers Handbook* by Eikelberner and Agadjanian, revised by Adele Bowden. D&P numbers refer to *The Collector's Guide to Candy Containers* by Doug Dezso and Leon and Rose Poirier (Collector Books).

Airplane, Army Bomber, 15-P-7 on right wing, D&P 76/E&A 6/L 328 .**40.00**

Airplane, Liberty Motor, West Glass Co, D&P 78/E&A 10 ....**3,000.00**

Airplane, Spirit of St Louis, many variants, D&P 85/E&A 9, $500 to..**700.00**

Barney Google by Barrel, King Features Syndicate, D&P 188/E&A 71.**1,500.00**

Bell, Liberty w/Hanger; bl glass, wire bail, D&P 95/E&A 85 ....**60.00**

Bird on Mound, orig whistle, ca 1920, D&P 3/E&A 95...........**1,000.00**

Boat, Battleship; open base w/3 sections, D&P 99/E&A 97 ....**30.00**

Boat, Colorado; TH Stough, orig superstructure, D&P 101/E&A 102/L 334..**400.00**

Bottle, Maud Muller Candies, 4 in cb crate, D&P 110................**250.00**

Bus, Chicago; open base w/no dividers, D&P 149/E&A 118 ......**450.00**

Bus, Country Club; tin bk closure, metal wheels, D&P 150/E&A 117.**1,400.00**

Candelabrum, 2 glass shakers in metal stand, D&P 317/E&A 174/L 202.**45.00**

Cannon, Muzzle Loader; silver metal carriage, D&P 381/E&A 130/L 452.**1,000.00**

Car, Air Flow; Victory Glass, Jeannette PA, all orig, D&P 158/E&A 61.**650.00**

Car, Coupe - Long Hood w/Glass Wheels; D&P 161 ....**175.00**

Car, Electric Runabout - Open Top; D&P 163/E&A 47/L 356 (+) ..**80.00**

Car, Green Taxi; gr wheels, Westmoreland Specialty, D&P 183 (+) .**1,200.00**

Car, Little Sedan; blown, tin or cork closure, D&P 171/E&A 31 .**35.00**

Car, Sedan w/6 Vents; Victory Glass Co, no mks, G pnt, D&P 176/E&A 37.**125.00**

Cash Register, open bottom, tin closure, D&P 420/E&A 135/L 244.**600.00**

Cat, Winking Stretched Neck; screw-on closure, D&P 6 ....**5,000.00**

Chick in Shell Auto w/Balloon Tires, tin closure, D&P 9 ....**725.00**

Child, Naked; hand under chin, orig closure, VGCO..., D&P 197/E&A 546.**90.00**

Clock, Candy Bank; red plastic hands, Van Brode, D&P 479 ....**50.00**

Clock, Lynne Bank; 2-pc tin w/glass base, D&P 481/E&A 159 ..**600.00**

Clock, Octagon; deep open base, paper dial, D&P 484/E&A 163 ..**225.00**

Dog, Scottish Terrier, metal cap closure, D&P 34.........................**75.00**

Dog by Barrel, yel screw cap on bbl, LE Smith, D&P 19/E&A 190/L 13.**250.00**

Duck on Rnd Base, gold-tone closure, USA, D&P 40/E&A 200/L 26..**625.00**

Fire Engine, Fire Dept No 99, mk VG (Victory Glass), D&P 252/E&A 214..**125.00**

Fire Engine, Little Boiler #1, bl w/gr tin closure, D&P 256/E&A 218.**150.00**

Fire Engine, 1914 Stough, orig wheels, mk Pat Pending, D&P 262/E&A 223 .**175.00**

Flapper, paper face glued inside, Des Pat No 84161, D&P 203/E&A 227.**75.00**

Flossie Fisher's Bed, tin w/glass cover, D&P 299......................**3,500.00**

Fox, Learned; swallow-tail suit, metal closure, D&P 45/E&A 470..**100.00**

Golf Club, mk DRGM on shaft, D&P 425/E&A 244....................**75.00**

Gun, Grooved Barrel; X-hatching on grip, D&P 392 ....**35.00**

Gun, Whistling Jim - Waisted Grip, open bbl, D&P 403/E&A 248.**25.00**

Horn, Millstein 1948; plastic bell & mouthpc, D&P 449/E&A 311.**35.00**

Horn, Musical Clarinet No 515a, whistle cap, D&P 452/E&A 315..**150.00**

Hound w/Lg Glass Hat, push-in closure: TH Stough..., D&P 27/E&A 182..**25.00**

Jack-o'-Lantern, Big Straight Eyes; bail hdl, D&P 264/E&A 347/L 160.**275.00**

Lamp, Candlestick Base; paper-cup shade, TH Stough, D&P 322/E&A 370..**350.00**

Lamp, Hobnail; cb shade, TH Stough, all orig, D&P 329/E&A 365.**500.00**

Lamp, Library; mk Pat Pending on metal base, D&P 334/E&A 372.**525.00**

Lamppost, pewter stand, glass top, D&P 341/L 553 ....**110.00**

Lantern, Beaded #1, beaded ribs, mk USA, D&P 347/E&A 404 ..**40.00**

Lantern, Japanese Paper Type; metal lid, bail hdl, D&P 354/E&A 389..**500.00**

Lantern, Tiny Pear Shaped; tin top w/bail hdl, D&P 368..............**25.00**

Lantern on Stand, 6-panel, wire stand, bail hdl, D&P 358/L 571.**55.00**

Locomotive, Am Type 23, bl, 4-4-0 wheels/3 stacks, D&P 489/E&A 480..**150.00**

Locomotive, Curved Line 888; 4-4-0 wheels, open base, D&P 490/E&A 483..**45.00**

Locomotive, Lithographed Closure #3, West Bros, D&P 494/E&A 498..**100.00**

Locomotive, Man in Window 888, 4-4-0 wheels, M.**400.00**

Locomotive, Stough's Musical Toy, whistle cap, D&P 506...........**35.00**

Locomotive, Two Stacker #23, 4-4-0 wheels, D&P 512/E&A 479/L 603..**150.00**

Mail box, Letters US Mail, tin closure, Westmoreland, D&P 216/E&A 521..**250.00**

Mug, Eagle; ruby flashed, D&P 431/E&A 543 ....**75.00**

Nurser, Lynn Doll; rubber nipple mk Hygeia, D&P 122/E&A 550.**35.00**

Nurser, Plain Oval; lipped opening, Crosetti Co, D&P 124 ....**30.00**

Piano, ruby flashed, tin slide-on closure, D&P 460/E&A 577.....**400.00**

Pipe, Fancy Bowl; cut-glass pattern, Trade Mark, D&P 436/E&A 583..**125.00**

Powder Horn, blown, mk Pat Appd For, D&P 411/E&A 589/L 265..**95.00**

Pumpkin Head Witch, wire bail, G pnt, D&P 272/E&A 594/L 165.**950.00**

Rabbit, Peter; clover between legs, Jeannette..., D&P 60/E&A 618/L 55.**30.00**

Rabbit by Stough, heavily striated 'fur,' ca 1948, D&P 53/E&A 617.**45.00**

Racer, Pointed Front; 9-vent sides, pk body, D&P 471/E&A 638.**3,500.00**

Racer #12, 2-vent sides, disc wheels, D&P 476/E&A 642/L 432..**220.00**

Refrigerator, coil top, VG (Victory Glass), D&P 309/E&A 650/L 266.**6,500.00**

Santa Claus, Victory Glass, mk Avor 3½ oz, D&P 285, rare ...**7,500.00**

Santa Claus in Long Coat, gold-tone cap, REGDNO716934, D&P 279.**350.00**

Swing, Porch; metal, bag ties to seat, D&P 315/E&A 468..........**200.00**

Telephone, Flat Top Hinge; wood receiver, D&P 225/E&A 737...**65.00**

Telephone, Lynne - Sunken Dial; candlestick, complete, D&P 232/E&A 741.**60.00**

Telephone, Pewter Top #1; blown, blk wood receiver, D&P 236/E&A 756.**150.00**

Telephone, Redlich's Screw Top #1; glass/metal/wood, D&P 241/E&A 742 ..450.00
Telephone, Stough's Ringed Base, wht cap, red whistle, D&P 247/E&A 732..40.00
Train, Coal Car - No Couplers; tin wheels, D&P 518 ....500.00
Train, Parlor Car, open top, NY Central atop windows, D&P 516 .325.00
Village Bank, tin litho w/insert, D&P 133/E&A 804/L 76E........275.00
Village Drug Store, tin litho w/insert, D&P 137/E&A 810 ....150.00
Village Log Cabin, tin litho w/insert, D&P 140/E&A 816/L 765 ..400.00
Wagon, Circus; blown, metal screw-on cap, D&P 527/L 439 ......250.00
Wagon, US Express, metal wheels, wire hdl, D&P 530/E&A 821 .750.00
Windmill, 5 Window; open base/screw cap/orig blades, D&P 535/E&A 844 ..500.00

Miscellaneous

These types of candy containers are generally figural. Many are holiday related. Small sizes are common; larger sizes are in greater demand. Because of eBay's influence, prices have dropped and remain soft. Our prices reflect this trend. Our advisor for this category is Jenny Tarrant; she is listed in the Directory under Missouri. See also Christmas; Easter; Halloween.

Key: pm — papier-mache

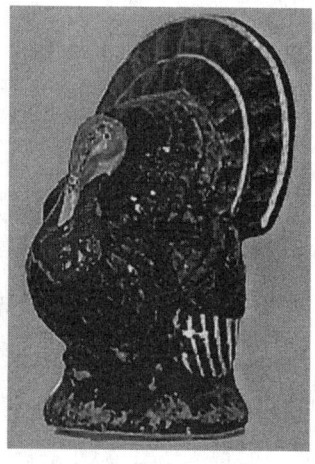

Turkey, plaster and composition with bottom cardboard closure, EX: 3", $55.00; 4", $58.00; 5", $78.00; 6", $110.00.

Bulldog, compo, cream w/orange hat, Germany, 4", VG 100.00
Cat, pm w/gesso, mc pnt, glass eyes, red ribbon, rpt, 6" 190.00
Cat, seated, pm w/gesso, worn flocking, glass eyes, rpr, 4" 175.00
Cat in shoe, compo & gesso w/mc pnt, rpr, 4" 150.00
Doll, bsk open dome head, crepe-paper/cb cylinder body, Germany, 6"..120.00
Dove, compo w/gray pnt, pk-pnt metal fr, orange glass eyes, 4½x8"..150.00
Elephant, pm, glass tusks, Germany, ca 1885-1920, 6" L 155.00
English Bobby, pm, EX pnt, Pat No 208063, 12" 160.00
Geo WA, compo, stands on rnd box w/silk flag, Germany, 5".....195.00
Geo WA bust, bottom plug, compo, 2-3" 95.00
Geo WA bust, bottom plug, compo, 4-6" 150.00
Geo WA w/tree stump, compo, Germany, 3-4" 150.00
Geo WA w/tree stump, compo, Germany, 5-7" 225.00
Horse, pm, head removes, 4½", VG 85.00
Pig, pm, gr w/HP features, Made in Germany, 5¼x5½x3" 90.00
Pig, pm, sleeping, worn/soiled pk flocking, 5⅝" 90.00
Pigeon, compo w/metal ft, gray/wht/irid purple, 4½x6" 75.00
Pigeon, compo w/metal ft, yel/red/brn pnt, lt ft wear, 4½x4¾" 75.00
Rooster, compo w/metal ft, yel/red/brn pnt, lt ft wear, 4½x4¾" .120.00
St Patrick's Day, Irish man bust, w/plug, compo, Germany, 3-4" ...95.00
St Patrick's Day, Irish man bust, w/plug, compo, Germany, 5-6" .150.00
St Patrick's Day, Irish man on candy box, compo, Germany, 3½" .155.00
St Patrick's Day, pig, flocked gr, plug in tummy, wood legs, 3-5"...95.00
St Patrick's Day, pk, pk w/shamrock, compo, Germany, 4-6" 95.00

St Patrick's Day, potato, compo, Germany, 3-4" 50.00
Stag, compo w/metal rack, brn flock, yel glass eyes, Germany, 10", VG .465.00
Stork w/baby, spun cotton & paper, lifts leg, Germany, 1930s, 6½"..95.00
Turkey, compo w/metal ft, head removes, Germany, 5" 150.00
Turkey, compo w/metal legs, head removes, Germany, 3½"...........70.00
Watermelon w/face, molded cb w/celluloid body, Austria, 4¼" ..125.00

Canes

Fancy canes and walking sticks were once the mark of a gentleman. Hand-carved examples are collected and admired as folk art from the past. The glass canes that never could have been practical are unique whimseys of the glassblower's profession. Gadget and container sticks, which were produced in a wide variety, are highly desirable. Character, political, and novelty types are also sought after as are those with handles made of precious metals.

Because our line length is limited, the values we suggest are midrange. Expect to pay as much as 25% more or less than prices listed.

For more information we recommend *American Folk Art Canes, Personal Sculpture,* by George H. Meyer, Sandringham Press, 100 West Long Lake Rd., Suite 100, Bloomfield Hills, MI 48304. Other possible references are *Canes in the United States* by Catherine Dike and *Canes From the 17th – 20th Century* by Jeffrey Snyder. For information concerning the Cane Collectors Club, see the Directory under Clubs, Newsletters, and Catalogs. Our advisor for this category is Bruce Thalberg; he is listed in the Directory under Connecticut.

Bloodstone L hdl w/gold/rubies & silver o/l, hardwood shaft..1,200.00
Cigarette lighter gadget crook hdl, blk hardwood shaft, ca 1911 .2,500.00
Ebony pug dog w/glass eyes on pillow hdl, silver collar, ebony shaft ..900.00
Gold-filled GAR hdl, ebony shaft, wht metal/iron ferrule, ca 1890 ...600.00
Hearing aid gadget blk enamel hdl, bamboo shaft, ca 1860...2,500.00
Horn elephant hdl w/glass eyes, malacca shaft, 1880s, from $400 to ..700.00
Imari porc ball finial w/chrysanthemums, blk shaft, English, 1880s..1,200.00
Ivory Art Deco hdl w/tortoise shell inlay, hardwood shaft, 1920s.1,250.00
Ivory bulldog w/glass eyes hdl, stepped partridgewood shaft, ca 1917...900.00
Ivory cat hdl w/gr glass eyes, ebony shaft, horn ferrule, 1900s ..850.00
Ivory elephant hdl removes for 12½" sword, bamboo shaft, 1840s..1,200.00
Ivory hdl w/silver tiger cap, birch shaft, iron/brass ferrule, 1895 .800.00
Ivory nude maiden hdl (EX detail), ebony shaft, rpl ferrule, 1880s .2,850.00
Ivory rose hdl, coconutwood shaft, brass/iron ferrule, ca 1945.1,000.00
Jade & rock crystal hdl, silver collar, ebony shaft, Am, ca 1900 ...1,200.00
Lapis w/silver o/l cherubs, ebony shaft, brass/iron ferrule, 1900s..1,300.00
Mahog harmonica hidden in hdl, cvd shaft w/ivory separator, 1890s .2,200.00
Obsidian rhino head hdl, gold collar, ebony shaft, horn ferrule, 1900s..3,900.00
Pepperbox gun w/dagger forms gadget hdl, malacca shaft, ca 1895 .5,250.00
Porc cockerel head hdl, thick malacca shaft, horn ferrule, 1860s .1,050.00
Porc hdl w/red HP scenes on wht, gold collar, malacca shaft, 1880s ..850.00
Porc w/HP putti & flowers w/silver o/l ball hdl, hardwood shaft, 1890s .900.00
Porc w/HP scene & silver o/l hdl, snakewood shaft, horn ferrule, 1870s .1,250.00
Silver Art Nouveau peacock w/sapphires & dmn, snakewood shaft, ca 1904.3,900.00
Silver drinking glass & flask in hdl, hardwood shaft, horn ferrule ..850.00
Silver Masonic unfolding ball hdl, ebonized shaft, ca 1891 .....2,700.00
Silver Unger Bros Am Indian hdl, partridgewood shaft, ca 1890..2,000.00
Wedgwood bl Jasper hdl w/wht feathers, wooden shaft, ca 1930s .2,500.00
Whalebone 8-sided hdl, rosewood shaft, brass ferrule, 1850s ...1,100.00
Wood, folk-art guardsman atop roses/springs/shamrocks, mc stain, 1900s .1,400.00
Wood, primitive bird hdl w/mc stain, beaded eyes, lt wear 150.00
Wood cvd fist hdl, detailed rattlesnake on shaft, lt wear, 35"......325.00
Wood cvd sheepdog hdl w/amber glass eyes, malacca shaft, ca 1895..500.00
Wood dog w/wagging tongue hdl, cherrywood shaft, brass ferrule, 1880s..1,100.00
Wood/ivory Fr bulldog hdl w/glass eyes, palmwood shaft, ca 1900..625.00

Canton

Canton is a blue and white porcelain that was first exported in the 1790s by clipper ships from China to the United States. Importation continued into the 1920s. Canton became very popular along the East Coast where the major ports were located. Its popularity was due to several factors: it was readily available, inexpensive, and (due to the fact that it came in many different forms) appealing to homeowners.

The porcelain's blue and white color and simple motif (teahouse, trees, bridge, and a rain-cloud border) have made it a favorite of people who collect early American furniture and accessories. Buyers of Canton should shop at large outdoor shows and up-scale antique shows. Collections are regularly sold at auction and many examples may be found on eBay. Collectors usually prefer a rich, deep tone rather than a lighter blue. Cracks, large chips, and major repairs will substantially affect values. Prices of Canton have escalated sharply over the last twenty years, and rare forms are highly sought after by advanced collectors. Our advisor for this category is Hobart D. Van Deusen; he is listed in the Directory under Connecticut.

Bottle, water; ovoid w/long neck, hairlines, 7⅝" 300.00
Bowl, lobed, 10x8¼" 800.00
Bowl, serving; 8-sided, shallow, prof rpr, 2x13x10¾" 330.00
Bowl, vegetable; berry finial, 5¾x10", VG 500.00
Bowl, vegetable; fruit finial, 9½" L 550.00
Bowl, vegetable; invected corners, fruit finial, rpr, 10" 300.00

Candlesticks, nineteenth century, 7½", $2,200.00 for the pair.

Creamer, bull-nose spout, flared rim, 3¾", NM 220.00
Creamer, helmet shape w/hooked crosses on ft, swirls on hdl, 4⅛".580.00
Creamer, high hdl, 3¼" 220.00
Gravy tureen, boars' head hdls, bud finial, 5x7", VG 500.00
Pie plate, shallow flakes, 10⅛" 400.00
Pitcher, thin hdl w/molded fan terminal, 6", NM 880.00
Platter, octagonal, flake, 14¼x11½" 500.00
Platter, octagonal, geometric line borders, 15½", EX 750.00
Platter, octagonal, staple rpr, 19x15¾" 350.00
Platter, octagonal, 12" 300.00
Soup tureen, boars' head hdls, leaf finial, 11" L, EX 1,200.00
Sugar bowl, hdls w/appl decor, fruit finial, 4½" 500.00
Teapot, branch hdl, berry finial, rpr/flakes, 5⅛" 200.00
Warming dish, high base, fruit finial, 5x9⅜" 660.00

Capodimonte

The relief style, highly colored and defined porcelain pieces in this listing are commonly called and identified in our current marketplace as Capodimonte. It was King Ferdinand IV, son of King Charles who opened a factory in Naples in 1771 and began to use the mark of the blue crown N (BCN). When the factory closed in 1834, the Ginori family at Doccia near Florence, Italy, acquired what was left of the factory and continued using its mark. The factory continued until 1896 when it was then combined with Societa Ceramica Richard of Milan which continues today to manufacture fine porcelain pieces marked with a crest and wreaths under a blue crown with R. Capodimonte.

Boxes and steins are highly sought after as they are cross collectibles. Figurines, figure groupings, flowery vases, urns, and the like are also highly collectible, but most items on the market today are of recent manufacture. In the past several years, Europeans have been attending U.S. antique shows and auctions in order to purchase Capodimonte items to take back home, since many pieces were destroyed during the two world wars. This has driven up prices of the older ware. Our advisor for this category is James Highfield; he is listed in the Directory under Indiana.

Floral Style

Bowl of bsk flowers, 4¾x5" 35.00
Candle holders, pk rose, 2x4x3", pr 40.00
Mirror, cherubs, 22x13" 45.00
Pedestal planter w/orchids, 37" 175.00
Sunflower on leaves, 5x2½" 25.00
Telephone w/red rose, 7x8" 21.00
Vase, dbl hdl, single rose, 7½x5" 25.00

Relief Style

Box, cherubs, R Capo mk, 2½x3¼" sq 15.00
Box, Neptune on lid, BCN, 3x4½" dia 250.00
Box, 4 ladies harvesting on lid, BCN, 1¾x3½x2¾" 200.00
Casket, brass spires & ft, BCN France, 6½x13x9½" 3,000.00
Casket, mythological scenes, BCN, 9½x15x9" 2,500.00
Centerpc, cherubs w/grapes in 4 corners, BCN, 10x13x11" 850.00
Cup, bearded face, BCN, 4x4½" 75.00
Cup & saucer, gr & gold vine hdl, BCN, 2¼x4½", set of 6 .... 560.00
Figurine, beggar woman, BCN, 6¼" 65.00
Figurines, band members, BCN, 4½", 6-pc set 100.00
Jardiniere, ram head hdls, no mk, 8x10" 360.00
Plaque, draped male, Bernini mk, 14¼" dia 60.00
Plates, center coat of arms, 8¾", set of 4 .... 300.00
Stein, cherub procession, eagle finial on lid, BCN, 12x7½" 450.00
Tray, harvesting by river scene, BCN, 15¾x11½" 250.00
Triptych, religious scenes, BCN, 10x12" 375.00
Urn, battle scene, plumed helmet finial, BCN, 14¼x6" 175.00
Urn, wine scenes, w/lid, BCN Saxony, 6¼x3½", pr 125.00

Carlton Ware

Carlton Ware was the product of Wiltshaw and Robinson, who operated in the Staffordshire district of England from about 1890. During the 1920s, they produced ornamental ware with enameled and gilded decorations such as flowers and birds, often on a black background. In 1958 the firm was renamed Carlton Ware Ltd. Their trademark was a crown over a circular stamp with 'W & R, Stoke on Trent,' surrounding a swallow. 'Carlton Ware' was sometimes added by hand.

Ashtray, Rouge Royale, 2 rests, 7" L 39.00
Basket, Water Lily, gr 140.00
Biscuit bbl, Oak Tree, wicker hdl, 6½" 155.00
Bookends, Oak Tree, 6½", pr 145.00
Bowl, birds (1 flying/1 on branch), blk/wht on orange, 7¾" 110.00
Bowl, Bleu Royale, bird & tree on bl, #1608, 12x7½" 210.00

Bowl, Hazelnut, swirled shallow oval, #2277, 9½x6½" 60.00
Bowl, Oak Tree, hdls, bl mk, 2½x11x7" 110.00
Bowl, Rosetta, orange ground, #3505, 8" 315.00
Bowl, Rouge Royale, New Stork, #4340, 2x5¼x8½" 65.00
Bowl, Rouge Royale, spider web decor on red, 2x10½x8½" 160.00
Bowl, serving; Foxglove, yel, 2½x7¼x11" 95.00
Chamberstick, Anemone, yel, 1 hdl 190.00
Coffeepot, bright orange w/emb ribs, slim, 1970s retro style, 12" ..90.00
Coffeepot, gold swirls & trim, 7½x8½" 200.00
Coffepot, Paradise Bird & Tree, #3154, 9" 500.00
Cruet set, 3 shell shapes on shell tray, brn & wht 65.00
Cruet set, Oak, shakers & mustard on tray, #1185 ....165.00
Cruet set, pear/apple/lemon shapes on banana-shaped tray 75.00
Cruet set, robins (2) on 5¾" L tray 75.00
Cruets, shell forms (3), lime gr on blk shell tray 85.00
Cup, Walking Ware, gr shoes w/gr & wht plaid socks 60.00
Cup, Walking Ware, maroon shoes w/wht socks w/gr dots, 5" 75.00
Cup & saucer, Buttercup, pk 160.00
Cup & saucer, Foxglove, yel 90.00
Cup & saucer, Primula, 3x3", 5½" 80.00
Cup & saucer, Water Lily, #1786, 2½x3½", 6" 90.00
Dish, grapefruit; Buttercup, pk, 4" dia, 5½" underplate 100.00
Dish, grapefruit; Water Lily, pk, 5x6" 110.00
Dish, Rouge Royale, Kingfisher, 11x6" 190.00
Egg cup, Walking Ware, blk shoes, wht socks w/red circles, 1973 .65.00
Egg cup set, 4 bird-form cups, 2¾", on 13" tray 110.00
Figurine, Beefeater Yeoman, 16⅛" 135.00
Figurine, Guiness Zoo Keeper, My Goodness, My Guiness on base, 4" .170.00
Figurines, stylized toucans w/2 pints of Guiness in beaks, set of 3 ...350.00
Fleshpots, Laurel & Hardy, hats form lids, 9¾", 8½", pr 210.00
Ginger jar, lyre-tail birds, flowers & fruit baskets, #2979, 4¾" 105.00
Ginger jar, Rouge Royale, fantasy forest & storks, w/lid, 7½" 320.00
Jar, Fantasia, w/lid, #3421, 7" 420.00
Jar, Paradise Bird & Tree, w/lid, 11" 540.00
Knife, Foxglove, gr, 4½" 68.00
Mug, coffee; bright orange, '70s retro style, slim, tall, 6 for 80.00
Mug, Hangman, wording on bk, 4" 40.00
Mug, Hangman, 1940, 3" 45.00
Pen holder, peacock seated on tree stump 175.00
Pitcher, Bell, gilded, 6¾" 825.00
Pitcher, bl mottle, MOP int, Deco shape, sticker, 6½" 100.00
Pitcher, hot water; bl chrysanthemums on cream, 6¼" 165.00
Pitcher, Rabbits at Dusk, #4247, 5½" 280.00
Pitcher, Rouge Royale, Mikado, 5⅞" 140.00
Pitcher, Walking Ware, bl shoes, zigzag-pattern socks, 3¼x5" 60.00
Pitcher & bowl, Paradise Bird & Tree, #3154, 2½x3¼", 3½x4" .250.00
Plate, Buttercup, sm hdl, #1395, 4½x3¾" 40.00
Plate, O Lovely Guiness...What a Wonderful Guiness You Are, 7½" .110.00
Plate, Rouge Royale, stork & tree, 10½" 200.00
Plate, Walking Ware, yel shoes & wht socks w/bl dots, 10" 150.00
Platter, burnt orange/yel/red/gr slip glaze design, oblong, 5x5" 25.00
Preserve pot, Fruit Basket, w/lid & underplate, #712, 4x6" 100.00
Salad servers, plain leaf design, scarce, 7½" 45.00
Shakers, English Beefeater figurals, orange, mk, 4", pr 40.00
Shakers, lady 1 side, reverse: man, 3½", pr 30.00
Sugar sifter, cottage design, wht w/orange roof, 5½x3" 135.00
Tea set, Windstream, pot+cr/sug+jelly jar w/lid+underplate+spoon.250.00
Teacup, Walking Ware, yel shoes, checked socks, 1980, 4½" 120.00
Teapot, Austin Cooper car figural, Peace/floral/Love, 4½x8½" ..110.00
Teapot, Buttercup, pk, 6-cup, w/lid 525.00
Teapot, Foxglove, #1883/3, 5" 235.00
Teapot, prop plane w/pilot, Union Jack flag on side, 6x8" 100.00
Teapot, Walking Ware, yel shoes w/wht socks w/bl dots, 3½" 135.00
Tray, Hydrangea, shaped as from lapping leaves, 9x7" 110.00

Tray, Poppy, 3 flowers form shallow wells, 11" L 80.00
Tray, Rouge Royale, spider web, 8½" L 112.00
Urn, Chinese Tea Garden, tall ped ft, #2936, 7x7½" 260.00
Vase, Cherry, #3272, 10¼" 675.00
Vase, Chinese pagoda scenes on bl, w/gilt, 6" 220.00
Vase, Floral Comets, mc floral on gr, 1 hdl, 6⅝" 480.00
Vase, Geometric Tree, 3-ftd, 3-hdld, bullet form, 9½" 775.00
Vase, lyre-tail birds, stick neck, #2969, 8" 105.00
Vase, Mandarin Tree, gr, ped ft, #3719, 6" 525.00
Vase, Persian, mc & gilt on cobalt, 10½" 675.00
Vase, Rouge Royale, Chinese people, mk #0/2840 & #3675, 10¼" .680.00
Vase, Rouge Royale, no pattern, 3¼x3½" 50.00
Vase, Rouge Royale, spider web decor, 5" 175.00
Vase, Stork, mc floral on blk, flared neck, 10½" 290.00
Vase, tulips, mauve & pk in cream, sq, hdls, 5x5" 80.00
Vase, Tutankhamen, enamel & gilt on cobalt, 6" 765.00
Vase, Zig Zag, lightning motif, dk bl/bronze copper lustre/gilt, 6"..320.00

Carnival Collectibles

Carnival items from the early part of this century represent the lighter side of an America that was alternately prospering and sophisticated or devastated by war and domestic conflict. But whatever the country's condition, the carnival's thrilling rides and shooting galleries were a sure way of letting it all go by — at least for an evening.

For further information on chalkware figures, we recommend *The Carnival Chalk Prize* by our advisor, Thomas G. Morris, who is listed in the Directory under Oregon.

In the shooting gallery target listings below, items are rated for availability from 1, commonly found, to 10, rarely found (these numbers appear just before the size), and all are made of cast iron. Our advisors for shooting gallery targets are Richard and Valerie Tucker; their address is listed in the Directory under Texas.

Chalkware Figures

Abe Lincoln bust, 1940-50, 12" 55.00
Alice the Goon, from Popeye, 1930-40, 10" 165.00
Apache Babe, orig mks, 1936-45, 15" 85.00

Betty Boop, Fleisher Studios, 1930 – 40, 14½", $375.00.

Boy, w/top hat/tux/cane/spats, 1930s, 8" 45.00
Bulldog, sitting, 1925-35, 10¼" 65.00
Charlie McCarthy, seated, 1930-40, 9½" 55.00
Donald Duck, head bank, Disney, 1940-50, 10½" 80.00
Felix the Cat, 1922-40, 12½" 245.00
Frenchie, Jenkins, 1924, rare, 15" 195.00

Kewpie, jtd arms, mohair wig, 1920s, 12½" 165.00
Lighthouse, 1935-40, 12¼" 45.00
Little Sheba, orig feathers, HP, 1920s, 13" 165.00
Mae West, w/lg hat & parasol, 1930-40, 14" 125.00
Maggie & Jiggs, 1920-35, 8¼" & 9½", pr....................265.00
Ming Toy, Jenkins, 1924, 13" 185.00
Nude bust, lamp, Art Deco style, 1930-40, 8½" 135.00
Piano baby, 1910-25, 10½" 120.00
Popeye, saluting, 1930-40, 11½"..115.00
Sailor girl, Jenkins, 1934, 13½" 80.00
Shirley Temple, ca 1935-45, 14½" 190.00
Sitting lady, pk chalk, HP, ca 1920, 6½" 65.00
Snow White, 1937-50, 14" 85.00

Shooting Gallery Targets

Battleship, worn wht pnt, Mangels, 5, 6¼x11⅜", $200 to 300.00
Birds (8) on bar, worn pnt, Mangels, 9, 3½x41½", $700 to 800.00
Bull's-eye w/pop-up duck, old pnt, Quakenbush, 7, 12" dia, $500 to .600.00
Clown, worn red/wht pnt, Mangels, 9, 19x9½"+movable arms, minimum.1,000.00
Clown standing, bull's-eye, mc pnt, Evans or Hoffman, 20½", minimum..1,000.00
Dbl star spinner, worn mc pnt, Mangels, 6, 8x2¾", $200 to 300.00
Dog running, worn wht pnt, Smith or Evans, 6, 6x11", $100 to.200.00
Duck, detailed feathers, old pnt, Parker, 8", 3¾x5½", $100 to ...200.00
Duck, detailed feathers, worn pnt, Evans, 4", 5½x8½", $100 to.200.00
Eagle w/wings wide, mc pnt, Smith or Evans, 6, 14¾", $650 to..750.00
Elephant, worn red pnt, King, 10, 17x19", minimum value 1,000.00
Greyhound, bull's-eye, old patina, Parker, 8", 26" W, minimum.1,000.00
Indian chief, worn mc pnt, Hoffmann or Smith, 10, 20x15", minimum..1,000.00
Monkey, standing, worn pnt, 10, 9¾x8½", $300 to....................400.00
Owl, bull's-eye, wht traces, Evans, 6, 10¾x5⅛", $400 to 500.00
Pipe, old patina, Smith, 1, 5⅜x1¾", value less than 50.00

**Rabbit running, bull's-eye, old patina, Parker, 8, 12x25x1",
minimum value $1,000.00.** (Photo courtesy Richard and Valerie Tucker)

Rabbit standing, worn pnt, Smith or Mueller, 8, 18x10", $900 to..1,000.00
Reindeer (elk), wht pnt (worn/rusty), 7", 10x9", $300 to............400.00
Saber-tooth tiger, old patina, Mangels, 7, 7¾x13", $300 to 400.00
Soldier w/rifle, pnt traces/old patina, Mueller, 5, 9x5", $100 to ..200.00
Squirrel running, old patina, Smith, 4, 5⅛x9¼", $100 to...........200.00
Swan, worn wht pnt, Mueller, 7, 5¾x5", $100 to 200.00

Carnival Glass

Carnival glass is pressed glass that has been coated with a sodium solution and fired to give it an exterior lustre. First made in America in 1905, it was produced until the late 1920s and had great popularity in the average American household, for unlike the costly art glass produced by Tiffany, carnival glass could be mass produced at a small cost. Colors most found are marigold, green, blue, and purple; but others exist in lesser quantities and include white, clear, red, aqua opalescent, peach opalescent, ice blue, ice green, amber, lavender, and smoke.

Companies mainly responsible for its production in America include the Fenton Art Glass Company, Williamstown, West Virginia; the Northwood Glass Company, Wheeling, West Virginia; the Imperial Glass Company, Bellaire, Ohio; the Millersburg Glass Company, Millersburg, Ohio; and the Dugan Glass Company (Diamond Glass), Indiana, Pennsylvania. In addition to these major manufacturers, lesser producers included the U.S. Glass Company, the Cambridge Glass Company, the Westmoreland Glass Company, and the McKee Glass Company.

Carnival glass has been highly collectible since the 1950s and has been reproduced for the last twenty-five years. Several national and state collectors' organizations exist, and many fine books are available on old carnival glass, including *The Standard Encyclopedia of Carnival Glass* by Bill Edwards and Mike Carwile, *Dugan & Diamond Carnival Glass, 1909 – 1931*, *Imperial Carnival Glass*, and *Northwood Carnival Glass, 1908 – 1925*, all by Carl O. Burns.

Acorn (Fenton), plate, marigold, rare, 8½" 1,350.00
Acorn Burrs (Northwood), butter dish, amethyst, w/lid..............300.00
Adam's Rib (Dugan/Diamond), tumbler, ice gr 60.00
American (Fostoria), tumbler, gr, rare 140.00
Apple Blossom (Diamond), bowl, bl, 6" 150.00
Apple Tree (Fenton), pitcher vase whimsey, bl, rare 9,000.00
Arcadia Basket, plate, marigold, 8" 50.00
Asters, bowl, bl...100.00
Aurora Pearls, bowl, amethyst, decor, 2-szs 700.00
Australian Swan (Crystal), bowl, amethyst, 9" 450.00
Aztec (McKee), rose bowl, clambroth 400.00
Bamboo Bird, jar, marigold, complete...800.00
Band of Roses, tray, marigold 75.00
Banded Crystal (Crystal), pitcher, amethyst, very rare.............1,250.00
Banded Drape (Fenton), pitcher, gr...500.00
Banded Moon & Stars (Jain), tumbler, marigold, rare.................225.00
Barbella (Northwood), plate, marigold...70.00
Basketweave & Cable (Westmoreland), creamer, gr, w/lid..........100.00
Beaded Bull's Eye (Imperial), vase, amethyst, 14" 235.00
Beaded Mirrors Variant (Jain), tumbler, marigold, rare...............250.00
Beaded Shell (Dugan), bowl, amethyst, ftd, 5"..............................40.00
Beaded Spears (Jain), pitcher, marigold, rare 560.00
Beaded Swirl (English), compote, bl..60.00
Bellaire Souvenir (Imperial), bowl, marigold, scarce 125.00
Bells & Beads (Dugan), gravy boat, amethyst, hdld......................70.00
Big Basketweave (Dugan), vase, peach opal, 8"-14" 425.00
Big Fish (Millersburg), bowl, gr, 8½"...725.00
Birds & Cherries (Fenton), bonbon, gr 80.00
Blackberry (Fenton), spittoon whimsey, bl, rare 3,600.00
Blackberry Block (Fenton), tumbler, vaseline 350.00
Blackberry Spray (Fenton), compote, marigold..............................40.00
Blocks & Arches (Crystal), tumbler, amethyst, rare 90.00
Blueberry (Fenton), pitcher, bl, scarce.......................................2,000.00
Boggy Bayou (Fenton), vase, amethyst, 6"-11".............................125.00
Bow & Knot, perfume, marigold..45.00
Braziers Candies (Fenton), plate, amethyst, handgrip 1,000.00
Brocaded Acorns (Fostoria), cake tray, ice bl, center hdl 200.00
Brocaded Daffodils (Fostoria), bonbon, ice gr 90.00
Brocaded Palms (Fostoria), ice bucket, ice gr...............................250.00
Brocaded Roses (Fostoria), wine goblet, ice gr.............................200.00
Broken Arches (Imperial), punch bowl, marigold, w/base 1,100.00
Bubbles, lamp chimney, horehound...50.00
Bull's Eye (US Glass), oil lamp, marigold.......................................210.00
Bull's Eye & Loop (Millersburg), vase, gr, rare, 7"-11"................400.00
Butterflies (Fenton), card tray, bl..60.00

Butterfly & Berry (Fenton), bowl, gr, ftd, 10" 200.00
Butterfly & Berry (Fenton), pitcher, wht 1,500.00
Butterfly & Tulip (Dugan), bowl whimsey, amethyst, rare 2,500.00
Butterfly Bush & Waratah, compote, marigold 200.00
Buzz Saw (Cambridge), cruet, gr, scarce, 4" 800.00
Cambridge Hobstar (Cambridge), napkin ring, marigold 165.00
Camellia Loop, vase, marigold, 5¾" 150.00
Cane & Daisy Cut (Jenkins), basket, smoke, hdld, rare 250.00
Cannonball Variant, pitcher, bl 285.00
Captive Rose (Fenton), compote, gr 100.00
Carolina Dogwood (Westmoreland), bowl, marigold, 8½" 80.00
Cartwheel #411 (Heisey), bonbon, marigold 60.00
Chain & Star (Fostoria), butter dish, w/lid, rare 1,500.00
Chatelaine (Imperial), pitcher, amethyst, very scarce 3,000.00
Checkerboard (Westmoreland), wine, marigold, rare 300.00
Checkers, rose bowl, marigold 85.00
Cherry (aka Hanging Cherries) (Millersburg), bowl, gr, 7" 165.00
Cherry (Dugan), banana bowl, amethyst 300.00
Cherry & Cable (Northwood), bowl, marigold, scarce, 9" 110.00
Cherry Blossoms, tumbler, bl 40.00
Cherry Chain Variant (Fenton), plate, bl, 9½" 225.00
Chesterfield (Imperial), compote, marigold, 6½" 35.00
Chevrons, vase, marigold 325.00
Circled Rose, plate, marigold, 7" 95.00
Classic Arts, vase, marigold, very scarce, 7½" 425.00
Coin Dot (Fenton), rose bowl, bl 140.00
Colonial (Imperial), sugar bowl, marigold, open 30.00
Columbine (Fenton), tumbler, gr 55.00
Concave Diamonds (Northwood), pitcher, olive gr, w/lid 450.00
Concord (Fenton), plate, amethyst, rare, 10" 2,400.00
Coral (Fenton), bowl, wht, 9" 400.00
Corn Vase (Northwood), pulled husk, gr, rare 13,000.00
Cosmos & Cane (US Glass), basket, honey amber, 2-hdld, rare .1,000.00
Cosmos & Cane (US Glass), rose bowl whimsey, amethyst 1,500.00
Country Kitchen (Millersburg), creamer, gr 750.00
CR (Argentina), ashtray, bl 300.00
Crosshatch (Sowerby), sugar bowl, marigold, open 75.00
Curtain Optic (Fenton), tumbler, vaseline 150.00
Cut Arcs (Fenton), bowl, gr, 7½"-10" 120.00
Cut Ovals (Fenton), candlesticks, marigold, pr 270.00
Czech Interior Swirl, pitcher, lemonade; marigold 175.00
Dahlia (Dugan), sugar bowl, amethyst 100.00
Daisy & Cane (Brockwitz), decanter, marigold, rare 100.00
Daisy & Plume (Northwood & Dugan), compote, gr, stemmed 60.00
Daisy Dear (Dugan), bowl, amethyst 45.00
Daisy Squares, goblet, amethyst, rare 750.00
Dandelion (Northwood), mug, bl opal 750.00
Decorama, pitcher, marigold 550.00
DeVilbiss, perfumer, marigold 65.00

Diamond & Daisy Cut (US Glass), tumbler, marigold, rare 50.00
Diamond & Fan, compote, peach opal 100.00
Diamond & Rib (Fenton), vase, amethyst or gr, 7"-12" 60.00
Diamond Checkerboard, bowl, marigold, 9" 40.00
Diamond Cut Shields, pitcher, marigold 475.00
Diamond Lace (Imperial), bowl, gr, 5" 50.00
Diamond Point (Northwood), vase, bl, 7"-14" 250.00
Diamond Point Columns (Late), powder jar, marigold, w/lid 40.00
Diamond Ring (Imperial), bowl, fruit; amethyst, 9½" 90.00
Diamond Star, mug, marigold, 2 szs 125.00
Dianthus (Fenton), pitcher, ice gr 475.00
Dogwood Sprays (Dugan), compote, amethyst 225.00
Dotted Diamonds & Daisies, tumbler, marigold 55.00
Double Diamond, pin tray, marigold 60.00
Double Dolphin (Fenton), vase, fan; celeste bl 90.00
Double Stem Rose (Dugan), bowl, peach opal, dome base, 8½".175.00
Dragon & Lotus (Fenton), bowl, gr, flat, 9" 190.00
Dragon's Tongue (Fenton), bowl, marigold, scarce, 11" 1,200.00
Drapery (Northwood), candy dish, aqua 200.00
Duckie, powder jar, marigold, w/lid 20.00
Dugan Many Ribs (Dugan), vase, marigold 60.00
Duncan (National Glass), cruet, marigold 600.00
Early American (Duncan & Miller), plate, marigold 75.00
Egyptian Lustre (Dugan), plate, blk amethyst 85.00
Elektra, butter dish, marigold 150.00
Elks (Fenton), bowl, Atlantic City; scarce 1,300.00
Embroidered Mums (Northwood), bowl, bl, 9" 500.00
Enameled Crocus, pitcher, bl 175.00
Enameled Double Daisy, tumbler, wht 30.00
Enameled Grape (Northwood), pitcher, bl 400.00
Enameled Lotus (Fenton), pitcher, ice gr 450.00
Enameled Stork (German), tumbler, marigold 50.00
English Button Band (English), creamer, marigold 45.00
Engraved Floral (Fenton), tumbler, gr 95.00
Estate (Westmoreland), bud vase, smoke, 6" 75.00
Exchange Bank, bowl, advertising; amethyst 850.00
Fan-Tail (Fenton), plate, bl, ftd, rare 6,000.00
Fanciful (Dugan), plate, bl, 9" 600.00
Fashion (Imperial), bowl, smoke, 9" 55.00
Feathered Serpent (Fenton), bowl, gr, 10" 90.00
Fenton #643, compote, marigold 50.00
Fenton #9, candy jar, marigold, w/lid 35.00
Fenton Cherries, banana boat, marigold, very rare 3,000.00
Fentonia Fruit (Fenton), bowl, ftd, bl, 10" 175.00
Fern (Fenton), bowl, bl, rare, 7"-9" 1,100.00
Field Flower (Imperial), bowl, marigold, 6"-10" 50.00
File (Imperial & English), bowl, amethyst, 7"-10" 50.00
Filed Rib (Federal), plate, marigold, 10¾" 65.00
Fine Cut & Roses (Northwood), candy dish, gr, ftd 70.00
Fine Cut Rings (English), celery dish, marigold 160.00
Fine Rib (Fenton), plate, gr, 9" 120.00
Fir Cones (Finland), tumbler, bl 350.00
Fishnet (Dugan), epergne, amethyst 300.00
Five Panel, candy jar, marigold, stemmed 70.00
Flashing Stars, tumbler, bl, rare 275.00
Flora (English), float bowl, bl 200.00
Floral & Grape Variant (Fenton), pitcher whimsey, bl, very rare .4,500.00
Floral Fan, vase, marigold, etched 50.00
Florentine (Fenton & Northwood), candlesticks, olive gr, lg, pr..160.00
Flowering Dill (Fenton), hat, gr 65.00
Flowers & Beads (Dugan), plate, salad; amethyst, 6-sided, 7½"..110.00
Flute (Fenton), vase, bl, 7"-12" 45.00
Flute (Northwood), ring tree, marigold, rare 175.00
Flute & Cane (Imperial), wine, marigold 60.00

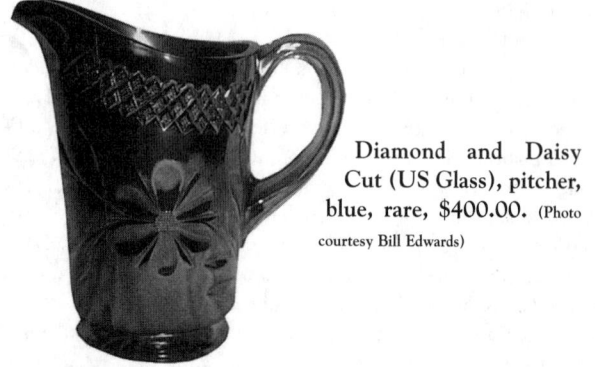

Diamond and Daisy Cut (US Glass), pitcher, blue, rare, $400.00. (Photo courtesy Bill Edwards)

Flute #700 (Imperial), toothpick, vaseline, no hdl 300.00
Folding Fan (Dugan), compote, amethyst 75.00
Forks, cracker jar, marigold, very rare 1,750.00
Four Flowers (Dugan), banana bowl, amethyst, scarce 400.00
Frosted Block (Imperial), bowl, marigold, 9" 30.00
Frosted Ribbon, tumbler, marigold 30.00
Fruit Lustre, tumbler, marigold.......................................35.00
Garden Path (Dugan), plate, chop; peach opal, rare 7,500.00
Garland & Bows (English), butter dish, marigold, w/lid..............75.00
George (Brockwitz), compote, marigold, 3 szs, minimum value 75.00
Giant Lily (Czech), vase, marigold...................................250.00

Grape and Gothic Arches (Northwood), bowl, amethyst, 10", $95.00. (Photo courtesy Bill Edwards)

Golden Bird, nappy, marigold, ftd, hdld 300.00
Golden Honeycomb, compote, marigold 35.00
Golden Pineapple & Blackberries, plate, marigold, 10"..............500.00
Good Luck (Northwood), plate, bl, 9"...............................1,950.00
Gooseberry Spray (US Glass), compote, amethyst, rare 225.00
Grape & Cable (Fenton), bowl, gr, ball ftd, 7"-8½" 85.00
Grape & Cable (Northwood), bowl, ice cream; lav, 11" 350.00
Grape & Cable Banded (Northwood), banana bowl, bl.............600.00
Grape & Cable Variant (Northwood), plate, marigold, handgrip, scarce.165.00
Grape & Cable w/Thumbprint (Northwood), pitcher, gr, tankard style.2,500.00
Grape & Gothic Arches (Northwood), spooner, bl 70.00
Grape Delight (Dugan), rose gowl, wht, ftd, 6".......................65.00
Grape Leaves (Northwood), bowl, gr, ruffled or 3-in-1 edge, 8½" ..85.00
Grape Wreath (Millersburg), bowl, gr, 5"............................165.00
Grecian Daisy, tumbler, marigold, scarce.............................60.00
Greek Key (Northwood), tumbler, amethyst, rare 235.00
Halloween, spitton, marigold..600.00
Harvest Flower (Dugan), pitcher, marigold, rare 2,800.00
Hattie (Imperial), bowl, amethyst 295.00
Headdress, compote, bl...75.00
Heart & Vine (Fenton), plate, gr, very scarce, 9" 625.00
Hearts & Flowers (Northwood), bowl, aqua opal, 8½" 1,500.00
Heavy Diamond (Imperial), sugar bowl, marigold......................35.00
Heavy Grape (Imperial), plate, amethyst or gr, 8" 200.00
Heavy Iris (Dugan), tumbler, amethyst 105.00
Heavy Vine, lamp, marigold..250.00
Heisey Colonial, dresser tray, marigold.............................100.00
Heisey Flute, toothpick holder, marigold............................150.00
Heron (Dugan), mug, amethyst, rare..................................150.00
Hex Optic (Honeycomb)(Jeannette, Depression era), creamer, marigold..20.00
Hobnail (Millersburg), pitcher, gr, rare..........................4,000.00
Hobnail Variant (Millersburg), rose bowl, marigold, rare...........800.00
Hobstar (Imperial), bowl, fruit; gr, w/base........................150.00
Hobstar & Cut Triangles (English), plate, amethyst.................100.00
Hobstar & Feather (Millersburg), bowl, gr, rnd, rare, 5" 1,400.00
Hobstar Band, pitcher, marigold, 2 shapes, scarce..................250.00
Hobstar Reverse (English), rose bowl, amethyst 95.00
Holly (Fenton), compote, bl 45.00

Holly Sprig (Millersburg), bowl, gr, tri-cornered, 7"-8" 325.00
Holly Sprig (Millersburg), nappy, amethyst, tri-cornered 95.00
Holm Spray, atomizer, marigold......................................65.00
Honeycomb & Clover (Fenton), spooner, marigold, rare............100.00
Horses' Head (Horse Medallion)(Fenton), nut bowl, marigold, scarce.80.00
Humpty-Dumpty, mustard jar, marigold...............................75.00
Illinois Daisy (English), cookie jar, marigold, w/lid................60.00
Imperial #107½A, compote, marigold.................................65.00
Imperial #3939, punch cup, gr, scarce...............................50.00
Imperial #5, bowl, amethyst, 8".....................................50.00
Imperial #641, cheese plate, marigold...............................50.00
Imperial Grape, compote, gr...75.00
Imperial Grape, tumbler, marigold, ftd 30.00
Imperial Jewels, bowl, gr, 7"-10"...................................45.00
Intaglio Daisy (Dugan/Diamond), bowl, marigold, 7½"................50.00
Interior Flute, creamer, marigold...................................50.00
Interior Swirl, tumbler, gr...70.00
Inverted Coin Dot (Fenton), pitcher, marigold, rare 650.00
Inverted Coin Dot (Fenton), tumbler, marigold, scarce...............75.00
Inverted Feather (Cambridge), cookie jar, gr, w/lid................300.00
Inverted Strawberry (Cambridge), bowl, amethyst, 5"................115.00
Inverted Strawberry (Cambridge), spooner, bl, rare.................425.00
Inverted Thistle (Cambridge), bowl, amethyst or gr, rare, 5"......150.00
Inverted Thistle (Cambridge), pitcher, marigold, rare 3,000.00
Ivy, claret, marigold, stemmed......................................85.00
Jacobean (Inwald), decanter, marigold 200.00
Jacobean Ranger (Czech & English), tumbler, juice; marigold....125.00
Jasmine & Butterfly (Czech), tumbler, marigold 25.00
Jenkin Lattice (#336), spooner, marigold 75.00
Jewel (Dugan), vase, bl...175.00
Jeweled Heart (Dugan), pitcher, marigold, rare 900.00
Kangaroo (Australian), bowl, marigold, 5"..........................100.00
Kittens (Fenton), cup, bl, scarce...................................500.00
Kiwi & Variant (Australian), bowl, amethyst, rare, 10"...........1,000.00
Kookaburra & Variants (Australian), bowl, marigold, 5"............175.00
Laco, oil bottle, marigold 80.00
Large Kangaroo (Australian), bowl, amethyst, 10"...................450.00
Late Enameled Strawberry, tumbler, lemonade; marigold 75.00
Late Sunflower (Jeannette), pitcher, marigold 50.00
Lattice & Daisy (Dugan), pitcher, marigold.........................250.00
Lattice & Sprays, vase, marigold, 10½"..............................50.00
Laurel Leaves (Imperial), plate, smoke 65.00
Leaf & Beads (Northwood), nut bowl, bl, ftd, scarce 475.00
Leaf Chain (Fenton), plate, yel, 9¼".............................5,100.00
Leaf Rosette & Beads (Dugan), bowl, amethyst, 6"-7"................60.00
Leaf Tiers (Fenton), bowl, marigold, ftd, 5".......................30.00
Lightning Flowers (Northwood), nappy, marigold, rare.............125.00
Lined Lattice (Dugan), vase, peach opal, 8"-12"....................250.00
Lion (Fenton), plate, marigold, rare, 7½" 1,300.00
Little Fishes (Fenton), bowl, amethyst, flat or ftd, 10" 425.00
Little Stars (Millersburg), bowl, amethyst or gr, scarce, 8"-9" 450.00
Long Hobstar (Imperial), compote, marigold 65.00
Lotus (Fenton), tumbler, marigold...................................35.00
Lotus & Grape Variant (Fenton), bowl, gr, ftd, 6" 90.00
Louisa (Westmoreland), rose bowl, amethyst 70.00
Lovely (Northwood), bowl, gr, ftd.................................1,100.00
Lucile, pitcher, marigold, rare...................................1,200.00
Lustre & Clear (Imperial), butter dish, marigold 65.00
Lustre Flute (Northwood), punch cup, marigold or gr 20.00
Lustre Rose (Imperial), fernery, amethyst...........................200.00
Magnolia Rib (Fenton), bowl, berry; marigold, lg 55.00
Malaga (Dugan), plate, amber, rare, 10" 400.00
Many Fruits (Dugan), punch cup, gr..................................40.00
Maple Leaf (Dugan), spooner, bl.....................................70.00

Marilyn (Millersburg), tumbler, amethyst, rare 225.00
Massachusetts (US Glass), vase, marigold, very scarce 175.00
Maypole, vase, gr 60.00
Memphis (Northwood), bowl, berry; amethyst, 10"-12" 350.00
Meydam (Leerdam), cake stand, marigold.....................................95.00
Miniature Hobnail, pitcher, marigold, rare, 6" 250.00
Miniature Shell, candle holder, clear, ea 75.00
Minnesota (Late), mug, marigold 100.00
Mirrored Lotus (Fenton), rose bowl, bl, rare 500.00
Moonprint (Brockwitz), banana boat, marigold, rare...................135.00
Moonprint (Brockwitz), jar, marigold, w/lid.................................65.00
Mt Gambier (Crystal), mug, marigold..100.00
Multi-Fruits & Flowers (Millersburg), tumbler, gr, rare 1,200.00
Nautilus (Dugan-Northwood), creamer, peach opal, scarce 200.00
Near Cut (Northwood), compote, amethyst 150.00
Nesting Swan (Millersburg), bowl, gr, sq, rare 1,500.00
Niagara Falls (Jeannette), pitcher, marigold 50.00
Nola (Scandanavian), pitcher, marigold, squat............................300.00
Northern Star (Fenton), card tray, marigold, 6" 40.00
Northwood #699, cheese dish, vaseline..100.00
Nu-Art Homestead (Imperial), plate, gr, scarce 3,000.00
Number 270 (Westmoreland), compote, bl opal............................150.00
Nutmeg Grater, butter dish, amethyst 125.00
Octagon (Imperial), cordial, marigold...250.00
Octagon (Imperial), wine, gr 150.00
Ohio Star (Millersburg), vase, aqua opal, very scarce 25,000.00
Omera (Imperial), rose bowl, clambroth 60.00
Open Edge Basket (Basketweave)(Fenton), plate, bl, rare 1,400.00
Open Rose (Imperial), bowl, marigold, flat, 9" 40.00
Optic & Buttons (Imperial), goblet, marigold................................60.00
Optic Flute (Imperial), bowl, smoke, 10" 35.00
Orange Tree (Fenton), creamer whimsey, wht, made from cup mold..195.00
Orange Tree (Fenton), mug, gr, 2 szs...475.00
Orange Tree (Fenton), pitcher, bl...600.00
Orange Tree (Fenton), wine, gr 300.00
Orebro (Sweden), bowl, bl, oval 185.00
Oval & Round (Imperial), bowl, gr, sm 40.00
Painted Castle, shade, marigold 65.00
Palm Beach (US Glass), banana bowl, honey amber...................175.00
Panama (US Glass), goblet, marigold, rare 150.00
Paneled Dandelion (Fenton), pitcher, gr......................................500.00
Paneled Palm (US Glass), wine, marigold, rare 150.00
Pansy (Imperial), dresser tray, amethyst 175.00
Panther (Fenton), bowl, amethyst, ftd, 5" 225.00
Papini Victoria (Argentina), tumbler, marigold 75.00
Parquet, creamer, marigold 70.00
Peach & Pear (Dugan), banana bowl, bl 600.00
Peacock (Millersburg), bowl, ice cream; amethyst, 5" 300.00
Peacock & Grape (Fenton), plate, gr, ftd, 9" 425.00
Peacock & Urn & Variants (Millersburg), bowl, bl, 9½".........2,500.00
Peacock at the Fountain (Northwood), bowl, gr, 9" 350.00
Peacock at the Fountain (Northwood), tumbler, ice bl 165.00
Peacock Tail (Fenton), compote, wht..55.00
Peacock Tail Variant (Millersburg), compote, amethyst, scarce ..150.00
Peacocks (On the Fence)(Northwood), bowl, gr, 8¾" 1,000.00
Pebbles (Fenton), bonbon, amethyst 45.00
Perfection (Millersburg), pitcher, gr, rare 6,000.00
Persian Gardens (Dugan), bowl, fruit; marigold, w/base............675.00
Persian Medallion (Fenton), hair receiver, bl...............................85.00
Petal & Fan (Dugan), bowl, amethyst, 8"-9".................................250.00
Philox (Northwood), pitcher, marigold..400.00
Pillar & Flute (Imperial), creamer, marigold 35.00
Pine Cone (Fenton), plate, gr, 6¼" 325.00
Pineapple (English), compote, bl...60.00

Plain & Fancy (Heisey), tumbler, marigold, very scarce 125.00
Plain Jane (Imperial), bowl, gr, 10"-12"......................................100.00
Plain Rays, bowl, marigold, 9" 40.00
Poinsettia (Imperial), pitcher, milk; amethyst 2,000.00
Pond Lily (Fenton), bonbon, bl 60.00
Poppy (Millersburg), salver, amethyst, rare 1,700.00
Poppy Show (Northwood), plate, marigold, scarce, 9" 1,300.00
Portland (US Glass), bowl, marigold, 8" 170.00
Potpourri (Millersburg), pitcher, milk; amethyst, rare 4,500.00
Premium Swirl (Imperial), candlesticks, marigold, pr 50.00
Pretty Panels (Fenton), tumbler, ice gr, w/hdl..............................90.00
Primrose (Millersburg), bowl, gr, ruffled, 8¾" 200.00
Princely Plumes, candle holder, amethyst 300.00
Prism & Daisy Band (Imperial), vase, marigold 25.00
Prism Columns, bowl, marigold, low, 7¾" 55.00
Proud Puss (Cambridge), bottle, marigold....................................85.00
Puritan (McKee), plate, marigold, rare, 6" 150.00
Question Marks (Dugan), bonbon, lav 80.00
Radiance, bowl, marigold, 8" 85.00
Rainbow (Northwood), compote, gr...80.00
Rambler Rose (Dugan), tumbler, bl 65.00
Ranger (Imperial), sherbet, marigold, ftd 55.00
Ranger (Mexican), shot glass, marigold, rare 450.00
Raspberry (Northwood), pitcher, amethyst 325.00
Rays & Ribbons (Millersburg), bowl, amethyst or gr, sq, scarce..600.00
Rex, pitcher, buttermilk; marigold 75.00
Ribbed Ellipse (Higbee), tumbler, marigold 250.00
Ribbed Swirl, pitcher, gr...225.00
Ribbon Tie (Fenton), bowl, amethyst, 8¼" 275.00
Ripple (Imperial), vase, funeral; gr, 15"-21" 400.00
Rock Crystal (McKee), punch cup, amethyst, rare 75.00
Roll, shaker, marigold, rare..45.00
Rolling Ridges, tumbler, marigold..25.00
Rosalind (Millersburg), compote, jelly; bl, rare, 9"................15,000.00
Rose Bouquet, bonbon, wht, rare...400.00
Rose Garden (Sweden & German), bowl, marigold, 8¼" 150.00
Rose Show (Northwood), bowl, gr, 8¾" 2,000.00
Rosetime, vase, marigold, 7½" 100.00
Royal Lustre (Dugan), bowl, console; ice gr 60.00
Ruffled Rib, spittoon, aqua opal, ruffled, rare 2,000.00
Rustic (Fenton), vase, peach opal, standard, 8"-13" (+3" base)..1,400.00
S-Repeat (Dugan), tumbler, amethyst 125.00
Sawtooth Band, pitcher, marigold 375.00
Scale Band (Fenton), plate, red, flat, 6½"....................................425.00
Scales (Westmoreland), bowl, Persian Blue, 7"-10" 100.00
Scroll Embossed (Imperial), bowl, amethyst, 4"-7" 65.00
Scroll Embossed (Imperial), plate, gr, 9" 125.00
Seacoast (Millersburg), pin tray, gr, scarce 800.00

Seaweed (Millersburg), bowl, green, 9", $400.00. (Photo courtesy Bill Edwards)

Seaweed, lamp, ice bl, rare, 8½" 400.00
Serrated Ribs, shaker, marigold 60.00
Shell (Imperial), plate, amethyst, 8½" 1,000.00
Signature (Jeannette), parfait, marigold, tall 25.00
Silver Queen (Fenton), pitcher, marigold 250.00
Singing Birds (Northwood), creamer, gr.....................125.00
Single Flower (Dugan), hat, amethyst 45.00
Six Petals (Dugan), bowl, gr or peach opal, 8½" 75.00
Ski Star (Dugan), banana bowl, amethyst...................175.00
Slim Jim, vase, marigold, 13" 45.00
Small Rib (Fenton), compote, gr, 4½" 50.00
Smooth Panels (Imperial), vase, funeral; marigold, 15"-18" 125.00
Smooth Rays (Imperial), custard cup, marigold 15.00
Smooth Rays (Imperial), wine, smoke, 2 szs 40.00
Smooth Rays (Westmoreland), rose bowl, amethyst 70.00
Soda Gold (Imperial), pitcher, marigold 200.00
Soutache (Dugan), bowl, peach opal, rare, 10½" 350.00
Sowerby Frog, flower frog, marigold, ftd, scarce 125.00
Spanish Moss, hatpin holder, marigold, rare, 5½" 200.00
Spicer Beehive (Spicer Studios), honey pot, amethyst, w/catch plate .95.00
Spiral (Imperial), candlesticks, gr, pr.........................195.00
Split Diamond (English), creamer, marigold, sm............25.00
Springtime (Northwood), tumbler, gr, rare 120.00
Stag & Holly (Fenton), plate, marigold, scarce, 13".....1,000.00
Star & File (Imperial), bonbon, marigold.....................35.00
Star & File (Imperial), tumbler, lemonade; marigold, rare 800.00
Star Center, plate, amethyst, 9" 80.00
Star Medallion (Imperial), butter dish, marigold 100.00
Star Medallion (Imperial), plate, clambroth, 10" 85.00
Starbright, vase, gr, 6½" 55.00
Starburst (Finland), spittoon, bl 175.00
Stars & Bars, rose bowl, marigold 130.00
Stippled Diamond Swag (English), compote, bl............60.00
Stippled Petals (Dugan), basket, peach oal, hdld.........170.00
Stippled Rays (Fenton), bonbon, gr............................50.00
Stork & Rushes (Dugan), bowl, marigold, 10" 40.00
Strawberry (Northwood), plate, marigold, stippled, 9".............2,100.00
Strawberry w/Checkerboard (Jenkins), butter dish, marigold........85.00
Strawberry Wreath (Millersburg), compote, gr, scarce.................400.00
Stream of Hearts (Fenton), goblet, mariglld, rare 225.00
Strutting Peacock (Westmoreland), rose bowl whimsey gr, ...150.00
Sunflower (Millersburg), pin tray, amethyst or gr, scarce............600.00
Sunk Daisy (aka Amerika) (Sweden), bowl, bl.............275.00
Sunray, compote, peach opal 60.00
Swirl (Imperial), plate, marigold 80.00
Swirl Variant (Imperial), epergne, gr.........................200.00
Swirled Rib (Northwood), pitcher, marigold................165.00
Sword & Circle, tumbler, juice; marigold, rare 225.00
Szea (aka Sweden), plate, bl, 6" 210.00
Taffeta Lustre (Fostoria), candlesticks, gr, rare, pr.......350.00
Ten Mums (Fenton), bowl, amethyst, flat, 8"-10" 275.00
Thin & Wide Rib (Northwood), vase, marigold, ruffled 35.00
Thistle (Fenton), plate, marigold, very scarce, 9" 6,700.00
Thistle Banana Boat (Fenton), banana boat, gr, ftd, scarce........450.00
Three Diamonds (Dugan), vase, amethyst, 6"-10" 50.00
Three Fruits (Northwood), plate, amethyst or gr, 9"....400.00
Three-In-One (Imperial), bowl, amethyst, 8¾" 60.00
Thunderbird (Australian), bowl, marigold, 9½" 350.00
Tiger Lily (Imperial), pitcher, marigold 140.00
Tornado (Norhtwood), vase, amethyst, plain, 2 szs......425.00
Tree Bark (Imperial), candlesticks, marigold, 4½", pr....40.00
Tree Bark (Imperial), plate, marigold, 8" 50.00
Tree of Life, tumbler, marigold 30.00
Tree Trunk (Northwood), vase, funeral; gr, 12"-22".....4,250.00

Trout & Fly (Millersburg), plate, lav, rare, 9".............6,000.00
Tulip Panels, ginger jar, marigold............................125.00
Twins (Imperial), bowl, gr, 9" 50.00
Twitch (Bartlett-Collins), sherbet, marigold 45.00
Two Row (Imperial), vase, amethyst, rare................1,150.00
US #310 (US Glass), candy dish, ice gr, w/lid 90.00
US #310 (US Glass), mayonnaise set, ice gr 95.00
Utah Liquor (Fenton), plate, advertising; amethyst, scarce 1,350.00
Venetian, sugar bowl, marigold, rare.........................625.00
Vineyard (Dugan), tumbler, amethyst 50.00
Vining Twigs (Dugan), hat, marigold..........................40.00
Vintage (Fenton), rose bowl, bl 125.00
Vintage (Millersburg), bowl, gr, rare, 9" 825.00
Vintage Banded (Dugan), tumbler, marigold, rare 600.00
Waffle Block (Imperial), bowl, marigold, 7"-9" 30.00
Waffle Block (Imperial), vase, clambroth, 8"-11" 55.00
Water Lily (Fenton), bonbon, marigold........................40.00
Water Lily & Cactus (Fenton), bowl, tri-corner; marigold, 6" 35.00
Water Lily & Cattails (Northwood), tumbler, bl 700.00
Western Thistle, pitcher, cider; bl 350.00
Wheat (Northwood), sherbet, amethyst, very rare 6,000.00
Wide Panel (Fenton), glass, lemonade; marigold, hdld....30.00
Wide Panel (Imperial), bowl, marigold milk glass, 7"-10" 125.00
Wide Panel (Northwood), compote, marigold, #645 .....40.00
Wide Rib (Dugan), vase, squat; marigold, 4"-6" 30.00
Wild Loganberry (Westmoreland), sugar bowl, irid moonstone, rare..100.00
Wild Rose (Millersburg), lamp, gr, rare, sm 1,100.00
Wild Strawberry (Northwood), bowl, amethyst, rare, 6"...........150.00
Wildflower (Millersburg), compote, jelly; amethyst, rare 1,700.00
Windmill (Imperial), bowl, fruit; marigold or gr, 10½"..............40.00
Wine & Roses (Fenton), goblet, wine; bl......................100.00
Wishbone & Spades (Dugan), plate, amethyst, rare, 10½".......2,000.00
Wreathed Cherry (Dugan), bowl, amethyst, oval, 5" 40.00
Wreathed Cherry (Dugan), sugar bowl, marigold..........70.00
Zippered Heart (Imperial), bowl, marigold, 5" 40.00
474 (Imperial), compote, amethyst, rare, 7"................275.00
474 (Imperial), vase, red, rare, 7" 3,200.00
49er Variant (Inwald), tray, marigold, scarce...............95.00

Carousel Figures

For generations of Americans, visions of carousel horses revolving majestically around lively band organs rekindle wonderful childhood experiences. These memories are the legacy of the creative talent from a dozen carving shops that created America's carousel art. Skilled craftsmen brought their trade from Europe where American carvers took the carousel animal from a folk art creation to a true art form. The golden age of carousel art lasted from 1880 to 1929.

There are two basic types of American carousels. The largest and most impressive is the 'park style' carousel built for permanent installation in major amusement centers. These were created in Philadelphia by Gustav and William Dentzel, Muller Brothers, and E. Joy Morris who became the Philadelphia Toboggan Company in 1902. A more flamboyant group of carousel animals was carved in Coney Island, New York, by Charles Looff, Marcus Illions, Charles Carmel, and Stein & Goldstein's Artistic Carousel Company. These park-style carousels were typically three, four, and even five rows with forty-five to sixty-eight animals on a platform. Collectors often pay a premium for the carvings by these men. The outside row animals are larger and more ornate and command higher prices. The horses on the inside rows are smaller, less decorated, and of lesser value.

The most popular style of carousel art is the 'country fair style.' These carousels were portable affairs created for mobility. The horses are smaller and less ornate with leg and head positions that allow for stacking and easy loading. These were built primarily for North Tonawanda, New York, near Niagara Falls, by Armitage Herschell Company, Herschell Spillman Company, Spillman Engineering Company, and Allen Herschell. Charles W. Parker was also well known for his portable merry-go-rounds. He was based in Leavenworth, Kansas. Parker and Herschell Spillman both created a few large park-style carousels as well, but they are better known for their portable models.

Horses are by far the most common figure found, but there are two dozen other animals that were created for the carousel platform. Carousel animals, unlike most other antiques, are oftentimes worth more in a restored condition. Figures found with original factory paint are extraordinarily rare and bring premium amounts. Typically, carousel horses are found in garish, poorly applied 'park paint' and are often missing legs or ears. Carousel horses are hollow. They were glued up from several blocks for greater strength and lighter weight. Bass and poplar woods were used extensively.

If you have an antique carousel animal you would like to have identified, send a clear photograph and description along with a LSASE to our advisor, William Manns, who is listed in the Directory under New Mexico. Mr. Manns is the author of *Painted Ponies*, containing many full-color photographs, guides, charts, and directories for the collector.

Key:
IR — inside row
MR — middle row
OR — outside row
PTC — Philadelphia Toboggan Company

Coney Island-Style Horses

Carmel, IR jumper, unrstr	4,800.00
Carmel, MR jumper, unrstr	7,900.00
Carmel, OR jumper w/cherub, rstr	17,000.00
Illions, IR jumper, rstr	5,200.00
Illions, MR stander, rstr	9,200.00
Looff, IR jumper unrstr	3,200.00
Looff, OR jumper, unrstr	14,000.00
Stein & Goldstein, IR jumper, unrstr	4,700.00
Stein & Goldstein, MR jumper, rstr	8,000.00
Stein & Goldstein, OR stander w/bells, unrstr	18,000.00

European Horses

Anderson, English, unrstr	2,500.00
Bayol, French, unrstr	2,500.00
Heyn, German, unrstr	3,000.00
Hubner, Belgian, unrstr	2,000.00
Savage, English, unrstr	2,500.00

Menagerie Animals (Non-Horses)

Dentzel, bear, unrstr	20,000.00
Dentzel, cat, unrstr	22,000.00
Dentzel, deer, unrstr	13,500.00
Dentzel, lion, unrstr	35,000.00
Dentzel, pig, unrstr	8,000.00
E Joy Morris, deer, unrstr	10,000.00
Herschell Spillman, cat, unrstr	11,000.00
Herschell Spillman, chicken, portable, unrstr	7,000.00
Herschell Spillman, dog, portable, unrstr	6,500.00
Herschell Spillman, frog, unrstr	15,000.00
Looff, camel, unrstr	10,000.00
Looff, goat, rstr	13,500.00
Muller, tiger, rstr	32,000.00

Philadelphia-Style Horses

Dentzel, IR 'topknot' jumper, unrstr	4,100.00
Dentzel, MR jumper, unrstr	7,800.00
Dentzel, OR stander, female cvg on shoulder, rstr	20,000.00

Dentzel, outside row stander, flowing mane, double eagle-back saddle, worn paint, minor separations, unrestored, $10,350.00. (Photo courtesy Skinner, Inc.)

Dentzel, prancer, rstr	8,000.00
Morris, IR prancer, rstr	4,500.00
Morris, MR stander, unrstr	7,000.00
Morris, OR stander, rstr	13,500.00
Muller, IR jumper, rstr	5,000.00
Muller, MR jumper, rstr	7,500.00
Muller, OR stander, rstr	18,000.00
Muller, OR stander w/military trappings	30,000.00
PTC, chariot (bench-like seat), rstr	7,500.00
PTC, IR jumper, rstr	4,000.00
PTC, MR jumper, rstr	8,500.00
PTC, OR stander, armored, rstr	35,000.00
PTC, OR stander, unrstr	19,000.00

Portable Carousel Horses

Allan Herschell, all aluminum, ca 1950	500.00
Allan Herschell, half & half, wood & aluminum head	1,200.00
Allan Herschell, IR Indian pony, unrstr	2,200.00
Allan Herschell, OR, rstr	3,200.00
Allan Herschell, OR Trojan-style jumper	3,000.00
Armitage Herschell, track-machine jumper	2,800.00
Dare, jumper, unrstr	3,000.00
Herschell Spillman, chariot (bench-like seat)	3,800.00
Herschell Spillman, IR jumper, unrstr	2,400.00
Herschell Spillman, MR jumper, unrstr	2,900.00
Herschell Spillman, OR, eagle decor	4,500.00
Herschell Spillman, OR, park machine	10,000.00
Parker, MR jumper, unrstr	4,200.00
Parker, OR jumper, park machine, unrstr	6,500.00
Parker, OR jumper, rstr	5,800.00

Carpet Balls

Carpet balls are glazed china spheres decorated with intersecting lines or other simple designs that were used for indoor games in the British Isles during the early 1800s. Mint condition examples are rare. Our values are for those in excellent to near-mint condition.

Allover concentric bl circles, minor wear, 3" **175.00**
Crossed yel stripes, minor wear, 3" **200.00**
Overall stars, red/wht, 3" **240.00**
Plaid w/blk stripes & bl/gr bands, wear, 3" **120.00**
Sponged, bright cobalt on wht, 3¼" **100.00**
Sponged, red/dk gr, 3" **550.00**
Swirled red w/crossed blk stripes, 2½" **100.00**

Cash Registers

From 1884 until 1916, the National Cash Register Company dominated the field with a massive over-choice of styles and functions. Before the termination of the 'antique styles,' 1,600,000 registers had been built. An inexpensive, painted-on woodgrain patterned steel cabinet replaced the ornate plates, though the mechanisms remained unchanged. Serial numbers were consecutive, making dating simple. Many registers were chopped up for brass shell casings in the two world wars, and as a result, those that remained became more attractive to collectors. Of the NCRs, scholars speculate that about half of them survive. Add to that the many other existing brands, and it is estimated that there are nearly two million registers to discover.

Register values are fixed by a machine's scarcity and charm, including add-on fixtures such as brass or glass topsigns, clocks, and personalized nameplates. National used eight designs on metal registers and four on inlaid wood machines.

The condition code of registers in this column is quite simple: good (G), very good (VG), and mint (M), restored by a professional. About 20% variation in prices can be attributed to geography and buyer/seller differences.

Internet web pages have jumped into the pricing fray, sometimes creating a carnival-like frenzy when prices aren't fixed. *Schroeder's* will provide a standard but also be mindful of changes generated by the 'net. For further information we recommend *Antique Cash Registers, 1880 – 1920*, by Bartsch and Sanchez.

Dial, emb brass, emb pattern on drw, 25", EX **6,500.00**
Monitor #1A, wood w/CI Amount of Sale sign, ca 1900, 9x13x14", VG..**415.00**
NCR #1, Am detail adder, VG..**2,650.00**
NCR #2 or #3, inlaid oak or mahog, scarce **2,250.00**
NCR #3, mahog inlay, deep wood drw, ca 1886, VG **4,500.00**
NCR #5, narrow scroll, glass topsign, M **2,750.00**
NCR #7 or #8, detail adder, fleur-de-lis, VG................................**850.00**
NCR #13 or #14, Ionic CI, 1899, G..**750.00**
NCR #30, bronze, total adder, 13 keys, VG..............................**2,000.00**
NCR #33, 1903, VG **900.00**
NCR #47, oak w/mahog inlay, up to $6, VG **2,250.00**
NCR #50, Renaissance design, orig clock, M **2,500.00**
NCR #52 or #52¼, Renaissance design, extended base, no clock, VG...**2,500.00**
NCR #52, Renaissance design, orig clock, extended base, VG...**2,900.00**
NCR #64, Bohemian pattern, iron, 25-key, 1901, VG **600.00**
NCR #78, custom built to eliminate bk window, NP, 1902, VG.**950.00**
NCR #129-130, bronze, VG **950.00**
NCR #130, Art Nouveau cabinet, M..**1,600.00**
NCR #135, Art Nouveau pattern, CI, 31-key, 1905, VG............**600.00**
NCR #215 or #216, bronze fleur-de-lis, VG.............................**1,200.00**
NCR #226, rare bilingual topsign, VG..**900.00**
NCR #250 or #251, bronze, VG **1,200.00**
NCR #312, #313, or #317, dolphin pattern, VG **800.00**
NCR #322, #323, or #327, marble 3 sides, extended base, M..**2,500.00**
NCR #322, #323, or #327, marble 3 sides, extended base, VG..**1,500.00**
NCR #324, bronze plated, wood base, $2 till, rstr, 21x16x13½".**920.00**
NCR #324, VG **700.00**
NCR #332, #333 or #349, orig topsign, M.................................**1,150.00**

NCR #332, #333 or #349, orig topsign, VG...............................**550.00**
NCR #336, brass, M..**950.00**
NCR #337, dolphin design, M...**950.00**
NCR #338, dogwood pattern, English numerals, CA, 1910-16, VG...**475.00**
NCR #359-G, fleur-de-lis pattern, brass w/marble tray, 1906, EX+......**200.00**
NCR #360, 37 keys, rings to $60, 1908-09, M.........................**1,500.00**
NCR #441 or #442, Empire design w/quartered-oak base, M...**1,750.00**
NCR #441E, electric, VG..**1,250.00**
NCR #442E-L, EX orig **1,800.00**
NCR #452E, electric, M..**2,000.00**
NCR #522, 2-drw, electric bar model, 1910-16, M...................**2,500.00**
NCR #522, 2-drw, electric bar model, 1910-16, VG **1,800.00**
NCR #711-#717, mahog-grain finish on steel, M........................**275.00**
NCR #1054, glass automatic w/box attachment, 1910-16, M..**1,200.00**

Cast Iron

In the mid-1800s, the cast-iron industry was raging in the United States. It was recognized as a medium extremely adaptable for uses ranging from ornamental architectural filigree to actual building construction. It could be cast from a mold into any conceivable design that could be reproduced over and over at a relatively small cost. It could be painted to give an entirely versatile appearance. Furniture with openwork designs of grapevines and leaves and intricate lacy scrollwork was cast for gardens as well as inside use. Figural doorstops of every sort, bootjacks, trivets, and a host of other useful and decorative items were made before the 'ferromania' had run its course. For more information, we recommend *Antique Iron* by Kathryn McNerney (Collector Books). See also Kitchen, Cast-Iron Bakers and Kettles; and other specific categories.

Architectural element, 4-part acanthus leaf, old wht pnt, 10x10x3" ..**185.00**
Architectural figure, dove, wht pnt traces, early 19th C, 8x12x10" .**980.00**
Bench, geometric apron/seat, 3-panel bk w/rosette crests, arms, 45" L .**380.00**
Bench (44" L)+2 side chairs, vintage openwork bk/apron, leaf legs ..**415.00**
Garden chair, rtcl vintage bks, vine/leaf legs, sm sz, 28", pr **125.00**

Garden statues, finely modeled whippets on oval plinths, nineteenth century, 17½", $3,500.00 for the pair.

Hitching post, horse head w/defined mane, old blk pnt, late 19th C .**325.00**
Hitching post, jockey, pnt clothing, thin sq base, 24" **250.00**
Hitching post caps, horse's head & pineapple, 10½", pr.............**635.00**
Horse, running, copper & zinc, att LW Waltham, ca 1880s, 16x31"..**2,300.00**
Sprinkler, w/figural wood duck, EX detail, mc pnt w/lt wear, 13½" .**650.00**
Sugar nippers, stamped leaves at rivet, 9½", EX **275.00**
Sugar nippers, tooled flower at pivot point, 10" **635.00**
Umbrella stand, bkplate as figure of Admiral Nelson, titled, 31" .**700.00**
Umbrella stand, molded seated spaniel, old blk pnt, 23½".........**125.00**
Urn, half fluted, on sq plinth w/wreaths, Spicer & Peckham, 42" .**550.00**
Urns, cherub w/urn on shoulder, rnd base, late 20th C, 53", pr ..**865.00**
Urns, lobed bottom w/loop hdls, sq base, Spicer & Peckham, 23", pr.**700.00**

Castor Sets

Castor sets became popular during the early years of the eighteenth century and continued to be used through the late Victorian era. Their purpose was to hold various condiments for table use. The most common type was a circular arrangement with a center handle on a revolving pedestal base that held three, four, five, or six bottles. A few were equipped with a bell for calling the servant. Frames were made of silverplate, glass, or pewter. Though most bottles were of pressed glass, some of the designs were cut, and on rare occasion, colored glass with enameled decorations was used as well. To maintain authenticity and value, castor sets should have matching bottles. Prices listed below are for those with matching bottles and in frames with plating that is in excellent condition (unless noted otherwise). Note: Watch for new frames and bottles in clear, cranberry, cobalt, and vaseline Inverted Thumbprint as well as reproductions of Czechoslovakian cut glass bottles. These have recently been appearing on the market. Our advisors for this category are Barbara and Steve Aaronson; they are listed in the Directory under California.

3-bottle, Am Shield; pewter fr w/eagle, mini, child sz **165.00**
4-bottle, cranberry, orig stoppers; pressed glass holder **275.00**

4-bottle, rose amber, Inverted Thumbprint, faceted stoppers, Mt. Washington; Acme Silverplate Co. frame, $2,000.00. (Photo courtesy John A. Shuman III)

5-bottle, clear/sq; revolving SP #2165 fr **650.00**
5-bottle, etched floral w/cutting, much decor; Meriden ft...........**450.00**
5-bottle, pressed glass; rstr Meriden fr w/cherub hdl revolves......**525.00**
5-bottle, sq; SP #2165 fr revolves **650.00**
6-bottle, mold-blown casters w/ribbed acorn stoppers, Sandwich, 8"..**585.00**
6-bottle, pressed; 18" Simpson-Hall-Miller fr w/EX SP **550.00**
7-bottle, cut crystal; lg ped-ft Gleason fr w/doors.....................**1,650.00**

Catalina Island

Catalina Island pottery was made on the island of the same name, which is about twenty-six miles off the coast of Los Angeles. The pottery was started in 1927 at Pebble Beach, by Wm. Wrigley, Jr., who was instrumental in developing and using the native clays. Its principal products were brick and tile to be used for construction on the island. Garden pieces were first produced, then vases, bookends, lamps, ashtrays, novelty items, and finally dinnerware. The ware became very popular and was soon being shipped to the mainland as well.

Some of the pottery was hand thrown; some was made in molds. Most pieces are marked Catalina Island or Catalina with a printed incised stamp or handwritten with a pointed tool. Cast items were sometimes marked in the mold, a few have an ink stamp, and a paper label was also used. The most favored colors in tableware and accessories are 1) black (rare), 2) Seafoam and Monterey Brown (uncommon), 3) matt blue and green, 4) Toyon Red (orange), 5) other brights, and 6) pastels with a matt finish.

The color of the clay can help to identify approximately when a piece was made: 1927 to 1932, brown to red (Island) clay (very popular with collectors, tends to increase values); 1931 to 1932, an experimental period with various colors; 1932 to 1937, mainly white clay, though tan to brown clays were also used on occasion.

Items marked Catalina Pottery are listed in Gladding McBean. For further information we recommend *Catalina Island Pottery Collectors' Guide* by Steven and Aisha Hoefs, and *The Collector's Encyclopedia of California Pottery, Second Edition,* by Jack Chipman (Collector Books). Our advisor for this category is Steven Hoefs; he is listed in the Directory under Georgia.

Ashtray, fish shape, wht w/blk features, 6⅞x5" **195.00**
Bowl, gray, patterned rim, #721, 14"...............................**110.00**
Bowl, wht, fluted to rim, 3x8" **75.00**
Candlestick, bl & brn on red clay, 5¼" **240.00**
Creamer & sugar bowl, gr, art Deco style, creamer mk #63, sugar w/lid.**145.00**
Cruet, vinegar; gray, gourd shape, 4½" **75.00**
Cup & saucer, yel, red clay, sq hdl **45.00**
Flower frog, tannish yel, gear shape, 3-pc, 3¼x5¼" **60.00**
Jardiniere, wht w/pk flowers & gr leaves, bulbous, 3⅝x4⅝" dia..**145.00**
Pin, flyfish figural, Catalina on bk, 3½", MIB...........................**45.00**
Pitcher, beverage; Mandarin Manchu Yellow, 7½" **200.00**
Plate, dinner; yel, rolled rim, 9⅞".....................................**50.00**
Plate, ivory, 12½" **50.00**
Plate, red sea horse on bl w/yel border, 12½" dia **1,840.00**
Plate, Submarine Garden, mc scene w/gr border, 12½"...........**1,500.00**
Plate, turq, pierced bk for hanging, 10½" **60.00**
Platter, gr, ruffled, 14⅛" dia **175.00**
Platter, med gr, 16" dia **175.00**
Teapot, bl, Art Deco style, #65, 4¼x7⅜" **790.00**
Vase, yel, Art Deco style, #636, 7"....................................**165.00**

Catalogs

Catalogs are not only intriguing to collect on their own merit, but for the collector with a specific interest, they are often the only remaining source of background information available, and as such they offer a wealth of otherwise unrecorded data. The mail-order industry can be traced as far back as the mid-1800s. Even before Aaron Montgomery Ward began his career in 1872, Laacke and Joys of Wisconsin and the Orvis Company of Vermont, both dealers in sporting goods, had been well established for many years. The E.C. Allen Company sold household necessities and novelties by mail on a broad scale in the 1870s. By the end of the Civil War, sewing machines, garden seed, musical instruments, even medicine, were available from catalogs. In the 1880s Macy's of New York issued a 127-page catalog; Sears and Spiegel followed suit in about 1890. Craft and art supply catalogs were first available about 1880 and covered such varied fields as china painting, stenciling, wood burning, brass embossing, hair weaving, and shellcraft. Today some collectors confine their interests not only to craft catalogs in general but often to just one subject. There are several factors besides rarity which make a catalog valuable: age, condition, profuse illustrations, how collectible the field is that it deals with, the amount of color used in its printing, its size (format and number of pages), and whether it is a manufacturer's catalog verses a jobber's catalog (the former being the most desirable).

Acme White Lead & Color, Acme paints, 1920s, 106 pgs, VG **35.00**
Allis Chalmers, Model WC Tractor, 1937, 4 pgs, G **14.00**
American Crayons Co, art supplies, 1926, 16 pgs, VG **10.00**
Arthur Edward Johnstone, orchestra instruments, 1917, 63 pgs, VG+...**40.00**

AW Staub Co, Quaker City Grinding Mills, 1927, 24 pgs, G+ **16.00**
Barcola Mfg Co, bedding/sleeping equipment, 1929, 56 pgs, G.....**32.00**
Barnhart Bros & Spindler, printing supplies, 1925, 719 pgs, VG...**125.00**
Binghamton Scale Co, scales, 1880, 26 pgs, VG......................**74.00**
BL Gilbert Magic Co, supplies, 1924, 48 pgs, G+ **19.00**
Bradley Knitting, Fall & Winter clothes, 1922, 24 pgs, VG **34.00**
Brown Fayrd Co, mining equipment, 1951, 40 pgs, G **24.00**
Cedar Rapid Pump & Supplies, 1924, 524 pgs, VG **32.00**
Cedar Rapids Tanning Co, leather tanning/mfg, 1928, 36 pgs, G .**64.00**
Central Felt Co, clothing, 1952, 16 pgs, VG..........................**15.00**
CF Martin & Co, guitars, 1977, 32 pgs, VG+ **48.00**
CJ Lundstrom Mfg Co, furniture, 1941, 36 pgs, VG **21.00**
Cleveland & Whitehill Co, clothing, 1907, 12 pgs, VG+............**85.00**
Colt's Patent Fire Arms, ca 1930, 16 pgs, VG **41.00**
Colt's Patent Fire Arms Mfg, 1927, 64 pgs, VG+ **110.00**
David C Cook Publishing, Sunday School supplies, 1911, 50 pgs, G+ .**24.00**
De La Vergne Refrigeration, machines & ice making, 1898, 128 pgs, VG+ ...**86.00**
Duluth Showcase Co, showcases, ca 1929, 32 pgs, G+ **36.00**
E Butterick & Co, sewing, 1872, 34 pgs, G **38.00**
Emil J Paidar Co, barber/beauty supplies, 1928, 124 pgs, G+ **365.00**
EP Gilkinson Sons Co, camp trailers, 1935, 2 pgs, G+ **19.00**
FAO Schwarz, toys, 1961, 96 pgs, G- **34.00**
Fender Musical Co, guitars, banjos, etc, 1972, 15 pgs, VG+ **37.00**
Franklin Railway Supply, fire doors, 1900s, 16 pgs, G...............**12.00**
Frantz Mfg Co, builder's hardware, 1926, 73 pgs, G.................**23.00**
Frost Mfg, machinery, 1905, 31 pgs, G **46.00**
George C Goodwin & Co, drugs, 1885, 384 pgs, G+ **420.00**
George H Tay & Co, tin & iron wares, 1887, 154 pgs, G...........**63.00**
Grand Rapids Band Instruments, brass section, 1927, 18 pgs, VG+..**32.00**
H Von Der Linden, bicycles, 1894, 32 pgs, VG+ **125.00**
H&A Selmer Inc, brass & woodwind instruments, 1958, 30 pgs, VG+ ..**44.00**
HB Nims & Co, Little Gem Health Exerciser, 1905, 14 pgs, VG .**43.00**
HI Sackett Electric Co, coffee mills, 1920, 6 pgs, VG **28.00**
HL Judd Co, hardware, 1909, 309 pgs, G............................**110.00**
Horton Mfg Co, flooring, 1920, 16 pgs, G...........................**38.00**
IA Sheppard & Co, stoves, 1880, 130 pgs, G+ **145.00**
Ihling Bros & Everard, lodge/Masonic supplies, 1898, 52 pgs, G ..**31.00**
Illinois Surgical Supply Co, 1929, 98 pgs, VG **46.00**
Jackson & Co, ice products, 16 pgs, G+ **48.00**
Jamestown Specialty Co, canoes & kayaks, 1939, 15 pgs, G+.......**74.00**
Jewel Electric & Mfg Co, fountains & accessories, 1917, 64 pgs, G+ ..**34.00**
Jewett & Root, stoves, 1877, 79 pgs, VG **225.00**
Johnson Smith & Co, novelties, 1940, 624 pgs, G **38.00**
Jones, Post & Co, farm implements/supplies, 1910, 850 pgs, G.....**96.00**
JR Wood & Sons, 1911, jewelry, 19 pgs, G+ **30.00**
King Novelty Co, curios/incense/oils/roots, 1942, 48 pgs, G+.......**26.00**
LE Waterman Co, The Pen Prophet Vol XV #2, 1927, 24 pgs, VG..**48.00**
Lewis Sports & Hobby, fishing equipment, 1948, 13 pgs, G+ **33.00**
LL Bean Inc, outdoor items, Fall 1956, 108 pgs, VG **21.00**
Locke Regulator Co, 1928, 72 pgs, VG **19.00**
Lowe & Campbell AG Co, Athletic Goods, Fall/Winter 1926, 130 pgs, G..**42.00**
LS Knoek & Co, hardware & tools, #6, 1913, 152 pgs, G.........**58.00**
Lussky, White & Coolridge, cabinet/drapery hardware, 1938, 281 pgs, VG..**48.00**
Luthe Hardware Co, 1937, 698 pgs, VG+ **97.00**
Maher Publications, guitars, October 1956, 50 pgs, G.............**125.00**
Maine Beauty & Barber Supply Co, 1930, 20 pgs, VG **37.00**
Martin Metal Mfg Co, sheet metal, 1922, 591 pgs, VG............**31.00**
Montgomery Wards & Co, photographic equipment, 1953, 104 pgs, G..**18.00**
Mosaic Tile Co, architecture, 1929, 12 pgs, G **63.00**
MS Young & Co, toys/hardware/paints, 1919, 130 pgs, VG+.......**98.00**
Nashua Mfg Co, household, 1929, 46 pgs, VG **21.00**
National Cloak & Suit Co, clothes, Fall & Winter 1915, 500 pgs, G+ .**57.00**
Ornamental Stamping Works, sheet metal ornaments, 1898, 112 pgs, G..**120.00**
PA Grier Co, appliances, 1929, 16 pgs, VG+ **22.00**

Pittsburgh Steel Co, fencing & gates, 1911, 48 pgs, VG+ **20.00**
RC Nichols Corp, hunting/fishing/camping, Fall/Winter 1946, 34 pgs, G+..**18.00**
RE Dodge & Co, shell jewelry supplies, 1908, 58 pgs, G...........**41.00**
Rochester Can Co, Iron Horse Brand metalware, 1917, 99 pgs, VG..**64.00**
Roger & Gallet, Paris perfume wholesale, 1914, 45 pgs, VG+ **125.00**
Rookwood Pottery Co, Rookwood's History, ca 1930, 16 pgs, VG+...**33.00**
S Stanley Hawbaker, trapping equipment, 1956, 48 pgs, G...........**19.00**
Sanders Mfg Co, advertising specialties, 1937, 34 pgs, VG **21.00**
Schack Artificial Flower, Christmas wreaths/garland, 1932, 24 pgs, VG..**46.00**
Schneitter Fireworks, 1923, 40 pgs, G **52.00**
Schwarze Electric Co, electrical supplies, 1924, 15 pgs, VG.........**23.00**
Sears, Roebuck & Co, Seroco Paints Catalog, 1925, 20 pgs, G.....**17.00**
Smith & Wesson Inc, military & police issue guns, 1925, 40 pgs, VG..**98.00**
Southwestern Milling Co, cooking, 1911, 32 pgs, G.................**14.00**
Sperry & Hutchinson, S&H Green Stamp redemption, 1956, 44 pgs, VG.**24.00**
Stanberry Parade Products Inc, float accessories, 1935, 16 pgs, G.**51.00**
Stone & Tar Products Co, home decor, 1932, 40 pgs, VG **12.00**
Taylor Instrument Co, thermometer/barometers etc, 1927, 92 pgs, VG...**86.00**
Theo A Kochs Co, barber supplies, 1926, 164 pgs, VG..............**305.00**
Thomas Kane & Co, boats & canoes, 1885, 44 pgs, G+ **475.00**
Thos Mills & Bro, nut foods/popcorn equipment, 1930, 24 pgs, VG+...**47.00**
Unadilla Silo Co Inc, yard & garden accessories, 1927, 32 pgs, VG ..**47.00**
United States Electical Tools, #21, 1923, VG+ **42.00**
Van Meter Co, electrical appliances, 1958, 100+ pgs, G+...........**32.00**
Wheeler-Van Label Co, Blue Bird Paper products, 1924, 16 pgs, VG...**53.00**
White Paper Box Co, druggist's pill & powder boxes, 1926, 38 pgs, VG .**74.00**
William Rott Inc, adult games & novelties, 1940, 36 pgs, G **76.00**
World Railway Publ Co, Westinghouse Air Brakes, 1903, 102 pgs, G+.**14.00**
WS Darley & Co, police supplies, 1960s, 122 pgs, VG................**54.00**
Yale & Towne Mfg Co, hardware, 1921, 450 pgs, VG+...............**145.00**

Caughley Ware

The Caughley Coalport Porcelain Manufactory operated from about 1775 until 1799 in Caughley, near Salop, Shropshire, in England. The owner was Thomas Turner, who gained his potting experience from his association with the Worcester Pottery Company. The wares he manufactured in Caughley are referred to as 'Salopian.' He is most famous for his blue-printed earthenwares, particularly the Blue Willow pattern, designed for him by Thomas Minton. For a more detailed history, see Coalport.

Bowl, Oriental figures in garden, floral border, 1820, 8", NM **300.00**
Jug, Oriental figural landscape, floral borders, 6½".....................**400.00**

Cauldon

Formerly Brown-Westhead, Moore & Co., Cauldon Ltd. was a Staffordshire pottery that operated under that name from 1905 until 1920, producing dinnerware that was most often transfer decorated. They company operated under the title Cauldon Potteries Ltd. from 1920 until 1962.

Bowl, Blue Onion (pattern called Meissen), 2x9"..........................**42.00**
Cake plate, pk w/gold bellflowers, vine/leaf hdls, ca 1885, 11" ...**200.00**
Cup & saucer, bone china, orange floral w/gold on wht, Made in England .**28.00**
Cup & saucer, salmon bands w/gold flowers on wht **25.00**
Egg cup, Jacobean-style floral transfer, dbl, 1895, 3½"..................**50.00**
Jug, 2 dragons/floral reserves, bl on wht, diaper rims, 4".............**125.00**
Plate, Delft style, scenes in reseves, bl on wht, 8"........................**100.00**
Plate, game bird by Birbeck, scallop/gilt rim, mk Tiffany, 9", 12 for.**3,175.00**
Platter, red/pk floral on wht, 1800s, 15" **225.00**

Ceramic Art Company

Jonathan Coxon, Sr., and Walter Scott Lenox established the Ceramic Art Company in 1889 in Trenton, New Jersey, where they produced fine belleek porcelain. Both were experienced in its production, having previously worked for Ott and Brewer. They hired artists to hand paint their wares with portraits, scenes, and lovely florals. Today artist-signed examples bring the highest prices. Several marks were used, three of which contain the 'CAC' monogram. A green wreath surrounding the company name in full was used on special-order wares, but these are not often encountered. Coxon eventually left the company, and it was later reorganized under the Lenox name. See also Lenox. Our advisor for this category is Mary Frank Gaston.

Bell, tulip form, silver decor on wht, unmk......................................150.00
Bowl, finger; gold leaves & flowers on gr, scalloped rim..............130.00
Buttonhook, mc floral w/gold, factory decor, unmk, 7¾"............285.00
Cream soup cup & saucer, Tridacna w/gold, 2", 5½"...................150.00
Creamer, gold floral, hdl & trim, mk, 3¾"....................................135.00
Cup, chocolate; bl beading & gold on ivory, ped ft.......................75.00
Cup, loving; roses on gr, 3 pk hdls w/gold, purple mk, 8"............350.00
Decanter, scotch, cobalt w/silver o/l, silver hdl & stopper, 4".....300.00
Humidor, lilies, red-orange on orange, ca 1897, 6x5½"................350.00
Jug, yel & purple pansies, artist sgn, gold spout/hdl, mk, 6" dia ..300.00
Mug, gr hops, artist sgn, palette mk, 4¾"......................................75.00
Mug, monk holding open box on brn, gr mk, 5¾"..........................110.00
Mug, strawberries, emb hdl & base, palette mk, 6"........................95.00
Pitcher, cider; 3-color grapes, beaded hdl, lg...............................165.00
Pitcher, tankard; pines & full moon on dk gr, gr mk....................265.00
Salt cellar, gold 4-leaf clover in center, palette mk, 1½", 4 for......35.00
Salt cellar, scalloped rim, palette mk..25.00
Stein, monk eating in cellar, copper/sterling lid, mk, ½-liter......600.00
Vase, begonias, shouldered, 12½"..500.00
Vase, birds on branch over lily pond, hairline, 9x5½"................500.00
Vase, crysanthemums, bulbous, sgn, 7½".....................................725.00
Vase, floral, sgn Frill, stick neck, palette mk, 1894-1906, 12½x6"..465.00
Vase, lady's portrait medallion w/gold, mk, 11½".......................285.00
Vase, roses, yel on pk, slim neck, gold hdls, 1889, 12½".............295.00
Vase, shell form w/snail hdls & emb decor, no pnt decor, 6x7"...300.00
Vase, 3 heron reserves, iris on blk at neck, mk, 22"....................575.00

Ceramic Arts Studio, Madison

The Ceramic Arts Studio Company began operations sometime prior to the 1940s, but it was about then that Betty Harrington started marketing her goods through this company. Betty Harrington was the designer primarily responsible for creating the line of figurines and knickknacks that has become so popular with collectors. There were two others — Ulli Rebus, who not only designed several of the animals and various other pieces but taught Betty the art of mold-making as well; and Ruth Planter, who's work may have been limited to 'Sonny' and Honey.' About 65% of these items are marked, but even unmarked items become easily recognizable after only a brief study of their distinctive styling and glaze colors. At least eight different marks were used, among them the black ink stamp and the incised mark: 'Ceramic Arts Studio, Madison, Wisc.' A paper sticker was used in the early years.

After the 1955 demise of the company in Madison, the owner (Ruben Sand) went to Japan where he continued production under the same name using many of the same molds. After a short time, the old molds were retired, and new and quite different items were produced. Most of the Japan pieces can be found with a Ceramic Arts Studio backstamp. The Japan identification was often on a paper label and can be missing. Japan pieces are never marked Madison, Wisc., but not all Madi-

son pieces are either. Red or blue backstamps are exclusively Japanese.

Another company that also produced figurines operated at about the same time as the Madison studio. It was called Ceramic Art (no 's') Studio; do not confuse the two.

A second and larger building in the C.A.S. complex in Madison was for the exclusive production of metal accessories. The creator and designer of this related line was Zona Liberace, Liberace's stepmother, who was art director for the line of figurines as well. These pieces are rising fast in value and because they weren't marked can sometimes be found at bargain prices. They were so popular that other ceramic companies bought them to complement their own lines, so they may also be found with ceramic figures other than C.A.S.'s.

Our advisor for this category is BA Wellman; his address can be found under Massachusetts. Mr. Wellman encourages collectors to e-mail him with any new information concerning company history and/or production. See also Clubs, Newsletters, and Catalogs.

Ashtray, hippo, 3½"...135.00
Bank, Mr & Mrs Blankety Blank, 4½", pr.................................325.00
Bell, Lillibelle, 6½"...165.00
Birdbath, 4½"...125.00
Blade bank, Tony the Barber..165.00
Bowl, Bonita, paisley shape, 3¾" L..65.00
Candle holder, Triad Girl, center, 5".......................................165.00
Candle holder, Triad Girl, right or left; from $90 to.................145.00
Candle holders, Bedtime Boy & Girl, 4¾", pr...........................225.00
Figurine, Adonis and Aphrodite, 9", 7¾", pr, from $650 to........695.00
Figurine, Annie, baby elephant, 3¼"..85.00
Figurine, Archibald, dragon, 8", minimum value.......................425.00
Figurine, Bali-Hai, standing, 8"...145.00
Figurine, Bird of Paradise, 3"..95.00
Figurine, blk bear, mother, realistic, 3¼"..................................135.00
Figurine, Blythe, 6½"..135.00
Figurine, Bright Eyes, cat, looking forward, 3"...........................65.00
Figurine, bunny baby, 2¼"...40.00
Figurine, Burmese Man, 4½"..125.00
Figurine, Butch (Boxer), dog, snuggle, 3"...................................95.00
Figurine, Caddy, mountain goat, 5¼".......................................245.00
Figurine, Calico Cat, 3"..45.00
Figurine, child w/towel, 5"...145.00
Figurine, cockatoo, female, tail up, 5"......................................110.00
Figurine, Comedy & Tragedy, 10", pr.......................................265.00
Figurine, Cupid, 5"...145.00
Figurine, Daisy, donkey, 4¾"...150.00
Figurine, Dem, donkey, 4½"..125.00
Figurine, donkey mother, 3¼"..100.00
Figurine, Drum Girl, 4½", from $165 to....................................185.00
Figurine, Dutch Boy & Girl, 4½", pr, from $50 to........................95.00
Figurine, Egyptian man & woman, rare, 9½", pr........................695.00
Figurine, Fifi, poodle, standing, 3"..80.00
Figurine, fish, head up, 3½"..65.00
Figurine, fish, str tail, lg..80.00
Figurine, Frisky, colt, 3¾"...135.00
Figurine, Gingham Dog, 2¾"..45.00
Figurine, giraffe mother, 6½"...110.00
Figurine, Guatar Man, on stool, scarce, 6½".............................235.00
Figurine, Gypsy Man, 6½"...95.00
Figurine, Harem Girl, kneeling, 4½"...95.00
Figurine, Isaac, 10"...195.00
Figurine, jaguar mother, stylized, scarce, 5" L..........................200.00
Figurine, Japanese Kabuki Man & Woman, 8½", 6", pr............675.00
Figurine, Jester, flutist man, 12"..195.00
Figurine, kid's band, 8-pc, from $1,395 to..............................1,450.00
Figurine, lamb, plain...50.00

Figurine, leopards, fighting, 3½", 6¼" L, pr, from $250 to 300.00
Figurine, Lightning, stallion, 5¾" 190.00
Figurine, lion, 5½" 200.00
Figurine, Lover Boy, 4½" 85.00
Figurine, Madonna w/golden halo 195.00
Figurine, Minnehaha 165.00
Figurine, Our Lady of Fatima 195.00
Figurine, Pekingese, 3" 95.00
Figurine, Pete & Polly, parrots, 7½", pr, from $170 to............245.00
Figurine, Peter Pan & Wendy, 5¼", pr 295.00
Figurine, Petrov & Petruska, 5", 5¼", pr 100.00
Figurine, Pied Piper, 6¼" 125.00
Figurine, Pioneer Sam & Suzie, 5½", 5", pr 145.00
Figurine, pixie sitting on bowl, 4½" 145.00
Figurine, Pomeranian, dog, standing, 3" 80.00
Figurine, Praise Angel, hand up, 6" 125.00
Figurine, Rhumba Man, 7¼" 95.00
Figurine, Rose, ballerina tying shoe 125.00
Figurine, Sambo, 3½" 365.00
Figurine, Santa Claus, 2¼" 145.00
Figurine, seal mother, 6" L 225.00
Figurine, Spring Sue, 5" 85.00
Figurine, Squeaky, squirrel, 3¼" 95.00
Figurine, squirrel w/jacket, 2¼" 95.00
Figurine, St George on charger, 8½", from $225 to 325.00
Figurine, Swan Lake Man, 7" 295.00
Figurine, Tembina, elephant baby, 2½" 95.00
Figurine, Water Man & Woman, 11½", pr 525.00
Figurine, Wee Chinese boy & girl 3", pr..........................65.00
Figurine, Wee Pig Girl, 3½" 39.00
Figurine, zebra, 5", from $195 to 225.00
Figurine, Zulu Man, 5½" 295.00

Figurines, Cinderella and Prince, any colorway, from $195.00 to $225.00 for the pair.

Head vase, Barbie, 7" 195.00
Head vase, Becky, 5¼" 195.00
Head vase, Bonnie, 7" 195.00
Head vase, Svea & Sven, 6", pr 425.00
Lamp, Fire Man on base, very scarce 625.00
Lamp, Manchu lantern holder, scarce 395.00
Miniature, Aladdin's lamp, 2" L 75.00
Miniature, teapot, appl swan, open 65.00
Plaque, Attitude & Arabesque, pr, from $135 to 195.00
Plaque, Goosey Gander, scarce, 4½" 165.00
Plaque, Hamlet & Ophelia, 8¼", pr 495.00
Plaque, Harlequin & Columbine, pr 245.00
Plaque, Lotus, lantern woman, 9" 125.00
Plaque, Zor & Zorina, 9", pr 145.00
Razor blade bank, Tony, #319, 4¾" 95.00
Shakers, Blackamoor, 4¾", pr 185.00
Shakers, covered wagon & oxen, ea 3" L, pr....................135.00

Shakers, dog & doghouse, snuggle, pr..........................165.00
Shakers, horse's heads, pr 95.00
Shakers, monkey mother & baby, snuggle, pr 185.00
Shakers, Sabu (Black boy) & elephant, pr 395.00
Shakers, sea horse & coral, pr 175.00
Shelf sitter, Banjo Girl, 4", from $80 to.....................175.00
Shelf sitter, canary, left or right, 5" 95.00
Shelf sitter, Chinese Boy & Girl, 3½", pr......................65.00
Shelf sitter, Collie mother, 5"................................95.00
Shelf sitter, Fluffy & Tuffy, cats, 7", pr....................225.00
Shelf sitter, Mo-Pi, chubby woman, 6", from $40 to.............60.00
Shelf sitter, Sun-Li & Su-Lin, chubby, 5½", pr.................95.00
Vase, bud; bamboo, 6" 45.00
Vase, Flying Ducks, rnd, 2"....................................95.00

Metal Accessories

Arched window for religious figure, 6½" 95.00
Artist palette w/shelves, left & right, 13" W 125.00
Beanstalk for Jack, rare 185.00
Birdcage w/perch, 14" 125.00
Box, dmn shape, 15½x14" 125.00
Corner spider web for Miss Muffet, flat bk, 4" 165.00
Frame w/shelf, 22" sq 95.00
Garden shelf, for Mary Contrary, 4x12" 125.00
Musical score, flat bk, 14x12" 125.00
Pocket step shelf, w/planter, rnd, 8" 75.00
Pyramid shelf...95.00
Rainbow arch w/shelf, blk, 13½x19x5½".........................135.00
Sofa, for Maurice & Michelle, from $60 to 85.00
Star for angel, flat bk 80.00
Triple ring for birds (shelf sitting), 15" 135.00

Chalkware

Chalkware figures were a popular commodity from approximately 1860 until 1890. They were made from gypsum or plaster of Paris formed in a mold and then hand painted in oils or watercolors. Items such as animals and birds, figures, banks, toys, and religious ornaments modeled after more expensive Staffordshire wares were often sold door to door. Their origin is attributed to Italian immigrants. Today regarded as a form of folk art, nineteenth century American pieces bring prices in the hundreds of dollars. Carnival chalkware from this century is also collectible, especially figures that are personality related. For those, see Carnival Collectibles

Cat, seated, blk spots/tail, red/yel ears, yel eyes/base, rpr, 7x4"....635.00
Cat, seated, gray w/blk spots/ears, yel eyes/base, red collar, rpr, 5" .550.00
Fruit basket, mantel ornament, imperfections, 8½x7" 750.00
Poodle, molded coat/ears, on base, 4-color detail, chips/touch-up, 5" ..465.00
Rabbit, worn rpt, 8x5½" 275.00
Ram, raised dots on coat, blk eyes/ears/horns w/red accents, 9x6", G...250.00
Squirrel, brn pnt w/blk details, chips, 6½" 160.00
Stag, recumbent w/open front leg, ribbed base, mc details, 9x8", EX...650.00
Stag's head in oval fr w/wire hanging loop, grn/tan/blk, PA, 14x7"..325.00

Chase Brass & Copper Company

Chase introduced this logo in 1928. The company was incorporated in 1876 as the Waterbury Manufacturing Company and was located in Waterbury, Connecticut. This location remained Chase's principal fabrication plant, and it was here that the 'Specialties' were made.

CHASE

In 1900 the company chose the name Chase Companies Inc., in honor of their founder, Augustus Sabin Chase. The name encompassed Chase's many factories. Only the New York City sales division was called Chase Brass and Copper Co., but from 1936 on, that name was used exclusively.

In 1930 the sales division invited people to visit their new Specialties Sales Showroom in New York City 'where an interesting assortment of decorative and utilitarian pieces in brass and copper in a variety of designs and treatments are offered for your consideration.' Like several other large companies, Chase hired well-known designers such as Walter Von Nessen, Lurelle Guild, the Gerths, Russel Wright, and Dr. A Reimann. Harry Laylon, an in-house designer, created much of the new line.

From 1930 to 1942 Chase offered lamps, smoking accessories, and housewares similar to those Americans were seeing on the Hollywood screen — generally at prices the average person could afford.

Besides chromium, Chase manufactured many products in a variety of finishes, some even in silver plate. Many objects were of polished or satin-finished brass and/or copper; other pieces were chromium plated.

After World War II Chase no longer made the Specialties line. It had represented only a tiny fraction of this huge company's production. Instead they concentrated on a variety of fabricated mill items. Some dedicated Chase collectors even have shower heads, faucet aerators, gutter pipe, and metal samples. Is anyone using Chase window screening?

Chase products are marked either on the item itself or on a screw or rivet. Because Chase sold screws, rivets, nails, etc. (all with their logo), not all items having these Chase-marked components were actually made at Chase. It should also be noted that during the 1930s, China produced good quality chromium copies; so when you're not absolutely positive an item is Chase, buy it because you like it, understanding that its authenticity may be in question. Remember that if a magnet sticks to it, it's not Chase. Brass and copper are not magnetic, and Chase did not use steel.

Prior to 1933 Chase made smoking accessories for the Park Sherman Co. Some are marked 'Park Sherman, Chicago, Illinois, Made of Chase Brass.' Others carry a Park Sherman logo. It is believed that the 'heraldic emblem' was also used during this period. Many items are identical or very similar to Chase-marked pieces. Produced in the 1950s, National Silver's 'Emerald Glo' wares look very similar to Chase pieces, but Chase did not make them. It is very possible that National purchased Chase tooling after the Chase Specialties line was discontinued.

For further study we recommend *Chase Complete, Chase Catalogs 1934 & 1935, 1930s Lighting — Deco & Traditional by Chase;* and *The Chase Era, 1933 and 1942 Catalogs of the Chase Brass & Copper Co.* all by Donald-Brian Johnson and Leslie Pina (Schiffer); and *Art Deco Chrome, The Chase Era,* by Richard Kilbride; and *Art Deco Chrome* by James Linz (Schiffer).

In the listings that follow, examples are polished unless noted satin. A co-advisor for this category is Barbara Endter; she is listed in the Directory under New York. Donna and John Thorpe are our advisors for Chase lighting; they are listed in the Directory under Wisconsin.

Key:
Ge — Gerth
LG — designed by Lurelle Guild
RW — Russel Wright
VN — designed by Von Nessen

Assembly Smokers' Set, chromium w/colored tray, Ackerman, #850, 4-pc .**125.00**
Autumn Leaf Ash Reciever, chromium or copper, #28009, 5⅛" ...**42.50**
Candlepc, 4-light, satin copper or brass, Reimann, #21005, $1,200 to..**1,500.00**
Carefree Set, chromium, #8003, 4 cup holders+tray, from $125 to ..**150.00**
Cat Bookends, polished brass on blk nickel base, #17042, 7⅜x4"....**500.00**
Circlet Tray, chromium & ivory compo, #90060, 7"...................**175.00**
Crown Ashtray, chromium w/red trim, dumping feature, #811, lg, $40 to..**55.00**
Devonshire Pitcher, polished copper or chromium, RW, #90025 ..**80.00**
Dinner Gong, chromium, Ge, #11251, 8½x6¼", from $150 to ..**175.00**
Drum Bank, brass w/red plastic, #90156b, 3½x3" dia, from $80 to..**90.00**
Duplex Server, 2-tier, chromium or satin copper, #9005, 12", $85 to..**95.00**

Electric Table Chef, #17087, chromium with white plastic, designed by Walter Von Nessen, from $150.00 to $175.00. (Photo by Dale Endter/courtesy Barbara Endter)

Fiesta Candlesticks, chromium w/blk wood, Ge, #29001, 8⅜x3⅞", pr ..**170.00**
Flowerpot Holder, brass or copper, w/saucer, #11155, 4½x5¾" **55.00**
Imperial Bowl, copper w/silver int, blk nickel base, #15003, 4x8½" .**125.00**
Jungle Coasters, satin copper or chromium, #8002, 4 for $80 to .**100.00**
Lamp, Glow, #01001, chrome w/blk, cone shade, 8", M..............**100.00**
Lamp, Glow, #01001, copper & brass, cone shade, 8", M..............**50.00**
Lamp, Glow, #01001, copper w/wht, cone shade, 8", M..............**100.00**
Light, Binnacle; #25002, wired, colored glass, from $50 to............**65.00**
Light, Binnacle; #25002, wired, 1933-34 Chicago Expo, from $100 to .**120.00**
Light, Colonel's Lady; #27014, head is bulb, 9⅜", M, from $150 to..**250.00**
Meridian Tray, chromium w/wht hdls, #17078, 7⅞", from $40 to .**65.00**
Nob-Top Ashtray, chromium w/colored knob center, #810, 6½" dia .**40.00**
Pelican Smokers' Stand, English Bronze, VN, #17056, 21x8¼" dia.**375.00**
Piccadilly Cigarette Box, chromium-plate & wht, #867, ¾x8¾x3" ...**95.00**
Smokeless Ashtray, polished brass w/mc enameling, #537, from $60 to .**70.00**
Sphere Smokers' Set, chromium & enamel, #858, 4 pcs on 8¼" tray.**130.00**
Star Ashtray, copper w/3-point chromium star, #870, 3½" dia base ..**110.00**
Sugar Sphere, chromium, RW, #90078, 2⅞x2⅝", from $45 to......**55.00**
Sunday Morning Waffle Set, chromium, compo hdls, #90059, 4-pc, $225 to .**250.00**
Sunday Supper Candle Holders, blk nickel, #24002, 4 for..........**100.00**
Sunshine Watering Can, brass & copper, Ge, #5003, 5x8½", $30 to .**40.00**
Tavern Pitcher, polished copper, brass hdl, VN, #17026, 10¼" ..**250.00**
Three-Layer Candy Box, apple & leaves on lid, chromium, #90104, 5⅝"..**85.00**
Triple Flower Stand, brass & copper, #11228, 14½x16" **175.00**
Tripod Ashtray, copper & brass, 3-leg, VN, #301, from $50 to **60.00**
Trowel, brass w/blk hdl, VN, #90015, 10", from $80 to **100.00**
Watering Can, copper w/brass hdl/spout, Ge, #11173, from $65 to .**75.00**
Weather Vane, brass arrow, #90030, 12x12", from $225 to **250.00**

Chelsea Dinnerware

Made from about 1830 to 1880 in the Staffordshire district of England, this white dinnerware is decorated with lustre embossings in the grape, thistle, sprig, or fruit and cornucopia patterns. The relief designs vary from lavender to blue, and the body of the ware may be porcelain, ironstone, or earthenware. Because it was not produced in Chelsea as the name would suggest, dealers often prefer to call it 'Grandmother's Ware.' For more information we recommend *Collector's Encyclopedia of English China* by Mary Frank Gaston, our advisor for this category.

Grape, bowl, 8" **35.00**
Grape, cake plate, emb ribs, 10" dia, from $25 to **30.00**
Grape, cake plate, w/copper lustre, 10" sq, from $25 to **30.00**
Grape, coffeepot, stick hdl, 2-cup, 7"..**75.00**
Grape, creamer, 5½"..**55.00**
Grape, cup & saucer, from $25 to **35.00**
Grape, egg cup, 2¼", from $35 to **50.00**
Grape, pitcher, milk; 40-oz **60.00**

Grape, plate, 6", from $12 to......................................**15.00**
Grape, plate, 7"......................................**18.00**
Grape, plate, 8", from $22 to......................................**25.00**
Grape, plate, 9½"......................................**22.50**
Grape, sugar bowl, w/lid......................................**55.00**
Grape, teapot, octagonal, 10"......................................**165.00**
Grape, teapot, octagonal, 8½", from $125 to......................................**150.00**
Grape, teapot, 2-cup......................................**75.00**
Grape, waste bowl......................................**40.00**
Sprig, cake plate, 9"......................................**40.00**
Sprig, cup & saucer......................................**40.00**
Sprig, pitcher, milk......................................**60.00**
Sprig, plate, dinner......................................**25.00**
Sprig, plate, 7"......................................**18.00**
Thistle, butter pat......................................**15.00**
Thistle, cake plate, 8¾", from $25 to......................................**30.00**
Thistle, cup & saucer, from $30 to......................................**35.00**
Thistle, plate, 6", from $6 to......................................**8.00**
Thistle, plate, 7"......................................**15.00**
Thistle, sugar bowl, 8-sided, w/lid, 7½"......................................**45.00**

Chelsea Keramic Art Works

In 1866 fifth-generation Scottish potter Alexander Robertson started a pottery in Chelsea, Massachusetts, where his brother Hugh joined him the following year. Their father James left the firm he partnered to help his sons in 1872, teaching them techniques and pressing decorative tiles, an extreme rarity at that early date. Their early production consisted mainly of classical Grecian and Asian shapes in redware and stoneware, several imitating metal vessels. They then displayed influences from Europe's most important potteries, such as Royal Doulton and Limoges, in underglaze and barbotine or Haviland painting. Hugh's visit to the Philadelphia Centennial Exposition introduced him to the elusive sang-de-boeuf or oxblood glaze featured on Ming porcelain, which he would strive to achieve for well over a decade at tremendous costs.

James passed away in 1880, and Alexander moved to California in 1884, leaving Hugh in charge of the pottery and his oxblood glaze experiments. The time and energy spent doing research were taken away from producing saleable artwares. Out of funds, Hugh closed the pottery in 1889.

Wealthy patrons supported the founding of a new company, the short-lived Chelsea Pottery U.S., where the emphasis became the production of Chinese-inspired crackleware, vases, and tableware underglaze-painted in blue with simplified or stylized designs. The commercially viable pottery found a new home in Dedham, Massachusetts, in 1896, whose name it adopted. Hugh died in 1908, and the production of crackleware continued until 1943.

The ware is usually stamped CKAW within a diamond or Chelsea Keramic Art Works/Robertson & Sons. Our advisors for this category are Suzanne Perrault and Dave Rago; they are listed in the Directory under New Jersey. See also Dedham Pottery.

Bottle, oxblood, experimental by Hugh Robertson, mk, E/A 29, 8x3½".**2,500.00**
Bottle, oxblood/slate gray, CKAW, 6½x4"......................................**1,725.00**
Charger, emb nude on waves/butterflies, gr gloss, mk/HCR, 10¾"..**4,300.00**
Pilgrim flask, girl/geese, teal/gr, CKAW/Robertson-Sons, mfg flaw, 9"..**1,800.00**
Pilgrim flask, pine boughs/flowers, amber, sgn Ferrity, CKAW, 7½"..**1,500.00**
Plate, crackleware w/gr sponging to rim, experimental, CPUS, 8¾"...**450.00**
Vase, cvd violets, bl on gr, pillow form w/scroll ft, mk/sgn, 4", NM....**865.00**
Vase, emb honeycomb, sheer teal gloss, bottle form, mk, rstr, 9x4"..**700.00**
Vase, emb honeycomb/3 cvd daisy motifs, teal, bottle form, mk/rstr, 9"..**800.00**
Vase, incised florals/stems, khaki gr gloss, CKAW/JD, 6¼x3½"..**600.00**
Vase, 4-sided, 2 w/emb bird/bee/florals, amber gloss, mk, 7x2½", EX.**750.00**

Chicago Crucible

For only a few years during the 1920s, the Chicago (Illinois) Crucible Company made a limited amount of decorative pottery in addition to their regular line of architectural wares. Examples are very scarce today; they carry a variety of marks, all with the company name and location.

Vase, mottled green, twisted mushroom form, factory chips on base, 9", $1,500.00. (Photo courtesy Craftsman Auctions)

Figure, frog, mottled dk gr, 4¾x5"......................................**400.00**
Match holder, fireplace; frog figural, blk matt, 5x6x6"......................................**415.00**
Vase, mottled gr matt finish, 4 side openings, 9"......................................**740.00**
Vase, spade leaves on swirled stems, curdled med gr matt, 9x6".**1,600.00**

Children's Books

Children's books, especially those from the Victorian era, are charming collectibles. Colorful lithographic illustrations that once delighted little boys in long curls and tiny girls in long stockings and lots of ribbons and lace have lost none of their appeal. Some collectors limit themselves to a specific subject, while others may be far more interested in the illustrations. First editions are more valuable than later issues, and condition and rarity are very important factors to consider before making your purchase. For further information we recommend *Collector's Guide to Children's Books, 1850 – 1950, Volumes I, II,* and *III,* and *Boys' and Girls' Book Series,* all by Diane McClure Jones and Rosemary Jones. All are available from Collector Books or your local bookstore. Values are for examples in excellent condition, unless otherwise described within the line.

Key:
brds — boards   ed — edition
dj — dust jacket

Adventures of Sherlock Holmes, AC Doyle, Whitman, 1965, hardcover ..**7.50**
American Indian Tales & Legends, Hulpach, London, 1966, hardcover.**20.00**
Andy Panda's Rescue, Lantz, Whitman Authorized ed 1949...........**8.50**
At Daddy's Office, RJ Mirsch, Alfred A Knopf, c 1946, hardcover...**12.50**
Bambi's Children, Story of...Family; Salten, Grosset & Dunlap, 1939 ..**15.00**
Barbara & 5 Little Purrs, EL Gould, Caldwell, c 1908, pictorial cover..**20.00**
Black Cauldron, L Alexander, Holt Rinehart, 1965 2nd ed, VG ..**12.00**
Bobbsey Twins & Their Schoolmates, LL Hope, Grosset & Dunlap, 1928..**15.00**
Children's Music Box, Webster, Morrow, 1945, 1st ed, VG...........**35.00**
Children's Picture Atlas of World, Bacon editor, Golden Press.....**10.00**
Clue of Leaning Chimney, C Keen, Grosset & Dunlap, 1967, 176-pg ..**7.50**
Complete Tales of Winnie-the-Pooh, AA Milne, 1928 2nd ed, 344-pg.**28.00**

Dear Mr Henshaw, B Cleary, Morrow, 1983, 5th printing, 134-pg, VG ..**16.00**
Don't Go Out Tonight, B Cole, Starlight, Doubleday, pop-up, 1982, VG..**30.00**
Easter Bunny Are You for Real, H Myra, Thos Nelson Inc, 1979, 32-pg.**10.00**
Easy Drawing Book, P White, Gramercy Pub, 1966, hardcover **12.50**

Ef You Don't Watch Out, James Whitcomb Riley, Bobbs Merrill, 1908, EX, from $50.00 to $75.00.

Egg in the Hole Book, R Scarry, Golden Book, 1967, 16 cb pgs ...**15.00**
Emma, J Stevenson, Greenwillow Books, 1985 1st ed, 30-pg **12.50**
Ernie's Telephone Call, Sipherd, Golden Tell-A-Tale, 1978............**5.00**
Flyaways & Goldilocks, AD Hardy, Grosset & Dunlap, c 1925, hardcover.**15.00**
Golden Trail, P Berton, MacMillan, 1962, 147-pg, NM **12.00**
Helen Keller, Story of My Life; H Keller, Pendulum Press, 1969...**12.50**
Hope for the Flowers, T Paulus, Paulist Press, 1972, 151-pg.........**12.50**
Jemima & Welsh Rabbit, Avery, Reindeer Book, 1974, pictorial brds ..**22.00**
JoJo, M Barrows, Rand McNally Glowing Eye Book, pop-up, 1944.**55.00**
Journey to Japan, UNICEF, Viking, pop-up, 1986, VG+ **16.00**
Jr Girl Scout Handbook, Nat'l Council of Girl Scouts, 1975, 371-pg.**8.00**
Kidnapped, RL Stevenson, Pendulum Press, 1969, elephant ed....**12.50**
Lassie & Cub Scout, F Michelson, Whitman Tell-A-Tale, 1966...**10.00**
Leonardo Da Vinci, Provensen, Viking, pop-up, 1984, VG..........**22.00**
Lewis Carroll: Biography; A Clarke, Schocken Books, 1979, 284-pg..**25.00**
Little by Little, O Optic, Donohue, no date, hardcover, 245-pg, VG..**10.00**
Lucky Starr & Oceans of Venus, Asimov, Twayne, 1978, 186-pg, VG .**12.00**
Mad About Madeline, Bemelmans, 1939, hardcover, 316-pg **28.00**
Mystery Candlestick, J Bothwell, Dial, 1970, 1st ed, 148-pg, VG.**25.00**
Nancy Drew & Crooked Banister, C Keene, Grosset & Dunlap, 1971..**7.50**
Night Before Christmas, CC Moore, Random House, 1975, Picturebk series.**8.00**
Our Wild Animals, EL Moseley, Appleton & Co, 1927 1st ed......**16.50**
Paddington's London, Bond, London, pop-up, 1986, shaped brds, VG.**50.00**
Pink Panther & Sons: Fun at Picnic, Beris, Golden Book, 1985 .....**6.00**
Pinocchio: Tale of a Puppet, Collodi, Donohue, no date, 264-pg .**20.00**
Rainbow Book of People & Places, M Mead, World Pub, 1972 printing..**17.50**
Real Princess, HC Anderson, Whitman, 1932, 1st ed, 14-pg, VG ..**110.00**
Saggy Baggy Elephant, K&B Jackson, Golden Press, 1973, 22nd printing..**8.50**
Steadfast Tin Soldier, HC Anderson, Little Brown & Co, 1983 ...**27.50**
Stories From Hans Anderson, HC Anderson, London, 1972, 182-pg, NM.**35.00**
Stories Julian Tells, Cameron, Pantheon, 1981, 3rd ed, 71-pg, VG.**28.00**
Strike-Out King, J De Vries, World Publishing, 1948, hardcover, VG..**9.00**
Teeny Tiny Witches, J Wahl, GP Putnam's Sons, Weekly Reader, 1979.**12.00**
That Julia Redfern, Cameron, Dutton, 1982, 1st ed, 133-pg, NM ..**35.00**
There's a Mouse in Our House, E Wynn, Whitman Tiny-Tot-Tale, 1966 ..**18.50**
Toby Tyle or 10 Weeks w/Circus, J Otis, Harper & Bros, no date, 265-pg..**35.00**
Why Corn Is Golden, V Blackmore, London, 1984, 1st UK ed, VG.**28.00**
Witch's Daughter, Bauden, London, 1968, dj by S Hughes, NM...**15.00**
Witches Four, M Brown, Parents Magazine Press, 1980, hardcover ..**14.00**
Young McKinley, Butterworth, Appleton, 1905, 1st ed, 307-pg, VG.**30.00**
12 Days of Christmas, Schlindler illus, Harper Collins, 1991 1st ed.**10.00**
3 Boys & Lighthouse, Agle & Wilson, Scribners, 1967 reprint, VG..**10.00**
365 Bedtime Stories, 2-pg author list, Whitman, c 1944, hardcover.**55.00**

Children's Things

Nearly every item devised for adult furnishings has been reduced to child size — furniture, dishes, sporting goods, even some tools. All are very collectible. During the late seventeenth and early eighteenth centuries, miniature china dinnerware sets were made both in China and in England. They were not intended primarily as children's playthings, however, but instead were made to furnish miniature rooms and cabinets that provided a popular diversion for the adults of that period. By the nineteenth century, the emphasis had shifted, and most of the small-scaled dinnerware and tea sets were made for children's play.

Late in the nineteenth century and well into the twentieth, toy pressed glass dishes were made, many in the same pattern as full-scale glassware. Today these toy dishes often fetch prices in the same range as those for the 'grown-ups'!

Our advisors for this category are Margaret and Kenn Whitmyer; you will find their address in the Directory under Ohio. See also A B C Plates; Blue Willow; Clothing; Stickley; etc.

Key: ds — doll size

China

Bowl, Blue Banded Ironstone, 8-sided, England, 4" **25.00**
Bowl, Blue Willow, England, 2" **42.50**
Bowl, Calico, brn & wht, oval, England, 4" **35.00**
Bowl, Livesley Fern & Floral, Livesley Powell & Co, mid-1800s, 3⅞"..**37.50**
Bowl, Myrtle Wreath, bl & wht, oval, JM&S, 5"............................**35.00**
Bowl, soup; Animals & Birds, Fr, 4⅜"...**32.50**
Bowl, soup; Kite Fliers, bl & wht, England, early 1800s, 3½" **67.50**
Bowl, soup; Twin Flowers, flow bl, England................................**65.00**
Bowl, vegetable; Athens, bl & wht, Davenport, mid-1800s, w/lid, 2¾".**90.00**
Bowl, vegetable; Gaudy Floral, England, 4"...................................**65.00**
Canister, Blue Banded, Germany, 2½"..**30.00**
Casserole, Forget-Me-Not, bl & wht, England, 4¾"....................**180.00**
Casserole, Pembroke, bl & wht, Bistro England, 5¼"...................**55.00**
Casserole, Rhodesia, floral w/gold, Ridgway's, 1900s, 5½".............**55.00**
Casserole, Spirit of Children, England, 4" **32.00**
Cold cream jar, Autumn, Germany **55.00**
Comport, Pastel Blue Majolica, England, 3¼"............................**170.00**
Creamer, Acorn, brn & wht, Cork Edge & Malkin, 2⅛" **22.50**
Creamer, Amherst Japan, England, 2½"..**47.50**
Creamer, Basket, flow bl, England **70.00**
Creamer, Blue Portrait, Germany, 2¾"...**35.00**
Creamer, Chinaman, Japan, 2¼"...**45.00**
Creamer, Joseph Mary & Donkey, Germany, 3" **42.50**
Creamer, Nursery Rhymes, red & wht, W&Co, 1886-1892 ....**30.00**
Creamer, Orient, bl & wht, England **32.00**
Creamer, Silhouette Children, Victoria/Czechoslovakia, 2⅛".......**15.00**
Cup, Buster Brown, Germany, 2½"...**45.00**
Cup, Girl w/Pets, Charles Allerton & Sons, 2⅛" **18.00**
Cup, Holly, Germany, 1900s **25.00**
Cup, Pink Banded Floral, England, 2¼" **7.50**
Cup, Punch & Judy, bl & wht, England, 1⅞" **37.50**
Cup, Water Hen, bl & wht, England, 2" **22.50**
Gravy boat, Gold Floral, England, 5½"..**65.00**
Gravy boat, Kite Fliers, bl & wht, England, 3½" **125.00**
Gravy boat, Rosamond, bl & wht, Bistro England, 2½" **65.00**
Ladle, Greek Key, brn & wht, RSR (Ridgway Sparks & Ridgway), 5" ...**18.00**
Mug, A Present for a Good Boy, red transfer, lustre rim, Staffordshire .**460.00**
Mug, Blue Willow, Coalport/Made in England, 1⅞".......................**27.50**
Mug, Bridesmaid, Germany, 2⅝" **120.00**
Plate, Angel w/Shining Star, Germany...**20.00**

Plate, Athens, bl & wht, Davenport, mid-1800s, 3" **10.00**
Plate, Blue Acorn, RSR (Ridgway Sparks & Ridgway), 3¾" **10.00**
Plate, Bridesmaid, Germany, 6½" **12.00**
Plate, Copeland's Blue Animal, Copeland, early 1900s, 5" **30.00**
Plate, Flow Blue Dogwood, Minton, 4" **27.50**
Plate, Gaudy Floral, England, 2¾" **10.00**
Plate, Gaudy Ironstone, England, 6" **55.00**
Plate, Humphrey's Clock, bl & wht, Ridgway's England, 4½" **18.00**
Plate, Nursery Scenes, Germany **5.50**
Plate, Pagodas, England, 4½" **17.50**
Plate, Red & White Rose, Germany, 5" **9.00**
Plate, Scenes From England, bl & wht, 3⅛" **45.00**
Plate, Silhouette, Noritake, 4¼" **8.00**
Plate, Sunset, Made in Japan, 4¼" **5.00**
Plate, Tan Luster & White, England, 3¼" **6.50**
Plate, Twin Flower, flow bl, England, 3¾" **25.00**
Platter, Blue Banded Ironstone, England, 5⅛" **25.00**
Platter, Fancy Loop, cream & gr, England, 5" **26.00**
Platter, Fishers, dk gr & wht, CE&M, 3¾" **32.50**
Platter, Flow Blue Dogwood, Minton, 5" **62.50**
Platter, Maiden-Hair-Fern, Ridgway, late 1800s, 7¼" **25.00**
Saucer, Acorn, brn & wht, Cork Edge & Malkin, 4¾" **4.00**
Saucer, Amherst Japan, England, mid-1800s, 4½" **15.00**
Saucer, Father Christmas & the Children, Germany, 4¼" **6.50**
Saucer, Mary Had a Little Lamb, Staffordshire, 3¾" **3.00**
Saucer, Standing Pony, gr lustre, Germany, 4¼" **6.00**
Saucer, Stick Spatter, Staffordshire, 4½" **6.50**
Sugar bowl, Barnyard Animals, w/lid, Germany, 4" **22.50**
Sugar bowl, Blue Onion, w/lid, England **40.00**
Sugar bowl, Dimmock's Blue Banded, w/lid, Thomas Dimmock, 3¾" ..**95.00**
Sugar bowl, floral, w/lid, Nippon, 3" **15.00**
Sugar bowl, Nursery Rhymes, w/lid, W&Co, ca 1886-92, 3½" **38.00**
Sugar bowl, Orient, bl & wht, w/lid, England, 3½" **40.00**
Sugar bowl, Sunset, w/lid, Made in Japan, 3⅛" **16.00**
Sugar bowl, Teddy Bear, w/lid, Germany, 4" **52.50**
Teapot, Butterfly, England, 4¼" **58.00**
Teapot, Dimmock's Blue Banded, Thomas Dimmock, 3¾" **90.00**
Teapot, Humphrey's Clock, bl & wht, Ridgway's England, 4½" **85.00**
Teapot, Lady Standing by Urn, purple & wht, England, 4½" **160.00**
Teapot, Mary Had a Little Lamb, Staffordshire, 3½" **70.00**
Teapot, Pink Rose, Germany, 6¼" **68.00**
Teapot, Roman Chariots, bl & wht, w/lid, Caldon England, 3⅜" .**150.00**
Teapot, Standing Pony, gr lustre, Germany, 6" **90.00**
Toothbrush holder, Pink Lustre, England, 1¼x3⅛" **55.00**
Tray, Dimity, gr & cream, rectangular, England, 5¾" **35.00**
Tray, dresser; Bluebird & Floral, hdls, England, 4¾" **45.00**
Tureen, Blue Acorn, RSR (Ridgway Sparks & Ridgway), 6½" **44.00**
Tureen, Rhodesia, floral w/gold, Ridgway's, 1900s, 4¾" **65.00**
Underplate, Maiden-Hair-Fern, Ridgway, late 1800s, 5" **18.00**
Waste bowl, Gaudy Ironstone, England, 2⅞" **120.00**
Waste bowl, Stick Spatter, Staffordshire, 2½" **80.00**
Waste bowl, Water Hen, bl & wht, England, 2½" **62.50**

Furniture

Examples with no dimensions given are child size unless noted doll size.

Armchair, birch w/orig mellow brn, 3-slat bk, rush seat, 27" ..**250.00**
Armchair, maple/ash, 3 arched slats, orig red, rpl woven seat, 1790s.**435.00**
Armchair, slat-bk, yel over early red, rpl rush seat, 1790s, 25" ..**350.00**
Armchair, Windsor, red pnt w/gr seat, repro by DT Smith & Co, 32".**330.00**
Armchair, 3 arched slats w/knob finials, old red, splint seat, 1790s...**575.00**
Bed, Arts & Crafts, oak, headbrd: doll images/ftbrd: 2 cutouts, 16x29".**230.00**
Bed, mahog Sheraton high-post w/acorn finials, rpr, 70x69x34".**2,000.00**

Bed steps, gray-pnt pine, 2-step w/shaped sides, dvtl, 1800s, 10x16x9".**635.00**
Bin w/lower drw, red-pnt pint, hinged top, NE/1700s, 21x21".**1,175.00**
Blanket chest, poplar w/bright red pnt, dvtl, 1-brd 30x15" top ...**990.00**
Chair, potty; gray pnt, New England, early 19th C, 21" **300.00**
Chair, side; Windsor bow-bk, later blk pnt, New England, 1790s, 29" ..**700.00**
Chest, cherry Country, 2-part, trn wood pulls, chip-cvd edge, 29x19" ..**660.00**
Chest, pine w/orig red, 6-brd, New England, 18th C, 19x33x15".**1,380.00**
Chest, poplar/cherry vnr Emp, 4 dvtl drws, rpl ft/rfn, 26x24x15".**880.00**
Chest, walnut 4-drw, trn legs/pilasters w/cvd acanthus, dvtl, 36x33".**935.00**
Chest, walnut/cherry Emp, ½-spiral trn pilasters, sq nails, 27x29" ..**1,400.00**
Chest, 3 graduated dvtl drws, paneled ends, Bennington-type pulls, 13".**325.00**

Chest of drawers, red-stained pine, split drawers over two graduated drawers with wooden pulls, bun feet, nineteenth century, 16x13x7", $4,025.00. (Photo courtesy Skinner, Inc.)

Cradle, old bl rpt, cutout hdls, dvtl, 19x40x19" **330.00**
Cradle, pnt soft wood, 19½" **130.00**
Crib, walnut Renaissance Revival, canopy, cvd children, burl, 45" L.**15,700.00**
Cupboard, old red pnt, door opens to single shelf, ca 1880s, 26x18".**2,875.00**
Desk, cherry/poplar QA, slant lid, 18th C, rfn, 27x23x14" **4,115.00**
Desk, maple, slant-lid, grpt drw, old rfn, rstr brasses, 37" **4,300.00**
Desk, pine/poplar, hinged top, 2 drws, sq legs, orig bl pnt, 19th C.**1,035.00**
Dresser, poplar, 2-drw, orig pnt w/swag decor, wire nails, 16x10x5" .**110.00**
Dry sink, pine/poplar, 1 drw/1 door, built from old wood, 25x24x14" ..**275.00**
Highchair, maple, 3 arched slats, rush seat, orig brn pnt, 1700s, 37".**12,650.00**
Highchair, maple/hickory/walnut, 2-slat bk, trn arms, splint seat, 34".**220.00**
Highchair, PA decor (roses) on salmon pnt, trn legs, 3-spindle bk.**2,000.00**
Highchair, Windsor, vestiges of stippled red/blk pnt, NE/1840s, 32".**765.00**
Highchair, 2-slat bk, orig brn pnt, rush seat, 1750s, 38" **2,185.00**
Highchair, 3-slat ladderbk, dk gr pnt, trn legs, woven tape seat, 38".**3,800.00**
Rocker, arm; plank seat, single splat, bamboo supports/legs, 21" ...**75.00**
Rocker, dk blk finish, scrolled arms, cane seat, 22", VG.............**175.00**
Rocker, Lincoln style; cane bk & seat, curved arms, 26" **100.00**
Rocker, Lincoln; cane bk & seat, scrolled/curved arms, dk finish, 26".**100.00**
Rocker, platform; walnut w/uphl seat/bk/arm pads, Victorian, 30".**350.00**
Sea chest, pnt pine & poplar, beck hdls, hinged lid, dvtl, 1850s.**1,380.00**
Sideboard, walnut, mirror top, candle shelves, 2 doors, 38" H **525.00**

Glass

Acorn, butter dish, 4" **315.00**
Acorn, spooner, crystal frosted....................................**265.00**
Arched Panel, pitcher, 3¾" **36.50**
Arched Panel, tumbler, cobalt, 2" **32.00**
Austrian No 200, butter dish, chocolate **840.00**
Austrian No 200, creamer, canary, 3¼" **210.00**
Austrian No 200, sugar bowl, w/lid, 3¾" **187.50**
Baby Thumbprint, candlestand, tall, 3" **115.00**
Baby Thumbprint, compote, w/lid, 4" **182.50**
Bead & Scroll, butter dish, amber, 4" **315.00**
Bead & Scroll, sugar bowl, w/lid, 4" **132.00**
Beaded Swirl, butter dish, cobalt, 2⅜" **155.00**

Beaded Swirl, creamer, 2¼"...32.00
Betty Jane, bread baker, crystal w/red trim, rectangular, #256.......32.50
Betty Jane, pie plate, crystal 18.00
Block, butter dish, bl..192.50
Block, spooner, amber, 3"..115.00
Braided Belt, butter dish, wht w/decor, 2¼"............................315.00
Braided Belt, spooner, 2⅝"...95.00
Bucket (Wooden Pail), butter dish, 2¼"................................295.00
Bucket (Wooden Pail), creamer, 2½"....................................62.50

Butterfly, mug, Bryce Hibgee, 2x2", from $40.00 to $50.00.
(Photo courtesy Doris Anderson Lechler)

Button Panel No 44, butter dish, crystal w/gold, 4"....................125.00
Button Panel No 44, sugar bowl, w/lid, 4⅝" 95.00
Buzz Saw No 2697, butter dish, 2⅜"....................................36.50
Buzz Saw No 2697, sugar bowl, w/lid, 2⅞"..............................34.00
Cherry Blossom, plate, pk, 5⅞" (+) 12.50
Cherry Blossom, sugar bowl, Delphite, 2⅝" (+).........................50.00
Chimo, butter dish, 2⅜" (+)...130.00
Clear & Diamond Panel, butter dish, gr, 2⅞"...........................70.00
Clear & Diamond Panel, sugar bowl, bl, w/lid, 3½" 57.50
Cloud Band, butter dish, milk glass w/decor, 3¾"......................192.50
Cloud Band, sugar bowl, w/lid, 4"......................................85.00
Colonial No 2630, butter dish, olive or emerald gr, 2½" 57.50
Colonial No 2630, sugar bowl, w/lid, 3"...............................26.50
Diamond Ridge, butter dish 200.00
Diamond Ridge, sugar bowl, w/lid, 4⅝".................................157.50
Doric & Pansy, cup, ultramarine, 1½"..................................50.00
Doric & Pansy, saucer, pk, 4½"...7.00
Drum, mug, 2½"..40.00
Drum, spooner, 2⅝"..72.50
Dutch Boudoir, candlestick, bl opaque, 3".............................130.00
Fernland, creamer, 2⅜" 22.00
Fernland No 2635, butter dish, cobalt, 2⅝"............................62.50
Fine Cut Star & Fan, butter dish, 2½".................................36.50
Fine Cut Star & Fan, spooner, 2¼" 34.00
Grapevine w/Ovals, butter dish, 2½"...................................115.00
Grapevine w/Ovals, spooner, 1⅞".......................................75.00
Hawaiian Lei, cake plate 52.50
Hawaiian Lei, creamer, 2"...22.00
Homespun, cup, crystal, 1⅝"...17.50
Homespun, plate, pk, 4½"..12.00
Inverted Strawberry, bowl, master berry; 1⅝"..........................68.00
Inverted Strawberry, punch bowl, 3⅜" (+)..............................57.50
Kidibake, bread baker, clear opal, #1928, 5".........................70.00
Kidibake, grill plate, bl, 8½" 37.50
Lamb, creamer, 2⅞"..75.00
Lamb, sugar bowl, w/lid, 4⅛"..125.00
Laurel, creamer, Jade Green, 2⅝" 35.00
Laurel, plate, French Ivory, 5⅞" 8.00
Laurel, sugar bowl, Scottie decal, 2⅜"................................115.00
Lion, butter dish, crystal frost, 4¼" 147.50
Lion, cup, crystal w/frosted head, 1¾"................................62.50

Moderntone, creamer, wht, 1¾" 17.50
Moderntone, cup, Sunny Yellow, 1¾"....................................7.00
Moderntone, teapot, maroon, w/lid, 3½"................................70.00
Nearcut, pitcher, 3⅛"...32.50
Nearcut, tumbler, 2"..7.50
Oval Star No 300, punch bowl 57.50
Palm Leaf Fan, cake stand, 5"...47.50
Pattee Cross, bowl, master berry; 1¾".................................42.50
Pattee Cross, punch cup, gold trim, 1⅛"...............................30.00
Peacock Feather, cake stand, 3".......................................100.00
Peacock Feather, creamer 52.50
Pennsylvania, butter dish, gr...235.00
Pennsylvania, creamer, 2½"..47.50
Pennsylvania, sugar bowl, gr, w/lid, 4"...............................182.50
Pert, butter dish, 2¾"..130.00
Pert, spooner, 3"...130.00
Pointed Jewel (Long Diamond), butter dish.............................178.00
Pointed Jewel (Long Diamond), sugar bowl, w/lid, 3⅞".................135.00
Pyrexette, bread baker, 3x4¾"...24.00
Pyrexette, custard, 3½"...3.00
Rex (Fancy Cut), creamer, 2½"...28.50
Rex (Fancy Cut), pitcher, 3½"...62.50
Rooster, butter dish, 2¾"...210.00
Rooster, nappy, 3"..147.50
Sandwich Ivy, creamer, amethyst, 2⅜"..................................130.00
Sandwich Ivy, sugar bowl, 3¼"...85.00
Sawtooth, butter dish, 3"...52.50
Sawtooth, spooner, 3¼"..42.50
Stippled Raindrop & Dewdrop, butter dish, amber or cobalt, 1¾" ..152.50
Stippled Raindrop & Dewdrop, creamer, 2¼".............................62.50
Sultan, creamer, gr or gr frost, 2½".................................125.00
Sultan, spooner, chocolate, 2½".......................................365.00
Sunbeam (Twin Snowshoes), butter dish, 2"............................147.50
Sunbeam (Twin Snowshoes), sugar bowl, w/lid, 3⅛".....................122.50
Sunny Suzy, baker, hdls, 10-oz..12.00
Sunny Suzy, boxed set, 7-pc...150.00
Sunny Suzy, casserole, w/lid, 10-oz...................................12.00
Sweetheart, butter dish, 2"...22.00
Sweetheart, sugar bowl, w/lid, 3".....................................22.00
Twist, butter dish, 3⅝"...28.50
Twist No 137, butter dish, crystal frost, 3⅝".........................72.50
Twist No 137, sugar bowl, bl opal, w/lid, 3⅞".........................200.00
Wee Branches, cup, 1⅝"..47.50
Wee Branches, plate, 3"...62.50
Whirligig No 15101, butter dish, 2½"..................................28.50
Whirligig No 15101, punch bowl, 4¾"...................................36.50
Wild Rose, candlestick, 4¼"...130.00

Miscellaneous

Bucket, staved, yel w/bl-pnt tin bands, stenciled stars/chicks, 4", VG....650.00
Carriage, for twins, wicker w/rolled arms/bk rail, Heywood, 54x58"...2,500.00
Hobby horse, burlap on cvd wood, w/mane/tail, canvas saddle, 28" ..500.00
Noah's ark, mc pnt wood, cvd animal figures, Germany, 19th C, 7x12x5".1,380.00
Noah's ark, pnt & litho wood, 29 cvd pnt animals, 17" L 950.00
Sled, oak w/hickory & iron runners, HP floral/gold stencil, wear, 31"..500.00
Sled, Paris Mfg Co...ME USA on bl pnt wood, wood/iron runners, 38", EX .800.00
Sleigh, rpt w/scrollwork & foliage on red, yel borders, bl int, 29" L.385.00

Chintz

'Chintz' is the generic name for English china with an allover floral transfer design. This eye-catching china is reminiscent of chintz dress fabric. It is colorful, bright, and cheery with its many floral designs and reminds one of an English garden in full bloom. It was produced in England during the first half of this century and stands out among other styles of china. Pattern names often found with the manufacturer's name on the bottom of pieces include Florence, Blue Chintz, English Roses, Delphinium, June Roses, Hazel, Eversham, Royalty, Sweet Pea, Summertime, and Welbeck, among others.

The older patterns tend to be composed of larger flowers, while the later, more popular lines can be quite intricate in design. And while the first collectors preferred the earthenware lines, many are now searching for the bone china dinnerware made by such firms as Shelley. You can concentrate on reassembling a favorite pattern, or you can mix two or more designs together for a charming, eclectic look. Another choice may be to limit your collection to teapots (the stacking ones are especially nice), breakfast sets, or cups and saucers.

Though the Chintz market remains very active, prices for some pieces have been significantly compromised due to their having been reproduced. For further information we recommend *Charlton Book of Chintz, I, II,* and *II,* by Susan Scott. Our advisor is Mary Jane Hastings; she is listed in the Directory under Illinois. See also Shelley.

Lorna Doone, biscuit barrel with silver lid and handle, Wilkinson, $695.00; Lorna Doone, milk jug, Wilkinson, 4¼", $495.00. (Photo courtesy Mary Jane Hastings)

Anemone, bowl, Lord Nelson, 1½x5½x3¾" 25.00
Anemone, creamer & sugar bowl, Lord Nelson, ea 2¼" 100.00
Apple Blossom, cup & saucer, James Kent 45.00
Bedale, canoe, allover transfer, Royal Winton 240.00
Bedale, teapot, Countess shape, Royal Winton, 5½" 325.00
Blue Paisley, candy box, Royal Winton, 5½x3¾" 130.00
Blue Paisley, cup & saucer, Wade Heath 60.00
Blue Pansy, plate, serving; center hdl, Lord Nelson, 10" dia..........75.00
Brama, cake plate, chrome base, Midwinter 105.00
Brama, creamer, Midwinter, 2½" 90.00
Chelsea, bowl, Royal Winton, 5" sq+hdls 50.00
Clyde, teapot & trivet, Royal Winton, 6-cup..............................100.00
Cotswold, bonbon dish, w/lid, Gordon shape, Royal Winton 890.00
Crocus, coffeepot, Albans shape, Royal Winton, prof rpr............500.00
DuBarry, jug, James Kent, 3" 85.00
DuBarry, nut dish, ruffled rim, James Kent 45.00
DuBarry, sugar bowl, w/lid, James Kent, 3½" 120.00
DuBarry, teapot, James Kent, 4½x9½" 525.00
DuBarry, trio, James Kent..105.00
English Rose, pin dish, Royal Winton, 4½x3½" 80.00
Green Paisley, cup & saucer, Royal Winton 35.00
Hazel, butter dish, Royal Winton, 1930s, 6¼x4¼"....................125.00
Hazel, plate, Royal Winton, 7" sq..140.00
Hazel, platter, Royal Winton, 11"...495.00
Heather, cheese keeper, slant lid, Lord Nelson 200.00
Heather, cup & saucer, Lord Nelson 75.00

Heather, jam set, Lord Nelson, 4-pc...190.00
Hydrangea, plate, James Kent, 9" 75.00
Kew, comport, ftd, Royal Winton, 3x7" 220.00
Kew, cup & saucer, Royal Winton 90.00
Kew, plate, Royal Winton, 7" 60.00
Lilac Time, plate, Empire, 7" 45.00
Lorna Doone, creamer, Barker Bros, 3¾" 50.00
Lorna Doone, jug, Barker Bros, 5" 125.00
Lorna Doone, jug, Barker Bros, 5¾" 175.00
Lorna Doone, sugar bowl, Barker Bros, 2¼x4¼".........................40.00
Lorna Doone, tidbit tray, 3-tier, Barker Bros............................115.00
Majestic, canoe, Royal Winton, 10¾".......................................325.00
Majestic, creamer & sugar bowl, Stuart shape, Royal Winton 225.00
Marguerite, breakfast/tea set, Royal Winton, 1928, 6-pc...........950.00
Marguerite, cup & saucer, Royal Winton, from $55 to 65.00
Marguerite, jug, breakfast; Royal Winton, 2½" 50.00
Marguerite, plate, Ascot shape, Royal Winton, 6" 28.00
Marguerite, plate, Royal Winton, 8" 80.00
Marguerite, plate, 8-sided, Royal Winton, 5" 30.00
Marigold, bowl, fluted oval, James Kent, 13x6½" 120.00
Marina, bowl, hdls, Lord Nelson, 1½x6½x4" 40.00
Marina, bud vase, Lord Nelson, 5¼x2" 125.00
Marina, cake plate, Lord Nelson, 10¾" 125.00
Marina, creamer & sugar bowl, Lord Nelson 65.00
Marina, jug, globular, Lord Nelson, 4½", NM............................140.00
Marina, plate, Lord Nelson, 6½" 55.00
Marina, plate, Lord Nelson, 8½" 80.00
Marina, teacup & saucer, Lord Nelson 45.00
Marion, cup & saucer, Royal Winton..120.00
Mille Fleurs, plate, dinner; 8-sided, James Kent, 10"...................95.00
Old Cottage, condiment jar, Royal Winton, 4¼x3" 125.00
Old Cottage, jam pot & underplate, Royal Winton 125.00
Old Cottage, jug, Royal Winton, 4"...215.00
Old Cottage, plate, dinner; Royal Winton, 10" 125.00
Old Cottage, plate, Royal Winton, 8" 120.00
Old Cottage, sugar bowl, Royal Winton......................................55.00
Pebbles, plate, Royal Winton, 6¼" 25.00
Pekin, condiment set, Royal Winton, cr/sug+jam/mustard jar+rnd tray .625.00
Pelham, cup & saucer, Royal Winton..35.00
Pelham, jam pot, Rheims shape, Royal Winton 55.00
Pelham, teapot, Royal Winton, 8½"...225.00
Persian, plate, Royal Doulton, 8½" 120.00
Persian, trio, Royal Doulton..120.00
Pink Peony, cake plate, Colclough..50.00
Pink Peony, cup & saucer, Colclough..50.00
Primula, cup & saucer, Crown Ducal...50.00
Primula, plate, Crown Ducal, 9" 42.00
Primula, teapot, Crown Ducal, 5" 250.00
Queen Anne, bowl, Royal Winton, 9" 100.00
Queen Anne, plate, Royal Winton, 6" 45.00
Queen Anne, teapot, Royal Winton, 6-cup 225.00
Rosalynde, bowl, serving; James Kent, 5x7" 150.00
Rosalynde, plate, salad; James Kent, 8"......................................40.00
Rosalynde, shell dish, James Kent..100.00
Rosalynde, tray, James Kent, 1½x13x6½"................................135.00
Rose Brocade, cup & saucer, demi; Royal Winton 32.50
Rosetime, bowl, Lord Nelson, 5¾" 22.00
Rosetime, pin tray, Lord Nelson, 3½"...22.00
Rosetime, plate, Triangular, Lord Nelson, 5½x5½" 32.00
Royal Brocade, creamer & sugar bowl, Lord Nelson 75.00
Royal Brocade, plate, 3-part; Lord Nelson, 1¼x7¾" 125.00
Royal Brocade, tea set, stacking; Lord Nelson, 3-pc..................500.00
Royal Brocade, teapot, Lord Nelson, 8".....................................250.00
Royalty, basket, Hampton shape, Royal Winton, 4x4¼"..............500.00

Royalty, breakfast set, Royal Winton, ca 1934, 6 pcs on 10" tray .2,250.00
Royalty, butter dish, Royal Winton 250.00
Royalty, cup & saucer, Royal Winton...90.00
Royalty, mint boat, no liner, Royal Winton...............................155.00
Royalty, sugar bowl, Hector shape, Royal Winton 95.00
Royalty, teacup, Raleigh shape, Royal Winton............................75.00
Royalty, teapot, Royal Winton, 6-cup 800.00
Somerset, canoe, Royal Winton, 11"...230.00
Summertime, butter dish, Ascot shape, Royal Winton..............150.00
Summertime, creamer & sugar bowl, w/lid, Royal Winton 180.00
Summertime, cup & saucer, Royal Winton, 2¼", 5½" 100.00
Summertime, plate, dinner; Royal Winton, 10".........................165.00
Summertime, tea set, Royal Winton, pot+sugar bowl+milk jug..900.00
Summertime, teapot, Royal Winton, 8-cup..............................350.00
Summertime, teapot, stacking; Royal Winton 450.00
Summertime, toast rack & tray, Royal Winton..........................295.00
Summertime, trio, Royal Winton 145.00
Sunshine, creamer & sugar bowl, breakfast; Royal Winton.........100.00
Sunshine, creamer & sugar bowl, Royal Winton...........................65.00
Sunshine, teapot, Royal Winton, 6-cup 350.00
Sweet Pea, cup & saucer, grandfather's; Royal Winton 240.00
Sweet Pea, plate, sandwich; rectangular, Royal Winton, 10x6" ..200.00
Tapestry, creamer & sugar bowl, w/lid, Royal Winton 175.00
Thistle, cup, Regency 50.00

Chocolate Glass

Jacob Rosenthal developed chocolate glass, a rich shaded opaque brown, sometimes referred to as caramel slag, in 1900 at the Indiana Tumbler and Goblet Company of Greentown, Indiana. Later, other companies produced similar ware. Only the latter is listed here. See also Greentown. Our advisors for this category are Jerry and Sandi Garrett; they are listed in the Directory under Indiana.

Bowl, Beaded Triangle, 4½" 375.00
Bowl, Geneva, oval, 10½" 450.00
Bowl, nappy; Chrysanthemum Leaf...675.00
Box, dresser; Venetian 450.00
Butter dish, Chrysanthemum Leaf...1,500.00
Butter dish, File, Royal Glass..2,500.00
Butter dish, Touching Squares 3,000.00
Celery tray, Jubilee, 10"...350.00
Celery vase, Chrysanthemum Leaf, 6"..875.00
Compote, Melrose, Royal Glass, 6" 250.00
Creamer, Rose Garland..1,350.00
Creamer, Wild Rose w/Bowknot 250.00
Pickle dish, Aurora, violin shape, Royal.....................................200.00
Pitcher, Chrysanthemum Leaf 3,000.00
Pitcher, Fleur-de-Lis, Royal Glass..1,250.00

Pitcher, Geneva,
$1,000.00. (Photo
courtesy James Measell)

Salt cellar, Honeycomb, master, 3½" 650.00
Shaker, Big Rib...575.00
Spooner, Chrysanthemum Leaf..600.00
Spooner, Geneva...200.00
Sugar bowl, Aldine, w/lid 1,850.00
Toothpick holder, Kingfisher 1,200.00
Tray, dresser; 6⅝x4⅛" 400.00
Tumbler, Chrysanthemum Leaf...575.00
Tumbler, File, Royal Glass..650.00
Vase, Beaded Triangle, 6¼" 250.00
Vase, Wild Rose w/Bowknot, 10½" 450.00

Christmas Collectibles

Christmas past . . . lovely mementos from long ago attest to the ostentatious Victorian celebrations of the season.

St. Nicholas, better known as Santa, has changed much since 300 A.D. when the good Bishop Nicholas showered needy children with gifts and kindnesses. During the early eighteenth century, Santa was portrayed as the kind gift-giver to well-behaved children and the stern switch-bearing disciplinarian to those who were bad. In 1822 Clement Clark Moore, a New York poet, wrote his famous *Night Before Christmas*, and the Santa he described was jolly and jovial — a lovable old elf who was stern with no one. Early Santas wore robes of yellow, brown, blue, green, red, white, or even purple. But Thomas Nast, who worked as an illustrator for *Harper's Weekly*, was the first to depict Santa in a red suit instead of the traditional robe and to locate him the entire year at the North Pole headquarters.

Today's collectors prize early Santa figures, especially those in robes of fur or mohair or those dressed in an unusual color. Some early examples of Christmas memorabilia are the pre-1870 ornaments from Dresden, Germany. These cardboard figures — angels, gondolas, umbrellas, dirigibles, and countless others — sparkled with gold and silver trim. Late in the 1870s, blown glass ornaments were imported from Germany. There were over 6,000 recorded designs, all painted inside with silvery colors. From 1890 through 1910, blown glass spheres were often decorated with beads, tassels, and tinsel rope.

Christmas lights, made by Sandwich and some of their contemporaries, were either pressed or mold-blown glass shaped into a form similar to a water tumbler. They were filled with water and then hung from the tree by a wire handle; oil floating on the surface of the water served as fuel for the lighted wick.

Kugels are glass ornaments that were made as early as 1820 and as late as 1890. Ball-shaped examples are more common than the fruit and vegetable forms and have been found in sizes ranging from 1" to 14" in diameter. They were made of thick glass with heavy brass caps, in cobalt, green, gold, silver, red, and occasionally in amethyst.

Although experiments involving the use of electric light bulbs for the Christmas tree occurred before 1900, it was 1903 before the first manufactured socket set was marketed. These were very expensive and often proved a safety hazard. In 1921 safety regulations were established, and products were guaranteed safety approved. The early bulbs were smaller replicas of Edison's household bulb. By 1910 G.E. bulbs were rounded with a pointed end, and until 1919 all bulbs were hand blown. The first figural bulbs were made around 1910 in Austria. Japan soon followed, but their product was never of the high quality of the Austrian wares. American manufacturers produced their first machine-made figurals after 1919. Today figural bulbs (especially character-related examples) are very popular collectibles. Bubble lights were popular from about 1945 to 1960 when miniature lights were introduced. These tiny lamps dampened the public's enthusiasm for the bubblers, and manufacturers stopped providing replacement bulbs.

Feather trees were made from 1850 to 1950. All are collectible. Watch for newly manufactured feather trees that have been reintroduced.

For further information concerning Christmas collectibles, we recommend *Christmas Ornaments, Lights, and Decorations, A Collector's Identification and Value Guide, Volumes I* through *III,* by George Johnson, available from Collector Books or your local bookstore.

Note: Values are given for bulbs that are in good paint, with no breaks or cracks, and in working order. Examples termed 'mini' measure no more than 1½". When no condition is mentioned in the description, assume values are for examples in EX/NM condition except paper items; those should be assumed NM/M.

Bulbs

Angel standing, clear glass, Japan, ca 1925, 2½"	70.00
Angelfish, milk glass, wide body, Japan, 2"	60.00
Banana, clear glass, 2¾"	30.00
Bear sitting, milk glass, Japan, ca 1950, 2¾"	85.00
Betty Boop, milk glass, Japan, ca 1930, '35 & '55, 2¼"	35.00
Bird in birdhouse, milk glass, Japan, 1935-50, 1½"	20.00
Bulldog sitting on ball, clear glass, Japan, ca 1925, 2¼"	20.00
Candle, emb flame, standard base, 4½"	20.00
Cat begging, milk glass, ribbon at neck, lg eyes, Japan, 2½"	30.00
Cats (2) in basket, milk glass, Japan, 2¼"	65.00
Clown w/mask, milk glass, Japan, ca 1950, 3"	25.00
Cube w/stars, silvered, Japan, 1½"	35.00
Dragon on lantern, milk glass, Japan, 2¼"	15.00
Duck, milk glass, dressed, arms crossed, Japan, 1920-55, 2¼"	25.00
Ear of corn, milk glass, Japan, 4"	30.00
Elephant, milk glass, trunk up, 3"	30.00
Flapper girl, milk glass, slim shape, Japan, ca 1950, 2¾"	65.00
Flower in seashell, milk glass, Japan, 2¼"	85.00

Indented ball, Germany, 2½", from $30.00 to $40.00. (Photo courtesy George Johnson)

Indian chief, clear glass, headdress & tomahawk, Europe, 3¼"	275.00
Jiminy Cricket, milk glass, Walt Disney, Japan, ca 1970, 2¾"	18.00
Lantern, carriage; clear glass, exhaust tip, 2¼"	75.00
Lion, clear glass, on haunches, detailed mane, 2¼"	175.00
Man in cap, dbl-face egg shape, ca 1950, 1¾"	175.00
Man in moon on star, milk glass, Japan, ca 1950, 2"	25.00
Monkey w/stick, clear glass, 2¼"	100.00
Mother Goose, milk glass, Paramount, Japan, 2¾"	25.00
Mushroom, milk glass, thick stalk, 2"	25.00
Old Woman in Shoe, Paramount Nursery Rhymes	25.00
Owl-headed girl, frosted glass, 2½"	90.00
Pear, milk glass, 1¾"	10.00
Pig in dress, milk glass, Japan, 2"	75.00
Plum, clear glass, ca 1920, 1¾"	30.00
Putto angel, clear glass, German, 2¼"	250.00
Red Riding Hood, milk glass, Paramount, Japan, 2½"	25.00
Santa, milk glass, dbl-faced, common, Japan, 3½"	15.00

Santa, milk glass, 3-faced, emb ball shape, Japan, 2¼"	30.00
Santa face in pine cone, milk glass, Japan, 2¾"	20.00
Santa w/satchel & tree, standard base, 4"	175.00
Smitty, milk glass, Japan, ca 1955, 2½-2¾"	35.00
Snow White, Walt Disney, ca 1940, 2¾"	225.00
Snowman w/bag, milk or clear glass, 2½", ea	12.00
Snowman w/stick, milk glass, Japan, 4"	25.00
Songbird, clear glass, sitting, 2¾"	15.00
Tadpole, milk glass, Japan, ca 1950, 2½"	100.00
WWI tank, milk glass, Japan, ca 1950, 2½"	200.00

Candy Containers

Animal Crackers boxes, szs vary, early (+), from $15 to	25.00
Baby in shoe, cb & cotton batting, head removes, 3", from $125 to	150.00
Banjo, cb body w/appl neck, string strings, bk opens, 9", $95 to	110.00
Bell, chenille on cb, Japan, 4", from $90 to	110.00
Book, cb, opens along pages edge, 3", from $30 to	40.00
Butterfly, fabric w/pastels, tinsel hoop, 2½", from $25 to	35.00
Butterfly, stiffened velour w/realistic pnt, Germany, 5", from $40 to	50.00
Drum, cb w/red/wht/bl dmns, emb drumsticks at top, 2½" dia, $75 to	100.00
Parasol, cb w/wooden hdl & lace/lace trim, top lifts up, 2½" dia	175.00
Potato, cb w/emb eyes, opens at seam, 2½", from $45 to	55.00
Snowman, spun cotton w/hollow tube inside, 4", from $125 to	150.00
Steinway grand piano, cb w/floral pattern on lid, 3 rnd legs, 2" W	200.00
Stocking, printed felt, 1930s (+), from $15 to	30.00
Top hat, fabric over cb, bag inside for candy, 2", from $175 to	200.00

Ornaments

Ali Baba in bbl, mold-blown, Germany, 4", from $275 to	300.00
American lantern, mold-blown, emb star in ea of 4 panels, 2¾"	4.00
Anchor, tin, flat, faceted indents, Germany, 2½-3¼", from $70 to	110.00
Angel, molded wax, seated, needle in bk is fastener, Germany, 3"	125.00
Angel, wax, spun glass wings, fabric skirt, mohair wig, Germany, 3"	75.00
Angel w/cornucopia, scrap w/tinsel, Germany, 8x4½x5", from $55 to	65.00
Apple, mold-blown, unsilvered, Germany, 1½", from $15 to	25.00
Baby in bunting, mold-blown, scrap face, 2½-3½", from $125 to	175.00
Bacchus, mold-blown, face emb in grapes, Germany, 2½" (+)	150.00
Barrel, mold-blown, staves & end-hoop details, 2¼" (+)	30.00
Basket of flowers on disc, mold-blown, bumpy edge, 1¾" dia	15.00
Bear w/stick, mold blown, Germany, 2-2½", ea from $50 to	110.00
Bee on flower, mold-blown, 2"	50.00
Bell, crushed glass on spun cotton, Germany, 1¾-3½", from $10 to	20.00
Bird on pine cone, mold blown, facing right, Germany, old, 3" (+)	45.00
Birdcage, mold blown, rnd, bird molded on side, 3", from $20 to	30.00
Black boy squatting, mold-blown, flat cap, Germany, 3¼"(+)	200.00
Boat, Sebnitz, wire/foil, scrap rider, 3", from $60 to	70.00
Boy on swing, Sebnitz, wax/cotton/plastic/wire, from $200 to	225.00
Boy-head rattle (dbl-faced), mold- & free-blown, clips on, 6½"	275.00
Bust of Jesus, mold-blown, flowing hair, Germany, 3" (+)	450.00
Buster Brown head, mold-blown, 2¾", from $250 to	275.00
Butterfly, tin, emb teardrop shapes, Germany, 2", from $35 to	45.00
Camel, Dresden, 3-D, gold/silver, 1-hump, silk tassel at chin, 3"	225.00
Carousel w/rnd top, mold-blown, 6-panel, 3½", from $40 to	50.00
Chicken, mold-blown, EX details, clips on, Germany, 2", from $100 to	125.00
Cinderella carriage, mold-blown & tinsel, Germany, 3", from $50 to	60.00
Clown in drum, mold-blown, Germany, 1½" dia (+), from $35 to	45.00
Coffeepot w/rose, mold-blown, 3¼", from $25 to	35.00
Cross, mold-blown, Germany or Czech, old, from $40 to	50.00
Daisy basket, mold-blown, Germany, 2-2¾"	30.00
Daisy on heart, mold-blown, radiating petals, 2¼", from $8 to	12.00
Dolly Dingle head, mold-blown, little expression/detail, 3", $150 to	175.00
Duck in egg, mold blown, Germany, 3¼", from $175 to	200.00

Eagle atop ball, mold blown, Germany, old, 5½" (+) **125.00**
Father Christmas head, mold-blown, Germany, mini, 1" (+) **30.00**
Fish basket, tin, 3-D, soldered corners, Germany, 2" L, from $40 to ..**55.00**
Fish w/emb waves, mold-blown, 4½" **60.00**
Flower bowl, Sebnitz, foiled cb, bead legs, artificial flowers, 2½" ..**55.00**
Girl soldier, mold-blown, sword at side, Germany, 4¼", $275 to..**350.00**
Girl w/doll, scrap/tinsel/crepe-paper, 10x8", from $100 to..........**125.00**
Goldilocks, mold-blown, right hand at collar, Germany, 3" (+)....**60.00**
Grapes on heart, mold-blown, ornate sides, 3", from $20 to..........**30.00**
Greyhound, Dresden, 3-D, natural, appl tail & ears, 3¼" **350.00**
Greyhound, free-blown milk glass w/annealing, Germany, 1920s, 3½" .**30.00**
Harp w/emb angel, mold-blown, Germany, 3½" (+), from $40 to..**50.00**
Horse, Dresden, flat, gold/silver, 4½" W, from $90 to..................**110.00**
Icicle, free-blown, hollow, 10" (+), from $20 to **30.00**
Icicle, free-blown, hollow, 2-4" (+), from $1 to **5.00**
Icicle, solid glass, 8" (+), from $15 to **25.00**
Indian head, mold-blown, full headdress, Germany, 3" (+).........**120.00**
Jesus on cross, mold-blown, emb figure on disc shape, 1½" dia..**55.00**
Joey clown w/accordion, mold-blown, Germany, 3¼" (+), from $40 to .**50.00**
Kugel, ball, cobalt, copper hanger, lt wear, 4½" **55.00**
Kugle, grapes, bl (faint silvering), brass hanger, 5¾" **190.00**
Lotus, mold-blown, 6-leaf base, 2" **25.00**
Miss Liberty, mold-blown, peaked cap, Germany, 3", from $200 to...**225.00**
Monkey in clown suit, mold-blown, 3"..**225.00**
Mushroom, free-blown, Germany, 1-2" (+), from $10 to **15.00**
Mushroom girl, mold-blown, ruffled collar, Germany, 3½", $70 to..**90.00**
Orange, mold-blown ball shape w/emb dimples, 1¾" (+).............**30.00**
Owl, mold blown w/spun-glass tail, clips on, 2½-3", from $20 to .**35.00**
Peacock, mold- & free-blown w/spun-glass tail, Germany, 3-4", ea...**20.00**
Pocketwatch, mold-blown, Roman numerals, hands at 10 o'clock, 1¾"..**60.00**
Rabbit in egg, mold-blown, clips on, early, 3-3½", from $150 to..**225.00**
Rooster, Dresden, 3-D, natural or gold/silver, 3x2¼", $275 to **300.00**
Roping, tinsel, many colors found, Germany, 8-18', ⅜x2⅛" W, $5 to..**8.00**
Rose bud, free-blown egg shape, Germany, ca 1920, 2½" **35.00**
Rosette, spun glass, scrap angel 1 side only, 6" (+), from $50 to ...**60.00**
Rosette, spun glass, sm scrap Santa head ea side, 2" (+)................**40.00**
Saddle shoe, mold-blown, emb laces & decor, Germany, 1950s....**50.00**
Sailboat, Dresden, gold or silver, flat, loop for hanging, 4x3¾" **90.00**

Swan, tin, flat swimming position, 2 faceted indents, 1¾", $50 to ..**65.00**
Teddy bear, sitting, mold-blown, Germany, old, 2" (+), from $50 to..**60.00**

Miscellaneous

Bubble light, Alps, Japan, 1954, working **55.00**
Bubble light, Noma Biscuit, 1946-60, common C6, from $3 to.......**5.00**
Bubble light, Noma Rocket, 1961-62 ....**30.00**
Bubble light, Paramount, oil, C7½, 1947-48...................................**50.00**
Bubble light, Peerless, w/or w/o clip, 1950-55 ....**5.00**
Bubble light, Reliance Spark-L-Light, 1949-51 ....**8.00**
Bubble light, Royal, ca 1947-54 ....**5.00**
Bubble light, Seda Snap-On, ca 1950, set of 7, MIB **700.00**
Bubble light, World Wide, 1973-74 ....**5.00**
Celluloid light, apple, 1¾" dia **40.00**
Celluloid light, baby head in ruffled bonnet, 1¾"..........................**75.00**
Celluloid light, grapes cluster, 2"..**35.00**
Celluloid light, monkey, squatting w/hands up to face, 2¼"..........**85.00**
Celluloid light, rooster, sitting, wings folded, 2½" **60.00**
Light, dmn pattern, clear, Depose BS Lyon on base, 2¾" **80.00**
Light, harlequin pattern, milk glass, RD 291933 on base, 3½" **90.00**
Light, 12-Diamond, lt amethyst, folded rim, 3" **110.00**
Light, 16 right-swirl ribs, amethyst, folded rim, 3⅛" **150.00**
Light cover, Dresden glass, ball of yarn, 3".....................................**75.00**
Light cover, Dresden glass, 3¾" **90.00**
Light cover, Kristal Star, metal, Japan, ca 1935, 2¾" **2.00**
Light cover, Noma, Glass-Glo-Light Candle, 3" **8.00**
Light cover, Santa face on bell, Dresden glass, 3¼" **60.00**
Light reflector, cb & glitter, old tarnish, 3½" **1.00**
Light reflector, Mirostar, Berwick, 5-point star, 2½" **1.00**
Light reflector, multi-layered foil, Germany, plain, 3½-4½" dia.......**1.50**
Light reflector, tin/lead, ca 1920, 3"...**12.00**
Light shade, Merry-Go-Light, Am, ca 1933, 2"................................**7.00**
Light shade, Noma Bell, plastic, Christmas scene **7.00**
Light shade, Whirl-Glo, paper, Am, 2"...**5.00**
Santa, Belsnickle, chalk, blk base/gr hooded coat w/mica, no tree, 5"..**275.00**
Santa, Belsnickle, comp, red robe/fur beard/feather tree, 1922, 16" .**1,375.00**
Santa, Belsnickle, compo, wht robe w/mica, tree missing/damage, 9" **660.00**

Santa carrying toys, color litho, paper, tinsel, scrap, and cotton, grocer advertising, 1900, 9", EX, $40.00.

Santa in sleigh pulled by reindeer, papier-mache and cloth figure, wicker and wood sleigh, cloth-covered papier-mache deer with glass eyes, clockwork nodder, early twentieth century, 36" long, $2,300.00.

Santa in airplane, mold-blown, Germany, 3" (+), from $20 to......**25.00**
Santa in auto, mold-blown, open car w/toys, 3¼", from $250 to ...**300.00**
Santa in holly holds sm girl in hands, scrap, 6¾" (+)....................**45.00**
Santa w/basket, mold-blown, no tree, Germany, early, 3½" **70.00**
Santa w/children, scrap w/tinsel, 7½x10¼", from $110 to **125.00**
Snow angel w/tree, scrap, Germany, ca 1887-1927, 8", from $35 to...**45.00**
Song bird w/berry, mold blown, loop in beak w/plaster berry, 4"..**55.00**
Stork, mold- & free-blown, orange pnt, Germany, 3" (+) **40.00**
Swan, mold- & free-blown milk glass, Germany, 1920s, 2¾" **35.00**

Sheep, compo w/wht coats & paper collars, mk Germany, 2" - 3", 8 for...**220.00**
Tree, feather; Germany, Japan or US, 6", ea from $50 to...............**75.00**
Tree, feather; Germany, Japan or US, 7-18", ea, from $80 to......**100.00**
Tree, feather; Germany, Japan or US, 24-30", ea from $125 to...**250.00**
Tree, feather; Germany, Japan or US, 48-54", ea from $300 to...**350.00**
Tree, feather; Germany, Japan or US, 84-90", ea from $600 to...**800.00**
Tree stand, bronzed cast metal w/geometrics, 1928, 5x13½" sq ..**150.00**
Tree stand, CI, 3 legs resemble tree roots, Austrian, ca 1911, lg ...**75.00**

Tree stand, CI w/Merry Christmas cast into side, 12" **25.00**
Tree stand, metal, cone shape, Noma, 1928, 13" **200.00**
Tree stand, metal standard type, 3 thumb screws, old, 11".............**15.00**
Tree stand, rotates/plays Jingle Bells, Cameo/Handy Things, 1960s..**25.00**
Tree stand, 4-leg w/lights, Deco style, North Bros, 1920s **60.00**
Tree stand, 4-leg w/water well, IXL, 1928, 14" **15.00**
Tree top, angel, compo & fabric, Noma Electric, 1940s-50s, 8¼".**15.00**
Tree top, angel, Dresden, gold/silver, flat, cone-like skirt, 6½" ...**160.00**
Tree top, angel, plastic/compo w/paper-foil wings, Am, 7¼" **15.00**
Tree top, angel standing, spun glass wings, Dresden crown, 8½" ...**200.00**
Tree top, Angel-Glo w/magic wand, plastic, Glo-Light, 1949, 7"..**15.00**
Tree top, Color Point Star, Noma, metal & plastic, ca 1948, 9" ...**10.00**
Tree top, glass points w/single or dbl ball, common, 9-14", $2 to....**8.00**
Tree top, Matchless Wonderstar, clear/amber glass, 1939-40, 3½"..**650.00**
Tree top, Santa chimes, metal, mechanical, Germany.................**600.00**
Tree top, Santa face, plastic on glass ball, cb hat, Germany, 1930s..**60.00**
Tree top, Santa w/arms in sleeves, molded & free-blown, 9".......**175.00**

Chrysanthemum Sprig, Blue

This is the blue opaque version of Northwood's popular pattern, Chrysanthemum Sprig. It was made at the turn of the century and is today very rare, as its values indicate. Prices are influenced by the amount of gold remaining on the raised designs. Our advisors for this category are Betty and Clarence Maier; they're listed in the Directory under Pennsylvania.

Creamer, from $350.00 to $450.00; Sugar bowl, with lid, from $450.00 to $600.00.

Bowl, berry; ind, M gold, 2⅝x5x3¾", from $165 to **250.00**
Bowl, master fruit; 10½" W, from $450 to...............................**600.00**
Butter dish...**1,250.00**
Butter dish, lt in color...**500.00**
Celery, from $400 to...**550.00**
Compote, jelly **600.00**
Condiment tray, rare, VG gold **750.00**
Cruet, EX gold, from $975 to **1,200.00**
Pitcher, water **1,100.00**
Shakers, pr **450.00**
Spooner, from $300 to...**350.00**
Toothpick holder, NM gold & decor, 2¾", from $450 to **550.00**
Tumbler, 3¾", NM gold **185.00**

Cincinnati Art Pottery

One of the very first art potteries in the country, the Cincinnati Art Pottery was developed by T.J. Wheatley at the Coultry Pottery in 1879. Wheatley left in 1882, and only after his departure was the Cincinnati

Pottery name used. The seminal company produced Asian-shaped wares decorated in underglaze-painting, barbotine, and applied designs as well as several distinct lines: Hungarian Faience, with enamel-type decoration; Portland Blue Faience, named after the famous Wedgwood vase and covered in dark blue glaze; and Kezonta, ivory-ground ware painted with flowers and gold scrolls. Blanks were also sold to independent china painters for home decoration. The pottery closed in 1891.

All pieces are not marked. The ones that are may bear a printed C.A.P. Co. stamp or KEZONTA with or without a turtle figure. Our advisors for this category are Suzanne Perrault and Dave Rago; they are listed in the Directory under New Jersey.

Vase, appl apple blossom branch on encrusted surface, 7½", EX............**170.00**
Vase, floral emb/pnt on bl to ivory, Limoges style, 12" **150.00**
Vase, mc floral, ftd, hdls, Limoges style, sgn FMD, 8¼" **100.00**
Vase, winter cathedral scene, Limoges style, 9", EX......................**80.00**

Circus Collectibles

The 1890s were the golden age of the circus. Barnum and Bailey's parades transformed mundane city streets into an exotic never-never land inhabited by trumpeting elephants with jeweled gold headgear strutting by to the strains of the calliope that issued from a fine red- and gilt-painted wagon extravagantly decorated with carved wooden animals of every description. It was an exciting experience. Is it any wonder that collectors today treasure the mementos of that golden era? See also Posters.

Key:
B&B — Barnum & Bailey   RB — Ringling Bros.

Advertisement, PT Barnum's Greatest..., clipped from newspaper, 1900s.**70.00**
Blotter, Sells-Floto Circus...Human Cannonball, 1920s, EX **35.00**
Catalog/souvenir book, RB & B&B, 70+ pgs, 1975, EX **22.50**
Popcorn bag, RB & B&B, unused, 1930s, M...................................**12.50**
Postcard, RB & B&B, Winter Quarters, linen, 1954, EX **10.00**
Poster, B&B, lions & lady dancing, litho, 1915, 17x24", EX ...**1,000.00**
Poster, B&B, 1,000 Skits by 50 Original Clowns, 24x40", EX.......**35.00**
Program, B&B, 1910, 52 pgs, VG-...**25.00**
Program, RB & B&B, 1921, 10 pgs, 10x6¾", VG.......................**18.00**
Program, RB & B&B, 1932, clown on cover, 10x7", EX **70.00**
Program, RB & B&B, 1935, 8½x11", EX...................................**45.00**
Program, RB & B&B, 1937, 10 pgs, 8½x11", VG+ **40.00**
Program, RB & B&B, 1940, EX...**15.00**
Program, RB & B&B, 1945, 68 pgs, EX....................................**15.00**
Program, RB & B&B, 1948, 76 pgs, 8½x11", VG+ **25.00**
Program, RB & B&B, 1950, 76 pgs, 8½x11", EX........................**35.00**
Program, RB & B&B, 1952, 16 pgs, EX...................................**15.00**
Program, RB & B&B, 1955, 76 pgs, 8¼x11", EX........................**30.00**
Puppet, Tom Thumb, RB & B&B in bl on red shirt, EX **20.00**
Route book, B&B, 66 pgs, 1947, 8½x5", M **30.00**
Sheet music, Under the Big Tent, B&B, 1913, VG+.....................**55.00**
Souvenir folder/postcard, Mrs Gargantua (gorilla), EX................**150.00**
Stock certificate, RB & B&B, bl, 1969, M.................................**300.00**
Stock certificate, RB & B&B, red, 1960s, unissued, M.................**210.00**
Tour book, B&B, Day by Day, 112 pgs, 1903-04, VG..................**260.00**
Toy, RB & B&B, whistling billboard, enameled steel, 1948, MIB....**225.00**
Wagon panel, cvd/pnt wooden relief-cvd lion, ca 1875, 30x74x2½"...**2,300.00**

Cleminson

A hobby turned to enterprise, Cleminson is one of several California potteries whose clever hand-decorated wares are attracting the attention of today's collectors. The Cleminsons started their business at their El Monte home in 1941 and were so successful that eventually they expanded to a modern plant that employed more than 150 workers. They produced not only dinnerware and kitchen items such as cookie jars, canisters, and accessories, but novelty wall vases, small trays, plaques, etc., as well. Though nearly always marked, Cleminson wares are easy to spot as you become familiar with their distinctive glaze colors. Their grayed-down blue and green, berry red, and dusty pink say 'Cleminson' as clearly as their trademark. Unable to compete with foreign imports, the pottery closed in 1963. For more information we recommend *The Collector's Encyclopedia of California Pottery, Second Edition*, by Jack Chipman (Collector Books).

Bowl, Galagray, 4x11x9" 65.00
Bowl, Gram's, w/lid, 2½" H (w/out lid) 27.50
Cleanser shaker, Kate, 6½" 40.00
Clothes sprinkler bottle, Oriental man, 8¾", EX 75.00
Cookie canister, Galagray 90.00
Cookie canister, PA Dutch 80.00
Cookie jar, Carrot Head 165.00
Cookie jar, Cookstove, HP decor 175.00
Cookie jar, King, 10½x8" 550.00
Cookie jar, PA Dutch, brn Distlefink line 80.00
Cookie jar, Pig, HP decor 275.00
Cookie jar, Potbellied Stove, 9x6½" 225.00
Cookie jar, Way to a Man's Heart 175.00
Creamer, rooster figural, 5½", from $40 to 50.00
Creamer & sugar bowl, Distlefink 25.00
Cup, clown's head form, hat is lid, mc, from $60 to 80.00
Cup & saucer, There's Something About a Soldier 30.00
Darner, lady figural, Darn It, HP decor, from $50 to 60.00
Marmalade, HP flowerpot form, strawberry finial, w/spoon, 3-pc set..25.00
Match holder, Cherry, wall mt 40.00
Mug, Morning After, w/lid 22.00
Pin holder, Bobbie Guard, 4x2¾" 50.00
Pitcher, Distlefink, 9½" 28.00
Plaque, man w/scissors, lady w/basket, 4x5", pr 55.00

Plaque, No Matter Where I Place My Guests They Always Like My Kitchen Best, $25.00.

Plate, lady's portrait, brunette w/bl bonnet, floral rim, 7½" ...12.00
Plate, rooster crowing, yel decor rim, 9½" 22.50
Razor bank, man w/lathered face in relief, from $30 to 40.00
Ring holder, bulldog, tail up (holder), from $32 to 40.00
Shakers, Cherry, 6", pr 40.00
Shakers, Distlefink, lg, pr 35.00
Spoon rest, Cherry 20.00
Spoon rest, floral decor, 3-lobed, 8½" 27.00
Spoon rest, stylized floral on gray, 8½" 20.00
String holder, You'll Always Have a 'Pull'..., heart shape 50.00
Tray, partridge figural, floral deco on brn, 5x13x6½" 45.00
Wall pocket, coffeepot form, 'Let's Have Another...,' from $30 to..40.00

Wall pocket, mortgage bank 27.50
Wall pocket, Take Time for Tea, 7¾x6⅝" 50.00

Clewell

Charles Walter Clewell was a metal worker who perfected the technique of plating an entire ceramic vessel with a thin layer of copper or bronze treated with an oxidizing agent to produce a natural deterioration of the surface. Through trial and error, he was able to control the degree of patina achieved. In the early stages, the metal darkened and if allowed to develop further formed a natural turquoise-blue or green corrosion. He worked alone in his small Akron, Ohio, studio from about 1906, buying undecorated pottery from several Ohio firms, among them Weller, Owens, and Cambridge. His work is usually marked. Clewell died in 1965, having never revealed his secret process to others.

Prices for Clewell have advanced rapidly during the past few years along with the Arts and Crafts market in general. Right now, good examples are bringing whatever the traffic will bear.

Bowl, brn-to-copper patina, riveted, 3¾x2" 160.00
Lamp base, copper clad, orig bl/gr/red patina, minor flaking, 25"..1,000.00
Lamp base, copper clad, 2-socket, bulbous bottom, #357 ....475.00
Pitcher, brn patina, 6-panel body, unmk, 6x3½" 300.00
Vase, copper clad, orange/red/gr/bl patina, 3¾" 600.00
Vase, copper w/verdigris, invt rim, broad shoulders, 11¼x8½" ..2,750.00
Vase, emb leaves, EX copper patina, 11", EX 1,300.00
Vase, orange/gr/bl patina, shouldered, #320-24, 6¼" 900.00
Vase, raspberries & leaves, EX orig patina, minor lines, 8" 325.00
Vase, rust to mottled gr, #402-210, wear/lt flaking, 9x12" ...1,265.00
Vase, 3 emb poppy buds at rim/lg bloom, much rtcl, 13¼x5½" ..4,250.00

Clews

Brothers Ralph and James Clews were potters who operated in Cobridge in the Staffordshire district from 1817 to 1835. They are best known for their blue and white transfer-printed earthenwares, which included American Views, Moral Maxims, Picturesque Views, and English Views. A series called *Three Tours of Dr. Syntax* contained thirty-one different scenes with each piece bearing a descriptive title. Another popular series was *Pictures of Sir David Wilkie* with seven prints. (Though we once thought that the *Don Quixote* series was made by Clews, new information seems to indicate that it was made instead by Davenport.) Both printed and impressed marks were used, often incorporating the pattern name as well as the pottery. See also Staffordshire, Historical.

Plate, Valentine, dark blue transfer, Wilkie Series, 9", NM, $250.00.

Bowl, soup; Chase After a Wolf, Indian Sporting Series, 9½" 600.00
Bowl, vegetable; Dr Syntax setting Out on First Tour, sq, 11" ..950.00
Cup plate, Coronation, fruits & flowers, bl transfer, 3⅝" dia...105.00

Pitcher, Chameleon Ware, angled hdl, 7½" 150.00
Pitcher, Water Girl, dk bl transfer, floral ground, 7" 580.00
Plate, child's; Dr Syntax Sketching the Lake, 6½" 525.00
Plate, Death of Bears, Indian Sporting Series, bl transfer, 10".....460.00
Plate, Dr Syntax Returns From His Tour, 8¾" 550.00
Plate, Dr Syntax Turned Nurse, bl transfer, 7⅞" 575.00
Plate, Escape of the Mouse, Wilkie, 10" 425.00
Plate, The Valentine, woman fighting man over card, bl transfer, 10" ..525.00
Plate, toy; creamware w/red line at border, 2½" 55.00
Plate, 2 men, 1 on donkey, look bk at bridge, med bl transfer, 9¾"...270.00
Platter, creamware w/gr feather edge, combed bk, 16x13" 380.00
Platter, Dr Syntax Advertisement for a Wife, bl transfer, 15" 580.00
Platter, Dr Syntax Amused w/Pat in Pond, dk bl, 19x14¼", $1,850 to .2,000.00
Platter, Peace & Plenty, bl transfer, 19x14½" 1,800.00
Platter, toy; creamware w/red line at rim, 4½" 120.00
Sugar bowl, girl fishing, dk bl transfer, w/lid 500.00
Teapot, lady at well, w/lid, VG+ 425.00
Teapot, shepherd w/sheep & dog, prof rpr to lid rim, lg 700.00
Vase, Chameleon Ware, bl w/brns & oranges, #22/116, 4¼" 140.00

Cliff, Clarice

Between 1928 and 1935 in Burslem, England, as the director and part owner of Wilkinson and Newport Pottery Companies, Clarice Cliff and her 'paintresses' created a body of hand-painted pottery whose influence is felt to the present time.

The name for the oevre was Bizarre Ware, and the predominant sensibility, style, and appearance was Deco. Almost all pieces are signed. There were over 160 patterns and more than 400 shapes, all of which are illustrated in *A Bizarre Affair — The Life and Work of Clarice Cliff*, published by Harry N. Abrams, Inc., written by Len Griffen and Susan and Louis Meisel.

Note: Non-hand-painted work (transfer printed) was produced after World War II and into the 1950s. Some of the most common names are 'Tonquin' and 'Charlotte.' These items, while attractive and enjoyable to own, have little value in the collector market. Our advisors for this category are Wilfred and Dolli Cohen; they are listed in the Directory under California.

Bowl, Delecia Citrus, flambe drip beneath fruit, 3½x8½" 460.00
Candle holder, Blue Chintz, 7" 975.00
Coffee set, Crocus, pot+cr/sug+6 c/s 915.00
Creamer, Aureau (Rodanthe variant), 3¼" 210.00
Creamer & sugar bowl, Sungleam Crocus 425.00
Cup & saucer, Picasso Flower, red 445.00
Dish, Sunshine, triangular, Bizarre, 3½" 250.00
Honey pot, Crocus, notched lid w/bee finial, 4½" 450.00
Jam jar, Avignon, mc decor, w/lid, 1931, 3½" 765.00
Jug, Lotus, Crocus, hdls, 12x10", NM 1,100.00
Jug, Lotus, Delecia Citrus, emb ribs, 12x8½", NM 1,500.00
Jug, Lotus, Trees & House, gr roof, 1930, 12" 1,265.00
Jug, milk; Idyll, Bon-Jour shape 460.00
Pin jar, Gayday, 3¼x2¾" 250.00
Pitcher, Patina, 8-sided, 8" 380.00
Planter, Sungleam, crocuses, #515, 4¾x5⅞" sq 710.00
Plate, Autumn Tree, orange-red band, 8¾".................................650.00
Plate, Biarritz, landscape, rectangular, Bizarre, 6½x5¼".............430.00
Plate, Biarritz, mc flowers on cream, oblong w/rnd well, 1933, 10⅜" ...450.00
Plate, Biarritz, red-roofed cottage, rectangular, 6½x5½" 450.00
Plate, Blue Crocus, Bizarre, 9" 350.00
Plate, Broth, orange w/bubbles & mc cobwebs, 7¾"....................350.00
Plate, Cafe Au Lait, scalloped corners, 8" 375.00
Plate, clown in center of crowd border, Laura Knight, 6⅝" 600.00

Plate, Crocus, 9" 500.00
Plate, Palemo, mc floral, 13"..4,215.00
Plate, Triple Star, Cerulean Blue ground, 10", NM.....................375.00
Plate, Tulip, 8-sided, orange band, 7¼" 300.00
Plate, 2 circus horses in center, Laura Knight, 6⅝" 530.00
Platter, Rhondanthe, 6-sided, 9½x7¼" 315.00
Pot, Morocco, ball finial, 3-ftd, wicker over emb hdl, 6x6¾" 715.00
Shakers, Autumn Crocus, 3", pr 295.00
Shakers, Double Diamond, pr 475.00
Sugar sifter, mc floral on wht, conical, #489, 5½" 950.00
Tea-for-2 set, Bon-Jour, teapot+cr/sug+2 c/s+snack plate.........1,100.00
Teapot, Autumn Crocus, w/yel lid, 5¼" 495.00
Teapot, Teepee, Indian spout, totem pole hdl, moose/leaf decor.495.00

Tea set, Fantasque Appliqué Design, 1930s, teapot, cup and saucer, slop bowl, sugar basin, cream jug, and two small plates, $750.00.

Toast rack, Water lily, 2 shallow reservoirs, ca 1938, 8" 175.00
Vase, Crocus, shouldered w/flared ft, 5¾" 530.00
Vase, Delecia, orange flowers w/blk leaves, 5¾x5" 495.00
Vase, Fantasque, house & trees, reds/oranges/wht, 6" 2,520.00
Vase, Inspiration, abstract flowers on turq, ca 1928, 6⅞" 750.00
Vase, Inspiration, overlapping flowers on periwinkle, 9½" 950.00
Vase, Lotus Flower, flower form, 5x8½" 220.00
Vase, Nasturtium, stepped-down sides, Bizarre, 6" 1,250.00
Vase, Rhodanthe, cylindrical, #613, 12½" 730.00

Clifton

Clifton Art Pottery of Clifton, New Jersey, was organized ca 1903. Until 1911 when they turned to the production of wall and floor tile, they made artware of several varieties. The founders were Fred Tschirner and William A. Long. Long had developed the method for underglaze slip painting that had been used at the Lonhuda Pottery in Steubenville, Ohio, in the 1890s. Crystal Patina, the first artware made by the small company, utilized a fine white body and flowing, blended colors, the earliest a green crystalline. Indian Ware, copied from the pottery of the American Indians, was usually decorated in black geometric designs on red clay. (On the occasions when white was used in addition to the black, the ware was often not as well executed; so even though two-color decoration is very rare, it is normally not as desirable to the collector.) Robin's Egg Blue, pale blue on the white body, and Tirrube, a slip-decorated matt ware, were also produced.

Ewer, birds, brn on tan matt, fat, 5" 60.00
Teapot, Crystal Patina, squat, 3½"...165.00
Vase, Crystal Patina, yel/buff mottle, 4-sided flared neck, 7" 275.00
Vase, Indian Ware, commas in shaped band, squat body, #206, 4¾" ..300.00
Vase, Indian Ware, contrasting ovals on bulbous base, #231, 11½" 600.00
Vase, Indian Ware, dmns on Xs, 3-color, Little Colorado, #226, 5x6"..400.00
Vase, Indian Ware, stovepipe neck, spherical body, Mississippi, 12x9"..950.00

Vase, Indian Ware, stylized feathers, 4-Mile Ruin, #160, 5½x6"..**275.00**
Vase, Indian Ware, 2 interlocking lines of waves, #238, 6x5" **325.00**
Vase, lt gr, dbl-gourd w/sm waist hdls, #011, 4"..........................**125.00**

Clocks

In the early days of our country's history, clock makers were influenced by styles imported from Europe. They copied the European's cabinets and reconstructed their movements — needed materials were in short supply; modifications had to be made. Of necessity was born mainspring motive power and spring clocks. Wooden movements were made on a mass-production basis as early as 1808. Before the middle of the century, brass movements had been developed.

Today's collectors prefer clocks from the eighteenth and nineteenth centuries with pendulum-regulated movements. Bracket clocks made during this period utilized the shorter pendulum improvised in 1658 by Fromentiel, a prominent English clock maker. These smaller square-face clocks usually were made with a dome top fitted with a handle or a decorative finial. The case was usually walnut or ebony and was sometimes decorated with pierced brass mountings. Brackets were often mounted on the wall to accommodate the clock, hence the name. The banjo clock was patented in 1802 by Simon Willard. It derived its descriptive name from its banjo-like shape. A similar but more elaborate style was called the lyre clock.

The first electric novelty clocks were developed in the 1940s. Lux, who was the major producer, had been in business since 1912, making wind-up novelties during the '20s and '30s. Another company, Mastercrafter Novelty Clocks, first obtained a patent to produce these clocks in the late 1940s. Other manufacturers were Keebler, Westclox, and Columbia Time. The cases were made of china, Syroco, wood, and plastic; most were animated and some had pendulettes. Prices vary according to condition and rarity.

Except for the novelty clocks whose values are on the increase, clock prices have been stable for several years. Unless noted otherwise, values are given for eight-day time only clocks in excellent condition. Clocks that have been altered, damaged, or have had parts replaced are worth considerably less.

Our advisor is Bruce A. Austin; he is listed in the Directory under New York.

Key:
br — brass	reg — regulator
dl — dial	rswd — rosewood
esc — escapement	TS — time & strike
mcr — mercury	wt — weight
mvt — movement	vnr — veneer
OG — ogee	2nds — seconds
pnd — pendulum	

Calendar Clocks

Ingraham, parlor, BB Lewis calendar, walnut case, 1881, 21½", G...**900.00**
Ithaca, #10 Farmer's, dbl dl, walnut case, rpl pnd, 1880, 25".......**400.00**
Ithaca, #8 Shelf Library, rstr dl, NP pnd, walnut case, 1880, 26", VG..**800.00**
Ithaca, #9 Shelf Cottage, old rpl dl, walnut case, 1880, 13", G...**500.00**
Ithaca, Cottage #5 variant, walnut panels, orig dl, 1875, 21"......**800.00**
S Thomas, Parlor #1, 8-day wt, rswd vnr, 1866, 33", G-..............**525.00**
S Thomas, Parlor #3, repapered dl, rswd vnr, ca 1875, 26¾", G ..**600.00**
S Thomas, Parlor #5, rpl hands, pnt loss, walnut case, 1886, 20"..**750.00**
Southern, Fashion #2, rpt dls, rfn walnut case, 1875, 30½" **650.00**
Waterbury Peru, walnut, figure-8, 21½" **900.00**

Novelty Clocks

Fr, Aboriginal, spelter figure w/clock in belly, 1910, 11½" **900.00**
Fr, Cyclist, Victorian man w/Penny-Farthing bicycle, 1880s, 15½"..**10,000.00**
Fr, Eiffel tower, 1-day mvt, porc dl, 1890s, 12½" **400.00**
Fr, Jester, bell-ringer alarm, ca 1900, 11½", EX **2,000.00**
Fr, Lighthouse, gong, pnd, br case, 1880s, 24" **11,500.00**
Fr, Windmill, sm platform time mvt, 1880s, 17½" **2,700.00**
Lux, banjo, NP, 30-hr rear-wind mvt, ca 1930, 6", M.................**250.00**
Lux, Happy Days, beer drinker lifts mug, 1935, 3¾", VG **175.00**
Lux, violin, NP, sgn dl, 30-hr rear-wind mvt, 6½", M **400.00**
Oswold, Scotty, revolving eyes tell time, 1959, 6", EX **300.00**
St Charles...Cream, bronze cow figural, 30-hr lever mvt, 1930s, 8½".**500.00**
United, Bartender, shakes canister, wht metal case, 1930s, 9½", G .**225.00**
United, 4 dancers on carousel, plastic/br, #990, 1950s, 11".........**150.00**
Welch, Little Grip, pot-metal suitcase w/rpl hdl, 1891, 2½x3"...**350.00**

Shelf Clocks

Aaron Willard, Fed, TS, rvpt tablet, br paw front ft, 1817, 35"...**7,475.00**
Aaron Willard, Fed mahog w/inlay, recoil esc, old rfn, 1815, 38"..**32,000.00**
Ansonia, bronzed metal, jeweled bezel, porc dl, 1910, 11"..........**225.00**
Ansonia, Crystal Reg #3, yel irid, 1915, 17½", EX...................**2,750.00**
Ansonia, Greenwich, metal case, porc dl, TS, ca 1901, rprs, 8½".**165.00**
Ansonia, Monmouth, Colonial br finish over iron, 1901, 11", VG..**200.00**
B Morrill, birch box-cased watchman's, pnt iron dl, 1860s, 54½".**2,875.00**
Benson, Ship's Wheel, red brass case, lever mvt, rear wind, 1930, 14".**1,100.00**
Black Forest, cuckoo, lg 3-D bird atop, many cvd leaves/fence, 22".**1,285.00**
Black Forest, lg mtn goats on rocky ledge, 19"............................**785.00**
Black Forest, lg stag/recumbent deer atop, leaves/birds in base, 40".**5,880.00**
Boston, Delphus, crystal reg, porc dl, tandem wind mvt, 1890s, 10½".**850.00**
Brewster & Ingrahams, beehive, rswd case, orig esc & lock, 1845, 19"..**450.00**
Brewster & Ingrahams, iron front w/HP decor, br springs, 1850, 17".**750.00**
Chelsea/Hardy & Hayes, mahog 'Drum on Base,' 1906, 16½".**2,500.00**
Chelsea/Spaulding & Co, red brass 'Drum on Base,' 1916, 13½".**1,900.00**
Chelsea/Tiffany, Bambro #32, mahog tambour, 1916, 11x24" **975.00**
Chelsea/Tiffany, Emp #1, house strike, gong, 6½" dl, 1912, 16"..**900.00**
Chelsea/Tiffany, Mahog Gothic, 8" silvered dl, rstr, 1912, 18"....**900.00**
Chelsea/Tiffany, Yacht Wheel, 6" dl, mahog base, 1922, 18½".**1,800.00**
David Wood, Fed mahog w/much inlay, br 60-hr mvt, 1815, 34"..**12,650.00**
Eli Terry & Sons, Fed mahog vnr Pillar & Scroll, rvpt, 1810s, 31"..**1,950.00**
Forestville Hdw & Clock Co, mini steeple, mahog/rswd, ca 1854, 13".**1,000.00**
Forrestville Manufg..., acorn dl, spring mvt, rvpt tablet, 1845, 25".**7,450.00**
Fr, bronzed spelter Brise d' Autumn statue, swinger, 1890s, 38½".**4,000.00**
G Parker, Fed mahog w/inlay, kidney-shaped dl, 1810, rfn, 35"..**26,450.00**
Ingraham, Admiral Dewey, rfn case, rstr, 1899, 23" **350.00**

Isidore Grenot Paris, Classical ormolu mantel type with winged figure, enamel dial, ca 1815, 19x14x4½", EX, $5,000.00.

Junghans, swinging arm on onyx & ormolu stand, ca 1910, 10¼" .1,200.00
Marble w/gilt mts & globe, Fr bronze seated child, Oudin, 15" .1,900.00
R&JB Terry, triple decker, pnt losses, all orig, 1835, G................450.00
Royal Bonn, floral case, open esc, 13½" 1,400.00
S Thomas, Emp #1 Extra, porc dl, pnd, 1909, 11", G.................175.00
S Thomas, Emp #4, crystal reg, porc dl, pnd, 1910, 10½", EX 525.00
S Thomas, Fed mahog, TS, 30-hr mvt, rvpt panels, rstr, 1820, 30".1,725.00
S Thomas, Mini Cottage, flat top, rpl dl, D mvt, pnd, rswd case, 9".225.00
S Thomas, Tudor #3, 8-day cottage, T mvt, rfn rswd case, 1860s, 10" .400.00
Terry & Andrews, steeple on steeple, rpl dl/hands, rstr, 1850s, 25"...850.00

Tall Case Clocks

Austrian, oak, simple lines, dl mk Joh Wolkenstein, 1900s, 80x15x10".2,645.00
B Monroe, Fed mahog w/inlay, pierced fretwork, rstr, 1810s, 86".17,625.00
B Monroe, Fed mahog w/inlay, pierced fretwork/br finials, 1800s..26,000.00
B Willard, cherry, br dl/spandrels, calendar, TS, 1771, rfn, 82"...12,650.00
Cherry/figured vnrs, waisted, broken arch pediment, br works, 96" .2,695.00
Curly maple, broken arch crest w/rosettes, HP house scene, 95" ..440.00
D Munroe, Fed mahog, br ball finials, rpt dl/rstr, 1810s, 93"....5,300.00
E Taber, Fed mahog vnr, pnt CI dl, calendar, 2nds, 1815, rfn, 92".48,875.00
Elliot mvt, Westminster/Whittington chimes, oak w/lions/wolves, 94x26" .11,700.00
Gilbert, Reg #7, walnut case, orig lyre pnd, 1881, 102", EX ..12,000.00
HW Plumstead, cherry, broken-arch crest w/cvg, Fr ft, 1820s, 96" .6,000.00
Isaac Brokaw (att), cherry, pyramidal top w/rocking ship mvt, 94", EX....11,500.00
J Wilder Hingham, mahog & mahog vnr dwarf, rpl crest, 1810s, 47½" .28,750.00
JW Todd Glasgow, mahog/figured vnrs on pine, stepped waist, pnd, 84".2,975.00
MA, Fed mahog w/inlay, pierced fretwork, 1810s, 87", EX 14,000.00
Mahog, bonnet top/br ball finials, cvd case, wt driven, claw ft, 99"..3,900.00
Mulliken, cherry, stepped cornice, br spandrels, rfn/rstr, 1760, 90".12,925.00
Mulliken, mahog/cherry, broken arch, wt-driven mvt, rfn, 1770s, 88"..7,650.00
Mulliken, walnut, eng br dl, flat cornice above arch, 1760s, 86"..7,650.00
Noah Ranlet Golmanton 1796, pine & rvpt TS dwarf, rpl crest, 49".18,400.00
PA, cvd tiger maple, pull-up br mvt, rfn/rstr, ca 1800, 101"...10,925.00
Read-Watson, cherry, 30-hr mvt w/strike, wooden works, 90", VG .2,200.00
Reuben Tower Kingston, pine dwarf w/mahog columns & pnt decor, 41".12,650.00
Seth Thomas, oak, claw ft/shell cvgs, 3-wt, bonnet top, 94"....3,900.00
Simon Willard, Fed mahog w/inlay, TS, pierced fretwork, 1800, 94"..37,375.00
Waterbury Regulator #71, quarter-sawn oak, pnd, 1905, 96¼"..10,500.00
Watson, cherry/mahog/flame vnr, broken arch w/scrolls & finial, 96" .2,000.00

Wall Clocks

A Chandler, Fed cvd mahog vnr lyre, 1825, rfn, 43" 17,250.00
A Willard Jr, Fed mahog w/giltwood, rvpt naval scene, 1820, 39".13,800.00

Abel Stowell, Federal
mahogany carved lyre
banjo timepiece, ca 1837,
40", EX, $7,000.00.

Ansonia General, rfn, walnut, 2-wt T only, prof rstr dl, 1900, 68", VG.....3,500.00
B Morrill, dk pine, TS, mirror glass, rvpt tablet, 1825, 30"....10,350.00
B Morrill, Late Fed, gilt & rvpt, wheelbarrow mvt, rstr, 1825, 31".3,750.00
Black Forest, cuckoo, 3-D eagle pediment, many leaves/stag/fox, 60".6,720.00
Black Forest, cuckoo & quail, 3-train mvt, deer finial, 1920, 33" .375.00
Curtis & Dunning, Fed giltwood & rvpt banjo, 1815, 33½" .5,175.00
Dyer, mahog Fed banjo, br bezel, pnt dl, rvpt scene, 1815, 33" ...2,800.00
E Currier, Fed mahog w/gilt, rvpt tablet, rstr, 1820, 42" 3,335.00
E Howard #20 Reg, walnut figure-8, rpt baffle, 1890, 33", G...6,300.00
E Howard #58-8 Reg, walnut, prof rpt/rstr, 1890, 40".........4,500.00
E Howard #60 Reg, blk walnut, rubbed dl, 1880, 80", VG+ ..34,000.00
E Howard #95, Reg reissue, x-banding, geometric tablets, 1982, 42", M.1,350.00
G Becker Vienna Reg, 2-wt, 1905, 49", G+.............................1,000.00
Gilbert #10 Reg, oak, rfn dl/case, front-hung pnd, rstr, 1901, 52".2,400.00
Gilbert Shield, walnut, prof rpl arch top/finial, TS, 1881, 29"....625.00
Ingraham Treasure Island banjo, silvered dl/orig tablets, 1928, 39"..475.00
Japy Freres RA Reg, walnut w/pnd, 1880, 37", VG 400.00
Junghans, walnut w/ornate shell & leaf cvgs, TS, br pnd, 38".....525.00
Junghans RA Reg, walnut w/br trim, steel gong, 1910, 41", VG.875.00
Kitchen, Ansonia, walnut w/mirrored side panels, gilt putti figures,..140.00
Kroeber #27 Reg, walnut, Swiss pinwheel mvt, porc dl, rfn, 1974, 89".11,500.00
Kroeber Cabinet #1, cherry w/incised front, pnd, 1885, 12", VG.350.00
LW Noyes, mahog Fed banjo, br bezel, rvpt harbor scene, 1825, 32".2,475.00
Monroe's Pat Suspension, Fed gilt mahog, br side arms, 1820s, 33".1,500.00
Munroe & Whiting, Fed gilt mahog, pnt dl, rvpt ships, 1808-17, 33" .1,880.00
New Haven Washington banjo, rpl tablets, chimes, 1928, 42", VG..525.00
R Whiting, Fed gilt mahog banjo, rvpt village scene, rstr, 33".1,850.00
S Thomas, Flora, ebony, 2-wt TS, pnd, 1884, 38" 2,000.00
Sawin & Dyer, Fed mahog cvd/gilt rvpt lyre, 1820s, 40"........13,800.00
Sawin & Dyer, Fed gilt mahog banjo, br bezel, 1822-28, rprs, 29" .1,880.00
Sawin & Dyer, Fed giltwood & rvpt banjo, ca 1825, 33" 4,000.00
Simon Willard, Fed mahog w/giltwood inlay, rvpt throat/tablet, 34".10,350.00
TE Burleigh Jr, Fed-style giltwood & mahog girandole banjo, 47" .9,400.00
Waltham lever banjo, WA/Mt Vernon tablets, sm touch-up, ¾-sz, 31".600.00
Waterbury Augusta, oak, 2 dragons on top, ornate crest, 1893, 60", VG.3,000.00
Waterbury Kendal Reg, walnut, 30-day, rpl finials, 1896, 52", VG.3,100.00
Welsch, Spring & Co #3 Reg, all orig, 1880, 35" 4,700.00
Willard, Fed mahog w/inlay, rvpt: throat/Willard's Pat tablet, 32".15,275.00
Wm Cummens, Fed rvpt & gilt mahog banjo, rstr, 34"............6,325.00

Cloisonne

Cloisonne is a method of decorating metal with enameling. Fine metal wires are soldered onto the metal body following the lines of a pre-determined design. The resulting channels are filled in with enamels of various colors, and the item is fired. The final step is a smoothing process that assures even exposure of the wire pattern. The art is predominately Oriental and has been practiced continuously, except during war years, since the sixteenth century. The most excellent examples date from 1865 until the turn of the century. The early twentieth century export variety is usually lightweight and the workmanship inferior. Modern wares are of good quality and are produced in Taiwan as well as China.

Several variations of the basic art include plique-a-jour, achieved by removing the metal body after firing, leaving only the transparent enamel work; foil cloisonne, using transparent or semitranslucent enameling over a layer of embossed silver covering the metal body of the vessel; wireless cloisonne, made by removing the wire dividers prior to firing; and cloisonne executed on ceramic, wood, or lacquer rather than metal.

Figure, brass w/mc chrysanthemum-decor robe, 15¾", EX 200.00
Figure, Korean warrior, dk patina w/mc enamel coat, holds bow, 16".375.00
Horse, phoenixes/florals on turq, saddle removes, 20th C, 21" ...400.00
Jardiniere, geometrics/chrysanthemums w/relief scene int, rpr, 10x13" ...220.00

Plate, horse in center, gray on bl, dk bl flower border, 10" **165.00**
Stamp box, bl background, hinged lid, 4-ftd, 2x3½" **60.00**
Vase, geometrics/florals on turq, trumpet neck/base, 20th C, 16", pr.**250.00**

Clothing and Accessories

The field of collectable, vintage, and antique clothing is an often confusing, especially for the novice collector or nonspecialty dealer. Prices vary enormously, depending on where you are — the Midwestern and Southern states still harbor the best deals, sometimes as much as 70% below book value — and the individual article of clothing in question. Prior to 1940 almost all apparel was custom made, therefore each garment is unique in both design and quality of construction. Specialty gowns, i.e. dresses which can be worn by modern-day brides or for special events, fetch the highest prices. Civil War re-enactors have driven up the prices of authentic Civil War apparel. Dresses with intact bustles continue to be rare finds. Young collectors are creating a demand for wearable 1950s – 1970s clothing, although prices in these categories still remain reasonable. A first-time collector needs to do thorough research to understand vintage clothing construction techniques before venturing into this field because of the many reproductions and mismarked items now finding their way onto the market. For example, reproductions of Victorian dresses usually close with a zipper instead of the traditional hooks and eyes. Zippers were not commonly used until after 1935.

For further information we recommend *Collector's Guide to Vintage Fashions* by Kristina Harris (an easy-to-use guide for dating women's clothing); *Vintage Hats and Bonnets, 1770 – 1970,* by Susan Langley; *Ladies' Vintage Accessories,* by LaRea Johnson Bruton; and *Antique & Vintage Clothing: A Guide to Dating and Valuation of Women's Clothing, 1850 – 1940,* by our advisor, Diane Snyder-Haug. (Ms. Snyder-Haug is listed in the Directory under Florida.) Vintage denim values are prices realized at Flying Deuce Auctions, who specialize not only in denims but Hawaiian shirts, souvenir jackets, and various other types of vintage clothing. They are listed in the Directory under Auction Houses. Our values are for items of ladies' clothing unless noted 'man's' or 'child's.' Assume them to be in excellent condition unless otherwise described.

Key:
cap/s — cap sleeves   ms — machine sewn
embr — embroidery   n/s — no sleeves
hs — hand sewn   plt — pleated
l/s — long sleeves   s/s — short sleeves

Apron, bl & wht check homespun, skirt length w/embr at hem ...**50.00**
Bathing suit, red/wht/bl linen, 1-pc w/attached bloomers, 1910s...**315.00**
Bed jacket, printed satin w/lace trim, l/s, 1920s, EX **55.00**
Blouse, ectu net lace w/Irish crochet lace insert, l/s, 1910-20........**95.00**

Blouse, white batiste with lace inserts, pin tucks and embroidery, long sleeves, ca 1900, EX, $95.00. (Photo courtesy Neal Auction Company)

Cape, embr silk w/silk lining, Chantilly lace inserts, tassels, 1870s..**325.00**
Coat, toddler's, ribbed cotton, dbl-breasted, wide collar, 1920s....**38.00**
Dress, acrylic Hawaiian floral print, n/s, scoop neck, zipper, 1960s..**26.00**
Dress, bl silk, l/s bodice w/fringe, boned, peplum, full skirt, 1860s..**995.00**
Dress, bl taffeta, V neck w/lace, cap/s, appl plastic flowers, 1950s.**70.00**
Dress, blk brocade w/cummerbun, peplum, s/s, Edith Flagg, 1960s.**65.00**
Dress, blk crepe, shirred bias bodice, cap/s, V neck, 1950s **95.00**
Dress, blk crepe knit, beaded front, s/s, Charlotte of CA, 1960s ...**45.00**
Dress, blk crepe top, s/s, tweed wool skirt, 1950s **55.00**
Dress, blk crushed velvet w/wht collar & cuffs, 1930s, M............**125.00**
Dress, blk knit, draped neck, dropped waist, flared skirt, n/s, 1980s.**25.00**
Dress, blk knit, halter top, Emp waist, long bell skirt, 1960s **25.00**
Dress, blk lace, n/s, low bk, +l/s lace jacket+satin petticoat, 1930s .**255.00**
Dress, blk silk/net lace/beading, l/s, 2-pc, ca 1900, EX **345.00**
Dress, crepe print, wide/s, blouson bodice, plt circle skirt, 1970s..**27.50**
Dress, dbl-knit print, ¾/s, sweetheart neck, flared skirt, 1980s......**27.50**
Dress, floral acetate, scoop neck, cap/s, princess line, 1950s..........**55.00**
Dress, girl's, cotton print, s/s w/ruffle, piping, hand sewn, 1850s.**185.00**
Dress, girl's, ivory cotton w/gr drop-waist plt skirt, n/s, 1920s **85.00**
Dress, girl's, cream silk, lined n/s bodice w/piping, smocking, 1890s..**95.00**
Dress, girl's, peach silk flapper style w/ribbons & lace, n/s, 1920s ..**155.00**
Dress, girl's, printed calico, s/s w/ruffle, glass buttons, 1890s **110.00**
Dress, girl's, printed silk, s/s, gathers at hips, tie blet, 1920s **100.00**
Dress, gr linen, lined sheath w/side ties, s/s, Parade NY, 1960s......**40.00**
Dress, gray gabardine, ¾/s, Bateau neck w/piping, dolman/s, 1950s..**60.00**
Dress, hand-crochet wool, l/s, A-line, boat neck, 1960s **30.00**
Dress, Irish linen w/lace appliques/beads, s/s, scoop neck, 1950s...**45.00**
Dress, ivory brocade sheath, A-line, 1970s..................................**65.00**
Dress, lav knit, n/s, flared skirt, 1950s, +boxy l/s jacket..................**50.00**
Dress, maternity, checked organdy, princess neck, cap/s, 1950s.....**60.00**
Dress, nylon velveteen knit, l/s, crossover bodice, belt, 1970s.......**28.00**
Dress, pk silk, s/s, pintuck yoke, butterfly appliques, 1950s............**55.00**
Dress, princess A-line wrapper type, l/s w/cuffs, lined, 1870s **200.00**
Dress, printed acetate, ¾/s, shirtwaist, pockets, 1950s **22.50**
Dress, printed knit, l/s, V neck, Emp waist, long skirt, 1970s........**27.50**
Dress, printed moire silk, ¾ dolman/s, scoop neck, lined, 1950s...**60.00**
Dress, printed rayon silk, ¾/s, scoop neck, piped waist, 1950s **70.00**
Dress, printed silk, n/s, +s/s jacket w/blk velvet collar, 1960s........**60.00**
Dress, printed silk, n/s, bias-cut skirt, wide collar, 1920s **115.00**
Dress, printed silk, s/s, shoulder pads, peplum, 1930s, +jacket **145.00**
Dress, purple knit, s/s, scoop neck, ½-circle skirt, 1970s................**27.50**
Dress, purple velvet, lined, pleat-tuck strap, fitted top, 1950s **60.00**
Dress, rayon w/lining, n/s, collar, +s/s jacket w/collar, 1960s **30.00**
Dress, red bandana-print cotton, halter tie neck, Dorian, 1950s...**85.00**
Dress, striped cotton wrapper w/full/s, ruffled hem, tie belt, 1900s...**245.00**
Dress, wht cotton w/machine embr, MOP buttons, ca 1906, EX.**215.00**
Dress, wool crepe, l/s jacket w/lg buttons, str skirt, late 1950s.......**40.00**
Dress/robe, wht check cotton w/piping, hand sewn, loose fit, 1850s...**150.00**
Dressing gown, printed cotton, elbows w/frill, princess line, 1890s.**385.00**
Duster, man's, ecru linen, 2 lg pocket, drop shoulders, 1900s......**195.00**
Fur muff, child's, dk fur w/cotton lining, 1890-1910, sm................**45.00**
Gym suit, blk cotton w/ribbon trim, rnd neck, s/s, 2-pc, 1900s...**150.00**
Hat, blk felt w/feather cockade to side, designer label, 1940s, $50 to..**75.00**
Hat, blk widow's bonnet, beadwork & ribbons, Victorian, from $100 to..**125.00**
Hat, metallic lace over purple velvet w/beading, late 1910s, $200 to.**225.00**
Hat, navy fur-felt helmet cloche, 1920s, from $95 to **125.00**
Hat, olive drab silk, padded brim, floral trim, Victorian, $200 to ..**250.00**
Hat, pk lace w/pearls & sm feather, brimless, sm, 1950s, from $25 to..**35.00**
Hat, 3-color satin turban, Haggarty's label, 1960s, from $20 to.....**35.00**
Jacket, Alaska 49th State souvenir tour, reversible, rare, EX......**925.00**
Jacket, blk silk w/allover sequins, Minelli label, ca 1960, EX **50.00**
Jacket, campus style, fake fur, leopard print, w/hood, 1960s, med...**275.00**
Jacket, Hercules, pony leather, crown zipper, sz 44, G **50.00**
Jacket, ivory lamb's wool w/beads & sequins, l/s, 1960s **80.00**

Jacket, Japan souvenir tour, EX embr front/bk, 1950s, M **410.00**
Jacket, Vietnam souvenir tour, EX embr, 1970-71, med **270.00**
Jumpsuit, blk polyester knit w/gold braid, V-neck, bellbottoms, 1960s..**30.00**
Jumpsuit, knit leopard print, zip front, bellbottoms, late 1960s **50.00**
Kimono, printed silk w/much embr, gold braid, 1930s, 54" L **235.00**
Knickers, check linen, 4 bone buttons, ca 1918-25, EX **115.00**
Knickers, pk crepe romala w/lace inserts & hand embr, 1930s **30.00**
Leisure suit, pk/wht denim western style, flared pants, Wrangler, '70s.**50.00**
Nightgown, bias-cut ivory satin, scalloped hem, embr flowers, 1930s.**155.00**
Nightgown, ivory rayon & lace, silk ribbon at top, 1930s, 44" L ..**70.00**
Nightgown, printed rayon & lace, V neck w/lace trim, ca 1930, 55" L.**125.00**
Nightgown, wht cotton w/frilled collar & cuffs, MOP buttons, 1900s.**150.00**
Nightgown, wht linen w/frills at neck, l/s, 1870s, EX **165.00**
Pantaloons, drawstring waist, lace trim, ca 1915, EX **75.00**
Pants, cotton corduroy bellbottoms, 4 patch pockets, 1970s **16.00**
Pants, cotton pique, 4-pocket, flat front, metal zipper, 1960s **15.00**
Pants, man's, corduroy, 2-pocket flares, elastic bk, 1960s...............**15.00**
Pants, man's, corduroy bellbottoms, 4 patch pockets, 1970s..........**16.00**
Pants, man's, cotton, flat front, 4-pocket, Levis Sta-Prest, 1960s ..**15.00**
Pants, man's, gabardine, dbl pleats, 1950s, VG **28.00**
Pants, man's, maroon cotton, cuffed bellbottoms, Dickies, 1970s .**30.00**
Pants, man's, slubby silk, 4-pocket, tapered legs, 1960s.................**16.00**
Pants, polyester crepe, 43" elephant bellbottoms, pockets, 1970s .**20.00**
Pants, red corduroy capris, Robin D, 1950s **16.00**
Pants, wool & spandex stretch gabardine, stirrups, 1960s............**25.00**
Pants suit, drapey floral print, l/s jacket+bellbottoms, 1970s........**38.00**
Pants suit, polyester, s/s wrap jacket, bellbottoms w/pockets, 1970s.**30.00**
Petticoat, roller-print cotton, quilted over wool batting, ca 1800..**375.00**
Shawl, blk Chantilly lace, ca 1875, 23x114".............................**295.00**
Shift, wht homespun, l/s, drawstring at neck, 18th C, EX...........**475.00**
Shirt, Aloha, topless hula girl, vintage, rare................................**160.00**
Shirt, California Beachwear, cotton, '50s modern print, lg, M....**110.00**
Shirt, man's, corduroy, red/blk speckled, 1940s, sm, EX.................**90.00**
Shirt, man's, cotton w/tucked front, l/s, neckband, 1860s **50.00**
Shirt, man's, shiny nylon tricot geometric print, l/s, 1960s............**15.00**
Shirt, sheer printed polyester crepe, l/s, 1960s **20.00**
Shorts, cotton Hawaiian print broadcloth, metal bk zipper, 1950s.**17.50**
Shorts, crochet hip-hugger hot pants, laced fly, 1970s...................**35.00**
Shorts, man's, cotton Hawaiian print, drawstring, flap pocket, 1960s..**16.50**
Shorts, man's, plaid polyester cotton, 1960s **16.00**
Shorts, man's, slubby rayon print, flap pocket, shell buttons, 1950s.**18.50**
Skirt, ecru linen, 2 lg pockets, ca 1900-18 ....**50.00**
Skirt, pleated cotton w/bustle bk & underskirt, 1870s, VG.........**315.00**
Slip, peach satin w/embr, shoestring straps, 1920s, 44" L **125.00**
Stole, ivory silk Maltese lace, ca 1900, 9½x78"........................**275.00**
Suit, aqua knit, s/s shell+jacket w/¾/s+str skirt, 1960s **68.00**
Suit, check gabardine, split-cuff jacket, mid-calf skirt, 1930s......**225.00**
Suit, cocktail; satin brocade, shell+¾/s jacket+long skirt, 1950s ...**150.00**
Suit, hand knit, bell/s, glass buttons top+mid-calf skirt, 1930s......**70.00**
Suit, orlon knit, V-neck collar top w/embr, str skirt, 1950s **50.00**
Suit, plaid wool jersey, l/s V-neck jacket, str skirt, 1960s...............**55.00**
Suit, printed rayon bouclé, s/s cardigan+mini skirt+n/s shell, 1960s.**28.00**
Suit, rayon blend, ¾/s jacket w/shoulder pads, str skirt, 1940s....**100.00**
Suit, synthetic 2-color Princess n/s A-line dress+l/s blk coat, 1960s.**60.00**
Suit, twilled jersey, l/s jacket w/split cuffs, gored skirt, 1940s **135.00**
Suit, wool military-style jacket, fur collar, str skirt, 1930s, $45 to.**75.00**
Suit, wool tweed, l/s 3-button jacket, str skirt, lined, 1950s **85.00**
Suit, yel knit, l/s placket-neck top, long bell skirt, sash, 1970s......**25.00**
Sweater, angora cardigan w/embr flowers & sequins, Komal, 1980s.**32.50**
Sweater, cotton crochet tunic-length cardigan, V neck, 1960s **20.00**
Sweater, man's, acrylic dmn-pattern cardigan, 2-pocket, 1960s.....**28.00**
Sweater, man's, alpaca bouclé knit golf-style cardigan, 1960s........**28.00**
Sweater, man's, garter-stitch knit, dbl-breasted cardigan, 1960s....**22.00**
Sweater, man's, suede leather front & yoke, knit l/s, 2 pockets, 1970s.**32.00**

Sweater, man's, wool knit, Danish-style patterned yoke, l/s, 1960s..**30.00**
Sweater, mohair & wool bouclé knit, ¾/s, pullover, 1960s............**18.00**
Sweater, red/wht/bl wool ski type, Charles Wolf, 1960s.................**23.00**
Sweater, wool cardigan w/embr floral on front & l/s, 1960s..........**28.00**
Sweater vest, acrylic w/openwork crochet pattern, 3-color, 1970s..**20.00**
Sweater vest, crochet granny sqs, 1960s **21.00**
Sweater vest, man's, tan acrylic w/blk/wht trim, 2 pockets, 1960s.**14.00**
Sweater vest, openwork knit, drawstring waist, button front, 1970s .**15.00**
Teddy, pk silk w/ivory lace bodice, silk flowers/ribbons, 1920s **75.00**
Vest, man's, blk velvet w/woven design, dbl breasted, 1850s, VG .**150.00**
Vest, man's, silk damask, covered buttons, lined, 1850-50s **220.00**

Vintage Denim

Jacket, Lee, big button/long L, rare label on collar, slanted e, EX..**200.00**
Jacket, Lee 91-B, Union Made, deadstock, sz 36....................**200.00**
Jacket, Levi E, med/dk, sz 26, M **75.00**
Jacket, Levi 501 E, dk, sz 40, M **80.00**
Jacket, workwear, union made SPG, EX color, crop pocket, 1930s, 38/40.**275.00**
Jeans, Foremost, cowboy's, single stitched red lines, med/dk, 36x31".**130.00**
Jeans, Lee Riders, sanforized, Union Made label, leather patch, VG ..**145.00**
Jeans, Levi, orange tag E, slim fit, indigo, peg leg, 1970s..............**45.00**
Jeans, Levi, printed patchwork bellbottoms, wht tag, 1970s, EX.**100.00**
Jeans, Levi e, indigo, single stitched, EX color contrast, 29x32", EX...**35.00**
Jeans, Levi 501, red lines, #6 button, NM **70.00**
Jeans, Levi 501, red lines, dk, G...**25.00**
Jeans, Levi 501 e, indigo single stitching, very dk, 37x29", M **185.00**
Jeans, Levi 501 E, med hege, 34x30", EX **190.00**
Jeans, Levi 501 E, very dk, 36x30"......................................**250.00**
Jeans, Levi 501 E A patch, single-stitch waistband, deadstock, 28x31".**325.00**
Jeans, Levi 501 E A patch, single-stitched waistband, 29x31", NM ..**245.00**
Jeans, Levi 501 E S patch, 38x30", M **230.00**
Jeans, Levi 501 S XX, EX contrast/hedge, rare denim pockets, WWII, EX.**2,300.00**
Jeans, Levi 501 XX, EX color/grainy effect, great hege, rprs, 31x31"...**525.00**
Jeans, Levi 501 XX, full paper patch, med-dk/G contrast, 33x32", EX.**700.00**
Jeans, Levi 501 XX, med color w/good contrast, 31x33" **310.00**
Jeans, Levi 501 XX, very dk, no rivets in bk pockets, 36x32" **385.00**
Jeans, Levi 501 Z XX, full leather patch, supple/very dk, 35x30"..**1,200.00**
Jeans, Levi 505, single stitched, med color, 32x31", NM...............**80.00**
Jeans, Levi 505, single stitched, red lines, dk, 34x32", EX...........**110.00**
Jeans, Levi 505 E, full red lines, slight hege/G contrast, 29x29" .**200.00**
Jeans, Levi 517, single stitched, dk, 36x29", NM......................**30.00**
Jeans, Levi 646, single stitched, dk, 1970s, 34x34", NM **30.00**
Shirt, Roebuck's, western style, dk, 1950s, med **95.00**
Shirt, US Army PW, 1930s, med, M.....................................**300.00**

Cluthra

The name cluthra is derived from the Scottish word 'clutha,' meaning cloudy. Glassware by this name was first produced by J. Couper and Sons, England. Frederick Carder developed cluthra while at the Steuben Glass Works, and similar types of glassware were also made by Durand and Kimball. It is found in both solid and shaded colors and is characterized by a spotty appearance resulting from small air pockets trapped between its two layers.

Bowl, finger; dk amethyst, 2⅝x5" dia...**290.00**
Bowl, wht w/pk int, no mk, 10" **100.00**
Plate, pk to opal mottle, att Monart, 7"...**35.00**
Vase, gr, spherical, Kimball, 5"..**250.00**
Vase, opal & amethyst mottle, att Kimball, 4¾" **250.00**
Vase, tomato red to wht to clear, free-form, 5½" **150.00**
Vase, wht mottled on teal, Kimball, 6½" **265.00**

Coca-Cola

J.S. Pemberton, creator of Coca-Cola, originated his world-famous drink in 1886. From its inception the Coca-Cola Company began an incredible advertising campaign which has proven to be one of the most successful promotions in history. The quantity and diversity of advertising material put out by Coca-Cola in the last one hundred years is literally mind-boggling. From the beginning, the company has projected an image of wholesomeness and Americana. Beautiful women in Victorian costumes, teenagers and schoolchildren, blue- and white-collar workers, the men and women of the Armed Forces and even Santa Claus have appeared in advertisements with a Coke in their hands. Some of the earliest collectibles include trays, syrup dispensers, gum jars, pocket mirrors, and calendars. Many of these items fetch prices in the thousands of dollars. Later examples include radios, signs, lighters, thermometers, playing cards, clocks, and toys — particularly toy trucks.

In 1970 the Coca-Cola Company initialed a multimillion-dollar 'image-refurbishing campaign' which introduced the new 'Dynamic Contour' logo, a twisting white ribbon under the Coca-Cola and Coke trademarks. The new logo often serves as a cut-off point to the purist collector. Newer and very ardent collectors, however, relish the myriad of items marketed since that date, as they often cannot afford the high prices that the vintage pieces command. For more information we recommend *Petretti's Coca-Cola Collectibles Price Guide* (available from Nostalgia Publications whose address you will find under Auctions in the Directory); *B.J. Summers' Guide to Coca-Cola* and *B.J. Summers' Pocket Guide to Coca-Cola*; also *Coca-Cola Commemorative Bottles, Second Edition*, by Bob and Debra Henrich. You may wish to call our advisor for this category, Craig Stifter, at 630-789-5780; he is listed in the Directory under Illinois.

Key:
CC — Coca-Cola   sf — self-framed
dc — diecut   tm — trademark

Reproductions and Fantasies

Beware of reproductions! Prices are given for the genuine original articles, but the symbol (+) at the end of some of the following lines indicate items that have been reproduced. Warning! The 1924, 1925, and 1935 calendars have been reproduced. They are identical in almost every way; only a professional can tell them apart. These are *very* deceiving! Watch for frauds: genuinely old celluloid items ranging from combs, mirrors, knives, and forks to doorknobs that have been recently etched with a new double-lined trademark. Still another area of concern deals with reproduction and fantasy items. A fantasy item is a novelty made to appear authentic with inscriptions such as 'Tiffany Studios,' 'Trans Pan Expo,' 'World's Fair,' etc. In reality, these items never existed as originals. For instance, don't be fooled by a Coca-Cola cash register; no originals are known to exist! Large mirrors for bars are being reproduced and are often selling for $10.00 to $50.00.

Of the hundreds of reproductions (designated 'R' in the following examples) and fantasies (designated 'F') on the market today, these are the most deceiving.

Belt buckle, no originals thought to exist (F), up to 10.00
Bottle, dk amber, w/arrows, heavy, narrow spout (R)....................10.00
Bottle carrier, wood, yel w/red logo, holds 6 bottles (R)...............10.00
Clock, Gilbert, regulator, battery-op, ¾-sz, NM+ (R)................175.00
Cooler, Glascock Jr, made by Coca-Cola USA (R).....................300.00

Doorknob, glass etched w/tm (F) 3.00
Knife, bottle shape, 1970s, many variations (F), ea..................5.00
Knife, fork or spoon w/celluloid hdl, newly etched tm (F)............5.00
Letter opener, stamped metal, Coca-Cola for 5¢ (F) 3.00
Pocket watch, often old watch w/new face (R) 10.00
Pocketknife, yel & red, 1933 World's Fair (F) 2.00
Sign, cb, lady w/fur, dtd 1911, 9x11" (F) 3.00
Soda fountain glass holder, word 'Drink' on orig (R) 5.00
Thermometer, bottle form, DONASCO, 17" (R) 10.00
Trade card, copy of 1905 'Bathtub' foldout, emb 1978 (R)...........25.00

The following items have been reproduced and are among the most deceptive of all:
Pocket mirrors from 1905, 1906, 1908, 1909, 1910, 1911, 1916, and 1920
Trays from 1899, 1910, 1913, 1914, 1917, 1920, 1923, 1925, 1926, 1934, and 1937
Tip trays from 1907, 1909, 1910, 1913, 1914, 1917, and 1920
Knives: many versions of the German brass model
Cartons: wood versions, yellow with logo
Calendars: 1924, 1925, and 1935
These items have been marketed:
Brass thermometer, bottle shape, Taiwan, 24"
Cast-iron toys (none ever made)
Cast-iron door pull, bottle shape, made to look old
Poster, Yes Girl (R)
Button sign, has one round hole while original has four slots, most have bottle logo, 12", 16", 20" (R)
Bullet trash receptacles (old cans with decals)
Paperweight, rectangular, with Pepsin Gum insert
1930 Bakelite radio, 24" tall, repro is lighter in weight than the original, of poor quality and cheaply made
1949 cooler radio (reproduced with tape deck)
Tin bottle sign, 40"
Fishtail die-cut tin sign, 20" long
Straw holders (no originals exist)
Coca-Cola bicycle with cooler (F): the piece has been totally made-up, no such original exists
1914 calendar top, reproduction, 11¼x23¾", printed on smooth-finish heavy ivory paper
Countless trays — most unauthorized (must read 'American Artworks; Coshocton, OH.')

Centennial Items

The Coca-Cola Company celebrated its 100th birthday in 1986, and amidst all the fanfare came many new collectible items, all sporting the 100th-anniversary logo. These items are destined to become an important part of the total Coca-Cola collectible spectrum. The following pieces are among the most popular centennial items.

Bottle, gold-dipped, in velvet sleeve, 6½-oz..................................75.00
Bottle, Hutchinson, amber, Root Co, ½-oz, 3 in case..................375.00
Bottle, International, set of 9 in plexiglas case.........................400.00
Bottle, leaded crystal, 100th logo, 6½-oz, MIB.........................150.00
Medallion, bronze, 3" dia, w/box 100.00
Pin set, wood fr, 101 pins 300.00
Scarf, silk, 30x30" 40.00
Thermometer, glass cover, 14" dia, M...................................35.00

Coca-Cola Originals

Ad, Ladies' Home Journal, ski scene, Thirst Knows the Season, 1922, EX..10.00
Ad, Massengale, lady & maid, magazine pg, 1906, EX 110.00

Apron, Enjoy Ice Cold Coke on bib, 1941, EX 65.00
Ashtray, metal, molded holder w/4 rests, rectangular, EX 30.00
Ashtray, tin, High in Energy, Low in Calories, 4 rests, 1950s, EX .30.00
Banner, King Size, paper, 1958, 36x20", NM 110.00
Banner, paper, Santa, The Gift for Thirst, horizontal, 1952, G 50.00
Banner, 24-bottle case, area at bottom for price, canvas, 9' H, EX .150.00
Belt, vinyl, Drink CC blocks, wht, 1960, EX 20.00
Blotter, I Think It's Swell, girl, 1942, EX 35.00
Blotter, Pause That Refreshes, 1929, EX 110.00
Blotter, Pure Drink of Natural Flavors, 1929, EX 150.00
Book, Wonderful World of CC, NM 85.00
Booklet, Romance of CC, 1916, EX 95.00
Bottle, amber, script CC on shoulder, vertical arrow, 1910s, 6-oz, EX.135.00
Bottle, amber, 75th Anniversary, Thomas Bottling Co, 1974, G ..55.00
Bottle, aqua, block print emb in circle, Sedalia MO, 6½", EX 40.00
Bottle, aqua, block print emb on base, 6½-oz, EX 35.00
Bottle, clear, block print emb on base, fluted sides, 7-oz, EX 40.00
Bottle, gr, block print emb on shoulder, 32-oz, EX 75.00
Bottle, porc flange, Enjoy CC in Bottles, rare, 1948, EX 950.00
Bottle carrier, cb, triangular, 1950s, M 65.00
Bottle carrier, cb, 24-bottle case, 1950s, EX 50.00
Bottle carrier, Masonite, 6-pack, 1940s, EX 95.00
Bottle carrier, plastic, wht letters on red, 6-pack, 1950s, EX 15.00
Bottle carrier, wooden, cut-out hand hold, 6-pack, 1940s, EX 165.00
Bottle hanger, Ice Cold CC King Size, red/wht/gr, M 8.00
Bottle topper, lady w/yel scarf, gr parasol, 1927, 10x8", EX......2,000.00
Bottle topper, We Let You See the Bottle, plastic, 1950s, NM ...600.00
Calendar, Out Fishin', boy on stump, Rockwell, 24x12", M (+).750.00
Calendar, 1904, Lillian Nordica standing by table w/glass, 15x7", EX.2,700.00
Calendar, 1912, Drink CC Delicious & Refreshing, King, G- 750.00
Calendar, 1914, Betty, full pad, EX+ 400.00
Calendar, 1942, Am Love It or Leave It, drum & fife, monthly pads, G...75.00
Calendar, 1952, Coke Adds Zest, full pad, EX 150.00
Calendar, 1961, Coke Refreshes You Best, lady w/bottle, full pad, M ...85.00
Calendar, 1964, Things Go Better..., lady on couch/man w/bottle, EX.75.00
Calendar, 1968, girl w/bottle looks at 45 rpm record, full pad, M .75.00
Calendar, 1972, Lillian Nordica, cloth, VG 10.00
Clock, light-up counter-top, Serve Yourself, 1940-50s, EX..........750.00
Clock, light-up glass front, wht letters on red button, 1950s, NM..600.00
Clock, neon, bottle in octagon w/logo, metal case, 1942, 16" sq, EX ..1,250.00
Clock, oak regulator, pendulum, key wound, 1980s, 23", M........225.00
Clock, plastic electric, wood-grain effect, 1960s, EX 35.00
Coaster, metal, Hilda Clark artwork, EX 8.00
Coaster, metal, Santa, wht...8.00
Cooler, metal picnic, bottle in hand decal, 1940-50s, 8x13x12", EX..110.00
Coupon, This Card Entitles You to 1 Glass..., 1903, EX 400.00
Cutout for Children, Circus, fr, 1921, 10x15", NM 200.00
Decal, Drink, fishtail logo, foil, NM 35.00
Decal, Drink CC Ice Cold, 1960, G 30.00
Door push, metal & Plastic, Have a Coke!, 1930, NM 155.00
Door push, porc, Iced CC Here, yel/wht/red, Canadian, 1950s, 30", NM..250.00
Fan, cb w/rolled paper hdl, Drink CC...Refreshed, 1930, EX 175.00
Fan, Quality Carries On, bottle in hand, 1950, EX......................65.00
Ice pick, wood hdl w/bottle opener finial, 1930, EX 40.00
Jug, clear glass w/dmn paper label, 1910, 1-gal, EX....................250.00
Jug, syrup; clear glass, appl label, 1950, 1-gal, VG 25.00
Knife, bone hdl, 2-blade, Delicious & Refreshing, 1920, VG 110.00
Knife, pearl hdl, Serve CC, 1940s, EX 175.00
Knife, pearl hdl w/corkscrew blade & opener, 1930s, EX 125.00
Lighter, bottle shape, 1950, M 30.00
Lighter, musical, 1960s, EX 200.00
Menu board, cb stand-up, Refreshing You Best, 1950s, EX 175.00
Menu board, metal, Silhouette Girl in lower corner, 1939, NM .450.00
Menu board, tin diecut, Drink CC Be Refreshed, Canadian, 1950, EX..325.00

Needle case, 1924, lady holds bottle, promotional giveaway, 3x2", EX+, $80.00. (Photo courtesy Past Tyme Pleasures)

Note pad, celluloid, 1902, 5x2½", EX 600.00
Note pad, leather covered, 1905, 4½x2¾", EX 225.00
Opener, metal, flat, 1950s, EX 35.00
Opener, metal lion head, 1910-30s, EX 160.00
Opener, steel, blk w/red, outing style, 1910-20s, EX 100.00
Plate, brunette lady w/draped gown, Western CC Bottling Co, 1908, 10"..400.00
Plate, sandwich; Drink CC, Knowles China, 1931, NM 775.00
Playing cards, Drink CC, party scene, 1960, M..........................75.00
Playing cards, Sign of Good Taste, girl in pool, 1959, EX.............80.00
Pocket mirror, celluloid & metal, Relieves..., 1907, 1¾" sq, EX .600.00
Pocket mirror, folding cb cat's head, Drink..., 1920, EX 825.00
Postcard, Bobby Allison race car, 1973, EX................................15.00
Postcard, Fulton CC Bottling Co, 1909, EX 150.00
Postcard, Weldmech truck, 1930, EX 25.00
Radio, can w/dynamic wave, 1970s, EX......................................45.00
Radio, cooler design, upright, 1980s, EX 75.00
Service pin, 15 yrs, EX 90.00
Sign, cb, All Set at..., boy w/6-pack carrier, horizontal, 1943, EX ..650.00
Sign, cb, Autumn Girl, orig wooden fr, 1941, 27x16", EX 875.00
Sign, cb, Drink CC...Refreshing, cowboy w/bottle, 1941, 27x16", EX...550.00
Sign, cb, girl at refrigerator, 1940, 36x20", EX 600.00
Sign, cb, Hospitality in Your..., lady serving tray, 1948, 20x36", G ..250.00
Sign, cb, Nothing Refreshes..., couple on bicycles, vertical, 1943, EX.1,700.00
Sign, cb, Planning Hospitality, hand at 6-pack, 16x27", EX 375.00
Sign, cb, Play Refreshed, girl in cowboy hat, horizontal, 1951, EX..375.00
Sign, cb, Santa, Real Holidays..., 1970s, 36", EX 35.00
Sign, cb, Santa at bench, Bring Home the..., 1956, 28x14", EX .225.00
Sign, cb, Things Go Better..., food & bottle, vertical, 1960s, EX+ .125.00
Sign, cb, Weissmuller & O'Sullivan, 1934, 29½x13½", EX+ ..2,900.00
Sign, cb, Welcome Pause, tennis girl by vendor, 1940s, 27x16", EX ...300.00
Sign, cb carton insert, Coke Is a Natural, EX 15.00
Sign, cb carton insert, Take Home This Handy..., 1936, EX 95.00
Sign, cb diecut, food scene & bottles, 1939, 42x31", VG............275.00
Sign, cb diecut, girl in swimsuit, in fr/under glass, 1938, 22", NM...2,700.00
Sign, cb diecut, lady w/6-pack, 60", EX....................................250.00
Sign, cb diecut, service woman in uniform w/bottle, 1944, 64x25", NM.600.00
Sign, cb litho, circus performers, fr, 1936, 27x18", EX................275.00
Sign, cb stand-up, Santa w/toy bag at feet, button logo, 1945, 13", EX.250.00
Sign, cb 3-D, Boy Oh Boy, boy w/bottle by cooler, 1937, 34x36", VG..850.00
Sign, fiberboard, Please Pay When Served, Kay Displays, 13" dia, VG.600.00
Sign, Good Pause..., lady in trapeze swing, 1954, 20x36", EX 500.00
Sign, masonite, Drink CC, wht on red, oval, 1940, 5½x13", EX.275.00
Sign, metal, fishtail, pnt Drink CC, wht on red, 1960s, 8x14", VG.140.00
Sign, neon, Coke w/Ice, 3-color, 1980s, EX 400.00
Sign, paper, Home Refreshment, 3 pcs of products, 1940s, NM..215.00
Sign, porc, Come In!, Have a CC, yel & wht, 1940s, 54", NM .1,200.00
Sign, porc, Drink CC on botton over bottle, 1950s, 28x18", NM.550.00
Sign, porc button, Drink CC, 24", NM......................................400.00
Sign, sidewalk; metal, CC Ice Cold Sold Here, 1931, 28x20", VG.275.00
Sign, tin, Cold Drinks, fishtail in center, 1960s, 15x24", NM.....300.00
Sign, tin, Drink CC fishtail, self-fr, 1960s, 20x28", EX 250.00

Sign, tin, Drink over bottle, CC under, 1930s, 13x5", EX...........375.00
Sign, tin, ribbon diecut, Sign of Good Taste, 1957, 36", NM 275.00
Sign, tin, 6-pack diecut, King Size CC, 1960s, G 225.00
Sign, tin button, Drink CC in Bottles, wht on red, 1954, 12", EX...250.00
Sign, tin button, Drink CC Sign of..., yel/wht letters, 1950s, 16", NM.425.00
Sign, tin flange, Drink CC, 1941, 21x24", EX 400.00
Sign, trolley car; cb, lady on hammock w/glass, 1912, EX........3,900.00
Sign, wood, Silhouette Girl, metal hanger, 1940, G-.................150.00
Sign, wood & Masonite, Beverage Department & Sprite Boy, 1950s, EX .625.00
Thermometer, glass front, Enjoy..., dial, red/wht, 1960s, 12" dia, EX.155.00
Thermometer, masonite, Thirst Knows No Season, 1940s, 17x6¾", NM...455.00
Thermometer, metal, Enjoy CC, wht on red, rnd, EX.................110.00
Thermometer, porc, Silhouette Girl, red & gr, 1939, 18x5½", EX...625.00
Thermometer, wooden, Drink CC...Everywhere, Paris IL, 1910s, VG.675.00
Toy, Frisbee, plastic w/wave logo, 1960s, EX 15.00
Toy, petal car, wht lettering on red, 1940-50, 36", EX.............1,300.00
Toy, top, plastic, Coke Adds..., 1960s, VG 15.00
Toy truck, Buddy L #5646, GMC loader w/loading line, yel, 1950s, EX...450.00
Toy truck, Chevy delivery, tin, Smokeyfest Estb 1930, 1995, MIB...250.00
Tumbler, clear bell, Enjoy CC, 1970s.................................8.00
Tumbler, clear w/syrup line, arrow flare, wht lettering, 1912-13 .875.00
Wallet, leather, blk w/gold emb lettering, 1907, EX 95.00
Writing tablet, landmarks of the USA, 1960s, EX 10.00

Trays

Values are given for trays in excellent plus condition (C8+). Those that have been reproduced are marked with a (+). The 1934 Weismuller and O'Sullivan tray has been reproduced at least three times. To be original, it will have a black back and must say 'American Artworks, Coshocton, Ohio.' It was not reproduced by Coca-Cola in the 1950s.

All 10½x13½" original serving trays produced from 1910 to 1942 are marked with a date, Made in USA, and the American Artworks Inc., Coshocton Ohio. All original trays of this format (1910 – 40) had REG TM in the tail of the C.

1897, Victorian Lady, 9¼" dia, VG........................15,000.00
1901, Hilda Clark, 9¾", VG....................................4,000.00
1903, Hilda Clark, oval, 18½x15", EX........................6,000.00
1905, Lillian Russell, glass or bottle, 10½x13¼", EX.......3,500.00
1906, Juanita, glass or bottle, oval, 13¼x10½", EX.........2,200.00
1907, Relieves Fatigue, 10½x13¼", NM 4,000.00
1907, Relieves Fatigue, 13½x16½", EX 3,600.00
1908, Topless, Wherever Ginger Ale..., 12¼" dia, NM 11,500.00
1909, St Louis Fair, 10½x13¼", EX 1,800.00
1909, St Louis Fair, 13½x16½", NM 3,000.00
1910, Coca-Cola Girl, Hamilton King, 10½x13¼", EX+ 1,200.00
1914, Betty, oval, 12¼x15¼", EX+ 400.00
1914, Betty, 10½x13¼", EX+ 600.00
1916, Elaine, 8½x19", NM 600.00
1920, Garden Girl, oval, 10½x13¼", EX+.........................800.00
1921, Autumn Girl, oval, 10½x13¼", EX+ 800.00
1922, Summer Girl, 10½x13¼", NM 1,100.00
1923, Flapper Girl, 10½x13¼", NM 500.00
1924, Smiling Girl, brn rim, 10½x13¼", NM 650.00
1924, Smiling Girl, maroon rim, 10½x13¼", EX+.................1,050.00
1925, Party, 10½x13¼", NM 650.00
1926, Golfers, 10½x13¼", EX+ 800.00
1927, Curbside Service, 10½x13¼", EX 750.00
1928, Bobbed Hair, 10½x13¼", NM 650.00
1929, Girl in Swimsuit w/Glass, 10½x13¼", EX+ 450.00
1930, Swimmer, 10½x13¼", EX 425.00
1930, Telephone, 10½x13¼", NM 650.00
1931, Boy w/Sandwich & Dog, 10½x13¼", NM....................1,100.00

1932, Girl in Swimsuit on Beach, Hayden, 10½x13¼", EX+ 625.00
1933, Francis Dee, 10½x13¼", NM 900.00
1934, Weismuller & O'Sullivan, 10½x13¼", NM 1,200.00
1935, Madge Evans, 10½x13¼", NM 575.00
1936, Hostess, 10½x13¼", NM 600.00
1937, Running Girl, 10½x13¼", NM 375.00
1938, Girl in the Afternoon, 10½x13¼", NM 275.00
1939, Springboard Girl, 10½x13¼", NM...........................350.00

1940, Sailor Girl, 10½x13¾", NM, $480.00.

1941, Ice Skater, 10½x13¼", NM..................................450.00
1942, Roadster, 10½x13¼", NM+..................................500.00
1950s, Girl w/Wind in Hair, screen bkground, 10½x13¼", M...100.00
1950s, Girl w/Wind in Hair, solid bkground, 10½x13¼", NM ...225.00
1955, Menu Girl, 10½x13¼", M.....................................65.00
1957, Birdhouse, 10½x13¼", NM...................................125.00
1957, Rooster, 10½x13¼", NM.......................................175.00
1957, Umbrella Girl, 10½x13¼", M.................................375.00
1961, Pansy Garden, 10½x13¼", NM................................30.00

Vendors

Though iterest in Coca-Cola machines of the 1949 – 1959 era rose dramatically over the last decade, values currently seem to have leveled off. The major manufacturers of these curved-top, 5¢ and 10¢ machines were Vendo (V), Vendorlator (VMC), Cavalier (C or CS), and Jacobs. Prices are for machines in excellent or better condition, complete and working. They vary greatly according to geographical location.

Cavalier, model #CS72, EX orig......................................1,600.00
Cavalier, model #CS72, M rstr.......................................3,200.00
Cavalier, model #C27, M rstr..2,800.00
Cavalier, model #C27, orig..1,200.00
Cavalier, model #C51, EX orig...950.00
Cavalier, model #C51, M rstr...2,000.00
Jacobs, model #26, EX 1,200.00
Jacobs, model #26, M rstr..2,500.00
Vendo, model #23, EX orig..900.00
Vendo, model #39, EX orig...1,100.00
Vendo, model #39, M, rstr...2,700.00
Vendo, model #44, EX orig...2,000.00
Vendo, model #44, M rstr..3,200.00
Vendo, model #56, EX orig...1,400.00
Vendo, model #56, M rstr..3,000.00
Vendo, model #80, EX orig...600.00
Vendo, model #80, M rstr..1,250.00
Vendo, model #81, EX orig...1,400.00
Vendo, model #81, M rstr..3,200.00
Vendorlator, model #27, EX orig....................................1,200.00

Vendorlator, model #27, rstr (w/stand) 2,750.00
Vendorlator, model #27A, EX orig 900.00
Vendorlator, model #27A, M rstr 2,000.00
Vendorlator, model #33, EX orig 1,100.00
Vendorlator, model #33, M rstr 2,250.00
Vendorlator, model #44, EX orig 1,250.00
Vendorlator, model #44, M rstr 2,300.00
Vendorlator, model #72, EX orig 1,000.00
Vendorlator, model #72, M rstr 1,800.00

Coffee Grinders

Coffee mills continue to be a popular collectible and interest grows annually as more people discover the beauty of their intricate designs and variety of materials from which they are made. Interest remains high even among seasoned collectors. This is largely due to the fact that there is such a wide variety of makers and models of both US and European mills that no one person could ever assemble a collection that would encompass them all.

Prices remain strong on attractive mills that display well and continue to rise on scarce or rare mills that turn up from time to time. The value of common, incomplete, or damaged mills remains low. The majority of values have gone up; but as more mills enter the market, some prices have come down as supply outstrips demand. There are many nice mills that can be added to a collection for less than $100.00. Mills fall into only a few categories — side mills, wall mills, box mills, and uprights; these can be table, counter, or floor-standing and have any combination of cranks and/or wheels. The last type of mill to appear is the electric. These were first produced in the early 1900s for industrial use. The first electric coffee mill made made for home use was not, as many believe, the Kitchen Aid/Hobart of the mid-1930s, but rather a Hamilton-Beach model produced and sold around 1915. These are very scarce and rarely turn up. When they do they are quickly purchased.

In the last few years several large and important collections have come on the market and added to the mill collecting frenzy as they have been dispersed around the country. The Internet continues to play an important role as many never-before-seen mills and scarce items are offered for sale or auction. Mills can be found on the many auction sites and for sale at online malls and shops. As always, buyer beware. There are unknowing or untrustworthy sellers trying to pass off fantasy or reproduction items as authentic old mills. Doing research is key, and there are many fine books on the market that address coffee mills in particular. We recommend joining online collector clubs, website chat rooms, or a collector organization to learn more. (See Association of Coffee Mill Enthusiasts listed under Clubs, Newsletters, and Catalogs in the Directory.)

Key: adj — adjustment

A Kenrick & Sons No 1, lap, CI w/brass hopper, CI drw, EX 125.00
Adams Pat, lap, pewter hopper, wood w/orig knob 155.00
Arcade, glass catchers, mk Arcade Freeport Illinois....................135.00
Arcade Crystal #9010, CI, Art Deco, glass hopper, EX 175.00
Arcade Crystal #9010, CI, w/orig mk cup, NM 285.00
Arcade Imperial, table, closed CI hopper, wood box 125.00
Arcade Imperial No 999, decal, 1-lb box, EX 155.00
Arcade IXL, table, ornate CI hopper, hdl on side, 1-lb, EX 395.00
Arcade Jewel, canister, rectangular glass hopper, w/lid, EX 695.00
Arcade No 3, canister, CI w/glass hopper, orig lid, EX 155.00
Arcade No 4, canister, CI, glass hopper, orig lid, wall mt, EX.....175.00
Arcade No 5, side, CI, Pat June '94, VG.................................95.00
Arcade No 700, lap, w/dust cover, Sears 1908 catalog, EX............135.00
Arcade Our Baby (toy), label, mini, EX 110.00
Arcade Queen, glass canister & receiver, CI works, EX 395.00
Arcade Royal, canister, CI cup, tin hopper, EX.........................95.00

Arcade Telephone, canister, CI front, Pat Sept 25, '88, EX 575.00
Arcade Telephone, early motif, CI & wood, EX 625.00
Arcade X-Ray, CI works, wood hopper w/glass, EX 175.00
Bell, canister, similar to Golden Rule, CI & wood, EX 650.00
Belmont Lightning No 23, canister, tin & CI, EX....................225.00
Blacksmith-made, funnel shape, 1-hdl, open hopper, wall mt.....375.00
Bronson-Walton Ever Ready No 2, w/cup, Pat 1905, EX 185.00
Bronson-Walton Silver Lake, canister, glass hopper, EX 675.00
Cavanaugh Bros, table, front fill, 1-lb, EX 300.00
Cavanaugh's, table, CI, ornate legs, wood box, EX 675.00
Clawson & Clark No 1, CI, dbl grind, Pat 1886, 6" wheel 750.00
Coles Mfg No 7, counter, CI, Pat 1887, 16" wheels, 27", EX......900.00
Coles No 00, CI, wall mt w/CI cup, NM...............................295.00
Crescent, CI, Rutland VT, orig pnt, 15" wheels, EX..................775.00
Daisy No 867 (toy), CI top, wood box & drw, orig decal, mini, EX..85.00
Elgin Nat'l, floor, silver hopper, 24" wheels 1,500.00
Elgin Nat'l No 44, CI, red, w/eagle & pan, 15" wheels, 24".......850.00
Elgin Nat'l No 46, orig pnt/decals, 12" wheels, EX...................795.00
Enterprise Baby No 2, orig pnt & decals, 2 wheels, 7½", EX...1,050.00
Enterprise Boss, floor, CI, closed hopper, 1873, 39" wheels......3,675.00
Enterprise No 1, counter, open hopper, hdl, Pat 1873, 11", VG...275.00
Enterprise No 16, floor, CI, orig pnt, CI hopper.......................3,500.00
Enterprise No 2, orig pnt/decal, 2 8¾" wheels, EX 950.00
Enterprise No 212, floor, CI, 2 wheels, orig pnt, 30½", EX 3,000.00
Enterprise No 3, counter, CI, wood drw, orig pnt/decals 785.00
Enterprise No 300, very heavy, wall mt, w/catcher, EX 495.00
Enterprise No 50, single-wheel grist mill, NM........................115.00
Enterprise No 6, brass hopper, 2 wheels, rstr, NM 1,100.00
Enterprise No 7, counter, CI, orig pnt, 17" wheel w/eagle, VG ..850.00
Fairbanks Morse, floor, CI, brass hopper, 2 wheels, 27", EX.....2,750.00
Fisher, J; dvtl mahog, pewter hopper, orig drw, handmade 275.00

Golden Rule, cast-iron canister, dovetailed wood box with tin screw-top lid, wall mount, EX, $425.00. (Photo courtesy Buffalo Bay Auction Co.)

Grand Union Tea, table, CI sq base, rnd hopper, mfg Griswold..650.00
Hart, Henry C; Detroit MI, CI, wall mt, NM 115.00
L'il Tot (toy), CI hopper & drw front, wood box, decal, mini 95.00
Landers, Frary & Clark, canister, CI & tin, Pat 1905, VG 80.00
Landers, Frary & Clark, CI, rnd, sq base, ornate, Pat 1875 ....700.00
Landers, Frary & Clark Crown No 11, CI, decals, side crank, EX .300.00
Landers, Frary & Clark Crown No 20, counter, 8" wheels, EX ...900.00
Landers, Frary & Clark No 50, counter, CI, 12" wheels, EX+ .1,100.00
Landers, Frary & Clark Regal No 44, canister, CI/tin, orig 95.00
Logan & Strobridge Franco-American, lap, ornate CI hopper....125.00
Logan & Strobridge Queen, glass canister, CI works, EX 395.00
Luther, side, CI, tin hopper, brass plate, Pat 1843.....................395.00
MJB, tin canister, wall mt w/lid & cup, EX.............................175.00
Nat'l Specialty, CI, brass hopper, 2 12½" wheels.....................1,100.00

Nat'l Specialty, CI, single crank, 12", EX......................475.00
Nat'l Specialty No 0, table, CI, covered hopper, clamps on........225.00
Nat'l Specialty No 7, CI, 16½" wheels, EX.............................1,000.00
New Model, lap, CI w/CI drw, bottom open all 4 sides, EX........150.00
None Such, Bronson Co Cleveland OH, table, tin, pnt, EX.......125.00
Olde Thompson, lap, orig drw, EX...65.00
Parker (mk CPCo) No 1350, CI, wall mt, NM.........................85.00
Parker Challenge Fast Grind No 555, table, orig, 1-lb, EX.........145.00
Parker Eagle No 50, side, CI, Pat 1860, EX..............................85.00
Parker No 260 Columbia, table, side grind, 1-lb, EX.................375.00
Parker No 3000, drw, eagle on top, 11" wheels, orig.................900.00
Parker No 350, side, orig lid, Pat 4/1876, EX...........................165.00
Parker No 446, wall mt...185.00
Parker No 5000, counter, CI, Pat 1897, 12" wheels, 17", VG.....850.00
Parker No 555, screw cap, label, 1-lb, EX.................................135.00
Parker Union, side, CI, gear drive, Pat 1855, EX.....................145.00
Peck, Stow & Wilcox Internat'l #360, lap.................................175.00
PS&W No 3500, side, CI, orig lid, EX.......................................165.00
PS&W Standard No 31, lap, CI open hopper, wood box.............155.00
PS&W Vortex No 40, lap, wood box, CI hopper........................185.00
Queen (toy), CI hopper & drw front, wood box, decal, mini.....115.00
Richmond, side, CI, Chatham Conn (2 szs made), EX, ea..........345.00
Royal Blue, Supplee Hdwe Co, CI, tin hopper, EX....................225.00
Russell & Erwin Diamond, CI, bronze finish, scarce..................475.00
Russell & Erwin Mfg Co No 1008, CI hopper, wood box...........115.00
S&H, counter, CI, w/drw, 19" wheels, 21", VG........................750.00
Selsor, Cook & Co, lap, name on hdl, Pat 1859.......................185.00
Silvers No 1, CI, dbl-grind, w/cup, EX......................................825.00
Simmon's Defiance, label, CI fill lid, 1-lb box, EX....................155.00
Simmon's Hdwe, Delmar Coffee, table, CI cover........................295.00
Star, canister, tin w/CI works, Pat 1910, VG...........................120.00
Star No 7, counter, CI, w/pan, 2 wheels, VG...........................650.00
Steinfield, canister, CI works, glass jar, orig lid, EX..................175.00
Stuttle, Henry; #2, CI, tin hopper, Pat 2/20/77, EX.................395.00
Sun Mfg No 1080, orig lid & drw, 1-lb box, EX/NM.................125.00
Sun Success No 25, cylinder, 2 different szs, EX, ea...................495.00
Swift No 13, counter, orig tin drw, red pnt, 12" wheels, 19".......475.00
Swift No 15, counter, orig decals/pnt, Pat 1875, 19" wheels....1,100.00
Swift No 26, Lane Brothers, floor, CI, 2 wheels.....................2,700.00
Tillmann's Hawaiian Coffee, CI, wall mt, EX............................215.00
Universal No 109, blk tin w/gr decal, Pat 1905, NM...................75.00
Vandergrift, side hinged, CI, ca 1870, complete, EX.................395.00
Waddel A-17, CI, sunflower design, wall mt, EX........................280.00
Waddel A-9, orig drw & label, box type, EX..............................125.00
Wilson Increase, side, CI & tin...75.00
Wright, John; CI, red or gr, ca 1968, 2 6¾" wheels, NM...........250.00
Wrightsville Hdwe Brighton, label, 1-lb box, EX.......................110.00
Wrightsville Hdwe Peerless No 200, canister, CI/glass, EX.........170.00
WW Weaver Warranted, dvtl walnut, pewter hopper, ca 1830...225.00

Coin-Operated Machines

Coin-operated machines may be the fastest-growing area of collector interest in today's market. Many machines are bought, restored, and used for home entertainment. Older examples from the turn of the century and those with especially elaborate decoration and innovative features are most desirable.

The www.GameRoomAntiques.com website and *Antique Amusements*, *Slot Machine, and Jukebox Gazette* are excellent sources of information for those interested in coin-operated machines; see the Clubs, Newsletters, and Catalogs section of the Directory for publishing information. Jackie and Ken Durham are our advisors; they are listed in the Directory under the District of Columbia.

Arcade Machines

ABT Target Skill Shooting, 1¢ = 10 shots, 1930s, rstr................975.00
Ask Me Another About Your Fortune, 1940s, G working.............595.00
Atlas 5¢ Tilt Test, balls roll down ramp, 1950s, EX..................295.00
Baseball, gumball w/penny return, rpt case, 1950s, 16x9x8".......365.00
Bat a Ball, flip & catch, rpt case, 25x16x11".............................895.00
Booz Barometer, skill game, 1950s, G orig.................................300.00
Bouncer, flip skill game, 1940s, rpt case...................................975.00
Clam Shell Mutoscope, w/reel, all orig, EX.............................6,850.00
Gottlieb Grip Tester, 1940s, rstr case..300.00
Junior Deputy Sheriff Pistol Range 5¢, 1940s-50s, G................895.00
Mills Seal, flip game, rpt case, 1930s, 30x15x12"..................2,500.00
Over the Top, work penny to top, wall machine, 1920s, 20", rstr..1,295.00
Punt Return 5¢, 1950s, VG...595.00
Smiley the Clown, silk-screen graphics, 1940s, rstr....................795.00
Steam Shovel, rpl marque & paper, 1930s, mini, rstr..............3,000.00

Jukeboxes

The coin-operated phonograph of the early 1900s paved the way for the jukeboxes of the '20s. Seeburg was first on the market with an automatic eight-tune phonograph. By the 1930s Wurlitzer was the top name in the industry with dealerships all over the country. As a result of the growing ranks of competitors, the '40s produced the most beautiful machines made. Wurlitzers from this era are probably the most popularly sought-after models on the market today. The model #1015 of 1946 is considered the all-time classic and often brings prices in excess of $8,000.00.

AMI #500, 1949, 65"..800.00
AMI Continental VV, chrome plated, 1961, rstr......................9,995.00
Ristaucrat, table-top, 5¢ play, holds 10 45 records, 1950s, sm..1,300.00
Rockola #490 Supersound, EX orig..1,500.00
Rockola #1422, EX orig..6,000.00
Rockola #1493 Princess, EX orig..4,500.00
Scopitone, shows movies, 1950s, rstr...4,000.00
Seeburg #100C, walnut veneer case, 1950s, rstr......................6,000.00
Seeburg #100G, chrome pilasters, metal grill, 1953, rstr..........7,000.00
Seeburg Q-160, worn chrome, 1959, G working.......................1,150.00
Seeburg SMC1, Disco, visible record mechanism, 1978, EX orig.2,000.00
Seeburg SPS160, Olympian, 1972, purple, orange or bl, NM..1,200.00
Seeburg SPS2, Matador, 1973, EX orig...................................1,500.00
Seeburg STD 4, Mardi Gras, 1977, rstr....................................1,600.00
Seeburg USC 2, Band Shell Firestar, 1971, rstr.......................1,800.00
Seeburg V-200, rstr..7,000.00
Stoner Theater, 8-column, 73x30x15", rstr..............................6,000.00

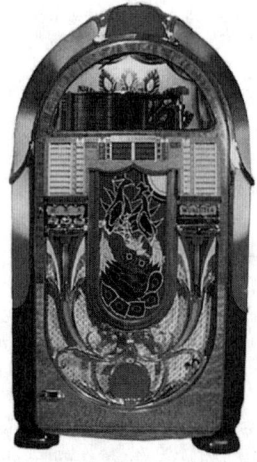

Wurlitzer #850, Peacock, 66x41", EX original, $15,000.00.

Wurlitzer #1015, Bubbler, plays 78s, 60", VG 7,500.00
Wurlitzer #1610, 33 & 45 rpms, VG 2,400.00
Wurlitzer #2304, 1955, EX...3,000.00
Wurlitzer #2610, 100 selections, rpt, 1962, EX.......................2,600.00

Pinball Machines

Bally Black Pyramid, electronic, 1984, G working.......................875.00
Bally Carnival Queen, bingo machine, 1958, G working............950.00
Bally Circus Queen, bingo machine, 1960, G working 1,200.00
Bally Dude Ranch, bingo machine, 1953, G working.................750.00
Bally Fireball II, electronic, 1981, G working.........................750.00
Bally Kiss, electronic, 1979, G working 2,500.00
Bally Laguna Beach, bingo machine, 1960, G working............1,400.00
Bally Strikes & Spares, electronic, 1978, G working.................850.00
Bally Yacht Club, bingo machine, 1953, G working...................650.00
Gottlieb Fair Lady, 1956, EX+...1,300.00
Gottlieb The Games, electronic, 1984, G working......................900.00
Williams Cyclone, electronic, 1988, G working.......................1,600.00
Williams Pin Bot #N-7, clean, rubbered, G working................1,250.00
Williams Star Series Pitch & Bat Baseball, wood rail, 1949, G working..1,800.00

Slot Machines

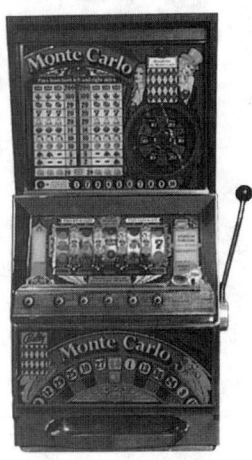

Bally 25¢ Monte Carlo, EX original, working, $2,500.00.

Bally 5¢ console, 1948, rstr..2,500.00
Dewey, upright color wheel, ornate Albert Pick case, 1900s, EX...15,000.00
Evans 5¢, horse-race console, rstr..3,000.00
Jennings Silver Dollar Red Sun Chief, w/light-up stand, M rstr..4,600.00
Jennings 1¢ Little Duke, gumball side vendor, 1933, EX orig..4,000.00
Jennings 25¢ Nevada Club Light-Up, 1950s-60s, M rstr..........3,500.00
Keeney 25¢ Sweet Shawnee, console, 1960s, EX orig 800.00
Keeney 5¢ Black Dragon, console, 3 can play, EX orig 1,800.00
Mills $1 Golden Nugget, w/jackpot, EX, rare 7,000.00
Mills Futurity, gold award tokens, EX orig 5,300.00
Mills Silver Dollar Black Golden Nugget, 1945, old rstr..........6,000.00
Mills 25¢ Bursting Cherry, chrome plated, 1938-42, M rstr.....3,200.00
Mills 25¢ Extra Bell, M rstr 3,200.00
Mills 25¢ Hightop Bonus, 1948, EX orig 3,500.00
Mills 25¢ Lion Head (aka Wolf's Head), str drop, 1932, M rstr.3,200.00
Mills 25¢ War Eagle, 5-coin visible escalator, 1931, M rstr.....3,200.00
Mills 5¢ Lion Front, rstr..3,000.00
Mills 5¢ Skyscraper, 1936, EX rstr 3,200.00
Mills 5¢ Vest Pocket, 1938, 8" cube, EX orig 800.00
Mills 50¢ Black Hightop, 1946-51, M rstr 3,500.00
United Coin 25¢ Big Six, console, color wheel, EX orig 2,000.00
Victor, upright color wheel, EX, rare.....................................19,000.00

Trade Stimulators

Ad Lee Crystal Gazer Dice, globe lights up, electric, 1932, 12", EX..875.00
B&O Hit the Target, penny drop, w/gumball dispenser, 1950s, 20x9x10".250.00
Bally Baby Bell, ca 1938, 12½x8½x7½", rstr..............................685.00
Bomb Hit, penny drop, WW II motif, 15¼x12¼x6¾", EX 975.00
Daval Reel dice, ca 1936, 10x9x9", rstr case 685.00
Exhibit Supply Little Gypsy, penny drop, 1920s, 17x8x5", rstr.1,295.00
Groetchen Punchet, nickel coin slide, VG 895.00
High Card Challenge/Poker, penny drop, 1930s, rpt case 650.00
Indoor Striker Skill, aluminum, gumballs, 1930s, EX..............1,500.00
Mills Kounter King, w/gum dispenser, 1930s, EX orig 895.00
Rockola Radio wizard, single reel, playing cards, 1930s, rstr case .850.00
Twins Dice, w/gumball dispenser, remade award card, rstr case...495.00

Vendors

Vending machines sold a product or a service. They were already in common usage by 1900 selling gum, cigars, matches, and a host of other commodities. Peanut and gumball machines are especially popular today. The most valuable are those with their original finish and decals. Older machines made of cast iron are especially desirable, while those with plastic globes have little collector value. When buying unrestored peanut machines, beware of salt damage.

ASCO 5¢ Hot Nut, heating element not working, 21", EX rstr .400.00
Ask Yogi/Madam X Dbl Fortune Napkin Holder, 1950s, VG......495.00
Aspirin 10¢, w/packets/plastic cup, 20", VG 475.00
Atlas Bantam Tray 5¢, peanuts, 1940s, 11x8x10", rstr.................395.00
Coast Baseball, gumball w/pinball feature, 1950s, rstr 395.00

Diamond Matches One Cent, round variation, minor wear, 13½x10½x7½", EX, $550.00. (Photo courtesy Buffalo Bay Auction Co.)

Hawkeye 1¢, glass globe, rstr decal, bell rings w/10th vend, 1930s...495.00
Miles Wilbur Succhard, chocolate, 1930s, 14x9x4", rstr 650.00
Northwestern 1¢, peanuts, porc w/frosted globe, 1930s, 15", VG ..400.00
Play Baseball 1¢, gumball, 14", rstr...185.00
Radio 1¢, hot nuts, aluminum, Femachen Mfg, 1930s, 18" 495.00
Schemach Sanitary Postage Station, CI, dbl machine, EX..........595.00
Silver King 5¢, peanuts, bl, 11", EX 295.00
Swarmi 1¢ Fortune Napkin Holder, w/100 slips, 1950s, VG 345.00
Uncle Sam, stamps, porc front, wall type, 1950s-60s, EX............165.00
Vendo Coke coin changer, gives nickels, 1950s, 11x16", rstr.....2,500.00
Victor 1¢ Model V, gum/candy, 15", rstr.....................................245.00
Victor 1¢ Topper, red/blk w/glass globe, 1950s, 11", rstr.............195.00

Cole, A. R.

A second generation North Carolina potter, Arthur Ray Cole opened his own shop in 1926, operating under the name Rainbow Pottery until 1941 when he adopted his own name for the title of his business. He remained active until he died in 1974. He was skilled in modeling the pottery and highly recognized for his fine glazes.

Birdhouse, gr lead gloss & matt, earthenware, 1940s-50s, 6½" **60.00**
Bowl, mc splotches on wht, earthenware, 1941-62, 2⅞x11" **150.00**
Candle holder, owl figural, gr gloss & matt, earthenware, 1950s, 5"..**70.00**
Churn, aqua & turq gloss, w/lid & dasher, 1979, 14" **70.00**
Jar, apothecary; Chrome Red, incised lines, split hdls, att, 5⅛"..**130.00**
Jug, chrome red, streaky, att Nel Graves, 5" **40.00**
Lamp base, gr lead gloss & mass, coiled-ring hdls, 1940s, 11¼"..**130.00**
Pitcher, Rebekah; cobalt w/yel & dk gr streaks, earthenware, 1976, 13" .**70.00**
Plate, gr matt w/dk gloss, 9½" **80.00**
Teapot, Huckleberry gloss, earthenware, 1950s, 5½x8¼"...........**120.00**
Vase, Chrome Red, scalloped, earthenware, 1940s, 5" **110.00**
Vase, gr cystalline over brn, cylindrical neck, att, 9½" **110.00**
Vase, gr lead gloss & matt, incurvate rim, 1940s-50s, 15½" **130.00**
Vase, gr lead gloss & matt, rim-to-hip hdls, earthenware, 1940s, 20"..**450.00**
Vase, gr/yel/brn crystalline, 2 split hdls, att, 15", EX **325.00**
Vase, wht semi-matt w/subtle crackle, spherical, circular stamp, 5x6" .**60.00**

Compacts

The use of cosmetics before WWI was looked upon with disdain. After the war women became liberated, entered the work force, and started to use makeup. The compact, a portable container for cosmetics, became a necessity. The basic compact contains a mirror and a powder puff.

The vintage compacts were fashioned in a myriad of shapes, styles, materials, and motifs. They were made of precious metals, fabrics, plastics, and in almost any other conceivable medium. Commemorative, premium, patriotic, figural, Art Deco, plastic, and gadgetry compacts are just a few of the most sought-after types available today. Those that are combined with other accessories (music/compact, watch/compact, cane/compact) are also very much in demand. Vintage compacts are an especially desirable collectible since the workmanship, design, techniques, and materials used in their execution would be very expensive and virtually impossible to duplicate today.

Our advisor, Roselyn Gerson, has written several highly informative books: *Vintage and Contemporary Purse Accessories*; *Vintage & Vogue Ladies' Compacts*; and *The Estée Lauder Solid Perfume Compact Collection*. She is listed in the Directory under the state of New York. For further information we recommend *Collector's Encyclopedia of Compacts, Carryalls, and Face Powder Boxes* by Laura M. Mueller. See Clubs, Newsletters, and Catalogs for information concerning the compact collectors' club and their periodical publication, *The Powder Puff*.

Ball, Loves Me Loves Me Not, gold-tone/plastic, Henriette, 2"..**200.00**
Basket, brass-colored metal, swing hdl, metal int, K&K, 2⅛" dia ...**100.00**
Bracelet, gold-tone w/filigree, hinged band, FJ Co, 1⅞" dia........**325.00**
Cuff bracelet, medallions on gold-tone, Flamand-Fladiu, 2¼" dia .**300.00**
Music box, silver eng, resembles hand mirror, lipstick in hdl, Germany..**200.00**
Necessaire, blk/ivorene Bakelite w/rhinestones, 4x1¾", +cord/tassel..**425.00**
Novelty, gold-tone faux watch w/rhinestones on hands, 3" dia **50.00**
Novelty, gold-tone hand w/wht lace mitt, Volupte, 4½x2" **225.00**
Novelty, gold-tone suitcase w/leather cover, metal hdl, Atomette, 3"..**100.00**
Novelty, harlequin mask, polished gold-tone, E Arden, 3x1⅝" ..**150.00**
Novelty, mc enameled telephone dial, I Like Ike/US map **225.00**
Novelty, plastic US Navy hat form w/gold-tone insignia, 3x1¼"..**85.00**
Novelty, rnd maroon hatbox w/USN emblem on lid, Zell, 3" **165.00**
Novelty, silver vanity faux cigarette lighter, A Dunhill, 1⅞" **275.00**
Novelty, 2 dials set appointments, gold-tone/plastic, Fr, 2½x3"..**165.00**
Oblong, 3 cigarette packet transfers on brushed gold-tone, 3½x2"..**115.00**
Pendant, Sphinx enameling, fitted int, chain, 1⅜" dia **125.00**

Petit-point city scene & brushed gold-tone, Elgin, 3½x3" **100.00**
Purse-like, dk grained gold-tone w/bl stone, chain, 2¾x1¾" **90.00**
Rnd, avocado plastic w/beads & rhinestones, 3½x4¼", +cord/tassel ..**335.00**
Rnd, bl enamel/gold-tone, perfume well, Austria, 2½" **475.00**
Rnd, bl silk w/embr, tassel, cord w/ojimi bead, Vantine, 1920s ..**150.00**
Rnd, cloisonne Fr scene on gold-tone, Schildkraut, 2½" **60.00**
Rnd, gold-tone astrological signs on bl enamel, 3¾" **110.00**
Rnd, gold-tone w/mc enameled Eastern Star emblem, Elgin, 3"....**50.00**
Rnd, lav cloisonne lid w/flowers, finger ring, Sterling hallmk, 2"..**250.00**
Rnd, Lucite lid encloses HP lady on swing on irid ground, Fr, 2½"..**200.00**
Rnd, molded dog w/appl head on pearlized plastic lid, Britain, 3"..**115.00**
Rnd, pnt flamenco dancer w/appl lace skirt on gold-tone, 2¾"..**100.00**
Rnd, Silver Queen, resembles gold ball, De Corday, 2"..............**40.00**
Scalloped oval, gold-tone w/enamel & Fr ivory miniature, Italy, 1900s..**200.00**
Semi-scalloped, pastoral scene on bl w/gold, eng bl lid, 2¾x2¾"..**225.00**
Souvenir, Paris, gold-tone & blk enamel, Fr, 3½x2¾"...............**150.00**
Souvenir, WA DC attractions on gold-tone heart shape, 2¾x3"..**50.00**
Sq, brushed gold-tone w/appl mc stones, Trifari, 3" **175.00**
Sq, brushed gold-tone w/lg emerald stones on lid, Eisenberg Orig, 3"..**175.00**
Sq, clear Lucite, insert photo behind removeable mirror, 3¼" **80.00**

Square, clear Lucite with golden molded and painted sunburst medallion, mirror and compartment inside, Roger & Gallet, 4x4", $225.00. (Photo courtesy Alvin Gerson)

Sq, gilt-metal w/filigree lid & mc stones/pearls, Fr, 2¼" **200.00**
Sq, mink covered, Volupté, 3"..**90.00**
Tango chain vanity, gr cloisonne w/pk roses, lipstick tube/perfume .**600.00**
Tango chain w/lipstick, brushed silver w/gold-tone flowers, 3½" dia .**185.00**
Triangular, wht figure on pk enameled gold-tone, Schiaparelli, 2" .**80.00**
Vanity, antique gold-tone filigree w/mc stones, fitted int, 2x1¼"..**400.00**
Vanity, blk suede & brass heart shape, top opens, Fr, 3½x5½x2"..**350.00**
Vanity, blk/wht enamel & gold-tone domino, Coty, 3¾x2¼".....**200.00**
Vanity, bolster w/silhouette/polka dots, lipstick in tassel, 1920s..**275.00**
Vanity, brushed gold-tone w/mc stones & filigree plaque, chain, 3x2".**135.00**
Vanity, coral Bakelite w/HP floral/rhinestones, lipstick in tassel.**265.00**
Vanity, emb leather, resembles book, Raquel, 2x3" **110.00**
Vanity, floral on lav, mirror & compartments, 2x1½"..................**50.00**
Vanity, floral on yel enamel, fitted int, 2¼x1¾" **65.00**
Vanity, gilt inlay Asian scene, finger ring, 3½x2¾" **250.00**
Vanity, gilt-metal w/mc intaglio/red stones/pearls, Fr, ca 1900....**250.00**
Vanity, gold-tone horseshoe shape w/mc intaglio, Fr, 1900s........**250.00**
Vanity, gold-tone w/photo insert in lid, fitted int, 1930s, 2" dia ...**90.00**
Vanity, gold-tone/MOP book shape w/tube in spine, 2x2½x½"....**80.00**
Vanity, gr/off-wht/silver-tone champleve, finger ring, 2¼" dia....**115.00**
Vanity, lamè covered saddle bag, tube sleeve, comb pocket, 4x3¼"..**150.00**
Vanity, marbleized plastic w/mc flowers, ogime button, 1920s **300.00**
Vanity, pnt Robin Hood scene on silver-tone, chain, Fisher, 3"..**225.00**
Vanity, pyramidal, red/blk stripes, fraternal emblem, Fillkwik, 1¾"..**85.00**
Vanity, silver-tone powder grinder, fitted int, SGDG, Fr, 2x2"......**80.00**
Vanity & floral enamel, 4½x2½x1½"+lipstick holder on chain ..**275.00**
Vanity cigarette case, brushed gold-tone w/enamel, 3x5" **165.00**

Consolidated Lamp and Glass

The Consolidated Lamp and Glass Company of Coraopolis, Pennsylvania, was incorporated in 1894. For many years their primary business was the manufacture of lighting glass such as oil lamps and shades for both gas and electric lighting. The popular 'Cosmos' line of lamps and tableware was produced from 1894 to 1915. (See also Cosmos.) In 1926 Consolidated introduced their Martelé line, a type of 'sculptured' ware closely resembling Lalique glassware of France. (Compare Consolidated's 'Lovebirds' vase with the Lalique 'Perruches' vase.) It is this line of vases, lamps, and tableware which is often mistaken for a very similar type of glassware produced by the Phoenix Glass Company, located nearby in Monaca, Pennsylvania. For example, the so-called Phoenix 'Grasshopper' vases are actually Consolidated's 'Katydid' vases.

Items in the Martelé line were produced in blue, pink, green, crystal, white, or custard glass decorated with various fired-on color treatments or a satin finish. For the most part, their colors were distinctively different from those used by Phoenix. Although not foolproof, one of the ways of distinguishing Consolidated's wares from those of Phoenix is that most of the time Consolidated applied color to the raised portion of the design, leaving the background plain, while Phoenix usually applied color to the background, leaving the raised surfaces undecorated. This is particularly true of those pieces in white or custard glass.

In 1928 Consolidated introduced their Ruba Rombic line, which was their Art Deco or Art Moderne line of glassware. It was only produced from 1928 to 1932 and is quite scarce. Today it is highly sought after by both Consolidated and Art Deco collectors.

Consolidated closed its doors for good in 1964. Subsequently a few of the molds passed into the hands of other glass companies that later reproduced certain patterns; one such reissue is the 'Chickadee' vase, found in avocado green, satin-finish custard, or milk glass. Our advisor for this category is Jack D. Wilson, author of *Phoenix and Consolidated Art Glass, 1926 – 1980*; he is listed in the Directory under Arizona.

Allover Ivy, pitcher, gr over wht casing	300.00
Bird of Paradise, fan vase, amethyst, rare, 10½x9⅝"	455.00
Bird of Paradise, fan vase, yel wash, 10"	350.00
Bird of Paradise, plate, yel wash, 8¼"	45.00
Bird of Paradise, vase, gr & frost, sq, 9¾"	285.00
Bird of Paradise, vase, gr wash, 10"	250.00
Bittersweet, lamp, reverse ruby stain on crystal	150.00
Bittersweet, vase, amber irid on milk glass, rare	325.00
Bittersweet, vase, reverse ruby stain, 10"	200.00
Bittersweet, vase, ruby stain on crystal	150.00
Bittersweet, vase, sepia (brn) cased	275.00
Blackberry, umbrella vase, gr cased	1,200.00
Blackberry, umbrella vase, red, rare	1,500.00
Catalonian, basket, honey, sm hdl, 4¼"	117.50
Catalonian, bowl, Jade Green, #1186, 9½"	110.00
Catalonian, bowl, rainbow bl/pk/gr, #1130, 9½"	315.00
Catalonian, bowl, rainbow bl/pk/gr, #1186, 9½"	500.00
Catalonian, bowl, salad; rainbow bl/pk/gr, #1115, 3½x8½"	280.00
Catalonian, candlestick, rainbow bl to crystal	75.00
Catalonian, carafe, rainbow bl/pk/gr, #1168, 7¾"	360.00
Catalonian, console bowl, Reuben Blue, #1186, 9½", +#1124 sticks	1,125.00
Catalonian, fan vase, bl cased irid stretch	225.00
Catalonian, flower bowl, yel	85.00
Catalonian, goblet, rainbow bl/pk/gr, #1120, 5"	188.00
Catalonian, pitcher, rainbow bl/pk/gr, #1109, 7¾"	765.00
Catalonian, toilet bottle, honey wash, #1175, popped bubble on lid	110.00
Catalonian, whiskey jug, emerald gr	250.00
Catalonian (Monterey), ceiling modernizer w/fitter, gr, 25x10x4"	600.00

Catalonian (Monterey), wall sconces, honey, pr	862.50
Chickadee, vase, sepia (brn) wash on crystal	125.00
Chrysanthemum, vase, 2-color on satin milk glass, 12"	150.00
Chrysanthemum, vase, 3-color on satin custard, 12"	175.00
Cockatoo, candlestick, purple wash	225.00
Cockatoo, light shade, hanging; pk cased, 4" fitter, rare	600.00
Cockatoo, vase, reverse gr on crystal, Martele label	275.00
Cockatoo, vase, straw opal, ormolu mts	450.00
Dancing Girls, vase, bl on satin milk glass, 12"	525.00
Dancing Girls, vase, 3-color on satin custard, 12"	550.00
Dancing Nymph, fan vase, crystal	125.00
Dancing Nymph, palace bowl, honey, 4x16⅝", EX	2,145.00
Dancing Nymph, palace platter, Reuben Blue, 17"	2,025.00
Dancing Nymph, plate, Fr crystal, 6"	65.00
Dancing Nymph, plate, lt ceramic bl, beveled edge, 8⅜"	260.00
Dancing Nymph, plate, pk frosted, 10"	175.00
Dancing Nymph, plate, reverse ruby stain, rare	250.00
Dancing Nymph, sherbet, crystal	35.00
Dogwood, vase, bl on wht cased w/faint irid	400.00

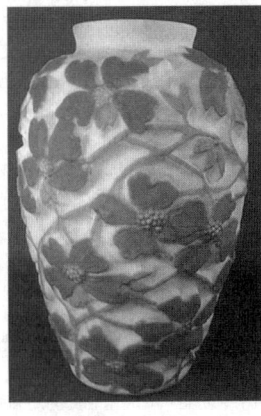

Dogwood, vase, three-color on satin custard, 11", $185.00. (Photo courtesy John A. Shuman III)

Dogwood, vase, yel cased	300.00
Dolphin, candlestick, gr wash, Santa Maria Line	450.00
Dragon Fly, vase, purple cased on straw opal, 7"	200.00
Dragon Fly, vase, reverse bl highlights on satin milk glass, 7"	135.00
Dragon Fly, vase, satin milk glass (no highlighting), 7"	50.00
Fish, tray, gr wash	200.00
Five Fruits, plate, russet wash (rare), ormolu mts, 12"	295.00
Five Fruits, plate, sepia (brn) wash, 12"	95.00
Five Fruits, tumbler, Fr crystal, ftd	35.00
Five Fruits, tumbler, gr wash, ftd	35.00
Floral, vase, 3-color on satin milk glass	125.00
Florentine, vase, coffee-brn, etch	250.00
Florentine, vase, gr, urn shape	175.00
Florentine, vase, gr, 7"	195.00
Foxglove, vase, amber over wht cased w/faint irid	300.00
Foxglove, vase, red satin, 10"	450.00
Hollyhock, lamp vase, reverse gr on crystal	150.00
Hummingbird, puff box, bl wash on crystal, 5"	110.00
Hummingbird, puff box, mc highlights on milk glass, 7"	125.00
Hummingbird, vase, gr wash on crystal	75.00
Iris, candlestick, pk wash	125.00
Iris, jug, gr over wht casing, ½-gal	350.00
Jonquil, vase, rose & gr on satin custard	95.00
Jonquil, vase, yel & gr on satin custard	75.00
Jonquil, 2-color highlights on satin milk glass	125.00
Katydid, fan vase, gr wash	195.00
Katydid, vase, bl on satin milk glass, ovoid	225.00
Katydid, vase, reverse gr on milk glass, ovoid	250.00

L'Ora, ginger jar, no lid, 7½"..360.00
Line 700, plate, service; amber wash, 10"...............................135.00
Line 700, plate, service; bl frost, 10"...................................145.00
Line 700, vase, bl frost w/clear bl ribs, #701, 11x10"..................350.00
Line 700, vase, brn wash w/clear, #701, 11x10".........................395.00
Line 700, vase, dk Reuben Blue, #701, 11x10"...........................950.00
Line 700, vase, red w/satin bkground, 7"................................350.00
Line 700, vase, reverse dk bl on crystal, 6½"...........................175.00
Line 700, vase, reverse russet on custard, 6½"..........................225.00
Love Bird, banana boat, 3-color on custard, ormolu mts............550.00
Love Bird, candlesticks, wiped gr wash (gr on birds, unusual), pr..859.00
Love Bird, glove box, gr wash, rare......................................350.00
Love Bird, powder jar, yel wash..80.00
Love Bird, vase, gold on straw opal......................................400.00
Love Bird, vase, ruby stain on crystal, ornate surmount..............375.00
Love Bird, vase, straw opal, ormolu mts.................................400.00
Love Bird, vase, 3-color on satin custard................................375.00
Nuthatch, planter vase, purple wash......................................175.00
Nuthatch, planter vase, 3-color highlights on satin milk glass....225.00
Olive, bowl, reverse bl highlighting (rare color)........................125.00
Olive, lamp, 3-color highlighting, rare...................................300.00
Olive, plate, yel wash, 8"..45.00
Olive, vase, gr & yel on satin custard....................................165.00
Orchids, bowl, console; gray wash, rare.................................275.00
Orchids, candlestick, yel wash..95.00
Pine Cone, vase, brn & gr on satin milk glass..........................145.00
Pine Cone, vase, red..350.00
Pine Cone, vase, reverse rose on glossy custard.......................150.00
Pine Cone, vase, straw opal...185.00
Poppy, vase, bl wash (rare color)..225.00
Poppy, vase, purple cased...400.00
Poppy, vase, reverse ruby stain..200.00
Regent Line, vase, ash-rose pk on wht opal casing, #1174B........125.00
Regent Line, vase, Pine Cone decor, faint irid.........................125.00
Regent Line, vase, violets decor...45.00
Ruba Rombic, bowl, bouillon; Sunshine................................275.00
Ruba Rombic, candle holder, lav...200.00
Ruba Rombic, creamer, jade...250.00
Ruba Rombic, plate, salad; jade, 8"......................................125.00
Ruba Rombic, relish tray, smoky topaz.................................195.00
Ruba Rombic, toilet bottle, Sunshine....................................950.00
Ruba Rombic, tumbler, Jungle Green, 9-oz............................135.00
Ruba Rombic, vase, amethyst w/lt opal in valleys, #800, 6½", EX.4,495.00
Ruba Rombic, vase, jade, #800, blk smudge on glass, 6¼".......2,075.00

Ruba Rombic, vase, smoky topaz, 9½", $2,900.00. (Photo courtesy Gene Florence)

Ruba Rombic, vase, Sunshine, #800, 6¼", EX...........................1,500.00
Ruba Rombic, whiskey decanter, smoky topaz.........................2,000.00
Ruba Rombic, whiskey tray, Fr crystal, #825, 12x10¼", NM...3,125.00

Ruba Rombic, whiskey tray, jade, #825, 11⅜x9⅞", NM.........3,665.00
Santa Maria, console bowl, lt brn (sand), NM, +2 dolphin candlesticks.3,750.00
Santa Maria, dolphin candlesticks, gr, pr, NM.......................1,975.00
Screech Owls, vase, bl & salmon on satin custard....................145.00
Screech Owls, vase, gold on milk glass.................................135.00
Screech Owls, vase, orange & gr on satin custard....................145.00
Sea Gull, vase, gold on milk glass.......................................275.00
Sea Gull, vase, gr cased...425.00
Sea Gull, vase, orange on satin custard................................275.00
Sea Gull, vase, rose & bl on custard....................................275.00
Tropical Fish (Gold Fish), vase, bl matt, Reuben Line label, 9"..275.00
Tropical Fish (Gold Fish), vase, red, 9"................................450.00
Tropical Fish (Gold Fish), vase, reverse ruby stain on clear, 9"..250.00
Tropical Fish (Gold Fish), vase, rose & bl on milk glass, 9"........275.00

Cookbooks

Cookbooks from the nineteenth century, though often hard to find, are a delight to today's collectors both for their quaint formats and printing methods as well as for their outmoded, often humorous views on nutrition. Recipes required a 'pinch' of salt, butter 'the size of an egg' or a 'walnut,' or a 'handful' of flour. Collectors sometimes specialize in cookbooks issued as advertising premiums. Especially desirable are the figurals that were shaped like a jar, a slice of bread, or some other form relative to the product. Others with unique features such as illustrations by well-known artists or references to famous people or places are priced in accordance. Cookbooks written earlier than 1874 are the most valuable and when found command prices as high as $200.00; figurals usually sell in the $10.00 to $15.00 range.

As is true with all other books, if the original dust jacket is present and in nice condition, a cookbook's value goes up by at least $5.00. Right now, books on Italian cooking from before circa 1940 are in demand, and bread-baking is important this year. For further information we recommend *A Guide to Collecting Cookbooks* by Col. Bob Allen and *Price Guide to Cookbooks and Recipe Leaflets* by Linda Dickinson. Our advisor for this category is Charlotte Safir; she is listed in the Directory under New York.

Key: CB — cookbook

After 60 CB, D Hamilton, Castle Books, w/dust jacket, 1974, 377-pg..8.50
Alice Bradley Menu-CB..., Macmillan, cloth cover, dust jacket, 1948...22.50
American Frugal Housewife, Lydia Child, 334th ed, 1860, 130-pg, G...150.00
Appledore CB, M Parloa, 1880, 240-pg, G-.................................40.00
Art of Creole Cookery, Kaufman & Cooper, Doubleday, dust jacket, 1962.18.00
Art of Fine Baking, P Peck, James Beard intro, illus, c 1961, 320-pg..15.00
Auto Vacuum Freezer Recipes, folded phamplet, 1910, 32-pg, VG..15.00
Avon International CB, hardbound, 1983, 95-pg...........................9.00
Baker's Best Chocolate Recipes, W Baker & Co, color illus, 1932, 60-pg.12.50
Better Homes & Gardens Best Buffets, 1st ed, 1963, 110 recipes....7.00
Better Homes & Gardens Jr CB, color cover, 1972 ed...................20.00
Better Homes & Gardens So-Good Meals, 1st ed, 1963.................5.00
Better Meals...Meatless Menus for Victory, Review & Herald Pub, 1930..22.00
Betty Crocker Hostess CB, 1st ed, 2nd printing, 1967...................10.00
Betty Crocker's 101 Delicious Bisquick..., General Mills, 1833, 32-pg.9.00
Book of Merry Eating, Food Editors of McCalls, softcover, 1989, 64-pg..6.00
Boston Cooking School CB, Fannie Merritt Farmer, 1916, 648-pg, VG.25.00
Bubby's CB, Jody Cameron, Berkeley Medallion, 1971, 150 recipes.7.00
Calendar of Dinners w/615 Recipes, MH Neil, w/Story of Crisco, 1917, G..15.00
Casserole Cookery, Tracy, Viking Press, 1952, 154-pg.....................8.00
CB for Family Camping, Williams, Golden Press, paperback, 1972, 180-pg.7.50
Chinese Stand-Up CB, B Frank, PSI Assoc, wire spiral, 1986.........8.00
Coffee Cuisine, D De Lorne, MacMillan, softcover, 1972, 125-pg..5.00
Complete Book of Mexican..., EL Ortiz, M Evans, 3rd printing, 1967.15.00

Cooking Is Easy: Hostess Handbook, Grace Kohl, blk/wht illus, 1939..22.00
Cow Brand Baking Soda CB, Dwight's Baking Soda, 1916, 33-pg, G..10.00
Creative Cook, Campbell Soup Co, red hard cover, 1978, 172-pg.12.50
Creative Holiday Recipes, Pillsbury Classics No 22, 1982 ....9.50
Dainty Desserts for Dainty People, Knox Gelatin, mc illus, 1924, 41-pg..16.50
Diet for a Small Planet, FM Lappe, Ballantine, 1977 revised ed, 411-pg.8.50
Duham's Cocoanut...Desserts, Mrs Sarah Tyson Rorer, 1900, 32-pg, VG .20.00
Electric Epicure's CB, Poppy Cannon, Crowell, 1961, 340-pg 25.00
Enterprising Housekeeper, HL Johnson, 1906, 96-pg, VG.............30.00
Fish 'N Fowl CB, Food Editors of McCalls, softcover, 1978, 64-pg .6.00
Fleichmann's Recipes, 1916, 48-pg, G 12.00
Fondue CB, Ed Callahan Pacific Productions, 1968, 5½x8¼" 13.00
Fun-Filled Butter Cookie CB, Pillsbury, color wraps, no date, 48-pg .8.50
FW McNess' CB, Furst-McMess Co, recipes in 15 languages, 1933..38.00
Glorious Stew, D Ivens, Harper & Row, cloth cover, 1st ed, 1969 .13.00
Gold Metal Flour CB, Washburn-Crosby Co, 1904, 70-pg, G-..12.00
Good Housekeeping's Book of Cookies, Chicago, softcover, 1958, 68-pg.14.50
Grace Harelty's Southern CB, Doubleday, 1st ed, 1976, w/dust jacket .40.00
Graham Kerr CB, Galloping Gourmet, Doubleday, 8th printing, 1969 .9.00
Great Chicken Recipes, Family Circle, Cowles Ed Corp, hardcover, 1968 .8.00
Henry's Household Companion, JF Henry & Co, 1880s, 32-pg, EX .30.00
Housewife's Library, Hubbard Bros, 1883, 644-pg, VG+ 75.00
How To Use Spices, Watkins, color wraps, 1958.............................9.50
Ida Bailey Allen's Time-Saving CB, Rand McNally, 1940, 192-pg.12.50
International CB, Margaret Heywood, 1929 ....20.00

Jell-O The Dainty Dessert,
1905, $75.00. (Photo courtesy
Colonel Bob Allen)

Jewish Cookery, LW Leonard, Crown Pub, dust jacket, 1949/1975 .12.50
Josie McCarthy's TV Recipe Book, 1st ed, Prentice Hall, 1958, 250-pg..18.00
Kerr Home Canning Book, c 1945, 50+pgs, 6½x9½" 6.00
Kraft CB, Kraft Kitchens, 3-ring binder, 3rd printing, 1978, 224-pg..15.00
Ladies Aid CB, B Vaughan, S Green Press, blk/wht illus, 1971, 186-pg..15.00
Le Chocolate, M Jolly (translated), Pantheon, w/jacket, 1985, 149-pg .20.00
Learn To Bake You'll Love It, General Foods, c 1947 ....5.00
M Rudkin Pepperidge Farm CB, Grosset & Dunlap, 1963/1981 printing ..15.00
Micro Menus CB, Whirlpool, Meredith Corp, 1982, 192-pg............8.50
Milk Made Candies, Evaporated Milk Assoc, 1951, 15-pg, 6x9"...14.00
Mr & Mrs Roto-Broil CB, blk/wht illus, 1953, 256-pg, EX 12.00
Our New CB & Household Receipts, S Annie Frost, 1883, 454-pg, VG..100.00
Passion for Chocolate, Bernachon, translated, 1st ed, 1989, 397-pg.20.00
Penn Family Recipes, hardbound, dust jacket, 1966, 213-pg, EX ..19.00
Peter Hunt's Cape Cod CB, Gramercy Pub, c 1954 & 1962, 181-pg .11.50
Pillsbury's 14th Grand Nat'l..., color wraps, no date (1963), 96-pg..10.00
Practical CB, Mrs Bliss, 1850, 273-pg, VG 175.00
Pure Food CB, Mrs Mary J Lincoln (editor), 1907, 79-pg, VG 25.00
Quaker Oats Teen Cooks CB, 1930s, 39-pg booklet, 5½x4⅜" 12.00
Ransom's Family Receipt Book 1912, D Ransom, orange cover, 1912, 32-pg.12.50
Rawleigh's Good Health Guide Almanac CB, products/recipes/hints, 1925..8.00
Rumford CB, Fannie Merritt Farmer, 1908, 48-pg, VG 22.00

Rumford Common Sense CB, LH Wallace, Rumford, 1920, 64-pg .10.00
Rumford Complete CB, hardbound, 1950, 215-pg, 5x7½" 16.00
See & Do Book of Cooking..., HJ Fletcher, c 1959, dust cover, 100-pg..10.00
Simple New England..., E Beilenson, Peter Pauper Press, 1962, 62-pg..10.00
Smorgasbord CB, AO Coombs, AA Wyn Ny, 3rd printing, 1949, 240-pg..9.50
Spice Sampler CB, EM Barber, 1st ed, 1950, 62-pg, 5½x8½", EX..17.00
Tempting Low-Calorie Recipes, M De Proft, Culinary Arts Inst, 1965..6.50
Vinegar Book, E Thacker, Treco Pub, 6th ed, 1995, 66-pg 8.50
Vital Foods for Health..., B Jensen, C 1950, 11th printing, 1962 ....8.00
White House CB, Zeimann & Gillette, Saalfield, 1904, 590-pg, G..30.00
20th Century CB Candy Making, 1st ed, Geographical Publishing, 1921..19.00

Cookie Cutters

Early hand-fashioned cookie cutters have recently been command-ing stiff prices at country auctions, and the ranks of interested collectors are growing steadily. Especially valuable are the figural cutters; and the more complicated the design, the higher the price. A follow-up of the carved wooden cookie boards, the first cutters were probably made by itinerant tinkers from leftover or recycled pieces of tin. Though most of the eighteenth-century examples are now in museums or collections, it is still possible to find some good cutters from the late 1800s when changes in the manufacture of tin resulted in a thinner, less expensive material. The width of the cutting strip is often a good indicator of age; the wider the strip, the older the cutter. While the very early cutters were 1" to 1½" deep, by the '20s and '30s, many were less than ½" deep. Crude, spotty soldering indicates an older cutter, while a thin line of sol-der usually tends to suggest a much later manufacture. The shape of the backplate is another clue. Later cutters will have oval, round, or rectan-gular backs, while on the earlier type the back was cut to follow the lines of the design. Cookie cutters usually vary from 2" to 4" in size, but gin-gerbread men were often made as tall as 12". Birds, fish, hearts, and tulips are common; simple versions can be purchased for as little as $12.00 to $15.00. The larger figurals, especially those with more imaginative details, often bring $75.00 and up. The cookie cutters listed here are tin and handmade unless noted otherwise.

Baby chicken, flat bk, ca 1930, 3¾x5" 25.00
Baker Man, flat bk, ca 1930, 5x3"..25.00
Bird, aluminum, red riveted hdl, Holey Tole, VG..........................18.00
Bird, flat bk, 4½x3" 25.00
Bird in flight, w/bk & strap hdl, 3¾x2½".....................................20.00
Bird w/long neck, flat bk, 5" 40.00
Bunny, ca 1880, 7½x4¼" 45.00
Bunny, flat bk, no hdl, 1920s, 2⅝" 22.50
Chick, flat bk, soldered loop hdl, 1930s, 2½x2½"..........................13.00
Chick, flat bk, strap hdl, ca 1930, 3¾x5" 20.00
Chicken, flat bk, no hdl, 1920s, 2x2"..22.50
Chicken, flat bk, 3x4" 30.00
Church w/2 Gothic arches, window in steeple, hdl, 6¼x1½" 110.00
Crescent moon, mk Nutbrown Product...England, 1930s, 3"...........8.50
Cupid, red plastic, Amscan-Harrison...Hong Kong, 4x3"................8.00
Davis Baking Powder, horse, open bk, 3¾x3" 35.00
Diamond w/scalloped edge, aluminum, gr wood hdl, 3⅜x2¼" 12.50
Donald Duck, yel plastic, Hallmark, 1970s, 4½", MIP 18.00
Dutchman, w/bk & strap hdl, 5¼x2¾" 40.00
Eagle, stylized, flat bk, 6"...65.00
Elephant, Campaign Cookie Cutter, 1920s, EXIB 25.00
Elephant, flat bk, loose seams, 7¼"...85.00
Elf w/pointed hat, no hdl, 8¾x3¾x½"...55.00
Fish, flat bk, 2¼x4"...40.00
Formay Shortening, rabbit, aluminum, 6" 25.00
Gingerbread man, red plastic, Betty Crocker, 3⅞".........................15.00

Gingerbread man, stamped Nutbrown Product...England, 1930s, 5"..20.00
Guitar, flat bk, 1¾x4" 45.00
Hansel & Gretel, red plastic, w/house, witch & tree, 1947, NMIB .25.00
Heart, appl hdl, 6x4¾" 55.00
Heinz pickle, loop hdl, 5½" 8.50
High-heeled boot, handmade, 1800s, 4⅝" 45.00
Horse, flat bk, primitive, 7¾" 105.00
Horse, flat bk, 4x7" 70.00
International Harvester, logo in mold, 3" dia 13.50
Lady w/long skirt, flat bk, 4" 50.00
Leslie's Baking Powder, circle, metal w/wrapped hdl, 3½" 25.00
Lizard, hdl, 3⅛x6½" 45.00
Man, metal, Germany, 5¾" 50.00
Man & woman, flat bk, 5", pr 40.00
Man w/hat, flat bk, 9⅞" 50.00
Man w/hat, standing, flat bk, German mk, 5¾", from $45 to........55.00
Noah's Ark w/dove in corner, 10x7½x⅜" 50.00
Penguin standing, w/bk & strap hdl, 3⅝x2½" 25.00
Powder flask, 4x2⅛x1½" 60.00
Rabbit running, w/bk & strap hdl, 4x2⅛" 18.00
Reindeer, rectangular bk, appl hdl, 6¼x4¾" 65.00
Rnd cutter w/multiple shapes inside, flat bk, 6¼" dia 65.00
Rocking horse, flat bk, hdl, 10x14¼" 200.00
Rooster, flat bk, 2x3" 23.50
Sailor in profile, no hdl, 10" 155.00
Santa, open bk, no hdl, Germany, 8½x4⅛" 55.00
Santa head, red plastic, Aunt Chicks, 5x3" 8.00
Santa w/bag, aluminum, gr wood hdl, 3½", from $10 to............15.00
Santa w/Christmas tree, rectangular bk, lg hdl, 6¼x3¼" 85.00
Scalloped circle, aluminum, gr wood hdl, 2⅝" dia....................12.50
Scalloped circle, strap hdl, 4" dia 25.00
Stag, stylized, flat bk, 6½" 135.00
Swan, w/bk & strap hdl, 2⅞x2¾" 35.00
Swan's Down, heart, aluminum, flat bk, 2½x2¾" 15.00
Tulip w/scalloped leaf, flat bk, 4¾" 50.00
Turkey, aluminum, hdl, 3x4" 5.00
Turkey w/tail wide, flat bk, no hdl, 1870s, 4½" 55.00
Uncle Sam, flat bk, GMTCo Germany, 12⅝" 600.00
Witch on broomstick, copper-colored aluminum, 5¼" 17.00
5 shapes on rolling type, aluminum, Made in West Germany, 3½x2¼".32.50

Cookie Jars

The appeal of the cookie jar is universal; folks of all ages, both male and female, love to collect 'em! The early '30s heavy stoneware jars of a rather nondescript nature quickly gave way to figurals of every type imaginable. Those from the mid to late '30s were often decorated over the glaze with 'cold paint,' but by the early '40s underglaze decorating resulted in cheerful, bright, permanent colors and cookie jars that still have a new look fifty years later.

Stimulated by the high prices commanded by desirable cookie jars, a broad spectrum of 'new' cookie jars are flooding the marketplace in three categories: 1) Manufactures have expanded their lines with exciting new designs specifically geared toward attracting the collector market. 2) Limited editions and artist-designed jars have proliferated. 3) Reproductions, signed and unsigned, have pervaded the market, creating uncertainty among new collectors and inexperienced dealers. One of the most troublesome reproductions is the Little Red Riding Hood jar marked McCoy. Several Brush jars are being reproduced, and because the old molds are being used, these are especially deceptive. In addition to these reproductions, we've also been alerted to watch for cookie jars marked Brush-McCoy made from molds that Brush never used. Remember that none of Brush's cookie jars were

marked Brush-McCoy, so any bearing the compound name is fraudulent. For more information on cookie jars and reproductions, we recommend *The Collector's Encyclopedia of Cookie Jars, Books I, II,* and *III,* by Fred and Joyce Roerig; they are listed in the Directory under South Carolina. Another good source is *An Illustrated Guide to Cookie Jars, Books I* and *II,* by Ermagene Westfall. Our advisors for this category are Fred and Joyce Roerig; they are listed in the Directory under South Carolina.

The examples listed below were made by companies other than those found elsewhere in this book; see also specific manufacturers.

Apple, red glossy, unmk Pantry Parade 25.00
Ark, Treasure Craft c Made in USA on lid 60.00
Avon Cookie Jar, lady at door..125.00
Badcock Cookies, cylinder, fired-on decal on bottom, 1993.........35.00
Bear, brn w/pk ft pads, #896, California Originals 35.00
Bear on Blocks, ABC Cookies (on blocks), 1967 ....275.00
Bud, Army man, brn, RRPCo, 1942-43, 12", from $150 to.........175.00
Bugs Bunny, on tree stump, c Warner Bros Inc 1981 ....375.00
Buick Convertible, Appleman, 1981-87 ....1,000.00
Calypso Mammy, fruit on apron & turban, Made in Indonesia 50.00
Case Steam Engine, 150th Anniversary, 1992 ltd ed..................125.00
Catfish, Clay Art, 1990 ....45.00
Chef, Lot'sa Goodies on brn apron, WH Hirsch Mfg...................275.00
Children on Windmill, flower finial, mk Tulip Tyme 19261 ....45.00
Churn, red & gr flower on brn, mk USA (American Bisque), 1958..35.00
Churn Boy, unmk Regal China...375.00
Cinderella, JC Napco 1957 K2292 ....175.00
Coffeepot, brn w/gold, Treasure Craft c Made in USA 25.00
Cookie Monster, c Muppets Inc Newcor USA..............................45.00
Cooky Girl, Os in Cooky are eyes, unmk 50.00
Corn, yel & gr, Terrace Ceramics USA 4299 ....45.00
Cow in Overalls, cream w/red & blk, mk USA APCO 35.00
Cow Jumped Over Moon, unmk RRPCo, 1949, 1957-59, 11", $125 to .150.00
Cow on Moon, mk J 2 USA, Doranne of California 375.00
Daisy Cow, copyright OCI (Omnibus) 60.00
Davy Crockett, raccoon on stump beside, Sierra Vista, 10⅞"..1,200.00
Derby Dan, Pfaltzgraff Pottery Co..250.00
Dog on Drum, Sierra Vista California...50.00
Dog w/Cookie, Snoopy-like, yel hat lid, Japan.............................25.00
Donald Duck, cylinder, Walt Disney, California Originals 50.00
Dutch Girl, gold trim, RRPCo Roseville Ohio, 1956, 12", from $250 to .275.00

Elephant, Sierra Vista California, from $100.00 to $125.00. (Photo courtesy Joyce and Fred Roerig)

Famous Amos, cookie bag, Treasure Craft 75.00
Fat Lady, Fitz & Floyd, mc c OCI, from $100 to.............................125.00
Gigantic Clown, Maurice of Calif USA JA 10 ....225.00

Gingerbread House, brn w/gr & wht, unmk Hirsch Mfg...............60.00
Glass Bowl Santa, tummy is glass, Treasure Craft...USA.............195.00
Goose, red vest & gr bow tie, Made in Mexico on paper label......40.00
Haunted House, Fitz & Floyd c FF 1987, from $150 to 175.00
Hen w/Basket of Eggs, wht w/mc, mk CJ 103, Doranne of California, 1984..50.00
Hen w/Chick, mc, mk USA (American Bisque), 8⅞x9½", $100 to...125.00
Hobo, Treasure Craft Compton, California Made in USA............45.00
Hortense, lady w/wht apron, Hortense Tastesetter c Sigma.........175.00
Indian (chief), sgn R Nickerson, c 1950 Lane & Co..., 10⅛" 950.00
Jack in Box, mk USA (American Bisque), 1958 ....125.00
Jack Rabbit, gr, Doranne of California, 15" 50.00
John Deere Moline Ill, cylinder, USA, 8" 40.00
Ken-L-Ration Dog, F&F Mold & Die Works.........................140.00
Kitchen Witch, brn broom, bl apron, unmk..............................60.00
Kitten & Beehive, mk USA (American Bisque), 1958 ....45.00
Kittens & Yarn, mk ABC (American Bisque)............................75.00
Lamb, For My Little Lamb on tummy, DeForest of California......50.00
Log w/Squirrel, mk RRPCo Roseville O, from $250 to 300.00
Lunch box, dk & lt bl, unmk Doranne of California 45.00
Mammy, wht w/blk & bl details, Artistic Potteries Inc Calif USA 31 .675.00
Milk Can, After School Snacks, bell in lid, USA (American Bisque) ...60.00
Monk, brn robe, mk Japan 30.00
Moon Rocket, bl or gray, mk USA (American Bisque)...............325.00
Mother Goose, bl bonnet, yel apron w/bl dots, Gilner USA G-720 .300.00
Mother Goose, gr w/gold, mk CJ 16 USA, Doranne of California, 1960s .175.00
Mr & Mrs Pig Turnabout, unmk Am Pottery Co.......................225.00
Nick at Nite Television, Treasure Craft for Nickelodeon 600.00
Nun, brn & wht, WH Hirsch Mfg Co Calif USA 275.00
Owl, Fitz & Floyd Inc C MCMLXXVII FF, from $40 to................50.00
Paradise Bakery Logo, Ken Auster, 1890s-early 90s 175.00
Peck o' Cookies, chicken w/head down, William H Hirsch 175.00
Peter Peter Pumpkin Eater, gold trim, RRPCo, 1957-59, 8½", $225 to.250.00
Pig, brn w/'Goodies' on tummy, DeForest of California, 1956.....100.00
Pillsbury Best Flour Sack, Benjamin & Medwin, Taiwan, 1993 ....45.00

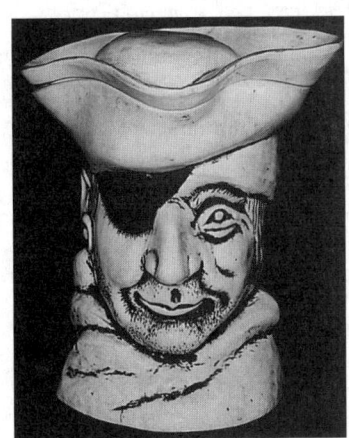

Pirate Bust, Treasure Craft c Made in USA, from $275.00 to $325.00. (Photo courtesy Joyce and Fred Roerig)

Polka Dot Kitty, mk Pat Design ABCO 131 USA.........................70.00
Porky Pig, in gr chair, Warner Bros, 1975 ....110.00
Professor Owl, brn, flower-like eyes, Japan 20.00
Rabbit in Basket, mk Patent Pending (early American Bisque) 45.00
Rabbit in Hat, brn w/mc details, DeForest of Calif c USA............50.00
Ranger Bear, DeForest of California 45.00
Rocking Chair Santa, mk 54-193 House of Lloyd for Christmas...35.00
Rocking Horse, Treasure Craft, c Made in USA 45.00
Santa, Scioto mold, Orig Sculpture by Don Winton...................225.00
Santa Head (Black), 50 Wolfe Studio, Cookie Jars Et Cetera.......60.00
Santa in Easy Chair, unmk Alberta's mold, Don Winton Creation .50.00
Seal, brn & tan, mk USA 17, Doranne of California 35.00

Sentry, guard w/in arch, mk #743 USA (American Bisque)..........95.00
Sheriff, brn stain, mk USA (California Originals).......................45.00
Sheriff Pig, glazed bottom, unmk RRPCo, 1954-59, 12", from $100 to .125.00
Smokey Bear, 50th Anniversary, Treasure Craft, 1994 ltd ed......500.00
Snoopy Doghouse, Benjamin & Medwin, c '58 '66 UFS, Made in Taiwan.40.00
Spaceship, space man finial, Napco....................................900.00
Special Angel, Richard Simmons through Fingerhut....................60.00
Sphinx, Luxor Las Vegas, Made in Thailand...............................50.00
Spuds, dog w/Mr Cookie on sweater, Taiwan 175.00
Stan Laurel, CW mk (Cumberland Ware), California Originals..775.00
Stella Strawberry, FKR 1942 PD & Co Inc 65.00
Strawberry Shortcake, Am Greetings Corp, MCML XXXIII 450.00
Tat-L-Tale, 'crier' in lid, Helen's Tat-L-Tale Helen Hutula Original ...750.00
Teakettle, blk, mk USA (American Bisque) 35.00
Thomas the Tank Engine & Friends, Schmid, Sri Lanka, 1994 ....70.00
Tigers, on striped cylinder, RRPCo Roseville OH 386.................50.00
Tom & Jerry, c Metro Goldwyn Mayer...1981, Made in Japan ...325.00
Train, smiling face, Sierra Vista California 65.00
Train Engine, Cookie RR on side, #200, ABC............................50.00
Wilbur the Blue Ribbon Pig, brn w/bl ribbon at neck, unmk........45.00
Wilma on the Telephone, mk USA (American Bisque), 11⅝" ..950.00
Wind in the Willows, cottage, Aeriel Inc '81 Sigma the Tastesetter .100.00
Windmill, bl & wht, mk FAPCo USA 25.00
Winnie the Pooh Hunny Pot, Walt Disney, #907, California Originals..175.00
Woody Woodpecker, c Walter Lantz...980 USA, California Originals.950.00
1957 Chevrolet, convertible, Made in Portugal 150.00

Cooper, Susie

A twentieth-century ceramic designer whose works are now attracting the attention of collectors, Susie Cooper was first affiliated with the A.E. Gray Pottery in Henley, England, in 1922 where she designed in lustres and painted items with her own ideas as well. (Examples of Gray's lustreware is rare and costly.) By 1930 she and her brother-in-law, Jack Beeson, had established a family business. Her pottery soon became a success, and she was subsequently offered space at Crown Works, Burslem. In 1940 she received the honorary title of Royal Designer for Industry, the only such distinction ever awarded by the Royal Society of Arts solely for pottery design. Miss Cooper received the Order of the British Empire in the New Year's Honors List of 1979. She was the chief designer for the Wedgwood group from 1966 until she resigned in 1972. After 1980 she worked on a free-lance basis until her death in July 1995.

Bowl, Glen Mist, 3¾x8"...55.00
Bowl, Swansea Spray, pk, 1½x6¼" 45.00
Bowl, vegetable; Dresden Spray, oval, 7x10" 60.00
Butter pat, Swansea Spray, 3"...50.00
Charger, Patricia Rose, 14½" 110.00
Coffee set, Kestrel, gr & tan bands, coffee jug+6 c/s...................300.00
Coffeepot, Black Fruit, w/gr lid..150.00
Coffeepot, Diablo (for Wedgwood), w/lid.................................120.00
Coffeepot, Dresden Spray, w/lid, 7½".......................................145.00
Coffeepot, Nebula Old Gold, w/lid, 8" 65.00
Coffeepot, Nosegay, Kestrel shape, 7".......................................450.00
Coffeepot, Tyrol, 8" 65.00
Coffeepot, Wedding Band, Kestrel shape, 7½".............................60.00
Cream jug & sugar basin, Sunflower, C2002 ....60.00
Creamer, Highland Grass, 3½"..40.00
Creamer, orange/yel/lemon/gray//blk bands, 3½" 45.00
Creamer, pk rose on bl, mk #8415, 2x4" 80.00
Cup & saucer, Crescent Sgraffito..70.00
Cup & saucer, Dresden Spray...85.00

Cups and saucers, orange, yellow, or turquoise with black circles, $45.00 each; Hand-painted vase, Jazz Age design, 7½", $380.00; Jug, Cubist pattern, Paris shape, 4¼", $280.00. (Photo courtesy J. David Ehrhard)

Cup & saucer, Patricia Rose......................................235.00
Cup & saucer, Pineapple, 2¼", 5"..............................25.00
Cup & saucer, Tiger Lily, demi...................................70.00
Egg cup, Dresden Spray, 1¾" from $25 to 35.00
Gravy boat, Susan's Red, 6"..60.00
Gravy boat, Swansea Spray, w/underplate 75.00
Jam jar, Foliage, abstract leaves in lav/peach/gr, 2½" 70.00
Jug, cottage scene, 1830-50, 5"...............................300.00
Jug, Dresden Spray, 4½"..100.00
Jug, milk; Susan's Red, 4"...80.00
Jug, milk; Swansea Spray, 5".......................................80.00
Jug, Tiger Lily, Kestrel shape, 4¼"..............................70.00
Jug, water; Crescent Sgraffito, 7"..............................300.00
Lamp, Nosegay, sq body & orig shade, 1932, 5¾x7¾x3" 145.00
Pitcher, stag & abstracts; bk: ram, 1930s, 8½x7" 300.00
Plate, Hampton, 7¾"..95.00
Plate, Longleaf, 6"..30.00
Plate, Longleaf, 7"..40.00
Plate, Patricia Rose, 10", from $40 to 60.00
Plate, ski scene on wht w/red & orange border, 5½" 245.00
Plate, stylized fox & trees, red border, 11½" 735.00
Platter, Corn Poppy, red rose w/2 bulbs on wht, oval, 14½x10"....40.00
Platter, Green Flowers, 16x12½" 60.00
Platter, Longleaf, oval, 10½x8¾"...............................60.00
Platter, mixed flowers in center, gr rim, 16x12½" 60.00
Soup bowl & plate, Tiger Lily.....................................55.00
Sugar bowl, Highland Grass, w/lid..............................65.00
Sugar bowl, pk rose on bl, w/hdls, open, mk #8415, 2x5"......85.00
Sugar bowl, Tiger Lily, open, 1¾x3½" dia....................65.00
Teapot, Dresden Spray, gr, Kestrel shape #1017, from $150 ....185.00
Teapot, Patricia Rose, pk rose on wht, #1844 ....310.00
Teapot, Polka Dot, w/drip plate 80.00
Tray, martini glass w/olive on cerulean bl, 2¼x7"........440.00
Tureen, Dresden Spray, Kestrel shape, w/lid, 8" dia 130.00
Tureen, Dresden Spray, 8"..125.00
Vase, blk & brn scrolls under matt aubergine glaze, 6x5¼".........165.00
Vase, Deco box & abstract decor on deep bl, 6¼x5"....................300.00

Coors

The firm that became known as Coors Porcelain Company in 1920 was founded in 1908 by John J. Herold, originally of the Roseville Pottery in Zanesville, Ohio. Though still in business today, they are best known for their artware vases and Rosebud dinnerware produced before 1939.

Coors vases produced before the late '30s were made in a matt finish; by the latter years of the decade, high-gloss glazes were also being used. Nearly fifty shapes were in production, and some of the more common forms were made in three sizes. Typical colors in matt are white, orange, blue, green, yellow, and tan. Yellow, blue, maroon, pink, and green are found in high gloss. All vases are marked with a triangular arrangement of the words 'Coors Colorado Pottery' enclosing the word 'Golden.' You may find vases (usually 6" to 6½") marked with the Colorado State Fair stamp and dated 1939. For such a vase, add $10.00 to the suggested values given below.

Our advisor for this category is Jo Ellen Winther; she is listed in the Directory under Colorado.

Rosebud

Apple baker, w/lid..55.00
Basket, 9¼"..60.00
Bowl, pudding; 2-pt, from $35 to 40.00
Bowl, vegetable; deep 35.00
Cake plate, from $40 to 45.00
Casserole, Dutch; lg...95.00
Cookie jar, deluxe, rope hdls, w/lid..........................110.00
Creamer, 3"...30.00
Cup & saucer...45.00
Dish, fruit/sauce 15.00
Egg cup...50.00
Pie plate, 10"..35.00
Pitcher, water; w/lid..150.00
Plate, used under muffin cover, 6"..............................35.00
Plate, 5"..8.00
Plate, 7", from $10 to..12.00
Platter, 12x9", from $42 to 48.00
Refrigerator set 130.00
Shakers, kitchen; slanted or pillar style, lg, pr.............65.00
Shakers, 2½", pr..85.00
Teapot, 2-cup..200.00
Tumbler, ftd or w/hdl, from $105 to.........................130.00
Water server, cork stopper, 6-cup.............................120.00

Miscellaneous

Cake knife, Hawthorne, decalcomania.......................90.00
Casserole, Open Window, decalcomania, str sides, w/lid, lg........125.00
Creamer, Mello-Tone or Rockmount...........................15.00
Cup & saucer, Mello-Tone or Rockmount 15.00
Mortar & pestle, cobalt...55.00
Pitcher, Open Window, decalcomania, w/lid lg 125.00
Shakers, Coorado, gr, pr..50.00
Shakers, Mello-Tone or Rockmount, pr.......................15.00
Stein, Rocky Mountain Legend series, 1993, M..........27.50
Teapot, Tulip, decalcomania.....................................150.00
Vase, Beehive, orange matt, sm rings, 6" 45.00
Vase, Brighton, yel matt, bulbous, 8"..........................70.00
Vase, bud; yel high gloss, 8".......................................30.00
Vase, Deco style, wht, low hdls, 12" 345.00
Vase, Golden, bl matt, integral hdls, 6"......................55.00
Vase, Golden, burgundy high gloss, integral hdls, 6"......45.00
Vase, Leadville, gr matt, angle hdls, 8"........................70.00
Vase, Matchless, gr matt, emb ribs, 8"........................70.00
Vase, Trinidad, wht matt w/turq int, hdls, 12" 125.00

Copper

Handcrafted copper was made in America from early in the eighteenth century until about 1850, with the center of its production in

Pennsylvania. Examples have been found signed by such notable coppersmiths as Kidd, Buchanan, Babb, Bently, and Harbeson. Of the many utilitarian items made, teakettles are the most desirable. Early examples from the eighteenth century were made with a dovetailed joint which was hammered and smoothed to a uniform thickness. Pots from the nineteenth century were seamed. Coffeepots were made in many shapes and sizes and along with mugs, kettles, warming pans, and measures are easiest to find. Stills ranging in sizes of up to fifty-gallon are popular with collectors today. Mary Frank Gaston has compiled a lovely book, *Antique Brass and Copper*, with many full-color photos and current market values.

Architectural element, lion's head, EX verdigris, Am, 19th C, 14x14" .375.00
Brandy warmer, conical, 12½" 225.00
Coffeepot, Deco-shaped cylinder, wood hdl/finial, 13" 150.00
Finial, pyramidal top, fluted shaft, floral decor, verdigris, 57" ..6,900.00
Flower holder, hammered, flower w/spiral for insert, hangs, 9" 50.00
Glue pot, brass hdls & burner attachment, electric, 6½" 150.00
Jar, emb rings, brass base & lid, tinned int, Deco style, 1920s, 5x4" .65.00
Jardiniere, repousse decor, ftd, Victorian, 25x28" 3,000.00
Kettle, apple butter; dvtl, iron hdl, lg...100.00
Kettle, broad, flat hdl, brass finial, English, 19th C, 8½x6" 225.00
Kettle, preserving; lg iron hdls, mid-1800s, 4x8" dia 150.00
Kettle, stewing; bail hdl, 5½x8"...160.00
Measure, haystack, dvtl, lg ear hdl, mk Gallon, crown mk w/in, 11"....275.00
Measure, hot liquid; stick hdl, 7" 150.00
Pail, jelly; tin lined, 11x12½" 325.00
Pan, roasting; dmn shape, English, 19th C, 7x27x20" 500.00
Pitcher, cylindrical, tin lined, mk, 1800s, 9" 65.00
Pitcher, milk; hinged lid, Russian, 19th C, 7½" 240.00
Planter, brass hdls & paw ft, 9x10" dia 175.00
Plaque, repousse classical figures & Nouveau flowers, English, 26x22"..550.00
Saucepan, dvtl, 8" dia..50.00
Shower head, pierced work around rim, 8" dia............................110.00
Teakettle, domed lid, brass finial, G Tryon, 11x7" dia.............1,150.00
Teakettle, dvtl, wrought iron tripod base & hdl, dome lid, dents, 11".55.00
Teakettle, gooseneck spout, domed lid w/brass finial, Hunneman..., 10"..460.00
Teakettle, gooseneck spout, hammered, mid-1800s, 11" 225.00

Teakettle, gooseneck spout, hinged copper handle marked Shindler, cone-shaped finial, five-quart, 11½x13¾", EX, $1,000.00. (Photo courtesy Horst Auctioneers)

Tray, emb berries & leaves, 20½x9¼" 160.00
Tray, warming; Alex Boyd & Son...London, 33x9½" 375.00
Warming oven, hinged lid, English, 11x23½"..............................500.00
Wash boiler, tin lid, Rochester, 13½x26½".................................165.00
Water jug, hammered w/dvtls, ovoid w/str neck, Mid-Eastern, 20" ..135.00

Copper Lustre

Copper lustre is a term referring to a type of pottery made in Staffordshire after the turn of the nineteenth century. It is finished in a metallic rusty-brown glaze resembling true copper. Pitchers are found in abundance, ranging from simple styles with dull bands of color to those with fancy handles and bands of embossed, polychromed flowers. Bowls are common; goblets, mugs, teapots, and sugar bowls much less so. It's easy to find, but not in good condition. Pieces with hand-painted decoration and those with historical transfers are the most valuable.

Bowl, banded monochrome floral motif, 5½"..................................35.00
Butter pat, cobalt & wht center scene, 4" 45.00
Commode, wht w/gold band at rim/bottom/hdl, floral spray decor, 5x10"..95.00
Creamer, bl & copper bands, horse & chariot scene, w/lid, 5" 100.00
Goblet, water; floral band on wht, 2-hdld, English, 1850s, 4½x6" ..55.00
Jug, bl & wht floral on yel w/yel band at top, 6" 40.00
Jug, bl band w/rose decor, bulbous w/tall flared neck, 5½" 90.00
Jug, cherub scenes, wht band at top, 1830s, 4½" 75.00
Jug, clock face, bk: Oriental figures, scroll hdl, ftd, 7⅝".............650.00
Jug, copper floral decor on bl band, 6¼" 45.00
Jug, Cornwallis resigns sword, bk: Lafayette, fruit spout, 6⅜", NM..1,400.00
Jug, lions decor, rpr, 7½"...100.00
Jug, man plays flute to lady, 7¼", NM...250.00
Master salt, bl band, ftd, English, 1840s, 2x3".............................70.00
Sherbet, floral band, 4"..55.00
Teapot, pk floral on wht band on body & lid, English, 1840s, 9" ..95.00
Vase, floral decor on bl band, English, 1840s, 3½x5" 45.00

Coralene Glass

Coralene is a unique type of art glass easily recognized by the tiny grains of glass that form its decoration. Lacy allover patterns of seaweed, geometrics, and florals were used, as well as solid forms such as fish, plants, and single blossoms. (Seaweed is most commonly found and not as valuable as the other types of decoration.) It was made by several glasshouses both here and abroad. Values are based to a considerable extent on the amount of beading that remains. Our advisors for this category are Betty and Clarence Maier; they are listed in the Directory under Pennsylvania.

Bowl, pk satin w/gold seaweed, Webb, 2⅞x4½" 400.00
Sweetmeat, pk Dmn Quilt w/yel-gold seaweed, Webb, metal mts, 4½"..500.00
Vase, bl cased satin w/mc floral, tapered neck, 4½"....................360.00
Vase, bl flowers w/gr leaves, amber highlights, appl 5-point ft, 5"..300.00
Vase, bl MOP Dmn Quilt w/mc butterfly & flowering branches, 9½" .400.00
Vase, cream w/allover orange coral, shouldered, 5"....................225.00
Vase, gr w/orange & pk floral, 5" 105.00
Vase, pk cased w/yel seaweed, bulbous w/long neck, 9¾" 635.00
Vase, pk Dmn Quilt MOP w/seaweed, stick neck, 6¾" 225.00
Vase, pk Moire MOP w/rows of sm bl/yel flowers, 4-lobe body, 8"..1,035.00

Vase, pink satin cased with yellow seaweed, 5x3½", NM, $260.00. (Photo courtesy James Julia)

Vase, pk satin w/yel seaweed, tapered neck, 12".........................750.00
Vase, pk Snowflake MOP w/gold snowflake coralene, slight loss, 5" .200.00
Vase, pk Snowflake MOP w/gold wheat & wht dotted rim, flat sides, 6" .225.00
Vase, pk/wht Dmn Quilt w/beading over mc floral decor, ruffled/ftd, 7"...345.00

Cordey

The Cordey China Company was founded in 1942 in Trenton, New Jersey, by Boleslaw Cybis. The operation was small with less than a dozen workers. They produced figurines, vases, lamps, and similar wares, much of which was marketed through gift shops both nationwide and abroad. Though the earlier wares were made of plaster, Cybis soon developed his own formula for a porcelain composition which he called 'Papka.' Cordey figurines and busts were characterized by old-world charm, Rococo scrolls, delicate floral appliqués, ruffles, and real lace which was dipped in liquefied clay to add dimension to the work.

Although on rare occasions some items were not numbered or signed, the 'basic' figure was cast both with numbers and the Cordey signature. The molded pieces were then individually decorated and each marked with its own impressed identification number as well as a mark to indicate the artist-decorator. Their numbering system began with 200 and in later years progressed into the 8000s. As can best be established, Cordey continued production until sometime in the mid-1950s. Boleslaw Cybis died in 1957, his wife in 1958.

Due to the increased availability of Cordey on the Internet over the last year, values of the more common pieces have fallen off. Our advisor for this category is Sharon A. Payne; she is listed in the Directory under Washington.

Key: ff — full figure

#312, bust of lady in pk shawl w/flowers exposed, mk MB Cybis, 8½"..60.00
#324, mallards, 14", pr..295.00
#861, wall sconces w/roses, pr 120.00
#1949, bust of lady, drilled for lamp, 7" 80.00
#4034, lady in lt bl dress w/pk roses, matching hat, ff, 8¼" 85.00
#5002, bust of lady in pk w/roses at base & in hair, 5¾" 45.00
#5005, bust of lady in pk w/bl roses at base & in hair, 6" 60.00
#5009, bust of lady, bl Fedora-style hat, 6" 45.00
#5011, bust of lady in wht w/lg collar, gold rose at base & hair, 6".45.00
#5020, bust of man in pk w/lg wht curls, 2 roses at base, 6½" 60.00
#5025, bust of lady, 6" 60.00
#5026, bust of Madonna w/wht shawl, gold at base, 6" 65.00
#5030, bust of lady in bl shawl w/pk roses, lg hat w/bl ribbon, 8" .70.00
#5034, Raleigh, bust of man, gr shirt, blk vest, 8½" 70.00
#5036, bust of lady in silver gown, bl hat w/pk roses, 8½" 85.00
#5037, bust of lady (¾) in bl dress w/red roses in hair, 9½" 65.00
#5042, Monsieur DuBarry, ff, bl coat, pk pants, 11"..................125.00
#5042, Victorian man, bl coat & pk breeches, 11" 125.00
#5051, bust of lady in cream dress, bl ribbon at neck, bl hat w/roses..75.00
#5054, bust of lady (¾) in wht w/roses at base & in hair, 9" 75.00
#5084, Madame DuBarry, in bl & pk, ff, 11" 125.00
#5138, bust of lady w/bl bow on dress & bl Fedora hat, Papka curls, 6" .65.00
Lamp, lady in kimono, 11¼" figure, 24½" overall 90.00
Lamps, ladies' high-button shoes, appl flowers, brass base, 30", pr.225.00

Corkscrews

The history of the corkscrew dates back to the mid-1600s, when wine makers concluded that the best-aged wine was that stored in smaller containers, either stoneware or glass. Since plugs left unsealed were often damaged by rodents, corks were cut off flush with the bottle top and sealed with wax or a metal cover. Removing the cork cleanly with none left to grasp became a problem. The task was found to be relatively simple using the worm on the end of a flintlock gun rod. So the corkscrew evolved. Endless patents have been issued for mechanized models. Handles range from carved wood, ivory, and bone to porcelain and repousse silver. Exotic materials such as agate, mother-of-pearl, and gold plate were also used on occasion. Celluloid ladies' legs are popular.

For further information, we recommend *The Ultimate Corkscrew Book* and *Bull's Pocket Guide to Corkscrews* by Donald Bull, our advisor for this category. He is listed in the Directory under Virginia. In the following descriptions, values are for examples in excellent condition, unless noted otherwise.

All-Ways Handy Combination, AW Stephens, MA, from $20 to..50.00
Barrel, chromed, closed, hdl mk Italy, from $30 to 40.00
Boar's head w/Walker 1893 Pat bell held by hollow tube over shank ..450.00
Clough, wooden sheath w/advertising, Oct 16, 1900, from $10 to ..50.00
Clough's 1876 Pat, mk Williamson's on wire wrap, 3¾" hdl, $25 to..35.00
Codd type, boxwood hdl, J&W Roper of Birmingham, from $100 to..150.00
Combination can opener, Vaughan, w/stamped price, from $5 to .10.00
Dbl lever, Magic Lever Cork Drawer, from $100 to 125.00
Figural, lady's legs, celluloid, mini, 1⅞", from $650 to 850.00
Figural, Mannekin Pis, holding worm w/1 or 2 hands, ea from $10 to .100.00
Figural, Scottie, folding tail in center, from $250 to 300.00
Finger pull, 2-finger, direct pull, unmk, from $20 to 30.00
Finger pull, 3-finger (eyebrow hdls), unmk, 2¼-3¼", ea, $5 to.....25.00
Flynut, brass, Edwin Jay Made in Italy, from $75 to....................100.00
Flynut champagne cork puller, from $30 to 50.00
Frame, ivory or bone hdl, unmk, mini, from $100 to...................300.00
Frame, John Coney's 1854 English Pat, 2-post, threaded stem, $700 to..1,000.00
Frame, Wulfruna, Stephen Plant's 1884 English Pat, from $150 to..200.00
Frame, 3-pillar w/ivory hand gripping bar, 19th C, $2,000 to ..3,000.00
Frame, 4-column, brass, hdl mk Italy, from $70 to 80.00
Nifty, beer advertising, from $10 to 50.00
Ornate cast fr w/spring & wood hdl, from $200 to 300.00
Ornate fr, verdigris w/gold-tone finish, roll-over hdl, from $80 to .100.00
Perfume opener, silver tiger-head hdl, Birmingham 1896, from $300 to .400.00
Picnic, brass hex head, machined-in cap lifter, unmk, from $25 to .35.00
Pocket, silver w/various hdls, English or Dutch, 19th C, from $900 to .1,500.00
Pocket folding, So-Ezy Made in USA Pat Pend, from $40 to........50.00
Pocket folding, Turkey Foot, cap lifter & sm spoon, from $125 to..150.00
Prong puller, swivel cap lifter, mk For Crown Corks...British Made...100.00
Sardine key, w/folding fork, from $150 to................................200.00
Scissors style, ornate German silver hdls, from $800 to 1,000.00
Single lever, Lund & Hipkins, single worm, 1854, from $100 to..250.00
Spring bbl w/paper-clip stop, W Sommers, Pat 1895, from $90 to..120.00
Spring type, all steel, unmk, from $60 to 100.00
Spring type, Dunisch & Scholer, Pat 1883, Am Walker hdl, $100 to..150.00
T-hdl, metal, clawfoot hdl w/bulbed shank, from $100 to 125.00
T-hdl, metal, slight 2-finger grip, mk Jacques Perille, from $100 to .150.00
T-hdl, trn ivory, unmk, 3-4½", ea, from $125 to........................150.00
Tusk hdl cvd w/cavorting putto vintners, ca 1900, 10½" 550.00
Waiter's friend, Davis Pat, knife blade atop hdl, from $125 to....175.00
Waiter's friend, w/bottle cap lifter, from $5 to...........................25.00
Whistle in sm horn hdl, Fr, from $100 to................................150.00
Williamson's Don't Swear, catalin sheath, from $25 to................50.00
Wm Rockwell Clough 1876 Pat, 2 pcs wrapped wire, from $15 to ..50.00
Wood dbl-action, Copex Made in France, from $30 to 40.00
15 Tools in One, Natian Jenkins, 1930, from $150 to 200.00

Cosmos

Cosmos, sometimes called Stemless Daisy, is a patterned glass tableware produced from 1894 through 1915 by Consolidated Lamp and Glass Company. Relief-molded flowers on a finely crosscut background were painted in soft colors of pink, blue, and yellow. Though nearly all were made of milk glass, a few items may be found in clear glass with the designs painted on. In addition to the tableware, lamps were also made.

Bottle, cologne; orig stopper, rare, from $275 to	300.00
Butter dish, 5x8"	275.00
Creamer	150.00
Lamp, bouquet; kerosene, 24"	575.00
Lamp, bouquet; slender base, rnd globe, all orig, 16"	525.00
Lamp, mini: 8", from $400 to	450.00
Lamp, 10"	450.00
Pickle castor, mk SP fr, from $600 to	700.00
Pitcher, milk; 5"	250.00
Pitcher, syrup; 6"	300.00
Pitcher, water; 9"	350.00
Shakers, tall, orig lids, pr	175.00
Spooner	125.00
Sugar bowl, open	150.00
Sugar bowl, w/lid	185.00
Sugar shaker	400.00
Tumbler, 3¾"	75.00

Cottageware

You'll find a varied assortment of novelty dinnerware items, all styled as cozy little English cottages or huts with cone-shaped roofs; some may have a waterwheel or a windmill. Marks will vary. English-made Price Brothers or Beswick pieces are valued in the same range as those marked Occupied Japan, while items marked simply Japan are considerably less pricey. Our advisor for this category is Grace Klender; she is listed in the Directory under Ohio. All of the following examples are Price Brothers/Kensington unless noted otherwise.

Bank, dbl slot, 4½x3½x5"	95.00
Bell, minimum value	150.00
Biscuit jar, wicker hdl, Maruhon Ware, Occupied Japan, 6½"	92.50
Bowl, salad	65.00
Butter dish	65.00
Butter dish, cottage int (fireplace), Japan, 6¾x5"	85.00
Butter dish, oval, Burlington Ware, 6"	60.00
Butter dish, rnd, Beswick, England, w/lid, 3½x6", from $75 to	100.00
Butter pat, emb cottage, rectangular, Occupied Japan	20.00
Chocolate pot	148.00
Condiment set, mustard, 2½" s&p on 5" hdld leaf tray	85.00
Condiment set, mustard pot, s&p, row arrangement, 6"	50.00
Condiment set, mustard pot, s&p, tray, row arrangement, 7¾"	50.00
Condiment set, 3-part cottage on shaped tray w/appl bush, 4½"	85.00
Cookie jar, pk/brn/gr, sq, Japan, 8½x5½"	75.00
Cookie jar, windmill, wicker hdl	165.00
Cookie jar/canister, cylindrical, rare sz, 8x3¾"	275.00
Cookie jar/canister, cylindrical, 8½x5"	140.00
Cookie/biscuit jar, Occupied Japan	95.00
Creamer, windmill, Occupied Japan, 2⅝"	30.00
Creamer & sugar bowl, 2½x4½"	50.00
Cup & saucer, chocolate; str-sided cup, 3½x2¾", 5½"	45.00
Cup & saucer, 2½", 4½"	50.00
Demitasse pot	110.00
Dish w/cover, Occupied Japan, sm	40.00
Egg cup set, 4 on 6" sq tray	65.00
Gravy boat & tray, rare	275.00
Grease jar, Occupied Japan, from $25 to	38.00

Hot water pot, Westminster, England, 8½x4"	50.00
Marmalade	45.00
Marmalade & jelly, 2 conjoined houses	85.00
Mug, 3⅞"	55.00
Pin tray, 4" dia	22.00

Pin tray, 5", $22.00; Teapot, 6¼", $65.00.

Pitcher, emb cottage, lg flower on hdl	150.00
Pitcher, tankard; rnd, 7⅞"	138.00
Platter, oval, 11¾x7½"	65.00
Reamer, Japan	65.00
Sugar box, for cubes, 5¾" L	50.00
Tea set, Japan, child's, serves 4	165.00
Teapot, Keele Street, w/creamer & sugar	95.00
Teapot, Occupied Japan, 6½"	60.00
Teapot, Ye Olde Fireside, Occupied Japan, 9x5"	85.00
Toast rack, 3-slot, 3½"	75.00
Toast rack, 4-slot, 5½"	85.00
Tumbler, Occupied Japan, 3½", set of 6	65.00

Coverlets

The Jacquard attachment for hand looms represented a culmination of weaving developments made in France. Introduced to America by the early 1820s, it gave professional weavers the ability to easily create complex patterns with curved lines. Those who could afford the new loom adaptation could now use hole-punched pasteboard cards to weave floral patterns that before could only be achieved with intense labor on a draw-loom.

Before the Jacquard mechanism, most weavers made their coverlets in geometric patterns. Use of indigo-blue and brightly colored wools often livened the twills and overshot patterns available to the small-loom home weaver. Those who had larger multiple-harness looms could produce warm double-woven, twill-block, or summer-and-winter designs.

While the new floral and pictorial patterns' popularity had displaced the geometrics in urban areas, the mid-Atlantic, and the Midwest by the 1840s, even factory production of the Jacquard coverlets was disrupted by cotton and wool shortages during the Civil War. A revived production in the 1870s saw a style change to a center-medallion motif, but a new fad for white 'Marseilles' spreads soon halted sales of Jacquard-woven coverlets. Production of Jacquard carpets continued to the turn of the century.

Rural and frontier weavers continued to make geometric-design coverlets through the nineteenth century, and local craft revivals have continued the tradition through this century. All-cotton overshots were factory produced in Kentucky from the 1940s, and factories and professional weavers made cotton-and-wool overshots during the past decade. Many Jacquard-woven coverlets have dates and names of places and people (often the intended owner — not the weaver) woven into corners or borders. In the listings that follow, examples are blue and white and in excellent condition unless noted otherwise. When dates are included, they appear on the coverlet itself as part of the woven design.

Key: mdl — medallion   vt — variant

Jacquard

Agriculture...Independence mottos, borders: eagle/Masonic/deer, 78x79"..**700.00**
Bird of Paradise corners, red/wht, 1-pc, lt stains, 86x76".............**415.00**
Central rayed mdl/foliage, red/lt & dk olive/natural, Beiderwand, 86"..**300.00**
Double Rose & Tie, tulip border, summer/winter dbl weave, sgn/1839, NM..**500.00**
Floral grid, natural/navy/salmon, IN, 1860s, 2-pc, dbl weave, 86x75"..**360.00**
Floral mdl, navy/red/gr/natural, Biederwand, 1854, rprs, 58x86"..**550.00**
Floral mdl, red/bl/gr/cream, A Kump, PA, 1852, 90x81".............**800.00**
Floral mdl/triangles, gr/red, 1-pc, summer/winter, sm rpr, 78x84"..**440.00**
Floral mdls, eagle/flower border, navy/natural, dbl weave, 84"....**400.00**
Floral mdls, mustard/salmon/navy/natural, Bierderwand, 1-pc, 84x96"..**485.00**
Floral mdls, natural/navy/red/gr, PA, 1842, 1-pc, 67x100", VG ..**385.00**
Floral mdls, princess feathering, 1848, 2-pc, rprs, 68x83"............**250.00**
Floral mdls & dbl borders, wht/gr/dk & med bl, 2-pc, dbl weave, 74x84"...**500.00**
Floral mdls w/hearts & grapevines, bl/red/wht, MD, 2-pc, 84x87"...**325.00**
Floral mdls w/vining tulip border, 4-color, sgn/1842, 92x71", VG ..**440.00**
Floral mdls/borders, bl/red/wht, 2-pc, OH, 1850, 72x79"............**500.00**
Floral mdls/dmns/stars, natural/gr/bl/red, PA, 1865, 1-pc, 78x81", G..**300.00**
Floral mdls/strawberry pot borders, red/gr/wht, 2-pc, 1848, 72x76"..**415.00**

Floral medallions and stars, double-row floral border with star corners, red, navy blue, olive-tan, and natural white, one-piece, single weave, dated 1857, 78x85", moth damage and stains, $385.00.

Floral mdls/sunbursts, gr/bl/red/wht, OH, 1855, 2-pc, 71x90", VG ..**440.00**
Floral mdls/sunbursts, natural/navy/red/olive, OH, 1845, 2-pc, 72x88"...**600.00**
Flowers/grapes/eagles/leaves, bl/red/brn/wht, 2-pc, 1843, 77x90", G.**250.00**
Flowers/stars/birds, navy/bl/faded bl, sgn/1840, 2-pc, 94x80".......**385.00**
Geometrics, pine tree border, dbl weave, fringe loss/sm hole, 82x90".**300.00**
Independence Hall/Masonic symbols/etc, 1826, 82x98"............**1,950.00**
Leaf mdl (20)/vine borders, 5-color 2-pc single, rpr/stains, 80x95" ..**700.00**
Leaf mdls/stars/dmns/tulips, red/bl/yel/natural, 1-pc, 1846, 76x91", G.**300.00**
Lilies/star mdl, eagles/birds/willow tree borders, dbl weave, 86x76".**715.00**
Mdls amid seaweed & conch shells, navy/wht, 2-pc, IN, 1850s, 88x80"..**550.00**
Roses mdls, 1837, 2-pc, dbl weave, rprs, 74x82".........................**330.00**
Snowflake & rose center, eagle/tree border, 1837, 98x83"............**550.00**
Star mdl/tulips/roses, wht/navy/burgundy/olive, 1-pc, 69x77", G ..**275.00**
Star/rose mdls, Piqua 8X ea side/1848 in corners, 2-pc, rpr, 74x85"....**880.00**
Tulip mdls, vine borders, 2-pc dbl, lt stains/rstr, 78x78" **110.00**
Windows vt w/pine tree border, coral/dk bl/naural, dbl weave, G .**235.00**

Overshot

Diamond bands, natural/salmon/navy, 2-pc, 51x72" **85.00**
Grid pattern, red/navy/gr, wavy border, rpr, 78x82" **200.00**
Navy/salmon red/aqua on natural, edge ware, 78xx72" **275.00**

Optic, natural/pk-red/navy, fringe, 68x78" **415.00**
Optic (intricate), natural/purple/cinnamon, 74x106" **495.00**
Optical geometric, red/bl/wht, fringe, 2-pc, dbl weave, 68x78"..**450.00**
Plaid, natural/butterscotch, CT, 2-pc, fringe, 78x88", VG..........**250.00**
Sm blocks: 5 sqs & geometric borders, summer/winter, rebound, 94x74" ..**220.00**
6-sq blocks alternate w/sqs of wavy lines, red/dk bl/teal, wht, 84x67" ..**275.00**

Cowan

Guy Cowan opened a small pottery near Cleveland, Ohio, in 1913, where he made tile and artware on a small scale from the natural red clay available there. He developed distinctive glazes — necessary, he felt, to cover the dark red body. After the war and a temporary halt in production, Cowan moved his pottery to Rocky River, where he made a commercial line of artware utilizing a highly fired white porcelain. Although he acquiesced to the necessity of mass production, every effort was made to insure a product of highest quality. Fine artists, among them Waylande Gregory, Thelma Frazier, and Viktor Schreckengost, designed pieces which were often produced in limited editions, some of which sell today for prices in the thousands. Most of the ware was marked 'Cowan,' except for the 1930 mass-produced line called 'Lakeware.' Falling under the crunch of the Great Depression, the pottery closed in 1931.

The use of an asterisk (*) in the listing below indicates a nonfactory name that is being provided as a suggested name for the convenience of present-day collectors. One example is the glaze *Original Ivory, which is a high-gloss white that resembles undecorated porcelain. It was used on many of Cowan's lady 'flower figures' (Cowan's more graceful term for what some collectors call frogs).

Our advisor for this category is Mark Bassett; he is listed in the Directory under Ohio. With Victoria Naumann, Mark is the author of *Cowan Pottery and the Cleveland School*, a detailed history of Cowan Pottery and of Guy Cowan's students, colleagues, and designers. Our prices are for marked examples in mint condition, unless noted otherwise.

Ashtray, Ram, E Eckhardt, Oriental Red, #T-2, 5¼" **300.00**
Bookends, Boy & Girl, F Wilcox, *Original Ivory, #519, 6½" **375.00**
Bookends, Sunbonnet Girls, K Jenkins, Antique Green, #521, 7½".**375.00**
Bowl, Debutante, W Gregory, April, 6-petal leaf shape, #946, 11"..**150.00**
Candelabrum, Swirl Dancer (figure), RG Cowan, Special Ivory, #745, 9"..**650.00**
Candlesticks, Figural Pr, RG Cowan, Special Ivory, #744-L, #744-R, 12"..**1,500.00**
Candlesticks, Unicorn, W Gregory, Caramel, #970, 5½", pr **300.00**
Compote, Normandy, RG Cowan, Black/Silver, #834-A, 7x4¼x2¼"...**140.00**
Creamer & sugar bowl on tray, Colonial, Special Ivory, #X-24/25/33 ..**120.00**
Decanter, Arabian Night, #X-16, 10½", +4 matching cups **500.00**
Figurine, flamingo, W Gregory, ivory gloss, 11" **400.00**
Figurine, Nocturne (Radio Figure), Special Ivory, att Sinz, 9x7" ..**5,000.00**
Figurine, Torso, W Gregory, Parchment, rstr glaze, 17½".........**1,500.00**
Flower frog, Awakening, RG Cowan, Special Ivory, #F-8, 9" **650.00**
Flower frog, Duet, RG Cowan, Special Ivory, #685, 7½" **400.00**
Flower frog, Kneeling Nude, W Sinz, *Original Ivory, no mk, 6".**500.00**
Flower frog, Laurel, RG Cowan, *Original Ivory, #721, 10"........**800.00**
Flower frog, Mayflower Stag, W Gregory, Special Ivory, #905, 8¼".**500.00**
Flower frog, Swirl Dancer, RG Cowan, *Original Ivory, #720, 10"..**850.00**
Humidor, 6-sided w/goat finial, E Eckhardt, Oriental Red, 8".....**300.00**
Lamp, Art Deco Nude, W Gregory, Shadow White, #433, 11"...**750.00**
Lamp, Foliage, #L-16, 13" **200.00**
Lamp, Larkspur, #419, 12"...**160.00**
Lamp, Peach, RG Cowan, #L-22 (based on shape #V-47), 11½".**250.00**
Lamp, Squirrel & Pheasant, W Gregory, Peach, #L-17 (shape #V-19), 9".**350.00**
Lamp base, emb maple-like leaves, Shadow White, 12x7"..........**250.00**
Lamp base, emb upright leaves, Antique Green, ftd, 11x7" **225.00**
Paperweight, Elephant, M Postgate, Black, #D-3, 4½" **450.00**
Plaque, Arabesque, W Atchley, Drypoint Guava & Black, #X-10-B, 11"...**500.00**

Plaque, Hunt, V Schreckengost, Russet Brown, #X-44, 11½" .**1,200.00**
Strawberry jar, RG Cowan, April Green #SJ-3, 12" **450.00**
Trivet, Floral Vines, Special Ivory, #X-19.............................**85.00**
Vase, Arabian, RG Cowan, #V-30, 4¾" **100.00**
Vase, Azure, #546, 6" **100.00**
Vase, bud; Sea Horse, Delphinium, #725, 7½"......................**65.00**
Vase, Chinese Bird Vase, RG Cowan, Special Ivory, #747, 11¼".**375.00**
Vase, Copper, #544, 6" **120.00**
Vase, Delphinium, #509, no mk, 9½"..................................**80.00**
Vase, Delphinium, #649-A, 6¾"..**60.00**
Vase, Floral Fan, Egyptian Blue, #755, 8¾"...........................**90.00**
Vase, Foliage, #V-15, 12" **275.00**
Vase, Foliage, #916, 7" **130.00**

Vase, Logan, Larkspur,
#649-B,   8¼x7x3",
$125.00.

Vase, Maple Leaf, W Gregory, Caramel, #V-32, 11" **300.00**
Vase, Mother o' Pearl, RG Cowan, #822, 9" **200.00**
Vase, Oriental Red, strong mottling, #V-25, 6¾" **225.00**
Vase, Squirrel & Pheasant, W Gregory, Mother o' Pearl, #V-19, 9".**700.00**
Vase, 2 Deco hdls, Azure, #V-63, 10¾" **200.00**

Cracker Jack

Kids have been buying Cracker Jack since it was first introduced in the 1890s. By 1912 it was packaged with a free toy inside. Before the first kernel was crunched, eager fingers had retrieved the surprise from the depth of the box — actually no easy task, considering the care required to keep the contents so swiftly displaced from spilling over the side! Though a little older, perhaps, many of those same kids still are looking — just as eagerly — for the Cracker Jack prizes. Point of sale, company collectibles, and the prizes as well have over the years reflected America's changing culture. Grocer sales and incentives from around the turn of the century — paper dolls, postcards, and song books — were often marked Rueckheim Brothers (the inventors of Cracker Jack) or Reliable Confections. Over the years the company made some changes, leaving a trail of clues that often help collectors date their items. The company's name changed in 1922 from Rueckheim Brothers & Eckstein (who had been made a partner for inventing a method for keeping the caramelized kernels from sticking together) to The Cracker Jack Company. Their Brooklyn office was open from 1914 until it closed in 1923. The first time the sailor Jack logo was used on their packaging was in 1919. The sailor image of a Rueckheim child (with red, white, and blue colors) was introduced by these German immigrants in an attempt to show support for the United States during the time of heightened patriotism after WW I. For packages and 'point of sale' dating, note that the word 'prize' was used from 1912 to 1925, 'novelty' from 1925 to 1932, and 'toy' from 1933 on.

The first loose-packed prizes were toys made of wood, clay, tin, metal, and lithographed paper (the reason some early prizes are stained). Plastic toys were introduced in 1946. Paper wrapped for safety purposes in 1948, subjects echo the 'hype' of the day — yoyos, tops, whistles, and sports cards in the simple, peaceful days of our country, propaganda and war toys in the '40s, games in the '50s, and space toys in the '60s. Few of the estimated 15 billion prizes were marked. Advertising items from Angelus Marshmallow and Checkers Confections (cousins of the Cracker Jack family) are also collectible. When no condition is indicated, the items listed below are assumed to be in excellent to mint condition. 'CJ' indicates that the item is marked. Note: An often-asked question concerns the tin Toonerville Trolley called 'CJ.' No data has been found in the factory archives to authenticate this item; it is assumed that the 'CJ' merely refers to its small size. For further information see *Cracker Jack Toys, The Complete, Unofficial Guide for Collectors*, by Larry White. Our co-advisors for this category are Wes Johnson (listed in the Directory under Kentucky) and Harriet Joyce (under Florida). Also look for *The Prize Insider* newsletter listed in the Directory under Clubs, Newsletters, and Catalogs.

Dealer Incentives and Premiums

Badge, pin-bk, celluloid, lady w/CJ label reverse, 1905, 1¼" **100.00**
Bat, baseball; wood, Hillerich & Bradsby, CJ, full sz.....................**85.00**
Blotter, CJ question mk box, yel, 7¾x3¾".................................**185.00**
Book, pocket; jester on cover, CJ Riddles.................................**30.00**
Book, pocket; riddle/sailor boy/dog on cover, RWB, CJ, 1919.......**45.00**
Book, recipe; Angelus, 1930s **22.00**
Book, Uncle Sam Song Book, CJ, 1911, ea................................**40.00**
Cart w/2 movable wheels, wood dowel tongue, CJ **50.00**
Corkscrew/opener, metal plated, CJ/Angelus, 3¾" tube case **85.00**
Golf tee set, wood tees in paper 'matchbook' folder, CJ, 1920s .**725.00**
Harmonica, full scale, emb CJ, early, 5⅛" **365.00**
Jigsaw puzzle, CJ or Checkers, 1 of 4, 7x10", in envelope.............**35.00**
Marbles, Akro set of 12 in box w/instructions, CJ, 1929 ....**950.00**
Mask, Halloween; paper, CJ, series, 10" or 12", ea......................**28.00**
Match holder, hinged, eng gold-tone case, CJ, 2½x1⅞" **650.00**
Mirror, oval, Angelus (redhead or blond) on box **89.00**
Palm puzzle, mirror bk, CJ, mk Germany/RWB, 1910-14, 1½" ...**110.00**
Pen, ink; w/nib, tin litho bbl, CJ **485.00**
Pencil top clip, metal/celluloid, oval boy & dog logo **220.00**
Pencil top clip, metal/celluloid, tube shape w/pkg **220.00**
Postcard, bear, 1 of 16, CJ, 1907, ea....................................**35.00**
Puzzle, metal, CJ/Checkers, 1 of 15, '34, in envelope, ea.............**14.00**
Riddle card, 2 series of 20, w/pkg/from factory, CJ, 1907, ea **10.00**
Tablet, school; CJ, 1929, 8x10"..**195.00**
Thimble, aluminum, CJ Co/Angelus, red pnt, rare, ea **165.00**
Truck, steel, wood wheels for CJ pkg, unmk.............................**125.00**
Wings, air corps type, silver or blk, stud-bk, CJ, 1930s, 3", ea.......**55.00**

Packaging

Box, popcorn; Question Mark box end for CJ 'Toy,' 1933-34......**250.00**
Box, popcorn; red scroll border, CJ 'Prize,' 1912-25, ea **150.00**
Box, popcorn; store display, CJ 'Novelty,' 1925-32, ea..................**90.00**
Canister, tin, CJ Candy Corn Crisp, 10-oz **75.00**
Canister, tin, CJ Coconut Corn Crisp, 1-lb **55.00**
Canister, tin, CJ Coconut Corn Crisp, 10-oz **65.00**
CJ Commemorative canister, mc scene, 1990s, ea **9.00**
CJ Commemorative canister, wht w/red scroll, 1980s, ea **8.00**
Crate, shipping; wood, CJ, Rueckheim Bros Eck, 1902-22, lg.....**165.00**

Prizes, Cast Metal

Badge, shield, CJ Jr Detective, silver, 1931, 1¼".......................**50.00**
Badge, 6-point star, mc CJ Police, silver, 1931, 1¼" **55.00**
Button, stud bk, Me for Cracker Jack, boy & dog, oval **55.00**

Button, stud bk, Xd bats & ball, CJ pitcher/etc series, 1928 ....130.00
Chair, T (Tootsie), 3 different sectional pcs, pnt, mini, ea 12.00
Coins, Presidents, 31 series, CJ, mk cancelled on bk, 1933, ea 12.00
Coins, Presidents, 31 series, CJ, 1933, ea 4.00
Dollhouse items; lantern, mug, candlestick, etc; no mk, ea 6.50
Horse & wagon, CJ, 3-D, silver or gold, early, 2½", ea................250.00
Pistol, soft lead, inked, CJ on bbl, early, rare, 2⅛"......................180.00
Ring, alphabet letter setting (series), unmk, ea 4.00
Rocking horse, no rider, 3-D, inked, early, 1⅛" 25.00
Rocking horse w/boy, 3-D, inked, early, 1½"..................................32.00
Spinner, early pkg in center, 'More You Eat...,' CJ, rare 295.00
Tootsietoy series: boats, cars, animals; 1931, ¾"-1½", ea................7.00

Prizes, Paper

Baseball CJ score counter, 3⅜" L...130.00
Book, Animals (or Birds), to color, Makatoy, unmk, 1949, mini...35.00
Book, Bess & Bill on CJ Hill, series of 12, 1937, mini................105.00
Book, Birds We Know, CJ, 1928, mini 105.00
Book, Chaplin flip book, CJ, 1920s, ea 140.00
Book, drawing w/tracing paper, CJ, 1920s, mini 110.00
Book, Twigg & Sprigg, CJ, 1930, mini 105.00
Booklet, stickers/wisecracks/riddles, Borden, CJ, 1965 on...............3.00
Decal, cartoon or nursery rhyme figure, 1947-49, CJ 12.00
Disguise, ears, red (out of carrier), unmk, 1950, pr 18.00
Disguise, ears, red (still in carrier), CJ, 1950, pr............................22.00
Disguise, glasses, hinged, cello lenses, CJ Where Ever..., 1933 ......65.00
Disguise, glasses, hinged, w/eyeballs, unmk, 1933............................6.00
Disguise, mustache, blk/brn, in carrier, CJ, 1949...........................30.00
Fan, lady's, folding, mc, unmk 20.00
Fortune Teller, boy/dog on film in envelope, CJ, 1920s, 1¾x2½".80.00
Fortune wheel, 2-pc litho, turn for fortune, CJ, 1¾" 70.00
Game, Midget Auto Race, wheel spins, CJ, 1949, 3⅜" H 15.00
Game spinner, ...baseball at home, rectangle, CJ, 2¾" W 125.00
Game spinner, ...baseball at home, unmk, 1946, 1½" dia 60.00
Hat, fold out, More You Eat/More You Want, CJ, early.................75.00
Hat, Indian headdress, CJ, 1910-20, 5⅜" H................................275.00
Hat, Indian headdress, CJ, 1931, 2½" H 125.00
Hat, Me for CJ, early, ea...120.00
Hat visor, baseball, tie-on string, red, gr or bl, CJ, 1931 ....120.00
Magic game book, erasable slate, CJ, series of 13, 1946, ea 25.00
Movie, boy at blkboard, turn wheel: draws/erases, CJ, 1931, 2" ..175.00
Movie, Goofy Zoo, trn wheel(s): change animals, unmk, 1939.....25.00
Movie, pull tab for 2nd picture, series, CJ, 1943, 1¼", ea 105.00
Movie, pull tab for 2nd picture, yel, early, 3", in envelope..........125.00
Paper dolls, Boggie, Betty & Billie...125.00
Sand toy pictures, pours for action, series of 14, 1967, ea..............65.00
Top, golf game, wood stick center, CJ, 1933.................................57.00
Top, string; Rainbow Spinner, 2-pc, cb, different designs, ea 45.00
Transfer, iron-on, sport figure or patriotic, CJ, 1939, ea.................22.00
Transfer, iron-on, sport figure or patriotic, unmk, 1939, ea.............6.00
Whistle, Blow for More, CJ box/boy/dog, yel, 1931, ea 55.00
Whistle, Blow for More, CJ/Angelus pkgs, 1928, '31 or '33, ea.....45.00
Whistle, pressed paper, series of 10, 1948-49, CJ, 1¼x2", ea.........34.00
Whistle, Razz Zooka, C Carey Cloud design, CJ, 1949 ....25.00

Prizes, Plastic

Animals, standup, letter on bk, series of 26, Nosco, 1953, ea 4.00
Animals, standup on base, assorted, Nosco or CJ, 1947 on, ea........2.00
Baseball players, 3-D, bl or gray team, 1948, 1½", ea.......................8.00
Disc, emb comic character, series of 12, 1954, unmk, 1½" 16.00
Disc, emb fish plaque, oval, series of 10, 1956, unmk, ea..............14.00
Dog, 3-D, hollow base, series of 10, CJCO, 1954, ea 6.00
Figure, circus; stands on base, 1 of 12, Nosco, 1951-54.....................3.00
Figure on rocking base, semi-flat, 1 of 9, Cloud design, '56 ....4.00
Fob, alphabet letter w/loop on top, 1 of 26, 1954, 1½"....................4.00
Magnifying glass, many designs/shapes, from 1961, ea 1.00
Palm puzzle, ball(s) roll into holes, dome or rnd, from 1966............6.00
Palm puzzle, ball(s) roll into holes, rectangle, CJ, 1920s, ea..........55.00
Palm puzzle, ball(s) roll into holes, sq, CJ, 1920s, ea 45.00
Pinball game, lever shoots ball/score in holes, 1964 to recent.........5.00
Ships in a bottle, 6 different, unmk, 1960, ea...................................6.00
Signs, road; Stop, Caution, etc, yel, series of 10, 1954-60, ea..........5.00
Spinner, tops varied colors, 10 designs, from 1948, ea 2.50
Toys, take apart/assemble, variety, from '62, assembled, ea 2.00
Toys, take apart/assemble, variety, from '62, unassembled, ea..........5.00
Whistle, tube w/animals on top, CJ, series, 1950-53, 1⅜" 5.00

Prizes, Tin

Badge, boy & dog diecut, complete w/bend-over tab, CJ 150.00
Badge, boy & dog diecut, w/o tab at top, CJ 95.00
Badge, emb/plated CJ officer, 2⅜" or 1⅝", early, ea.....................110.00
Badge, litho, red/wht/bl, boy/dog, CJ, 1920s, 1¼" dia 150.00
Bank, 3-D book form, red/gr/or blk, CJ Bank, early, 2"...............120.00
Bookmark, dogs, 4 different, 1941, 3", ea 18.00
Brooch or pin, various designs on card, CJ/logo, early, ea 125.00
Cash register, litho, More You Eat, CJ, early, 1⅞" 275.00
Clicker, 'Noisy CJ Snapper,' pear shape, aluminum, 1949 ....14.00
Clicker, CJ Telegraph, Pat 1897, inked, 1¾" dia, ea...................145.00
Doll dishes, tin plated, CJ, '31, 1¾", 1⅞", & 2⅛" dia, ea.............35.00
Fortune Wheel, 2-pc litho, CJ, 1939-41, 1¾"...............................105.00
Helicopter, yel propeller, wood stick, unmk, 1937, 2⅝" 27.00
Horse & wagon, litho diecut, CJ & Angelus, 2⅛"........................65.00
Horse & wagon, litho diecut, gray/red mks, CJ, 1914-23, 3⅛"....395.00
Model T Ford, License: NY 1915 #999, blk/wht, CJ, rare, 2"......410.00
Pocket watch, silver or gold, CJ as numerals, 1931, 1½" 45.00
Sled, tin plated, CJ, 1931, 2" L 35.00
Small box shape; garage litho, unmk, 1⅛" 60.00
Small box shape: Elect Alarm Clock litho, unmk, 1⅛" 75.00
Small box shape: electric stove litho, unmk, 1⅛" 80.00
Small box shape: radio litho, bl, unmk, 1⅛" 60.00
Soldier, litho, die-cut standup, officer/private/etc, unmk, ea 17.00
Spinner, wood stick, Always on Top, red/wht/bl, CJ, 1½" dia.......25.00
Spinner, wood stick, Fortune Teller Game, red/wht/bl, CJ, 1½" ...90.00
Spinner, wood stick, Question Mark Box at center, CJ 50.00
Spinner, wood stick, 2 Toppers, red/wht/bl, Angelus/Jack, 1½" 85.00
Stand up, comic character, 1 of 10, CJ, 1936-46, ea 60.00
Stand up, oval Am Flag, series of 4, unmk, 1940-49, ea 18.00
Stand up, rectangle litho, boy & dog, ca 1916, lg or sm, ea 155.00
Tall box shape: Frozen Foods locker freezer, '47, unmk, 1¾" 75.00
Tall box shape: Refrigerator Car, CJ, 1947, 1¾" L.......................125.00
Tall box shape: grandfather clock, unmk, 1947, 1¾" 65.00
Tall box shape: radio, Tune in w/CJ, brn/yel, 1939, 1¾" 125.00
Train, engine & tender, litho, CJ Line/512 ....125.00
Train, litho coach only, red, unmk, 1941...24.00
Train, litho engine only, red, 1941, unmk 20.00
Train, Lone Eagle Flyer cars, unmk 65.00
Train, Lone Eagle Flyer engine, unmk 60.00
Tray, emb, litho w/early pkg, 2¼x1¾" 95.00
Truck, litho, RWB, CJ/Angelus, 1931, ea 65.00
Wagon shape: Playtime Trailer (auto trailer), unmk, 1947 ....50.00
Wagon shape: Tank Corps No 57, gr & blk, 1941...........................30.00
Wagon shape: Caterpillar tractor, unmk, 1931, 1¾" L....................35.00
Wagon shape: CJ Shows, yel circus wagon, series of 5, ea 175.00
Wagon shape: tank, orange/red/gr camouflage, unmk 65.00
Wheelbarrow, tin plated, bk leg in place, CJ, 1931, 2½" L 35.00

Miscellaneous

Ad, comic book, CJ, ea 14.00
Ad, Saturday Evening Post, mc, CJ, 1919, 11x14" 18.00
Hat, ball park vendor cap, CJ, 1930s 30.00
Lunch box, tin, 2 hdls, CJ, 1980s, 4½x5x6" 40.00
Lunch box, tin emb, CJ, 1970s, 4x7x9" 30.00
Medal, CJ salesman award, brass, 1939, scarce 125.00
Pocket mirror, bl-on-wht graphics, oval, EX 300.00

Poster, trolley car, early 1910s, 10½x20½", EX, $400.00. (Photo courtesy Harriet Joyce)

Sign, bathing beauty, 5-color cb, CJ, early, 17x22" 460.00
Sign, boy or girl w/box of CJ, 5-color cb, early, 17x22", ea 460.00
Sign, Jack & Bingo, die-cut litho, easel standup, CJ, early..........450.00
Sign, Jack & Bingo, standing on early CJ pkg, mc cb, rare 520.00
Sign, Santa & prizes, mc cb, Angelus, early, lg 220.00
Sign, Santa & prizes, mc cb, Checkers, early, lg 1,000.00
Sign, Santa & prizes, mc cb, CJ, early, lg 265.00

Crackle Glass

Though this type of glassware was introduced as early as the 1880s (by the New England Glass Co.), it was made primarily from 1930 until about 1980. It was produced by more than five hundred companies here (by Benko, Rainbow, and Kanawah, among others) and abroad (by such renown companies as Moser, for example), and its name is descriptive. The surface looks as though the glass has been heated then plunged into cold water, thus producing a network of tight cracks. It was made in a variety of colors; among the more expensive today are ruby red, amberina, cobalt, cranberry, and gray. For more information we recommend *Crackle Glass, Identification and Value Guide, Book I* and *Book II* (Collector Books), by Stan and Arlene Weitman, our advisors this category; they are listed in the Directory under New York. See also Moser.

Cruet, amber, 2-ball stopper, Rainbow, 1940s-60s, 4¼", pr...........80.00
Cruet, ruby, amber hdl & teardrop stopper, Pilgrim, 6½" 75.00
Decanter, amberina, Rainbow, mushroom-form stopper, 1940s-60s, 7¾".100.00
Decanter, crystal w/olive gr top, Blenko, 1940s-50s, 10½"..........80.00
Decanter, tangerine, stick neck, tall teardrop top, Blenko, 1960s, 13"...100.00
Decanter, topaz, ball stopper, Rainbow, 1940s-60s, 8½" 100.00
Goblet, wine; olive gr, 5¾" 75.00
Jar, apothecary; topaz, 2-ball stopper, att Blenko, 9¼"..................85.00
Mug, amber, 1950s-early 1960s, 6¼" 30.00
Pitcher, amberina, drop-over hdl, bulbous, Rainbow, 1940s-60s, 4¾".55.00
Pitcher, amberina w/clear hdl, slightly bulbous, Pilgrim, 1949-69, 4".35.00
Pitcher, bl, drop-over hdl, flared cylinder, sq top, 4" 45.00
Pitcher, charcoal, drop-over hdl, bulbous, 4½" 55.00
Pitcher, emerald gr, drop-over hdl, Pilgrim, 1949-69, 4"..............30.00

Pitcher, gr, pulled-bk hdl, Williamsburg Glass label, 1950-60, 4¾" .60.00
Pitcher, Lemon Lime, pulled-bk hdl, sm mouth, Pilgrim, 1949-69, 4¼" .30.00
Pitcher, ruby, clear hdl, trumpet neck, Pilgrim, 1949-69, 3½".35.00
Pitcher, tangerine, drop-over hdl, Pilgrim, 1949-69, 3½" .35.00
Pitcher, topaz, drop-over hdl, waisted, Pilgrim, 1949-69, 3¾"..30.00
Pitcher, wheat, drop-over hdl, Blenko, 1960s, 9¾" 75.00
Tumbler, liqueur: topaz, clear drop-over hdl, Pilgrim, 1949-69, 4" .45.00
Tumbler, topaz, slim cylinder, 6¾" 50.00
Vase, amberina (tangerine), waisted, Blenko, 1961, 7" 85.00

Vase, black amethyst (rare color), unknown maker, ca 1940s, 8¼", $150.00. (Photo courtesy Stan and Arlene Weitman)

Vase, bl, appl rigaree, Pilgrim, 1949-69, 5" 65.00
Vase, bud; orange, ruffled rim, 8" 45.00
Vase, emerald gr, stick neck, Hamon, 1940s-70s, 9¾" 75.00
Vase, Lemon Lime, pinched, Pilgrim, 1949-69, 5" 40.00
Vase, ruby, scalloped rim, bulbous base, 5" 75.00
Vase, ruby, 3-scallop rim, trumpet neck, Rainbow, 1940s-70s, 5¼" .75.00
Vase, Smoke Gray w/appl serpentine at waist, Pilgrim, 1949-69, 11¼" .125.00

Cranberry Glass

Cranberry glass is named for its resemblance to the color of cranberry juice. It was made by many companies both here and abroad, becoming popular in America soon after the Civil War. It was made in free-blown ware as well as mold-blown. Today cranberry glass is being reproduced, and it is sometimes difficult to distinguish the old from the new. Ask a reputable dealer if you are unsure.

For further information we recommend *American Art Glass* by John A. Shuman III, available from Collector Books or your local bookstore. See also Cruets; Salts; Sugar Shakers; Syrups.

Basket, ruffled rim, clear twist hdl 230.00
Bottle, gold stars, star cut in base, w/stopper, 6x3" 165.00
Bottle, gold/wht dots & bands, clear cut stopper, 8½x2½" 175.00
Bowl, appl yel/clear decor, ftd, sq, 5" 175.00
Bowl, finger; amber threading on ruffled rim 135.00
Box, mc floral garlands/scrolls, brass hinges, 4x4" 375.00
Casket, jewelry; brass enclosure, 4x5½x3½" 200.00
Celery vase, Invt T'print, tapered sides, mc floral, Am, 7" 100.00
Compote, mc florals & gold berries, clear ped, 4x6⅛" 135.00
Decanter, clear wafer ft, rope hdl, clear finial, 10¾" 195.00
Decanter, wine; lt ribbing, clear ft/hdl/stopper, 12x3" 180.00
Ewer, mc floral, clear hdl, 8½x4¼" 300.00
Loving cup, gold threads & decor, crystal base, 11¼"..................200.00
Pitcher, clear glass ice bladder, 10x5" 210.00

Pitcher, Dmn Quilt, ruffled, clear hdl, 9" 350.00
Pitcher, feathered/ribbed, bulbous, 8" 160.00
Pitcher, Invt T'print, bulbous, 8" 215.00
Plate, 8"...55.00
Shakers, mc daisies, in SP fr...225.00
Sweetmeat jar, HP decor, rstr SP lid/hdl, 4½" dia.......................250.00
Vase, wht lilies of the valley w/gold leaves, 7½" 135.00

Crown Devon

Devon and Crown Devon were trade names of S. Fielding and Company, Ltd., an English firm founded after 1879. They produced majolica, earthenware mugs, vases, and kitchenware. In the 1930s they manufactured an exceptional line of Art Deco vases that have recently been much in demand.

Bowl, Fruits, mc on cobalt, #165, G Brouch, 2¾x10" 575.00
Bowl, John Peel, fox figural hdls, 5x9" 135.00
Cigar box, George VI/Elizabeth Comm, musical, castle decor, #813582 .....1,620.00
Condiment set, Garden Path, shakers & mustard on tray 150.00
Decanter, Auld Lang Syne, Scottish man on wht, w/gr hdl, 8¼" 430.00
Jug, bl flowers w/brn stems & gr leaves on beige, musical, #M275, 9".....585.00
Jug, John Peel, musical, #755789, 8" 250.00
Jug, Killarney, people on carriage rise & landscape, musical, 7¾" 500.00
Jug, Rouge Royale, floral on brn, #438, 4" 100.00
Stein, tandem bicycle, red rose on hdl, musical, 6¼" 165.00
Teapot, Garden Path, yel w/gr trim, w/lid, 2-cup, 4½x6" 200.00
Toby jug, Guardsman, 8¼" 95.00
Vase, mc floral on cobalt, ribbed tab hdl, #2060, 5x6½" 100.00
Vase, Memphis, Colin Melbourne, #CM8, 10¾" 125.00
Vase, wht cattails & flying geese on blk, 11"................................100.00
Wall plaque, Irish Terrier head, brn w/blk nose 220.00

Crown Ducal

The Crown Ducal mark was first used by the A.G. Richardson & Co. pottery of Tunstall, England, in 1925. The items collectors are taking a particular interest in were decorated by Charlotte Rhead, a contemporary of Suzie Cooper and Clarice Cliff, and a member of the esteemed family of English pottery designers and artists.

Bowl, Marigolds, mk Crown Ducal Ware England, #1063, 3½x9" .110.00
Bowl, serving; Bristol, bl, oval, 10" L...55.00
Bowl, vegetable; Bristol, red & pk transferware, w/lid 160.00
Bowl, yel duck in center on wht w/Who Said Dinner? on border, 6½" .200.00
Celery plate, Chintz, 11x5" 95.00
Cup & saucer, Florida, pheasant & flower design 65.00
Jardinere, Chintz on ivory, scalloped rim, 5x4" 70.00
Muffin dish, Orange Tree, 4x8" dia...170.00
Mug, Little Boy Blue, C Rhead, 3" 165.00
Plate, Bristol, 8¾"..50.00
Plate, Grey Fruit w/yel border, 8½" sq 25.00
Plate, Queen Elizabeth II, maroon border w/floral, 10" 200.00
Plate, serving; Chintz w/gold bkground, 10¼x8⅞" 95.00
Plate, 3 shell-shape sections w/rose in center, gold border, 8x8" ...40.00
Platter, Bristol, scalloped edge, 12½x9½" 65.00
Platter, Bristol, 16x12" 90.00
Snack set, Orange Tree, plate w/indent & cup 95.00
Teapot, Rimula, w/lid, 5" 390.00
Teapot, Rosalie, w/lid, 5½x9¾" 265.00
Toast rack, Orange Tree, in shape of face, 6x6" 250.00
Vase, Persian Rose, 8-sided, C Rhead, 5x7" 200.00
Vase, Poppy, 9" 170.00

Crown Milano

Crown Milano was a line of decorated milk glass (or opal ware) introduced by the Mt. Washington Glass Co. of New Bedford, Massachussetts, in the early 1890s. It had previously been called Albertine Ware. Some pieces are marked with a 'CM,' and many had paper labels. This ware is usually highly decorated and will most likely have a significant amount of gold painted on it. The shiny pieces were recently discovered to have been called 'Colonial Ware' and have a laurel wreath and a crown. This ware was well received in its day, and outstanding pieces bring high prices on today's market. Advisors for this category are Wilfred and Dolli Cohen; they are listed in the Directory under California.

Biscuit jar, allover bamboo on pnt burmese, SP mts, 6" 900.00
Biscuit jar, gold apple blossom branches, rope hdl 750.00
Biscuit jar, pansies/other flowers, scrolls around rim, 8" 700.00
Biscuit jar, peonies on wht w/gold, bulbous, mk lid, to top of hdl: 8" ..1,350.00
Bonbon, Colonial Ware, mc pansies, #3610, 1¾x5¼" 275.00
Bowl, Dmn Quilt, pnt Burmese w/floral, sq top, 4"....................495.00
Box, gold maidenhair fern on gr tint, heart shape, w/lid, 3x6x5" ..975.00
Bride's bowl, floral on ivory, sq/shaped rim; hdld Webster ped ft, 10".575.00
Bride's bowl, florals, int: gold scrolls, tricon shaped rim, 9½" .1,250.00
Cup & saucer, demitasse; floral vines/gilt/blk dots, 2", 5" 1,750.00
Ewer, Colonial Ware, floral w/gold, rope hdl, 6½x7½" 835.00

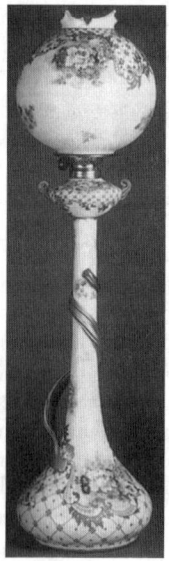

Lamp, matching base, font, and ball shade with hand-painted floral decoration and applied gilt ribbons, original fluid burner, 38", $12,650.00.

Pitcher, gold mums in blown-out reserves, reeded hdl, 8¼" 800.00
Plate, Colonial Ware, floral clusters/gold scrolls on wht, 7" 450.00
Plate, Colonial Ware, florals/gold scroll rim reserves, 8¾" 450.00
Salt cellar, Colonial Ware, mums/etc, emb gold scrolls, 2½" dia..250.00
Sweetmeat, acorns/peach swirl ribs on ivory, 5" 495.00
Sweetmeat, Colonial Ware, flowers/scrolls on ribbed wht, gilt mts..485.00
Sweetmeat, Dmn Quilt w/gold oak leaves/jewels, SP lid, branch hdl, 5" .900.00
Sweetmeat, floral, gold on pk to cream, SP lid, 4½" 1,000.00
Sweetmeat, line scrolls/jewels, shadow florals, turtle on lid, 5" dia.545.00
Syrup, Colonial Ware, Dresden floral on melon-rib body, gold scrolls...950.00
Syrup, 6 gilt-lined panels of roses, SP #d mts, 4" 695.00
Vase, cherubs w/gold/jewels, #503, sm rstr, 19x8" 1,725.00
Vase, Colonial Ware, mums, gold scrolls border pk areas, petal rim, 5" ..375.00
Vase, floral, 4-fold neck on swirled bulbous body, 6x5¾".........1,485.00
Vase, forget-me-nots, bulbous, 4-fold top, 24 swirling ribs, 6x5¾".1,350.00
Vase, Jack-in-the-pulpit; floral on pnt burmese, crimped, 9¾" ..750.00

Vase, oak leaves, mc on shaded tan, bulbous, petal top, 5¾" .1,300.00
Vase, pansies w/gold, petticoat shape, 10½"...............................750.00
Vase, petit-point iris/scrolls on lt tan, 8-rib, petal top, 4½" 850.00
Vase, thistles, gold on cream to melon, shadow thistles, str sides, 9" ...985.00
Vase, thistles w/gold, 3-hdl, triangular stick form, 9¼" 1,000.00
Vase, wild roses etc, gold on peach/yel mottle, jewels, 5x7".....1,150.00

Cruets

Cruets, containers made to hold oil or vinegar, are usually bulbous with tall, narrow throats, a handle, and a stopper. During the nineteenth century and for several years after, they were produced in abundance in virtually every type of glassware available. Those listed below are assumed to be with stopper and mint unless noted otherwise. Our advisor for this category is Elaine Ezell; she is listed in the Directory under Maryland.

See also specific manufacturers.

Ada #2577, TeePee body w/cut neck, Cambridge, ca 1903, 8-oz...60.00
Aladdin, cut, faceted top, Pitkins & Brooks................................120.00
Amazon, bar-in-hand stopper, ftd, 8½" 185.00
Amber w/sapphire bl hollow stopper, hdl & pontil, 4 indents, 7¾"..95.00
Amberette 90.00
Arched Ovals, gr 130.00
Art..60.00
Bead Swag, milk glass w/gold beading 250.00
Bubble Lattice Paneled Sprig, wht opal.....................................325.00
Button Arches, ruby stain, bulbous, ribbed stopper 250.00
Cane Column 45.00
Cathedral, amber..125.00
Chrysanthemum Base Swirl, bl opal 250.00
Cut Log, lg 70.00
Daisy & Fern, wht opal, Northwood 225.00
Dewey...65.00
Dewey, canary..195.00
Diamond Quilt, bl satin MOP 210.00
Duncan Homestead 50.00
Everglades, bl opal 500.00
Feather 60.00
Feather, gr 250.00
Flora, bl opal..795.00
Florette, pk satin, frosted hdl & stopper....................................235.00
Galloway 55.00
Georgia Gem, custard w/gold..295.00
Gr spatter w/emb leaves 200.00
Heart w/Thumbprint 65.00
Heisey #300 Colonial, made in 5 szs, ea from $50 to....................85.00
Hidalgo, frosted...70.00
Hobnail, rubena verde, Hobbs-Brockunier 595.00
Honeycomb w/Star 50.00
Intaglio, vaseline opal 795.00
Inverted Thumbprint, reverse amberina, amber hdl & stopper, 7½"...400.00
Ivy Scroll, gr 125.00
Jacob's Ladder 95.00
King's Block #312, amber, ped ft, clear Maltese Cross top, 1890s.220.00
Magnolia, str sides w/etch, mushroom top, Cambridge, 6x2" 50.00
Michigan..65.00
Nailhead, rose satin 295.00
New Garland #284, amber, tall melon-ribbed stopper, Fostoria, 9" ..300.00
New Jersey...50.00
Ohio Star 85.00
Paneled Forget-Me-Not..55.00
Paneled Herringbone, gr 125.00

Paneled Thistle..60.00
Pennsylvania..45.00
Plume 40.00
Prize, gr 225.00
Rose Point, loop hdl, Cambridge, 5-oz.....................................150.00

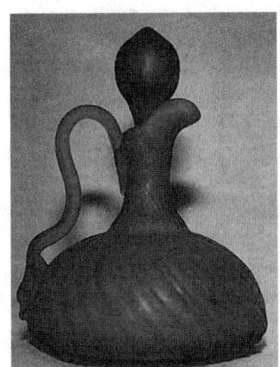

Satina Swirl, sapphire satin, Hobbs-Brockunier, $250.00. (Photo courtesy Neila and Tom Bredehoft)

Royal Crystal, ruby stain, sm...295.00
Seaweed, bl opal satin 475.00
Spanish Lace, bl opal, Northwood, clear cut stopper................595.00
Starburst, etch florals, notched neck, faceted top, 6½" 70.00
Stripe, wht opal 175.00
Tiny Optic, amethyst w/decor...125.00
Wild Bouquet, bl opal, opal hdl, clear stopper, 7¼" 395.00
Wisconsin..95.00
Zipper..45.00

Cup Plates, Glass

Before the middle 1850s, it was socially acceptable to pour hot tea into a deep saucer to cool. The tea was sipped from the saucer rather than the cup, which frequently was handleless and too hot to hold. The cup plate served as a coaster for the cup. It is generally agreed that the first examples of pressed glass cup plates were made about 1826 at the Boston and Sandwich Glass Co. in Sandwich, Cape Cod, Massachusetts. Other glassworks in three major areas (New England, Philadelphia, and the Midwest, especially Pittsburgh) quickly followed suit.

Antique glass cup plates range in size from 2⅝" up to 4¼" in diameter. The earliest plates had simple designs inspired by cut glass patterns, but by 1829 they had become more complex. The span from then until about 1845 is known as the 'lacy period,' when cup plate designs and pressing techniques were at their peak. To cover pressing imperfections, the backgrounds of the plates were often covered with fine stippling which endowed them with a glittering brilliance called 'laciness.' They were made in a multitude of designs — some purely decorative, others commemorative. Subjects include the American eagle, hearts, sunbursts, log cabins, ships, George Washington, the political candidates Clay and Harrison, plows, and beehives. Of all the patterns, the round George Washington plate is the rarest and most valuable — only four are known to exist today.

Authenticity is most important. Collectors must be aware that contemporary plates which have no antique counterparts and fakes modeled after antique patterns have had wide distribution. Condition is also important, though it is the exceptional plate that does not have some rim roughness. More important considerations are scarcity of design and color.

The book *American Glass* by George and Helen McKearin has a section on glass cup plates. The definitive book is *American Glass Cup Plates* by Ruth Webb Lee and James H. Rose. Numbers in the listings that follow refer to the latter. When attempting to evaluate a cup plate, remember that minor rim roughness is normal.

Note: Most of the values listed below are prices realized at auction. See also Staffordshire; Pairpoint.

R-41, scarce, G+ **38.00**
R-44, Sunflower, acanthus rim, att Sandwich, roughness, 3¼" **85.00**
R-72, rare, VG+ **78.00**
R-81, heart center, sprig border, greenish opal, rim flakes, 3¾" ..**440.00**
R-82, Acorn & Maple leaf, silver-bl, edge roughness, 3⅝" **1,880.00**
R-85, rosette w/floral rim, silver-bl, 2 lg rim chips, 3⅜" **700.00**
R-86, swirled w/rope rim, opaque bl, 3 lg chips, 3⅜" **550.00**
R-103, rare, G **62.00**
R-164-A, EX **40.00**
R-216, quatrefoil w/vesica cuts, bull's eye rim, bl, 3⅜", G **1,400.00**
R-236, G **28.00**
R-262, Scroll w/Lily, quatrefoil/trefoil border, bl, 3⅜", NM **400.00**
R-291, Rosette, bl, 3" **235.00**
R-333, Starburst w/star & palmetto border, lt bl, rim chips, 3⅜" .**175.00**
R-342, G **14.00**
R-396, Rayed Star, bl, several shallow edge cracks, 3¼" **175.00**
R-425, G **21.00**
R-440b, Pierced Hearts, lyre rim, cobalt, few chips, 3½" **200.00**
R-440b, Pierced Hearts, lyre/scrolled leaf border, 3½", EX..........**175.00**
R-465j, Rosette w/13-Heart rim, bl-violet, ¾" rim crack, 3½".....**60.00**
R-465j, Rosette w/13-Heart rim, opal, rim chips/roughness, 3½"..**60.00**
R-522, Sunburst, amethyst, att Sandwich, few chips, 3⅜" **115.00**
R-530, Sunburst, amethyst, 3¼" **350.00**
R-531, Sunburst, bull's-eye rim, lt gr, several sm chips, 3⅝" **145.00**
R-565, Henry Clay, bl, rim roughness, 3½" **400.00**
R-565b, Henry Clay, bl, few rim chips, 3½" **235.00**
R-590, G **28.00**

R-600c, log cabin, 3⅜", EX, $3,100.00; R-671, eagle, 3⁷⁄₁₆", roughness, $330.00.

R-594, beehive & bees, Midwest, rim roughness, 3⅛" **60.00**
R-610c, VG- **40.00**
R-610a, ship in center, bl, several sm rim chips, 3⅝" **295.00**
R-615a, Steamboat & Hairpin, several chips, 3½" **26.50**
R-651a, Eagle w/in concentric circles, 3", G **470.00**
R-654a, Eagle & Shield, acorn/oak leaf border, Midwest, roughness, 3"...**400.00**
R-661, VG **39.00**
R-662, Eagle w/5 stars, opal, few rim chips, 3½"........................**200.00**
R-677a, Eagle, Palmette/Roman Rosette rim, bl, Midwest, 3¼", EX.**470.00**
R-677e, Eagle & Shield, octagonal, Midwest, several chips, 3⅝"...**1,050.00**
R-677g, Eagle & Shield, octagonal, Midwest, several chips, 3⅝"...**350.00**
R-679, VG **34.00**

Cups and Saucers

The earliest utensils for drinking were small porcelain and

stoneware bowls imported from China by the East India Company in the early seventeenth century. European and English tea bowls and saucers, imitating Chinese and Japanese originals, were produced from the early eighteenth century and often decorated with Chinese-type motifs. By about 1810, handles were fitted to the bowl to form the now familiar teacup, and this form became almost universal. Coffee in England and on the Continent was often served in a can — a straight-sided cylinder with a handle. After 1820 the coffee can gave way to the more fanciful form of the coffee cup.

An infinite variety of cups and saucers are available for both the new and experienced collector, and they can be found in all price ranges. There is probably no better way to thoroughly know and understand the various ceramic manufacturers than to study cups and saucers. Our advisors for this category, Susan and Jim Harran, have written a series entitled *Collectible Cups and Saucers, Identification and Values, Books I, II,* and *III,* published by Collector Books. Book II contains more than eight hundred full-color photos; it is divided into six collectible eras: early years (1700 – 1875), cabinet cups, nineteenth and twentieth century dinnerware, English tablewares, miniatures, and mustache cups and saucers. The Harrans are listed in the Directory under New Jersey.

Bouillon, floral on lt gr w/gold, w/lid, Limoges, 1900-41, $75 to...**85.00**
Breakfast, floral borders w/in & w/out, gold loop hdl, Austria, 1900 ...**60.00**
Breakfast, majolica, emb fruit, Societe de...Salens, ca 1880 ....**125.00**
Chocolate, floral w/gold, fluted/molded cup, Haviland Limoges, 1904-25 ...**55.00**
Chocolate, floral w/gold, str cup w/loop hdl, Limoges, 1895, $40 to.**50.00**
Coffee, bl jasper w/classic figures, broken loop hdl, Wedgwood, 1860s..**950.00**
Coffee, HP daisies on pk, bucket-shaped can, Bodley, 1875+, $50 to ...**65.00**
Coffee, HP floral, swirled can w/loop hdl, Dresden, 1893-1916..**115.00**
Coffee, HP flower garlands, snake hdl, 3-ftd, Dresden, 1893-1916...**375.00**
Coffee, pearlware w/bl romantic transfer, 12-sided, loop hdl, 1840s+.**50.00**
Coffee, red floral w/gilt, can w/ring hdl, Minton, 1811, $150 to.**190.00**
Demi, cobalt w/gold leafy garlands & urns, Royal Doulton, 1920s .**200.00**
Demi, floral tapestry, quatrefoil w/kicked loop hdl, BankoWare, 1930s.**125.00**
Demi, gold floral on lt yel, gold wash in cup, Royal Crown Derby, 1891 .**225.00**
Demi, gold floral w/bl, Royal flute shape, Geo Jones, 1890s, $65 to.**75.00**
Demi, gold lace on cobalt & wht, Venezia, 1880s, from $150 to...**200.00**
Demi, HP floral w/bl-lined rim, Adams Titian Ware, 1896-1920s.**35.00**
Demi, HP floral w/gold, bucket w/loop hdl, Royal Worcester, ca 1887..**125.00**
Demi, HP floral w/much gold, Bute cup w/unusual hdl, KPM, 1890s....**250.00**
Demi, HP pk roses w/gr leaves, Royal Flute cup, Meissen, 1924-34.**150.00**
Demi, portrait reserve w/gold beads/wht jewels, beehive mk, 1885-1920.**200.00**
Mini, bird & flowers, Eberthal Qualitats Porzellan, 1949-70s **50.00**
Mini coffee, floral w/gold, loop hdl, Limoges, 1920s, from $100 to..**125.00**
Mini tea, floral transfer, ribbed cup, Royal Sutherland, 1947-59...**75.00**
Mini tea, floral transfer w/gold rim, Royal Adderly, 1955+, $50 to .**75.00**
Mini tea, gr leafy transfer, loop hdl, WT Copeland, 1940-56, $75 to...**100.00**
Mini tea, paisley chintz, Grosvenor China Ltd, 1961-69, $75 to .**100.00**
Snack, bl floral (dainty) w/gold, scalloped tray, Haviland, 1876-1930 ....**125.00**
Tea, bl forget-me-nots, Paragon, 1957+, from $45 to.....................**60.00**
Tea, Cannonball pattern, bl/wht, ftd bowl, Worcester, 1775, $250 to.**300.00**
Tea, cherubs, gold int, ftd, loop hdl, Capodimonte, 1930s, $45 to.**60.00**
Tea, Christmas candles & holly, Bavaria, 1969 to present, from $45 to .**60.00**
Tea, cobalt w/fruit int, gold trim, Oban shape, Aynsley, 1930s..**125.00**
Tea, cream w/gold rims & hdl, 6-sided, angle hdl, Lenox, 1920s, $60 to.**75.00**
Tea, floral transfer, waisted cup w/ped ft, Cauldon, 1950-62, $30 to ..**40.00**
Tea, floral transfer w/gold garlands, Collingwood Bros, 1937-57 ...**40.00**
Tea, floral w/gold, Pickard on Nippon blank, 1895-98, $90 to....**115.00**
Tea, floral transfer w/HP accents, Foley, 1930+, from $35 to **45.00**
Tea, fruit clusters, gold trim, Schumann, 1950s to present, $35 to.**45.00**
Tea, gr lady & landscape transfer, English stepped hdl, unmk, 1830s ..**75.00**
Tea, Lily of the Valley, Shelley, 1925-40, from $90 to...............**125.00**
Tea, Nova Scotia Tartan, ftd cup, Paragon, 1957+, from $40 to.**50.00**

Tea, Olde Avesbury, gold on wht, Royal Crown Derby, 1969, $50 to ..**60.00**
Tea, Oriental blk/wht transfer paneled bowl, Wm Adams & Sons, 1819-64 .**100.00**
Tea, pearlware bowl w/stylized flowers, Challinor, 1860-90, $60 to ...**90.00**
Tea, Persian-type floral w/gold, scalloped, Aynsley, 1891-1910, $95 to...**125.00**
Tea, roses HP on lt gr, dbl-ear hdl, T&V Limoges, 1892-1907, $50 to...**70.00**
Tea, scattered flowers on wht, ftd, Rosenthal, 1949-54, from $50 to..**60.00**
Tea, turq & wht w/gold leaves, low Doris shape, Aynsley, 1950s...**40.00**

Currier & Ives by Royal

During the 1950s dinnerware decorated with transfer-printed scenes taken from prints by Currier and Ives was manufactured by Royal China and distributed as premiums through A&P stores. Though it was also made in pink and green, blue is by far the easiest to find and the most popular. Pie plates have been found in black and brown, and dinnerware items have been reported in black as well. Occasionally the blue line has been found decorated with a hand-painted pattern. Currier and Ives has become a very popular collectible at malls and flea markets around the country. Included in our listings are pieces from Hostess sets by Royal which should be of great interest to collectors. The 11½" round platter with the 'Rocky Mountains' scene is very rare. This piece does not have tabs but is round like the 12" platter. An interesting note: There are five different (decal) variations of the teapot. Our advisors for this category are Treva and Jack Hamlin; they are listed in the Directory under Ohio.

Ashtray, 5½" **15.00**
Bowl, cereal; tab hdl, 6¼" **48.00**
Bowl, cereal; 6¼" **15.00**
Bowl, dessert; 5½" **5.00**
Bowl, soup; 8" **14.00**
Bowl, vegetable, 9" **20.00**
Bowl, vegetable; deep, 10" **30.00**
Butter dish, Fashionable decal **55.00**
Butter dish, Road Winter decal **40.00**
Casserole, angle hdls **100.00**
Casserole, tab hdls, knob turned 90 degrees **200.00**
Clock, 10" plate, bl #s, 2 decals **200.00**
Creamer, angle hdl **8.00**
Cup, angle hdl **4.00**
Cup, rnd hdl, tall, 9" **10.00**
Gravy boat, pour spout **20.00**
Gravy boat, tab hdls **58.00**
Gravy ladle, all wht **45.00**
Lamp, candle; w/globe **300.00**
Mug, coffee; reg **35.00**
Mug, coffee; rnd hdl **30.00**
Pie baker, 9 decals, 10" **30.00**
Plate, bread; 6½" **5.00**
Plate, calendar; 10" **20.00**
Plate, chop; Getting Ice, 11½" **45.00**
Plate, chop; Rocky Mountains, 11½" **100.00**
Plate, chop; 12¼" **30.00**
Plate, dinner; 10" **5.00**
Plate, luncheon; 9" **25.00**
Plate, salad; 7¼" **15.00**
Plate, snack; w/cup well, 9" **75.00**
Platter, oval, 13" **35.00**
Platter, tab hdls, 10½" dia **25.00**
Platter, 13" dia **75.00**
Saucer, 6⅛" **2.00**
Shakers, pr **30.00**
Spoon rest, wall hanging **75.00**

Sugar bowl, flared top, no handle, $48.00; Creamer, tall, $48.00. (Photo courtesy Jack and Treva Hamlin)

Sugar bowl, hdld, w/lid **18.00**
Sugar bowl, no hdls, str sides, w/lid **30.00**
Teapot, 5 different decal variations **125.00**
Tray, gravy boat; regular **20.00**
Tray, gravy boat; wht tabs, like 7" plate **75.00**
Tumbler, iced tea; 12-oz, 5½" **12.00**
Tumbler, juice; 5-oz, 3½" **12.00**
Tumbler, old fashion; 7-oz, 3¼" **12.00**
Tumbler, water; 8½-oz, 4¾" **12.00**

Hostess Set Pieces

Bowl, candy; 7¾" **25.00**
Bowl, dip; 4⅜" **20.00**
Pie baker, 11" **50.00**
Plate, cake; flat, 10" **40.00**
Plate, cake; ftd, 10" **150.00**
Plate, serving; 7" **18.00**
Tray, deviled egg **200.00**

Custard Glass

As early as the 1880s, custard glass was produced in England. Migrating glassmakers brought the formula for the creamy ivory ware to America. One of them was Harry Northwood, who in 1898 founded his company in Indiana, Pennsylvania, and introduced the glassware to the American market. Soon other companies were producing custard, among them Heisey, Tarentum, Fenton, and McKee. Not only dinnerware patterns but souvenir items were made. Today custard is the most expensive of the colored pressed glassware patterns. The formula for producing the luminous glass contains uranium salts which imparts the cream color to the batch and causes it to glow when it is examined under a black light.

Argonaut Shell, bowl, master berry; gold & decor, 10½" L **275.00**
Argonaut Shell, bowl, sauce; ftd, gold & decor **75.00**
Argonaut Shell, butter dish, gold & decor **350.00**
Argonaut Shell, butter dish, no gold **300.00**
Argonaut Shell, compote, jelly; gold & decor, scarce **165.00**
Argonaut Shell, creamer, gold & decor **155.00**
Argonaut Shell, creamer, no gold **110.00**
Argonaut Shell, cruet, gold & decor **850.00**
Argonaut Shell, pitcher, water; gold & decor **475.00**
Argonaut Shell, shakers, gold & decor, pr **435.00**
Argonaut Shell, spooner, gold & decor **275.00**
Argonaut Shell, sugar bowl, w/lid, gold & decor **235.00**
Argonaut Shell, tumbler, gold & decor **110.00**
Bead Swag, bowl, sauce; floral & gold **50.00**
Bead Swag, goblet, floral & gold **65.00**

Bead Swag, tray, pickle; floral & gold, rare.................................300.00
Bead Swag, wine, floral & gold 60.00
Beaded Circle, bowl, master berry; floral & gold.................350.00
Beaded Circle, butter dish, floral & gold.............................500.00
Beaded Circle, creamer, floral & gold...................................180.00
Beaded Circle, pitcher, water; floral & gold.........................750.00
Beaded Circle, shakers, floral & gold, pr..........................1,000.00
Beaded Circle, spooner, floral & gold....................................200.00
Beaded Circle, tumbler, floral & gold, very rare.................175.00
Cane Insert, berry set, 7-pc...450.00
Cane Insert, table set, 4-pc...450.00
Cherry & Scales, bowl, master berry; nutmeg stain 145.00
Cherry & Scales, butter dish, nutmeg stain.........................250.00
Cherry & Scales, creamer, nutmeg stain 125.00
Cherry & Scales, pitcher, water; nutmeg stain, scarce 350.00
Cherry & Scales, spooner, nutmeg stain, scarce.................125.00
Cherry & Scales, sugar bowl, w/lid, nutmeg stain, scarce 150.00
Cherry & Scales, tumbler, nutmeg stain, scarce 75.00
Chrysanthemum Sprig, bowl, master berry; gold & decor 300.00
Chrysanthemum Sprig, bowl, master berry; no gold...........175.00
Chrysanthemum Sprig, bowl, sauce; ftd, gold & decor 60.00
Chrysanthemum Sprig, butter dish, gold & decor.................450.00
Chrysanthemum Sprig, celery vase, gold & decor, rare..............700.00
Chrysanthemum Sprig, compote, jelly; gold & decor 150.00
Chrysanthemum Sprig, compote, jelly; no decor...................100.00
Chrysanthemum Sprig, creamer, gold & decor 135.00
Chrysanthemum Sprig, cruet, gold & decor, 6¾".................495.00
Chrysanthemum Sprig, pitcher, water; gold & decor............485.00
Chrysanthemum Sprig, pitcher, water; no decor...................350.00
Chrysanthemum Sprig, shakers, gold & decor, pr 300.00
Chrysanthemum Sprig, spooner, gold & decor.......................135.00
Chrysanthemum Sprig, spooner, no gold..................................75.00
Chrysanthemum Sprig, sugar bowl, gold & decor.................250.00
Chrysanthemum Sprig, toothpick holder, gold & decor 325.00
Chrysanthemum Sprig, toothpick holder, no decor 175.00
Chrysanthemum Sprig, tray, condiment; gold & decor, rare 595.00
Chrysanthemum Sprig, tumbler, gold & decor........................80.00
Dandelion, mug, nutmeg stain 175.00
Delaware, bowl, sauce; pk stain 65.00
Delaware, creamer, breakfast; pk stain 75.00
Delaware, tray, pin; gr stain 85.00
Delaware, tumbler, pk stain 65.00
Diamond w/Peg, bowl, master berry; roses & gold.............225.00
Diamond w/Peg, bowl, sauce; roses & gold.............................50.00
Diamond w/Peg, butter dish, roses & gold............................275.00
Diamond w/Peg, creamer, ind; no decor..................................35.00
Diamond w/Peg, creamer, ind; souvenir...................................50.00
Diamond w/Peg, creamer, roses & gold....................................85.00
Diamond w/Peg, mug, souvenir..50.00
Diamond w/Peg, napkin ring, roses & gold, rare.................175.00
Diamond w/Peg, pitcher, roses & gold, 5½"..........................275.00
Diamond w/Peg, sugar bowl, w/lid, roses & gold.................175.00
Diamond w/Peg, toothpick holder, roses & gold.................175.00
Diamond w/Peg, tumbler, roses & gold.....................................75.00
Diamond w/Peg, water set, souvenir, 7-pc.............................650.00
Diamond w/Peg, wine, roses & gold...65.00
Diamond w/Peg, wine, souvenir..55.00
Everglades, bowl, master berry; gold & decor......................215.00
Everglades, bowl, saucer; gold & decor.....................................60.00
Everglades, butter dish, gold & decor....................................395.00
Everglades, creamer, gold & decor..155.00
Everglades, cruet, EX gold & decor......................................1,200.00
Everglades, shakers, gold & decor, pr.....................................375.00
Everglades, spooner, gold & decor...160.00

Everglades, sugar bowl, w/lid, gold & decor 235.00
Everglades, tumbler, gold & decor...100.00
Fan, bowl, master berry; good gold...200.00
Fan, bowl, sauce; good gold..60.00
Fan, butter dish, good gold...345.00
Fan, creamer, good gold...110.00
Fan, ice cream set, good gold, 7-pc...500.00
Fan, pitcher, water; good gold..300.00
Fan, spooner, good gold...100.00
Fan, sugar bowl, w/lid, good gold..175.00
Fan, tumbler, good gold...85.00
Fan, water set, good gold, 7-pc..725.00
Fine Cut & Roses, rose bowl, fancy int, nutmeg stain 100.00
Fine Cut & Roses, rose bowl, plain int......................................85.00
Geneva, bowl, master berry; floral decor, ftd, oval, 9" L............110.00
Geneva, bowl, master berry; floral decor, rnd, 9" 130.00
Geneva, bowl, sauce; floral decor, oval.....................................50.00
Geneva, bowl, sauce; floral decor, rnd......................................50.00
Geneva, butter dish, floral decor...250.00
Geneva, butter dish, no decor 145.00
Geneva, compote, jelly; floral decor..95.00
Geneva, creamer, floral decor...115.00
Geneva, cruet, floral decor..475.00
Geneva, pitcher, water; floral decor..275.00
Geneva, shakers, floral decor, pr...280.00
Geneva, spooner, floral decor...100.00
Geneva, sugar bowl, open, floral decor.....................................85.00
Geneva, sugar bowl, w/lid, floral decor..................................175.00
Geneva, syrup, floral decor..500.00
Geneva, toothpick holder, floral w/M gold 375.00
Geneva, tumbler, floral decor...60.00
Georgia Gem, bowl, master berry; good gold 135.00
Georgia Gem, bowl, master berry; gr opaque........................115.00
Georgia Gem, butter dish, good gold......................................200.00
Georgia Gem, celery vase, good gold......................................145.00
Georgia Gem, creamer, good gold..100.00
Georgia Gem, creamer, no gold..60.00
Georgia Gem, cruet, good gold...295.00
Georgia Gem, mug, good gold..45.00
Georgia Gem, powder jar, w/lid, good gold..............................80.00
Georgia Gem, shakers, good gold, pr......................................140.00
Georgia Gem, spooner, souvenir...55.00
Georgia Gem, sugar bowl, w/lid, no gold.................................95.00
Grape (& Cable), bottle, scent; orig stopper, nutmeg stain.........650.00
Grape (& Cable), bowl, banana; ftd, nutmeg stain..............350.00
Grape (& Cable), bowl, master berry; flat, nutmeg stain............200.00
Grape (& Cable), bowl, orange; ftd, flat top, nutmeg stain.........400.00
Grape (& Cable), bowl, orange; ftd, nutmeg stain 500.00
Grape (& Cable), bowl, sauce; nutmeg stain, ftd.....................50.00
Grape (& Cable), butter dish, nutmeg stain..........................300.00
Grape (& Cable), compote, jelly; open, nutmeg stain..........150.00
Grape (& Cable), compote, nutmeg stain, 4½x8"..................300.00
Grape (& Cable), cracker jar, nutmeg stain...........................850.00
Grape (& Cable), creamer, breakfast; nutmeg stain................80.00
Grape (& Cable), humidor, bl stain, rare................................950.00
Grape (& Cable), nappy, nutmet stain, rare..............................60.00
Grape (& Cable), pitcher, water; nutmeg stain 550.00
Grape (& Cable), plate, nutmeg stain, 7" 50.00
Grape (& Cable), plate, nutmeg stain, 8" 65.00
Grape (& Cable), powder jar, nutmeg stain............................350.00
Grape (& Cable), punch bowl, w/base, nutmeg stain.........1,900.00
Grape (& Cable), spooner, nutmeg stain.................................155.00
Grape (& Cable), sugar bowl, breakfast; open, nutmeg stain........85.00
Grape (& Cable), sugar bowl, w/lid, nutmeg stain................225.00

Grape (& Cable), tray, dresser; nutmeg stain, scarce, lg 375.00
Grape (& Cable), tray, pin; nutmeg stain 150.00
Grape (& Cable), tumbler, nutmeg stain 75.00
Grape & Gothic Arches, bowl, master berry; pearl w/gold..........200.00
Grape & Gothic Arches, bowl, sauce; pearl w/gold, rare 80.00
Grape & Gothic Arches, butter dish, pearl w/gold 235.00
Grape & Gothic Arches, creamer, pearl w/gold, rare..................100.00
Grape & Gothic Arches, favor vase, nutmeg stain 80.00
Grape & Gothic Arches, goblet, pearl w/gold..............................75.00
Grape & Gothic Arches, pitcher, water; pearl w/gold 300.00
Grape & Gothic Arches, spooner, pearl w/gold 85.00
Grape & Gothic Arches, sugar bowl, w/lid, pearl w/gold 135.00
Grape & Gothic Arches, tumbler, pearl w/gold............................65.00
Grape Arbor, vase, hat form..90.00
Heart w/Thumbprint, creamer 90.00
Heart w/Thumbprint, lamp, good pnt, scarce, 8" 450.00
Heart w/Thumbprint, sugar bowl, ind....................................95.00
Honeycomb, wine..65.00
Horse Medallion, bowl, gr stain, 7"......................................85.00
Intaglio, bowl, master berry; gold & decor, ftd, 9" 250.00
Intaglio, bowl, sauce; gold & decor......................................50.00
Intaglio, butter dish, gold & decor, scarce..............................300.00
Intaglio, compote, jelly; gold & decor...................................125.00
Intaglio, creamer, gold & decor..125.00
Intaglio, pitcher, water; gold & decor....................................395.00
Intaglio, shakers, gold & decor, pr.......................................250.00
Intaglio, spooner, gold & decor..135.00
Intaglio, sugar bowl, w/lid, gold & decor................................180.00
Intaglio, tumbler, gold & decor...95.00
Inverted Fan & Feather, bowl, master berry; gold & decor..........275.00
Inverted Fan & Feather, bowl, sauce; gold & decor 75.00
Inverted Fan & Feather, butter dish, gold & decor.....................400.00
Inverted Fan & Feather, compote, jelly; gold & decor, rare 500.00
Inverted Fan & Feather, creamer, gold & decor.........................175.00
Inverted Fan & Feather, cruet, gold & decor, scarce, 6½" 1,100.00
Inverted Fan & Feather, pitcher, water; gold & decor 700.00
Inverted Fan & Feather, punch cup, gold & decor 250.00
Inverted Fan & Feather, shakers, gold & decor, pr 750.00
Inverted Fan & Feather, spooner, gold & decor.........................165.00
Inverted Fan & Feather, sugar bowl, w/lid, gold & decor 250.00
Inverted Fan & Feather, tumbler, gold & decor.........................115.00
Jackson (Alaska Variant), bowl, master berry; good gold, ftd......150.00
Jackson (Alaska Variant), bowl, sauce; good gold..........................50.00
Jackson (Alaska Variant), creamer, good gold..............................85.00
Jackson (Alaska Variant), pitcher, water; good gold...................250.00
Jackson (Alaska Variant), pitcher, water; no decor.....................175.00
Jackson (Alaska Variant), shakers, good gold, pr.......................195.00
Jackson (Alaska Variant), tumbler, good gold..............................50.00
Louis XV, bowl, master berry; good gold.................................250.00
Louis XV, bowl, sauce; good gold, ftd.......................................50.00
Louis XV, butter dish, good gold..250.00
Louis XV, creamer, good gold...85.00
Louis XV, pitcher, water; good gold.......................................250.00
Louis XV, spooner, good gold..110.00
Louis XV, sugar bowl, w/lid, good gold...................................165.00
Louis XV, tumbler, good gold...65.00
Maple Leaf, bowl, master berry; gold & decor, scarce.................350.00
Maple Leaf, bowl, sauce; gold & decor, scarce............................50.00
Maple Leaf, butter dish, gold & decor.....................................350.00
Maple Leaf, compote, jelly; gold & decor, rare 475.00
Maple Leaf, creamer, gold & decor..150.00
Maple Leaf, cruet, gold & decor, rare...................................3,000.00
Maple Leaf, pitcher, water; gold & decor.................................400.00
Maple Leaf, shakers, gold & decor, very rare, pr.....................1,000.00

Maple Leaf, spooner, gold & decor..175.00
Maple Leaf, sugar bowl, w/lid, gold & decor.............................250.00
Maple Leaf, tumbler, gold & decor..100.00
Panelled Poppy, lamp shade, nutmeg stain, scarce......................900.00
Peacock & Urn, bowl, ice cream; nutmeg stain, sm.......................80.00
Peacock & Urn, bowl, ice cream; nutmeg stain, 10".....................350.00
Punty Band, shakers, pr..175.00
Punty Band, spooner, floral decor...100.00
Punty Band, tumbler, floral decor, souvenir...............................65.00
Ribbed Drape, bowl, sauce; roses & gold...................................45.00
Ribbed Drape, butter dish, scalloped, roses & gold....................400.00
Ribbed Drape, compote, jelly; roses & gold, rare.......................200.00
Ribbed Drape, creamer, roses & gold, scarce............................180.00
Ribbed Drape, cruet, roses & gold, rare..................................700.00
Ribbed Drape, pitcher, water; roses & gold, rare.......................365.00
Ribbed Drape, shakers, roses & gold, rare, pr...........................400.00
Ribbed Drape, spooner, roses & gold......................................195.00
Ribbed Drape, sugar bowl, w/lid, roses & gold..........................250.00
Ribbed Drape, toothpick holder, roses & gold...........................475.00
Ribbed Drape, tumbler, roses & gold.......................................75.00
Ribbed Thumbprint, wine, floral decor.....................................80.00
Ring Band, bowl, master berry; roses & gold.............................200.00
Ring Band, bowl, sauce; roses & gold.......................................50.00
Ring Band, butter dish, roses & gold......................................300.00
Ring Band, compote, jelly; roses & gold, scarce.........................195.00
Ring Band, creamer, roses & gold..125.00
Ring Band, cruet, roses & gold, scarce....................................500.00
Ring Band, cruet, roses decor, clear stopper.............................175.00
Ring Band, shakers, roses & gold, pr......................................155.00
Ring Band, spooner, roses & gold..125.00
Ring Band, syrup, roses & gold, scarce....................................475.00
Ring Band, table set, 4-pc...600.00
Ring Band, toothpick holder, roses & gold...............................155.00
Ring Band, tray, condiment; roses & gold.................................200.00

Ring Band, water set with enameled roses: Pitcher, $375.00; Tumbler, from $75.00.

Singing Birds, mug, nutmeg stain..85.00
Tarentum's Victoria, bowl, master berry; gold & decor................200.00
Tarentum's Victoria, butter dish, gold & decor, rare...................350.00
Tarentum's Victoria, celery vase, gold & decor, rare...................300.00
Tarentum's Victoria, creamer, gold & decor, scarce....................135.00
Tarentum's Victoria, pitcher, water; gold & decor, rare...............375.00
Tarentum's Victoria, spooner, gold & decor..............................135.00
Tarentum's Victoria, sugar bowl, w/lid, gold & decor..................175.00
Tarentum's Victoria, tumbler, gold & decor...............................75.00
Vermont, butter dish, bl decor..195.00
Vermont, toothpick holder, bl decor......................................175.00
Vermont, vase, floral decor, jeweled.....................................125.00
Wide Band, bell, roses...195.00
Wild Bouquet, bowl, sauce; gold & decor...................................60.00

Wild Bouquet, butter dish, gold & decor, rare 750.00
Wild Bouquet, creamer, no gold 145.00
Wild Bouquet, spooner, gold & decor.................................250.00
Wild Bouquet, tumbler, no decor...................................100.00
Winged Scroll, bowl, master berry; gold & decor, 11" L.............250.00
Winged Scroll, bowl, sauce; good gold...............................50.00
Winged Scroll, butter dish, good gold 235.00
Winged Scroll, butter dish, no decor..............................175.00
Winged Scroll, celery vase, good gold, rare 400.00
Winged Scroll, cigarette jar, scarce................................195.00
Winged Scroll, compote, ruffled, rare, 6¾x10¾"....................495.00
Winged Scroll, cruet, good gold, rpl clear stopper 400.00
Winged Scroll, hair receiver, good gold.............................135.00
Winged Scroll, pitcher, water; bulbous, good gold 400.00
Winged Scroll, shakers, bulbous, good gold, rare, pr.....................400.00
Winged Scroll, shakers, str sides, good gold, pr 300.00
Winged Scroll, sugar bowl, w/lid, good gold.........................175.00
Winged Scroll, syrup, good gold 450.00
Winged Scroll, tumbler, good gold...................................75.00

Cut Glass

The earliest documented evidence of commercial glass cutting in the United States was in 1810; the producers were Bakewell and Page of Pittsburgh. These first efforts resulted in simple patterns with only a moderate amount of cutting. By the middle of the century, glass cutters began experimenting with a thicker glass which enabled them to use deeper cuttings, though patterns remained much the same. This period is usually referred to as Rich Cut. Using three types of wheels — a flat edge, a mitered edge, and a convex edge — facets, miters, and depressions were combined to produce various designs. In the late 1870s, a curved miter was developed which greatly expanded design potential. Patterns became more elaborate, often covering the entire surface. The Brilliant Period of cut glass covered a span from about 1880 until 1915. Because of the pressure necessary to achieve the deeply cut patterns, only glass containing a high grade of metal could withstand the process. For this reason and the amount of handwork involved, cut glass has always been expensive. Bowls cut with pinwheels may be either foreign or of a newer vintage, beware! Identifiable patterns and signed pieces that are well cut and in excellent condition bring the higher prices on today's market. For more information, we recommend *Evers' Standard Cut Glass Value Guide* (Collector Books). See also Dorflinger; Hawkes; Libbey; Tuthill; Val St. Lambert; other specific manufacturers.

Basket, Daisy, Pitkins & Brooks, 8", from $475 to 525.00
Basket, Zesta, Pitkins & Brooks, 7", from $300 to 350.00
Bell, Buzz Star, call bell, from $200 to 250.00
Bonbon, Adonis, TB Clark & Co, from $85 to 100.00
Bonbon, Crescent, Pitkins & Brooks, 4¾", from $60 to...............70.00
Bonbon, Thelma, JD Bergen, 9", from $75 to 90.00
Bottle, cologne; Jewel, rnd, TB Clark & Co, 8-oz, from $75 to ..100.00
Bottle, scent; Russian & Bar, 8".....................................100.00
Bottle, worchestershire; Delmar, Pitkins & Brooks, 8", from $125 to.150.00
Bowl, Ambrose, JD Bergen, 9", from $200 to...........................250.00
Bowl, Coronet, Higgins & Seiter, 8", from $100 to 125.00
Bowl, finger; Cut Star, Higgins & Seiter, from $20 to 25.00
Bowl, finger; Rajah, Pitkins & Brooks, from $40 to.....................50.00
Bowl, grapefruit; Topaz, Pitkins & Brooks, 7½", from $125 to........150.00
Bowl, Monarch, Higgins & Seiter, 8", from $75 to......................100.00
Bowl, salad; Cleo; Pitkins & Brooks, 8", from $200 to 250.00
Bowl, salad; Mikado, Pitkins & Brooks, 8", from $200 to...........250.00
Bowl, whipped cream; Liberty, Averbeck, 4½x7", from $125 to .150.00
Butter tub & plate, Manhattan, TB Clark & Co, from $200 to..250.00

Butterette, Lady Curzon, Averbeck, 3½", from $25 to.................30.00
Candlestick, Victoria, JD Bergen, 7", from $125 to 150.00
Carafe, Atlas, JD Bergen, qt, from $100 to 125.00
Carafe, Roland, JD Bergen, qt, from $175 to 200.00
Carafe, Tornado, Higgins & Seiter, from $150 to 175.00
Celery dip, Oval, Pitkins & Brooks, 1⅞", from $8 to.................10.00
Celery tray, Bowa, Pitkins & Brooks, 12", from $200 to..............225.00
Celery tray, Premier, JD Bergen, 5x11", from $200 to................250.00
Celery tray, Winola, TB Clark & Co, from $75 to 100.00
Cheese dish, Manhattan, TB Clark & Co, from $250 to 300.00
Comport, Beacon, JD Bergen, 6", from $125 to 150.00
Comport, Heart, Pitkins & Brooks, 7½", from $200 to...............225.00
Comport, Radium, Averbeck, tall stem, 6", from $150 to 175.00
Cordial set, Glenwood, JD Bergen, decanter+6 cordials+tray, $750 to.1,000.00
Creamer & sugar bowl, Belmont, Pitkins & Brooks, from $125 to.150.00
Creamer & sugar bowl, Vienna, Averbeck, from $100 to............125.00
Creamer & sugar bowl, Webster, Higgins & Seiter, from $100 to.125.00
Cruet, Garland, JD Bergen, ½-pt, from $175 to 200.00
Cruet, Premier, JD Bergen, ½-pt, from $125 to 150.00
Cup, Garland, Pitkins & Brooks, from $25 to..........................30.00
Cup, Monticello, JD Bergen, from $30 to..............................35.00
Cup, Wabash, JD Bergen, from $30 to.................................35.00
Decanter, Aladdin, Pitkins & Brooks, from $200 to....................250.00
Decanter, Golf, JD Bergen, 1-pt, from $150 to 200.00
Decanter, Liberty, Averbeck, from $250 to............................300.00
Decanter, Marie, JD Bergen, 1-qt, from $350 to 400.00
Goblet, Belmont, Pitkins & Brooks, from $40 to.......................50.00
Goblet, Florida, Averbeck, from $40 to...............................50.00
Goblet, Marie, JD Bergen, from $55 to................................60.00
Hair receiver, Aladdin, Pitkins & Brooks, 4½", from $200 to.....225.00
Hatpin holder, Vivian, Pitkins & Brooks, 7", from $125 to.........150.00
Humidor, Seaside, JD Bergen, 25 cigars, from $250 to................300.00
Ice tub & plate, Napoleon, Higgins & Seiter, from $250 to.......300.00
Jug, Georgia, Averbeck, 9¾x7½", from $200 to 250.00
Jug, Jewel, wide mouth, TB Clark & Co, qt, from $125 to..........150.00
Jug, Palmetto, Flemish style, TB Clark & Co, from $150 to 250.00
Knife rest, Hexagon, Pitkins & Brooks, 4", from $15 to 18.00
Lamp, Chrysanthemum, electric, 32 prisms, Pitkins & Brooks, 17", up to..1,750.00
Lamp, Oro, electric, Pitkins & Brooks, 14", from $1,200 to 1,500.00
Nappy, Canton, Averbeck, 7", from $110 to 125.00
Nappy, Gem, hdl, Averbeck, 5", from $40 to 60.00
Nappy, Jewel, TB Clark & Co, 6", from $55 to.........................70.00
Nappy, Marietta, hdl, Averbeck, 6", from $60 to 70.00
Pickle dish, Nellore, Pitkins & Brooks, 7", from $150 to 175.00
Pitcher, Bedford, tankard, JD Bergen, 2-qt, from $250 to...........300.00
Pitcher, claret; Syrott, Higgins & Seiter, 3-pt, from $250 to.......300.00
Pitcher, Vienna, Averbeck, 3-pt, from $200 to 250.00

Plate, brilliant cuttings on heavy scalloped blank, 14½", $3,565.00.

Plate, Boston, Averbeck, 7", from $70 to..................................80.00
Plate, Delaware, JD Bergen, 9", from $300 to 350.00
Puff box, Electra, Pitkins & Brooks, from $175 to.....................200.00
Punch bowl, Corsair, JD Bergen, 14", from $500 to...................550.00
Punch bowl, Elgin, JD Bergen, 14", from $700 to......................900.00
Punch bowl, Golf, ftd, JD Bergen, 12", from $1,000 to............1,200.00
Punch bowl, Plymouth, ftd, Pitkins & Brooks, 12", from $850 to.1,000.00
Punch bowl, Rajah, ftd, Pitkins & Brooks, 10", from $750 to.....900.00
Salt cellar, Amelia, Pitkins & Brooks, 3⅛", from $8 to.................10.00
Saucer, Beaver, Pitkins & Brooks, 5", from $70 to.......................85.00
Spoon dish, Baltic, JD Bergen, from $100 to 125.00
Spoon dish, Naples, Averbeck, from $150 to 175.00
Spoon holder, Empress; Jewel, TB Clark & Co, from $100 to.....125.00
Spooner, Ruby, Averbeck, from $100 to.......................................120.00
Spooner, Webster, Higgins & Seiter, from $125 to 150.00
Tray, comb & brush; Electra, Pitkins & Brooks, 11", from $450 to..500.00
Tray, ice cream; Adonis, TB Clark & Co, from $400 to..............450.00
Tray, ice cream; Renaissance, Averbeck, 8x12", from $75 to.......100.00
Tumbler, Evans, JD Bergen, from $30 to.......................................35.00
Tumbler, Golf, JD Bergen, from $35 to...40.00
Tumbler, Nellore, Pitkins & Brooks, from $25 to........................30.00
Tumbler, Saratoga, Averbeck, from $22 to 25.00
Vase, Everett, Higgins & Seiter, 8", from $65 to.........................75.00
Vase, Florida, Averbeck, 12", from $175 to..................................200.00
Vase, Glee, Pitkins & Brooks, 8", from $350 to 400.00
Vase, Liberty, Averbeck, 10", from $125 to 150.00
Whiskey set, Manilla, Higgins & Seiter, decanter+6 shots+tray.750.00

Cut Overlay Glass

Glassware with one or more overlying colors through which a design has been cut is called 'Cut Overlay.' It was made both here and abroad. Watch for new imitations!

Bottle, cordial; cranberry to clear, late 1800s, 14x4½" 450.00
Bottle, scent; cobalt to clear, dmn cuttings, cylindrical, 7¼" 150.00
Bottle, scent; gr to clear, 3" 270.00
Bottle, scent; ruby to clear, vertical stripes, sq sides, 3⅛", pr 450.00
Bowl, brn to yel, flowers & fruit, sm ft, 19th C, 4¼x8¾" 350.00
Bowl, finger; gr to clear, Honeycomb w/rayed base, 2x4¼" 40.00

Comport, green to white with gold, 6¼x7¼", $475.00.

Compote, cobalt/clear, geometrics, appl clear stem, flint, 4½x9" .275.00
Decanter, amber to clear, vintage cuttings, 12"............................200.00
Decanter, bl/wht/clear w/trefoils & ovals, neck panels, 1890s, 10", pr.490.00
Decanter, cobalt to wht, slim, 11¾" 425.00
Decanter, gr to clear, slim neck w/cutting, 14¾", pr....................275.00
Flacon, bl/wht/red, long windows, metal neck & lid, 4⅛".........935.00
Hand cooler, wht to cobalt, floral repousse silver lid, 4½" L.......300.00

Newel post, bl to clear, 12-pointed stars, brass hardware, 8¼" 100.00
Pitcher, caramel/wht/clear, 4¾" 90.00
Vase, cranberry to wht w/HP floral & gold, ftd, 12x9", pr...........975.00

Cut Velvet

Cut Velvet glassware was made during the late 1800s. It is characterized by the effect achieved through the execution of relief-molded patterns, often ribbing or diamond quilting, which allows its white inner casing to show through the outer layer.

Ewer, Dmn Quilt, pk, shouldered, 7½".....................................160.00
Rose bowl, Dmn Quilt, pk, pinched rim, 3 clear frosted ft, 6¾" .550.00
Tumbler, Dmn Quilt, yel w/pk int, 4"...100.00

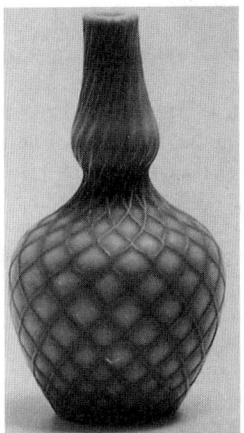

Vase, Diamond Quilt, blue, 6", $150.00.

Vase, Dmn Quilt, bl, spherical w/short can neck, 5¼", from $90 to..115.00
Vase, Dmn Quilt, gr, stick neck, 6"...125.00
Vase, Dmn Quilt, pk, fold-over ruffled rim, 7½"........................250.00
Vase, Dmn Quilt, pk, ruffled/folded rim, Mt WA, 5" 320.00
Vase, Dmn Quilt, pk, stick neck, 6½"...150.00
Vase, Dmn Quilt, robin-egg bl, stick neck, 7" 150.00
Vase, jack-in-the-pulpit; dk pk, fold-down lip, 9¾" 675.00
Vase, rose, bulbous w/tall knopped neck & ruffled/lobed/flared lip, 7".285.00
Vase, vertical ribs, pk, ruffled/folded rim, 8"...............................230.00
Vase, vertical ribs, pk & wht, 6" 180.00

Cybis

Boleslaw Cybis was a graduate of the Academy of Fine Arts in Warsaw, Poland, and was well recognized as a fine artist by the time he was commissioned by his government to paint murals in the Polish Pavilion's Hall of Honor at the 1939 World's Fair. Finding themselves stranded in America at the outbreak of WWII, the Cybises founded an artists' studio, first in Astoria, New York, and later in Trenton, New Jersey, where they made fine figurines and plaques with exacting artistry and craftsmanship entailing extensive handwork. The studio still operates today producing exquisite porcelains on a limited edition basis.

Adoration, #2158, 1982 ....250.00
Allegra, #4005, 1978-81 ....250.00
Aphrodite, #4088, 1983 ....975.00
Baa Baa Blacksheep, 34036, 1981..275.00
Baby Owl, #334, 1957 ....75.00
Barnaby Bear, #686, 1975-77 ....125.00
Bedtime Beth, #5025, 1983..200.00

Bedtime Jody, #5026, 1983......................................200.00
Betty Blue, #479, 1974..250.00
Bird Watcher, #4730, 1970-85..............................225.00
Bluebirds Nesting, #386, 1978..............................225.00
Boy Potter Seller, #5080, 1980-85........................475.00
Calla Lily, #515, 1968-74..995.00
Carmencita, #5373, 1986-93...................................150.00
Carousel Horse, #645, 1973....................................850.00
Cheerful Dragon, bust, #4029, 1979.....................250.00
Cinderella at the Ball, #4033, 1980.......................475.00
Colonial Basket, #527, 1976-78.........................1,900.00
Columbia, #447, 1967-72....................................1,200.00
Cybele, #672, 1973..900.00
Dainty Lady, #4934, 1974-85..................................475.00
David, shepherd boy, 1983.......................................250.00
Dress Maker, #4700, 1970-93.................................280.00
Eagle atop Palisades, #911, 1976...........................450.00
Edith, #4007, 1978-81...250.00
Elizabeth Anne, #490, 1976....................................285.00
Fitzgerald, burro, #632, 1964..................................145.00
Fleurette, #4048, 1981...950.00
Free Spirit, Pegasus colt, #665, 1980 ....475.00
Girl From Valencia, #4841, 1973............................175.00
Girl w/Lamb, #4505, 1969...95.00
Girl w/Pig, #1011, 1969...70.00
Goldfinch, #341, 1961-659......................................275.00
Good Queen Anne, #4001, 1978.............................975.00
Gretel, #476, 1974-76..250.00
Guinevere, #448, 1967-71....................................1,200.00
Heidi, #432, 1962-73..250.00
Hiawatha, #701, 1969...925.00
Holiday Child w/panda, #4024, 1980.....................200.00
Jayne Eyre, #4047, 1981..950.00
Karina, ballerina, #4053, 1981................................500.00
Kristina, #4074, 1982...500.00
Little Blue Heron, #347, 1960-71...........................975.00
Little Duck, #4553, 1969..75.00
Little Girl w/Cat, #1187, 1972-89..........................270.00
Lolita, #5372, 1986-93..150.00
Lotus Blossom, bust, #4030, 1980 ....285.00
Madonna, #2153, 1972-75, 5".................................120.00
Mariko, #1421, 1982-95..1,050.00
My Buddy, #7609, 1989-90 ....350.00
Nancy & Ned, #4003, 1978.....................................265.00
Oceana, #694, 1977...1,275.00
Old Man w/Violin, #4622, 1969-82........................450.00
On Cue, ballerina, #423, 1963-70..........................500.00
Oriental Girl, #4840, 1973-97.................................395.00
Pollyanna, #465, 1971-75...350.00
Priscilla, #489, 1976...875.00
Queen Esther, #644, 1974.......................................950.00
Romeo & Juliet, #4750, 1971 ....850.00
Rumples the Clown, #4014, 1979...........................400.00
Satin, #662, 1978-81..1,100.00
School Days, #7604, 1988-89...................................525.00
Sharpening Cutlery, #5204, 1984-88......................450.00
Shepherd w/Lamb, #4676, 1969...............................80.00
Skylarks (2), #344, 1958-70.................................1,200.00
Spring Bouquets, #7603, 1987-88...........................595.00
Springtime, #427, 1963-69......................................185.00
Suzanne, girl w/kitten, #4016, 1980 ....265.00
Tabitha, kitten, #684G, 1975-77............................190.00
Thumbelina, #434, 1957..125.00
Valencian Lady, #1304, 1974..................................395.00

Wendy, w/doll, #433, 1957......................................275.00
Woman carrying water, #1212, 1973-83................350.00
Wood Duck, #368, 1975-77.....................................425.00
Woody Owl, #20388, 1983.......................................115.00

Czechoslovakian Collectibles

Czechoslovakia came into being as a country in 1918. Located in the heart of Europe, it was a land with the natural resources necessary to support a glass industry that dated back to the mid-fourteenth century. The glass that was produced there has captured the attention of today's collectors, and for good reason. There are beautiful vases — cased, ruffled, applied with rigaree or silver overlay — fine enough to rival those of the best glasshouses. Czechoslovakian art glass baskets are quite as attractive as Victorian America's, and the elegant cut glass perfumes made in colors as well as crystal are unrivaled. There are also pressed glass perfumes, molded in lovely Deco shapes, of various types of art glass. Some are overlaid with gold filigree set with 'jewels.' Jewelry, lamps, porcelains, and fine art pottery are also included in the field.

More than seventy marks have been recorded, including those in the mold, ink stamped, acid etched, or on a small metal nameplate. The newer marks are incised, stamped 'Royal Dux Made in Czechoslovakia' (see Royal Dux), or printed on a paper label which reads 'Bohemian Glass Made in Czechoslovakia.' (Communist controlled from 1948, Czechoslovakia once again was made a free country in December 1989. Today it no longer exists; after 1993 it was divided to form two countries, the Czech Republic and the Slovak Republic.) For a more thorough study of the subject, we recommend *Made in Czechoslovakia* and *Made in Czechoslovakia, Book 2,* by our advisor, Ruth A. Forsythe. Other fine books are *Czechoslovakian Glass & Collectibles, Volumes I* and *II,* by Dale and Diane Barta and Helen M. Rose; *Czechoslovakian Perfume Bottles and Boudoir Accessories* by Jacquelyne Y. Jones North, and *Czechoslovakian Pottery* by Bowers, Closser, and Ellis. In the listings that follow, when one dimension is given, it refers to height; decoration is enamel unless noted otherwise. See also Amphora; Erphila.

Candy Containers

Autumn mottled colors, ruffled rim, crystal thorn hdl w/str top, 6½" .200.00
Bl mottled w/yel ruffle, twisted jet hdl, 8"......................................300.00
Blk w/silver mica, bl int, blk hdl, 8" 350.00
Gr varicolored w/red opaque o/l, gr hdl, 8½"..................................275.00
Lt gr varicolored, matching hdl, 8"..200.00
Red & yel mottle, crystal str-top hdl, 8½".......................................125.00
Red & yel mottle, simple crystal hdl, 6½".......................................175.00
Red & yel mottle, twisted thorn hdl, 7"...220.00
Red solid w/blk rim, 6-scallop, simple crystal hdl, 6½"...............200.00
Yel solid w/blk rim, simple crystal hdl, 6½"....................................200.00
3-color mottle, crystal twisted thorn hdl, 6½" 225.00

Cased Art Glass

Bowl, red w/pnt geometric decor, lg, 3" H.......................................125.00
Candlestick, autumn mottled colors, slim, 8½"................................75.00
Decanter, orange w/exotic bird silver o/l, stick neck, 12" 135.00
Mayonnaise jar, bl varicolored, w/lid, 5½".......................................175.00
Pitcher, orange w/enameled bird & flowers, blk hdl, 11½" 285.00
Vase, bl cased, pleated/ruffled rim, crystal hdls, 8¼"....................110.00
Vase, blk w/exotic bird silver o/l, hdls, 11¾" 175.00
Vase, gr cased w/appl gr ornaments, 5½"...95.00
Vase, gr mottle on blk, metal flower arranger, squat, 4¼" 120.00
Vase, gr w/blk o/l at ft & lower body, 8½".....................................125.00
Vase, med bl w/bl o/l ft & lower body, 10".....................................175.00

Vase, mottled colors, stick form, 8½" 165.00
Vase, orange w/blk rim, ftd urn form, 7¼" 85.00
Vase, pk casing & hdls, canes & partial red o/l, 7" 375.00
Vase, red w/gr aventurine, gourd shape, 7¼" 180.00
Vase, wht w/red mottle low on body, appl ornaments, 8" 275.00
Vase, yel, trumpet neck, ftd, 7¾" 75.00
Vase, yel w/blk decor, 3 blk angle hdls, squat, 3½" 675.00
Vase, yel w/blk serpentine, blk edge on ruffled rim, 10" 120.00
Vase, yel w/blk trim at ruffled rim, slim, 8½" 75.00
Vase, yel w/mottling on lower third, slim, 6¼" 85.00

Cut Glass Perfume Bottles

Amber half-doughnut shape, crystal stopper w/eng figure, 5½" ..450.00
Bl, can neck, crystal teardrop stopper, 3½" 145.00
Bl, shouldered form, simple bl stopper, 7½" 850.00
Bl, 2-pc bottle, crystal flower-shaped stopper, 5¾" 465.00
Blk opaque w/stepped sides, crystal faceted stopper, 5⅞" 250.00

Crystal faceted irregular hexagon base, pink stopper with intaglio-cut lady holding flowering branch, signed, 6¼", $600.00.
(Photo courtesy Monsen and Baer)

Blk transparent w/jewels, matching plain stopper, 4½" 750.00
Crystal, flared shoulders, fan-shaped stopper, 3⅞" 145.00
Crystal, gr-cut-to clear floral stopper, 3⅝" 160.00
Crystal, pyramidal, tall yel prism stopper, 6½" 165.00
Gr, 4-ftd low form, crystal sphere-shaped eng stopper, 7¼" 220.00
Gr waisted form, matching stopper w/diagonal cuttings, 5⅜" 250.00
Pk, shouldered, low, lg pk 16-petal cut stopper, 5½" 200.00
Pk pyramidal base, frosted floral stopper, 6⅛" 225.00

Lamps

Boudoir, lady figural, porc, glass flower skirt & bodice, 10¼" ..1,200.00
Boudoir, mc mottled satin base & shade, 12½" 80.00
Chandelier, yel-gr w/alabaster segments, 12 yel-gr arms, 1930s, 23x29" ..750.00
Desk, metal base, acid-cut shade, 10" 600.00
Perfume, enameled florals, 4" 350.00
Sconce, crystal, 2-arm, prisms, 14½" 300.00
Shade, mottled colors, globular, cased, 5¾" 150.00
Shade, mottled colors, globular, cased, 7¼" 200.00
Student, metal base, acid-cut shade, 21" 1,000.00
Table, Art Deco geometric base & matching conical shade.....1,000.00
Table, basket, mc fruit in bl beaded base, 8" 900.00
Table, basket form, bl flowers, crystal beaded base, 8½" 800.00
Table, basket form, mc nuts & fruit, crystal beaded base, 10¾"...1,200.00
Table, beaded shade, 7" 110.00
Table, Deco figure (gold-tone metal) beside crystal paperweight, 9" .800.00
Table, dk bl lustre, rpl shade, 13¼" 200.00
Table, milk glass w/HP decor, kerosene, 12¾" 200.00
Table, peacock figural, brass w/beaded glass tail/blk onyx base, 12" .1,400.00

Table, pnt decor on clear base & globe shade, 8¾" 500.00

Mold-Blown and Pressed Bottles

Atomizer, bl, shouldered, 3" 45.00
Atomizer, crystal frost w/HP decor, tall ft, 6½" 175.00
Atomizer, orange cased w/blk decor, bulb missing, 5" 85.00
Atomizer, pk cased, bulb missing, 5⅞" 125.00
Cranberry opal Hobnail, bulbous, 5½" 225.00
Crystal w/jewel ornaments, 1½" 145.00
Crystal w/overall jewels, 2¼" 250.00
Gr frosted, shouldered cylinder, w/Deco enameling, 6" 65.00
Gr w/overall jewels, 2⅜" 250.00
Pk, conical w/jewel stopper, 7¼" 110.00
Topaz tinted w/jewel ornaments, 2¼" 100.00

Opaque, Crystal, Colored Transparent Glass

Candy jar, geometric mc decor on clear, 3¾" 175.00
Candy jar, gr, appl apricot base w/3 buttressed ft, w/lid, 6" 275.00
Cocktail shaker, violet-pk, 8¼" 95.00
Decanter, gr w/pnt vertical stripes, 7⅝" 75.00
Decanter, topaz tinted, HP scene, sgn HP by Borokistol..., 10¼" .140.00
Pitcher, bl bubbly, bulbous, 4-bead stopper, 8⅝" 200.00
Vase, bl, trumpet neck, bulbous, 7" 100.00

Vase, cased pink, white, and brown aventurine, 5", $75.00. (Photo courtesy Dale and Diane Barta and Helen M. Rose)

Vase, bl lustre, ftd, flared rim, 5⅞" 750.00
Vase, crystal w/blk & red o/l, 8¼" 200.00
Vase, crystal w/mc canes & yel decor, 5¾" 375.00
Vase, crystal w/red spiral threading, ftd cylinder, 8⅞" 200.00
Vase, fan; orange w/yel o/l, 8" 200.00
Vase, mc mottle on red, stick neck, 8⅛" 85.00
Vase, milky wht opal w/opal ball hdls, 8⅝" 275.00
Vase, pk & bl varicolored, bulbous, sm neck w/flared rim, 7¾" ..200.00
Vase, pk lustre, bl lustre King Tut decor, 3½" 2,500.00
Vase, pk mottled, slim fan-like form, 8¼" 250.00
Wine tumbler, amber, 2⅞" 25.00
Wine tumbler, gr bubbly, HP decor, 4¼" 55.00

Pottery and Porcelain

Ashtray, wht w/bl anchor & wht rope in center, 2x4" 35.00
Basket, blk & wht bands on yel, blk trim at rim & hdl, 4¼" 45.00
Basket, floral on gray w/blk rim & hdl, 3¾" 45.00
Candlestick, blk & wht bands on bright orange, flared base, 10", pr.130.00
Candlestick, wht lustre w/dk bl trim, sq base, 4" 35.00
Chocolate pot, orange lustre, ear-type hdl, 9½" 55.00

Coaster, single flower center, red & wht, 3" 25.00
Creamer, bright red w/wht hdl, spout & rim, bulbous, 4" 35.00
Creamer, mc flowers on yel w/blk trim, bulbous, 3¾" 65.00
Creamer, moose head, antlers form rim, 3½" 60.00
Cup & saucer, orange-yel lustre w/bl-gray lustre int, 2¼", 5¼" 20.00
Egg cup, flowers & butterfly on wht, bl sponge band at top, 3¾" .50.00
Figurine, goose, wht w/gold trim, 5¼" 45.00
Figurine, horse, blk w/turq mane, tail & hooves, 8" 60.00
Flowerpot, turq w/yel leaf band at top, 3½" 25.00
Pitcher, church scene w/orange & blk trim, ornate hdl, 7¾" 75.00
Pitcher, mc Deco floral on wht, orange trim, 5½" 50.00
Pitcher, milk; pnt scenic design, orange rim & hdl, cobalt at ft, 7"...60.00
Plate, salad; majolica, leaf in lt gr/brn/yel, 7" 50.00

Teapot, lady with fruit basket, 8", $185.00. (Photo courtesy Dale and Diane Barta and Helen M. Rose)

Sugar bowl, shell shape, wht pearl lustre, 4-ftd, 2¾" 55.00
Teapot, wht pearl lustre w/gr hdl, finial & accents, bulbous, 4" 45.00
Toothpick holder, elephant figural, wht w/gr seat, 3½" 45.00
Vase, bl irid w/blk rim, slim, 9¼" 65.00
Vase, blk Deco medallion & lower band on beige crackle-look, hdls, 10" .100.00
Vase, boy & girl silhouette reserve on dk orange-red, 5½" 75.00
Vase, floral band on blk & wht stripes, 4½" 45.00
Vase, floral on wht w/blk & orange trim, bulbous, 4¾" 55.00
Vase, flower garland on orange, fan shape w/low hdls, 5¾" 35.00
Vase, gray pearl lustre, blk rim & angle hdls, 5½" 30.00
Vase, mc floral medallion on red w/blk trim, flared/scalloped rim, 5".60.00
Vase, roses on brn to ivory, hdls, 5⅜" 30.00
Vase, varicolored w/blk linear design, ftd wedge shape, 11¾" 115.00

D'Argental

D'Argental cameo glass was produced in France from the 1870s until about 1920 in the Art Nouveau style. Browns and tans were favored colors used to complement floral and scenic designs developed through acid cuttings. Our advisor for this category is Don Williams; he is listed in the Directory under Missouri.

Cameo

Box, floral, maroon on amber, cylindrical, 3⅝x3" 880.00
Ceiling shade, pine cones/needles, rpl sockets, minor rim flakes, 18" .1,860.00
Vase, floral, red on amber, trumpet neck, 10" 865.00
Vase, maple leaves & seeds, orange/brn on amber, ovoid, 10" .1,035.00
Vase, morning glories, amber/red/rust, long slim neck, low width, 10" ..750.00
Vase, roses, red on yel, slim, flared ft, 14" 1,900.00
Vase, seed pod branches, plum/wine on dk amber, ovoid, 12"..1,600.00

Vase, seed pods/leafy branches, plum/wine on dk amber, 12"...1,600.00

Daum Nancy

Daum was an important producer of French cameo glass, operating from the late 1800s until after the turn of the century. They used various techniques — acid cutting, wheel engraving, and handwork — to create beautiful scenic designs and nature subjects in the Art Nouveau manner. Virtually all examples are signed. Daum is still in production, producing many figural items. Our advisor for this category is Don Williams; he is listed in the Directory under Missouri.

Cameo

Bottle, scent; floral cut/pnt on textured purple, w/lid, 3" 800.00
Bowl, berries/thorn branches, vitrified bl-gr/yel on lav/yel frost, 8"..2,000.00
Bowl, floral, cut/pnt on yel & brn mottle, 3-sided, 5½" 850.00
Bowl, irises cut/pnt on frost, 3½" 900.00
Bowl, magnolias, mocha on gray frost w/tinge of tan, incurvate, 11"..2,000.00
Bowl, violets, cut/pnt, 2½" H 2,475.00
Bowl vase, tiger lilies, orange/red on umber, cross mk, 7x11" 4,000.00
Box, delicate floral or thistle repeats, pnt/gilt on amethyst, sq, 5"..1,250.00
Dish, barren trees, cut/pnt, rim w/3 scalloped sides, 4" W..........920.00
Inkwell, floral on all 4 sides, blk on red-orange, matching lid, 5x4"..1,955.00
Jar, sailboats cut/pnt on orange & yel mottle, w/lid, 2" 1,100.00
Lamp, grapevines, on dome shade/shaped base w/flaring ft, 19" .12,000.00
Lamp, leaves, brn on mottled orange flaring 11" shade/tall base, 23" .12,880.00
Lamp, tobacco plants, orange/red on apricot 9" shade/base, 18".12,000.00
Lamp, winter trees cut/pnt on dome shade/slim base (rpr/chips), 14"..4,400.00
Salt cellar, palm trees/ocean scene, 2" L 1,440.00
Salt cellar, wooded scene cut/pnt on gr, 2" L 1,800.00
Sconce, comma shapes, gold/mc on 6" gray shade; lg 3-D metal bird mt..1,725.00
Snuff bottle, windmills/church/winter landscape, 2¼" 1,265.00
Tumbler, rain/windblown trees, cut/pnt, 3½" 3,600.00
Vase, berries/leaves, gr on pk to gr martele, ftd, 7½" 1,200.00
Vase, berries/leaves, wine on ivory, rnd w/stick neck, 2" 800.00
Vase, berries/leaves cut/pnt on frost to red, cylindrical, 4" 1,100.00
Vase, berries/leaves/stems cut/pnt on mottled yel, frost & brn, 15"..1,600.00
Vase, boats/windmill cut/pnt on wht frost, stick neck, mini, 3" ...1,200.00
Vase, bud; lilies/floral medallions, amethyst to clear w/gold, 9".1,380.00
Vase, daffodils, wht (yel in refractive light), trumpet form, 13"..6,000.00
Vase, daisies, bl on mottled frost, wheel-cvd, tumbler form, 7" .2,000.00
Vase, dandelions, pk on gr martele, 10" 3,500.00
Vase, Dutch village/winter scene, cut/pnt, 11½x6" 5,175.00
Vase, floral, amethyst on bl opal w/lt martele, ftd, cross mk, 4"...2,000.00
Vase, floral, red on mottle, 4-sided, 5" 1,150.00
Vase, floral cut/pnt on brn & yel mottle, cylindrical, 5" 1,100.00
Vase, floral w/leaves, bl to yel & rose, slim, 20" 5,500.00
Vase, flowers/butterfly cut/pnt on orange & gr, shouldered, ftd, 4" .1,200.00
Vase, fuchsias cut/pnt on bl & wht mottle, tumbler form, 5"...1,495.00
Vase, landscape cut/pnt on brn to orange, 8" 2,000.00
Vase, leaves, brn on mc mottle, shouldered w/flaring ft, 12"...1,150.00
Vase, mtns/trees cut/pnt on wht frost, stick neck, 3" 1,500.00
Vase, nasturtiums, brn/red on apricot/gray frost, slim w/bun ft, 20" .3,500.00
Vase, orchids cut/pnt on brn & yel mottle, long slim neck, 8"..2,500.00
Vase, orchids cut/pnt on frost & lt gr, cylindrical, 3½" 1,100.00
Vase, peasant/farm, cut/pnt, gilt/pnt relief briars at long neck, 10"..2,130.00
Vase, river scenic cut/pnt on yel, mini, 1¼" 550.00
Vase, sailing ships, cut/pnt, tumbler form, 5" 1,100.00
Vase, serrated leaves on vines, brn on purple mottle/gray, 14".2,350.00
Vase, snow scene w/trees cut/pnt on frost, mini, 2" W...........1,250.00
Vase, storks/pond lilies, cut/pnt on apricot to gray, 3 hdls, 7"..5,750.00
Vase, summer scene, yel/bl/gr, pillow form w/4-lobe rim, 4x7".2,600.00
Vase, thistles, gr on pk martele, 1895-1920, 8¾"...................2,000.00

Vase, tobacco blossoms, plum on butterscotch mottle, floriform, 6" .2,300.00
Vase, trees cut/pnt on ivory mottle, shouldered w/bun ft, 16"..4,760.00
Vase, trees in landscape, gr on amber to yel, ftd, 15½" 3,250.00
Vase, trees/brush, blown-out, dk on lt brn, 11½".....................7,000.00
Vase, trees/mtn shoreline, dk umber on yel, shouldered, 10½".2,350.00
Vase, winter scene on orange to yel, banjo shape, 20x10½"....9,200.00
Vase, winter trees/blk birds, cut/pnt on wht, bottle form, 2½"..3,395.00

Enameled Glass

Pitcher, Dutch scene w/people/windmill/etc, enamel on frost, 5"..850.00
Vase, Dutch windmill pnt on frost, mini, 2" 1,250.00
Vase, landscape, brn/amber, wide mouth/swollen cylinder, 4⅝".1,115.00
Vase, poppies pnt on frost & gr w/gold, silvered ft, 5" 600.00
Vase, sailboats on mottled amber, swollen cylinder, 8".............2,235.00
Vase, trees/path/windmill, blk on lt gray, egg shaped, 3" 1,035.00
Vase, windmill/ship on wht opal, onion form w/long slim neck, 6½" ..1,150.00

De Vez

De Vez was a type of acid-cut French cameo glass produced by Cristal-lerie de Pantin in Paris around the turn of the century. Our advisor for this category is Don Williams; he is listed in the Directory under Missouri.

Cameo

Lamp base, mtn lake, bl/yel on gray, metal fittings, 10"...............285.00

Vase, lake scene with trees and mountains, four-color, 14", $2,500.00. (Photo courtesy Don Williams)

Vase, castle landscape, pk/yel/gr, 8¼x5".................................1,175.00
Vase, leafage, amethyst on pk, gourd form, mini, ¾" 345.00
Vase, leaves/acorns, gr on frost, short neck, 6½"..........................425.00
Vase, lg floral blooms, rose/wine on amber, full body w/can neck, 12".2,400.00
Vase, mtn scene, bl on yel/lav, shouldered, 6¼" 1,000.00
Vase, mums, red on frost to amber, short neck, 7½" 400.00
Vase, roses/trees/mtns, gr over yel, tapered, 10½".....................1,600.00
Vase, trees/village/mtns, amber/olive/bl/frost, ovoid, 10"..........1,800.00
Vase, windmills/ships/clouds, brn/orange/frost/yel, 7½"............1,200.00

De Vilbiss

Perfume bottles, atomizers, and dresser accessories marketed by the De Vilbiss Company are appreciated by collectors today for the various types of lovely glassware used in their manufacture as well as for their pleasing shapes. Various companies provided the glass, while De Vilbiss made only the metal tops. They marketed their merchandise not only here but in Paris, England, Canada, and Havana as well. Their marks were acid stamped, ink stamped, in gold script, molded in, or on paper labels. One is no more significant than another. Our advisor for this category is Randy Monsen; he is listed in the Directory under Virginia.

Atomizer, acid etched & bl enamel, orig ball w/crochet cover, 7".100.00
Atomizer, amber irid, hexagonal, rpl ball/tassel, 6¾"..................255.00
Atomizer, amber trumpet form w/gold flower trellis, rpl ball, 10".550.00
Atomizer, bl Aurene trumpet form, Steuben, rpl ball/tassel, 7" .600.00
Atomizer, bl irid trumpet form, Durand, rpl ball/tassel, 8½" 600.00
Atomizer, bl w/wht pull-up waves, rpl ball, 7⅝" 275.00
Atomizer, blk w/gold leaves & berries in band, rpl ball, 6⅜" 185.00
Atomizer, blk w/metal attachment, Industrial Modern style, 2½".145.00
Atomizer, clear hexagonal bell w/intaglio thistles, rpl ball, 4½" ...90.00
Atomizer, clear w/cut facets, star-cut bottom, rpl ball/tassel, 10".220.00
Atomizer, electric bl w/cut leaves, 6⅛", pr..................................220.00
Atomizer, frosted w/emb leaves & berries, rpl ball/tassel, 6½" 415.00
Atomizer, gold dots on wht satin w/coralene glass buttons, 5½" ...85.00
Atomizer, gold scrolls at top & along base on clear, all orig, 4¾"..200.00
Atomizer, gr to wht opal, violet stones, gold ft, ball missing, 6¾"..3,000.00
Atomizer, irid w/gold metal holder w/3 ft, Le Moderne #510, 3¼" ...355.00
Atomizer, mercury glass w/yel crackle o/l, all orig, 4x4" 150.00
Atomizer, mirrored crackle, all orig, 4⅞x3" (base) 145.00
Atomizer, peach w/enameled peach & gold bands, rpl ball, 6½"..120.00
Atomizer, pk cone, metal attachment, orig ball, 2½" 45.00
Atomizer, pk/blk/gold geometrics, acorn finial, 10" 2,400.00
Atomizer, wht w/clear bull's eye, rpl cord & ball, 5¼" 115.00
Bottle, blk on chrome ped base, chrome/blk glass medallion dropper, 6"..385.00
Bottle, blk w/gold scrolled ft, glass dropper, 6¼"........................300.00
Bottle, clear & bl flashed, triangular, cut leaves, 6½" 385.00
Bottle, lt amber irid w/metal neck & dropper, 5⅜", NM.............100.00
Bottle, orange enamel w/gold roses, metal neck/dropper, 6¼" 385.00
Bottle, pk teardrop on brass fr, hex base, Debutant #315, 6".......385.00
Bottle, purple irid, gold-tone pump sprayer & cap, 4"...................90.00
Bottle, yel satin cone w/gold ring, 6"..155.00
Bottle & atomizer, violet w/blk & gold sqs, 6¾", pr 880.00
Ginger jar, amber & satin w/gold & wht florals, 6¼" 330.00
Lamp, perfume; nymph riding waves under moon, 7¾" 465.00
Lamp, perfume; 2 glass panels w/gold birds ea side, 8½"............440.00
Tray, gold enamel w/etched birds & flowers, 10½" 145.00
Vase, bird/branches, cut-bk/gold enameled, fan form, 8½"..........400.00

Decanters

Ceramic whiskey decanters were brought into prominence in 1955 by the James Beam Distilling Company. Few other companies besides Beam produced these decanters during the next ten years or so; however, other companies did eventually follow suit. At its peak in 1975, at least twenty prominent companies and several on a lesser scale made these decanters. Beam stopped making decanters in mid-1992. Now only a couple of companies are still producing these collectibles.

Liquor dealers have told collectors for years that ceramic decanters are not as valuable, and in some cases worthless, if emptied or if the federal tax stamp has been broken. Nothing is further from the truth. Following are but a few of many reasons you should consider emptying ceramic decanters:

1) If the thin glaze on the inside ever cracks (and it does in a small percentage of decanters), the contents will push through to the outside. It is then referred to as a 'leaker' and worth a fraction of its original value.

2) A large number of decanters left full in one area of your house poses a fire hazard.

3) A burglar, after stealing jewelry and electronics, may make off with some of your decanters just to enjoy the contents. If they are empty,

chances are they will not be bothered.

4) It is illegal in most states for collectors to sell a full decanter without a liquor license.

Unlike years ago, few collectors now collect all types of decanters. Most now specialize. For example, they may collect trains, cars, owls, Indians, clowns, or any number of different things that have been depicted on or as a decanter. They are finding exceptional quality available at reasonable prices, especially when compared with many other types of collectibles.

We have tried to list those brands that are the most popular with collectors. Likewise, individual decanters listed are the ones (or representative of the ones) most commonly found. The following listing is but a small fraction of the thousands of decanters that have been produced.

These decanters come from all over the world. While Jim Beam owned its own china factory in the U.S., some of the others have been imported from Mexico, Taiwan, Japan, and elsewhere. They vary in size from miniatures (approximately two-ounce) to gallons. Values range from a few dollars to more than $3,000.00 per decanter.

Most collectors and dealers define a 'mint' decanter as one with no chips, no cracks, and label intact. A missing federal tax stamp or lack of contents have no bearing on value. All values are given for 'mint' decanters. A 'mini' behind a listing indicates a miniature. All others are fifth or 750 ml unless noted otherwise. Our advisor for this category is Roy Willis; he is listed in the Directory under Kentucky.

Aesthetic Specialties (ASI)

Kentucky Derby	45.00
Stanley Steamer 1909, blk or gr	65.00
Stanley Steamer 1911, blk	80.00

Ballantine

Fisherman	25.00
Golf Bag	25.00
Knight	10.00

Beam

Casino Series, Barney's Slot Machine	40.00
Casino Series, Binion's Horseshoe	15.00
Casino Series, Harold's Club Pinwheel	45.00
Centennial Series, Civil War North	29.00
Centennial Series, Civil War South	45.00
Centennial Series, Edison Light Bulb	20.00
Centennial Series, Reno	6.00
Centennial Series, San Diego	5.00
Executive Series, 1958, Gray Cherub	125.00
Executive Series, 1959, Tavern Scene	40.00
Executive Series, 1973, Phoenician	12.00
Executive Series, 1974, Twin Cherubs	18.00
Executive Series, 1987, Twin Doves	18.00
Executive Series, 1988, Holiday Carolers	40.00
Foreign Series, Australia, Hobo (Swagman)	20.00
Foreign Series, Australia, Magpies	18.00
Foreign Series, Germany, 1970	10.00
Foreign Series, Italy, Boys Town	9.00
Foreign Series, Seoul, Korea	20.00
Foreign Series, Thailand	6.00
Organization Series, Ducks Unlimited #11	65.00
Organization Series, Ducks Unlimited #12	60.00
Organization Series, Ducks Unlimited #13	40.00
Organization Series, Ducks Unlimited #14	45.00
Organization Series, Ducks Unlimited #15	90.00
Organization Series, Homebuilders	25.00

Organization Series, LVNH Owl	18.00
Organization Series, Marine Devil Dog	45.00
Organization Series, Pearl Harbor, 1976	12.00
Organization Series, Shrine, Moila w/Camel	20.00
Organization Series, Shrine, Moila w/Sword	25.00
Organization Series, Telephone #1, Wall	25.00
Organization Series, Telephone #3, French cradle	25.00
Organization Series, Telephone #5, Pay Phone	60.00
People Series, John Henry	35.00
People Series, King Kamehameha	18.00
People Series, Leprechaun	20.00
Political Series, 1968 Clown, Republican or Democrat	12.00
Political Series, 1972 on Football, Republican or Democrat	15.00
Regal China Series, AC Sparkplug	35.00
Regal China Series, Black Canasta, 1957	12.00
Regal China Series, Canteen	25.00
Regal China Series, Coffee Mill	15.00
Regal China Series, Franklin Mint	10.00
Regal China Series, Grand Canyon	10.00
Regal China Series, Jug, 1978, brn or oatmeal	6.00
Regal China Series, King Kong	20.00
Regal China Series, London Bridge	10.00
Regal China Series, New York World's Fair, 1964	15.00
Regal China Series, Pony Express	10.00
Regal China Series, Redwood	6.00
Regal China Series, Tombstone	10.00
Regal China Series, Yosemite	5.00
Wheel Series, Bass Boat	38.00

Wheel Series, Corvette, 1953, white, 1989, $175.00.

Wheel Series, Chevy '57 Bel Air Hot Rod	110.00
Wheel Series, Corvette, 1968, bl	70.00
Wheel Series, Corvette, 1968, maroon	70.00
Wheel Series, Dodge Challenger, 1970 Hot Rod	60.00
Wheel Series, Dump Truck, Gravel	50.00
Wheel Series, Fire Chief Car, 1934	80.00
Wheel Series, Ford 1903 Model A, blk or red	50.00
Wheel Series, Ford 1913 Model T, blk or gr	50.00
Wheel Series, Ford 1929 Phaeton	75.00
Wheel Series, Ford 1956 Thunderbird, blk or gray	100.00
Wheel Series, Space Shuttle	65.00
Wheel Series, Stutz Bearcat, gray or yel	50.00
Wheel Series, Thomas Flyer, bl or ivory	65.00

Brooks

American Legion, Hawaii	15.00
Bear, Golden	8.00
Bowler	15.00
Cable Car	6.00
Cannon	9.00
Charolais Bull	15.00
Clown w/Accordion	30.00

Elephant, Big Bertha 20.00
Greensboro Open, 1972 ....28.00

Indy Racer #21, 1970, $45.00.

Hog, Razorback, 1969 ....22.00
Jester 10.00
Ontario Racer #10 ....35.00
Silver Dollar 9.00
Tractor, Fordson, 1971 ....20.00
West Virginia Mountain Lady 22.00
West Virginia Mountain Man 65.00

Double Springs

Cord, 1937 ....35.00
Owl, brn or red 15.00
Peasant, Boy or Girl 5.00
Tiger on Ball 20.00

Famous Firsts

Hurdy Gurdy 18.00
Phonograph 45.00
Renault Racer #3A 65.00
Riverboat, Robert E Lee 65.00
Telephone, Floral 25.00
Telephone, French 40.00
Telephone, Johnny Reb 35.00

Hoffman

Aesop's Fable, 6 different, ea 25.00
Bird, Turkey (Gaither), mini 40.00
CM Russell Series, Red River Breed 45.00
CM Russell Series, Red River Breed, mini 15.00
Dogs, 1978, 6 different, mini, ea 30.00
Dogs, 1981, 6 different, mini, ea 22.00
Generation Gap Pair, mini 25.00
Indy Commemorative, 1973 ....50.00
Indy 500 Commemorative, 1972 ....30.00
Mr Lucky Series, Mr Cobbler 29.00
Mr Lucky Series, Mr Cobbler, mini 15.00
Mr Lucky Series, Mr Doctor 40.00
Mr Lucky Series, Mr Doctor, mini 18.00
Mr Lucky Series, Mr Sandman 25.00
Mr Lucky Series, Mr Sandman, mini 12.00
Wildlife Series, Falcon & Rabbit 60.00
Wildlife Series, Falcon & Rabbit, mini 15.00
Wildlife Series, Owl & Chipmunk 55.00
Wildlife Series, Owl & Chipmunk, mini 15.00

Kontinental

Gandy Dancer 25.00

Homesteader 30.00
Innkeeper 30.00
Medicine Man 50.00
Pharmacist 40.00
Prospector 40.00
Prospector, mini 20.00
Saddle Maker 35.00
Sadele Maker, mini 20.00

Lionstone

Annie Christmas 25.00
Betsy Ross 30.00
Blacksmith 30.00
Buccaneer 25.00
Calamity Jane 28.00
Dancehall Girl 60.00
Engineer, Railroad 30.00
Falcon 25.00
Gambler 20.00
Gambler, mini 15.00
Jesse James 25.00
Lonely Luke 30.00
Lonely Luke, mini 18.00
Lucky Buck 30.00
Lucky Buck, mini 18.00
Molly Brown 25.00
Mountain Man 22.00
Paul Revere 30.00
Quail 25.00
Roadrunner 25.00
Roadrunner, mini 15.00
Sheriff 25.00
Sheriff, mini 15.00
Sodbuster 20.00
Stage Driver 25.00
Tinker 25.00
Vigilante 20.00
Woodhawk 25.00

McCormick

Bicentennial Series, Ben Franklin 25.00
Bicentennial Series, Ben Franklin, mini 18.00
Bicentennial Series, John Hancock 25.00
Bicentennial Series, John Hancock, mini 18.00
Bicentennial Series, Thomas Jefferson 25.00
Bicentennial Series, Thomas Jefferson, mini 18.00
Caio Baby 25.00
Carver, George Washington 30.00
Edison, Thomas 30.00
Elvis, Designer I 150.00
Elvis, Designer II 190.00
Elvis, Designer III 250.00
Elvis, Silver Anniversary 175.00
Ewing, JR 60.00
Gunfighter Series, 8 different, ea 40.00
Gunfighter Series, 8 different, mini, ea 25.00
Houston, Sam 35.00
Lobsterman 30.00
Missouri, china 10.00
Missouri, glass 7.00
Packard, 1937, blk or cream 50.00
Pocahontas 90.00

Shrine, Midian..12.00
Strouger Telephone.................................45.00
Thelma Lu...40.00
Thelma Lu, mini.....................................20.00
Twain, Mark...30.00

Old Bardstown

Foster Brooks...25.00
Surface Miner...25.00
Tiger...35.00

Old Commonwealth

Coal Miner #3, w/Lump of Coal...............55.00
Coal Miner #3, w/Lump of Coal, mini......25.00
Coal Miner #5, Coal Shooter....................35.00
Coal Miner #5, Coal Shooter, mini..........20.00
Fireman, Volunteer #5.............................75.00
Fireman, Volunteer #5, mini....................30.00
Fireman, Volunteer #6.............................75.00
Fireman, Volunteer #6, mini....................30.00
Horses of Ireland....................................38.00
Irish Lore...32.00
Lumberjack...35.00
Oktoberfest...45.00

Old Fitzgerald

Old Ironsides..5.00
Pheasant Rising..7.00
Ram, Bighorn...7.00
Texas 'Hook 'em Horns'...........................25.00
Tree of Life..5.00
Venetian...4.00

Old Mr. Boston

Anthony Wayne.......................................10.00
Molly Pitcher...15.00
Nathan Hale...10.00
Race Car #9, red or yel...........................50.00

Ski Country

Antelope, Pronghorn...............................60.00
Basset Hound..65.00
Basset Hound, mini.................................40.00
Buffalo Stampede.....................................60.00
Buffalo Stampede, mini............................25.00
Caveman...30.00
Caveman, mini..20.00
Chicadees...70.00
Chicadees, mini......................................35.00
Condor..55.00
Condor, mini...30.00
Ducks Unlimited, Bufflehead....................70.00
Ducks Unlimited, Bufflehead, mini...........35.00
Ducks Unlimited, Oldsquaw......................70.00
Ducks Unlimited, Oldsquaw, mini.............35.00
Eagle, Easter Seals..................................60.00
Eagle, Easter Seals, mini.........................30.00
Falcon, Gyrafalcon...................................85.00
Falcon, Gyrafalcon, mini..........................35.00

Falcon, Peregrine....................................90.00
Falcon, Peregrine, mini............................20.00
Falcon, Peregrine, 1-gal.........................300.00
Fox Family..70.00
Fox Family, mini.....................................40.00
Hawk Eagle...160.00
Hawk Eagle, mini....................................75.00
Indian, Ceremonial Dancer #1, Eagle......175.00
Indian, Ceremonial Dancer #1, Eagle, mini...35.00
Indian, Ceremonial Dancer #2, Buffalo....180.00
Indian, Ceremonial Dancer #2, Buffalo, mini...45.00
Kangaroo...40.00
Kangaroo, mini..30.00
Labrador w/Mallard Duck........................125.00
Labrador w/Mallard Duck, mini................45.00
Meadowlark...60.00
Meadowlark, mini....................................30.00
Owl, Horned..90.00
Owl, Horned, mini...................................90.00
Peacock...100.00
Peacock, mini..60.00
Penguin Family..70.00
Penguin Family, mini...............................35.00
Polar Bear...60.00
Polar Bear, mini......................................30.00
Raccoon..60.00
Raccoon, mini...38.00
Ringmaster..35.00
Ringmaster, mini.....................................25.00
Swan, Black...65.00
Swan, Black, mini....................................45.00
Woodpecker, Gila.....................................75.00
Woodpecker, Gila, mini............................35.00

Series III, #12, Turkey and Skunks, 1986, $125.00.

Wild Turkey

Crystal, Baccarat...................................250.00
Crystal, Wedgwood.................................195.00
Flask, silver, plastic-covered...................10.00
Flask, stainless steel, leather-covered......20.00
Mack Truck...28.00
Series I, #1..250.00
Series I, #2..150.00
Series I, #3..65.00
Series I, #4..65.00
Series I, #5..30.00
Series I, #6..28.00
Series I, #7..28.00
Series I, #8..45.00
Series II, Lore #1.....................................25.00
Series II, Lore #2.....................................35.00
Series II, Lore #3.....................................48.00

Decoys

American colonists learned the craft of decoy making from the Indians who used them to lure birds out of the sky as an important food source. Early models were carved from wood such as pine, cedar, and balsa and a few were made of canvas or papier-mache. There are two basic types of decoys: water floaters and shorebirds (also called 'stick-ups'). Within each type are many different species, ducks being the most plentiful since they migrated along all four of America's great waterways. Market hunting became big business around 1880, resulting in large-scale commercial production of decoys which continued until about 1910 when such hunting was outlawed by the Migratory Bird Treaty.

Today decoys are one of the most collectible types of American folk art. The most valuable are those carved by such artists as Laing, Crowell, Ward, and Wheeler, to name only a few. Each area, such as Massachusetts, Connecticut, Maine, the Illinois River, and the Delaware River, produces decoys with distinctive regional characteristics. Examples of commercial decoys produced by well-known factories — among them Mason, Stevens, and Dodge — are also prized by collectors. Though mass produced, these nevertheless required a certain amount of hand carving and decorating. Well-carved examples, especially those of rare species, are appreciating rapidly, and those with original paint are more desirable. In the listings that follow, all decoys are solid-bodied unless noted hollow.

Key:
CG — Challenge Grade
DDF — Dodge Decoy Factory
DG — Detroit Grade
MDF — Mason's Decoy Factory
OP — original paint
ORP — old repaint

OWP — original working paint
PDF — Pratt Decoy Factory
PG — Premier Grade
SG — Standard Grade
WDF — Wildfowler Decoy Factory
WOP — worn original paint

Black duck, Chauncey Wheeler, trn head, WOP w/some RP, prof rpr ..575.00
Black duck, in the manner of Barber or Baldwin, glass eyes, EX OP .100.00
Black duck, MDF, CG, WOP, inlet weight, checks/shot..............275.00
Black duck, Tom Fitzpatrick, hollow, EX OP, structurally fine.1,600.00
Black duck pr, Cigar Daisey, glass eyes, NM OP, branded 1,050.00
Black-Bellied Plover, Harry V Shourds, EX OP, shot, ca 1900.2,800.00
Black-Bellied Plover, Harry V Shourds, taken down OP w/old RP, shot ..950.00
Black-Breasted Plover, MDF, tack eyes, nail bill, 1905, EX......5,750.00
Bluebill, Ward Bros, spooney bill, WOP, shot/check in tail, 1930s-40s ..1,400.00
Bluebill drake, Charles McCoy, hollow, dry EX OP, minor split .700.00
Bluebill drake, Harvey Stevens, old RP w/some OP, wear/dents, ca 1880s ..650.00
Bluebill drake, Ira Hudson, rusted tack eyes, WOP, chip.............275.00
Bluebill drake, MDF, glass eyes, WOP, shot scar, rpl filler 175.00
Bluebill drake, Paul Gibson, OP w/sm chips, early 150.00
Bluebill hen, Ben Schmidt, trn head, wing cvg, EX OP 350.00
Bluebill hen, Robert Wm Dixon, EX OP, solid 125.00
Bluewing Teal hen, Davey Nichol, EX OP.................................400.00
Bluewing Teal hen, MDF, SG, pnt eyes, EX OP, rprs/hairline 800.00
Bluewing Teal pr, Davey Nichol, NM OP, structurally EX 1,300.00
Brant, MDF, CG, G- OP, rpr...725.00
Bufflehead drake, MDF, glass eyes, VG OP, rpl neck filler..........325.00
Bufflehead drake, primitive, 2-pc pegged body, WOP.................200.00
Canada goose, Ken Harris, trn cedar head/cork body, NMOP, rough bill.600.00
Canada goose, Willie Leduc, solid body, appl wing tips, EX OP .700.00
Canvasback drake, Benjamin Schmidt, OP w/some working RP, crack..550.00
Canvasback drake, HA Stevens, WOP, prof rpr bill, 1880s.........800.00
Canvasback drake, MDF, Detroit Grade, tack eyes, OP w/touchup .250.00
Canvasback drake, MDF, glass eyes, EX OP, rough 400.00
Canvasback drake, MDF, PG, G OP, rpl filler, removed weight ..575.00

Canvasback drake, MDF, PG Seneca Lake model, WOP, split, shot ..300.00
Canvasback drake, Ward Bros 1948 Model, trn head, RP, Lem Ward, 1967 .1,350.00
Canvasback hen, AE Crowell, EX OP, brand, mini..................1,300.00
Canvasback hen, MDF, glass eyes, WOP, cracked neck filler 200.00
Canvasback hen, MDF, PG, WOP, shot scars/brands...................475.00
Canvasback pr, Ralph Reghi, EX OP, chip, structurally VG........750.00
Chesapeake goose, att Travis Ward, pegged head, some OP, shot ..450.00
Coot, Charles Schoenheider Jr, hollow, mellow OP, cracked bill....275.00
Crow, Charles Perdew, tack eyes, wire legs, hollow, 3-pc, EX OP ...850.00
Golden Plover, Joseph Lincoln, winter plumage, G OP, shot...1,500.00
Golden Plover, New England style, papier-mache, EX OP, rprs, VG ..350.00
Goldeneye drake, MDF, glass eyes, OP, rpl filler, chips 275.00
Goldeneye drake, Rosh Douglas, NM OP, filled lamp hole in bk, shot...100.00
Goldeneye drake, Stevens, tack eyes, WOP, shot struck..............800.00
Goldeneye hen, MDF, WOP, cracked filler, shot.........................250.00
Goose, Herbert Hancock, preening w/Xd wings, EX OP, checks.375.00
Goose, MDF, PG, glass eyes, RP w/some OP, checks/chews 1,650.00
Greenwing Teal drake, Perry Wilcoxen, WOP, rpr, never weighted..900.00
Greenwing Teal drake, Tom Schroeder, EX OP, half-sz, on wooden mt.1,900.00
Greenwing Teal hen, Dr Edgar Burke, cork w/wood head, WOP, ca 1943.1,900.00
Greenwing Teal pr, Ben Schmidt, EX OP, sgn, rare..................9,500.00
Knot, partial OP w/old RP, cvd breast ridge, full body, shot.....1,200.00
Knot or dowitcher, JH Birch, 2-pc, EX OP old RP, 1850s-60s .2,300.00
Mallard drake, Cooper Berkley, raised V wing cvg, fluted tail, NM OP .300.00
Mallard drake, Downeast Sportcraft, EX OP, solid body..............550.00
Mallard drake, Heck Whittington, metal tail spring, trn head, EX OP ..700.00
Mallard drake, MDF, glass eyes, EX OP, chips/missing filler/checks .250.00
Mallard drake, MDF, PG, snakey head, solid, EX OP, ca 1900, shot...800.00
Mallard hen, Bert Graves, dry WOP, sm chip...........................3,850.00
Mallard hen, John Wells, WOP, tight fracture/chip, ca 1900......900.00
Mallard hen, Will Birk, preening, raised wings, EX OP, 1963 .....250.00
Mallard pr, Walter 'Tube' Dawson, WOP, crack/hairline..........1,800.00
Merganser drake, MDF, CG, OP w/wear, narrow checks, rare..1,400.00
Merganser hen, Bob Kerr, glass eyes, EX OP, minor rubs.............375.00
Merganser hen, Orrin Hiltz, old in-use RP, lightly shot 1,600.00
Oldsquaw pr, Holger Smith, EX OP, branded, pr, EX 425.00
Pintail drake, Billy Ellis, NM OP w/EX detail & patina, sm dents...700.00
Pintail drake, Hays, glass eyes, OP w/some RP, crack 325.00
Pintail drake, MDF, CG, OP (possibly taken down), missing filler .500.00
Pintail drake, R Madison Mitchell, high head, EX OP, rubs/dings 1,800.00

Pintail hen, Harold Haertel, 1971, tail repair, minor paint wear, 6½x15¼", $2,200.00. (Photo courtesy Skinner, Inc.)

Pintail drake, Robert Elliston, WOP, loose head, chip, late 1800s...850.00
Pintail hen, Hays, glass eyes, EX OP, cracked filler, early, rare 800.00
Pintail hen, Horace 'Hie' Crandal, EX OP, narrow crack.........1,100.00
Pintail hen, MDF, PG, WOP w/chips, ca 1905........................2,700.00
Plover, EF 'Frank' Adams, NM OP, outstanding detail.............1,200.00
Plover, Herbert Randall, trn head, EX OP, sap stain...................125.00
Red-Breasted Merganser drake, att Miles Hancock, WOP, bill rpr/shot .400.00
Redhead drake, James Look, pnt eyes, molded wings, EX OP, shot/crackle..900.00
Redhead drake, MDF, CG, G OP, missing sliver/checks, wear 325.00

Redhead drake, Robert Elliston, EX OP w/fine detail, dents, 1880s..18,000.00
Redhead hen, MDF, CG, WOP w/minor rpt, shot/filler missing.350.00
Redhead hen, MDF, PG, G OP 1,800.00
Ringbill drake, Mark McNair, trn head, EX OP 1,000.00
Sea gull, Holger Smith, EX OP, dings....150.00
Shoveler drake, Norris Pratt, EX OP by Lem Ward, tiny dings, 1966..425.00
Surf scoter, Geo Boyd, EX OP, minor dings, mini....3,400.00
Swan, Madison Mitchell, EX OP, hollow, ca 1950, crazing/flaking..3,600.00
Tern, Elmer Crowell, standing, split tail, NM OP, dent 4,500.00
Widgeon drake, AE Crowell, EX OP, mellow patina, brand, mini.1,300.00
Widgeon drake, Herter, glass eyes, EX OP, 1893 stamp 150.00
Widgeon drake, MDF, glass eyes, OP w/touch up, rpl filler 325.00
Wigeon, Ken Harris, NM OP, chip/crack 575.00
Wood duck drake, Ward Bros, glass eyes, layered/tacked feathers, 1940s..12,500.00
Yellowlegs, Thomas Gelston, cork, WOP, minor chip, ca 1900 ..550.00

Dedham Pottery

Originally founded in Chelsea, Massachusetts, as the Chelsea Keramic Works, the name was changed to Dedham Pottery in 1895 after the firm relocated in Dedham, near Boston, Massachusetts. The ware utilized a gray stoneware body with a crackle glaze and simple cobalt border designs of flowers, birds, and animals. Decorations were brushed on by hand using an ancient Chinese method which suspended the cobalt within the overall glaze. There were thirteen standard patterns, among them Magnolia, Iris, Butterfly, Duck, Polar Bear, and Rabbit, the latter of which was chosen to represent the company on their logo. On the very early pieces, the rabbits face left; decorators soon found the reverse position easier to paint, and the rabbits were turned to the right. (Earlier examples are worth from 10% to 20% more than identical pieces manufactured in later years.) In addition to the standard patterns, other designs were produced for special orders. These and artist-signed pieces are highly valued by collectors today.

Though their primary product was the blue-printed, crackle-glazed dinnerware, two types of artware were also produced: crackle glaze and flambé. Their notable volcanic ware was a type of the latter. The mark is incised and often accompanies the cipher of Hugh Robertson. The firm was operated by succeeding generations of the Robertson family until it closed in 1943. Our advisor for this category is Dale MacLean; he is listed in the Directory under Massachusetts.

See also Chelsea Keramic Art Works.

Ashtray, cigar; Rabbit, stamped/registered, 6½" dia....450.00
Ashtray, Rabbit, flared rim, stamped, 3¾"....165.00
Bacon rasher, Lobster, stamped twice, 10" dia 1,000.00
Bowl, Lotus, paneled, stamped, 2x5" 825.00
Bowl, Poppy (bending), V notches in rim, registered/D, 3¾x9".1,000.00
Bowl, Rabbit, sm ft, stamped/registered, 3¾x9", EX....300.00
Bowl, Rabbit, stamped, 1½x6"....250.00
Bowl, Rabbit, stamped/registered, 2x4½" 200.00
Bowl, rice; Elephant, stamped, 2x3" 660.00
Bowl, sauce; Pond Lily, stamped/registered, 1½x5½" 475.00
Bowl, soup; Rabbit; stamped, 1½x8½", EX....200.00
Butter pat, Pansy, stamped, 3½" 275.00
Candle snuffer, Rabbit, unmk, 2"....900.00
Charger, Lobster, stamped/registered, 12¼" 1,325.00
Child's dish, Rabbit, stamped, 7¾"....800.00
Coffeepot, Rabbit, cylindrical, angled hdl, stamped/registered, 10"..800.00
Creamer, Elephant & Baby, stamped, mini, 3x3", EX....550.00
Creamer & sugar bowl, Rabbit, stamped, 4", 3¼"....550.00
Cup & saucer, demi; Rabbit, stamped, 2", 4¼" 400.00
Cup & saucer, Rabbit, stamped, 2", 5¼" 325.00
Cup plate, Swan, stamped/registered, NM 385.00
Egg cup, Elephant & Baby, unmarked, 3½" 800.00
Flower frog, Rabbit, figure on domed base, stamped, 6x4½" 1,000.00
Pickle dish, Rabbit, stamped, 2¼x9½", EX....325.00
Pitcher, Night & Morning, stamped/incised D4, tiny flaw, 5x5¼"..600.00
Pitcher, Rabbit, bulbous, stamped, 5x6" 500.00
Pitcher, Rabbit, 3¼"....300.00
Pitcher, refined scrolls, emb ribs, 1850 style, stamped, 5x4"....900.00
Pitcher, Swan, bulbous, stamped, 5x6" 800.00
Plate, Bird in Potted Orange Tree, imp, 8½" 500.00
Plate, Butterfly, stamped, 8½", EX....500.00
Plate, Crab, stamped/imp, 8½" 750.00
Plate, Elephant, stamped/registered, 7½" 800.00
Plate, Elephant & Baby, stamped/imp, 6" 700.00
Plate, Grape, Davenport rebus, stamped, 6" 275.00
Plate, Grape, stamped, slight warp, 8¼"....300.00
Plate, Horse Chestnut, imp, 6" 200.00
Plate, Iris, stamped/imp, 6", EX....225.00
Plate, Landscape & Boat, stamped, 6" 700.00
Plate, Lily, stamped/imp, 6"....750.00
Plate, Lion Tapestry, stamped/registered/imp, 9¾" 1,000.00
Plate, Lobster, stamped, 6⅛"....560.00
Plate, Lobster, stamped, 8¼"....650.00
Plate, Lunar Moth, imp, 6", EX 550.00
Plate, Magnolia, Davenport rebus, stamped/imp, 6" 275.00
Plate, Magnolia, stamped, 6"....250.00

Plate, Nasturtium, stamped and impressed marks, 8¾", $2,600.00.

Plate, Mushroom, stamped/imp, 10⅛"....700.00
Plate, Polar Bear, stamped/imp, 9¾"....880.00
Plate, Pond Lily, Davenport rebus, stamped/imp, 6" 275.00
Plate, Pond Lily, stamped/imp, 10" 400.00
Plate, Poppy, stamped/imp, 8¼"....700.00
Plate, Rabbit, Davenport rebus, stamped, 10" 300.00
Plate, Rabbit, stamped, 6" 195.00
Plate, Snowtree, imp, 10¼" 360.00
Plate, Snowtree, stamped, 6"....220.00
Plate, Swan, stamped/registered, 7½" 475.00
Plate, Swan, stamped/registered/imp, 6" 400.00
Plate, Tufted Duck, imp, 10"....475.00
Plate, Turkey, stamped/registered, 7½" 425.00
Platter, Rabbit, rectangular, stamped/2 imp rabbits, 10" 950.00
Shakers, Rabbit, globular, unmk, 3", pr 450.00
Star dish, Rabbit, 5-sided, stamped, 6x6" 700.00
Stein, Rabbit, tiny rabbit at base of hdl, stamped, 5½x6" 500.00
Sugar bowl, Rabbit, stamped/1931, 4⅞"....375.00
Teapot, Rabbit, stamped/registered, 5½x7"....1,200.00
Tile, Magnolia & Vine, stamped/imp, 3¾x3¾"....1,000.00
Vase, Swan, stamped/registered, 3⅞"....575.00

Degenhart

The Crystal Art Glass factory in Cambridge, Ohio, opened in 1947 under the private ownership of John and Elizabeth Degenhart. John had previously worked for the Cambridge Glass Company and was well known for his superior paperweights. After his death in 1964, Elizabeth took over management of the factory, hiring several workers from the defunct Cambridge Company, including Zack Boyd. Boyd was responsible for many unique colors, some of which were named for him. From 1964 to 1974, more than twenty-seven different moulds were created, most of them resulting from Elizabeth Degenhart's work and creativity, and over 145 official colors were developed. Elizabeth died in 1978, requesting that the ten moulds she had built while operating the factory were to be turned over to the Degenhart Museum. The remaining moulds were to be held by the Island Mould and Machine Company, who (complying with her request) removed the familiar 'D in heart' trademark. The factory was eventually bought by Zack's son, Bernard Boyd. He also acquired the remaining Degenhart moulds, to which he added his own logo.

In general, slags and opaques should be valued 15% to 20% higher than crystals in color.

Beaded Oval Toothpick, Bittersweet...30.00
Beaded Oval Toothpick, Crystal 12.00
Bird w/Cherry Salt, Blue Fire 20.00
Bird w/Cherry Salt, Daffodil 20.00
Bird w/Cherry Salt, Orchid 20.00
Bow Slipper, Milk Blue..20.00
Bow Slipper, Opal to clear..15.00
Buzz Saw Wine, Amberina/Sunset...20.00
Chick Salt, Amber..15.00
Chick Salt, Milk White...20.00
Colonial Drape Toothpick, Cobalt 20.00
Daisy & Button Toothpick, Baby Blue Slag 20.00
Daisy & Button Toothpick, Milk Blue...15.00
Forget Me Not Toothpick, Bluebell 16.00
Forget Me Not Toothpick, Buttercup Slag (very red) 30.00
Forget Me Not Toothpick, Dogwood 35.00
Forget Me Not Toothpick, Old Lavender 20.00
Gypsy Pot Toothpick, Amberina..20.00
Gypsy Pot Toothpick, Fawn 17.50
Gypsy Pot Toothpick, Lavender Blue 37.50
Hand, Crown Tuscan..10.00
Hand, Sapphire 6.00
Hat, Amethyst Satin 18.00
Hat, Vaseline Satin 18.00
Heart Toothpick, Gray Tomato...23.00
Hen Covered Dish, Bluebell, 5"...50.00
Hen Covered Dish, Custard, 5"..50.00
Hen Covered Dish, Honey, 5"...30.00
Hen Covered Dish, Sparrow, 3"..25.00
Hen Covered Dish, Vaseline, 5"..30.00
Hobo Baby Shoe, Caramel Custard Slag 20.00
Lamb Covered Dish, Bernard Boyd's Ebony 75.00
Owl, Amberina...35.00
Owl, Bernard Boyd's Ebony 50.00
Owl, Bloody Mary #2...100.00
Owl, Chad's Blue 40.00
Owl, Cobalt #3 ....25.00
Owl, Cobalt Carnival 125.00
Owl, Dark Heliotrope 75.00
Owl, Dark Rose Marie 20.00
Owl, Gray Green Slag 35.00
Owl, January Blizzard (w/Green Slag) 100.00
Owl, Lemon Opal 30.00
Owl, Light Bluefire 30.00
Owl, Mauve 30.00

Owl, Opalescent 20.00
Owl, Seafoam Green 35.00
Owl, Spice Brown 40.00
Owl, Vaseline...25.00
Pooch, Cobalt Carnival 35.00
Pooch, Gun-Metal Blue 20.00
Portrait Plate, Cobalt...40.00
Pottie Salt, Chocolate Creme Slag 15.00
Pottie Salt, Milk White 10.00
Priscilla Doll, Amethyst 80.00
Priscilla Doll, Dark Rose Marie...100.00

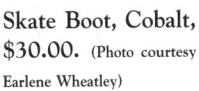

Skate Boot, Cobalt, $30.00. (Photo courtesy Earlene Wheatley)

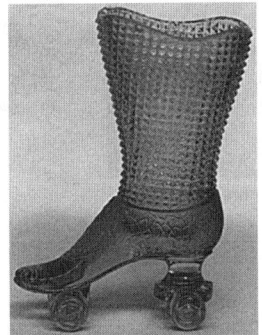

Priscilla Doll, Milk Blue 80.00
Texas Boot, Amethyst 15.00
Texas Boot, Baby Green 20.00
Tomahawk, Cobalt Satin...30.00
Tomahawk, Crown Tuscan..35.00
Tomahawk, Custard...40.00
Tomahawk, Pink Carnival 50.00
Turkey Covered Dish, Dark Heliotrope 75.00

Delatte

Delatte was a manufacturer of French cameo glass. Founded in 1921, their style reflected the influence of the Art Deco era with strong color contrasts and bold design. Our advisor for this category is Don Williams; he is listed in the Directory under Missouri.

Vase, azaleas, pk on pk/gr, classic form on bun ft, 13x5".............900.00
Vase, azaleas/butterflies, aubergine/pk on gray frost, ovoid, 16"..2,235.00
Vase, iris, amethyst on wht mottle, 10" 660.00

Delft

Old Delftware, made as early as the sixteenth century, was originally a low-fired earthenware coated in a thin opaque tin glaze with painted-on blue or polychrome designs. It was not until the last half of the nineteenth century, however, that the ware became commonly referred to as Delft, acquiring the name from the Dutch village that had become the major center of its production. English, German, and French potters also produced Delft, though with noticeable differences both in shape and decorative theme.

In the early part of the eighteenth century, the German potter, Bottger, developed a formula for porcelain; in England, Wedgwood began producing creamware — both of which were much more durable. Unable to compete, one by one the Delft potteries failed. Soon only one remained. In 1876 De Porcelyne Fles reintroduced Delftware on a hard white body with blue and white decorative themes reflecting the Dutch countryside, windmills by the sea, and Dutch children. This manufacturer is the most well known of several operating today. Their products are now produced under the Royal Delft label.

For further information we recommend *Discovering Dutch Delftware, Modern Delft and Makkum Pottery*, by Stephen J. Van Hook (Glen Park Press, Alexandria, Virginia). Examples listed here are blue on white unless noted otherwise. See also specific manufacturers. Our advisor is Ralph Jaarsma; he is listed in the Directory under Iowa.

Bowl, Dutch, cherub design, shallow, mid-18th C, rpr, 1½x8½"..250.00
Bowl, Dutch, peacock, yel rim, mid-18th C, 1½x7¾", EX..........385.00
Bowl, English, elaborate floral/int band & floral, mc, 1775, 9", G..940.00
Bowl, English, house/garden, mc, 1770, 9", EX........................1,175.00
Charger, English, Chinaman sits by flowering tree, 1750s, 14", VG.645.00
Charger, English, floral scene, insect/floral border, 1750s, 12", EX .350.00
Charger, English, lg floral urn, foliage border, 14", EX 550.00
Charger, English, urn of flower/fan of feathers, yel rim, 14", EX .750.00
Charger, Holland (Boch), sleigh scene, scalloped border, 15¼"..155.00
Charger, Rembrandt, bl floral border, mk Royal Bonn Delft, 19¾"..275.00
Clock, French, flowers, sailboats, windmill, brass works, recent, 12"..100.00
Flower brick, English, rtcl top/floral sides, 1760, 5½" L, G 440.00
Plaque, cartouch form w/windmill & canal, ca 1900, #1/A, 19x14"..545.00

Plaque, Dutch, windmill and water scene, 1880s, 22x18½", EX, $1,000.00. (Photo courtesy Collectors Auction Service)

Plate, Dutch, vintage, mid-18th C, flakes/rprs, 8¾" 165.00
Plate, English, floral, mc w/blk outlining on wht, 18th C, 14", EX.765.00
Plate, English, oak leaves, mid-18th C, flakes, 7⅝" 55.00
Plate, English, Oriental scenes, octagonal, mid-18th C, 7⅝"......600.00
Platter, English, war bonnet design, 8-sided, late 18th C, 11½x8"..550.00
Punch bowl, English, Napoleon portrait, 1793, 5¾x12", EX 635.00
Tile, flying goose, 5-color, 4x12", EX...175.00
Tiles, Dutch, dog & cat, molded walnut fr: 11⅜x6½", pr............825.00

Depression Glass

Depression Glass is defined by Gene Florence, author of several bestselling books on the subject, as 'the inexpensive glassware made primarily during the Depression era in the colors of amber, green, pink, blue, red, yellow, white, and crystal.' This glass was mass produced, sold through five-and-dime stores and mail-order catalogs, and given away as premiums with gas and food products.

The listings in this book are far from being complete. If you want a more thorough presentation of this fascinating glassware, we recommend *The Collector's Encyclopedia of Depression Glass, The Pocket Guide to Depression Glass, Elegant Glassware of the Depression Era, Very Rare Glassware of the Depression Years*, and *Treasures of Very Rare Depression Glass*, all by Gene Florence, whose address is listed in the Directory under Kentucky. See also McKee; New Martinsville.

Key: AOP — allover pattern   PAT — pattern at top

Adam, bowl, cereal; pk or gr, 5¾"..55.00
Adam, bowl, pk, oval, 10"...35.00
Adam, candlesticks, gr, 4", pr..115.00
Adam, pitcher, pk or gr, 32-oz, 8"...45.00
Adam, plate, grill; gr, 9"..23.00
Adam, sugar bowl, pk, w/lid...50.00
Adam, vase, pk, 7½"..435.00
American Pioneer, bowl, gr, hdld, 9"..38.00
American Pioneer, coaster, crystal, pk or gr, 3½".......................35.00
American Pioneer, goblet, wine; gr, 3-oz, 4"..............................55.00
American Pioneer, lamp, crystal or pk, 8½"..............................125.00
American Pioneer, plate, gr, hdld, 11½".....................................40.00
American Pioneer, tumbler, crystal or pk, 12-oz, 5"....................50.00
American Pioneer, vase, gr, round, 9".......................................250.00
American Sweetheart, bowl, cereal; smoke & other trims, 6".......50.00
American Sweetheart, bowl, console; red, 18" 1,100.00
American Sweetheart, bowl, soup; pk, flat, 9½".........................75.00
American Sweetheart, lamp shade, cremax................................495.00
American Sweetheart, plate, luncheon; monax, 9"......................12.00
American Sweetheart, plate, salver; bl, 12" 265.00
American Sweetheart, saucer, monax 2.00
American Sweetheart, sugar bowl, red, open, ftd.......................165.00
American Sweetheart, tidbit, pk or monax, 2-tier, 8" & 12".........60.00
Aunt Polly, bowl, gr or irid, 1-hdl, 5½"......................................15.00
Aunt Polly, butter dish, bl, w/lid...250.00
Aunt Polly, plate, sherbet; bl, 6"..15.00
Aunt Polly, tumbler, bl, 8-oz, 3⅝"..38.00
Aurora, creamer, cobalt or pk, 4½"...25.00
Aurora, tumbler, cobalt or pk, 10-oz, 4¾"...................................27.50
Avocado, bowl, relish; crystal, ftd, 6" 9.00
Avocado, cup, gr, ftd, 2 styles, ea..38.00
Avocado, plate, sherbet; pk, 6⅜"..16.00
Avocado, tumbler, pk..195.00
Beaded Block, bowl, crystal, pk, gr or amber, deep, 6" dia...........25.00
Beaded Block, creamer, colors other than crystal, pk, gr or amber...45.00
Block Optic, bowl, salad; gr or pk, 7¼".....................................175.00
Block Optic, candy jar, pk, w/lid, 6¼"......................................150.00
Block Optic, pitcher, gr, 54-oz, 8½"...65.00
Block Optic, shakers, gr, squatty, pr...125.00
Block Optic, tumbler, gr, 3-oz, 2⅝"...25.00
Block Optic, whiskey, gr or pk, 2-oz, 2¼"....................................32.00
Bowknot, bowl, berry; gr, 4½"...25.00
Bowknot, sherbet, gr, low ftd..25.00
Cameo, bowl, salad; gr, 7¼"...65.00
Cameo, candy jar, yel, w/lid, low, 4"..110.00
Cameo, creamer, gr, 3¼"...25.00
Cameo, goblet, wine; pk, 4"...245.00
Cameo, pitcher, juice; gr, 36-oz, 6"...68.00
Cameo, plate, yel, closed hdls, 10½"...14.00
Cameo, sherbet, pk, molded, 3⅛"..75.00
Cameo, vase, gr, 5¾"..250.00
Cherry Blossom, bowl, flat soup; pk, 7¾"..................................100.00
Cherry Blossom, creamer, Delphite...22.00
Cherry Blossom, plate, grill; gr, 9"..34.00
Cherry Blossom, platter, pk or gr, oval, 11"................................60.00
Cherry Blossom, tumbler, Delphite, AOP, ftd, 4-oz, 3¾".............25.00
Cherryberry, bowl, berry; crystal or irid, 4"..................................6.50
Cherryberry, creamer, crystal or irid, lg, 4⅝"..............................18.00
Cherryberry, olive dish, pk or gr, 1-hdl, 5"..................................22.00
Cherryberry, plate, salad; crystal or irid, 7½"...............................8.00
Cherryberry, tumbler, pk or gr, 9-oz, 3⅝"...................................40.00
Chinex Classic, bowl, soup; brownstone or plain ivory, 7¾"........12.50
Chinex Classic, creamer, decal decor...10.00
Chinex Classic, sherbet, castle decal, low ftd...............................27.50

Circle, bowl, gr, 5¼" 20.00
Circle, pitcher, gr, 80-oz 35.00
Circle, plate, gr, 9½" 12.00
Circle, plate, luncheon; pk, 8¼" 10.00
Cloverleaf, bowl, dessert; pk, gr or yel, 4" 40.00
Cloverleaf, shakers, blk, pr 100.00
Cloverleaf, tumbler, yel, ftd, 10-oz, 5¾" 40.00
Colonial, bowl, cereal; gr, 5½" 100.00
Colonial, cup, wht 8.00
Colonial, platter, pk, oval, 12" 35.00
Colonial, sherbet, pk, 3" 25.00
Colonial, tumbler, juice; crystal, 5-oz, 3" 15.00
Colonial Block, bowl, crystal, 4" 4.00
Colonial Block, creamer, wht 8.00
Colonial Block, goblet, pk or gr 14.00
Colonial Fluted, bowl, berry; gr, 4" 12.00
Colonial Fluted, cup, gr 8.00
Colonial Fluted, plate, sherbet; gr, 6" 4.00
Columbia, bowl, cereal; crystal, 5" 18.00
Columbia, butter dish, crystal, w/lid 20.00
Columbia, cup, pk 25.00
Coronation, bowl, berry; pk or Royal Ruby, hdld, 4¼" ...7.00
Coronation, bowl, pk or gr, no hdls, 8" 195.00
Coronation, sherbet, gr 85.00
Cube, bowl, salad; pk, 6½" 14.00
Cube, coaster, pk or gr, 3¼" 10.00
Cube, plate, luncheon; gr, 8" 10.00
Cube, tumbler, pk, 9-oz, 4" 75.00
Diamond Quilted, bowl, pk or gr, 1-hdl, 5½" 7.50
Diamond Quilted, compote, pk or gr, w/lid, 11½" ...95.00
Diamond Quilted, goblet, cordial; pk or gr, 2-oz ...12.00
Diamond Quilted, plate, salad; bl or blk, 7" 11.00
Diamond Quilted, saucer, bl or blk 6.00
Diamond Quilted, whiskey, pk or gr, 1½-oz 8.00
Diana, bowl, cream soup; amber, 5½" 20.00
Diana, bowl, crystal, scalloped edge, 12" 16.00
Diana, cup, pk 20.00
Diana, platter, amber, oval, 12" 15.00
Diana, sherbet, crystal 3.00
Dogwood, bowl, fruit; monax & cremax, 10¼" 125.00
Dogwood, coaster, pk, 3¼" 595.00
Dogwood, plate, grill; plate, pk, AOP, 10½" 25.00
Dogwood, plate, luncheon; gr, 8" 10.00
Dogwood, sugar bowl, gr, flat, thin, 2½" 45.00
Doric, bowl, berry; pk, lg, 8¼" 30.00
Doric, butter dish, pk, w/lid 80.00

Doric, pitcher,
green, 32-ounce,
5½", $37.50.

Doric, creamer, pk, 4" 20.00
Doric, plate, sherbet; gr, 6" 7.00
Doric, relish tray, gr, 4x4" 12.00
Doric, tray, gr, hdld, 10" 30.00

Doric & Pansy, bowl, berry; gr or teal, lg, 8" 95.00
Doric & Pansy, cup, gr or teal 16.00
Doric & Pansy, plate, dinner; pk or crystal, 9" 15.00
Doric & Pansy, tumbler, gr or teal, 9-oz, 4½" 120.00
English Hobnail, ashtray, pk or gr, 3" 20.00
English Hobnail, bowl, nappy; pk or gr, cupped, 8" ...30.00
English Hobnail, bowl, pk or gr, ftd, 8" 55.00
English Hobnail, bowl, turq or ice bl, rolled edge, 11" ...80.00
English Hobnail, pitcher, pk or gr, str sides, 32-oz ...185.00
English Hobnail, plate, pk or gr, rnd, 8" 12.50
English Hobnail, rose bowl, pk or gr, 4" 50.00
English Hobnail, straw jar/vase, pk or gr, 10" 110.00
English Hobnail, vase, flip; pk or gr, 7½" 85.00
Englsish Hobnail, compote, sweetmeat; pk or gr, ball stem, 8" ...60.00
Fire-King Philbe, bowl, cereal; crystal, 5½" 20.00
Fire-King Philbe, creamer, bl, ftd, 3¼" 150.00
Fire-King Philbe, plate, luncheon; pk or gr, 8" 37.50
Fire-King Philbe, plate, salver; pk or gr, 10½" 65.00
Fire-King Philbe, sherbet, crystal, no stem, 3¾" 75.00
Fire-King Philbe, tumbler, iced tea; crystal, ftd, 15-oz, 6½" ...50.00
Floral, bowl, vegetable; pk, oval, 9" 25.00
Floral, creamer, Delphite, flat 77.50
Floral, refrigerator dish, Jadite, w/lid, 5" sq 50.00
Floral, tumbler, gr, ftd, 3-oz, 3½" 175.00
Floral & Diamond Band, butter dish, pk, w/lid 140.00
Floral & Diamond Band, plate, luncheon; pk or gr, 8" ...45.00
Floral & Diamond Band, tumbler, water; pk or gr, 4" ...25.00
Florentine No 1, ashtray, crystal or gr, 5½" 22.00
Florentine No 1, butter dish, pk, w/lid 160.00
Florentine No 1, pitcher, cobalt bl, ftd, 36-oz, 7½" ...850.00
Florentine No 1, plate, salad; yel, 8½" 12.00
Florentine No 1, tumbler, crystal or gr, ftd, 4-oz, 3¼" ...16.00
Florentine No 1, tumbler, iced tea; yel or pk, ftd, 12-oz, 5¼" ...30.00
Florentine No 2, bowl, cream soup; crystal or gr, 4¾" ...18.00
Florentine No 2, candy dish, pk, w/lid 145.00
Florentine No 2, pitcher, yel, 48-oz, 7½" 265.00
Florentine No 2, plate, yel, w/indent, 6¼" 32.00
Florentine No 2, saucer, amber 15.00
Florentine No 2, tumbler, yel, ftd, 9-oz, 5" 35.00
Flower Garden w/Butterflies, bowl, orange; blk, ftd, 11" ...225.00
Flower Garden w/Butterflies, candy dish, amber, flat, w/lid, 6" ...130.00
Flower Garden w/Butterflies, comport, blk, ftd, 7" ...175.00
Flower Garden w/Butterflies, cup, pk, gr or bl-gr ...75.00
Flower Garden w/Butterflies, vase, bl or canary yel, 10½" ...235.00
Fortune, bowl, pk or crystal, rolled edge, 5¼" 22.00
Fortune, saucer, pk or crystal 5.00
Fruits, bowl, berry; gr, 4½" 35.00
Fruits, saucer, gr 5.50
Fruits, sherbet, gr or pk 12.00
Hex Optic, bowl, berry; pk or gr, ruffled, 4¼" 9.00
Hex Optic, bowl, mixing; pk or gr, 10" 28.00
Hex Optic, pitcher, pk or gr, ftd, 48-oz, 9" 50.00
Hex Optic, plate, luncheon; pk or gr, 8" 5.50
Hex Optic, saucer, pk or gr 3.00
Hex Optic, tumbler, pk or gr, ftd, 5¾" 10.00
Hobnail, bowl, salad; crystal, 7" 4.50
Hobnail, pitcher, crystal, 67-oz 28.00
Hobnail, saucer/sherbet plate, pk 5.00
Hobnail, tumbler, cordial; crystal, ftd, 5-oz 6.00
Homespun, bowl, berry; pk or crystal, lg, 8¼" 30.00
Homespun, saucer, pk or crystal 5.00
Homespun, tumbler, pk or crystal, ftd, 15-oz, 6⅜" ...35.00
Homespun, tumbler, pk or crystal, str, 7-oz, 3⅛" ...24.00
Indiana Custard, bowl, cereal; French Ivory, 6½" ...30.00

Indiana Custard, plate, luncheon; French Ivory, 8⅞" 20.00
Indiana Custard, sugar bowl, French Ivory, w/lid 37.00
Iris, bowl, cereal; crystal, 5" 115.00
Iris, bowl, fruit; crystal, str edge, 11" 65.00
Iris, bowl, sauce; crystal, ruffled, 5" 10.00
Iris, cup, demi; irid 150.00
Iris, goblet, irid, 4-oz, 5½" 225.00
Iris, plate, luncheon; crystal, 8" 110.00
Iris, tumbler, crystal or irid, ftd, 6" 20.00
Iris, vase, transparent gr or pk, 9" 225.00
Jubilee, bowl, fruit; yel, hdld, 9" 125.00
Jubilee, creamer, pk 35.00
Jubilee, cup, pk 40.00
Jubilee, tumbler, iced tea; yel, 12½-oz, 6⅛" 150.00
Jubilee, vase, pk, 12" 350.00
Lace Edge, bowl, salad; pk, ribbed, 7¾" 60.00
Lace Edge, butter dish, pk, w/lid 70.00
Lace Edge, cookie jar, frosted, w/lid 60.00
Lace Edge, plate, pk, solid lace, 13" 65.00
Lace Edge, tumbler, pk, flat, 5-oz, 3½" 150.00
Laced Edge, bowl, fruit; opal, 4⅜" to 4¾" 30.00
Laced Edge, bowl, vegetable; opal, 9" 110.00
Laced Edge, creamer, opal 40.00
Laced Edge, plate, bread & butter; opal, 6½" 18.00
Laced Edge, platter, opal, 13" 185.00

Laced Edge, tumbler, blue or green opalescent, footed, nine-ounce, $55.00.
(Photo courtesy Gene Florence)

Lake Como, bowl, vegetable; wht w/bl scenes, 9¼" 50.00
Lake Como, platter, wht w/bl scenes, 11" 75.00
Laurel, bowl, berry; Jade Green or decor rim, 4¾" 15.00
Laurel, bowl, vegetable; Poudre Blue, oval, 9¾" 55.00
Laurel, cup, Poudre Blue 22.00
Laurel, plate, sherbet; White Opal or French Ivory, 6" 10.00
Laurel, shakers, Jade Green or decor rim, pr 85.00
Lincoln Inn, ashtray, cobalt bl or red 17.50
Lincoln Inn, comport, cobalt bl or red 30.00
Lincoln Inn, plate, colors other than cobalt bl or red, 8" 10.00
Lincoln Inn, tumbler, cobalt bl or red, ftd, 9-oz 30.00
Little Jewel, bowl, crystal, 6½" 10.00
Little Jewel, jug, colors, tankard style, 1-pt 45.00
Little Jewel, vase, bouquet; crystal, 6" 12.00
Lorain, bowl, salad; crystal or gr, 7¼" 50.00
Lorain, plate, sherbet; yel, 5½" 12.50
Lorain, saucer, crystal or gr 4.50
Lorain, tumbler, yel, ftd, 9-oz, 4¾" 30.00
Madrid, ashtray, amber, 6" sq 350.00
Madrid, bowl, berry; amber or pk, lg, 9⅜" 20.00
Madrid, gravy boat, amber 1,000.00
Madrid, Lazy Susan, amber, wooden, cold-cut coasters 995.00
Madrid, pitcher, gr, 60-oz, 8" sq 125.00

Madrid, pitcher, gr, 80-oz, 8½" 200.00
Madrid, plate, dinner; bl, 10½" 75.00
Madrid, tumbler, amber, 5-oz, 3⅞" 13.00
Manhattan, ashtray, crystal, rnd, 4" 12.00
Manhattan, bowl, crystal, closed hdls, 8" 25.00
Manhattan, plate, salad; pk, 8½" 195.00
Manhattan, relish tray, crystal or pk, 5-part, 14" 85.00
Mayfair Federal, bowl, sauce; amber, 5" 9.00
Mayfair Federal, cup, gr 15.00
Mayfair Federal, plate, dinner; crystal, 9½" 12.00
Mayfair Federal, tumbler, amber, 9-oz, 4½" 35.00
Mayfair/Open Rose, bowl, console; pk or gr, 3-legged, 3⅛x9" ..5,500.00
Mayfair/Open Rose, bowl, fruit; bl, scalloped, deep, 12" 110.00
Mayfair/Open Rose, candy dish, yel, w/lid 495.00
Mayfair/Open Rose, cookie jar, bl, w/lid 295.00
Mayfair/Open Rose, goblet, claret; pk, 4½-oz, 5¼" 1,000.00
Mayfair/Open Rose, pitcher, gr, 80-oz, 8½" 800.00
Mayfair/Open Rose, plate, grill; yel, hdld, 11½" 125.00
Mayfair/Open Rose, shakers, pk, ftd, rare, pr 10,000.00
Mayfair/Open Rose, sherbet, bl, flat, 2¼" 165.00
Mayfair/Open Rose, tumbler, water; pk, 9-oz, 4¼" 36.00
Mayfair/Open Rose, vase, sweetpea; gr 325.00
Miss America, bowl, cereal; crystal, 6¼" 10.00
Miss America, bowl, fruit; pk, str, deep, 8¾" 85.00
Miss America, bowl, Royal Ruby, shallow, 11" 900.00
Miss America, candy jar, crystal, w/lid, 11½" 65.00
Miss America, creamer, Royal Ruby, ftd 225.00
Miss America, goblet, water; pk, 10-oz, 5½" 55.00
Miss America, plate, dinner; pk, 10¼" 38.00
Miss America, plate, sherbet; Royal Ruby, 5¾" 55.00
Miss America, shakers, pk, pr 67.50
Miss America, tumbler, water; pk, 10-oz, 4½" 37.50
Moderntone, bowl, cereal; cobalt or amethyst, 6½" 75.00
Moderntone, platter, cobalt, oval, 12" 85.00
Moderntone, tumbler, amethyst, 9-oz 30.00
Moondrops, bowl, soup; bl or red, 6¾" 90.00
Moondrops, candlesticks, bl or red, triple light, 5¼", pr 150.00
Moondrops, decanter, bl or red, lg, 11¼" 100.00
Moondrops, gravy boat, colors other than bl or red 100.00
Moondrops, saucer, colors other than bl or red 3.00
Moondrops, tumbler, bl or red, 9-oz, 4⅞" 20.00
Mt Pleasant, bowl, rose; pk or gr, 4" opening 18.00
Mt Pleasant, cup, amethyst, blk or cobalt 14.00
Mt Pleasant, mayonnaise, amethyst, blk or cobalt, 3-ftd, 5½" 30.00
Mt Pleasant, tumbler, amethyst, blk or cobalt, ftd 28.00
New Century, bowl, berry; gr or crystal, 4½" 30.00
New Century, cup, pk, cobalt or crystal 20.00
New Century, goblet, cocktail; gr or cobalt, 3¼-oz 33.00
New Century, plate, sherbet; gr or crystal, 6" 8.00
New Century, tumbler, pk, cobalt or amethyst, 9-oz, 4¼" 20.00
Newport, bowl, cream soup; cobalt, 4¾" 25.00
Newport, plate, luncheon; cobalt, 8½" 16.00
Newport, plate, sandwich; amethyst, 11¾" 45.00
Newport, tumbler, amethyst, 9-oz, 4½" 40.00
No 610 Pyramid, bowl, berry; crystal, 4¾" 20.00
No 610 Pyramid, pitcher, gr 265.00
No 612 Horseshoe, bowl, salad; gr or yel, 7½" 25.00
No 612 Horseshoe, plate, luncheon; yel, 9⅜" 125.00
No 612 Horseshoe, tumbler, gr, ftd, 12-oz 165.00
No 616 Vernon, creamer, gr, ftd 30.00
No 616 Vernon, saucer, crystal 3.00
No 616 Vernon, tumbler, gr or crystal, ftd, 5" 45.00
No 618 Pineapple & Floral, ashtray, crystal, 4½" 17.50
No 618 Pineapple & Floral, comport, amber or red, dmn shape......8.00

No 618 Pineapple & Floral, plate, crystal, w/indent, 11½" 25.00
No 618 Pineapple & Floral, sherbet, crystal, ftd 18.00
Normandie, bowl, berry; amber, 5" 10.00
Normandie, cup, pk 14.00
Normandie, plate, salad; pk, 7¾" 14.00
Normandie, sherbet, irid 7.00
Old Cafe, bowl, berry; crystal or pk, tab hdls, 5½" 35.00
Old Cafe, olive dish, crystal or pk, oblong, 6" 10.00
Old Cafe, pitcher, crystal or pk, 80-oz 150.00
Old Cafe, vase, Royal Ruby, 7¼" 50.00
Old English, bowl, pk, gr or amber, flat, 9½" 35.00
Old English, pitcher, pk, gr or amber, w/lid.................................135.00
Old English, vase, pk, gr or amber, ftd, 8x4½" 55.00
Ovide, candy dish, blk, w/lid..45.00
Ovide, shakers, blk or gr, pr...27.50
Ovide, tumbler, decor wht..17.50
Oyster & Pearl, bowl, crystal or pk, heart shape, 1 hdl, 5¼" 15.00
Oyster & Pearl, plate, sandwich; Royal Ruby, 13½" 55.00
Parrot, bowl, soup; gr, 7" 55.00
Parrot, creamer, amber, ftd 85.00
Parrot, plate, grill; gr, rnd, 10½" 33.00
Parrot, sherbet, amber, ftd cone 22.50
Patrician, bowl, berry; amber or crystal, 5" 14.00
Patrician, butter dish, gr, w/lid..140.00
Patrician, plate, salad; amber, crystal or pk, 7½" 15.00
Patrician, saucer, amber, crystal or gr 9.50
Patrician, tumbler, pk, 14-oz, 5½" 45.00
Patrick, bowl, console; pk, 11" 165.00
Patrick, goblet, cocktail; pk or yel, 4" 80.00
Patrick, plate, sherbet; yel, 7" 12.00
Patrick, tray, yel, w/hdls, 11" 60.00
Pebbled Rim, bowl, all colors, oval, 9½" 28.00
Pebbled Rim, creamer, all colors 13.00
Petalware, bowl, berry; crystal, lg, 9" 8.50
Petalware, bowl, cream soup; cremax or monax (plain), 4½".........12.00
Petalware, plate, salad; pk, 8" 7.00
Petalware, sherbet, red floral trim, low ftd, 4½" 38.00
Pillar Optic, creamer, amber, gr or pk, ftd 50.00
Pillar Optic, pretzel jar, crystal, 130-oz 60.00
Pillar Optic, tumbler, Royal Ruby, ftd, 10-oz, 5¼" 35.00
Primo, bowl, yel or gr, 4½" 25.00
Primo, plate, yel or gr, 6¼" 12.00
Primo, tumbler, yel or gr, 9-oz, 5¾" 20.00
Princess, ashtray, gr, 4½" 75.00
Princess, coaster, pk 85.00
Princess, plate, grill; gr or pk, 9½" 20.00
Princess, plate, salad; gr or pk, 8" 18.00
Princess, sherbet, topaz or apricot, ftd...35.00
Princess, tumbler, pk, ftd, 12½-oz, 6½" 90.00
Queen Mary, ashtray, crystal, rnd, 3¼" 3.00
Queen Mary, bowl, lug soup; pk, hdls, 5½" 30.00
Queen Mary, coaster, pk, 3½" 6.00
Queen Mary, creamer, pk, #471, oval, 5½".....................................14.00
Queen Mary, plate, salad; crystal, #438, 8¾" 5.50
Queen Mary, tumbler, juice; crystal, 5-oz, 3½" 4.00
Queen Mary, vase, crystal, #441, 6½" 10.00
Raindrops, bowl, fruit; gr, 4½" 6.00
Raindrops, sherbet, gr 7.00
Raindrops, sugar bowl, gr, w/lid..47.50
Ribbon, bowl, berry; gr, 4" 35.00
Ribbon, plate, luncheon; blk, 8" 45.00
Ribbon, plate, sherbet; gr, 6¼" 3.00
Ribbon, tumbler, gr, 10-oz, 6" 35.00
Ring, bowl, berry; crystal, 5" 4.00

Ring, cocktail shaker, crystal...20.00
Ring, pitcher, w/decor or gr, 80-oz, 8½" 35.00
Ring, plate, sandwich; w/decor or gr, 11¼" 14.00
Ring, sherbet, crystal, ftd, 4¾" 6.00
Ring, tumbler, water; crystal, ftd, 5½" 6.00
Rock Crystal, bowl, crystal, scalloped edge, 4½" 20.00
Rock Crystal, bowl, relish; crystal, 6-part, 14" 50.00
Rock Crystal, bowl, salad; red, scalloped edge, 9" 125.00
Rock Crystal, candy dish, red, rnd, w/lid.......................................195.00
Rock Crystal, cup, colors other than red, 7-oz...............................27.50
Rock Crystal, lamp, electric; red...695.00
Rock Crystal, plate, crystal, scalloped edge, 9" 18.00
Rock Crystal, salt dip, crystal 60.00
Rock Crystal, spooner, crystal 45.00
Rock Crystal, tumbler, juice; red, 5-oz 57.50

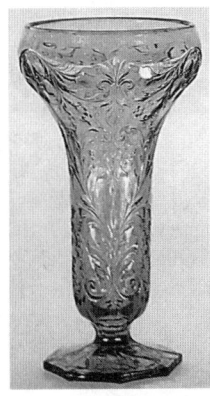

Rock Crystal, vase, red, footed, 11", $225.00.

Rose Cameo, bowl, gr, str sides, 6" 30.00
Rose Cameo, tumbler, gr, ftd, 2 styles, 5".....................................25.00
Rosemary, bowl, berry; amber, 5" 18.00
Rosemary, cup, gr 9.50
Rosemary, tumbler, pk, 9-oz, 4¼" 75.00
Roulette, crystal, cup 4.00
Roulette, tumbler, old fashioned; pk or gr, 7½-oz, 3¼"................45.00
Round Robin, creamer, gr, ftd 12.50
Round Robin, saucer, gr or irid..2.00
Round Robin, sugar bowl, gr 12.50
Roxana, bow, yel, 4½x2⅜" 15.00
Roxana, plate, yel, 5½" 12.00
Royal Lace, bowl, cream soup; crystal, 4¾" 17.50
Royal Lace, bowl, vegetable; bl, oval, 11" 70.00
Royal Lace, candlesticks, pk, rolled edge, pr 155.00
Royal Lace, pitcher, pk, w/o ice lip, 64-oz, 8" 110.00
Royal Lace, saucer, gr 10.00
Royal Lace, tumbler, crystal, 9-oz, 4⅛" 16.00
Royal Ruby, bowl, Coronation, w/hdls, 4½" 7.00
Royal Ruby, bowl, Sandwich, scalloped, 8¼" 50.00
Royal Ruby, goblet, ball stem 12.00
Royal Ruby, saucer, rnd..2.50
S Pattern, plate, luncheon; crystal, 8¼" 7.00
S Pattern, tumbler, yel, amber or crystal w/trims, 10-oz, 4¾" 12.00
Sandwich, bowl, amber or crystal, 6" 4.00
Sandwich, bowl, console; pk or gr, 9" 40.00
Sandwich, butter dish, teal bl, domed, w/lid 155.00
Sandwich, plate, bread & butter; amber or crystal, 7".....................4.00
Sandwich, plate, sandwich; teal bl, 13" 24.00
Sandwich, puff box, amber or crystal...16.00
Sandwich, wine, red, 4-oz, 3" 12.50
Sharon, bowl, cream soup; amber, 5"..28.00

Sharon, bowl, fruit; gr, 10½" 42.50
Sharon, creamer, gr, ftd 22.50
Sharon, pitcher, pk, w/ice lip, 80-oz 195.00
Sharon, shakers, pk, pr 60.00
Sharon, tumbler, amber or pk, thin, 12-oz, 5¼" 55.00
Ships, ice bowl, bl & wht 40.00
Ships, tumbler, shot; bl & wht, 2-oz, 2¼" 225.00
Ships, tumbler, water; bl & wht, str, 9-oz, 3¾" 14.00
Sierra, bowl, berry; pk, lg, 8½" 35.00
Sierra, pitcher, pk, 32-oz, 6½" 135.00
Sierra, shakers, pk or gr, pr 45.00
Sierra, tumbler, gr, ftd, 9-oz, 4½" 90.00
Spiral, bowl, mixing; gr, 7" 15.00
Spiral, plate, luncheon; gr, 8" 3.50
Spiral, shakers, gr, pr 35.00
Spiral, vase, gr, ftd, 5¾" 55.00
Starlight, bowl, salad; crystal or wht, 11½" 28.00
Starlight, plate, sandwich; pk, 13" 18.00
Starlight, relish dish, crystal or wht 15.00
Strawberry, bowl, salad; crystal or irid, deep, 6½" 15.00
Strawberry, creamer, crystal or irid, lg, 4⅝" 22.50
Strawberry, pitcher, pk or gr, 7¾" 210.00
Strawberry, tumbler, pk or gr, 8-oz, 3⅝" 40.00
Sunburst, bowl, crystal, 10¾" 27.50
Sunburst, cup, crystal 10.00
Sunburst, tumbler, crystal, flat, 9-oz, 4" 33.00
Sunflower, ashtray, pk, center design only, 5" 9.00
Sunflower, saucer, gr 10.00
Swirl, bowl, salad; pk, 9" 30.00
Swirl, butter dish, ultramarine, w/lid 285.00
Swirl, candy dish, pk, open, 3-legs 15.00
Swirl, platter, Delphite, oval, 12" 38.00
Swirl, tumbler, ultramarine, 9-oz, 4" 35.00
Tea Room, bowl, banana split; gr or pk, flat, 7½" 200.00
Tea Room, creamer, amber, ftd, 4½" 100.00
Tea Room, parfait, gr or pk 100.00
Tea Room, saucer, gr or pk 30.00
Tea Room, sugar bowl, gr, flat, w/lid 200.00
Tea Room, tumbler, pk, ftd, 12-oz 70.00
Thistle, bowl, cereal; pk, 5½" 33.00
Thistle, plate, cake; gr, heavy, 13" 225.00
Tulip, decanter, amethyst or bl, w/stopper 495.00
Tulip, plate, crystal or gr, 6" 10.00
Twisted Optic, bowl, salad; bl or canary yel, 7" 25.00
Twisted Optic, cup, colors other than bl or canary yel 5.00
Twisted Optic, plate, sandwich; bl or canary yel, 10" 20.00
Twisted Optic, saucer, colors other than bl or canary yel ...2.00
US Swirl, comport, gr 35.00
US Swirl, pitcher, gr or pk, 48-oz, 8" 85.00
US Swirl, vase, pk, 6½" 25.00
Victory, bonbon, blk, amber, pk or gr, 7" 11.00
Victory, bowl, console; bl, 12" 65.00
Victory, cup, blk, amber, pk or gr 30.00
Victory, goblet, bl, 7-oz, 5" 95.00
Vitrock, bowl, cream soup; wht, 5½" 16.00
Vitrock, cup, wht 6.00
Vitrock, plate, dinner; wht, 10" 10.00
Waterford, ashtray, crystal, 4" 7.50
Waterford, butter dish, pk, w/lid 235.00
Waterford, goblet, pk, Miss America shape, 5½" 125.00
Waterford, pitcher, juice; crystal, tilted, 42-oz 24.00
Waterford, plate, dinner; pk, 9⅝" 25.00
Waterford, shakers, crystal, 2 styles, pr 9.00
Windsor, candy jar, crystal, w/lid 20.00

Windsor, plate, chop; gr, 13⅝" 42.00
Windsor, tray, pk, no hdls, 4⅛x9" 60.00
Windsor, tumbler, crystal, ftd, 7¼" 18.00
Windsor, Windsor, bowl, pk, pointed edge, 8" 60.00

Desert Sands

As early as the 1850s, the Evans family, living in the Ozark Mountains of Missouri, produced domestic clay products. Their small pot shop was passed on from one generation to the next. In the 1920s it was moved to North Las Vegas, Nevada, where the name Desert Sands was adopted. Succeeding generations of the family continued to relocate, taking the business with them. From 1937 to 1962 it operated in Boulder City, Nevada; then it was moved to Barstow, California, where it remained until it closed in the late 1970s.

Desert Sands pottery is similar to Mission Ware by Niloak. Various mineral oxides were blended to mimic the naturally occurring sand formations of the American West. A high-gloss glaze was applied to add intensity to the colorful striations that characterize the ware. Not all examples are marked, making it sometimes difficult to attribute. Marked items carry an ink stamp with the Desert Sands designation. Paper labels were also used.

Vase, 7¾", $70.00. (Photo courtesy David Gifford)

Bowl, incurvate rim, 3¼x7" 40.00
Bowl, w/lid, ped ft, 6½x4½" 80.00
Butter dish, w/lid, 3½x6" 85.00
Candle holder, bowl-like bottom w/rnd top, 3½x5" 30.00
Cup & saucer 40.00
Planter, w/drip bowl, 4" 60.00
Tumbler, 4¼" 25.00
Vase, flared rim, 5" 35.00
Vase, 4¾" 45.00

Documents

Although the word 'document' is defined in the general sense as 'anything printed or written, etc., relied upon to record or prove something. . .,' in the collectibles market, the term is more diversified with broadsides, billheads, checks, invoices, letters and letterheads, land grants, receipts, and waybills some of the most sought after. Some documents in demand are those related to a specific subject such as advertising, mining, railroads, military, politics, banking, slavery, nautical, or legal (deeds, mortgages, etc.). Other collectors look for examples representing a specific period of time such as colonial documents, Revolutionary, or Civil War documents, early western documents or those from a specific region, state, or city.

Aside from supply and demand, there are five major factors which determine the collector-value of a document.

These are

1) Age — Documents from the eastern half of the country can be found that date back to the 1700s or earlier. Most documents sought by collectors usually date from 1700 to 1900. Those with twentieth-century dates are still abundant and not in demand unless of special significance or beauty.

2) Region of origin — Depending on age, documents from rural and less-populated areas are harder to find than those from major cities and heavily populated states. The colonization of the West and Midwest did not begin until after 1850, so while an 1870s billhead from New York or Chicago is common, one from Albuquerque or Phoenix is not, since most of the Southwest was still unsettled.

3) Attractiveness — Some documents are plain and unadorned, but collectors prefer colorful, profusely illustrated pieces. Additional artwork and engravings add to the value.

4) Historical content — Unusual or interesting content, such as a letter written by a Civil War soldier giving an eye-witness account of the Battle of Gettysburg or a western territorial billhead listing numerous animal hides purchased from a trapper, will sell for more than one with mundane information.

5) Condition — Through neglect or environmental conditions, over many decades paper articles can become stained, torn, or deteriorated. Heavily damaged or stained documents are generally avoided altogether. Those with minor problems are more acceptable, although their value will decrease anywhere from 20% to 50%, depending upon the extent of damage. Avoid attempting to repair tears with scotch tape — sell 'as is' so that the collector can take proper steps toward restoration.

Foreign documents are plentiful; and though some are very attractive, resale may be difficult. The listings that follow are generalized; prices are variable depending entirely upon the five points noted above. Values here are based upon examples with no major damage. Common grade documents without significant content are found in abundance and generally have little collector value. These usually date from the late 1800s to mid-1900s. It should be noted that the items listed below are examples of those that meet the criteria for having collector value. There is little demand for documents worth less than $5.00. For more information we recommend *Owning Western History* by our advisor Warren Anderson. His address and ordering information may be found in the Directory under Utah.

Key:
illus — illustrated   vgn — vignette

Account, Adams Co/1864, attempted murder/shooting, handwritten, 7x12"..22.00
Affidavit, NY/1871, soldier died of typhoid...1862, handwritten, 5x8"..23.00
Bank draft, Whitewood DS/1897, Devil's Tower vgn, blk on bl paper..18.00
Bill, Franktown/1875, costs due to laborer, handwritten 30.00
Bill, ID, wagon rprs, horse & horseshoe vgn, ca 1917....................10.00
Bill of health, KS cattle/1885, pre-printed, 5x7" 25.00
Bill of sale for slave, Boston, 17?5, tear/minor stains, 8x12"........200.00
Billhead, AZ Territory/1905, Thomas Wilson...Powder Co, pre-printed.22.00
Billhead, McFarlane & Co...CO/1901, vgn, pre-printed, 5x8" 15.00
Billhead, San Francisco/1865, Reynolds & Murray, produce, 7x9".17.00
Certificate, Kansas City/1893, Boiler Inspector's Office, 8x9" 10.00
Certificate of appeal, OK Supreme Court/1908, Fort Smith & Western RR..17.00
Certificate of marriage, MS/1864, printed on bl, sgn, 4x7", VG......8.00
Certificate of matriculation, Tulane University/1886, sgn, 4x8"......7.00
Check, Raymond-IL Mining Co/1909, blk on wht, 3x8" 8.00
Complaint, 1907, weapon assault w/intent to cause harm, sgn......13.00
Complaint, 1911, drunk & disorderly man disturbing peace, sgn..13.00
Cover, CA Wells-Fargo/1870s, emb orange 3¢ stamp, 3x5" 40.00
Deed, quit claim; Gr Mtn Falls CO, pre-printed, 1902, 11x17" 12.50
Indenture, SC, 1793, for acreage in St Paul's Parrish, 18x24" 300.00
Ledger/registry, lists sales/bonds/slaves/etc, VA, 1793-1835.........700.00
Letter, Bureau of Mines/1910, explosion news, typed, 1-pg, 8x11".18.00
Letter, CO Wells Fargo/1902, purple print & vgn, payment enclosed.25.00

Letter, from former slave to Vice President A Stephens, 1876, 1½-pg...400.00
Letter, ID/1911, late for payments, handwritten, 1-pg, 6x9"..........10.00
Letter, Nicholia (ID Territory)/1886, bbl of bad whiskey, 8x10" ...30.00
Letter, OK/1919, to judge about officer failing to serve papers, 2-pg.12.00
Letter, re: time checks for miners, ca 1881, 1-pg, 8x10" 18.00
Letterhead, Assay Office...AZ Territory, business matters, 1896, 1-pg .18.00
Letterhead, Continental Wire Co...St Louis/1896, info & charges, 8x11".25.00
Letterhead, DA Rowland...CO/1912, Ford convertible vgn, stock sale...20.00
Muster roll, US Colored Civil War troops, FL, 1865, 21x31" 375.00
Notice of Enrollment, NY, Civil War era, 4½x8" 90.00
Order, Fort Apache AZ/1891, freight goods, rubber stamped, 5x8", VG...40.00
Order, ID Territory/1888, beer & tobacco, 1-pg, 5x8" 25.00
Pamphlet, Observations on Slavery..., anti-slavery, 1823, 19-pg, EX.230.00
Pass, Nemaha Valley (KS) Fair Assoc/1889, admits couple w/buggy, 3x4" .16.00
Pay order, Chicago & W MI RR, days worked/amount paid, 2¢ tax stamp..8.00
Policy, Monmouth Mutual Fire Ins Co/1845, house & barn, pre-printed .28.00
Poster, Reward $500, arrest of murderers, CA, 1896, 13x9½"..........250.00
Price list, CA Wine Assoc/1900, lists over 60, 9x13" 25.00
Promissory note, CA/1878, 15% interest, pre-printed, 7x8".........20.00
Promissory note, Kimberly UT/1907, pre-printed, 4x7"................18.00
Promissory note, Pawhuska OK/1919, payment to Wah-kon-tah-he-um-pa, EX..22.00
Prospectus, Internat'l Mining Co of NY/1933, 8-pg, 8x11" 15.00
Receipt, AZ Coop Merc Inst/1895, pre-printed, elk head vgn, 3x8".15.00
Receipt, AZ Territory/1906, Indian vgn, blk on wht printing 12.00
Receipt, El Paso TX/1899, H Lesinsky Wholesale Grocers, vgn, 3x8"...8.00
Receipt, Sacramento/1881, title/ passenger train vgn, issued/sgn, 3x8".10.00
Receipt, Silver Star MT/1876, registered letter, pre-printed, 4x5" ...25.00
Receipt, UT Territory/1885, liquor/cigars, pre-printed, 3x8".........22.00
Receipt, WY Territory/1889, vet services, pre-rpinted, 3x5" 28.00
Report, Cyclops Assay Office of Central City/1903, pre-printed, sgn..22.00
Statement, NE cattle sale/1892, cattle vgn, 8x11" 28.00
Statement, San Bernadino CA/1896, supply delivery, pre-printed, 6x9"....15.00

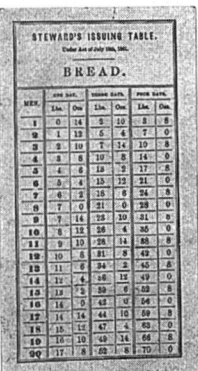

Steward's Issuing Table, bread rations, 1861, black print on white card stock, 6¼x3½", EX, $75.00. (Early American History Auctions)

Summons, Johnston County/1923, court appearance, legal-sz pg 6.00
Summons, Reading MA town meeting, lists agenda, 1764, 25x17".600.00
Voucher, discharge; VA/1862, Civil War soldier, pre-printed, 1862..25.00
Warrant, WV/1925, arrest for trespass of B&O RR Co 12.50
Warrant, 1925, couple (cousins) cohabiting out of wedlock, legal sz .15.00
Will, KY, 1838, pay debts/free 2 slaves, 9½x7¾" 350.00

Dollhouses and Furnishings

Dollhouses were introduced commercially in this country late in the 1700s by Dutch craftsmen who settled in the East. By the mid-1800s, they had become meticulously detailed, divided into separate rooms, and lavishly furnished to reflect the opulence of the day. Originally intended for the amusement of adults of the household, by the late 1800s their status had changed to that of a child's toy. Though many early dollhouses were lovingly hand-fashioned for a special little girl, those made commercially by such companies as Bliss and Schoenhut are highly valued.

Furniture and furnishings in the Biedermeier style featuring stenciled Victorian decorations often sell for several hundred dollars each. Other early pieces made of pewter, porcelain, or papier-mache are also quite valuable. Certainly less expensive but very collectible, nonetheless, is the quality, hallmarked plastic furniture produced during the '40s by Renwal and Acme, and the Petite Princess line of the 60s produced by Ideal. In the listings that follow, dollhouses are litho paper on wood, unless otherwise noted. For more information, see *Schroeder's Collectible Toys, Antique to Modern*. Our advisor for this category is Barbara Rosen; she is listed in the Directory under New Jersey. See also Miniatures.

Furnishings

Acme/Thomas, seesaw, red w/yel horse heads 10.00
Acme/Thomas, stroller, pk w/bl or wht wheels................................6.00
Acme/Thomas, swing, single, red w/gr, yel ropes............................18.00
Allied/Pyro, hutch, aqua or red...4.00
Allied/Pyro, radio, yel floor model 8.00
Allied/Pyro, tub, lt bl...4.00
Arcade, GE Refrigerator, red-pnt CI w/decal, 7", NM................700.00
Arcade, sofa & lounge chair, rose-pnt CI w/maroon, NM..........850.00
Fisher-Price, armoire, wht..5.00
Fisher-Price, bedroom set, w/bed & dresser w/mirror, #255.............6.00
Fisher-Price, cradle, wht 5.00
Fisher-Price, lounge chair & grill, #272, MOC 4.00
Fisher-Price, rocker, #273, MOC 4.00
Ideal, chair, bedroom; bl w/pk skirt......................................30.00
Ideal, chair, living room 15.00
Ideal, cradle, bl or pk, ea..45.00
Ideal, hamper, ivory 4.00
Ideal, potty chair, bl..15.00
Ideal, refrigerator, ivory w/blk..15.00
Ideal, stove, ivory w/blk..15.00
Ideal Petite Princess, bed, pk, #4416-4...................................25.00
Ideal Petite Princess, buffet, complete 25.00
Ideal Petite Princess, chair, hostess dining; #4415-6 ....8.00
Ideal Petite Princess, hamper, #4499-0....................................30.00
Ideal Young Decorator, bed, rose-colored spread 35.00
Ideal Young Decorator, sink, bathroom; yel w/bl..........................40.00
Kilgore, buffet, bl-pnt CI..50.00
Kilgore, sink, bathroom; bl-pnt CI..50.00
Marx, bread box, red...4.00
Marx, chair, kitchen; hard plastic, ivory or wht, ½" scale...............3.00
Marx, highboy, hard plastic, bright yel, ½" scale 3.00
Marx, laundry basket, chartreuse, soft plastic 3.00
Marx, stove, hard plastic, wht, ½" scale 3.00
Marx, vanity, hard plastic, bright yel or tan, ½" scale....................3.00
Mattel Littles, armoire 8.00
Mattel Littles, dresser & lamp, MIB 12.00
Plasco, grandfather clock, lt brn swirl w/cb face.........................15.00
Plasco, nightstand, brn or marbleized......................................3.00
Plasco, table, dining room; dk brn, +4 chairs 22.00
Plasco, table, kitchen; lt bl..5.00
Renwal, carpet sweeper 85.00
Renwal, chair, club; dk gr w/brn base 10.00
Renwal, chair, rocker; yel w/red 8.00
Renwal, china closet, brn, stenciled 15.00
Renwal, dining set, red-brn w/ivory, table+4 chairs+china closet .32.00
Renwal, highchair, ivory...30.00
Renwal, sink, wht w/blk nonopening door 18.00
Renwal, table, cocktail; metallic red.....................................15.00
Strombecker, baby grand piano, walnut.....................................20.00

Strombecker, bed, walnut, 1936, 1" scale 18.00
Strombecker, lamp, table; yel or gr w/ivory shade, ¾" scale 15.00
Strombecker, sink, aqua or ivory, ¾" scale................................8.00
Strombecker, sofa, red..10.00
Strombecker, toilet, ivory, ¾" scale......................................10.00
Tootsietoy, chair, bedroom rocker; pk.....................................18.00
Tootsietoy, lamp, table; bl..45.00
Tootsietoy, tub, Little Lady Blue, hard plastic, 6"........................5.00
Wolverine, bed w/headboard...12.00
Wolverine, desk, turq or off-wht..3.00
Wolverine, highboy, brn or turq...3.00
Wolverine, sofa, pk..3.00

Houses, Shops, and Single Rooms

Arcade, Laundry Set, washer+wringer+dbl sinks+bench+chair, #716, NM.2,500.00
Bliss, 1½-story w/attic, paper litho on wood, red roof, 20x18", G..1,800.00
Bliss, 2-story, paper litho on wood, bl roof, brick front, sm, EX..300.00
Bliss, 2-story Colonial mansion, litho on wood, hinged dbl doors, 18"..325.00
Fisher-Price, 3-story light-up w/5 rooms, spiral stairs, #280, MIB..50.00
German, shop, pnt/papered wood, 16 drws, accessories, 25x29x11", EX.1,600.00
German, 2-story, litho paper/pnt wood, window glass, electric, 27x24"..1,350.00
German, 2-story/balcony/porch, litho on wood, 1890s, 31x26", G..1,600.00
German, 3-story warehouse w/hoist, 2-horse dray, bl roof, 22x11x9", VG..2,000.00
Jayline, 2-story/5-room, litho tin, purple roof, 1949, 15x19", VG.50.00
Marklin, bathroom, 3-sided, tin, w/tub/sink/toilet, 7x14", VG ...950.00
Marx, Little Red Schoolhouse, 1950s, 16", +plastic furniture & figures .450.00
Marx, Modern Kitchen Set, litho tin, complete, NMIB.............250.00
Marx, Newlyweds Parlor, litho tin room, 1925, +furniture, 3x5x3", MIB 250.00
Marx, split level, w/pool, doorbell, light fixtures, +60 pcs furniture .125.00
Marx, 2-story/7-room, litho tin, patio/breezeway, clapboard/stone, 38" ..95.00
Meritoy, Cape Cod, litho tin, red roof, plastic windows, 1949, 21", M..200.00
Ohio Art, Midget Manor, 2-story/4-room, litho tin, 1949, 5x8", MIB ..300.00
Rich, 6-room bungalow, litho fiberbrd, Arts & Crafts type, 1930s, 33"..200.00
Schoenhut, 2-room bungalow, cb roof, electric, ea side opens, 17", EX..550.00

Schoenhut, two-room cottage, window boxes on front porch windows, electrified, EX, $375.00. (Photo courtesy Yorktown Auctions)

Schoenhut, 2-story/8-room w/attic, wood & fiberbrd, 1923, 27", EX.2,400.00
Wolverine, Corner Grocer, litho tin, w/shelves & products, 12½", G 350.00

Dolls

To learn to invest your money wisely as you enjoy the hobby of doll collecting, you must become aware of defects which may devaluate a doll. In bisque, watch for eye chips, hairline cracks and chips, or breaks on any part of the head. Composition should be clean, not crazed or cracked. Vinyl and plastic should be clean with no pen or crayon marks. Though a quality replacement wig is acceptable for bisque dolls, composition and hard plastics should have their original hair in uncut condition. Original clothing is a must except in bisque dolls, since it is unusual to find one in its original costume.

It is important to remember that prices are based on condition and rarity. When no condition is noted, either in the line listing or the subcategory narrative, dolls are assumed to be in excellent condition. In relation to bisque dolls, excellent means having no cracks, chips, or hairlines, being nicely dressed, shoed, wigged, and ready to to be placed into a collection. Some of our values are for dolls that are 'mint in box' or 'never removed from box.' As a general rule, a mint-in-box doll is worth twice as much (or there about) as one mint, no box. The same doll, played with and in only good condition, is worth half as much (or even less) than the mint-condition doll. Never-removed-from-box examples sell at a premium; allow an additional 10% to 20% over MIB prices for a doll in this pristine condition.

For a more thorough study of the subject, refer to *Modern Collectible Dolls,* and *Doll Values, Antique to Modern,* by Patsy Moyer; *Collector's Guide to Dolls of the 1960s and 1970s* by Cindy Sabulis; *Scouting Dolls through the Years* by Sydney Ann Sutton wih Patsy Moyer; *Encyclopedia of Nancy Ann Storybook Dolls* by Elaine M. Pardee and Jackie Robertson; *Nippon Dolls* by Joan F. Van Patten and Linda Lau; *Small Dolls of the 1960s and 1970s* by Cindy Sabulis; *Collector's Guide to Horsman Dolls* by Don Jensen; and *Collector's Guide to Celebrity Dolls,* by David Spurgeon. Several other book are referenced throughout this category. All are published by Collector Books. Except for the subcategories where another expert is noted, our general advisor for this category is author Patsy Moyer; she is listed in the Directory under New Mexico.

Key:
bjtd — ball-jointed	OC — original clothes
blb — bent limb body	o/m — open mouth
bsk — bisque	p/e — pierced ears
c/m — closed mouth	pnt/e — painted eyes
hh — human hair	pwt/e — paperweight eyes
hp — hard plastic	RpC — replaced clothes
jtd — jointed	ShHd — shoulder head
MIG — Made In Germany	ShPl — shoulder plate
NC — no clothes	SkHd — socket head
o/c/e — open closed eyes	str — straight
o/c/m — open closed mouth	trn — turned

American Character

AC or Petite mk, compo w/baby body, OC, 14", NM	185.00
AC or Petite mk mama, compo/cloth, hh or mohair wig, crier, OC, 16", M.	275.00
Annie Oakley, hp walker, embr skirt, 14", M	400.00
Baby, hp & vinyl, bottle, OC, 12", MIB	250.00
Campbell Kid, jtd compo, forehead curl, Petite Doll, OC, 1928, 12", M.	350.00
Carol Ann Beery, compo, sleep eyes, cm, OC, 1935, 13", NM	415.00
Chuckles, compo & cloth, o/c/e, o/m, Am Character, 1930s-49s, 20", EX.	250.00
Eloise, cloth w/orange yarn hair, crooked smile, 1950s, 15", NM.	260.00
Little Miss Echo, vinyl, talker, OC, 1964, 30", MIB	300.00
Puggy, compo, jtd, pnt/e & hair, OC, 1928, 13", EX	200.00
Sally, compo ShPl, o/m, o/c/e, S Temple look-alike, OC, 1934, 24", M.	375.00
Sally, compo/cloth, pnt or o/c/e, crier, OC, 1930, 14", NM/M.	400.00
Sally Joy, compo ShPl, cloth body, o/c/e, o/m, curly wig, OC, 24", M.	400.00
Sweet Sue, hp, OC, 1953-61, 15", G	55.00
Tiny, vinyl head, rooted hair, ca 1958, 10½", M	195.00
Tiny Tears, hp & vinyl, nude, 1950-62, 13", G	65.00
Tiny Tears, hp & vinyl, OC, 1950-62, 13", M	225.00
Tiny Tears, vinyl, 1963, OC, 9", M	80.00
Toodle-Loo, Magic Foam plastic body, jtd, blond rooted hair, 1961, M.	190.00
Toodles, vinyl, w/wardrobe & accessories, 1960, 29", MIB	350.00
Tressy, vinyl, high heels, OC, 1963-65, 11", MIB	200.00

Annalee

Barbara Annalee Davis has been making her dolls since 1950. What began as a hobby, very soon turned into a commercial venture. Her whimsical creations range from tiny angels atop powder puff clouds to funky giant frogs, some 42" in height. In between there are dolls for every occasion (with Christmas being her specialty), all characterized by their unique construction methods (felt over flexible wire framework) and wonderful facial expressions. Naturally, some of the older dolls are the most valuable (though more recent examples are desirable as well, depending on scarcity and demand), and condition, as usual, is very important. To date your doll, look at the tag. If made before 1986, that date is only the copyright date. (Dolls made after 1986 do carry the manufacturing date.) Dolls from the '50s have a long white red-embroidered tag with no date. From 1959 to 1964, that same tag had a date in the upper right-hand corner. From 1965 until 1970, it was folded in half and sewn into the seam. In 1970, a satiny white tag with a date preceded by a copyright symbol in the upper right-hand corner was used. In 1975, the tag was a long white cotton strip with a copyright date. This tag was folded over in 1982, making it shorter. Our advisor for Annalees is Jane Holt; she is listed in the Directory under New Hampshire.

Abraham Lincoln, Folk Hero series, #746, 14", M in dome	70.00
Abraham Lincoln, 1989, 10"	150.00
Angel tree topper, 1980, 7"	35.00
Annie Oakley, 1985, 10"	200.00
Baby mouse w/bottle, 1987, 7"	35.00
Back-to-School kid, logo w/pin, 1992, 7"	60.00

Bear with Honey Pot and Bee, 1986, 18", M, $125.00. (Photo courtesy Margaret Fox Mandel)

Bellhop, 1963, 24"	1,200.00
Bob Cratchet, w/Tim (7"), 1974, 18"	250.00
Bride & groom, 1985, 10", pr	125.00
Caroler woman, 1966, 9"	75.00
Clown kid, logo w/pin, 1990, 7"	80.00
Deer w/Christmas pkgs on bk, 1982, 32", NM	125.00
Disco mouse, 1979, 7"	60.00
Duck w/raincoat, 1986, 5"	45.00
Earth Day mouse, 1991, 7"	45.00
Elephant-head pick, 1972	100.00
Elf, red, wht or gr, 1987, 10", ea	20.00
Fishing Santa ornament, 1994	35.00
Flood Relief mouse, 1993, 7"	40.00
Headless Horseman, 1993, 10"	75.00
Huck Finn, 1988, 10"	150.00
Jack Frost, 1977, 22"	75.00
Johnny Appleseed, 1984, 10"	250.00
Monk, wht beard, blk hooded robe & skullcap, 1962 tag, 9"	150.00
Mouse cheerleader, 7"	50.00
Mouse jogger, 1980, 7"	25.00

Mouse w/cheese, 1996, 3"..20.00
Mouse w/metal mailbox, 1970, 7"..................................125.00
Mouse witch, 1985, 7"..25.00
Mr & Mrs Fireside Couple, 1970, 18", pr.........................75.00
Pilot duck, 1983, 5"...40.00
PJ kid, 1990, 18"...50.00
Polar bear, w/plaque, 1989, 7".......................................30.00
Santa, 1978, 48"..500.00
Santa Fox, Designer series, 1981, 18"............................125.00
Santa in chair, w/2 18" children, 1984, 30".................300.00
Santa in chef's hat & apron holds mixing bowl & spoon, 1988, 18" .75.00
Santa Mouse w/sack, 1977, 29"....................................250.00
Santa w/chef's hat & apron holds pie, 1988, 18" 85.00
Scarecrow, 1977, 42" 500.00
Sherlock Holmes, 1988, 10"..150.00
Snow Woman, holder, 1972, 29" 350.00
Two for Tea, logo, 1997, 7"..30.00
Woodchopper, 1971, 7"..40.00

Armand Marseille

#225, character child, bsk SkHd, jtd compo, o/m/teeth, RpC, 14", EX..3,600.00
#231, Fany, child, toddler or baby, molded hair, 1912, 17", VG .3,150.00
#251, SkHd, o/c/m, RpC, ca 1912, 17", EX 2,000.00
#259, bsk SkHd, o/m, glass eyes, bent-leg baby, RpC, 15", EX....425.00
#310, Just Me, bsk SkHd, compo, flirty eyes, c/m, RpC, 13", EX ..2,100.00
#328, bsk SkHd, o/m, glass eyes, bent-leg baby, RpC, 21", VG...525.00
#341, My Dream Baby, bsk SkHd, cloth body, c/m, wig, RpC, 10", VG ..185.00
#345, Kiddiejoy, bsk ShHd, glass eyes, c/m, RpC, 1926, 11", EX...275.00
#352, bsk dome SkHd, wig, glass eyes, c/m, OC, 1926, 16", EX..525.00
#370, Duchess, kid body, o/m, glass eyes, RpC, ca 1900, 12", VG ..125.00
#372, Kiddiejoy, ShHd, pnt eyes, o/c/m, kid body, RpC, 1925, 21", VG..775.00
#390, Floradora, bsk, compo body, o/m, glass eyes, RpC, 1900s, 18", EX...375.00
#449, pnt eyes, c/m, RpC, ca 1930, 18", EX 1,200.00
#520, domed head, compo body, glass eyes, o/m, RpC, ca 1910, 12", EX..775.00
#560, character, domed head, pnt eyes, o/c/m, RpC, 1910s, 14", VG...600.00
#600, character, domed head, pnt eyes, c/m, RpC, 10", EX.........850.00
#1890, bsk ShHd or SkHd, kid body, glass eyes, o/m/teeth, RpC, 12" ..125.00

#1894, open mouth with teeth, brown glass eyes, nicely dressed, 21", EX, $575.00. (Photo courtesy McMasters Auctions)

#1900, bsk ShHd or SkHd, kid body, glass eyes, o/m/teeth, RpC, 22", EX..350.00
Alma, kid body, RpC, 15", EX 200.00
AM (no #), bsk SkHd, jtd compo, o/m, glass eyes, wig, RpC, 17", VG ..300.00
Baby Betty, bsk, compo body, bent-leg baby, RpC, 16", VG........500.00
Baby Gloria, solid dome, o/m, pnt hair, RpC, 15", EX................675.00
Rosebud, bsk, compo body, RpC, 17", EX 375.00

Barbie Dolls and Related Dolls

Though the face has changed three times since 1959, Barbie is still as popular today as she was when she was first introduced. Named after the young daughter of the first owner of Mattel, the original Barbie had a white iris but no eye color. These dolls are nearly impossible to find, but there is a myriad of her successors and related collectibles just waiting to be found.

For further information we recommend *The Story of Barbie, Second Edition*, by Kittarah B. Westenhouser; *A Decade of Barbie Dolls and Collectibles, 1981–1991*, by Beth Summers; *Barbie, The First Thirty Years*, by Stefanie Deutsch; *Collector's Encyclopedia of Barbie Doll Exclusives and More*, by J. Michael Augustyniak; *The Barbie Doll Years* by Patrick C. and Joyce L. Olds; and *Barbie Fashion, Vol. I, II, and III*, by Sarah Sink Eames, which gives a complete history of the wardrobes of Barbie, her friends, and her family. *Schroeder's Toys, Antique to Modern*, is another good source for current market values. All these are published by Collector Books.

Allan, 1964, pnt red hair, str legs, MIB, from $125 to................150.00
Barbie, #1, 1958-59, blond or brunette, MIB, ea from $5,000 to .6,500.00
Barbie, #2, 1959, blond or brunette, MIB, ea from $5,000 to ..6,000.00
Barbie, #3, 1960, blond (extra long), orig swimsuit, NM.........1,100.00
Barbie, #3, 1960, blond or brunette, orig swimsuit, NM.............950.00
Barbie, #4, 1960, blond or brunette, orig swimsuit, M, from $450 to .500.00
Barbie, #5, 1961, blond, MIB, from $550 to...............................650.00
Barbie, #5, 1961, red hair, orig swimsuit, NM.............................375.00
Barbie, #6, blond, orig swimsuit, EX...250.00
Barbie, #6, brunette, MIB, from $525 to.....................................600.00
Barbie, American Airline Stewardess, 1963, NRFB.....................700.00
Barbie, American Girl, 1964, platinum hair, orig swimsuit, NM..650.00
Barbie, Ballerina..on Tour, 1976, NRFB.....................................125.00
Barbie, Barbie Celebration, 1987, NRFB.......................................30.00
Barbie, Bubble-Cut, 1962, blond or brunette, NRFB..................400.00
Barbie, Deluxe Quick Curl, Jergens, 1976, NRFB.......................100.00
Barbie, Dinner at Eight, 1964, NRFB..600.00
Barbie, Eskimo, Dolls of the World, 1982, NRFB........................100.00
Barbie, Gold Metal Skater, 1975, NRFB..75.00
Barbie, Hawaiian Superstar, 1977, MIB......................................110.00
Barbie, Holiday, 1988, NRFB, minimum value............................500.00
Barbie, Knitting Pretty (pk), 1964, NRFB..................................1,265.00
Barbie, Knitting Pretty (royal bl), 1965, NRFB...........................635.00
Barbie, Malibu (Sunset), 1971, NRFB..65.00
Barbie, Miss America, Kellogg Co, 1972, NRFB...........................175.00
Barbie, Perfume Party, 1988, NRFB...30.00
Barbie, Scottish, Dolls of the World, 1981, NRFB 140.00
Barbie, Sports Star, 1979, NRFB..25.00
Barbie, Swirl Ponytail, blond or brunette, 1964, NRFB 650.00
Barbie, Ten Speeder, 1973, NRFB..30.00
Barbie, Twist 'N Turn, 1966, brunette, orig swimsuit, NM..........275.00
Barbie, Twist 'N Turn, 1969, lt brn flip, NRFB.............................900.00
Barbie, Winter Fantasy, FAO Schwarz, 1990, NRFB....................200.00
Casey, Twist 'N Turn, 1968, blond or brunette, NRFB 350.00
Christie, Beauty Secrets, 1980, MIB...60.00
Christie, Golden Dream, 1980, MIB...50.00
Christie, Superstar, 1977, MIB...95.00
Francie, Growin' Pretty hair, orig clothes, 1970, NM.................150.00
Ginger, Growing UP, 1977, MIB...95.00
Kelley, Quick Curl, 1972, NRFB 175.00
Ken, Arabian Nights, 1964, NRFB..420.00
Ken, Crystal, 1984, NRFB...40.00
Ken, Fashion Jeans, 1982, MIB..35.00
Ken, King Arthur, 1964, NRFB..500.00
Ken, Party Time, 1977, NRFB 35.00
Ken, pnt blond, bendable legs, 1965, NRFB................................650.00
Ken, pnt blond, orig clothes, bendable legs, 1965, M.................225.00
Ken, pnt blond, 1963, ¼" shorter, NRFB.......................................200.00
Ken, pnt blond or brunette, 1962, NRFB.....................................200.00
Ken, Superstar, 1977, MIB 95.00

Midge, blond or red hair, bendable legs, 1963, MIB 500.00
Midge, Japanese, brunette, str legs, orig swimsuit, rare, NM 1,250.00
Nikki, Animal Lovin', 1989, NRFB..30.00
PJ, Free Moving, 1976, MIB..85.00
PJ, Sunsational Malibu, 1982, MIB..40.00
Scott, Skipper's boyfriend, 1980, MIB 55.00
Skipper, Growing Up, 1976, MIB..100.00
Skipper, Music Lovin', 1985, NRFB...65.00
Skipper, Workout Teen Fun, 1988, NRFB...................................30.00
Tutti, blond, OC, 1974, EX...60.00
Tutti, brunette, OC, 1966, NM..85.00

Barbie Gifts Sets and Related Accessories

Unless otherwise indicated, the items listed below are assumed to be mint and in the original box or package (if one was issued). Items in only excellent condition may be worth 40% to 60% less.

Case, Barbie, Francie & Skipper, plastic, rare, NM, from $75 to..100.00
Case, Barbie & Stacey, vinyl, 1967, NM, from $65 to 75.00
Case, Circus Star Barbie, FAO Schwarz, 1995, M 25.00
Clothes, Barbie All Turned Out, #482, 1984, NRFP 20.00
Clothes, Barbie Crusie Stripes, #918, 1959, NRFP 150.00
Clothes, Barbie Student Teacher, #1622, 1965, M 250.00
Clothes, Francie Hip Knits, #1265, 1966, NRFB..........................225.00
Clothes, Ken Hiking Holiday, #1412, 1965, NRFP 250.00
Clothes, Skipper Tea Party, #1924, 1966, NRFP..........................250.00
Furniture, Barbie Dream Glow Vanity, 1986, MIB.........................20.00
Furniture, Go-Together Chair, Ottoman & End Table, MIB.......100.00
Furniture, Susy Goose Canopy Bed, 1962, MIB............................150.00
Gift set, Barbie's Olympic Ski Village, MIB 75.00
Gift set, Golden Groove Barbie, Sears Exclusive, 1969, NRFB..2,000.00
Gift set, Skipper Party Time, 1964, NRFB 500.00
Room, Skipper Dream, 1964, MIB 300.00
Shop, Barbie Unique Boutique, Sears Exclusive, 1971, MIB.......185.00
Vehicle, Barbie Silver 'Vette, MIB...30.00
Vehicle, Ken's Hot Rod, Sears Exclusive, 1964, MIB 900.00
Vehicle, Star 'Vette, red, 1977, MIB..100.00

Belton Type

Bru-type face, EX bsk, o/c/m or c/m, wig, RpC, 14", EX 2,400.00
Bru-type face, EX bsk, o/c/m or c/m, wig, RpC, 18", EX 2,925.00
French-type face, EX bsk, o/c/m or c/m, wig, RpC, 9", EX........1,200.00
French-type face, EX bsk, o/c/m or c/m, wig, RpC, 16", EX.....2,350.00
French-type face, EX bsk, o/c/m or c/m, wig, RpC, 20", EX.....3,050.00
French-type face, EX bsk, o/c/m or c/m, wig, RpC, 24", EX.....3,700.00
German-type face, EX bsk, o/c/m or c/m, wig, RpC, 9", EX.....1,100.00
German-type face, EX bsk, o/c/m or c/m, wig, RpC, 12", EX...1,250.00
German-type face, EX bsk, o/c/m or c/m, wig, RpC, 18", EX...1,950.00
German-type face, EX bsk, o/c/m or c/m, wig, RpC, 23", EX...2,750.00
German-type face, EX bsk o/c/m or c/m, wig, RpC, 25", EX....3,000.00

Betsy McCall

Am Character, hp, peg-jtd knees, OC, 1957-63, 8", NM 375.00
Am Character, Linda McCall, vinyl, rooted hair, RpC, 36", NM .350.00
Am Character, Sandy McCall, vinyl, o/c/e, OC, 1959, 39", NM ..350.00
Am Character, vinyl, rooted hair, flirty eyes, RpC, 1959, 19-20", NM .500.00
Am Character, vinyl, swivel waist or 1-pc torso, OC, 1958, 14", NM .500.00
Horsman, vinyl/hp, o/c/e, OC, 1974, w/accessories, 12½", M 50.00
Horsman, vinyl/hp, o/c/e, side part, c/m, OC, 1974, 29", M .275.00
Ideal, vinyl, blk rooted hair, brn o/c/e, OC, 1952-53, 14" 165.00
Uneeda, vinyl, rooted hair, o/c/e, OC, 1964, 11½", M, minimum 95.00

Boudoir Dolls

Boudoir dolls, often called bed dolls, French dolls, or flapper dolls were popular from the late teens through the forties. The era of the 1920s and 1930s was the golden age of boudoir dolls.

More common boudoir dolls are usually found with composition head, arms, and high-heeled feet. Clothes are nailed on (later ones have stapled-on clothes). Wigs are usually mohair, human hair, or silk floss. Smoking boudoir dolls were made in the late teens and early twenties. More expensive boudoir dolls were made in France, Italy, and Germany, as well as the U.S. Usually they are all cloth with elaborate sewn or pinned-on costumes and silk, felt, or velvet painted faces. Sizes of boudoir dolls vary, but most are around 30". These dolls were made to adorn a lady's boudoir or sit on a bed. They were not meant as children's playthings. Our advisor for this category is Bonnie Groves; she is listed in the Directory under Texas.

Anita, trn head, all orig, 30", EX, minimum value 425.00
Black, OC, EX, minimum value 600.00
Blossom, cloth, 1930, 30", G...255.00
Blossom, Pierrette, 1930, 30", EX, minimum value......................900.00
Bride, all orig, 1940s, 29", VG 125.00
Bucalla kit for making boudoir doll costume, EX, minimum value .125.00
Cloth (possibly Gerling), 1920s, 27", VG 275.00
Compo, OC, 1915-40, 25", EX 245.00
Compo, OC, 1915-40, 28", EX 375.00
EX quality, glass eyes, OC, 1915-40, 15", EX 300.00
EX quality, glass eyes, OC, 1915-40, 28", VG 175.00
EX quality, glass eyes, OC, 1915-40, 32", VG 200.00
Felt, Pierrot, all orig, 23", G...315.00
Felt, Pierrot, possibly EHA, 30", VG 450.00
Lenci, Fadette, smoker, 25", VG, minimum value 3,000.00
Lenci, Fadette, 17", EX, minimum value....................................2,000.00
Lenci, salon lady, oll orig, 25", EX, minimum value 3,000.00
Lenci, 1915-40, 18-26", EX, ea, minimum value 2,250.00
Shoes for doll, 3", EX, pr..45.00
Silk face, bsk arms & legs, Fr, 33", VG......................................600.00
Smoker, cloth, OC, 1915-40, 16", EX 285.00
Smoker, cloth, OC, 1915-40, 25", EX 525.00
Smoker, jtd compo, Cubeb, 1925, 25", VG, minimum value 400.00
Standard quality, OC, ca 1915-40, 16", EX 125.00
Standard quality, OC, 1915-40, 28", EX 175.00
Standard quality, OC, 1915-40, 32", EX 235.00
Sterling, all orig, 1930, 27", VG 185.00
W-K-S, Gypsy, all orig, 25", VG 185.00

Bru

Bru Jne, swivel head, paperweight eyes, nicely dressed, 19", $12,700.00 at auction. (Photo courtesy McMasters Auctions)

Bebe Automate (breather/talker), key/lever in torso, RpC, 124", EX..**17,000.00**
Bebe Baiser (kiss thrower), pull-string mechanism, RpC, 1892, 11"..**4,100.00**
Bebe Brevete, swivel head ShPl, pwt/e, c/m, RpC, 1879-80, 19", EX.**18,500.00**
Bebe Merchant, walker, clockwork mechanism, jtd body, RpC, 17", EX.**6,800.00**
Bebe Teteur, o/m w/insert bottle, key on bk of head, RpC, 14", EX.**7,000.00**
Bru Jne, swivel head, cork pate, pwt/e, o/c/m/teeth, RpC, 12", EX..**11,500.00**
Bru Jne, swivel head, pwt/e, o/c/m/teeth, RpC, 17", EX.........**17,000.00**
Bru Jne R, swivel head, cork pate, pwt/e, c/m, RpC, 14", EX ..**3,800.00**
Bru Jne R, swivel head, cork pate, pwt/e, o/m/teeth, RpC, 16", EX.**2,100.00**
Circle Dot Bebe, swivel head, pwt/e, o/c/m/teeth, RpC, 11", EX .**12,000.00**
Fashion type (poupee), smiler, pwt/e, kid body, RpC, 13", EX.**3,000.00**
Fashion type (poupee), smiler, pwt/e, wood body, RpC, 16", EX.**6,000.00**
Fashion type (poupee), swivel head, ShPl, kid body, wig, RpC, 12", EX..**3,050.00**

Celebrity

Ben Cartright/Lorne Green, Am Character, 1965, 8", EX.............**75.00**
Buckwheat/Billy Thomas, Effanbee, 1989, 12", MIB **25.00**
Cowardly Lion/Bert Lahr, Multi Toy Corp, 1988, 12", MIB, M **20.00**
Dick Clark, Juro, 1958, 26½", M..**200.00**
DJ Tanner/Candace Cameron, Tiger Toys, 1993, 5½", MIB..........**50.00**
Doctor Dolittle/Rex Harrison, talker, Mattel, 1967, 22", MIB....**150.00**
Ed Grimley/Martin Short, talker, Tyco, 1989, 18", EX **10.00**
Elly May Clampett/Donna Douglas, Unique, 1964, 12", M.........**125.00**
Gene Simmons of KISS/Eugene Klein, Mego, 1978, 12½", EX ...**95.00**
Jeannie/Barbara Eden, Libby, 1966, rare, 20", EX......................**75.00**
JJ Evans/Jimmie Walker, talker, Shindana, 1975, 21", M..............**60.00**
John-Boy Walton/Richard Thomas, Mego, 1975, 8", M...............**45.00**
Laurie Partidge/Susan Dey, Remco, 1973, 19", EX.....................**100.00**
Louis Armstrong, Effanbee, 1984, 15½", MIB.............................**25.00**
Marie Osmond Modeling Doll, w/patterns, Mattel, 1976, 30", M.**75.00**
Marilyn Monroe, new face mold, 2nd issue, Tristar, 1982, 11½", M ..**35.00**
Miss Hannigan/Carol Burnett, Knickerbocker, 1982, 7", MIB **35.00**
Mr T/BA Baracus of A-Team, Galoob, 1983, 12", MIB.................**25.00**
Pollyanna/Hayley Mills, Uneeda, 1960, 30", EX **75.00**
Princess Diana, in wedding gown, Effanbee Fan Club, 1982, 16½", MIB..**225.00**
Shari Lewis, Madame Alexander, 1959, 21", M............................**400.00**

China

Agnes, cloth body, molded blouse w/gold lettering, RpC, 9", EX ..**110.00**
Child, swivel neck, ShPl, china limbs, RpC, 14", EX..............**2,850.00**
Child or boy, short blk or blond hairdo, exposed ears, RpC, 13", EX..**260.00**
Covered Wagon, center part w/sausage curls, wooden body, RpC, 17", EX.**2,850.00**
French, glass or pnt/e, open crown/cork pate, kid body, RpC, 14", EX.**3,150.00**
Japanese, mk or unmk, blk or blond hair, RpC, 1910-20, 10", EX .**125.00**
Kling, mk w/bell & #, RpC, 13", EX.......................................**350.00**
KPM, man w/brn hair, mk, 1869, 23", G (auction value) **7,000.00**
KPM, pk-tint lady w/Latchmann 1847 body, 19", G (auction value).**5,100.00**
Man w/curls, RpC, 19", EX..**1,850.00**
Queen Victoria, young, RpC, 16", EX......................................**1,600.00**
Spill curls w/or w/o headband, RpC, 13", EX.............................**435.00**
Swivel neck, flange type, RpC, 10", EX **2,100.00**
1840 style, brn hair in bun, ShHd w/long neck, RpC, 16", EX .**3,500.00**
1840 style, Covered Wagon, center part w/sausage curls, RpC, 10", EX...**275.00**
1840 style, Covered Wagon, center part w/sausage curls, RpC, 17", EX .**475.00**
1850 style, Alice in Wonderland, snood/headband, RpC, 12", EX .**300.00**
1850 style, bald head, hh or mohair wig, RpC, 14", EX **750.00**
1850 style, Greiner type, glass eyes, various hairdos, RpC, 13", EX ..**3,200.00**
1850 style, Greiner type, pnt/e, various hairdos, RpC, 15", EX, ea...**750.00**
1860 style, flat-top blk hair w/center part, side curls, RpC, 14", EX.**245.00**
1860 style, flat-top blk hair w/center part, side curls, RpC, 7", EX..**100.00**
1860 style, highbrow w/high forehead & curls, rnd face, RpC, 15", EX.**535.00**
1860 style, Mary Todd Lincoln, blk hair gold snood, RpC, 15", EX.**625.00**

1870 style, Adelina Patti, center part/ringlets, RpC, 20", EX......**550.00**
1870 style, bangs, aka Highland Mary, blk hair, RpC, 14"...........**300.00**
1870 style, Jenny Lind, blk hair in bun or coronet, RpC, 15", EX.........**1,550.00**
1880 style, Dolly Madison, blk hair w/ribbon, pnt eyes, RpC, 18", EX..**475.00**
1880 style, overall curls, narrow shoulders, china legs, RpC, 22", EX .**475.00**
1890 style, common or low brow, printed body, RpC, 10", EX....**115.00**
1890 style, jeweled necklace, RpC, 20", EX **325.00**

Cloth

A cloth doll in very good condition will display light wear and soiling, while one assessed as excellent will be clean and bright.

Alabama Indestructible, Black Baby, 1905, 20", EX **6,200.00**
Babyland Rag, Black, 1893-1928, 14½", EX **480.00**
Babyland Rag, Buster Brown, 1893-1928, 17", VG.....................**300.00**
Babyland Rag, molded/pnt face, 1893-1928, 13", EX..................**700.00**
Baybyland, color litho, 1893-1928, 14½", VG............................**175.00**
Beecher missionary rag, needle-sculptured features, ca 1900, 20", EX.**2,000.00**
Bing Art, pnt hair, cloth or felt, 1921-32, 13", EX **550.00**
Bing Art, wig, cloth or felt, 1931-32, 10", EX **350.00**
Black, pnt or embr features, 1930s, 15", EX, minimum value......**165.00**
Black, Topsy Turvy, oil pnt, EX..**650.00**
Chad Valley, child, pnt/e, 1917-1930+, 14", EX **625.00**
Chad Valley, Prince Edward Duke of Windsor, EX..................**1,500.00**
Chad Valley, Red Riding Hood, 14", VG...................................**125.00**
Chase, baby, pnt hair, jtd shoulders, 1899-1930+, 16", EX..........**575.00**
Chase, unusual hairdo, molded bun, 1899-1930+, 15", VG.....**2,200.00**
Columbian, HP features, stitched fingers & toes, 1891+, 15", EX.**4,500.00**
Deans Rag Book Co, child, 1905+, 16", VG...............................**185.00**
Drayton, Chocolate Drop, brn cloth, yarn hair, 1932, 14", EX ...**550.00**
Drayton, Dolly Dingle, printed features, mk torso, 1923, 15", EX.**550.00**
Gund, character, cloth mask face, pnt features, 1898+, 19", EX.**300.00**
Krueger, child, oil-pnt mask face, yarn or mohair wig, 1917+, 16", EX.**195.00**
Mollye, child, mask face, 1929-30+, 22", EX **200.00**
Philadelphia Baby, ShHd, pnt features, stockinette, 1860-1935, 18", EX.**3,500.00**
Printed cloth, Black child, ca 1876+, 16", VG **150.00**
Printed clothing, cut & sewn, ca 1903, 14", EX..........................**200.00**
Raynal, felt, cloth or celluloid head, 1922-30+, 14½", EX..........**450.00**
Walker, pressed mask w/oil-pnt, stockinette, late 1800s, 20", VG..**6,600.00**
Wellings, child, glass eyes, 1926-30+, 18", EX **850.00**

Effanbee

Bernard Fleischaker and Hugo Baum became business partners in 1910, and after two difficult years of finding toys to buy, they decided to manufacture dolls and toys of their own. The Effanbee trademark is a blending of their names, Eff for Fleischaker and bee for Baum. The company still exists today.

Baby Bud, composition, pnt features, o/c/m, jtd, RpC, 1918+, 6", VG.**50.00**
Baby Effanbee, compo & cloth, RpC, 1925, 12-13", EX..............**165.00**
Baby Grumpy Gladys, compo ShHd, cloth body, RpC, 1923, 15", EX.**350.00**
Barbara Lou, o/m, separated fingers, RpC, 1936-39+, 21", EX **900.00**
Brother, compo/cloth, pnt/e, OC, 1943, 6", EX **235.00**
Bubbles, compo ShHd, o/c/m, pnt teeth, molded hair, RpC, 1924, 16", EX.**375.00**
Charlie McCarthy, ca 1937, 17", EX **775.00**
Grumpykins, compo/cloth, orig Amish costume, 1936, 12", EX .**300.00**
Happy Birthday, compo, music box/heart bracelet, 1940, 17", VG.**1,050.00**
Harmonica Joe, cloth body, w/rubber ball, RpC, 1923, 15", EX..**350.00**
Historical, jtd compo, hh wig, pnt/e, fancy OC, 1939+, 16", EX..**600.00**
Howdy Doody, compo/cloth, brn o/c/e, o/c/m, OC, 1947-49, 20", EX.**275.00**
Johnny Tu-Face (face front & bk), pnt hair, OC, 16", EX...........**325.00**
MaMa, compo ShHd, wig, cloth body, crier, RpC, 1921+, 18", EX.**350.00**

Mary Jane, bsk head w/compo & wood, o/c/e, RpC, ca 1920, 20", EX.**700.00**
Mary Lee/Ann Shirley, compo, o/m, OC, 1935-40, 16", EX **500.00**
Pat-o-pat, compo/cloth, pnt/e, clapping mechanism, 1925+, 13", VG..**50.00**
Patsy Baby Tinyette, compo, bent legs, pnt/e, RpC, 1934, 61/2", EX..**300.00**

Patsy Lou, composition, open/close eyes, closed mouth, original clothes, 22", $675.00. (Photo courtesy McMasters Auctions)

Peggy Lou, compo, c/m, holds gloves & purse, OC, 1936-39+, 20½", EX.**1,800.00**
Sweetie Pie, compo bent limbs, o/c/e, caracul wig, RpC, 1939, 20", VG.**85.00**
Whistling Jim, compo/cloth, sewn-on shoes, RpC, 1916, 15", EX...**350.00**

Half Dolls

Half dolls were never meant to be objects of play. Most were modeled after the likenesses of lovely ladies, though children and animals were represented as well. Most of the ladies were firmly sewn on to pincushion bases that were beautifully decorated and served as the skirts of their gowns. Other skirts were actually covers for items on milady's dressing table. Some were used for parasol or brush handles or for tops to candy containers or perfume bottles. Most popular from 1900 to about 1930, they will most often be found marked with the country of their origin, especially Bavaria, Germany, France, and Japan. You may also find some fine quality pieces marked Goebel, Dressel and Kester, KPM, and Heubach.

Arms away, china or bsk, bald head w/wig, 4", EX......................**140.00**
Arms away, holding item, 4", EX..**185.00**
Arms away, holding item, 6", EX..**275.00**
Arms away, mk by maker or mold #, 4", EX.................................**200.00**
Arms away, mk by maker or mold #, 8", EX.................................**400.00**
Arms in, close to figure, bald head w/wig, 4", EX.......................**80.00**
Arms in, close to figure, bald head w/wig, 6", EX **115.00**
Arms in, decor bodice, necklace, fancy hair or holding article, 3", EX..**135.00**
Arms in, hands attached, 3", EX...**35.00**
Arms in, hands attached, 7", EX...**70.00**
Arms in, mk by maker or mold #, 5", EX......................................**135.00**
Arms in, papier-mache or compo, 4", EX......................................**35.00**
Arms in, w/legs, dressed, fancy decor, 5", EX **300.00**
German mk, 4", EX..**200.00**
German mk, 6", EX..**500.00**
Japan mk, 3", EX...**15.00**
Japan mk, 6", EX...**50.00**
Jtd shoulders, china or bsk, molded hair, 5", EX **145.00**
Jtd shoulders, solid dome, mohair wig, 4", EX.............................**220.00**
Man or child, 4", EX **120.00**
Man or child, 6", EX **160.00**

Handwerck, Heinrich

#69, child, bsk SkHd, o/m, o/c or set eyes, wig, RpC, 21", EX **700.00**
#79, bsk ShHd, c/m, o/c/e, wig, RpC, 15", EX..........................**1,800.00**
#89, bsk SkHd, c/m, o/c/e, wig, RpC, 18", EX **2,200.00**

#89, child, blk SkHd, o/c or set eyes, wig, RpC, 15", EX.............**575.00**
#99, child, bsk SkHd, o/m, o/c/e, wig, RpC, 24", EX..................**775.00**
#139, child, bsk SkHd, o/m, o/c/e, wig, RpC, 15", EX................**625.00**
#189, bsk SkHd, o/m, wig, RpC, 15", EX..................................**800.00**
#199, child, bsk SkHd, c/m, o/c/e, wig, RpC, 40", EX.............**3,400.00**
No mold #, child, bsk SkHd, o/m, o/c/e, wig, RpC, 29", EX **1,000.00**
No mold #, child, o/m, o/c/e, wig, RpC, 11", EX **500.00**
No mold #, kid body, ShHd, o/m, RpC, 17", EX........................**330.00**

Hertel, Schwab and Company

#127, character child, molded hair, o/c/e, o/m, RpC, 1915, 15", EX .**1,350.00**
#130, baby, bsk head, molded hair or wig, o/c/m/teeth, 9", EX....**325.00**
#136, character, o/m, mk Made in Germany, RpC, 1912, 24", EX.**1,000.00**
#140, character, glass eyes, laughing o/c/m, RpC, 1912, 12", EX .**3,400.00**
#141, character, pnt/e, o/c/m, RpC, 12", EX.............................**3,200.00**
#150 or #151, baby, bsk head, molded hair, o/c/m/teeth, RpC, 11", EX..**450.00**
#152, baby, bsk head, wig, o/m/teeth, o/c/e, bent legs, RpC, 22", EX .**900.00**
#154, character, molded hair, glass eyes, o/m, RpC, 1912, 20", VG..**1,900.00**

Heubach, Ernst

#250, child, kid body, o/m, RpC, 19", EX....................................**425.00**
#250, child, o/m, kid body, RpC, 13", EX....................................**250.00**
#267, baby, SkHd, 5-pc compo body, o/m, glass eyes, RpC, 11", EX..**250.00**
#275, child, ShHd, kid body, o/m, RpC, 27", EX........................**675.00**
#320, baby, SkHd, 5-pc compo body, o/m, glass eyes, RpC, 20", EX .**550.00**
#338, newborn, solid dome, cloth body, compo hands, RpC, 12", VG..**300.00**
#340, newborn, molded hair, cloth body, glass eyes, c/m, RpC, 15", EX .**700.00**
#444, Black newborn, molded hair, cloth body, glass eyes, c/m, 12", VG..**300.00**
#1900, child, kid or cloth body, glass eyes, o/m, RpC, 12", EX ...**150.00**
#1900, child, kid or cloth body, glass eyes, o/m, RpC, 22", EX ...**415.00**

Heubach, Gebruder

#5636, character, SkHd, laughing o/c/m/teeth, RpC, ca 1912, 13", EX..**2,000.00**
#5730, Santa, SkHd, RpC, 16", EX...**1,700.00**
#5777, Dolly Dimple, SkHd, o/m, RpC, ca 1913, 16", EX.......**2,500.00**
#6688, character child, ShHd, molded hair, intaglio eyes, c/m, 10", VG...**450.00**
#6692, character child, ShHd, intaglio eyes, c/m, RpC, 14", EX..**875.00**
#6736, character child, pnt/e, laughing, RpC, 16", EX.............**1,900.00**
#6894 or #7759, SkHd, molded hair, intaglio eyes, c/m, RpC, 9", EX..**500.00**
#6969, character, SkHd, glass eyes, c/m, RpC, 12", EX............**2,000.00**
#6970, character, glass eyes, c/m, RpC, 13", EX **2,300.00**
#7247, character, glass eyes, c/m, RpC, 15", EX **3,500.00**
#7622 or #7623, intaglio eyes, c/ or o/c/m, RpC, 16", EX **1,200.00**
#7644, character child, pnt/e, laughing o/c/m, RpC, 17", EX ..**1,200.00**
#7850, Coquette, o/c/m, RpC, 15", EX **1,100.00**
#7925, lady, ShHd, glass eyes, smiling o/m, RpC, 15", EX **2,000.00**
#7975, Baby Stuart, glass eyes, removable bsk bonnet, RpC, 13", EX..**1,900.00**
#8192, character, o/c/e, o/m, RpC, 13", EX..............................**900.00**
#8381, Princess Juliana, molded hair/ribbon, pnt/e, RpC, 14", VG .**5,000.00**
#8774, Whistling Jim, smoker/whistler, cloth body, RpC, 14", EX........**985.00**
#9355, glass eyes, o/m, sq mk, RpC, ca 1914, 13", EX **850.00**
#11010, Revalo, o/c/e, o/m, for Gebr Ohlhaver, RpC, 24", EX ...**850.00**
Heubach mk/no #, o/c/e, o/c/m, dimples, RpC, 18", EX...........**4,450.00**
Heuback mk/no #, adult, smile, pnt/e, RpC, 15", EX **3,500.00**
Hubach mk/no #, adult, o/m, glass eyes, RpC, 14", EX **4,500.00**

Ideal

Two of Ideal's most collectible lines of dolls are Crissy and Toni. For more information, refer to *Collector's Guide to Ideal Dolls, Second Edition*, by Judith Izen (Collector Books).

Baby, compo, molded hair, pnt eyes, OC, 1913, 12", EX, minimum .**100.00**
Baby Coos, hp w/magic skin body, o/c/e, pnt hair, c/m, OC, 14", EX.**75.00**
Baby Crissy, jtd vinyl, pnt teeth, brn o/c/e, OC, c 1972, 24", EX.**150.00**
Child or toddler, compo, o/c/e, wig, OC, 1915+, 15", EX, minimum...**150.00**
Daddy's Girl, vinyl/plastic, bl o/c/e, smiling c/m, OC, 1961, 38", EX.**1,200.00**
Flexy, Black, compo/wood, tube arms/legs, OC, 1938-42, 13½", EX...**325.00**
Flexy Clown, compo/wood, tube arms/legs, OC, 1938-42, 13½", EX...**225.00**
Flossie Flirt, compo/cloth, flirty eyes, o/m/teeth, crier, OC, 22", EX..**300.00**
Jiminy Cricket, compo/wood, OC, 1940, 9", EX.........................**500.00**
Liberty Boy (Dough Boy), compo, molded uniform, 1918+, 12", EX...**250.00**
Little Miss Revlon, vinyl, strung, rooted hair, o/c/e, OC, 10½", EX.**175.00**
Mama, compo/cloth, molded hair, o/c/e, crier, 1921+, 20", EX..**300.00**
Saucy Walker, hp, walks/head turns, flirty eyes, teeth, OC, 16", EX.**225.00**
Snoozie, compo/hard rubber/cloth, yawning o/m, OC, 1933+, 16", EX..**250.00**
Snow White, mask face, pnt/e, cloth body, hh wig, OC, 1938, 16", EX.**550.00**
Soozie Smiles, 2-headed (smile/frown), compo, OC, 1923, 15-17", EX ..**300.00**
Strawman, cloth, yarn hair, all orig, 1939, 17", EX **1,000.00**

Tammy, MIB, $85.00.

(Photo courtesy Cindy Sabulis)

Toni, jtd hp, nylon wig, c/m, w/wave set & curlers, OC, 14", EX..**475.00**
Uneeda Kid, pnt/e, molded yel hat, OC, 1916, 11", EX **300.00**

Jumeau

The Jumeau factory became the best known name for dolls during the 1880s and 1890s. Early dolls were works of art with closed mouths and paperweight eyes. When son Emile Jumeau took over, he patented sleep eyes with eyelids that drooped down over the eyes. This model also had flirty (eyes that move from side to side) eyes and is extremely rare. Over 98% of Jumeau dolls have paperweight eyes. The less-expensive German dolls were the downfall of the French doll manufacturers, and in 1899 the Jumeau company had to combine with several others in an effort to save the French doll industry from German competition.

#306, Princess Elizabeth, SkHd, flirty eyes, Unis Label, RpC, 18", EX.**2,100.00**
#1907, child, o/c/e, o/m, jtd Fr body, RpC, 14", EX.................**1,850.00**
BL Bebe, SkHd, pwt/e, c/m, wig, jtd compo, p/e, RpC, 20", EX.**4,200.00**
Depose E (sz #) J, RpC, 26", EX **8,000.00**
Depose Jumeau, bsk head, compo/wood body, pwt, c/m, RpC, 18", EX..**5,900.00**
Depose/E (sz #) J, RpC, 19", EX **5,850.00**
EJ Bebe, bsk SkHd, pwt/e, jtd body, wig, RpC, 17", EX **10,250.00**
EJ w/sz # between, RpC, 20", EX..**7,200.00**
EJ w/sz # between, 15", EX...**6,200.00**
EJ w/sz # between, 23", EX...**8,000.00**
Fashion type, #d swivel head, c/m, pwt, p/e, RpC, 17", EX...**3,800.00**
Fashion type, #d swivel head, wood body, bsk lower arms, RpC, 16", EX .**5,100.00**
Portrait, almond eyes, wig, RpC, 13½", EX...........................**12,500.00**
Portrait, wood body, RpC, 20", EX.......................................**8,500.00**

Tete Jumeau, child, SkHd, glass eyes, c/m, jtd compo, RpC, 12", EX.**3,500.00**
Tete Jumeau, child, SkHd, glass eyes, c/m, jtd compo, RpC, 23", EX.**5,000.00**

Kammer and Reinhardt

#117, Mein Liebling, glass eyes, c/m, RpC, 15", EX **4,400.00**
#118 or #118A, baby, o/c/e, o/m, RpC, 18", EX.......................**2,275.00**
#121, baby, o/c/e, o/m, RpC, 24", EX....................................**1,300.00**
#126, Mein Liebling Baby, flirty eyes, bent-leg baby, RpC, 18", EX..**1,000.00**
#135, baby, o/c/e, o/m, RpC, 13", EX **850.00**
#191, Dolly Face child, o/m, o/c/e, jtd body, RpC, 17", EX.........**865.00**
#192, Dolly Face child, o/m, o/c/e, jtd body, RpC, 18", EX......**1,100.00**
#214, ShHd, pnt eyes, c/m, muslin body, RpC, rare, 12", VG..**2,600.00**

Kestner

Johannes D. Kestner made buttons at a lathe in a Waltershausen factory in the early 1800s. When this line of work failed, he used the same lathe to turn doll bodies. Thus the Kestner company began. It was one of the few German manufacturers to make the complete doll. By 1860, with the purchase of a porcelain factory, Kestner made doll heads of china and bisque as well as wax, worked-in-leather, celluloid, and cardboard. In 1895 the Kestner trademark of a crown with streamers was registered in the U.S. and a year later in Germany. Kestner felt the mark was appropriate since he referred to himself as the 'king of German dollmakers.'

#128, bsk SkHd, glass eyes, pouty c/m, wig, bjtd, RpC, 15", EX.**1,000.00**
#142, bsk SkHd, glass eyes, o/m, bjtd, RpC, 18", EX **950.00**
#143, Dolly Face child, o/m, glass eyes, jtd, RpC, 8", EX **700.00**
#145, bsk ShHd, glass eyes, o/c/m, kid body, wig, RpC, 17", EX.**800.00**
#148, bsk ShHd, glass eyes, o/m, RpC, 21", EX **500.00**
#155, Dolly Face child, o/m, glass eyes, 5-pc body, RpC, 7½", EX .**925.00**
#161, Dolly Face child, o/m, glass eyes, jtd compo/wood, RpC, 23", EX..**1,100.00**
#172, Gibson Girl, ShHd, c/m, glass eyes, kid body, RpC, 10", EX ..**850.00**
#175, character child, SkHd, glass eyes, c/m, wig, jtd, 15", EX .**4,000.00**
#210, character baby, ShHd, o/c/e, o/c/m, RpC, 12", EX.............**700.00**
#211, character baby, SkHd, glass eyes, o/m, wig, RpC, 12", EX ..**775.00**
#243, Oriental baby, o/c/e, o/m, RpC, 15", EX **5,400.00**
#257, SkHd, o/c/e, o/m, RpC, 14", EX **900.00**
#257, SkHd, o/c/e, o/m, RpC, 17", EX **1,025.00**
#257, toddler, SkHd, o/c/e, o/m, RpC, 16", EX **950.00**
#260, character baby, SkHd, glass eyes, o/m, wig, RpC, 18", EX..**1,000.00**
#263, character baby, SkHd, solid dome, glass eyes, RpC, 18", EX..**1,000.00**
Sz # only, trn ShHd, glass eyes, c/m, RpC, 22", EX.....................**900.00**

Lenci

Characteristics of Lenci dolls include seamless, steam-molded felt heads, quality clothing, childishly plump bodies, and painted eyes that glance to the side. Fine mohair wigs were used, and the middle and fourth fingers were sewn together. Look for the factory stamp on the foot, though paper labels were also used. The Lenci factory continues today, producing dolls of the same high quality. Values are for dolls in excellent condition — no moth holes, very little fading. Dolls from the 1940s, 1950s, and beyond generally bring the lower prices; add for tags, boxes, and accessories. Mint dolls and rare examples bring higher prices. Dolls in only good condition are worth approximately 25% of one rated excellent.

Aviator girl, felt helmet, pre-1940s, OC, 18", EX....................**3,200.00**
Baby, OC, pre-1940s, 13", EX..**1,500.00**
Bali Dancer, pre-1940s, OC, 15", EX **1,500.00**
Child, hard face, 1940s-50s, plainer costume, 15", EX **500.00**
Child, softer face, fancy costume, 1920s-30s, 17", EX **2,500.00**
Child, softer face, 1920s-30s, fancy costume, 21", EX **2,750.00**

Fadette, adult face, flapper type w/slim limbs, pre-1940s, OC, 17", EX .1,050.00
Flirty glass eyes, pre-1940s, OC, 15", EX 2,200.00
Flower girl, ca 1930, OC, 20", EX......................................1,000.00
Jack Dempsey, pre-1940s, OC, 18", EX................................3,500.00
Mascotte, swing legs, pre-1940s, OC, 8½", EX 325.00
Merry widow, pre-1940s, OC, 20", EX................................1,450.00
Miniature, child, pre-1940, OC, 9", EX.....................................400.00
Smoker, pnt eyes, pre-1940s, OC, 28", EX............................2,400.00
Spanish girl, ca 1930, OC, 14", EX 800.00

Liddle Kiddles

From 1966 to 1971, Mattel produced Liddle Kiddle dolls ranging in size from ¾" to 4". They were all poseable and had rooted hair that could be restyled. There were various series of the dolls, among them Animiddles, Zoolery Jewelry Kiddles, extraterrestrials, and Sweet Treats, as well as many accessories. Our advisor for this category is Paris Langford; she is listed in the Directory under Louisiana. Please send SASE for information or contact Paris by e-mail: bbean415@aol.com.

Aqua Funny Bunny, #3532, complete, EX....................................35.00
Baby Rockaway, #3819, MIP...95.00
Blue Funny Bunny, #3532, MIP...100.00
Chitty Chitty Bang Bang, #3597, 1968, MOC 250.00
Dainty Deer, #3637, complete, M 45.00
Greta Grape, #3728, 1968-69, M...50.00
Heart Pin Kiddle, #3741, MIP 75.00
Howard Biff Biddle, #3520, complete, M 75.00
Kiddle & Kars Antique Fair Set, #3806, NRFB 300.00
Kleo Kola, #3729, complete, M..50.00
Lenore Limousine, #3743, complete, M 65.00
Liddle Kiddle Kottage, #3534, EX..25.00
Liddle Lion Zoolery, #3661, complete, M...................................125.00
Limey Lou Spoonfuls, #3815, MIP...75.00
Lorelei Locket, #3717, MP..75.00
Lucky Locket Jewel Case, #3542, M 75.00
Nurse 'N Totsy Outfit, #LK7, MIP..25.00
Playhouse Kiddles Bedroom, MIB..175.00
Rolly Twiddle, #3519, complete, M 175.00
Sleep 'N Totsy Outfit, #LK5, MIP...25.00

Madame Alexander

Beatrice Alexander founded the Alexander Doll Company in 1923 by making an all-cloth, oil-painted face, Alice in Wonderland doll. With the help of her three sisters, the company prospered; and by the late 1950s there were over six hundred employees making Madame Alexander dolls. The company still produces these lovely dolls today. For more information, refer to *Madame Alexander Collector's Doll Price Guide* and *Madame Alexander Store Exclusives and Limited Editions*, both by Linda Crowsey and published by Collector Books.

In the listings that follow, values represent dolls in mint to near-mint condition.

Active Miss, hp, Violet/Cissy, 1954 only, 18" 850.00
Alexander-Kins, Flowergirl, bend-knee walker, 1956-65, 8"........875.00
American Indian, compo, Little Betty, 1938-39, 9" 350.00
Ballerina, compo, Little Betty, 1935-41, 9" 375.00
Betty, compo, 1938-41, 19-21", ea..550.00
Bride, compo, Little Betty, 1936-41, 9-11", ea 325.00
Bridesmaid, compo, Little Betty, 1937-39, 9" 350.00
Cinderella, compo, Wendy Ann, 1935-37, 13"...........................395.00
Clover Kid, compo, Tiny Betty, 1935-36, 7" 375.00
Cousin Karen, hp, bend-knee walker, Wendy Ann, 1956 only, 8", minimum.1,800.00

Dionne Quintuplets, 7½" dolls, all original, complete with accessories and bed, M, $2,500.00 at auction. (Photo courtesy McMasters Auctions)

Dressed for Opera, hp, Margaret, 1953 only, 18", minimum value .1,800.00
Elise, hp/vinyl, street clothes, 1957-64, 16½", minimum value ..450.00
Flora McFlimsey, compo, Little Betty, 1938-41, 9" 425.00
Godey Bride, hp, Margaret, lacy satin gown w/train, 1950, 14", minimum ..1,000.00
Hansel, compo, Tiny Betty, 1935-72, 7" 300.00
Janie, toddler, #1156, 1964-66, 12" 275.00
Klondike Kate, hp, Portrette (Cissette), 1963 only, 10", minimum..1,400.00
Little Genius, compo/cloth, 1935-40, 1942-46, 12-14", ea..........200.00
Little Shaver, cloth, 1940-44, 10", minimum............................450.00
Maggie Teenager, hp, 1951-53, 15-18", ea, from $475 to 600.00
Mary Mine, vinyl/cloth, 1977-89, 21" 125.00
Mrs March Hare, cloth/felt, mid-1930s 625.00
Peasant, compo, Tiny Betty, 1936-37, 7"...................................275.00
Queen Alexandrine, compo, Wendy Ann, 1939-41, 21", minimum value..1,975.00
Rosebud, cloth/vinyl, 1952-53, 15-19", ea.................................150.00
Scarlett O'Hara, gr gown w/braid, Nancy Drew, 1981-85, 12" 125.00
Southern Belle, hp, str-leg non-walker, wht dress, 1953, 8", minimum ...750.00
Tommy, hp, Lissy, 1962 only, 12"..1,000.00
Vietnam, hp, Wendy Ann, #788, 1968-69, 8" 275.00
Yolanda, Brenda Starr, 1965 only, 12" 375.00

Mattel

For more information refer to *Talking Toys of the 20th Century* by Kathy and Don Lewis. Our values are for examples in near-mint to mint condition.

Baby Pattaburp, vinyl, drinks/burps, OC, 1964-66, 16" 200.00
Baby's Hungry, battery-op, eyes move/lips chew, 1967-68, 17" 30.00
Baby Secret, vinyl, stuffed body, whispers 11 phrases, 1966-67, 18" ..75.00
Baby Tender Love, realistic skin, wets, OC, 1970-73, 13" 65.00
Baby Tender Love Brother, anatomically correct, OC, 11½" 50.00
Baby 1st Step, battery-op walker, rooted hair, o/c/e, OC, 1965-67, 18" ..150.00
Big Jim, vinyl action figure, blk hair, 9½" 150.00
Captain Kangaroo, talker, Sears only, 1967, 19" 50.00
Chatty Baby, red pinafore over rompers, 1962-64, 18"..................75.00
Chatty Cathy, Black, brn eyes, 1960-65, 20" (auction value) 885.00
Chatty Cathy, vinyl/hp, blond, 1960-63, 20" 350.00
Cheerful Tearful, vinyl, blond hair, arm changes face, OC, 7" 100.00
Drowsy, vinyl head, stuffed body, pull-string talker, OC, 15½" ..175.00
Guardian Goddess, 1979, 11½" 50.00
Julia, Twist 'N Turn, OC, 1969, 11½" 250.00
Shrinkin' Violet, cloth, yarn hair, pull-string talker, OC, 16" 350.00
Tippee Toes, battery-op, OC, 1968-70, 17" 80.00

Papier-Mache

1820-60s milliner's type, braided bun w/side curls, RpC, 15", EX.1,600.00
1820-60s milliner's type, center part & sausage curls, RpC, 21", EX.950.00

1820-60s milliner's type, molded bonnet, kid body, RpC, rare, 15", VG .**1,700.00**
1820-60s milliner's type, topknot & side curls, RpC, 10", EX .**850.00**
1835-50 Fr type, solid dome ShHd, glass eyes, pnt hair, RpC, 13", EX .**1,000.00**
1835-50 Fr type, solid dome ShHd, pnt/e, pnt blk hair, RpC, 16", EX.**1,000.00**
1840s-60s, ShHd, cloth body/wooden limbs, glass eyes, RpC, 18", EX .**1,700.00**
1840s-60s, ShHd, cloth body/wooden limbs, pnt/e, RpC, 21", EX ..**1,150.00**
1840s-60s, ShHd, cloth body/wooden limbs, pnt/e, RpC, 9", EX ..**450.00**
1840s-60s, ShHd w/long curls, cloth body/wood limbs, RpC, 16", EX .**1,550.00**
1844-92 M&S Superior, #1020, ShHd, molded hair, pnt/e, RpC, 17", EX.**425.00**
1844-92 M&S Superior, ShHd, glass eyes, RpC, 16", EX **700.00**
1879-1900s, trn ShHd, solid dome, glass eyes, c/m, RpC, 22", EX.**925.00**
1879-1900s, washable ShHd, glass eyes, RpC, EX quality, 15", EX.**550.00**
1879-1900s, washable ShHd, glass eyes, RpC, G quality, 10", EX .**150.00**
1920s+, Fr, bright coloring, wig, ethnic OC, 9", EX **125.00**
1920s+, German, bright coloring, wig, OC, 10", EX.....................**80.00**

Parian

Alice in Wonderland, molded headband or comb, RpC, 19", EX .**750.00**
Dolly Madison, RpC, 22", EX..**1,600.00**
Irish Queen, Limbach, clover mk, #8552, RpC, 14", EX **575.00**

Lady, fancy hairdo with molded blue tiara, painted eyes, pierced ears, replaced clothes, 24", $1,900.00.
(Photo courtesy McMasters Auctions)

Lady, fancy molded hair, pnt/e, ears not pierced, RpC, 13", EX ..**700.00**
Lady, fancy molded hair, pnt/e, p/e, RpC, 16", EX.......................**900.00**
Lady, fancy molded hair, swivel neck, glass eyes, RpC, 15", EX.**2,700.00**
Lady, simple molded hair w/no decor, RpC, 10", EX....................**175.00**
Lady, simple molded hair w/no decor, RpC, 21", EX....................**425.00**
Man or boy, center part, decor shirt & tie, glass eyes, RpC, 16", EX.**2,825.00**
Man or boy, center part, decor shirt & tie, pnt/e, RpC, 13", EX.**775.00**
Molded bodice, fancy trim, RpC, 17", EX **800.00**
Molded hat, blond or blk pnt hair, glass eyes, RpC, 17", EX....**3,000.00**
Molded hat, blond or blk pnt hair, pnt/e, RpC, 16", EX **2,300.00**

Schoenhut

Albert Schoenhut left Germany in 1866 to go to Pennsylvania to work as a repairman for toy pianos. He eventually applied his skills to wooden toys and later designed an all-wood doll which he patented on January 17, 1911. These uniquely jointed dolls were painted with enamels and came with a metal stand. Some of the later dolls had stuffed bodies, voice boxes, and hollow heads. Due to the changing economy and fierce competition, the company closed in the mid-1930s.

#100, girl, cvd hair, solemn face, pnt/e, RpC, 1911-12, 16", EX.**3,000.00**
#100, girl, no iris outline, RpC, 1911-12, 16", EX **1,500.00**
#102, girl, cvd hair w/braids, RpC, 19-21", 1912-16, EX, ea..**2,100.00**
#102, girl, short cvd bob, no iris outline, RpC, 1911-16, 16", EX.**2,400.00**
#105, girl, short cvd bob w/cvd ribbon, RpC, 1912-16, 19-21", EX, ea.**2,100.00**
#107/#107W (walker), bent-limb toddler, RpC, 1917-26, 11", EX.**700.00**

#107/#107W (walker), toddler, elastic strung, RpC, 1924-26, 14", EX..**750.00**
#108/#108W (walker), toddler, cloth body, crier, RpC, 1924-28, 17", EX.**550.00**
#201, boy, cvd hair, iris outline, RpC, 1911-12, 16", EX..........**1,500.00**
#202, boy, cvd hair w/forelock, pnt/e, RpC, 1911-12, 16", EX.**3,000.00**
#206, boy, cvd hair, covered ears, RpC, 1912-16, 19", EX **2,600.00**
#305, girl, wig braids, face of #303, RpC, 1911-12, 16", EX.....**1,500.00**
#307, girl, long curly wig, smooth eye, RpC, 1911-16, 16", EX...**850.00**
#310, girl w/long curly wig, same as #105 face, RpC, 1912-16, 19", EX..**825.00**
#314, girl, long curls, wide face, smooth eye, RpC, 1912-16, 19", EX.**725.00**
#316, Miss Dolly, o/m/teeth, wig, pnt/e, RpC, 1915-25, 21", EX..**675.00**
By-Lo Baby, cloth baby, c/m, o/c/m, Grace S Putnam stamp, RpC, 13", EX ..**2,400.00**
Maggie, cartoon character, 9", EX **525.00**
Schnickel-Fritz, cvd hair, grinning o/c/m/4 teeth, RpC, 15", EX.**3,000.00**
Teddy Roosevelt, OC, 8", EX **1,600.00**
Tootsie Wootsie, cvd hair, o/c/m/2 teeth, lg ears, RpC, 15", EX.**3,400.00**

SFBJ

By 1895 Germany was producing dolls at much lower prices than the French dollmakers could, so to save the doll industry, several leading French manufacturers united to form one large company. Bru, Raberry and Delphieu, Pintel and Godshaux, Fleischman and Bodel, Jumeau, and many others united to form the company Society Francaise de Fabrication de Bebes et Jouets (SFBJ).

#226, character, bsk SkHd, glass eyes, c/m, RpC, 20"...............**2,400.00**
#226, character, bsk SkHd, glass eyes, c/m, RpC, 20"...............**2,400.00**
#230, character, bsk SkHd, o/m/teeth, glass eyes, RpC, 17", EX..**1,900.00**
#235, character, bsk SkHd, glass eyes, o/c/m, RpC, 18", EX ...**1,800.00**
#237, character, bsk SkHd, glass eyes, o/c/m, RpC, 16", EX **1,700.00**
#252, character, bsk SkHd, glass eyes, pouty c/m, RpC, 15", EX .**4,000.00**
#301, lady, bsk SkHd, kiss thrower, RpC, 22", EX....................**1,700.00**

Shirley Temple

Prices are suggested for dolls complete and in at least near-mint condition. Add up to 25% (depending on her outfit) if mint with box. A played-with doll in only very good condition would be worth only about half of listed values.

Bsk, 6", Japan, unlicensed variant, OC, NM................................**250.00**
Celluloid, 13", open crown, o/c/e, Dutch costume, mk head, NM.**350.00**
Celluloid, 5", Japan, unlicensed variant, OC, 5", NM.................**185.00**
Compo, 13", Ideal, jtd body, o/m/teeth, mohair wig, OC, 1934+, NM..**750.00**
Compo, 17", Ideal, jtd body, o/c/e, o/m/teeth, wig, OC, 1934+, NM ...**875.00**
Compo, 22", Ideal, jtd body, o/c/e, o/m/teeth, wig, OC, 1934+, NM.**1,200.00**
Compo, 7½", Japan, molded hair, pnt eyes, o/c/m/teeth, OC, NM..**300.00**
Vinyl, 12", o/c/e, rooted wig, o/c/m/teeth, OC, mk ST/12", NM, minimum..**350.00**
Vinyl, 16", red dot Stand Up & Cheer outfit, 1963, NM...........**165.00**
Vinyl, 17", flirty eyes, OC, mk ST//15", 1958-61, NM...............**500.00**
Vinyl, 35", jtd wrists, OC, mk ST-35-38-2, 1960, NM............**2,100.00**

Simon and Halbig

Simon and Halbig was one of the finest German makers to operate during the 1870s into the 1930s. Due to the high quality of the makers, their dolls still command large prices today. During the 1890s a few Simon & Halbig heads were used by a French maker, but these are extremely rare and well marked S&H.

#719, child, o/c/e, c/m, p/e, jtd compo wood body, RpC, 18", EX ..**3,700.00**
#729, laughing face, glass eyes, o/c/, RpC, ca 1888, 16", EX **2,550.00**
#749, SkHd, glass eyes, c/m, p/e, RpC, ca 1888, 21", EX **3,100.00**
#758, child, RpC, ca 1888, 20", EX..**2,100.00**

#852, Oriental, swivel head, glass eyes, c/m, wig, RpC, 5½", EX **1,100.00**
#939, bsk SkHd, glass eyes, o/m, p/e, RpC, ca 1888, 11", EX **925.00**
#949, glass eyes, c/m, RpC, ca 1888, 16", EX...........................**2,350.00**
#1009, bsk SkHd, o/c/e, o/m/teeth, p/e, wig, kid body, RpC, 19", EX.**525.00**
#1010, child, ShHd, RpC, 18", EX..**575.00**
#1039, bsk w/compo walking body, glass eyes, o/m, RpC, 13", EX.**2,000.00**
#1160, Little Women, ShHd, glass eyes, c/m, RpC, ca 1894, 7", EX.**350.00**
#1199, Oriental, SkHd, o/m, glass eyes, compo/wood body, OC, 16", EX.**8,000.00**
#1248, Santa, o/m, glass eyes, RpC, ca 1898, 6", EX **650.00**
#1250, dolly face, ShHd, RpC, ca 1898, 15", EX **550.00**
#1294, character baby, glass eyes, o/m, RpC, 1910+, 16", EX **750.00**
#1428, character baby, glass eyes, o/c/m, RpC, 1914, 13", EX..**1,600.00**
#1469, flapper, glass eyes, c/m, RpC, ca 1920, 15", EX.............**3,500.00**
#1489, character baby, solid dome, pnt/e, o/c/m, RpC, 1920, 20", VG.**4,200.00**
S&H (no #), child, ShHd, molded hair, RpC, 1870s, 19", EX..**1,700.00**

Steiner, Jules

Jules Nicholas Steiner established one of the earliest French manufacturing companies (making dishes and clocks) in 1855. He began with mechanical dolls with bisque heads and open mouths with two rows of bamboo teeth; his patents grew to include walking and talking dolls. In 1880 he registered a patent for a doll with sleep eyes. This doll could be put to sleep by turning a rod that operated a wire attached to its eyes.

A Series child, bisque socket head, blue paperweight eyes, closed mouth, replaced human hair wig, jointed composition body, antique dress, replaced undies and shoes, 22", EX, $3,100.00. (Photo courtesy McMasters Auctions)

Bebe le Parisian, SkHd, cb pate, pwt/e, c/m, wig, 1895+, 21", EX..**4,100.00**
Bebe w/A or C series mk, SkHd w/cb pate, pwt/e, c/m, RpC, 14", EX..**8,500.00**
Bebe w/figure mks, SkHd, glass eyes, c/m, wig, RpC, 1887+, 13", EX..**3,500.00**
Bebe w/figure mks, SkHd, o/c/m/dimples, RpC, 1887+, 16", EX.**3,500.00**
Motschmann-type baby, solid dome, glass eyes, c/m, wig, RpC, 14", EX..**4,800.00**
Unmk bebe, bsk SkHd, pwt/e, o/m/teeth, p/e, wig, RpC, 18", EX..**6,000.00**

Vogue

This is the company that made the Ginny doll. Composition was used during the '40s, but vinyl was the preferred material throughout the decade of the '50s. An original mint-condition composition Ginny would be worth a minimum of $450.00 on the market today (played-with about $90.00). The last Ginny came out in 1969. Another Vogue doll that is becoming very collectible is Jill, whose values are steadily climbing. Our advisor for Jill dolls is Bonnie Groves; she is listed in the Directory under Texas.

Accessories, charm bracelet & wristwatch **36.00**
Accessories, vinyl belt, purse & collar, MIP **15.00**
Accessory, poodle purse, MIP...**35.00**

Baby Dear, hp/plastic, plays tune/wiggles, OC, 1962-63, 18", EX.....**150.00**
Baby Dear, hp/vinyl, rooted hair, OC, 1959-64, 18", EX **325.00**
Brikette, hp/vinyl, flirty eyes, orange hair, OC, 1959-61, 22", MIB.**250.00**
Clothes, Jill jeans outfit & Coke bottle, #3333, MIB **93.00**
Clothes, Jill outfit, 1957, MIB..**80.00**
Cynthia, compo, o/c/e, o/m, wig, 3-pc compo body, RpC, 1940s, 13", EX.**350.00**
Dora Lee, compo, o/c/e, c/m, OC, 11", EX...............................**375.00**
Ginnette, vinyl, pnt/e, o/m, jtd, OC, 1955-69, 8", EX **250.00**
Ginny, hp, bent-knee walker, o/c/e, wig, OC, 1957-62, 8", EX...**175.00**
Ginny, hp, Davy Crockett outfit, 1954-56, 8", MIB **935.00**
Ginny, hp, str-leg walker, o/c/e, pnt lashes, OC, 1953-54, 8", MIB..**2,000.00**
Ginny, hp, 7-pc body, o/c/e, wig, OC, 1954-56, 8", EX **225.00**
Ginny, hp walker, o/c/e, dynel wig, OC (common dress), 1850-54, 8", EX .**350.00**
Ginny, pnt hp, molded hair w/wig, OC, 1948-50, 8", EX............**375.00**
Ginny, vinyl, mk Dakin, OC, 1986-95, 8", M............................**25.00**
Ginny, vinyl, non-walker, o/c/e, rooted hair, OC, 1972-77, 8", EX...**50.00**
Ginny, vinyl/hp, o/c/e, rooted hair, OC, 1963-65, 8", EX.............**50.00**
Ginny baby, vinyl, o/c/e, drinks/wets, OC, 1959-82, 18", EX........**50.00**
Ginny Crib Crowd baby, curved legs, o/e/c, caracul wig, OC, 8", EX..**650.00**
Ginny from Far-Away Lands, vinyl, OC, Hong Kong, 1977-82, 8", EX.**35.00**
Ginny Sasson, vinyl, jtd, rooted hair, o/c/e, Lesney, OC, 1981, 8", EX.**35.00**
Jan, vinyl, RpC, 10½" **38.00**
Jan, vinyl, 6-pc body, swivel waist, OC, 1958-60, 10½", EX.......**150.00**
Jeff, all orig, 10", VG..**40.00**
Jeff, nude, 10", G..**10.00**
Jeff, RpC, 10", VG in box **49.00**
Jeff, vinyl, 5-pc rigid body, pnt hair, OC, 1958-60, 11", EX **100.00**
Jeff, w/3 tagged outfits, 10", EX......................................**78.00**
Jill, Bride, all orig, 1952, 10", VG...................................**195.00**
Jill, Bride, all orig, 1957, 10", VG....................................**40.00**
Jill, hp teenager, 7-pc body, walker, OC, 1957-60, 10½", MIB ..**225.00**
Jill, in #7401, all orig, 10", VG.......................................**95.00**
Jill, nude, 10", G..**30.00**
Jill, OC, wrist tag, 1957, MIB...**239.00**
Jill, orig bra & panties, 10", MIB......................................**100.00**
Jill, tagged outfit, 10", G...**50.00**
Jimmy, vinyl, pnt/e, o/m, OC, 1958, 8", EX.............................**60.00**
Li'l Imp, vinyl, walker, o/c/e, orange hair, OC, 1959-60, 10½", EX..**75.00**
Little Miss Ginny, vinyl pre-teen, 1-pc body, OC, 1965-71, 12", EX.**40.00**
Love Me Linda, vinyl, pnt/e, long hair, OC, 1965, 15", NM.........**65.00**
Miss Ginny, vinyl, 2-pc body, swivel waist, OC, 1962-65, 15", EX..**45.00**
Toddles, pnt/e, mohair wig, jtd body, OC, 8", EX **425.00**
Wee Imp, hp, orange wig, gr eyes, OC, 1960, 8", EX..................**400.00**

Wax, Poured Wax

Bride, rose wax ShHd, glass eyes, c/m, wig, kid body, RpC, 15", VG.**1,650.00**
Over compo, Alice in Wonderland style w/molded headband, RpC, 16", EX..**525.00**
Over compo, ShHd, molded hair, glass eyes, cloth body, RpC, 15", EX..**300.00**
Over compo, 2-faced (laughing/crying), RpC, 1880s+, 15", EX..**900.00**
Over compo ShHd, child, o/m, glass eyes, cloth body, RpC, 17", EX..**350.00**
Over compo ShHd, slit-head, glass eyes, RpC, 1830-60s, 18", EX..**1,300.00**
Over compo/reinforced, child, glass eyes, cloth body, RpC, 14", EX ...**1,000.00**
Over papier-mache, bellows, glass eyes, pnt hair, o/m, RpC, 18", VG.**2,000.00**
Poured, baby, ShHd, glass eyes, c/m, cloth body, RpC, 17", EX..**1,500.00**
Poured, baby, ShHd, glass eyes, c/m, cloth body, wig, RpC, 25", EX .**2,250.00**
Poured, child, ShHd, glass eyes, wax limbs/cloth body, RpC, 13", EX.**1,100.00**
Poured, lady, ShHd, glass eyes, wax limbs/cloth body, RpC, 15", EX...**1,100.00**

Door Knockers

Door knockers, those charming precursors of the doorbell, come in an intriguing array of shapes and styles. The very rare ones come from

England. Cast-iron examples made in this country were often produced in forms similar to the more familiar doorstop figures.

Alsatian wolf dog (German shepherd), brass, 5x4", EX 60.00
Birdhouse, cream w/mc, cream bkplate, Hubley #629, 3⅜x2⅝" 425.00
Butterfly, mc, under pk rose, cream & purple bkplate, 3½x2½"..525.00
Cardinal on twigs, pnt CI, rare, 5x3", M 285.00
Cottage in woods, wht w/red roof, gr trees, Judd #629, 3¼", $300 to...350.00
Daisies tied w/bow, pnt CI, 4½x2¾", VG+................................105.00
Dragon, tooled wrought iron, w/strike, 6½" 115.00
Highlander w/bagpipes, brass, mk Made in Great Britain, 6" 85.00
Ivy pot, pnt CI, Hubley #123, EX..160.00
Mammy w/laundry basket on head, mc, breasts are knocker, rare, 7¼"..1,750.00
Parrot, mc pnt on CI, ca 1890, 4½x3", EX 125.00
Parrot on branch, mc pnt, Hubley, 4¾x2¾" 125.00
Pear, pnt CI, flower bkplate, rare, 4¼x3", M 360.00
Rooster, wht variation, 4½x3", EX 275.00
Roses (3) tied w/bl ribbon, pnt CI, Judd Co #626, 4x3", EX 55.00
Woman wearing bonnet, detailed profile, Judd #619, 4", EX 425.00
Zinnias, mc, mk Pat Pend LVL, rare, 3¾x2½" 550.00

Doorstops

Although introduced in England in the mid-1800s, cast-iron doorstops were not made to any great extent in this country until after the Civil War. Once called 'door porters,' their function was to keep doors open to provide better ventilation. They have been produced in many shapes and sizes, both dimensional and flat-backed, and in the past few years have become a popular, yet affordable collectible. While cast-iron examples are the most common, brass, wood, and chalk were also used. An average price is in the $100.00 to $200.00 range, though some are valued at more than $400.00. Doorstops retained their usefulness and appeal well into the '30s.

In some areas of the country, it it may be necessary to adjust prices down about 25%. When no condition code is present, items are assumed to be in exceptional original condition, flat-backed unless noted full-figured, and cast iron unless another material is mentioned. To evaluate a doorstop in only very good to excellent paint, deduct at least 35%. Values for examples in poor to good paint drop dramatically.

Key: ff — full figured

Cosmos, Hubley, 17¾x10¼" (largest flower doorstop made), EX, $700.00.

Apple Blossoms, in woven basket, Hubley #329, 7⅝x5⅜", $100 to.150.00
Aunt Jemima, red/blk/wht, arms akimbo, 13¼x8", from $425 to...600.00
Beagle, seated, looking right, 8x6½", from $200 to 275.00
Bellhop, bl uniform, #1244, 8⅞x4⅝", from $275 to....................350.00
Bobby Blake, boy w/teddy, Hubley, #46, 9½x5¼", from $425 to.550.00
Boston Terrier, Begging; ff, 8¾x5", from $300 to........................375.00
Boston Terrier, Sm; looking right, 9⅞x8¼", from $65 to 125.00
Boy w/Fruit Basket, top hat, 9¼x3⅞", from $375 to 450.00
Buster Brown, in sailor suit, on base, 7¾x5¼", from $425 to.......475.00
Cape Cod, cottage w/flowers, Albany Foundry, 5¾x8¾", from $125 to..200.00
Colonial Woman, w/purse & bonnet, Littco (others), 10¼", $175 to.225.00
Crossed Out, man w/arms & legs crossed, 7⅛x5⅝", from $650 to.850.00
Deco Nude, stands before elevated circle, 9¼", from $200 to 275.00
Deco Woman, hands to hair, front-wrap dress, 17x6½", $475 to .550.00
Dolly Dimple, ff, wide-brim bonnet, Hubley, 7¾x3¾", $325 to...450.00
Dutch Girl, head bowed, ff, 6x3¾", from $150 to 225.00
Dutch Girl w/Big Shoes, 9¾x9¼", from $325 to.........................400.00
Elephant, on base, pnt blanket, 5x8", from $100 to.....................175.00
Flower Bowl, rubber knobs at bk, B&H, 5⅞x5", from $225 to.....275.00
Frog, open mouth, 6½x4½", from $100 to...................................150.00
Girl Holding Dress, B&H #7798, 13x6¾", from $750 to.........1,000.00
Grapes & Leaves, Albany Foundry, 7¾x6½", from $125 to........200.00
Huckleberry Finn, w/stick & pail, Littco Products, 12½", $550 to ..650.00
Humpty Dumpty, ff, on short wall, #661, 4½x3½", from $300 to..375.00
Jonquil, 3 flowers on base, Hubley, #534, 7x6", from $175 to 250.00
Lamb, ff, wht, ft wide, 6¾x9¼", from $275 to............................350.00
Lighthouse, Light of the World, 9½x6½", from $100 to 175.00
Lighthouse, rubber, 9¾x9⅜", from $250 to.................................300.00
Little Dutch Woman, arms akimbo, ff, 4x2⅜", from $100 to....125.00
Log Cabin, among trees, National Foundry, 4⅝x10", from $150 to .225.00
London Royal Mail Coach, Pat Pending, 7x12¼", up to..............85.00
Mad Hatter, ff, seated on base, #666, 6⅝x2⅞", from $275 to................350.00
Monkey, seated, sm base, 13½x5⅝", from $350 to 425.00
Owl, perched on log, 9x5½", from $275 to 350.00
Pan & Nymph, on base, 9¼x14", from $850 to........................1,000.00
Peacock on Fence, National Foundry, #56, 13x7⅜", from $250 to..300.00
Penguin w/Top Hat, ff, Hubley, 10½x3¾", from $350 to 475.00
Peter Rabbit, eating carrot, facing left, Hubley, #96, 9½" 450.00
Pirate Girl, w/sword & treasure, 13⅞x7¼", from $250 to...............300.00
Poppies & Daisies, in vase, Hubley, #491, 7¼x6", from $125 to...175.00
Rooster, ff, head high, on sq base, 15⅜x6⅛", from $325 to.....375.00
Rumba Dancer, slim, ruffled skirt, 11⅛x6⅝", from $600 to................850.00
Saddled Horse, ff, walking w/head up, 10x11½", from $175 to...275.00
Sax Player, Black man w/instrument on base, 6⅞x6", from $500 to .650.00
Scottish Highlander, w/spear, rocky base, 15½x13", from $275 to ..325.00
Setter, ff, blk & wht, on point, Hubley, 8¾x15⅞", from $175 to.275.00
Spanish Girl, w/fan & comb, skirt held wide, 9⅞", from $325 to ...400.00
Spanish Guitarist, ff, Pat Pend, 11x3⅜", from $600 to 750.00
Tiger Lilies, 3 lg blooms on base, Hubley, #472, 10½x6", $200 to.275.00
Topsy, wedge, Hubley, 6x4", from $275 to 300.00
Tulip Pot, 5 flowers, National Foundry, 8¼x7", from $175 to...250.00
Twin Cats, dressed, Hubley, #73, 7x5¼", from $325 to 400.00
Windmill, National Foundry, mk 10 Cape Cod, 6¾x6⅞", from $100 to .150.00
Wine Man, w/many bottles, on base, 9½x7", from $650 to.........850.00
Woman Holding Flower Baskets, cJo, #1270, 8x4¾", from $200 to 275.00
Woman w/Ruffled Skirt, unmk, 6⅜x4⅞", from $150 to.............225.00
Zinnias, in vase, Hubley, #316, 9¾x8½", from $150 to..............250.00

Dorchester Pottery

Taking its name from the town in Massachusetts where it was organized in 1895, the Dorchester Pottery Company made primarily utilitarian wares, though other types of items were made as well. By 1940 a line of decorative pottery was introduced, some of which was painted by hand with scrollwork or themes from nature. The buildings were destroyed by fire in the late 1970s, and the pottery was never rebuilt. In the listings that follow, the decorations described are all in cobalt unless otherwise noted. Our advisor for this category is Dale MacLean; he is listed in the Directory under Massachusetts.

Key: CAH — Charles A. Hill (noted artist)

Bed warmer, stoneware, no decor, mk, 5x11" 100.00
Bowl, Blueberry, CAH, N Ricci, 4x8" 150.00
Bowl, cereal; Pine Cone, 6" 100.00
Bowl, emb scalloped sides w/bl stripes, CAH, 2¾x5½" 100.00
Bowl, Grape, leaves on hdls, sgn, mk, 4x6" 165.00
Bowl, Pine Cone, 2x6" 110.00
Bowl, Ship & Seascape, decor rim, sgn RB/N Ricci, 3x9", NM ..325.00
Bowl, Whale, sgn CAH, 2¼x5½", +Swirl underplate 150.00
Casserole, Blueberry, open, CAH, N Ricci, 3½x6" 200.00
Casserole, Blueberry, w/lid, mk, 1-qt, 4x6" dia 200.00
Casserole, Colonial Lace, CAH, 4½x7½" 275.00
Charger, Fruit, mk, 12½" 400.00
Charger, Spiral, mk, 13" 350.00
Coffeecup, Blueberry 95.00
Creamer & sugar bowl, Strawberry, CAH/Denisons, 3¼", 3½", EX..200.00
Cup & saucer, Geometric Floral, K Denisons 125.00
Dish, Tear Drop, CAH, 4½x7½" 150.00
Jam jar, Clipper Ship, K Denisons, 3x2¼", NM 100.00
Mug, Apple, CAH, 3", set of 4 ....250.00
Mug, Bell, striped hdl, paper label, 4½x3⅜" 165.00
Mug, Blueberry, mk, 4½x3½" 95.00
Mug, Full Scroll, CAH, 4½" 110.00
Mug, Swirls, mk, 4½x3½" 110.00
Pitcher, Grape, w/lid, CAH, N Ricci, 7", EX 150.00
Pitcher, Pilgrim, stamped, RT (Robert Trotter) under hdl, 7½", EX .250.00
Plate, Fruit, strawberries & pear, sgn, 7½", EX 200.00
Plate, Pine Cone, CAH, 7¼" 175.00
Plate, Whale, CAH, 10¼" 275.00
Sugar bowl, Blueberry, w/lid 110.00
Sugar jar, Polka Dot, sgn RB (Robert Brake), 3½" 100.00
Syrup, Half Scroll, bulbous, 5¼x4½" 150.00
Syrup, Pine Cone, overall decor, mk, 4¼x3½" 150.00

Dorflinger

    C. Dorflinger was born in Alsace, France, and came to this country when he was ten years old. When still very young, he obtained a job in a glass factory in New Jersey. As a young man, he started his own glassworks in Brooklyn, New York, opening new factories as profits permitted. During that time he made cut glass articles for many famous people including President and Mrs. Lincoln, for whom he produced a complete service of tableware with the United States Coat of Arms. In 1863 he sold the New York factories because of ill health and moved to his farm near White Mills, Pennsylvania. His health returned, and he started a plant near his home. It was there that he did much of his best work, making use of only the very finest materials. Christian died in 1915, and the plant was closed in 1921 by consent of the family.

    Dorflinger glass is rare and often hard to identify. Very few pieces were marked. Many only carried a small paper label which was quickly discarded; these are seldom found today. Identification is more accurately made through a study of the patterns, as colors may vary.

Bottle, scent; Montrose, gr cut to clear, att, 7¾" 660.00
Bowl, finger; Picket Fence, w/underplate 100.00
Bowl, punch; Marlboro, ornate pattern, 2-pc, 11½x14½" 2,300.00
Celery dish, Marlboro, 2⅛x4½x12½" 230.00
Compote, Kalana, ftd, 3½x5¼" 125.00
Cordial, Kalana Lily, ftd, 3¾" 85.00

Decanter, floral cutting with Rococo above band of nailhead diamonds, rayed base, 6¼", $3,400.00.

Ferner, Picket Fence, cut 85.00
Goblet, wine; Prince of Wales, teardrop stem, 2¾" 165.00
Grapefruit server, Kalana Lily, stemmed, 5⅜" 120.00
Nappy, cranberry cut to clear w/X-cut dmns, strawberry dmn & fan.750.00
Pitcher, water; Colonial, 7½"...300.00
Plate, American, cut, scalloped & serrated rim, 7½" 95.00
Plate, Picket Fence, cut, 6¼" 55.00
Salt cellar, Parisian, paperweight style, master 140.00
Sherbet, Kalana Lily, 3¼x4⅛" 115.00
Tumbler, Old Colony, 3¾" 200.00
Vase, Kalana Lily, ftd, tapered, 9" 165.00
Vase, Kalana Pansy, 6" 125.00
Wine, Colonial, knobbed stem, ca 1893 ....95.00

Dragon Ware

    Dragon ware is fairly accessible and is still being made today. New dragon ware is distinguishable by the lack of detail in the application of the dragon. In the older pieces, much care is given to the slipwork of the dragon itself, including the eyes, wings, scales, and pearl. The new ware tends to be flat, lacking personality and detail. Many pieces were made for souvenirs and will carry the name of the place or attraction they commemorate.

    The color referred to in our descriptions is the primary color found on the piece. This usually tends to be black or gray with splashes of pink and blue found on these pieces. The newer pieces are generally glossier than their older counterparts, except for lusterware items. Older colors tend to be more vibrant, while many of the newer colors are pastels. In addition to the primary colors, splashes of other colors are often found, creating a cloud effect behind the dragon. At this writing, pieces that are older and not the typical black/gray are commanding slightly higher prices and attention.

    Primary colors are applied in several ways, the most common method being a wide band of color on the top and bottom of each piece. The 'cloud' effect is achieved when the primary color (and often the only color besides those of the dragon) is swirled on, creating a cloud-like backdrop for the dragon. Lustreware items have very shiny, almost pearl-like backgrounds, and solid-color pieces are those completely done in one color except for the dragon, clouds, and pearl.

    Many cups have lithophanes depicting the face of a geisha girl. Nude lithophanes can also be found, although they are harder to find. The newer the lithophane, the less detail it seems to have.

    Items listed below are unmarked unless noted otherwise. Ranges are given to take into consideration the age and quality of the piece. Examine a piece carefully to determine if it is old or new. The Internet offers various sites for Dragon Ware enthusiasts —

www.dragonware.com is especially informative. For information about a collector club, see Clubs, Newsletters, and Catalogs (under Dragon Ware).

Key:
MIJ — Made in Japan   MIOJ — Made in Occupied Japan

Biscuit jar, orange, ftd, 6", from $35 to 50.00
Bowl, gray, unmk, 10½", from $75 to 100.00
Box, trinket; blk, MIJ mk, 3½x5½", from $10 to..........................60.00
Box, trinket; pk lustre, 1½x5", from $10 to 45.00
Chocolate set, brn/red, MIJ mk, pot+6 c/s, from $125 to 175.00
Cigarette box, gr, MIJ mk, 4x3½", from $15 to........................45.00
Cigarette box, gray, HP mk, +2 ashtrays, from $50 to 150.00
Cigarette box, gray, MIJ mk, +2 ashtrays, from $15 to....................25.00
Cigarette box, pk lustre, unmk, 1¾x5x4", +2 ashtrays, from $30 to .75.00
Cigarette/match/ashtray holder, brn elephant, HP MIJ mk, 6½", up to ..350.00
Cookie jar, gray, ftd, Nippon, from $300 to...............................450.00
Creamer, gray, unmk, from $20 to 45.00
Creamer & sugar bowl, brn elephant, HP MIJ mk, 4½x6½", $75 to .125.00
Cup & saucer, child's, yel, from $10 to 15.00
Cup & saucer, child's, yel, MIOJ mk, from $12.50 to 20.00
Cup & saucer, coffee; orange, from $15 to 45.00
Cup & saucer, coffee; orange, MIJ mk, from $20 to.....................35.00
Cup & saucer, demi; bl, MIJ mk, from $10 to 25.00
Cup & saucer, demi; blk, lithophane, unmk, from $25 to..............50.00
Cup & saucer, demi; gr, unmk, from $15 to.................................25.00
Cup & saucer, demi; gray, lithophane, MIJ mk, from $25 to 40.00
Cup & saucer, demi; gray w/lustre, MIJ mk, 12 pcs, from $60 to ..120.00
Cup & saucer, demi; pk, from $7.50 to 15.00
Cup & saucer, demi; yel, MIJ mk, from $15 to.............................25.00
Cup & saucer, gray, 6-sided, from $10 to 25.00
Cup & saucer, pk & blk, Shafford, from $15 to...........................35.00
Demitasse set, bl or gr, MIOJ mk, 6 c/s+carrier, 13-pc, from $75 to .125.00
Ginger jar, orange, 6", from $25 to 75.00
Lamp, bl/gr, unmk, 20½x5", from $125 to 175.00
Lamp, mini; bl lustre, Napco, from $15 to.................................20.00
Mug, gray, MIJ mk, pr, from $40 to 50.00
Nappy, bl, from $20 to..60.00
Plate, gray, 4-compartment, sq w/wicker hdl, Noritake, 9", $50 to .125.00
Sake set, bl cloud, kitten center, whistles, unmk, 7-pc, from $75 to ..125.00
Sake set, gray, kitten center, whistles, Japan, 7 pcs+tray, $150 to ..200.00
Sake set, orange, Japan, dispenser+5 cups, from $75 to 125.00
Sake set, orange cloud, dispenser+6 cups, MIJ mk, from $75 to ..125.00
Sake set, wht/gold, whistles, unmk, dispenser+6 cups, from $50 to .75.00
Shakers, blk, Japan mk, pr+tray, from $25 to 55.00
Shakers, gray, unmk, 6", pr, from $15 to......................................45.00
Shakers, orange, MIJ mk, pr+tray, from $25 to 75.00
Shakers+cr/sug, VA souvenir, bl lustre, 4 pcs, from $15 to 20.00
Shoe, gray, from $20 to..25.00
Sugar bowl, gray, unmk, from $20 to 45.00
Tea set, gr, unmk, pot+cr/sug w/lids+5 c/s, from $350 to 425.00
Tea set, gr cloud, dragon spouts, lithophane, 17-pc, from $175 to .225.00
Tea set, gray, dragon spout, unmk, pot+cr/sug w/lids+4 c/s, $75 to .100.00
Tea set, gray, lithophane, Japan, 17 pcs, from $125 to.................175.00
Tea set, orange cloud, unmk, pot+cr/sug w/lids+6 c/s, from $250 to ..300.00
Tea set, red, gold dragon, wicker hdl, no mk, 23 pcs, from $175 to ..225.00
Tea set, wht lustre, dragon spout, Japan, 21-pc, from $125 to 175.00
Tea set, wht lustre, no mk, pot+cr/sug+6 c/s, from $50 to 75.00
Tea/coffee set, gray, MIJ mk, 2 pots+cr/sug w/lids+12 c/s, $250 to .325.00
Teapot, gray, unmk, from $45 to 75.00
Trio, coralene, wht lustre, unmk, plate+coffee c/s, from $30 to.....80.00
Trio, gray, lithophane, plate+coffee c/s, from $30 to.....................80.00
Trio, orange, Nikonik China, plate + demitasse c/s, from $25 to ..45.00

Vase, bl, trumpet neck, Niagara Falls souvenir, Japan, 6¼" 20.00
Vase, blk, bulbous, unmk, 3¼" 45.00
Vase, orange, floating dragon head, no mk, 5" 20.00
Vase, yel, w/hdl, 3", from $10 to 25.00
Wall pocket, bl & yel lustre, MIJ, 8½" 30.00
Wall pocket, orange, MIJ, 7¼", from $20 to 45.00

Dresden

The city of Dresden was a leading cultural center in the seventeenth century and in the eighteenth century became known as the Florence on the Elbe because of its magnificent baroque architecture and its outstanding museums. Artists, poets, musicians, philosophers, and porcelain artists took up residence in Dresden.

In the late nineteenth century, there was a considerable demand among the middle classes for porcelain. This demand was met by Dresden porcelain painters. Between 1855 and 1944, more than two hundred painting studios existed in the city. The studios bought porcelain white ware from manufacturers such as Meissen and Rosenthal for decorating, marketing, and reselling throughout the world. The largest of these studios include Donath & Co., Franziska Hirsch, Richard Klemm, Ambrosius Lamm, Carl Thieme, and Helena Wolfsohn.

Most of the Dresden studios produced work in imitation of Meissen and Royal Vienna. Flower painting enhanced with burnished gold, courting couples, landscapes, and Cupids were used as decorative motifs. As with other hand-painted procelains, value is dependent upon the quality of the decoration. Sometimes the artwork equaled or even surpassed that of the Meissen factory.

Some of the most loved and eagerly collected of all Dresden porcelains are the beautiful and graceful lace figures. Many of the figures found in the maketplace today were not made in Dresden but in other areas of Germany. For more information, we recommend *Dresden Porcelain Studios,* by Jim and Susan Harran, our advisors for this category. They are listed in the Directory under New Jersey.

Beethoven at piano flanked by five figures on oval base with pair of putti, 8½x22x11", from $2,500.00 to $2,800.00.

Basket, mint; appl/HP flowers w/gold, C Thieme, 1920s, 2½" 70.00
Candy dish, mc flowers & gold on wht, sq, F Hirsch, 1901-20, 5½" .175.00
Chamberstick, flowers & gold, R Wehsner, 1895-1918, mini, 1½x3" ..180.00
Chocolate pot, reserve of maid in wht apron, much gold, w/lid, 7½" .500.00
Figurine, ballerina, lacy dress, arms out, crown mk, 1900s, 5" 225.00
Figurine, ballerina sitting, much lace, appl rose, 1945+, 3½" ...165.00
Figurine, couple at tea, dog beside, average quality, 1955-70, $250 to..275.00
Figurine, dog barking, HP, C Thieme, 1930-50s, 5¼", from $125 to .150.00
Figurine, lady curtsying, lace trim, Von Schierholz, 1907-20, 9¼"..325.00
Figurine, lady in chair, lacy dress & ruffles, crown mk, 1900s, 4"..225.00
Figurine, Spanish dancer, 6-tier lacy dress, lace bra, 1900s, 9" 475.00
Figurine, 4 figures w/musical instruments, Wolfsohn, 1886-1900 ..1,100.00

Ginger jar, nineteenth-C figures, emb gold flowers on gr, R Klemm, 3¼" .**275.00**
Jardiniere, bold flowers w/gold, scalloped, hdls, F Hirsch, 8x8" .**385.00**
Mirror, oval w/allover appl/HP florals, 3-D cherub atop, 1870, 10" .**600.00**
Place card holder, flowers & gold bows on wht, ftd, F Hirsch, $35 to .**50.00**
Plate, Leda & Swan w/gold decor border, A Lamm, 1887-1914, 10¼" .**375.00**
Plate, shaped lattice rim, floral sprays, gilt, 1900, 9", 12 for ...**1,175.00**
Sweetmeat dish, Cupid leans at side, appl/HP flowers, Thieme, 1930s..**265.00**
Toothpick holder, flowers & gold, hat shape, H Wolfsohn, ca 1886 .**85.00**
Vase, lg mc flowers w/gold, tapered cylinder, R Klemm, 1891-1914, 8"..**165.00**

Dresser Accessories

Dresser sets, ring trees, figural or satin pincushions, manicure sets — all those lovely items that graced milady's dressing table — were at the same time decorative as well as functional. Today they appeal to collectors for many reasons. The Victorian era is well represented by repousse silver-backed mirrors and brushes and pincushions that were used to display ornamental pins for the hair, hats, and scarves. The hair receiver — similar to a powder jar but with an opening in the lid — was used to hold long strands of hair retrieved from the comb or brush. These were wound around the finger and tucked in the opening to be used later for hair jewelry and pictures, many of which survive to the present day. (See Hair Weaving.)

Celluloid dresser sets were popular during the late 1800s and early 1900s. Some included manicure tools, pill boxes, and buttonhooks, as well as the basic items. Because celluloid tends to break rather easily, a whole set may be hard to find today. (See also Plastics.) With the current interest in anything Art Deco, sets from the '30s and '40s are especially collectible. These may be made of crystal, Bakelite, or silver, and the original boxes just as lavishly appointed as their contents.

Box, amber satin glass, rose finial, 1930s, 3¾x5" dia **65.00**
Box, brass filigree w/4 cherubs forming legs, peach glass lid **125.00**
Box, celluloid, emb cherub & flowers, w/8 pcs+10-pc manicure set.**545.00**
Box, china, violets on bl-gr w/gold, unmk, ca 1910, 2¼x4½" **185.00**
Box, gr celluloid, silk lining, sq, EX **60.00**
Box, pill; sterling, 1½" dia..**85.00**
Casket, copper color on wht metal, sgn JB, ca 1915, 3x8x3" **150.00**
Clothes brush, flapper lady figural, brush is skirt, Germany, 6½"..**150.00**
Hairbrush, gilt metal w/portrait on bk, +hand mirror.................**235.00**
Jar, brilliant cuttings, silver Pairpoint lid w/cherub, 1903, 3x4"..**450.00**
Jar, brilliant cuttings, sterling Arts & Crafts lid, 3x4" dia **350.00**
Jar, panelled glass, Nouveau SP lid, 3¾x2¾" **98.00**
Jar, Paul & Virginia (pattern) silver lid, glass base, Foster & Bailey.**750.00**
Jar, Zipper cutting, sterling lid w/floral & ribbon decor, 3x3½" ..**300.00**
Jars, pressed glass, bronze lid, 2x3", 2¾x3¾", pr **80.00**
Mirror, gilt iron, Rococo w/scrolled acanthus, oval beveled glass, 22".**70.00**
Mirror & brush, sterling, hammered w/emb florals, mk att Whiting, 9" .**490.00**

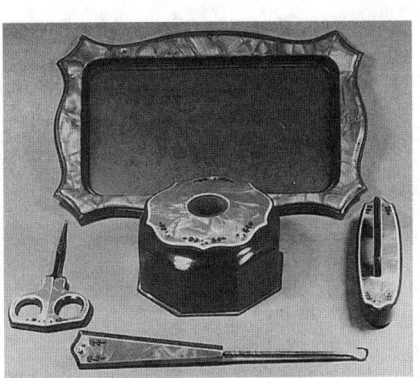

Set, amber and blue pearlescent celluloid, five pieces: tray, hair receiver, buttonhook, nail buffer, and scissors, marked Germany, $50.00.
(Photo courtesy Keith Lauer and Julie Robinson)

Set, china, blk & red Deco design, MIG USA Pat 45776, 6-pc set .**135.00**
Set, china, floral on wht, Austria, 1920s, 3 pcs on 12½x8¾" tray .**255.00**
Set, china, HP floral on wht, Elgin, 8½" mirror+brush+trinket box..**110.00**
Set, china, HP poppies, sgn/1893, M...Redon...Limoges, 2 boxes+tray..**550.00**
Set, metal, gr tones on bright gold-tone, 1930s, box+jar+mirrored tray.**60.00**
Set, plastic, pearlized gr w/blk decor, 9-pc **125.00**
Set, silver, Art Nouveau, Foster & Bailey, 1880s, 10" hand mirror+jar..**795.00**
Set, silver gilt w/enamel plaques w/enamel ladies, Wm Kerr & Co, 13-pc .**5,875.00**
Set, vaseline glass, mk Shari, 4-pc on 2x7" tray...........................**165.00**
Tray, china, bl & gold floral on ivory, unmk, 10x15½".................**75.00**
Tray, china, mc flowers w/gold, Dresden, 22½x6½" **395.00**
Tray, china, putti w/in rose wreath w/gold, Silesia Germany, 1880s.**135.00**

Dryden

World War II veteran, Jim Dryden founded Dryden Pottery in Ellsworth, Kansas, in 1946. Starting in a Quonset hut, Dryden created molded products which he sold at his father's hardware store in town. Using Kansas clay from the area and volcanic ash as a component, durable glossy glazes were created. Soon Dryden was selling pottery to Macy's of New York and the Fred Harvey Restaurants on the Santa Fe Railroad.

After ten years, six hundred stores stocked Dryden Pottery. However direct sales to the public from the pottery studio offered the most profit because of increasing competition from Japan and Europe. Using dental tools to make inscriptions, Dryen began to offer pottery with personalized messages and logos. This specialized work was appreciated by customers and is admired by collectors today.

In 1956 the interstate bypassed the pottery and Dryden decided to move to Hot Springs National Park to find a broader and larger tourist base. Again, local clays and quartz for the glazes were used. Later, in order to improve consistency, commercial clay (that fired bone white) and controlled glazes were used. Sometimes overlooked by collectors who favor the famous potteries of the past, Jim Dryden, son Kimbo, and grandsons Zach, Cheyenne, and Arrow, continue to develop new glazes and shapes in the studio in Hot Springs, Arkansas. Glazes comparable to those created by Fulper, Grueby, and Rookwood can be found on pottery for sale there. Dryden was the first to use two different glazes successfully at the same time.

In 2001 The Book Stops Here published the first catalog and history of Dryden pottery. The book shows the evolution of Dryden art pottery from molded ware to unique hand-thrown pieces; the studio illustrations show the durable and colorful glazes that make Dryden special.

Kansas pieces have a golden tan clay base and were made between 1946 and 1956. Arkansas pieces made after 1956 were made from bone white clay. Dryden pottery has a wide range of values. Many collectors are interested in the early pieces while a fast-growing number search for wheel-thrown and hand-decorated pieces made within the past twenty years. One-of-a-kind specialty pieces can exceed $500.00. Our advisor for this category is Ralph Winslow; he is listed in the Directory under Missouri.

Kansas Dryden (1946 – 1956)

Ashtray, souvenir, #17A **18.00**
Boot, #19, 6½"..**98.00**
Borl, rose, #115 ....**25.00**
Bowl, gr, 7E, 7" **22.00**
Ewer, blk, #715 ....**35.00**
Figurine, lion, brn **65.00**
Figurine, panther, blk **98.00**
Jug, souvenir, 3" **17.00**
Juice set, yel, 7-pc **49.00**
Pitcher, #98, 5½"...**12.00**

Shakers, gr, 6" **29.00**
Tankard, #70, +6 #4 tumblers **65.00**
Vase, #100 ....**18.00**
Vase, Madonna, #87, 4½" **45.00**
Vase, souvenir, #17 ....**22.00**
Vase, 4H **25.00**
Wall pocket, #887 ....**27.00**

Arkansas Dryden (1956 to Present)

Vase, vining decoration on pink to green to pink, wheel thrown, J.K. Dryden, 9", $40.00. (Photo courtesy Ralph Winslow)

Ashtray, maj-lis, 8½" **28.00**
Bell, JBS, 3½" **28.00**
Bowl, apple, 8½" **10.00**
Bowl, pnt, 5½" **35.00**
Candle holder, mc, 3½" **15.00**
Mug, J Dryden, 5" **25.00**
Mug, JK Dryden 82, 3¾" **22.00**
Pitcher & bowl, 1982, 9½" **17.00**
Planter, brn, 1984, 5" **17.00**
Teapot, mc, 5½" **25.00**
Vase, deer, mc, 8¾" **16.00**
Vase, TL, 5½" **16.00**
Vase, wheel thrown, LOI178, 6¾" **21.00**

Duncan and Miller

The firm that became known as the Duncan and Miller Glass Company in 1900 was organized in 1874 in Pittsburgh, Pennsylvania, a partnership between George Duncan, his sons Harry and James, and his son-in-law Augustus Heisey. John Ernest Miller was hired as their designer. He is credited with creating the most famous of all Duncan's glassware lines, Three Face. (See Pattern Glass.) The George Duncan and Sons Glass Company, as it was titled, was only one of eighteen companies that merged in 1891 with U.S. Glass. Soon after the Pittsburgh factory burned in 1892, the association was dissolved, and Heisey left the firm to set up his own factory in Newark, Ohio. Duncan built his new plant in Washington, Pennsylvania, where he continued to make pressed glassware in such notable patterns as Bagware, Amberette, Duncan Flute, Button Arches, and Zippered Slash. The firm was eventually sold to U.S. Glass in Tiffin, Ohio, and unofficially closed in August 1955.

In addition to the early pressed dinnerware patterns, today's Duncan and Miller collectors enjoy searching for opalescent vases in many patterns and colors, frosted 'Satin Tone' glassware, acid-etched designs, and lovely stemware such as the Rock Crystal cuttings. Milk glass was made in limited quantity and is considered a good investment. Ruby glass, Ebony (a lovely opaque black glass popular during the '20s and

'30s), and, of course, the glass animal and bird figurines are all highly valued examples of the art of Duncan and Miller.

Expect to pay at least 25% more than values listed for other colors, for ruby and cobalt, as much as 50% more in the Georgian, Pall Mall, and Sandwich lines. Pink, green, and amber Sandwich is worth approximately 30% more than the same items in crystal. Milk glass examples of American Way are valued up to 30% higher than color, 50% higher in Pall Mall. Chartreuse Canterbury is worth 10% to 20% more than crystal. Add approximately 40% to 50% to listed prices for opalescent items. Etchings, cuttings, and other decorations will increase values by about 50%. For further study we recommend *The Encyclopedia of Duncan Glass* by Gail Krause; she is listed in the Directory under Pennsylvania. Several Duncan and Miller lines are shown in *Elegant Glassware of the Depression Era* by Gene Florence. See also Glass Animals and Figurines. Our advisor is Roselle Schleifman; she is listed in the Directory under New York.

Canterbury, crystal, ashtray, 5" **10.00**
Canterbury, crystal, basket, crimped, 3x4" **27.50**
Canterbury, crystal, bowl, crimped, 2¾x8" **22.50**
Canterbury, crystal, bowl, salad dressing; 2-part, 5x3¼" **14.00**
Canterbury, crystal, bowl, sweetmeat; star, hdls, 2x6" **10.00**
Canterbury, crystal, celery, hdls, 1¼x9x4" **22.50**
Canterbury, crystal, cup **8.00**
Canterbury, crystal, mayonnaise, 3¼x6" **22.50**
Canterbury, crystal, plate, dinner; 11¼" **27.50**
Canterbury, crystal, plate, 7½" **9.00**
Canterbury, crystal, stem, water; #5115, 10-oz **20.00**
Canterbury, crystal, tray, sandwich; center hdl, 5¼x12" **47.50**
Canterbury, crystal, tumbler, juice; flat, 5-oz **8.00**
Canterbury, crystal, vase, flared, 12" **75.00**
Canterbury, crystal, vase, violet, crimped, 3" **15.00**
Caribbean, bl, ashtray, 4-indent, 6" **32.50**
Caribbean, bl, cruet **95.00**
Caribbean, bl, plate, luncheon; 8½" **35.00**
Caribbean, bl, punch bowl, 10" **475.00**
Caribbean, bl, relish, 4-part, oblong, 9½" **65.00**
Caribbean, bl, server, center hdl, 5¾" **55.00**
Caribbean, bl, tray, 12¾" **50.00**
Caribbean, bl, vase, ruffled top, ftd, 9" **225.00**
Caribbean, crystal, bowl, finger; 4½" **16.00**
Caribbean, crystal, creamer **14.00**
Caribbean, crystal, ice bucket, hdls, 6½" **75.00**
Caribbean, crystal, plate, salad; 7½" **15.00**
Caribbean, crystal, relish, 2-part, 6" dia **12.00**
Caribbean, crystal, stem, sherbet; ftd, 4¼" **12.00**
First Love, crystal, ashtray, #30, 3¼x5" **24.00**
First Love, crystal, bowl, hdls, #111, 2½x8½" sq **60.00**
First Love, crystal, butter or cheese dish, #111, 1¼x7" sq **130.00**
First Love, crystal, candle holder, 2-light, #30, 6" **35.00**
First Love, crystal, comport, w/lid, #111, 5½x8¾" **135.00**
First Love, crystal, ice bucket, #30, 6" **110.00**
First Love, crystal, mayonnaise, hdls, ftd, #111, 2½x5½" **35.00**
First Love, crystal, nappy, hdls, #111, 1¾x6" **22.00**
First Love, crystal, plate, #111, 7½" sq **19.00**
First Love, crystal, plate, torte; rolled edge, #111, 12" **40.00**
First Love, crystal, relish tray, #115, 11¾" **45.00**
First Love, crystal, stem, sauce champagne; #5111½, 5" **18.00**
First Love, crystal, tumbler, whiskey; #5200, 1½-oz **65.00**
Lily of the Valley, crystal, ashtray, 6" **35.00**
Lily of the Valley, crystal, bowl, 12" **55.00**
Lily of the Valley, crystal, celery, 10½" **35.00**
Lily of the Valley, crystal, mayonnaise ladle **8.00**
Lily of the Valley, crystal, plate, 9" **45.00**
Lily of the Valley, crystal, stem, cordial **80.00**

Lily of the Valley, crystal, sugar bowl	25.00
Nautical, bl, ashtray, 3"	30.00
Nautical, bl, cigarette holder	55.00
Nautical, bl, creamer	45.00
Nautical, bl, plate, 10"	100.00
Nautical, bl, tumbler, whiskey & soda; 8-oz	25.00
Nautical, crystal, ashtray, 3"	8.00
Nautical, crystal, cigarette holder	15.00
Nautical, crystal, ice bucket	55.00
Nautical, crystal, shakers, pr	35.00
Nautical, crystal, tumbler, orange juice; ftd	15.00
Sandwich, crystal, basket, loop hdl, 6½"	135.00
Sandwich, crystal, bonbon, heart shape, ring hdl, 5"	15.00
Sandwich, crystal, bowl, console; oblong; 12"	40.00
Sandwich, crystal, bowl, fruit salad; 6"	12.00
Sandwich, crystal, bowl, grapefruit; w/fruit cup liner, ftd, 5½"	17.50
Sandwich, crystal, bowl, salted almond; 2½"	11.00
Sandwich, crystal, cake stand, plain ped, ftd, 13"	90.00

Sandwich, crystal, candy dish, 6" square, $395.00. (Photo courtesy Gene Florence)

Sandwich, crystal, comport, low ft, crimped, 5½"	30.00
Sandwich, crystal, comport, 2¼"	15.00
Sandwich, crystal, cup, tea; 6-oz	10.00
Sandwich, crystal, Lazy Susan, w/turntable, 16"	125.00
Sandwich, crystal, plate, dessert; 7"	9.00
Sandwich, crystal, plate, ice cream; rolled edge, 12"	60.00
Sandwich, crystal, shakers, metal lids, 3¾", pr on 6" tray	30.00
Sandwich, crystal, stem, champagne; 5-oz, 5¼"	20.00
Sandwich, crystal, stem, cocktail; 3-oz, 4¼"	15.00
Sandwich, crystal, tray, pickle; oval, 7"	15.00
Sandwich, crystal, tumbler, iced tea; ftd, 12-oz, 5¼"	20.00
Sandwich, crystal, vase, epergne; threaded base, 7½"	65.00
Spiral Flutes, amber, gr or pk, bowl, bouillon; 3¾"	15.00
Spiral Flutes, amber, gr or pk, bowl, cereal; sm flange, 6½"	35.00
Spiral Flutes, amber, gr or pk, bowl, oval vegetable; 2 styles, 10"	45.00
Spiral Flutes, amber, gr or pk, candle holder, 3½"	25.00
Spiral Flutes, amber, gr or pk, console stand, 1½x4⅝"	12.00
Spiral Flutes, amber, gr or pk, mug, 9-oz, 6½"	30.00
Spiral Flutes, amber, gr or pk, pitcher, ½-gal	195.00
Spiral Flutes, amber, gr or pk, plate, dinner; 10⅜"	22.50
Spiral Flutes, amber, gr or pk, platter, 13"	60.00
Spiral Flutes, amber, gr or pk, stem, wine; 3½-oz, 3¾"	17.50
Spiral Flutes, amber, gr or pk, sugar bowl, oval	8.00
Spiral Flutes, amber, gr, or pk, tumbler, juice; ftd (no stem), 4⅜"	14.00
Spiral Flutes, amber, gr or pk, vase, 10½"	40.00
Tear Drop, crystal, bottle, bar; w/stopper, 12"	135.00
Tear Drop, crystal, bowl, fruit nappy; 6"	8.00
Tear Drop, crystal, bowl, low ft, crimped, 12"	40.00
Tear Drop, crystal, bowl, salad; 9"	30.00
Tear Drop, crystal, candlestick, ball loop center, 2-light, 7"	30.00
Tear Drop, crystal, celery dish, hdls, 1-part, 11"	22.50
Tear Drop, crystal, creamer, 6-oz	6.00

Tear Drop, crystal, marmalade, w/lid, 4"	40.00
Tear Drop, crystal, pitcher, milk; 16-oz, 5"	55.00
Tear Drop, crystal, plate, salad; 7½"	5.00
Tear Drop, crystal, plate, torte; rolled edge, 13"	30.00
Tear Drop, crystal, relish, 6-part, 12" dia	40.00
Tear Drop, crystal, stem, ale; 8-oz, 6¼"	16.00
Tear Drop, crystal, tray, center hdl, 7¾"	12.50
Tear Drop, crystal, tumbler, ftd, 9-oz, 4½"	10.00
Tear Drop, crystal, tumbler, iced tea; flat, 12-oz, 5¼"	15.00
Terrace, cobalt or red, bowl, ftd, 4¾x10¼"	145.00
Terrace, cobalt or red, candy urn, w/lid	425.00
Terrace, cobalt or red, creamer, 10-oz, 3"	45.00
Terrace, cobalt or red, plate, 11"	90.00
Terrace, cobalt or red, plate, 6"	25.00
Terrace, cobalt or red, relish, 5-part, w/lid, 12"	295.00
Terrace, cobalt or red, stem, saucer champagne; #511½, 5-oz, 5"	50.00
Terrace, cobalt or red, sugar bowl, 10-oz, 3"	45.00
Terrace, crystal or amber, bowl, finger; #5111½, 4¼"	30.00
Terrace, crystal or amber, butter or cheese dish, 1¼x7" sq	120.00
Terrace, crystal or amber, comport, 3½x4¾"	30.00
Terrace, crystal or amber, plate, hdls, 11"	30.00
Terrace, crystal or amber, plate, torte; rolled edge, 13"	37.50
Terrace, crystal or amber, plate, 7"	17.50
Terrace, crystal or amber, stem, wine; #5111½, 3-oz, 5¼"	32.50

Durand

Durand art glass was made by the Vineland Flint Glass Works of Vineland, New Jersey. Victor Durand Jr. was the sole proprietor. The division called the 'fancy shop' was geared to the production of fine hand-blown art glass in the style of Tiffany and Steuben. Crystal, amber-gis, and opal glass were each used as a basis to create such patterns as King Tut, Heart and Vine, Peacock Feather, and Egyptian Crackle. Cased glass was used to produce cut designs. Production of art glass began in 1924 and continued until 1931. Although much of this art glass was unsigned, when it was, it was generally signed within the pontil 'Durand' or 'Durand' written across the top of a large letter V, all in silver script. The numbers that sometimes appear along with the signature indicate the shape and height of the object. Owner Victor Durand employed the owner and several workers from the failed Quezal Art Glass and Decorating Co. This is why early Durand may sometimes look similar to Quezal art glass. In 1926 Durand art glass was awarded a medal of honor at the Sesquicentennial International Exposition in Philadelphia, Pennsylvania. Our advisor for this category is Edward J. Meschi, author of *Durand — The Man and His Glass* (Antique Publications); he is listed in the Directory under New Jersey.

Bowl, King Tut, bl/gold irid, gold int, unmk, 10½"	840.00
Bowl, King Tut, 3-color on opal, gold irid int, appl ft, 7½"	2,100.00
Bowl gold irid, thick ped ft, 5½x10"	500.00
Candlestick, King Tut, bl/gold, wafer between cup & stem, 10"	1,035.00
Console set, peacock feathers, wht on red, bowl+mushroom candlesticks	1,725.00
Ginger jar, King Tut, gr/gold, amber floret on lid, 9"	4,085.00
Goblet, feathers, wht on red, amber ft w/eng band, 4½"	320.00
Jar, bl lustre w/opal hearts & vines, #1964-8 B, 9", NM	2,465.00
Jar, feathers, wht on gold irid, lined in bl w/allover threads, 8"	2,000.00
Jar, red & wht crackle on ambergris, 6"	2,500.00
Lamp, King Tut insert w/4-ftd metal base, 10"	600.00
Lamp, Moorish Crackle, red/wht on amber, cylinder on metal ft, 11"	800.00
Plate, bl, scalloped/ribbed edge, unmk, 8½"	115.00
Plate, red, 8½"	160.00
Shade, King Tut, bl on marigold irid, 6" H w/2¼" fitter	535.00
Sherbet, gold irid, unsgn, 3½"	145.00

Vase, amber w/gold lustre irid, #1710-4, 4¼" 315.00
Vase, amber w/red-gold lustre, beehive form w/stepped neck, 12".2,300.00
Vase, ambergris w/silvery irid, bulbous w/stick neck, unsgn, 18".2,500.00
Vase, bl irid, classic form, 6½" 400.00
Vase, bl irid, stepped beehive, 12" 1,500.00
Vase, bl irid, trumpet form, gold disk ft, 10"...............................810.00
Vase, bl lustre w/appl threading, cylinder, #1968, 6⅛" 525.00
Vase, coils, gr & bl on opal, 9" 1,900.00
Vase, coils, silver-bl on dk bl, dbl band at ft, trumpet form, 14".2,600.00
Vase, feathers, bl w/gold tips on opal, gold threading/ft/int, 13".2,185.00
Vase, feathers, wht w/gr tips on gold, allover gold threads, 12", EX ..1,035.00
Vase, feathers, wht/gold w/gr tips on gold, allover threading, 12x10".3,565.00
Vase, feathers, wht/gr on gold, allover threading, unmk, 8½".2,185.00
Vase, gold irid, ovoid w/stepped shoulder, 8½" 980.00
Vase, gold irid w/woodland scene cameo band, 14" 4,600.00
Vase, gold/orange irid, much gold threading, squat w/trumpet neck, 10".750.00
Vase, hearts/vines, bl on gold irid, 5½" 1,035.00
Vase, hearts/vines, gr/gold on opal, allover gold threading, 12" ..750.00
Vase, hearts/vines, silver-bl on bl, 10" 2,200.00
Vase, hearts/vines, wht on bl irid, 10" 1,800.00
Vase, King Tut, bl irid on gr, gold int, ovoid, #1968, 6" 1,265.00

Vase, King Tut, blue, gold, and marigold on opal, 10", $1,950.00.
(Photo courtesy Edward J. Meschi)

Vase, King Tut, bl on orange, gold int, no mk, 9½" 1,380.00
Vase, King Tut, bl/orange, shaped/slim w/low hdls, disk ft, unmk, 13".1,550.00
Vase, King Tut, gr on amber w/gold irid, #1722-8, 8" 1,265.00
Vase, King Tut, wht on bl, gold disk ft, #2011-10R, 10" 3,000.00
Vase, King Tut, wht on gold lustre, ovoid, flared rim, 10¼" 2,500.00
Vase, Moorish Crackle, bl/wht on amber, rnd w/petal rim & can ft, 9".2,300.00
Vase, 4-color o/l cut to clear w/geometric decor, sgn 1971-10, 10½".2,700.00

Easter

In the early 1900s to the 1930s, Germany made the first composition candy containers in the shapes of Easter rabbits, ducks, and chicks. A few were also made of molded cardboard. In the 1940s West Germany made candy containers out of molded cardboard. Many of these had spring necks to give a nodding effect. From the 1930s and into the 1950s, United States manufacturers made Easter candy containers out of egg-carton material (pulp) or pressed cardboard. Ducks and chicks are not as high in demand as rabbits. Rabbits with painted-on clothes or attached fabric clothes bring more than the plain brown or white rabbits. When no condition is mentioned in the description, assume that values reflect excellent to near mint condition for all but paper items; those assume to be in near mint to mint condition. Our advisor for this category is Jenny Tarrant; she is listed in the Directory under Missouri.

Note: In the candy container section, measurements given for the rabbit and cart or rabbit and wagon containers indicate the distance to the tip of the rabbits' ears.

Candy Containers

German, begging rabbit, brn w/glass eyes, compo, 1900-30s, 5" 95.00
German, begging rabbit, brn w/glass eyes, compo, 1900-30s, 6" ..125.00
German, begging rabbit, brn w/glass eyes, compo, 1900-30s, 7" ..150.00
German, begging rabbit, brn w/glass eyes, compo, 1900-30s, 8" ..175.00
German, begging rabbit, brn w/glass eyes, compo, 1900-30s, 9" ..250.00
German, begging rabbit, mohair covered, compo, 1900-30s, 4" ..135.00
German, begging rabbit, mohair covered, compo, 1900-30s, 5" ..150.00
German, begging rabbit, mohair covered, compo, 1900-30s, 6" ..195.00
German, begging rabbit, mohair covered, compo, 1900-30s, 7" ..200.00
German, duck, yel w/glass eyes, compo, 1900-30s, 5" 110.00
German, duck or chick, pnt-on clothes, compo, 1900-30s, 3-4" ..125.00
German, duck or chick, pnt-on clothes, compo, 1900-30s, 5" 145.00
German, duck or chick, pnt-on clothes, compo, 1900-30s, 6" 185.00
German, duck or chick, pnt-on clothes, compo, 1900-30s, 7" 200.00
German, egg, molded cb, 1900-30, 3-7", from $65 to 45.00
German, egg, molded cb, 1900-30, 8"...65.00
German, egg, tin, 1900-10, EX, 2-3"..55.00
German, rabbit (dressed) in car, compo, 1900-30s, from $250 to ..325.00
German, rabbit (dressed) in shoe, compo, 1900-30s, from $250 to ..275.00
German, rabbit (dressed) on egg, compo, 1900-30s, from $200 to ..250.00
German, rabbit (dressed) on log, compo, 1900-30s, from $200 to ..250.00
German, rabbit pulling wood cart, mohair covered, 1900-30s, 4" ..175.00
German, rabbit pulling wood cart, mohair covered, 1900-30s, 5" ..225.00
German, rabbit pulling wood cart, mohair covered, 1900-30s, 6" ..295.00
German, rabbit pulling wood cart, mohair covered, 1900-30s, 7" ..325.00
German, rabbit pulling wood wagon, brn compo, 1900-30s, 4" ...150.00
German, rabbit pulling wood wagon, brn compo, 1900-30s, 5" ...175.00
German, rabbit pulling wood wagon, brn compo, 1900-30s, 6" ...195.00
German, rabbit pulling wood wagon, brn compo, 1900-30s, 7" ...225.00
German, rabbit w/fabric clothes, compo, 1900-30s, 4" 250.00
German, rabbit w/fabric clothes, compo, 1900-30s, 5" 300.00
German, rabbit w/fabric clothes, compo, 1900-30s, 6" 325.00
German, rabbit w/fabric clothes, compo, 1900-30s, 7" 350.00
German, rabbit w/glass beading, compo, 1900-30s, 6" 150.00
German, rabbit w/pnt-on clothes, compo, 1900-30s, 4" 150.00
German, rabbit w/pnt-on clothes, compo, 1900-30s, 5" 200.00
German, rabbit w/pnt-on clothes, compo, 1900-30s, 6" 225.00
German, rabbit w/pnt-on clothes, compo, 1900-30s, 7" 250.00
German, sitting rabbit, brn w/glass eyes, compo, 1900-30s, 5" 95.00
German, sitting rabbit, brn w/glass eyes, compo, 1900-30s, 6" 110.00
German, sitting rabbit, brn w/glass eyes, compo, 1900-30s, 7" 125.00
German, sitting rabbit, mohair covered, compo, 1900-30s, 4" 140.00
German, sitting rabbit, mohair covered, compo, 1900-30s, 5" 160.00
German, sitting rabbit, mohair covered, compo, 1900-30s, 6" 175.00
German, standing rabbit (Ma), pnt-on clothes, molded cb, 10½" ..250.00
German, standing rabbit (Pa), pnt-on clothes, molded cb, 10½" ..250.00
German, walking rabbit, brn w/glass eyes, compo, 1900-30s, 5" ..110.00
German, walking rabbit, brn w/glass eyes, compo, 1900-30s, 6" ..125.00
German, walking rabbit, brn w/glass eyes, compo, 1900-30s, 7" ..135.00
German, walking rabbit, brn w/glass eyes, compo, 1900-30s, 8" ..150.00
German, walking rabbit, brn w/glass eyes, compo, 1900-30s, 9" ..175.00
German, walking rabbit, mohair covered, compo, 1900-30s, 4" ..150.00
German, walking rabbit, mohair covered, compo, 1900-30s, 5" ..185.00
German, walking rabbit, mohair covered, compo, 1900-30s, 6" ..225.00
German, walking rabbit, mohair covered, compo, 1900-30s, 7" ..245.00
German, walking rabbit, wht compo, 1900-30s, 6" 125.00
German, wht w/pnt on clothes, compo, 1900-30s, 3" 175.00
US, begging rabbit, pulp, 1940-50, w/base....................................55.00

US, sitting rabbit, pulp, brn w/glass eyes, Burk Co, 1930 ....85.00
US, sitting rabbit, pulp, no basket, 1940-50.................................45.00
US, sitting rabbit next to lg basket, pulp, 1930-50 ....75.00
US, sitting rabbit w/basket on bk, pulp, 1940-50.........................75.00
W German/US Zone, dressed chick, cb, spring neck, 1940-50......65.00
W German/US Zone, dressed rabbit, cb, spring neck, 1940-50.....80.00
W German/US Zone, egg, molded cb, 1940-60, 3-8", $25 to........40.00
W German/US Zone, plain rabbit, cb, spring neck, 1940-50 ....60.00

Miscellaneous

Celluloid chick or duck, dressed, 3-5", M...............................45.00
Celluloid chick or duck, dressed, 6-8", M...............................75.00
Celluloid chicken pulling wagon w/rabbit, M..........................125.00
Celluloid rabbit, dressed, 3-5", M...65.00
Celluloid rabbit, dressed, 6-8", M...75.00
Celluloid rabbit, plain, 3-5", M...20.00
Celluloid rabbit, plain, 6-7", M...30.00
Celluloid rabbit & chick in swan boat, M..............................150.00
Celluloid rabbit driving car, M 150.00
Celluloid rabbit pulling wagon, M..125.00
Celluloid rabbit pushing or pulling cart, lg, M.......................125.00
Celluloid rabbit pushing or pulling cart, sm, M.......................75.00
Celluloid windup toy, Japan or Occupied Japan, M..................150.00

Celluloid windup toy, mother bunny pushing baby in basket, M, $175.00. (Photo courtesy David Longest)

Cotton batten rabbit w/paper ears, Japan, 1930-50, 2-5".............30.00
Cotton batten rabbit w/paper ears, Japan, 1930-50, 6" 45.00

Egg Cups

Egg cups, one of the fastest growing collectibles, have been traced back to the ruins of Pompeii. They have been made in almost every country and in almost every conceivable material (ceramics, glass, metal, papier-mache, plastic, wood, ivory, even rubber and straw). Popular categories include Art Deco, Black Memorabilia, Chintz, Characters/Personalities, Golliwoggs, Railroadiana, Steamship, Souvenir Ware, etc.

Still being produced today, egg cups appeal to collectors on many levels. Prices can range from quite low to many thousands of dollars. Those made prior to 1840 are scarce and sought after, as are the character/personality egg cups of the 1930s.

For a more thorough study of egg cups we recommend *Egg Cups: An Illustrated History and Price Guide* (Antique Publications) by Brenda Blake, our advisor. You will find her address listed in the Directory under Maine.

Key:
bkt — bucket, a single cup   hoop — hoop, a single open
    without a foot   cup with waistline

dbl — two-sided with small end   inst. dbl — large custard cup shape
    for eating egg in shell,   set — tray or cruet
    large end for mixing egg   (stand, frame, or basket)
    with toast and butter   with two to eight cups
fig — figural, an egg cup   sgl — single, with a foot;
    actually molded into the   goblet shaped
    shape of an animal, bird,
    car, person, etc.

American China/Pottery

Dbl, Adam Antique, emb, Steubenville, ca 1948 ....18.00
Dbl, Autumn Leaf, Hall's Autumn Leaf Collector's Club gift, 1997 .65.00
Dbl, Ballerina, khaki-gr, Universal 14.00
Dbl, Bride, Cleminson, ca 1940s..30.00
Dbl, Colonial, ribbed, red, Stangl, ca 1926 ....15.00
Dbl, Frost Flowers, Eva Zeisel, Hall, 1950s............................28.00
Dbl, Golden Harvest, Stangl, ca 1953-72 ....15.00
Dbl, Juvenile, Chick, Roseville, ca 1917 ....275.00
Dbl, Mexicana, Cable shape, red rim, Homer Laughlin...............38.00
Dbl, Mexicana, dk gr, Homer Laughlin 65.00
Dbl, Passion Flower, Stangl 15.00
Dbl, Starburst, Franciscan 38.00
Dbl, Virginia Rose, Homer Laughlin 90.00
Sgl, Duet, Franciscan, ca 1956 ....30.00
Sgl, Florida, Lenox, ca 1922..30.00
Sgl, Juvenile, Chick, Roseville, ca 1917................................800.00
Sgl, yel ware, no decor, ca 1880..325.00

Characters/Personalities

Bkt, Lone Ranger, molded face against stump, Keele St Pottery, 1961 .105.00
Bkt, Tonto, molded face against stump, Keele St Pottery, 1961 ....80.00
Bkt, Yogi Bear in hammock...20.00
Fig, Happy, WD Ent, 1937..150.00
Fig, Humpty Dumpty, Mansell, 1985 ....35.00
Fig, Minnie Mouse, orange ears, Foreign, 1930s 125.00
Fig, Pink Panther, plastic, Hong Kong, 1974............................25.00
Fig, Popeye, squatting, w/pipe, Japan....................................100.00
Fig, Prince Harry, Spitting Image 30.00
Fig, Prince William, Spitting Image, 1982................................65.00
Fig, Ronald Reagan, Spitting Image, 1980s 90.00
Fig, Snow White, standing by sgn cup, WD Enterprises, 1937....350.00
Fig, Swee' Pea, yel, KFS, 1980 ....70.00
Set, Muppets, Statler+Waldorf+Zoot+Sam, Sigma, ca 1981 ....200.00
Sgl, Elvis Presley, 2 views in circle.......................................38.00
Sgl, Field Marshall Roberts, ca 1903......................................55.00
Sgl, Lloyd George, The Patriotic Fowl, ca 1920........................50.00
Sgl, Lord Kitchener, ca 1903...80.00
Sgl, Paddington, Good Morning series 14.00
Sgl, Prince Ranier/Princess Grace of Monaco, wedding, Limoges, 1950s .100.00

Figurals

Black cat, male, all blk, Japan...15.00
Black face, earrings, bow tie, Foreign, early 1900s......................125.00
Boat, orange, Honiton...22.00
Butler holding cup on tray, Silver Crane Co, 1988.......................65.00
Chicken, yel, hoisting wht cup, gr base, tall.............................15.00
Dog, standing, gr hat, Japan 12.00
Female face, Goebel, ca 1930s 60.00
Financial Times newspaper, soap egg head 15.00
Grandmother, hdld, gray boots, Japan 15.00
Lion seated, brn pottery...10.00

Miss Priss, Lefton 30.00
Mr Shifter, PG Chimp, plastic, w/lid 25.00
Oriental boy w/dog, Occupied Japan 40.00
Pig, seated, orange hat band, tie, Foreign 60.00
Quaker Oats Man, Wood & Sons, 1920s...........60.00
Train (whistler), lustre, Foreign 110.00
Volkswagen, Devon Ceramics, 1959................22.00
Wellies, Carlton 85.00

Foreign

Bkt, OEUF, orange & blk rim band, France 10.00
Dbl, Alpine Peasant Ware, Germany.................15.00
Dbl, floral, JP/L France, Limoges, ca 1910.......22.00
Dbl, geometric gold band, T&V Limoges 25.00
Dbl, peasant, yel & gr, floral panels, HB Quimper 50.00
Dbl, Rooster, Holt Howard, Japan, 1961 ....20.00
Sgl, Devon Motto-Ware, Torquay.....................30.00
Sgl, floral, Japan 7.00
Sgl, floral, Lefton 12.00
Sgl, grapes & leaves emb, Revoi, France, ca 2000........10.00
Sgl, lamb & skating bear, Royal Stuart Ireland, child sz ...15.00
Sgl, mini w/egg, Limoges 25.00
Sgl, owl base, wht cup, Sarreguemines 110.00
Sgl, Rose Medallion, ca 1860 ....75.00
Sgl, Shamrock, Belleek, 2nd blk mk 135.00

Glass

Dbl, Birch Leaf, bl, NF, ca 1878......................70.00
Dbl, clambroth, opaline, ca 1970s....................85.00
Dbl, jadite, gr 30.00
Dbl, Palmette, Burlington Glass, ca 1870s 55.00
Fig, chicken, red & blk beak, Vallerysthal.........30.00
Fig, rooster, milk glass w/red trim, Westmoreland, ca 1930s 17.00
Fig, swan, scalloped rim, Fenton 28.00
Sgl, Bohemian o/l, Biedermeier, ca 1890-1920....125.00
Sgl, Candlewick, beaded ft, Imperial 70.00
Sgl, cobalt, blown, flared rim, ca 1870 ....100.00
Sgl, Cremax, red to wht....................................7.50
Sgl, mercury glass, gold-wash lining, ca 1910 ...70.00
Sgl, slag, gr, brn & wht marbleized, scalloped rim & ft........75.00

Railroad

Dbl, Prairie Mountain Wildflower, Southern Pacific, 1940s........350.00
Inst dbl, Challenger, Union Pacific, Syracuse 75.00
Inst dbl, Tri-Link, Richmond, Fredericksburg & Potomac, ca 1927 .550.00
Sgl, Canadian Pacific, dining car service............125.00
Sgl, Denver & Rio Grande, bl logo, recent.........15.00
Sgl, Mercury, NYC, NY Central RR.................150.00
Sgl, Reading, SP, Rowley Mfg Co 400.00

Souvenir

Bkt, London, wht letters on bl ground, Old Foley........8.00
Bkt, Syria, eng brass 8.00
Bkt, Western Airlines, solid wht 6.00
Dbl, BPOE #30, gr elk 40.00
Dbl, Columbia Gas System, bl logo....................28.00
Dbl, Hotel Paso Del Norte, El Paso 20.00
Dbl, US Navy anchor, bl rim band 25.00
Fig, Harrods' Doorman, Wade, 1990s 30.00
Fig, Tower of London, ca 1928..........................95.00

Set, Ireland, wooden wall rack w/4 sgl cups, egg timer 28.00
Sgl, Aruba, windmill scene, Delft, recent...........................9.00

Single, Condit's Dance Ball Room, Revere Beach, Massachusetts, ceramic, unmarked, 2⅜", $35.00. (Photo courtesy Laurence W. Williams)

Sgl, Euro Disney, Mickey Mouse painting 1992, Porzellan/W Germany, 1992.20.00
Sgl, Evesham, crest, Goss 50.00
Sgl, Ford Motor Co, logo, ca 1960s.................38.00
Sgl, HMS Dreadnought, ca 1920s....................70.00
Sgl, Hotel Grand Osaka, gold logo, Noritake.....16.00
Sgl, Plymouth Rock, Plymouth MA, Germany, ca 1900...............40.00
Sgl, Soldier's Monument, Gettysburg PA 38.00

Staffordshire

Bkt, Autumn Crocus, Clarice Cliff....................125.00
Bkt, Crocus, Clarice Cliff.................................60.00
Bkt, Orange Tree, Decvo, Crown Ducal 38.00
Dbl, Bristol, red, Crown Ducal, 1931.................25.00
Dbl, Chinese Garden, Adams 30.00
Dbl, Cornishware, bl bands, TC Green, 1930s....55.00
Dbl, Friendly Village, Johnson Bros 25.00
Dbl, Madras, flow bl, Royal Doulton, ca 1900 ...110.00
Dbl, Mr Snowman w/dish hat, Royal Doulton....90.00
Dbl, Non-Pareil, flow bl, Burgess & Leigh, ca 1891 ....270.00
Dbl, Vista, red, Mason's...................................30.00
Set, Selkirk, 4 bkts on tray, Royal Winton 65.00
Sgl, Chelsea Gardens, red floral, fluted edge, Copeland/Spode ...100.00
Sgl, creamware, rtcl, 18th C 1,150.00
Sgl, Japan, Mason's, ca 1820 ....200.00
Sgl, Normandy, flow bl, Johnson Bros, ca 1900 ....350.00
Sgl, Tango, Deco, Royal Doulton, 1930s 65.00

Miscellaneous

Dbl, chrome, wht porc insert 12.00
Dbl, Teleflora, yel, 1982 ....10.00
Hoop, Cunard, Queen Mary, ca 1950s...............75.00
Hoop, graniteware, red horse, Austria, 1930s 40.00
Hoop, Lloyd, North German Line 125.00
Inst dbl, Admiral Oriental Line 25.00
Set, mini (dollhouse) stand, metal, w/4 sgl cups, ca 1998.............15.00
Set, oak & SP, hdld stand, 4 bkt cups+2 spoons+open salt, ca 1880s .225.00
Set, toast holder, silver, 2 sgl cups+pr shakers, ca 1920s.............350.00
Sgl, egg cutter, silver, w/lid, England, 1902 ......240.00
Sgl, marble, yel swirls, Taiwan..........................8.00
Sgl, thermoplastic, stylized, yel, A Antonuccio design, Italy, 1998 ..14.00
Sgl, wire, blk, ca 1990s...................................10.00

Elfinware

Made in Germany from about 1920 until the 1940s, these miniature vases, boxes, salt cellars, and miscellaneous novelty items are characterized by the tiny applied flowers that often cover their entire surface. Pieces with animals and birds are the most valuable, followed by the more interesting examples such as diminutive grand pianos, candle holders, etc. Items covered in 'spinach' (applied green moss) can be valued at 75% to 100% higher than pieces that are not decorated in this manner. See also Salts, Open.

Basket, appl bl floral w/much spinach, 5¼x4⅞x3⅛" 90.00
Basket, mc flowers, 2 Xd hdls w/center rose, 2⅛x2½" 65.00
Box, 2 puppies peer out of basket, appl bl flowers & spinach, 1¾x2" .165.00
Chair, appl flowers, 2¾x1½" 50.00
Grand piano, appl roses/pansies/daisies/spinach, 5x6½" 260.00
Pen holder, bell shaped w/forget-me-nots, 4¼x3¾" 55.00
Poodle, standing on base w/gr grass, 4½" 125.00
Pot, lavender rose on front w/appl lilacs & much spinach, 2⅛x3" .50.00
Salt cellar, swan w/appl flowers & spinach, 2¼" 50.00
Shoe, high-heel, appl flowers & spinach, 3" 65.00
Shoe, pointed toe, appl flowers & spinach, 2¼x5¼" 100.00
Shoe, slipper style, appl pk & bl flowers w/much spinach, 1¼x4⅜" .75.00
Teapot, appl flowers & spinach, 3¾" 65.00

Epergnes

Popular during the Victorian era, epergnes were fancy centerpieces often consisting of several tiers of vases (called lilies), candle holders, dishes, or a combination of components. They were made in all types of art glass, and some were set in ornate plated frames. Our advisors for this category are Barbara and Steven Aaronson; they are listed in the Directory under California.

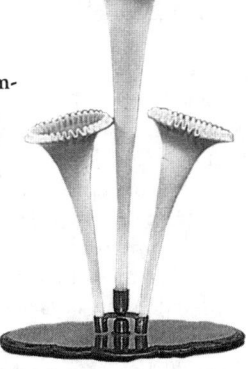

Burmese, three crimped trumpet vases on beveled oval, mirrored base, Mt. Washington, 19" overall, $2,500.00.
(Photo courtesy Early Auctions)

Silver, rtcl eagle head hdls, cherubs & flowers at sides, 12x11½" .575.00
Silver w/rtcl cherubs/fruit/etc, GR hallmk, 12x11½" 575.00
SP, figural cherub ea side, repousse bowl, Reed & Barton 1,100.00
SP, lg posey holder+6 sm vases on meandering Nouveau vine, 10x19" .145.00
SP, vase+4 arms for either candle cup or bowl, Victorian, 19" .1,725.00
SP cherub holds receptacle for 2 clear vases, Reed & Barton #1490 .950.00

Erickson

Carl Erickson of Bremen, Ohio, produced hand-formed glassware from 1943 until 1960 in artistic shapes, no two of which were identical. One of the characteristics of his work was the air bubbles that were captured within the glass. Though most examples are clear, colored items were also made. Rather than to risk compromising his high stan-

dards by selling the factory, when Erickson retired, the plant was dismantled and sold.

Ashtray, pipe; smoke w/clear raised center, cupped sides, 3x8½" ..90.00
Ashtray, wht & clear layer w/controlled bubbles, gr int, 6½" 75.00
Bookend/vases, brn/purple w/controlled bubbes, 5¾", pr 160.00
Bowl, clear w/brn rising from bottom, oviod, 3¾x6½x10½" 80.00
Bowl, emerald gr w/bubbles, free-form, 2½x7x7" 50.00
Bowl, smoke, on clear paperweight base w/controlled bubbles, 6½" ..130.00
Compote, gr w/clear paperweight base, sm 75.00
Compote, smoke, on clear base w/controlled bubbles, flared top, 6¼" .100.00
Compote+pr candlesticks, smoke, on clear base w/controlled bubbles .190.00
Decanter, cobalt bl w/clear stopper, controlled bubbles, 16" 225.00
Decanter, honey amber w/clear stopper, 3 connected balls, 14½" .165.00
Pitcher, amber, on clear paperweight base, 11" 235.00
Pitcher, bl, clear appl hdl, 10" 230.00
Tumbler, clear w/gr flame at bottom, 5½x3" 25.00
Vase, champagne w/bubbles, incurvate rim, 11" 195.00
Vase, clear w/gr flame bottom, 7¼x3" 40.00
Vase, gr, on clear paperweight base w/controlled bubbles, 11¾" .125.00

Erphila

The Erphila trademark was used by Ebeling and Ruess Co. of Philadelphia between 1886 and the 1950s. The company imported quality porcelain and pottery from Germany, Czechoslovakia, Italy, and France. Pieces more readily found are from Germany and Czechoslovakia. A variety of items can be found and pieces such as figural teapots and larger figurines are moving up in value. There are a variety of marks, but all contain the name Erphila. One of the earlier marks is a green rectangle containing the name Erphila Germany. In general, Erphila pieces are scarce, not easily found.

Bookends, ram's heads, Czech, 6x7½", pr 145.00
Bowl, spaghetti-ware sides w/wht sq in center w/floral, 2⅝x8x8" .85.00
Box, cream w/roses, gold trim, #3729, w/lid, 3½x4x3" 150.00
Creamer, lemon color & texture w/gr leaves, Czech, 4x4½" 65.00
Dresser doll, Nancy Pert, #5859, lime gr dress w/blk hair, Germany .85.00
Dresser jar, Madame Pompadour, purple dress, Germany, 5" 50.00
Figurine, bloodhound, blk & brn, 5x7" 80.00
Figurine, Borzoi, blk & wht, seated, #15, 4½x8" 85.00
Figurine, bulldog pr, blk & wht, #7522, Germany, 4x5" 55.00
Figurine, bunny, gray, Germany, 2¾" 30.00
Figurine, Great Dane, blk & wht w/gold collar, Germany, 9½x9" ..85.00
Figurine, wht cat playing w/gold ball, Germany, 7" 55.00
Flower frog, scarf dancer w/leg bk, Fayence Germany, 7x5" 200.00
Jug, Bumble, Colonial man w/wht shirt, red coat & blk hat, Dickens, 4" .55.00
Jug, lady in red coat & hat w/wht apron, Dickens, 4" 60.00
Lemonade set, floral on wht, pitcher w/lid +5 tumblers, Czech 80.00
Napkin ring, girl in sunbonnet, Czech, 4" 75.00
Pitcher, begging dog, seated, blk & wht, #6702B, 8" 55.00
Pitcher, cat, blk & pk-to-wht, #6700B, 8" 35.00
Pitcher, dachshund, #6703B, Germany, 8" 140.00
Pitcher, poodle, gray, #734, 8¼" 140.00
Pitcher, red/orange flowers w/gr foliage on wht, Czech, 7⅝" 50.00
Pitcher, rooster, Czech, 7½" 175.00
Pitcher, rose w/wht cat hdl, Erphila Fayence Germany, #757/III, 8" .235.00
Pitcher, toucan, Czech, 7½" 210.00
Pitcher, wht w/gr polka dots & band at top, w/lid, Czech...............28.00
Plate, wht w/gr leaves, #1132/2, Germany, 12" 90.00
Plate, yel w/pk fruit & gr leaves raised, gr border, Black Forest, 8" .55.00
Reamer, orange shape & color, gr leaf hdls, Czech, 7" 290.00
Shakers, boy w/accordion & girl w/parasol, Czech, 3" & 3½", pr ..40.00

Shakers, Mrs Gump & Pickwick, Dickens characters, pr..............40.00
Teapot, cow, bell on collar is spout...240.00
Teapot, pig, #AK 722, 7½" 185.00

Tea set, marked Dorset Cherry Chintz Germany, 7" pot, three-piece set, $150.00.

Vanity jar, lady in bl costume party gown, 8" 165.00
Vase, mc abstract design, 9" 150.00
Vase, red & wht plaid, #2236, Czech, 8⅛" 65.00

Eskimo Artifacts

While ivory carvings made from walrus tusks or whale teeth have been the most emphasized articles of Eskimo art, basketry and wood-working are other areas in which these Alaskan Indians excel. Their designs are effected through the application of simple yet dramatic lines and almost stark decorative devices. Though not pursued to the extent of American Indian art, the unique work of these northern tribes is beginning to attract the serious attention of today's collectors.

Awl, bone, ca 1900, 6x½", in orig sealskin pouch..........................40.00
Basket, coiled, fish skin/seal gut lid decor, 1900s, 9x10½" 200.00
Basket, coiled, mc design, w/lid, Yupik, ca 1940, 6x8"................140.00
Basket, coiled oval w/fragmented wool design, 1910s, 7x11x14"...60.00
Basket, fine-weave split grass w/X design, w/lid, 1920s, 6x8½" .275.00
Basket, Kipnuk covered, seal gut imbrications, 1900s, 11x12½".300.00
Basket, storage; finely coiled, simple decor, Hooper Bay, 1920s, 8x11" ..225.00
Basket, storage; imbricated crosses & animals, 1900s, 12x14".....300.00
Blanket, sewn & beaded child's story on bl wool, 1950, 36x60" .600.00
Cribbage board, cvd walrus tooth w/fish/walrus/seal/etc, ca 1910, 12"..750.00
Cvg, gr soapstone, Eskimo & seal, A Temela, ca 1940, 9½x6½x11" .150.00
Cvg, gr soapstone, seal, w/Inuit provenance, ca 1970, 3½x8" 50.00
Cvg, gr soapstone, seated figure, ca 1940, 3½x5½" 45.00
Cvg, gray soapstone, musk ox, ca 1940, 14¾x7x2"......................250.00
Cvg, ivory scrimshaw, 7 sled dogs+sled & driver, 1950s, 17" L ...550.00
Cvg, scrimshaw ivory, walrus, full figure w/EX details, 1970s, 6".375.00
Cvg, soapstone, lady & 2 babies, T Ugjuk, 1940s, 12x6x4½" 200.00

Face Jugs, Contemporary

The most recognizable form of Southern folk pottery is the face jug. Rich alkaline glazes (lustrous greens and browns) are typical, and occasionally shards of glass are applied to the surface of the ware which during firing melts to produce opalescent 'glass runs' over the alkaline. In some locations clay deposits contain elements that result in areas of fluorescent blue or rutile; another variation is swirled or striped ware, rem-

iniscent of eighteenth-century agateware from Staffordshire. Collector demand for these unique one-of-a-kind jugs is at an all-time high and is still escalating. Choice examples made by Burlon B. Craig and Lanier Meaders sometimes bring over $1,000.00 on the secondary market. If you're interested in learning more about this type of folk pottery, contact the Southern Folk Pottery Collectors Society; their address is in the Directory under Clubs, Newsletters, and Catalogs. Our advisor for this category is Billy Ray Hussey; he is listed in the Directory under North Carolina.

China plate teeth, concave eyes/blk-gr Albany slip, R Armfield, 7½"..80.00
China plate teeth, pop eyes, crushed glass on swirlware, Craig, 4¾" .850.00
Dbl: Am Indian man/lady, redware, wht clay eyes, gr hair, Crocker, 10".165.00
Devil w/short horns, long lashes, 3 spouts, AG Meaders 19, 10"..250.00
Monkey, wht clay teeth, dbl-face, stoneware, B Henson, 1993, 11½" .1,350.00
Monkey, wht clay teeth, olive feldspathic gloss, Ferrell, 10" 350.00
Mossy Creek Monster #15, gr ash glaze, Cleater Meaders Jr, 11¼".415.00
Perplexed/concerned look, orange peel, cobalt salt glaze, BH, 1998, 8"..400.00
R Nixon caricature, rock teeth/wht clay eyes, L Meaders, 1970s, 11" .800.00
Squarish w/sm features, gr, unglazed eyes/teeth, R Meaders, 8¾".275.00
Upside-down Frankenstein-like, gr ash glaze, Cleater Meaders, 12".250.00
Wht clay eyes & teeth, incised whiskers, gr ash glaze, C Meaders, 13".385.00
Wht clay teeth & eyes, brn feldspatic gloss, J Brock, ca 1988, 9⅛"..225.00
Wht clay teeth & eyes, lashes, matt & gloss, L Meaders, late 1980s, 9" .1,000.00
Wht glaze teeth & eyes, plump, olive gloss, C Meaders, 1988, 12".400.00

Fairings

Fairings are small, brightly colored nineteenth-century hard-paste porcelain objects, largely figural groups and boxes. Most figural fairings portray amusing (if not risque) scenes of courting couples, marital woes, and political satire complete with appropriate base captions.

Fairing boxes, also referred to as trinket boxes, sometimes had captions just like the figural fairings with the same figures on top. These items were originally sold at 'Fairs' thus giving them the name Fairings.

Conta & Boehme of Poessneck, Germany, was the originator and leading manufacturer (1814 – 1931). Not all fairings were marked. Those that were, were given a model number along with the company logo depicting an arm holding a sword/dagger inside a shield. Those that did not get the Conta shield received an incised model number.

For more information, we recommend *Victorian Trinket Boxes* by Janice and Richard Vogel, and their latest book, *Conta & Boehme Porcelain*, published by the authors (See Directory, Florida). Other good 'out of print' references are *Victorian Fairings* by W.S. Bristow and *Victorian Fairings and Their Value* by Margaret Anderson. Items listed below reflect values for examples in very good to excellent condition.

Figurals

Animated Spirits, #3311, minimum value....................................400.00
Awkward Interruption, #2879, spill vase, from $125 to..............200.00
Cancan, #3301, from $300 to...400.00
Caught in the Act, match striker, #2855, from $300 to 400.00
Fair Play Boys, #2878, from $300 to 400.00
Favourable Opportunity, #2887, from $200 to 300.00
Good Templars, #3330, from $125 to 200.00
He Don't Like His Pants, minimum value....................................400.00
If Youth Knew, #2870, from $300 to...400.00
In Chancery, #3355, minimum value 600.00
Long Pull & a Strong Pull, #3335, from $300 to 400.00
Oh! What a Differente (sic) in the Morning, from $125 to........200.00
Oyster Day, #3331, from $75 to...125.00

Fairings (continued)

Power of Love, #2864, from $125 to **200.00**
Some Contributors To Punch, #3360, from $700 to **800.00**
Taking the Cream, #3347, from $125 to **200.00**
To Epsom, #2884, minimum value..**400.00**
Twelve Months After Marriage, #2858, from $75 to **125.00**
Waiting for a Bus, minimum value **400.00**
Who Is Coming?, #3382, from $125 to **200.00**
You Dirty Girl, #1456, 6½", from $75 to..................................**125.00**

Trinket Boxes

Dresser, boy w/2 pups, #130, from $125 to **175.00**
Dresser, cat & dog, #2998, from $100 to **150.00**
Dresser, cat on mantel of fireplace, #3520, from $125 to............**175.00**
Dresser, Centennial, #1997, from $150 to..................................**200.00**
Dresser, child looking in mirror, #1997, 4¼", from $75 to **125.00**
Dresser, girl reading to dog, #3560, from $125 to........................**175.00**
Dresser, girl w/doll, #3591, from $150 to **225.00**
Dresser, homing pigeon w/letter, #3518, from $75 to...................**125.00**
Dresser, pocket watch, #499, sz II, from $75 to **100.00**
Dresser, tea set, #479, sz II, from $75 to **100.00**
Lg, tea set, unmk, 4¾x6½", from $200 to **250.00**
Man/lady on bicycles, from $400 to **500.00**
3-spot, American eagle & flag, from $200 to **300.00**
3-spot, child w/dog, from $50 to **100.00**

Fans

The Japanese are said to have invented the fan. From there it went to China, and Portuguese traders took the idea to Europe. Though usually considered milady's accessory, even the gentlemen in seventeenth-century England carried fans! More fashionable than practical, some were of feathers and lovely hand-painted silks with carved ivory or tortoise sticks. Some French fans had peepholes. There are mourning fans, calendar fans, and those with advertising.

Fine antique fans (pre-1900) of ivory or mother-of-pearl are highly desirable. Those from before 1800 often sell for upwards of $1,000.00. Fans are being viewed as works of art, and some are actually signed by known artists. Our advisor for this category is Vicki Flanigan; she is listed in the Directory under Virginia.

Blk lacquer sticks (22) w/gold Oriental decor strung w/ribbon, 1850s .**300.00**
Courting scenes litho sgn JM Kibbe, rtcl ivory fr, 14x19"+Deco case ..**415.00**
Feathers, goose; HP roses, cvd ivory sticks, China, 1830s, 9" **700.00**
Feathers, ostrich; tortoise shell sticks, w/tassel **345.00**
Feathers, peacock; tortoise shell sticks, early 20th C, 23" **300.00**

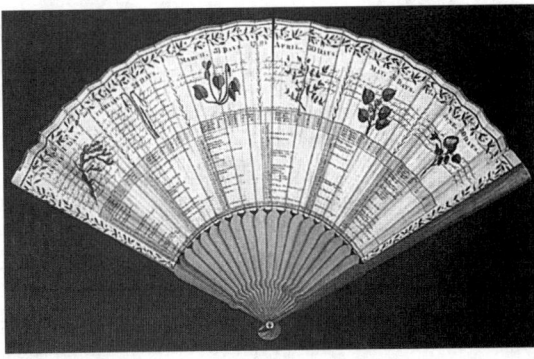

Hand-colored etching of almanac for 1794 and spring flowers, wooden sticks, with Duty stamp, English, 11", $400.00.

HP bronze silk panels w/Oriental flowers & birds, rtcl wood sticks ..**300.00**
HP gauze w/floral, sgn Bellini, MOP sticks, 1890s, 13" **250.00**
HP gauze w/roses, ca 1890, 13" **150.00**
HP paper, ships scene, pierced/ivory sticks, China trade, 1850s, 25" .**5,000.00**
HP silk, lady w/crown on table, eng/enameled ivory fr, 24" **440.00**
HP silk w/lady & 2 men in garden, ivory sticks, 17", EX+ **300.00**
Ivory brise, cvd/pierced w/figures/animals/etc, Canton, 1820s, 7"..**550.00**
Lace flowers appl to blk net, tortoise-shell sticks, 1870s, 11" **350.00**
Satin printed w/romantic scene, rtcl ivory sticks, Fr, 1900, 15", +box .**460.00**

Farm Collectibles

Country living in the nineteenth century entailed plowing, planting, and harvesting; gathering eggs and milking; making soap from lard rendered on butchering day; and numerous other tasks performed with primitive tools of which we in the twentieth century have had little first-hand knowledge. Our advisor for this category is Lar Hothem; his address is listed in the Directory under Ohio. See also Cast Iron; Lamps, Lanterns; Woodenware; Wrought Iron.

Bee smoker, canvas bellows, Woodman's Famous Bingham..., EX.**35.00**
Bridle, mule; brass rosettes, w/lg iron broken bit, 1860s, EX **175.00**
Cart, wood w/orange & gr pnt, yel line decor, 2-wheel, 1800s, 50" L.**1,000.00**
Corn husker, hook on leather strap, EX....................................**17.50**
Corn husker, hook w/leather strap, Boss Huskers...Illinois, EX......**10.00**
Corn husker, peg type, wood & leather (dry), EX **30.00**
Corn sheller, David Bradley C87, hand crank............................**65.00**
Corn sheller, Keystone Invincible, hand crank, wooden **140.00**
Corn sheller, sq-cut nails, trn hdl, old red pnt, 2-pc, 22" L **110.00**
Corn sheller, unmk, CI, wood hdl, 11" **98.00**
Cow bell, Holstein Bell #1, Blon Mfg **210.00**
Cow bell, wrought iron, orig clapper, traditional shape, 7½" **40.00**
Cranberry scoop, wood & tin, 19th C, 10x18x20" **345.00**
Feed sack, bluebells & flowers on wht, 44x34"............................**20.00**
Feed sack, navy leaves on bright pk, 36x44" **22.00**
Grain shredder, CI & wood, operable...**75.00**
Guide book, Farm Life...S Plains of TX, ca 1940, EX **18.50**
Hames, wrought iron, EX gr pnt, VG...**85.00**
Hames & collar, mule; wrought iron & leather, EX **85.00**
Handbook, Livestock Judging, Nordby, Beeson & Fourt, 1945, 350-pg..**5.00**
Hay fork, mechanical, primitive, 36x18".....................................**145.00**
Hay hook, wrought iron, 5¼", w/orig 8" wooden hdl **12.00**
Hay knife, Brades Mills, 22" saw blade w/14" wooden hdl, EX......**70.00**
Hay knife, wrought iron w/wood hdl, Brades Mills, 22" blade, 14" hdl..**70.00**
Haystack measure, dvtl wood, stamped: 1 Gallon, EX patina, 10" .**350.00**
Horse comb, brass w/wood hdl..**25.00**
Key, wrought iron, ca 1600s, 7"..**28.00**
Manual, McCormick Deering/International Harvester 3-Bar Rake, EX.**14.00**
Prickly pear burner, brass, B&H Pear Burner Co, 1900s, 22" **100.00**
Pump, hand; Red Jacket, CI, orig blk pnt, 15½"...........................**70.00**
Root cutter, Banner, Thompson...1894, 37x28x24", EX..............**250.00**
Wagon seat, dbl; hardwood, 3-slat bk, splint seat, 32x36x21", VG..**550.00**
Wagon seat, mixed hardwoods, 2-part arrow bk, rabbit-ear finials, 33"..**220.00**
Yoke, oxen; dbl, wood w/iron rings, 51" **135.00**
Yoke, shoulder; cvd w/orig 3-color pnt w/stenciled pineapples, 40"..**135.00**

Fenton

The Fenton Art Glass Company was founded in 1905 by brothers Frank L. and John W. Fenton. In the beginning they were strictly a decorating company, but when glassware blanks supplied by other manufacturers became difficult to obtain, the brothers started their own glass manufactory. This factory remains in operation today; it is located in Williamstown, West Virginia.

Early Fenton consisted of pattern glass, custard glass, and carnival glass. During the 1920s and 1930s, Fenton introduced several Depression-era glass patterns, including a popular line called Lincoln Inn, along with stretch glass and glassware in several popular opaque colors — Chinese Yellow, Mandarin Red, and Mongolian Green among them.

In 1939 Fenton introduced a line of hobnail glassware after the surprising success of a hobnail cologne bottle made for Wrisley Cologne. Since that time hobnail has remained a staple in Fenton's glassware line. In addition to hobnail, other lines such as coin spot, the crested lines, and thumbprint have been mainstays of the company, as have their popular opalescent colors such as cranberry, blue, topaz, and plum. Their milk glass has been very successful as well. Glass baskets in these lines and colors are widely sought after by collectors and can be found in a variety of different sizes and shapes.

Today the company is being managed by third- and fourth-generation family members. Fenton glass continues to be sold in gift shops and retail stores. Additionally, exclusive pieces are offered on the television shopping network, QVC. Desirable items for collectors include limited edition pieces, hand-painted pieces, and family signature pieces.

For further information we recommend *Fenton Art Glass, 1907 – 1939,* and *Fenton Art Glass Patterns, 1939 – 1980,* by Margaret and Kenn Whitmyer; *Fenton Glass, The Third Twenty-Five Years,* by William Heacock (with 1998 value guide); and *Fenton Glass: The 1980s Decade* by Robert E. Eaton, Jr. (1997 values). Additionally, two national collector clubs, the National Fenton Glass Society (NFGS) and the Fenton Art Glass Collectors of America (FAGCA) promote the study of Fenton art through their respective newsletters, *The Fenton Flyer* and *The Butterfly Net* (see Clubs, Catalogs, and Newsletters in the Directory). Our advisors for this category are Laurie and Richard Karman; they are listed in the Directory under Illinois.

See Also Carnival Glass; Custard Glass; Stretch Glass.

Hobnail, fairy lamp, plum opal, 9", from $275.00 to $325.00. (Photo courtesy Lee Garmon)

Apple Blossom, basket, #7336, 1960-61, 6½" 150.00
Apple Blossom, vase, dbl-crimped, #7258, 1960-61, 8" 85.00
Apple Tree, vase, blk, crimped or flared, #1561, 10" 165.00
Aqua Crest, basket, #703, 1941-43, 7" 85.00
Aqua Crest, bowl, salad; low, #7220, 1948-53, 10" 80.00
Aqua Crest, plate, #7219, 1942-43, 6½" 15.00
Basket Weave w/Open Edge, bowl, blk, #1092, 1935-36, 5½" 35.00
Basket Weave w/Open Edge, candlestick, gr, #1091, 1936 ....28.00
Basket Weave w/Open Edge, candlestick, jade or ruby 48.00
Basket Weave w/Open Edge, vase, gr opal, flared rim, 5½" 90.00
Big Cookies, basket, amber, #1681, 1933, 10½" 100.00
Big Cookies, basket, Moonstone, #1681, 1933, 10½" 215.00
Big Cookies, macaroon jar, Chinese Yellow, #1681, 1933, 7" 250.00
Black Crest, fairy lamp, #7392, early 1970s, from $175 to...........200.00
Black Crest, tidbit tray, 2-tier, #7294, 1970s 150.00

Black Rose, hurricane lamp, #7398, 1953-55 ....325.00
Blue Crest, bowl, dbl-crimped, #7321, 1963, 11½" 87.50
Blue Ridge, pitcher, #187, ca 1939 ....350.00
Blue Ridge, top hat, #1920, ca 1939, 12" 300.00
Cactus, basket, milk glass, #3437, 1959-60...........................30.00
Cactus, vase, fan; milk glass, #3459, 1959-60, 6" 22.00
Cameo Opal, puff box, #53, 1927 ....62.50
Coin Dot, basket, bl opal, #1522, ca 1947-51, 10" 155.00
Coin Dot, candle holder, Fr opal, #1524, 1947-54 ....75.00
Coin Dot, candy jar, cranberry opal, w/lid, #1522, 1947-51 ....325.00
Coin Dot, rose bowl, topaz opal, 1959-60, 4" 85.00
Coin Dot, top hat, cranberry opal, #1294, 1948-54, 5" 73.00
Coin Dot, vase, bl opal, crimped, #194, 1948-53, 6" 55.00
Coin Dot, vase, Honeysuckle, #1925, 1948-49, 6" 110.00
Crystal Crest, bowl, dbl-crimped, #1523, 13½" 125.00
Crystal Crest, vase, regular, #192, 9½" 80.00
Daisy & Button, bootee, rose pastel, #1994, 1954-55 ....32.50
Daisy & Button, bowl, milk glass, crimped, ftd, #1924, 1954-60...22.50
Daisy & Button, vase, fan; turq opaque, ftd, #1959, 1955-56, 9" ..45.00
Daisy & Button #1900, ashtray, Royal Blue, 1937-39 ....15.00
Daisy & Button #1900, creamer, vaseline, 1937-39 ....15.00
Daisy & Button #1900, vase, fan; crystal, 1937-39, 10" 22.00
Dancing Ladies, bowl, Chinese Yellow, oval, #900, 11".........235.00
Dancing Ladies, vase, fan; Mandarin Red, #901, 1934, 9".........600.00
Dancing Ladies, vase, Mongolian Green, cupped, #901, 8½" 325.00
Dancing Ladies, vase, Pekin Blue, hdls, #901, 1933, 6" 115.00
Dancing Ladies, vase, ruby, #901, 1933, 9" 265.00
Dancing Ladies, vase, topaz opal, crimped, #901, 8½" 625.00
Diamond Lace, candlestick, Fr opal, low, #1948, 1950-54 ....22.00
Diamond Lace, comport, Fr opal w/aqua crest, dbl-crimped, #1948..75.00
Diamond Lace, epergne set, Fr opal w/emerald crest, 12" bowl, 4-pc..250.00
Diamond Optic, basket, aquamarine, #1616, 1928, 6½" 62.50
Diamond Optic, bonbon, Orchid, flared, #1502, 1927, 6" 32.50
Diamond Optic, bottle, cologne; ruby o/l, squat, #192, 1942-49...65.00
Diamond Optic, creamer, gr, #1502, 1927 ....18.00
Diamond Optic, cup, rose, #1502, 1927 ....10.00
Diamond Optic, cup, ruby, #1502, 1933 ....18.00
Diamond Optic, dresser set, aqua, #1502, 1927-38, 4-pc...........200.00
Diamond Optic, jug, Mulberry, #1353, 1942, 70-oz 450.00
Diamond Optic, mayonnaise & ladle, gr or rose, 1927-38.............40.00
Diamond Optic, plate, Jade Green, 8-sided, #1502, 1927, 8" 8.00
Diamond Optic, vase, fan; Tangerine, #1502, 1927, 8½" 95.00
Diamond Optic, vase, ruby o/l, dbl-crimped, #192, 1942-49, 6"...30.00
Diamond Optic, vase, tulip; Mulberry, #192, 1942, 6" 70.00
Dolphin, bonbon, Jade Green, flared, ftd, #1502, 6" 42.50
Dolphin, bonbon, ruby, flared, ftd, #1502, 6" 36.00
Dolphin, bowl, Lilac, deep, oval, 10½" 165.00
Dolphin, candlestick, gr, #1623 ....57.50
Elizabeth #1639, bowl, salad; Royal Blue, 9½" 32.50
Elizabeth #1639, mint jar, blk, w/lid 157.50
Emerald Crest, bowl, soup; #680/#7320, 1949-56, 5½" 37.50
Emerald Crest, sherbet, ftd, #680/#7226, 1949-56 ....27.50
Flame, bowl, shallow, cupped, #601, 1924, 10" 65.00
Flame, candlestick, bl base, #649, 1924, 10" 155.00
Flame Crest, cake plate, ftd, #7213, 1963, 13" 160.00
Flower Windows, tumbler, iced tea; ruby, #1720, 1937-38.............52.50
Georgian #1611, plate, compartment; aquamarine, 1931-42, 11" .32.50
Gold Crest, basket, #1923, 1943-44, 7" 85.00
Gold Crest, vase, dbl-crimped, regular, #192, 1943-44, 6".........24.00
Hanging Hearts, bonbon, #3037, from $850 to........................950.00
Hanging Hearts, vase, #3000, 11", from $900 to 1,200.00
Hobnail, basket, bl opal, #3830, 1940-55, 10" 155.00
Hobnail, basket, Peach Blow, #3837, 1952-57, 7" 75.00
Hobnail, basket, turq opaque, #3837, 1955-59, 7"....................40.00

Hobnail, bonbon, cranberry, dbl-crimped, #3926, 1940-57, 6" 18.00
Hobnail, bottle, cologne; gr opal, #389, 1940-41 ....115.00
Hobnail, bottle, cologne; topaz opal, 1941-44 ....110.00
Hobnail, bowl, milk glass, low ft, #3623, 1961-65, 10½" 100.00
Hobnail, candle bowl, plum opal, #3771, 1959 ....125.00
Hobnail, candle holder, bl pastel, #3974, 1954-55 ....22.00
Hobnail, candle holder, rose pastel, #3974, 1955-57 ....22.00
Hobnail, comport, Fr opal, ftd plate, 1941-43, 8" 57.50
Hobnail, cruet, rose o/l, 1943 ....85.00
Hobnail, decanter, cranberry, 1941-50 ....385.00
Hobnail, goblet, wine; Fr opal, 1940-57 ....22.50
Hobnail, jug, milk glass, 1953-69, 80-oz 100.00
Hobnail, jug, tankard; bl opal, 1940-44, 48-oz 275.00
Hobnail, punch bowl, milk glass, 1958-59, 7-qt 265.00
Hobnail, slipper, gr pastel, #3995, 1954-56 ....30.00
Hobnail, tray, crescent; Fr opal, 1948-50, 6½" 32.50
Hobnail, tumbler, amber, #3949, 1959-60, 9-oz 13.00
Hobnail, tumbler, crystal, ftd, ca 1940, 12-oz 12.50
Hobnail, tumbler, topaz opal, 1941-44, 12-oz 37.50
Hobnail, vase, Apple Green, o/l, #3752, 1961-62, 11" 85.00
Hobnail, vase, cranberry, flared bottle form, 1941-44, 10" 250.00
Hobnail, vase, flip; Fr opal, 1941, 8½" 175.00
Hobnail, vase, gr opal, dbl-crimped, flared sq cup, 1940-41, 4½" .27.50
Hobnail, vase, hand; bl opal, 1942-43, 6" 75.00
Hobnail, vase, lime gr opal, dbl-crimped, 1952-55, 4½" 27.50
Hobnail, vase, rose o/l, dbl-crimped, 1943, 9" 40.00
Horizon, candle holder, amber, w/insert, 1959, 5" 12.00
Horizon, vase, Jamestown Blue, hangs, w/thong, 1959 ....80.00
Ivory Crest, vase, crimped, #186, 1940-42, 8½" 35.00
Jade Green, aquarium, turtle base w/Coin Spot top, #1538, 1929 .425.00
Jade Green, bowl, cupped, #847, 1932, 6" 17.50
Lace Edge, bowl, banana; turq opaque, #9024, 1955-56 ....52.50
Lace Edge, bowl, milk glass, 1954-59, 8" 20.00
Lace Edge, comport, bl pastel, ftd, #9029, 1954-55 ....45.00
Lace Edge, plate, rose pastel, #9018, 1954-55, 8" 18.00
Lace Edge/Scroll & Eye, bowl, #9025, gr pastel, 1955-56 ....27.00
Lamb's Tongue, candy jar, turq, #4381, 1954-55 ....85.00
Lamb's Tongue, shakers, milk glass, #4306, 1954-46, pr 62.50
Lamp, free-hand Hanging Hearts 1,350.00
Lilac, basket, wicker hdl, #1684, 1933 ....225.00
Lilac, vase, fan; #857, 1933, 8" 60.00
Lincoln Inn, comport, aqua, flat plate 22.50
Lincoln Inn, plate, Emerald Green, 12" 28.00
Lincoln Inn, tumbler, Royal Blue, ftd, 12-oz 42.50
Mandarin Red, bowl, shallow, cupped, #601, 1933, 10" 47.50
Mandarin Red, candlestick, cornucopia; #950, 1934 ....47.50
Ming, basket, gr, wicker hdl, #1684, 1935-36, 9" 90.00
Ming, bowl, rose, crimped, ftd, #857, 1935-36, 10" 45.00
Ming, mayonnaise jar, crystal, 1935-36 ....75.00
Ming, pitcher, rose, #1653, 1935-36, 10" 170.00
Mongolian Green, bowl, crimped, #847, 1934, 6" 36.00
Mongolian Green, vase, flared, #1093, 5½" 90.00
Mosaic, bonbon, high ft, #3035, minimum value 1,500.00
Mosaic, bowl, ftd, #30169, from $300 to 350.00
Peach Crest, basket, #201, 1940-47, 10" 155.00
Peach Crest, bowl, 8-point, #1522, 1940-41, 10" 80.00
Peach Crest, jug, hdld, #192A, 1943-49, 9" 70.00
Peach Crest, puff box, #192-A, 1943-48 ....55.00
Peacock, vase, milk glass, cupped, flared, 1933-35, 4" 200.00
Peacock, vase, Mongolian Green, flared, 8" 85.00
Pekin Blue, bottle, cologne; #53, 1932, 5" 150.00
Pineapple, bonbon, crystal satin, triangular, 1938, 6½" 20.00
Pineapple, bowl, rose satin, flared, flat, 11¼" 60.00
Pineapple, candlestick, ruby, dbl-branch, 1938, 5½" 60.00

Plymouth, cocktail shaker, Royal Blue 225.00
Plymouth, jigger, ruby 55.00
Plymouth, tumbler, old fashioned; Fr opal, 7-oz 27.50
Rib Optic, bowl, cranberry, 1953-55, 12" 115.00
Rib Optic, bowl, Fr opal, #1522, 1939, 10" 60.00
Rib Optic, cruet, bl satin, #815, 1952-55 ....225.00
Rib Optic, vase, pinch; rose satin, #1720, 1952-53, 7½" 75.00
Rib Optic, wine, cranberry, 1953-55 ....85.00
Rib Optic, wine bottle, lime opal, 1953-54 ....275.00
Ring Optic, bottle, Stiegel Blue opal, ca 1939, 5" 75.00
Ring Optic, tumbler, cranberry, ca 1939, 10-oz 45.00
Rose Crest, candle holder, #1523, 1946-48 ....40.00
Rose Crest, vase, dbl-crimped, cupped, flared, #203, 1946-48, 4½".30.00
Royal Blue, candlestick, cornucopia; #950, 1934 ....47.50
Ruby, bowl, flared rim, #857, 1933-35, 11" 60.00
San Toy, bonbon, crystal, flared, #107, 1936, 7" 15.00
San Toy, ginger jar, crystal, #893, 1936 ....125.00
San Toy, vase, gr, oval, #349, 1936 ....85.00
Sheffield, bonbon, aquamarine, shallow, 3-ftd, 1936-38, 7½" 20.00
Sheffield, mayonnaise bowl, Gold, 1936-38, 5" 10.00
Sheffield, vase, crystal satin, sq, flared, 1936-38, 8" 12.00
Silver Crest, bottle, cologne; squat, #192, 1943-49 ....45.00
Silver Crest, creamer, #680/#7261, , 1948-67, 3¼" 35.00

Silver Crest, jug pitcher, #7467, 70-ounce, from $300.00 to $350.00. (Photo courtesy Gene Florence)

Silver Crest, punch cup, #7247, 1956-63 ....18.00
Silver Crest, vase, dbl-crimped, #7258, 1943-67, 8" 20.00
Silver Turquoise, cake plate, ftd, #7213, 1956-59, 13" 85.00
Silvertone, bowl, Wisteria, triangular, #1008, 1934-38, 7" 22.50
Silvertone, plate, amber, #1009, 1934-38, 8" 15.00
Silvertone Etch, bowl, crytal, cloverleaf, #950, 1937-38 ....32.50
Silvertone Etch, pitcher, iced tea; crystal, #1352, 1937-38 ....165.00
Silvertone Etch/Sheffield, vase, bl, #1800, 1937-38, 10" 57.50
Spiral Optic, bowl, cranberry, crimped, #1522, 1938-40, 10" 100.00
Spiral Optic, candlestick, cranberry, 31523 ....95.00
Spiral Optic, hurricane lamp, Fr opal, #170, 1939, w/base 190.00
Spiral Optic, pitcher, Stiegel Blue, ice lip, #1353, 1939, 9" 265.00
Spiral Optic, rose bowl, gr, #201, 5" 75.00
Spiral Optic, rose bowl, topaz opal, crimped, #201, 1939-40 ....68.00
Spiral Optic, top hat, gr opal, #1920, 1939, 12" 265.00
Spiral Optic, tumbler, Stiegel Blue, #1353, 1939, 9-oz 45.00
Spiral Optic, vase, cranberry, cupped, #188, 1938-40, 7½" 75.00
Stretch, basket, Celeste Blue, #1903, 6½" 300.00
Stretch, bonbon, Persian Pearl, crimped, #106, 6½" 24.00
Stretch, bowl, Tangerine, shallow, #1512, 1927-29, 9½" 115.00
Stretch, candlestick, ruby, #249, 1920s, 6" 165.00
Stretch, candy jar, topaz, #736, 1921, 1-lb 55.00
Stretch, cigarette holder, Florentine Green, #556, ca 1917-28 ......87.50
Stretch, comport, Grecian Gold, cupped, #736, 1930s, 6½" 28.00
Stretch, cup & saucer, Celeste Blue, plain 110.00
Stretch, nut cup, Wisteria, #923, 1921-28, ind 42.50

Stretch, sherbet, Celeste Blue, #103 ....**30.00**
Stretch/Diamond Optic, bowl, Velva Rose, dolphins, #1504, 10" .**190.00**
Stretch/Diamond Optic, creamer, aquamarine, #1502, ca 1950 ....**22.50**
Swirl, bowl, milk glass, deep, 1954-55, 11" **22.50**
Swirl, mayonnaise set, rose pastel, #7004, 1954-55 ....**42.00**
Swirl, puff box, gr pastel, 1945-56 ....**45.00**
Swirl, shakers, bl pastel, #7001, 1954-55, pr **37.50**
Swirl, vase, Jamestown Blue, 1957-59, 6" **45.00**
Swirled Feather, bottle, cologne; gr satin, 1953-55 ....**225.00**
Swirled Feather, candy jar, bl satin, 1953-55 ....**275.00**
Swirled Feather, cruet, cranberry satin, 1953-54 ....**475.00**
Teardrop, candle holder, milk glass, 1957-59 ....**15.00**
Teardrop, condiment set, Goldenrod, 1956-57 ....**215.00**
Venetian Red, ashtray, #1566, 1927 ....**75.00**
Venetian Red, candy jar, #735, 1926, ½-lb **75.00**
Wisteria, creamer, #349, 1937-38 ....**30.00**
Wisteria, jug, #1355, 1937-38 ....**185.00**
Wisteria, vase, fan; #857, 1937-38, 8" **48.00**

Fiesta

Fiesta is a line of dinnerware that was originally produced by the Homer Laughlin China Company of Newell, West Virginia, from 1936 until 1973. It was made in eleven different solid colors with over fifty pieces in the assortment. The pattern was developed by Frederick Rhead, an English Stoke-on-Trent potter who was an important contributor to the art-pottery movement in this country during the early part of the century. The design was carried out through the use of a simple band-of-rings device near the rim. Fiesta Red, a strong red-orange glaze color, was made with depleted uranium oxide. It was more expensive to produce than the other colors and sold at higher prices. During the '50s the color assortment was gray, rose, chartreuse, and dark green. These colors are relatively harder to find and along with medium green (new in 1959) command the highest prices.

Fiesta Kitchen Kraft was introduced in 1939; it consisted of seventeen pieces of kitchenware such as pie plates, refrigerator sets, mixing bowls, and covered jars in four popular Fiesta colors.

As a final attempt to adapt production to modern-day techniques and methods, Fiesta was restyled in 1969. Of the original colors, only Fiesta Red remained. This line, called Fiesta Ironstone, was discontinued in 1973.

Two types of marks were used: an ink stamp on machine-jiggered pieces and an indented mark molded into the hollow ware pieces.

In 1986 HLC reintroduced a line of Fiesta dinnerware in five colors: black, white, pink, apricot, and cobalt (darker and denser than the original shade). Since then yellow, turquoise, seafoam green, 'country' blue, lilac, persimmon, sapphire blue, chartreuse, gray, juniper, cinnabar, plum, sunflower yellow, and shamrock have been added.

In the listings below, 'original colors' indicates only three of the original six — light green, turquoise, and yellow (or those remaining after specific original colors have been priced). Red, ivory, and cobalt values are listed separately. Turquoise was the last original color to be introduced, so the items that were discontinued in 1946 are harder to find in that color (since it had a shorter production run), and values fall into the price range of red, cobalt, and ivory. These are designated with an asterisk.

For more information we recommend *The Collector's Encyclopedia of Fiesta, Harlequin, and Riviera, 9th Edition,* by Sharon and Bob Huxford, and *Post86 Fiesta* by Richard Racheter, both by Collector Books.

Dinnerware

Ashtray, '50s colors **88.00**
Ashtray, orig colors **48.00**

Ashtray, red, cobalt or ivory **65.00**
Bowl, covered onion soup; cobalt or ivory **725.00**
Bowl, covered onion soup; red **750.00**
Bowl, covered onion soup; turq, minimum value **8,000.00**
Bowl, covered onion soup; yel or lt gr **650.00**
Bowl, cream soup; '50s colors **75.00**
Bowl, cream soup; med gr, minimum value **4,200.00**
Bowl, cream soup; orig colors **45.00**
Bowl, cream soup; red, cobalt or ivory **62.00**
Bowl, dessert; '50s colors, 6" **52.00**
Bowl, dessert; med gr, 6" **600.00**
Bowl, dessert; orig colors, 6" **40.00**
Bowl, dessert; red, cobalt or ivory, 6" **52.00**
Bowl, fruit; '50s colors, 4¾" **40.00**
Bowl, fruit; '50s colors, 5½" **40.00**
Bowl, fruit; med gr, 4¾" **525.00**
Bowl, fruit; med gr, 5½" **80.00**
Bowl, fruit; orig colors, 4¾" **28.00**
Bowl, fruit; orig colors, 5½" **28.00**
Bowl, fruit; orig colors, 11¾" **275.00**
Bowl, fruit; red, cobalt or ivory, 4¾" **35.00**
Bowl, fruit; red, cobalt or ivory, 5½" **35.00**
Bowl, fruit; red, cobalt or ivory, 11¾" * **340.00**
Bowl, ftd salad; orig colors **340.00**
Bowl, ftd salad; red, cobalt or ivory * **400.00**
Bowl, ind salad; med gr, 7½" **120.00**
Bowl, ind salad; red, turq or yel, 7½" **90.00**
Bowl, nappy; '50s colors, 8½" **65.00**
Bowl, nappy; med gr, 8½" **145.00**
Bowl, nappy; orig colors, 8½" **42.00**
Bowl, nappy; orig colors, 9½" **52.00**
Bowl, nappy; red, cobalt or ivory, 8½" * **58.00**
Bowl, nappy; red, cobalt or ivory, 9½" * **65.00**
Bowl, Tom & Jerry; ivory w/gold letters **260.00**
Bowl, unlisted salad; red, cobalt, or ivory **1,200.00**
Bowl, unlisted salad; yel **110.00**
Candle holders, bulb; orig colors, pr **110.00**
Candle holders, bulb; red, cobalt or ivory, pr * **140.00**
Candle holders, tripod; orig colors, pr **485.00**
Candle holders, tripod; red, cobalt or ivory, pr * **650.00**
Carafe, orig colors **255.00**
Carafe, red, cobalt or ivory * **340.00**
Casserole, '50s colors **300.00**
Casserole, French; standard colors other than yel **725.00**
Casserole, French; yel **300.00**
Casserole, med gr **900.00**
Casserole, orig colors **165.00**
Casserole, red, cobalt or ivory **225.00**
Coffeepot, '50s colors **350.00**
Coffeepot, demi; orig colors **425.00**
Coffeepot, demi; red, cobalt or ivory * **550.00**
Coffeepot, orig colors **195.00**
Coffeepot, red, cobalt or ivory **255.00**
Compote, orig colors, 12" **150.00**
Compote, red, cobalt or ivory, 12" * **200.00**
Compote, sweets; orig colors **80.00**
Compote, sweets; red, cobalt or ivory * **100.00**
Creamer, '50s colors **40.00**
Creamer, ind; red **365.00**
Creamer, ind; yel **80.00**
Creamer, med gr **90.00**
Creamer, orig colors **22.00**
Creamer, red, cobalt or ivory **35.00**
Creamer, stick hdld, orig colors **48.00**

Creamer, stick hdld, red, cobalt or ivory * 72.00
Cup, demi; '50s colors 375.00
Cup, demi; orig colors...68.00
Cup, demi; red, cobalt or ivory 80.00

Egg cup: '50s colors, $160.00; original colors, $60.00; red, cobalt, or ivory, $72.00.

Lid, for mixing bowl #1-#3, any color, minimum value 770.00
Lid, for mixing bowl #4, any color, minimum value 1,000.00
Marmalade, orig colors..245.00
Marmalade, red, cobalt or ivory * 325.00
Mixing bowl, #1, orig colors...180.00
Mixing bowl, #1, red, cobalt or ivory * 245.00
Mixing bowl, #2, orig colors...115.00
Mixing bowl, #2, red, cobalt or ivory * 130.00
Mixing bowl, #3, orig colors...125.00
Mixing bowl, #3, red, cobalt or ivory * 135.00
Mixing bowl, #4, orig colors...130.00
Mixing bowl, #4, red, cobalt or ivory * 160.00
Mixing bowl, #5, orig colors...160.00
Mixing bowl, #5, red, cobalt or ivory * 185.00
Mixing bowl, #6, orig colors...215.00
Mixing bowl, #6, red, cobalt or ivory * 275.00
Mixing bowl, #7, orig colors...350.00
Mixing bowl, #7, red, cobalt or ivory * 410.00
Mug, Tom & Jerry; '50s colors 100.00
Mug, Tom & Jerry; ivory w/gold letters 65.00
Mug, Tom & Jerry; orig colors...60.00
Mug, Tom & Jerry; red, cobalt or ivory...............................82.00
Mustard, orig colors..210.00
Mustard, red, cobalt or ivory * 265.00
Pitcher, disk juice; gray, minimum value.........................3,000.00
Pitcher, disk juice; Harlequin yel 60.00
Pitcher, disk juice; red..600.00
Pitcher, disk juice; yel...48.00
Pitcher, disk water; '50s colors 280.00
Pitcher, disk water; med gr, minimum value 1,200.00
Pitcher, disk water; orig colors 125.00
Pitcher, disk water; red, cobalt or ivory 170.00
Pitcher, ice; orig colors..140.00
Pitcher, ice; red, cobalt or ivory * 160.00
Pitcher, jug, 2-pt; '50s colors 150.00
Pitcher, jug, 2-pt; orig colors...88.00
Pitcher, jug, 2-pt; red, cobalt or ivory 120.00
Plate, '50s colors, 6" 9.00
Plate, '50s colors, 7" 13.00
Plate, '50s colors, 9" 22.00
Plate, '50s colors, 10" 52.00
Plate, cake; orig colors...900.00
Plate, cake; red, cobalt or ivory * 1,000.00
Plate, calendar; 1954 or 1955, 10" 45.00
Plate, calendar; 1955, 9"...50.00

Plate, chop; '50s colors, 13" 100.00
Plate, chop; '50s colors, 15" 145.00
Plate, chop; med gr, 13" 375.00
Plate, chop; orig colors, 13" 42.00
Plate, chop; orig colors, 15" 50.00
Plate, chop; red, cobalt or ivory, 13" 60.00
Plate, chop; red, cobalt or ivory, 15" 80.00
Plate, compartment; '50s colors, 10½" 75.00
Plate, compartment; orig colors, 10½" 40.00
Plate, compartment; orig colors, 12" 55.00
Plate, compartment; red, cobalt or ivory, 10½" 45.00
Plate, compartment; red, cobalt or ivory, 12" 60.00
Plate, deep; '50s colors...58.00
Plate, deep; med gr 140.00
Plate, deep; orig colors...38.00
Plate, deep; red, cobalt or ivory...60.00
Plate, med gr, 6" 20.00
Plate, med gr, 7" 32.00
Plate, med gr, 9" 45.00
Plate, med gr, 10" 135.00
Plate, orig colors, 6" 5.00
Plate, orig colors, 7" 9.00
Plate, orig colors, 9" 12.00
Plate, orig colors, 10" 32.00
Plate, red, cobalt or ivory, 6" 7.00
Plate, red, cobalt or ivory, 7" 10.00
Plate, red, cobalt or ivory, 9" 18.00
Plate, red, cobalt or ivory, 10" 40.00
Platter, '50s colors...58.00
Platter, med gr 175.00
Platter, orig colors...35.00
Platter, red, cobalt or ivory..45.00
Relish tray, gold decor, complete 250.00
Relish tray base, orig colors...75.00
Relish tray base, red, cobalt or ivory * 100.00
Relish tray center insert, orig colors 50.00
Relish tray center insert, red, cobalt or ivory * 60.00
Relish tray side insert, orig colors 50.00
Relish tray side insert, red, cobalt or ivory * 60.00
Sauce boat, '50s colors..78.00
Sauce boat, med gr 180.00
Sauce boat, orig colors..48.00
Sauce boat, red, cobalt or ivory...85.00
Saucer, '50s colors..6.00
Saucer, demi; '50s colors...110.00
Saucer, demi; orig colors...18.00
Saucer, demi; red, cobalt or ivory......................................22.00
Saucer, med gr 12.00
Saucer, orig colors..4.00
Shakers, '50s colors, pr 45.00
Shakers, med gr, pr 185.00
Shakers, orig colors, pr 22.00
Shakers, red, cobalt or ivory, pr...30.00
Sugar bowl, ind; turq 365.00
Sugar bowl, ind; yel 125.00
Sugar bowl, w/lid, '50s colors, 3¼x3½" 75.00
Sugar bowl, w/lid, med gr, 3¼x3½" 225.00
Sugar bowl, w/lid, orig colors, 3¼x3½" 48.00
Sugar bowl, w/lid, red, cobalt or ivory, 3¼x3½" 58.00
Syrup, orig colors 375.00
Syrup, red, cobalt or ivory * 425.00
Teacup, '50s colors..38.00
Teacup, med gr 60.00
Teacup, orig colors..25.00

Teacup, red, cobalt or ivory 35.00
Teapot, lg; orig colors 210.00
Teapot, lg; red, cobalt or ivory * 260.00
Teapot, med; '50s colors 325.00
Teapot, med; med gr, minimum value 1,200.00
Teapot, med; orig colors 165.00
Teapot, med; red, cobalt or ivory 225.00
Tray, figure-8; cobalt 100.00
Tray, figure-8; turq or yel 400.00
Tray, utility; orig colors 38.00
Tray, utility; red, cobalt or ivory * 42.00
Tumbler, juice; chartreuse, or dk gr 600.00
Tumbler, juice; orig colors 40.00
Tumbler, juice; red, cobalt or ivory 60.00
Tumbler, juice; rose 65.00
Tumbler, water; orig colors 65.00
Tumbler, water; red, cobalt or ivory * 85.00
Vase, bud; orig colors 85.00
Vase, bud; red, cobalt or ivory * 125.00
Vase, orig colors, 8" 600.00
Vase, orig colors, 10" 850.00
Vase, orig colors, 12", minimum value 1,100.00
Vase, red, cobalt or ivory, 8" * 700.00
Vase, red, cobalt or ivory, 10" * 950.00
Vase, red, cobalt or ivory, 12", minimum value * 1,300.00

Kitchen Kraft

Bowl, mixing; lt gr or yel, 6" 72.00
Bowl, mixing; lt gr or yel, 8" 85.00
Bowl, mixing; lt gr or yel, 10" 115.00
Bowl, mixing; red or cobalt, 6" 78.00
Bowl, mixing; red or cobalt, 8" 95.00
Bowl, mixing; red or cobalt, 10" 125.00
Cake plate, lt gr or yel 55.00
Cake plate, red or cobalt 65.00
Cake server, lt gr or yel 145.00
Cake server, red or cobalt 155.00
Casserole, ind; lt gr or yel 150.00
Casserole, ind; red or cobalt 160.00
Casserole, lt gr or yel, 7½" 85.00
Casserole, lt gr or yel, 8½" 105.00
Casserole, red or cobalt, 7½" 90.00
Casserole, red or cobalt, 8½" 115.00
Covered jar, lg; lt gr or yel 320.00
Covered jar, lg; red or cobalt 325.00

Covered jar, medium: light green or yellow, $280.00; red or cobalt, $295.00.

Covered jar, sm; lt gr or yel 285.00
Covered jar, sm; red or cobalt 300.00
Covered jug, lt gr or yel 280.00
Covered jug, red or cobalt 290.00

Fork, lt gr or yel 125.00
Fork, red or cobalt 135.00
Metal frame for platter 26.00
Pie plate, lt gr or yel, 9" 45.00
Pie plate, lt gr or yel, 10" 45.00
Pie plate, red or cobalt, 9" 48.00
Pie plate, red or cobalt, 10" 48.00
Pie plate, Spruce gr 305.00
Platter, lt gr or yel 70.00
Platter, red or cobalt 75.00
Platter, spruce gr 350.00
Shakers, lt gr or yel, pr 100.00
Shakers, red or cobalt, pr 110.00
Spoon, ivory, 12", minimum value 500.00
Spoon, lt gr or yel 135.00
Spoon, red or cobalt 145.00
Stacking refrigerator lid, ivory 225.00
Stacking refrigerator lid, lt gr or yel 75.00
Stacking refrigerator lid, red or cobalt 85.00
Stacking refrigerator unit, ivory 210.00
Stacking refrigerator unit, lt gr or yel 48.00
Stacking refrigerator unit, red or cobalt 58.00

Fifties Modern

Postwar furniture design is marked by organic shapes and lighter woods and forms. New materials from war research such as molded plywood and fiberglass were used extensively. For the first time, design was extended to the masses and the baby-boomer generation grew up surrounded by modern shape and color, the perfect expression of postwar optimism. The top designers in America worked for Herman Miller and Knoll Furniture Company. These include Charles Eames, George Nelson, and Eero Saarinen.

Unless noted otherwise values are given for furnishings in excellent condition; glassware and ceramic items are assumed to be in mint condition. This information was provided to us by Richard Wright.

See also Italian Glass.

Key:

alum — aluminum	plwd — plywood
cntl — cantilevered	ss — stainless steel
fbrg — fiberglass	uphl — upholstered
lcq — lacquered	vnr — veneer
lm — laminated	

Armchair, Jacobsen/Hansen, Egg, wht vinyl uphl, alum/ss fr, swivels 1,700.00
Armchair, McArthur, anodized alum alloy fr, reuphl, 33x20x24", VG 1,500.00
Armchair, Saarinen/Knoll, uphl seat, molded walnut legs, 33", G, 4 for 200.00
Armchair, Wegner/Knoll, teak fr w/dvtl detailed bkrest, uphl seat, pr 1,000.00
Bench, Nelson/Miller, birch slat top, 3 ebonized legs, 14x102x19" 1,100.00
Bench, Nelson/Miller, slat birch top, ebonized legs, 14x68x18½" 550.00
Bookcase, Rohde, burled vnr drop door, ebonized shelves, 27x60x17" 1,300.00
Bowl, Architectural Pottery, bl glaze, 1958, 12" dia 180.00
Bowl, G Nylund, brn matt w/lt bl gloss int, short cylinder, 2x7⅛" 115.00
Breakfront, Rohde/Miller, Paldao, burl wood/ebonized, 2-pc, 73x66x15" 2,200.00
Cabinet, Nelson/Miller, birch, 2 sliding glass doors/wood door, 30x56" 425.00
Cabinet, Nelson/Miller, Thin Edge, rosewood, 4 drws, 30½x34x18½" 3,000.00
Cabinet, Nelson/Miller, Thin Edge, rosewood, 5 drws, 41x40x18½" 4,500.00
Cabinet, Nelson/Miller, walnut, lm sliding doors, file drw, 26x60x19" 600.00
Cabinet, stereo; Esherick, walnut, cvg/dowels, 2 lift tops, 25x42x22" 18,000.00
Cabinet, stereo; Nelson/Miller, birch, center door, 35x57x18½" 500.00
Chair, after Eames, molded rswd vnr, leather uphl, alum base, +ottoman 750.00
Chair, Bertoia/Knoll, Diamond, chromed steel, rubber mts, 38x44x32" 750.00

Chair, Breuer/Knoll, Wassily, blk leather, chromed tubular steel fr ..375.00
Chair, Eames/Miller, birch lm, chrome fr, orig glides, 29" 200.00
Chair, Eames/Miller, blk molded seat/bk/fr, shock mts, 30" 300.00
Chair, Eames/Miller, blk wire seat, wooden dowel legs, bikini pads .1,000.00

Chair, Eames/Miller, Eiffel Tower, black wire, original leather bikini cover, label, 32", EX, $500.00. (Photo courtesy Treadway Gallery, Inc.)

Chair, Eames/Miller, gray Zenith shell, zinc wire cage base 800.00
Chair, Eames/Miller, molded ash, blk rod fr, shock mts, 29" 140.00
Chair, Eames/Miller, molded walnut seat/bk/fr, shock mts, 29", pr .900.00
Chair, Eames/Miller, parchment fbrg shell, blk rod legs, 36" 425.00
Chair, easy; B Mogensen, high-bk oak fr, cane seat, 37" 1,035.00
Chair, Eero Aarnio, Tomato, red pnt molded plastic, 1970......2,650.00
Chair, Jacobsen/Hansen, Ant, molded seat over chrome legs, 30½", pr.475.00
Chair, Jacobsen/Hansen, Swan, red uphl, alum 4-point base, 33x29x20".1,200.00
Chair, Laverne, Lily, clear plastic, purple uphl loose seat, 36" .2,100.00
Chair, lounge; Knoll, Parallel Bar, vinyl uphl, chrome fr/blk supports ..425.00
Chair, lounge; Plantner/Knoll, turq uphl, chrome wire base, +ottoman..700.00
Chair, lounge; Robsjohn-Gibbings/Widdicomb, beech, uphl seat/bk, VG.1,000.00
Chair, McArthur, Biltmore, alum fr w/rubber ft pads, uphl seat, 32".1,000.00
Chair, molded walnut, chrome fr w/nylon glides, shock mts, 29" .190.00
Chair, Nelson/Miller, Coconut, red reuphl Miller hopsack, chrome fr.5,000.00
Chair, Nelson/Miller, Tri-Swivel (Flying Duck), yel wool uphl, casters..500.00
Chair, Paulin/Artifort, Donut, gray uphl, 25x34x34" 600.00
Chair, Saarinen/Knoll, Grasshopper, lm bentwood fr, 39x23x31".2,300.00
Chair, side; Wormley/Dunbar #5527, lm ash w/brass spindles, uphl seat.900.00
Chair, swivel lounge; Kagan, uphl, Lucite X base, 32x30x36" .1,200.00
Chair, swivel; Columbo/Comfort, Elda, fbrg shell, leather uphl .2,500.00
Chair, swivel; Eames/Miller Time Life, purple wool uphl, 29", 4 for .1,300.00
Chair, swivel; H Miller, molded plastic seat, gr uphl, 38¼" 235.00
Chair, swivel; Panton, Cone, enameled bent wire, reuphl, 31x24x25".1,300.00
Chair, valet; Hansen/Wegner, teak & oak, flip-up panel seat, 37¼" ..4,350.00
Chair, Wegner, Papa Bear, gr textured uphl w/tufted bk, 40x35x36"..1,300.00
Chair, womb; Eero Saarinen, fbrg, red uphl, chrome legs, 1947, 35½".1,000.00
Chair set, Eames/Saarinen/Knoll, orange uphl, lm walnut, 31", 6 for.1,000.00
Chair set, McCobb/Directional, mahog w/brass, 4 side+2 arm..1,000.00
Chair set, Wegner/Hansen, teak fr, cord seat, thru tenons, 30", 6 for .850.00
Chairs, Breuer/Sendig, Wassily, tan leather, chrome fr, 28½", pr.2,500.00
Chest, blanket; Nelson/Miller, birch, lift lid, steel legs, 48".....1,600.00
Chest, Knoll, birch w/3 wht drws, blk metal legs, 28x36x18" 800.00
Clock, Miller, cork body, blk & orange hands, 11½" dia.............325.00
Clock, Nelson/Miller, Asterisk, cherry spikes, 13" dia, VG.........800.00
Clock, Nelson/Miller, Asterisk, wht metal face, blk hands, 10" dia .300.00
Clock, Nelson/Miller, Ball, wht balls on brass spindles, 13" dia ..800.00
Clock, Nelson/Miller, Dish, wooden knobs for hour markers, 9" dia.700.00
Clock, Nelson/Miller, Paddle Wheel, yel center, blk hands, 1952 .2,235.00
Clock, Nelson/Miller, Spike, tapered walnut hour markers, 1947 .700.00
Clock, Nelson/Miller, Starburst, blk wood spikes w/blk/orange/gray..400.00
Compote, Architectural Pottery, yel, 12" dia 325.00
Covered dish, Raymor, duck figural, brn & blk, 1959, 9x15" 125.00

Credenza, Kagan, cherry/ebonized wood, curved legs, 32x80x22"..4,000.00
Credenza, Loewy DF2000, molded plastic drw fronts, 30x80x22".3,500.00
Daybed, Gray, chromed tubular steel fr, blk leather uphl, 24x75x38"..3,750.00
Daybed, Nelson/Miller, birch fr, hairpin legs, G- cushions, 27x75x27".1,700.00
Daybed/sofa, Wegner/Getama, teak, gold uphl, bk adjusts, 30x77x34".2,000.00
Desk, Bel Geddes/Simmons, brn enameled metal, 3-drw, 30x44½" ..200.00
Desk, executive; Platner/Knoll, leather top, 2 leather-covered drws ..1,900.00
Desk, Heywood-Wakefield, birch w/wheat finish, 3 drw ea side, 50" L.660.00
Desk, Heywood-Wakefield, 1-drw table type, birch w/wheat finish, 40" L..315.00
Desk, Platner/Leopold, Pedestal, walnut-fr leather, bronze ped, 60" W.1,600.00
Dresser, Nakashima/Widdicomb, walnut, 12-drw in 3 rows, rpr, 32x106".2,500.00
Figurine, Raymor, cat, dressed in bl suit & red tie, partial label, 7".125.00
Figurine, Raymor, musk ox, cream w/orange & blk, appl horns, 4x5"..65.00
Flatware, Gio Ponti, Fraser, stainless, 1951, 29 pcs...................3,200.00
Headboard, Nakashima/Widdicomb, laurel woood vnr/walnut, king sz.950.00
Headboard, Wormley/Dunbar #4588A, drop-arms for reading, mahog fr.3,500.00
Lamp, Arteluce, plastic tubular form in ivory, 11½" 250.00
Lamp, floor; Castiglioni/Flos, stainless arc & shade, marble base, 95" .1,000.00
Lamp, floor; Nelson/Miller, Bubble, 24x12" 550.00
Lamp, floor; 3 conical enameled alum shades on arms, 1957, 60" .225.00
Lamp, hanging; Nelson/Miller, Bubble, 14x10" 270.00
Lamp, table; Von Nessen, brushed ss, swing arm, weighted base, 19x20"..70.00
Lamp, table; Von Nessen, polish ss, swing-arm, weighted base, 17".130.00
Magazine tree, Wormley/Dunbar #4765, birch & walnut, 25x28x16" .1,800.00
Ottoman, Nelson/Miller, Coconut, orig vinyl uphl, chrome fr, 16x24x18"..1,200.00
Plate, M Heaton, textured glass w/infused yel/gr/charcoal design, 7" .50.00
Rocker, Longhi-Parma, leather sling, walnut fr, cushion, +ottoman..500.00
Rocker, M Nissan, curved crest & armrests, rust cushions, 38" ...225.00
Runner, E Fields, wool, wht w/alternating mc bands, 27½x190"..315.00
Screen, Eames/Miller, 8 birch panels w/canvas webbing, 69x100"..3,000.00
Sculpture, JA Burlini, chromed bronze rings, walnut base, 33x20" .1,500.00
Settee, Jacobsen/Hansen, Swan, dk red uphl, alum base, 31x57x22" .4,000.00
Settee, Knolle, Parallel Bar, flame-stitch uphl, chrome fr, 58" W.1,000.00
Sideboard, Knoll #119 W, walnut w/4 caned doors, leather pulls, 77"..900.00
Sideboard, McCobb/Directional, mahog case in brass fr, travertine top..1,200.00
Sofa, Eames/Miller, Alum Group, vinyl slab seat & bk, alum fr, 73".3,500.00
Sofa, Eames/Miller, red reuphl, chrome-steel legs, 35x72x30" .1,300.00
Sofa, Fornasetti, HP faux bamboo metal fr, reuphl cushions, 32x72x24" .3,500.00
Sofa, Hans Wegner, teak bk fr/armrests, uphl bk/seat/arm cushions, 82".700.00
Sofa, Hoffman, tufted blk leather, blk/silver wood ft, 29x82x30" ..2,300.00
Sofa, Nelson/Miller, Marshmallow, 18-cushion, blk chrome fr, 32x51x34" .15,000.00
Sofa, Paulin/Artifort, Wave, purple uphl on steel fr, 23x63x28"..2,500.00
Sofa, Wilkes/Miller, Modular Group, foam-covered fr, dk bl uphl, 61"..550.00
Sofa, Wormley/Dunbar, 4 loose bk & 2 tufted seat cushions, 89", G ..650.00
Sofa, Wormley/Dunbar #5512, plaid reuphl, brass legs, 28x114x35".3,250.00
Stand, telephone; Hansen, formica top, 2 slide-out trays, 2 short drw .475.00
Stool, Eames/Miller, Time-Life, walnut, orig finish, 15x13" dia .1,400.00
Stool, rocking; Noguchi/Knoll, walnut w/chromed wire fittings, 17x14" .5,000.00
Table, bed; Knoll, wht lam top, walnut shelf/drw/fr, 18x19½" sq .200.00
Table, cocktail; Nelson/Miller, wht enamel 4-point base, lm top, 42".200.00
Table, coffee; Frankl/Johnson, bimorphic cork top, 3 mahog legs, 72" .2,400.00
Table, coffee; Frankl/Johnson, cork top, mahog bases, 48" dia .1,600.00
Table, coffee; Kagan, walnut triform base, glass top, 16x42" dia .9,500.00
Table, coffee; Robsjohn-Gibbings/Widdicomb, glass w/3-leg mahog base ..1,600.00
Table, coffee; Wormley/Dunbar, lm ash w/brass trim, marble top, 32" .900.00
Table, coffee; Wormley/Dunbar #5424, mosaic Murano glass tiles, 46" L.2,500.00
Table, console; Frankl/Johnson, cork top, 2 bleached oak bases, 40" W.1,100.00
Table, Eames/Miller, blk lm 'surfboard' top, zinc rod base, 10x89x29" .3,500.00
Table, Eames/Miller, cherry vnr, alum/blk enamel segmented base, 48" .400.00
Table, end; Wormley/Dunbar #5403, ash fr, blk lm top, shelf, 34x54x23" .500.00
Table, Gray E1027, chrome-plated ss tubular fr w/adjustable glass top.500.00
Table, Hansen, removable teak tray-top, ebonized folding legs, 24" dia .175.00
Table, Nakashima, Frenchman's Cove, walnut, central base, 29x50x49" .4,500.00
Table, Nelson/Miller, Swagged Leg, walnut, chrome legs, rpr, 30x54x32".1,600.00

Table, Robsjohn-Gibbings/Widdicomb, mahog, 2-tier, 22x30x30" ..**550.00**
Table, side; Platner/Knoll, glass top in bronze wire base, 18x16" dia.**325.00**
Table/desk, Knoll, woodgrain lav, blk metal fr, 29½x66x32".......**425.00**
Tapestry, abstract angular shapes, mc wool, sgn SD, 81x56" **2,350.00**
Tapestry, M Mood, Floral Summer Garden Modern, 55x50".......**950.00**
Tea cart, Kagan/Dreyfuss, wht lm lift-up top, walnut fr, 38x48x20"....**3,500.00**
Tray, Bel Geddes/Revere, chrome, 14½" **135.00**
Vanity, Loewy DF2000, red plastic drw fronts, 30x41x21".......**1,200.00**
Vase, Palshus Denmark, pottery, bl-gr mottle on bottle form, 8¼"...**460.00**
Vase, Raymor, mc patches & volcanic drips, att Fontani, 8x7½".**125.00**
Wall bracket, Wormley/Dunbar #4903, wall-mt ½-moon console w/drw..**1,200.00**
Wall hanging, Angelo Testa, 3-D wool suspensions on Lucite rod, 75x48".**2,000.00**
Wall unit, Platner/Knoll, 3 oak shelves over leather-covered credenza ..**2,600.00**
Wastebasket, McArthur, alum alloy, 14x12x12", VG **500.00**

Finch, Kay

Kay Finch and her husband, Braden, operated a small pottery in Corona Del Mar, California, from 1939 to 1963. The company remained small, employing from twenty to sixty local residents who Kay trained in all but the most requiring tasks, which she herself performed. The company produced animal and bird figurines, most notably dogs, Kay's favorites. Figures of 'Godey' type couples were also made, as were tableware (consisting of breakfast sets) and other artware. Most pieces were marked, but ink stamps often came off during cleaning.

After Kay's husband, Braden, died in 1962, she closed the business. Some of her molds were sold to Freeman-McFarlin of El Monte, California, who soon contracted with Kay for new designs. Though the realism that is so evident in her original works is still strikingly apparent in these later pieces, none of the vibrant pastels or signature curliques are there. Kay Finch died on June 21, 1993.

For further information we recommend *Kay Finch Ceramics, Her Enchanted World* (Schiffer), written by our advisors for this category, Mike Nickel and Cynthia Horvath; they are listed in the Directory under Michigan. *The New Kay Finch Ceramics Identification Guide* (published in 1996), containing many reprints of original catalog pages, is available from Frances Finch Webb; she is listed in the Directory under California. See also Clubs, Catalogs, and Newsletters.

Note: Original model numbers are included in the following descriptions — three-digit numbers indicate pre-1946 models. After 1946 they were assigned four-digit numbers, the first two digits representing the year of initial production. Unless otherwise described, our prices are for figurines decorated in multiple colors, not solid glazes.

Box, heart; #B5051, bird on lid, 2½" **75.00**
Canister, emb raspberry vines, purple/gr on wht, 9½" **125.00**
Canister, Santa, 10½" **125.00**
Figurine, Afghan Dog, sitting, #5553, 5¼"......................**550.00**
Figurine, Ambrosia, cat, #155, 10½", minimum value **495.00**
Figurine, Angel, #144a, #144b or #144c, ea **40.00**
Figurine, Bride & Groom, #204, 6½", 6", pr....................**450.00**
Figurine, Butch & Biddy, rooster & hen, #177, #178, he: 8½", pr.**175.00**
Figurine, Camel, w/ or w/out saddle, #465, 5", ea **395.00**
Figurine, Chanticleer, rooster, #129, 11" **250.00**
Figurine, Cherub, head, #212, 2¼"...............................**60.00**
Figurine, Choir Boy, kneeling, #211, 5½"........................**65.00**
Figurine, Cocker Spaniel, sitting, #5201, 8"...................**300.00**
Figurine, Cubby & Tubby, playful bears, #3837, #4848, 4¼", pr.**350.00**
Figurine, Dickey Bird, Mr & Mrs, #4905a, #4905b, ea **150.00**
Figurine, Dickey Bird, Mr or Mrs, w/skis, ea **500.00**
Figurine, Dog Show Boxer, #5025, 5x5"..........................**500.00**
Figurine, Doves, #5101 (tail down), #5102 (tail up), lustre glaze, pr...**200.00**
Figurine, Godey Man & Lady, #122, 9½", pr **150.00**

Figurine, Grumpy, pig, #165, 6x7½"............................**200.00**
Figurine, Happy Monkey, #4903, 11" **700.00**
Figurine, Hippo, eating tropical flower & w/bow, #5019, 5¾" **400.00**
Figurine, Hoot, owl, #187, 8½"................................**175.00**
Figurine, Jezebel, contented cat, #179, 6x9"..................**200.00**
Figurine, Littlest Angel, #4803, 2½" **125.00**
Figurine, Mermaid, #161, 6½" **400.00**

Figurine, Mitzi, Pomeranian, #465, pink, 10", from $600.00 to $700.00.

Figurine, Mr & Mrs Bird, #454, #453, 4½", 3", pr **175.00**
Figurine, Mumbo, sitting elephant, #4840, 4½"..................**125.00**
Figurine, Peasant Boy & Girl, #113, #117, 6¾", pr.............**85.00**
Figurine, Peep & Jeep, ducks, #178a, #178b, pr **75.00**
Figurine, Pekingese, #154, 14" L..............................**400.00**
Figurine, Persian Hunter (#5162), Persian Dancer (#5163), 9½", pr..**450.00**
Figurine, Polly Penguin, #467, 4¾"............................**150.00**
Figurine, Prancing Lamb, #168, 10½"...........................**475.00**
Figurine, Sassy, pig, looking up, #166, 3¾x4"..................**75.00**
Figurine, Sleepy Bear, #5004, 4½"............................**150.00**
Figurine, Squirrel Family, #108a/b/c, 3½" parents, 1¾" baby **125.00**
Figurine, Toot, owl, #188, 5¾"................................**75.00**
Figurine, Turkey, #5843, 4½" **125.00**
Figurine, Vicki, dog, pk & wht, #455, 11" **1,000.00**
Figurine, Violet, elephant, #190, 17".........................**2,500.00**
Planter, Animal Book series, #B5145, 6½", ea **75.00**
Plaque, Baby Fish, 2¼x3"......................................**60.00**
Plate, Santa face, 6½" **75.00**
Toby mug, Santa, w/hat lid, 5½" **150.00**
Tureen, Turkey, #5361, platinum/gray, 9", w/ladle **450.00**
Vase, Elephant, #B5155, 6"....................................**95.00**
Wall pocket, Girl & Boy, #5501, 10", ea.......................**350.00**

Findlay Onyx and Floradine

Findlay, Ohio, was the location of the Dalzell, Gilmore, and Leighton Glass Company, one of at least sixteen companies that flourished there between 1886 and 1901. Their most famous ware, Onyx, is very rare. It was produced for only a short time beginning in 1889 due to the heavy losses incurred in the manufacturing process.

Onyx is layered glass, usually found in creamy white with a dainty floral pattern accented with metallic lustre that has been trapped between the two layers. Other colors found on rare occasions include a light amber (with either no lustre or with gilt flowers), light amethyst (or lavender), and rose. Although old tradepaper articles indicate the company originally intended to produce the line in three distinct colors, long-time Onyx collectors report that aside from the white, production was very limited. Other colors of Onyx are very rare, and the few examples that are found tend to support the theory that production of colored Onyx ware remained for the most part in the experimental stage. Even three-layered items have been found (they are extremely rare) decorated with three-color flowers. As a rule of thumb, using white Onyx prices as a basis for evaluation, expect to pay five to ten times more for colored examples.

Floradine is a separate line that was made with the Onyx molds. A single-layer rose satin glassware with white opal flowers, it is usually valued at twice the price of colored Onyx.

Chipping around the rims is very common, and price is determined to a great extent by condition. Our advisors for this category are Betty and Clarence Maier; they are listed in the Directory under Pennsylvania. Unless noted otherwise, our prices are for examples in near-mint condition.

Floradine

Bowl, fluted, squat bulbous base, 4"	950.00
Celery vase, fluted cylinder neck, bulbous body, 6½"	1,800.00
Celery vase, fluted cylinder neck, bulbous body, 6½", EX	1,000.00
Creamer, bulbous, 4⅝"	950.00
Mustard pot	1,550.00
Spooner, 4¾"	1,285.00
Sugar bowl, bulbous, w/lid, 5½"	1,200.00
Sugar shaker	1,500.00
Syrup pitcher	2,500.00
Toothpick holder, 2½"	1,500.00
Tumbler, slightly bulbous, 3⅝"	1,000.00

Onyx

Bowl, wht w/raspberry decor, fluted top, 2½x4½"	2,000.00
Bowl, wht w/silver decor, 2¾x8"	350.00
Butter dish, wht w/silver decor, 3x6"	1,250.00
Celery vase, wht w/silver decor, 6¾"	485.00
Covered dish, wht w/silver decor, 5½"	1,000.00
Creamer, wht w/silver decor, 4½"	485.00
Lamp, oil; blk opaque base, sm rpr to collar, 7¼"	6,500.00
Mustard, wht w/raspberry decor, hinged metal lid, 3¼"	2,900.00
Pitcher, apricot w/orange decor, 4½"	4,200.00
Pitcher, water; wht w/silver decor, 8"	1,200.00
Shaker, wht w/silver decor, minor wear, 2¾"	650.00
Shaker, wht w/silver decor, Pat 2/23/1889, 2¾"	800.00
Spooner, raisin w/wht decor, rare color, 4", EX	1,500.00

Spooner, raisin with white decor, 4", NM, $2,250.00. (Photo courtesy John A. Shuman III)

Spooner, wht w/orange decor, 4"	1,500.00
Spooner, wht w/silver decor, 4", EX	250.00
Spooner, wht w/silver decor, 4"	525.00
Sugar bowl, wht w/silver decor, 5½", EX	475.00
Sugar shaker, wht w/silver decor, brass mts, mfg defects, 5½"	335.00
Sugar shaker, wht w/silver decor, 5½", from $400 to	550.00
Syrup, gr (unusual color) w/silver decor, 7¾	3,000.00
Syrup, wht w/silver decor, 7¾", from $850 to	1,150.00
Toothpick holder, wht w/silver decor, from $325 to	500.00

Tumbler, wht w/apricot decor, lt line unseen from w/in, bbl	2,300.00
Tumbler, wht w/silver decor, bbl shape, 3½", EX	450.00
Tumbler, wht w/silver decor, thin str sides (rare), 3¾"	1,250.00

Fire Marks

The earliest American fire marks date back to 1752 when 'The Philadelphia Contributionship for the Insurance of Houses From Loss By Fire' (the official name of this company, who is still in business) used a plaque to identify property they insured. Early fire marks were made of cast iron, sheet brass, lead, copper, tin, and zinc. The insignia of the insurance company appeared on each mark, and they would normally reward the volunteer fire department who managed to be the first on the scene to battle the fire. (Altercations occasionally broke out between firefighting companies vying for the chance to earn the reward!)

Fire marks were first used in Great Britain about 1780 and were more elaborate than U.S. marks. The first English examples were made of lead and carried a policy number. They were used to identify insured property to the fire brigades maintained by the insurance companies. Most copper and brass fire marks are of European origin.

During the latter half of the nineteenth century, municipalities replaced the volunteer fire companies and fire brigades with paid fire departments. No longer was there a need for fire marks, so the companies discontinued their use (though some companies still use fire marks for advertising purposes). See *The Fire Mark Circle of America*, listed under Clubs, Catalogs, and Newsletters in the Directory.

Prices listed are for legitimate fire marks in good to excellent condition. Reproductions are identified when possible. Many fire marks have been and continue to be widely reproduced in cast iron and aluminum. They are sold legitimately as decorator items and collectible reproductions. Fantasy items, on the other hand, are not reproductions, as they depict items that never existed in the first place. They are twentieth-century fabrications and never existed in their present form prior to this recent production. They appear in cast iron, aluminum, and other mediums.

Baltimore Equitable Society...MD, pnt CI, 1794, 9⅜x10"	1,300.00
British Fireman's Insurance Co of Baltimore MD, pnt CI, 11¾"	325.00
City Insurance Co Cin, CI, 12½" L	850.00
Eagle in oval, gold & blk rpr, bk: Issued 1830 by Ins Co of NA, 11"	275.00
German Freeport Ill, pnt tin, 2½x7", EX, from $100 to	150.00
Insured Home New York, tin, 5¼x8⅛", VG	80.00
London Assurance Co AD 1720, tin, British, common, 10x11¾", EX	75.00
Mutual Insurance of Phila, gr tree type on wooden shield	100.00
Ohio Farmers Ins Co in Leroy OH, tin	75.00
Phoenix, copper, many varieties, worn	90.00
Royal Exchange Assurance London, gold traces, issued 1835, 8⅞x4"	200.00
Tree form, CI, gr pnt, 11¼x8"	175.00
Valiant Hose No 2, pnt CI, 19th C, fantasy item, 10⅝"	15.00

Firefighting Collectibles

Firefighting collectibles have always been a good investment in terms of value appreciation. Many times the market will be temporarily affected by wild price swings caused by the 'supply and demand principle' as related to a small group of aggressive collectors. These collectors will occasionally pay well over market value for a particular item they need or want. Once their desires are satisfied, prices seem to return to their normal range. It has been noticed that during these periods of high prices, many items enter the marketplace that otherwise would remain in collections. This may (it has in the past) cause a price depression (due again to the 'supply and demand principle' of market behavior).

The recent phenomenon of Internet buying and selling of firefighting collectibles and antiques has caused wild swings in prices for some fire collectibles. The cause of this is the ability to reach into vast international markets. It appears that this has resulted in a significant escalation in prices paid for select items. The bottom-line items still languish price wise, but at least continue to change hands. This marketplace continues to be active, and many outstanding items have appeared recently in the fire antiques and collectibles field. But when all is said and done, the careful purchase of quality, well-documented firefighting items will continue to be an enjoyable hobby and an excellent investment opportunity.

Today there is a large, active group of collectors for fire department antiques (items over 100 years old) and an even larger group seeking related collectibles (those less than 100 years old). Our advisors for this category (except grenades) are H. Thomas and Patricia Laun; they are listed in the Directory under New York. (SASE required.)

Fire grenades preceded the pressurized metal fire extinguishers used today. They were filled with a mixture of chemicals and water and made of glass thin enough to shatter easily when thrown into the flames. Many varieties of colors and shapes were used. Not all the grenades listed contain salt-brine solution, some, such as the Red Comet, contain carbon tetrachloride, a powerful solvent that is also a health hazard and an environmental threat. (It attacks the ozone layer.) It is best to leave any contents inside the glass balls. The source of grenade prices are mainly auction results; current retail values will fluctuate. Our fire grenades advisor is Willy Young; he is listed in the Directory under Nevada.

Key:
ALF — American LaFrance   s&a — soda & acid
CCL4 — carbon tetrachloride

Gong, Gamewell, 15" brass bell in fancy oak case, ca 1880, 38", EX+, $4,200.00.

Ashtray, chrome, Mack bulldog in center........................30.00
Axe, Viking style, wooden hdl (rpl), G.........................300.00
Badge, Asst Foreman Hook & Ladder..., steel w/helmet/trumpets at top ...45.00
Badge, Lowell FD, silver w/high eagle helmet/trumpets/etc...........65.00
Badge, Whitman FD H&L 1 Foreman, eng.........................40.00
Bell, muffin; brass, trn wood hdl, 3½", VG.....................250.00
Belt, parade; Washington on wht leather, EX w/keeper................85.00
Book, Am La France Operator's Manual, detailed apparatus engravings ...150.00
Book, How To Become a Fireman, Chief Publishing Co of NY, 1909, EX ..85.00
Bookends, Hartford Fire Ins Co, elk figural, pr RI,........................75.00
Box, ballot; w/blk & wht marbles, complete, EX 75.00
Bucket, leather, blk w/gold letters: C Goodall No 1, rpr, VG 425.00
Bucket, leather, Boston Street...Salem 1826, 10¾", VG..........2,415.00
Bucket, leather, gold banner: Wiscasset Fire Society...1883, VG..825.00
Bucket, leather, gr/blk pnt over orig red w/name & 1843, wear, 20" 825.00
Bucket, leather, Leonidas H Titcomb Jr 1820..., rpl hdls, 13" ..3,200.00
Bucket, leather, mustard pnt w/banner & lettering, complete, EX .1,050.00
Bucket, leather, name & 1806 in oval w/winged goddess, 11x9¼", VG .2,000.00

Bucket, leather, Warren Fire Club...1829, pnt, broken hdl, 12"...2,415.00
Bucket, leather w/blk pnt lettering & 1929 in cartouch, 12", EX...4,400.00
Bucket, leather w/gilt stenciled name, rpl hdl, wear, 12½" 150.00
Can, Minimax Refill, tin, graphics on front, G.........................40.00
Cap, dress; tan w/gold braid & VFA, gold-tone FD buttons 15.00
Clip, London Assurance, NY branch, early................................35.00
Decanter, Mack 1911 rotary fire pumper on wht ceramic, dog stopper...45.00
Drawing, chemical horse-drawn wagon, pen & ink, dtd 1935, 10x20"..150.00
Extinguisher, DC Ranger, complete 35.00
Extinguisher, Pyrene CTC, brass, hand pumped 15.00
Extinguisher, Waterloo Chemical Dry Powder, Reed & Campbell, 20-oz.75.00
Frontispc, leather, high front, blk & wht raised letters: Engine 1 OFD..225.00
Frontispc, leather, low, for New Yorker by Cairns, Fairmont 1 Lansdale ..15.00
Frontispc, leather, low, Lieutenant FW FC, single trumpet 15.00
Frontispc, leather, wht high front, 2nd Asst Engineer, VG 300.00
Grenade, Harden, aqua-gr, quilted, pt 400.00
Grenade, Harden, aqua-gr quilted pnt.................................500.00
Grenade, Harden Improved, clear, 2-pc 950.00
Grenade, Harden's Star, (flat/twisted star), turq, English, pt 500.00
Grenade, Harden's Star, cobalt, qt....................................500.00
Grenade, Harden's Star, Cornflower Blue, qt 450.00
Grenade, Harden's Star, yel-gr, pt....................................650.00
Grenade, Harkness, cobalt 500.00
Grenade, Hayward's, aqua, pleated, ⅔-qt...............................250.00
Grenade, Hayward's, turq, pleated, pt 500.00
Grenade, Hayward's Diamond, cobalt (lt), pt 650.00
Grenade, HSN, Nuttings, golden amber 250.00
Grenade, Imperial, lime gr w/crown on top, English 250.00
Grenade, Santa Fe Route, clear......................................1,000.00
Grenade, Swift, smoky-clear, English 1,000.00
Grenade, UNIC, amber, Fr 650.00
Helmet, aluminum, leather front: Engine 2 HFD, w/liner...........125.00
Helmet, aluminum, leather front: Wiscasset 14, VG 75.00
Helmet, aluminum, metal frontispc: Lieut WFD, w/liner 125.00
Helmet, blk composite, high front w/Machais (ME), Bullard Co SF USA..25.00
Helmet, brass w/brass front: fire ball/castle, VG.....................125.00
Helmet, leather, high eagle, aluminum frontispc: #1, Cairns, w/liner....450.00
Helmet, leather, high eagle, Citizen's Hose 6, w/liner, VG..........225.00
Helmet, leather, high eagle, front shield; Sea Grit 1 Fire Co, VG..350.00
Helmet, leather, high eagle, frontispc: Chief, sm rpr 450.00
Helmet, leather, high eagle, frontispc: HHFD 60 Bunn, VG 225.00
Helmet, leather, high eagle, frontispc: Lambert...NY, w/liner, VG..575.00
Helmet, leather, high eagle, Phoenix Hose 5 HFD.....................825.00
Helmet, leather, high eagle, tin front, Anderson & Jones..., 1850s..635.00
Helmet, leather, high eagle, 32 comb, frontispc: VFA NSFD, Cairns, VG .600.00
Helmet, leather, high eagle, 64 combs, frontispc, VG 450.00
Helmet, parade; Friendship & HP scene on blk, flat brim, 1860s, EX.....8,850.00
Helmet, salesman's sample, Cairns mini w/red frontispc.............250.00
Helmet, silver-tone w/leather liner 65.00
Holder, nozzle; metal, lg 65.00
Key, alarm system; brass, Gamewell, VG 65.00
Lantern, Dietz Fire King, blk pnt, clear globe, mixed metals, EX ..150.00
Lantern, Dietz Fire King, NP brass w/red globe, VG..................225.00
Lantern, Dietz Fire King, red pnt, tin w/copper tank, 14", G 140.00
Lantern, Dietz Fire King Dept, tin/nickel, Am LaFrance, complete, EX..300.00
Lantern, Dietz Tubular, tin, slide over cage/clear globe, 1881-93, EX ..265.00
Lantern, hand, Vulture No 4/Quincy, brass, 1851, EX+ 850.00
Lantern, wrist; Joseph S Abbott eng globe, ca 1884.................1,500.00
Lantern, wrist; SP, eng RAPFD in globe, 13", VG....................650.00
Mug, Defiance #5 1908 in bl on wht ceramic, EX 75.00
Mug, Firemen's Assoc Of...PA 1907, silver print on wht ceramic, EX ...55.00
Nozzle, brass, playpipe w/1" tip, mk Am La France....................125.00
Nozzle, fog; brass, shut-off, Akron, 9½".............................35.00
Nozzle, Underwriters, cord wrap, Powhattan B&I Works, VG.......75.00

Paperweight, Monarch Fire Insurance..Cleveland, pewter-like, 5½".100.00
Photo, steam fire engine, Boston FD, 7½x9½"+mat 150.00
Playpipe, brass & copper, cord wrap, short underwriter's type 100.00
Rattle, alarm; wooden, single reed, 9¼" L, VG...........................100.00
Rattle, alarm; wooden w/single reed, lg 125.00
Spanner wrench, 6-function, 4 house fittings/1 hex in center, P1699...60.00
Strainer, NP brass, 17x5" dia...45.00
Trumpet, presentation; emb florals/high-eagle helmet/etc, 19th C, 18".1,050.00
Trumpet, presentation; eng florals/steamer, 20" 1,100.00
Wrench, brass, 7-function, 12¾x3¼" 98.00

Fireplace Accessories and Implements

In the colonial days of our country, fireplaces provided heat in the winter and were used year round to cook food in the kitchen. The implements that were a necessary part of these functions were varied and have become treasured collectibles, many put to new use in modern homes as decorative accessories. Gypsy pots may hold magazines; copper and brass kettles, newly polished and gleaming, contain dried flowers or green plants. Firebacks, highly ornamental iron panels that once reflected heat and protected masonry walls, are now sometimes used as wall decorations. By Victorian times the cook stove had replaced the kitchen fireplace, and many of these early utensils were already obsolete; but as a source of heat and comfort, the fireplace continued to be used for several more decades. See also Wrought Iron.

Andirons, bell metal & iron, lemon finials, spurred legs, 19th C, 18".750.00
Andirons, brass, ball finial/chamfered column/spurred legs, 1830, 21"..1,100.00
Andirons, brass, ball ft, scalloped cabriole legs, ring trn, 18" ..350.00
Andirons, brass, ball top, dbl spur legs, ball ft, MA, 1800s, rpr, 15" ..460.00
Andirons, brass, Geo III, spured cabriole legs, ball/claw ft, 22" .285.00
Andirons, brass & iron, lemon finials, trn shafts/slipper ft, Am, 17"..750.00
Andirons, brass & iron baluster form, ribbed/faceted shaft/plinth, 22" .700.00
Andirons, brass Chpndl w/spiral finial, hex block, claw & ball ft, 24" ...5,750.00
Andirons, brass w/iron knife-blade shaft, urn finial, 1780s, 22" ..940.00
Andirons, CI, Geo WA figures, standing, in waistcoat & boots, pnt, 15".1,750.00
Andirons, CI, upright cat w/gr glass eyes, 16", VG 200.00
Andirons, wrought iron, gooseneck polyhedron finials, ca 1800, 18"....500.00
Andirons, wrought iron, serpentine scroll bases, basketweave columns...300.00
Bellows, blk over cream smoke decor, fruit/foliage on front, rstr, 18"..385.00
Bellows, gr pnt w/mc floral on leather, 17x7" 60.00
Bellows, turtle-bk, HP bl-gray bird, yel bands, brass nozzle, 18", VG..385.00
Bellows, turtle-bk, HP fruit on yel, worn leather/pnt, 17" 600.00
Bellows, turtle-bk, stenciled fruit on blk rpt, faded, 17", VG 220.00
Broiler, wrought iron, rotary type, scrollwork, 32" L 150.00
Broiler, wrought iron, tripod base, penny ft, adjusts, 28" H.........300.00
Coal box, copper, urn finial, ftd, brass fittings, English, 16x16"..500.00
Coal bucket, brass, emb floral & fruit, English, late 1800s, G ..275.00
Coal hod, brass, punched design, emb ft, English, mid-1800s, 22"...700.00
Coal scuttle, lacquered copper, 16" 275.00

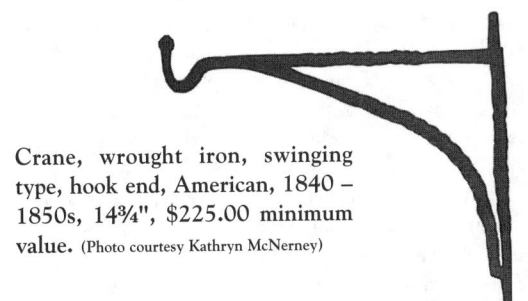

Crane, wrought iron, swinging type, hook end, American, 1840 – 1850s, 14¾", $225.00 minimum value. (Photo courtesy Kathryn McNerney)

Fender, brass, bowed front w/vertical wire rods & decorative weaving ...500.00
Fender, brass, rtc/ribbed base w/reeded divisions, 6 finals, 11x47"...220.00
Fender, brass & wire D-form w/swag & scrollwork, 1800s, 24x40x14" ...1,850.00
Fender, brass & wire D-form w/wirework screen, 1830s, 15x49x15".1,400.00
Fender, brass & wire D-form w/3 urn finials, ca 1900, 18x46x16" ..700.00
Fender, brass Emp style, paw ft, pierced aprons, 20th C, 8x57x14"...110.00
Fender, brass rim over entwined wirework, late 1700s, 12x50" ...550.00
Fireback, brass, cut-out flowers & birds, English, 1870s, 18x19" .1,200.00
Fireback, CI w/tavern scene, wrought log rack, brass finials, 26x25" ...330.00
Frying pan, iron & sheet metal, tripod base, ca 1800, 22x32".....285.00
Insert, Fed style, brass finials, bow front, sgn Wyer & Noble 350.00
Kettle rack, wrought iron, 4 arms w/scrolled ends........................85.00
Log bin, brass w/acorn finial dome lid, tripod w/paw ft, 1860s, 20x14"...700.00
Pan, wrought iron, 3-legged, 6½"+11" hdl................................200.00
Roasting jack, brass & iron, Chesterman's Pat..., 19th C, 19" drop..700.00
Screen, cvd walnut w/pierced crest, lovers needlework, 1850s, 45x30" .865.00
Surround, gilt & patinated Louis XVI style, urn finials w/putto, 57"....4,250.00
Toaster, wrought iron, spiral arch design, 1700s, 16" 250.00

Fisher, Harrison

Harrison Fisher (1875 – 1934), noted illustrator and creator of the Fisher Girl, was the son of landscape artist, Hugh Antoine Fisher. His career began in his teens in San Francisco where he did artwork for the Hearst papers. Later in New York his drawings of beautiful American women attracted much attention and graced the covers of the most popular magazines of the day such as *Puck, Ladies' Home Journal, Saturday Evening Post,* and *Cosmopolitan.* He also illustrated novels, and his art books are treasured. His drawings appeared on thousands of postcards and posters. His creation of the Fisher Girl and his panel of six scenes of the *Greatest Moments in a Woman's Life* made him the most sought-after and well-paid illustrator of his day.

Book, American Beauties, Bobbs Merrill, 1909, VG+ 285.00
Book, Bachelor Bells, Dodd Mead & Co, pictorial cover, 1908, EX ...160.00
Book, Hiawatha, Bobbs Merrill, pictorial cover, 1906, VG 165.00
Postcard, Autumn's Beauty, Reinthal & Newman #937, unused, EX ..35.00
Postcard, Behave, Reinthal & Newman #302, G+............................9.00
Postcard, By Right of Conquest, Reinthal & Newman #860, unused, EX ..40.00
Postcard, Chocolate, Reinthal & Newman #2048, unused, EX ..40.00
Postcard, Contentment, Reinthal & Newman Watercolor Series #383, VG .22.00
Postcard, Engagement Days, Reinthal & Newman #103, VG+.....25.00
Postcard, Evening Hour, Reinthal & Newman #861, unused, EX.45.00
Postcard, First Evening in Their Own Home, Reinthal & Newman #189, EX..35.00
Postcard, Honeymoon, Reinthal & Newman #189, unused, EX ..35.00
Postcard, Kiss, Reinthal & Newman #108, VG+ 20.00
Postcard, Miss Santa Claus, Reinthal & Newman #182, unused, EX..50.00
Postcard, My Hero, Reinthal & Newman #977, unused, EX+ 200.00
Postcard, Peggy, Reinthal & Newman #871, unused, EX..............40.00
Postcard, Proposal, Reinthal & Newman #186, unused, EX+ 35.00
Postcard, Reflections, Reinthal & Newman Series 101, VG 9.00
Postcard, Sense of Smell, Reinthal & Newman Watercolor Series #701, EX.45.00
Postcard, Trousseau, Reinthal & Newman #187, unused, VG+/EX..28.00
Postcard, Wedding, Reinthal & Newman #188, unused, EX.........35.00
Postcard, What To See in America, Reinthal & Newman #2054, unused, EX.40.00
Print, Buttercup Fairy, EX 25.00
Print, Celandine Fairy, holding yel flowers, sm 20.00
Print, Danger, lady w/hatpin, 1908, 10¾x8¾", +orig fr................85.00
Print, Eyes Under the Cowl, 1909, 10x8", VG 30.00
Print, In Days of Old, couple w/in heart, 1909, 10x8", VG 25.00
Print, In the Toils w/Cupid, 10x8", VG.......................................30.00
Print, Leisure Moments, brunette w/cat, 1909, 10x8", EX.............42.50
Print, Odd Moments, lady w/rose & playful kitten, 7x5", EX........27.50

Print, Penelope & Randolph, horsewoman w/man & dog, 1907, 11x8⅝".20.00
Print, Rich Man's Children, couple at piano, 9¾x7¼", EX...........35.00
Print, Roses, lady in pk w/long-stem rose, 11⅜x9", EX 50.00
Print, Strollers, 1907, 9x6", VG..17.50
Print, Sweetheart, lady in fancy hat & long curls, 1909, 10x8", VG ...30.00
Print, Tempted by the Devil, 1907, 9¾x7¼", EX 30.00
Print, Those Bewitching Eyes, lady glancing to side, 10x8", VG ..30.00
Print, Wanted an Answer, couple & dog on porch, 11x8⅝", EX ...30.00

Fishing Collectibles

Collecting old fishing tackle is becoming more popular every year. Though at first most interest was geared toward old lures and some reels, rods, advertising, and miscellaneous items are quickly gaining ground. Values are given for examples in excellent or better condition and should be used only as a guide. For more information we recommend *19th-Century Fishing Lures* by Arlan Carter; *Fishing Lure Collectibles, Vol. 1*, by Dudley Murphy and Rick Edmisten, and *Fishing Lure Collectibles, Vol. 2*, by Dudley and Deanie Murphy; *Collector's Encyclopedia of Creek Chub Lures and Collectibles, Second Edition*, by Harold E. Smith, MD; *Commercial Fish Decoys* by Frank R. Baron; *The Heddon Legacy* by Bill Roberts and Rob Pavey; *Captain John's Fishing Tackle* by John A. Kolbeck and Russel E. Lewis; and *Modern Fishing Lure Collectibles* by Russel E. Lewis. All are published by Collector Books. Our advisor for this category is Dave Hoover; he is listed in the Directory under Indiana.

Creel, AE Nelson, split willow/leather, old snap closure, VG 330.00
Creel, Turtle Trade Mark brand, wicker w/cvd wood turtle latch, EX.550.00
Creel, wicker w/leather straps, Made in Japan label, NM 60.00

Creel, woven whole willow, carved turtle latch, built-in ruler in lid, stamped Turtle Trade Mark, EX, $2,000.00.

Decoy, Bear Creek Bait Co, Type III, from $25 to 35.00
Decoy, Bethel, critter, from $35 to...50.00
Decoy, Brown Brothers, from $35 to...45.00
Decoy, Frankln Discher, lg, from $70 to 90.00
Decoy, Martin Kroph, from $50 to..75.00
Decoy, Moonlight/Paw Paw Bait Co, from $125 to 175.00
Decoy, Randal Decoy Co, from $25 to 75.00
Decoy, sunfish, wood w/metal fins, Leroy Howell, early 20th C, 4¼".825.00
Decoy, trapping; Eagle Claw, from $250 to...................................350.00
Decoy, trapping; Gabriel Fish Trap, from $125 to 150.00
Fish grabber, from $25 to 35.00
Ice saw, from $25 to..35.00
Lure, CB Hibbard, heart shape, Pat March 25 84...No 3, from $100 to .150.00
Lure, Creek Chub, Ding Bat #5100, 2 trebles, 1937, 2", from $30 to.50.00
Lure, Creek Chub, Husky Musky #600, 2 trebles, 1925, 5", from $100 to .150.00
Lure, Creek Chub, Wiggle Fish #2400, 2 trebles, 1925, 3½", $40 to..50.00
Lure, Enterprise Mfg, Climax Bass Bait, non-luminous, ca 1894-1900 ..125.00
Lure, Enterprise Mfg, Fine Mottled Pearl Spoon, 1894-1900, $30 to.40.00
Lure, Enterprise Mfg, Floating Meadow Frog, 1899, from $75 to .125.00
Lure, Enterprise Mfg, frog, gimp leader, #712, ca 1900, from $50 to .75.00
Lure, GM Skinner, weedless casting spoon, brass or copper, from $20 to.30.00

Lure, Heddon, Baby Vamp #7400, 2 trebles, 1935, 3½", from $40 to..60.00
Lure, Heddon, Crab Wiggler #1800, 2 trebles, 1916, 4", from $50 to..75.00
Lure, Heddon, Fat Killer Wooden Minnow, 5 trebles, 1912, 3¾"...375.00
Lure, Heddon, King Zig-Zag #8350, 2 trebles, 1939, 5", from $50 to .75.00
Lure, Hill & Hibbard, spring holds spinner from shaft, dbl, $75 to ..100.00
Lure, Jamison, Bill's Bass Getter, 2 dbls, 1927, 2¾", from $150 to..200.00
Lure, Jamison, Muskie Nemo Bait, 3 dbls, 1912, 4", from $300 to .400.00
Lure, JB McHarg, dmn-pattern kidney spoon, solid swivel, #3, $250 to .300.00
Lure, JB McHarg, Kidney Bat, reflective ball, Pat 1886, from $20 to.40.00
Lure, JT Buel, Buel's Kidney Fly Spoon, made in 11 szs, ea from $30 to ...40.00
Lure, JT Buel, SP copper spoon shape, mk Pat...Buel Whitehall 1854.850.00
Lure, Keeling, Bass Kee-Wig, 2 trebles, glitters, 1920s, 3", $70 to ...80.00
Lure, Keeling, Flat Expert, 4 special dbls/1 treble, 1915, 3⅝" 175.00
Lure, Keeling, Top Water Bait, 2 trebles, 1925, 3½", from $70 to....80.00
Lure, Moonlight, Open Mouth Eat-Us, 1 treble, 1926, 2", from $50 to.75.00
Lure, Moonlight, Wilson Wobbler, 3 trebles, 1921, 4", from $40 to .60.00
Lure, Paw Paw, McGingy, 1 treble, twirling action, 1930, 2", $25 to .40.00
Lure, Paw Paw, Trout Caster, 2 trebles, 1936, 3½", from $50 to....75.00
Lure, Pflueger, Bearcat #6400, 2 trebles, 1924, 4½", from $150 to..200.00
Lure, Pflueger, Kent Floater, 3 trebles, 1915, 2¾", from $150 to.200.00
Lure, Pflueger, Simplex Minnow, 1 treble, 1907, 1¾", from $100 to.150.00
Lure, Pflueger, Wizard Wiggler #4700, 2 trebles, 1925, 3½", $30 to..50.00
Lure, Sea Witch Jr #6553, 2 trebles, 1930, 3¼", from $75 to.......100.00
Lure, Shakespeare, Metal-Plated Minnow #33, 3 trebles, 1915, 3" ..225.00
Lure, Shakespeare, Revolution, 3 trebles, acorn shape, 1909, 3½".80.00
Lure, Shakespeare, Submarine Minnow #42, 3 trebles, 1925, 3¾"..90.00
Lure, South Bend, Coast-Oreno #985, 1 single, 1924, 4½", $30 to.45.00
Lure, South Bend, Mouse-Oreno #949, 1 treble, 1932, 2¾", $30 to...60.00
Lure, South Bend, Surface Minnow, 3 trebles, 1910, 3⅝", $125 to..150.00
Lure, South Bend, Underwater Minnow #905, 5 trebles, 1935, 3⅝".90.00
Lure, TH Bate & Co, No 3 Lake Spoon, mk TH Bate NY, from $200 to.250.00
Lure, TH Bate & Co, Serpentine Minnow, Pat appl for, sz #1 (lg).350.00
Lure, WD Chapman, Allure, stamped 1-pc metal blade, from $100 to.125.00
Lure, WD Chapman, brass fish shape, 3½", from $250 to...........300.00
Lure, WD Chapman, fly rod spinner, short blades (less than 1"), $50 to..75.00
Lure, WD Chapman, Perfect Bait, willow-leaf pattern, 2⅝", $125 to .225.00
Lure, WD Chapman, Safe Deposit Minnow, NP, 1897, 4½", minimum..2,500.00
Lure, Wilson, Bassmerizer, 2 trebles, 1917, 3⅝", from $100 to....150.00
Lure, WTJ Lowe, New Fly Spoon, burnished brass, made in 4 szs, $20 to..30.00
Reel, Acme-Pat Jan'y 29...84, Ferris wheel type skeleton, 2½", VG...825.00
Reel, F Godfrey, high quality, drag lever (unusual), 3⅜", EX 350.00
Reel, Garcia #1422, Landex Fly, med width, 4", EXIB..................85.00
Reel, Hardy St Geo Jr Trout, agate line guide, 2¾", NMIB.....1,025.00
Reel, Hardy Uniqua Trout, click type, Duplicated Mark II stamp, 2⅝"..360.00
Reel, Leonard Mills, German silver/hard rubber, raised pillar, 4", EX...660.00
Reel, Otto Zwarg #400, hand-made German silver, sz 2/0, 3⅜", EX .1,650.00
Reel, Seamaster Mark II, hand made, anti-reverse, 3¼", EX.......770.00
Reel, Thompson #100 Fly, free spool, 2 drag controls, brass ft, 3¼".385.00
Reel, Thos J Conroy...Pat Oct 8' '89, aluminum/German silver, 1⅞" .990.00
Rod, Garrison #201 Trout, 2-pc, 2-tip, orig plug, 7', EX w/bag .5,600.00
Rod, Goodwin Granger Co Trout, 3-pc, 1-tip, 9', VG in bag......110.00
Rod, Leonard, 3-pc, 2-tip, rfn, 9½', M in case 200.00
Rod, Orvis Battenkill Trout, 2-pc, 2-tip, dirty hdl, 7½', EX in bag ..550.00
Rod, Orvis Equinox Trout, 2-pc, 1 tip, screw down lock, 8', EX.440.00
Rod, Orvis Impregnated Pat Pending, detachable hdl, 6½', NM in bag.165.00
Rod, Orvis Superfine Trout, 2-pc, 2-tip, cork, 6½', EX in bag .600.00
Rod, Payne Trout, 2-pc, 2-tip, 6½', M rstr................................3,300.00
Rod, Pezon et Michel Parabolic Supreme Trout, 2-pc, 1 tip, 8½', M..220.00
Rod, Thomas & Thomas, 2-pc, 2-tip, 4 weight line, walnut, 6½', NM..1,200.00
Rod, Thomas & Thomas Graphite Vagabone Briefcase Trout, 7-pc, 8', M.385.00
Rod, W Mitchell...1883 Trout, 3-pc, 3-tip, hdl removes, 11', VG ..715.00
Spear, eel; whistle shape, from $75 to...100.00
Spear, Pflueger, from $10 to 20.00
Spear, Shurkatch, from $5 to 20.00

Flags of the United States

Over the past few years the popularity of vintage flags has grown dramatically, and prices have risen greatly as a result. The pending restoration of the Fort McHenry Flag (The Star Spangled Banner) has also created greater public interest in flag collecting.

The brevity and imprecise language of the first Flag Act of 1777 allowed great artistic license for America's early flag makers. This resulted in a rich variety of imaginative star formations which coexisted with more conventional row patterns. In 1912 inviolate design standards were established for the new 48-star flag, but the banners of our earlier history continue to survive:

The 'Great Star' pattern — configured from the combined stars of the union, appeared in various star denominations for about 50 years, then gradually disappeared in the post-Civil War years.

The utilitarian 'scatter' pattern — created through the random placement of stars, is traceable to the formative years of our nation and remained a design influence through most of the nineteenth century.

The 'wreath' pattern — first appearing in the form of simple single-wreath formations, eventually evolved into the elegant double- and triple-wreath medallion patterns of the Centennial period.

Acquisition of specific star denominations is also a primary consideration in the collecting process. Pre-Civil War flags of 33 stars or less are very scarce and are typically treated as 'blue chip' items. Civil War-era flags of 34 and 35 stars also stand among the most sought-after denominations. Market demand for 36-, 37-, and 38-star flags is strong but less broad-based, while interest in the unofficial 39-, 40-, 41-, and 42-star examples is largely confined to flag aficionados. The very rare 43 remains in a class by itself and is guaranteed to attract the attention of the serious collector.

Row-patterned flags of 44, 45, and 46 stars still turn up with some frequency and serve as a source of more modestly priced vintage flags. Ordinary 48-star flags flood the flea markets and are priced accordingly, while the short-lived 49 is regarded as a legitimate collectible. Thirteen-star flags, produced over a period of more than 200 years, surface in many forms and must be assessed on a case-by-case basis.

Many flag buffs favor sizes that are manageable for wall display, while others are attracted to the more monumental proportions. Allowances are typically made for the normal wear and tear — it goes with the territory. But severe fabric deterioration and other forms of excessive physical damage are legitimate points of negotiation.

The dollar value of a flag is by no means based upon age alone. The wide price swings in the listing below have been influenced by a variety of determining factors related to age, scarcity, and aesthetic merit. In fact, almost any special feature that stands out as unusual or distinctive is a potential asset. Imprinted flags and inscribed flags; 8-point stars, gold stars, and added stars; extra stripes, missing stripes, tricolor stripes, and war stripes are all part of the pricing equation. And while political and military flags may rank above all others in terms of prestige and price, any flag with a significant and well-documented historical connection has 'star' potential (pardon the pun). Our advisor for this category is Ryan Cooper; he is listed in the Directory under Massachusetts.

13 stars, Dmn pattern, hand sewn, early 1800s, 32x38"	8,365.00
13 stars, hand/machine sewn, Centennial	850.00
13 stars, printed glazed muslin, 1880s, 7x11"	300.00
13 stars, str rows, hand/machine sewn, Civil War era, 40x50"	1,800.00
13 stars, US Naval boat insignia, 1880, 50x96"	750.00
15 stars, union jack from War of 1812, rare, 35x62"	23,000.00
15 stars, 15 stripes, all machine sewn, ca 1912, 48x72"	375.00
16 stars, Great Star, hand sewn, 1850s, 54x78"	9,500.00
19 stars, 16 orig+3, sewn scrap fabric, 39x66"	7,500.00
20 stars, oval pattern, ship's flag, 1818, worn, 64x128"	6,500.00
21 stars, Commissioning pennant, ship 'Herald,' 1819, 50-ft	8,500.00

25 stars, oval pattern w/central star, ship's flag, 96x200"	6,700.00
25 stars, row pattern, Civil War, 90x175"	2,200.00
26 stars, Great Star, embr on sewn silk, 30x43"	8,500.00
26 stars, Great Star, printed cotton, 12x17"	3,885.00
29 stars, entirely hand sewn, poor condition, 43x68"	4,500.00
30 stars, gold stars/fringe, silk, delicate, 52x68"	4,500.00
31 stars, Great Star, hand-sewn silk, 14'	4,000.00
31 stars, row pattern, hand-stitched bunting, 104x247"	2,500.00
31 stars, Scatter Star pattern, hand sewn, 45x68"	4,480.00
32 stars, dbl wreath of inset stars, hand sewn, 36x48"	5,200.00
33 stars, Great Star, hand-sewn muslin, 60x96"	5,000.00
33 stars, hand-/machine-sewn wool bunting, 66x92"	2,250.00
33 stars, in rows, printed bunting, 28x44", G-	1,200.00
34 stars, dbl-wreath pattern, printed silk, 18x28"	1,600.00
34 stars, Great Star, from Albany RR Depot, 116x175"	6,500.00
34 stars, Great Star, printed cotton, 25x39"	3,500.00
34 stars, printed linen, 3 sewn sections, 22x48"	600.00
34 stars, random pattern, hand sewn, 66x140"	1,600.00
35 stars, dbl-wreath pattern, printed, sized muslin, 19x28"	1,500.00
35 stars, recruiting flag, sewn bunting, 50x116"	1,800.00
35 stars, row pattern, hand/machine sewn, 96x180"	1,500.00
36 stars, cut-in, in rows, machined stripes, 25x50"	1,000.00
36 stars, inscr parade flag, muslin print, 6x9"	350.00
36 stars, sailing ship's, inscr & dtd, 75x142"	950.00
37 stars, medallion pattern, printed/sewn muslin, 48x87"	550.00
37 stars, printed silk, 32x40"	300.00
37 stars, row pattern, hand-sewn silk, poor, 60x80"	350.00
37 stars, row pattern, stitched bunting, 30x48"	600.00
38 stars, medallion-wreath pattern, printed cotton, 12x17"	550.00
38 stars, printed silk w/ribbon ties, 30x47"	350.00
38 stars, row pattern, clamp dyed in 3 sections, 60x120"	325.00
38 stars, row pattern, hand/machine-stitched bunting, 71x116"	450.00
38 stars, unique wreath pattern, sewn, 89x134"	1,200.00
38 stars, 1776-1876 pattern, printed linen, 27½x46"	1,800.00
39 stars, Centennial 'International Flag,' 16x24"	275.00
39 stars, row pattern, all machine-stitched bunting, 40x84"	450.00
39 stars, row pattern variation, printed silk, 12x24"	200.00
39 stars (6-5 pattern), printed gauze bunting, 19x34"	200.00
40 stars, row pattern, hand-sewn bunting, lg, 98x204"	270.00
40 stars, row pattern, printed/sewn British import, 55x106"	250.00
41 stars (rare), printed cotton sheeting, 15x24"	375.00
42 stars, sewn cotton, from Ft Hamilton NY, 120x177"	275.00
42 stars, 7-row pattern, printed cotton, 12x17"	125.00
43 stars, machine-sewn bunting, extremely rare, 29x70"	1,500.00
44 stars, machine-sewn cotton bunting, 53x82"	200.00
44 stars, triple-wreath pattern, printed cotton, 23x26"	350.00
45 stars, HP w/sewn stripes, 38x70"	120.00
45 stars, machine-sewn cotton bunting, 80x108"	55.00
45 stars, printed silk w/red ribbon ties, 32x46"	45.00
45 stars, row pattern variant, printed muslin, 9x13"	25.00
46 stars, machine-sewn wool bunting, 72x138"	60.00
46 stars, printed silk, GAR Post in gold, 32x45"	350.00
47 stars, unofficial, sewn bunting, 108x137"	350.00
48 stars, all crocheted, dtd 1941, 20x38"	85.00
48 stars, machine-sewn cotton bunting, 60x96"	50.00
48 stars, printed cotton w/GAR surprint, 11x16"	40.00
48 stars, sewn to form 'USA,' unauthorized WWI, 45x69"	300.00
48 stars, USN Union Jack, machine-sewn wool, 23x33"	35.00
48 stars in gold, sewn WWII casket flag, 58x118"	95.00
49 stars, embr, sewn stripes, 36x60"	45.00
49 stars, 3 uncut flags, printed cotton sheet, 37x36"	25.00
50 stars, early prototype 'June 1959,' 52x66"	220.00
50 stars, hand-knitted coverlet w/fringe, 30x51"	30.00
51 stars, printed flaglette for DC statehood, 4x6"	15.00

Florence Ceramics

Figurines marked 'Florence Ceramics' were produced in the '40s and '50s in Pasadena, California. The quality of the ware and the attention given to detail are prompting a growing interest among today's collectors. The names of these lovely ladies, gents, and figural groups are nearly always incised into their bases. The company name is ink stamped. Examples are evaluated by size, rarity, and intricacy of design. For more information we recommend *The Collector's Encyclopedia of California Pottery, Second Edition,* by Jack Chipman, who is listed in the Directory under California; *The Florence Collectibles* by Doug Foland; and *The Complete Book of Florence Ceramics: A Labor of Love* by Sue and Jerry Kline and Margaret Wehrspaun. Our advisor for this category is Jerry Kline; he is listed in the Directory under Vermont.

Abigail, beige dress w/red hair, 8", from $170 to...........................200.00
Amber, 9¼", from $700 to 750.00
Ann, pk & wht w/gold trim, 6", from $60 to.....................................70.00
Annette, 8¼", from $500 to 550.00
Ava, wht-to-brn-gr dress w/gr basket on head, 10½", from $300 to .350.00
Blue Boy, 11¾", from $400 to 450.00
Bride, rare, 8¾", from $1,800 to 2,000.00
Charles, lamp, wht, from $450 to 500.00
Chinese couple, blk & wht w/yel flowers, 8½", pr.....................125.00
Cindy, 8", from $425 to 475.00
Delia, gray dress w/burgundy trim, brn hair, 7¼", from $135 to ..150.00
Delia, ycl, hand showing, 7¼", from $350 to 375.00
Edward, wht tux w/gold, blk hat, seated in purple chair, 7", $450 to .500.00
Elaine, gr, 6", from $60 to...70.00
Grace, bl, plain, 10", from $250 to 300.00
Her Majesty, regal lady in fancy wht gown, w/crown, 7", from $200 to ..250.00
Irene, pk dress, 6" , from $60 to 70.00
Josephine, 9", from $350 to 375.00
June, pk w/bl floral dress, flower holder, 7", from $50 to 60.00
Kay, wht dress w/pk & bl flowers, flower holder, 7", from $60 to ..70.00
Lady Diana, lav dress w/lace at neck, 10", from $1,250 to 1,400.00

Louis XV and Madame Pompadour, $800.00 for the pair.

Louise, 7½", from $175 to..200.00
Marilyn, carrying hat box, violet, 8", from $500 to 550.00
Matilda, rose dress, muff in right hand, 8½", from $165 to.........190.00
May, flower holder, from $60 to 70.00
Melanie, gray dress w/Royal Red trim, from $135 to 150.00
Mermaid, from $175 to 200.00
Mimi, wht dress w/gold trim, flower holder, 6¼", from $70 to 80.00
Oriental couple, in aqua & wht, 7¾", pr, from $150 to.............175.00
Our Lady of Grace, wht w/gold trim, 9½", from $250 to............300.00
Patrice, wht w/gold trim, 7¼", from $200 to...............................225.00
Patsy, pk, flower holder, 6", from $45 to 50.00
Pinkie, wht dress w/pk belt & hat w/ribbon, 11½", from $400 to .450.00

Polly, pk & wht, flower holder, 6", from $50 to...........................60.00
Rhett, beige trimmed in gr, 9", from $325 to 375.00
Rhett, gold trim, 9", from $325 to 375.00
Rhett, violet, 9", from $325 to 375.00
Sally, wht dress, hat in left hand, flower holder, 6", from $65 to ...70.00
Scarlett, beige dress w/gr trim, brn hair, 9", from $200 to 250.00
Shirley, 8", from $250 to 350.00
Sue Ellen, pk dress, holding flowers, 8¼", from $175 to.............200.00
Suzanne, wht dress w/gold trim, matching hat, 9¼", from $550 to ..600.00
Suzette, 6", from $140 to 160.00
Vivian, coral dress, hat & parasol, 10", from $350 to 400.00
Wynkin & Blynkin, fancy, 5½", pr, from $400 to 450.00
Yvonne, bl dress w/wht purse & hat w/gold trim, 8¾", from $425 to..500.00

Flow Blue

Flow Blue ware was produced by many Staffordshire potters; among the most familiar were Meigh, Podmore and Walker, Samuel Alcock, Ridgway, John Wedge Wood (who often signed his work Wedgewood), and Davenport. It was popular from about 1825 through 1860 and again from 1880 until the turn of the century. The name describes the blurred or flowing effect of the cobalt decoration, achieved through the introduction of a chemical vapor into the kiln. The body of the ware is ironstone, and Oriental motifs were favored. Later issues were on a lighter body and often decorated with gilt. For further information we recommend *The Collector's Encyclopedia of Flow Blue China* (1st and 2nd series) by Mary Frank Gaston (Collector Books).

Abbey, plate, dessert; Petrus-Regout, 7".......................................47.50
Abbey, plate, Petrus-Regout, 10" 85.00
Alaska, bowl, oval, Grindley, 9" 140.00
Aldine, bone dish, Grindley, 6½" L...50.00
Aldine, tureen, ftd, Grindley, 8x12"...375.00
Amoy, plate, Davenport, 9¼", NM 100.00
Amoy, sugar bowl, w/lid, Davenport, 8½" 800.00
Anemone, platter, 23x17"...895.00
Anemone, sauce bowl, ped ft, hdls, Lockhart & Arthur.............500.00
Arabesque, plate, Mayer, 10" 175.00
Arcadia, cup & saucer, Wilkinson, 2¼", 5½" 100.00
Arundel, bowl, salad; silver rim, Doulton..................................275.00
Ashburton, cup, demitasse; ped base, Grindley 85.00
Ashburton, plate, Grindley, 9" 90.00
Asiatic Pheasants, plate, Adams, 11"...195.00
Aster & Grapeshot, cup plate, hexagonal, Clementson, 4", EX..125.00
Aster & Grapeshot, plate, hexagonal, Clementson, 10½" 250.00
Astoria, bowl, oval, Upper Hanley Pottery, 11½x6½" 150.00
Atlantic, sauce dish 30.00
Baltic, plate, Grindley, 10" 90.00
Beatrice, gravy boat, Maddock, 9"...100.00
Belmont, wash bowl & pitcher, Grindley..................................2,000.00
Bentick, gravy boat & underplate, Cauldon, 8½x6¼" 275.00
Bentick, platter, Ridgway, 17x14"...1,000.00
Bisley, plate, Grindley, 9" 85.00
Blue Rose, bowl, fruit/dessert; Grindley, 5"................................35.00
Botanical, toothbrush holder, w/lid, Minton 450.00
Brooklyn, cup & saucer, Johnson Bros, 2", 6" 100.00
Brunswick, cup & saucer, New Wharf Pottery, 3½", 5¾"...........100.00
Burslem Berries, gravy boat, ped ft, Newport Pottery 100.00
Buttercup, toothbrush holder, Doulton, 6"................................275.00
California, teapot, att Podmore Walker, 8½"...............................900.00
Campion, wash bowl & pitcher, Grindley 1,800.00
Campion, waste jar, Grindley..600.00

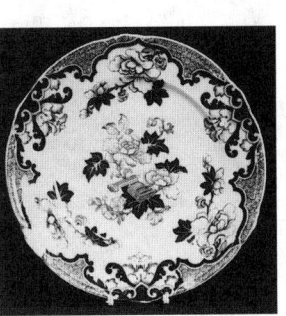

Candia, plate, Cauldon, 10", $85.00.

Canton, cup, demitasse; Maddock, 2½" 110.00
Cashmere, bowl, soup; Morley, 9" 150.00
Cashmere, plate, Morley, 10½" 250.00
Cashmere, plate, Morley, 9" 200.00
Cashmere, plate, Ridgway & Morley, 7" 120.00
Cashmere, plate, scalloped, Morley, 10½" 300.00
Cashmere, tea bowl & saucer, Morley, 3", 5¾" 150.00
Cattle Scenery, bowl, oval, Adams & Sons, mid-1800s, 19x14".1,000.00
Celeste, platter, Alcock, 10x7" 350.00
Celestial, pitcher, Ridgway, ca 1841, 7" 800.00
Chatsworth, plate, Ford & Sons, 10¼" 85.00
Chatsworth, soap dish, oval, Keeling, 9½x6" 110.00
Chiswick, plate, Ridgways, 10" 85.00
Chusan, pitcher, ped base, C Collinson & Co, 11" 1,200.00
Claremont, bowl, vegetable; w/lid, gold trim, Johnson Bros........325.00
Clarendon, platter, oval, Alcock, 18x13½" 450.00
Cleopatra, compote, fruit; Walley, 9x13" 1,100.00
Clive, pitcher, T Rathbone & Co, 8" 450.00
Coburg, cup plate, John Edwards, 4½" 140.00
Coburg, relish, fluted & scalloped, Edwards, 9x5" 275.00
Crescent, cake plate, Grindley, 14x13¼" 160.00
Crescent, soup plate, gold trim, Grindley 85.00
Cyprus, bowl, Ridgway, Bates & Co, 10½" 160.00
Cyprus, soup tureen, w/lid, +15½x10" tray & 10½" ladle 800.00
Delamere, cup, gold trim, att Alcock, 2½" 60.00
Delmar, plate, Grindley, 9¾" 100.00
Delph, cake stand, ped ft, gold trim, unmk, 7½" 300.00
Devon, bowl, vegetable; w/lid & 10x8" underplate, Ford & Sons....625.00
Doreen, chamber pot, w/lid, Grindley 400.00
Doreen, shaving mug, Grindley 175.00
Doreen, toothbrush holder, Grindley 275.00
Duchess, wash bowl, Wood & Son, 17¼" 750.00
Dunkeld, plate, bread & butter; Frank Beardmore & Co, 7½" 35.00
Eagle, platter, Podmore Walker, 13½x10½" 450.00
Eagle & Shield, creamer, Hammersley, 4½", from $175 to..........200.00
Edgar, gravy boat, New Wharf Pottery, 3½x9" 150.00
Excelsior, teapot, ped ft, Thomas Fell 900.00
Fallow Deer, bowl, serving; w/lid, sq, Wedgwood......................375.00
Fallow Deer, plate, Wedgwood, 10" 150.00
Fibre, plate, Globe Pottery, ca 1917, 6" 35.00
Florian, platter, oval, Burgess & Leigh, lg 500.00
Gainsborough, bowl, vegetable; w/lid, Ridgway, 3½x11¼x7¾"..350.00
Geisha, sugar bowl, w/lid, Upper Hanley Potteries 275.00
Genevese, plate, Edge Malkin & Co, 9¼" 150.00
Gladiolus, pitcher, cylindrical, Doulton, 9" 700.00
Grasshopper & Flowers, pitcher, hinged metal lid, att Meigh, 11"....1,200.00
Grecian Scroll, pitcher, bearded-head spout, Mayer, 6" 700.00
Halford, plate, Ford & Sons Ltd, 10" 75.00
Harvard, plate, Alfred Meakin, 10" 90.00
Hindustan, platter, Maddock, 16x12½", from $1,000 to..........1,200.00
Homestead, saucer, J&G Meakin, 6" 40.00
Hong Kong, waste bowl, Meigh 450.00

Iris, cheese dish, Doulton, 9½x9" 600.00
Iris, platter, oval, AJ Wilkinson, 13x9½" 250.00
Iris, vase, gold trim, hdls, 7½" 225.00
Iris, vase, hexagonal, gold trim, 9½" 215.00
Ivanhoe, cup & saucer, Wedgwood, mini, 2", 4" 120.00
Ivy, pitcher, gold trim, unmk, 8" 500.00
Kaolin, sugar bowl, ped ft, w/lid, Podmore Walker 800.00
Kelvin, dessert set (c/s+sm plate), Meakin...............................195.00
Kendal, plate, gold trim, Ridgway, 10" 85.00
Kin Shan, wash bowl, scalloped rim, 5x13½" 300.00
Kirkee, tea bowl & saucer, Meir, 3", 5¾" 100.00
Ladas, cake plate, gold trim, Ridgways, 9" sq............................80.00
Le Pavot, plate, Grindley, 10" 80.00
Lily, vase, gold tapestry work/sponging, bulbous, hdls, Adderly, 9"...500.00
Lotus, bowl, vegetable; Grindley, 10¼x8" 130.00
Louise, bowl, vegetable; oval, New Wharf Pottery 150.00
Madras, platter, Doulton, 18x14½" 1,000.00
Manilla, bowl, vegetable; Podmore Walker, 8x12x9¾" 650.00
Manilla, plate, Podmore Walker, 9½" 115.00
Manilla, teapot, pumpkin shape, Podmore Walker, 8¾" 1,000.00
Manilla, tureen, att Podmore Walker, 6x9⅛x4¼" 1,200.00
Matlock, bowl, vegetable; w/lid, ca 1890, 5½x11½x7" 175.00
Meissen, bowl, fruit/cereal; Furnival 50.00
Messina, bowl, vegetable; w/lid, Alfred Meakin........................350.00
Montana, plate, Johnson Bros, 10" 70.00
Morning Glory, rose bowl, gold trim, Thomas Hughes & Son, 6".175.00
Norfolk, bowl, simple border, Doulton, 8" 75.00
Norfolk, plate, pictorial border, Doulton, 10" 85.00
Normandy, toothbrush holder, Meakin, 6x3½" 130.00
Old Castles, plate, Henry Alcock, ca 1913, 10" 150.00
Old English Rural Scenes, plate, Wm Adams & Sons, 10" 100.00
Oregon, cup & saucer, gold trim, Johnson Bros, 2⅜", 6" 100.00
Oregon, pitcher, 6-paneled, Mayer, 6¾" 650.00
Oregon, plate, Johnson Bros, 8¾" 70.00
Oregon, plate, Mayer, 7½" 100.00
Oriental, plate, Samuel Alcock, 10½" 140.00
Ormonde, wash bowl & pitcher, Alfred Meakin, 5½x16¾", 13¼"..1,800.00
Pansy, pitcher, gold trim, att Johnson Bros, early 1900s, 9".........550.00
Pekin, plate, gold trim, Davenport, 10½" 140.00
Pelew, plate, Challinor, 10" 200.00
Pembroke, soup plate, Bishop & Stonier, 10" 70.00
Poppy, bowl, W Adams & Co, ca 1881, 10" 90.00
Poppy, pitcher, Doulton, 6⅝" 325.00
Poppy, plate, New Wharf Pottery, 8¾" 70.00
Rebecca, plate, Geo Jones & Sons, 8½" 75.00
Regal, casserole, hdls, w/lid, Leighton, 5½x11" 165.00
Regent, plate, mk England, 9" 80.00
Rhine, sauce tureen, w/lid & ladle 700.00
Rhoda Gardens, plate, Hackwood, 9½" 150.00
Ripon, tea tile, Wood & Hulme, 8x6½", NM 60.00
Rock, saucer, Challinor 45.00
Rose, gravy boat & undertray, gold trim, WH Grindley 150.00
Roslyn, plate, Alfred Colley, 10" 80.00
Salisbury, wash bowl & pitcher, Ford & Sons, 16" dia, 12" 2,000.00
Savoy, platter, oval, Empire Porcelain Co, 13½x10½" 275.00
Saxon, platter, 16x12" 98.00
Scinde, bowl, vegetable; J&G Alcock, 3x11¾x9", NM 375.00
Scinde, cup & saucer, Alcock, 3", 5¼" 150.00
Scinde, plate, dbl-scalloped corners, Alcock, 16¼x12¾" 350.00
Scinde, punch cup, 12-paneled, J&G Alcock, 2¾" 215.00
Scinde, sugar bowl, J&G Alcock, w/lid, 8" 425.00
Scinde, tea bowl & saucer, J&G Alcock, EX 125.00
Shanghai, cup & saucer, unidentified maker.............................150.00
Shanghai, sugar bowl, ped ft, w/lid, Furnival...........................800.00

Shapoo, pitcher, unmk, 8"..**800.00**
Siva, platter, polychromed, illegible mk, lg **450.00**
Stanley, saucer, gold trim, Johnson Bros, 6½" **25.00**
Superior, plate, 9" **65.00**
Sutton, plate, gold trim, Ridgways, 9"....................**80.00**
Temple, cup & saucer, handleless; Podmore Walker, 3", 6" **175.00**
Temple, plate, paneled, Podmore Walker, 9¾" **175.00**
Temple, plate, Podmore Walker, 8¾" **145.00**
Tonquin, plate, Adams & Sons, 8½" **150.00**
Touraine, bowl, serving; Stanley, 3x10½" **200.00**
Touraine, bowl, soup; Henry Alcock, 10⅛" **90.00**
Touraine, bowl, vegetable; w/lid, Alcock, 6¼x11¼x7⅛" **550.00**
Touraine, bowl, vegetable; w/lid, Alcock, 6x10½x6½" **400.00**
Touraine, creamer, Alcock, 4½" **250.00**
Touraine, cup & saucer, Stanley, 3¼", 6" **65.00**
Touraine, sugar bowl, w/lid, Stanley, 6½".............**300.00**
Turkey, platter, oval, unmk, 18x13½".....................**500.00**
Tuscan Rose, tureen, brn transfer, 1814-37 ....**495.00**
Tyne, saucer, Bridgwood & Son, 5½"......................**25.00**
Venus, platter, oval, Till & Sons, lg.......................**300.00**
Victoria, bowl, center; Wood & Sons, 10" **115.00**
Waldorf, creamer, New Wharf Pottery, 3½"...........**275.00**
Warwick, teapot, ped ft, att Podmore Walker, 8¼" **900.00**
Watteau, platter, Doulton, 13½x11".......................**300.00**
Watteau, saucer, full pattern, Doulton, 5½" **35.00**
Wellbeck, bowl, Sampson Hancock & Sons, w/lid, 7x11x5".......**275.00**
Whampoa, pitcher, att Mellor Venables & Co, 1830s, 7¼" **800.00**
York, plate, Couldon England, 9"...........................**75.00**

Flue Covers

When spring housecleaning started and the heating stove was taken down for the warm weather season, the unsightly hole where the stovepipe joined the chimney was hidden with an attractive flue cover. They were made with a colorful litho print behind glass with a chain for hanging. In a 1929 catalog, they were advertised at 16¢ each or six for 80¢. Although scarce today, some scenes were actually reverse painted on the glass itself. The most popular motifs were florals, children, animals, and lovely ladies. Occasionally flue covers were made in sets of three — one served a functional purpose, while the others were added to provide a more attractive wall arrangement. They range in size from 7" to 14", but 9" is the average.

Babes in the woods, lady and three cherubs, unsigned Clappsaddle, 9", $95.00.

Basket of Grapes, spilling over, 6½x8¼", from $75 to **85.00**
Basket of Strawberries, spilling from tipped basket, 7x8¼", $75 to ..**85.00**
Birds (2) w/wht flowers, scrolled border, ca 1900, 13" **50.00**
Box of Violets, w/purple bow on lid, 9½", from $75 to..................**85.00**
Boy & girl, he w/arm over her shoulder, MIG, 9¾"....................**230.00**
Boy & girl ice skating, 9⅝"..**110.00**

Dancing the Reel, 2 girls in pk & red, 9½", from $85 to..............**95.00**
Dreaming, lady sniffs rose, sgn Harrison Fisher, 1910, 9½", up to..**100.00**
Ducks (2) in flight w/ferns & flowers border, ca 1898, 13" **40.00**
Duet, man w/accordion, she w/sheet music, 9½", from $50 to **60.00**
Feeding King, lady in red jacket offers apple to horse, 9½", $75 to ..**85.00**
Feline Love, lady w/rose in hair holds wht cat, 7¾", from $90 to...**100.00**
Game of Croquet, pup chews ball, 2 kittens watch, 9½", $100 to.**110.00**
Girl holds wreath of roses around face, 9⅞"...........................**130.00**
Girl in big red hat w/daisies in hair, 9½".................................**110.00**
Heaven's Pleasure, classical lady in gr on swing w/cherubs, 8¾" ...**95.00**
Holding Felix, girl holds kitten, 4⅝", from $55 to **65.00**
Just One Nanny?, sm blond girl wants a grape, 9¾" dmn shape, $75 to..**85.00**
Ladies, 1 in bl, 1 in pk, w/rose garland, 9¼" **105.00**
Lady dressed in blk dress w/blk hat, pearl necklace, 9¼"............**145.00**
Lady in flowing wht dress stands beside roses, 9¾"....................**160.00**
Lady w/iris, yel gown, 9½", from $85 to **95.00**
Lady w/red flowers in hair, oval, 9½x8" **125.00**
Ladykin, Victorian brunette lady w/curly updo, 9½", from $50 to..**60.00**
Mother's Helpers, 4 children in interior, sepia tone, 6½x8½".......**55.00**
Over the Wall, courting couple at stone wall, 9½", from $55 to...**65.00**
Parasol, Oriental child w/colorful parasol, 9½", from $50 to........**60.00**
Pink Wisteria, in red vase, 8¼x7", from $50 to **60.00**
Please Stay, Psyche begging Cupid, 15½", from $110 to **120.00**
Sabrina's Poppies, brunette girl w/poppy in hair, 8", from $75 to ..**85.00**
Sir Winston, blk horse's portrait, facing left, 9½", from $70 to **80.00**
Springtime, lady in floral archway, 8", from $55 to.......................**65.00**
Strawberries in basket spilling onto table, 9½" **105.00**
Tulip Garden, cottage scene w/many flowers, 6¾x8¼", from $50 to..**60.00**
Victorian boy in bl shirt & red cap, finger in mouth, 9½" **145.00**
Victorian girl in pk w/flowers in hair, 14" **150.00**
Victorian girl profile, gray & wht border, 6½" **100.00**
Whispering Cherubs, sweet winged girls among clouds, 9¼", $60 to.**70.00**
Winter scene, snowy landscape w/house & figure, 6½x9", from $50 to..**60.00**
Young Master, boy w/wht curls & frilly collar, 7¾", from $50 to...**60.00**

Folk Art

That the creative energies of the mind ever spark innovations in functional utilitarian channels as well as toward playful frivolity is well documented in the study of American folk art. While the average early settler rarely had free time to pursue art for its own sake, his creative energy exemplified itself in fashioning useful objects carved or otherwise ornamented beyond the scope of pure practicality. After the advent of the Industrial Revolution, the pace of everyday living became more leisurely, and country folk found they had extra time. Not accustomed to sitting idle, many turned to carving, painting, or weaving. Whirligigs, imaginative toys for the children, and whimsies of all types resulted. Though often rather crude, this type of early art represents a segment of our heritage and as such has become valued by collectors.

Values given for drawings, paintings, and theorems are 'in frame' unless noted otherwise. See also Baskets; Decoys; Frakturs; Samplers; Trade Signs; Weather Vanes; Wood Carvings.

Alligator, concrete over steel, C Peterson, ca 1900, 92" L **6,325.00**
Birdhouse, pnt gourd, old iron screw-in perch, 12½"....................**35.00**
Birdhouse, pnt wood, wht w/red & blk, gr roof, ca 1900, 22x16x18"..**435.00**
Charcoal drawing on paper, Am Indian ladies by cabin, 12-3-81, 19x14".**495.00**
Coconut, rtcl dancers/crowned lions/man on bull/etc, European, 1800s.**690.00**
Elephant, laminated/pegged wood, dk rpt, wht tusks, rope tail, 28" L ...**55.00**
Frame, appl heart at ea mitered corner, 7x5⅞" opening, 12x10"..**475.00**
Ink drawing, Model-T by train tracks, farm beyond, 1920s, 29x18"..**185.00**
Lamp base, wooden pyramid w/mc marbles set into sides, 1950s, 23" ...**85.00**
Lighthouse, cvd/pnt wood, by cottage/rowboat/fence, 20th C, 28x22x12" .**1,850.00**

Limestone cvg, owl w/sq, Xd-out eyes, Nixon on base, E Reed, 5⅜".**250.00**
Oil on academy brd, walnuts in red bowl, sgn/dtd 1930, 31x15"...**70.00**
Oil on canvas, peaches & plums on table, F Miller, 15½x21½".**1,725.00**
Penmanship instruction, calligraphy w/cat at top, 18x22" **1,650.00**

Pipe, folk-carved and detailed, Union Forever, American, mid-nineteenth century, $1,300.00. (Photo courtesy Aston Americana Auctioneers & Appraisers)

Sandstone cvg, Indian chief in relief, E Popeye Reed, 1976, 16x12x2" .**700.00**
Spencerian drawing, dove w/banners, sgn, 1906-07, 17x17" in matted fr.**550.00**
Spencerian drawing, eagle w/banner, in fr: 16x18" **220.00**
Theorem on paper, flowers in vase, sgn/1818, on Bristol paper, 14x11"..**400.00**
Theorem on paper, watercolor fruit, G colors, stains/foxing, 9x7", +fr.**350.00**
Theorem on velvet, flowers in basket, unsgn, fr: 22x24½"..........**550.00**
Theorem on velvet, fruit basket on wht, EX art, 1800s, 14x11".**1,645.00**
Theorem on velvet, watercolor, distlefinks/fruit, Bill Rank, 17x19".**275.00**
Utensil rack, 2 well-cvd birds on stippled bk, 6 wire hooks, 7x11"..**330.00**
Whirligig, Black lady churning butter, wood w/old pnt, 1930s, 17x12".**135.00**
Whirligig, chicken, sheet copper, mc pnt/verdigris, early 20th C, 20" .**425.00**
Whirligig, duck, mc pnt on wood, rotating wings, 20th C, 39" L..**350.00**
Whirligig, farmer milking & lady churning, wood/metal, old pnt, 16"..**450.00**
Whirligig, man cranking blades, mc pnt on wood, 20th C, merchant's ad..**575.00**
Whirligig, man w/paddle arms, mc pnt/EX details, Am, 1890s, 15x4".**2,000.00**
Whirligig, policeman, cap w/metal visor, paddle arms, pnt details, 14".**2,470.00**
Whirligig, soldier, pnt wood, 19th C, 9⅝" **500.00**
Whirligig, windmill, pnt wood, 2 men working at base, 20th C, 56x31"..**2,750.00**
Whirligig, witch, pnt wood w/iron paddle arms, ca 1900, 22x17".**4,400.00**
Whirligig, witch on broomstick, pnt pine, 1940s, 8x8x3" on iron rod.**225.00**
Whirligig, workshop w/press operator/carpenter/blksmith, old pnt, 47" ..**2,750.00**

Fostoria

The Fostoria Glass Company was built in 1887 at Fostoria, Ohio, but by 1891 it had moved to Moundsville, West Virginia. During the next two decades, they produced many lines of pressed patterned tableware and lamps. Their most famous pattern, American, was introduced in 1915 and was produced continuously until 1986 in well over two hundred different pieces. From 1920 to 1925, top artists designed tablewares in colored glass — canary (vaseline), amber, blue, orchid, green, and ebony — in pressed patterns as well as etched designs. By the late '30s, Fostoria was recognized as the largest producer of handmade glassware in the world. The company ceased operations in Moundsville in 1986.

Many items from both the American and Coin Glass lines have been reproduced by Lancaster Colony. In some cases the new glass is superior in quality to the old. Since the 1950s, Indiana Glass has produced a pattern called 'Whitehall' that looks very much like Fostoria's American, though with slight variations. Because Indiana's is not handmade glass, the lines of the 'cube' pattern and the edges of the items are sharp and untapered in comparison to the fire-polished originals. Three-footed pieces lack the 'toe' and instead have a peg-like foot, and the rays on the bottoms of the American examples are narrower than on the Whitehall counterparts. The Home Interiors Company offers several pieces of American look-alikes which were not even produced in the United States. Be sure of your dealer and study the books suggested below to become more familiar with the original line.

Coin Glass reproductions are flooding the market. Among items you may encounter are an 8" round bowl, 9" oval bowl, 8¼" wedding bowl, 4½" candlesticks, urn with lid, 6¼" candy jar with lid, footed comport, sugar and creamer; there could possibly be others. Colors in production are crystal, green, blue, and red. The red color is very good, but the blue is not the original color, nor is the emerald green. Buyer beware!

For further information see *Elegant Glassware of the Depression Era* by Gene Florence; *Fostoria Glassware, 1887 – 1982,* by Frances Bones; *Fostoria Stemware, The Crystal for America Series* (there are four books); *The Fostoria Value Guide* by Milbra Long and Emily Seate; and *Fostoria, Volume II,* by Ann Kerr.

See also Glass Animals and Figurines.

Alexis, crystal, bowl, nappy, 8" **22.50**
Alexis, crystal, bowl, nut **15.00**
Alexis, crystal, cup, custard **10.00**
Alexis, crystal, oil, 9-oz **45.00**
Alexis, crystal, salt cellar, flat, ind **12.50**
Alexis, crystal, stem, cordial; 1-oz **15.00**
Alexis, crystal, stem, water; 10-oz **15.00**
Alexis, crystal, tray, pickle...**22.50**
Alexis, crystal, tumbler, water; ftd, 8½-oz **20.00**
American, crystal, appetizer tray w/6 inserts, 10½".................**32.50**
American, crystal, ashtray, oval, 5½"...**20.00**
American, crystal, bottle, cologne; w/stopper, 6-oz, 5¾" **72.50**
American, crystal, bottle, condiment/ketchup; w/stopper **145.00**
American, crystal, bowl, fruit; flared rim, 4¾" **15.00**
American, crystal, bowl, jelly; 4¼x4¼" **15.00**
American, crystal, bowl, lemon; w/lid, 5½" **55.00**
American, crystal, bowl, pickle; oblong, 8" **15.00**
American, crystal, bowl, punch; high ft base, 2-gal, 14"............**395.00**
American, crystal, bowl, wedding; sq, ped ft, w/lid, 8x6½" **110.00**
American, crystal, butter dish, ¼-lb **25.00**
American, crystal, candlestick, twin; 4⅛x8½"............................**60.00**
American, crystal, comport, 5¼x9½"...**85.00**
American, crystal, goblet, fruit; hex ft, #2056, 4½-oz, 4¾" **9.00**
American, crystal, goblet, low sherbet; 4½-oz, 4½" **10.00**
American, crystal, ice dish insert **10.00**
American, crystal, marmalade, w/lid & chrome spoon **50.00**
American, crystal, pitcher, w/o ice lip, ½-gal............................**295.00**
American, crystal, plate, salad; 8½"...**12.00**
American, crystal, punch cup, flared rim....................................**11.00**
American, crystal, rose bowl, 5" **30.00**
American, crystal, shakers, 3", pr...**20.00**
American, crystal, soap dish...**975.00**
American, crystal, toothpick holder **25.00**
American, crystal, tray, oval, hdls, 6" **35.00**
American, crystal, tray, service; hdls, 9½" **35.00**
American, crystal, tumbler, juice; 5-oz.......................................**13.00**
American, crystal, vase, str sides, 6" **35.00**
American, crystal, vase, swung; 14" **250.00**
Baroque, bl, bowl, celery; 11"...**45.00**
Baroque, bl, pitcher, 6½"...**800.00**
Baroque, bl, stem, water; 9-oz..**40.00**
Baroque, bl, vase, 7" **175.00**
Baroque, crystal, candelabrum, 16-lustre, 2-light, 8¼" **150.00**
Baroque, crystal, candlestick, 3-light, 6"....................................**32.50**
Baroque, crystal, plate, 7½"...**8.00**
Baroque, crystal, tray, oval, 12½"..**40.00**
Baroque, yel, bowl, cream soup **77.50**
Baroque, yel, candlestick, 4"...**35.00**
Baroque, yel, comport, 6½"..**40.00**

Baroque, yel, platter, oval, 12" 52.50
Baroque, yel, tumbler, water; ftd, 9-oz.............................25.00
Brocade Grape, bl, bowl, console; #2375, 12" 115.00
Brocade Grape, bl, bowl, cupped rose; #2339, 7½" 85.00
Brocade Grape, gr, bonbon, #2375....................................40.00
Brocade Grape, gr, bowl, flat, shallow, #2297, 12½"......100.00
Brocade Grape, orchid, bowl, deep, rolled rim, #2297, 10½" 120.00
Brocade Oakleaf, crystal, bowl, cornucopia hdls, #2398, 11" 100.00
Brocade Oakleaf, crystal, bowl, finger; #869.....................60.00
Brocade Oakleaf, gr or rose, bowl, console; #2375, 12" ...115.00
Brocade Oakleaf, gr or rose, bowl, scroll hdls, #2395, 10" 145.00
Brocade Oakwood, orchid or azure, bonbon, #2375.........50.00
Brocade Oakwood, orchid or azure, bowl, centerpc; #2375, 11"..185.00
Brocade Palm Leaf, rose or gr, bowl, scroll hdls, #2395, 10" 200.00
Brocade Palm Leaf, rose or gr, bowl, 3-toed, flared rim, 12" 150.00
Brocade Paradise, gr or orchid, bowl, centerpc, rnd, #2329, 13" .140.00
Brocade Paradise, gr or orchid, bowl, 3-ftd, #2297, 10½" 95.00

Chintz, platter, #2496, rare, $125.00. (Photo courtesy Gene Florence)

Coin, amber, ashtray, center coin, 7½" 20.00
Coin, amber, cake salver, ftd, 6½" 110.00
Coin, amber, candle holders, 4½", pr 30.00
Coin, amber, cruet, w/stopper, 7-oz..................................65.00
Coin, amber, lamp, coach; oil burning, 13½" 145.00
Coin, bl, ashtray, 10" 50.00
Coin, bl, bowl, oval, 9" 175.00
Coin, bl, lamp, patio; electric, 16⅝" 275.00
Coin, bl, lamp chimney, coach or patio...........................60.00
Coin, bl, sugar bowl, w/lid...45.00
Coin, bl, vase, bud; 8" 40.00
Coin, crystal, candle holders, 4½", pr 40.00
Coin, crystal, creamer..10.00
Coin, crystal, nappy, hdl, 5⅜"..15.00
Coin, crystal, plate, 8" 20.00
Coin, crystal, punch cup..35.00
Coin, crystal, stem, wine; 5-oz, 4" 35.00
Coin, crystal, tumbler, iced tea; 14-oz, 5¼"....................38.00
Coin, crystal, tumbler, water/scotch & soda; 9-oz, 4¼" ...30.00
Coin, gr, ashtray, oblong..25.00
Coin, gr, cigarette urn, ftd, 3⅜"......................................50.00
Coin, gr, pitcher, 32-oz..55.00
Coin, gr, shakers, chrome tops, 3¼", pr............................90.00
Coin, olive, bowl, ftd, 8½"...25.00
Coin, olive, condiment set, tray+2 shakers+cruet...........250.00
Coin, olive, nappy, hdl, 5⅜"...18.00
Coin, olive, stem, sherbet; 9-oz, 5¼"...............................45.00
Coin, ruby, ashtray, 7½" dia 20.00
Coin, ruby, candy jar, w/lid, 6¼" 50.00
Coin, ruby, pitcher, 32-oz...150.00
Coin, ruby, stem, wine; 5-oz, 4" 100.00
Coin, ruby, tumbler, iced tea; 14-oz 75.00
Colony, crystal, bowl, console; rolled rim, 9" 40.00

Colony, crystal, bowl, console; 13" 40.00
Colony, crystal, bowl, oval, 2-part, 10½".........................55.00
Colony, crystal, bowl, 4½" 12.00
Colony, crystal, candlestick, prisms, 9¾"........................100.00
Colony, crystal, cup, ftd, 6-oz...7.50
Colony, crystal, pitcher, ice lip, 48-oz............................210.00
Colony, crystal, plate, dinner; 9" 27.50
Colony, crystal, plate, torte; 18" 110.00
Colony, crystal, stem, wine; 3¼-oz, 4¼"..........................22.00
Colony, crystal, tumbler, ftd, 12-oz, 5¾"..........................22.00
Colony, crystal, vase, str, 12"..195.00
Fairfax #2375, amber, bonbon...9.00
Fairfax #2375, amber, bowl, grapefruit.............................18.00
Fairfax #2375, amber, butter dish.....................................80.00
Fairfax #2375, amber, plate, salad; 8¾".............................7.00
Fairfax #2375, amber, sugar bowl lid................................20.00
Fairfax #2375, gr or topaz, bottle, salad dressing 110.00
Fairfax #2375, gr or topaz, bowl, cream soup; ftd 15.00
Fairfax #2375, gr or topaz, mayonnaise ladle...................25.00
Fairfax #2375, gr or topaz, plate, canape..........................10.00
Fairfax #2375, gr or topaz, platter, oval, 12" 45.00
Fairfax #2375, gr or topaz, whipped cream pail 50.00
Fairfax #2375, rose, bl or orchid, baker, oval, 9" 45.00
Fairfax #2375, rose, bl or orchid, bowl, centerpc; 12" 50.00
Fairfax #2375, rose, bl or orchid, ice bucket.....................95.00
Fairfax #2375, rose, bl or orchid, plate, canape 20.00
Fairfax #2375, rose, bl or orchid, platter, oval, 12" 65.00
Fairfax #2375, rose, bl or orchid, sugar pail 80.00
Fuchsia, crystal, bowl, #2395, 10" 95.00
Fuchsia, crystal, comport, low, #2470, 6" 40.00
Fuchsia, crystal, stem, cordial; #6004, ¾-oz.....................65.00
Fuchsia, wisteria, oyster cocktail, #6004, 4½-oz 35.00
Fuchsia, wisteria, stem, cocktail; #6004, 3-oz 65.00
Fuchsia, wisteria, tumbler, juice; ftd, #6004, 5-oz 45.00
Hermitage, amber, gr or topaz, ashtray holder, #2449......8.00
Hermitage, amber, gr or topaz, candle holder, #2449, 6"...22.00
Hermitage, amber, gr or topaz, icer, #2449 ....18.00
Hermitage, amber gr or topaz, sherbet, low ft, 7-oz, 3".....8.00
Hermitage, amber gr or topaz, tumbler, old fashioned; 6-oz, 3¼" 6.00
Hermitage, azure, bowl, fruit; #2449½, 5" 15.00
Hermitage, azure, decanter, w/stopper, #2449, 28-oz......150.00
Hermitage, azure, pitcher, #2449, 3-pt.............................150.00
Hermitage, azure, stem, water goblet; #2449, 9-oz, 5¼"....25.00
Hermitage, crystal, bowl, deep, ped ft, #2449, 8"............17.50
Hermitage, crystal, mug, ftd, #2449, 9-oz 15.00
Hermitage, crystal, relish, pickle; #2449, 8".......................8.00
Hermitage, crystal, tumbler, iced tea; #2449, 12-oz, 5¼" 10.00
Hermitage, wisteria, comport, #2449, 6"..........................40.00
Hermitage, wisteria, sugar bowl, ftd, #2449,....................30.00
Hermitage, wisteria, tumbler, #2449½, 13-oz, 5⅞"...........40.00
June, crystal, bowl, Grecian, 10" 50.00
June, crystal, creamer, ftd...15.00
June, crystal, cup, AD...25.00
June, crystal, pitcher..275.00
June, crystal, sauce boat...40.00
June, rose or bl, bowl, bouillon; ftd..................................50.00
June, rose or bl, candlestick, 3" 50.00
June, rose or bl, plate, grill; 10¼" 125.00
June, rose or bl, plate, lemon...30.00
June, rose or bl, sugar pail 250.00
June, topaz, cake plate, hdls, no indent, 10".....................45.00
June, topaz, candlestick, Grecian, 5"................................45.00
June, topaz, parfait, 5¼"...75.00
June, topaz, platter, 15" 135.00

June, topaz, vase, fan; ftd, 8½" 175.00
Kashmir, bl, bowl, fruit; 5" 25.00
Kashmir, bl, candlestick, 5" 27.50
Kashmir, bl, cup, AD; ftd 55.00
Kashmir, bl, plate, luncheon; 9" 15.00
Kashmir, bl, sandwich tray, center hdl 40.00
Kashmir, bl, sugar bowl, ftd 20.00
Kashmir, yel or gr, bowl, cream soup 22.00
Kashmir, yel or gr, candlestick, 2" 15.00
Kashmir, yel or gr, plate, salad; rnd or sq, 7" 6.00
Kashmir, yel or gr, stem, cocktail; ftd, 3½-oz 22.00
Kashmir, yel or gr, tumbler, tea; ftd, 16-oz 35.00
Lafayette, burgundy, bowl, sauce; oval, 6½" 50.00
Lafayette, burgundy, mayonnaise, 2-part, 6½" 55.00
Lafayette, crystal or amber, bowl, cream soup..........................22.50
Lafayette, crystal or amber, plate, 7¼" 8.00
Lafayette, Empire Green, bowl, relish; 2-part, 6½" 45.00
Lafayette, Empire Green, creamer, ftd, 4½" 40.00
Lafayette, Regal Blue, bonbon, hdls, 5" 35.00
Lafayette, Regal Blue, bowl, oval baker, 10" 75.00
Lafayette, rose, gr or topaz, bowl, sweetmeat; 4½" 22.50
Lafayette, rose, gr or topaz, plate, 10¼" 27.50
Lafayette, wisteria, bowl, olive; 6½" 50.00
Lafayette, wisteria, cup, demitasse...22.50
Navarre, crystal, bowl, floating garden; oval, #2496, 10" 67.50
Navarre, crystal, bowl, hdls, #2496, 4⅜" 17.50
Navarre, crystal, candlestick, triple, #2496, 6" 65.00
Navarre, crystal, creamer, ftd, #2440, 4¼" 20.00
Navarre, crystal, relish, 3-part, #2496, 10x7½" 55.00
Navarre, crystal, salad; #2440, 7½" 16.00
Navarre, crystal, shakers, ftd, #2375, 3½", pr 125.00
Navarre, crystal, stem, sherbet, low, #6106, 6-oz, 4⅝" 25.00
New Garland, amber or topaz, bottle, salad dressing.................135.00
New Garland, amber or topaz, candlestick, 3" 17.50
New Garland, amber or topaz, decanter 125.00
New Garland, amber or topaz, mint dish, 5½" 12.50
New Garland, amber or topaz, shakers, pr 40.00
New Garland, amber or topaz, stem, cordial; #6002 ....30.00
New Garland, rose, bowl, baker, 10" 45.00
New Garland, rose, creamer, ftd 17.50
New Garland, rose, ice dish 25.00
New Garland, rose, plate, 9" 35.00
New Garland, rose, tumbler, ftd, #6002, 10" 17.50
Pioneer, azure or orchid, comport, 8" 35.00
Pioneer, bl, bowl, fruit; shallow, 5" 15.00
Pioneer, bl, bowl, oval baker, 9" 45.00
Pioneer, bl, cup, ftd...15.00
Pioneer, bl, urn 55.00
Pioneer, crystal, amber or gr, bowl, bouillon; ftd 10.00
Pioneer, crystal, amber or gr, creamer, ftd 9.00
Pioneer, crystal, amber or gr, plate, chop; 12" 18.00
Pioneer, ebony, ashtray, 3¾" 18.00
Pioneer, ebony, comport, 8" 30.00
Pioneer, ebony, sugar bowl, ftd..10.00
Pioneer, rose or topaz, ashtray, deep, lg 22.00
Pioneer, rose or topaz, comport, 8" 30.00
Pioneer, rose or topaz, relish, 3-part, rnd 15.00
Rogene, crystal, comport, #5078, 5" 30.00
Rogene, crystal, jug, #4095, 7" 195.00
Rogene, crystal, nappy, ftd, #5078, 7" 30.00
Rogene, crystal, plate, 8" 15.00
Rogene, crystal, shakers, glass (pearl) top, #2283, pr 60.00
Rogene, crystal, stem, grapefruit; #945½ 30.00
Rogene, crystal, tumbler, flat, hdl, #837, 12-oz 25.00

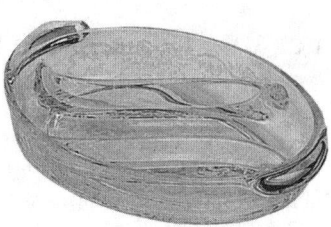

Romance, relish, three-part, 10", $75.00. (Photo courtesy Gene Florence)

Royal, amber or gr, bowl, cereal; #2350, 6½" 25.00
Royal, amber or gr, bowl, cream soup; flat, #2350 ....18.00
Royal, amber or gr, candlestick, #2324, 9" 75.00
Royal, amber or gr, creamer, fat, ftd, #2315½ 18.00
Royal, amber or gr, plate, chop; #2350, 13" 35.00
Royal, amber or gr, stem, water; #869, 9-oz 23.00
Seville, amber, bowl, vegetable; #3150 ....22.00
Seville, amber, butter dish, rnd, #2350 ....210.00
Seville, amber, egg cup, #2350 ....30.00
Seville, amber, plate, chop; 13¾" 30.00
Seville, amber, tumbler, ftd, #2084, 9-oz 15.00
Seville, gr, bowl, flared rim, ftd, #2315, 10½" 30.00
Seville, gr, candlestick, #2324, 4" 22.00
Seville, gr, cup, AD; #2350 ....30.00
Seville, gr, plate, dinner; #2350, 9½" 13.50
Seville, gr, stem, water; #870 ....240.00
Seville, gr, vase, 32292, 8" 95.00
Sun Ray, crystal, bowl, salad; 12" 35.00
Sun Ray, crystal, candlestick, 5½" 27.50
Sun Ray, crystal, creamer, ind 12.00
Sun Ray, crystal, pitcher, 64-oz 75.00
Sun Ray, crystal, plate, sandwich, 12" 35.00
Sun Ray, crystal, stem, cocktail; ftd, 4-oz, 3" 12.00
Trojan, rose, bowl, centerpc; ftd, #2394, 12" 85.00
Trojan, rose, bowl, cream soup; ftd, #2375 ....40.00
Trojan, rose, goblet, water; #5299, 10-oz, 8¼" 42.50
Trojan, rose, plate, salad; #2375, 7½" 12.00
Trojan, rose, shakers, ftd, #2375, pr 130.00
Trojan, topaz, tray, center hdl, #2375, 11" 50.00
Trojan, topaz, tumbler, ftd, #5099, 12-oz, 6" 40.00
Trojan, topaz, whipped cream pail, #2378 ....125.00
Versailles, bl, bowl, lemon 22.00
Versailles, bl, creamer, ftd, #2357½ 25.00
Versailles, bl, parfait, #5098 or #5099 ....95.00
Versailles, bl, plate, luncheon; #2375, 8¾" 25.00
Versailles, pk or gr, bowl, baker; #2375, 9" 95.00
Versailles, pk or gr, candlestick, #2394, 2" 35.00
Versailles, pk or gr, goblet, water; #5098 or #5099, 3-oz, 5¼" 100.00
Versailles, pk or gr, platter, #2375, 15" 160.00
Versailles, yel, bowl, centerpc; scroll hdls, #2395, 10" 90.00
Versailles, yel, bowl, grapefruit; 35082½ 40.00
Versailles, yel, relish, #2375, 8½" 38.00
Versailles, yel, tumbler, ftd, #5098 or #5099, 12-oz, 6" 40.00
Vesper, amber, bowl, cereal; rnd or sq, #2350, 6½" 35.00
Vesper, amber, butter dish, #2350 ....850.00
Vesper, amber, oyster cocktail, #5100 ....30.00
Vesper, amber, stem, wine; #5093, 2¾" 40.00
Vesper, bl, bowl, fruit; #2350, 5½" 30.00
Vesper, bl, comport, 8" 85.00
Vesper, bl, pickle dish, #2350 ....50.00
Vesper, bl, tumbler, ftd, #5100, 2-oz...70.00
Vesper, gr, bowl, bouillon; ftd, #2350 ....20.00
Vesper, gr, candlestick, #2394, 3" 23.00
Vesper, gr, cup, #2350 ....15.00
Vesper, gr, plate, dinner; 10½" 45.00

Fostoria Glass Specialty Company

The Fostoria Glass Specialty Company was founded in Fostoria, Ohio, in 1899. In 1910 they were purchased by General Electric. The new owners had an interest in developing a high-quality lustre-type art glass able to complete with the very successful glassware produced by Tiffany. They hired Walter Hicks, who had previously worked for Tiffany, to help develop the line they called Iris. Their efforts were extremely successful. The art glass they developed was cased and iridescent, very similar to Steuben's Aurene. Colors included green, tan, white, blue, yellow, and rose. It was made in several patterns, including Heart and Leaf, Leaf and Tendrils, Heart and Spider Webbing, and Lustred Dot. Although the main thrust of their production was lamp shades, vases and bowls were made as well. Iris was made for only four years, since gold was required in its production and manufacturing costs were very high. It was marked with only a paper label, without which identification is sometimes difficult. Look for a pronounced, well-finished pontil that shows the glass layers represented. Most items show a layer of white, which Fostoria called Calcite, as did Steuben. Very little has been written on the history of this company, but for more information refer to *The Collector's Encyclopedia of Art Glass* by John Shuman (Collector Books), and *Fostoria Ohio Glass, Vol II*, by Melvin L. Murray (self published).

Our advisor for this category is Frank W. Ford; he is listed in the Directory under Massachusetts.

Rose bowl, Iris, gold lustre leaves on opal, ovoid 500.00
Shade, feathers, gr on opal, gold lining, ruffled 300.00
Shade, festoons, gr on opal, 7" 250.00
Shade, leaves & vines, gr & gold on opal, 4-sided 250.00
Shade, leaves & vines on pearly wht, gold int, bell form, 4½" ...300.00
Shade, opal w/gold zipper over gr pulled decor, 7¼" 430.00
Vase, Iris, gold lustre, pinched-in sides, narrow neck, ftd, 4½" ...600.00
Vase, Iris, gold lustre w/gr leaves/vines, sq top, 12" 2,000.00

Frakturs

Fraktur is a German style of black letter text type. To collectors the fraktur is a type of hand-lettered document used by the people of German descent who settled in the areas of Pennsylvania, New Jersey, Maryland, Virginia, North and South Carolina, Ohio, Kentucky, and Ontario. These documents recorded births and baptisms and were used as bookplates and as certificates of honor. They were elaborately decorated with colorful folk-art borders of hearts, birds, angels, and flowers. Examples by recognized artists and those with an unusual decorative motif bring prices well into the thousands of dollars; in fact, some have sold at major auction houses well in excess of $10,000.00. Frakturs made in the late 1700s after the invention of the printing press provided the writer with a prepared text that he needed only to fill in at his own discretion. The next step in the evolution of machine-printed frakturs combined woodblock-printed decorations along with the text which the 'artist' sometimes enhanced with color. By the mid-1800s, even the coloring was done by machine. The vorschrift was a handwritten example prepared by a fraktur teacher to demonstrate his skill in lettering and decorating. These are often considered to be the finest of frakturs. Those dated before 1820 are most valuable.

The practice of fraktur art began to diminish after 1830 but hung on even to the early years of this century among the Pennsylvania Germans ingrained with such customs. Our advisor for this category is Frederick S. Weiser; he is listed in the Directory under Pennsylvania. (Mr. Weiser has provided our text, but being unable to physically examine the frakturs listed below cannot vouch for their authenticity, age, or condition. When requesting information, please include a self-addressed

stamped evelope.) These prices were realized at various reputable auction galleries in the East and Midwest. Unless otherwise noted, values are for examples in excellent condition. Note: Be careful not to confuse frakturs with prints, calligraphy, English-language marriage certificates, Lord's Prayers, etc.

Key:
lp — laid paper
pr — printed
p/i — pen and ink
wc — watercolored
wp — wove paper

Birth Record

Birth and baptism certificate titled Welentines, pen and ink with watercolor parrots and flowers, records 1828 birth, printed in 1831, 7½x10¼" in old painted frame, $1,980.00.

Cut-out/pin-prick design w/wc flowers, 1883, 14x15" +fr............220.00
P/i/wc, hearts/cherubs/x-hatching, 1814-70, IN, JC Jartin, 16x20"..1,100.00
P/i/wc, Martin Brechal, G colors, PA, 1808, minor damage, 13x8" +fr.1,100.00
P/i/wc, scalloped heart/2 birds, att Krebs, 1805, 8x12", +fr......1,155.00
P/i/wc, tulips/hearts/text, PA, 1820, minor damage, 12x14" +fr..740.00
P/i/wc/lp, floral/heart/text, PA, 1782, wear/rpr, 13x15" +fr 385.00
P/i/wc/lp, title & floral garland, 1819, 8½x12"+fr, EX................800.00
P/i/wc/wp, heart/parrots/tulips/fans, PA, 1820, 13x16" 2,500.00
Pr/i/wc, Berks Co PA, Weidner/1852, orig decor fr, 10x12" 330.00
Pr/wc, Gerburts und Taufschein, Ritter, PA, 1798, 16x13" +fr....150.00

Miscellaneous

Bookplate, i/wc/lp, 2 birds on tulip, script, in fr w/some curl, 7x6" .245.00
Bookplate, p/i/wc, inscription/name, floral garland, 4x4", +burl fr .350.00
Bookplate, p/i/wc, script/flowers/wreath, foxing/stains, vnr fr, 5x6" .385.00
Bookplate, wc/lp, flowers, dtd 1800, stains/wear/split, +fr, 6x4½" .600.00
Drawing, p/i/wc, bird/floral branch, yel/bl borders, fr: 5½x4½" ..440.00
Drawing, wc, exotic bird on floral branch, +fr, 4⅝x3¾", VG 650.00

Frames

Styles in picture frames have changed with the fashion of the day, but those that especially interest today's collectors are the deep shadow boxes made of fine woods such as walnut or cherry, those with Art Nouveau influence, and the oak frames decorated with molded gesso and gilt from the Victorian era.

As is true in general in the antiques and collectibles fields, the influence of online trading is greatly affecting prices. Many items once considered difficult to locate are now readily available in the .com world; as a result, values have declined. Our advisor for this category is Michael Hinton; he is listed in the Directory under Pennsylvania.

Note: Unless another era is given, frames described in the following listings are from the nineteenth century.

Brass, cherubs playing instruments w/scrolls & flowers, 12½x9½" .95.00
Brass, open scrollwork, easel bk, 12½x9½" 95.00

Brass, oval, convex glass, 14x20"	70.00
Brass filigree, gilt, 5" dia	150.00
Brass-plated CI, pierced foliage, Victorian, 13x10"	85.00
Cast brass, Cupid design, 20x12"	225.00
Chip cvd, old red pnt & natural, easel bk, 7x6"	250.00
Cvd cherry: eagle/US in star/acorns, bk: geometric lines, 5" W, 22x20"	770.00
Gesso, gold leaf, inner/outer liners w/emb foliage, 30x25"	200.00
Grpt, red rosewood on pine, beveled, 12x16"	125.00
Grpt, red/blk, mortise/tenon built, 6" W, 18x20"	135.00
Molded walnut w/ebonized & gilt borders, Victorian, 16x14"	75.00
Oak w/gesso, emb florals, 18x24"	125.00
Sterling w/etched flowers in corner, standing, 2x3"	85.00
Walnut w/gilt & marbleized inner borders, 15x17"	110.00

Frances Ware

Frances Ware, produced in the 1880s by Hobbs, Brockunier and Company of Wheeling, West Virginia, is a term refering to the decoration or finish used in the production of some of their glassware lines. Hobnail (Dewdrop) is the most commonly found of these lines, though Swirl and on occasion Quartered Block with Stars were also finished with the frosted surface and amber-stained band that defines the Frances Ware indication. Though in general collectors also tend to regard examples in crystal with simply an amber-stained band as Frances Ware, according to *Hobbs, Brockunier & Co. Glass* by Nelia and Tom Bredehoft, this is incorrect. The company called this finish 'decorated #7.' To evaluate examples in crystal with amber stain, deduct 10% from the values given below, which are strictly for the frosted finish. Our advisors for this category are Betty and Clarence Maier; they are listed in the Directory under Pennsylvania.

Hobnail, bowl, ftd, berry pontil, 6x10"	150.00
Hobnail, bowl, no flange, 9" sq	85.00
Hobnail, bowl, oblong, 8"	75.00
Hobnail, bowl, shell ftd, 8" dia	250.00
Hobnail, bowl, sq, 7½"	70.00
Hobnail, bowl, 2½x5½"	30.00
Hobnail, bowl, 7½", from $65 to	75.00
Hobnail, bowl, 8" dia	75.00
Hobnail, bowl, 8" sq	75.00
Hobnail, bowl, 10"	90.00
Hobnail, butter dish, from $80 to	120.00

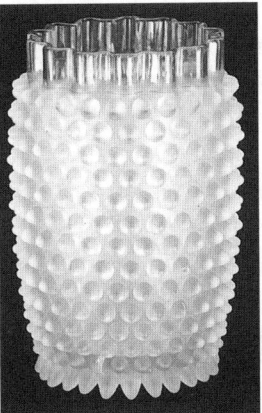

Hobnail, celery vase, 7", $125.00.

Hobnail, chandelier, amber font, brass fr, 14" dia	950.00
Hobnail, creamer, from $40 to	60.00
Hobnail, cruet, from $425 to	500.00

Hobnail, finger bowl, 4", from $25 to	35.00
Hobnail, molasses can	375.00
Hobnail, nappy, 4½" sq	25.00
Hobnail, pickle jar	175.00
Hobnail, pitcher, milk	175.00
Hobnail, pitcher, water; sq top, 8½"	195.00
Hobnail, sauce dish, sq, 4"	28.00
Hobnail, shakers, very rare, pr	300.00
Hobnail, sugar bowl, w/lid, from $65 to	80.00
Hobnail, syrup, pewter lid	375.00
Hobnail, toothpick holder/toy tumbler	60.00
Hobnail, tray, cloverleaf, 12", from $90 to	125.00
Hobnail, tumbler, water	45.00
Hobnail, vase, ruffled top	165.00
Quartered Block w/Stars, bowl, oval, 10"	65.00
Quartered Block w/Stars, butter dish	95.00
Quartered Block w/Stars, goblet	140.00
Quartered Block w/Stars, sugar bowl, w/lid	75.00
Swirl, bowl, 4"	25.00
Swirl, bowl, 8"	90.00
Swirl, butter dish	95.00
Swirl, celery, ind	35.00
Swirl, cruet, from $250 to	295.00
Swirl, mustard jar, from $90 to	125.00
Swirl, pitcher, water	225.00
Swirl, plate, 6"	30.00
Swirl, shakers, pr	165.00
Swirl, sugar bowl, w/lid	80.00
Swirl, sugar shaker, orig lid	195.00
Swirl, syrup, Pat dtd	295.00
Swirl, toothpick holder	160.00
Swirl, tumbler	45.00

Franciscan

Franciscan is a trade name used by Gladding McBean and Co., founded in northern California in 1875. In 1923 they purchased the Tropico plant in Glendale where they produced sewer pipe, gardenware, and tile. By 1934 the first of their dinnerware lines, El Patio, was produced. It was a plain design made in bright, attractive colors. El Patio Nouveau followed in 1935, glazed in two colors — one tone on the inside, a contrasting hue on the outside. Coronado, a favorite of today's collectors, was introduced in 1936. It was styled with a wide, swirled border and was made in pastels, both satin and glossy. Before 1940 fifteen patterns had been produced. The first hand-decorated lines were introduced in 1937, the ever-popular Apple pattern in 1940, Desert Rose in 1941, and Ivy in 1948. Many other hand-decorated and decaled patterns were produced there from 1934 to 1984.

Dinnerware marks before 1940 include 'GMcB' in an oval, 'F' within a square, or 'Franciscan' with 'Pottery' underneath (which was later changed to 'Ware'). A circular arrangement of 'Franciscan' with 'Made in California USA' in the center was used from 1940 until 1949. At least forty marks were used before 1975; several more were introduced after that. At one time, paper labels were used.

The company merged with Lock Joint Pipe Company in 1963, becoming part of the Interpace Corporation. In July of 1979 Franciscan was purchased by Wedgwood Limited of England, and the Glendale plant closed in October 1984.

Note: Due to limited space, we have used a pricing formula meant to be only a general guide, not a mechanical ratio on each piece. Rarity varies with pattern, and not all pieces occur in all patterns. Our advisors for this category are Mick and Lorna Chase (Fiesta Plus); they are listed in the Directory under Tennessee. See also Gladding McBean.

Coronado

Both satin (matt) and glossy colors were made including turquoise, coral, celadon, light yellow, ivory, and gray (in satin); and turquoise, coral, apple green, light yellow, white, maroon, and redwood in glossy glazes. High-end values are for maroon, yellow, redwood, and gray. Add 10 – 15% for gloss.

Bowl, casserole; w/lid, from $45 to	90.00
Bowl, cereal; from $10 to	15.00
Bowl, cream soup; w/underplate, from $25 to	40.00
Bowl, fruit; from $6 to	12.00
Bowl, nut cup; from $8 to	12.00
Bowl, onion soup; w/lid, from $25 to	40.00
Bowl, rim soup; from $14 to	25.00
Bowl, salad; lg, from $20 to	35.00
Bowl, serving; oval, 10½", from $20 to	33.00
Bowl, serving; 7½" dia, from $12 to	18.00
Bowl, serving; 8½" dia, from $10 to	17.00
Bowl, sherbet/egg cup; from $10 to	15.00
Butter dish, from $25 to	35.00
Cigarette box, w/lid, from $40 to	75.00
Creamer, from $8 to	12.00
Cup & saucer, demitasse; from $20 to	32.00
Cup & saucer, jumbo	32.00
Demitasse pot, from $100 to	150.00
Fast-stand gravy, from $25 to	35.00
Jam jar, w/lid, from $45 to	60.00
Pitcher, 1½-qt, from $25 to	45.00
Plate, chop; 12½" dia, from $18 to	32.00
Plate, chop; 14" dia, from $20 to	30.00
Plate, crescent hostess; w/cup well, no established value	
Plate, crescent salad; lg, no established value	
Plate, ind crescent salad; from $22 to	32.00
Plate, 6½", from $5 to	8.00
Plate, 7½", from $7 to	10.00
Plate, 8½", from $8 to	11.00
Plate, 9½", from $10 to	15.00
Plate, 10½", from $12 to	18.00
Platter, oval, 10", from $12 to	20.00
Platter, oval, 13", from $24 to	36.00
Platter, oval, 15½", from $25 to	45.00
Relish dish, oval, from $12 to	25.00
Shakers, pr, from $15 to	30.00
Sugar bowl, w/lid, from $10 to	20.00
Teacup & saucer, from $8 to	12.00
Teapot, from $45 to	75.00
Tumbler, water; no established value	
Vase, 8", no established value	

Desert Rose

Ashtray, ind	12.00
Ashtray, oval	95.00
Ashtray, sq	195.00
Bell, Danbury Mint	95.00
Bell, dinner	95.00
Bowl, bouillon; w/lid	395.00
Bowl, cereal; 6"	15.00
Bowl, divided vegetable	45.00
Bowl, fruit	7.00
Bowl, mixing; lg	175.00
Bowl, mixing; med	165.00
Bowl, mixing; sm	155.00
Bowl, porringer	175.00
Bowl, rimmed soup	25.00
Bowl, salad; 10"	95.00
Bowl, soup; ftd	32.00
Bowl, vegetable; 8"	32.00
Bowl, vegetable; 9"	40.00
Box, cigarette	95.00
Box, egg	115.00
Box, heart shape	165.00
Box, rnd	165.00
Butter dish	45.00
Candle holders, pr	95.00
Candy dish, oval	225.00
Casserole, 1½-qt	75.00
Casserole, 2½-qt, minimum value	395.00
Coffeepot	75.00
Coffeepot, ind	395.00
Compote, lg	55.00
Compote, low	125.00
Cookie jar	295.00
Creamer, ind	40.00
Creamer, regular	15.00
Cup & saucer, coffee	85.00
Cup & saucer, demitasse	45.00
Cup & saucer, jumbo	45.00
Cup & saucer, tall	35.00
Cup & saucer, tea	15.00
Egg cup	35.00
Ginger jar	225.00
Goblet, ftd	195.00
Gravy boat	30.00
Heart	145.00
Hurricane lamp	325.00
Jam jar	125.00
Long 'n narrow, 15½x7¾"	495.00
Microwave dish, oblong, 1½-qt	225.00
Microwave dish, sq, 1-qt	195.00
Microwave dish, sq, 8"	195.00
Mug, bbl, 12-oz	35.00
Mug, cocoa; 10-oz	95.00
Mug, 7-oz	25.00
Napkin ring	65.00
Piggy bank	295.00
Pitcher, jug	195.00
Pitcher, milk	65.00
Pitcher, water; 2½-qt	95.00
Plate, chop; 12"	65.00
Plate, chop; 14"	95.00
Plate, coupe dessert	65.00
Plate, coupe party	125.00
Plate, coupe steak	195.00
Plate, divided; child's	195.00
Plate, grill	125.00
Plate, side salad	35.00
Plate, TV	175.00
Plate, 6½"	6.00
Plate, 8½"	12.00
Plate, 9½"	20.00
Plate, 10½"	18.00
Platter, turkey; 19"	295.00
Platter, 12¾"	35.00
Platter, 14"	45.00
Relish, oval, 10"	35.00
Relish, 3-section	65.00

Salt and pepper shakers, tall, $45.00 for the pair; Pitcher, syrup, $75.00.

Shaker & pepper mill, pr	295.00
Shakers, rose bud, pr	15.00
Sherbet	20.00
Soup ladle	75.00
Sugar bowl, open, ind	75.00
Sugar bowl, regular	25.00
Tea canister	225.00
Teapot	125.00
Thimble	75.00
Tidbit tray, 2-tier	125.00
Tile, in fr	50.00
Tile, sq	35.00
Toast cover	195.00
Trivet, fluted, rnd	325.00
Tumbler, juice; 6-oz	45.00
Tumbler, 10-oz	32.00
Tureen, soup; flat bottom	495.00
Tureen, soup; ftd, either style	695.00
Vase, bud	75.00

For other hand-painted patterns, we recommend the following general guide for comparable pieces (based on current values):

Daisy	-20%
October	-20%
Cafe Royal	Same as Desert Rose
Forget-Me-Not	Same as Desert Rose
Meadow Rose	Same as Desert Rose
Strawberry Fair	Same as Desert Rose
Strawberry Time	Same as Desert Rose
Fresh Fruit	Same as Desert Rose
Bountiful	Same as Desert Rose
Desert Rose	Base Line Values
Apple	+10%
Ivy	+20%
Poppy	+50%
Original (small) Fruit	+50%
Wild Flower	200% or more!

There is not an active market in Bouquet, Rosette, or Twilight Rose, as these are scarce, having been produced only a short time. Our estimate would place Bouquet and Rosette in the October range (-20%) and Twilight Rose in the Ivy range (+20%).

There are several Apple items that are so scarce they command higher prices than fit the above formula. The Apple ginger jar is valued at $600.00+, the 4" jug at $195.00+, and any covered box in Apple is at least 50% more than Desert Rose.

Apple Pieces Not Available in Desert Rose

Bowl, batter; minimum value	450.00
Bowl, str sides, lg	55.00
Bowl, str sides, med	45.00
Casserole, stick hdl & lid, ind	65.00
Coaster	65.00
Jam jar, redesigned	425.00
Shaker & pepper mill, wooden top, pr	395.00
½-apple baker, from $125 to	195.00

Franciscan Fine China

The main line of fine china was called Masterpiece. There were at least four marks used during its production from 1941 to 1977. Almost every piece is clearly marked. This china is true porcelain, the body having been fired at a very high temperature. Many years of research and experimentation went into this china before it was marketed. Production was temporarily suspended during the war years. More than 170 patterns and many varying shapes were produced. All are valued about the same with the exception of the Renaissance group, which is 25% higher.

Bowl, vegetable; serving, oval	50.00
Cup	20.00
Plate, bread & butter	18.00
Plate, dinner	30.00
Plate, salad	25.00
Saucer	12.00

Starburst

Ashtray, ind	20.00
Ashtray, oval, lg	50.00
Bonbon/jelly dish	22.00
Bowl, crescent salad	40.00
Bowl, divided, 8"	25.00
Bowl, fruit; ind	13.00
Bowl, salad; ind	25.00
Bowl, soup/cereal	13.00
Bowl, vegetable; 8½"	45.00
Butter dish	45.00
Candlesticks, pr, from $175 to	200.00
Casserole, lg	100.00
Coffeepot	150.00
Creamer	15.00
Cup & saucer	25.00
Gravy boat, from $20 to	30.00
Gravy boat, w/attached undertray	40.00
Gravy ladle	30.00
Jug, water; 10"	90.00
Mug, sm	60.00
Mug, tall	95.00
Oil cruet	75.00
Pepper mill	150.00
Pitcher, water; 10"	85.00
Pitcher, 7½", from $50 to	75.00
Plate, chop; from $55 to	65.00
Plate, dinner	12.00
Plate, 11"	45.00
Plate, 6"	6.00
Plate, 8"	8.00
Platter, 15"	80.00
Shakers, bullet shape, lg, pr	50.00
Shakers, sm, pr	20.00

Snack/TV tray w/cup rest, 12½", from $75 to.............................100.00
Sugar bowl...25.00
Tumbler, 6-oz, from $40 to 50.00
Vinegar cruet..75.00

Frankart

During the 1920s Frankart, Inc., of New York City, produced a line of accessories that included figural nude lamps, bookends, ashtrays, etc. These white metal composition items were offered in several finishes including verde green, jap black, and gunmetal gray. The company also produced a line of caricatured animals, but the stylized nude figurals have proven to be the most collectible today. With few exceptions, all pieces were marked 'Frankart, Inc.' with a patent number or 'pat. appl. for.' All pieces listed are in very good original condition unless otherwise indicated. Our advisor for this category is Walter Glenn; he is listed in the Directory under Georgia.

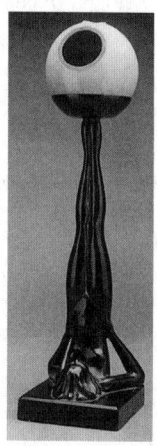

Ash receiver, inverted nude balances ash ball on toes, 12", $650.00.

Aquarium, nude sits atop wrought-iron stand, sq, aqua, 14" 1,050.00
Ashtray, ballet girl in center of 8" rnd onyx tray, 10" 625.00
Ashtray, dancing nude holds tray on side, box on base, 10" 750.00
Ashtray, nude on pointe, 3 trays form ballerina's tutu, 10" 725.00
Ashtray, nude on tiptoe arches bk, holds 4" tray..........................675.00
Ashtray, seated nude w/matchbox holder, 5½" 650.00
Ashtray, stylized duck holds tray in outstretched wings, 5" 275.00
Bookends, caricatured cowboys in chaps, 8", pr 350.00
Bookends, nude sits atop human skull, 8", pr..............................950.00
Bookends, standing nude, arms bk to support, 7½", pr...............285.00
Bookends, standing nude 'peek-a-boos' around books, 8", pr.....525.00
Bookends, stylized parrot on arched perch, 7", pr 275.00
Clock, 2 nudes kneel & hold 10" rnd glass clock, 12½" 2,550.00
Fruit bowl, 2 bk-to-bk kneeling nudes hold 8" dish, 6".............975.00
Incense burner, standing nude holds tray in front, 10" 675.00
Lamp, kneeling nude gazes into 5" rnd globe, 7"..........................875.00
Lamp, seated nude, leg extended, 2 cylinders on sides, 8"........1,575.00
Lamp, standing nude silhouettes against glass fan, 10"............1,750.00
Lamp, 2 bk-to-bk dancing nudes hold sq glass cylinder, 13" 1,850.00
Lamp, 2 bk-to-bk nudes hold 8" ball globe, 21"......................1,350.00
Lamp, 2 kneeling nudes embrace 8" crackle glass globe, 9"......1,050.00
Lamp, 2 nudes stand either side rectangular glass panel, 10½" ..1,850.00
Mirror, kneeling nude holds 6" gold-bk mirror, 11" 850.00
Smoke set, seated nude, cigarette box in base, tray in ea arm, 9" ..775.00
Smoke stand, nude sits atop wrought-iron stand, 36" 850.00
Vase, dancing nude holds 10" flower vase on hip, 12½" 1,250.00
Vase, 2 bk-to-bk standing nudes hold 7" glass vase, 13" 975.00

Frankoma

The Frank Pottery, founded in Oklahoma in 1933 by John Frank, became known as Frankoma in 1934. The company produced decorative figurals, vases, and such, marking their ware from 1936 to 1938 with a pacing leopard 'Frankoma' mark. These pieces are highly sought. The entire operation was destroyed by fire in 1938, and new molds were cast — some from surviving pieces — and a similar line of production was pursued. The body of the ware was changed in 1955 from a honey tan (called 'Ada clay,' referring to the name of the town near the area where it was dug) to a red brick clay (known as Sapulpa), and this, along with the color of the glazes (over fifty have been used), helps determine the period of production. A Southwestern theme has always been favored in design as well as in color selection.

In 1965 they began to produce a limited-edition series of Christmas plates, followed by a bottle vase series in 1969. Considered very collectible are their political mugs, bicentennial plates, Teenagers of the Bible plates, and the Wildlife series. Their ceramic Christmas cards are also very popular items with today's collectors.

Frankoma celebrated their fiftieth anniversary in 1983. On September 26 of that same year, Frankoma was again destroyed by fire. Because of a fire-proof wall, master molds of all 1983 production items were saved, allowing plans for rebuilding to begin immediately.

Frankoma filed for Chapter 11 in April 1990, and eventually sold to a Maryland investor in February of 1991, thereby ending the family-ownership era. For a more thorough study of the subject, we recommend that you refer to *Frankoma Treasures* and *Frankoma and Other Oklahoma Potteries* by Phyllis and Tom Bess, our advisors; you will find their address in the Directory under Oklahoma.

Ashtray, recumbent cocker spaniel at side, Ada clay, 7⅜", $175 to .200.00
Beverage set, blk, #8L, 7½" pitcher+4 #26DC tumblers................38.00
Bookends, Charger Horse, blk, leopard mk, pr...........................385.00
Casserole, Aztec, Sapulpa clay, #7W, 10" 40.00
Christmas card, 1944, from $400 to...500.00
Christmas card, 1947-48, from $95 to 115.00
Christmas card, 1949, from $85 to...95.00
Christmas card, 1950-51, from $125 to 150.00
Christmas card, 1952, Donna Frank, from $150 to 200.00
Christmas card, 1952, from $125 to..140.00
Christmas card, 1953, from $90 to 110.00
Christmas card, 1954...110.00
Christmas card, 1957...70.00
Christmas card, 1958-60..65.00
Christmas card, 1969-71..40.00
Christmas card, 1972...35.00
Christmas card, 1973-75..30.00
Christmas card, 1976-82..25.00
Christmas plate, Flight Into Egypt, Della Robia White, J Frank, 1968 ....60.00
Cookie jar, Barrel, Prairie Green, NM...50.00
Head vase, Phoebe, wht, Sapulpa clay, 7x5"................................75.00
Horn of Plenty (cornucopia), Desert Gold, #222, 12" 60.00
Mug, Donkey, Plum, 1983...45.00
Mug, Donkey, yel, 1975..42.50
Mug, Elephant, brn, 1973...40.00
Mug, Elephant, 1968, from $45 to 75.00
Mug, Elephant, 1969, from $40 to 65.00
Mug, Elephant, 1974, from $30 to 40.00
Mug, Elephant or Donkey, 1975-76, from $30 to..........................40.00
Mug, Elephant or Donkey, 1977-90, from $20 to..........................30.00
Pitcher, Aztec, Desert Gold, 2-qt..57.50
Pitcher, Barrel, Desert Gold, #97D, ½-gal....................................95.00
Pitcher, Flame Red, #8, 7¼" 115.00

Pitcher, Prairie Green, Ada clay, #835, 8" 50.00
Pitcher, water; Prairie Green, w/ice lip, 96-oz, 8" 75.00
Planter, Swan, wht, 7½" 37.50
Plaque, Indian Head, #132, 4⅛x2¼" 60.00
Platter, Plainsman, Prairie Green, med...40.00
Sculpture, Bucking Bronco, Ivory, ca 1942, 5¾"...................300.00
Sculpture, Gardener Girl, Prairie Green w/yel & wht, #700, 1942-52.165.00
Sculpture, Indian Maiden, Desert Gold, Willard Stone, 12½" ...75.00
Sculpture, Madonna, Desert Gold, Willard Stone, 14½" 45.00
Sculpture, Peter Pan, Jade Green, 1942, 6"..............................110.00
Shakers, Guernsey jug, Cherokee Red, 1936-42, ##93H, pr..........55.00
Tray, palm leaf & Club Trade Winds advertising, Sapulpa clay, 17"...85.00
Vase, collector; V-1, from $125 to 150.00
Vase, collector; V-2, 1970, 12", from $80 to................................90.00
Vase, collector; V-4, 1972 ....85.00
Vase, collector; V-5, 1973, 13" 85.00
Vase, collector; V-6, from $80 to..90.00
Vase, collector; V-7, 13" 80.00
Vase, collector; V-8, w/stopper, 13"..75.00
Vase, collector; V-9, w/stopper, 13"..65.00
Vase, collector; V-10 & V-11, ea, from $40 to................................50.00
Vase, collector; V-12, 13" 65.00
Vase, collector; V-14, from $75 to...80.00
Vase, collector; V-15, 13", from $85 to..100.00
Vase, Crocus, Brown Satin, #43..50.00
Vase, Prairie Green, Ada clay, #28, 9" 45.00
Vase, ram's head, ivory, #28, 1936-42, 9¼"................................125.00
Vase, Shell Fan, Prairie Green, Ada clay, #54, 6" 40.00

Fraternal Organizations

Fraternal memorabilia is a vast and varied field. Emblems representing the various organizations have been used to decorate cups, shaving mugs, plates, and glassware. Medals, swords, documents, and other ceremonial paraphernalia from the 1800s and early 1900s are especially prized. Our advisor for Odd Fellows is Greg Spiess; he is listed in the Directory under Illinois. Information on Masonic and Shrine memorabilia has been provided by David Smies, who is listed under Kansas. Assistance concerning Elks collectibles was provided by David Wendel; he is listed in the Directory under Missouri.

Elks

Whiskey nip, elk's tooth form, white china with brown wash, American, 1890 – 1910, $1,250.00.

Ashtray, brass, 3 elks' heads & 3 rests, brass, 4½" 20.00
Badge, Medford Oregon, elk's head logo w/apple & fruit pendant, 1912.110.00
Belt & buckle, brass w/bl enameled elk's head & insignia, MIB.30.00
Book, Ritual BLO Elks, 1946, EX 30.00
Card case, elk's head w/garnet eye, enameled clock, mk sterling..120.00

Cookbook, Bicentennial; G Washington & Liberty Bell, 82 pgs, 1970s..20.00
Doorknob, clock w/BPOE on both ends, brass.............................125.00
Flask, carmel-colored ceramic, clock & elk's head, 6⅛x3" 70.00
Match safe, BPOE, clock & elk's head, sterling silver, 2⅜x2" 55.00
Match safe, 2 emb elks' heads, silver filigreed horn top & bottom.215.00
Mug, elk's head & logo w/wht bkground on purple, WH Tatler, 5" ..45.00
Pendant, Elk's Carnival Fair, Erie Lodge, heart shape, gr stone center..35.00
Pennant, bl w/BPOE 1912 Portland w/elk's head, 29x11½", EX...20.00
Pin, hot-air balloon w/bl enameled La Grange OR, #443, shield pendant.90.00
Pin, reunion; elk's head on bar w/bell pendant w/clock center, 1907.30.00
Plate, Grafton Lodge, wht w/insignia, Syracuse China, 9"............50.00
Poker chip, BPOE 310 on 1 side w/elk's head on other, clay........12.00
Ring, 14k wht gold w/elk's head, star & BPOE in silver on blk enamel.60.00
Spoon, BPOE, logo/elk's head enameled in bowl, historic events on hdl.180.00
Spoon, sterling, BPOE & elk's head in bowl, buffalo on end.......45.00
Toothpick holder, Cincinnati, emb elk's head w/BPOE, SP, 2¼" ..55.00
Watch fob, BPOE & logo w/elk's head on 14k gold w/2 teeth, w/chain 200.00

Masons

Apron, symbols & devices litho on silk w/HP details, 1850s, 16x14" ..400.00
Apron, wht w/cobalt satin & gold decor, presentation, 1934, 14x17"...85.00
Cane, cvd lizard, metal tip, emblem & eagle knob, 33½" 350.00
Collar covers, arrowhead shape w/insignia in center, 1¾", pr 12.50
Columns, cvd symbols, mc pnt, ca 1900, 98½x18", pr.............1,380.00
Cuff links, cvd cameo type w/Gs, ca 1890s, pr+tie clip 150.00
Gavel, walnut w/2 eng silver fittings, 11¾" 170.00
Goblet, amethyst glass w/etch St Paul MN 1908, ftd, 5¼"...........60.00
Pendant, roadrunner w/rose in mouth & insignia, 1⅝" dia 15.00
Pendant/fob, hammered 14k rose gold w/bl & wht enameling, early, 1".110.00
Pitcher, flow bl, Portland ME 1806-1906, logo, Royal Doulton, 8½".........200.00
Sign, symbols pnt on wood shield shape w/gilt fr, 19th C, 34x29" .3,000.00
Tobacco jar, lead sides w/pnt inscriptions, ship/etc, 1820s, 7"..1,175.00

Odd Fellows

Banner, symbols on bl, gold braid, 30x18", EX................................90.00
Book, souvenir; paperbk, 1922 Convention, EX..............................30.00
Collar, scarlet w/sateen lining, silver trim, fringe, EX 75.00
Emblem, horseshoe w/dove atop, pnt CI, 7½x6x1" 75.00
Gameboard, blk/gold metallic sqs, chain links/symbols, 20x20", VG...330.00
Prospectus, re: publishing books about order, 1845, 1 pg, 8x10" .15.00
Report, response to request to join, refused for drunkenness, 1846..13.00
Shaving mug, eye & 3 rings, initials, ca 1920, 3¾", EX 80.00

Shrine

Buckle, brass w/inset red stones, fez shape, custom made, 2x3" 40.00
Buckle, gold-tone metal w/emblem, 1½" dia, EX...........................25.00
Collar tips, gold-tone w/mc inlay, 1" triangles, pr 15.00
Fez, Khiva, w/tassel pin, red w/mc rhinestones & lg sphinx front .35.00
Money clip, enameled metal, dollar-sign shape, EX.......................15.00
Planter, fez w/symbols, Klay Kraft, 4"..30.00
Ring, 10k yel gold w/blk & red stones 125.00
Tie bar, copper-tone metal w/alligator clip, 3"...............................10.00
Tie bar, hanging medallion, Hickok, 1950s, EX 10.00

Miscellaneous

Almas Temple, guest badge, emb images, ca 1923, 1½x2"............40.00
Am Legion, medal, 14th Nat'l Convention, OR 1932, 4", VG.....28.00
Am Legion, pin-bk button, devil on red, Whitehead & Hoag, 1¼", EX.25.00
Daughters of the Nile, pin, saber w/insignia & rose 12.50
Eastern Star, creamer & sugar bowl, Lefton.................................50.00

Eastern Star, ring, 14k wht gold w/emblem on top, dainty filigree..**125.00**
Kiwanis, cuff links, 2-toned enamel w/lg K, 1" dia, pr.................**27.50**
Knight's Templar, plate, Grand Master Gobin portrait, 1889-92, 8"..**40.00**
Knights of Golden Eagle, flag holder, CI, memorial, 19th C, 18½"...**110.00**
Knights of Pythias, pin, triangular w/blk C on yel.....................**15.00**
Maccabees, photo, 11 men in robes w/helmets/etc, 1911, 25½x22½"...**85.00**
Scottish Rite, hat, 32nd Degree, blk w/gold trim, eagle front........**45.00**

Fraunfelter

Charles Fraunfelter organized his company in Zanesville, Ohio, in 1915. It was known as the Ohio Pottery Company until 1923. During this period their main product was a line of utilitarian articles for chemical laboratories made of hard-paste porcelain. In 1918 they used the same body to produce a brown and white line called 'Petruscan.' By 1920 a line of hotel ware was added. The company organized in 1923 and became known and Fraunfelter China Company; but after the death of Fraunfelter in 1925, the business fell into hard times and eventually closed altogether in 1939.

Casserole, poppies on wht, rnd, w/lid **50.00**
Creamer & sugar bowl, HP violets, gold trim.........................**37.50**
Custard cup, orange lustre **3.00**
Jug, bl gloss, w/lid, 5" **50.00**
Teapot, Deco style, yel & cream w/silver trim, dmn mk.............**125.00**
Vase, trees & cliff beside ocean & sailboats, gold on gr, 6x4¼".**415.00**
Waffle set, Bird of Paradise decal, syrup+batter bowl+tray .**325.00**

French Enameled Ware

In France during the 1880s, it became commonplace to decorate metalware items, decorative as well as utilitarian, with enameling that was often embellished with birds, flowers, and various other devices. The work was done by hand and was often very detailed and intricate.

Bud vase, portrait of lady in landscape, ovoid on trumpet ft, 5", EX **400.00**
Patch box, 18k yel/rose gold, Venus & Eros reserves, 1700s, 3" dia ...**2,400.00**

Fruit Jars

As early as 1829, canning jars were being manufactured for use in the home preservation of foodstuffs. For the past twenty-five years, they have been sought as popular collectibles. At the last estimate, over four thousand fruit jars and variations were known to exist. Some are very rare, perhaps one-of-a-kind examples known to have survived to the present day. Among the most valuable are the black glass jars, the amber Van Vliet, and the cobalt Millville. These often bring prices in excess of $20,000.00 when they can be found. Aside from condition, values are based on age, rarity, color, and special features. For more information, we recommend *1,000 Fruit Jars* by Bill Schroeder. Our advisor for this category is John Hathaway; he is listed in the Directory under Maine.

Acme (on shield w/stars & stripes), clear, pt.........................**15.00**
Acme Seal (in script), qt...**50.00**
Air Tight, pt...**125.00**
Atlas (HA in stippled circle) Mason, Mascot Cooler label, ½-gal..**9.00**
Atlas (HA in stippled circle) Mason, pt..............................**5.00**
Atlas E-Z Saal, ½-pt..**3.00**
Atlas E-Z Seal, aqua, bell shape, pt.................................**3.00**
Atlas E-Z Seal, gr, pt, w/gr lid.....................................**18.00**
Atlas E-Z Seal, gr, qt...**15.00**

Atlas E-Z Seal, 58-oz..**48.00**
Atlas Mason Patent, aqua, qt...**4.00**
Atlas Strong Shoulder Mason, bl, pt.................................**12.00**
Atlas Whole Fruit, qt..**2.00**
Ball (leaning Ls) Perfect Mason, bl, qt.............................**12.00**
Ball (underlined) Perfect Mason, bl, 9 ribs, ½-gal.................**15.00**
Ball (3 L loop) Improved Mason, aqua, qt............................**4.00**
Ball Eclipse, base: Pat 7-14-08, qt..................................**4.00**
Ball Eclipse Wide Mouth, pt..**6.00**
Ball Freezer Jar, 10-oz..**2.00**
Ball Ideal, bl, rnd, ½-gal..**12.00**
Ball Ideal, bl, ½-pt..**65.00**
Ball Ideal Pat'd July 14 1908, bl, pt...............................**5.00**
Ball Ideal Pat'd July 14 1908, bl, qt...............................**2.00**
Ball Improved, bl, pt...**12.00**
Ball Mason, bl, pt...**2.00**
Ball Perfect Mason, bl, sq, qt......................................**10.00**
Ball Perfect Mason, pk, pt..**40.00**
Ball Perfect Mason (undropped A), 8 ribs, circle: 1932, bl, qt........**9.00**
Ball Perfect Mason Made in USA, bl, 8 ribs, qt......................**25.00**
Ball Perfection, bl, pt, no closure................................**100.00**
Ball Special, 8 ribs, rnd or sq, pt.................................**5.00**
Ball Standard, aqua, wax sealer w/tin lid, qt.......................**20.00**
Ball Sure Seal, bl, qt...**3.00**
Beaver (beaver chewing log), ½-gal.................................**60.00**
Bernardin (script, underlined) Mason, pt...........................**10.00**
Best (arched), qt...**30.00**
Boston Trade Mark Dagger (dagger) Brand, lt gr, qt.................**250.00**

Burns Mf'g Co...Patd. June 29th 1884, aquamarine, clear lid, quart, bail missing, rare, $450.00.

Brighton, sun-colored amethyst, orig clear lid, repro clamp, qt...**125.00**
Carroll's Sure Seal, pt...**58.00**
Chef Trade (chef) Mark (in stippled fr), ½-pt......................**125.00**
Clark's Peerless, aqua, pt..**6.00**
Cohansey (arched), aqua, pt...**75.00**
Crown (crown), aqua, qt...**4.00**
Crown (crown) Imperial, aqua, qt....................................**5.00**
Crown (crown) Tall Narrow Crown, aqua, midget......................**40.00**
Crown Cordial & Extract & Co New York, ½-gal.......................**12.00**
Crown Crown (ring crown), aqua, qt.................................**17.00**
Crown Mason, qt...**2.00**
Crystal, aqua, qt...**125.00**
Daisy, pt...**20.00**
Dexter Improved (around circle of fruit), aqua, qt.................**125.00**
Double Safety (script), ½-pt.......................................**12.00**
Double Seal, pt...**28.00**
Drey Improved Ever Seal Pat 1920, pt...............................**5.00**
Drey Sq Mason (in carpenter's sq), ½-gal...........................**20.00**
Eagle, aqua, qt, orig..**175.00**

Economy, base: Portland Ore, sun-colored amethyst, qt 10.00
Electric Trade Mark (in circle), aqua, ½-gal 75.00
Empire (in stippled cross), pt...5.00
Erie Lightning, aqua, qt..75.00
Eureka (script), lt gr, base: Eureka Jar Co...WVa, qt 25.00
Everlasting Jar, aqua, pt...35.00
Franklin Fruit Jar, aqua, orig band, ½-gal....................................75.00
Gem, aqua, midget..40.00
Genuine (Mason script in flag), aqua, qt.......................................12.00
Ghosted Economy, aqua, wax sealer, tin lid, qt 25.00
Globe, amber, qt...125.00
Green Mountain (in fr), pt 12.00
Hamilton, ½-gal..100.00
Hazel Atlas E-Z Seal, aqua, pt...20.00
Hazel Preserve Jar, ½-pt...40.00
Hero (over lettered cross), aqua, qt 40.00
Improved Crown (all in script), lt gr, qt, clear lid.........................18.00
Improved Crown Crown, aqua, qt..12.00
Improved Gem Made in Canada, pt 10.00
Improved Mason Jar (2 lines), qt..15.00
Jewel Jar (block letters in fr), qt...15.00
Kerr 'Self Sealing' Mason, amber, qt...40.00
Kerr 'Self Sealing' Trade Mark Patented Mason, ½-gal...................5.00
Lafayette (in script), aqua, pt..300.00
Lindell Glass Co (base), amber, wax sealer, tin lid, qt, M 250.00
Lynchburg Standard Mason, aqua, qt...35.00
Mason, teal, qt..50.00
Mason (on slant over cattails), bl, ½-gal......................................200.00
Mason's (cross) Improved, reverse: circle, aqua, qt 25.00
Mason's (Keystone in circle) Patent Nov 30th 1858, aqua, midget.....50.00
Mason's (3 dot) Patent Nov 30th 1858, base: L&W, aqua, qt.......45.00
Mason's CFJ Improved, aqua, midget...25.00
Mason's CFJ Patent Nov 30th 1858, aqua, ½-gal 12.00
Mason's CFJ Patent Nov 30th 1858, w/CFJ zinc lid, midget 35.00
Mason's Cross Improved, aqua, midget 50.00
Mason's G (lg) Patent Nov 30th 1858, aqua, whittled, ½-gal.......50.00
Mason's III Patent Nov 30th 1858, aqua, midget.........................175.00
Mason's Patent, aqua, ½-gal 10.00
Mason's Patent Nov 30th 1858, aqua, midget 35.00
Mason's Patent Nov 30th 1858, reverse: HGW, aqua, qt...............25.00
Mason's Patent Nov 30th 58 (Christmas Mason), bl, pt 100.00
Mason's SGCo Patent Nov 30th 1858, aqua, qt...............................8.00
Mason's 20 Patent Nov 30th 1858, aqua, qt..................................30.00
Millville WTCo Improved, aqua, correct grape insert, qt...........110.00
Mountain Mason, rnd, qt..22.00
Mrs Chapin's Mayonnaise Boston Mass, pt......................................6.00
Pet, aqua, whittled, ½-gal...150.00
Presto, ½-pt...35.00
Princess, qt..18.00
Putnam (on base), aqua, 7⅜"...75.00
Regal (in circle), sun-colored amethyst, wax sealer, tin lid, pt, EX.112.00
Safe Seal (arched) Block Letters, qt...150.00
Safe Seal (in circle), bl, pt..5.00
Security Seal FG Co (in triangle), pt..8.00
Simplex Mason, correct glass lid, qt..150.00
Smalley's Nu-Seal Trade Mark in Diamonds, ½-pt 75.00
Solidex (in oval), gr, liter...65.00
Star (star, R is curled), qt...50.00
The Daisy FE Ward & Co, aqua, qt 25.00
The Gem, aqua, 24-oz 75.00
The Gem Reverse Hourglass, aqua, qt..25.00
The Ideal Imperial, aqua, qt..35.00
The Mason Jar of 1858 TM (in circle & sq), aqua, qt 65.00
The Pearl, aqua, qt..75.00

The Queen, aqua, ½-gal...40.00
Tight Seal (in circle), bl, ½-gal..20.00
Trade Mark 'The Smalley' Self Sealer, qt..6.00
Trade Mark Lightning, amber, ½-gal...120.00
Trade Mark Lightning, golden amber, qt.......................................95.00
Trademark No 1 Lightning, aqua, qt..135.00
Union No 2, aqua, 3-pc mold, qt...865.00
Victory (in shield on lid), twin side clamps, pt................................6.00
Victory (in shield on lid), twin side clamps, ½-pt..........................20.00
Victory Circle by Patd Feb by 9th 1864 Reisd June 22 1867, aqua, qt..80.00
Wears (in oval), aqua, qt...12.00

Fry

Henry Fry established his glassworks in 1901 in Rochester, Pennsylvania. There, until 1933 when it was sold to the Libbey Company, he produced glassware of the finest quality. In the early years they produced beautiful cut glass; and when it began to wane in popularity, Fry turned to the manufacture of occasional pieces and oven glassware. He is perhaps most famous for the opalescent pearl art glass called 'Foval.' It was sometimes made with blue or jade green trim in combination. Because it was in production for only a short time in 1926 and 1927, it is hard to find. Our advisor for this category is Ron Damaska; he is listed in the Directory under Pennsylvania. See also Kitchen Collectibles, Glassware.

Ashtray, Rose pk, 4 buttressed ft, 4 rests......................................50.00
Baker, pearl ovenware, #1919, 6"..20.00
Baker, pearl ovenware, #1932, 12"..75.00
Basket, floral (unnamed) cutting, uptrn sides, from $500 to 575.00

Basket, Foval, cobalt handle and stem, 1920s, 8½", $275.00. (Photo courtesy John A. Shuman III)

Bean pot, pearl ovenware, #1924, 1-qt 85.00
Bowl, cream soup; Emerald, w/underplate 40.00
Bowl, cream soup; pearl ovenware, hdls, #1970, w/underplate 50.00
Bowl, cream soup; Royal Blue, hdls, w/underplate 50.00
Bowl, cut Hobstars & Canes, 4½x8¾"..200.00
Bowl, Emerald, petal ft, clear swirl connector..............................185.00
Bowl, flat soup; Foval, silver trim, 1½x7½"..................................150.00
Bowl, fruit; Foval, Delft ft, #2505, 12"..475.00
Bowl, fruit; Foval w/Jade Green trim & connector, rolled edge, 10"...350.00
Bowl, Pinwheel cuttings, 8" dia 150.00
Bowl, Royal Blue, petal ft, clear swirl connector, 3½x6".............165.00
Cake plate, pearl ovenware, sq, #1947...25.00
Candle holders, amber w/gold trim, orig paper labels, pr..............65.00
Candlestick, Foval, Jade Green threading & ft, 12" 395.00
Carafe, 3-Stemmed Rose etching, rpl stopper 85.00
Casserole, gr, w/lid, #1938, 7"..110.00
Casserole, pearl ovenware, etched lid, #1938, w/metal holder 8" ..50.00
Casserole, pearl ovenware, etched lid, #1954, metal holder 55.00
Casserole, pearl ovenware, w/lid, 11" dia......................................50.00

Casserole, pearl ovenware w/leaf cutting, w/lid, #37 ....40.00
Comport, Foval festooning & Delft Blue stem, #2502, 5½".........350.00
Compote, amethyst w/crystal stem, 3½x7⅞" 75.00
Compote, Foval, Jade Green stem & ft, 6⅞x6" 250.00
Console set, Azure Blue w/colored bands, bowl+2 candlesticks ..150.00
Creamer & sugar bowl, Azure Blue, Diamond Optic 55.00
Creamer & sugar bowl, Foval, Jade Green hdls, 3¼", 3" 275.00
Creamer & sugar bowl, Foval, Stippled, Delft Blue hdls.............300.00
Creamer & sugar bowl, Foval w/festooning, Delft Blue hdls 350.00
Creamer & sugar bowl, Ivy cutting, from $225 to.......................250.00
Creamer & sugar bowl, Vienna cutting, from $225 to 250.00
Cruet, Nashville cutting, from $165 to 200.00
Cup & saucer, AD; Foval w/Delft Blue hdl, #2003 ....100.00
Cup & saucer, AD; Fuchsia or Royal Blue, ea 75.00
Cup & saucer, Azure Blue, 2x4½", 6" 30.00
Cup & saucer, coffee; Emerald 30.00
Ferner, Albert cutting, 3-ftd, from $175 to.................................225.00
Ferner, Frederick cutting, triangular, 3-ftd, from $285 to.............335.00
Goblet, Emerald w/needle etching, ftd 20.00
Goblet, water; quilted rose-pk bowl w/gr twisted stem...................45.00
Grapefruit, Rose etching (bowl only), ftd.....................................60.00
Grill plate, amber, 3-compartment 45.00
Grill plate, Emerald, 3-compartment...50.00
Ivy bowl, blk, clear swirl connector, blk ft....................................95.00
Jelly dish, pearl ovenware, custard type, from $20 to....................25.00
Lamp base, water; amber 125.00
Mayonnaise set, Pershing cutting, from $270 to 325.00
Measuring cup, pearl ovenware, 1 spout, #1933, 1-cup................55.00
Meat loaf pan, pearl ovenware w/emb grapes on lid, #1928, 9" 40.00
Nappy, Wilhelm cutting, hdls, from $230 to 280.00
Pickle dish/relish, Prince cutting, 1 hdl, from $135 to................175.00
Pie plate, pearl ovenware w/orange trim, #1916, 9" 35.00
Pitcher, Carnation cutting, from $265 to 325.00
Pitcher, clear crackle w/Jade Green hdl & finial, 9¼x7".............225.00
Pitcher, Sunbeam cutting, from $300 to 350.00
Plate, Sunbeam cutting, 8", from $150 to 200.00
Platter, fish; pearl ovenware, oval, #1958, 14", from $30 to 35.00
Platter, meat; pearl ovenware w/floral leaf cutting, in metal holder ...70.00
Platter, pearl ovenware, 14x8¾" 28.00
Platter/liner, pearl ovenware w/Thistle etching, from $50 to 60.00
Punch bowl & base, Frederick cutting, from $900 to 1,200.00
Ramekin, pearl ovenware, #1923, w/metal holder, 4" 25.00
Relish, Trojan cutting, oval, 10", from $150 to............................185.00
Sherbet, Azure Blue, Optic 20.00
Sherbet, quilted rose-pk bowl w/gr twist stem 45.00
Sherbet, rose pk w/etched panels, ftd, 4¾x3½"............................18.00
Sherbet, Royal Blue w/clear swirl connector & ft 30.00
Snack set, pearl ovenware, #1968, from $45 to 50.00
Spice tray, Rose, center fleur-de-lis hdl, 3-compartment................75.00
Teapot, etched Japanese Maid pattern, from $300 to...................350.00
Teapot, Foval, gold enameling, #2000, 6-cup 300.00
Teapot, Foval, Jade Green hdl, spout & finial, #2002.................325.00
Teapot, pearl ovenware, #2002, 2-cup..275.00
Tray, biscuit; pearl ovenware, #1934 ....20.00
Tray, lemon; Foval, Delft Blue center hdl, 6" 250.00
Tray, sandwich; Emerald, center hdl 35.00
Trivet, pearl ovenware, #1959, 8"...30.00
Tumbler, iced tea; etched floral spray, hdld, w/underplate, $60 to.80.00
Tumbler, juice; Foval, Jade Green ft, 3½"....................................90.00
Tumbler, rose-pk, cut panels (16), ftd, 4½x3½" 18.00
Vase, bud; Azure Blue, ruffled rim 200.00
Vase, bud; pearlware, ruffled rim, #814, 10" 175.00
Vase, Foval, Delft ft, flared rim, #1657, 12" 350.00

Vase, Foval w/festooning, Jade Green trim, Bulging II shape, 7".450.00
Vase, Foval w/Rose festooning, cylindrical, 10" 550.00
Vase, Honeysuckle etching, slim, 12" 75.00
Vase, Ivy cutting, slim, 12", from $225 to 325.00
Vase, jack-in-pulpit; Foval w/Delft Blue trim, #821, 10" 300.00
Vase, wht opal, scalloped sq top, bulbous, ftd, 8½".....................110.00

Fulper

Throughout the nineteenth century the Fulper Pottery in Flemington, New Jersey, produced utilitarian and commercial wares. But it was during the span from 1902 to 1935, the Arts and Crafts period in particular, that the company became prominent producers of beautifully glazed art pottery. Although most pieces were cast rather than hand decorated, the graceful and classical shapes used together with wonderful experimental glaze combinations made each piece a true work of art.

The company also made dolls' heads, Kewpies, figural perfume lamps, and powder boxes. Their lamps with the colored glass inserts are extremely rare and avidly sought by collectors. Examples prized most highly by collectors today are those produced before the devastating fire in 1929 and subsequent takeover by Martin Stangl (see Stangl Pottery).

Several marks were used: a vertical in-line 'Fulper' being the most common in ink or incised, an impressed block horizontal mark, Flemington, Rafco, Prang, and paper labels. Unmarked examples often surface and can be identified by shape and glaze characteristics. Values are determined by size, desirability of glaze, and rarity of form. Our advisor for this category is Douglass White; he is listed in the Directory under Florida.

Bowl, brn gloss w/gr streaks, pre-1920, 2½x9"...........................60.00
Bowl, Chinese Bl & ivory flambé, ribbed rim, shallow, label, 2¾x13"..315.00
Bowl, combed ext, gr/bl/ivory flambé, integral flower frog, 11½" ..200.00
Bowl, fish/waves, Copper Dust/mahog/Leopard Skin crystalline, 11", NM.750.00
Bowl, gr gloss, invt rim, #4072, ca 1915, 3¼x13" 200.00
Bowl, gr matt, invt rim, 1915, 2¾x10¾" 230.00
Bowl, ivory flambé over dk mustard matt, shallow, 9½" 85.00
Candlesticks, Leopard Skin crystalline, 6", pr 600.00
Candlesticks, Mirror Bl crystalline, stepped base, 3", pr 150.00
Jardiniere, Mission Brn matt, hdls, 7½" 850.00
Lamp, Chinese Bl flambé, 15" mushroom shade w/inset stained glass .10,000.00
Lamp, gunmetal & brn crystalline drip, bulbous, 22½".........700.00
Luminer, parrot figural, perched on knob base, mc, 1930s, 12¼" ..700.00
Pilgrim flask, amber/turq crystalline (EX glaze), scroll hdls, 10x8"..900.00
Pilgrim flasks, Flemington Gr, scroll hdls, 10x7½", pr (1 NM)...400.00
Vase, bl crystalline, hdls, 6½" 200.00
Vase, bl crystalline on olive gr, 1930s, 8x5" 495.00

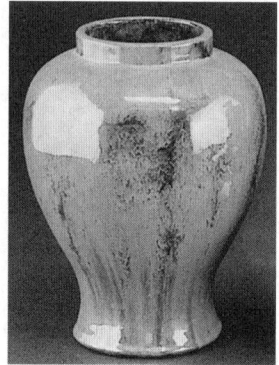

Vase, blue, green, and cobalt flambé mirrored glaze, racetrack mark, 11½x8½", $900.00. (Photo courtesy David Rago)

Vase, blk/bl/mahog frosty flambé, incurvate sides, 7½x4¼" 600.00
Vase, butterscotch flambé, 3 short rim hdls, 6¾x7¾" 250.00

Vase, Cat's Eye flambé, faceted classic form, 11x5" **325.00**

Vase, Cat's Eye flambé, shouldered cylinder, rstr drill hole, 16x6"..**1,000.00**

Vase, Cat's Eye flambé, squat w/tall trumpet neck, 10½", pr (1 NM) .**750.00**

Vase, Cat's Eye w/bl flambé, bullet shape, 9¾x6½" **550.00**

Vase, Cat's Eye w/bl flambé, emb ridges, sm hdls, 12½x8½".......**700.00**

Vase, Chinese Bl & caramel flambé, flaring toward base, 11½x9"..**950.00**

Vase, Chinese Bl crystalline flambé, prunts at shoulder, 7" **250.00**

Vase, Chinese Bl crystalline flambé, upright 'riveted' rim hdls, 12x9" ..**1,000.00**

Vase, Chinese Bl flambé, short collar rim, 10x10" **1,300.00**

Vase, Chinese Bl flambé dripping over mahog gloss, hdld urn form, 8".**500.00**

Vase, Chinese Bl mottled flambé, urn form, 13½" **3,200.00**

Vase, Chinese Bl/frothy gr dripping over wht matt, 8½x5" **500.00**

Vase, Copper Dust crystalline, tapering w/squat base, bar hdls, 9½"..**1,200.00**

Vase, Elephant's Breath flambé, sides flare, drilled, 13x7" **350.00**

Vase, Elephant's Breath to Leopard Skin crystalline, Prang, 7x5".**1,700.00**

Vase, Famille Rose dripping over gr/pk microcrystalline, 12x7" ..**600.00**

Vase, Flemington Gr flambé, 4 tapered buttresses, squat base, 13x10".**2,100.00**

Vase, frothy bl/gr flambé, classic shape, 13¼x6½", NM **800.00**

Vase, frothy bl/ivory/Mirror Blk flambé, shouldered, 12x9" **1,400.00**

Vase, frothy cucumber to ivory crystalline flambé, flared panels, 10" .**600.00**

Vase, frothy Indigo intermingled w/lt bl, bulbous w/shoulder hdls, 12".**1,300.00**

Vase, frothy ivory/mahog/Mirror Blk flambé w/prunts, classic form, 7"..**475.00**

Vase, frothy Mission Verde/turq/wht flambé, paneled, rim w/emb sqs, 8"..**425.00**

Vase, gr & aubergine poured over rose semigloss, buttress hdls, 7"..**475.00**

Vase, gr & brn drip, quatrefoil rim, ca 1915, 10¼" **350.00**

Vase, gunmetal/gr/bl w/dripping, 4-sided, Prang, 8¼x3½" **550.00**

Vase, ivory/bl/Mirror Blk flambé, teardrop w/3 horn-like hdls, 7x6" .**750.00**

Vase, ivory/brn/bl flambé, baluster form, 9½x5¾" **300.00**

Vase, Leopard Skin crystalline, bulbous w/4 shoulder hdls, rstr, 13"..**2,600.00**

Vase, Leopard Skin crystalline, paneled/shouldered, emb sqs in rim, 8"..**550.00**

Vase, Leopard Skin to amber flambé, spherical, incurvate, 5½x7".**650.00**

Vase, Mirror Bl/Gr flambé, bottle form w/flared rim, rstr drill, 15x7"..**500.00**

Vase, Mirror Blk & Indigo dripping onto Famille Rose flambé, 7½x8"..**850.00**

Vase, Mirror Blk crystalline, panelled classic shape, 11x5"..........**350.00**

Vase, Mirror Blk over Chinese Bl crystalline flambé, 7¾x10½".**1,600.00**

Vase, Mirror Blk to dk bl/ivory flambé, shouldered, 7½x8"..........**500.00**

Vase, Mirror Blk-to-Copper Dust crystalline flambé, teardrop, 13x7" ...**2,600.00**

Vase, mottled bl/amber/mahog/caramel, urn form w/lg hdls, 12x7" .**1,400.00**

Vase, mottled gr/purple/bl, Prang, glaze bubbles, 7½x5" **1,000.00**

Vase, mushrooms/2 cutouts, ivory to Elephant's Breath flambé, 10", EX.**500.00**

Vase, purple gloss to Famille Rose, str sides/closed rim, 7¾x5", pr.**650.00**

Vase, umber to Chinese Bl crystalline flambé, faceted sides, 11x5" ...**425.00**

Vase, umber/gr/cobalt matt, spherical w/6 wide melon ribs, 4x5"..**1,000.00**

Vase, wisteria, purple on magenta gloss, 9½x6¼" **525.00**

Wall pocket, Greek Key band, gr matt, U-form, 8" **550.00**

Furniture

Aside from its obvious utility, furniture has always been a symbol indicating wealth, taste, and social position. Each period of time has wrought distinct changes in style, choice of wood, and techniques — all clues that the expert can use to determine just when an item was made. Regional differences as well as secondary wood choice give us clues as to country and locale. The end of the Civil War brought with it the Industrial Revolution and the capability of producing man-made furniture. With this came the Victorian period and the many revival styles.

Important to the collector (and dealer) is the ability to recognize furniture on a 'good, better, best' approach. Age alone does not equal value. During a recessionary market the 'best' of forms always seem to do well. The 'better' or middle market will show a drop in value, and the 'good' or lower end of the marketplace will suffer the most. Many of this year's values emphasize what has been going on in the marketplace. Auction estimates for part of the year were way off the mark due to unforseen

economic factors. The marketplace struggles to recover and astute shoppers are finding wonderful buys. Value is based on scarcity, form, and technique, as well as what is fashionable in the marketplace at the time. Some pieces are timeless classics and will always have a place in the antiques marketplace. Others are strictly fashionable at the time, and value is speculative at best.

Still popular and continuing to rise are the mahogany classic copies from the early twentieth century. This includes the styles of Queen Anne, Duncan Phyfe, Chippendale, Sheraton, and Hepplewhite. The English counterparts are also enjoying popularity. Turn-of-the-century European inlaid and carved furniture is still rising in value. Stronger in the marketplace is the 'decorator trade,' who realize this type of furniture is a sound investment and can be refinished (without any loss of value) to suit the client's needs. Upholstered pieces that are 'floor ready' are bringing stronger prices at auction. Frames for sofas, chairs, and benches needing new upholstery and some work are being sold reasonably to eager collectors and dealers. They realize that when the work is completed, they will have a unique, well-made item at a reasonable price.

Items that have sold at auction for at least 25% lower than their normal market values will be designated with (*). Items listed in the lines that are designated with (**) are pieces in the best of form and of museum quality.

Please note: If a piece actually dates to the period of time during which its style originated, we will use the name of the style only. For example: 'Hepplewhite' will indicate an American piece from roughly the late 1700s to 1815. The term 'style' will describe a piece that is far removed from the original time frame. 'Hepplewhite style' refers to examples from the turn of the century. When the term 'repro' is used it will mean that the item in question is less than thirty years old and is being sold on a secondary market. When only one dimension is given for blanket chests, dry sinks, tables, settees, sideboards, and sofas, it is length.

Condition is the most important factor to consider in determining value. It is also important to remember that *where* a piece sells has a definite bearing on the price it will realize, due simply to regional preference. Our advisor for this category is Suzy McLennan Anderson, ISA CAPP, of Heritage Antiques and Anderson Auctions, LLC, whose address is listed in the Directory under New Jersey. (Photo and SASE required; no phone appraisals.) To learn more about furniture, we recommend *The Collector's Encyclopedia of American Furniture, Vol. 3*, by Robert and Harriet Swedberg; *Heywood-Wakefield Modern Furniture* by Steve and Roger Rouland; *Antique Oak Furniture* by Conover Hill; *American Oak Furniture, Book II*, and *Victorian Furniture, Our American Heritage, Books I and II*, by Kathryn McNerney; and *Early American Furniture* by John Obbard.

See also Art Deco; Art Nouveau; Arts and Crafts; Fifties Modern; Limbert; Nutting, Wallace; Shaker; Stickley.

Key:

Am — American	grpt — grainpainted
bj — bootjack	hdbd — headboard
brd — board	hdw — hardware
Chpndl — Chippendale	Hplwht — Hepplewhite
Co — Country	mar — marriage
cvd — carved	mahog — mahogany
cvg — carving	NE — New England
c&b — claw and ball	QA — Queen Anne
do — door	R/R — Renaissance Revival
drw — drawer	rswd — rosewood
Emp — Empire	trn — turning, turned
Fed — Federal	uphl — upholstered/upholstery
Fr — French	vnr — veneer
ftbd — footboard	Vict — Victorian
G — good	W/M — William and Mary
Geo — Georgian	: — over (example: 1 do:2 drw)

Armoires, See Also Wardrobes

Am Classical, single do w/inset panels, cvd paw ft, 1830s, 86x42"..**2,000.00**
Mahog Am Late Fed, anthemion cvd cornice:cvd dbl do:base, 94x61"..**3,675.00**
Mahog Art Nouveau w/fruitwood inlay, mirror, 2 panel do:drw, 83x69" *..**2,150.00**
Oak Louis XV w/EX cvg, old rfn, brass hinges, 92x66x25" **4,125.00**
Rswd Am, cvd mirrored dbl do w/ebony inlay:drw, 1850s........**3,450.00**
Walnut Vict, arch cornice w/anthemion cartouch, 98x70" ..**1,725.00**
Walnut vnr Fr w/ornate cvg, breakdown, appl Rococo cvgs, rpr, 96x54"...**935.00**

Beds

American Rococo carved mahogany bed with turned and faceted posts, paneled headboard with scrolling and central shell above cabochon egg and draped fruit and foliage, mid-nineteenth century, 80x66", $6,000.00. (Photo courtesy Neal Auction Company)

Burl walnut R/R, lg cvd crest, EX trn, paneled ft/hdbd, 1870, 93x61" ..**4,480.00**
Cherry w/maple hdbd, tall posts, arched sides, 1830s, 93x54x72"..**3,225.00**
Curly/bird's-eye maple 4-poster Am Classical, acorn finials, 1820, 82"..**5,750.00**
Day, pnt Louis XVI style w/cvd crest, reuphl, 33x48x79"............**920.00**
Fed style, 4-poster w/lg cvd eagle in hdbd, 1880, 60x57".........**2,800.00**
Field, birch Fed w/red wash traces, 1815-20, tester: 82"...........**1,150.00**
Hired man's, curly maple, well-trn posts w/acorn finials, 38x36"...**330.00**
Maple Fed, 4 tall octagonal tapering posts, arched tester, 76".....**920.00**
Oak, 4-post, pedimented plank hdbd, 8-sided posts, LA, 70x37x84"..**2,300.00**
Red-stained birch Classical tall post, acorn/vase/ring-trn posts, 1825.**1,000.00**
Rope, cherry/maple PA, shaped hdbd w/rolling-pin top, trn posts, EX..**450.00**
Rope, curly maple, well-trn posts w/acorn finials........................**880.00**
Rope, low post, old bl pnt, early trn, EX **300.00**
Rope, poplar Co, ball finials, scalloped hdbd, 45½x52x69" **250.00**
Sleigh, mahog Charles X, figured scroll crest, 43x67x38"............**750.00**
Tall-post tester, mahog Fed, arch canopy fr, spiral cvgs, 61x72x46" *..**1,765.00**
Tester, tiger maple Fed, trn/cvd, NE, 1810s, 82½x50x72"........**1,850.00**
Walnut Co Sheraton, high posts/rolled crest, 83x77x56", VG+ .**880.00**
Walnut Vict, ornate crest, floral-cvd medallion, 89x63" **800.00**

Benches

Arrowbk, bamboo trn legs/arms, 2-brd seat w/rain gutter, 20th C, 35"..**275.00**
Bucket, pine, orig bl-gray pnt, 18th C, 24x31x9½" **.............**2,185.00**
Bucket, pine w/gr pnt, sq nails, bj ends, 2 shelves, 31x42" **650.00**
Fireside, oak/pine/yew, shoe ft, seat:2 panel do, 52x73x19", VG ..**550.00**
Fireside, pumpkin pine, inset panels, lift lid, pegged, rfn, 40x46x19" ..**2,100.00**
Kneeling, pine w/old rfn, cutouts, sq nails, nailed split, 7½x50"..**165.00**
Mahog Fed w/mahog vnr, velvet slip seat:scrolls:casters, 17x24x20" ..**350.00**
Mahog w/2 scroll supports w/acanthus leaves, caned inserts, 48" L..**350.00**
Mammy's, mellow brn w/11-spindle bk, scrolled arms, rprs, 29x43" ..**770.00**

PA decor Windsor, natural arms, plank seat, fruit/leaf crest, 34x71"..**1,000.00**
Pine w/bl pnt, arched cutouts on legs, early 19th C, 19x61x11".....**400.00**
Pine/walnut w/smoke decor traces, mortised, splay legs, 27x25x18"..**140.00**
Walnut Am Renaissance, cvd crest, shaped arms, tapered legs, 39x80" ..**460.00**
Wash, pine, 2-brd ends w/bj cutouts, 1 lower shelf, 32x48".........**440.00**

Blanket Chests, Coffers, Trunks, and Mule Chests

Chest on drws, tiger maple/pine Chpndl, rstr, late 18th C, 39½x36"..**1,950.00**
Chestnut/pine w/blk over red grpt, scalloped cut-out ends, 30x42", VG..**880.00**
Curly maple/cherry Co Sheraton, 2 raised panels on front/ea side, 43"..**1,595.00**
Dower, walnut w/inlay, lidded till, dvtl, rfn/rpl, late 18th C, 25" ...**4,900.00**
Grpt, gold/burnt sienna (fanciful), 6-brd, dvtl, 1830s, 50" L....**2,400.00**
Grpt pine, hinged top:well:drw in cut-out base, 40x39x18" **825.00**
Grpt/decor, 6-brd, scratch-beaded till, 1790s, 25x47x18".........**2,300.00**
Oak English, mortised, 4-panel top/bk/front, 25x46x19".............**450.00**
PA decor w/tulips & stars, mc on bl, 2 drws, bracket ft, 50" L.**4,950.00**
Pine, 6-brd, shaped cutouts on side, 22x40x16" **200.00**
Pine Co Chpndl, dvtl drw, 1-brd top, bracket ft, rpr/rpl, 38x19"...**880.00**
Pine Co Chpndl w/orig bl, 3 dvtl drw, rstr/rpl, 27x52x23¼"..**1,200.00**
Pine Co Chpndl-style (copy), worn bl pnt, dvtl, till, 14x22x11"..**500.00**
Pine grpt dome top, yel-pnt initials/floral, 28" L........................**235.00**
Pine w/bl pnt, 6-brd, dvtl case w/pnt reserve, 1800s, 17x42x19", VG .**1,035.00**
Pine w/mc vines on mustard, dvtl drw, brass pulls, 1-brd top, 38x37"..**2,300.00**
Pine w/old bl pnt, 6-brd, hinged lid, dvtl case, 1850s, 18x35x15"...**975.00**
Pine w/red over mustard vinegar decor, dvtl, dtd 1862, 49" L, VG.**600.00**
Pine w/red pnt, bracket ft/molded base, 1-brd 46x20" top, T-head nails .**700.00**
Pnt red w/3 gr recessed panels bordered in yel, lift lid, 1800s, 36" L .**4,995.00**
Poplar w/blk:red sponging, pegged, 1-brd lid, rpr, 24x38x19"..**495.00**
Poplar/pine w/flame grpt, 2-drw w/decor fronts, rpr, 29x50x23"..**825.00**
Quartersawn wht oak w/cvd inset panels, dk stain, rstr/rpl, 24x49x21"..**935.00**
Softwood, dvtl, robin's egg bl pnt, molded bracket ft...................**175.00**
Vinegar & putty pnt w/mc accents, 6-brd, ca 1800, 14x36x18"....**1,840.00**
Vinegar decor: uniform vertical gr sponged lines, 50" L, EX **3,300.00**
Walnut Chpndl, dvtl, w/till, rstr, 14x12x37"................................**600.00**

Bookcases

Fruitwood vnr European, 8-pane dbl do w/X mullions, rpl hinges, 64x36"...**1,500.00**
Mahog, 6-do, 2 figured cvd lower panels, cvd/fluted columns, att Pabst...**6,000.00**
Mahog English Hplwht style w/inlay, cornice:2 do:drw, 2-pc, 78"..**1,750.00**
Oak, trim on 2 outer do encircles 4-drw center, mirror/spindle gallery .**4,480.00**
Oak, 3-do, bowed center, cvd top/base bands, claw ft, 1885, 66x74x20" .**7,800.00**
Oak, 3-do, glazed bow-front center, acorn/leaf cvgs, 1890s, 78x70".**6,700.00**
Oak, 3-do, reeded pilasters, cvd crest, dentil molding, 65x60"..**1,550.00**
Pine Co, dvtl w/2 drw, old red wash, 27x32x10" **600.00**
Pnt-decor satinwood, Adams style, revolving plinth, 34x24" dia.**1,035.00**
Walnut, ornate crest:2 do w/shaped glass panels:2 drw, 104x50"..**2,800.00**
Walnut Renaissance, 2 do ea side lg center area, lion pulls, 75x123" ..**8,900.00**
Walnut Vict, 3 glass do, appl ornaments, 3-drw base, 3-pc, 73x66" **4,200.00**

Cabinets

Apothecary, orig red w/brn stripes over wht, 35 dvtl drws, 24x64" ...**5,725.00**
Apothecary, pine w/Co decor, 24 dvtl drws, rpl pulls, 27x47x9" .**3,300.00**
Beverage, Art Deco walnut & ash, Fr, ca 1930, 37x33" **1,035.00**
Breakfront, bird's-eye maple Geo style, 4 glass do:4 panel do, 83" .**3,450.00**
China, oak bow-front w/old blk pnt, trn/reeded legs, rprs, 68x37x17" .**1,125.00**
China, oak Co, bow-front, cvd crest, rstr leg, 69x38x12"............**600.00**
China, oak Vict, winged griffins crest, bowed glass sides & do, 71x48"..**3,200.00**
Corner, cvd walnut, Ombelles pattern, Majorelle, 68x39".....**16,450.00**
Corner, walnut/cherry, paw ft, 2 panel do w/rope twist columns, 82".**1,870.00**
Curio, Fr w/gold rpt/cvd Rococo/gesso, high scroll ft/aprons, 72x35" .**880.00**
Music, cherry, Aesthetic, lion pulls/floral cvd panels, att Pabst, 37" .**4,000.00**

Music, mahog, lion-head mirrored top, Nouveau panel do, 1890, 61x25"...**1,400.00**
Music, rswd R/R, satinwood int, cvd gallery, 41x28x15" **1,000.00**
Parlor, gilt & ebony Am Renaissance w/marquetry & brass, 52x48x20"..**5,750.00**
Parlor, walnut Aesthetic, canted shelves flank decorated panel, 57x48"..**1,850.00**
Press, mahog, marble top:2 do w/Gothic panels, cvd capitals, 42x48x25" .**2,400.00**
Serving, mahog, raised panel do/rtcl & appl cvgs, 1910, 42x21", pr.**1,100.00**
Vitrine, glazed center do, foliate cvd stiles/ft, att Majorelle, 63" **5,750.00**

Candlestands

Butternut Fed, sq top:trn post:tripod:spade ft, rfn, 25x17x17"..**120.00**
Cherry, cross base, tray top, old rfn, CT, ca 1800, 27x15x14"..**1,495.00**
Cherry, cvd tray-top:tripod w/cvd knees, old rfn, 1790s, 26x16x16"...**2,875.00**
Cherry, dish top, old finish, att CT, ca 1800, 26x16" **1,150.00**
Cherry, drw, old rfn, att CT, late 1700s, 28x16x18" **2,875.00**
Cherry, drw, old rfn, CT, late 18th C, 26x17x18" **1,265.00**
Cherry Fed, sq top w/ovolo corners:trn post:3 legs, rfn, 39x14x13.**1,950.00**
Cherry/walnut Chpndl, 1-brd top:trn column:tripod, rprs/rfn, 27x16"..**3,000.00**
Mahog, tilt-top:ring-trn post:tripod cabriole legs, rfn/rpr, 1770s..**1,380.00**
Mahog Co Chpndl, 1-brd tilt top, cabriole legs, rfn, 27x16x14" .**470.00**
Mahog Fed, pnt/stenciled dish top, striping on legs, 1790s, 29x16"..**4,600.00**
Mahog Fed, serpentine top:tripod cabrole legs:pad ft, rfn, 26x17x17"..**2,645.00**
Maple, rnd top:vase & ring-trn post:tripod cabriole legs, 1750s 25x16"....**460.00**
QA, un-shaped post, snake ft, rprs, 38x17x17" **635.00**
Tiger maple Fed, sq 18" top w/ovolo corners, trn post, scroll legs..**1,000.00**
Walnut Chpndl, 2-brd 20" dia tilt top, urn-trn column w/sm birdcage .**2,035.00**
Walnut Fed, tilt-top:urn & ball shaft:cabriole legs:pad ft **900.00**
Walnut Fed, tilt-top, urn-shaped legs, tiny spade ft, 37x20x14" .**2,750.00**
Windsor, mixed wood, tripod base, trn column, 11" dia top adjusts .**550.00**

Chairs

Arm, Belter Fountain Elms/cornucopia pattern, crushed velvet uphl, 45".**12,650.00**
Arm, blk-pnt banister-bk, arched crest, dbl arms, 18th C, 45"..**1,265.00**
Arm, Co QA wing-bk, reuphl, blk-on-red decor base, 50" **440.00**
Arm, fruitwood Regency style, curved bk members, spike ft....**1,035.00**
Arm, mahog Art Nouveau, cvd floral bk/legs, att Majorelle, 37" ..**785.00**
Arm, mahog Chpndl, damask uphl, NE, old rfn, 1760-80, 46" ..**6,325.00**
Arm, mahog Flemish style, scrolled legs, needlepoint uphl, 47".**1,150.00**
Arm, mahog Hplwht style, cvd shield bk, needlepoint seat, 37".**220.00**
Arm, mahog QA wing-bk, cabriole legs, old rfn, reuphl, 18th C, 48"..**34,500.00**
Arm, mahog QA-style wing-bk, red velvet uphl, 20th C, 47" **400.00**
Arm, maple QA, cvd Spanish ft, old rfn, late 18th C, 41" **2,650.00**
Arm, oak, cvd lions/Northwind heads, uphl seat/bk panel, 50" ..**560.00**
Arm, oak w/Northwind head, lion posts, claw ft, 1890s, 39" **335.00**
Arm, Rswd Am Rococo, floral-cvd/rtcl crest & skirt scroll arms...**460.00**
Arm, satinwood Edwardian w/decor, trn crest:pierced rail:cane seat .**635.00**
Arm, tiger maple Sheraton, lyre bk, balloon seat, 34", VG **100.00**
Arm, walnut, lg 3-D griffins w/lion crest, uphl seat, 1875, 35" .**3,350.00**
Arm, walnut, lg 3-D putti/EX cvgs, uphl bk/seat panel, 1870, 50" .**3,900.00**
Arm, walnut Jacobean style w/cvg, scroll arms, reuphl, 1900s, 52x17"..**935.00**
Arm, walnut QA, reuphl, old rfn/rprs, 44x32x24" **1,150.00**
Arm, walnut w/cvd standing griffin sides, winged maid crest, massive ..**7,280.00**
Arm, 5-slat ladder-bk, old blk pnt, DE River Valley, late 18th C, 45".**1,400.00**
Arm, 5-slat ladder-bk w/old blk, rpl rush seat, late 1700s, 47" .**3,000.00**
Blk-pnt QA, gilt striping, yoked crestrail, vasiform splat, 1750s, 42".**650.00**
Club, Art Deco, Bauchausen uphl, Madagascar ebony base, pr..**3,450.00**
Corner, mahog Chpndl, ornate urn-shaped splats, slip seat, fine rstr.**1,875.00**
Corner, red over dk brn pnt, pillow-bk crest, NY, 18th C, 29" .**4,000.00**
Corner, W/M style, salmon-color pnt, 32x17" **400.00**
Corner, walnut QA w/cvg, uphl seat, old rfn, 32½" **1,200.00**
Gentleman's, walnut Am Rococo w/much cvg, reuphl, 47x29x39".**1,850.00**
Lolling, Fed mahog, reverse serpentine crest, old rfn, 1790s, 43" .**6,900.00**
Lolling, mahog QA style, bowed seat, shaped arms, uphl, 43", pr.**440.00**

Office, oak R/R, cvd crest/c&b base/burl panels/tufted leather, 54" .**3,000.00**
Rocker, mahog, figural lion pierced/cvd bk, 1890, 37"................**750.00**
Rocker, red pnt w/gold stencil/yel & blk striping, PA, 1830-40, 30" ...**230.00**
Rocker arm, bentwood spirals, pressed bk & seat, Thonet, 39"...**585.00**
Side, banister bk, Spanish ft, blk pnt, NE, 1790s, rprs, 45" **750.00**
Side, birch/maple Chpndl, cvd crest/splat, slip seat, rfn, 38" ...**2,500.00**
Side, curly maple Emp, vase splat, 33", EX................................**385.00**
Side, grpt banister-bk, old rush seat, MA, 1750s, 42" **2,415.00**
Side, mahog Chpndl, cabriole legs w/acanthus knees, c/b ft/shell crest .**2,200.00**
Side, mahog Chpndl, cvd fan in shaped crestrail/scroll splat, 1750s ** .**10,575.00**
Side, mahog QA, ornate bk splat/crest, slip seat, rpr/rpl seat, 38" .**3,300.00**
Side, mahog QA style, modified Spanish ft, paper rush seat, 40" .**225.00**
Side, maple QA, cvd crest & formed splat, crewelwork seat, cvd ft .**920.00**
Side, maple QA, yoked crest:slip seat:cabriole front legs, rfn, 40"..**4,000.00**
Side, maple QA, yoked/spooned crest, rush seat, Spanish ft, 1780s, 40".**800.00**
Side, walnut, serpentine crest w/cvd shell, shell-cvd legs, PA/1760 .**6,400.00**
Side, walnut Chpndl, pierced splat, reuphl seat, old rfn, rstr bk legs.**1,150.00**
Side, walnut QA, yoked crest:vasiform splat:slip seat, 39½" **9,200.00**
Windsor, clerk's, 7-spindle, ash, shaped saddle seat, NE 1790, 41" .**1,500.00**
Windsor, continuous arm, incised crestrail/scroll-cvd hand holds, 1790 .**1,295.00**
Windsor arrow-bk rocker arm, floral on grpt w/yel border, 43" .**635.00**
Windsor birdcage, 7-spindle, bamboo trn, mk Horton, rpl leg, 34" .**385.00**
Windsor birdcage, 7-spindle, bamboo trn, rfn, 33", EX, pr **700.00**
Windsor bow-bk arm, 8-spindle, mixed hardwoods, English, 45¾"..**660.00**
Windsor bow-bk side, yel-gr over red, bamboo-trn, NE/1810, EX ..**1,175.00**
Windsor bow-bk side, 9-spindle, bamboo trn, 2 legs rpl, 37".......**330.00**
Windsor bow-bk side 9-spindle, vase/ring trn, rfn/rstr **385.00**
Windsor brace-bk arm, rswd grpt w/gilt stripes, PA, 1700s, 43"..**3,400.00**
Windsor brace-bk side, 7-spindle, dk brn wash, seat w/rain gutter..**770.00**
Windsor brace-bk side, 9-spindle, blk pnt, baluster/ring-trns ..**935.00**
Windsor brace-bk w/continuous arms, gr rpt, CT, 1780s, 37"......**975.00**
Windsor fan-bk, dk gr rpt, shield-shaped seats, 38", pr **700.00**
Windsor fan-bk, 7-spindle, red pnt, shield seat w/rain gutter, 35" .**875.00**
Windsor fan-bk arm, old yel pnt, rpr, NE, 1780s, 44" **1,500.00**
Windsor fan-bk side, branded J Mansfield, 1780s **1,500.00**
Windsor fan-bk side, old red pnt, NE, 1780s, 40" **865.00**
Windsor fan-bk side, serpentine crest w/cvd ears, pnt traces, 1780s..**1,265.00**

Windsor fan-back side, seven-spindle, ash and maple, shaped crest rails, saddle seats, refinished, ca 1780s, 35½", $1,600.00 for the pair.

Windsor fan-bk side, vase/ring-trn stiles, old dk finish, 37" **1,500.00**
Windsor fan-bk side, 7-spindle, bl pnt over red, worn, 37" **990.00**
Windsor sack-bk arm, old red pnt, rprs, New England, 1780-90, 38"..**2,530.00**
Windsor sack-bk arm, rpt, vase/ring trn, H-stretcher, rpr, 27"..**1,760.00**
Windsor sack-bk arm, worn gr pnt, CT, 1780-90, 35½"...........**3,750.00**
Windsor sack-bk side, old gr pnt, saddle seat, late 18th C, 36".**2,185.00**
Windsor writing arm, drw under arm, old rfn, CT, 1780s, 39".**2,000.00**
Wing, mahog Chpndl style, acanthus cvg, c&b ft, high bk, EX..**475.00**

Chair Sets

Art Deco mahog, curved crest, uphl drop-in seat, 39½", 8 for..**1,495.00**

Co QA, dk rfn w/orig red traces, rpl rush seats, 40", 6 for........**4,000.00**
Hitchcock, fruit/flower stencil on blk, rush seat, 35", 6 for **635.00**
Mahog Centennial Geo, ribbon-bks, 2 arm+10 side **4,200.00**
Mahog English Sheraton style, reuphl/rfn, 37", 2 arm+4 side ..**1,550.00**
Mahog/walnut English Chpndl style, pegged, slip seat, 2 arm+8 side ..**2,750.00**
Oak Lancashire style, cvd fan crest, uphl seat, 2 arm+8 side ...**1,650.00**
PA decor, blk on red w/floral panels & gilt, 5 for **3,600.00**
PA decor, flame grpt w/gr & blk hearts & leaves, wht lines, 6 for..**2,300.00**
Rswd, portrait cvd crests, 1885, 2 48" arms+2 sides, 4 for........**2,240.00**
Windsor, blk crackled pnt, vase/ring trn, DR Dimes brand, repro, 6 for ..**3,100.00**
Windsor, rabbit ear, old mustard rpt, 4-spindle bks, 34", 10 for .**880.00**

Chests (Antique), See Also Dressers

Birch/bird's-eye maple Fed w/mahog inlay, bow-front, 1810, rfn, 41x47" ..**8,625.00**
Burled yew Geo III style w/inlay, 2 short:3 long drw:bracket ft, 36"..**865.00**
Cherry Chpndl, ogee ft, reeded quarter columns, 10-drw, 70x39x43" ..**10,725.00**
Cherry Chpndl, 3 scratch-beaded drw, reeded columns, claw ft, 35x38"..**7,050.00**
Cherry Chpndl, 4 grad drw, lambrequin corners, c&b ft, rfn, 38x42x18"..**9,400.00**
Cherry grpt Chpndl, 4-drw, rpl brass, sm rpr, 37x39x29" **1,440.00**
Cherry Sheraton, 4-drw, beaded edges, rpl 35x19" 2-brd top, 38"..**1,980.00**
Cherry w/curly maple vnr drw fronts Hplwht, 8-drw, line inlay, 63x42"..**4,400.00**
Cherry/bird's-eye maple vnr Fed bow-front, X-banding, MA/1800, 36x39"..**4,995.00**
Cherry/curly maple vnr Sheraton, 4 dvtl drw, 2-brd top, 41x40"..**1,750.00**
Cherry/pine Hplwht, Fr ft/shaped apron/band inlay, 4-drw, rstr, 40x40"..**2,000.00**
Cherry/poplar Hplwht, 4-drw, high bracket ft/scalloped aprons, 38x42" ...**1,870.00**
Cherry/red stain, cove-molded cornice, beaded fr, PA/1830s, 66x45x22"..**2,900.00**
Cherry/tiger maple Chpndl, 4 grad drws, 39x38x20"................**1,325.00**
Cherry/vnr Chpndl bow-front, ogee ft w/scroll returns, 4-drw, 37x42"..**6,300.00**
Chpndl serpentine w/extensive fan inlay, drop pendant, MA/1780, 34x38"..**21,150.00**
Curly maple Chpndl, 4-drw, high scalloped bracket ft, 39x36" ..**8,250.00**
Faux bamboo bird's-eye maple, 6 grad drw, 1875, 62x35".........**5,750.00**
Figured mahog vnr/pine/English Hplwht, bow-front, 6-drw, rpl, 41x46"..**1,200.00**
Gentleman's, burl walnut R/R, 6-drw, cvd fronts, 1870, 62x42"..**3,360.00**
Mahog Chpndl, block front, 4 grad drw, rpl c&b ft, rfn, 30x33x18"..**8,500.00**
Mahog Chpndl serpentine, 4-drw, c&b ft, very heavy, MA/1770, 32x37"..**11,600.00**
Mahog Fed, orig pressed glass & brass pulls, old rfn, 50x42x20"..**750.00**
Mahog Fed w/figure, drw:3 grad:paw ft, cvd ½-columns, 1830s, 50x49"..**4,300.00**
Mahog Hplwht, bow-front, 4 grad drw, 3-line inlay, Fr ft, 34x37"..**1,600.00**
Mahog Late Georgian, 2 short:3 long drw:bracket ft, 1830s, 43x40x20"..**1,495.00**
Mahog serpentine vnr Chpndl, 4 bow-front drw, old finish, 36x41"..**13,800.00**
Oak Geo III, molded top:2 short:3 drw:plinth, 36x41x22" .**1,035.00**
OH Amish cherry/oak, dk pnt bars on varnish w/DM & 1897, 51x44"..**1,100.00**
Pine, 3 molded drw:scrolled skirt, old blk pnt, rpl/rpr, 18h C, 34"..**5,465.00**
Pine Hplwht, bow-front, 4 dvtl drw, high ft, rfn/rstr, 38x40x22" ..**1,800.00**
Poplar Sheraton w/red pnt, 4-drw, trn legs/scalloped apron, 40x21"..**2,000.00**
Tiger/bird's-eye maple Fed, 4 grad drw:trn ft, rfn/rpl, 1820s, 42x42" ..**4,000.00**
Walnut Fed, 4-drw w/barber-pole inlay, Fr ft, rpl/rstr, 38x42x20" ..**1,600.00**
Walnut PA, 4 grad drw w/rosette & bail brasses, ogee ft, 37x37x19"..**7,000.00**
Walnut PA Sheraton, 4 scratch-beaded drw, tall trn legs, rpl/rfn...**750.00**

Cupboards, See Also Pie Safes

Cherry/poplar red-wash Co, high/scalloped base, 8-pane top do, 82x42"..**4,000.00**
Cherry/walnut Co, 2 6-pane do:shelf:4 drw:2 panel do, 2-pc, OH, 92x65"..**19,800.00**
Chimney, pine w/bl-gr pnt, molded base/cornice, panel do, 72x29" ..**880.00**
Corner, cherry Chpndl, 2-pc, glazed do:3 drw:2 do, bracket ft, 85x41"..**3,300.00**
Corner, cherry Co, cornice:12-pane glass do:2-do base, 90x46" .**5,800.00**
Corner, cherry Co, 1-pc, 2 panel do:short dvtl drw:2 base do, 82x47"..**2,640.00**
Corner, cherry Co, 2 panel do:2 shelves:2 panel do, 18th C, 76x42", VG..**2,125.00**
Corner, cherry/poplar/pine, reeded detail ea side glazed do:2 do, 83"..**2,860.00**
Corner, mahog, cornice:2 dmn-pane do:base w/drw:2 drw, 1820s, 80x37"..**3,550.00**
Corner, pine, old red/gr pnt, dbl do:dbl do, rosehead nails, 1-pc, 84"..**2,650.00**
Corner, pine, 2 raised panel do:2, H hinges, sq nails, 77x36"..**2,200.00**

Corner, pine Co, 2 10-pane do:2 panel, 2-pc, 18th C, 94x54x29", G..**1,050.00**
Corner, poplar, arched 8-pane do:panel do, old gr pnt, 18th C, 85"..**10,925.00**
Corner, softwood, 2 8-pane do:2 panel do:base molding, 2-pc, rfn.**1,500.00**
Corner, walnut Co, cornice:2 raised panel do:2, rfn, 1-pc, 81x46"..**2,300.00**
Corner, walnut/pine Southern, 2 8-pane do:drw:2 panel do, rfn, 84x47"..**4,125.00**
Corner/hanging, pine, top: scalloped triangle w/sm shelf:do, 40x24"..**550.00**
Corner/hanging, salmon pnt/bl striping, scrolled bkbrd, 1830s, 31x18"..**2,470.00**
Hanging, oak English Gothic style, 2 do w/cvd decor, 20th C, 30x24x8"..**300.00**
Hanging, pine Co, red stain, cornice:do:base, PA, 1830s, 30x24x10" ..**765.00**
Hanging, walnut, 2-do:shelf, 33x32x12" **880.00**
Jelly, PA mustard pnt, bracket ft/bj ends, 2 drw:2 panel drw, 58x45"..**3,600.00**
Jelly, pine/poplar w/red over amber pnt decor, pegged, att Rupp, 52" ..**3,400.00**
Jelly, poplar Co, 2 drw:2 panel do, 1-brd ends & top, sq nails, 50x45"..**1,875.00**
Mahog Fed, 2 drw w/rnded fronts:3 grad drw, cvd capitals, 44x44" ..**600.00**
Pantry, walnut/poplar Co Sheraton, 2 drw:2 panel do, CI hinges, 67x48"..**2,200.00**
Pewter, pine, 1-pc, 4 step-bk shelves:do w/2 raised panels, 75x38"..**1,100.00**
Pewter, pine Co, step-bk, red pnt traces, rpr, 78x37x18"..........**3,000.00**
Pine, primitive, 1-do, scraped to gray over red, sq nails, 70x36" .**360.00**
Pipe/polar/yel pine Co, 2-pc, 3 bracket ft, cove-mold cornice, 116" L ..**5,225.00**
Poplar/pine w/mustard comb/grpt over earlier red, PA, 72x26x21" ..**1,200.00**
Step-bk, glazed pine (old rfn), 2-part, PA, 1825-35, 87x52x20" ...**3,225.00**
Step-bk, red pnt, 4-do, angled ft, 73x38x17" **3,450.00**
Step-bk, walnut/poplar, 2 6-pane do:2 panel do, 2-pc, rfn, 90x49"..**2,300.00**
Walnut vnr QA style, 2-arch top w/10-pane do:2 drw:2 do, 19th C, 86"..**4,000.00**
Walnut/poplar, 2 8-pane do:2 raised panel do, OH, 1-pc, rpr, 87x21"..**10,725.00**

Desks

Birch Chpndl oxbow, slant-lid, fitted int, old rfn/rpl brass, 44" ...**4,600.00**
Birch/pine Chpndl, slant-lid, dvtl case w/4 drw, rstr, 44x40" ...**1,925.00**
Cherry Hplwht, slant lid, 4-drw, Fr feet, 10 int drw, 44x44" **2,200.00**
Cherry/maple, slant lid, arch molded case, 2 short dw:2 long, 1730s..**3,350.00**
Cherry/pine QA, slant lid:4 drw+19 int drw, rpl lid/ft/trim, 43x38" ..**2,090.00**
Cherry/pine/poplar Co Sheraton, slant lid, 3-drw, rstr, 38x37" ...**990.00**
Comb-grained, dbl 2-shelf int:lid, old yel/red pnt, ME, 1820s, 46x27"..**3,225.00**
Curly maple Hplwht w/inlay, slant lid, 4-drw, fitted int, 43x30"..**12,100.00**
Ebonized Modern Gothic, brass mts, att Kimbel & Cabus, 58x35x21"..**6,700.00**
Executive, mahog/oak Chpndl style, 4-drw, Kittinger, 31x72x36"...**1,600.00**

Fancy oak drop-front desk with open carved and mirrored gallery, applied carvings, 60x29x15", $1,200.00.

Lap, figured mahog, folding, felt-lined int, ca 1840-80, 9x22x11" ...**385.00**
Mahog, kidney shape, 7 dvtl drw, leather top, Colonial Mfg, 46"..**220.00**
Mahog Chpndl, slant lid, cvd shell drw:4 grad, orig hdw, 45x38x20" **...30,000.00**
Mahog Chpndl, slant lid, fitted int, ogee bracket ft, RI/1780s, 45x38".**4,100.00**

Mahog/mahog flame vnr Hplwht style w/inlay, Wms-Kemp...MI, 38x28"..**825.00**
Mahog/mahog flame vnr Sheraton lady's, hinged top, rope legs, 37x30"..**1,500.00**
Mahog/pine Chpndl, slant-front, dvtl drws, rpl hinges/rstr, 43x39x21"..**3,575.00**
Mahog/vnr/oak English Chpndl, slant lid, fitted int, 41x40" ...**1,700.00**
Maple Chpndl, slant lid, 4-drw, fitted int, NE, rstr, 41x36" **3,575.00**
Oak Vict, elaborate spindled galleries/cvgs, drop front, 67x30"..**2,500.00**
On fr, grpt pine, hinged lid:single drw:sq tapered legs, 36x24x21"..**4,850.00**
On fr, pine, slant lid:beaded fr:trn legs, old rfn, late 1700s, 43x30"..**2,415.00**
Partner's, mahog, 8 lion heads, lg claw ft, cvd top, 1885, 54"..**1,300.00**
Partner's, walnut Chpndl style, 4 dvtl drw, kneehole w/cvg, 30x48"..**1,000.00**
Plantation, poplar/pine Co w/old wash, fold-out top, 2-pc, rstr, 76"..**990.00**
Poplar/pine Co, slant-lid w/comb pnt, rpl pulls, OH, 38x34x27"..**440.00**
Primitive, pine w/old gr pnt, slant-lid, short gallery, 18x36x20"..**385.00**
Roll-top, oak, inset panels, 5-drw base, fitted int, 52x54x30"..**1,750.00**
Tambour, mahog Fed w/chevron inlay, rpl brasses, rfn, 35x37x19"....**11,750.00**
Walnut Co Sheraton, dvtl drw, rfn/rpr, 31x23x20" **330.00**
Walnut European w/inlay, 4 dvtl drw, brass pulls, leather top, 33x46"..**300.00**
Walnut Fed, inlaid slant top, 4 grad cock-beaded drw, Fr ft, rstr, 44" ..**3,000.00**
Walnut Fed, slant-front, 8 valance drw, 4-drw case, PA, rstr, 37" W .**4,000.00**
Walnut Renaissance, drop front, oval burl panels, fitted int, 70x34"..**2,240.00**
Walnut/well-figured vnr European Chpndl, slant lid, rstr, 4xx41x22" ..**2,750.00**
Wooton, Eastlake rotary w/incised panels, 3-hinge, 1874, 67x42"...**7,800.00**
Wooton, oak, dbl rotary peds w/files, roll top, 52x60x34" .**5,300.00**
Wooton, oak, dbl rotary peds w/files, tooled leather 60x33" top .**2,240.00**
Wooton, Standard grade, arched burl panels, ornate gallery, 72x42"..**9,500.00**
Wooton, Standard grade, 3-hinge, burl panels, Renaissance gallery .**8,900.00**

Dressers (Machine Age), See Also Chests

Mahog, 3-D female nudes/cherubs, oval swivel mirror, 77x60"..**3,350.00**
Rswd/marble Renaissance, domed jewelry caskets, telescoping mirror, lg.**3,000.00**
Walnut Vict, drop-down desk, grape-cvd pulls, mirror, 77x45" ..**1,500.00**

Dry Sinks

Cherry, plain gallery, panel do, trn ft, 1820, 30x38x21" **2,000.00**
Cherry/walnut, 3-brd 50x21" top:3 drw: 2 do ea w/2 panels, wood pulls..**1,150.00**
Pine/poplar w/worn bl over red, 2 panel do, rstr/rpl brd, 32x45x20" ..**1,450.00**
Poplar, scraped to wht, bracket ft, arched aprons, 2 panel do, 48" L.**1,375.00**
Poplar, 2 panel do, sm dvtl drw, old rfn, pieced rstr, 43¾x43" **880.00**
Walnut, 17" end brds, bj cutouts, sq nails, 2 open shelves, 32x38" .**700.00**
Walnut, 2 panel do w/CI latch/brass lever, dvtl drw at side, 42x48".**1,450.00**

Hall Pieces

Bench, oak, cvd 3-D storks, Northwind bk, c&b ft, 1880 ....**3,000.00**
Chair, oak, bk: cvd owl in ornate openwork surround, 41" **1,400.00**
Coat rack, Black Forest fox head w/glass eyes, 16"......................**700.00**
Coat rack, Black Forest ram's head w/glass eyes, leaves/branches, 32" .**950.00**
Mirror, mahog Fed w/gold cornucopias w/fruit, 107x27" **4,000.00**
Table, mahog Emp, thick scroll front legs, 1840, 35x39x19" ..**1,300.00**
Table, mahog QA style w/cvd knees & apron, 20th C, 30x72x22"..**475.00**
Tree, Black Forest, cvd glass-eye bears, bear atop holds antlers, 76"..**4,480.00**
Tree, Black Forest, simple branch/leaf detailing, mirror bk, 72x44"..**1,300.00**
Tree, CI w/old dk finish, Rococo details, 6 hooks, ca 1900, 78x29" .**1,100.00**
Tree, mahog w/brass lions, spindle/latticework bk, Hunzinger, 86"..**11,200.00**
Tree, mahog w/lg cherubs/etc, shaped mirror, att Horne, 94x70" **..20,000.00**
Tree, walnut, Vict, cvd, mirror, umbrella well, 86" **995.00**
Tree, walnut/marble Vict, deer/oak limbs, Mitchell/Rammelsberg ** .**23,000.00**

Highboys

Burl walnut vnr/inlay QA, scroll top, 3-part skirt, MA, 88" ..**57,500.00**
Cherry QA, 7 grad drw:4:cabriole legs, pegged, rfn/rpl, 71½"..**6,000.00**

Cherry/maple QA, 2 short:4 grad dw:3-drw base, att DE Water Gap, 72" ..**6,325.00**
Chpndl style, 2-part, cvd knees/shell drws/flame finials, Horner, 90" .**4,200.00**
Mahog, broken-arch top, 3 flame finials, c&b ft, Marlo, 85x38x19" ..**1,600.00**
Mahog Chpndl style, 3 short drw:5 grad, acanthus leaf cvgs, 81" .**1,100.00**
Maple QA, cornice w/concealed drw:4 grad:2 long in base, 71x36"..**31,000.00**
Maple QA, deeply scalloped aprons, 2 drw:4 grad: ½ in base, rfn, 74" .**3,000.00**
Maple QA, 5 grad:3 grad:base, 80x40x20" **11,750.00**
Maple/poplar QA, cornice:5 grad drw:case of 3 drw:skirt, red pnt, 70" .**5,465.00**
Oak W/M, 5 dvtl drw w/rpl brasses, rstr/old varnish, 65x40x20" .**2,000.00**
Tiger maple QA, NH Dunlop style w/cvd fan, 2-pc, 81" **24,150.00**
Tiger maple W/M, split drw:3:case w/3 sm drw:skirt:ball ft, 63" .**12,650.00**
Walnut Chpndl, cornice:3 drw:2:3 grad:cvd apron:legs w/c&b ft, 67" .**11,000.00**
Walnut QA, cornice w/drw:4 grad:long:3 short:skirt:cabriole legs, 69" .**10,925.00**
Walnut QA, scalloped aprons, 3 sm drw:4+1 in base, rstr/rpl, 70x38"..**4,100.00**

Lowboys

Mahog QA style, 2 drw:3 (center w/shell cvg), batwing brasses, 30x36" .**660.00**
Maple/pine, cabriole legs/scalloped aprons, 4-drw, rpl top, RI, 30x32" .**1,760.00**
Oak QA, button ft, mortised, dvtl drw, old rfn, 2-brd top, 28x33x20" ...**1,200.00**
Walnut Geo II QA, sm drw amid 1 sq ea side, rpl hdls, rstr, 39x26x15" .**2,650.00**

Pie Safes

Hanging, pine, 1 do, punched tin w/flowers in scallop reserve, 36x24" .**1,100.00**
Mixed woods w/bl pnt, punched tins w/2-color pnt GA state seal, 67x41"..**2,200.00**
Pine Co w/pierced tin inserts, EX patina, ME, 19th C, 59x34x17" .**1,035.00**
Poplar, 12 punched tin panels w/stars & corner fans, 57x42" ..**1,100.00**

Red polychrome pine pie safe, flat molded cornice, paneled punched tin doors and sides, two drawers, nineteenth century, $1,000.00.

Walnut, top drw:2 do, ea w/2 punched tin panels, +3 in ends, 50x40".**5,290.00**
Walnut/poplar Southern, 2 do w/tin panels:2 drw:2 do, KY, rstr, 74" ..**2,850.00**

Secretaries

Butler's, curly maple/walnut/poplar, 3 short drw:do:3 drw, 58x48x23" .**1,875.00**
Butler's, mahog, 2-part w/bookcase top, 3-drw, NY, 106x46x21" .**17,250.00**
Butler's, mahog w/inlay, bookcase top, cvd crest, NY, 106x46x21".**17,250.00**
Cherry Chpndl, scroll pediment/appl fan, desk int, RI/1770, 80x38" **..55,800.00**
Curly maple Co Chpndl, 2 do:drop-front:4 grad drw, rstr/rpl .**8,250.00**
Fr style, cherubs/roses/scrolls rpt, 2 do:slant lid:3 drw, 2-pc, 79" .**2,750.00**
Mahog Chpndl style, 4-drw, fan-cvd center do, bonnet top, 84x38" ..**440.00**
Mahog English QA, bookcase top, deep base, ball ft, rstr, 84x39" .**4,200.00**
Mahog Sheraton w/inlay, 3-part, 8-drw, ornate orig brasses, 81" .**5,000.00**
Oak, glazed do ea side drop-down desk, 2 mirrors, much cvg, 82x63" .**3,100.00**
Oak, Wooton-style upright w/roll top, cvd gallery, 1885, 70x42" .**4,750.00**
Walnut German Baroque w/inlay, 3-part, rams' head brasses, 75x49x26" .**7,500.00**

Walnut S German Baroque w/inlay, ram's-head brasses, 3-part, 75x49x26"..**7,475.00**
Walnut Vict, side-by-side, cvd do, ornate gallery, 1885, 73x50x15" .**2,000.00**

Settees

Fr Louis XVI style, delicate cvd fr w/acanthus arms, 33" H..**1,150.00**
Gold rpt Louis XVI-style, bbl bk, old wht uphl, ca 1900, 35x54x30".**1,450.00**
Maple/ash/hickory birdcage Windsor, bamboo trn, rfn/rpl seat, 32"..**2,415.00**
Walnut English Chpndl w/needlepoint uphl, shell cvg, 40x59x23", EX..**5,750.00**
Walnut Fr style w/acanthus cvgs, shell knees, old crewel uphl, 39" H...**880.00**
Walnut QA style, scrolled arms:cvd legs, reuphl, ca 1900, 42x62" .**330.00**

Shelves

Corner, brn pnt, 4 bow-front shelves joined by trn pegs, 17" to 12" W..**220.00**
Grad set of 3 attached by rope, med bl pnt, rpr, bottom: 30" L..**110.00**
Mahog, whale ends, 4-tier, dvtl base, 33x27"..............................**1,650.00**
Mahog, whale shapes support 4 shelves, New England, 1800s, 32x32x9"..**1,400.00**
Oak, 3-D owl supports, 1890, 15x41x12"..................................**2,350.00**
Pine w/brn grpt, 4 grad shelves, scalloped sides, 34x27x8"..........**330.00**
Pine w/red pnt, rose/sq-head nails, 3-shelves, box styling, 36x36".**600.00**
Walnut, scalloped sides, dvtl corners, 3-shelf, 25x24x6" **495.00**

Sideboards

Mahog, 3 vnr drw:4 panel do, cvd capitals, J Needles, 1820s, 51"..**4,900.00**
Mahog Fed w/serpentine inlay, 5-part facade, att John Shaw, 38x72" ** **74,000.00**
Mahog Hplwht style w/flower inlay top, serpentine front, 20th C, 72"..**2,400.00**
Mahog Hplwht w/inlay, bow-front center, VA, rfn, 53x71x22"..**2,500.00**
Mahog inlaid Hplwht, bow-front, lg bksplash, rfn/sm rstr, 53x71x22".**2,500.00**
Mahog/figured vnrs Emp, paw ft, break front, 3 drw:4 do, 42x74x23".**1,550.00**
Oak, griffins support cvd lion head crest, mirror, 3 ornate do, 78x72"..**6,100.00**
Oak Art Nouveau w/emb copper panel, copper/brass pulls, 82x48x22".**1,175.00**
Oak cvd high-bk w/scrolls, griffin-cvd supports, swell front, 83x54"..**1,900.00**
Walnut Modern Gothic, drop-down desk, spindle gallery w/Minton tiles.**560.00**
Walnut Vict, marble top, eagle-head brackets, 78x54"..............**2,000.00**
Walnut w/allover cvg: scenic panels/giffins/atlas supports/etc, 94x70" ..**13,500.00**
Walnut/figured vnrs English Hplwht, 8-leg, 6-drw, 99" L.........**3,850.00**

Sofas

Mahogany Empire lyre-frame sofa, gold velvet reupholstery, paw feet with carving, reeded crest with pineapple finials, 34x77x27", $1,430.00.

Am Sheraton, rectangular padded bkrest/seat, trn ft, scroll arms, 72".......**4,300.00**
Chpndl style camelbk, Hickory Chair Co, 34x79".......................**550.00**
Fainting couch, mahog vnr Emp, rnd crest, reuphl, 39x53x26" ..**1,875.00**
Fed, cvd w/claw ft, horn of plenty arms, str crest, 34x90" **3,100.00**
Louis XV style, medallion bk, tapestry uphl, old rstr, 44x70x29" **550.00**
Mahog Am Classic, anthemion/rosette cvd paw ft, scroll crest/arms, 37" **4,600.00**
Mahog Am Classical, scroll arms/legs, rectangle top rail, 90" ..**4,000.00**
Mahog Chpndl style, camel-bk, reuphl, Century Furniture, 31x83x35"......**500.00**

Mahog cvd fr Transitional Sheraton to Emp, scroll arms, 70" **550.00**
Mahog Empr w/flame vnr panels, scrolled/cvd arms, reuphl, 36x89x25"..**3,400.00**
Mahog English Hplwht w/inlay, brass ft, reuphl, 38x77x26" **1,800.00**
Mahog Fed w/inlay, ring-trn reeded arm supports, NH, 1810, 33x75"....**3,500.00**
Mahog NY Sheraton, cvd crest, reeded arms, 32x73x30" **7,500.00**
Mahog Sheraton, cvd crest, reeded arm/rail, brass caster ft, old uphl.**7,475.00**
Mahog Sheraton style, 3-panel bk, scroll arms, old uphl, 35x77x31" .**850.00**
Recamier, mahog vnr Fed w/cvg, muslin uphl, rfn, 33x73x23"...**1,000.00**
Rswd, cvd/rtcl floral crest & apron, Roux, 1865, 43x70".......**3,600.00**
Rswd, cvd/rtcl triple bk, grotesques/florals, ornate, Boudoin, 78"..**5,600.00**
Rswd laminate, arched serpentine bk, cvd legs, reuphl, Belter, 83" **4,250.00**
Rswd Vict, triple bk w/openwork & cvd bk & apron, 46x77"..**2,240.00**
Walnut Emp, lyre fr w/paw ft & swan arms, horsehair uphl, 66", G .**1,100.00**

Stands

Basin, mahog, aproned top:shelf w/drw:shelf, England, 18th C, rfn, 33".**800.00**
Bedside, burl walnut w/floral inlay, marble top, Herter, 1885, 32"..**6,700.00**
Bedside, walnut Vict, marble top, appl fluting/leaves, 31x18" ...**545.00**
Birch Adirondack, stretcher w/3-D mc bird, 30x15x15".........**1,380.00**
Birch w/bird's-eye maple vnr, 1-drw, NE, 19x17" top w/biscuit corners.**1,375.00**
Birch/butternut Fed, tray top:skirt:4 tapered legs, rfn, 25x18x18" .**925.00**
Canterbury, mahog Fed, trn posts, 5 dividers:drw:4 casters, 17x19x14".**1,725.00**
Canterbury, mahog Sheraton style, drw, trn legs w/casters, 18x20x14"..**165.00**
Chamber, mahog, old rfn/rstr, England, ca 1800, 32x14x14" **300.00**
Cherry w/blk pnt, vase/ring-trn post, cabriole legs, NE, 1780s, 25" **590.00**
Cherry w/string inlay, tripod cabriole legs, rfn, 19th C, 27x19x12"..**2,500.00**
Curly maple Co Sheraton, 1-drw, dtd 1767, 20" sq top, 27" ..**2,000.00**
Curly maple Co Sheraton, 2-dw, 1-brd 24x17" top, ring-trn legs ...**2,090.00**
Curly maple/bird's-eye Hplwht, 1-drw, 1-brd top.....................**1,500.00**
Fern, Euro w/gilt gesso scrolls & acanthus leaves, marble top, 31x20".**450.00**
Kettle, mahog, tray top, candle slide:Marlborough legs, 1790s, 39x12".**1,035.00**
Mahog, tilt-top, cabriole leg tripod base, late 18th C, 29x24x17".**1,380.00**
Music, cast brass, molded base, bk adjusts, for table top, 9x12x11"..**165.00**
Music, walnut/rswd vnr Fed w/cvg, brass sconce ea side, old rfn, 47".**865.00**
Nightstand, oak, heavily cvd upper/lower cabinets, marble top, 33x20"..**2,800.00**
Plant, Art Deco wrought iron, 3 tiers, 1930s, 28x7½x25"..........**575.00**
Plant, mahog, full standing male as std, 37"................................**900.00**
Plant, spiral-trn legs, lower spindle gallery, Hunzinger, 36x20"..**900.00**
Plant, teakwood w/marble top, pierced/cvd skirt & apron, 1890, 32".**335.00**
Sewing, burl walnut R/R, sliding rtcl basket, cabriole legs, 31x22x16".**785.00**
Sewing, mahog M Washington, 3 dvtl drw, ½-rnd compartments, 20th C ..**220.00**
Tiger maple Fed, tilt-top, tripod w/scrolled legs, rfn, 29x22x16".**865.00**
Tiger maple Sheraton, 3 grad drw, trn legs, rpl pulls, 38x23x17" ..**3,000.00**
Walnut Co Sheraton w/figured mahog, 2 dvtl drw, trn legs, 30x21x17".**300.00**
Work, grpt Fed, 2 drw:sq ped:platform:bracket ft, 29x24x19" **700.00**
Work, tiger maple Fed, 2 grad drw:skirt:tapered legs, rfn, 39x20x16"......**1,950.00**

Stools

Footstool, mortised hardwood, scalloped apron, shaped legs, sm ..**100.00**
Footstool, pine w/orig grpt, fringed wool uphl, ca 1850, 8x13x9" .**1,265.00**
Mahog Sheraton, uphl top:rope-trn legs:ball ft, 13x16" oval, pr..**2,600.00**
Piano, mahog Fed, rfn, MA, 20x13" dia **700.00**
Piano, mahog w/spiral trn columns/legs, shaped seat, Hunzinger, pr.**1,680.00**
Piano, oak, 4 legs w/rectangular cvgs, WD Allison, adjusts 20 - 26" ...**90.00**
Tavern, pine, slant top/box stretcher/cut nails, EX patina, 31x14x12".**230.00**
Vanity, walnut Fr, floral cvg, velvet uphl, 20th C, 19x25" **110.00**
Walnut Baroque, yel velvet uphl, late 1800s, 19x21x15".........**2,500.00**
Windsor, olive gr pnt w/blk striping, bamboo-trn, NE/1810, 18" ..**600.00**

Tables

Banquet, mahog, drop-leaf extension type, banded, 1930, 118" L **1,800.00**

Banquet, mahog w/vnr aprons, reeded legs, Baltimore, 1800s, 52"+leaves ...**7,750.00**
Breakfast, mahog Boston Fed, drop-leaf, concave ends, 53" open ...**4,300.00**
Card, mahog Fed w/inlay, semi-elliptical, 30x36x18" **925.00**
Card, mahog w/rope legs, spindled shelf, c&b ft, Hunzinger, 1885.**1,100.00**
Card, walnut Vict 36" flip top, serpentine rose-cvd skirt/basket ..**1,800.00**
Center, Am R/R, much marquetry/bronze mts, Marcotte, top: 43x31".**6,000.00**
Center, burl/ebonized w/gold incising, 43x31" marble top, att Jeliff .**6,000.00**
Center, gilt Fr w/12" Sevres portrait+12 sm in border, ornate, 29x22" .**8,900.00**
Center, mahog, marble top:sq vnr ped:shaped base:4 scroll ft, 32" dia.**1,000.00**
Center, walnut R/R, ebonized trim, lg ornate center urn, 50" L ..**2,185.00**
Center, walnut Vict, 27x27 glass:cvd apron:ornate acanthus leaf legs .**1,150.00**
Chair, pine/maple, red wash traces, New England, 1800, 27x46" .**2,750.00**
Coffee, lacquered Regency style w/Oriental bird & flower, 20x42" dia .**1,600.00**
Cricket, maple/pine, tripod base:trn legs, 1-brd top, rprs, 27x23" ...**880.00**
Dining, mahog Chpndl, drop-leaf:cabriole legs:c&b ft, 38x52x18"+leaves.**6,600.00**
Dining, mahog Duncan Phyfe style, 2 tripod peds, Kittinger, 72"....**1,700.00**
Dining, mahog Emp, 5-column base, claw ft, 54" dia **1,900.00**
Dining, mahog Regency style, X-band top, brass paw ft, +1 leaf, 52".**1,000.00**
Dining, mahog Sheraton style w/inlay, dbl ped w/pineapple cvgs, 20th C..**5,000.00**
Dining, sycamore QA, old rfn, NE, 1740-60, 27x36x38" **3,335.00**
Dressing, faux bamboo bird's-eye maple, Vict, 1875, 58x43" ..**5,400.00**
Dressing, figured chestnut, 2 sm drw on 48x22" top w/2 lg drw, Herter ..**1,500.00**
Dressing, grpt, trn logs, scrolled bk splash, ME, 35x33x15", VG..**300.00**
Dressing, maple QA, overhanging top:3 short drw:cabriole legs, 28x30" ..**9,200.00**
Dressing, walnut QA, drw:3 short:skirt:cabriole legs, 30x30x17" ..**14,950.00**
Dressing, walnut QA w/inlay, 3 beaded drw:apron:pad ft, 1710s, 29x30" .**1,265.00**
Drop-leaf, cherry Fed w/much inlay, att Lombard, MA/1800, 35" rnd drop ..**11,750.00**
Drop-leaf, cherry Fed w/much inlay, MA/1800, 31" drop.........**6,400.00**
Drop-leaf, cherry Sheraton, ring-ball trn legs, rpl 20x30" top **360.00**
Drop-leaf, grpt Fed, hinged leaves, ped:platform:ball ft/casters, 40"..**925.00**
Drop-leaf, mahog Chpndl, curved skirt:cabriole legs:c&b ft, rfn, 47".**4,600.00**
Drop-leaf, rswd, lg fruit basket center finial, top: 29x26" **1,950.00**
End, walnut English, 2 urn-trn supports, appl cvgs, 21x26x17"...**275.00**
Game, mahog Fed w/inlay & water-leaf-cvg, MA, 30x36x16" ...**4,900.00**
Game, mahog Fed w/inlay at top & legs, Boston, rfn, 39x36x18" ..**7,000.00**
Game, mahog Sheraton, swivel top:str front:rope-twist legs........**300.00**
Game, Moroccan leather top, bone & wood inlay, 32x30x16", pr...**1,800.00**
Gate-leg, tiger maple/maple, drw, trn ft, rpl pull, old rfn, 45" ..**1,500.00**
Hunt, mahog, old rfn, att Ireland, ca 1800, 39½x85x54" **4,900.00**
Hutch, cherry, hinged oval top:compartment:shoe ft, late 1700s, 27x40".**4,000.00**
Lamp, spiral-trn column on platform w/c&b ft, 24" sq top, Hunzinger .**1,500.00**
Library, walnut w/highly cvd legs, lg claw ft, cvd apron, 1-drw, 86"..**3,000.00**

Nesting, rock maple, Heywood-Wakefield, ca 1940s – early 1950s, 25x21x15" (largest), $350.00. (Photo courtesy Robert W. and Harriett Swedberg)

Parlor, mahog Rococo, 39" marble turtle-top, shaped/cvd skirt & knees..**1,100.00**
Parlor, rswd/marble Rococo, lg 3-D figures/ornate base/apron, 40"..**3,360.00**
Pembroke, mahog Fed w/inlay, 1 working/1 faux drw, rfn, 38x38x20" ..**5,750.00**
Pembroke, mahog Hplwht w/inlay, brass casters, drw, 38x29x18"+2 leaves .**1,500.00**
Pembroke, mahog w/floral inlay Am Fed, bowed drw, 1820s, top: 44x33"...**8,912.00**

Refectory, oak, stretcher w/cvd supports, 3-brd top, 1900s, 31x72x28"..**1,500.00**
Sawbuck, pine w/red & wht pnt traces, sq nails, 1-brd 32x19" top.**990.00**
Sawbuck, primitive, old red rpt w/blk top, sq nails, 28x24x15"...**550.00**
Sawbuck, red-pnt pine, scrubbed 3-brd top, early 19th C, 28x60x29".**4,600.00**
Side, 1-drw, spiral-trn legs, stick/ball apron, Hunzinger, 24x24" top.**900.00**
Sofa, walnut/marble Renaissance, gold incising, figural pulls, 72"..**3,000.00**
Tavern, blk-pnt vase & ring-trn stretcher base, old rpt, 1790s ...**4,000.00**
Tavern, cherry/maple, 1-drw, rpl pine 24x41" breadbrd top.........**550.00**
Tavern, maple Co QA w/old red pnt base, rfn top, 27x36x27".**1,980.00**
Tavern, maple/pine/birch QA, rpl 1-brd 27x20" top, trn legs......**990.00**
Tavern, pine/maple, oval top, splay legs, rfn, 18th C, 24x33x25".**2,300.00**
Tea, cherry Chpndl, 4-brd scalloped 32" sq rpl top.....................**385.00**
Tea, mahog QA, tray top, old rfn, rprs, 38x28x19" **6,325.00**
Tea, Majorelle, inlaid foliage/berries, 3-tier w/drop leaves, 33x28"..**2,000.00**
Tea, QA style, red pnt tray top, NE, 27x29x17".......................**2,500.00**
Tea, walnut Georgian, tilt-top:birdcage, rfn, England, 39x33" ..**5,175.00**
Tea, walnut QA tilt-top, trn center post, 3 snake ft, 38x3½x32", EX..**4,600.00**
Tea, 28x28" pie-crust tilt top, cvd knees, c&b ft, 1789, 43", G.....**1,200.00**
Tilt-top, mahog Chpndl style w/pie-crust edge, tripod, rstr, 29x29"........**350.00**
Tilt-top, walnut Italian w/ivory & ebony inlay, ped:3 legs, 30x36"..**1,495.00**
Work, walnut, 2 long dvtl drw, 3-brd removable top, 33x140x42", EX.**3,200.00**
Work, walnut Sheraton, lift lid w/fitted int, false drw:drw, trn legs.**400.00**
Writing, cherry Am Louis XV style, 2-drw, late 1900s, 30x57x30" ...**1,400.00**
Writing, satinwood/ebonized w/bird's-eye maple top, att Marcotte, 54".....**2,240.00**

Wardrobes

Chiffonier, mahog European w/figured vnr, 6-drw, rstr/frn, 62x41x18" .**1,925.00**
Linen press, cherry, panel do:3 drw:molded base:ogee ft, rfn, 87x50"....**4,600.00**
Linen press, mahog/poplar Chpndl, 2 panel do:3 drw, rstr, 75x44"..**3,850.00**
Poplar w/orig mc pnt, cornice:2 panel do:bracket ft, OH, 66x22" ..**880.00**
Poplar w/orig red & overvarnish, scalloped ends, 1-drw, OH, 80x42"..**2,200.00**

Washstands

Corner, cherry/pine/poplar Sheraton, bow-front, dvtl drw, rstr, 30x18" ..**880.00**
Figured mahog vnr Sheraton, 17x22" top w/3 cutouts +2 sm shelves:drw .**550.00**
Mahog, gallery:compartment:drw:trn legs:shelf, MD, 1825-40, 33x30x22".**400.00**
Pnt Am, mustard w/red pinstripes, gallery, grpt drw, low shelf, 37"..**625.00**
Smoke/pnt decor, shaped bksplash, medial shelf w/drw, NE/1830s, 30"..**1,000.00**
Tiger maple Fed, drw in lower shelf, high gallery, old rfn, 1820s, 37"..**975.00**
Tiger maple Fed w/inlay, scalloped splashbrd, 1 drw, 22" L **2,300.00**
Walnut Eastlake w/cvg, 3-drw, 1 do, lion-head pulls, rfn, 37x28x17"...**300.00**
Walnut Sheraton, drw, 4 trn legs, shelf, 33x30x17"....................**400.00**
Walnut Sheraton, 1-drw, bksplash, trn legs, 33x30x17" **400.00**
Walnut Vict, marble top w/splash & candle shelves; drw:2 do....**525.00**

Miscellaneous

Bed steps, mahog, commode combination, serpentine front, 17x18½", G..**325.00**
Bed steps, walnut Sheraton, trn ft, 3-step, 28x22x28" **880.00**
Cellarette, figured mahog Georgian, hinged lid, late 19th C, 18x20x17" ..**330.00**
Cellarette, mahog Fed w/inlay, 8-sided top, rfn, 25x22x17" **2,800.00**
Etagere, bamboo/faux bamboo, ball finials, 4-shelf, English, 47x21" ...**230.00**
Etagere, rswd Am Rococo, fleur-de-lys crest/curving marble top, 85x48"..**5,450.00**
Etagere, rswd/marble, floral bonnet top, serpentine, att Meeks, 106"..**36,000.00**
Etagere, stick/ball sides/apron, Northwind gallery, 1890, 64x43" ..**1,500.00**
Fire screen, walnut Renaissance Revival, rtcl crest, silk panel, 75" .**5,600.00**
Fire screen, walnut Vict w/lg 3-D griffins & cherubs, c&b ft, 48" .**10,600.00**
Library ladder, poles w/brass-studded leather, fruitwood rungs, 91"..**1,295.00**
Parlor set, Art Deco rswd, Fr, 1925, library cabinet+desk+chair.**11,500.00**
Parlor set, lion-head arms, claw ft, att Herter, 55" sofa+armchair.**4,480.00**
Parlor set, rswd, Hartford pattern, Meeks, 50x70" sofa+arm+side chair ..**28,000.00**
Pedestal, burled walnut R/R, ornate cvd panels, 45x18x18" **3,000.00**

Pedestal, lg cvd 3-D seated winged griffin support, 1885, 46"..**2,240.00**
Pedestal, mahog, cvd drapery column, claw ft, 1885, 37x15" dia.**1,800.00**
Pedestal, mahog w/cvd acanthus, lg claw ft, 1890, 35"............**1,250.00**
Pedestal, oak, Cupid heads/cvd columns/marble tops, 1880s, 57x26" sq..**2,500.00**
Pedestal, onyx/bronze, swivel top, reeded pillars, claw ft, 31x16" dia.**3,000.00**
Pedestal, walnut R/R, bold cvg, w/ebony & gold, 43x19x19"..**5,300.00**
Pipe rack, dvtl pine, triangular, drw w/trn pull, red traces, 18x15".**385.00**
Pole screen, pnt vnr w/tripod ft, oval sections w/fabric, Fr, 56", pr.**880.00**
Tea cart, oak, spoked wheels, Ferguson Bros, 29x28x18"+2 drop leaves...**440.00**
Umbrella stand, oak, 2 open sides, 2 sides w/oval cutouts, 28x12x10"...**90.00**

Galle

Emile Galle was one of the most important producers of cameo glass in France. His firm, founded in Nancy in 1874, produced beautiful cameo in the Art Nouveau style during the 1890s, using a variety of techniques. He also produced glassware with enameled decoration, as well as some fine pottery — animal figurines, table services, vases, and other objets d' art. In the mid-1880s he became interested in the various colors and textures of natural woods and as a result began to create furniture which he used as yet another medium for expression of his artistic talent. Marquetry was the primary method Galle used in decorating his furniture, preferring landscapes, Nouveau floral and fruit arrangements, butterflies, squirrels, and other forms from nature. It is for his furniture and his cameo glass that he is best known today. All Galle is signed.

In the listings below, 'fp' indicates items that have been fire polished. Our advisor for this category is Don Williams; he is listed in the Directory under Missouri.

Cameo

Bowl, floral sprigs, brn/lime on pk to gray, rim w/4 pulled points, 8"....**920.00**
Ewer, floral, orange/brn on tan w/silver foil, amber stem/hdl, 9"..**1,725.00**
Jardiniere, maple leaves, rust on topaz mottle, fp, cylindrical 6"...**4,400.00**
Lamp base, fruit/leafy stems, cinnamon on bl-gray, slender/ftd, 17"..**1,380.00**
Pitcher, floral, amber on clear martele, amber tendril hdl, 11"...**3,000.00**
Powder box, scenic lid, leaves on bottom, 5¾" dia **1,035.00**
Vase, bud; flower & bud, purple on amber, stick neck, 3⅝".......**375.00**
Vase, crocus, 2-tone yel w/brn on lt citron, bulbous, mold blown, 9"..**6,000.00**
Vase, ferns, dk gr on frost to lt gr, stick neck, 12½"................**2,300.00**
Vase, ferns, lt gr on pk, rnd w/very tall & slim neck, 12".........**2,500.00**
Vase, floral, bl on bl to frost to yel, slim, ftd, 10"....................**2,400.00**
Vase, floral, bl/purple on yel & frost, 8"..................................**1,800.00**
Vase, floral, purple on yel, stick neck, 6½"..............................**650.00**
Vase, floral, red/gr on yel frost, band at neck, 12½"................**4,250.00**
Vase, floral, red/orange on wht, bulbous/waisted gourd form, 5"...**1,095.00**
Vase, floral, rust/burgundy on salmon, ovoid, 6½"....................**2,050.00**
Vase, floral stems, amethyst on gray/bl, rnd w/long pencil neck, 13"..**2,000.00**
Vase, floral stems, amethyst on martele frost, cylinder, petal ft, 12"..**2,500.00**
Vase, floral stems, cherry red/maroon on amber, shouldered, 14"..**4,825.00**
Vase, floral stems, red on lt gr, fp, cylinder w/bun base, 18"..**3,235.00**
Vase, floral vines, yel/brn on dk peach, slim, 9½"...................**1,200.00**
Vase, floral/leaves, amethyst on frost, cylinder w/wide ft, 14½"....**1,550.00**
Vase, grapevines/leaves, brn on gray frost, 10".......................**2,000.00**
Vase, irises, lav on gray frost, cylindrical w/bun ft, 18".............**3,500.00**
Vase, irises, lav on opal, shouldered w/incurvate sides, 16"......**3,700.00**
Vase, leaves, amethyst on amber to frost, shouldered cylinder, 14"..**1,250.00**
Vase, leaves/vines, 2-tone gr on opal/tan, cylindrical w/wide ft, 24"...**4,200.00**
Vase, lg trees before lake, rust/umber on citron frost, 15½".....**3,500.00**
Vase, lg trees/town beyond, 4-color, 12¾"..............................**2,360.00**
Vase, lilies, pk on gr, can neck, ftd sphere, 10½".....................**5,275.00**
Vase, maple leaves/pods, yel frost to amber, stick neck, 6½".......**600.00**

Vase, orchids/foliage, rust on amber, shouldered, 8".................**1,800.00**
Vase, pond plants, orange/brn/cream, rnd w/short collar neck, 3½".**550.00**

Vase, rhododendrons, dark amethyst on yellow-amber, spherical, 1925, 10¼", $12,000.00. (Photo courtesy Skinner, Inc.)

Vase, river scene, brn/gr on bl/yel/frost, 13"............................**2,000.00**
Vase, roses, orange/red on amber, U-form, 9¾".......................**3,500.00**
Vase, thistles, chartreuse on gray/pk, invt trumpet form, 16"..**1,380.00**
Vase, thistles cut/pnt on textured topaz w/lt ribs, 7"...............**2,350.00**
Vase, trees/pond, 4-color, 13"...**2,530.00**
Vase, trumpet flowers, opaque ochre/mauve, tapered cylinder, 11".....**2,750.00**
Vase, vines/pods, gr/lime on apricot to gray, rnd w/neck hdls, 8x7"....**5,750.00**
Vase, 3 floral bands on gr, conical w/bun ft, 4".......................**320.00**

Enameled Glass

Vase, clear crackle w/HP stemmed flowers, hdls, squat, 4½x6".........**230.00**
Vase, florals/diagonal band w/floral medallion on lt brn, lg hdls, 10"...**1,500.00**
Vase, flower bud/blossoms, purple/pk/brn/gr on frost, cylinder, 6½".**320.00**
Vase, lg floral, cranberry/gr/wht on clear, ribbed, 7".................**1,000.00**
Vase, pendant flowers, maroon/rose on textured frost, 5½x5".**1,200.00**
Vase, topaz w/mc trumpet flowers & gold, dbl bulb, 9"............**1,850.00**
Vase, vining thistles on diagonal swirls w/pinched rim & disk ft, 10"..**1,350.00**

Marquetry, Wood

Cabinet, mahog, cvd & inlaid florals & scenic, mk, 36x25"....**6,000.00**
Table, shaped 29" top w/inlaid mums/leaves, lower inlay shelf, 30"...**3,600.00**
Table, 2-tier, butterfly/floral, serpentine legs, 28x25x16".........**3,500.00**
Tray, lg sailboats w/figures, shaped open hdls, 16x24".............**2,300.00**

Pottery

Figurine, upright lion by castle tower, banner/shield, 17"........**1,100.00**
Plate, man in ragged cloak, icicle trim, shield form, 7x8½"........**500.00**
Vase, dbl upright fish form, 6"..**1,495.00**
Vase, iris/butterfly, bl/gr/gold, ribs/dimples, drilled, 10"..............**550.00**

Gambling Memorabilia

Gambling memorabilia from the infamous casinos of the West and items that were once used on the 'Floating Palace' riverboats are especially sought after by today's collectors.

Ashtray, Carson City Nugget, clear glass w/wht center, EX........**195.00**
Ashtray, Fabulous Flamingo, clear glass w/wht & red center, 1940s, EX...**65.00**
Ashtray, Sans Couci, clear glass w/wht center w/red letters, EX .**100.00**
Ashtray, Silver Palace, Downtown Las Vegas, rectangular, EX....**150.00**
Ashtray, Wilbur Clark Desert Inn & Country Club, rnd, EX........**75.00**

Card case, 2 decks w/chips, hardwood box, Club Reno, EX **45.00**
Card shuffler, metal w/wood hdl/grip, Johnson Mfg Co, 1950s, EXIB..**30.00**
Chip, Flamingo Hotel, purple, 50¢, 1967, EX....................**140.00**
Chip, Hacienda, clay, $1, 1960s, 1½", EX....................**180.00**
Chip, scrimshawed ivory w/star & leaf, 1850s, EX....................**185.00**
Chip, Sphinx, clay w/brn celluloid insert w/wht letters, 1940s, EX .**110.00**
Chip, SS Rex, California gambling boat in 1938-39, clay, red & wht, EX .**110.00**
Chip, Star Dust, maroon, 25¢, EX....................**250.00**
Chip caddy, Catalin, yel w/brn, holds 8 stacks, w/141 chips, EX...**220.00**
Chips, Mermaid Casino, emb mermaid, 184 in wooden rack w/cover, EX....**50.00**
Dice, M&M Club, ivory w/blk dots & red M&M, 1940s-50s, M ..**65.00**
Dice cage, NP brass w/parchment paper ends, Napier, 4½", EX....**90.00**

Folding faro layout and card press, Geo. Mason & Co., Denver, ca 1880, layout: 17x40"; Card press: 3x7", holds five decks, all original, EX+, $550.00 for all.

Game, roulette, w/8" wheel/ball/chips/felt mk Loze, 1940s, EXIB ..**50.00**
Plate, dinner; Flamingo Hotel, 2 abstract flamingos decor, 10" ..**30.00**
Punch board, Fortunes, magician w/crystal ball on front, A Master, NM..**30.00**
Punch board, 26 Girl, pinup girl diecut, 1940s, unused, NM **35.00**
Table, roulette; BS Williams, w/wheel, chips & ball, 1930s, EX ...**4,200.00**
Wheel, orig red/yel pnt w/dice emblems, OH, 20" dia................**415.00**
Wheel, pnt wood on wood stand, 19th C, 25x16" dia **2,000.00**
Wheel, pnt wood w/stencils/flowers/etc, 30" dia.........................**475.00**

Game Calls

Those interested in hunting and fishing collectibles are beginning to take notice of the finer specimens of game calls available on today's market.

Crow, Charles H Perdew, walnut w/silver band, 5¼"....................**235.00**
Crow, Duc-Em Crow Call, wooden, Oliveros, 5", NM (EX box) ..**45.00**
Crow, Herter's #204, EXIB **35.00**
Crow, Inman Turpin, wooden, 1970s..............................**290.00**
Crow, Olt's Model E1, EXIB.......................................**20.00**
Crow, Pull-Em Crow Call, oak, Oliveros Manufacturing Co, 5", EXIB.**30.00**
Crow, wood w/bone tip, 3", VG....................................**125.00**
Crow/duck, H Perdew Henry III Pat Nov 2, 1909, 4½" **170.00**
Deer, Herter's #903, NM (VG+ box)...............................**45.00**
Duck, Bean Lake E Stofer, EX.....................................**80.00**
Duck, Cajun #4317, wooden, cvd rings **30.00**
Duck, Charles Perdew, cvd/checkered walnut, ca 1920............**1,600.00**
Duck, Cree, wooden, 1970s, MIB **80.00**
Duck, Duc-Em Duck Call, wooden, Oliveros, 1950s, orig box **30.00**
Duck, Dupe a Duck, Bakelite, 5⅞"................................**375.00**
Duck, FA Allen, wooden body w/metal reed & mouthpc..............**40.00**
Duck, Faulk's Duck Call 1954-55 on label, 12x3¼" dia.................**60.00**
Duck, HE McMahon, clear plastic, EX...............................**50.00**

Duck, Herter's #272, original box **40.00**
Duck, Herter's Indian Glodo #139, orig box **35.00**
Duck, John 'Sandy' Morrow, checkered, early 20th C, 7", EX .**1,100.00**
Duck, Kinney & Harlow, wood/leather duck head w/shell in mouth, 6½" ..**10,350.00**
Duck, Perry Wade, wooden w/cvd rings, 1950s.........................**250.00**
Duck, PS Olt B-4, plastic shell w/hard rubber plug, EX..............**115.00**
Duck, PS Olt D-2, NMIB..**55.00**
Duck, Ralph True, wooden w/metal reed, 1950s **80.00**
Duck, Sta-Dri, plastic, 3-pc, 5" **35.00**
Duck, tinplate, w/crank, mk Pat March 28 1905, EX................**65.00**
Goose, Fuller's, 2-pc, slide outer sleeve to change tone, 5" **105.00**
Goose, Olt #800, 1970s, orig box & papers.......................**30.00**
Goose, PS Olt Model No A-5, hard rubber, 1960s, 4½"...............**60.00**
Mountain lion, Herter's World Famous Predator Call, 1960s, orig box.**35.00**
Shorebird whistle, R Woodman Mfg, ca 1890, 4" **200.00**

Gameboards

Gameboards, the handmade ones from the eighteenth and nineteenth century, are collected more for their folk art quality than their relation to games. Excellent examples of these handcrafted 'playthings' sell well into the thousands of dollars; even the simple designs are often expensive. If you are interested in this field, you must study it carefully. The market is always full of 'new' examples. Well-established dealers are often your best sources; they are essential if you do not have the expertise to judge the age of the boards yourself. Our advisor for this category is Louis Picek; he is listed in the Directory under Iowa.

Checkers, blk/gray w/red lines, 1850s, 14x14" **1,035.00**
Checkers, blk/red sqs w/wht surround, Am, 1900-50, 19x25"..**1,265.00**
Checkers, gr/brn, red/bl-gr/wine borders, blk appl molding, 1861, 15" ..**770.00**
Checkers, incised/HP sqs on slate, late 1800s, 19½" sq............**1,650.00**
Checkers, mc pnt, appl fr, pull-out drw w/pcs, 1870s, 17x29"..**2,000.00**
Checkers, mc w/allover marbleized surface, appl fr, 1880s, 19x31"....**3,450.00**
Checkers, mustard/blk on pine w/appl oak trim, sq nails, 19" sq .**1,050.00**
Checkers, pnt wood w/appl fr, floral decals, 1890s, 20" sq **3,000.00**
Checkers, pnt/inlaid, appl fr, ca 1890, 16" sq........................**1,725.00**
Checkers, scribed/mc pnt, chamfered edges, ca 1900, 8x11"..**1,950.00**
Checkers, 2-sided, mc pnt, mortised & tenoned, late 1800s, 16x18"...**1,035.00**
Checkers/backgammon, appl fr, yel/bl/gr/red pnt, dbl sided, 20" sq **1,645.00**
Checkers/backgammon, mc pnt, folding, Am, 14½x15½"..........**575.00**
Checkers/backgammon, mc pnt on brd, folds, ca 1880, 17x19" .**1,265.00**
Checkers/backgammon/parcheesi (reverse), mc pnt, ca 1900, 17x24"..**1,840.00**
Checkers/Old Mill, pnt wood (split), ca 1900, 24x30".............**1,265.00**
Checkers/parcheesi, mc pnt, stars/leaves/etc decor, 1900, 18x30"..**1,400.00**
Checkers/parcheesi, mc pnt w/fleur-de-lis, appl fr, late 1800s, 27" sq.**5,465.00**
Checkers/parcheesi, pnt brd, appl molding/fr, ca 1900, 19x21" ..**3,000.00**
Checkers/unknown w/pnt cards, mc pnt w/abstract floral, 1890s, 15x29".**3,000.00**
Chinese checkers, mc pnt box w/rnd cutouts, 20th C, 24½" sq ..**1,100.00**
Darts, red/wht/bl pnt canvas over pine brd, 1930s, 18x19" .**1,850.00**
Marbles, dmn pattern, mc arched fr w/gutters, 1890s, 12x22" ..**980.00**
Parcheesi, bird's eye maple laminated over mahog, 4-color wash, 15x22".**465.00**
Parcheesi, bk: Checkers, 6-color, molded edges, 1875, 18x18", G..**1,120.00**
Parcheesi, mc box w/game-pc drw, ca 1920, 15½x16"..............**1,725.00**
Parcheesi, mc pnt, early 1900s, 15x18"...........................**1,750.00**
Parcheesi, mc pnt, 2 compartments w/sliding lids, 1900s, 19x31"..**5,750.00**
Parcheesi, mc pnt on artist brd, ca 1900, 20" sq.......................**1,150.00**
Parcheesi, paper on brd, mc, late 1800s, appl fr, 18" sq............**1,265.00**
Parcheesi, stenciled gilt scroll & florals, appl fr, 1880s, 27" sq....**4,000.00**
Parcheesi/fox & geese, mc pnt on wood, breadboard ends, 19th C, 18" sq.**2,300.00**
Penny pitch, red & wht pinwheel panels, appl fr, 1900, 18" dia.....**3,750.00**
Unknown w/flag motifs, mc pnt, folds, appl fr, 1920s, 25" sq...**2,300.00**

Games

Collectors of antique games are finding it more difficult to find their treasures at shows and flea markets. Most of the action these days seems to be through specialty dealers and auctions. The appreciation of the art on the boards and boxes continues to grow. You see many of the early games proudly displayed as art, and they should be. The period from the 1850s to 1910 continues to draw the most interest. Many of the games of that period were executed by well-known artists and illustrators. The quality of their lithography cannot be matched today. The historical value of games made before 1850 has caused interest in this period to increase. While they may not have the graphic quality of the later period, their insights into the social and moral character of the early nineteenth century are interesting.

Twentieth-century games invoke a nostalgic feeling among collectors who recall looking forward to a game under the Christmas tree each year. They search for examples that bring back those Christmas-morning memories. While the quality of their lithography is certainly less than the early games, the introduction of personalities from the comic strips, radio, and later TV created new interest. Every child wanted a game that featured their favorite character. Monopoly, probably the most famous game ever produced, was introduced during the Great Depression.

For further information, we recommend *Schroeder's Collectible Toys, Antique to Modern*; available from Collector Books.

The Wide World and a Journey Round It, Parker Brothers, 1896, EXIB, $525.00 at auction.

$64,000 Dollar Question Jr Edition, Lowell, 1956, EXIB 30.00
ABC Education, card game, Ed-U-Cards, 1959, EX+ (EX box)....10.00
Across the Continent, Parker Bros, 1952, NM (EX box) 40.00
All American Skittle Score-Ball, Aurora, 1974, EX (EX box)......35.00
American Boys, McLoughlin Bros, early 1900s, EX (EX box).....200.00
Animal Talk, Mattel, 1964, MIB...150.00
Apple's Way, Milton Bradley, 1974, EX (EX box).........................25.00
Astro Launch, Ohio Art, 1963, EXIB..75.00
Auto Racing, Milton Bradley, 1930s, VG (VG box) 225.00
Automobile Race, McLoughlin Bros, 1904, EX (EX box)........1,800.00
Bandersnatch, Mattel, 1969, NMIB..70.00
Barnstormer, Marx, 1970, EX (EX box)...35.00
Battle Line, Ideal, 1964, EX (EX box)...40.00
Battleboard, Ideal, 1972, NMIB...30.00
Battleship, Whitman, 1940, EX (EX box).......................................65.00
Beach Head Invasion, Built-Rite, 1950s, EX (EX box)..................40.00
Behind the 8 Ball, Selchow & Righter, 1969, EX (EX box).........25.00
Big Town News Reporting, Lowell, 1950s, rare, NMIB 75.00
Black Hole Space Alert, Whitman, 1979, MIB 35.00
Blockade, Corey Games, 1941, VG (VG box) 85.00
Boom or Bust, Parker Bros, 1951, EX (EX box) 250.00
Boots & Saddles, Gardner, 1958, EX (EX box)..............................50.00
Break the Bank, Bettye-B, 1955, EX (EX box)...............................35.00
Bucket of Fun, Milton Bradley, 1968, EX (EX box)......................35.00

Burke's Law, target game, Transogram, 1964, EX (EX box) 45.00
Cabby, Selchow & Righter, 1950s, EX (EX box) 75.00
Camp Granada, Milton Bradley, 1965, EX (EX box)....................35.00
Chiclets Gum Village, Hasbro, 1959, EX (EX box) 30.00
Chiromagica, McLoughlin Bros, 1890, VG (VG wood & glass box)..300.00
Civil War Game of 1963, Parker Bros, 1961, NM (NM box)........50.00
Crazy Clock, Ideal, 1964, NM (NM box) 100.00
Crow Hunt, Parker Bros, 1930, VG (VG box)...............................65.00
Dice Ball, Milton Bradley, 1934, VG (VG box) 60.00
Dino the Dinosaur, Transogram, 1961, MIB.................................75.00
Down & Out, Milton Bradley, EX (worn box)..............................75.00
Dream Date, Transogram, 1963, EX (EX box) 50.00
FBI, Transogram Landmark Game Series, MIB 75.00
Fireball XL5 Magnetic Dart Game, Magic Wand, 1963, EX (EX box) .150.00
Flip-A-Lid, Hassenfeld Bros, 1950s, VG (VG box) 35.00
Flying Aces, Selchow & Righter, 1940s, EX (EX box) 100.00
Funny Finger, Ideal, 1968, EX (EX box)..25.00
Game of Bagatelle, McLoughlin Bros, 1890s, VG (VG box) 400.00
Game of Bounce, McLoughlin Bros, late 1800s, EX (EX box)....650.00
Game of Philippine, McLoughlin Bros, 1900, EX (EX box)........300.00
Game of Steeple Chase, McLoughlin Bros, 1889, EX (worn box).350.00
Game of the Crusaders, McLoughlin Bros, 1888, EX (G box) 300.00
Game of Up & Down, Whitman, 1959, EX (EX box)...................35.00
Gay Purr-ee, Whitman, 1962, EX (EX box)...................................70.00
Gee-Whiz Race, Wolverine, EX (EX box) 85.00
Gypsy Fortune Telling Game, Milton Bradley, 1920, NMIB 150.00
Hands Down, Ideal, 1964, EX (EX box)..20.00
Honey West, Ideal, 1955, MIB 175.00
Hungry Henry, Ideal, 1969, EX (EX box).....................................30.00
Jumpy Tinker, Toy Tinkers, 1918, EX (worn box).......................75.00
Kentucky Derby, Whitman, 1969, NMIB......................................30.00
Kookie Chicks, Milton Bradley, 1964, EX (EX box)....................20.00
Last Straw, Schraper, 1966, EX (EX box)......................................30.00
Lippy the Lion Flips, Transogram, 1962, EX (EX box) 95.00
Little Fireman, McLoughlin Bros, EX (EX wood box) 2,800.00
Lost Heir, Milton Bradley, 1905, VG (G box) 125.00
Lucky Louie, Transogram, 1968, EX (EX box).............................30.00
Magic Robot, J&L Randall/England, 1950s, EX (EX box) 125.00
Mansion of Happiness, Ives, 1864, VG (VG box) 300.00
Marathon Tinker, Toy Tinkers, 1925, EX (EX box)....................150.00
Merry Milkman, Hasbro, 1955, EX (EX box)..............................100.00
Miss America, Parker Bros, 1974, EX (EX box) 45.00
Monster Old Maid, Milton Bradley, 1964, EX (EX box).............35.00
Mouse Trap, Ideal, 1963, 1st issue, EX (EX box)........................65.00
Mystery Pistol Target Master, Ohio Art, 1960s, EX (EX box).....100.00
Mystic Skull Game of Voodoo, Ideal, 1960s, EX (EX box)...........65.00
Nurses, Ideal, 1963, EX (EX box) 70.00
Patty Playpal, Ideal, 1961, EX (EX box).......................................35.00
People Magazine Trivia, Parker Bros, 1984, EX (EX box) 20.00
Picture Lotto, McLoughlin Bros, 1888, VG (VG wood box) 300.00
Pivot Golf, Milton Bradley, MIB 125.00
Pop Yer Top, Milton Bradley, 1968, EX (EX box).......................25.00
Poppin Hoppies, Ideal, 1968, EX (EX box) 20.00
Pot O-Gold, All-Fair, 1940s, EX (EX box)....................................30.00
Pow-Cannon, Milton Bradley, 1964, NMIB.................................65.00
Ranger Commandos, Parker Bros, 1944, EX (EX box) 70.00
Restless Gun, Milton Bradley, 1959, NMIB 50.00
Ring My Nose, Milton Bradley, EX (EX box)...............................50.00
Rock, Paper & Scissors, Schaper, 1961, EX (EX box)..................25.00
Rock-Em Sock-Em Robots, Marx, 1966, MIB............................200.00
Sea Raiders, Parker Bros, 1945, EX (EX box)...............................55.00
See New York 'Round the Town, Transogram, 1964, EX (EX box) 85.00
Simon Says, 1964, EX (EX box) 25.00
Skatterbug, Parker Bros, 1951, EX (EX box)................................45.00

Skill-Drive Raceway, Tarco, 1960s, NMIB 45.00
Smack-A-Roo, Mattel, 1964, EX (EX box) 60.00
Sonar Sub Hunt, Mattel, 1961, EX (EX box) 65.00
Sports Arena, Milton Bradley, 1962, EX (EX box) 50.00
Sprint, Holland Crafts, 1930s, EX (EX box) 75.00
Spy Detector, Mattel, 1960, NMIB 40.00
Stock Exchange, Milton Bradley, 1910, EX (EX box) ...75.00
Supercar Magnetic Target, Wand, 1962, EX (EX box), from $300 to ...400.00
Swamp Fox, Parker Bros, 1960, NMIB 75.00
Talking Football, Mattel, 1971, NMIB 100.00
Tickle Bee, Schaper, 1959, EX (EX box) 35.00
Tin Pin Tinker, Toy Tinkers, 1925, EX (worn box) 75.00
Tinkerdux, Toy Tinkers, 1919, EX (worn box) 60.00
Top Secret, National Games, 1956, EX (EX box) 75.00
Wanted Dead or Alive, Lowell, 1959, EX (EX box) 100.00
Whirling Jockey Race, McDowell, early 1900s, EX (worn box) ..325.00
Whyoo, Milton Bradley, 1906, EX (EX box) 100.00
Zoo Games, Milton Bradley, 1920s, EX (worn box) 55.00

Personalities, Movies, and TV Shows

Adventures of Popeye, Transogram, 1957, EX (EX box) 50.00
Annie Oakley Game Gems/T Cohn, 1965, EX (EX box) 50.00
Bat Masterson, Lowell, 1958, EX (EX box) 65.00
Batman & Robin Target, Hasbro, 1966, MIB 200.00
Batman's Cave Maze, Pressman, scarce, NM (NM box) 350.00
Beatles Flip Your Wig, EX (EX box) 250.00
Ben Casey, Transogram, 1961, EX (EX box) 30.00
Bewitched, Stymie card game, Milton Bradley, 1964, EX (EX box) ...45.00
Bonanza Rummy, Parker Bros, 1964, EX (EX box) 35.00
Bozo the Clown TV Lotto, Ideal, 1960, EX (EX box) 30.00
Buffalo Bill Jr's Cattel Roundup, Built-Rite, 1956, EX (EX box) ..35.00
Bullwinkle Motorized Target, Parks, 1961, EX (EX box) 200.00
Captain America, Milton Bradley, 1966, MIB 100.00
Carol Burnett's Spoof, Milton Bradley, 1964, EX (EX box) 40.00
Casper's Picture Lotto, Built-Rite, 1959, EX (EX box) 30.00
Chitty-Chitty Bang-Bang Electric Movie Quiz, Remco, 1968, EX (EX box) .75.00
Davy Crockett Indian Scouting, Whitman, NMIB, from $65 to .85.00
Dennis the Mennis, Standard-Toykraft, 1960, EX (EX box) 75.00
Dick Tracy Crime Stopper, Ideal, 1963, NMIB 75.00
Dick Tracy Electronic Target, 1961, NMIB 100.00
Dick Tracy Target, Marx, 1930s, 17" dia, NMIB 400.00
Doc Holiday Wild West, Transogram, 1960, NMIB 65.00
Dr Dolittle, Mattel, 1967, EX (EX box) 45.00
Dr Kildare, Ideal, 1962, NMIB 65.00
Elvis Welcomes You to His World, Duff, 1978, NMIB 125.00
Family Affair, Remco, 1968, MIB 100.00
Felix the Cat, Milton Bradley, 1960, EX (EX box) 50.00
Fess Parker Trail Blazers, Milton Bradley, 1964, EX (EX box) 75.00
Flash Gordon, Game Gems/T Cohn, 1965, EX (EX box) 100.00
Flintstones Brake Ball, 1962, EX (EX box) 85.00
Flintstones Just for Kicks, Transogram, 1962, EX (EX box) 50.00
Flipper, card game, Hinkosha/Japan, 1960s, MIB 60.00
Flying Nun Bagatelle, Hasbro, 1967, M 85.00
Frankenstein Mystery, Hasbro, 1963, NM (NM box) 150.00
Gene Autry's Dude Ranch, Built-Rite, 1956, EX (EX box) 65.00
Gentle Ben Animal Hunt, Mattel, 1967, EX (EX box) 40.00
George of the Jungle, Parker Bros, 1968, NMIB 50.00
Gidget Fortune Teller, Milton Bradley, 1966, EX (EX box) 35.00
Godzilla, Ideal, 1963, EX (EX box) 300.00
Gomer Pyle, Transogram, 1964, EX (EX box) 50.00
Gumby & Pokey Playful Trails, MIB 100.00
Hansel & Gretel, Lowell, 1963, EX (EX box) 50.00
Heckle & Jeckle 3-D Target, Aldon Industries, 1950s, MOC 50.00

Hee Haw, Dooley Inc, 1975, EX (G box) 20.00
Hogan's Heros Bluff Out, Transogram, 1966, EX (EX box) 100.00
Hollywood Squares, Watkins-Strathmore, 1966, EX (EX box) 25.00
Hopalong Cassidy, Milton Bradley, 1950, EX (EX box) 150.00
Hopalong Cassidy Canasta, Pacific Playing Cards, 1950, EX (EX box)..75.00
Howdy Doody TV Game, Milton Bradley, 1950s, EX (EX box) .100.00
Huckleberry Hound Spin-O, Bardell, 1959, EX (EX box) 50.00
Jackie Robinson Baseball, Gotham, 1950s, EX (EX box) 275.00
Jetsons Out of This World, Transogram, 1962, EX (EX box) 125.00
Johnny Quest, card game, Milton Bradley, 1963, MIB 100.00
Katzenjammer Kids Hockey, Jaymar, 1950s, missing few pcs, EX (EX box).25.00
King Kong, Milton Bradley, 1966, EX (EX box) 150.00
Laugh-Ins Knock Knock Jokes, Saalfield, 1969, NM (NM box) ...50.00
Leave It To Beaver Ambush, Hasbro, 1959, EX (EX box) 75.00
Let's Make a Deal, Ideal, 1964, EX (EX box) 25.00
Little Lulu, Milton Bradley, 1946, EX (EX box) 200.00
Lone Ranger, card game, 1938, MIB, from $75 to 125.00
Lone Ranger & Tonto, 1967, NMIB, from $75 to 125.00
Lone Ranger Ring-Toss, 1943, NMIB, from $350 to 450.00
Lost in Space, Milton Bradley, 1965, EX (EX box) 75.00
Ludwig Von Drake Tiddley Winks, Whitman, EX (EX box) 35.00
Man From Uncle, Ideal, 1965, EX (EX box) 50.00
Marlin Perkin's Zoo Parade, Cadaco, 1955, NMIB 60.00
Mary Poppins Carousel, Parker Bros, 1964, MIB (sealed) 50.00
McHale's Navy, Transogram, 1962, EX (EX box) 50.00
Mickey Mouse Circus, Marks Bros/WDE, 1930s, EX (EX box), from $750 to..950.00
Mickey Mouse Scatter Ball, Marks Bros, 1935, NM (EX box) 250.00
Mickey Mouse Tidley Winks, Chad Valley, 1948, EX (EX box) .125.00
Monkees, Transogram, 1967, EX (EX box) 150.00
Mr Magoo at the Circus, target game, Knickerbocker, 1956, EX (EX box).150.00
Nancy & Sluggo, Milton Bradley, 1944, EX (EX box) 75.00
Our Gang Tipple-Topple, All-Fair, 1930, EX (EX box) 400.00
Patty Duke, Milton Bradley, 1963, EX (EX box) 50.00
Pebbles Flintstone, Transogram, 1962, NMIB, minimum value 65.00
Peter Pan, Selchow & Righter, 1927, EX (EX box) 175.00
Pinocchio Target, Am Toy Works/WDP, 1940, EX (EX box), from $350 .450.00
Popeye Shooz-It, Ideal, 1963, EX (EX box) 65.00
Price Is Right, Lowell, 1958, EX (EX box) 40.00
Quick Draw McGraw Private Eye, Milton Bradley, 1960, NMIB..50.00
Rifleman, Milton Bradley, 1959, EX (EX box) 75.00
Roy Rogers Magic Play-Around, Amsco, 1955, EX (EX box)...125.00
Snow White & the Seven Dwarfs, Milton Bradley, 1937, rare, NMIB .200.00
Snow White & the Seven Dwarfs Target, Am Toy Works, 1930s, EX (EX box).250.00
Superman & Superboy, Milton Bradley, 1967, EX (EX box).......100.00
Superman Calling, Transogram, 1954, EX (EX box) 150.00
Terrytoons Hide 'N Seek, Transogram, 1960, EX (EX box)...........65.00
Three Musketeers, Milton Bradley, 1950, NMIB 60.00
Tom & Jerry, Transogram, 1965, NMIB, from $75 to 100.00
Touche Turtle, Transogram, 1962, EX (EX box) 125.00
Twiggy, Milton Bradley, 1967, EX (EX box).....................100.00
Underdog, Milton Bradley, 1964, EX (EX box)...................50.00

Voyage to the Bottom of the Sea, Milton Bradley, MIB, $70.00.

Walt Disney's Three Little Pigs, Einson-Freeman, 1933, scarce, NMIB..**200.00**
Wild Bill Hickok's Calvary & the Indians, Built-Rite, 1956, NMIB.**100.00**
Welcome Back Kotter, card game, Milton Bradley, 1976, NMIB..**15.00**
Yogi Bear Circus Bagatelle, Marx, 1960, EX (EX box) **50.00**
Zorro Target, Superior/T Cohn, 1960, EX (EX box)....................**175.00**

Garden City Pottery

Founded in 1902 in San Jose, California, by the end of the 1920s this pottery had grown to become the largest in Northern California. During that period production focused on stoneware, sewer pipe, and red clay flowerpots. In the late '30s and '40s, the company produced dinnerware in bright solid colors of yellow, green, blue, orange, cobalt, turquoise, white, and black. Royal Arden Hickman, who would later gain fame for the innovative artware he modeled for the Haeger company, designed not only dinnerware but a line of Art Deco vases and bowls as well. The company endured hard times by adapting to the changing needs of the market and during the '50s concentrated on production of garden products. Foreign imports, however, proved to be too competitive, and the company's pottery production ceased in 1979.

Because none of the colored-glazed products were ever marked, to learn to identify the products of this company, you'll need to refer to *Sanford's Guide to Garden City Pottery* by Jim Pasquali, our advisor for this category, who is listed in the Directory under California. Values apply to items in all colors (except black) and all patterns, unless noted otherwise. Due to relative rarity, 20% should be added for any item found in black.

Artichoke plate...**45.00**
Bean pot, plain, 1-qt...**25.00**
Biscuit jar..**65.00**
Bowl, batter; lg...**65.00**
Bowl, Bulb, 10"...**45.00**
Bowl, Low Swirl, 9"...**25.00**
Bowl, mixing; #24..**30.00**
Bowl, nappy, #1..**10.00**
Bowl, nappy, #4..**25.00**
Bowl, soup...**25.00**
Bowl, Succulent, 11"...**60.00**
Casserole, Narrow Ring, 7"..**35.00**
Casserole, Wide Ring, 9"...**45.00**
Crock, 2-gal...**45.00**
Cup, custard; w/lid..**30.00**
Cup, punch...**15.00**

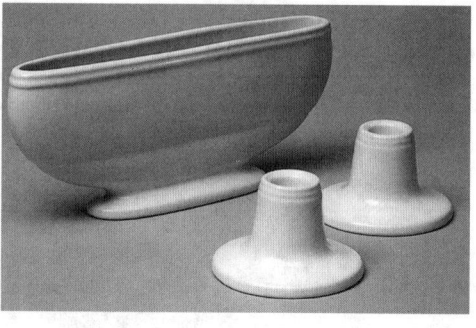

Deco vase, 4¹/₂ x 10", $85.00; Candle holders, pair, $45.00.
(Photo courtesy Jim Pasquali)

Frog, sm...**15.00**
Jardiniere, Ribbed, 10" **45.00**
Mug..**20.00**
Mug, chowder; w/lid..**45.00**
Oil jar, hand thrown, mini, 5½"..**150.00**

Pitcher, 2-qt...**55.00**
Plate, dinner; 10"..**20.00**
Plate, salad; 7"...**10.00**
Rose bowl, 4"..**25.00**
Teapot, Deco, 6-cup..**125.00**
Vase, Ribbed Cylinder, 8"...**35.00**

Gas Globes and Panels

Gas globes and panels, once a common sight, have vanished from the countryside but are being sought by collectors as a unique form of advertising memorabilia. Early globes from the 1920s (some date back to as early as 1912), now referred to as 'one-piece globes,' were made of molded milk glass and were globular in shape. The gas company name was etched or painted on the glass. Few of these were ever produced, and this type is valued very highly by collectors today.

A new type of pump was introduced in the early 1930s; the old 'visible' pumps were replaced by 'electric' models. Globes were changing at the same time. By the mid-teens a three-piece globe consisting of a pair of inserts and a metal body was being produced in both 15" and 16½" sizes. Collectors prefer to call globes that are not one-piece or plastic 'three-piece glass' (Type 2) or 'metal body, glass inserts' (Type 3). Though metal-body globes (Type 3) were popular in the 1930s, they were common in the 1920s, and some were actually made as early as 1915. Though rare in numbers, their use spans many years. In the 1930s Type 2 and Type 3 globes became the replacements of the one-piece globe. The most recently manufactured gas globes are made with a plastic body that contains two 13½" glass lenses. These were common in the '50s but were actually used as early as 1932.

In the listings that follow, values are for examples with both sides in excellent condition: no chips, wear, or other damage.

Note: Standard Crowns with raised letters are one-piece globes that were made in the 1920s; those made in the 1950s (no raised letters), though one-piece, are not regarded as such by today's collectors. Our advisor for this category is Scott Benjamin; he is listed in the Directory under Ohio.

Type 1, Plastic Body, Glass Inserts (Inserts 13½") — 1931 – 1950s

D-X Marine, rare, EX...**1,400.00**
Dixie, plastic band, EX..**250.00**
DX Lubricating Gasoline, tan body, EX **300.00**
Fleet-Wing, EX...**500.00**
Frontier Gas, Rarin' To Go, w/horse, EX **1,000.00**
Kendal Deluxe, Capcolite body w/red pnt, 13½", EX.......**350.00**
Kendall Polly Power, Capcolite body, 13½" dia, EX...........**400.00**
Marathon, no runner, EX..**200.00**
Never Nox Ethyl, EX...**450.00**
New State 88, EX..**1,000.00**
Phillips 66, EX..**350.00**
Phillips 66 Flite-Fuel, EX..**400.00**
Sinclair H-C Gasoline, red & gr on wht, EX **300.00**
Skelly Keotane, EX...**300.00**
Spur, Oval body, EX...**350.00**
Sunray Estyl Corp, EX **1,500.00**
Texaco Diesel Chief, Capcolite body, 13½", EX.................**1,350.00**
Viking, pictures Viking ship, EX...**2,200.00**

Type 2, Glass Frame, Glass Inserts (Inserts 13½") — 1926 – 1940s

Aerio, gr gill ripple body, 13½" dia, EX **8,500.00**
Aladdin Gasoline, 1 lens w/side body, EX **600.00**
American, gill body, 12½", EX...**450.00**

Amoco, gill body, 13½", EX................................450.00
Atlantic, glass body, 13½" dia, EX......................325.00
Atlantic Imperial, gill body, 13½", EX..................450.00
Barnsdall Be Square Gasoline, 2 lenses in wide body, EX...........500.00
Capitol Gasoline Ethyl Corp, EX 500.00
Capitol Kerosene Oil Co, EX 600.00
Derby, EX..450.00
Esso, EX 325.00
Frontier Gas, Double Refined, EX 400.00
Globe Gasoline, metal base ring, EX.................1,600.00
Guyler Brand, milk glass, EX...........................1,000.00
Kan O Tex, gill body, metal base ring, EX...............900.00
Lion, single lens, metal base, EX.....................2,200.00
Lion (only), metal base, EX............................1,600.00
Pitman Streamlined, bl gill rippled body, 13½", EX....8,500.00
Pure, EX..500.00
Sinclair Dino, milk glass, EX 300.00
Sinclair H-C Gasoline, narrow milk glass body, EX........500.00
Sinclair Pennant, wide glass body, EX................1,000.00
Sky Chief, gill body, 13½", EX...........................500.00
Standard Crown, bl, EX 800.00
Standard Crown, gr, EX 1,000.00
Standard Crown, gray, EX...............................1,200.00
Standard Crown, wht, red or gold, EX, ea................400.00
Standard Flame, EX..500.00
Texaco Ethyl, EX..2,000.00
United Hi-Test Gasoline, red/wht/bl, EX..................450.00
White Flash, gill body, EX.................................450.00
WNAX, w/radio station pictured, EX 3,500.00

Type 3, Metal Frame, Glass Inserts (Inserts 15" or 16½") — 1915 – 1930s

Aero Mobilgas, new metal body, rare, 15", EX 2,800.00
Atlantic Ethyl, 16½", EX.....................................950.00
Atlantic White Flash, 16½", EX 750.00
Blue Anti-Knock Gasoline, Interstate Oil Gas, EX........1,200.00
Farmer's Union High Octane, red/wht/bl, high profile metal body, 15"...1,000.00
General Ethyl, 15" fr, complete, EX 1,200.00
Kendal Gasoline, airplane, metal body, rare, 15", EX...........7,000.00

Magnolia Gasoline, 16½", EX, $3,000.00.
(Photo courtesy B.J. Summers and Wayne Priddy)

Marathon, low profile metal body, 15", EX.............1,300.00
Mobilgas Ethyl, 16½", EX 600.00
Oil Creek Gas, drake well & derrick, 15", EX 4,500.00
Phillips Benzo, low profile metal body, 15", EX 4,000.00
Purol Gasoline, w/arrow, porc body, EX..................900.00
Red Crown Ethyl, EX.......................................950.00

Royal Maine, high profile metal body, 15", EX..........2,500.00
Signal, old stoplight, 15", EX.............................4,500.00
Skelly It's Better Gasoline, high profile metal body, 15", EX...2,500.00
Stanolined Aviation, rare, 16½", EX......................5,000.00
Texaco Leaded, glass panels, complete globe, EX 5,000.00
White Star, 15" fr, complete, EX.........................1,500.00

Type 4, One-Piece Glass Globes, No Inserts, Co. Name Etched, Raised, or Enameled — 1912 – 1931

Atlantic, chimney cap, EX 4,500.00
Dixie, etched..2,500.00
Mobil Gargoyle, gargoyle pictured, oval, EX.............2,300.00
Pierce Pennant, etched, EX 3,500.00
Republic, 3-sided, EX.....................................2,500.00
Shell, rnd, etched, EX 1,000.00
Super Shell, clam shape, EX 1,800.00
Super Shell, rnd, etched, EX 4,000.00
Texaco, etched letters, wide body, EX....................3,000.00
Texaco Ethyl, EX..2,200.00
That Good Gulf..., emb, orange & blk letters, EX.........1,500.00
White Eagle, blunt nose, 20¾", EX........................1,600.00
White Eagle, detailed eagle, 20¾", EX....................2,000.00
White Rose, boy pictured, pnt, EX.......................4,000.00

Gaudy Dutch

Inspired by Oriental Imari wares, Gaudy Dutch was made in England from 1800 to 1820. It was hand decorated on a soft-paste body with rich underglaze blues accented in orange, red, pink, green, and yellow. It differs from Gaudy Welsh in that there is no lustre (except on Water Lily). There are seventeen patterns, some of which are War Bonnet, Grape, Dahlia, Oyster, Urn, Butterfly, Carnation, Single Rose, Double Rose, and Water Lily. Unless otherwise noted, values are given for items with minimal wear and no obvious damage.

Butterfly, cup plate 880.00
Butterfly, plate, butterfly on side, 7¼" 825.00
Carnation, cup plate..715.00
Carnation, plate, 8⅜".......................................855.00
Cybis, cup plate, butterfly on side, unmk 165.00
Dahlia, plate, 8"...880.00
Double Rose, creamer..660.00
Double Rose, plate, mint; 9"................................990.00
Double Rose, toddy plate, rare, 4½".........................825.00
Dove, creamer, helmet; rare..............................1,400.00
Dove, teapot...1,100.00
Grape, plate, 6⅜"...410.00
Grape, soup plate, 8⅜"......................................500.00
Leaf, tea bowl & saucer.....................................800.00
Oyster, plate, 5⅝"..400.00
Primrose, plate, impressed Riley, 8¾".......................610.00
Single Rose, cup plate......................................440.00
Single Rose, plate, 6⅜".....................................525.00
Single Rose, tea bowl & saucer, minor flakes................550.00
Strawflower, soup plate.....................................880.00
Urn, creamer..385.00
Urn, teapot 660.00
War Bonnet, plate, 6⅜"......................................635.00
War Bonnet, tea bowl & saucer, stain 495.00
War Bonnet, toddy plate, 6".................................685.00
Zinnia, plate, 6⅜"..660.00

Gaudy Welsh

Gaudy Welsh was an inexpensive hand-decorated ware made in both England and Wales from 1820 until 1860. It is characterized by its colors — principally blue, orange-rust, and copper lustre — and by its uninhibited patterns. Accent colors may be yellow and green. (Pink lustre may be present, since lustre applied to the white areas appears pink. A copper tone develops from painting lustre onto the dark colors.) The body of the ware may be heavy ironstone (also called Gaudy Ironstone), creamware, earthenware, or porcelain; even style and shapes vary considerably. Patterns, while usually floral, are also sometimes geometric and may have trees and birds. Beware! The Wagon Wheel pattern has been reproduced.

Our advisor for this category is Cheryl Nelson; she is listed in the Directory under Minnesota.

Note: Prices are rising. Each day more collectors enter. For the first time British auction houses are picturing and promoting Gaudy Welsh. Demand for Columbine, Grape, Tulip, Oyster, and Wagon Wheel is slow. We should also mention that the Bethedsa pattern is very similar to a Davenport jug pattern. No porcelain Gaudy Welsh was made in Wales.

Abutilon, creamer, 4"	450.00
Abutilon, teapot, 9"	800.00
Cherry Tree, plate, 7½"	350.00
Chinoiserie, child's mug	195.00
Conway, vase, 7¼"	800.00
Cornucopia, jug, 6"	585.00
Denbigh, jug, 6"	775.00
Dogtooth Violet, creamer, 4"	395.00
Feather, plate, 7½"	175.00
Flower Basket, jug, 6½"	525.00
Geranium, toddy/cockle plate, 4½"	300.00
Ghent, jug, 5¾"	465.00
Lantern, plate, 7½"	300.00
Lilypond, jug, 5½"	515.00
Pagoda, bowl, ftd, 8½"	900.00
Pen-y-ddraig, ewer & basin, mini, 5¾"	725.00
Poppy, jug, 6¼"	350.00

Powys, creamer, 5", $285.00. (Photo courtesy John A. Shuman III)

Rose & Butterfly, teapot, 9"	775.00
Ross, jug, 6¼"	700.00
Royal Family, cup & saucer	280.00
Swan, jug, 7"	800.00
Tibet, cup & saucer	250.00
Urn, plate, 7¾"	265.00
Verbena, mug, 3¼"	295.00
Village, cup & saucer	250.00
ZigZag, jug, 5¾"	465.00

Geisha Girl

Geisha Girl Porcelain was one of several key Japanese china production efforts aimed at the booming export markets of the U.S., Canada, England, and other parts of Europe. The wares feature colorful, kimono-clad Japanese ladies in scenes of everyday Japanese life surrounded by exquisite flora, fauna, and mountain ranges. Nonetheless, the forms in which the wares were produced reflected the late nineteenth- and early twentieth-century Western dining and decorating preferences: tea and coffee services, vases, dresser sets, children's items, planters, etc.

Over a hundred manufacturers were involved in Geisha Girl production. This accounts for the several hundred different patterns, well over a dozen border colors and styles, and several methods of design execution. Geisha Girl Porcelain was produced in wholly hand-painted versions, but most were hand painted over stencilled outlines. Be wary of Geisha ware executed with decals. Very few decaled examples came out of Japan. Rather, most were Czechoslovakian attempts to hone in on the market. Czech pieces have stamped marks in broad, pseudo-Oriental characters. Items with portraits of Oriental ladies in the bottom of tea or sake cups are *not* Geisha Girl Porcelain, unless the outside surface of the wares are decorated as described above. These lovely faces, formed by varying the thickness of the porcelain body, are called lithophanes and are collectible in their own right.

The height of Geisha Girl production was between 1910 and the mid-1930s. Some post-World War II production has been found marked Occupied Japan.

The ware continued in minimal production during the 1960s, but the point of origin of the later pieces was Hong Kong. These productions are discerned by the pure whiteness of the porcelain; even, unemotional borders; lack of background washes and gold enameling; and overall sparseness of detail. A new wave of Nippon-marked reproduction Geisha emerged in 1996. If the Geisha Girl productions of the 1960s – 80s were overly plain, the mid-1990s repros are overly ornate. Original Geisha Girl porcelain was enhanced by brush strokes of color over a stenciled design; it was never the 'color perfectly within the lines' type of decoration found on current reproductions. Original Geisha Girl porcelain was decorated with color washes; the reproductions are in heavy enamels. The backdrop decoration of the current reproductions feature solid, thick colors, and the patterns feature too much color; period Geisha ware had a high ratio of white space to color. The new pieces also have bright shiny gold in proportions greater than most period Geisha ware. The Nippon marks on the reproductions are wrong. Some of the Geisha ware created during the Nippon era bore the small precise decaled green M-in-Wreath mark, a Noritake registered trademark. The reproduction items feature an irregular facsimile of this mark. Stamped onto the reproductions is an unrealistically large M-in-Wreath mark in shades of green ranging from an almost neon to pine green with a wreath that looks like it has seen better days, as it does not have the perfect roundness of the original mark. Reproductions of mid-sized trays, chunky hatpin holders, an ornate vase, a covered bottle, and a powder jar are among the current reproductions popping up at flea and antique markets.

Many of our descriptions contain references to border colors and treatments. This information is given immediately preceding the mark and/or size. Our advisor for this category is Elyce Litts; she is listed in the Directory under New Jersey.

Ashtray, Teample A, spade-shaped, mc	25.00
Berry set, Dragon Boat, cobalt w/gold, master+5 ind	85.00
Biscuit jar, Basket of Mums B, melon ribs, red w/gold	49.00
Biscuit jar, Flower Gathering B, red w/gold, 6½"	55.00
Bowl, berry; Fan A, cobalt/brick red/gold, scalloped, mk	22.00
Bowl, Carp, red w/gold, 6"	18.00

Bowl, Chinese Coin, Battledore/etc scenes, hdls, mk, 10"............**85.00**
Butter pat, Fan A, red border, 4¼"...**8.00**
Butter pat, Flower Gathering B, red-orange, 3¼"....................**8.00**
Cake set, River's Edge, master+6 ind plates........................**75.00**
Cocoa pot, Basket A, 4 ladies gather shells at river, 8"...............**55.00**
Cocoa set, Bamboo Trellis, red-orange, pot+6 c/s.................**125.00**
Creamer, Boy w/Scythe, cobalt w/gold..................................**15.00**
Creamer, Chrysanthemum Garden, red, toy sz......................**15.00**
Creamer, Porch, red-orange, modern....................................**10.00**
Cup, bouillon; Garden Bench J, w/lid & drip plate, mk.............**55.00**
Cup, Doll's Tea Party, Emery-Birel-Thayer, dtd 1916.............**30.00**
Cup, tea; Garden Bench C, apple gr w/gold, patterned int.............**4.00**
Cup & saucer, tea; Geisha in Sampan A, gold..........................**15.00**
Cup & saucer, tea; Peacock on Flowered Stone Roof, cobalt/gold...**25.00**
Cup & saucer, Temple A, mc, Japan mk toy sz........................**20.00**
Egg cup, Cherry Blossom Ikebana, flowers in pot, cobalt.............**18.00**
Egg cup, dbl; Mother & Son A, bl-gr..**20.00**
Ewer, Garden Beach H, red w/gold lacing...............................**35.00**
Hatpin holder, Rendezvous, vine & leaves, Kutani mk................**75.00**
Jug, Cherry Bossom, red-orange edge, 6½"..............................**35.00**
Lemonade set, Garden Bench D, mc border, pot+6 c/s+6 plates.**175.00**
Mint dish, Seamstress, floral shape, hdls, Japan mk, 5¼x4"........**14.00**
Muffineer, Parasol C, wavy red, bulbous, Made in Japan...........**35.00**
Nut dish, Feather Fan, ftd, Nippon...**48.00**
Pancake server, So Big, boy gesturing Kutani mk, 9½x3½".........**150.00**
Plate, Butterfly Dancers, red w/gold, 7"...................................**35.00**
Plate, Fan w/Fan Dance reserves, red-orange, toy sz, 4½"..........**15.00**
Plate, Geisha in Sampson A, brn w/gold, 9½"..........................**25.00**
Plate, Inside the Teahouse, apple gr, swirl fluted, 8½"...............**28.00**
Plate, Writing A, scalloped cobalt w/gold lacing, Japan, 7⅜".......**28.00**
Sauce dish, Meeting B, dk apple gr...**12.00**
Shakers, Child Reaching for Butterfly, bl top/red border, pr.........**20.00**
Tea set, Visitor to the Court, cobalt w/gold, Ozan mk, 3-pc.........**65.00**
Teapot, Fan Dance A, pk w/gold, Kutani mk............................**125.00**
Teapot, Kite A, brn w/gold..**28.00**
Toothpick holder, Court Lady, 3 blk-lined reserves, melon shape.**28.00**
Vase, bud; Watching the Carp, red-orange, 4½".........................**18.00**

Georgia Art Pottery

In Cartersville, Georgia, in August 1935, W.J. Gordy first fired pottery turned from regional clays. By 1936 he was marking his wares 'Georgia Art Pottery' (GP) or 'Georgia Art Pottery' (GAP) and continued to do so until 1950 when he used a 'Hand Made by WJ Gordy' stamp (HM). There are different configurations of the GAP mark, one being a three-line arrangement, another that is circular and thought to be the earlier of the two. After 1970 his pottery was signed. Known throughout the world for his fine glazes, he won the Georgia Governor's Award in 1983. Examples of his wares are on display in the Smithsonian. His father W.T.B. and brother D.X. are also well-known potters.

Basket, blk irid, fluted edge, dbl hdl, 3x7".................................**95.00**
Jug, brn, mk Georgia, 3"...**85.00**
Pitcher, brn, HM mk, 5¾x5"..**160.00**
Pitcher, cream; bl, mk GAP, 3"..**75.00**
Pitcher, cream; Dogwood, mk DX Gordy, 3½x4".......................**165.00**
Vase, brn matt, elongoated ovoid, WJ Gordy, 1935, 9½"............**435.00**
Vase, cornucopia; wht, GP mk, 5x5"..**125.00**
Vase, flower frog; blk, slots (instead of holes), 3x4½"..................**70.00**
Vase, gr w/bl specs, GP mk, 5"...**125.00**
Vase, Mountain Gold base w/mc overglazes, HM mk, 5½x3½"..**150.00**
Vase, Mountain Gold w/bl interior, incurvate neck, 3½"............**135.00**

German Porcelain

Unless otherwise noted, the porcelain listed in this section is marked simply 'Germany.' Products of other German manufactures are listed in specific categories.

See also Bisque; Pink Paw Bears; Pink Pigs; Elfinware.

Bowl, floral w/sculptured wht & yel leaves on gr border, 3x10½...**90.00**
Cake plate, spring bouquet, amethyst scrolling border, open hdls, 10".**55.00**
Chocolate pot, wht w/red/gold geometric floral reserves, 10", +4 c/s..**315.00**
Figurine, 18th-C figures toasting (5), Adolph Sache, 1910s, 11x19x12".**1,750.00**
Figurine, fan dancer, Herwig & Co, 1930s, 12"..........................**335.00**

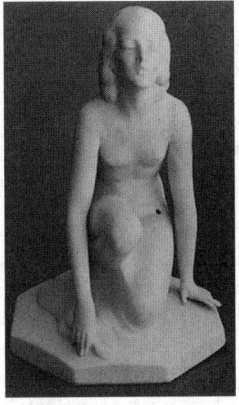

Figurine, kneeling nude shedding drape, white matt, signed Poerzl, late 1920s, 10", $900.00.
(Photo courtesy Mary Frank Gaston)

Plate, Rose, lady's portrait, gr/gold border, beehive/Germany, 8".....**375.00**
Vase, Ruth (portrait) on violet lustre, beehive/Germany script, 5¾"....**430.00**

Gladding McBean and Company

This company was established in 1875 in Lincoln, California. They first produced only clay drainage pipes, but in 1883 architectural terra cotta was introduced, which has been used extensively in the United States as well as abroad. Sometime later a line of garden pottery was added. They soon became the leading producers of tile in the country. In 1923 they purchased the Tropico Pottery in Glendale, California, where in addition to tile they also produced huge garden vases. Their line was expanded in 1934 to include artware and dinnerware.

At least fifteen lines of art pottery were developed between 1934 and 1942. For a short time they stamped their wares with the Tropico Pottery mark; but the majority was signed 'GMcB' in an oval. Later the mark was changed to 'Franciscan' with several variations. After 1937 'Catalina Pottery' was used on some lines. (All items marked 'Catalina Pottery' were made in Glendale.) For further information we recommend *The Collector's Encyclopedia of California Pottery, Second Edition*, by Jack Chipman (Collector Books). See also Franciscan Ware. Our advisor for this category is Kathy Eichert; she is listed in the Directory under California.

Bowl, aqua, emb scrolls on low ft, Catalina Pottery USA, 3½x13".**125.00**
Bowl, Redwood, stick hdl w/finger ridges, GMB, 5"....................**12.00**
Bowl, shell form, wht w/coral int, USA, 15" L.............................**75.00**
Bowl, sunbonnet form, pk, Catalina Pottery, 4½x10x8½"............**32.00**
Bowl, wht, fluted/lobed oval, GMB label, 9" L...........................**70.00**
Bowl, wht w/aqua int, Deco, Catalina Pottery #C-341, 2x10"......**68.00**
Carafe, orange, w/lid, GMB, 7½"..**100.00**
Carafe, yel, wood hdl attaches at neck, Catalina Rancho, 9".......**110.00**
Cup & saucer, demi; assorted solid colors, GMB, set of 6............**75.00**

Dish, leaf shape, bl w/tan underneath, California Pottery, 14" L...50.00
Mug, assorted colors, in metal fr w/hdl, GMB, 3¾", set of 6 ....85.00
Pitcher, yel, ball shape, GMB, 6½x8x6" 55.00
Plate, Rolled Edge, solid color, Catalina Pottery, 10" 15.00
Platter, lt gr, Catalina Pottery USA, 11½" 35.00
Tray, tan w/bl int, scalloped/lobed rectangle, Catalina Pottery, 10" L.....40.00
Vase, bl, ovoid w/sm collar rim, Catalina Pottery USA, 8x6" 110.00
Vase, bl w/wht int, wide bottle form, GMB, 6" 32.00
Vase, bust of girl in scarf, hands hold receptacle, salmon matt, 7" ...75.00
Vase, bust of lady in scarf, hands hold receptacle, HP decor, 7"..100.00
Vase, Cielito, ruby w/wht int, GMB #114, 8¾" 200.00
Vase, emb morning glories/horizontal rings, peach, ft, GMB, 5" ...70.00
Vase, nautilus shell form, ivory w/coral int, Catalina Pottery #C-926....85.00
Vase, oxblood w/celadon int & top edge, ftd, GMB USA, 6" 195.00
Vase, sunfish form, wht w/bl int, Catalina Pottery, #C-362 USA, 8x9".....235.00
Vase, upright conch shell form, wht w/rose-pk int, Catalina #C-353, 8" 80.00
Vase, yel w/oxblood int, lobed gourd form, Catalina Pottery #C-252, 6" 60.00
Vase, yel w/wht int, Ming shape, GMB, 8½" 95.00

Glass Animals and Figurines

These beautiful glass sculptures have been produced by many major companies in America, in fact, some are still being made today. Heisey, Fostoria, Duncan and Miller, Imperial, Paden City, Tiffin, and Cambridge made the vast majority, but there were many others involved on a lesser scale. Some, but not all, marked their animals.

As many of the glass companies went out of business, molds were often sold to others still active who used them to reproduce their own line of animals. While some are easy to recognize, others can be very confusing. For example, Summit Art Glass now owns Cambridge's 6½", 8½", and 10" swan molds. We recommend *Glass Animals of the Depression Era* by Lee Garmon and Dick Spencer, if you're thinking of starting a collection or wanting to identify and evaluate the glass animals you already have. Both are our advisors for this category and are listed in the Directory under Illinois.

Note: Heisey Collectors of America stopped using the plug horse and have adopted the rabbit paperweight as the new yearly mascot. Viking collectors should also be made aware that crystal Viking pieces are much harder to find than colored ones.

Cambridge

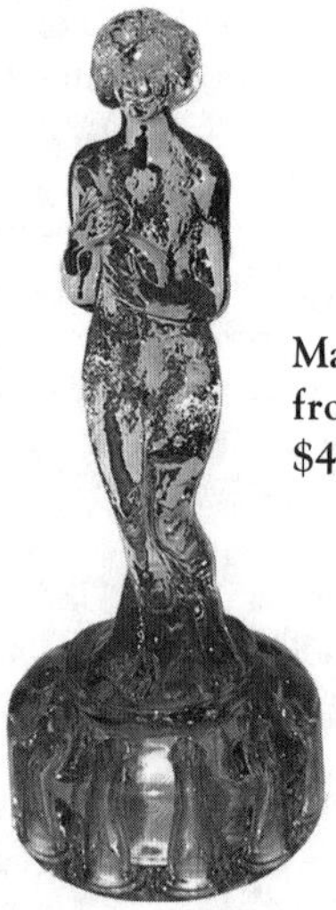

Mandolin Lady, flower frog, light emerald, $400.00.

Bashful Charlotte, flower frog, crystal, 11½"...........................150.00

Bashful Charlotte, flower frog, Moonlight Blue, 11½" 800.00
Bird, crystal satin, 2¾" L 35.00
Blue jay, flower holder, crystal 150.00
Buddha, amber, 5½" 250.00
Draped Lady, flower frog, crystal frost, 13¼" 175.00
Draped Lady, flower frog, Dianthus, 13¼" 250.00
Draped Lady, flower frog, Dianthus, 8½" 125.00
Draped Lady, flower frog, Gold Krystol, 8½" 200.00
Draped Lady, flower frog, gr frost, 8½" 125.00
Draped Lady, flower frog, lt emerald, 8½" 125.00
Frog, crystal satin 35.00
Heron, crystal, lg, 12" 150.00
Lion, bookend, crystal, ea 150.00
Melon Boy, flower frog, Dianthus 750.00
Rose Lady, flower frog, amber, 8½" 225.00
Rose Lady, flower frog, crystal satin, tall base, 9¾" 200.00
Rose Lady, flower frog, gr, 8½" 250.00
Swan, #1 style, 10½" 115.00
Swan, Carmen, 6½" 250.00
Swan, Crown Tuscan, 3" 45.00
Swan, Crown Tuscan, 8½" 135.00
Swan, ebony, 3" 65.00
Swan, ebony, 8½" 250.00
Swan, ebony, 10½" 300.00
Swan, ebony, 12½" 350.00
Swan, emerald, 3" 55.00
Swan, emerald, 8½" 175.00
Swan, milk glass, #3 style, 8½" 300.00
Swan, milk glass, 8½" 200.00
Turkey, pk, w/lid 400.00
Two Kids, flower frog, amber, oval base, 9¼" 350.00
Two Kids, flower frog, amber satin, 9¼" 400.00

Duncan and Miller

Bird of Paradise, crystal 700.00
Dove, crystal, head down, 11½" L 175.00
Duck, ashtray, red, 7" 275.00
Goose, crystal, fat, 6x6" 300.00
Heron, crystal satin, 7" 120.00
Swan, bl opal, W&F, spread wings, 10x12½" 265.00
Swan, chartreuse, open bk, 7" 65.00
Swan, crystal, solid, 5" 45.00
Swordfish, crystal 275.00
Sylvan swan, bl or pk, 5½" 95.00
Sylvan swan, yel opal, 5½" 165.00
Sylvan swan, yel opal, 7½" 225.00

Fenton

Airedale, Rosalene, 1992 issue for Heisey 100.00
Alley cat, Teal Marigold, 11" 85.00
Bunny, pale yel...25.00
Cardinal head, ruby, 6½" 175.00
Elephant, periwinkle, whiskey bottle, 8" 450.00
Filly, Rosalene, head front, 1992 issue for Heisey 125.00
Fish, bookend, Rosalene, ea 95.00
Fish, red w/amberina tail & fins, 2½" 55.00
Gazelle, Rosalene..125.00
Giraffe, Rosalene 125.00
Happiness Bird, Rosalene 40.00
Hen, Rosalene, 1992 issue for Heisey 75.00
Peacock, bookends, crystal satin, 5¾", pr...................................200.00
Rabbit, paperweight, Rosalene, 1992 issue for Heisey...................75.00

Fostoria

Buddha, bookends, blk, pr 525.00
Cat, lt bl, 3¾" 35.00

Chanticleer, crystal, 1950 – 58, 10¾", $250.00.

Chinese Lute, ebony w/gold, 12½" 300.00
Deer, bl, sitting or standing, ea 55.00
Dolphin, bl, 4¾" 35.00
Duckling, crystal, head down (+) 20.00
Eagle, bookend, crystal, 7½", ea 125.00
Frog, bl, lemon or olive gr, 1⅞", ea 40.00
Goldfish, crystal, vertical 110.00
Madonna, Silver Mist, orig issue, 10" (+) 50.00
Mermaid, crystal, 11½" 125.00
Pelican, amber, 1991 commemorative 55.00
Polar Bear, crystal, 4⅝" 65.00
Rebecca at Well, candle holder, crystal frost, ea 125.00
Seal, topaz, 3⅞" 125.00
Squirrel, amber, sitting 45.00
Stork, bl, lemon or olive gr, 2", ea 35.00

Heisey

Airedale, crystal 1,400.00
Asiatic pheasant, crystal, 7½" L 400.00
Bull, crystal, sgn, 4x7½" 2,400.00
Bunny, crystal, head down or up, 2½" 275.00
Chick, crystal, head down or up, ea 100.00
Colt, amber, rearing 650.00
Colt, cobalt, rearing 1,500.00
Colt, crystal, kicking 225.00
Colt, crystal, rearing 250.00
Dolphin, candlesticks, crystal, #110, pr 400.00
Dolphin, candlesticks, Moongleam, #110, pr 700.00
Duck, ashtray, crystal 100.00
Duck, flower block, crystal 140.00
Elephant, amber, lg or med, ea 2,400.00
Elephant, crystal, lg or med, ea 450.00
Elephant, crystal, sm 275.00
Filly, crystal, head bkwards 1,500.00
Filly, crystal, head forward 1,200.00
Fish, bowl, crystal, 9½" 550.00
Fish, candlestick, crystal, 5", ea 175.00
Flying Mare, crystal 4,800.00
Giraffe, crystal, head bk 275.00
Giraffe, crystal, head to side 275.00
Goose, crystal, wings down 475.00
Goose, crystal, wings up 100.00
Hen, crystal, 4½" 400.00
Horse head, frosted, bookend, ea 125.00

Irish setter, ashtray, Flamingo 45.00
Mallard, crystal, wings half 225.00
Mallard, crystal, wings up 200.00
Plug horse, cobalt 1,200.00
Pouter pigeon, crystal, 7½" L 1,000.00
Rabbit mother, crystal, 4½x5½" 1,600.00
Ram head, stopper, crystal, 3½" 175.00
Ringneck pheasant, crystal, 11¾" 175.00
Rooster, crystal, 5½x5" 450.00
Rooster, vase, crystal, 6½" 110.00
Rooster head, cocktail shaker, crystal, 1-qt 75.00
Scottie, crystal 170.00
Sea horse, cocktail, crystal 160.00
Sow, crystal, 3x4½" 1,200.00
Swan, crystal 1,300.00
Swan, master nut, crystal, #1503 .... 45.00
Tropical fish, crystal, 12" 2,200.00
Wood duck, crystal, floating 225.00
Wood duck, crystal, standing 225.00

Imperial

Airedale, Ultra Blue 75.00
Bulldog-type pup, milk glass, 3½" 65.00
Chick, milk glass, head down 20.00
Chick, milk glass, head up 20.00
Clydesdale, Salmon 200.00
Colt, amber, balking 140.00
Colt, caramel slag, balking 140.00
Colt, Sunshine Yellow, standing 75.00
Cygnet, blk, 2½" 45.00
Cygnet, caramel slag 40.00
Donkey, caramel slag 55.00
Donkey, Meadow Green carnival 65.00
Elephant, caramel slag, sm 75.00
Elephant, Meadow Green carnival, #674, med 75.00
Elephant, Nut Brown, sm 100.00
Fish, bookend, ruby, ea 340.00
Fish, match holder, Sunshine Yellow satin, 3" 20.00
Flying mare, amber, NI mk, extremely rare 1,500.00
Gazelle, blk, 11" 300.00
Giraffe, amber, ALIG mk, extremely rare 200.00
Mallard, caramel slag, wings down 200.00
Mallard, caramel slag, wings up 40.00
Mallard, lt bl satin, wings down 35.00
Owl, Hootless; caramel slag 50.00
Owl, jar, caramel slag, 16½" 75.00
Owl, purple slag, shiny 95.00
Piglet, amber, standing 40.00
Plug horse, pk, HCA, 1978 .... 40.00
Ring-neck pheasant, amber, extremely rare 320.00
Rooster, pk, fighting 175.00
Scolding bird, Cathay Crystal 175.00
Scottie, milk glass, 3½" 55.00
Terrier, Parlour Pup, amethyst carnival, 3½" 45.00
Tiger, paperweight, caramel slag 95.00
Wood duck, caramel slag 65.00
Wood duckling, caramel slag, sitting, 4½" 45.00
Wood duckling, standing, Sunshine Yellow satin ... 20.00

L.E. Smith

Camel, crystal 50.00
Elephant, crystal, 1¾" 20.00

Goose Girl, crystal, orig, 6" 25.00
Horse, bookend, amber, rearing, ea.........................38.00
Horse, bookend, ruby, rearing, ea............................55.00
King Fish, aquarium, gr, 7¼x15".............................325.00
Queen fish, aquarium, gr, 7x15"..............................250.00
Scottie, pipe rest, fired-on blk, 5½" L......................20.00
Swan, milk glass w/decor, 8½" 45.00
Thrush, bl frost..30.00

New Martinsville

Bear, baby, crystal, head trn or str, 3"....................40.00
Bunny, crystal, head up, scarce, 1" H.......................75.00
Chick, frosted, 1"...35.00

Elephant, bookend, crystal, 5½", $90.00 each.

German shepherd, lamp base, pk............................125.00
Horse, crystal, head up, 8" 95.00
Pelican, crystal..100.00
Piglet, crystal, standing..125.00
Rabbit, mama, crystal..350.00
Seal, baby w/ball, crystal...60.00
Seal, candlesticks, crystal, lg, pr.............................150.00
Ship, bookend, crystal, ea..45.00
Swan, sweetheart candy dish, red, 5" 35.00
Wolfhound, crystal, 7"..95.00

Paden City

Bunny, cotton-ball dispenser, bl frost, ears bk 250.00
Bunny, cotton-ball dispenser, crystal frost, ears bk......150.00
Bunny, cotton-ball dispenser, milk glass, ears bk.........200.00
Dragon swan, crystal, 9¾" L...................................225.00
Horse, crystal, rearing...150.00
Pheasant, Chinese; bl...180.00
Pheasant, Chinese; med bl, 13¾", from $175 to........180.00
Pheasant, lt bl, head bk, 12"....................................195.00
Pony, blk, 12"...350.00
Pouter pigeon, bookend, crystal, 6¼" 95.00
Rooster, Barnyard; crystal, 8¾"...............................85.00
Rooster, Chanticleer; crystal, 9½"............................95.00
Squirrel on curved log, crystal, 5½"..........................65.00
Starfish, bookends, crystal, pr 200.00

Tiffin

Cat, blk satin, raised bumps, #9445, 6¼" 400.00
Cat, Sassy Suzie, milk glass 300.00
Fawn, flower floater, Copen Blue..............................500.00
Frog, candle holders, blk satin, pr............................225.00
Pheasants, Copen Blue, paperweight bases, male & female pr 650.00

Viking

Angelfish, blk, 6½" 150.00
Bird, candy dish, med gr, w/lid, 12"..........................50.00
Bird, moss gr, tail up, 12"...35.00
Bird, Orchid, 9½"...50.00
Cat, gr, sitting, 8"...55.00
Duck, crystal, standing, Viking's Epic Line, 9"...........65.00
Duck, orange, rnd, ftd, 5" 35.00
Duck, vaseline, 5"...40.00
Egret, orange, 12"...50.00
Hound dog, crystal, 8"..50.00
Owl, amber, Viking's Epic Line.................................45.00
Penguin, crystal, 7"...45.00
Rabbit (Thumper), crystal, 6½"................................45.00
Seal, Persimmon, 9¾" L...25.00
Swan, orange, fluted, 6½x4" 45.00

Westmoreland

Butterfly, Blue Mist, 2½"..35.00
Butterfly, Green Mist, 2½".......................................25.00
Butterfly, Smoke, 3½"...25.00
Owl, dk bl, shiny eyes, 5½".......................................65.00
Pig, amberina 85.00
Porky Pig, milk glass, hollow, 3" L..........................10.00
Robin, crystal, 5⅛"...20.00
Robin, rcd, 5⅛"...27.50
Turtle, ashtray, crystal...15.00
Turtle, flower block, gr, 7 holes, 4" L.......................55.00
Wren, Crystal Mist, 2½"...20.00
Wren, Pink Mist, 2½"..25.00
Wren, smoke, 2½"..25.00

Miscellaneous

Co-Operative Flint, elephant, crystal, 13"................375.00
Co-Operative Flint, elephant, pk, 4½x7"....................85.00
Haley, horse, crystal, jumping, 9½" L.......................65.00
Haley, Lady Godiva, bookend, crystal, 1940s, ea.......45.00
Indiana, horse head, bookends, milk glass, 6", pr........70.00
Indiana, panther, bl, walking 400.00
Indiana, pouter pigeon, bookend, crystal frost, ea......40.00
LG Wright, trout, crystal...150.00
New Martinsville by Mirror Images, baby bear, ruby....95.00
New Martinsville by Mirror Images, mama bear, ruby 150.00
New Martinsville by Mirror Images, wolfhound, ruby carnival ...150.00

Glass Knives

Glass knives were manufactured from about 1920 to 1950, with distribution at its greatest in the late '30s and early '40s. Colors generally followed Depression glass dinnerware: crystal, light blue, light green, pink (originally called rose), and more rarely amber, forest green, and white (opal). Many glass knives were hand painted in fruit or flower designs. Knife blades were ground to a sharp edge. Today knives are usually found with blades nicked through years of use or bumping in silverware drawers or reground, which is acceptable to collectors as long as the original knife shape is maintained.

Many glass knives were engraved for gift-giving, personalized with the recipient's name and, on occasion, with a greeting. Originally presented in boxes, most glass knives were accompanied by a paper insert extolling the virtues of the knife and describing its care.

Boxes printed with World's Fair logos are fun to find, though not rare. Butter knives, which are smaller than other glass knives, typically were made in Czechoslovakia and sometimes match the handle patterns of glass salad sets. Knife lengths often vary slightly because the knives were snapped off the molded glass and the end ground during manufacture.

Several styles of knives (i.e. Vitex, Dur-X, Cryst-O-Lite) were manufactured by the thousands and are therefore found more often. Prices have become volatile due to the popularity of online, Internet auctions and the competition that results. Values reflect knives with minimal blade roughness or resharpening.

Aer-Flo, amber, 7½", from $300 to...350.00
Aer-Flo, gr, 7½", from $70 to..75.00
BKCo, crystal, 9¼", from $15 to..18.00
Block, crystal, 8¼", from $12 to..20.00

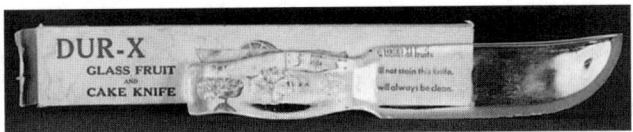

Dur-X (three-leaf), crystal, 8½", MIB, $20.00.

Dur-X, 3-leaf, gr, 8½", from $35 to...50.00
Dur-X, 3-leaf, lt amber, 9¼", from $200 to 225.00
Dur-X, 5-leaf, bl, 8½", from $35 to...50.00
Dur-X, 5-leaf, crystal, 8½", from $25 to.......................................40.00
Plain hdl, gr, 9¼", from $32 to...40.00
Rose Spray, amber, 8½", from $225 to..275.00
Rose Spray, pk, 8½", from $200 to...250.00
Star, bl, 9¼", from $32 to...35.00
Star, pk, 8½", from $32 5o..35.00
Steel-ite, pk, from $80 to..90.00
Thumbguard, crystal, from $25 to..40.00

Glass Shoes

Little shoes made of glass can be found in hundreds of styles, shapes, and colors. They've been made since the early 1800s by nearly every glasshouse, large and small, in America. To learn more about them, we recommend *Shoes of Glass II* (newly updated) by our advisor Libby Yalom, who is listed in the Directory under Maryland. Numbers in the listings refer to her book. Another reference is *Collectible Glass Shoes, Second Edition,* by Earlene Wheatley, published by Collector Books.

See also Boyd; Degenhart.

#3, Daisy & Button, mesh sole, bl, Duncan, lg...............................55.00
#24, Daisy & Button, amber..45.00
#47, Daisy & Button, bl, Pat'd Oct 19, 1886, 7¼"........................75.00
#89, crystal frost, mk Gillinder & Sons Centennial Exhibition, 5½".47.00
#101, Cane, crystal, solid heel, 1880s, 4⅝" 85.00
#109A, boot, Daisy & Square, vaseline, 1880s, scarce, 3" 105.00
#127, boot, Daisy & Button, crystal, Duncan & Sons, 4¾" 95.00
#128, high heel w/scalloped edge, crystal, Gillinder & Sons, 4¼".135.00
#136, boot w/spur, blk, att Challinor Taylor, 1890s, 4" 75.00
#141, boot, Daisy & Button, bl w/clear/solid toe & heal, 3⅜" 125.00
#157, roller skate, Daisy & Button, vaseline, Central Glass, 5¼".85.00
#179, high shoe roller skate, dmn-mesh upper, amber, 3½"...........40.00
#200, boot w/spur, Daisy & Button, crystal, 1880s, 5¼"..............150.00
#212, bootee, dk amber, King Glass, 1880s, 3⅝"..........................70.00

#251, jockey boot, hollow sole & heel, bl, 1880s, 4" 75.00
#276A, lady's, flat bow & stippling, lt marigold carnival, 4⅜" 85.00
#319, Dutch style, bl, 8¼" 125.00
#323, boot, cased spangle, 5-color 175.00
#344, frosted mc millefiori w/crystal heel, Murano label, 5⅝" 90.00
#385, Dutch style, crystal, 3 ridges on vamp, 3 buttons, 7" 55.00
#395, boot match holder, gr, Bryce Higbee & Co, 1880s, 4½".......45.00
#477, boot, emb leaves, plain band at top, lt bl, 1880s, 2¾".......125.00
#494, boot, crystal, etched Murphy...Peel St, 2½".........................40.00
#522, boot, wht opaque, appl heel, somewhat crude, 3⅜".............50.00
#549, boot pitcher, pk & wht slag, 1⅜"...30.00
#584, boot, crystal, cut decor, appl heel, ca 1890, ½-liter 150.00
#743, high heel w/rnd heel plate, amethyst, no Pat date, 1880s, 3¾".110.00
#758, pump, crystal, slightly shaped as left shoe, 5¼"..................60.00
#789, boot w/turned-up toe, gold opal, Venetian, 3⅜" 50.00
#813, man's, crystal over cranberry w/gold traces, 3⅜" 175.00
#851, boot, crystal, on oval ped, 1880s, 3⅝" 95.00

Glidden

Genius designer Glidden Parker established Glidden Pottery in 1940 in Alfred, New York, having been schooled at the unrivaled New York State College of Ceramics at Alfred University. Glidden pottery is characterized by a fine stoneware body, innovative forms, outstanding hand-milled glazes, and hand decoration which make the pieces individual works of art. Production consisted of casual dinnerware, artware, and accessories that were distributed internationally.

In 1949 Glidden Pottery became the second ceramic plant in the country to utilize the revolutionary Ram pressing machine. This allowed for increased production and for the most part eliminated the previously used slip-casting method. However, Glidden stoneware continued to reflect the same superb quality of craftsmanship until the factory closed in 1957. Although the majority of form and decorative patterns were Mr. Parker's personal designs, Fong Chow and Sergio Dello Strologo also designed award-winning lines.

Glidden will be found marked on the unglazed underside with a signature that is hand incised, mold impressed, or ink stamped. Interest in this unique stoneware is growing as collectors discover that it embodies the very finest of Mid-Century High Style. Our advisor is David Pierce; he is listed in the Directory under Ohio.

Ashtray, Alfred Stoneware, #821 ....35.00
Ashtray, Fish (Fred Press), #275 ....25.00
Ashtray, Green Mesa, #274-U...25.00
Ashtray, Leaves (Fred Press), #274 ....25.00
Ashtray, Loop Artware, #904-U...55.00
Ashtray, Safex, dbl sq..20.00
Bowl, Cobalt, #23 ....30.00
Bowl, Counterpane, #622...20.00
Bowl, Early Pink, #38 ....35.00
Bowl, Plaid, #27 ....35.00
Bowl, Turq Matrix, #21 ....15.00
Bowl, Turq Matrix, #26 ....12.00
Bowl, Viridian, lug soup, #467 ....15.00
Bowl, Viridian, oval, #417 ....25.00
Candle bench, Afrikans 100.00
Canister, Garden, w /lid & bail, #601 ....75.00
Casserole, Pear, w/lid, #165 ....45.00
Casserole, Ric Rac, yel, #167 ....18.00
Casserole, Turq Matrix, #162 ....12.00
Casserole, Viridian, 3165..30.00
Casserole, Will O' the Wisp, #167 ....15.00
Coaster, Mexican Cock, #19 ....10.00

Creamer & sugar bowl, Feather, w/lid, #144/#143 ....35.00
Creamer & sugar bowl, Pear, w/lid, #144/#143.............................45.00
Creamer & sugar bowl, Turq Matrix, w/lid, #1430/#1440..............30.00
Creamer & sugar bowl, Yellowstone, w/lid, #1430/#1440..............25.00
Cup & saucer, Boston Spice, #441A/#442.....................................25.00
Cup & saucer, Feather, #441A/#442 ....15.00
Cup & saucer, Turq Matrix, #141/#142 ....10.00
Pitcher, Turq Matrix, #617...55.00
Planter, Charcoal & Rice, bird form...160.00
Planter, Sage & Sand, #122 ....12.00
Plate, Marine Fantasia, Lucent Green, #431..................................85.00
Plate, Mexican Cock, #35..20.00
Plate, Plaid, #65, salad sz 25.00
Plate, Turn of the Century, #35, 5½"...30.00
Teapot, Flourish, #140 ....70.00
Teapot, Yellowstone, #240...50.00
Vase, Cobalt, ball form, #49...55.00
Vase, Early Pink, pillow form, #128 ....25.00

Goebel

F.W. Goebel founded the F&W Goebel Company in 1871, located in Rodental, West Germany. They produced thousands of different decorative and useful items over the years, the most famous of which are the Hummel figurines first produced in 1935 based on the artwork of a Franciscan nun, Sister Maria Innocentia Hummel.

The Goebel trademarks have long been a source of confusion because all Goebel products, including Hummels, of any particular time period bear the same trademark, thus leading many to believe all Goebels are Hummels. Always look for the Hummel signature on actual Hummel figurines (these are listed in a separate section).

There are many, many other series — some of which are based on artwork of particular artists such as Disney, Charlot Byj, Janet Robson, Harry Holt, Norman Rockwell, M. Spotl, Lore, Huldah, and Schaubach. Miscellaneous useful items include ashtrays, bookends, salt and pepper shakers, banks, pitchers, inkwells, perfume bottles, etc. Figurines include birds, animals, Art Deco pieces, etc. The Friar Tuck monks and the Co-Boy elves are especially popular.

The date of manufacture of a particular piece is determined by the trademark. The incised date found underneath the base on many items is the mold copyright date. Actual date of manufacture may vary as much as twenty years or more from the copyright date.

Most Common Goebel Trademarks and Approximate Dates Used
1.) Crown mark (may be incised or stamped, or both): 1923 – 1950
2.) Full bee (complete bumble bee inside the letter 'V'): 1950 – 1957
3.) Stylized bee (dot with wings inside the letter 'V'): 1957 – 1964
4.) 3-Line (stylized bee with 3 lines of copyright info to the right of the trademark): 1964 – 1972
5.) Goebel bee (word Goebel with stylized bee mark over the last letter 'e'): 1972 – 1979
6.) Goebel (word Goebel only): 1979 – Present

Our advisors for this category are Gale and Wayne Bailey; they are listed in the Directory under Georgia.

Cardinal Tuck (Red Monk)

Ashtray, ZF-43/0...225.00
Bank...500.00
Calendar holder...325.00
Egg timer, single..250.00
Match holder 275.00
Pitcher, S-14/0, TMK-3, 4" 135.00

Pourer..230.00
Shakers, pr, w/Bibles & tray 250.00

Charlot BYJ Redheads and Blonds

Atta Boy, BYJ-7, TMK-4...85.00
Bird Watcher, BJY-84..105.00
Bongo Beat, 5"..110.00
Girl w/2 dachshunds following her, BYJ-25...........................120.00
Little Miss Coy, BYJ-4...125.00
Off Beat, 5½"..115.00
Off Key, BYJ-22..85.00
Springtime, BYJ-10...115.00
Sunbonnet Girl, BYJ-12..100.00
Trim Lass, BYJ-49...110.00

Co-Boy Figurines

Al the Trumpet Player, 6"...60.00
Bit the Bachelor, TMK-4, 7¾"..80.00
Brad the Clock 225.00
Brum the Lawyer, w/owl 65.00
Chuck the Chimney Sweep 255.00
Fritz the Happy Boozer, 1971, 8"..80.00
Gilda, w/baby doll, 2" 70.00
Jack the Pharmacist 60.00
Mark the Gnome, ready for beach, 8"...50.00
Rob the Vegetarian, TMK-6...80.00
Rosi & Rolf, 3½x4¼"..110.00
Ted the Gnome Tennis Player, EX..75.00
Walter the Jogger, w/tag 50.00

Cookie Jars

Cat, TMK-5, from $100 to...175.00
Dog, TMK-5, from $100 to..125.00
Friar Tuck, K-29, TMK-5 ....350.00
Owl, TMK-5, from $70 to..80.00
Panda Bear, TMK-5, from $70 to..80.00
Parrot, TMK-5, from $70 to..80.00
Pig, TMK-5, from $100 to..125.00

Friar Tuck (Brown Monk)

Bank, marked SD-29 Goebel W. Germany, 4½", $75.00. (Photo courtesy Jim and Beverly Mangus)

Bowl/ashtray, ZF-42/II, TMK-3, 4½" dia 65.00
Candle holders, TMK-3, 3", pr...75.00
Clock, 8½x7½" 235.00
Cookie jar, TMK-2...350.00

Cordial set, KL91, TMK-3 ....350.00
Creamer, S-141/0, TMK-2, 3½" 30.00
Decanter, musical, KL-93 ....500.00
Egg cup, E-95/A, TMK-3...48.00
Egg timer, 2 monks hold rope w/timer in middle, 3½" 125.00
Matchbox holder, RX-111, TMK-3, 3"..................100.00
Mug, T-740/0, TMK-2 ....35.00
Mustard, S-183, TMK-2, 3¾" 35.00
Napkin ring, X-98, 1½" dia......................................85.00
Oil & vinegar cruets, M-80, TMK-2, 5½"............250.00
Pitcher, S-141-3/0, TMK-2...75.00
Shakers, musicians, 5", pr...125.00
Shakers, TMK-2, pr...35.00
Sugar bowl, M-43B...60.00
Wine glass, 5"...60.00

Shakers

Bears, 3", pr...25.00
Bride & groom, Goebel, 3½", pr.............................48.00
Cat & dog, TMK-1, 2⅝", pr...................................65.00
Chef w/apron & 2 pots (shakers), M-31, 3-pc set, from $120 to.160.00
Dogs, 2½", pr...25.00
Lobsters, red-orange w/blk & gray, #18A, pr 38.00
Man, w/4-leaf clover-type badge on chest, red scarf, 3", pr...........40.00
Peppers, 1 gr/1 red, pr...32.00
Poodles, blk & wht, ca 1960, 3½", pr.......................18.00
Skunks, 1 sitting up, 2nd on all 4s, pr.....................30.00
Swiss boy & girl, Goebel, 2¾", pr...........................20.00
Turkeys, P-98, pr..42.50

Miscellaneous

Bird, crested, Deco style, #38-938-25, c 1984, 10½", NM.............85.00
Figurine, barmaid w/beer steins, #15-007-76, TMK-6, 6¾" 38.00
Figurine, boxer dog, CH-570, TMK-5, 3½x4"..........35.00
Figurine, cat, wht, #31-037-15, TMK-6, 6½x6" 42.00
Figurine, ducklings (2), #32055, TMK-6, 1¾x4¼" 30.00
Figurine, monkey, #541, TMK-6, 3½" 32.00
Figurine, owl trio, #38340-07, TMK-6, 3¼x4½".......30.00
Figurine, redstart, TMK-5, 3½x3"...........................35.00
Figurine, robin on branch, CV-61, TMK-6, 3½"........32.00
Figurine, titmouse on trunk w/flowers, CV-241, TMK-5, 5"..........40.00
Figurine, yel wagtail, #CV-32, TMK5, 3¾x3" 40.00
Planter, swan, ZV-103/IV, TMK-5, 4½x6".................27.50

Goldscheider

The Goldscheider family operated a pottery in Vienna for many generations before seeking refuge in the United States following Hitler's invasion of their country. They settled in Trenton, New Jersey, in the early 1940s where they established a new corporation and began producing objects of art and tableware items. (No mention was made of the company in the Trenton City Directory after 1950, and it is assumed that by this time the influx of foreign imports had taken its toll.) In 1946 Marcel Goldscheider established a pottery in Staffordshire where he manufactured bone china figures, earthenware, etc., marked with a stamp of his signature. Larger artist-signed examples are the most valuable with the Austrian pieces bringing the higher prices.

A wide variety of marks has been found: 1.) Goldscheider USA Fine China; 2.) Original Goldscheider Fine China; 3.) Goldscheider USA; 4.) Goldscheider-Everlast Corp.; 5.) Goldscheider Everlast Corp. in circle; 6.) Goldscheider Inc. in circle; 7.) Goldcrest Ceramics Corp. in circle; 8.) Goldcrest Fine China; 9.) Goldcrest Fine China USA; 10.) A Goldcrest Creation; and 11.) Created by Goldscheider USA.

Our co-advisors are Randy and Debbie Coe (listed in the Directory under Oregon) and Darrell Thomas (listed under Wisconsin).

Ad photos w/info/prices/etc, 1942 postmk, Trenton...USA, 8x10", 7 for ...800.00
Box, woman on top, flower decals on bl, ball ft, 1940s, USA, 5x7" ..295.00
Bust, lady w/crown, bl top, #663A, USA #9 mk, 6x4¾" 75.00
Bust, lady w/curly hair, hands by face, #7653, Austria, 15½"...1,350.00
Bust, Madonna, gray w/maroon, #664, USA #9 mk, 6¾x4½" 65.00
Bust, man w/turban, gr w/yel top, #1188, USA, 8x5" 90.00
Busts, Chinese heads, gr/yel on gray, detailed, Lindloff, USA, 5", pr ..250.00
Clock, man on horse w/maiden, brass face, F Goldscheider/Austria, 13"..1,800.00
Figurine, Anne Boleyn, gr & maroon outfit, #1199, USA #7 mk, 10¾"..195.00
Figurine, Bachelor Carnation, man w/cane, #317, USA #8 mk, 7½" ...98.50
Figurine, Balinese dancing girl, sgn B Baldwin, USA, 17" 295.00
Figurine, bat girl w/spiders/butterflies, EX color, Lorenzl, 20x16x6".7,500.00
Figurine, Borzoi dog, recumbent, Austria, 17" L 495.00
Figurine, Caroline, lady in pk, gr cape, #1230, USA #7 mk, 10½"..145.00
Figurine, Country Girl, sgn HIG, Hapsburg seal, #d, pre WWI, 14", EX..1,350.00
Figurine, couple, wht w/gold, she: hoop skirt, USA mks, 8", 8½", pr..200.00
Figurine, Deco dancing girl, 15" W skirt, sgn Dakon, 16½" 3,600.00
Figurine, dogs (2) pull at joined leash, orange/wht, USA, 4½x5½"..85.00
Figurine, Europa, Nouveau nude, Schmidt & Kester mk (removed), 14x8x7"...4,500.00
Figurine, Fr lady, pk & detailed, artist sgn, #405, 1895, 14".....2,600.00
Figurine, girl plays violin, book at ft, #861, 9" 145.00
Figurine, harem girl, Lorenzel, #5921/74/15, 18" 5,500.00
Figurine, Henry VII, gr & maroon outfit, #1198, USA #7 mk, 10½" ..195.00
Figurine, horses, 1 w/head up, 2nd: head down, brn/wht spots, USA, 6"..150.00
Figurine, lady dancer w/1 leg held up, Austria, 20½"...............1,600.00
Figurine, lady in bl/gr w/new hat, USA, 5¾" 75.00
Figurine, lady w/parasol, gr outfit, USA, 8¼"..................................95.00
Figurine, man in tuxedo, violets under coat, Deco style, Austria, 12".1,900.00
Figurine, Marie Antoinette, sgn Peggy Porscher, USA, 6½"..........125.00
Figurine, Oriental lady w/tilted head, gr, #823, USA #5 mk, 10¼"...135.00
Figurine, Oriental man w/lute, gray, #822, USA #5 mk, 10½" ...125.00
Figurine, Pierrot placing shawl on lady, domed base, 15" 325.00
Figurine, Southern belle w/flowers on pk base, P Porscher, USA, 12x13".....350.00
Figurine, Westie dog, wht w/bl eyes, Austria Wein mks, 4".........195.00
Lamp, dancing couple by lamppost, detailed/mc, Dakon, w/shade, 15" ...2,450.00
Lamp, lady seated by column, Austria, 16" 595.00
Mask, bl/gray/pk/orange mottle, sgn MZ, sticker/gold tag, no mk, 7" 1,100.00
Mask, Medusa, mc w/snaky bl-blk hair, 14" 2,500.00
Mask, terra cotta, blk curly hair, gr/wht scarf, #2976, rubbed mk, 10" 400.00
Mask, woman w/fruits, long face, EX mc details on terra cotta, 12" 2,000.00
Masks, boy & girl, yel curls/bl eyes/plaids, '40s, stamped/#d, 7", 6" 800.00
Plaque, boy, #8814-2, Austria, 4" 75.00
Plaque, girl, #8815-2, Austria, 4" 75.00
Vase, abstracts, mc, Clarice Cliff designs, Austria mk, 12" 500.00

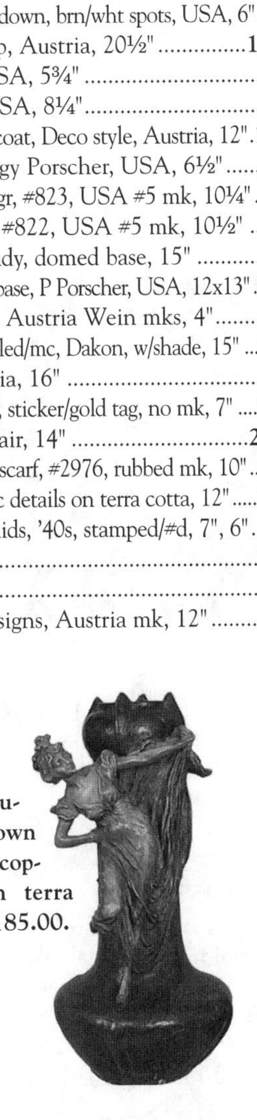

Vase, Victorian Nouveau-style lady in flowing gown stands at side, allover coppery-bronze finish on terra cotta, 28", NM, $1,185.00.

(Photo courtesy James Julia)

Vase, vines & feathers, wht on bl-purple, sgn Doblinger, Fr, 16x7"..**750.00**
Vase, 3-D draped nude w/lyre before vase w/emb face/leaves, Wien, 25" ..**10,575.00**

Gonder

Lawton Gonder grew up with clay in his hands and fire in his eyes. Gonder's interest in ceramics was greatly influenced by his parents who worked for Weller and a close family friend and noted ceramic authority, John Herold. In his early teens Gonder launched his ceramic career at the Ohio Pottery Company while working for Herold. He later gained valuable experience at American Encaustic Tile Company, Cherry Art Tile, and the Florence Pottery. Gonder was plant manager at the Florence Pottery until fire destroyed the facility in late 1941.

After years of solid production and management experience, Lawton Gonder established the Gonder Ceramic Art Company, formerly the Peters and Reed plant, in South Zanesville, Ohio. Gonder Ceramic Arts produced quality art pottery with beautiful contemporary designs which included human and animal figures and a complete line of Oriental pottery. Accentuating the beautiful shapes were unique and innovative glazes developed by Gonder such as flambé (flame red with streaks of yellow), 24k gold crackle, antique gold, and Chinese crackle. (These glazes bring premium prices.)

All Gonder is marked with the company name and mold number. They include 'Gonder U.S.A' in block letters, 'Gonder' in script, 'Gonder Original' in script, and 'Gonder Ceramic Art' in block letters. Paper labels were also used. Some of the early Gonder molds closely resemble RumRill designs that had been manufactured at the Florence Pottery; and because some RumRill pieces are found with similar (if not identical) shapes, matching mold numbers, and Gonder glazes, it is speculated that some RumRill was produced at the Gonder plant. In 1946 Gonder started another company which he named Elgee (chosen for his initials LG) where he manufactured lamp bases until a fire in 1954 resulted in his shifting lamp production to the main plant. Operations ceased in 1957.

Wall mask, white, 8", $150.00.

Bowl, sunflower, #523, 2x9" 40.00
Candle holders, blk w/wht drip glaze, label, 2x3½", pr.................35.00
Ewer, gr w/brn & pk highlights, #J-25, 11x5" 50.00
Ewer, mottled oxblood, #682, 10" 70.00
Figurine, Basque Dancer, man w/2 jugs in outstretched hands, gr, 12"..35.00
Figurine, elephant, head up w/trunk curled bk, gr/brn, 6x7" 80.00
Figurine, horse's head, maroon & gold blend, #873, 6½x15" 85.00
Figurine, lady in European-style clothes, bl-gr, #765, 12" 55.00
Figurine, panther, walking, oxblood, #205, 3⅛x12¼" 70.00
Figurine, semi-nude Oriental man w/2 jugs on yoke, yel, 13½" 60.00
Lamp, sailing ship figural, brn-wht volcanic glaze, 13⅜"...............50.00
Planter, clam shell shape, gray w/pk int, #505, 7½x15".................60.00
Planter, leaping gazelle, yel, #215, 4x8½" dia............................45.00
Vase, angelfish, gray w/pk int, #522 ....50.00

Vase, ball shape, tan w/drip glaze, #514-B, 3¼x4" 70.00
Vase, cornucopia; yel w/brn highlights, #692, 4⅝" 40.00
Vase, cornucopia; 2 fish on front, Coral Lustre, #558.................140.00
Vase, deer (female) head, mauve drip glaze, #518 ....65.00
Vase, dk purple w/pk int, attached geese at base, 8¼" 35.00
Vase, log shape w/sea gull w/13¼" wingspan, #514, 11½" 68.00
Vase, Pegasus decor, gr w/brn highlights & pk int, #526, 10½".....95.00
Vase, sq w/geometric design, bl-gr, #534, 10½" 45.00
Vase, swan shape, purple w/wht drip glaze, #802, 9½" 35.00
Wall pocket, crashing waves design, Pistachio glaze, 5½x4x10½".115.00
Wall pocket, Happy & Sad (theatre masks), dk gr, #519, 10x5x6" 85.00

Goofus Glass

Goofus glass is American-made pressed glass with designs that are either embossed (blown out) or intaglio (cut in). The decorated colors were aerographed or hand applied and not fired on the pieces. The various patterns exemplify the artistry of the turn-of-the-century glass crafters. The primary production dates were ca 1908 to 1918. Goofus was produced by many well-known manufacturers such as Northwood, Indiana, and Dugan.

When no condition is given, our values are for examples in mint original paint. Our advisor for this category is Steve Gillespie of the *Goofus Glass Gazette*; he is listed in the Directory under Missouri. See also Clubs, Catalogs, and Newsletters.

Basket, Diamond & Daisy, hdld, 6½", EX 55.00
Bowl, Butterfly, red & gold, ruffled, 2½x10½", EX+ 75.00
Bowl, Cherry, red & gold, Dugan, 2¼x10⅛"................................85.00
Bowl, cherry, ruffled rim, 3¼x10", NM 95.00
Bowl, Jeweled Heart, 2x9", NM 70.00
Bowl, Poppy, red & gold, ftd, 4x9", EX.....................................60.00
Compote, Butterfly, 6⅞x10¼", EX 80.00
Lamp, oil; Grape & Leaf, minor flaking, 13¼" 275.00
Lamp, oil; Wild Rose, Riverside, finger loop, 15" overall 250.00
Plate, Chrysanthemum, frosted ground, 6¼", EX.........................60.00
Plate, Little Bo Peep, minor gold flaking, 6½"...........................135.00
Plate, rose in base amid 8 long-stem roses, red/gold, 10¾", EX 55.00
Plate, Temple of Music, Pan Am Expo Buffalo NY, 7¼", EX......120.00
Shakers, Vintage, dk gr & gold on milk glass, G orig lids, 3¼", pr.55.00
Vase, Corn, Dugan, 1905, 7¾", NM...110.00
Vase, Crested Love Birds, Indiana Glass, 10½x5", EX.................60.00
Vase, Dogwood, baluster, 15", EX+ 90.00
Vase, Flower Bouquet, wine & gr, 15½", NM 110.00
Vase, flowers (2) & leaves, red/gr/gold, 9½", EX........................110.00
Vase, Iris, purple on gr, 12½x5", NM.......................................85.00
Vase, Parrot, 12½", EX 75.00
Vase, Peaches, gold/red/gr, 9", EX 50.00
Vase, Peacock in Tree, gr w/gold, 15", NM 150.00
Vase, Peacock in Tree, red/gr/gold, 15", EX..............................195.00
Vase, Statue of Liberty, gold/gr, cylindrical, 12½x5" 85.00
Vase, Water Lily, 12", EX 65.00

Goss and Crested China

William Henry Goss received his early education at the Government School of Design at Somerset House, London, and as a result of his merit was introduced to Alderman William Copeland, who owned the Copeland Spode Pottery. Under the influence of Copeland from 1852 to 1858, Goss quickly learned the trade and soon became their chief designer. Little is known about this brief association, and in 1858 Goss left to begin his own business. After a short-lived partnership with a Mr. Peake, Goss opened a pottery on John Street, Stoke-on-Trent, but by 1870 he had moved to his business to a location near London Road. This pottery became the famous Falcon Works. Their mark was a spread-wing falcon (goss-hawk) centering a narrow, horizontal bar with 'W.H. Goss' printed below.

Many of the early pieces made by Goss were left unmarked and are difficult to discern from products made by the Copeland factory, but after he had been in business for about fifteen years, all of his wares were marked. Today unmarked items do not command the prices of the later marked wares.

Adolphus William Henry Goss (Goss's eldest son) joined his father's firm in the 1880s. He introduced cheaper lines, though the more expensive lines continued in production. Shortly after his father's death in 1906, Adolphus retired and left the business to his two younger brothers. The business suffered from problems created by a war economy, and in 1936 Goss assets were held by Cauldon Potteries Ltd. These were eventually taken over by the Coalport Group, who retained the right to use the Goss trademark. Messrs. Ridgeway Potteries bought all the assets in 1954 as well as the right to use the Goss trademark and name. In 1964 the group was known as Allied English Potteries Ltd. (A.E.P.), and in 1971 A.E.P. merged with the Doulton Group. Now it remains to be seen if Goss ware will ever be produced again. Values are all for items in mint condition.

Ancient Urn, Arms of Goss **50.00**
Birth of Venus figurine, turq trim, 8" **325.00**
Caer Worgron salt cellar...**15.00**
Coggeshall Abbey radio horn, 3¾x2" dia **55.00**
Essex Regt bowl, 2¼x5" **125.00**
Haddington cup & saucer, Bagware, 2", 4" **35.00**
Kitcheners Army (Bravo! & flag) posey vase, 5 fingers **50.00**
Robert Burns cottage, 1½x2½" **72.50**
Rock of Ages, Cheddar crest...**60.00**
Thistle vase, Edinburgh crest, 3"...**55.00**
West Hartlepool vase, 3½" **45.00**
Woolwich toothpick holder **10.00**

Crested China

Arcadia, Eli Priory **80.00**
Arcadia, Wimbourne Minster in Dorset, 2½x5" **90.00**
Willow Art, Maidstone elephant, 2x3".................................**35.00**
Willow Art, Royal Army Medical Corps book, 2¼x2¼" **45.00**

Gouda

Gouda is an old Dutch market town in the province of South Holland. Famous for its cheese, Gouda's ceramics industry had its beginnings in the early sixteenth century and was fueled by the growth in the popularity of smoking tobacco. Initially learning their craft from immigrant potters from England who had settled in the area, the clay pipe makers of Gouda were soon regarded as the best. While some authorities give 1898 (the date the Zuid-Holland factory began operations) as the initial date for the manufacturing of decorative pottery in Gouda, C.W. Moody, author of Gouda Ceramics, indicates the date was ca 1885. Gouda was not the only town in the Netherlands making pottery; Arnhem, Schoonhoven, and Amsterdam also had earthenware factories, but technically the term 'Gouda pottery' refers only to pieces made within the town of Gouda. Today, no Gouda-style factories are active within the city's limits, but in the first quarter of the twentieth century there were several firms producing decorative pottery there — the best known being Zuid, Regina, Zenith, Ivora, and Goedewaagen. At present Royal Goedewagen is making three patterns of limited editions. They are well marked as such.

This information was provided to us by Adela Meadows; she is listed in the Directory under California.

For further information we recommend The World of Gouda Pottery by Phyllis T. Ritvo (Front & Center Press, Weston, Massachussets).

Bowl, abstracts, florals & vines, Tokio, Holland, 1910s, 2¼x10"...**165.00**
Bowl, Deco-style tulips, Zuid Holland, ca 1927, 2¼x9½" **260.00**
Bowl, florals & leaf-like abstracts, Royal Zuid, 1953, 8¾"...........**100.00**
Bowl, flowers & stripes on cobalt, Madeleine, Holland, 1929, 3x12".**250.00**
Bowl, geometric abstracts w/cobalt, Rhodian, 1923, 3x10½" **195.00**
Bowl, peacock feathers, Dorian Holland, 1925, 3¾x7¾" **250.00**
Bowl, thistle-like flowers & abstracts, Regina, 1925, 3x10" **195.00**
Candlestick, stylized flowers, PZH, 1929, 7½x4½" **360.00**
Candlesticks, Deco floral, dbl-gourd top, Royal Metz, 11¼", pr..**225.00**
Candlesticks, Gager, scalloped drip tray, PZH, 1931, 12x5½", pr.**385.00**
Candlesticks, Nouveau motif, ruffled drip pan, artist sgn, 18", pr ..**435.00**
Chamber stick, brn/wht abstract on lav mottle, Zuid Holland, 1930, 7" ...**250.00**
Charger, flowers & leaves on cobalt, PZH, 1929, 2¼x14"...........**880.00**
Clock, tulips, beveled glass face, gold trim, PZH, ca 1900-10, 20x7" **2,400.00**
Ewer, vertical trails/dots/accents, Corona, Holland, 1918, 15¾" ..**825.00**
Inkwell, arches & stripes, 6-sided, Dorian, 1920s, 3¾x4" **195.00**
Inkwell, ochre/wht swirls w/blk borders, Ivora, ca 1926, 4½x6½" ..**360.00**
Inkwell, tulips & abstracts on cobalt, Cobo, Holland, 1921, 2¼x9"..**165.00**
Jar, Pikan, floral w/dotted gold, Holland, 1927, 6" **165.00**
Lamp base, butterfly motif, mc on matt, ovoid, AJK Holland, 12"...**290.00**
Lantern, floral in Rhodian-type colors, electrified, PZH, 9½".....**385.00**
Matchbox holder, floral, sq w/angular hdl, PZH, 1919, 3½x5" ...**220.00**
Pitcher, abstracts & dots on sage gr, Décor Bos, Holland, 9¼", NM ...**250.00**
Pitcher, abstracts & florals on ivory, Holland, 1927, 8x6"...........**140.00**
Pitcher, floral abstracts, Cyprus Holland, 1906-17, 9¾x5" **250.00**
Pitcher, floral abstracts, Rhodian Holland, 1906-17, 9¾x5" **275.00**
Pitcher, Maas/Massa, abstract dots/lines on cobalt, PZH, 1918, 5x4" ..**385.00**
Pitcher, Nouveau pansies & buds on mocha tan, Zuid Holland, 7x6½".**470.00**
Pitcher, wht swirls w/gold on brn, bulbous, Roma, 5½x4"...........**140.00**
Planter, arching abstracts & spattered brn, hdls, Lolette, 11" L **165.00**
Planter, Lydia pattern, florals/abstracts, Regina, hangs, 6x7½"......**80.00**
Plaque, floral, rtcl, sgn Brigette, Holland, 1940s-50s, 14"...........**220.00**
Plaque, Nouveau abstracts, sgn Verwaal, Holland, #1165, 17½".**600.00**
Plaque, peacock on branch, Regina, 1920s, 17" **715.00**
Plate, Deco bird/flowers/tree, Ivora, Holland, #407, 5¼" **200.00**
Plate, lovebirds, Xs & Os, Rutoro Goedenwaagen Holland, 8" **70.00**
Tazza, Nanette, mc w/blk borders, PZH, 1927, 6½x6½".............**220.00**
Tray, Nadra, 3 lg flowers, Holland, ca 1930, 10" dia **255.00**
Urn, flowers & leaves w/cobalt, Pico, 1926, 17½x9" **1,500.00**
Vase, abstracts, spherical body, Rhodian Holland, 1903, 12⅛x5"..**360.00**
Vase, butterfly & flowers, jug form, Zuid, 1925, 5⅛x3½"............**220.00**
Vase, butterfly & flowers on gray-bl, Zuid Holland, 4¾x3½" **140.00**
Vase, cascading leaves & flowers, chalice form, Corona Zuid, 6½"..**275.00**
Vase, chrysanthemums on lt bl, dbl gourd, Rolly, 1928, 6¾x4" ..**220.00**

Vase, country scene with figures, Zuid Holland house mark, 1906 – 17, 19", $1,100.00. (Photo courtesy Skinner, Inc.)

Vase, cvd ice skaters/countryside, bulbous w/long neck, Distel, 10" ..**175.00**
Vase, daisies & pineapple-style decor, Holland, 1902, 12", NM.**140.00**
Vase, Damascus, florals & pinwheels, Holland, 1910-25, 11½x7" ...**525.00**
Vase, Deco hearts on gray, Miehigan, PZH, 1902, 7x4¼" **140.00**
Vase, Flora, floral on wht, 1 hdl, Holland, #735, 6½"................**90.00**
Vase, floral abstracts (wht), Blanca, Holland, 8¼x5" **470.00**
Vase, floral on ivory w/turq rim, gr ft, Tudor, Holland, 1925, 10½".**300.00**
Vase, floral sbstracts & leaves, mc on matt, ovoid, Zuid, 10¾"....**400.00**
Vase, floral/abstract on brn, slim neck, Tonny, Holland, 1924, 10½".**550.00**
Vase, flower border at shoulder, circles in field, PZH, 1928, 8¼x5".**140.00**
Vase, flowing leaves & mini flowers on gray to gr, Holland, rstr, 9".**300.00**
Vase, irises, dbl bulb w/basket hdl, Zuid, 13"............................**920.00**
Vase, lg tulips, squat w/neck flanked by integral hdls, Distel, 8".**520.00**
Vase, Norma, flame-like design, Holland, 1923, rstr, 7¾x4¾"....**140.00**
Vase, Nouveau abstract floral, classic shape, Rhodian, 1926, 10¾".**495.00**
Vase, Nouveau abstracts w/gold on bl, Ajoul, Holland, 1920s, 6½x5".**275.00**
Vase, Nouveau floral on turq, emb ribs, Holland, 6½x3" **220.00**
Vase, orchids on gr to blk, long neck, Ivora, 1920s, 6¼x3" **600.00**
Vase, pheasant in landscape, looped hdls, Liberty & Co Holland, 6x5".**440.00**
Vase, poppies & leaves, buttressed hdls, Klaproos, Goedewaagen, 7".**250.00**
Vase, Rembrandt, feather designs/abstracts, Holland, rstr, 10½".**300.00**
Vase, Roer, mc floral, wide mouth, Schoonhaven, 1920s, 6¼x6".**300.00**
Vase, stylized lilies, mc gloss, invt trumpet form, 1898, 20", pr.**575.00**
Vase, transcending circles on cobalt, Remo, Schoonhoven, 1920s, 6", NM.**185.00**
Vase, tulips, pansies & abstracts, Holland, 1924, 4x5½" **220.00**

Graniteware

Graniteware, made of a variety of metals with enamel coatings, derives its name from its appearance. The speckled, swirled, or mottled effect of the vari-colored enamels may look like granite — but there the resemblance stops. It wasn't especially durable! Expect at least minor chipping if you plan to collect.

Graniteware was featured in 1876 at Phily's Expo. It was mass produced in quantity, and enough of it has survived to make at least the common items easily affordable. Condition, color, shape, and size are important considerations in evaluating an item; cobalt blue and white, green and white, brown and white, and old red and white swirled items are unusual, thus more expensive. Pieces of heavier weight, seam constructed, riveted, and those with wooden handles and tin or matching graniteware lids are usually older. Pieces with matching granite lids demand higher prices than ones with tin lids.

For further study we recommend *The Collector's Encyclopedia of Graniteware, Book II*, by our advisor, Helen Greguire. It is available from the author and Collector Books. For information on how to order, see her listing in the Directory under South Carolina. For the address of the National Graniteware Society, see the section on Clubs, Newsletters, and Catalogs.

Note: Unless noted otherwise, our values are for pieces in mint or near-mint condition; appropriate deductions must be made if damage is present.

Baking pan, bl & wht lg swirl w/blk trim, oblong, 2¼x17" L......**295.00**
Bean pot, bl solid, wht int, perforated lid, 7¾x5¾"..................**125.00**
Bed pan, bl & wht lg mottle w/blk trim, 2⅛x10¾", EX **115.00**
Bidet, cobalt & wht lg mottle, 4x18⅝x11⅝", G- **350.00**
Biscuit sheet, brn & wht mottle, Onyx Enamel Ware, 11¼x16¼", VG.**1,100.00**
Bowl, fruit; cobalt & wht lg mottle, ped ft, 7½x8"..................**1,350.00**
Bowl, salad; bl & wht med mottle, wht int, 2¾x10⅝", EX.........**145.00**
Bucket, blk & wht lg swirl w/blk trim, bail hdl, seamed, 7½", EX ..**575.00**
Bucket, dk gr & wht lg mottle w/cobalt trim, Chrysolite, w/lid, 5¾".**575.00**
Bucket, gr veins w/wht lumpy effect, gr trim, w/lid, 10x8¼", EX...**325.00**
Butter dish, gray lg mottle w/metal trim, w/insert, 7x5" dia.....**1,050.00**
Candlestick, gray med mottle, riveted ring, 2", EX.....................**395.00**

Chamber pot, bl & wht lg swirl w/blk trim, wood bail, seamless, 12".**295.00**
Coal hod, bl-gray solid, seamed, emb GM, 15x10½x18", EX......**250.00**
Coffee basket, lt gray solid, stemmed, 4¾", EX **45.00**
Coffee biggin, red & wht med mottle w/red trim, 4-pc, 9¼".......**625.00**
Coffee biggin, red solid w/blk trim, 5-pc, 10½".......................**155.00**
Coffee boiler, brn & bl-gray lg swirl, seamed, bail hdl, 12x9½" ..**595.00**
Coffee boiler, gr & wht lg swirl w/cobalt, Emerald Ware, 11¾", M .**1,750.00**
Coffeepot, bright bl to lt bl w/blk trim & hdl, seamless, 9¼x6", EX ...**325.00**
Coffeepot, cream w/gr trim, weld hdl, seamed, 7¾x5½" **95.00**
Coffeepot, gray-bl & wht lg mottle w/blk, seamed, 9½x6½", EX.**195.00**
Coffeepot, lt bl & wht lg swirl, riveted/seamless, 10½x6⅝"........**525.00**
Coffeepot, lt bl & wht med swirl, blk trim & hdl, 6¾", EX **160.00**
Coffeepot, red & wht med swirl w/cobalt trim, seamless, 9½", EX.**1,995.00**
Coffeepot, sea gr to moss gr, seamless, 9x5¼" **395.00**
Cream can, bl & wht lg swirl w/cobalt trim, Bl Dmn Ware, 7¾x4" ..**950.00**
Creamer, red & wht lg mottle w/blk trim, ca 1980, 3¼x4" **65.00**
Cup, custard; cream w/gr trim, 2¼x3⅜" **55.00**
Dbl boiler, aqua & wht lg swirl w/cobalt, seamed/riveted, 8½x9¾".**310.00**
Dbl boiler, bl & wht lg swirl w/blk trim & hdl, seamed, 7¼x6⅝" ..**475.00**
Dipper, bl & wht lg mottle w/blk trim & flat hdl, 5" dia, EX **75.00**
Dipper, gr & wht lg swirl w/blk trim, wht int, Emerald Ware, 15¼" L.**795.00**
Dustpan, gray lg mottle, Haberman's Steel Enamel Ware label, 14", G+ **850.00**
Egg pan, red solid, 7-eye, hdls, 1⅛x9⅞"....................................**110.00**
Fry pan, bl & wht lg mottle, wht int, 1⅞x10¼", EX **375.00**
Fry pan, red & wht lg swirl w/blk trim & hdl, 1970s, 6⅝" dia **185.00**
Funnel, bl & wht med mottle, gray int, seamed spout, 4¾x3¾", EX ..**165.00**
Grater, dk gray solid, 11¾x4⅞", EX **675.00**
Kettle, preserve; bl & wht swirl w/blk, Azure Enamelware label, 5x11".**295.00**
Ladle, wht solid w/blk trim & hdl, perforated bottom, 13¼" L, EX ..**45.00**
Measure, aqua & wht lg swirl w/cobalt trim, riveted/seamed, 4⅞"..**450.00**
Milk can, bl & wht lg swirl w/blk bail & trim, seamed, 8¾", EX...**975.00**
Milk can, dk bl & wht mottled relish w/cobalt trim, bail hdl, 8⅞".**395.00**
Mold, melon, gr & wht relish, tin lid emb NO 80, 4¾x9⅛x6⅜" ..**240.00**
Mold, ribbed tube, cobalt w/wht int, 2⅞x8¼", EX **95.00**
Mold, ring, yel w/wht int, 2¼x8⅛", EX **65.00**
Mold, turk's head, bl & wht med mottle, gray int, 8½" dia, EX...........**295.00**

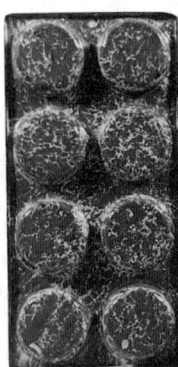

Muffin pan, cobalt blue, white mottle, eight cups, $425.00; Sugar bowl, cobalt blue, white mottle, with lid, $495.00. (Photo courtesy Helen Greguire)

Muffin pan, lav-cobalt & wht med swirl w/blk trim, 8-cup, 14¼" L .**650.00**
Mug, camp/mush; bl & wht wavy mottle w/blk trim, seamless, 4⅜x6" ...**175.00**
Mug, red & wht lg swirl w/cobalt, wht int, seamless, old, 3⅛x3¼"...**895.00**
Mug, yel & wht lg swirl w/blk trim, seamless, 1950s, 3⅛" **50.00**
Pail, chamber; wht & lt bl lg mottle w/blk, bail hdl, 11¼x10½" .**250.00**
Pail, water; bl & wht fine mottle w/cobalt, L&G Mfg label, 8x10"..**250.00**
Pail, water; bl & wht lg mottle, wht int, blk trim, wood bail, 9x11".**275.00**
Pitcher, milk; brn w/wht specks/fine mottle, seamless, 8½x5⅜"...**200.00**
Pitcher, milk; gray lg mottle, weld hdl, seamless, squatty, 7x4½".**325.00**
Pitcher, molasses; dk to lt brn, seamless, covered spout, 6x3½", EX.**375.00**
Pitcher, molasses; sea gr to moss gr, seamless, 6x3⅜"..................**495.00**
Pitcher, molasses; wht solid w/cobalt hdl & trim, 5½x3½"........**175.00**

Pitcher, water; brn shading to gold, brn hdl & trim, 9¾x7¼", EX .225.00
Pitcher, water; burgundy w/mc chicken wire, Elite..., 8⅜x6¾" ...1,250.00
Platter, bl & wht lg swirl w/cobalt, Bl Dmn Ware, 18x14¼" 445.00
Potty, gray lg mottle, EL-AN-GE... label, child sz, 3¾x6½" 145.00
Pudding pan, bl & wht lg swirl w/blk trim, wht int, 3¼x9⅝", G+ .195.00
Pudding pan, red solid w/blk trim, narrow rim, 2¾x9¾" 30.00
Pudding pan, wht w/cobalt trim, Tru-Bl Quality... label, 7" dia.....35.00
Roaster, red solid w/cobalt trim & hdls, wire inset, w/lid, 11⅝" L ..110.00
Saucepan, red-orange w/wht int, blk trim & hdl, 1960s, 6" dia, EX..20.00
Scoop, bl solid, wht int, 2⅜" dia, 5¼" L 155.00
Scoop, wht solid, seamless, 2¾x9¼x2⅝", EX 135.00
Spatula, wht & lt bl med mottle chicken wire, flat hook hdl, 15", EX.165.00
Spoon, brn & wht lg swirl, wht bowl int, 13⅜" L, NM 195.00
Strainer, lt bl & wht lg mottle, perforated, 6⅝" dia+hdl, EX......315.00
Strainer, tea; red & wht lg mottle, perforated, 1x4" dia, G 395.00
Strainer, toddy; gray med mottle, perforated shell shape, 6" L, EX .795.00
Sugar bowl, gray lg mottle w/metal mts & lid, 8½x5⅛" 595.00
Sugar bowl, red solid w/blk trim, 1970s, 5x3⅜", EX 30.00
Teakettle, brn & wht lg swirl, wht int, seamed, 7x7⅜", EX 995.00
Teakettle, dk gr & wht med swirl, Chrysolite, 7¼x7⅞", EX....1,050.00
Teakettle, dk gray med mottle, Savory Sterling label, 6½x9¼" ..265.00
Teakettle, gr vanes w/wht lumpy effect & gr trim, 7½x9½", G...130.00
Teakettle, pk & wht lg marbleized w/blk trim, Bakelite knob, 7x9" .525.00
Teakettle, redipped lav w/wht flecks & wht lg mottle, 8¾x10", EX..265.00
Teapot, dk gr & wht lg mottle w/blk trim, Chrysolite, 9¼x5¾" .525.00
Teapot, gray lg mottle, metal trim, 6¾x3¾" 495.00
Tray, gray lg mottle, L&G Mfg Co mk, ⅝x13⅜x9½" 155.00
Trivet, wht solid w/fancy cutouts, ftd, 7¾" dia...........................110.00
Tumbler, yel & wht lg swirl w/blk trim, 1950s, 4x3" 95.00
Tureen, gray mottle, seamless, domed lid w/cutout, 10½x16x13", EX.225.00
Wash basin, bl & wht lg spatter, wht int, blk trim, 10¼", EX.....145.00
Wash basin, gr & wht lg swirl w/cobalt trim, Emerald Ware, 10¾", EX..195.00
Wash basin, gray lg mottle, Hooser Gray Columbian... label, 2½x11" ...85.00
Wash basin, red & wht lg swirl w/cobalt trim, old, 3½x12¼".....950.00
Wash bowl & pitcher, bl & wht lg swirl w/cobalt, seamless, Columbian .2,350.00
Water carrier, gray lg mottle, seamless, wooden bail, 8x8½" 550.00

Green Opaque

Introduced in 1887 by the New England Glass Works, this ware is very scarce due to the fact that it was produced for less than one year. It is characterized by its soft green color and a wavy band of gold reserving a mottled blue metallic stain. It is usually found in satin; examples with a shiny finish are extremely rare. Values depend to a large extent on the amount of the gold and stain remaining. Our advisors for this category are Betty and Clarence Maier; they are listed in the Directory under Pennsylvania.

Bowl, EX stain & gold, w/lid, 4x6"..1,250.00
Bowl, EX stain & gold, 3½x8" 995.00
Bowl, M stain & gold, 4x8" 1,150.00
Bowl, VG stain & gold, w/lid, 6⅜"...900.00
Celery vase, worn stain & gold, 6½" 450.00
Creamer, EX stain & gold 950.00
Cruet, M stain & gold, orig stopper 1,950.00
Cruet, VG stain, orig stopper 1,500.00
Mug, EX stain & gold, 2¼"..500.00
Mug, M stain & gold, 2½" 700.00
Punch cup, M stain & gold...750.00
Punch cup, worn stain & gold, 2½" 225.00
Shaker, M stain & gold, 2½" 400.00
Spooner, EX stain/gold, lt ribbing, 4" 925.00
Sugar bowl, EX stain & gold 500.00
Toothpick holder, EX gold 900.00
Toothpick holder, M gold 1,150.00
Tumbler, EX stain at rim, 3½" 350.00
Tumbler, lemonade; w/hdl, M stain & gold, 5" 950.00
Tumbler, w/hdl, EX stain & gold, 3½"...800.00
Vase, flared, M stain & gold, 6" 900.00

Greenaway, Kate

Kate Greenaway was an English artist who lived from 1846 to 1901. She gained worldwide fame as an illustrator of children's books, drawing children clothed in the styles worn by proper English and American boys and girls of the very early 1800s. Her book, *Under the Willow Tree*, published in 1878, was the first of many. Her sketches appeared in leading magazines, and her greeting cards were in great demand. Manufacturers of china, pottery, and metal products copied her characters to decorate children's dishes, tiles, and salt and pepper shakers as well as many other items.

What some collectors/dealers call Kate Greenaway items are not actual Kate Greenaway designs but merely look-alikes. Genuine Kate Greenaway items (metal, paper, cloth, etc.) must bear close resemblance to her drawings in books, magazines, and special collections.

See also Napkin Rings.

Shakers, girl with book, boy in long coat, unmarked, 4¾", $145.00.

Biscuit jar, ceramic, boy w/tinted features, w/lid 165.00
Book, A Apple Pie, Warne, 1940, w/dust jacket, VG 28.00
Book, Almanack for 1884, printed by Edmund Evans, EX 135.00
Book, Birthday Book for Children, 1880, VG 160.00
Book, Day in a Child's Life, Routledge, 1st ed, VG 150.00
Book, Greenaway's Babies, Saalfield Muslin Book, 1907, G+ 40.00
Book, Kate Greenaway Pictures, London, Warne, 1st ed, 1921, VG..300.00
Book, Kate Greenaway's Alphabet, London, 1880, EX...............190.00
Book, Kate Greenaway's Book of Games, Routledge, 1st ed, 1889, NM....475.00
Book, Language of Flowers, Routledge, 1st ed, picture board, VG.100.00
Book, Little Ann & Other Poems, by Taylor, VG 50.00
Book, Marigold Garden, London, 1888, VG 60.00
Book, Mother Goose, London, later print of 1st ed, VG 150.00
Book, Pied Piper of Hamlin, NM..85.00
Book, Sunshine for Little Children, 1884, EX 80.00
Book, Under the Willow, Routledge, 1st ed, orig cloth 165.00
Bowl, Daisy & Button, amber; Reed & Barton SP fr w/girl & dog .525.00
Butter pat, children playing transfer, pre-1910..............................40.00
Calendar, chromolithograph, 1884, Routledge, 7⅜x9½", EX........60.00
Combination set, shakers/napkin ring/stand, Middleton Plate, $350 to..500.00
Cup & saucer, children transfer, pk lustre trim, pre-1910...........125.00
Engraving, Harper's Bazaar, Jan 1879, full-pg 25.00
Figurine, seated girl tugs on lg hat, bsk, pre-1910, sm 75.00
Handkerchief, ca 1890-1900, 17x16", VG.......................................55.00
Hatpin holder, SP, figural girl, Meriden, 4" 125.00
Inkwell, boy & girl, bronze...215.00

Match holder, ornate SP, girl in fancy clothes, Tufts 195.00
Paperweight, CI Victorian girl in lg bonnet, pre-1910, 3x2¾"....110.00
Pencil holder, pnt porc, pre-1910 ....100.00
Pickle castor, bl; SP fr w/2 girls, blown-out florals 455.00
Plate, ABC, girl in lg hat, Staffordshire, 7" 105.00
Plate, children at play, fruits, birds & flowers, 9" 100.00
Salt cellar, Little People, bsk, arms over basket, 3¾".....................10.00
Scarf, children on silk, early, EX..65.00
Tea set, semiporc, floral motif, pre-1910, 3-pc, child sz.................95.00
Toothpick holder, bsk, girl sits on stump, basket on bk.................40.00
Toothpick holder, clear glass, 2 girls by basket 100.00
Toothpick holder, SP, girl holds amberina cup, ornate base, 5"..785.00
Toothpick holder, SP child stands by Sandwich glass holder w/crane ...750.00
Wall pocket, ceramic, 6 girls on open book form, 6x9x3" 137.00

Greentown Glass

Greentown glass is a term referring to the product of the Indiana Tumbler and Goblet Company of Greentown, Indiana, ca 1894 to 1903. Their earlier pressed glass patterns were #75 (originally known as #11), a pseudo-cut glass design; #137, Pleat Band; and #200, Austrian. Another line, Dewey, was designed in 1898. Many lovely colors were produced in addition to crystal. Jacob Rosenthal, who was later affiliated with Fenton, developed his famous chocolate glass in 1900. The rich, shaded opaque brown glass was an overnight success. Two new patterns, Leaf Bracket and Cactus, were designed to display the glass to its best advantage, but previously existing molds were also used. In only three years Rosenthal developed yet another important color formula, Golden Agate. The Holly pattern was designed especially for its production. The dolphin covered dish with a fish finial is perhaps the most common and easily recognized piece ever produced. Other animal dishes were also made; all are highly collectible. There have been many repros — not all are marked! The symbol (+) at the end of some of the following lines was used to indicate items that have been reproduced.

Our advisors for this category are Jerry and Sandi Garrett; they are listed in the Directory under Indiana. See the Pattern Glass section for clear pressed glass; only colored items are listed here.

Teardrop and Tassel, butter dish, cobalt, $325.00.

Animal dish, bird w/berry, Golden Agate 2,500.00
Animal dish, cat on hamper, canary, tall (+) 875.00
Animal dish, cat on hamper, chocolate, low 775.00
Animal dish, dolphin, amber, sawtooth rim (+) 825.00
Animal dish, dolphin, cobalt, beaded rim...............................1,500.00
Animal dish, fighting cocks, emerald gr............................2,000.00
Animal dish, hen, wht opaque...225.00
Animal dish, rabbit, cobalt 800.00
Animal dish, chocolate ....
Austrian, bowl, canary, 8" 325.00
Austrian, bowl, nappy; chocolate, w/lid 350.00
Austrian, butter dish, chocolate, child sz 800.00
Austrian, cake stand, canary 450.00

Austrian, rose bowl, canary, lg...325.00
Austrian, vase, Nile Green, 6"...450.00
Brazen Shield, bowl, bl, 7½"...175.00
Brazen Shield, pitcher, bl..275.00
Brazen Shield, sauce bowl, bl, 4⅜"..45.00
Brazen Shield, tumbler, bl...75.00
Cactus, bowl, chocolate, 7¼"...140.00
Cactus, butter dish, chocolate...175.00
Cactus, compote, chocolate, 7¼"...200.00
Cactus, sauce dish, chocolate, flat...125.00
Cactus, toothpick holder, chocolate (+)..65.00
Cord Drapery, bowl, cobalt, ftd, 8¼"...225.00
Cord Drapery, compote, amber, 8½"...250.00
Cord Drapery, mug, emerald gr, ftd..225.00
Cord Drapery, pitcher, amber..325.00
Cord Drapery, wine, cobalt...500.00
Cupid, butter dish, wht opaque..200.00
Cupid, creamer, Nile Green..425.00
Cupid, spooner, chocolate..350.00
Cupid, sugar bowl, chocolate, w/lid...500.00
Dewey, butter dish, cobalt..550.00
Dewey, cruet, amber, w/stopper..150.00
Dewey, plate, emerald gr..75.00
Dewey, sugar bowl, amber, w/lid, 2¼"..75.00
Dewey, tumbler, canary..85.00
Diamond Prisms, tumbler, chocolate...675.00
Early Diamond, dish, rectangular, cobalt, 8x5"...........................275.00
Early Diamond, pitcher, emerald gr...350.00
Early Diamond, tumbler, canary...275.00
Greentown Daisy, butter dish, frosted emerald gr.......................125.00
Greentown Daisy, mustard pot, chocolate, w/lid.........................275.00
Herringbone Buttress, bowl, emerald gr, 9¼"..............................425.00
Herringbone Buttress, cracker jar, emerald gr.............................475.00
Herringbone Buttress, mug, chocolate...75.00
Herringbone Buttress, vase, emerald gr, 10".................................325.00
Holly Amber, bowl, oval, ped ft..1,750.00
Holly Amber, bowl, 8½"...725.00
Holly Amber, butter dish, ped ft...3,000.00
Holly Amber, compote, w/lid, 8¼"...3,000.00
Holly Amber, creamer..850.00
Holly Amber, mug, 4" (+)..500.00
Holly Amber, sugar bowl, w/lid...1,250.00
Holly Amber, toothpick holder (+)...450.00
Leaf Bracket, bowl, chocolate, 8"..85.00
Leaf Bracket, butter dish, cobalt...1,500.00
Leaf Bracket, pitcher, chocolate..450.00
Leaf Bracket, toothpick holder, chocolate...................................350.00
Mug, indoor drinking scene, Nile Green, 5".................................165.00
Mug, outdoor drinking scene, lt cobalt..350.00
Mug, Serenade, amber..125.00
Novelty, buffalo, wht opaque, dtd 1901.......................................850.00
Novelty, Connecticut Skillet, chocolate...................................1,400.00
Novelty, hairbrush, Nile Green..900.00
Novelty, mitted hand, chocolate...1,400.00
Novelty, Scotch Thistle, Nile Green..900.00
Novelty, wheelbarrow, teal bl..225.00
Paneled, pitcher, water; chocolate...600.00
Pattern #75, bowl, emerald gr, rectangular, 8x6½".....................100.00
Pattern #75, relish tray, cobalt, 6"..175.00
Pattern #75, vase, emerald gr, 10"..100.00
Pleat Band, cordial, canary..250.00
Ruffled Eye, pitcher, water; amber or emerald gr, ea....................200.00
Scalloped Flange, tumbler, chocolate..150.00
Shuttle, tumbler, chocolate..150.00

Teardrop & Tassel, bowl, cobalt, 7¼" 200.00
Teardrop & Tassel, compote, Nile Green, 7½" 400.00
Teardrop & Tassel, salt shaker, amber............................400.00
Teardrop & Tassel, sugar bowl, wht opaque, w/lid 185.00
Toothpick holder, dog head, amber frost 325.00
Toothpick holder, picture fr, amber 275.00
Toothpick holder, sheaf of wheat, chocolate (+) 1,250.00
Toothpick holder, witch head, Nile Green (+) 300.00

Grueby

William Henry Grueby joined the firm of the Low Art Tile Works at the age of fifteen and in 1894, after several years of experience in the production of architectural tiles, founded his own plant, the Grueby Faience Company, in Boston, Massachusetts. Grueby began experimenting with the idea of producing art pottery and had soon perfected a fine glaze (soft and without gloss) in shades of blue, gray, yellow, brown, and his most successful, cucumber green. In 1900 his exhibit at the Paris Exposition Universelle won three gold medals.

Grueby pottery was hand thrown and hand decorated in the Arts and Crafts style. Vertically thrust tooled and applied leaves and flower buds were the most common decorative devices. Tiles continued to be an important product, unique (due to the matt glaze decoration) as well as durable. Grueby tiles were often a full inch thick. Many of them were decorated in cuenca, others were impressed and filled with glaze, and some were embossed. Later, when purchased by Pardee, they were decorated in cuerda seca.

Incompatible with the Art Nouveau style, the artware production ceased in 1907, but tile production continued for another decade. The ware is marked in one of several ways: 'Grueby Pottery, Boston, USA'; 'Grueby, Boston, Mass.'; or 'Grueby Faience.' The artware is often artist signed. Our advisors for this category are Suzanne Perrault and Dave Rago; they are is listed in the Directory under New Jersey.

Key: c — cuenca

Bowl, curdled bl-gray, leaves, curled edges, R Erickson, 2x6½" ..1,500.00
Bowl, gr, glossy coiled int, low, 7", from $400 to............................600.00
Bowl, leathery gr, closed-in rim, 1½x4"..700.00
Bowl, leathery gr, leaves, gloss int, W Post, 4-sided, 3½x6", EX+.3,450.00
Bowl, leathery gr w/yel & lime water lilies & pads, JE, 4x9½", NM ..47,500.00
Bowl vase, leathery gr, wide leaves between buds, glaze flecks, 6x8".5,500.00
Flowerpot, leathery gr, conical w/raised rim, mfg hole/hairlines, 3x6"..550.00
Jardiniere, feathered gr, widely spaced thin ribs, rstr/spider, 5x8" .750.00
Trivet, 5 butterflies, curdled oatmeal w/pk & gr, MD, 10½", VG..18,000.00
Vase, curdled dk gr w/wide pointed leaves, spherical, label, 4½" ..4,000.00
Vase, feathered gr, squat base w/wide leaves, long flaring neck, 7x5"..2,100.00
Vase, feathered gr, yel buds alternate w/leaves, rstr rim chips, 9x4".6,325.00
Vase, frothy gr, triangular leaves, tear form, 6¾x3¾" 4,600.00
Vase, frothy gr, 2 rows of short leaves overlap at base, WP, 13", EX .3,250.00
Vase, frothy gr w/yel, bl or burgundy daffolids (3X), LFH, 11x5"..11,000.00
Vase, frothy med-gr, wide leaves (nondimensional), rim touch-ups, 4x4" ...950.00
Vase, gr, cylinder w/tooled panels, R Erickson, 5¾x2½", NM.1,200.00
Vase, gr, lappet leaves, att ER Farrington, ca 1902, 13¾" 7,475.00
Vase, gr, leaves, squat w/long cylinder neck, WP, sm base chips, 8".2,130.00
Vase, gr, tapered, flared lip, paper label, 7" 1,250.00
Vase, gr, tooled leaves, squat, 5¾", NM 3,750.00
Vase, gr, tooled/appl leaves, bulbous, 1908, 8", NM....................925.00
Vase, gr w/broad leaves & yel trefoils, 1" hairline, 6½x3½" 6,500.00
Vase, leathery brn, ovoid w/tooled panels, 8x5" 3,500.00
Vase, leathery gr, leaves, W Post, can neck/bulbous base, 16½x10"..10,350.00
Vase, leathery gr, short/tall leaves, W Post, bbl shape, 8½x7", VG....3,500.00
Vase, leathery gr, 3 full-height leaves, ovoid, 7½x3¾", NM 2,875.00

Vase, leathery gr, 3-ridge shoulder band, squat w/sm rim, 3½x6".1,300.00
Vase, leathery gr w/lime pod-bearing stems, wide leaves, ER, 10x4"..850.00

Vase, leathery green with yellow trefoils on long stems alternating with leaves, Wilhemina Post, EX mold, perfectly fired, #188A, 18", $92,000.00. (Photo courtesy Dave Rago Auctions)

Vase, med gr, lg leaves w/curled-out tips between buds, CP, 7½x5" ..2,400.00
Vase, mottled yel, buds & leaves, bulbous, 1908, 6¼" 5,285.00
Vase, ochre, cylindrical w/bulbous base, partial label, 7", NM 800.00
Vase, pulled/feathered gr, short lg leaves between yel buds, 10½x4"..4,800.00
Vase, thick/curdled gr, lg leaves/yel buds, 3-lobe rim, 7x4", EX ...2,500.00
Vase, yel, incurvate rim, squat, 4" W..950.00

Tiles

Candlestick w/snuffer, gr/yel/brn, EX mold, 6" 10,000.00
Monk, sitting/reading/ curdled ochre matt on red clay, no mk, 6", EX..460.00
Oak tree/grass/clouds, c, 5-color, EN, 6x6½", EX 4,885.00
Oak tree/grassy/clouds, c, 3-color, LeBoutiller, 12x12"..........43,150.00
Pines, tree scenic, grs/bls/brn, HH, corner flakes, 6" 3,500.00
Ship w/sails, c, 4-color, GM, 8" 1,725.00

Gustavsberg

Gustavsberg Pottery, founded near Stockholm, Sweden, in the late 1700s, manufactured faience, creamware, and porcelain in the English taste until the end of the nineteenth century. During the twentieth century, the factory has produced some inventive modernistic designs, often signed by their artists. Wilhelm Kage (1889 – 1960) is best remembered for Argenta, a stoneware body decorated in silver overlay, introduced in the 1930s. Usually a mottled green, Argenta can also be found in cobalt blue and white. Other lines included Cintra (an exceptionally translucent porcelain), Farsta (copper-glazed ware), and Farstarust (iron oxide geometric overlay). Designer Stig Lindberg's work, which dates from the 1940s through the early 1970s, includes slab-built figures and a full range of tableware. Some pieces of Gustavsberg are dated.

Our advisors for this category are Suzanne Perrault and Dave Rago; they are listed in the Directory under New Jersey.

Bowl, Farsta, emb stars, red-brn/lt olive/ochre, Kage, 1940, 8⅝"..1,400.00
Bowl, Farsta, incised decor, yel ochre/brick red, Kage, 1952, 10"..2,295.00
Bowl, Farsta, radiating lines, red & bl, Kage, 1957, low, 8⅜" 1,070.00
Bowl, imp rows of petals, bl/amber mottle matt, W Kage, 3x12", $400 to..600.00
Bowl, Vaga, wht, ruffled rim, 1950, 2⅞x7" 200.00
Bowl, Verkstad, bl haresfur, Kage, 1950s, 1⅞x7¼" 250.00
Bud vases, ea w/fish o/l, mk, 6", 7"..515.00
Figurine, lion, Africa series, Lisa Larson, 15x16" 535.00
Vase, Argenta, silver circles & crisscross decor, Kage, 5¾x4" 500.00
Vase, Argenta, silver fish, top & bottom rim, flat sides, Kage, 5" ..510.00

Vase, Argenta, silver flower sprigs, 1935, 8x6¾"............**230.00**
Vase, Argenta, silver geometrics, anchor mk, 1932, 10¼"..........**650.00**
Vase, Argenta, silver geometrics, sq sides, 1948, 11⅜"............**1,225.00**
Vase, Argenta, silver linear decor, 4-ftd, #A47 R, 1948, 8¾".......**445.00**
Vase, Argenta, silver mermaid & top & bottom rim, 3-ftd, Kage, 8x4"..**800.00**
Vase, Argenta, silver mermaid decor, Kage, #1045, 9x8" dia ...**2,650.00**
Vase, Argenta, silver nude figures, 1930-50s, 7½"......................**800.00**
Vase, Argenta, sivlver swordfish/bubbles, pillow form, 7½", EX, $250 to ...**350.00**
Vase, bl w/emb linear decor, cylindrical, 1959, 12¼"..............**2,350.00**
Vase, dk gr, bulbous w/sm flared neck, Friberg, 3¾"...................**360.00**
Vase, dk turq w/dk bl & gray sgraffito, Lindberg, sm neck, 2½"..**390.00**
Vase, Domino, stoneware, blk on buff, ribbed, Lindberg, 3¾x3½"..**250.00**
Vase, Farsta, bl, bottle shape, Kage, 1957, 12¼"......................**1,950.00**
Vase, Farsta, bl-gray drip, ftd teardrop, Kage, 1955, 9"............**1,900.00**
Vase, Farsta, cross-hatched dmns, ftd, Kage, 1947, 4⅜"...........**1,000.00**
Vase, Farsta, emb triangles, red-brn & cream, Kage, 1950, 6"..**1,285.00**
Vase, Farsta, linear decor, lt olive to brn, Kage, 1959, 11½"....**2,500.00**
Vase, Farsta, turq drip on brn, emb ribs, Kage, #182, 1945, 5½"..**1,100.00**
Vase, gr w/yel/wht edging, sq shoulder w/sm opening, Friberg, 3½".**435.00**
Vase, pale bl w/gr/turq overshot, bulbous w/flared neck, Friberg, 4".**290.00**
Vase, Vaga, wht, ruffled rim, 1950, 4¾"..........................**200.00**
Vase, Vaga, wht, 2-neck, ruffled rims, 1950, 2⅞".................**650.00**
Vase, Verkstad, bl haresfur, bulbous, Kage, 1950s, 6¾x5¾"......**580.00**
Vase, Verkstad, bl haresfur, emb ribs, 1950s, 10¼"................**500.00**
Vase, wht w/silver o/l, Grazia #219 DN, 1945, 8"....................**215.00**
2 pcs, Argenta pen tray, 2½x10", & paper clip, from $150 to.........**250.00**
4 pcs, 3 gr: 7" vase w/fish, box w/birds, dish; +bl vase, from $400 to....**500.00**
6 pcs, set of 5 lions by L Larsson, +brn bulbous 9" vase..............**375.00**

Hadley, M.A.

Founded by artist-turned-potter Mary Alice Hadley, this Louisville, Kentucky, company has been producing handmade dinnerware and decorative items since 1940. Their work is painted freehand in a folksy style with barnyard animals, whales, sailing ships, and several other patterns. The palette is predominately blue and green. Each piece is signed with Hadley's first two initials and her last name, and her artwork continues to be the inspiration for modern designs. Among collectors, horses and other farm animals are popular subject matters. Older pieces are generally heavier and, along with the more unusual items, command the higher prices. Our advisor for this category is Lisa Sanders; she is listed in the Directory under Indiana.

Bank, bunny, 5½"...**28.00**
Bowl, basket of strawberries, 8"......................................**30.00**
Bowl, chicken, 5½"...**14.00**
Bowl, duck (lg/front view) in center int, 5x8".......................**40.00**
Butter dish, rearing horse, dome lid, 6½" dia **40.00**
Coaster, Graduation, 4"..**14.00**
Coaster, Happy New Home, 4"...**15.00**
Cup & saucer, puppy **20.00**
Drw pulls, various animals, 1¼" dia, set of 8.......................**80.00**
Mug, duck (lg/front view), flaring sides, 12-oz **18.00**
Mug, Happy Birthday, 8-oz...**28.00**
Night light, lighthouse shape, 8½"....................................**75.00**
Pitcher, frog (lg/front view), 7½x6"..................................**35.00**
Plaque, fish form, 10x6"...**25.00**
Plate, cat (lg/side view), 11"...**25.00**
Plate, cow, 11"...**25.00**
Plate, cow, 9"..**20.00**
Plate, downhill skier, 9"..**20.00**
Plate, lighthouse, 8"..**25.00**
Platter, fisherman sitting under tree, 10½"..........................**42.00**

Platter, rodeo cowboy, 8½"..**30.00**
Refrigerator magnet, fish shape, 3x3¾"..............................**14.00**
Spoon rest, pig shape, 3x5"...**14.00**
Trivet, snowman, 6"..**20.00**
Vase, cat figural, 14½"..**95.00**
Wall pocket, hen, V-shape, 8x8"......................................**50.00**

Hagen-Renaker

Best known for their line of miniature animal figures, Hagen-Renaker was founded in Monrovia, California, in 1946. It is estimated that perhaps as many as eighty different dogs were produced. In addition to the animals, they made replicas of characters from several popular Disney films under license from the Disney Studio. The firm relocated to San Dimas in 1962, where they remain active to the present time. Their wares are sometimes marked with an incised 'HR,' a stamped 'Hagen-Renaker' or part of the name, or paper labels. For more information, we recommend *The Collector's Encyclopedia of California Pottery, Second Edition*, by Jack Chipman; *Charlton Standard Catalog of Hagen-Renaker, Second Edition*; *Disneyana Collector's Guide to Californian Pottery, 1938 – 1960*, by Devin Frick and Tamara Hodge; and *Hagen-Renaker Pottery: Horses and Other Figurines* by Nancy Kelly (Schiffer). Another source of information is Hagen-Renaker Collectors Club (HRCC), listed in the Directory under Clubs, Newsletters, and Catalogs.

Bank, Lady (of Lady & the Tramp), Disney, #5071, 1956, 5½", EX ..**350.00**
Figurine, Am, Siamese from Lady & Tramp, Disney, 1950s, 1¾"..**80.00**
Figurine, Amir, stallion, rose-gray, 6" **170.00**
Figurine, Beanbag, dachshund, sitting, 2"............................**45.00**
Figurine, Choo San, Siamese cat, 10¾"...............................**55.00**
Figurine, Comella, thoroughbred mare, 1950s, 5½x8¼", EX **500.00**
Figurine, dancing frogs on lily, #3052, 1992, 3½" **35.00**
Figurine, Dumbo, elephant baby, Disney, 1950s, 1½" **60.00**
Figurine, elephant mama, #2053, discontinued, 2¾" **25.00**
Figurine, Fantail, fish, Aurasperse coloring, ⅞".....................**50.00**
Figurine, Fantail, goldfish, A-426, 1950-65, ⅞" **25.00**
Figurine, Fluffy, pup from Lady & Tramp, Disney, 1950s, ½" **25.00**
Figurine, Forever Amber, Morgan mare, B-703, 5" **150.00**
Figurine, fox, DW sticker, 9½" **175.00**
Figurine, giraffe, #3036, 1991, 3¼"...................................**35.00**

Figurines, good fairies from Sleeping Beauty, tallest: 2", $500.00 for the set. (Photo courtesy Joel Cohen)

Figurine, grizzly bear, brn matt, A-328, 1¼"................................**35.00**
Figurine, Happy Trails, rearing palomino, special run, 2000, 4½".**90.00**
Figurine, Jock, Scottie from Lady & Tramp, Disney, #5007, 1950s, 1½".**35.00**
Figurine, Khitti Kat, Siamese kitten, B-530, DW sticker, 2¼" **30.00**
Figurine, Lady, dog from Lady & Tramp, Disney, 1950s, 1½"........**25.00**
Figurine, Lippit, Morgan palomino stallion, 6" **150.00**

Figurine, Little Horrible Helping Hand, 1959 only, 2½" **75.00**
Figurine, Metalchex, quarterhorse stallion, 1982, 11½x13", EX .**400.00**
Figurine, Michael Darling (of Peter Pan), Disney, unmk, 1950s, 1"..**65.00**
Figurine, Mickey, Pomeranian, H-1535, bl label, 1956-68, 3½"....**35.00**
Figurine, Mistweaver, Thoroughbred stallion, #3273, 1998, 2⅜" ..**30.00**
Figurine, Molly, mama rabbit, brn, B-570, DW sticker, 1956, 4"...**50.00**
Figurine, Old English Sheepdog, wht w/orange tongue, 1958-72, 3½"...**50.00**
Figurine, Papa Bear, A-10, 1949-50, 2"......................................**30.00**
Figurine, Pedro, chihuahua from Lady & Tramp, Disney, 1950s, 1⅜" ..**75.00**
Figurine, Pip Emma, cocker spaniel, H-1013, 1953, 2½" **25.00**
Figurine, Sassy, tabby kitten, ca 1959-60 ....**70.00**
Figurine, Scamper, Morgan foal, wht, B-562/DW sticker, 1954-58, 3", NM...**165.00**
Figurine, Scooter, pup from Lady & Tramp, Disney, 1950s, 1" **25.00**
Figurine, Siamese, climbing cat, B-525, DW sticker, 1952-75, 6½" L .**30.00**
Figurine, Siamese cat, watching tail, B-526, 1952-54, 3", NM **55.00**
Figurine, Silver, Persian cat, B-694, DW sticker, 1958-68, 9½" ..**100.00**
Figurine, Sleepy, dwarf from Snow White, Disney, 1950s, 1¼" **75.00**
Figurine, Thunder, Morgan stallion, B-549, 1953-58, DW sticker, 5½"..**125.00**
Figurine, triceratops, adult, #3151, mid-1990s, 2⅜" **45.00**
Figurine, Trusty, Bloodhound from Lady & Tramp, Disney, 1950s, 2" .**65.00**
Figurine, unicorn, Designer series, 1980, 4x6" **60.00**
Figurine, Zilla, foal, dk-rose gray matt, Monrovia sticker, 5", EX ..**200.00**

Hagenauer

Carl Hagenauer founded his metal workshops in Vienna in 1898. He was joined by his son Karl in 1919. They produced a wide range of stylized sculptural designs in both metal and wood.

Figurine, stylized female skater, bronze, 1935, 3" **175.00**
Sculpture, horse's head, cvd wood, bronze base, orig finish, 12½"..**1,200.00**

Hair Weaving

A rather unusual craft became popular during the mid-1800s. Human hair was used to make jewelry (rings, bracelets, lockets, etc.) by braiding and interlacing fine strands into hollow forms with pearls and beads added for effect. Wreaths were also made, often using hair from deceased family members as well as the living. They were displayed in deep satin-lined frames along with mementoes of the weaver or her departed kin. The fad was abandoned before the turn of the century. The values suggested below are for mint condition examples. Any fraying of the hair greatly lowers value. For further information, we recommend *Collector's Encyclopedia of Hairwork Jewelry* by C. Jeanenne Bell (Collector Books). See also Mourning Collectibles.

Key:
p-w — palette work   t-w — table work

Brooch, brown and blond hair, table worked, with gold mounts, 1850s, 4½", $400.00.

Bracelet, open t-w, p-w clasp, sewn-on hair flowers, ca 1852 ....**675.00**
Bracelet, t-w elastic weave w/central gold compartmented plaque, 1850s...**500.00**

Bracelet, t-w flat braid w/heart-shaped drop containing hair, 1840s **395.00**
Bracelet, t-w rows (4) in 2 weaves, gold clasp (no locket), 1840-70.....**400.00**
Bracelet, t-w rows (5) in 2 weaves, gold glasp w/pk stone, 1850-80....**450.00**
Bracelet, t-w rows (7) in 2 weaves, locket clasp w/dag, 1840s **500.00**
Bracelet, 10 braided links w/gold ends, gold clasp, 7", VG **230.00**
Brooch, braid under beveled glass, pearls surround, 1837, 1½" ...**375.00**
Brooch, gold w/onyx/seed pearls, compartment in bk, 1870s, 1½x1"..**375.00**
Brooch, gold-filled revolving style w/tintype/hair, 1860s, 2⅜" **375.00**
Brooch, p-w, gold-plated brass w/flowers/tombstone, 1790-1810, 1⅝" ...**375.00**
Brooch, p-w, hair flowers/seed pearls, 1790-1830, 1¼" **750.00**
Brooch, p-w curls on milk glass, gold-filled/gold-plated, 1840s, 2"..**325.00**
Brooch, p-w flower basket (ornate) on milk glass, gold fr, 2x1⅝" ...**700.00**
Brooch, p-w hair w/in crescent shape w/seed pearls, 1840-60s, 2¼" .**800.00**
Brooch, t-w, wound pattern w/gold-plated mts, 1860s-80s, ¾x2⅛" .**165.00**
Brooch, t-w crescent w/dangles, gold-filled mts, 1850-70s, 2x1¼" ...**300.00**
Brooch, t-w oval w/in gold fr w/leaf & rope twist decor **100.00**
Brooch, t-w tubular bow w/gold mts, 1850s-70s, 2½x3" **350.00**
Brooch, woven under glass, gold-filled w/blk enamel, 1850s, 1½" ..**175.00**
Charm, t-w horseshoe w/gold-filled mts, 1860-90, ⅝x⅞" **150.00**
Earrings, t-w acorns w/gold mts, 1850-70s, 1¼x⅜", pr **375.00**
Earrings, t-w balls, 2-color, all orig, 1850-70s, 1½x½", pr **400.00**
Earrings, t-w blond acorn dangles, 1850-70s, rpl wires, 1½", pr ..**350.00**
Earrings, t-w ovoids w/gold mts, 1840-70, 1¾", pr **300.00**
Necklace, t-w, tubular, dangling cross w/gold ends, 14" **200.00**
Necklace, t-w, 3 rows in 2 weaves, 1840-60s, ¾x14" **450.00**
Necklace, t-w balls w/silk ties, gold-filled mts, 1840-60s, 16½" ..**250.00**
Necklace, t-w flat chain, gold clasp, 1840-60, ⅜x16" **275.00**
Necklace, t-w panband weave w/t-w heart, gold mts, ½x13" **550.00**
Pendant, t-w cross w/amethysts & pearls, gold mts, 1840-60s **675.00**
Pendant, t-w cross w/gold caps, EX...**100.00**
Pendant locket, gold-filled w/horse & rider, hair under glass, 2"..**400.00**
Ring, eng gold w/braid in compartment, 1830s, dainty sz...........**165.00**
Ring, gold band w/t-w insert, ca 1850-90, ⅜" **325.00**
Ring, gold mt w/hair under crystal w/pearls, Georgian, ½x¼" **425.00**
Ring, gold urn w/jet, compartment for hair, late 1700s, ½x½" **450.00**
Ring, p-w flowers on opaline on gold mt, 1790 – 1830, ¾x⅝" ...**500.00**
Stickpin, gold & enameling w/center compartment, 1840s-80s, $150 to.**200.00**

Hall

The Hall China Company of East Liverpool, Ohio, was established in 1903. Their earliest products were whiteware toilet seats, mugs, jugs, etc. By 1920 their restaurant-type dinnerware and cookingware had become so successful that Hall was assured of a solid future. They continue today to be one of the country's largest manufacturers of this type of product.

Hall introduced the first of their famous teapots in 1920; new shapes and colors were added each year until about 1948, making them the largest teapot manufacturer in the world. These and the dinnerware lines of the '30s through the '50s have become popular collectibles. For more thorough study of the subject, we recommend *The Collector's Encyclopedia of Hall China, Third Edition,* by Margaret and Kenn Whitmyer; their address may be found in the Directory under Ohio.

Blue Bouquet, baker, French; fluted..**20.00**
Blue Bouquet, bowl, cereal; D-style, 6"..**22.00**
Blue Bouquet, bowl, Radiance, 6"..**18.00**
Blue Bouquet, cake plate...**45.00**
Blue Bouquet, creamer, modern **30.00**
Blue Bouquet, custard, Thick Rim...**30.00**
Blue Bouquet, drip jar, Radiance **200.00**
Blue Bouquet, gravy boat, D-style **65.00**
Blue Bouquet, percolator, electric **700.00**
Blue Bouquet, pie baker...**70.00**

Blue Bouquet, plate, D-style, 6" 6.00
Blue Bouquet, pretzel jar 240.00
Blue Bouquet, spoon 135.00
Blue Bouquet, teapot, Boston...225.00
Cameo Rose, bowl, E-style, oval, 10½" 25.00
Cameo Rose, bowl, flat soup; E-style, 8" 14.00
Cameo Rose, creamer, E-style 11.00
Cameo Rose, gravy boat, E-style, w/underplate 32.00
Cameo Rose, plate, E-style, 9¼" 9.50
Cameo Rose, platter, E-style, oval, 13¼" 22.00
Cameo Rose, sugar bowl, E-style, w/lid 20.00
Christmas Tree & Holly, bowl, E-style, oval..........................60.00
Christmas Tree & Holly, bowl, plum pudding; E-style, 4½" 30.00
Christmas Tree & Holly, cookie jar, E-style, Zeisel 350.00
Christmas Tree & Holly, saucer, E-style 4.00
Crocus, bowl, fruit; D-style, 5½" 10.00
Crocus, bowl, salad; 9" 22.00
Crocus, bread box, metal...130.00
Crocus, coffee dispenser, metal......................................35.00
Crocus, coffeepot, Deco 850.00
Crocus, coffeepot, Waverly (Drip-O-Lator).............................75.00
Crocus, drip jar, #1188, open 47.00
Crocus, mug, tankard style 75.00
Crocus, plate, D-style, 6" 8.00
Crocus, saucer, D-style 2.50
Crocus, soup tureen, Thick Rim or Clover 300.00
Crocus, sugar bowl, w/lid, modern 30.00
Crocus, teapot, Streamline 1,800.00
Five Band, batter bowl, red or cobalt................................60.00
Five Band, jug, colors other than red or cobalt, 5" 25.00
Game Bird, ball jug, #3 ....300.00
Game Bird, bowl, E-style, oval 65.00
Game Bird, mug, Tom & Jerry 27.00
Game Bird, saucer, E-style 4.00
Golden Oak, bowl, fruit; D-style, 5¼" 5.00
Golden Oak, bowl, salad 12.00
Golden Oak, saucer, D-style 1.50
Heather Rose, bowl, fruit; 5¼" 5.00
Heather Rose, cake plate 18.00
Heather Rose, gravy boat & underplate 32.00
Heather Rose, teapot, New York......................................135.00
Homewood, bowl, flat soup; S-style, 8½" 14.00
Homewood, bowl, Radiance, 6" 16.00
Homewood, teapot, New York...175.00
Medallion, bowl, Lettuce, #4, 7¼" 16.00
Medallion, reamer, Chinese Red......................................500.00
Mums, bowl, D-style, rnd, 9¼" 45.00
Mums, casserole, Medallion 50.00
Mums, creamer, Medallion 25.00
Mums, jug, Simplicity..220.00
Mums, platter, D-style, oval, 11¼" 35.00

Mums, pretzel jar, $225.00. (Photo courtesy Margaret and Kenn Whitmyer)

Mums, shaker, w/hdl, ea 25.00
Mums, teapot, New York..200.00
No 488, bowl, flat soup; D-style, 8½" 35.00
No 488, bowl, Radiance, 10" 50.00
No 488, bowl, salad; 9" 40.00
No 488, casserole, Five Band 75.00
No 488, creamer, Meltdown 32.00
No 488, drip jar, Medallion, w/lid 45.00
No 488, jug, Simplicity 300.00
No 488, plate, D-style, 7" 12.00
No 488, punch bowl, Tom & Jerry 950.00
No 488, sugar bowl, New York, w/lid 50.00
Orange Poppy, ball jug, #3 ....125.00
Orange Poppy, bowl, cereal; C-style, 6" 25.00
Orange Poppy, bowl, salad; 9" 20.00
Orange Poppy, casserole, #76, rnd....................................40.00
Orange Poppy, condiment jar, Radiance..............................900.00
Orange Poppy, drip jar, Radiance, w/lid 35.00
Orange Poppy, match safe, metal 100.00
Orange Poppy, pie baker 55.00
Orange Poppy, plate, C-style, 9" 30.00
Orange Poppy, teapot, Bellevue, 2-cup.............................1,800.00
Orange Poppy, teapot, Streamline 350.00
Orange Poppy, wastebasket, metal 100.00
Pastel Morning Glory, ball jug, #3 or #4.............................210.00
Pastel Morning Glory, bowl, fruit; D-style, 5½" 7.50
Pastel Morning Glory, bowl, Radiance, 9" 40.00
Pastel Morning Glory, coffeepot, Terrace 125.00
Pastel Morning Glory, condiment jar, Radiance 250.00
Pastel Morning Glory, drip jar, #1188, open..........................45.00
Pastel Morning Glory, jug, Donut....................................350.00
Pastel Morning Glory, plate, D-style, 6" 5.00
Pastel Morning Glory, pretzel jar 225.00
Pastel Morning Glory, sugar bowl, Art Deco, w/lid...................35.00
Pastel Morning Glory, tea tile 120.00
Pastel Morning Glory, teapot, Boston................................300.00
Prairie Grass, bowl, cereal; 6¼" 10.00
Prairie Grass, cup 8.00
Prairie Grass, tidbit, 3-tier...75.00
Primrose, ashtray..10.00
Primrose, cup 7.00
Primrose, plate, 6½" 3.50
Primrose, sugar bowl, w/lid...16.00
Radiance, bowl, red or cobalt, #2, 5¼" 18.00
Radiance, casserole, ivory..25.00
Red Poppy, baker, French, fluted.....................................26.00
Red Poppy, bowl, fruit; D-style, 5½" 9.00
Red Poppy, bowl, Radiance, 7½" 22.00
Red Poppy, cake safe, metal, w/gold trim............................65.00
Red Poppy, coffeepot, Daniel 62.00
Red Poppy, custard..20.00
Red Poppy, drip jar, Radiance, w/lid 37.00
Red Poppy, leftover, sq 250.00
Red Poppy, mixer cover, plastic......................................45.00
Red Poppy, napkin, linen 25.00
Red Poppy, saucer, D-style 3.00
Red Poppy, shakers, hdls, ea 22.00
Red Poppy, teapot, Aladdin 155.00
Red Poppy, tray, metal, rectangular 50.00
Red Poppy, tumbler, clear glass 40.00
Red Poppy, wax paper dispenser, metal..............................125.00
Ribbed, bowl, salad; Russet, 9¾"......................................22.00
Ribbed, onion soup, Chinese Red, w/lid 45.00
Sear's Arlington, bowl, fruit; 5¼" 4.50

Sear's Arlington, sugar bowl, w/lid................16.00
Sear's Fairfax, creamer 8.00
Sear's Fairfax, plate, 7¼" 5.50
Sear's Fairfax, saucer 2.00
Sear's Monticello, bowl, cereal; 6¼" 9.00
Sear's Monticello, plate, 9¼"....................9.00
Sear's Mount Vernon, bowl, fruit; 5¼" 6.00
Sear's Mount Vernon, cup 7.00
Sear's Mount Vernon, saucer 2.00
Sear's Richmond/Brown-Eyed Susan, bowl, fruit; 5¾"....4.50
Sear's Richmond/Brown-Eyed Susan, gravy boat & underplate.....25.00
Sear's Richmond/Brown-Eyed Susan, saucer...........1.50
Serenade, bowl, cup, D-style 9.00
Serenade, bowl, Radiance, 9" 20.00
Serenade, bowl, salad; 9" 16.00
Serenade, fork..................................125.00
Silhouette, bowl, flat soup; D-style, 8½" 20.00
Silhouette, bread box, metal 75.00
Silhouette, casserole, Medallion....................40.00
Silhouette, custard, Medallion 27.00
Silhouette, drip coffeepot, Kadota, all china..........250.00
Silhouette, jug, Simplicity........................150.00
Silhouette, saucer, D-style 2.50
Silhouette, sugar bowl, Medallion, w/lid............25.00
Silhouette, tea tile, 6" 95.00
Silhouette, waffle iron 150.00
Springtime, bowl, D-style, oval....................22.00
Springtime, cake plate 16.00
Springtime, platter, D-style, oval, 13¼" 32.00
Springtime, teapot, French........................85.00
Sundial, batter jug, red or cobalt 210.00
Sundial, teapot, Art Glaze colors, 6-cup............275.00
Tab-Handled, bean pot, Chinese Red, tab hdls........110.00
Tab-Handled, drip jar, Cadet......................12.00
Teapot, Airflow, Black Satin, from $80 to............90.00
Teapot, Airflow, Canary, standard gold, from $60 to......65.00
Teapot, Aladdin, Blue Turquoise, standard gold, from $100 to ...125.00
Teapot, Aladdin, Maroon, from $75 to..............85.00
Teapot, Albany, Chinese Red, from $225 to 250.00
Teapot, Albany, Mahogany, standard gold, from $45 to.........55.00
Teapot, Automobile, Delphinium or Dresden, standard decor, from $500 to...550.00
Teapot, Baltimore, Emerald, no gold, from $65 to 75.00
Teapot, Basket, Cobalt, no decor, from $225 to..........245.00
Teapot, Basketball, Maroon, Turquoise, Warm Yellow, from $450 to..500.00
Teapot, Bellevue, common solid colors, 6- or 10-cup, from $45 to ..55.00
Teapot, Birdcage, Maroon, no decor, from $300 to..........350.00
Teapot, Boston, Cadet or Rose, no gold, 1- to 3-cup, from $30 to ...35.00
Teapot, Cleveland, Emerald, standard gold, from $70 to 80.00
Teapot, Cleveland, Turquoise or Warm Yellow, standard gold, $75 to ..85.00
Teapot, Danielle, Maroon, from $185 to 200.00

Teapot, Donut, Cadet, Canary or Delphinium, no decor, from $300 to.....350.00
Teapot, Football, Black, Cadet or Canary, standard decor, from $500 to ...600.00
Teapot, French, Blue Turquoise, Canary or Marine, 8-cup, from $35 to..45.00
Teapot, Globe (no-drip), Camellia, Rose or Turquoise, no gold, $45 to..55.00
Teapot, Globe (reg spout), Cadet or Chartreuse, standard gold, $100 to .125.00
Teapot, Hollywood, Cadet, Canary or Chartreuse, no gold, from $40 to..50.00
Teapot, Hollywood, Chinese Red, from $185 to 225.00
Teapot, Hook Cover, Emerald or Turquoise, standard gold, from $65 to.75.00
Teapot, Lipton, French shape, from $40 to................65.00
Teapot, McCormick, wht w/gr band, 6-cup, from $45 to 55.00
Teapot, Melody, Black, standard gold, from $125 to.................155.00
Teapot, Melody, Emerald, no gold, from $200 to 225.00
Teapot, Moderne, Chinese or Indian Red, solid color, from $125 to.145.00
Teapot, Nautilus, Cobalt, no gold, from $300 to............350.00
Teapot, New York, Marine, Maroon or Canary, standard gold, from $35 to.40.00
Teapot, Newport, Pink, no gold, from $45 to 55.00
Teapot, Parade, Marine, Maroon or Turquoise, standard gold, $60 to..70.00
Teapot, Philadelphia, Dresden or Emerald, no gold, 1- to 4-cup, $40 to..45.00
Teapot, Reagan, from $100 to 125.00
Teapot, Rhythm, Cadet, Maroon or Turquoise, no gold, from $120 to..140.00
Teapot, Sherlock Holmes, from $200 to 225.00
Teapot, Star, Cadet, Delphinium or Pink, standard gold, from $110 to .125.00
Teapot, Streamline or Cobalt, no gold, from $110 to 125.00
Teapot, Sundial, Cobalt, Dresden or Emerald, standard gold, $85 to .95.00
Teapot, Surfside, Delphinium or Dresden, standard gold, from $180 to..200.00
Teapot, Teamaster, Cadet, Canary, or Warm Yellow, gold decor, $100 to..120.00
Teapot, Windshield, Cadet, Dresden or Turquoise, standard gold, $50 to..55.00
Tulip, bowl, D-style, rnd, 9¼" 35.00
Tulip, bowl, Radiance, 9" 30.00
Tulip, canister set, metal, 4-pc....................120.00
Tulip, casserole, Radiance........................45.00
Tulip, custard, Thick Rim.........................20.00
Tulip, plate, D-style, 9".........................13.00
Wildfire, bowl, cereal; D-style, 6" 13.00
Wildfire, casserole, partially bl, str sides, 6"..........22.00
Wildfire, coffee dispenser, metal 30.00
Wildfire, gravy boat, D-style 25.00
Wildfire, teapot, Streamline.......................600.00
Yellow Rose, bowl, Radiance, 6" 16.00
Yellow Rose, bowl, salad; 9" 27.00
Yellow Rose, bowl, vegetable; D-style, rnd, 9¼" 35.00
Yellow Rose, creamer, Norse 22.00

Zeisel Designs, Hallcraft

Century Fern, ashtray 8.00
Century Fern, ladle 22.00
Century Fern, shakers, ea 15.00
Century Garden of Eden, bowl, fruit; 5¾"............7.00
Century Garden of Eden, casserole..................55.00
Century Sunglow, bowl, vegetable; 10½" 27.00
Century Sunglow, teapot, 6-cup....................195.00
Tomorrow's Classic Arizona, ashtray 9.00
Tomorrow's Classic Arizona, casserole, 8"............40.00
Tomorrow's Classic Arizona, vase 75.00
Tomorrow's Classic Bouquet, ashtray 13.00
Tomorrow's Classic Bouquet, gravy boat.............45.00
Tomorrow's Classic Bouquet, jug, 1¼-qt.............35.00
Tomorrow's Classic Bouquet, vinegar bottle 95.00
Tomorrow's Classic Buckingham, bowl, celery; oval 24.00
Tomorrow's Classic Buckingham, creamer, AD 16.00
Tomorrow's Classic Buckingham, vinegar bottle 95.00
Tomorrow's Classic Caprice, bowl, fruit; 5¾" 7.00
Tomorrow's Classic Caprice, candlestick, 8" 40.00

Teapot, Donut, Blue Garden, from $1,200.00 to $1,400.00. (Photo courtesy Margaret and Kenn Whitmyer)

Tomorrow's Classic Caprice, vinegar bottle 75.00
Tomorrow's Classic Dawn, butter dish 190.00
Tomorrow's Classic Dawn, plate, 11" 14.00
Tomorrow's Classic Fantasy, bowl, coupe soup; 9" 10.00
Tomorrow's Classic Fantasy, egg cup 47.00
Tomorrow's Classic Fantasy, teapot, 6-cup 195.00
Tomorrow's Classic Flair, ashtray 10.00
Tomorrow's Classic Flair, platter, 15" 37.00
Tomorrow's Classic Frost Flowers, ashtray 9.00
Tomorrow's Classic Frost Flowers, butter dish 160.00
Tomorrow's Classic Frost Flowers, egg cup 47.00
Tomorrow's Classic Frost Flowers, plate, 6" 5.50
Tomorrow's Classic Harlequin, casserole, 2-qt 65.00
Tomorrow's Classic Harlequin, coffepot, 6-cup 120.00
Tomorrow's Classic Harlequin, teapot, Thorley 300.00
Tomorrow's Classic Holiday, ashtray 11.50
Tomorrow's Classic Holiday, cup 11.00
Tomorrow's Classic Holiday, ladle 22.00
Tomorrow's Classic Holiday, vase 90.00
Tomorrow's Classic Lyric, bowl, cereal; 6" 7.00
Tomorrow's Classic Lyric, creamer 13.00
Tomorrow's Classic Lyric, gravy boat 40.00
Tomorrow's Classic Lyric, vase 75.00
Tomorrow's Classic Mulberry, candlestick, 4½" 32.00
Tomorrow's Classic Mulberry, plate, 6" 6.00
Tomorrow's Classic Mulberry, vinegar bottle 80.00
Tomorrow's Classic Peach Blossom, ashtray 9.00
Tomorrow's Classic Peach Blossom, bowl, fruit; E-style, 5¼" 6.50
Tomorrow's Classic Peach Blossom, coffeepot, 6-cup 105.00
Tomorrow's Classic Peach Blossom, plate, 11" 13.00
Tomorrow's Classic Pinecone, ashtray 9.00
Tomorrow's Classic Pinecone, candlestick, 8" 40.00
Tomorrow's Classic Pinecone, cup, E-style 11.00
Tomorrow's Classic Pinecone, gravy boat 35.00
Tomorrow's Classic Pinecone, platter, E-style, 11¼" 25.00
Tomorrow's Classic Pinecone, platter, 17" 38.00
Tomorrow's Classic Satin Black/Hi-White, bowl, coupe soup; 9"..16.00
Tomorrow's Classic Satin Black/Hi-White, marmite, w/lid............37.00
Tomorrow's Classic Spring/Studio 10, bowl, fruit; 5¾" 6.50
Tomorrow's Classic Spring/Studio 10, creamer 13.00
Tomorrow's Classic Spring/Studio 10, jug, 1¼-qt..................28.00
Tomorrow's Classic Spring/Studio 10, sugar bowl, w/lid 22.00

Hallmark

Hallmark introduced a line of artplas (molded plastic) ornaments in 1973 which quickly became popular with collectors. The Hallmark Keepsake Ornament Collectors Club was organized in 1987 and offered exclusive limited edition ornaments to club members only. Hallmark has produced miniature ornaments since 1988 and added a line of Easter (now known as Spring) ornaments beginning in 1991. All these ornaments are very collectible.

Our advice for this category is from the Baggage Car; you will find them listed in the Directory under Iowa. Values are for ornaments in mint condition and with their original boxes.

1973, HXD110-2, Betsy Clark, 1st edition, glass ball, dtd............125.00
1973, XHD103-5, Elves, glass ball, MIB..................................99.00
1974, QX100-1, Mrs Santa, yarn..................................24.50
1974, QX109-1, Charmers, glass ball, dtd 55.00
1975, QX133-1, Betsy Clark, 3rd edition, glass ball, dtd 75.00
1975, QX161-1, Drummer Boy, handcrafted 300.00
1975, QX166-1, Norman Rockwell, satin ball 65.00

1976, QX178-1, Tree Treats, Reindeer, handcrafted, dtd, MIB ...150.00
1976, QX197-1, Currier & Ives, glass ball, dtd, MIB 50.00
1976, QX203-1, Bicentennial '76 Commemorative, satin ball, dtd ..75.00
1977, QX153-5, Charmers, satin ball, dtd, MIB 65.00
1977, QX312-2, Drummer Boy, acrylic, Holiday Highlights..........75.00
1978, QX146-3, Carousel, 1st edition, handcrafted, dtd, MIB 395.00
1979, QX130-7, Angel Delight, handcrafted 95.00
1979, QX1419, Snoopy & Friends, 1st edition, panorama ball, MIB.....165.00
1979, QX302-7, Christmas Tree, acrylic, Holiday Highlights, dtd...80.00
1980, QX140-1, Caroling Bear, handcrafted, dtd 175.00
1980, QX352-1, Dove, handcrafted, dtd 350.00
1981, QX408-2, Clothespin Drummer Boy, handcrafted 45.00
1981, QX504-2, 25th Christmas Together, acrylic, dtd..................29.50
1982, QX455-3, Baby's First Christmas, handcrafted, dtd............50.00
1982, QX494-6, Embroidered Tree, fabric 40.00
1983, QX432-9, First Christmas Together, brass locket, dtd.........40.00
1983, QX440-1, Betsy Clark, porc 35.00
1984, QLX707-1, Brass Carousel, brass, lighted, MIB..................95.00
1985, QX470-5, Candy Apple Mouse, dtd 65.00
1985, QX482-2, Frosty Friends, Kayak, dtd 75.00
1986, QX4243, Acorn Inn 32.50
1987, QX473-7, Crayola Mice, Bright Xmas Dreams, dtd 87.50
1989, QLX7342, First Christmas Together, lighted 47.50
1989, QX4492, Baby's 1st Bear, dtd, MIB 70.00
1989, QX4545, Mary's Angels, Bluebell, 2nd in series 125.00
1990, QX4426, Cinnamon Bear w/Christmas Tree, 8th in series ..35.00
1990, QLX7246, Baby's 1st Christmas, light & motion 75.00
1991, QLX7249, Bringing Home the Tree, light & motion, dtd ...65.00
1992, QX467-4, Dad, handcrafted, dtd..................................22.50

Halloween

Though the origin of Halloween is steeped in pagan rites and superstitions, today it is strictly a fun time, and Halloween items are fun to collect. Pumpkin-head candy containers of papier-mache or pressed cardboard, noisemakers, postcards with black cats and witches, costumes, and decorations are only a sampling of the variety available.

Here's how you can determine the origin of your jack-o'-lantern:

American
1940 – 1950s

German
1900 – 1930s

— items are larger
— made of egg-carton material
— bottom and body are one piece

— items are generally small
— made of cardboard or composition
— always has a cut-out triangular nose; simple, crisscross lines in mouth; blue rings in eyes
— have attached cardboard bottoms

For further information we recommend *More Halloween Collectibles, Anthropomorphic Vegetables and Fruits of Halloween*, by Pamela E. Apkaria Russell (Schiffer). Other good reference books are *Halloween in America* by Stuart Schneider, and *Halloween Collectables* by Dan and Pauline Campanelli.

Our advisor for this category is Jenny Tarrant; she is listed in the Directory under Missouri. See Clubs, Catalogs, and Newsletters for information concerning *Trick or Treat Trader*, a quarterly newsletter. Unless noted otherwise, values are for examples in excellent to near mint condition except for paper items, in which case assume the condition to be near mint to mint.

American

Most American items were made during the 1940s and 1950s, though a few date from the 1930s as well. Lanterns are constructed either of flat cardboard or the pressed cardboard pulp used to make the jack-o-lantern shown on the left.

Jack-o'-lantern, pressed cb pulp w/orig face, 4" 95.00
Jack-o'-lantern, pressed cb pulp w/orig face, 4½" 110.00
Jack-o'-lantern, pressed cb pulp w/orig face, 5" 115.00
Jack-o'-lantern, pressed cb pulp w/orig face, 5½" 125.00
Jack-o'-lantern, pressed cb pulp w/orig face, 6" 130.00
Jack-o'-lantern, pressed cb pulp w/orig face, 6½" 135.00
Jack-o'-lantern, pressed cb pulp w/orig face, 7" 150.00
Jack-o'-lantern, pressed cb pulp w/orig face, 8", minimum value ..175.00
Lantern, cat, pressed cb pulp w/orig face 155.00
Lantern, cat (full body), pressed cb pulp, 7x6½" 350.00
Lantern, cb w/tab sides, any 75.00
Lantern, pumpkin man (full body), pressed cb pulp 350.00
Plastic Halloween car 250.00
Plastic pumpkin stagecoach, witch & cat 450.00
Plastic witch holding blk cat w/wobbling head, 7" 150.00
Plastic witch on rocket, upright, 7" 250.00
Plastic witch on rocket, 4" 95.00
Plastic witch on rocket, 5" 250.00
Tambourine, tin litho/paper, Ohio Art, 1930s, 6" dia 75.00
Tin noisemaker, bell style 38.00
Tin noisemaker, can shaker 38.00
Tin noisemaker, clicker..35.00
Tin noisemaker, fry pan style...55.00
Tin noisemaker, horn...55.00
Tin noisemaker, sq spinner 38.00
Tin noisemaker, tambourine, Chein 75.00
Tin noisemaker, tambourine, Kirkoff 95.00

Celluloid (German, Japanese, or American)

Blk cat, plain, M...150.00
Egg-shape house, M..400.00
Long-leg veggie rattle, M 300.00
Owl, plain, M...85.00
Owl on pumpkin, M 175.00
Owl on tree, M 200.00
Pumpkin-face man, M...350.00
Pumpkin-face pirate, M...400.00
Scarecrow, M 175.00
Witch, plain, M...175.00
Witch in auto, M...450.00
Witch in corncob car, M..450.00
Witch pulling cart w/ghost, M 400.00
Witch pulling pumpkin cart w/cat, M 400.00
Witch sitting on pumpkin, M 350.00

German

As a general rule, German Halloween collectibles date from 1900 through the early 1930s. They were made either of composition or molded cardboard, and their values are higher than American-made items. In the listings that follow, all candy containers are made of composition unless noted otherwise.

Candy container, blk cat walking, glass eyes, head removes, 3-4"..225.00
Candy container, blk cat walking, glass eyes, head removes, 5-6"..250.00
Candy container, cat, glass eyes, 4-6" 250.00
Candy container, cat, w/mohair, 5" 350.00
Candy container, cat, 3-5", from $175 to 285.00
Candy container, lemon-head man, pnt compo, 7" 575.00
Candy container, pumpkin-head man (or any vegetable), on box, 3"..175.00
Candy container, pumpkin-head man (or any vegetable), on box, 4"..185.00

Candy container, pumpkin-head man with hat, 5", $225.00. (Photo courtesy Dunbar Gallery)

Candy container, pumpkin-head man (or any vegetable), on box, 6" ...275.00
Candy container, witch, pumpkin people, devil, ghost, etc, 3"..225.00
Candy container, witch, pumpkin people, devil, ghost, etc, 4"..250.00
Candy container, witch, pumpkin people, devil, ghost, etc, 5"..275.00
Candy container, witch, pumpkin people, devil, ghost, etc, 6"..300.00
Candy container, witch or pumpkin man, head removes, 4".......225.00
Candy container, witch or pumpkin man, head removes, 5".......250.00
Candy container, witch or pumpkin man, head removes, 6".......300.00
Candy container, witch or pumpkin man, head removes, 7".......350.00
Diecut, bat, emb cb, from $95 to 125.00
Diecut, cat, emb cb, from $55 to...95.00
Diecut, devil, emb cb, from $95 to 150.00
Diecut, jack-o'-lantern, emb cb...65.00
Diecut, pumpkin man or lady, emb cb, 7½" 125.00
Jack-o'-lantern, compo w/orig insert, 3" 225.00
Jack-o'-lantern, compo w/orig insert, 3½"...................................250.00
Jack-o'-lantern, compo w/orig insert, 4" 250.00
Jack-o'-lantern, compo w/orig insert, 4½"...................................275.00
Jack-o'-lantern, compo w/orig isnert, 5" 350.00
Jack-o'-lantern, molded cb w/orig insert, 3" 95.00
Jack-o'-lantern, molded cb w/orig insert, 3½" 100.00
Jack-o'-lantern, molded cb w/orig insert, 4" 125.00
Jack-o'-lantern, molded cb w/orig insert, 4½" 140.00
Jack-o'-lantern, molded cb w/orig insert, 5" 155.00
Jack-o'-lantern, molded cb w/orig insert, 5½" 175.00
Jack-o'-lantern, molded cb w/orig insert, 6" 185.00
Jack-o'-lantern, molded cb w/orig insert, 6½", minimum value ..200.00
Lantern, cat, cb, molded nose, bow under chin, 3-5", from $275 to..375.00
Lantern, cat, cb, simple rnd style...225.00
Lantern (ghost, skull, devil, witch, etc), molded cb, 3-4", minimum ...300.00
Lantern (ghost, skull, devil, witch, etc), molded cb, 5"+, minimum 350.00

Lantern (skull, devil, witch, etc), compo, 3", minimum value **375.00**
Lantern (skull, devil, witch, etc), compo, 4", minimum value **400.00**
Lantern (skull, devil, witch, etc), compo, 5", minimum value **450.00**
Noisemaker, cat (3-D) on wood rachet..**95.00**
Noisemaker, cb figure (flat) on rachet **95.00**
Noisemaker, db paddle w/diecut face **95.00**
Noisemaker, devil (3-D) on wood rachet **95.00**
Noisemaker, pumpkin head (3-D) on wood rachet **95.00**
Noisemaker, tin frying pan paddle, 5" L **125.00**
Noisemaker, tin horn, 3" **75.00**
Noisemaker, veggie (3-D) horn (w/pnt face) **125.00**
Noisemaker, veggie or fruit (3-D) horn (no face), ea...................**65.00**
Noisemaker, witch (3-D) on wood rachet **95.00**
Noisemaker, wood & paper tambourine **150.00**

Hampshire

The Hampshire Pottery Company was established in 1871 in Keene, New Hampshire, by James Scollay Taft. Their earliest products were redware and stoneware utility items such as jugs, churns, crocks, and flowerpots. In 1878 they produced majolica ware which met with such success that they began to experiment with the idea of manufacturing art pottery. By 1883 they had developed a Royal Worcester type of finish which they applied to vases, tea sets, powder boxes, and cookie jars. It was also utilized for souvenir items that were decorated with transfer designs prepared from photographic plates.

Cadmon Robertson, brother-in-law of Taft, joined the company in 1904 and was responsible for developing their famous matt glazes. Colors included shades of green, brown, red, and blue. Early examples were of earthenware, but eventually the body was changed to semiporcelain. Some of his designs were marked with an M in a circle as a tribute to his wife, Emoretta. Robertson died in 1914, leaving a void impossible to fill. Taft sold the business in 1916 to George Morton, who continued to use the matt glazes that Robertson had developed. After a temporary halt in production during WWI, Morton returned to Keene and re-equipped the factory with the machinery needed to manufacture hotel china and floor tile. Because of the expense involved in transporting coal to fire the kilns, Morton found he could not compete with potteries of Ohio and New Jersey who were able to utilize locally available natural gas. He was forced to close the plant in 1923.

Interest is highest in examples with the curdled, two-tone matt glazes, and it is the glaze, not the size or form, that dictates value. The souvenir pieces are not particularly of high quality and tend to be passed over by today's collectors. Our advisors for this category are Suzanne Perrault and David Rago; they are listed in the Directory under New Jersey.

Bowl, dk gr matt w/artichoke overlapping leaves, 2¾x4½".........**440.00**
Ewer, gr matt, slim neck, flattened spherical body, 6½x6" **200.00**
Lamp base, gr matt, buds/leaves, 11", orig hdw, wicker shade ..**1,265.00**
Lamp base, gr matt, 5 repeating tulips, bulb, #0015, 11" **925.00**
Pitcher, brn w/Art Nouveau motif, EX, from $75 to....................**125.00**
Pitcher, gr matt, scroll hdl, 12", VG, +(EX) 5½" mug, from $200 to..**300.00**
Tankard, gr matt, emb rings, scroll hdls, 2 rstrs, 9x5", from $200 to..**300.00**
Vase, bl & gr matt, tapered cylinder, #38, 8"................................**650.00**
Vase, bl & rose mottled matt, slightly shouldered, #1813, 7x4½"..**650.00**
Vase, bl volcanic matt w/tan veining, brn/gr blended rim, 5¼"....**660.00**
Vase, bl/rose mottled matt, leaves, squat w/tall neck, 10x7", EX- ...**690.00**
Vase, blk matt w/red-brn mottle, faint shoulder, 7x4½" **385.00**
Vase, cerulean bl & sea gr, emb Deco sqs, #59, 5¼x5½".............**660.00**
Vase, cerulean bl w/pk & ivory mottling, shouldered, 9½x8" ..**1,750.00**
Vase, cucumber gr matt w/dk veins, bulbous, 8¾x7" **770.00**
Vase, feathered bl/gr, 4x5"...**550.00**
Vase, frothy gr matt, 3 panels w/leaves, ovoid, #157, 6¾", EX....**400.00**

Vase, gr frothy matt, 3 leafy panels, #157, 6¾" **350.00**
Vase, gr matt, dandelions w/long stems, jagged leaves, 6x5¼"....**600.00**
Vase, gr matt, ears of corn, bulbous, 5¾", EX..............................**550.00**
Vase, gr matt, incised linear/scroll band, ca 1910, 2¾x4½" **700.00**
Vase, gr matt, incised water lilies, W King, 2¼x5½" **770.00**
Vase, gr matt, lily pads, stems encircle trumpet form, 87/M, 15"..**1,380.00**
Vase, gr matt, raspberries & branch, #125, 3¾x3¼"....................**500.00**
Vase, gr matt, tulips w/long stems, shouldered, rpr, 15¼x8½" .**1,750.00**
Vase, gr matt, upright ear of corn/leaves, glaze bubbles, 5¾" **475.00**
Vase, gr matt, water lilies & leaves, C Robertson, ca 110, 7x5½"..**635.00**
Vase, gr mottled matt, elongated ovoid, C Robertson, #38, 7½" ...**575.00**

Vase, leathery green and blue matt, marked and numbered, 8¾x9¾", **$2,645.00**. (Photo courtesy Dave Rago Auctions)

Vase, midnight blk w/gunmetal sheen, bulbous, 8½x6¼" **440.00**
Vase, red-brn mottle on midnight bl, navy int, paneled, 4½x3¼"..**715.00**
2 pcs, ea gr matt: 7" chamberstick (EX) & 4" vase emb w/rnd panels....**375.00**

Handel

Philip Handel was best known for the art glass lamps he produced at the turn of the century. His work is similar to the Tiffany lamps of the same era. Handel made gas and electric lamps with both leaded glass and reverse-painted shades. Chipped ice shades with a texture similar to overshot glass were also produced. Shades signed by artists such as Bailey, Palme, and Parlow are highly valued.

Teroma lamp shades were created from clear blown glass blanks that were painted on the interior (reverse painted), while Teroma art glass (the decorative vases, humidors, etc. in the Handel Ware line) is painted on the exterior. This type of glassware has a 'chipped ice' effect achieved by sand blasting and coating the surface with fish glue. The piece is kiln fired at 800 degrees F. The contraction of the glue during the cooling process gives the glass a frosted, textured effect. Some shades are sand-finished, adding texture and depth.

Both the glassware and chinaware decorated by Handel are rare and command high prices on today's market. Many of Handel's chinaware blanks were supplied by Limoges.

Key: chp — chipped/lightly sanded

Handel Ware

Unless noted china, all items in the following listing are glass.

Candlesticks, HP windmill scene, inv't trumpet shape, 8", pr..**1,450.00**
Humidor, Indian chiefs on front & lid, brn/gr cylinder body, mk, 6"....**700.00**
Vase, gr mosserine, concave cylinder, 10½" **560.00**
Vase, Teroma, birch trees, sgn Bedigie/#4222, corseted, 8" **1,200.00**
Vase, Teroma, palm trees, sgn Bedigie/#4214, petal top, ped ft, 10" ...**1,680.00**
Vase, Teroma, trees/flying birds, #4216, shouldered, ped ft, 11" .**1,800.00**
Vase, Teroma, trees/mtns, sgn Broggi, shouldered, 7½" **1,300.00**
Vase, Teroma, woodland, sgn Gubisch/#4220, shouldered, 8x4" ...**1,300.00**

Lamps

Base only, elephant-ft style w/dk brn & gr patina, orig font, 20" ...**900.00**
Base only, stem w/emb vines, brn patina, mk, 15" **290.00**
Base only, urn shape w/molded panels, 3-socket, bronze patina, 23"...**500.00**
Boudoir, HP 13" lake scene shade #6850; sgn oval base w/dk patina .**2,800.00**
Boudoir, HP 7" shade w/floral sprigs on yel-orange to plum; 13" .**1,600.00**
Boudoir, lily-form shade w/naturalistic stem, 1-light, 13" **460.00**
Boudoir, molded 7" shade w/HP florals, sgn KW/#6704, gilt sgn std ..**2,000.00**
Boudoir, rvpt 7" flaring floral shade; tan-washed ivory-pnt base, 13" .**1,100.00**
Boudoir, rvpt 7" flower-basket shade w/shaped rim; swollen std.**1,400.00**
Boudoir, rvpt 7" rose stems/butterflies bowl shade; gold ribbed std.**16,800.00**
Chandelier, cast brass sq mt w/5 pendant slag glass & o/l 6" shades..**5,465.00**
Desk, caramel glass globe w/in geometric o/l; curved arm adjusts...**1,450.00**
Desk, HP tan swirls on etched opal ½-cylinder; 4-sided grooved base .**1,200.00**
Desk, HP 10" gr shade w/yel geometrics; bronzed metal std, 10"..**900.00**
Desk, HP 8" pine needle brn cylinder shade; textured brass-tone base.**780.00**
Desk, ldgl 5" floral shade; bronzed foliate std, 13" **650.00**
Desk, o/l 6" bell shade w/gridwork; base adjusts, 15" **1,340.00**
Desk, rvpt 8" cylinder shade w/woodland scene; shoe-form base .**2,200.00**
Floor, o/l 24" 8-sided shade w/palm trees; bronze std, 67" **6,500.00**
Floor, rvpt 10" scenic shade; simple harp std, 57" **6,150.00**
Floor, 10" alligatored orange irid shade w/wht int; mk harp std, 58" ..**2,645.00**
Hanging, HP 10" ball shade w/trees & birds sgn Bedigie, ceiling mt .**3,000.00**
Piano, ldgl 6" brickwork pendant shade; fluted base & curved arm ..**1,800.00**
Sconce, HP 5½x4½" narcissus shade; simple wall mt, pr........**1,500.00**
Shade, o/l 2-color 8-panel w/pnt oak leaves, 23" **5,000.00**
Shade, o/l 9-panel w/tropical trees, 20" **7,475.00**
Table, dbl arms w/hanging gr-over-caramel shades, 21x21"......**2,900.00**
Table, Goodnight Owls on globe, Many a Time (owl) on hdld base, 7" .**1,900.00**
Table, HP 18" sponged shade w/floral border; slender Arts & Crafts std..**4,200.00**
Table, HP 18" trees/mtns textured shade; brn leaf/bud EX std #979664 .**2,400.00**
Table, HP/rvpt 17" dk woodland scene on red; pear-form emb #929664 std.**9,000.00**
Table, ldgl 12" lily (multipetaled) shade; leafy base w/1 glass bud ..**1,230.00**
Table, ldgl 15½" floral shade; floriform bronzed metal std, 20" **2,300.00**
Table, ldgl 18" dome shade w/fruit baskets on tilework (EX); mk base.**1,380.00**
Table, ldgl 2 6" lily (multipetaled) shades; 2-arm std w/faux rivets ..**1,450.00**
Table, ldgl 20" tilework shade (EX); gr matt organic pottery base..**5,750.00**
Table, ldgl 20" tilework shade w/wide floral apron; bulbous std, VG .**2,500.00**
Table, ldgl 22" brickwork shade w/vines & flowers; 5-socket base ..**8,000.00**
Table, ldgl 22" floral shade w/irregular border; sgn organic std..**14,000.00**
Table, ldgl 24" multi-panel gr shade w/pk dmns inset at rim; urn base.**4,480.00**
Table, mushroom 12" gr shade w/HP 'lead lines' & cherries; gilt base .**865.00**
Table, o/l 15" 7-panel shade w/delicate vines & roses; sgn std, 21" .**3,600.00**
Table, o/l 18" bent-panel shade w/simple pattern; sgn base......**1,200.00**
Table, o/l 18" shade, ivory w/wide gr border & leaf pattern; 24"..**3,600.00**
Table, o/l 18" 7-panel shade w/cattails; bronze std, 23" **4,800.00**
Table, o/l 20" curved panel shade w/bamboo; vasiform hdld std/rtcl ft..**6,150.00**
Table, o/l 20" geometric-tile shade w/grapevines; bronze std....**1,950.00**
Table, rtcl brass-finish metal 12" shade; prisms on stem of ftd base .**1,000.00**
Table, rvpt 17" hex shade w/vine & berry border; textured gr/brn base..**4,400.00**
Table, rvpt 18" birch trees/stream shade; fluted column/rtcl base, 23".**5,300.00**
Table, rvpt 18" butterflies/floral shade; bottle std on rtcl vine ft..**16,200.00**
Table, rvpt 18" Columbian River scene shade; bronze-finish urn base..**8,000.00**
Table, rvpt 18" daffodils shade; vasiform base w/emb band, stepped ft..**8,100.00**
Table, rvpt 18" floral shade w/4 birds of paradise; rtcl platform ft .**16,800.00**
Table, rvpt 18" lake/trees shade; Japanesque w/etched birds & prunus .**8,950.00**
Table, rvpt 18" Olympic Rain Forest shade; bronzed vasiform base, 26"...**10,350.00**
Table, rvpt 18" parrots shade; panelled gourd on rtcl/cvd ft, 24" ..**28,000.00**
Table, rvpt 18" Persian-design shade; base w/3 stylized hdls, 25" ..**5,600.00**
Table, rvpt 18" poppies/butterfly shade; floral-emb base w/rtcl bun ft.**56,000.00**
Table, rvpt 18" ripple-glass aquarium shade; bronzed 3-D mermaid base.**64,400.00**
Table, rvpt 18" riverbed #6752 shade sgn GM; sgn lotus base, 25"..**25,200.00**
Table, rvpt 18" roses/butterfly #6688 shade; stepped std, 23" ..**16,000.00**

Table, rvpt 18" summer scene sgn shade; gold-finish base (VG), 24" ..**7,475.00**
Table, rvpt 18" sunset scene shade; tree trunk base, 24" **4,945.00**
Table, rvpt 18" Treasure Island shade; unsgn shouldered columnar std ..**11,700.00**
Table, Teroma 18" veined shade; VG ovoid base w/emb lotus & leaves ..**1,265.00**
Torchieres, rvpt 4" dia cylinder shade w/daisies; stick base, 9", pr ..**3,360.00**

Harker

The Harker Pottery was established in East Liverpool, Ohio, in 1840. Their earliest products were yellow ware and Rockingham produced from local clay. After 1900 whiteware was made from imported materials. The plant eventually grew to be a large manufacturer of dinnerware and kitchenware, employing as many as three hundred people. It closed in 1972 after it was purchased by the Jeannette Glass Company. Perhaps their best-known lines were their Cameo wares, decorated with white silhouettes in a cameo effect on contrasting solid colors. Floral silhouettes are standard, but other designs were also used. Blue and pink are the most often found background hues; a few pieces are found in yellow. For further information we recommend *The Best of Collectible Dinnerware* by Jo Cunningham (Schiffer). Our advisor for this category is Ted Haun; he is listed in the Directory under Indiana.

Amy, Spoon, $45.00; Dinner plate, $16.00; Cake lifter, $45.00.

Advertising, rolling pin, Kelvinator, w/cork, 15" **125.00**
Bamboo, bowl, vegetable; rnd, from $20 to **22.00**
Bamboo, cup...**8.00**
Bamboo, plate, dinner; from $16 to **18.00**
Bamboo, plate, salad; from $12 to **14.00**
Bouquet, plate, bread & butter; 6¼" **12.50**
Cactus Blooms, cheese plate, 11"...**42.50**
Cameo Rose, bowl, serving; bl, 8¼", from $18 to **22.00**
Cameo Rose, plate, dinner; bl, 10¼"...**16.00**
Cameo Rose, platter, bl, oval, 11"...**22.00**
Cameo Rose, rolling pin, bl, 15"...**95.00**
Chesterton, bowl, vegetable; 9" **15.00**
Chesterton, creamer **15.00**
Chesterton, plate, dinner **12.00**
Chesterton, platter, 12"...**15.00**
Chesterton, platter, 13½"...**22.00**
Chesterton, sugar bowl, w/lid **18.00**
Colonial Homestead, cup & saucer...**10.00**
Colonial Homestead, plate, salad; 7⅛".......................................**12.00**
Corinthian, snack cup & plate, 8¼"...**10.00**
Currier & Ives, cake plate, 12¼", from $15 to **20.00**
Currier & Ives, plate, dinner..**19.00**
Dogwood, plate, dinner; 10" **15.00**
Dogwood, platter, 11½x10¾"..**15.00**
Dogwood, set, service for 8, 49-pc **160.00**

Dogwood, shakers, pr..15.00
Dogwood, sugar bowl, w/lid..12.00
Gadroon, platter, lime gr, 11½"..28.00
Heritage, plate, salad..12.00
Heritance, bowl, soup..20.00
Heritance, bowl, 2-part, w/lid...32.00
Heritance, creamer & sugar bowl..12.00
Heritance, cup & saucer..20.00
Heritance, plate, bread & butter; 6"...................................14.00
Heritance, plate, dinner; 10"...24.00
Heritance, plate, luncheon; 8"...20.00
Heritance, sugar bowl, w/lid..20.00
Intaglio Wheat, bowl, serving; 8¾".....................................10.00
Intaglio Wheat, creamer & sugar bowl................................18.00
Intaglio Wheat, cup & saucer 8.00
Intaglio Wheat, plate, dinner; 10".......................................10.00
Intaglio Wheat, platter, 13x11"...18.00
Iris, cake lifter...40.00
Ivy, bowl, soup..12.00
Ivy, drippings jar...28.00
Ivy, gravy boat...16.00
Ivy, platter, 12¼"..16.00
Ivy, platter, 16"...30.00
Ivy, shakers, range sz, pr..15.00
Ivy, teapot...75.00
Laurelton, bowl, fruit/dessert..9.00
Laurelton, butter dish...32.00
Laurelton, coffeepot..55.00
Laurelton, creamer...20.00
Laurelton, cup & saucer..12.00
Laurelton, sauce boat, attached underplate 18.00
Laurelton, sauce boat, 6½"...10.00
Laurelton, shakers, pr..22.00
Magnolia, bowl, fruit/dessert; 6"..16.00
Mallow, pie baker, 9¾"..36.00
Modern Tulip, bowl, soup; 7½"...9.00
Modern Tulip, bowl, vegetable; 8¼".....................................16.00
Modern Tulip, casserole, w/lid, 8⅝".....................................36.00
Modern Tulip, cookie jar, oval..68.00
Modern Tulip, platter, 13¾"...28.00
Pate Sur Pate, bowl, vegetable; oval 18.00
Pate Sur Pate, platter, 13½"...20.00
Pate Sur Pate, sauce boat...16.00
Pate Sur Pate, shakers, pr...18.00
Persian Key, bowl, fruit/dessert 9.00
Persian Key, plate, dinner...12.00
Petit Fleurs, bowl, divided vegetable, 10½x7½" 20.00
Petit Fleurs, bowl, soup/cereal...10.00
Petit Fleurs, bowl, vegetable; rnd, 8¾"................................16.00
Petit Fleurs, bowl, vegetable; w/lid, 4x9".............................27.00
Petit Fleurs, creamer...12.00
Petit Fleurs, plate, dinner; 10"...10.00
Petit Fleurs, platter, 11⅜x9⅝"..22.00
Petit Fleurs, platter, 13¼x11⅜"..27.00
Petit Point, bowl, mixing; 9"...25.00
Petit Point, cake lifter 45.00
Petit Point, canister, paneled, 6x5¾"................................100.00
Petit Point, casserole, steam hole in lid, 8½" 40.00
Petit Point, jug, paneled, 6"...100.00
Petit Point, pie baker, 9"...30.00
Petit Point, plate, dinner; 10¼"...20.00
Petit Point, plate, luncheon; 9⅜"..15.00
Petit Point, plate, utility; 11"...22.00
Petit Point, platter, 14"...28.00

Petit Point, rolling pin, w/cork, 15".....................................95.00
Petit Point, spoon & fork, 8½", 8¾"..................................110.00
Pine Cone, bowl, cereal; 6¼"..8.00
Pine Cone, creamer..15.00
Pine Cone, cup..12.00
Pine Cone, plate, dinner...8.00
Pine Cone, plate, salad; 8½"...8.00
Pine Cone, sugar bowl, w/lid..18.00
Rooster Cameo, platter, 13¼x11⅜".....................................18.00
Silhouette, bowl, serving; 3x8½", NM..................................18.00
Silhouette, bowl, 9¼"...32.00
Silhouette, pie lifter..24.00
Silhouette, rolling pin, woman & fireplace, w/cork, 15"......125.00
Snow Leaf, platter, 13½"...32.00
Tulip, rolling pin, w/cork, 15"..95.00
White Daisy, plate, salad...10.00
Wild Rose, bowl, fruit/dessert...12.00
Wild Rose, platter, 13½"...15.00

Harlequin

Harlequin dinnerware, produced by the Homer Laughlin China Company of Newell, West Virginia, was introduced in 1938. It was a lightweight ware made in maroon, mauve blue, and spruce green, as well as all the Fiesta colors except ivory (see Fiesta). It was marketed exclusively by the Woolworth stores, who considered it to be their all-time bestseller. For this reason they contracted with Homer Laughlin to reissue Harlequin to commemorate their 100th anniversary in 1979. Although three of the original glazes were used in the reissue, the few serving pieces that were made were restyled, and collectors found the new line to be no threat to their investments.

The Harlequin animals, including a fish, lamb, cat, penguin, duck, and donkey, were made during the early 1940s, also for the dime-store trade. Today these are very desirable to collectors of Homer Laughlin china.

In the listings that follow, use the high side of the range of values for colors other than turquoise and yellow. Unless priced, for medium green, double the higher values on all items other than flat items and small bowls. *The Collector's Encyclopedia of Fiesta* (Collector Books, 2001 values) by Sharon and Bob Huxford contains a more thorough study of this subject and includes specific pricing for many medium green examples.

Animals, maverick, gold trim...50.00
Animals, non-standard color..325.00
Animals, standard color...195.00
Ashtray, basketweave, from $40 to..60.00
Ashtray, regular, from $38 to...53.00
Ashtray/saucer, from $55 to...68.00
Bowl, '36s oatmeal; from $16 to..28.00
Bowl, '36s; from $28 to..40.00
Bowl, cream soup; from $25 to...32.00
Bowl, cream soup; med gr, minimum value 900.00
Bowl, fruit; 5½", from $8 to...11.00
Bowl, ind salad; from $28 to..42.00
Bowl, mixing; Kitchen Kraft, mauve bl, 8".........................125.00
Bowl, mixing; Kitchen Kraft, red or lt gr, 6", ea..................90.00
Bowl, mixing; Kitchen Kraft, yel, 10".................................125.00
Bowl, nappy; 9", from $28 to...40.00
Bowl, oval baker, from $27 to..42.00
Butter dish, cobalt, ½-lb..300.00
Butter dish, ½-lb, from $115 to...135.00
Candle holders, pr, from $250 to..300.00
Casserole, w/lid, from $95 to..160.00
Creamer, high lip, any color, ea..135.00

Creamer, ind; from $20 to..35.00
Creamer, novelty, from $28 to...42.00
Creamer, regular, from $14 to..20.00
Cup, demitasse; from $42 to...110.00
Cup, lg, any color, ea...185.00
Cup, tea; from $9 to...11.00
Egg cup, dbl, from $20 to..28.00
Egg cup, single, from $25 to..35.00
Marmalade, from $225 to...265.00
Nut dish, basketweave, from $15 to...................................20.00
Perfume bottle, any color, ea...140.00

Pitcher, service water; high-end colors, up to
$105.00; Tumbler, high-end colors, up to, $58.00;
turquoise or yellow, minimum value, $45.00.

Pitcher, 22-oz jug, from $50 to...70.00
Pitcher, 22-oz jug, med gr..800.00
Plate, deep; from $20 to..30.00
Plate, deep; med gr..90.00
Plate, 6", from $4 to..5.50
Plate, 7", from $6 to..8.00
Plate, 9", from $10 to..14.00
Plate, 10", from $24 to..40.00
Platter, med gr, 11"...210.00
Platter, med gr, 13"...300.00
Platter, 11", from $20 to...27.00
Platter, 13", from $24 to...34.00
Relish tray, mixed colors...335.00
Sauce boat, from $22 to..35.00
Saucer, demitasse; from $18 to...30.00
Saucer, demitasse; med gr, minimum value 175.00
Saucer, from $2 to...4.00
Shakers, pr, from $18 to..26.00
Sugar bowl, w/lid, from $20 to...32.00
Sugar bowl, w/lid, med gr, minimum value.....................135.00
Syrup, red or yel..250.00
Syrup, spruce gr or mauve 340.00
Teapot, from $90 to..155.00
Tumbler, car decal...65.00
Tumbler, from $45 to...58.00

Hatpin Holders

Most hatpin holders were made from 1860 to 1920 to coincide with the period during which hatpins were popularly in vogue. The taller types were required to house the long hatpins necessary to secure the large hats that were in style from 1890 to 1914. They were usually porcelain, either decorated by hand or by transfer with florals or scenics, although some were clever figurals. Glass examples are rare, and those of slag or carnival glass are especially valuable.

If you are interested in collecting or dealing in hatpins or hatpin holders, you will enjoy *Hatpins and Hatpin Holders* by Lillian Baker, with beautiful color illustrations and current market values. For information concerning the American Hatpin Society, see the Clubs, Newsletters, and Catalogs section of the Directory. Our advisor for this category is Virginia Woodbury; she is listed in the Directory under California. (SASE required.)

Bsk, lady's portrait reserve, hanging cone form, S&V, 6¾", $275 to..375.00
Bsk, Nouveau face & decor, glass beads, S&V mk, ca 1905, 5½" ..250.00
China, City of York crest, bl/wht, Goss, 3½" 120.00
China, crocus figural, 16 holes, Royal Bayreuth, 4¾" 650.00
China, HP hunt scene, Royal Doulton, 1902-22, 4¾" 225.00
China, HP Nouveau decor w/much gold, HP Pickard mk, 4¾" ..250.00
China, Nouveau floral w/gold o/l, ftd, Pickard, 4¾" 250.00
China, Sunbonnet Babies washing, Royal Bayreuth, 4¾" 750.00
China, transfer w/HP o/l & gold, 14-hole, Limoges, 4½" 375.00
Chocolate glass, emb floral decor, ca 1905, 7⅞x2⅝" dia.............500.00
Gr jasper w/vining fruit, 12-hole, Volkstedt, 5⅜x2⅛" sq 250.00
Moriage butterflies w/gold beading, Nippon mk, 5⅛" 150.00
Porc, HP w/gold o/l, ftd, Nouveau floral mold, Austria, 4¾" 100.00
Porc, King George V transfer, pearlized, souvenir, 1910s, 4½"....100.00
Porc, Nouveau lady & peacock, 7-hole, LP Limoges, 3⅝", $250 to.275.00
Porc, Ophelia portrait on cream w/gr trim, Royal Doulton, 5", $350 to.475.00
Porc, portrait tapestry, 15-hole, Royal Bayreuth, 4½", $495 to ...595.00

Hatpins

A hatpin was used to securely fasten a hat to the hair and head of the wearer. Hatpins, measuring from 4" to 12" in length, were worn from approximately 1850 to 1920. During the Art Deco period, hatpins became ornaments rather than the decorative functional jewels that they had been. The hatpin period reached its zenith in 1913 just prior to World War I, which brought about a radical change in women's head-dress and fashion. About that time, women began to scorn the bonnet and adopt 'the hat' as a symbol of their equality. The hatpin was made of every natural and manufactured element in a myriad of designs that challenge the imagination. They were contrived to serve every fashion need and complement the milliner's art. Collectors often concentrate on a specific type: hand-painted porcelains, sterling silver, commemoratives, sporting activities, carnival glass, Art Nouveau and/or Art Deco designs, Victorian gothics with mounted stones, exquisite rhinestones, engraved and brass-mounted escutcheon heads, gold and gems, or simply primitive types made in the Victorian parlor. Some collectors prefer the long pin-shanks while others select only those on tremblants or nodder-type pin-shanks.

If you are interested in collecting or dealing in hatpins, see the information in the Hatpin Holders introduction concerning a national collectors' club. For further study we recommend *Hatpins and Hatpin Holders* by Lillian Baker, available at your local bookstore or from Collector Books. Our advisor for this category is Virginia Woodbury; she is listed in the Directory under California. (SASE required.)

Amethyst (faceted) gilt brass mt w/openwork, 1900s, 2½", $185 to .225.00
Brass w/4 topaz-colored bezeled stones, 2¾", 12" brass pin, $175 to..250.00
Brass wire-work fr w/faceted amethyst-like stone, 1905, 2", 10" pin ...120.00
Garnet cabachon tops 1" gilt head, 5½" gilt pin, from $125 to ..150.00
Gilt brass w/peacock-eye cabochon top, ca 1905, 1", 7½" steel pin.115.00
Gr stone circled by brillants, ca 1895, 1x1", 9" brass pin, $85 to .110.00
Ivory, hollow-cvd floral design, screws to pin, 1", 7⅜" pin..........225.00
Metallic mtd dbl-fr mosaic w/granular trim, 1875, 1¼", 7" brass pin..155.00

Peacock Eye glass oval, ca 1905,⅞", on 7½" steel pin, from $65 to.**95.00**
Plastic, molded geometric Egyptian design, 1922, 2x2", 5" steel pin ..**85.00**
Satsuma, dragon w/gold & cinnabar, 1" dia, 8" pin, from $165 to.**250.00**
Satsuma, HP floral, 1¾", on 10" steel pin, from $165 to **250.00**
Satsuma, tortoise pear-shape w/ribbon piquè work, 1¼", 8" steel pin.**275.00**
Silver, Billiken figural, Trade Mark Billiken, 1x1½", 8" brass pin.**250.00**
Sterling, Dutch shoe, hand wrought, ca 1900,¾", 8" steel pin **75.00**
Sterling, Nouveau lady w/repousse work, ca 1905, 1", 8¾" steel pin .**120.00**
Wht metal mt w/brilliants, triangular, 1895, 1¼", 12" steel pin....**85.00**

Haviland

The Haviland China Company was organized in 1840 by David Haviland, a New York china importer. His search for a pure white, nonporous porcelain led him to Limoges, France, where natural deposits of suitable clay had already attracted numerous china manufacturers. The fine china he produced there was translucent and meticulously decorated, with each piece fired in an individual sagger.

It has been estimated that as many as 60,000 chinaware patterns were designed, each piece marked with one of several company backstamps. 'H. & Co.' was used until 1890 when a law was enacted making it necessary to include the country of origin. Various marks have been used since that time including 'Haviland, France'; 'Haviland & Co. Limoges'; and 'Decorated by Haviland & Co.' Various associations with family members over the years have resulted in changes in management as well as company name. In 1892 Theodore Haviland left the firm to start his own business. Some of his ware was marked 'Mont Mery.' Later logos included a horseshoe, a shield, and various uses of his initials and name. In 1941 this branch moved to the United States. Wares produced here are marked 'Theodore Haviland, N.Y.' or 'Made In America.'

Though it is their dinnerware lines for which they are most famous, during the 1880s and 1890s they also made exquisite art pottery using a technique of underglaze slip decoration called Barbotine, which had been invented by Ernest Chaplet. In 1885 Haviland bought the formula and hired Chaplet to oversee its production. The technique involved mixing heavy white clay slip with pigments to produce a compound of the same consistency as oil paints. The finished product actually resembled oil paintings of the period, the texture achieved through the application of the heavy medium to the clay body in much the same manner as an artist would apply paint to his canvas. Primarily the body used with this method was a low-fired faience, though they also produced stoneware. Numbers in the listings below refer to pattern books by Arlene Schleiger. For further information we recommend Mary Frank Gaston's *Encyclopedia of Limoges Porcelain, Third Edition* (the first two editions are out of print), which offers examples and marks of the Haviland Company.

Plate, cake; small multicolored flowers with bird and butterflies, gold trim, H&CO, 11", from $220.00 to $240.00. (Photo courtesy Mary Frank Gaston)

Basket, bird/flower transfer, rtcl bowl/ped ft, Theo Haviland, 1892 ....**500.00**
Cake plate, Moss Rose, w/border, hdls, H&Co, 1879-89, 9½" **150.00**

Charger, HP cherries, H&Co mk, 1894-1931, 13½" **350.00**
Chocolate pot, floral on lt to dk brn w/gold, H&Co, 1894-1931, 12".**250.00**
Cup & saucer, floral border, Vermicelle blank, H&Co, 1879-89 ...**65.00**
Cup & saucer, Papillon (butterfly), HP holly/berries, H&Co, 1894-1931.**100.00**
Gravy/sauce tureen, floral w/gold, attached tray, w/lid, H&Co, ca 1887.**165.00**
Humidor, roses border on brn, 4-lobe, H&Co, 1894-1931, 7".....**275.00**
Plate, peacocks on flowering limb w/gold, H&Co, dtd 1887, 8" .**125.00**
Plate, pk roses w/gold, scalloped, H&Co, 1894-1931, 10" **50.00**
Shell fish plate, floral w/gold, 5-cup, H&Co, 1889-96, 8" **225.00**
Soup tureen, lg floral sprays w/gold, w/lid, Theo Haviland, ca 1892 .**500.00**
Sugar bowl, floral w/bl borders & gold, w/lid, H&Co, 1879-89, 7" ...**165.00**
Tea set, floral transfer w/gold, H&Co, 1865-75, 3-pc **475.00**
Vase, floral, emb/pnt gold on tan, ftd, 7", NM **200.00**

Hawkes

Thomas Hawkes established his factory in Corning, New York, in 1880. He developed many beautiful patterns of cut glass, two of which were awarded the Grand Prize at the Paris Exposition in 1889. By the end of the century, his company was renowned for the finest in cut glass production. The company logo was a trefoil form enclosing a hawk in each of the two bottom lobes with a fleur-de-lis in the center. With the exception of some of the very early designs, all Hawkes was signed. (Our values are for signed pieces.)

Ashtray, cut, stars & eagle in base, 1½x6½x4¼" **75.00**
Bottle, scent; bl, w/silver o/l, 4½" **110.00**
Bottle, scent; Brazilian, cylinder, 7" **225.00**
Bottle, scent; Chrysanthemum, sterling stopper, 6½" **440.00**
Box, intaglio cutting, silver finial, 3x4⅜" L **495.00**
Candlestick, intaglio cutting w/ribbons & flowers, hollow stem, 14"..**750.00**
Compote, intaglio cutting, silver ft, 5x5½", pr **600.00**
Creamer & sugar bowl, rose bud band w/bl & gold decor, 1900-30 .**195.00**
Mustard jar, eng decor, ftd, sterling lid, 4½" **165.00**
Nappy, cut, stars, swags & flowers, ca 1910-35............................**115.00**
Pitcher, lemonade; brilliant cut, silver trim, early 20th C........**2,900.00**
Plate, eng ship, smooth rim, 10¼" **95.00**
Punch bowl, cut rim, miter star-cut pattern, 2-pc, 13x14½' **1,840.00**
Punch bowl, Thumbprint, ftd, dtd 1905, 10x11", +12 matching cups..**1,000.00**
Toothpick holder, cut geometrics, silver ft, 3¾x3x1½" **45.00**

Head Vases

Vases modeled as heads of lovely ladies, delightful children, clowns, famous people — even some animals — were once popular as flower containers. Today they represent a growing area of collector interest. Most of them were imported from Japan, although some American potteries produced a few as well.

For more information, we recommend *Head Vases, Identification and Values,* by Kathleen Cole; and *The World of Head Vase Planters* by Mike Posgay and Ian Warner.

Our advisor for this category is Larry G. Pogue (L&J Antiques and Collectibles); he is listed in the Directory under Texas.

Baby, blond, over-sz dk eyes, unmk, 5¼" **45.00**
Baby, blond, pk bonnet w/bl bow, Relpo #K1866, 7" **75.00**
Baby, blond in ruffled bonnet, lg pale bl bow, unmk, 5½" **65.00**
Baby, blond sucking finger, Relpo #459B, 5" **65.00**
Baby, lt brn hair, dk eyes, holding bottle, Sampson #313A, 5½" ..**60.00**
Boy, blond, head bowed & hands folded in prayer, Inarco #E1575, 5¾" ..**85.00**
Boy, blond w/bl cap, Hummel-like, Relpo #K1018A, 8"..............**225.00**
Clown, wht w/red nose & mouth, sm blk hat, Inarco #E5071, 4½" .**85.00**

Couple, extremely rare, Vcagco #8170A, 5½", $275.00. (Photo courtesy Larry G. Pogue)

Famous people, Ben Franklin, wht shirt & blk collar, 6" 125.00
Famous people, Jackie Kennedy, blk glove, Inarco #E1852, 5½"..650.00
Girl, blond, pk bonnet w/flower, flowered bodice, unmk, 5" 65.00
Girl, blond, winking, flowered hat, lg bow at neck, unmk, 5" 75.00
Girl, blond in Christmas hat & coat, Inarco #E1247, 4" 65.00
Girl, blond ponytail w/bow in hair, hand up, Napcoware #C5037, 6" .125.00
Girl, blond w/lg yel scarf, Lefton, 6" 75.00
Girl, brn updo w/flowers & ponytail, Wales Label, Japan, 6" 95.00
Girl w/umbrella, scarf over brn hair, unmk, #S1725A, 5" 135.00
Girl w/umbrella, unmk, very rare sz, 3½" 200.00
Lady, blond, Art Deco, flowers at shoulder, Marti Hollywood, 9½" ..200.00
Lady, blond, floral pillbox hat/gloved hands up, Relpo #A-1229, 6½"..75.00
Lady, blond, gloved hand/pearls/daisies at neck, Napcoware #C6428, 6" .125.00
Lady, blond, gloved hands folded/flat hat/pearls, Napco #C5046, 4½".95.00
Lady, blond, thick lashes, pearls, Inarco #E969/S, 4½" 75.00
Lady, blond, yel hair bows & bodice, pearls, Rubens #4121, 5½"..85.00
Lady, blond flip, open eyes, pk bodice, Inarco #E2782, 6" 90.00
Lady, blond in brn top hat, high collar, Rubens #530, rare, 6" 175.00
Lady, blond in ruffled bonnet, thick lashes, pk bodice, unmk, 5½" .175.00
Lady, blond updo, pearls, hands up, Enesco, 8" 295.00
Lady, blond w/hand to face, Sampson Import #381A, 1959, 6½"..110.00
Lady, blond w/poodle, unmk, 6" 110.00
Lady, blond w/rose in hair, hand up, pearls, Inarco #E193/M, 6" ...200.00
Lady, frosted updo, thick lashes, pearls, Inarco #E1062, 6" 155.00
Lady, lt brn updo, dbl pearls, Inarco #1608, 10" 675.00
Lady, Mary Lou, blk hat, yel ruffled bodice, thick lashes, 5½" .250.00
Lady, wht long curls, ruffled bodice, Relpo #K1335, 8" 375.00
Lady w/poodle, unmk, 6" 95.00
Madonna & Child, pastels, Napcoware label, #R7076, 6½" 75.00
Man, blk hair, winking, gr hat & jacket, bow tie, unmk, 4½".......45.00
Nun w/Bible, thick lashes, Inarco #E188/M, 1961, 6" 60.00
Nun w/hands crossed, thick lashes, Relpo label, 6½" 55.00
Oriental lady w/ornate headress, pastels w/gold, Japan, 5"............50.00
Teen girl, blk hair, flat hat, pearls, Tremont label, 6¼" 225.00
Teen girl, blk hair w/yel bow, pnt bl eyes, Enesco label, 5½" 95.00
Teen girl, blond curls, dk eyes, pearls, Inarco #E5623, 6½".........125.00
Teen girl, blond frosted flip, bow at neck, Caffco label, 7" 225.00
Teen girl, blond frosted hair, pearls, lacy bodice, Enesco, 5½" 95.00
Teen girl, blond pageboy, blk hat, pearls, Relpo #K1947, 5½" 175.00
Teen girl, blond ponytail, brn derby hat, hand up, unmk, 6½" 90.00
Teen girl, blond side-swept hair, pearls, Ardco label, #C3259, 5½".85.00
Teen girl, blond w/bl bow, flower on bodice, Japan, 5½" 85.00
Teen girl, blond w/curls & bows, ruffled collar, Inarco #E3523, 7" .265.00
Teen girl, blond w/gr bow, 1 pearl earring, gr bodice, unmk, 7" ..375.00
Teen girl, blond w/lg curls, dk eyes, blk bodice, Relpo #1695, 7" ..275.00
Teen girl, blond w/lg curls, pearl earrings, blk bodice, unmk, 6" ...95.00
Teen girl, blond w/phone, yel headband & bodice, Inarco #E3548, 5½"..70.00
Teen girl, blond w/pk tam & coat, gloved hand, Relpo #K1694/S, 5½"..95.00
Teen girl, blond w/pk-lined hood over hair, Rubens #4135, 5½" ..150.00
Teen girl, blond w/red bow, hand up, pearls, gr bodice, unmk, 7"..275.00
Teen girl, blond w/sunglasses & ponytails, unmk, 7½"................450.00

Teen girl, brn hair, flowered hat, pearls, Napco #C4556C, 6¼" 95.00
Teen girl, Nancy Pew, brn hair, lav hat w/wht bow, #7410, 6½"..150.00
Teen girl graduate, blond w/diploma, gold trim, Napco #C4072G, 6" .100.00
Uncle Sam, pastel gr overall, unmk, 6½" 45.00

Heintz Art Metal Shop

Founded by Otto L. Heintz in Buffalo, New York, ca 1909, the Heintz Art Metal Shop (HAMS) succeeded the Art Crafts Shop (begun in 1903) and featured a new aesthetic. Whereas the Art Craft Shop offered products of hammered copper with applied color enamel and with an altogether somewhat cruder or more primitive and medieval-looking appearance, HAMS presented a refined appearance of applied sterling silver on bronze. Most pieces are stamped with the manufacturer's mark — the letters HAMS conjoined within a diamond, often accompanied by a Aug. 27, 1912, patent date — although paper labels were pasted on the bottom of lamp bases. Original patinas for Heintz pieces include a mottled brown or green (the most desirable), as well as silver and gold (less desirable). Desk sets and smoking accessories are common; lamps appear less frequently. The firm, like many others, closed in 1930, a victim of the Depression. Silvercrest, also located in Buffalo, produced products similar though not nearly as valuable as Heintz. Please note: Cleaning or scrubbing original patinas diminishes the value of the object. Our advisor for this and related Arts & Crafts subjects is Bruce A. Austin; he is listed in the Directory under New York.

Bowl, leafy branches, sterling on verdigris bronze, HAMS, 8" 425.00
Box, bronze, etched golfer on lid, 6½x9½"................................1,400.00
Frame, trees & house, sterling on bronze, oval window, 5x8"......900.00
Golf trophy, geometrics, sterling on bronze, mk HAMS, 9x8" 275.00
Humidor, abstract on lid, sterling on dk bronze patina, sq, 5½x6" 375.00
Humidor, fox-hunt on lid, sterling on verdigris bronze, HAMS, 3x9x4"....500.00
Inkwell, floral, sterling on bronze, att, 7¼" 375.00

Lamp, bronze mushroom shape with silver overlay berries and leaves, three-socket base, marked HAMS with patent, 17x15", $9,500.00. (Photo courtesy Craftsman Auctions)

Lamp, floral, sterling on bronze; 9" shade w/metal floral o/l 1,100.00
Lamp, simple silver o/l on copper shade & base, unmk, 12"........900.00
Vase, cornflowers, sterling on bronze, shouldered, bun base, 8x3".325.00
Vase, peacock on branch, sterling on bronze, cylindrical, 1912, 9"..325.00
Vase, rose stem, sterling on verdigris bronze, #3809B, 12x5" 700.00

Heisey

A.H. Heisey began his long career at the King Glass Company of Pittsburgh. He later joined the Ripley Glass Company which soon became Geo. Duncan and Sons. After Duncan's death Heisey became half-owner in partnership with his brother-in-law, James Duncan. In 1895 he built his own factory in Newark, Ohio, initiating production in 1896 and continuing until Christmas of 1957. At that time Imperial Glass Corporation bought some of the molds. After 1968 they removed the old 'Diamond H' from any they put into use. In 1985 HCA purchased all of Imperial's Heisey molds with the exception of the Old Williamsburg line.

During their highly successful period of production, Heisey made fine handcrafted tableware with simple, yet graceful designs. Early pieces were not marked. After November 1901 the glassware was marked either with the 'Diamond H' or a paper label. Blown ware is often marked on the stem, never on the bowl or foot.

For more information we recommend *Collector's Encyclopedia of Heisey Glass, 1925 – 1938*, by Neila Bredehoft and *Heisey Glass, 1896 – 1957*, by Neila and Tom Bredehoft.

For information concerning Heisey Collectors of America, see the Clubs, Newsletters, and Catalogs section of the Directory.

See also Glass Animals and Figurines.

Charter Oak, crystal, candle holder, acorn, 1-light, #130 ....100.00
Charter Oak, crystal, stem, parfait; #3362, 4½-oz 15.00
Charter Oak, Flamingo, candlestick, Tricorn, 3-light, #129, 5" 90.00
Charter Oak, Flamingo, plate, luncheon/salad; acorn & leaves, 7" ..12.00
Charter Oak, Hawthorne, bowl, floral; oak leaf, 3116, 11" 85.00
Charter Oak, Hawthorne, stem, luncheon goblet; low ft, #3362, 8-oz ..95.00
Charter Oak, marigold, comport, ftd, #3362, 7" 175.00
Charter Oak, marigold, tumbler, flat, #3362, 12-oz 35.00
Charter Oak, Moongleam, comport, low ft, #3362, 6" 60.00
Charter Oak, Moongleam, stem, sherbet; low ft, #3362, 6-oz 22.00
Chintz, crystal, bowl, preserve; hdls, ftd, 5½" 15.00
Chintz, crystal, mayonnaise, dolphin ft, 5½" 35.00
Chintz, crystal, platter, oval, 14" 35.00
Chintz, crystal, stem, water; #3389, 9-oz 17.50
Chintz, crystal, tumbler, iced tea; #3389, 12-oz 16.00
Chintz, Sahara, bowl, pickle/olive; 2-part, 13" 35.00
Chintz, Sahara, pitcher, dolphin ft, 3-pt 300.00
Chintz, Sahara, shakers, pr 85.00
Chintz, Sahara, sugar bowl, 3 dolphin ft 45.00
Crystolite, crystal, ashtray, w/book match holder, 5" 45.00
Crystolite, crystal, bowl, leaf pickle; 9" 30.00
Crystolite, crystal, cigarette lighter 30.00

Crystolite, crystal, cup and saucer, $28.00. (Photo courtesy Gene Florence)

Crystolite, crystal, ice tub, SP hdl 120.00
Crystolite, crystal, plate, buffet/punch liner, 20" 125.00
Crystolite, crystal, plate, torte; 11" 40.00
Crystolite, crystal, stem, sherbet/saucer champagne; #5003, 6-oz ..18.00
Crystolite, crystal, sugar bowl, regular 30.00
Empress, Alexandrite, bowl, nappy, dolphin ft, 7½" 350.00
Empress, Alexandrite, creamer, dolphin ft 250.00
Empress, Alexandrite, plate, 6" 40.00
Empress, Alexandrite, sugar bowl, ind 210.00
Empress, Alexandrite, tray, buffet relish; 4-part, 16" 160.00

Empress, cobalt, ashtray 300.00
Empress, cobalt, bowl, nasturtium; dolphin ft, 7½" 350.00
Empress, cobalt, plate, 8" 70.00
Empress, Flamingo, bowl, cream soup 30.00
Empress, Flamingo, bowl, mint; dolphin ft, 6" 35.00
Empress, Flamingo, bowl, vegetable; oval, 10" 50.00
Empress, Flamingo, cup 30.00
Empress, Flamingo, plate, 7" 12.00
Empress, Flamingo, stem, oyster cocktail; 2½" 30.00
Empress, Moongleam, bonbon, 6" 30.00
Empress, Moongleam, bowl, grapefruit; sq top, 6" 25.00
Empress, Moongleam, bowl, relish; triplex, 10" 65.00
Empress, Moongleam, plate, rnd or sq, 7" 17.00
Empress, Moongleam, stem, sherbet; 4-oz 35.00
Empress, Moongleam, vase, flared rim, 8" 190.00
Empress, Sahara, bowl, nappy, 8" 375.00
Empress, Sahara, bowl, preserve; hdls, 5" 25.00
Empress, Sahara, cup, custard/punch; 4-oz 35.00
Empress, Sahara, mustard, w/lid 80.00
Empress, Sahara, plate, rnd or sq, 10½" 100.00
Empress, Sahara, tumbler, tea; 12-oz 65.00
Greek Key, crystal, bowl, almond; ftd, ind 45.00
Greek Key, crystal, bowl, jelly; shallow, low ft, 4½" 40.00
Greek Key, crystal, bowl, nappy, 6½" 70.00
Greek Key, crystal, bowl, orange; 12" 500.00
Greek Key, crystal, candy dish, w/lid, 1-lb 170.00
Greek Key, crystal, cup, punch; 4½" 20.00
Greek Key, crystal, ice tub, tab hdls, lg 150.00
Greek Key, crystal, oil bottle, squat, w/#8 stopper, 2-oz 100.00
Greek Key, crystal, pitcher, jug form, 1-pt 130.00
Greek Key, crystal, puff box, #1 or #3 ....175.00
Greek Key, crystal, sherbet, flared or str rim, ftd, 4½" 30.00
Greek Key, crystal, stem, claret; 4½-oz 170.00
Greek Key, crystal, tray, celery; oval, 9" 50.00
Greek Key, crystal, tumbler, str sides, 12-oz or 13-oz 100.00
Ipswich, Alexandrite, stem, goblet; knob in stem, 10-oz 750.00
Ipswich, cobalt, bowl, floral; ftd, 11" 450.00
Ipswich, crystal, bowl, floral; ftd, 11" 80.00
Ipswich, crystal, creamer 35.00
Ipswich, crystal, sherbet, ftd, knob in stem, 4-oz 15.00
Ipswich, gr, cocktail shaker, strainer, #86 stopper, qt 400.00
Ipswich, gr, plate, 7" sq 70.00
Ipswich, gr, sugar bowl 125.00
Ipswich, pk, bowl, finger; w/underplate 90.00
Ipswich, pk, candy jar, ½-lb 325.00
Ipswich, pk, stem, goblet, knob in stem, 10-oz 85.00
Ipswich, Sahara, candlestick, 1-light, 6" 200.00
Ipswich, Sahara, pitcher, ½-gal 550.00
Ipswich, Sahara, tumbler, soda; ftd, 12-oz 70.00
Kalonyal, crystal, bottle, oil; hdl, 6-oz 130.00
Kalonyal, crystal, bowl, shallow, 6" 35.00
Kalonyal, crystal, celery tray, 12" 65.00
Kalonyal, crystal, cup, punch; 3-oz 26.00
Kalonyal, crystal, pickle jar, w/lid 195.00
Kalonyal, crystal, plate, fruit; 8" 55.00
Kalonyal, crystal, stem, sherbet; scalloped, 3½-oz 40.00
Lariat, crystal, bowl, nut; ind, 4" 32.00
Lariat, crystal, bowl, salad; hdls, 10½" 38.00
Lariat, crystal, candlestick, 2-light 40.00
Lariat, crystal, creamer 20.00
Lariat, crystal, plate, dinner; 10½" 125.00
Lariat, crystal, tray, center hdl w/ball finial 165.00
Lariat, crystal, vase, fan; ftd, 7" 30.00
Narcissus, crystal, bottle, oil; #1519 ....175.00

Narcissus, crystal, candlestick, 3-light, #1519 ....65.00
Narcissus, crystal, plate, luncheon; #1519, 8" 16.00
Narcissus, crystal, relish, oval, 3-part, #1519, 11" 40.00
Narcissus, crystal, stem, wine; #3408, 2-oz 26.00
New Era, crystal, ashtray/ind nut bowl 30.00
New Era, crystal, creamer 37.50
New Era, crystal, plate, 9x7" 25.00
New Era, crystal, relish, 3-part, 13" 25.00
New Era, crystal, stem, claret; 4-oz 18.00
New Era, crystal, stem, wine; 3-oz 25.00
New Era, crystal, sugar bowl 37.50
New Era, crystal, tumbler, low, ftd, 10-oz 11.00
Octagon, crystal, bowl, cream soup; hdls 10.00
Octagon, crystal, mayonnaise, ftd, #1229, 5½" 10.00
Octagon, crystal, plate, sandwich; #1229, 10" 15.00
Octagon, crystal, sugar bowl, #500 ....10.00
Octagon, Flamingo, bowl, flat soup; 9" 15.00
Octagon, Flamingo, bowl, jelly; #1229, 5½" 30.00
Octagon, Flamingo, plate, luncheon; 8" 10.00
Octagon, Flamingo, plate, 14" 25.00
Octagon, Hawthorne, basket, #500, 5" 450.00
Octagon, Hawthorne, bowl, frozen dessert; #500 ....35.00
Octagon, Hawthorne, plate, sandwich; center hdl, 10½" 70.00
Octagon, Marigold, bowl, mint; #1229, 6" 30.00
Octagon, Marigold, ice tub, #500 ....150.00
Octagon, Moongleam, bowl, mint; #1229, 5½" 25.00
Octagon, Moongleam, cup, AD 25.00
Octagon, Moongleam; saucer, AD 10.00
Octagon, Sahara, bonbon, sides up, #1229, 6" 25.00
Octagon, Sahara, bowl, vegetable; 9" 25.00
Octagon, Sahara, plate, muffin; sides up, #1229, 10" 30.00
Old Colony, Sahara, bowl, cream soup; hdls 22.00
Old Colony, Sahara, bowl, floral; hdls, ftd, 8½" 60.00
Old Colony, Sahara, bowl, nappy, 4½" 14.00
Old Colony, Sahara, cup 32.00
Old Colony, Sahara, cup, bouillon; hdls, ftd 25.00
Old Colony, Sahara, pitcher, dolphin ft, 3-pt 240.00
Old Colony, Sahara, plate, muffin; hdls, 12" 75.00
Old Colony, Sahara, plate, rnd or sq, 7" 20.00
Old Colony, Sahara, shakers, pr 125.00
Old Colony, Sahara, stem, cocktail; #3390, 3-oz 20.00
Old Colony, Sahara, tray, hors d'oeuvre; hdls, 13" 75.00
Old Colony, Sahara, tumbler, iced tea; ftd, #3390, 12-oz 27.00
Old Sandwich, cobalt, ashtray, ind 45.00
Old Sandwich, cobalt, creamer, 12-oz 575.00
Old Sandwich, cobalt, stem, claret; 4-oz 150.00
Old Sandwich, crystal, candlestick, 6" 60.00

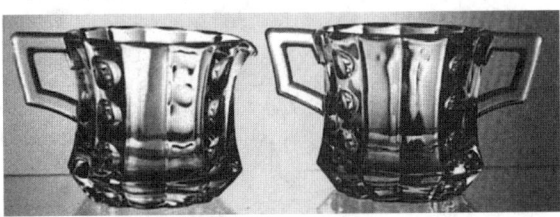

Old Sandwich, crystal, creamer and sugar bowl, $50.00.

Old Sandwich, crystal, mug, beer; 12-oz 50.00
Old Sandwich, crystal, parfait, 4½-oz 15.00
Old Sandwich, crystal, stem, sherbet; 4-oz 7.00
Old Sandwich, Flamingo, bowl, finger 50.00

Old Sandwich, Flamingo, floral block, #22 ....25.00
Old Sandwich, Flamingo, shakers, pr 65.00
Old Sandwich, Flamingo, tumbler, bar; 1½-oz 130.00
Old Sandwich, Flamingo, tumbler, low ft, 10-oz 40.00
Old Sandwich, Moongleam, bottle, catsup; w/#3 stopper (like lg cruet) .225.00
Old Sandwich, Moongleam, candlestick, 6" 150.00
Old Sandwich, Moongleam, pitcher, regular, ½-gal 185.00
Old Sandwich, Moongleam, stem, sherbet; 4-oz 20.00
Old Sandwich, Sahara, bowl, popcorn; ftd, cupped 110.00
Old Sandwich, Sahara, decanter, #98 stopper, 1-pt 200.00
Old Sandwich, Sahara, pilsner, 8-oz 32.00
Old Sandwich, Sahara, tumbler, juice; 5-oz 15.00
Pleat & Panel, crystal, marmalade, 4¾" 10.00
Pleat & Panel, crystal, pitcher, 3-pt 45.00
Pleat & Panel, crystal, plate, dinner; 10¾" 15.00
Pleat & Panel, Flamingo, bowl, chow chow; 4" 11.00
Pleat & Panel, Flamingo, marmalade, 4¾" 30.00
Pleat & Panel, Flamingo, plate, luncheon; 8" 12.50
Pleat & Panel, Flamingo, tray, compartmented spice; 10" 25.00
Pleat & Panel, Moongleam, bowl, bouillon; hdls, 5" 17.50
Pleat & Panel, Moongleam, pitcher, ice lip, 3-pt 165.00
Pleat & Panel, Moongleam, plate, bread; 7" 10.00
Pleat & Panel, Moongleam, vase, 8" 100.00
Provincial/Whirlpool, crystal, bonbon, uptrn sides, hdls, 7" 12.00
Provincial/Whirlpool, crystal, bowl, nappy, hdl, 5½" 20.00
Provincial/Whirlpool, crystal, candlestick, 2-light 80.00
Provincial/Whirlpool, crystal, plate, cheese; ftd, 5" 20.00
Provincial/Whirlpool, crystal, stem, wine; 3½" 20.00
Provincial/Whirlpool, crystal, tumbler, iced tea; ftd, 12-oz 20.00
Provincial/Whirlpool, Limelight Green, bowl, nut/jelly; ind 40.00
Provincial/Whirlpool, Limelight Green, bowl, relish; 4-part, 10" .150.00
Provincial/Whirlpool, Limelight Green, sugar bowl, ftd 95.00
Provincial/Whirlpool, Limelight Green, vase, violet; 3½" 95.00
Queen Ann, crystal, ashtray 30.00
Queen Ann, crystal, bowl, cream soup; w/sq liner 25.00
Queen Ann, crystal, bowl, floral; lion head, 10" 250.00
Queen Ann, crystal, bowl, grapefruit; w/sq liner 20.00
Queen Ann, crystal, bowl, nasturtium; dolphin ft, 7½" 35.00
Queen Ann, crystal, comport, ftd, 6" 25.00
Queen Ann, crystal, plate, sandwich; hdls, 12" 30.00
Queen Ann, crystal, plate, 6" 5.00
Queen Ann, crystal, shakers, pr 50.00
Queen Ann, crystal, sugar bowl, ind 20.00
Queen Ann, crystal, tray, buffet relish; 4-part, 16" 35.00
Ridgeleigh, crystal, ashtray, sq 10.00
Ridgeleigh, crystal, bottle, bitters; w/tube, 5-oz 130.00
Ridgeleigh, crystal, bowl, floral; oblong, 14" 70.00
Ridgeleigh, crystal, bowl, lemon; w/lid, 5" 65.00
Ridgeleigh, crystal, bowl, salad; 9" 50.00
Ridgeleigh, crystal, cigarette box, 6" 35.00
Ridgeleigh, crystal, mayonnaise, w/underplate 55.00
Ridgeleigh, crystal, plate, sq, 6" 24.00
Ridgeleigh, crystal, stem, claret; pressed 50.00
Ridgeleigh, crystal, stem, sherry; blown, 2-oz 90.00
Ridgeleigh, crystal, tumbler, bar; pressed, 2½-oz 45.00
Ridgeleigh, crystal, tumbler, soda; pressed, #1469½, 12-oz 50.00
Saturn, crystal, bowl, baked apple 25.00
Saturn, crystal, bowl, whipped cream; 5" 15.00
Saturn, crystal, creamer 25.00
Saturn, crystal, pitcher, ice lip, blown, 70-oz 65.00
Saturn, crystal, stem, 10-oz 20.00
Saturn, crystal, vase, str sides, 8½" 55.00
Saturn, Zircon or Limelight Green, bowl, finger 65.00
Saturn, Zircon or Limelight Green, candelabrum, 2-light 500.00

Saturn, Zircon or Limelight Green, marmalade, w/lid 500.00
Saturn, Zircon or Limelight Green, pitcher, juice 500.00
Saturn, Zircon or Limelight Green, stem, saucer champagne; 6-oz...95.00
Saturn, Zircon or Limelight Green, tumbler, juice; 5-oz 80.00
Stanhope, crystal, ashtray, ind 25.00
Stanhope, crystal, bowl, floral; w/or w/o T knobs, hdls, 11" 80.00
Stanhope, crystal, bowl, jelly, w/or w/o rnd knobs, hdl, 6" 25.00
Stanhope, crystal, plate, 7" 20.00
Stanhope, crystal, relish, hdls, 5-part, 12" 55.00
Stanhope, crystal, stem, cocktail; pressed, 3½-oz 20.00
Sunburst, crystal, bottle, molasses; 13-oz 175.00
Sunburst, crystal, bottle, water 75.00
Sunburst, crystal, bowl, scalloped, 5" 25.00
Sunburst, crystal, pitcher, bulbous, 3-pt 150.00
Sunburst, crystal, tray, pickle; 6" 35.00
Sunburst, crystal, tumbler 40.00
Sunburst, crystal; bowl; punch; w/stand, 15" 160.00
Twist, Alexandrite, bowl, floral, 4-ftd, oval, 12" 550.00
Twist, crystal, bottle, French dressing 50.00
Twist, crystal, bowl, grapefruit; ftd 15.00
Twist, crystal, bowl, nasturtium; oval, 8" 45.00
Twist, crystal, plate, relish; 3-part, 13" 10.00
Twist, crystal, tumbler, iced tea; ftd, 12-oz 20.00
Twist, Flamingo, bowl, cream soup/bouillon 25.00
Twist, Flamingo, bowl, floral; oval, 4-ftd, 12" 100.00
Twist, Flamingo, mayonnaise 65.00
Twist, Flamingo, tumbler, soda; ftd, 6-oz 25.00
Twist, Marigold, baker, oval, 9" 60.00
Twist, Marigold, bowl, mint; hdls, 6" 30.00
Twist, Marigold, creamer, hotel; oval 50.00
Twist, Marigold, plate, cream soup liner 15.00
Twist, Marigold, tumbler, soda; str or flared, 8-oz 40.00
Twist, Moongleam, bonbon, ind 40.00
Twist, Moongleam, candlestick, 1-light, 2" 50.00
Twist, Moongleam, ice tub 110.00
Twist, Moongleam, tray, pickle; 7" 35.00
Twist, Sahara, bowl, mint; hdls, 6" 20.00
Twist, Sahara, ice tub 125.00
Twist, Sahara, shakers, pr 140.00
Victorian, crystal, bowl, finger 25.00
Victorian, crystal, cigarette box, 6" 100.00
Victorian, crystal, cup, punch; 5-oz 10.00
Victorian, crystal, plate, sandwich; 13" 90.00
Victorian, crystal, stem, sherbet; 5-oz 18.00
Victorian, crystal, tumbler, old fashioned; 8-oz 35.00
Victorian, crystal, vase, flared rim, ftd, 9" 140.00
Waverly, crystal, bowl, lemon; oval, w/lid, 6" 45.00
Waverly, crystal, bowl, salad; 7" 20.00
Waverly, crystal, butter dish, 6" sq 65.00
Waverly, crystal, candle epergnette, 6½" 15.00
Waverly, crystal, comport, low, ftd, 6" 20.00
Waverly, crystal, cup 14.00
Waverly, crystal, shakers, pr 60.00
Waverly, crystal, vase, violet; 3½" 60.00
Yeoman, crystal, bowl, cream soup; hdls 12.00
Yeoman, crystal, bowl, vegetable; hdls, w/lid, 9" 35.00
Yeoman, crystal, plate, 10½" 20.00
Yeoman, crystal, plate/coaster, 4½" 3.00
Yeoman, crystal, tray, rectangular, 7x10" 26.00
Yeoman, Flamingo, bowl, banana split; ftd 23.00
Yeoman, Flamingo, bowl, bonbon; hdls, 6½" 10.00
Yeoman, Flamingo, creamer 25.00
Yeoman, Flamingo, plate, relish, 4-part, 11" 27.00
Yeoman, Flamingo, stem, champagne; 6-oz 16.00

Yeoman, Hawthorne, bowl, finger 27.50
Yeoman, Hawthorne, comport, low ft, deep, 6" 42.00
Yeoman, Hawthorne, plate, cream soup underliner 14.00
Yeoman, Hawthorne, sugar bowl, w/lid 70.00
Yeoman, Howthorne, platter, oval, 12" 33.00
Yeoman, Marigold, bowl, jelly; low, ftd, 5" 40.00
Yeoman, Marigold, marmalade jar, w/lid 65.00
Yeoman, Marigold, saucer 10.00
Yeoman, Marigold, sugar bowl, w/lid 40.00
Yeoman, Moongleam, bottle, cologne; w/stopper 160.00
Yeoman, Moongleam, bowl, fruit; oval, 9" 45.00
Yeoman, Moongleam, pitcher, qt 140.00
Yeoman, Moongleam, plate, 7" 14.00
Yeoman, Moongleam, stem, soda; 5-oz 20.00
Yeoman, Moongleam, tumbler, iced tea; 12-oz 30.00
Yeoman, Sahara, bowl, nappy, 4½" 10.00
Yeoman, Sahara, oil cruet, 2-oz 80.00
Yeoman, Sahara, plate, cheese; hdls 13.00
Yeoman, Sahara, plate, grapefruit bowl; 6½" 15.00
Yeoman, Sahara, stem, sherbet; 4½-oz 10.00

Herend

Herend, Hungary, was the center of a thriving pottery industry as early as the mid-1800s. Decorative items as well as tablewares were made in keeping with the styles of the times. One of the factories located in this area was founded by Moritz Fisher, who often marked his wares with a cojoined MF. Items described in the following listings may be marked simply Herend, indicating the city, or with a manufacturer's backstamp.

Bone dish, flowers w/gold, molded basketweave, crescent, 7⅜" 95.00
Candelabra, triple; Chinese Bouquet, w/gold, 6¼", pr 370.00
Coffeepot, Fruit & Flowers, #476½, 9x7" 310.00
Figurine, Canadian ducks (2) on woodpile, #15341, 8x12" 725.00
Figurine, nude combing her hair, sgn Elek Lux, 14¼" 380.00
Ice bucket, butterflies/flowers, flowers inside bottom, hdls, 6⅜" .265.00
Plate, castle scene, rtcl edge, 10" 520.00
Plate, chop; Fortuna, coral-colored floral on wht, hdls, 14" 525.00
Platter, Market Garden, fruits & vegetables on wht, #101, 16x12"..400.00
Tray, butterflies & flowers, Queen Victoria collection, #400, 11x16"..310.00
Tureen, soup; birds & butterflies, #1005/RO, 11x9x15" 780.00
Tureen, soup; birds/butterflies/insects, ½-lemon finial, 4x8" 450.00

Heubach

Gebruder Heubach is a German company that has been in operation since the 1800s, producing quality bisque figurines and novelty items. They are perhaps most famous for their doll heads and piano babies, most of which are marked with the circular rising sun device containing an 'H' superimposed over a 'C.' Items with arms and hands positioned away from the body are more valuable, and color of hair and intaglio eyes affect price as well. Our advisor for this category is Grace Ochsner; she is listed in the Directory under Illinois. See also Dolls, Heubach.

Babies (2) in wht sit on grassy base, 4½x5" 575.00
Baby boy sitting, wht outfit w/gr ribbon, 7¾", from $400 to 500.00
Baby in bunny suit beside egg, 5½" 625.00
Baby in gr tub w/1 ft in mouth, 4½x5½" 1,000.00
Baby in wht, crawling, 7", EX, from $300 to 400.00
Baby in wht w/bl ribbon, crawling, 7" 275.00
Bather in gr china tub, ft to mouth, 4½x5½" 1,150.00
Boy (girl) on bk w/arms & legs up, 5½", pr 475.00

Boy & girl on bks w/arms & legs up, rpr, 5½", pr, from $500 to..**600.00**
Boy in wht w/gr ribbon, sitting/playing w/toes, 7¾", pr..............**700.00**
Child in Easter bunny outfit, attached egg at bk, 5½", from $500 to..**600.00**
Nude baby w/hands covering ears, kneeling, 6½x4½"..................**575.00**

Hickman, Royal Arden

Born in Willamette, Oregon, Royal A. Hickman was a genius in all aspects of design interpretation. Mr. Hickman's expertise can be seen in the designs of the lovely Heisey figurines, Kosta crystal, Bruce Fox aluminum, Three Crowns aluminum, Vernon Kilns, and Royal Haeger Pottery, as well as handcrafted silver, furniture, and paintings.

Hickman (as a designer), Harvey Hamilton (his son-in-law), and Frank Petty (also as a designer), all worked for Haeger potteries from 1939 through 1944. Hickman and his son-in-law left Haeger, moved to Tennessee in 1944 and started Royal Hickman Industries. Frank Petty left Haeger in 1938 and founded Petty Pottery in Louisiana. He returned to Haeger in 1940, and then joined Hickman and Hamilton in Tennessee.

The Petty glazes are fantastic! Watch for them. Frank Petty has really not received the recognition he truly deserves, as he was an extremely talented artist. Hickman noted this and was the one who started the practice of putting the Petty Glaze sticker on those designs.

Because Mr. Hickman moved around during much of his lifetime (as with all designers), his influence has been felt in all forms of the media. Designs from his independent companies include 'Royal Hickman Pottery and Lamps' (sold through Ceramic Arts Inc., of Chattanooga, Tennessee), 'Royal Hickman's Paris Ware,' 'Royal Hickman — Florida,' and 'California Designed by Royal Hickman.' The following listings will give examples of pieces bearing the various trademarks.

Our advisor for this category is Lanette Clarke; she is listed in the Directory under California. See also Garden City Pottery; Royal Haeger.

Bruce Fox Aluminum

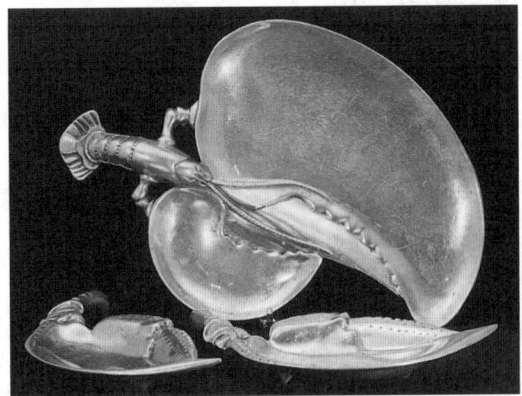

Lobster party service, large tray, $95.00; small trays, $25.00 each.

Bowl, leaf shape, stem hdl, 8¾x16¼"...**55.00**
Candle holders, triple; curved ribbon-like base, 5¾" high end, pr ..**100.00**
Candlesticks, daffodil blossom w/2 leaves, 10⅜x3", pr **110.00**
Tray, charging bull, SP-77, 9x14½" **110.00**
Tray, fish form, 22½x7" **85.00**
Tray, leaf form, 3-lobe, 15½x12"..**45.00**
Tray, leaf form, 4 cast ft, long/slender, RH-5, 15½x6" **75.00**
Tray, leaf form, 4 cast ft, RH-5, 26x5" **65.00**
Tray, leaf form, 5-lobe w/long stem (hdl), 5-ftd, 9½x11"+stem.....**80.00**
Tray, lobster, RH-20, 14½"...**40.00**
Tray, pineapple shape, leaf hdl, 13x6½" **32.00**

Tray, serving; banana-leaf shape, 5 petals, 21x9"............................**65.00**
Tray, serving; basketweave w/maple-leaf edging, 8¾x15¾" **60.00**
Tray, wood w/aluminum fr & horse's head in center, 27½x18"......**75.00**
Tray, 2-acorn oak, 14½" **45.00**

California, Designed by Royal Hickman

Figurine, deer, apple gr w/wht spots, appl eyes, 15" **75.00**
Lamp base, flying geese, 17" **250.00**
Planter, elephant figural, gr to gray, trunk up, 7x12", NM.............**80.00**
Vase, fish on wave, brn w/frosty wht, orig label, 9" **157.50**

Royal Hickman — Florida

Tray, silver, banana-leaf hdls, 15" L **220.00**
Vase, classic ftd shape w/ornate hdls, pk mottle, #342, 12" **145.00**
Vase, 3 dolphin figures, 14k gold decor, crown signature label, 13" **300.00**

Miscellaneous Signatures

Lamp base, Petty Crystal Glaze, mauve/purple/maroon, unmk, 14½"..**95.00**
Tray, 3 heart-shaped leaves, center blossom, SP metal, 3x8½"....**167.50**
Urn, Petty Crystal Glaze, bl/gr/mauve/cream, ball on sq base, #450, 6".**125.00**
Vase, angelfish, Royal Kickman Florida, #521, 9½" **75.00**
Vase, bl mottle, shouldered, Royal Hickman USA, #544, 11½".**165.00**
Vase, crystal, sea horse figural, Royal Hickman USA, #468, 8"....**75.00**
Vase, dk red w/shades of gr, shouldered, USA mk, #202, 7½".....**275.00**
Vase, Fluted, dusty mauve w/seafoam gr drip, USA mk, 1940, 7"..**100.00**
Vase, Petty Crystal Glaze, bl & cream mottle, ftd, USA mk, #458, 8" ...**75.00**
Vase, sailfish figural, gray w/blended mc, FL mk, 6¼x11½" **45.00**
Vase, swan form, Petty Crystal Glaze, USA mk, #475, 16⅝"......**125.00**

Higgins

Contemporary glass artists Frances and Michael Higgins designed high-quality glassware from the late 1940s until his death on February 13, 1999. (Frances continues with her staff.) Their designs were often created by fusing layers of glass together, though sometimes colored ground glass was used to 'paint' the decoration onto the surface. Molds were used, and through a process called 'slumping,' the glass was fired to a very high temperature, causing it to soften and take on the predetermined shape. Their work is ultramodern and is more readily found in metropolitan areas.

The earliest mark was an engraved signature on the bottom of the glass — either 'Frances Stewart Higgins' or 'Michael Higgins' or both, which was dropped in favor of just 'Higgins' with a raised 'Higgins Man.' From approximately 1957 to 1964, the Higgins signature was embossed in gold on the top. After 1964 the signature again appeared on the bottom and was engraved in the glass. Recent items produced at the Higgins studio in Riverside, Illinois, were marked 'Higgins' and for a period of time were dated (example: Higgins 99); but with some exceptions, this is no longer the case. For more information we recommend *Higgins, Adventures in Glass,* by Donald-Brian Johnson and Leslie Pina (Schiffer). Our advisor is Dennis Hopp; he is listed in the Directory under Illinois.

Ashtray, gr & gold radiating lines, 2 rests, 7½" sq **260.00**
Ashtray, mc checkered pattern, 4 rests, 1x13⅞x10"....................**190.00**
Ashtray, red/bl/gold/blk web-like pattern, free-form, 9" L **140.00**
Bowl, bl radiating lines, gr-gold circles along rim, 2¼x9"............**125.00**
Bowl, radiating bands: beige/wht/gray w/gold-stripe accents, sq, 9"..**100.00**
Bowl, wht globular spokes & gold spirals in clear, 12¼"...............**95.00**
Bowl, yel/orange/silver stripes, 4-sided, 10".................................**280.00**

Bowl, 2-tone gr radiating bands w/in, gr & bl band ext, 8¼".......100.00
Bowl, 4-color counterclockwise pinwheel, wide rim, 4½x17½"..365.00
Bowl/platter, 3 abstract flowers among forked branch on bl, 13½" sq.......235.00
Chandelier, 3-arm, orange 12" panels w/lt orange & wht inner shades.....265.00
Charger, mc bubbles/swirls in clear w/gold, 15" 265.00
Charger, radiating design, purple/lt & dk pk in clear, 11½" 75.00
Figurine, angel, flat w/wire halo/hands/ft, 13½".........................85.00
Mobile, 31 mc glass pcs & copper mts, 41x22" dia.................2,000.00
Pendant, abstract design, Michael Higgins, 1¾x2¼" 120.00
Plaque, ear of corn on golden yel, 10x4" 100.00
Plate, radiating spear shapes in purple, 11⅜" 85.00
Plate, 10-point star, mc w/gold, controlled bubbles, 8¼"..............85.00
Tray, birds, red/wht/blk w/golden sun & branches, 1x14½x12"...125.00
Tray, fish (5) w/hook & line, bl/gold in clear, 14x10" 150.00
Tray, globular wht spots/gold spiral in clear, 2-part, 7x14"..........170.00
Tray, golden sand dollars in lav & bl, 10x7" 140.00
Tray, red/orange/gr radiating design w/gold spirals, 10x5" 95.00
Tray, red/wht/yel/orange geometric w/gr border, 7x14" 175.00
Tray, stylized birds & sun w/gold, 12x7½" 80.00
Vase, bl w/gr & wht striations, controlled bubbles, 3x3¾"..........100.00
Vase, Drop-Out, silver-bl/gr/silver-lav on lav, wide rim, 3½x4¼"..140.00

Historical Glass

Glassware commemorating particularly significant historical events became popular in the late 1800s. Bread trays were the most common form, but plates, mugs, pitchers, and other items were also pressed in clear as well as colored glass. It was sold in vast amounts at the 1876 Philadelphia Centennial Exposition by various manufacturers who exhibited their wares on the grounds. It remained popular well into the twentieth century.

In the listings that follow, L numbers refer to a book by Lindsey, a standard guide used by many collectors. Our advisor for this category is Darlene Yohe; she is listed in the Directory under Arkansas.

See also Bread Plates; Pattern Glass.

Ale glass, Centennial...60.00
Bank, Liberty Bell..38.00
Bottle, Columbus, milk glass, w/stopper 600.00
Bowl, Frosted Eagle (Old Abe), braid trim, w/lid, 8".................395.00
Bust, Dewey, Manila 1898, 5"...145.00
Butter dish, American Shield 195.00
Celery, Independence Hall...65.00
Covered dish, Pope Leo, milk glass, L-241, very scarce 40.00
Creamer, Peace & Plenty, milk glass, pontil scar, 4⅝".................500.00
Cup, Harrison & Morton, bl..235.00
Flask, McKniley & Hobart, Distilled Protection, 7" 475.00
Flask, Washington & Jackson, dk amber 495.00
Goblet, Emblem Centennial, L-61..45.00
Goblet, Pittsburgh Centennial 95.00
Hat, 1908 Presidential Campaign, milk glass w/red pnt 125.00
Jar, Statue of Liberty, L-530..70.00
Lamp, Goddess of Liberty, 1887 Centennial 125.00
Match holder, T Roosevelt, etched, top-hat form 90.00
Mug, Assassination..60.00
Mug, beer; Philadelphia Centennial 65.00
Mug, Centennial, waisted..90.00
Mug, Christopher Columbus, L-1..45.00
Mug, Columbus/Washington, L-2..175.00
Mug, Geo Peabody hdl 35.00
Mug, Lincoln & Garfield, Our Country's Martyrs, L-272 ....95.00
Mug, McKinley..30.00
Mug, Tennessee, L-102..55.00

Mustard dish, Dewey bust, Xd flags on lid, milk glass, 4¼" 55.00
Paperweight, Cleveland sulfide medallion, 3½".........................195.00
Paperweight, Geo Washington, frosted center, rnd, Gillinder.....295.00
Paperweight, Lincoln, L-275...175.00
Paperweight, Memorial Hall, frosted, L-495.............................150.00
Paperweight, Ruth the Gleaner, frosted, Gillinder......................125.00
Pickle dish, E Pluribus Unum...45.00
Pin tray, McKinley bust, frosted base, L-297.............................110.00
Pitcher, Admiral Dewey, Gridly You May Fire..., 9¼".................140.00
Pitcher, Garfield Drape, scarce...145.00
Plate, Atlantic City Lighthouse, Egg & Dart border, 5¼" 22.00
Plate, Battleship Maine, openwork border, 5½".........................16.00
Plate, CA Gold Rush, Eureka 50.00
Plate, Frieda Hepel, Egg & Dart border, 5¼"............................40.00
Plate, Mary Had a Little Lamb, Egg & Dart border, 5¼"..............25.00
Plate, Old Glory, Egg & Dart border, 5¼".................................32.00
Plate, Present From the Isle of Man, 10" 60.00
Plate, Texas Campaign, lt bl, 9½"..200.00
Plate, US Grant Patriot & Soldier, clear/frosted, 9¼" 250.00
Plate, Yankee Doodle, Egg & Dart border, 5¼".........................35.00
Platter, Centennial Hall...65.00
Platter, Washington Centennial, clear/frosted, dtd hdls 95.00
Shaker, Centennial, boot...27.00
Spooner, Log Cabin, L-184...115.00
Statuette, Ruth the Gleaner, frosted, 1876 Phila Expo, Gillinder...175.00
Stein, Centennial, hdl...60.00
Sugar shaker, Proclaim Liberty Throughout the Land 195.00
Toothpick holder, Preparedness, gold on soldier & sailor 225.00
Tumbler, Admiral Dewey, L-398..55.00
Tumbler, America, L-48...25.00
Tumbler, Lincoln Tribute, L-282..25.00
Tumbler, Pan Am Buffalo Exposition 22.00
Tumbler, Rock of Ages, L-227..25.00
Wine, Washington Centennial 65.00

Hobbs, Brockunier & Co.

Hobbs and Brockunier's South Wheeling Glass Works was in operation during the last quarter of the nineteenth century. They are most famous for their peachblow, amberina, Daisy and Button, and Hobnail pattern glass. The mainstay of the operation, however, was druggist items and plain glassware — bowls, mugs, and simple footed pitchers with shell handles.

Basket, Hobnail, rubena verde, Meriden frame with leaves, 7½" diameter, $495.00.

Bottle, bar; Polka Dot...225.00
Bottle, bitters; Coral (Seaweed) Opal, #308 ....400.00
Bottle, water; Opal Swirl, #325...385.00
Bowl, Daisy & Button, 6½" sq 40.00
Bowl, finger; Dew Drop 25.00

Bowl, fruit; Neopolitan..325.00
Bowl, Leighton, ruby w/crystal rigaree, w/lid, 8" 500.00
Bowl, nappy, Dew Drop, 4½" (rnd or sq)......................25.00
Bowl, Tree of Life, 10"..50.00
Butter dish, Mario, ruby stain w/eng.............................100.00
Canoe, Daisy & Button..80.00
Celery vase, Dew Drop..70.00
Celery vase, Dolphin...120.00
Comport, Goat's Head, low ft, all crystal, 9"................350.00
Cranberry dish, Daisy & Button 35.00
Cup, custard; sapphire bl, shell hdl................................10.00
Goblet, Hobbs' Block..155.00
Jug, Venetian, wht loopings w/ruby or bl threading, minimum value....1,800.00
Molasses can, Murano..115.00
Molasses can, Polka Dot, 12-oz.....................................175.00
Pickle dish, Maltese & Ribbon 30.00
Pitcher, tankard, Leaf & Flower, amber stain.................150.00
Salt cellar, turtle figural, ca 1875..................................75.00
Sugar bowl, Craquelle, w/lid, #305.................................45.00
Sugar bowl, Dolphin, w/lid...375.00
Tray, water; Dew Drop..90.00
Tumbler, Swirl, ruby opal...185.00
Vase, spangle, clear-cased dk bl w/mica flakes, 7¾x5¼"..............245.00

Holt Howard

Novelty ceramics marked Holt Howard were produced in Japan from the 1950s into the 1970s, and these have become quite collectible. They're not only marked, but most are dated as well. There are several lines to reassemble — the rooster, the white cat, figural banks, Christmas angels and Santas, to name only a few — but the one that most Holt Howard collectors seem to gravitate toward is the pixie line. For more information see *Garage Sale and Flea Market Annual* (Collector Books).

Cookie jar, Rooster, from $100.00 to $135.00.

Ashtray, golfer figural, 5½" 95.00
Ashtray, lady w/bottle 110.00
Ashtray, Santa, med 25.00
Bank, Coin Kitty, bobbing head finial, from $100 to......150.00
Bank, piggy, w/polka-dotted neck ribbon, 3x4" 40.00
Bookends, eagle w/uplifted wings, pr.............................150.00
Bowl, cereal; Rooster, 6" 9.00
Butter dish, Kozy Kitten, cats peeking out on side, ¼-lb, $100 to..125.00
Butter dish, Rooster, ¼-lb, from $40 to 50.00
Butter pats, holly leaves & berries, 2¾", set of 4.............32.00
Candle holder, double; 3 choir boys hold lg song book..............38.00
Candle holder, girl kneeling, 2-light 20.00
Candlestick, Santa hdl—

Candlesticks, Pixieware, pr, from $50 to..........................65.00
Candy container, w/pop-up Santa, 4¼"............................50.00
Christmas tree, electric, 10" 70.00
Cocktail onions, Pixieware, onion-head finial, from $160 to......175.00
Cocktail shaker, bartender theme, +4 tumblers.................75.00
Coffeepot, Rooster, electric, from $50 to..........................70.00
Cottage cheese keeper, Kozy Kitten, 2 cats on lid, from $45 to.....55.00
Creamer & sugar bowl, Kozy Kitten, stackable, from $85 to.......100.00
Creamer & sugar bowl, Rooster, from $30 to.....................45.00
Cup & saucer, Rooster..15.00
Dish, Christmas tree form, 9⅞"..15.00
Dish, Santa face, 7¼x5½"..35.00
Honey jar, Pixieware, very rare, from $400 to..................500.00
Jam & jelly jar, Pixieware, flat-head finial, from $65 to.............85.00
Jam & jelly jar, Rooster, from $40 to 50.00
Ketchup bottle, Pixieware, tomato-face finial, 6", from $80 to ...110.00
Lipstick holder, Ponytail Princess, from $50 to 65.00
Match holder, pk mouse w/cane, unmk, 6".......................40.00
Match holder, Santa w/bongo drums, 4½" 30.00
Mug, Christmas tree w/Santa hdl......................................10.00
Mugs, Blue Willow, set of 4...45.00
Mustard jar, Pixieware, yel head finial, from $80 to.........110.00
Mustard jar, Rooster, w/lid..35.00
Napkin holder, Rooster...40.00
Note pad holder, 3-D lady's hand.....................................45.00
Olive jar, Pixieware, winking gr head finial, from $100 to 125.00
Pencil sharpener, whale figural, sharpener in mouth.........55.00
Pitcher, water; Rooster, flaring sides, tail hdl, tall 50.00
Plant feeder, bird form...25.00
Planter, candy cane..20.00
Plate, Rake 'N Spade, MIB..20.00
Plate, Rooster, 8½", from $15 to.......................................22.00
Platter, Rooster, oval, from $28 to....................................35.00
Relish jar, Pixieware, gr flat-head finial.............................250.00
Russian dressing bottle, Pixieware, minimum value.........200.00
Shakers, bride & groom, pr 30.00
Shakers, Christmas tree w/Santa, pr 25.00
Shakers, goose & golden egg, pr..40.00
Shakers, Kozy Kitten, cat's head, pr 30.00
Shakers, Kozy Kitten, tall cats w/noisemakers, pr.............45.00
Shakers, mice in wicker baskets, pr...................................35.00
Shakers, Ponytail Princess..45.00
Shakers, poodle & cat, 4½", 4", pr....................................40.00
Shakers, Santa & his bag, Santa: 3", pr.............................35.00
Shakers, Santa & Rudolph in bed, 3-pc 55.00
Snack set, tomato cup & lettuce leaf plate.........................25.00
Spice set, stacking; Kozy Kitten, from $150 to..................175.00
String holder, Kozy Kitten, head only, from $40 to...........50.00
Tape measure, Kozy Kitten, cat on cushion 85.00
Tray, butler (Jeeves), 4¾" wide...150.00
Tray, dbl; Ponytail Girl, 2 joined flower cups, girl between, $50 to..65.00
Tray, Rooster, facing left, from $15 to...............................20.00
Tray, Santa, beard forms tray, 7¾" 25.00
Vase, bud; Kozy Kitten, cat in plaid cap & neckercheif, from $75 to..100.00
Votive candle holder, pig, pastel, dtd 1958, 5½"................45.00
Votive candle holder, Santa, dtd 1968, 3" 20.00
Wall pocket, Kozy Kitten, 7½", from $40 to 50.00

Homer Laughlin

The Homer Laughlin China Company of Newell, West Virginia, was founded in 1871. The superior dinnerware they displayed at the Centennial Exposition in Philadelphia in 1876 won the highest award of excellence. From that time to the present, they have continued to produce quality dinnerware and kitchenware, many lines of which are becoming very popular collectibles. Most of the dinnerware is marked with the name of the pattern and occasionally with the shape name as well. The 'HLC' trademark is usually followed by a number series, the first two digits of which indicate the year of its manufacture. For further information we recommend *The Collector's Encyclopedia of Fiesta, Ninth Edition*, by Sharon and Bob Huxford; and *The Collector's Encyclopedia of Homer Laughlin China* by Joanne Jasper (both available from Collector Books). Another fine source of information is *Homer Laughlin, A Giant Among Dishes*, by Jo Cunningham (Schiffer). Our advisors for Virginia Rose are Jack and Treva Hamlin; they are listed in the Directory under Ohio.

Our values are base prices. Very desirable patterns on the shapes named in our listings may increase values by as much as 75%. See also Blue Willow; Fiesta; Harlequin; Riviera.

Century

For English Garden or Sun Porch, add from 50% to 75%; Mexican lines are at least double.

Bowl, deep, 1-pt, from $23 to	32.00
Bowl, fruit; from $8 to	10.00
Bowl, nappy, 8", from $22 to	26.00
Butter dish, from $125 to	150.00
Jug, 2½-pt, from $65 to	80.00
Plate, 8", from $11 to	14.00
Plate, 10", from $18 to	21.00
Platter, 10", from $22 to	26.00
Sugar bowl, w/lid, from $28 to	38.00
Teapot, from $100 to	150.00

Debutante

For Suntone, add 20%; add 25% for Karol China gold-decorated items.

Bowl, nappy, 8", from $10 to	12.00
Casserole, w/lid, from $30 to	35.00
Coffeepot, from $50 to	60.00
Plate, chop; 15", from $16 to	20.00
Sugar bowl, w/lid, from $12 to	18.00
Teapot, from $40 to	50.00

Eggshell Georgian

Bowl, cream soup; from $22 to	28.00
Cup & saucer, from $14 to	21.00
Egg cup, dbl; from $30 to	40.00
Plate, sq, 8", from $16 to	22.00
Sugar bowl, from $25 to	30.00
Teapot, from $65 to	95.00

Eggshell Nautilus

Baker, 10", from $24 to	32.00
Bowl, rim soup; deep, from $12 to	18.00
Creamer, from $15 to	25.00
Cup & saucer, AD; from $13 to	20.00
Plate, 8", from $9 to	12.00
Sugar bowl, w/lid, from $20 to	30.00

Empress

Add 25% for solid colors. See also Bluebird China.

Bowl, fruit; 6", from $6 to	8.00
Creamer, from $12 to	16.00
Gravy boat, from $20 to	28.00
Sauce tureen, from $45 to	55.00
Sugar bowl, w/lid, from $18 to	25.00
Teapot, from $75 to	95.00

Marigold

Bowl, flat soup; from $12 to	18.00
Bowl, oatmeal; from $12 to	17.00
Casserole, w/lid, from $60 to	80.00
Cup & saucer, tea; from $14 to	22.00
Platter, from $20 to	30.00
Sauce boat, from $24 to	35.00

Nautilus

Baker, 10", from $22 to	28.00
Bowl, onion soup (lug); from $14 to	16.00
Bowl, oval vegetable; from $18 to	24.00
Butter dish, Jade, from $50 to	65.00
Cup & saucer, from $14 to	22.00
Plate, dinner; 10", from $12 to	15.00

Rhythm

Add 25% for American Provincial.

Casserole, w/lid, from $40 to	50.00
Creamer, from $14 to	20.00
Plate, 9", from $12 to	15.00
Platter, from $20 to	22.00
Sauce boat, from $25 to	30.00
Sugar bowl, w/lid, from $20 to	25.00

Swing

Add 30% for Oriental patterns and Mexicali.

Creamer and sugar bowl with lid, Mexicali, $45.00; 13½" platter, $50.00.

Baker, from $25 to	32.00
Bowl, fruit; from $9 to	12.00
Bowl, serving; from $25 to	35.00
Bowl, soup; from $15 to	18.00
Plate, 9", from $12 to	15.00
Sauce boat, from $25 to	35.00
Teapot, from $85 to	125.00

Virginia Rose

Use the high end of the price range to evaluate popular patterns such as JJ59 and VR128.

Baker, 9", from $18 to	26.00
Bowl, coupe soup; from $20 to	25.00
Bowl, lug soup; from $20 to	25.00
Bowl, nappy, 8", from $24 to	35.00
Casserole/covered dish, from $85 to	135.00
Cup & saucer, tea; from $13 to	21.00
Egg cup, dbl (Cable); from $75 to	100.00
Jug, 7½", from $115 to	155.00
Mug, coffee; from $25 to	40.00
Plate, 7", from $8 to	11.00
Plate, 9", from $12 to	18.00
Platter, 10½", from $24 to	28.00

Wells

Add 25% for solid colors Sienna Brown, French Rose, or Leaf Green.

Casserole, from $35 to	45.00
Creamer, from $10 to	14.00
Muffin cover, from $55 to	75.00
Plate, dinner; from $12 to	14.00
Platter, 15", from $18 to	22.00
Sauce boat, from $15 to	18.00
Sugar bowl (open), from $10 to	14.00
Teapot, from $50 to	60.00

Hull

The A.E. Hull Pottery was formed in 1905 in Zanesville, Ohio, and in the early years produced stoneware specialities. They expanded in 1907, adding a second plant and employing over two hundred workers. By 1920 they were manufacturing a full line of stoneware, art pottery with both airbrushed and blended glazes, florist pots, and gardenware. They also produced toilet ware and kitchen items with a white semi-porcelain body. Although these continued to be staple products, after the stock market crash of 1929, emphasis was shifted to tile production. By the mid-'30s interest in art pottery production was growing, and over the next fifteen years, several lines of matt pastel floral-decorated patterns were designed, consisting of vases, planters, baskets, ewers, and bowls in various sizes.

The Red Riding Hood cookie jar, patented in 1943, proved so successful that a whole line of figural kitchenware and novelty items was added. They continued to be produced well into the '50s. (See also Little Red Riding Hood.) Through the '40s their floral artware lines flooded the market, due to the restriction of foreign imports. Although best known for their pastel matt-glazed ware, some of the lines were high gloss. Rosella, glossy coral on a pink clay body, was produced for a short time only; and Magnolia, although offered in a matt glaze, was produced in gloss as well.

The plant was destroyed in 1950 by a flood which resulted in a devastating fire when the floodwater caused the kilns to explode. The company rebuilt and equipped their new factory with the most modern machinery. It was soon apparent that the matt glaze could not be duplicated through the more modern processes, however, and soon attention was concentrated on high-gloss artware lines such as Parchment and Pine and Ebb Tide. Figural planters and novelties, piggy banks, and dinnerware were produced in abundance in the late '50s and '60s. By the mid-'70s dinnerware and florist ware were the mainstay of their business.

The firm discontinued operations in 1985.

Our advisor, Brenda Roberts, has compiled a lovely book, *The Collector's Encyclopedia of Hull Pottery,* with full-color photos and current values, available from Collector Books.

Special note to Hull collectors: reproductions are on the market in all categories of Hull pottery — matt florals, Red Riding Hood, and later lines including House 'n Garden dinnerware.

Athena, vase, cornucopia; #608, 8½", from $30 to	40.00
Athena, wall pocket, #61, 8½", from $130 to	165.00
Blossom Flite, bowl, console; #T-10, 16½", from $115 to	165.00
Blossom Flite, planter, 10½", from $95 to	135.00
Bow-Knot, candle holder, #B-17, 4", from $140 to	175.00

Bow-Knot, cornucopia, B-5, 7½", from $225.00 to $265.00.

Bow-Knot, jardiniere, #B-19, 9⅜", from $950 to	1,200.00
Bow-Knot, vase, cornucopia; #B-5, 7½", from $225 to	265.00
Bow-Knot, wall pocket, pitcher from, #B-26, 6", from $275 to	325.00
Butterfly, bonbon, #B-4, 6½", from $30 to	45.00
Butterfly, pitcher, #B-11, 8¾", from $155 to	215.00
Butterfly, vase, bud; #B-1, 6¼", from $50 to	70.00
Calla Lily, candle holder, gr to pk, unmk, 2¼", from $100 to	130.00
Calla Lily, ewer, pk to bl, #506, 10", from $380 to	480.00
Camellia, vase, bud; pk, low hdls, #129, 7", from $175 to	225.00
Camellia, vase, swan form, pk, #118, 6½", from $175 to	215.00
Capri, swan, #23, 1961, 8½", from $40 to	60.00
Capri, vase, urn form, #50, 9", from $45 to	65.00
Cinderella Kitchenware (Blossom), casserole, open, #21, 7½", up to	45.00
Cinderella Kitchenware (Blossom), pitcher, #29, 16-oz, from $45 to	70.00
Cinderella Kitchenware (Bouquet), grease jar, #24, 32-oz, $50 to	75.00
Cinderella Kitchenware (Bouquet), shaker, #25, 3½", from $20 to	30.00
Continental, consolette, 13¼", from $80 to	115.00
Continental, flower bowl, 9¼", from $35 to	45.00
Coronet, flowerpot, #204, 4", from $10 to	12.00
Coronet, window box, #207, 8", from $15 to	20.00
Dogwood, vase, cornucopia, cream to bl, #522, 3¾", from $110 to	135.00
Dogwood, vase, pk to bl, long hdls, #513, 6½", from $140 to	165.00
Early Art, jardiniere, turq w/emb decor on semi-porc, #546, 7"	140.00
Early Art, vase, emb ribs, slim, #39, 8"	155.00
Early Utility, bowl, yel w/brn band, #106, 1920s, 6"	35.00
Early Utility, mug, gr, 1930s, 4½"	35.00
Ebb Tide, basket, #E-11, 16½", from $210 to	265.00
Ebb Tide, pitcher, #E-10, 14", from $210 to	295.00
Ebb Tide, vase, angelfish form, #E-6, 9¼", from $150 to	200.00
Ebb Tide, vase, twin fish form, #E-7, from $155 to	165.00
Fiesta, ewer, #48, 8¾", from $75 to	100.00
Fiesta, flowerpot, #40, 4¼", from $20 to	30.00
Fiesta, vase, #45, 8½", from $85 to	125.00
Heritageware, cookie jar, #0-18, 9¼", from $100 to	145.00
Heritageware, cruet, USA, 6¼", from $25 to	35.00
Heritageware, grease jar, #A-3, 5¾", from $30 to	50.00
House 'n Garden, baker, #543, 10", from $20 to	30.00

House 'n Garden, bean pot, #510, 2-qt, from $30 to **40.00**
House 'n Garden, bowl, divided vegetable; #542, 10¾", from $25 to..**35.00**
House 'n Garden, canister set, 6-9", 4-pc, from $375 to.............**475.00**
House 'n Garden, casserole, Fr; w/lid, #579, 3-pt, from $55 to......**80.00**
House 'n Garden, casserole, w/lid, #544, 10", from $35 to **50.00**
House 'n Garden, casserole, w/lid, #548, 10", from $40 to **65.00**
House 'n Garden, coffee carafe set, #528, 2-cup, from $35 to **50.00**
House 'n Garden, coffeepot, #522, 8-cup, from $40 to **50.00**
House 'n Garden, cookie jar, 3523, 94-oz, from $50 to.................**75.00**
House 'n Garden, Dutch oven, #568, 3-pt, from $30 to **40.00**
House 'n Garden, jar, #551, 12-oz, from $25 to...........................**30.00**
House 'n Garden, jug, water; #509, 5-pt, from $50 to **80.00**
House 'n Garden, mug, #502, 9-oz, from $4 to **6.00**
House 'n Garden, plate, 10", from $8 to **12.00**
House 'n Garden, shakers, #515/#516, pr, from $14 to **18.00**
House 'n Garden, soup 'n sandwich set, from $20 to **25.00**
House 'n Garden, steak plate, #541, 11¾", from $20 to................**25.00**
House 'n Garden, teapot, #549, 5-cup, from $25 to......................**35.00**
House 'n Garden, vase, bud; 9", from $20 to.................................**30.00**
Imperial, basket, #F-38, 1960s, 6¾", from $25 to **35.00**
Imperial, ewer, #F-480, late 1960s, 10½", from $40 to **60.00**
Imperial, planter, Carnation Pink, #F-24, 12½", from $22 to........**32.00**
Imperial, vase, Carnation Pink, #413, 8¾", from $16 to **24.00**
Imperial, vase, urn form, #454, 5", from $16 to...........................**22.00**
Iris, candle holder, pk to bl, #411, 5", from $125 to **155.00**
Iris, vase, pk to bl, ornate hdls, shaped top, #414, 10½", $325 to .**410.00**
Iris, vase, yel to pk, hdls, scalloped top, #406, 8½", from $210 to..**250.00**
Kitchenware (Crescent), shaker, #B-4, 3¾", from $16 to.............**22.00**
Kitchenware (Crescent), teapot, #B-13, 7½", from $65 to **95.00**
Kitchenware (Debonair), cookie jar, pk, #0-8, 8¼", from $75 to...**105.00**
Kitchenware (Floral), bowl, salad; #49, 10", from $60 to **85.00**
Kitchenware (Floral), grease jar, #43, 5¾", from $40 to **50.00**
Kitchenware (Vegetable), cookie jar, #28, 8¾", from $350 to **450.00**
Magnolia, gloss; basket, #H-14, 10½", from $400 to **450.00**
Magnolia, gloss; console bowl, #H-23, 13", from $125 to............**165.00**
Magnolia, gloss; teapot, #H-20, 6½", from $175 to **225.00**
Magnolia, gloss; vase, low hdls, #H-13, 10½", from $140 to **180.00**
Magnolia, matt; ewer, #18, 13½", from $375 to...........................**435.00**
Magnolia, matt; lamp base, 12½" pottery sections+metal ft, $350 to .**450.00**
Magnolia, matt; teapot, #23, 6½", from $250 to...........................**275.00**
Magnolia, matt; vase, dbl cornucopia; #6, 12", from $205 to **255.00**
Magnolia, matt; vase, low hdls, #9, 10½", from $235 to **275.00**
Mardi Gras, bowl, mixing; unmk, 1940, 10¼" **55.00**
Mardi Gras/Granada, ewer, #31, 10", from $150 to **185.00**
Mardi Gras/Granada, vase, cream, ftd/loop hdls, #216, 1947, 9", $50 to..**75.00**
Mayfair, wall pocket, mandolin shape, #84, 7", from $35 to..........**45.00**
Novelty, basket, #72, 8", from $80 to **125.00**
Novelty, cat figurine, unmk, ca 1940, 7", from $300 to **400.00**
Novelty, clown planter, #82, 6¼", from $45 to **65.00**
Novelty, flowerpot, emb rings, yel, #95, 1940, 4½", from $15 to ..**20.00**
Novelty, leaf dish, #85, 13", from $35 to **45.00**
Novelty, piggy bank, solid satin, 1958, 3½", from $250 to **325.00**
Novelty, planter, Basket Girl, glossy, #954, mid-1940s, 8", $35 to..**45.00**
Novelty, poodle planter, #114, 8", from $50 to **75.00**
Orchid, basket, pk to bl, #305, 7", from $750 to...........................**850.00**
Orchid, vase, bl, trumpet neck, hdls, #301, 10", from $425 to **525.00**
Parchment & Pine, ashtray, #S-14, 14", from $145 to **185.00**
Parchment & Pine, bowl, console; unmk, 16" L, from $95 to **145.00**
Parchment & Pine, teapot, #S-15, 8", from $175 to....................**225.00**
Poppy, basket, yel to pk, #601, 12", from $1,300 to..................**1,600.00**
Poppy, vase, bl to pk, sm scroll hdls, #606, 10½", from $450 to..**550.00**
Rainbow, leaf dish, #86, 10", from $20 to.....................................**30.00**
Regal, planter, #303, 5", from $10 to **15.00**
Rosella, lamp base, ivory w/gr, #L 3, 1946, 11", from $400 to **500.00**

Rosella, sugar bowl, ivory w/gr, R-4, 5½", from $45 to **65.00**
Rosella, vase, cornucopia, ivory w/gr, R-13, 8½" L, from $125 to ...**165.00**
Royal Imperial, jardiniere, #75, 7", from $35 to **55.00**
Royal Imperial, window box, #82, 12½", from $25 to....................**35.00**
Royal Woodland, basket, #W-9, 8¾", from $95 to **150.00**
Royal Woodland, vase, cornucopia; #W-10, 11", from $65 to.......**95.00**
Royal Woodland, wall pocket, #W-13, 7½", from $90 to...........**125.00**
Serenade, basket, #S-14, 12x11½", from $400 to **500.00**
Serenade, mug, S-22, 8-oz, from $75 to.....................................**100.00**
Sueno Tulip, vase, bl, ring hdls, #101-33, 9", from $325 to........**380.00**
Sueno Tulip, vase, bud; pk to bl, #104-33, 6", from $140 to **165.00**
Sunglow, ewer, #90, 5½", from $40 to **55.00**
Sunglow, vase, dk pk gloss, #100, 1952, 6½", from $55 to............**85.00**
Sunglow, wall pocket, iron shape, unmk, 6", from $165 to..........**210.00**
Sunglow, wall pocket, whisk broom shape, #82, 8¼", from $125 to ..**160.00**
Thistle, vase, pk, angle hdls, #52, 6½", from $130 to...................**150.00**
Tokay/Tuscany, basket, #11, 10½", from $120 to **170.00**
Tokay/Tuscany, candy dish, #9, 7x8½", from $130 to **175.00**
Tokay/Tuscany, creamer, #17, from $75 to..................................**105.00**
Tokay/Tuscany, leaf dish, #19, 13", from $30 to **50.00**
Tropicana, ewer, #56, 12½", from $575 to **675.00**
Water Lily, candle holder, #L-22, 4½", from $85 to **125.00**
Water Lily, ewer, #L-17, 13½", from $525 to **650.00**
Water Lily, jardiniere, #L-23, 5½", from $130 to **170.00**
Water Lily, vase, cornucopia; #L-7, 6½", from $115 to **150.00**
Wildflower, basket, pk to yel to bl, #W-16, 10½", from $375 to .**425.00**
Wildflower, candle holder, pk to yel, unmk, from $60 to..............**85.00**
Wildflower (# series), creamer, #73, 4¾", from $240 to **275.00**
Wildflower (# series), ewer, #W-2, 5½", from $105 to................**140.00**
Woodland, gloss (post-1950); teapot, 2-tone, #W-16, 6½", $140 to ...**185.00**
Woodland, gloss (post-1950); window box, 2-tone, #W-14, 10", $60 to..**90.00**
Woodland, matt (1949); basket, #W-22, 10½", from $850 to..**1,100.00**
Woodland, matt (1949); vase, cornucopia; #W-2, 5½", from $105 to..**145.00**
Woodland, matt (1949); vase, low hdls, #W-16, 8½", from $230 to...**295.00**

Hummel

Hummel figurines were created through the artistry of Berta Hummel, a Franciscan nun called Sister M. Innocentia. The first figures were made about 1935 by Franz Goebel of Goebel Art Inc., Rodental, West Germany. Plates, plaques, and candy dishes are also produced, and the older, discontinued editions are highly sought collectibles. Generally speaking, an issue can be dated by the trademark. The first Hummels, from 1935 to 1949, were either incised or stamped with the 'Crown WG' mark. The 'Full Bee in V' mark was employed with minor variations until 1959. At that time the bee was stylized and represented by a solid disk with angled symetrical wings completely contained within the confines of the 'V.' The Three-Line mark, 1964 – 1972, utilized the stylized bee and included a three-line arrangement, 'c by W. Goebel, W. Germany.' Another change in 1972 saw the 'Stylized Bee in V' suspended between the vertical bars of the 'b' and 'l' of a printed 'Goebel, West Germany.' Collectors refer to this mark as the 'Last Bee' or 'Goebel Bee.' The mark in use from 1979 to 1990 omits the 'bee in V.' The New Crown mark, in use from 1991 to 1999 is a small crown with 'WG' initials, a large 'Goebel,' and a small 'Germany' signifying a united Germany. The current Millennium Mark came into use in the year 2000 and features a large bee. For further study we recommend *Hummel, An Illustrated Handbook and Price Guide*, by Ken Armke; *Hummel Figurines and Plates, A Collector's Identification and Value Guide*, by Carl Luckey; *The No. 1 Price Guide to M.I. Hummel* by Robert L. Miller; and *The Fascinating World of M.I. Hummel* by Goebel. These books are available through your local book dealer.

See also Limited Edition Plates.

Key:
ce — closed edition
CM — Crown Mark
cn — closed number
FB — Full Bee
LB — Last Bee
MB — Missing Bee

MM — Millennium Mark
NC — New Crown Mark
oe — open edition
SB — Stylized Bee
tw — temporarily withdrawn
3L — Three-Line mark

#305, The Builder,
Last Bee Mark,
5½", $225.00.

#II/111, Wayside Harmony, table lamp, FB, ce, 7½" 325.00
#II/112, Just Resting, table lamp, CM, ce, 7½" 430.00
#III/110, Let's Sing, box, CM, ce, 6¼" 540.00
#III/38/I, Angel, Joyous News w/Lute, candle holder, CM, ce, 2½".215.00
#III/63, Singing Lesson, box, CM, ce, 5¾" 540.00
#2/0, Little Fiddler, CM, ce, 6" 505.00
#5, Strolling Along, FB, ce, 5¼" 360.00
#6/0, Sensitive Hunter, CM, ce, 4¾" 470.00
#8, Book Worm, CM, ce, 4¼" 505.00
#11/0, Merry Wanderer, CM, ce, 5" 375.00
#12, Chimney Sweep, CM, ce, 6" 540.00
#14 A&B, Book Worm, boy & girl, bookends, FB, ce, 5½", pr...470.00
#15/0, Hear Ye, Hear Ye, MB, ce, 5" 175.00
#16, Little Hiker, FB, ce, 5½" 325.00
#18, Christ Child, SB, ce, 3¾x6½" 160.00
#20, Prayer Before Battle, FB, ce, 4¼" 250.00
#21/0, Heavenly Angel, 3L, ce, 4½" 120.00
#23, Adoration, CM, ce, 9" 1,150.00
#24/I, Lullaby, candle holder, SB, ce, 3½x5¼" 200.00
#26, Child Jesus, font, CM, ce, 3x5¾" 250.00
#27/I, Joyous News, FB, ce, 2¾" 180.00
#29/0, Guardian Angel, FB, ce, 2⅞x6" 935.00
#30/I A&B, Ba-Bee-Ring, CM, ce, red rings, 5¼x6", pr 5,760.00
#32/0, Little Gabriel, SB, ce, 5¼" 160.00
#33, Joyful, ashtray, 3L, ce, 3½x6" 145.00
#35/I, Good Shepherd, font, FB, ce, 2¾x5¾" 200.00
#36/0, Child w/Flowers, font, FB, ce, 3¼x4¼" 90.00
#42/I, Good Shepherd, FB, ce, 7½" 4,320.00
#43, March Winds, 3L, ce, 5¼" 145.00
#44B, Out of Danger, table lamp, CM, ce, 9" 360.00
#47/0, Goose Girl, 3L, ce, 5" 215.00
#48/II, Madonna, plaque, CM, ce, 4¾x5¾" 395.00
#49/I, To Market, 3L, ce, 6¼" 360.00
#50/I, Volunteers, FB, ce, 6¾" 540.00
#52/0, Going to Grandma's, SB, ce, 4¾" 290.00
#53, Joyful, FB, ce, 4" 160.00
#54, Silent Night, candle holder, FB, ce, 3½x4¾" 395.00
#56/A, Culprits, FB, ce, 6½" 360.00
#57/I, Chick Girl, CM, ce, 4¼" 540.00
#58, Playmates, CM, ce, 4¼" 575.00

#60 A&B, Farm Boy/Goose Girl, bookends, CM, ce, 4¾", pr....685.00
#62, Happy Pastime, ashtray, CM, ce, 3½x6¼" 325.00
#64, Shepherd's Boy, FB, ce, 6" 290.00
#65/0, Farewell, SB, ce, 3¾" 3,600.00
#66, Farm Boy, FB, ce, 5½" 290.00
#67, Doll Mother, SB, ce, 4½" 235.00
#70, Holy Child, 3L, ce, 7¼" 235.00
#71, Stormy Weather, SB, ce, 6½" 470.00
#73, Little Helper, FB, ce, 4½" 180.00
#74, Little Gardener, FB, ce, 4¼" 160.00
#79, Globe Trotter, 3L, ce, 5¼" 200.00
#80, Little Scholar, FB, ce, 5½" 270.00
#81 2/0, School Girl, SB, ce, 4½" 160.00
#82/0, School Boy, LB, ce, 5½" 180.00
#84/V, Worship, FB, ce, 13" 1,080.00
#85/II, Serenade, FB, ce, 7¼" 540.00
#86, Happiness, CM, ce, 4¾" 290.00
#88, Heavenly Protection, FB, ce, 9¼" 935.00
#89/I, Little Cellist, SB, ce, 5¾" 235.00
#91 A&B, Angels at Prayer, font, FB, ce, 3⅜x5" 145.00
#92, Merry Wanderer, plaque, FB, ce, 4¾x5¼" 200.00
#93, Little Fiddler, plaque, SB, ce, 4½x5" 160.00
#94, Surprise, CM, ce, 5¾" 575.00
#95, Brother, CM, ce, 5½" 430.00
#96, Little Shopper, FB, ce, 4¾" 200.00
#98, Sister, FB, ce, 5¾" 250.00
#100, Shrine, table lamp, CM, ce, 7½" 5,760.00
#102, Volunteers, table lamp, CM, ce, 7½" 5,750.00
#104, Eventide, table lamp, CM, ce, 7½" 5,760.00
#106, Merry Wanderer, plaque w/wood fr, CM, ce, 6x6" 2,160.00
#109/II, Happy Traveler, SB, ce, 7½" 360.00
#110, Let's Sing, CM, ce, 4" 340.00
#111/I, Wayside Harmony, FB, ce, 5¼" 325.00
#112/I, Just Resting, CM, ce, 5¼" 470.00
#113, Heavenly Song, candle holder, CM, ce, 3½x4¾" 4,320.00
#114, Let's Sing, SB, ce, 3½x6¼" 160.00
#116, Girl w/Fir Tree, advent candle holder, FB, ce, 3½" 80.00
#118, Little Thrifty, bank, FB, ce, 5¼" 290.00
#123, Max & Moritz, CM, ce, 5¼" 470.00
#124/I, Hello, FB, ce, 7" 325.00
#126, Retreat to Safety, plaque, FB, ce, 5x5" 290.00
#127, Doctor, CM, ce, 5" 325.00
#128, Baker, FB, ce, 5" 250.00
#130, Duet, FB, ce, 5¼" 395.00
#132, Star Gazer, SB, ce, 4¾" 235.00
#134, Quartet, plaque, FB, ce, 5½x6¼" 380.00
#136/I, Friends, SB, ce, 5¼" 235.00
#137A, Child in Bed, plaque, CM, ce, 3x3" 3,600.00
#138, Tiny Baby in Crib, plaque, FB, cn, 2¼x3" 2,880.00
#140, The Mail Is Here, plaque, FB, ce, 4¼x6¾" 325.00
#141/X, Apple Tree Girl, LB, ce, 32" 10,800.00
#142/X, Apple Tree Boy, SB, ce, 30" 12,240.00
#143/I, Boots, FB, ce, 6¾" 430.00
#144, Angelic Song, FB, ce, 4" 200.00
#146, Angel Duet, font, CM, ce, 3½x4¾" 125.00
#150 2/0, Happy Days, 3L, ce, 4¼" 160.00
#151, Madonna Holding Child, FB, ce, bl, 12½" 1,440.00
#152/0 A, Umbrella Boy, SB, ce, 4¾" 610.00
#152B, Umbrella Girl, CM, ce, 8" 2,880.00
#153, Auf Wiedersehen, CM, ce, 7" 650.00
#154/0, Waiter, FB, ce, 6¼" 270.00
#163, Whitsuntide, FB, ce, 6¾" 610.00
#165, Swaying Lullaby, plaque, CM, ce, 4½x5¼" 575.00
#167, Angel w/Bird, font, FB, ce, 3¼x4⅛" 110.00

#169, Bird Duet, CM, ce, 4" 305.00
#170/I, School Boys, 3L, ce, 7½" 1,115.00
#172/0, Festival Harmony (Mandolin), SB, ce, 8" 360.00
#174, She Loves Me, She Loves Me Not, FB, ce, 4¼" ...250.00
#176/I, Happy Birthday, FB, ce, 5½" 395.00
#177, School Girls, CM, ce, 9½" 2,880.00
#178, The Photographer, SB, ce, 5" 310.00
#179, Coquettes, CM, ce, 5¼" 575.00
#180, Tuneful Good Night, plaque, SB, ce, 5x3¾" 250.00
#182, Good Friends, CM, ce, 4¼" 395.00
#183, Forest Shrine, SB, ce, 9" 505.00
#184, Latest News, FB, ce, 5¼" 395.00
#186, Sweet Music, CM, ce, 5¼" 395.00
#188, Celestial Musician, FB, ce, 7" 610.00
#191, Old Man Walking to the Market, cn, 6¾" 10,800.00
#193, Angel Duet, candle holder, CM, ce, 5" 970.00
#194, Watchful Angel, FB, ce, 6½" 470.00
#195 2/0, Barnyard Hero, 3L, ce, 4" 160.00
#196/0, Telling Her Secret, FB, ce, 5¼" 430.00
#197/I, Be Patient, SB, ce, 6¼" 305.00
#199/I, Feeding Time, SB, ce, 5¾" 305.00
#200/I, Little Goat Herder, FB, ce, 5¼" 325.00
#201, Retreat to Safety, CM, ce, 6" 720.00
#203 2/0, Signs of Spring, FB, ce, 4" 305.00
#204, Weary Wanderer, CM, ce, 5¾" 505.00
#205, MI Hummel Dealer's Plaque, German, FB, ce, 5½x4¼" ...720.00
#206, Angel Cloud, font, SB, ce, 3¼x4¾" 145.00
#217, Boy With Toothache, FB, ce, 5¼" 305.00
#218/0, Birthday Serenade, FB, ce, 5¼" 630.00
#220, We Congratulate (w/base), FB, ce, 4" 235.00
#222, Madonna Plaque, FB, ce, 4x5" 540.00
#223, To Market, table lamp, SB, ce, 9½" 470.00
#224/I, Wayside Harmony, table lamp, FB, ce, 7½" 395.00
#226, Mail Is Here, FB, ce, 4½x6¼" 790.00
#228, Good Friends, table lamp, FB, ce, 7½" 470.00
#229, Apple Tree Girl, table lamp, FB, ce, 7½" 650.00
#231, Birthday Serenade, table lamp, FB, ce, 9¾" ..1,440.00
#232, Happy Days, table lamp, FB, ce, 9¾" 865.00
#238B, Angel With Accordion, SB, ce, 2¼" 70.00
#240, Little Drummer, FB, ce, 4¼" 215.00

Hutschenreuther

The Porcelain Factory C.M. Hutschenreuther operated in Bavaria from 1814 to 1969. After the death of the elder Hutschenreuther in 1845, his son Lorenz took over operations, continuing there until 1857 when he left to establish his own company in the nearby city of Selb. The original manufactory became a joint stock company in 1904, absorbing several other potteries. In 1969 both Hutschenreuther firms merged, and that company still operates in Selb. They have distributing centers in both France and the United States.

Casserole, Richelieu, bow finial on lid, gold trim, 8" dia 185.00
Figurine, Borzoi, lying down, 10½" L 265.00
Figurine, Bremen Town Musicians, 4-animal totem, 7½" 200.00
Figurine, cherubs (2) reading, Tutter, 5x4⅝" 165.00
Figurine, Chihuahua, brn, Granget, 4x4" 140.00
Figurine, collie, standing, 4½x6½" 120.00
Figurine, eagle, wings up, perched on rock base, 16¾x9½" 415.00
Figurine, Finale, ballerina on knee, att Tutter, 11½x12" 400.00
Figurine, fox pr, facing opposite directions, 6½x11½" 410.00
Figurine, leopard, open mouth, 18" L 360.00
Figurine, lion, male, head raised, open mouth, #1814, 7x11" 210.00

Figurine, nude lady w/flowers, fawn behind, US Zone, 9¼" 330.00
Figurine, nude on horseback, Tutter, 12½x10½" 400.00
Figurine, nude on unicorn, Tutter, 9x8" 310.00

Figurine, nude standing on a gilded ball, hexagonal basin, 9x7" diameter, $500.00.
(Photo courtesy Neal Auction Gallery)

Figurine, rabbit, jumping over log base, Achtziger, 3x7" 340.00
Figurine, rearing filly, 6¾x4" 125.00
Figurine, rearing stallion, Tutter, 12¼" 215.00
Figurine, 2 bear cubs wrestling, 3¼x5" 155.00
Plate, angel in long robe w/lg wings, gold trim, #3 of 4, ltd ed, 8" ...100.00
Plate, Unicorns in Dreamer's Garden, 6¾" 65.00
Platter, Blue Onion, scalloped edge, #22, 15" 190.00

Imari

Imari is a generic term which covers a broad family of wares. It was made in more than a dozen Japanese villages, but the name is that of the port from whence it was shipped to Europe. There are several types of Imari. The most common features a design with panels of birds, florals, or people surrounding a central basket of flowers. The colors used in this type are underglaze blue with overglaze red, gold, and green enamels. The Chinese also made Imari wares which differ from the Japanese type in several ways — the absence of spur marks, a thinner-type body, and a more consistent control of the blue. Imari-type wares were copied on the continent by Meissen and by English potters, among them Worcester, Derby, and Bow. Unless noted otherwise, our values are for Japanese ware.

Bowl, fish/birds/flowers among central spread-wing bird, ftd, 5x12" ..865.00
Bowl, flowering design, exotic bird cartouches, ftd, 6½x11½" 700.00
Bowl, grass & flowers w/3-petal bl center, scalloped, 4x10" 157.00
Charger, birds/flowers/serpent panels, bl border, unmk, 18" 575.00
Charger, vignettes among flowers & birds, EX color, 24½" 1,000.00
Charger, 4 wht reserves: bird/branch/2 w/foo dogs, w/gilt, 22" 650.00
Dish, florals in cobalt/orange, much gilt, lobed/scalloped, 12" 400.00
Plate, chop; dragons & foliage in panels, lt bl/red/wht, 12" 110.00
Punch bowl, carnations/mums/pheasants, int: flower vase, 16", +teak ft.440.00
Urn, floral panels w/pheasants & cranes, 36½" 2,100.00

Imperial Glass Company

The Imperial Glass Company was organized in 1901 in Bellaire, Ohio, and started manufacturing glassware in 1904. Their early products were jelly glasses, hotel tumblers, etc., but by 1910 they were making a name for themselves by pressing quantities of Carnival glass, the iridescent glassware that was popular during that time. In 1914 NuCut was introduced to imitate cut glass. The line was so popular that it was made in crystal and colors and was reintroduced as Collector's Crystal in the 1950s. From 1916 to 1924 they used the lustre process to make a line called Art Glass, which today some collectors call Imperial Jewels. Free-Hand ware, art glass made entirely by hand using no molds, was made from 1923 to 1924. From 1925 to 1926, they made a less expensive line of art glass called Lead Lustre. These pieces were mold blown and have similar colors and decorations to Free Hand ware.

The company entered bankruptcy in 1931 but was able to continue operations and reorganize as the Imperial Glass Corporation. In 1936 Imperial introduced the Candlewick line, for which it is best known. In the late thirties the Vintage Grape milk glass line was added, and in 1951 a major ad campaign was launched, making Imperial one of the leading milk glass manufacturers.

In 1940 Imperial bought the molds and assets of the Central Glass Works of Wheeling, West Virginia; in 1958 they acquired the molds of the Heisey Company and in 1960 the molds of the Cambridge Glass Company of Cambridge, Ohio. Imperial used these molds, and after 1951 they marked their glassware with an 'I' superimposed over the 'G' trademark. The company was bought by Lenox in 1973; subsequently an 'L' was added to the 'IG' mark. In 1981 Lenox sold Imperial to Arthur Lorch, a private investor (who modified the L by adding a line at the top angled to the left, giving rise to the 'ALIG' mark). He in turn sold the company to Robert F. Stahl, Jr., in 1982. Mr. Stahl filed for Chapter 11 to reorganize, but in mid-1984 liquidation was ordered, and all assets were sold. A few items that had been made in '84 were marked with an 'N' superimposed over the 'I' for 'New Imperial.'

For more information, we recommend *Imperial Glass Encyclopedia, Vols I, II, and III*, edited by James Measell; and *Imperial Carnival Glass* by Carl O Burns.

See also Candlewick; Carnival Glass; Glass Animals and Figurines; Stretch Glass.

Ashtray, fish, milk glass, 4" 18.00
Ashtray, heart shape, ruby slag, #294, 4½" 25.00
Baked apple, Cape Cod, Ritz Blue 25.00
Basket, Crocheted Crystal, 9" 45.00
Basket, Monticello, crystal, 10" 20.00
Bottle, bitters; Reeded, any color, 3-oz 35.00
Bottle, cologne; Cape Cod, crystal, w/stopper, #1601 ......60.00
Bottle, condiment; Cape Cod, crystal, #160/224, 6-oz 65.00
Bottle, cordial; Cape Cod, crystal, #160/256, 18-oz 90.00
Bottle, ketchup; Cape Cod, crystal, #160/237, 14-oz 225.00
Bowl, Amelia, Clambroth, sq, 5½" 25.00
Bowl, Atterbury Scroll, milk glass, 3-toed 25.00
Bowl, Beaded Block, crystal, pk, gr or amber, rnd, flared, 7¼" 30.00
Bowl, Cape Cod, crystal, hdls, #160/51F, 6" 33.00
Bowl, Cape Cod, crystal, oval, divided, #160/125, 11" 80.00
Bowl, console; Crocheted Crystal, 11" 30.00
Bowl, console; Twisted Optic, amber, 10½" 25.00
Bowl, cream soup, Twisted Optic, bl or yel, 4¾" 25.00
Bowl, Dmn Quilt, blk, crimped, 7" 35.00
Bowl, finger; Cape Cod, crystal, #1602, 4" 12.00
Bowl, finger; Mt Vernon, crystal, 5" 12.00
Bowl, Hobnail, purple slag, #641, 8½" 95.00
Bowl, Laced Edge, opal, 5½" 37.50
Bowl, mint; Cape Cod, crystal, hdls, #160/51F, 6" 22.00
Bowl, Monticello, crystal, rnd, 7" 12.50
Bowl, nappy, Amelia, smoke, rnd, 6" 40.00
Bowl, nappy, Fancy Colonial, any color, 6" 20.00
Bowl, Pipe, ruby slag, #1605, 7½" 40.00
Bowl, Rose, jade slag, #52c, 8" 65.00
Bowl, Rose, jade slag, #62c, 9" 75.00

Bowl, salad; Cape Cod, crystal, 11" 60.00
Bowl, salad; Crocheted Crystal, 10½" 27.50
Bowl, salad; Twisted Optic, bl or yel, 9¼" 40.00
Bowl, soup; Katy, gr opal, 7" 80.00
Bowl, Twisted Optic, gr, crimped, 7" 20.00
Box, dog, purple slag, #822 ....185.00
Box, duck, purple slag, 3823 ....185.00
Butter dish, Cape Cod, crystal, #160/161, ¼-lb, w/lid 45.00
Butter dish, Cape Cod, crystal, ¼-lb 45.00
Butter dish, Fancy Colonial, any color, w/lid 75.00
Butter tub, Mt Vernon, crystal, 5" 15.00
Cake salver, Open Lace, milk glass, 12" 25.00
Cake stand, Cape Cod, crystal, #160/103D, 11" 85.00
Cake stand, Crocheted Crystal, ftd, 12" 40.00
Candle holder, Cape Cod, crystal, #160/170, 3" 26.50
Candle holder, Cape Cod, crystal, Aladdin style, 4" 150.00
Candle holder, center pc; Cape Cod, crystal, 6" 95.00
Candle holder, Crocheted Crystal, Narcissus bowl shape 25.00
Candlestick, Free-Hand, heart/vine, wht on clear, bl cup, 10" 400.00
Candlestick, Rose, jade slag, 3½" 75.00
Candlesticks, Dolphin, caramel slag, #779, 5", pr 65.00
Candy box, Reeded, any color, ftd, w/cone lid 50.00
Carafe, wine; Cape Cod, crystal, #160/185, 26-oz 195.00
Celery, Crocheted Crystal, oval, 10" 25.00
Celery, Flute & Cane, crystal, oval, 8½" 25.00
Celery tray, Huckabee, pk, oval, 8¼" 32.50
Champagne, Cape Cod, amber, #1602 ....18.00
Cigarette holder, Cape Cod, crystal, ftd, #1602 ....12.50
Claret, Cape Cod, Azalea, #1602 ....20.00
Claret, Cape Cod, crystal, #1602, 5-oz 12.00
Claret, Fancy Colonial, any color, deep, 5-oz 30.00
Coaster, Cape Cod, crystal, flat, #160/1R, 4½" 9.00
Coaster, Cape Cod, crystal, w/spoon rest, #160/76 ....10.00
Cocktail, Cape Cod, crystal, #160b 12.00
Cocktail, Cape Cod, ruby, #160 ....27.00
Comport, Cape Cod, crystal, #160F, 5¼" 27.50
Comport, Cape Cod, crystal, ftd, w/lid, 6" 80.00
Comport, Lace edge, milk glass, 4-toed, 7" 25.00
Cookie jar, Cape Cod, crystal, wicker hdl, w/lid, #160/195, 6½" ..100.00
Cordial, Collector's Crystal, #612 ....14.00
Cordial, Fancy Colonial, pk, #582, 1-oz 50.00
Creamer, Amelia, crystal 20.00
Creamer, Cape Cod, crystal, ftd 15.00
Creamer, Crocheted Crystal, ftd 20.00
Creamer, Fancy Colonial, any color, ftd 25.00
Cruet, Collector's Crystal, caramel slag, #505 ....50.00
Cruet, Octagon, jade, w/stopper, #505 ....75.00
Cup, coffee; Cape Cod, crystal, #160/37 ....7.00
Cup, coffee; Mt Vernon, crystal 8.00
Cup, punch; Crocheted Crystal, closed hdl 5.00
Cup, punch; Crocheted Crystal, open hdl 7.00
Cup, Reeded, any color 20.00
Decanter, bourbon; Cape Cod, crystal, #160/260 ....80.00
Decanter, Cask #1, Antique Blue 50.00
Decanter, Grape, Heather, #8 ....55.00
Egg cup, Cape Cod, crystal, #160/225 ....32.50
Egg cup, Grape, milk glass, #1952/225 ....12.00
Goblet, cafe parfait; Fancy Colonial, any color, low ft 25.00
Goblet, Cape Cod, Evergreen, #160, 14-oz 55.00
Goblet, Chroma, Midwest Custard, #123 ....35.00
Goblet, Mt Vernon, crystal, 9-oz 10.00
Goblet, water; Monticello, crystal 15.00
Goblet, wine; Amelia, Rubigold 50.00
Goblet, wine; Atterbury Scroll, milk glass 12.00

Goblet, wine; Crocheted Crystal, 4½-oz, 5½" 25.00
Goblet, wine; Dmn Quilt, pk or gr, 2-oz................................12.00
Ice bucket, Cape Cod, crystal, #160/63, 6½" 195.00
Ice tub, Reeded, any color..55.00
Jar, pokal; Cape Cod, crystal, #160/128, 11" 85.00
Jelly, Beaded Block, crystal, pk, gr or amber, stemmed/flared, 4½"...25.00
Ladle, marmalade; Cape Cod, crystal...................................10.00
Ladle, punch; Cape Cod, crystal 35.00
Lamp, Free-Hand, heanging hearts 1,350.00
Lamp, hurricane; Crocheted Crystal, 11" 65.00
Mayonnaise, Monticello, crystal, 3-pc...................................30.00
Mayonnaise, Open Border, milk glass, #1950/23, 3-pc.........25.00
Mayonnaise, Twisted Optic, bl or yel.....................................50.00
Mint dish, Cape Cod, crystal, heart shape, #160/49, 5" 25.00
Muddler, Reeded, any color, 4½" 10.00
Mug, Cape Cod, crystal, hdls, #160/188, 12-oz 50.00
Mug, supper; Eagle, Antique Blue...35.00
Nappy, Pansy, caramel slag, hdl, 5" 35.00
Nut dish, Cape Cod, crystal, hdls, #160/184, 4" 30.00
Parfait, Cape Cod, crystal, #1602, 6-oz................................12.00
Pickle jar, Mt Vernon, crystal, w/lid......................................35.00
Pickle tray, Fancy Colonial, any color, oval, 8" 30.00
Pitcher, Atterbury Scroll, milk glass 60.00
Pitcher, Cape Cod, crystal, #160/24, 2-qt...........................100.00
Pitcher, Cape Cod, crystal, ice lip, 40-oz.............................85.00
Pitcher, Dew Drop, opal, #624, 56-oz...................................65.00
Pitcher, Windmill, red slag, satin..55.00
Plate, Beaded Block, yel, sq, 7¾" 30.00
Plate, bread & butter; Cape Cod, #160/1D, 6½" 8.00
Plate, buffet; Twisted Optic, gr, 14" 25.00
Plate, Cape Cod, crystal, #160/3D, 7" 8.00
Plate, crescent salad; Cape Cod, crystal, 8" 75.00
Plate, Crocheted Crystal, 17"..40.00
Plate, dinner; Cape Cod, crystal, #160/10D, 10" 37.50
Plate, Flute & Cane, 6"...20.00
Plate, luncheon; Dmn Quilt, bl or blk, 8" 15.00
Plate, Monticello, crystal, rnd, 12" 35.00
Plate, Mt Vernon, crystal, rnd, 8" 10.00
Plate, salad bowl liner; Crocheted Crystal, 13" 22.50
Plate, salad; Katy, bl opal, 8" 32.00
Plate, salad; Laced Edge, opal, 8" 35.00
Plate, salad; Reeded, any color, belled rim, 8" 20.00
Plate, sandwich; Twisted Optic, bl or yel, 10" 20.00
Plate, torte; Cape Cod, crystal, #1608F, 13" 37.50
Puff box, Cape Cod, crystal, #1601, w/lid.............................50.00
Punch bowl, Crocheted Crystal, 14"......................................65.00
Relish, Cape Cod, crystal, 5-part, #160/102, 11"...................70.00
Relish, Crocheted Crystal, 3-part, 11½"................................25.00
Rose bowl, Black Suede, 6" 90.00
Rose bowl, Wide Panel, marigold on milk glass 210.00
Salt cellar, ruby slag, 4-ftd, #61 ....20.00
Shakers, Atterbury Scroll, crystal, ea.....................................15.00
Shakers, Cape Cod, crystal, sq, #160/109, pr........................25.00
Shakers, Cape Cod, Fern Green, #160/117, pr.......................35.00
Shakers, Monticello, crystal, w/glass tops, ea........................20.00
Shakers, Mt Vernon, crystal, pr...22.00
Sherbet, Crocheted Crystal, 6-oz, 5".....................................10.00
Sherbet, Dmn Quilt, bl or blk..16.00
Sherbet, Huckabee, pk, ftd..30.00
Sherbet, Twisted Optic, bl or yel..10.00
Stem, cocktail; Cake Cod, crystal, 3½-oz.................................6.00
Sugar bowl, Cape Cod, crystal, #160/30..................................7.00
Sugar bowl, Crocheted Crystal, ftd..20.00
Sugar bowl, Fancy Colonial, any color, w/lid..........................30.00

Tidbit, Laced Edge, opal, 2-tier, 8 & 10" plates....................110.00
Toothpick holder, Octagon, caramel slag, #505 ....25.00
Tumbler, fruit juice; Crocheted Crystal, ftd, 6-oz, 6"..............10.00
Tumbler, iced tea; Cape Cod, crystal, #160, 12-oz................12.50
Tumbler, iced tea; Crocheted Crystal, 12-oz, 7⅛"..................25.00
Tumbler, iced tea; Mt Vernon, crystal, 12-oz.........................12.50
Tumbler, water; Atterbury Scroll, milk glass...........................15.00
Tumbler, water; Cape Cod, crytal, 10-oz..................................8.00
Tumbler, water; Fancy Colonial, any color, 10-oz 18.00
Tumbler, water; Flute & Cane, crystal, 9-oz 30.00
Tumbler, water; Katy, gr opal, 9-oz..55.00
Tumbler, whiskey; Cape Cod, Ritz Blue, #160, 2½-oz............60.00
Vase, ball; Reeded, any color, 4"...17.50
Vase, bud; Free-Hand, hearts/vines, lt gr on opal, 8½"..........350.00
Vase, Cape Cod, crystal, ftd, #160/21, 11½" 70.00
Vase, Cape Cod, crystal, urn form w/hdls, #160/186, 10½".........195.00
Vase, Crocheted Crystal, 8"...20.00
Vase, Free-Hand, bl irid w/opal pulled swags, cylindrical, 11½"..350.00
Vase, Free-Hand, bronze w/waves of bl & orange, waisted shape, 10½"..750.00
Vase, Free-Hand, drag loops, wht on cobalt, 10½" 345.00
Vase, Free-Hand, draped swags, gr-bl on marigold irid, 11½" ..1,000.00
Vase, Free-Hand, hearts/vines, bl on orange, ruffled, 5x6¾".......400.00
Vase, Free-Hand, hearts/vines, bl on orange irid swollen cylinder, 11"..750.00
Vase, Free-Hand, hearts/vines, lt bl on clear irid, bl rim, 10"...1,100.00
Vase, Free-Hand, hearts/vines, orange on dk bl, 5¾" 900.00
Vase, Free-Hand, leaves, gr on cream w/gold irid, ca 1925, 10½"..800.00
Vase, Free-Hand, loops, bl on wht, baluster, att, ca 1925, 6¾" ...300.00
Vase, Free-Hand, mc swirls in cobalt, orange int, stick neck, 9¾"..500.00
Vase, Free-Hand, swags, bl on opal, orange int, shouldered, 7½"..550.00
Vase, Free-Hand, swags, orange irid w/bl, shouldered, 6¾" 225.00
Vase, Free-Hand, wht/bl/gray marbleized w/bl int, cylindrical, 9"..500.00
Vase, Jade slag, tricorn, 8½"..160.00
Vase, Mosaic, cobalt shaded & swirled w/opal, orange int, 6½"..490.00
Vase, Nuart, irid aquamarine, shouldered/incurvate, 6¾"...........125.00
Vase, Reeded (Spun), red, 9" 75.00

Imperial Porcelain

The Blue Ridge Mountain Boys were created by cartoonist Paul Webb and translated into three-dimension by the Imperial Porcelain Corporation of Zanesville, Ohio, in 1947. These figurines decorated ashtrays, vases, mugs, bowls, pitchers, planters, and other items. The Mountain Boys series were numbered 92 through 108, each with a different and amusing portrayal of mountain life. Imperial also produced American Folklore miniatures, twenty-three tiny animals one inch or less in size, and the Al Capp Dogpatch series. Because of financial difficulties, the company closed in 1960.

American Folklore Miniatures

Cat, 1½", from $80 to 100.00
Cow, 1¾", from $80 to..100.00
Hound dogs, from $80 to...100.00
Plaque, store ad, Am Folklore Porcelain Miniatures, 4½", $350 to..400.00
Sow, from $80 to 100.00

Blue Ridge Mountain Boys by Paul Webb

Ashtray, #101, man w/jug & snake, from $90 to....................120.00
Ashtray, #103, hillbilly & skunk, from $90 to.......................120.00
Ashtray, #105, baby, hound dog & frog, from $100 to...........135.00
Ashtray, #106, Barrel of Wishes, w/hound, from $85 to.........115.00
Ashtray, #92, 2 men by tree stump, for pipes, from $100 to........125.00

Box, cigarette; #98, dog atop, baby at door, sq, from $135 to......165.00
Dealer's sign, Handcrafted Paul Webb Mtn Boys, rare, 9", from $500 to...700.00
Decanter, #100, outhouse, man & bird, from $100 to 125.00
Decanter, #104, Ma leaning over stump, w/baby & skunk, from $125 to.145.00
Decanter, man, jug, snake, & tree stump, Hispch Inc, 1946, $100 to.125.00
Figurine, #101, man leans against tree trunk, 5", from $100 to...125.00
Figurine, man on hands & knees, 3", from $100 to 130.00
Figurine, man sitting, 3½", from $120 to 145.00
Figurine, man sitting w/chicken on knee, 3", from $100 to.........130.00
Jug, #101, Willie & snake, from $80 to 95.00
Mug, #94, Bearing Down, 6", from $80 to.......................................95.00
Mug, #94, dbl baby hdl, 4¼", from $80 to.......................................95.00
Mug, #94, ma hdl, 4¼", from $80 to...95.00
Mug, #94, man w/bl pants hdl, 4¼", from $80 to...........................95.00
Mug, #94, man w/yel beard & red pants hdl, 4¼", from $80 to 95.00
Mug, #99, Target Practice, boy on goat, farmer, 5¾", from $80 to .95.00
Pitcher, lemonade; from $150 to...200.00
Planter, #100, outhouse, man & bird, from $100 to 125.00
Planter, #105, man w/chicken on knee, washtub, from $100 to..130.00
Planter, #110, man, w/jug & snake, 4½", from $80 to 95.00
Planter, #81, man drinking from jug, sitting by washtub, from $80 to ..95.00
Shakers, Ma & Old Doc, pr, from $85 to 115.00

Indian Tree

Indian Tree is a popular dinnerware pattern produced by various potteries from the early 1800s to recent times. Although backgrounds and borders vary, the Oriental theme is carried out with the gnarled, brown branch of a pink-blossomed tree. Among the manufacturers' marks, you may find represented such notable firms as Coalport, S. Hancock and Sons, Soho Pottery, and John Maddock and Sons.

See also Johnson Brothers.

Bonbon, fluted, Coalport, 6¼"...20.00
Bowl, Aynsley, 2¾x8¾" 60.00
Bowl, cream soup; scalloped, Spode...45.00
Bowl, fruit; Johnson Bros, 5" 9.00
Bowl, fruit; Morley, sm...8.00
Bowl, fruit; Spode, 5¼" 28.00
Bowl, Myott, 8"..20.00
Bowl, scalloped, Coalport, 1½x6"...40.00
Bowl, soup; Johnson Bros, 7¼" 14.00
Bowl, vegetable; John Maddock & Sons, ca 1935, w/lid, 8" dia....55.00
Bowl, vegetable; Johnson Bros, 8½" 25.00
Bowl, vegetable; Noritake, ca 1930s, w/hdls & lid, 10½" W 50.00
Butter pat, scalloped, #2/916, 4¼" 18.00
Candy dish, scalloped edge, gr mk, 5¼" L 20.00
Coffee can & saucer, Maddock, 2¼"...18.00
Creamer & sugar bowl, Coalport, bone china mk, late.................40.00
Cup & saucer, AD; Minton..25.00
Cup & saucer, Spode 35.00
Dinner service, Coalport, serves 10+8 serving pieces, 144-pc 750.00
Egg cup, flat base, Johnson Bros, 1¾", set of 4 ....70.00
Gravy boat, w/attached underplate, Spode..................................145.00
Jar, Sadler, fancy shape, w/lid, 4½" 55.00
Pitcher, Coalport, 4¾" 65.00
Plate, cookie; Coalport, 10½" 55.00
Plate, dessert; ruffled rim, 8"...30.00
Plate, dinner; scalloped, Coalport, 10" 40.00
Plate, luncheon; Copeland Spode, 9" 35.00
Plate, luncheon; Minton, #5185, 9¼", set of 8 ....100.00
Plate, luncheon; Staffordshire, 9"..12.00
Plate, Maddock, 8"...8.00
Plate, salad; scalloped, Coalport, 7¾", set of 6...............................85.00
Plate, sandwich; closed scroll hdls, Coalport, sq, 10" W 55.00
Platter, Ashworth, 14½"...90.00
Platter, John Maddock & Son, 14" 35.00
Tazza, scalloped ft, Coalport, 3¼x8" 75.00

Teacup and saucer, Coalport, ca 1891 – 1920, from $45.00 to $60.00. (Photo courtesy Jim and Susan Harran)

Teacup & saucer, cone shape, scalloped, Coalport, gr mk.............32.00
Teapot, Burgess & Lee 60.00
Tray, mc w/gold accents, Coalport, 10¾x8½" 85.00
Tray, octagonal, scalloped rim, Copeland, 8" 65.00
Tray, serving; fluted, w/hdls, 10½", EX 48.00

Inkwells and Inkstands

Receptacles for various writing fluids have been used since ancient times. Through the years they have been made from countless materials — glass, metal, porcelain, pottery, wood, and even papier-mache. During the eithteenth century, gold or silver inkstands were presented to royalty; the well-known silver inkstand by Philip Syng, Jr., was used for the signing of the Declaration of Independence, and impressive brass inkstands with wells and pounce pots (sanders) were proud possessions of men of letters. When literacy vastly increased in the nineteenth century, the dip pen replaced the quill pen, and inkwells and inkstands were widely used and produced in a broad range of sizes in functional and decorative forms from ornate Victorian to flowing Art Nouveau and stylized Art Deco designs. However, the acceptance of the ballpoint pen literally put inkstands and inkwells 'out of business.' But their historical significance and intriguing diversity of form and styling fascinate today's collectors.

For further information we recommend *Collector's Encyclopedia to Inkwells, Books I* and *II*, by Veldon Badders (Collector Books).

See also Bottles, Ink.

Bakelite, blk w/press glass font, Carter's, 1930s, 3¼" L 50.00
Bakelite inserts/pen holder, clambroth glass base, Am, early 20th C...80.00
Black Forest cvd figural owl reading book on naturalistic base, 8½" .600.00
Blown, dome shape, Britannia top, Am, 1860, 3¾" dia................45.00
Blown/cut, bl, faceted/HP floral, 8-sided, silver lid, 1870s, sm....800.00
Blown/cut, cobalt 8-sided teakettle, brass filigree w/jewels, 1890s .700.00
Blown/cut, vaseline, faceted, hinged brass mts, late 19th C, 2¾" ..600.00
Brass, cast chestnut leaf & nut, hinged lid, glass insert, 1900s....250.00
Brass, cast female heads on panels, ceramic insert, 1890s, 3x2¼"...300.00
Brass, cast Renaissance style, ceramic insert, Am, 1900-10.........180.00
Brass, neo-Japanese teapot w/appl flowers, brass insert, 1890s, 1⅞"...125.00
Brass, sheet, dome w/pattern glass insert, Am, 1900-10, 3¼" dia..50.00
Britannia, cast pierced base, 2" sq swirl glass well, 1800s 200.00
Bronze, lg greyhound chained to fencepost between 2 glass wells, 12" ..800.00
Bronze, Nouveau leaf/berry motif, tray w/2 wells & pen recession, 13"...460.00

Bronze, nude w/harp sits on bk, naturalistic modeling, Godet, 14" .1,175.00
Bronze, Rococo w/lion's head crest, dolphin ft, 2 wells/tray, 14" L .460.00
Bronzed sheet metal, Deco look, pressed glass well, 4½" W 50.00
Chrome w/blk compo base, glass insert, Deco style, 1920s, 4⅞" dia .80.00
CI, elk head & leaves, gilt, pattern glass well, Am, 1900s, 6½" L...200.00
CI, Gothic style, low relief decor, pen rest, glass well, 1880-90 ..195.00
CI, owl form, blk pnt, metal insert, Iron Art, #146, 20th C, 9" W.140.00
CI, Rococo manner, blk pnt, pressed glass well, 1890s-1900, 5¼" W.140.00
Copper, camel, cast, gilt traces, glass well, 3¼x4¼" 250.00
Copper, chased floral w/pierced decor, Art Nouveau, 1900-15, 5½" L ..140.00
Copper, cherub on dolphin, cast, gold rpt, cut glass well, 4½" 220.00
Crystal, blown & cut, swivel lid w/Greetings plaque, 1¾" sq 50.00
Cut, amethyst to clear, dome, hinged silver lid, 1900s, 3½" dia..500.00
Cut, bl, 8-sided, brass mts, Am, 1900-10, 2¾" 450.00
Faience, reserves on 3-leaf clover form, Fr, 1900s, 2¾x5¼" 210.00
Faience, tin glaze w/HP decor, 3 quill holes, Rouex, 1900s, 2x3x3⅛".180.00
Hand blown/cut w/int striations, European, 1890s, 1¾x1" dia....150.00
Metal, cast camel w/saddle lid, milk glass insert, 1910-15, 5¾" L..175.00
Metal, cast horse & child between 2 glass wells, ornate base, 10" L..5,000.00
Metal lily-pad emb/rtcl hdld tray w/letter rack, 2 Loetz glass wells.1,550.00
Mold-blown, bottle gr, funnel opening, Am, 1830s-40s, 1⅝" dia.250.00
Pattern glass, clear, brass mts, plastic lid, early 20th C, 2½" 40.00
Pattern glass, 6-sided star bottom, Am, 20th C.............................65.00
Pattern molded, gr aquamarine, 16 vertical ribs, pontil, 1⅞" 475.00
Porc, HP bird & nest, sq top w/flowers, Germany, 1890s, 2¾x2" sq ..90.00

Porcelain, hand-painted landscape reserve with gilt decor, English, early nineteenth century, 3¼x7½", $425.00 to $550.00.

Porc, Oriental figures in relief, Japanese Export, 1900s, 5x3" sq .220.00
Porc, owl figural, HP, Noritake mk, early 20th C, 3⅜x2¾" 120.00
Porc, Rococo decor, maroon w/gold, dome lid, Fr, 1890s, 2½x2" dia .85.00
Porc, shamrocks, gray/brn/bl, 2 pen rests, Ireland, 1¾x3⅛" sq....140.00
Pottery, Dutch shoe form, bl/wht, Delft, early 20th C, 1¾x3⅞".120.00
Pottery, mc floral/armorial decor, conical, Rouen, 1860s, 2x3" dia .190.00
Pottery, shoe form, brn Rockingham, mid-19th C, 1⅝x4½" 300.00
Pressed glass, brass collar w/hinged floral lid, early 1900s 90.00
Pressed glass swirls, hinged brass lid, Fr, late 19th C...................110.00
Pressed milk glass, lt gr swirl w/HP flowers (worn), 2¼x1¾" sq....80.00
Soapstone, hand-cvd, Am, early 20th C, 2½" sq 35.00
SP wht metal, Georgian style, cameo on hinged lid, Am, 1920s...60.00
Wood, cvd owl figural w/clear glass insert, yel glass eyes, 3½" 60.00
Wood, 2 nuts & leaves cvg, att Germany, 1890-1900, 10" L.......200.00
Wood base w/pen rests, sq pressed glass well & lid, 20th C, 7" sq...150.00

Insulators

The telegraph was invented in 1844. The devices developed to hold the electrical transmission wires to the poles were called insulators. The telephone, invented in 1876, intensified their usefulness; and by the turn of the century, thousands of varieties were being produced in pottery, wood, and glass of various colors. Even though it has been rumored that red glass insulators exist, none have ever been authenticated. There are amber-colored insulators that appear to have a red tint to the amber, and those are called red-amber. Many insulators are embossed with patent dates.

Of the more than 3,000 types known to exist, today's collectors evaluate their worth by age, rarity of color and, of course, condition. Aqua and green are the most common colors in glass, dark brown the most common in porcelain. Threadless insulators (for example, CD #701.1), made between 1850 and 1865, bring prices well into the hundreds, sometimes even the thousands, if in mint condition.

In the listings that follow, the CD numbers are from an identification system developed in the late 1960s by N.R. Woodward.

Those seeking additional information about insulators are encouraged to contact Line Jewels NIA #1380 (whose address may be found in the Directory under Clubs, Newsletters, and Catalogs) or attend a club-endorsed show. (For information see Directory under Florida for Jacqueline Linscott Barnes.) In the listings that follow those stating 'no name' have no company identification, but do have embossed numbers, dots, etc. Those stating 'no embossing' are without raised letters, dots, or any other markings. Please note: Our values are for insulators in mint condition.

Key:
* (asterisk) — Canadian
BE — base embossed
CB — corrugated base
CD — Consolidated Design
FDP — flat drip points
RB — rough base
RDP — round drip points
SB — smooth base
SDP — sharp drip points

Threaded Pin-type and Threadless Glass Insulators

CD 102, NW&BIT CO, SB, purple 500.00
CD 1038, Cutter Pat April 26 04, SB, aqua...............................300.00
CD 110, Brookfield, SB, aqua..150.00
CD 113, Whitall Tatum/No 13, SB, lt straw 5.00
CD 121, AT&T Co, SB, lt aqua 3.00
CD 121, WGM Co, SB, purple 30.00
CD 123, EC&M Co, SB, lime gr..1,000.00
CD 130, Cal Elec Works, SB, bl 350.00
CD 133, City Fire Alarm, SB, lt aqua...75.00
CD 135.5, ERW, SB, ice bl 1,200.00
CD 141.8, Buzby, SB, aqua 20,000.00
CD 145, Am Insulator Co, BE, aqua 50.00
CD 150, Barclay, SDP, aqua...3,000.00
CD 153, Brookfield, SB, aqua 40.00
CD 154, Hemingray-42, RDP, aqua 1.00
CD 154, Hemingray-42, SB, Hemingray Blue 30.00
CD 154, Maydwell-42/USA, RDP, straw 2.00
CD 154.5, Derflingher, RDP, aqua 20.00
CD 160, Brookfield/New York, SB, gr..5.00
CD 160.6, Am Tel & Tel Co, SB, lt yel-gr 2,500.00
CD 161, California, SB, purple 30.00
CD 162, Hemingray, No 19, SDP, aqua 8.00
CD 163, Hemingray-19, SDP, clear...1.00
CD 190/CD 191, both: Hemingray-50, SB, aqua 15.00
CD 190/CD 191, 2-pc/transposition, SB, milky aqua 400.00
CD 194/CD 195, Hemingray-54 A&B, SB, purple 150.00
CD 197, Whitall Tatum/No 15, SB, clear..2.00
CD 203, Armstrong TW, SB, clear 1.00
CD 213, Hemingray, No 43, RDP, aqua..10.00
CD 214, Armstrong's No 10, SB, clear 2.00
CD 217, Armstrong's 51 C3, SB, root beer amber 10.00
CD 226, No 115, SB, aqua..30.00
CD 231, Hemingray-820, CB, clear...25.00
CD 236, Brookfield, SB, dk aqua 500.00
CD 238, Hemingray-514, CB, honey amber 325.00
CD 239, Kimble, CB, clear...5.00
CD 250, NEGM Co, SB, aqua..1,250.00
CD 252, No 2 Cable, RB, orange-amber.....................................300.00

CD 253, Knowles Cable, SB, lt aqua **40.00**
CD 254, No 3 Cable, SB, aqua **30.00**
CD 257, Hemingray, No 60, RDP, bl aqua **20.00**
CD 262, No 2 Columbia, SB, lt bl aqua **175.00**
CD 263, Columbia, SB, lt aqua **200.00**
CD 267.5, NEGM Co, SB, emerald gr **200.00**
CD 269, Jumbo, SB, aqua **500.00**
CD 299.7, Lowex, D-514, SB, lt lemon **5,000.00**
CD 317, Chambers/Pat Aug 14 1877, SB, lt aqua **500.00**
CD 321, Registered Trade Mark, SB, aqua **30.00**
CD 322, Corning Pyrex, SB, carnival **125.00**
CD 729.4, Mulford & Biddle/83 John St NY, SB, aqua **1,250.00**
CD 734.8*, (no embossing), SB, olive blk glass **300.00**
CD 735, Chester/NY, SB, aqua **600.00**
CD 736, NY&ERR, SB, lt gr aqua **3,000.00**
CD 742.3, MTCo, BE, lt teal bl **600.00**

Irons

History, geography, art, and cultural diversity are all represented in the collecting of antique pressing irons. The progress of fashion and invention can be traced through the evolution of the pressing iron.

Over seven hundred years ago, implements constructed of stone, bone, wood, glass, and wrought iron were used for pressing fabrics. Early ironing devices were quite primitive in form, and heating techniques included inserting a hot metal slug into a cavity of the iron, adding hot burning coals into a chamber or pan, and placing the iron directly on hot coals or a hot surface.

To the pleasure of today's collectors, some of these early irons, mainly from the period of 1700 to 1850, were decorated by artisans who carved and painted them with regional motifs typical of their natural surroundings and spiritual cultures.

Beginning in the mid-1800s, new cultural demands for fancy wearing apparel initiated a revolution in technology for types of irons and methods to heat them. Typical of this period is the fluter which was essential for producing the ruffles demanded by the nineteenth-century ladies. Hat irons, polishers, and numerous unusual iron forms were also used during this time, and provided a means to produce crimps, curves, curls, and special fabric textures. Irons from this time-frame are characterized by their unique shapes, odd handles, latches, decorations, and even revolving mechanisms.

Also during this time, irons began to be heated by burning liquid and gaseous fuels. Gradually the new technology of the electrically heated iron replaced all other heating methods, except in the more rural areas and undeveloped countries. Even today the Amish communities utilize gasoline fuel irons.

In the listings that follow, prices are given for examples in best possible as-found condition. Damage, repairs, plating, excessive wear, rust, and missing parts can dramatically reduce value. For further information we recommend *Irons By Irons, More Irons By Irons,* and *Even More Irons by Irons* by our advisor Dave Irons; his address and information for ordering these books are given in the Directory under Pennsylvania.

Box, Empire Co, flowers on corners, lift-up top, late 1800s, $200 to **250.00**
Box, English, brass w/wigglework decor, mid-1800s, 5½", $200 to **300.00**
Box, European, all iron, charcoal, late 1700s, 7½", from $200 to **300.00**
Box, European, dolphin posts, iron, charcoal, 1900s, 6⅝", $100 to **150.00**
Box, European, rnd bk, iron joints, lift gate w/cutout, 1850s, over **500.00**
Box, India, brass, vent holes/front latch/bk hinge, 1880s+, $100 to **150.00**
Buttonhole, Pat June 1904..., removable hdl, button slot, $200 to **300.00**
Flatiron, cast, dbl-pointed, late 1800s, 9", from $150 to **200.00**
Flatiron, cold slant hdl, ca 1900, 7⅛", from $150 to **200.00**
Flatiron, J Smart...NY #9, cast, late 1800s, 7", from $40 to **50.00**

Flatiron, SD #10, FR, cast, late 1800s, 7⅞", from $100 to **125.00**
Flower, J Alente NY, brass top/iron base, late 1800s, 9½", $100 to **125.00**
Fluter, combination, Patd Aug 2 70, Myron H Knapp, 6⅝", $100 to **150.00**
Fluter, Eagle Pat...1875...PA, decal, 5⅛" roll, from $150 to **200.00**
Fluter, rocker, Pat Appd For, brass, ca 1875, 5⅜", from $200 to **300.00**
Fluter, Royal Perin & Gaff...1876, decals, 5¾" roll, from $150 to **200.00**
Gas jet, WF Shaw's Patent...1857, holes in top, 6¼", from $150 to **200.00**
Gasoline, Diamond...Made in USA, early 1900s, 7½", from $50 to **70.00**
Gasoline, Sunshine...Pat Pending, early 1900s, 7½", from $70 to **100.00**
Goffering, dbl, European, wrought iron, monkey-tail spiral, 1700s, over **750.00**
Goffering, English, brass bbl, iron std/base, late 1800s, 11", $200 to **300.00**
Goffering, English, brass Queen Anne style, late 1800s, from $200 to **300.00**
Goffering, European, iron bbl, brass std, CI base, 1850s, 11", $300 to **500.00**
Goffering, European, wrought iron, tripod base, 1700s, 6⅛", $300 to **500.00**
Goffering, triple, English, brass, sm bbls on arms, 1850s, 13", over **1,000.00**
Hat, shackle, iron, flat bottom, late 1800s, 5⅛", from $100 to **125.00**
Hat, tolliker, MCO, smooth bottom, early 1900s, 5½", from $100 to **125.00**
Mushroom, European, mid-1800s, 10", from $70 to **100.00**
Natural gas, Central Flat Iron Mfg...April 23 '07..., 6¼", $100 to **150.00**
Natural gas, Uneedit Gas...Pat Pending, early 1900s, 6½", $100 to **150.00**
Ox tongue, Aver Wein, slug or gas jet, lift-up gate, ca 1900, $100 to **150.00**
Ox tongue, European, brass w/CI hdl, lift-out gate, mid-1800s, $200 to **300.00**
Ox tongue, slug, brass, late 1800s, 5", from $150 to **200.00**
Poking stick, English, all iron, early 1800s, 12½", from $200 to **300.00**
Polisher, #8, rough bottom, late 1800s, 6⅜", from $70 to **100.00**
Polisher, Carron 2, English, rnd bottom, late 1800s, 4⅝", $100 to **125.00**
Polisher, vertical, brass hdl, late 1800s, 5⅜", from $150 to **200.00**

Polishers: W. Cross, round bottom, late 1800s, 5¾"; No. 1, J&JS, round bottom, early 1900s, 4¼", from $100.00 to $125.00 each. (Photo courtesy Dave Irons)

Rocker fluter, late 1800s, 1⅞", from $200 to **300.00**
Rope hdl, ca 1900, 4½", from $50 to **70.00**
Seam, Pat Apd For, hdl opens/folds bk, late 1800s, 6¾", $200 to **300.00**
Sleeve, English, mid-1800s, 6¼", from $70 to **100.00**
Sleve, #1 Sensible...NY...1887 on hdl, 6⅞", from $30 to **50.00**
Slug, #2, English, brass, lift-up gate, late 1800s, 3⅞", $150 to **200.00**
Slug, English, brass, animal face at ea post, floral eng, 1743, over **750.00**
Slug, English, brass, heart cutout at hdl, late 1800s, 7½", up to **750.00**
Slug, European, brass, eng flowers/hinged gate, 1835, 5¼", $500 to **750.00**
Slug, European, ca 1900, 3½", from $100 to **150.00**
Slug, swan latch, top lifts for slug, Pat Apd For...1877, 7", over **750.00**
Smoothing board, European, horse hdl, mid-1800s, 25", from $300 to **500.00**
Split chimney, Spanish/Portuguese, hinged bk, 1880s, 6½", $100 to **125.00**
Standing egg, European, ornate cast base, mid-1800s, 4½", $200 to **300.00**
Standing egg, Fr, ca 1900, 12¾", from $150 to **200.00**
Swan figural, Ray M Harpel...PA, cast, early 1900s, 3⅜", $300 to **500.00**
Tailor, Sensible...Sept 6 '87, cold removable hdl, 9½", $200 to **300.00**
Tailor, steam, Koening New Jersey, early 1900s, 11¼", $70 to **100.00**
Tailor, wrought, hdl forged w/body, early 1800s, 11¼", $100 to **150.00**
Wire hdl, FR, thin base, early 1900s, 3⅜", from $70 to **100.00**

Ironstone

During the last quarter of the eighteenth century, English potters began experimenting with a new type of body that contained calcinated flint and a higher china clay content, intent on producing a fine durable whiteware — heavy, yet with a texture that would resemble porcelain. To remove the last trace of yellow, a minute amount of cobalt was added, often resulting in a bluish-white tone. Wm and John Turner of Caughley and Josiah Spode II were the first to manufacture the ware successfully. Others, such as Davenport, Hicks and Meigh, and Ralph and Josiah Wedgwood, followed with their own versions. The latter coined the name 'Pearl' to refer to his product and incorporated the term into his trademark. In 1813 a fourteen-year patent was issued to Charles James Mason, who called his ware Patented Ironstone. Francis Morley, G.L. Asworth, T.J. Mayer, and other Staffordshire potters continued to produce ironstone until the end of the century. While some of these patterns are simple to the extreme, many are decorated with in-mold designs of fruit, grain, and foliage on ribbed or scalloped shapes. In the 1830s transfer-printed designs in blue, mulberry, pink, green, and black became popular; and polychrome versions of Oriental wares were manufactured to compete with the Chinese trade. See also Mason's Ironstone. Our advise for this category comes from Home Place Antiques, whose address is listed in the Directory under Illinois.

Bone dish, Crescent, Wilkinson, 3x6¼", EX....55.00
Bowl, punch; plain, rosettes on hdls, Furnival, ca 1851-90, 6x9½"....315.00
Bowl, punch; plain, W&E Corn, ca 1870, 7x9½"....260.00
Bowl, sauce; w/lid, Red Cliff..., ca 1960, 6½x4¾"....130.00
Bowl, vegetable; fruit finial, hdls, Cockson Chetwynd & Co, 6x11"....195.00
Bowl, vegetable; President, oval, w/lid....145.00
Coffeepot, Grape Clusters, Davenport, 1870s, EX....295.00
Coffeepot, Lily, Burgess....275.00
Compote, Sydenham, w/lid, T&R Boote, 1854, 9x9", NM....195.00
Creamer, Square Ridged, Iona shape, Powell, Bishop & Stonier, ca 1886....165.00
Creamer, Wheat, Ceres shape, Elsmore & Forster, 1859, 3¼x6½"....175.00
Cup, syllabub; emb leaves, ped ft, 4", 4 for....120.00
Cup & saucer, handleless; Niagara, Walley, ca 1856....95.00
Cup & saucer, handleless; Wheat, Furnival, ca 1860s....65.00
Drainer, oval, unmk, 10x7¼"....45.00
Gravy boat, Ceres, Elsmore & Forster, EX....145.00
Gravy boat, floral design at thumb rest, Pankhurst, ca 1870, 9" L....110.00
Ladle, leaf design, twisted hdl, 12"....165.00
Mold, geometric design, Am, ca 1900, 5½x7½"....95.00
Mold, rabbit, unmk Am, ca 1900, 3x7¼"....135.00
Mold, strawberries, ca 1900, 2½x6" dia, NM....275.00
Mold, tiger lilies, late 1800s, 2½x7x5½"....295.00
Nappy, Internat'l Pottery Co, ca 1897, 12¾", NM....275.00
Pitcher, batter; emb leaf band, bail hdl, unmk, 9x9"....225.00
Pitcher, milk; Olympic, Elsmore & Forster, 9⅜"....275.00
Pitcher, water; Meakin, ca 1890, 12½"....225.00
Pitcher, water; Wheat, melon ribs, W&E Corn, 1864-91, 12"....245.00
Plate, Bellflower, Edwards, 9¾"....55.00
Plate, Fluted Pearl shape, bordered rim, J Wedge Wood, 9½"....50.00
Plate, President shape, James Edwards, 9½"....65.00
Plate, Sydenham shape, T&R Boote, 1853, 7"....45.00
Plate, True Scallop, James Edwards, 1845, 10"....75.00
Plate, Western Shape, Hope & Carter, mini, 5"....30.00
Platter, Ceres shape, Elsmore & Forster, 1860s, 10½x8¼"....75.00
Platter, octagonal, Pankhurst, ca 1852-82, 15¼x12", NM....165.00
Platter, plain, rectangular, Meakin, ca 1865, 15½x11"....130.00
Platter, Wheat, Ceres shape, Elsmore & Forster, 1859, 13¾x10¾"....145.00
Platter, Wheat, Jacob Furnival, ca 1860, 17¾x12½"....165.00
Platter, Wheat & Clover, Turner & Tomkinson, 1860-72, 16½", NM....160.00
Relish, plain, J&G Meakin, ca 1890, 6x8¾", NM....40.00
Shaving mug, Berlin Swirl....165.00
Teapot, Full Ribbed, unmk, mini, 5¾"....175.00
Teapot, Lily of the Valley, Anthony Shaw....320.00

Teapot, Wheat, 11", $245.00.

Tureen, Baltic shape, ear-of-corn finial, J Meir, 1855, 7x10½", NM....200.00
Tureen, fluted, John Wedgewood, 1850s, 7x13"....175.00
Tureen, Vintage shape, w/lid, E&C Challinor, 1865, 7x12"....125.00
Tureen, Wheat, Ceres shape, w/lid, Elsmore & Forster, ca 1853, 11"....255.00
Wash bowl, Hyacinth, unmk, 13"....120.00
Wash bowl & pitcher, Sydenham shape, T&R Boote....350.00
Wash pitcher, Corn & Oats....195.00
Waste bowl, Tuscan, unmk, 5¼" dia....85.00

Patterned Ironstone

Bowl, vegetable; Carrare, pk transfer, unmk, 1⅝x7⅜x5⅜"....110.00
Butter dish, Castle Scenery, bl transfer, Furnival, 5½x7¼"....160.00
Creamer, Princess Feather, bl transfer, Challinor, 5¼"....120.00
Creamer & sugar bowl, Spray, bl transfer, JWP&Co, w/lid....125.00
Cup & saucer, Cleopatra, brn transfer....35.00
Cup & saucer, Rose, purple transfer, Challinor....45.00
Cup & saucer, Zamara, red transfer....50.00
Pitcher, milk; Tyrol, purple transfer, Wedgwood, 8¾", NM....95.00
Plate, Ailanthus, purple transfer, C&WHK, 6½", NM....30.00
Plate, Canella, gr transfer, unmk, 10"....35.00
Plate, Eon, purple & brn transfer, Wooliscroft, 9⅞"....70.00
Plate, Priory, bl transfer, Challinor, 8¾"....40.00
Platter, Gipsy, bl transfer, 17⅜x13½", NM....85.00
Platter, Palestine, bl transfer, Ridgway, 13x10⅝"....105.00
Relish, Venus, bl transfer, Podmore Walker, 8¾x5½",....45.00
Waste bowl, Roselle, pk transfer, Meier, 3¾x5½"....55.00

Italian Glass

Throughout the twentieth century, one of the major glassmaking centers of the world was the island of Murano. From the Stile Liberte work of Artisi Barovier (1890 – 1920s) to the early work of Ettore Sottsass in the 1970s, they excelled in creativity and craftsmanship. The 1920s to 1940s featured the work of glass designers like Ercole Barovier for Barovier and Toso and Vittorio Zecchin, Napoleone Martinuzzi and Carlo Scarpa for Venini. Many of these pieces are highly prized by collectors.

The 1950s saw a revival of Italy as a world-reknown design center for all of the arts. Glass led the charge with the brightly colored work of Fulvio Bianconi for Venini, Dino Martens for Aureliano Toso, and Ercole Barovier for Barovier and Toso. The best of these pieces are extremely desirable. The '60s and '70s have also seen many innovative designs with work by the Finnish Tapio Wirkkala, the American Thomas Stearns, and many other designers.

Unfortunately, amongst the great glass, there was a plethora of commercial ashtrays, vases, and figurines produced that, though having some value, do not compare in quality and design to the great glass of Murano.

Venini: The Venini company was founded in 1921 by Paolo Venini, and he led the company until his death in 1959. Major Italian designers worked for the firm, including Vittorio Zecchin, Napoleone Martinuzzi, Carlo Scarpa, and Fulvio Bianconi. After his death, his son-in-law, Ludovico de Santillana, ran the factory and employed designers like Toni Zucchieri, Tapio Wirkkala, and Thomas Stearns. The company is known for creative designs and techniques including Inciso (finely etched lines), Battuto (carved facets), Sommerso (controlled bubbles), Pezzato (patches of fused glass), and Fascie (horizontal colored lines in clear glass). Until the mid-'60s, most pieces were signed with acid-etched 'Venini Murano ITALIA.' In the '60s they started engraving the signatures. The factory still exists.

Barovier: In the late 1920s, Ercole Barovier took over the Artisti Barovier and started designing many different vases. In the 1930s he merged with Ferro Toso and became Barovier and Toso. He designed many different series of glass including the Barbarico (rough, acid-treated brown or deep blue glass), Eugenio (free-blown vases), Efeso, Rotallato, Dorico, Egeo (vases incorporating murrine designs), and Primavera (white etched glass with black bands). He designed until 1974. The company is still in existence. Most pieces were unsigned.

Aureliano Toso: The great glass designer Dino Martens was involved with the company from about 1938 to 1965. It was his work that produced the very desirable Oriente vases. This technique consisted of free-formed patches of green, yellow, blue, purple, black, and white stars and pieces of zanfirico canes fused into brilliantly colored vases and bowls. His El Dorado series was based on the same technique but was not opaque. He also designed pieces with alternating groups of black and white filigrana lines. Pieces are unsigned.

Seguso: Flavio Poli became the artistic director of Seguso in the late 1930s and remained until 1963. He is known for his Corroso (acid-etched glass) and his Valve series (elegant forms of two to three layers of colored glass with a clear glass casing).

Archimede Seguso: In 1946 Archimede Seguso left the Seguso Vetri D'Arte to open a new company and designed many innovative pieces. His Merlatto (thin white filigrana suspended three dimensionally) series is his most famous. The epitome of his work is where a colored glass (yellow or purple) is windowed in the merlotti. His Macchia Ambra Verde is yellow and spots on a gold base encased in clear glass. The A Piume series contained feathers and leaves suspended in glass. Pieces are unsigned.

Alfredo Barbini: Barbini was a designer known for his sculptures of sea subjects and his amorphic-shaped vases with an inner core of red or blue glass with a heavy layer of finely incised outer glass. He worked in the 1950s to the 1960s, and some pieces are signed.

Vistosi: Although this glassworks was started in the 1940s, fame came in the 1960s and 1970s with the birds designed by Allesandro Pianon and the early work of the Memphis school designer, Ettore Sottsass. Pieces may be signed.

AVEM: This company is known for its work in the 1950s and 1960s. The designer, Ansolo Fuga, did work using a solid white glass with inclusions of multicolored murrines.

Cenedese: This is a postwar company led by Gino Cenedese with Alfredo Barbini as designer. When Barbini left, Cenedese took over the design work and also used the free-lanced designs of Fulvio Bianconi. They are known for their figurines and vases with suspended murrines.

Cappellin: Venini's original partner (1921 – 25), Giacomo Cappellin, opened a short-lived company (1925 – 32) that was to become extremely important. His chief designer was the young Carlo Scarpa who was to create many masterpieces in glass both for Cappellin and then Venini.

Ettore Sottsass: Sottass founded the Memphis School of Design in the 1970s. He is an extremely famous modern designer who designed several series of glass for the Vistosi Glass Company. The pieces were created in limited editions, signed and numbered, and each piece was given a name.

Our advisor for this category is Howard Lockwood, publisher of *Vetri: Italian Glass News*. For further information concerning Mr. Lockwood or this publication, see the Directory under New Jersey.

Venini Glass

A Machie vase, sgn, 9½"	11,000.00
Battuto purple dbl-gourd vase	11,325.00
Bird, gr irid	720.00
Bolle, vase, orange & amber	920.00
Canoe, red & blk murrines w/inner bl core	7,550.00
Colletto amber vase w/deep amber collar	865.00
Demode marbleized vase w/sq top	485.00
Fasce orrizontalli gr vase w/yel lattimo fasce	645.00
Fasce orrizontalli gray bottle w/yel band	415.00
Fasce verticale gr lattimo & red transparent vase	7,280.00
Fasce verticale gr/clear/red striped pitcher	1,150.00
Fascemurrine gray vase w/band of murrines	1,780.00
Fazzoletto blk ext/gray int	1,380.00
Fazzoletto red & wht zanfirico	430.00
Figurine, Mrs Tartaglia	2,922.00
Fish, various colors, Ken Scott, 3 for	1,215.00
Forato bl pitcher w/single lg hole	1,300.00
Hourglass, gray/bl	865.00
Hourglass, yel/gray	1,150.00
Incalmo gr w/red stripes w/stopper bottle	1,240.00
Incalmo transparent bl bottle w/wht latticino band	700.00
Inciso gr triangular bottle	1,200.00
Inciso lt gr stoppered bottle	635.00
Lattimo bl bowl w/wht ft	4,745.00
Mezza filigrana flared wht cylindrical vase	7,120.00
Mezza filigrana wht vase w/rnd to sq top	5,550.00
Murrine battuto bowl in opaque murrines, red w/blk	26,950.00
Murrine bowl, red & orange murrines	3,545.00
Nautilus shell, clear irid	7,000.00
Pezzato bottle vase, red/bl/wht	9,775.00
Pezzato pinched cylinder-shaped vase	3,290.00
Pezzato triangular bowl	4,875.00
Pezzato vase, red/bl/straw/gr	10,785.00
Rilievi rose-colored vase w/bubbles & serpent ft	1,888.00
Sirene, rose, arms over head	6,425.00
Sommerso bollicine brn vase	1,525.00
Sommerso gr bird w/gold inclusions	833.00
Spicchi vase, lt bl/aubergine/pk canes	3,525.00
Tessuto vase: red/wht, red/plum	865.00
Zanfirico wht latticino vase	1,235.00

Non-Venini Glass

A Seguso, clear vase w/red core	465.00
A Seguso, Laguna pk vase	1,075.00
A Seguso, Macchia Ambre Verde vase & bowl	735.00
Aldo Nason Hokohma: 2 spouts	4,315.00
Aureliano Toso, Bianca Nera ashtray	475.00
Aureliano Toso, Cactus: 4 appl uplifted arms	2,350.00
Aureliano Toso, Frammentati vase, mc	4,200.00
Aureliano Toso, Oriente vase, no pinwheel	900.00
Aureliano Toso, Oriente 2-hdld pitcher	9,700.00
AVEM Fuga incalmo murrine vase	3,776.00
AVEM Nason vase w/3 spouts & internal decor	3,220.00
AVEM Reazione polychrome sm pitcher w/bl murrines	2,415.00
Barbini, charger, clear w/2 fish in center	725.00
Barbini, Inciso Sasso, red core, no base	3,235.00
Barbini, Martinuzzi inciso triangular gray vase	1,055.00
Barbini, Martinuzzi triangular orange vase	1,221.00
Barovier, Argo wht & aubergine cylindrical vase	5,551.00
Barovier, Barbarico pinched vase	1,265.00
Barovier, Crepuscolo bucket-shaped vase	4,315.00

Barovier, Dorico Corniola cylindrical vase **4,045.00**
Barovier, Graffito gr & clear vase **1,945.00**
Barovier, Lenti irid clear vase **4,045.00**
Barovier, Pelugoso 2-hdld pk vase **335.00**
Barovier, Primavera vase w/blk lip wrap **23,500.00**
Barovier, Spacchi vase, blk w/wht fold..**5,125.00**
Cenedese, DaRos II Momento clear w/amber core **978.00**
Cenedese, Fish block w/2 fish **450.00**
Cenedese, Fish block w/6 sm fish **2,498.00**
Cenedese, Sommerso vase, lime yel & bl **550.00**
Fratelli Toso, E Toso Millepunti bl vase w/gr **5,050.00**
Fratelli Toso, E Toso Tiffany vase of sqd murrines **11,865.00**
Fratelli Toso, Murrine 2-hdld vase **555.00**
Fratelli Toso, Perelda Stellato cylindrical vase.....................**5,895.00**
Fratelli Toso, Zanfirico lg cylindrical ftd vase **2,115.00**
IVR Mazzega Scarpa Croce vase, clear w/internal decor **1,350.00**
Salviati, Asti Clio red filigrana vase **730.00**
Salviati Gaspari Sasso: clear vase w/red & aubergine **1,565.00**
Seguso Vetri D'Arte, Sommerso gr bowl **800.00**
Seguso Vetri D'Arte, Sommerso red w/amber decanter **400.00**
Sottsass stepped vase, blk w/gr top **1,150.00**
Tagliapietra vase, yel w/canes **1,575.00**
Vistosi, Incalmo squashed apple-shaped vase **915.00**
Vistosi, Pulcino, J-shaped, gr **1,495.00**
Vistosi, Pulcino: globular model: orange w/prunts **1,775.00**
Zecchin-Martinuzzi, Rosso e Nera vase.................................**16,185.00**

Ivory

Ivory has been used and appreciated since Neolithic times. It has been a product of every culture and continent. It is the second most valuable organic material after pearls. Ivory is defined as the dentine portion of mammalian teeth. Commercially the most important ivory comes from elephant and mammoth tusks, walrus tusks, hippo teeth, and sperm whale teeth. The smaller tusks of boar and warthog are often used whole.

Ivory has been used for artistic purposes as a palette for oil paints, as inlay on furniture, and especially as a medium for sculptures. Some are in the round, others in the form of plaques. Ivory also has numerous utilitarian uses such as cups and tankards; combs; handles for knives and medical tools; salt and pepper shakers; chess, domino, and checker pieces; billiard balls; jewelry; shoehorns; snuff boxes; brush pots; and fans.

There are a number of laws domestically and internationally to protect endangered animals including the elephant, walrus, and whale. However ivory taken and used before the various enactment dates is legal within the country in which it is located, and can be shipped internationally with a permit. Ivory from mammoths, hippopotamus, wart hog, and boar is excepted from all bans.

Prices have been stable for the last ten years, rising slightly in the last year. Prices are highest for European, Japanese, and Chinese ivories. Prices are lowest for African and Indian ivories. As with all collectibles, the very best pieces will appreciate most in the years to come. Small, poorly carved pieces will not appreciate to any extent. Our advisor for this category is Robert Weisblut; he is listed in the Directory under Maryland.

Bust of Voltaire on marble plinth, France, 19th C, 10" **7,500.00**
Children, carving, Communist Chinese era, 9½" **1,250.00**
Figures, wise man w/fruit, lady w/cherry blossoms, 1910, 12", pr.**600.00**
Goddess, multi-armed, w/sitar, Indian, 20th C, 6½" **125.00**
Grouping of gods & children, Chinese, early 20th C, 10" **2,650.00**
Hippo tooth carving of village scene, Chinese, 1980s, 16".........**325.00**
Horse-drawn carriage, 20th C, 12" **1,750.00**
Lantern, Chinese, late 19th C, 28" **4,500.00**

Narwhal tusk shakers, scrimshawed, 2½", pr.............................**350.00**
Snuff bottle, deep relief, China, 19th C, 5" **1,250.00**
Study of rose branch, Japan, early 20th C, 13" **1,750.00**
Table screen on stand, Ming era, 11" **2,200.00**
Tusk, full, cvd procession of people, African, mid-19th C..........**775.00**
Vases, set of 2, w/basket, early 19th C, Chinese, 8"................**2,000.00**
Village scene, Japanese, ca 1900, 5½" **2,000.00**
Walrus sailing vessel w/full sails, Eskimo, 1950s, 10" **1,500.00**
Woman w/weaving implements, Chinese, early 20th C, 9".........**675.00**

Jack-in-the-Pulpit Vases

Popular novelties at the turn of the century, jack-in-the-pulpit vases were made in every type of art glass produced. Some were simple, others elaborately appliquéd and enameled. They were shaped to resemble the lily for which they were named.

Amethyst w/clear spiral rigaree & 8 petal ft, 14" **220.00**
Cranberry, 6½" **60.00**
Emerald to wht, tightly crimped rim w/Hobnails on flange, 11" .**175.00**
Gr opal w/appl red flower on crystal stem, 5 appl clear ft, 6" **115.00**
Pk opal striped w/clear & wht opal striped dome ft, 12", pr **550.00**
Rainbow w/Hobnails & HP floral, 3-ftd, bowl form, 6x10½"....**460.00**
Rubena verde, appl wht flower, crimped 4-point rose rim, 6 ft, 8".**200.00**
Wht opal, long stem w/spiral twist, disk ft, 19" **145.00**
Yel w/pk int, appl ribbed ft, 9½" **145.00**
Yel/wht satin stripes, tightly ruffled top/ft rim, English, 14" **115.00**

Jewelry

Jewelry as objects of adornment has always been regarded with special affection. Today prices for gems and gemstones crafted into antique and collectible jewelry are based on artistic merit, personal appeal, pure sentimentality, and intrinsic value. Note: In general, diamond prices have gone up more than 20% in the past year, and platinum is becoming popular again, so retail prices are rising. Diamond prices vary greatly depending on cut, color, clarity, etc., and to assess the value of any diamond of more than a carat in weight, you will need to have information about all of these factors. Values given here are for diamond jewelry with a standard commercial grade of diamonds that are most likely to be encountered.

Our advisor for fine jewelry is Rebecca Dodds; her address may be found in the Directory under Florida. Marcia 'Sparkles' Brown is our advisor for costume jewelry and the author of *Unsigned Beauties of Costume Jewelry* and *Signed Beauties of Costume Jewelry, Books 1 and 2* (Collector Books); she is also the host of the video *Hidden Treasures, A Collector's Guide to Antique and Vintage Jewelry of the 19th and 20th Centuries*. Mrs. Brown is listed in the Directory under Oregon. Other good references are *Collectible Costume Jewelry* by Cherri Simonds; *Costume Jewelry, A Practical Handbook & Value Guide*, and *Collectible Silver Jewelry* by Fred Rezazadeh; *100 Years of Collectible Jewelry*, *Fifty Years of Collectible Fashion Jewelry* and *Plastic Jewelry of the Twentieth Century* by Lillian Baker; *Vintage Jewelry for Investment and Casual Wear* by Karen L. Edeen; *Brilliant Rhinestones* by Ronna Lee Aikens; and *Painted Porcelain Jewelry and Buttons*, by Dorothy Kamm (all available from Collector Books). See also American Painted Porcelain; Hair Weaving.

Key:
cab — cabochon g-t — gold-tone
ct — carat k — karat
dmn — diamond plat — platinum
dwt — penny weight r/stn — rhinestone
Euro — European cut stn — stone

fl — filigree
gf — gold filled
gp — gold plated
grad — graduated
gw — gold washed

tw — total weight
wg — white gold
yg — yellow gold
ygf — yellow gold filled

Bar pin, plat fl w/.23ct (GIA-D VVS-1) dmn+4 sm dmns, 2½" L..**650.00**
Bar pin, 14k yg/wg fl w/.10ct dmn amid 2 sq-cut sapphires (4.4mm)..**375.00**
Bracelet, bangle; 14k wg w/62 1.75ct tw dmns & 7mm pearl ..**1,000.00**
Bracelet, bangle; 14k yg, Art Nouveau swallows, seed pearls, 1907 .**750.00**
Bracelet, bangle; 14k yg, 12 5.55ct tw sapphires+3 .06ct dmns...**950.00**
Bracelet, bangle; 14k yg w/floral eng **200.00**
Bracelet, cuff; Spratling, 2 ridged bands of silver w/dk brn shells..**1,850.00**
Bracelet, cuff; Taxco, hinged, silver w/lapped leaves & beads **175.00**
Bracelet, Kalo, hammered silver w/vines & cherries, 1x7" L.......**800.00**
Bracelet, silver, elephants form links, toggle-&-ring catch, 8" **115.00**
Bracelet, Taxco, alternating silver cross & X links......................**200.00**
Bracelet, Tiffany, 14k yg/rose gold, flexible, retro style.............**1,950.00**
Bracelet, yg fl w/9 9.7ct tw emeralds+126 (12.5ct tw) dmn melees ..**7,500.00**
Bracelet, 14k yg, blk enamel & dmns (1ct tw), Antebellum style ..**950.00**
Bracelet, 14k yg cat motif, Ardian Corp NY, 25.4 dwt, 6½" **725.00**
Bracelet, 14k yg dbl loop, 15", 21.79 dwt................................**350.00**
Bracelet, 14k yg fl w/4 jade pi disks, 34 dwt, 7¼" **550.00**
Bracelet, 14k yg fl w/7 turq cabs, 20.1 dwt.................................**350.00**
Bracelet, 14k yg links w/lg citrine & .42ct tw dmn melees, 43.7 dwt..**750.00**
Bracelet, 14k yg snakes, 4 ruby eyes & 1.25ct (G-H VSI) dmns, 18.7 dwt.**1,250.00**
Bracelet, 14k yg stiff band w/S scroll & beading, 1880s, 40 dwt..**3,450.00**
Bracelet, 14k yg w/20 1.25ct tw rnd dmns (J SI1), 50 dwt **500.00**

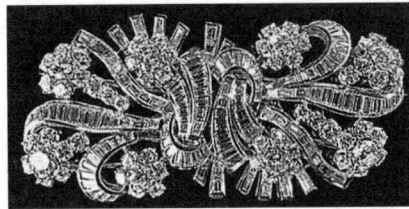

Brooch, Art Deco platinum with 62 full-cut diamonds, 128 straight and tapered baguette diamonds, 12 carats total weight, separates into a pair of clips, $13,000.00. (Photo courtesy Neal Auction Company)

Brooch, Georg Jensen, silver flower & bud w/oval moonstone cabs, 3".**450.00**
Brooch, plat, 8.1ct emerald+28 emerald 1.55ct tw melee+200 tiny dmns....**7,475.00**
Brooch, plat, 8.2ct emerald+28 1.55ct tw emeralds+200 10ct tw dmns, 3"..**7,500.00**
Brooch, plat bow & spray w/80 sm dmns, center 1.40ct dmn, 3ct tw.**4,675.00**
Brooch, plat fl bar w/31 dmns 5.70ct tw (VVSI, E) **5,450.00**
Brooch, yg star w/21 2.75ct tw mine-cut dmns & enameling, 1870s ...**1,850.00**
Brooch, 14k yg, beige & wht shell cameo, 23 dwt, 2¼" **250.00**
Brooch, 14k yg frog w/6 sm dmns on bk/2 ruby eyes/sm gr stones, 1890s .**700.00**
Brooch, 14k yg swirl w/.20ct dmn amid 6 .05ct dmns w/in 42 sm dmns ..**850.00**
Brooch, 18k yg, lg turq, 14.6 dwt.......................................**400.00**
Brooch, 18k yg, sm turq cabs & 5 .15ct tw melees (G SI1), 21.3 dwt..**450.00**
Brooch, 18k yg, 2 .40ct tw rubies+2 .20ct sapphires+15 sm rnd dmns.**1,750.00**
Brooch, 18k yg foo dog w/.15ct emerald eyes, onyx nose & sm dmns..**1,250.00**
Brooch, 18k yg turtle w/tiny turq & 6 .33ct tw dmns **650.00**
Brooch, 18k yg turtle w/1.0ct tw rubies, Italy, 8.5 dwt.................**400.00**
Brooch & earrings, 14k yg leaf shapes, sgn **1,265.00**
Earrings, gold w/.50ct dmn in ea (I, J-K) **1,200.00**
Earrings, gold w/flower drop, ea: .10ct dmn+.30ct dmn (SI2 - I, J-K).**750.00**
Earrings, yg, ea w/9-dmn cluster of 1.06ct tw, pr......................**1,035.00**
Earrings, 14k yg, 2 1.5ct tw rnd-cut (IJ S1) dmns, stud bks, pr...**2,650.00**
Earrings, 14k yg, 2 7.5mm cultured pearls, lever bks, pr **200.00**

Earrings, 14k yg w/rose-cut dmns, ca 1900, 6.0 dwt.....................**600.00**
Lapel pin, Spratling, silver, 2 clasped hands over N&S Am, ¾x1"..**375.00**
Necklace, coral beads w/2 gold clasps & cvd cameos, 13" **400.00**
Necklace, cultured pearls, 5-strand, wg clasp w/rubies & sm dmns.**4,600.00**
Necklace, faceted citrine beads, 14k yg clasp, 24ct tw.................**350.00**
Necklace, Liberty, gold chain w/10 jade beads+5 opal-set 'spades,' 26"...**1,600.00**
Necklace, pearls, unknotted grad Baroque South Sea, 11.2mm to 15.6.**8,000.00**
Necklace, pearls, 5-strand (58-69 in ea), from 5.7-6mm, 148 yg clasp...**650.00**
Necklace, R Pearson, silver ribbed 'spinning top'; amber cab on strap .**375.00**
Necklace, yg Cleopatra style w/5 oval+6 pear peridot+4 sm pearls, 1900..**2,400.00**
Necklace, 14k yg, clasp: sapphire cab & dmn melees of 1.0 ct, 35 dwt .**865.00**
Necklace, 14k yg, 25 .66 ct tw (G-H) dmns, 10 dwt **600.00**
Necklace, 14k yg, 45 4-5mm garnet melees, 56 dwt **575.00**
Necklace, 14k yg chain w/fl octagon locket & gp beads, 37 dwt..**500.00**
Necklace, 14k yg chain w/leopards' heads, 4 1.0ct tw rubies, pave dmns..**3,450.00**
Necklace, 14k yg link graduating collar w/etch design, 25 grams tw .**130.00**
Necklace, 15k yg Georgian chain w/interwoven links, jeweled clasp, 44"..**2,500.00**
Necklace, 18k yg, coral ram's head w/.08ct dmn eye on 14k 30" chain.**1,100.00**
Necklace, 18k yg, turq clusters, gross weight: 65 dwt, 16"........**1,200.00**
Necklace, 18k yg braided links, 18", 49.8 dwt............................**800.00**
Necklace, 18k yg fl, 60 dwt, 36" **950.00**
Necklace, 18k yg granulated pomegranate motif, 65.7 dwt, 17" ..**1,250.00**
Necklace/belt, 22k yg leopard head links w/124 6.0ct tw dmns, 240 dwt.**5,750.00**
Pendant, JB&B Co, hammered/cut silver 1" crest-like shape w/enamel cab.**500.00**
Pendant, Margaret Rogers, 14k gold w/mc stones, on chain........**825.00**
Pendant, 14k wg heart outline w/18 dmn (SI2, I-J) tw 1.40........**650.00**
Pendant, 14k yg, 50ct pk kunzite+15 rnd .33ct tw dmns, 18.6 dwt..**750.00**
Pendant, 14k yg bull (Taurus) w/ruby eyes, 18 dwt.....................**250.00**
Pendant, 14k 2-tone gold cross w/scallped ends, 1870-80, 5.5 dwt ..**635.00**
Pendant, 18k yg crab, 53 dwt..**650.00**
Pendant, 22k yg, lg cvd carnelian surrounded by antelopes, 36 dwt.....**750.00**
Ring, cocktail; 18k yg, 12 2.75ct rnd rubies+6 old Euro 1.33ct tw dmns .**1,250.00**
Ring, Eastern Star, 21 dmns, star points: sapphire/ruby/emerald/topaz.**150.00**
Ring, gold, .40ct dmn (G-H) +6 .10ct dmn (G-H, VS1), custom mount .**950.00**
Ring, gold, 15x9mm teardrop opal+sm accent dmn, +9x5mm opal earrings..**850.00**
Ring, gold, 2.5ct orange-brn dmn (SI-2) +6 dmn tw .40ct **2,585.00**
Ring, gold w/row of 3 flowers, 8 dmns tw .36cts+13 rubies tw .35cts ..**350.00**
Ring, man's, 2-tone gold w/1ct dmn (H-J)................................**2,500.00**
Ring, plat, pear-shape 2.5ct (K) dmn amid 10 sm H dmns **5,750.00**
Ring, plat, 2.30ct dmn & 2 tapered baguettes **6,600.00**
Ring, plat, 2ct Euro dmn (I-J) & 2 sm baguettes **5,500.00**
Ring, plat, 29.3ct emerald-cut aquamarine+50 sm dmns, gross 16.9 dwt...**6,500.00**
Ring, 10k yg, sq onyx w/center dmn....................................**25.00**
Ring, 10k yg, 15 sm dmns in 5 swirl motifs on band...................**100.00**
Ring, 10k yg w/sm marquise emerald amid 12 dmn chips............**125.00**
Ring, 12k yg, 5.5ct bl topaz+24 .75ct tw dmns (J-K, I), 4.1 dwt....**200.00**
Ring, 14k wg, pear-shaped bl star sapphire w/14 sm dmns...........**100.00**
Ring, 14k wg, turq cab amid 2.5ct tw dmns (G-I VSI), 5.8 dwt ..**1,925.00**
Ring, 14k wg, 30ct aquamarine & 8 1.25ct tw (H) dmns......**2,185.00**
Ring, 14k wide band w/cluster of 13 dmn tw .90ct **650.00**
Ring, 14k yg, .60ct Euro dmn (VS1 H), .50ct amethyst ea side ..**900.00**
Ring, 14k yg, eng, onyx marquise w/cvd wht cameo......................**75.00**
Ring, 14k yg, heart-shaped dmn cluster, .60ct center dmn, 1.24ct tw..**2,750.00**
Ring, 14k yg, smoky-quartz topaz, scalloped edge, +matching earrings..**175.00**
Ring, 14k yg, 1.25 ct dmn (I1 HC)...**1,800.00**
Ring, 14k yg, 15x13mm moss-in-snow jade stone w/18 sm 90ct tw dmns.**700.00**
Ring, 14k yg, 3 dmns+12 sm, 1.23ct tw **1,400.00**
Ring, 14k yg, 5 rows containing 45 dmn tw 1.50ct....................**750.00**
Ring, 14k yg, 7 cab opals & 12 sm rubies in cluster.....................**250.00**
Ring, 14k yg lion head, sapphire eyes/ruby ears, dmns in mouth & mane.**1,400.00**
Ring, 14k yg w/1928 2½ dollar Indian Head gold pc+24 1ct tw dmns ..**750.00**
Ring, 16k wg, 3.45ct dmn (S12 S/L) solitaire...........................**6,350.00**
Ring, 18k wg, Euro-cut .55ct dmn (VVS1, I) amid 8 sm dmns & fl..**950.00**
Ring, 18k wg, 1.25 ct (VSI-VS2), pear-cut dmn amid 12 .45ct tw dmns ..**2,000.00**

Ring, 18k yg, 12 rnd 2.75ct tw rubies+5 Euro-cut 1.33ct tw dmns.**1,250.00**
Ring, 18k yg, 9.3ct emerald (SI1 G) solitaire+36 dmns 3ct tw **11,500.00**
Ring, 18k yg w/wht tips, 1.85ct tw dmns, 1930s......................**2,100.00**
Stickpin, Liberty, silver w/interlocking loops, 1¾" **200.00**
Stickpin, yg, angel-skin coral teardrop, late Victorian, from $45 to..**75.00**
Stickpin, yg lover's knot w/med-sz pearl, Edwardian, from $50 to.**75.00**

Costume Jewelry

Rhinestone jewelry is a very popular field of collecting. Rhinestones are foil-backed, leaded crystal, faceted stones with a sparkle outshining diamonds. Copyrighting jewelry came into effect in 1955. Pieces bearing a copyright mark (post-1955) are considered 'collectibles,' while pieces (with no copyright) made before then are regarded as 'antiques.' Fur clips are two-pronged, used to anchor fur stoles. Dress clips have a spring clasp and are used at the dress neckline. Look for signed and well-made, unmarked pieces for your collections and preserve this American art form. Our advisor for costume jewelry is Marcia Brown (see introductory paragraphs for information on her books and videos).

Brooches, a collection of Eisenberg original bows, ranging in value from $350.00 to $800.00 each. (Photo courtesy Marcia Brown)

Bracelet, Bakelite, floral cvg, gr, hinged, 1", VG **155.00**
Bracelet, Bakelite, gr w/red band, dimple cvg, brass studs, 1¼"...**900.00**
Bracelet, bangle; Bakelite, apple juice, reverse-cvd diagonals, ¾" .**145.00**
Bracelet, bangle; Bakelite, cvd butterstotch w/2 red cvd chanels, ¾".**160.00**
Bracelet, clear r/stns in 6 strands.......................................**79.00**
Bracelet, cuff; amethyst facet r/stns, hinged **65.00**
Bracelet, cuff; multi-shaped lav r/stns, wide **75.00**
Bracelet, g-t Persian trellis fr (4) w/colored r/stns **65.00**
Bracelet, Kafin, rnd metal links, from $25 to **40.00**
Bracelet, Leru, gp floral design, from $50 to..................................**75.00**
Bracelet, M Haskell, wht glass beads (3 strands), r/stns in clasp .**135.00**
Bracelet, tennis; sm bezel-set topaz chatons **28.00**
Bracelet, tennis; sq enamel boxes w/aquamarine r/stns, 1920s.......**85.00**
Bracelet & earrings, Tara, g-t w/red plastic inserts, from $30 to....**45.00**
Brooch, Bakelite, clown, 4-color, hinged/articulated, 3"..............**375.00**
Brooch, Bakelite, fish pr, cvd bodies w/wood wing-like fins, 2¼" ..**100.00**
Brooch, Bakelite, 2 red beets w/cvd wooden tops, 4½", VG **150.00**
Brooch, bird, g-t w/bl glass belly, r/stn details............................**35.00**
Brooch, bow tie w/mc r/stns, 1940s, sm, from $18 to....................**24.00**
Brooch, butterfly, bl r/stn w/gp fringe **55.00**
Brooch, Coro, rhodium-plated floral w/clear & bl r/stns, from $60 to...**85.00**
Brooch, Emmons, g-t stylized horse, dainty, from $25 to **35.00**
Brooch, fish, sterling silver w/reverse-cvd Lucite belly **225.00**
Brooch, gr navette r/stn sunburst w/clear r/stns scattered, lg.......**185.00**
Brooch, Jeanne, g-t rooster w/red & wht r/stns, lg, from $50 to....**75.00**
Brooch, lizard, gp w/mc navettes...**35.00**
Brooch, pk marble glass beads, aurora borealis r/stns, gold chains.**78.00**
Brooch, r/stns in 5 rows of various shapes, 4½" dia **135.00**
Brooch, ram's head, gp w/faux turq & coral, r/stns at neck...........**45.00**

Brooch, ribbon, g-t w/r/stns in knot...**58.00**
Brooch, snowflake, SP w/various sz chaton r/stns, very lg..............**55.00**
Brooch, sterling silver w/cut emerald gr glass stones, 1940s.........**125.00**
Brooch, Van Dell, 12k gf, flowers & bow w/pearl accents, $45 to.**60.00**
Brooch & earrings, Austrian, yel to Chinese red r/stns.................**65.00**
Brooch & earrings, Danecraft, sterling vermeil & cultured pearl grapes...**125.00**
Brooch & earrings, Eisenberg Ice, topaz & clear r/stns, from $150 to.**200.00**
Brooch & earrings, flowers w/mc r/stns on satin-finish gp.............**48.00**
Brooch & earrings, gr r/stns w/aurora borealis navettes **60.00**
Brooch & earrings, Hollycraft, mc vari-shaped r/stns, 1953, $60 to..**95.00**
Brooch & earrings, Napier, silver-metal grapes, lg, from $70 to..**100.00**
Brooch & earrings, Weiss, Maltese cross w/amber r/stns, from $125 to.**175.00**
Brooch/pendant, Panetta, lg aquamarine on g-t fl w/r/stns, from $65 to..**95.00**
Earrings, aurora borealis cluster, pr...**38.00**
Earrings, clear baguettes trio w/5 sm chaton guards, pr.................**54.00**
Earrings, colored button type rimmed w/r/stns, pr, from $12 to.....**18.00**
Earrings, faux emerald sqs w/lt gr teardrop, pr **38.00**
Earrings, faux pearls w/r/stn accents, dainty **15.00**
Earrings, flower, yel plastic, held by r/stn center, pr **14.00**
Earrings, flowers w/fringed leaves, plastic w/r/stns, clips, 1940s.....**45.00**
Earrings, Kramer, cultured pearls, pr, from $40 to **60.00**
Earrings, loops, gold w/r/stn center, pr **18.00**
Earrings, open pod, g-t w/r/stns inside, pr **28.00**
Earrings, Schiaparelli, sculptured stones & pearls, from $60 to **95.00**
Earrings, sterling silver w/pk & gr chatons & clear r/stns, pr.........**68.00**
Earrings, Vendome, mc beads & r/stns, pr, from $25 to **40.00**
Earrings, Weiss, dbl rows of brilliant r/stns, pr, from $70 to.........**100.00**
Earrings, wreath & bw, bl r/stns on SP, pr....................................**18.00**
Necklace, Bakelite, red floral medallion in rope reserve, brass chain ..**40.00**
Necklace, Coro, g-t floral w/r/stn, from $45 to..............................**60.00**
Necklace, Corocraft, g-t w/clear baguette r/stns, from $85 to......**135.00**
Necklace, Egyptian collar, silver w/r/stns in 2 rows......................**95.00**
Necklace, faux pearls, 3-strand w/lg faux pearl & gr r/stns **25.00**
Necklace, Florenza, HP porc in enameled fr on chain, from $60 to .**95.00**
Necklace, lav & amethyst r/stn 5-row bib **98.00**
Necklace, lg chain w/cab-studded locket w/faux turq center **28.00**
Necklace, Lisner, faux pearls & r/stns, from $35 to......................**50.00**
Necklace, M Haskell, pearls, single strand, typical, from $100 to ...**150.00**
Necklace, mesh chain w/blk & wht cabs in center w/r/stns...........**30.00**
Necklace, Richelieu, faux pearls, 2-strand, from $15 to.................**25.00**
Necklace, Vendome, floral pendant w/red & bl r/stns, from $80 to .**140.00**
Necklace, Whiting & Davis, glass cameo pendant, from $50 to ...**80.00**
Necklace & bracelet, g-t w/plastic flower inserts & r/stns, $60 to ...**90.00**
Necklace & earrings, Coro, SP w/aurora borealis stones, from $65 to ..**95.00**
Necklace & earrings, faceted aurora borealis beads, 3-strand **95.00**
Necklace & earrings, r/stn chatons (2 strands), w/lg navettes.......**48.00**
Necklace & earrings, Star, silver-tone w/bl plastic inserts, $40 to ..**50.00**
Necklace & earrings, wht glass cabs w/r/stns.................................**40.00**
Ring, bl chaton amid clear r/stn circle..**35.00**
Ring, clear r/stns & ruby navettes on rhodium-plate **28.00**
Ring, cocktail; gp woven bands & pave, opens to reveal watch **85.00**
Ring, Emmons, faux pearls & turq form cluster, from $30 to .**45.00**
Ring, gp dmn shape w/filled w/clear r/stns....................................**28.00**
Ring, opalene clusters on gp..**45.00**

Johnson Brothers

A Staffordshire-based company operating since well before the turn of the century, Johnson Brothers has produced many familiar lines of dinnerware, several of which are becoming very collectible. Some of their patterns were made in both blue and pink transfer as well as in polychrome. One of the more familiar patterns is Friendly Village, which is still being produced, though the pattern is much more limited than it once was.

Values below range from a low base price for patterns that are still in production (i.e., Friendly Village) or less collectible to a high that would apply to very desirable patterns such as Tally Ho, English Chippendale, Wild Turkeys, Strawberry Fair, Historic America, Harvest Fruit, etc. Mid-range lines include Coaching Scenes, Millsteam, Old English Countryside, Rose Bouquet (and there are others).

For more information on marks, patterns, and pricing, we recommend *Johnson Brothers Dinnerware Pattern Directory and Price Guide* by Mary J. Finegan, who is listed in the Directory under North Carolina.

Old Britain Castles (old), dinner plate, 25.00.

Bowl, cereal/soup; rnd, sq or lug, ea, from $10 to **15.00**
Bowl, soup; rnd or sq, 7", from $12 to **16.00**
Bowl, vegetable; oval, from $30 to upwards of **40.00**
Chop/cake plate, from $50 to **70.00**
Coffee mug, from $20 to upwards of **25.00**
Coffeepot, from $90 to upwards of **100.00**
Covered butter dish, from $50 to **60.00**
Demitasse set, 2-pc, from $20 to **24.00**
Egg cup, from $15 to **20.00**
Pitcher/jug, from $45 to upwards of **55.00**
Plate, salad; sq or rnd, from $10 to upwards of **18.00**
Platter, med, 12-14", ea, from $45 to **55.00**
Sauce boat/gravy, from $40 to upwards of **48.00**
Shakers, pr, from $40 to **48.00**
Sugar bowl, open, from $30 to **35.00**
Teacup & saucer, from $15 to **24.00**
Teapot, from $90 to upwards of **100.00**
Turkey platter, 20½", from $200 to **300.00**

Josef Originals

Figurines of lovely ladies, charming girls, and whimsical animals marked Josef Originals were designed by Muriel Joseph George of Arcadia, California, from 1945 to 1985. Until 1960 they were produced in California, but costs were high and copies of her work were being made in Japan. To remain competitive, she and her partner, George Good, found a company in Japan to build a factory and produce her designs to her specifications. Muriel retired in 1982; however, Mr. Good continued production of her work and made some design changes on some figurines. The company was sold in late 1985; the name is currently owned by Dakin/Applause, and a limited amount of figurines with the Josef Originals name are being made. Those made during the ownership of Muriel are the most collectible. They can be recognized by these characteristics: The girls have a high-gloss finish, black eyes, and most are signed on the bottom. As of the late 1970s, bisque finish was making its way into the lineup, and by 1980 glossy girls were fairly scarce in the product line. Brown-eyed figurines date from 1982 through 1985. Applause uses a red-brown eye, although they are starting to release 'copies' of early pieces that are signed Josef Originals by Applause or by Dakin. The animals

were nearly always done in a matt finish and bore paper labels only. In the mid-1970s they introduced a line of fuzzy flocked-coat animals with glass eyes. Our advisors, Jim and Kaye Whitaker (see the Directory under Washington, no appraisal requests please) have written three books: *Josef Originals, Charming Figurines, Revised Edition*; *Josef Originals, A Second Look*; and *Josef Originals, Figurines of Muriel Joseph George*. These are all currently available, and each has no repeats of items shown in the other books. Please note: All figurines listed here have black eyes unless specified otherwise. As with many collectibles, values have been negatively impacted to a measurable extent since the advent of the Internet.

Birthday Girls, 1 through 16, Japan, ea **30.00**
Birthstone Dolls, Jan - Dec, w/jewels, Japan, 3½", ea **20.00**
Buggy Bugs series, various poses, wire antenna, Japan, 3¼", ea **20.00**
Camel, standing, Japan, 6¼" **45.00**
Career Girls series, Nurse, in yel holding baby, Japan, 5¾" **55.00**
Champions (dogs) series, Japan, 5", ea **20.00**
Character Cats series, Japan, 4", ea **12.00**
Christmas music box, girl decorating tree, Japan, 7" **45.00**
Colonial Days series, Jeanne, Japan, 9" **95.00**
Country series, Greece or Spain, California, 10¼", ea **90.00**
Doll of the Month, tilted head, Jan - Dec, California, 3¼", ea **45.00**
Elephant w/tusks, Japan, 6¾" **40.00**
Farmer's Daughter, girl w/hen & basket of eggs, Japan, 5" **30.00**
First Love series, Tony & Tina, Japan, 5" **50.00**
First Time series, New Hat, Japan, 4½" **40.00**
Flower Girl series, Rose, girl w/flower hat, Japan, 4¼" **35.00**
Happy Home w/Dove Greeting Angel, Japan, 3¾" **35.00**
Hunter, beautiful horse standing, Japan, 6" **25.00**
International series, various countries, 4¾", ea **40.00**
It's a Wonderful World series, Japan, 3½", ea **30.00**
Italian Aristocrats, lady & escort, Japan, 7", ea **75.00**
Joseph's Children, Johnny, w/marbles, California, 4¾" **85.00**
Kennel Club series, Yorkshire, etc, Japan, 3", ea **15.00**
Little Jewels series, Ruby, girl w/'ruby' set in crown, Japan, 3½" ... **25.00**
Love Makes the World Go Round series, 8½", ea **90.00**
Make Believe series, Japan, 4½", ea **30.00**
Mama Ballerina, California, 7" **75.00**
Mary Ann & Mama, California, 4", 7", pr **95.00**
Mermaid lipstick holder, wht w/beige trim, Japan, 4" **75.00**
Mice, varous styles, 2¾", ea **12.00**
Missy, girl in bonnet, several colors, California, 4" **40.00**
Monkeys, mama & papa, Japan, 3" **15.00**
Music box, Happy Anniversary, Japan, 7¼" **55.00**
Nanette, half doll w/jewels, several colors, California, 5½" **65.00**
Nursery Rhymes series, Miss Mary, Japan, 4" **45.00**
Ostrich babies, 1", ea **25.00**
Ostrich mama, 5" **45.00**
Parasol Girl series, 3 in set, Japan, 6¾" **60.00**
Pixies, various poses, gr w/red & gold trim, Japan, 2-3¼", ea **25.00**
Poodle from 'Poodle & Siamese,' Japan, 4¼" **25.00**
Romance series, Love Letter from Love Story, Japan, 8" **90.00**
Rose Garden series, brn eyes, Japan, 5¼", 6 different, ea **55.00**
Secret Pal, girl w/fan, various colors, California, 3½" **35.00**
Skunk w/wht hair tuft on head, Japan, 2½" **18.00**
Sports Angels series, angels playing various sports, Japan, 2¾", ea .. **35.00**
Three Kings, Japan, 8½-11", set of 3 .... **70.00**
Wall plaque, cat, gray, California **50.00**
Watusi Luau series, hunter in pot, Natives, etc, Japan, 5" **50.00**
Wee Ching & Wee Ling, Chinese boy & girl w/dog & cat (copied), CA **50.00**
Wee Folk, various poses, Japan, 4½", ea **20.00**
World Greatest series, bowler, boxer, etc, Japan, 4½", ea **25.00**
Zodiac Girls series, Japan, 4¾" **35.00**

Judaica

The items listed below are representative of objects used in both the secular and religious life of the Jewish people. They are evident of a culture where silversmiths, painters, engravers, writers, and metal workers were highly gifted and skilled in their art. Most of the treasures shown in recently displayed exhibits of Judaica were confiscated by the Germans during the late 1930s up to 1945; by then eight Jewish synagogues and fifty warehouses had been filled with Hitler's plunder. Judaica is currently available through dealers, from private collections, and the annual auction held in Israel, New York City, and Boston.

Candelabrum, sabbath; brass, German, 19th C, 15x15" 1,200.00
Candelabrum, sabbath; chrome-plated, Farberware, 1950s, 13½x12½"..165.00
Candlesticks, brass, E Europe, 5-branch, 19th C, 12x12" 235.00
Candlesticks, sabbath; brass, E Europe, 3-branch, 19th C, 12½"..225.00
Candlesticks, sabbath; German silver, Baroque style, 19th C, 12", pr..2,200.00
Candlesticks, sabbath; Polish, brass, 19th C, 12", pr 450.00
Etrog container, SP, Continental Europe, 20th C, 5x6" 375.00
Kiddush cup, German silver, late 18th C, 3" 400.00
Kiddush cup, Mexican silver, w/semi-precious stones, 20th C, 8¼" ..575.00
Kiddush cup, Russian niello & silver, 19th C, 2½" 575.00
Kiddush cup, Russian silver, beaker style, 19th C, 3" 300.00
Kiddush cup, Russian silver, stem style, 19th C, 3½" 300.00
Kiddush cup, Russian silver, 2" 200.00
Kiddush cup, silver w/turq stones, Israel, 1960s, 6½"...................495.00
Menorah, Bezalel, brass, 1920, 11x9¾".......................................2,500.00

Menorah, silver, marked P.W.G. Rzeszow, Hungarian, 1787, stepped circular base with leaves and berries, graduated foliate tubular arms with sconces, lacks servant light, 20", $17,500.00.

Mezuzah, sterling & glass, R Landau design, 4½" 170.00
Spice tower, rosewater, brass, N Africa, 20th C, 14½x12¾"..150.00
Spice tower, silver, Continental Europe, 19th C, 9½" 1,200.00
Spice tower, SP, USA, 20th C, 9"..375.00

Jugtown

The Jugtown Pottery was started about 1920 by Juliana and Jacques Busbee, in Moore County, North Carolina. Ben Owen, a young descendant of a Staffordshire potter, was hired in 1923. He was the master potter, while the Busbees experimented with perfecting glazes and supervising design and modeling. Preferred shapes were those reminiscent of traditional country wares and classic Oriental forms. Glazes were various: natural-clay oranges, buffs, Tobacco-spit Brown, Mirror Black, white, Frog Skin Green, a lovely turquoise called Chinese Blue, and the traditional cobalt-decorated salt glaze. The pottery gained national recognition, and as a result of their success, several other local potteries were established. The pottery closed for a time in the late 1950s due to the ill health of Mrs. Busbee (who had directed the business after her husband died in 1947) but reopened in 1960. Jugtown is still in operation; howev-

er, they no longer use their original glaze colors which are now so collectible and the circular mark is slightly smaller than the original.

Bowl, Chinese Blue, flared, ftd, 11½"...500.00
Bowl, Chinese Blue, Korean, stoneware, B Owen, 1940s, 3x9¼".400.00
Bowl, Chinese Blue, Oriental, B Owen, 1940s, 5x5¼" 2,800.00
Bowl, Chinese White, Oriental, B Owen, late 1930s, 4¼x7" 150.00
Bowl, mirror blk, earthenware, incised lines, B Owen, 1930s, 7" .200.00
Bowl, Tobacco Spit Brown, Oriental, B Owen, late 1930s, 4¼x12⅜"...175.00
Candlesticks, orange lead, earthenware, Ben Owen, 1930s, 12", pr.275.00
Chamberstick, butter gloss, earthenware, B Owen, 1930s, 2x6⅞"....130.00
Charger, orange, abrasion/surface flakes, 15" 200.00
Dish, Chicken Pie, orange w/chicken decor, V Owen, 1960s, 12½" .250.00
Pitcher, buttermilk; salt glaze, Ben Owen, 1920s, 8¼" 120.00
Vase, Chinese Blue, bulbous, 5½" 600.00
Vase, Chinese Blue, cylindrical, incurvate rim, 5½"....................475.00
Vase, Chinese Blue, egg form, B Owen, 1940s, 4" 250.00
Vase, Chinese Blue, Han Dynasty style, hdls, B Owen, 1940s, 8½" ..3,600.00
Vase, Chinese Blue, tapered cylinder, 5" 500.00
Vase, Chinese White, angular, stoneware, B Owen, 1930s, 5½".250.00
Vase, Chinese White, dbl gourd, V Owen, ca 1960s, 8" 150.00
Vase, Chinese White, Dragon Head, stoneware, B Owen, 1930s, 15"...1,700.00
Vase, Chinese White, Han Dynasty style, B Owen, late 1930s, 9" .2,200.00
Vase, Lily, Chinese White, earthenware, B Owen, 1930s, 9½" ...950.00
Vase, Sung, butter on orange lead, 3-hdl, B Owen, 1930s, 6⅛" ..425.00
Vase, turq mottle, pear shape w/raised rim, mid-20th C, 6" 635.00

K. P. M. Porcelain

The original KPM wares were produced from 1823 until 1847 by the Konigliche Porzellan Manfaktur, located in Berlin, Germany. Meissen used the same letters on some of their porcelains, as did several others in the area. The mark contains the initials KPM. Watch for items currently being imported from China; they are marked KPM with the eagle but the scepter is not present. Our advisor for this category is Don Williams; he is listed in the Directory under Missouri.

Cup saucer, floral 75.00
Figurine, cat sleeping, orange & bl bow, gold trim, mk, 12¾", NM .140.00
Plaque, Aurora, figures/horse/cherub, Bierschneider, in fr, 5¼x10"..3,450.00
Plaque, Cupid, after Raphel, sight: 6½x4½", +oval wood fr 800.00
Plaque, First Snowfall, grandfther/2 children in doorway, 10", gilt fr.4,300.00
Plaque, lady in scanty purple dress, oval 4½x3½" image in fr.....525.00
Plaque, semi nude draped in dk bl wrap reading book, 6⅜x9", +fr.4,000.00
Plaque, Sistine Madonna after Raphael, 12x10", in gilt fr 3,500.00
Plaque, Sistine Madonna after Raphael, 17", giltwood fr in shadow box ...4,000.00
Plaque, Una Gitana, lady draped in purple, 4½x3½" 525.00
Plate, fruit decor center on wht, ca 1920, 7½" dia 190.00

Kayserzinn Pewter

J.P. Kayser Sohn produced pewter decorated with relief-molded Art Nouveau motifs in Germany during the late 1800s and into the twentieth century. Examples are marked with 'Kayserzinn' and the mold number within an elongated oval reserve. Items with three-dimensional animals, insects, birds, etc., are valued much higher than bowls, plates, and trays with simple embossed florals, which are usually priced at $100.00 to about $200.00, depending on size.

Basket, Nouveau floral, simple hdl, 3¾x6x4" 150.00
Bowl, flowers & dragonflies, #4245, ca 1900, 2x10" 125.00
Bowl, Nouveau floral, H Leven, ca 1890s, #4133, 5x9¾" 185.00

Bowl, swallowtail butterflies (4), #4278, 3½x4½" 125.00
Candlestick, Nouveau floral, drip plate, #4018, 1890s, 11½x5½" ..145.00
Knife rest, dachshund, 3½" L 45.00
Pitcher, Nouveau flowers & devil's face, twig hdl, #27, 13x8" 350.00
Pitcher, satyr's face/iris design, #4061, 12½" 325.00
Plate, anemones & interwining stems, 10" 100.00
Platter, emb bat heads & berries, mk/#d, 18½x8" 225.00
Stopper, dog's head in profile 1 side, fox on reverse, ca 1920 ....45.00
Tray, Nouveau floral, H Leven, #4436, ca 1907, 13¾x6¼" 200.00
Tureen, birds, flowers, fruit & berries, hdls, w/lid & base, 10" L .300.00
Vase, dragonflies & flowers, ftd, #4310, 7¾" 165.00

Keeler, Brad

Keeler studied art for a time in the 1930s; later he became a modeler for a Los Angeles firm. By 1939 he was working in his own studio where he created naturalistic studies of birds and animals which were marketed through giftware stores. They were decorated by means of an airbrush and enhanced with hand-painted details. His flamingo figures were particularly popular. In the mid-'40s, he developed a successful line of Chinese Modern housewares glazed in Ming Dragon Blood, a red color he personally developed. Keeler died of a heart attack in 1952, and the pottery closed soon thereafter. For more information, we recommend *The Collector's Encyclopedia of California Pottery, Second Edition*, by Jack Chipman (Collector Books).

Ashtray, duck figural, 2½x3¾", pr 45.00
Charger, fish & 2 lures & lines emb, turq, #141, 11" 150.00
Creamer & sugar bowl, fish form, w/lid, #14?/#149, pr 250.00
Dish, tomato centered on cabbage leaves, 3½x9½" dia.................50.00
Figurine, bird on branch, bl & pk, #718, 5" 65.00
Figurine, bird on branch, rose pk, #710, 5" 65.00
Figurine, bird on branch, rose pk, #720, 4⅜" 65.00
Figurine, bird on stump, rose pk, #18, 8¼" 70.00
Figurine, bird perched on stump, lt rose, #17, 6" 70.00
Figurine, bird perched on stump, yel w/red head, #17, 6" 70.00
Figurine, cardinal, 9¼" 85.00
Figurine, cockatoo w/wings up, #30, w/sticker, 10¾" 100.00
Figurine, cocker spaniel pup, blk & gray, #748, 4½" 60.00
Figurine, flamingo, #2 in mold, 10" 135.00
Figurine, flamingo, head down, #2, 7½" 125.00
Figurine, flamingo, head up, 7½" 150.00
Figurine, Little Miss Muffet, Pryde 'n Joy line, 4" 70.00
Figurine, pheasant female on branch, #21, 6½" 65.00
Figurine, Siamese cat, #771, 9¼" 85.00

Figurine, Siamese cat, #798, $75.00. (Photo courtesy Jack Chipman)

Figurine, swallow, on branch, bl w/wht-tipped wings, 10¾" 80.00
Figurines, deer family, 5¼", 3", 3", set of 3 ....75.00

Figurines, kittens at play, blk w/gray, #772/#773, 7" & 8" L, pr...140.00
Pitcher, rooster, mc, #228, 6" 225.00
Plate, lobster on leaves, 9" 25.00
Platter, fish shape, #136, 18½" 250.00
Shakers, range; fish figural, turq & beige, label, #149, 4", pr.......125.00
Tray, lobster on gr leaves, 6 compartments, #873, 14" 95.00
Tray, wht w/red lobster center hdl, #865, 12x8½".........................80.00

Keen Kutter

Keen Kutter was the brand name chosen in 1870 by the Simmons Firm for a line of high-grade tools and cutlery. The trademark was first applied to high-grade axes. A corporation was formed in 1874 called Simmons Hardware Company. In 1922 Winchester merged with Simmons and continued to carry a full line of hardware plus the Winchester brand. The merger terminated in March of 1929 and converted back to the original status of Simmons Hardware Co. It wasn't until July 1, 1950, that Simmons Hardware Co. was purchased by Shapleigh Hardware Company. All Simmons Hardware Co. trademark lines were continued, and the business operated successfully until its closing in 1962. Today the Keen Kutter logo is owned by the Val-Test Company of Chicago, Illinois. For further study we recommend *Collector's Guide to E. C. Simmons Keen Kutter Cutlery Tools*, an illustrated price guide by our advisors for this category, Jerry and Elaine Heuring, available at your favorite bookstore or public library. The Heurings are listed in the Directory under Missouri. See also Knives.

Auger bit set, KSR116, from ⁴⁄₁₆" to ¹⁴⁄₁₆", in pouch 100.00
Axe, broad; EC Simmons w/lg logo, 13" cutting edge 150.00
Axe, Michigan pattern, Keen Kutter on hdl, 7¼x4½" head.......100.00
Bit brace, ratchet, KBB14, 14" sweep 45.00
Bottle, oil; bl glass, 4x1½" 45.00
Box, axe; held 12 KBW 3½" western dbl-bit axes, dvtl 65.00
Brace bit, ratchet, KBC10, 10" sweep 45.00
Breast drill, lg gear wheel, 5" dia, 16" overall 100.00
Cabinet, tool; oak, wall hung, dbl-door, 31x22½x8" 500.00
Calendar, The Future Champion, 1950 ....150.00
Calipers, outside; K38, 8" 50.00
Can opener, logo type...25.00
Can opener, logo type, w/bottle opener attachment 150.00
Carving set, stag hdls, logo on sterling ferrules, 3-pc 65.00
Catalog, No R1, revised prices, 1922, 153-pg 125.00
Catalog, Shapleigh, Dmn Edge & KK, 29-section, 1942 ....300.00
Clock, EC Simmons, electric, K530, 15" sq, EX 750.00
Corn mill, clamps to table, CI, Pat Aug 9 '09 ....150.00
Dandelion weeder..40.00
Dividers, 6" 40.00
File, mill bastard; flat single cup, various szs...............................10.00
Flashlight battery, mk Shapleigh Keen Kutter.............................90.00
Fork, spading; KHSD..45.00
Gauge, marking; wooden, rosewood w/brass strips, 8"..................75.00
Gimlet, blade extends through hdl, single or dbl cut...................35.00
Glass cutter, KK on hdl 50.00
Hammer, blacksmith shop; Shapleigh, 48-oz 65.00
Hammer, EC Simmons, curved claw, hexagon neck, 16-oz 40.00
Hammer, EC Simmons, curved claw, rnd neck, K514, 5-oz.........175.00
Hammer, saw setting; w/orig sticker, 7-oz, M 200.00
Hatchet, claw; w/label, M 200.00
Hatchet, flooring; EC Simmons, w/nail slot 55.00
Hatchet, rig builder's 55.00
Hedge trimmer, electric, KK57...55.00
Jigsaw, electric, KK249 ....55.00
Key, skeleton; brass, emblem shape..10.00

Key chain, plastic, hardware store name on bk, sm........................60.00
Knife, butcher; N622, 8¼" blade 15.00
Knife, hunting; blk hard rubber hdl w/guard, KBK25, 9½" 75.00
Lawn mower, revolving wheel, 5 blades, 16" cut..........................30.00
Letterhead w/invoice of hardware store 15.00
Level, adjustable, brass top, dbl duplex plates, KK30, 30" 100.00
Level, adjustable, dbl duplex plates, KK45 ....200.00
Level, Shapleigh, cast aluminum, 24" 65.00
Magazine ad, Better Tools Make Better..., mc, 11½x8¼" 35.00
Meet grinder, clamps to table, K105, family sz 20.00
Nippers, K26-6........................30.00
Notebook holder, w/metal folding clip, 12½x9" 100.00
Order-by-mail form, KK logo at top 10.00
Padlock, EC Simmons, St Louis USA 125.00
Paper holder, wood & CI, holds 12" roll 175.00
Pin, lapel; axe shape, shield emblem 225.00
Pincers, farrier's nail cutting; 12" 30.00
Plane, block; iron, w/lever adjustment, KK103 ....50.00
Plane, circular; cuts concave or convex, K200........................600.00
Plane, iron w/corrugated bottom, K3, 8" 200.00
Plane, jack; smooth bottom, +fence & jointer attachment 175.00
Plane, jointer; iron, smooth bottom, K8 ....125.00
Plane, scraper & chamfer; KK212 ....275.00
Plane, wood bottom, K31, 24" 85.00
Pliers, combination; middle cutter, K51, various szs.....................30.00
Pliers, diagonal cutting; K45, 5" 40.00
Pliers, heavy pattern, raised side cutter, 8½" 40.00
Pliers, rnd nose; K66-6 ....40.00
Postcard, MO street scene w/KK sign on storefront, ca 1908 ....80.00
Punch, Shapleigh, various szs, ea 10.00
Rack, garden tool; metal, on casters 175.00
Rake, garden 35.00
Rasp, half-round wood; various szs 10.00
Razor, corn; celluloid hdl, mk Germany 70.00
Razor, straight; wht celluloid hdl, full gold-etch blade, K746........45.00
Razor strop, EC Simmons, dbl swing, K82 ....75.00
Reamer (for wood), sq blade, K115........................50.00
Rule, boxwood, 4-fold, 1" W, 24" 55.00
Rule, folding zigzag, w/Pat date, K603, 3"........................200.00
Saw, dehorning; CI, wood hdl........................70.00
Saw, hack; adjustable for 8-12" blades, K188A........................45.00
Saw, hand; EC Simmons, buttons have axe head w/KK, 28" blade....60.00
Scissors, embroidery; fancy, 3½" 40.00
Scissors, nail; rnd bows, 4" 15.00
Scissors; stork-bird shaped, 8½" 150.00
Screwdriver, beaded hardwood hdls, mk Blue Brand, 5½" blade...20.00
Screwdriver, steel ferrule through hardwood hdl, 3-10" 20.00
Shears, barber's; Germany, 7½" 20.00
Shears, hedge; KS, 8½" 20.00
Shotgun, 16 guage, Simmons Hardware mk (twice), KK on side...350.00
Shovel, dirt; KRD2B........................25.00
Sign, EC Simmons, porc, dbl-sided, 13½", EX 1,700.00
Slick, beveled edge, wood hdl, blade: 16", 3½" W 350.00
Square, combination; mk blade, maroon hdl, 12" 80.00
Square, copper finish, KC3........................35.00
Square, sliding T-bevel; CI hdl, KK/logo on top, 6" 75.00
Square, take down; KT100........................250.00
Steel, knife; emblem-shaped guard, 10-14" 40.00
Tack claw, K5, 7" 25.00
Ticket punch 80.00
Tobacco cutter, CI 300.00
Vise, hand; K49, 7" removable pin 200.00
Wagon, KK Rocket........................250.00
Wrench, adjustable; Shapleigh KK, K12 ....50.00

Wrench, bicycle; K94 ....70.00
Wrench, engineer's; K31, 7/16" 40.00
Wrench, general purpose; KK on end, various szs 35.00
Wrench, pipe; KK on hdl, 36" 200.00
Yard stick, hardware store give-away........................30.00

Kellogg Studio

Stanley Kellogg (1908 – 1972) opened the Kellogg Studio in Petoskey, Michigan, in 1948. It remained in operation until 1976, producing a wide range of both decorative and functional ceramics including dinnerware, vases, and figurines. Most pieces are glazed in rich, solid colors and are marked 'Petoskey' as well as 'S. Kellogg Studio' or 'Kellogg's.' Stanley Kellogg began as a sculptor, and it was while working on an outdoor monument with the great Swedish-American sculptor, Carl Milles, that Stanley suffered the back injury which forced him to turn to studio work. In addition to naturalistic treatments of Michigan wildlife, Kellogg developed some angular, architectural forms in his molded art pottery. Our co-advisors for this category are Walter P. Hogan and Wendy L. Woodworth; they are listed in the Directory under Michigan.

Ashtray, brn, leaf shape w/floral design, 5" 20.00
Ashtray, gr, sq w/personalized name........................15.00
Ashtray, yel, sq, 4" 15.00
Bowl, brn w/wht int, 1" 8.00
Bowl, shadow type, gr, bulbous, cut-out chickadees, 7" 150.00
Box, metallic glaze, w/lid, 3x5" 50.00
Dish, teardrop shape, lt gr w/tiny flower frog insert, 3½" 15.00
Figurine, crouching rabbit, blk, 2" 95.00
Figurine, great-horned owl on branch, brn & ivory, 7¼"..............65.00
Figurine, owl chick standing, blk, 5" 95.00
Flower frog vase, yel, spherical, 3¼", w/separate 4" rnd base.........55.00
Mug, bl, sq hdl, 5"........................20.00
Pitcher, bl, curved hdl, 9"........................40.00
Plate, gr, w/flowers & personalized name, 11" 12.00
Plate/charger, brn w/yel pears, 10" 45.00
Vase, bl, bulbous w/cylindrical neck & slanted rim, 3" 35.00
Vase, blk gourd shape w/irregular vertical grooves, 16"................90.00

Kelva

Kelva was a trademark of the C.F. Monroe Company of Meriden, Connecticut; it was produced for only a few years after the turn of the century. It is distinguished from the Wave Crest and Nakara lines by its unique Batik-like background, probably achieved through the use of a cloth or sponge to apply the color. Large florals are hand painted on the opaque milk glass; and ormolu and brass mounts were used for the boxes, vases, and trays. Most pieces are signed. Our advisors for this category are Dolli and Wilfred Cohen; they are listed in the Directory under California.

Humidor, cigars and flowers on green, 5¼x6¼", $895.00; Box, pastel panels, 6" diameter, $750.00. (Photo courtesy Dolli and Wilfred Cohen)

Box, Bishop's Hat, wild roses on gr w/grayed border, 3x4" 500.00
Box, floral, red & wht, plain mold, 5½" dia.................................650.00
Box, roses, pk on gr, fuchsia trim, wht dots, mk, 3½x6" 700.00
Box, watch; daisies, pk on bl..450.00
Box, wild roses, pk on gr, hinged lid, sq, 2¾x4" 425.00
Ferner, floral on pk, ogee sides, 7½" dia....................................795.00
Napkin ring, floral on waisted hexagon form, rare......................450.00
Pin dish, floral, pk on gr, SP mts, flared 6-panel bowl, 3¾" dia ..195.00
Tray, Crown mold, floral on moss gr, 6" dia...............................350.00
Tray, daisies on maroon, rnd w/emb metal rim, rope hdl, 3½" 275.00
Vase, floral on rose, trumpet form w/4 ormolu ft, 6x2" 450.00
Vase, lg roses on gr, ornate ormolu hdls & 4-ftd base, 16" 3,500.00
Whisk broom holder, floral on red, ornate ormolu bkplate 1,750.00

Kenton Hills

Kenton Hills Porcelain was established in 1940 in Erlanger, Kentucky, by Harold Bopp, former Rookwood superintendent, and David Seyler, noted artist and sculptor. Native clay was used; glazes were very similar to Rookwood's of the same period. The work was of high quality, but because of the restrictions imposed on needed material due to the onset of the war, the operation failed in 1942. Much of the ware is artist signed and marked with the Kenton Hills name or cipher and shape number.

Lamp, stylized leaves, turq, 10" 1,100.00
Vase, geometrics, mc on wht, Dickman, flaws, 5¼" 150.00
Vase, prunts, wht on mirrored umber, cylindrical, Hentschel, 7x4¾"...700.00

Kentucky Derby Glasses

Kentucky Derby glasses are the official souvenir glasses sold at Churchill Downs filled with mint juleps on Derby Day. Many folks from all over the country who attend the Derby take home the souvenir glass, and thus the collecting begins. The first glass (1938) is said to have either been given away as a souvenir or used for drinks among the elite at the Downs. This one, the 1939 glass, two glasses from 1940, the 1940 – 41 aluminum tumbler, the 'Beetleware' tumblers from 1941 to 1944, and the 1945 short, tall, and jigger glasses are the rarest, most sought-after glasses, and they command the highest prices. Some 1974 glasses incorrectly listed the 1971 winner Canonero II as just Canonero; as a result, it became the 'mistake' glass for that year. Also, glasses made by the Federal Glass Company (whose logo, found on the bottom of the glass, is a small shield containing an F) were used for extra glasses for the 100th running in 1974. There is also a 'mistake' and a correct Federal glass, making four to collect for that year. Another mistake glass was produced this year as about 2,070 were made with the 1932 winner Burgoo King listed incorrectly as a Triple Crown winner instead of the 1937 winner of the Triple Crown, War Admiral.

The 1956 glass has four variations. On some 1956 glasses the star which was meant to separate the words 'Kentucky Derby' is missing making only one star instead of two stars. Also, all three horses on the glass were meant to have tails, but on some of the glasses only two have tails making two tails instead of three. To identify which 1956 glass you have, just count the number of stars and tails.

In order to identify the year of a pre-1969 glass, since it did not appear on the front of the glass prior to then, simply add one year to the last date listed on the back of the glass. This may seem to be a confusing practice, but the current year's glass is produced long before the Derby winner is determined.

The prices on older glasses remain high. These are in high demand, and collectors are finding them extremely hard to locate. Values listed here are for absolutely perfect glasses with bright colors, all printing and

gold complete, no flaws of any kind, chipping, or any other damage. Any problem reduces the price by at least one-half. Our advisor for this category is Betty Hornback; she is listed in the Directory under Kentucky.

1938...4,000.00
1939...6,500.00
1940, aluminum...800.00
1940, French Lick, aluminum 800.00
1940, glass tumbler, 2 styles, ea, minimum value.............10,000.00
1941-44, Beetleware, from $2,500 to...................................4,000.00
1945, jigger...1,000.00
1945, regular...1,600.00
1945, tall...450.00
1946-47, ea...100.00
1948, clear bottom...225.00
1948, frosted bottom 250.00
1949...225.00
1950...450.00
1951...650.00

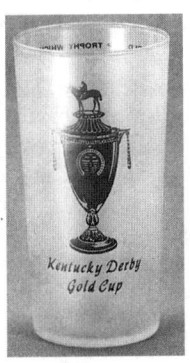

1952, Gold Cup, $225.00.

1953 ....175.00
1954 ....200.00
1955 ....150.00
1956, 1 star, 2 tails..275.00
1956, 1 star, 3 tails..400.00
1956, 2 stars, 2 tails..200.00
1956, 2 stars, 3 tails..250.00
1957, gold & blk on frosted 125.00
1958, Gold Bar 175.00
1958, Iron Leige..225.00
1959-60, ea...100.00
1961...110.00
1962, Churchill Downs, red, gold & blk on clear 80.00
1963 ....70.00
1964, ea...55.00
1965 ....75.00
1966-68, ea..60.00
1969...65.00
1970...70.00
1971...50.00
1972...45.00
1973...55.00
1974, Federal, regular & mistake, ea............................200.00
1974, Libbey, mistake, Canonero in 1971 listing on bk.................18.00
1974, regular, Canonero II in 1971 listing on bk 16.00
1975...16.00
1976...16.00
1976, plastic 16.00
1977...14.00
1978-79, ea..16.00

1980 ....22.00
1981-82, ea..14.00
1983-85, ea..12.00
1986 ....14.00
1986 (1985 copy)...20.00
1987-89, ea..12.00
1990-92, ea..10.00
1993-95, ea..9.00
1996-97, ea..8.00
1998-99, ea..6.00
2000-02, ea..5.00
2003, mistake, 1932 incorrectly listed as Derby Triple Crown Winner..8.00
2003-04 ....3.00

Keramos

Keramos (Austria) produced a line of decorative items including vases, bowls, masks, and figurines that were imported primarily by the Ebeling & Ruess Co. of Philadelphia from the late 1920s to the 1950s. The figurines they manufactured were of high quality and very detailed, similar to those made by other Austrian firms. Their glazes were very smooth, though today some crazing is present on older pieces.

Most items were marked and numbered, and some bear the name or initials of the artist who designed them. In addition to Ebeling & Ruess (whose trademark includes a crown), other importers' stamps and labels may be found as well. Knight Ceramics employed a shield mark, and many of the vases produced through the 1940s are marked with a swastika; these pieces are turning up with increasing frequency at shops as well as Internet auction sites. Although the workmanship they exhibit is somewhat inferior, the glazes used during this period are excellent and are now attracting much attention among collectors.

Detail is a very important worth-assessing factor. The more detailed the art figures are, the more valuable. Artist-signed pieces are quite scarce. Many artists were employed by both Keramos and Goldscheider. The molds of these two companies are sometimes very similar as well, and unmarked items are often difficult to identify with certainty.

Items listed below are considered to be in excellent, undamaged condition unless otherwise stated. Our advisor for this category is Darrell Thomas; he is listed in the Directory under Wisconsin.

Bookends, Franciscan monk w/Bible, older triangle mk, 7x4½", pr 250.00
Ewer, butterfly decal above flowers, mc, KKK triangle, 1930s-40s, 24"..395.00
Figurine, beagle pup, sad look, 7x8"..65.00
Figurine, birds (2) on flowering dogwood branch, mc, 1940s mk, 9"..125.00
Figurine, child feeding fawn, sgn Dakon, older mks, 9" 450.00
Figurine, children in Deco tennis clothes, Dakon, 10", pr 1,000.00
Figurine, dog, various/series of; 1940s, shield mk, ea from $50 to..75.00
Figurine, German shepherd, realistic, #2208, shield mk, 7" L 225.00
Figurine, Greta Garbo style, red knickers, sgn Dakon, 1930s mk, 14"..750.00
Figurine, horses (2) rearing on base, gray on gr, Wein Keramos, 13"....165.00
Figurine, kingfisher, brush details, lifelike, 1930s mk, 6x7", 4 for..95.00
Figurine, lion male/female, lg mane, grassy base, shield mks, 1940s ..75.00
Figurine, Madonna w/halo holds sheep, detailed, 1930s mks, 18"...225.00
Figurine, maiden w/pail, hands up, Dakon, #1228/14/2, KKK mk, 13"..385.00
Figurine, nude, no colors, sgn Dakon, older mks, 1920s, 11" ...1,750.00
Figurine, nude harem dancer, similar to W Werkstatte, Austria/mk, 15" ..2,000.00
Figurine, penguin, realistic/detailed, #1203, triangle mk, 4½" 75.00
Figurine, poodle, sitting, wht w/pnt collar, #5119, 12½x14¾"......85.00
Figurine, sparrows, lifelike/detailed, 1940s mk, 2" L, set of 14 ....175.00
Figurine, tigers fighting, lifelike, E&R labels, 1940s-50s, 8", pr.....85.00
Mask, Deco abstract design, slit eyes, orange lips, sgn WW, old mk.1,500.00
Mask, realistic mc face, bright scarf, banner mks, 1940s, 10" oval..185.00
Pitcher, red w/gold, squat, gold shield mks, 1940s style, 8x12"......85.00

Plaque, lady's head, feather in hat, mc, flaw, Wein Keramos, 7"....45.00
Vase, bud; frog at base of flower form, wht, #457, 8½", pr 110.00
Vase, floral, swollen cylinder, #1847, 12" 280.00

Kew Blas

The Union Glass Company was founded in 1854, in Somerville, Massachusetts, an offshoot of the New England Glass Co. in East Cambridge. They made only flint glass — tablewares, lamps, globes, and shades. Kew Blas was a trade name they used for their iridescent, lustered art glass produced there from 1893 until about 1920. The glass was made in imitation of Tiffany and achieved notable success. Some items were decorated with pulled leaf and feather designs, while others had a monochrome lustre surface. The mark was an engraved 'Kew Blas' in an arching arrangement.

Vase, opal glass cased to iridescent gold with green pulled feathers on double-bulbed form, 6¾", $1,500.00; Vase, classic oval form with four green and gold pulled feathers, gold iridescent handles, 5¾", $1,600.00; Jack-in-the-pulpit vase, amber with stretched gold iridescence, 12¼" with 8" diameter flower, $1,495.00.

Candlesticks, gold irid, swirled stem, 10", pr..............................825.00
Candlesticks, gold irid w/striped swirls, scalloped tops, 8", pr 700.00
Plate, gold irid, ribbed/scalloped flange, 6¾" 110.00
Tumbler, gold irid w/bl highlights, ribbed, flaring sides, 3¾".......275.00
Vase, draped loops, gold on yel, stick form w/wide ft, 6x5" dia ...750.00
Vase, feathers, gr/gold on wht irid, gold int, concave sides, 5" 720.00
Vase, feathers on alabaster, flared wide rim, 12" 2,000.00
Vase, King Tut-like mc decor on caramel-gold, 4-ruffle rim, 8" ..1,000.00
Vase, swirls/waves, gr on ivory w/gold zigzag, petal-top cylinder, 11"..1,200.00

Kindell, Dorothy

Yet another California artist that worked during the prolific years of the 1940s and 1950s, Dorothy Kindell produced a variety of household items and giftware, but today she is best known for her nudes. One of her most popular lines consisted of mugs, a pitcher, salt and pepper shakers, a wall pocket, bowls, a creamer and sugar set, and champagne glasses, featuring a lady in various stages of undress, modeled as handles or stems (on the champagnes). In the set of six mugs, she progresses from wearing her glamorous strapless evening gown to ultimately climbing nude, head-first into the last mug. These are relatively common but always marketable. Except for these and the salt and pepper shakers, the other items from the nude line are scarce and rather pricey. Collectors also vie for her island girls, generally seminude and very sensuous.

Ashtray, Beachcombers, 2 nudes under 7½" hat, common, from $60 to .75.00
Champagne glass, blk w/gold-colored nude stem, 6x4½" dia 275.00

Champagne glass, nude stem..150.00
Creamer & sugar bowl, nude hdls, 3½x3"......................290.00
Figurine, foal, grazing, 3½"..30.00
Figurine, island girl in form-fitting strapless dress, 8"......75.00
Head vase, Black native girl, red lips & necklace, 5", from $75 to...100.00
Ice bucket, nude on ea side, 5x11½" dia........................185.00
Mug, nude hdl, 1 of series of 6, common, 5¼-6", ea from $35 to..40.00
Mug, old cowboy w/wht hair/beard/mustache, gray hat, 4½"......135.00
Pitcher, water; nude hdl..325.00
Shakers, nude hdls, 3x1¼", pr, from $50 to........................65.00
Shelf sitter, nude w/red cold-pnt head band & towel at waist, 11" .375.00
Turtle box, 12" W...165.00
Wall pocket, nude from mug series, rare...........................295.00

King's Rose

King's Rose was made in Staffordshire, England, from about 1820 to 1830. It is closely related to Gaudy Dutch in body type as well as the colors used in its decoration. The pattern consists of a full-blown, orange-red rose with green, pink, and yellow leaves and accents. When the rose is in pink, the ware is often referred to as Queen's Rose.

Coffeepot, dome lid, minor wear, 11¾"............................700.00
Creamer, minor wear & stain, 4¾"..................................190.00
Cup plate, 3½", EX...110.00
Pitcher, dk red rose, bl/yel flowers w/gr leaves, wear, 5⅜"........220.00
Plate, orange rose, pk lustre X-hatched rim, 5¾", pr.........135.00
Plate, pk rose, vine border, shaped rim, 7", NM...............160.00
Plate, Queen's, 4-color, vine border, scalloped, 8"............180.00
Plate, scalloped, Rogers, 8½"...200.00
Plate, solid border, 9¾", EX...135.00
Plate, toddy; Queen's, scalloped, 5½"..............................110.00
Plate, 6¼", EX..85.00
Tea bowl & saucer, pearlware, 3¾", 6⅜"..........................185.00
Tea bowl & saucer, Queen's, pk & gr w/mc floral border, unmk..125.00
Teapot, sectional border, lt wear, 6"................................350.00

Kitchen Collectibles

During the last half of the 1850s, mass-produced kitchen gadgets were patented at an astonishing rate. Most were ingeniously efficient. Apple peelers, egg beaters, cherry pitters, food choppers, and such were only the most common of hundreds of kitchen tools well designed to perform only specific tasks. Today all are very collectible.

For further information we recommend *Kitchen Glassware of the Depression Years* and *Anchor Hocking's Fire-King & More, Second Edition*, both by Gene Florence; and *Kitchen Antiques, 1790 – 1940*, by Kathryn McNerney.

See also Appliances; Butter Molds and Stamps; Cast Iron; Cookbooks; Copper; Glass Knives; Molds; Pie Birds; Primitives; Reamers; String Holders; Tinware; Trivets; Wooden Ware; Wrought Iron.

Cast Kitchen Ware

Be aware that cast-iron counterfeit production is on the increase. Items with phony production numbers, finishes, etc., are being made at this time. Many of these new pieces are the popular miniature cornstick pans. To command the values given below, examples must be free from damage of any kind or excessive wear. Waffle irons must be complete with all three pieces and the handle. The term 'EPU' in the description lines refers to the **Erie PA, USA** mark. The term 'block mark' refers to the lettering in the large logo that was used ca 1920 until 1940; 'slant logo' refers to the lettering in the large logo ca

1900 to 1920. 'PIN' indicates 'Product Identification Numbers.' Victor was Griswold's first low-budget line (ca 1875). Skillets #5 and #6 are uncommon, while #7, #8, and #9 are easy to find. For further information contact our advisor, Grant S. Windsor (SASE required); he is listed in the Directory under Virginia. See also Keen Kutter; Clubs, Catalogs, and Newsletters.

Key:
FW — full writing   TM — trade mark

Ashtray, Griswold #00, PIN 570, rnd, w/matchbook holder, from $10 to...15.00
Ashtray, Wagner C #1050, from $5 to................................10.00
Bundt cake pan, Griswold, PIN 935, from $800 to.............900.00
Bundt cake pan, Wagner Ware B, from $100 to.................150.00
Cake mold, lamb, Griswold, PIN 866, from $75 to.............100.00
Cake mold, Santa, Griswold, from $400 to........................500.00
Display rack, Griswold Griddle, Griswold Plate, metal, from $450 to ..500.00
Double broiler, Griswold, PINs 875 & 876, from $175 to...........225.00
Dutch oven, Favorite Piqua Ware #7, Stylized TM, from $40 to ..60.00
Dutch oven, Favorite Piqua Ware #8, Stylized TM, from $30 to ..50.00
Dutch oven, Griswold #8, Early Tite-Top, Block TMs, FW lid, $40 to.60.00
Dutch oven, Griswold #8, Tite-Top Baster, Slant/EPU TM, from $50 to ...75.00
Dutch oven, Griswold #9, Early Tite-Top, Block TMs, FW lid, $40 to.60.00
Dutch oven, Griswold #9, Late Tite-Top, Block TMs, w/trivet, $50 to.80.00
Dutch oven, Griswold #10, Tite-Top Baster, Slant/EPU TM, from $125 to...150.00
Dutch oven lid, Griswold #8, hinged, from $25 to...............30.00
Gem pan, Griswold #3, Slant TM & PIN 942, from $250 to......300.00
Gem pan, Griswold #11, Fr roll pan, mk NES NO 11, from $30 to .50.00
Gem pan, Griswold #11, Fr roll pan, mk NES oN (sic) 11, $40 to ..60.00
Gem pan, Griswold #12, Slant/EPU TM, from $300 to.............350.00
Gem pan, Griswold #16, wide band, aluminum, from $500 to....600.00
Gem pan, Griswold #18, popover, wide hdl, 6 cups, from $50 to..70.00
Gem pan, Griswold #19, fully mk, 6-cup golf ball, from $250 to ...300.00
Gem pan, Griswold #24, breadstick, PIN 957, from $400 to.......450.00
Gem pan, Griswold #240, turk's head, from $230 to 260.00

Gem pan, Griswold #262, miniature, 4x8½", from $50.00 to $75.00. (Reproductions outnumber the real thing by as many as 20 to one or more. Buyer Beware!)

Gem pan, Griswold #273, cornstick, from $15 to 20.00
Gem pan, Griswold #2700, wheatstick, from $275 to.............325.00
Gem pan, Wagner Ware T, cutouts, turk head, 12 cups, from $100 to ..150.00
Griddle, Griswold #8, Slant/EPU TM, X bar support, hdl, from $20 to .40.00
Griddle, Griswold #12 Gas or Vapor, mk Erie Gas Griddle, from $275 to...325.00
Griddle, Wagner #8, Stylized TM, C #1108, hdl, from $20 to 30.00
Griddle, Wapak #8, oval, Early TM, from $50 to......................75.00
Juice extractor, Wagner Ware #453, aluminum, from $20 to.........40.00
Loaf pan, Griswold, PIN 877, w/lid PIN 859, from $800 to 900.00
Muffin pan, Filley #10, 11 cups, from $75 to 100.00
Muffin pan, Griswold #3, mk #3 & #943 only, 11 cups, from $150 to .175.00
Muffin pan, Griswold #11, Fr roll, wide band, 12 cups, from $30 to ..40.00
Muffin pan, Griswold #32, Danish cake, fully mk, 7 cups, from $30 to .40.00
Muffin pan, Griswold #100, heart & star, 5 cups, from $600 to ..800.00

Paperweight, Griswold, Pup, mk 30 GRISWOLD PUP, from $200 to ..**300.00**
Patty molds, Griswold #2, MIB, set, from $25 to **35.00**
Roaster, Griswold #3, oval, Block TMs, w/lid mk Oval Roaster, $475 to .**525.00**
Roaster, Griswold #5, oval, Block TMs, mk lid, +trivet, $350 to .**400.00**
Roaster, Griswold #9, oval, Block TMs, FW lid, from $425 to....**475.00**
Roaster, Wagner, #7, oval, Stylized TM, incised writing lid, $175 to..**225.00**
Sandwich toaster, Wagner, w/low bailed base, sq, from $125 to..**150.00**
Scoop, coffee; Wagner Ware #2, C#912, from $10 to....................**20.00**
Skillet, breakfast; Cliff Cornell, from $75 to...............................**125.00**
Skillet, Griswold #2, Block TM, no heat ring, chrome, from $200 to..**250.00**
Skillet, Griswold #2, Block TM, no heat ring, from $300 to.......**350.00**
Skillet, Griswold #2, Slant/EPU TM, heat ring, from $375 to....**425.00**
Skillet, Griswold #2, Slant/EPU TM, Rau Brothers, from $500 to .**600.00**
Skillet, Griswold #3, Block TM, no heat ring, from $10 to...........**20.00**
Skillet, Griswold #3, Slant/Erie TM, from $30 to **40.00**
Skillet, Griswold #3, Square Fry Skillet, PIN 2103 (+), from $75 to..**125.00**
Skillet, Griswold #4, Block TM, heat ring, from $375 to............**425.00**
Skillet, Griswold #4, Block TM, no heat ring, from $40 to...........**60.00**
Skillet, Griswold #4, Slant/ERIE TM, NP, from $40 to **60.00**
Skillet, Griswold #5, sm TM, grooved hdl, from $10 to **15.00**
Skillet, Griswold #6, Block TM, heat ring, from $50 to **75.00**
Skillet, Griswold #6, Block TM, no heat ring, from $10 to...........**20.00**
Skillet, Griswold #7, Block TM, heat ring, from $45 to **55.00**
Skillet, Griswold #8, Block TM, no heat ring, from $10 to...........**20.00**
Skillet, Griswold #8, extra deep, Block TM, no heat ring, $50 to.**75.00**
Skillet, Griswold #8, Small TM, extra deep, w/hinge, from $35 to..**45.00**
Skillet, Griswold #8, Spider TM, from $1,100 to **1,400.00**
Skillet, Griswold #8, Victor, fully mk, from $35 to **45.00**
Skillet, Griswold #9, Block TM, heat ring, from $40 to **60.00**
Skillet, Griswold #10, Block TM, heat ring, from $50 to **75.00**
Skillet, Griswold #10, Block TM, no heat ring, from $40 to.........**60.00**
Skillet, Griswold #11, Slant/EPU TM, from $250 to...................**300.00**
Skillet, Griswold #12, Block TM, from $75 to **100.00**
Skillet, Griswold #12, Slant/EPU TM, from $125 to...................**175.00**
Skillet, Griswold #13, Block TM, from $1,400 to **1,600.00**
Skillet, Griswold #13, Slant/EPU TM, from $800 to **1,000.00**
Skillet, Griswold #14, Block TM, chrome, from $100 to **125.00**
Skillet, Griswold #14, Block TM, from $125 to.........................**175.00**
Skillet, Griswold #15, oval, from $250 to.................................**300.00**
Skillet, Griswold Sq Utility, PIN 768, w/iron lid: PIN 769, $275 to..**300.00**
Skillet, Merit #3, from $20 to **30.00**
Skillet, Vollrath #5, from $15 to **25.00**
Skillet, Wagner, Bacon & Egg Breakfast; Stylized TM, from $15 to .**25.00**
Skillet, Wagner #2, Stylized TM, from $50 to..........................**75.00**
Skillet, Wapak #5, Z TM, from $35 to **45.00**
Skillet, Wapak #8, Early TM, from $25 to **35.00**
Skillet, Wapak #9, Tapered TM, from $25 to.............................**35.00**
Skillet lid, Griswold #3, high smooth dome, from $150 to..........**200.00**
Skillet lid, Griswold #6, high dome smooth, Block TM, from $50 to..**75.00**
Skillet lid, Griswold #8, high dome smooth, sm TM, from $20 to...**30.00**
Skillet lid, Griswold #10, high dome smooth, Block TM, from $40 to..**60.00**
Skillet lid, Wapak #9, mk 9 only, recessed basting dots, from $30 to..**50.00**
Teakettle, Griswold #8, Spider TM top, from $400 to.................**500.00**
Trivet, Classic Sad Iron, from $50 to **75.00**
Trivet, Griswold, Family Tree, P #1726, lg/decorative, from $10 to ..**20.00**
Trivet, Griswold #9, Dutch oven, P #207, from $25 to................**35.00**
Trivet, Old Lace (coffeepot), PIN 1739, lg, from $75 to **125.00**
Wafer iron, Griswold, side-hdl base, from $300 to......................**400.00**
Waffle iron, Griswold #2, sq, from $650 to **700.00**
Waffle iron, Griswold #7, finger hinge, low hdl base, from $100 to .**125.00**
Waffle iron, Griswold #8, Fr (3 sets of paddles), finger hinge, up to..**800.00**
Waffle iron, Griswold #11, sq, low bailed base, ball hinge, $175 to .**225.00**
Waffle iron, Griswold #19, Heart & Star, low bailed base, $250 to..**300.00**
Wax ladle, Griswold, ERIE TM, PIN 964, from $125 to **150.00**

Egg Beaters

Egg beaters are unbeatable. Ranging from hand-helds, rotary-crank, and squeeze power to Archimedes up-and-down models, egg beaters are America's favorite kitchen gadget. A mainstay of any kitchenware collection, in recent years egg beaters have come into their own — nutmeg graters, spatulas, and can openers will have to scramble to catch up! At the turn of the century, everyone in America owned an egg beater. Every household did its own mixing and baking — there were no pre-processed foods. And every inventor thought he/she could make a better beater. Thus American ingenuity produced more than one thousand egg beater patents, dating back to 1856, with several hundred different models being manufactured over the years. As true examples of Americana, egg beaters saw a steady increase in value over the years, though they have leveled off and even decreased in the past year due to a proliferation of Internet sales. Some very rare beaters will bring more than $1,000.00, including the cast-iron, rotary crank 'Dodge Race Course egg beater.' But the vast majority stay under $50.00. Just when you think you've seen them all, new ones always turn up, usually at flea markets or garage sales. For further information, we recommend our advisor (author of the definitive book on egg beaters) Don Thornton, who is listed in the Directory under California. (SASE required.)

A&J, Ekco Products...Pat Apld for, red wood hdl & knob, 12½" .**10.00**
A&J, High Speed Super Centerdrive Beater, red T-shaped hdl.......**5.00**
A&J...Pat Oct 9 1923, red wood hdl, 10¾"...................................**10.00**
Androck, rotary, gr Bakelite hdls **30.00**
Christy Knife **435.00**
Edlund Co Burlington VT, rotary, gr wood hdl...............................**5.00**

Express or 'Fly Swatter,'
Pat Oct 15, 1887, 11½",
$1,200.00. (Photo courtesy Diane Thornton© 1999)

H-L No 0 Tarrytown NY, cast wheels, loop-type hdl, wood knob, 9"..**30.00**
Holt-Lyon, side hdl...**400.00**
Ladd Beater No 1...1908...1915, coiled wire knob, 11", EX...........**10.00**
Maynard, chrome/stainless, yel crank hdl, 1950s.............................**8.00**
PD&Co, EX **800.00**
Taplin Mfg...Light Running Pat Nov 24 08, wood knob, 10½".....**25.00**
Turbine Egg Beater...1912...Cassity Fairbank..., EX....................**15.00**

Glass

Bottle, water; cobalt, Hazel-Atlas, 64-oz, 10", from $60 to...........**65.00**
Bottle, water; Criss Cross, gr, 32-oz, from $150 to **165.00**
Bottle, water; Forest Green, w/top, Hocking, from $65 to.............**75.00**
Bottle, water; gr, centered screw-on lid, Hocking, from $30 to **35.00**
Bowl, batter; Fruits, milk glass, Anchor Hocking, hdl & spout...**225.00**
Bowl, batter; yel opaque, Hocking, from $110 to........................**125.00**
Bowl, bl opaque, rnd w/sq base, Pyrex, 12", from $35 to...............**38.00**

Bowl, cereal; bl opaque, Pyrex, 5¾"..3.50
Bowl, cobalt, Hazel-Atlas, 10⅜", from $85 to.................................95.00
Bowl, crystal ribs w/red fired-on rim, Federal, 5", from $8 to.........10.00
Bowl, Delphite Blue, horizontal ribs, 7½", from $75 to.................85.00
Bowl, drippings; Ships, red on wht, 8-oz, from $50 to.................55.00
Bowl, Jennyware, pk, 10½", from $85 to.......................................95.00
Bowl, mixing; amber, US Glass, 9", from $35 to...........................37.50
Bowl, mixing; Butter-Print Cinderella, Pyrex, 9¾", from $12 to...14.00
Bowl, mixing; Delphite Blue, 9", from $110 to............................125.00
Bowl, mixing; Fruits, Splash Proof, Anchor Hocking, 2-qt, from $65 to.75.00
Bowl, mixing; gr, paneled, Hocking, 11½", from $55 to...............60.00
Bowl, mixing; Modern Tulip, 3-qt, from $18 to.............................20.00
Bowl, mixing; Skating Dutch, Hazel-Atlas, 9", from $27.50 to.....30.00
Bowl, mixing; Swedish Modern, turq bl, 7¼", 2-qt, from $30 to...35.00
Bowl, salad; Emerald-Glo, gold-tone metal ft, from $40 to...........45.00
Bowl w/spout (egg beater), gr jadite, Jeannette, from $55 to.........60.00
Butter box, pk, emb B, Jeannette, 2-lb, from $200 to...................225.00
Butter dish, Chalaine Blue, ribbed, tab hdls, from $425 to.........450.00
Butter dish, Criss Cross, pk, Hazel-Atlas, 1-lb, from $60 to..........65.00
Butter dish, dk jadite, Jeannette, from $65 to................................70.00
Butter dish, gr, Hocking, from $50 to..55.00
Butter dish, Jennyware, ultramarine, Jeannette, from $175 to.....195.00
Canister, Coffee, blk letters on custard, McKee, from $65 to........75.00
Canister, Dutch Decal on wht, Hocking, from $20 to...................22.00
Canister, gr fired-on color, ribbed, from $35 to............................40.00
Canister, Sugar, Delphite Blue, 40-oz, from $400 to...................425.00
Canister, Zipper, gr, lg, from $225 to...250.00
Casserole, fired-on color, Glasbake, McKee, ind, w/lid, from $6 to..8.00
Casserole, Peach Blossom, milk glass, Anchor Hocking, 1½-qt....25.00
Casserole, Sapphire Blue, Anchor Hocking, ind, 10-oz, from $11 to...13.00
Coffeepot, crystal w/silver rings, McKee, from $15 to..................18.00
Coffeepot, red, Silex, from $175 to...200.00
Cookie jar, blk, LE Smith, from $95 to..110.00
Cookie jar, Peacock Blue, LE Smith, from $100 to.....................125.00
Cruet, Mayfair, yel, from $100 to..150.00
Cruet, Twist, pk, Heisey, 2½-oz, from $75 to................................85.00
Cup, custard; Sapphire Blue, Anchor Hocking, 6-oz, either style....5.00
Cup, wht w/red fired-on hdl, from $4 to..5.00
Drawer pull, blk, from $18 to...20.00
Drawer pull, Chalaine Blue, dbl, from $30 to................................35.00
Egg cup, amber, Paden City, from $15 to......................................18.00
Egg cup, blk, from $20 to...25.00
Gravy boat, amber, 2-spout, Cambridge, from $40 to..................50.00
Ice bucket, Mt Vernon, red, Cambridge, from $85 to.................100.00
Ice tub, Emerald Glo insert, w/tongs, from $65 to........................70.00
Jug, batter; cobalt, McKee, from $150 to....................................160.00
Jug, batter; Forest Freen, New Martinsville, from $125 to...........135.00
Measure cup, crystal, Glasbake, McKee, 1-cup, from $20 to..........25.00
Measure cup, crystal, McKee Glasbake Scientific, 2-cup, from $20 to..25.00
Measure cup, fired-on gr, 2-cup, from $25 to................................30.00
Measure cup, gr, Hocking, 1-cup, from $75 to..............................80.00
Measure cup, gr, Sunflower bottom, Jeannette, 2-cup, from $110 to...125.00
Measure cup, gr, 3-spout, Federal, from $40 to............................45.00
Measure cup, milk glass, Hocking, w/lid, 2-cup, from $55 to........60.00
Measure cup, yel opaque, 2-spout, McKee, 1-cup, from $180 to .200.00
Measure pitcher, Delphite Blue, McKee, 4-cup, from $600 to.....650.00
Measure pitcher, yel opaque, McKee, 2-cup, from $130 to..........140.00
Mug, cobalt, Cambridge, from $50 to...60.00
Mug, gr clambroth, from $35 to..40.00
Parfait, gr, Paden City, from $18 to..20.00
Pitcher, Chalaine Blue, ftd, from $225 to...................................250.00
Pitcher, Chesterfield, amber, Imperial's #600, from $120 to........125.00
Refrigerator dish, Dots, red on custard, McKee, 5x8", from $35 to ...38.00
Refrigerator dish, gr jadite, Jeannette, 4x4", from $25 to............30.00

Refrigerator dish, Jennyware, crystal, rnd, Jeannette, 70-oz, $30 to...35.00
Refrigerator dish, Ships, red on wht, 4x5", from $22.50 to...........25.00
Refrigerator stack set, Skating Dutch, Hazel-Atlas, 3-pc, $65 to...75.00
Rolling pin, gr w/wooden hdls, from $500 to..............................550.00
Rolling pin, Peacock Blue, from $275 to.....................................295.00
Rolling pin, wht clambroth w/wooden hdls, from $125 to..........135.00

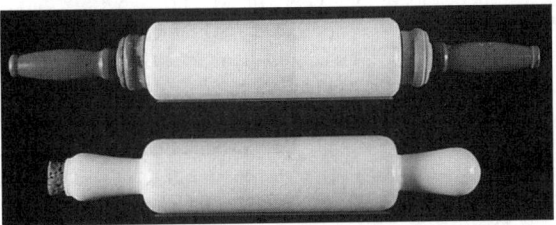

Rolling pins: Milk glass, marked Cambridge, one wooden handle replaced, 20½", from $50.00 to $60.00; Blown white opaque glass with cork stopper, unknown maker, 15", from $120.00 to $130.00. (Photo courtesy Betty Newbound)

Shakers, Chalaine Blue, pr, from $125 to....................................135.00
Shakers, Dots, gr or bl on wht, pr, from $60 to.............................70.00
Shakers, Dutch boy (red) on wht, pr, from $25 to.........................30.00
Shakers, gr clambroth, Hocking, 8-oz, pr, from $40 to.................45.00
Shakers, labels on gr, screw-on lid, Hocking, pr, from $40 to........45.00
Skillet, Range-Tec, McKee, from $12.50 to..................................15.00
Stack set, Hex Optic, pk, Jeannette, 3 bases+1 lid, from $65 to ...75.00
Sugar bowl, Criss Cross, crystal, Hazel-Atlas, from $20 to...........25.00
Sugar shaker, fired-on red, Gemco, from $25 to...........................27.50
Tumbler, Jennyware, pk, Jeannette, 8-oz, from $45 to..................50.00
Warming dish, gr, 2 inserts, from $75 to.......................................90.00

Miscellaneous

Apple corer, cream plastic w/red wood hdl, mk Pat Pend....USA, 4½"..12.00
Apple cutter, Rollman Mfg, cores & cuts into 8 sections, 5½"......16.00
Apple peeler, Reading Hardware...PA, CI, blk wood hdl................48.00
Apple peeler, Sinclair Scott Co of Baltimore, CI, EX....................85.00
Can opener, Dazey DeLuxe Model 80, wall mt, red hdls, 1950s, EX..25.00
Can opener, Ecko USA, punch type, red hdl..................................13.00
Can opener, Model 80, red & wht, wall mt, 1950s, EX................25.00
Canisters, Kromex, blk letters on aluminum, 4-pc set...................40.00
Canisters, Westbend, copper-tone w/blk graphics & lids, 3-pc set...20.00
Cherry seeder, Enterprise #18, CI, Pat Mar 31 1883....................32.00
Cherry seeder, New Standard, wobbly wheel.................................85.00
Chopper, Ahol Machine Co, Pat May 23 1865, CI, 10x15x19", EX..285.00
Chopper, clear glass w/metal top, red-pnt wooden hdl, 8" H.........35.00
Chopper, dbl steel rocker blades, CI shanks, wood hdl, 6x7" 20.00
Chopper, nut; 1½-cup clear base, spring-loaded, Bakelite hdl.......14.00
Chopper, 5½" steel blade pinned into wood hdl, EX.....................35.00
Churn, Dandy, Hazel-Atlas jar, 1-gal, EX.....................................85.00
Churn, Dazey, unmk jar, 4-qt...95.00
Churn, Dazey #10, beveled edge, 1-qt..750.00
Churn, Dazey #10, bull's eye, 1-qt 700.00
Churn, Dazey #20...200.00
Churn, Dazey #30, Pat 1922...225.00
Churn, Dazey #40...150.00
Churn, Dazey #60...165.00
Churn, Dazey #80...250.00
Clothes sprinkler bottle, clothespin, plastic, mc, from $20 to........40.00
Clothes sprinkler bottle, iron w/gr ivy, ceramic, from $50 to........75.00
Clothes sprinkler bottle, Sprinkle Plenty, chinaman, ceramic, $95 to..150.00

Colander, tinware, cone in fr, early 1900s, EX **45.00**
Cracker pricker/cutter, tin, fluted cutting edge, 1900s, 2¼" dia **45.00**
Cutter, slaw; walnut w/brass blade, chip-cvd ends, sm **50.00**
Diffuser, flat metal circle (to set on burner), red hdl.....................**15.00**
Fork, all metal, 3-prong, 16¼" **16.00**
Fork, meat; 2-prong, antler hdl **14.00**
Grater, Arrow Aluminum Products, ½-rnd, 12" **10.00**
Grater, Wonder Shredder Pat Pend, tin w/lg holes, 8⅜x4⅛"..........**7.50**
Grinder, #810, CI, red wood hdl, clamps to table, 10", EX...........**18.00**
Grinder, Griscer...USA, CI, tin conical drum, rotary, gr wood hdl, 9"..**35.00**
Grinder, Griswold #1, CI, w/4 blades, 40" **25.00**
Ice cream freezer, Dazey, 1-qt **700.00**
Ice crusher, Ice-O-Mat, yel plastic & chrome, crank hdl, 1950s ..**50.00**
Ice crusher, Swing Away, wht plastic, crank hdl, 1960s, EX **24.00**
Jar opener, Yo-Ho Monticello IA, metal w/orange rubber (cracked), 8" .**7.50**
Ladle, metal w/red/wht/gr pnt wood hdl **12.00**
Lemon squeezer, Gotham Metal Specialties Co NY, EX **5.00**
Masher, loopy wires, wht wood hdl, 6" **10.00**
Meat cleaver, steel blade, wooden hdl, 12", EX............................**25.00**
Meat cleaver, w/tenderizer attached, Superior Warranted, 11"......**24.00**
Meat tenderizer, hatchet-like w/wooden hdl, 11"...........................**12.50**
Meat tenderizer, wood w/gr pnt hdl **17.50**
Melon baller, scoop ea end, red wood hdl w/wht stripe, 8" **9.00**
Mincer, Acme, rotary type, red hdl, MIB **15.00**
Nut sheller, York, metal pliers type **15.00**
Nutmeg grater, silver, Birmingham 1807 hallmks, 1¾" **360.00**
Nutmeg grater, wooden acorn form, top screws off, 3¼x1⅜" **365.00**
Nutmeg grinder, dk tin w/wooden hdl, 3½x4½", EX.....................**135.00**
Pastry blender, Androck, 6 bent wires, blk wood hdl **15.00**
Pastry blender, Androck Stainless Steel..., red Catalin hdl............**14.00**
Peeler, curved blade w/slot, gr wood hdl **9.00**
Pot scrubber, metal rings on wire hdl, early 1900s **37.50**
Rolling pin, curly maple, dk color/EX patina, 17" **275.00**
Rolling pin, trn wood, 1-pc, 16¼" **22.50**
Sifter, Androck Hand-i-Sift, wheat/goodies on tin, red hdl, EX....**25.00**
Sifter, Bromwell's, wht-pnt tin, crank hdl, EX................................**22.00**
Sifter, Watkins, tin w/blk bands, wood hdl, EX.............................**25.00**
Slicer, cheese; metal w/wire cutter, gr Bakelite roller, unmk, 5" **7.50**
Slicer, crinkle-cut blade, red-pnt wood hdl, 6½".............................**12.50**
Slicer, tomato; wire cutters, red wood hdl, 10", L **12.00**
Slicer, vegetable; metal blades, wooden fr & hdl, 4½x12"..............**20.00**
Slicer, vegetable; Universal, Landers Frary & Clark, CI, 13" **65.00**
Spoon, A&J, red hdl, 12"...**10.00**
Spoon, stuffing; SP pewter bowl, 800 silver hdl, 9½" **100.00**
Spreader, Androck, stainless w/butterscotch Bakelite hdl, 11"......**24.00**
Strainer, coiled wore in rnd fr, gr Bakelite hdl, 8½", VG **18.50**
Strainer, tea; metal, hook opposite hdl, Germany, 2" bowl...........**32.50**
Strainer, tea; metal, Pat NB Co Mar 1910, 6½" L **35.00**
Vegetable lifter, Androck, metal pliers type w/spring, MIB **14.00**
Warming oven, blk-pnt steel, penny ft, domed top, 39x14x10", EX...**400.00**
Whisk, coiled wire, red wood hdl, 8¾"...**30.00**
Whisk, Tomado Holland, coiled wires, wood hdl, 1930s-40s, 11" .**12.50**

Knife Rests

Knife rests were used to prevent the tablecloth from becoming soiled by used knives. As the table was cleared after each course, the only utencil allowed to remain was the knife, thus the knife rest was a necessity. Many types have been made in Europe — porcelain, Delft, Majolica, and pottery. European companies made knife rests to match their dinnerware patterns, a practice not pursued by American manufacturers. Research has found only one company, Mackenzie-Childs of New York, who made a pottery knife rest.

Several scholars feel that porcelain knife rests originated in Germany and France; from there, their usage spread to England. Though there were glasshouses in Europe making pressed and cut glass, often blanks were purchased from American companies, cut by European craftsmen, and shipped back to the States. American consumers regarded the European cut glass as superior. When economic woes forced the Europeans to come to the U.S., many brought their motifs and patterns with them. American manufacturers patented many of the designs for their exclusive use, but in some cases as the cutters moved from one company to another, they took their patterns with them.

Knife rests of pressed glass, cut crystal, porcelain, sterling silver, plated silver, wood, ivory, and bone have been collected for many years. Signed knife rests are especially desirable. It was not until the Centennial Exhibition in Philadelphia in 1876 that the brilliant new cut glass rests, deeply faceted and shining like diamonds, appeared in shops by the hundreds. There were sets of twelve, eight, or six that came in presentation boxes. Sizes vary from 1¼" to 3¼" for individual knives and from 5" to 6" for carving knives. Glass knife rests were made in many colors such as purple, blue, green, vaseline, pink, and cranberry. It is important to note that prices may vary from one area of the country to another and from dealer to dealer. For further information we recommend our advisor, Beverly Schell Ales; she is listed in the Directory under California.

Boar's tusk w/brass mts, glass base, 6x3½" **275.00**
Book, Knife Rests, Virginia Neas, 1987, from $25 to....................**75.00**
China, Bing & Grondahl, sea horse, bl & wht, 1870-90, 3¾" H, lg..**145.00**
China, Meissen, mk X w/sword logo on end, pr.............................**165.00**
China, Royal Copenhagen, 1/134, Denmark, bl & wht **150.00**
Glass, Bimini, gr striped, ftd, early 1990s, 4¾", from $30 to **50.00**
Glass, cut, prism ends (8 stars per end), 4¾x1½", from $35 to **55.00**
Glass, cut; Hawkes, lapidary ends, 5"...**100.00**
Glass, cut; Hawkes, prisms, 1889 catalog, 3½", from $100 to **150.00**
Glass, cut; Hoare, prisms, 1853 catalog, 5¾", from $100 to........**200.00**
Glass, cut; Libbey; lapidary ends, 3¾", from $50 to.....................**100.00**
Glass, cut; overall Brilliant cuttings, knob ends, 5½" **185.00**
Glass, cut; squash form **75.00**
Glass, cut; star on end of ball, 1½x4¾" **85.00**
Glass, cut; Waterford, rnd shaft, sq ends, 2½x7⅛", from $50 to ...**70.00**
Glass, Lalique France, mk, frosted end **95.00**
Glass, lapidary cut; rnd ball, 3½" **40.00**
Glass, pressed; Baccarat, bar, new mk, 3", from $20 to **25.00**
Glass, pressed; Baccarat, clear, 4¾", from $25 to **50.00**
Glass, pressed; Baccarat, frosted baby's head ea end, 4x2" **32.00**
Glass, pressed; Baccarat, triangle mk, 3", 12 in box.....................**180.00**

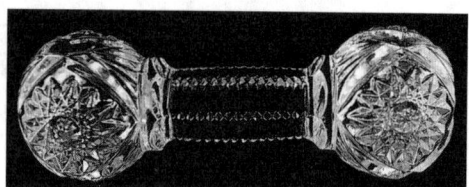

Glass, pressed; Cambridge, Nearcut, Hobstar With Fans, #2749, 4¼x1½", $40.00. (Photo courtesy Beverly Schell Ales)

Glass, pressed; gr, 3½", pr...**60.00**
Glass, pressed; Heisey, dmn & H mk, 3¼", from $100 to............**150.00**
Glass, pressed; Imperial, milk glass, mk, 3½", from $35 to **45.00**
Glass, pressed; Imperial, mk, 3½", from $18 to **25.00**
Glass, pressed; IRENA, Poland, doorknob, 24%, from $10 to.......**20.00**
Glass, pressed; Marjorie, Cambridge, plain shaft, 4x1", from $25 to ..**30.00**
Glass, pressed; w/dbl salt, Duncan/Ripley, 4", from $70 to **100.00**

Glass, Sabino, bl w/duck end, from $15 to **50.00**
Glass, Val St Lambert Belquigue, amber, 1963............................**100.00**
Metal, Carvel Hall, silver, 6 in box..**30.00**
Metal, fruit & flowers, 3¾", set of 6 (ea different)........................**85.00**
Metal, gold-tone, horse on base, 2¾" L..**75.00**
Pearlware, dk bl w/heart-shaped ends, Meir, 1812-36, 3¾" **350.00**
Porc, flow bl, SP side ft, 3½x1"..**48.00**
Pottery, Quimper, #499, 1950s, from $40 to **65.00**
Pottery, Quimper, bl, Hb, #797, ca 1883 ....**75.00**
SP, children hopping over stile **125.00**
SP, sphinx ea end..**75.00**
SP, squirrel w/lg bar on tail, Simpson, Hall & Miller..................**195.00**
Transferware, Staffordshire, bl floral, 1830s....................................**195.00**

Knives

Knife collecting as a hobby began in earnest during the 1960s when government regulations required for the first time that knife companies mark their products with the country of origin. The few collectors and dealers aware of this change at once began stockpiling the older knives made before this law was enacted. Another impetus to the growing interest in this area came with the Gun Control Act of 1968, which severely restricted gun trading. Frustrated gun dealers transferred their attention to knives. Today there are collectors' clubs in many of the states.

The most sought-after pocketknives are those made before WWII. However, as time goes on knives no older than twenty years are collectible if in mint condition. Most collectors prefer knives in 'as found' condition. Do *not* attempt to clean, sharpen, or in any way 'improve' on an old knife.

Please note: Length is measured with blades *closed*. Our values are for knives in used/excellent condition (unless specified 'mint'). Most old knives are usually not encountered in mint condition. Therefore to give a mint price could mislead the novice collector. If a knife has been used, sharpened, or blemished in any way, its value decreases. It is common to find knives made in the 1960s and later in mint condition. Knives made in the 1970s and 1980s may be collectible in mint condition, but not in used condition. Therefore a used knife thirty years old may be be worth no more than a knife for use. For further information refer to *The Standard Knife Collectors Guide; Cattaragus Cutlery Co.;* and *Big Book of Pocket Knives* by Ron Stewart and Roy Ritchie. All are published by Collector Books. Our advisor for this category is Bill Wright, author of *Theatre-Made Military Knives of World War II* (Schiffer). Mr. Wright is listed in the Directory under Indiana.

Key:
alum — aluminum   jack — jacknife
bd — blade   lb — lockback
gen — genuine   pat — pattern
imi — imitation   wb — winterbottom

A Davy & Sons (Sheffield England), 2-bd, Liberty & Union bolster...**700.00**
Aerial Cutlery Co, 2-bd jack, bone hdl, 3⅜"..................................**60.00**
Anheuser-Busch, red & gold emb hdl, w/peephole & picture **250.00**
Barnett Tool Co, bone hdl, bd+punch+pliers **175.00**
Boker, Heinrich (German), 1-bd, bone hdl, 4½" **65.00**
Boker (German), 4-bd congress, bone hdl, 4"..............................**125.00**
Boker (USA), 3-bd stockman, imi pearl hdl, 4"..............................**40.00**
Boker (USA), 4-bd congress, bone hdl, 3¾"..................................**65.00**
Bulldog Brand (Germany), 3-bd whittler, gen abalone hdl, 5⅛"..**150.00**
Case, Tested XX, 5202½, 2-bd, gen stag hdl, 3⅜" **100.00**
Case, Tested XX, 61093, 1-bd, gr bone hdl, toothpick pat, 5".....**200.00**
Case, Tested XX, 6150sab, 1-bd, gr bone hdl, Coke Bottle, 5⅜"...**300.00**
Case, Tested XX, 62031½, 2-bd, gr bone hdl, 3¾" **150.00**

Case, Tested XX, 6220, 2-bd, rough blk hdl, peanut pat, 2⅜".....**100.00**
Case, Tested XX, 6392, 3-bd, gr bone hdl, stockman pat, 4"........**175.00**
Case, Tested XX, 8383, 3-bd, gen pearl hdl, whittler pat, 3½" ...**500.00**
Case, Texted XX, 62100, 2-bd, gr bone hdl, saddlehorn pat, 4⅜" ..**675.00**
Case, XX, 2-bd, bone hdl, muskrat pat, 3⅜" **150.00**
Case, XX, 3347hp, 3-bd, yel compo hdl, stockman pat, 3⅜".........**85.00**
Case, XX, 5254, 2-bd, gen stag hdl, trapper pat, 4⅛" **300.00**
Case, XX, 5375, 3-bd, gen red stag hdl, long pull, stockman, 4¼"...**1,000.00**
Case, XX, 6185, 1-bd, bone hdl, doctor's pat, 3¾" **125.00**
Case, XX, 62009, 1-bd, bone hdl, barlow pat, 3⅜".........................**70.00**
Case, XX, 6231½, 2-bd, bone hdl, 3¾"..**100.00**
Case, XX, 6250, 2-bd, bone hdl, sunfish pat, 4½" **200.00**
Case, XX, 6294, 2-bd, bone hdl, cigar pat, 4¼" **250.00**
Case, XX, 6308, 3-bd, bone hdl, whittler pat, 3¼" **125.00**
Case, XX, 6488, 4-bd, bone hdl, congress pat, 4⅛" **500.00**
Case, XX, 6565sab, 2-bd, bone hdl, folding hunter pat, 5¼" **125.00**
Case, XX USA, 52131, 2-bd, gen stag hdl, canoe pat, 3⅜", M...**350.00**
Case, XX USA, 5354, 2-bd, gen stag hdl, trapper pat, 4⅛", M...**375.00**
Case, XX USA 10 dots, 6111½, 1-bd, bone hdl, lb, 4⅜", M **325.00**
Case Bros, Little Valley NY, 2-bd, wood hdl, 3¼" **100.00**
Case Bros, Little Valley NY, 5321, 3-bd, stag hdl, 3¾" **200.00**
Case Bros, Springville NY, 8250, 2-bd, pearl hdl, sunfish pat..**3,000.00**
Cattaraugus, D2589, 4-bd, bone hdl, Official Scout Emblem, 3½" ..**200.00**
Cattaraugus, 12839, 1-bd, bone hdl, King of the Woods, 5⅜" **500.00**
Cattaraugus, 22346, 2-bd, wood hdl, jack pat, 3⅜"........................**85.00**
Cattaraugus, 22919, 2-bd, bone hdl, cigar pat, 4¼" **400.00**
Cattaraugus, 3-bd+nail file, gen pearl hdl, lobster gun stock, 3" .**150.00**
Cattaraugus, 32145, 3-bd, bone hdl, stockman pat, 3⅜" **200.00**
Challenge Cutlery, 1-bd, bone hdl, lb pat, 4¾" **200.00**
Challenge Cutlery, 3-bd, bone hdl, cattle pat, 3⅜"......................**125.00**
Diamond Edge, 2-bd, bone hdl, jack, 3⅜" **75.00**
Diamond Edge, 2-bd, pearl celluloid hdl, gun stock, 3" **100.00**
Frost Cutlery Co (Japan), 3-bd, bone hdl, lb whittler, 4" **15.00**
H&B Mfg Co, 3-bd, buffalo horn hdl, whittler, 3⅜" **150.00**
Hammer Brand, NY Knife Co, 2-bd, bone hdl, 3⅜"........................**85.00**
Hammer Brand, 1-bd, bone hdl, NYK on bolster, lb, 5¼"............**375.00**
Hammer Brand, 1-bd, tin shell hdl, powder-horn pat, 4¾" **25.00**
Hammer Brand, 2-bd, bone hdl, dog-leg pat, 3¾" **225.00**
Hammer Brand, 2-bd, wood hdl, jack, 3¾" **85.00**
Henckels, JA; 3-bd, bone hdl, whittler pat, 3¼" **65.00**
Henckels, JA; 4-bd, bone hdl, congress pat, 4" **150.00**
Hibbard, Spencer, Bartlett & Co, 2-bd, bone hdl, barlow, 3⅜"......**85.00**
Hibbard, Spencer, Bartlett & Co, 2-bd, bone hdl, dog-leg, 3⅜" .**100.00**
Holley Mfg Co, 1-bd, wood hdl, 5"..**140.00**
Holley Mfg Co, 3-bd, pearl hdl, whittler pat, 3¼" **225.00**
Holley Mfg Co, 4-bd, bone hdl, congress pat, 3½" **375.00**
Honk Falls Knife Co, 1-bd, bone hdl, 3" **125.00**
I*XL (Sheffield England), 4-bd, gen stag hdl, congress, 4"..........**350.00**
I*XL (Sheffield), 2-bd, wood hdl, heavy jack, 4"..........................**125.00**
Imperial Knife Co, 2-bd, bone hdl, dog-leg pat, 3⅜" **50.00**
Imperial Knife Co, 2-bd, mc hdl, 3¼"..**35.00**
John Primble, Belknap Hdw Co, 3-bd, bone hdl, 4" **75.00**
John Primble, Belknap Hdw Co, 4-bd, bone hdl, 3¾"....................**85.00**
John Primble, India Steel Works, 2-bd, gen stag hdl, 4¼" **500.00**
John Primble, India Steel Works on bolster, celluloid hdl, 3" **125.00**
Ka-Bar, Union Cutlery, knife & fork, bone hdl, 5¼"....................**300.00**
Ka-Bar, Union Cutlery, 2-bd, gen stag hdl, dog head, 5¼"..........**300.00**
Ka-Bar, Union Cutlery, 3-bd, bone hdl, whittler, 3¾"..................**150.00**
Ka-Bar, 2-bd, gen stag hdl, Old Time Trapper, 4⅛" **85.00**
Ka-Bar, 3-bd, bone hdl, cattle pat, 3⅜" **100.00**
Keen Kutter, EC Simmons, 1-bd, bone hdl, lb, 4¼" **200.00**
Keen Kutter, EC Simmons, 1-bd, bone hdl, 3¼" **50.00**
Keen Kutter, EC Simmons, 2-bd, bone hdl, trapper, 3⅜"............**250.00**
Keen Kutter, EC Simmons, 2-bd, colorful celluloid hdl, 3⅜"........**70.00**

Keen Kutter, EC Simmons, 2-bd, pearl hdl, doctor pat, 3⅜" 250.00
Keen Kutter, EC Simmons, 2-bd, wood hdl, jack, 3¼" 75.00
Keen Kutter, EC Simmons, 3-bd, bone hdl, whittler, 3⅜" 75.00
Keen Kutter, 1-bd, bone hdl, TX toothpick, 5" 125.00
Keen Kutter, 2-bd, bone hdl, barlow, 3⅜" 75.00
Keen Kutter, 2-bd, bone hdl, folding hunter, 5¼" 125.00
LF&C, 2-bd, jigged hard rubber hdl, jack, 3⅜" 75.00
LF&C, 3-bd, gen pearl hdl, whittler, 3½" 125.00
Maher & Grosh, 2-bd, bone hdl, jack, 3⅜" 150.00
Marbles, 1-bd, gen stag hdl, Safety Folding Hunter, lg 700.00
Marbles, 1-bd, gen stag hdl, Safety Folding Hunter, sm 500.00
Miller Bros, 2-bd, bone hdl, jack, 3½" 100.00
Miller Bros, 2-bd, screws in bone hdl, 4¼" 500.00
Miller Bros, 3-bd, gen stag hdl, stockman, 4" 350.00
Miller Bros, 3-bd, screws in gen pearl hdl, 3⅜" 250.00
Morley, WH & Sons; 3-bd, bone hdl, whittler, 3¼" 65.00
MSA Co, Marbles, 2-bd, pearl hdl, sunfish, rare, 4" 3,500.00
Napanoch Knife Co, X100X, 1-bd, bone hdl, very rare, 5⅜" ..2,500.00
Napanoch Knife Co, 2 lg bd, bone hdl, 3⅜" 250.00
Napanoch Knife Co, 4-bd, bone hdl, 3¼" 150.00
Northfield Knife Co, 2-bd, bone hdl, dog-leg pat, 3¾" 500.00
Northfield Knife Co, 2-bd, bone hdl, jack, 3⅜" 165.00
Pal, 2-bd, bone hdl, easy-open, 3⅜" 85.00
Pal, 3-bd, bone hdl, jack, 3⅜" 60.00
Parker, Eagle (Japan), 1-bd, bone hdl, lb, 4½", M 25.00
Parker, Eagle (Japan), 4-bd, gen abalone hdl, congress, 3⅜", M .100.00

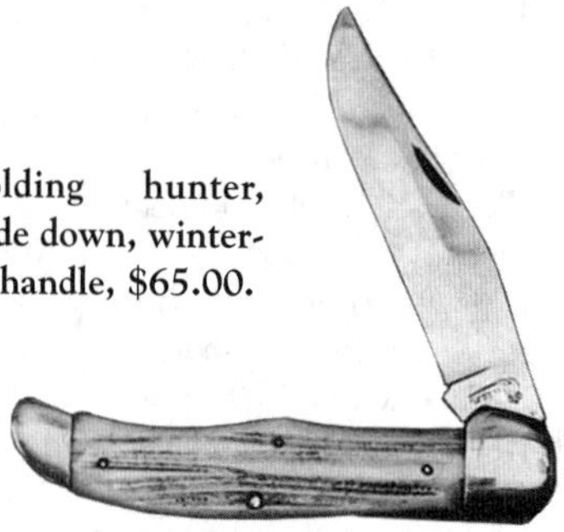

Queen, folding hunter, stamped upside down, winter-bottom bone handle, $65.00.

Queen, #18, 2-bd, wb bone hdl, jack, 3¹¹⁄₁₆" 50.00
Queen, #19, 2-bd, wb bone hdl, trapper, 4⅛" 150.00
Remington, RB43, 2-bd, bone hdl, barlow, 3⅜" 75.00
Remington, RS3333, 4-bd, bone hdl, scout shield, 3¾" 125.00
Remington, R1123, (old) 2-bd, silver bullet on bone hdl, 4½"...750.00
Remington, R1153, 2-bd, bone hdl, jack, 4½" 250.00
Remington, R1225, 2-bd, wht compo hdl, 4¼" 125.00
Remington, R1306, (old) gen stag hdl, lb, silver bullet, 4⅜" 600.00
Remington, R173, 2-bd, bone hdl, teardrop jack, 3¾" 150.00
Remington, R3054, 3-bd, gen pearl hdl, stockman, 4" 300.00
Remington, R555, 2-bd, candy stripe celluloid hdl, 3¼" 125.00
Remington, R775, 2-bd, red/wht/bl hdl, 3½" 185.00
Robeson, Shuredge, 2-bd, gen pearl hdl, jack, 3½" 150.00
Robeson, Shuredge, 2-bd, strawberry bone hdl, jack, 3¾" 100.00
Robeson, Shuredge, 3-bd, bone hdl, stockman, 3⅜" 125.00
Rodgers, Jos & Sons, multi-bd, stag hdl, sportsman's 350.00
Rodgers, Jos & Sons, 2-bd, gen stag hdl, jack, 3⅜" 125.00
Rodgers, Jos & Sons, 3-bd, bone hdl, stockman, 4" 150.00
Russell, 2-bd, bone hdl, barlow, 3⅜" 125.00
Russell, 2-bd, bone hdl, barlow, 5" 200.00
Schatt & Morgan, (current) 1-bd, w/bone hdl, lb, 5¼", M 100.00
Schatt & Morgan, (old) 2-bd, bone hdl, jack, 3⅜" 150.00
Schrade Walden, 2-bd, peach seed bone hdl, 4¼" 250.00
Schrade Walden, 3-bd, peach seed bone hdl, 3⅜" 75.00

Ulster Knife Co, 1-bd, bone hdl, barlow, 5", M 200.00
Ulster Knife Co, 4-bd, imi bone hdl, scout/campers 30.00
Wade & Butcher (Germany), 3-bd, gen stag hdl, whittler 125.00
Wade & Butcher (Sheffield England), 4-bd, gen stag hdl, 4" 500.00
Walden Knife Co, 1-bd, bone hdl, toothpick pat, 5" 200.00
Wards, 4-bd, bone hdl, cattle pat, 3⅝' 85.00
Winchester, 1920, (old) 1-bd, bone hdl, 5¼" 650.00
Winchester, 2046, (old) 2-bd, bone hdl, trapper, 3⅜" 350.00
Winchester, 2046, (old) 2-bd, celluloid hdl, jack, 3¾" 85.00
Winchester, 2974, (old) 2-bd, bone hdl, dog-leg jack, 3½" 125.00
Winchester, 3350, (old) 3 bd, gen pearl hdl, whittler, 3¼" 125.00
Winchester, 3960, (old) 3-bd, bone hdl, stockman, 4" 275.00
Winchester, 3971, dtd 89 (1989), 3-bd, bone hdl, whittler 75.00

Sheath Knives

Over the past several years knife collectors have noticed that the availability of quality old pocketknives has steadily decreased. Many collectors have now started looking for sheath knives as an addition to their hobby. In many cases the same makers of pocketknives also made quality hunting and sheath knives. Listed below is a small sampling of collectible sheath knives available.

Length is given for overall knife measurement; price includes original sheath and reflects the value of knives in excellent used condition.

Case, (XX) 516-5, stacked leather hdl, 9" 35.00
Case, (XX) 523-5, gen stag hdl, 9¼" 85.00
Case (Bradford PA), bk of tang: Case's Tested XX, 8¼" 150.00
Case (WR & Sons), bone hdl, Bowie knife, 11" 400.00
Case (XX USA), gen stag hdl, Kodiak hunter, 10¾" 125.00
Case (XX), V-44, blk Bakelite hdl, WWII, 14½" 350.00
Cattaraugus, gen stag hdl, alum pommel, 10¼" 85.00
Cattaraugus, 225Q, stacked leather hdl, WWII, 10⅜" 45.00
I*XL (Sheffield), Bowie knife, ca 1845, 14" 2,000.00
I*XL (Sheffield), leather hdl w/stag, ca 1935, 10" 100.00
Ka-Bar, Union Cutlery Co, jigged bone hdl, 9¾" 150.00
Ka-Bar, Union Cutlery Co, leather hdl w/stag, 8½" 125.00
Ka-Bar, USMC, stacked leather hdl, WWII, 12¼" 100.00
Keen Kutter, EC Simmons, K1050-6, Bowie knife, 10" 500.00
Marbles, Ideal, all gen stag hdl, 10" 275.00
Marbles, Ideal, stacked leather hdl w/alum, 9" 100.00
Marbles, Ideal, stacked leather hdl w/stag, 11⅜" 500.00
Marbles, Woodcraft, stacked leather hdl w/alum, 8¼" 125.00
Randall, Springfield MA, leather hdl, WWII, 13" 1,750.00
Randall, stacked leather hdl w/alum, 10¼" 300.00
Remington, RH36, stacked leather hdl w/alum, 10½" 150.00
Remington, RH40, stacked leather hdl w/alum, rare, 14½" 1,500.00
Remington, RH73, gen stag hdl, 8" 75.00
Ruana, alum w/elk horn hdl, skinner, current, 7½" 100.00
Ruana, RH; alum w/elk horn hdl, ca 1980, 6½" 200.00
Ruana, RH; M stamp, alum w/elk horn hdl, skinner, 9¼" 275.00
Winchester, W1050, jigged bone hdl, Bowie knife, 10" 1,200.00
Wragg, SC (Sheffield); stag hdl, Bowie knife, 13½" 1,500.00
WWII, theater knife, mc Bakelite hdl, 12" 200.00
WWII, theater knife, mc hdl, Bowie knife, 12¾" 125.00
WWII, theater knife, mc hdl, dagger, 11" 150.00
WWII, theater knife, Plexiglas hdl w/picture, 12" 175.00

Kosta

Kosta glassware has been made in Sweden since 1742. Today they are one of that country's leading producers of quality art glass. Two of their most important designers were Elis Bergh (1929 – 1950) and Vicke

Lindstrand, artistic director from 1950 to 1973. Lindstrand brought to the company knowledge of important techniques such as Graal, fine figural engraving, Ariel, etc. He influenced new artists to experiment with these techniques and inspired them to create new and innovative designs. Today's collectors are most interested in pieces made during the 1950s and 1960s. Our advisor for this category is Abby Malowanczyk; she is listed in the Directory under Texas.

Bowl, clear w/etched horse racing scene in purple, LG425, 2x8".....**275.00**
Bowl, clear w/red well, free-form, LH1005, 7x4½x3" **105.00**
Figurine, giraffe, clear etching, Lindstrand, #95729, 11½" **165.00**
Paperweight, clear w/etched ballet dancers, triangular, Lindstrand, 4".**145.00**
Paperweight, clear w/etched birds in flight, triangular, #01415, 4x3" ..**80.00**
Vase, clear w/dk purple well w/dangling strand, LH1412, 10" **375.00**
Vase, clear w/tapering bl/gr lines, LH1591, 11x4" **820.00**
Vase, clear w/thin blk twisting lines, LH1260, 6" **190.00**
Vase, clear w/wht & dk red looping bands, free-form, LH1116, 4¾" ..**235.00**
Vase, gr w/orange overcased in clear, Schildt, #05780, 5" **450.00**
Vase, obelisk form, blk overcased in clear, LS563, 11½" **175.00**
Vase, twilight bl, ovoid w/encased teardrop int, LH1606, 7" **180.00**

Kutani

Kutani, named for the Japanese village where it originated, was first produced in the seventeenth century. The early ware, Ko Kutani, was made for only about thirty years. Several types were produced before 1800, but these are rarely encountered. In the nineteenth century, kilns located in several different villages began to copy the old Kutani wares. This later, more familiar type has large areas of red with gold designs on a white ground decorated with warriors, birds, and flowers in controlled colors of red, gold, and black.

Vase, festival scene and foliate borders, ovoid, nineteenth century, 18", $2,250.00.

Bowl, swimming bird form, early 19th C, 4½x9", pr, NM **880.00**
Bowl, women in garden/birds on wht w/gold, hdls, w/lid, 7x8" ...**385.00**
Charger, sages under waterfall, ca 1930s, NM **295.00**
Figurine, bijin (lovely lady) in fine attire, ca 1912-26, 14" **650.00**
Figurine, Hotei in sm boat, bright colors, pre-1900, 4x8¼" **400.00**
Figurine, kitten, gilt fur, red collar, Taisho (1912-26), 1x1½" **195.00**
Figurine, samurai, seated in armor, holds fan & dish, ca 1860, 12½" .**1,195.00**
Figurines, temple dogs, turq & brn, pre-1900, 12x7x5", pr.......**625.00**
Plate, cockerel & flowers, wide abstract border, ca 1880, 8⅜" ...**275.00**
Plate, figure in landscape, pie-crust rim, mk, ca 1810s, 5¾"........**300.00**
Platter, scenes on 3 open fans, gold trim, late 19th C, 14½" **480.00**
Vase, aviary/floral/geometrics w/gold, stick neck, 19th C, 6x3¼" ..**400.00**

Labels

Before the advent of the cardboard box, wooden crates were used

for transporting products. Paper labels were attached to the crates to identify the contents and the packer. These labels often had colorful lithographed illustrations covering a broad range of subjects. Eventually the cardboard box replaced the crate, and the artwork was imprinted directly onto the carton. Today these paper labels are becoming collectible — primarily for the art, but also for their advertising appeal. Our advisor for this category is Cerebro; their address is listed in the Directory under Pennsylvania.

Ann Arundel Pride, horse-drawn wagon w/tomatoes, M **10.00**
Can, Casserole Oysters, bowl of oysters in cream, M **5.00**
Can, Cherry Hill, Indian holding arrows, teepee, M.....................**7.00**
Can, Commercial Floor Paint, int view of house, 6x9", EX..........**12.00**
Can, Delight Malt Syrup, man smiling while holding can, 1929, EX ...**18.00**
Can, Dinette Pork & Beans, 2 fancy bowls of beans, M **2.00**
Can, Eventide, peas in pod, M...**1.00**
Can, Four H, girl surrounded by fruit, M......................................**12.00**
Can, Gaspe Shore, lobster on coast, Canadian, early, M...............**25.00**
Can, Gold Camel, camel in desert, pyramid, 1922, EX **40.00**
Can, Ibex, ibex on summit, mountains, pear, M **40.00**
Can, Kamo Shrimp, mallard duck on water, 1923, EX **30.00**
Can, Lucky Dutchman, smiling Dutchman holding can, 1930, EX....**20.00**
Can, Marigold, peach & flowers, red, 1927, EX **14.00**
Can, Monarch Chicken Soup, head of lion, 1922, EX **25.00**
Can, Norwood Corn Syrup, country roads, gr, EX **12.00**
Can, Osseo Early Peas, 2 prospectors, knight on horse, M............**25.00**
Can, Peacock Apricot & Apple, mc peacock & fruit, M...............**15.00**
Can, Peter Pan Sugar Peas, Peter playing flute, M........................**15.00**
Can, Quail Grapefruit, grapefruit half, bowl of pineapple, 1922, EX..**25.00**
Can, Rice Lake, packing house on lake, sugar peas, 1928, EX.......**30.00**
Can, Royal Star, spinach plant, red star w/rays, EX **15.00**
Can, Sun-Lite Prunes, prunes, jars & bottles, EX **15.00**
Can, Tide Rim Oysters, 2 oysters, waves on ocean, M..................**20.00**
Can, W-G Brand, pineapples, head of Washington, M.................**40.00**
Can, Yankee Brand, smiling Uncle Sam sitting on stool, M.........**30.00**
Cigar box, inner; A-New-Deal, stars, red/wht/bl stripes, M **15.00**
Cigar box, inner; Aim Hi, bust of Jefferson, 1924, EX.................**75.00**
Cigar box, inner; Apollo, sculptured bust of Apollo, EX **18.00**
Cigar box, inner; Ben Ali, fierce looking Arab, M.......................**12.00**
Cigar box, inner; Blue Poll, young woman, M **50.00**
Cigar box, inner; Canadian Beauties, 2 women, EX.....................**65.00**
Cigar box, inner; Cigarros Primeros, Grecian men wrestling, EX..**50.00**
Cigar box, inner; Covered Wagon, cowboys & wagons crossing desert, M....**85.00**
Cigar box, inner; Darby, ram & gold coins, M **15.00**
Cigar box, inner; Edel-Falke, falcon at night, M.........................**25.00**
Cigar box, inner; Empire State, New York Skyscraper, M **12.00**
Cigar box, inner; First National, bank, cars, trolley, M.................**15.00**
Cigar box, inner; Hemazon, 3 lg dice, M.....................................**25.00**
Cigar box, inner; Lyon's Special, majestic lion, M **12.00**
Cigar box, inner; Politano, bust of woman, M **25.00**
Cigar box, inner; Subway Perfecto, coat of arms, EX...................**15.00**
Cigar box, inner; Wedding Veil, bride, wedding ceremony, EX.....**40.00**
Cigar box, outer; After Dinner, men playing cards, M.................**150.00**
Cigar box, outer; Crusader, M...**20.00**
Cigar box, outer; El Cavalo, cavalier, M......................................**20.00**
Cigar box, outer; Grand Ouvert, men playing cards, M...............**50.00**
Cigar box, outer; John Selden, portrait of patriot, M...................**20.00**
Cigar box, outer; Lissy, woman, M..**12.00**
Cigar box, outer; Mutuel, image of Black man, M **15.00**
Cigar box, outer; Red Cloud, Indian chief on horseback, EX........**20.00**
Cigar box, outer; Wild Flower, woman, M...................................**20.00**
Crate, apple; Big Chief, Indian, M...**25.00**
Crate, apple; Yakima Chief, Indian chief, 1930, M......................**15.00**
Crate, CA lemon; Fido, cartoon of sm wht dog, 1930, M............**35.00**

Crate, CA lemon; Spray, lemon red bkground, M 60.00
Crate, cranberry; Santa Claus Brand, blk, red & wht Santa, G.....20.00
Crate, FL citrus; Chow, face of dog, 7x7", M.............................85.00
Crate, FL citrus; Whip, whip, grapefruit & orange, VG 40.00
Crate, pear; American Beauty, lg red rose, 1920, EX 85.00
Crate, pear; Peacock, bird, blk bkground, M 15.00
Crate, yam; Jaguar, jaguar on savannah, M.................................5.00

Labino

Dominick Labino was a glassblower who until mid-1985 worked in his studio in Ohio, blowing and sculpting various items which he signed and dated. A ceramic engineer by trade, he was instrumental in developing the heat-resistant tiles used in space flights. His glassmaking shows his versatility in the art. While some of his designs are free-form and futuristic, others are reminiscent of the products of older glasshouses. Because of problems with his health, Mr. Labino became unable to blow glass himself; he died January, 10, 1987. Work coming from his studio since mid-1985 has been signed 'Labino Studios, Baker,' indicating ware made by his protegee, E. Baker O'Brien. In addition to her own compositions, she continues to use many of the colors developed by Labino. Our advisor for this category is Kathy Hall; she is listed in the Directory under Ohio.

Bowl, gold ruby, 1968, 7½" 450.00
Cane, crystal w/twisted rib design, 1969, 39"...........................3,000.00
Cup, smoky w/red trim, 1967, 3½" 250.00
Fountain, bl w/gold veil, twisted rim, 1969, 8½" 6,500.00
Goblet, amber, int-twist air-trap stem, 1971, 6¾"........................300.00
Paperweight, opal, tulip, 1968...450.00
Paperweight, pulled mc decor/bubbles on lt bl, 1966, 3x2¾"......295.00
Sculpture, Emergence, bubble forms & veils, #12, 1974, 7"......5,000.00
Sculpture, Emergence, dbl veil & encased air, 1976, 6" 6,100.00
Sculpture, Rendezvous, w/veil, arrow piercing a bubble, 1979, 6" ...2,000.00

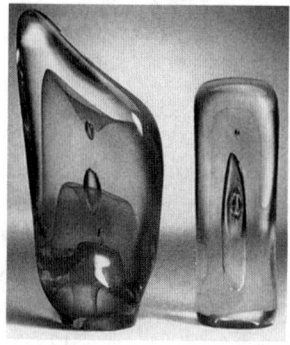

Emergence sculptures: Crystal with internal veils of pink and orange with four bubbles at core, D Labino 9-1971, 9¼", $6,325.00; Vertical oblong shape, crystal with internal veil of pink and orange, large central teardrop bubble flanked by two smaller, D Labino 3 1972, 7", $4,890.00. (Photo courtesy Skinner Auctions)

Tumbler, smoky red, ribbed sides, 1976, 4" 200.00
Vase, avocado gr w/bubbles, ovoid w/tiny opening, 1968, 4".......400.00
Vase, bl/gr w/thick walls & air bubbles, 1967, 6" 495.00
Vase, bl/yel/gr/pk opal, bulbous base w/pillared sides, 7-1971, 8"...850.00
Vase, bud; pk swirl, 1968, 5½" 250.00
Vase, cobalt w/appl dripping ribs & tooling, 1981, 6½" 450.00
Vase, copper ruby, continuous prunts, #2, 1971, 11½" 950.00
Vase, crystal sphere w/bl & yel inclusions, #6, 1972, 4" 500.00
Vase, gr, sm bubbles, 1970, 5½x4⅛"...400.00
Vase, peach w/clear panelled sides, loop design, 1980, 6½" 750.00
Vase, ruby shading to gr, bottle form, 1971, 13"...........................800.00
Vase, silver schmeltz w/mc swirls, 1978, 7½" 1,200.00
Vase, yel 'ferns' on caramel w/int petal motif, 1982, 5½" 650.00
Vase, yel-gr w/pulled prunts at bulbous base, 1976, 7¼".............875.00

Lace, Linens, and Needlework

Two distinct audiences vie for old lace and linens. Collectors seek out exceptional stitchery like philatelists and numismatists seek stamps or coins — simply to marvel at its beauty, rarity, and ties to history. Collectors judge lace and linens like figure skaters and gymnasts are judged: artist impression is half the score, technical merit the other. How complex and difficult are the stitches and how well are they done? The 'users' see lace and linens as recyclables. They seek pretty wearables or decorative materials. They want fashionable things in mint condition, and have little or no interest in technique. Both groups influence price.

Undiscovered and underpriced are the eighteenth-century masterpieces of lace and needle art in techniques which will never be duplicated. Their beauty is subtle. Amazing stitches often are invisible without magnification. To get the best value in any lace, linen, or textile item, learn to look closely at individual stitches, and study the design and technique. The finest pieces are wonderfully constructed. The stitches are beautiful to look at, and they do a good job of holding the item together.

Key: embr — embroidered

Bedcover, wht cotton w/wht embr flowers, 1900s, 84x96" 250.00
Bedcover, 2-color satin w/embr flowers, cotton lined, 1940s, queen sz....285.00
Bedspread, drawn lace w/embr pastel flowers & Fr knots, 84x100", EX..115.00
Boudoir cap, ivory filet lace w/satin ribbon & silk roses, 1920s.....75.00
Buffet cloth, wht linen w/embr butterflies & cutwork, 1900s, 33x23" ..60.00
Collar, handmade Brussels lace, ca 1880s, 6½x48" 185.00
Collar, wht Irish Crochet lace, ca 1885, 4" deep at bk, 12" W......80.00
Coverlet, homespun, cream w/bl & brn stripes, summer/winter, 102x96"...175.00
Curtain, ivory Fr lace, ca 1900, 105x41" 275.00
Curtain, wht English cotton floral lace, 1920s, 130x70" 275.00
Curtains, wht English Nottingham lace, ca 1920, 93x45", pr 325.00
Doily, crochet lace w/Bread in center of oval, 1930s, 7x13".........45.00
Doily, linen, handmade lace center & edge, 1900s, 10" sq 50.00
Doily, linen damask w/wide handmade scalloped lace, 1890s, 8x10"...25.00
Doily, linen damask w/3" scalloped lace edging, 1900s, 11½" dia........40.00
Doily, linen w/Chemical lace surround w/8 angels, 1920s, 11½" 55.00
Doily, Pineapple crochet, ca 1940, 16" dia 30.00
Doily, wht damask w/2" lace trim, ca 1900, 12" 45.00
Doily, wht linen w/embr, Princess lace trim, 1920s, 9", 11", pr 50.00
Doily, wht ribbed cotton w/embr flowers & lace inserts, 1920s, 8x11"..30.00
Hot biscuit cover, embr Hot Biscuit on wht, Portugal, 1930s........48.00
Lappets, Bedfordshire Maltese lace, ca 1890s, 4x35".....................85.00
Luncheon set, pk linen, 1930s, 8 place mats+8 napkins 95.00
Napkins, cocktail; wht linen w/emb monogram, 1930s, 5x8½", 8 for.........80.00
Napkins, ecru silk damask w/orchids, Made in Japan, 1940s, 16", 8 for...65.00
Napkins, irish linen dbl damask, monogram, 1900s, 22" sq, 8 for...110.00
Napkins, wht Madeira linen w/bl embr corners, 1930s, 16" sq, 12 for ..95.00
Needlework, Death of Sylvia's Stag..., sgn, 19thC, 24x25" 14,950.00
Needlework, fallen knight & ladies, EX details, ivory fr, 53x59" ..1,450.00
Needlework, flowers in basket, wool, England, 1890s, 18x16" 400.00
Needlework, lady w/dog at river bank, 19thC, mat & fr: 17x16".............450.00
Needlework, minstrel couple & verse, mc on silk, LA, 1836, 16x20" ...12,925.00
Needlework, shepherdess/sheep in landscape on linen, in 15" dia fr...475.00
Needlework, ship Essex, 3-masted ship scene, 19x28"................2,500.00
Needlework, view of Mt Vernon, silk w/HP details, 1800s, 20x24"...10,000.00
Needlework family register, ME, 1826, walnut fr, 10x16".........2,500.00
Nightdress bag, wht linen w/wht embr, ca 1900, 14x19" 55.00
Nightdress case, wht linen w/crochet lace edge, ca 1895, 19x23" .60.00
Pillowcase, wht organdy w/wht embr hearts/flowers, MOP buttons, 1930s ...50.00
Pillowcases, wht cotton w/embr His & Hers, lace trim, 1930s, 32", pr...65.00
Pillowcases, wht cotton w/floral embr, tatted edge, 1940s, 31x21", pr....55.00
Pillowcases, wht linen w/fine lace w/lemon yel edge, ca 1920, 33"..65.00

Pillowcases, wht linen w/wht embr flowers, ca 1900, 33x24", pr.**145.00**
Runner, ecru linen w/embr daffodils, Torchon lace ends, 1890s, 74x15" **110.00**
Runner, ivory Maderia lace w/hand embr, ca 1930, 32x14"...........**55.00**
Runner, Madeira linen w/hand embr, ca 1930, 30x15" **45.00**
Runner, wht cotton lace w/3 roundels in center, 1920s, 33x15½" **65.00**
Runner, wht linen w/embr flowers ea end, 1930s, 40x15" **50.00**
Runner, wht linen w/wht floral embr, scalloped, 1900s, 50x17"....**75.00**
Scone cover, wht linen w/padded satin stitch embr, 1900s, 18x18"..**80.00**
Sheet, Fr linen w/embr monogram, ca 1890, 88x128" **255.00**
Show towel, homespun, X-stitch urns of flowers/bird/etc, sgn/1810, 54"...**440.00**
Show towel, yarn crewelwork flowers/potted tree/etc, ER/1840, 58".........**385.00**
Table center, embr Scottish Thistles & lace trim, ca 1890, 20x26" ..**85.00**
Table center, wht linen w/embr butterflies, 1900s, 23" dia **60.00**
Table topper, wht linen w/embr & cutwork edges, 1900s, 34" sq ..**55.00**
Tablecloth, bl/wht homespun, tied fringe, 43½x33½" **55.00**
Tablecloth, crochet, ecru floral rondells & rosettes, 1900s, 120x80"....**300.00**
Tablecloth, embr linen w/cutwork, ca 1900, 88x68" +6 15" napkins ...**175.00**
Tablecloth, embr wht linen w/needle lace inserts, 66" dia...........**145.00**
Tablecloth, Irish dbl damask linen w/Arts & Crafts design, 132x64"...**275.00**
Tablecloth, lace w/embr & drawnwork linen panels, 102x68" **200.00**
Tablecloth, Madeira hand-embr lace, 1930s, 42" sq, +6 napkins ...**265.00**
Tablecloth, pk & wht linen w/rose pattern, ca 1930, 72x104" **175.00**
Tablecloth, wht Irish linen w/embr, scalloped edge, 1900s, 50x42"....**125.00**
Tablecloth, wht Irish linen w/floral embr, scalloped, 1900s, 42x50"..**125.00**
Tablecloth, wht linen w/embr flower garland corners, 1890s, 48" sq ..**105.00**
Tea cloth, Irish linen w/hand lace inserts, 4" border, 1890, 30" sq......**130.00**
Tea cloth, ivory linen w/appliqued flowers & leaves, 1930s, 34" sq ..**85.00**
Tea cloth, wht linen w/embr butterflies ea corner, ca 1900, 34" sq..**95.00**
Tea cosy, crochet lace w/removable cover & thick pad, 1900s, 11x12"....**700.00**
Tea cosy, wht linen w/embr Scottish thistles & lace trim, 1900s...**70.00**
Towel, damask w/embr monogram, 3" lace ea end, 1900s, 39x18" **50.00**
Towel, homespun linen, embr hearts/flowers/1848, fringe, 72x15"...**245.00**
Towel, Irish linen w/embr monogram, 3" lace ea end, 1900s, 43x22"..**60.00**
Towel, linen w/hand embr, 3" lace ruffle, 1890s, 38" **50.00**
Towel, wht damask w/gr floral woven design, fringe, 1920s, 42" ...**60.00**
Towel, wht linen w/embr Guest & wreaths, ca 1930, 19x13"........**45.00**
Towel, wht linen w/embr monogram, 6" lace ea end, 1890s, 50x21"..**65.00**
Towel, wht linen w/pk/gray flower embr, 1930s, 20x14", pr...........**65.00**
Tray cloth, crochet, Staff of Life worked in center, ca 1915, 10x15" ..**35.00**
Tray cloth, linen & lace w/drawnwork, embr monogram, 1900s, 16x20"..**65.00**
Tray cloth, linen w/drawnwork border, 1890s, 13x20" **50.00**
Tray cloth, wht Irish linen dbl damask w/2" lace trim, 1900s, 29" sq...**55.00**
Tray cloth, wht Irish linen w/drawnwork, ca 1900, 18x26" **50.00**
Tray cloth, wht Irish linen w/2" crochet lace border, 1890s, 19x28" ..**60.00**
Tray cloth, wht Irish linen w/3" hand lace trim, 1890s 20x25" **60.00**
Tray cloth, wht linen w/drawn/cutwork, 1900s, 16x19" **50.00**
Tray cloth, wht linen w/drawn/cutwork & embr, ca 1900, 14x20"....**40.00**
Tray cloth, wht linen w/embr florals, 3½" lace edge, 1900s, 21x27" **65.00**
Tray cloth, wht linen w/embr flower baskets, 1900s, 11x21" **55.00**
Tray cloth, wht linen w/embr flower baskets/butterflies, 1900s, 14x19"...**55.00**
Tray cloth, wht linen w/much embr, drawnwork border, 1900s, 14x20"..**30.00**
Tray cloth, wht linen w/3" crochet lace edge, 1890s, 19x25" **55.00**
Tray cloth, wht linen w/8" crochet lace edge, 1890s, 28x34" **90.00**

Lacy Glassware

Lacy glass became popular in the late 1820s after the development of the pressing machine. It was decorated with allover patterns — hearts, lyres, sheaves of wheat, etc. — and backgrounds were completely stippled. The designs were intricate and delicate, hence the term 'lacy.' Although Sandwich produced this type of glassware in abundance, it was also made by other eastern glassworks as well as in the Midwest. By 1840, its popularity on the wane and a depressed economy forcing manufac-

turers to seek less expensive modes of production, lacy glass began to be phased out in favor of pressed pattern glass.

For more information refer to *Sandwich Glass* by Ruth Webb Lee. When no condition is indicated, the items listed below are assumed to be without obvious damage; minor roughness is normal.

See also Salts, Open; Sandwich.

Bowl, Daisy, minor rim chips, 9" **85.00**
Bowl, Daisy, 8" **130.00**
Bowl, Log Cabin Industry, stipped ground, rim chips, 6" **165.00**
Compote, Gothic Arch, Heart & Leaf border, rim/base chips, 6x11" ...**4,400.00**
Compote, Heart Sheaf & Shield, minor chips, 4x6½" **1,000.00**
Compote, Peacock Feather (Eye), hex ft, minor chips, 6½x10"...........**1,400.00**
Dish, Lyre, edge chips/roughness, 7" **40.00**
Dish, Lyre, rectangular, minor rim roughness, 9" L **400.00**
Dish, Nectarine, scalloped rim, rectangular, lt roughness, 8" L ...**115.00**
Dish, Shield & Anchor, minor rim roughness, 7" **585.00**
Nappy, Log Cabin Industry, rim chips, 6" **175.00**
Nappy, Peacock Eye, rim chips, 7½" **175.00**
Nappy, Peacock Feather (Eye) & Thistle, chip/roughness, 8" ...**145.00**
Nappy, Peacock Feather Medallion, lg chips/roughness, 12" **470.00**
Nappy, Princess Feather Medallion, dmn/iron X in heart, 10", G **200.00**
Nappy, Shield & Anchor, edge roughness, 8" **140.00**
Nappy, Thistle & Rose, edge roughness, 8" **130.00**

Plate, cobalt with sunburst center design, ca 1830 – 1850, 8⅛", EX+, $200.00. (Photo courtesy Glass-Works Auctions)

Plate, Gothic Arch, cobalt, very minor imperfections, 5" **320.00**
Toddy, Roman Rosette, dk amethyst, ftd, 5¾" **330.00**

Lalique

Having recognized her son's talent at an early age, Rene Lalique's mother apprenticed him at the age of 21 to a famous Paris jeweler. In 1885 he opened his own workshop, and his unique style earned him great notoriety because of his use of natural elements in his designs — horn, ivory, semi-precious stone, pearls, coral, enamel, even plastic or glass.

In 1900 at the Paris Universal Exposition at the age of 40, he achieved the pinnacle of success in the jewelry field. Already having experimented with glass, he decided to focus his artistic talent on that medium. In 1907 after completing seven years of laborious work, Lalique became a Master Glassmaker and designer of perfume bottles for Francois Coty, a chemist and perfumer, who was also his neighbor in the Place Vendome area in Paris. All in all he created over two hundred fifty perfume bottles for Roger et Gallet, Coty, Worth, Forvil, Guerlain, D'Orsay, Molinard, and many others. In the commercial perfume bottle collecting field, Rene Lalique's are those most desired. Some of his one-of-a-kind experimental models have gone for over $100,000.00 at auction in the last few years.

At the height of production his factories employed over six hundred workers.

Seeking to bring art into every day life, he designed clocks, tableware, stemware, chandeliers, inkwells, bowls, statues, dressing table items, and, of course, vases. Lalique's unique creativity is evident in his designs through his polishing, frosting, and glazing techniques. He became famous for his use of colored glass in shades of blue, red, black, gray, yellow, green, and opalescence. His glass, so popular in the 1920s and 1930s, is still coveted today.

Lalique's son Marc assumed leadership of the company in 1948, after his father's death. His designs are made from full lead crystal, not the demi-crystal Rene worked with. Designs from 1948 on were signed only 'Lalique, France.' The company was later taken over by Marc's daughter, Marie-Claude, and her designs were modern, clear crystal accented with color motifs. The Lalique company was sold in 1995, and Marie-Claude Lalique retired shortly thereafter.

Condition is of extreme importance to a collector. Grinding, polished out chips, and missing perfume bottle stoppers can reduce the value significantly, sometimes by as much as 80%.

Czechoslovakian glassware bearing fradulent Lalique signatures is appearing on all levels of the market. Study and become familiar with the various Lalique designs before paying a high price for a fraudulent piece. Over the past five years Lalique-designed glass has been showing up in a deep purple-gray color. These are clear glass items that have been 'irradiated' to change their appearance. Buyer beware.

Our advisor for this category is John Danis; he is listed in the Directory under Illinois.

Key:
cl/fr — clear and frosted   RL — signed R. Lalique
L — signed Lalique   RLF — signed R. Lalique, France
LF — signed Lalique France

Ashtray, Irene, fr bird border, sgn, 3¾" dia.....................85.00
Bookends, nude kneels, rests head on hands, cl, paper label, 9"..900.00
Bottle, scent; Coeur des Calices, bl w/bee stopper, RL.............2,500.00
Bottle, scent; Dans la Nuit, star motif w/moon stopper, RL, 8"...500.00
Bottle, scent; Grecian maidens, amber antique, brn wash, RL....900.00
Bottle, scent; Le Jane, gr opal, snuff bottle form......................2,500.00
Bottle, scent; Molinard, 12 nudes, brn wash, RL, 5"...................800.00
Bottle, scent; Phalene, nude w/wings, amber, w/box................3,000.00
Bottle, scent; roses/columns, roses finial, peach patina, RLF, 4"..575.00
Bottle, scent; Sirenes, 10 mermaids, gr wash, RL, 6¾".............1,300.00
Bowl, centerpc; Nemours, daisies, blk enamel on sepia, RLF, 4x10"...650.00
Bowl, Fleurons, 6 wavy line swirls in relief, opal, RLF, 3x8"........200.00
Bowl, Marguerites, flowers on rim, fr, L Cristal F, 14"...................465.00
Bowl, molded as 2 lg leaves, cl/fr, label/LF, 18" L.........................490.00
Bowl, 2 lg leaves, cl, LF, late 20th C, 7⅜x18x10"........................765.00
Box, Cigales, cicadas, opal, RL, 2x10", w/compo box..............1,100.00
Box, puff; Houppes, milkweed, opal, RLF, lt wear, 5½" dia.........350.00
Candlesticks, Chantilly, leaves, cl, sq on short base, RL, 2⅛".........345.00
Carafe, Lotus, leaves overlap, enameled stopper, RLF, 6½".........385.00
Charger, Algues, seaweed, opal, RLF, 15⅜"................................800.00
Clock, Inseparables, lovebirds ea side, opal, sq, RLF, 4½"........3,500.00
Compote, row of fr birds on cl ftd U-form, LF, 4¾"....................175.00
Dish, Roscoff, fish, RLF, 14"...1,410.00
Figure, Sirene, mermaid, opal, RL, 4".......................................1,950.00
Figure, toad, Gregoire, LF, 3"...290.00
Hatpin, Feuilles, spiral leaves, salmon wash, L, 10¾".............1,265.00
Ice bucket, 2 nudes on foliate ground, cl/fr, label/LF, 9".............550.00
Mascot, Coq Nain, crouching rooster, #1135, RLF, 8"................600.00
Mascot, Grande Libellule, dragonfly, amethyst tint, RL/RLF, VG...3,235.00
Mascot, Grande Libellule, dragonfly, gr-tone cl, RL, 8"............2,800.00
Mascot, Tete D' Aigle, eagle head, cl/fr, LF, 1928, 4⅜".............250.00
Mascot, Tete D' Aigle, eagle's head on rnd chrome base, RL, 4"....800.00
Pendant, Lys, lilies, dk red wash, triangular, RL, 2⅛"................685.00
Plafonnier, Dahlias, wht opal bowl, conical ceiling mt, 12", 19" drop..3,000.00

Shade, ceiling; apples/leaves, honey-color, RLF, 5x15" dia.......1,900.00
Vase, Acanthes, cl/fr, ovoid, RLF, 11".......................................1,200.00
Vase, Aigrettes, birds in flight, grey fr, RLF, 9¾", EX................4,700.00
Vase, Antilopes, fr w/cl rnd cabachons, bulbous, RL, 10½"......4,700.00
Vase, Bacchantes, frieze of nudes, cl/fr, label/LF, 9½"...............800.00
Vase, Baguette, birds in foliage, cl, LF, late 20th C, 6¾"............200.00

Vase, Chamarande, flowerheads and thorny branches on opal, Model #974, R. Lalique France, 1926, 19½", $1,400.00. (Photo courtesy Butterfields)

Vase, Chardons, thistles ea corner, bulbous, RLF, 7"...................475.00
Vase, Domremy, thistles, fr, bulbous, RLF, 8½"........................1,295.00
Vase, Domremy, thistles, opal, bulbous, RLF, 8½".....................1,765.00
Vase, Font-Romeu, tapered/beaded ribs on flaring U form, LF, 9", EX..1,175.00
Vase, Graines, seed pod rows at base, alexandrite, RL, 8".........2,800.00
Vase, Grimpereaux, birds on branches, wht patina, RL, 8¼x6⅛"..............1,495.00
Vase, Languedoc, overlapped/relief leaves, gr, RL, 9", EX......10,575.00
Vase, Milan, repeating leaves, gr, RLF, 10x11".........................3,575.00
Vase, Montmorency, rows of cherries, smoke, V-form, RLF, 8½".........3,000.00
Vase, Ormeaux, leaves, fr w/amber, RLF, 7x7", EX....................600.00
Vase, Poissons, perch, opal, spherical, RLF/#925, 9".................3,820.00
Vase, Royat, chains, cl/fr, tabs at rim, ca 1936, 6".......................288.00
Vase, Sauterelles, grasshoppers, bl/fr, RLF, 11".......................3,200.00
Vase, Tuileries, sparrows at bottom, bl-gr wash, RL, 11".........2,860.00

Lamps

The earliest lamps were simple dish containers with a wick that hung over the edge or was supported by a channel or tube. Grease and oil from animal or vegetable sources were the first fuels used. Ancient pottery lamps, crusie, and Betty lamps are examples of these early types. In 1784 Swiss inventor Ami Argand introduced the first major improvement in lamps. His lamp featured a tubular wick and a glass chimney. During the first half of the nineteenth century, whale oil, burning fluid (a highly explosive mixture of turpentine and alcohol), and lard were the most common fuels used in North America. Many lamps were patented for specific use with these fuels.

Kerosene was the first major breakthrough in lighting fuels. It was demonstrated by Canadian geologist Dr. Abraham Gesner in 1846. The discovery and drilling of petroleum in the late 1850s provided an abundant and inexpensive supply of kerosene. It became the main source of light for homes during the balance of the nineteenth century and for remote locations until the 1950s.

Although Thomas A. Edison invented the electric lamp in 1879, it was not until two or three decades later that electric lamps replaced kerosene household lamps. Millions of kerosene lamps were made for every purpose and pocketbook. They ranged in size from tiny night or miniature lamps to tall stand or piano lamps. Hanging varieties for homes commonly had one or two fonts (oil containers), but chandeliers for churches and public buildings often had six or more. Wall or bracket lamps usually had silvered reflectors. Student lamps, parlor lamps (now called Gone-With-the-Wind lamps), and patterned glass lamps were designed to complement the popular furnishing trends of the day. Gaslight, introduced in the early nineteenth century, was used mainly in homes of the wealthy and public places until the early twentieth century. Most fixtures were wall or ceiling mounted, although some table models were also used.

Few of the ordinary early electric lamps have survived. Many lamp manufacturers made the same or similar styles for either kerosene or electricity, sometimes for gas. Top-of-the-line lamps were made by Pairpoint, Phoenix, Tiffany, Bradley and Hubbard, and Handel. See also these specific sections.

When buying lamps that have been converted to electricity, inspect them very carefully for any damage that may have resulted from the alterations; such damage is very common, and when it does occur, the lamp's value may be lessened by as much as 50%. Lamps seem to bring much higher prices in some areas than others, especially the larger cities. Conversely, in rural areas they may bring only half as much as our listed values. One of our advisors for lamps is Carl Heck; he is listed in the Directory under Colorado. Advice for miniature lamps comes from Bob Culver (who is listed in the Directory under Michigan), and Jeff Bradfield (in Virginia) is our advisor for pattern glass lamps. See also Stained Glass.

Key: col — cut overlay

Aladdin Lamps, Electric

Bed, #2305 SS, whip-o-lite fluted & flocked shade, EX, from $200 to..250.00
Bedroom, P-071, ceramic, from $25 to 35.00
Boudoir, G-10, glass, 1934, from $40 to..50.00
Boudoir, G-15, crystal, floral base, from $150 to 200.00
Boudoir, G-49, Alacite, from $40 to...50.00
Boudoir, G-92, moonstone, 1937, from $50 to................................60.00
Figurine, G-16, lady, crystal, etched, EX, from $600 to 700.00
Figurine, G-163, dbl nudes, NM, from $3,000 to 3,500.00
Glass Urn, G-213A, Alacite, closed urn, from $225 to 275.00
Pin-up, G-354, Alacite, from $125 to...150.00
Pin-up, P-057, Gun-n-Holster, ceramic, EX, from $125 to..........150.00
Ranch House, G-378C, Bullet, Alacite, lit/decaled urn, EX, $325 to....375.00
Table, E-310, #784 vase, from $275 to 325.00
Table, G-2, marble-like glass, from $300 to...................................350.00
Table, G-98, moonstone, from $100 to..125.00
Table, G-178, opalique, from $100 to..150.00

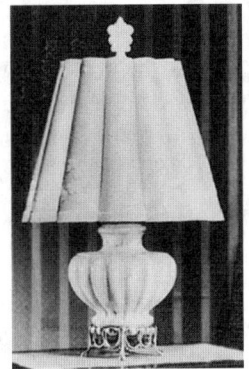

Table, G-195, Alacite, Whip-o-Lite shade, 1940 – 41, Lamp base (common), from $60.00 to $80.00; Shade, EX, from $50.00 to $100.00; Finial, EX, from $25.00 to $40.00. (Photo courtesy J.W. Courter)

Table, G-223, Alacite, from $75 to..100.00
Table, G-233, Alacite, illuminated base (same as G-95), $100 to....125.00
Table, G-331, Alacite, illuminated base, from $60 to 80.00
Table, M-463, ivory ceramic w/blk iron base, from $30 to............40.00
Table, P-408, ceramic, planter, from $75 to 100.00
Table, P-424, ceramic, from $50 to 60.00
TV, M-384, shell, ceramic, from $50 to 60.00
TV, M-469, metal, w/shade, from $25 to 30.00
TV, MT-520, cherry & brass base, NM, from $400 to..................500.00

Aladdin Lamps, Kerosene

From 1908 Aladdin lamps with a mantle became the mainstay of rural America, providing light that compared favorably with the electric light bulb. They were produced by the Mantle Lamp Company of America in over eighteen models and more than one hundred styles. During the 1930s to the 1950s, this company was the leading manufacturer of electric lamps as well. Still in operation today, the company is now known as Aladdin Mantle Lamp Co., located in Clarksville, Tennessee. For those seeking additional information on Aladdin Lamps, we recommend *Aladdin — The Magic Name in Lamps*, *Aladdin Electric Lamps Collector's Manual & Price Guide #3*, and *Aladdin Collector's Manual and Price Guide #20*, all written by our advisor for Aladdins, J. W. Courter; he is listed in the Directory under Kentucky. Mr. Courter has also published a book called *Angle Lamps, Collector's Manual and Price Guide*.

Caboose, Model B, B-400, brass font, from $150 to.....................250.00
Floor, Model #12, bl & gold, 1928-29, EX, from $200 to 250.00
Floor, Model B-265, ivory & rose gold, 1935, EX, from $175 to .250.00
Floor, Model B-293, Antique Ivory lacquer, 1939-42, from $175 to ...225.00
Foreign, Model #8, table, London, from $250 to 300.00
Foreign, Model C-164, glass font, shelf lamp, Brazil, from $100 to ..125.00
Hanging, Model #2, w/#203 shade, EX, from $375 to 475.00
Hanging, Model #11, w/#516 shade, EX, from $275 to 350.00
Hanging, Model #23, brass w/glass shade, several types, ea, $60 to 100.00
Parlour, Practicus, polished brass or Old English, NM, from $500 to ...600.00
Table, Model #6, satin brass or nickel, from $75 to 100.00
Table, Model #10, nickel, from $300 to 400.00
Table, Model #12 Crystal Vase, Bengal Red, from $500 to..........600.00
Table, Model #12 Florentine Vase, Rose Moonstone, EX, from $2,800 to ...3,200.00
Table, Model A Venetian, rose, EX, from $150 to 200.00
Table, Model B Cathedral, Flesh moonstone, EX, from $400 to .450.00
Table, Model B-49 Washington Drape, amber crystal, bell stem, $350 to.....375.00
Table, Model B-52, Washington Drape, amber, filigree stem, $125 to......175.00
Table, Model B-61 Short Lincoln Drape, amber crystal, EX, $3,000 to ...3,500.00
Table, Model B-80 Beehive, clear crystal, from $80 to 100.00
Table, Model B-98, rose moonstone, NM, from $400 to 450.00
Table, Model B-125, Corinthian, moonstone, wht w/rose ft, from $250 to ..300.00
Wall bracket, Model #2, from $400 to...450.00
Wall bracket, Model #12, from $125 to...175.00

Angle Lamps

The Angle Lamp Company of New York City developed a unique type of kerosene lamp that was a vast improvement over those already on the market; they were sold from about 1896 until 1929 and were expensive for their time. Nearly all Angle lamps are hanging lamps and wall lamps. Table models are uncommon. Our Angle lamp advisor is J.W. Courter; he is listed in the Directory under Kentucky. See the narrative for Aladdin Lamps for information concerning popular books Mr. Courter has authored.

Note: Old glass pieces for Angle lamps are scarce to rare; unless noted otherwise, the lamp values that follow are for examples with no glass.

Gas adaptor, polished brass, no glass, EX..................................850.00
Glass, chimney top, clear, petal-top, EX....................................200.00
Glass, chimney top, wht, petal-top, EX 85.00
Glass, chimney top, wht opal, petal-top, NM 250.00
Glass, elbow globe, clear w/birds, NM.......................................275.00
Glass, elbow globe, clear w/wreath & torch band, NM 275.00
Hanging, #263, polished brass, old glass, EX 475.00
Hanging, #283, antique copper, 2-burner, EX 375.00
Hanging, #352, polished brass, 3-burner, no glass, EX 600.00

Hanging, Classic, antique gold, 2-burner, NM..........................2,000.00
Hanging, EG-22, extended grape, 2-burner, EX..........................375.00
Table, Classic #1, antique gold, NM 2,000.00
Wall, #103, nickel, old glass, NM..265.00
Wall, #103, plain can, nickel, EX 275.00
Wall, #125, Pinwheel, nickel no glass, EX 350.00
Wall, #182, fleur-de-lis pattern, antique copper, NM 300.00
Wall, Classic #3, antique gold, no glass, EX.............................1,000.00
Wall, Leaf & Vine, nickel, old glass, EX 400.00
Wall, MW 966-NF, leaf & vine, nickel, EX 325.00

Banquet Lamps

Brass w/blk glazed ceramic ft, amber swirled globe, w/burner 150.00
Cranberry shade/font w/florals & gilt, marble/ormolu ped, 24", pr....2,000.00
Flow Bl, pear & leaf decor, etched ball shade, electrified, 28".....925.00
Milk glass w/HP cherubs scene ball shade sgn Baccarat, 23"....1,150.00
Pk cased, 3-part, brass mts, plated ft, Consolidated, 25½", VG+ 460.00
Slag panel shade w/brass grill work; zinc/brass decor base, 32"....400.00

Chandeliers

Bronze, floral Rococo, 6-arm, 28" dia 600.00
Bronze acanthus 4-arm mt w/prisms, glass beaded shade, 25"......800.00
Bronze w/6 swans holding candle cups, central blk-pnt dish, Fr, 23"..........3,165.00
Floral-emb bronze mts for bowl shade/ceiling, 4 sm pendant shades, 30" ..2,300.00
Fr pk mottle art glass, lg bowl shade+4 lilies; wrought mt w/leaves 800.00
Gilt-bronze, 12-light, ornate scroll chains/font/arms, Fr/1900, 56x26" ..860.00
Wood, 8 baluster-trn arms w/candle holders, Am, 1800s, 21x28" dia..3,250.00
Wrought steel w/scrolls & spirals, 16 electric candles, 42x33x47" 1,450.00

Decorated Kerosene Lamps

When only one color is given in a two-layer cut overlay lamp description, the second layer is generally clear; in three-layer examples, the second will usually be white, the third clear. Exceptions will be noted.

Note: Kerosene lamp values are for lamps with correct burners.

Cut overlay, two-color (white to green) trefoil and oval cuttings on font and standard, stepped brass and marble bases, 15", NM, $2,300.00.

Bl alabaster w/gold loops, 2-step milk glass std w/gold, 13", VG .800.00
Cobalt w/wht spirals, stepped marble base w/brass column/stem, 12"...900.00
Col (2-layer), amethyst, fluted std, marble base, Sandwich, 11" 2,500.00
Col (2-layer), cobalt, circle/X motif, marble base w/brass trim, 11" 220.00
Col (2-layer), cobalt w/gilt, wht opaque std, Sandwich, 13⅝"..........1,265.00
Col (2-layer), cranberry, rosettes/gilt, milk glass 2-step std, 13"...1,000.00
Col (2-layer), gr, tall fluted brass/marble stepped std, prisms, 21"..345.00
Col (2-layer), jade gr w/leaf band, milk glass base, 8"..................780.00
Col (2-layer), red, clear wafer, reeded brass std, marble base, 13" 1,150.00
Col (2-layer), red, oval cut std on stepped marble base, 15½" 2,400.00
Col (2-layer), red, wht Baroque base, Sandwich, 12¾"............1,380.00
Col (2-layer), wht, circles, brass stem, dk slate ft, 8" 230.00
Col (2-layer), wht invt pear font w/floral, fluted brass/onyx ft, 10"..520.00
Col (2-layer), wht/bl w/ovals, brass stem, 2-step marble base, 11"....800.00
Col (2-layer), wht/cranberry, alabaster base w/3 dolphins, 13", EX...1,150.00
Col (3-layer), bl/wht, ovals/circles/etc, marble base, 10" 460.00
Col (3-layer), bl/wht, ovals/stars/etc, marble base (G), 13" 515.00
Col (3-layer), cranberry/wht, marble base, brass std, 13¾" 650.00
Col (3-layer), dk pk, brass/marble std, acid-cut bowl shade, 20", VG..8,800.00
Col (3-layer), pk, fishbowl shade w/transfers, marble base, 19", EX 500.00
Col (3-layer), pk/cranberry, wht marble base, brass hdw, 12", EX...550.00
Col (3-layer), red, wht opaque std, Baroque base, NE Glass, 14"...1,150.00
Col (3-layer), red font & stem, clear ft, #3 collar, 14", EX..........800.00
Col (3-layer), rose w/windows, milk glass base, worn gold, 12".....1,000.00
Cut crystal w/gilt font, brass stem, 2-step marble base, 14" 575.00
Milk glass w/lady's profile reserve, milk glass base, worn gold, 11" ...400.00
Ruby flashed vintage, orig burners, brass std, marble base, 15" ...400.00
Wht opal satin w/mc band, gr opaque base, 10"..........................375.00

Fairy Lamps

Amber opal, pressed swirl, Clarke base, pyramid sz, 3⅝" 110.00
Bl opal, mk Clarke Fairy Pyramid base, 4¾" 135.00
Bl shaded satin w/deep emb molding, 6½x6½"............................480.00
Burmese, clear Clarke cup, Webb, ca 1890, 4", EX......................200.00
Burmese, clear Clarke Pyramid base, Webb, 4¾"........................335.00
Burmese, dome shade in lg floral-decor porc bowl, 6½x8" 1,380.00
Burmese, pleated skirt, Thomas Webb...Queen's..., Cricklite, 5¾" 985.00
Burmese, Tunnicliffe base, sgn Webb Pyramid..., 4¾x6" 1,250.00
Burmese, 4-fold burmese base, clear Clarke cup, 6x5¼" 1,800.00
Cranberry w/Mary Gregory decor, ruffled top, optic rib base, 7¼"...........575.00
Cranberry w/wht spiral threading, ribbed, Clarke base, 3" 400.00
Gr w/Mary Gregory decor, Czechoslovakia sticker, 5½" 85.00
Lithophane scenes (3), cup mk S Clarke's Fairy Trade Mk, 3⅜x3¼" 575.00
Mc spatter shade, pressed base, Clarke's...Cricklite, 5" 125.00
Nailsea, bl/wht dome shade, plain bl base w/raised bl/wht center, 6x9" ..985.00
Nailsea, citron/wht, Clarke base, 5x5½" 835.00
Nailsea, cranberry/wht w/pinched/ruffled bowl base, 7x8"...........795.00
Nailsea, red/wht, Clarke cup (chipped), ruffled bowl base, 5½x6".........600.00
Nailsea, red/wht, clear Clarke base, Cricklite sz, 6x7" 975.00
Nailsea, red/wht dome shade over 2nd tier of 4 on clear base..2,200.00
Nailsea, rose/wht, on clear Cricklite base, 4¼"...........................230.00
Owl's head, gr frosted, clear Clarke base, 4½x3⅜" 340.00
Three Face, cat/dog/owl, pnt porc, 4x4"...................................1,200.00
Wht satin Swirl w/bl, 2-part base, 6¾x5½" 378.00
Yel Swirl MOP, on matching crimped-edge holder, 4¾" 300.00

Gone-With-the-Wind Lamps

Arabian camel rider/palms on blown-out shade/base, metal ft, 22"..785.00
Corn & leaves emb on shade/base, 10" globe, rtcl metal ft, 25"..560.00
Poppies, red on pastel mottle, ball shade/base on sq 4-ftd metal base ..425.00
Red glass globe/base w/HP leaves & flowers, gilt metal mts, 25".......1,100.00
Roses on ball shade & base, electrified, 26", VG 575.00

Hanging Lamps

Astral, brass font in brass 3-arm ring, no burner, o/w EX 800.00
Clear globe w/cut floral, emb brass mts, smoke bell, 28" 600.00
Cranberry Hobnail shade, rpl font, jewel fr, prisms, 15" dia 900.00
Cranberry shade w/opal net, brass fr, clear prisms, 14" dia 1,200.00
Peachblow melon-rib 14" shade/font, rtcl brass fr, Sandwich...2,000.00
Slag glass 21" 6-panel shade w/metal palm tree o/l..................1,000.00

Lanterns

Dietz Little Wizard, tin, red globe, EX..85.00
Glass onion globe, tin font/base/top/ring hdl, pierced top, 9"+hdl......385.00
Miner's, iron/brass w/brass font & hasp, Thomas & Williams, 9¾".........100.00
Oak/pine, orig dk finish, pegged, wrought iron hdw, 15"............575.00
Pine, copper deflector, glass door, wire bail, 14"............................250.00
Punched sheet brass w/faceted glass jewels, CT, 11½"................250.00
Reeded wooden posts, iron nails, staple hinges, 7", G................500.00
Skaters, brass w/clear globe, wire hdl, gold traces, 7"................110.00
Tin, Paul Revere type, punched, pnt blk, 1900, 17" 165.00
Tin, Rococo detail, 6 rvpt panes, candle socket, rpt, 18", VG.....400.00
Tin, 4 glass panes, peaked top w/vents & ring hdl, 8½" 245.00
Tin, 4 glass panes, punched stars in base, wire hoop protectors, 16"...170.00
Wood w/copper wire bail, nailed top/base, insect damage, 12"....220.00
Wooden post fr, staple hinges, punched tin, 12¾"......................650.00

Lard Oil/Grease Lamps

Pottery w/Albany slip, saucer base/strap hdl/2 sm spouts on rnd font ..1,870.00
Redware w/Albany slip, pinch spout/strap hdl/saucer base, 4½" 750.00
Tin, petticoat style, rnd pan base w/lg ring hdl on side of column, 9"..245.00
Wrought-iron rush light, arched tripod base w/penny ft, 14" 525.00
Wrought-iron rush light, 3-leg w/sm ft, 5-sided counterweight, 9"...385.00

Miniature Lamps, Kerosene

Miniature oil lamps were originally called 'night lamps' by their manufacturers. Early examples were very utilitarian in design — some holding only enough oil to burn through the night. When kerosene replaced whale oil in the second half of the nineteenth century, 'mini' lamps became more decorative and started serving other purposes. While mini lamps continue to be produced today, collectors place special value on the lamps of the kerosene era, roughly 1855 to 1910. Four reference books are especially valuable to collectors as they try to identify and value their collections: *Miniature Lamps* by Frank and Ruth Smith, Schiffer Publishing, 1968 (referred to as SI); *Miniature Lamps II* by Ruth Smith, Schiffer Publishing 1982 (SII); *Miniature Victorian Lamps* by Margorie Hulsebus (source of the H numbers below), Schiffer Publishing, 1996; and *Price Guide for Miniature Lamps* by Marjorie Hulsebus, Schiffer Publishing, 1998 (contains 1998 values for all the above books). References in the following listings correlate with each lamp's plate number in these books. Our advisor is Bob Culver; he is listed in the Directory under Michigan.

Cranberry with gold and orange enameling, nutmeg burner, S-440, 8½", EX, $975.00. (Photo courtesy James D. Julia Inc.)

Beaded Drape, bl satin, ball shade/onion base, S-400, 9", EX 300.00
Beaded Swirl cranberry, shade w/upright ruffle, S-369, 8½", EX 150.00

Bl opaline, ½-ribbing/emb flowers, ball shade/can base, S-408, 8"......690.00
Cosmos, milk glass, SI-286, 7½", EX...150.00
Cranberry Invt T'print, ball shade/base, Fenton/Wright, 8½" 150.00
Cranberry Invt T'print, umbrella shade, Fenton/Wright, 7½", EX.........290.00
Cranberry w/emb overlapping leaves, ball shade/base, S-443, 8½", EX 750.00
Cranberry w/optic panels, ruffle-top shade, appl clear ft, 9½", VG........460.00
Defender, gr opaque, ball shade, shaped 4-sided base, S-240, 9", VG 375.00
Drape, gr satin, ball shade/sq base, S-231, 8¾", VG 375.00
Leon's Rib, bl opaque, SI-177, 6"..210.00
Lincoln Drape, clear, frosted shade, SI-143, 5½" 50.00
Med bl opal, shade w/upright ruffle, base w/5 clear appl ft, S-514, VG...865.00
Milk glass, paneled/HP floral, ball shade/onion base, S-310, 8", EX........345.00
Milk glass, reclining elephant, pnt traces, wht globe, SI-488 ......150.00
Milk glass, w/red fleur-de-lis decor, SI-274, no chimney, 7¾" 250.00
Milk glass pnt brn w/wht & red flowers, gone w/wind shape, 8½" 300.00
Milk glass w/emb acanthus & swirl, fired-on pk/gr, S-273, 9", EX..........345.00
Milk glass w/emb beaded panels & HP flowers, umbrella shade, SII-257 ..300.00
Milk glass w/HP bl & gray windmill scenes, ball shade/base, S-333, 8" ..575.00
Milk glass w/pastel emb, umbrella shade/sq base, S-244, 8".........235.00
Milk glass w/pk & gr pnt, artichoke shade, ribbed base, S fig III, 8"... 120.00
Milk glass w/yel-gold acanthus leaves & swirls, ball shade/base, S-230.....200.00
Pk opaline w/emb reserves, ball shade/cylinder base, #409, 8¾", EX 490.00
Pk satin pansy-emb cased ball shade, melon-rib base, S-389, 7", EX ..690.00
Red satin, ball shade w/fancy emb, SI-397, 8¼" 110.00
Red satin w/emb swirls, onion shade/base, S-401, 7½" 240.00
Sapphire bl ball shade/base w/overlapping emb leaves, S-443, 8½" 865.00
Yel Dmn Quilt ruffled-top shade on leaf/floral-emb brass base, 9", EX....200.00
Yel spatter, tulip shade, swirl-rib sqd base (H-150 style), 8", EX .230.00

Motion Lamps

Animated motion lamps were made as early as 1920 and as late as 1980s. They reached their peak during the 1950s when plastic became widely used. They are characterized by action created by the heat of a light bulb which causes the cylinder to revolve and create the illusion of an animated scene. Some of the better-known manufacturers were Econolite Corp., Scene in Action Corp., and LA Goodman Mfg. Co. As with many collectible items, prices are guided by condition, availability, and collector demand. Collectors should be aware that reproductions of lamps featuring cars, trains, sailing ships, fish, and mill scenes are being made. Values are given for original lamps in mint condition. Any damage or flaws seriously reduce the price. As has been true in many areas of collecting, Internet auctions have affected the prices of motion lamps. Erratic ups and downs in prices realized have resulted in a market that is often unpredictible. For additional information, we recommend *Collector's Guide to Motion Lamps* by Sam and Anna Samuelian. Our advisors for motion lamps are Kaye and Jim Whitaker; they are listed in the Directory under Washington.

Annie, Johnson Co, 1981, 11"...35.00
Antique Autos, Econolite, 1957, 11" (+).....................................110.00
Bicycles, Econolite, 11"...175.00
Boy & Girl Scouts, Econolite, 10"...150.00
Butterflies, Econolite, 1954, 11"...110.00
Christmas Trees, gr/red/bl/wht (paper), 1950s, 10-24", ea, $55 to .95.00
Colonial Fountain, glass/metal, Scene in Action, 1930s, 10"......135.00
Davy Crockett 130.00
Disneyland Express, red or yel plastic, Econolite, 1955, 11"........150.00
Elephant Lady Fortune Teller, chalk, S&S, 1930s, 12" 150.00
Elvgrin Pin-up Girls 250.00
Firefighters, LA Goodman, 1957, 11"...195.00
Fireplace, Econolite, 1958, 11" 110.00
Fish, Salt Water; Econolite, 1950s, 11" (+)..................................110.00
Forest Fire, Econolite, 1955, 11"...110.00

Forest Fire, Rotovue Jr, 1949, 10" **95.00**
Forest Fire, Scene in Action, 1931, 10"................................130.00
Fountain of Youth, Rotovue Jr, 1950, 10" 110.00
Indian Warrior, Gritt Inc, 1920s, 11"..................................**95.00**
Japanese Twilight, Scene in Action, 1931, 13" 150.00
Jet Planes, Econolite, 1958, 11"...175.00
Merry Go Round, Rotovue Jr, 1949, 10" 85.00
Miss Liberty, Econolite, 1957, 11" 175.00
More Here Than Meets the Eye, Hawaiian girl, paper front, 1952, 12" ...150.00
Niagara Falls, Econolite, 1955, 11"......................................80.00
Niagara Falls, glass w/paper wrap picture, Scene in Action, 1931, 10" ..110.00
Niagara Falls, Rotovue Jr, 1949, 10"...................................60.00
Old Mill, Econolite, 1965, 11" (+) **95.00**
Op Art Lamp, Visual Effects, 1970s, 13" (reproduced in 1990s) ...40.00
Oriental Fantasy, LA Goodman, 1957, 11" **95.00**
Oriental Scene, Econolite, 1959, 11" 110.00
Sailboats, LA Goodman, 1954, 14" **95.00**
Sailing Ships, Econolite (+)...110.00
Seattle World's Fair, Econolite...160.00
Snow Scene, church or cabin, Econoolite, 1957, 11" 145.00
Snow Scene, LA Goodman...80.00
Steamboats, Econolite, 1957, 11".......................................110.00
Totville Train, Econolite, 1948, 11".....................................110.00
Trains, Econolite, 1956, 11" (+)..110.00
Tropical Fish, Econolite, 1954, 11".......................................80.00
Truck & Bus, Econolite, 1962, 11" 150.00
Venice Canal, Econolite, 1963, 11" 150.00
White Christmas, flat front, Econolite, 11"..........................150.00
Why You Should Never Drink the Water, paper front, 1946-49, 4 szs, ea...**135.00**

Pattern Glass Lamps

The letter/number codes in the following descriptions refer to *Oil Lamps, Books I , II,* and *III,* by Catherine Thuro (book, page, item number or letter). Our advisor for this section is Jeff Bradfield who is listed in the Directory under Virginia.

Acorn, fine-rib bkground, 1860s, T2-67g, 9" 300.00
Aster Band, wht Gem base, hand lamp w/appl hdl, T2-83h, from $150 to ..250.00
Basketweave w/Medallions, ftd hand lamp, T2-109-g..................325.00
Bow & Rib, pressed, composite, T2-71f, 10", from $175 to.........250.00
Bull's Eye Band Entwined, Gem w/Leaf base, T2-37o, from $300 to ...350.00
Chadwick, pressed, wht opaque pressed base, T2-79i, from $225 to ...325.00
Checkered Star Band, stand lamp, T2-106b, 6½", from $150 to.........175.00
Coolidge Drape or Bellevue, bl opaque, T2-125h 750.00
Daisy, Westmoreland Specialty Co, T2-119i.................................125.00
Heart-Top Panel, transfer/pnt stem on wht opaque base, T2-32a ...400.00
Hearts & Stars, wht translucent base, T2-41-c, 9¼" 275.00
Hobbs Fruit Medallion, all glass, T3-117f, minimum value.........150.00
King Melon Optic, opal stand lamp, T2-103m 175.00
Lion & Baboon, T2-119j, 9½" to collar 300.00
Moon & Crescents, amethyst, T2-59d, 12½".........................1,500.00
Pineapple & Fan/Shepherd's Plaid, T2-123l, 16½", w/shade.......700.00
Plume, hand lamp, T2-99x...125.00
Riverside Ring & Rib, T2-111j, 8¼" 90.00
Roulette, allover design, T2-114a, 8½" 125.00
Shell & Dart, mold blown, sq base, T2-63i, 7⅞", from $175 to 275.00
Star Brooch, sq pressed base, T2-75h, 8", from $200 to...............300.00
Veronica, Hobbs plunger pressed, clinch connector, T3-110a, minimum ...175.00
Waffle & Thumbprint, wide flat base, T2-62a, 10⅛", from $175 to.............275.00

Peg Lamps

Col (3-layer), pk, cloverleaves, frosted peg/clear wafer, 4½" 440.00

Cranberry col, cylinder font, brass stem, marble, ft, 9", EX.........450.00
Cranberry w/frosted rubena cut shade, orig burner, 13" 315.00
Robin's egg bl shade & font w/emb decor, brass base, 15" 750.00
Yel swirl ribbed font & shade, brass candlestick, 21½"................460.00

Reverse-Painted Lamps

A&R Co, 18" trees/foliage/water hemisphere shade; scroll-emb std ...920.00
Classique, 6½" red roses/bl bows shade; gilt swirled/ribbed stem.........900.00
Jefferson, 14" hexagonal tree scenic shade; simple coppery base, 22" ...1,565.00
Jefferson, 16" flaring shade w/open top, comma shapes/circles; +base ...2,240.00
Jefferson, 18" daisy shade; 2-tone brn metal std w/appl decor, 24"...2,000.00
Jefferson, 18" trees/lake scene #8233; bronzed base w/shaped column...2,245.00
Jefferson (att), 14½" sailing ships shade; bronzed metal std, 21" 1,500.00
Moe Bridges, 8" palm tree/rock piles shade; hdld blk vase #62028 base .1,850.00
Moe Bridges, 18" shade w/temple ruins+2 more scenes; coppery vase base ..3,600.00
Phoenix, 16" trees/lake unmk shade; floral-emb base #1876, 22" ...1,035.00
Phoenix, 18" hillside woodland scene on cone shape; emb base 2,675.00
Pittsburgh, desk lamp, 9" L scenic shade; brass-finish base..........980.00
Pittsburgh, 7" snowy trees ribbed shade; metal std w/emb foliage, 14" 635.00

Pittsburgh (attributed), 8" shade with ducks, lake, and mountains; tree trunk-form standard with patinated metal base, 15½", $1,100.00.

Pittsburgh, 9" rib-molded shade w/figural scene; ribbed std/flared ft...1,400.00
Pittsburgh, 14" rose border shade w/6 butterflies; sq gold dore base 1,235.00
Pittsburgh, 16" band of roses on picket fence shade; wide emb ft...1,800.00
Pittsburgh, 16" swans/trees shade; base w/floral stem & flaring ft...3,300.00
Pittsburgh, 18" autumn leaf dome shade in red/gold; gilt vase std..3,000.00
Pittsburgh, 18" lake scene shade; melon rib base, 25" 2,800.00
Pittsburgh, 18" trees/mtns shade #1595; ornate ribbed patinated std........1,950.00
Pittsburgh, 23" shade w/Indian by stream (2X); Indian-motif base, 23"...5,600.00
Unmk, 6" scenic bell-form shade; VG weighted brass base, 13" 345.00
Unmk, 14" windmill/trees shade; vasiform base w/incised flowers #2500..1,000.00
Unmk, 16" moonlit winter/cabin scene shade; copper-finish columnar std....1,000.00
Unmk, 17" village/trees shade; matching glass base w/metal o/l, 24".......1,150.00
Unmk, 18" tree scene 6-reserve shade w/metal o/l; 4-reserve glass base ...1,450.00
Unmk, 18" winding road/mtns/trees shade w/metal o/l; ornate base, 22" ..1,200.00

Student Lamps, Kerosene

Brass, Apollo Duplex EM & Co, acorn-shaped fonts, 25" 990.00
Brass, dbl, rnd stepped base/urn stem, cased gr shades, electric, 23" ..875.00
Brass, Manhattan Brass Co, milk glass shade, electrified, 23" 325.00
NP, Cleveland Safety...1871, w/old milk glass shade, 20" 350.00

TV Lamps

When TV viewing became a popular pastime during the 1940s, TV lamps were developed to provide just the right amount of light — not bright enough to compromise the sharpness of the picture, but just enough to prevent the eyestrain it was feared might result from watching TV in a darkened room. Most were made of ceramic, and many were figurals such as cats, owls, ducks, and the like, or made in the shape of Conestoga wagons, sailing ships, seashells, etc. Some had shades and others were made as planters. Few were marked well enough to identify the maker without some study. *TV Lamps* by Tom Santiso (Collector Books) provides many photos and suggested value ranges for those who want more information.

All lamps listed below are ceramic unless otherwise described. See also Maddux; Morton Pottery; Rosemeade; other specific manufacturers.

Ballet dancer (male), pnt plaster/Fiberglas shade, Am Statuary, $65 to ... **85.00**
Bulldog w/flock coating, eyes glow, from $40 to **60.00**
Cats (2), brn airbrushed near-porc, eyes light up, Kron, from $75 to ... **100.00**
Coach (ornate), metal w/Fiberglas shade, 9", from $40 to **65.00**
Deco fawn w/planter, gr or brn, ceramic, from $50 to **75.00**
Deco horse head, blk w/wht-streaked mane, ceramic, from $50 to .. **75.00**
Doves (pr), airbrushed bl & wht, porc-like material, from $40 to .. **65.00**
Duck flying, brn & turq, ceramic w/wooden base, from $82 to **97.00**
Duck flying (mallard), w/planter, ceramic, Lane Co, from $65 to .. **90.00**
Horse & colt on grassy base, brn, ceramic, from $60 to **85.00**
Horses' heads (2) w/dbl planters, gr wash, ceramic, from $225 to .. **45.00**
Leaf, airbrushed plaster, from $35 to **55.00**
Madonna, airbrushed ceramic, from $60 to **85.00**
Oriental figures w/cart & pagoda, wht metal, from $50 to **75.00**
Oriental lady seated, bl w/mc/gold, plaster w/Fiberglas shade, $75 to .. **95.00**
Panther, blk, ceramic, w/removable Fiberglas shade, from $40 to . **65.00**
Panther crouching, w/planter, solid color (red rare), ceramic, $40 to .. **65.00**
Rooster w/rising sun, bl-gr, ceramic, from $95 to **125.00**
Sailing ship, ceramic w/metal sails, portholes light up, from $50 to ... **75.00**
Sailing ship, plaster w/airbrushed decor, from $50 to **75.00**
Sailing ship (Viking style), pnt plaster, from $50 to **75.00**
Stag (dying) & lg flower (light inside), airbrushed plaster, $75 to. **100.00**
Swan, gr ceramic, holes in wings light up, from $55 to **80.00**
Swordfish, gr or blk w/gold, ceramic, from $50 to **75.00**
Tower of Pisa, soapstone, lights inside, windows light up, $100 to ... **135.00**

Whale Oil/Burning Fluid Lamps

Clear, paneled font, early replacement burner, Sandwich, 1850s, 11x4½", $150.00.

Amethyst, Bigler, 8-sided std, sq base, #2097, 10", EX **2,100.00**
Bl opaque pressed Sunflower font, baluster stem, flat ft, 7⅝" **200.00**
Clambroth w/Star & Punty, stand lamp, pewter mts, 10", pr, EX **2,875.00**
Clear, cylinder font cut/frosted w/floral, ornate hollow stem, 10", pr .. **800.00**
Clear, free-blown elongated conical font, emb cup-plate base, 5½" **1,250.00**
Clear, free-blown font, hollow spiral-rib stem, plain base, 10", EX **2,500.00**
Clear, free-blown invt pear font w/cut panels, #2062, 11", pr, VG ... **375.00**

Clear, free-blown rnd font, short wine stem, saucer base, 5" **2,300.00**
Clear, free-blown teardrop font, emb stem, 8-sided lacy ft, 8½" **300.00**
Clear, free-blown urn-shape font, hollow stem w/wafer, saucer base, 4" . **700.00**
Clear, lacemaker's, invt pear font, hollow stem w/hdl, folded rim, 9" **250.00**
Clear, lacemaker's, stem w/expanded rings & hdls, folded rim on ft, 9" ... **350.00**
Clear, waisted Loop font, flaring hex base, 11", pr, EX **500.00**
Cobalt, Bigler, 8-sided std, sq base, #2097, 10", EX **2,150.00**
Cobalt, 4-printie block font, flaring hex base, #2104, 11", EX ... **2,500.00**
Col (2-layer), gr, clear hex base & std, #2358, 10", VG **300.00**
Lt bl, 3-printie, octagonal std, sq base, 10", EX, pr **1,880.00**
Pk/wht/clear, latticinio font w/wht & clear std, Sandwich, 10" ... **3,200.00**
Wht opal, Loop, hand lamp w/hdl, #2107, 3¼" **1,495.00**

Miscellaneous

Argand, blk posts/arm, stepped ft, vasiform top, complete, 14", pr .. **1,000.00**
Argand, brass, repolished/lacquered, imported by Morton, 16", pr .. **1,300.00**
Astral, cut/etch shade w/prisms on brass font, marble base, 22" **1,600.00**
Astral, etch shade w/vintage, sq wht marble base, brass column, 22" ... **245.00**
Austrian bronze, frog w/upstretched arms raised beaded/rtcl shade, 15" .. **4,115.00**
Bent slag 17" shade w/filigree village scene, ornate iron base, 22" **400.00**
Bent slag 22" shade w/filigree lattice & florals, gilt patina, 25" ... **575.00**
Floor, metal o/l 23" shade w/6 HP scenic panels, pine needle border ... **12,300.00**
Pittsburgh, 13" molded drapery shade w/etch flowers; fluted base, 20" ... **1,200.00**
Slag glass 12" shade/base w/intricate metal o/l, paw ft, 24" **690.00**
Slag glass/palm tree o/l; draped swags on gold/blk metal std, 24x18" **900.00**
Solar, brass font/ruby col stem/stepped marble ft/vine-cut shade, 24" .. **2,300.00**

Lang, Anton

Anton Lang (1875 – 1938) was a German studio potter and an actor in the Oberammergau Passion Plays early in the twentieth century. Because he played the role of Christ three times, tourists brought his pottery back to the U.S. in suitcases, which accounts for the prevalence of smaller examples today. During 1923 – 1924 Anton Lang and the other 'Passion Players' toured the U.S. selling their crafts. Lang would occasionally throw pottery when the cast passed through a pottery center such as Cincinnati, where Rookwood was located. The pots thrown at Rookwood are easy to identify as Lang hand signed the side of each piece and they have a 1924 Rookwood mark on the bottom. Lang visited the U.S. only once, and contrary to popular belief, he was never employed by Rookwood. His pottery, marked with his name in script, is fairly scarce and highly valued for its artistic quality. His son Karl (1903 – 1990), also a gifted potter, designed most of the Art Deco shapes and conducted glaze experiments. Only pieces bearing a hand-written signature (not a facsimile) are certain to be Anton Lang originals instead of the work of Karl or the Langs' assistants. Anton and Karl also made pieces together; Karl might design a piece and Anton decorate it. Postcards, programs, prints, and photographs depicting Lang are also collectible. Karl was managing the day-to-day operations of the pottery by 1934, and he continued to operate it as Anton Lang Pottery after his father's death in 1938. The pottery is now owned and operated by Karl's daughter, Barbara Lampe, who took over for her father in 1975. The facsimile 'Anton Lang' signature was used until 1995 when the name was changed to Barbara Lampe Pottery. Her mark is an interlocked 'BL' in a circle. Pieces with a facsimile signature and an interlocked 'UL' in a circle were made by Lampe's former husband, Uli Lampe, and date from 1975 to 1982. The 'Anton Lang' mark is not sharp on pieces made in 1975 and later. The bottoms are brick red clay with three lighter circular tripod marks. The later pieces are considerably heavier than the earlier work. Our advisor for this category is Clark Miller; he is listed in the Directory under Minnesota.

Cup, gr, 3¼" **25.00**
Ewer, floral emb on body, gr, 8x5" **75.00**
Ewer, turq w/yel int, twist hdl, 6½" **75.00**
Figurine, elephant, bl, 2¼x3¼" **90.00**
Figurine, pelican, mc, 5¾x9¾x6" **180.00**
Figurine, puppies sleeping, wht, 2¾x6¾" **115.00**
Lamp, mc Fulper-style glaze, 11x6" **200.00**
Medallion, bronze, Lang as Christ, 1924, 2x1½" **67.00**
Photo, Lang as Christ, autographed/inscribed, dtd 1900, 4½x6¾" .**37.50**
Photo, Lang as Jesus w/5 of his children, autographed, dtd 1930, 7x5" ..**92.50**
Photo, Lang in street clothes, autographed, 1900, 6½x4" **110.00**
Pin dish, Cross design, mc, script signature, ½x3" **45.00**
Pitcher, bl & brn fuzzy stripes on tan, 4" **22.50**
Plate, Lang as Christ, by Rosenthal, 1924 ....**22.50**
Postcard, Lang in street clothes, autographed, 1934 ....**8.00**
Stein, pewter lid, motto & flowers, bl & mc, 6x6½" **110.00**
Stereo card, Lang w/Henry Ford **40.00**
Time magazine, Lang on cover, December 12, 1923 ......**20.00**

Vase, blue with yellow flowers, hand signed, 15¾x6½", $1,250.00.
(Photo courtesy Clark Miller)

Vase, Greek Key band, red & gr on cobalt, sgn in script, 3" **200.00**
Vase, mc flowers, sgn in script, dtd 1910, 4¾" **265.00**
Vase, red-orange crystalline, 5½x5" **127.50**
Vase, yel triangle band on bl, sgn in script, 3½x2¾" **58.00**
Wall plaque, turq, 14½" **78.00**
Wall pocket, female face, mc, 4¾x3½" **50.00**
Wedding vase, hearts & flowers, mc on bl, 6¼x7" **155.00**

Le Verre Francais

Le Verre Francais was produced during the 1920s by Schneider at Epinay-sur-Seine in France. It was a commercial art glass in the cameo style composed of layered glass with the designs engraved by acid. Favored motifs were stylized leaves and flowers or geometric patterns. It was marked with the name in script or with an inlaid filigrane. Our advisor for this category is Don Williams; he is listed in the Directory under Missouri.

Cameo

Bowl, flowers/leaves, dk bl to orange on yel mottle, orange bun ft, 9" .**1,380.00**
Lamp, hanging; poppies, orange/brn on gray w/yel mottle, 11" bowl ...**2,300.00**
Pitcher, disks, red on orange/red mottle, blk serpent hdl, 13" ..**2,350.00**
Vase, berries/vines, burgundy/cranberry, slim/ftd, 15" **980.00**
Vase, butterflies, crimson/dk bl on gray w/turq mottle, hdls, 18" **6,670.00**
Vase, cascading fruit/leaves, brn/orange, invt trumpet w/bun ft, 18" ..**1,265.00**

Vase, columbine, cranberry to cobalt on wht/bl frost, ftd, 12" .**1,550.00**
Vase, florals & geometrics, brn on orange, dbl bulb, 6¾" **880.00**
Vase, flowering yucca plants, orange/brn on gray w/yel, bulbous, 16" .**4,370.00**
Vase, geometric leaves, bl-gray on orange, gourd shape, 8" **800.00**
Vase, leaves/beads/sprials, orange/amethyst on gray w/opal mottle, 11" **800.00**
Vase, lg leaves, amethyst w/bl mottle on gray w/amber streaks, 12½" **3,000.00**
Vase, orchids, red on yel & bl mottle, goblet form w/red ft, 10" **1,500.00**
Vase, poppies, red/brn on gray w/yel mottle, bulbous, flared rim, 10" .**1,600.00**
Vase, stylized asters, brn over orange mottle, ovoid w/bun ft, 8" .**690.00**
Vase, vertical floral 'ribs,' orange shoulder band on yel mottle, 15" ..**2,000.00**

Leeds, Leeds Type

The Leeds Pottery was established in 1758 in Yorkshire and under varied management produced fine creamware, often highly reticulated and transfer printed, shiny black-glazed Jackfield wares, polychromed pearlware, and figurines similar to those made in the Staffordshire area. Little of the early ware was marked; after 1775 the impressed 'Leeds Pottery' mark was used. From 1781 to 1820, the name 'Hartley Greens & Co.' was added. The pottery closed in 1898.

Today the term 'Leeds' has become generic and is used to encompass all polychromed pearlware and creamware, wherever its origin. Thus similar wares of other potters (Wood for instance) is often incorrectly called 'Leeds.' Unless a piece is marked or can be definitely attributed to Leeds by confirming the pattern to be authentic, 'Leeds-Type' would be a more accurate nomenclature.

Key:
cw — creamware   pw — pearlware

Bowl, roses, bl/yel w/gold buds & gr & brn leaves, int: gold bud, 7" ...**550.00**
Charger, lg yel urn w/2 hdls & brn swags holding mc flowers, 15", NM ..**1,265.00**
Coffeepot, pw, Oriental brn transfer, dome lid, 11", EX **210.00**
Creamer, tulip, yel w/brn & gr, umber/gr sprigs, brn stripe **795.00**
Figurine, horse, short docked tail, brn w/wht saddle, on base, 5", NM ..**4,000.00**
Figurine, pw, wht lamb w/brn legs etc on lt gr base, 3½" L, VG **165.00**
Figurine, pw, woman as Spring, minor wear, 4¼" **110.00**
Figurine, seated dog, pw, brn/gold spots, 3¼x2⅞", EX **500.00**
Plate, peafowl in tree, bl/gold/yel w/gr leaves, 7", NM **495.00**
Plate, peafowl in tree, bl/gold/yel w/gr leaves, 10" **650.00**
Plate, peafowl on tree branch, 6-color, gr feather edge, 9½" **1,700.00**
Sugar bowl, pw, 2 3-color narrow bands, hexagonal, swan finial, 6", EX ..**385.00**
Tea bowl & saucer, floral swags/4-color, brn rim band, VG **135.00**
Tea bowl & saucer, pw, floral, gold w/gr & brn leaves, mini **275.00**
Tea bowl & saucer, pw, peafowl, bl/gold/yel, on branch, rpr, mini **190.00**
Tea bowl & saucer, 4-color floral, brushed crescent mk **220.00**
Teapot, Oriental figures in reserve, cell bkground, 7½", VG **585.00**
Teapot, pw, gaudy bl floral, 7½" **300.00**
Waste bowl, bl band w/4-color leaves, 3x4" **110.00**
Waste bowl, gr/gold leaves w/bl, hairlines/stains, 6" **110.00**

Lefton China

The Lefton China Company was the creation of Mr. George Zoltan Lefton who migrated to the United States from Hungary in 1939. In 1941 he embarked on a new career and began shaping a business that sprang from his passion for collecting fine china and porcelains. Though his funds were very limited, his vision was to develop a source from which to obtain fine porcelains by reviving the postwar Japanese ceramic industry, which dated back to antiquity. As a trailblazer, George Zoltan Lefton soon earned the reputation as 'The China King.'

Counted among the most desirable and sought-after collectibles of today, Lefton items such as Bluebirds, Miss Priss, Angels, all types of dinnerware and tea-related items are eagerly acquired by collectors. As is true with any antique or collectible, prices may vary, dependent on location, condition, and availability. For additional information on the history of Lefton China, its factories, marks, products, and values, readers should consult the *Collector's Encyclopedia of Lefton China, Books I, II,* and *III,* and *Lefton Price Guide* by our advisor, Loretta DeLozier, who is listed in the Directory under Florida. All are published by Collector Books.

Ashtray, milk china w/appl roses, 2 rest, #844, 3½", from $12 to..........**15.00**
Ashtray, wht porc w/appl bird & flowers, oval, #262, 5", from $25 to..**30.00**
Bank, lion wearing glasses, #13384, 6", from $52 to **58.00**
Bell, appl Forget-Me-Nots on pk, #8293, 3", from $25 to.............**30.00**
Bell, figures in relief, bsk w/brn wash, #295, 5½", from $14 to.........**18.00**
Bell, Green Holly, #787, 3½", from $13 to.....................................**18.00**
Bowl, Green Holly, sleigh form, #1346, 8", from $45 to **55.00**
Bowl, pastel gr bsk w/appl roses, ftd, #773, 9¼", from $240 to........**280.00**
Box, Spring Bouquet, hinged lid, rnd or sq, #8134, 4", from $40 to..**50.00**
Butter dish, Pear N Apple, #2739, 7½", from $12 to **15.00**
Cake plate, Green Heritage (roses), #719, 7¼", from $22 to **28.00**
Candle holder, Christmas angel votive, #5286, 4", from $7 to......**10.00**
Candle holders, Green Holly, #717, pr, from $25 to **30.00**
Candle holders, lily form, #2499, 3¾", pr, from $25 to...............**30.00**
Candle holders, milk china w/appl roses at base, #825, 4", pr, $55 to...**65.00**
Candle holders, pk china w/sponge gold & Lily of the Valley, #285, pr...**58.00**
Candy basket, pk porc w/appl roses, center hdl, #2085, 6", $45 to ...**50.00**
Candy box, egg shape w/roses decals, #2209, 5½", from $25 to........**30.00**
Canister, Harvest Pansy, #7975, 10", from $45 to **55.00**
Canisters, Pear N Apple, #4131, 4-pc, from $85 to **95.00**
Cheese dish, Miss Priss, #1505, 5½", from $200 to......................**225.00**
Child's set, Miss Priss, bowl & mug, #3553, from $90 to **110.00**
Coaster, Festival (grapes), #2630, 3½", from $3 to........................**5.00**
Coffeepot, Magnolia, #2518, 5-cup, from $125 to **165.00**
Compote, Heavenly Rose, rtcl rim & ft, #109, 7", from $32 to.....**38.00**
Compote, Mardi Gras, appl floral, ftd, #20438, 5½", $95 ....**105.00**
Cookie jar, Dainty Miss, #040, 7½", from $150 to.......................**200.00**
Cookie jar, White Holly, #6054, 7½", from $85 to.......................**105.00**
Creamer & sugar bowl, Miss Priss, hat lid, #1508, from $55 to.....**65.00**
Creamer & sugar bowl, Poinsettia, #4384, w/lid, from $45 to **55.00**
Creamer & sugar bowl, Rose Chintz, w/lid, #663, from $30 to **40.00**
Creamer & sugar bowl, Violet Chintz, w/lid, #661, from $60 to ...**70.00**
Cup & saucer, demi; floral reserves on gr w/gold, #801, from $25 to .**30.00**
Cup & saucer, Elegant Rose, ftd, #2125, from $30 to **35.00**
Cup & saucer, Green Heritage (roses), #3067, from $25 to...........**30.00**
Egg cup, Golden Wheat, #20121, 3", from $15 to **20.00**
Figurine, angel climber, #389, 4", from $30 to **35.00**
Figurine, Angel of the month - April, #1987, 3", from $45 to **55.00**
Figurine, Colonial lady w/basket, #869, 8", from $80 to **90.00**

Figurine, Fifi (lady), ruffled gown/umbrella, #5742, 7½", $120 to.......**150.00**
Figurine, French lady, Dubonnet w/stones, #10337, 6", from $65 to **75.00**
Figurine, girl in bonnet & apron, #5153, 5½", from $15 to...........**20.00**
Figurine, girl w/flower basket, fine pnt details, #5050, 6¾" **50.00**
Figurine, girl w/hat & stole, gold trim, #461, 6¼", from $70 to..........**80.00**
Figurine, goldfinch, naturalistic base, #395, 5", from $25 to..........**35.00**
Figurine, heron on leafy base, #1532, 5½", from $45 to **55.00**
Figurine, January, flower girl of the month, #985, 5", from $28 to...**32.00**
Figurine, Kewpie, 3 poses, bsk, #228, 4½", ea from $40 to **50.00**
Figurine, Kewpie of the month - January, #130, 4½", from $35 to........**40.00**
Figurine, lion, realistic, 1 paw raised, #7286, 7", from $13 to..........**18.00**
Figurine, Madonna bust, lace-trim head covering, glazed, #3207, 4½".........**20.00**
Figurine, Madonna w/Child, #1416, 7", from $70 to **80.00**
Figurine, Napoleon on horse, #4908, 11", from $285 to.................**315.00**
Figurine, pheasant, realistic, #670, 8¼", from $30 to....................**35.00**
Figurine, Pinkie (girl) and Blue Boy, glazed, #3049, 8", pr, $90 to..........**120.00**
Figurine, Provincial man/lady, flower baskets, #4141, 12", pr, $400 to....**450.00**
Figurine, Pussy Cat Pussy Cat, girl w/blk cat, #1474, 4½", $55 to.........**75.00**
Figurine, rooster w/long tail, on stump, #1057, 10", from $125 to.......**145.00**
Figurine, squirrel, realistic, bsk, #4749, 5", from $35 to **38.00**
Flower holder, hand holding fan, wht china w/roses, #282, $95 to ..**105.00**
Jam jar, grapes on leaf, #3023, 4", from $30 to **40.00**
Lamp, Elegant Rose, #931, 13½", from $125 to **175.00**
Lipstick holder, French Rose, #3381, 3¼" dia, from $9 to.............**11.00**
Mug, Blue Aster, #6496, 4", from $8 to **10.00**
Mug, George Washington, hat feather forms hdl, #1110, 4¼", $35 to..........**45.00**
Mug, Rustic Daisy, gr hdl, #4468, 3¾", from $8 to........................**12.00**
Picture frame, appl cherubs, oval, #7221, 7¼", from $65 to...........**75.00**
Picture frame, w/appl roses & rhinestones, #90511, 4", from $16 to ..**20.00**
Pin box, heart shape, appl flowers on lid, pastels, #2443, 2½" **40.00**
Pitcher, Mushroom Forest, #6466, 6¾", from $19 to.....................**21.00**
Pitcher & bowl, Forget-Me-Not, #4189, 5½", 7¼", from $35 to **45.00**
Planter, ivory bsk w/brn wash, ftd, #722, 5", from $18 to **20.00**
Planter, peacock w/tail down, mc matt, #892, 6½", from $32 to........**38.00**
Planter, Santa w/bag, #3656, 8", from $23 to **27.00**
Planter, violin form w/appl flowers, #1734, 7¼", from $15 to **18.00**
Plaque, fruit, rtcl decor at rim w/gold, #268, 8", from $15 to........**18.00**
Plaque, To Mother, w/roses, rtcl hearts at rim, #508, 7¾", $18 to.........**22.00**
Plate, Blue Paisley, #2337, 9¼", from $20 to.................................**25.00**
Plate, Christmas tree, #1096, 8", from $28 to.................................**32.00**
Shakers, Brown Heritage (roses), #613, 2¾", pr, from $25 to........**30.00**
Shakers, dog w/rhinestone eyes, #30404, 3", pr, from $18 to.........**22.00**
Shakers, Fruit Basket, #1657, 2¾", pr, from $22 to.......................**28.00**
Shakers, Green Holly, #1353, pr, from $22 to................................**28.00**
Shakers, Rustic Daisy, #3857, 3¼", pr, from $12 to **15.00**
Snack set, Wheat, #2768, 8", from $10 to......................................**12.00**
Tea bag holder, Blue Paisley, #2354, from $15 to..........................**20.00**
Tea set, Dresden-type roses, stacking pot+cr/sug, #985, 3-pc, $150 to...**165.00**
Teapot, Green Heritage (roses), #792, 6-cup, from $130 to **165.00**
Teapot, Green Holly, #1357, 6-cup, from $75 to............................**85.00**
Teapot, Heirloom Rose, #1075, from $145 to **185.00**
Teapot, Miss Priss, #1516, from $145 to **195.00**
Tidbit tray, Crimson Rose, metal center hdl, #651, from $14 to ...**18.00**
Tidbit tray, Holly Garland, center metal hdl, #2094, from $20 to..**25.00**
Toothbrush holder, French Rose, holds 4, #2646, 3¾", from $15 to........**20.00**
Vase, bud; wht bsk w/appl flowers, #1847, 4", from $13 to...........**17.00**
Vase, cherubs support lg flower, pearlized bsk, #924, 10", $800 to......**950.00**
Vase, child by tree trunk, birds/nest at top, pastel bsk, #970, 6½".......**120.00**
Vase, egg form w/appl flowers & ft, #4342, 4½", from $9 to..........**12.00**
Vase, ewer form w/appl fruit, #7363, 7½", from $45 to..................**50.00**
Vase, Forget-Me-Not trim, #7295, 7", from $80 to **90.00**
Vase, pineapple form w/appl pk roses, #7283, 5", from $60 to........**70.00**
Vase, pitcher form w/appl flowers, #4209, 7", from $22 to.............**24.00**
Wall pocket, Dainty Miss, #6767, 5", from $95 to **125.00**

Figurines, Colonial man and woman, painted bisque, #337, 10", $350.00 for the pair.

(Photo courtesy Loretta DeLozier)

Legras

Legras and Cie was founded in St. Denis, France, in 1864. Production continued until the 1930s. In addition to their enameled wares, they made cameo art glass decorated with outdoor scenes and florals executed by acid cuttings through two to six layers of glass. Their work is signed 'Legras' in relief and in enamel. Our advisor for this category is Don Williams; he is listed in the Directory under Missouri.

Cameo

Vase, floral, gr on pk to gr 'chipped ice,' slim, 7" 375.00
Vase, fruit/leaves on trailing vines, gr on yel/rose, onion base, 24" ..2,645.00
Vase, grapes/vines on cream, 22" 700.00
Vase, lake/woodland, gr/bl on orange, 9" 750.00
Vase, leafy branches, burgundy enamel on textured clear, ovoid, 11" .500.00
Vase, lg trees/lake, cut/gr enameled on gray w/pk hues, cylinder, 8" 485.00
Vase, seaweed, cut/pnt on gray to mauve, cylinder w/bulb base, 14"...635.00
Vase, tall trees above forest/lake, gr on rose amber, 24", pr 4,000.00
Vase, triangles made of 4 sm triangles, crimson on clear texture, 11"...545.00
Vase, underwater plants on gray to mauve, flaring sides, 14".......800.00

Miscellaneous

Vase, pk to gr w/HP purple violets, angle shoulder/bun base, 4", pr....430.00
Vase, winter trees/snow, HP, concave, 4-sided, slim, 13¾" 230.00
Vase, winter trees/snow/figure/cabin, HP, unmk, 13¼", pr 375.00

Lenox

Walter Scott Lenox, former art director at Ott and Brewer, and Jonathan Coxon founded The Ceramic Art Company of Trenton, New Jersey, in 1889. By 1906 Cox had left the company, and to reflect the change in ownership, the name was changed to Lenox Inc. Until 1930 when the production of American-made Belleek came to an end, they continued to produce the same type of high-quality ornamental wares that Lenox and Coxon had learned to master while in the employ of Ott and Brewer. Their superior dinnerware made the company famous, and since 1917 Lenox has been chosen the official White House China. Our advisor for this category is Mary Frank Gaston. See also Ceramic Art Company.

Basket vase, Lenox Rose J300, #81, ca 1930-52, 5x6¾" 135.00
Bowl, fruit; Imperial, gold trim........................25.00
Bowl, fruit/dessert; Arcadia R311........................32.00
Bowl, fruit/dessert; Hadley, 1¾x5¾"........................30.00
Bowl, fruit/dessert; Noblesse........................40.00
Bowl, oval vegetable; Alaris, lg........................125.00
Bowl, oval vegetable; Royal Peony, 10¼"........................145.00
Bowl, oval vegetable; Wind Chimes, lg........................75.00
Bowl, rim soup; Winslow Castle, 8¼"........................85.00
Coffeepot, Alaris 175.00
Coffeepot, Fire Flower 45.00
Coffeepot, Versailles........................250.00
Cream soup & saucer, Ming 55.00
Cream soup & saucer, Royal Peony 90.00
Creamer, Castle Garden 90.00
Creamer, Fair Lady 100.00
Cup & saucer, Adrienne........................35.00
Cup & saucer, Brookdale, platinum trim 50.00
Cup & saucer, Clarion........................55.00
Cup & saucer, Desire 35.00
Cup & saucer, Ebony Rose 32.00

Cup & saucer, Fair Lady 60.00
Cup & saucer, Forever 40.00
Cup & saucer, Imperial, gold trim........................30.00
Cup & saucer, Interlude 50.00
Cup & saucer, Mandarin 40.00
Cup & saucer, Meadow Song 42.00
Cup & saucer, Summer Wind 12.50
Cup & saucer, Versailles........................55.00
Cup & saucer, Winslow Castle........................85.00
Gravy boat, Patriot, w/attached tray........................195.00
Jug, golfing scene, belleek, mk CAC/Lenox, sterling silver cap, 6x5" ...4,175.00
Pepper mill, Lido, 7"........................70.00
Plate, bread & butter; Alaris........................20.00
Plate, bread & butter; Castle Garden 22.00
Plate, bread & butter; Forever........................16.00
Plate, bread & butter; Imperial 14.00
Plate, bread & butter; Meadow Song........................20.00
Plate, bread & butter; Rhythm........................16.00
Plate, bread & butter; Wind Chimes 8.00
Plate, dinner; Autumn, gr bkstamp........................48.00
Plate, dinner; Brookdale, platinum trim 65.00
Plate, dinner; Castle Garden 38.00
Plate, dinner; Cinderella 22.50
Plate, dinner; Clarion 55.00
Plate, dinner; Desire 30.00
Plate, dinner; Ebony Rose 30.00
Plate, dinner; Heiress........................34.00
Plate, dinner; Meadow Song 40.00
Plate, dinner; Ming 50.00
Plate, dinner; Repertoire 40.00
Plate, dinner; Serenade........................40.00
Plate, dinner; Snow Lily 50.00
Plate, dinner; Summer Wind........................20.00
Plate, dinner; Tea Garden 22.00
Plate, luncheon; Mandarin 35.00
Plate, salad; Arcadia R311 ....29.00
Plate, salad; Clarion........................30.00
Plate, salad; Hadley........................20.00
Plate, salad; Interlude 32.00
Plate, salad; Ming 12.00
Plate, salad; Prairie Blossoms........................15.00
Plate, salad; Snow Lily........................16.00
Plate, salad; Versailles........................32.00
Platter, Fair Lady, oval, 16"........................225.00
Platter, Hadley, 13¾"........................95.00
Platter, Heiress, 13½"........................165.00
Platter, Interlude, 16¼"........................185.00
Platter, Noblesse, 16"........................200.00
Shakers, Georgian Shell, pr........................70.00
Sugar bowl, Castle Garden, w/lid........................110.00
Sugar bowl, Mandarin, w/lid........................80.00
Sugar bowl, Royal Peony, w/lid........................100.00
Vase, birds & flowers on creamy wht w/gold, globular, 7¼x8"........................125.00
Vase, birds & flowers on wht cylinder, sgn, #1718, ca 1906-16, 10x3" ...250.00
Vase, cornucopia; Lenox Rose J300, #70, ca 1934-52, 4¾" 105.00
Vase, Deco shape w/emb linear design, cream bsk, 1906-30 mk, 11"..185.00
Vase, HP classical ladies in landscape, prof decor, gold hdls, 10"...600.00
Vase, HP florals & 24k gold, 1987 Mother's Day ltd ed, 6½"........75.00
Vase, pillow; celadon gr, 1960s, 6½x10x2⅛"........................110.00
Vase, Regal, cream, fluted rim, gold trim, post-1952, 8¾"..........250.00
Vase, shepherdess & sheep, Mt St Vincent written on bk, prof decor, 8" ..500.00
Vase, springer spaniel portrait on wht, sgn Baker, 8¼"................550.00
Vase, wht classic shape w/floral relief & emb ribs, gold stamp, 7½".........30.00
Vase, yel, flared rim, ca 1906-30 mk, 8½x7¼"........................275.00

Letter Openers

Made in a wide variety of materials and designs, letter openers make an interesting collection, easy to display and easy on the budget as well. For further information we recommend *Collector's Guide to Letter Openers, Identification & Values*, by Everett Grist (Collector Books); Mr. Grist is listed in the Directory under Tennessee.

Brass, eagle (wings wide) hdl, mk 7-46 Virginia Metal Crafters **20.00**
Brass, eagle w/cornucopia hdl, antiqued finish **15.00**
Brass, grasshopper 3-D paperweight hdl, shiny **20.00**
Brass, hammered hdl w/2 rivets **6.00**
Brass, lizard figural, tail is blade, antiqued finish, mk China **10.00**
Brass, owl on perch figural hdl, ring for hanging, shiny **10.00**
Brass, red-pnt floral on sleek design, mk India **6.00**
Brass, stag hdl, shiny..**12.00**
Brass w/Bakelite & aluminum wire inlay, stainless blade, mk........**45.00**
Brass w/enameled flowers, China **15.00**
Bronze, rampant lion w/scepter, royal seal, old patina....................**10.00**
Bronze-colored metal, pelican hdl, stainless blade, Gulf Shores **8.00**
Copper, Scottie hdl, State Capitol Atlanta GA............................**10.00**
Copper-colored metal, rifle form, Washington DC **8.00**
Copper-colored metal, stag w/tree hdl, Cherokee Reservation, Japan...**10.00**
Gold-color metal, dagger form, Home of FDR, Hyde Park NY........**6.00**
Gold-plated metal, jeweled hdl **8.00**
Ivory, cvd crocodile figural **85.00**
Leather hdl w/gold stamping, mk Italy..**6.00**
Lucite, liquid-filled w/shells/seaweed/sea horse, FL souvenir **15.00**
Lucite hdl w/reverse-cvd/pnt fish, Golf Shores AL **15.00**
Magnifier, clear w/red plastic sheath, also ruler, Bausch & Lomb....**3.00**
Magnifier, red plastic w/brass shield, Annapolis, mk SP, Made in USA..**6.00**
MOP hdl w/HP orange & blossoms, metal blade, FL souvenir **15.00**
Onyx hdl w/brass blade, Penn Turnpike, mk Germany.................**10.00**
Pewter & brass, curved dagger shape, Carnival, New Orleans, Rex 1902...**20.00**
Pewter & steel, fish hdl, w/clipper & file, MO shield w/mule **10.00**
Pewter plate, buffalo hdl, sm, M **10.00**
Plastic, Aztec god (gr) inset in wht..**4.00**
Plastic, red & wht hdl w/steel blade, Italy **4.00**
Plastic, thunderbird hdl, brilliant turq, sm..**3.00**
Plastic & brass, pen & magnifier, Laguna Beach souvenir..............**12.00**
Silver, dagger, mk Silver, sm..**20.00**
SP, Pella IA souvenir **6.00**
SP, souvenir of Natches MS, Rosalie..**8.00**
Steel, Olympic torch hdl **5.00**
Steel, pen knife hdl, Harry Hall, Tailords ad, Cheapside **30.00**
Tortoise shell, 3-D bird's claw w/movable tortoise marble, Victorian ...**125.00**
Wood, HP flowers, souvenir **20.00**
Wood, needlepoint look **15.00**

Libbey

The New England Glass Company was established in 1818 in Boston, Massachusetts. In 1892 it became known as the Libbey Glass Company. At Chicago's Columbian Expo in 1893, Libbey set up a ten-pot furnace and made glass souvenirs. The display brought them worldwide fame. Between 1878 and 1918, Libbey made exquisite cut and faceted glass, considered today to be the best from the brilliant period. The company is credited for several innovations — the Owens bottle machine that made mass production possible and the Westlake machine which turned out both electric light bulbs and tumblers automatically. They developed a machine to polish the rims of their tumblers in such a way that chipping was unlikely to occur. Their glassware carried the patented Safedge guar-

antee. Libbey also made glassware in numerous colors, among them cobalt, ruby, pink, green, and amber. Our advisors for this category are Don and Anne Kier; they are listed in the Directory under Ohio.

Bottle, water; cut, Imperial **300.00**
Bowl, cut, Hobstar, 9" **125.00**
Bowl, cut, Hobstar & Fan, 6-petal notched rim, 8", EX **135.00**
Bowl, nappy; cut, Heart, 7" **200.00**
Compote, amberina, 4½x6" **985.00**
Compote, cut, Colonna, 5½x10" **450.00**
Compote, cut, gr to clear, 8x7" **575.00**
Cruet, cut, Hobstar & X-cut Dmn, 6" **150.00**
Decanter, Spillane, w/stopper & St Louis dmn strap hdl, 8½x5¾" **510.00**
Dish, Columbus' ship Santa Maria, 1893 expo souvenir, 6½"........**595.00**
Jug, milk; cut, Venetia, 2-qt, 7" **425.00**
Maize, bowl, gr husks on wht opaque, 4x8¾" **275.00**
Maize, butter dish, bl husks on irid **650.00**
Maize, butter dish, bl husks w/gold outlines, 6½x7" **1,000.00**
Maize, butter dish, gr husks on custard **165.00**
Maize, celery vase, gold-tipped gr husks on oyster-wht, 6½" **265.00**
Maize, celery vase, gr husks on custard **200.00**
Maize, celery vase, lt gold irid on clear, 6⅝" **185.00**
Maize, condiment set, gr husks on custard, 3-pc, +tray w/metal lid...**565.00**
Maize, pickle castor, amber stain **595.00**
Maize, pickle castor, gr husks on custard, SP fr **495.00**
Maize, pitcher, gold-yel husks on wht, 8¾x5½" **525.00**
Maize, shakers, bl husks w/gold edge on custard, pr **200.00**
Maize, sugar shaker, gold husks on oyster-wht, 5½" **335.00**
Maize, sugar shaker, gold-tipped gr husks on oyster-wht, 5½"........**485.00**
Maize, syrup, gold irid cob, bl husks, pewter lid, 6".....................**600.00**

Maize, syrup, pewter top, green husks on custard, 7½", $350.00. (Photo courtesy John A. Shuman III)

Maize, toothpick holder, gr husks w/gold edge on custard **345.00**
Maize, tumbler, bl husks on gold irid...**110.00**
Maize, tumbler, bl husks on irid..**135.00**
Maize, tumbler, gr husks on irid **175.00**
Maize, vase, yel/gold husks on custard, 6½" **210.00**
Parfait, ribbed, crystal w/int draped lime gr threading, Nash, 4¾" **135.00**
Stem, champagne flute; bear, wht opal, 5½"...................................**185.00**
Stem, champagne; squirrel, wht opal, 6" **165.00**
Stem, claret; bear, blk, 5½" **155.00**
Stem, cordial; Embassy, tall **100.00**
Stem, cordial; monkey, wht opal, 5" **145.00**
Stem, cordial; whippet/greyhound, wht opal **175.00**
Stem, goblet; cat, wht opal **200.00**
Stem, goblet; monkey, wht opal, 1930s **180.00**
Stem, iced tea; cut, Artic Rose, 6⅜"...**25.00**
Stem, iced tea; Halifax, 6⅜" **15.00**
Stem, sherbet; squirrel, wht opal, 4" **150.00**

Stem, wine; giraffe, wht opal, 6" 120.00
Stem, wine; kangaroo, wht opal.................................230.00
Stem, wine; monkey, frosted, 5" 85.00
Tray, cut, Neola, 12" 2,000.00
Tray, ice cream; Anita, scalloped edges, 2¼x11½x7¾"....265.00
Tray, Senora, 12" dia 875.00
Tumbler, amberina, 2" 175.00
Tumbler, Colonna, hobnails/fans/stars, 3⅞" 95.00
Vase, amberina, onion form on tall slim stem, 10½".......1,550.00
Vase, bud; amberina, lt ribbing, 11½" 900.00
Vase, floral intaglio, 14x4⅞" 200.00
Vase, Jack-in-pulpit; amberina, #3000, 10x6" 2,450.00
Water set, cut, geometric floral, 8½" jug+4 3¾" tumblers.............625.00

Lightning Rod Balls

Used as ornaments on lightning rods, the vast majority of these balls were made of glass, but ceramic examples can be found as well. Their average diameter is 4½", but it can vary from 3½" up to 5½". Only a few of the available pattern-and-color combinations are listed here. The most common measure 4½" and are found in sun-colored amethyst and milk glass. Some patterns are being reproduced without marking them as such, and some new patterns are available as well. Collectors are cautioned to look for signs of age (stains) and/or to learn more before investing in a 'rare' lightning rod ball. Our advisor is Rod Krupka, author of a book on this subject. Anyone interested in his book may write to him for more information; he is listed in the directory under Michigan.

Amber, Doorknob, faint stain, 4¼x4" 110.00
Amber, Shinn-Belted, emb Mfg Co, copper caps, 5x4⅜" 95.00
Blue opaque, Mast, EX collars, 5¾x5" 125.00
Blue opaque, plain rnd, 3½" 30.00
Clear, Dodd & Struthers, faint stain, copper end caps................80.00
Cobalt, Pleat-Round, copper end caps, 5x4½" 120.00
Gold mercury, plain rnd, orig cube/caps, 5¼x5" 125.00
Gray-green, Ribbed Grape, aluminum caps, 5x4⅜" 350.00
Green opaque, plain rnd, 5½x4½" 85.00
Green opaque, Ribbed Grape, aluminum caps, strong color, 5x4⅜".....130.00
Milk glass, Chestnut, aluminum caps..............................30.00
Milk glass, Electra Cone (boldly emb), 5x4½" 40.00
Milk glass, Moon & Star, 5x4½"..................................42.50
Red flashed, SLRCo, short wide collar 100.00
Root beer, unemb (Dodd & Struthers), bubbly glass, rare...........225.00
Rust-orange, Hawkeye, old aluminum caps, 5¼x4½"............800.00
Silver mercury, National, rnd, correct tube/caps, 5x4½" 400.00
Sun-colored amethyst, Electra Round, 5x4¾"...................75.00
Sun-colored amethyst, plain rnd, 5½x4½" 25.00

Limbert

Charles P. Limbert formed his firm in 1894 in America's furniture capital, Grand Rapids, Michigan, and from 1902 until 1918, produced a line of Arts & Crafts furniture. While his wide-ranging line of furniture is not as uniformly successful as Gustav Stickley, the Limbert pieces that do exhibit design excellence stand among the best of American Arts & Crafts examples. Pieces featuring cutouts, exposed construction elements (e.g., key and tenon), metal and ebonized wood inlays, and asymmmetric forms are among the most desirable. Less desirable are the firm's Outdoor Designs that show exposed metal screws and straight grain, as opposed to quarter-sawn oak boards. His most aesthetically successful forms mimic those of Charles Rennie Mackintosh (Scotland) and, to a lesser extent, Joseph Hoffmann (Austria). Usually signed with a rectan-

gular mark (as a paper label, branded in the wood, or as a metal tag) showing a man planing wood, and with the words Limbert's Arts Craft Furniture Made in Grand Rapids and Holland. The firm continued to produce furniture until 1944. Currently, only his Arts & Crafts style furniture holds any interest among collectors.

Please note: Furniture that has been cleaned or refinished is worth less than if its original finish has been retained. Our advisor for this and related Arts & Crafts objects is Bruce A. Austin; he is listed in the Directory under New York.

Key: b — brand

Armchair, flat arms w/corbels, scooped apron, oversz, wear, 33x32x34" .2,700.00
Armchair, inlaid mission bell/geometrics, drop-in seat, 41x28x26" 4,750.00
Bench, Inglenook, lift seat, leather uphl, overcoated/wear, 47x48x20"...1,500.00
Bookcase, #321, 2-door, leaded glass at top of ea, keyed tenons, 54" 4,250.00
Bookcase, #343, 2-doors w/single mullon on ea, open shelf ea side, rfn..2,600.00
Bookcase, 2 glazed doors, ea over 3 adjustable shelves, 58x41" ..2,600.00
Chair, side; arched crest & bk panel w/ebony inlay, cane seat, b, 39" ..1,100.00
Chair, side; like #811, arched crest over 2 vertical slats, unmk, pr 400.00
Chairs, side; 1 vertical bkslat, tacked-on leathers, set of 4.......1,400.00
Chest, #487¼, 5-drw, arched toebrd, thru tenons, 50x36x20" 2,100.00
China cabinet, #1308, 2-over-3 pane doors, 1 per side, 3-shelf, 56x31"...3,250.00
China cabinet, #1463, single door, orig hdw, 58x32x15" 1,100.00
China cabinet, 3 glass panes over lg pane, open shelf ea side, 59x45"...5,500.00
Desk, inlaid dk sqs/caned panels, drw, rfn/chips, 35x36x20", +chair 2,200.00
Desk, overhanging 36x24" top, 1-drw w/copper drops, VG......1,000.00
Desk, postcard; dbl, trn posts, owl-motif slag shade, rfn, 66x36x40" .8,000.00
Footstool, cricket; #200, central cutout, flared ft, b, 1906-18, 18" 350.00

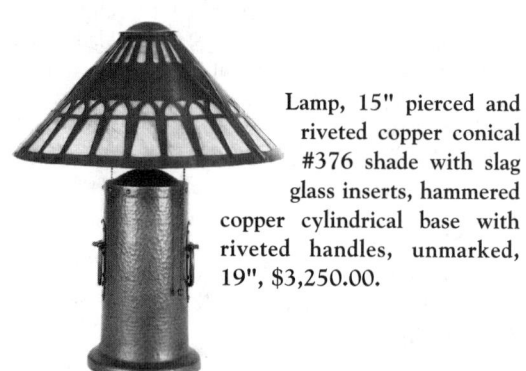

Lamp, 15" pierced and riveted copper conical #376 shade with slag glass inserts, hammered copper cylindrical base with riveted handles, unmarked, 19", $3,250.00.

Lamp, 23" 6-panel floral o/l slag shade; 6-side bottle form copper std ...3,750.00
Plant stand, 4 flaring sides w/oval cutouts, shelf, 30x20" sq 6,000.00
Rocker, #644, curved rail, flat arms, seat missing, b, 39" 1,100.00
Settle, #880, drop arms, 8-slat bk, partial rfn, b, 40x80x30" 1,800.00
Sideboard, #459 (similar), orig copper hdw, 42x54x21", VG...1,900.00
Stool, tacked-on brn canvas top, drw, arched apron, 13x18x12", VG...1,100.00
Table, #172, corbelled, drw at ends, orig hdw, 29x46x34"........3,000.00
Table, arched stretchers mortised through tapered posts, rfn, 42" dia ..1,300.00
Table, dining; 54" dia top on 4-sided ped base, heavy overcoat............2,000.00
Table, lamp; #148, oak, X base w/sq cutouts, rfn, unmk, 30" dia...............2,350.00
Table, library; #106, 2-tiered open shelves ea end, drw, b, 29½x48".........1,100.00
Table, library; oval 45x40" top, arched aprons, sq side cutouts, rfn...1,500.00
Table, library; overhanging 60x32" top, 3-drw, copper pulls 1,600.00
Table, library; tacked-on 42x26" naugahyde top, 3 sm corbels ea side......950.00
Table, library; 2-drw, long corbels/wide shelf, 48x34" top, worn/chips ..1,200.00
Table, pagoda style, 34" sq w/2 sq cutouts ea side of base, overcoated...12,000.00
Table, side; overhanging 30x22" top, arched apron, rfn, VG 900.00
Table, 18½" dia top, tapered posts, sq shelf, rfn, 22" 950.00
Table, 4 18x16½" sides, ea w/2 sq cutouts, overhanging top 2,300.00

Limited Edition Plates

Current values of some limited edition plates have risen, while many others have fallen. Prices charged by plate dealers in the secondary market vary greatly; we have tried to suggest an average.

Since Goebel Hummel plates have been discontinued, values have started to decline. While those who are trying to complete the series continue to buy them, few seem interested in starting a collection. As for the Danish plates, Royal Copenhagen and Bing and Grondahl, more purchases are for plates that commemorate the birth year of a child or a wedding anniversary than to add to a collection.

Bing and Grondahl

1895, Behind the Frozen Window	6,250.00
1896, New Moon	2,300.00
1897, Christmas Meal of Sparrows	1,500.00
1898, Roses & Star	850.00
1899, Crows Enjoying Christmas	1,800.00
1900, Church Bells Chiming	1,000.00
1901, 3 Wise Men	450.00
1902, Gothic Church Interior	375.00
1903, Expectant Children	350.00
1904, View of Copenhagen From Fredericksberg Hill	175.00
1905, Anxiety of the Coming Christmas Night	175.00
1906, Sleighing to Church	100.00
1907, Little Match Girl	135.00
1908, St Petri Church	100.00
1909, Yule Tree	105.00
1910, Old Organist	100.00
1911, Angels & Shepherds	100.00
1912, Going to Church	100.00
1913, Bringing Home the Tree	100.00
1914, Amalienborg Castle	95.00
1915, Dog on Chain Outside Window	130.00
1916, Prayer of the Sparrows	90.00
1917, Christmas Boat	90.00
1918, Fishing Boat	90.00
1919, Outside the Lighted Window	85.00
1920, Hare in the Snow	85.00
1921, Pigeons	85.00
1922, Star of Bethlehem	85.00
1923, Hermitage	85.00
1924, Lighthouse	90.00
1925, Child's Christmas	90.00
1926, Churchgoers	90.00
1927, Skating Couple	120.00
1928, Eskimos	85.00
1929, Fox Outside Farm	90.00
1930, Tree in Town Hall Square	100.00
1931, Christmas Train	100.00
1932, Lifeboat at Work	100.00
1933, Korsor-Nyborg Ferry	85.00
1934, Church Bell in Tower	85.00
1935, Lillebelt Bridge	85.00
1936, Royal Guard	85.00
1937, Arrival of Christmas Guests	100.00
1938, Lighting the Candles	150.00
1939, Old Lock-Eye, The Sandman	190.00
1940, Delivering Christmas Letters	215.00
1941, Horses Enjoying Meal	225.00
1942, Danish Farm on Christmas Night	190.00
1943, Ribe Cathedral	190.00
1944, Sorgenfri Castle	120.00
1945, Old Water Mill	135.00
1946, Commemoration Cross	115.00
1947, Dybbol Mill	120.00
1948, Watchman	100.00
1949, Landsoldaten	105.00
1950, Kronborg Castle at Elsinore	120.00
1951, Jens Bang	105.00
1952, Old Copenhagen Canals & Thorsvaldsen Museum	110.00
1953, Royal Boat	110.00
1954, Snowman	115.00
1955, Kaulundborg Church	115.00
1956, Christmas in Copenhagen	150.00
1957, Christmas Candles	150.00
1958, Santa Claus	125.00
1959, Christmas Eve	125.00
1960, Village Church	185.00
1961, Winter Harmony	115.00
1962, Winter Night	105.00
1963, Christmas Elf	110.00
1964, Fir Tree & Hare	60.00
1965, Bringing Home the Tree	55.00
1966, Home for Christmas	50.00
1967, Sharing the Joy	50.00
1968, Christmas in Church	45.00
1969, Arrival of Guests	35.00
1970, Pheasants in Snow	30.00
1971, Christmas at Home	30.00
1972, Christmas in Greenland	27.00
1973, Country Christmas	35.00
1974, Christmas in the Village	30.00
1975, The Old Water Mill	25.00
1976, Christmas Welcome	25.00
1977, Copenhagen Christmas	25.00
1978, A Christmas Tale	25.00
1979, White Christmas	35.00
1980, Christmas in the Woods	35.00
1981, Christmas Peace	35.00
1982, The Christmas Tree	40.00
1983, Christmas in Old Town	35.00
1984, Christmas Letter	35.00
1985, Christmas Eve, Farm	35.00
1986, Silent Night	40.00
1987, Snowman's Christmas	45.00
1988, In King's Garden	55.00
1989, Christmas Anchorage	55.00
1990, Changing Guards	55.00
1991, Copenhagen Stock Exchange	75.00
1992, Pastor's Christmas	75.00
1993, Father Christmas in Copenhagen	90.00
1994, Day in Deer Park	85.00
1995, Towers of Copenhagen	85.00
1996, Winter at the Old Mill	85.00
1997, Country Christmas	85.00
1998, Santa the Storyteller	85.00

M. I. Hummel

The last issue for M.I. Hummel annual plates was made in 1995. Values listed here are for plates in mint condition with original boxes.

1971, Heavenly Angel	600.00
1972, Hear Ye, Hear Ye	65.00
1973, Glober Trotter	150.00

1974, Goose Girl	55.00
1975, Ride Into Christmas	55.00
1976, Apple Tree Girl	55.00
1977, Apple Tree Boy	60.00
1978, Happy Pastime	55.00
1979, Singing Lesson	45.00
1980, School Girl	50.00
1981, Umbrella Boy	65.00
1982, Umbrella Girl	125.00
1983, The Postman	185.00
1984, Little Helper	60.00
1985, Chick Girl	60.00
1986, Playmates	120.00
1987, Feeding Time	200.00
1988, Little Goat Herder	120.00
1989, Farm Boy	110.00
1990, Shepherd's Boy	175.00
1991, Just Resting	145.00
1992, Meditation	155.00
1993, Doll Bath	155.00
1994, Doctor	155.00
1995, Come Back Soon	155.00

Royal Copenhagen

1908, Madonna & Child, minimum value	3,500.00
1909, Danish Landscape	265.00
1910, Magi	180.00
1911, Danish Landscape	175.00
1912, Christmas Tree	200.00
1913, Frederik Church Spire	160.00
1914, Holy Spirit Church	170.00
1915, Danish Landscape	190.00
1916, Shepherd at Christmas	130.00
1917, Our Savior Church	110.00
1918, Sheep & Shepherds	110.00
1919, In the Park	110.00
1920, Mary & Child Jesus	105.00
1921, Aabenraa Marketplace	100.00
1922, 3 Singing Angels	100.00
1923, Danish Landscape	100.00
1924, Sailing Ship	140.00
1925, Christianshavn Street Scene	100.00
1926, Christianshavn Canal	90.00
1927, Ship's Boy at Tiller	150.00
1928, Vicar's Family	100.00
1929, Grundtvig Church	100.00
1930, Fishing Boats	155.00
1931, Mother & Child	145.00
1932, Frederiksberg Gardens	145.00
1933, Ferry & Great Belt	190.00
1934, Hermitage Castle	200.00
1935, Kronborg Castle	275.00
1936, Roskilde Cathedral	265.00
1937, Main Street of Copenhagen	300.00
1938, Round Church of Osterlars	425.00
1939, Greenland Pack Ice	550.00
1940, Good Shepherd	595.00
1941, Danish Village Church	475.00
1942, Bell Tower	535.00
1943, Flight Into Egypt	700.00
1944, Danish Village Scene	375.00
1945, Peaceful Scene	625.00
1946, Zealand Village Church	260.00

1947, Good Shepherd	350.00
1948, Nodebo Church	265.00
1949, Our Lady's Cathedral	280.00
1950, Boeslunde Church	335.00
1951, Christmas Angel	500.00
1952, Christmas in Forest	185.00
1953, Frederiksberg Castle	185.00
1954, Amalienborg Palace	185.00
1955, Fano Girl	225.00
1956, Rosenborg Castle	200.00
1957, Good Shepherd	165.00
1958, Sunshine Over Greenland	165.00
1959, Christmas Night	200.00
1960, Stag	165.00
1961, Training Ship	175.00
1962, Little Mermaid	300.00
1963, Hojsager Mill	85.00
1964, Fetching the Tree	85.00
1965, Little Skaters	70.00
1966, Blackbird	60.00
1967, Royal Oak	55.00
1968, Last Umiak	50.00
1969, Old Farmyard	50.00
1970, Christmas Rose & Cat	50.00
1971, Hare in Winter	35.00
1972, In the Desert	35.00
1973, Train Home Bound	40.00
1974, Winter Twilight	45.00
1975, Queens Palace	35.00
1976, Danish Watermill	40.00
1977, Immervad Bridge	35.00
1978, Greenland Scenery	35.00
1979, Choosing Tree	60.00
1980, Bringing Home Tree	45.00
1981, Admiring Tree	50.00
1982, Waiting for Christmas	85.00
1983, Merry Christmas	65.00
1984, Jingle Bells	65.00
1985, Snowman	70.00
1986, Wait for Me	65.00
1987, Winter Birds	70.00
1988, Christmas Eve Copenhagen	90.00
1989, Old Skating Pond	105.00
1990, Christmas in Tivoli	155.00
1991, St Lucia Basilica	100.00
1992, Royal Coach	85.00
1993, Arrival Guests by Train	350.00
1994, Christmas Shopping	95.00
1995, Christmas at Manorhouse	425.00
1996, Lighting Street Lamps	95.00
1997, Roskilde Cathedral	90.00
1998, Welcome Home	190.00

Limoges

From the mid-eighteenth century, Limoges was the center of the porcelain industry of France, where at one time more than forty companies utilized the local kaolin to make a superior quality china, much of which was exported to the United States. Various marks were used; some included the name of the American export company (rather than the manufacturer) and 'Limoges.' After 1891 'France' was added. Pieces signed by factory artists are more valuable than those decorated outside the factory by amateurs. The listings below are hand-painted pieces unless noted otherwise.

For a more thorough study of the subject, we recommend you refer to *The Collector's Encyclopedia of Limoges Porcelain, Third Edition* (with beautiful illustrations and current market values), by our advisor, Mary Frank Gaston.

Please note: Limoges porcelain is totally French in origin, but one American china manufacturer, The Limoges China Company, marked its earthenware 'Limoges' to reflect its name. For information concerning this American earthenware, we recommend *American Limoges* by Raymonde Limoges. Both this book and Mrs. Gaston's are available from Collector Books.

Biscuit jar, poppies, sgn C Stouffer, JPL mk, Pat Jan 23rd 1906, 6"..**325.00**
Bowl, plums w/gold, ftd, T&V, ca 1907, 3x7¼" **215.00**
Box, dresser; cherubs in relief on cobalt, pate-sur-pate, 7"...........**175.00**
Box, dresser; roses on wht, bud finial, T&V, ca 1907....................**145.00**
Cache pot, roses, 4 gold ball ft, gold hdls, Guerin, ca 1900, 9¼" **595.00**
Cake plate, roses, gold trim & hdls, T&V, ca 1907, 10¼"...........**110.00**
Candlesticks, roses, mc on wht, gold trim, slim, T&V, 5¼", pr **245.00**
Candlesticks, roses on wht, ftd, Haviland mk, 7½", pr.................**335.00**
Charger, chrysanthemums, sgn AA, T&V, 1907, 17" in 19½" fr **1,400.00**
Charger, grapes & leaves, gold trim, T&V, ca 1907, 11½" **495.00**
Charger, wild roses on bl to cream, gold scalloped rim, ca 1922, 9"....**295.00**
Chocolate pot, roses at otp, sgn J Marsey, dbl mk, 9" **515.00**
Creamer & sugar bowl, roses on wht w/gold, 1981-1932, sugar: 5"....**225.00**
Cup & saucer, roses, pk on gr, sgn Lucien, mk Elite, ca 1900, 2", 6"..**75.00**
Ferner, roses on bl to pk to gr, 4 gold ft, 4½x6¾" **575.00**
Fish service, sgn R Solange, AKCD, 24" platter, sauce boat, 10 plates ...**975.00**
Jardiniere, roses on bl/peach/cream mottle, bulbous, 8¾" **1,100.00**
Jardiniere, violets on lav to wht, 4 sm ft, 1890-1900, 3¾x8½" **550.00**
Long dish, violets ea side, T&V, 2x10x4½" **150.00**
Pitcher, cider; cherries w/gold, mk B&C, ca 1915, +6 cups **1,100.00**
Pitcher, currants allover, gold hdl, D&C over France mk, 7x7"....**450.00**
Pitcher, tankard, vintage w/gold, gr base, Guerin mk, 1900-30, 15"..**700.00**
Pitcher, water lilies allover, Paroutaud Freres mk #2, 6x8" **565.00**

Plaque, hunting dog and elk, signed Gilbert, 13", from $400.00 to $500.00; Charger, roses blossoms, rose red and pink on dark green shading to white, signed Rousset, 12½", from $375.00 to $425.00.

Plaque, lady's portrait, sgn IF Shaler, T&V, 1907, 11x8½", +orig fr ...**1,800.00**
Punch bowl, chrysanthemums, int/ext, T&V, ca 1907, 5x10½" **885.00**
Punch bowl, grapes in & out, T&V, 14", separate 9" ped.........**3,000.00**
Rose bowl, roses w/gold, dbl mk, ca 1896-1905, 5"....................**185.00**
Sweetened condensed milk set, currants, ca 1900, 3-pc **295.00**
Tankard, grape clusters, gr Guerin mk, 14" **450.00**
Teapot, roses, ca 1891 mk, 4¾", +cr/sug....................................**550.00**
Teapot, roses on wht, artist sgn, Guerin mk, 10½" **450.00**
Tray, orchids, artist sgn, T&V, dtd 1906, 16¼x13½"...................**495.00**
Tray, roses on wht (EX art), artist sgn, T&V, dtd 1901, 14½x13.........**495.00**
Tray, roses w/gold-paste trim, hdls, T&V, ca 1907, 14¾x12¾" **495.00**
Vase, egrets & cattails, tapered cylinder, 12"..............................**125.00**
Vase, irises, tapered cylinder w/flared rim, gr Guerin mk, 14" **450.00**

Vase, Nouveau chrysanthemums w/gold, 1900-14 mk, 15¼"................**1,100.00**
Vase, peacock on flowering branch on pk to bl lustre, Bernardaud, 14"...**300.00**
Vase, people in landscape scenes transfers on cobalt w/gold, 26½" **525.00**
Vase, pillow; roses allover, gold hdls, JPL mk, 1891-1932, 8x7"...**550.00**
Vase, roses, wht on wht, artist sgn, 3 gold hdls, dtd 1939, 10½" **1,295.00**
Vase, roses allover, bulbous, GDA mk, 5x6½" **465.00**
Vase, standing gent, silver-foil attire, gr w/gold neck/floral, 7½"..........**745.00**
Vase, vintage, mc on cream, artist sgn, JPL mk, ca 1910, 14" ..**1,250.00**

Lithophanes

Lithophanes are porcelain panels with relief designs of varying degrees of thickness and density. Transmitted light brings out the pattern in graduated shading, lighter where the porcelain is thin and darker in the heavy areas. They were cast from wax models prepared by artists and depict views of life from the 1800s, religious themes, or scenes of historical significance. First made in Berlin about 1803, they were used as lamp shade panels, window plaques, and candle shields. Later steins, mugs, and cups were made with lithophanes in their bases. Japanese wares were sometimes made with dragons or geisha lithophanes. See also Dragon Ware; Steins.

Panel, Christ as youth among angels, bronze fr, Am, 1856, 19" ..**800.00**
Panel, hunter scene, cast metal fr, candle holder behind, mini, 5"...**725.00**
Panel, maidens, foliate metal fr w/candle holder behind, 1850s, 15" ...**2,300.00**
Panel, robed lady w/mask, Meissen, brass fr, 1854, 11x8".........**1,600.00**
Panel, women & courtier, foliate fr, candle holder behind, 1850s, 15"..**2,600.00**

Little Red Riding Hood

Though usually thought of as a product of the Hull Pottery Company, research has shown that a major part of this line was actually made by Regal China. The idea for this popular line of novelties and kitchenware items was developed and patented by Hull, but records show that to a large extent Hull sent their whiteware to Regal to be decorated. Little Red Riding Hood was produced from 1943 until 1957.

For further information we recommend *The Collector's Encyclopedia of Hull Pottery* by our advisor Brenda Roberts, and *The Collector's Encyclopedia of Cookie Jars Vol. I, II,* and *III,* by Joyce and Fred Roerig. All are published by Collector Books.

Bank, standing, 7", from $900 to.................................**1,350.00**
Butter dish, from $350 to **400.00**
Canister, cereal...**1,375.00**
Canister, coffee, sugar or flour; ea from $600 to.........**700.00**
Canister, salt..**1,100.00**
Canister, tea...**700.00**
Casserole, red w/emb wolf, RRH, Grandma & axe man, 11¾", $1,800 to...........**2,500.00**
Cookie jar, closed basket, from $450 to........................**650.00**
Cookie jar, full skirt, from $750 to..............................**850.00**
Cookie jar, open basket, from $400 to..........................**500.00**
Cracker jar, unmk, from $600 to.................................**750.00**
Creamer, side pour, from $150 to................................**225.00**
Creamer, top pour, no tab hdl, from $400 to..................**425.00**
Creamer, top pour, tab hdl, from $350 to **375.00**
Dresser jar, 8¾", from $350 to **425.00**
Lamp, from $2,000 to...**2,650.00**
Match holder, wall hanging, from $800 to **850.00**
Mustard jar, w/orig spoon, from $375 to.......................**460.00**
Pitcher, 7", from $450 to...**675.00**
Pitcher, 8", from $550 to...**850.00**
Planter, wall hanging, from $400 to.............................**500.00**
Shakers, Pat design 135889, med sz, pr (+), from $800 to...........**900.00**

Shakers, 3¼", pr, from $95 to **140.00**
Shakers, 5½", pr, from $180 to **235.00**
Spice jar, sq base, ea, from $650 to **750.00**
String holder, from $1,800 to **2,500.00**
Sugar bowl, crawling, no lid, from $300 to.....................**450.00**
Sugar bowl, standing, no lid, from $175 to......................**225.00**
Sugar bowl, w/lid, from $350 to **425.00**
Sugar bowl lid, minimum value **175.00**
Teapot, from $400 to **450.00**
Wolf jar, red base, from $925 to **1,000.00**
Wolf jar, yel base, from $750 to **850.00**

Liverpool

In the late 1700s Liverpool potters produced a creamy ivory ware, sometimes called Queen's Ware, which they decorated by means of the newly perfected transfer print. Made specifically for the American market, patriotic inscriptions, political portraits, or other States themes were applied in black with colors sometimes added by hand. (Obviously their loyalty to the crown did not inhibit the progress of business!) Before it lost favor in about 1825, other English potters made a similar product. Today Liverpool is a generic term used to refer to all ware of this type.

Tureen, figure with coat-of-arms shields, black transfer, 9½x12¼", $1,095.00. (Photo courtesy Skinner, Inc.)

Bowl, British ship/verse, blk transfer, 7⅛"..........................**300.00**
Bowl, Hope/3-masted Am ship, 6 reserves, blk transfer w/red trim, 11" ...**800.00**
Bowl, Poor Jack/Billy's Farewell/creatures/etc, blk transfer, 10⅞"............**550.00**
Jug, Am eagle/E Pluribus Unum/Am ship, blk transfer w/mc, 8", VG...**700.00**
Jug, Apotheosis of Washington/Am ship, blk transfer, 8¾" **925.00**
Jug, Boston Fusiliers, officer w/flag, in wreath w/eagle atop, 10".......**11,165.00**
Jug, By Virtue & Valor We Have.../soldier/lion/ship, blk transfer, 10"...**825.00**
Jug, Commodore Prebles Squadron.../Salem Shipyard scene, 8¾".........**2,300.00**
Jug, courtship scene/sailing ship, blk transfer, 9¼", EX **1,150.00**
Jug, gamecocks/grapes/ribbon, blk transfer w/gold, 8⅝"...............**600.00**
Jug, Great Britain & Ireland United MDCCC, blk transfer, 9" ..**265.00**
Jug, Hope/3-masted Am ship, motto, blk w/gold, 14¼" **6,325.00**
Jug, Hope/3-masted Am ship/Jefferson quote, blk transfer, 1804, 9"...**3,750.00**
Jug, Independence/As he tills.../stanza, blk transfer, 8¼" **1,150.00**
Jug, Joiners Arms/3-masted ship, 11½".......................................**865.00**
Jug, L'Insurgent & Constellation/Shipbuilding, blk transfer, 7¾" **1,880.00**
Jug, L'Insurgent & Constellation/Success..., blk transfer, 9", EX **1,650.00**
Jug, Massachusetts (ship)/Newburyport Harbor map, blk w/gold, 11¾".........**14,950.00**
Jug, O Liberty Thou Goddess/15 states named on ribbon, blk, 8"..**1,100.00**
Jug, Peace Plenty & Independence, blk transfer, 10¾"................**765.00**
Jug, Peace Plenty & Independence/3-masted ship, blk transfer, 10", EX..**925.00**
Jug, Proscribed Patriots/Success to Am..., blk w/mc, 1802, rpr, 10" ..**3,225.00**
Jug, Sailor's Adieu w/compass & verse, blk transfer, 7¼" **750.00**
Jug, Sailor's Return/Sailor's Life's..., blk transfer, 8" **545.00**
Jug, Shipbuilding/timber-cutting scene, blk transfer, 8¾" **1,000.00**
Jug, Shipwright's Arms, blk transfer, 8⅛", VG...............................**600.00**
Jug, The Farewell/Chorus, blk transfer, 7".................................**550.00**

Jug, Tom Truelove Going to Sea/3-masted ship, blk transfer, 8⅝".........**1,100.00**
Jug, WA, Liberty & Franklin w/map/ship, blk transfer w/mc, 9" .**975.00**
Jug, WA in Glory, America in Tears/ship, eagle under spout, 10", EX..**1,259.00**
Jug, WA/Virtue & Valour, blk transfer, 10¼"..............................**300.00**
Jug, World in Planisphere/Fleet of Smugglers..., blk transfer, 9½" **900.00**
Jug, World in Planisphere/Sportsman's Festival, blk transfer, 10" ..**825.00**
Jug, wounded officer & aides/British Man of War, blk transfer, 10½" **1,650.00**
Plate, Returning Hopes, blk transfer, 10", 11 for **1,500.00**

Lladro

Lladro porcelains are currently being produced in Labernes Blanques, Spain. Their retired and limited edition figurines are popular collectibles on the secondary market.

Baby's Outing, #4938, 1976, MIB.....................................**625.00**
Children on the Sofa, #5229, MIB.....................................**325.00**
Closing Scene, #4935, retired **500.00**
Clown w/Alarm Clock, #01005056, early 1970s mk....................**675.00**
Clown w/Violin, #01001126, 1978.....................................**600.00**
Dancing Class, #5741..**115.00**
Family Roots, Black Legacy, #5371, retired, MIB, from $550 to .**750.00**
Father Time, #6696, retired millennium edition, MIB **375.00**
Fishing w/Gramps, #5215, 1st edition, 1984, from $500 to **600.00**
German Shepherd & Puppies, #6454, 1997, retired, MIB..........**450.00**
Happy Anniversary, #6475, retired, MIB................................**255.00**
Harmony, #5159G, 1982...**465.00**
Lap Full of Love, #5739, MIB..**300.00**
Little Traveler, #7602, 1986, from $700 to............................**800.00**
Love's First Light, #1862, retired, MIB.................................**1,450.00**
Magic, clown w/girl, #4605, 1969..**800.00**
Man w/Violin, #4622, 1969..**475.00**
Mile of Style, clown, #998, retired, MIB................................**335.00**
Milky Way, #6569, retired, MIB **600.00**
Pacific Beauty, nude lady, #2403, 1999, retired, MIB....................**550.00**
Prince of the Sea, #1821, retired, MIB..................................**400.00**
Puppies in a Box, #1121G, 1971...**750.00**
Reading w/Daddy, retired, MIB..**325.00**
Serene Moment, #6708, retired, MIB.....................................**465.00**
Shelley, #1357, MIB...**230.00**
Snow Man, #5713, MIB..**250.00**
Springtime in Japan, #1445, 1983, M...................................**875.00**
Sweethearts, #4598, retired...**465.00**
Torso in White, #4512..**265.00**
Tranquility, #6677, retired, MIB **950.00**
Trying on the Hat, #5011G...**230.00**
Young Mozart, #5915, retired, MIB......................................**685.00**

Locke Art

By the time he came to America, Joseph Locke had already proven himself many times over as a master glassmaker, having worked in leading English glasshouses for more than seventeen years. Here he joined the New England Glass Company where he invented processes for the manufacture of several types of art glass — amberina, peachblow, pomona, and agata among them. In 1898 he established the Locke Art Glassware Co. in Mt. Oliver, adjacent to Pittsburgh, Pennsylvania. Locke Art Glass was produced using an acid-etching process by which the most delicate designs were executed on crystal blanks. All examples are signed simply 'Locke Art,' often placed unobtrusively near a leaf or a stem. Some pieces are signed 'Jo Locke,' and some are dated. Most of the work was done by hand. The business continued into the 1920s. For further study we recommend *Locke Art Glass, Guide for Collectors*, by Joseph and Janet Locke, available at your local bookstore.

Our advisor for this category is Richard Haigh; he is listed in the Directory under Virginia.

Cup, ice cream; Kalana Poppy etch, ftd..75.00
Goblet, Ivy etch...95.00
Pitcher, Otus & Ephialts w/Mars eng w/title panel, amberina, 12"....875.00
Plate, Poinsettia etch, 7"..125.00
Sherbet, fruits etch..125.00
Sherbet, Vintage, saucer base..135.00
Tray, ice cream; eng flowers, 16x8"..290.00
Tumbler, brandy; etch flowers & leaves, rare, 3¼"........................95.00
Tumbler, eng sheaves of wheat, 2¾"...110.00
Vase, Buds & Poppies, flared rim, 5"..300.00
Vase, Rose, tinted rose/gold leaves, cylindrical, 10¾".................875.00
Vase, Rose etch, flared rim, 6¼"..450.00

Locks

The earliest type of lock in recorded history was the wooden cross bar used by ancient Egyptians and their contemporaries. The early Romans are credited with making the first key-operated mechanical lock. The ward lock was invented during the Middle Ages by the Etruscans of Northern Italy; the lever tumbler and combination locks followed at various stages of history with varying degrees of effectiveness. In the eighteenth century the first precision lock was constructed. It was a device that utilized a lever-tumbler mechanism. Two of the best known of the early nineteenth-century American lock manufacturers are Yale and Sargent, and today's collectors value Winchester and Keen Kutter locks very highly. Factors to consider are rarity, condition, and construction. Brass and bronze locks are generally priced higher than those of steel or iron. Our advisor for this section is Joe Tanner; he is listed in the Directory under California.

Key:
bbl — barrel   st — stamped

Brass Lever Tumbler

Anchor, 6-lever, emb, 3⅛"...85.00
Belknap, emb, 3⅛"...25.00
Blue Grass, emb, 3"...85.00
Cleveland 4 Way, Cleveland 4 Way emb on front, 3⅝"..................80.00
Cotterill Birmingham Eng, st, 5⅛"..400.00
Duplex Yale & Towne Mfg Co, st, 2⅞"......................................200.00
Geo B Bahr & Co Lou Ky, st, 3⅛"...70.00
GW Co, 1929, emb, 3"...60.00
Jackson's, st Jackson's on front, 2½"...35.00
Keen Kutter, shape of KK emblem, KK emb on front, 4¾".........125.00
Motor, Motor emb on body, 3¼"..35.00
P Fister Cin O, st, 2½"..60.00
Romer & Co, Romer & Co st on dust cover, 3"..............................55.00
Safe, Safe emb in scroll on front, 2⅜"...20.00
Simmons, emb, 2¼"...18.00
Tooker & Reeves (seal lock), st, 5¼"..400.00
Tower & Lyon NY, st, 3"..25.00
W Bohannan & Co, SW emb in scroll on front, 2⅜"......................30.00
Winchester, Winchester emb on front, 3"..................................160.00

Combinations

Canton Lock Co, emb, iron, 3⅜"...425.00
Clark, st, brass, 2¼"...300.00

Edwards Mfg Co No-Key, st on lock, brass, 2¾"..........................60.00
Karco st on body, 2½"..50.00
No Kee, st, brass, 2"...45.00
Number or letter disk, st, 3-disk, iron, 2".....................................20.00
Number or letter disk, st, 4-disk, brass, 4½"..............................250.00
Number or letter disk type (4 disks), brass, 2¾".........................130.00
Quaint Mfg Co, st on lock case, 4¼"...200.00
Sq lock case of steel, st Pat Germany, 4-wheel, 3¼"..................110.00
Vulcana Push Lock Corp, st on lock case, 3¼".............................75.00
WA Harrison, Inc, st, brass, 2½"...100.00

Eight-Lever Type

Armory, brass, Armory 8-Lever st on front....................................30.00
Electric, steel, Electric st on front...30.00
Goliath, steel, Goliath 8-Lever st on front....................................25.00
Mastadon, st, steel, 4½"...15.00
Miller, steel, Miller 8-Lever st on front..18.00
Samson, brass, 8-Lever st on front...18.00

Iron Lever Tumbler

Automobile, st, 2⅞"...50.00
Bronco, emb, 3¼"...45.00
Bulldog, word Bulldog & face of dog emb on front, 2¾".............35.00
Dan Patch, Dan Patch emb on front, horseshoe on bk, 2¾".......150.00
Eagle, word Eagle emb on body, 4⅜"...40.00
G Merkel, st, 3"..30.00
Indian Head, Indian head emb on front, 3"................................140.00
Karo, word Karo emb on front, CI, 3⅛"..25.00
Lever Buckle Co, emb, 4½"...90.00
Moose head, emb, 2¾"..20.00
Owl, emb, 2¼"..30.00
Rough Rider (horse & rider), emb, 3"...90.00
S Andrews, st, 2⅝"...200.00
Thoroughbred, emb, 2⅛"..35.00
Victory, emb, 3⅛"...45.00
W Hall & Co, st, 4½"...400.00
Yale & Towne, lion face emb on front, shackle mk Y&T, 3".......150.00

Lever Push Key

Achilles, emb, iron, 3⅝"...120.00
Belknaps 6-Lever, emb, iron, 2¼"..40.00
California, emb, brass, 2½"...300.00
Champion, emb Champion 6-Lever, brass push-key type, 2¼".........25.00
Climax, emb Climax 6-Lever, iron push-key type, 2¼"................35.00
Crank, emb, iron, 2⅞"...25.00
Dash, emb Dash 6-Lever, iron push-key type, 2¼".......................25.00
Eagle, 3-Lever, emb, brass, 2"...50.00
Elm City 4-Lever, emb, brass, 3"...35.00
Excelsior, emb Excelsior 6-Lever, brass push-key type, 2¼"...........25.00
Harvard, emb Harvard 4-Lever, brass push-key type, 2".................50.00
IXL, emb IXL on body, 2¼"...110.00
Keystone, emb Keystone 6-Lever, brass push-key type, 2¼"..........40.00
Morley, emb, iron, 2½"...150.00
National Lock Co, emb, brass, 2½"..150.00
SB Co, emb SB Co on body, 3¼"..60.00
Supplee, emb, iron, 2½"..100.00
Ten Star, emb Ten Star 6-Lever, 2¼"...60.00

Logo — Special Made

Brass pancake push key emb US Internal Revenue, 2¼"............225.00

Canada Custom, emb, iron, 2¾" 225.00
Coca-Cola, st, brass, 2⅝" 50.00
D&H, emb, brass, 2½" 170.00
Georgia Power Co, st, brass, 3" 15.00
Heart-shape brass lever type emb Shults Co, bbl key, 2¾" 55.00
International Harvester Co, emb, brass, 2½" 100.00
John Deere, st, brass 50.00
Lilly, st, brass, 2½" 15.00
Okla State Pen, st, brass, 2⅝" 70.00
Property of Syracuse Univ, st, brass, 2⅝" 40.00
Sq brass pin-tumbler case st Regd US Mail, int counter, 2¾" 140.00
Sq Yale-type brass pin tumbler, st US/A/tree/Forest Svc, 2⅞" 200.00
Swift & Co, st, iron, 2¼" 20.00
University of Notre Dame, emb, brass, 2½" 400.00
USBIA, st, brass, 3¾" 80.00
USGS, emb, iron, 2½" 40.00
USMC, st, brass, 2½" 100.00
West Baking Co, emb, brass, 2½" 200.00

Pin-Tumbler Type

Corbin, brass, Corbin in oval st on body, 3⅝" 25.00
Eagle, brass, Eagle st on body, 2⅞" 20.00
Eagle, emb, iron, 2¾" 20.00
Hickory, emb, iron, 2¾" 150.00
Hope, brass, emb Hope on body, 2½" 20.00
Il-A-Noy, emb, iron, 2¾" 40.00
Il-A-Noy, emb Il-A-Noy on body, 2½" 40.00
Pearl, brass, emb Pearl on body, 2⅛" 30.00
Sargent, brass, emb Sargent on body, 3" 15.00
Shapleigh, emb Shapleigh on body, 2⅝" 30.00
Simmons, emb, iron, 2⅝" 30.00
Yale, brass, emb Yale on body, Yale & Towne on shackle, 2⅝" 25.00
Yale, emb, iron, 2¼" 60.00

Scandinavian (Jail House) Type

Bull Dog, emb, brass, 2½" 150.00
JHW Climax Co, iron, 2⅞" 50.00
Pear, emb, iron, 3⅓" 40.00
Romer, st, iron, 4" 70.00
Star, iron, 2½" 70.00
999 Miller, emb 999, brass, 2½" 70.00

Six-Lever Type

Bon-Ton, st, iron, 3" 15.00
Edwards, iron, Edwards st on body 18.00
Oak Leaf Six-Lever, st, iron, 3¼" 15.00
Safe, brass, Safe st on body 18.00
Yale, brass, Yale emb on front 12.00

Story and Commemorative

AYPEX Seattle (Alaska Yukon Pacific Expo), emb tin/iron, 3" ..300.00
CI, emb ornate scroll motif throughout body of lock, 3½" 400.00
CQD/sinking ship Titanic & SOS waves emb on brass, 2¾" 120.00
Eagle & stars/shield & stars, emb CI, Eagle Liberty, 2½" 300.00
Missouri Seal, brass, 2¼" 150.00
National Hardware Co (NHCo), emb Mercury figure, iron, 2" ..250.00
New York to Paris, brass, 2⅝" 200.00
Russell & Erwin (R&E), em Ganesha form, iron, 3" 700.00
Russell & Erwin (R&e), emb vase, iron, 3¼" 800.00
1904 World's Fair, iron & brass, 3⅝" 400.00

Warded Type

Aetna, emb, brass, 2¼" 35.00
Bramah's Patent VR, 5" 60.00
Enders, st, brass, 1½" 25.00
Globe, iron sq lock case, emb US on bk, 2⅜" 20.00
Jewel, emb, iron, 2½" 18.00
Lucky, emb, brass, 2½" 45.00
Red Seal, emb, brass, 2" 20.00
Ruby, emb, brass, 2⅛" 20.00
Safety First, brass pancake type, emb letters, 2¾" 15.00
Secure, iron pancake type, emb letters, 2⅝" 20.00
Sprocket, brass oval shape, emb letters, 2⅛" 50.00
Try Me, iron pancake type, emb letters, 2½" 25.00
Van Guard, emb, iron, 2⅞" 18.00
Winchester, brass sq case, st letters, 2¾" 135.00

Wrought Iron Lever Type (Smokehouse Type)

DM&Co, bbl key, 4¼" 20.00
Improved Warranted, 3½" 35.00
MW&Co, bbl key, 2⅝" 10.00
MW&Co, flat key, 3½" 20.00
R&E, 4½" 40.00
S&Co, bbl key, 3" 8.00
VR, 3½" 30.00
Waines, 4⅜" 40.00
WT Patent, 3¼" 20.00

Loetz

The Loetz Glassworks was established in Klostermule, Austria, in 1840. After Loetz's death the firm was purchased by his grandson, Johann Loetz Witwe. Until WWII the operation continued to produce fine artware, some of which made in the early 1900s bears a striking resemblance to Tiffany's, with whom Loetz was associated at one time. In addition to the iridescent Tiffany-style glass, he also produced threaded glass and some cameo. The majority of Loetz pieces will have a polished pontil. Our advisor for this category is Don Williams; he is listed in the Directory under Missouri.

Atomizer, cameo, leaves/flowers, bl on yel, no stopper, 7" 400.00
Bowl, frosted w/appl bl prunts, ped ft shades to gr, 5x11" 1,175.00
Cup, gold w/mc irid, shallow, 3¾" 290.00
Lamp, amber & gold dome shade on tripod supports, att, 16½" 1,550.00
Lamp, owl figural, appl beak/eyes/wings, metal ft, 17", EX.......3,000.00
Pitcher, gr irid, long vertical 'comma' ribs, 6" 70.00
Vase, amber irid, 4-sided top w/swirled design, 4¼" 250.00
Vase, amber irid w/cranberry drapery, overall gold oil spots, 8" ...635.00
Vase, amber w/overall oil spots, appl hdls, ftd cone, 7¼" 550.00
Vase, amber w/pk & bl irid, appl tendrils, long neck, 9" 900.00
Vase, amber/pk/gr irid, loop hdls, 7½" 650.00
Vase, amber/rose w/oil spots, leaves/trailings, pinched/shaped rim, 3" ..2,000.00
Vase, bl irid, U-form w/pinched-in sides, 4-lobe top, 6½" 460.00
Vase, bl irid over amber, ftd trumpet form w/wide rolled-down top, 10"...575.00
Vase, bl irid waves on dk gold, wide U-form w/4-pinch rim, 5"...1,600.00
Vase, bl/pk irid swirl on yel, ovoid, 3½" 1,265.00
Vase, cameo, narcissus/butterfly, burgundy on pk/lav mottle, 12½" ...1,495.00
Vase, cameo, tulip on long stem, purple on textured gr, AC68, 8" 600.00
Vase, cobalt w/pulled lines forming patches in silver-bl surface, 4" ..430.00
Vase, damascene design w/rainbow irid, flared rim, 7½" 1,400.00
Vase, dk bl irid w/oil spots, amber buttress hdls, 10" 1,500.00
Vase, dk to lt amber shading w/oil spots, 3 clear hdls, unmk, 10x8" ..2,235.00

Vase, feathers, lt amethyst/gold irid, swollen shoulder/flared lip, 6"....**2,000.00**
Vase, frost w/pk swirls & oil spots, ruffled/pinched rim, pk int, 5"..**350.00**
Vase, gold irid stripes, squat, flared rim, 4".....................**500.00**
Vase, gold irid tree trunk form w/pierced body, 10½" **600.00**
Vase, gold irid w/gr & bl pulled design, pinched, 7½" **700.00**
Vase, gr textured w/much irid, shouldered, 6¾".......................**300.00**
Vase, gr w/bl & pk pulled design, pinched bottom, folded rim, 12½" **900.00**
Vase, gr w/bl-gr irid, long swollen neck on onion base, 9¾" **430.00**
Vase, gr w/purple & bl irid drape pattern, ruffled rim, 10½" **950.00**
Vase, gray w/amethyst irid & bl oil spots, ovoid, 3¾"..................**865.00**
Vase, lt gr w/lt bl disks & hdls, 5¾"....................................**500.00**
Vase, lt gr w/4 bl appl circles & serpentine at neck, 8¼" **475.00**
Vase, pulled & damascene decor, flower form, 6½" **3,000.00**
Vase, purple & bl irid swirls, fluted form w/pinched rim, 9".....**1,200.00**
Vase, red waves w/bl irid, pinched sides, invt cone w/ped ft, 4" **1,325.00**
Vase, silver o/l poppies on gold irid, dbl-bulbed gourd, 7"........**1,265.00**
Vase, silver o/l poppies on gold lustre, ovoid, 9⅝"..................**2,530.00**
Vase, silver o/l Vs on cased amethyst w/oil spots, unmk, 8" **3,525.00**
Vase, silver o/l w/bl oil spots, 3".......................................**850.00**
Vase, silver o/l w/bl oil spots & appl glass tendrils, 3"..................**850.00**
Vase, yel irid w/SP hdls & 'cage,' Apollo Silver, 6" **1,000.00**
Vase, yel w/horizontal panels of undulating gold irid, shouldered, 8"...**1,035.00**

Lomonosov Porcelain

Founded in Leningrad in 1744, the Lomonosov porcelain factory produced exquisite porcelain miniatures for the Czar and other Russian nobility. One of the first factories of its kind, Lomonosov produced mainly vases and delicate sculptures. In the 1800s Lomonosov became closely involved with the Russian Academy of Fine Arts, a connection which has continued to this day as the company continues to supply the world with these fine artistic treasures. In 1992 the backstamp was changed to read 'Made in Russia,' instead of 'Made in USSR.'

Bathing Beauty, hands to hair, towel beside, 1950s, 7" **145.00**
Bears inkwell, 1950s, 5"..**65.00**
Chinese girl, kneeling, early USSR mk, 3½" **35.00**
Cook & Cat, cat stealing meat, early mk, 7"................................**55.00**
Dachshund, standing w/tail up, early mk, 4½x5½"........................**35.00**
Eskimo girl w/flower & book, ca 1950, 7¾" **50.00**
Giraffe, recumbent w/head up, 1970s mk, 12".............................**45.00**
Girl in pajamas w/teddy bear, early mk, 4¾" **75.00**
Girl w/basket, early USSR mk, 4x4¼" **60.00**
Happy Childhood, girl w/doll, 1950s, 4½" **50.00**
Kitten, early USSR mk, 5½x5"...**35.00**
Moose, early mk, 13"...**45.00**
Penguin, early USSR mk, 6½"...**35.00**
Rabbit & flower, 1970s USSR mk, 4"......................................**50.00**
Shire horse, red USSR mk, 5¼x6½".......................................**55.00**
Tiger w/meat, 1940s, 7¼" L..**85.00**

Longwy

The Longwy workshops were founded in 1798 and continue today to produce pottery in the north of France near the Luxembourg-Belgian border under the name 'Societe des Faienceries de Longwy et Senelle.' The ware for which they are best known was produced during the Art Deco period, decorated in bold colors and designs. Earlier wares made during the first quarter of the nineteenth century reflected the popularity of Oriental art, cloisonne enamels in particular. The designs were executed by impressing the pattern into the moist clay and filling in the depressions with enamels. Examples are marked 'Longwy,' either impressed or paint-

ed under glaze. Our advisors for this category are Suzanne Perrault and Dave Rago; they are listed in the Directory under New Jersey.

Bowl, exotic bird/flowers, ftd, rpr & rim nick, 2¾x10¼", $350 to...............**500.00**
Bowl, flowers/stork, mc w/gilt, ftd, #23, 2¾x10½", EX, $500 to...............**750.00**
Box, purple & wht flowers on bl, 2x4" dia **160.00**
Charger, floral/3 storks, 14¼", from $650 to **950.00**
Charger, phoenix/flowers, D279/35, 13¾", EX, from $500 to...........**700.00**
Cigarette box/ashtray, box w/tray on ea side, floral decor, 7x4x1½" **290.00**

Compote, allover enameled florals, marked and numbered, 5½x13¼", from $500.00 to $750.00. (Photo courtesy Dave Rago Auctions)

Lamp, floral sprigs, red/wht on bl, Hinks font/burner, 25" **1,950.00**
Nut dish, squirrel w/nut center, bl paneled border, octagonal, 1x4" **160.00**
Plate, floral/2 swallows in marsh, 4-sided, 12¾x12", EX, $650 to.........**950.00**
Plate, mc floral, bird/floral center scene, 10"...............................**195.00**
Plate, mc floral decor on bl, 9" **250.00**
Tile, red, wht & purple flowers on bl w/purple border, 8x8"........**120.00**
Tray, lg mc floral center flower surrounded by sm floral, 7½x6"....**245.00**
Vase, floral, flared/scalloped rim, 9¾x5½", from $350 to...............**450.00**
Vase, mc floral on bl, bulbous bottom w/trumpet neck, 7" **110.00**
Vase, triple bud; mc floral, 3 joined cylinders, #792, 5½" **325.00**
Wine flask, birds/floral, rope hdl, #1115 16/D486, 11½x7, $400 to **600.00**

Losanti

Mary Louise McLaughlin, who had previously experimented in trying to reproduced Haviland faience in the 1870s and 'American faience' (a method of inlaying color by painting the inside of the mold before the vessel was cast) in the mid-1890s, developed a type of hard-paste porcelain in which the glaze and the body fused together in a single firing. Her efforts met with success in 1900, and she immediately concentrated on glazing and decorating techniques. The ware she perfected was called Losanti, most of which was decorated with Nouveau florals, either carved or modeled. By 1906 she had abanonded her efforts. Examples are marked with several ciphers, one resembling a butterfly, another with the letters MCL superimposed each upon the other, and L. McL in a linear arrangement. Other items were marked Losanti, sometimes in the Oriental manner. Our advisors for this category are Suzanne Perrault and Dave Rago; they are listed in the Directory under New Jersey.

Bowl, scrolled wreath cvg, wht on dk bl mottle, sgn/#65, 2¾x4".........**1,250.00**
Trivet, celadon w/emb floral, 6", VG, from $500 to.....................**750.00**
Vase, grain-of-rice floral, wht w/oxblood wash, sgn/#55, 4¾x3½" **25,875.00**
Vase, peacock feathers, beige/oxblood crackle, 4x4", EX, $2,750 to...**3,750.00**

Lotton

Charles Lotton is a contemporary glass artist. He began blowing glass and developing original designs thirty years ago and now has work on display in many major glass museums and collections, among them the Smithsonian, the Art Institute of Chicago, the Museum of Glass, and the Chrysler Museum. He has become famous for his unique lamps. Every piece is signed and dated. His three sons, David, Daniel, and John, each work in their own studios. All four artists produce distinctive work. They sell their glass at antique shows and in their showroom in Crete, Illinois. For further information read *Lotton Art Glass* by Charles Lotton and Tom O'Conner; see the Directory under Illinois.

Lamp, Multi Flora, signed Charles Lotton, 24", $2,300.00.

Bowl, wht w/gr leaf & vine decor, dk gr interior, Charles, 6½x11"..........1,100.00
Paperweight, bl, teal & wht swirls, 1974, 2x2½" 180.00
Perfume bottle, Multi Flora, lt pk w/rose/wht floral, Charles, 6½" 500.00
Vase, Multi Flora, lavender, Charles, 10" 1,800.00
Vase, neodymium irid w/purple tulipticus, Daniel, 12x8".........2,200.00
Vase, opaque bl w/gold irid, cvd floral, bulbous, 1973, 3½x2½" 370.00
Vase, paperweight; wht w/lt bl & cobalt floral w/gr leaves, 1973, 6" 670.00
Vase, pulled drape, irid yel, Charles, 1977, 10x5½" 440.00
Vase, purple w/silver swirls, curved fluted neck, Charles, 1977, 12"..415.00
Vase, red w/gold heart & vine design, 1973, 7½x4½" 315.00
Vase, wht w/bl morning glories & gr leaves, bl interior, David, 9½" 700.00
Vase, wht w/purple stripes w/overlayed silver webbing, David, 5x6" 400.00
Vase, Wisteria, bl & copper opal, cobalt interior, Charles, 5¾x6" 550.00

Lotus Ware

Isaac Knowles and Issac Harvey operated a pottery in East Liverpool, Ohio, in 1853 where they produced both yellow ware and Rockingham. In 1870 Knowles brought Harvey's interests and took as partners John Taylor and Homer Knowles. Their principal product was ironstone china, but Knowles was confident that American potters could produce as fine a ware as the Europeans. To prove his point, he hired Joshua Poole, an artist from the Belleek Works in Ireland. Poole quickly perfected a Belleek-type china, but fire destroyed this portion of the company. Before it could function again, their hotel china business had grown to the point that it required their full attention in order to meet market demands. By 1891 they were able to try again. They developed a bone china, as fine and thin as before, which they called Lotus. Henry Schmidt from the Meissen factory in Germany decorated the ware, often with lacy filigree applications or hand-formed leaves and flowers to which he added further decoration with liquid slip applied by means of a squeeze bag. Due to high production costs resulting from so much of the fragile ware being damaged in firing and because of changes in tastes and styles of decoration, the Lotus Ware line was dropped in 1896. Some of the early ware was marked 'KT&K China'; later marks have a star and a crescent with 'Lotus Ware' added. Our advisor for this category is Mary Frank Gaston.

Bowl, coastal scene, triangular panels of appl gold fishnet, 4", EX 300.00
Bowl, Columbia, appl bl floral w/gold, ruffled rim, 1890-1905, 4x5" ..600.00
Bowl, Columbia, appl filigree openwork, no pnt, 4¾", from $700 to........900.00
Bowl, finger; gold sponging on ruffled border, 2¾x5¼", $150 to...............200.00

Chocolate jug, gold-paste florals, Quincy design, ca 1890-1905, 9" ..800.00
Cracker jar, fishnet & beadwork alternating panels, 7½"...........600.00
Creamer & sugar bowl, Chestnut, gold-paste florals, pr...............550.00
Cup & saucer, AD; Mecca, lt gr geometrics w/gold stippling, $125 to...150.00
Cup & saucer (4½"), gold florals in panels on lt yel, cylindrical...........235.00
Flower bowl, gold leaves w/red veins, bl accents, 1890-1905, 4½"...700.00
Jardiniere, scalloped gold top w/bl beading & rtcl hdls, HP floral, 4" ..235.00
Jug, globe; roses w/gold, dk gr hdl, 5x7", from $700 to 800.00
Jug, leaf; pk & gr florals w/gold sponging, 5x7", from $800 to.....900.00
Loving cup/trophy vase, appl floral, 3-hdl, no pnt, 7", $1,200 to..1,400.00
Match holder, rtcl body w/beadwork & gold, 4" L, from $700 to ..900.00
Orange dish, roses transfer w/gold, emb designs, 3½x11½" 400.00
Perfume ewer, gilt/lt gr & lt yel enamel, rtcl, twig hdl, 3½", VG 200.00
Pin tray, draped nude w/lg fan behind, HP finish, 6" L, from $1,200 to ...1,500.00
Rose jar, Avignon, filigree openwork, no pnt, 6¾x6½", $1,400 to 1,600.00
Shell tray, Nouveau tulips w/gold leaves & trim, 5½x6", $450 to 500.00
Shell tray, Victorian lady transfer, gold trim, 7½x8¾", $500 to...............600.00
Tea set, pk & bl floral panels w/gold florals, non-factory decor, 3-pc ...700.00
Teacup, dainty florals inside, from $70 to................................90.00
Teapot, wht w/triangular fishnet panels, 4", +cr/sug 485.00
Tray, gilt trim/HP floral on yel, shell shape w/3 twig ft, 8" 235.00
Vase, Arcanian, appl flowers, celadon on wht, hdls, 8½", $1,800 to.........2,000.00
Vase, Cremonian, HP floral, gr at neck, gold trim, 6¼", $500 to.................600.00
Vase, Egyptian, bl floral w/gold-paste leaves, gold hdls, ftd, 15"....4,500.00
Vase, Grecian, pk/lav flowers w/gr leaves, pate-sur-pate neck, 6" .800.00
Vase, Parmian, HP Colonial couple dancing on lt gr, gold trim, 10" ...1,200.00
Vase, Thebian, lady/2 children in garden, gold hdls, non-factory, 9" ...1,200.00
Vase, Tuscan, HP flowers & leaves w/filigree, non-factory, 8½" 2,000.00

Lu Ray Pastels

Lu Ray Pastels dinnerware was introduced in the early 1940s by Taylor, Smith, and Taylor of East Liverpool, Ohio. It was offered in assorted colors of Persian Cream, Sharon Pink, Surf Green, Windsor Blue, and Chatham Gray in complete place settings as well as many service pieces. It was a successful line in its day and is once again finding favor with collectors of American dinnerware. For further information we recommend *Collector's Guide to Lu Ray Pastels* by Bill and Kathy Meehan. Our advisor for this category is Shirley Moore; she is listed in the Directory under Oklahoma.

Bowl, '36s oatmeal 60.00
Bowl, coupe soup; flat..18.00
Bowl, cream soup 70.00
Bowl, fruit; Chatham Gray, 5" 16.00
Bowl, fruit; 5" 5.00
Bowl, lug soup; tab hdld 24.00
Bowl, mixing; 5½" 125.00
Bowl, mixing; 7" 125.00
Bowl, mixing; 8¾" 100.00
Bowl, mixing; 10¼" 150.00
Bowl, salad; any color other than yel................................65.00
Bowl, salad; yel 55.00
Bowl, vegetable; oval, 9½" 20.00
Butter dish, any color other than Chatham Gray, w/lid...............50.00
Butter dish, Chatham Gray, rare color, w/lid.......................90.00
Calendar plates, 8", 9" & 10", ea 40.00
Casserole 140.00
Chocolate cup, AD; str sides..80.00
Chocolate pot, AD; str sides...400.00
Coaster/nut dish 65.00
Coffee cup, AD 20.00
Coffeepot, AD 200.00

Creamer 8.00
Creamer, AD, ind 40.00
Creamer, AD, ind, from chocolate set 92.00
Egg cup, dbl 30.00
Epergne 125.00
Jug, water; ftd 150.00
Muffin cover 140.00
Muffin cover, w/8" underplate 165.00
Nappy, vegetable; rnd, 8½" 20.00
Pitcher, any color other than yel, bulbous w/flat bottom 125.00
Pitcher, juice 200.00
Pitcher, yel, bulbous w/flat bottom 95.00
Plate, cake 70.00
Plate, Chatham Gray, rare color, 7" 16.00
Plate, chop; 15" 38.00
Plate, grill; compartment 35.00
Plate, 6" 3.00
Plate, 7" 12.00
Plate, 8" 25.00
Plate, 9" 10.00
Plate, 10" 25.00
Platter, oval, 11½" 20.00
Platter, oval, 13" 24.00
Relish dish, 4-part 95.00
Sauce boat 28.00
Sauce boat, any other color than yel, fixed stand 35.00
Sauce boat, yel, fixed stand 22.50
Saucer, coffee; AD 8.50
Saucer, coffee/chocolate 30.00
Saucer, cream soup 28.00
Saucer, tea 2.00
Shakers, pr 18.00
Sugar bowl, AD; w/lid, from chocolate set 92.00
Sugar bowl, AD; w/lid, ind 40.00
Sugar bowl, w/lid 15.00
Teacup 8.00
Teapot, curved spout, w/lid 125.00
Teapot, flat spout, w/lid 160.00
Tray, pickle 28.00
Tumbler, juice 50.00
Tumbler, water 80.00
Vase, bud 400.00

Lunch Boxes

Early twentieth century tobacco companies such as Union Leader, Tiger, and Dixie sold their products in square, steel containers with flat, metal carrying handles. These were specifically engineered to be used as lunch boxes when they became empty. (See Advertising, specific companies.) By 1930 oval lunch pails with colorful lithographed decorations on tin were being manufactured to appeal directly to children. These were made by Ohio Art, Decoware, and a few other companies. In 1950 Aladdin Industries produced the first 'real' character lunch box — a Hopalong Cassidy decal-decorated steel container now considered the beginning of the kids' lunch box industry. The other big lunch box manufacturer, American Thermos (later King Seely Thermos Company) brought out its 'blockbuster' Roy Rogers box in 1953, the first fully lithographed steel lunch box and matching bottle. Other companies (ADCO Liberty; Landers, Frary & Clark; Ardee Industries; Okay Industries; Universal; Tindco; Cheinco) also produced character pails. Today's collectors often tend to specialize in those boxes dealing with a particular subject. Western, space, TV series, Disney movies, and cartoon characters are the most popular. There are well over five hundred different lunch boxes

available to the astute collector. For further information we recommend *Collector's Guide to Lunch Boxes* by Carole Bess White and L.M. White (Collector Books), and *The Illustrated Encyclopedia of Metal Lunch Boxes* by Allen Woodall and Sean Brickell. In the following listings, lunch boxes are metal unless noted vinyl or plastic, and values include thermoses only when they are mentioned within the descriptions.

As indicated in the lines, our values are for examples in exceptional condition; remember to discount sharply for wear and damage beyond the stated conditions.

Adam-12, 1972, VG 50.00
Airport Control Tower, 1972, vinyl, EX 150.00
Aladdin Cable Car, 1962, dome top, VG 250.00
Alvin & the Chipmunks, 1963, w/thermos, vinyl, EX ...125.00
Astrokids, 1988, w/robot thermos, plastic, M 50.00
Atom Ant, 1966, G 60.00
Barbarino, brunch bag, 1977, zipper closure, vinyl, NM ...100.00
Barbie & Francie, 1965, w/thermos, vinyl, NM 200.00
Batman & Robin, 1966, G 95.00
Battlestar Galactica, 1978, w/thermos, EX 75.00
Beatles, 1965, bl, VG 200.00
Bedknobs & Broomsticks, 1972, VG 30.00
Benji, 1974, plastic, EX 15.00
Big Jim, 1972, dome top, w/thermos, plastic, M 125.00
Blondie, 1968, w/thermos, EX 125.00
Bonanza, 1963, gr rim, EX 150.00
Bozo the Clown, 1963, dome top, w/thermos, NM 250.00
Brady Bunch, 1969, w/thermos, NM 200.00
Bugaloos, 1971, EX 100.00
Campbell Kids, 1975, NM 275.00
Care Bear Cousins, 1985, w/thermos, VG 15.00
Casey Jones, 1960, dome top, w/thermos, NM 400.00
Casper the Ghost, 1966, bl background, vinyl, NM 300.00
Chiclets Chewing Gum, 1987, w/thermos, plastic, M 30.00
CHiPs, 1977, dome top, plastic, NM 45.00
Cracker Jack, 1979, EX 50.00
Davy Crockett & Kit Carson, 1955, EX 225.00
Deputy Dawg, 1964, vinyl, NM, from $300 to 325.00
Dick Tracy, 1967, w/thermos, NM 200.00
Disney Express, 1979, VG 20.00
Disney World, 1970, w/thermos, EX 40.00
Dr Seuss, 1970, VG+ 95.00
Duchess, 1960, w/thermos, EX+ 135.00
Dukes of Hazzard, 1980, EX 35.00
Dynomutt, 1976, EX 50.00
Empire Strikes Back, 1980, w/thermos, VG 35.00
Family Affair, 1969, w/thermos, EX 135.00
Flags of the United Nations, 1954, w/thermos, NM 250.00
Flintstones & Dino, 1962, orange, VG 140.00
Flying Nun, 1968, EX 60.00
Fox & the Hound, 1982, EX 25.00
Ghostland, 1977, EX 50.00
Girl Scout, 1960, w/thermos, vinyl, EX 175.00
Great Wild West, 1959, w/thermos, NM 500.00
Green Hornet, 1960s, w/thermos, EX 400.00
Gremlins, 1984, w/thermos, M 95.00
Gunsmoke, 1959, EX 150.00
Hardy Boys Mysteries, 1977, w/thermos, NM 65.00
Hector Heathcote, 1963, w/thermos, NM 200.00
Hogan's Heros, 1966, dome top, VG 150.00
Holly Hobbie, 1989, w/thermos, plastic, M 45.00
How the West Was Won, 1978, w/thermos, EX 60.00
Incredible Hulk, 1978, w/thermos, EX 65.00
James Bond 007, 1966, EX 250.00

Jet Patrol, 1957, VG..175.00
Keebler Cookie, 1987, w/thermos, plastic, M.................30.00
KISS, 1979, w/thermos, NM..150.00
Kung Fu, 1974, w/thermos, NM...................................100.00
Laugh-In, 1968, EX...100.00
Lawman, 1961, vinyl, VG+..85.00
Little Dutch Miss, 1959, w/thermos, NM......................225.00
Little Orphan Annie, 1973, dome top, w/thermos, plastic, NM ...95.00
Mary Poppins, 1973, vinyl, VG......................................50.00
Mickey Mouse, 1988, head figure, w/thermos, plastic, NM 25.00
Monkees, Canadian, 1967, w/thermos, plastic, EX.........275.00
Monroes, 1967 EX..225.00
Munsters, 1965, w/thermos, NM...................................250.00
Pink Panther, 1980, vinyl, EX..95.00
Popeye, 1964, EX+...100.00
Porky's Lunch Wagon, 1959, dome top, EX 400.00
Rat Patrol, 1967, EX...145.00
Rifleman, 1960, VG...200.00
Sesame Street, 1980, yel gingham, vinyl, EX...................25.00
Sigmund & the Sea Monsters, 1974, w/thermos, NM 150.00
Snoopy, 1968, dome top, EX..65.00
Steve Canyon, 1959, EX...275.00
Sunnie Miss, 1972, EX..45.00
Supercar, 1962, w/thermos, VG...................................275.00
Superman, 1980, plastic, EX+..30.00
Swan Lake, 1960, vinyl, EX...150.00
Tom Corbett, 1954, VG..250.00
Tropicana Orange Juice, 1989, w/thermos, plastic, M.........65.00
Wild Wild West, 1969, EX...225.00
World of Barbie, 1971, pk, vinyl, EX...............................35.00

Maddux of California

One of the California-made ceramics now so popular with collectors, Maddux was founded in the late 1930s and during the years that followed produced novelty items, TV lamps, figurines, planters, and tableware accessories.

Ashtray, #7001, 12" dia 10.00
Ashtray, fish, #7134, 6" L..20.00
Ashtray, pig form, natural colors, #7204, 7" L.................12.00
Ashtray, triangular, gunmetal gray, #731, 10½"................20.00
Bank, smiling pig, red or gr, 12" L.................................25.00
Bowl, cabbage leaf design, 4x13" L................................25.00
Bowl, creamy wht, flared rim, #3093, 2x5½" 16.00
Bowl, ftd, #2102...10.00
Bowl, ped w/6 ind servers, #3905A................................25.00
Bowl, shell form, wht, #3017..15.00
Bowl, vegetable; emb swirls, wht w/turq lid, #3066B, 4½x7¾" 25.00
Bowl set, Contempo, wht satin, #1047, 16½".................20.00
Centerpiece, flamingos (2) & pond, #1024, 7¼" & 10" birds 90.00
Clock, astrology design, Westclox, #718R, 12" dia 75.00
Cookie jar, Baby Birds on Bough, from $45 to 55.00
Cookie jar, California King, #2103, 14½"......................175.00
Cookie jar, Chipmunk on Stump, C Romanelli, from $130 to ...140.00
Cookie jar, Queen, #2104, from $150 to 175.00
Cookie jar, Strawberry..25.00
Figurine, bulls, head up/head down, #972/#973, 11", L, pr 75.00
Figurine, Chinese pheasant, #527, 11½"........................20.00
Figurine, cockatoos (2) on limb, #112, 10" wingspan, 10"............75.00
Figurine, doe, #907, 12½"...15.00
Figurine, elephant sitting, #984, 18" 25.00
Figurine, flamingo, wings wide, 12" 95.00

Figurine, flamingo flying, natural colors, #970, 11".........45.00
Figurine, flamingos, #400/#401, pr...............................50.00
Figurine, horses rearing/charging, #925/#926, pr.............20.00
Figurine, parrots (2) on branch, yel on dk gr, 10x9½x4" 75.00
Figurine, pheasants, wht w/brushed gold, 6¼x11¾", pr.............115.00
Figurine, puppy, #300, 6x5½"..15.00
Figurine, rooster, #932, 10½"..30.00
Figurine, stag standing, natural, #914, 12½"....................20.00
Lamp, table; cockatoos (pr) at base, parchment shade.................55.00
Planter, bird, #3304...20.00
Planter, bird in flight, #536, 11½"...................................20.00
Planter, birds (2) in flight, pk & blk, #528, 10"................20.00
Planter, Chinese Bell Tower, #206A, 8" 20.00
Planter, cockatoo, pk & bl, #612....................................25.00
Planter, flamingos, pk, #515, 10½"..................................75.00
Planter, parrots (2) above marsh, #535/60, 6½" wingspan, 10½" ...70.00
Planter, swallow, pk & gray, $628....................................35.00
Planter, swan, #150, 11"..18.00
Relish, gr pepper, w/lid & side bowls, #3275....................15.00
TV lamp, basset hound, #896, 12"................................140.00
TV lamp, deer (1) on rocky base, natural, 12x10" 50.00
TV lamp, deer running (2), natural, #829, 10½"...............45.00
TV lamp, head of Christ, 3-D planter, #841.....................45.00
TV lamp, mallard flying, natural, #839, 11¼"....................45.00
TV lamp, prairie schooner (covered wagon), #844, 11" 35.00
TV lamp, rooster, orange, #519, 13"...............................75.00
TV lamp, sampan w/wht sail, 11½", NM 55.00
TV lamp, shell, pearl tone, #850, 13"..............................40.00
TV lamp, shell (malibu), pearl tone, 10½"........................25.00
TV lamp, Siamese cat, airbrushed, 12½"........................125.00
TV lamp, swan planter, wht porc, #828, 12½"..................45.00
TV lamp, swans w/planter, wht porc, #825.......................45.00
TV lamp, Toro (bull), ft on mound, #859, 11½".................50.00
TV lamp, Toro (bull) charging, walnut, #894, 11¼".............40.00
Vase, flamingos (2), #529, 5", from $50 to 60.00
Vase, horse's head top, str-sided body, aqua, #225, 12"............20.00
Vase, Siamese cat, airbrushed, 8¾x3½"..........................40.00
Vase, swan, wht, #221, 12"...20.00

Magazines

Magazines are collected for their cover prints and for the information pertaining to defunct companies and their products that can be gleaned from the old advertisements. In the listings that follow, items are assumed to be in very good condition unless noted otherwise.

For more information, we recommend *Old Magazines* by Richard E. Clear. See also Movie Memorabilia; Parrish, Maxfield.

Key:
M — mint condition, in original wrapper
EX — excellent condition, spine intact, edges of pages clean and straight
VG — very good condition, the average as-found condition

Allure, 1991, March, Stephanie Seymore cover, premier issue, EX.8.00
Cosmopolitan, 1981, May, Kelly Emberg cover, EX...........12.00
Cosmopolitan, 1985, October, Terry May cover, VG...........6.00
Cosmopolitan, 1989, September, Cindy Crawford cover, VG 8.00
Elle, 1986, April, Ashley Richardson cover, EX..................12.00
Elle, 1987, May, Elle MacPherson cover, VG 5.00
Entertainment Weekly, 1990, March 2, Sean Connery cover, EX.10.00
Entertainment Weekly, 1990, May 4, Patricia Wettig cover, EX...10.00
Esquire, 1985, January, Dubious Achievements of 1984, EX 10.00
Esquire, 1987, July, McEnroe & O'Neal w/baby, EX 10.00

Glamour, 1948, July, Ricki Van Dusen cover, VG.........................15.00
Glamour, 1950, July, Annual Beauty issue, VG.........................15.00
Glamour, 1954, April, Jean Patchett cover, Marilyn inside, EX....18.00
Glamour, 1978, September, Cheryl Tiegs cover, EX.......................15.00
GQ, 1980, March, Richard Gere cover, EX............................10.00
GQ, 1984, October, Peter Jennings cover, G..........................8.00
Harper's Bazaar, 1971, April, China Machado cover, EX.............18.00
Harper's Bazaar, 1976, February, Cheryl Tiegs cover, EX.............25.00
Harper's Bazaar, 1979, November, Elizabeth Taylor cover, EX.......20.00
Harper's Bazaar, 1983, August, Victoria Principal cover, EX 15.00
Life, 1940, July 15, Rita Hayworth cover, EX.........................30.00
Life, 1940, June 3, Statue of Liberty cover, VG.........................18.00
Life, 1941, April 21, US Cavalryman cover, EX.........................25.00
Life, 1941, October 13, Lana Turner & Clark Gable cover, VG ...18.00
Life, 1942, March 30, Shirley Temple Grows Up cover, VG 18.00
Life, 1943, October 25, Mary Martin cover, EX.........................18.00
Life, 1944, April 17, Esther Williams cover, VG.........................18.00
Life, 1945, November 12, Ingrid Bergman cover, EX.....................25.00
Life, 1946, February 11, Lincoln Memorial cover, VG 15.00
Life, 1951, February 26, Debbie Reynolds cover, EX.....................15.00
Life, 1952, February 18, Queen Elizabeth II cover, EX 15.00

Life, 1954, November 1, Dorothy Dandridge cover, EX, $40.00.
(Photo courtesy P.J. Gibbs)

Life, 1955, August 15, General Douglas MacArthur cover, VG+ .12.00
Life, 1958, July 21, Roy Campanella cover, EX.............................18.00
Life, 1963, December, Kennedy Memorial edition, VG.................20.00
Life, 1967, February 24, Elizabeth Taylor cover, foldout, EX 18.00
Life, 1969, November, Paul & Linda McCartney cover, EX..........35.00
Life, 1970, January 23, Johnny Carson cover, EX 10.00
Mademoiselle, 1980, September, Carol Alt cover, VG 10.00
Mademoiselle, 1989, January, Stephanie Seymour cover, EX 10.00
Modern Screen, 1956, May, Elizabeth Taylor cover, G 8.00
Modern Screen, 1975, May, B Streisand, Ali MacGraw & Steve McQueen, EX...15.00
Motion Picture, 1946, February, Gregory Peck cover, VG+ 20.00
Movie Mirror, 1933, September, Claudette Colbert cover, VG.....25.00
Movie World, 1961, March, Debbie Reynolds & Sandra Dee cover, EX..15.00
National Geographics, 1915-16, ea...15.00
National Geographics, 1917-24, ea...9.00
National Geographics, 1925-29, ea...8.00
National Geographics, 1930-45, ea...7.00
National Geographics, 1946-55, ea...6.00
National Geographics, 1956-57, ea...5.50
National Geographics, 1968-89, ea...4.50
National Geographics, 1990-present, ea 2.00
Newsweek, 1966, January 24, Truman Capote cover, EX 20.00
Newsweek, 1986, February, David Letterman cover, VG 8.00
Newsweek, 1988, October, John Lennon cover, EX.......................15.00
People, 1975, March 17, Alan Alda cover, EX 12.00
People, 1977, March 21, David Carradine cover, EX.....................15.00

People, 1978, October 2, Battlestar Galactica cover, EX 18.00
Photoplay, 1945, January, Ingrid Bergman cover, EX 25.00
Photoplay, 1972, May, Chad Everett & Dean Martin cover, EX ...15.00
Radio Mirror, 1939, March, Annabella & Tyrone Power, VG+ 30.00
Rolling Stone, 1974, January, Richard Nixon & Statue of Liberty, EX+ .10.00
Rolling Stone, 1974, September, Tanya Tucker cover, VG............10.00
Rolling Stone, 1975, December, Bonnie Rait cover, EX 15.00
Rolling Stone, 1975, March, Linda Ronstadt cover, EX 15.00
Rolling Stone, 1976, June, Paul & Linda McCartney cover, EX ...20.00
Saturday Evening Post, 1941, June 26, Rockwell cover, EX 30.00
Saturday Evening Post, 1955, April 23, Dodgers cover, VG+ 30.00
Saturday Evening Post, 1963, May 25, Nasser by Rockwell cover, VG...6.00
Saturday Evening Post, 1964, August 8, Beatles cover, VG+ 20.00
Saturday Evening Post, 1973, November/December, Waltons cover, EX..10.00
Screen Romances, 1947, September, Clark Gable & Deborah Kerr, EX...30.00
Screen Stories, 1966, April, David McCallum cover, EX 15.00
Seventeen, 1956, November, Sandy Brown cover, VG.................10.00
Seventeen, 1957, March, Delores Hawkins cover, VG 8.00
Seventeen, 1958, November, Romanna Swan cover, G.................6.00
Sports Illustrated, 1957, January 28, Boston Bruins cover, VG 15.00
Sports Illustrated, 1965, December 20, Sandy Koufax cover, EX...50.00
Sports Illustrated, 1967, June, Bill Casper (gold) cover, VG+.......12.00
Sports Illustrated, 1969, February 3, Bobby Orr cover, EX.............25.00
Time, 1951, December 31, Groucho Marx cover, EX 50.00
Time, 1956, September 24, John D Rockefeller Jr cover, G.............5.00
Time, 1957, February 18, Martin Luther King cover, VG..............10.00
Time, 1959, January 26, Fidel Castro cover, VG 10.00
Time, 1961, April 21, Yuri Gagarin space cover, EX.....................25.00
Time, 1962, April 6, Sophia Loren cover, VG 15.00
Time, 1963, September 27, Governor G Wallace cover, EX............15.00
Time, 1964, February 14, Marina Oswold cover, VG+ 20.00
TV Guide, 1966, Oct 30, Addams Family cover, EX 80.00
TV Guide, 1975, June 7, Little House on Prairie cover, VG.........10.00
TV Guide, 1976, January 24, M*A*S*H cover, VG......................6.00
TV Guide, 1977, January 29, Lynda Carter as Wonder Woman cover, EX..30.00
TV Mirror, 1976, June, cast of Mary Hartman Mary Hartman cover, EX.15.00
Vogue, 1943, May 1, model by pool cover, Burns & Allen inside, VG.50.00
Vogue, 1972, August 15, Lauren Hutton cover, EX 25.00

Majolica

Majolica is a type of heavy earthenware, design-molded and decorated in vivid colors with either a lead or tin type of glaze. It reached its height of popularity in the Victorian era; examples from this period are found in only the lead glazes. Nearly every potter of note, both here and abroad, produced large majolica jardinieres, umbrella stands, pitchers with animal themes, leaf shapes, vegetable forms, and nearly any other design from nature that came to mind. Not all, however, marked their ware. Among those who sometimes did were Minton, Wedgwood, Holdcroft, and George Jones in England; Griffin, Smith and Hill (Etruscan) in Phoenixville, Pennsylvania; and Chesapeake Pottery (Avalon and Clifton) in Baltimore.

Color and condition are both very important worth-assessing factors. Pieces with cobalt, lavender, and turquoise glazes command the highest prices. For further information we recommend *The Collector's Encyclopedia of Majolica* by Mariann Katz-Marks (see Directory, Pennsylvania). Unless another condition is given, the values that follow are for pieces in mint condition. Our advisor for this category is Hardy Hudson; he is listed in the Directory under Florida.

Basket, Bird's Nest, 8½", NM 300.00
Basket, cat playing at base, Minton, 6", NM 2,750.00
Basket, Sunflower, begonia-leaf hdl, 12" L 700.00

Bottle, liquor; dog w/gun, 12" 1,600.00
Bottle, liquor; fox w/horn & bbl, prof rpr, 12" 2,100.00
Bowl, Lettuce Leaf, sq, 8" 125.00
Box, boar's head, cobalt base, Geo Jones, 5x8½" 7,000.00
Bread tray, Wheat, Eat Thy Bread w/Thankfulness, 13" 325.00
Butter dish, Pineapple, cow finial, sm prof rpr 450.00
Butter pat, Chrysanthemum, cobalt, Wedgwood 175.00
Butter pat, fan shape, cobalt, Eureka 150.00
Butter pat, Maple Leaf on yel plate, Etruscan 100.00
Butter pat, pk pearlware shell, Wedgwood 60.00
Butter pat, Wild Rose, cobalt 120.00
Cache pot, Calla Lily, EX color & detail, Geo Jones, 7½x8½", NM ..850.00
Cake stand, leaves & ferns on turq, EX 200.00
Cake stand, Maple Leaves on pk, Etruscan 150.00
Cake stand, Napkin, cobalt fringe on yel basket, low, 8¾" 250.00
Cake stand, Shell & Seaweed, Etruscan 800.00
Candle holder, Pond Lily, EX detail, 7½" 325.00
Centerpiece, bowl held by 4 winged lions, Wilhelm & Schiller, 9x16"..1,000.00
Centerpiece, putti fishermen (2) w/net & fish, Copeland, 10x13½"..2,750.00
Centerpiece, shell supported by merman w/staff, Minton, 8", NM..1,200.00
Charger, stylized floral, Minton, prof rim rpr, 14½" 500.00
Cheese keeper, Fish in Seaweed, cboalt, 7" 3,750.00
Cheese keeper, Picket Fence, Geo Jones, prof rpr 1,700.00
Cheese keeper, Picket Fence & Apple Blossom, Geo Jones, 11", NM.2,000.00
Cheese keeper, Water Lily, Cattail & Dragonfly, cobalt, Geo Jones, NM.6,000.00
Comport, Fishnet & Shell, turq, Fielding, EX 450.00
Comport, Pond Lily, storks on ft, 3x9¼" 130.00
Comport, Shell, shells & coral on base, cobalt, Holdcroft, 7¼x11"..550.00
Comport, Strawberry, cobalt, Fielding, 5½x9½" 375.00
Comport, Sunflower, ftd, twig hdls, 10¼" 75.00
Comport, 3 putti w/instruments, rtcl basket top, Wedgwood, 16"..2,750.00
Creamer, Beaded Melon, Holdcroft 90.00
Creamer, frog atop eggplant, Minton, rare, 4" 5,500.00
Creamer, Strawberry, vine hdl, Geo Jones 425.00
Cup & saucer, Cauliflower, Etruscan 150.00
Ewer, Heron & Fish, Minton, prof rpr, 21" 9,000.00
Figure, man carrying 2 baskets, much cobalt, Minton, 16½" ...4,250.00
Fish plate, Argenta, Wedgwood, 8¾" 200.00
Flask, elk in relief, 3¾" 200.00
Game dish, dead game & fish on basketweave base, Geo Jones, 12¾".6,000.00
Game dish, dead game w/vines, yel rope, rabbit finial, Wedgwood, 10"..800.00
Game dish, quail on turq, wheat around base, Geo Jones, NM.2,000.00
Garden seat, Bamboo w/turq ribbon & bow, 1892, 18½", NM ...700.00
Humidor, frog w/red smoking jacket, prof rpr, 7½" 425.00
Humidor, Indian head, 8" 125.00
Jardiniere, Picket Fence & Blackberry, turq, twig ft & hdls, 8" ...400.00
Match striker, Black man, advertising Cuba Fina 300.00
Match striker, Black man carrying melon 400.00
Match striker, Black man w/accordion, EX detail, NM 400.00
Match striker, cat w/top hat & umbrella, EX detail, 8" 350.00
Meat dish, winged fish supports shell, 5x6½" 325.00
Muffin dish/cheese keeper, Apple Blossom, Geo Jones 3,250.00
Pitcher, Acorn, Oak Leaf & Bark, snail hdl, 4½" 550.00
Pitcher, Bamboo & Wheat, 8" 160.00
Pitcher, bear figural, seated, brn, 5¼", NM 150.00
Pitcher, Bird in Hand Is Worth Two in Bush, 6¼" 100.00
Pitcher, Bird's Nest w/Begonia Leaf spout, 9¾" 200.00
Pitcher, birds feeding young in nest, 6" 160.00
Pitcher, Corn, EX color, 7½" 175.00
Pitcher, Corn, 5½" 120.00
Pitcher, dog figural, EX detail, Geo Dreyfus, 8¾" 1,800.00
Pitcher, Dogwood on brn, Holdcroft, 4½" 200.00
Pitcher, elephant figural, Onnaing, 9" 400.00
Pitcher, Fern, cobalt, prof rim rpr 375.00

Pitcher, Fern, Etruscan, 8" 900.00
Pitcher, Fish, cobalt & turq, flat-sided, Holdcroft, 8½"...........1,200.00
Pitcher, Floral, cobalt flowers, 6" 40.00
Pitcher, frog figural, English, 8" 400.00

Pitcher, grapes figural, Brown, Westhead, Moore & Co., minor professional rim repair, 8½", $6,500.00. (Photo courtesy Michael Strawser)

Pitcher, pig waiter figural, Onnaing, 10½" 350.00
Pitcher, Pineapple, 7" 140.00
Pitcher, robin on branch, turq (rare color), 7¼" 400.00
Pitcher, Stork in Marsh, cobalt, sq top, 9", NM 300.00
Pitcher, syrup; Basketweave & Leaf, pewter top, 5" 175.00
Pitcher, syrup; Dogwood on turq, pewter top, Holdcroft, 5½" 225.00
Pitcher, syrup; Pond Lily, pewter top, Holdcroft, 4¼" 225.00
Pitcher, wheat figural w/chicken & rooster, 7" 550.00
Pitcher, Wheat, cobalt, Geo Jones, 5½", NM 2,100.00
Planter, girl playing w/cat & ball of string, Continental, 4¾" 65.00
Plaque, 3 fish on gr leaf, Renoleau, Palissy, prof rpr, 12" 2,000.00
Plate, Bamboo, Etruscan, 8" 120.00
Plate, Begonia Leaf, pk border, 8¼" 300.00
Plate, bird & branch, Eureka, 8¼" 250.00
Plate, Cauliflower, Etruscan, 9" 175.00
Plate, Chestnut Leaf & Napkin, Geo Jones, 9" 450.00
Plate, Fish & Daisy, turq, Holdcroft, 8½" 350.00
Plate, leaves, fern & floral, EX color, 8¾" 110.00
Plate, Leaves & Fern, pk ground, Geo Jones, 8½", NM 850.00
Plate, Maple Leaf on Basket (pk), Etruscan, 9" 300.00
Plate, Overlapping Begonia Leaf, Etruscan, 9" 200.00
Plate, Pansy, Choisy-le-Roi, 8" 125.00
Plate, Pineapple, 9" 180.00
Plate, Pond Lily, Holdcroft, 8¼" 400.00
Plate, Pond Lily, turq center, Minton, prof rpr, 8" 750.00
Plate, Quail, cobalt, rtcl border, Wedgwood, prof rim rpr, 9" 700.00
Plate, Shell & Seaweed, Etruscan, 8", NM 150.00
Plate, Shell & Seaweed, Etruscan, 9¼" 210.00
Plate, Strawberry, blossoms on wht border, Geo Jones, 8¼" 300.00
Plate, Strawberry, cobalt, Geo Jones, 8¼" 400.00
Plate, Strawberry, turq, Geo Jones, 9½" 700.00
Plate, Strawberry, w/dipping well, Minton, NM 800.00
Plate, Strawberry & Apple, cobalt, Etruscan, 9" 400.00
Plate, Strawberry & Apple, lav, Etruscan 300.00
Plate, Strawberry & Napkin w/pk accents, Geo Jones, 8" 400.00
Platter, Bird & Fan, Bamboo border, Wardle, 13", NM 250.00
Platter, Bird & Fan, fan shape, minor prof rim rpr, 16" 375.00
Platter, Bird in Flight, turq, 13¼" 170.00
Platter, Classical Urn & Sunflower, Samuel Lear, 14½" 300.00
Platter, Deer & Dog, 11" 110.00
Platter, Dog & Doghouse, 11" 140.00
Platter, Pear & Apple, 12½" 225.00
Platter, Picket Fence & Floral, turq border, 10" 140.00
Platter, Shell & Coral, Wedgwood, 19" 1,000.00
Salt cellar, shell on coral, 5" 325.00
Sardine box, fish on lid, shells on corners, cobalt 600.00
Sardine box, Pineapple, attached undertray 650.00

Sardine box, wooden boat, Geo Jones, prof rpr............................900.00
Server, Asparagus Basket, Fr, 12½"..100.00
Server, Bird & Shell, 3-part, cobalt accents, NM 950.00
Spooner, Grape & Leaf, Copeland...125.00
Strawberry server, Basketweave & Floral, twig hdl, 10½"............350.00
Sugar bowl, Cauliflower, Etruscan, w/lid 370.00
Syrup, Blackberry, Bennett, 7½"...140.00
Tea set, Pineapple, teapot+cr/sug+2 c/s+tray, NM.................1,700.00
Tea set, Shell & Seaweed, Etruscan, 4-pc, NM.........................700.00
Tea set, Shell & Seaweed, turq, Wedgwood, 3-pc 2,250.00
Teapot, Chinaman w/coconut, att Holdcroft 1,500.00
Teapot, dragon hdl & spout, cobalt, Wedgwood, 5¼"..............3,500.00
Teapot, fish on cobalt, bail hdl, 7½"......................................550.00
Toothpick holder, moth on pk, 1½" 175.00
Tray, Chestnut Leaf, twig hdl...300.00
Tray, Dragonfly on Leaf, 11¼" 135.00
Tray, oak leaf, unmk, 12"...185.00
Tray, Owl & Fan, 12"..500.00
Tureen, rabbit & mallard duck, cobalt, Minton, 1876, 18", NM .35,000.00
Urn, Dickens portrait, laurel swags, foliate scrolls, Minton, 20", NM..1,500.00
Vase, Art Nouveau winged lady w/harp, 6¾"..............................600.00
Vase, peacock figural, Continental, 8½" 150.00
Vase, Strawberry, Continental, 12"...150.00
Wall pocket, monkey figural, Palissy, sm rpr, 8" 850.00
Waste bowl, Blackberry & Basketweave, 5½" 75.00
Waste bowl, Cauliflower, Etruscan..100.00

Malachite Glass

Malachite is a type of art glass that exhibits strata-like layerings in shades of green, similar to the mineral in its natural form. Some examples have an acid-etched mark of Moser/Carlsbad, usually on the base. However, it should be noted that in the past fifteen years there have been reproductions from Czechoslovakia with a paper label.

Bottle, scent; blk glass w/gold, gr malachite stopper, 5½" 715.00
Inkstand, bronze w/malachite base, flit-up top, Fr, 1850-80s, 9¾" L.350.00
Vase, draped nudes in relief, Ingrid label, 9½" 350.00

Mantel Lustres

Mantel lustres are decorative vases or candle holders made from all types of glass, often highly decorated and usually hung with one or more rows of prisms. In the listings that follow, values are given for a pair.

Apple gr Bristol w/gold decor, 7 cut prisms ea, 9⅝"......................450.00
Flashed ruby w/floral, 7 sm/7 lg prisms, gilt rop, 15", pr, EX........200.00
O/l, gr cut to wht, medallions, HP florals & gold, prisms, 11" 295.00
O/l, wht cut to cobalt w/HP florals & gilt, prisms, 9" 265.00
Pk w/enamel, waisted top, 2 rows prisms w/ball drops, 15"..........600.00
Ruby w/gold decor, castellated rim, prisms, 11½" 435.00

Maps and Atlases

Maps are highly collectible, not only for historical value but also for their sometimes elaborate artwork, legendary information, or data that since they were printed has been proven erroneous. There are many types of maps including geographical, military, celestial, road, and railroad. Nineteenth-century maps, particularly of U.S. areas, are increasing in popularity and price. Rarity, area depicted (i.e. Texas is more sought after than North Dakota), and condition are major price factors. World globes

as a form of round maps are increasingly sought after. Our advisor for this category is Murray Hudson; he is listed in the Directory under Tennessee.

Key: hc — hand colored

Atlases

AT Andreas' Illustrated...State of Iowa 1875, 558 pgs, VG+ 625.00
Atlas of Sommerset County Maine, 1883, 75 maps, 17x14", VG+..310.00
Cram's Universal..., 657 gilt-edge pgs, 1899, 12x14½", VG+ 175.00
Gray's Atlas of the US, general maps, 175 pages, 1873, VG 990.00
Mitchell's New General Atlas, 84 maps +26 pgs, 1863, EX.....1,175.00
Mitchell's School Atlas, 32 maps, 9 geographical tables, 1852, EX..270.00
New Popular Family Atlas...World, 582 pgs, ca 1890, VG 100.00
Official Topographical Atlas of Massachusetts, 1871, G.............420.00

Maps

Colton's ME, GW & CB Colton, NY, 1869, 12¾x16" 75.00
Ipswich Bay, JFW Desbarre, 1776, 42½x30¼"...........................1,495.00
Johnson's NY, Johnson & Ward, NY, 1866, 17x23" 75.00
Monumenthensis Comitatus Vernacule Monmouthshire, J Blaeu, 15x20"+fr.635.00
MS & La Louissiane, places/rivers/Indian tribes, Paris, 1718, 28x22" .550.00
New Mappe of Roman Empire, John Speed London/G Humble, 1626, 16x20"....1,500.00
NY Bay & Harbor & Environs, US survey published 1845, 32x42"..635.00
Plan of Town of Boston Attack on Bunker Hill...1775, J Norman, 11x7".2,000.00
West Indies/Caribbean Islands/Am coast, de Wit, 1680, 19¼x22¼" ..800.00

Marblehead

What began as therapy for patients in a sanitarium in Marblehead, Massachusetts, has become recognized as an important part of the Arts and Crafts movement in America. Results of the early experiments under the guidance of Arthur E. Baggs in 1904 met with such success that by 1908 the pottery had been converted to a solely commercial venture. Simple vase shapes were sometimes incised with stylized animal and floral motifs or sailing ships. Some were decorated in low relief; many were plain. Simple matt glazes in soft yellow, gray, wisteria, rose, tobacco brown, and their most popular, Marblehead blue, were used alone or in combination. They also produced fine tiles decorated with ships, stylized floral or tree motifs, and landscapes. Early examples were lightly incised and matt painted (these are the most valuable) on 1"-thick bodies. Others, 4" square and thinner, were matt painted with landscapes in indigoes, in the style of Arthur Wesley Dow.

The Marblehead logo is distinctive — a ship with full sail and the letters 'M' and 'P.' The pottery closed in 1936.

Our advisors for this category are Suzanne Perrault and Dave Rago; they are listed in the Directory under New Jersey. Unless noted otherwise, all items listed below are marked and in the matt glaze.

Bookends, sailing ships, midnight bl, wedge shape, 5⅜", pr........700.00
Bowl, dk gr, globular, 3½x5" 715.00
Bowl, lotus pattern on dk bl ext, bl-gray int, flaring, 8" 250.00
Bowl vase, floral wreath, pk/gr on dk bl, sm rstr, 4x4", $1,400 to..1,900.00
Candle holder, rose, flared rim, long shaft, 4x4½" 300.00
Flowerpot, mustard speckle on red clay, flaring cylinder, 7" 300.00
Tile, potted topiaries, gr/brn/bl on gray, rstr corners/bubbles, 6" .2,760.00
Tile, sailboat, bl on gray, wax resist, rstr chip/firing line, 6" 3,220.00
Tile, trees, lt & dk gr, ca 1908, 6¼" sq..1,380.00
Vase, amber mottle, Baggs, cylindrical, early, 3½x2¼"..............490.00
Vase, antique verde w/brn speckles, cylindrical neck, 5x3¼" 715.00
Vase, band of geese, bl/gray on flecked gray, cylinder, drilled, 6x6"..4,025.00
Vase, blueberries & leaves, 4-color, Hannah Tutt, 1912, 6"...12,650.00

Vase, bud; dk gr, cylinder w/flared base, 4½x2¾" 550.00
Vase, floral, brn on gr, wide mouth, swollen cylinder, ca 1912, 10"..21,850.00
Vase, floral, indigo on gray, experimental, Baggs, cylinder, 2x2¼".....1,380.00
Vase, floral, 2-tone indigo on gray speckle, H Tutt, bbl shape, 4½"..4,025.00
Vase, floral (8 repeats), 3-color, Hannah Tutt, 1912, 4⅜x3⅞"..4,885.00
Vase, floral band w/trailing stems, 4-color, Hannah Tutt, 5⅛x3¼"..1,150.00
Vase, floral w/long twist stems, cobalt on lt gray w/bl specks, 9x4"..9,900.00
Vase, florals & geometrics, olive on lt gr, Hannah Tutt, 1912, 8"..13,800.00
Vase, fruit trees, amber/brn on gray, H Tutt, cylindrical, 4x3¾" ..20,700.00
Vase, fruit trees, gr/orange/bl, tapering oval, 1915, 7¼", NM ..4,850.00
Vase, geese flying in band, 2-color, swollen cylinder, ca 1912, 3⅜" .3,225.00
Vase, geometrics, dk gr on deep bl, wide neck, bulbous, A Biggs, 4x4"..2,415.00
Vase, geometrics, dk olive-grn on gr, invt rim, bulbous, 3x4" ..1,265.00
Vase, gr w/slight irid texture (watermelon rind), ca 1908, 5x3¼" ..1,100.00
Vase, gr/bl mottle, wide swollen shoulder, 2½" 115.00
Vase, grapes/leaves wreath, gray/bl on gray speckle, ovoid, 5x4", NM .1,725.00
Vase, lav, wht int, ovoid, ship logo, 3½x2¾" 300.00
Vase, lav mottled semimatte, curved rim, widening at base, 1935-36, 7"..650.00
Vase, leaves & berries, cvd/pnt on bl, bowl form, 4" 2,100.00
Vase, leaves on stems, brn/indigo on dk bl, 6x5" 1,955.00
Vase, rose pk, powder wht int, ovoid, 5½x3¼" 360.00
Vase, speckled bl matt/gr, floral by A Baggs, cylindrical, 8¾", EX....880.00
Vase, speckled caramel, oatmeal int, mk/paper label, 3½x2¼" ...300.00
Vase, speckled caramel, oatmeal int, ovoid, 3⅝x3" 440.00
Vase, stylized cvg, blk on bl-gr speckle, H Tutt, beaker shape, 6"..8,050.00

Vase, stylized flowers, umber, black, and cream on speckled matte green, marked with an impressed ship, signed Hannah Tutt, 6¾", $120,750.00. (Photo courtesy Dave Rago Auctions)

Vase, trees (8 connecting), brn on bl, bulbous, Hannah Tutt, 3½"..6,900.00
Vase, trees/fruit, gr/red on dk bl speckle, label, 7x4¼", $4,500 to .6,500.00
Wall pocket, dk bl speckled w/turq int, flaring U form, 5x6½"...450.00

Marbles

Marbles have been popular with children since the mid-1800s. They've been made in many types from a variety of materials. Among some of the first glass items to be produced, the earliest marbles were made from a solid glass rod broken into sections of the proper length which were placed in a tray of sand and charcoal and returned to the fire. As they were reheated, the trays were constantly agitated until the marbles were completely round. Other marbles were made of china, pottery, steel, and natural stones. Below is a listing of the various types, along with a brief description of each.

Agates: stone marbles of many different colors — bands of color alternating with white usually encircle the marble; most are translucent.

Ballot Box: handmade (with pontils), opaque white or black, used in lodge elections.

Bloodstone: green chalcedony with red spots, a type of quartz.

China: with or without glaze, in a variety of hand-painted designs — parallel bands or bull's-eye designs most common.

Clambroth: opaque glass with outer evenly spaced swirls of one or alternating colors.

Clay: one of the most common older types; some are painted while others are not.

Comic Strip: a series of twelve machine-made marbles with faces of comic strip characters, Peltier Glass Factory, Illinois.

Crockery: sometimes referred to as Benningtons; most are either blue or brown, although some are speckled. The clay is shaped into a sphere, then coated with glaze and fired.

End of the Day: single-pontil glass marbles — the colored part often appears as a multicolored blob or mushroom cloud.

Goldstone: clear glass completely filled with copper flakes that have turned gold-colored from the heat of the manufacturing process.

Indian Swirls: usually black glass with a colored swirl appearing on the outside next to the surface, often irregular.

Latticinio Core Swirls: double-pontil marble with an inner area with net-like effects of swirls coming up around the center.

Lutz Type: glass with colored or clear bands alternating with bands which contain copper flecks.

Micas: clear or colored glass with mica flecks which reflect as silver dots when marble is turned. Red is rare.

Onionskin: spiral type which are solidly colored instead of having individual ribbons or threads, multicolored.

Peppermint Swirls: made of white opaque glass with alternating blue and red outer swirls.

Ribbon Core Swirls: double-pontil marble — center shaped like a ribbon with swirls that come up around the middle.

Rose Quartz: stone marble, usually pink in color, often with fractures inside and on outer surface.

Solid Core Swirls: double-pontil marble — middle is solid with swirls coming up around the core.

Steelies: hollow steel spheres marked with a cross where the steel was bent together to form the ball.

Sulfides: generally made of clear glass with figures inside. Rarer types have colored figures or colored glass.

Tiger Eye: stone marble of golden quartz with inclusions of asbestos, dark brown with gold highlights.

Vaseline: machine-made of yellowish-green glass with small bubbles.

Prices listed below are for marbles in near-mint condition unless noted otherwise. When size is not indicated, assume them to be of average size, ½" to 1". Polished marbles have greatly reduced values. (We do not list tinted marbles because there is no way of knowing how much color the tinting has, and intensity of color is an important worth-assessing factor.)

For a more thorough study of the subject, we recommend *Antique and Collectible Marbles, 3rd Edition; Machine-Made and Contemporary Marbles, 2nd Edition;* and *Big Book of Marbles, Second Edition,* all by Everett Grist (published by Collector Books); you will find his address in the Directory under Tennessee. Our advisors for this category are Robert and Stan Block; they are listed in the Directory under Connecticut.

Agate, contemporary, carnelian, 1¾" 20.00
Akro Agate, bl slag 1.00
Akro Agate, corkscrew 2.00
Akro Agate, egg yoke/oxblood swirls on custard, ⅝"+, NM........150.00
Akro Agate, Popeye corkscrew 25.00
Akro Agate, Popeye corkscrew, red/wht/bl (rare), ⅝" 125.00
Akro Agate, sparkler 45.00
Banded Opaque, gr & wht, 2" 1,200.00
Banded Opaque, gr w/red bands, wht & bl streaks, 1¾", EX.......160.00
Banded Opaque, red & wht, 1¾" 1,200.00
Banded Opaque, red & wht, ¾" 125.00
Banded Transparent Swirl, bl, ¾" 45.00

Banded Transparent Swirl, lt gr, 1¾".............................300.00
Bennington, bl, 1¾"..15.00
Bennington, bl, ¾"..1.00
Bennington, brn, 1¾"..15.00
Bennington, fancy, 1¾"..40.00
Bennington, fancy, ¾"..2.00
China, decorated, glazed, apple, 1¾"...........................750.00
China, decorated, glazed, rose, 1¾"............................750.00
China, decorated, glazed, wht w/geometrics, 1¾"..............75.00
China, decorated, unglazed, geometrics & flowers, ¾"......125.00
Christensen Agate, Bloodie..80.00
Christensen Agate, clear Cobra, ⅝", NM+......................145.00
Christensen Agate, flame..400.00
Christensen Agate, Guinea..500.00
Christensen Agate, slag...25.00
Christensen Agate, swirl..25.00
Clam broth, opaque, bl & wht, 1¾".............................1,500.00
Clambroth, opaque, bl & wht, ¾"................................200.00
Clambroth, pk (red)/bl/gr swirls, ⅝", EX......................130.00
Comic, Andy Gump...80.00
Comic, Betty Boop..250.00
Comic, Cotes Bakery, advertising.................................900.00
Comic, Kayo, rare...450.00
Comic, Little Orphan Annie...150.00
Comic, Moon Mullins...300.00
Comic, set of 12...1,500.00
Comic, Skeezix..80.00
End of Day, bl & wht, 1¾"..450.00
Goldstone, ¾"..12.50
Indian Swirl, 1¾"..2,500.00
Indian Swirl Lutz-type, gold flakes, ¾".......................1,200.00
Line Crockery, clay, 1¾"...20.00
Lutz type, clear/bl/gold swirls, 1⁵⁄₃₂"...........................300.00
Marble King, bumblebee..1.00
Marble King, watermelon..400.00
MF Christensen, bl opaque..250.00
MF Christensen, bl slag...5.00
Mica, bl, ¾"..30.00
Mica, gr, 1¾"...500.00
Millefiori flowers, tight pattern, pontil mk, 1½", EX.......575.00
Onionskin, w/mica, 1¾"...1,200.00
Onionskin, w/mica, ¾"..110.00
Onionskin, 16-lobe, unusual, 1¾"..............................3,000.00
Onionskin, 2 wht panels w/bl streaks & 2 yel w/red streaks, 2¼"..1,125.00
Onionskin, ¾"..80.00
Opaque Swirl, gr, ¾"...40.00
Opaque Swirl, red/yel/bl/wht, pontil mk, 2⅜", EX...........995.00
Opaque Swirl Lutz-type, bl/yel/gr, ¾"..........................325.00
Peltier Glass, Golden Rebel...500.00
Peltier Glass, National line...25.00
Peltier Glass, NLR Revel, much aventurine, ¹¹⁄₁₆", M......200.00
Peltier Glass, Peerless Patch...5.00
Peltier Glass, slag..15.00
Peltier Glass, Superman..150.00
Peppermint Swirl, opaque, red/red/wht/bl, 1¾".............2,000.00
Peppermint Swirl, opaque, red/wht/bl, ¾"....................125.00
Pottery, 1¾"...20.00
Ribbon Core Lutz-type, red, 1¾".................................1,500.00
Solid Opaque, gr, 1¾"..300.00
Solid Opaque, ¾"..40.00
Sulfide, angel, full body, w/halo, little detail, 1¾".........750.00
Sulfide, angel face w/wings, 1¾"...............................1,200.00
Sulfide, baboon playing bass fiddle, 2⅛"....................1,200.00
Sulfide, baby in basket (Moses in Bullrushes), 1¾"..........800.00

Sulfide, bear cub on all 4s, detailed, 1¼".....................100.00
Sulfide, billy goat, 1½"...100.00
Sulfide, bird, 2"...100.00
Sulfide, boar, 1⅞"...165.00
Sulfide, boy in short pants crawling, 1¾".....................600.00
Sulfide, boy in top hat & dress clothes, gr glass, 1¾"....4,000.00
Sulfide, buffalo, little detail, 1¾"................................300.00
Sulfide, camel, 1-hump, on grassy mound, 1½"..............200.00
Sulfide, child (girl) w/hammer, EX detail, 1¾"................600.00
Sulfide, child sitting, 1¾"..600.00
Sulfide, circus bear, 2"...140.00
Sulfide, coin, face ea side, 1¾"..................................1,500.00
Sulfide, crane w/fish, 1¾"...250.00
Sulfide, crucifix, 1¾", M..600.00
Sulfide, deer, 1¼"...175.00
Sulfide, dog howling, 1⅜"...140.00
Sulfide, dog on grass mound, HP/3-color, pontil, 1¼"....3,500.00
Sulfide, dog w/bird in mouth, 1¾"...............................400.00
Sulfide, dove, 1⅝"...165.00
Sulfide, doves (facing pr), EX details, gr glass, 1¾".......5,000.00
Sulfide, eagle w/closed wings, 1⅞"..............................200.00
Sulfide, elephant, head erect, 'bang' tail, 1¾"...............300.00
Sulfide, elephant standing, sea gr glass, 1¾".................400.00
Sulfide, elephant w/long trunk, 1¼".............................140.00
Sulfide, fish, 1¾"..175.00
Sulfide, fox, 1½", EX..130.00
Sulfide, George Washington, bust, 2⅜"......................2,000.00
Sulfide, gnome, 1½", EX..615.00
Sulfide, hen, 1⅛"...150.00
Sulfide, horse rearing, 1⅞"..175.00
Sulfide, horse standing, 2", EX.....................................130.00
Sulfide, lamb, 1¾"..125.00
Sulfide, lion, standing male, 1½"..................................125.00
Sulfide, Little Boy Blue, 1¾", M...................................450.00
Sulfide, monkey seated on drum, 1⅜"...........................200.00
Sulfide, Nipper dog, 1¾", EX.......................................200.00
Sulfide, numeral 1, 1¾"...400.00
Sulfide, owl, wings spread, detailed feathers, 1¾"..........350.00
Sulfide, owl w/closed wings, 1¾"..................................150.00
Sulfide, papoose, 1¾"...300.00
Sulfide, parrot, 1½", EX..100.00
Sulfide, peacock, tricolor in clear glass, 1¾"................8,000.00
Sulfide, pony trotting through grassy field, EX detail, 1¾"....200.00
Sulfide, poodle on hind legs, 1⅛".................................100.00
Sulfide, rabbit crouching, EX detail, 1¾"......................250.00
Sulfide, rabbit running, lg/offset/sm bubble, 1½", M-......110.00
Sulfide, razor-bk hog, 1½"...150.00
Sulfide, rooster, 1¾"...150.00
Sulfide, sheep grazing, 1¼"...150.00
Sulfide, squirrel standing, 1¾", EX...............................170.00
Sulfide, woman (Kate Greenaway), 1½"........................300.00
Transitional, Leighton, 1"..1,000.00

Marine Collectibles

Vintage tools used on sea-going vessels, lanterns, clocks, and memorabilia of all types are sought out by those who are interested in preserving the romantic genre that revolves around the life of the sea captains, their boats and their crews; ports of call; and the lure of far-away islands.

See also Steamship Collectibles; Telescopes; Scrimshaw; Tools.

Air pump, Bishop & Babcock Cleveland OH, VG.................300.00
Anchor, CI, iron ring at top, mtd on later iron brackets, 107x56"...825.00

Battle rattle, trn maple, w/provenance, 10"............................650.00
Beckets, knotwork, blk pnt, scarce, pr..............................300.00
Bell, brass, 8¼" dia, VG..25.00
Bell, ship's; cast bronze, J Warner & Sons London 1855, 14x13"..1,175.00
Bell, ship's; cast bronze, linear raised bands, 19th C, 17x14"......550.00
Bell, ship's; cast bronze w/verdigris, 1945 on shoulder, 16x14"...450.00
Billet head, cvd wood w/scrolled foliate design, 19th C, 38x7½"..2,500.00
Billet head, cvd/pnt wood w/scrolled foliate design, 195h C, 24x8"..700.00
Binnacle, ES Ritchie Boston, brass, w/compass & lanterns, ca 1876, 25"..1,400.00
Binnacle, mahog w/brass hood & iron compass compensation, stands, 51"..650.00
Binnacle, sky light; Kelvin-White Boston, brass, 1898, 12½"..1,000.00
Binnacle, Wilcox & Crittendon, chrome dome, w/compass, 8", EX...200.00
Cask lifter, CI, lg iron ring in center, EX..........................425.00
Chest, blk pnt, strap hinges, knotwork becket hdls, 14x37x17"..400.00
Chest, camphor wood, 2-part, 47x42x20", EX.....................2,600.00
Chest, carpenter's, wood w/brass trim, canvas-covered base, 9-drw, 38"..900.00
Chest, stencilled name, knotwork beckets, EX......................950.00
Chronometer, presentation; Waltham Watch Co, brass, 8-day, 1950s..1,000.00
Chronometer, TS&JD Negus New York No 3587, 56-hr indicator.2,500.00
Chronomoter, Russian, brass bound w/gimbal mechanism, 56-hr, EX..750.00
Compass, sighting; Stopanni, brass, 2 sight vanes, 3¼x3½", +case..125.00
Desk, captain's traveling, mahog, side drw, leather top, 1850s, 18"..300.00
Dividers, eng solid silver, unmk, mid-1800s, closed: 8"..............350.00
Fid, whalebone, orig rope, 12¼", EX................................750.00
Fid, whelebone, hole for rope, ivory inlay on top, 7½"..............200.00
Float, mk Beaver Harbor, wood w/orig gr & wht pnt.................60.00
Fog horn, Siebe Gorman Ltd London, brass, foot-operated, EX..450.00
Fog horn, Tyfon, brass, mtd on wooden base, 24".................130.00
Gauge, pressure; Ashton Valve Co Boston, copper, 12"..............100.00
Gun, flare; brass fr, octagon-to-rnd bbl, wood grips, AH Fox, 8", EX..425.00
Gun, harpoon; Greener, for dbl-flute harpoon, A Russel & Son..., 54"..11,000.00
Gun, harpoon; S Eggers...Mass, brass, Pat 1878, 37", VG........5,000.00
Half model, builder's; laminated mahog & other wood, on panel, 6x30"..2,000.00
Half model, builder's; pine w/blk & gilt, 19th C, 11x42".........9,400.00
Harpoon, Temple iron, Dean & Driggs, 17th C, 33"..............1,100.00
Hatchet, whale boat; HN Dean, ca 1850s, orig hdl, EX...........4,000.00
Helmet, diving; copper & brass, 3-light, 3-bolt, Russian, VG..1,000.00
Horn, dbl fog; w/alarm bell, brass, on wooden base, 20" L..........125.00
Jumper, lifesaving service, wht w/whalebone buttons, EX......12,000.00
Kettle, solid copper w/splayed bottom, tight cover, 9¾" dia........150.00
Knife, diver's; Morse Diving Equip Co, screws into brass sheath.350.00
Lamp, buoy; brass & copper, ruby red 360-degree lens, 20" H....550.00
Lamp, hand; metal, clear 360-degree lens, converted, 15"+hdl...250.00
Lamp, masthead; metal w/clear ribbed lenses, w/burner, 21".......225.00
Lamp, salon; brass w/milk glass shade, gimbal mt at tip, EX........550.00
Lamp, starboard; W Nunn & Co, brass, chips in bl lens, 17"+hdl..85.00
Lance, killing; 31", mtd on short pole, 56" overall......................750.00
Lantern, copper w/clear ribbed lens (mk Croning), electric, 15"..100.00
Lantern, hand; brass w/5 rnded glass panels, 11½"................125.00
Lantern, mast; Robert Findley...NY, lacks font, clear lens, 10"+hdl.175.00
Lantern, onion; Perkins, galvanized & brass w/red globe, 15".....250.00
Lantern, Perco, solid brass, clear 180 degree lens, w/burner, 18".300.00
Lantern, Perko, brass, converted to electric, 13"+base..............125.00
Lantern, Peter Gray, 3 clear ribbed lenses, 30", VG...................825.00
Log, John Bliss & Co Taffrail Log, used, chip in porc dial..........100.00
Log book, Ship Indian Chief, Hempstead Master, ca 1847, worn cover..17,250.00
Mallet, sail maker's; scrimshawed whalebone, multiple turnings..1,100.00
Model, Saga Marastal, 3-masted barquentine, 1930s-40s, 58" L..4,300.00
Model, Spanish galleon w/sails, EX details, 34"....................3,500.00
Model, 3-masted ship, pnt/cvd wood w/metal fittings, 19th C, 20x31"...600.00
Model, 4-masted sailing ship/buildings/etc in 10" bottle............375.00
Octant, Browning Boston, ebony w/ivory scales, early 1800s, 14", VG..500.00
Octant, solid brass w/ivory scales, complete, EX in case............650.00
Octant, Wilkinson & Sons London, ebony/ivory/brass, 1820s, 16", VG..650.00

Oiler, brass, long spout, w/cap, 11"..................................40.00
Palm, sewing; sail maker's, leather, EX..............................20.00
Plug, cannon muzzle, solid brass, 5-pointed star in center, 6" dia.150.00
Scribe, whalebone w/iron blade, ca 1800, 5x11", EX..............3,600.00
Sextant, Spencer Barret & Co London, brass, silver scale, w/box..850.00
Sextant, Stanley London, solid brass, ca 1890, 4¼" dia, EXIB..1,250.00
Sextant, Tamaya & Co, brass & alumnium, EX in dvtl case.......150.00
Sextant, Troughton London #429, eng scale, 1790s, VG.........1,000.00
Shadow box, Annie May (sloop), cvd/pnt wht on seascape, 22x27"..765.00
Sink, cabin; mahog & steel, folding, 2-door, 50x21x9", VG.......975.00
Sounder, brass w/lead weight, Thos Walker & Sons, 7", +dvtl case.500.00
Spoke shave, whalebone wear plate & wedge, 13", VG..............120.00
Telegraph, yacht; Chas Cory & Son...NY, brass, complete, 36"..700.00
Trumpet, captain's; solid brass, dtd 1866, EX......................950.00
Whaling lance, iron w/wood pole, maker's mk, 1800s, 116½"....295.00
Wheel, solid brass, 16", EX..125.00
Wheel, walnut, orig finish w/varnish traces, 8 spokes & hdls, 47".330.00
Wheel, walnut & hickory, 8 trn spokes & hdls, worn, 43½".......220.00
Wheel, wooden, w/drum, 42" dia, EX................................550.00
Wheel, wooden w/iron hub & brass band, 42", VG..................900.00

Martin Bros.

The Martin Bros. were studio potters who worked from 1873 until 1914, first at Fulham and later at London and Southall. There were four brothers, each of whom excelled in their particular area. Robert, known as Wallace, was an experienced stonecarver. He modeled a series of grotesque bird and animal figural caricatures. Walter was the potter, responsible for throwing the larger vases on the wheel, firing the kiln, and mixing the clay. Edwin, an artist of stature, preferred more naturalistic forms of decoration. His work was often incised or had relief designs of seaweed, florals, fish, and birds. The fourth brother, Charles, was their business manager. Their work was incised with their names, place of production, and letters and numbers indicating month and year.

Though figural jars continue to command the higher prices, decorated vases and bowls have increased a great deal in value. Our advisors for this category are Suzanne Perrault and David Rago; they are listed in the Directory under New Jersey.

Vase, painted and incised with birds and oak branches, 1883, restored hairline, 20", from $4,500.00 to $6,500.00. (Photo courtesy Dave Rago Auctions)

Bird jar, bl & wht w/gold beak, 15½"...............................30,000.00
Bird jar, dk brn w/gold-tone beak & ft, head cocked, 7¾".......1,400.00
Bird jar, droopy beak, sleepy eyes, 11½xx5½"....................9,500.00
Bird jar, lid is head, gr/bl/brn, sgn/dtd, 9".......................7,000.00
Clock, Gothic Revival architectural design, mk 1876, 12x7"..2,625.00
Ewer, flying ducks & swimming fish, bulbous base, flared neck, 9½".870.00
Figurine, fish, mtd on 2 wire supports, wood base, 5x10½x2"....720.00
Jug, detailed grotesque face, disk shape w/shoulder hdls, 1901, 9x7"..3,450.00

Jug, Gothic-style scrollwork, ram's head atop hdl, 9".................700.00
Jug, parrot on branch w/2 in flight, cvd, 8½"...............480.00
Master salt, Gothic style w/creature on ea corner, 3¾x4x4"....1,050.00
Pitcher, thistles cvg, tapered, cylindrical, 8⅝".................340.00
Plaque, Father of Sir Drummond, oval w/bust profile, dtd 1897, 6x4"...500.00
Vase, bl-gr oxide wash, ovoid w/crimped flared neck, 8¼".......1,125.00
Vase, brn mottle w/ribbing, hexagonal ovoid form, 4¾x3½"...1,025.00
Vase, dragons/creatures, ovoid w/flared neck, 10x6¼".............720.00
Vase, poppies cvd on brn, sq tapered body, rstr, 8¾"..............940.00

Mary Gregory

Mary Gregory glass, for reasons that remain obscure, is the namesake of a Boston and Sandwich Glass Company employee who worked for the company for only two years in the mid-1800s. Although no evidence actually exists to indicate that glass of this type was even produced there, the fine colored or crystal ware decorated with figures of children in white enamel is commonly referred to as Mary Gregory. The glass, in fact, originated in Europe and was imported into this country where it was copied by several eastern glasshouses. It was popular from the mid-1800s until the turn of the century. It is generally accepted that examples with all-white figures were made in the U.S.A., while gold-trimmed items and those with children having tinted faces or a small amount of color on their clothing are European. Though amethyst is rare, examples in cranberry command the higher prices. Blue ranks next; and green, amber, and clear items are worth the least. Watch for new glass decorated with screen-printed children and a minimum of hand painting. The screen effect is easily detected with a magnifying glass.

Beaker, gr, boy, pk cheeks, 4⅛x2⅝"...............................85.00
Bell, cobalt, boy w/bird & mtns, 5½".............................135.00
Bell, gr, boy in outdoor scene, 5½"................................80.00
Bowl, cranberry, girl in winter scene, globular, 6".............450.00
Box, jewel; blk amethyst, girl, Middletown #34, 2½x5x4".........850.00
Cruet, cranberry, mc Victorian child, bk: From a Friend/1895, 6½"..275.00
Cup & saucer, gr, boy, ped ft, fat loop hdl....................50.00
Decanter, gr, boy, late 1880s, 9½"+clear stopper...............325.00
Mantle lusters, cobalt, girl on swing, gold trim, pr...........350.00
Pickle castor, cranberry, boy in landscape, Meriden #304 SP fr, 9¾"..1,500.00
Pickle castor, cranberry, girl, rstr Meriden Britannia #273 fr, 11"..1,100.00
Pitcher, clear, lady w/apron among trees, worn gold, 8"........145.00
Pitcher, clear, winged angel, wht among mc flowers, 8".........75.00
Pitcher, gr, girl picking flowers, 11¾".........................250.00
Tumbler, bl, girl, sgn Jessie, World's Fair 1893 on bk..........165.00
Tumbler, gr, lady dancing.......................................65.00
Vase, bl, lady beside churn, amber ft, ca 1890, 4½x2¼"..........75.00
Vase, bl, lady w/bird, cylindrical, 10x2¾", pr.................600.00
Vase, cobalt, badminton player, stick neck, 8".................175.00
Vase, cobalt, girl, crimped top, 8½"...........................275.00
Vase, cranberry, boy w/bird & mtns, 8x4½"......................325.00
Vase, cranberry, boy w/bird in flight, ftd, ruffled rim, 9½x9"..595.00
Vase, cranberry, boy w/birds & mtns, scrollwork, 11x5½".........465.00
Vase, cranberry, girl (EX details), trumpet neck, ftd, 6¼".....375.00
Vase, emerald gr, mc male hunter, ribs, vertical clear rigaree, 11..110.00

Mason's Ironstone

In 1813 Charles J. Mason was granted a patent for a process said to 'improve the quality of English porcelain.' The new type of ware was in fact ironstone which Mason decorated with colorful florals and scenics, some of which reflected the Oriental taste. Although his business failed for a short time in the late 1840s, Mason re-established himself and con-

tinued to produce dinnerware, tea services, and ornamental pieces until about 1852, at which time the pottery was sold to Francis Morley. Ten years later, Geo. L. and Taylor Ashworth became owners. Both Morley and the Ashworths not only used Mason's molds and patterns but often his mark as well. Because the quality and the workmanship of the later wares do not compare with Mason's earlier product, collectors should take care to distinguish one from the other. Consult a good book on marks to be sure. The Wedgwood Company now owns the rights to the Mason patterns and is reproducing Vista. Note: Blue Vista is generally valued at 15% to 20% above prices for pink/red.

Bowl, Flying Bird, mc on wht w/blk transfer, 1890, 10¼"...........175.00
Bowl, fruit; Vista, red, scalloped, ftd, 1890-1900, 4¼x10¼".......300.00
Bowl, Landscape Scroll, mc, scalloped, hdls, 1840s, 10¾" L.......450.00
Bowl, Mogul, mc, flared rim, 1818, 1½x9¾".......................275.00
Bowl, NangPo, mc, gold scroll hdls, 1818, 1x10¾x7¾", EX.........225.00
Bowl, nesting; Vista, red, 8-sided, 1925-30, 3¼x6½"..............125.00
Bowl, soup; Japan, mc, 1813-25, 1½x9½".........................200.00
Bowl, Watteau, red, dragon hdls, 1925-30, 2¼x10½"...............175.00
Chamber pot, Flying Bird, mc, 1830-35, 6x9"....................400.00
Compote, Landscape Scroll, mc, scalloped, ftd, 1840s, 4½x10¼"..950.00
Creamer, Am Marine, red, scalloped rim, 1890-1900, 3½x4", EX..125.00
Cup & saucer, chowder; Vista, red, 1890-1900, 3¼x6", 8½".......150.00
Cup & saucer, demi; Bandana, blk & wht on burnt-orange, 1860s.150.00
Cup & saucer, demi; Jardiniere, ca 1870........................325.00
Egg cup, Vista, red, 1890-1900, 4x3"............................30.00
Jug, dragon, burnt orange, serpent hdl, 1890, 6¼x4½"...........300.00
Jug, Gay Japan/House, mc, dragon hdl, much gold, att, ca 1840s, 4½".650.00
Jug, Real Old Canton, bl, Ashworth, 6¾", EX....................125.00
Jug, Scale, red, 1840s, 4¼x4"..................................400.00
Jug, Vista, red, 8-sided, serpent hdl, 1890-1900, 5¼x4".........175.00
Pitcher, hunt scene, relief molded, 1850s, 8½x8"...............350.00
Plate, Am Marine, bl, scalloped, 1890-1900, 8"..................60.00
Plate, Bandana, blk, 1880-1889, 8".............................350.00
Plate, Fruit Basket, mc on wht, 1890-1900, 7¾", 3 for..........70.00
Plate, NangPo, mc, 1813-25, 8"..................................225.00
Plate, Persiana, mc on cream, 1930, 10⅝".......................80.00
Plate, Table & Flowerpot, mc, ca 1818, 7¼"......................175.00
Plate, Vista, brn, 1890-1900, 7¾"...............................25.00
Plate, Vista, red, 1890-1900, 9"................................30.00
Plate, Water Lily, gold o/l throughout, 1813-25, 6⅛"............250.00
Plate, Wood Pigeon, maroon w/mc o/l, 1900-20, 9¼"...............40.00
Platter, Mogul, mc, early Canton-comb bk, 1818, 12½x9¼", EX..200.00
Platter, NangPo, mc, early Canton-comb bk, 1840s, 9x6½", EX...175.00
Platter, Table & Flowerpot, mc, 1813-25, 9x6¼".................325.00
Platter, Vase & Trophies, mc, scalloped, 1840s, rpr, 10¾x8½"...125.00
Platter, Vista, red, 1925-30, 15¼x12½", EX......................175.00
Teapot, Vista, red, bulbous, 1890-1900, 6¾x9"..................300.00
Teapot, Willow, bl, 1890-1900, 7¼".............................300.00
Trivet, Vista, red, 1925-30, 6x6"...............................150.00
Vase, Landscape Scroll, mc on wht, scalloped, 1835, 6½"........450.00

Massier

Clement Massier was a French artist-potter who in 1881 established a workshop at Golfe Juan, France, where he experimented with metallic lustre glazes. (One of his pupils was Jacques Sicardo, who brought the knowledge he had gained through his association with Massier to the Weller Pottery Company in Zanesville, Ohio.) The lustre lines developed by Massier incorporated nature themes with allover decorations of foliage or flowers on shapes modeled in the Art Nouveau style. The ware was usually incised with the Massier name, his initials, or the location of the pottery. Massier died in 1917.

Vase, stylized floral in lustre and metallic glazes, paper label, 8¼", $950.00.

(Photo courtesy Cincinnati Art Gallery)

Vase, foliate design, metallic irid, tall cyllinder, #10, 19½", NM ..**1,175.00**
Vase, gold swallows on lemon w/gold sponging, 12x5", NM, pr ..**275.00**

Match Holders

John Walker, an English chemist, invented the match more than one hundred years ago, quite by accident. Walker was working with a mixture of potash and antimony, hoping to make a combustible that could be used to fire guns. The mixture adhered to the end of the wooden stick he had used for stirring. As he tried to remove it by scraping the stick on the stone floor, it burst into flames. The invention of the match was only a step away! From that time to the present, match holders have been made in amusing figural forms as well as simple utilitarian styles and in a wide range of materials. Both table-top and wall-hanging models were made — all designed to keep matches conveniently at hand. The prices in this category are very volatile due to increased interest in this field and the fact that so many can be classified as a cross or dual collectible.

Caution: As prices for originals continue to climb, so do the number of reproductions. Know your dealer. Our advisor for this category is Ron Damaska; he is listed in the Directory under Pennsylvania. See also Advertising.

Brass, coat of arms/flags/helmet/2 drums (holders), heavy **85.00**
Brass, devil figure, scrolled wall mt, early **55.00**
Bronze, bear on stump, mk Dodge Inc **85.00**
Bronze, pnt oriental man on flying carpet **225.00**
Bronze, sentry w/musket, caped uniform & kepi, 19th C, EX **135.00**
Bsk, girl w/NY paper & lg pipe, 3 compartments, German/R in dmn, 9".**595.00**
Bsk, street urchin on stump smoking cigar, pastels, 7½" **115.00**
Ceramic, Apollinaris Table Water, striker neck, 3x4½" **80.00**
Ceramic, blk cat w/glass eyes, sanded striker, Goebel **85.00**
Ceramic, bulldog head figural, sgn, Victoria Austria......................**75.00**
China, chamberstick w/matchbox holder, Dresden.....................**110.00**
CI, arched top, hinged lid, striker plate, hangs, 7x4x2⅛"..............**25.00**
CI, frog figural, hinged lid w/striker, stove advertising.................**150.00**
CI, openwork scroll bk, 2 urn-shape holders, 1867, 5x7½x1¼" **65.00**
CI, rctl bkplate, 2-compartment, 7"..**45.00**
CI, urn w/hdls, on sq base, 3"..**75.00**
Compo, Indian in full headdress, mc pnt, 7½x4⅞x3½" **50.00**
Metal, hunting dog & tree stump, old bronze pnt, 2½x4½" **160.00**
Porc, girls playing near fence, Germany **125.00**
Pot metal, elk & stump, VG pnt, 4x6½"..................................**80.00**
SP, antique auto form, flip lid, WB Mfg Co Pat 1907, minimum value .**375.00**
Spelter, Dickens-like character w/oversz top hat extended, 5¾".**250.00**
Walnut Blk Forest type, terrier w/top hat in mouth, wall mt, 9".**175.00**
Walnut wood, bbl w/leaded mechanical base, 5½x4¾x3" **85.00**
Wht metal, pnt Oriental man on flying carpet **85.00**

Match Safes

Before the invention of the safety match in 1855, matches were carried in small pocket-sized containers because they ignited so easily. Aptly called match safes, these containers were used extensively until about 1920, when cigarette lighters became widely available. Some incorporated added features (hidden compartments, cigar cutters, etc.), some were figural, and others were used by retail companies as advertising giveaways. They were made from every type of material, but silver-plated styles abound. Both the advertising and common silver-plated cases generally fall in the $50.00 to $100.00 price range.

Beware of reproductions and fakes; there are many currently on the market. Know your dealer. Our advisor for this category is Ron Damaska; he is listed in the Directory under Pennsylvania. See also Advertising.

Brass, emb Gothic design of St George & dragon, EX.................**185.00**
Brass, emb Oriental fish scene, Japan, ca 1900, 2x1¼" **210.00**
Brass, emb Oriental scene w/birds in flight, ca 1895, 2⅝x1½" ...**225.00**
Brass, World's Fair 1918, bk: Marne Argonne St Mihiel, 2½".......**50.00**
Copper, emb/pnt Nouveau flowers, hinged lid, striker, 2½x1½".**350.00**
Metal, emb horse & rider, 2⅞x1½x½" **80.00**
Silver, emb Art Nouveau decor, w/striker, 1½x1½" **165.00**
Silver, emb ferns, ca 1895, 2⅜x1¼" **235.00**
Silver, folds bk in 2 places for easy access, Sterling E-Z Open, 1916 ...**185.00**
Silver, hidden photo type, att Battin & Co, Pat 1/10/99, 2½" **265.00**
Silver, Masonic emblems, 10th Anniversary...05, mk Sterling, 2½".**235.00**
Silver, monogram, Birmingham hallmarks, ca 1905, 1¾x1¾" **150.00**
Silver, Victorian styling, opens at top, mk Sterling, 2¼ **145.00**
SP, Belfast seal, mk EPNS, 2¼x2¾" **95.00**
SP, chased foliage, striker, English mk, ca 1900, 2x1½" **110.00**
Tin, New Process Gas Range Saves..., printed, stove graphics, 3¼" ..**200.00**

Mauchline Ware

Mauchline ware is the generic name for small, well-made, and useful wooden souvenirs and giftware from Mauchline, Scotland, and nearby locations. It was made from the early nineteenth century into the 1930s. Snuff boxes were among the earliest items, and tea caddies soon followed. From the 1830s on, needlework, stationery, domestic and cosmetic items were made by the thousands. Today, needlework items are the most plentiful and range from boxes of all sizes made to hold supplies to tiny bodkins and buttons. Napkin rings, egg cups, vases, and bowls are just a few of the domestic items available.

The wood most commonly used in the production of Mauchline ware was sycamore. Finishes vary. Early items were hand decorated with colored paints or pen and ink. By the 1850s, perhaps even earlier, transfer ware was produced, decorated with views associated with the place of purchase. These souvenir items were avidly bought by travelers for themselves as well as for gifts. Major exhibitions and royal occasions were also represented on transferware. An alternative decorating process was initiated during the mid-1860s whereby actual photos replaced the transfers. Because they were finished with multiple layers of varnish, many examples found today are still in excellent condition.

Tartan ware's distinctive decoration was originally hand painted directly on the wood with inks, but in the 1840s machine-made paper in authentic Tartan designs became available. Except for the smallest items, each piece was stamped with the Tartan name. The Tartan decoration was applied to virtually the entire range of Mauchline ware, and because it was favored by Queen Victoria, it became widely popular. Collectors still value Tartan ware above other types of decoration, with transferware being their second choice. Other types of Mauchline decorations include Fern ware and Black Lacquer with floral or transfer decorations.

When cleaning any Mauchline item, extreme care should be used to avoid damaging the finish! Mauchline ware has been reproduced for at least twenty-five years, especially some of the more popular pieces and finishes. Collectors should study the older items for comparison and to learn about the decorating and manufacturing processes.

Album, photograph; Victoria Street, bk: Bridge of Cree, +12 photos .115.00
Autograph book, Gannochy Bridge, bk: Rock of Skea, 1880s 65.00
Box, hairpin; violets & retailer's address, 3½", +orig pins 95.00
Box, Mauchline transfer, brass clasp, hinged, 2¾x6½x4½" 215.00
Box, McPherson, Tartan Ware, 1¾x3½x2⅝" 115.00
Box, pencil; A Pleasantry (poem) & flowers, 2x9¼x3¼" 70.00
Box, ring; Tartan Ware, Caledonia, w/tiny 14k gold ring 250.00
Box, studs; Holkham, domed lid, 1x3½x2½" 90.00
Crochet hook set, 6 hooks+trn bone hdl, in 4" case w/Osborn House, EX...450.00
Emery, Squirrel Island ME, 2" 110.00
Inkwell/pen holder, boat form, Palavas Le Casion decal, 6¾" L .315.00
Match holder, Enniskillen, coronet shape, 2-tone sycamore 165.00
Match safe, Ann Hathaway's Cottage, 2¼" 145.00
Match striker, Vesta, Fern Ware, 2½x2½" 150.00
Needle book, Conway Castle & Bridge, fabric int, 3x2¼" 115.00
Page turner, Mt Pleasant House, 11x1½" 110.00
Ruler, geometric design, 9" 150.00
Sewing egg, McBeth, Tartan Ware, orig thimble inside..............165.00
Tatting shuttle, Fern Ware, conch shells & sea grass decor 230.00
Whistle, Lake Worth (FL) scene, 4½" 125.00

McCoy

The third generation McCoy potter in the Roseville, Ohio, area was Nelson, who with the aid of his father, J.W., established the Nelson McCoy Sanitary Stoneware Company in 1910. They manufactured churns, jars, jugs, poultry fountains, and foot warmers. By 1925 they had expanded their wares to include majolica jardinieres and pedestals, umbrella stands, and cuspidors, and an embossed line of vases and small jardinieres in a blended brown and green matt glaze. From the late '20s through the mid-'40s, a utilitarian stoneware was produced, some of which was glazed in the soft blue and white so popular with collectors today. They also used a dark brown mahogany color and a medium to dark green, both in a high gloss. In 1933 the firm became known as the Nelson McCoy Pottery Company. They expanded their facilities in 1940 and began to make the novelty artware, cookie jars, and dinnerware that today are synonymous with 'McCoy.' More than two hundred cookie jars of every theme and description were produced.

More than a dozen different marks have been used by the company; nearly all incorporate the name 'McCoy,' although some of the older items were marked 'NM USA.' For further information consult *The Collector's Encyclopedia of McCoy Pottery* (with recently updated values) by Sharon and Bob Huxford; or *McCoy Pottery Collector's Reference & Value Guide, Vol. I, II, and III*, by Margaret Hanson, Craig Nissen, and Bob Hanson (all published by Collector Books). Also available is *Sanfords Guide to McCoy Pottery* by Martha and Steve Sanford (Mr. Sanford is listed in the Directory under California.)

Alert! Stimulated by the high prices commanded by desirable cookie jars, a broad spectrum of 'new' cookie jars have flooded the marketplace in three categories: 1) Manufacturers have expanded their lines with exciting new designs to attract the collector market. 2) Limited editions and artist-designed jars have proliferated. 3) Reproductions, signed and unsigned, have pervaded the market, creating uncertainty among new collectors and inexperienced dealers. After McCoy closed its doors in the late 1980s, an entrepreneur in Tennessee tried (and succeeded for nearly a decade) to adopt the McCoy Pottery name and mark. This company reproduced old McCoy designs as well as some classic designs of other defunct American potteries, signing their wares 'McCoy' with a mark which very closely approximated the old McCoy mark. Legal action finally put a stop to this practice, though since then this company has used other fraudulent marks as well: Brush-McCoy (the compound name was never used on Brush cookie jars) and B.J. Hull.

Note: Still under pressure from Internet exposure and the effects of a slow economy, the cookie jar market remains soft. High-end cookie jars are often slow to sell.

Cookie Jars

Animal Crackers..100.00
Apollo Age, minimum value 1,000.00
Apple, 1950-64..50.00
Apple, 1967..60.00
Apples on Basketweave 70.00
Asparagus..50.00
Astronauts..850.00
Bananas...125.00
Barnum's Animals..150.00
Barrel, Cookies sign on lid 75.00
Baseball Boy..200.00
Basket of Eggs 40.00
Basket of Potatoes...40.00
Bear, cookie in vest, no 'Cookies' 85.00
Betsy Baker (+)...300.00
Black Kettle, w/immovable bail, HP flowers 40.00
Black Lantern 65.00
Blue Willow Pitcher 75.00
Bobby Baker..65.00
Bugs Bunny...150.00
Burlap Bag, red bird on lid 50.00
Caboose...150.00
Cat on Coal Scuttle 175.00
Chairman of the Board (+).................................550.00
Chef Head, from $175 to 200.00
Chilly Willy 85.00
Chipmunk..125.00
Christmas Tree...800.00
Churn, 2 bands..35.00
Circus Horse, blk...250.00
Clown Bust (+) 75.00
Clown in Barrel, yel, bl or gr..............................85.00
Clyde Dog..250.00
Coalby Cat...375.00
Coca-Cola Can...100.00
Coca-Cola Jug...85.00
Coffee Grinder...45.00
Coffee Mug...45.00
Colonial Fireplace..85.00
Cookie Bank, 1961...165.00
Cookie Barrel, from $35 to.................................45.00
Cookie Boy..225.00
Cookie Cabin...80.00
Cookie Jug, dbl loop..35.00
Cookie Jug, single loop, 2-tone gr rope................35.00
Cookie Jug, w/cork stopper, brn & wht 40.00
Cookie Log, squirrel finial..................................45.00
Cookie Mug...45.00
Cookie Pot, 1964...40.00
Cookie Safe...65.00
Cookstove, blk or wht 35.00
Corn, row of standing ears, yel or wht, 1977.........85.00
Corn, single ear 175.00

Covered Wagon 95.00
Cylinder, w/red flowers 45.00
Dalmatians in Rocking Chair (+) 275.00
Davy Crockett (+) 500.00
Dog in Doghouse, from $225 to 250.00
Dog on Basketweave 90.00
Drum, red 90.00
Duck on Basketweave 90.00
Dutch Boy 65.00
Dutch Girl, boy on reverse, rare 250.00
Dutch Treat Barn 50.00
Eagle on Basket, from $35 to 50.00
Early American Chest (Chiffoniere) 85.00
Elephant 200.00
Elephant w/Split Trunk, rare, minimum value 300.00
Engine, blk 175.00
Flowerpot, plastic flower on top 500.00
Football Boy (+), from $245 to 275.00
Forbidden Fruit 90.00
Fortune Cookies 50.00
Freddy Gleep (+), minimum value 500.00
Friendship 7 ....200.00
Frog on Stump 75.00
Frontier Family 55.00
Fruit in Bushel Basket 85.00
Gingerbread Boy 75.00
Globe 275.00
Grandfather Clock 90.00
Granny 120.00
Hamm's Bear (+) 225.00
Happy Face 80.00
Hen on Nest 95.00
Hillbilly Bear, rare, minimum value (+) 900.00
Hobby Horse, brn underglaze (+) 150.00
Hocus Rabbit 45.00
Honey Bear, rustic glaze 80.00
Hot Air Balloon 40.00
Ice Cream Cone 45.00
Indian, brn (+) 350.00
Indian, majolica 400.00
Jack-O'-Lantern 500.00
Kangaroo, bl 300.00
Keebler Tree House 70.00
Kettle, bronze, 1961 ....40.00
Kissing Penguins, from $100 to 125.00
Kitten on Basketweave 90.00
Kittens (2) on Low Basket 600.00
Kittens on Ball of Yarn 85.00
Koala Bear 85.00
Kookie Kettle, blk 35.00
Lamb on Basketweave 90.00
Lemon 75.00
Leprechaun, minimum value (+) 1,800.00
Liberty Bell 75.00
Little Clown 75.00
Lollipops 80.00
Mac Dog 95.00
Mammy, Cookies on base, wht w/cold pnt (+) 150.00
Mammy w/Cauliflower, G pnt, minimum value (+) ...1,100.00
Milk Can, Spirit of '76 ....45.00
Modern 65.00
Monk 50.00
Mother Goose 150.00
Mouse on Clock 40.00

Mr & Mrs Owl 90.00
Mushroom on Stump 55.00
Nursery, decal of Humpty Dumpty, from $70 to 80.00
Oaken Bucket, from $25 to 45.00
Orange 55.00
Owl, brn 50.00
Pear, 1952 ....85.00
Pears on Basketweave 70.00
Penguin, yel or aqua 200.00
Pepper, yel 40.00
Picnic Basket 75.00
Pig, winking 300.00
Pine Cones on Basketweave 70.00
Pineapple 80.00
Pineapple, Modern 90.00
Pirate's Chest, from $125 to 145.00
Popeye, cylinder 200.00
Potbelly Stove, blk 30.00
Puppy, w/sign 85.00
Quaker Oats, rare, minimum value 700.00
Raggedy Ann 110.00

Red Barn, cow in door, rare, $350.00 minimum value. (Photo courtesy Joyce Roerig)

Rooster, wht, 1970-1974 ....60.00
Rooster, 1955-1957 ....95.00
Round w/HP Leaves 40.00
Sad Clown 85.00
Snoopy on Doghouse (+), mk United Features Syndicate ...200.00
Snow Bear 75.00
Spaniel in Doghouse, bird finial 250.00
Stagecoach, minimum value 800.00
Strawberry, 1955-57 ....65.00
Strawberry, 1971-1975 ....45.00
Teapot, 1972 ....60.00
Tepee, slat top 350.00
Tepee, str top (+) 300.00
Thinking Puppy, #0272 ....40.00
Tilt Pitcher, blk w/roses 50.00
Timmy Tortoise 45.00
Tomato 60.00
Touring Car 100.00
Traffic Light 50.00
Tudor Cookie House 125.00
Tulip on Flowerpot 150.00
Turkey, gr, rare color 300.00
Turkey, natural colors 250.00
Upside Down Bear, panda 50.00
WC Fields 200.00
Wedding Jar 90.00
Windmill 100.00
Wishing Well 40.00
Woodsy Owl 300.00

Wren House, side lid 175.00
Yellow Mouse (head) 45.00
Yosemite Sam, cylinder 150.00

Miscellaneous

Ashtray, Feb 20 Space Capsule, from $40 to 50.00
Ashtray, top hat form, yel, from $20 to 25.00
Basket planter, Floraline, wht, #561L, 7x7½", from $25 to 35.00
Bowl, Garden Club, scalloped rim/ped ft, 1950s-60s, 7x7", from $30 to ..35.00
Centerpiece, antelope on blk or gr base, 1955, 12" W, from $350 to ..450.00
Coffee server, Sandstone, 1978, from $30 to 50.00
Creamer, Mediterranean Line, 1980, from $12 to 15.00
Cup & saucer, Brown Antique Rose, 1959, from $25 to 35.00
Deviled egg plate, chicken shape, yel, 1973, from $20 to 30.00
Dutch oven, gr gloss w/emb rings, stoneware, 1920s-30s, 9¾", $75 to ...100.00
Flowerpot, wavy lines on gr, w/saucer, 1960s, 4-6", ea from $25 to..40.00
Frog w/lotus planter, common color, 1940s, from $15 to 20.00
Jar, oil; burgundy mottle, stoneware, unmk, 1920s-30s, 25", $400 to ..500.00
Jar, oil; drip-style glaze, stoneware, unmk, 1920s-30s, 18", $350 to ..400.00
Jar, porch; leaves & berries on blended matt, 14", from $1,200 to ...1,500.00
Jardiniere, emb swirling pattern, Model 431L, 6½x8½", $25 to ...35.00
Jardiniere, gr onyx, unmk, 1930s-40s, 6", from $35 to 40.00
Jardiniere, Holly, brn onyx, unmk, 1930s, 10½", from $85 to.....100.00
Jardiniere & ped, Basketweave, gr or wht, 8½", 12½" 250.00
Jardiniere & ped, Holly, brn & gr, 8½", 12½", from $200 to 250.00
Jardiniere & ped, Leaves & Berries, brn/gr, unmk, 10½, 18½" ...650.00
Jug, Happytime Line, children decal, 1974, from $20 to 25.00
Matchbox holder, wht w/bl speckles, mk, 1970s, 5¾x3¼" 40.00
Mug, beer advertising on wht w/gold rim, from $25 to 30.00
Mug, Similac for Ross Coffee, yel or gr, from $10 to.....................20.00
Pitcher, donkey form, gr or yel, 1940s, 7", from $250 to.............300.00
Pitcher, fish figural, gr/brn blended, 1949, 7", from $650 to........800.00
Pitcher, Western Wear, brn woodgrain look, 1979, 2½-qt, $50 to ...75.00
Planter, Artisan Line, wht, mk, 1965, 7½", from $35 to 45.00
Planter, baby rattle, wht w/cold pnt, 1954, 3x5½", from $90 to .110.00
Planter, caterpillar figural, wht, Model 416L, 13½" L, from $30 to ..45.00
Planter, dog w/cart, blk, 8½", from $80 to...................................90.00
Planter, Happy Face, 1970s-80s, from $25 to 35.00
Planter, lamb, wht w/gold bow, 1954, 8½", from $90 to..............110.00
Planter, leaves emb on gr, mk, 1950s, 7" L, from $35 to...............45.00
Planter, Madonna, Floraline, wht, 7x6", from $200 to 250.00
Planter, Sunburst Gold, mk, 1950s-60s, 9½", from $30 to............35.00
Planting dish, Capri, bl w/pk int, 1950-60s, 14½", from $40 to 50.00
Shoe planter, Floraline, yel, #530, 3x8½", from $18 to 25.00
Stein, Schlitz Malt Liquor, #6020, 1973, from $25 to...................35.00
Tankard, emb floral, stoneware, unmk, 1920s-30s, 8½", from $70 to .90.00
Tea set, Pine Cone, bl (unusual color), 1940s-50s, 3-pc, $100 to .125.00
Tidbit tray, Morano Line, 2-tier, #915, 1966, from $35 to 40.00
Tumbler, gr, emb rings, flared, stoneware, 1920s-30s, 5", from $40 to..50.00
Vase, bud; bird details, blended gr & brn, 1940s-50s, 8", $35 to ...50.00
Vase, bud; Floraline, turq, 6", from $12 to 18.00
Vase, bud; Vesta, yel w/trim, unmk, 1963, 8", from $20 to 25.00
Vase, Crestwood, yel w/gold, cylindrical, mk, 1964, 14½", $60 to..70.00
Vase, Floraline Fineforms, dk mauve, unmk, #0488FF, 12½x9", $50 to...75.00
Vase, gr w/emb rings, hdls, shield mk, 7½", from $80 to 100.00
Vase, gr w/scrolling ft, 1959, 14", from $75 to............................100.00
Vase, hand form, opening in palm, cold-pnt fingernails, 1940s, 6½" ..175.00
Vase, peacock emb on gr, hdls, 1948, 8", from $50 to 60.00
Vase, red roses decal on wht, hdls, 1950s, 8", from $35 to 45.00
Vase, Ribbed Pedestal, dk gr, #407, 6½x3¾", from $15 to 20.00
Vase, Square Top, any standard color, #446, 9", from $20 to.........25.00

Vase, yel w/low gold hdls, 1950s, 9", from $85 to 120.00
Wall pocket, fan form, bl, mid-1950s, 8½x8", from $75 to...........90.00
Wall pocket, flower, common glaze, late 1940s, 6", from $35 to ...50.00
Wall pocket, lady w/bonnet, mk, 8", from $75 to 200.00
Wall pocket, leaves w/berries, mk, 1940s, very rare, 9" 1,000.00
Wall pocket, lovebirds, mk, 1950s, 8½", from $100 to...............150.00
Wall pocket, umbrella, gr, mk, 1950s, 8¾", from $90 to 100.00
Wall pocket, violin, mk, 1950s, 10¼", from $150 to 200.00

McCoy, J. W.

The J.W. McCoy Pottery Company was incorporated in 1899. It operated under that name in Roseville, Ohio, until 1911 when McCoy entered into a partnership with George Brush, forming the Brush-McCoy Company. During the early years, McCoy produced kitchenware, majolica jardinieres and pedestals, umbrella stands, and cuspidors. By 1903 they had begun to experiment in the field of art pottery and, though never involved to the extent of some of their contemporaries, nevertheless produced several art lines of merit. Their first line was Mt. Pelee, examples of which are very rare today. Two types of glazes were used, matt green and an iridescent charcoal gray. Though the line was primarily mold formed, some pieces evidence the fact that while the clay remained wet and pliable it was pulled and pinched with the fingers to form crests and peaks in a style not unlike George Ohr.

The company rebuilt in 1904 after being destroyed by fire, and other artware was designed. Loy-Nel Art and Renaissance were standard brown lines, hand decorated under the glaze with colored slip. Shapes and artwork were usually simple but effective. Olympia and Rosewood were relief-molded brown-glaze lines decorated in natural colors with wreaths of leaves and berries or simple floral sprays. Although much of this ware was not marked, you will find examples with the die-stamped 'Loy-Nel Art, McCoy,' or an incised line identification.

Corn, tankard, majolica-type glaze, 1910 ....350.00
Loy-Nel-Art, bowl, flat, w/hdls, lg 150.00
Loy-Nel-Art, jardiniere & ped, 22", from $500 to 750.00
Loy-Nel-Art, vase, daffodils, 5"...145.00
Mt Pelee, dish, gr, 1902, 3½x12", from $2,000 to 3,500.00
Mt Pelee, pitcher, #10, 1902, 8", from $700 to 950.00
Olympia, mug, #33, 1905, from $75 to..150.00
Olympia, oil lamp, early 1900s, from $125 to 200.00
Olympia, pitcher, 4", from $125 to...250.00
Rosewood, ewer, emb grapes & leaves, 10" 350.00
Rosewood, vase, #7, 8", from $90 to..175.00
Rosewood, vase, #10, 1904, 9", from $125 to 200.00

McKee

McKee Glass was founded in 1853 in Pittsburgh, Pennsylvania. Among their early products were tableware of both the flint and non-flint varieties. In 1888 the company relocated to avail themselves of a source of natural gas, thereby founding the town of Jeannette, Pennsylvania. One of their most famous colored dinnerware lines, Rock Crystal, was manufactured in the 1920s. Production during the '30s and '40s included colored opaque dinnerware, Sunkist reamers, and 'bottoms up' cocktail tumblers as well as a line of black glass vases, bowls, and novelty items. All are popular items with today's collectors, but watch for reproductions. The mark of an authentic 'bottoms up' tumbler is the patent number 77725 embossed beneath the feet. The company was purchased in 1916 by Jeannette Glass, under which name it continues to operate. See also Animal Dishes with Covers; Carnival Glass; Depression Glass; Kitchen Collectibles; Reamers.

Bottoms Up, coaster, cream ivory (custard), from $50 to **50.00**
Bottoms Up, coaster, Jade-ite..**200.00**
Bottoms Up, tumbler, butterscotch opal.......................................**80.00**
Bottoms Up, tumbler, cream ivory (custard), from $90 to...........**100.00**
Bottoms Up, tumbler, crystal frost **60.00**
Bottoms Up, tumbler, custard...**75.00**
Bottoms Up, tumbler, Jade-ite **125.00**
Bottoms Up, tumbler, Jade-ite, split legs.....................................**285.00**
Bottoms Up, tumbler, lt opal...**65.00**
Bottoms Up, tumbler, vaseline, w/coaster, 3½x3¾".....................**65.00**
Bowl, Pres Cut, milk glass, 3-leg, 1921-30, 3x7".........................**20.00**
Card receiver, Fancy Arch, rolled on 2 sides, 6½" L.....................**45.00**
Celery tray, Pres Cut in raised circle, 7½x4½"..............................**45.00**
Comport, Innovation, milk glass, ftd, ca 1918, 6x6".....................**30.00**
Comport, Sunburst (aka Aztec Sunburst), ca 1910, 7½x6¼".........**25.00**
Console set, Brocade, gr, 11½" bowl+2 2x4½" candlesticks **190.00**
Cup & saucer, Snowflake, bl on milk glass, ftd, 4¾", 5½".............**20.00**
Dish, Pres Cut, ca 1903-51, 7⅜" L..**28.00**
Orange bowl, Innovation Line #412, milk glass, ca 1918, 14½" ...**75.00**
Pitcher, Prism, scalloped top, 8"...**55.00**
Pitcher, Sunburst, ca 1910, 4⅛"...**35.00**
Punch bowl set, Tom & Jerry, wht w/blk, 11½" bowl+8 3½" mugs..**125.00**
Sherbet, Laurel, French Ivory...**8.00**
Vase, Champion, ca 1894, 10" **30.00**

Medical Collectibles

The field of medical-related items encompasses a wide area from the primitive bleeding bowl to the X-ray machines of the early 1900s. Other closely related collectibles include apothecary and dental items. Many tools that were originally intended for the pharmacist found their way to the doctor's office, and dentists often used surgical tools when no suitable dental instrument was available. A trend in the late 1800s toward self-medication brought a whole new wave of home-care manuals and 'patent' medical machines for home use. Commonly referred to as 'quack' medical gimmicks, these machines were usually ineffective and occasionally dangerous. Our advisor for this category is Jim Calison; he is listed in the Directory under New York.

Amputation saw, Civil War era, H&C Disston Co, 18¼", EX....**195.00**
Apothecary chest, comb grpt, 64 sm drw+3 lg drw, 1850s, 39x43x14"..**10,500.00**
Blood pressure gauge, Lifetime Baumanometer, WA Baum, 1928, EXIB..**110.00**
Book, Atlas of Congential Cardiac Disease, hardcover, 1936, 14x11"...**35.00**
Book, Prevention & Cure of Disease, hardcover, 1151 pgs, 1877, VG+..**30.00**
Book, Principles of Physiology...Education, Combs, 1839, VG+ ...**25.00**
Bullet probe, Civil War era, mk KLAR, 9½", EX **50.00**
Dental tool sterilizer, mahog w/NP brass fittings, alchol burner, 12"..**230.00**
Doctor's Apothecary Traveling Kit, J&J first aid products, leather bag.**90.00**
Doctor's bag, brn leather, Emdee by Schnell on brass tag, 1950s, EX..**300.00**
Doctor's Forehead Mirror, English, 1920s, hinged case, EX **65.00**
Eye cup, mk E-Z Pat 1-19-37, emb eye, clear glass, 2⅛", EX.......**25.00**
Fountain syringe, Rexall Victoria, complete, 2-qt, EXIB **70.00**
Hearing aid, Zenith Super Extended Range, EX **25.00**
Hearing aid (ear trumpet), sgn Rockhausen, 15⅜x3¾" dia.........**360.00**
Instrument, blood letting; cvd brass, hand-tooled leather case, VG+..**175.00**
Invalid feeder, wht w/Red Cross insignia, English, 2½x5"............**50.00**
Lancet, walnut hdl, slight rust, 2" blade, 5¾" overall **30.00**
Oscilloclast, ca 1914-20, wooden box, mk #1770, EX **450.00**
Quack device, Dr Charles Body Battery, EXIB...........................**150.00**
Quack device, Revigator Radium Ore, crock, metal spigot, 1912, 12"..**480.00**
Stethoscope, Ford's Bell, ca 1885, EX **50.00**
Syringe case, Lily's Ever-Aseptic Iletin; complete, #24344, EXIB..**45.00**
Thermometer holder, MOP tube w/chain & pin, 4½"..................**80.00**

Thermometer set, Weinhagen & Hespe, oral & rectal, ca 1935, EXIB..**25.00**
Tin, Scott's Blood Tablets, Victorian lady, 3x2", EX+..................**30.00**

Meissen

The Royal Saxon Porcelain Works was established in 1710 in Meissen, Saxony. Under the direction of Johann Frederick Bottger, who in 1708 had developed the formula for the first true porcelain body, fine ceramic figurines with exquisite detail and tableware of the highest quality were produced. Although every effort was made to insure the secrecy of Bottger's discovery, others soon began to copy his ware; and in 1731 Meissen adopted the famous crossed swords trademark to identify their own work. The term 'Dresden ware' is often used to refer to Meissen porcelain, since Bottger's discovery and first potting efforts were in nearby Dresden. See also Onion Pattern.

Centerpc, appl flowers & putti support pierced basket, Xd swords, 21".**4,600.00**
Cup & saucer, battle scene, Xd swords, ca 1735, 2⅝", 5⅛" **2,600.00**
Cup & saucer, floral on wht, gold border & trim, 3", 6" dia........**385.00**
Cup & saucer, navy bl w/gold gilt & trim on wht, Xd swords **150.00**
Cup & saucer, yel dragon on wht, gilded, Xd swords **150.00**
Desk set, sm mc flowers on wht, 2 inkwells (1½") & tray (8¾x6")..**225.00**
Figurine, Arch Duke Frederick & Maria Theresa, Xd swords, 11½"..**2,225.00**
Figurine, Athena, Goddess...Wisdom, in purple w/book, Xd swords, 7"..**1,025.00**
Figurine, baby in carriage, Dresden, 5x5" **475.00**
Figurine, cherub w/cameo & flowers in hands, #1546, Xd swords, 17"..**1,825.00**
Figurine, cockatoo on stump, wht w/red head feathers, Xd swords, 9".**575.00**
Figurine, Friede, nude w/bl blanket w/sm cherub at ft, Xd swords, 23"..**1,650.00**
Figurine, gardening couple, both mk #68, Xd swords, 8", pr **1,825.00**
Figurine, girl playing ball, Xd swords, ca 1900, 14½" **2,025.00**
Figurine, hen w/chicks tucked under wings, Xd sword, 8½" L.**1,325.00**
Figurine, lad in chair, head bk daydreaming, Xd swords, ca 1880, 7"..**1,375.00**
Figurine, lady feeding chicken & chicks, 5x3"............................**440.00**
Figurine, lady in lt lav w/lamb at ft, Xd swords, ca 1750, 8" ...**1,650.00**
Figurine, lady in pk playing spinet piano, Xd swords, 5x3¼x3¼".**1,050.00**
Figurine, lady musician w/cage on bk, Xd swords, ca 1940, 7½"..**1,520.00**

Figurine, lovers, musicians, and cherubs on rocky landscape, multicolor with gold, crossed swords mark, 14", NM, $3,700.00.

Figurine, lovers under a tree w/lamb/dog/bird, Xd swords, 9x7¼" .**1,050.00**
Figurine, man/lady play chess, losses to lace, 20th C, 9x12" **285.00**
Figurine, Monkey Band triangle player, Xd swords, ca 1850, 5⅞".**940.00**
Figurine, nude seated on blanket, all wht, Xd swords, 12¾" **650.00**
Figurine, parrot on stump, Xd swords, 11" **1,500.00**
Figurine, peasant lady in bl w/head scarf, Xd swords, 4" **500.00**
Figurine, Pluto w/Proserpina on shoulder, mk 1797, Xd swords, 8"..**2,875.00**
Figurine, 2 children w/birdcage, Xd swords, 5¾" **1,325.00**
Figurine, 3 winged cherubs painting on easel, Xd swords, ca 1780, 7".**2,525.00**
Lamp, parrot on 4-scroll ft on C-arm stem w/allover flowers, 21"..**500.00**

Plate, gr floral center on wht, gold scalloped rim, 9¾" 100.00
Plate, 2 cherubs w/globe & telescope, Xd swords, 9" 1,200.00
Relish dish, wht w/gr vine border, leaf-based hdl, 3-part, 8x9" ...410.00
Tray, sm mc flowers on wht, 22k gilt, Xd swords, 11½x6" 150.00
Vase, appl flower garlands & cherubs w/gold wings, Xd swords, 14½"..460.00
Vase, potpourri; panels of lovers, dog & birds on bottom, 9½" 1,275.00
Wall shelf, 4 ornate pillars w/cherubs & urns join 2 wood shelves, 20".350.00

Mercury Glass

Silvered glass, commonly called mercury glass, was a major scientific achievement of the nineteenth century. It was developed by the glass industry, who was searching for an inexpensive substitute for silver. Though very fragile, it was lightweight and would not tarnish. Mercury glass was made with two thin layers, either blown with a double wall or joined in sections, with the space between the walls of the vessel filled with a silvering compound, the perfecting of which involved much experimentation. Colored glass was also silvered. Green, blue, and amber were favored. Occasionally, colors were achieved using clear glass by adding certain chemicals to the compound. Besides hollow ware items, flat surfaces were silvered as well, through a process whereby small facets were cut on the underneath side, then treated with the silvering compound. Sometimes mercury glass was decorated by engraving; it was also hand painted. Besides decorative items such as vases and candlesticks, for instance, utilitarian items — doorknobs, curtain tiebacks, and reflectors for lamps — were also popular. Silvered Christmas ornaments were produced in large quantities.

Condition is an issue, though opinions are divided. While some prefer their acquisitions to be in mint condition, others accept items with flaked silvering. Watch for reproductions marked Made in China. In the listings that follow, all examples are silver unless noted another color.

Bowl, 3 clear appl ft, 4¾x9½" 125.00
Candlestick, HP leaves & flowers, gold top, 9" 115.00
Centerpc, spherical top, rnd base, baluster stem, 10"..................100.00
Doorknobs, pr 70.00
Drawer pulls, 1¼" dia, matching set of 6.........................80.00
Match holder 70.00
Mug, clear appl hdl, 3" 40.00
Pitcher, water; eng lacy floral, clear hdl, bulbous, 1840s, scarce..350.00
Rolling pin...120.00
Toothpick holder 50.00
Vase, HP bird, 7½" 70.00
Witch ball, w/stand, scarce, 18" 240.00

Merrimac

Founded in 1897 in Newburyport, Massachusetts, the Merrimac Pottery Company primarily produced gardenware. In 1901, however, they introduced a line of artware that is now attracting the interest of collectors. Marked examples carry an impressed die-stamp or a paper label, each with the firm name and the outline of a sturgeon, the definition of the Indian word, Merrimac.

Bowl, gr, wht drips on caramel int, invt ruffled rim, 3x7" 770.00
Jardinere, gr matt, melon ribbed w/incurvate rim, rstr rim/base, 8x12"..1,500.00
Vase, feathered gr matt, shouldered w/heavy wide rim, 4¼x3½", NM...325.00
Vase, gr, elephant hdls, 5" 425.00
Vase, gr matt drips over bright yel, hdls, glaze burst to base, 4x8".1,100.00
Vase, gr textured on dk gr, shouldered, pinched neck, unmk, 13x6½".1,980.00
Vase, mottled apple gr semi-matt, shouldered, 3x3¾" 1,000.00
Vase, thick bl mottle, classic form, ca 1915, unmk, 5½" 90.00

Metlox

Metlox Potteries was founded in 1927 in Manhattan Beach, California. Before 1934 when they began producing the ceramic housewares for which they have become famous, they made ceramic and neon outdoor advertising signs. The company went out of business in 1989.

Well-known sculptor Carl Romanelli designed artware in the late 1930s and early 1940s (and again briefly in the 1950s). His work is especially sought after today.

Some Provincial dinnerware lines can be confusing. There are two 'rooster' lines, Red Rooster (red, orange, and brown) and California Provincial (dark green and burgundy), and there are three 'homestead' lines, Colonial Heritage (red, orange, and brown like the Red Rooster pieces), Homestead Provincial (dark green and burgundy like California Provincial), and Provincial Blue (blue and white). For further information we recommend *Collector's Encyclopedia of Metlox Potteries, Second Edition,* by our advisor Carl Gibbs, Jr.; he is listed in the Directory under Texas.

Cookie Jars

Apple, red, 3½-qt, 9½", from $75 to 85.00
Barrel (aka Cookie Barrel), w/cookie lid, 11", from $100 to 125.00
Barrel (aka Pretzel Barrel), w/pretzel lid, 11", from $125 to 150.00
Barrel (aka Squirrel Nut Barrel), w/squirrel & nuts lid, 11", $100 to.110.00
Basket, natural, w/gr apple lid, from $40 to 50.00
Basket, wht, w/fruit lid (natural colors), from $40 to....................50.00
Basket (aka Cookie Basket), natural, w/cookie lid, 10½", $40 to .50.00
Bear, Circus, from $400 to 450.00
Bear, Koala, from $100 to...125.00
Bear, Panda (w/o lollipop), from $80 to 100.00
Bear, Roller, from $100 to 125.00
Bear, Teddy, w/red heart, from $200 to..250.00
Bluebird on Pinecone, stain finish, 3-qt, from $65 to 75.00
Candy Girl, 9", from $275 to 300.00
Cat, Calico, cream w/bl ribbon, from $140 to................................150.00
Chickadee, Cookie Creations, 2-qt, from $65 to 85.00
Chicken, Mother Hen, wht, from $100 to.....................................125.00
Clown, yel, 3-qt, from $125 to...150.00
Cow, Purple, pk flowers/butterfly, yel bell, $425 to......................450.00
Daisy Cookie Canister, 3½-qt, from $50 to....................................55.00
Dog, Fido, cream, from $150 to 175.00
Dog, Scottie, blk, from $175 to..200.00
Duck, Puddles, yel or wht raincoat, from $75 to............................100.00
Dutch Boy, from $375 to..400.00
Eagle Provincial, 2nd series, bl, 1776 date, from $35 to.................45.00
Elephant, 11", minimum value 350.00
Feathered Friends, Cookie Creations, 2-qt, from $65 to...............85.00
Gingerbread, bsk, 3½-qt, from $100 to 125.00
Goose, Mother, 2-qt, from $225 to..250.00
Grapefruit, 3-qt, from $150 to 175.00
Happy the Clown, 11", minimum value...350.00
Hippo, Bubbles, yel & gr, minimum value 350.00
Intaglio, from $35 to..45.00
Lamb w/Flowers, 2½-qt, from $275 to..300.00
Lion, yel, 2-qt, from $150 to 175.00
Little Red Riding Hood, minimum value..1,250.00
Mammy, Cook, yel, from $425 to 450.00
Mediereè, any color, 2½-qt, from $35 to.......................................45.00
Miller's Sack, from $50 to 75.00
Mona-Monoclonius, Year of the Dinosaur, from $150 to...............175.00
Mouse Mobile, bsk, from $75 to 100.00
Noah's Ark, color glaze, from $225 to 250.00
Orange, 3½-qt, from $90 to 100.00

Parrot, minimum value..350.00
Pelican, Salty, from $200 to.......................................225.00
Piggy, Little, decor, from $125 to................................150.00
Pinocchio, 3-qt, 11", from $325 to..............................350.00
Pretty Anne, 2½-qt, from $175 to................................200.00
Rabbit, clover bloom finial, from $175 to.....................200.00
Rabbit, Mrs Bunny, holding carrot, from $100 to............125.00
Rag Doll, Boy, 1¾-qt, from $200 to.............................225.00
Rose, 2¾-qt, from $375 to..400.00
Santa, standing, solid chocolate, minimum value...........900.00
Seal, Sammy, from $475 to..500.00
Space Rocket, 12⅞", minimum value...........................750.00
Sun, from $150 to...175.00
Tulip, from $375 to...400.00
Tulip Time, Cookie Creations, 2-qt, from $65 to.............85.00
Watermelon, from $300 to..325.00
Whale, bl, from $475 to..500.00

Dinnerware

#200 series (aka Poppy Trail), cup, jumbo; from $22 to.................25.00
#200 series (aka Poppy Trail), grease jar, 1-pt, from $50 to...........55.00
#200 series (aka Poppy Trail), plate, rimmed salad; 7¼", $10 to...12.00
#200 series (aka Poppy Trail), platter, oval, 13¾", from $40 to.....45.00
#200 series (aka Poppy Trail), relish dish, 9½", from $30 to.........35.00
#200 series (aka Poppy Trail), tumbler, 10-oz, from $80 to............85.00
Antique Grape, bowl, divided vegetable; sm, 8½", from $45 to....50.00
Antique Grape, compote, ftd, 8½", from $75 to.............................80.00
Antique Grape, cup & saucer, 7-oz, 6⅛", from $16 to...................18.00
Antique Grape, jam & jelly, 8⅛", from $55 to..............................60.00
Blueberry Provincial, butter dish, from $50 to..............................55.00
Blueberry Provincial, gravy, 1-pt, from $32 to..............................35.00
Blueberry Provincial, mug, lg, 1-pt, from $28 to...........................30.00
Blueberry Provincial, plate, dinner; 10½", from $12 to.................13.00
California Aztec, coaster, from $35 to...38.00
California Aztec, plate, luncheon; from $45 to..............................48.00
California Aztec, platter, oval, 11", from $75 to...........................80.00
California Aztec, shakers, pr, from $60 to.....................................64.00
California Ivy, bowl, salad; 11¼", from $90 to.............................95.00
California Ivy, cup & saucer, AD; from $30 to..............................35.00
California Ivy, egg cup, from $35 to...38.00
California Ivy, gravy, 12-oz, from $35 to......................................38.00
California Ivy, plate, dinner; 10¼", from $16 to...........................18.00
California Ivy, soup tureen, w/lid, minimum value......................850.00
California Peach Blossom, creamer, from $32 to............................35.00
California Peach Blossom, cup & saucer, from $16 to....................19.00
California Peach Blossom, pitcher, water; from $85 to..................95.00
California Peach Blossom, plate, dinner; from $16 to....................18.00
California Peach Blossom, platter, sm, from $45 to.......................50.00
California Provincial, bowl, soup; 8", from $28 to........................30.00
California Provincial, candle holder, from $55 to..........................60.00
California Provincial, canister, coffee; from $75 to.......................80.00
California Provincial, coffee carafe, 44-oz, 7-cup, from $140 to..150.00
California Provincial, hen on nest, from $145 to...........................155.00
California Provincial, plate, bread & butter; 6⅜", from $10 to.....11.00
California Strawberry, bowl, fruit; 5⅜", from $12 to...................14.00
California Strawberry, cup & saucer, 7-oz, 6", from $12 to...........14.00
California Strawberry, pitcher, 1¼-qt, from $50 to.......................55.00
California Strawberry, plate, salad; 8", from $9 to........................10.00
Della Robbia, bowl, soup; 8⅜", from $20 to................................22.00
Della Robbia, gravy w/faststand, 1-pt, from $35 to......................40.00
Della Robbia, oval baker, 12⅛", from $45 to..............................50.00
Della Robbia, plate, dinner; 10⅝", from $14 to...........................15.00
Homestead Provincial, bowl, vegetable; 7⅛", from $50 to...........55.00

Homestead Provincial, coffeepot, 42-oz, 7-cup, from $125 to.....135.00
Homestead Provincial, cup & saucer, from $18 to........................20.00
Homestead Provincial, gravy, 1-pt, from $45 to...........................50.00
Homestead Provincial, pitcher (aka milk pitcher), 1-qt, from $75 to...85.00
Homestead Provincial, soup tureen ladle, from $60 to..................65.00
Homestead Provincial, sugar bowl, w/lid, 8-oz, from $35 to.........38.00
La Mancha, butter dish, from $50 to...55.00
La Mancha, coffeepot, 8-cup, form $80 to.....................................90.00
La Mancha, creamer, 9-oz, from $20 to...22.00
La Mancha, mug, 10-oz, from $18 to..20.00
La Mancha, plate, bread & butter; 6½", from $7 to........................8.00
Lotus, banana leaf, 11", from $40 to...45.00
Lotus, cup & saucer, demi; from $26 to..30.00
Lotus, gravy, from $38 to...40.00
Lotus, plate, dinner; 10½", from $15 to..16.00
Lotus, shakers, pr, from $28 to...30.00
Lotus, shell server, ind, from $30 to..35.00
Navajo, bowl, lug soup; from $20 to...22.00
Navajo, chop plate, 13", from $60 to..65.00
Navajo, coaster, from $20 to..22.00
Navajo, cup & saucer, from $14 to...16.00
Navajo, mug, cocoa; 8-oz, from $20 to...22.00
Navajo, pepper mill, from $35 to..40.00
Provincial Blue, bowl, lug soup; ind, 5", from $32 to...................35.00
Provincial Blue, buffet server (aka chop plate), 12¼", from $80 to..85.00
Provincial Blue, butter dish, from $75 to......................................80.00
Provincial Blue, mug, w/lid, lg, 1-pt, from $65 to........................70.00
Provincial Blue, pipkin set, minimum value...............................425.00
Provincial Blue, plate, salad; 7½", from $14 to............................15.00
Provincial Blue, sugar bowl, w/lid, 8-oz, from $35 to..................38.00
Red Rooster, ashtray, 10", from $30 to...35.00
Red Rooster, bread server, 9½", from $60 to.................................65.00
Red Rooster, canister, tea; from $55 to...60.00
Red Rooster, creamer, 6-oz, from $25 to.......................................28.00
Red Rooster, cruet set, 5-pc, from $180 to..................................195.00
Red Rooster, cup & saucer, 7-oz, 6⅛", from $14 to......................16.00
Red Rooster, egg cup, from $32 to..35.00
Red Rooster, kettle casserole, w/lid, 2-qt 12-oz, $125 to............135.00
Red Rooster, plate, dinner; 10", from $13 to................................15.00

Sculptured Grape, Bread and butter plate, from $10.00 to $11.00; Butter dish, from $60.00 to $65.00.

(Photo courtesy Carl Gibbs, Jr.)

Sculptured Grape, bowl, soup; 8⅛", from $22 to...........................25.00
Sculptured Grape, creamer, 10-oz, from $28 to.............................30.00
Sculptured Grape, mug, 8-oz, from $25 to....................................28.00
Sculptured Grape, pitcher, 2¼-qt, from $75 to.............................80.00
Sculptured Grape, plate, bread & butter; 6⅜", from $10 to..........11.00
Sculptured Zinnia, cup & saucer, 7-oz, 6⅛", from $14 to.............16.00
Sculptured Zinnia, gravy w/faststand, 1-pt, from $35 to...............40.00
Sculptured Zinnia, mug, 8-oz, from $22 to...................................25.00
Sculptured Zinnia, sugar bowl, w/lid, 10-oz, from $30 to.............32.00
Vineyard, bowl, vegetable; 8¼", from $32 to...............................35.00
Vineyard, buffet server, 14¼" dia, from $55 to.............................60.00
Vineyard, creamer, 8-oz, from $25 to...28.00

Vineyard, mug, 8-oz, from $22 to 25.00
Vineyard, pitcher, 1-qt, from $50 to 55.00
Woodland Gold, plate, dinner; 10¼", from $12 to 13.00
Woodland Gold, sugar bowl, w/lid, 12-oz, from $30 to 32.00
Woodland Gold, teapot, 6-cup, from $100 to 110.00
Woodland Gold, tumbler, 12-oz, from $28 to 30.00
Yorkshire, ashtray, from $18 to 20.00
Yorkshire, bowl, salad; 12", from $60 to 65.00
Yorkshire, cup & saucer, from $13 to 16.00
Yorkshire, egg cup, from $28 to 30.00
Yorkshire, pitcher, 2-qt, from $60 to 65.00
Yorkshire, plate, luncheon; 9", from $12 to 15.00

Disney Figurines

Bambi, jumbo, from $1,000 to 1,500.00
Bambi w/butterfly, from $225 to 250.00
Cinderella, formal, from $400 to 450.00
Dog house, mini, 2½", from $125 to 150.00
Donald Duck w/guitar, from $275 to 300.00
Dumbo, lying on ear, from $125 to 150.00
Dumbo, mini, 1¾", from $175 to 200.00
Dumbo, standing, from $200 to 225.00
Dwarf, any, from $200 to 250.00
Faline, looking str ahead, lg, from $140 to 165.00
Figaro, any position, from $175 to 225.00
Hippo, Fantasia figure, from $325 to 400.00
Jiminy Cricket, from $550 to 600.00
Jiminy Cricket, mini, 1¼", from $175 to 225.00
Jock (dog from Lady & Tramp), mini, 1¾", from $200 to 250.00
Jose, Panchito or Donald as in 3 Caballeros, ea, from $325 to 350.00
Mamma Mouse (Cinderella), from $175 to 200.00
Michael, from $150 to 180.00
Peter Pan, from $400 to 450.00
Pig, (of 3 Little Pigs), mini, 1¼", ea, from $150 to 200.00
Pinocchio, from $400 to 450.00
Scamp Pup (from Lady & Tramp), mini, ¾", from $200 to.........250.00
Snow White, #220, from $425 to 500.00
Snow White, mini, 3", from $550 to 600.00
Sprite, Fantasia Figure, 1940, from $175 to................................250.00
Timothy Mouse, from $175 to 250.00
Timothy Mouse, mini, 1¼", from $200 to 250.00
Tweedle Dum or Tweedle Dee, ea from $225 to.........................250.00
White Rabbit, from $250 to..275.00

Miniatures

Canary on stump, 4⅝", from $75 to 125.00
Crane, 6¼", from $50 to 80.00
Dodo bird, 6", from $100 to 140.00
Elephant, running, 6½", from $175 to......................................225.00
Gay Caballero, minimum value 475.00
Indian rhinoceros, from $125 to 175.00
Mexican peasant, comical, minimum value 450.00
Scottie, 6½" L, from $50 to...80.00
Ship, 2½", from $50 to...80.00

Nostalgia Line

Reminiscent of the late nineteenth and early twentieth centuries, the Nostalgia line contained models of locomotives, gramophones, early autos, stage coaches, and baby carriages. There were also wagons and carts pulled by horses or donkeys, sometimes with separate drivers and passengers. The line was produced from the late 1940s through the 1960s.

American Royal Horses, Clydesdale, 9x9", minimum value........250.00
American Royal Horses, mustang, lg, 10x8", from $180 to 190.00
American Royal Horses, palomino, 6x6", from $165 to 175.00
Auto, Old Ford, from $75 to...85.00
Bathtub, 3¼x7½x4½", from $55 to..60.00
Coachman, from $65 to..70.00
Dr's buggy, 9", from $65 to 70.00
Drum table, from $40 to 45.00
Ice wagon, from $70 to 80.00
Locomotive, from $60 to 65.00
Perambulator, from $60 to 65.00
Santa, from $85 to 90.00
Stagecoach, from $90 to 100.00

Poppets

From the mid-'60s through the mid-'70s, Metlox produced a line of 'Poppets,' eighty-eight in all, representing characters ranging from royalty and professionals to a Salvation Army group. They came with a name tag; some had paper labels, others backstamps.

Barney, bather boy, 8½", from $45 to 55.00
Emma the cook, 8", from $45 to 55.00
Grace, princess, from $45 to...55.00
Hawaiian girl, 4¾", from $40 to 50.00
Melinda, tennis girl w/4" bowl, from $60 to 70.00
Minnie, mermaid, form $55 to...65.00
Sally, girl w/baby, 6¾", from $40 to 50.00
Salty the sea captain, 5¼", from $45 to......................................55.00
School marm w/4" bowl, from $70 to 80.00
Tony the cart peddler, 7⅛", from $45 to.....................................55.00

Romanelli Artware

Cowboy, 10¾", minimum value...500.00
Rooster, 8¼", from $100 to..125.00
Silhouette, Dancing Girl, 9¼", from $250 to...............................275.00
Silhouette, Stylized Geese, 9", from $135 to...............................155.00
Tropical Fish vase, 8½", from $75 to 90.00
Vase, Aquatic, 7⅜", from $175 to 200.00
Vase, Sail Fish, 9", from $140 to..160.00
Vase, Zodiac sign, 8x4x3", ea, from $175 to...............................200.00

Mettlach

In 1836 Nicholas Villeroy and Eugene Francis Boch, both of whom were already involved in the potting industry, formed a partnership and established a stoneware factory in an old restored abbey in Mettlach, Germany. Decorative stoneware with in-mold relief was their specialty, steins in particular. Through constant experimentation, they developed innovative methods of decoration. One process, called chromolith, involved inlaying colorful mosaic designs into the body of the ware. Later underglaze printing from copper plates was used. Their stoneware was of high quality, and their steins won many medals at the St. Louis Expo and early world's fairs. Most examples are marked with an incised castle and the name 'Mettlach.' The numbering system indicates size, date, stock number, and decorator. Production was halted by a fire in 1921; the factory was not rebuilt.

Key:
L — liter   PUG — print under glaze
POG — print over glaze   tl — thumb lift

#168, pokal, relief: spiral scene, set-on lid, 20" 675.00
#280, stein: transfer/HP: crest, pewter lid, .5L 300.00
#284, stein, tranfer/HP: monkey, cat & boar w/verse, pewter lid, .5L..235.00
#376, stein, tree trunk w/branch hdl, inlaid lid, early, .5L, NM ..300.00
#675, stein, bbl w/figural drinking cavalier lid, early, .5L, NM ...400.00
#1053, stein, etch: dwarfs drinking, inlaid lid, 1L..........................775.00
#1130, stein, etch/glazed: eagle, Munich child inlay lid, .5L.......865.00
#1155, stein, etch/glazed: repeating design, inlaid lid, .5L.........380.00
#1288, stein, etch/glazed: repeating leaves & acorns, inlaid lid, .5L..325.00
#1376, charger, cvd/pnt: maiden, 10½" dia..........................130.00
#1394, stein, etch: German cards, inlaid lid, .5L 500.00
#1395, stein, etch: Fr cards, inlaid lid, .5L 525.00
#1396, stein, etch: cherub drinking, Warth, inlaid lid, .5L 485.00
#1494, stein, etch: man drinks/sits on bbl, pewter lid, 5.6L 1,950.00
#1525, stein, relief: fox picking grapes, inlaid lid, .25L, EX.........105.00
#1526, stein, HP: Borussia Sei's Panier, pewter lid, ca 1898, .25L.515.00
#1526, stein, HP: Glaxonia Sei's Panier, pewter lid, ca 1930, .5L .255.00
#1526, stein, transfer/HP: family crest, pewter lid, dtd 1896, .5L .365.00
#1526, stein, transfer/HP: 3 blk cats, pewter lid w/dents, .5L.....265.00
#1526-1076, stein, PUG: hunter, pewter lid w/target, .5L...........185.00
#1526-1502, stein, PUG: military scene, inlaid lid, flaw, .5L 345.00
#1526-629, stein, PUG: boy serving, pewter lid, .25L, NM.........185.00
#1527, stein, etch: cavaliers drinking, inlaid lid, Warth, .5L.......400.00
#1530-581, stein, PUG: student smoking pipe, inlaid lid, .5L.....400.00
#1566, stein, etch: man on high-wheeler, SP lid, .5L, NM 575.00
#1648, stein, etch/tapestry: man drinking, pewter lid, rpr strap, 1L .300.00

#1676, charger, bird on branch, flower cluster, signed Hein, 19", $1,300.00.

#1741, stein, etch: Tubingen, Warth, old rpl pewter lid, .5L.......475.00
#1809, stein, pnt relief: barmaid & cavaliers, inlaid lid, .5L, NM ...700.00
#1855-622, stein, PUG: man playing bagpipes, pewter lid, .5L...400.00
#1856, stein, etch/glazed: Post eagle, ornate pewter lid, 1L, NM.1,665.00
#1863, stein, etch: Stuttgart, inlaid lid, EX color, .5L 600.00
#1872, stein, relief: woman w/children, inlaid lid, 2L.................350.00
#1883, vase, incised/pnt: floral, 6", pr..........................450.00
#1909, stein, PUG: Schonblick (building), pewter lid, .4L 345.00
#1909, stein, PUG: tapestry, SP lid w/pewter hinge, .5L............600.00
#1909-1038, stein, PUG: frogs fill steins in pond, pewter lid, .5L.800.00
#1909-1078, stein, PUG: man smoking, Schlitt, pewter lid, .4L.235.00
#1909-1102, stein, PUG: people drinking, Munich child lid, .5L..280.00
#1909-732, stein, PUG: drunken man sleeping, Schlitt, pewter lid, .5L.245.00
#1909-943, stein, PUG: knights & innkeeper, pewter lid, .5L...........375.00
#1934, stein, etch: military uniforms, eagle inlay lid, .5L.........1,065.00
#1946, stein, etch: lovers, old rpl pewter lid, .5L 190.00
#1981, vase, etch: floral, 3¼x4½"..........................170.00
#1995, stein, etch: musician drinking, inlaid lid, .5L...................365.00
#2001C, stein, etch/relief: scholars, inlaid lid, .5L....................845.00
#2001F, stein, etch/relief: architecture, inlaid lid, flat, .5L 800.00
#2001I, stein, etch/relief: theology, inlaid lid, .5L 1,450.00
#2001K, stein, etch/relief: Commerce, inlaid lid, scratches, .5L..725.00
#2005, stein, etch: people eating at table, inlaid lid, .5L.............415.00

#2007, stein, etch: blk cat, night watchman pewter lid, .5L........545.00
#2027, stein, etch: Gambrinus, inlaid lid, .5L..........................725.00
#2035, stein, etch: festive scene, inlaid lid, .5L..........................345.00
#2050, stein, etch: wedding, figural lid w/slipper finial, .5L......1,200.00
#2052, stein, etch: Munich child/children, inlaid lid, .25L.........345.00
#2074, stein, etch: bird in cage, inlaid lid, .5L..........................3,350.00
#2075, stein, etch/glazed: telegraph, inlaid lid, .5L..................1,725.00
#2087, stein, etch: people in cellar, inlaid lid, .5L, ...500.00
#2090, stein, etch; man at table, Schlitt, inlaid lid, .5L..............435.00
#2093, stein, etch/glazed: cards, inlaid lid, .5L..........................575.00
#2100, stein, etch: Germans meeting Romans, inlaid lid, .5L.....800.00
#2140, stein, PUG: Lowenbrau Munchen, pewter lid, .5L.......1,325.00
#2140-840, stein, PUG: Fus Rgt Nr 37, pewter lid, .5L.............715.00
#2140-941, stein, PUG: beer barometer, pewter lid, .5L.............300.00
#2177-1085, stein, PUG: children picnic, pewter lid, .25L.........350.00
#2192, stein, etch: Etruscan scene, Schlitt, inlaid lid, .5L, EX....265.00
#2209, vase, etch: Lohengrin, female hdls, 17½".................12,300.00
#2231, stein, etch: cavaliers drinking, inlaid lid, .5L, NM 460.00
#2238, stein, etch: 7th Regt Armory, inlaid lid, .5L.................1,000.00
#2327, beaker, PUG: Old Vienna Atlantic City, .25L, NM 115.00
#2327-1200, beaker, PUG: Montreal, .25L 430.00
#2327-1200, beaker, PUG: Sverige, .25L 335.00
#2327-1290H, beaker, PUG: Suede, .25L 160.00
#2402, stein, etch: Siegfried, inlaid lid, .5L.............................750.00
#2435, vase, etch: Nouveau floral, 4" 400.00
#2449, vase, cameo: scene of ladies, 2 men on bk, 7½"...............715.00
#2500, stein, etch: drunken cavaliers, inlaid lid, 1L, EX 575.00
#2532, stein, etch: Gasthaus scene, Quidenus, inlaid lid, .5L......475.00
#2582, stein, etch: jester entertaining, inlaid lid, .5L 725.00
#2583, stein, etch: Egyptian design/Blk Whale of Ascolon, 1L.1,450.00
#2608, stein, cameo, 3 scenes of people, Stahl, inlaid lid, .3L...365.00
#2692, stein, etch: Art Nouveau hops, inlaid lid, hairline, .5L...230.00
#2765, stein, etch: knight on wht horse, tower body, inlaid lid, .5L...1,850.00
#2767, stein, Munich child w/bl, rpl inlay on lid, .5L 460.00
#2778, stein, etch: carnival scene, Schlitt, inlaid lid, .25L..........700.00
#2778, stein, etch: carnival scene, Schlitt, inlaid lid, 1L 1,900.00
#2780, stein, etch: lovers, inlaid lid, sm rpr, 1L 300.00
#2789-6134, stein, Rookwood: man smoking pipe, pewter lid, .5L ..575.00
#2839, ash holder, etch: Art Nouveau, 3 women smoking, 2x5"..395.00
#2872, stein, etch: Cornell University, inlaid lid, rpr, .5L 345.00
#2902-1014, vase, PUG: Munich child, Schlitt, 14" 500.00
#2913, vase, etch: Art Nouveau, 13¾"..........................800.00
#2921, stein, etch: campfire scene, inlaid lid, 2.8L..................600.00
#2937, stein, etch: nightwatchman, Quidenus, inlaid lid, 1L......845.00
#2938, stein, etch: hunter, Quidenus, inlaid lid, 1L 1,025.00
#2939, stein, etch: barmaid, Quidenus, inlaid lid, .5L...............625.00
#2939, stein, etch: barmaid, Quidenus, inlaid lid, 1L...............1,080.00
#2948, sugar bowl, etch: Art Nouveau, orig lid, 4" 200.00
#2950, stein, cameo: Bavarian crest, helmet pewter lid, 1L.......785.00
#2957, stein, etch: bowling scene, inlaid lid, .5L....................385.00
#2965, bowl, etch: Art Nouveau, 7½"..........................285.00
#2994, stein, etch: Art Nouveau, inlaid lid, rpr, .5L 275.00
#3003, stein, etch: man reads paper, Ringer, pewter lid, .5L, EX.200.00
#3081-533, beaker, PUG/POG: girl holding stein, .25L, NM 220.00
#3081-533, beaker, PUG/POG: girl holding stein, .5L 220.00
#3089, stein, etch: Diogenes, inlaid lid, 1L..........................1,435.00
#3142, stein, etch: Bavarian couple dancing, inlaid lid, rpl tl, .5L..400.00
#3185-1359, stein, PUG: hiker eats under tree, inlaid lid, .4L 485.00
#3194IV, pitcher, cameo: musician, 7½" 285.00
#3220, stein, etch: lovers, Quidenus, inlaid lid, .5L.................975.00
#3244, stein, relief: Art Nouveau, inlaid lid, flake, .5L 515.00
#3507, stein, relief: Munich child, 1/32-L.............................130.00
#5006, stein, faience: Nurnberg, pewter lid, flaw, .5L................460.00
#5006-5189, stein, man w/pipe & goblet, pewter lid, .5L...........345.00

#5015, stein, faience: bird & floral, pewter lid, 1.35L **1,325.00**
#7002, vase: phanolith: ladies/men/children on bl, 9½".............**635.00**
#7011, vase, phanolith: roman scene of men, Stahl, 11" **865.00**

Microscopes

The microscope has taken on many forms during its 250-year evolutionary period. The current collectors' market primarily includes examples from England, surplus items from institutions, and continental beginner and intermediate forms which sold through Sears, Roebuck & Company and other retailers of technical instruments. Earlier examples have brass main tubes which are unpainted. Later, more common examples are all black with brass or silver knobs and horseshoe-shaped bases. Early and more complex forms are the most valuable; these always had hardwood cases to house the delicate instruments and their accessories. Instruments were never polished during use, and those that have been polished to use as decorator pieces are of little interest to most avid collectors.

Acme, brass & iron, +14" case, EX...**350.00**
Bausch & Lomb, dissecting, w/filters & holders...........................**200.00**
Bausch & Lomb, single lens, Y base, 1896, EX **725.00**
Bausch & Lomb, 2 brass objectives, Y base, 1902, 12", EX **795.00**
Bulloch, Chicago, brass, complex, Y base, 1880, 15", +case **1,100.00**
English, student, brass, ca 1870, 12", +case/accessories **450.00**
Ernest Leitz, 3 brass objectives, rpl mirror, 1910, VG+...............**650.00**
Ernest Leitz, 3 brass objectives, 4x eyepc, rpl mirror, 1925, EX...**895.00**
German, student, rnd base, ca 1860, G, +case **125.00**
Hand-held, simple form, 1890, 3", G..**45.00**
M Moreau, brass drum type, ca 1850, 7x2" dia, EX **995.00**
Made in Germany, CI/brass, 3 brass objectives, 1890s, EXIB......**450.00**
Queen, brass & iron, Y base, 14", G, +case.................................**325.00**
Tolles, Boston, brass, Y base, ca 1880, 16", G, +case **750.00**
Unmk mini drum, compound lens, brass base, 1840s, 6⅛", EXIB..**495.00**
Unmk mini drum, compound lens screwed on bottom, 1840s, 3¾" body ...**395.00**
Zentmeyer, brass, complex, dbl pillar, tripod base, 18", G........**1,250.00**

Militaria

Because of the wide and varied scope of items available to collectors of militaria, most tend to concentrate mainly on the area or areas that interest them most or that they can afford to buy. Some items represent a major investment and because of their value have been reproduced. Extreme caution should be used when purchasing Nazi items. Every badge, medal, cap, uniform, dagger, and sword that Nazi Germany issued is being reproduced today. Some repros are crude and easily identified as fakes, while others are very well done and difficult to recognize as reproductions. Purchases from WWII veterans are usually your safest buys. Reputable dealers or collectors will normally offer a money-back guarantee on Nazi items purchased from them. There are a number of excellent Third Reich reference books available in bookstores at very reasonable prices. Study them to avoid losing a much larger sum spent on a reproduction. Our advisor for this category is Ron L. Willis; he is listed in the Directory under Florida.

Key: insg — insignia

Imperial German

Backpack, Army, gray canvas w/leather fittings, dtd 1919, EX....**115.00**
Badge, wound; NM blk lacquer...**30.00**
Book, Deutschland's Taten Zur See, naval content, Stein, 1915, EX...**25.00**
Canteen, Army, pnt steel, lacks stopper & cover, VG **25.00**

Frock coat, officer's, bl wool, dbl-breasted, NP buttons, prewar, EX ..**250.00**
Greatcoat, Infantry officer's, gray wool w/dk bl collar, prof rprs ..**350.00**
Helmet, fire; brass w/top comb, neck visor, lacks liner, 1870s, G .**200.00**
Helmet, spike; Bavarian Artillery enlisted, ball spike finial, VG..**550.00**
Helmet, spike; Bavarian enlisted, front plate, modern replacements, G..**350.00**
Helmet, spike; Bavarian Infantry, gilt front plate, w/liner, EX+ ..**775.00**
Helmet, spike; Prussian NCO, brass furniture, pre-1887 pattern, EX..**275.00**
Magazine, Illustrated Zeitung, patriotic themes, 1914, EX **25.00**
Medal, Baden WWI War Service, gray metal, rpr, w/ribbon **25.00**
Medal, Kaiser Jubilee, bronze, Wilhelm profile, dtd 1797-1897, NM.**25.00**
Medal, Kaiser's 90th Birthday, brass, dtd Mar 22 1887, EX **25.00**
Medal, Prussian 1915 War Service, gray metal, w/ribbon, EX **30.00**
Newspaper, Bismark Death Notice, Berlin paper, 1898, EX **25.00**
Postcard, emb 1914 Iron Cross, EX..**25.00**
Stickpin, 1813 Iron Cross, 2nd class, EX patina, rare **850.00**
Stickpin, 1914 Iron Cross, crown designation, VG......................**25.00**
Tunic, Shooting Assoc, dk gr w/silver buttons, 1870s, EX..........**350.00**

Third Reich

Backpack, Army M1934, gray canvas w/leather straps, dtd 1937, EX..**55.00**
Badge, Army Tank Assault, worn bronze, solid bk, old rpr **75.00**
Badge, Luftwaffe Glider Pilot, detailed eagle, EX........................**150.00**
Badge, Navy U-Boat Combat, worn gilt...................................**175.00**
Bar, Army Close Combant, bronze, hallmk, EX...........................**115.00**
Binoculars, Army, blk-pnt aluminum, 6x30 power, clear optics, EX...**55.00**
Canteen, Army, aluminum w/wool cover, Bakelite cup, VG **35.00**
Cap, folding side; Luftwaffe Forestry Troops NCO, lined dk gr wool, EX.**175.00**
Cap, Luftwaffe, gray fleece w/natural fleece lining, insg, EX **100.00**
Collar tab, Luftwaffe Medical Troops officer, 3 gulls/wreath on bl..**30.00**
Helmet, Army M1935/40, field gray w/eagle insg, w/liner, VG ...**150.00**
Helmet, Lufschutz M38 Gladiator factory guard, 1-pc, olive gr pnt, EX .**175.00**
Helmet, M35 style battlefield relic w/bullet holes, G- **45.00**
Identification card, DAF, w/gear & swastika motif, 1939, EX **25.00**
Insignia, Army Jager Troops, oak leaves on gr cloth, EX **25.00**
Insignia, Eagle (Breast), Veteran Assoc, pin-bk, metal, hallmk.....**25.00**
Lapel pin, Armed Forces Worker's Eagle, silvered, wreath planchet, EX..**25.00**
Medal, War Service Cross 2nd class, w/swords & ribbon, EX........**35.00**
Medal, 1939 Iron Cross 2nd class, G **25.00**
Pitcher, coffee; Luftwaffe Mess Hall, wht porc, dtd 1941, 9½", EX ...**75.00**
Plate, Army mess, wht porc, Eagle proofmk, 9" **25.00**
Shell carrier, Army Artillery, wicker w/leather, metal base, EX.....**50.00**
Shoulder boards, Fire Service, Meister rank, silver & blk on rose wool ...**25.00**
Stickpin, Freiheits Spende 1938, bronze oval w/rising sun swastika ..**25.00**
Stickpin, RLB Membership, swastika on silver starburst, hallmk ..**25.00**
Stove, field; cylinder w/top hdl, complete, 7½", EX **250.00**
Trousers, Navy fatigue, brn linen, gray metal buttons, 1941, EX.**150.00**
Work permit, Eastern Territories, w/eagle & ink stamp, EX **35.00**

Japanese

Badge, Military Veteran, silver w/gilt star insg, WWII era, EX......**80.00**
Badge, Proficiency, gold-washed aluminum, WWII era **60.00**
Belt plate, brass fr, push-button release, late 1800s, EX **100.00**
Buckle, 2-pc, silver fr w/bronze border, animals/insects, 3¼", EX.**200.00**
Camera, aerial; machine gun style, pistol grip, WWII era, G.......**235.00**
Dog tags, WWII era...**65.00**
Fatigue shirt & pants, heavy, WWII era, VG **75.00**
Goggles, pilot's, folding frames, cotton mask, WWII era, NM **100.00**
Grenade, model 97, EX..**65.00**
Holster, baby Nambu, brn leather, clip pouch removed, WWII, VG..**365.00**
Insignia, Army Air Corps wings, aluminum wire/gilt on bl, WWII era.**30.00**
Leaflet, anti-US propaganda, EX **50.00**
Medal, Order of Golden Kite 7th class, M in case.......................**190.00**

Medal, Order of Rising Sun breast star, silver w/gilt medallion, M.1,000.00
Medal, Order of Rising Sun 5th class, silver w/gilt & enameling, EX .185.00
Medal, Order of Sacred Treasure 1st class, EX 225.00
Medal, Red Cross, silver planchet, w/ribbon, WWII era, NM.......40.00
Medal ensemble, Order of Sacred Treasure 8th class, M in case .100.00
Mess kit, aluminum w/brn khaki finish, WWII, M 35.00
Photograph, Emperor Hirihoto, WWII era, 18x15", EX in orig fr.1,500.00
Raincoat, Army, waterproof khaki twill, dbl-breasted, WWII era, EX..400.00
Shoulderbrds, Navy ensign, gold bullion/purple on bl, WWII era, EX..40.00
Stick, swagger; officer's, telescoping bamboo stick, WWII era, 27"..40.00
Uniform, WWII, blouse & trousers w/belt/patches/etc, EX.........175.00

Russia/Soviet

Backpack, Army, rigid style, canvas over wood fr, WWII era, EX .125.00
Badge, Alexis Military School, cross w/swords, Imperial era, EX..285.00
Badge, Army sniper, rifle w/scope, brass, WWII, rare 125.00
Badge, breast; Order of St Vladimir 4th Class, w/o swords, 1917, EX .450.00
Beret, blk woold w/red enamel star & gilt wreath, 1980s...............25.00
Book, Russia & the Golden Horde, Halperin, 1985, EX................25.00
Buckle, Army, brass w/star insg, 1970s......................................25.00
Cabinet photo, Cossack officer & 2 civilians, 6¼x4½" 50.00
Cabinet photo, Imperial Russian officer in full regalia, 1880s, 4"..25.00
Canteen, gr glass, lacks cover, WWII era, EX 120.00
Cap, Dragoon NCO, gr w/red piping, Imperial era, EX 350.00
Hat, brimmed; Army Tropical, khaki cotton twill, star insg, 1980s...35.00
Hat, fur; Army officer's, brn leather & Persian lamb's fur, star insg.195.00
Hat, visor; Air Force officer's, bl twill w/wool piping/crown, 1980s ..25.00
Hat, visor; Naval, blk twill w/wht piping, gilt wreath, 1980s 25.00
Helmet, Army, olive drab, w/leather strap & liner, WWII era, EX..55.00
Helmet, flight; blk twill, earphones/throat microphones, 1970s, EX..35.00
Identification book, aircraft, silhouettes of Allied planes, 1956, EX.35.00
Identification book, red cover w/gilt CCCP, 1980s, unissued 25.00
Leaflet, dropped on German troops, late WWII, rare, EX...........165.00
Map case, Army, brn waterproof material, leather straps, EX 25.00
Medal, Military Service Cross (Caucasus), bronze, Xd swords, 1864, EX.115.00
Mess kit, Army, aluminum w/blk finish, WWII era, EX 35.00
Plaque, Stalin portrait, aluminum, WWII era, EX 45.00
Pouch, AK-47, khaki canvas, 1970s, EX 25.00
Propaganda card, anti-German, WWII era, scarce, EX.................40.00
Radio, field; Army, metal w/M khaki pnt, complete w/earphones & case ..45.00
Seal, Artillery Regiment, brass, rampant lion, ca 1910, rare 180.00
Shoulder boards, Army medical, star devices, 1980s, EX...............25.00
Tunic, Army Combat, khaki cotton, epaulettes, compo buttons, 1980s, EX.25.00
Tunic, KGB general's, olive wool twill, WWII era, rare, EX 600.00
Uniform, snow camo, drawstring waist, WWII era, scarce 500.00
Wall hanging, Stalin, pnt linen, WWII era, 38x33", EX.............125.00

United States

Badge, Army Expert Qualification, silver cross w/laurel wreath, EX.10.00
Badge, pilot's wings, silver, EX patina, Korean War era, EX 25.00
Belt, cartridge; woven canvas, japanned buckle, Indian Wars era, G..365.00
Belt, money; khaki cotton w/4 pockets, leather trim, WWI era, EX..30.00
Book, Decisive Battles of USA, Fuller, 29 maps, 1942, EX............25.00
Book, Rough Riders, T Roosevelt, orig drawings/etc, 1899, EX 30.00
Bridal rosette, Cavalry, US brass ornaments, ca 1905, G..............30.00
Canteen, blk compo screw camo w/chain & cup, canvas cover, 1944, EX.25.00
Canteen, brn twill cover, tin spout, copper chain, Civil War era, EX.365.00
Canteen, bull's eye design, cloth strap, mk Hadden-Porter-Booth .300.00
Canteen, Militia, tin w/emb ribs, tin cap/cup, 1860s, 11½", G...125.00
Canteen, wood cask w/stepped spout, Revolutionary War era, 12x7".250.00
Canteen, wood drum w/riveted iron securing straps, War of 1812, G.275.00
Cap, Navy sailor's, bl wool w/gold embr, WWII era, M................25.00

Cap, Navy USS Dekalb, dk bl wool w/blk silk band, gold bullion, 1900s .95.00
Cap, overseas; Army officer's, dk khaki wool w/gold piping, WWII, VG.25.00
Cap, overseas; General's, brn twill w/gold piping, WWII, unissued, M...25.00
Cartridge box, CW, cross belt & eagle plate, mk Calhoune, complete ..880.00
Collar disc, enlisted, bronze w/Xd rifles, WWI era, EX.................25.00
Dispatch case, tin, w/lid & carrying loops, Civil War era, 7", G ...75.00
Engraving, General Burnside portrait, Civil War era, 8x5¾" 40.00
Epaulettes, Artillary, gold bullion, red silk trim, Indian Wars era, G.135.00
Flag, Air Force Systems Command, bl w/gold fringe, Vietnam War era, M.65.00
Flight suit, Air Force, khaki cotton twill, WWII era, M...............30.00
Frock coat, Militia, dk bl wool, gold bullion at cuffs, 1880s, VG .295.00
Greatcoat, Army, bl wool, dbl breasted, w/cape, Indian Wars era, EX..615.00
Hat, contract Boonie; desert night khaki twill, dtd 1986, EX 25.00
Hat, rain; Marine Corps, blk rubberized canvas, 1917, EX..........300.00
Hat, visor; Air Force, bl twill, Vietnam War era, M 25.00
Hat, visor; Army enlisted, olive drab w/brass insg, WWII era, EX .35.00
Hat, visor; Model 1895 'Train Conductor' style, Spanish-Am War era, EX.75.00
Haversack, US stencil on brn khaki, flapped tab, VG....................25.00
Headband, nurse, wht cotton w/red cotton cross, WWI era, EX ...30.00
Helmet, Army, blk pnt w/gr pnt insg, WWI, G 25.00
Helmet, pilot's, brn leather, compo snaps, flab tabs, WWII era, EX.150.00
Helmet, pilot's flight, blk leather w/fleece lining, 1930s, EX.........95.00
Helmet, pith; Army Tropical, compo w/cotton cover, WWII era, EX .35.00
Insignia, cap; brass eagle w/shield, 1840s, rare, 3x3" 150.00
Insignia, hat; brass Model 1872, Xd sabers, Indian Wars era, EX ..25.00
Knife, survival raft; Navy, curved w/yel wood grip, scabbard, WWII, EX..55.00
Lantern, field; tinned iron w/glass lenses, 1880s, G 125.00
Lapel pin, Selective Service System, bronze, eagle, EX 25.00
Leggings, Marine Corps, khaki canvas w/bronze fittings, WWII era, EX.50.00
Leggings, officer's, brn leather, brass buckle, WWI era, NM..........30.00
Lithograph, General Pershing in full uniform, WWI era, 23x15", EX..100.00
Manual, Armed Forces officer's, Dept of Defense, 1950, M..........25.00
Map, survival; AAF, colored silk, ca 1945, VG 25.00
Medal, Army Expert Rifleman, gold w/Xd rifles, Meyer, 1920s, EX.40.00
Medal, China Relief Expedition, bronze, w/ribbon, 1930s, EX ...100.00
Medal, MA Volunteer Infantry, Civil War era, 2½", EX 90.00
Microphone, aircrafty type MT-425, w/plug-in cord, dtd 1946, EX..25.00
Mittens, gauntlet style, buffalo fur, Indian Wars era, G 125.00
Padlock, Army Security, Miracle mfg, US hallmk, 1980s, +2 keys .10.00
Pennant, Infantry, 1-sided swallow-tail style, WWII, 27x18"+staff, M.150.00
Raincoat, olive drab canvas, dbl-breasted, WWI era, VG 50.00
Saddle, McClellan, natural rawhide, brass pommel shield, 1860s, EX..400.00
Sash, dress; Militia, cross-shoulder, red cotton, 1880s, 3" W, M....90.00
Shako, West Point Band, gray cotton twill, w/plume, WWI era, NM..600.00

Snare drum, 36th RegT Mass Vols in arch, repainted, replaced rope strap, head missing, $4,370.00. (Photo courtesy Skinner, Inc.)

Spurs, brass, Confederate, Leech & Ridgon style, 4" 110.00
Spurs, NP, pinwheel rowels, leather straps, Indian Wars era, EX...95.00
Sword belt, CW officer's, blk leather w/stitched motif, sword hangers .660.00
Tunic, Army, khaki twill, 4 flap pockets, WWI era, G 35.00
Tunic, Militia, bl waistcoat, brass buttons w/blk frogs, 1870s, VG.395.00
Uniform, Currier Service, dk bl wool w/brass buttons, 2-pc, ca 1900, G..150.00

Miscellaneous

Austria, helmet, Dragoon, metal w/brass furniture, Imperial Era, EX..**1,200.00**
Austria, shako, officer's, blk wool body, gold insg, Imperial era...**685.00**
Britain, helmet, Army, khaki finish, lacks liner, WWII era, VG...**25.00**
Britain, helmet, Army, olive drab, w/liner, WWII era **25.00**
Britain, helmet, spike; Foreign Service, wht cotton w/brass, EX .**150.00**
Britain, helmet, turtle style, blk finish, w/liner, EX.......................**25.00**
Britain, medal, WWI Victory, bronze, inscribed, w/ribbon, VG **25.00**
Canada, badge, Officer Training Corps, bimetal, WWI, EX..........**25.00**
Canada, beret, Westminster Regiment, beaver insg, 1970s, EX.....**25.00**
Croatia, medal, Order of Iron Trefoil 3rd class, EX.....................**275.00**
Finland, medal, Bravery 2nd class, bronze, w/ribbon, dtd 1939, EX ..**80.00**
France, helmet, Army, khaki finish, front badge, WWII era, relic..**25.00**
France, Resistance, bronze cross w/swords & ribbon, WWII, EX ..**25.00**
Germany, beret, Army, red wool w/blk, unit metal insg, 1980, EX .**25.00**
Greece, beret, Army enlisted, khaki wool, 1940s, EX **30.00**
Iraq, helmet, Army, tan compo w/webbed strapping, Gulf War era, G .**60.00**
Latvia, fire helmet, khaki finish, front plate w/star, 1930s, EX......**40.00**
Poland, medal, Order of Polonia Restituta neck cross, 1918, EX .**325.00**
Spain, helmet, tanker; blk leather, eagle badge, 1940s, VG...........**70.00**
Switzerland, helmet, Army M1918, bl-gray sand finish, EX **75.00**
Yugoslavia, medal, Army 20 Yr Commemorative, silver, soldier, 1961 .**50.00**

Milk Glass

Milk glass is the current collector's name for milk-white opaque glass. The early glassmaker's term was Opal Ware. Originally attempted in England in the eighteenth century with the intention of imitating china, milk glass was not commercially successful until the mid-1800s. Pieces produced in the U.S.A., England, and France during the 1870 – 1900 period are highly prized for their intricate detail and fiery, opalescent edges.

For further information we recommend *Collector's Encyclopedia of Milk Glass, An Identification & Value Guide*, by Betty and Bill Newbound. (CE numbers in our listings refer to this publication.) Another highly recommended book is *The Milk Glass Book* by Frank Chiarenza and James Slater. The newest reference, published in 2001, is *Milk Glass Imperial Glass Corporation* by Myrna and Bob Garrison. Our advisor for this category is Rod Dockery; he is listed in the Directory under Texas. See also Animal Dishes with Covers; Bread Plates; Historical Glass; Westmoreland.

Key:
B — Belknap   G — Garrison
CE — Newbound   MGB — Milk Glass Book
F — Ferson

Bone dish, Lacy Edge, CE-343, 6¼", from $30 to **35.00**
Bookend, bear upright, Northwood's Luna Glass, 1916, CE-192, 8¾".**300.00**
Bottle, Atterbury Duck, 1871, CE-3, 11½"+stopper, from $750 to.**850.00**
Bottle, Columubs Column, ca 1893, CE-7, 13"+7" metal statue, $800 to..**950.00**
Bottle, Dawes Dog, Pat Oct 1, 1872, F-31, 11½", from $850 to..**875.00**
Bowl, Daisy & Button panels, wing-like hdls, unmk, CE-31, 8½x12".**25.00**
Bowl, open lacy edge, ftd, Atterbury, CE-25, 10¼", from $30 to ..**35.00**
Box, cigarette; Santa Maria emb lid, Consolidated, CE-50, 3¾x5".**130.00**
Box, glove; scrolls & flower decals, CE-35, 4x10⅜", from $55 to...**65.00**
Box, powder; emb florals, Fostoria, CE-41, 4x4¾" dia, from $40 to..**45.00**
Butter press, HP flowers on top, pineapple pattern, CE-415, 4½".**95.00**
Candlestick, Crucifix, Cambridge, CE-71, 10⅛", from $65 to **75.00**
Candlesticks, Dolphin, Westmoreland, CE-65, 9¼", pr, from $70 to.**75.00**
Candy jar, Pocket Watch, Imperial, G-1950/260, Pg 126, 5¾" dia..**70.00**
Clock, cherub above clock face, Pat June 12...1900, CE-431, 8"..**325.00**
Compote, Atlas (stem), lace edge, CE-95, 8¼", from $100 to.......**125.00**
Compote, Bird Pedestal, scalloped rim, CE-87, 4⅛x7", from $50 to.**55.00**

Compote, Lace & Dew Drop, Kemple, w/lid, CE-98, 8½", from $40 to.**50.00**
Coupe plaque, Kewpie baby, gold scrolls, CE-252, 10⅛", from $30 to.**35.00**
Covered dish, Baby Moses, cattail or reed base, unmk, B-160, 6¼".**250.00**
Covered dish, Baseball, unmk, 1940s-50s, CE-188, 3⅛" dia, $35 to ..**40.00**
Creamer, Sunflower (emb), CE-299, 4½", from $50 to **55.00**
Creamer & sugar bowl, Betsy Ross, Fostoria, CE-294, 4", 3⅝"......**40.00**
Decanter, Capitol Building, ca 1976-77, CE-21, from $10 to........**15.00**
Figurine, rooster, opal comb, Summit, CE-200, 3", from $12 to....**15.00**
Goblet, Dewberry, Kemple, CE-218, 6", from $12 to **15.00**
Honey dish, Beehive w/Vines, Vallerysthal, CE-55, 5½", $100 to.**125.00**
Jar, biscuit; Golden Poppy HP, LG Wright, SP hdl mk Canada, CE-180..**80.00**
Jar, ginger; Roses & Ribbons (emb), bulbous, w/lid, CE-58, 6¼"..**40.00**
Jar, Old Abe Eagle, E Pluribus Unum banner, Crystal Co, F-568, 6½".**125.00**
Ladle, curved hdl, ice lip, CE-223, 13¾", from $45 to **50.00**
Lamp, Mission Octagon, US Glass, CE-244, 6½", from $100 to..**125.00**
Lamp, Plain Jane (no decor), CE-241, 8" to shoulder, from $50 to **75.00**
Light, Taxicab, MGB-264, 11½" L **90.00**
Mug, Cathedral Arches & Roses, gold pnt, CE-209, 3¼" **50.00**
Paperweight, horse head, pnt, MGB-298 ....**135.00**
Pitcher, Owl, glass eyes, Challinor Taylor, CE-313, from $185 to..**200.00**
Pitcher, syrup; Flower Swirl, w/lid, CE-316, from $85 to **90.00**
Plate, Baltimore Oriole decal, Club & Shell border, CE-260, 9½".**35.00**
Plate, Bluebird, beaded edge, Westmoreland, CE-246, 7½", $20 to.**25.00**
Plate, Daisies, beaded edge, Westmoreland, CE-248, 7½", $18 to..**20.00**
Plate, Dutch girl scene, Sheaf of Wheat border, CE-267, 6", $20 to.**25.00**
Plate, Easter Chicks, Leaf & Loop border, Westmoreland, CE-278...**35.00**
Plate, Pennsylvania Turnpike, MGB-203, 8¼" **95.00**
Plate, Taft campaign, eagles/flags/stars border, CE-273, 7½" **125.00**
Platter, Retriever (emb), lily pad border, CE-336, 13¼", $95 to .**100.00**
Punch bowl set, grape pattern, Imperial, G-1950/128, 15 pc.......**185.00**
Spittoon, HP floral (worn), CE-399, 5⅜x7¼", from $30 to..........**35.00**
Spooner, Strawberry, Bryce Bros, C-304, from $60 to **65.00**
Sugar shaker, Tulip (emb), CE-284, 4", from $60 to **65.00**
Tray, butterfly shape w/HP florals & much gold, CE-347, 5½x4" .**25.00**
Tray, dresser; HP roses & gold scrolls, rectangular, CE-354, 9¾" ..**25.00**
Tray, Fleur de Lis & Scroll, beaded circle center, CE-346, 4½" sq..**10.00**
Tray, Hand w/Fan, Atterbury, CE-331, 9¼", from $75 to **80.00**
Vase, Horse & Foliage, LE Smith for M Walrath, ca 1981, CE-366..**15.00**
Vase, Lily of the Valley, Westmoreland, CE-371, 7½", from $25 to ..**30.00**

Millefiori

Millefiori was a type of art glass produced during the 1800s. Literally the term means 'thousand flowers,' an accurate description of its appearance. Canes, fused bundles of multicolored glass threads such as are often used in paperweights were cut into small cross sections, arranged in the desired pattern, refired, and shaped into articles such as cruets, lamps, and novelty items. It is still being produced, and many examples found on the market today are fairly recent in manufacture. See also Paperweights.

Cruet, mc on lt aqua bl, appl hdl, old, 8" **300.00**
Decanter, mc, teardrop stopper, 12"..**220.00**
Shade, 17" flared bell shape, mc w/border having bl bkground...**1,400.00**
Vase, lt bl & dk purple bands of flowers, 6"...................................**130.00**
Vase, mc canes on gr, burnt-orange int, swirled form w/ruffle, 8¼"..**385.00**
Vase, mc random canes, flared rim, ftd, 5x4" **195.00**
Vase, patterned flower canes on bl, hdls, 3½" **215.00**
Vase, random mc canes, slim neck, ornate hdls, 1940s, 6" **175.00**

Miniature Portraits

Miniature works of art vary considerably in value depending on many criteria: as with any art form, those that are signed by or can be attributed to a well-known artist may command prices well into the thousands of dollars. Collectors find paintings of identifiable subjects especially interesting, as are those with props, such as a child with a vintage toy or a teddy bear or a soldier in uniform with his weapon at his side. Even if none of these factors come to bear, an example exhibiting fine details and skillful workmanship may bring an exceptional price. Of course, condition is important, and ornate or unusual frames also add value.

Admiral Dewey in uniform, on ivory, sgn Verrcet, brass fr: 7x5"..**635.00**
Boy beside tree w/dog, on ivory, EX color, 2¾"+fr **1,100.00**
Boy on classical sofa w/column, on ivory, 3½x2½", +leather case ...**1,645.00**
Child w/bl ribbon & riding crop, on ivory, in orig fr, 3x2¼".......**460.00**
Gentleman (identified), on ivory, sgn Fratelli, mid-19th C, 3x2½" ..**495.00**
Geo & Martha WA, on ivory, Gainsborough, pr in 4¾x6⅜" ivory fr .**1,950.00**
Geo WA, watercolor on ivory, 1800s, 3x2", in oval thermoplastic fr.**450.00**
Lady, ink/watercolor on paper, att R Porter (1792-1884), in mat: 5x4"..**1,100.00**
Lady (well done), on ivory, +fr w/brass liner, 4¾x3¾" **600.00**
Lady in bl w/lace collar, on ivory, 1⅞x1½"+gilt-metal fr **230.00**
Lady in blk dress, wht collar/sleeves, on paper, blk fr: 6x5".........**220.00**
Lady in blk w/ruffles & ornate hairdo, on paper, orig fr, 6x5" **600.00**
Lady in brn, lace collar/bl ribbons, watercolor on paper, 1800s, 9x8"..**345.00**
Lady in fine attire/jewels, watercolor on paper, early 1800s, fr:6x5".**2,000.00**
Lady in powdered wig & lace cap, on ivory, sgn Augustine, Fr, 1¾"...**265.00**
Lady w/elaborate updo w/comb & ribbon, on ivory, 1800s, gilt fr: 3x2".**1,000.00**
Lady w/flowers in hair, low-cut dress, on ivory, Dumont, +5x4" case..**330.00**
Lady w/lace collar & curls, on ivory, EX color, 2¾"+fr................**385.00**
Lady w/long curls/elegant attire, on ivory, bk: hair, 2¾x2", +fr.**2,000.00**
Lady w/wht collar & red gem jewelry, on ivory, blk compo fr: 5x5".**500.00**
Lady wearing tortoiseshell comb, watercolor on paper, 1840s, 4¾".**350.00**
Man in blk frock coat, blk curly hair, on paper, orig fr, 6x5".......**440.00**
Man's profile on wax, in 5" dia leatherized paper/velvet case......**110.00**
Man seated on red chair, on paper, 3⅞x2½"+grpt fr **260.00**
Man w/brn hair & eyes, blk coat, on ivory, brass fr w/hair swatch, 3"..**550.00**
Man w/hair in ringlets, on ivory, wear, emb brass fr, 3½x2¾".....**275.00**
Military officer, watercolor on ivory, 1800s, 3x2", +ebonized wood fr .**1,000.00**
Seaman in coat/view of ship, bk: braid of hair, on ivory, 4x3", +fr.**2,900.00**
Young man, identified, on ivory, sgn Mercer, 1800-33, 7x6", + gilt fr ..**650.00**
Youth in great coat, bk: braided hair, on ivory, 2¾x2", +leather fr ..**900.00**

Miniatures

There is some confusion as to what should be included in a listing of miniature collectibles. Some feel the only true miniature is the salesman's sample; other collectors consider certain small-scale children's toys to be appropriately referred to as miniatures, while yet others believe a miniature to be any small-scale item that gives evidence to the craftsmanship of its creator. For salesman's samples, see specific category; other types are listed below. See also Dollhouses and Furnishings; Children's Things.

Armoire, figured walnut vnr, Fr style, dvtl drw in base, 19x13" ..**660.00**
Blanket chest, cherry, tall trn ft, old surface, 8x13x7" **325.00**
Blanket chest, dk gr pnt, dvtl, molded base/lid, till lid gone, 13" L.**495.00**
Blanket chest, PA decor: house/trees/flowers, att J Weber; 10" L, EX+.**15,400.00**
Blanket chest, PA decor: house/trees/name, att J Weber, 10¾", G.**2,750.00**
Blanket chest, PA decor: metallic fruit on mustard, rstr/rpr, 24" L.**800.00**
Blanket chest, softwood w/pnt vine decor, New England style, E Wheeler.**175.00**
Chest, cherry, 4-drw, glass knobs, trn legs, paneled ends, 17x15x9" **515.00**
Chest, Fr-style bombè, 3-drw, high ft, cast pulls, 20th C, 10x15x8" **140.00**
Chest, mahog Sheraton, 3 graduated drws, reeded stiles, 13x12x7".**2,800.00**
Chest, mahog/cherry, intricate floral cvg, ivory inlay, sgn, 7x7x10".**1,500.00**
Chest, oak, dvtl w/shaped bracket ft, molded edges, English, 10", VG.**385.00**
Chest, pnt pine, 3-drw, shaped skirt, brass pulls, 1800s, 11x14x7" **235.00**

Chest, walnut, 4-drw, panel ends, cvd ft, 17x16x11½"................**450.00**
Chest, walnut/tiger maple Hplwht style, 4-drw, 23x19x11".........**575.00**
Chest, 1-drw box top, fancy bk splash, 2 lower drws, 20x17x9", VG..**375.00**
Cupbrd, corner; tiger maple, 1-pc w/lg panel do & 2 drw, 20th C, 20" ...**230.00**
Cupbrd, spice; step-bk, 15-drw w/foreign wht letters, rope trn, 11x10"..**300.00**
Kayak, animal skin stitched over wood fr, 33" L **175.00**
Sampler, 3 ABCs/trees/etc on linen, NH, 1808, 4¾x3¾"+fr..**2,585.00**
Table, dressing; cherry/maple Sheraton, marble top, drw, rpr, 14x10x6".**440.00**
Table, hutch; 3-brd curly maple top, dvtl drw, pegged joints, 9½".**550.00**
Table, mahog w/flame vnr on drw front, inlay on legs, 12x9x9" .**190.00**

Minton

Thomas Minton established his firm in 1793 at Stoke-on-Trent and within a few years began producing earthenware with blue-printed patterns similar to the ware he had learned to decorate while employed by the Caughley Porcelain Factory. The Willow pattern was one of his most popular. Neither this nor the porcelain made from 1798 to 1805 was marked (except for an occasional number series), making identification often impossible.

After 1805 until about 1816, fine tea services, beehive-shaped honey pots, trays, etc., were hand decorated with florals, landscapes, Imari-type designs, and neoclassic devices. These were often marked with crossed 'Ls.' It was Minton that invented the acid gold process of decorating (1863), which is now used by a number of different companies. From 1816 until 1823, no porcelain was made. Through the 1920s and 1930s, the ornamental wares with colorful decoration of applied fruits and florals and figurines in both bisque and enamel were usually left unmarked. As a result, they have been erroneously attributed to other potters. Some of the ware that was marked bears a deliberate imitation of Meissen's crossed swords. From the late '20s through the '40s, Minton made a molded stoneware line (mugs, jugs, teapots, etc.) with florals or figures in high relief. These were marked with an embossed scroll with an 'M' in the bottom curve. Fine parian ware was made in the late 1840s, and in the 1850s Minton experimented with and perfected a line of quality majolica which they produced from 1860 until it was discontinued in 1908. Their slogan was 'Majolica for the Millions,' and for it they gained widespread recognition. Leadership of the firm was assumed by Minton's son Herbert sometime around the middle of the nineteenth century. Working hand in hand with Leon Arnoux, who was both a chemist and an artist, he managed to secure the company's financial future through constant, successful experimentation with both materials and decorating methods. During the Victorian era, M.L. Solon decorated pieces in the pate-sur-pate style, often signing his work; these examples are considered to be the finest of their type. After 1862 all wares were marked 'Minton' or 'Mintons,' with an impressed year cipher.

Many collectors today reassemble the lovely dinnerware patterns that have been made by Minton. Perhaps one of their most popular lines was Minton Rose, introduced in 1854. The company itself once counted forty-seven versions of this pattern being made by other potteries around the world. In addition to less expensive copies, elaborate hand-enameled pieces were also made by Aynsley, Crown Staffordshire, and Paragon China. Solando Ware (1937) and Byzantine Range (1938) were designed by John Wadsworth. Minton ceased all earthenware production in 1939.

See also Majolica.

Bowl, berry; Ardmore, 5½", 8 for..**70.00**
Bowl, cereal; Lady Devonish, S520..**65.00**
Bowl, cream soup & saucer, Corinthian, H5218.......................**105.00**
Bowl, rimmed soup; Rose, globe bkstamp, 8⅜" **40.00**
Bowl, soup; Gold Laurentian, H5184 ....**70.00**
Bowl, vegetable; Bellemeade, w/lid, 6x12" **285.00**
Bowl, vegetable; Rose, globe bkstamp **300.00**

Candlesticks, draped nudes hold columns, lt gr/celadon, 16½", pr.**1,750.00**
Coffeepot, Adam, w/lid, 4-cup, 7" **200.00**
Cup & saucer, Adam, ftd....**35.00**
Cup & saucer, Alabaster & Gold....**89.00**
Cup & saucer, demitasse; Buckingham, K159....**110.00**
Cup & saucer, Grosvenor....**85.00**
Cup & saucer, Rose, ftd, stripe hdl, globe mk....**40.00**
Dish, mc floral on wht, oval, mk Marlow, 8½x5⅜"....**300.00**
Egg cup, dbl; Rose, globe bkstampe, 3¾"....**60.00**
Figurine, Miranda, nude seated on stump, John Bell, 1850, 16"..**710.00**
Jug, ERVII 1901, Secessionist, 7½", NM....**285.00**
Plate, bread & butter; Penrose....**49.00**
Plate, cake; Winter Harvest....**85.00**
Plate, dinner; Cockatrice, 1916....**180.00**
Plate, dinner; Gold Rose, H4680....**90.00**
Plate, dinner; Vermont, S365....**95.00**
Plate, luncheon; Ardmore, 8"....**40.00**
Plate, luncheon; Rose, globe bkstamp, 8⅞"....**30.00**
Plate, oyster; 6 yel wells divided by seaweed & shells, majolica, 9"..**5,400.00**
Plate, salad; Laurentian, S659....**56.00**
Plate, wheat gatherers w/mountains, gilt scalloped border, 5¾"..**470.00**
Plates, various portraits on wht w/gold berries, sgn ASI, 9", 4 for..**345.00**
Platter, Bala, S570, lg....**295.00**
Platter, Rose, globe bkstamp, 14½" dia....**150.00**
Platter, Saint James, bone china, sm....**175.00**
Teapot, Acanthus, w/lid, 4-cup, 5⅛"....**100.00**
Teapot, Bridal Veil....**250.00**
Teapot, Vermont, S365....**275.00**

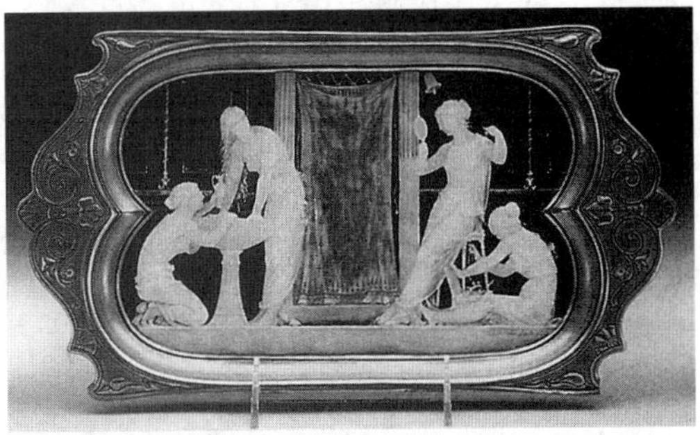

Tray, pate-sur-pate, female figures with Cupid behind curtain, Louis Solon Hildesheim, made for the Paris Exhibition of 1878, 13", $5,000.00.

Tureen, soup; Ancestral, Fife shape, scalloped sides, gold trim, 3-pc .**900.00**
Vase, gr leaves/purple berries on turq, pk int, 2 hdld, #722, 4" ...**580.00**
Vase, pk floral 'cloisonne,' moon flask shape, ca 1900, 7¾"....**1,175.00**
Vase, squeezebag pheasant feathers, gr/lav, oviod, #2707, 13x5½" .**1,900.00**

Mirrors

The first mirrors were made in England in the thirteenth century of very thin glass backed with lead. Reverse-painted glass mirrors were made in this country as early as the late 1700s and remained popular throughout the next century. The simple hand-painted panel was separated from the mirrored section by a narrow slat, and the frame was either the dark-finished Federal style or the more elegant, often-gilded Sheraton.

Mirrors changed with the style of other furnishings; but whatever type you purchase, as long as the glass sections remain solid, even broken or flaking mirrors are more valued than replaced glass. Careful resilvering is acceptable if excessive deterioration has taken place. In the listings that follow, items are from the nineteenth century unless noted otherwise. The term 'style' (example: Federal style) is used to indicate a mirror reminiscent of but made well after the period indicated. Obviously these retro styles will be valued much lower than their original counterparts. As with most other items in antiques and collectibles, the influence of online trading is greatly affecting prices. Many items once considered difficult to locate are now readily available in the .com world. Our advisor for this category is Michael Hinton; he is listed in the Directory under Pennsylvania.

Key:
Chpndl — Chippendale
Emp — Empire
Fed — Federal
QA — Queen Anne
Vict — Victorian
vnr — veneer

Black Forest, oak, cvd foxes/leaves/snail/fly in openwork fr, 50" .**850.00**
Blk-pnt Chinoiserie, scrolled crest w/figure in garden, 1760s, 20x11"..**3,500.00**
Blk-pnt gesso, cvd bird/basket of fruit, rtcl cartouch, 1780s, 22".**500.00**
Blk-pnt QA, beaded/shaped, beveled glass, 18th C, 24x13" **2,185.00**
Bronze, ornate Rococo design, rnd beveled glass, 41x32"....**900.00**
Bronze Louis XVI style w/torch & quiver decor, 1890s, 25"....**1,100.00**
Burlwood vnr w/floral inlay corners, birds inlaid on 4 sides, 34x28" .**1,880.00**
Cheval, faux bamboo (maple/bird's eye maple), att Horner, 1885, 77x35..**5,600.00**
Cheval, mahog w/ornate cvd acanthus leaves, pineapple finials, 73"..**1,200.00**
Courting, NE pnt decor, sun crest & stars, CT, 11x6"....**925.00**
Courting, pnt wood fr around molded inner fr w/rvpt floral, 19x13"..**1,400.00**
Curly maple fr, beveled/appl to pine, appl int molding, 29x23" ..**440.00**
Dressing, mahog Fed w/scrolled supports on stand, rpl brass, 23x28x5".**1,265.00**
Flame mahog Am Fed, divided mirror, all orig, 1830-40, 32x16½"..**745.00**
Gilt, allover elaborate cvgs/scalloped crest, L Uter, 77x60....**3,100.00**
Gilt architectural fr, rope twists/ball drops/rvpt farmhouse, 20x13"..**525.00**
Gilt gesso, fans/scrolls/flowers, Fr, 1800s, 112x68....**2,950.00**
Gilt gesso, Fr Baroque, ornate scrolled acanthus, 1800s, 40x28".**350.00**
Gilt gesso, ½-trn, molded ivy liner, rosette blocks, 24x18" **165.00**
Gilt gesso & walnut Chpndl, phoenix in rtcl crest, scroll fr, 37x20" .**890.00**
Gilt gesso Am Rococo, floral crest, pierced vines, 1850s, 89x45" .**4,600.00**
Gilt gesso Fed, rvpt farmer/cattle, cornice w/appl balls, 35x20"...**1,000.00**
Gilt gesso Fed, split balusters, relief cornucopia, 1825, 40x18" ...**940.00**
Gilt gesso Regency style w/floral cvgs, shells in corners, 75x38"..**1,100.00**
Gilt gesso Rococo, scrolls/rtcl crest w/gilt device, beaded fr, 38x15" ..**765.00**
Giltwood & compo, acanthus/leaves/florals in corners, 1860, 45x35" .**1,095.00**
Giltwood Am Fed, corner rosettes, ring trn/acanthus, 46x32" .**2,750.00**
Giltwood Am Fed, cornice w/cone ends, row of acorn drops, 50x30"..**2,500.00**
Giltwood Am Fed w/cvg, rvpt cottage scene, ca 1820, 46x22" .**1,725.00**
Giltwood Baroque style w/cvg & ebonized recessed panels, 45x40".**7,000.00**
Giltwood Bell Epoque, cherubs/cartouches, marble base, 108x40", pr...**1,400.00**
Giltwood cvd cartouch form, late 1800s, 45x29"....**975.00**
Giltwood Fed, cornice w/14 spherules, rvpt landscape, 1810s, 31x18" ..**1,600.00**
Giltwood Fed, rope-twist cvg, rvpt naval scene, ca 1815, 32x21" .**2,500.00**
Giltwood Rococo, rocaille crest w/bust of goddess, Continental, 17" .**470.00**
Girondole Fed, eagle crest w/2 snakes, sea horse pendant, 44"...**10,350.00**
Mahog Chpndl w/phoenix crest, sm rpr, 37"....**925.00**
Mahog Emp, half-trn pilasters & X pc at base, rpl bk, 35x17" **300.00**
Mahog Fed w/mitred string-inlay liner, NE/1800, 31x18" **1,500.00**
Mahog Fed w/much cvg, old rfn, NY, 1820s, 48x21"....**700.00**
Mahog QA style, scrolled cutouts on crest, 20th C, 48x17"....**250.00**
Mahog vnr Chpndl, line inlay, scroll bottom/top w/bird, 46x24"..**1,870.00**
Mahog vnr Chpndl, molded liner, orig glass, 21x13"....**450.00**
Mahog vnr Chpndl, pierced crest, gilt ho-ho bird, regilded, 37x19" .**1,150.00**
Mahog vnr Chpndl, top/bottom well scalloped w/rtcl leaf in top, 29x17" .**1,045.00**
Mahog vnr on pine w/line inlay, Chpndl to Hplwht, orig glass, 39x21" .**1,300.00**
Mahog vnr QA, tightly scrolled crest/ears, molded liner, 41x23" .**880.00**
Mahog vnr w/gilt, ogee molded fr w/molded borders, NE, 1925, 33x23" ..**470.00**
Mahog w/figured vnr Chpndl-style, ornate crest w/eagle, 40x23" ..**1,150.00**
Mahog/gilt gesso Chpndl, scrolled fr, pierced crest, rpl/rfn, 28x15" .**1,150.00**

Mahog/giltwood late Classic, cove-molded fr, 1830, 28x60" **1,600.00**
Mahog/mahog vnr 2-part Fed, rvpt country house, 35x19" **440.00**
Mahog/parcel-gilt Geo style, swan's neck crest w/eagle, 19th C, 59x27" ..**350.00**
Over-mantel, gilt gesso & wood Fed, 1825-30, 36x50" **2,185.00**
Over-mantel, giltwood & gesso, rocaille crest w/swags/grapes, 75x50".**7,500.00**
Over-mantel, pnt/giltwood Am Fed, cvd ½-columns, rpl glass, 23x46".**925.00**
Pier, ebonized & cvd giltwood Am Fed, gilt bronze rosettes, 77x38"..**5,175.00**
Pier, giltwood Am Fed, cornice w/acorns pendant, colonettes, 63x25".**2,300.00**
Pier, mahog Fed, 2 lg cvd fruit cornucopias, 107x27" **4,000.00**
Pine w/mahog vnr QA, gesso liner, canted top corners, 18x12"..**330.00**
Pine/parcel gilt QA, bold crest, olive gr pnt, 1740-70, 24x13", EX.**16,000.00**
Shaving, mahog vnr w/inlay, bow-front, ogee ft, dvtl drws, rfn.....**220.00**
Shaving, mahog w/swivel mirror on 4-leg base, Hagen, 68x16x16".**1,600.00**
Tabernacle, gilt gesso Fed, molded cornice, 1-part, 31x14" **865.00**
Table plateau, silvered brass, rosette/rtcl oval gallery, 18x13" **145.00**
Trumeau, giltwood Geo III style, appl cvg, landscape scene, 1850s, 70".**2,875.00**
Walnut & gilt gesso Chpndl, scrolled fr w/phoenix cvd crest, 44x23"..**400.00**
Walnut Chpndl, scalloped crest & base, appl scroll, rprs, 18x12"...**300.00**
Walnut Chpndl, scrolled fr w/gilt gesso foliage in crest, 33x18", EX.**1,295.00**
Walnut QA, scrolled crest, rstr glass, 22½x10½" **1,200.00**
Walnut Vict, appl scrolls w/leaves etc, once on chest, 63x59".**1,500.00**
2-Part, brn/ochre mottle pnt w/gilt, rvpt steamship, Portland, Co, 29".**2,350.00**
2-Part, red/yel vinegar pnt, worn rvpt floral, trn crest finials, 24"..**600.00**

Mocha

Mochaware is utilitarian pottery made principally in England (and to a lesser extent in France) between 1780 and 1840 on the then prevalent creamware and pearlware bodies. Initially, only those pieces decorated in the seaweed pattern were called 'Mocha,' while geometrically decorated pieces were referred to as 'Banded Creamware.' Other types of decorations were called 'Dipped Ware.' During the last thirty to forty years the term 'Mocha' has been applied to the entire realm of 'Industrialized Slipware' — pottery decorated by the turner on his lathe using coggle wheels and slip cups.

Mocha was made in numerous patterns — Tree, Seaweed or Dandelion, Rope (also called Worm or Loop), Cat's-eye, Tobacco Leaf, Lollypop or Balloon, Marbled, Marbled and Combed, Twig, Geometric or Checkered, Banded, and slip decorations of rings, dots, flags, tulips, wavy lines, etc. It came into its own as a collectible in the latter half of the 1940s and has become increasingly popular as more and more people are exposed to the rich colorings and artistic appeal of its varied forms of abstract decoration. (Please note: Values hinge to a great extent on vivid coloration, intricacy of pattern, and unusual features.)

The collector should take care not to confuse the early pearlware and creamware Mocha with the later kitchen yellow ware, graniteware, and ironstone sporting mocha-type decoration that was produced in America by such potters as J. Vodrey, George S. Harker, Edwin Bennett, and John Bell. This type was also produced in Scotland and Wales and was marketed well into the twentieth century.

Our values are prices realized at auction, where nearly every example was in exceptional condition. Unless a repair, damage, or another rating is included in the description, assume the item to be in EX+ to NM condition.

Beaker, rust/lt & dk brn/wht combed marbling, 3" **2,720.00**
Bowl, bl/blk/wht scroddled dots on rust, rouletted rim band, rpr, 5"....**940.00**
Bowl, bl/brn/wht scroddled dots on rust, gr rouletted band, 7", EX.**1,000.00**
Bowl, bl/rust/wht/brn marbling on mustard below gr rim, 3⅝x7⅜".**4,115.00**
Bowl, blk/bl/rose/wht earthworm on bl, rose bands, wht ft, 5" **825.00**
Bowl, dk bl/tan/dk brn marbling on wht, gr reeded rim, 7", VG .**885.00**
Bowl, marbled rust/dk brn/buff, cream bands, rpr, 8½" **825.00**
Bowl, rust band w/lg zigzag device of blk 'spiders,' 7" **2,350.00**

Bowl, rust/bl/dk brn/wht combed marbling, blk/wht check band, 7", G-..**900.00**
Bowl, waste; earthworm, 3-color on brn, hairline, 2½x5" **330.00**
Creamer, balloons, pk/bl/wht on gr band, leaf hdl, wear/hairlines, 5" .**440.00**
Jug, blk & bl bands w/wht & bl rick-rack/circles/twigs, leaf hdl, 7".**5,875.00**
Jug, blk trees on rust, brn/rust/gr rouletted upper band, ovoid, 7"...**2,585.00**
Jug, brn band ea side gray band, marbled/trailed brn/rust/wht, 10".**6,465.00**
Jug, cat's eye band+earthworm band ea side band w/16-dot dmns, rpr, 9".**5,525.00**

Jug, central seaweed band on rust and olive above brown and white stripes, 6", $2,000.00. (Photo courtesy Skinner Auctions, Inc.)

Jug, earthworm, bl on gray & bl bands w/blk stripes, 5", EX **330.00**
Jug, earthworm, bl/blk/wht on ocher, bbl form, 1840s, 7½", EX ..**1,850.00**
Jug, earthworm bands ea side wide band w/wht & blk 'branches,' 8", VG.**3,525.00**
Jug, engine-trn bands: 3 blk w/dots & dashes, 2 bl w/arrows, 2 gr, 6".**3,175.00**
Jug, gr/rust/bl bands w/twigs/dots/rick-rack, leaf hdl, ovoid, 8", VG ..**6,465.00**
Jug, marbled orange/bl/gr/wht/med & dk brn, rpr hdl, 4¾".......**1,175.00**
Jug, rust band ea side bl band, seaweed on all, ovoid, 5½", G .**2,940.00**
Mug, bl/brn/tan/wht earthworm on ochre/brn/gr rouletted bands, 6", EX..**5,525.00**
Mug, bl/brn/wht 3-loop earthworm, tan/brn/gr/blk bands, 6", VG .**2,820.00**
Mug, blk stripes/tan band w/wht waves, leaf hdl, stains, 4⅝"......**550.00**
Mug, brn/tan/wht scroddled dots on rust, brn/ochre bands, 6", G- ..**1,175.00**
Mug, dk brn/tan/gray/wht earthworm band, brn cat's eye band, 6".**5,290.00**
Mug, dmn pattern of bl/rust/blk earthworm on gray, rust bands, 6", EX ..**2,350.00**
Mug, gray/tan/brn/wht earthworm on bl, 2 bl rouletted bands, 5", EX ..**2,900.00**
Mug, marbled bl/dk brn/ochre/wht on rust, glued hdl, 4¾" **2,585.00**
Mug, olive/rust/tan bands, wide wht engine-trn band w/blk sqs, 6", VG..**1,765.00**
Mug, pk/bl/blk marbling, hairlines, 3½x4⅛"..............................**350.00**
Mug, rust w/brn dots, bisecting lines cut to wht, rpr, child's, 2½"..**825.00**
Mug, seaweed, blk on ochre w/blk & bl hdls, 1820s, 3⅞", EX.**1,400.00**
Mug, wht w/blk engine-trn geometrics, bl bands, leaf hdl, 6", EX..**1,500.00**
Mug, wht w/2 gr rouletted bands, engine-trn gridwork band, 6", EX.**885.00**
Mug, 2 bl bands, wide buff engine-trn band w/recessed ovals, 6", EX.**3,000.00**
Mug, 2 rows bl/brn/rust/wht earthworm, wht bands, foliate hdl, 6", VG.**1,700.00**
Mustard pot, brn/rust/gray/wht earthworm on bl, w/lid, 2½", VG..**1,295.00**
Mustard pot, earthworm/4-color on bl, tooled bl band, leaf hdl, 4", EX..**1,300.00**
Mustard pot, rust w/seaweed, brn bands, acorn finial, rpr, 3½" .**1,645.00**
Salt cellar, dk brn ribs on wht, bl rim band, 2½" **590.00**
Salt cellar, dk brn seaweed on brn, gr reeded band, 2¾", VG **560.00**

Molds

Food molds have become popular as collectibles — not only for their value as antiques, but because they also revive childhood memories of elaborate ice cream Santas with candy trim or barley sugar figurals adorning a Christmas tree. Ice cream molds were made of pewter and came in a wide variety of shapes and styles. Chocolate molds were made in fewer shapes but were more detailed. They were usually made of tin or copper, and then were nickel plated to keep them from tarnishing or rusting, and also for sanitary reasons. Hard candy molds were usually metal, although primitive maple sugar molds (usually simple hearts, rabbits, and other animals) were carved from wood. (Unless otherwise indicated, the hard candy molds in our listings are cast aluminum or stainless steel.) Cake molds were made of cast iron or cast aluminum and were most common in the shape of a lamb, a rabbit, or Santa Claus. Our advisors for this category are Dale and Jean Van Kuren; they are listed in the Directory under New York.

Chocolate Molds

Alligator, 2-pc, Anton Reiche #10766, 5"..................................135.00
Boy w/arm raised, 2-part, Anton Reiche #14796, 5¼" 100.00
Bride & groom, hinged, 5¼x5"..150.00
Clown, 2-pc, Anton Reiche #15538, 12½x6¼" 215.00
Devil, 2-pc w/clamps, #4224, 6¼x3".......................................260.00
Devil w/club & length of chain, mk ___Fon Wien 14 & lg #7, 5¼"..115.00
Donkey standing, 2-pc, Anton Reiche #26907, 4¾x5¼" 80.00
Dove in flight, #1825, 9x10"...150.00
Dutch man & woman, Anton Reiche #13147 & #13148, 7¼", pr..185.00
Fish, 2-pc, 9x6½" (makes 8" fish) 98.00
Girl standing by rabbit, hinged, 2 clamps, 8x7½" 195.00
Girl toddler (Kewpie like), 2-pc, Anton Reiche #20407S, 5" 70.00
Halloween witch, 2-pc w/6 clamps, 9x7".....................................325.00
Horse, 3-pc, #1436, 9½x10"...140.00
Lamb, hinged, 2-pc..60.00
Man on bicycle, 2-pc, w/ring clips, dolphin mk, #1519, 9x11" ...175.00
Popeye the Sailor, H Walter, Made in Germany #9006, 7" 235.00
Postcard w/Season's Greetings, Santa in sleigh scene, 3⅝x5⅛"..175.00
Rabbit dressed w/apron, basket on bk, 2-pc, Dehaeck #8342, 12¾"..260.00
Rabbit on high-wheeler, 2-pc w/clamps, 4½"..............................160.00
Rabbit on toadstool, 2-pc, Germany, #3106, 1920s-40s, 8" 75.00
Rabbit w/basket & egg at ft, hinged, NY NY US, 9¾x5"................80.00
Rabbit w/short pants & basket, Anton Reiche #29485, 12¾x4¼" .335.00
Rabbits (4) sitting in a row, hinged, overall 1¼x9x3¼" 80.00
Red Riding Hood & wolf in woods/she w/wolf under bed (bk), Germany, lg..550.00
Sailor, 2-pc, w/clip, Anton Reiche #23133, 6¼x3".....................75.00
Santa, 2-pc, #7837, 10x5½"...190.00
Santa, 2-pc, Van Emden #8036, 8x3" 165.00
Santa (Belsnickel type), 2-pc, Germany, #1020, ca 1900, 11".....165.00
Santa (Belsnickel type), 2-pc w/clips, 5x3"...............................200.00
Santa & reindeer, 2-pc, #8130, 2½x6"......................................215.00
Santa in sleigh pulled by reindeer, Anton Reiche #27620, 2½x4½".300.00
Santa riding donkey, 2-pc, Germany, #170, 1930s-30s, 6"...........110.00
Santa w/bag of toys, #22633S, ca 1920, 6¼x3"..........................390.00
Santa w/bag of toys, Anton Reiche #25876, 9"...........................155.00
Santa w/long beard & lantern, 2-pc, #5933, 8x4"........................215.00
Santa w/teddy bear, hinged, Anton Reiche #13308, 5¾x2¾".......75.00
Snail, hinged, #606, 1¾"..100.00
Snowman, hinged, Germany, 5½"..215.00
Spirit of St Louis, New York to Paris 1 side, 2-pc, 11" L............110.00
Star of David (2), pre-WWII, Mle Cerf Koln #27614, 8" L........215.00
Steam locomotive, hinged, Anton Reiche #9954, 4½x6½" 85.00
Sun w/face, copper, 2¾x11½"...215.00
Turtle, 4-pc, Anton Reiche #8422...115.00
Valentine heart box, 3-pc, Anton Reiche, 5¼" 150.00
Valentine hearts (6) in row, 2-pc, Germany, #4018, 13¼" W 75.00
Witch on broom, hinged, 3 metal clips, ca 1970, 6"....................215.00
Witch standing, 2-pc, #16345, 5¼x2¾".....................................65.00
Yellow Kid, hinged, #476, 4¾", EX 315.00
Zeppelin, Anton Reiche #25647, 11½x10⅞" 240.00

Ice Cream Molds

American flag, hinged, #282 ....90.00
Army commander (fat), 2-pc, Anton Reiche #14785, 4x3" 85.00
Battleship Maine, 2 stacks, #513, 2½x6"...................................110.00
Becassine (lady), 2-part, Letang Fils, 4⅜x2½" 110.00
Bird w/spread wings, 2-pc, Anton Reiche #10734, 6¾x4½" 120.00
Boy mountain dweller, 2-pc, Anton Reiche, 3⅛x2¼" 65.00
Bride & groom, E&Co, #M1201, 3x5½" 150.00
Butterfly, hinged, E&Co #679, 3x5"..75.00
Christmas candlestick (in holder), 3-pc, E&Co #932, 5x4" 80.00
Christmas tree, E-1154, 5½x3½"...120.00
Christmas wreath, #1146, ca 1930-40s, 5" dia............................140.00
Colonial man's bust (Geo Washington?), E-108, 3x3"..................110.00
Conch shell, C&MCo, 2½x4"..95.00
Igloo, cast aluminum, 4½x9x8"...135.00
Poinsettia, #1144, 5x5"..165.00
Revolutionary war soldier, S&Co #504, 5⅛x2¼" 85.00
Santa, E-427, 4½x2"...160.00
Sea shell (scallop), hinged, S&Co #524, 4¾" L..........................140.00
Wedding bells, 3"...42.50

Maple Sugar Molds

Beaver, hand cvd, EX detail, 5x9"..75.00
Cow in 2 parts, varnished, 4½x7"..68.00
Figures/animals ea side, 21x3¼"...250.00
Fruit & foliage, hardwood, 2-part, 5½x8"...................................28.00
Heart & clover, primitive, 5x17½"...60.00
Openwork on rnd fluted cups, CI, 1840s, 12 in 11x16" fr 115.00
Rabbit sitting, EX cvg, 1¼x6½x5"..55.00
Strawberry, deeply cvd pine, rtcl, 1830s, 1¾x5½x9" 165.00

Miscellaneous

Aluminum, German shepherd dog head on base, 2¾x4½" dia 25.00
Copper, cross & orb, Reg April 22 186?, 5½x5½" 265.00
Copper, ear of corn, 3¾x6x3"..100.00
Copper, fish, brass hanger, ca 1950-60, 5x13".............................8.00
Copper, flower, 3x11½"...155.00
Copper, grape cluster, EX patina, 4½x10¼"...............................205.00
Copper, rabit w/carrot, 1¾x7x5¾"...145.00
Copper, rnded/hammpered peaks, 19th C, 2⅜x6½" dia..............275.00
Copper, rope-patterned top, 'ladyfingers' along sides, oval, 9½".375.00
Copper, 2-tier crown w/12 'fingers' around central funnel, 5½" dia.240.00
Copper, 6-pointed star, bundt type, 4x11¾" dia.........................205.00
Pottery, ram, 2-part, moss gr glaze, ftd base, hdls ea part, 12"......110.00

Monmouth

The Monmouth Pottery Company was established in 1892 in Monmouth, Illinois. It was touted as the largest pottery in the world. Their primary products were utilitarian: stoneware crocks, churns, jugs, water coolers, etc. — in salt glaze, Bristol, spongeware, and Albany brown. In 1906 they were absorbed by a conglomerate called the Western Stoneware Company. Monmouth Pottery Co. became their number one plant and until 1930 continued to produce stoneware marked with the Western Stoneware Company's maple leaf logo. Items marked 'Monmouth Pottery Co.' were made before 1906. Western Stoneware Co. introduced a line of artware in 1926. The name chosen for the artware was Monmouth Pottery. Some stamps and paper labels add ILL to the name.

Bowl, batter; lt gr, 4¾x8" dia 85.00
Bowl, salt glazed, brn int, base mk, 2-gal....................................200.00
Churn, #3, cobalt on salt glaze, 3-gal, 13"..................................250.00
Churn, #5, cobalt on salt glaze, 5-gal 325.00
Churn, Bristol, Maple Leaf mk, 2-gal 250.00

Churn, cobalt on salt glaze, 6-gal.................................400.00
Churn, salt glaze, mini, 4"..................................1,200.00
Churn, salt glaze, 3-gal...350.00
Churn, 2 Men in a Crock stencil, 5-gal.................1,000.00
Cooler, ice water; bl & wht sponge, w/lid & spigot, 8-gal........1,500.00
Cooler, ice water; bl & wht sponge, 5-gal..............1,500.00
Cooler, ice water; bl & wht spongeware, mini..........1,000.00
Cow & calf, brn, mk Monmouth Pottery Co.............3,000.00
Crock, Bristol, Albany slip int, 4-gal........................85.00
Crock, Bristol, Maple Leaf mk, 2-gal.........................75.00
Crock, Bristol, mini, 2½"...600.00
Crock, Bristol, 10-gal...100.00
Crock, Bristol, 20-gal...100.00
Crock, Bristol, 60-gal...1,500.00
Crock, Bristol Monmouth Pottery Co, bl stencil, 1-qt.............250.00
Crock, early dull Bristol w/cobalt stencil.................300.00
Crock, salt glaze, Albany slip int, 3-gal....................95.00
Crock, salt glaze, hand decor, base mk, 2-gal.........250.00
Crock, salt glaze, unmk, 2-gal...............................60.00
Crock, salt glaze, 3-gal...150.00
Crock, stencil, bl on dk brn Albany slip, 3-gal.........300.00
Crock, stencil, bl on dk brn Albany slip, 6-gal.........600.00
Crock, 2 Men in a Crock stencil, 10-gal..................500.00
Dog, Monmouth Pottery Co, mk, Albany slip..........5,000.00
Hen on nest, bl & wht spongeware.......................1,200.00
Jug, Bristol, bl stencil (early rectangle), 5-gal.........250.00
Jug, Bristol, Maple Leaf mk, 5-gal..........................200.00
Jug, Bristol w/Albany slip top, mini, 2½"................500.00
Letterhead, 1898 letter...45.00
Pig, brn, mk Monmouth Pottery Co.....................1,000.00
Pig, Monmouth Pottery Co, Bristol......................1,500.00
Snuff or preserve jar, wax seal...............................350.00
Tobacco jar, monk, brn Albany slip........................300.00
Vase, bl matt, incised shoulder band, 16x10".........495.00

Mont Joye

Mont Joye was a type of acid-cut French cameo glass produced by Cristallerie de Pantin in Paris around the turn of the century. It is accented by enamels. Our advisor for this category is Don Williams; he is listed in the Directory under Missouri.

Bowl, chestnuts on branches, 3-color on icy ground w/gold, 8"..525.00
Bowl, iris int, incurvate rim, ftd, 3½x9¾x7"..............435.00
Bowl, poppies on red, 12", +matching 12" vases......3,000.00
Rose bowl, violets/leaves on gr, 4¾x5½".................300.00
Vase, acorns/leaves, gold/silver on textured emerald, 13x9".....1,000.00

Vase, enameled and silvered acorns with gold and silvered oak leaves on dark gilt ground, swollen top on narrow stem with flared foot, ca 1900, 19¾", $4,000.00. (Photo courtesy Skinner, Inc.)

Vase, floral, purple/gold, gold leaves/silver buds as base, 19"....1,850.00
Vase, floral on purple, 7¾x3¼"..............................700.00
Vase, gr textured w/gold flowers, rectangular, 5".......320.00
Vase, hollyhock w/gr leaves on golden-brn frost, 10"....1,200.00
Vase, irises, gold on frost, cylindrical w/flaring base, 15"....485.00
Vase, violets/gold leaves on gr chipped ice, 10".......345.00

Moon and Star

Moon and Star was originally produced in the 1880s by John Adams & Company of Pittsburgh. In the 1960s, Joseph Weishar of Wheeling, West Virginia, owner of the Island Mould & Machine Company, reproduced some of the original molds and incorporated the pattern into approximately forty new and different items. Two of the largest distributors of this line were L.E. Smith of Mt. Pleasant, Pennsylvania, who pressed their own glass, and L.G. Wright of New Martinsville, West Virginia, who had theirs pressed by Fostoria, Fenton, and Westmoreland. Both companies carried a large and varied assortment of shapes and colors. Several other companies were involved in its manufacture as well, especially of the smaller items.

Over the years the glassware has been pressed in amberina (yellow shading to orange- or ruby-red), green, amber, crystal, light blue, and ruby. Pieces in ruby and light blue are most collectible and harder to find than the other colors, which seem to be abundant. Purple, pink, cobalt, amethyst, tan slag, and light green and blue opalescent were made, too, but on a lesser scale.

In 1992 the Weishar company introduced a new color, teal green, which was followed in 1993 with sapphire blue opalescent, and in 1994 with cranberry ice. These items (and those being made today) carried the Weishar mark and were made primarily for collectors. Currently the company is producing water sets, salt and pepper shakers, creamers and sugars, spoon holders, and various relish trays in Delphite and Delphite carnival, Crown Tuscan and Crown Tuscan carnival, Colonial Blue, Millennium Rose (pink), and various other colors such as amethyst and cobalt on a more limited basis. Miniature water sets have been made in more than thirty colors, the newest being amethyst slag and amethyst slag carnival. Unless another color is noted, our values are given for vintage glassware in ruby and light blue. For amberina, green, and amber, deduct 20%.

Banana boat, allover pattern, moons form scallops at rim, 12"......40.00
Basket, allover pattern, moons form scallops, solid hdl, 9", $50 to...60.00
Bell, patterned sides, plain rim & hdl.........................35.00
Butter dish, allover pattern, scalloped ft, patterned lid, 5½" dia...45.00
Cake plate, allover pattern, low collared base, 13" dia, from $50 to...60.00
Cake stand, allover pattern, plate removes from std, 2-pc, 11" dia...75.00
Candle holders, allover pattern, flared/scalloped ft, 6", pr...........40.00
Candy dish, allover pattern on base & lid, ftd ball shape, 6".........20.00
Canister, allover pattern, 1-lb or 2-lb, ea..................12.00
Chandelier, ruffled dome w/allover pattern, amber, 10"................65.00
Compote, allover pattern, scalloped rim, ftd, 7x10"......35.00
Creamer & sugar bowl (open), disk ft, sm...................25.00
Epergne, allover pattern, 1-lily, flared bowl, scalloped ft, minimum..95.00
Goblet, wine; plain rim & ft, 4½"..............................9.00
Jelly dish, allover pattern, patterned lid/stemmed ft, 10½", $55 to..60.00
Lamp, mini, gr...135.00
Lamp, oil; allover pattern, all orig, common, 12", from $50 to.....65.00
Relish, allover pattern, 1 plain hdl, 2x8" dia.............35.00
Salt cellar, allover pattern, scalloped rim, sm flat ft.........6.00
Soap dish, allover pattern, oval, 2x6".......................9.00
Sugar bowl, allover pattern, patterned lid, flat ft, 5¼x4"........35.00
Sugar shaker, allover pattern, metal lid, 4½x3½".......45.00
Tumbler, iced tea; no pattern at rim or on disk ft, 11-oz, 5".........18.00
Tumbler, no pattern at rim or disk ft, 7-oz, 4¼".........12.00

Moorcroft

William Moorcroft began to work for MacIntyre Potteries in 1897. At first he was the chief designer but very soon took over their newly created Art Pottery department. His first important design was the Aurelian Ware, part transfer and part hand painted. Very shortly thereafter, around the turn of the century, he developed his famous Florian Ware, with heavy slip, done in mostly blue and white. Since the early 1900s there has been a succession of designs, most of them very characteristic of the company. Moorcroft left MacIntyre in 1913 and went out on his own. He had already well established his name, having won prizes and gold medals at the St. Louis World's Fair as well as in Paris. In 1929 Queen Mary, who had been collecting his pottery, made him 'Potter to the Queen,' and the pottery was so stamped up until 1949. William Moorcroft died in 1945, and his son Walter ran the company until recent years. The factory is still in existence. They now produce different designs but continue to use the characteristic slipwork. Moorcroft pottery was sold abroad in Canada, the United States, Australia, and Europe as well as in specialty areas such as the island of Bermuda.

Moorcroft went through a 'Japanese' stage in the early teens with his lovely lustre glazes, Oriental shapes and decorations. During the mid-teens he began to produce his most popular Pomegranate Ware, and Wisteria (often called 'Fruit'). Around that time he also designed the popular Pansy line as well as Leaves and Grapes. Soon he introduced a beautiful landscape series called variously Hazeldine, Moonlit Blue, Eventide, and Dawn. These wonderful designs along with Claremont (Mushrooms) seem to be the most sought after by collectors today. It would be possible to add many other designs to this list.

During the 1920s and 1930s, Moorcroft became very interested in highly fired Flambé (red) glazes. These could only be achieved through a very difficult procedure which he himself perfected in secret. He later passed the knowledge on to his son.

Dating of this pottery is done by knowledge of the designs, shapes, signatures, and marks on the bottom of each piece; an experienced person can usually narrow it down to a short time frame. Prices escalated for this 'rediscovered' pottery in the late 1980s but have now leveled off. This is true mainly of the pre-1935 designs of William Moorcroft, as it is items from that era that attract the most collector interest. Prices in the listings below are for pieces in mint condition unless noted otherwise; no reproductions are listed here. Advisors for this category are Wilfred and Dolli Cohen; they are listed in the Directory under California.

Bowl, anemones, mc on teal, MIE, 2¼x9¾" 195.00
Bowl, clematis, gr/bl, w/lid, 4½x6½" 175.00
Bowl, hibiscus on gr, 5¾" 125.00
Bowl, pomegranates on cobalt, low ft, 3¼x8¼" 500.00
Candlesticks, wisteria on cobalt, Tudric pewter cup & base, 5¾", pr.... 900.00
Creamer, Florian Ware, bl floral on bl, MacIntyre, 3" 725.00
Humidor, pomegranates on blk, w/lid, 6x5" 680.00
Jar, spring flowers on gray to teal, w/lid, 1940s, 4¾x3½" 360.00
Pitcher, spring flowers, mc on teal, MIE, 6x6" 360.00
Tazza, pansies on bl, Tudric pewter base, 3¼x6⅞" 695.00
Vase, Alhambra, gilted, baluster, MacIntyer, 11⅞" 1,250.00
Vase, anemones, lg band on teal, MIE, 7¼x4¾" 500.00
Vase, anemones, magenta/sage gr on cobalt, MIE, 1920s-40s, 5x3"..385.00
Vase, anemones, mc on cobalt, MIE, 1920s, 5¼x5¼" 415.00
Vase, berries & leaves, yel/tan/caramel, 9" 650.00
Vase, blackberries on cobalt & magenta, MIE, 1920-30s, 4½"....415.00
Vase, Claremont, mushrooms, gr/brn on gr, 6" 3,330.00
Vase, clematis on bl, 14½" 480.00
Vase, clematis on cobalt, stick neck, MIE, 1940s, 8¼x5" 525.00
Vase, fish & seaweed, slim baluster form, 12½" 2,975.00
Vase, Florian Ware, bl cornflowers on wht, 11", pr 800.00

Vase, hibiscus, coral on gr, 1953-78, label, 4¼" 235.00
Vase, hills/trees/clouds on red, MIE, 8¼" 1,140.00
Vase, leaf & fruit on gr, U-form on rnd ft, 7½" 550.00
Vase, leaves & berries, mc on cobalt, slim neck, paper label, 12½"...550.00
Vase, orchids & flowers on cobalt, MIE, 1920s-40s, 5x4½" 500.00
Vase, orchids on cream to cobalt, 10½" 1,380.00
Vase, pansy & bud, MIE, mk M49, 1914, 6½" 1,650.00
Vase, pomegranates, celedon gr hdls, 3⅛x3½" 630.00
Vase, pomegranates on blk, ca 1915, 9" 800.00
Vase, pomegranates on cobalt, ca 1918-29, 8¾" 725.00
Vase, pomegranates on tan, 15¾" 1,280.00
Vase, poppies, bl on wht ovoid w/flared lip, ftd, MIE, 3x1¾" 725.00
Vase, poppies, dk red flambe, shouldered, 12½x6¾" 2,000.00
Vase, swags of roses & forget-me-nots on wht, loop hdls, 8" 775.00
Vase, waving corn on wht, 2-hdl, 8" 650.00
Vase, weeping willow, pale gr/beige on wht, 9" 2,700.00

Morgantown Glass

Incorporated in 1899, the Morgantown Glass Works experienced many name changes over the years. Today 'Morgantown Glass' is a generic term used to identify all glass produced there. Purchased by Fostoria in 1965, the factory was permanently closed in 1971.

Golf Ball is the most recognized design with crosshatched bumps equally distributed along the stem (very similar to Cambridge #1066, identified with alternating lines of dimples between rows of crosshatching). Color identification is difficult and further information is provided by Gene Florence in his book *Stemware Identification* (Collector Books). Prices for Golf Ball with ranges begin with lower values referring to colors other than Steigel Green, Spanish Red, or Ritz Blue with the high range reflecting values for those colors. For further information we also recommend *Elegant Glassware of the Depression Era* by Gene Florence (Collector Books).

Golf Ball, other colors, candlestick, Jacobi (top flat rim), 4" 135.00
Golf Ball, other colors, stem, champagne; 5" 27.50
Golf Ball, other colors, stem, wine; 3-oz 35.00
Golf Ball, other colors, tumbler, juice; ftd, 5-oz 22.00
Golf Ball, other colors, vase, Charlotte, crimped rim, 8" 175.00
Golf Ball, Ritz Blue, candlestick, torch; 6" 220.00
Golf Ball, Ritz Blue, pilsner, 9⅛" 182.50
Golf Ball, Ritz Blue, stem, cordial; 3½" 55.00
Golf Ball, Ritz Blue, stem, sherbet/sundae; 4⅛" 32.50
Golf Ball, Ritz Blue, tumbler, water; 9-oz 44.00
Golf Ball, Steigel Green or Spanish Red, creamer 175.00
Golf Ball, Steigel Green or Spanish Red, stem, cafe parfait; 4-oz ..100.00
Golf Ball, Steigel Green or Spanish Red, stem, oyster cocktail; 4⅜"...60.00
Golf Ball, Steigel Green or Spanish Red, stem, water; 9-oz........... 50.00
Golf Ball, Steigel Green or Spanish Red, tumbler, iced tea; ftd, 12-oz..50.00
Golf Ball, Steigel Green or Spanish Red, vase, #79 Montague, 11"..450.00
Golf Ball, Stiegel Green or Spanish Red, bell............................... 125.00
Queen Louise, crystal w/Anna Rose, bowl, finger; ftd 225.00
Queen Louise, crystal w/Anna Rose, plate, salad 150.00
Queen Louise, crystal w/Anna Rose, stem, cocktail; 3-oz........... 375.00
Queen Louise, crystal w/Anna Rose, stem, sherbet; 5½-oz.......... 300.00
Queen Louise, crystal w/Anna Rose, stem, water; 9-oz............... 400.00
Queen Louise, crystal w/Anna Rose, stem, wine; 2½-oz.............. 375.00
Sunrise Medallion, bl, creamer 325.00
Sunrise Medallion, bl, plate, sherbet; 5⅞" 18.00
Sunrise Medallion, bl, saucer 22.50
Sunrise Medallion, bl, sugar bowl 300.00
Sunrise Medallion, bl, tumbler, ftd, 5-oz... 65.00
Sunrise Medallion, bl, vase, bud, slim, 10" 400.00
Sunrise Medallion, crystal, cup 40.00

Sunrise Medallion, crystal, plate, salad; 7½" 15.00
Sunrise Medallion, crystal, sherbet, cone 20.00
Sunrise Medallion, crystal, tumbler, ftd, 11-oz, 5½" 35.00
Sunrise Medallion, crystal, tumbler, ftd, 2½" 25.00
Sunrise Medallion, pk or gr, cup 80.00
Sunrise Medallion, pk or gr, plate, 8⅜" 22.50
Sunrise Medallion, pk or gr, stem, cordial; 1½-oz 225.00
Sunrise Medallion, pk or gr, stem, water; twist stem, 8¼" 55.00
Sunrise Medallion, pk or gr, vase, 6x5" 395.00
Tinkerbell, Azure or gr, bowl, finger; ftd.................100.00
Tinkerbell, Azure or gr, night bottle set, 4-pz...........600.00
Tinkerbell, Azure or gr, stem, cocktail; 3½-oz............125.00
Tinkerbell, Azure or gr, stem, cordial; 1½-oz.............175.00
Tinkerbell, Azure or gr, stem, goblet; 9-oz..............150.00
Tinkerbell, Azure or gr, stem, wine; 2½-oz...............135.00
Tinkerbell, Azure or gr, vase, plain top, ftd, #36 Uranus, 10"......350.00

Mortars and Pestles

Mortars are bowl-shaped vessels used for centuries for the purpose of grinding drugs to a powder or grain into meal. The masher or grinding device is called a pestle.

Ash burl w/G figure, 6½x5", +trn wooden pestle 220.00
Brass, flared rim, wear, 3¼", +pestle 50.00
Brass, 2-hdl, flared rim, 4½", +dbl-ended pestle...........90.00
Burl, trn bands, 2 filled cracks, 5x6", wood-hdl ceramic-head pestle.110.00

Mortens Studio

Oscar Mortens was already established as a fine sculptural artist when he left his native Sweden to take up residency in Arizona. During the 1940s he developed a line of detailed animal figures which were distributed through the Mortens Studios, a firm he co-founded with Gunnar Thelin. Thelin hired and trained artists to produce Mortens' line, which he called Royal Designs. More than two hundred dogs were modeled and over one hundred horses. Cats and wild animals such as elephants, panthers, deer, and elk were made, but on a much smaller scale. Bookends with sculptured dog heads were shown in their catalogs, and collectors report finding wall plaques on rare occasions. The material they used was a plaster-type composition with wires embedded to support the weight. Examples were marked 'Copyright by the Mortens Studio' either in ink or decal. Watch for flaking, cracks, and separations. Crazing seems to be present in some degree in many examples. When no condition is indicated, the items listed below are assumed to be in near-mint condition, allowing for minor crazing.

Beagle pup, seated, 3¾" 65.00
Boston terrier pup, seated, 3x3½" 50.00
Boxer (male) dog, standing, 5½" 165.00
Chihuahua, standing, 1¾" 55.00
Cocker spaniel, recumbent, 3x6½" 55.00
Cocker spaniel, seated, 3" 45.00
Cocker spaniel head plaque, 5x5½" 95.00
Cocker spaniel pup, 2½" 25.00
Collie, recumbent, 5¼x5¼" 135.00
Doberman pinscher, standing, #659 w/label, 6x7" 110.00
Doberman pinscher, standing, 7¼x8½" 135.00
English setter, mini 55.00
English setter, w/label, 6¼x10¾" 95.00
English Springer Spaniel, blk ink stamp, 2¾" 65.00
Great Dane, golden tan w/brn muzzle, w/label, #72, 8" 75.00

Horse, American Saddlebred, bay, stretched stance, 8" 110.00
Horse, American Saddlebred, palomino, stretched stance, 8" 85.00
Horse plaque, #651, 7x8½" 125.00
Irish setter, on point, 3⅝", EX 55.00
Irish setter plaque, 7x8½".................................90.00
Kerry bl terrier, decal, 4¾x6" 140.00
Pekingese, #740, 3½" 75.00
Poodle, w/label, 3½".......................................65.00
Pug dog, w/label, 4½x5½"...................................85.00
Sealyham terrier, w/label 125.00
Spaniel, blk & wht, standing w/head up, 5x8½".............125.00
Wild stallion (on base), #718, 9½", from $95 to 110.00

Morton Pottery

Six potteries operated in Morton, Illinois, at various times from 1877 to 1976. Each traced its origin to six brothers who immigrated to America to avoid military service in Germany. The Rapp brothers established their first pottery near clay deposits on the south side of town where they made field tile and bricks. Within a few years, they branched out to include utility wares such as jugs, bowls, jars, pitchers, etc. During the ninety-nine years of pottery operations in Morton, the original factory was expanded by some of the sons and nephews of the Rapps. Other family members started their own potteries where artware, gift-store items, and special-order goods were produced. The Cliftwood Art Pottery and the Morton Pottery Company had showrooms in Chicago and New York City during the 1930s. All of Morton's potteries were relatively short-lived operations with the Morton Pottery Company being the last to shut down on September 8, 1976. For a more thorough study of the subject, we recommend *Morton's Potteries: 99 Years, Vols. I* and *II*, by Doris and Burdell Hall; their address can be found in the Directory under Illinois.

Morton Pottery Works — Morton Earthenware Co. (1877 – 1917)

Bowl, rice nappy, brn Rockingham, fluted, 10" 65.00
Bowl, rice nappy, yel ware, fluted, 8" 80.00
Coffeepot, dripolator, brn Rockingham, lg infuser, 8-cup 70.00
Coffeepot, dripolator, brn Rockingham, sm infuser, 10-cup...........90.00
Cuspidor, brn Rockingham, urn shape, 7" 45.00
Cuspidor, cobalt, urn shape, 7"...........................55.00
Miniature, coffee dripolator, brn Rockingham, 3" 70.00
Miniature, creamer, brn Rockingham, 1¾" 35.00
Miniature, creamer, jade gr, 1¾" 40.00
Miniature, milk jug, cobalt, 4¼" 60.00
Stein, yel ware, 2 bl slip stripes top & bottom 50.00
Teapot, brn Rockingham, +cr/sug & std spooner............125.00
Teapot, Rebecca in shield, brn Rockingham, bulbous, 2½-pt........50.00

Cliftwood Art Potteries, Inc. (1920 – 1940)

Chocolate/lemonade set, pitcher and six mugs, chocolate drip, **$150.00.** (Photo courtesy Doris and Burdell Hall)

Bean pot, old rose, ind...10.00
Bookends, elephant, bl/mulberry, 3¼", pr 125.00
Bowl, sweetmeat; yel/gr drip, w/lid, 2x4¾x4¾" 40.00
Creamer, cow figural, tail hdl/mouth spout, chocolate drip, 3¾x6" .85.00
Dresser set, apple gr, tray+jar+powder box+2 candle holders 65.00
Figurine, American eagle, natural colors spray glaze, 8½" 150.00
Flower bowl insert, water lily pad #1, rose glaze, 2x4" 18.00
Flower bowl insert, water lily pad #2, med bl, 2x6"..........24.00
Lamp, bulb w/emb lovebirds, jade gr, w/harp, 20" 60.00
Lamp, fluted bulb/hdls, bl/mulberry, Art Deco #31, 10⅝" 48.00
Lamp, pillar base, star-emb globe, wht, Art Deco #23, 8½" 40.00
Planter, police dog, open bk, wht matt, 5" 30.00
Reamer, Herbage gr, rare 55.00
Vase, rectangular w/simulated palm fronds, turq matt, 14" 30.00
Vase, wht matt/old rose spray, dolphin base, 9"...............75.00
Waffle set, pk/orchid drip, pitcher+syrup w/lid+tray...................150.00
Wall pocket, tree trunk w/3 openings, chocolate drip, 8½"..........80.00

Midwest Potteries, Inc. (1940 – 1944)

Bookend (1 only), leaping deer, bl, Deco design, 7¾" 40.00
Candle holder, Jack-be-nimble type, hdl, lime gr, 7" 24.00
Figurine, bird of paradise, bl/brn spray, 12"..........................25.00
Figurine, canaries (2) on stump, yel w/gold, 4" 30.00
Figurine, gull in flight, wht w/gold, 12"..............................35.00
Figurine, Irish setter, brn drip, gr base, 4½"......................35.00
Figurine, tiger stalking, HP natural colors, 7x12"...........50.00
Pitcher, cow, tail hdl, wht w/gold, 4½"............................25.00
Pitcher, fish, jade gr, 9½" 34.00
Planter, broken egg, tripod base, gr, 6" 20.00
Planter, elephant, bl/yel drip, 4"...................................12.00
Plaque, African native, female w/gold neck rings & ear bones......40.00
Plaque, African native, male, blk, glossy, 9" 30.00

Morton Pottery Company (1922 – 1976)

Ashtray, Meuhlebach Hotel, Kansas City, burgundy.....................15.00
Bank, Scottie dog, blk, 7"..22.00
Bookends, bald eagle, brn & wht, pr...................................30.00
Bowl, mixing; yel ware, wht slip bands, Hohulin..., IL 70.00
Cookie jar, circus animals, cylindrical, yel & orange 45.00
Cookie jar, fruit basket, natural-color fruit in gr basket 45.00
Easter rabbit in bonnet, bl egg at side, 9½"......................20.00
Easter rabbit in top hat, yel egg at side, 9½".....................20.00
Easter rabbit pushing cart, brn & wht, 7"..........................30.00
Honey jug, underglaze flowers & bee, Herm's Honey 30.00
Lamp, TV; gondola, gray w/blk, removable planters, 18" L 55.00
Lamp, TV; horse's head, brn, 18" 45.00
Lapel stud, stein, brn Rockingham, We Want Beer, std hdl, 1".....50.00
Night light, teddy bear, wht w/bl or pk paws, brn ears...................40.00
Planter, covered wagon, Compliments of Weidman's Store...........30.00
Stein, bbl form, brn Rockingham, advertising emb on side 24.00
Stein, cylindrical, brn Rockingham, emb advertising 28.00
Wall pocket, harp, wht w/underglaze florals 20.00
Wall pocket, lady gardener w/hoe (or watering can), ringed pot front ..25.00
Water fountain figure, fish, pk 40.00

American Art Potteries (1947 – 1963)

Bottle, crown shape, yel/gray spray, 6" 24.00
Console set, mauve/pk spray, 10x6¾" bowl+2 1¾" candle holders..30.00
Creamer, bird figural, tail forms hdl, spray glaze, 4" 24.00
Doll parts, head, arms & legs, HP, rare, 1¾", 3½" dia 66.00
Doll parts, head, arms & legs, HP, 3½", 6" dia 72.00

Doll parts, head, arms & legs, HP, 7½", 12" dia..........................110.00
Flower bowl, bullet form, blk/gray spray, 3½x12"........................15.00
Flower bowl, S shape, yel/wht, 2x10"....................................14.00
Flower frog, titmouse on raised disk, mauve/yel spray, 8"................24.00
Lamp, TV; cardinals on planter, mauve/gray spray, 12".................40.00
Lamp, TV; 2 Afghan hounds, blk, 15".....................................75.00
Planter, fish, mauve/pk spray, 4".......................................16.00
Planter/vase, cowboy boot, gray/pk spray, 5"...........................24.00
Vase, bulbous w/molded flower clusters, brn/yel spray, 12½".........50.00
Vase, pitcher, wht w/rust spackling, 14"................................24.00
Vase, swan w/elongated neck, gr/yel spray w/gold, 11"..................25.00
Vase, 6-sided, pk w/bl int, 10"..18.00
Wall pocket, elongated flower, mauve petals/gr leaves, 8½"..........24.00

Moser

Ludwig Moser began his career as a struggling glass artist, catering to the rich who visited the famous Austrian health spas. His talent and popularity grew and in 1857 the first of his three studios opened in Karlsbad, Czechoslovakia. The styles developed there were entirely his own; no copies of other artists have ever been found. Some of his original designs include grapes with trailing vines, acorns and oak leaves, and richly enameled, deeply cut or carved floral pieces. Sometimes jewels were applied to the glass as well. Moser's animal scenes reflect his careful attention to detail. Famed for his birds in flight, he also designed stalking tigers and large, detailed elephants, all created in fine enameling.

Moser died in 1916, but the business was continued by his two sons who had been personally and carefully trained by their father. The Moser company bought the Meyr's Neffe Glassworks in 1922 and continued to produce quality glassware.

When identifying Moser, look for great clarity in the glass; deeply carved, continuous engravings; perfect coloration; finely applied enameling (often covered with thin gold leaf); and well-polished pontils. Our advisor for this category is Don Williams; he is listed in the Directory under Missouri. Items described below are enameled unless noted otherwise. If no color is mentioned in the line, the glass is clear.

Bottle, amber w/centaurs/warriors frieze, 8½", +9" tray.............360.00
Bottle scent; cranberry w/aquatic scene, appl fish, 4", pr.........1,600.00
Bowl, crystal to gr w/heavy random gold enamel, boat shaped, 12" L..275.00
Box, birds/mythical creatures/floral on cobalt, 6½x2½x4¼".......530.00
Box, cobalt w/etched gold elephant, 3x5" dia 375.00
Champagne, heavy gold, set of 6..1,200.00
Compote, pk opaline, oak leaves, amber tree branch ft, 7½"...1,725.00
Cruet, bl, wht/gold lilies of the valley, faceted stopper 325.00
Cruet, clear w/8 appl ruby panels & 8 alternating gilt/leaf strips, 6"..585.00
Cruet, cranberry, heavy gold o/l, 5" 400.00
Cruets, cranberry w/bl & wht flowers, pr, in EC Webs SP fr 750.00
Cup & saucer, cranberry w/heavy gold intricate floral.................350.00
Decanter, amethyst, rectangular, w/matching stopper, 7" 315.00
Decanter, gr w/gilt, 6-sided, clear stopper, 15", +6 matching cordials...710.00
Goblet, bl stain w/gilt floral, appl prunts on stem, 1890s, 8".......425.00
Goblet, bowl w/fluted int & floral, amber stem, 1890s, 7", NM..115.00
Goblet, marriage; cranberry w/allover decor & gold 500.00
Loving cup, citron to ruby, bl/gold daisies & scrolls, citron hdls, 5" ..500.00
Mug, cranberry, appl acorns/mc leafage 450.00
Pitcher, florals, gold band, 2⅜"...200.00
Pitcher, pk w/gold floral, int fluted body, 1890s, 12¾" 665.00
Rose bowl, cranberry, floral roundles w/in gold partitions, silver ft..400.00
Rose bowl, cranberry w/florals/butterfly/appl acorns, gold ft, 3½" ...750.00
Tankard, lt emerald to crystal w/silver & gilt scrolled florals, 12" ..400.00
Vase, alexandrite, heavy cutting, 3-wafer bottom, flaring top, 6"...345.00
Vase, alexandrite frost w/cherubs, 3⅛x2¼" 150.00

Vase, amber, relief gold bands w/soldiers, 5¾" 150.00
Vase, amethyst, wheat stalks & flowers, snake hdl, 9½" 575.00
Vase, amethyst w/etched & gilt warriors & cut facets, ca 1920, 9¼" .625.00
Vase, bl w/wht floral & gold, scalloped rim, 15" 600.00
Vase, cobalt w/armed men in gold band, 5x4¾" 180.00
Vase, cranberry w/fishscale decor & floral band, gold, 13" 460.00
Vase, cranberry w/mc ferns, cornucopia form, ped ft, 12" 1,495.00
Vase, gr w/fireflies & flowers, SP fr w/nymphs & goats, 10½" 500.00
Vase, gr w/gold & yel floral, ruffled trumpet form, 16" 165.00
Vase, jack-in-the-pulpit; lt gr w/wht & gold floral, 5¾" 415.00
Vase, olive craquelle, fish & plants, 4 appl pods, 6", NM 300.00
Vase, ruby, w/sprig of oak leaves & 1 appl acorn, crystal hdls, 3" ...175.00
Vase, ruby facets, unmk, 3⅞" 125.00
Vase, vaseline to gr opal w/florals & scrolls, ruffled, 7x10" 365.00
Water set, gr w/Mary Gregory boys & girls, 15½" pitcher+4 tumblers.1,200.00
Wine, gr w/gold enamel decor, air-twist stem, 7" 200.00

Moss Rose

Moss Rose was a favorite dinnerware pattern of many Staffordshire and American potters of the mid-1800s. In America the Wheeling Pottery of West Virginia produced the ware in large quantities, and it became one of their bestsellers, remaining popular well into the '90s. The pattern was colored by hand; this type is designated 'old' in our listings to distinguish it from the more modern Moss Rose design of the twentieth century, which we've also included. It's not hard to distinguish between the two. The later ware you'll recognize immediately, since the pattern is applied by decalcomania on stark white backgrounds. It has been made in Japan to a large extent, but companies in Germany and Bavaria have produced it as well. Today, there is more interest in the twentieth-century items than in the older ware.

Bowl, Japan, 1950s, 4x7" 20.00
Bowl, soup; Pompadour, Rosenthal, US Zone 42.00
Bowl, sterling knob on lid, Pompadour, Rosenthal, 3¾x5⅛" 40.00
Bowl, vegetable; w/lid, Pompadour, Rosenthal...........................150.00
Cake/sandwich plate, Royal Albert..45.00
Candle holders, Japan, 3", pr...15.00
Coffeepot, Pompadour, Rosenthal, 11".....................................150.00
Creamer & sugar bowl, Haviland & Co, sugar: 7" to finial 90.00
Cruets, oil & vinegar; Japan sticker, pr......................................25.00
Cup & saucer, Japan, 2½", 5½"...10.00
Cup & saucer, Royal Albert..22.50
Egg boiler, electric, NM..55.00
Egg coddler, Apco, Japan, paper labels, w/clamp & lid, 3½" 32.00
Lamp, oil; 2-hdl, Japan, 7½"...30.00
Mustache cup, gold accents, Haviland, from $225 to 275.00
Pitcher, gold trim, Limoges, 8", from $250 to.............................300.00
Place setting, plate+bread plate+berry bowl+c/s, 5-pc set, Japan ..30.00
Plate, dinner; Johann Haviland Bavaria, 10", from $10 to 15.00
Plate, dinner; Royal Albert, 11¼" 15.00
Plate, 12-sided, Limoges, 9¼" 30.00
Platter, Pompadour, Rosenthal, 13" dia 70.00
Platter, Ucagco, rare, 12", from $65 to 85.00
Shakers, Pompadour, Rosenthal, 5", pr......................................60.00
Shakers, Royal Albert, 3", pr..30.00
Soap dish, w/lid & drainer, gold trim, Haviland, 5x4", from $175 to..200.00
Tea tile, Haviland, 6½" dia, from $125 to...................................150.00
Teapot, whistling, electric, Japan, 6"...15.00
Tidbit, 2-tier, Japan...20.00
Tray, Pompadour, Rosenthal, 13x10" 65.00
Tureen, w/lid, Pompadour, Rosenthal, 7¼x12" 105.00
Wall pocket, violin shape, marked Japan, 9x4" 58.00

Mother-of-Pearl Glass

Mother-of-Pearl glass was a type of mold-blown satin art glass popular during the last half of the nineteenth century. A patent for its manufacture was issued in 1886 to Frederick S. Shirley, and one of the companies who produced it was the Mt. Washington Glass Company of New Bedford, Massachusetts. Another was the English firm of Stevens and Williams. Its delicate patterns were developed by blowing the gather into a mold with inside projections that left an intaglio design on the surface of the glass, then sealing the first layer with a second, trapping air in the recesses. Most common are the Diamond Quilted, Raindrop, and Herringbone patterns. It was made in several soft colors, the most rare and valuable is rainbow — a blend of rose, light blue, yellow, and white. Occasionally it may be decorated with coralene, enameling, or gilt. Watch for twentieth century reproductions, especially in the Diamond Quilted pattern. Our advisors for this category are Betty and Clarence Maier; they are listed in the Directory under Pennsylvania. See also Coralene; Stevens and Williams.

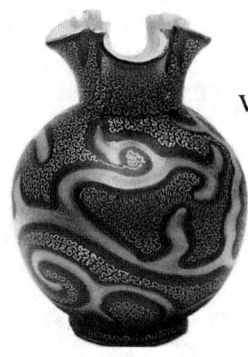

Vase, Federzeichnung (Octopus) brown pearl satin with gilt tracery and internal decor, 6¼", $2,500.00.

Basket, herringbone, bl w/crystal hdl, 5½x4¼"..........................150.00
Biscuit barrel, Zipper, raspberry, metal hdld rim/lid, 5½x5¼"..1,225.00
Bottle, scent; Peacock Eye, yel, sphere w/stick neck, SP mts, 7½" 750.00
Bowl, Coin Spot, pk to red at rim, bl-trimmed pinched rim, 4x8½" .260.00
Bowl, Dmn Quilt, rainbow, pinched rim, 5".................................230.00
Celery vase, Herringbone, bl, shaped 4-lobe rim, vertical ribs, 5" .175.00
Cheese dish, Dmn Quilt, apricot, frosted tray/thorn finial, 9½x9".1,200.00
Creamer & sugar bowl (open), Dmn Quilt, rose/pk, tightly crimped, lg.1,345.00
Ewer, Dmn Quilt, bl to wht, crimped/flared rim forms spout, Mt WA, 7"..285.00
Finger bowl, Dmn Quilt, dk crimson to peach, 8-crimp rim, +plate ...975.00
Lamps, Dmn Quilt, pk, ruffled bowl shades/ribbed ovoid fonts, 18", pr .3,800.00
Pitcher, Coin Spot, rose to pk, crimped rim, bulb w/waisted neck, 9".400.00
Rose bowl, Dmn Quilt, apricot to wht, box-pleated top, 6" dia ..345.00
Rose bowl, Dmn Quilt, rainbow, 3¾x4" 1,095.00
Rose bowl, Herringbone, bl, finger-pinched rim, 3¼x4"................90.00
Rose bowl, Herringbone, bl, finger-pinched rim, 5¼" dia 175.00
Rose bowl, Herringbone, chartreuse, 4"....................................125.00
Rose bowl, Herringbone, pk, 8-crimp rim, 3½"............................70.00
Spooner, Dmn Quilt, apricot w/mc floral, tightly ruffled rim, 6".250.00
Tumbler, T'print, rainbow, 3¾" 290.00
Vase, Coin Spot, yel to caramel, long neck, 4 dimples in rnd body, 9".145.00
Vase, Dmn Quilt, bl, egg shape w/finger-crimped rim, 3 frosted ft, 6"...260.00
Vase, Dmn Quilt, bl w/brn & gold leaves & flowers, Mt WA, 9".345.00
Vase, Dmn Quilt, pk, ruffled 3-lobe rim, Mt WA, 10½" 345.00
Vase, Dmn Quilt, pk, stick neck, 10"...115.00
Vase, Dmn Quilt, yel, teardrop w/elongated neck, 9½" 70.00
Vase, Dmn Quilt, yel, 2 lg thorny satin hdls, tightly crimped rim, 10" ..285.00
Vase, Dotted Swiss, pk, flared/petaled rim, Mt WA, 9½" 460.00
Vase, Federzeichnung, 4-lobe ruffled rim, mk Pat, 6½"...........2,500.00
Vase, Fleur-de-Lis, mc insect/foliage in pointillism style, ovoid, 5" ..515.00

Vase, Flower & Acorn, wht w/gold branches, dimpled, 3-lobe neck, 8"..**800.00**
Vase, Herringbone, lt pk, ribbed/ftd, flaring ruffled top, 9" **175.00**
Vase, Herringbone, pk, bulbous w/short can neck, 4½" **70.00**
Vase, Herringbone, rose to pk, crimped/ruffled, bulbous, long neck, 9".**485.00**
Vase, Hobnail, pk, sq-folded rim, 6½" **250.00**
Vase, Melon Ribbed, bl, cupped pinched-in top, 6½" **145.00**
Vase, Raindrop, butterscotch, ruffled camphor edge, Mt WA, 8" ..**375.00**
Vase, Raindrop, wht, ruffled rim, Mt WA, 6½x3", pr **550.00**
Vase, Raindrop w/Hobnail effect, clear to tan, sq top, 6" **375.00**
Vase, Ribbon, bl, ruffled/crimped, ovoid w/hollow base, Mt WA, 8x4".**325.00**
Vase, Swirl, yel, bulbous w/trumpet top, 6½" **240.00**

Mountainside

John Kovaks operated a ceramic studio from the late 1920s until about 1939 in Mountainside, New Jersey, where through extensive experimentation he produced stoneware and earthenware items glazed with colors of his own formulation. Our advisors for this category are Suzanne Perrault and Dave Rago; they are listed in the Directory under New Jersey.

Bust of woman, ivory, 8½x5¾", NM **145.00**
Vase, burnt orange/celadon mottled gr matt, hdld gourd form, 7x5½".**400.00**
Vase, face figural, strong features, gr matt, sgn MP, 4½x5" **195.00**
Vase, mottle blk dripping on yel gloss, tear shape, 14x9", EX, $100 to.**200.00**

Mourning Collectibles

During the eighteenth and early nineteenth centuries, ladies made needlework pictures, samplers, painting on ivory plaques, watercolor drawings, etc., to commemorate the death of a loved one. Elements contained in nearly all examples are the tomb, mourners, a weeping willow tree, and data relating to the deceased. Often plaits of hair were included. Today these are recognized and valued as a valid form of folk art.

Cut paper, monument flanked by willows, inscribed/1890s, 23x28"..**1,295.00**
Needlework, lady by column & trees, oval, 10½" H....................**275.00**
Needlework, lady by monument w/lg urn, willow, sgn/1815, 31x25"..**5,390.00**
Needlework, lady w/book, monument, mixed media, English/1800s, 13" dia.**1,175.00**
Needlework & watercolor, monuments/urns, 1820, 24x24" **4,700.00**
Silk, figures w/photographic faces at monument, 1856, 30x34".**16,000.00**

Movie Memorabilia

Movie memorabilia covers a broad range of collectibles, from books and magazines dealing with the industry in general to the various promotional materials which were distributed to arouse interest in a particular film. Many collectors specialize in a specific area — posters, pressbooks, stills, lobby cards, or souvenir programs (also referred to as premiere booklets). In the listings below, a one-sheet poster measures approximately 27" x 41", three-sheet: 41" x 81", and six-sheet: 81" x 81". Window cards measure 14" x 22". Values are for examples in NM condition unless noted otherwise. Our advisor for this category is Robert Doyle; he is listed in the Directory under New York.

See also Autographs; Cartoon Art; Magazines; Paper Dolls; Personalities; Rock 'n Roll Memorabilia; Sheet Music.

Insert card, Beach Blanket Bingo, F Avalon/A Funicello, 1965, EX ..**85.00**
Insert card, Wake of the Red Witch, John Wayne, 1949, EX......**350.00**
Lobby card, Beyond the Valley of the Dolls, Sharon Tate, 1967, EX ..**125.00**
Lobby card, Big Shot, Humphrey Bogart w/gun, 1942, EX..........**250.00**
Lobby card, Bus Stop, Marilyn Monroe in bed, 1956, EX **200.00**

Lobby card, Dr Jekyl & Mr Hyde, Spencer Tracy in scene, 1941, EX.**175.00**
Lobby card, Greatest Show on Earth, Stewart as clown, 1952, EX ..**125.00**
Lobby card, High Society, F Sinatra/B Crosby/G Kelley, 1956, EX..**95.00**
Lobby card, High Society, F Sinatra/Crosby closeups, 1956, EX .**150.00**
Lobby card, House on Haunted Hill, Vincent Price, 1959, EX ...**175.00**
Lobby card, King of Underworld, Humphrey Bogart, 1939, EX ..**250.00**
Lobby card, Mummy's Curse, Lon Chaney, 1944, EX **450.00**
Lobby card, Quiet Man, J Wayne w/flowers, 1951, EX...............**175.00**
Lobby card, Rio Rita, Abbot & Costello, 1942, EX.....................**150.00**
Lobby card, River of No Return, M Monroe/R Mitchum, 1954, EX...**150.00**
Lobby card, To Catch a Thief, C Grant/G Kelly, 1955, EX.........**125.00**
Lobby card, Yankee Doodle Dandy, James Cagney, 1942, EX......**250.00**
Poster, Abbott & Costello Meet Dr Jekyl & Mr Hyde, 1953, 1-sheet, EX..**295.00**
Poster, Bedlam in Paradise, 3 Stooges, 1955, 1-sheet, EX............**975.00**
Poster, Beyond the Valley of the Dolls, 8 sexy ladies, 1-sheet, EX ..**250.00**
Poster, Big Jim McClain, John Wayne, 1952, 1-sheet, EX...........**200.00**
Poster, Bird Man of Alcatraz, B Lancaster, 1962, 1-sheet, EX **450.00**
Poster, Bowery at Midnight, Bela Lugosi, 1942, ½-sheet, EX......**375.00**
Poster, Challenge the Dragon, Tarng Long, 1982, 1-sheet, M **25.00**
Poster, Chinatown, Jack Nicholson w/cigarette, 1971, 1-sheet, NM.**395.00**
Poster, Dr Zhivago, style A, 1965, 1-sheet, EX **150.00**
Poster, East of Eden, Julie Harris/James Dean, 1955, 1-sheet, EX.**850.00**
Poster, Exorcist, silhouette figure, blk/wht w/bl, 1972, 1-sheet, NM ...**150.00**
Poster, Funny Lady, Streisand at piano, 1975, 1-sheet, NM **45.00**
Poster, Godfather, hand w/marionette strings, 1972, 1-sheet, EX ..**300.00**
Poster, House of Dark Shadows, characters on lawn, 1970, 1-sheet, EX...**200.00**
Poster, House of Psychotic Women, Paul Naschy, 1973, 1-sheet, G...**80.00**
Poster, Interlude, June Allyson/Rossano Brazzi, 1957, ½-sheet, VG...**25.00**
Poster, King of Carnival, Republic serial, 1955, 1-sheet, G **50.00**
Poster, Let It Be, Beatles in 4 blocks on blk, 1970, 1-sheet, EX..**450.00**
Poster, Lure of Swamp, Marshal Thompson/Joan Vohs, 1957, 1-sheet, EX ...**40.00**
Poster, Man From Laramie, James Stewart, 1955, 1-sheet, NM ..**315.00**
Poster, Man of Thousand Faces, James Cagney, 1957, ½-sheet, EX.**250.00**
Poster, Man w/Golden Gun, Roger Moore (James Bond), 1974, 1-sheet, VG...**40.00**
Poster, Marnie, T Hedren/S Connery, 1964, linen mt, 3-sheet, EX...**650.00**
Poster, Marriage on Rocks, Sinatra/D Kerr/D Martin, 1965, 1-sheet, EX...**45.00**
Poster, McHale's Navy, caricatures on boat, 1964, 1-sheet, EX...**250.00**
Poster, Moonraker, Roger Moore (James Bond), 1979, 1-sheet, EX.**40.00**
Poster, Poseidon Adventure, explosive scene, 1972, 1-sheet, EX...**250.00**
Poster, Rear Window, James Stewart, 1962 re-release, 1-sheet, EX.**475.00**
Poster, Shane, A Ladd/J Arthur/V Heflin, portraits, 1953, 1-sheet, EX...**275.00**
Poster, Sound of Music, J Andrews/C Plummer/etc, 1965, 1-sheet, EX...**250.00**
Poster, Star Wars, figures w/ghostly Darth Vader behind, 1977, 1-sheet.**375.00**
Poster, Star Wars, wht-line letters on bl, 1977, 1-sheet, NM **250.00**
Poster, Sting, Newman/Redford, 1974, ½-sheet, NM..................**285.00**
Poster, The Bat, Vincent Price, 1959, 1-sheet, EX......................**295.00**
Poster, The Spoilers, M Dietrich/R Scott/J Wayne, 1-sheet, 1942, EX.**650.00**
Poster, Three Stooges Meet Hercules, 1961, 1-sheet, EX **225.00**
Poster, Tomorrow Is Forever, Colbert/Welles/Brent, 1945, ½-sheet, EX..**425.00**
Poster, Virgin Island, John Cassavetes/Virginia Maskell, ½-sheet, VG...**75.00**
Poster, Without Love, S Tracy/K Hepburn, 1945, ½-sheet, EX...**275.00**
Poster, Wizard of Oz, Judy Garland, 1955 release, 1-sheet, EX....**875.00**
Poster, 101 Dalmatians, dogs on yel, Disney, 1961, 1-sheet, EX..**750.00**
Poster, 3 Came To Kill, Cameron Mitchell, 1960, 1-sheet, VG **35.00**
Press kit, Rescuers, w/10 stills, 1977, NM......................................**30.00**
Press kit, Sea of Love, w/12 stills, 1989, NM................................**28.00**
Press kit, Swing Shift, w/13 stills, 1984, NM................................**35.00**
Press kit, War of Roses, w/13 stills, 1989, NM **32.50**
Pressbook, Abbott & Costello Meet the Mummy, 1954, EX.......**150.00**
Pressbook, Detroit 9000, A Rocco/H Rhodes/V McGee, 1973, NM..**10.00**
Pressbook, Rose of Rancho, John Boles/G Swarthout, 1935, EX.....**7.00**
Program, Superman I, 8-pg preview w/silver cover, 1978, NM.......**20.00**
Title card, Actress, Spencer Tracey/Jean Simmons, 1953, EX.......**85.00**
Title card, An Affair To Remember, Cary Grant/Deborah Kerr, 1957, EX.**275.00**

Title card, Cinderella, coach in street, Disney, 1950, EX 295.00
Title card, Fatal Hour, Boris Karloff, 1940, EX.....................325.00
Title card, Man at Large, Geo Reeves/M Weaver/R Derr, 1941, EX .200.00
Title card, Monkey Business, C Grant/M Monroe/G Rogers, 1952, EX..425.00
Title card, Once Upon a Honeymoon, C Grant/G Rogers, 1941, EX ...295.00
Title card, Pirate, Judy Garland/Gene Kelly, 1948, EX 375.00
Title card, She Wore a Yel Ribbon, John Wayne, 1949, EX........350.00
Title card, Shiver My Timbers, Little Rascals, 1951 re-release, EX .250.00
Title card, Voodoo Man, Bela Lugosi, 1944, EX.....................295.00
Window card, Comin' Round the Mtn, Abbot/Costello, 1951, EX ..195.00
Window card, From Russia w/Love, Sean Connery, 1964, EX 395.00
Window card, How to Marry a Millionare, Monroe/Grable/Bacall, EX..350.00
Window card, Mad Doctor, Basil Rathbone, 1940, 1-sheet, EX..350.00

Mt. Washington

The Mt. Washington Glass Works was founded in 1837 in South Boston, Massachusetts, but moved to New Bedford in 1869 after purchasing the facilities of the New Bedford Glass Company. Frederick S. Shirley became associated with the firm in 1874. Two years later the company reorganized and became known as the Mt. Washington Glass Company. In 1894 it merged with the Pairpoint Manufacturing Company, a small Brittania works nearby, but continued to conduct business under its own title until after the turn of the century. The combined plants were equipped with the most modern and varied machinery available and boasted a working force with experience and expertise rival to none in the art of blowing and cutting glass. In addition to their fine cut glass, they are recognized as the first American company to make cameo glass, an effect they achieved through acid-cutting methods. In 1885 Shirley was issued a patent to make Burmese, pale yellow glassware tinged with a delicate pink blush. Another patent issued in 1886 allowed them the rights to produce Rose Amber, or amberina, a transparent ware shading from ruby to amber. Pearl Satin Ware and Peachblow, so named for its resemblance to a rosy peach skin, were patented the same year. One of their most famous lines, Crown Milano, was introduced in 1893. It was an opal glass either free-blown or pattern-molded, tinted a delicate color and decorated with enameling and gilt. Royal Flemish was patented in 1894 and is considered the rarest of the Mt. Washington art glass lines. It was decorated with raised, gold-enameled lines dividing the surface of the ware in much the same way as lead lines divide a stained glass window. The sections were filled in with one or several transparent colors and further decorated in gold enamel with florals, foliage, beading, and medallions.

For more information, we recommend *Mt. Washington Art Glass* by Betty B. Sisk. Our advisors for this category are Betty and Clarence Maier; they are listed in the Directory under Pennsylvania.

See also Amberina; Cranberry; Salt Shakers; Burmese; Crown Milano; Mother-of-Pearl; Royal Flemish; etc.

Bowl, cranberry to clear base w/lt bl ruffled rim, 4¾x11½x9" 265.00
Bride's basket, wht w/pk int, gold scalloped rim, ornate SP fr, 6x4"..460.00
Celery vase, pk to clear insert w/HP birds & flowers; Tufts hdld ped ..490.00
Condiment set, floral, mustard & shakers in Wilcox fr, lt wear, 6½".235.00
Cracker jar, camels/pyramids on #d opal sq, Pairpoint mt #3910, 8".2,760.00
Cracker jar, man/lady w/in gold scrolls on wht, squat, hdl rpr.....460.00
Cracker jar, mums, pk/gr/rose on yel, 5" sq, to top of hdl: 10½".460.00
Fernery, mums/gold on lt gray tracery, 8" dia 1,000.00
Goblet, Rose Amber, amberina.....................................250.00
Jar, lilies of the valley, cylindrical, metal lid w/3-D butterfly, 6" .230.00
Pickle jar, Timothy Canty floral on ribbed clear ovoid, SP lid, 6" .575.00
Plate, Butterfly & Daisy, 8".......................................200.00
Shades, Russian cut cranberry o/l, bowl shape, 8" dia, EX, pr.1,550.00
Shaker, chick head, cosmos on wht egg shape, metal head 735.00
Shakers, bl to wht satin w/red floral, cylindrical, 3", pr 125.00
Shakers, bluerina, Hartford SP fr, pr...............................400.00

Shakers, Tomato, 1 floral on bl, 2nd gr, 2¼", pr 90.00
Sugar shaker, daisies on lemon yel to wht satin, egg form, 4¼" ..350.00
Sugar shaker, floral below lid, melon ribbed, 3¼" dia.................115.00
Sugar shaker, flowers on wht satin, egg form, 4¼x3⅜"...............310.00
Sugar shaker, holly leaves/red berries on wht, egg form, 4¼" 145.00
Sugar shaker, Pillar Ribbed, cream w/purple/bl pansies, 1890s, 5½"..390.00
Sugar shaker, wht w/pansies on mushroom form, 3x6" dia 350.00
Sweetmeat, flowers/jewels on melon-rib pnt burmese, mk lid, 5½" dia .800.00
Sweetmeat, gold/beaded floral on diagonal swirl, label, to hdl top: 7" ...575.00
Toothpick holder, pale yel custard w/ferns & flowers, 1⅞x2½" ...470.00
Vase, aquatic scene on clear, sponged gilt scalloped rim, 5x5" 360.00
Vase, canary yel, Arch, gauffered rim, hex base, tall ft, 11", pr, VG.1,175.00
Vase, floral outlined w/gold & silver on pk, #918, 9" 1,250.00
Vase, Lava, appl hdls, 4½x5".....................................2,500.00
Vase, Lava, blk w/mc multi-sz 'chips,' broken blister, 5⅜x4⅛" ...2,500.00
Vase, Napoli, chicks in the rain, 8¾"..............................1,400.00
Vase, Swirl, pk satin w/wht int, ruffled/lobed rim, 10"...............230.00
Vase, Verona, drayon decor, cylindrical, 14"......................1,900.00

Mulberry China

Mulberry china was made by many of the Staffordshire area potters from about 1830 until the 1850s. It is a transfer-printed earthenware or ironstone named for the color of its decorations, a purplish-brown resembling the juice of the mulberry. Some pieces may have faded out over the years and today look almost gray with only a hint of purple. (Transfer printing was done in many colors; technically only those in the mauve tones are 'mulberry'; color variations have little effect on value.) Some of the patterns (Corean, Jeddo, Pelew, and Formosa, for instance) were also produced in Flow Blue ware. Others seem to have been used exclusively with the mulberry color. Our advisor for this category is Mary Frank Gaston.

Alpine Amusements, platter, Davenport, 14½" 675.00
Antiquarian, soup plate, Davenport, 10" 275.00
Asia, plate, Heath, 9" 200.00
Athens, cup...45.00
Athens, plate, Adams & Sons, 7⅝"....................................70.00
Athens, sugar bowl, w/lid, Adams, EX................................225.00
Blantyre, platter, Meigh & Son, 21½x17".............................450.00
Bochara, relish, fluted/scalloped, Edwards, 9x5"......................125.00
Bochara, sauce tureen, Edwards, w/lid & ladle........................650.00
Bochara, teapot, Edwards, rpr, 9x10" 200.00
Brunswick Star, plate, 7½"..125.00
Bysham Abbey, plate, dessert; Davenport, 7" 85.00
Calcutta, plate, Challinor, 8½".......................................110.00
Canova, platter, Mayer, 13" 450.00
Castle Garden, plate, medallion-floral border, 7⅞"....................85.00
Castle Scenery, plate, Furnival, 6⅛".................................50.00
Castle Scenery, plate, Furnival, 7½".................................65.00
Cologne, plate, Stevenson, 9¾".......................................85.00
Corean, cup & saucer 75.00
Corean, gravy boat 275.00
Corean, plate, Podmore Walker, 7⅝" 65.00
Corean, plate, Podmore Walker, 9⅞" 90.00
Corean, teapot 600.00
Cyprus, creamer...250.00
Cyprus, teapot, Davenport, 8½".....................................225.00
European Scenery, plate, Enoch Wood, 9¼".............................95.00
Excelsior, plate, Wooliscroft, 8½"....................................65.00
Foliage, bowl, serving; w/lid, Edwards & Walley, 7½x9" 425.00
Foliage, platter, mk A Walley, 15¼"..................................300.00
Harp, plate, Stevenson, 8"..85.00
Hong, pitcher, 2-qt 500.00

Horticultural, plate, 9" 85.00
Jeddo, bowl, soup; Adams & Sons, ca 1850 ....195.00
Jeddo, bowl, vegetable; w/lid, Adams.......................535.00
Jeddo, cup & saucer, Adams.......................................140.00
Jeddo, plate, 14-panel, Adams, 9¼" 130.00
Jeddo, teapot, Adams 475.00
Marble, creamer, Wedge Wood, 5⅝"..........................100.00
Marble, platter, Wedge Wood, 17¼x14".....................495.00
Nankin, creamer, Davenport......................................225.00
Neptune, plate, 6½" 40.00
Ning-Po, plate, Hall, 1890s, 9"..................................110.00
Panama, platter, Challinor, 13½x10½" 250.00
Pelew, bowl, vegetable; w/lid, Challinor....................525.00
Pelew, plate, Challinor, 8½"..90.00
Pelew, platter, Challinor, 18".....................................275.00
Pomerania, cup plate, Ridgway, 4".............................110.00
Rhone Scenery, cup & saucer, handleless....................65.00
Rhone Scenery, saucer, Mayer, 6" 25.00
Rhone Scenery, sugar bowl, w/lid 155.00
Rose, pitcher, Walker, 2-qt...375.00
Rose, plate, Challinor, 8½"...50.00
Singan, creamer, ca 1850, 5¾".....................................250.00
Strawberry, platter, dbl scalloped corners, Walker, 16½x13" 350.00
Tavoy, platter, 15" 175.00
Tavoy, teapot 275.00
Tillenberg, teapot, prof rstr, 1840s, EX 295.00
Vincennes, bowl, vegetable; w/lid...............................395.00
Vincennes, cup & saucer, handleless; Alcock, ca 1860..................75.00
Vincennes, plate, Alcock, 7"...50.00
Vincennes, relish 195.00
Vincennes, sauce trueen..295.00
Virginia Waters, plate, Stevenson lace border, 7½" 55.00
Washington Vase, bowl & pitcher, Podmore Walker....................750.00
Washington Vase, cup plate, 4¼", NM 75.00
Washington Vase, plate, Podmore Walker, 10⅜" 90.00
Washington Vase, teapot, 8¾".....................................375.00
Wreath, bowl, vegetable; w/lid, 11".............................425.00
Zoological, soup plate, Robinson Wood & Brownfield, 9" 100.00

Muller Freres

Henri Muller established a factory in 1900 at Croismare, France. He produced fine cameo art glass decorated with florals, birds, and insects in the Art Nouveau style. The work was accomplished by acid engraving and hand finishing. Usual marks were 'Muller,' 'Muller Croismare,' or 'Croismare, Nancy.' In 1910 Henri and his brother Deseri formed a glassworks at Luneville. The cameo art glass made there was nearly all produced by acid cuttings of up to four layers with motifs similar to those favored at Croismare. A good range of colors was used, and some later pieces were gold flecked. Handles and decorative devices were sometimes applied by hand. In addition to the cameo glass, they also produced an acid-finished glass of bold mottled colors in the Deco style. Examples were signed 'Muller Freres' or 'Luneville.' Our advisor for this category is Don Williams; he is listed in the Directory under Missouri.

Cameo

Dish, sailboats/mtn lake, brn on orange mottle, boat shape, 5½" L...635.00
Vase, floral, amethyst on frost, 3¼" 145.00
Vase, floral/leaves, gr on wht, fire polished, 7½".........980.00
Vase, lake/trees/figure in boat, cut/pnt, 14½x5" 1,325.00
Vase, landscape, brn & gr on peach & frost, 3½" 750.00
Vase, morning glories, red/rose on gr/gray mottle, ovoid, 8" 3,000.00

Vase, Oriental scenes in three reserves, dark red on white frost, 17", $9,500.00. (Photo courtesy Don Williams)

Vase, orchids, 2-tone bl on yel & amber mottle, globular, 6"...1,200.00
Vase, rasperries/branches, fluogravure, brn/wht on citron, 4½".2,200.00
Vase, trees/lake, wine-blk on mauve/lav, camphor hdls, flat sides, 11".6,000.00

Miscellaneous

Basket, Chapelle iron fr w/appl florals, +mottled bowl, 9" 750.00
Basket, Chapelle iron fr w/scrollwork & appl leafage, +bowl, 18" L...1,495.00
Chandelier, wht shades w/lav & gr mottle, lg bowl+3 lilies, leafy mt.2,400.00
Lamp, 10" shade molded w/skyscraper styling & rosettes; iron base, 19" ..1,095.00
Vase, bl/wht mottle w/sm areas of pk/gr/brn, early 20th C, 9" 400.00

Muncie

The Muncie Pottery was established in Muncie, Indiana, by Charles O. Grafton; it operated there from 1922 until about 1935. The pottery they produced is made of a heavier clay than most of its contemporaries; the styles are sturdy and simple. Early glazes were bright and colorful. In fact, Muncie was advertised as the 'rainbow pottery.' Later most of the ware was finished in a matt glaze. The more collectible examples are those modeled after Consolidated Glass vases — sculptured with lovebirds, grasshoppers, and goldfish. Their line of Art Deco-style vases bear a remarkable resemblance to the Consolidated Glass Company's Ruba Rombic line. Vases, candlesticks, bookends, ashtrays, bowls, lamp bases, and luncheon sets were made. A line of garden pottery was manufactured for a short time. Items were frequently impressed with MUNCIE in block letters. Letters such as A, K, E, or D and the numbers 1, 2, 3, 4, or 5 often found scratched into the base are finishers' marks. For more information, we recommend *Collector's Encyclopedia of Muncie Pottery* by Jon Rans and Mark Eckelman (Collector Books).

Bowl, gr matt drip over lav, 'Rhombic shape,' 9" 375.00
Bowl vase, lt bl froth over med bl, 5½x6" 125.00
Ewer, #136, gr over lilac, mk 2A, 10½"..65.00
Vase, #100, pumpkin w/gr drip, mk 1A, 5¾".................................65.00
Vase, #105, gloss gr, 5⅞" 55.00
Vase, #261, orange, 6-sided, 8¼" 95.00
Vase, #411, lav w/dk gr drip, 3½x5½" 50.00
Vase, #480, gr w/bl drip, bulbous, 3⅞"..80.00
Vase, lav w/gr drip, trumpet shape w/turned-in neck, mk 3H, 5¾"..60.00
Vase, med bl w/lt bl drip, 5½"...125.00

Musical Instruments

The field of automatic musical instruments covers many different categories ranging from watches and tiny seals concealing fine early musical movements to huge organs and orchestrions which weigh many hundreds of pounds and are equivalent to small orchestras. Music boxes, first made in the early nineteenth century by Swiss watchmakers, were produced in both disc and cylinder models. The latter type employs a cylinder with tiny pins that lift the teeth in the comb of the music box (producing a sound much like many individual tuning forks), and music results. The value of a cylinder music box depends on the length and diameter of the cylinder, the date of its manufacture, the number of tunes it plays (four or six is usually better than ten or twelve), whether it has multiple cylinders, if it has extra instruments (like bells, an organ, or drum), and its manufacturer. Nicole Freres, Henri Capt, LeCoultre, and Bremond are among the the most highly regarded, and the larger boxes made by Mermod Freres are also popular. Examples with multiple cylinders, extra instruments (such as bells or an organ section), and those in particularly ornate cabinets or with matching tables bring significantly higher prices. Early cylinder boxes were wound with a separate key which was inserted on the left side of the case. These early examples are known as 'keywind' boxes and bring a premium. While smaller cylinder boxes are still being made, the larger ones (over 10" cylinders) typically date from before 1900. Disc music boxes were introduced about 1890 but were replaced by the phonograph only twenty-five years later. However, during that time hundreds of thousands were made. Their great advantage was in playing inexpensive interchangeable discs, a factor that remains an attraction for today's collector as well. Among the most popular disc boxes are those made by Regina (USA), Polyphon, Mira, Stella, and Symphonion. Relative values are determined by the size of the discs they play, whether they have single or double combs, if they are upright or table models, and how ornate their cases are. Especially valuable are those that play multiple discs at the same time or are incorporated into tall case clocks.

Player pianos were made in a wide variety of styles. Early varieties consisted of a mechanism which pushed up to a piano and played on the keyboard by means of felt-tipped fingers. These use sixty-five note rolls. Later models have the playing mechanism built in, and most use eighty-eight note rolls. Upright pump player pianos have little value in unrestored condition because the cost of restoration is so high. 'Reproducing' pianos, especially the 'grand' format, can be quite valuable, depending on the make, the size, the condition, and the ornateness of the case; however the market for 'reproducing' grand pianos has been very weak in recent years. 'Reproducing' grand pianos have very sophisticated mechanisms and are much more realistic in the reproduction of piano music. They were made in relatively limited quantities. Better manufacturers include Steinway and Mason & Hamlin. Popular roll mechanism makers include AMPICO, Duo-Art, and Welte.

Coin-operated pianos (orchestrions) were used commercially and typically incorporate extra instruments in addition to the piano action. These can be very large and complex, incorporating drums, cymbals, xylophones, bells, and dozens of pipes. Both American and European coin pianos are very popular, especially the larger and more complex models made by Wurlitzer, Seeburg, Cremona, Weber, Welte, Hupfeld, and many others. These companies also made automatically playing violins (Mills Violin Virtuoso, Hupfeld), banjos (Encore), and harps (Whitlock); these are quite valuable.

Collecting player organettes is a fun endeavor. Roller organs, organettes, player organs, grind organs, hand organs — whatever the name — are a fascinating group of music makers. Some used wooden barrels or cobs to operate the valves, or metal and cardboard discs or paper strips, paper rolls, metal donuts, or metal strips. They usually played from fourteen to twenty keys or notes. Some were pressure operated or vacuum type. Their heyday lasted from the 1870s to the turn of the century. Most were reed organs, but a few had pipes. Many were made in either America or Germany. They lost favor with the advent of the phonograph, as did the music box. Some music boxes were built with little player organs in them. Any player organette in good working condition with some music and in their original finish should be worth from $200.00 to $600.00,

depending on the model. Generally the more keying it has and the larger and fancier the case, the more desirable it is. Rarity plays a part too. There are a handfull of individuals who make new music rolls for these player organs. Some machines are very rare, and music for them is nearly impossible to find. For further information on player organs we recommend *Encyclopedia of Automatic Musical Instruments* by Bowers.

Unless noted, prices given are for instruments in fine condition, playing properly, with cabinets or cases in well-preserved or refinished condition. In all instances, unrestored instruments sell for much less, as do those with broken or missing parts, damaged cases, and the like. On the other hand, particularly superb examples in especially ornate case designs and those that have been particularly well kept will often command more. Our advisor for mechanical instruments is Martin Roenigk; he is listed in the Directory under Arkansas.

Key:
c — cylinder   d — disc

Mechanical

Box, Capital B, w/7 cuffs, lt rstr, EX, scarce 7,200.00
Box, Criterion, 10⅝" d, cherry case, EX orig...........................1,450.00
Box, Criterion, 15½" d, walnut case, EX, +10 d.....................3,000.00
Box, Empress, dbl comb, 12" d, mahog 4-ftd case, 11x21x18", EX.2,400.00
Box, Euphonia, 15" d, NM 3,600.00
Box, Imperator #27, 5½" d, single comb, 1904 fair decal, 5x8x7"...500.00
Box, Lochmann, 17" d w/saucer bells, table model, nonworking.7,500.00
Box, Lochmann 78-20, 24½" d, tubular bells, rpl base/rstr 16,800.00
Box, Mermod Freres, 6 24½" c, cvd oak case w/drws, EX+....46,000.00
Box, Mira, 18½" d, dbl comb, cvd console, EX 8,500.00
Box, Nicole, 12" c, keywind, 6-tune, EX...............................1,800.00
Box, Nicole Freres, keywind, 10¾x3⅛" c, 4-tune, inlaid lid, EX.7,000.00
Box, Orpheus, oak, 8 interchangeable c, 10½x28x13", +matching table.8,950.00
Box, Paillard Sublime Harmonie Tremolo Zither, dbl spring, 17" c, EX...3,700.00
Box, Perfection, 14" d, needs rstr 1,350.00
Box, Piano, Melodica, 30-key, EX, +6 books of music..............4,800.00
Box, Polyphon, 24" d, burled walnut, coin-op, 79x33", EX ...14,000.00
Box, Polyphon #45, 15½"d, ornate case, rstr 5,800.00
Box, Regina, tall clock, 15" d movement, dbl comb, EX 12,000.00
Box, Regina, 15½" d , coin-op, oak table model, EX 3,200.00
Box, Regina, 15½" d, dbl comb, automatic changer, EX........18,000.00
Box, Regina, 15½" d, dbl comb, oak case, coin-op, VG...........3,500.00
Box, Regina, 20½" d, w/base cabinet, NM 7,500.00
Box, Regina, 20¾" d, flat front, auto changer, nonworking...16,000.00
Box, Regina #33 (late), 27" changer, cvd dragons, EX, +12 d..21,000.00
Box, Regina Console #40, short bedplate/Rookwood pnt finish, EX, +12 d ..8,500.00

Box, Regina Corona, mahogany changer, with twelve 27" disks, etched glass, EX working condition, 14x19", $18,250.00.
(Photo courtesy James Julia)

Box, Reginaphone, 20¾" d, NP horn, matching base 8,000.00
Box, Stella, 17¼" d, dbl comb, mahog table model, EX...........4,000.00
Box, Stella, 17¼" d, mahog console, VG, +12 d 5,500.00
Box, Symphonion, d, dbl comb, walnut case w/appl molding, 14¼x11".400.00
Box, Symphonion, 14½" d, walnut case, EX orig, +7 d...........2,300.00
Box, Symphonion, 7½" d, EX...500.00
Box, Thibouville-Lamy, 11" c, VG...1,150.00
Box, Thornward, 15½" d, single comb, 12½x25x19", EX........2,500.00
Nickelodeon, Chicago Electric A Roll, EX...............................3,500.00
Nickelodeon, Encore Banjo, automatic, EX 32,000.00
Nickelodeon, Englehardt, w/pipes, art glass, Mission-style case, EX...9,800.00
Nickelodeon, Link, pictorial glass doors, 1900s, 77" L, EX 8,500.00
Nickelodeon, Peerless #44, rfn oak case, M rstr, +20 rolls 10,500.00
Nickelodeon, Wurlitzer, piano only, EX 2,400.00
Orchestrion, Coinola C-2, EX..27,000.00
Orchestrion, Coinola X, older rstr 12,000.00
Orchestrion, Seeburg K, eagle art glass, rstr...........................11,000.00
Organ, band; N Tonawanda Military, 18 brass trumpets, VG...24,000.00
Organ, band; Wurlitzer #125, all orig, rstr 20,000.00
Organ, barrel; Frati, 38-key, w/trumpet/piccolo pipes, rstr 13,900.00
Organ, fairground; Gavioli, 65-key, EX..................................45,000.00
Organ, monkey; Molinari, 20-key, EX....................................4,500.00
Organ, monkey; Zimmerman Harmonipan, exposed pipes, EX+ ..6,500.00
Organ, Wilcox & White Symphony, oak, w/shutters, rstr........1,500.00
Organette, Artiston, 13" d, EX 400.00
Organette, Celestina, roll operated, EX.................................800.00
Piano, grand; Chickering Ampico, rfn, 1916, 68", EX 6,000.00
Piano, grand; Knabe Ampico, 64", M 3,500.00
Piano, grand; Mason & Hamlin B Ampico, rstr, 84"..............13,000.00
Piano, grand; Stroud Duo-Art, tubed sides, recent, NM 3,300.00
Piano, Louis Caspli/Gaston Fritch, bbl style, 10-tune, EX...........700.00
Piano, upright; Chickering Ampico, EX orig.........................1,500.00
Piano forte, Joseph Haskey, mahog/maple/rswd, sq w/lyre peds, 1830s...4,500.00
Piano/orchestrion, Lion-Healy, w/pipes, EX.........................9,000.00
Violin, Mills Single Virtuoso, M 22,500.00

Non-Mechanical

Banjo, AC Fairbanks White Lady's #7, MOP Inlay, ca 1900s, 37", EX...4,315.00
Banjo, Gibson UB-1 Melody, 9" rim, 14" scale neck, 18 frets, 1920s, EX ..650.00
Banjo, Vega, 4-string tenor, rstr neck 300.00
French horn, Con 8D, nickel-silver, NM in case.....................2,185.00
Guitar, Epiphone Spartan, natural spruce arch top, ca 1943, EX .975.00
Guitar, Gibson #EtG-150, 4-string tenor, arch top, electric, 1958, EX..1,000.00
Guitar, Gibson L-7, 16" arch top, pearl inlay fingerboard, 1933, EX.4,250.00
Guitar, Gibson TG-00, flat top tenor, all blk, 1930s, VG 1,250.00
Guitar, Harmony Stella, flat top tenor, faux grain finish, 1950s, VG .85.00
Guitar, Martin 1-28, herringbone trim/ivory binding, 1917, EX..3,550.00
Guitar, Washburn Delux, sunburst top, ebony/pearl inlay, 1930s, EX ..995.00
Guitar/banjo, Gibson GB-3, early ball-bearing tone ring, ca 1925, VG ..2,450.00
Harmonica, M Hohner #64 w/4 chromatic octaves, prof model, 7", MIB .100.00
Mandolin, Bacon Style C, 10" rim, V-shaped neck, 1930s, VG..350.00
Mandolin, CF Martin, 1970s, NM in case 685.00
Mandolin, Gibson A-1, arch top, prof rfn, str neck/frets, ca 1918, VG...850.00
Mandolin, Supertone, spruce top, perloid fingerboard, 1930s, VG .145.00
Organ, parlor; AB Chase...OH, walnut molded case w/candle shelves, G...150.00
Piano, cvd oak w/figural griffin supports, 56x66" 2,800.00
Saxophone, Buescher Harwood Str C Soprano, satin SP, ca 1925, EX..985.00
Saxophone, Conn, chrome-plated, EX in velvet-lined case 300.00
Saxophone, Conn Ltd Str Neck C-Melody, gold-plate, ca 1923, NM.1,485.00
Saxophone, Conn Transitional E-flat Alto, brass patina, ca 1932, EX+.1,450.00
Saxophone, King Zephyr Special Tenor, orig lacquer, 1945, NM in case.2,750.00
Ukelele, Gretsch soprano, bl-gray sunburst, rnd body, 1950s, VG ..125.00
Ukelele, Martin Style 0, mahog, all orig, 1920s, EX 695.00

Ukelele, Regal triple, 10-string, marquetry trim/spruce top, 1920s, VG..550.00
Violin, Jacobus Stainer, spruce top, 2-pc bk, ca 1900, full sz, VG..395.00

Mustache Cups

Mustache cups were popular items during the late Victorian period, designed specifically for the man with the mustache! They were made in silverplate as well as china and ironstone. Decorations ranged from simple transfers to elaborately applied and gilded florals. To properly position the 'mustache bar,' special cups were designed for the 'lefties.' These are the rare ones! Our advisor for this category is Robert Doyle, he is listed in the Directory under New York.

Barber portrait, blk/wht w/red trim hdl/rim, Susie Cooper, +saucer 215.00
Floral, mc w/gold on wht, Copeland...England, 2½", +6" saucer ...230.00
Floral panels alternate w/bl, gold trim, Elite France, +saucer 85.00
Floral w/gold on pale yel, Germany, 3", 5¾" saucer 50.00
Roosevelt/Grant/Lincoln w/in wreath, gold trim, wht porc, 4" 65.00
Roses & A Present in banner on wht w/gold, Germany, +saucer..45.00
Roses borders w/gold, Haviland Limoges, 1876-1910, +saucer 150.00
Roses HP on wht, RM Bavaria, 1920s, +saucer...........................60.00
Sister Dora monument on pk lustre, bucket shape, Germany, +saucer..75.00
SP, eng floral, Quadruple Plate Stevens..., 2¾", 5⅝" saucer........110.00
Wild roses HP on wht w/gold Rococo, Rosenthal, 2½", 6½" saucer..225.00

Nailsea

Nailsea is a term referring to clear or colored glass decorated in contrasting spatters, swirls, or loops. These are usually white but may also be pink, red, or blue. It was first produced in Nailsea, England, during the late 1700s but was made in other parts of Britain and Scotland as well. During the mid-1800s a similar type of glass was produced in this country. Originally used for decorative novelties only, by that time tumblers and other practical items were being made from Nailsea-type glass. See also Lamps.

Bowl, rose; cranberry w/wht loops, ruffled/inverted rim, 3x4½"..420.00
Bowl, rose; lt bl w/wht loops, 3x5"...210.00
Flask, clear w/wht loops, flattened oval, 1850-70, 6x4" 110.00
Pitcher, turq opaque w/raspberry loops, dbl molded rings, 12" 650.00
Rolling pin, bl aquq w/wht loops, pontil scar, 1880-1910, 18" 150.00
Rolling pin, clear w/red & wht loops, 17" 320.00
Witch ball, clear w/wht loopings, +stand, 14x7½", VG 880.00

Nakara

Nakara was a line of decorated opaque milk glass produced by the C.F. Monroe Company of Meriden, Connecticut, for a few years after the turn of the century. It differs from their Wave Crest line in several ways. The shapes were simpler; pastel colors were deeper and covered more of the surface; more beading was present; flowers were larger; and large transfer prints of figures, Victorian ladies, cherubs, etc., were used as well. Ormolu and brass collars and mounts complemented these opulent pieces. Most items were signed; however, this is not important since the ware was never reproduced. Our advisors for this category are Dolli and Wilfred R. Cohen; their address is listed in the Directory under California.

Box, Bishop's Hat (scarce), floral on pk/yel, wht beadwork, 6¾" dia.795.00
Box, cherubs transfer on lid, shades of olive w/wht beadwork, 6" dia..675.00
Box, Collars & Cuffs, Gibson girl transfer 2,950.00
Box, floral, pk in shaped bl reserve on lid, shaped wht panels, 3x5" L.475.00
Box, florals/wht beadwork rim on shaded bl, no embossing, 8" dia.800.00

Box, Kate Greenaway figures on lid, pk shades w/wht beadwork, 4" W .500.00
Box, lg floral, pk/wht on olive, crown mold, 8½" dia 800.00
Box, mums, pk/wht on shades of bl, beadwork accents, hexagon, 3¼" W .350.00
Box, roses, pk/wht on gr, crown mold, rpl lining, 8½" dia 1,550.00
Box, roses, red/wht on pk to gr w/wht beadwork, 6" dia 700.00
Box, Spindrift, floral, pk/wht on bl to yel, emb scrolls, 8" dia ..1,250.00
Box, X in wht beadwork/bl floral on pk to yel, mirror, 5" dia......875.00
Box, 18th-C courting couple on peach (scarce color), 6" dia......950.00

Card holder, floral on blue, $550.00; Box, flowers and white beading on blue, 6", $695.00; Tray, Puffy, flowers on blue, rectangular, rare form, $550.00. (Photo courtesy Wilfred and Dolli Cohen)

Cigar holder, floral on gr/wht, ormolu hdld rim/base w/4 ft, rare ...750.00
Hair receiver, wht beadwork/floral on pk to yel, ormolu rim/hdl, open .375.00
Humidor, floral, pk/wht on dk bl, Tobacco at lower front 775.00
Humidor, Old Sport, bulldog transfer on brn, ovoid, 7" 575.00
Humidor, owl/tree transfer on shades of brn, Cigars on lid, rare, 6".1,200.00
Match holder, floral, wht on pk to yel, ormolu rim w/hdls 495.00
Pin tray, floral, pk/wht on pk to gr, ormolu rim w/pointed hdls, 6" L ..225.00
Sweetmeat, fall leaves on bl, shaped body, metal lid/hdl, 5½" W ..475.00
Tray, wht beadwork/floral on pk to yel, mirror in ormolu frwork ...750.00
Vase, floral, pk/wht on shaded gr w/wht beadwork, much ormolu, 9x6".1,100.00
Vase ornament, floral reserve on pk, ormolu rim/collar/hdls/ft, sm ..425.00

Napkin Rings

Napkin rings became popular during the late 1800s. They were made from various materials. Among the most popular and collectible today are the large group of varied silver-plated figurals made by American manufacturers. Recently the larger figurals in excellent condition have appreciated considerably. Only those with a blackened finish, corrosion, or broken and/or missing parts have maintained their earlier price levels. When no condition is indicated, the items listed below are assumed to be all original and in very good to excellent condition. Check very carefully for missing parts, solder repairs, marriages, and reproductions.

A timely warning: Inexperienced buyers should be aware of excellent reproductions on the market, especially the wheeled pieces and cherubs. However, these do not have the fine detail and patina of the originals and tend to have a more consistent, soft pewter-like finish. These are appearing at the large, quality shows at top prices, being shown along with authentic antique merchandise. Beware!

Key:
gw — gold washed   SH&M — Simpson, Hall &
R&B — Reed & Barton   Miller

Baby in cradle, Tufts #1620, minimum.....................1,500.00
Boy on base crouches by ring, Meriden #250 ....650.00
Boy w/begging dog, plain base, Meriden Britannia #199 ....495.00
Boy w/cookie plays w/dog atop ring, Rogers #19 ....500.00
Brooms (curling) & wreath by ring, Meriden Britannia #647 .....450.00
Bud vase by turtle w/ring on bk, ftd base, Derby #342.................550.00
Bull in harness pulls ring on plain sled, Middletown #84............750.00

Butterfly on leafy base by basketweave ring, Tufts #1542, up to..200.00
Chair w/'bentwood' bk supports ring, Simons & Miller #18, up to..200.00
Cherub body intersected by ring, Meriden #224 ....450.00
Cherub holds cup & donut away from lg rat, Middletown #70 ...650.00
Cherub pulls sled w/ring, fox emb on runners, Meriden #284.....650.00
Cherub sits on ped & holds bud vase, R&B #1285.................850.00
Cherub w/lyre sits before ring, Aurora #9..........................350.00
Cherub w/wings beside ring w/appl florals, unmk 350.00
Chick by eng ring on ornate base, Van Bergh Silver Plate #80, up to ...100.00
Cockatiel w/lg flower & branch around ring, unmk SH&M 450.00
Cockatoo on sunflower stem on domed base by ring, Derby #370..450.00
Cockatoo perches on ball w/scrollwork before ring, Pairpoint #8..250.00
Combination set, cherub w/salt cellar by ring, Meriden #238.....450.00
Combination set, ring/salt & pepper, ornate hdl, Wilcox #1659.350.00
Combination set, Spaniard amid shaker & holder, Taunton #310..350.00
Combination set, vase atop ring amid 2 shakers, Rockford #33..550.00
Coral & shell at base of ring, Meriden Britannia #227................350.00
Deer (2) w/ring on bks, held by antlers, Webster #158...............450.00
Dog (hunting) crouches w/holder on bk, SH&M #019 ....450.00
Dog on base, cat w/tail up atop ring, Rogers #262 ....750.00
Dog w/glass eyes beside scroll holder, unmk, #382 ....450.00
Dolphins (2) hold ring w/tails, Pairpoint #30 ....350.00
Egyptian kneels w/ring on bk, R&B #1508 ....450.00
Elephant w/ring on bk, stepped base, Tufts #1681 ....750.00
Fawn w/garland around neck by ruffled ring, R&B #1807.........850.00
Flowers & leaves hold elevated ring, Aurora #38, up to.............200.00
Girl w/basket before ring, ornate base, Pelton Bros.................1,200.00
Girl w/braid & apron pushes ring, Meriden Britannia #280........750.00
Gnomes carry bbl-shaped ring on poles, SH&M #016 ....850.00
Greenaway-type baby on chair before ring, Middletown #98, minimum..1,500.00
Greenaway-type boy (4½") before ring, Rogers Smith #251 ....850.00
Greenaway-type boy & girl w/chair (legs form ring), SH&M #036, minimum...3,500.00
Greenaway-type boy on horse beside ring, SH&M #225, minimum.2,700.00
Greenaway-type girl sits beside ring, Derby #316.......................500.00
Greenaway-type girl ties bonnet by ring, unmk 950.00
Greenaway-type lady on toboggan w/ring in lap, Wilcox #4342, minimum.3,000.00
Hen beside ring, Meriden Britannia #268 ....550.00
Heron w/leaf in beak beside ring, R&B #1126............................500.00
Lady w/arms akimbo & bare ft beside ring, Rogers #10 ....500.00
Lion (rampant) w/front ft on ring, Meriden Britannia #153 ....350.00
Log & branches support ring, Tufts #1593, under 200.00
Monkey plays horn before ornate ring, unmk, #064.................1,500.00
Morning glories on bud vase beside ring, Webster & Bro #168...350.00
Owl w/glass eyes on branch beside ring, Osborn & Co #706 ......850.00
Palmer Cox Brownie rests hands on ring, Pairpoint #37 ....550.00
Parakeet on stem w/leaves (forming base), unmk SH&M 350.00
Parakeet perched by ring, vase opposite, Webster & Bro #169 ...350.00
Parrot w/long tail atop ring, sm base, R&B #1136 ....350.00
Peacock w/tail down atop ring, ornate base, Pelton Bros............650.00
Sadiron shape w/open sides, Tufts #1636, up to 200.00
Sheep rests beside ring on short ped, Aurora #35 ....750.00
Squirrel on base beside emb ring, Knickerbocker #7 ....350.00
Squirrel w/nut facing away from ring, SH&M #09 ....300.00
The (maple leaf) Forever motto/swords, Meriden Britannia #642, under.200.00

Nash

A. Douglas Nash founded the Corona Art Glass Company in Long Island, New York. He produced tableware, vases, flasks, etc. using delicate artistic shapes and forms. After 1933 he worked for the Libbey Glass Company.

Candlesticks, gold irid w/bl highlights, #651, 4", pr....................690.00
Parfait, gold irid, shell stem, slightly pinched rim, sgn/#543, 4½" .300.00

Vase, cobalt w/irid stripes, ovoid, flared lip, 5¼" **520.00**
Vase, floriform; gold irid, stretched/ruffled rim tapers to disk, 9" ..**900.00**
Vase, gold irid, cone shape on appl ft, #547, 5x6½" **435.00**

Natzler, Gertrude and Otto

The Natzlers came to the United States from Vienna in the late 1930s. They settled in Los Angeles where they continued their work in ceramics, for which they were already internationally recognized. Gertrude created the forms; Otto formulated a variety of interesting glazes, among them volcanic, crystalline, and lustre. Our advisor for this category is Abby Malowanczyk; she is listed in the Directory under Texas.

Bowl, blk to dk brn, wide mouth, 8⅛" **1,725.00**
Bowl, bright bl w/purple & ivory mottling, 5" **1,300.00**
Bowl, bright gr w/brn accents, low, #6357, 4" **900.00**
Bowl, brn/blk metallic flake, ftd/folded, rstr, 1¾x5" **475.00**
Bowl, lime gr, oval, 2x5½" **1,000.00**
Bowl, ochre w/free-from wht opal bands, ⅞x5⅜", NM **400.00**
Bowl, volcanic verdigris, 1½x5½" **1,600.00**
Bowl, yel over slightly ribbed tan clay, 4" **475.00**
Candle cup, pierced w/holes, Hebrew script, rust/brn, 5" **565.00**
Vase, lt bl gloss, 2½" **950.00**
Vase, yel/bl/brn flambé, wide cupped top, 5½x3" **1,575.00**

Naughties and Bathing Beauties

These daring all-bisque figurines were made in various poses, usually in one piece, in German and American factories during the 1920s. Admired for their fine details, these figures were often nude but were also made with molded-on clothing or dressed in bathing costumes. Items below are all in excellent undamaged condition.

For further information we recommend *Doll Values, Antique to Modern,* by Patsy Moyer (Collector Books). Our advisors for this category are Don and Anne Kier; they are listed in the Directory under Ohio.

Action figure, w/wig, 7" **650.00**
Action figure, 5" **450.00**
Action figure, 7½" **650.00**
Elderly woman in suit w/legs crossed, rare, 5¼" **1,800.00**
Glass eyes, 5" **400.00**
Glass eyes, 6" **650.00**
Glass eyes, 6" **650.00**
Japan mk, 3" **55.00**
Japan mk, 5-6", ea **95.00**
Japan mk, 9" **140.00**
Pnt eyes, 3" **165.00**
Pnt eyes, 6" **325.00**
Swivel neck, 5" **625.00**
Swivel neck, 6" **700.00**
With animal, 5½" **1,200.00**
2 modeled together, 4½-5½", ea **1,600.00**

New Geneva

In the early years of the nineteenth century, several potteries flourished in the Greensboro, Pennsylvania, area. They produced utilitarian stoneware items as well as tile and novelties for many decades. All failed well before the turn of the century.

Pitcher, floral on tanware, device of short lines on neck, rpr, 9" .**245.00**

Pitcher, floral on tanware, int: dk brn matt, 6⅝", EX **440.00**
Pitcher, floral on tanware w/dk matt glaze, tooled lines, 7" **465.00**
Pitcher, floral/stripes on red-tanware, brn glaze int, chips, 9½" ..**385.00**
Pitcher, wavy lines/brushed flourishes on red-tan w/brn gloss, 6", EX .**520.00**

New Martinsville

The New Martinsville Glass Company took its name from the town in West Virginia where it began operations in 1901. In the beginning years, pressed tablewares were made in crystal as well as colored and opalescent glass. Considered an innovator, the company was known for their imaginative applications of the medium in creating lamps made entirely of glass, vanity sets, figural decanters, and models of animals and birds. In 1944 the company was purchased by Viking Glass, who continued to use many of the old molds, the animals molds included. They marked their wares 'Viking' or 'Rainbow Art.' Viking recently ceased operations and has been purchased by Kenneth Dalzell, president of the Fostoria Company. They, too, are making the bird and animal models. Although at first they were not marked, future productions are to be marked with an acid stamp. Dalzell/Viking animals are in the $50.00 to $60.00 range. Values for cobalt and red items are two to three times higher than for the same item in clear.

See also Depression Glass; Glass Animals and Figurines.

Addie, blk, cobalt, jade or red, creamer, ftd **14.00**
Addie, blk, cobalt, jade or red, tray, sandwich; hdls......................**35.00**
Addie, blk, cobalt, jade or red, tumbler, water; ftd, 9-oz..............**22.50**
Addie, crystal or pk, candlestick, 3½" **20.00**
Addie, crystal or pk, sherbet, ftd **10.00**
Addie, crystal or pk, tumbler, water; ftd, 9-oz............................**15.00**
Bowl, Sunglow, 28-rib, 8-scallop rim, 2x5"................................**165.00**
Janice, bl or red, bonbon, hdls, 4x6"..**33.00**
Janice, bl or red, bowl, flared rim, 11" **90.00**
Janice, bl or red, bowl, 10" **75.00**
Janice, bl or red, bowl, 6-crimp, 12" **125.00**
Janice, bl or red, celery, 11"..**45.00**
Janice, bl or red, creamer, tall **45.00**
Janice, bl or red, mayonnaise plate, 6" **12.50**
Janice, bl or red, plate, 13"..**70.00**
Janice, bl or red, platter, oval, 13"..**90.00**
Janice, bl or red, sherbet..**25.00**
Janice, bl or red, vase, ftd, 7" **75.00**
Janice, crystal, basket, 9x6½"..**75.00**
Janice, crystal, bowl, cupped, 9½"..**35.00**
Janice, crystal, bowl, oval, 11"..**40.00**
Janice, crystal, bowl, salad; scalloped rim, 12" **50.00**
Janice, crystal, candlestick, 1-light, 6x4½" **37.50**
Janice, crystal, ice pail, hdld, 10" **85.00**
Janice, crystal, pitcher, berry cream; 15-oz................................**50.00**
Janice, crystal, plate, rolled rim, ftd, 11"....................................**27.50**
Janice, crystal, platter, oval, 13"..**40.00**
Janice, crystal, tumbler..**14.00**
Janice, crystal, vase, ball from, 9"..**55.00**
Lions, blk, candy dish, w/lid..**95.00**
Lions, blk, creamer, #34 Addie **35.00**
Lions, blk, plate, 12"..**40.00**
Lions, crystal, candle holder, #37 Moondrops **25.00**
Lions, crystal, creamer, #37 Moondrops......................................**15.00**
Lions, pk or gr, candlestick, #34 Addie..**35.00**
Lions, pk or gr, cup..**25.00**
Lions, pk or gr, saucer..**7.50**
Meadow Wreath, crystal, bowl, crimped, 10" **40.00**
Meadow Wreath, crystal, bowl, punch; 5-qt................................**135.00**
Meadow Wreath, crystal, bowl, relish; 2-part, 7" **18.00**

Meadow Wreath, crystal, cheese & cracker, 11" 50.00
Meadow Wreath, crystal, punch ladle...55.00
Meadow Wreath, crystal, vase, crimped, 10" 55.00
Moondrops, color other than red or bl, bowl, berry; 5¼" 12.00
Moondrops, color other than red or bl, bowl, divided relish; 3-ftd .20.00
Moondrops, color other than red or bl, candle holders, ruffled, 2", pr.25.00
Moondrops, color other than red or bl, comport, 4" 18.00
Moondrops, color other than red or bl, goblet, cordial, 2⅞" 30.00
Moondrops, color other than red or bl, goblet, 8-oz, 5¾"..............20.00
Moondrops, color other than red or bl, plate, luncheon; 8½" 14.00
Moondrops, color other than red or bl, tumbler, shot; 2¾" 10.00
Moondrops, red or bl, bowl, celery, boat shape, 11".....................37.00
Moondrops, red or bl, bowl, cream soup; 4¼" 100.00
Moondrops, red or bl, bowl, vegetable; oval, 9¾" 75.00
Moondrops, red or bl, butter dish 500.00
Moondrops, red or bl, candlesticks, 3-light, 5¼", pr.....................150.00
Moondrops, red or bl, creamer, regular, 3¾"..................................16.00
Moondrops, red or bl, decanter, 8½"...75.00
Moondrops, red or bl, goblet, 8-oz, 5¾"..40.00
Moondrops, red or bl, gravy boat..195.00
Moondrops, red or bl, pitcher, no lip, 53-oz, 8⅛" 185.00
Moondrops, red or bl, plate, sandwich; 14" dia 45.00
Moondrops, red or bl, sherbet, 4½" 30.00
Moondrops, red or bl, tumbler, 7-oz, 4⅜" 16.00
Moondrops, red or bl, vase, ruffled rim, flat base, 7¾"..................60.00
Radiance, amber, bowl, bonbon; 6"..17.50
Radiance, amber, bowl, flared rim, 10" 25.00
Radiance, amber, bowl, pickle; 7" 20.00
Radiance, amber, comport, 6"...22.00
Radiance, amber, cup, ftd 12.00
Radiance, amber, honey jar, w/lid..75.00
Radiance, amber, plate, punch bowl; 14".......................................50.00
Radiance, amber, tray, oval..25.00
Radiance, Ice Blue or red, bowl, bonbon, ftd, 6".............................35.00
Radiance, Ice Blue or red, bowl, crimped rim, 10" 60.00
Radiance, Ice Blue or red, bowl, nut; hdls, 5" 20.00
Radiance, Ice Blue or red, candy dish, flat, w/lid 100.00
Radiance, Ice Blue or red, cruet, ind..80.00
Radiance, Ice Blue or red, lamp, 12" 140.00
Radiance, Ice Blue or red, plate, luncheon; 8" 16.00
Radiance, Ice Blue or red, vase, flared or crimped, 12"................175.00
Top Notch (Sunburst), any color, creamer 25.00
Top Notch (Sunburst), any color, cup 20.00
Top Notch (Sunburst), any color, serving tray 35.00
Top Notch (Sunburst), sugar bowl..25.00

Newcomb

The Newcomb College of New Orleans, Louisiana, established a pottery in 1895 to provide the students with first-hand experience in the fields of art and ceramics. Using locally dug clays — red and buff in the early years, white-burning by the turn of the century — potters were employed to throw the ware which the ladies of the college decorated. From 1897 until about 1910, the ware they produced was finished in a high glaze and was usually surface painted. After 1905, some carving was done as well. On today's market, even a small piece of carved high glaze ware generally brings a minimum of $4,000.00. After 1912 a matt glaze was favored; these pieces are always carved. Soft blues and greens were used almost exclusively, and decorative themes were chosen to reflect the beauty of the South. The end of the matt-glaze period and the art-pottery era was 1930.

Various marks used by the pottery include an 'N' within a 'C,' sometimes with 'HB' added to indicate a 'hand-built' piece. The potter often incised his initials into the ware, and the artists were encouraged to sign their work. Among the most well-known artists were Sadie Irvine, Henrietta Bailey, and Fannie Simpson.

Newcomb pottery is evaluated to a large extent by era (early, transitional, or matt), decoration, size, and condition. In the following descriptions, unless noted otherwise, all decoration is carved and painted on matt glaze. The term 'transitional' defines a period of two to three years (ca 1910 to 1912) between earlier and later work, and signifies changes to the glazes, colors, and style of decoration. Our advisors for this category are Suzanne Perrault and Dave Rago; they are listed in the Directory under New Jersey.

Key: hg — high glaze

Bowl, crocuses on purple, AF Simpson, 1926, 3x9", from $2,000 to ..3,000.00
Bowl, daisy band, AF Simpson, transitional, 1914, 3¼x5¼" ...2,185.00
Bowl, florals on shoulder, pk on mauve, S Irvine, 1919, 2¼x7¾".1,300.00
Bowl, irises, pk/gr on med bl, AF Simpson, 1923, 3¼x9¼", EX....1,400.00
Bowl, jonquils, wht/gr on bl, H Bailey/J Meyer, #LA89, 11"....1,880.00
Bowl, pk irises & gr leaves on med bl, AF Simpson, 1923, 3¼x9¼".1,400.00
Bowl, roses, yel/wht/bl to gr, S Irvine, #DY49, 5½".................2,100.00
Bowl vase, crocuses at shoulder, AF Simpson, 1922, 4x4¾", NM .2,500.00
Bowl vase, narcissus at sloped neck, Littlejohn/Meyers, 1914, 3x6".1,265.00
Bowl vase, trillium, bl/yel on bl, S Irvine, 4-hdl, EX, 4x5½" ...3,000.00

Chocolate pot, high glaze, stylized landscape on blue-green, Lucia Jordan, 1907, NC/LJ/JM/BN33/Q, 11x6", $20,700.00. (Photo courtesy Dave Rago Auctions)

Inkwell, band of children, bl/gr hg, Ayars/Meyers, open, 2⅜".6,600.00
Jar, covered; oak trees w/Spanish moss on bl, AF Simpson, 1929, 5x4"..7,500.00
Jar, paperwhites on bl, H Bailey, 1920, 6x6", EX, from $4,000 to .6,000.00
Pitcher, berries in 2 bands, spherical, AR Urquhart, NC XX84, 5⅛".3,175.00
Pitcher, Deco floral, C Chalaron, 1923, 8x5½", from $3,000 to ...4,000.00
Pitcher, floral neck panels, hg, L Nicholson, 1906, 8", from $6,000 to...9,000.00
Plate, lg magnolia blossom/leaves, Ayars/Meyers/ED 89, 1910, 5½"..3,450.00
Salt cellar, Blk-eyed Susan band, Ayars/Meyers/ED 90, cylinder, 1x2"..1,495.00
Trivet, swirl of wht blossoms on gr, H Bailey, 1912, 3¾" dia ...1,100.00
Urn, dripping turq over ivory, ribbed, 2-hdl, 12" 650.00
Vase, artichokes, gr/bl on striated med bl, hg, O Webster, 9x6", EX.17,250.00
Vase, bl to gray matt, shouldered, 4¾" 375.00
Vase, cicada band at bottom, hg, L Nicholson, 1906, 7x2½"..12,000.00
Vase, daffodils, mc on bl, S Irvine, #LP92, 6"...........................2,750.00
Vase, dogwood branches on pk to bl, S Irvine, 1914, bulbous, 8x6"...9,775.00
Vase, floral, bl/bl-gr/lt yel, H Bailey, 7" 2,600.00
Vase, floral, mc on bl, S Irvine, flared cylinder, PL39, 6½"......2,000.00
Vase, floral, pk/yel on bl, AF Simpson, JQ65/#171, invt trumpet, 6"...1,840.00
Vase, floral at shoulder, gr/wht on bl, H Bailey, 1910s, 4x4¼".1,600.00
Vase, floral band on bl, S Irvine, bulbous, SW25, 8½" 3,500.00
Vase, floral on bl, AF Simpson, bulbous, 1924, 4½x5".............1,600.00
Vase, floral shoulder band, AW/Meyers/FS 65, 1913, 4" 920.00
Vase, floral w/long stems, S Irvine/JB Hunt, #329 RL54, 1929, 6"...1,765.00

Vase, geometrics on bl, Sabrina Wells, SS30, 9½", NM **16,000.00**
Vase, grape clusters on bl-gr satin, S Irvine, 1912, 7½"............**2,400.00**
Vase, gunmetal, gr & yel, bulbous w/2 buttress hdls, NC/JM/FR, 8x9"..**2,500.00**
Vase, hibiscus, att AC Arbo, transitional, 10½x4½", $8,000 to .**11,000.00**
Vase, iris stalks on bl, S Irvine, cylindrical, 6½"............**2,185.00**
Vase, irises, S Irvine, 1925, 10½x4½", from $7,500 to **10,000.00**
Vase, landscape, rose/cobalt, S Irvine, QP16, 4" W............**2,700.00**
Vase, lotus, wht on dk bl-gr, sgn (?), transitional, 1910, 8x4½" ..**5,460.00**
Vase, moon/live oaks, S Irvine, 6½x3¾" **3,450.00**
Vase, moon/moss/oaks, AF Simpson, 1926, 7½x4", EX, from $2,500 to.**3,500.00**
Vase, moon/moss/oaks, AF Simpson, 1930, NC/SN43/131/JH/AFS, 11x5"...**14,000.00**
Vase, moon/moss/oaks, S Irvine, 1932, 3½x4½" **2,300.00**
Vase, moon/moss/trees, S Irvine/Hunt/SL5/#500, 1930, 6x6" ..**8,335.00**
Vase, moon/pine trees, AF Simpson, 1930, ovoid, 9x4" **13,800.00**
Vase, moss/tall trees, H Bailey, ovoid, 11½" **7,500.00**
Vase, mossy oaks, AF Simpson, transitional, 1913, 8x6¼".......**8,600.00**
Vase, mossy oaks bl, AF Simpson, QB53, 4½"............**2,800.00**
Vase, narcissus, AF Simpson, 1924, 8x3¾"............**3,335.00**
Vase, organic design on bl, Nickolson, 9", NM **14,000.00**
Vase, pendant abutilon blossoms, bl on ivory, S Frackelton, 6¾", EX.**18,000.00**
Vase, pk orchids on med bl, S Irvine, 1920, 2½x3"............**1,600.00**
Vase, sailboats reflecting on water, bl & gr on ivory, Roman, 6½" ..**11,000.00**
Vase, turq drip on ivory hg, ribbed, hdld urn form, 12x5", EX **650.00**
Wall pocket, rose buds/leaves border on bl, H Bailey/1905, 10¼" .**10,350.00**

Newspapers

People do not collect newspapers simply because they are old. Age has absolutely nothing to do with value — it does not hold true that the older the newspaper, the higher the value. Instead, most of the value is determined by the historic event content. In most cases, the more important to American history the event is, the higher the value. In over two hundred years of American history, perhaps as many as 98% of all newspapers ever published do not contain news of a significant historic event. Newspapers not having news of major events in history are called 'atmosphere.' Atmosphere papers have little collector value. (See price guide below.)

To learn more about the hobby of collecting old and historic newspapers, be sure to visit our mega-websight on the Internet at www.history buff.com/. The e-mail address for the NCSA is help@historybuff.com/. See Newspaper Collector's Society of America in Clubs, Catalogs, and Newsletters for more information.

1800-1820, Atmosphere editions, from $5 to **10.00**
1821-1859, Atmosphere editions, from $4 to **8.00**
1836, Texas declares independence, from $60 to **85.00**
1845, Annexation of Texas, from $35 to **45.00**
1846, Start of Mexican War, from $25 to **35.00**
1846-1847, Major battles of Mexican War, from $25 to **30.00**
1847, End of Mexican War, from $30 to **40.00**
1860, Lincoln elected 1st term, from $115 to **225.00**
1861, Lincoln's inaugural address, from $140 to **275.00**
1861-1865, Atmosphere editions: Confederate titles, from $110 to..**165.00**
1861-1865, Atmosphere editions: Union titles, from $8 to **15.00**
1861-1865, Civil War major battle, Confederate report, $225 to ..**350.00**
1861-1865, Civil War major battle, Union 1st report, $60 to.....**120.00**
1862, Emancipation Proclamation, from $85 to **225.00**
1863, Gettysburg Address, from $165 to **380.00**
1865, April 29 edition of Frank Leslie's, from $175 to **225.00**
1865, April 29 edition of Harper's Weekly, from $150 to............**200.00**
1865, Capture & death of J Wilkes Booth, from $85 to **165.00**
1865, Fall of Richmond, from $85 to............**275.00**
1865, NY Herald, Apr 15 (Beware: reprints abound), from $600 to..**900.00**

1865, Titles other than NY Herald, Apr 15, from $125 to **375.00**
1866-1900, Atmosphere editions, from $3 to **5.00**
1876, Custer's Last Stand, later reports, from $30 to............**80.00**
1876, Custer's Last Stand, 1st reports, from $100 to............**250.00**
1881, Billy the Kid killed, from $130 to **350.00**
1881, Garfield assassinated, from $60 to **115.00**
1881, Gunfight at OK Corral, from $175 to **400.00**
1882, Jesse James killed, later report, from $60 to............**120.00**
1882, Jesse James killed, 1st report, from $165 to............**385.00**
1898, Sinking of Maine, from $25 to............**70.00**
1901, McKinley assassinated, from $45 to **100.00**
1903, Wright Brother's flight, from $200 to **500.00**
1906, San Francisco earthquake, other titles, from $25 to............**50.00**
1906, San Francisco earthquake, San Francisco title, from $300 to...**500.00**
1912, Sinking of Titanic, later reports, from $25 to **50.00**
1912, Sinking of Titanic, 1st reports, from $100 to **250.00**
1915, Sinking of Lusitania, later reports, from $25 to............**65.00**
1915, Sinking of Lusitania, 1st reports, from $40 to **125.00**
1927, Babe Ruth hits 60th home run, from $50 to **125.00**
1927, Lindbergh arrives in Paris, 1st reports, from $65 to **125.00**
1929, St Valentine's Day Massacre, from $100 to **225.00**
1929, Stock market crash, from $75 to............**180.00**
1931, Al Capone found guilty, from $40 to **80.00**
1931, Jack 'Legs' Diamond killed, from $30 to **45.00**
1933, Machine Gun Kelley captured, from $25 to **45.00**
1934, Baby Face Nelson killed, from $30 to............**60.00**
1934, Bonnie & Clyde killed, from $125 to **250.00**
1934, Dillinger killed, from $100 to **250.00**
1934, Pretty Boy Floyd killed, from $25 to............**45.00**
1937, Hindenburg explodes, from $75 to **150.00**
1939-45, WWII major battles, from $20 to **50.00**
1941, Honolulu Star-Bulletin, Dec 7, 1st extra (+), from $300 to ..**600.00**
1941, Other titles, Dec 7, w/Pearl Harbor news, from $30 to........**60.00**
1945, Hitler dead, from $35 to............**50.00**
1948, Chicago Daily Tribune, Nov 3, Dewey Defeats Truman, from $500 to..**800.00**
1953, Truce signed to end Korean War, from $25 to............**35.00**
1960, JFK elected, from $10 to............**25.00**
1961, Alan Shephard 1st astronaut in space, from $15 to **30.00**
1961, Bay of Pigs, from $20 to **50.00**
1961, Roger Maris hits 61st home run, from $20 to............**40.00**
1963, JFK assassination, Nov 22, Dallas title, from $70 to **100.00**
1963, JFK assassination, Nov 22, titles other than Dallas, from $3 to ..**8.00**
1967, Super Bowl I, from $15 to............**30.00**
1968, Assassination of Martin Luther King, from $15 to............**25.00**
1968, Assassination of Robert Kennedy, from $5 to **20.00**
1969, Moon landing, from $5 to **20.00**
1974, Nixon resigns, from $15 to............**20.00**

Nicodemus

Chester R. Nicodemus was born near Barberton, Ohio, August, 17, 1901. He started Pennsylvania State University in 1920, where he studied engineering. Chester got a share of a large paper route and attended Cleveland Art School where he studied under Herman Matzen, sculptor, and Frank Wilcox, anatomy illustrator, graduating in 1925. That fall Chester was hired to start the sculpture department at the Dayton Art Institute.

Nicodemus moved from Dayton to Columbus, Ohio, in 1930 and started teaching at the Columbus Art School. During this time he made vases and commissioned sculptures, water fountains, and limestone and wood carvings. In 1941 Chester left the field of teaching to pursue pottery making full time, using local red clay containing a large amount of iron. Known for its durability, he called the ware Ferro-stone. He made teapots and other utility wares, but these goods lost favor, so he started producing animal and bird sculptures, nativity sets, and Christmas ornaments, some bearing Chester's and Florine's names as personalized cards for his customers and friends. Chester died in 1990.

His glaze colors were turquoise or aqua, ivory, green mottle, pink pussy willow, and golden yellow. The glaze was applied so that the color of the warm red clay would show through, adding an extra dimension to each piece. His name is usually incised in the clay in an arch, but paper labels were also used. For more information, we recommend *Sanford Guide to Nicodemus, His Pottery and His Art*, by James Riebel.

Figurine, French Poodle, brn, #28, 6½".......................................400.00
Figurine, owl, Ferro-Stone, 4½"..125.00
Figurine, squirrel, #139, hand-sgn Nicodemus/label/stamp, 3"....215.00
Flower block, geometric decor, rectangular, #561, 4x6x3".............90.00
Vase, curdled brn, #43, 5½x2½"...135.00

Niloak

During the latter part of the 1800s, there were many small utilitarian potteries in Benton, Arkansas. By 1900 only the Hyten Brothers Pottery remained. Charles Hyten, a second generation potter, took control of the family business around 1902. Shortly thereafter he renamed it the Eagle Pottery Company. In 1909 Hyten and former Rookwood potter Arthur Dovey began experimentation on a new swirl pottery. Dovey had previously worked for the Ouachita Pottery Company of Hot Springs and produced a swirl pottery there as early as 1906. In March 1910, the Eagle Pottery Company introduced Niloak — kaolin spelled backwards.

In 1911 Benton businessmen formed the Niloak Pottery Corporation. Niloak, connected to the Arts and Crafts Movement and known as 'mission' ware, had a national representative in New York by 1913. Niloak's production centered on art pottery characterized by accidental, swirling patterns of natural and artificially colored clays. Many companies through the years have produced swirl pottery, yet none achieved the technical and aesthetic qualities of Niloak. Hyten received a patent in 1928 for the swirl technique. Although most examples have an interior glaze, some early Mission Ware pieces have an exterior glaze as well; these are extremely rare.

In 1934 Hyten's company found itself facing bankruptcy. Hardy L. Winburn, Jr., along with other Little Rock businessmen, raised the necessary capital and were able to provide the kind of leadership needed to make the business profitable once again. Both lines (Eagle and Hywood) were renamed 'Niloak' in 1937 to capitalize on this well-known name. The pottery continued in production until 1947 when it was converted to the Winburn Tile Company, which exists to this day in Little Rock.

Be careful not to confuse the swirl production of the Evans Pottery of Missouri with Niloak. The significant difference is the dark brown matt interior glaze of Evans pottery.

For further information we recommend *Collector's Encyclopedia of Niloak Pottery* by David Edwin Gifford (Collector Books). Our advisor for this category is Lila Shrader; she is listed in the Directory under California. All items listed below bear the Niloak mark unless noted otherwise.

Key:
HN — Hywood by Niloak   NI — Niloak (impressed) mark
N — N mark   NL — Niloak (in low relief) mark
NB — Niloak (block letters) mark

Mission Ware

Ashtray, str outward sloping sides/3 notches, 2nd art mk, 4¾x1¾"...135.00
Bowl, flower; invt rim, 2nd art mk, 1½x6½" 88.00
Bowl, flower/frog; invt rim, punched flower stems, 2½x5" 100.00
Candlestick, flared ft, bl/gray/cream, 1st art mk, 10⅛".................249.00

Candlestick, no hdl, saucer-like base, unmk, 4x4¾"....................118.00
Candlestick/bud vase, flared base+3 'rings' on neck, 2nd art mk, 9"..135.00
Chamberstick, flared base/hdl, dk brn/deep bl/tan, 1st art mk, 4¾" ..265.00
Flower frog, unmk, 1¼x3¼"..55.00
Goblet, flared ft & rim, brn/bl/cream, 2nd art mk, 7½" 258.00
Humidor, int indented for sponge, dk colors, 1st art mk, 6".......585.00
Jug, dk bl/dk brn/tan, no hdl, missing stopper, 2nd art mk, 7" 355.00
Mug, flared base, cream/brick/gray, 1st art mk, 4".....................310.00
Pin tray, lt bl/cream/tan, rectangular, 2nd art mk, 3¼x1⅞"..........96.00
Pitcher, lemonade; bulbous, 1st art mk, 7x6½"..........................945.00
Punch bowl, brn/tan/bl, corseted ped base, 11x13½", NM 3,250.00
Punch cups, 2x3½", set of 6...2,100.00
Stein, flared base, 1st art mk, 7½"...480.00
Tankard, bl/brn/tan/cream, 2nd art mk, 10½" 1,155.00
Thimble, bl/cream/tan, unmk, ⅞"...65.00
Tumbler, extremely wavy composition, 2nd art mk, shot sz, 2¼" .165.00
Tumbler, flared rim, Patent Pending, 5" 197.00
Vase, bud; bulbous base, 2nd art mk+metallic sticker, 8½".........172.00
Vase, bulbous, 1st art mk, 3½"...89.00
Vase, classic shape, rolled rim, dk brick red/brns, 1st art mk, 8½" .288.00

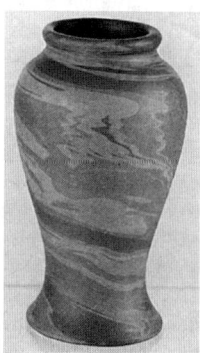

Vase, classic shape, 1st art mark, 9", $300.00. (Photo courtesy David Edwin Gifford).

Vase, classic shape w/flared rim, bl/cream/brns, 2nd art mk, 8" ...160.00
Vase, classic shape w/flared rim, brn/brick/cream/bl, 2nd art mk, 9"..278.00
Vase, classic shape w/flared rim, brn/cream/brick, 1st art mk, 5½".94.00
Vase, classic shape w/wide flared rim, 2nd art mk, 3½" 78.00
Vase, conical, flared ft, bl/brn/cream, 2nd art mk, 5¼" 180.00
Vase, conical, flared ft, bl/tan/cream, 2nd art mk, 8" 325.00
Vase, corseted, dk brn/deep bl/brick red, Patent Pending, 6⅛"...167.00
Vase, cylindrical, no rim, bl/dk brn/tan/cream, 1st art mk, 7⅞"..160.00
Vase, cylindrical, no rim, tan/brn/cream/bl, 2nd art mk, 6".........130.00
Vase, fan; flared ft, bl paper sticker, 5½" 200.00
Vase, high shoulders, no rolled rim, gray/lt bl/lt brn, 2nd art mk, 6" .125.00
Vase, high shoulders, rolled rim, brn/gray/bl, 2nd art mk, 8½" ...210.00
Vase, high shoulders, squat w/incurvate rim, 2nd art mk, 2⅞" 96.00
Vase, high shoulders/rolled collar, tan/gray/bl/cream, 2nd art mk, 10" ...300.00
Vase, pear shape, bl/gray/tan/cream, 2nd art mk, 3½-4", $50 to....68.00
Vase, rose bowl shape, 2nd art mk, 4" opening, 5¼" 135.00
Vase, teardrop shape, dk colors, 1st art mk, 1¾" at neck, 10½"..455.00
Wall pocket, rolled rim, brns/bls, unmk, 9" 310.00
Water bottle w/drinking glass cover, dk colors, 2nd art mk, 7⅞" ...885.00

Miscellaneous

Ashtray, canoe shape w/2 rests, Ozark Blue, NB, 4½" 33.00
Bowl, flower; flat, fluted edge, matt, unmk, 9½" dia.....................18.00
Bowl, Peter pan on edge, NL, 7½", from $24 to 29.00
Canoe, Ozark Dawn, NB, 3½x11"...45.00
Cookie jar, Ozark Blue, tab hdls, unmk, 9½".............................165.00
Cornucopia, wht matt, EX details, raised base, NI, 6" 21.00
Cornucopia vase, almost upright, semigloss, NI, 7½" 24.00

Creamer, cow figural, tail hdl, high-gloss, unmk, 4½" 55.00
Creamer, Fox Red, Aladdin lamp style, unmk but w/sticker, 2¾" .16.00
Cup & saucer, tobacco spit, cup unmk, saucer NB, 5¾" dia..........18.00
Dish, 1" W ribbing & scallops at top opening, N, 1½x3¾" 11.00
Ewer, gr-brn tobacco spit, graceful arc hdl, NI, 7¾" 22.00
Ewer, Ozark Blue, graceful spout, NI, 16½" 145.00
Ewer, silhouettes ea side, elongated spout & hdl, NL, 10¼" 55.00
Figurine, donkey w/ears up looking bk, unmk, 3½" 165.00
Figurine, razor-bk hog on base, maroon, unmk, NB, 3¾" 250.00
Figurine, Southern Belle, Ozark Blue or Ozark Dawn, NL, 10"...185.00
Figurine, Trojan horse on base, ivory matt, 2nd art mk, 9" 185.00
Flower frog, duck on wing, Ozark Dawn, unmk, 6" 70.00
Head vase, Southern Belle, Ozark Blue, unmk, 7" 155.00
Jug, mini; Ozark Dawn, unmk, 3", from $12 to 22.00
Mug, Bouquet dinnerware line, NI, 3½", from $4 to 9.00
Pitcher, ball form, NL, 7½" 27.00
Pitcher, bull's-eye decor, 1st HN, 6" 67.00
Pitcher, hand thrown, high-gloss, w/lid, 2nd art mk, 6½" 95.00
Pitcher, maroon, graceful hdl, str sides, 2nd art mk, 3" 19.00
Planter, deer & fawn on woodsy base, high-gloss, NL, 7½" 32.00
Planter, elephant, Ozark Dawn, NB, 4½" 29.00
Planter, Fox Red, attached drip tray, rectangular, 6" 12.00
Planter, fox resting w/tail over bk, high-gloss, NL, 4x7" 38.00
Planter, parrot perched on side of dish, NL, 4½", from $40 to......58.00
Planter, pouter pigeon, Ivory, NI, 9" 185.00
Planter, seal resting on side, Lewis glaze, NL, 4½" 62.00
Planter, swan, Lewis Ivory, NI, 7½" 14.00
Relish, Fox Red, triangular w/3 sections, unmk, 9¾"....................65.00
Shakers, penguins, Ozark Blue, unmk but w/sticker, 2¾", pr.........22.00
Strawberry jar, Mirror Black, gracefully curved top, 1st HN, 9½"...185.00
Teapot, Fox Red, Aladdin lamp style, unmk, 6½" 92.00
Tumbler, Peacock Blue, unmk, 5" 44.00
Vase, appl spaghetti-like hdls run length, 2nd art mk, 11½".......235.00
Vase, fan; forest gr & brn, ribbed, low G-shape hdls, 5x6" 55.00
Vase, maroon, tri-fluted, NI, 7¾" 88.00
Vase, Mirror Black, high sloping shoulders w/2 tiny hdls, 1st HN, 9" ..165.00
Vase, tulip; 7 openings, NB, 8" 27.00
Vase, Winged Victory, Fox Red, low-slung wing-like hdls, NB, 7½"..24.00
Vase, Winged Victory, high-gloss, wing-like hdls, NI, 7½"............32.00
Wall pocket, Bouquet, half cup attached to 5½" saucer, high-gloss, NL..35.00
Wall pocket, half pitcher, tobacco spit, NL, 5" 65.00

Nippon

Nippon generally refers to Japanese wares made during the period from 1891 to 1921, although the Nippon mark was also used to a limited extent on later wares (accompanied by 'Japan'). Nippon, meaning Japan, identified the country of origin to comply with American importation restrictions. After 1921 'Japan' was the acceptable alternative. The term does not imply a specific type of product and may be found on items other than porcelains. For further information we recommend *The Collector's Encyclopedias of Nippon Porcelain* (there are seven in the series) by our advisor, Joan Van Patten; you will find her address in the Directory under New York. In the following listings, items are assumed hand painted unless noted otherwise. Numbers included in the descriptions refer to these specific marks:

Key:
#1 — China E-OH
#2 — M in Wreath
#3 — Cherry Blossom
#4 — Double T Diamond in Circle
#5 — Rising Sun
#6 — Royal Kinran
#7 — Maple Leaf
#8 — Royal Nippon, Nishiki
#9 — Royal Moriye Nippon

Ashtray, long-billed bird at side, #2..1,200.00
Ashtray, pipe & matches pnt inside, 3 rests, #2, 5¼" H..............175.00
Basket, wht w/Deco floral int, gold hdl, #2, 5½" 100.00
Basket vase, floral tapestry w/gold, #7, 8½" 2,100.00
Bowl, coralene floral, inverted rim, 3-ftd, oval, mk, 3½" H........800.00
Bowl, Egyptian portrait reserve, mc geometric border, hdls, #2, 7¾" ..350.00
Bowl, grapes, simple gold hdls, #2, 8½"......................................175.00
Bowl, river scenic w/boats & windmill, #2, 6½" 175.00
Bowl, roses on wht, simple gold rim, mk, 9½"............................250.00
Cake plate, river scenic w/cottage, hdls, #2, 11"........................235.00
Candlestick, Egyptian figure in relief, brn tones, #2, 8¾" 1,900.00
Candlestick, floral w/moriage trim, flared ft, #2, 6" 300.00
Celery dish, floral reserves w/cobalt & gold, scalloped, #7, 13" L ..550.00
Chamberstick, floral on gr, curled hdl, scalloped base, #7, 6" dia...230.00
Charger, lion's head in relief, brn tones, gr #2, 14"..................3,500.00
Chocolate set, floral band on wht, #2, 9" pot+6 c/s....................315.00
Chocolate set, geisha girls, HP mk, 9½" pot+6 c/s 375.00
Chocolate set, gold design on wht, #7, 10" pot+6 c/s..................675.00
Chocolate set, roses w/gold, #7, pot+6 c/s................................1,750.00
Condensed milk container, roses w/gold, bl #7, w/underplate 300.00
Creamer & sugar bowl, floral on shaded pk w/gold, w/lid, unmk..175.00
Creamer & sugar bowl, floral w/heavy gold beading, #6, sugar: 5½" .400.00
Creamer & sugar bowl, landscape scenic, w/lid, #2 ....125.00
Ewer, floral reserve w/gold, bolted, 2-pc, #2, 14" 1,750.00
Ewer, scenic band, cobalt & gold, bulbous, #7, 6½" 600.00
Ferner, floral band w/cobalt & gold, 4-ftd, hdls, #7, 10¼" W 875.00
Ferner, floral w/gold, lion-head hdls, #2, 5¾" 465.00
Figurine, bird on stump, blk mk, 4" 350.00
Hair receiver, floral on wht w/gold, #2, 4½" dia 75.00
Hatpin holder, floral w/gold, hangs, #7, 7"..................................500.00
Humidor, Chief Joseph reserve, wht beading, #2, 6" 1,600.00
Humidor, scenic moriage, 3-hdl, #2, 5¾" 1,200.00
Humidor, woodland scene, sq, #7, 6¼" 1,500.00
Mug, horses & hunting dogs, #2, 5¾" 400.00
Mustard pot, dainty floral on wht w/gold, #2, 3½", w/underplate .65.00
Pancake dish, floral w/cobalt & gold, oval, w/lid, #7, 8¾" 675.00
Pitcher, roses w/gold, ftd, unmk, 8"..425.00
Plaque, cat looking from window, HP mk, 9½" 650.00
Plaque, Indian in canoe, geometric border, #2, 10" 525.00
Plaque, irises (pastel), #2, 10" 350.00
Plaque, lady's portrait, coralene floral rim, US Pat mk, 11" 3,500.00
Plaque, owl in woodland scene, #2, 8¾" 385.00
Plaque, portrait reserve, geometric border, #7, 10½" 1,200.00
Plaque, river scenic w/tree, gr #2, 9"..335.00
Plaque, still life of fruit, #2, 12"..600.00
Plaque, windmill scene w/ornate border, #7, 9"..........................350.00
Plate, scenic w/flowers & gold, Mt Ranier souvenir, 8½"............250.00
Potpourri jar, swallows, bl on wht, mk, 5½"................................235.00
Powder box, river scenic, #2, 3¼" dia...75.00
Reamer, dainty floral on wht w/gold, 2-pc, #2, 4¾" W 175.00
Stein, floral w/moriage trim on blk, gr moriage hdl, #7, 7" 750.00
Tankard, floral reserve on wht w/gold, ornate hdl, #7, 11½".......875.00
Tankard, moriage flowers & leaves on shaded brn, #7, 10½"...1,300.00
Tea set, Wedgwood, bl, #2, 6" pot+cr/sug 1,100.00
Toast rack, floral on wht, 2-slice, #5, 5" L..................................175.00
Urn, coralene floral, gold trim, w/lid, US Pat mk, 15" 400.00
Urn, irises, gold hdls, bolted, 2-pc, #7, 14"..............................1,500.00
Urn, mtn scenic, cobalt & gold, w/lid, #7, 8¾".........................1,750.00
Urn, swans scenic reserve w/much gold, w/lid, 2-pc, #7, 24" .14,000.00
Vase, autumn leaves in relief, bulbous top, #2, 10"..................1,100.00
Vase, autumn leaves in relief, shouldered, #7, 9¼"...................1,000.00
Vase, bird on branch w/flowers, ring hdls, HP mk, 12"...............350.00
Vase, coaching scene, angle hdls, #2, 5½"..................................700.00
Vase, cobalt w/floral silver o/l, bottle neck, hdls, mk, 10" 850.00

Vase, coralene floral, gold hdls & trim, ornate rim, US Pat mk, 8¾".1,150.00
Vase, coralene scenic, cylindrical, mk removed, 10¼" 1,000.00
Vase, coralene water lilies, gold rim, mk, 8" 800.00
Vase, dragon moriage, trumpet neck, #2, 10" 600.00
Vase, Dutch lady w/umbrella, cylindrical, #2, 7¼" 565.00
Vase, floral, ornate gold at top & base, #7, 25" 5,000.00
Vase, floral band w/cobalt & gold, bulbous, angle hdls, #7, 5¼".350.00
Vase, floral on blk, angle hdls, gr #2, 13" 400.00

Vase, floral reserve and chinoiserie on urn shape, square mouth, green mark, 16", from $850.00 to $1,000.00. (Photo courtesy Joan Van Patten)

Vase, floral tapestry, gold rim & ft, bulbous, #7, 5½" 1,500.00
Vase, floral tapestry w/gold, hdls, #7, 10" 1,600.00
Vase, floral w/gold, integral hdls, bulbous, #7, 5" 300.00
Vase, floral w/heavy gold beading, bulbous, Oriental China mk, 4"..350.00
Vase, floral w/heavy gold beading, slim, mk removed, 11" 800.00
Vase, floral w/moriage trim & hdls, in basket, #7, 8¼"...............900.00
Vase, iris tapestry, gold uptrn hdls, #7, 9¼" 2,350.00
Vase, irises, resembles Rookwood, hdls, gr #7, 12" 665.00
Vase, lady w/stick & geese, integral hdls, #2, 5½" 625.00
Vase, lilies, slim neck, Royal Kinjo, mk, 10" 575.00
Vase, moriage birds & ocean waves, hdls, #7, 10" 1,700.00
Vase, moriage dragon, Del Water Gap PA souvenir, hdls, ftd, #2, 5¼"..275.00
Vase, moriage flowers, gold hdls, bottle neck, unmk, 10½".........550.00
Vase, moriage gulls at sunset, sm curled hdls, #7, 10" 1,700.00
Vase, mtn & sampan scene, cylindrical, Royal Kinjo, mk, 10"....500.00
Vase, mums w/gold, cylindrical, bl #7, 12½" 875.00
Vase, portrait reserve w/cobalt & gold, cylindrical, #7, 6½" 1,100.00
Vase, portrait reserve w/cobalt & gold, uptrn hdls, #7, 7½".....1,300.00
Vase, portrait reserve w/gold, ring hdls, unmk, 5¼" 825.00
Vase, river scenic w/flowers & gold, dragon hdls, #7, 12½" 775.00
Vase, scenic band, cobalt w/gold, bottle neck, #2, 14" 1,750.00
Vase, scenic tapestry, cylindrical, #7, 8" 2,000.00
Vase, swan scenic in earth tones, sm neck, #2, 9" 325.00
Vase, water lilies, 3-ftd, brn hdls, #2, 7" 285.00
Vase, wht woodland scene w/moriage trim & hdls, #2, 5" 825.00
Vase, winter scenic, sq sides, angle hdls, Imperial mk, 6½".........230.00
Wine jug, cottage beside river, gold hdl, bl #2, 11" 1,400.00
Wine jug, pine cones, brn angle hdl, #2, 9½" 1,000.00

Nodders

So called because of the nodding action of their heads and hands, nodders originated in China where they were used in temple rituals to represent deity. At first they were made of brass and were actually a type of bell; when these bells were rung, the heads of the figures would nod. In the eighteenth century, the idea was adopted by Meissen and by French manufacturers who produced not only china nodders but bisque as well. Most nodders are individual; couples are unusual. The idea

remained popular until the end of the nineteenth century and was used during the Victorian era by toy manufacturers. Our advisor for nodders is Barry Larkins; he is listed in the Directory under Florida.

Augustinian monk, bsk/terra cotta, Portugal, ca 1900, 9" 150.00
Bear, dressed/holding tennis racket, bsk, mk, #9884, minimum value ..100.00
Boy w/derby hat & cigar, ...Be a Man on base, S&V mk, 4", minimum ...375.00
Chinese couple, bsk porc, 3-color, Germany, 1⅝", pr 75.00
Dutch barge captain w/lunch pail/wife w/broom, porc, 7½", pr, up to..350.00
English pointer on point, pewter, head on steel strap, 1900s, 9" L ..175.00
Falconer by tree-trunk candle holder, bsk, Conta & Boehme, 6½"..225.00
Mandarin man seated, pnt/fired bsk, unmk, 4½" 125.00
Oriental lady in fine kimono, post nodder, 10", from $125 to.....175.00
Oriental lady sitting cross-legged w/lg fan behind, porc, Germany, 6".795.00
Oriental man seated w/opium pipe, porc, unmk E Bohne Sohne, 3".200.00
Oriental peasant holds basket w/turnip, by lg basket, 8½", minimum..100.00
Policeman drawing saber, sways 2 ways, Portugal, 1901, 9¼", up to.150.00
Russian child in fur coat & hat, seated, porc, E Bohne Sohne, 2¼"..125.00
Santa sitting atop chimney, spring neck, Vcago, Japan, 5¾", $50 to..75.00
Skeleton, spring legs, stands on tray, bsk, Japan, post WWII, up to....75.00
Snoopy, pnt papier-mache, United Features Syndicate, ca 1958, 3"..125.00
Victorian lady in chair, w/cap/apron, porc, 4½x4¼", from $150 to..200.00

Nordic Art Glass

Finnish and Swedish glass has recently started to develop a following, probably stemming from the revitalization of interest in forms from the 1950s. (The name Nordic is used here because of the inclusion of Finnish glass — the term Scandinavian does not refer to this country.) Included here are Flygsfors, Hadeland, Holmegaard, Iittala, Maleras, Motzfeldt, Nuutajarvi, and Strombergshyttan.

Our suggested prices are fair market values, developed after researching the Nordic secondary markets, the current retail prices on items still being produced, and American auction houses and antique stores.

Our advisor for this category is William L. Geary; he is listed in the Directory under Colorado.

Flygsfors Glass Works, Sweden

Flygsfors Glass Works was established in 1888 and continued in production until 1979 when the Orrefors Glass Group, which had acquired this entity, ceased operations.

Flygsfors is well known for art glass designed by Paul Kedelv, who joined the firm in 1949 with a contract to design light fittings, a specialty of the company.

Their 'Coquille' series, which utilizes a unique overlay technique combining opaque, bright colors, and 'Flamingo' have become very desirable on today's secondary market. Other internationally known artists/designers include Prince Sigvard Bernadotte and the Finnish designer Helene Tynell.

Bowl, Coquille, cranberry & wht, oblong w/flared ends, Kedelv, 11"..195.00
Bowl, Coquille, pk w/cobalt to clear o/l, pinched, Kedelv, 5x3"....75.00
Lamp, gr w/clear o/l, tall stem, flared base, 11" 285.00
Vase, bull & sun motif, mold-blown, rectangular, Bernt, 8" 55.00
Vase, Coquille, bl/red, flared wings, Kedelv, 10¼" 190.00
Vase, Coquille, maroon/gr, flared wings, Kedelv, 13" 265.00
Vase, Flamingo, teardrop w/woven gr/brn/wht threads, Kedelv, 10½"..245.00

Hadeland Glassverk, Norway

Glass has been produced at this glassworks since 1765. From the beginning, their main product was bottles. Since the 1850s they have made small items — drinking glasses, vases, bowls, jugs, etc., and for the last forty years, figurines, souvenirs, and objects of art.

Important designers include Willy Johansson, Arne John Jutrem, Inger Magnus, Severin Brorby, and Gro Sommerfelt.

Bowl, pk w/blk rim & ft, I Magnus, #10747, 8" **225.00**
Bowl, presentation; clear w/eng cranes & stylized leaves, 8x11⅝" ..**150.00**
Plate, clear w/brn & bl, A Jon Jutrem, #10814, 23½" **295.00**
Plate, opal w/amber center, textured underside, Gro Sommerfelt, 9½" ..**65.00**
Sculpture, polar bear, cast technique, 4¾" **45.00**
Vase, bud; pk underlay, gr speckled base w/wht & blk threads, 6½" ...**65.00**
Vase, cranberry teardrop form, W Johansson, 11½" **50.00**

Holmegaard Glassvaerk, Denmark

This company was founded in 1825. Because of a shortage of wood in Denmark, it became necessary for them to use peat, the only material available for fuel.

Their first full-time designers were hired after 1923. Orla Juul Nielson was the first. He was followed in 1925 by Jacob Band, an architect. Per Lukin became the chief designer in 1941. His production and art glass incorporates a simple yet complex series of designs. They continue to be popular among collectors of Scandinavian glass.

During 1965 the company merged with Kastrup and became Kastrup Holmegaard AS; a merger with Royal Copenhagen followed in 1975.

Bowl, wht w/orange o/l, flattened form, Michael Bang, 2x7" **25.00**
Jar, gr, sq w/short neck, Per Lukin, 6½x5⅞" **35.00**
Vase, Flame, gr w/clear o/l, Per Lukin, 9⅛x3½" **100.00**
Vase, wht opal w/purple lines/2 musical notes, cylinder, Lukin, 6¾" ..**50.00**
Vase, wht w/orange o/l, flared body w/short neck, O Bauer, 4¾x6" ..**65.00**

Iittala Glass Works, Finland

This glassworks was founded in 1881; it was originally staffed by Swedish workers who produced glassware of very high quality. In 1917 Ahiststrom OY bought and merged Iittala with Karhula Glass Works. After 1945 Karhula's production was limited to container glass. In 1946 Tapio Wirkkala, the internationally known artist/designer, became Iittala's chief designer. Timo Sarpeneva joined him in 1950. Jointly they successfully spearheaded the promotion of Finnish glass in the international markets, winning many international awards for their designs. Today, Oiva Toikka leads the design team.

Sculpture, Dancing Leaves, clear w/paste-on bk ground, Sundsrrom, 9" ..**40.00**
Sculpture, Dog Listens to Rain, Marko Salo, 8¼" L **275.00**
Sculpture, Raven (bird) O Toikka, 4¼x6½" **350.00**
Vase, Aalto Flower, clear, 4 forms, Alvar Aalto.......................**1,575.00**
Vase, Claritas, blk/opal/clear, Timo Sarpaneva, 10¼" **1,000.00**
Vase, Kantarelli, Tapio Wirkkala, 8"...**825.00**
Vase, Marcel, ltd ed, Timo Sarpaneva, 11¾" **1,000.00**
Vase, Orkidea, clear crystal, T Sarpaneva, in production since 1953 ..**325.00**

Maleras Glass Works, Sweden

The first glassworks at Maleras was founded in 1890. The city of Maleras was an important railway junction in Smaland, the Kingdom of Crystal, where articles from many of the glasshouses were shipped to the Swedish cities of Stockholm, Goteborg, and Malmo.

During the 1940s the company built a reputation throughout Sweden as one of the leading manufacturers of lead crystal. In 1975 the company joined the Royal Krona Group. Six years later, under the leadership of Mats Jonasson, the glassblowers and members of the community bought the factory from the existing management.

During the last twenty years, the company has produced first-class crystal sculptures of wildlife, which are sold around the world. Mats Jonasson is the master designer, and his wildlife images and engraving techniques are superb. Two other designers, artists Erika Hoglund and Lars Goran Tinback, are also important elements in this company's success.

Sculpture, Agitator, ltd ed, Mats Jonasson................................**3,200.00**
Sculpture, Bears, clear, ltd ed, Mats Jonasson **2,100.00**
Sculpture, Feather Dreamer, female form, red/crystal, Hoglund, 14½" .**550.00**
Sculpture, Owl, clear, ltd ed, Mats Jonasson, 13" **2,100.00**
Sculpture, Plura, Erika Hoglund, 9¼" **875.00**
Sculpture, Sharks, clear, Mats Jonasson, 7¼" **190.00**
Vase, Navarra, red underlay teardrop w/blk pulled up neck, Tinback ..**265.00**
Vase, Twister, red/wht/bl, Klas-Goran Tinback **490.00**

Benny Motzfeldt, Norwegian Glass Artist

Benny Motzfeldt, a graduate of the Arts and Crafts School of Oslo, Norway, started her career in glass in 1954 by responding to an ad for a designer of engraving and decoration at Christiania Glassmagasin and Hadeland Glassverk. After several years at Hadeland, she joined the Plus organization and managed their glass studio in Frederikstad. She is acknowledged as one of the leading exponents of Norwegian art glass and is recognized internationally. She challenged the rather sober Norwegian glass designs with a strong desire to try new ways, using vigorous forms and opaque colors embedded with silver nitrate patterns.

Bottle, clear w/wht shards, short neck, sgn, 6" **65.00**
Bowl, bl & gr w/bubbled glass applications w/wht & blk shards, 3x5" .**95.00**
Bowl, orange w/int bubbles, sgn, 9¾x6⅛" **75.00**
Vase, wht underlay w/gold frit bands & vertical lines, 7¼x4¼" ..**100.00**
Vase, yel w/orange band at rim & bottom, ftd, sgn, 7x7" **100.00**

Nuutajarvi Glass Works, Finland

Bowl, dk gray-bl bowl in flower shape, Jaako Neimi, 1¾" **75.00**
Bowl, pk heart shape, Kan Franck, 4"...**65.00**
Goblet, yel cup on wht stem & ft, Kaj Franck, 8½" **185.00**
Vase, amber underlay, bubbles surround, rnd, Gunnel Nyman, 4" .**775.00**
Vase, clear w/purple circle, apple form w/short neck, S Hopea, 3½" ..**295.00**
Vase, Kupla, bl to clear base w/low turq bubble, Saara Hopea, 7" ..**350.00**
Vase, Serpentine, clear w/wht winding glass ribbon, G Nyman, 18¼" ..**2,950.00**

Strombergshyttan, Sweden

The original factory, Lindefors, was founded in 1876. Although the factory was modernized in the 1920s, it closed in 1931. In 1933 Edvard Stromberg bought the factory; Gerda Stromberg designed for the company until 1942. In 1945 the factory was purchased by Stromberg's son Eric and his wife Asta. She designed for them until 1976. Edvard worked with Eric, who was a chemist, and together they developed a new color of glass with a distinctive bluish-silver hue which became the factory's speciality.

Gunnar Nylund, famous for his copper wheel-engraved forms, was at the glassworks from 1952 until 1975.

After a renovation in 1962, the factory suffered a serious fire and due to economic conditions was sold to Orrefors Glass Works; it operated under that title until it closed in 1979.

Sculpture, girl & deer w/trees, cast crystal, 7x6" **65.00**
Vase, bl-silver teardrop w/eng girl & flying bird, Nylund, 10" **225.00**
Vase, dk gray, B963, Stromberg, 14½" **110.00**
Vase, gray w/circles of air, Ariel technique, B943 Stromberg, 5" .**210.00**

Noritake

The Noritake Company was first registered in 1904 as Nippon Gomei Kaisha. In 1917 the name became Nippon Toki Kabushiki Toki. The 'M in wreath' mark is that of the Morimura Brothers, distributors with offices in New York. It was used until 1941. The 'tree crest' mark is the crest of the Morimura family.

The Noritake Company has produced fine porcelain dinnerware sets and occasional pieces decorated in the delicate manner for which the Japanese are noted. (Two dinnerware patterns are featured below, and a general range is suggested for others.)

Authority Joan Van Patten has compiled a lovely book, *The Collector's Encyclopedia of Noritake*, with many full-color photos and current prices; you will find her address in the Directory under New York. For more information, we recommend *Collector's Encylopedia of Early Noritake* by Aimee Nef Alden, also available from Collector Books. In the following listings, examples are hand painted unless noted otherwise. Numbers refer to these specific marks:

Key:
#1 — Komaru	#3 — N in Wreath
#2 — M in Wreath	

Azalea

The Azalea pattern was produced exclusively for the Larkin Company, who gave the lovely ware away as premiums to club members and their home agents. From 1916 through the 1930s, Larkin distributed fine china which was decorated in pink azaleas on white with gold tracing along edges and handles. Early in the '30s, six pieces of crystal hand painted with the same design were offered: candle holders, a compote, a tray with handles, a scalloped fruit bowl, a cheese and cracker set, and a cake plate. All in all, seventy different pieces of Azalea were produced. Some, such as the fifteen-piece child's set, bulbous vase, china ashtray, and the pancake jug, are quite rare. One of the earliest marks was the Noritake 'M in wreath' with variations. Later the ware was marked 'Noritake, Azalea, Hand Painted, Japan.' Our advisor for Azalea is Linda Williams; she is listed in the Directory under Massachusetts.

Basket, mint; Dolly Varden, #193 ....**165.00**
Bonbon, #184, 6¼" **60.00**
Bowl, #12, 10" **42.50**

Bowl, candy/grapefruit; #185, $210.00. (Photo courtesy of Linda Williams)

Bowl, cream soup; #363 ....**175.00**
Bowl, deep, #310 ....**68.00**
Bowl, fruit; #9, 5¼" **12.00**
Bowl, fruit; shell form, #188, 7¾" **385.00**
Bowl, fruit; scalloped, glass **95.00**
Bowl, oatmeal; #55, 5½" **28.00**
Bowl, soup; #19, 7⅛" **28.00**
Bowl, vegetable; divided, #439, 9½" **295.00**

Bowl, vegetable; oval, #101, 10½" 60.00
Bowl, vegetable; oval, #172, 9¼" 58.00
Butter chip, #312, 3¼" 120.00
Butter tub, w/insert, #54 ....48.00
Cake plate, #10, 9¾" 40.00
Candle holders, glass, 3½", pr 100.00
Candy jar, w/lid, #313 ....750.00
Casserole, gold finial, w/lid, #372 ....425.00
Casserole, w/lid, #16 ....95.00
Celery tray, #444, closed hdls, 10" 330.00
Celery/roll tray, #99, 12" 55.00
Cheese/butter dish, #314 ....135.00
Cheese/cracker, glass 110.00
Child's set, #253, 15-pc 2,500.00
Coffeepot, AD; #182 ....695.00
Compote, #170 ....98.00
Compote, glass 95.00
Condiment set, #14, 5-pc 65.00
Creamer & sugar bowl, #7 ....45.00
Creamer & sugar bowl, AD; open, #123, from $125 to 140.00
Creamer & sugar bowl, gold finial, #401 ....155.00
Creamer & sugar bowl, scalloped, ind, #449 ....395.00
Creamer & sugar shaker, berry; #122 ....150.00
Cruet, #190 ....210.00
Cup & saucer, #2 ....20.00
Cup & saucer, AD; #183 ....195.00
Cup & saucer, bouillon; #124, 3½" 28.00
Egg cup, #120 ....40.00
Gravy boat, #40 ....48.00
Jam jar set, #125, 4-pc 155.00
Mayonnaise set, scalloped, #453, 3-pc 525.00
Mustard jar, #191, 3-pc 38.00
Olive dish, #194 ....30.00
Pickle/lemon set, #121 ....24.50
Pitcher, milk jug; #100, 1-qt 225.00
Plate, #4, 7½" 10.00
Plate, bread & butter; #8, 6½" 10.00
Plate, breakfast/luncheon; #98 ....28.00
Plate, dinner; #13, 9¾" 22.00
Plate, grill; 3-compartment, #38, 10¼" 195.00
Plate, salad, 7⅝" sq 85.00
Plate, scalloped sq, salesman's sample 950.00
Plate, tea; #4, 7½" 10.00
Platter, #17, 14" 60.00
Platter, turkey; #186, 16" 525.00
Platter, #56, 12" 58.00
Platter, cold meat/bacon; #311, 10¼" 195.00
Refreshment set, #39, 2-pc 48.00
Relish, #194, 7⅛" 65.00
Relish, oval, #18, 8½" 20.00
Relish, 2-part, #171 ....58.00
Relish, 2-part, loop hdl, #450 ....390.00
Relish, 4-section, #119, rare, 10" 160.00
Saucer, fruit; #9, 5¼" 10.00
Shakers, bell form, #11, pr 30.00
Shakers, bulbous, #89 ....42.00
Shakers, ind, #126, pr 32.00
Spoon holder, #189, 8" 115.00
Syrup, #97, w/underplate & lid 110.00
Tea tile 40.00
Teapot, #15 ....110.00
Teapot, gold finial, #400 ....495.00
Toothpick holder, #192, from $115 to 120.00
Vase, bulbous, #452 ....1,500.00

Vase, fan form, ftd, #187 ....**185.00**
Whipped cream/mayonnaise set, #3, 3-toed, 3-pc **38.50**

Tree in the Meadow

Another of their dinnerware lines has become a favorite of many collectors. Tree in the Meadow is a scenic hand-painted pattern which features a thatched cottage in a meadow with a lake in the foreground. The version accepted by most collectors will have a tree behind the cottage and will not have a swan or a bridge. The colors resemble a golden sunset on a fall day with shades of orange, gold, and rust. This line was made during the 1920s and 1930s and seems today to be in good supply. A fairly large dinnerware set with several unusual serving pieces can be readily assembled. Our advisor for Tree in the Meadow is Linda Williams; she is listed in the Directory under Massachusetts.

Basket, Dolly Varden **125.00**
Bowl, cream soup; 2-hdl **35.00**
Bowl, fruit; shell form, #210 ....**285.00**
Bowl, oatmeal **15.00**
Bowl, oval, 9½" **48.00**
Bowl, oval, 10½" **58.00**
Bowl, soup **38.00**
Bowl, vegetable; 9" **35.00**
Butter pat **25.00**
Butter tub, open, w/drainer **35.00**
Cake plate, open hdl **35.00**
Candy dish, octagonal, w/lid, 5½" **425.00**
Celery dish **35.00**
Cheese dish **75.00**
Coffeepot, demitasse **250.00**
Compote **95.00**
Condiment set, 5-pc **45.00**
Creamer & sugar bowl, berry **125.00**
Cruets, vinegar & oil; cojoined, #319 ....**325.00**
Cup & saucer, breakfast **18.00**
Cup & saucer, demitasse **48.00**
Demitasse creamer & sugar bowl **125.00**
Egg cup **30.00**
Gravy boat **50.00**
Jam jar/dish, cherries on lid, 4-pc **125.00**
Lemon dish **15.00**
Mayonnaise set, 3-pc **48.00**
Plate, dinner; 9¾" **120.00**
Plate, salad; 8" **12.00**
Plate, 6½" **8.00**
Plate, 7⅝" sq, rare **75.00**
Platter, 10" **125.00**
Platter, 11¾x9" **58.00**
Platter, 13¾x10¼" **65.00**
Relish, divided **35.00**
Snack set (cup & tray), 2-pc **60.00**
Teapot **95.00**

Miscellaneous

Ashtray, cigarette & matches on brn, 4 rests, #2, 4¼" sq **90.00**
Ashtray, Deco-style lady smoking, #2, 1¾" **110.00**
Ashtray, flowers on shaded cream, 4 rests, #2, 5¾" **50.00**
Ashtray, harlequin figure seated at side, mc lustre, 32, 5" **375.00**
Ashtray, Indian chief's portrait, 3 rests, #2, 5½" **150.00**
Ashtray, pipe sits on club shape, #2, 5¼" **140.00**
Basket vase, gold o/l on cobalt, mk, 8¾" **350.00**
Basket vase, red w/floral int, gold hdl, #2, 5½" **140.00**
Bowl, floral rim w/cobalt on wht, gold hdls, #2, 8" **70.00**

Bowl, gold-lined floral, orange lustre rim, hdls, mk, 9½" **50.00**
Bowl, nappy, floral on wht w/gold, 1 pierced gold hdl, #2, 6½" **45.00**
Bowl, parrot on branch, blk rim, #2, 10" **85.00**
Bowl, river scenic on yel, gold hdls, #2, 7" **60.00**
Bowl, river scenic w/windmill, hdls, #2, 7" **65.00**
Bowl, salad; yel w/various vegetables on wht int, #2, 9¾" **125.00**
Bowl, sauce; floral w/exotic bird & tan lustre, #2, 4½", +ladle **50.00**
Cake plate, exotic birds, pk border w/gold, #2, 8¼" **70.00**
Candlesticks, floral on bl mottle w/cobalt & gold, sq ft, #2, 9", pr..**260.00**
Candlesticks, floral/exotic bird reserve on lustre, #2, 9¼", pr **240.00**
Candy dish, river scenic, 8 scallops, center hdl, #2, 7½" **50.00**
Candy jar, scenic reserve on lustre, w/lid, #2, 6½" **225.00**
Celery set, celery on shaded brn, hdls, #2, 12", +6 3¾" salts **140.00**
Chamberstick, floral band on orange lustre, #2, 4¾" **100.00**
Chocolate set, exotic bird w/gold, #2, 8¾" pot+6 c/s **350.00**
Cigarette holder, floral on bell shape, bird finial, #2, 5" **200.00**
Compote, man on camel w/cobalt & gold, ftd, mk, 3½x8½" **325.00**
Compote, 3 ladies form standard that supports bowl, #2, 7" **1,100.00**
Condensed milk container, Deco floral w/gold, #2, 5¼", +tray..**160.00**
Demitasse set, Deco floral w/red band, #2, pot+tray+cr/sug+6 c/s..**300.00**
Demitasse set, floral on wht w/orange lustre, pot+tray+cr/sug+6 c/s..**300.00**
Dresser set, bl band on wht w/gold decor, #2, 12½" tray +6 pcs .**260.00**
Dresser tray, scenic reserves in gold band on burgundy, mk, 13" L.**120.00**
Egg cup, fruit compote & gold on wht, #2, 3½" **45.00**
Ferner, red leaves & blk berries, triangle w/3 posts, #2, 6" **160.00**
Game set, deer in forest, geometric border, #2, 16" platter+8 plates..**2,000.00**
Honey jar, hive figural w/appl bees, #2, 5½" **140.00**
Humidor, couple smoking, yel band, gr #2, 6¾" **650.00**
Humidor, geometric floral on bl, pipe finial, #2, 3¾" **200.00**
Humidor, horse w/in horseshoe in relief, brn tones, #2, 7" **575.00**
Humidor, lion killing python in relief on red, #2, 6¾" **650.00**
Lemon dish, blossoms & leaves on yel, oval, #2, 6½" **40.00**
Mantle set, ornate Deco florals w/gold, #2, 9" bowl+2 9" candlesticks.**425.00**
Match holder, horses' heads on brn bell shape, #2, 3½" **150.00**
Mug, river scenic, #2, 3¼" **80.00**
Mustard jar, floral, bl on wht w/gold, #2, 3½", w/undertray **40.00**
Napkin ring, roses, mc on wht, #2, 2¼" **45.00**
Nut dish, nuts in relief, silver trim, #2, 8" L................................**100.00**
Plaque, elk in relief, brn tones, #2, 10½" **500.00**
Plate, sandwich; river scenic, center hdl, #2, 8" **65.00**
Playing card holder, horse's head on lustre, ftd, #2, 3¾" **150.00**
Potpourri jar, floral on bl, bud finial, #2, 6½" **130.00**
Punch bowl, sunset scene w/gold & cobalt, scroll hdls/ft, #2, 14" W..**750.00**
Punch set, peacock reserve w/gold on pk, #2, 9x16" bowl+8 cups ...**1,200.00**
Snack set, floral on cream w/yel border, #2, cup+7½" tray.........**65.00**
Sugar bowl, parrots on red, gold hdls, w/lid, #2, 3¼" **35.00**
Syrup, Deco-style floral on wht w/gold, undertray, #2, 4½"...........**75.00**
Tea set, floral on blk w/gold, #2, 6" pot+cr/sug **165.00**
Tea set, river scenic w/ornate gold, mk, 6¾" pot+cr/sug+6 c/s.....**525.00**
Tray, horses' heads emerging from trees, hdls, #2, 12" L...............**100.00**
Trinket box, lady w/whippet, ftd, gold finial, #2, 3" lI **200.00**
Trinket dish, desert scene, earth tones, center hdl, mk, 2¼" **25.00**
Vase, bird by tree trunk, mc lustres, #2, 5⅛" **275.00**
Vase, cottage by lake scene, sm angle hdls, #2, 6¼" **140.00**
Vase, Deco-style florals, 4 integral hdls, #2, 7¼", pr...................**275.00**
Vase, geometric band on orange lustre, waisted, #2, 8¾" **145.00**
Vase, leaping gazelles on blk w/flowers, hdls, #2, 10" **260.00**
Vase, swan scenic w/cobalt & gold, hdls, mk, 7½", pr **350.00**
Wall pocket, musician w/wide ruffled collar on lustre, #2, 6".......**300.00**

Various Dinnerware Patterns, ca. 1933 to Present

So many lines of dinnerware have been produced by the Noritake company that to list them all would require a volume in itself. In fact, just such a book is available — *The Collector's Encyclopedia of Early Noritake* by Aimee Neff Alden (Collector Books). And while many patterns had specific names, others did not, so you'll probably need the photographs the book contains to help you identify your pattern. Outlined below is a general guide for the more common pieces and patterns. The high side of the range will represent lines from about 1933 until the mid-1960s (including those marked 'Occupied Japan'), while the lower side should be used to evaluate lines made after that period.

Bowl, berry; ind, from $8 to	12.00
Bowl, soup; 7½", from $12 to	16.00
Bowl, vegetable; rnd or oval, ca 1945 to present, from $28 to	38.00
Butter dish, 3-pc, ca 1933-64, from $40 to	50.00
Creamer, from $18 to	28.00
Cup & saucer, demi; from $12 to	17.50
Gravy boat, from $35 to	45.00
Pickle or relish dish, from $18 to	28.00
Plate, bread & butter; from $8 to	12.00
Plate, dinner; from $15 to	30.00
Plate, luncheon; from $10 to	18.00
Plate, salad; from $10 to	15.00
Platter, 12", from $25 to	40.00
Platter, 16" (or larger), from $40 to	60.00
Shakers, pr, from $15 to	25.00
Sugar bowl, w/lid, from $18 to	30.00
Tea & toast set (sm cup & tray), from $18 to	28.00
Teapot, demi pot, chocolate pot, or coffeepot, ea, from $45 to	60.00

Norse

The Norse Pottery was established in 1903 in Edgerton, Wisconsin, by Thorwald Sampson and Louis Ipson. A year later it was purchased by A.W. Wheelock and moved to Rockford, Illinois. The ware they produced was inspired by ancient bronze vessels of the Norsemen. Designs were often incised into the red clay body. Dragon handles and feet were favored decorative devices, and they achieved a semblance of patina through the application of metallic glazes. The ware was marked with model numbers and a stylized 'N' containing a vertical arrangement of the remaining letters of the name. Production ceased after 1913. Our advisor for this category is John Danis; he is listed in the Directory under Illinois.

Bowl, band of cvd waves, 3 dragon-head ft, 4x7½"	325.00
Bowl, incised rising sun, dragon-head hdls, #50, 7½" L	250.00
Bowl, owls in relief, blk w/verdigris & gold, #30, 4x6"	400.00
Bowl, stylized animal hdls, #14, 6x11"	1,200.00
Candlestick, blk w/gold snake looped at base, #54, 12", pr	275.00
Chamberstick, bronze colored, 5", NM	125.00
Jardiniere, incised snake, 3 Viking head ft, verdigris, #62, 7x9"	500.00
Mug, incised decor, blk w/bronze wash, #51, 5"	150.00
Vase, angle shoulder w/2 lg dragons as hdls, #6, 7½x14½"	1,500.00
Vase, flat shoulder w/cvd geometrics, zigzag hdls, 7x3"	170.00
Vase, geometrics at top, gold remnants, #45, 4½"	95.00
Vase, slash mks at shoulder, #43, 9x1¾"	100.00
Wall pocket, dmn shape w/lizards, #72, 11"	2,500.00

North Dakota School of Mines

The School of Mines of the University of North Dakota was established in 1890, but due to a lack of funding it was not until 1898 that Earle J. Babcock was appointed as director, and efforts were made to produce ware from the native clay he had discovered several years earlier. The first pieces were made by firms in the East from the clay Babcock

sent them. Some of the ware was decorated by the manufacturer; some was shipped back to North Dakota to be decorated by native artists. By 1909 students at the University of North Dakota were producing utilitarian items such as tile, brick, shingles, etc., in conjunction with a ceramic course offered through the chemistry department. By 1910 a ceramic department had been established, supervised by Margaret Kelly Cable. Under her leadership, fine artware was produced. Native flowers, grains, buffalo, cowboys, and other subjects indigenous to the state were incorporated into the decorations. Some pieces have an Art Nouveau/Art Deco style easily attributed to her association with Frederick H. Rhead, with whom she studied in 1911. During the '20s the pottery was marketed on a limited scale through gift and jewelry stores in the state. From 1927 until 1949 when Miss Cable announced her retirement, a more widespread distribution was maintained with sales branching out into other states. The ware was marked in cobalt with the official seal — 'Made at School of Mines, N.D. Clay, University of North Dakota, Grand Forks, N.D.' in a circle. Very early ware was sometimes marked 'U.N.D.' in cobalt by hand. Our advisor for this category is William M. Bilsland III; he is listed in the Directory under Iowa.

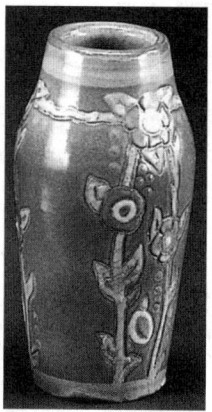

Vase, stylized flowers on long stems, red, blue, and green on blue, Reinert 1938, 7½x3¼", $1,800.00.

Bowl, geometrics on bl, #252, 3x7"	520.00
Bowl, lt to dk brn, built-in flower frog, sgn WRS, 4¼x6"	80.00
Bowl vase, birds of paradise/cornflowers band, yel/bls/gr on bl, 4x8"	1,765.00
Coaster, cvd cyote, gr matt, ink stamp, 3½"	275.00
Cookie jar, Mammy, 2-tone brn, M Cable, 10½x6¾"	1,645.00
Figurine, rabbit, tan gloss, sgn Billy, 4" L	350.00
Trivet, band of rabbits, periwinkle/dk bl, J Mattson, 6½"	1,295.00
Trivet, pears/grapes in bl/gr/brn on ivory w/dk bl border, 4¾" dia	235.00
Vase, acorn band, cvd/stylized, gr/brn matt, J Mattson, 3x3¼"	700.00
Vase, band of prairie roses, beige & blk on brn, Huckfield, 4½x4"	1,050.00
Vase, cowboy/cactus cvd band, 2-tone brn, flared sides, Mattson, 4x5"	850.00
Vase, cowboys, brn, ovoid, J Mattson, ink stamp, 7¼x5"	1,000.00
Vase, cvd flickertail, gr matt, JM (Mattson), 4½"	1,150.00
Vase, cvd panels w/fawn in forest, lt brn, Bjerken, 3½x5"	330.00
Vase, cvd wheat band, orange matt, ink stamp/incised ND Wheat, 3x4"	450.00
Vase, Deco florals, mc on bl, bulbous, Huckfield, 3x3¾"	495.00
Vase, floral emb on pk gloss, sgn FLH, 3"	450.00
Vase, Indian motif, yel & blk on red, ink stamp, 4x5"	175.00
Vase, jonquils, gr matt, M Cable, ink stamp, 5½x5½"	2,935.00
Vase, mustard yel, bulbous w/3 bands at top, 3"	45.00
Vase, olive gr matt, swollen, sgn SEW, 6"	325.00
Vase, pioneers/covered wagons in band on brn gloss, Huck, 4½x3½"	1,880.00
Vase, stylized floral, brn, Sorenson, 1942, 7x6"	2,235.00

North State

In 1924 the North State Pottery of Sanford, North Carolina, began small-scale production, the result of the extreme fondness Mrs. Rebecca Copper had for potting. With the help of her husband Henry and the abundance of suitable local clay, the pottery flourished and became well known for lovely shapes and beautiful glazes. They shared the knowledge they gained from their glaze experiments with the ceramic engineering department of North Carolina University; and during summer vacation, they often employed some of the university students. Salt glazed stoneware was produced in the early years but was quickly abandoned in favor of Henry's vibrant glazes. Colors of copper red, Chinese Red, moss green, and turquoise blue were used alone and combination, producing bands of blending colors. Some swirl ware was made as well. The pottery was in business for thirty-five years; most of its ware was sold in gift and craft shops throughout North Carolina. Items in the following descriptions are earthenware unless noted stoneware within the line.

Bowl, turq on flambé, 1-hdl, 1930s-40s, 2⅛x5" sq 9.00
Candlestick, turq w/rust specks, 2x4½" 25.00
Flower jug, turq dbl-dip/burgundy flambé, hdl, '30s, W Owen, 3½" ..175.00
Jug, buggy; orange-brn, single hdl, W Owen, 1940s-50s, 4⅞x6" ...40.00
Jug, lava-like turq dbl-dip/turq/flambé burgundy, '38, W Owen, 7"..500.00
Pitcher, bl-blk gloss on feldspathic gray, stoneware, J Owen, '26, 7" .450.00
Pitcher, cobalt gloss over gray, W Owen, ca 1920s, 3¾" 500.00
Pitcher, multi-gr dbl-dip burgundy/flambé reduction, '40s, W Owen, 7" ..200.00
Pitcher, Rebekah, brn matt over glossy brn, Elvin Owen, 1950s, 6⅛" ..50.00
Tea set, yel gloss, W Owen, 1940s-50s, 6½" pot+cr/sug 200.00
Teapot, lava-like turq/red/oxblood/burgundy flambé, W Owen, 7" L, NM...550.00
Teapot, low-gloss Chrome Red, unmk, 1930s, 8" L, EX...............225.00
Teapot, turq on flambé, W Owen, 1930s-40s, 6¼", EX 175.00
Vase, aqua-turq dbl dip on brn, W Owen, 1950s, 7¼", NM..........60.00
Vase, burgundy/turq flambé, W Owen, simple shape, late '30s, 7½" ..550.00
Vase, Chrome Red, pinched fan form, W Owen, 1930s-40s, rstr, 5½"..90.00
Vase, flambé gloss over celadon, pinched sides, W Owen,7".......400.00
Vase, multi-gr semigloss, 3 rim hdls, 1930s, CB Craven, 7".........275.00
Vase, orange-brn, fan form, W Owen, 1940s-50s, 3¾x6½" 60.00
Vase, red/burgundy w/turq flambé, hdls, stoneware, W Owen, 10", G..300.00
Vase, red/rose w/lt gr flambé, hdls, stoneware, W Owen, '30s, 6", EX...175.00
Vase, turq dbl-dip/burgundy flambé, simple form, ca '30, W Owen, 4".350.00
Vase, turq on flambé, 3-hdl, W Owen, 1930s, rpr, 15" 600.00
Wall sconce, moss gr w/slightly dk drip, bottle shape, 7½x3¾" 20.00

Northwood

The Northwood Company was founded in 1896 in Indiana, Pennsylvania, by Harry Northwood, whose father, John, was the art director for Stevens and Williams, an English glassworks. Northwood joined the National Glass Company in 1899 but in 1901 again became an independent contractor and formed the Harry Northwood Glass Company of Wheeling, West Virginia. He marketed his first carnival glass in 1908, and it became his most popular product. His company was also famous for its custard, goofus, and pressed glass. Northwood died in 1923, and the company closed. See also Carnival; Custard; Goofus; Opalescent; Pattern Glass.

Bowl, berry; Regent (Leaf Medallion), amethyst w/gold, lg.........190.00
Bowl, berry; Royal Oak, crystal & frosted, 7½"..............................60.00
Bowl, sauce; Posies & Pods, emerald gr w/gold................................30.00
Butter dish, #12 Semi-Cut, gr w/gold 200.00
Butter dish, Regal, gr w/gold 145.00
Butter dish, Regent (Leaf Medallion), gr w/gold..........................400.00
Butter dish, Royal Oak, frosted rubena..425.00
Creamer, Grape & Gothic Arches, emerald gr w/gold...................60.00
Creamer, Leaf Medallion, gr w/gold...95.00
Creamer, Royal Ivy, rainbow frost, crystal hdl, 4¾" 125.00
Creamer, Royal Oak, crystal & frosted 75.00

Cruet, Alaska, emerald gr w/clear stopper, 6"............................200.00
Cruet, Regent (Leaf Medallion), cobalt w/gold............................900.00
Cruet, Royal Ivy, lt cranberry w/clear hdl & stopper, 6½"...........600.00
Nut dish, Drapery, ice gr, 3½x7"..160.00
Pitcher, Cherry Lattice, crystal w/decor...75.00
Pitcher, Dandelion, gr w/gold...400.00
Pitcher, Flute, gr w/gold 145.00
Pitcher, Grapevine & Cherry Sprig, crystal w/satin fruit 95.00
Pitcher, Oriental Poppy, bl w/gold...425.00
Pitcher, Panelled Holly, gr w/gold, ftd...300.00
Pitcher, Peach, gr w/gold..225.00
Pitcher, Plums & Cherries (aka Two Fruits), crystal w/decor.........90.00
Pitcher, Posies & Pods, emerald gr w/gold...................................195.00
Pitcher, Regent (Leaf Medallion), amethyst 500.00
Pitcher, Regent (Leaf Medallion), gr w/gold 450.00
Pitcher, Teardrop Flower, amethyst w/gold.................................325.00
Shaker, Scroll w/Acanthus, lt gr..225.00
Shakers, Royal Ivy, rubena, 2¾", pr...165.00
Spooner, Royal Oak, crystal & frosted...45.00
Sugar bowl, Atlas, crystal w/gold & maiden's blush, w/lid............75.00
Sugar bowl, Grape & Gothic Arches, gr w/gold, w/lid...................75.00
Sugar bowl, Peach, gr w/gold, w/lid...150.00
Sugar shaker, Royal Ivy, rainbow craquelle, metal lid, 4¼" 400.00
Syrup, S-Repeat, amethyst, 4"..140.00
Toothpick holder, Leaf Umbrella, bl, 2½".....................................240.00
Toothpick holder, Royal Oak, frosted rubena................................165.00
Toothpick holder, Scroll w/Acanthus, bl w/gold............................150.00
Toothpick holder, Scroll w/Acanthus, purple slag, 2½".................160.00
Tumbler, Oriental Poppy, gr w/gold...60.00
Tumbler, Panelled Holly, gr w/gold..80.00
Tumbler, Peach, gr w/gold...45.00
Tumbler, Teardrop Flower, amethyst w/gold 65.00
Vase, pull-ups, rust & yel w/pk casing, bulbous w/long neck, 13" ..500.00
Vase, pull-ups, wht/turq on cream, ruffled, 3½x4" 350.00

Nutcrackers

The nutcracker, though a strictly functional tool, is a good example of one to which man has applied ingenuity, imagination, and engineering skills. Though all were designed to accomplish the same end, hundreds of types exist in almost every material sturdy enough to withstand sufficient pressure to crack the nut. Figurals are popular collectibles, as are those with unusual design and construction. Patented examples are also desirable. Our advisor for this category is Susan Otto; she is listed in the Directory under Ohio. For more information, we recommend *Nutcrackers* by Robert Mills.

Bear figural, cvd wood w/appl glass eyes, Zermatt, Switzerland, 8"..165.00
Bird, cvd wood, screw type, English, mid- to late 19th C, 6⅝"...125.00
Bird's head, pnt wood, long beak (levers), England, ca 1900, 8½"..200.00
Dog face, brass, English, late 1800s, 5½x1½x1½" 90.00
Dragon, CI w/old gold pnt, English, 1900-10, 5½x14x3⅛".........350.00
Eagle, cvd head w/glass eyes, ca 1900, 7½x3½x1½".................150.00
Elephant, pnt CI, nut crushed in mouth, Am, 1920s-30s, 4¾x9¾"..75.00
Girl w/hoop skirt, brass, screw type, England, ca 1956, 3½" 150.00
Grandfather's clock, brass, Made in England, ca 1925, 5½x1¼x¾"..25.00
Man in long coat, pnt CI, wooden base, Am, Pat 1870, 9¾x6½"..450.00
Man w/bowler hat, cvd boxwood, English, mid- to late 19th C, 8½".275.00
Parrot, pnt aluminum, tail lever, mid-20th C, 10" L....................20.00
Peasant figure, cvd wood, Spanish, attached tray, 1930s-40s, 10½"..90.00
Peasant woman, cvd wood figural, stands, Breton, 1920s-30s, 8½"..125.00
Ram, ornately cvd wood, Swiss or Tyrolean, ca 1900, 8¼" 225.00
Skull & X bones, NP CI, Banks..., Made in England, 1928, 6"...100.00

SP, non-figural w/eng hdls, mk Wallace Bros, ca 1900, 5¾".........**40.00**
Wolf or dog head, NP CI, Am, Pat 1920, 10" (including lever) ...**75.00**

Nutting, Wallace

Wallace Nutting (1861 – 1941) was America's most famous photographer of the early twentieth century. A retired minister, Nutting took more than 50,000 pictures, keeping 10,000 of his best and destroying the rest. His popular and bestselling scenes included exterior scenes (apple blossoms, country lanes, orchards, calm streams, and rural American countrysides), interior scenes (usually featuring a colonial woman working near a hearth), and foreign scenes (typically thatch-roofed cottages). His poorest selling pictures, which have become today's rarest and most highly collectible, are classified as miscellaneous unusual scenes and include categories not mentioned above: animals, architecturals, children, florals, men, seascapes, and snow scenes. Process prints are 1930s machine-produced reprints of twelve of Nutting's most popular pictures. These have minimal value and can be detected by using a magnifying glass.

Nutting sold literally millions of his hand-colored platinotype pictures between 1900 and his death in 1941. He started in Southbury, Connecticut, and later moved his business to Framingham, Massachusetts. The peak of Wallace Nutting picture production was 1915 – 1925. During this period Nutting employed nearly two hundred people, including colorists, darkroom staff, salesmen, and assorted office personnel. Wallace Nutting pictures proved to be a huge commercial success and scarcely an American household was without one by 1925.

While attempting to seek out the finest and best early American furniture as props for his colonial interior scenes, Nutting became an expert in early American antiques. He published nearly twenty books in his lifetime, including his 10-volume *State Beautiful* series and various other books on furniture, photography, clocks, stools, chairs, settles, settees, tables, stands, desks, mirrors, beds, chests of drawers, cabinet pieces, and treenware. He made furniture as well, which he clearly marked with a distinctive paper label that was glued directly onto the piece, or a block or script signature brand which was literally branded into the furniture.

The overall synergy of the Wallace Nutting name — on pictures, books, and furniture — has made anything 'Wallace Nutting' quite collectible.

Our advisor for this category is Michael Ivankovich, author of many books concerning Nutting. Those currently available are *Collector's Guide to Wallace Nutting Pictures*; *Collector's Guide to Early 20th Century American Prints*; *The Wallace Nutting Expansible Catalog*; *The Alphabetical and Numerical Index to Wallace Nutting Pictures*; *The Guide to Wallace Nutting Furniture*, *Wallace Nutting General Catalog, Supreme Edition*; *Wallace Nutting: A Great American Idea*; *Wallace Nutting's Windsors: Correct Windsor Furniture*; and *The Guide to Wallace Nutting-Like Photographers of the Early 20th Century*. Also available through Mr. Ivankovich is *The History of The Sawyer Pictures* by Carol Begley Gray. Mr. Ivankovich's address and ordering information are listed in the Directory under Pennsylvania.

Prices below are for pictures in good to excellent condition. Mat stains or blemishes, poor picture color, or frame damage can decrease value significantly.

Wallace Nutting Pictures

As It Was in 1700, 10x12" **250.00**
Birch Grove, 9x11" **165.00**
Chair for John, 11x14" **325.00**
Coming Out of Rosa, 13x16" **350.00**
Hawthornside, 13x16" **475.00**
Honeymoon Cottage, 10x12" **165.00**
In Tenderleaf, 11x17" **175.00**

Little River, 13x22" **250.00**
New Hampshire Drive, 11x17" **195.00**
Nuttinghome Blossoms, 12x14" **315.00**
Orchard Heights, 11x14" **195.00**
Patti's Favorite Walk, 10x12" **250.00**

Quilting Party, 16x20", $375.00.
(Photo courtesy Michael Ivankovich)

River's Song, 11x14" **185.00**
Rock Creek Banks, 10x12" **195.00**
Stitch in Time, 11x14" **295.00**
Summer Wind, 11x14" **185.00**
Turn of the River, Berkshires, 13x16" **235.00**
Untitled, girl at piano, 7x11" **145.00**
Untitled, swirling seas, 7x9" **185.00**
Warm Spring Day, 15x22" **425.00**
Whitsunday, 11x17" **195.00**

Wallace Nutting Books

England Beautiful, 2nd ed **45.00**
Maine Beautiful, 1st ed **45.00**
Maine Beautiful, 2nd ed **40.00**
New Hampshire Beautiful, 1st ed **45.00**
New Hampshire Beautiful, 2nd ed **40.00**
New York Beautiful, 2nd ed **45.00**
Vermont Beautiful, 2nd ed **40.00**

Wallace Nutting Furniture

Butterfly table, #625...**2,200.00**
Country Dutch chair, 3461 ....**400.00**
Country Dutch maple armchair, 3461 ....**750.00**
Game table w/rotating top **850.00**
Hutch table, pine...**825.00**
Ladder-bk side chair, 4-rung, #392, block brand **475.00**
Maple drop-leaf chair, 3603 ....**950.00**
Maple slat-bk chair, #374 ....**350.00**
Mirror, gold, 3-feather, #761, impressed brand **575.00**
NE ladderbk armchair, #492 ....**770.00**
NE ladderbk side chair, #490 ....**825.00**
Pembroke table, #628..**1,600.00**
Pilgrim armchair, 3493..**1,050.00**
Table, oak refractory, #601, block brand......................**935.00**
Table, trestle **500.00**
Wild Rose side chair, 3365 ....**440.00**
Windsor armchair, low-bk, #414, block brand, paper label..........**525.00**
Windsor candlestand, tripod, #17, block brand............**525.00**
Windsor side chair, bent-run bow-bk, bamboo trns, #305, block brand..**800.00**
Windsor side chair, fan-bk, old finish, brand/label, 44"..........**1,100.00**
Windsor stand, 3-leg, $605 ....**600.00**
Windsor stool, rnd, #104, block brand **300.00**
Windsor writing armchair, #451 ....**1,600.00**

Major Wallace Nutting-Like Photographers

Although Wallace Nutting was widely recognized as the country's leading producer of hand-colored photographs during the early twentieth century, he was by no means the only photographer selling this style of picture. Throughout the country literally hundreds of regional photographers were selling hand-colored photographs from their home regions or travels. The subject matters of these photographers was very comparable to Nutting's, including interior, exterior, foreign, and miscellaneous unusual scenes. The key determinants of value include the collectability of the particular photographer, subject matter, condition, and size. Keep in mind that only the rarest pictures in the best condition will bring top prices. Discoloration and/or damage to the picture or matting can reduce value significantly.

Several photographers operated large businesses, and although not as large or well known as Wallace Nutting, they sold a substantial volume of pictures which can still be readily found today. The vast majority of their work was photographed in their home regions and sold primarily to local residents or visiting tourists. It should come as little surprise that three of the major Wallace Nutting-like photographers — David Davidson, Fred Thompson, and the Sawyer Art Co. — each had ties to Wallace Nutting.

David Davidson: Second to Nutting in overall production, Davidson worked primarily in the Rhode Island and Southern Massachusetts area. While a student at Brown University around 1900, Davidson learned the art of hand-colored photography from Wallace Nutting, who happened to be the minister at Davidson's church. After Nutting moved to Southbury in 1905, Davidson graduated from Brown and started a successful photography business in Providence, Rhode Island, which he operated until his death in 1967.

Sawyer: A father and son team, Charles H. Sawyer and Harold B. Sawyer, operated the very successful Sawyer Art Company from 1903 into the 1970s. Beginning in Maine, the Sawyer Art Company moved to Concord, New Hampshire, in 1920 to be nearer their primary market of New Hampshire's White Mountains. Charles H. Sawyer briefly worked for Nutting in 1902 – 03 while living in southern Maine. Sawyer's production volume ranks #3 behind Wallace Nutting and David Davidson.

Fred Thompson: Frederick H. Thompson and Frederick M. Thompson were another father and son team that operated the Thompson Art Company (TACO) from 1908 to 1923, working primarily in the Portland, Maine, area. We know that Thompson and Nutting had collaborated because Thompson widely marketed an interior scene he had taken in Nutting's Southbury home. The production volume of the Thompson Art Company ranks #4 behind Nutting, Davidson, and Sawyer.

Davidson, Easter Bonnet, 5x7"	**75.00**
Davidson, Old Ironsides, 7x9"	**115.00**
Davidson, Roadside Mirror, 14x17"	**160.00**
Davidson, Snow Basin, 5x7"	**110.00**
Sawyer, San Juan, Capistrano, 10x13"	**235.00**
Thompson, Fireside Dreams, 7x9"	**125.00**

Minor Wallace-Like Photographers

Hundreds of other smaller local and regional photographers attempted to market hand-colored pictures comparable to Nutting's during the 1900 – 1930s time period. Although quite attractive, most were not as appealing to the general public as Wallace Nutting pictures. However, as the price of Wallace Nutting pictures has escalated, the work of these lesser-known Wallace Nutting-like photographers have become increasingly collectible.

A partial listing of some of these minor Wallace Nutting-like photographers include Babcock; J.C. Bicknell; Blair; Ralph Blood (Portland, Maine); Bragg; Brehmer; Brooks; Burrowes; Busch; Carlock; Pedro Caciola; Croft; Currier; Depue Bros; Derek; Dowly; Eddy; May Farini (hand-colored colonial lithographs); Geo. Forest; Gandara; Gardner (Nantucket, Bermuda, Florida); Gibson; Gideon; Gunn; Bessie Pease Gutmann (hand-colored colonial lithographs); Edward Guy; Harris; C Hazen; Knoffe; Haynes (Yellowstone Park); Margaret Hennesey; Charles Higgins; Hodges; Homer; Krabel; Kattleman; La Bushe; Lake; Lamson (Portland, Maine); M. Lightstrum; Machering; Rossiler Mackinae; Merrill; Meyers; William Moehring; Moran; Murrey; Lyman Nelson; J. Robinson Neville (New England); Patterson; Owen Perry; Phelps; Phinney; Reynolds; F. Robbins; Royce; Fred'k Scheetz (Phila., Pennsylvania); Shelton; Standley (Colorado); Stott; Summers; Esther Svenson; Florence Thompson; Thomas Thompson; M.A. Trott; Sanford Tull; Underhill; Villar; Ward; Wilmot; Edith Wilson; and Wright.

A very general breakdown of prices for works by these minor Wallace Nutting-like photographers would be as follows: larger pictures, greater than 14" x 17", from $75.00 to over $200.00; medium pictures, from 11" x 14" to 14" x 17", from $50.00 to $200.00; smaller pictures, 5" x 7" to 10" x 12", from $10.00 to $75.00.

The same pricing guidelines that apply to Wallace Nutting pictures typically apply to Wallace Nutting-like pictures.

1.) Exterior scenes are the most common.

2.) Some photographers sold colonial interior scenes as well.

3.) Subject, matter, condition, and size are all important determinants of value.

Gibson, Lover's Road, 13x15"	**85.00**
Gibson, Old Apple Tree, 11x14"	**75.00**
Harris, Ausable Chasm, 6x10"	**85.00**
Harris, Chapel Nombre de Dios, Fountain of Youth...Fla, 8x10"	**110.00**
Harris, Fountain of Youth, St Augustine Fla, 8x10"	**135.00**
Harris, Mt Lake Sanctuary & Singing Tower, Fla, 7x17"	**110.00**
Harris, Oldest House in US, St Augustine Fla, 4x8"	**125.00**
Harris, Oldest School House, St Augustine Fla, 7x9"	**125.00**
Harris, Watkins Glen NY, 4x8"	**75.00**
Haynes, Sylvan Lake & Top Notch Peak, 5x8"	**110.00**
Higgins, Pine Road, 13x15"	**145.00**

Occupied Japan

Items marked 'Occupied Japan' have become popular collectibles in the last few years. They were produced during the period from the end of World War II until April 18, 1952, when the occupation ended. By no means was all of the ware exported during that time marked 'Occupied Japan'; some was marked 'Japan' or 'Made In Japan.' It is thought that because of the natural resentment felt by the Japanese toward the occupation, only a fraction of these wares carried the 'Occupied' mark. Even though you may find identical 'Japan'-marked items, because of its limited use, only those with the 'Occupied Japan' mark are being collected to any great extent. Values vary considerably, based on the quality of workmanship. Generally, bisque figures command much higher prices than porcelain, since on the whole they are of a finer quality.

For those wanting more information, we recommend *Occupied Japan Collectibles* by Gene Florence; he is listed in the Directory under Kentucky. Our advisor for this category is Florence Archambault; she is listed in the Directory under Rhode Island. She represents the Occupied Japan Club, whose mailing address may be found in the Directory under Clubs, Newsletters, and Catalogs. All items described in the following listings are common ceramic pieces unless noted otherwise.

Ashtray, Georgia, shape of state, from $12.50 to	**20.00**
Ashtray, metal, football shape, from $5 to	**6.00**
Ashtray, metal, horse head in center, from $10 to	**12.50**

Candy dish, metal, 3-part, center hdl, from $10 to **12.50**
Christmas decoration, reindeer, celluloid, 7x7½", from $12.50 to..**15.00**
Christmas decoration, Santa, red papier-mache, from $40 to........**50.00**
Cigarette box, Moss Rose decor on wht, rectangular, from $8 to..**10.00**
Cigarette lighter, metal gun w/pearl hdls, from $17.50 to.............**25.00**
Cigarette lighter, metal knight figural, from $10 to **25.00**
Creamer, Blue Willow, child sz, 1½-2", from $12.50 to **15.00**
Crumb pan, emb metal, NY scenes, from $10 to............................**20.00**
Cup & saucer, daisy on wht, ornate hdl, ftd, from $10 to.............**15.00**
Cup & saucer, demitasse; floral on wht, from $10 to **12.00**
Cup & saucer, dragon on bl, Lucky China mk, from $17.50 to.....**20.00**
Cup & saucer, lg pk roses, high gold hdl, scalloped rims, $12.50 to..**20.00**
Cup & saucer, pk chintz, mk Merit, from $10 to............................**25.00**
Cup & saucer, wht w/blk & wht checkerboard border, from $5 to...**10.00**
Dinnerware, complete set for 4, w/3 szs plates+cr/sug+cereal/soups..**200.00**
Dinnerware, complete set for 6, as for 4+gravy & platter............**250.00**
Dinnerware, complete set for 8, as for 6+sm platter....................**350.00**
Dinnerware, complete set for 12, as for 4+3 platters & serving bowl..**500.00**
Doll, celluloid, baby in molded snowsuit, jtd, from $40 to **50.00**
Doll, celluloid, crocheted suit, 7", from $45 to.............................**50.00**
Doll, celluloid, football player, 6", from $12 to **20.00**
Doll, celluloid, nude, strung shoulders, 4¾", from $12.50 to.........**15.00**
Egg timer, Dutch girl stands beside sand timer, 3½", complete **30.00**
Figurine, angel w/mandolin, blond boy on base, 6⅜", from $25 to.**30.00**
Figurine, ballerina, arms up/away, net dress, 5¾", from $35 to......**40.00**
Figurine, bird on stump, mc, 7⅞", from $30 to **35.00**
Figurine, Black band member, 2¾", from $20 to...........................**22.50**
Figurine, Black shoeshine boy, 5½", from $50 to **55.00**
Figurine, blue jay, 2½", from $4 to..**5.00**
Figurine, boy w/saxophone, red hair, bl pants, 4⅝", from $8 to **10.00**
Figurine, bride & groom on base, traditional pose, pnt bsk, 6⅛" ..**50.00**
Figurine, cherub w/tambourine, pastels, on base, 7¼", from $75 to.**85.00**
Figurine, clown in striped suit, 5¼", from $35 to **40.00**
Figurine, Colonial man, bsk, pastels, 15½", from $150 to **175.00**
Figurine, Colonial man, on sm base, bsk, 7", from $27.50 to........**30.00**
Figurine, Colonial man in tricorner hat, 10", from $30 to............**35.00**
Figurine, Cupid beside lg open flower, mc pastels, 4", from $30 to.**35.00**
Figurine, dog, spaniel type, seated, 4⅜", from $20 to....................**25.00**
Figurine, duck, mallard-like, 3x5", from $12.50 to.......................**15.00**
Figurine, frog w/violin, pastels, 4¼", from $20 to.........................**22.00**
Figurine, girl w/book & basket, mc, 3¾", from $6 to **8.00**
Figurine, girl w/doll, blond standing, 4¼", from $12.50 to **15.00**
Figurine, horse on base, wht, 2¼", from $4 to...............................**5.00**
Figurine, horses jumping, brn pr on base, 5", from $35 to **45.00**
Figurine, lady seated & reading book, 5⅜", from $40 to...............**45.00**
Figurine, lion pride (3 lions) on base, brn tones, 4⅛", $45 to.......**50.00**
Figurine, man w/cape, bsk, pastels, 6", from $25 to.......................**30.00**
Figurine, Mexican man w/sombrero, 5¼", from $17.50 to.............**20.00**
Figurine, Oriental boy & girl kissing, lying on tummies, pr, $30 to.**35.00**
Figurine, Oriental lady w/basket on head, 7⅞", from $20 to..........**25.00**
Fish bowl decoration, castle atop bridge, from $10 to...................**12.00**
Fish bowl decoration, cat poised to hang from rim of bowl, from $20 to.**25.00**
Fish bowl decoration, sailing ship, from $7.50 to **9.00**
Ice bucket, lacquerware, 7⅝", from $50 to **60.00**
Lady bug (clothed) w/ball bat, 2¼", from $6 to **8.00**
Planter, boy pulling cart, bsk, pastels, 7", from $75 to **85.00**
Planter, cat beside, 3⅝", from $6 to **8.00**
Planter, couple w/rabbits sit before planter, bsk, mc, 5¼x7¼" **150.00**
Planter, dog w/bow at neck, blk spots, 4⅝", from $6 to **8.00**
Planter, duck w/cart, 3x5", from $6 to **7.50**
Planter, Oriental girl w/lg hat stands amid 2 baskets, 5⅛"............**17.50**
Plate, blackberries on stem, 6", from $12.50 to **15.00**
Plate, floral center, pierced rim, Rosetti, 8¼", from $22.50 to **25.00**
Plate, roses, mc on shaded ground, 7", from $25 to......................**35.00**

Shakers, seated Middle-Eastern figures; Windmills, $22.00 for each pair. (Photo courtesy Helen Guarnaccia)

Tea set, floral, pot+cr/sug+2 c/s, child sz, from $30 to **45.00**
Vase, angel boy supports flower-form (vase), pastels, 7½", $55 to.**60.00**
Vase, lacquerware, fern leaves, 13", from $125 to **150.00**

Ohr, George

George Ohr established his pottery in the 1880s in Biloxi, Mississippi. The first pottery burned down and was subsequently rebuilt. Ohr, among other things, was a master of the wheel. This mastery enabled him to create unique forms of unbelievable thinness, verging at times on Abstraction and looking far ahead toward many art movements of the twentieth century. In addition to Abstraction, by studying Ohr, one can discover elements of Expressionism and Fauvism (the wild use of color often seemingly at odds with the piece being glazed) and Dada (meaning shock the bourgeosie). An Ohr piece may be rooted in the functional form of a teapot, but following his manipulation it becomes a sculpture for which the functional form serves only as a take-off point for the finished piece. Ohr was also a master of glazes. Highly esteemed are his volcanic and gunmetal glazes. He was not well received in his day and sold few pieces of his art pottery — a van Gogh-like tale. Ohr decorated his pieces with snakes and lizards and sometimes with asymmetrical handles. He believed that like all things on earth, no two things should be alike. This dictum was applied to his pottery making. He signed his pieces either in impressed letters or florid script. In the early 1900s Ohr ceased making pottery and became a motorcycle dealer and ultimately sold automobiles. His pottery was stored away to be rediscovered many years later. Ohr died in 1918. Our advisors for this cateogry are Dave Rago and Suzanne Perrault; they are listed in the Directory under New Jersey.

Ashtray/pipe knocker, amber speckle, glaze drip/kiln kiss, 2¼x5"..**520.00**
Bowl, aventurine, deep vertical crimps on tapered body, ftd, 4x5", NM.**4,000.00**
Bowl, aventurine, horizontal dimples/folds, 3x4"....................**2,100.00**
Bowl, bsk, pinched/dimpled, 3-lobe opening, 3x5¼", NM.......**4,300.00**
Bowl, bsk w/dk iron flashes, gourd shape, 4¾x4¾" **2,070.00**
Bowl, mirror blk on amber, 4 pinched dimples in shoulder, 3x5"..**3,500.00**
Bowl, speckled ochre semimatt, rim swoops up on 1 side, 2¾x4".**3,000.00**
Bowl vase, bsk w/4 indents, 5½" dia..**600.00**
Chamberpot, brn/blk sponge, w/contents, opposing short lines, EX, 4"..**920.00**
Chamberstick, gunmetal, dimpled base, ribbed neck, 5x3¾"...**1,500.00**
Cup, brn gunmetal, lg triangular pinched/cut-out hdl, 3½".....**1,900.00**
Curio, shell/curlicues on notched bk, amber, 3¾x4½", VG, $1,000 to..**1,500.00**
Inkwell, artist palette w/2 pnt tubes+2 brushes+well, gr/gunmetal, VG..**4,000.00**
Jug, puzzle; brn/gr, incised wheat & landscape, 1899, 8x6¾" ...**1,400.00**
Mug, puzzle; brn rtcl circular pattern, rabbit hdl, twist base, 3½"..**1,150.00**
Mug, rose matt, gunmetal int, ear-shape hdl, 3¾x5", from $3,000 to.**4,000.00**
Pitcher, brn/amber mottle, incised bird of paradise/landscape, 7½"..**5,500.00**
Pitcher, cobalt glossy, scalloped side, 4½x4¾".........................**9,500.00**
Pitcher, pk/gr/red/wht sponged matt, scrolled ribbon hdl, 6½".**7,000.00**
Pitcher, tan/buff swirls, pinched spout/hdl, 2 lg rim chips, 5"..**3,250.00**
Pourer, khaki gr gloss, crimped rim, loop hdl, 1½x5"..............**1,980.00**

Puzzle mug, gunmetal & olive, stamped w/faux screw on bottom, 3¼".**1,840.00**
Teapot, brn/blk/gr/orange, in-body twist, serpent spout, 3⅞"...**6,750.00**
Teapot, gr speckle gloss, minor rstr spout/rim/lid, 4¼x6½".......**5,460.00**
Teapot, red/pk/wht sponge on amber, snake-like spout, 5½x12" L..**54,625.00**
Vase, amber, folded rim, dimpled body, tapered, 4x3" **3,340.00**
Vase, aventurine, 2nd side: blk, pinched/folded/dimpled, 4¾x3¾" ...**9,775.00**
Vase, bl/gr/gray/lav sponged (rare), dimpled base, folded rim, 5x6".**16,100.00**
Vase, bl/raspberry/gr sponge gloss, baluster, 5x2" **4,885.00**
Vase, blk/gr drip on cucumber, 3 khaki ft, yel int, 2¾x3¾" **1,550.00**
Vase, bottle gr semimatt w/powder deposits, ruffled/ftd, 3½x5", EX..**1,035.00**
Vase, brn bsk, flared mouth, invt cone, ped ft, 4x3" **1,045.00**
Vase, bsk, bowl form top tier on squat bulbous body, 4⅝" **2,000.00**
Vase, bsk, deep in-body twist, firing lines, 2¼x3¾" **2,100.00**
Vase, cadmium yel/lav/gr/pk volcanic, bulbous, 4x3¾" **2,700.00**
Vase, cobalt gloss, cupped rim, in-body twist, 3½x3¾".............**3,250.00**
Vase, dk bl drip gloss, bulbous w/twisted top, 4½x4½" **2,000.00**
Vase, gr mottle, asymetrical, folded/twisted rim, 3⅜x4½", NM ...**2,300.00**
Vase, gr/bl matt, cobalt/gr int, in-body twist, 4¼x4" **3,750.00**
Vase, gr/gunmetal, dbl-lobed top, pear-shaped body, 5x2½" **3,250.00**
Vase, gunmetal, corseted base, cupped rim, 3¾x2¼"..................**750.00**
Vase, hunter gr, oatmeal yel int, tulip-like form, 3½x2½" **1,300.00**
Vase, khaki to brn, twisted/pinched flowerpot form, 4¼", NM.**1,725.00**
Vase, mirror blk w/squat gunmetal base, flared/crumpled neck, 4½"..**6,000.00**
Vase, mottled dk brn/gunmetal, thrown off-center, can neck, 4½x3"..**2,000.00**
Vase, pebbly blk-gr gloss w/blk dots, 3-gourd shape, 4¾x2¾"..**2,250.00**
Vase, pk w/sponged-on gr & gunmetal band, folded/scalloped, 6x5".**17,000.00**
Vase, raspberry/blk speckle, gr rim flashes, ruffled, 3½x3¾", EX...**9,200.00**
Vase, raspberry/dk bl/gray, pinched/folded w/bulbous middle, 4½".**8,050.00**
Vase, red bsk, bulbous w/flared lip, 4⅜" **1,800.00**
Vase, red/amber/dk gr mottle gloss, pinched rim, in-body twist, 5x4"..**19,550.00**
Vase, speckled brn/amber, bulbous w/cinched waist, folded rim, 3x4"..**2,800.00**
Vase, tomato/dk gr speckle, amber/gr int, twisted w/cupped rim, 4x4"..**34,500.00**
Vase, yel/br/brn mottle, rnd w/short neck, 4".............................**3,680.00**

Old Ivory

Old Ivory dinnerware was produced from 1882 to 1920 by Herman Ohme, of Lower Salzbrunn in Silesia. The patterns are referred to by the numbers stamped on the bottom of many items. (Some early patterns are marked Old Ivory and are not numbered, but the vast majority bears the tiny blue fleur-de-lis/crown mark with Silesia or Germany beneath. Handwritten numbers signify something other than pattern.) Patterns #16 and #84 are the easiest to find and come in a wide variety of table items. Values are about the same for both patterns. Other floral designs include pink, yellow, and orange roses; holly; and lavender flowers — all on the same soft ivory background. Our price ranges are intended to represent a nationwide average, though you may have to pay a little more in some areas. Minor damage and gold wear can lower these prices by as much as 25%. Holly pieces command from 50% to 100% more than those listed below. Novice collectors should be aware of copy-cat versions from the turn of the century that are much heavier and of a coarser material. They are marked 'Old Ivory' without the blue trademark. They are not included in this listing.

Another area gaining in popularity is the vases from Ohme usually featuring portraits of Edwardian children. There are a few other forms with portraits, and these are very pricey, with 4" to 5" vases going in the range of $450.00 to $600.00, and 8" and 9" vases about $800.00 to $1,200.00.

Prices realized on the Internet for Old Ivory now rival RS Prussia. With so many collectors now buying on eBay, prices for common patterns have dropped while the rare patterns and pieces have skyrocketed in price. As prices have risen, many collections have come on the market, resulting in a drop in the prices of common pieces. Because of climbing values for Old Ivory, interest is growing for the clear-glazed pieces by Ohme, which

are still reasonable, though escalating in price. In comparison, while an Old Ivory open-handled cake plate might sell for $124.00 to $145.00, a comparable clear-glazed example might go for $45.00 to $55.00 with the same mark and mold. It should be noted that the same items with differing pattern numbers bring widely differing prices. For further information we recommend *Collector's Encyclopedia of Old Ivory China, The Mystery Explored,* by Alma Hillman (our advisor), David Goldschmitt, and Adam Szynkiewicz. Ms. Hillman is listed in the Directory under Maine.

Bowl, ftd, #28, 6", from $100 to.................................**150.00**
Bowl, oatmeal; #75, 6½", from $55 to.....................**95.00**
Celery dish, #10, 11¼", from $100 to.....................**195.00**
Compote, #42, 9", from $300 to.............................**500.00**
Cup & saucer, chocolate; #16, 2¼", from $95 to.......**125.00**
Cup & saucer, demitasse; #84, 2½", from $100 to.....**150.00**
Cup & saucer, tea; #7 , 3¼", from $65 to................**85.00**
Demitasse pot, #33, 7½", from $400 to....................**600.00**
Dish, 3-lobed, #200, 6", from $50 to.......................**95.00**
Egg cup, #16, 2½", from $450 to............................**700.00**
Jam jar, #200, 3½", from $250 to...........................**350.00**
Plate, bread & butter; #15, 7", from $30 to..............**75.00**
Plate, coupe; #75, 6¼", from $50 to.......................**75.00**
Plate, dinner; #11, 9½ or 10", from $200 to.............**275.00**
Plate, soup; #7, 10", from $175 to..........................**250.00**
Platter, #16, 21", from $500 to...............................**600.00**
Porringer, #32, 6¼", from $75 to............................**125.00**
Sugar bowl, #22, 5½", from $100 to........................**200.00**
Trinket box, portrait, 3", from $300 to.....................**600.00**

Old Paris

Old Paris porcelains were made from the mid-eighteenth century until about 1900. Seldom marked, the term refers to the area of manufacture rather than a specific company. In general, the ware was of high quality, characterized by classic shapes, colorful decoration, and gold application.

Bottle, scent; bird & scroll decor, sq, w/stopper, 3x3"................**110.00**
Censers, period couple on floral scrolled bases, 10", pr.............**385.00**
Figurines, lady & gentleman, ornate costumes, 1850s, 9", pr......**250.00**
Fruit stand, rtcl, scalloped border, gilt paw ft, 4½x9" **250.00**
Ice pail, mc floral bouquet on wht w/reeded gilt bands, lion hdls, 8" ..**1,150.00**
Pitcher, pk bands w/gold highlights on wht, 9" **100.00**
Platter, appl gr border, gilt edge, cut corners, 1850s, 15" L..........**230.00**
Urn, campagna; courting scene, mask hdls, 1840s, 9", pr.........**2,300.00**
Vase, chinoiserie figure in landscape, leaf/scroll hdls, gilt, 16", pr..**690.00**
Vase, gold w/reserve of lady w/putto, hdls, ftd, rstr, 13", pr **1,725.00**
Vase, mc floral w/gold, 13x9"...**300.00**
Vase, transfer: wedding (2nd w/baby), griffin hdls, drilled, 16", pr..**440.00**

Old Sleepy Eye

Old Sleepy Eye was a Sioux Indian chief who was born in Minnesota in 1780. His name was used for the name of a town as well as a flour mill. In 1903 the Sleepy Eye Milling Company of Sleepy Eye, Minnesota, contracted the Weir Pottery Company of Monmouth, Illinois, to make steins, vases, salt crocks, and butter tubs which the company gave away to their customers. A bust profile of the old Indian and his name decorated each piece of the blue and gray stoneware. In addition to these four items, the Minnesota Stoneware Company of Red Wing made a mug with a verse which is very scarce today.

In 1906 Weir Pottery merged with six others to form the Western Stoneware Company in Monmouth. They produced a line of blue and white ware using a lighter body, but these pieces were never given as flour premiums. This line consisted of pitchers (five sizes), steins, mugs, sugar bowls, vases, trivets, and mustache cups. These pieces turn up only rarely in other colors and are highly prized by advanced collectors. Advertising items such as trade cards, pillow tops, thermometers, paperweights, letter openers, postcards, cookbooks, and thimbles are considered very valuable. The original ware was made sporadically until 1937. Brown steins and mugs were produced in 1952. Our advisor for this category is Jim Martin; he is listed in the Directory under Illinois.

Barrel, flour; orig paper label, 1920s......................................1,000.00
Barrel, grapevine-effect banding...2,500.00
Barrel, oak w/brass bands 3,000.00
Barrel label, Chief Strong Bakers..., 16", EX+...........................170.00
Barrel label, mk Chief/Strong Bakers, image in center, 16", NM...200.00
Blanket, horse; w/logo, EX..1,000.00
Butter crock, Flemish bl & gray..650.00
Cabinet, bread display; Old Sleepy Eye etched in glass 950.00
Calendar, 1904, NM..375.00
Cookbook, Indian on cover, Sleepy Eye Milling Co, 4¾x4".......300.00
Cookbook, loaf of bread shape, NM 120.00
Coupon, for ordering cookbook 200.00
Dough scraper, tin/wood, To Be Sure, EX................................300.00
Fan, diecut image of Old Sleepy Eye, EX+ 200.00
Flour sack, cloth, mc Indian, red letters 345.00
Flour sack, paper, Indian in blk, blk lettering, NM....................125.00
Hot plate/trivet, bl & wht 3,500.00
Ink blotter..125.00
Letter opener, bronze..600.00
Match holder, pnt...800.00
Match holder, wht...850.00
Mug, bl & gray, 4¼"..300.00
Mug, bl & wht, 4¼"...150.00
Mug, verse, Red Wing, EX..1,200.00
Paperweight, bronzed company trademk 300.00
Pillow cover, Sleepy Eye & tribe meet President Monroe 350.00
Pillow cover, trademk center w/various scenes, 22", NM 800.00
Pin-bk button, Indian, rnd face 250.00
Pitcher, #1, 4"..200.00
Pitcher, #2...250.00
Pitcher, #3...275.00
Pitcher, #3, w/bl rim...1,000.00
Pitcher, #4...300.00
Pitcher, #5...350.00
Pitcher, bl & gray, 5"...300.00
Pitcher, bl on cream, 8", M..220.00
Pitcher, brn on yel, Sesquicentennial, 1981, from $100 to.........125.00
Pitcher, standing Indian, good color.......................................1,100.00
Postcard, colorful trademk, 1904 Expo Winner 185.00

Postcard, Indian Artist, one of a set of nine, M, $60.00.
(Photo courtesy Postcards International)

Ruler, wooden, 15" 700.00
Salt crock, Flemish bl & gray, 4x6½"..600.00

Sheet music, in fr...200.00
Sign, emb tin litho, ...Flour & Cereal Products, profile, rstr, 28x19"...760.00
Sign, self-fr tin, Old Sleepy Eye Flour, 20x24".......................3,000.00
Sign, sf tin, portrait w/multiple scenes around border, 24x20", G.2,300.00
Sign, tin litho die-cut Indian, ...Flour & Cereals, 13½"...........1,650.00
Spoon, demitasse; emb roses in bowl, Unity SP..........................60.00
Spoon, Indian-head hdl..70.00
Stein, bl & wht, 7¾"..600.00
Stein, Board of Directors, all yrs, 40-oz 265.00
Stein, Board of Directors, 1969, 22-oz.....................................350.00
Stein, brn, 1952, 22-oz...200.00
Stein, brn & wht..1,000.00
Stein, brn & yel, Western Stoneware mk 1,000.00
Stein, chestnut, 40-oz, 1952..225.00
Stein, cobalt...900.00
Stein, Flemish, bl on gray..600.00
Stein, ltd edition, 1979-84, ea 125.00
Sugar bowl, bl & wht, 3"..500.00
Thermometer, front rpl 600.00
Vase, cattails, all cobalt...800.00
Vase, cattails, bl & wht, good color, 9"......................................600.00
Vase, cattails, brn on yel, rare color 1,000.00
Vase, cattails, gr & wht, rare..2,500.00
Vase, Indian & cattails, Flemish, 8½"..370.00

O'Neill, Rose

Rose O'Neill's Kewpies were introduced in 1909 when they were used to conclude a story in the December issue of *Ladies' Home Journal*. They were an immediate success, and soon Kewpie dolls were being produced worldwide. German manufacturers were among the earliest and also used the Kewpie motif to decorate chinaware as well as other items. The Kewpie is still popular today and can be found on products ranging from Christmas cards and cake ornaments to fabrics, wallpaper, and metal items.

For further information we recommend *Doll Values, Antique to Modern*, by Patsy Moyer (Collector Books). In the following listings, 'sgn' indicates that the item is signed Rose O'Neill. Values are for examples in excellent condition with no chips. The copyright symbol, ©, is also a good mark on items. Unsigned items can be of interest to collectors; many are authentic and collectible, some are too small to sign.

Our advisors for this category are Don and Anne Kier; they are listed in the Directory under Ohio.

Book, The Goblin Woman, 345 pgs, 1st ed, 1930, VG+ 65.00
Book, They Wanted Jell-O, recipes, 1908, 4½x4½", VG.............40.00
Booklet, the Jell-O Girl Entertains, ca 1920s, 16-pg, 5¼x7", EX..42.50
Card, The Kewpies Think-That To Win Anything...After It, 1920s.50.00
Christmas card, Kewpie in chair, folds to stand up, ca 1915, 4x3"..55.00
Christmas card calendar, Kewpie, Campbell, 1916, closed: 3x4½", EX..170.00
Christmas plate, Let Joy Be Everywhere You Are, Cameo, 1973, 10¾" ...15.00
Creamer, 3 Kewpies w/floral top border, Bavaria, 3x5¼"...............85.00
Cup & saucer, Kewpie transfers, R O'Neill Wilson Kewpie Germany.50.00
Inkwell, Kewpies (2) stand on sides of glass well, pewter, 3x5"...165.00
Kewpie, bsk, Black Hottentot, Germany, 5", EX.........................625.00
Kewpie, bsk, immobile, bl wings, pnt hair, Germany, 2", EX/NM.110.00
Kewpie, bsk, immobile, bl wings, pnt hair, Germany, 4½", EX ...150.00
Kewpie, bsk, immobile, bl wings, pnt hair, Germany, 6", EX.......300.00
Kewpie, bsk, jtd hips & shoulders, Germany, 5", EX 695.00
Kewpie, bsk, jtd hips & shoulders, Germany, 10", EX 175.00
Kewpie, bsk, jtd shoulders, Germany, 2", EX............................105.00
Kewpie, bsk, jtd shoulders, Germany, 5¼", EX 275.00
Kewpie, bsk, jtd shoulders, Germany, 7".................................350.00
Kewpie, bsk, jtd shoulders, Germany, 10", EX..........................625.00

Kewpie, bsk, jtd shoulders, molded clothes, Germany, 2½", EX..200.00
Kewpie, bsk, jtd shoulders, molded clothes, Germany, 6", EX/NM .330.00
Kewpie, bsk, jtd shoulders, molded clothes, Germany, 8", EX.....375.00
Kewpie, bsk, nude holding drawstring bag, #4882, 4½" 1,095.00
Kewpie, bsk action figure, arms folded, Germany, 6" 575.00
Kewpie, bsk action figure, Blunderboo (falling), Germany, 1¾", EX...465.00
Kewpie, bsk action figure, bride & groom, Germany, 3½", EX, ea .350.00
Kewpie, bsk action figure, carpenter, Germany, 8½", EX 1,100.00
Kewpie, bsk action figure, cowboy, Germany, 10", EX 850.00
Kewpie, bsk action figure, farmer, Germany, 6½", EX 900.00
Kewpie, bsk action figure, kneeling, Germany, 4" 750.00
Kewpie, bsk action figure, laying on bk, kicking ft, Germany, 4", EX...200.00
Kewpie, bsk action figure, minister, Germany, 5", EX 250.00
Kewpie, bsk action figure, pen in hand, Germany, 4", EX 550.00
Kewpie, bsk action figure, seated in chair, Germany, 4", EX 400.00
Kewpie, bsk action figure, seated w/basket & ladybug, Germany, 4", EX..1,800.00
Kewpie, bsk action figure, soldier in egg, 3½", VG 6,600.00
Kewpie, bsk action figure, soldier w/helmet, Germany, 4½", EX.600.00
Kewpie, bsk action figure, Thinker, Germany, 5", EX 275.00
Kewpie, bsk action figure, w/Doodle Dog, Germany, 2½", EX 250.00
Kewpie, bsk action figure, w/jack-o'-lantern, Germany, 2", EX ...500.00
Kewpie, bsk shoulder head, cloth body, 7", EX 575.00
Kewpie, celluloid, bride & groom, 4", EX, ea 40.00
Kewpie, celluloid, jtd arms, heart label, 8" 50.00
Kewpie, celluloid, jtd arms, heart on chest, 12", EX 325.00
Kewpie, chalk, jtd shoulders, 13", EX.......................................165.00
Kewpie, china, perfume holder, 1-pc, opening in head, 4½", EX..1,100.00
Kewpie, china, salt shaker, 1¼", EX..165.00
Kewpie, cloth, Richard Krueger Cuddle Kewpie, w/tag, 12".......325.00
Kewpie, compo, Hottentot, heart decal, ca 1946, 11", EX 575.00
Kewpie, compo, jtd body, bl wings, 11", EX................................375.00
Kewpie, compo, jtd shoulders, Jesco, 1966, 24", EXIB...............250.00
Kewpie, compo, jtd shoulders, flange neck, tagged dress, 11", EX 875.00
Kewpie, hard plastic, all orig, 1950, 8½", MIB 385.00
Kewpie, soap figure w/cotton batting, mk RO Wilson 1917, 4", EX..110.00
Kewpie, soft rubber, Cameo, sgn, 9½" 45.00
Kewpie Doodle Dog, bsk, Germany, 3", EX/NM.......................1,350.00
Kewpie Kutout pgs, ca 1912, set of 8 w/12 corresponding story pgs, VG+....85.00
Kewpo, compo, jtd shoulders, rnd bl base, 13" 325.00
Lamp, Kewpie (4½") on lamppost, mk, 8" 575.00
Magazine ad, Kewpie Garter Belts, 1915, 10x14½", VG+ 35.00
Magazine article, Kewpies & Little Mermaid, 3-pg, 8½x11", VG.45.00
Newspaper comic, Tom, Dick & Harry Meet Kewpies, full-pg, 1918.40.00
Plate, Happy Days Are Here Again, features band, gold trim, 8¼"...25.00
Plate, Kewpies on bl, copyright on bk, Royal Rudolstadt, 7".........75.00
Plate, 6 action Kewpies, Germany, early 1900s, 8¼" 130.00
Postcard, advertising for jersey & plush Kewpies by Krueger, 1936, EX..75.00
Tea set, angel Kewpies, +cr/sug & 6 c/s, Germany, 5¼" pot, 17 pcs ..1,265.00

Onion Pattern

The familiar pattern known to collectors as Onion acquired its name through a case of mistaken identity. Designed in the early 1700s by Johann Haroldt of the Meissen factory in Germany, the pattern was a mixture of earlier Oriental designs. One of its components was a stylized peach, which was mistaken for an onion; as a result, the pattern became known by that name. Usually found in blue, an occasional piece may also be found in pink and red. The pattern is commonly associated with Meissen, but it has been reproduced by many others including Villeroy and Boch and Royal Copenhagen.

Many marks have been used, some of them fraudulent Meissen marks. Study a marks book to become more familiar with them. In our listings, 'Xd swords' indicates first-quality old Meissen ware. Meissen in

an oval over a star was a mark of C. Teichert Stove and Porcelain Factory of Meissen; it was used from 1882 until about 1930. Items marked simply Meissen were produced by the State's Porcelain Manufactory VEB after 1972. The crossed swords indication was sometimes added. Today's market abounds with quality reproductions.

Blue Danube is a modern line of Onion-patterned dinnerware produced in Japan and distributed by Lipper International of Wallingford, Connecticut. At least one hundred items are available in porcelain; it is sold in most large stores with china departments.

Bell, wood ringer, Xd swords, 4½" 225.00
Bowl, Blue Danube, 2x4½" 14.00
Bowl, divided, Blue Danube, 7½x11" 70.00
Bowl, mk Meissen #56, 9¾" 35.00
Bowl, oval, Blue Danube, 10"..45.00
Bowl, rimmed soup; scalloped rim, single arrow, 8⅞"......................60.00
Bowl, Royal Copenhagen, 1½x7½"..30.00
Bowl, scalloped rim, Blue Danube, 2½x9"......................................60.00
Bowl, scalloped rim, Blue Danube, 3x10" 65.00
Bowl, scalloped rim, Kensington, 3x8⅞"...35.00
Bowl, scalloped rim, oval, Xd swords, 1½x10¼x7⅜".........................80.00
Bowl, soup; Blue Danube, 7½"..18.00
Bowl, soup/cereal; Hutschenreuther, 2x6" 20.00
Bowl, sq, Cauldon, 3x9" 40.00
Bowl, Xd swords, 2½x7¼" sq 55.00
Butter dish, attached underplate, Xd swords, 7" dia......................300.00
Butter dish, Blue Danube, w/lid, rnd, 3¾x8".................................60.00
Butter pat, Meissen in oval w/star, 3"...40.00
Candlestick, rnd, Xd swords, 7½"...60.00
Candlesticks, Rococo style, Xd swords, 7", pr...............................330.00
Candy dish, ped ft, sq, Blue Danube, 8½x5¼"................................55.00
Canister, Barley in center, bbl shape, mk #53, 6x4"........................45.00
Canister, Flour in wht band, bbl shape, mk GKT Bro, 8¼".............60.00
Canister, full pattern, w/lid, Blue Danube, 8½"..............................45.00
Casserole, Blue Danube, w/hdls, 9"...45.00
Casserole, Blue Danube, w/lid, 1½-qt, 8" W....................................90.00
Cigar jar, scrolled border, 4-ftd on base, Xd swords, 3½x3".........110.00
Coasters, Vienna Woods, set of 12,⅝x3⅝".......................................50.00
Coffeepot, bulbous, Hutschenreuther, 5" 75.00
Coffeepot, sq, Wedgwood, 9" 40.00
Coffeepot, w/lid, Blue Danube, 8½"..65.00
Compote, rtcl, Xd swords, 6x7¼"..175.00
Cookie jar, Blue Danube, w/lid, 8½x5" 75.00
Creamer, cat figural, Blue Danube, 5x6" 40.00
Creamer, open, Xd swords, 2"...40.00
Cup & saucer, gilded, scalloped rim & sides, Xd swords, ca 1890 ..200.00
Dish, rtcl edges, Xd swords, ca 1890, shallow, 8¼" 170.00
Dish, scalloped rim, single arrow, 6¾x10½"...................................35.00
Dish, 2 open hdls, Hutschenreuther, oval, shallow, 11" 60.00
Egg coddler, metal lid, Xd arrows, 4⅛x2¾", w/3⅞" underplate.....85.00
Egg cup, Xd swords, 1½" 80.00
Jam pot, notched lid, Hutschenreuther,4x3" 50.00
Jar, Granulated Sugar on wht band, mk Germany, 8½"..................130.00
Jar, Oatmeal on wht band, 7¼" 100.00
Knife, dinner; Gorham blade, 8½"...45.00
Ladle, Blue Danube, 9½"..55.00
Mustard spoon, Xd swords, 4" 65.00
Napkin ring, rectangular, Blue Danube 10.00
Pitcher, Blue Danube, 24-oz, 6¾"..60.00
Plate, bread & butter; Royal Copenhagen, 6¼"..............................15.00
Plate, bread & butter; rtcl edges, mk Meissen, MIG, 6" 20.00
Plate, cake; open hdls, Hutschenreuther, 11½" 100.00
Plate, cake; rnd, Meisssen in oval w/star, 10¾"..............................55.00
Plate, gold rim, Xd swords, 1x6⅞"...35.00

Plate, Hutschenreuther, 10" 50.00
Plate, rtcl, hole for wall hanging, Hutschenreuther, 8½" 80.00
Plate, rtcl, mk #57, 8¼" 50.00
Plate, rtcl, Xd swords, 6" 80.00
Plate, Xd swords, 6⅜" 40.00
Plate, Xd swords, 9¾" 60.00
Platter, Blue Danube, oval, 10x8¾" 50.00
Platter, scalloped rim, Hutschenreuther, oval, 14x9½" 60.00
Platter, 2 open heart-shaped hdls, single arrow, Meissen, 11" 60.00
Rolling pin, wooden hdls, mk GMT & B & Germany, 2¾" dia, 15" L.150.00
Salad spoon & fork, Blue Danube, 11½" ea 45.00
Salt box, wooden lid, Blue Danube, 4x4½" 55.00
Saucer, scalloped rim, Xd swords, 5½" 22.50
Shakers, Vienna Woods, pr 35.00
Stein, beer; metal lid, Hutschenreuther, 5x4½" 50.00
Sugar bowl, w/lid, rnd, Hutschenreuther 60.00
Tazza, 5 rtcl medallions, swirls/foliage on ft, gilt, Meissen, 9x9"..300.00
Teapot, Blue Danube, #99183, 6x9" 70.00
Toothpick holder, shoe shape, Xd swords, 1¼x3¾x1⅛" 65.00
Tray, cheese/bread; hole for hanging, Xd swords, 10x6" 160.00
Trivet, Blue Danube, 5½x10¼" 45.00
Trivet, scalloped rim, Blue Danube, 6" 25.00
Tureen, swirled finial, Meissen, 6½x8½" sq 200.00
Tureen, Xd swords, 8½x12", w/12¾x9½" plate & ladle 345.00
Underpate, Blue Danube, 9¾x13" 35.00
Warming plate, porc in metal fr, Germany, hdls, 12" 110.00
Watering can, Sprinkler on side, Xd arrows, 6½" 185.00

Opalescent Glass

First made in England in 1870, opalescent glass became popular in America around the turn of the century. Its name comes from the milky-white opalescent trim that defines the lines of the pattern. It was produced in table sets, novelties, toothpick holders, vases, and lamps. Note that American-made sugar bowls have lids; sugar bowls of British origin are considered to be complete without lids. For further information we recommend *Standard Encyclopedia of Opalescent Glass* by Bill Edwards and Mike Carwile (Collector Books).

Acorns Burrs (& Bark), bowl, master; bl 75.00
Adonis Pineapple, bottle, claret; amber 425.00
Alaska, bowl, sauce; wht 30.00
Alaska, creamer, vaseline or canary 85.00
Alhambra, syrup, cranberry 590.00
Argonaut Shell (Nautilus), butter dish, bl 325.00
Argonaut Shell (Nautilus), shakers, vaseline or cranberry, pr 100.00
Ascot, creamer, bl 85.00
Autumn Leaves, banana bowl, gr 70.00
Banded Neck Scale Optic, vase, wht 55.00
Beaded Block, creamer, wht 45.00
Beaded Drape, rose bowl, gr, ftd 55.00
Beaded Moon & Stars, bowl, gr 45.00
Beaded Ovals in Sand, cruet, gr 300.00
Beaded Stars & Swag, rose bowl, bl or gr 60.00
Beatty Honeycomb, bowl, master; bl 50.00
Beatty Honeycomb, sugar bowl, bl 125.00
Beatty Rib, cracker jar, wht 100.00
Beatty Rib, toothpick holder, bl 65.00
Beatty Swirl, butter dish, bl 175.00
Beatty Swirl, tray, water; vaseline or canary 110.00
Berry Patch, bowl, novelty; gr 45.00
Blackberry, plate, amethyst, 6" 85.00
Blooms & Blossoms, nappy, bl or gr, hdld..................................50.00

Blown Diamonds, pitcher, vaseline or canary, scarce 300.00
Blown Twist, pitcher, cranberry 900.00
Brideshead, basket, bl 90.00
Bubble Lattice, creamer, gr or wht 50.00
Bull's-Eye, bottle, water; cranberry 265.00
Button Panels, rose bowl, bl 45.00
Calyx, vase, wht, scarce 50.00
Cherry, spooner, bl, LG Wright 45.00
Chippendale, basket, vaseline or canary 65.00
Christmas Pearls, cruet, gr 280.00
Chrysanthemum Base Swirl, tumbler, wht..................................75.00
Circled Scroll, butter dish, gr 275.00
Circled Scroll, pitcher, bl 325.00
Coinspot (includes variants, prices averaged), bowl, sauce; bl.......30.00
Colonial Stairsteps, creamer, bl 100.00
Concave Columns, vase, vaseline or canary 100.00
Consolidated Crisscross, butter dish, cranberry 725.00
Contessa, pitcher, amber 265.00
Coronation, creamer, vaseline or canary 40.00
Crown Jewels, tumbler, bl 60.00
Daffodils, lamp, oil; gr 300.00
Daisy & Fern, cruet, cranberry 525.00
Daisy & Fern, pickle castor, bl 325.00
Daisy & Plume, bowl, bl, ftd 50.00
Daisy Block, rowboat, gr, 4 szs 100.00
Daisy in Crisscross, pitcher, bl 300.00
Daisy Intaglio, basket, gr 185.00
Davidson Shell, spill vase, vaseline or canary 125.00
Diamond Optic, compote, bl 50.00
Diamond Point & Fleur de Lis, nut bowl, gr 65.00
Diamond Spearhead, creamer, gr, mini 75.00
Diamond Spearhead, sugar bowl, bl or vaseline or canary 125.00
Diamond Stem, vase, bl, JIP shape, rare 115.00
Dogwood Drape (Palm Rosette), compote, wht...........................120.00
Dolly Madison, pitcher, gr 295.00
Dolphin Petticoat, candlesticks, vaseline or canary, pr...............165.00
Double Greek Key, creamer, bl 85.00
Double Stemmed Rose, bowl, bl, variant, rare 85.00
Drapery, Northwood's; bowl, sauce; bl 30.00
Duchess, cruet, bl 225.00
Dugan, Jack-in-the-Pulpit, vase, bl, 4½" 50.00
Dugan's #1013 (Wide Rib), vase, gr 75.00
Ellen, vase, gr 55.00
Elson Dew Drop, mug, wht 50.00
English Spool, vase, bl 75.00
Everglades, creamer, bl 95.00
Fan, gravy boat, gr 50.00
Feathers, vase, bl 35.00
Fenton #370, bonbon, amber 50.00
Fern, butter dish, bl 195.00
Finecut & Roses, bowl, novelty; bl 45.00
Fishscale & Beads, bowl, wht 30.00
Flora, compote, jelly; bl, vaseline or canary 125.00
Floral Eyelet, tumbler, bl 100.00
Fluted Scroll w/Vine, vase, bl, ftd 100.00
Fluted Scrolls (Klondyke), puff box, wht.....................................50.00
Frosted Leaf & Basketweave, spooner, vaseline or canary 135.00
Gonderman (Adonis) Swirl, shade, amber 100.00
Gossamer Threads, bowl, finger; bl 55.00
Grecian Urn, vase, bl, 4½"..65.00
Heart-Handle Open O's, ring tray, bl 100.00
Herringbone, pitcher, bl..575.00
Hobnail (Hobbs), celery vase, rubena 225.00
Hobnail (Hobbs), tumbler, rubena..125.00

Hobnail & Panelled Thumbprint, butter dish, wht 145.00
Hobnail in Square, barber bottle, wht..............................120.00
Hobnail 4-Footed, butter dish, cobalt..............................225.00
Holly, bowl, wht 175.00
Honeycomb (Blown), tumbler, bl......................................80.00
Honeycomb & Clover, creamer, gr, Fenton 75.00
Inside Ribbing, bowl, sauce; wht......................................20.00
Inside Ribbing, syrup, bl...155.00
Intaglio, sugar bowl, bl...125.00
Intaglio (Dugan), bowl, wht, 7"-10", ea 120.00
Interior Panel, vase, fan; amethyst..................................100.00
Inverted Coindot, rose bowl, wht......................................55.00
Inverted Fan & Feather, bowl, master; cranberyy 200.00
Inverted Fan & Feather, rose bowl, gr...............................85.00
Iris w/Meander, compote, jelly; bl....................................55.00
Jackson, bowl, master; bl...100.00
Jackson, tumbler, vaseline or canary.................................70.00
Jazz, vase, bl...50.00
Jefferson Wheel, bowl, gr 50.00
Jewel & Flower, butter dish, vaseline or canary 325.00
Jewelled Heart, plate, bl, sm...75.00
King Richard, compote, wht 150.00
Lady Caroline, spill, bl..65.00
Lattice & Points, vase, wht 75.00
Leaf & Beads, rose bowl, gr 70.00
Leaf Mold, bowl, master; cranberry 140.00
Lily Pond, epergne, wht 250.00
Linking Rings, glass, juice; bl...40.00
Lords & Ladies, butter dish, bl..100.00
Lustre Flute, custard cup, wht 30.00
Many Loops, bowl, bl, ruffled...50.00

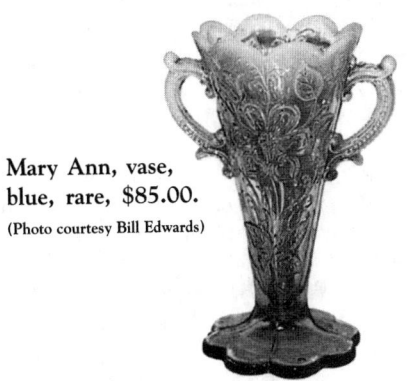

Mary Ann, vase, blue, rare, $85.00.
(Photo courtesy Bill Edwards)

Meander, bowl, bl 60.00
Nesting Robin, bowl, wht 300.00
Northern Star, bowl, banana; gr..70.00
Opal Loops, decanter, wht 160.00
Opal Loops, flask, wht 195.00
Over-All Hob, bowl, sauce; vaseline or canary...................25.00
Over-All Hob, tumbler, bl...65.00
Palm Beach, compote, jelly; bl...135.00
Panelled Holly, bowl, master; bl.......................................200.00
Panelled Holly, tumbler, wht...70.00
Peacocks (On the Fence), bowl, bl, scarce 300.00
Picadilly, basket, bl, sm...100.00
Pinecones & Leaves, bowl, wht 70.00
Plain Panels, vase, gr 40.00
Poinsettia, tumbler, bl...75.00
Polka Dot, cruet, cranberry 400.00
Pressed Coinspot, (#617 or Concave Columns), card tray, wht 50.00

Princess Diana, tumbler, vaseline or canary.......................40.00
Pump & Trough, trough, bl 75.00
Queen Victoria, plate, bl, ruffled 150.00
Quilted Pillow Sham, creamer, bl 75.00
Rayed Jane, nappy, bl..50.00
Regal (Northwood's), tumbler, gr.......................................70.00
Reverse Swirl, bowl, master; bl..70.00
Reverse Swirl, mustard pot, vaseline or canary 75.00
Ribbed Coinspot, creamer, cranberry, rare........................500.00
Ribbed Lattice, cruet, bl..225.00
Ribbed Lattice, spooner, wht...65.00
Ribbed Spiral, cup & saucer, wht.......................................60.00
Ribbed Spiral, vase, funeral; bl, 15"-22", ea.....................100.00
Richelieu, cracker jar, bl, w/lid..200.00
Richelieu, tumbler, wht...20.00
Ripple, vase, gr..110.00
Rose (also called Rose & Ruffles), pomade, bl..................100.00
Rose Show, bowl, wht, rare 100.00
Roulette, plate, gr 100.00
Ruffles & Rings, rose bowl, gr 60.00
Sachews, bowl, gr 45.00
Scottish Moor, cracker jar, wht..225.00
Scroll w/Acanthus, creamer, bl 85.00
Seaweed, butter dish, wht 125.00
Seaweed, sugar shaker, cranberry 425.00
Shell Beaded, bowl, sauce; gr 65.00
Shell Beaded, toothpick holder, gr...................................400.00
Silver Overlay, vase, wht 75.00
Sir Lancelot, bowl, gr, ftd 60.00
Snowflake, lamp, hand; wht...275.00
Spanish Lace, bride's basket, cranberry, 2 szs, ea 200.00
Spanish Lace, jam jar, bl..300.00
Spatter, vase, bl, 9"...95.00
Speckled Stripe, barber bottle, bl.....................................290.00
Squirrel & Acorn, bowl, gr 175.00
Stars & Stripes, pitcher, cranberry.................................1,150.00
Strawberry, bowl, amethyst 125.00
Stripe, pitcher, cranberry...575.00
Stripe (Wide), tumbler, cranberry....................................100.00
Sunk Hollyhock, bowl, vaseline or canary, scarce..............100.00
Swag w/Brackets, bowl, gr 45.00
Swag w/Brackets, toothpick holder, wht 150.00
Swirl, cheese dish, cranberry 400.00
Swirl, lamp, finger; cranberry...600.00
Swirling Maze, bowl, salad; gr 70.00
Thorn Lily, epergne, vaseline or canary............................300.00
Thousand Eye, shakers, wht, pr...75.00
Thousand Eye, spooner, wht...75.00
Three Fingers & Panel, bowl, sauce; bl, rare 40.00
Tiny Tears, vase, bl..50.00
Trafalger Fountain, epergne, amber 350.00
Tree of Love, compote, wht 55.00
Trellis, tumbler, vaseline or canary....................................65.00
Twist (Miniatures), butter dish, bl....................................200.00
Twister, bowl, bl..50.00
Victoria & Albert, biscuit jar, wht....................................110.00
Vintage (Northwood, Dugan), rose bowl, gr.......................65.00
War of the Roses, bowl, bl...75.00
Waterlily & Cattails, gravy boat, amethyst, hdld................80.00
Waterlily & Cattails, spooner, bl..80.00
White Chapel, bowl, bl..35.00
Wild Bouquet, bowl, sauce; gr...50.00
Wild Daffodils, mug, bl...85.00
William & Mary, butter dish, bl, w/lid.............................200.00

Windflower, bowl, wht, rare..................................125.00
Windows (Plain), tumbler, bl.................................55.00
Windows (Swirled), bowl, master; cranberry..................100.00
Windows (Swirled), spooner, cranberry......................225.00
Winged Scroll, nappy, vaseline or canary, rare.............150.00
Woven Wonder, bowl, novelty; bl.............................55.00
Wreath & Shell, ivy ball, wht, rare.........................95.00
Zipper & Loops, vase, gr, ftd...............................70.00

Opaline

A type of semiopaque opal glass, opaline was made in white as well as pastel shades and is often enameled. It is similar in appearance to English bristol glass, though its enamel or gilt decorative devices tend to exhibit a French influence.

Bottle, scent; gr w/gold, Fr, 1860s, chip on stopper, 7½"............525.00
Box, pasty HP floral, Bohemian, ca 1850, 4¾x3", NM..............825.00
Vase, gray w/bl & brn bird/branch, flat-sided ftd flask form, 10", pr..115.00
Vase, pk w/gold lilies, 3 crimped hdls extend from rim to width, 10".90.00

Optical Items

Collectors of Americana are beginning to appreciate the charm of antique optical items, and those involved in the related trade find them particularly fascinating. Anyone, however, can appreciate the evolution of technology apparent when viewing a collection of old eye wear and at the same time admire the primitive ingenuity involved in their construction.

Magnifier, lace maker's; blown globe on trn wood stand, 24"........60.00
Magnifying glass, herringbone patterned bone hdl w/cvd cats, 3x7"..75.00
Magnifying glass, metal w/wooden hdl, 4" dia, 8½"..................50.00
Magnifying glass, sterling silver hdl w/flower & scrolls, ca 1900, 3".50.00
Magnifying glass, sterling silver w/eng hdl, 4" dia, 12"............60.00
Magnifying glass, swings out of case, figural owl on top, 3"........40.00
Opera glasses, abalone at rims, mk Henry Kahn/Lemaire Paris, EX..210.00
Opera glasses, brass & MOP, Le Roi of Paris, EX...................110.00
Opera glasses, floral enamel w/scrolls, MOP at lens, NM...........500.00
Opera glasses, leather wrapped, mk Vendome Paris, VG...............35.00
Opera glasses, MOP allover including hdl, Lemaire...Paris, EX....175.00

Orientalia

The art of the Orient is an area of collecting currently enjoying strong collector interest, not only in those examples that are truly 'antique' but in the twentieth-century items as well. Because of the many aspects involved in a study of Orientalia, we can only try through brief comments to acquaint the reader with some of the more readily available examples. We suggest you refer to specialized reference sources for more detailed information. See also specific categories.

Key:
Ch — Chinese	hdwd — hardwood
cvg — carving	Jp — Japan
drw — drawer	Ko — Korean
Dy — Dynasty	lcq — lacquer
E — export	mdl — medallion
FR — Famille Rose	rswd — rosewood
FV — Famille Verte	tkwd — teakwood
gb — guard border	

Bronze

Bell, hand; cylindrical, vajra surmount, Java, 14th C, 6¼"........285.00
Bowl, holy water; inlaid weyang figures, Bali, 18th C, 5" H.......115.00
Bowl, quatrefoil, 4-ftd, w/stand, Ming Dy, 3¼x5".................275.00
Bracelet, Singa motifs, thick gr patina, Sumatra, 19th C.........285.00
Buddha, gr-gray patina, Thailand, 17th C, 6½".....................350.00

Censer, samurai finial, squat baluster with dragon handles, molded and pierced wave bands at rim and base, nineteenth century, 43¾", $2,000.00.

Figure, Bodhistava, lotus throne, semi-precious stones/gilt, 8", EX.1,000.00
Figure, Chintamani Lokeshvara, gilt, T'ang period, Ch, 2¼"......230.00
Figure, Ganesha, 10-armed divinity w/goddess, Indian, 15th C, 2½"...315.00
Figure, Kabuki dancer, coppery birds on robe, gilt fan, '30s, 12".275.00
Figure, Vishnu, 4 arms, S India, 14th C, 3".......................865.00
Incense burner, canted sides w/relief dragons, foo dog finial, 12"...165.00
Jar, raised circles, ftd, EX patina, Thai, 9th C, 6½x8"..........700.00
Palace urns, birds/Foo dogs/leaves relief, appl dragons, 1900, 24", pr..750.00
Pendant, monkey playing w/ring, Thailand, 17th C, 2"............145.00
Vase, geometric base/mid band, att Shang Dy, corrosion/sm hole, 10".600.00

Furniture

Armchair, cvd splat, wood seat, curved arms, box stretcher, 44".230.00
Armchair, pierced cvd bk, blk lcq w/uphl seat, 42"................165.00
Armchair, tkwd, pierced cvgs, mdl splat, mortised, rprs, 43"......360.00
Bench, relief cvd vines/panels/scrolls/etc, lift lid, 56x64x26"..1,750.00
Cabinet, cvd tkwd, 3 drws, 2 doors, brass hdw, 38x43x34"..........460.00
Chair, side; rswd w/cvd dragons/fruit leaves, claw/ball ft, Ch, 19th C.500.00
Chest, camphor wood w/inlay, brass hinges, dvtl, bracket ft, 17x31x16"..330.00
Curio, rswd, disk shape w/irregular cubbyholes, 1945, 36" dia.....200.00
Screen, cvd scenes w/mc pnt, splits/crazing, 4-part, 53x64"........550.00
Stand, cvd rswd w/rose marble insert top, cvd skirt, 33x23" dia..700.00
Stand, fern; tkwd, cabriole legs, cvd/pierced apron, soapstone top..300.00
Stand, fern; tkwd, foliage cvgs, pierced cvd flowers, 8-sides, 36", EX.250.00
Stand, rswd w/pierced heart cvgs, shelf, 30x12" dia, EX.............350.00
Table, alter; 2-plank top, trestle legs w/much cvg, old, 38x82x17".5,400.00
Table, red lcq top, relief cvgs w/dragons, Ch, 19th C, 13x28x17"...300.00
Table, side; Lao Hung Mu wood, appl fretwork aprons, early, 33x58x25".2,500.00

Hardstones

Celadon Nephrite, Quanyin w/fly whisk, attendant on rock, recent, 6".115.00
Gray Nephrite, bowl, pear form w/floral cvg, brn/blk areas, 1800s, 6".115.00
Jade, bird, celadon w/bright areas, 20th C, 8", on stand, pr........700.00
Jade, bowl, spinach-gr, early 20th C, 9", on wood stand.............230.00
Jade, ewer, Kuang form, dk spinach gr, Ch, 20th C, 12x13"..........800.00
Jade, figure, Lan Tsai Ho, pale gr w/gray, late 19th C, 6"..........230.00

Jade, foo dog, yel-gr, Ch, 19th C, 2¾x3"......................**300.00**
Jade, maid w/rose (2nd w/flower basket), wht/lt amber, 20th C, 5", pr..**200.00**
Jade, phoenix, mottled/dk gr, cvd rswd base, 1900s, 16", pr........**500.00**
Jade, pomander box, pierced shou & 8 precious emblems, 18th C, 6"..**500.00**
Jade, Soo Chow foo dog w/4 puppies, brn tones, 1¼x3½"..........**400.00**
Jade, vase, olive gr, cvd tao-tie masks, Ch, 19th C, 5¼"............**115.00**
Jade, 1-horned beast, dk gr nephrite, late 20th C, 9" L..............**575.00**
Jade Chrysophase, seated Buddha, gray-gr, wood base, 20th C, 7½".**460.00**
Jadeite, boulder w/int figure of Guanyin, lt gr w/amber int, 1900, 13"...**800.00**
Jadeite, Ch gods in garden setting, polished wht/lav/gr, 1900, 16"...**1,000.00**
Jadeite, Ch princess/royal attendants in garden setting, 1900, 24", EX.**1,150.00**
Jadeite, figural jar, Buddhist/leaves, polished lav/gr, 1900, lid, 11"...**1,000.00**
Jadeite, heron, 200+ appl feathers, on wood plinth, 20th C, 76", pr.**1,150.00**
Jadeite, wise man w/scroll, polished wht/lav/gr, 1900, 18".......**1,495.00**
Nephrite, bowl, lt gr/wht, Qing Dy style, 1900s, 6½"...............**900.00**
Nephrite jade, female in garden setting, 1900, 7", rswd base, EX.**115.00**
Nephrite jade, pr of phoenixes on rockery base, polished, 20th C, 12"..**690.00**
Rock crystal, elephant, transparent Burmese crystal, Ch, 1890s, 4".**115.00**
Wht jade, man w/robe holds hands in front, 14".........................**175.00**

Lacquer

Lacquerware is found in several colors, but the one most likely to be encountered is cinnabar. It is often intricately carved, sometimes involving hundreds of layers built one at a time on a metal or wooden base. Later pieces remain red, while older examples tend to darken.

Box, aquatic plants, gilt hiramaki-e & aogai, Meiji, 5x9x6"....**1,275.00**
Box, sewing, E, scenic panels, brass bail hdls, 19th C, 6x17x12"...**500.00**
Inro, blk & cinnabar, cvd scholars in mtns, 4-compartment, 19th C, 2"..**550.00**
Inro, blk w/silver & gold boat scene, 4-compartment, 19th C, 3".**1,600.00**
Inro, relief-cvd fan medallions, 4-compartment, 19th C, 3½"....**435.00**
Tea caddy, blk/gold w/figural panels, serpentine, 1850s...............**425.00**

Netsukes

A netsuke is a miniature Japanese carving made with two holes called the Himitoshi, either channeled or within the carved design. As kimonos (the outer garment of the time) had no pockets, the Japanese man hung his pipe, tobacco pouch, or other daily necessities from his waist sash. The most highly valued accessory was a nest of little drawers called an Inro, in which they carried snuff or sometimes opium. The netsuke was the toggle that secured them. Although most are of ivory, others were made of bone, wood, metal, porcelain, or semiprecious stones. Some were inlaid or lacquered. They are found in many forms — figurals the most common, mythological beasts the most desirable. They range in size from 1" up to 3", which was the maximum size allowed by law. Many netsukes represented the owner's profession, religion, or hobbies. Scenes from the daily life of Japan at that time were often depicted in the tiny carvings. The more detailed the carving, the greater the value.

Careful study is required to recognize the quality of the netsuke. Many have been made in Hong Kong in recent years; and even though some are very well carved, these are considered copies and avoided by the serious collector. There are many books that will help you learn to recognize quality netsukes, and most reputable dealers are glad to assist you. Use your magnifying glass to check for repairs. In the listings that follow, netsukes are ivory unless noted otherwise; 'stain' indicates a color wash.

Candy maker stirring pot, 19th C.....................................**350.00**
Daikoku & Jurojin w/bag of wealth, Tamamitsu, 19th C............**400.00**
Daikoku w/hammer & bag of wealth, 19th C.......................**700.00**
Daruma stretching his arm, staghorn, 19th C......................**350.00**

Dragon boat w/Daikoku & Hoi tei, late 19th C, on sgn MOP plaque...**115.00**
European in tiger-pattern robe, inlaid horn eyes, 18th C, 3¾"...**9,775.00**
Fan dancer (ivory) w/in persimmon section, EX patina, 19th C, 1½"..**350.00**
Foreigner w/drum in long gown & tall hat, amber stain, 19th C.....**1,265.00**
Frog caught by crab on lotus pad, wooden, 18th C, 2"...............**635.00**
Goddess w/fan, 19th C..**700.00**
Kappa in lotus pond, boxwood, 19th C............................**375.00**
Karako w/bib, boxwood w/ivory inlay, 19th C....................**350.00**
Mask, wooden, sgn Deme Shokei, 18th C..........................**230.00**
Okame holding gourds, 19th C....................................**230.00**
Oni w/gong & rosary, pigment traces, 19th C....................**350.00**
Sennin w/dbl gourd, 18th C, 3¾"...................................**925.00**
Tiger, sgn, 19th C..**700.00**
Woman w/sake cup, 19th C...**350.00**
Youthful woman, Ryoichi Yosuichi, 19th C........................**175.00**

Porcelain

Chinese export ware was designed to appeal to Western tastes and was often made to order. During the eighteenth century, vast amounts were shipped to Europe and on westward. Much of this fine porcelain consisted of dinnerware lines that were given specific pattern names. Rose Mandarin, Fitzhugh, Armorial, Rose Medallion, and Canton are but a few of the more familiar.

Bottle, water; Fitzhugh, E, mc floral w/animals/etc, Ch, 19th C, 15"..**750.00**
Bowl, celadon, birds, butterflies & flowers, scalloped, rprs, 11"...**235.00**
Bowl, E, Cabbage, 1800s, 8" dia....................................**500.00**
Bowl, E, FR, birds/butterflies/vegetables/etc, 8", 6 for..............**360.00**
Bowl, E, hunt scene, Ch, 19th C, 4x11¼", EX......................**635.00**
Bowl, E, hunters/horses/dogs, dmn diaper, floral rim, 1780s, rpr, 11".**1,000.00**
Bowl, E, Orange Fitzhugh, geometric border, 6x18¾"................**715.00**
Bowl, FR, E, celadon, cut corners, Ch, 19th C, 4⅝x9⅞"..........**575.00**
Bowl, grisaille floral swag & flower sprays, Ch, ca 1800, 4½x10"..**500.00**
Bowl, salad; FR, E, cut corners, Ch, 19th C, 5x9½"..................**375.00**
Box, brush; celadon, Rose Medallion palette, 19th C, 2½x7½x3"....**385.00**
Candle holder, lotus scrolls & 8 Precious Emblems, 1735-96, 31".**2,200.00**
Charger, E, armorial, spearhead bordered well, gilt, 1730s, rpr, 17".**5,000.00**
Charger, E, Cabbage, mc border w/floral reserves, 1800s, 15½"..**590.00**
Charger, E, figures in gazebo view egrets, floral border, Ch, 14", EX.**400.00**
Charger, E, flowers & armorial designs w/birds, 16½"..............**4,750.00**
Charger, E, FR, cranes/plants/rocks, Ch, 18th C, 14", pr.........**2,400.00**
Incense burner, 7 sages & attendants, Kutani-Ko-zan, Meiji, 4½".**300.00**
Jug, cider; floral w/gold, foo dog finial, ca 1800, 11", +9 syllabubs.**475.00**
Mug, Orange Fitzhugh, gold trim, leaf-molded hdl, 4½".............**220.00**
Plate, chop; Blue Fitzhugh, center medallion, rstr, 20x17"..........**500.00**
Plate, E, FR, flowers/ribbons, cell diapered rim, 1770s, 9", pr......**115.00**
Plate, FR, E, mandarin figures, 19th C, 9½".........................**765.00**
Plate, gr celadon w/dbl petal design, foliate sprig center, Ming, 8"..**200.00**
Plate, ships & island w/egret borders, bl & wht, Ming, 10¼".....**200.00**
Platter, cealdon, Rose Canton, oval, 15¾x13¼"....................**650.00**
Platter, E, FR, 2 lg reserves w/figures, 1 w/nude, 1780, 9".......**90,000.00**
Platter, E, FR, 4 Chinese figures alternate w/flowers, 1840, 17"..**1,000.00**
Punch bowl, E, FR, Compagnie des Indes, ext/int florals, 1770, 9".**175.00**
Shrimp dish, celadon, bird/butterfly/floral decor, 19th C, 10x9¾"..**325.00**
Soap dish, celadon, Rose Medallion border, 3-part, w/lid, 2½x5x4"..**265.00**
Stand, FV, cloverleaf shape, cabriole legs, K'ang Hsi, 1662-1722.**1,380.00**
Teapot, E, VR, florals/cherries, strawberry finial, 1780, 6"..........**150.00**
Tray, ice cream; celadon, Rose Canton decor, hdls, 7x14"..........**600.00**
Vase, celadon, paneled bird & floral decor, hdls, 12¾", EX........**385.00**
Vase, E, FR, foo dog hdls & gecko decor, 35½"....................**4,550.00**
Vase, E, FR, warriors, appl dragons on shoulders, dragon hdls, 18"..**230.00**
Vase, scenic w/eagle/trees/rocks, bl/wht, 2-part, 46", pr............**1,500.00**
Warming dish, E, Fitzhugh, 19th C, 9¾"...........................**325.00**

Pottery

Bowl, floral, wht on chalky bl, Ming, shallow, 15".........................345.00
Figurine, elder in bl/rose, floral base, 1800s, mk, 9½"..................135.00
Garden stool, butterflies/mums/gold bird band/lion masks, 19"...300.00
Jar, grass gr w/emb flowers, 6 lugs, old rprs, Ming, 10".................115.00
Teapot, terra cotta, gr enamel spout/hdl, branch on lid, 4x7".......50.00
Vase, phoenix birds/beading on crackleware, 1880s, 10".............55.00

Rugs

The 'Oriental' or Eastern rug market has enjoyed a renewal of interest as collectors have become aware of the fact that some of the semi-antique rugs (those sixty to one hundred years old) may be had at a price within the range of the average buyer.

Ahar Heriz, wide midnight bl border, ivory spandrels on red, 96x132"..825.00
Akstafa prayer, serrated hex lattice of palmettes on dk bl, 67x32", G.650.00
Armenian Kazak, column of 4 serrated shield mdl on navy, 108x65", VG..3,400.00
Baluch, 3 concentric hooked mdl on camel, fine border, 65x36", EX+.350.00
Caucasian, dk rust w/multiple borders, 72x76"............................470.00
Dagestan prayer, ivory w/multi borders, dtd 1895, 41x54", VG...600.00
Ersari Chuval, 2 rows of 4 radiating dmns, 58x38", G.................500.00
Ersari Main, 3 columns: 7 gulli-guls on rust-red, similar gb, 96x106"..1,295.00
Gabbeh, florals, brn/ivory, bk/ivory checked border, 84x48".......225.00
Gorovan, midnight bl gb/ivory spandrels on rust, 140x98".......1,400.00
Hamadan runner, hooked mdl on brick red w/bl borders, 72x45"..275.00
Heriz, blk border, ivory spandrels on dk burgundy, 96x132"........825.00
Heriz, lg serrated leaves/palmettes/rosettes on red, 140x99", VG.1,880.00
Kapatrang, multiple borders, bl spandrels on dk red, 127x210"...550.00
Karabagh, lg keyhole mdl inset w/4 octagons on royal bl, 114x48", EX..940.00
Karadja, 5 gabled sqs/2 hooked mdl w/vines on red, 1940s, 120x38", NM..1,500.00
Kashan, dk burgundy ground w/golden-brn border, sm rpr, 132x267"..5,400.00
Kazak, red/bl gb, red/tan/camel/ivory on bl, rstr, 80x32".............220.00
Kazak, rows of stepped polygons, dk bl border, mc on red, 78x44".1,765.00
Kazak, 2 lg hex mdl ea w/8 cloud bands on red, 82x56", VG...2,235.00
Konaghend, arabesque lattice on midnight bl, kufic border, 66x40", VG.590.00
Lillihan, bl border on red w/florals, wear/ends frayed, 300x30".3,000.00
Lillihan, open florals on midnight bl, red border, wear, 84x34"..1,155.00
Luristan, ivory/abrash bl borders, red spandrels on dk bl, 52x108"..300.00
Musel, florals, pk/rose/brn on dk bl, 84x54"...................................200.00
NW Persian, rows of botech & rosettes on midnight bl, 118x46", G.890.00
NW Persian, rows of stylized florals on dk brn, 140x40", VG..1,175.00
Perisan Heriz, 8-point mdl, ivory spandrels, rose/celadon/brn, 13x10"..1,200.00
Persian Heriz, radiating star mdls, wht/crimson/brn, 120x90".....700.00
Persian Lilihan, stylized flowers/vines in multiple borders, 72x39"...600.00
Persian Saraband runner, vines cartouch, red/brn/tan, 120x45"..275.00
Persian Tabriz, ivory/bl spandrels on burgundy, wide border, 108x150"..600.00
S Caucasian, keyhole mdl w/octagons, ivory border, VG, 63x45"..1,880.00
S Persian, 3 hooked dmn mdl w/bird motifs on navy, 108x77", EX..1,880.00
Sarouk, bl border/spandrels, floral mdl on red, 76x47"............1,925.00
Sarouk, deep magenta w/midnight bl border w/ivory & pk, 140x142"..2,750.00
Sarouk, dk bl border/ground, dk dusty pk spandrels, rebound, 48x84".385.00
Sarouk, dk bl w/rust red border, floral w/mdl & urns, 37x60"......715.00
Sarouk, midnight bl gb on red mottle, 144x108".....................3,740.00
Senneh, dmn mdl/lg spandrels w/Herati motif on dk bl, 72x51", G..890.00
Serenend, ivory gb, red ground, pile has wear, 54x36"................275.00
Sparta, gr/bl border+camel border on burgundy, wear, 84x132"..385.00
Tabriz, wide red-brn border on dk bl ground, wear, 114x144".....660.00
Tekke Ensi, quartered rust garden plan w/plant motifs, 53x43", G..470.00
Turkish Bergama, string graphics w/ivory border, bl sqs, 45x63".1,125.00
Yomund Chuval, 9 chuval guls on rust-red, ivory border, 48x31", EX..700.00
Yomund Ensi, 10 columns of triangle prs on aubergine, 62x50", G-.1,100.00

Snuff Bottles

The Chinese were introduced to snuff in the seventeenth century, and their carved and painted snuff bottles typify their exquisite taste and workmanship. These small bottles, seldom measuring over 2½", were made of amber, jade, ivory, and cinnabar; tiny spoons were often attached to their stoppers. By the eighteenth century, some were being made of porcelain, others were of glass with delicate interior designs tediously reverse painted with minuscule brushes sometimes containing a single hair. Copper and brass were used but to no great extent.

Agate, rvpt children, coral glass stopper, Ch, early 1900s, 3"......115.00
Amber, dbl form cvd w/prunus plants, coral/jade stoppers, 2".....400.00
Amber, deeply hollowed, honey-colored swirls, Ch, 19th C, 2¾"...115.00
Ivory, cvd in rnd as boy w/immortals attributes, Ch, 19th C, 4".350.00
Jade, celadon gr basket form, well hollowed, Ch, 18th C, 2¼"...800.00
Porc, mc relief decor, Ch, late 19th C, 3"...................................115.00
Porc, molded as lotus plant, gr color, Ch, late 19th C, 2¾"........115.00
Rose quartz, cvd birds & flowers, European bronze mts, Ch, 20th C, 4"...115.00

Textiles

Pictorial, silk, circle of Gopis/god Krishna, 1900, 25x26"............690.00
Pictorial, silk, courtesan in elaborate costume, 19th C, 28x20"..345.00
Pictorials, silk, parade/participants; dignitaries, 1900, 18x16", pr..1,800.00
Robe, Mandarian Imperial court; embr silk w/dragons/bats/etc, 47", EX..2,750.00

Miscellaneous

Cvg, teakwood plaque w/red wash & gold detail, Mandarin scenes, 20x16"..385.00
Dr's figure, cvd ivory nude stands on wood ped, 7½"..................330.00
Figure, God of War, cvd, gilt/red enamel, horsehair beard, 15"...100.00
Foo dogs, cvd wood w/cinnabar, gilt & blk pnt, 20th C, 17", pr.1,375.00
Panel, Gelugpa lama w/flower & chakra, pnt, Tibet, 18th-19th C, 17x18".1,150.00
Panel, rswd, pr of peacocks on flowering tree (deeply cvd), 23x16"...100.00
Rose water sprinkler, mesh ware w/silver mts, Persia, 18th-19th C, 9".485.00
Trunk, camphor wood w/blk leather & HP floral, brass tacks/mts, 25" L..550.00

Orrefors

Orrefors Glassworks was founded in 1898 in the Swedish province of Smaaland. Utilizing the expertise of designers such as Simon Gate, Edward Hald, Vicke Lindstrand, and Edwin Ohrstrom, it produced art glass of the highest quality. Various techniques were used in achieving the decoration. Some were wheel engraved; others were blown through a unique process that formed controlled bubbles or air pockets resulting in unusual patterns and shapes. Our advisor for this category is Abby Malowanczyk; she is listed in the Directory under Texas.

Vase, Poseideon and mermaid in turbulent waters supporting massive sailboat, Orrefors Landberg Expo 3451 L2Ei, ca 1955, 12", $7,150.00.

Charger, cobalt, blown, Palmquist, 2½x20½" 620.00
Vase, Ariel, rows of clear sqd bubbles, cobalt int layer, #174, 5½" ..865.00
Vase, clear cased w/vertical bubble bars in amethyst, Ohrstrom, 6¾" .925.00
Vase, clear w/eng fish/seaweed/bubbles, Lindstrand, 1939, 7½" ..360.00
Vase, clear w/eng sailing ship & waves, heavy ft, Lindstrand, 10¾" ..360.00
Vase, clear w/etched fish, gr seaweed & bubbles, Lindstrand, 7½" ..360.00
Vase, clear w/etched Romeo & Juliet, rectangular, Landberg, 7¾" .520.00
Vase, clear w/horizontal ribs, eng mermaid, blk base, Gate, 9"....800.00
Vase, clear w/swirling amethyst int, hexagonal, Hald, 1952, 13¾" ..1,800.00
Vase, cobalt, blown, bulbous, EXPO AU 139-59/Palmquist, 6" ..355.00
Vase, Expo, gray pencil neck blown to clear teardrop, Landberg, 14" .440.00
Vase, Graal, clear w/gr fish & seaweed, ovoid, Hald, 6" 500.00
Vase, gray facet-cut body eng w/nude, Gate, ca 1934, 8"............460.00

Ott and Brewer

The partnership of Ott and Brewer began in 1865 in Trenton, New Jersey. By 1876 they were making decorated graniteware, parian, and 'ivory porcelain' — similar to Irish belleek though not as fine and of different composition. In 1883, however, experiments toward that end had reached a successful conclusion, and a true belleek body was introduced. It came to be regarded as the finest china ever produced by an American firm. The ware was decorated by various means such as hand painting, transfer printing, gilding, and lustre glazing. The company closed in 1893, one of many that failed during that depression. In the listings below, the ware is belleek unless noted otherwise. Our advisor for this category is Mary Frank Gaston.

Bowl, lt gr w/gold, fluted, hdls w/shell terminals, 2x6½x3¼" 195.00
Cake plate, floral, fluted rim w/gold, tab hdls, 1882-93, 10½" 125.00
Coffeepot, floral transfer w/gold, non-beleek, 1867-92, 9½" 75.00
Cup, flowers/leaves/butterfly, gold paste on wht ribbed, 1882-92 .150.00
Cup & saucer, bouillon; gold acorns on branch hdls 195.00
Ewer, gold stylized leaves, cactus hdl, 8½" 1,250.00
Vase, calla lily form, gold highlights, 1884-94, 7" 500.00
Vase, leaves & butterfly, gold paste on matt, hdls, 5½" 600.00

Overbeck

The Overbeck Studio was established in 1911 in Cambridge City, Indiana, by four Overbeck sisters. It survived until the last sister died in 1955. Early wares were often decorated with carved designs of stylized animals, birds, or florals with the designs colored to contrast with the background. Others had tooled designs filled in with various colors for a mosaic effect. After 1937, Mary Frances, the last remaining sister, favored handmade figurines with somewhat bizarre features in fanciful combinations of color. Overbeck ware is signed 'OBK,' frequently with the designer's and potter's initials under the stylized 'OBK.'

Bowl, hunter gr on red clay, mahog flambé on butterscotch int, 3x6" ...770.00
Brooch, blond in full skirt, 4-color, 2" dia 265.00
Brooch, bluebird in flowering tree, mc, metal bk, 1½" 325.00
Figurine, couple in Southern 19th-C attire, 5", pr, NM 400.00
Figurine, dog (spaniel), OBK, 1½" 225.00
Figurine, woodpecker, OBK, 2½" 350.00
Jardiniere, repetitive flowers, gr-grn on tan, 5x7", NM 4,500.00
Vase, hummingbirds (16), brn/gr, cut-out hdls, EF, 6x5" 5,500.00
Vase, pine cones cvd in panels, pk-gr ground, sgn EF, 4¾" 1,200.00

Overlay Glass

Art glass having layers of more than one type or color of glass is sometimes called overlay or cased glass. Very often glassware of this type has applied decorations such as fruit, flowers, leaves, or ruffles (rigaree), such as is commonly identified with Stevens and Williams. See also Stevens and Williams.

Basket, rose to pk, wht int, appl gr leaves/amber stem & ft, 11" .300.00
Bowl, pk cased w/appl leaves & bl strawberry, thorn hdls, English, 9" ...175.00
Bowl, pk on wht w/appl 3-color floral/leaves/ft, 5½" H..............635.00
Bowl, rose to pk w/wht int, appl amber ft & stem w/3 wht flowers, 6" .200.00
Pitcher, orange to wht shaded, ruffled, clear hdl, 7¼" 175.00
Rose bowl, bl, HP florals w/gold, 8-crimp, 3½x4¼" 100.00
Vase, gr, appl amber stem/4 red cherries, bk: flowers, 4 amber ft, 10" ..260.00
Vase, pk to wht w/lg appl flowers & leaves, folded/ruffled rim, 9½" .230.00
Vase, red, HP florals, cut scallops w/gold, gold hdls, 8½" 165.00

Overshot

Overshot glass originated in sixteenth century Venice, and the ability to make this ware eventually spread to Bohemia, Spain, and elsewhere in Europe. Sometime prior to 1800, the production of this glass seems to have stopped.

The Englishman Apsley Pellatt, owner of the Falcon Glass Works, is credited with reviving this decorative technique around 1845 – 1850. He acknowledged the origin of this technique by calling his product 'Venetian Frosted Glass' or 'Anglo-Venetian Glass.' Later it would be called by other names, such as frosted glassware, ice glass, or craquelle glass.

It is important to understand the difference between crackle glass and overshot glass. All crackle is not overshot, and all overshot is not crackle. However, most overshot is also crackle glass. Two different processes or steps were involved in making this glassware.

Crackle glass was produced by dipping a partially blown gob of hot glass in cold water. The sudden temperature change caused fissures or cracks in the glass surface. The gob was then lightly reheated and blown into its full shape. The blowing process enlarged the spaces between fissures to create a labyrinth of channels in varying widths. When cooled in the annealing lehr, the surface of the finished object had a crackled or cracked-ice effect.

Overshot glass was made by rolling a partially inflated gob of hot glass on finely ground shards of glass that had been placed on a steel plate called a marver. The gob was then lightly reheated to remove the sharp edges of the ground glass and blown to its final shape. Most overshot pieces were immersed in cold water before application of the ground glass, and such glassware can be considered both crackle and overshot.

Sometimes an object was blown to full size before being rolled over the glass shards. As Barlow and Kaiser explained in *The Glass Industry in Sandwich, Vol. 4*, 'The ground particles adhered uniformally over the entire surface of the piece, showing no roadways, because the glass was not stretched after the particles had been applied. Overshot glass produced by this second method is much sharper to the touch' (page 104).

Overshot glass produced by the first method — with the 'roadways' — has been mistaken for the Tree of Life Pattern. However, this pattern is pressed glass, whereas overshot is either free-blown or mold-blown.

Overshot pieces could be further embellished, requiring a third decorative technique at the furnace, such as the application of vaseline glass designs or fine threads of glass that were picked up and fused to the object. The latter decorative style, called Peloton, was patented in 1880 by Wilhelm Kralik in Bohemia.

Boston & Sandwich, Reading Artistic Glass Works, and Hobbs Brockunier were among the companies that manufactured overshot in the United States. Such products were quite utilitarian — vases, decanters, cruets, bowls, water pitchers with ice bladders, lights, lamps, and other shapes. Colored overshot was produced at Sandwich, but research has shown that the applied ground glass was always crystal. Czechoslovakia is known to have made overshot with colored ground glass. Many such pieces are acid stamped 'Czechoslovakia.' Undamaged, mint conditon overshot is extremely hard to find and expensive.

Our advisors for this category are Stan and Arlene Weitman; they are listed in the Directory under New York.

Basket, cranberry to crystal, thorn hdl, rectangular, 10x7½".......750.00
Bowl, lt gr w/appl rigaree & flower, 4x6"..................................350.00
Mug, rubena w/emb pattern, clear ft & hdl, 4⅛x2¾".................175.00
Pitcher, clear, Sandwich, 4½"...350.00
Pitcher, cranberry, reeded hdl, water sz................................550.00
Salt cellar, clear, Reed & Barton SP fr....................................95.00
Tumbler, gr to clear, 3¾x2¾"...82.50
Tumbler, rubena, swirled, 3¾"..165.00
Vase, cranberry w/4 crystal ft, 5¾".......................................450.00
Vase, metallic gold, indented sides, slight twist to 6" neck, 10"....60.00

Owen, Ben

Ben Owen worked at the Jugtown Pottery of North Carolina from 1923 until it temporarily closed in 1959. He continued in the business in his own Plank Road Pottery, stamping his ware 'Ben Owen, Master Potter,' with many forms made by Lester Fanell Craven in the late 1960s. His pottery closed in 1972. He died in 1983 at the age of 81.

The pottery was reopened in 1981 under the supervision of Benjamin Wade Owen II. One of the principal potters was David Garner who worked there until about 1985. This pottery is still in operation today with Ben II as the main potter.

Baker, Tobacco Spit Brown, emb rings in bottom, hdls, 2⅜x14½" L ..90.00
Bean Pot, Tobacco Spit Brown, Master Potter, 1960s, 6⅞", NM .150.00
Bowl, dk brn-red, Ben Owen Pottery, 1980s, 2⅝x7½" 80.00
Candlesticks, bright orange, Ben Owen I, 11½", pr................650.00
Candlesticks, Crimson Red, Ben Owen III, 9th Annual...1990, 15", pr..375.00
Casserole, warm orange, Ben Owen I, 1961-62, 4¼x8" 70.00
Creamer & sugar bowl, cobalt/salt glaze, ...Master Potter, 3½" 90.00
Jar, apothecary; Frogskin, F Craven, late 1960s, 4¾" 40.00
Jug, Frogskin, F Craven, late 1960s, 4½"................................60.00
Rice bowl, Frogskin Albany slip, F Craven, 1960s, 4¾" 30.00
Ring jug/canteen, salt glaze w/orange peel on top side, Ben Owen III.50.00
Soap dish/ashtray, orange-red, Ben Owen Pottery, 1980s, 2x4¾"..80.00
Tray, Bent; Tobacco Spit Brown, B Owen III, 1986, 3x10¼x13½"..60.00
Vase, Egg, Chinese White, ca 1959-60, 4⅝" 70.00
Vase, Egg, Chinese White, David Garner, ca 1981-85, 2⅞".........50.00

Owens Pottery

J.B. Owens founded his company in Zanesville, Ohio, in 1891, and until 1907, when the company decided to exert most of its energies in the area of tile production, made several quality lines of art pottery. His first line, Utopian, was a standard brown ware with underglaze slip decoration of nature studies, animals, and portraits. A similar line, Lotus, utilized lighter background colors. Henri Deux, introduced in 1900, featured incised Art Nouveau forms inlaid with color. (Be aware that the Brush McCoy Pottery acquired many of Owens's molds and reproduced a line similar to Henri Deux, which they called Navarre.) Other important lines were Opalesce, Rustic, Feroza, Cyrano, and Mission, examples of which are rare today. The factory burned in 1928, and the company closed shortly thereafter. Values vary according to the quality of the artwork and subject matter. Examples signed by the artist bring higher prices than those that are not signed. For further information we recommend *Owens Pottery Unearthed* by Kristy and Rick McKibben and Jeanette and Marvin Stofft. Mrs. Stofft is listed in the Directory under Indiana.

Cyrano, planter, rtcl band around body, corseted, 7x8", EX, $500 to..750.00

Lotus, pitcher, 2 floating blossoms, #1, 8⅝" 400.00
Majolica, jard & ped, putti/dolphins/dragons/sea creatures, G, $300 to .400.00
Matt Green, vase, bulbous w/buttress hdls, rtcl neck, #115, 6½", VG..485.00
Matt Green, vase, Celtic motif, stamped mk, 9x6½"..................485.00
Matt Green, vase, geometrics, 6"...325.00
Matt Green, vase, rtcl neck w/Greek Key incised pattern, 7x8" .550.00
Matt Green, vase, shoulder w/openings, emb swan panels, #1025, 12"..1,495.00
Matt Green, vase, tapered w/incised dragonflies, Pollock, 4x5½" .450.00
Matt Utopian, vase, chrysanthemums, TS, 13x6½", EX, from $250 to.350.00
Matt Utopian, vase, nasturtiums, FC, 13½", from $300 to..........500.00

Matt Utopian, vase, portrait of a cat, Mae Timberlake, minor flecks to body, 10½", $3,450.00. (Photo courtesy Dave Rago Auctions)

Tile, rose & leaves, pk on gr matt, 5½" sq, EX............................550.00
Utopian, lamp base, leaves & berries, post-factory, 10½"............250.00
Utopian, letter opener, daisies, pillow form w/4 toes, 5x4½" 350.00
Utopian, pitcher, 3 tulips, mc on gold to brn, cylinder, mk, 12¼"..495.00
Utopian, vase, autumn leaves, Timberlake, cylindrical, 10½x5".565.00
Utopian, vase, carnations, Mary Pierce, twisted, 5x3½", EX, $200 to..300.00
Utopian, vase, clover blossoms, bottle shape, 15".........................550.00
Utopian, vase, nasturtiums, 12x4", EX, from $250 to..................350.00
Utopian, vase, pansies, AJ/#219, 8½".....................................260.00
Utopian, vase, poppy, tapered, #014, 12½" 345.00
Utopian, vase, rose, LT, 13¼x6", from $200 to...........................300.00
Utopian, vase, roses, bulbous, 7x3¼", EX, from $200 to.............300.00
Utopian Light, jug, plum branch, HR, 6¾x4¾", NM, from $150 to ..250.00

Pacific Clay Products

The Pacific Clay Products Company got its start in the 1920s as a consolidation of several smaller southern California potteries. The main Los Angeles plant had been founded in 1890 to make kitchen stoneware, ollas, and similar items. Terra cotta and brick were later produced.

In 1932 Hostess Ware, a vividly colored line of dinnerware, was introduced to compete with Bauer's Ring Ware. Coralitos, a lighter-weight, pastel-hued dinnerware line was first marketed in 1937, and a similar but less expensive line called Arcadia soon followed. Art ware including vases, figurines, candlesticks, etc., was produced from 1932 to 1942, at which time the company went into war-related work and pottery manufacture ceased. A limited amount of hand-decorated dinnerware was also made. For further information we recommend *Collector's Encyclopedia of California Pottery, 2nd Edition*, by Jack Chipman; he is listed in the Directory under California.

Baker, orange, Hostessware, #205, 1930-42 ....30.00
Bowl, fruit; yel, Hostessware, #601, 1930-42, 5½" 27.50
Mug, yel, metal bands & wooden hdl, Hostessware, #411, 4¼" 32.50
Planter, Martha Washington cameo, 1930s, 5½x3½"...................15.00
Plate, orange, 9" 15.00

Vase, fan; lt bl, 7½x6½" **65.00**
Vase, lime gr, emb branches on ft, Deco shape w/hdls, 8x5" **130.00**
Vase, lt pk, 8x5½" **55.00**
Vase, pk w/horned antelope in reserve, 10x7½" **225.00**

Paden City

Paden City Glass Mfg. Co. was founded in 1916 in Paden City, West Virginia. It made both mold-blown and pressed wares and is most remembered today for its handmade wares in bright colors with fanciful etchings. A great deal of Paden City's business was in supplying decorating companies and fitters with glass; therefore, Paden City never marked their glass with a trademark of any kind, and the company's advertisements were limited to trade publications, rather than retail. In 1948 the management of the company opened a second plant to make utilitarian, machine-made wares such as tumblers and ashtrays, but the move was ill-advised due to a glut of similar wares already on the market. The company remained in operation until 1951 when it permanently closed the doors of both factories as a result of the losses incurred by Plant No. 2. (To clear up an often-repeated misunderstanding, dealers and collectors alike should keep in mind that The Paden City Glass Mfg Co. had absolutely no connection with the Paden City Pottery Company, other than their identical locale.)

Today Paden City is best known for its numerous acid-etched wares that featured birds, but other ornate etchings were also produced — some of which are well documented in print, while others have yet to be documented in publications that are widely available. Peacock and Rose and Cupid are two of the most commonly found etched patterns. Currently, collectors especially seek out examples of Paden City's most detailed etching, Orchid, and its most appealing etching, Cupid. However, pieces bearing undocumented etchings or documented etchings on shapes and/or colors on which that etching has not previously been seen are fetching the highest prices from advanced collectors. Pieces in the company's plainer pressed dinnerware lines, however, have remained affordable, even though some patterns are quite scarce.

Below is a list of Paden City's colors. Names in capital letters indicate original factory color names where known, followed by a description of the color.

Amber — several shades
Blue — early 1920s color, medium shade, not cobalt
Cheriglo — pink
Copen, Neptune, Ceylon — various shades of light blue
Crystal — clear
Ebony — black
Emeraldglo — thinner dark green, not as deep as Forest Green
Forest Green — dark green
Green — various shades, from yellowish to electric green
Mulberry — amethyst
Opal — white (milk glass)
Primrose — amber with reddish tint (rare)
Rose — dark pink (rare)
Royal or Ritz Blue — cobalt
Ruby — red
Topaz — yellow

Collectors seeking more information on Paden City would do well to consult the following: *Paden City, The Color Company*, by Jerry Barnett (out of print, privately published, 1979); *Colored Glassware of the Depression Era 2* by Hazel Marie Weatherman (Glassbooks, 1974); and *Price Trends to Colored Glassware of the Depression Era 2* by Hazel Marie Weatherman (Glassbooks, Editions in 1977, 1979, and 1981). Also available are *Paden City Company Catalog Reprints from the 1920s* (Antique Publica-

tions, 2000) and *Paden City Glassware* by Paul and Debora Torsiello and Tom Arlene Stillman (Schiffer, 2002). There is also a quarterly newsletter currently being published by the Paden City Glass Collectors Guild; this group is listed the Directory under Clubs, Newsletters, and Catalogs. Our advisor for this category is Michael Krumme; he is listed in the Directory under California. If no color is listed, the item is crystal.

Ardith (etched), bowl, console; ruby..............................**150.00**
Ardith (etched), bowl, console; yel or blk, from $85 to................**95.00**
Ardith (etched), cake salver, yel or blk, low ft, from $75 to.........**85.00**
Ardith (etched), candy box, yel or blk, sq **150.00**
Ardith (etched), cheese & cracker set, pk or gr, from $85 to.......**95.00**
Ardith (etched), comport, yel or blk, from $75 to **95.00**
Ardith (etched), creamer & sugar bowl, yel or blk **125.00**
Ardith (etched), decanter, cordial; pk, +6 shot glasses in metal stand .**275.00**
Ardith (etched), mayonnaise set, yel or blk, 3-pc.....................**150.00**
Ardith (etched), tray, pk or gr, center hdl **85.00**
Ardith (etched), tray, yel or blk, hdls, from $75 to **85.00**
Ardith (etched), tumbler, pk, blown..................................**75.00**
Ardith (etched), vase, pk or gr, elliptical, sm, 5" **150.00**
Ardith (etched), vase, yel or blk, squarish, 9", from $175 to.......**200.00**
Black Forest (etched), bowl, serving; blk, hdls..........................**100.00**
Black Forest (etched), cake salver, pk or gr, low ft, from $85 to....**95.00**
Black Forest (etched), candle holders, pk or gr, mushroom style, pr..**125.00**
Black Forest (etched), candy dish, blk, ftd............................**150.00**
Black Forest (etched), cheese & cracker set, pk or gr..................**110.00**
Black Forest (etched), comport, pk or gr, from $85 to **95.00**
Black Forest (etched), creamer & sugar bowl, from $85 to............**95.00**
Black Forest (etched), cup & saucer, #991 shape........................**100.00**
Black Forest (etched), cup & saucer, blk, #210 shape..................**100.00**
Black Forest (etched), decanter, gr **450.00**
Black Forest (etched), ice bucket, amber, metal bail **150.00**
Black Forest (etched), ice tub, pk or gr, tab hdls....................**125.00**
Black Forest (etched), mayonnaise set, pk or gr, 3-pc.................**150.00**
Black Forest (etched), tray, amber, center hdl........................**75.00**
Black Forest (etched), tray, pk or gr, hdls, from $65 to..............**75.00**
Black Forest (etched), vase, blk, cylindrical, 9", from $175 to **200.00**
Black Forest (etched), vase, pk or gr, bulbous, 10", from $150 to ..**175.00**
Crow's Foot Round, bowl, console; ruby, flat rim, 3-ftd **95.00**
Crow's Foot Round, bowl, serving; ruby or cobalt, hdls **65.00**
Crow's Foot Round, candle holders, single, pr..........................**65.00**
Crow's Foot Round, candle holders, triple, ruby or cobalt, pr **150.00**
Crow's Foot Round, candy dish, 3-ftd, from $85 to.....................**95.00**
Crow's Foot Round, cheese & cracker set, ruby, from $85 to.........**95.00**
Crow's Foot Round, comport, ruby or cobalt, tall stem..................**65.00**
Crow's Foot Round, mayonnaise & liner, ruby or cobalt, 3-ftd......**85.00**
Crow's Foot Round, plate, ruby, 6", from $8 to **10.00**
Crow's Foot Round, plate, ruby, 8", from $10 to **12.00**
Crow's Foot Round, plate, ruby, 9", from $25 to **35.00**
Crow's Foot Round, tray, amber, center hdl............................**50.00**
Crow's Foot Round, tray, amber, hdls..................................**35.00**
Crow's Foot Round, tumbler, amber.....................................**40.00**
Crow's Foot Round, tumbler, ruby or cobalt............................**75.00**
Crow's Foot Square, bowl, console; cobalt, from $55 to **65.00**
Crow's Foot Square, bowl, cream soup; ruby, from $15 to.............**20.00**
Crow's Foot Square, bowl, oval vegetable; ruby, from $30 to.........**40.00**
Crow's Foot Square, bowl, serving; ruby, hdls, from $45 to............**65.00**
Crow's Foot Square, cake salver, opal, low ft.........................**95.00**
Crow's Foot Square, candle holders, blk, mushroom style, pr **85.00**
Crow's Foot Square, candle holders, ruby, keyhole style, pr...........**95.00**
Crow's Foot Square, candy dish, ruby or cobalt, cloverleaf shape ..**150.00**
Crow's Foot Square, candy dish, yel, sq **125.00**
Crow's Foot Square, cheese & cracker set, ruby **85.00**
Crow's Foot Square, comport, mulberry, low stem......................**45.00**

Crow's Foot Square, creamer & sugar bowl, opal 85.00
Crow's Foot Square, cup & saucer, ruby, from $15 to..........20.00
Crow's Foot Square, mayonnaise set, ruby, 3-pc 95.00
Crow's Foot Square, plate, ruby, 6", from $8 to 10.00
Crow's Foot Square, plate, ruby, 8", from $10 to 12.00
Crow's Foot Square, platter, cobalt, oval 50.00
Crow's Foot Square, tray, amber, hdls, from $30 to 35.00
Crow's Foot Square, tray, blk, center hdl 45.00
Crow's Foot Square, vase, ruby, cupped, 10" 110.00
Cupid (etched), bowl, console; pk or gr, 13" 185.00
Cupid (etched), bowl, pk or gr, oval 225.00
Cupid (etched), cake salver, pk or gr, low ft 125.00
Cupid (etched), candy dish, pk or gr, ftd 275.00
Cupid (etched), comport, pk or gr 150.00
Cupid (etched), creamer & sugar bowl, pk or gr 175.00
Cupid (etched), ice bucket, pk or gr, metal bail 195.00
Cupid (etched), mayonnaise set, pk or gr, 3-pc 225.00
Cupid (etched), plate, pk or gr, oval, ftd 125.00
Cupid (etched), salver, pk or gr, low ft 150.00
Cupid (etched), tray, center hdl 125.00
Delilah Bird (etched), bowl, console; pk 125.00
Delilah Bird (etched), bowl, console; ruby 350.00
Delilah Bird (etched), cake salver, yel, low ft 85.00
Delilah Bird (etched), candle holders, pk, keyhole style, pr........150.00
Delilah Bird (etched), comport, low ft 95.00
Delilah Bird (etched), vase, blk, cylindrical, 9" 250.00
Delilah Bird (etched), vase, pk or gr, squat, 7" 175.00
Eden Rose (etched), top hat, 6" 85.00
Eden Rose (etched), vase, blk, cylindrical, 9" 150.00
Eden Rose (etched), vase, gr or pk, bulbous, 12" 175.00
Gazebo (etched), bowl, console; from $45 to 50.00
Gazebo (etched), candy dish, lt bl, ftd................95.00
Gazebo (etched), creamer & sugar bowl, from $40 to...........45.00
Gazebo (etched), mayonnaise bowl & liner, from $35 to 40.00
Gazebo (etched), tray, center hdl 45.00
Gazebo (etched), tray, hdls....................40.00
Gazebo (etched), vase, bulbous, 10" 75.00
Gothic Garden (etched), bowl, console; yel or blk, flat rim, $65 to...75.00
Gothic Garden (etched), cake salver, pk or gr, low ft 95.00
Gothic Garden (etched), candle holders, yel or blk, key hole style, pr...135.00
Gothic Garden (etched), candy box, pk or gr, sq.............150.00
Gothic Garden (etched), cheese & cracker set, yel or blk 125.00
Gothic Garden (etched), comport, pk or gr, from $85 to 95.00
Gothic Garden (etched), creamer & sugar bowl, yel or blk 125.00
Gothic Garden (etched), mayonnaise set, yel, 3-pc 150.00
Gothic Garden (etched), tray, pk or gr, hdls, from $75 to 85.00
Gothic Garden (etched), tray, yel or blk, center hdl, from $65 to...85.00
Gothic Garden (etched), vase, pk or gr, squarish, 9" 300.00
Largo, bowl, console; lt bl, 3-ftd....................65.00
Largo, bowl, serving; lt bl, hdls, from $50 to 65.00
Largo, cake salver, lt bl, high ft 50.00
Largo, cheese & cracker set, ruby....................85.00
Largo, comport, amber....................25.00
Largo, creamer & sugar bowl, amethyst or forest gr 150.00
Largo, creamer & sugar bowl, lt bl or ruby, from $50 to...........65.00
Largo, cup & saucer, ruby 35.00
Largo, mayonnaise bowl & liner 35.00
Largo, tray, center hdl....................35.00
Largo, tray, lt bl, hdls....................50.00
Lela Bird (etched), cake salver, pk or gr, low ft, from $95 to.......110.00
Lela Bird (etched), candle holders, pk or gr, mushroom style, pr...125.00
Lela Bird (etched), comport, pk or gr, ftd, lg..............125.00
Lela Bird (etched), mayonnaise bowl, pk or gr.............85.00
Lela Bird (etched), pk or gr, center hdl, from $75 to 85.00

Lela Bird (etched), vase, blk, elliptical, 8", from $100 to 125.00
Lela Bird (etched), vase, blk w/gold etching, bulbous, 12".........225.00
Lela Bird (etched), vase, pk or gr, bulbous, 10", from $125 to 150.00
Maya, bowl, console; 3-ftd....................40.00
Maya, cheese & cracker set, lt bl, dome lid................75.00
Maya, comport, ruby, tall....................95.00
Maya, creamer & sugar bowl 35.00
Maya, cup & saucer, lt bl....................30.00
Maya, tray, lt bl, center hdl....................50.00
Nora Bird (etched), candle holders, pk or gr, mushroom style, pr...125.00
Nora Bird (etched), creamer & sugar bowl, pk or gr....................150.00
Nora Bird (etched), mayonnaise set, 3-pc 95.00
Nora Bird (etched), tumbler, gr, blown, 5", from $75 to 100.00
Orchid (etched), bowl, console; pk 150.00
Orchid (etched), bowl, ruby, hdls....................250.00
Orchid (etched), cheese & cracker set, pk 200.00
Orchid (etched), comport, ruby, low ft................200.00
Orchid (etched), cup & saucer, from $75 to 100.00
Orchid (etched), mayonnaise comport 45.00
Orchid (etched), tray, gr, center hdl 100.00
Orchid (etched), tray, hdls....................50.00
Orchid (etched), tray, ruby, center hdl................125.00
Orchid (etched), tray, ruby, hdls....................200.00
Orchid (etched), vase, blk, elliptical, sm, 5"............150.00
Orchid (etched), vase, bulbous, 12"..................200.00
Orchid (etched), vase, ruby, flared, 10"................450.00
Party Line, banana split dish, gr..................30.00
Party Line, bowl, console; lt bl, rolled edge..............50.00
Party Line, cake salver, pk or gr, high ft 150.00
Party Line, candle holders, gr, flat ft, pr.................45.00
Party Line, candle holders, med bl, dome ft, pr............40.00
Party Line, cocktail shaker, gr....................125.00
Party Line, cologne bottle, pk, long dauber..............65.00
Party Line, comport, amethyst 40.00
Party Line, creamer & sugar bowl, pk or gr, from $25 to 30.00
Party Line, ice bucket, pk or gr, metal bail 75.00
Party Line, ice tub, pk or gr, tab hdls, from $35 to.........45.00
Party Line, pitcher, pk, w/lid....................95.00
Party Line, powder jar, amber, flat 30.00
Party Line, shakers, ruby or cobalt, pr.................95.00
Party Line, stem, champagne, pk or gr.................15.00
Party Line, stem, low sherbet, pk or gr 10.00
Party Line, stem, tulip sundae, pk or gr 25.00
Party Line, sugar pourer, pk or gr....................100.00
Party Line, syrup, gr, metal lid....................85.00
Party Line, tray, pk or gr, center hdl 30.00
Party Line, tumbler, ftd, 6"....................20.00
Party Line, tumbler, pk or gr, 4"....................15.00
Party Line, vase, lt bl, fan shape 50.00
Party Line, vase, pk or gr, blown hourglass, crimped top, 8", $35 to...45.00
Party Line, water bottle, gr....................45.00
Peacock & Rose (etched), bowl, console; pk or gr, 13" 150.00
Peacock & Rose (etched), bowl, pk or gr, oval 250.00
Peacock & Rose (etched), candy dish, pk or gr, ftd 225.00
Peacock & Rose (etched), comport, pk or gr 125.00
Peacock & Rose (etched), creamer & sugar bowl (no peacock), pk or gr....200.00
Peacock & Rose (etched), ice bucket, amber, metal bail............100.00
Peacock & Rose (etched), ice tub, pk or gr, tab hdls............125.00
Peacock & Rose (etched), mayonnaise set, pk or gr, 3-pc 175.00
Peacock & Rose (etched), salver, low ft................125.00
Peacock & Rose (etched), tray, pk or gr, center hdl 95.00
Peacock & Rose (etched), vase, ebony, bulbous, 10"..................200.00
Penny Line, bowl, serving; cobalt, hdls 55.00
Penny Line, creamer & sugar bowl, cobalt, from $40 to...............45.00

Penny Line, creamer & sugar bowl, ruby, from $25 to 30.00
Penny Line, cup & saucer, ruby 15.00
Penny Line, decanter, ruby..85.00
Penny Line, goblet, ruby, high ft, from $30 to.............................35.00
Penny Line, goblet, ruby, low ft, from $15 to...............................20.00
Penny Line, plate, ruby, 8", from $8 to.......................................10.00
Penny Line, sherbet, forest gr, low...15.00
Penny Line, shot glass, ruby, from $8 to......................................10.00
Penny Line, tray, amethyst, center hdl...45.00
Penny Line, tumbler, ruby, 6"...25.00
Spring Orchard (etched), bitters bottle......................................125.00
Spring Orchard (etched), cocktail shaker....................................150.00
Spring Orchard (etched), decanter, cordial, hdld tilt style 50.00
Spring Orchard (etched), decanter, flat sided, cog stopper, $55 to...65.00
Spring Orchard (etched), stem, cocktail; hourglass shape 20.00
Spring Orchard (etched), stem, cordial 25.00
Spring Orchard (etched), stem, wine...15.00
Spring Orchard (etched), tumbler, whiskey...................................20.00
Utopia, candy box, lt bl, heart shape..150.00
Utopia, relish dish, 3-part..45.00
Utopia, vase, lt bl, bulbous, 10"...125.00
Utopia, vase, squarish, 9"..150.00

Pairpoint

The Pairpoint Manufacturing Company was built in 1880 in New Bedford, Massachusetts. It was primarily a metalworks whose chief product was coffin fittings. Next door, the Mt. Washington Glassworks made quality glasswares of many varieties. (See Mt. Washington for more information concerning their artware lines.) By 1894 it became apparent to both companies that a merger would be to their best interest.

From the late 1890s until the 1930s, lamps and lamp accessories were an important part of Pairpoint's production. There were three main types of shades, all of which were blown: puffy — blown-out reverse-painted shades (usually floral designs); ribbed — also reverse painted; and scenic — reverse painted with scenes of land or seascapes (usually executed on smooth surfaces, although ribbed scenics may be found occasionally). Cut glass lamps and those with metal overlay panels were also made. Scenic shades were sometimes artist signed. Every shade was stamped on the lower inside or outside edge with 1) The Pairpoint Corp., 2) Patent Pending, 3) Patented July 9, 1907, or 4) Patent Applied For. Bases were made of bronze, copper, brass, silver, or wood and are always signed. (In our listings all information before the semicolon pertains specifically to the shade.)

Because they produced only fancy, handmade artware, the company's sales lagged seriously during the Depression, and as time and tastes changed, their style of product was less in demand. As a result, they never fully recovered; consequently part of the buildings and equipment was sold in 1938. The company reorganized in 1939 under the direction of Robert Gundersen and again specialized in quality hand-blown glassware. Isaac Babbit regained possession of the silver departments, and together they established Gundersen Glassworks, Inc. After WWII, because of a sharp decline in sales, it again became necessary to reorganize. The Gundersen-Pairpoint Glassworks was formed, and the old line of cut, engraved artware was reintroduced. The company moved to East Wareham, Massachusetts, in 1957. But business continued to suffer, and the firm closed only one year later. In 1970, however, new facilities were constructed in Sagamore under the direction of Robert Bryden, sales manager for the company since the 1950s.

In 1974 the company began to produce lead glass cup plates which were made on commission as fund-raisers for various churches and organizations. These are signed with a 'P' in diamond and are becoming quite collectible. See also Burmese; Napkin Rings.

Glass

Bowl, bright bl w/lg clear pinwheel, 3½x11½", EX 500.00
Box, Russian cut, SP vertical bars & lid, 7¼" dia 460.00
Candlesticks, Viscaria, teardrop stems, 9", pr 235.00
Ice bucket, eng polar bear, SP mts, 9x4¾" 345.00
Pokal, old English Hobnail cutting, domed lid w/finial, 14"........415.00
Vase, Ambero, landscape/2 figures/house, 11½" 1,725.00
Vase, ruby, bubble ball & ruby ft, 13" 180.00
Vase, Tavern Glass, bubbly w/enamel bouquet of flowers in bowl, 6½"...145.00
Vase, Tavern Glass, bubbly w/enamel ship, str flared sides, 8¼" .260.00

Lamps

Base only, 4-sided shaft, lobed base, bronze patina, B-3040, 15".345.00
HP/rvpt 10" dome shade w/autumn leaves; 4 rtcl supports on emb base ..2,520.00
HP/rvpt 16" winter night scene shade w/moon on water; simple std..2,600.00
Puffy candelabra w/5 floral shades; classically styled gilt base .31,000.00
Puffy 5" rose bonnet shade w/butterflies; tree trunk base 12,300.00
Puffy 8" shade w/orange/yel mums; silvered base w/3 curved arms, 18"...15,100.00
Puffy 8" shade w/4 floral panels; emb floral sq-base std #3050, 15" ..3,640.00

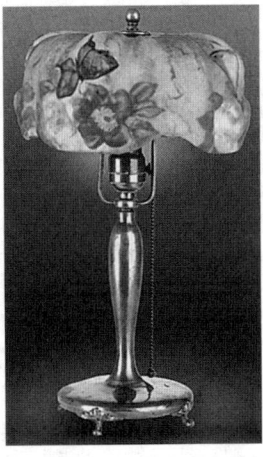

Puffy 8½" roses and butterflies shade; gilded base, $5,000.00. (Photo courtesy Fontaine's Auction Gallery)

Puffy 9" tulips shade; silvered sq-ft std w/4 legs & emb stem ...7,280.00
Puffy 10" azalea shade; intricate floral-arm/floral emb SP base ...21,800.00
Puffy 10" peony Torino shade; 4-sided rtcl inv't trumpet base, 19" ..17,350.00
Puffy 10" roses shade; invt trumpet base w/leaves & floral-rtcl arms..7,840.00
Puffy 10" shade w/4 lg roses, 4-lobe border; simple std 2,500.00
Puffy 12" grape clusters/autumn leaves shade; SP grapevine base ..44,800.00
Puffy 12" grapes/vines sgn shade; sgn tree trunk organic base .10,600.00
Puffy 12" red & wht poppy shade; silver/gold-tone base w/etch floral .24,600.00
Puffy 14" butterflies/roses shade; silver base #3086 w/rtcl, 21".5,750.00
Puffy 14" humingbirds/roses/gr swirls closed shade; rtcl #3086 base..14,000.00
Puffy 14" ribbed shade w/mums & hummingbird; trn column/stepped ft.6,900.00
Puffy 14" Stratford shade w/roses & hummingbirds; sqd std/base..5,000.00
Puffy 16" Marlborough shade w/various florals; rtcl base w/etch tulip..6,700.00
Puffy 16" roses/4 butterflies Papillon shade; vintage-emb base, 16" .4,480.00
Rvpt 4½" floral shade, wht/purple, faceted glass/marble stem, pr .17,900.00
Rvpt 8" cone shade w/wide band of stylized flowers; vasiform base ..950.00
Rvpt 8½" shade w/quail; #3040 highly decorated base, 15" 2,800.00
Rvpt 9" cone shade /w2 lg poppies; spiral-wrap section in ftd base ..1,568.00
Rvpt 11" Carlisle shade w/landscape; 2-hdld urn-form bronzed std, 26" .1,850.00
Rvpt 12" melon-section shade w/rose panels; gold vasiform base.4,760.00
Rvpt 13" draped shade w/4 lg red flowers on red; vase base C3047 .4,200.00
Rvpt 15" shade w/fisherman in boat; silvered 3-arm std w/glass/marble ..5,300.00
Rvpt 15" shade w/3 clipper ships sgn Durand; 3-dolphin base, 22" .4,590.00
Rvpt 16" autumn scene Bombay shade; mahog urn-shape unsgn base .3,000.00

Rvpt 16" Directorie shade w/mc floral on blk; 3-scroll support...**3,360.00**
Rvpt 16" Garden of Allah Chesterfield shade; 4-arm/sqd/emb SP base.**11,200.00**
Rvpt 16" Italian garden Seville shade; bubble-ball/onyx/marble base.**3,475.00**
Rvpt 16" pastoral scene Copley shade sgn Fisher (EX); baluster base.**1,840.00**
Rvpt 16" Venetian harbor shade; base #3038 w/egg-form stem, 22"..**3,350.00**
Rvpt 18" exotic bird/floral Bombay shade; SP 3-strap base, 3-sided ft.**4,480.00**
Rvpt 18" shade w/4 parrots & fronds; silvered 3-leg std w/center stem..**4,480.00**
Rvpt 20" cone shade w/country-scene band; mahog base w/gold filigree..**1,900.00**

Paper Dolls

No one knows quite how or when paper dolls originated. One belief is that they began in Europe as 'pantins' (jumping jacks). During the nineteenth century, most paper dolls portrayed famous dancers and opera stars such as Fanny Elssler and Jenny Lind. In the late 1800s, the Raphael Tuck Publishers of England produced many series of beautiful paper dolls. Retail companies used paper dolls as advertisements to further the sale of their products. Around the turn of the century, many popular women's magazines began featuring a page of paper dolls.

Most familiar to today's collectors are the books with dolls on cardboard covers and clothes on the inside pages. These made their appearance in the late 1920s and early 1930s. The most collectible (and the most valuable) are those representing celebrities, movie stars, and comic-strip characters of the '30s and '40s.

When no condition is indicated, the dolls listed below are assumed to be in mint, uncut, original condition. Cut sets will be worth about half price if all dolls and outfits are included and pieces are in very good condition. If dolls were produced in die-cut form, these prices reflect such a set in mint condition with all costumes and accessories.

For further information we recommend *Tomart's Price Guide to Lowe and Whitman Paper Dolls*, and *Tomart's Price Guide to Saalfield and Merrill Paper Dolls*, by Mary Young, our advisor for this category; she is listed in the Directory under Ohio. We also recommend *Schroeder's Collectible Toys, Antique to Modern* (Collector Books).

Ann & Joe, MA Donohue & Co, #80C, EX uncut **50.00**
Army Nurse & Doctor, Merrill #3425, 1942, EX **125.00**
Ballet Dancers, Merrill #3447, 1947, M **50.00**
Betsy McCall Around the World, ca 1962, VG **10.00**
Bette Davis, Merrill #4816, 1942, NM **250.00**
Betty & Dick Tour the USA, Standard Toykraft, 1940, NM........**22.00**
Blondie, Whitman #993, family figures+dogs, 1945, EX uncut **88.00**
Blondie in the Movies, Whitman #979, book type, 1941, EX.......**95.00**
Bob Hope & Dorothy Lamour, Whitman #976, 1942, M uncut .**300.00**
Carmen Miranda, cut, EX **60.00**
Chitty Chitty Bang Bang, Whitman #1952, 1968, NM.................**22.50**
Deanna Durbin, Merrill #3480, 1940, M uncut **185.00**
Dollies To Dress Like Father & Mother, Platt & Munk #225, EX.**22.50**
Dolly Dingle Gives a Thanksgiving Dinner, EX uncut **27.50**
Donna Reed, Saalfield/Artcraft #5197, 1960, M uncut **75.00**
Dorothy, Playtime House #313, NM in VG box **15.00**
Dotty & Danny on Parade, Burton #875, 1935, EX uncut **25.00**
Double Wedding, Merrill #3472, partially punched/cut, 1939, EX.**75.00**
First Ladies of White House, Saalfield #2164, 1937, M uncut.......**55.00**
Gigi Perreau, Saalfield #1542, 1951, EX uncut **50.00**
Gone w/the Wind, Merrill #3405, 1940, M uncut.......................**350.00**
Gulliver's Travels, Saalfield #1261, 1939, M uncut....................**150.00**
Jackie & Caroline Wonderful Paper Dolls, Magic/Wand, 1960s ...**65.00**
Janet Leigh, Abbott #1805, 1958, EX uncut **60.00**
Joan's Wedding, Whitman #990, 1942, EX uncut........................**75.00**
Judy Garland, Whitman #999, 1940, M uncut............................**125.00**
Kewpies, Saalfield #4461, 1968, M **27.50**
Let's Play Paper Dolls, McLoughlin, 1938, EX uncut...................**40.00**

Liberty Belles, Merrill #3477, 1943, uncut **125.00**
Magic Doll, Parker Bros, ca 1948, EX..................................**20.00**
Mary Frances Housekeeper, JC Winston, ca 1914, EX uncut **200.00**
Munster's Paper Dolls, Whitman #1959, 1966, NM uncut...........**75.00**
My Dolly Sister Nan, Sam Gabriel Sons #D-90, EX **35.00**
Natalie Wood, Whitman #2086, 1958, NM uncut **150.00**
Pat Boone, Whitman #1968, 1959, EX uncut **65.00**
Prince & Princess, Saalfield #2706, 1949, EX uncut **75.00**
Rita Hayworth, Saalfield #2712, 1948, NM uncut.....................**125.00**
Shirley Temple Magnetic Doll, Gabriel #303, NM uncut.............**65.00**
Snow White & 7 Dwarfs, Whitman #1998, ca 1970, EX **18.00**
Tarzan of the Apes, 1933 figure set, M **57.00**
Three Sisters, Whitman #1174, Sally, Sue & Dot, 1942, complete cut set ..**25.00**
War Girls, Samuel Lowe #529, 1943, EX uncut **85.00**
Ziegfeld Girl, Merrill #3466, 1941, M uncut...............................**400.00**
1964 World's Fair, M uncut...**35.00**

Paperweights

Glass paperweight collecting has grown in intensity over the past ten years. Many glass artists in the marketplace today are creating beautiful examples that generally sell for less than $100.00. There are hundreds of artisans in the U.S. and factories in China, Italy, and Scotland who produce these 'gift range' paperweights.

Astute collectors are beginning to piece together collections of the old Chinese paperweights that were imported into this country during the 1930s. These were basically unrefined imitations of the lovely and unique French weights of the mid-1800s. When viewed some seventy years later, however, one can appreciate the beauty and craftsmanship these weights exhibit. Murano weights, especially those from the 1960s and 1970s, represent another area of concentrated interest. Prices are beginning to escalate in both categories. With the demise of Perthshire Paperweights of Scotland, collectors began scrambling for their high-end 'annual collection' and annual Christmas paperweights. Interest is increasing in frit weights, Victorian portrait paperweights, and early advertising weights as well — all of which are relatively inexpensive and abundant. Collectors with a large budget can search for the antique French paperweights from the classic period (1845 – 1860), the wonderful English or American weights from the 1850s, or choose to collect the high quality contemporary artistry of master glass artists.

Baccarat, St. Louis, Clichy, and Pantin (names synonymous with classic French paperweights) as well as some American factories stopped making paperweights between the 1880s and 1910 due to a decline in their popularity. In the 1950s Baccarat and St. Louis revived paperweight production and continue today to make lines of high quality, limited production weights. In the 1960s many glass studios began to spring up due to the development of smaller glass furnaces, thereby allowing more freedom for the individual glassmaker to design and fabricate a piece of glass from the fire to the annealing kiln. Such success stories are evident in the creative glass produced by Lundberg Studios, Orient & Flume, and Lotton Studios, to name only a few.

Many factors determine value, particularly of antique weights, and auction-realized prices of contemporary weights usually differ from issue price. Even if two paperweights seem to be identical, their values may not be. Size, faceting, fancy cuts on the base, the inclusion of a seemingly innocuous piece of frit, or a tear in a lampworked leaf can affect cost. And, of course, supply and demand affect prices as well, as do Internet auctions. Antique paperweights have steadily increased in value as has the work of many now deceased glass artists (i.e., Paul Ysart, Joe St. Clair, Charles Kazian, and Del Tarsitano).

The dimension given at the end of the line is diameter. Prices are for weights in perfect or near-perfect condition unless otherwise noted. Our advisors for this category are Betty and Larry Schwab, The Paperweight Shoppe; they are listed in the Directory under Illinois. See Clubs, Newsletters, and Catalogs in the Directory for the Paperweight Collector's Associations, Inc., with chapters in many states. They offer assistance to collectors at all levels.

Key:
con — concentric
fct — faceted
gar — garland
grd — ground
jsp — jasper
latt — latticinio
mill — millefiori
sil — silhouette

Ayotte, Rick

Daisies and blueberries on branch, 1998 limited edition, 3½", $2,300.00.
(Photo courtesy Skinner, Inc.)

Butterfly above sm yel & wht flowers, ltd ed, 1993, 3½" 1,800.00
Daisies & blueberries on branch, 1999, 3¾"...............................2,300.00
Hummingbirds & fuchsia blossoms, ltd ed, 1999, 3½" 1,400.00

Baccarat, Antique

Butterfly w/mil wings amid gr & wht gar, star-cut base, 3".......2,800.00
Clematis (dbl/wht) w/2 buds, fcts, 2⅜" 1,250.00
Con mc mill in clear, 2⅜"...450.00
Con mill w/complex mc canes, 2½"...375.00
Macedoine, mc, filigree, 2"...475.00
Mushroom, close pack w/bl torsade, 3" 4,000.00
Pansy & buds on stems, 7 side fcts, star-cut base, 2¾"..................800.00
Pansy w/gr leaves in clear, star-cut base, 1845-60, 2¾"................700.00
Trefoil gar, complex mill on clear, 3"...775.00

Banford, Bob

Clematis (dbl) w/2 buds on lattice grd, 3" 800.00
Cruciform w/central flower & 52 gr leaves, 3" 600.00
Dueling snakes & ladybug on speckled sandy grd, 3⅛" 950.00
Purple iris bouquet w/gr leaves in basket, dmn-cut base, 2¾"..1,200.00
Rose bouquet on upset muslin, red/wht/bl torsade, 2¾" 700.00
Striped snake coiled around pk flower on rock grd, 3" 750.00

Banford, Ray

Irises (3, different colors), star-cut base, 2⅞" 900.00
Pk rose & 2 buds w/foliage on wht lace, mc spiral torsade, 3" 650.00

Buzzini, Chris

Flowers & butterfly, smoke over wht grd, 1977, 2¾" 200.00
Paphiopedilum orchid, roots, on clear, ltd ed of 40, 1991, 3⅛" ..1,100.00
Yel flowers & dk bl vines on bl irid, 2⅝" 200.00

Caithness

Chai (Life) symbol, bubbles on bl grd, front fct, 3¼" 210.00

Jubilee Floating Crown, Colin Terris, ltd ed, 1977 ....210.00
Jubilee Moonflower, 1977 ltd ed...90.00
Star of David, cobalt gr w/sm bubbles, front fct, 3¼" 110.00

Clichy, Antique

Bl & wht swirl w/complex pk/wht center cluster, 2⅜" 1,750.00
Chequer w/pk rose & pastry mold canes, 2¾" 2,000.00
Con mill w/pk & gr Clichy rose in clear, 2⅝"..............................700.00
Open con mill w/mc canes on bl opaque, 1-6 fcts, 2½" 1,600.00
Pk & gr rose amid spaced mill in clear, 2"....................................900.00
Pk rose center, fcts & flute cut, 3"..4,800.00
Purple/turq/wht swirl w/pk complex center cane, 2½".............2,000.00
Scattered mill w/gr/wht Clichy rose on ruby grd, 2½"...............2,600.00
Scramble w/mill canes including pk rose, 3" 1,000.00
Spaced canes in clear w/6 lg pk & gr roses, 2¾" 2,700.00

Kaziun, Charles

Bl aventurine heart among mc mill & mc gar on wht opaque grd, 2⅛"..600.00
Clematis w/mill center & gr leaves, yel jsp grd, 1½" 600.00
Clematis w/3 gr leaves on gr opaque, 1-6 fcts, 2½" 600.00
Mc con mill amid mc twisted gar on turq opaque grd, 2⅛".........600.00
Morning glory/bud/vine on wht trellis on amethyst grd, 2¼" ..1,100.00
Pansy w/gr leaves & gold bee, bl opaque grd, 2" 1,750.00
Roses (4), pk w/gr foliage amid mc gar on lt bl opaque, 2"..........800.00
Snake, mc w/blk head, coiled by pk rose w/gold bee on wht opaque, 2".1,200.00

Lundberg Studios

Apple on cushion, 1993, 3⅛" 200.00
Crane & bamboo, Steven, 1998, 3½" 475.00
Poinsettia, encircled w/6 Clichy-type roses, wht grd, Salazar, 2⅝" ..300.00
Spider, gr above bl web, Steven, 1969, 2¾" 250.00
Wild Rose Thicket, compound, Steven, 1995, 3¼"......................450.00

New England Glass, Antique

Con mc mill w/spaced air bubbles, 2½".......................................800.00
Con mc mill w/6 heart sil canes, swirl latt grd, fcts, 2⅝"............750.00
Nosegay w/3 blossoms & 4 gr leaves, 2" 400.00
Nosegay w/3 mill cane flowers & 4 leaves, 1¾", EX 250.00
Red poinsettia w/central mill cane on dbl latt, 2¾" 750.00
5 pears/4 cherries in latt basket, 3" 750.00

Perthshire

Complex canes in bl-gr grd, 1-8 fcts, mini, 1¼" 200.00
Con mill w/11 radial twist canes, 1-5 fcts, 2⅜"...........................170.00
Toucan on branch, clear grd, 1-6 fcts, ltd ed of 250, 2½"............400.00
Tudor Rose, ltd ed of 400, 1975, 3⅛" 550.00

Rosenfeld, Ken

Flowers (red/purple/wht) on bl transparent, '93, 9/25, 3½" 435.00
Mc bouquet w/buds on gr stems on bl, 1993, 3¼" 485.00
Monarch butterfly on leafy stem, red flower/3 buds, KR 2001, 2⅝" ..345.00

St. Louis, Antique

Cherries on branch w/gr leaves, fcts, 2⅜" 2,500.00
Fuchsia w/gr leaves, dbl spiral latt, 3".......................................3,500.00
Nosegay, 6 side facets, strawberry-cut base, 2⅞" 1,000.00
Nosegay w/cane flowers in clear, multi-fcts, 2½" 475.00

Nosegay w/mill gar on amber grd, 2⅞" 1,100.00
Patterned mill on muslin grd, 3" 1,000.00
Pk dahlia, star-cut base, 2¼" 5,000.00
Scrambled, 2½" 700.00
Upright bouquet w/bl torsade, 3⅛" 3,450.00

Stankard, Paul

Flowering seed pod w/insects & berries, 'Seeds,' & 'Fertile,' 3¼" ..3,220.00
Flowers & bud w/exposed roots & red ant, 1998, 3⅛" 2,600.00
Morning glory (2/bl), bee on hive, 3 orange berries/2 yel flowers, 3" .2,875.00
Orchids (2) on stems w/leaves, 1981, 2⅞" 1,950.00

Miscellaneous

Czechoslovakia, memorial sulfide portrait of young man, fcts, 4" ..300.00
Donofrio, Aquatic, boy w/3 fish, 1999, 3½" 1,200.00
Dupont, looped gar w/mc mill, central red/wht/bl canes, 3" 500.00
Gentile, John; striped snake & lady bug on brn earth grd, 3⅜" ..575.00
Hamon, Robert; red clematis w/2 buds & gr leaves, 1-6 fcts, 2¼" ...295.00
Hansen, Ron; cherries & leaves on lt bl grd, 2" 150.00
Orient & Flume, cherries on branch, clear cased, 1982, 3½" 450.00
Orient & Flume, iris (irid), 1984, 3¼" 285.00
Parabelle, close pack, 1977, 2¾" 650.00
Smith, strawberries on dk bl grd, 1983, 2¾" 600.00
St Louis, lily of the valley, ltd ed of 200, 1983, 3³⁄₁₆" 650.00
Trabucco, Victor; purple pansy/bud/leaf stem on wht lace, 1998, 3½" ...800.00
Whitefriars, Christmas Wise Men, Christmas 1976, 3¹⁄₁₆" 550.00
Whittemore, Francis; pk crimped rose, ped ft, 2¾" H 400.00
Ysart, striped flower on jsp, PY cane, 3½" 1,200.00

Parian Ware

Parian is hard-paste unglazed porcelain made to resemble marble. First made in the mid-1800s by Staffordshire potters, it was soon after produced in the United States by the U.S. Pottery at Bennington, Vermont. Busts and statuary were favored, but plaques, vases, mugs, and pitchers were also made.

Mercury, after Thorwaldson, Robinson, and Leadbeater, late 1800s, 22⅜", EX+, $975.00. (Photo courtesy Skinner, Inc.)

Bust, Jenny Lind, attached to separately cast base, E&B/Enere, 15" ..200.00
Cupid in naturalistic setting, carrying quiver, English, 8½" 460.00
Geo Washington w/hatchet & chopped wood, unmk, 8½" 100.00
Girl gathering wheat, holds sm pot, 22", EX 650.00
Group, Ariande & Panther, Minton, 15x13" 2,875.00
Group, Babes in Wood, 2 sleeping children/bird, Minton, loss, 12½" ..750.00
Group, Innocence Protected, warrior, maid & child, att Beattie, 20" ...2,350.00
Group, Naomi & Daughters-in-law, Minton, 1860, 13" 880.00
Group, Una & the Lion, nude seated on lion, John Bell, 14" ..2,450.00
Harvest couple, she w/grain he w/sheaf, unmk, 11" 100.00
Mending the Net, seated female, Copeland, 1874, rpr, 17" 500.00
Solitude, seated female, crane beside, Minton, line/chip, 20" 700.00
Sunshine, draped female w/sheaf of wheat, Staffordshire, 18", EX ..400.00

Parrish, Maxfield

Maxfield Parrish (1870 – 1966), with his unique abilities in architecture, illustrations, and landscapes, was the most prolific artist during the golden years of illustrators. He produced art for more than one hundred magazines, painted girls on rocks for the Edison-Mazda division of General Electric, and landscapes for Brown & Bigelow. His most recognized work was 'Daybreak' that was published in 1923 by House of Art and sold nearly two million prints. Parrish began early training with his father who was a recognized artist, studied architecture at Dartmouth, and became an active participant in the Cornish artist colony in New Hampshire where he resided. Due to his increasing popularity, reproductions are now being marketed.

In our listings, values for prints apply to those that are in their original frames (or very nice and appropriate replacement frames) unless noted otherwise. For further information we recommend *Collector's Value Guide to Early 20th Century American Prints* by Michael Ivankovich. Bobby Babcock, our advisor for this category, is listed in the Directory under Texas.

Key: BB — Brown & Bigelow

Ad page, Dutch Boy, Colgate, Cashmere Bouquet, 18x12", +dbl matt .60.00
Book page, Autumn, from A Golden Treasury, 1911, 9¼x7" overall 20.00
Bookplate, Aladdin, dbl matt, 11x8½" 30.00
Bookplate, Cassim, 11x8½" overall, +dbl matt 30.00
Bookplate, City of Brass, 11x8½" overall, +dbl matt 30.00
Bookplate, Pierrot, 10x8" overall, +dbl matt 30.00
Bookplate, Third Voyage of Sinbad, 11x8½", +dbl matt 30.00
Calendar, Contentment, 1928, complete, 19x8½", EX 650.00
Calendar, Dreamlight, 1925, 22½x14½" (cropped), VG 1,000.00
Calendar, Golden Hours, 1929, 22½x14½" (cropped), EX 900.00
Calendar, Golden Hours, 1929, 37½x18", complete, EX 2,000.00
Calendar, Moonlight, 1934, complete, 19x9", NM 1,200.00
Calendar, Primitive Man, 1921, complete, 37½x18", EX 4,000.00
Calendar, Prince Agib, Dodge Pub, 1925, 6x8" 150.00
Calendar, Reveries, 1927, 22x14½" (cropped), EX 700.00
Calendar, Solitude, 1932, complete, 19x8½", EX 750.00
Calendar, Venetian Lamplighter, 1924, complete, 19x8½", EX..1,350.00
Calendar, Venetian Lamplighter, 1924, partial pad, 37½x18", EX .2,750.00
Calendar, Waterfall, 1931, complete, 19x8½", EX 600.00
Calendar, Waterfall, 1931, complete, 37½x18", NM (w/tube)..3,000.00
Frontispiece, Bellerophon, Collier's, 1908, 18½x14½" overall, EX .80.00
Magazine, Charlestown, Life, December 2, 1899, 10¾x8½" 200.00
Magazine, Circus Bedquilt, Ladies' Home Journal, 1905, 16x11¼", NM.60.00
Magazine, Story of Snow Drop, Hearst's, August 1912, complete, EX...450.00
Magazine, Sunset on River cover, Progressive Farmer, 1952, complete...80.00
Magazine cover, Balloon Man, Collier's, December 26, 1908, EX.75.00
Magazine cover, Harper's Round Table, December 1896 ....150.00
Magazine cover, Hermes, Hearst's, 1912, EX 325.00
Magazine cover, Milking Time, Collier's, May 19, 1906, EX 75.00
Magazine page, Mother Goose, The Wond'rous Wise Man, 9½x7¼" ...50.00
Plate, Sawdust & Sin, from Golden Age 50.00
Playing cards, Broadmoor Hotel, 1950s, M, sealed 110.00
Playing cards, Ecstasy, Edison-Mazda, 1930, M in wrapper 275.00
Playing cards, Waterfall, Edison-Mazda, NM 125.00
Postcard, Broadmoor Hotel, 1920s, M 65.00
Poster, Nat'l Authority on Amateur Sport, 12¼x16" overall...2,000.00
Print, Air Castles, 1904, 16x12", +old oak fr 275.00

Print, Aladdin, 11x9" (15¼x12" w/fr)............................325.00
Print, At Close of Day, BB, Executive print, 1943, 12x16" overall..225.00
Print, Atlas, 1908, 11½x9½", +orig fr............................325.00
Print, Aucassin, Scribner's, 1905, 17x11½"+margins, NM..........900.00
Print, Cadmus, 1909, 9x11" 200.00
Print, Cassim, 1906, 9x11" 175.00
Print, Centaur, 1910, 9¼x11½".................................150.00
Print, Daybreak, 1922, 10x6", +orig rpt fr, EX 125.00
Print, Dreaming, 1928, 30x18", EX............................1,400.00
Print, Dreamlight, Edison-Mazda, cropped to: 14¾x24" 1,400.00
Print, Dreamlight, Edison-Mazda, 6¼x10½" (cropped) 385.00
Print, Early Autumn, BB, 22x18" overall (cropped) 200.00
Print, Enchantment, Edison-Mazda, 1926, 14½x19½" (cropped)..1,500.00
Print, Frog & Prince, King of Hearts full page, 16x13", +dbl matt ..50.00
Print, Lampseller of Bagdad, Edison-Mazda, cropped to: 6½x8¾".495.00
Print, New Moon, BB, 1958, 16x12" overall (cropped)..............200.00
Print, Old King Cole, ca 1896, 6½x25", EX....................1,200.00
Print, Path of Home, BB, Executive print, 1946, 16x11" overall...250.00
Print, Peace of Evening, BB, Executive print, 1953, 16x11" overall..250.00
Print, Peaceful Valley, BB, 1936, 16x11", +rpl fr 300.00
Print, Peaceful Valley, BB, 1936, 18x15" (cropped)..............200.00
Print, Primitive Man, Edison-Mazda, 8¼x6" (cropped), EX 300.00
Print, Reveries, Edison-Mazda, 14½x22⅛" (cropped) 795.00
Print, Rubiayat, 1917, 8x30".....................................750.00
Print, Thy Templed Hills, BB, 1942, 24x30" overall 300.00
Print, Twilight Houre, BB, Executive print, 1951, 16x11" 250.00
Print, When Day Is Dawning, BB, Executive print, 1954, 16x11"..250.00
Print, White Birch, BB, 1955, 16x11", EX.........................250.00
Sheet music, Djer-Kiss Waltz, 1925, EX 195.00
Stamp, Brill Brothers, 1915, 1½x2½", +dbl matt 75.00

Pate-De-Verre

Simply translated, pate-de-verre means paste of glass. In the manufacturing process, lead glass is first ground, then mixed with sodium silicate solution to form a paste which can be molded and refired. Some of the most prominent artisans to use this procedure were Almaric Walter, Daum, Argy-Rouseau, and Decorchemont. See also specific manufacturers.

Bowl, 6 red berries on gr ground yel w/mc striations, Decorchemont, 4".1,600.00
Pendant, pine cones/needles, gr/yel on wht, sq, on knotted cord.1,000.00
Plaque, dragon, pk w/bl eyes on wht, 8" L........................575.00
Scarab, gray mottled w/amethyst, sgn Decorchemont, 3x4½".....865.00
Skull mask, dull gray-gr, sgn Poetavera, 7½"....................525.00

Pate-Sur-Pate

Pate-sur-pate, literally paste-on paste, is a technique whereby relief decorations are built up on a ceramic body by layering several applications of slip, one on the other, until the desired result is achieved. Usually only two colors are used, and the value of a piece is greatly enhanced as more color is added.

Box, cupid/doves/butterflies, cobalt, sgn Haufman, 1½x3" L 115.00
Box, dresser; cherubs in clouds w/cobalt & gold, Tharaud Limoges, 7" L..175.00
Powder box, St Geo & dragon on bl lid, gold scrolls, Limoges, 6" W.125.00
Vase, children panels on brn w/gold, Minton, rpr, 4x5x4" 575.00
Vase, children playing w/gold, rtcl border, scroll ft, 4x5x4".........575.00
Vase, classical scene, wht/bl reserve on bl & wht, Limoges, 9x7" ..550.00
Vase, lady & cherub medallion on gr, hdls, 9¼" 400.00
Vase, seaweed, gr/blk on bl mottle, Tharaud Limoges, 12".......1,200.00
Vase, winged Victory, wht on dk bl, Limoges, 7½x3" 450.00

Pattern Glass

Pattern glass was the first mass-produced fancy tableware in America and was much prized by our ancestors. From the 1840s to the Civil War, it contained a high lead content and is known as 'flint glass.' It is exceptionally clear and resonant. Later glass was made with soda lime and is known as non-flint. By the 1890s pattern glass was produced in great volume in thousands of patterns, and colored glass came into vogue. Today the highest prices are often paid for these later patterns flashed with rose, amber, canary, and vaseline; stained ruby; or made in colors of cobalt, green, yellow, amethyst, etc. Demand for pattern glass declined by 1915, and glass fanciers were collecting it by 1930. No other field of antiques offers more diversity in patterns, prices, or pieces than this unique and historical glass that represents the Victorian era in America.

Our advisor for this category is Darlene Yohe; she is listed in the Directory under Arkansas. For a more thorough study on the subject, we recommend *Field Guide to Pattern Glass* by Mollie Helen McCain; *Standard Encyclopedia of Pressed Glass, 1860 – 1930, Identification & Values*, by Bill Edwards and Mike Carwile; and *Much More Early American Pattern Glass* by Alice Hulett Metz. All are available from Collector Books.

See also Bread Plates; Cruets; Historical Glass; Salt and Pepper Shakers; Salts, Open; Sugar Shakers; Syrups; specific manufacturers such as Northwood.

Note: Values are given for open sugar bowls and compotes unless noted 'w/lid.'

Acorn, celery vase 25.00
Acorn, goblet..50.00
Acorn Band, compote, open 25.00
Acorn Band, wine...15.00
Actress, bowl, 6"..50.00
Actress, cake stand 175.00
Actress, relish, any sz..40.00
Ada, butter dish...75.00
Ada, shaker..20.00
Admiral Dewey, See Dewey; See Also Greentown Dewey
Adonis, cake plate 25.00
Adonis, tumbler..15.00
Alabama, bowl, 8" 50.00
Alaska, bowl, berry; lg 40.00
Alaska, rose bowl 45.00
Alaska, spooner..35.00
Almond, wine, stemmed..25.00
Almond, wine decanter 65.00
Amazon, bowl, w/lid, 5-7", ea 35.00
Amazon, claret...25.00
Amberette, butter dish...150.00
Amberette, See Also Klondike
Amberette, tumbler 45.00
Amboy, berry bowl, sm..15.00
Amboy, goblet..35.00
Amboy, pickle dish...15.00
American Beauty, creamer 20.00
American Beauty, jelly compote 30.00
Angular, compote, w/lid 45.00
Angular, pitcher...85.00
Arcadia Lace, jelly compote 25.00
Arcadia Lace, plate, 11"...30.00
Arch & Forget-Me-Not Bands, berry bowl, lg 35.00
Arched Fleur-de-Lis, cake stand..................................40.00
Arched Fleur-de-Lis, mug...40.00
Arched Grape, butter dish..55.00
Arched Grape, sauce bowl, flat or ftd............................10.00

Arched Ovals, compote, w/lid................................45.00
Arched Ovals, relish...25.00
Arched Ovals, sugar bowl...................................25.00
Argent, goblet...35.00
Argent, tumbler..20.00
Argus, ale glass...50.00
Argus, celery vase..30.00
Argus, champagne..25.00
Arrowhead-in-Oval, butter dish............................80.00
Arrowhead-in-Oval, punch bowl..........................125.00
Art, butter dish...70.00
Art, compote, open...40.00
Art, pitcher..85.00
Artichoke, bobeche...40.00
Artichoke, celery vase..35.00
Ashman, bowl..25.00
Aurora, compote, w/lid.......................................55.00
Aurora, tumbler...25.00
Austrian, banana stand.......................................65.00
Austrian, cordial..25.00
Baby Face, champagne.......................................125.00
Baby Face, wine...175.00
Balder, See Pennsylvania
Baltimore Pear, bowl, w/lid, 5-9", ea, from $25 to.......60.00
Baltimore Pear, cake stand..................................45.00
Bamboo Beauty, butter dish.................................90.00
Bamboo Beauty, tumbler.....................................25.00
Banded Buckle, bowl..30.00
Banded Buckle, cordial.......................................20.00
Banded Buckle, goblet..40.00
Banded Diamond Point, berry bowl, lg.....................35.00
Banded Diamond Point, sugar bowl.........................35.00
Banded Diamond w/Peg, butter dish........................45.00
Banded Diamond w/Peg, tumbler............................20.00
Banded Fleur-de-Lis, celery vase............................20.00
Banded Fleur-de-Lis, milk pitcher...........................60.00
Banded Star, compote, w/lid, low............................55.00
Banded Star, sauce bowl......................................10.00
Bar & Block, finger bowl......................................15.00
Bar & Block, tumbler..25.00
Barley, cordial...25.00
Barley, platter, oval, scarce..................................70.00
Barrel Huber, See Huber
Bead & Scroll, butter dish....................................55.00
Bead & Scroll, tumbler..25.00
Beaded Chain, celery vase....................................25.00
Beaded Chain, sugar bowl....................................30.00
Beaded Diamond, butter dish................................55.00
Beaded Diamond, tumbler....................................20.00
Beaded Medallion, jelly compote............................30.00
Beaded Medallion, sugar bowl...............................25.00
Beaded Tulip, champagne.....................................25.00
Beaded Tulip, pickle dish, oval..............................20.00
Bearded Head, See Viking
Bevelled Star, bowl, 9"...35.00
Bevelled Star, celery tray.....................................35.00
Bird & Strawberry, chop plate..............................150.00
Blazing Cornucopia, nappy...................................30.00
Bleeding Heart, compote, w/lid, 7-9", ea...................60.00
Bleeding Heart, waste bowl...................................20.00
Block & Circle, goblet...40.00
Block & Circle, sugar bowl...................................30.00
Block & Fan, butter dish......................................65.00
Block & Fan, cracker jar......................................55.00

Block & Fan, waste bowl......................................20.00
Blockade, goblet..45.00
Blockade, pitcher..85.00
Blue Jay, See Cardinal Bird
Bow Tie, jam jar...35.00
Bow Tie, punch bowl...150.00
Brazen Shield, creamer or spooner..........................25.00
Brazen Shield, wine..20.00
Brazilian, butter dish..65.00
Brazilian, finger bowl...20.00
Brazilian, pickle jar..30.00
Brittanic, banana stand..85.00
Brittanic, custard cup...10.00
Broken Column, cake stand...................................40.00
Broken Column, wine carafe..................................50.00
Bryce Ribbon Candy, cake plate.............................35.00
Bryce Ribbon Candy, cup & saucer..........................30.00
Buckle w/Star, celery vase....................................25.00
Buckle w/Star, goblet..30.00
Bull's-Eye & Daisy, goblet....................................25.00
Bull's-Eye & Daisy, wine......................................20.00
Bull's-Eye & Fan, cake stand.................................55.00
Bull's-Eye & Fan, mug..30.00
Bull's-Eye Band, See Reverse Torpedo
Bull's-Eye in Heart, See Heart w/Thumbprint
Button Arches, jelly compote.................................30.00
Button Arches, pitcher..75.00
Buzz-Star, butter dish...65.00
Buzz-Star, salt cellar..15.00
Cabbage Rose, basket, hdld...................................75.00
Cabbage Rose, celery vase....................................20.00
Cabbage Rose, milk pitcher...................................70.00
California, See Beaded Grape
Cane, goblet..20.00
Cane, pickle dish...20.00
Cane Pinwheel, cologne bottle...............................45.00
Cane Pinwheel, creamer or spooner.........................25.00
Cannonball Pinwheel, celery vase...........................25.00
Cannonball Pinwheel, olive dish, sq.........................25.00
Cardinal Bird, cake stand.....................................40.00
Cardinal Bird, honey dish, w/lid.............................60.00
Cathedral, bowl, 5-6", ea......................................20.00
Cathedral, goblet...45.00
Cathedral, tumbler..20.00
Centennial, See Liberty Bell
Chain w/Star, butter dish......................................55.00
Chain w/Star, creamer...27.50
Chain w/star, wine...20.00
Chandelier, butter dish..95.00
Chandelier, inkwell, lettered & dtd.........................110.00
Cherry & Cable, compote......................................55.00
Cherry & Cable, punch bowl, rare...........................250.00
Cherry & Fig, compote, w/lid.................................55.00
Cherry & Fig, pickle dish......................................20.00
Cherry & Fig, wine...20.00
Chippendale, creamer or spooner............................25.00
Chippendale, pitcher...75.00
Church Windows, butter dish.................................65.00
Church Windows, sardine dish................................25.00
Church Windows, sugar bowl.................................25.00
Classic, butter dish...200.00
Classic, celery vase, either style............................125.00
Classic, goblet..275.00
Classic, sauce bowl, flat or ftd...............................35.00

Cleopatra, See Egyptian

Clio, pitcher..90.00

Clio, sauce bowl, 2 szs, ea................................20.00

Coin, See US Coin

Colorado, bowl, 3-corner..................................20.00

Colorado, cheese dish, ftd................................20.00

Colorado, cup, eng..25.00

Comet, butter..55.00

Comet, goblet..40.00

Compact, See Snail

Connecticut, basket..35.00

Connecticut, goblet..30.00

Cord Drapery, berry bowl, lg..............................35.00

Cord Drapery, goblet..30.00

Cord Drapery, mug..45.00

Cornucopia, butter dish....................................35.00

Cornucopia, pitcher..85.00

Cosmos, lemonade set......................................125.00

Cosmos, shaker..20.00

Cottage, banana stand......................................35.00

Cottage, cup..10.00

Cottage, milk pitcher..45.00

Croesus, bowl, purple, 8"..................................155.00

Croesus, cake stand..60.00

Croesus, shaker..50.00

Crossed Shield, compote, 4 szs, ea, from $20 to..........55.00

Crossed Shield, goblet......................................45.00

Crossed Shield, wine..10.00

Crow's Foot, See Yale

Crown Jewels, See Chandelier

Crystal Queen, berry bowl, lg..............................55.00

Crystal Queen, milk pitcher`................................80.00

Crystal Queen, vase..30.00

Crystal Wedding, berry bowl, 4½" sq......................20.00

Crystal Wedding, compote, flat, 3-szs, ea, from $35 to....60.00

Cube w/Fan, See Pineapple & Fan

Cupid & Venus, compote, open, low or high..............55.00

Cupid & Venus, tumbler....................................30.00

Cupids, compote, low, 8"....................................65.00

Cupids, relish..20.00

Currier & Ives, bowl, oval, 10".............................40.00

Currier & Ives, plate, 10"..................................25.00

Curtain Tie-Back, celery vase..............................20.00

Curtain Tie-Back, goblet....................................35.00

Curtain Tie-Back, water tray................................30.00

Cut Log, biscuit jar..45.00

Cut Log, honey dish..35.00

Dahlia (Canton), cake stand, various, ea, from $25 to....40.00

Dahlia (Canton), jam jar....................................30.00

Dahlia (Canton), relish......................................10.00

Daisy & Button (Hobbs), butter pat........................30.00

Daisy & Button (Hobbs), parfait............................20.00

Daisy & Button w/Crossbars, catsup bottle................40.00

Daisy & Button w/Crossbars, mug, 2 szs, ea..............25.00

Daisy & Button w/V Ornament, butter dish................65.00

Daisy & Button w/V Ornament, milk pitcher..............50.00

Daisy & Scroll, berry bowl, sm............................15.00

Daisy & Scroll, tumbler....................................20.00

Daisy-in-Square, butter dish................................45.00

Daisy-in-Square, sugar bowl................................20.00

Dakota, bottle, cologne......................................85.00

Dakota, cake basket, flat or ftd............................210.00

Dart, bowl..25.00

Dart, sauce bowl..15.00

Deer & Dog, butter dish....................................150.00

Deer & Dog, wine..80.00

Delaware, banana bowl......................................35.00

Delaware, compote..40.00

Delaware, pin tray..20.00

Dew & Raindrop, creamer or spooner......................20.00

Dewey, butter dish..120.00

Dewey, See Also Greentown, Dewey

Diamond, berry bowl, lg....................................35.00

Diamond, compote..35.00

Diamond Lattice

Diamond Lattice, berry bowl, lg............................40.00

Diamond Lattice, pickle dish................................20.00

Diamond Medallion, See Grand

Diamond Spearhead, celery vase............................20.00

Diamond Spearhead, jelly compote..........................30.00

Diamond Spearhead, mug....................................25.00

Diamond Thumbprint, butter dish..........................200.00

Diamond Thumbprint, decanter..............................175.00

Diamond Thumbprint, mug..................................200.00

Diamond w/Peg, butter dish................................65.00

Diamond w/Peg, pickle dish................................15.00

Doric, See Feather

Double Pinwheel, butter dish................................60.00

Double Pinwheel, creamer or spooner......................25.00

Double Ribbon, egg cup......................................20.00

Double Ribbon, sauce bowl, ftd............................25.00

Duncan's #40, bowl, various, ea from $10 to..............35.00

Duncan's #40, cup..10.00

Duncan's #40, tumbler......................................20.00

Duncan's Late Block, butter dish............................75.00

Duncan's Late Block, jelly compote..........................35.00

Duncan's Late Block, sugar bowl............................35.00

Egg in Sand, cake stand....................................35.00

Egg in Sand, goblet..35.00

Egyptian, bowl..60.00

Egyptian, celery vase..85.00

Elephant, See Jumbo

Emerald Green Herringbone, See Florida

English Colonial, butter dish................................50.00

English Colonial, decanter..................................50.00

Esther, compote, w/lid, tall................................50.00

Esther, jelly compote..30.00

Esther, shaker..25.00

Eyewinker, banana dish......................................30.00

Eyewinker, bowl, w/lid......................................55.00

Eyewinker, honey dish......................................25.00

Fairfax Strawberry, See Strawberry

Falling Leaves, pitcher......................................70.00

Falling Leaves, sugar bowl..................................25.00

Fan & Star, berry bowl, sm................................15.00

Fan & Star, pitcher..65.00

Fancy Loop, bonbon 35.00
Fancy Loop, champagne 25.00
Fancy Loop, sherry 15.00
Fandango, bar bottle 35.00
Fandango, custard cup 10.00
Fandango, salver 40.00
Feather, cordial 25.00
Feather, pitcher 70.00
Feather Duster, goblet 30.00
Feather Duster, tumbler 15.00
Festoon, bowl, various, ea 30.00
Festoon, finger bowl 30.00
Festoon, waste bowl 25.00
File, banana dish, 8" 30.00
File, vase, 7" 25.00
Fine Cut & Block, butter dish, 2 styles, ea, from $80 to 95.00
Fine Cut & Block, punch cup 10.00
Fine Cut & Fan, bowl, heart shape 30.00
Fine Cut & Fan, sauce bowl 10.00
Fishscale, pickle scoop, tapered 20.00
Florida, cordial 20.00
Florida, goblet 45.00
Flower Band, butter dish 55.00
Flower Band, milk pitcher 65.00
Flower Pot, compote, w/lid 45.00
Flower Pot, goblet 45.00
Flute, compote 40.00
Flute, vase 25.00
Flute & Cane, berry bowl, lg 30.00
Flute & Cane, tumbler 15.00
Fringed Drape, bowl, deep, 6" 20.00
Fringed Drape, vase, ftd, 8-9", ea 35.00
Frosted Circle, butter dish 80.00
Frosted Circle, compote, w/lid 75.00
Frosted Eagle, celery vase 45.00
Frosted Eagle, pitcher 165.00
Frosted Stork, bowl, 9" 60.00
Frosted Stork, jam jar, w/lid 130.00
Galloway, basket 85.00
Galloway, ice jug 75.00
Garfield Drape, honey dish 18.00
Gem, See Nailhead
Good Luck, See Horseshoe
Gothic Windows, berry bowl, lg 40.00
Gothic Windows, goblet 45.00
Grand, bowl, ftd 35.00
Grand, goblet 40.00
Grape & Festoon, bowl 35.00
Grape & Festoon, wine 15.00
Grape w/o Vine, butter dish 65.00
Grape w/Thumbprint, butter dish 70.00
Grape w/Thumbprint, shaker 20.00
Grape w/Vine, bowl, lg 35.00
Grape w/Vine, creamer, spooner or sugar bowl, ea 25.00
Grasshopper, bowl, w/lid 45.00
Grasshopper, pickle dish 25.00
Grasshopper (deduct 50% if no insect is present)
Hand, cake stand 35.00
Hand, cordial 20.00
Hand, water tray 45.00
Hartley, bowl, 6-9", ea, from $20 to 40.00
Hartley, creamer or spooner 20.00
Hatpin, champagne, flint 78.00
Heart w/Thumbprint, berry bowl, lg 40.00

Heart w/Thumbprint, carafe 50.00
Henrietta, bowl, rectangular 30.00
Henrietta, sauce bowl 10.00
Hickman, bowl, various szs, ea, from $15 to 40.00
Hickman, pitcher, water 60.00
Hidalgo, berry bowl, lg 40.00
Hidalgo, water tray 25.00
Hobnail, bone dish 15.00
Hobnail, tumbler 20.00
Hobnail w/Fan, butter dish 60.00
Hobnail w/Fan, goblet 45.00
Hobstar, compote, 10-11", ea 40.00
Hobstar, goblet 50.00
Hobstar, orange bowl, 11" 35.00
Hobstar & Feather, cracker jar 150.00
Hobstar & Feather, sherbet 40.00
Holly, bowl, w/lid, 2 styles, ea 155.00
Holly, compote, w/lid, low 145.00
Holly, sauce bowl 15.00
Holly Amber, See Greentown, Holly Amber
Honeycomb w/Star, compote 30.00
Honeycomb w/Star, pitcher 85.00
Hops & Barley, See Wheat & Barley
Horseshoe, cake stand 40.00
Horseshoe, salt cellar, master, rare 65.00
Huber, bitters bottle 75.00
Huber, mug 40.00
Hummingbird, bowl, w/lid 60.00
Hummingbird, compote 50.00
Hummingbird, sauce bowl 25.00
Idaho, See Snail
Illinois, candlestick 30.00
Illinois, puff box 40.00
Indian Sunset, bonbon 25.00
Indian Sunset, pitcher 95.00
Indiana, catsup bottle 40.00
Indiana, tray, oblong 30.00
Inverted Feather, basket 50.00
Inverted Feather, pickle tray 35.00
Inverted Strawberry, bonbon, ftd 30.00
Inverted Strawberry, butter dish 85.00
Inverted Strawberry, oil bottle 65.00
Iris w/Meander, See Opalescent Glass
Jacob's Ladder, bowl, oblong, from $20 to 30.00
Jacob's Ladder, compote, 7½-10", ea, from $35 to 50.00
Jersey Swirl, bowl 25.00
Jersey Swirl, wine 10.00
Jewel & Dewdrop, cordial 25.00
Jewel & Dewdrop, wine 30.00
Job's Tear, See Art
Jubilee, celery tray 20.00
Jubilee, plate, 9" 20.00
Jumbo, compote, w/lid, 7-12", ea, from $450 to 900.00
Jumbo, spooner, Barnum head 150.00
Kentucky, bowl 25.00
Kentucky, sugar bowl 45.00
King's Crown, berry bowl, sm 15.00
King's Crown, fruit basket 40.00
King's Crown, saucer 15.00
Klondike, bowl, sq, 7-11", ea 45.00
Klondike, cake stand 175.00
Klondike, relish tray 35.00
Kokomo, butter dish 50.00
Kokomo, pitcher 85.00

La Clede, See Hickman
Lacy Dewdrop, bowl, w/lid, lg 55.00
Lacy Dewdrop, mug 20.00
Lattice, butter dish...65.00
Lattice, platter 35.00
Laverne, cake stand 40.00
Laverne, goblet..50.00
Laverne, sugar bowl 30.00
Leaf, See Maple Leaf
Leaf & Star, berry bowl, lg 35.00
Leaf & Star, custard cup 10.00
Leaf & Star, goblet...50.00
Leaf Bracket, See Greentown, Leaf Bracket
Leaf Medallion, See Northwood, Leaf Medallion
Liberty Bell, celery vase 45.00
Liberty Bell, tumbler 100.00
Lion Head, butter dish 225.00
Lion Head, sugar bowl 75.00
Lion w/Cable, compote, w/lid, high, 7-9", ea 145.00
Lion w/Cable, pitcher 275.00
Log Cabin, butter dish..325.00
Log Cabin, compote, 10½" 290.00
Loop, bowl, w/lid 35.00
Loop, carafe..45.00
Loop, egg cup 25.00
Loop & Dart w/Diamond Ornament, egg cup 15.00
Loop & Dart w/Diamond Ornament, pitcher 85.00
Loop w/Dewdrop, cake stand 40.00
Magic, See Rosette
Maple Leaf, butter dish...65.00
Maple Leaf, milk pitcher 55.00
Mardi Gras, bitters bottle 75.00
Mardi Gras, pitcher 90.00
Maryland, cake stand, 8-10", ea 40.00
Maryland, pickle dish 15.00
Masonic, custard cup 10.00
Masonic, wine..20.00
Massachusetts, cologne 40.00
Massachusetts, rum jug 80.00
Medallion Sunburst, jam jar....................................25.00
Medallion Sunburst, pitcher....................................85.00
Memphis, fruit bowl, on metal base 65.00
Memphis, pitcher..275.00
Michigan, lemonade, hdl...20.00
Michigan, tumbler 20.00
Minerva, butter dish...85.00
Minerva, champagne 25.00
Minnesota, humidor 150.00
Missouri, cake stand...35.00
Missouri, cordial..30.00
Moon & Star, cake stand...40.00
Moon & Star, waste bowl 20.00
Nail, berry bowl, lg 35.00
Nail, shaker 25.00
Nail, sugar bowl 30.00
Nailhead, cake stand 35.00
Nailhead, wine 15.00
New England Pineapple, butter dish.......................275.00
New England Pineapple, milk pitcher 550.00
New England Pineapple, spooner..............................70.00
New Hampshire, bowl, sq, 5-9", ea, from $15 to.........40.00
New Hampshire, celery vase 20.00
New Jersey, cake stand..45.00
New Jersey, fruit bowl on std, 9½-12½", ea, from $40 to 65.00

New Jersey, olive dish...25.00
Niagara, compote...30.00
Niagara, plate..25.00
Oaken Bucket, See Wooden Pail
Octagon, bowl, 11" 40.00
Octagon, punch bowl 85.00
Octagon, sherbet..20.00
Ohio Star, cider pitcher...200.00
Ohio Star, mint dish...40.00
One Hundred & One, creamer 55.00
One Hundred & One, vase 25.00
One-O-One, See One Hundered & One
Optical Tube, See Tile
Palmette, compote, w/lid, low 75.00
Palmette, relish, scoop shape...................................25.00
Palmette, shaker, lg 75.00
Panelled Diamond Blocks, carafe 30.00
Panelled Diamond Blocks, creamer or spooner 20.00
Panelled Forget-Me-Not, cake stand.........................45.00
Panelled Forget-Me-Not, wine 15.00
Panelled Strawberry, pitcher....................................65.00
Panelled Strawberry, tumbler 15.00
Panelled Thistle, berry bowl, lg................................35.00
Panelled Thistle, plate..25.00
Pennsylvania, cheese dish 85.00
Pennsylvania, oil bottle 45.00
Persian, butter dish 65.00
Persian, claret..15.00
Pineapple & Fan, celery tray 20.00
Pineapple & Fan, decanter.......................................35.00
Pineapple & Fan, rose bowl.....................................25.00

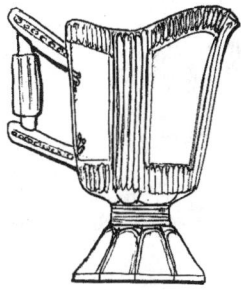

Pleat and Panel

Pleat & Panel, candy jar, w/lid.................................35.00
Pleat & Panel, water tray 25.00
Polar Bear, creamer...145.00
Polar Bear, ice bowl..95.00
Polar Bear, waste bowl..75.00
Portland, basket 50.00
Portland, epergne..175.00
Portland, mug..35.00
Prayer Rug, See Horseshoe
Pressed Leaf, bowl, oval..20.00
Pressed Leaf, spooner...25.00
Priscilla, compote, open, 5-9", ea, from $20 to...........40.00
Priscilla, plate..20.00
Priscilla, rose bowl...35.00
Prism, butter dish 45.00
Prism, pitcher..60.00
Queen Anne, creamer or spooner..............................20.00
Queen Anne, tumbler..20.00
Raindrop, finger bowl...15.00
Raindrop, water tray 30.00

Recessed Pillared Red Top, See Nail
Red Block, creamer or spooner **70.00**
Red Block, pitcher..**225.00**
Red Top, See Button Arches
Reverse Torpedo, banana dish **35.00**
Reverse Torpedo, fruit basket **50.00**
Rexford, cake stand **45.00**
Ribbed Palm, butter dish **50.00**
Ribbed Palm, compote, w/lid, 6" **140.00**
Ribbed Palm, egg cup **15.00**
Ribbon, berry bowl, sm **20.00**
Ribbon, tumbler **30.00**
Rising Sun, berry bowl, lg **35.00**
Rising Sun, pitcher..**75.00**
Rising Sun, sugar bowl, 3 shapes, ea **30.00**
Robin Hood, goblet **40.00**
Robin Hood, pickle dish **15.00**
Roman Key, bowl, 8-10", ea, from $30 to **45.00**
Roman Key, champagne **15.00**
Roman Rosette, butter dish................................**65.00**
Roman Rosette, celery vase **30.00**
Roman Rosette, goblet **45.00**
Romeo, See Block & Fan
Rose in Snow, bowl, w/lid, 8-9", ea **50.00**
Rose in Snow, pickle dish **20.00**
Rosette, creamer or spooner **20.00**
Rosette, sugar bowl **25.00**
Royal Ivy, See Northwood
Royal Oak, See Northwood
Ruby Diamond, goblet..**50.00**
Ruby Diamond, sugar bowl................................**40.00**
Ruby Thumbprint, See King's Crown
S-Repeat, butter dish **85.00**
S-Repeat, decanter **100.00**
S-Repeat, jelly compote....................................**40.00**
Saint Bernard, cake stand **35.00**
Saint Bernard, pitcher **85.00**
Sawtooth, butter dish **80.00**
Sawtooth, cordial..**45.00**
Sawtooth Band, See Amazon
Scalloped Daisy Red Top, See Button Arches
Scroll w/Flowers, cordial..................................**25.00**
Scroll w/Flowers, relish **25.00**
Seneca Loop, See Loop
Sequoia, celery boat **30.00**
Sequoia, wine **10.00**
Sheaf & Block, creamer or spooner **25.00**
Sheaf & Block, sugar bowl **30.00**
Shell & Jewel, butter dish **65.00**
Shell & Jewel, shaker **30.00**
Shell & Tassel, berry bowl, sm **15.00**
Shell & Tassel, compote, w/lid, 8 szs, ea, from $30 to..........**100.00**
Shelton Star, creamer or spooner **15.00**
Shelton Star, tumbler **15.00**
Sheraton, milk pitcher..**55.00**
Sheraton, platter, oblong, 8 panels **35.00**
Shuttle, cordial..**15.00**
Shuttle, mug..**20.00**
Shuttle, wine **10.00**
Snail, butter dish **80.00**
Snail, finger bowl..**55.00**
Snail, vase **50.00**
Snow Flake, butter dish **65.00**
Snow Flake, pitcher..**110.00**

Spirea Band, cake stand....................................**45.00**
Spirea Band, wine **20.00**
Star & Crescent, pickle dish **15.00**
Star & Crescent, pitcher **65.00**
Star & File, bowl, 7"..**20.00**
Star & File, ice cream bowl, stemmed **20.00**
Star in Bull's-Eye, butter dish **50.00**
Star Medallion, compote **35.00**
Star Medallion, tumbler **15.00**
Stars & Stripes, berry bowl, sm **45.00**
Stars & Stripes, vase **20.00**
Stars & Stripes, wine **18.00**
States, butter dish **70.00**
States, cup **15.00**
Stippled Chain, egg cup **15.00**
Stippled Chain, sugar bowl **30.00**
Stippled Cherry, creamer **25.00**
Stippled Cherry, plate, 6" **25.00**
Stippled Forget-Me-Not, cake stand, 9-12", ea, from $30 to **50.00**
Stippled Forget-Me-Not, cordial **20.00**
Stippled Medallion, cake plate **30.00**
Stippled Medallion, plate **20.00**
Strawberry, spooner **37.00**
Strawberry, wine **110.00**
Strawberry & Cable, butter dish **65.00**
Strawberry & Cable, wine **15.00**
Sunbeam, berry bowl, lg **45.00**
Sunbeam, tumbler..**20.00**
Sunk Daisy, butter dish **60.00**
Sunk Daisy, goblet **40.00**
Swirl & Ball, candlestick **30.00**
Swirl & Ball, plate, 6" **20.00**
Tarantum's Virginia, butter dish........................**50.00**
Tarantum's Virginia, cordial..............................**15.00**
Tarantum's Virginia, goblet **35.00**
Teardrop, candlestick..**25.00**
Teardrop, pickle dish **15.00**
Teardrop & Tassel, butter dish **85.00**
Teardrop & Tassel, tumbler **35.00**
Teasel, cake stand **35.00**
Teasel, pitcher..**100.00**
Texas, carafe **35.00**
Texas, horseradish jar, w/lid..............................**55.00**
Theatrical, See Actress
Thousand Eye, celery vase................................**40.00**
Thousand Eye, jelly glass **20.00**
Three Face, butter dish **165.00**
Three Face, milk pitcher..................................**225.00**
Three Panel, butter dish **60.00**
Three Panel, pitcher..**80.00**
Three-in-One, carafe **60.00**
Three-in-One, punch bowl................................**135.00**
Thumbprint, See Argus
Thumbprint Band, See Dakota
Thunderbird, See Hummingbird
Tile, cake stand **35.00**
Tile, decanter **40.00**
Tokyo, bowl, ftd, 9" **30.00**
Tokyo, pitcher, 2 styles, ea................................**85.00**
Tokyo, plate **25.00**
Torpedo, banana stand..**40.00**
Torpedo, cake stand **35.00**
Torpedo, tumbler..**20.00**
Tree of Life, See Portland

Truncated Cube, butter dish...80.00
Truncated Cube, pitcher 135.00
Tulip w/Sawtooth, barber bottle..55.00
Tulip w/Sawtooth, creamer or spooner 20.00
Tulip w/Sawtooth, decanter 135.00
Twin Snowshoes, creamer 20.00
Twin Snowshoes, pitcher..100.00
Twinkle Star, See Utah
Two Panel, bowl, 7-9", ea, from $20 to.............................45.00
Two Panel, pitcher..85.00
Two Panel, tray, w/hdls..35.00
US Coin, berry dish, 3¾"..175.00
US Coin, butter dish, clear 350.00
US Coin, butter dish, w/lid, 6½" base dia 515.00
US Coin, cake plate, ped ft, 6½x10"...................................500.00
US Coin, compote, frosted, high std, str rim, 8½" dia.........500.00
US Coin, compote, frosted, 7x7"...195.00
US Coin, compote, w/lid, 11½x7"..750.00
US Coin, compote, w/lid, 9¼x6"..750.00
US Coin, epergne...250.00
US Coin, kerosene lamp, 11"..975.00
US Coin, pickle dish, frosted, 7½x3¾"..............................220.00
US Coin, pitcher, milk; 8½x4"..975.00
US Coin, spooner, clear 200.00
US Coin, syrup, frosted 600.00
US Coin, toothpick holder, frosted, ftd, sq 100.00
US Coin, tray, 10x7"..745.00
US Coin, tumbler, frosted..200.00
US Sheraton, sundae dish 25.00
Utah, butter dish, 2 szs, ea, from $40 to 55.00
Utah, goblet...45.00
Venus, celery vase...20.00
Venus, tumbler...35.00
Viking, apothecary jar 75.00
Viking, casserole, w/lid 55.00
Waffle & Fine Cut, bowl 20.00
Waffle Variant, butter dish..30.00
Waffle Variant, ice cream tray...25.00
Wheat & Barley, butter dish..70.00
Wheat & Barley, tumbler...15.00
Wildflower, cake basket, oval..45.00
Wildflower, goblet..45.00
Willow Oak, celery vase...30.00
Willow Oak, mug..45.00
Wisconsin, bonbon...20.00
Wisconsin, butter dish...55.00
Wisconsin, cup & saucer..35.00
Wooden Pail, compote, w/lid...50.00
Wooden Pail, ice bucket...65.00
X-Ray, celery tray...50.00
X-Ray, jelly compote 30.00
Yale, cake stand 30.00
Yale, relish, oval 15.00
Yale, sauce bowl, flat or ftd...10.00
Zipper, cheese dish..65.00
Zipper, milk pitcher 65.00
Zippered Heart, bowl, sq..35.00
Zippered Heart, sherbet...15.00

Paul Revere Pottery

The Saturday Evening Girls was a group of young immigrant girls headed by philanthropist Mrs. James Storrow who started meeting with

them in the Boston library in 1899 for lectures, music, and dancing. Mrs. Storrow provided them with a kiln in 1906. Finding the facililties too small, they soon relocated. Because their new quarters were near the historical Old North Church, they chose the name Paul Revere Pottery. Their supervisor was Edith Brown. With very little training, the girls produced only simple ware. Until 1915 the pottery operated at a deficit, then a new building with four kilns was constructed on Nottingham Road. Vases, miniature jugs, children's tea sets, tiles, dinnerware, and lamps were produced, usually in soft matt glazes often decorated with incised, hand-painted designs from nature. Examples in a dark high gloss may also be found on occasion.

Several marks were used: 'P.R.P.'; 'S.E.G.'; or the circular device, 'Boston, Paul Revere Pottery' with the horse and rider.

The pottery continued to operate; and even though it sold well, the high production costs of the handmade ware caused the pottery to fail in 1946.

Our advisors for this category are Suzanne Perrault and Dave Rago; they are listed in the Directory under New Jersey.

Vase, trees in band, multi-color on brown, PRP logo, 8½", $2,300.00.

Bookends, ea w/different snowy scene, concave front, EM/626, 4x5x3" .1,035.00
Bowl, cereal; gr/gray bands on ivory, SEG, 1909, 6" 350.00
Bowl, Greek key band, tan/ivory on wht & brn, SEG/10-12/FL, 3x6".1,100.00
Bowl, lotus band on bl, tiny rstr, SEG/SG/5-17, 2½x8½" 660.00
Bowl, rooster reserve, yel/brn/navy/lime gr, stamped, 1¾x6".......660.00
Candlesticks, floral wreath, bl/yel/gr on teal, 1¾x4", pr, $400 to .600.00
Charger, bl crystalline, SEG, 12¼"...240.00
Child's bowl, duck/landscape, Elaine Her Bowl, PRP, 1924, 2¼x5½".745.00
Child's breakfast set, rabbits band, His Bowl..., plate & (VG) mug .1,380.00
Child's cup, racing rabbits overlapping on band on bl, SEG/12-18 .....600.00
Cup & saucer, landscape reserve on mottle, stamped, 2", 5½" 525.00
Honey pot, scenic landscape, 7-color, prof rstr, SEG/9/14/SG, 4½x3" .5,225.00
Mug, ducks band on ivory, SEG/1-11-13/JG, 3¼x4" 770.00
Pitcher, Greek key border in wht/gr/bl, SEG, 4¼"......................765.00
Plate, duck reserve, bl/ivory/blk, SEG/4-10-13/JG, 6¼" 990.00
Plate, geese, gr on bl, SEG/6-13/IG, 7⅝" 490.00
Plate, lotus, wht on bl-gray, SEG/11-14/AM, 10", EX 630.00
Plate, rooster reserve, muted yel/brn/gr, sgn HOS, 6½" 770.00
Plate, ship scene, teal/navy bands w/in mottled rim, PRP/1931/LS, 10" .1,100.00
Plate, swan reserve, mc on wht w/wide navy bl band, SEG/8-19/FL, 8".825.00
Tile, goat/grapevines cvg, blk-lined gr tones, LS/20-5-04, 5¼", +fr.3,000.00
Tile, Hull Street house, PRP, 3¾", NM, +fr.................................1,380.00
Tile, The Common, park scene, teal/navy/tan/brn, 3½" sq, NM.1,430.00
Vase, band w/lg oak trees & bl sky on bl-gr, rstr (sgn)/6/24, 4x4" ..980.00
Vase, bl crystalline, bulbous, SEG, 8" 600.00

Peachblow

Peachblow, made to imitate the colors of the Chinese Peachbloom porcelain, was made by several glasshouses in the late 1800s. Among them were New England Glass, Mt. Washington, Webb, and Hobbs, Brockunier and Company (Wheeling). Its pink shading was achieved through action of the heat on the gold content of the glass. While New England's peachblow shades from deep crimson to white, Mt. Washington's tends to shade from pink to blue-gray. Many pieces were enameled and gilded. While by far the majority of the pieces made by New England had a satin (acid) finish, they made shiny peachblow as well. Wheeling glass, on the other hand, is rarely found in satin. In the 1950s Gundersen-Pairpoint Glassworks initiated the reproduction of Mt. Washington peachblow, using an exact duplication of the original formula. Though of recent manufacture, this glass is very collectible. Our advisors for this category are Betty and Clarence Maier; they are listed in the Directory under Pennsylvania.

Bowl, gold branches/flowers, pinched rim, 2½x5" 865.00
Bowl, gold/wht foliage w/mc star jewels, heart shape, 11½" 345.00
Cracker jar, Webb, lg florals in bl/yel on lav/gr stems, SP mts, 8" ..300.00
Cruet, Wheeling, sm neck, 5½" 750.00
Cup & saucer, Gundersen, 3¼" H, 5¼" dia 60.00
Mustard, Wheeling, spherical, 3¼" 585.00
Pitcher, Webb, rigaree extends from hdl/forms leaf on side, 4½", EX..145.00
Pitcher, Wheeling, draped, wht cased, crystal hdl, 5" 400.00
Pitcher, Wheeling, protruding duck-bill spout, #324, 6½" 4,700.00
Pitcher, Wheeling, 319-#0 Jug, 5⅜" 975.00
Punch cup, Wheeling, amber hdl, 2¼" 350.00
Rose bowl, Stevens & Wms, Matsu No Ke, clear knobby base, 4½".750.00
Shaker, Wheeling, bulbous, 2¾" 500.00
Toothpick holder, NE Glass, shiny, cylindrical w/sqd top, 2¼" ...400.00
Tumbler, Wheeling, satin, 3¾" 350.00
Tumbler, Wheeling, 3¾" 350.00
Vase, Jack-in-pulpit; Mt WA, ruffled top, 7¾" 2,875.00
Vase, Morgan; Wheeling, glass griffin holder (VG), 10" 1,550.00
Vase, Morgan; Wheeling, plastic repro griffin holder, 10" 1,325.00
Vase, Morgan; Wheeling, satin, glass griffin holder (NM), 10".1,450.00
Vase, Morgan; Wheeling, satin, plastic repro griffin holder, 10"...980.00
Vase, Mt WA, rnd w/long vasiform neck, 8" 1,865.00
Vase, NE Glass, trumpet form, 18" 800.00
Vase, Webb, cascading vines/insect in gold/gray, bottle w/cup rim, 10".175.00
Vase, Webb, gold ferns/flowers, flat sides, draped rim, amber ft, 9".690.00
Vase, Webb, leafy branch, gr/gold, bulbous w/long neck, 10"...1,265.00
Vase, Wheeling, elongated bottle form, 9" 950.00
Vase, Wheeling, elongated teardrop form, 9" 965.00

Peloton

Peloton glass was first made by Wilhelm Kralik in Bohemia in 1880. This unusual art glass was produced by rolling colored threads onto the transparent or opaque glass gather as it was removed from the furnace. Usually more than one color of threading was used, and some items were further decorated with enameling. It was made with both shiny and acid finishes.

Pitcher, floral sprig on clear with green stringing, gold trim at rim, 5", $265.00.

Bowl, wht cased, mc strings, 4-crimp, 3¾x3½" 300.00
Pitcher, clear overshot w/mc strings, 6⅝x3⅝" 175.00
Pitcher, wl w/mc leaves/flowers/butterfly, 8" 465.00
Rose bowl, lav, ribbed, crystal pulled ft, 3" H............................185.00
Rose bowl, wht w/pastel strings, clear rim, scalloped ft, 4" 300.00
Vase, bl/red/yel/wht strings on glossy wht, ribbed, ruffled, 7" 325.00
Vase, pastel strings on cased wht, clear floret-emb ft, fan form, 4" ..200.00
Vase, pastel strings on wht, ribbed tumbler bottom, ruffled rim, 4¾.400.00

Pennsbury

Established in the 1950s in Morrisville, Pennsylvania, by Henry Below, the Pennsbury Pottery produced dinnerware and novelty items, much of which was sold in gift shops along the Pennsylvania Turnpike. Henry and his wife, Lee, worked for years at the Stangl Pottery before striking out on their own. Lee and her daughter were the artists responsible for many of the early pieces, the bird figures among them. Pennsbury pottery was hand painted, some in blue on white, some in multicolor on caramel. Pennsylvania Dutch motifs, Amish couples, and barbershop singers were among their most popular decorative themes. Sgraffito (hand incising) was used extensively. The company marked their wares 'Pennsbury Pottery' or 'Pennsbury Pottery, Morrisville, PA.'

In October of 1969 the company closed. Contents of the pottery were sold in December of the following year, and in April of 1971, the buildings burned to the ground. Items marked Pennsbury Glenview or Stumar Pottery (or these marks in combination) were made by Glenview after 1969. Pieces manufactured after 1976 were made by the Pennington Pottery. Several of the old molds still exist, and the original Pennsbury Caramel process is still being used on novelty items, some of which are produced by Lewis Brothers, New Jersey. Production of Pennsbury dinnerware was not resumed after the closing. Our advisor for this category is Shirley Graff; she is listed in the Directory under Ohio. Note: Prices may be higher in some areas of the country — particularly on the East Coast, the southern states, and Texas. Values for examples in the Rooster patterns apply to both black and red variations.

Ashtray, Pennsbury Inn, 8" 45.00
Ashtray, Solebury National Bank, 5" 30.00
Ashtray, Summerset, 1804-1954, 5" dia..30.00
Bookends, eagle, 8", pr 185.00
Bowl, Hex, 9" 40.00
Bowl, pretzel; Gay Ninety, 12x8" 95.00
Bowl, pretzel; Red Barn, 12x8" 150.00
Butter dish, Folkart, w/lid, 5x4" 35.00
Casserole, Hex, w/lid, 6½" 65.00
Chip & dip, Rooster, 11" 85.00
Coaster, Gay Ninety, 5" 35.00
Compote, holly decor, 5 ....25.00
Compote, Rooster, ftd, 5" 40.00
Cookie jar, Red Barn, w/lid..225.00
Cruets, oil & vinegar; Rooster, pr 150.00
Desk basket, National Exchange Club, 5" 40.00
Desk basket, Two Women Under Tree, 5" 50.00
Figurine, Audubon's Warbler, #122, 4" 160.00
Figurine, blue jay, #108, 10½" 400.00
Figurine, cardinal, #120, 6½" 175.00
Figurine, Marsh Wren, #106, 6½" 120.00
Figurines, rooster & hen, various colors, 12", pr 450.00
Mug, beer; Barbershop Quartet, 5"..25.00
Mug, beverage; Rooster, 5" 20.00
Mug, coffee; Amish, 3¼" 22.00
Mug, coffee; Eagle, 3¼" 20.00
Mug, coffee; Gay Ninety, 3¼" 25.00

Mug, coffee; Quartet, 3¼" 20.00
Mug, coffee; Red Barn, 3¼" 35.00
Pie plate, Rooster, 9" 60.00
Pitcher, Blue Dowry, 5" 55.00
Pitcher, Delft Toleware, 5" 55.00
Pitcher, Gay Ninety, 7¼" 125.00
Pitcher, Hex, 6¼" 65.00
Plaque, boy & girl, 6" 40.00
Plaque, Charles W Morgan, ship decor, 11x8" 110.00
Plaque, eagle, #P214, 22" 125.00
Plaque, General, train decor, 11x8" 55.00
Plaque, horse & carriage, 6" 50.00
Plaque, Iron Horse Ramble, Reading Railroad, 1960, 7¼x5¼" 60.00
Plaque, It's Making Down, 4" 25.00
Plaque, River Steamboat, 13½x10¼" 160.00
Plaque, Stourbridge Lion, 1829, 11x8" 55.00
Plaque, Swallow the Insult, 6" 25.00
Plaque, United States Steel, 1954, 8" 40.00
Plaque, Walking to Homestead, 6" 40.00
Plaque, Washington Crossing the Delaware, 5" dia 25.00
Plate, Amish, 9" 40.00
Plate, bread; Give Us This Day Our Daily Bread, 8" dia 40.00
Plate, bread; Give Us This Day Our Daily Bread, 9x6" 40.00
Plate, Harvest, 8" 40.00
Plate, Neshaminy Woods, 11½" 120.00
Plate, Pea Hen Over Heart, 11" 85.00
Plate, Rooster, 10" 35.00
Plate, Treetops Christmas, 1961 ....25.00
Plate, Two Birds Over Heart, 11" 85.00
Shakers, Amish man & woman, pr, from $30 to 45.00
Tray, cigarette; Eagle, 7½x5" 40.00
Tray, tulip decor, 7½x5" 40.00
Wall pocket, bellows shape, 6½x6½" 40.00
Wall pocket, floral in heart shape w/bl border, 6½" 50.00
Wall pocket, ship w/brn border, 6½" sq 50.00

Pens and Pencils

The first metallic writing pen was patented in 1809, and soon machine-produced pens with steel nibs gradually began replacing the quill. The first fountain pen was invented in 1830, but due to the fact that the ink flow was not consistent (though leakage was), they were not manufactured commercially until the 1880s. The first successful commercial producers were Waterman in 1884 and Parker with the Lucky Curve in 1888.

The self-filling pen of the early 1900s featured the soft, interior sack which filled with ink as the metal bar on the outside of the pen was raised and lowered. Variations of the filling mechanisms were tried until 1932 when Parker introduced the Vacuumatic, a sackless pen with an internal pump.

Prices below are for pens in near mint or better condition which have been professionally restored to full operating capacity. For unrestored as-found pens, approximagely one third should be deducted from the values below.

For more information we recommend *Fountain Pens, Past & Present*, by Paul Erano (Collector Books). Our advisor for this category is Gary Lehrer; he is listed in the Directory under Connecticut. For those interested in purchasing pens through catalogs, both our advisor, Mr. Lehrer, and Pen Fanciers (whose address can be found in the Directory under Clubs, Newsletters, and Catalogs) publish extensive catalogs.

Key:
AF — aeromatic filler
BF — button filler
CF — capillary filler
CPT — chrome-plated trim

HR — hard rubber
LF — lever filler
NPT — nickel-plated trim
PF — plunger filler

ED — eyedropper filler
GFM — gold-filled metal
GFT — gold-filled trim
GPT — gold-plated trim

PIF — piston filler
PKF — push knob filler
TD — touchdown filler
VF — vacumatic filler

Fountain Pens

Aiken Lambert, 1900, #2, ED, GF Gopheresque (rare), med, NM ..600.00
C Stewart, 1938, #15, LF, gr pearl, NPT, NM 75.00
C Stewart, 1951, #27, LF, silver candystripe, GFT, NM 175.00
C Stewart, 1951, #55, LF, gr marble, GFT, NM 150.00
C Stewart, 1952, #27, LF, Tiger's Eye, GFT, NM 250.00
C Stewart, 1955, #55, LF, bl marble, GFT, NM 200.00
C Stewart, 1955, #58, LF, gr pearl web, GFT, NM 185.00
C Stewart, 1956, #74, twist fill, red herringbone, fretwork band, NM .200.00
C Stewart, 1956, #76, LF, gr herringbone, GFT, NM....................200.00
C Stewart, 1956, #85, LF, bl pearl w/gold veins, GFT, NM 150.00
Carters, 1928, #6 sz INX, LF, ivory Pearltex, GFT, NM...............500.00
Carters, 1928, #7 sz INX, LF, bl pearl, GFT, NM.........................600.00
Carters, 1928, #7 sz INX, LF, coral, GFT, NM.............................825.00
Chilton, 1924, #6, sleeve fill, blk, GFT, NM................................300.00
Conklin, 1918, #20, CF, blk chased HR, GFT, NM......................175.00
Conklin, 1918, #40, crescent fill, blk chased HR, GFT, NM 250.00
Conklin, 1927, #2, LF, wht b/blk veins (rare), GFT, NM............300.00
Conklin, 1927, Endura Large, LF, blk, GFT, NM.........................400.00
Conklin, 1927, Endura Large, LF, sapphire bl, GFT, NM 650.00
Conklin, 1927, Endura Oversz, blk HR, long cap/section, GFT, NM .700.00
Conklin, 1927, Endura Standard, LF, Cardinal, GFT, NM..........225.00
Conklin, 1930, Endura Symetric Oversz, LF, blk/bronze, GFT, NM ..350.00
Conklin, 1932, Nozac, PF, gr pearl w/blk stripe, GFT, NM 300.00
Crocker, 1910, #2, blow filler, GF, NM......................................375.00
Crocker, 1932, #2, hatchet fill, blk chased HR, GFT, NM..........150.00
Dunn, 1921, #2, pump fill, ring top, blk chased HR, GFT, NM..100.00
Eclipse, 1931, #2, LF, Mandarin Yel w/jade ends, GFT, NM.........75.00
Esterbrook, 1949, LJ Pen, LF, red, NM...30.00
Esterbrook, 1949, SJ Pen, LF, red, NM...20.00
Esterbrook, 1950, Pastel Pen, LF, wht, NM...................................75.00
Esterbrook, 1950, Relief #12, LF, Tiger's Eye web, GVT, NM 275.00
Leboeuf, 1928, #4, sleeve fill, ring top, gr Pearltex, GFT, NM 250.00
Leboeuf, 1932, #8, sleeve fill, ring top, gr Pearlex, GFT, NM 250.00
Mabie Todd, 1925, #44 Eternal, LF, blk, NM.............................100.00
Mabie Todd, 1925, #44 Eternal, LF, jade, NM 175.00
Mabie Todd, 1938, Blackbird Bulb, gr & gold spiral, GFT, NM..175.00
Mabie Todd, 1939, #4, LF, silver pearl snakeskin, NM 175.00
Mabie Todd, 1947, Swan #3240, LF, dk gr, GFT, NM..................95.00
Montblanc, 1935, #20, blk, GFT, NM..600.00
Montblanc, 1935, #20, Coral Red, GFT, NM 500.00
Montblanc, 1935, #25, blk, GFT, NM..600.00
Montblanc, 1935, #25, Coral Red, GFT, NM 750.00
Montblanc, 1935, #30, blk, GFT, NM..800.00
Montblanc, 1935, #30, Coral Red, GFT, NM 850.00
Montblanc, 1937, #134, blk w/long window, nM.........................450.00
Montblanc, 1937, #333½, PIF, blk, GFT, NM 375.00
Montblanc, 1939, #139, PIF, blk, GF & sterling silver trim, NM .2,000.00
Montblanc, 1941, #25 Masterpiece, PIF, 12-sided brn marble, GFT, NM .1,250.00
Montblanc, 1947, #136, PIF, blk, GFT, NM.................................650.00
Montblanc, 1950, #146, PIF, gr stripe, GFT, NM 1,250.00
Montblanc, 1950, #246, PIF, blk, GFT, short window, NM.........450.00
Montblanc, 1950, #642N, silver striped, brushed chrome cap w/GFT, NM ...800.00
Montblanc, 1952, #142, PIF, blk, GFT, flat feed/telescoping filler, NM ..300.00
Montblanc, 1955, #82, PIF, GF pinstripe, M...............................275.00
Montblanc, 1955, #124, PF, GF, fluted, M 250.00
Montblank, 1927, #1266, PIF, chrome plate fluted, NM 200.00
Moore, 1925, L-96, LF, dk bl, GFT, NM......................................400.00

Moore, 1925, L-96, LF, maroon/burgundy, GFT, NM 500.00
Moore, 1941, #2, LF, gr pearl web, GFT, NM........................125.00
Moore, 1946, Fingertip, LF, dk gr, GFT, M.........................200.00
Parker, 1918, Black Giant, ED, blk HR, NP clip, NM 1,500.00
Parker, 1921, Duofold Jr, BF, red HR, bandless cap, NM 500.00
Parker, 1921, Duofold Sr, BF, red HR, bandless cap, MIB 1,400.00
Parker, 1928, Duofold Sr, BF, Mandarin Yel, GFT, NM............1,500.00
Parker, 1930, Duofold Special, BF, red, GFT, EX 250.00
Parker, 1932, BF, blk, bendless, NM..................................75.00
Parker, 1932, Thrift Time, BF, gray marble, GFT, NM 200.00
Parker, 1935, Victory, BF, bl marble, GFT, NM.....................300.00
Parker, 1937, Vacumatic Oversz, blk, GFT, NM.....................350.00
Parker, 1937, Vacumatic Oversz, brn banded, GFT, NM.............400.00
Parker, 1937, Vacumatic Oversz, gr banded, GFT, NM..............450.00
Parker, 1937, Vacumatic Oversz, gray banded, NPT, NM...........350.00
Parker, 1937, Vacumatic Oversz, red banded, GFT, NM.............550.00
Parker, 1937, Vacumatic Slender, red laminated, GFT, NM........125.00
Parker, 1939, Duofold Jr, BF, silver geometric, NPT, NM...........125.00
Parker, 1945, Vacumatic Major, silver laminated, NPT, dbl jeweled, EX..150.00
Parker, 1946, #51, AF, forest gr, brushed lustraloy cap, M 100.00
Parker, 1946, NS (new style) Duofold, gray, NPT, NM 300.00
Parker, 1948, #51, AF, Buckskin, GF cap w/pinstripe & plain panels, NM.125.00
Parker, 1948, #51, AF, plum, GF cap, NM 150.00
Parker, 1950, #51 Mark II, AF, rare later version, NM 125.00
Parker, 1951, #51, AF, plum, brushed lustraloy cap, NM............125.00
Parker, 1957, #61, wick fill, blk, 2-tone silver cap, NM.................75.00
Parker, 1960, #45, cartridge/converter, bronzed anodized, M 100.00
Parker, 1965, #75, sterling silver crosshatch (flat ends), NM 150.00
Parker, 1965, #75 Spanish Treasure LE, sterling silver crosshatch, MIB..1,300.00
Parker, 1970, #65 Titanium Ball (ballpoint) Pen, M 300.00
Parker, 1970, #75 Titanium, M 700.00
Parker, 1970, T-1 (Titanium), M 750.00
Parker, 1975, #75, sterling silver crosshatch (dimpled ends), NM ..100.00
Parker (Valentine), 1935, #2, BF, burgundy pearl web, GFT, rare, NM.150.00
Pelikan, 1937, #100N, gr pearl, GFT, NM 300.00
Pelikan, 1937, #100N, tortoise w/matching cap/derby, Palladium nib, NM..850.00
Pelikan, 1937, #100N, tortoise w/red cap, NM 900.00
Pelikan, 1938, #100N, gr pearl, chased GF band/clip, NM 325.00
Pelikan, 1938, IBIS, PIF, blk, GFT, NM................................175.00
Pelikan, 1950, #400, PIF, brn stripe, GFT, NM......................185.00
Pelikan, 1950, #400, PIF, gr stripe, GFT, NM 175.00
Pelikan, 1950, #400, PIF, gr V stripe, gr turning knob/section, NM.450.00
Salz, 1920, Peter Pan, LF, dk red w/blk veins, GFT, NM 110.00
Salz, 1925, Peter Pan, LF, blk HR, GFT, rare longer length, NM..70.00
Salz, 1925, Peter Pan, LF, tan/brn Bakelite, GFT, NM..................75.00
Sheaffer, 1930, Lifetime Balance Lg, brn stripe, LF, GFT, NM....300.00
Sheaffer, 1930, Lifetime Balance Lg, LF, Carmine Red stripe, GFT, NM.600.00
Sheaffer, 1930, Lifetime Balance Lg, LF, ebonized pearl, GFT, NM.500.00
Sheaffer, 1930, Lifetime Balance Lg, LF, gr stripe, GFT, NM 350.00
Sheaffer, 1930, Lifetime Balance Lg, LF, Roseglow stripe, GFT, NM..900.00
Sheaffer, 1936, Feather Touch #8 Lg Balance, PF, gray marble, NM...450.00
Sheaffer, 1937, Standard Sz Lifetime Balance, LF, blk, GFT, NM.75.00
Sheaffer, 1942, Lifetime Triumph, PF, silver laminated, NPT, EX.75.00
Sheaffer, 1950, Triumph Snorkel, GF, NM..........................150.00
Sheaffer, 1952, Clipper Snorkel, sage gr, chrome cap w/GFT, MIB..150.00
Sheaffer, 1954, Valiant Snorkel, burgundy, NM.......................30.00
Sheaffer, 1954, Valiant Snorkel, pk, NM...............................75.00
Sheaffer, 1958, Lady Skripsert, gold-plated, jeweled ring, EX........35.00
Sheaffer, 1959, PFM I, blk, blk cap, CPT, NM 150.00
Sheaffer, 1959, PFM II, blk, chrome cap, NM 175.00
Sheaffer, 1959, PFM II, burgundy, stainless steel cap, GFT, NM.200.00
Sheaffer, 1959, PFM III, blk, blk cap, GFT, NM.....................200.00
Sheaffer, 1959, PFM III, gray (rare), GFT, NM......................375.00
Sheaffer, 1959, PFM III Demonstrator, transparent, GFT, blk shell, NM.800.00

Sheaffer, 1959, PFM IV, blk, GF cap, GFT, NM 300.00
Sheaffer, 1959, PFM V, blk, polished chrome cap, GFT, NM......325.00
Soennecken, 1952, III Extra, PIF, gr herringbone, NM 600.00
Soennecken, 1952, III Superior, PIF, golden weave, NM.............400.00
Soennecken, 1952, 222 Extra, PIF, blk...............................250.00
Soennecken, 1952, 222 Superior, PIF, silver lizard, NM.............300.00
Wahl Eversharp, 1920, #0, LF, GF pinstripe, NM 55.00
Wahl Eversharp, 1927, Gold Seal, LF, rosewood, NM 350.00
Wahl Eversharp, 1929, #2, LF, rosewood, GFT, NM.................150.00
Wahl Eversharp, 1929, Equipoised, LF, blk & pearl, GFT, NM...350.00
Wahl Eversharp, 1929, Oversz Deco Band, LF, blk, GFT, NM....450.00
Wahl Eversharp, 1929, Oversz Deco Band, LF, Lapis, GFT, NM.650.00
Wahl Eversharp, 1929, Oversz Deco Band, LF, woodgrain, GFT, NM...450.00
Wahl Eversharp, 1934, #2 Doric, LF, Ice (blk w/pearl veins), NPT, NM.300.00
Wahl Eversharp, 1942, Skyline Jr, LF, blk Moderne stripe, GFT, NM..100.00
Wahl Eversharp, 1951, Symphony, LF, blk, GFT, M w/orig label ..65.00
Waterman, 1910, #18S Safety, ED, blk HR, rare, M 2,600.00
Waterman, 1915, #14, ED, blk chased HR, stanhope cap, NM..1,895.00
Waterman, 1915, #52, LF, blk chased HR, NPT, NM.................100.00
Waterman, 1915, #452½ LEC, LF, sterling Sheridan, NM...........450.00
Waterman, 1920, #055½ LEC, LF, GF Gothic, eng, NM............325.00
Waterman, 1920, #52½V, LF, Cardinal HR, GFT, NM 200.00
Waterman, 1924, #54, LF, blk HR, GFT, NM..........................110.00
Waterman, 1924, #452, LF, sterling Gothic, NM......................350.00
Waterman, 1925, #0552½, ED, Secretary in GF filigree, NM.....500.00
Waterman, 1925, #58, LF, blk HR, GFT, NM..........................875.00
Waterman, 1926, #5, LF, red ripple w/red band, GFT, NM+ 275.00
Waterman, 1927, #7, LF, red ripple, pk band, 1st yr model, NM ...400.00
Waterman, 1929, Patrician, LF, blk HR, GFT, NM 850.00
Waterman, 1929, Patrician, LF, moss agate 900.00
Waterman, 1929, Patrician, LF, Nacre (blk & pearl), GFT, M color.1,750.00
Waterman, 1929, Patrician, LF, Onyx (red cream), GFT, M color.1,500.00
Waterman, 1930, #94, LF, bl & cream, NPT, NM 225.00
Waterman, 1930, #94, LF, brn & cream (mahog), GFT, NM......225.00
Waterman, 1930, #94, LF, red ripple HP, GFT, NM 400.00
Waterman, 1940, #2 Model 513, LF (England), GFT, NM 125.00
Waterman, 1941, 100 Yr, blk, smooth cap/bbl, GFT, NM...........300.00

Mechanical Pencils

Anonymous, rifle shape, cocking mechanism, eng: Rin Tin Tin, NM.75.00
Autopoint, 1945, 2-color (blk/bl), w/clip, M...........................15.00
Conklin, 1929, Symetric, gr marble, GFT, no clip, EX 40.00
Cross/Tiffany, 1990, sterling silver pinstripe, clip: Tiffany, MIB ..100.00
Eversharp, 1940, blk snakeskin pattern leather cover, GFT, NM.100.00
Montblanc, 1924, #6, octagonal, blk HR, eng bbl, lg, rare, NM.900.00
Montblanc, 1930, #92 Repeater, blk HR, NPT, NM 125.00
Montblanc, 1939, #392 Repeater, blk HR, NM 80.00
Parker, 1929, Duofold Jr, jade, GFT, NM 50.00
Parker, 1929, Duofold Jr, Mandarin Yel, GFT, NM..................150.00
Parker, 1930, Duofold Vest Pocket, burgundy, GFT, w/opener taper, NM..150.00
Parker, 1948, Duofold Repeater, gray, GFT, worn imprint, NM ..150.00
Sheaffer, 1925, Balance, deep jade, GFT, NM+ 50.00
Sheaffer, 1925, Balance, gr marble, GFT, NM+ 40.00
Sheaffer, 1959, PFM III, blk, GFT, M w/orig decal 125.00
Wahl Eversharp, 1929, Oversz Deco Band, blk & pearl, GFT, NM.125.00
Wahl Eversharp, 1939, Coronet, blk w/smooth GF cap, NM........50.00
Wahl Eversharp, 1948, Coronet, bronze pearl, chrome cap w/blk, NM..70.00
Waterman, 1925, blk HR, GFT, M....................................150.00
Waterman, 1928, #52½ V, olive ripple, GFT, NM....................85.00

Sets

C Stewart, 1951, #27, LF, lav pearl web, GFT, +#37 pencil, NM.225.00

C Stewart, 1952, #14, LF, bl pearl, GFT, MIB..............................60.00
Montblanc, 1972, #1266, PIF, sterling, fluted, 18k wht gold nib, M..400.00
Parker, 1937, Depression, BF, red pearl, GFT, matching blind caps, NM..175.00
Parker, 1940, Vacuum Jr, gr/bronze/blk stripes, GFT, NM 125.00
Parker, 1957, #61, GF, alternating pinstripes & panels, M 200.00
Sheaffer, 1925, #2-25 Tall, LF, blk plastic, GFT, NM..................100.00
Sheaffer, 1936, Junior, LF, gray marble, NPT, NM 75.00
Sheaffer, 1952, Clipper Triumph Snorkel, bright red, chrome caps, MIB.175.00
Sheaffer, 1958, Lady Skripsert, GF filigree & bl, MIB 45.00
Sheaffer, 1959, PFM III, blk, GFT, MIB..............................325.00

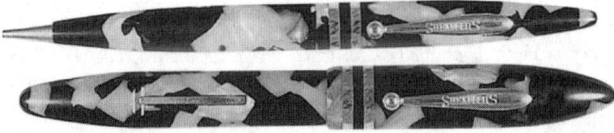

Sheaffer Lifetime Balance, 1932, pearl and black plastic, lever filler, unusual split cap bands, $350.00. (Photo courtesy Paul Erano)

Wahl Eversharp, #4, GF w/chased wave pattern, NM 175.00
Waterman, 1925, #52, LF, red ripple, GFT, NM 250.00

Personalities, Fact and Fiction

One of the largest and most popular areas of collecting today is character-related memorabilia. Everyone has favorites, whether they be comic-strip personalities or true-life heroes. The earliest comic strip dealt with the adventures of the Yellow Kid, the smiling, bald-headed Oriental boy always in a nightshirt. He was introduced in 1895, a product of the imagination of Richard Fenton Outcault. Today, though very hard to come by, items relating to the Yellow Kid bring premium prices.

Though her 1923 introduction was unobtrusively made through only one newspaper, New York's *Daily News*, Little Orphan Annie, the vacant-eyed redhead in the inevitable red dress, was quickly adopted by hordes of readers nationwide, and before the demise of her creator, Harold Gray, in 1968, she had starred in her own radio show. She made two feature films, and in 1977 'Annie' was launched on Broadway.

Other early comic figures were Moon Mullins, created in 1923 by Frank Willard; Buck Rogers by Philip Nowlan in 1928; and Betty Boop, the round-faced, innocent-eyed, chubby-cheeked Boop-Boop-a-Doop girl of the early 1930s. Bimbo was her dog and KoKo her clown friend.

Popeye made his debut in 1929 as the spinach-eating sailor with the spindly-limbed girlfriend, Olive Oyl, in the comic strip *Thimble Theatre*, created by Elzie Segar. He became a film star in 1933 and had his own radio show that during 1936 played three times a week on CBS. He obligingly modeled for scores of toys, dolls, and figurines, and especially those from the '30s are very collectible.

Tarzan, created around 1930 by Edgar Rice Burroughs, and Captain Midnight, by Robert Burtt and Willfred G. Moore, are popular heroes with today's collectors. During the days of radio, Sky King of the Flying Crown Ranch (also created by Burtt and Moore) thrilled boys and girls of the mid-1940s. Hopalong Cassidy, Red Rider, Tom Mix, and the Lone Ranger were only a few of the other 'good guys' always on the side of law and order.

But of all the fictional heroes and comic characters collected today, probably the best loved and most well known is Mickey Mouse. Created in the late 1920s by Walt Disney, Micky (as his name was first spelled) became an instant success with his film debut, 'Steamboat Willie.' His popularity was parlayed through wind-up toys, watches, figurines, cookie jars, puppets, clothing, and numerous other products. Items from the 1930s are usually copyrighted 'Walt Disney Enterprises'; thereafter, 'Walt Disney Productions' was used.

For more information we recommend *Schroeder's Collectible Toys, Antique to Modern*, by Sharon and Bob Huxford; *Cartoon Toys & Collectibles* by David Longest; *Collector's Guide to TV Toys & Memorabilia, Second Edition*, by Greg Davis and Bill Morgan; *Roy Rogers and Dale Evans Toys and Memorabilia* by P. Allan Coyle; *Peanuts Collectibles* by Andrea Podley with Derrick Bang; and *G-Men and FBI Toys and Collectibles* by Harry and Jody Whitworth are other great publications. All are available from Collector Books. See also Autographs; Banks; Big Little Books; Children's Books; Comic Books; Cookie Jars; Dolls; Games; Lunch Boxes; Movie Memorabilia; Paper Dolls; Pin-Back Buttons; Posters; Puzzles; Rock 'N Roll Memorabilia; Toys.

Addams Family, key chain, Thing, MOC..................................6.00
Alice in Wonderland, wristwatch, pk fabric strap, Ingersoll, EX, up to..350.00
Alvin & Chipmunks, Stuff & Lace Set, Hasbro, 1959, MIB..........75.00
Andy Panda, bank, tin litho, EX...65.00
Archies, Pick-Up Sticks, Ja-Ru, 1986, MOC...........................10.00
Bambi, Flower figure, Am Pottery, 1940s, 4½", M....................65.00
Bambi, wall clock, yel plastic, battery-op, 1970s, 11x11", NM......65.00
Banana Splits, flute set, plastic, Laramie, 1973, set of 3, MOC.....55.00
Banana Splits, Paint-by-Number 'N Frame Set, Hasbro, 1959, MIB...125.00
Banana Splits, tambourine, Laramie, 1973, MIP.......................40.00
Batman, Activity Box, Whitman, 1966, MIB............................65.00
Batman, balloons, National Latex/NPPI, 1966, set of 8, MIP 75.00
Batman, Batphone, red plastic, says 10 phrases, Marx, 1966, 8", MIB..400.00
Batman, bicycle ornament, plastic, spring clamp, Empire, 1966, 8", MOC .50.00
Batman, Colorforms, 1966, complete, NMIB..........................55.00
Batman, Electronic Project-A-Light, AHI/Canadian, 1978, MIB.55.00
Batman, film, Adventures of Batman, Columbia, 1950s, 8mm, EXIB..500.00
Batman, Flying Batplane, plastic, attached remote control, Remco, MIB .300.00
Batman, Official Batman Chute, NPPI, 1966, MOC....................40.00
Batman, Sky Hero, plastic figure/rubber-band launcher, Marx, 1977, MOC..45.00
Batman, toy watch, Marx, 1978, MOC....................................20.00
Batman, wristwatch, batwings keep time on rnd face, 1966, NMIB.850.00
Batman & Robin, pinball machine, Marx, 1966, 22x10", EX 100.00
Beany & Cecil, Beany-Copter, Mattel, 1960s, MOC 140.00
Betty Boop, Big Dress-Up Set, Colorforms, 1970s, MIB, from $35 to..45.00
Betty Boop, Bimbo Orchestra figures, Fleisher Studios, set of 3, MIB.500.00
Beverly Hillbillies, slide-tile puzzle, 1960s, MOC 60.00
Bionic Woman, Play-Doh Action Playset, Kenner, 1977, NMIB..25.00
Bionic Woman, Styling Boutique, Kenner, 1977, MIB, from $100 to.125.00
Blippy, jack-in-the-box, Mattel, M, from $100 to.........................150.00
Bozo the Clown, sticker board, 1983, MIB..............................15.00
Bozo the Clown, Stitch-a-Story, Hasbro, 1967, MOC..................50.00
Brady Bunch, Hex-A-Game, Laramie, 1973, MOC.....................45.00
Brady Bunch, jump rope, Larami, 1973, MIP, from $50 to............75.00
Brady Bunch, magic slate, lift-up film sheet, Whitman, 1973, NM ..75.00
Broom Hilda, bubble bath container, 1977, EX 30.00
Brothers Grimm, school kit, Hasbro, 1962, NMOC 50.00
Buck Rogers, Midget Caster Set, 1934, rare, VG (VG box)........750.00
Bugs Bunny, alarm clock, Ingraham, reclining w/carrot, 4x4", EX ..200.00
Bugs Bunny, Cartoon Kit, Colorforms, early, complete, NMIB 75.00
Bugs Bunny, jack-in-the-box, Mattel, 1962, NM, from $50 to 75.00
Bugs Bunny, poster, I Want You, as Uncle Sam, 22x16", EX 5.00
Bugs Bunny, Toot-A-Tune plastic figure, Warner Bros, NMIB, $100 to.150.00
Cap'n Crunch, hand puppet, vinyl, cereal premium, 1963, 9", M.35.00
Captain America, flashlight, plastic w/paper decal, Gordy, 1980, MIP...30.00
Care Bears, figure, any character, Kenner, 1984, 3", MOC...........15.00
Casper the Ghost, baseball & bat set, inflatable vinyl, MOC 15.00
Casper the Ghost, bubble bath container, Colgate Palmolive, EX...30.00
Charlie Brown, nodder, ceramic, baseball cap & mitt, Japan, NM ..60.00
Charlie McCarthy, compo doll, movable mouth, 1930s, 13", EX ..250.00
Charlie McCarthy, Mazuma Phony Money, 1950s, MIP...............50.00
Charlie's Angels, Hide-A-Way House, Hasbro, 1978, MIB, from $75 to .100.00

CHiPs, sunglasses, Fleetwood, 1977, MOC 15.00
CHiPs, wallet, vinyl w/badge & logo on front, Imperial, 1981, MIP..12.00
Cinderella, bank, Leeds, NM 85.00
Cinderella, character glasses, Disney/Libbey, 1950s-60s, set of 8.120.00
David Cassidy, wristwatch, photo image on face, 1970s, NM, $150 to ..200.00
Dennis the Menace, Joey doll, cloth, Presents, 1980s, EX.............25.00
Dennis the Menace, Play Dentist, Pressman, 1954, near complete, EX..175.00
Deputy Dawg, bop bag, vinyl w/weighted base, Doughboy, 1961, 54", NM.50.00
Dick Tracy, Bonnie Braids figure, plastic, Charmore, 1951,½", MOC..50.00
Dick Tracy, Breathless Mahoney canteen, MIB, from $20 to 30.00
Dick Tracy, Breathless Mahoney fanny pack, pk, 1990, M 25.00
Dick Tracy, Sparkle Paints, Kenner, 1963, MIB 50.00
Dick Tracy, Special Secret Agent Set, Laramie, 1972, NMIP 40.00
Donald Duck, crib toy, compo w/wire arms & legs, EX 225.00
Donald Duck, hat, mesh w/vinyl beak, quacks when squeezed, 10", EX .125.00
Donald Duck, jtd celluloid figure, 1930s, 3", NM......................450.00
Donald Duck, roly poly, jtd celluloid figure at top, 4", EX 325.00
Donald Duck, watering can, tin litho, Ohio Art/WDE, 1938, 3", NM .350.00
Donny Osmond, nodder, wht jumpsuit, w/microphone, NM, from $100 to.150.00
Dr Dolittle, Fun Sponge, Amsco, NM..30.00
Dr Dolittle, hat, animal-skin print, Jacobson, NM 20.00
Dr Dolittle, Spelling & Counting Board, Bar-Zim, NMIP.............35.00
Dr Seuss, Cat in Hat ring, gold-tone metal w/head view, NM.........5.00
Dr Seuss, See 'N Say Talking Storybook, Mattel, 1970, NM.......200.00
Dukes of Hazzard, backpack, denim-like w/General Lee picture, 1981, NM...40.00
Dukes of Hazzard, ID Set, Grand Toy, MOC................................10.00
Elmer Fudd, mask, cb, Warner Bros, NM, from $60 to 90.00
Emergency, fire helmet, plastic, Playco, 1975, EX+ 30.00
ET, yo-yo, glitter plastic/paper insert, slimline, 1980s, MIP...........22.00
Family Affair, Buffy Fashion Wig, Amsco, 1971, MIB...............100.00
Family Affair, Fun Box, Whitman, 1970, MIB............................50.00
Fearless Fly, kite, plastic, Roalex, 1967, MIP...........................200.00
Felix the Cat, drum, tin litho, 1930s, scarce, NM.....................200.00
Felix the Cat, slide-tile puzzle, Roalex, 1960, MOC......................30.00
Felix the Cat, TV Color Set, Lido, 1950s, NMIB.......................175.00
Ferdinand the Bull, Cut-Outs, WDP, unused, EX.......................200.00
Flintstones, Bamm-Bamm bubble pipe, Transogram, 1963, MOC.25.00
Flintstones, Barney doll, plush, Hanna-Barbera, 1960s, NM 55.00
Flintstones, Dino riding toy, plastic, 1960s, 18", EX 70.00
Flintstones, Fred figure, vinyl squeaker, Hanna-Barbera, 1982, 7", NM .65.00
Flintstones, Fred lamp, vinyl, 11", NM.....................................55.00
Flintstones, Paint 'Em Pals, Craftmaster, 1978, MIB (sealed)........25.00
Flintstones, Pebbles & Bamm-Bamm yo-yo, Festival, 1980, MIP..25.00
Flipper, Color-By-Number Set, Hasbro, 1966, NMIB, from $50 to..60.00
Flipper, jack-in-the-box, tin litho, Mattel, 1976, NM 150.00
Flipper, magic slate, lift-up film sheet, Whitman, 1967, NM 30.00
Flying Nun, Oil Painting-By-Numbers, Hasbro, 1967, NMIB, from $75 to .100.00
Fonze, wristwatch, photo image on face, Time Trends, 1976, MIB..75.00
G-Men, Secret Communication Set, NY Toy & Game, 1936, EX (EX box)..375.00
Garfield, Ball Darts, MIB, from $25 to 35.00
Garfield, jack-in-the-box, Pop Goes the Odie, MIB......................30.00
Garfield, slide-tile puzzle, MIP 5.00
Garfield, toothbrush holder, plastic, United Features, 1978 ....14.00
Garfield, vinyl figure, as Santa, 6" 25.00
Gilligan's Island, Gilligan's Floating Island, Playskool, 1977, MIB..150.00
Goofy, yo-yo, plastic tournament shape, Festival, 1960s, MIP.......25.00
Goose Bumps, rings, set of 4, MOC...35.00
Green Hornet, Oil Painting by Numbers Set, Hasbro, MIB, from $300 to.500.00
Green Hornet, Print Putty, Colorforms, 1966, MOC....................75.00
Green Hornet, rub-ons, Hasbro, rare, MIB 425.00
Green Hornet, Stardust Touch of Velvet Art, Hasbro, 1966, NMIB ..200.00
Gremlins, Colorforms Deluxe Set, MIB.....................................65.00
Gumby & Pokey, Lilly Pop-Up Puppet, 1967, MIB 65.00
Gumby & Pokey, Pokey bendy figure, Lakeside, 1965, MOC........55.00

Happy Days, Flip-A-Knot, 1977, MIP 15.00
Happy Days, Fonz Viewer, Larami, 1981, MOC.........................20.00
Happy Days, Fonzie Colorforms, EX (EX box)............................30.00
Happy Days, Fonzie guitar, 1976, MIB (sealed)..........................75.00
Hogan's Heroes, writing tablet, 1965, unused, NM.....................30.00
Howdy Doody, cowboy figure, soft vinyl, NM+ (G illus cello case).145.00
Howdy Doody, doll, beanbag body, EX 25.00
Howdy Doody, Magic Piano, w/friends on yel, Kagran, 15x10", EXIB.575.00
Howdy Doody, raft, inflatable vinyl, Ideal/Kagran, 9x9", MIP 200.00
Howdy Doody, shakers, figural, pr, NMIB.................................95.00
Howdy Doody, sparkler, lever action, Ja-Ru, 1987, MOC............10.00
Huckleberry Hound, bank, plastic figural, 1960, 10", EX 35.00
Huckleberry Hound, chalkboard, diecut at top, Pressman, 1966, EX..50.00
Huckleberry Hound, gumball bank, Transogram, 1960, NM (EX+ box).55.00
I Dream of Jeannie, Knitting & Embroidery Kit, Harmony, 1975, MOC .35.00
Incredible Hulk, Crazy Foam, 1979, w/contents, VG+ 25.00
Incredible Hulk, push toy, plastic, 1979, 7", EX.........................25.00
Incredible Hulk, Rub 'N Play, Colorforms, 1979, MIB 30.00
Incredible Hulk, Split Ring, inflatable vinyl, 1977, MIB..............20.00
James Bond, ID bracelet, Marvin Glass/Glidrose, 1965, 8", NMIB..75.00
Jetsons, Flip Disk Shooting Game, MOC.....................................8.00
Jetsons, George & Jane puffy magnets, 1970s, 4", EX, pr..............10.00
Josie & the Pussy Cats, chalkboard, 1970s, M, from $50 to...........75.00
Julia, Hospital Set, Transogram, 1970, NMIB, from $75 to.........100.00
Justice League of America, Paint-By-Number Set, Hasbro, 1967, EXIB.150.00
King Kong, Panoramic Play Set, Colorforms, 1976, EX (EX box)..25.00
Knight Rider, Adventure Set, Colorforms, 1982, MIB 35.00
Kr Kildare, telephone, plastic, Renzi, 1960s, NM 50.00
Krazy Kat, jdt wood figure, Chein, 1920s, 7", NM....................250.00
Krazy Kat, pull toy, tin litho w/wood & paper bellows, Chein, 7", EX...700.00
Land of the Lost, magic slate, lift-up film sheet, Whitman, 1975, M..40.00
Lassie, ring, Good Luck, EX...165.00
Lassie, Trick Trainer, Mousely Inc, 1945, NM (EX box) 275.00
Laurel & Hardy, Fuzzy Felt Playset, Standard Toykraft, 1962, NMIB..75.00
Laurel & Hardy, Stuff & Lace Dolls, Transogram, 1962, MIB 45.00
Laverne & Shirley, Secretary Set, Harmony, 1977, MOC, from $25 to .35.00
Linus the Lion-Hearted, bank, plastic figure, Transogram, 1965, EX..55.00
Little Bo Peep, tea set, tin litho, Ohio Art, 1930s, 9-pc, EX.......200.00
Little King, pnt wood figure, rubber-band walker, Jaymar, 1939, 4", EX....85.00
Little Orphan Annie, pull toy, sitting on 4-wheel wood base, 10", EX+.350.00
Little Orphan Annie, toy stove, metal w/upper oven/warmer, 1930s, NM...200.00
Little Orphan Annie & Sandy, jtd wood figures, Jamar, 5", EX ..165.00
Love Boat, Ship's Doctor Set, Fleetwood, 1979, MOC.................25.00
Ludwig Von Drake, figure set, Marx, 1960s, NMIB.....................95.00
Ludwig Von Drake, vinyl squeeze toy, WDP, 1960s, NM.............30.00
M*A*S*H, canteen, plastic, Tristar, 1981, EX.............................10.00
M*A*S*H, helicopter, Durham, 1975, EX (EX box)...............100.00
Magilla Gorilla, change purse, vinyl w/zipper, Estelle, 1960s, 3" dia..35.00
Marvel Super Heroes, notebook, Mead, 1970s, M 25.00
Masters of the Universe, Colorforms, EX (EX box)......................15.00
Mickey Mouse, baton, compo head, WD label, VG 300.00
Mickey Mouse, Big Little Set, WDE, 1930s, EX (EX box), from $75 to.100.00
Mickey Mouse, ceramic figure, w/tuba, Rosenthal, 3½", NM 200.00
Mickey Mouse, Kodak Theatre, MIB...35.00
Mickey Mouse, nodder, yel shirt/red pants/gr base, NM 75.00
Mickey Mouse, pocket watch, red plastic, Bradley, 1970s, 2" dia, EX..50.00
Mickey Mouse, pull toy, pulls axle w/bell, NN Hill Brass/WD, 1930s, EX.500.00
Mickey Mouse, Slugaroo, w/cb display sign, Gardner/WDP, NMIB..75.00
Mickey Mouse, top, tin litho, WDE, 1935, 9½" dia, VG 175.00
Mickey Mouse & Goofy, teacup, tin litho, Ohio Art, 1932, 1⅛", EX .55.00
Mickey Mouse & Minnie, party horn, Marks Bros/WDE, 1935, 7", EX .165.00
Mickey Mouse Club, Clubhouse, Hasbro/Romper Room, 1970s, MIB .125.00
Mickey Mouse Club, Magic Adder, battery-op, 1950s, NMIB.......65.00
Mighty Mouse, alarm clock, MM hands keep time, orange case, 1960s, NM.85.00

Minnie Mouse, bank, compo, in house, Japan/WDE, NM.............20.00
Minnie Mouse, bsk figure, hands on hips, Japan, 1930s, 2¾", EX.65.00
Minnie Mouse, doll, Sun Rubber, 1950s, 10", VG.........................65.00
Minnie Mouse, Minnie Picture Toast, Hoan Products, 1988, M (EX card).25.00
Mork & Mindy, Rub 'N Play Set, Colorforms, 1979, MIB.............25.00
Mork & Mindy, Shrinky Dinks, Colorforms, 1979, MIB (sealed).25.00
Mother Goose, dishes, plastic, Ideal, 1940s, 26 pcs, MIB...........150.00
Mother Goose, Nursery Pianette, Schoenhut, 1940s, VG (VG box).125.00

Munsters figures, Herman and Lily, Remco, 1964, $225.00 each.

(Photo courtesy June Moon)

Muppets, Great Gonzo Dress-Up Doll, clothes remove, Fisher-Price, MIB..15.00
Muppets, Miss Piggy Latch Hook Kit, MIB (sealed) 55.00
Mutt & Jeff, drum, tin litho, Converse, 1930, 8" dia, EX............200.00
New Zoo Revue, musical mobile, Young Designs, 1971, MIB, from $50 to..75.00
Oswald Rabbit, magic slate, lift-up plastic film, Saalfield, 1952, EX ..35.00
Partridge Family, bulletin board, red cork, 1970s, 18x24", EX, $75 to..100.00
Pater Pan, Television Studio, cb, Admiral TV Premium, 1952, M ..165.00
Peanuts, Linus figure w/blanket, 3", M.......................................8.00
Peanuts, Linus nodder, blk sq base, Lego, NM 95.00
Peanuts, Schroeder nodder, Lego, lg, NM 95.00
Peanuts, Snoopy & Woodstock piano, Determined, 1980s, MIB.125.00
Peanuts, Snoopy bank, compo, on rainbow, NM.......................25.00
Peanuts, Snoopy baseball player doll, PVC, 1984, 8½", NM, $35 to..45.00
Peanuts, Snoopy camera, soda can shape, Tomy, 1984, MIB, $100 to..125.00
Peanuts, Snoopy doll, cloth pillow type, 1963, VG 35.00
Peanuts, Snoopy See & Say, Mattel, VG....................................50.00
Peanuts, Snoopy Sing-Along Radio, Determined, EX 85.00
Peanuts, Snoopy tea set, plastic, Berwick, 1979, 19-pc set, MIB.100.00
Peanuts, Woodstock yo-yo, Festival, 1970s, NM...........................14.00
Phantom of the Opera, slide-tile puzzle, Ja-Ru, 1985, MOC.........25.00
Pinocchio, Honest John figure, bsk, Multi-Products, 1940s, 7", EX.75.00
Pinocchio, Puppet Show, Whitman, complete w/stage+8 figures, EXIB.125.00
Pinocchio, xylophone, battery-op, 1955, 8½", NM 250.00
Pixie & Dixie, Punch-O Punching Bag, Kestral, 1959, 18", NMIB.25.00
Pluto, Peppy Puppet, mini plastic marionette, Kohner, MOC.......55.00
Pluto, vinyl figure, inflatable, 1960s, 9", MIP................................50.00
Popeye, colored chalk, Am Crayon, EX (VG box), from $100 to .125.00
Popeye, floating toy, figure in vinyl boat, 1950s-60s, 6", NMIP 45.00
Popeye, Glow Putty, MOC..25.00
Popeye, Magic Play Around, Amsco, NMIB..............................300.00
Popeye, plaster figure, 7", EX 165.00
Popeye, pocket watch, characters between #s, Ingersoll, 1935, EX.650.00
Popeye, TV Eras-O-Board Set, Hasbro, 1958, EX (EX box)..........75.00
Popeye, wristwatch, chrome case, New Haven, 1935, VG, from $500 to.700.00
Popeye & Olive Oyl, Slinky pull toy, Linemar, 6½", EX.............800.00
Porky Pig, figure, rubber squeaker, Sun Rubber, NM 50.00
Prince Valiant, pressed wood figure on base, 1942, 6", NM 200.00
Raggedy Ann, iron, metal/plastic, Gabriel/Bobbs-Merrill, 1970, EX ..30.00
Raggedy Ann, nodder bank, mk A Penny Saved, NM 75.00
Raggedy Ann & Andy, phonograph, Vanity Fair, 1974, NMIB, from $45 to.55.00

Raggedy Ann & Andy, Shoeshine Kit, Janex/Bobbs-Merrill, 1974, NMIB.40.00
Raggedy Ann & Andy, tea set, tin litho, Chein, 1972, 89-pc, MIB..30.00
Raggedy Ann & Andy, tea set, Wolverine/Bobbs-Merrill, 1978, 26-pc, MIB.50.00
Robin Hood, iron-on patch, Johnson & Johnson, 1956, 3x3", MOC .25.00
Rocky & Bullwinkle, Bullwinkle Electric Quiz, 1971, MOC.........40.00
Rocky & Bullwinkle, Rocky, Natasha & Boris bendable figures, 1991, MOC...20.00
Rocky & Bullwinkle, spelling & counting board, Larami, 1969, MOC..28.00
Secret Squirrel, bubble bath container, Purex, 1966, rare, VG......45.00
Sesame Street, Big Bird doll, talks w/tape player, Ideal, 25", VG ..55.00
Sesame Street, Big Bird/Ernie Lacin' Puppets, Fisher-Price, 1984, MIP.10.00
Simpsons, air mattress, inflatable vinyl, Mattel, 72x30", MIP.......30.00
Simpsons, Bart doll, cloth & vinyl, Dandee, 16", MIB.................15.00
Simpsons, Bart flashlight, Happiness Express, 3-D figure on side, MOC.12.00
Simpsons, Bart rag doll, Dandee, 12", MOC...............................20.00
Simpsons, Barv Vs Homersaurus video game, hand-held, Tiger, MIP..35.00
Simpsons, Paint-By-Number Set, Rose Art, MIB........................10.00
Sleeping Beauty, Magic Bubble Wand, 1950s, MIP......................40.00
Smurfs, Papa Smurf ceramic figure, VG......................................30.00
Snow White & 7 Dwarfs, charms, celluloid, Japan, 1930s, set of 8, NM.75.00
Snow White & 7 Dwarfs, Doc figure, bsk, Japan, 1930s, 3", NM..50.00
Snow White & 7 Dwarfs, Happy figure, Shaw, 1950s, NM 115.00
Spider-Man, Code Breaker, Gordy, 1980, MOC 35.00
Spider-Man, roller skates, plastic, 1970s, MIP (sealed)..................40.00
Steve Canyon, school bag, yel canvas, 1959, EX 75.00
Superman, Fun Poncho, Ben Cooper, 1976, MIP (sealed) 30.00
Superman, Kiddie Paddlers, bl rubber swim fins, Superswim, 1956, NMIB.100.00
Superman, Muscle Building Set, Peter Puppet, 1954, EX (VG box)...400.00
Superman, wristwatch, image on face, gold-tone case, Bradley, EXIB.175.00
Tasmanian Devil, cloth doll, Mighty Stars, 1960s, EX..................40.00
Three Little Pigs, tea set, gr tin litho, WDE, 1930s, 15-pc, NM .500.00
Three Stooges, Larry flasher ring, EX 25.00
Tom & Jerry, jack-in-box, Mattel, M, from $75 to.....................100.00
Tom & Jerry, Music Maker, tin litho, Mattel, 1960s, NM, from $65 to..75.00
Underdog, bop bag, inflatable vinyl w/weighted base, MIB...........50.00
Underdog, harmonica, plastic w/emb images, 1957, 7", NM 70.00
Welcome Back Kotter, Kotter Kids Kit, Ideal Publishing, 1977, M..65.00
Welcome Back Kotter, Poster Art Kit, Board King, 1976, MIB.....45.00
Welcome Back Kotter, record player, Peerless Vid-Tronic Corp, 1976, NM..75.00
Wendy the Witch, bubble bath container, Colgate-Palmolive, 1960s, NM ..30.00
Winnie the Pooh, Tigger doll, stuffed plush, Sears, 1967s, EX 35.00
Wizard of Oz, Cowardly Lion flasher ring, M 40.00
Woody Woodpecker, character glass, W Lantz/Pepsi, 1970s, from $10 to.20.00
Woody Woodpecker, film, Castle Films, MIB, from $25 to 35.00
Yogi Bear, camera, 1960s, MIB...65.00
Yogi Bear, Play Fun Set, Whitman, 1964, NMIB........................50.00
Yogi Bear, Ranger Rick doll, stuffed cloth, Giacotelli, 10, NM 65.00
Yogi Bear, riding toy, stick w/plastic head, squeaker, AJ Renzi, 34"..50.00

Peters and Reed

John Peters and Adam Reed founded their pottery in Zanesville, Ohio, just before the turn of the century, using the local red clay to produce a variety of wares. Moss Aztec, introduced about 1912, has an unglazed exterior with designs molded in high relief and the recesses highlighted with a green wash. Only the interior is glazed to hold water. Pereco (named for Peters, Reed and Company) is glazed in semi-matt blue, maroon, cream, and other colors. Orange was also used very early, but such examples are rare. Shapes are simple with in-mold decoration sometimes borrowed from the Moss Aztec line. Wilse Blue is a line of high-gloss medium blue with dark specks on simple shapes. Landsun, characterized by its soft matt multicolor or blue and gray combinations, is decorated either by dripping or by hand brushing in an effect sometimes called Flame or Herringbone. Chromal, in much the same colors as Landsun, may be decorated with a realistic scenic, or the swirling application of colors may merely suggest one. Vivid, realistic Chromal scenics command much higher prices than weak, poorly drawn examples. (Brush-McCoy made a very similar line called Chromart. Neither will be marked; and due to the lack of documented background material available, it may be impossible make a positive identification. Collectors nearly always attribute this type of decoration to Peters and Reed.) Shadow Ware is usually a glossy, multicolor drip over a harmonious base color but occasionally seen in overall matt glaze. When the base is black, the effect is often iridescent.

Several other lines were produced, including Mirror Black, Persian, Egyptian, Florentine, Marbleized, etc., and an unidentified line which collectors call Mottled-Marbleized Colors. In this high-gloss line, the red clay body often shows through the splashed-on multicolors. At one time, the brown high-glaze artware line with 'sprigged' decoration was attributed to Peters and Reed. However, this line has recently been re-attributed to Weller pottery by the Sanfords in their latest book on Peters and Reed pottery. This conclusion was drawn due to the overwhelming number of shapes proven to be Weller molds. Since the decoration was cut out and applied, however, it is possible that Peters and Reed or yet another Zanesville company simply contracted for the Weller greenware and added their own decoration and finishes.

In 1922 the company became known as the Zane Pottery. Peters and Reed retired, and Harry McClelland became president. Charles Chilcote designed new lines, and production of many of the old lines continued. The body of the ware after 1922 was light in color. Marks include the impressed logo or ink stamp 'Zaneware' in a rectangle.

Basket, hanging, Moss Aztec, grapevines, 11½x9" 225.00
Cemetery urn, Moss Aztec, ivy leaves & berries, Ferrell, 9¾x4½" .195.00
Jardiniere, Moss Aztec, Ferrel, 8x9" 275.00
Jardiniere, terra cotta w/moss gr patina, emb pine cones, 4¼x7¼" .200.00
Vase, Chromal, clouds & landscape, yel/tan/brn, 7¾x3¾" 475.00
Vase, Chromal (Impressionistic), trees & landscape, 7½x4½" 250.00
Vase, Copper Mantene, ca 1920, 9½x6" dia 275.00
Vase, creamy ivory/brn/bl-gray/tan swirling matt, prof rstr, 11x4½" ..125.00
Vase, dk gr swirls form horizontal drip bands on gr, 9x4½" 275.00
Vase, Landsun, earth tones w/bl, mk #40-D, 11¾" 250.00
Vase, Landsun, gr/brn/tan/rust, bulbous w/flared neck, 5" 130.00
Vase, Moss Aztec, leaves & berries, 7⅝x4¾" 150.00
Vase, Shadow Ware, cobalt/yel/aqua drips on mocha, can neck, 8x5½" .275.00
Vase, Wilse Blue, ball shaped, 5⅛x6½" dia..................................55.00
Vase, Wilse Blue, corseted, 6⅜" 55.00
Window box, Moss Aztec, 12¼x5¼x6" 350.00

Pewabic

The Pewabic Pottery was formally established in Detroit, Michigan, in 1907 by Mary Chase Perry Stratton and Horace James Caulkins. The two had worked together since 1903, firing their ware in a small kiln Caulkins had designed especially for use by the dental trade. Always a small operation which relied upon basic equipment and the skill of the workers, they took pride in being commissioned for several important architectural tile installations.

Some of the early artware was glazed a simple matt green; occasionally other colors were added, sometimes in combination, one over the other in a drip effect. Later Stratton developed a lustrous crystalline glaze. (Today's values are determined to a great extent by the artistic merit of the glaze.) The body of the ware was highly fired and extremely hard. Shapes were basic, and decorative modeling, if used at all, was in low relief. Mary Stratton kept the pottery open until her death in 1961. In 1968 it was purchased and reopened by Michigan State University; it is still producing today. Several marks were used over the years: a triangle with 'Revelation Pottery' (for a short time only); 'Pewabic' with five maple leaves; and the impressed circle mark.

Bookends, rnd tops/platforms, comical rabbit reserve, bl/gr lustre, NM..350.00
Plate, rooster band, yel/red/gr on wht crackle, chips/glaze loss, 9" .800.00
Plates, for Household Arts/Columbia U, by Wesley, 25 pcs, EX, $850 to..1,250.00
Tile, boy riding dolphin, 90th Anniversary commemorative, 3x3" ..30.00
Tiles, lot of 4:, oxblood w/emb king, mustard w/scarab, etc, 2¾-4"..1,000.00
Vase, bronze/gr/bl, bottle shape, label, 9½x5" 1,500.00
Vase, crackled turq w/dk bl 'plumes,' 2"..225.00
Vase, cream drip on mottled mauve & cream lustre, sm shoulder, 4½" ..200.00
Vase, gr/tan matt flambe, drips at base, drilled, 10x8", $1,500 to..2,000.00
Vase, indigo/turq/gr lustre, 13¼x6¾", NM 2,875.00

Vase, lavender and green lustre over gold, horizontal ridges, marked, 8x6", $2,530.00. (Photo courtesy Dave Rago)

Vase, mauve lustre/dripping copper & turq, spherical, PP, 3½x4½" ..1,725.00
Vase, purple/turq mottled lustre, cylindrical, 1942, 3¾x3"..........225.00
Vase, tan/purple lustre crystalline, mfg flaw, unmk, 8x2½", $900 to..1,200.00
Vase, teal gloss, wide w/waisted upper body, horizontal ribs, 5½x5" .515.00
Vase, turq crackle w/bl plumes, PP, 2" 260.00
Vse, cobalt/gr lustre, 5¾x6¼" 1,380.00

Pewter

Pewter is a metal alloy of tin, copper, very small parts of bismuth and/or antimony, and sometimes lead. Very little American pewter contained lead, however, because much of the ware was designed to be used as tableware, and makers were aware that the use of lead could result in poisoning. (Pieces that do contain lead are usually darker in color and heavier than those that have no lead.) Most of the fine examples of American pewter date from 1700 to the 1840s. Many pieces were melted down and recast into bullets during the American Revolution in 1775; this accounts to some extent why examples from this period are quite difficult to find. The pieces that did survive may include buttons, buckles, and writing equipment as well as the tableware we generally think of.

After the Revolution makers began using antimony as the major alloy with the tin in an effort to regain the popularity of pewter, which glassware and china was beginning to replace in the home. The resulting product, known as britannia, had a lustrous silver-like appearance and was far more durable. While closely related, britannia is a collectible in its own right and should not be confused with pewter.

Key: tm — touch mark

Alms dish, RC tm, 17th C, 6" 595.00
Basin, Boardman Warranted tm w/eagle, wear, 1¾x8" 250.00
Basin, crown tm/Made in London, hammered booge, rpr split, 4x13"..150.00
Basin, Thomas Badger tm, minor scratches, 9¼".......................1,380.00
Candlesticks, Henry Hopper tm, ca 1842-47, 12", pr 635.00

Canister, milk; GNL tm, hand eng design, 12", EX 380.00
Chalices, att Sellew, dbl hdls, ca 1830-60, 5", pr 315.00
Charger, GFM tm w/moon & stars, central boss, 1730-50, 13½".700.00
Charger, Thomas Badger eagle tm, 12⅛" 300.00
Charger, Thos Danforth II tm, pitting/scratches, 13" 1,650.00
Chocolate pot, C Roessler tm w/Roman soldier, lighthouse, 1837, 8½".365.00
Coffeepot, A Porter tm, bulbous, 1830-40, 12" 515.00
Coffeepot, Dixon & Son tm, melon ribs, wood hdl & finial, 12".140.00
Coffeepot, F Porter tm, bulbous, tooled lines, stepped dome lid, 11".360.00
Coffeepot, H Homan tm, cast flower finial, 11" 220.00
Coffeepot, unmk Beverly Group, lighthouse style, 10¼".............230.00
Creamer & sugar bowl, Dixon & Sons tm, 1860s, 6½", 8½" 265.00
Deep dish, Danforth tm, surface scratches/minor pitting, 13"..1,035.00
Deep dish, Samuel Kilbourne tm, minor dents, 11" 650.00
Deep dish, WM Billings tm, scratches/minor pitting, 11⅜".....1,850.00
Flagon, Boardman eagle tm, domed hinged lid, S hdl, 11¼" 1,850.00
Flagon, unmk, Scottish style, very heavy, 1-liter, 9½", EX 675.00
Inkwell, wide flat base, yellowware insert, 3x7" dia 140.00
Ladle, J Danforth tm, sm rpr, 12¼" 300.00
Mug, Crown Rose tm, pear shape, 5x4"....................................110.00
Plate, Boardman Group lion tm, 9⅜"..260.00
Plate, eagle & Samuel Pierce tm, wear/scratches, 8" 360.00
Plate, Edward Danforth tm, minor rstr, 8" 385.00
Plate, Frederick Bassett tm, 8½" 325.00
Plate, T Danforth partial tm, minor damage, 9" 250.00
Plate, Thomas Badger tm, ca 1737-1815, set of 3 (3" to 8½") 925.00
Porringer, Gershom Jones tm, minor wear, 5½"........................1,850.00
Porringer, Melville tm, crown hdl w/spline support, 1755-93, 4¼"..1,500.00
Salt box, unknown mk, hinged lid, hangs, dtd 1825, 5x7½".......525.00
Sugar bowl, Boardman tm, flattened ball form w/chased foliage, w/lid.375.00
Tea set, Frederik Lunning mk, 1940s, 3-pc.................................160.00
Teapot, A Porter tm, horn finial wafer, squat w/ear hdl, sm dent, 6".330.00
Teapot, HB Ward & Co tm, ca 1810, 8¾", EX...........................225.00
Teapot, HB Ward tm, sample sz, 1840s, 6"..............................1,550.00
Teapot, Philip Ashberry & Sons tm, Sheffield #521, 7½" 145.00
Teapot, R Dunham tm, tapered form, hinged lid, 11½", VG 145.00
Teapot, Roswell Gleason tm, spire finial, scroll hdl, 1822-71, 7" .285.00
Teapot, Shaw & Fisher tm, cucumber vine & leaf finial, ca 1880-1900 ..350.00
Teapot, unmk, ornate spout & hdl, lt weight, 6", G 55.00
Tureen, Ulrich Orth tm, ftd, w/lid, ca 1700-30, 5⅜x8¾x5¼" 525.00

Pfaltzgraff

Pfaltzgraff has operated in Pennsylvania since the early 1800s making redware at first, then stoneware crocks and jugs, yellow ware and spongeware in the '20s, artware and kitchenware in the '30s, and stoneware kitchen items through the '40s. To collectors, they're best known for their Gourmet Royal (circa 1950s), a high-gloss dinnerware line of solid brown with frothy white drip glaze around the rims, and their giftware line called Muggsy, comic-character mugs, ashtrays, bottle stoppers, children's dishes, pretzel jars, cookie jars, etc. It was designed in the late 1940s and continued in production until 1960. The older versions have protruding features, while the features of later examples were simply painted on.

Their popular Village line, an almond-glazed pattern with a brown-stenciled folk-art tulip design, was discontinued a few years ago, and is today becoming very collectible. Yorktown and Folk Art are manufactured today only on a very limited basis, so discontinued items in those lines are attracting much interest as well. (In general, use Village prices to help you evaluate those two lines.) For more information on their dinnerware, we recommend *The Flea Market Trader* and *The Garage Sale and Flea Market Annual*, Collector Books. Our advisor for the Muggsy line is Judy Posner; she is listed in the Directory under Florida.

Gourmet Royale, baker, #321, oval, 7½", from $8 to....................10.00
Gourmet Royale, bean pot, #11-3, 3-qt..................................25.00
Gourmet Royale, bean pot, #11-4, 4-qt..................................35.00
Gourmet Royale, bowl, #241, oval, 7x10", from $10 to.............12.00
Gourmet Royale, bowl, cereal; #934SR, 5½" 3.50
Gourmet Royale, bowl, mixing; 8", from $10 to..........................12.00
Gourmet Royale, bowl, salad; tapered sides, 10", from $10 to.......14.00
Gourmet Royale, butter dish, #394, ¼-lb, stick type, from $9 to ..12.00
Gourmet Royale, casserole, hen on nest, 2-qt, from $65 to...........95.00
Gourmet Royale, casserole, stick hdl, 1-qt, from $9 to 12.00
Gourmet Royale, casserole, stick hdl, 4-qt, from $25 to 35.00
Gourmet Royale, casserole-warming stand 7.00
Gourmet Royale, chip 'n dip, #311, molded in 1 pc, 12", from $14 to..18.00
Gourmet Royale, coffeepot, #303, 10-cup, from $20 to 25.00
Gourmet Royale, cup, from $2 to..3.00
Gourmet Royale, gravy boat, w/stick hdl, 2-spout, from $8 to.......12.00
Gourmet Royale, ladle, 3½" dia bowl w/11" hdl, from $18 to.......20.00
Gourmet Royale, mug, #391, 12-oz, from $5 to............................7.00
Gourmet Royale, mug, #392, 16-oz, from $9 to..........................12.00
Gourmet Royale, plate, egg; holds 12 halves, 7¾x12½", $15 to ...20.00
Gourmet Royale, plate, grill; #87, 3-section, 11", from $9 to 12.00
Gourmet Royale, platter, #337, 16", from $18 to.........................20.00
Gourmet Royale, roaster, #326, oval, 16", from $20 to 28.00
Gourmet Royale, serving tray, rnd, 4-section, center hdl, $15 to ..20.00
Gourmet Royale, shirred egg dish, #360, 6", from $7 to 10.00
Gourmet Royale, teapot, #381, 6-cup, from $12 to......................18.00
Planter, donkey, brn drip, common, 10", from $15 to 20.00
Village, baker, #236, rectangular, tab hdls, 2-qt, from $10 to 12.00
Village, baker, #24, oval, 10¼", from $7 to 9.00
Village, baker, #240, oval, 7¾", from $6 to.................................8.00
Village, bowl, batter; w/spout & hdl, 8", from $22 to 28.00
Village, bowl, mixing; #453, 1-qt, 2-qt & 3-qt, 3-pc set, $45 to....50.00
Village, bowl, serving; #010, 7", from $8 to................................12.00
Village, bowl, vegetable; #011, 8¾"..12.00
Village, butter dish, #028...8.00
Village, casserole, w/lid, #315, 2-qt, from $18 to.........................22.00
Village, coffeepot, lighthouse shape, 48-oz, from $20 to 25.00
Village, cookie jar, #540, 3-qt, from $15 to 20.00
Village, cup & saucer, #001 & #002...3.50
Village, flowerpot, 4½", from $12 to..15.00
Village, gravy boat, #443, w/saucer, 16-oz, from $10 to..............12.00
Village, onion soup crock, #295, stick hdl, sm, from $5 to 7.50
Village, pedestal mug, #90F, 10-oz...3.50
Village, pitcher, #416, 2-qt, from $20 to.....................................25.00
Village, soup tureen, #160, w/lid & ladle, 3½-qt, from $40 to 45.00
Village, table light, #620, clear chimney, candle holder base, $12 to ..14.00

Muggsy Line

Ashtray 125.00
Cigarette server...125.00
Clothes sprinkler bottle, Myrtle, Black 275.00
Clothes sprinkler bottle, Myrtle, wht 250.00
Cookie jar, character face...250.00
Jar, utility; Handy Harry, hat w/short bill as flat lid 200.00
Mug, action figure (golfer/fisherman/etc), any 65.00
Mug, character face 35.00
Mug, shot sz, character face...50.00
Tumbler..60.00

Phoenix Bird

Blue and white Phoenix Bird china has been produced by various

Japanese potteries from the early 1900s. With slight variations the design features the Japanese bird of paradise and scroll-like vines of Kara-Kusa, or Chinese grass. Although some of their earlier ware is unmarked, the majority is marked in some fashion. More than 125 different stamps have been reported, with 'Made in Japan' the one most often found. Coming in second is Morimura's wreath and/or crossed stems (both having the letter 'M' within). The cloverleaf with 'Japan' below very often indicates an item having a high-quality transfer-printed design. Among the many categories in the Phoenix Bird pattern are several shapes; therefore (for identification purposes), each has been given a number, i.e. #1, #2, etc. Newer items, if marked at all, carry a paper label. Compared to the older ware, the coloring of the new is whiter and the blue more harsh; the design is sparse with more ground area showing. Although collectors buy even 'new' pieces, the older is, of course, more highly prized and valued.

The Flying Turkey is a pattern very similar to Phoenix Bird. Though there are several other differences, the phoenix bird's head is turned left, while the turkey is looking forward. Values are given for this line as well.

On today's market, prices fluctuate wildly, based on individual need and demand. While advanced collectors pass up common pieces, they may pay exorbitant amounts for those necessary to complete their collections. This creates an artificial high and low price structure. Some of our values are actual selling prices and include examples of both low and high-end sales.

For further information we recommend *Phoenix Bird Chinaware, Books I – V*, written and privately published by our advisor, Joan Oates; her address is in the Directory under Michigan. Join Phoenix Bird Collectors of America (PBCA) and receive the *Phoenix Bird Discoveries* newsletter, an informative publication that will further your appreciation of this chinaware. See Clubs, Newsletters, and Catalogs for ordering information.

Flying Turkey, chocolate pot #2, scalloped base	155.00
Flying Turkey, condensed milk container, w/lid	147.50
Phoenix Bird, batter jug, missing lid	85.00
Phoenix Bird, bowl, berry; scalloped, 8¾"	195.00
Phoenix Bird, bowl, bouillon; w/lid & saucer	40.00
Phoenix Bird, bowl, fruit/salad; 10"	80.00
Phoenix Bird, celery tray, 13¼" L	90.00
Phoenix Bird, coffee mugs, post-1970, pr	14.00
Phoenix Bird, condiment set, triangular, 3-pc	155.00
Phoenix Bird, hair receiver	40.00
Phoenix Bird, nut bowl & 6 nut cups, #2a	205.00
Phoenix Bird, plate, luncheon; 8"	14.00
Phoenix Bird, platter, scalloped, 12¼" L	85.00
Phoenix Bird, platter, 11" L	50.00
Phoenix Bird, platter, 13¾" L	50.00
Phoenix Bird, ramekin dishes, 4 for	46.00
Phoenix Bird, sugar bowl, #9	16.00
Phoenix Bird, tea strainer, ftd, #6	36.00
Phoenix Bird, teapot, #13A	105.00
Phoenix Bird, teapot, #7	38.50
Phoenix Bird, vase, #4, 4"	35.00

Phoenix Glass

Founded in 1880 in Monaca, Pennsylvania, the Phoenix Glass Company became one of the country's foremost manufacturers of lighting glass by the early 1900s. They also produced a wide variety of utilitarian and decorative glassware, including art glass by Joseph Webb, colored cut glass, Gone-With-the-Wind style oil lamps, hotel and barware, and pharmaceutical glassware. Today, however, collectors are primarily interested in the Sculptured Artware produced in the 1930s and 1940s. These beautiful pressed and mold-blown pieces are most often found in white milk glass or crystal with various color treatments or a satin finish.

Phoenix did not mark their Sculptured Artware line on the glass; instead, a silver and black (earliest) or gold and black (later) foil label in the shape of the mythical phoenix bird was used.

Quite often glassware made by the Consolidated Lamp and Glass Company of nearby Coraopolis, Pennsylvania, is mistaken for Phoenix's Sculptured Artware. Though the style of the glass is very similar, one distinguishing characteristic is that perhaps 80% of the time Phoenix applied color to the background leaving the raised design plain in contrast, while Consolidated generally applied color to the raised design and left the background plain. Also, for the most part, the patterns and colors used by Phoenix were distinctively different from those used by Consolidated.

In 1970 Phoenix Glass became a division of Anchor Hocking which in turn was acquired by the Newell Group in 1987. Phoenix has the distinction of being one of the oldest continuously operating glass factories in the United States. For more information refer to *Phoenix and Consolidated Art Glass, 1926 – 1980*, written by our advisor, Jack D. Wilson, who is listed in the Directory under Arizona. See also Consolidated Glass.

Bachelor Button, vase, wht pearlized, rare, 7"	275.00
Bicentennial, vase, spray pnt, machine made	50.00
Bicentennial, vase, wht spray w/gold highlights, machine made	50.00
Bluebell, vase, dk burgundy pearlized, 7"	125.00
Bluebell, vase, florist gr, KR Haley, 1948	250.00
Cosmos, vase, brn shadow, 7½"	145.00
Cosmos, vase, ivory pearlized, 7½"	125.00
Cosmos, vase, vase, pk w/pearlized design, 7½"	175.00
Daisy, vase, burgundy on pearlized, 9x9"	275.00
Daisy, vase, pk pearlized, 9x9"	275.00
Diving Girl, banana boat, bl on gr w/pearlized design	350.00
Diving Girl, banana boat, lt bl/purple w/frosted design	325.00
Fern, vase, aqua w/frosted design, 7"	125.00
Freesia, fan vase, brn w/milk glass design	170.00
Freesia, vase, aqua w/frosted design, 8"	140.00
Freesia, vase, burgundy w/milk glass design, 8"	160.00
Jewel, vase, bl pearlized	125.00
Jewel, vase, lt gr pearlized	125.00
Jewel, vase, med gr on milk glass, 5"	100.00
Lacy Dewdrop, bowl, caramel irid	125.00
Lacy Dewdrop, compote, pk decor on milk glass	145.00
Lacy Dewdrop, pitcher, heavy caramel irid, rare	700.00
Lily, vase, aqua wash (rare color), str sides, 8"	225.00
Lily, vase, aqua wash (rare color), 3-crimp	250.00
Madonna, vase, brn shadow, 10"	275.00
Madonna, vase, med gr on milk glass	200.00
Madonna, vase, peach on milk glass, 10"	250.00
Philodendron, vase, avocado gr w/satin, Davis-Lynch, 1960s	75.00
Philodendron, vase, rose shadow, 11½"	250.00
Phlox, ashtray, aqua wash	55.00
Phlox, ashtray, burgundy pearlized	65.00
Phlox, candy dish, rose pearlized	225.00
Primrose, vase, bl frosted, 8¾"	475.00
Star Flower, vase, blk stain on crystal, rare	450.00
Star Flower, vase, coral w/frosted design, 7"	145.00
Thistle, vase, lime gr pearlized, 18"	500.00
Thistle, vase, slate bl pearlized, 18"	550.00
Tiger Lily, bowl, amethyst frost, 11½"	350.00
Tiger Lily, bowl, purple & clear satin, 11½"	350.00
Wild Geese, vase, amber w/frosted design, 9"	275.00
Wild Geese, vase, bl-gray w/frosted design, 9x12"	200.00
Wild Geese, vase, lime gr pearlized, 9x12"	225.00
Wild Geese, vase, med gr on milk glass	175.00
Wild Geese, vase, wht pearlized, 9x12"	175.00
Wild Rose, vase, wht frost, 10½"	150.00
Zodiac, vase, tan on milk glass, 10½"	900.00

Phonographs

The phonograph, invented by Thomas Edison in 1877, was the first practical instrument for recording and reproducing sound. Sound wave vibrations were recorded on a tinfoil-covered cylinder and played back with a needle that ran along the grooves made from the recording, thus reproducing the sound. Very little changed to this art of record making until 1885, when the first replayable and removable wax cylinders were developed by the American Graphophone Company. These records were made from 1885 until 1894 and are rare today. Edison began to offer musically recorded wax cylinders in 1889. They continued to be made until 1902. Today they are known as brown wax records. Black wax cylinders were offered in 1902, and the earlier brown wax cylinders were discontinued. These wax two-minute records were sold until 1912. From 1912 until 1929, only four-minute celluloid blue amberol record cylinders were made. The first disc records and disc machines were offered by the inventor Berliner in 1894. They were sold in America until 1900, when the Victor company took over. In the 1890s, all machines played 7" diameter disc records; the 10" size was developed in 1901. By the early 1900s there existed many disc and cylinder phonograph companies, all offering their improvements. Among them were Berliner, Columbia, Zonophone, United States Phono, Wizard, Vitaphone, Amet, and others.

All Victor I's through VI's originally came with a choice of either brass bell, morning-glory, or wooden horns. Wood horns are the most valuable, adding $1,000.00 (or more) to the machine. Spring models were produced until 1929 (and even later). After 1929 most were electric (though some electric-motor models were produced as early as 1910). Unless another condition is noted, prices are for complete, original phonographs in at least fine to excellent condition. Note: Edison coin-operated cylinder players start at $7,000.00 and may go up to $20,000.00 each. All outside-horn Victor phonographs are worth at least $1,000.00 or more, if in excellent original condition. Machines that are complete, still retaining all their original parts, and with the original finish still in good condition are the most sought after, but those that have been carefully restored with their original finishes, decals, etc., are bringing high prices as well. Unless noted, values are for examples in excellent condition, sold at popular, repeated buying prices.

Key:
cyl — cylinder	NP — nickel plated
mg — morning glory	rpd — reproducer

Aretino, disc, orig gr mg horn, 3" center spindle 750.00
Berliner Trade Mark, disc, Clark-Johnson rpd, brass horn 5,000.00
Brunswick, cvd upright case w/moldings, lg 350.00
Brunswick Queen Anne, console, rpr motor, working 350.00
Cameraphone, disc, orig rpd, tortoise-shell resonator, oak 550.00
Colibri, disc, box-camera type, Colibri rpd, sound box, w/case ...350.00
Columbia AA, cyl, eagle rpd, blk horn, oak 1,000.00
Columbia AJ, disc, Columbia rpd, blk/brass bell horn, top crank .1,200.00
Columbia AK, disc, orig rpd, brass bell horn, 7¼" turntable.......800.00
Columbia AZ, cyl, Lyric rpd, repro blk/brass horn 500.00
Columbia BE Leader, cyl, Lyric rpd, mg, 6" mandrel, serpentine ..650.00
Columbia BF Peerless, cyl, Lyric rpd, NP horn, M case 800.00
Columbia BI Sterling, disc, Columbia rpd, oak horn 2,250.00
Columbia BI Sterling Graphophone, disc, brass mg horn, oak case, rstr.2,250.00
Columbia Eagle B Braphophone, cyl, 2-min, replica Trump horn, EX .695.00
Columbia Grafonola Mignon, disc, inside horn, floor model 200.00
Columbia Graphophone Q, cyl, oak case, repro horn, EX 350.00
Columbia K, disc, orig rpd, front mt 1,000.00
Columbia Q Busy Bee, yel, D rpd, 14" blk cone horn, keywind..300.00
Columbia Regent Desk, disc, Columbia rpd, inside horn, mahog..400.00
Edison A-250, floor model 600.00

Edison Amberola VIII, cyl, Dmn B rpd, internal horn, oak table model..400.00
Edison Business Phono D, cyl, Spectacle rpd, speaking tube, oak..335.00
Edison Concert C, cyl, R rpd, 30" brass bell, floor stand, M 2,500.00
Edison Dmn Disc S19, DD rpd, inside horn, oak, upright...........250.00
Edison Fireside A, cyl, 2-4 min, Dmn B rpd, cygnet horn, EX orig..1,395.00
Edison Fireside B, cyl, 4 min, Dmn B rpd, blk cygnet horn 1,000.00
Edison Gem D Maroon, cyl, 2-4 min, K rpd, 2-pc Fireside horn, EX .1,750.00
Edison Gem E Maroon, cyl, all orig 2,000.00
Edison Home, cyl, C rpd, bl mg horn w/bracket 725.00
Edison Home A, no rpd, all brass horn (poor solder), mahog case..750.00
Edison Home B, cyl, 2-min, lg mg horn, oak case w/orig decal, EX orig.695.00
Edison Home E, cyl, O rpd, oak cygnet horn, oak case 1,800.00
Edison Opera, Music Master horn, mahog case 6,750.00
Edison Standard Flat Top, cyl, VG 600.00
Edison Triumph, cyl, O rpd, oak cygnet horn, NM 2,500.00
Edison Triumph, cyl, 2-4 min repeater, O rpd, wood cygnet 2,800.00
Edison Triumph D, cyl, 2-4 min, H rpd, 23" bell horn 1,000.00

Graphophone, coin-operated Model S, table model, flaring 13" nickeled horn, reproducer, nickel play, oak case with banner transfer, ca 1899, EX, $2,700.00.

Kalamazoo Duplex, disc, Kalamazoo rpd, 2 blk/brass horns, rare .4,300.00
Klingsor, disc, Klingsor rpd, inside horn, ldgl doors.................2,000.00
Nirona box type, disc, Nirona rpd, sound reflector, red metal case, sm...550.00
Pathe Actuelle, disc, cone horn, mahog console 1,000.00
Pathe Coq, cyl, ebonite rpd, aluminum horn, walnut cover........425.00
Pathephone B, disc, walnut case, low-set mg horn, minor pnt rstr, EX .1,350.00
Puck Lyre, cyl, floating rpd, red mg horn 400.00
Regina Hexaphone #103, cyl, Hexaphone rpd, oak horn, rstr.7,500.00
Regina Hexaphone #104, cyl, Hexaphone rpd, oak horn, rstr.8,500.00
Standard A, disc, red mg horn, orig decal, EX 995.00
Standard A, disc, Standard rpd, bl mg horn, decal 650.00
Standard X, disc, Standard rpd, front mt brass bell w/support.....600.00
Thorens Excelda, disc, Escelda rpd, internal horn, camera type..285.00
United Symphony, disc, United rpd, inside horn, table model ...250.00
Victor II, disc, Exhibition rpd, metal horn...............................1,200.00
Victor II, disc, huge Searchlight horn, tiger-oak case, EX orig.1,495.00
Victor IV, disc, tiger oak case, no horn......................................425.00
Victor M Monarch, disc, Exhibition rpd, 11" horn, oak/composite .1,500.00
Victor MS Monarch specialty, disc, Exhibition rpd, oak horn .2,500.00
Victor V, disc, oak Music Master horn, orig decals, prof rstr 4,250.00
Victor VI, Exhibition rpd, quartersawn oak case, M rstr.............465.00
Victor VV-VI, disc, Exhibition rpd, inside horn, oak, table top..200.00
Victor VV-8-30, disc, Orthophonic rpd, inside horn, credenza .1,000.00
Victor VV-50, disc, #2 rpd, inside horn, oak portable..................150.00
Victor XXV, Schoolhouse, disc, oak schoolhouse horn, oak upright .4,500.00
Victrola Credenza, w/longest Victor horn, walnut, rare, VG.......800.00
Victrola VIA, disc, rstr rpd, Exhibition sound box, post-1918 style ..495.00
Zonophone A, disc, Concert rpd, brass horn, glass sides 2,500.00
Zonophone Parlor, disc, brass bell horn, rear crank.................1,100.00
Zonophone Royal Grand, disc, lg NP horn..............................2,200.00

Photographica

Photographic collectibles include not only the cameras and equipment used to 'freeze' special moments in time but also the photographic images produced by a great variety of processes that have evolved since the daguerrean era of the mid-1800s. For the most part, good quality images have either maintained or increased in value. Poor quality examples (regardless of rarity) are not selling well. Interest in cameras and stereo equipment is down, and dealers report that average-priced items that were moving well are often completely overlooked. Though rare items always have a market, collectors seem to be buying only if they are bargain priced.

Our advisor for this category is John Hess; he is listed in the Directory under Massachusetts.

Albumens

Bethlehem panoramic view, Bonfils, 1860, 2 joined: 8x21½" **250.00**
Black field workers gathering lilies in lg field, pre-1940, 7x9½" .**135.00**
Civil War Union soldier stands heavily armed, 9x7", hard paper mat..**175.00**
Crater of Architectural Geyser, Wm H Jackson, 1873, 9x13" **250.00**
Klondike miners on river, ca 1898, 9x7"+cb mt............................**285.00**
Paris, aerial view of streets & bridge, late 1800s, 4¾x7¼" **25.00**
Tower of St Jacques, Paris, 1880s, 11x8"..**42.50**
Yale football team, 1892-93, 4½x7½" **45.00**

Ambrotypes

An ambrotype is a type of photograph produced by an early wet-plate process whereby a faint negative image on glass is seen as positive when held against a dark background.

4th plate, infantry sergeant w/full gear, EX in G case **450.00**
4th plate, infantryman w/sword, +thermoplastic case w/cherub & stag.......**495.00**
4th plate, lady seated by table, +Habana monument case **285.00**
6th plate, cavalry man w/2 Colts, lt silver color w/wear **345.00**
6th plate, lady in fine attire, 1850s, +eagle Union case...............**150.00**
6th plate, lady in finery w/gold cross & wedding band, 1850s, +case......**75.00**
6th plate, man in formal suit, pk tint, +brass fr............................**145.00**
6th plate, sm girl in ruffled dress on chair, +brass fr....................**150.00**
6th plate, 2 soldiers arm-in-arm, in kepis, 1 w/Colt, +half-case **400.00**
9th plate, man in suit, chest up, 1850s, +floral Union case.........**110.00**

Cabinet Photos

Baby in carriage, 6¼x4" **40.00**
Broadway actress in full costume, NY, EX **25.00**
Family of 4 (unknown) studio background, VT, 6½x4¼"................**8.00**
Jefferson Davis, chest-up portrait, postwar, EX............................**350.00**
Lady posed by early bicycle, blk dress, overblouse w/vest & tie.....**35.00**
Prime Minister of Austria, uniform, mutton chops, 1874, 4⅛x2¾" ..**28.00**
Queen, AKC Black Labrador, G Yergers' prize winner, 1857, 10x8" .**15.00**
Salvation Army couple, 6½x4", EX..**20.00**
Sitting Bull, seated in wht shirt w/long pipe, info on bk, 1882 ...**800.00**

Cameras

Collecting antique cameras is very popular. The high-quality items have become harder to find. Most of the pre-1900 cameras will be found in the large format view cameras or studio camera types. There are quite a few of these that can be found in well-worn condition, but there is a large difference in value between an average-wear item and an excellent or mint-condition camera. It is rare indeed to find one of these early cameras in mint condition.

The types of cameras are generally classified into — large format, medium format, early folding, and box types, 35 mm single-lens-reflex (SLR), 35mm rangefinders, twin-lens reflex (TLR), miniature or subminiature, novelty, and even a few others. Collectors may specialize in a type, a style, a time period, or even in high-quality examples of the same camera.

In the 1900 to 1940 period, large quantities of various makes of box cameras and folding bellows type cameras were produced by many manufacturers, and the popular 35mm camera was introduced in the 1930s. Most have low values because they were made in vast numbers, but mint-condition cameras are prized by collectors. In the 1930 to 1955 period, the 35mm rangefinders and the SLR's and TLR's became the cameras of choice. The most prized of these are the early German or Japanese rangefinders such as the Leica, Canon, or Nikon. Earlier, German optics were favored, but after WWII, Japanese cameras and optics rivaled and/or even exceeded the quality of many German optics.

Now there are thousands of different cameras to choose from, and collectors have many options when selecting categories. Quality is the major factor; values vary widely between an average-wear working camera and one in mint condition, or one still in the original box and unused. This brief list suggests average prices for good working cameras with average wear. The same camera in mint condition will be valued much higher, while one with excessive wear (scratches, dents, corrosion, poor optics, nonworking meters or rangefinders) may have little value.

Buying, selling, and trading of old and late vintage cameras on the Internet, both in direct transactions and via e-mail auctions, have affected the number of cameras that are available to collectors. As a result, values have fluctuated as well. Large numbers of old, mass-produced box cameras and folding cameras have been offered; many are in poor condition and have been put up for sale by persons who know nothing about quality. So in general, prices have dropped, except for the mint quality offerings. Many common models in poor to average condition can be bought for $1.00 to $10.00. The collector is advised to purchase only quality cameras that will enhance his collection.

Note: To date, no appreciable collector's market has developed for most old movie cameras or projectors. The Polaroid type of camera has little value, although a few models are gaining in popularity among collectors, and values are expected to increase. Note that many fakes and copies have been made of several of the classic cameras such as the German Leica, and caution is advised in purchasing one of these cameras at a price too good to be true. Consult a specialist on high-priced classics if good reference material is not available. Our advisor for this category is Gene Cataldo; he is listed in the Directory under Alabama (e-mail: genecams@aol.com). SASE required for information by mail.

Agfa, Billy, early 1930s..**15.00**
Agfa, box type, 1930-50, from $5 to...**20.00**
Agfa, Isolette...**20.00**
Agfa, Karat-35, 1940...**35.00**
Agfa, Optima, 1960s, from $15 to..**35.00**
Aires, 35III, 1958...**35.00**
Alpa, Standard, 1946-52, Swiss...**1,500.00**
Ansco, Cadet **5.00**
Ansco, Folding, Nr 1 to Nr 10, ea, from $5 to **30.00**
Ansco, Memar, 1954-58...**20.00**
Ansco, Memo, 1927 type...**100.00**
Ansco, Speedex, Standard, 1950..**15.00**
Ansco, Super Speedex, 3.5 lens, 1953-58..................................**150.00**
Argoflex, Seventy-five, TLR, 1949-58 ....**7.00**
Argus A2F, 1940 ....**20.00**
Argus C3, Black brick type, 1940-50 ....**8.00**
Argus C4, 2.8 lens w/flash..**30.00**
Asahi Pentax, Original, 1957..**200.00**
Asahiflex 1, 1st Japanese SLR...**500.00**
Baldi, by Balda-Werk, 1930s **30.00**

Bell & Howell Dial-35 ....40.00
Bell & Howell Foton, 1948 ....700.00
Bolsey, B2 ....20.00
Braun Paxette I, 1952 ....30.00
Burke & James, Cub, 1914 ....20.00
Canon A-1 ....130.00
Canon AE-1, from $50 to 80.00
Canon AE-1P, from $70 to 125.00
Canon F-1 ....225.00
Canon IIB, 1949-53 ....250.00
Canon III 250.00

Canon IV SB, rangefinder with 50/fl.8 lens, 1952 – 55, from $300.00 to $500.00. (Photo courtesy C.E. Cataldo)

Canon J, 1939-44, from $4,000 to 5,000.00
Canon L-1, 1956-57 ....400.00
Canon P, 1958-61 ....300.00
Canon Rangefinder IIF, ca 1954 ....350.00
Canon S-II, Seiki-Kogaku, 1946-47, from $600 to 800.00
Canon S-II, 1947-49 ....375.00
Canon T-50, from $40 to 65.00
Canon TL, from $40 to 60.00
Canon TX 40.00
Canon VT, 1956-57 ....300.00
Canon 7, 1961-64 ....450.00
Canonet QL1, from $25 to 40.00
Ciroflex, TLR, 1940s 30.00
Compass Camera, 1938, from $1,000 to 1,300.00
Conley, 4x5 Folding Plate, 1905, from $90 to 140.00
Contessa 35, 1950-55, from $100 to 150.00
Contex II or III, 1936, from $200 to 400.00
Detrola Model D, Detroit Corp, 1938-40 ....20.00
Eastman Folding Brownie Six-20 ....12.00
Eastman Kodak Baby Brownie, Bakelite 10.00
Eastman Kodak Bantam, Art Deco, 1935-38 ....35.00
Eastman Kodak Medalist, 1941-48, from $140 to 175.00
Eastman Kodak Retina II 60.00
Eastman Kodak Retina IIa 80.00
Eastman Kodak Retina IIIc, from $125 to 180.00
Eastman Kodak Retina IIIC, from $250 to 375.00
Eastman Kodak Retinette, various models, ea, from $20 to 50.00
Eastman Kodak Signet 35 ....20.00
Eastman Kodak Signet 80 ....50.00
Eastman Kodak 35, 1940-51 ....25.00
Eastman Premo, many models exist, ea, from $30 to ...200.00
Eastman View Camera, early 1900s, from $100 to 200.00
Edinex, by Wirgen 30.00
Exakta, VX, 1951 ....85.00
Exakta II, 1949-50 ....130.00
FED 1, USSR, postwar, from $30 to 50.00
FED 1, USSR, prewar, from $70 to 120.00
Fujica, AX-3 ....80.00
Fujica AX-5 ....125.00
Fujica ST-701 ....60.00
Graflex Pacemaker Crown Graphic, various szs, ea, from $80 to ..150.00

Graflex Speed Graphic, various szs, ea, from $100 to ...200.00
Hasselblad 1000F, 1952-57, from $350 to 550.00
Herbert-George, Donald Duck, 1946 ....35.00
Kodak No 2 Folding Pocket Brownie, 1904-07 ....25.00
Konica Autoreflex TC, various models, ea, from $40 to ...70.00
Konica FS-1 ....60.00
Konica III Rangefinder, 1956-59 ....110.00
Kowa H, 1963-67 ....25.00
Leica II, 1963-67 ....425.00
Leica IID, 1932-38, from $250 to 400.00
Leica IIIf, 1950-56, from $300 to 400.00
Leica M3, 1954-66, from $500 to 1,000.00
Mamiya-Sekor 500TL, 1966 ....20.00
Mamiyaflex, TLR, 1951, from $100 to 150.00
Mercury Model II, CX, 1945 ....35.00
Minolta Autocord, TLR 100.00
Minolta HiMatic Series, various models, ea, from $15 to ...25.00
Minolta SR-7 ....50.00
Minolta SRT-101, from $40 to 65.00
Minolta SRT-202, from $50 to 90.00
Minolta X-700 ....135.00
Minolta XD-11, 1977 ....140.00
Minolta XG-1, XG7, EX-9, XG-A, ea, from $35 to 80.00
Minolta 35, early Rangefinder models, 1947-50, ea, from $250 to ...400.00
Minolta-16, mini, various models, ea, from $15 to 30.00
Minox B, spy camera 125.00
Miranda Automex II, 1963 ....70.00
Nikkormat (Nikon), various models, ea, from $70 to ...150.00
Nikon EM, from $45 to 75.00
Nikon F, various finders & meters, ea, from $150 to ...275.00
Nikon FG 115.00
Nikon FM 150.00
Nikon S Rangefinder, 1951-54, from $350 to 700.00
Nikon S2 Rangefinder, 1954-58, from $300 to 500.00
Nikon S3 Rangefinder, 1958-60, from $500 to 1,200.00
Olympus OM-1 ....120.00
Olympus OM-10 ....60.00
Olympus Pen EE, compact half-fr 35.00
Olympus Pen F, compact half fr SLR, from $150 to ...200.00
Pax M3, 1957 ....30.00
Pentax K-1000, from $70 to 90.00
Pentax ME 75.00
Pentax Spotmatic, many models, ea, from $40 to 130.00
Petri FT, FT-1000, FT-EE & similar models, ea 70.00
Petri-7, 1961 ....20.00
Plaubel-Makina II, 1933-39 ....200.00
Polaroid, most models, ea, from $5 to 10.00
Polaroid SX-70 ....35.00
Polaroid 110, 110A, 110B, ea, from $25 to 40.00
Polaroid 180, 185, 190, 195, ea, from $100 to 250.00
Praktica FX, 1952-57 ....30.00
Pratika Super TL 50.00
Realist Stereo, 3.5 lens 100.00
Regula, King, various models, fixed lens, ea 25.00
Regula, King, various models, interchangeable lens, ea ...75.00
Ricoh Diacord 1, TLR, built-in meter, 1958 ....75.00
Ricoh Singlex, 1965 ....80.00
Rollei 35, mini, Germany, 1966-70, from $175 to 275.00
Rollei 35, mini, Singapore, from $100 to 175.00
Rolleicord II, 1936-50, from $70 to 90.00
Rolleiflex Automat, 1937 model 125.00
Rolleiflex SL35M, 1978, from $75 to 100.00
Rolleiflex 3.5E 300.00
Samoca 35, 1950s 25.00

Sereco 4x5, Folding Plate, Sears, 1901, from $90 to.................**135.00**
Spartus Press Flash, 1939-50 ....**10.00**
Taron 35, 1955...**25.00**
Tessina, mini, from $300 to...**500.00**
Tessina, mini in colors, from $400 to......................................**700.00**
Topcon Super D, 1963-74 ....**125.00**
Topcon Uni..**35.00**
Tower 45, Sears, w/Nikkor lens..**200.00**
Tower 50, Sears, w/Cassar lens...**20.00**
Univex-A, Univ Camera Co, 1933 ....**25.00**
Voightlander Bessa, various folding models, 1931-49, ea, from $15 to..**35.00**
Voightlander Bessa, w/rangefinder, 1936.................................**140.00**
Voigtlander Vitessa L, 1954, from $150 to **200.00**
Voigtlander Vitessa T, 1957..**200.00**
Voigtlander Vito II, 1950 ....**40.00**
Yashica A, TLR **40.00**
Yashica Electro-35, 1966 ....**25.00**
Yashica FX-70 ....**60.00**
Yashicamat 124G, TLR, from $150 to......................................**230.00**
Zeiss Baldur Box Tengor, Frontar lens, 1935, from $35 to..........**150.00**
Zeiss Ikokn Nettar, folding Roll Film, various szs, ea, from $20 to..**35.00**
Zeiss Ikon Juwell, 1927-39 ....**500.00**
Zeiss Ikon Super Ikonta B, 1937-56..**150.00**
Zenit A, USSR, from $20 to **35.00**
Zorki, USSR, 1950-56, from $20 to **40.00**
Zorki-4, USSR Rangefinder, 1956-73 ....**50.00**

Carte De Visites

Among the many types of images collectible today are carte de visites, known as CDVs, which are 2¼" x 4" portraits printed on paper and produced in quantity. The CDV fad of the 1800s enticed the famous and the unknown alike to pose for these cards, which were circulated among the public to the extent that they became known as 'publics.' When the popularity of CDVs began to wane, a new fascination developed for the cabinet photo, a larger version measuring about 4½" x 6½". Note: A common portrait CDV is worth only about 50¢ unless it carries a revenue stamp on the back; those that do are valued at about $2.00 each.

Admiral Farragut, seated w/sword & hat on lap, Brady **200.00**
Baby seated on chair, VT, 4x2½"..**6.00**
Black-face banjo player from minstrel show w/pet dog at ft, EX .**300.00**
Boy on rocking horse, ca 1872, VG...**45.00**
Boy w/no arms, left hand at shoulder..**75.00**
Elizabeth wife of Emperor Francis Joseph of Austria, 1874............**32.00**
General Doubleday, Brady mk, VG..**55.00**
Greek Royal family (King Geo I & wife Olga w/others), 1874......**20.00**
Jefferson Davis, Anthony from Brady negative **445.00**
John Wilkes Booth, ¾-length, seated...**375.00**
Lady leaning on chair, VG, 8½x4" **8.00**
Red Bead Blackfoot, Huffman Studio, MT Territory, 1880s, 6¾x4¼"..**325.00**
Union officers (4 identified on bk), horizontal, EX **285.00**
US Grant in uniform seated by table, Anthony, Brady negative.**100.00**
Wm David 'Dirty Bill' Porter, Commodore of US Navy, in uniform.**100.00**

Daguerreotypes

Among the many processes used to produce photographic images are the daguerreotypes (made on a plate of chemically treated silver-plated copper) — the most-valued examples being the 'whole' plate which measures 6½" x 8½". Other sizes include the 'half' plate, measuring 4½" x 5½", the 'quarter' plate at 3¼" x 4¼", the 'sixth' plate at 2¾" x 3¼", the 'ninth' at 2" x 2½", and the 'sixteenth' at 1⅜" x 1⅝". (Sizes may vary slightly, and some may have been altered by the photographer.)

Half plate, youthful man, well dressed, ¾-length, +ornate metal fr ..**40.00**
6th plate, elderly couple, +brass fr & floral book-shaped case.....**100.00**
6th plate, husband & wife, seated, +single case, VG **125.00**
6th plate, lady in finery & lace gloves, +emb case **65.00**

Sixth-plate, lady with flowers holding book with eagle insignia on cover, hand-tinted details, in case, $125.00.

6th plate, lady w/husband's arm around her, gold details, +case **225.00**
6th plate, men (2) seated, 1 w/hand on other's lap, +brass fr **350.00**
6th plate, wrinkled man w/fierce stare, +brass fr **150.00**
9th plate, youth w/straw Bowler hat in hands, +case **75.00**

Photos

Astanihkyi (Come Singing) - Blood, sepia on paper, ES Curtis, 8x6"..**275.00**
Berry Picker - Clayoquot, photogravure, Curtis, 1915, 15½x11"...**250.00**
Chief Geronimo, Ft Sill OK; sepiatone, Hendrick, 1901, 7½x9½".**600.00**
Chief Pretty Voice Eagle, battle dress, photogravure, Wanamaker, 1913.**275.00**
Chief Running Fisher, photogravure, R Wanamaker, 1913, 9x13"..**225.00**
Columbia River Indian Fisherman, gold-tone on glass, Curtis, 14x11".**2,500.00**
General Wm T Sherman, photogravure, 9x7" mtd on 13½x10" sheet..**350.00**
Goes Ahead, Custer Scout - Crow; browntone, ca 1910, 6x4½"..**100.00**
Naranmo family of Santa Clara Pueblo, ca 1910, 25x16" in fr....**300.00**
Piegan Chief Duck on well-decorated horse, ca 1900, 6½x4½"....**80.00**
Sac-N-Fox men (2) in pose, browntone, fading, 1890s, 3½x2¾".**160.00**
Sailboats at sunset, photogravure, Brown & Bigelow, 1916, 6½x9".**17.50**
Snoqualmu Type, sepia on tissue, ES Curtis/Andrews, orig mat/mt, 15x9".**300.00**
Union officers in uniform, unidentified, salt print, 16½x19" **800.00**
US Grant standing by tree before tent, sepia-tone, 5½x3¾" **200.00**
White River Apache, photogravure, ca 1903, 7½x5½" **140.00**

Stereoscopic Views

Stereo cards are photos made to be viewed through a device called a stereoscope. The glass stereo plates of the mid-1800s and photo prints produced in the darkroom are among the most valuable. In evaluating stereo views, the subject, date, and condition are all-important. Some views were printed over a thirty- to forty-year period; 'first generation' prices are far higher than later copies, made on cheap card stock with reprints or lithographs, rather than actual original photographs.

It is relatively easy to date an American stereo view by the color of the mount that was used, the style of the corners, etc. From about 1854 until the early 1860s, cards were either white, cream-colored, or glossy gray; shades of yellow and a dull gray followed. While the dull gray was used for a very short time, the yellow tones continued in use until the late 1860s. Red, green, violet, or blue cards are from the period between 1865 until about 1870. Until the late 1870s, corners were square; after that they were rounded off to prevent damage. Right now, quality stereo views are at a premium.

Abraham Lincoln, Keystone #28016, biography on bk, EX.........**300.00**
American Falls, Anthony, 1859, EX **25.00**

Fort Darling (Rebel int view of defenses), Anthony #3352, EX..**150.00**
Fort Sumter (int view of wreckage), E& HT Anthony #3457, EX..**150.00**
Libby Prison, exterior view, Kilburn Bros, #891, EX **150.00**
Louisiana Purchase Expo, 1904, 6 for **32.00**
Manchurian street scene, Dainan Gate toward market, att Ponting ..**45.00**
Perils of Wilderness, man & bear, 1893, VG................................**17.50**
Southern views, JA Palmer, set of 18, EX....................................**400.00**
Zuni Indian girl w/water ola, O'Sullivan **60.00**

Tintypes

Tintypes, contemporaries of ambrotypes, were produced on japanned iron and were not as easily damaged.

Full plate, lumber mill w/logs in river, workers, etc, 8x10" **150.00**
Full plate, musician w/violin & dog, pk tint, G **200.00**
Half plate, dog resting on floor **150.00**
Half plate, lady in chair w/spaniel, G **200.00**
Half plate, man w/paint can & brush, EX **300.00**
4th plate, Civil War soldier w/sword & revolver, +flower-urn case **575.00**
4th plate, hunter w/gun & animal tails..**200.00**
4th plate, soldiers (2) w/whiskey flask, pk tint, +brass fr in case........**350.00**
4th plate, Union officer w/wife & baby at piano, +thermoplastic case......**350.00**
4th plate, 2 OH infantrymen, seated X-legged, tinted, +case **350.00**
4th plate, 2 soldiers seated X-legged in kepies/vests, +half case........**300.00**
6th plate, cavalryman, shell jacket w/gilt detail, bl pants, Colt gun **400.00**
6th plate, cavalryman w/bugle, Colt pistol in belt, +case **900.00**
6th plate, Confederate artillery man, ¾-length, in kepi **250.00**
6th plate, dog in costume, corncob pipe in mouth, EX................**200.00**
6th plate, enlisted man seated by table, in kepi w/sm flag, +half case **285.00**
6th plate, men (2 young) in suits, 8-sided case w/oval brass frs, VG **180.00**
6th plate, Union cadet stands w/hat in hand, studio setting........**115.00**
6th plate, Union sergeant, pk highlights, +brass fr in case **285.00**
9th plate, boy stands by baby sister (on chair), EX **25.00**
9th plate, Civil War soldier, bl/gold tint, w/gun, +thermoplastic case......**300.00**
9th plate, drummer boy, waist-up, +Ships Stern Union case......**450.00**
9th plate, father in military coat/wife & daughter, +case, VG......**135.00**
9th plate, infantryman holds hat w/feather & bugle insignia, +case **350.00**
9th plate, man in military shirt, pk tint, VG **250.00**
9th plate, Plateau chief holding pipe, full costume, EX **60.00**
9th plate, Union engineer, ¾-length, w/pistol/dagger, +case......**425.00**

Union Cases

From the mid-1850s until about 1880, cases designed to house these early images were produced from a material known as thermoplastic, a man-made material with an appearance much like gutta percha. Its innovator was Samuel Peck, who used shellac and wood fibers to create a composition he called Union. Peck was part owner of the Scoville Company, makers of both papier-mache and molded leather cases, and he used the company's existing dies to create his new line. Other companies (among them A.P. Critchlow & Company; Littlefield, Parsons & Company; and Holmes, Booth & Hayden) soon duplicated his material and produced their own designs. Today's collectors may refer to cases made of this material as 'thermoplastic,' 'composition,' or 'hard cases,' but the term most often used is 'Union.' It is incorrect to refer to them as gutta percha cases. Sizes may vary somewhat, but generally a 'whole' plate case measures 7" x 9⅛" to the outside edges, a 'half' plate 4⅞" x 6", a 'quarter' plate 3¾" x 4¾", a 'sixth' 3⅛" x 3⅝", a 'ninth' 2⅜" x 2⅞", and a 'sixteenth' 1¾" x 2". Clifford and Michele Krainik and Carl Walvoord have written a book, *Union Cases*, which we recommend for further study. Another source of information is *Nineteenth Century Photographic Cases and Wall Frames* by Paul Berg. Values are for examples in excellent condition unless noted otherwise.

Half plate, Am Country Life, Summer's Evening, K-8, +lady ambrotype.**575.00**
4rth plate, Chasse au Facon, K-32, +father & sons daguerreotypes **200.00**
4th plate, Clipper Ship & Fort, K-100, +man ambrotype............**300.00**
4th plate, officers standing at table, scroll border, +similar tintype **350.00**
4th plate, Roger de Coverly & Gypsies, K-29, +couple tintype, VG.........**100.00**
4th plate, Sweet Potato Dinner, K-17, +couple daguerreotype **200.00**
4th plate, Union & Constitution, K-27, +lady & 3 girls in ambrotype........**250.00**
6th plate, Chess Players, +man's portrait daguerreotype..............**175.00**
6th plate, Faithful Hound, K-89, +4 tintypes..............................**225.00**
6th plate, Geometric, K-226, +lady daguerreotype, VG **125.00**
6th plate, Hunter, K-131, +couple ambrotype, EX **350.00**
6th plate, Rebekkah at Well, K-155, +man & wife ruby ambrotypes **200.00**
6th plate, Volunteer Fireman, K-116, +couple ruby ambrotypes **250.00**
9th plate, Eagle & Flag, +soldier ambrotype, M........................**350.00**
9th plate, Geometric, K-467, VG **55.00**
16th plate, Indian Head Penny, K-617, +man tintype................**200.00**

Miscellaneous

Album, gr velvet cover w/celluloid flowers, Victorian photos, EX..**75.00**
Album, leather w/emb gilt, decorative clasp, 9x11x2½"..............**40.00**
Periscope, ivory, Lord's Prayer, 1x¼" **85.00**
Stanhope, nail set, ivory, Matlock Bath photos (6), 3-pc set **125.00**
Stereoscope-Graphoscope, wood/brass, 1896, G **160.00**

Piano Babies

A familiar sight in Victorian parlors, piano babies languished atop shawl-covered pianos in a variety of poses: crawling, sitting, on their tummies, or on their backs playing with their toes. Some babies were nude, and some wore gowns. Sizes ranged from about 3" up to 12". The most famous manufacturer of these bisque darlings was the Heubach Brothers of Germany, who nearly always marked their product; see Heubach for listings. Watch for reproductions. These guidelines are excerpted from one of a series of informative doll books by Patsy Moyer, published by Collector Books. Values are for examples in excellent condition.

Blk, bsk, 4", EX quality..**500.00**
Blk, bsk, 4", med quality, unmk **250.00**
Blk, bsk, 5", EX quality..**500.00**
Blk, bsk, 8", EX quality..**600.00**
Blk, bsk, 8", med quality..**400.00**
Blk, bsk, 9", EX quality..**500.00**
Blk, bsk, 12", EX quality..**995.00**
Blk, bsk, 12", med quality..**400.00**
Blk, bsk, 14", EX quality..**900.00**
Blk, bsk, 16", EX quality..**925.00**
Blk, bsk, 16", med quality..**950.00**
Bsk, may not have pnt finish on bk, unmk, 4", med quality........**225.00**
Bsk, may not have pnt finish on bk, unmk, 8", med quality........**275.00**
Bsk, may not have pnt finish on bk, unmk, 12", med quality......**350.00**
Bsk, molded hair, unjtd, molded-on clothes, 4", EX quality **525.00**
Bsk, molded hair, unjtd, molded-on clothes, 4", med quality **400.00**
Bsk, molded hair, unjtd, molded-on clothes, 6", EX quality **600.00**
Bsk, molded hair, unjtd, molded-on clothes, 8", EX quality **895.00**
Bsk, molded hair, unjtd, molded-on clothes, 8", med quality **500.00**
Bsk, molded hair, unjtd, molded-on clothes, 9", EX quality **700.00**
Bsk, molded hair, unjtd, molded-on clothes, 12", EX quality **975.00**
Bsk, molded hair, unjtd, molded-on clothes, 16", EX quality ...**1,125.00**
Bsk, w/animal/pot/flowers/etc, 4", EX quality **425.00**
Bsk, w/animal/pot/flowers/etc, 5", EX quality **450.00**
Bsk, w/animal/pot/flowers/etc, 8", EX quality **525.00**
Bsk, w/animal/pot/flowers/etc, 10", EX quality **525.00**

Bsk, w/animal/pot/flowers/etc, 12", EX quality 800.00
Bsk, w/animal/pot/flowers/etc, 16", EX quality, minimum value.1,125.00

Picasso Art Pottery

Pablo Picasso created some distinctive pottery during the 1940s, marking the ware with his signature.

Pitcher, smiling face, bk: devil's face, 5" 800.00
Plate, man in sombrero w/lance on horse, blk on wht, 1950s, 8½".650.00

Pickard

Founded in 1895 in Chicago, Illinois, the Pickard China Company was originally a decorating studio, importing china blanks from European manufacturers. Some of these early pieces bear the name of those companies as well as Pickard's. Trained artists decorated the wares with hand-painted studies of fruit, florals, birds, and scenics and often signed their work. In 1915 Pickard introduced a line of 24k gold over a dainty floral-etched ground design. In the 1930s they began to experiment with the idea of making their own ware and by 1938 had succeeded in developing a formula for fine translucent china. Since 1976 they have issued an annual limited edition Christmas plate. They are now located in Antioch, Illinois.

The company has used various marks. The earliest (1893 – 1894) was a double-circle mark, 'Edgerton Hand Painted' with 'Pickard' in the center. Variations of the double-circle mark (with 'Hand Painted China' replacing the Edgerton designation) were employed until 1915, each differing enough that collectors can usually pinpoint the date of manufacture within five years. Later marks included the crown mark, 'Pickard' on a gold maple leaf, and the current mark, the lion and shield. Work signed by Challinor, Marker, and Yeschek is especially valued by today's collectors. For further information we recommend *Collector's Encyclopedia of Pickard China* by Alan B. Reed, available from Collector Books.

Bonbon, Rose & Daisy (gold), gr ext, unsgn, 1925-30, ftd, 6" ...**100.00**
Bonbon, violets on gr w/gold, Marker, 1898-1903, JPL blank, 5½"..**135.00**
Bowl, cherry sprays & blossoms, Freidrich, 1903-05, 10".............**185.00**
Bowl, Gibson Narcissus, Gibson, 1903-05, JPL France blank, 9½"..**250.00**
Bowl, seashells/spider web, Krische, 1905-10, 9"..........................**225.00**
Bowl, Violet Supreme, Fisher, 1910-12, 10"..................................**450.00**
Cake plate, Trumpet Flowers & Trellis, Moore, 1905-10, 10½"..**125.00**
Celery dish, Tulip Conventional, unsgn, 1903-05, 13" L.............**275.00**
Charger, Plum Branch, Rean, 1903-05, CA France blank, 12½"...**385.00**
Charger, raspberries, Yesceck, pierced hdls, 1903-05, 10¼" **285.00**
Charger, Rean Pears, Rean, 1903-05, JPL France blank, 13".......**550.00**
Chocolate pot, Challinor Nasturtiums, Challinor, 1903-05, 6¼".**550.00**
Claret, Morning Glory Trellis, Stahl, 1903-05, GDA blank, 11½".**550.00**
Coffee set, Aura Argenta Linear, Podlaha, 1905-10, pot+cr/sug+6 c/s.**2,250.00**
Coffee set, Carnation Conventional, Tomas, 1903-05, T&V bank, 3-pc.**550.00**
Coffee set, Cornflower Conventional, sgn CK, 1905-10, pot+tray+4 c/s.**1,050.00**
Creamer & sugar bowl, Carnation & Platinum, sgn AP, 1905-10, w/lid.**325.00**
Creamer & sugar bowl, Rose Bower, Leon, 1903-05, GDA blank, w/lid.**250.00**
Cruet, Cyclamen, unsgn, 1903-05, T&V Limoges blank, 6½"....**350.00**
Cup & saucer, Encrusted Honeysuckle, unsgn, Aida, 1925-30....**125.00**
Cup & saucer, poppies on cream w/gold, Hessler, 1898-1903......**185.00**
Ewer, cherries on bl w/gold, LeRoy, 1903, T&V blank, 10¾" **600.00**
Goblet, Arab w/earring, unsgn, 1903-05, Willets blank, 11¼"..**1,350.00**
Goblet, Autumn Currants, Vokral, 1905-10, Willets blank, 5¾".**350.00**
Jardiniere, Carnation Garden, Yeschek, 1903-05, 3 gold ft, 6¾" dia.**1,300.00**
Jardiniere, roses on gr w/gold, Loba, ftd ped, 1894-98, 9¾" **5,500.00**
Mug, Falstaff, P Gasper, 1905-10, gold hdl, 7" **635.00**
Mug, monk w/maroon robe, Weiss, 1903-05, WG&Co blank, 6"...**650.00**

Pin/ring tray, Buttercup Conventional, Beutlich, 1905-10, 4½".**400.00**
Pitcher, lemonade; Lily Palmate, Shoner, 1905-10, Haviland blank, 8"..**500.00**
Pitcher, milk; Poppy & Daisy, Shoner, 1905-10, gold hdl, 6" **325.00**
Pitcher, Pond Lily, Leach, 1905-10, gold bamboo hdl, AKD blank, 8½"..**585.00**
Pitcher, strawberry clusters on band, Michel, 1898-1903, JPL blank, 5"..**525.00**
Pitcher, Twin Tulip, Shoner, Ranson, 1905-10, Haviland blank, 10"..**750.00**
Pitcher, White Poppy & Daisy, Gasper, 1910-12, Bavaria blank, 6"...**525.00**

Pitchers: **Apples and blossoms decor, signed Gifford, 1903 – 05 mark, 8", $1,100.00; Celtic decor, signed M, 1905 – 10, 9¾", $800.00; Crab Apples in gold on green matt, signed Cou, 1905 – 10 mark, 8¾", $600.00.** (Photo courtesy Joy Luke Fine Arts Brokers and Auctioneers)

Plate, currants w/gold, GP Leach, 1903-05, scalloped, 8"............**125.00**
Plate, gr apples, Gasper, 1918-19, Bavaria blank, 8¾"..................**160.00**
Plate, leaves/blackberries, gold border, Limoges blank, 8½"........**175.00**
Plate, Triple Tulip, Yeschek, 1912-18, Bavaria blank, 8½"..........**250.00**
Plate, Wight Tulips, Wight, 1905-10, Haviland blank, 8¾"........**125.00**
Vase, apple blossoms on blk w/gold, Rean, 1905-10, 8"...............**300.00**
Vase, Aura Mosaic, sgn Rosl, 1910-12, 13" **850.00**
Vase, Birches, vellum, Marker, 1918-19, Bavaria blank, 12" **800.00**
Vase, Butterfly, unsgn, 1903-05, pinched, 5½"............................**335.00**
Vase, Chrysanthemums, lustre/red, Rean, 1905-10, gold hdls, 11½".**800.00**
Vase, Cornflower Conventional, unsgn, 1903-05, gold hdls, 8½"..**600.00**
Vase, daisies on russet to gr, Jelinek, 1903-05, 7".........................**215.00**
Vase, Flora Geometrica, Kriesche, 1905-10, slim, 12" **600.00**
Vase, Fruits Linear, Tolphin, 1912-18, hdls, Noritake blank, 8½" .**400.00**
Vase, Hummingbird & Gold, unsgn, 1919-22, ruffled rim, 6¾" ...**175.00**
Vase, Iris Conventional, Lind, ftd, slim, 1898-1903, 10" **400.00**
Vase, Midnight, vellum, E Challinor, Gotham, 1912-18, 7½" **550.00**
Vase, nude blond & raven, gold hdls, Grane, 1898-1903, 19¾".**7,000.00**
Vase, Poppies, Gifford, St Denis, 1905-10, 6½" **335.00**
Vase, tulips on maroon, Challinor, 1938+, Pickard blank, 6¾" ..**375.00**
Vase, Water Lily Conventional, Fuchs, 1910-12, 10¼" **450.00**
Vase, Wisconsin Dells, vellum, E Challinor, 1912-18, slim, 10" .**600.00**

Pickle Castors

Affluent Victorian homes seemed to have something for everything, and a pickle castor was not only an item of beauty but of practicality. American Victorian pickle castors can be found in old catalogs dating from the 1860s through the early 1900s. (Those featured in catalogs after 1900 were made by silver manufacturers that were not part of the International Silver Company, which was formed in 1898 — for instance, Reed and Barton, Tufts, Pairpoint, and Benedict.)

Catalogs featured large selections to choose from, ranging from simple to ornate. Inserts could be clear or colored, pattern glass or art glass, molded or blown. Many of these molds and design were made by more than one company as they merged or as personnel took their designs with them from employer to employer. It is common to see the same insert in a variety of different frames and with different lids as viewed in these old catalogs.

Pickle Castors

Pickle castors are being reproduced today. Frames are being imported from Taiwan. New enameling is being applied to old jars; and new or old tumblers, vases, or spooners are sometimes used as jars in old original frames. The biggest giveaway in this latter scenario is that the replacement insert does not fit properly in the old frame. A good thing to remember is that old glass is not perfect glass.

In the listings below, the description prior to the semicolon refers to the jar (insert), and the remainder of the line describes the frame. Unless a color is mentioned, all glassware is clear. When no condition is indicated, the silver plate is assumed to be in very good to excellent condition, with the fork or tongs present. Glass jars are assumed near-mint.

Our advisor for this category is Barbara Aaronson; she is listed in the Directory under California.

Amber, Daisy & Button; rstr SP Wilcox #695 fr, 12", +tongs **395.00**
Amethyst w/decor; gold-leaf fr w/lt wear..................................**1,100.00**
Amethyst w/floral; rstr Meriden B #206 fr **2,100.00**
Bl, Cone; rstr Rockford #630 fr, pug dog finial............................**795.00**
Bl, Daisy & Button; ornate SP fr, eng lid, 12", +tongs................**395.00**
Bl, floral decor; rstr #263 fr, 10"...**850.00**
Bl, Hobnail; rstr Rogers Smith #156 fr, 11" **850.00**
Bl, Moire w/floral, flint; rstr 11" fr...**850.00**
Bl MOP, Raindrop; rstr Simpson Hall & Miller #192 fr, 13" ...**2,400.00**
Bl satin w/floral; unmk SP fr, 12"...**595.00**
Clear, Brazilian, Fostoria; rstr Meriden B #220 fr, 11½" **395.00**
Clear, bulbous w/etch; rstr Wm Rogers #480 fr, 10½" **550.00**
Clear, Daisy & Button, dbl; rstr Webster #38 fr, 11" **675.00**
Clear, Lorraine, Fostoria; rstr FB Rogers #499 fr, 10" **650.00**
Clear, panels w/etch leaves; rstr LB #741 fr w/fan & flowers, 11½" .**250.00**
Clear, pressed pattern, dbl; rstr Reed & Barton #1205 fr, 11"......**695.00**
Clear, pressed pattern; SP fr w/leaf details at ftd base, 13"...........**270.00**
Clear, swirl; rstr #0181 fr w/filigree bird & leaves, 10½" **250.00**
Clear frost w/floral; SP Middleton #128 fr, 11" **495.00**
Clear w/amber stain; rstr Pairpoint #661 fr, sm **495.00**
Clear w/emb floral; rstr Meriden B #653 fr, 12" **750.00**
Clear w/emb storks; rstr Middletown #129 fr, 11" **395.00**
Clear w/ornate etching; rstr SP fr, +fork **550.00**
Clear w/panels; rstr Meriden B #11 fr, 10¾" **250.00**
Clear w/pressed pattern; rstr Meriden #094 fr, 11" **250.00**
Clear w/pressed pattern; rstr Reed & Barton #1550 fr, 10½" **325.00**
Clear/frosted w/etch; Simpson Hall & Miller #85 fr w/cherubs, 10½" .**850.00**
Cobalt, floral on lantern shape; rstr SP fr, 10¼" **950.00**
Cobalt, Torquay; rstr SP fr, 8½" **1,500.00**
Colonial Ware, Mt WA, yel mums on rust, lt wear, 6"; Pairpoint fr ..**735.00**
Cranberry, Coin Spot w/floral; Benedict fr w/raised ft & appl floral ..**495.00**
Cranberry, Invt T'print, bowl shape; rstr Crown #405 fr, 11"......**675.00**
Cranberry, Invt T'print, corseted; rstr Monarch #357½ fr, 12½" .**650.00**
Cranberry, Invt T'print, dbl; rstr Meriden #613 fr, 11"...........**1,500.00**
Cranberry, Invt T'print w/floral; rstr Meriden Britannia #250 fr, 10" ..**775.00**
Cranberry, Invt T'print; Aurora SP fr w/berry finial on SP lid....**745.00**
Cranberry, Invt T'print; rstr SP fr, 10½" **550.00**
Cranberry, paneled w/floral; Meriden #97 fr................................**650.00**
Cranberry opal, Daisy & Fern; rstr Hamilton #58 fr **850.00**
Cranberry panels; rstr Derby #119 fr w/owl/fan/leaves hdl, 12" ...**895.00**
Cranberry potbelly (dbl); SP #62 fr w/center hdl, dtd 1890 ....**895.00**
Cranberry potbelly w/gold floral; SP New Amsterdam #120 fr, 11" ..**495.00**
Cranberry w/appl crystal rigaree; ornate SP Rogers #479 fr, 11" .**495.00**
Cranberry w/floral, 4⅞x3"; rstr Adelphi #100 fr, 10½" **695.00**
Cranberry w/floral; rstr Barbour #133 fr, 9½" **650.00**
Cranberry w/floral; rstr Barbour #140 fr, 10¾" **775.00**
Cranberry w/floral; rstr Derby #115 fr, 12¼" **795.00**
Cranberry w/floral; rstr Derby #347 fr w/pickles & leaves. 6"......**950.00**
Cranberry w/flowers & birds; rstr Colonial #108 fr, 11½" **750.00**
Cranberry w/Mary Gregory decor; Meriden #304 fr, 9¾".........**1,500.00**

Cranberry w/Mary Gregory decor; rstr Derby fr w/acorns/leaves, 12"..**1,500.00**
Cranberry w/Mary Gregory decor; rstr Meriden Britannia #273 fr, 10½"..**1,100.00**
Emerald gr, pressed pattern; rstr Monarch SP fr w/tall base, 12" .**695.00**
Emerald gr; rstr SP Tufts #2361 fr, 12"..**695.00**
Frosted w/floral, att Wavecrest; rstr Crescent #38 fr, 11"............**950.00**
Med bl satin w/wht floral; Wm Rogers fr w/ornaments at sides & hdl top ..**1,000.00**
Milk glass w/floral; rstr Homan #1060 fr, 11" **895.00**
Pigeon blood, paneled lantern shape; SP Crescent #4 fr **750.00**
Pigeon blood, Torquay; ornate SP fr, 9x4¼", +tongs **895.00**
Pk MOP, Dmn Quilt w/decor; rstr Adelphi #18 fr, butterfly finial, 12" .**2,400.00**
Pk opal, Hobnail; rstr Tufts #2374 fr, attached lid, 11" **1,200.00**
Pk opal, stripes, Mt WA; rstr Pairpoint #604 fr.............................**850.00**
Pk satin; rstr Meriden B #223 fr w/birds, 11¾" **950.00**
Purple slag; rstr Tufts #2361 fr, 12"...**1,100.00**
Rubena, Invt T'print w/floral; rstr Aurora #0650 fr, 12½" **850.00**
Rubena, Moire; rstr Barbour #290 fr **750.00**
Rubena; rstr #0666 fr...**775.00**
Ruby, Invt T'print; SP Aurora fr, 1890s..**695.00**
Ruby, paneled; SP Aurora #635 fr, +fork **550.00**
Sapphire bl, Daisy & Button; SP Britannia #640 fr, 11" **495.00**
Sapphire bl w/emb ribs; ornate SP St Louis Silver ftd fr, 12" **495.00**
Turq, Daisy & Button; SP Union Metal works ftd fr, 10½".........**450.00**
Vaseline, Beaded Dart; rstr Simpson, Hall & Miller fr **650.00**
Vaseline, Daisy & Button; SP Pairpoint fr, 10" **595.00**
Vaseline, Daisy & Peg, canoe; rstr SP fr, 8x11", +fork.................**680.00**

Pie Birds

A pie bird or pie funnel (pie vent) is generally made of pottery, glazed inside and out. Most are 3" to 5" in height with arches at the base to allow steam to enter. The steam is then released through an exit hole at the top.

The English pie funnel was as tall as the special baking dish was deep and held the crust even with the dish's rim, thereby lifting the crust above the filling so it would stay crisp and firm. These dishes came in several different sizes, which accounts for the variances in the heights of the pie birds.

The first deviations from the basic funnels were produced in the mid-1930s to late 1940s: the Clarice Cliff (signed Midwinter or Newport) pie bird (reg. no. on white base) and the signed Nutbrown elephant. Shortly thereafter (1940s – 1960s), figures of bakers and colorful birds were created for additional visual baking fun. From the 1980s to present, many novelty pie vents have been added to the market for the enjoyment of both the baker and collector. These have been made by commercial (including Far East importers) and local enterprises in Canada, England, and the United States. A new category for the 1990s includes an array of holiday-related pie vents. Basic tip: Older pie vents were air-brushed, not hand painted.

Incense burners (i.e., elephants and Oriental people), one-hole pepper shakers, dated brass toy bird whistle, egg timers (missing glass timer), and ring holders (i.e., elephant with clover on his tummy) should not be mistaken for pie vents.

Aluminum pie funnels, England, ea..**25.00**
Benny the Baker, w/pie crimper & cake tester, Cardinal, from $125 to.**135.00**
Bird, all blk or all wht, imported, up to 4" tall **4.00**
Bird, blk or wht, wide mouth, mk England....................................**35.00**
Bird, mc, Morton Pottery **20.00**
Bird on nest, Artesian Galleries, copyright mk, 1950s, from $200 to..**300.00**
Blackbird, wht head, teardrop eyes, Australia, from $40 to **60.00**
Boy, gr sombrero, mk Pie Boy **200.00**
Chef, The Servex; from $150 to **175.00**
Cutie Pie, Josef (or Lorrie Design), hen in bonnet, from $125 to.**150.00**
Decaled, mk New Devon Pottery, Made in England......................**50.00**
Dutch girl, multipurpose kitchen tool, from $150 to **195.00**

Eagle, mk Sunglow, golden color, from $75 to..............................85.00
Elephant, mk Nutbrown, wht, tan or gray, respectively, from $75 to.175.00
Fred the Flour Grater (orig has) dots for eyes, from $65 to............75.00
Funnel, pagoda, Gourmet Pie Cup, Reg No 369793 ....75.00
Funnel, terra cotta, mk Wales 35.00
Funnels, plain wht, szs vary, ea, from $15 to.................................25.00
Half-bird, blk, w/scalloped or triangular bottom, from $100 to...125.00
Mammy, multipurpose kitchen tool, outstretched arms, from $125 to.150.00
Rooster, mc, mk Cleminson or Cb..50.00
Rowland's Hygienic Patent, England 90.00
Songbird, Chick Pottery (Le Pere), cream & blk w/gold, from $125 to..150.00
TG gr motif/logo on wht funnel, 1993+ 15.00
Welsh lady, Cymru, from $75 to 95.00

Pierce, Howard

After Howard Pierce died on February 28, 1994, many values of his pieces increased greatly and items not seen before began to appear on the market. William Manker, a well-known ceramist, hired Mr. Pierce in 1938. This liaison lasted about three years and then Pierced opened a small studio in Laverne, California. He did not want to be in competition with Manker so he began making miniature animal figures, some of which he made into jewelry. Now, pewter miniature brooches, depending on the animal types, are selling for as much as $275.00. Howard married and he and his wife, Ellen (Van Voorhis), opened a small studio in Claremont, California. Polyurethane animals are high on collectors' lists as Howard, after creating in the early years only a few pieces using this material, realized he was allergic to it and had to discontinue its use. Polyurethane was used mostly to create a small number of roadrunners on bases, either standing or running, or birds on small, flat bases. The materials used by Pierce during his long career were varied, probably to satisfy his curiosity and many talents. He experimented with a Jasperware-type body, bronze, concrete, gold leaf, porcelain, Mt. St. Helens ash, and others. In November 1992, Pierce's health had continued to worsen and he and Ellen Pierce destroyed all the molds they had created over the years. Pierce began producing smaller versions of past porcelain wares and developing a few new items.

For further information we recommend *Collector's Encyclopedia of Howard Pierce Porcelain* by our advisor, Darlene Hurst Dommel; she is listed in the Directory under Minnesota.

Bowl, maroon w/gold int, 4x8½" dia 125.00
Box, mint gr w/wht gazelles, w/lid, 4x5" 125.00
Creamer & sugar bowl, pale bl w/dk bl shepherd & sheep 125.00
Figurine, bison, unmk, 9" 175.00
Figurine, blk cats (2) on base, mk Pierce 1965, 4" 150.00
Figurine, cat (faceless), 11x4¼" 175.00
Figurine, chipmunk, gray w/4 stripes down bk, stylized, 2¼x7".....35.00
Figurine, dachshund, stylized, 3¼x10"...100.00
Figurine, deer, recumbent, gold, 12", minimum value..................250.00
Figurine, duck, blk w/gray flecked stomach, 4½x9" 85.00
Figurine, elephant, pk, rare, 4½x4", minimum value....................200.00
Figurine, frog, warty-skinned, 3x3¾" 65.00
Figurine, gazelle, brn, stylized, 11¼x4" 125.00
Figurine, girl w/dog, 4½x3¼" 75.00
Figurine, koala bear, 1991, 4¼x4½" 85.00
Figurine, monkey, gray flecked, stylized, 6¼x3" 85.00
Figurine, pigeon, blk w/gray flecked stomach, 7¼x5½" 65.00
Figurine, raccoon, textured glaze, 5x5¼" 75.00
Figurine, red bird on blk rock, 6x4" 85.00
Figurine, rooster, brn, #251P, 9¼x6" 65.00
Figurine, songbird, dk gray w/etched feathers, 4", minimum value...250.00
Figurine, water bird, wht over red clay, 13¼" 70.00
Figurines, Eskimos, brn & wht, 7½x2½", 6½"x2½", pr.............175.00

Flower arranger, St Francis of Assisi w/birds, gr/brn-to-bl, 11x6"..150.00
Magnet, rabbit, brn, 3¼"..75.00
Planter, gr w/sm wht gazelle lying on side, #80P, 2½x10"............100.00
Planter, pale bl w/wht running gazelles on dk bl, 2½x9¾".........125.00
Planter, pale gr w/wht leaf motif on dk gr, 4½x6½"......................75.00
Planter, strawberry; yel & brn, 5x5"...125.00
Teapot, pale bl w/wht shepherd & sheep in dk bl circle, w/lid, 6".150.00
Whistle, bird, 2¾x2"..125.00

Pigeon Forge

Douglas J. Ferguson and Ernest Wilson started their small pottery in Pigeon Forge, Tennessee, in 1946. Using red-brown and gray locally dug clay and glazes which they themselves formulate, bowls, vases, and sculptures are produced there. Their primary target is the tourist trade.

Bowl, brn & orange, D Ferguson, 1½x6"......................................40.00
Candle holder, wht w/blk specks, E Wilson, 3¾" W 50.00
Figurine, baby duck, gray speckled, 3" 35.00
Figurine, bear, brn & wht w/brn eyes, D Ferguson, 6¼x8" 85.00
Figurine, bird, wht w/brn specks, sgn, 3½".....................................50.00
Figurine, hound dog, seated, brownish-red, 8" 110.00
Figurine, mouse, brn, 2"..25.00
Figurine, owl, wht w/brn specks, Ferguson, 9"...............................55.00
Figurine, rabbit, brn & wht specks, 5½" L.......................................60.00
Figurine, raccoon, brn & wht, D Ferguson, 3½x5½".......................50.00
Figurines, mother bear w/2 cubs, D Ferguson, 4", 3⅜".................90.00
Pitcher, pk w/wht dogwood flower, 1955, 3¾" 25.00
Pitcher, wht w/dogwood flowers, bl int, 5½".................................45.00
Plate, wht w/brn specks, D Ferguson, 1956, 10½" dia...................40.00
Teapot +cr/sug, bl w/brn drip, D Ferguson, 3-pc set 75.00
Vase, brn top over w/wht mottled bottom, D Ferguson, 12"..........35.00

Pilkington

Founded in 1892 in Manchester, England, the Pilkington pottery experimented in wonderful lustre glazes that were so successful that when they were displayed at exhibition in 1904, they were met with critical acclaim. They soon attracted some of the best ceramic technicians and designers of the day who decorated the lustre ground with flowers, animals, and trees; some pieces were more elaborate with scenes of sailing ships and knights on horseback. Each artist signed his work with his personal monogram. Most pieces were dated and carried the company mark as well. After 1913 the company became known as Royal Lancastrian.

Their Lapis Ware line was introduced in the late 1920s, featuring intermingling tones of color under a matt glaze. Some pieces were very simply decorated while others were painted with designs of stylized leafage, scrolls, swirls, and stripes. The line continued into the '30s. Other pieces of this period were molded and carved with animals, leaves, etc., some of which were reminiscent of their earlier wares.

The company closed in 1938 but reopened in 1948. During this period their mark was a simple P within the outline of a petaled flower shape.

Vase, flowers & leaves on mc streaks, tapered urn w/sm mouth, 3"..250.00
Vase, mc irid, tapered form w/spiraling snake, 3½", NM.............450.00
Vase, stylized flowers & leaves on red, squat, 2x2".....................300.00
Vase, 2 lizards appl to copper-brn bulbous form, 4"....................200.00

Pillin

Polia Pillin was born in Poland in 1909. She came to the U.S. as a teenager and showed an interest and talent for art, which she studied in Chicago. She married William Pillin, who was a poet and potter. They ultimately combined their talents and produced her very distinctive pottery from the 1950s to the mid-1980s. She died in 1993.

Polia Pillin won many prizes for her work, which is always signed Pillin with the loop of the 'P' over the full name. Some undecorated pieces are signed W&P, due to her husband's collaboration.

Her work is prized for its art, not for the shape of her pots, which for the most part are simple vases, dishes, bowl, and boxes. Wall plaques are rare. She pictured women with hair reminiscent of halos, girls, an occasional boy, horses, birds, and fish. After viewing a few of her pieces, her style is unmistakable. Some of her early work is very much like that of Picasso.

Her pieces are somewhat difficult to find, as all the work was done without outside help, and therefore limited in quantity. In the last few years, more and more people have become interested in her work, resulting in escalating prices. Our advisors for this category are Dolli and Wilfred Cohen; they are listed in the Directory under California.

Bowl, stylized horses, mc on mauve, 7⅛"	750.00
Box, lady in wht robe, child in pk leotards, blk shirt, 5½x4"	595.00
Compote, frieze of lady's faces on lt marigold w/turq wash, 5x6"	650.00
Dish, 2 full-length women, eliptical form, 17½"	2,100.00
Goblet, bust portrait of lady, bl/gr/tan on brn, 9"	750.00
Jug, blistered yel/brn gloss, 7¾x5½"	275.00
Pendant, female portrait on marigold, 3¼x2½"	500.00
Pendant, 4 songbirds, 3" H	650.00
Plaque, 5 dancers against gr wall, 15½" L	2,750.00
Plate, lady w/chicken & birds, mc on bl, 8½"	800.00
Plate, lady w/3 birds, mc on bl, 10½"	1,400.00
Tray, ballerinas, 3 in leotards/1 center front in wht tutu on bl, 9x9"	850.00
Tray, Madonna portrait on dk brn w/bl rim, rectangular, lg	775.00
Tray, 2 cats, free-form, 5" W	750.00
Tray, 2 women & bird, oval, 8½" L	925.00
Vase, avocado gr over lt seaweed gr, onion base, can neck, 6½"	250.00
Vase, cat/rooster, trees/female dancers on marigold, 4½x3¾"	665.00
Vase, chicken/horse/woman, bulbous w/stick neck, 8"	800.00
Vase, fish (9) on pastel sea, 6½x6"	495.00
Vase, horses (4), bottle neck, 5½" W	400.00
Vase, horses (4), bulbous, 4"	350.00
Vase, ladies, mc on bl, rectangular, 9", NM	850.00
Vase, lady, various pastel-colored sqs as bkground, 6x4½"	625.00
Vase, lady & birds/lady w/horse, bottle shape, 6½x2½"	550.00
Vase, lady holding bird, 2nd bird beside; bk: lady, 6¾"	550.00
Vase, lady/horse/goose on brn, 6¼x5", NM	550.00

Pin-Back Buttons

Buttons produced up to the early 1920s were made of a celluloid covering held in place by a ring (or collet) to the back of which a pin was secured. Manufacturers used these 'cellos' to advertise their products. Many were of exceptional quality in both color and design. Buttons were produced in sets featuring a variety of subjects. These were given away by tobacco, chewing gum, and candy manufacturers, who often packed them with their product as premiums. Usually the name of the button maker or the product manufacturer was printed on a paper placed in the back of the button. Often these 'back papers' are still in place today. Much of the time the button maker's name was printed on the button's perimeter, and sometimes the copyright was added. Beginning in the 1920s, a large number of buttons were lithographed on tin; these are referred to as tin 'lithos.' Nearly all pin-back buttons are collected today for their advertising appeal or graphic design. There are countless categories to base a collection on.

The following listing contains non-political buttons representative of the many varieties you may find. Our advisor for this category is Michael J. McQuillen; he is listed in the Directory under Indiana.

A Midnight Alarm, comic bedroom scene, mc, early 1900s, EX	15.00
Bruiser, wrestler's portrait, blk & wht, 1950s, lg, NM	15.00
Ceresota Four, cello w/gold-colored metal border, 1¾", M	65.00
Diamond C Hams, gift-wrapped ham on gr, cello, 1½", NM	65.00
Dixie Belle, Confederate flag, red/wht/bl, 1960s, M	5.00
Dizzy Dean portrait, mc, early, ⅞", EX	95.00
Ducks Unlimited, 1975, sgn Maass, mc, 2¼"	25.00
Gene Autry, portrait on wht, 1¾", w/5" ribbon, EX	45.00
Golden Guernsey Co, Am Cattle Club, cello w/paper insert, EX	40.00
High Admiral Cigarettes, Yellow Kid, #2, G	35.00
Hopalong Cassidy, portrait, cello cover, 2¼", EX	55.00
I Have Visited the Gerber Baby, baby's portrait, bl on wht, 1930s, M	10.00
I Like Bottled Carbonated Beverages, red & wht, 1930s, NM	5.00
I'm Not a Breakfast Battler - I Eat Holsum Bread, 2", EX	14.00
It's Naughty But Its Nice, lady, High Admiral Cigarettes, cello, EX	40.00
Jack Johnson Heavyweight Champion, boxing pose, blk & wht, 1¾", NM	85.00
Log Rollers, 1933 World's Fair, paper, blk on wht, 1", NM	15.00
Lou Gehrig Never Forgotton, portrait, blk & wht, 1940s, NM	50.00
Miller High Life Beer, cello w/Miller girl attachment, 1x3", EX	65.00
Miller's Cocoa, windmill, mc, ca 1900, EX	15.00
New Chevrolet Six, Queen of the Show, lady on bl, ca 1929, NM	65.00
Palmer Method, hand w/long pin, M	10.00
Peppy Flame, character on wht, cello front, Nipsco, 1960, 1¾", NM	45.00
Plymouth Rock The Corner Stone of a Nation, blk & wht, 1970s, M	5.00
Raggedy Ann & Andy on wht, 1971, 1¼", EX	10.00
Roper Snow Suits for Boys & Girls, children sledding, mc, 1900s, EX	15.00
Santa, cello w/orig cloth body, toy advertising, 2⅝x1¼", NM	165.00
Santa on phone at desk, store ad, mc on wht, 1¼", NM	50.00
Shirley Temple Doll, The World's Darling, smiling Shirley, 1930s, EX	25.00
Stand By for the 1934 Chevrolet, character w/flags on wht, G	30.00
State Capitol Building, Benicia CA, 1958 commemorative, 2", EX	2.50
Sun Drop & hot air balloon on gr, 2", EX	15.00
Uncle Sam, Home Improvement Society, cello on metal, 1¼", M	38.00
United for One Cause, men shaking hands, mc, 1960s, M	15.00

Use Peters Shells, hunting dog with quail in mouth, multicolor, EX, $600.00 at auction.

Wear Daisy Rubbers, daisy, mc, 1¼", NM	15.00
Wurlitzer Accordions Made in America, red/wht/bl, 1930s, EX	10.00
Ye Olde Mill, Atlantic City amusement ride, cello, 1¼", EX	95.00
Zorro, 7-Up, blk/red/wht, Walt Disney Productions, 1957, 1¼", M	15.00

Pine Ridge

In the mid-1930s, the Indian Bureau of Affairs and the Work Progress Administration offered the Native Americans living on the Pine Ridge Indian Reservation in South Dakota a class in pottery making. Originally, Margaret Cable (director of the University of North Dakota ceramics department) was the instructor and Bruce Doyle was director. By the early 1950s, pottery production at the school was abandoned. In 1955 the equipment was purchased by Ella Irving, a student who had been highly involved with the class since the late 1930s. From then until it closed in the 1980s, Ella virtually ran the pot shop by herself.

The clay used in Pine Ridge pottery was red and the decoration reminiscent of early Indian pottery and beadwork designs. A variety of marks and labels were used. For more information we recommend *Collector's Encyclopedia of the Dakota Potteries* by our advisor, Darlene Hurst Dommel; she is listed in the Directory under Minnesota.

Basket, hanging; cream-colored geometric motif on red, Woody, 5x7½"..300.00
Bowl, avocado gr, 2¼x7" 50.00
Bowl, cream-colored geometric motif on red, Firethunder, 2x10"..350.00
Bowl, dk bl, Ramona W Knee, 2¾x4" 75.00
Bowl, red w/incised motif, milky wht glaze, Cottier, 2½x4¾" 300.00
Creamer & sugar bowl, aqua, plain shape, 2½", 2" (open) 75.00
Cup & saucer, bl-gr, Ella Cox, 2", 5½" 75.00
Dish, wht drip over red, chartreuse int, sq, 1½x6" 50.00
Jardiniere, brn/tan/gray flowing glaze, Sioux Indian, 4¾x9¼" 500.00
Mug, gr w/brn wash at top, tapered side, Bernice Talbot, 3½" 50.00
Mug, gray drip over red w/turq int, 3" 75.00
Pitcher, glossy rust, Firethunder 80, 4½" 65.00
Pitcher, red-brn w/cream arrrowhead decor, +4 tumblers, minimum.600.00
Plate, cream-colored geometric motif on red, Firethunder, 10½" ..500.00
Plate, cream-colored geometric star motif on red, Irving, 7" 400.00
Platter, wht drip over red, turq int, 9x10½" 70.00
Shakers, cream-colored geometric motif on red, Cox, 2x2¼", pr..150.00
Teapot, gr w/brn wash, +matching cr/sug, Cox, 7½" 250.00
Vase, dk bl, Firethunder, 2½" 50.00
Vase, sgraffito cream-colored geometric motif on red, 7¼x5" 400.00

Pink Lustre Ware

Pink lustre was produced by nearly every potter in the Staffordshire district in the late eighteenth and first half of the nineteenth centuries. The application of gold lustre on white or light-colored backgrounds produced pinks, while the same over dark colors developed copper. The wares ranged from hand-painted plaques to transfer-printed dinnerware.

Bowl, ivy, pk lustre int, 5½" 35.00
Cake plate, pk rim band, mc floral/sprigs, #912, hdls, 10" 70.00
Cup & saucer, Queen Victoria/Prince Albert & family, 5½", EX ..100.00
Cup plate, church scene, bl transfer, lustre rim, 4" 250.00
Gravy boat, floral/leaves, lustre rim, 8" L 125.00
Jug, puce transfer: Peace Plenty Independence/lustre bands, 7½", EX .1,100.00
Mug, Sailor's Farewell, 3-D frog in bottom, 4¾", VG.................225.00
Pitcher, House, sq bldg w/shrubs, pk band, o/w copper lustre, 4½" ..90.00
Plate, pk band, mc floral sprigs, 9¾", +6 6" plates, EX 70.00
Saucer, scenic view transfer, pk rim band 35.00
Tea bowl & saucer, maroon transfer: boy hugging lamb................75.00
Teapot, cattle scenes, lustre rim w/gr dots, rose finial, 6", VG.....165.00

Pink Paw Bears

These charming figural pieces are very similar to the Pink Pigs described in the following category. They were made in Germany during the same time frame. The cabbage green is identical; the bears themselves are whitish-gray with pink foot pads. You'll find some that are unmarked while others are marked 'Germany' or 'Made in Germany.' In theory, the unmarked bears are the oldest, made prior to 1890 when the McKinley Tariff Act required imports to be marked with the country of origin. Those marked 'Made In' were probably produced after the revision of the Act in 1914.

1 by bean pot 135.00
1 by graphophone 150.00
1 by honey pot 145.00

1 by top hat...125.00
1 in front of basket 135.00
1 in roadster (car identical to pk pig car) 225.00
1 on binoculars 175.00
1 peaking out of basket..135.00
1 sitting in wicker chair 150.00
2 in hot air balloon 175.00
2 in purse 165.00
2 in roadster 225.00
2 on pin dish 175.00
2 on pin dish w/bag of coins 145.00
2 peering in floor mirror 150.00
2 sitting by mushroom 135.00
2 standing in wash tub 150.00
3 in roadster 250.00
3 on pin dish..160.00

Pink Pigs

Pink Pigs on cabbage green were made in Germany around the turn of the century. They were sold as souvenirs in train depots, amusement parks, and gift shops. 'Action pigs' (those involved in some amusing activity) are the most valuable, and prices increase with the number of pigs. Though a similar type of figurine was made in white bisque, most serious collectors prefer only the pink ones. They are marked in two ways: 'Germany' in incised letters, and a black ink stamp 'Made in Germany' in a circle. The unmarked pigs are the oldest, made prior to 1890 when the McKinley Tariff Act required imports to be marked with the country of origin. Those marked 'Made In' were probably produced after the revision of the Act in 1914.

1 beside lg pot emb Boston Baked Beans, match holder, 4" W ...135.00
1 beside stump, camera around neck, toothpick holder 185.00
1 coming out of cup, 2½" 95.00
1 driving touring car...185.00
1 holding cup by fence 140.00
1 in gr Dutch shoe 75.00
1 in money sack bank 95.00
1 on haunches, bottle, blk wood cork top, 2½" 110.00
1 on shoulder of gr ink bottle...115.00
1 putting letter in mailbox 125.00
1 sits by high-top boot 110.00
1 skating on bowling lane, tray, gold trim, 4¾" L 135.00
1 standing in oversz opera house box, gold trim, 3½"..............250.00
1 w/front ft in 3-part dish containing 3 dice, 1 ft on dice..........175.00
1 w/lg umbrella, picnic basket & water bucket, 5¼", NM.........150.00
2, mother & baby in bl blanket in tub, rabbit on board atop 175.00
2, 1 at telephone booth, 1 inside, 4½" 165.00
2 at pump & trough, 3¼" W 180.00
2 by eggshell...95.00
2 courting in touring car, trinket holder, 4½" W 225.00
2 in basket, gold trim, 3¾" W 90.00
2 in basket, Merry Squeelers, 3½x3" 135.00
2 in front of oval washtub w/hdls, 3" W 125.00
2 looking in phonograph horn, tray, 4½" W 200.00
2 on seesaw on top of pouch bank 175.00
2 singing, receptacle behind, gold trim, 4½", NM 365.00
2 teeter-tottering over log bank, 3½" L, NM 125.00
3, mother w/2 babies, The Dinner Bell, planter, 3¾" W 145.00
3 (center pig w/accordion) on tray, gold trim, 6½" L 530.00
3 dressed up on edge of dish 150.00
3 in horseless carriage, 4½" W 150.00
3 w/baby carriage, father & 2 babies, Wheeling His Own 225.00

Pisgah Forest

The Pisgah Forest Pottery was established in 1920 near Mount Pisgah in Arden, North Carolina, by Walter B. Stephen, who had worked in previous years at other locations in the state — Nonconnah and Skyland (the latter from 1913 until 1916). Stephen, who was born in the mountain region near Asheville, was known for his work in the Southern tradition. He produced skillfully executed wares exhibiting an amazing variety of techniques. He operated his business with only two helpers. Recognized today as his most outstanding accomplishment, his Cameo line was decorated by hand in the pate-sur-pate style (similar to Wedgwood Jasper) in such designs as Fiddler and Dog, Spinning Wheel, Covered Wagon, Buffalo Hunt, Mountain Cabin, Square Dancers, Indian Campfire, and Plowman. Stephen is known for other types of wares as well. His crystalline glaze is highly regarded by today's collectors.

At least nine different stamps mark his wares, several of which contain the outline of the potter at the wheel and 'Pisgah Forest.' Cameo is sometimes marked with a circle containing the line name and 'Long Pine, Arden, NC.' Two other marks may be more difficult to recognize: 1) a circle containing the outline of a pine tree, 'N.C.' to the left of the trunk and 'Pine Tree' on the other side; and 2) the letter 'P' with short uprights in the middle of the top and lower curves. Stephen died in 1961, but the work was continued by his associates. Our advisor for this category is R.J. Sayers; he is listed in the Directory under North Carolina.

Vase, red and green, three-handled, dated 1930, 17", firing line, $1,200.00; Vase, Cameo-style people around Christmas tree, blue and white, signed Stephen, red and blue body, dated, 8", $1,300.00. (Photo courtesy Treadway Gallery, Inc.)

Creamer & sugar bowl, feldspathic sea gr, mustard int, 3¼"..........20.00
Teapot, Cameo, wagon train, top dk bl/bottom wht, Stephen, 5½x9" .450.00
Vase, bl/silver/gr crystalline, waisted, Stephen, 6½" 225.00
Vase, Cameo, Indian on horse/camp scene, olive on gr crackle, 8x6".1,200.00
Vase, Cameo, wagon trail/dog/etc, gr matt on turq mottle, 7x5½" ..1,200.00
Vase, Cameo, wagon train, olive/bl-gr mottled gloss, Stephen, 4½x4".500.00
Vase, Cameo, wagon train, wht on bl, Stephen, 3¾" 375.00
Vase, Cameo, wagon train, wht on brn, Stephen, 3¾" 325.00
Vase, Cameo, wagon train on Wedgwood bl, Stephen, 1951, 5½x3¾" ..325.00
Vase, Cameo, wagon train w/man, olive band on bl crystalline, 12x8" .1,500.00
Vase, Cameo, wagon train/trees/etc, ⅓ is dk bl band on turq, 9x6" ...700.00
Vase, Cameo, wagon train/2 men on horse, lt gr/ivory, Stephen, 5x6" ..450.00
Vase, Cameo, wagon train/2 men on horse on Wedgwood bl, Stephen, 4x6"..325.00
Vase, feldspathic sea gr, slightly bulbous, 1983, 4⅞" 40.00
Vase, gr & silver w/crystalline, shouldered, 5½" 250.00
Vase, gr crystalline, 3-hdl, 5½" 325.00
Vase, gr streaks on aqua, rose int, 9¾x5½" 275.00
Vase, purple, flared swollen form, Stephen, 9" 250.00
Vase, silver/wht/gr/bl crystalline on ivory, bulbous, Stephen, '49, 6" ...375.00

Pittsburgh Glass

As early as 1797, utility window glass and hollow ware were being produced in the Pittsburgh area. Coal had been found in abundance, and it was there that it was first used instead of wood to fuel the glass furnaces. Because of this, as many as 150 glass companies operated there at one time. However, most failed due to the economically disastrous effects of the War of 1812. By the mid-1850s those that remained were producing a wide range of flint glass items including pattern-molded and free-blown glass, cut and engraved wares, and pressed tableware patterns. Our advisor for this category is Mark Vuono; he is listed in the Directory under Connecticut.

Bottle, bar; canary, 8-panel, appl bulbous lip, marble in stopper, 11"..1,500.00
Bottle, bar; cobalt, 8-panel, appl bulbous lip, marble in stopper, 11".1,045.00
Bottle, bar; cobalt, 8-panel, appl bulbous lip, pop-up in stopper, 11" ..880.00
Creamer, formed bands at rim, appl rings at shoulder, 4¾" 110.00
Creamer, sapphire bl, crimped base, 4½".....................................495.00
Decanter, waffle & pineapple cuttings, ball stopper, 9" 175.00
Pan, amethyst, 12 shaded ribs, folded rim, appl ft, 2x5¾"........4,400.00
Pan, lt amethyst, 8 shaded panels, folded-out lip, 1 flaw, 2x10½".1,700.00
Pitcher, Pillar Mold, appl rnd ft/scolled ear hdl, 11"....................990.00
Pitcher, Pillar Mold, scroll ear hdl, 9" 550.00
Vase, Ball & Groove, cobalt, deeply scalloped rim, 5¾", EX ...2,900.00
Vase, peacock gr on clear ft, appl ring at waist, 6¾" 2,000.00
Vase, pillar mold, appl ft/stem, 9⅝x5¾"..650.00
Vase, Pillar Mold, brilliant amethyst w/wht-edged ribs, ped ft, 10"..4,700.00

Plastics

Synthetic plastic was invented in 1868. Since then, many types have been developed, each with unique characteristics and uses. Among the earliest, those most familiar to us today are celluloid and French ivory; they were commonly used to make toiletry articles. In the early years of the century, buttons were made from Casein plastics, which could be made in a wide variety of colors and easily laminated and carved. The plastic jewelry that is so popular today had its heyday in the 1930s. The material used for its production was phenol formaldehyde. Two of the more recognizable tradenames for cast phenolics are Bakelite and Catalin. Buckles, buttons, radio and clock cases, cutlery handles, desk sets, and novelties were also made from this type of plastic. Vinyl and Lucite, acrylic resins, were used during the period between the two World Wars. There were many applications for vinyl, which is still commonly used. Lucite items that are particularly interesting to todays collectors are purses and jewelry. (See Jewelry.)

Today's collectors have adopted the term Bakelite to encompass any type of phenoic resin. There are two methods of testing used to identify genuine Bakelite: 1), using a cotton swab and Semichromeor 409, clean an inconspicuous area — oxidation on any color will tint the cotton ivory or light yellow; 2), hold the edge of item under very hot running water for at least twenty seconds; if it's genuine, it will smell like varnish or paint remover.

For more information we recommend *Celluloid Treasures of the Victorian Era* by Joan Van Patten and Elmer and Peggy Williams; and *Celluloid, Collector's Reference and Value Guide* by Keith Lauer and Julie Robinson. Both are published by Collector Books.

Bakelite/Catalin

Ashtray, blk-speckled brn, Pullman Co, ca 1940s, 5½" dia 80.00
Ashtray, butterscotch, stepped sides/wide bk, sq well, Carvcraft, NM.95.00
Barometer, Taylor, bl marbled w/alabaster Deco base, 10x14", NM.140.00
Box, amber w/brn corner trim/ft/sq knob, 3x2¾x4" L, NM 235.00
Box, butterscotch, includes Gem razor & manual, in orig cb box..350.00
Box, butterscotch base/final, blk lid, 4x4x6" L, EX+ 500.00
Box, red lid w/cvd line groupings, blk ft, 3x6" 160.00
Box, ring; emerald gr w/striations, curved lid, 1¼x2¾"...............175.00

Box, 1933 Century of Progress, blk, 6" L, NM 11.00
Button, banana shape, orange w/blk, 2½x⅝" 130.00
Camera, Coronet Midget, gr, 2¼x1" 165.00
Candlestick, red ring on blk post mtd on chrome stem, stepped ft, 6" .145.00
Candlesticks, brn marbleized, Deco style, Fr, 6½", pr 165.00
Candlesticks, funerary; Deco style, inlaid stds, 52", pr 425.00
Chess set, pcs in wht or ivory, in poor orig box 400.00
Cigar cutter, bust of man, put cigar in mouth, push down hat 95.00
Cigarette dispenser, dk red w/celluloid lid, Trigerette, 3¾" 125.00
Clock, car; Phinney-Walker, 30-hr, pull chain, MIB 150.00
Clock, GE #3H7, butterscotch, sq/scallped, 5x4¼", EX 45.00
Corn holders, Kob Knobs, butterscotch, set of 8, MIB...............60.00
Crib toy, clown, pk & bl w/apricot & gr, pnt details, 5½", VG...200.00
Crib toy, elephant, strung amber spools w/wht 3-D head, 3½"...265.00
Crib toy, female cat, flat body sections, 3-color, 3½", NM 200.00
Crib toy, Humpty Dumpty, stung amber beads, wht egg head, 4½"..210.00
Crib toy, little girl, strung tan/butterscotch beads & chunks, 6" ...95.00
Crib toy, man, red hat, rnd/cylindrical shapes for body/arms/legs, 4"..50.00
Dice, Caltex w/star on ivory, English, set of 5, MIB..................70.00
Dice cup, blk w/gold marbled bottom, 2" 80.00
Drawer pull, butterscotch swirl, bar style w/chrome bars 15.00
Figurine, greyhound, gray on gr marbled base, ca 1920s, 8" L 200.00
Flashlight, Dyna-lite, ivory, streamline styling, EX in box............95.00
Flatware, blk w/inlaid yel teardrop, GH Warranted, 6 sets in box .500.00
Flatware, SEB Perma Brite, 2-color hdls, 26 pcs including 2 servers..1,100.00
Flatware, various colors, 38 pcs, VG.......................................175.00
Flatware, yel hdls, service for 6 (4 pcs ea), no serving pcs...........100.00
Gavel, mc rings, 7½", EX..100.00
Gear shift knob/clock combo, blk/clear, New Haven, VG 100.00
Inkwell, stepped front, sides w/concentric arcs, butterscotch, EX.150.00
Napkin ring, comic profile of man, butterscotch marble, 2¾" 75.00
Pencil sharpener, chick cutout, yel mottle, 1⅜", NM 65.00
Poker chip caddy, yel mottle w/red knob, 2x2½x6½" L, +chips, EX..80.00
Poker chips, gr, 1930s, ⅛" thick, 1¼" sq, EX, 90 for..................125.00
Radio, Addison #5, lt gr w/maroon trim, EX 1,650.00
Radio, Addison #5, maroon/butterscotch, VG 1,400.00
Radio, Addison A-2 (Baby), blk marbled w/butterscotch trim, NM.1,450.00
Radio, Air King, gr/butterscotch marbled, horizontal grill, VG..1,300.00
Radio, ARIA (like Dewald #561), gr w/butterscotch, EX 1,000.00
Radio, Astor Valve (Football), cream, EX.................................350.00
Radio, Bendix #526, gr swirl, 11" L, EX 550.00
Radio, Crosley G-1465, red/orange, 9½" L, EX+ 2,600.00
Radio, De Wald Outline Grill, maroon/yel, EX 900.00
Radio, Dewald A-501, brn marbled, 7x7x9", VG 750.00
Radio, Dewald A-501, yel, EX 600.00
Radio, Dewald A-502, brn marbled/yel, 10" L, EX 1,100.00
Radio, EKCo SH-25 (Willow Trees), 18x17x10", EX..............950.00
Radio, Emerson #108 U-5A Tombstone, dk brn marbled, EX+ ..450.00
Radio, Emerson AU-190, yel, EX 1,100.00
Radio, Emerson Patriot, lt brn, VG 350.00
Radio, Emerson Tombstone, dk amber (yel), 10x7", EX+ 1,800.00
Radio, Emerson 5+1 EP-375, gr, 1941, VG- 2,000.00
Radio, Fada #1000 (Bullet), maroon/butterscotch, VG 525.00
Radio, Fada #1000 (Bullet), maroon/butterscotch, 1940s, EX .1,200.00
Radio, Fada #1000 (Bullet), wht w/red trim, 1945, EX 1,700.00
Radio, Fada #652, butterscotch w/clear swirl, 7x6x11" L, NM....700.00
Radio, Fada #652, maroon/butterscotch, NM 750.00
Radio, Fada #700 (Cloud), lime gr, EX 685.00
Radio, Fisk Radiolette, dk brn w/wht trim, 13x12x9", EX..........800.00
Radio, Globe, maroon, 1938, working, VG 1,450.00
Radio, Globe, yel w/tortoise vertical-bar grill, EX rstr.............2,200.00
Radio, Motorola #51-C, butterscotch marbled, 6x4x9" L, EX .1,450.00
Radio, Pye #323, 2-valve, 1929, EX.......................................650.00
Radio, RCA #66X8, red w/yel swirl, 15" L, EX........................500.00

Radio, RCA Bookshelf, molded row of books, dial on side, 10" L, VG...1,500.00
Radio, RCA Nipper #9TX, gr marbled w/brn/red/wht/etc, 4x5x9", NM .4,200.00
Radio, Sentinel #284, red/yel, EX/NM....................................1,100.00
Radio, Sentinel #284-NA, dk butterscotch marbled/yel grill, EX ..750.00
Radio, Sentinel #284-NI, butterscotch, 1946, EX.......................750.00
Radio, Sonora Coronet, orange/dk red, 6x5x9", VG 2,100.00
Radio, Stewart Warner #62T36, gr/wht/yel swirl, VG...............650.00
Roulette wheel, mc Catalin chips, wood pack, w/box, 1930s.......200.00
Shakers, gr, bbl shape on flat/ftd 4" L stand, Japan, pr...............125.00
Shakers, gr/yel marbleized, ball shape, NM, 1½", pr 50.00
Shakers, red or butterscotch, pr fits bk to bk on 1¾" rnd tray.......85.00
Shakers, various colors, W Germany, mini, ½", set of 4............100.00
Shakers, 3-pc barbell, shaker ea end, wine & yel, 4⅛" L 125.00
Steering wheel knob, amber w/inlaid scotty dog on wht, 1⅞" 180.00
Swizzle stick, butterscotch, star finial, 5¼"...............................30.00
Swizzle sticks, assorted styles/colors in case styled as a bar, VG...300.00
Table lighter, nude, pnt figure on bronze base, Dunhill 165.00
Toast rack, gr/orange, 3" rings, 6½" L, NM 800.00

Celluloid

Autograph album, cover emb w/Album in gold script, velour bk, 6x4"..85.00
Back comb, imitation grained ivory, crown-like openwork crest, 6x5".115.00
Back comb, imitation tortoise w/openwork cattail motif, 4x3¼" ..35.00
Box, handkerchief; lady's portrait on top, paper-covered sides, 3x5x5"..125.00
Candlestick, 5"...45.00
Clock, dresser; Deco shape w/wide base extension, 6" W 18.00
Collar, Challenge Valkyrie, EX 12.00
Comb, folding, elephant w/gr rhinestones eyes as hdl, pull ft to open...25.00
Dominoes, Hyatt Mfg Co, 1891, MIB......................................60.00
Dresser box, ivory grained w/scalloped gold-glitter top, 4" dia 20.00
Fan, mottled colors, rtcl sticks, souvenir, 3¼" L 15.00
Greeting card, emb design, 1900s...18.00
Hairpin, imitation tortoise shell, 5"...6.00
Hand mirror, emb swirling motif, ca 1880 ....25.00
Penholder, sq platform, blk w/pearlized top layer, ca 1930............18.00
Pitcure frame, oval opening, 3x2¾"..10.00

Playing Cards

Playing cards can be an enjoyable way to trace the course of history. Knowledge of the art, literature, and politics of an era can be gleaned from a study of its playing cards. When royalty lost favor with the people, Kings and Queens were replaced by common people. During the periods of war, generals, officers, and soldiers were favored. In the United States, early examples had portraits of Washington and Adams as opposed to kings, Indian chiefs instead of jacks, and goddesses for queens.

Tarot cards were used in Europe during the 1300s as a game of chance, but in the eighteenth century they were used to predict the future and were regarded with great reverence.

The backs of cards were of no particular consequence until the 1890s. The marble design used by the French during the late 1800s and the colored wood-cut patterns of the Italians in the nineteenth century are among the first attempts at decoration. Later the English used cards printed with portraits of royalty. Eventually cards were decorated with a broad range of subjects from reproductions of fine art to advertising.

Although playing cards are becoming popular collectibles, prices are still relatively low. Complete decks of cards printed earlier than the first postage stamp can still be purchased for less than $100.00. In the listings that follow, decks are without boxes unless the box is specifically mentioned. Information concerning the American Antique Deck Collectors Club, 52 Plus Joker, may be found in the Directory under Clubs, Newsletters, and Catalogs.

Key:
AC — ad card
C — complete
cts — courts
J — joker

SC — score card
std — standard
ws — wide scenic
XC — extra card

Advertising

Am Airlines & Ford Tri-Motor Airplane on red, M, sealed 12.50
Budweiser King of Beers, premium deck, USPC, M in wrapper 10.00
Elsie & Elmer on red, 52+J, MIB..25.00
Inland Homes of Piqua OH, dbl deck, M, sealed 25.00
Jack Daniels, men playing cards, 1960s, M, sealed 16.00
Kool Cigarettes, lovely lady, EXIB.......................................10.00
Royal Crown Best By Taste-Test, military eagle, ca 1945, VGIB ..10.00
Sunbeam, appliances on bks, ca 1950s, M, sealed 12.00
TWA, red logo w/plain bks, M, sealed.....................................15.00
William Grant's Scotch Whiskey, ads from 1928-40, G.................8.00
4 Roses, Congress, Cel-U-Tone finish, ca 1950s, 52+2 J, NM.......20.00

Souvenir

Harold's Club, Reno NV, Harold's Club or Bust w/wagon bks, M .15.00
Historical Facts about TX, mid-1960s, M, sealed 24.00
Homes of Longfellow & Emerson, dbl deck, ea: 52+2 J, EX..........25.00
Lone Star bks, pre-WWW TX scenes, ca 1915, 52+J, EX in G- box .32.00
NY State, scenic bks, Brown & Bigelow, 1950s, dbl deck, M, sealed .45.00
Republican Nat'l Convention 2000, dbl deck, MIP.......................15.00
Ringling Bros Barnum & Bailey Circus World, scenic bks, EX 12.50
Souvenir of Las Vegas...Fremont Street at Night, M, sealed..........22.00
St Regis, geisha bks, plastic coated, dbl deck, MIB.......................16.00

Transportation

American Air Lines, logo on wht, M, sealed...............................12.50
B&O Linking 13 Great States w/the Nation, dbl deck, 1943, EX.55.00
Braniff International, 52+J, M, sealed 10.00
C&O, Chessie & Peake (cats), dbl deck, EXIB 45.00
Catalina Island Steamship Line, Congress, 1940s, EXIB 45.00
Cats, Gladys Emerson Cook, USPC, dbl deck, EXIB.....................40.00
Delta Airlines, Miami scenic bks, M, sealed................................15.00
Denver & Rio Grande Western, 23 views/29 RR images, 52C, EXIB .95.00
Japan Air Lines, checkerboard bks, M, sealed 10.00
Pan-Am Engineering...Dallas TX, engine & tender bks, 1490s, M, sealed...20.00
Royal Viking Cruise Line, Heraclio Fournier, dbl deck, M in case .15.00

Miscellaneous

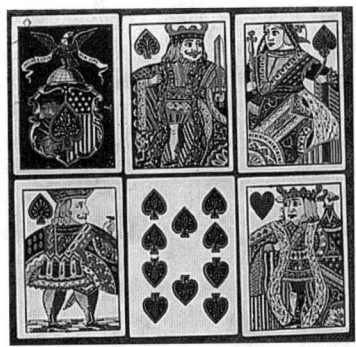

Lawrence & Cohen Illuminated Playing Cards, much gold on each card, ca 1863, fifty-two (complete), M in NM box, $2,200.00.

Al Moore pinup girls, c Esquire, dbl deck, M, sealed...................125.00
Boys Town, He Ain't Heavy..., Brown & Bigelow, 1940s, dbl deck, M..60.00

Clinton/Gore, 54 caricatures, Politicards, 2000, M, sealed 8.50
Congress, flying geese bks, dbl deck, ea: 52C, EX 15.00
Congress, lady w/dogs, dbl deck, ea: 52+2 J, MIB w/instructions ..28.00
Congress, poodle on bl, Cell-U-Tone finish, M 25.00
Congress #606, Std faces, Russell & Morgan Ace of Spades, 52C, EX..20.00
Duratone, fighting cocks, dbl set, ea w/52+2 J, VG 28.00
Elvgren Cuties, Seasons Greetings, dbl deck, EX..........................110.00
Elvgren pinup girl, service station advertising, Brown & Bigelow, EX ..95.00
Fish U&P & Drink Up, Washaw cartoon, 1950s, dbl deck, M......15.00
Marguerite #130, gold edges, Dougherty NY, 1896, 52+1J, NMIB.35.00
Nude photo bks, ca 1950s, MIB..22.50
Playboy nude Playmate, 1968, MIB w/cb sleeve............................48.00
Poodle w/bl bow on bks, Western Publishing, M, sealed 15.00
Port scenes by Lionel Barrymore, Brown & Bigelow, 1960s, dbl deck, M....45.00
Tarot, Brotherhood of Light, Egyptian, c Church of Light, 1964, MIB..100.00
Trip or Trap, drug info, WR Spence MD, Spenco, 1960, 52+2J, MIB...38.00
Virgo, symbol on bl, 52+J+1 Virgo XC, EXIB 12.50
Washington/Lincoln portrait bks by Eisenhower, 1960s, dbl deck, MIB..60.00

Political

Many of the most valuable political items are those from any period which relate to a political figure whose term was especially significant or marked by an important event or one whose personality was particularly colorful. Posters, ribbons, badges, photographs, and pin-back buttons are but a few examples of the items popular with collectors of political memorabilia.

Political campaign pin-back buttons were first mass produced and widely distributed in 1896 for the president-to-be William McKinley and for the first of three unsuccessful attempts by William Jennings Bryan. Pin-back buttons have been used during each presidential campaign ever since and are collected by many people. Some of the scarcest are those used in the presidential campaigns of John W. Davis in 1924 and James Cox in 1920.

Contributions to this category were made by Michael J. McQuillen, monthly columnist of *Political Parade,* which appears in *AntiqueWeek* newspapers; he is listed in the Directory under Indiana. Our advisor for this category is Paul J. Longo; he is listed under Massachusetts.

See also Autographs; Broadsides; Historical Glass; Watch Fobs.

Badge, Memphis Confederate Veterans Reunion, copper, 1909 ..250.00
Bandana, Alton B Parker/Henry G Davis, 1904, 24½x21½", EX..250.00
Bandana, Roosevelt/Fairbanks jugate, 3-color, 1904, 24½x21¾"...300.00
Bandana, T Roosevelt, Progressive Battle Flag, 1912, 21½x24", VG..200.00
Bandana, Union, Constitution & Flag, printed silk, Civil War era, 32".450.00
Bust, Eugene V Debs, sculpted metal, RR Hellvik, 1920, 4¾" 450.00
Engraving, Abraham Lincoln, Rudolf Lesch, NY, hand colored, 31x24" .275.00
Envelope, Lincoln rail-splitter theme, 1860, EX 150.00
Ferrotype, Lincoln, bk: Hamlin, in emb fr, campaign of 1860, ⅞", EX.350.00
Lapel pin, Confederate States of Am flags, 2½" L stickpin 250.00
Lithograph, Presidents of US, 1st 11 portraits, Baillie, 1844, 20x16"..600.00
Medal, campaign; Lincoln, shown as rail splitter, copper, EX 115.00
Medal, Washington Funeral Urn, copy in wht metal, pierced, 1799...900.00
Mug, New Deal, ceramic, golden-yel gloss, 4".............................85.00
Plaque, Lincoln, cast copper, 1909, 5½x3½"+walnut fr 200.00
Plaque, T Roosevelt, bronzed iron, JE Fraser, 1920, 13x10" 750.00
Plaque, Washington profile, bronze, EX patina, 1850s, 11" 500.00
Portrait, A Lincoln wax memorial, mtd on fabric, in 6x6" shadowbox fr..800.00
Poster, Garfield memorial, centered w/earlier presidents, 1881, 14x11" .200.00
Print, Declaration of Independence, eng by G Smith, 1937, 12x9¾".500.00
Ribbon, Lincoln mourning, lg vignette on silk, 5x2¼" 350.00
Ribbon, US Grant mourning, blk portrait/lettering, ca 1885, 6¼x2" .150.00
Ribbon, US Grant portrait on silk, Tschopf, 4½x1¼", EX..........230.00
Ribbon, Washington Monument commemorative, printed silk, 1847, 7½"..125.00

Pin-back Buttons

Al Gore Vice President, TN's Favorite Son, portrait, blk/wht/red/bl, M .**5.00**
All the Way w/Adlai, flasher, lg, M **15.00**
Bill Clinton for President, red/wht/bl, M...**4.00**
Bush/Quayle 88, red/wht/bl, M...**3.00**
Carter, smiling portrait, blk & wht, no lettering or slogan, M.........**4.00**
Carter for President, blk & wht portrait, sm, M **4.00**
Carter/Mondale, Carter portrait, red/wht/bl, lg, M **8.00**
Carter/Mondale in '76, blk & wht portraits on gr & wht, M...........**4.00**
Carter/Mondale 76, blk & wht portraits at right, M **4.00**
Citizens for Johnson & Humphrey, blk & wht portraits w/red & bl, M ..**6.00**
Clinton & Gore Deserve Four More, blk & wht portraits, M...........**2.00**
Dewey, bl lettering on wht, M..**5.00**
Draft Eisenhower for President, smiling portrait, red/wht/bl, lg, NM...**25.00**
Draft Pat Robertson for President 1988, mc portrait, bl/wht border, M .**3.00**
Emancipation Expo NY City 1913, Frederick Douglas portrait, EX ..**275.00**
Experience Counts, Elect Gerald R Ford in '75, blk/wht/red/bl, M .**5.00**
Fight Descrimination Defend Bill of Rights, cello, late 1940s, 1¼" .**50.00**
Ford for President, blk & wht portrait w/red lettering, sm, M **4.00**
Franklin D Roosevelt a Gallant Leader, blk & wht portrait, NM .**10.00**
Goldwater, bl letters on wht arrow on red, sm, M **4.00**
Goldwater in '64, blk & wht portrait, blk letters on gold, sm, M **6.00**
HHH, gr letters on wht w/bl border, M **3.00**
Hillary...Clinton, As Bad...She Wants.., portrait w/orange hair, M...**10.00**
Hoosiers for Reagan, portrait in western hat on wht, M **6.00**
I Like Ike, bl letters on wht center, red/wht/bl rim, M **5.00**
I'm for Nixon, flasher, lg, M..**8.00**
I'm for Nixon, red/wht/bl, sm, M **5.00**
I Signed the Perot Petition Have YOU, red/wht/bl, M...................**2.00**
I Want Roosevelt Again, red/wht/bl, EX **6.00**
If I Were 18 I'd Vote for Reagan '84, red & bl lettering on wht, M..**4.00**
Ike & Dick, They're for You, red/wht/bl, M...................................**5.00**
Jesse Jackson President, Bold Leadership New Direction, mc portrait, M ..**4.00**
John Kennedy, smiling portrait, blk & wht, M...............................**16.00**
Johnson & Humphrey in wht letters on bl, blk/wht portraits above, M..**6.00**
Keep Hope Alive, Jesse Jackson mc portrait w/rainbow behind, M.**4.00**
Kennedy/Johnson, Khruschev Does Not Want Kennedy, I Do, 2¼", NM..**35.00**
Lugar for President, bl/wht/yel, M..**2.00**
McGovern, orange & yel, 1972, M **4.00**
McGovern, Thank You for Your Support, bl & wht, sq, M..............**3.00**
McKinley/Hobart, National Wheelmen, star border, red/wht/bl, 2¼" .**165.00**

McKinley and T. Roosevelt with red, white, and blue ribbon, 2¼" diameter, $125.00.

Mondale/Ferraro, wht on bl w/swirling red & wht stripes, 1 wht star, M..**4.00**
Montgomery AL Civil War Reunion, cello, 1930, EX.................**75.00**
Nixon Agnew, portraits & names, bl & wht, sm, M **5.00**
Nixon for President, Progress for All, portrait, 4-color, M **8.00**
Read My Lips...Perot, flag behind name, red/wht/bl, M **2.00**
Reagan/Bush, mc portraits w/eagle & flags, Peace Through Strength, M.**5.00**
Reagan/Bush '84, mc portraits, M **6.00**
Reagan/Nancy portraits, Renew America's Strength..., mc, lg, M ..**5.00**
Roosevelt, FDR portrait, red/wht/bl, EX......................................**15.00**

Roosevelt/McKinley, jugate, 'stitching' at rim, 2", EX.................**135.00**
Stevenson, red/wht/bl w/bl letters on wht central stripe, M **4.00**
Students for Dukakis '88, blk/wht/bl/red, M **3.00**
Things Are Looking Up, Re-Elect President Reagan, baby's portrait, M.**6.00**
Vote Johnson, mc portrait, flasher, lg, M.......................................**8.00**
Wallace for President Stand Up for Am, portrait, red/wht/bl, M **3.00**
Wilson/Marshall, jugate, 1912 campaign, 1¼", G.........................**75.00**
WIN (Whip Inflation Now), red & wht, lg, M...............................**2.00**
Wings for Willkie America, bl plane, red letters on wht, EX **12.00**
Winning Team for Indiana, Bush/Mutz 88, race car, mc, oval, M ...**6.00**
Youth for Kennedy, full-face picture, red/bl on wht, 3", M..........**250.00**

Pomona

Pomona glass was patented in 1885 by the New England Glass Works. Its characteristics are an etched background of crystal lead glass often decorated with simple designs painted with metallic stains of amber or blue. The etching was first achieved by hand cutting through an acid resist. This method, called first ground, resulted in an uneven feather-like frost effect. Later, to cut production costs, the hand-cut process was discontinued in favor of an acid bath which effected an even frosting. This method is called second ground. Our advisors for this category are Betty and Clarence Maier; they are listed in the Directory under Pennsylvania.

Bowl, 1st ground, NM stain, 4½" dia **265.00**
Creamer & sugar bowl, 1st ground, Invt T'print, amber rim, 3-leg ..**600.00**
Cruet, 2nd ground, cornflowers, w/clear stopper, 6½" **400.00**
Finger bowl, 2nd ground, cornflowers, 5¼" **185.00**
Punch cup, 1st ground, Honeycomb, clear rim, 2¾x4"...................**35.00**
Punch cup, 1st ground, lt T'print, amber stain..............................**100.00**
Shakers, 2nd ground, cornflowers, cylindrical, SP fr w/center hdl, 7" .**1,150.00**
Tumbler, 2nd ground, blueberries/2 gold bands, 3⅝" **295.00**
Tumbler, 2nd ground, Dmn Quilt, cornflowers, 4"........................**165.00**
Tumbler, 2nd ground, Rivulet, ca 1900, 3¾" **320.00**
Vase, lily; 2nd ground, Optic Rib w/Dmn Quilt mouth, 10" **385.00**

Porcelier

The Porcelier Manufacturing Company, originally from East Liverpool, Ohio, started business in the late 1920s and moved to Greensburg, Pennsylvania, in the early 1930s. The company flourished until the late 1940s and finally closed its doors in 1954.

They produced an endless line of vitrified porcelain products including electric appliances, coffee makers, and light fixtures. These products were sold in many stores under a variety of names and carried over ten different types of marks and labels.

The prices below are for items in excellent condition with no chips, cracks, or excessive wear. For more information, we recommend *Collector's Guide to Porcelier China* by our advisor for this category, Susan E. (Grindberg) Lynn. If you have any questions or information regarding Porcelier, you may contact Mrs. Lynn; she is listed in the Directory under Nevada. (Queries require SASE.)

Andirons, VG, pr **700.00**
Appliance coasters, apple gr or wht, 6-sided, set of 4, lg...............**30.00**
Ashtray, 1939 New York World's Fair...**300.00**
Beverage cooler, bbl shape..**60.00**
Canister, Country Life series, ea...**80.00**
Coffeepot, Autumn Leaves, Fr drip, 6-cup **30.00**
Coffeepot, Colonial, no decor, 4-cup..**30.00**
Coffeepot, Dainty Rose, 4-cup..**40.00**

Coffeepot, Deco Ribbed, 6-cup **35.00**
Coffeepot, Diamond Leaf, 2-cup **32.00**
Coffeepot, Dogwood I, 4-cup **30.00**
Coffeepot, Dogwood II, blk, 4-cup **70.00**
Coffeepot, Dogwood II, 4-cup **30.00**
Coffeepot, Geometric Wheat, 6- or 8-cup **30.00**
Coffeepot, Hearth, 2- to 8-cup **30.00**
Coffeepot, Pears, 4- or 6-cup **25.00**
Coffeepot, Ribbed Bottom, 6-cup **30.00**
Coffeepot, Rose & Wheat, 4- or 6-cup **25.00**
Coffeepot, Southern Belle, 6-cup **40.00**
Coffeepot, Sunken Panel, 2-cup **32.00**
Coffeepot, 1939 New York World's Fair, 6- or 8-cup ...**250.00**
Creamer, Beehive Floral Spray **10.00**
Creamer, Leaf & Shadow **12.00**
Creamer, Orange Poppy Hostess **12.00**
Creamer, Pink Flower Hostess..**10.00**
Creamer, Tree Trunk...**25.00**
Lamp, table; Antique Rose decal **45.00**
Percolator, electric; Field Flowers....................................**70.00**
Percolator, Golden Wheat..**90.00**
Pitcher, ball jug; Beehive Crisscross **90.00**
Pitcher, disc; Flight **85.00**
Porchlight, blk w/clear glass globe (tapered sq)..............**80.00**
Sugar bowl, Flamingo **10.00**
Sugar bowl, Goldfinches...**15.00**
Sugar bowl, Medallion **10.00**
Sugar bowl, Silhouette Hostess **15.00**
Sugar bowl, Tulips...**25.00**
Urn, electric; Flower Pot Hostess....................................**125.00**

Postcards

Postcards are often very difficult to evaluate, since so many factors must be considered — for instance the subject matter or the field of interest they represent. For example: a 1905 postcard of the White House in Washington D.C. may seem like a desirable card, but thousands were produced and sold to tourists who visited there, thus the market is saturated with this card, and there are few collectors to buy it. Value: less than $1.00. However, a particular view of small town of which only five hundred were printed could sell for far more, provided you find someone interested in the subject matter pictured on that card. Take as an example a view of the courthouse in Hillsville, Virginia. This card would appeal to those focusing on that locality or county as well as courthouse collectors. Value: $3.00.

The ability of the subject to withstand time is also a key factor when evaluating postcards. Again using the courthouse as an example, one built in 1900 and still standing in the 1950s has been photographed for fifty years, from possibly a hundred different angles. Compare that with one built in 1900 and replaced in 1908 due to a fire, and you can see how much more desirable a view of the latter would be. But only a specialist would be aware of the differences between these two examples.

Postcard dealers can very easily build up stocks numbering in the 100,000s. Greeting and holiday cards are common and represent another area of collecting that appeals to an entirely different following than the view card. These types of cards range from heavily embossed designs to floral greetings and, of course, include the ever popular Santa Claus card. These were very popular from about 1900 until the 1920s, when postcard communication was the equivalent of today's quick phone call or e-mail. Because of the vast number of them printed, many have little if any value to a collector. For instance, a 1909 Easter card with tiny images or a common floral card of the same vintage, though almost one hundred years old, are virtually worthless. It's the cards with appeal and

zest that command the higher prices. One with a beautiful Victorian woman in period clothing, her image filling up the entire card, could easily be worth $3.00 and up. Holiday cards designed for Easter, Valentines Day, Thanksgiving, and Christmas are much more common than those for New Year's, St. Patrick's Day, the 4th of July, and Halloween. Generally, then, they're worth less, but depending on the artist, graphics, desirability, and eye appeal, this may not always be true. The signature of a famous artist will add significant value — conversely, an unknown artist's signature adds none.

In summary, the best way to evaluate your cards is to have a knowledgeable dealer look at them. For a list of dealers, send a SASE to the International Federation of Postcard Dealers, P.O. Box 1765, Manassas, VA 20108. Do not expect a dealer to price cards from a list or written description as this is not possible. For individual questions or evaluation by *photocopy (front and back)*, you may contact our advisor, Jeff Bradfield, 90 Main St., Dayton, VA 22821. You must include a SASE for a reply.

For more information we recommend *The Collector's Guide to Postcards* by Jane Wood and *Vintage Postcards for the Holidays* by Robert and Claudette Reed (Collector Books).

Posters

Advertising posters by such French artists as Cheret and Toulouse-Lautrec were used as early as the mid-1800s. Color lithography spurred their popularity. Circus posters by the Strobridge Lithograph Co. are considered to be the finest in their field, though Gibson and Co. Litho, Erie Litho, and Enquirer Job Printing Co. printed fine examples as well. Posters by noted artists such as Mucha, Parrish, and Hohlwein bring high prices. Other considerations are good color, interesting subject matter and, of course, condition. The WWII posters listed below are among the more expensive examples; 70% of those on the market bring less than $65.00. Values are for examples in excellent condition unless noted otherwise. See also Movie Memorabilia; Rock 'N Roll.

Advertising

Champagne Masse Per & Fils, man in wine cellar, 47x32", M....**700.00**
Cognac Jacquet, Bouchet, Vercasson Paris, sheet: 62½x45½" **940.00**
Cognac Monnet, Leonetto Cappiello, Davambez Paris, fr, sheet: 79x51".**350.00**
Edison Records, dancing couple, mc, 1930s, 26x30", NM...........**460.00**
Liqueur Cordial - Medoc, Henri le Monnier, Bedos & Cie, sheet: 62x45" ..**470.00**
Strand-Hotel, lady at table, yel/purple, 1930, 47x33", NM......**1,500.00**
Woodroffe's Engagement Rings, couple, Petty & Sons, 60x40", EX..**1,265.00**

Circus

Key:
B&B — Barnum and Bailey   RB — Ringling Brothers

AL G Barnes & Sells-Floto..., Old Mexico, 1937, 28x21", NM.**1,500.00**
B&B, Berta Beeson, high-wire artist, Strobridge, 1920s **920.00**
B&B, horse jumping through ring of fire, 1898, 29x19", EX....**1,850.00**
B&B, portraits, Greatest Show, Strobridge, 40x30"..................**1,400.00**
Cole Bros, Georgia Sweet, trick rider, 1947, 27x41", NM........**1,500.00**
Cole Bros, Getting Ready for the Ring, trapeze girl, 1930s, 49x29", EX .**1,850.00**
Cole Bros, girl on horse, 1936, 50x27", EX..............................**1,850.00**
Cole Bros, Great Gretonas, aerial high-wire stunts, 1930s, 41x27", NM.**2,500.00**
Cole Bros, Jennie O'Brien, bareback rider, 1935, 28x42", EX..**2,200.00**
Hunt Bros, Giant Siberian Tigers, snarling tiger, 1-sheet...............**95.00**
RB B&B, Francis Brunn, juggler, 1940s, 50x27", EX **875.00**
RB B&B, Miss Dorothy Herbert, trick rider, 1935, 41x27", NM.**1,500.00**
RB B&B, Miss Tommy Atkins, riding team, 1930, 28x42", EX ..**950.00**
Zimbral, bald clown w/ladder, Chippy, Fr, 1925, 61x23", EX **900.00**

Magic

Carter the Great, Modern Priestess of Delphi, 3-part, 78x42", EX .500.00
Chang & Fak-Hong's United Magicians Presents Elle, 1930s, 25x17", NM.750.00
Cortes & Mari, illusionists, Sevilla Spain, 1890s, 29x22", NM...800.00
George, Triumphant Am Tour, mc vignettes, USA, 1920s, 40x27", NM..1,500.00
Great Chang & Fak-Hong's United, Noe Ark, Valencia, 30x43", EX...375.00

Theatrical

Artist's Model, nude behind lg palette, Price, 1895, 88x57", EX ..2,500.00
Eldorado, Et Comment..!!, lady & Cupid, Kaub, 1890s, 32x24", EX.675.00
H'Lorolocer Amoureux, Buster Keaton, 31x24", EX 2,600.00
Jane Renouadt, lady in bkless gown, Stephen, Fr, 1920s, 60x46", M..2,750.00
La Veuve Joyeuse (Merry Widow), Georges Dola, M Eschig Paris, 47x31"...400.00
Maurice Chevalier La Voix de Son Maitre, Kiffer, 1937, 63x48", NM..2,500.00
Mistinguette, lady in bl, de Losques, 1911, 75x41", EX............2,000.00
Mora Y Manzano, Spanish lady dancer, Fr, 1900s, 55x39", EX ...950.00
Nijni et Stone, dancing couple, red/wht/blk, 1920s, 55x40", EX ..1,850.00
Othello, gazing down w/dagger, Anon, England, 1920s, 20x30", NM..750.00
Regina Bar, couple dancing, Schwarzen, Germany, 1927, 49x33", EX .7,500.00
Scala, La Troupe Viennoise, Fr, 1880s, 51x35", EX......................900.00
Simone Frevalles, lady in yel, Vertes, 1923, 49x34", NM.........1,500.00
T'en Auras Parisiana, sexy lady/well-dressed man, 1903, 24x16", NM..1,350.00
Walhalla, lady at window, Dupois, 1900, 42x31", NM.............4,500.00

Travel

A'Algèrie et la Tunisia par la Cie Gle Transatlantique, annon, 40x27".940.00
Am Airlines, cowgirl in lg hat, Kauffer, 1948, 40x30", NM 575.00
Australia, 90 Yrs-Progress, street scene, Northfield, 1930s, 40x50", M .7,000.00
Budapest, speeding train, Semizky, Kloss & Son, 1930, 37x25", NM..800.00
Fly to Nassau by Clipper, boat scene, Von Arenburg, 1950s, 42x28", NM..1,200.00
Geneve, sailboats & roses, Mahrer, 1930s, 39x26", EX 1,250.00
Join Fun on Ski Run in France, Dubois, Courbet Paris, 1950, 40x24" .385.00
Monte-Carlo, nude w/huge bouquet, Domergue, 1937, 39x25", NM.1,250.00
NY Central RR, Thorobreds, 3 locomotives, 1927, 19x24", EX+..1,035.00
Rome, British European Airways, coliseum, Casson, 1950s, 40x25".M.500.00
South Africa by Clipper, 4 scenes, 1951, 38x26", M 900.00
Sur la route de Namur, Gamy, Mabileau & Cie, 1913, sheet: 36x18".470.00

War

WWI, ...Menace of Seas, hand w/dagger, Grosse, 1917, 1917, 19x26", M.300.00
WWI, Americans All!, girl touches wreath, Christy, 1918, 40x28", EX.300.00
WWI, Be a US Marine, soldier before flag, Flagg, 1918, 40x28", EX...900.00
WWI, Boys Come Over Here..., D Allen & Sons, 1916, 40x50", EX..400.00
WWI, Christmas Roll Call?, Red Cross nurse, Fisher, 1918, 28x30", EX.250.00
WWI, Clear the Way...Bonds, mc, HC Christy, 39¾x19¼", VG...200.00
WWI, Credit National, ruins, Duval, Fr, 1915, 47x32", NM 600.00
WWI, Fight or Buy Bonds, girl w/flag, Christy, 1917, 41x30", EX.400.00
WWI, Forward!, horseman, Kemp-Welsh, 1915, 30x20", NM.2,000.00

WWI, Invest in the Victory Liberty Loan, submarine scene, 29¼x39", EX, $500.00.

WWI, I Want You for the Navy, Christy, 1917, 42x28", EX 250.00
WWI, Men Wanted for the Army, cannon scene, Whelan, 1909, 40x28", EX..850.00
WWI, Ring It Again...Bonds, bell & church, 30x20", EX...........135.00
WWI, See Him Through, 4-color, Nat'l Catholic War Council, 30x20".150.00
WWI, War Rages in France, villagers, US Food Administration, 30x20" .150.00
WWII, Am's Answer!, Production, hand w/wrench, 1942, 30x41", EX.1,850.00
WWII, Corn Food of Nation, lady & corn products, 30x21", NM ..485.00
WWII, Look's Who's Listening, Axis leaders, rpr, 30x23½", EX..400.00
WWII, Med Dept US Army, medic & soldier, 25x19", NM 1,265.00
WWII, Right in Der Fuehrer's Face, hand to Hitler's jaw, 21¼x14"..250.00
WWII, We French Workers Warn You, Shahn, 38½x40", NM..545.00
WWII, Woman's Place in War, lady soldier rprs radio, 38x25", EX...200.00

Pot Lids

Pot lids were pottery covers for containers that were used for hair dressing, potted meats, etc. The most common were decorated with colorful transfer prints under the glaze in a variety of themes, animal and scenic. The first and probably the largest company to manufacture these lids was F. & R. Pratt of Fenton, Staffordshire, established in the early 1800s. The name or initials of Jesse Austin, their designer, may sometimes be found on exceptional designs. Although few pot lids were made after the 1880s, the firm continued into the twentieth century.

American pot lids are very rare. Most have been dug up by collectors searching through sites of early gold rush mining towns in California. In the following listings, all lids are transfer printed; the color(s) mentioned describe the transfer. Minor rim chips are expected and normally do not detract from listed values. When no condition is given, assume that the value is based on an example in such condition.

American

Chlorine Detergent...WE Hagan, brn/wht, 2⅞", EX 350.00
Jules Hauel Perfumer..., purple/wht, 2¾", EX..............................195.00
Jules Hauel...Ambrosial Cream, red/wht, 3½", EX.......................425.00
Taylor's Saponaceous Compound, bl/wht, 4", EX.........................400.00
Taylor's Saponaceous Coumpound, blk/wht, 3⅜", EX 375.00
WA Batchelor's Dentifrice..., cobalt/wht, 2⅜x3⅝", EX..............425.00
Worsley's Saponaceous Shaving Compound, blk/wht, 4", NM....500.00

English

Allied Gens FM Lord Raglan, RL Robert, mc, 4¾", EX..............190.00
Almond Shaving Cream, gr/wht, 13¼", w/base 225.00
Arecua Nut Toothpaste, blk/wht, 3¼", w/base...........................145.00
Bears on Rock, mc, Pratt, ca 1860, EX 350.00
Bellevue, Pegwell Bay, lg estate, mc, 5", EX.............................140.00
Cherry Toothpaste, blk/wht, 2½" 125.00
Children of Flora, mc, Pratt, 4½", VG 275.00
England's Pride, mc, rare, 4¾", EX 180.00
Eye Ointment, blk/wht, 3¼" 95.00
Fedding the Chickens, mc, Pratt, 4¼", VG 275.00
Fortnum & Mason Chicken & Ham, blk/wht, 3x4" dia 110.00
Hauling in the Trawl, 4", EX...140.00
Klenzit Dental Plate Soap For Artificial Teeth Only, blk/wht, 3".175.00
Lobster Sauce, lobster/cat/fish, mc, 4½", EX.............................135.00
Pretty Kettle of Fish, mc, Pratt, EX 350.00
Royal Harbour Ramsgate, 4", EX 70.00
Snow Drift, mc, Pratt, 4¼", EX 325.00
Trafalgar Square, mc, 4", EX..65.00
Woods Areca Nut Toothpaste, blk/wht, 2½", VG 95.00

Powder Horns and Shot Flasks

Though powder horns had already been in use for hundreds of years, collectors usually focus on those made after the expansion of the United States westward in the very early 1800s. While some are basic and very simple, others were scrimshawed and highly polished. Especially nice carvings can quickly escalate the value of a horn that has survived intact to as high as $400.00. Those with detailed maps, historical scenes, etc., bring even higher prices.

Metal flasks were introduced in the 1830s; by the middle of the century they were produced in quantity and at prices low enough that they became a viable alternative to the powder horn. Today's collector regards the smaller flasks as the more desirable and valuable, and those made for specific companies bring premium prices.

Flask, brass, Colt type, emb eagle & revolver, rpr, 4⅜" **180.00**
Flask, brass, Colt type, emb eagle/shield/13 stars, 4½" **200.00**
Flask, brass, emb buffalo hunt scene, 9", VG **500.00**
Flask, brass, emb geometric scrolls, US Flask Co, 10½" **125.00**
Flask, brass, emb scrolls w/orig lacquer, 5¼" **150.00**
Flask, copper, emb Indian & game, 9¾", G **165.00**
Flask, copper, emb leaves, 2 compartments in base, 4¾" **100.00**
Flask, copper, emb lion chasing deer, 7¼" **150.00**
Flask, copper, emb shell & acanthus leaves, 5⅞" **110.00**
Flask, copper, emb stag/oak leaves/fox, orig lacquer, 5" **110.00**
Flask, glass, mold blown w/bird designs, 6½" **165.00**
Horn, Adam & Eve/village/lion, initialed GSM, 13" **1,750.00**
Horn, Am eagle/shield/banner, man/axe, animals/etc, mc wash, 1840, 16"...**3,000.00**
Horn, appl horn rings, screw tip, domed wooden plug, 14½" **775.00**
Horn, banner w/angel & sailing ship, sgn/1806, pine plug, 11".**2,500.00**
Horn, coat of arms/fort/windmill, pine plug dtd 1758, 15".......**3,575.00**
Horn, coat of arms/house/hunter/deer/dog, identified cvg, 12"..**1,550.00**
Horn, houses/trees/vines/flowers, maple plug, 12", EX **1,650.00**
Horn, lg tree/hunter & deer/etc, cvd panels/rings, sgn/1776, 12"..**3,500.00**
Horn, Masonic emblems/animals/etc, trn cherry plug, 13" **600.00**
Horn, name/geometrics, ca 1785, dome-like wooden plug, 18".**1,600.00**
Horn, NY scene w/men & animals (primitive), ca 1800, 7"...**1,150.00**
Horn, old red-orange stain, copper tacks, domed trn plug w/tack, 14" ..**110.00**
Horn, ships/building/figures/animals, 8" **700.00**
Horn, town/harbor/ships, sgn, ca 1760, 11" **1,750.00**
Horn, York County, screw tip, cherry plug, staple strap holders, 14" .**600.00**

Pratt

Prattware has become a generic reference for a type of relief-molded earthenware with polychrome decoration. Scenic motifs with figures were popular; sometimes captions were added. Jugs are most common, but teapots, tableware, even figurines were made. The term 'Pratt' refers to Wm. Pratt of Lane Delph, who is credited with making the first examples of this type, though similar wares were made later by other Staffordshire potters. Pot lids and other transfer wares marked Pratt were made in Fenton, Staffordshire, by F. & R. Pratt & Co. (See Pot Lids.)

Bank, house w/chimney, man stands at 1 side, lady at other, 5", VG ..**265.00**
Cradle, child inside, hooded, allover decor, 1800, rstr/chips, 8"..**585.00**
Flask, shell form, mc enamels, slight blemishes, 4" **765.00**
Mug, Britannia Looking to Sea/Sailor's Return, lg frog w/in, rstr, 4"..**875.00**
Pitcher, hunters/animals, emb oak leaves, feather edge spout/hdl, 6"..**935.00**
Pitcher, Old Mother Slipper Slopper, 5".......................**875.00**
Pitcher, Toby Philpots, bk: warrior, leaves at rim/base, 5½", EX.**650.00**
Teapot, molded/pnt classical designs, 1810-20s, sm rpr **295.00**

Pre-Columbian Artifacts

The term 'pre-Columbian' loosely refers to some time prior to 1492, when Columbus arrived in America. In particular, it indicates pre-1492 artifacts of Central and South America, some of which can be dated as early as 4000 B.C. Artifacts representing the cultures of the Inca, Maya, and Aztec Indians are avidly sought by the collector. These may be made of precious metals, hardstones, or pottery. Some were used in rituals and religious rites; some such as bowls and other utensils, though strictly utilitarian, nevertheless convey through form and decoration the craftsmanship of these early tribes.

Bowl, mc geometrics, fragmentary, Peruvian, 4½x9" **275.00**
Ceremonial head, cvd gr jadeite, Palenove Mexico, 3¼x2¾".....**550.00**
Figurine, human/animal, pottery, Costa Rican, rare, 8x6x4" **50.00**
Jar, mc decor, oval, Panama, 4½x5"..................................**50.00**
Knife, cvd jade, human head design, Huetar Culture, 6x1¾x½" .**800.00**
Stirrup vessel, phallic form, Peruvian, 6½x7" **250.00**
Vessel, bird effigy, mc, Incan, 7x2½" **100.00**
Vessel, crab effigy, Peruvian Chimu, 9x5½".............................**400.00**
Vessel, cvd redware, Peruvian, 6x6"...**130.00**
Vessel, human effigy, red geometrics on buff, Costa Rican, 6½x7"...**110.00**
Vessel, mc faces, w/lid, Mayan, 5½x9" **275.00**
Vessel, stirrup; pottery, human effigy, Madre, 6x7¼" **130.00**

Primitives

Like the mouse that ate the grindstone, so has collectible interest in primitives increased, a little bit at a time, until demand is taking bites instead of nibbles into their availability. Although the term 'primitives' once referred to those survival essentials contrived by our American settlers, it has recently been expanded to include objects needed or desired by succeeding generations — items representing the cabin-'n-corn-patch existence as well as examples of life on larger farms and in towns. Through popular usage, it also respectfully covers what are actually 'country collectibles.'

From the 1600s into the latter 1800s, factories employed carvers, blacksmiths, and other artisans whose handwork contributed to turning out quality items. When buying, 'touchmarks,' a company's name and/or location and maker's or owner's initials, are exciting discoveries.

Primitives are uniquely individual. Following identical forms, results more often than not show typically personal ideas. Using this as a guide (combined with circumstances of age, condition, desire to own, etc.) should lead to a reasonably accurate evaluation. For items not listed, consult comparable examples. Authority Kathryn McNerney has compiled several lovely books on primitives and related topics: *Primitives, Our American Heritage; Collectible Blue and White Stoneware;* and *Antique Tools, Our American Heritage.* You will find her address in the Directory under Florida. See also Butter Molds and Stamps; Boxes; Copper; Farm Collectibles; Fireplace Implements; Kitchen Collectibles; Molds; Tinware; Weaving; Woodenware; and Wrought Iron.

Bed warmer, brass, eng floral, copper rivets, wood hdl w/grpt, 43½" ..**225.00**
Bed warmer, brass pan w/eng scrollwork lid, trn wood hdl, 44½".**250.00**
Bed warmer, brass w/eng rooster on hill w/flowers, trn hdl, 42", EX ..**385.00**
Bin, pine, scrolling crest, drw, old gr pnt, 1850s-90s, 47x22x20" ...**750.00**
Bin, pine w/worn red pnt, 1-brd sides, 35x24x13" **385.00**
Bucket, staved, dk gr, tapered/copper tacks, Wilder & Sons, 14" .**550.00**
Bucket, staved, extended pc w/hanging hole, old pnt, 1800s, 13x9".....**700.00**
Bucket, staved, faded red, blk iron bands/finial, mk Pat Oct 27 85, 9".**220.00**
Bucket, staved, gr pnt over earlier tan, copper tacks, swing hdl, 14".....**400.00**
Bucket, staved, gray pnt, copper tacks, 16" w/hdl **700.00**

Bucket, staved, iron hoops, gr-blk pnt w/birds etc, bail, 5⅝" ...1,035.00
Bucket, staved, metal bands, mustard pnt w/blk stencil, bail, 11"..220.00
Bucket, staved, old brn patina w/dk varnish, rpr, 14½x15½"......250.00
Bucket, staved, orig alligatored red, wooden grip, 6x7" 750.00
Bucket, staved, tongue/grove, gray pnt, w/lid, mk WA Mfg, 4x5"..220.00
Candle mold, pine & tin, 12-tube, minor rprs, 15x24x4", VG....415.00
Candle mold, tin, 12-tube, ca 1800, 10⅝", VG 250.00
Candle mold, tin, 12-tube, ear hdls, ca 1830-50, EX 325.00
Candle mold, tin, 4-tube, ca 1800, 11", VG 165.00
Candle mold, tin, 60-tube, ear hdls, 17", EX.............................650.00
Canister, pressed fiber-brd, red pnt w/floral band, yel tulips, 5", VG ...245.00
Carrier, basket; stained slats, holds 6 pt boxes.............................45.00
Cheese mold, pierced tin, wire hdl, 19th C, 3½x4" dia..............165.00
Cheese mold, pierced tin heart, strap hdl, 2½x5x4½", EX 225.00
Chestnut roaster, rtcl brass lid, brass/tin pan, wrought hdl, 22" ..100.00
Chestnut roaster, tin w/pierced lid, brass knob, trn hdl w/red stain 165.00
Churn, oak w/iron bands, orig bl pnt, w/lid+dasher, 28", EX, $385 to..650.00
Churn, staved, 3 finger-lapped hoops, old bl pnt, 1800s, 34", w/dasher.2,000.00
Churn, staved pine w/rpl copper bands, lollipop hdl, tapered, rfn, 50".165.00
Churn, trn from single wood pc, wrought-iron band, w/dasher, 11x4¾".415.00
Door mat, steel woven w/rows of hearts, lt pitting, 25x15" 350.00
Door mat, steel woven w/rows of hearts, lt rust, 18x29½"...........400.00
Dough box, pine/poplar w/thin red wash, scalloped aprons, 38x18" top...330.00
Firkin, staved, red w/blk lapped bands, wht lettered name, 16x13", VG.350.00
Firkin, staved, 4 wooden bands, red pnt, iron bail, 7x9"..............265.00
Foot warmer, mortised wooden fr w/punched tin panels, 1840s, 6", EX+.350.00
Foot warmer, punched tin, mortised wood fr, rfn, bail hdl, 9" L..300.00
Glove stretcher, bone, rpl attachment pin, 6⅝" 55.00
Jar, Peaseware, bulbous, shaped finial, incised rings, ftd, 6x3½" .325.00
Jar, Peaseware, EX color, bail hdl, crack/rpr, 7½x7¼" 600.00
Jar, Peaseware, str sides w/stepped lid, urn finial, varnished, 4"...220.00
Jar, Peaseware, tooled lines on body & lid, chip/int age cracks, 6x3"..135.00
Jar, Peaseware, trn lid/body, EX patina, age crack, 7x6½" 660.00
Keg, staved, 6 finger-lapped hoops, leather strap, 1800s, 8¾x5½"..485.00
Kettle stand, pierced brass top/wrought-iron base, penny ft, 13x13x14"..275.00
Knitter's 3rd arm, curly maple whimsical fish w/inlaid eyes/tusks, 10"..875.00
Kraut cutter, hickory, well-shaped crest w/heart cut-out, 24x8" ..275.00
Pump, wood w/dk gr & red pnt, stenciled: Geo W Hackett...PA, 77" ..525.00
Rack, drying; 3 37x22½" sections, natural finish, Zoar, OH 300.00
Rack, herb drying; orig dk gr pnt, pegged mortise & tenons, 32x40"..220.00
Rack, quilt; pine, sm shoe ft, 3 X pcs mortised to post, rfn, 41x49".....250.00
Smoothing board, chip-cvd dmns/pinwheels/etc, EID 1928, dvtl hdl.660.00
Smoothing brd, cvgs: 8 hex signs/hearts, dtd 178?, bug damage, 28"...440.00
Spoon rack, pine w/old blk, scalloped ends, holds 15, early, 13x13x5"..415.00
Tinder lighter, pistol shape, flintlock striker, mahog/brass, 5" ..1,400.00
Tinderbox, tin, finger loop/candle socket, int damper/striker, 4½"...580.00
Tub, dk gr, yel int, chip-cvd edge, hdls w/heart cutouts, split, 3x4"..1,375.00
Tub, staved, worn red surface, sgn L Fisk on 1 hdl, 22x26" 1,000.00

Prints

The term 'print' may be defined today as almost any image printed on paper by any available method. Examples of collectible old 'prints' are Norman Rockwell magazine covers and Maxfield Parrish posters and calendars. 'Original print' refers to one achieved through the efforts of the artist or under his direct supervision. A 'reproduction' is a print produced by an accomplished print maker who reproduces another artist's print or original work. Thorough study is required on the part of the collector to recognize and appreciate the many variable factors to be considered in evaluating a print. Prices vary from one area of the country to another and are dependent upon new findings regarding the scarcity or abundance of prints as such information may arise. Although each collector of old prints may have their own varying criteria by which to judge condition,

for those who deal only rarely in this area or newer collectors, a few guidelines may prove helpful. Staining, though unquestionably detrimental, is nearly always present in some degree and should be weighed against the rarity of the print. Professional cleaning should improve its appearance and at the same time help preserve it. Avoid tears that affect the image; minor margin tears are another matter, especially if the print is a rare one. Moderate 'foxing' (brown spots caused by mold or the fermentation of the rag content of old paper) and light stains from the old frames are not serious unless present in excess. Margin trimming was a common practice; but look for at least ½" to 1½" margins, depending on print size.

When no condition is indicated, the items listed below are assumed to be in very good to excellent condition. See also Nutting, Wallace; Parrish, Maxfield. See also *Collector's Value Guide to Early 20th Century American Prints* by Michael Irankovich.

Audubon, John J.

Audubon is the best known of American and European wildlife artists. His first series of prints, 'Birds of America,' was produced by Robert Havell of London. They were printed on Whitman watermarked paper bearing dates of 1826 to 1838. The Octavo Edition of the same series was printed in seven editions, the first by J.T. Bowen under Audubon's direction. There were seven volumes of text and prints, each 10" x 7", the first five bearing the J.J. Audubon and J.B. Chevalier mark, the last two, J.J. Audubon. They were produced from 1840 through 1844. The second and other editions were printed up to 1871. The Bien Edition prints were full size, made under the direction of Audubon's sons in the late 1850s. Due to the onset of the Civil War, only 105 plates were finished. These are considered to be the most valuable of the reprints of the 'Birds of America Series.'

In 1971 the complete set was reprinted by Johnson Reprint Corp. of New York and Theaturm Orbis Terrarum of Amsterdam. Examples of the latter bear the watermark G. Schut and Zonen. In 1985 a second reprint was done by Abbeville Press for the National Audubon Society.

Although Audubon is best known for his portrayal of birds, one of his less-familiar series, 'Vivaparous Quadrupeds of North America,' portrayed various species of animals. Assembled in corroboration with John Bachman from 1839 until 1851, these prints are 28" x 22" in size. Several octavo editions were published in the 1850s. In the following listing, all measurements are actual print size unless stated otherwise.

Great-Footed Hawk, Plate 12 from Birds of North America, Bien, New York, 1860, elephant folio, EX, $900.00. (Photo courtesy Neal Auction Company)

American Badger, #10/Plate 47, Bowen, sheet: 21⅜x27¼" 1,380.00
Barnacle Goose, Autubon FRSFLS, octavo folio 100.00
Black Skimmer or Shearwater, #10-3/Plate 428, sheet: 25x39" ..1,725.00
Black Tern, #56/Plate 280, Havell, unfr, sheet: 38½x25".........2,415.00

Black-Tailed Deer, #16/Plate 78, Bowen, sheet: 21x27½" **500.00**
Black-Winged Hawk, #4-2/Plate 16, Bien, unmk, sheet: 38x26" ...**375.00**
Caribou or Am Rein Deer, JT Bowen, octavo folio **110.00**
Common Crossbill, #11-4/Plate 200, Bien, sheet: 39x25" **375.00**
Common Gallinule, #49/Plate 244, Havell, unfr, sheet: 25x38".**2,415.00**
Douglass Squirrel, #10/Plate 48, Bowen, sheet: 27½x21¼".........**575.00**
Eider Duck, #6-2/Plate 405, Bien, sheet: 26x39" **2,300.00**
Esquimaux Curlew, #42/Plate 208, Havell, plate: 12½x19⅜" **748.00**
Golden Eagle, JT Bowen, octavo folio..**120.00**
Great Cinereous Shrike or Butcher Bird, #39, Havell, plate: 26x21".**1,000.00**
Great Footed Hawk, #3/Plate 16, Havell, plate: 24x37½" **4,600.00**
Great White Heron, #6-1/Plate 368, Bein, sight: 25½x38" **3,000.00**
King Duck, JT Bowen, octavo folio **100.00**
Mallard drakes & hens, JT Bowen, sm folio **110.00**
Pied Oyster Catcher, #45/Plate 223, Havell, unfr, sheet: 25½x38"..**2,990.00**
Red-Tailed Squirrel, #11/Plate 55, Bowen, sheet: 27½x21½" **460.00**
Tawny Weasel, No #0, XLVII, Bowen, sight: 19x26" **460.00**
Uria Brunnichii, #49/Plate 245, Havell, unfr, sheet: 26x39" ...**1,895.00**
White Am Wolf, JT Bowen, octavo folio....................................**100.00**
Winter Wren, JT Bowen, 14½x11", prof fr & mt **50.00**
Yellow-Billed Cuckoo, #2-3/Plate 275, Bien, sheet: 24⅜x38" **750.00**

Currier and Ives

Nathaniel Currier was in business by himself until the late 1850s when he formed a partnership with James Merrit Ives. Currier is given credit for being the first to use the medium to portray newsworthy subjects, and the Currier and Ives views of nineteenth century American culture are familiar to us all. In the following listings, 'C' numbers correspond with a standard reference book by Conningham. Values are given for prints in very good condition; all are colored unless indicated black and white. Unless noted 'NC' (Nathaniel Currier), all prints are published by Currier and Ives. Our advisors for this category are John and Barbara Rudisill (Rudisill's Alt Print Haus); they are listed in the Directory under Maryland. See their Directory listing for information regarding a new Gallery website.

Four-In-Hand, 1861, C-2091, large folio, $2,200.00.

Admiral Porter's Fleet...Vicksburg April 16 1863, 1863, C-51, sm folio..**375.00**
American Clipper Ship, Witch of Wave; NC, undated, C-115, sm folio.**1,500.00**
American Country Life - May Morning, NC, 1855, C-121, lg folio.**2,500.00**
American Country Life - October Afternoon, NC, 1855, C-122, lg folio.**2,500.00**
American Country Life - Pleasures of Winter, NC, 1855, C-123, lg folio .**2,600.00**
American Country Life - Summers Evening, C-124, NC, lg folio .**2,400.00**
American Farm Scenes No 1, NC, 1853, C-133, lg folio.........**3,500.00**
American Farm Scenes No 2, NC, 1853, C-135, lg folio.........**3,500.00**
American Farm Scenes No 3, NC, 1853, C-134, lg folio.........**3,500.00**
American Fruit Piece, 1859, C-161, lg folio **2,200.00**
American Homestead - Autumn, 1869, C-168, sm folio **650.00**
American Homestead - Summer, 1868, C-171, sm folio **450.00**

American Winter Scenes, Morning; NC, 1854, C-208, lg folio ..**7,000.00**
American Winter Sports, Deer Shooting...; NC, 1855, C-209, lg folio.**7,500.00**
American Winter Sports, Trout Fishing...; NC, 1856, C-210, lg folio ...**7,600.00**
Arguing the Point, NC, 1855, C-265, lg folio **5,000.00**
Autumn in New England: Cider Making; 1866, C-322, lg folio..**1,400.00**
Boatswain, NC, undtd, C-580, sm folio..**275.00**
Bombardment of Fort Sumter - Charleston Harbor, undtd, C-597, sm folio.**350.00**
Bound Down the River, 1870, C-627, sm folio.........................**1,800.00**
Brook Trout Fishing, An Anxious Moment; 1862, C-703, lg folio ..**7,500.00**
Camping Out, Some of the Right Sort; NC, 1856, C-777, lg folio..**4,000.00**
Cares of a Family, NC, 1856, C-814, lg folio **4,000.00**
Celebrated Horse Dexter..., 1865, C-883, lg folio **1,850.00**
Celebrated Horse George M Panchen..., 1860, C-885, lg folio .**1,850.00**
Celebrated Mare Flora Temple..., 1860, C-892, lg folio **1,850.00**
Central Park, The Drive; 1862, C-951, med folio **2,200.00**
Champion Trotting Stallion Smuggler..., 1875, C-983, lg folio.**1,850.00**
City of New Orleans, undtd, C-1100, sm folio..........................**900.00**
Clipper Ship Dreadnought, NC, 1854, C-1143, lg folio..........**3,300.00**
Clipper Ship Dreadnought Off Tuskar..., NC, 1856, C-1144, lg folio ..**3,000.00**
Clipper Ship Great Republic, NC, 1853, C-1146, lg folio **3,000.00**
Clipper Ship Sovereign of the Seas, NC, 1852, C-1167, lg folio ..**5,600.00**
Crack Shots - In Position, 1875, C-1280, sm folio **200.00**
Deer Shooting in the Northern Woods, undtd, C-1539, sm folio..**700.00**
Eventide - October, Village Inn; 1867, C-1780, lg folio............**3,000.00**
Express Train, 1870, C-1792, sm folio......................................**2,200.00**
Farmer's Home - Autumn, 1864, C-1889, lg folio **2,600.00**
Farmer's Home - Harvest, 1864, C-1890, lg folio **2,500.00**
Farmyard in Winter, 1861, C-1881, lg folio **6,000.00**
Flora Temple & Lancet, NC, 1856, C-2018, lg folio................**1,900.00**
Flora Temple & Princess..., 1859, C-2019, lg folio.................**1,900.00**
Fording the River, NC, undtd, C-2081, med folio......................**600.00**
Four Seasons of Life: Middle Age, 1868, C-2097, lg folio **1,500.00**
Frozen Up, 1872, C-2155, sm folio...**2,200.00**
Garden Orchard & Vine, 1867, C-2221, lg folio **950.00**
Gem of the Atlantic, NC, 1849, C-2228, sm folio **750.00**
General Grant & Family, 1876, C-2273, sm folio........................**125.00**
Great West, 1870, C-2658, sm folio...**1,400.00**
Hero & Flora Temple, NC, 1856, C-2800, lg folio...................**2,000.00**
High Bridge at Harlem NY, 1845, C-2810, NC, sm folio **500.00**
Home in the Wilderness, 1870, C-2861, sm folio **650.00**
Home of Evangeline, 1864, C-2863, lg folio.............................**1,000.00**
Home of Washington, undtd, C-2874, med folio **400.00**
Home on the Mississippi, 1871, C-2876, sm folio......................**700.00**
Home to Thanksgiving, 1867, C-2882, lg folio **16,000.00**
Hunter's Shanty, In the Adirondacks; 1861, C-2993, lg folio ..**2,400.00**
Husking, 1861, C-3008, lg folio **12,000.00**
In Northern Wilds - Trapping Beaver, undtd, C-3073, sm folio..**550.00**
Ingleside Winter, undtd, C-3112, sm folio **700.00**
Lady Suffolk, NC, 1850, C-3387, med folio..............................**1,300.00**
Lady Suffolk & Lady Moscow, NC, 1850, C-3390, lg folio **1,800.00**
Lake Winnipiseogee...NH, undtd, C-3419, lg folio **3,000.00**
Life in the Country, Morning Ride; 1859, C-3512, lg folio.......**3,600.00**
Life of a Fireman...Muscle, 1861, C-3517, lg folio...................**3,000.00**
Life of a Sportsman, Camping in Woods; 1872, C-3523, sm folio .**500.00**
Life of a Sportsman, Going Out; 1872, C-3525, sm folio **500.00**
Maple Sugaring Early Spring in Northern Woods, 1872, C-3975, sm folio.**1,500.00**
Midnight Race on Mississippi, 1860, C-4116, lg folio..............**7,000.00**
Mr Bonner's Horse Joe Elliot..., 1873, C-4250, lg folio...........**1,600.00**
Mt Washington & White Mtns..., 1860, C-4242, lg folio.........**3,000.00**
New England Winter Scene, 1861, C-4420, lg folio.................**8,000.00**
Old Bull Dog on Right Track, 1864, C-4551, sm folio **350.00**
Old Farm House, 1872, C-4557, sm folio.................................**1,250.00**
Old Mill - In Summer, undtd, C-4571, sm folio........................**350.00**
Old Oaken Bucket, 1864, C-4576, lg folio **1,600.00**

Pigeon Shooting Playing the Decoy, 1862, C-4780, lg folio 3,200.00
Preparing for Market, NC, 1856, C-4872, lg folio 3,450.00
Prince & Lantern, NC, 1857, C-4925, lg folio 1,500.00
Rabbit Catching, Trap Sprung; undtd, C-5034, sm folio 700.00
Racquet River 'Adirondacks,' undtd, C-5049, sm folio 350.00
Rising Family, 1857, C-5151, lg folio 5,300.00
River Side, undtd, C-5161, sm folio 225.00
Road, Winter; NC, 1853, C-5171, lg folio.............................53,000.00
Roadside Mill, 1870, C-5175, sm folio 350.00
Rubber, NC, undtd, C-5247, med folio...............................1,200.00
Rysdyk's Hambletonian, 1876, C-5273, lg folio 2,500.00
Scenery of the Cattskills, undtd, C-5419, sm folio 350.00
Sleigh Race, 1859, C-5555, sm folio 3,000.00
Sluice Gate, undtd, C-5564, very sm folio 450.00
Snowy Morning, 1864, C-5582, med folio...........................2,600.00
Speeding on the Avenue, 1870, C-5644, lg folio....................6,000.00
Sperm Whale in a Flurry, NC, 1852, C-5648, sm folio 1,500.00
Spill Out on the Snow, 1870, C-5651, lg folio 4,500.00
Star of the Road, NC, 1849, C-5701, sm folio.........................850.00
State Street Boston Massachusetts, NC, 1849, C-5714, sm folio .500.00
Steamship Spain of the Nat'l Line, undtd, C-5794, sm folio.......350.00
Stopping Place on Road, Horse Shed; 1868, C-5821, lg folio..3,000.00
Summer Fruits, 1861, C-5857, med folio................................450.00
Summer Ramble, undtd, C-5874, med folio............................400.00
Tacony & Mac, NC, 1853, C-5943, lg folio...........................2,000.00
Through to the Pacific, 1870, C-6051, sm folio 1,500.00
Trials of Patience, undtd, C-6146, med folio...........................500.00
Trot for the Gate Money, 1869, C-6161, lg folio 1,500.00
Trotting Cracks at the Forge, 1869, C-6169, lg folio..............8,500.00
Trotting Mare Goldsmith Maid..., 1870, C-6189, lg folio 1,500.00
US Ship of Line Pennsylvania, NC, undtd, C-6334, sm folio.....500.00
Village Blacksmith, undtd, C-6460, med folio 800.00
Whale Fishery Laying On, NC, 1852, C-6626, sm folio 1,500.00
Wild Cat Banker...Secured...Public Stocks, NC, 1853, C-6663, sm folio...1,000.00
Wild Duck Shooting, Good Day's Sport; NC, 1854, C-6670, lg folio ...7,000.00
Wild Duck Shooting, On the Wing; 1870, C-6671, sm folio 600.00
Winter Evening, NC, 1854, C-6734, med folio.......................2,400.00
Winter Morning, 1861, C-6740, med folio 2,400.00
Winter Pastime, NC, 1855, C-6743, med folio........................3,000.00

Erte (Romain de Tirtoff)

Opium, emb silkscreen on wove paper, 1985, sheet: 34¼x26½"...1,060.00
Suitors, emb silkscrene on wove paper, 11½x15¼" 530.00
Twenties Remembered Again, 8 silkscreens, 17½x13", fr, w/portfolio..4,700.00

Fox, R. Atkinson

A Canadian who worked as an artist in the 1880s, R. Atkinson Fox moved to New York about ten years later, where his original oils were widely sold at auction and through exhibitions. Today he is best known, however, for his prints, published by as many as twenty print makers. More than thirty examples of his work appeared on Brown and Bigelow calendars, and it was used in many other forms of advertising as well. Though he was an accomplished artist able to interpret any subject well, he is today best known for his landscapes. Fox died in 1935. Our advisor for Fox prints is Pat Gibson whose address is listed in the Directory under California.

Aces All, #557, 8x10" 285.00
Andrew Jackson, 1923 calendar, #742, 8x5" 80.00
Cottage by the Sea, sgn, #412, 10½x14"..............................155.00
Dawn, #1, 18x10"...165.00
Discovery of the Mississippi, sgn, #395, 12x16", EX 200.00
Garden of Love, fountain, #42, orig fr, 10x12"......................125.00

Grover Cleveland, 1923 calendar, #711, 5x3½" 80.00
Monarch of the North, polar bears, #613, 14½x10" 350.00
Mountain Lake, #301, 8x11"..80.00
On the Meadow, #359, 6½x10"...125.00
Sentry, bear, sgn, #373, 16x12"..170.00
Spirit of Youth, #4, 18x10"..125.00
Tom & Jerry, horses, #583, 9x12"...245.00
Trusty Guardian, dog & lamb, #11, 11x14"..............................190.00

Gutmann, Bessie Pease (1876 – 1960)

Delicately tinted prints of appealing children sometimes accompanied by their pets, sometimes asleep, often captured at some childhood activity are typical of the work of this artist; she painted lovely ladies as well and was a successful illustrator of children's books. Her career spanned the five decades of the 1900s and she recorded over 800 published artworks. Our advisor for this category is Dr. Victor J.W. Christie; he is listed in the Directory under Pennsylvania.

Aeroplane, The; #266/#695, 14x21"...800.00
Always, #774, 14x21" 2,100.00
American Girl, The; #220, 13x18"..500.00
An Anxious Moment, #714, 14x21" 650.00
Annunciation, #705, 14x21" 900.00
Awakening, #664, 14x21"...125.00
Baby's First Christmas, #158 ....500.00
Bedtime Story, The; #712, 14x21" 750.00
Betty, #787, 14x21" 250.00
Blossom Time, #654, 14x21" 800.00
Blue Bird, The; #265/#666, 14x21"...650.00
Butterfly, The; #632, 14x18"...210.00
Call to Arms, A; #806, 14x21"..700.00
Caught Napping, #153, 9x12"...2,000.00
Chip of the Old Block, #728, 14x21".......................................600.00
Chuckles, #799, 11x14"...150.00
Chums, #665, 14x21"..350.00
Contentment, #781 ....90.00
CQD, #149, 9x12" 450.00
Cupid, After All My Trouble, #608, 16x20" 800.00
Cupid's Reflection, #602, 14x21"..800.00
Daddy's Coming, #644, 14x21"..495.00
Divine Fire, #722, 14x21"..550.00
Double Blessing, A; #643, 14x21"...500.00
Feeling, #19, 6x9"...250.00
Friendly Enemies, #215, 11x14"...155.00
Goldilocks, #771, 14x21"...1,100.00
Good Morning, #801, 14x21"...250.00
Guest's Candle, The; #651, 14x21"..500.00
Hearing, #22, 6x9"..250.00
Home Builders, #233/#655, 14x21"...185.00
In Arcady, #701, 14x21"...700.00
In Disgrace, #792, 14x21" 200.00
In Slumberland, #786, 14x21"..120.00
Kitty's Breakfast, #805, 14x21"...350.00
Knit Two - Purl Two, #657, 14x21" 850.00
Little Bit of Heaven, A; #650, 14x21".......................................125.00
Little Bo Peep, #200, 11x14" 150.00
Little Mother, #803, 14x21"..450.00
Lorelei, #645, 14x21"...1,700.00
Love's Harmony, #791, 14x21"...400.00
Madonna, The; #674, 14x21"...2,100.00
May We Come In, #808, 14x21"...385.00
Message of the Roses, The; #641, 14x21"..................................400.00
Mighty Like a Rose, #642, 14x21"...200.00

Mischief Brewing, #152, 9x12" **2,000.00**
Mothering Heart, The; #351, 14x21" **700.00**
My Honey, #756, 14x21" **1,200.00**
New Pet, The; #709, 14x21" **800.00**
Nitey Nite, #826, 14x21" **175.00**
Now I Lay Me, #620, 14x21" **1,800.00**
On Dreamland's Border, #692, 14x21" **155.00**
On the Up & Up, #796, 14x21" **190.00**
Our Alarm Clock, #150, 9x12" **250.00**
Perfect Peace, #809, 14x21" **300.00**
Popularity (Has Its Disadvantages), #825, 14x21" **150.00**
Priceless Necklace, A; #744, 14x21" **1,200.00**
Rosebud, #780, 14x21" **320.00**
Seeing, #122, 11x14" **250.00**
Smile Worth While, A; #180, 9x12" **800.00**
Snowbird, #777, 14x21" **650.00**
Sunkissed, #818, 14x21" **125.00**
Symphony, #702, 14x21" **650.00**
Tabby, #172, 9x12" **600.00**
Taps, #815, 14x21" **550.00**
Television, #821, 14x21" **110.00**
Thank You, God, #822, 14x21" **175.00**
To Love & To Cherish, #615, 14x21" **285.00**
Tom, Tom the Piper's Son, #219, 11x14" **175.00**
Touching, #210, 11x14" **150.00**
Verdict: Love for Life, The; #113, 9x12" **550.00**

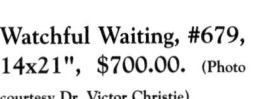
Watchful Waiting, #679, 14x21", $700.00. (Photo courtesy Dr. Victor Christie)

Who's Sleepy, #816, 14x21" **260.00**
Winged Aureole, The; #700, 14x21" **500.00**
Wood Magic, #703, 14x21" **750.00**

Icart, Louis

Louis Icart (1888 – 1950) was a Parisian artist best known for his boudoir etchings in the '20s and '30s. In the '80s prices soared, primarily due to Japanese buying. The market began to readjust in 1990, and most etchings now sell at retail between $1,400.00 and $2,500.00. Value is determined by popularity and condition, more than by rarity. Original frames and matting are not important, as most collectors want the etchings restored to their original condition and protected with acid-free mats.

Beware of the following repro and knock-off items: 1.) Pseudo engravings on white plastic with the Icart 'signature.' 2.) Any bronzes with the Icart signature. 3.) Most watercolors, especially if they look similar in subject matter to a popular etching. 4.) Lithographs where the dot-matrix printing is visible under magnification. Some even have phony embossed seals or rubber stamp markings. Items listed below are in excellent condition unless noted otherwise. Our advisor is William

Holland, author of *Louis Icart: The Complete Etchings*, and *The Collectible Maxfield Parrish*; he is listed in the Directory under Pennsylvania.

Autumn Storm, 9x7" in fr **1,050.00**
Coursing II, 15x25" in fr **3,200.00**
Eve, 1928, 14x19⅜", sheet: 22x27⅞", VG **1,800.00**
Lady of the Camelias, 1927, oval: 17x21", VG **1,600.00**
Martini, 13½x17½" in mat & fr **5,500.00**
Milkmaid, 1928, 20x13¼", sheet: 25⅞x18¾" **1,850.00**
Peonies, 1935, 14x17", VG in fr **1,600.00**
Perfect Harmony, 14x17½" in mat & fr **4,200.00**
Spanish Dance, 1929, 21x14", sheet: 26½x19¼" **885.00**
Symphony in Blue, 1936, 23½x19½", sheet: 29x24¾" ...**1,700.00**
Venus, 1928, 14x19½", sheet: 21⅞x27⅞", VG **1,900.00**
View of Paris, 1948, 5x8" **1,900.00**
Zest, 1928, 20x15", sheet: 25x19⅜" **2,800.00**

Kurz and Allison

Louis Kurz founded the Chicago Lithograph Company in 1833. Among his most notable works were a series of thirty-six Civil War scenes and one hundred illustrations of Chicago architecture. His company was destroyed in the Great Fire of 1871, and in 1880 Kurz formed a partnership with Alexander Allison, an engraver. Until both retired in 1903, they produced hundreds of lithographs in color as well as black and white. Unless noted otherwise, values are for prints in excellent condition.

Assault on Fort Sanders, 21x28" **600.00**
Battle of Champion Hills, 21x28" **550.00**
Battle of Chattanooga, 21x28" **600.00**
Battle of Five Forks VA, 21x28" **600.00**
Battle of Fort Donelson, 21x28" **600.00**
Battle of Stone River, 21x28" **650.00**
Battle of Williamsburg, 21x28", VG **550.00**
Battle of Wilson's Creek, 21x28" **550.00**
Capitulation & Surrender of Robert E Lee & His Army, uncolored, 21x28" .**450.00**
Fall of Petersburg, 21x28" **600.00**
Siege of Vicksburg, 21x28" **600.00**

McKenney and Hall

Chittee Yoholo, Seminole Chief, Greenough, 20x14⅜" **300.00**
J'Tcho-Tustinnuggee, Rice & Clark, sight: 19½x13¼" **345.00**
Kai-Pol-E-Quah, White Nosed Fox, Greenough, 20x14⅜" **300.00**
Pa-She-Nine, Chippewa Chief, Rice & Clark, 1843, 20x13¾", NM ..**800.00**
Wa-Baun-See, Pottawatomie Chief, FW Greenough, sight: 19¼x13¼" .**345.00**

Prang, Louis

Battle of Antietam, lg folio **125.00**
Battle of Shilo, lg folio **150.00**
Siege of Vicksburg, Thulstrup, 15x21½" **425.00**
Ulysses S Grant, 1885, 25x20" **150.00**

Yard Longs

Values for yard-long prints are given for examples in near mint condition, full length, nicely framed, and with the original glass. To learn more about this popular area of collector interest, we recommend *Those Wonderful Yard-Long Prints* and *More, More Wonderful Yard-Long Prints, Book 2*, and *Yard-Long Prints, Book 3*, by our advisors Bill and June Keagy, and Charles and Joan Rhoden. They are listed in the Directory under Indiana and Illinois respectively. A word of caution: Watch for reproductions; know your dealer.

American Beauty Roses, by Paul DeLongpre, c 1896 .... **300.00**
American Girl, Pabst, 1914 .... **400.00**
Battle of the Chicks, sgn Ben Austrian, c 1920 .... **300.00**
Beauty Among the Roses, Bowles Live Stock Commission, c 1912. **425.00**
Bride, sgn Rolf Armstrong, Pompeian, 1927 .... **400.00**
Butterick Pattern Lady, c 1930.......................... **500.00**
Carnation Symphone **250.00**
Cats & Kittens on a See-saw, Art Interchange Co, c 1893 .... **300.00**
Down on the Congo, c 1904, 2nd in series of 4 .... **450.00**
Girl w/the Laughing Eyes, by F Carlyle, Osborne Co NY, c 1910... **400.00**
Hula Girl on surfboard, sgn Gene Pressler **450.00**
In Grandmother's Garden, by Charles C Curran, c 1909 .... **375.00**
Lady in bl w/walking stick, Selz Good Shoes, 1925 .... **590.00**
Liberty Girl, by Forbes, Pompeian, 1919 .... **350.00**
Mother & Child, in swing, Selz Good Shoes, c 1915 .... **400.00**
Pabst Extract, different baby for ea month, 1904 .... **400.00**
Piggies in Clover, minimum value **600.00**
Priscilla, Schlitz Malt Extract, 1910 .... **500.00**
Stockman Bride, National Stockman & Farmer Magazine, 1912 .. **450.00**
Swallows over Lily Pads, by J Hoover & Sons, c 1897.................. **350.00**
Yard of Kittens, sgn Guy Bedford.......................... **350.00**

Purinton

With its bold colors and unusual shapes, Purinton Pottery is much admired by today's dinnerware collectors. In 1939 Bernard Purinton purchased the East Liverpool Pottery in Wellsville, Ohio, and re-named it the Purinton Pottery Company. One of its earliest lines was Peasant Ware, featuring simple shapes and bold, colorful patterns. It was designed by William H. Blair, who also designed what have become the company's most recognized lines, Apple and Intaglio. The company was extremely successful, and by 1941 it became necessary to build a new plant, which they located in Shippenville, Pennsylvania. Blair left Purinton to open his own pottery (Blair Ceramics), leaving his sister Dorothy Purinton (Bernard's wife) to assume the role of designer. Though never a paid employee, Dorothy painted many one-of-a-kind special-occasion items that are highly sought after by today's collectors who are willing to pay premium prices to get them. These usually carry Dorothy's signature.

Apple was Purinton's signature pattern; it was produced throughout the entire life of the pottery. Another top-selling pattern designed by Dorothy Purinton was Pennsylvania Dutch, featuring hearts and tulips. Other long-term patterns include the Plaids and the Intaglios. While several other patterns were developed, they were short-lived. One of the most elusive patterns, Palm Tree, was sold only through a souvenir store in Florida owned by one of the Purinton's sons.

In addition to dinnerware, Purinton also produced a line of floral ware, including planters for NAPCO. They did contract work for Esmond Industries and RUBEL, who were both distributors in New York. They made the Howdy Doody cookie jar and bank for Taylor Smith & Taylor; both items are highly collectible.

The pottery was sold to Taylor Smith & Taylor in 1958 and closed in 1959 due to heavy competition from foreign imports.

Most items are not marked, but collectors find their unusual shapes easy to identify. A small number of items were ink stamped 'Purinton Slip-ware.' Some of the early Wellsville pieces were hand signed 'Purinton Pottery,' and several have emerged carrying the signature 'Wm. H. Blair' or simply 'Blair.' Blair's pieces command a premium price.

Our advisor for this category is Joe McManus; he is listed in the Directory under Pennsylvania. Mr. McManus is also the editor of *Purinton News and Views*, see Clubs, Newsletters, and Catalogs for information.

Apple, beer mug.......................... **55.00**
Apple, bowl, fruit; scalloped border, 12"......................... **45.00**

Apple, butter dish, 6½".......................... **150.00**
Apple, canister, apartment sz, 5½", ea.......................... **50.00**
Apple, canister, short, oval, 5", ea **55.00**
Apple, canister, tall, oval, 9", ea.......................... **50.00**
Apple, chop plate, rnd, 12".......................... **30.00**
Apple, coffeepot, 8-cup **75.00**
Apple, creamer & sugar bowl, open, mini **30.00**
Apple, creamer & sugar bowl, w/lid **25.00**
Apple, cruets, Oil & Vinegar, sq, 5", pr.......................... **50.00**
Apple, cup & saucer **15.00**
Apple, jug, Dutch; 2-pt, 5¾".......................... **35.00**
Apple, jug, Dutch; 5-pt, 8".......................... **65.00**
Apple, marmalade.......................... **40.00**
Apple, pitcher, beverage.......................... **40.00**
Apple, plate, breakfast; 8½".......................... **20.00**
Apple, plate, dinner; 9½".......................... **18.00**
Apple, plate, salad; 6¾".......................... **15.00**
Apple, platter, 11".......................... **15.00**
Apple, relish, 3 rnd sections.......................... **25.00**
Apple, shakers, mini jug, pr.......................... **15.00**
Apple, shakers, Pour & Shake, pr.......................... **50.00**
Apple, teapot, domed, 6-cup.......................... **45.00**
Apple, wall pocket.......................... **65.00**
Brown Intaglio, butter dish, 6½".......................... **35.00**
Brown Intaglio, chop plate, 12".......................... **20.00**
Brown Intaglio, creamer & sugar bowl, w/lid.......................... **20.00**
Brown Intaglio, cruets, Oil & Vinegar, sq, 5", pr.......................... **25.00**
Brown Intaglio, platter, 12".......................... **20.00**
Brown Intaglio, shakers, mini mug, pr.......................... **12.00**
Cactus, plate, breakfast; desert scene, 8½".......................... **95.00**
Cactus, shakers, rnd, 2¾", pr.......................... **200.00**
Cactus Flower, teapot, 2-cup.......................... **125.00**
Chartreuse, canister, tall, oval, ea.......................... **60.00**
Chartreuse, lap plate & cup.......................... **35.00**
Crescent, jug, Dutch; 2-pt.......................... **50.00**
Crescent, jug, Oasis; rare, minimum value.......................... **750.00**
Crescent, teapot, 2-cup.......................... **50.00**
Dorothy Purinton sgn Blessing plate, 12", minimum value.......... **650.00**
Fruit, coffeepot, 8-cup.......................... **25.00**
Fruit, Dorothy Purinton sgn Fruit plate, 12", minimum value.....**650.00**
Fruit, jug, Dutch; 2-pt.......................... **15.00**
Fruit, jug, Dutch; 5-pt.......................... **25.00**
Fruit, jug, Oasis; rare, minimum value.......................... **750.00**
Fruit, shakers, mini jug, pr.......................... **10.00**
Heather Plaid, beer mug.......................... **40.00**
Heather Plaid, chop plate, 12".......................... **35.00**
Heather Plaid, creamer & sugar bowl, w/lid.......................... **25.00**
Howdy Doody bust bank.......................... **500.00**
Howdy Doody cookie jar.......................... **350.00**
Ivy (red), coffeepot, 8-cup.......................... **25.00**
Ivy (red), honey jug, 6¼".......................... **15.00**
Ivy (yel), honey jug, 6¼".......................... **18.00**
Ivy (yel), jug, Dutch; 2-pt.......................... **20.00**
Maywood, bowl, vegetable; w/lid.......................... **35.00**
Maywood, plate, dinner; 9½".......................... **30.00**
Maywood, shakers, mini jug, pr.......................... **35.00**
Maywood, teapot, 6-cup, 6".......................... **45.00**
Ming Tree, plate, salad; 6¾".......................... **25.00**
Ming Tree, sprinkler can, 7".......................... **50.00**
Mountain Rose, cookie jar, oval, 9".......................... **125.00**
Mountain Rose, plate, dinner; 9½".......................... **40.00**
Mountain Rose, teapot, 2-cup.......................... **15.00**
Normandy Plaid, canister, apartment sz, 5½".......................... **45.00**
Normandy Plaid, jug, Dutch; 5-pt.......................... **45.00**

Normandy Plaid, jug, Kent..25.00
Normandy Plaid, pitcher, beverage; 6¼" 45.00
Palm Tree, beer mug..150.00
Palm Tree, honey jug, 6¼"..75.00
Palm Tree, plate, dinner; 9½"...175.00
Palm Tree, shakers, Pour & Shake, pr.................................75.00
Peasant Garden, plate, dinner; 9½"....................................60.00
Peasant Garden, shakers, mini jug, pr.................................95.00
Peasant Lady candle holder, sgn Wm H Blair 500.00
Pennsylvania Dutch, chop plate, 12"................................125.00
Pennsylvania Dutch, cup & saucer.....................................20.00
Pennsylvania Dutch, honey jug, 6¼"...................................75.00
Pennsylvania Dutch, plate, salad; 6¼"................................18.00
Pennsylvania Dutch, shakers, mini jug, pr..........................60.00
Pennsylvania Dutch, shakers, Pour & Shake, pr 75.00
Pennsylvania Dutch, star candle holder 100.00
Petals, honey jug, 6¼"...15.00
Petals, jug, Dutch; 5-pt..50.00
Provincial Fruit, plate, dinner; 9½".....................................35.00
Provincial Fruit, tumbler, 12-oz...30.00
Saraband, beer mug 45.00
Saraband, platter, 12"...20.00
Tea Rose, creamer & sugar bowl, w/lid 95.00
Tea Rose, plate, dinner; 9½"...75.00
Turquoise Intaglio, plate, dinner; 9½".................................20.00
Turquoise Intaglio, platter, 12"...45.00
Turquoise Intaglio, shakers, mini jug, pr.............................40.00

Purses

Purses from the early 1800s are often decorated with small, brightly colored glass beads. Cut steel beads were popular in the 1840s and remained stylish until about 1930. Purses made of woven mesh date back to the 1820s. Chain-link mesh came into usage in the 1890s, followed by the enamel mesh bags carried by the flappers in the 1920s. Purses are divided into several categories by (a) construction techniques — whether beaded, embroidered, or a type of needlework; (b) material — fabric or metal; and (c) design and style. Condition is very important. Watch for dry, brittle leather or fragile material. For those interested in learning more, we recommend *Antique Purses, Second Edition*, by Richard Holiner; *More Beautiful Purses* and *Combs and Purses*, both by Evelyn Haertigi of Carmel, California; and *Ladies Vintage Accessories* by LaRee Johnson Bruton. An interesting related book is *Vintage Contemporary Purse Accessories* by Roselyn Gerson. Our advisor for this category is Veronica Trainer; she is listed in the Directory under Ohio.

Key: W&D — Whiting & Davis

Beaded, gold Bead-lite style, W&D fr, 3¼x2½"............................45.00
Beaded, long loops cover body, beaded hdl, no fr, 5¾x4¾"............75.00
Beaded, mc archway & garden scene, gold-tone fr, 6x6¼" 95.00
Beaded, mc cornucopia on gold, gold-tone str-top fr, 9½x6¾" ...110.00
Beaded, mc geometric pattern, loopy fringe, drawstring, 11½x7".150.00
Beaded, mc mixed flowers, 2-color loop fringe, enameled fr, 11x8".250.00
Beaded, Nouveau flowers on blk, loop fringe, simple fr, Fr, 10¼x7".190.00
Beaded, Nouveau roses on blk, drawstring top, tassle, 10¾x5¾"..85.00
Beaded, peacock & flowers on blk, blk fringe, gold-tone fr, 10x7".115.00
Blk silk, ornate 800 silver fr, Germany, 9¼x9½" 225.00
Blk silk, ornate 800 silver fr & ornate chain, 7½x7½"................300.00
Lucite, blk, clear-cut flower on lid, angle sides, Patricia of Miami.300.00
Lucite, blk w/gold 'confetti,' 3-lobe Deco top, Bags by Benne, lg.365.00
Lucite, cear top, amber body, 4 ball ft, 9 (w/hdl) x7½x3½".........165.00
Lucite, cutch, clear w/rhinestones & cvg 1 side, 5¼x1x8" 30.00

Lucite, gray w/gold confetti, clear hdl, 4 sm ft, clear hdl, 8½" L.215.00
Lucite, lt marbled lime, clear X-cut top/hdl, rectangular, Patricia..340.00
Lucite, tortoise w/lg brass initial plaque on front, Llewellyn, 8½" .265.00
Lucite, wht marbled, flat book shape w/hinge at bk, Wilardy, 9½" L.200.00
Mesh, abstract floral, scalloped fringe, gold W&D fr, chain hdl, 9x5".80.00
Mesh, abstract red/blk/gold-tone floral, metal fr, Germany, 6x4" ..75.00
Mesh, birds on branch, V scallops at bottom, Mandalian fr, 8x5" .190.00
Mesh, blk/gold-tone dmns, enameled German fr, 5¼x5½" 95.00
Mesh, blk/gold-tone floral, fringed V-shape bottom, Mandalian fr, 7x3"..80.00
Mesh, floral Bead-lite style, gold-tone W&D fr, 6¾x3¾" 95.00
Mesh, floral urn, fringed V-shaped bottom, Mandalian fr, 10½x4½" ..225.00
Mesh, geometric 4-color pattern, W&D fr, chain hdl, 12x9¼"...410.00
Mesh, gold, fringe, gold-tone fr w/faux jewel, Germany, 4x5¼" 50.00
Mesh, gold-tone, blk enamel on W&D fr, 5¾x5" 70.00
Mesh, gold-tone Bead-lite style, drawstring top, W&D, 5x3½" 55.00

Mesh, Mandalian, 7¾x4¼", $125.00.
(Photo courtesy of Richard Holiner)

Mesh, mc abstract design, triangular fringe, W&D fr, 6½x5" 110.00
Mesh, mc floral, gold fringe at V bottom, gold Mandalian fr, 7x4"..70.00
Mesh, mc floral, V scallops at bottom, W&D fr, 7½x5"...............100.00
Mesh, mc geometric, fringed V-shaped bottom, Mandalian fr, 9x4½".190.00
Mesh, mc geometric w/scalloped bottom, gold-tone W&D fr, 5¼x3¼".70.00
Mesh, silver/blk diagonal pattern, W&D fr, chain hdl, 12x7".....375.00
Mesh, sterling, dangles at bottom, ornate W&D fr, 6¼x3¾".....375.00
Tapestry, flowers & birds, sterling fr, 7¼x7".................................125.00
Tapestry, lovers scene, jeweled gold-tone fr, 8¼x7¼".................340.00
Tapestry, scenic reserve among flowers, jeweled fr, Austria, 7x7½".265.00
Tooled leather, fold-over clutch, Meeker, 5¼x9¼" 75.00
Tooled leather, metal fr, strap hdl, Jemco, 7½x9".......................125.00
Tooled leather, snap closure, leather hdl, F Kranz, Jemco, 8x6¾" .145.00
Tooled leather, snap closure, strap hdl, Meeker, 7x6½" 75.00
Wood, daisy w/lg amber jewel center on bl box, E Collins, EX...175.00
Wood, lg recumbent cat w/jewel collar on box, Glamor Puss, E Collins.300.00
Wood, Spring Bokay, jeweled flowers on tall box, E Collins, EX .135.00

Puzzles

'Jigsaw' puzzles have been around almost as long as games. The first examples were handcrafted from wood, and they are extremely difficult to find. Most of the early examples featured moral subjects just as the board games did. By the 1890s jigsaw puzzles had become a major form of home entertainment. During the Depression years jigsaw puzzles were set up on card tables in almost every home. The early wood examples are the most valuable.

Cube puzzles, or blocks, were often made by the same companies as the board games. Again, early examples display the finest quality lithography. While all subjects are collectible, some (such as Santa blocks) often command prices higher than games from the same period. In the miscellaneous subcategory below, all listing are for jigsaw puzzles (that are complete) unless noted otherwise.

Personalities, Movies, and TV Shows

Banana Splits, fr-tray, Whitman, 1969, set of 4, MIB 50.00
Bionic Woman, fr-tray, APC, 1976, complete, MIP, from $35 to..45.00
Bullwinkle, jigsaw, Whitman, complete, 1960s, EX (EX box).......25.00
Captain America, fr-tray, 1966, complete, EX........................25.00
Chatty Baby, fr-tray, Whitman, 1960s, MIP 30.00
Chipmunks, fr-tray, Whitman, 1964, complete, EX 25.00
Creatures of the Outer Limits, Milton Bradley, 1964, complete, EXIB.240.00
Dark Shadows, jigsaw, Barnabas in Graveyard, MIB.................75.00
Davy Crockett, fr-tray, Jaymar, 1950s, 11x14", complete, EX........75.00
Donald Duck, jigsaw, Whitman, 1965, 100 pcs, 8½x11", M (sealed box)..40.00
Donnie & Marie, jigsaw, Whitman, 1976, complete, MIB 35.00
Dr Strange, jigsaw, Third Eye, 1971, 500 pcs, MIB.....................100.00
Fantastic Four, jigsaw, Third Eye, 1971, 5 pcs, MIB....................100.00
Fantasy Island, jigsaw, HG Toys, 1977, complete, MIB................20.00
Fat Albert, jigsaw, Whitman, 1975, 100 pcs, EX (EX box)...........20.00
Flash Gordon, fr-tray, Milton Bradley, 1951, set of 3, VGIB 65.00
Flipper, jigsaw, Whitman, 1965, 100 pcs, MIB.........................25.00
Fonz, jigsaw, HG Toys, 1976, complete, EX (EX canister).............25.00
Grizzly Adams, jigsaw, House of Games, 1978, 100 pcs, MIB........15.00
Gulliver's Travels Picture Puzzles Set, jigsaw, Saalfield, 1939, EXIB.100.00
Gunsmoke, jigsaw, Whitman, 1950s, 63 pcs, NMIB 30.00

**Howdy Doody, set of three
different, Kagran, 1950s,
each 9x12", EXIB, $75.00.**

(Photo courtesy June Moon)

Howdy Goes West, fr-tray, Whitman, 1953, complete, EX............40.00
James Bond 007/Goldfinger, jigsaw, Milton Bradley, 1965, NMIB...60.00
Josie & the Pussycats, HG Toys, 1976, complete, MIB..................30.00
KISS, jigsaw, Casse-Tete, 1977, NMIB 25.00
Kristy McNichol, jigsaw, 1979, complete, MIB 20.00
Lassie, fr-tray, Whitman, 1966, complete, NM........................20.00
Love Boat, jigsaw, HG Toys, 1978, 15 pcs, MIB.......................20.00
Marvel Super Heroes, jigsaw, Milton Bradley, 1966, 100 pcs, MIB.125.00
Mary Poppins, jigsaw, Jaymar, 1964, complete, MIB...................40.00
Mork & Mindy, jigsaw, Milton Bradley, 1978, 250 pcs, MIB.........15.00
Munsters, jigsaw, Whitman, 1965, 100 pcs, EX (EX box).............35.00
Patty Duke, jigsaw, Whitman Jr, 1963, 100 pcs, MIB, from $35 to..45.00
Pinocchio, jigsaw, Jaymar, 300 pcs, complete, 14x22", VG (G box).38.00
Pokey Little Puppy, fr-tray, 1972, complete, 14x11", EX...............10.00
Road Runner, fr-tray, 1966, complete, NM 20.00
Rolling Stones Schmuzzle Puzzle, jigsaw, Musidor, 1983, NIB (sealed).70.00
Simpsons, jigsaw, Milton Bradley, 100 pcs, MIB (sealed) 16.00
Six Million Dollar Man, fr-tray, APC, 1976, complete, MIP...........35.00
Skippy, jigsaw, Consolidated Paper, 1933, set of 3, M (EX box) .125.00
Snow White, jigsaw, Whitman, 1938, complete (VG box) 125.00
Spider-man, fr-tray, Playskil, 1981, EX 18.00
Street Hawk, jigsaw, Salters, 1984, 150 pcs, complete, EXIB 35.00
Super Six, jigsaw, Whitman, 1969, complete, NMIB...................35.00
Tammy & Pepper, jigsaw, Ideal, 100 pcs, VG (VG box)................25.00
Tarzan, jigsaw, Whitman, 1968, complete, EX (EX box) 25.00
Tiny Chatty Twins, fr-tray, Whitman, 1960s, MIP....................30.00

Underdog, fr-tray, Whitman #4522, 1965, MIB (sealed) 23.00
Underdog, jigsaw, Whitman, 1975, 100 pcs, MIB......................25.00
Village People, jigsaw, APC, 1978, complete, MIB.....................85.00
Welcome Back Kotter, fr-tray, Whitman, 1977, MIP...................12.50
Zorro, fr-tray, Whitman, 1965, complete, 14x11", NM.................25.00

Miscellaneous

Ann Hathaway's Cottage, 1930s, plywood, 566 pcs, MIB..............75.00
Autumn, plywood, Parker Bros, 1909, 150 pcs, EX (EX box)........50.00
Bearing the Brunt, plywood, FAO Schwarz, 750 pcs, EX (EX box) .125.00
Bombs Away, Perfect Picture Puzzle, 375 pcs, NMIB....................40.00
Boy Eating Apples (Untitled), 1930s, plywood, 135 pcs, EX (orig box).25.00
Bundle of Joy, plywood, 380 pcs, 1930s, EX (rpl box)...................75.00
City of Worcester Picture Puzzle, McLaughlin Bros, 1889, EX (EX box)..950.00
Eiffel Tower, 1930s, plywood, 300 fantasy-knob pcs, EX (rpl box) .65.00
Fighters for Freedom, Whitman, 250 pcs, EX (EX box)...............35.00
Fire Engine Picture Puzzle, McLaughlin Bros, 1887, EX (EX wooden box).70.00
Grand Canyon, plywood, Venice, 255 pcs, 1930s, EX (EX box) ...50.00
Last Ray, plywood, 317 pcs, 1930s, G (G box).........................30.00
May Day, solid, 564 push-to-fit pcs, early 1900s, EX (EX box) ...100.00
Nature's Splender, plywood, Galles, 300 pcs, 1930s, EX (EX box) .75.00
Peaceful Retreat, plywood, 500 pcs, 1930-40, EX (EX box)........140.00
Progress for Democracy, Perfect Picture Puzzle, 375 pcs, NMIB....45.00
Tranquility, plywood, Perx Puzzle, 142 pcs, 1930s, EX (EX box)...25.00
Trouble Bruin, plywood, J Straus, 750 pcs, 1940-50, EX (EX box) .125.00
Wild West Picture Puzzle, McLaughlin Bros, 1890, complete, EX (G box)...400.00
Wings in the Night, All American by Dell, 1942, 280 pcs, EX (EX box) ..40.00

Pyrography

Pyrography, also known as wood burning, Flemish art, or poker work, is the art of burning designs into wood or leather and has been practiced over the centuries in many countries.

In the late 1800s pyrography became the hot new hobby for thousands of Americans who burned designs inspired by the popular artists of the day including Mucha, Gibson, Fisher, and Corbett. Thousands of wooden boxes, wall plaques, novelties, and pieces of furniture that they purchased from local general stores or from mail-order catalogs were burned and painted. These pieces were manufactured by companies such as The Flemish Art Company of New York and Thayer & Chandler of Chicago, who printed the designs on wood for the pyrographers to burn.

This Victorian fad developed into a new form of artistic expression as the individually burned and painted pieces reflected the personality of the pyrographers. The more adventurous started to burn between the lines and developed a style of 'allover burning' that today is known as pyromania. Others not only created their own designs but even made the pieces to be decorated. Both these developments are particularly valued today as true examples of American folk art.

By the 1930s its popularity had declined. Like Mission furniture, it was neglected by generations of collectors and dealers. The recent appreciation of Victoriana, the Arts and Crafts Movement, the American West, and the popularity of turn-of-the-century graphic art has rekindled interest in pyrography which embraces all these styles.

An informative book, *The Burning Passion — Antique and Collectible Pyrography*, by Carole and Richard Smyth, our advisors for this category, is currently available from the authors; they are listed in the Directory under New York.

Key: hb — hand burned

Bedroom set, hb/pnt, Wm Rogers/Forusville PA, 1905-07, 3-pc..**4,000.00**
Book rack, hb/pnt girl w/book, 5¾" W, extends to 15¾" L.........150.00
Box, flatware; factory burned/pnt poinsettias, Rogers, 9x11x5"...**195.00**

Box, floral decor, stamped design, 14½" sq.....................................40.00
Box, lady w/flowing hair, Flemish Art Co, 1909, 11¼x4¼"........120.00
Box, Miller Bros Steel Pens, 1900, stamped to look hb, 7" L, +contents...45.00
Catalog, Thayer-Chandler, Chicago, 1904, 92 pgs, 12 in full color .27.00
Chair-table, hb/pnt poinsettias, Rest-Ye... on chair bk, EX.........950.00
Checker/backgammon brd, red & gr decor/glass bead insets, 30x15".1,550.00
Chest, blanket; hb/pnt swans/lady's head/flowers/etc, ca 1890 ....850.00
Chest, medicine; hb/pnt Nouveau lady & vines, wall mt............450.00
Coat hanger, hb/pnt poppies & leaves, Mother Dearest................80.00
Cue holder, hb pool-hall scene, folk art, unique...........................650.00
Egg cup, hb/pnt, pr...60.00
Etching set, Snow White, Disney/Marks, 1938, electric pen, complete.175.00
Footstool, hb/pnt allover w/owl/branches/leaves...........................125.00
Frame, hb/pnt cherries, standing type, 7½x6", EX.......................85.00
Frame, hb/pnt chrysanthemums, Thayer-Chandler, 10½x8", EX ..85.00
Frame, hb/pnt flower garland, Thayer-Chandler, 8" dia.................85.00
Frame, owls in tree, 2 Is Company, 2 oval cutouts.......................145.00
Gameboard, hb/pnt ea side/edges, Flemish Art, 15" sq (open)....200.00
Humdior, trees & landscape on lid, gold & bl pnt on pine, 3x9x6".295.00
Knife rack, hb Lizzie Borden w/axe, 5 hooks below, rare.............550.00
Magazine stand, 4-shelf, burned/pnt florals, Thayer-Chandler, 48"..800.00
Mirror, hand; hb/pnt lady's head w/flowing hair, 13¼x6¾"........180.00
Nut bowl, hb/pnt squirrel on branch, Flemish Art Co #816, 5"....65.00
Panel, basswood, burned/pnt orange, Thayer-Chandler, 16x30".465.00
Panel, hb after painting: To the Feast, minor gold, 9x34"...........500.00
Pedestal, hb/pnt Nouveau flowers & vines, 45"...........................400.00
Plaque, cvd/burned/pnt strawberry basket, 3-ply, 12" dia...............70.00
Plaque, girl bathing puppies, #854, 14½".....................................125.00
Plaque, hb orange cat w/bow, paper 1912 calendar, 5¾" dia.........50.00
Plaque, Nouveau lady w/cherries, 19½".......................................150.00
Plaque, Oddfellows, hb I O O F in center, early 1900s, 16x10".....87.00
Plaque, Victorian couple, Parting by a Wall & flowers................145.00
Ribbon holder, hb/pnt Sunbonnet babies (3), 5x12"...................160.00
Screen, birds & foliage, mc pnt, 3-part, 63x73"...........................400.00
Spoon holder, geometric florals, wall hanging, 1915, 10x8"..........45.00
Tie rack, factory stamp, HP soldier/nurse/sailor, WWI motto.....125.00

Quezal

The Quezal Art Glass and Decorating Company of Brooklyn, New York, was founded in 1901 by Martin Bach. A former Tiffany employee, Bach's glass closely resembled that of his former employer. Most pieces were signed 'Quezal,' a name taken from a Central American bird. After Bach's death in 1920, his son-in-law, Conrad Vohlsing, continued to produce a Quezal-type glass in Elmhurst, New York, which he marked 'Lustre Art Glass.' Examples listed here are signed unless noted otherwise.

Bottle, scent; gold irid, 4-sided elongated teardrop, sgn Q Melba, 8".1,440.00
Bowl, gold irid w/bl highlights, ruffled, 6½"................................360.00
Bowl, King Tut, dk irid on orange, orange irid int, ftd, 8"........1,265.00
Ceiling shade, leaves/vines, gold/gr on 14" ivory irid bowl, brass mts.6,325.00
Hanging lamp, 5 yel irid shades; copper-wash scroll arms, 19x20".3,360.00
Shade, feathers, gold/gr/polychromatic, wide tulip rim, 8".......3,450.00
Shade, feathers, gr on gold, 5", pr...345.00
Shade, gold irid, ribbed, petal rim, 5"...250.00
Shade, King Tut, gold irid, globular, 5⅜".....................................690.00
Shade, lily; feathers, gr w/gold tips on opal, petal rim, 5"...........315.00
Vase, amber irid, slim/shouldered, unmk, 9½"............................460.00
Vase, bl irid, elongated w/disk ft, 7"...575.00
Vase, feathers, gr on bl, classic shape, 7¾"..................................980.00
Vase, feathers, gr w/gold outlines on wht, orange int, 3x3½"......750.00
Vase, gold irid, globular, 4½"...450.00
Vase, gold irid, long trumpet top, onion body, 10".....................575.00

Vase, gold irid, slim lily form w/4-lobe rim, sgn; bronze base, 20".4,000.00
Vase, gold irid, stretched/ruffled rim on trumpet form, bun base, 12".2,300.00
Vase, gold irid, wide ftd acorn shape, wide rim flange, 6"............660.00
Vase, gold irid w/gr/silver/cream waves, swollen, 1901-25, 8⅛"..3,750.00
Vase, gold irid w/mc pulled & hooked decor, #B846, 8"...........2,000.00
Vase, wht w/pulled gold & gr decor, slim neck, dbl-bulbed base, 7⅝"..2,115.00

Quilts

Quilts, while made of necessity, nevertheless represent an art form which expresses the character and the personality of the designer. During the seventeenth and eighteenth centuries, quilts were considered a necessary part of a bride's hope chest; the traditional number required to be properly endowed for marriage was a 'baker's dozen'! American colonial quilts reflect the English and French taste of our ancestors. They would include the classifications known as Lindsey-Woolsey and the central medallion appliqué quilts fashioned from imported copper-plate printed fabrics.

By 1829 spare time was slightly more available, so women gathered in quilting bees. This not only was a way of sharing the work but also gave them the opportunity to show off their best handiwork. The hand-dyed and pieced quilts emerged, and they are now known as sampler, album, and friendship quilts. By 1845 American printed fabric was available.

In 1793 Eli Whitney developed the cotton gin; as a result, textile production in America became industrialized. Soon inexpensive fabrics were readily available, and ladies were able to choose from colorful prints and solids to add contrast to their work. Both pieced and appliquéd work became popular.

Pieced quilts were considered utilitarian, while appliquéd quilts were shown with pride of accomplishment at the fair or used when itinerant preachers traveled through and stayed for a visit. Today many collectors prize pieced quilts and their intricate geometric patterns above all other types. Many of these designs were given names: Daisy and Oak Leaf, Grandmother's Flower Garden, Log Cabin, and Ocean Wave are only a few. Appliquéd quilts involved stitching one piece — carefully cut into a specific form such as a leaf, a flower, or a stylized device — onto either a large one-piece ground fabric or an individual block. Often the background fabric was quilted in a decorative pattern such as a wreath or medallions.

Amish women scorned printed calicos as 'worldly' and instead used colorful blocks set with black fabrics to produce a stunning pieced effect. To show their reverence for God, the Amish would often include a 'superstition' block which represented the 'imperfection' of Man!

One of the most valuable quilts in existence is the Baltimore album quilt. Made between 1840 and 1860 only three hundred or so still exist today. They have been known to fetch over $100,000.00 at prominent auction houses in New York City. Usually each block features elaborate appliqué work such as a basket of flowers, patriotic flags and eagles, the Oddfellow's heart in hand, etc. The border can be sawtooth, meandering, or swags and tassels.

During the Victorian period the crazy quilt emerged. This style became the most popular quilt ever in terms of sheer numbers produced and popularity. The crazy quilt was formed by random pieces put together following no organized lines and was usually embellished by elaborate embroidery stitches. Fabrics of choice were brocades, silks, and velvets.

Another type of quilting, highly prized and rare today, is trapunto. These quilts were made by first stitching the outline of the design onto a solid sheet of fabric which was backed with a second having a much looser weave. White was often favored, but color was sometimes used for accent. The design (grapes, flowers, leaves, etc.) was padded through openings made by separating the loose weave of the underneath fabric; a backing was added and the three layers quilted as one.

Besides condition, value is judged on intricacy of pattern, color effect, and craftsmanship. Examine the stitching. Quality quilts have from ten to twelve stitches to the inch. A stitch is defined as any time a needle pierces through the fabric. So you may see five threads but ten (stitches) have been used. In the listings that follow, examples rated excellent have minor defects, otherwise assume them to be free of any damage, soil, or wear. Values given here are auction results; retail may be somewhat higher.

Our advisor is Craig Ambrose; he is listed in the Directory under Iowa. For more information we recommend *Vintage Quilts, Identifying, Collecting, Dating, Preserving, and Valuing,* by Bobbie Aug, Sharon Newman, and Gerald Roy (Collector Books).

Key:
hs — hand sewn, sewing   mp — machine pieced
hq — hand quilted, quilting   ms — machine sewn

Amish

Log Cabin, many dk colors, striped flannel bk, 84x71" **325.00**
Log Cabin, salmon & blk, polished cotton bking, 72x77" **330.00**
Pineapple, red/bl wool w/brn thread, hq, 66x66", VG **935.00**
Pineapple Log Cabin, calicos, PA, 1880s, 96x84" **1,175.00**
Sunburst in sqs, wine/gr/dk bl-grey, wine flannel gathered border, lg.**135.00**
Sunshine & Shadow, bl/blk/bl-violet, wht bking, 72x72" **825.00**

Appliquéd

ABC, cat/duck etc, mc on wht w/bl bands, 36x54" **330.00**
Album, pcd w/appl mc prints & red plaid dividers, sgn/1850, 64x64".**1,870.00**
Bud & Rose Wreath, lt gr/red calico, hs w/princess feather hq, 91x88" ..**770.00**
Court House Sq, wide dbl border, sgn/1800s, stains, 86x86" **330.00**
Eagles in 9-block pattern on wht, eagle hq patterns, 20th C, 83x77".**2,300.00**
Fanciful flowers (4X), red sawtooth border, wht ground, 84x86", EX.**525.00**
Floral medallions (3X3), sawtooth edge, feather/scroll hs, 82x83", EX.**1,400.00**
Floral medallions (9), mc calico, Princess Feather hq, 79" sq, EX...**415.00**
Floral medallions+extra flowers, red/gr/goldenrod, hs dmn quilting.**1,200.00**
Flower rows w/leaves between, all red on wht, 71x84" **200.00**
Flowers, mc on wht w/embr centers, ca 1930s, 89x76", VG **250.00**
Grapevine border/medallions, puffed grapes, diagonal hs, 90x102, EX.**1,150.00**
Grapevines & grapes, gr/purple on wht, minor stains, 66x82" **770.00**
Iris bouquet center w/iris sprays on wht, 1940s, 92x79", EX........**350.00**
Kahili pattern w/center flower & plants, red on wht, 20th C, 80x92".**4,600.00**
Princess Feather, block border w/2-color triangles, hs, 76x80", EX...**660.00**
Princess Feather, 4 lg blocks, red/bl on wht, bl inner border, 74x72".**900.00**
Rose of Sharon, various calicos on wht, hs/fishscale hq, lt stain, 86".**990.00**
Rose of Sharon, 5-color calicos, scalloped border, 1840s, 88x90"..**1,500.00**
Roses & buds, hs diagonal hq, fading/stains, 70x100" **220.00**
Spread eagle in center w/vining tulips etc, 1930s, lt stains, 100x82".**1,375.00**
Star (7-point), sqs in red/gr, vining floral border, stains, 62x80".**495.00**
Swags & tassels among floral medallions, red/wht/gr/mustard, lg, EX.**325.00**
Tulips, hq flowers/feathering/dmns, 70x82" **770.00**
Turkey Tracks, bl on wht, ornate hq, stars in corners, 84" sq, VG+.**440.00**

Pieced

Alternating sqs w/HP flowers in pk & bl, vine borders, stains, 74x84".**220.00**
Aunt Eliza's Star VT, mc calicos/wht, hs, PA, stains, 78" sq........**385.00**
Basket, brn/wht alternate w/red sqs, triple border, hs, 76x88" **770.00**
Basket, printed fabrics, EX hq, 89x79" **250.00**
Bow Tie, bold printed florals & stripes w/solids, 1930s, 89x72", EX.**125.00**
Bow Tie, navy calicos & wht, hs, crib sz, 50x68" **140.00**
Bow Tie, zigzag border w/sawtooth edge, 4-petal flower hq, 74x74".**1,565.00**
Brickwork, sm mc printed rectangles alternate w/wht, stains, 116x82"..**990.00**
Bride's, lg medallion in sq, feather & dmn hq, hs, 1850, 81x68" ...**500.00**
Broken Star VT, red & wht calico, triple border, 88" sq, EX.......**275.00**
Cathedral, mc dmns w/in wht circles, hs, 92½x110" **300.00**
Chintz, overall exotic birds/urns/trees, floral print bking, 96x116" ..**1,430.00**
Chintz border, 9-patch VT sqs, dmn/floral hq, lt stains, 83x82".**1,500.00**
Chintz sqs alternate w/mc bow-tie sqs, hs, stains, 92x96" **1,300.00**

Crazy, embr animals/girls/etc, velvet border/bking, 62x62", EX ..**600.00**
Crazy, silks/velvets, geometrics, much embr, sgn/ca 1900, 63x62", EX.**1,265.00**
Crazy, silks/velvets w/embr, sawtooth border, 1884, wear, 69x71"..**700.00**
Crazy, wool/cotton, blocks w/fans & embr accents, sm holes, 68x76".**135.00**
Diamond 9-Patch & Block, mc on wht, 1840s, 90x92", G..........**350.00**
Diamonds & crosses, mc florals/prints/wht, 84x84" **400.00**
Dmn in Sq, yel/wht w/yel sawtooth border, hq, 73x75", VG.......**300.00**
Dolly Madison's Workbox VT, chintz border, lt stains/edge wear, 42x42"..**245.00**
Double Irish Chain, red & wht, hs, minor stains, 76x82" **415.00**
Drunkard's Path, red/yel calico, dbl border, hq, 74x70" **375.00**
Feathered Star, red/wht, sawtooth border, hq, 86" sq..................**500.00**
Flower blocks (12/embr), pk grid, 1920s, 72x96", M **315.00**
Flowers (4-petal), lt & dk yel/lt gr/wht, arches border, 84" sq.**4,956.00**
Flying Geese VT, mc w/gr calico border, 74x75", EX..................**250.00**
Grandmother's Flower Garden, mc/wht w/yel border, 1940s, 98x84", EX..**300.00**
Holly leaves & hearts, red/gr w/checked bking, hs, 68x82" **385.00**
House (in 20 blocks), mc on wht, no borders, minor stains, 68x70" .**165.00**
Irish Chain, mc w/appl swag & floral border, PA, early, 79" sq ...**600.00**
Irish Chain, red/gr on wht w/chintz border, stains/wear, 86x88".**1,650.00**
Irish Chain 4-Patch VT, bl/wht, dtd 1850, cut down, 44x35".....**275.00**
LeMoyne Stars, candy cane inner border, red/bl on wht, 1880s, 75x65".**900.00**
Log Cabin, dk mc wools, blk printed border, sm rprs, 82x78" **525.00**
Log Cabin, made of jockey silks from KY, yarn tied to silk bk, 91x100".**700.00**
Log Cabin, mostly printed wools, cotton bking, 70x70", EX.......**200.00**
Log Cabin in Sunshine & Shadow, bl/tan w/red, wear, 72x74".**575.00**
Lone Star, mc on wht, hs w/floral & leaf hq, 74" sq **250.00**
Lone Star w/sm stars in corners, mc calicos, bleeding, PA, 86" sq.**330.00**
Moon & Sars, woven rust & gr wool, twill binding, 19th C, 83x96".**765.00**
Ocean Waves, mc prints & calicos, hs, 82x86" **275.00**
Pineapple central medallion, mc calicos, hs, 92x92" **700.00**
Pineapple mdls (9)/floral vines, gr/orange/wht, hs/hq, 64x64" **550.00**
Pinwheel gr/pk sqs & red sqs alternate, dbl border, fishscale hq, 92".**300.00**
Postage Stamp, brns/wht/dk bls, hs, ca 1930, 85x77"...................**400.00**
Postage Stamp VT, mc calicos, triple border, 80x80", VG...........**200.00**
Robbing Peter To Pay Paul, red/wht w/gr border, hs, 37x43" **275.00**
Schoolhouse, red/orange/yel/tan on wht, EX hq detail, 1880s, 76x74"..**1,000.00**
Shoo Fly, dk red/gr/wht, wide border, PA, 83x85", EX.................**325.00**
Star, mc calico & wht trapunto blocks, hs, EX work, 78x92" ..**1,980.00**

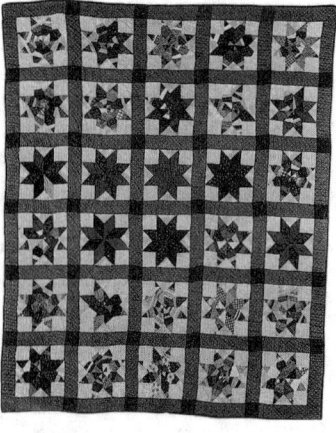

Star, multicolor prints, late 1800s, 77x65", EX, $450.00.

Star, red & wht w/burgundy prints, 1940s, 65x66" **250.00**
Star, red/wht/bl, red & bl border, 104x86", EX **1,000.00**
Star of Bethlehem, mc on wht w/2 borders, 1850s, 115x115", EX .**2,000.00**
State flowers (48) in 8 6-block rows w/needlework, red/wht/bl, 90x83".**1,380.00**
Triangles, mc silk w/wide claret border, feather hq, 1900s, 74x67", G .**110.00**
Triple Irish Chain, mc on yel, sgn/1923, 70x96" **300.00**
Tulip medallions/tulips, mc on wht, hq w/designs, 88" sq...........**770.00**
Turkey Tracks, red & red calico on wht, feather hq, hs, 75" sq ...**330.00**

Wedding, Princess Feather hq w/medallions on dmn pattern, 68" sq..**415.00**
Yo-yos (25 in sqs), pk ruffled border, 86x50", EX........................**200.00**
9-Patch, bl & brn calico on wht, hq, 68x84" **495.00**
9-Patch, chintz sqs/border, brn/bl/red on wht, 1850, lt stains, 84x86".**165.00**

Miscellaneous

Bride's, hs wht on wht w/leaf & nautilus design, 76x76" **440.00**
Chintz, printed w/Paisley border, rosebuds, hs, bed-post corners, 95" ...**600.00**
Wht on wht w/hq poppy medallion amid feathers/loops, lt stain, 80x74"..**300.00**

Quimper

Quimper pottery bears the name of the Breton town in northwestern France where it has been made for over three hundred years. Production began in 1690 when Jean-Baptiste Bousquet settled into a small workshop in the suburbs of Quimper, at Locmaria. There he began to make the hand-painted, tin enamel-glazed earthenware which we know today as faience. By the last quarter of the nineteenth century, there were three factories working concurrently: Porquier, de la Hubaudiere (the Grand Maison), and Henriot. All three houses produced similar wares which were decorated with scenes from the everyday life of the peasant folk of the region. Their respective marks are an AP or a P with an intersecting B (similar to a clover), an HB, and an HR (which became HenRiot after litigation in 1922).

The most desirable pieces were produced during the last quarter of the nineteenth century through the first quarter of the twentieth century. These are considered to be artistically superior to the examples made after World War I and II with the exception of the Odetta line, which is now experiencing a renaissance among collectors here and abroad.

Most of what was made was faience, but there was also a history of utilitarian gres ware (stoneware) having been produced there. In 1922 the Grande Maison HB revitalized this ware and introduced the line called Odetta, examples of which seemed to embody the bold spirit of the Art Deco style. The companion faience pieces of this period and genre are classified as Modern Movement examples and frequently bear the name of the artist who designed the mold.

Currently there are two factories still producing Quimper pottery. La Societe Nouvelle des Faienceries de Quimper is owned by Sarah and Paul Jenessens along with a group of American investors. Their mark is a stamped HB-Henriot logo. The other, La Faiencerie d'art Breton, is operated by the direct descendents of the HB and Henriot families. Their pieces are marked with an interlocked F and A conjoined with an inverted B. Other marks include HQF which is the Henriot Quimper France mark and HBQ, the HB Quimper mark. If you care to learn more about Quimper, we recommend *Quimper Pottery: A French Folk Art Faience* by Sandra V. Bondhus, our advisor for this category, whose address can be found in the Directory under Connecticut.

Bank, Bretonne lady, house form, red clay, Malicorne, PBs, 3x4x2¼" ...**150.00**
Benitier, Chateau de Quintin..., Vierge et l'Enfant, Porquier, 8"...**300.00**
Benitier, Virgin & Child, Ave Maria below figures, HenRiot 81, 8½" ...**325.00**
Bottle, Breton man figural, Modern Movement, HQ 140, 8"......**160.00**
Bowl, bl & gra a la touche garland, HRQ, flake, 3x5¼" **75.00**
Bowl, daisies/sheaf of wheat & leaves, Malicorne, 2½x10¼" **100.00**
Bust, Virgin, w/crown & veil, Renaissance style, Malicorne, PB, 5x4"...**350.00**
Cache pot, Breton couple, flower garlands, HenRiot 76, 5x8", EX ..**230.00**
Candlesticks, Breton couple, paisley swirl shape, Malicorne, 6x5", pr....**700.00**
Charger, Breton couple (detailed), Souvenir de Guerande, HB, 12½"...**450.00**
Charger, peasant lady, flower garlands, a la touche rim, unmk, 10½"...**350.00**
Cheese dish, peasants/Crest of Brittany, Malicorne, prof rpr, 7½" ...**200.00**
Coffeepot, Breton man w/pipe/Crest of Brittany/ermine tails, HB, 9".**325.00**
Condiment set, lad w/baskets, open basket at side, HB, 5¼x4"..**110.00**

Cup & saucer, Bretonne lady/bluet sprays, trefoil, PBx, NM.........**50.00**
Ewer, Breton musicians, de La Hubaudiere, HB, drilled for lamp, 18"..**2,050.00**
Ewer, Breton musicians/flowers, decor riche, Grecian form, HB, 18" ...**375.00**
Figurine, couple dancing Village Breton, Sevellec, 4" **300.00**
Figurine, man w/bottle assisted by wife, A Galland, pk clay, 3¼"...**350.00**
Figurine, Yann, boy w/walking stick, HenRiot, pk clay, 5½".......**175.00**
Flower arranger, lady listing flower basket, HenRiot/Maillard, 8x9"..**750.00**
Hand warmer, Crest of Guerande, book form, unmk, 4x3½" **195.00**
Hand warmer, inscr Brevaire de Rabelais, unmk, 2¼x3½"..........**350.00**
Inkwell, dbl; grandmother w/pipe, bagpipe form, decor riche, HR, 7x7" ..**700.00**
Inkwell, red geometrics/flower vine, 19th C, HB, 3½" sq, NM....**475.00**
Jardiniere, courting couple/cottage, decor riche, HenRiot, 7x20x10".**1,650.00**
Jardiniere, demi-fantasie couple, goemetrics, hdls, HR, 3¼x5" ...**675.00**
Jardiniere, girl seated w/flowers, loop hdls, ftd, HB, 5x9" L.........**650.00**
Match holder, Breton musician, envelope shape, unmk, 4½x2¼"..**155.00**
Menu, lady by hay bale, de la Hubaudiere, sm rstr, HB, 4x3"......**300.00**
Pitcher, Rouenesque pattern, Grecian helmet style, HB, 11" **625.00**
Plate, armorial w/fleur-de-lis, PBx, 9¼" **175.00**
Plate, asparagus, lady spinning, asparagus spear divider, HB, 8¾"..**300.00**
Plate, Breton bagpiper & bluets, demi-fantasie, HR, 9" **175.00**
Plate, Breton man (lady), 12-pointed rim, HenRiot, 8½", pr......**450.00**
Plate, Breton man (lady), 8-pointed star shape w/lattice, HRQ, pr..**850.00**
Plate, Bretonne scene, shield shape, PB, 5x5¼", pr..................**1,925.00**
Plate, butterfly, a la touch bands, HBQ, 7" **235.00**
Plate, coupe; lady w/distaff, chain-link border, HB, 6¾" **400.00**
Plate, couple/Crest of Brittany, decor riche, pierced, HenRiot, 9½" .**350.00**
Plate, delphiniums/roses/bird, linear border, HB (early), 8".........**350.00**
Plate, lady, bl & yel bands, Malicorne, 1899-1918, 8½", NM.....**125.00**
Plate, lady bl stick fence, lg pk blossom, bumblebee/ermines, HBQ, 9"..**750.00**
Plate, lady w/ornate coif, ajonc & bruyere border, HBQ, 9"........**375.00**
Plate, luncheon; naive man w/glass, HB, 19th C, 7¾"..............**150.00**
Plate, man in meadow w/walking stick, anjonc & bruyere border, HBQ, 9"..**350.00**
Plate, Rouen pattern w/cornucopias & flowers, xHB (early), 8" .**400.00**
Plate, scalloped coupe; hummingbird/wild roses, Porquier Beau, 10½"..**2,325.00**
Plate, tulip/floral spray, berry/leaves border, Malicorne, PBx, 9¼" ..**195.00**
Platter, Bretonnes dancing/bagpiper, nosegays/ermine tails, HB Q, 13".**1,650.00**
Platter, facing peasant couple, decor riche, HQ, 17¾x13", NM .**300.00**
Platter, fish; Breton couple on plain, Malicorne, PBx, 21¾x8"...**575.00**
Platter, naive couple, style of de la Hubaudiere, HB, 12¾x9½"..**550.00**
Platter, peasant couple & fir tree, HBQ, 11x8"...........................**250.00**
Platter, youth w/knapsack, scalloped, Malicorne, PBx, 14x9¼", EX..**145.00**
Snuff bottle, rooster & man, book shape, unmk, 3"....................**300.00**
Teapot, couple/sprays/bluets, sponged hdl, 6-sided, HR, chip, 6"..**325.00**
Tray, couple w/basket & pipe, decor riche, hdls, HB, 11", NM ...**160.00**
Trivet, Le Croisic, chain border, Malicorne, unmk PBx, 8" sq **85.00**
Vase, biniou player, acanthus band, fan shape, HB, 5x7¾".........**425.00**
Vase, boy by tree/Crest of Brittany, Malicorne, PBx, hdls, 3½", NM.**425.00**
Vase, Breton man (lady), flower sprays, biniou, HBQ, 11x7", pr..**800.00**
Vase, Breton w/walking stick/crest, fleur-de-lis shape, HR, 10x6", EX....**325.00**
Vase, musicians, Quimper & Brittany crests, hdls, HR, 13½"..**1,500.00**
Vase, quintal; Breton w/lg chevrette/flowers, PBx, 19th C, 7x5"..**240.00**
Vase, tulipiere; couple, demi-fantasie, 4-tube, HenRiot, 8½x8"..**525.00**
Vase, tulipiere; lady w/chevrette, ermine tails, 3-tube, HB, 7x7"..**145.00**
Wall pocket, Breton/flowers/dots, open letter form, HR, 4½x4", pr..**575.00**
Wall pocket, Bretonne lady at fence spinning, cornet, PBx, 10¼".**80.00**
Wall pocket, cornucopia w/snail shell tail, HB 1st Period mk, 13x9"..**1,300.00**
Wall pocket, lady knitting/Crest of Brittany, shoe form, HB, 8¼".**400.00**
Wall pocket, peasant couple, a la touche border, unmk, 11x6¾".**400.00**

Radford, Albert

Pottery associated with Albert Radford (1882 – 1904) can be categorized by three periods of production. Pottery produced in Tiffin, Ohio,

(1896 – 1899) consists of bone china (no marked examples known) and high-quality jasperware with applied Wedgwood-like cameos. Tiffin jasperware is often impressed 'Radford Jasper' in small block letters. At Zanesville, Ohio, Radford jasperware was marked only with an incised, two-digit shape number, and the cameos were not applied but rather formed within the mold and filled with a white slip. Zanesville Radford ware was produced for only a few months before the Radford pottery was acquired by the Arc-en-Ciel company in 1903. Production in Zanesville was handled by Radford's father, Edward (1840 – 1910), who remained in Zanesville after Albert moved to Clarksburg, West Virginia, where the Radford Pottery Co. was completed shortly before Albert's death in 1904. Jasperware was not produced in Clarksburg, and the molds appear to have been left in Zanesville, where some were subsequently used by the Arc-en-Ciel pottery. The Clarksburg, West Virginia, pottery produced a standard glaze, slip-decorated ware, Ruko; Thera and Velvety, matt glazed ware often signed by Albert Haubrich, Alice Bloomer, and other artists; and Radura, a semimatt green glaze developed by Albert Radford's son, Edward. The Clarksburg plant closed in 1912.

Our advisor for this category is James L. Murphy; he is listed in the Directory under Ohio. For pottery marked E. Radford, see Radford, Edward.

Jasper

Bowl, muses & vintage, fluted rim, imp mk **295.00**
Mug, vintage, gray, #25, 5" **165.00**
Pitcher, tankard, vintage, lt bl, #26, 12" **250.00**
Vase, cherubs & lion, #15, 6½" **325.00**
Vase, girl running, deep bl, flat & twisted, #53, 3½" **100.00**
Vase, Gladstone bust ea side, twisted form, 3" **125.00**
Vase, lady & cornucopia on bl, #59, 4" **165.00**
Vase, lady kneeling w/bird, gray, #24, 10½x4½" **250.00**

Miscellaneous

Candle holder, Ruko, floral, sgn/mk, rare, 7" **125.00**
Jardiniere, Ruko, floral, scalloped top, 8½", NM **370.00**
Vase, Radura, scalloped rim, 4-hdl, 10" **400.00**
Vase, Ruko, floral, 15" **325.00**
Vase, Thera, floral, mc on gr, #1453, 12½" **700.00**
Vase, Velvety, mums, mc on gr, sgn, bottle form, 10¼x3" **550.00**

Radford, Edward

Pottery marked 'E. Radford, Burslem,' or 'E. Radford, England,' includes a variety of earthenware designed by Edward Radford (1883 – 1968), first for H.J. Wood and later for himself in Burslem (production ending in 1948). A variety of floral patterns, cottage or tavern scenes, and Art Deco motifs distinguish this ware. His father, Edward Thomas Radford, worked at the Pilkington Tile and Pottery Co. in Manchester, England, and appears to have been a brother of Albert Radford. Items in the following listings are hand painted unless noted otherwise.

Ashtray, hummingbird at side, 5x6" **150.00**
Basket, floral on bl, pk int, 6x4½" **65.00**
Bowl, floral on wht, shallow, oval, 12" **100.00**
Bowl, kingfisher perched on side, leaves at rim, 4½x5" **150.00**
Candlesticks, floral on wht, 1¾x3½", pr, NM **75.00**
Creamer, wisteria, ca 1940, 4½" **145.00**
Dish, floral on wht 5-petal flower form, sm **30.00**
Jug, cottage scene, unmk, 11" **100.00**
Jug vase, floral, slim, scalloped top, swan-neck hdl, 1930s, 11" **75.00**
Pitcher, floral on wht, 5" **65.00**
Pitcher, poppies, ca 1935, 6" **155.00**
Platter, floral on wht, 11" dia **70.00**

Teapot, floral on pastel gr, 6", NM **90.00**
Vase, floral, pattern CJ, shape #195, 1920s **110.00**
Vase, lg flowers & leaves on pale bl, can neck, #202/PQ, 5⅛x4" .. **350.00**
Vase, mc flowers on wht, cylindrical, 9", NM **65.00**
Wall pocket, floral on Deco V shape, Burslem, 8" **90.00**

Radios

Vintage radios are very collectible. There were thousands of styles and types produced, the most popular of which today are the breadboard and the cathedral. Consoles are usually considered less marketable, since their size makes them hard to display and store. For those wishing to learn more about the subject, we recommend *Collector's Guide to Antique Radios, Fifth Edition*, by John Slusser and the staff of *Radio Daze*. For information on novelty radios, refer to *Collector's Guide to Novelty Radios* by Marty Bunis and Robert Breed. All of these publications are available through Collector Books.

Unless otherwise noted in the descriptions, **values are given for working radios in near mint to mint condition**. Our advisor for this category is Dr. E.E. Taylor; he is listed in the Directory under Indiana.

See also Plastics.

Key:
BC — broadcast	R/P — radio-phonograph
LW — long wave	s/r — slide rule
pb — push button	SW — short wave
phono — phonograph	tbl/m — table model

A-C Dayton, AC-63, tbl/m, wood, low rectangular case, 6-tube, 1928 . **110.00**
Admiral, #4E21, portable, gray plastic, 2-knob/4-tube, AC/DC, 1956 .. **30.00**
Admiral, #4V18, portable, plastic, ½-rnd dial, BC, AC/DC, 1952 .. **25.00**
Admiral #16-D5, tbl/m, ivory plastic, BC, 5-tube, AC/DC, 1940 . **110.00**
Air Castle, #9904, tombstone, wood, BC, 7-tube, AC, 1934 ...... **140.00**
Airline, #74BR-150B, tbl/m, walnut plastic, metal bk, s/r, 1947 ... **70.00**
Am Bosch, Cruiser, tbl/m, wood, window dial, battery, 1927 ...... **125.00**
Apex, #70, console, walnut highboy, cloth grill, 9-tube, AC, 1928 . **160.00**
Arvin, #518 Phantom Baby, tbl/m, wood, cloth grill, BC, SW, AC, 1937 ... **85.00**
Atwater Kent, #36, tbl/m, metal, low case, center logo, AC, 1927 . **125.00**
Atwater Kent, #545, tombstone, wood, airplane dial, BC, SW, AC, 1935 . **150.00**
Belmont, #575, tombstone, wood, shouldered, rnd dial, AC, 1934 .. **110.00**
Bendix, #114, tbl/m, plastic, wraparound bars, BC, AC/DC, 1948 . **275.00**
Brunswick, #1559, side table, wood, Fr Provincial styling, AC/DC, 1939 . **135.00**
Clarion, #91, console, wooden lowboy, cloth grill, 8-tube, 1931 . **150.00**
Colonial, #T345, cathedral, wood, quarter-rnd dial, cloth grill ... **175.00**
Crosley, #8H1, console, wood, cloth grill, rnd dial, BC, SW, AC, 1934 . **125.00**
Deforest, #D-6, tbl/m, wood, low case, 2-dial front, battery, 1922 .. **1,300.00**
Eagle, #K-2, tbl/m, wood, low case, 3-dial panel, battery, 1926 ... **145.00**
Echophone, #81, cathedral, wood, quarter-rnd dial, AC, 1932 ... **350.00**
Emerson, #AB-182, console, walnut, 14-tube, BC, SW, AC, 1937 . **125.00**
Emerson, #40, side table, walnut, Fr Provincial, 6-tube, AC/DC, 1933 . **125.00**
Emerson, #569, portable, plastic, s/r dial, BC, AC/DC/battery, 1948 . **50.00**
Fada, #652 Temple, tbl/m, Catalin, upper front dial, BC, AC/DC, 1946 . **550.00**
Firestone, #4-A-21, tbl/m, wood, s/r, 6 pushbuttons, BC, SW, AC, 1947 . **50.00**
Freshman, #6-F-5 Masterpc, tbl/m, mahog, 3-dial panel, battery, 1926 ... **135.00**
GE, #A-54, tbl/m, 2-tone walnut, step-down top, BC, SW, AC/DC, 1936 ... **35.00**
GE, #LB-603, portable, leatherette, fold-up front, AC/DC/battery, 1941 .. **35.00**
Globe, #456, portable, leatherette, s/r dial, hdl, BC, battery, 1948 . **20.00**
Kadette, #77, tombstone, wood, airplane dial, BC, SW, AC/DC, 1936 ... **90.00**
Lafayette, #BE-79, tbl/m, walnut plastic, 5-tube, BC, AC/DC, 1940 .. **125.00**
Majestic, #55 Duette, tbl/m, 2-tone wood, BC, SW, AC, 1933 .. **200.00**
Mohawk, #5A9M, portable, metal, flex hdl, BC, AC/DC/battery .. **40.00**
Motorola, #62B, tbl/m, plastic, 5 pushbuttons, BC, SW, AC/DC, 1939 .. **65.00**
Olympic, #7-638, console/record player, wood, s/r, AC, 1948 .... **50.00**
Philco, #38-116, console, wood, slant dial, BC, SW, AC, 1938 .. **200.00**

Philco, #42-100, console, wood, s/r dial, thumbwheel tuning, 1942..**125.00**
Pilot, #CG-184, console, wood, tuning eye, BC, SW, AC/DC, 1936...**125.00**
RCA, #$28B, tombstone, wood, rnd dial, 5-tube, BC, SW, 1933..**110.00**
RCA, #1-RA-25 Hardy, tbl/m, turq plastic, Nipper logo, AC/DC...**15.00**
RCA, #5X3, tbl/m, wood, top louvers, BC, SW, AC, 1936...........**85.00**
RCA, #7T, tombstone, wood, cloth grill, 7-tube, BC, SW, AC, 1936 .**110.00**

Royal, R-70, wooden cathedral, lower front window dial with escutcheons, upper grill with cutouts, three knobs, $200.00. (Photo courtesy Sue and Marty Bunis)

Silvertone, #3451, tbl/m, plastic, Deco, candy cane dial, 5-tube, BC ..**85.00**
Silvertone, #9000, tbl/m, plastic, graduated bars, BC, AC/DC, 1949.**50.00**
Stewart-Warner, #07-516 Fireside, chairside, shelf, AC/DC, 1939 ..**125.00**
Truetone, #D2210, tbl/m, wood-look metal w/chrome, 2 knobs, 1941.**135.00**
Western Electric, #4D, tbl/m, wood, 2-dial panel, battery, ca 1924..**600.00**
Westinghouse, #H-191, console/record player, wood, BC, FM, AC, 1949...**60.00**
Westinghouse, #WR-22, tombstone, wood, cloth grill, BC, SW, AC, 1934 ..**110.00**
Zenith, #4-B-422, tbl/m, plastic, wraparound bars, BC, battery, 1940..**75.00**

Novelty Radios

Annie, red & wht plastic, w/Sandy, AM, 1981, MIB.....................**70.00**
Beer barrel/keg, AM, Made in Japan, VG **50.00**
Big Foot 4X4 truck, AM/FM, Korea, Ertl, 6½x9⅜", EX **75.00**
Bozo the Clown, head & shoulders, AM, 1972, VG.......................**45.00**
Bugs Bunny, on mound of grass, AM, 6½x3¾", EX.......................**50.00**
Bumble Lion Wuzzle, AM, EX...**35.00**
Cabbage Patch Kids, purse style, Playtime Products, 1983, EX **25.00**
Carrier Air Conditioner, fat cylinder, AM, Hong Kong, 4x3½" .**125.00**
Champion Spark Plug, 1962, NM **165.00**
Del Monte Pineapple Spears Can, realistic, NM...........................**65.00**
Dick Tracy, wrist-band type, AM, Creative Creations, 1975, EX .**220.00**
Donald Duck, head shape, speaker in bk, AM, VG **30.00**
Fonze Jukebox, AM, G..**20.00**
Golden State Warriors, basketball shape, 1980s, 3½" dia, NM **45.00**
Internat'l Harvester Fleetrite Car Battery, plastic, VG **30.00**
Kent Cigarettes, pack w/strap, NM..**60.00**
Kraft Miracle Whip Jar, Hong Kong, ca 1970, M...........................**80.00**
Los Angeles Dodgers, baseball w/built-in strap, NM......................**45.00**
McDonald's Big Mac, GE, AM, 2¾x4", EX **60.00**
Miller High Life can, realistic, GE, 5", NM **50.00**
Mr T, photo front as BA Baracus, transistors, 1983, EX................**60.00**
Nestle Crunch Candy Bar, strap hdl, EX+......................................**60.00**
Owl w/baby bottle, wearing cap, blinking eyes, AM, 1970s, MIB .**25.00**
Pac Man, walkman type, w/headphones, NM **50.00**
Pinball Wizard, AM, Astra, 1981, MIB...**175.00**
Pinocchio, AM, Made in Hong Kong, W Disney, Philgee Internat'l, VG ...**50.00**
Pound Puppy, dog atop AM radio, 1987, EX..................................**20.00**
Punchy Hawaiian Punch Man, AM/FM, NM **65.00**
Ranier Beer Can, realistic, 5", NM **55.00**
Safeguard Deodorant Soap, bar shape, scarce, NM **70.00**
Santa Maria ship, AM, plastic w/brass trim, Japan, EX..................**35.00**
Shell Gasoline Pump, free-standing, 9¾", EX................................**75.00**
Snorky, space creature, Wallace Berrie, 1984, M **45.00**
Sonic Radio Man, transformer-like robot, MIB..............................**75.00**
Space Embassador Flying Saucer, transistor, NM **90.00**
Spiderman, AM wristwatch, Marvel Comic Group, Janex Corp, 1976, EX..**70.00**
Star Explorer Space Shipe, plastic, Hong Kong, AM/FM, NM **75.00**
Statue of Liberty, AM, Radio Shack, 1986, EX.............................**65.00**
Welch's Grape Juice Can, pull-up antenna, AM/FM, NM **60.00**

Transistor Radios

Post-World War II baby boomers, now in their fifties, are rediscovering prized possessions of youth, their pocket radios. The transistor wonders, born with rock 'n roll, were at the vanguard of miniaturization and futuristic design in the decade which followed their introduction to Christmas shoppers in 1954. The tiny receiving sets launched the growth of Texas Instruments and shortly to follow abroad, Sony and other Japanese giants.

The most desirable sets include the 1954 four-transistor Regency TR-1 and colorful early Sony and Toshiba models. Certain pre-1960 models by Hoffman and Admiral represented the earliest practical use of solar technology and are also highly valued. To avoid high tariffs, scores of two-transistor sets, boys' radios, were imported from Japan with names like Pet and Charmy. Many early inexpensive transistor sets could be heard only with an earphone. The smallest sets are known as shirt-pocket models while those slightly larger are called coat-pockets. Early collectible transistor radios all have civil defense triangle markings at 640 and 1240 on the frequency dial and nine or fewer transistors. Very few desirable sets were made after 1963. Model numbers are most commonly found inside. Our advisor for this category is Mike Brooks; he is listed in the Directory under California and welcomes questions. (Please include a SASE.)

Admiral, #Y821 Holiday, horizontal, clock, 8 transistors, AM, 1960...**15.00**
Admiral, #ZM16, horizontal, 7 transistors, yel/wht plastic, AM, 1958 .**50.00**
Aiwa, #AR-751, vertical, 7 transistors, AM, battery, 1965............**25.00**
Arvin, #65R98, horizontal, 12 transistors, AM/FM, battery, 1965..**15.00**
Channel Master, #6477, horizontal, 9 transistors, s/r, AM/FM, 1965...**20.00**
Continental, #TR-814, vertical, 8 transistors, AM, battery, 1964.**10.00**
Emerson, #847, horizontal, plastic, 6 transistors, AM, battery, 1956..**75.00**
GE, #P776B, horizontal, leather, 7 transistors, AM, battery, 1959 .**15.00**
GE, #677, horizontal, red plastic, 5 transistors, AM, battery, 1955 ..**150.00**
Global, #GR-711, vertical, 6 transistors, AM, Japan **90.00**
Golden Shield #7109 Ten Power, horizontal, 8 transistors, AM, battery...**35.00**
Hitachi, #TH-759, horizontal, 7 transistors, AM, battery, 1962....**45.00**
Hoffman, #KP706, Trans-Solar, horizontal, US, 1959 ....**95.00**
Juliette, #AA-64, horizontal, 6 transistors, AM, battery...............**15.00**
Mitchell, #1103, vertical, leather, 4 transistors, AM, battery, 1955 .**450.00**
Motorola, #AX4B, horizontal, bl/wht, 6 transistors, AM, battery, 1961 ..**25.00**
Norelco, #L4x05T, horizontal, 7 transistors, AM, battery, 1961....**35.00**
Philco, #NT-1004, horizontal, leather, 10 transistors, AM/FM, 1965 ..**15.00**
Philco, #T-88-124, horizontal, 8 transistors, AM, battery, 1962 ....**35.00**
RCA, #1-TP-1JE, vertical, 6 transistors, AM, battery, 1961..........**25.00**
Realtone, #TR-501, vertical, plastic, Japan, AM, battery.............**40.00**
Regency, #TR-5, horizontal, leather, AM, battery, 1958...............**55.00**
Seminole, #1030, horizontal, 10 transistors, s/r, AM/FM, battery, 1964 .**25.00**
Silvertone, #1060, horizontal tbl/m, 6 transistors, AM, battery, 1964...**15.00**
Standard, #SR-H438, horizontal, 8 transistors, Japan, AM, battery, 1965 .**100.00**
Tonecrest, #1051, horizontal, 10 transistors, AM/FM, battery, 1965 ..**20.00**
Toshiba, #8TH-428R, horizontal tbl/m, 8 transistors, AM, battery, 1963..**35.00**
Universal, #YT-161, vertical, 6 transistors, Japan, AM, battery **35.00**
Westinghouse, #H-858P12, horizontal, 12 transisters, AM/FM, 1963 ..**25.00**
Westinghouse, #H621P6 Cordless, horizontal, 6 transistors, AM, 1958 ..**55.00**
Zephyr, #ZR-620, vertical, 6 transistors, AM, 1962 ....**90.00**

Railroadiana

Collecting railroad-related memorabilia has become one of America's most popular hobbies. The range of collectible items available is almost endless; not surprising, considering the fact that more than 185 different railroad lines are represented. Some collectors prefer to specialize in only one railroad, while others attempt to collect at least one item from every railway line known to have existed. For the advanced collector, there is the challenge of locating rarities from short-lived railroads; for the novice, there are abundant keys, buttons, and passes. Among the most popular specializations are dining-car collectibles — flatware, glassware, dinnerware, etc., in a wide variety of patterns and styles. Railroad blankets are also collectible. Most common are Pullman blankets. The early ones had a cross-stitch pattern; these were followed by one in a solid cinnamon color; both are marked clearly with the Pullman name. Pullman, in the 1920s, put out a blue blanket, marked Pullman, specifically for ethnic use. There is one in the Sacramento railroad museum. Other railroads had their own 'marked' blankets that are even more desirable, such as the Soo line, the Chessie, and one marked 'Pheasant' (which was a private car on the Milwaukee Line that was reserved to carry special parties for hunting trips).

Another name among railroad dining collectors is Fred Harvey. From 1893 until after WWII, Fred Harvey masterminded all the dining halls and dining cars on the Santa Fe Railroad System from Chicago to the west coast. (A little known fact, he also had dining facilities on the Frisco railroad.) He had his famous Harvey girls, as portrayed by Judy Garland, and a lot of personal dining china, silver, and linens marked with his 'FH.'

Berth keys have become scarce and expensive as more and more collectors purchase private rail cars. This is also true of 'window lifters,' specially designed pry bars made of wood used to ram the windows open in the old wood coaches.

As is true in most collecting fields, scarcity and condition determine value. There is more interest in some railway lines than in others; generally speaking, it is greater in the region serviced by the particular railroad. American collectors prefer American-made products and items with ties to American railroads. For example, English switch lanterns, though of superior quality, usually sell at lower prices, as does memorabilia from Canadian railways such as Canadian Pacific or Canadian National.

Reproductions abound in railroadiana collectibles — from dinnerware and glassware to lanterns, keys, badges, belt buckles, timetables, and much more. Repro hand-executed, reverse-painted glass signs have been abundant throughout the country, most of them read 'Santa Fe,' but some say 'Whites Only.' Lately markets in the East have been inundated with Baltimore & Ohio reproductions: menus, glass water carafes, demitasse sets in the George Washington theme, and more. Beware! Also railroad drumheads are coming out of collections. A drumhead is a large (approximately 24" diameter) glass sign in a metal case. They were used on the back end of all railroad observation cars to advertise a special train or a presidential foray, etc. They're now beginning to surface, and a good one like the Flying Crow from the Kansas City Southern Railroad will go for $2,500.00, as will many others. When items of this value come out, the counterfeiters are right there. It is important to 'Know Thy Dealer.' For a more thorough study, we recommend *Railroad Collectibles, Fourth Revised Edition*, by Stanley L. Baker. The values noted for most of our dinnerware, glassware, linen, silverplate, and timetables are actual selling prices. However, because prices are so volatile, the best pricing sources are often monthly or quarterly 'For Sale' lists. Two you may find helpful may be ordered from Golden Spike, P.O. Box 422, Williamsville, NY 14221, and Grandpa's Depot, 6720 E. Mississippi Ave., Unit B, Denver, CO 80224. Our co-advisors for this category are Lila Shrader (See Directory, California) and John White (Grandpa's Depot, see Colorado).

Key:
BL — bottom logo
BS — bottom stamped
FBS — full back stamp
NBS — no back stamp
SL — side logo
SM — side mark
TL — top logo
TM — top mark

Dinnerware

Many railroads designed their own china for use in their dining cars or company-owned hotels or stations. Some railroads chose to use stock patterns to which they added their name or logo; others used the same stock patterns without the added identification. For more information, we recommend *Restaurant China, Volumes 1* and *2*, by Barbara J. Conroy (Collector Books).

Ashtray, GN, Mountains & Flowers, 4 rests, BS, 4" dia 88.00
Bowl, CRI&P, LaSalle, TL, NBS, 5½" 99.00
Bowl, Erie, Chataqua, oval, TL, NBS, 6x5" 275.00
Bowl, NP, Garnet, oval, BM, 6x4" 398.00
Bowl, oatmeal/chile; C&O, Russell, SL: Russell YMCA, 5" 46.00
Bowl, rim soup; B&O, Centenary, Lamberton, BS, 9" 89.00
Bowl, rim soup; MKT, Bluebonnet, BS, 8¾" 440.00
Bowl, soup/salad; CMStP&P, Traveler, flat, no rim, FBS, 7½" 75.00
Butter pat, ACL, Palmetto, TM, NBS 100.00
Butter pat, ATSF, Mimbreno, FBS w/Ancient Mimbreno Indian, 3½" ..90.00
Butter pat, CB&Q, Violets & Daisies, BS, Buffalo, 3¼" 148.00
Butter pat, CMStP&P, Traveler, NBS, 3", from $49 to 65.00
Butter pat, CRI&P, Golden State, TM, Buffalo, BS, from $185 to ..225.00
Butter pat, CRI&P, LaSalle, TM, Buffalo, BS 310.00
Butter pat, Erie, Starucca, TM, NBS, 3" 154.00
Butter pat, N&W, Cavalier, TM, Lamberton, NBS, 4" 68.00
Butter pat, NYC, Hudson, BS, Limoges, 3" sq 110.00
Children's ware, mug, GN, Rocky SL, monkey, hippo, etc 765.00
Chocolate pot, ATSF, California Poppy, NBS, from $127 to 149.00
Chocolate pot, B&O, Centenary, BM 585.00
Compote, ATSF, California Poppy, ped ft, BM, Bauscher, 3½x7" ...625.00
Creamer, ATSF, California Poppy, hdl, NBS, ind, 2¾" 188.00
Creamer, B&O, Centenary, BM, Lamberton, 4", from $86 to 108.00
Creamer, Fred Harvey, Webster, no hdl, NBS, ind, 2½" 44.00
Creamer, GN, Empire, no hdl, ind, 2¼", from $14 to 28.00
Creamer, N&W, Yellowbird, NBS, ind, 3⅛" 100.00
Creamer, NYC&StLFtW, SL, NBS, ind, 2" 135.00
Creamer, Pullman, Calumet, SL, 4" 198.00
Creamer, SP, Stanford, SL, Maddock, ind, 3" 500.00
Cup, bouillon; ATSF (Santa Fe), Mimbreno, hdls, BS, 2¼" 270.00
Cup, bouillon; B&O, Centenary, hdls, BS, 2¼" 155.00
Cup & saucer, Algoma Central Ry, Polar Bear, NBS 92.00
Cup & saucer, C&NW, Wild Rose, NBS, Syracuse 87.00
Cup & saucer, C&O, Silhouette, saucer BS, cup NBS 100.00
Cup & saucer, CMStP&P, Olympian, Mfg by Lenox, SL & TM ...100.00
Cup & saucer, coffee; Griffin, both BS, Bauscher 550.00
Cup & saucer, demi; MP, Eagle, SL & TL 210.00
Cup & saucer, demi; PRR, Allegheny, both BS, SWB 365.00
Cup & saucer, demi; SAL, Orange Blossom, NBS 725.00
Cup & saucer, GN, Glory of West, both BS 415.00
Cup & saucer, Seaboard, Palm Beach, TL & SL, NBS 625.00
Cup & saucer, SP, Sunset, TL & SL, NBS 455.00
Cup & saucer, tea; ATSF, Mimbreno, cup BS, saucer FBS 285.00
Cup & saucer, tea; NYC, TL & SL, cup BS 100.00
Cup & saucer, UP, Harriman Blue, both BS w/Overland logo 85.00
Egg cup, CMStP&P, Peacock, NBS, 2⅜" 192.00
Egg cup, GM&O, Rose, custard cup shape, SL, NBS, 3¼" 188.00
Egg cup, Pullman, Indian Tree, SL, 3¾" 190.00
Hot food cover w/vent, C&O, Geo Washington, 6¼" 400.00

Ice cream dish, PRR, Brown Keystone, tab hdl, TL, NBS..........146.00
Ice cream shell, SP, Golden State, tab hdl, 4¾" (w/hdl).............575.00
Mug, Canadian Railway News, Railway News, SL, 3" 66.00
Mug, UP, Harriman Blue, BS, heavily stained, 3" 49.00
Mustard pot, Atlanta & West Point, Montgomery, slotted lid, 2⅞"...42.00
Mustard pot, ATSF, California Poppy, slotted lid, NBS, 2¾" 290.00
Mustard pot, ATSF, Mimbreno, slotted lid, BS, 3¼" 495.00
Plate, CP, Maple Leaf, TL, 9"...60.00
Plate, grill; SP, PMWF, diagonal rib dividers, BS, 12½x7½" 200.00
Plate, IL Central, Pirate, NBS, 10"....................................128.00
Plate, NYNH&H, Merchants, Buffalo, BS, 9¾".......................90.00
Plate, service; C&NW, Flambeau, FBS, 10½"..........................740.00
Plate, service; C&O's Greenbrier Hotel, 24k gold vermeil, NBS, 10½"...735.00
Plate, service; CB&Q, AK-SAR-BEN, TL, Bauscher, NBS, 10½"..1,046.00

Plate, service; IC's Panama Limited Service, 10", $635.00. (Photo courtesy Stanley Baker)

Plate, service; ICRR, French Quarter, Clairbourne Court, BS, 10½"...1,725.00
Plate, service; IL Central, Creole, TL, 10" 525.00
Plate, service; MKT, Alamo, gr border, BS, 10" 382.00
Plate, service; SAL, Old Bay Line, legend on reverse, 10½" 360.00
Plate, Southern, Peach Blossom, TL, 9" 230.00
Plate, T&P, Eagle, TL, BS, 6½"...88.00
Platter, ACL, Palmetto, oval, TL, Buffalo, NBS, 11½"..............90.00
Platter, ATSF, Mimbreno, oval, FBS, 8", from $300 to...............500.00
Platter, Key Route, Oakland, TL, NBS, Limoges, 15½x10½".....680.00
Platter, Louisville & Nashville, Green Leaf, oval, NBS, 10½"......30.00
Platter, NP, Yellowstone, oval, TL, 8½" 135.00
Platter, Pullman, Calumet, oval, TM, 10½"............................125.00
Platter, Southern, Peach Blossom, TL, Lamberton, NBS, 11¼" .114.00
Platter, Southern, Pelican, oval, TL, 13½" 145.00
Platter, SP, Prairie-Mtns-Wildflowers, oval, NBS, 12½"..............100.00
Platter, UP, Harriman Blue, oval, TL, NBS, 13" 155.00
Relish, Lehigh Valley, Liberty Bell, TL, NBS, 10x4" 265.00
Relish, NYNH&H, Platinum Blue, TM, BS, 10x4¾".................36.00
Relish, Southern RR, Business, FBS, 12x5½" 235.00
Relish, SP, Golden State, oval, fluted, TL, NBS, Bauscher, 1924, 10"...398.00
Sherbet, ATSF, Mimbreno, ped ft, BS, 2½x3¾" 295.00
Teapot, CNR, Verde Green, cube shape, SL, BS, ind sz 68.00
Teapot, WP, Cobalt Blue, SL, NBS 375.00

Glass

Ashtray, B&O, clear w/bl logo & Capitol dome, 4½" 25.00
Ashtray, Burlington Zephyr, red pyro, 3½" dia...........................55.00
Ashtray, Pullman, oval, fits onto passenger car wall, mk 40.00
Ashtray, SF, clear w/wht center logo, oval, 5¼" 18.00
Bottle, disinfectant; emb PRR Disinfectant, brn, orig cork, 6-oz...55.00
Bottle, medicine; emb Southern Pacific Co Hospital Dept, +label, 5"..48.00
Bottle, milk; ATSF, Santa Fe in pyro, squarish, ½-pt.....................47.00
Bottle, milk; MP & buzz-saw logo in pyro, ½-pt, from $11 to 22.00
Bottle, milk; St Lous & San Francisco bl pyro logo, squarish, ½-pt..29.00

Brandy snifter, B&O, Capitol dome, 5 encircling lines, ftd, 4¼" ..70.00
Champagne, SF, Hock style, stemmed, 5"...................................60.00
Cordial, ATSF, Santa Fe in script/etched lines, stemmed, 3⅛" ...110.00
Cordial, NP, etched Yellowstone Park Line logo, 3¾" 175.00
Cruet, B&O, Linking 13 states, acid etch, w/stopper, 6¼" 42.00
Goblet, UP, frosted shield, pinstripe, stem, 5½".........................22.00
Goblet, UP, stemmed, tall 18.00
Roly poly, CRI&P, Route of the Rockets in red, Golden State emblem..25.00
Roly poly, EL, dtd 1969, 2¾" 10.00
Salt cellar, C&S emb on bottom, oval, 2¼x1½" 220.00
Shot glass, B&O, etched Capitol dome logo, 2½" 90.00
Shot glass, SL &SF, FRisco line in wht pyro, 2½" 14.00
Tumbler, Chicago, Indianapolis & Louisville, Hossier M SL, ftd, 4¾".57.00
Tumbler, CN, Bonaventure wht pyro logo, 4¼" 28.00
Tumbler, Erie, amethyst, slant sides, 3¼x3" 38.00
Tumbler, Frisco logo in bl, SM, 5" 15.00
Tumbler, ICRR, dmn logo, vertical grooves, SM, 5" 22.00
Tumbler, Lehigh Valley w/LV flag SL surrounded by wreath, 5½" ..118.00
Tumbler, UP, shield logo, str sides, 4½" 18.00
Wine, ATSF, Santa Fe etched script/encircling lines, stem, 4¼"...90.00
Wine, IC etched dmn logo, stem, 4¼" 70.00

Lamps

Backhead gauge, N&W, Tietze, ca 1930, M 50.00
Hand, GTW on side, steel/brass, 4 lenses, 12", VG 85.00
Hand, Kew-Light (Dewar), carbide burning, unmk, 10x5¾" dia...60.00
Inspector's, BR&P on brass plate, Dietz Ideal, VG......................95.00
Inspector's, Wabash, Dietz Acme, unmk Globe, rpt, EX...............85.00
Semaphore, B&A, 3 lenses, porc blade, style K 455.00
Semaphore, Lexan, 3 lenses, porc blade: 43" L 590.00
Vertical, Adlake, red & clear lenses, steel, worn pnt, sm...............50.00
Wall, caboose; UPRR, Aladdin, brass, steel mt, EX.....................60.00
Wall candle, Adams & Westlake 1907P, older style w/drilled top ..60.00

Lanterns

Before 1920 kerosene brakemen's lanterns were made with tall globes, usually 5⅜" high. These are most desirable to collectors and are usually found at the top of the price scale. Short globes from 1921 through 1940 normally measure 3½" in height, except for those manufactured by Dietz, which are 4" tall. (Soon thereafter, battery brakemen's lanterns came into widespread usage; these are not highly regarded by collectors and are generally not railroad marked.)

All lanterns should be marked with the name or initials of the railroad — look on the top, the top apron, or the bell base (if it has one). Globes may be found in these colors (listed in order of popularity): clear, red, amber, aqua, cobalt, and two-color. Any lantern's value is enhanced if it has a colored globe.

Key:
A&W — Adams and Westlake   bb — bell bottom

ATSF, A&W Adlake Kero, clear short globe, Pat dates 115.00
ATSF, Adlake Reliable, mk clear 5⅜" globe, Pat 1909, EX.........155.00
B&M RR, A&W Adlake Reliable, clear 5½" globe, wire ring base ..160.00
C of G, A&W Adlake No 100 Kero, Pat 1913, EX.....................150.00
Casey, T&P emb on clear globe, Pat 1902 & 1903, EX.............825.00
CCC&StL, Handlan Buck, red 5½" globe, insert pot, bb, 1909 .300.00
CI&SRR, A&W Adlake Reliable, tall globe, Pat 1897/1913 .....160.00
CPR, Hiram Piper Adlake Kero, short clear etch globe, EX........110.00
D&H, TM on apron, bb, mk clear globe, tall, complete..............350.00
D&RG, Dietz, bb, wood hdl, clear etch globe............................250.00
Dietz No 100, bl w/red globe, mk NY USA 45.00

GT, A&W Reliable, red Dietz Vulcan globe, VG 85.00
LV, Armspear, red cast 6" globe, complete, EX.............................165.00
OSL, A&W Adlake Reliable, tall mk globe, last Pat 1912 ....500.00
PRR Keystone, Adlake Kero, red K globe, Pat 1923, EX..............65.00
Pullman, A&W, eng P Co globe, orig NP, ca 1965-75, EX 725.00
SF, emb mk on bb, clear mk globe, tall, G................................300.00
TX & Pacific, Adlake Kero, short red mk globe, TM 80.00
WC, A&W, Soo Line 5⅜" etched globe, EX...............................200.00

Linens and Uniforms

Over the years the many railroad companies took great pride in their dining car table presentation. In the very early years of railroad dining car service, the linens used at the tables were of the finest quality white damask. Most railroads would add their company's logo, name, initials, or even a spectacular scene that would be woven into the cloth (white on white). These patterns were not evident unless the fabric was held at a particular angle to the light. The dining car staff's attire generally consisted of heavily starched blinding white jackets with shiny buttons.

In later years, post-World War II, color began to be used for table linens. Florida railroads created some delightfully colorful items for the table as well as for head-rests. The passenger train crew, the conductor, and the brakemen, were generally attired in black suits, white shirts, and black ties. Their head gear generally bore a badge denoting their position. These items have all become quite collectible. Sadly, however, replicas of badges and pins have been produced as well as 'fantasy' items (items that do not replicate an older item but are meant to mislead or deceive).

Key:
HCS — horizontal center stripe   w/w — white on white damask
RBH — reinforced buttonholes

Blanket, NP, tan/red/wht/stripes, 63x72" 275.00
Blanket, Pullman, cinnamon, woven-in logo, twin sz..................150.00
Cap, Railway Express Agency w/REA brass buttons....................100.00
Hat, Canadian Pacific in script on blk wool w/gold braid..............95.00
Hat, IA Central Station Agent (on brass badge), blk wool.........475.00
Hat, NYNH&H conductor, blk badge & gold braid on blk wool.155.00
Hat, T&P brakeman (passenger service), brass badge on blk wool ..110.00
Headrest cover, Norfolk & Western embr in script, 14x21", $10 to..17.50
Headrest cover, NP Monad on gray & blk band on ends, 14x22".32.50
Headrest cover, SCL, yel w/cut beach scenes, 24x16", from $10 to ..17.50
Headrest cover, SCL, yel/gr, beach scene 17.50
Jacket, NYC waiter, Empire State Express, wht w/bl lapels 45.00
Jacket, PRR waiter, yel cotton w/blk trim & PRR brass buttons.115.00
Jacket, SL&SF waiter, red cotton w/Meteor breast patch & SL&SF buttons...85.00
Napkin, GN, w/w w/YPL logo in center, 22" sq 34.00
Napkin, PRR embr on red bands at both ends, 14½" sq................24.00
Napkin, RG, wht on wht, speed letters, G-......................................10.00
Napkin, SL&SF, w/w, logo ea corner, 22x20".................................26.00
Napkin, SP, paper, sunset logo printed on corner, colorful 12.50
Napkin, SP, sunset logo in center, poppies border, linen, 1927, 21x21"..45.00
Napkin, SP, sunset logo on w/w, 22" sq...30.00
Napkin, UP's Portland Rose, pk w/rose woven into corner, 24" sq.38.00
Pants, Milwaukee waiter, purple stripe, EX......................................12.00
Pillowcase, CRI&P, wht cotton stamped w/RI's logo, 18x21" 9.00
Shop cloth, BR's logo w/safety slogans, blk & beige, 16x17" 7.00
Tablecloth, Amtrak, wht, stamped NRPC, 31x45" 10.00
Tablecloth, B&O, capital logo on w/w, 52x63"................................58.00
Tablecloth, Burlington Rte, logo on w/w, 43x45" 35.00
Tablecloth, CA Zephyr, oval logo on w/w, 43x53"...........................58.00
Tablecloth, MStP&SStM, Soo logo on w/w, 52x63 ....24.00
Tablecloth, NP's Monad logo on w/w, 45x54" 44.00
Tablecloth, SCL, w/w, VG 25.00

Tablecloth, SLSF logo on w/w, 56x42" 30.00
Towel, hand; ATSF, huck, bl stripe w/ATSF woven in, 26x14".....18.00
Towel, hand; CMStP&P woven in red at ea end+1918, 26x16" ...18.00
Towel, hand; CNR System woven in bl band through center, 15x22"..18.00
Towel, hand; Pullman woven in bl stripe w/various dates, from $7 to ..33.00
Towel, PRR, Thanks for Riding Pennsy, paper, fancy, sealed in bag..10.00
Towel, Pullman - Property of... woven in wht on bl stripe, 1929, 24" L..18.00

Locks

Brass switch locks (pre-1920) were made in two styles: heart-shaped and Keen Kutter style. Values for the heart-shaped locks are determined to a great extent by the railroad they represent and just how its name appears on the lock. Most in demand are locks with large embossed letters; if the letters are small and incised, demand for that lock is minimal. For instance, one from the Union Pacific line (even with heavily embossed letters) may go for only $45.00, while the same from the D&RG railroad could go easily sell for $250.00. Old Keen Kutter styles (brass with a 'pointy' base) from Colorado & Southern and Denver & Rio Grande could range from $600.00 to $1,200.00.

Steel switch locks (circa 1920 on) with the initials of the railroad incised in small letters — for example BN, L&H, and PRR — are usually valued at $20.00 to $28.00.

General use, Southern Pacific w/sunset logo, brass w/rnd bottom .125.00
Mail car, GNRy US Mail Car, sm brass heart shape 75.00
Shanty, CB&QRR, steel, sq w/brass rivets, w/chain.......................35.00
Signal, CRI&P Signal, USE No Oil, brass 25.00
Signal, GNRY, RACO, brass, w/wrench-type key............................30.00
Switch, B&MRR, Wilson Bohannan Co...USA, brass heart shape ..85.00
Switch, CGW Pat 204082, Adlake, steel 22.00
Switch, D&SF, Eagle Lock Co...USA, brass heart shape 200.00
Switch, GNRy, FS Hdwe Co..., steel, 1939 ....22.00
Switch, N&W R'Y Co (ornate), FS HDW Co, 1924, brass heart shape..125.00
Switch, PRRCo (ornate), Fraim 1911, Keystone, brass heart shape.250.00
Switch, Union Pacific, Switch CSI, Adlake, brass heart shape...210.00

Silver-Plated Flatware

The value of silver plate, hollow ware, or flatware, is influenced by the location of the logo or railroad name and, of course, by condition. A side- or top-marked piece is preferable to one with a bottom mark. Examine a prospective purchase carefully. Some unmarked flatware has been 'enhanced' with a rather crude stamping of the railroad's name. Authentic railway markings were done at the time of manufacture and were generally executed in a flawless manner.

Key:
G — Gorham   R&B — Reed & Barton
In'tl — International

Coffeepot, NP, ornate handle, side mark and bottom stamped, ca 1888, one-pint, 7", $250.00.
(Photo courtesy Stanley Baker)

Fork, dinner; NP, Winthrop, G, TM, 7½" **32.50**
Fork, dinner; NYC, Copley, BM, Int'l **22.50**
Fork, dinner; SAL, Cromwell, Int'l, TM, 7½" **28.00**
Fork, pickle; Fred Harvey, Albany, Int'l, BM, very early **24.00**
Fork, pickle; ICRR, Dartmouth, Int'l, 6" **22.50**
Fork, pickle; NYC, Commonwealth, Int'l, BS, 5¾" **55.00**
Fork, salad; PRR, Broadway, PRR TM, Int'l **42.00**
Fork, seafood; CMStP&P, Broadway, Int'l, BS, 5¾" **22.00**
Fork, seafood; CMStP&P, Sierra, TM, R&B, 5½" **26.00**
Fork, seafood; GN, Astoria, Wallace, TM, 5½" **50.00**
Fork, seafood; N&W, Troy, G, TM, 6½" **125.00**
Fork, seafood; NYC, Grecian, BM, Int'l, 5½" **25.00**
Iced-tea spoon, N&W, Holland, TL, G, 7¾" **52.00**
Iced-tea spoon, Union News Co, Puritan, TM Int'l, 7½" **40.00**
Knife, butter; B&O, Clovelly, TM, R&B, 8" **40.00**
Knife, butter; MP, Empire, BM, Int'l, 7⅛" **22.00**
Knife, dinner; CMStP&P, Broadway, BM, Int'l, 9¼" **18.00**
Knife, dinner; PRR, Kings w/full shell & stainless blade, Adams ..**22.00**
Knife, dinner; Pullman, Roosevelt, TM, 8½" **47.00**
Knife, dinner; SRR, DeSoto, BM, R&B, 9½" **20.00**
Knife, luncheon; Central RR of NJ, Cromwell, Meriden, 7⅜" **38.00**
Ladle, SL&SF, Chester, TM Frisco, G, 8½" **68.00**
Nut pick, ATSF, Windsor, Int'l, TM **48.00**
Spoon, bar; CP, Windsor, Rogers, TL, 8" **35.00**
Spoon, bouillon; PRR, Broadway, Int'l, 6" **20.00**
Spoon, condiment; CP, Windsor, Elkington, TM **34.00**
Spoon, condiment; ICRR, Alden, R&B, TL, BM, 4⅛" **155.00**
Spoon, condiment; NYC, Century, Int'l, TM, 4¼" **36.00**
Spoon, demitasse; N&W, Holland, TL, G, 4¼" **38.00**
Spoon, serving; D&RG, Navarre, TM, Rogers, 7¼" **68.00**
Spoon, soup; GN, Hutton, rnd bowl, Int'l, TL, 6" **42.50**
Spoon, soup; MStP&SStM, Empire, BM w/SOO, 7⅛" **32.00**
Sugar tongs, CMStP&P, SM, Int'l, 4" **180.00**
Sugar tongs, GN, resembles ice tongs, See America First, 4¼" ...**224.00**
Sugar tongs, NP, Embassy, Monad SL, BS, R&B **45.00**
Sugar tongs, SP, Grecian, Int'l, SL, 4" **62.50**
Tablespoon, CRI&P, Belmont, TM: RI, BM: Rock Island Lines ...**34.00**
Tea strainer, SP, TM w/Daylight logo on hdl, R&B, 4¼" **265.00**
Teaspoon, ATSF, Albany, BM, Int'l, 5¾" **22.00**
Teaspoon, GCL, Waverly, BM, Int'l, 5¾" **26.00**
Teaspoon, GN, Cromwell, TL, Int'l, 5¾" **26.00**
Teaspoon, Grand Trunk Pacific, Windsor, TL, Elkington, 5¾" **17.00**
Teaspoon, MP, Century (B), TM, Int'l, 6" **18.00**
Teaspoon, N&W, Holland, TL, G, 5⅞" **52.00**
Teaspoon, SP, Grecian, BM, Int'l, 6" **20.00**

Silver-Plated Hollow Ware

Bottle holder, B&O, BM, R&B, 5" **230.00**
Bowl, ATSF, SM, BS, R&B, 4¼", +underplate **135.00**
Bread tray, NP, oval, BM, Int'l, 10½x4¾" **80.00**
Butter icer, C&A, 2-pc, BS, R&B, 2¾"+tab hdls **385.00**
Butter pat, CRI&P, BS, G, 3¼" **22.00**
Chocolate pot, CM&O, hinged lid, BS, Int'l, 5" **88.00**
Chocolate pot, GN, hinged lid, SL, BS, Int'l, 5½" **135.00**
Coffeepot, NYC, hinged lid, SL, Int'l, ind, 5½" **135.00**
Coffeepot, Rio Grande, hinged lid, Curecanti logo SM, 12-oz **200.00**
Coffeepot, SP, hinged lid, SM+ball & wing finial, Int'l, 6½" **85.00**
Corn holders, MI Central, TM w/logo, 3", pr **75.00**
Crumber & scraper, GN, GNR intertwined TL, BS, 9" W **375.00**
Dish, NP, 2 sm hdls, YPL SL, Int'l, 1½x5½" **65.00**
Holder+3 shakers, Pullman, rtcl sides, SM sterling lids **270.00**
Ice bucket, CB&Q, hdls, BM, R&B, 7" **255.00**
Ice bucket, GTP SL, Toronto SP Co, 8" **175.00**

Menu holder, CMStP&P, The Milwaukee Road SL, Int'l **240.00**
Menu holder, CRI&P/SP, SL: Golden Rocket, Int'l, NBS **415.00**
Mustard fr, DL&W, hinged lid, clear glass insert, BS **365.00**
Mustard holder, UP Overland Route, BS, glass insert+spoon......**198.00**
Sauce boat, Pere Marquette, SL, Wallace, 2x4½" **275.00**
Server, Wabash, hdls, w/lid, BS, Int'l, 4x7½" **162.00**
Shakers, NPRy SL on lid, unmk glass, 2⅞", pr **335.00**
Sugar bowl, C&A, hdls, BS, 4x7" **280.00**
Sugar bowl, Lehigh Valley, BS w/flag & dmn **285.00**
Sugar bowl, NP, hdls, YPL SL, 4½" **80.00**
Syrup, D&H, attached underplate, hinged lid, SL, R&B, 5½" ...**125.00**
Teapot, ACL, hinged lid, ACL SL, Rogers Silver, 4" **120.00**
Teapot, MI Central, hinged lid, BS, 16-oz, 5¼" **145.00**
Teapot, MStP&SStM, hinged lid, elegant hdl, BS, 5" **195.00**
Teapot, Santa Fe Route in script, hinged lid, SM, Harrison, 4¾"..**785.00**
Teapot fr, CA Zephyr, hinged lid, Hall insert, BS **335.00**
Teapot fr, L&N, hinged lid, Hall insert, BS **315.00**
Tray, NP TM w/YPL logo, R&B, 12x9" **230.00**
Tray, T&P Eagle TL, rectangular, BS, Int'l, 7x10½" **115.00**
Tureen, Wabash, w/hdls & lid, BM, Int'l, 4x7½" **155.00**

Switch Keys

Switch keys are brass with hollow barrels and round heads with holes for attaching to a key ring. They were used to unlock the padlocks on trackside switches when the course of the tracks had to be changed. (Switches were padlocked to prevent them from being thrown by accident or vandals, a situation that could result in a train wreck.) A car key used to open padlocks on freight cars and the like is very similar to the switch key, except the bit is straighter instead of being specifically curved for a particular railroad and its accompanying switch locks. A second type of 'car' key was used for door locks on passenger cars, Pullmans, etc.; this type was usually of brass, but instead of having a hollow barrel, they were shaped like an old-fashioned hotel door key. In order for a key to be collectible, the head must be marked with a name, initials, or a railroad identification, with 'switch' generally designated by 'S' and 'car' by 'C' markings. Railroad, patina 'not polished,' and the presence of a manufacturer's mark other than Adlake all have a positive effect on pricing and collectibility.

A new precedent was set in 1995 when a Denver and South Park 'car' key went at a Missouri auction for $2,500.00. The key was marked DSP&P (an early Colorado road that stopped running in 1898); it was brass and had a hollow barrel and straight bit. Switch keys that only recently brought $15.00 to $17.00 are now bringing $35.00.

B&M, brass, Slaymaker, hollow bbl **30.00**
B&O, Adlake **30.00**
Burlington Rte, Adams & Westlake, steel, EX **35.00**
CRR, brass **22.50**
D&RGW, Adlake **30.00**
MOPAC, brass, hollow bbl **22.50**
NYNH&H, steel, EX **20.00**
SOO Line, brass, Adlake, hollow bbl **30.00**
UP, JHW Climax Co, Newark NJ **35.00**

Miscellaneous

Timetables and railroad travel brochures continue to gain in popularity and offer the collector vast information about the glory days of railroading. Annual passes continue to be favored over trip and one-time passes. Their value is contingent upon the specific railroad, its length of run, and the appearance of the pass itself. Many were tiny works of art enhanced with fancy calligraphy and decorated with unique vignettes.

Pocket calendars are popular as well as railroad playing cards. Pins, badges, and uniform buttons bearing the name or logo of a railroad are also sought after. The novice needs to be cautious about signs (metal as well as cardboard) and belt buckles. Reproductions flourish in these areas.

Key:
dd — double deck   sd — single deck

Advertising, CMStP&P, bronze bear: To Puget Sound Electrified, 5"..**130.00**
Advertising, mini ice tongs, GNRy, See America First **275.00**
Ashtray, GN, blk porc on CI, TM w/goat logo **125.00**
Badge, breast; CMStP&P&PEE RR Police, nickel star, 2⅝".......**175.00**
Badge, breast; GN Special Police, Northwestern Stamp Works..**255.00**
Badge, breast; IN Harbor Belt RR Police, brass star, 2⅝" **200.00**
Badge, breast; Seaboard Police, brass, star w/in rtcl shield, 2¾"..**165.00**
Badge, cap; DL&W, Lackawanna RR Station Officer, nickeled, 3¾x1".**235.00**
Badge, cap; GN Agent, nickel-plated, 3¾x1¼"..........................**175.00**
Badge, cap; NYC Train Announcer, silver-tone on brass, 3¾x1½"...**290.00**
Badge, cap; Pacific...Rail Motor Coach Operator, enamel on silver-tone.**135.00**
Badge, cap; PRR Messenger w/keystone logo unusual shape, 3⅛x1½"..**230.00**
Bell, locomotive; B&O, brass w/iron mt, 26x29" fr **1,330.00**
Bond, Jersey Junction RR, issued & signed by JP Morgan in 1886...**495.00**
Book, Appleton's...RR Guide, traveler's, fold-out map, 313-pg...**225.00**
Book, Complete Roster of Heavyweight Pullman Cars, 1981, 315-pg..**200.00**
Book, Panama RR & Pacific SS Co, lovely illus, hardbk, 1867, 5x8"..**80.00**
Book, 75 Yrs of Schwartzkopff RR Machinery (English), hardbk, 1927.**350.00**
Bookends, UP commemorating driving of golden spike, Bettendorf..**200.00**
Booklet, D&HRy, photos, no text, 1897, 8x10", 24-pg.................**35.00**
Booklet, Sketch...Geographical Rte...Great Railway..., 1829, 16-pg.**280.00**
Booklet, Western NC, tourist guide, fold-out map, 1886 ....**170.00**
Brake wheel, D&RG emb on CI...**100.00**
Brochure, CO Midland RR, Sights & Scenes, 1930s, 25-pg........**520.00**
Brochure, Pacific Electric Ry, Mt Lowe, 1920, 8¾x4"..............**155.00**
Brochure, Pacific Electric Ry, Mt Lowe Trail Trips, mc, 1913, 4-pg ..**80.00**
Bucket, coal; NYC System, w/bail & hdl, used in caboose..........**100.00**
Bulletin board, SRR w/logo, porc, 32x38".................................**660.00**
Caboose, fr+trucks+windows+doors+beams+rafters, etc, disassembled.**2,000.00**
Calendar, perpetual; MP, complete..**165.00**
Calendar, pocket; ATSF, Indian scene, 1989..............................**19.00**
Calendar, PRR, Grif Teller's, Mainline of Am Commerce, 1938, complete .**195.00**
Cattle car, D&RG, narrow gauge, 1870-80s, 10x30x8' **2,600.00**
Dater die, WVRy Co, Sagerton, TX, Witchita Valley Ry Co, brass ..**150.00**
Door hdl & plate, GN, TM, 6 holes for mounting, 3½x15" **155.00**
Figurine, Harvey Girl, plaster-like, PW Baston, 1946, 3" **165.00**
Gauge, Ashcroft, for air brakes on steam locomotive, 6" dia.......**195.00**
Gauge, Ashcroft, locomotove steam pressure, 1896, 6" dia **260.00**
Headlight, diesel locomotive, 74vdc, aluminum & brass, 24x14".**355.00**
Humidor, PRR, glass (BM), brass lid (TM), 1932, 5½"..............**220.00**
Ice pick, PRR, Save It w/Ice, all metal, SM in hdl, 8¼"...............**20.00**
Insulator, B&O, amethyst glass, Pat'd Dec 19, 1871....................**835.00**
Luggage tag, P&Ogd RR/ME Cent RR/Special, brass, 1⅜x1⅝"..**145.00**
Luggage tag, WStL&PRy/W Shore RR/via Grand Trunk Ry, brass, 1½" sq..**90.00**
Magazines, Trains, 20 yrs, 1940-60, complete, bound **935.00**
Manual, instruction; GM Electo-motive Div for NYO&WRR, 1945..**158.00**
Map, PRR, detailed regional, stations/phones/office+, 1957, 18x21".**138.00**
Map, UP, Panoramic Perspective...by Challenger Inn, 1930, 22x32".**75.00**
Mars light, SP, oscillating head lamp, inside mechanism, 23x14".**415.00**
Match safe, Monon's alligator (FL travel promo), CI, 9" L **140.00**
Menu, B&M/ME Central, Flying Yankee, 1930s.......................**168.00**
Menu, NYC, J Whitcomb Riley deluxe all coach streamliner, '40s, 7x10"..**110.00**
Menu, SP, children's, menu+activities, 1950s, 8-pg, 5x6¾" **42.50**
Pass, annual; Astoria & Columbia River RR Co, cardstock, 1907..**230.00**
Pass, annual; CO Midland Ry, ticket agent's, 1890.....................**350.00**
Pass, annual; CO Southern, ...stations on Ft Collins district, 1900..**350.00**
Pass, annual; CO Springs & Cripple Creek District Ry Co, 1904...**350.00**
Pass, annual; Elizabethtown & Paducah, unusually fine vignette, 1873 ..**355.00**

Pass, annual; Lehigh Valley, sgn Asa Packer founder, 1870.........**400.00**
Pass, annual; New Bedford & Taunton RR Fairhaven Branch, mc, 1873..**178.00**
Pass, annual; Newport & Sherman's Valley RR, yel cardstock, 1910.**155.00**
Pass, annual; Orange Belt Ry, Tarpon Rte, 1890.........................**450.00**
Pass, annual; Pittsburgh, Westmoreland & Somerset RR, cardstock, 1915.**190.00**
Pass, trip; Dunkirk, Allegheny Valley & Pittsburgh RR, 1903 ......**46.00**
Pass, trip; TPA silver, good on CO Midland, D&RG, UP, 1890..**3,000.00**
Photo, Grand Trunk RR Station, Bethel ME, 1908, mtd, 8x10"..**22.50**
Photo, Headquarters NPRR Tacoma, #254, Fr maker, mtd, 1889, 5x8" ..**80.00**
Photo, Montana RR yards+town, fr & hand tinted, 1900...........**140.00**
Plate, builder's; ATSF, 475 4-6-0, RI Loco Works, #3245, 1900 ..**2,575.00**
Plate, CN, brass number, #3496, 11x7⅛".....................................**800.00**
Plate, number; Shay locomotive, brass, Lima Machine Co, 15½" dia..**1,350.00**
Playing cards, GN, Julia Wades/Chief Wades, dd, slipcase w/TL goat...**75.00**
Playing cards, NYNH&H, RI & Cape Cod scenes, dd **120.00**
Playing cards, SP, Sunset, Shasta & Ogden Rt, scenics, sd, mk case ..**65.00**
Postcard, FEC, St Augustine, fold-out, ca 1900, 16-pg, 3½x5¼" ..**25.00**
Postcard, NYNH&H, real photo, locomotive on side, early 1900s.**65.00**
Postcard, SP, Glendale, real photo, train crew around train, 1940s...**24.00**
Poster, NP, Alaska scene by Sidney Lawrence, 1930s, 40x30" **490.00**
Poster, NP, Montana speeding steam train near Absoroka mtns, 30x40"...**670.00**
Poster, SP, West Coast of Mexico Route, Logan, 22x16".............**590.00**
Scales, platform; Southern RR, Chicago Scale Co, 300-lb max, 27½"..**100.00**
Shelf, luggage rack; Pullman, cast brass, 2-shelf, 11x28x10" **350.00**
Sign, B&O, Danger Run Slow, 1-sided porc, 6 grommets, 6x24"..**325.00**
Sign, CPR Telegraph & Cable Office, 1-sided porc, 6-holes, 12x21" .**315.00**
Sign, Nut Tree, mini RR on landing strip to restaurant, brass, 12" dia..**200.00**
Sign, photo of old steam locomotive on porc, no attribution, 24x36"..**520.00**
Sign, Railway Express, 1-sided porc, 4 grommets, 12x36" **355.00**
Sign, Seaboard logo, 1-sided pnt metal, 24" dia **360.00**
Sign, Wells Fargo & Co Express, 2-sided porc, 3 grommets, 21" sq..**550.00**
Spittoon, NC&StL Ry, emb NC&StL, enamel on CI **135.00**
Spoon, souvenir; Mt Lowe Incline Ry scene in bowl, sterling **25.00**
Steam injector, Penberthy, Model B 21 (STK249), brass, ¾" **380.00**
Step stool, IL Central, gridded rubber mat top, emb ICRR SM, $200 to.**250.00**
Step stool, NYC System, gridded top, rubber ft pads, SM, 18x20"..**300.00**
Stereoview, ORR, Columbia River View, Tooth Bridge, Watkins #1298.**100.00**
Stereoview, RR yards Chattanooga, TN, 1860s **400.00**
Stockholder's report, UP, fold-out map w/Indian Territory, 1882 ..**78.00**
Strong box, Property of Pacific Electric Ry on lid, nonworking lock.**155.00**
Telegraph key, D&RG RR, BM, early 1900s.................................**150.00**
Telegraph key, Xograph (Exograph) Morse Code, Canada, 1920 .**450.00**
Telephone, scissors; Western Electric decal, ...Pat'd...09 cord+stand ..**200.00**
Ticket, NP, employee's excursion, Tacoma to Centralia, 1889 ....**100.00**
Timetable, employee; CMStP&P Trans MO Division, #7, 1945 ...**17.50**
Timetable, employee; NC&StL Ry, Nashville Division 1948......**100.00**
Timetable, employee; Southern RR, Danville Division, #18, 1941, 12-pg.**10.00**
Timetable, employee; SP, Houston Division, #7, 1933.................**36.00**
Timetable, employee; SP, Lafayette Division, #82, 1935...............**44.00**
Timetable, public; Kansas Pacific Ry, includes map, 1874 ....**475.00**
Timetable, public; OH Central Lines, T&OCRy, K&MRy, 1899, 16-pg.**100.00**
Timetable, public; Toronto, Hamilton & Buffalo Ry, 1905, 23x15½".**280.00**
Timetable/map, public; MOPAC, 1883, unfolds to 23½x16¼" **92.50**
Token for ½ cord of wood, MI, Southern & N IN RR, E&N Division..**55.00**
Wax sealer, Maine Central, Hiram Station, brass **235.00**
Wax sealer, Southern Express Co, brass, mushroom shape **100.00**

Razors

As straight razors gain in popularity, prices of those razors also increase. This carries with it a lure of investment possibilities which can encourage the novice or speculator to make purchases that may later prove to be unwise. We recommend that before investing serious money in razors, you become familiar with the elements which make a razor valuable. As with other collectibles, there are specific traits which are desirable and which have a major impact on the price of a piece.

The following information is based on the second edition of *The Standard Guide to Razors* by Roy Ritchie and Ron Stewart (available from R&C Books, P.O. Box 151, Combs, KY 41729, $9.95 +$2.50 S&H, autographed). It describes the elements most likely to influence a razor's collector value and their system of calculating that value. (Their book is a valuable reference guide to both the casual and serious collector of razors.)

There are four major factors which determine a razor's collector value. These are the brand and country of origin, the handle material, the art work found on the handles or blades, and the condition of the razor. Ritchie and Stewart freely admit that there are other factors that may come into play with some collectors, but these are the major players in determining value. They have devised a system of evaluation which is based on these four factors.

The most important factor is the value placed on the brand and country of origin. This is the price of a common razor made by (or for) a particular company. It has plain handles, probably made of plastic, no art work, and is in collectible condition. It is the beginning value. Hundreds (thousands?) of these values are provided in the 'Listings of Companies and Base Values' chapter in the book.

The second category is that of handle material. This covers a wide range of materials, from fiber on the low end to ivory on the high end. The collector needs to be able to identify the different handle materials when he sees them. This often takes some practice, since there are some very good plastics that can mimic ivory quite successfully. Also, the difference between genuine celluloid and plastic can become significant when determining value. A detailed chart of these values is supplied in the book. The listing below can be used as a general guide.

The third category is the most subjective. Nevertheless, it is an extremely important factor in determining value. This category is artwork, which can include everything from logo art to carving and sculpture. It may range from highly ornate to tastefully correct. Blade etching as well as handle artistry are to be considered. Perhaps what some call the 'gotta have it' or the 'neatness' factors properly fall into this category. You must accurately determine the artistic merits of your razor when you evaluate it relative to this factor. Again, the book we referenced earlier provides a more complete listing of considerations than is used here.

Finally, the condition is factored in. The book's scales run from 'parts' (10% +/-) to 'Good' (150% +/-). Average (100% +/-) is classified as 'Collectible.' See chart D for details concerning condition guidelines for evaluation.

Samplings from charts:

Chart A: Companies and Base Values

Abercrombie & Finch, NY	14.00
Areial, USA	24.00
Boker, Henri & Co, Germany	14.00
Brick F, England	12.00
Case Mfg Co Spring Valley NY	40.00
Chores, James; England	13.00
Dahlqres, CW; Sweden	14.00
Diane, Japan	10.00
Electric Co, NY	15.00
Fautless, Germany	11.00
Fox Cutlery, Germany	11.00
Fredericks (Celebrated Cutlery), England	13.00
Gilbert Bros, England	11.00
Griffon XX, Germany	11.00
Henckels, Germany	15.00
Holly Mfg Co, CT	27.00
International Cutlery Co Ny/Germany	11.00

IXL, England	12.00
Jay, Jphn; NY	12.00
KaBar, Union Cut Co, USA	28.00
Kanner, J; Germany	11.00
Kern, R&W; Canada/England	12.00
LeCocltre, Jacque; Switzerland	12.00
Levering Razor Co, NY/Germany	18.00
McIntosh & Heather, OH	12.00
Merit Import Co, Germany	10.00
Monthoote, England	12.00
National Cut Co, OH	11.00
Oxford Razor Co, Germany	10.00
Palmer Brothers, Savannah, GA	20.00
Primble, John; Indian Steel Works, Louisville, KY	24.00
Queen City, NY	30.00
Querelle, A; Paris, France	12.00
Quigley, Germany	12.00
Radford, Joseph & Sons, England	12.00
Rattler Razor Co, Germany	10.00
Robeson Cut Co, USA	28.00
Salamander Works, Germany	11.00
Soderein, Ekilstuna Sweden	11.00
Taylor, LM; Cincinnati, OH	14.00
Tower Brand, Germany	16.00
Ulmer, Germany	11.00
US Barber Supply, TX	12.00
Vinnegut Hdw Co, IN	11.00
Vogel, Ed; PA	10.00
Wade & Butcher, England	24.00
Weis, JH; Supply House, Louisville, KY	15.00
Yankee Cutlery Co, Germany	11.00
Yazbek, Lahod; OH	11.00
Zacour Bros, Germany	10.00
Zepp, Germany	10.00

Chart B, as described below, is an abbreviated version of the handle materials list in *The Standard Guide to Razors*. It is an essential category in the use of the appraisal system developed by the authors.

Ivory	550%
Tortoise Shell	500%
Pearl	400%
Stag	400%
Bone	300%
Celluloid	250%
Composition	150%
Plastic	100%

Chart C deals with the artistic value of the razor. As pointed out earlier, this is a very subjective area. It takes study to determine what is good and what is not. Taste can also play a significant role in determining the value placed on the artistic merit of a razor. The range is from superior to nonexistent. Categories generally are divided as follows:

Exceptional	650%
Superior	550%
Good	400%
Average	300%
Minimal	200%
Plain	100%
Nonexistant	0%

Chart D is also very subjective. It determines the condition of the razor. You must judge accurately if the appraisal system is to work for you.

Good	150%

Does not have to be factory mint to fall within this category. However, there can be no visible flaws if it is to be calculated at 150%.

            Collectible   100%

May have some flaws that do not greatly detract from the artwork or finish.

            Parts   10%

Unrepairable, valuable as salvageable parts.

Razors may fall within any of these categories, ie. collectible + 112%.

Now to determine the value of your razor, multiply A times B, then multiply A times C. Add your two answers and multiply this sum times D. The answer you get is your collector value. See the example below.

(a) Brand and Origin Base Value	(b) Handle Material % Value	(c) Artwork % Value	(d) Condition % Value	(e) Collector Value
Wade & Butcher England $24.00	Iridescent Pearl Handles 24 x 400% $96.00	Carved handles 24 x 500% $120.00	Cracked handle at pin Collectible- 80%	$96+$120=$216 $216 x 80%= **$172.80**

Reamers

The reamer market is very active right now, and prices are escalating rapidly. They have been made in hundreds of styles and colors and by as many manufacturers. Their purpose is to extract the juices from lemons, oranges, and grapefruits. The largest producer of glass reamers was McKee, who pressed their products from many types of glass — custard; Delphite and Chalaine Blue; opaque white; Skokie Green; black; caramel and white opalescent; Seville Yellow; and transparent pink, green, and clear. Among these, the black and the caramel opalescents are the most valuable.

The Fry Glass Company also made reamers that are today very collectible. The Hazel Atlas Crisscross orange reamer in pink is valued at $300.00 to $325.00 or more — the same in blue, $350.00. Hocking produced a light blue orange reamer and, in the same soft hue, a two-piece reamer and measuring cup combination. Both are considered rare and very valuable with currently quoted estimates at $1,000.00 and up for the former and $1,800.00 and up for the latter. In addition to the colors mentioned, red glass examples — transparent or slag — are rare and costly. Prices vary greatly according to color and rarity. The same reamer in crystal may be worth three times as much in a more desirable color.

Among the most valuable ceramic reamers are those made by American potteries. The Spongeband reamer by Red Wing is valued in excess of $500.00; Coorsite reamers with gold or silver trim are worth $300.00 and up. Figurals are popular — Mickey Mouse and John Bull may bring $600.00 to $1,000.00. Others range from $55.00 to $350.00. Fine china one- and two-piece reamers are also very desirable and command very respectable prices.

A word about reproductions: A series of limited edition reamers is being made by Edna Barnes of Uniontown, Ohio. These are all marked with a 'B' in a circle. Other reproductions have been made from old molds. The most important of these are Anchor Hocking two-piece two-cup measure and top, Gillespie one-cup measure with reamer top, Westmoreland with flattened handle, Westmoreland four-cup measure embossed with orange and lemons, Duboe (hand-held darning egg), and Easley's Diamonds one-piece.

Our advisor for this category is Dee Long; she is listed in the Directory under Illinois. For more information concerning reamers and reproductions, contact our advisor or the National Reamer Collectors Association (see Clubs, Newsletters, and Catalogs). Be sure to include an SASE when requesting information.

Ceramic

Baby's, chicks jumping rope, pk 120.00
Child's face, red & wht, Japan mk, 2-pc, 3" 120.00
Chintz, wht w/red floral, 2-pc, MIJ, 6" dia 40.00
Citrus face on teapot, pk sponging w/mc details, Napco Japan ...150.00
Clown, mc lustre, Japan, ca 1940s, 4¾" 125.00
Clown, Sourpuss, w/saucer, 4¾" 125.00
Clown, wht w/mc details, Mikori Ware, 1940s, 7¼" 145.00
Clown, wht w/much orange, 1930s-40s, 7" 145.00
Clown, wht w/red, mc pointed cap, Japan, 1940s, 6" 110.00
Dog, beige w/red & blk trim, 2-pc, 8" 225.00
Duck, wht w/mc features, MIJ, 2-pc, 3½" 70.00
Floral, red & blk, Japan, 2-pc, 5½" 70.00
Girl's face 135.00
Mexican w/cactus, mc Japan 200.00
Orange, Erphila...Czecho-Slovakia, pre-1917, 6" 100.00
Pitcher style, wht w/gr floral decor, Moriyama, MIJ, EX 40.00
Puddinhead, 2-pc, 6" 200.00
Sailboat, yel or red, 3", ea 125.00
Swan, cream w/rose flowers, gr base, Japan, 2-pc, 4" 75.00
Teapot, English cottage scene decor, 2-pc 75.00
Teapot, floral, yel & maroon on wht, Nippon, 2-pc, 3¼" 90.00
Triangular, bl plaid, MIJ, 6x8" 35.00
Windmill, Japan, 4½" 75.00

Glass

Anchor Hocking, gr, Circle, pitcher w/reamer top....................70.00
Cambridge, amber, from $600 to 650.00
Cambridge, cobalt, sm tab hdl 300.00
Federal, amber, 6-sided cone, vertical hdl 275.00
Federal, gr, pointed cone, from $25 to 28.00
Federal, wht opal, sq...200.00
Fenton, gr opaque, pitcher & reamer.......................................800.00
Foreign, amber, from $80 to 85.00
Fry, Azure Blue, str sides, from $1,800 to 2,000.00
Fry, canary, fluted jell-o mold, from $375 to...........................400.00
Fry, canary (vaseline), str sides, from $65 to 75.00
Hazel-Atlas, cobalt, tab hdl, lemon, from $325 to 345.00
Hazel-Atlas, cobalt, tab hdl, orange, from $295 to 325.00
Hazel-Atlas, cobalt, 2-cup pitcher+top, from $295 to 325.00
Hazel-Atlas, gr, tab hdl, from $25 to.......................................28.00
Hazel-Atlas, yel, 2-cup pitcher & reamer set, from $350 to 375.00
Hocking, gr, tab hdl, from $25 to..27.50
Hocking, milk glass, tab hdl, from $100 to.............................110.00
Indiana, amber, hdl & spout opposite, from $300 to 325.00
Jeannette, Delphite Blue, sm...75.00
Jeannette, gr, lg, from $30 to..35.00
Jeannette, gr, tab hdl, from $25 to..28.00
Jeannette, lt jadite, sm, from $45 to 50.00
Jeannette, lt jadite, 2-cup pitcher+top, from $75 to 80.00
Jennyware, ultramarine, from $125 to 135.00
McKee, blk, grapefruit, from $1,200 to 1,350.00
McKee, custard, emb McK, 6", from $30 to 35.00
McKee, Delphite Blue, sm, from $100 to 115.00
McKee, milk glass, grapefruit, from $250 to 350.00
McKee, milk glass, sm, from $25 to 30.00
Orange Juice Extractor, pk, unemb, from $200 to....................250.00
Saunders, blk, from $1,400 to..1,600.00
Sunkist, blk, from $700 to...750.00
Sunkist, caramel custard, from $375 to 400.00
Sunkist, gray, from $175 to 185.00
Sunkist, milk glass, from $10 to 15.00

Tricia, blk, 2-pc, from $1,400 to **1,500.00**
Tufglas, gr, from $100 to **110.00**
US, gr, 4-cup pitcher & reamer set, from $140 to **150.00**
Valencia, amber, unemb, from $325 to **350.00**
Valencia, milk glass, from $120 to **150.00**
Westmoreland, amber, from $300 to......................................**325.00**
Westmoreland, pk, 2-pc, from $200 to **225.00**

Records

Records of interest to collectors are often not the million-selling hits by 'superstars.' Very few records by Bing Crosby, for example, are of any more than nominal value, and those that are valuable usually don't even have his name on the label! Collectors today are most interested in records that were made in limited quantities, early works of a performer who later became famous, and those issued in special series or aimed at a limited market. Vintage records are judged desirable by their recorded content as well; those that lack the quality of music that makes a record collectible will always be 'junk' records in spite of their age, scarcity, or the obsolescence of their technology.

Records are usually graded visually rather than aurally, since it is seldom if ever possible to first play the records you buy at shows, by mail, at flea markets, etc. Condition is one of the most important determinants of value. For example, a nearly mint-condition Elvis Presley 45 of 'Milk Cow Blues' (Sun 215) has a potential value of over $1,500.00. A small sticker on the label could cut its value in half; noticeable wear could reduce its value by 80%. A mint record must show no evidence of use (record jackets, in the case of EPs and LPs, must be equally choice). Excellent condition denotes a record showing only slight signs of use with no audible defects. A very good record has noticeable wear but still plays well. Records of lesser grades may be unsaleable, unless very scarce and/or highly sought-after.

While the value of most 78s does not depend upon their being in appropriate sleeves (although a sleeveless existence certainly contributes to damage and deterioration!), this is not the case with most EPs (extended play 45s) and LPs (long-playing 33⅓ rpm 'albums'), which must have their jackets (cardboard sleeves), in nice condition, free of disfiguring damage, such as writing, stickers, or tape. Often, common and minimally valued 45s might be collectible if they are in appropriate 'picture sleeves' (special sleeves that depict the artist/group or other fanciful or symbolic graphic and identify the song titles, record label, and number), e.g. many common records by Elvis Presley, The Beatles, and The Beach Boys.

Promotional copies (DJ copies) supplied to radio stations often have labels different in designs and/or colors from their commercially issued counterparts. Labels usually bear a designation 'Not for Sale,' 'Audition Copy,' 'Sample Copy,' or the like. Records may be pressed of translucent vinyl; while most promos are not particularly collectible, those by certain 'hot' artists, such as Elvis Presley, The Beach Boys, and The Beatles are usually premium disks.

Many of the most desirable and valuable 45s have been 'bootlegged' (counterfeited). For example, there are probably more fake Elvis Presley *Sun* records in circulation than authentic copies — certainly in higher grades! Collectors should be alert for these often deceptive counterfeits.

Our advisor for this category is L.R. Docks, author of *American Premium Record Guide*, which lists 60,000 records by over 7,000 artists, in its sixth edition. He is listed in the Directory under Texas. In the listings that follow, prices are suggested for records that are in excellent condition; worn or abused records may be worth only a small fraction of the values quoted and may not be saleable at all.

Blues, Rhythm and Blues, Rock 'N Roll, Rockabilly

Adams, Charlie; Black Land Blues, Columbia 21524, 45 rpm.......**10.00**
Adkins, Katherine; Individual Blues, Okeh 8363, 78 rpm.............**50.00**

Alderson, Mozelle; & Blind James Beck; Room Rent Blues, Black Patti label (extremely rare) 8004, $1,000.00 or more. (Photo courtesy L.R. Docks)

Anka, Paul; Diana, ABC Paramount 420, LP **20.00**
Avalon, Frankie; Young Frankie Avalon, Chancellor 5002, LP.....**20.00**
Bachelors, Delores, Earl 101, 45 rpm **30.00**
Belmonts, Tell Me Why, Sabrina 500, 45 rpm.............................**15.00**
Big Connie, Mumble Blues, Groove 0142, 45 rpm **15.00**
Blue Dots, You've Got To Live for Yourself, De Luxe 6052, 45 rpm...**30.00**
Bogan, Lucille; New Way Blues, Brunswick 7051, 78 rpm **100.00**
Bowman, Cecil; Man-A Waitin', D 1048, 45 rpm **10.00**
Buchanan & Goodman, Flying Saucer, Luniverse 100, 45 rpm.......**8.00**
Carnations, Long Tall Girl, Lescay 3002, 45 rpm........................**30.00**
Carolina Slim, Pleading Blues, Acorn 319, 78 rpm.....................**10.00**
Chantels, I Love You So, End 1010, 45 rpm................................**8.00**
Cleftones, Heart & Soul, Gee 705, LP **100.00**
Contenders, Whenever I Get Lonely, Saxony 1001, 45 rpm.........**30.00**
Cruisers, If I Knew, V-Tone 207, 45 rpm **15.00**
Davis, Link; Grasshopper Rock, Starday 242, 45 rpm.................**20.00**
Davis, Walter; I Just Can't Help It, Bullet 341, 78 rpm **10.00**
Derringers, Sheree; Capitol 4532, 45 rpm **10.00**
Dorsey, Lee; Ya Ya, Fury 1002, LP...**50.00**
Eagles, Please Please, Mercury 70391, 45 rpm.........................**12.00**
Everly Brothers, Bird Dog, Cadence 1350, 78 rpm....................**30.00**
Fidelity's, Memories of You, Baton 256, 45 rpm **10.00**
Five Royales, Take All of Me, Apollo 443, 45 rpm **20.00**
Flamingos, I Really Don't Want To Know, Parrot 811, 78 rpm **75.00**
Gavin, Tony; It's Never Seven or Eleven, Sims 165, 45 rpm........**10.00**
Gordon, Slim; Leg Iron Blues, Vocalion 1743, 78 rpm **100.00**
Gray, Geneva; Fortune Teller Blues, Okeh 8449, 78 rpm **50.00**
Hawkins, Buddy Boy; Yellow Woman Blues, Paramount 12558, 78 rpm.**150.00**
Hawks, Candy Girl, Imperial 5266, 45 rpm.................................**50.00**
Holly, Buddy; Peggy Sue, Coral 61885, 78 rpm **75.00**
Inspirations, Raindrops, Apollo 494, 45 rpm **30.00**
Jenkins, Robert & Trio; Steelin' Boogie, Parkway 103, 78 rpm.....**75.00**
Jewels, Please Return, Imperial 5362, 45 rpm...........................**12.00**
Kansas City Kitty, Scorchin', Vocalion 1632, 78 rpm **100.00**
Kaye, Anne; Every Fortune Teller Knows Me, Gee 1015, 45 rpm...**8.00**
Lamplighters, Part of Me, Federal 12149, 45 rpm **50.00**
Linthecome, Joe; Humming Blues, Gennett 7131, 78 rpm..........**200.00**
Little Johnny, Shelby County Blues, Aristocrat 405, 78 rpm **100.00**
Majestics, Pennies for a Beggar, Knight 105, 45 rpm **15.00**
Martin, Sara; Papa Papa Blues, Okeh 8231, 78 rpm **125.00**
Mr String Bean, Pass the Juice Miss Lucy; Herald 418, 45 rpm.....**20.00**
Nelson, Ricky; More Songs by Ricky, Imperial 9059, LP..............**40.00**
Nelson, Romeo; Head Rag Hop, Vocalion 1447, 78 rpm **200.00**
Nichols, Nick; Frankie & Johnny, Columbia 2071-D...................**50.00**
Peacocks, I Want You To Know, Nobel 711, 45 rpm **60.00**
Pigmeat Terry, Black Sheep Blues, Champion 50043, 78 rpm.......**40.00**
Presley, Elvis; Clambake, RCA Victor 3893, LP **75.00**
Price, Lloyd; Mr Personality, ABC Paramount 297, LP **25.00**
Rays, Silver Starlight, XYZ 608, 45 rpm.....................................**10.00**
Robinson, Alexander; My Baby, Paramount 12649, 78 rpm........**150.00**

Rodgers, Jimmie; Honeycomb, Roulette 4015, 78 rpm **20.00**

Sam the Sham & the Pharoahs, Wooly Bully, XL 906, 45 rpm **20.00**

Spiders, I'll Stop Crying, Imperial 5280, 45 rpm **25.00**

Starr, Andy; I Love My Baby, Arcade 115, 45 rpm **50.00**

Sugarman, Which Woman Do I Love, Sittin' In With 609, 78 rpm.**15.00**

Thayer, Frank; Evening Shadows, Outlaw 1, 45 rpm **20.00**

Tokens, Doom-Long, Gary 1006, 45 rpm **25.00**

Too Tight Henry, Charleston Contest, Columbia 14374D, 78 rpm...**100.00**

Velaries, Roll Over Beethoven, Jamie 1198, 45 rpm **12.00**

Washburn, Alberta; Hoboken Prison Blues, Superior 2826, 78 rpm..**300.00**

Willie Mae, I'd Rather Drink Muddy Water, Vocalion 03404, 78 rpm.**25.00**

Willis, Ralph; Shake That Thing, Lee 105, 78 rpm **40.00**

Wilson, Sonny; The Rainy Day Blues, Dee Gee 4000, 78 rpm......**30.00**

Woods, Eva; He's My Man, Silvertone 3557, 78 rpm **100.00**

Woody, Don; Bird Dog, Decca 30277, 45 rpm **20.00**

Young, Farron; The Object of My Affection, Capitol 1004, LP **30.00**

Country and Western

Alabama Four, Looking This Way, Broadway 8209, 78 rpm **25.00**

Allen Brothers, Slide Daddy Slide, Victor 23590, 78 rpm **50.00**

Armstrong & Ashley, No More Dying, Paramount 3291, 78 rpm.**50.00**

Barlow, Jerry; Louisiana Baby, OT 103, 78 rpm **7.00**

Boone County Entertainers, Arkansas Traveler, Supertone 9163, 78 rpm...**8.00**

Boyd, Aaron; Santa Barbara Earthquake, Champion 15652, 78 rpm.**18.00**

Boyd, Jim & Audrey Davis; Get Aboard That..., Vocalion 02873, 78 rpm...**100.00**

Butcher, Dwight; Lonesome Cowboy, Victor 23772, 78 rpm **50.00**

Carlisle, (Smiling) Bill; Rattle Snake Daddy, Vocalion 02520, 78 rpm..**25.00**

Cartwright Brothers, Kelly Waltz, Columbia 15220-D, 78 rpm.....**10.00**

Clark, Orla; I Want Some Home Brew, Gennett 6424, 78 rpm..**150.00**

Cross, Ballard; My Poodle Dog, Vocalion 5359, 78 rpm **15.00**

Davis & Nelson, I Shall Not Be Moved, Paramount 3186, 78 rpm..**30.00**

Denmon, Morgan; Naomi Wise, Okeh 45075, 78 rpm **10.00**

Dupree, Melvin; Augusta Rag, Gennett 6988, 78 rpm..................**100.00**

Floyd County Ramblers, Barn Dance, Victor 23759, 78 rpm.........**75.00**

Green, Jerry; Naggin' Women & Braggin' Men, Specialty 712, 78 rpm..**12.00**

Happy Valley Family, Going Down to the Valley, Vocalion 04484, 78 rpm...**8.00**

Hart Brothers, Empty Cradle, Paramount 3176, 78 rpm **15.00**

Hughey, Dan; Fatal Wedding, Champion 15428, 78 rpm **10.00**

Jones Brothers, Little Green Valley, Melotone 12179, 78 rpm **8.00**

Lambert & Hillpot, My Carolina Home, Paramount 3013, 78 rpm...**7.00**

Mack, Bill; Big Bad Daddy, Imperial 8151, 78 rpm **10.00**

Martin Brothers, Whistling Rufus, Paramount 3217, 78 rpm **50.00**

McGuire, Leon; When Blue Eyes Meet Brown, Vocalion 5393, 78 rpm.**10.00**

Miller, Emmett; I Never Had the Blues, Okeh 40545, 78 rpm....**100.00**

Moore, John; Columbus Prison Fire, Broadway 8188, 78 rpm.......**12.00**

Paradise Joy Boys, Cemetary Sal, Brunswick 4268, 78 rpm...........**50.00**

Peck's Male Quartet, Home Over There, QRS 9030, 78 rpm........**30.00**

Poindexter, Doug; Now She Cares No More, Sun 202, 78 rpm.....**75.00**

Red Headed Fiddlers, Rag Time Annie, Brunswick 288, 78 rpm...**20.00**

Rice, Edd; Cricket on the Hearth, Vocalion 5220, 78 rpm............**15.00**

Rochford & Peggs, Hawaiian Blues, Vocalion 5207, 78 rpm **50.00**

Stanley, Fred; The Tie That Binds, Columbia 15559-D, 78 rpm...**12.00**

Taggart, Charles Ross; Sister Sorrowful, Edison 51448, 78 rpm.....**10.00**

Taylor & Bunch, Six Months Ain't Long, Supertone 9352, 45 rpm..**12.00**

Turner, Cal; Only a Tramp, Champion 15587, 78 rpm **18.00**

Virginia Dandies, God's Getting Worried, Crown 3145, 78 rpm...**20.00**

Jazz, Dance Bands, Personalities

Alabama Red Jackets, You Can't Cry...Shoulder, Champion 15229, 78 rpm..**12.00**

Arcadia Peacock Orchestra of St Louis, Dream Boat, Okeh 40044, 78 rpm....**12.00**

Atlanta Syncopators, That Wicked Stomp, Grey Gull 1888, 78 rpm..**30.00**

Benson Orchestra of Chicago, Go Emmaline, Victor 19484, 78 rpm..**8.00**

Boots & His Buddies, Riffs, Bluebird 6081, 78 rpm **10.00**

Boswell, Connie; I'm Gonna Cry, Victor 19639, 78 rpm **30.00**

Brown, Henry; Twenty-First Street Stomp, Paramount 12825, 78 rpm.**200.00**

Cardinal Dance Orchestra, My Mammy Knows, Cardinal 504, 78 rpm.**20.00**

Cellar Boys, Barrel House Stomp, Vocalion 1503, 78 rpm **200.00**

Charleston Chasers, Delirium, Columbia 1076D, 78 rpm **20.00**

Cotton Pickers, Jimtown Blues, Brunswick 2766, 78 rpm **12.00**

Curran, Joe & His Orchestra; Louise, Parlophone PNY-41231, 78 rpm ..**40.00**

Dixie Washboard Band, Livin' High, Columbia 14128-D, 78 rpm ..**40.00**

Etting, Ruth; What Is Sweeter, Brunswick 6671, 78 rpm **12.00**

Fallon, Owen & Californians; If You Hadn't...Away, Sunset 1133, 78 rpm.**50.00**

Finley, Bob & His Orchestra; Audition Blues, Cameo 9105, 78 rpm.**15.00**

Fuller, Bob; Spread Yo' Stuff, Ajax 17091, 78 rpm **25.00**

Gold, Lou & His Orchestra; Love Light Lane, Cameo 713, 78 rpm ..**8.00**

Gray, Russell & His Orchestra; Sugar, Okeh 40938, 78 rpm **60.00**

Handy, Katherine; Loveless Love, Paramount 12011, 78 rpm **60.00**

Harmonians, Some Sweet Day, Harmony 863-H, 78 rpm..............**10.00**

Henderson, Edmonia; Black Man Blues, Paramount 12084, 78 rpm.**100.00**

Jones-Smith Inc, Shoe-Shine Boy, Vocalion 3441, 78 rpm **15.00**

Kirk, Andy & His 12 Clouds; Once or Twice, Brunswick 4863, 78 rpm...**30.00**

Langford, Francis; When Mother Played the Organ, Victor 24191, 78 rpm..**15.00**

Lentz, Al & His Orchestra; Sweet Thing, Banner 1812, 78 rpm...**10.00**

Lyman, Abe & Ambassador Orch; Those Longing..., Nordskog 3019, 78 rpm..**50.00**

Marvin, Johnny; Memphis Blues, Edison 51709, 78 rpm **15.00**

Miller, Ray & His Orchestra; Lots O' Mama, Brunswick 2613, 78 rpm.**8.00**

Moonlight Revelers, Alabama Shuffle, Grey Gull 1775, 78 rpm...**50.00**

New Orleans Lucky Seven, Goose Pimples, Okeh 8544, 78 rpm ..**75.00**

Original Dixieland Five, Tiger Rag, Victor 25524, 78 rpm **10.00**

Paulson's Night Hawks, Ol' Man Sunshine, Supertone 9041, 78 rpm ..**50.00**

Pendleton, Andy; Sweet Emmaline, Okeh 8625, 78 rpm **30.00**

Preer, Evelyn; Sunday, Banner 1895, 78 rpm...............................**12.00**

Ramblers, She Knows Her Onions, Romeo 266, 78 rpm **8.00**

Rocky Mountain Trio, Freakish Blues, Gennett 3002, 78 rpm **15.00**

Smith & West Orchestra, I Need Lovin' Broadway 1486, 78 rpm..**10.00**

Stuart, Hal & His Gang; Hot Coffee, Bell 602, 78 rpm.................**20.00**

Vallee, Rudy & His CT Yankees; Shame on You, Bluebird 5175, 78 rpm..**15.00**

Waters, Ethel; All the Time, Black Swan 14155, 78 rpm **50.00**

Welk, Lawrence & Novelty Orch; Spiked Beer, Gurney 20341, 78 rpm..**150.00**

Williams, Bill & His Gang; Doo Wacka Doo, Champion 15011, 78 rpm..**12.00**

Red Wing

The Red Wing Stoneware Company, founded in 1878, took its name from its location in Red Wing, Minnesota. In 1906 the name was changed to the Red Wing Union Stoneware Company after a merger with several of the other local potteries. For the most part they produced utilitarian wares such as flowerpots, crocks, and jugs. Their early 1930s catalogs offered a line of art pottery vases in colored glazes, some of which featured handles modeled after swan's necks, snakes, or female nudes. Other examples were quite simple, often with classic styling. After the addition of their dinnerware lines in 1935, 'Stoneware' was dropped from the name, and the company became known as Red Wing Potteries, Inc. They closed in 1967.

The pottery was reopened several years ago, and handmade and decorated salt-glazed stoneware is again being produced. Each piece is stamped with the potters' initials and the year of production.

Our artware advisors are Wendy and Leo Frese (Three Rivers Collectibles); they are listed under Texas. For further study we recommend *Red Wing Stoneware* and *Red Wing Collectibles* by Dan DePasquale, Gail Peck, and Larry Peterson; and *Red Wing Art Pottery, Book II*, and *Collector's Encyclopedia of Red Wing Art Pottery* by B.L. and R.L. Dollen. All are published by Collector Books. Another good reference is *Red Wing Art Pottery* by Ray Reiss (privately published).

Commercial Art Ware and Miscellaneous

Bowl, brn w/orange int, flat, #414, 7" 40.00
Bowl, English Garden, turq w/brn/wht wash, #1188, 12" L 40.00
Candle holders, gray gloss w/coral int, petal shape, #B1411, 4", pr..30.00
Candle holders, leaf motif, turq gloss, #1286, 8", pr............30.00
Compote, Nile Blue fleck w/Colonial Buff int, #5022, 7"..............50.00
Jug, genie type, bl gloss, stamped, 8¾".........................125.00
Planter, loops emb on Zephyr Pink fleck gloss, bowl form, #643, 4"...40.00
Planter, yel fleck w/lt gr int, #1552, 6".........................25.00
Shell bowl, Monarch line, Nile Blue fleck gloss, #M1567, 9" 25.00
Vase, cactus flowers, bl, Brushed Ware, RWUS mk, 8" 75.00
Vase, cattails, Brushed Ware, dk gr cylinder, 7" 150.00
Vase, Classic Group, bl/wht stippled, 5 scallops, #500, 5½" 75.00
Vase, cloverleaf shape, Zepher Pink fleck gloss, #1556, 6".............30.00
Vase, contoured front, bl gloss, #1202, 5½"........................25.00
Vase, Egyptian, gr semimatt, hdls, stamped, 12"...........................135.00
Vase, figures & flowers emb on pk, hdls, #1159, 8"..................50.00
Vase, floral emb, ivory w/brn wash, hdls, #1165, 8¾" 50.00
Vase, Grecian style, aqua matt/wht gloss, hdls, #641, 7"................35.00

Vases, King and Queen chess pieces, oatmeal with lavender interior, 13", from $200.00 to $250.00 each.

Vase, leaf emb on pk semimatt, hdls, #1174, 7" 35.00
Vase, lions & foliage, sage gr & bl semigloss, 7⅝" 150.00
Vase, Neo-Classic, ivory/gr semimatt, #668, 10" 175.00
Vase, peacock panels emb on lt gr gloss, cylindrical, #187, 7½" .125.00
Vase, pk w/emb ribs, dbl loop hdls, #1111, 7½".........................35.00
Vase, Renaissance Group, aqua/wht semimatt, #522, 6" 40.00
Vase, swirls emb on bl gloss, flared rim, #952, 6" 40.00
Vase, tan w/brn leaf trim, gr int, #1103, 8¼".........................35.00
Vase, trophy style, maroon gloss, #871, 7½"........................75.00
Vase, tulip shape, orange semimatt, #886, 7½" 35.00
Wall pocket, Magnolia, ivory semimatt w/brn wash, #1630, 7"...125.00
Wall pocket, sconce type, pk semimatt, #1254, scarce, 7" 50.00

Cookie Jars

Be aware that there is a very good reproduction of the King of Tarts. Except for the fact that the new jars are slightly smaller, they are sometime difficult to distinguish from the old.

Bob White, unmk...200.00
Carousel, unmk...350.00
Crock, wht..80.00
Dutch Girl (Katrina), yel w/brn trim.................................175.00
Friar Tuck, cream w/brn, mk..175.00
Friar Tuck, gr, mk..175.00
Friar Tuck, yel, unmk..150.00
Grapes, cobalt or dk purple, ea...275.00
Grapes, gr..135.00
Jack Frost, short, unmk..250.00

Jack Frost, tall, unmk...300.00
King of Tarts, mc, mk (+)...325.00
King of Tarts, pk w/bl & blk trim, mk...............................300.00
King of Tarts, wht, unmk..200.00
Peasant design, emb/pnt figures on aqua 110.00
Peasant design, emb/pnt figures on brn 120.00
Pierre (chef), bl, brn or pk, unmk, ea.............................150.00
Pineapple, yel..135.00

Dinnerware

Dinnerware lines were added in 1935, and today collectors scramble to rebuild extensive table services. Although interest is obvious, right now the market is so volatile, it is often difficult to establish a price scale with any degree of accuracy. Asking prices may vary from $50.00 to $200.00 on some items, which indicates instability and a collector market trying to find its way. (One guide currently on the market, for instance, lists Midnight Rose dinner plates at $15.00 to $20.00, while another terms them 'rare,' and values them at $145.00 each.) Sellers seem to be unfamiliar with pattern names and proper identification of the various pieces that each line consists of. There were many hand-decorated lines; among the most popular are Bob White, Tropicana, and Round-up. But there are other patterns that are just as attractive and deserving of attention. The Dollen books referenced both have dinnerware sections, and Ray Reiss has published a book called *Red Wing Dinnerware, Price and Identification Guide*, which shows nearly one hundred patterns on its back cover alone.

Town and Country, designed by Eva Zeisel, was made for only one year in the late 1940s. Today many collectors regard Zeisel as one of the most gifted designers of that era and actively seek examples of her work. Town and Country was a versatile line, adaptable to both informal and semiformal use. It is characterized by irregular, often eccentric shapes, and handles of pitchers and serving pieces are usually extensions of the rim. Bowls and platters are free-form comma shapes or appear tilted, with one side slightly higher than the other. Although the ware is unmarked, it is recognizable by its distinctive shapes and glazes. White (often used to complement interiors of bowls and cups), though an original color, is actually more rare than Bronze (metallic brown, also called gunmetal), which enjoys favored status; Gray is unusual. Other colors include Rust, Dusk Blue, Sand, Chartreuse, Peach, and Forest Green. Pieces have also shown up in Mulberry and Ming Green and are considered quite rare. (These are Red Wing Quartelle colors!) Note: Eva Zeisel recently gave permission to reissue a few select pieces of Town and Country; these are being made by World of Ceramics. In 1996 salt and pepper shakers were reproduced in new colors not resembling Red Wing colors. In 1997 the mixing bowl and syrup were reissued. All new pieces are stamped EZ96 or EZ97 and are visibly different from the old, as far as glaze, pottery base, and weight.

Charles Alexander (who is listed in the Directory under Indiana) advises us on the Town and Country market. Our advisor for the remainder of this category is Brenda Dollen; she is listed in the Directory under Minnesota.

Blossom Time, bowl, rim soup...10.00
Blossom Time, teapot 50.00
Bob White, cruet 30.00
Bob White, gravy boat, w/lid & stand 55.00
Brittany, bowl, coupe soup; 8"...20.00
Brittany, chop plate, 14"...55.00
Capistrano, bowl, rim soup 12.00
Capistrano, platter, 15"...25.00
Desert Sun, platter, 15"...24.00
Frontenac, shakers, pr...22.50
Hearthside, bowl, rim soup..16.00
Hearthside, cup & saucer 12.50
Iris, egg plate, w/lid..85.00

Iris, shakers, pr 14.00
Lexington Rose, celery dish..............................15.00
Lexington Rose, supper tray 12.50
Lotus, coffee cup 10.00
Lotus, shakers, pr 12.50
Lute Song, bread tray.......................................28.00
Midnight Rose, teapot.......................................80.00
Normandy, candle holders, pr 65.00
Normandy, creamer 20.00
Orleans, casserole, w/lid 20.00
Orleans, plate, chop; 12" 40.00
Orleans, shakers, pr..30.00
Pepe, bowl, vegetable.......................................20.00
Pepe, cup & saucer, AD....................................15.00
Pink Spice, bowl, buffet....................................40.00
Pink Spice, shakers, pr 20.00
Random Harvest, bowl, salad; 12" 35.00
Random Harvest, plate, 6½" 6.50
Random Harvest, platter, 13"............................22.50
Round-Up, bowl, salad; 12"...............................80.00
Round-Up, bowl, salad; 5½"...............................30.00
Round-Up, plate, 10½".......................................40.00
Smart Set, bowl, rim soup 16.00
Smart Set, cup & saucer....................................15.00
Tampico, bowl, rim soup...................................15.00
Tampico, sugar bowl, w/lid 35.00
Town & Country, bowl, mixing; 9" 90.00
Town & Country, bowl, salad; 13" 95.00
Town & Country, creamer..................................35.00
Town & Country, mustard jar, w/lid 125.00
Town & Country, pitcher, 2-pt..........................95.00
Town & Country, platter, 11x7½".......................55.00
Town & Country, sugar bowl, w/lid 55.00
Turtle Dove, bowl, vegetable............................22.00
Turtle Dove, cup & saucer 10.00
Two Step, bowl, salad; 9" 20.00
Two Step, cup & saucer.....................................12.50
Village Green, bowl, salad; sm 18.00
Village Green, chop plate, 14" 35.00
Village Green, creamer & sugar bowl, w/lid 25.00
Zinnia, butter dish 50.00
Zinnia, chop plate...40.00

Stoneware

Key:

c/s — cobalt on stoneware	RW — Red Wing
MN — Minnesota	RWUS — Red Wing Union
NS — North Star	Stoneware

Bean pot, Albany slip, bail hdl, NS, 1-gal....................................140.00
Bean pot, Boston style, Albany slip, MN, 1-gal 150.00
Bowl, Greek Key, bl & wht, 10" 175.00
Bowl, Spongeband on wht, RWUS, 12"...1,500.00
Butter jar, Albany slip, high, MN, ½-gal...60.00
Butter jar, Albany slip, low, MN, 10-lb..100.00
Butter jar, Albany slip, low, NS, 2-lb..125.00
Chamber pot, bl bands on wht, RW 200.00
Chamber pot, brn sponging, RW 300.00
Churn, #10/2 birch leaves, c/s, RWUS, 10-gal.............................1,600.00
Churn, #3/birch leaf, c/s, MN, 3-gal..1,500.00
Churn, #5/leaf, c/s, unsgn, 5-gal..600.00
Churn, #5/red wing on wht, RWUS, 5-gal.......................................300.00
Combinette, emb decor, bl to wht, complete, RW..........................350.00

Cooler, #5/dbl leaves, c/s, RW, 5-gal..3,500.00
Cooler, #6/Ice Water/flower, c/s, RW, 6-gal................................10,000.00
Cooler, #52/Ice Water/4 leaves, c/s, RWUS, 25-gal 900.00
Crock, #2/dbl P (aka rib cage), c/s, MN, 2-gal..............................200.00
Crock, #4/dbl P (aka rib cage), c/s, MN, 4-gal..............................700.00
Crock, #8/elephant ear leaves, cobalt on wht, MN, 8-gal 150.00
Crock, #10/dbl set of birch leaves, cobalt on wht, RWUS, 10-gal....800.00
Crock, #20/elephant ear leaves, cobalt on wht, MN, 20-gal 300.00
Crock, #30/butterfly, c/s, RW, 30-gal...3,000.00
Filter, Success; incised decor/bl bands, c/s, MN, 4-gal.............1,400.00
Flowerpot, Albany slip, MN, 7"..375.00
Jar, packing; #3/red wing on wht, bail hdl, 3-gal.........................400.00
Jar, preserve/snuff; Albany slip, MN, 1-gal 75.00
Jar, preserve/snuff; wht, MN, 1-gal..75.00
Jar, wax sealer; Albany slip, MN, ½-gal..60.00
Jug, beehive; #5, Albany slip, RW, 5-gal.......................................900.00
Jug, bl bands on wht, cone top, RW, 1-gal....................................450.00
Jug, common, wht, MN, ½-gal..75.00
Jug, fancy, red wing on wht w/Albany slip top, 2-gal...................800.00
Jug, fancy, wht w/brn ball top, RW, 1-gal.....................................200.00
Jug, molded seam, Albany slip, bail hdl, MN, 1-gal......................300.00
Jug, molded seam, wht, bail hdl, MN, 1-gal..................................100.00
Jug, molded seam, wht, bail hdl, RW, ½-gal..................................100.00
Jug, shoulder; #3/birch leaves, cobalt on wht, MN, 3-gal...........175.00
Jug, shoulder; brn & salt glaze, cone top, RW, ½-gal...................375.00
Jug, shoulder; brn & salt glaze, pear top, NS, 2-gal.....................400.00
Jug, shoulder; brn & salt glaze, std top, RW, 1-gal......................150.00
Jug, shoulder; wht, cone top, RW, 1-gal..75.00
Jug, shoulder; wht, std top, MN, ½-gal...75.00
Jug, syrup; wht, cone top, MN, ½-gal..100.00
Jug, threshing; #5/birch leaves, cobalt on wht, 5-gal...............1,000.00
Pitcher, mustard; Albany slip, NS..350.00
Salt box, Spongeband on wht, w/lid, RWUS................................1,300.00
Spittoon, German style, incised decor/bl bands on salt glaze, unsgn .700.00
Spittoon, salt glzae, plain, unmk...350.00
Wash bowl & pitcher, Lily (emb), bl & wht, RW...........................900.00

Redware

The term redware refers to a type of simple earthenware produced by the Colonists as early as the 1600s. The red clay used in its production was abundant throughout the country, and during the eighteenth and nineteenth centuries redware was made in great quantities. Intended for utilitarian purposes such as everyday tableware or use in the dairy, redware was simple in design and decoration. Glazes of various colors were used, and a liquid clay referred to as 'slip' was sometimes applied in patterns such as zigzag lines, daisies, or stars. Plates often have a 'coggled' edge, similar to the way a pie is crimped or jagged, which is done with a special tool. In the following listings, EX (excellent condition) indicates only minor damage. Our advisor for this category is Barbara Rosen; she is listed in the Directory under New Jersey.

Bowl, brn mottle, w/spout, ribbed hdl, teacup shape, 3¾x6", VG ..220.00
Bowl, milk; running brn w/blk specks & seaweed-like pattern, 9⅝"..200.00
Butter mold, lady standing/wearing bonnet, yel glaze, 4½" 55.00
Crock, #4, gr w/orange spots, thick rim, dbl hdls, Galena, 13x13"...880.00
Crock, manganese runs, 2 incised wavy borders, str sides, 8¾" ...300.00
Dish, goose shape w/some cvg, pinched rim, blk runs/gr tinge, 4", VG.1,100.00
Dish, 3-line yel slip wavy zigzag, coggled, sm flake, rare sz, 5".....770.00
Figure, cat, seated, wht w/brn sponging & gr daubs, 3½", VG....220.00
Figure, lamb reclining, dk gold pnt over wht, 9½" 100.00
Figure, lion on base, hollow molded, pnt details, 14x11x6¾", EX.1,200.00
Figure, rooster, incised details, gr running slip, 15" 200.00

Figure, spaniel, gold pnt, mk Speese & Son, Gettysburg PA, 9½", EX..**1,700.00**
Flowerpot, Rockingham-type mottle, attached saucer, John W Bell, 5"..**875.00**
Jar, canning; mottled dk brn stripes, incised line, Medinger, 6" ..**495.00**
Jar, gr/orange spotted glaze, slightly ovoid, Galena, 7½" **1,075.00**
Jar, reddish-brn, wide mouth, unmk, ca 1830, ½-gal **45.00**
Jar, running brn, 5 emb bands w/geometrics & stars decor, 8".....**440.00**
Jar, tiny blk spots, ovoid w/raised rim, John Bell, 5½", EX..........**325.00**
Jug, dk brn alkaline, ca 1820s, ½-gal **65.00**
Jug, manganese glase, dbl spout, appl strap hdl (reattached), 11".**230.00**
Jug, peppered tan/dk brn, tooled decor, S Bell & Son, ca 1835, 9"..**1,980.00**
Loaf dish, yel slip decor, Alfred Jones, 1850s, 10x12½" **1,265.00**
Mold, blk mottled rim, raised beaded edge, melon ribbed, 1½x4" ..**275.00**
Mold, manganese sponging at rim, 2¼x7¼", EX **55.00**
Mold, Turk's head, mk John Bell, 8¾", EX.....................................**700.00**
Mug, gr ash, tooled line, Lanier Meaders, 3¾", EX.......................**55.00**
Mug, yel & brn drip on brn speckled, appl ribbed hdl, 19th C, 4", EX..**4,300.00**
Pie plate, yel slip decor resembling 4 dbl flags, coggled rim, 9" ...**385.00**
Pie plate, yel slip stylized Vs, coggled rim, 6¼", EX....................**440.00**
Pie plate, yel slip wavy lines & flourishes, crazing/chips, 8" **400.00**
Pie plate, yel waves/dot clusters, coggled rim, chip/2 hairlines, 10"..**385.00**
Pie plate, yel 3-line waves & 4 flag-like devices, coggled rim, 10" .**1,045.00**
Pie plate, 2 yel/gr 2-arc devices, wavy line, coggled rim, 10" ...**7,590.00**
Pie plate, 3 sets of wavy yel slip lines, coggled, 11", EX..............**600.00**
Pie plate, 3 sets of 3-line yel slip waves, coggled, 11" **935.00**
Pie plate, 3-line yel slip waves & flourishes, coggled, 8", EX.......**990.00**
Pitcher, Albany slip, sgraffito: Independence Pottery etc, 11", VG .**1,375.00**
Pitcher, dk brn mottle, clay strands form ribs at top, 1820s, 9½" .**275.00**
Pitcher, lt yel & gr brushed streaks, strap hdl, wooden lid, PA, 6"..**550.00**
Pitcher, manganese splotches, appl strap hdl, w/lid, 6½x6½" **325.00**
Pitcher, sgraffito flower on yel, strap hdl, 7¼", EX.......................**220.00**
Pitcher, yel slip leaves under sawtooth arches w/scrolls, 6" **250.00**
Plate, manganese w/6 yel slip lines, 8", EX...................................**150.00**
Plate, 3-line yel slip waves, early 1800s, set of 4 from 6-10" **1,725.00**
Strainer, manganese, ovoid w/3 ft, 2 appl hdls, 7x6" dia, EX **400.00**

Regal China

Located in Antioch, Illinois, the Regal China Company open for business in 1938. Products of interest to collectors are James Beam decanters, cookie jars, salt and pepper shakers, and similar novelty items. The company closed its doors sometime in 1993. The Old MacDonald Farm series listed below is especially collectible, so are the salt and pepper shakers.

Note: Where applicable, prices are based on excellent gold trim. (Gold trim must be 90% intact or deductions should be made for wear.)

Our advisor for this category is Judy Posner; she is listed in the Directory under Florida.

See also Decanters.

Cookie Jars

Cat, from $340 to **385.00**
Churn Boy **250.00**
Clown, gr collar, from $650 to **675.00**
Davy Crockett, from $450 to **600.00**
Diaper Pin Pig, from $450 to **540.00**
Dutch Girl, from $600 to **655.00**
Dutch Girl, peach trim...**720.00**
FiFi Poodle, from $600 to **655.00**
Fisherman, from $650 to **720.00**
French Chef, from $350 to..**405.00**
Goldilocks (+) **340.00**
Harpo Marx **1,080.00**

Hobby Horse, from $250 to...**270.00**
Hubert Lion, from $720 to...**855.00**
Humpty Dumpty, red...**250.00**
Little Miss Muffet, from $315 to...**350.00**
Majorette, from $350 to **400.00**
Oriental Lady w/Baskets, from $585 to...**630.00**

Peek-a-Boo (has been reproduced), from $1,350.00 to 1,440.00.

Quaker Oats..**115.00**
Three Bears..**175.00**
Toby Cookies, unmk, from $675 to **700.00**
Tulip, from $200 to **225.00**
Uncle Mistletoe...**765.00**

Old McDonald's Farm

Butter dish, cow's head...**175.00**
Canister, flour, cereal, coffee; med, ea, from $225 to **275.00**
Canister, pretzels, peanuts, popcorn, chips, tidbits; lg, ea, $325 to..**375.00**
Canister, salt, sugar, tea; med, ea, from $225 to **275.00**
Canister, soap, cookies; lg, ea, from $350 to.................................**425.00**
Cookie barn, from $250 to...**300.00**
Creamer, rooster, from $110 to **125.00**
Grease jar, pig, from $200 to **250.00**
Pitcher, milk...**350.00**
Shakers, boy & girl, pr...**80.00**
Shakers, churn, gold trim, pr...**95.00**
Shakers, feed sacks w/sheep, pr..**150.00**
Spice jar, assorted lids, sm, ea, from $125 to **150.00**
Sugar bowl, hen..**135.00**
Teapot, duck's head, from $250 to...**275.00**

Shakers

A Nod to Abe, 3-pc nodder, from $300 to.....................................**350.00**
Bendel, bears, wht w/pk & brn trim, pr, from $125 to **150.00**
Bendel, bunnies, wht w/blk & pk trim, pr from $125 to...............**150.00**
Bendel, kissing pigs, gray w/pk trim, lg, pr, from $350 to............**375.00**
Bendel, love bugs, burgundy, lg, pr, from $150 to **185.00**
Bendel, love bugs, gr, sm, pr...**65.00**
Cat, sitting w/eyes closed, wht w/hat & gold bow, pr **225.00**
Clown, pr..**250.00**
Dutch Girl, pr, from $200 to..**225.00**
FiFi, pr..**450.00**
Fish, mk C Miller, 1-pc..**55.00**
French Chef, wht w/gold trim, pr, from $250 to **350.00**
Humpty Dumpty, pr...**95.00**
Peek-a-Boo, red dots, lg, pr (+), from $450 to **500.00**

Peek-a-Boo, red dots, sm, pr, from $250 to...............................275.00
Peek-a-Boo, wht solid, sm, pr...200.00
Pig, pk, mk C Miller, 1-pc..95.00
Tulip, pr...50.00
Van Tellingen, bears, brn, pr, from $25 to.............................28.00
Van Tellingen, boy & dog, Black, pr 125.00
Van Tellingen, boy & dog, wht, pr...75.00
Van Tellingen, bunnies, solid colors, pr, from $28 ....32.00
Van Tellingen, ducks, pr..38.00
Van Tellingen, Dutch boy & girl, from $45 to 50.00
Van Tellingen, Mary & lamb, pr..60.00
Van Tellingen, sailor & mermaid, pr, from $225 to 260.00

Relief-Molded Jugs

Early relief-molded pitchers (ca 1830s – 1840s) were made in two-piece molds into which sheets of clay were pressed. The relief decoration was deep and well defined, usually of animal or human subjects. Most of these pitchers were designed with a flaring lip and substantial footing. Gradually styles changed, and by the 1860s the rim had become flatter and the foot less pronounced. The relief decoration was not as deep, and foliage became a common design. By the turn of the century, many other types of pitchers had been introduced, and the market for these early styles began to wane.

Watch for recent reproductions; these have been made by the slip-casting method. Unlike relief-molded ware which is relatively smooth inside, slip-cast pitchers will have interior indentations that follow the irregularities of the relief decoration. Values below are for pieces in excellent condition. Our advisor for this category is Kathy Hughes; she is listed in the Directory under North Carolina.

Key: Reg — Registered

Dickens, mc, unknown maker, ca 1860, 7½" 225.00
Fern, wht, Brownfield, Reg Nov 5, 1859, 8½" 225.00
Foxes & Hounds, gray-gr, Minton, ca 1831, 8¼".........................475.00

Gipsey (sic), pictorial white body in raised relief, unglazed, Edward Walley, mid-1800s, 10", $350.00.

Gleaner, tan, Edward Walley, Reg Nov 11, 1858, 10¾" 500.00
Loyal Volunteers, wht, Sanford Pottery, Reg Sept 28, 1860, 10½"...550.00
Medallions & Swags, wht, unknown maker, ca 1865, 8¼".........225.00
Monkey, tan, unknown maker, ca 1840, 8" 325.00
Nesting Birds, greenish tan, Mason, ca 1845, 7½".....................300.00
Prince Consort, wht, Old Hall, Reg April 9, 1862, 8" 600.00
Toby Philpot, tan, unknown, ca 1840, 7¼"................................375.00
Vertical leaves, tan, Elijah Jones, Reg Sept 1, 1838, 7" 450.00
Wisdom & Providence, lav & wht, Alcock, ca 1851, 6¼"...........550.00

Restraints

Since the beginning of time, many things from animals to treasures have been held in bondage by hemp, bamboo, chests, chains, shackles, and other constructed devices. Many of these devices were used to hold captives who awaited further torture, as if the restraint wasn't torturous enough. The study and collecting of restraints enables one to learn much about the advancement of civilization in the country or region from which they originated. Such devices at various times in history were made of very heavy metals — so heavy that the wearer could scarcely move about. It has only been in the last sixty years that vast improvements have been made in design and construction that afford the captive some degree of comfort. Our advisor for this category is Joseph Tanner; he is listed in the Directory under California.

Key:
bbl — barrel
d-lb — double lock button
K — key
Kd — keyed

lc — lock case
NST — non-swing through
ST — swing through
stp — stamped

Foreign Handcuffs

Czechalaviak, ST, Ralken flat K, modern ST 150.00
East German, aluminum, single lg hinge, ST, bbl K....................70.00
English, Chubb, NST, hi-security 10-slider lock mechanism.......300.00
German, Swartiger, steel, NST, bbl K goes in at end of cuffs 700.00
German, 3-lb steel set, 2⅝" thick, center chain, bbl K 175.00
German Clejuso, oval design, ST, dbl-cuff weight, 22-oz 100.00
German Darby, adjusts, well finished, NST, sm 120.00
Hiatt, English Darby, like US CW Darby, stp Hiatt & #d.............75.00
Italian, stp New Police, modern Peerless type, ST, sm bbl K........35.00
Russian modern ST, blued bbl K, unmk, crude............................80.00
Spanish, stp Alcyon/Star, modern Peerless type, flat K.................40.00
Spanish, stp Alcyon/Star, modern Peerless type, ST, sm bbl K......40.00

Foreign Leg Shackles

East German, aluminum, lg hinge, cable amid 4 cuffs, bbl K 100.00
German Clejuso, sq lc, adjusts/NST, d-bl on side, bbl K 125.00
Hiatt English combo manacles, handcuff/leg irons w/chain 325.00
Hiatt English non-adjust screw K Darby style, uses screw K........100.00
Hiatt Plug leg irons, same K-ing as Plug-8 cuffs, w/chain............400.00

U.S. Handcuffs

Adams, teardrop lc, bbl Kd, NST, usually not stp.......................300.00
Bean-Cobb, sm rnd lc, removable cylinder, d-lb, NST, 1899 ......100.00
Civil War padlocking type, various designs w/loop for lock 225.00
Flexibles, steel segmented bows, NST Darby type, screw K.........300.00
H&R Super, ST, shaft-hinge connector takes hollow titted K 150.00
Judd, NST, used rnd/internally triangular K, stp Mattatuck........150.00
Palmer, 2" steel bands, 2 K-ways (top & center), NST stp..........400.00
Peerless, ST, takes sm bbl K, stp Mfg'ered by S&W Co................75.00
Pratt combo, 1 cuff connnects w/nipper/claw, ST, mk Pratt........400.00
Rankin, steel NST, mk screw K 400.00
S&W 94 Maximum Security, ST, takes Ace-type K, stp S&W...120.00
Tower Dbl Lock, NST, takes bbl-bitted K, usually stp Tower 110.00
Tower Single Lock, NST, bbl-bit K, K-way slanted on lc, sm......125.00

U.S. Leg Shackles

American Munitions, as handcuffs 55.00

Harvard, as handcuffs 75.00
Leg lock brace, metal brace, ankle to knee, lever locked............225.00
Providence Tool Co, stp, NST.....................................250.00
Tower, bottom K, as handcuffs....................................150.00
Tower Detective, as handcuffs....................................200.00

Various Other Restraining Devices

African slave padlocking or riveted forged iron shackles.............170.00
English figure-8 nipper, claws open by lifting top lock tab 80.00
Gale finger cuff, knuckle duster, non-K, mk GFC 150.00
Hiatt High Security, hinged bbl K & pin-tumbler K (2 key) 150.00
Jay Pee, thumb cuffs, mk solid body, bbl K 15.00
Korean, hand chain model, blk, bbl K.............................60.00
Korean, hand hinged model, blk, bbl K............................70.00
Mighty-Mite, thumb cuffs, solid body, ST, mk, bbl K 110.00
New Model Russian, chain bbl K, blued 125.00
New Model Russian, hinged, bbl K, blued 140.00
Phillips nipper, claw, flip lever on top to open 90.00
Thomas Nipper, claw, push button top to open 90.00
Tower Lyon, thumb cuffs, solid body, NST, dbl-bit center K.......300.00

Reverse Painting on Glass

Verre eglomise is the technique of painting on the underside of glass. Dating back to the early 1700s, this art became popular in the nineteenth century when German immigrants chose historical figures and beautiful women as subjects for their reverse glass paintings. Advertising mirrors of this type came into vogue at the turn of the century.

Geo Washington, wht wig, blk coat, flakes, old fr, 30x24" 550.00
Lady in bl dress w/wht collar on gr ground, 15x11⅝" +fr............550.00
Sinking of Titanic w/rafts at water, dk, 15½x19½", EX..............150.00
Victorian seated at table w/book, 13½x10½" +fr.....................135.00
Well-dressed man & woman, identified, China Trade, 8x6" oval+fr, pr..925.00

Richard

Richard, who at one time worked for Galle, made cameo art glass in France during the 1920s. His work was often multilayered and acid cut with florals and scenics in lovely colors. The ware was marked with his name in relief. Our advisor for this category is Don Williams; he is listed in the Directory under Missouri.

Vase, palms and buildings with distant mountains, red and dark maroon on yellow, ovoid, 14¼", $6,000.00.

Stem, champagne; floral, gr/purple on yel, ped ft, 4½" 300.00
Vase, berries & leaves, mottled bl on orange, bulbous, 4¼" 375.00
Vase, castle/trees/mtns/shoreline, amethyst on gray/rose mottle, 23"..1,500.00
Vase, floral, bl on pale yel, conical, 4½" 375.00

Ridgway

As early as 1792, the Ridgway brothers, Job and George, produced fine quality earthenwares in Shelton, Staffordshire, marking their products 'Ridgway, Smith & Ridgway,' and later 'Job & George Ridgway.' Around 1800 the brothers split, and each had his own firm, both at Shelton. They were joined in the business by various members of the Ridgway family, and, in fact, their descendants still operate there today.

The two firms created by the split were the Bell Works and the Cauldon Pottery. Bell produced stone china and earthenware decorated with blue transfer printing. Their mark was 'J. & W. Ridgway' or J. & W.R.' (John and William) until 1848 when 'William Ridgway' was used. The Cauldon Pottery made earthenware, stone china, and high quality porcelains fine enough to win them the distinction of being appointed potters to the Queen. From 1830 their wares attest to this fact, bearing the Royal Arms mark with 'J.R.' within the crest. In 1940 '& Co.' was added. Most examples of Ridgway's wares found today are transfer-printed historical scenes.

See also Staffordshire, Transferware; and Flow Blue.

Biscuit barrel, Coaching Days, The Meet at an Inn, 5" 175.00
Bowl, Etruscan Festoon, 2-color transfer, hdls, ca 1930, 12" L....650.00
Bowl, rimmed soup; Rutland 30.00
Bowl, vegetable, Windsor, mc, 8".................................30.00
Candlestick, Etruscan Festoon, blk & pk transfer, 10" 675.00
Cup & saucer, English Garden #4424..............................29.00
Cup & saucer, Hawthorne, ca 1912................................36.00
Cup & saucer, Meadowsweet, bl transfer 22.00
Cup plate, Pomerania, mulberry transfer, 1830s, 4" 95.00
Gravy boat, Windsor, mc transfer, w/underplate 55.00
Gravy boat, Woodland, brn transfer, attached underplate.............50.00
Jug, Tyrolean, teal gr transfer, 1835, 4" 225.00
Mustard pot, Coaching Days, 2½" 60.00
Plate, Bay of Naples scene, Royal Ambrosial Ware, pierced to hang...50.00
Plate, Beauties, gr transfer, 1830-41, 9¼" 175.00
Plate, dessert; Helical, gr & bl transfer, ca 1830, 6½" 85.00
Plate, dinner; Devon Fruit, brn transfer.........................25.00
Plate, dinner; Historic Castles, red transfer 45.00
Plate, dinner; Oriental, gr transfer 40.00
Plate, Oriental, purple transfer, 1830-40, 9"....................90.00
Plate, Persian, brn transfer, 1830-34, 10½" 135.00
Plate, Rural Scenery, bl transfer on pearlware, 1820s, 10"..........475.00
Plate, soup; Oriental, red transfer, 1835-45, 10" 110.00
Plate, Tuscan Rose, purple transfer, 1814-37, 5¾" 95.00
Platter, Clifton, bl transfer, sm 40.00
Platter, Oriental Birds, bl transfer on pearlware, 1830, 11" 350.00
Platter, Persian, brn transfer, 1830-40, 18¾x15"..................750.00
Platter, Willow, ca 1927, 15¾x12½", EX..........................250.00
Sugar bowl, English Garden #4424, w/lid.........................45.00
Tankard, Coaching Days, Taking Up the Mail, 12" 120.00
Tankard, Coaching Days, Watering the Horses, 9½".................100.00
Teapot, Byzantium, purple transfer, 1844-54, 11¼" 595.00
Tureen, Tuscan Rose, brn transfer, w/lid, 1814-37 ....495.00

Rie, Lucie

Lucie Rie was born in 1902. She moved to London in 1938 and shared her studio with Hans Coper from 1946 to 1958. Her ceramics look modern; however they are based on shapes from many world cultures dating back to Roman times. Lucie Rie is best known for the use of metallic oxides in her clay and glazes. She specializes in the hand throwing of thin porcelain bowls, which is a very difficult process. Her works are in the world's best museums. All of her ceramics are impressed with a seal mark on the bottom, a cojoined 'L & R' within a rectangular reserve. Recently, when her work is offered at auction, it has been bringing prices that are sometimes double the presale estimates.

Bowl, incised lines, dk brn matt, 5⅞" 880.00
Bowl, incised lines, wht & brn gloss w/bl specks, 6" 1,000.00
Bowl, vertical inlaid lines, pk/bronze/aqua, 2⅛x4⅝" 3,250.00

Riviera

Riviera was a line of dinnerware introduced by the Homer Laughlin China Company in 1938. It was sold exclusively by the Murphy Company through their nationwide chain of dime stores. Riviera was unmarked, lightweight, and inexpensive. It was discontinued sometime prior to 1950. Colors are mauve blue, red, yellow, light green, and ivory. On rare occasions, dark blue pieces are found, but this was not a standard color. For further information we recommend *The Collector's Encyclopedia of Fiesta* (2001 values) by Sharon and Bob Huxford, available from Collector Books.

Batter set, complete, from $290 to 315.00
Batter set, ivory, w/decals, complete, from $170 to 185.00
Bowl, baker; 9", from $25 to 30.00
Bowl, cream soup; w/liner, ivory, from $75 to 80.00
Bowl, fruit; cobalt, 5½", from $34 to 38.00
Bowl, fruit; 5½", from $12 to 14.00
Bowl, nappy; 7¼", from $25 to 30.00
Bowl, oatmeal; 6", from $38 to 42.00
Bowl, utility; ivory, from $48 to 52.00
Butter dish, cobalt, ½-lb, from $300 to 325.00
Butter dish, cobalt, ¼-lb, from $250 to 280.00
Butter dish, colors other than cobalt, turq or ivory, ¼-lb, $135 to..150.00
Butter dish, colors other than cobalt, ½-lb, from $120 to 130.00
Butter dish, ivory, ¼-lb, from $175 to 185.00
Butter dish, turq, ¼-lb, from $290 to 310.00
Casserole, from $110 to 120.00
Creamer, from $11 to 13.00
Cup & saucer, demitasse; ivory, from $80 to 90.00
Jug, w/lid, from $130 to 145.00
Pitcher, juice; mauve bl, from $210 to 225.00
Pitcher, juice; yel, from $120 to 135.00
Plate, deep, from $22 to 25.00
Plate, 6", from $7 to 9.00
Plate, 7", cobalt, from $35 to 45.00
Plate, 7", from $10 to 14.00
Plate, 9", from $16 to 20.00
Plate, 10", from $55 to 65.00
Platter, closed hdls, 11¼", from $24 to 28.00
Platter, cobalt, 12", from $70 to 80.00
Platter, 11½", from $22 to 25.00
Platter, 15", from $55 to 65.00
Sauce boat, from $22 to 27.00
Saucer, from $4 to 5.00
Shakers, pr, from $18 to 20.00
Sugar bowl, w/lid, from $18 to 20.00
Syrup, w/lid, from $160 to 180.00
Teacup, from $8 to 11.00

Teapot, from $155 to 165.00
Tidbit, ivory, 2-tier, from $70 to 75.00
Tumbler, hdl, from $70 to 75.00
Tumbler, hdl, ivory, from $135 to 145.00
Tumbler, juice; from $52 to 55.00

Robertson

Fred H. Robertson, clay expert for the Los Angeles Pressed Brick Company and son of Alexander Robertson of the Roblin Pottery, experimented with crystalline glazes as early as 1906. In 1934 Fred and his son George established their own works in Los Angeles, but by 1943 they had moved operations to Hollywood. Though most of their early wares were turned by hand, some were also molded in low relief. Fine crackle glazes and crystallines were developed. Their ware was marked with 'Robertson,' 'F.H.R.,' or 'R.,' with the particular location of manufacture noted. The small pottery closed in 1952. Our advisors for this category are Suzanne Perrault and David Rago; they are listed in the Directory under New Jersey.

Vase, blue and green crackle glaze with blooming crystals, stamped Los Angeles/FHR, 4½x3", from $1,000.00 to $1,500.00. (Photo courtesy David Rago Auctions)

Vase, ivory crackle, mini, 2¾" 30.00
Vase, pk shaded, mk, possibly missing lid, 5¾x3", from $200 to .300.00
2 pcs: 9x7" box w/rose finial, NM; 10½" charger w/gazelle, Hollywood..3,000.00

Robineau

After short-term training in ceramics in 1903, Adelaide Robineau (with the help of her husband, Samuel) built a small pottery studio at her home in Syracuse, New York. She was adept in mixing the clay and throwing the ware, which she often decorated by incising designs into the unfired clay. Samuel developed many of the glazes and took charge of the firing process. In 1910 she joined the staff of the American Women's League Pottery at St. Louis, where she designed the famous Scarab Vase. After this pottery failed, she served on the faculty of Syracuse University. In the 1920s she worked under the name of Threshold Pottery. She was also the founder and publisher of *Keramic Studio* magazine. Her work was and is today highly acclaimed for the standards of excellence to which she aspired. Our advisors for this category are Suzanne Perrault and David Rago; they are listed in the Directory under New Jersey.

Pitcher, mc rooster on wht crackle, Threshold, 4", +6" bowl, $4,000 to ..6,000.00
Vase, brn/robins'-egg bl crystalline, slim, cvd sgn, 6x2" 6,500.00
Vase, yel crackle w/cvd decor at top, bulbous, #16, 1914, 5½" W ..7,000.00

Robj

Robj was the name of a retail store that operated in Paris for only a few years, from about 1925 to 1931. Robj solicited designs from the best French artisans of the period to produce decorative objects for the home. These were executed mostly in porcelain but there were glass and earthenware pieces as well. The most well known are the figural bottles which were particularly popular in the United States. However, Robj also promoted tea sets, perfume lamps, chess sets, ashtrays, bookends, humidors, powder jars, cigarette boxes, figurines, lamps, and milk pitchers. Robj objects tend to be whimsical, and all embody the Art Deco style. Items listed below are ceramic unless noted otherwise. Our advisors for this category are Randall Monsen and Rod Baer; their address is listed in the Directory under Virginia.

Bookends, Adam & Eve, seated, bsk, 6½x7", pr........................1,500.00
Bottle, French priest, blk hat forms stopper, 10½x4"...............365.00
Bottle, man in hat holding umbrella & case, 10".........................550.00
Bottle, Scotsman in uniform, mc, 10½", VG 250.00
Bottle, 3-faced sailor, 11¾"..2,500.00
Cocktail shaker, golfer figural, bl & wht 1,200.00
Decanter, lady in gr dress w/wht apron, 10¾" 260.00
Decanter, musical, Russian man, hat forms stopper, 12" 350.00
Inkwell, Blackamoor in gold/wht robe holds well, 6".................350.00
Perfume burner, wht-robed Oriental, X-legged on steps, 8".........550.00
Powder box, Oriental lady holding fan, Liane, 7¼"....................465.00

Roblin

In the late 1800s, Alexander W. Robertson and Linna Irelan established a pottery in San Francisco, combining parts of their respective names to coin the name Roblin. Robertson was responsible for potting and firing the ware, which often reflected his taste for classic styling. Mrs. Irelan did much of the decorating, utilizing almost every method but favoring relief modeling. Mushrooms and lizards were her favorite subjects. Vases were a large part of their production, all of which were made from native California red, buff, and white clays. The ware was well marked with the firm name or the outline of a bear. Robin Pottery was destroyed in the earthquake of 1906.

Mug, bsk, AWR/SF 97, att, 3½" 350.00
Vase, bl speckled, bbl shape, mk, 2¼x1¾"..............................515.00
Vase, crackled bl/gray/gr, classic form, 4½x3", NM......................300.00

Rock 'N Roll Memorabilia

Memorabilia from the early days of rock 'n roll recalls an era that many of us experienced firsthand; these listings are offered to demonstrate the many and various aspects of this area of collecting. Beware of reproductions! Many are so well done even a knowledgeable collector will sometimes be fooled.

Our advisor for Elvis memorabilia is Rosalind Cranor, author of *Elvis Collectibles* and *Best of Elvis Collectibles* (Overmountain Press); she is listed in the Directory under Virginia. The remainder is under the advisement of Bob Gottuso, author of Beatles, KISS, and Monkees sections in *Garage Sale Gold II* by Tomart; see Pennsylvania.

See also Decanters.

Alice Cooper, concert poster, blk on pk, 1969, M 150.00
Allman Brothers, pin, mushroom shape, metal, 1970s, 1½x1½", NMOC.30.00
Andy Gibb, spiral notebook, Rock On, 1979, M 60.00

Animals, concert flyer, 1966 tour, blk & wht................................75.00
Bad Company, mirror, Bad Co & dice, 1979, 12x12", M.............25.00
Beatles, air mattress, UK by Lilo, inflatable vinyl, 1964, M 900.00
Beatles, animation cel, HP, from cartoon show, 1960s, ea from $750 to.1,000.00
Beatles, balloon, United Industries, 1964, sealed in orig pkg.........75.00
Beatles, blow-up doll, inflatable vinyl, US, 14", set of 4, M........150.00
Beatles, book binder, gray cloth cover, UK, 1964, M..................375.00
Beatles, Booty Bag, printed vinyl, drawstring, w/insert, 1964, M..175.00
Beatles, bracelet, 4 photo charms on chain, Randall, 1964, M (+)..100.00
Beatles, coin, silver w/ad, UK, 1966 ....250.00
Beatles, comb, plastic w/sticker on front, Lido, 1964, M (+) 300.00
Beatles, display, Paul...plays a Hofner..., Paul w/guitar, 1966, M .800.00

Beatles, figural mugs, Royal Doulton, 1984, M, set of four, $800.00. (Photo courtesy June Moon)

Beatles, Hummer, color portraits, 11", 1964, EX..........................185.00
Beatles, magazine, Newsweek, Bugs About Beetles, 1964, M.........35.00
Beatles, magazine, The Original Beatles Book, 1964, M................30.00
Beatles, necklace, G-clef on chain, Randall/Press-Initial, 1964, M.250.00
Beatles, necklace, 2" wooden disk pendant w/brass figures, US, 1964, M..300.00
Beatles, ornament, blown glass/plastic guitar, 1964, set of 4, MIB ..900.00
Beatles, pin-bk, I'm Bugs About the Beatles, 3½", M....................50.00
Beatles, poster, Ringo for President, 1964, M..............................200.00
Beatles, poster, Rubber Soul, LP promotional, 1965, M 800.00
Beatles, record carrying case, red or gr, Air Flite, 1964, M..........700.00
Beatles, sheet music, various songs, 1960s, M, ea, from $15 to......25.00
Beatles, socks, ironed-on emblems on wht, 1964, rare, pr, M......600.00
Beatles, swim ring, inflatable vinyl, United Artists, 1965, 22" dia, M..3,000.00
Beatles, tumbler, rubber-coated glass, Ringo blk/wht photo 225.00
Bee Gees, fan club kit, complete w/45 single, 1979, M 100.00
Bee Gees, mirror, Sgt Pepper, M 50.00
Bee Gees, scrapbook, St Pepper's Lonely Hearts Club Band the Movie, M.95.00
Bee Gees, tour program, 1979, M 50.00
Bobby Sherman, Paint & Color Album, 1970s, 10x13", NM........50.00
Bobby Sherman, record cutout, from cereal box, 1970s, M 12.00
David Bowie, program, Glass Spider tour, 1987, M.......................20.00
Doors, calendar, Morrison in blk, spiral bound, 1987, NM............20.00
Doors, Doors, poster, faces on blk, Elektra, 1967, 28x19", NM.1,000.00
Doors, N CA Folk-Rock Festival, Morrison, 1968, 21¾x14½", EX.250.00
Elton John, poster, Don't Shoot Me..., MCA Records, 1972, M.400.00
Elton John, tour program, 1980, M...20.00
Elvis, bookend, bronzed head-to-waist figure w/guitar, EPE, 1956, M.425.00
Elvis, doll, wht jumpsuit, EP Enterprises, Eugene, 1984, MIB.......60.00
Elvis, flasher pin, w/guitar on yel, red trim, Vari-Vue, 1956, 3", M..35.00
Elvis, game, Game That Allows...To Live On!, EP Enterprises, 1987, MIB.75.00
Elvis, lei & medallion, M...225.00
Elvis, menu from Las Vegas Hilton, 1974, M 45.00
Elvis, necklace, dogtag, M on card...80.00
Elvis, overnight case, bl, EP Enterprises, 1956, M 650.00
Elvis, overnight case, brn, EP Enterprises, 1956, M 650.00
Elvis, pillow, Love Me Tender, EP Enterprises, 1956, M.............400.00
Elvis, pin-bk, Blue Suede Shoes, late 1950s, ⅞", M........................50.00

Elvis, punching bag balloon from King Galahad promo, M 100.00
Elvis, ring, portrait top, adjustable, reissue of orig, M 75.00
Elvis, T-shirt, w/guitar & lg record on wht, EP Enterprises, 1956, M.460.00
Frank Zappa, comic book, 1970s, EX..20.00
Grateful Dead, poster, skeleton & roses, 1983, 54x45", EX 250.00
KISS, back pack, Thermos, 1979, M 250.00
KISS, belt buckle, w/face picture, 1970s, M 80.00
KISS, Colorforms set, 1979, MIB 125.00
KISS, doll, Ace or Peter, complete, M (no box) 150.00
KISS, fan club kit, Kiss Army, complete, M 85.00
KISS, game, On Tour, Aucoin, 1978, MIB.....................................150.00
KISS, jigsaw puzzle, Milton Bradley, 1977-78, MIB, from $65 to .100.00

KISS, lunch box, EX, $125.00. (Photo courtesy June Moon)

KISS, pin-bk, KISS Army, M...25.00
KISS, shoelaces, logo, unknown mfg, 1979, M...............................60.00
KISS, spiral notebook, 1970s, M, from $30 to................................45.00
KISS, transistor radio, KISS/Aucoin, 1977, MIB........................250.00
Led Zeppelin, T-shirt, 1977 US Tour, M...60.00
Madonna, bandanna, Blond Ambition tour, 1990, M.....................50.00
Madonna, concert poster, promo from 1st tour, 1984, 36x24", M .75.00
Madonna, pillow, Desperately Seeking Susan, 1986, M.................75.00
Madonna, pin-bk, in blk lingerie w/head bk, Boy Toy, lg, M.........15.00
Madonna, Poster Book, 9 posters, Button Up, 1990, M.................30.00
Madonna, Sex Book, Warner Bros, 1992, opened, M 75.00
Madonna, stationery, Dream Idol, Star Stationery, 1986, M sealed...60.00
MC Hammer, Simplicity clothing pattern, 1991, M in pkg...........15.00
Michael Jackson, belt, portrait buckle on blk leather, 1984, M.....30.00
Michael Jackson, doll, Am Music Awards, LJN, 1984, 12", M......60.00
Michael Jackson, Pepsi can, World Tour 84, M 15.00
Michael Jackson, socks, MJ/LA Gear on blk, pr, M 15.00
Michael Jackson, stuffed toy, Muscles (snake), Ideal, 1987, M......90.00
Monkees, ballpoint pen, Raybert, 1967, M 30.00
Monkees, book, Monkees Annual, Raybert Productions, 1967, M..60.00
Monkees, car, Monkeemobile, Corgi, 1967-68, 6", MIB..............300.00
Monkees, key chain, Raybert, 1966, M 40.00
Monkees, pin-bk, I Love Mike, red/wht/blk, Raybert, 1967, 1", M..10.00
Monkees, pin-bk, I'm a Special...Fan, bl/wht/blk, Raybert, 1966, M..10.00
Monkees, record cutouts, Golgems, Post Cereal, 1967-68, ea........20.00
Monkees, toy guitar, plastic wind-up, Mattel, 1966, 14", M........150.00
Pink Floyd, poster, The Wall, MGM Studios, M in fr 150.00
Rolling Stones, book cover, Musidor, 1981, M................................15.00
Rolling Stones, clock, Mick Jagger performing, clock inset, 1980s, M.60.00
Rolling Stones, doll, oversz vinyl head, Play Pal, 1963, M, ea 150.00
Rolling Stones, key chain, lg red tongue, 1983, M 15.00
Rolling Stones, license plate, Steel Wheels tour, 1989, M 15.00
Rolling Stones, pin-bk button, Elect Mick Jagger, ca 1980, M........8.00
Rolling Stones, wallet, red tongue on blk, M 15.00
Ted Nugent, tour program, no shirt, suspenders, 1979/80, M 20.00
Village People, toy guitar, Carnival Toys, 1978, 36", M 200.00

Rockingham

In the early part of the nineteenth century, American potters began to prefer brown- and buff-burning clays over red because of their durability. The glaze favored by many was Rockingham, which varied from a dark brown mottle to a sponged effect sometimes called tortoise shell. It consisted in part of manganese and various metallic salts and was used by many potters until well into the twentieth century. Over the past two years, demand and prices have risen sharply, especially in the East.

See also Bennington.

Baker, flat bottom, rnded rim, 3x13⅛x10⅞".................................300.00
Bottle, flower urn relief ea side, EX detail, 10⅜" 375.00
Bowl, mixing; mini, 1¾x4¼", EX 55.00
Bowl, mush; flared sides, #169, 2¼x8"..60.00
Bowl, shallow, 3¼x11½"..135.00
Bowl, tub shape, 6¼" 200.00
Cuspidor, molded shells, 7½" 125.00
Cuspidor, 4 sides w/molded eagles, 4x6½x6½" 300.00
Figure, Spaniel puppy, seated on oval base, crack, 13x13x9".......395.00
Flask, mermaid, sm rpr, 7x4" 80.00
Inkwell, recumbent dog figural, 4x6¼x2⅞", EX 350.00
Mold, Turk's head, swirled int, scalloped rim, 9¼" 125.00
Pie plate, 9⅝"...135.00
Pitcher, emb peacock & palm tree, C-shaped hdl, 8", EX 250.00
Pitcher, hunt scene, 9⅞"...325.00
Pitcher, tulips in relief, 7" 195.00
Planter, duck figural, 6¼x14¾x5½"...375.00
Plate, flared sides, illegible mk, 1⅛x8½"......................................150.00
Soap dish, vertical ribs, pierced top, 2¼x4¾x3½"...........................90.00
Teapot, molded Chinamen, paneled, prof rpr to lid, 9¾" 145.00
Teapot, molded leaves, 1800s, 10" 465.00
Toby pitcher, 7⅛"...195.00

Rockwell, Norman

Norman Rockwell began his career in 1911 at the age of seventeen doing illustrations for a children's book entitled *Tell Me Why Stories*. Within a few years he had produced the *Saturday Evening Post* cover that made him one of America's most beloved artists. Though not well accepted by the professional critics of his day who did not consider his work to be art but 'merely' commercial illustration, Rockwell's popularity grew to the extent that today there is an overwhelming abundance of examples of his work or those related to the theme of one of his illustrations.

The figurines described below were issued by the Rockwell Museum and Museum Collections Inc. (formerly Rockwell Museum). For Rockwell listings by Gorham see the 2002 edition of *Schroeder's Antiques Price Guide*. Our advisor for this category is Barb Putratz; she is listed in the Directory under Minnesota.

A Walkin' & a Whistlin', 1986...70.00
Adventures Between Adventures, 1986 ....100.00
All Wrapped Up, 1984..100.00
Almost Grown Up, 1982...175.00
America's Artist, ltd ed 5,000, 1983 ....195.00
Another Masterpiece by Norman Rockwell, ltd ed of 5,000, 1985.210.00
Apple for the Teacher, Museum Collections Inc, 1986...................70.00
Artist, The; Museum Collections Inc, ltd ed 2,500, 1986 ....195.00
At the Circus, 1982...190.00
Baby's First Step, 1979..175.00
Barefoot Boy, Museum Collections Inc, ltd ed 5,000, 1986.........110.00
Bedtime, LCF series, ltd ed 1,000, 1982 ....225.00

Bicycle Boys, 1981...120.00
Big Race, The; 1984..100.00
Birthday Party, The; 1980...150.00
Bored of Education, 1984..95.00
Bottom of the Sixth, Museum Collections Inc, ltd ed 5,000, 1986.200.00
Boy Meets His Dog, A; 1986.....................................100.00
Bride & Groom, 1981..140.00
Bringing Home the Christmas Tree, 1982....................125.00
Celebration, 1982...190.00
Checking His List, 1980..90.00
Christmas Prayers, 1985...95.00
Circus Comes to Town, The; 1982............................125.00
Cobbler, LCF Series, ltd ed 1,000, 1982....................225.00
Cobbler, The; 1979..80.00
Collect Fine Porcelain Figurines (ad stand), 1984........140.00
Courageous Hero, 1982...185.00
Dollhouse for Sis, A; 1979..80.00
Downhill Racer, 1981...120.00
Dreams in the Antique Shop, Museum Collections Inc, 1986......80.00

Dreams in the Antique Shop, 1982, $100.00.

Drummer's Friend, The; 1982...................................125.00
First Car in Town, The; ltd ed 2,500, 1985.................235.00
First Haircut, The; 1979...150.00
First Prom, The; 1979..125.00
For a Good Boy, 1980..90.00
Freedom of Fear, ltd ed 5,000, 1982..........................350.00
Freedom of Speech, ltd ed 5,000, 1982......................350.00
Freedom of Worship, ltd ed 5,000, 1982.....................350.00
Giving Thanks, 1982..200.00
Goin' Fishin', 1984..95.00
Good Food Good Friends, 1982.................................225.00
Happy Birthday, Dear Mother, 1979..........................140.00
Helping Mother, 1982...120.00
High Stepping, 1982...110.00
Home for Fido, A; Museum Collections Inc, 1986.........75.00
Homerun Slugger, 1982..145.00
Late Night Dining, Museum Collections Inc, 1986........80.00
Letterman, The; Museum Collections Inc, ltd ed 2,500, 1986....165.00
Lighthouse Keeper's Daughter, The; LCF series, ltd ed 1,000, 1982..225.00
Little Mother, 1980..135.00
Little Patient, 1981..120.00
Little Salesman, 1982...185.00
Lovely in Lipstick, Museum Collections Inc, 1988.........75.00
Memories, LCF series, ltd ed 1,000, 1983...................225.00
Memories, 1980...90.00
Mom's Helper, ltd ed 15,000, 1986............................120.00
Mom's Helper, 1986...90.00
Mother's Little Helpers, 1981...................................140.00
Music Master, The; 1980..90.00
Mysterious Malady, Museum Collections Inc, 1986......100.00

New Arrival, Museum Collections Inc, 1981................160.00
Off to School, LCF series, ltd ed 1,000, 1981..............115.00
Out Fishin', Museum Collections Inc, ltd ed 25,000, 1985........100.00
Outward Bound, ltd ed 5,000, 1984...........................200.00
Partygoers, Museum Collections Inc, ltd ed 2,500, 1984.............235.00
Pest, The; 1982...125.00
Playing Pirates, ltd ed 2,500, 1984............................235.00
Practice Makes Perfect, Museum Collections Inc, ltd ed 2,500, 1987..170.00
Pride of Parenthood, 1986..100.00
Puppy Love, 1983..95.00
Report Card, Museum Collections Inc, 1986.................80.00
Rosie the Riveter, Museum Collections Inc, ltd ed 2,500, 1987.165.00
Santa Takes a Break, Museum Collections Inc, ltd ed 3,500, 1987.110.00
Saturday's Hero, 1984...105.00
Sneezing Spy, Museum Collections Inc, ltd ed 2,500, 1986........160.00
Soda Jerk, The; ltd ed 5,000, 1986............................205.00
Space Age Santa, 1984...115.00
Space Pioneers, 1982..185.00
Special Treat, A; 1982..100.00
Spirit of America, The; ltd ed 5,000, 1982..................185.00
Spring Fever, 1981...100.00
Student, The; 1980...165.00
Summer Fun, 1982...120.00
Sunday Morning, Museum Collections Inc, ltd ed 2,500, 1986..225.00
Sweet Dreams, 1981...190.00
Sweet Sixteen, 1979...125.00
Tattoo Artist, Museum Collections Inc, ltd ed 2,500, 1987........170.00
Toymaker, The; LCF series, ltd ed 1,000, 1982............225.00
Toymaker, The; 1979..95.00
Trumpeter, The; Museum Collections Inc, ltd ed 2,500, 1986.2,000.00
Vacation's Over, 1981...120.00
Visiting the Vet, Museum Collections Inc, 1988............85.00
Waiting for Santa, 1982..135.00
We Missed You Daddy, 1981......................................190.00
Weighty Matters, ltd ed 5,000, 1986..........................180.00
Wet Behind the Ears, Museum Collections Inc, 1986.....80.00
Winter Fun, 1982..95.00
Words of Wisdom, 1982..130.00
Wrapping Christmas Presents, 1980...........................130.00

Rogers, John

John Rogers (1829 – 1904) was a machinist from Manchester, New Hampshire, who turned his hobby of sculpting into a financially successful venture. From the originals he meticulously fashioned of red clay, he had bronze master molds made from which plaster copies were cast. He specialized in five different categories: theatrical, Shakespeare, Civil War, everyday life, and horses. His large detailed groupings portrayed the life and times of the period between 1859 and 1892. In the following listings, examples are assumed to be in very good to excellent condition. Our advisor for this category is George Humphrey; he is listed in the Directory under Maryland.

Balcony...1,500.00
Bath...2,000.00
Bushwacker..2,000.00
Charity Patient..650.00
Checkers Up at the Farm, 1865, 20½x17½x12".............575.00
Chess...1,200.00
Country Post Office..750.00
Courtship in Sleepy Hollow, Pat date.........................550.00
Faust & Marguerite, Leaving the Garden...................1,200.00
Fetching the Doctor..750.00

First Ride..725.00
Frolic at the Old Homestead, 1887, 22½"....................800.00
Going for the Cows 450.00
Home Guard...800.00
Mail Day..2,000.00
Matter of Opinion 600.00
One More Shot...550.00
Parting Promise...475.00

The Photographer, signed and dated 1878, 18¾", $4,000.00. (Photo courtesy Neal Auction Company)

Picket Guard..750.00
Referee 800.00
Rip Van Winkle — At Home...325.00
Slave Auction 2,000.00
Taking the Oath & Drawing Rations, sgn, 23" 525.00
Village Schoolmaster..850.00
Wounded Scout, ca 1864 ....750.00

Rookwood

The Rookwood Pottery Company was established in 1879 in Cincinnati, Ohio. Its founder was Maria Longworth Nichols daughter of a wealthy family who provided the backing necessary to make such an enterprise possible. Ms. Nichols hired competent ceramic artisans and artists of note, who through constant experimentation developed many lines of superior art pottery. While in her employ, Laura Fry invented the airbrush-blending process for which she was issued a patent in 1884. From this, several lines were designed that utilized blended backgrounds. One of their earlier lines, Standard, was a brown ware decorated with underglaze slip-painted nature studies, animals, portraits, etc. Iris and Sea Green were introduced in 1894 and Vellum, a transparent mat-glaze line, in 1904. Other lines followed: Ombroso in 1910 and Soft Porcelain in 1915. Many of the early artware lines were signed by the artist. Soon after the turn of the twentieth century, Rookwood manufactured 'production' pieces that relied mainly on molded designs and forms rather than freehand decoration for their esthetic appeal. The Depression brought on financial difficulties from which the pottery never recovered. Though it continued to operate, the quality of the ware deteriorated, and the pottery was forced to close in 1967.

Unmarked Rookwood is only rarely encountered. Many marks may be found, but the most familiar is the reverse 'RP' monogram. First used in 1886, a flame point was added above it for each succeeding year until 1900. After that a Roman numeral added below indicated the year of manufacture. Impressed letters that related to the type of clay utilized for the body were also used — G for ginger, O for olive, R for red, S for sage green, W for white, and Y for yellow. Artware must be judged on an individual basis. Quality of the artwork is a prime factor to consider. Portraits, animals, and birds are worth more than florals; and pieces signed by a particularly renowned artist are highly prized.

For more information see *Rookwood Pottery* by the Treadway Gallery and *Rookwood Pottery* by Nick and Marilyn Nicholson and Jim Thomas (both by Collector Books). Our advisors for this category are Suzanne Perrault and David Rago; they are listed in the Directory under New Jersey.

Aerial Blue

Pitcher, maiden among grasses, B Horsfall, #769, 1895, 3" 1,300.00
Vase, violets, L Asbury, X158X, 5" 1,900.00

Black Opal

Bowl, magnolias & geometrics, S Sax, #2258, 1926, 13" dia ...1,200.00
Vase, roses on stems, HE Wilcox, #2789, 1924, 11" 2,100.00

Cameo

Bowl, berry; cherry blossoms, S Toohey, #481W, 9" 300.00
Cup & saucer, floral, A Valentien, #291, W, 1890, 3⅛" dia........300.00
Plate, cherry blossoms, S Toohey, #317BW, 1888, 8"...................160.00
Plate, floral, G Young, #336BW, 7½" 150.00

Iris

Vase, Blk, cherry blossom branches, K Shirayamadani, #951C, 1906, 10"..7,500.00
Vase, Blk, grasses, K Shirayamadani, #900B, 1900, 9½", NM..5,000.00
Vase, cherry blossoms, I Bishop, #1120, 1906, 4" 1,100.00
Vase, cherry blossoms, L Epply, 1911, Xd but M, 8¼x3¾" 1,100.00
Vase, cherry blossoms on blk to peach, I Bishop, 1907, 5½x4½"..1,100.00
Vase, clover, OG Reed, #917, 1900, 5½" 800.00
Vase, clover blossoms on gray to peach, R Fechheimer, 1903, 7¾" .1,000.00
Vase, dogwood, pk/gr on shaded gray, L Asbury, X, 1905, 11x5½" .1,265.00
Vase, dogwood blossoms on gray to wht, L Asbury, 1905, Xd, 10½x6"..1,100.00
Vase, fish (5) in water scene, S Coyne, #918E, X, 1911, 6" 1,200.00
Vase, floral, F Rothenbusch, #925CC, 1903, 8"........................1,600.00
Vase, flowers (detailed), S Sax, #786C, 1901, 10" 3,500.00
Vase, hawthorn branches, LE Lindeman, #9265, 1903, 6" 1,700.00
Vase, hydrangeas, AR Valentien, #907C, 1902, 14".................7,000.00
Vase, iris blossoms, L Asbury, #907D, 1905, 11¼" 4,700.00
Vase, irises, C Schmidt, #732B, 1908, 10½", NM 4,500.00
Vase, irises, C Schmidt, #732C, 1900, 6" 900.00
Vase, irises w/silver o/l, A Valentien, #879C, 1904, 14½" 11,000.00
Vase, lilies, I Bishop, #950E, 1906, 6¾", NM 300.00
Vase, lily-of-the-valley, C Schmidt, EX art, 1909, 8½x4½" 2,530.00
Vase, magnolias, L Asbury, #915C, 1906, 7".............................3,750.00
Vase, pansies, C Baker, #927E, 1902, 6½" 1,800.00
Vase, pansies (EX art), S Sax, #905E, 1911, 6¾" 1,500.00
Vase, pine cones & needles, R Fechheimer, #913, 1901, 5" 850.00
Vase, poppies, C Schmidt, #940DW, 1908, 9½"........................6,500.00
Vase, poppies (EX art), C Schmidt, #905E, X, 1901, 6¼"........1,100.00
Vase, roses, E Diers, #932D, 1903, 8½".....................................3,500.00
Vase, sweet peas, E Lincoln, 1910, rim rstr, 6¼x3" 750.00
Vase, thistles, S Sax, #909G, 1906, 8½" 2,600.00
Vase, thistles on stems, S Coyne, #904E, 1904, 6½" 1,200.00
Vase, tulips, S Sax, #935C, 1906, 8½" 2,800.00
Vase, Virginia Creepers, F Rothenbusch, #902D, 1902, 7".......1,200.00

Limoges

Dish, pie crust; bamboo trees, w/gilt, M Daly, 1883, 6½", $250 to..350.00
Ewer, Oriental swallows & grasses, M Rettig, #101, 1883, 11"....750.00
Humidor, spiders/bats, ML Nichols, 1882, dbl lid, 6x6", EX 2,200.00
Humidor, spiders/bats on brn mottle, NL Nichols, 1882, 6x6", EX .1,900.00
Jug, bamboo/butterfly on mc ground w/gilt, NJ Hirschfeld, 1883, 4½"..400.00

Jug, butterflies/bamboo, brn/gr on tan w/much gilt, A Valentien, 8x7"..**700.00**
Pitcher, swallows among clouds, unknown artist, #123, 1882, 6¾"..**425.00**
Plate, floral w/gold, unsgn, #87, 1887, 6½" **220.00**
Tankard, dogwood blossoms on cobalt, ETK, 1883, 9½", EX **850.00**
Vase, ships at night, MFG, pocket form, 1882, rpr, 4⅛" **375.00**
Water jug, butterflies/bamboo on bsk w/gilt, AR Valentien, 1844, 8"..**1,000.00**

Mat

Note: Both incised mat and painted mat are listed here. Incised mat descriptions are indicated by the term 'cvd' within the line; all others are hand-painted mat ware.

Bowl vase, pine boughs, brown and green on green, Lorinda Epply, 1908, 2¼x6½", $2,415.00. (Photo courtesy David Rago)

Bowl, cvd peacock feathers, W Hentschel, #494B, 1912, 8½"..**1,200.00**
Figurine, deer, Abel, #6170, 1945, 6" **200.00**
Figurine, elephant, Wm McDonald, #6124, 1931, 7" **275.00**
Vase, apple blossoms, C Covalenco, #2831, 1925, 5¼" **750.00**
Vase, cvd abstract floral, CS Todd, vivid colors, 1917, 7x5" **1,265.00**
Vase, cvd Arts & Crafts design, gr & yel, C Todd, #966, 1915, 3½"..**1,000.00**
Vase, cvd Arts & Crafts leaves, S Toohey, #919, 1905, 4"...........**800.00**
Vase, cvd geometric rim, brn ombroso, W Hentschel, #77A, 1915, 8¼"..**1,400.00**
Vase, cvd pods on hammered ground, W Hentschel, 1910, 11x4½"..**2,075.00**
Vase, cvd poppies, bl & brn ombroso, C Todd, #130, 1915, 6½" W.**2,200.00**
Vase, daisies, MH McDonald, #1358F, 1916, 6" **450.00**
Vase, dogwood, M McDonald, S, 1936, 5½" **550.00**
Vase, floral, multi-tone bl, K Jones, #952F, 1926, 6½" **500.00**
Vase, floral, 5-color, W Rehm, #2077, 1932, 6½".......................**950.00**
Vase, floral branches w/berries, OG Reed, #1124E, 7" **1,000.00**
Vase, flower garlands, C Todd, #1870, 1911, 6¼" **900.00**
Vase, geometrics, E Barrett, #6306, 1944, 7".............................**400.00**
Vase, geometrics, Mat Moderne, E Barrett, #6201D, 1931, 6¾".**950.00**
Vase, grapes, gr & bl mat, C Todd, #218B, 1915, 10½" **1,900.00**
Vase, leaves & berries, Mat Moderne, E Barrett, #2914, 1929, 8½".**700.00**
Vase, nasturtiums, AM Valentien, #223Z, 1901, 4½" **1,100.00**
Vase, organic squeezebag, Mat Moderne, W Hentschel, #614C, 1927, 13"..**2,200.00**
Vase, panels w/flying birds, bl on brn, CS Todd, 1911, 7x3¾".**1,300.00**
Vase, pine cones, M Mitchell, #1096, 1905, 4¾"..........................**800.00**

Porcelain

Vase, daffodils, ET Hurley, #907F, 1925, 7½" **1,700.00**
Vase, deer (3) & raised design, E Barrett, S, 1934, 7" **1,300.00**
Vase, ducks & geese (oriental style), A Conant, #905A, 1920, 19"..**5,000.00**
Vase, Jewel, blueberries & leaves, L Epply, #5194F, 1943, 5"......**475.00**
Vase, Jewel, floral, L Holtkamp, #5525, 1953, 4¾"......................**250.00**
Vase, Jewel, floral (unusual color), C McLaughlin, #999C, 1919, 9½"..**2,750.00**
Vase, Jewel, floral bands, S Sax, #553C, 1918, 10"...................**2,000.00**
Vase, Jewel, geometric leaves, S Sax, #2996, 1930, X, 8½", EX..**500.00**
Vase, Jewel, iris, C Schmidt, #356F, 1923, 5½" **2,500.00**
Vase, Jewel, mtns/eucalyptus, M McDonald, drilled, 15x7", $2,000 to.**3,000.00**
Vase, Jewel, mtns/trees, bl/gr/brn on ivory, McDonald, drilled, 15x7"..**1,700.00**

Vase, Jewel, peacocks/apple blossoms/flowers, A Conant, 1919, 17x8"..**12,650.00**
Vase, Jewel, peonies & landscape, A Conant, #356F, 1920, 5½".**3,500.00**
Vase, Jewel, snowdrops floral on pk, Shirayamadani, 1928, 5x3".**2,300.00**
Vase, Jewel, wht birds, gr-lined on dk bl, J Jensen, 1944, 6½x5".**1,150.00**
Vase, sailboats on water, C Schmidt, #913D, 1923, 7½"..........**4,500.00**
Vase, stylized roses band, S Sax, #975BT, 1918, 9" **3,750.00**
Vase, water lilies, S Coyne, #2551, 1924, rpr drill hole, 13½".**4,500.00**

Sea Green

Tray, leaf w/copper o/l, K Shirayamadani, #308Z, 1901, 7" **1,600.00**
Vase, Hercules parsnips, AR Valentien, #578, 1895, 14½" **5,500.00**
Vase, leaves (EX art), M Daly, #749CW, 1894, 6½" **2,200.00**

Standard

Chamberstick, violets, J Swing, 1894, 3"......................................**345.00**
Chocolate pot, rose branches, AM Valentien, 1891, rstr, 9x7", EX...**315.00**
Ewer, leaves, L Lincoln, #754, 1900, 6½".....................................**350.00**
Ewer, red maple leaves, R Fecheimer, #584C, 1898, 5½" **300.00**
Ewer, water lily, LN Lincoln, #611B, 1902, 10" **850.00**
Humidor, Pueblo Man, G Young, #683, 1901, 6" **3,750.00**
Inkwell, violets, lid w/appl frog, R Fecheimer, #418A, 1899, 6", NM ..**750.00**
Pitcher, holly, LN Lincoln, #40, 1899, 5½" **550.00**
Pitcher, Light, daisies, leaf hdl, C Baker, squat, 1890, 3¾" **250.00**
Pitcher, tiger lilies, S Toohey, #838C, 1899, 10x6"..................**1,035.00**
Tea caddy, mums/bee on speckled olive gr, AR Valentien, 1885, rstr, 5"..**400.00**
Vase, bird in tall grasses, K Shirayamadani, #30D, 1895, 9".....**3,750.00**
Vase, carnations (intricate), K Shirayamadani, #496AW, 1891, 13", NM.**900.00**
Vase, cherries & leaves, L Van Briggle, #304C, 1900, 7½" **850.00**
Vase, clover, flat rtcl form, AM Valentien, #452, 1892, 7½" dia..**900.00**
Vase, daffodils, M Daly, #901B, 1902, 11½".................................**550.00**
Vase, floral, K Shirayamadani, #469W, 1894, 11"....................**1,100.00**
Vase, floral, L Asbury, #749C, 1898, 7" **450.00**
Vase, floral w/silver o/l, A Sprague, #481W, 1892, 9", NM......**2,100.00**
Vase, floral w/silver o/l, K Hickman, #809#, 1898, 6" **2,100.00**
Vase, flowers & leaves, K Shirayamadani, #292BW, 1891, 14", NM..**1,100.00**
Vase, hawthorn, L Asbury, #749C, 1898, 6½" **400.00**
Vase, holly w/silver o/l, J Zettel, #514FW, 1892, 4½"..............**2,600.00**
Vase, Japanese quince (EX art), J Zettel, squat, 1894, 6" W........**550.00**
Vase, Light, irises, C Bonsall, 1901, 7½x3½", NM.....................**750.00**
Vase, nasturtiums w/ornate silver o/l, LN Lincoln, #565, 1896, 8".**5,750.00**
Vase, pansies, SE Coyne, #698E, 1899, 4"....................................**400.00**
Vase, persimmons, A Van Briggle, #534C, 1889, 6¾", NM **550.00**
Vase, poppies, C Baker, #846C, 1899, 10½x4½"......................**1,035.00**
Vase, tulips, J Zettel, #909, 1901, drilled, 9" **650.00**

Tiger Eye

Vase, exotic bird, W McDonald, #S1353, 1989, 8¼" **2,400.00**
Vase, frog, AR Valentien, #806D, 1898, 6¼" **600.00**
Vase, sea horses cvd on Empire Green, ET Hurley, #295D, 1923, 9¼".**3,500.00**
Vase, swan, W McDonald, #562, R, 1892, 9½", NM..................**500.00**

Vellum

Bowl vase, bluebirds on mauve, S Sax, 1917, 4½x8" **1,600.00**
Plaque, Across the Lake, F Rothenbusch, 6x8"+orig gold fr **5,500.00**
Plaque, birches & stream, ET Hurley, 1939, 12x7"+fr..............**5,000.00**
Plaque, End of the Woods, FR, fr, 10⅜x13⅝" **6,900.00**
Plaque, islands & palm trees, K Van Horn, 1914, 8x5", +orig fr..**4,000.00**
Plaque, Lake in Mtns, 8x4", +orig fr **2,875.00**
Plaque, landscape, L Asbury, 1922, 9½x12"+fr.........................**8,000.00**
Plaque, landscape w/houses & water, F Rothenbusch, 1935, 9x12"+fr..**7,000.00**

Plaque, Penacook Lake, Concord NH, ED, fr, 8¾x14¼" 8,625.00
Plaque, river landscape, E Diers, 1916, 11x8½"+orig fr 6,500.00
Plaque, sailboat w/shore beyond, C Schmidt, 1912, 7½x4"+fr..3,750.00
Plaque, tree silhouettes/river, S Coyne, bl/gr/yel, label, 11x9", +fr.4,000.00
Plaque, trees, bushes & mtns, F Rothenbusch, 1917, 11x9½"+fr..6,500.00
Plaque, trees & lake landscape, E Diers, 1919, 9½x14½"+fr.10,000.00
Plaque, trees & mtns at river, ET Hurley, 1948, 12x10"+fr......5,000.00
Plaque, trees/fall foliage/river, E Diers, 1916, 9x12½", + new fr...6,900.00

Plaque, trees by pond at dusk, Lenore Asbury, 9¼x12½", in new Arts & Crafts oak frame, $9,200.00. (Photo courtesy David Rago and Suzanne Perrault)

Plaque, waterfall scene, F Rothenbusch, 1927, 9x7"+fr............9,000.00
Plaque, Winter Twilight, E McDermott, 1910, 9x11½"+orig fr.7,500.00
Plaque, wooded landscape, F Rothenbusch, 1922, 9⅝x11½"+fr..7,000.00
Vase, anemones, K Shirayamadani, #6601, 1936, 9½" 1,600.00
Vase, begonias, pk on gray, E Diers, mfg flaws/no 2nd mk, 8" 925.00
Vase, birch trees & water, ET Hurley, #1660A, 1912, 16" 7,500.00
Vase, birch trees/lake/sky, ET Hurley, 1915, 7¾x3½", EX 1,950.00
Vase, cranes in flight, K Shirayamadani, #907DD, 1906, rpr, 10"...3,750.00
Vase, dragonflies/tall grass, Shirayamadani, 1907, glaze misses, 9x6".2,100.00
Vase, fish (5), ET Hurley, #162D, 1904, flaw, 5½" 1,100.00
Vase, fishing boats/Venetian harbor, C Schmidt, 1926, uncrazed, 8x3" ..3,450.00
Vase, floral, MG Denzler, #1872, 1914, 8" 400.00
Vase, flowers & buds on stems, L Epply, #907A, 1920, 21"......4,500.00
Vase, irises, H Van Horne, #1655F, 1905, 6½" 1,000.00
Vase, irises on shaded apricot, C Schmidt, 1905, 8¼x3½" 2,530.00
Vase, lake & trees, E Diers, #7023C, 1923, 10½" 3,750.00
Vase, lake & trees, ET Hurley, #951E, 1940, 7½" 3,500.00
Vase, lake & trees at dusk, L Epply, #1023C, X GV, 1911, 10½"..5,000.00
Vase, lake & trees at sunset, C Schmidt, #977, 1917, 11".......4,750.00
Vase, landscape, E Diers, #940D, 1917, 10½", NM..................2,500.00
Vase, landscape, F Rothenbusch, #2996, 1931, 8½".................3,000.00
Vase, landscape, L Asbury, #952, 1915, 7¾" 1,300.00
Vase, landscape, L Epply, #1930, 1913, 7" 1,100.00
Vase, mariposa lily at shoulder, K Shirayamadani, #2831, 1926, 5½".1,500.00
Vase, mtns & lake, F Rothenbusch, #907B, 1918, 17½" 7,500.00
Vase, nasturtiums, K Van Horne, #1348, 1909, 6" W 550.00
Vase, peonies (EX art), S Sax, #904C, 1905, 11¾" 4,250.00
Vase, poppies, K Shirayamadani, #6578, 1936, 8¼" 1,700.00
Vase, poppies, S Coyne, 1908, 8¼x4½", from $900 to.............1,400.00
Vase, Romanesque scene beside lake, E Diers, #1663D, 1910, flaw, 9".3,250.00
Vase, sailboats & tugboat scene at night, ET Hurley, #938D, 1912, 7".3,500.00
Vase, sailboats/Venetian port, C Schmidt, 1922, 12x5", from $4,500 to..6,500.00
Vase, seascape w/gulls, ET Hurley, #1126C, 1907, 9" 3,500.00
Vase, sunset scene, A Conant, #900D, 1922, 7" 1,100.00
Vase, sunset scene, F Rothenbusch, #1550D, 1919, 9" 3,000.00
Vase, trees/meadow, E Diers, 1921, bottle shape, 7¼x3½".......1,950.00
Vase, trees/meadow, F Rothenbusch, 1919, 7½x3½", EX, $1,500 to.2,000.00
Vase, trees/mtns/water, F Rothenbusch, #2251, 1926, 14" 9,000.00
Vase, trout on pk/ivory/teal, E Noonan, 1908, 4x5" 1,500.00
Vase, winter landscape, E Diers, #1856B, 1909, drilled, 13½" .1,900.00
Vase, wooded landscape, E Diers, #30E, 1918, 8½".................3,250.00

Wax Mat

Bottle, chrysanthemums, E Lincoln, #2825A, 1926, 16½x7" ..3,750.00
Bowl, mums/flowers, red/pk on yel butterfat, E Lincoln, hdls, 5x10"..1,100.00
Bowl vase, abstract, gr/purple on bl, A Pons, 1907, 4x8½" 630.00
Mask, Art Deco face, L Abel, #6244, 1931, 9½" 1,900.00
Vase, abstract flowers, J Jensen, #906E, 1930, X, 9¼x4" 1,400.00
Vase, abstract flowers, jewel tones on dk red, S Coyne, 1927, 13x6"..2,075.00
Vase, daffodils on yel to gr, Lincoln, 1927, 11x4" 1,000.00
Vase, floral, red/yel/bl on bl-gr butterfat, CST, 1921, 3¾x4" ...1,150.00
Vase, floral, thorny stems, MH McDonald, #2672, 1926, 8" 600.00
Vase, floral on imp pattern, red/bl/gr, E Lincoln, 9x4½" 1,150.00
Vase, floral/leaves, gr/blk/yel/red on bl & yel, M McDonald, 6x5", EX..630.00
Vase, peacock feather band, bl/gr on pk, Lincoln, 1920, 9x4" .1,200.00
Vase, repeating florals, C Covalenco, #614B, 1925, 15"...........1,800.00
Vase, stylized flowers, K Shirayamadani, #6644E, 1927, 6" 1,200.00
Vase, water lilies, S Coyne, #614D, 1930, 10¾x5" 2,000.00

Miscellaneous

Bookends, #2446, 1927, child on park pench, bl mat, 5½", pr ...650.00
Bookends, 1923, owl on books, indigo crystalline, 6x4x3", pr.....345.00
Bookends, 1941, water lilies emb, rose mat, 3¾x5¼", pr 230.00
Bowl, #1265, 1921, ivy, pk mat, 8" 100.00
Bowl, #2132, 1921, stylized decor, bl mat, 5½", NM 90.00
Bowl, #2133, 1915, Arts & Crafts design, bl mat, 4½".................150.00
Bowl, #2157, 1928, stylized decor, pk mat, 8" 225.00
Bowl vase, #214C, 1911, emb Greek key, Z-line, lt gr, 3¼x5¾".350.00
Box, #6466, 1936, emb floral lid, ivory mat, 1½x4" 110.00
Bud vase, 1929, ivory mat w/gr int, 7", pr 300.00
Candlesticks, #822D, 1917, bl mottled mat, 6½" 200.00
Figurine, #6405, 1936, rook, bl mat, 4½" 375.00
Flower frog, #2281, 1921, nude female w/mushrooms, gr gloss, 6½"..325.00
Ginger jar, #1321-E, 1929, cutouts on lid, pk mat, 3-pc, 4" 200.00
Planter, #1159, Faience, floral/fruit wreaths on gray crackle, 10", EX.300.00
Tile, Faience, thatched roof cottage/trees, rstr, 12", in Roycroft fr..2,000.00
Tray, #7192, 1961, cattails, 3-color, oval, 17"............................375.00
Trivet, #1794, 1929, rook among lattice, mc, 5¾" sq, NM 225.00
Trivet, #1987, 1917, bird among flowers, mc, 5½" sq, NM 375.00
Trivet, #3077, 1921, parrot among flowers, 6-color, 5½" sq 225.00
Trivet, 1919, Dutch peasant w/bucket, bl/ivory matt cuenca, 5", EX..300.00
Vase, #927D, 1929, leafy branches, bl/wht/brn butterfat, WEH, 9x6".1,500.00
Vase, #1322, 1920, ftd, cut-out lid, tan mat, 5½" 275.00
Vase, #1780, 1920, gray & gr mottled mat, shouldered, 6½"........150.00
Vase, #1795, 1922, rook, purple mat, 4¾"..................................600.00
Vase, #1889, 1924, pine cone, gr mat, 6¾" 500.00
Vase, #1894, 1919, dragonflies, pk mat, 6½", NM......................175.00
Vase, #1905, 1919, peacock feathers, gr mat, 7¾" 425.00
Vase, #1907, 1921, floral panels, gr mat, 5½" 150.00
Vase, #1907, 1928, floral panels, pk & gr mat, 5½" 200.00
Vase, #1908, 1927, swirls, purple mat, 5" 350.00
Vase, #2072, 1925, butterflies, lt bl mat, 6", NM 125.00
Vase, #2088, 1928, berries, purple mat, 5¼" 250.00
Vase, #2093, 1915, bl mat, ftd, 3½"..100.00
Vase, #2095, 1909, Arts & Crafts leaves, bl mat, 5" 250.00
Vase, #2123, 1925, maple leaves, brn mat, 5½" 250.00
Vase, #2136, 1921, wheat, yel mat, 6¼" 400.00
Vase, #2136, 1922, organic decor, gr mat, 6¼" 475.00
Vase, #2190, 1923, tapered, bl-gr mat, 5" 100.00
Vase, #2216, 1920, owl, lt tan mat, 8½" 375.00
Vase, #2312, 1921, yel mat, 6½"...275.00
Vase, #2327, 1921, geometric cvgs, yel mat, 7" 350.00
Vase, #2413, 1931, floral, turq mat, 7½" 400.00
Vase, #2425, 1919, cvd stylized design, bl mat, 7" 200.00

Vase, #2518, 1921, nymphs/Pan emb on turq porc, pk int, L Abel, 11x6"..**460.00**
Vase, #2562, 1928, lt bl matt, hdls, 5¼"...**125.00**
Vase, #2584, 1924, floral, 6-sided, 9½" **250.00**
Vase, #2873, 1926, cvd stylized design at top, pk mat, 3½".........**110.00**
Vase, #6031, 1928, cvd roses, turq mat, 7" **400.00**
Vase, #6548, 1937, birds, wht on yel, 3½"...**225.00**
Vase, #6762, 1941, figures in SW landscape, bl gloss, 6" **120.00**
Vase, #6833, 1949, water lilies, red gloss, 6" **210.00**
Vase, 1920, stylized tulips, pk/gr butterfat, Xd for scaling, 11" **200.00**
Wall pocket, #1395, 1919, peacock feathers, bl mat, 11½".........**450.00**
Wall pocket, #2957, 1928, faceted form, gr mottled mat, 6½"....**225.00**

Rorstrand

The Rorstrand Pottery was established in Sweden in 1726 and is today Sweden's oldest existing pottery. The earliest ware, now mostly displayed in Swedish museums, was much like old Delft. Later types were hard-paste porcelains that were enameled and decorated in a peasant style. Contemporary pieces are often described as Swedish Modern. Rorstrand is also famous for their Christmas plates.

Bowl, blk & gray mottled, Stalhane, 2½x7⅝" **185.00**
Bowl, gondola shape, mottled Robin Egg, Nylund, 3x3" **160.00**
Figurine, polar bear, wht, 8½x6½" **260.00**
Pitcher, wht speckled, teardrop shape w/slanted top, hdld, 9½" .**180.00**
Vase, bl & multi-toned purple matt, uneven rim, Nylund, 7½"..**375.00**
Vase, blk, cylindrical w/tapered middle, Stalhane, 12x2" **210.00**
Vase, chocolate mottled, Stalhane, 13½" **315.00**

Rose Mandarin

Similar in design to Rose Medallion, this Chinese Export porcelain features the pattern of a robed mandarin, often separated by florals, ladies, genre scenes, or butterflies in polychrome enamels. It is sometimes trimmed in gold. Elaborate in decoration, this pattern was popular from the late 1700s until the early 1840s.

Covered temple jar, China, 24", $3,850.00.

Bowl, scalloped rim, 9½"..**385.00**
Coffeepot, 19th C, 10¼" **1,500.00**
Cup & saucer, spur-hdld cup, ca 1840, 6¼" dia saucer **280.00**
Dish, rtcl borders, oval, lt wear, ca 1830s, 8x9½", pr..................**800.00**
Lamp, kerosene; porc cylinder w/brass base & fixture, 12" **600.00**
Platter, lt wear, 19th C, 15¾" **1,100.00**
Punch bowl, scenes w/in & w/out, 1840s, lt wear, 11" **1,000.00**
Punch bowl, well decorated, ca 1780, 10⅜" **2,000.00**

Sauce boat, intertwined hdl, 19th C, 8¼"......................................**300.00**
Umbrella stand, wrapped bamboo form, 19th C, 24" **1,495.00**
Vase, figures/inscriptions, bulbous middle, 1840s, 12", EX..........**800.00**
Vase, sq baluster w/gilt hdls, 19th C, 11", EX, pr....................**1,645.00**

Rose Medallion

Rose Medallion is one of the patterns of Chinese export porcelain produced from before 1850 until the second decade of the twentieth century. It is decorated in rose colors with panels of florals, birds, and butterflies that form reserves containing Chinese figures. Pre-1850 ware is unmarked and is characterized by quality workmanship and gold trim. From about 1850 until circa 1860, the kilns in Canton did not operate, and no Rose Medallion was made. Post-1860 examples (still unmarked) can often be recognized by the poor quality of the gold trim or its absence. In the 1890s the ware was often marked 'China'; 'Made in China' was used from 1910 through the 1930s.

Basin, 19th C, 5x15", NM **635.00**
Bottle, water; paneled, 16"...**1,150.00**
Bowl, canted corners, 4½x9½"+hardwood stand........................**385.00**
Bowl, fruit; ca 1860, 14½x11"...**1,375.00**
Bowl, punch; mandarin scenes w/gold, ftd, 6¼x15¾", EX **600.00**
Bowl, rice; 4x5" dia, w/matching spoon..**140.00**
Bowl, soup; mandarin scenes, wide rim, 8"...................................**120.00**
Bowl, 19th C, base hairline, 4¾x12"..**400.00**
Bowl, 19th C, 1½x10x8" **275.00**
Bowl, 19th C, 2⅝x9⅞"..**290.00**
Box, rnd, w/lid, 2½"...**140.00**
Butter pat, ca 1890, 2½x3"...**40.00**
Charger, ca 1800, 16" dia...**955.00**
Charger, court scene, 13½"...**700.00**
Compote, ped ft, ca 1900, 3x7¾"...**400.00**
Creamer & sugar bowl, 19th C, 5", 5¾" w/lid **275.00**
Cup & saucer, w/gold, ca 1790...**350.00**
Dish, shrimp; ca 1780, birds & floral, 10⅜x9½" dia **2,400.00**
Dish, sq, 1½x7½"..**225.00**
Dish, 19th C, 1x8½"...**175.00**
Lamps, tapered neck, ca 1840, 22", pr..**1,895.00**
Mustard pot, bulbous, appl gilt peach finial, 19th C, 3¾"...........**175.00**
Pitcher, birds/floral & court scene panels, 7⅝"............................**675.00**
Pitcher, cream; snout-shaped spout, ca 1860, 4x6½"...................**200.00**
Plate, ca 1840, 7⅞" **160.00**
Plate, 19th C, 6¼"..**70.00**
Plate, 19th C, 7¾"..**90.00**
Platter, ca 1890, oval, 17" **1,250.00**
Platter, mandarin scenes, orange peel, 12x9" **300.00**
Sauce boat, ovoid, 3½x8½x7", +10¾x7¾" underplate...............**600.00**
Sauce boat, twig hdls, ca 1860, 3" **450.00**
Spoon, gold trim, ca 1855, 5¾"...**95.00**
Teapot, domed lid, squat, gold trim, 8"...**765.00**
Teapot, late, 5⅝x7"...**110.00**
Tray, landscapes alternating w/birds & flowers, 9⅛x9⅛"............**300.00**
Tray, triangular w/scalloped edges, ca 1810, 11x14½" **1,695.00**
Tureen, floral/court scenes, w/lid, 6⅜x8", +9⅝" undertray **1,000.00**
Tureen, garden/court scene, twisted strap hdls, w/lid, 11x14"..**1,000.00**
Vase, dragon & ring hdls, ca 1860s, 10" **400.00**
Vase, dragons & foo dogs, 1840s, 17¼".......................................**1,125.00**
Vase, floral/court scenes, gilt dragon hdls, 1840s, 11¾"............**450.00**
Vase, floral/court scenes, gilt dragon/foo dog hdls, late, 18" **600.00**
Vase, gilt dragon hdls, ca 1840, 5½"..**175.00**
Wash bowl, 2" flat rim, 5¼x16½"...**700.00**
Water bottle, w/lid, 19th C, 15½"...**550.00**

Roselane

William and Georgia Fields began Roselane Pottery in their home in 1938. They moved several times over the years, but when William died in 1973, Georgia sold Roselane to Prather Engineering Corporation and the operation moved to Long Beach where it remained until its final closing in 1977.

Roselane had various lines that included several different glazes and treatments. Chinese-Modern is not as popular as some of Roselane's other products. Certain pieces of Chinese-Modern are plentiful and do not bring high values. In the mid-1940s until the early 1950s, Aqua Marine was a buffet serving line with pieces such as large, deep bowls and trays created in a sgraffito technique. The fish or snowflakes motifs are in demand today. The Sparkler series, created in the 1950s, was a popular product for the company. The airbrushed, decorated semi-porcelain children and animals fascinate collectors even though there are some reproductions on the market. Originally the Sparklers had rhinestone eyes, but the later ones were made of plastic. The deer and deer groups on a single base are sought after. Their muted glazes and their lifelike appearances have many collectors trying to amass all of them. William 'Doc' Fields created beautiful animals on walnut bases. The animals were generally a high-gloss white. When they became available the public did not buy them in any quantity and they were discontinued shortly after their introduction. Today collectors avidly look for items in this line and prices reflect that demand.

Bowl, gray geometric floral on pk, #A9, 2x9" dia 40.00
Bowl, salad; blk swirling fish on pk, #25 ....70.00
Coffee warmer, blk swirling fish on pk, #34, w/metal stand 125.00
Console bowl, speckled chartreuse, angelfish in seaweed centerpc, EX ..60.00
Dish, turq sq design w/blk shading, oblong, 18¾x5" 55.00

Figurine, angelfish, 7½", $75.00. (Photo courtesy Jack Chipman)

Figurine, angelfish, Sparkler, 4½", from $20 to 25.00
Figurine, Basset hound pup, Sparkler, 2", from $12 to 15.00
Figurine, bird w/wings outstretched, pale yel w/pk highlights, 5x8" ..35.00
Figurine, cat, stylized, #275, 17½" L 110.00
Figurine, cat mother holding babies, Sparkler, 5", from $40 to ..45.00
Figurine, cat sitting, head trn right/tail out, Sparkler, from $25 to .28.00
Figurine, deer, stylized, gr w/brn, 8" 30.00
Figurine, deer, 1 head up, 1 down, gold w/brn specks, 8", 6", pr .45.00
Figurine, deer leaping, bl/gray, #127, 6¼" 35.00
Figurine, elephant sitting on hind quarters, Sparkler, 6" 28.00
Figurine, gazelle, long horns, 16" 115.00
Figurine, horse, wht, stylized, 7¾", pr 90.00
Figurine, kitten sitting, Sparkler, 1¾" 12.00
Figurine, man on bk of water buffalo, chartreuse, 6x8" 40.00
Figurine, owl, Sparkler, 7" 30.00

Figurine, owl w/2 sm owls under wings, brn w/gold 25.00
Figurine, pouter pigeon, Sparkler, 3½" 20.00
Figurine, roadrunner, 4x8½" 35.00
Platter, cranberry, #115, 15x7¾" 20.00
Salad fork & spoon, swirling fish decor, ceramic w/wooden ends ..30.00
Tray, wht w/gr int, #312, 2¼x12x7¼" 18.00

Rosemeade

Rosemeade was the name chosen by Wahpeton Pottery Company of Wahpeton, North Dakota, to represent their product. The founders of the company were Laura A. Taylor and R.J. Hughes, who organized the firm in 1940. It is most noted for small bird and animal figurals, either in high gloss or a Van Briggle-like matt glaze. The ware was marked 'Rosemeade' with an ink stamp or carried a 'Prairie Rose' sticker. The pottery closed in 1961. Our advisor for this category is Bryce L. Farnsworth; he is listed in the Directory under North Dakota. For more information we recommend *Collector's Encyclopedia of Rosemeade Pottery* by Darlene Hurst Dommel (Collector Books).

Ashtray, chickadee at side of gr tray, 4 rests, 5", from $200 to 250.00
Ashtray, English toy spaniel (head) on side, 7", minimum value .300.00
Ashtray, mallard on side, North Dakota, gr, 5" 225.00
Ashtray, pheasant on side, Corn Palace, Mitchell SD, 5" 200.00
Ashtray, tepee in bottom, Chihinkapa Park, 2 rests, 5½", $150 to .200.00
Ashtray, yel duck in center of blk 8-sided tray, 4½", from $125 to .175.00
Bank, blk bear, 3¼x5¾", minimum value 400.00
Bank, hippopotamus, gr, 2¾x5¾", minimum value 500.00
Bell, peacock figural, 5½", from $250 to 300.00
Bell, tulip, any color, 3¾", from $125 to 150.00
Box, cigarette; horse emb on lid, 2¼x4½", from $250 to 300.00
Candy dish, shell form, wht/ice bl, 2¾x4½" 50.00
Cotton dispenser, rabbit, 4¾x2½", from $150 to 200.00
Covered dish, hen on basket, blk & wht, 5½x5½", from $350 to .400.00
Figurine, bison, solid, recumbent, 2x3¾", minimum value 500.00
Figurine, cock strutting, wht w/red on gr dome base, 3¾", $125 to ..150.00
Figurine, dolphin, tail up, 2½", from $75 to 100.00
Figurine, dove, wht, sticker, 4½x6¼", from $250 to 300.00
Figurine, frog, solid, gr w/blk spots, 1¼x1¼", from $150 to 175.00
Figurine, koala bear mother & cub, wht gloss, 5½", minimum value ..300.00
Figurine, pheasant, Golden Chinese cock; 2¾x4", from $150 to .200.00
Figurine, pheasant cock, mc, 9¼x14", from $400 to 450.00
Figurine, potato, 1½x2½", from $100 to 125.00
Figurine, walrus, blk & wht, 4½x6½" 500.00
Flower holder, fawn prancing, 6¼x5½", from $50 to 75.00
Jam jar, bbl w/strawberries finial, 5" 150.00
Mug, prairie rose, 3¾", from $40 to 50.00
Pin, goldfinch, rare, 1¾", minimum value 1,200.00
Pitcher, 2-color swirl, 3", from $150 to 200.00
Planter, circus horse, lt bl, 5x6½" 100.00
Planter, rooster, flat, rare, 7½x5", minimum value 300.00
Plaque, bird w/wings wide, flat, very rare, 8x5¾", minimum value ..600.00
Plaque, bluegill fish, 3½x6", from $300 to 500.00
Plaque, lg-mouth bass, 3½x6", from $300 to 500.00
Plaque, pheasants, cock: 6x7½", hen: 4¾x7", pr, minimum value .1,200.00
Plate, leaves emb, 4½", minimum value 200.00
Plate, Theodore Roosevelt, Nat'l Memorial Park, 8½", from $400 to ..450.00
Shakers, badgers, 1x2¾", pr, minimum value 600.00
Shakers, bear cubs, 3½", 3", pr 75.00
Shakers, bluegill fish, 2½x4", pr, from $400 to 500.00
Shakers, doves, wht, 1¾x2¾", pr, from $500 to 600.00
Shakers, ducklings, blk, 2¼", 2½", pr 100.00
Shakers, fighting cocks, mini, 1", 1½", pr 100.00

Shakers, flamingos on nests, 3", 3¾", pr, from $200 to...............**250.00**
Shakers, Fort Abercrombie blockhouse, 1¼", pr, minimum value.**750.00**
Shakers, Indian God of Peace, St Paul Minn, 4", pr, from $350 to.**400.00**
Shakers, mallard drake & hen, 3½", 2", pr, from $75 to.............**100.00**
Shakers, Trojan seed corn, ear figural, 4½", pr, from $450 to......**500.00**
Shakers, turkey gobbler & hen, mini, 1½", 1", pr, from $300 to.**400.00**
Shakers, wire-haired fox terrier (head), tan ears, 2", pr **50.00**
Spoon rest, prairie rose, 4½", from $70 to...................................**100.00**
Spoon rest, tulip, many colors, 5", from $80 to...........................**100.00**
TV lamp, horse, all blk, 9½x8¾", minimum value.....................**800.00**
TV lamp, panther, forest gr or bl, 7x13", minimum value...........**700.00**
Vase, ducks/fish (Egyptian style), gr, 5x5½", from $250 to.........**350.00**
Wall pocket, deer, aqua or pk, 5", from $40 to..............................**60.00**
Wall pocket, lovebirds in crescent moon, 6¼x6¼", minimum value..**400.00**

Rosenthal

In 1879 Phillip Rosenthal established the Rosenthal Porcelain Factory in Selb, Bavaria. Its earliest products were figurines and fine tablewares. The company has continued to operate to the present decade, manufacturing limited edition plates. Our advisor for this category is Raphael Wise; he is listed in the Directory under Florida.

Bowl, lady's portrait, heavy gold trim, 10¾", $135.00.

Cup & saucer, gold band w/butterflies, gilt eagle hdl, ca 1900....**175.00**
Figurine, Alsatian puppy, seated, Karner, #1533, 5¼" **225.00**
Figurine, Blackamoor w/jug & platter of fish, 7½" **240.00**
Figurine, Blackamoor w/platter of pears, 7¼".............................**240.00**
Figurine, blk poodle standing up, begging, Heidenreich, #5155, 8" .**450.00**
Figurine, bulldog, ca 1920, 6x9¼" **475.00**
Figurine, Chinese goldfish (2) in seaweed, sgn, 15x9x5"..........**2,000.00**
Figurine, dachshund puppy, brn, seated, Karner, #1347, 6x6¾" ...**200.00**
Figurine, doe & fawn, recumbent, Handgemalt, #1117, 5x7"......**225.00**
Figurine, elephant, gray w/1 leg raised, 6x10" **230.00**
Figurine, Eros, 2 kissing nudes kneeling, Aigner, 13½x7x8" **3,500.00**
Figurine, faun w/2 jugs, Himmelstoss, #K682, 7¼" **650.00**
Figurine, female snake charmer w/snake in basket, #956, 10½"..**315.00**
Figurine, Fox Terrier, Fritz, #1243, 6" **185.00**
Figurine, frog prince offering gold to nude princess, Fritz, 12x5" .**1,500.00**
Figurine, German Shepherd, brn w/blk, Fritz, #980, 5¾x4" **235.00**
Figurine, goat on ball, #808, 5½x5"..**200.00**
Figurine, gray cat playing w/yel ball, Karner, 3¾x6½" **900.00**
Figurine, greyhound, wht, Karner, 1930, 6¼", EX **895.00**
Figurine, Hannibal, horse's head, wht, #1609, 9¼x7½" **350.00**
Figurine, lady w/roses, Caasmann, #303, 10"..............................**350.00**
Figurine, little girl feeding rabbits, Handgemalt, #1639, 4x5x2".**230.00**
Figurine, minstrel lady in wht w/bl/gr trim, 12x13x7"..............**2,300.00**
Figurine, nude boy walking w/bird in hand, Himmelstoss, 6½" ..**235.00**

Figurine, nude crouched down w/1 hand on floor, Klimsh, 12x6x7" .**550.00**
Figurine, nude drinking from her hands, Wenck, 7½x6".............**150.00**
Figurine, nude female shot-putter, L Adam, #756, 17½x7" **1,500.00**
Figurine, nude holding drape behind, WV Heider, 16x7x5" **3,000.00**
Figurine, nude running, E Seger, #937, 12x12x3½" **1,750.00**
Figurine, panther on ball, Schliepstein, 4x8½".............................**200.00**
Figurine, parrot, mc on wht ped, #150, 6½".................................**300.00**
Figurine, peacock, Heidenreich, #1161, 7½x9" **250.00**
Figurine, pekingese, gray & wht, 1 paw raised, Flinsch, 5½x6"...**290.00**
Figurine, puppy, wht w/brn features, Karner, #1123, 2⅝x5¾".....**185.00**
Figurine, racing ostrich w/nude rider, Liebermann, 18x22x4½"...**7,500.00**
Figurine, setter, blk & wht, Heidenreich, 7x10½" **350.00**
Figurine, Spanish dancer w/hands behind head, LFG, 16½x9x5".**3,000.00**
Goblet, wine; Papyrus, 7¾" **40.00**
Lamp, Korean dancer w/red, bl & gold, C Holzer-Defanti, 32" .**1,500.00**
Plate, Chippendale, bird of paradise w/silver flowers, 13"............**250.00**
Plates, dinner; Baroco, 10½", 6 for..**260.00**
Tankard, lady profile w/long flowing hair, #55, 12".....................**425.00**
Tureen, soup; floral on wht, gold hdls, mk Sanssouci, 8x9".........**200.00**
Vase, floral, gold & wht on bl w/allover feather-leaves, 12x3½".**100.00**

Roseville

The Roseville Pottery Company was established in 1892 by George F. Young in Roseville, Ohio. Finding their facilities inadequate, the company moved to Zanesville in 1898, erected a new building, and installed the most modern equipment available. By 1900 Young felt ready to enter into the stiffly competitive art pottery market. Roseville's first art line was called Rozane. Similar to Rookwood's Standard, Rozane featured dark blended backgrounds with slip-painted underglaze artwork of nature studies, portraits, birds, and animals. Azurean, developed in 1902, was a blue and white underglaze art line on a blue blended background. Egypto (1904) featured a matt glaze in a soft shade of old green and was modeled in low relief after examples of ancient Egyptian pottery. Mongol (1904) was a high-gloss oxblood red line after the fashion of the Chinese Sang de Boeuf. Mara (1904), an iridescent lustre line of magenta and rose with intricate patterns developed on the surface or in low relief, successfully duplicated Sicardo's work. These early lines were followed by many others of highest quality: Fudjiyama and Woodland (1905 – 06) reflected an Oriental theme; Crystalis (1906) was covered with beautiful frost-like crystals. Della Robbia, their most famous line (introduced in 1906), was decorated with designs ranging from florals, animals, and birds to scenes of Viking warriors and Roman gladiators. These designs were worked in sgraffito with slip-painted details. Very limited but of great importance to collectors today, Rozane Olympic (1905) was decorated with scenes of Greek mythology on a red ground. Pauleo (1914) was the last of the art-ware lines. It was varied — over two hundred glazes were recorded — and some pieces were decorated by hand, usually with florals.

During the second decade of the century until the plant closed forty years later, new lines were continually added. Some of the more popular of the middle-period lines were Donatello, 1915; Futura, 1928; Pine Cone, 1931; and Blackberry, 1933. The floral lines of the later years have become highly collectible. Pottery from every era of Roseville production — even its utility ware — attest to an unwavering dedication to quality and artistic merit.

Examples of the fine art pottery lines present the greatest challenge to evaluate. Scarcity is a prime consideration. The quality of artwork varied from one artist to another. Some pieces show fine detail and good color, and naturally this influences their values. Studies of animals and portraits bring higher prices than the floral designs. An artist's signature often increases the value of any item, especially if the artist is one who is well recognized.

The market is literally flooded with imposter Roseville that is coming into the country from China. An experienced eye can easily detect these fakes, but to a novice collector, they may pass for old Roseville. Study the marks. If the 'USA' is missing or appears only faintly, the piece is most definitely a reproduction. Also watch for lines with a mark that is not correct for its time frame; for example, Luffa with the script mark, and Woodland with the round Rozane stamp from the 1917 line.

For further information consult the newly revised *Collector's Encyclopedia of Roseville Pottery, First* and *Second Series,* by Sharon and Bob Huxford and Mike Nickel (Collector Books). Other books on the subject include *Collector's Compendium of Roseville Pottery, Volumes I, II,* and *III,* by R.B. Monsen (see Directory, Virginia); and *Roseville in All Its Splendor With Price Guide* by Jack and Nancy Bomm (self-published). Our advisor for this category is Mike Nickel; he is listed in the Directory under Michigan.

Apple Blossom, bowl, #326-6, gr or pk, 2½x6½", from $175 to .**200.00**
Apple Blossom, vase, #390-12, gr or pk, 12½", from $400 to......**450.00**
Apple Blossom, window box, #368-8, gr or pk, 2½x10½", from $175 .**200.00**
Artcraft, jardiniere, glossy red, 4", from $150 to **175.00**
Artcraft, jardiniere, 6", from $450 to......................................**500.00**
Artwood, planter, #1054, 6½x8½", from $85 to.........................**95.00**
Artwood, 3-pc planter set, 2 #1050/1 #1051, 4" & 6", from $110 to.**125.00**
Aztec, vase, tapering, sgn R, 11", from $800 to..........................**900.00**
Azurean, candlestick, floral, V Adams, 9", from $1,000 to **1,100.00**
Azurean, vase, floral, #822/7, Leffler, 15½", from $2,500 to **3,000.00**

Baneda, vase, green, handles, 6½", from $750.00 to $825.00.
(Photo courtesy Craftsman Auctions)

Baneda, vase, #594, gr, 9", from $1,000 to **1,100.00**
Baneda, vase, #594, pk, 9", from $750 to **800.00**
Baneda, vase, #603, gr, 4½", from $625 to **675.00**
Baneda, vase, #603, pk, 4½", from $400 to **450.00**
Bittersweet, cornucopia, #857-4, 4½", from $100 to **125.00**
Bittersweet, vase, #888-16, 15½", from $450 to...........................**500.00**
Blackberry, hanging basket, 4½x6½", from $800 to **900.00**
Blackberry, jardiniere, 7", from $650 to......................................**750.00**
Bleeding Heart, plate, #381-10, bl, 10½", from $200 to.............**225.00**
Bleeding Heart, vase, #968-9, bl, 8½", from $375 to..................**425.00**
Bleeding Heart, vase, #968-9, gr or pk, 8½", from $325 to **350.00**
Bushberry, dbl cornucopia, #155-8, bl, 6", from $200 to.............**225.00**
Bushberry, vase, #39-14, bl, 14½", from $550 to..........................**650.00**
Cameo II, flowerpot, 5½", from $350 to **450.00**
Cameo II, wall pocket, from $500 to **600.00**
Capri, ashtray, #598-9, 9", from $40 to.......................................**50.00**
Capri, leaf dish, #532-16, 16", from $35 to..................................**45.00**
Capri, window box, #569-10, 3x10", from $45 to **55.00**
Carnelian I, console bowl, 14", from $150 to...............................**200.00**
Carnelian I, loving cup, 5", from $100 to....................................**125.00**
Carnelian II, bowl vase, hdld, 5", from $225 to **275.00**
Carnelian II, ewer, 12½", from $1,000 to **1,200.00**
Carnelian II, planter, hdld, 3x8", from $125 to..........................**150.00**
Cherry Blossom, hanging basket, #350, brn, 8", from $400 to **500.00**
Cherry Blossom, hanging basket, #350, pk/bl, 8", from $2,000 to.**2,250.00**

Clemana, vase, #112, bl, 7½", from $450 to **500.00**
Clemana, vase, #112, gr, 7½", from $350 to **400.00**
Clematis, center bowl, #456-6, brn or gr, 9", from $125 to **150.00**
Clematis, flower arranger vase, #192-5, bl, 5½", from $100 to....**125.00**
Columbine, bookend planters, #8, bl or tan, 5", pr, from $350 to .**400.00**
Columbine, cornucopia, #149-6, pk, 5½", from $175 to **200.00**
Corinthian, candlestick, 8", from $100 to...................................**125.00**
Corinthian, compote, 5x10" dia, from $150 to.............................**175.00**
Corinthian, hanging basket, 8", from $200 to.............................**250.00**
Cosmos, flower frog, #39, bl, 3½", from $200 to.........................**250.00**
Cosmos, flower frog, #39, tan, 3½", from $150 to........................**175.00**
Cosmos, vase, #134-4, gr, 4", from $150 to **175.00**
Cremona, bowl, sq, 9" W, from $125 to **150.00**
Cremona, fan vase, 5", from $125 to **150.00**
Cremona, urn, 4", from $150 to...**175.00**
Dahlrose, candlesticks, #1069, 3½", pr, from $175 to.................**225.00**
Dahlrose, vase, 4-sided, 6", from $450 to **500.00**
Dahlrose, window box, #377, 6x12½", from $450 to....................**500.00**
Dawn, #833-12, gr, 12", from $500 to..**600.00**
Dawn, ewer, #834-16, gr, 16", from $650 to.................................**750.00**
Dawn, vase #833-12, pk or yel, 12", from $600 to **700.00**
Dogwood I, bowl, 2", from $75 to..**100.00**
Dogwood I, vase, 9", from $175 to...**200.00**
Dogwood II, hanging basket, 7", from $250 to.............................**300.00**
Dogwood II, vase, 6", from $200 to...**225.00**
Donatello, basket, 15", from $600 to...**750.00**
Donatello, pitcher, 6½", from $375 to..**425.00**
Dutch, pitcher, 7½", from $225 to..**275.00**
Dutch, tankard, 11½", from $175 to...**200.00**
Dutch, toothbrush holder, 4", from $100 to.................................**125.00**
Earlam, candlesticks, #1080, 4", pr, from $600 to.......................**650.00**
Earlam, planter, #89, 5½x10½", from $400 to..............................**450.00**
Earlam, vase, #521-7, from $450 to **500.00**
Egypto, pitcher, 7", from $700 to...**750.00**
Egypto, pitcher vase, 11", from $1,750 to **2,000.00**
Falline, candlesticks, #1092, bl, 4", pr, from $1,250 to.............**1,500.00**
Falline, candlesticks, #1092, tan, 4", pr, from $800 to..............**1,000.00**
Falline, vase, #647, tan, 7½", from $600 to.................................**700.00**
Ferella, bowl/frog, #211, red, 5", from $1,100 to.....................**1,200.00**
Ferella, vase, #498, red, 4", from $550 to **600.00**
Ferella, vase, #498, tan, 4", from $350 to **400.00**
Florane, basket, 8½", from $300 to...**350.00**
Florane, dbl bud vase, gate-type, 5", from $125 to **150.00**
Florentine, bowl, 9" dia, from $75 to...**100.00**
Florentine, dbl bud vase, gate-type, 6", from $100 to **125.00**
Foxglove, flower frog, #46, bl or pk, 4", from $125 to **150.00**
Foxglove, tray, #424, 15" W, gr/pk, from $350 to **400.00**
Freesia, center bowl, #464-6, bl, 8½", from $125 to **150.00**
Freesia, flowerpot & saucer, #670-5, tangerine, 5½", from $185 to..**210.00**
Freesia, vase, #463-5, gr, from $225 to..**250.00**
Fuchsia, candlesticks, #1132, bl, 2", pr, from $175 to.................**200.00**
Fuchsia, vase, #897-8, brn/tan, 8", from $300 to.........................**350.00**
Futura, fan vase, #82, 6", from $550 to..**650.00**
Futura, vase, #394, 12½", from $1,000 to **1,100.00**
Futura, vase, #431, 10", from $1,500 to.....................................**1,750.00**
Gardenia, basket, #610-12, 12", from $350 to.............................**400.00**
Gardenia, bowl, #641-5, 5", from $125 to **150.00**
Gardenia, tray, #631-14, 15", from $200 to **250.00**
Imperial I, basket, 13", from $350 to **400.00**
Imperial I, planter, 14x16, from $350 to......................................**400.00**
Imperial II, bowl, 4½", from $300 to..**350.00**
Imperial II, vase, gr, bulbous, 4", from $500 to...........................**550.00**
Iris, pillow vase, #922-8, bl, 8½", from $325 to **375.00**
Iris, pillow vase, #922-8, pk or tan, 8½", from $175 to...............**200.00**

Iris, vase, #928-12, bl, 12½", from $550 to 650.00
Iris, vase, #928-12, pk or tan, 12½", from $300 to..................... 350.00
Ivory II, cornucopia, #2, 5½x12", from $75 to.......................... 95.00
Ivory II, jardiniere, 6", from $50 to.. 75.00
Ixia, basket, #346, 10", from $300 to... 350.00
Ixia, bowl, #327, 6", from $150 to.. 175.00
Ixia, hanging basket, 7", from $250 to....................................... 300.00
Jonquil, candlesticks, #1082, 4", pr, from $450 to...................... 550.00
Jonquil, center bowl, #219, 3½x9", from $325 to........................ 375.00
Jonquil, vase, #529, 8", from $500 to... 600.00
Juvenile, bowl, bear, 6", from $900 to....................................... 1,000.00
Juvenile, cake plate, chicks, 9½", from $700 to......................... 800.00
Juvenile, egg cup, rabbit, ped ft, 3", from $1,500 to 2,000.00
Juvenile, milk pitcher, chicks, from $175 to.............................. 200.00
Juvenile, mug, chick, 3½", from $200 to..................................... 250.00
Juvenile, mug, fancy cat, 3", from $1,500 to............................. 2,000.00
Juvenile, plate, Little Bo Peep, rolled edge, 8", from $175 to...... 200.00
La Rose, bowl, 6" dia, from $100 to.. 125.00
La Rose, dbl bud vase, gate type, from $150 to........................... 175.00
Laurel, vase, #674, gold, 9½", from $400 to................................ 500.00
Laurel, vase, #674, gr, 9½", from $650 to................................... 750.00
Lotus, pillow vase, #L4-10, 10½", from $275 to........................ 325.00
Luffa, candlesticks, #1097, brn or gr, 5", pr, from $500 to 600.00
Luffa, lamp, bl/rose or bl/gr, 9½", from $1,200 to..................... 1,400.00
Luffa, vase, brn or gr, 15½", from $2,000 to.............................. 2,500.00
Lustre, basket, 10", from $200 to... 250.00
Lustre, bowl, 5", from $95 to.. 125.00
Magnolia, conch shell, #453-6, 6½", from $95 to........................ 110.00
Magnolia, ewer, #14-10, 10", from $175 to................................ 200.00
Mayfair, jardiniere, #1109-4, 4", from $60 to............................. 75.00
Mayfair, vase, #1106-12, 12½", from $90 to................................ 110.00
Ming Tree, basket, #509-12, 13", from $275 to........................... 300.00
Ming Tree, bookends, #559, 5½", pr, from $200 to...................... 235.00
Ming Tree, window box, #569-10, 4x11", from $125 to 150.00
Mock Orange, pillow vase, #930-8, 7", from $150 to................... 175.00
Mock Orange, planter, #932, 4x10½", from $125 to..................... 150.00
Mock Orange, vase, #985-12, 13", from $350 to.......................... 450.00
Moderne, compote, #297-6, 6", from $250 to 275.00
Moderne, triple candlestick, #1112, 6", from $275 to................. 350.00
Mongol, mug, 3-hdld, 6", from $700 to 850.00
Mongol, vase, #C-16, 10½", from $3,000 to................................ 3,500.00
Montacello, vase, #564, bl, 9", from $1,300 to........................... 1,500.00
Montacello, vase, #564, tan, 9", from $1,000 to......................... 1,100.00
Morning Glory, candlesticks, #1102, gr, 5", pr, from $750 to 850.00
Morning Glory, pillow vase, #120, gr, 7", from $550 to.............. 600.00
Morning Glory, pillow vase, #120, ivory, 7", from $400 to.......... 450.00
Moss, candlesticks, #1109, bl, 2", pr, from $150 to 175.00
Moss, candlesticks, #1109, orange/gr or pk/gr, 2", pr, from $200 to. 225.00
Moss, pillow vase, #781, orange/gr or pk/gr, 8", from $350 to 400.00
Mostique, bowl, 7", from $150 to.. 175.00
Mostique, hanging basket, 7", from $400 to................................ 500.00
Mostique, jardiniere, 8", from $250 to.. 300.00
Orian, center bowl, #275, red, 5x12", from $375 to 425.00
Orian, center bowl, #275, turq, 5x12", from $325 to................... 375.00
Orian, vase, #742, yel, 12½", from $525 to................................. 575.00
Pauleo, vase, cylindrical w/squatty 3-ftd bottom, 12", from $1,500 to.. 1,750.00
Pauleo, vase, long trumpet neck w/squatty base, 19", from $2,000 to. 2,500.00
Pauleo, vase, pnt berries on leafy branch, 17", from $2,000 to.. 2,500.00
Peony, bookends, #11, 5½", pr, from $200 to............................. 250.00
Peony, planter, #387-8, 10", from $85 to..................................... 95.00
Persian, bowl, 3-hdld, 3½", from $175 to.................................... 200.00
Persian, jardiniere, from $350 to.. 400.00
Pine Cone, ashtray, #499, brn, 4½", from $175 to...................... 200.00
Pine Cone, ashtray, #499, gr, 4½", from $100 to........................ 125.00

Pine Cone, bowl, #320-5, gr, 4½", from $150 to......................... 175.00
Pine Cone, pitcher, #485-10, bl, 10½", from $950 to 1,150.00
Pine Cone, planter, #124, bl, 5", from $250 to 300.00
Pine Cone, vase, #908-8, bl, 8", from $650 to........................... 750.00
Poppy, basket, #348-12, gray/gr, 12½", from $500 to................ 550.00
Poppy, basket, #348-12, pk, from $650 to................................. 750.00
Poppy, bowl, #336-10, pk, 12", from $275 to 300.00
Poppy, bowl, #336-10, tan, 12", from $400 to............................ 450.00
Primrose, #761-6, tan, 6½", from $150 to.................................. 175.00
Primrose, vase, #761-6, bl or pk, 6½", from $175 to.................. 200.00
Raymor, covered butter, #181, 7½", from $75 to........................ 100.00
Raymor, shirred egg, #200, 10", from $40 to.............................. 45.00
Rosecraft, pillow vase, gr, 6", from $250 to............................... 300.00
Rosecraft Blended, bud vase, #36-6, 6", from $90 to 110.00
Rosecraft Blended, vase, #35, 10", from $125 to........................ 150.00
Rosecraft Hexagon, candlestick, brn, 8", from $375 to.............. 425.00
Rosecraft Hexagon, dbl bud vase/gate, glossy bl, rare, 5", $575 to.. 625.00
Rosecraft Panel, pillow vase, brn, 8", from $250 to.................... 275.00
Rosecraft Panel, pillow vase, gr, 6", from $350 to..................... 400.00
Rosecraft Panel, window box, gr, 6x12", from $550 to............... 600.00
Rosecraft Vintage, bowl, 3½" dia, from $75 to........................... 100.00
Rosecraft Vintage, candlestick, 8", from $250 to........................ 300.00
Rosecraft Vintage, vase, 5", from $175 to................................... 200.00
Rozane, bud vase, #841/3, MN, 7½", from $175 to..................... 225.00
Rozane, chocolate pot, floral, #936/7, sgn, 9½", from $550 to.... 650.00
Rozane, ewer, floral, #857/x, 7½", from $175 to......................... 200.00
Rozane, jardiniere, 3-ftd bowl, floral, 9½", from $175 to 225.00
Rozane, letter holder, floral, C Neff, 3½", from $275 to............. 325.00
Rozane, vase, floral, #872, 5½", from $200 to............................ 225.00
Rozane Light, bud vase, floral, #831, 6", from $125 to............... 150.00
Rozane Light, pillow vase, floral, 6½", from $400 to.................. 500.00
Rozane Light, tobacco jar, pipe motif, Walter Myers, 6", from $500 to. 600.00
Rozane 1917, basket, gr, 8", from $250 to.................................. 300.00
Rozane 1917, candlestick, ivory, 6", from $100 to..................... 125.00
Russco, triple cornucopia, 8x12½", from $300 to....................... 350.00
Russco, vase, flared rim & base, 7", from $175 to...................... 200.00
Silhouette, dbl planter, #757-9, 5½", from $125 to.................... 150.00
Silhouette, vase, #789-14, 14", from $350 to 400.00
Snowberry, ewer, #1TK-15, bl or pk, 16", from $600 to............ 700.00
Snowberry, ewer, #1TK-15, gr, 16", from $525 to..................... 575.00
Sunflower, bowl, #208, 4", from $600 to 700.00
Sunflower, candlesticks, 4", pr, from $1,000 to......................... 1,200.00
Sunflower, vase, #619, 6", from $1,250 to................................. 1,500.00
Sunflower, window box, 3½x11", from $2,000 to...................... 2,500.00
Teasel, vase, #888-12, dk bl or rust, 12", from $500 to 600.00
Teasel, vase, #888-12, lt bl or tan, 12", from $450 to 550.00
Thorn Apple, bowl vase, #305-6, 6½", from $200 to................. 250.00
Thorn Apple, dbl bud vase, #1119, 5½", from $175 to.............. 225.00
Thorn Apple, hanging basket, 7" dia, from $300 to 350.00
Thorn Apple, triple bud vase, #1120, 6", from $200 to............. 250.00
Topeo, center bowl, bl, 13", from $400 to.................................. 450.00
Topeo, center bowl, red, 13", from $250 to................................ 300.00
Topeo, dbl candlesticks, red, 5", pr, from $300 to..................... 350.00
Tourmaline, candlesticks, 5", pr, from $175 to........................... 200.00
Tourmaline, cornucopia, 7", from $75 to.................................... 100.00
Tourmaline, pillow vase, 6", from $100 to.................................. 125.00
Tuscany, console bowl, gray/lt bl, 11", from $125 to.................. 150.00
Tuscany, console bowl, pk, 11", from $150 to 175.00
Tuscany, flower-arranger vase, gray/lt bl, 5", from $100 to........ 125.00
Tuscany, flower-arranger vase, pk, 5", from $125 to.................. 150.00
Velmoss, bowl, #266, bl, 3x11", from $225 to............................ 275.00
Velmoss, vase, #719, tan (rare), 9½", from $450 to.................... 500.00
Velmoss Scroll, compote, 9x4" dia, from $200 to....................... 250.00
Velmoss Scroll, vase, cylindrical, 6", from $175 to 200.00

Vista, basket, 12", from $1,500 to...1,750.00
Vista, vase, #121-15, 15", from $1,000 to...............................1,200.00
Water Lily, candlesticks, #1155-4 ½, rose w/gr, 5", pr, from $225 to..250.00
Water Lily, vase, #78-9, brn, 9", from $300 to 325.00
White Rose, basket, #362-8, 7½", from $200 to 250.00
White Rose, dbl bud vase, #148, gate-type, 4½", from $85 to.......95.00
White Rose, dbl candlesticks, #1143, 4", pr, from $200 to 250.00
White Rose, vase, #992-15, 15½", from $300 to 400.00
Wincraft, basket, #210-12, 12", from $500 to 600.00
Wincraft, bookends, #259, 6½", pr, from $175 to 225.00
Windsor, center bowl, bl, 3½x10½", from $450 to 550.00
Windsor, vase, #546, 6", bl, from $400 to.................................450.00
Windsor, vase, #546, 6", from $300 to......................................350.00
Wisteria, bowl vase, #632, bl, 5", from $550 to 650.00
Wisteria, hanging basket, #351, tan, 7½", from $700 to..............800.00
Wisteria, hanging basket, #351, 7½", from $1,250 to..............1,500.00
Woodland, bud vase, floral, 4-sided, 7", from $550 to 650.00
Woodland, vase, geometrics, tapers to flat bottom, 13", from $3,500 to.4,000.00

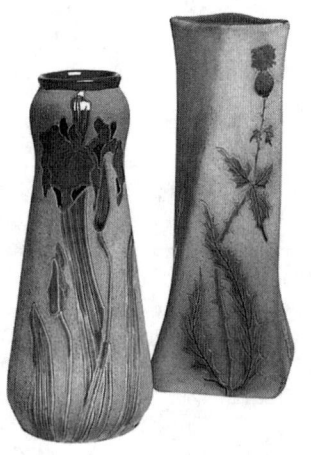

Woodland vases: Irises, 9",
$1,000.00; Thistles (all four
sides), 10", from $900.00 to
$1,000.00.

Zephyr Lily, fan vase, #205-6, brn, 6½", from $150 to.................175.00
Zephyr Lily, hanging basket, bl, 7½", from $350 to.....................400.00

Rowland and Marsellus

Though the impressive back stamp seems to suggest otherwise, Rowland and Marsellus were not Staffordshire potters but American importers who commissioned various English companies to supply them with the transfer-printed crockery and historical ware that had been a popular import commodity since the early 1800s. Plates (both flat and with a rolled edge), cups and saucers, pitchers, and platters were sold as souvenirs from 1890 through the 1930s. Though other importers — Bawo & Dotter, and A. C. Bosselman & Co., both of New York City — commissioned the manufacture of similar souvenir items, by far the largest volume carries the R. & M. mark, and Rowland and Marcellus has become a generic term that covers all twentieth-century souvenir china of this type. Their mark may be in full or 'R. & M.' in a diamond. Though primarily made with blue transfers on white, other colors may occasionally be found as well.

Note: Show prices may be as much as 25% higher than our values, which are based on eBay sales. Our advisor for this category is David Ringering; he is listed in the Directory under Oregon.

Key:
r/e — rolled edge   v/o — view of
s/o — souvenir of

Cup & saucer, farmer's...45.00
Pitcher, Discovery of America, 3 major scenes, 7½"...................400.00
Plate, Asbury Park, r/e, s/o, 10"...75.00
Plate, Atlantic City, v/o, 9"...60.00
Plate, Battle of Lake Erie, fruit & flower border.........................50.00
Plate, Cape Cod, fisherman's portrait, 9"....................................50.00
Plate, Cincinnati OH, v/o, 9"...50.00
Plate, Cleveland OH, r/e, s/o, 10"...70.00
Plate, Denver CO, v/o, 10" coupe...60.00
Plate, Hartford CT, 1906, r/e, v/o, 10".......................................55.00
Plate, Hermitage, fruit & flower border, 9¾"..............................50.00
Plate, Hudson River, s/o, 10"..55.00
Plate, Los Angeles CA, r/e, 10¼"..75.00
Plate, Myles Standish, r/e, 10"..65.00
Plate, New Bedford MA, r/e, s/o, 10"..70.00
Plate, New York, Statue of Liberty, r/e, v/o, 10".........................70.00
Plate, Niagara Falls, r/e, 10"...50.00
Plate, Philadelphia, r/e, s/o..65.00
Plate, Portland OR, s/o, 10" coupe 60.00
Plate, Robert Burns, r/e, 10"...55.00
Plate, Seattle WA, r/e, s/o, 10"...75.00
Plate, Sherbrooke, s/o, 10"...85.00
Plate, Syracuse NY (Indian), r/e, s/o, 10¼".................................140.00
Plate, Teddy Roosevelt, r/e, 10"..95.00
Plate, Waterbury CT, r/e, s/o, 10"...75.00
Plate, Zanesville OH, r/e, s/o, 10"...75.00
Sugar bowl, Plymouth, American Pilgrims...................................55.00
Tumbler, Fall River MA, v/o...85.00
Tumbler, Ottawa Canada...85.00
Tumbler, Plymouth, 1906, v/o...65.00

Royal Bayreuth

Founded in 1794 in Tettau, Bavaria, the Royal Bayreuth firm originally manufactured fine dinnerware of superior quality. Their figural items, produced from before the turn of the century until the onset of WWI, are highly sought after by today's collectors. Perhaps the most abundantly produced and easily recognized of these are the tomato and lobster pieces. Fruits, flowers, people, animals, birds, and vegetables shapes were also made. Aside from figural items, pitchers, toothpick holders, cups and saucers, humidors, and the like were decorated in florals and scenic motifs. Some, such as the very popular Rose Tapestry line, utilized a cloth-like tapestry background. Transfer prints were used as well. Two of the most popular are Sunbonnet Babies and Nursery Rhymes (in particular, those decorated with the complete verse).

Caution: Many pieces were not marked; some were marked 'Deponiert' or 'Registered' only. While marked pieces are the most valued, unmarked items are still very worthwhile. Our advisors for this category are Judy White from California and Dee Hooks from Illinois; they are listed in the Directory under their home states.

Figurals

Ashtray, clown, bl mk, 4¾" 385.00
Ashtray, elk, bl mk, 2x6"...295.00
Biscuit jar, grapes, pearlized, bl mk 315.00
Bowl, grapes, wht lustre, bl mk, 9" L, NM...................................200.00
Bowl, tomato, w/lid, bl mk, 3"..85.00
Candlestick, nautilus shell, bl mk, 2¾x6"....................................350.00
Cup & saucer, demi; pear...275.00
Cup & saucer, demi; poppy..203.00
Cup & saucer, demi; tulip 525.00
Cup & saucer, demi; violet...455.00

Dish, lobster, bl mk, 4¾x7⅞x5⅞" 325.00
Dish, lobster, w/lid, bl mk, 4¾x5x4" 325.00
Dish, pear, w/lid, 4x3" 535.00
Gravy boat, tomato, bl mk, 6¼" 175.00
Inkwell, elk, bl mk 475.00
Match holder, clown, wall hanging, bl mk, 5¼" 525.00
Mustard, lobster, bl mk, w/spoon 67.00
Pitcher, apple, red, bl mk, cream sz, 3¾" 150.00
Pitcher, apple, yel, bl mk, cream sz, 3¾" 210.00
Pitcher, Art Nouveau, yel, bl mk, water sz, 6" 2,500.00
Pitcher, bull's head, gray, bl mk, cream sz, 3¾" 245.00
Pitcher, butterfly, open wings, bl mk, cream sz, 3¾" 425.00
Pitcher, cat, blk, bl mk, cream sz, 4¾" 210.00
Pitcher, chimpanzee, gray-blk, Deponiert, cream sz, 4¼" 315.00
Pitcher, clover, bl mk, cream sz, 3¾" 778.00
Pitcher, clown, gr, bl mk, cream sz, 4" 585.00
Pitcher, clown, red, bl mk, cream sz, 3¾" 335.00
Pitcher, coachman, bl mk, water sz, 7" 465.00
Pitcher, cow, brn, unmk, cream sz, 6½" L 188.00
Pitcher, crow, blk, bl mk, cream sz 175.00
Pitcher, dachshund, bl mk, milk sz 725.00
Pitcher, dachshund, brn, bl mk, cream sz, 4" 300.00
Pitcher, Devil & Cards, bl mk, cream sz 180.00
Pitcher, Devil & Cards, bl mk, milk sz, 5" 435.00
Pitcher, duck, bl mk, water sz, 6¾" 595.00
Pitcher, frog, brn, bl mk, cream sz, 2½" 345.00
Pitcher, geranium, pearlized, Deponiert, water sz, 6¼" 1,400.00
Pitcher, grapes, wht, unmk, cream sz, 3¾" 245.00
Pitcher, lady bug, bl mk, water sz, 6½" 3,000.00
Pitcher, lamplighter, gr, bl mk, milk sz, 5½", NM 425.00
Pitcher, lemon, bl mk, cream sz, 3¾" 175.00
Pitcher, lemon, bl mk, milk sz, 4¾" 325.00
Pitcher, lettuce & lobster, bl mk, cream sz, 4" 150.00
Pitcher, lobster, bl mk, water sz, 6¾" 475.00
Pitcher, lobster, unmk, milk sz, 4¾" 225.00
Pitcher, maple leaf, mc, bl mk, cream sz, 3½" 410.00
Pitcher, monk, unmk, cream sz, 4⅝" 315.00
Pitcher, mouse, bl mk, water sz 4,650.00
Pitcher, oak leaf, wht, bl mk, milk sz, 4¾" 360.00
Pitcher, Old Man of the Mtn, mc, gr mk, cream sz, 3¾" 125.00
Pitcher, orange, bl mk, cream sz, 4½" 300.00
Pitcher, owl, unmk, cream sz, 4¾" 475.00
Pitcher, pansy, bl mk, cream sz, 4" 425.00
Pitcher, poppy, red, bl mk, cream sz, 3¾" 225.00
Pitcher, rabbit, bl mk, cream sz, 4½" 2,425.00
Pitcher, rooster, bl mk, cream sz, 4⅜" 475.00
Pitcher, rooster, mc, bl mk, water sz, 7x9" 2,000.00
Pitcher, rose bud, bl mk, cream sz, 4" 225.00
Pitcher, Santa, red, bl mk, milk sz, 5" 3,200.00
Pitcher, Santa, red, bl mk, water sz, 6" 7,100.00
Pitcher, shell w/lobster hdl, bl mk, cream sz, 2¾" 125.00
Pitcher, spiky shell, pearl lustre, bl mk, 4½" 175.00

Pitcher, squirrel, blue mark, cream size, 4¾", $5,000.00.

(Photo courtesy Judy White)

Pitcher, strawberry, bl mk, cream sz, 4" 225.00
Pitcher, tomato, orange leaves, leaves spout, bl mk, cream sz, sm..125.00
Pitcher, turtle, bl mk, cream sz, 2½" 500.00
Pitcher, turtle, bl mk, milk sz, 4½" 700.00
Plate, lettuce leaf, bl mk, 6" 25.00
Powder jar, spiky shell, gr mk, 3½x4¼" L 90.00
Shaker, cherry, red, bl mk 330.00
Shaker, corn, yel, bl mk 330.00
Shakers, cucumber, bl mk, pr 725.00
Tea strainer, flower, bl mk, 5¾" 545.00
Toothpick holder, spiky shell, wht pearlized, 3-ftd, bl mk 200.00
Wall pocket, tomato, wall hanging, bl mk, 9½" 835.00

Nursery Rhymes

Bell, Jack & Beanstalk, w/rhyme & clapper, bl mk 350.00
Bowl, Jack & Jill, bl mk, 5¾" 135.00
Box, Jack & Jill, bl mk, w/lid 250.00
Candlestick, Jack & Jill, bl mk, ring hdl 215.00
Chamberstick, Little Jack Horner, bl mk.......................................185.00
Cup & saucer, Jack & the Beanstalk, bl mk 195.00
Dutch shoe, Little Bo Peep, bl mk 450.00
Mug, Jack & Beanstalk, w/verse, bl mk, lg 250.00
Mug, Ring Around the Rosies, bl mk 175.00
Pitcher, Jack & the Beanstalk, bl mk, cream sz, 3½" 195.00
Plate, Little Bo Peep, bl mk, 6¼" 175.00
Sugar bowl, Little Boy Blue, bl mk 215.00
Sugar bowl, Little Miss Muffet, bl mk 215.00
Vase, Babes in the Woods, bl mk, 4" 385.00
Vase, Jack & Jill, hdls, bl mk 85.00

Scenics and Action Portraits

Bowl, musicians, 3-ftd, bl mk, 2x5" 145.00
Box, Dutch woman, shell shape, bl mk, 1½x3x2¾" 140.00
Charger, portrait reserve w/gold, bl mk, 10" 500.00
Dish, boy w/donkey, clover shape, bl mk, 4½" 120.00
Dish, pin; cavaliers, bl mk, 2½x5¾x3¼" 195.00
Hair receiver, storks (4) on yel, bl mk, 2¾" 350.00
Mug, beer; tavern scene, bl mk, 4¾" 175.00
Pin tray, polar bears, w/molded cork, 4¾x3½" 1,325.00
Pitcher, cattle in autumn, bl mk, cream sz, 4¼" 300.00
Pitcher, cattle scene, bl mk, cream sz, 4" 145.00
Pitcher, Corinthian, blk, bl mk, milk sz, 5" 175.00
Pitcher, hunt scene, bl mk, cream sz 80.00
Pitcher, hunting dogs chasing moose on orange, bl mk, 6¼" 105.00
Pitcher, jester, bl mk, cream sz, 3½" 450.00
Pitcher, Sand Babies, bl mk, cream sz, 4¼" 295.00
Pitcher, women gathering harvest, split hdl, bl mk, 5" 128.00
Plaque, cavaliers, bl mk, 11½" 275.00
Plate, Brittney Girls at seashore, bl mk, 7½" 120.00
Toothpick holder/vase, birds, silver-gilt rim, 3-hdl, bl mk, 3¼" ..165.00
Vase, fisherman smoking clay pipe, unmk, 4¾" 55.00
Vase, goats in field on orange, 3-hdl, bl mk, 4¼" 95.00
Vase, hunting scene, low hdls, bl mk, 3" 195.00
Vase, kangaroo in landscape, hdls, bl mk, 3¾" 300.00
Vase, pheasant scene, ruffled rim, bl mk, 3¾" 175.00

Sunbonnet Babies

Bowl, cereal; sweeping, bl mk, 5¼" 335.00
Bowl, washing, bl mk, 9" 400.00
Cake plate, washing, bl mk, 10¼" 350.00
Candlestick, cleaning, shield bk, bl mk 650.00

Chamberstick, sewing, ring hdl, bl mk 415.00
Cheese dish, w/lid, mini, 1½x3½x2¼" 660.00
Cup & saucer, fishing, bl mk 375.00
Hair receiver, sewing, bl mk 385.00
Hair receiver, washing, 4-leg, bl mk 425.00
Nappy, washing, w/hdl, bl mk, 6" L 230.00
Pitcher, cleaning, bl mk, 4" 335.00
Pitcher, cleaning windows & floors, bl mk, cream sz, 3¼" 335.00
Pitcher, scrubbing floor, bl mk, cream sz 345.00
Pitcher, washing, bl mk, 4½" 335.00
Tumbler, cleaning, bulbous, 3½" 450.00
Vase, sewing, ewer shape, bl mk 325.00

Tapestries

Box, dresser; Colonial scene, bl mk, 2¼x3¼" 300.00
Box, pin; courting scene, bl mk, 2½x4½" L 265.00
Chocolate set, Rose Tapestry, bl mk, pot+4 c/s 3,950.00
Hair receiver, Rose Tapestry, bl mk, 2½x4" dia 375.00
Lady's shoe, high top w/laces, chrysanthemums, 3¼" 1,465.00
Pitcher, goats in meadow, bl mk, milk sz, 4" 475.00
Pitcher, Rose Tapestry, bl mk, cream sz, 3½" 250.00
Plaque, cavaliers, bl mk, 1½x9½" dia 495.00
Toothpick holder, Rose Tapestry, bl mk 525.00
Vase, castle scene, bottle neck, bl mk, 3½" 350.00
Vase, Rose Tapestry, bl mk, 4x2¼" 325.00
Vase, tavern scene, bottle neck, hdls, bl mk, 4⅝x2" 345.00

Royal Bonn

Royal Bonn is a fine-paste porcelain, ornately decorated with scenes, portraits, or florals. The factory was established in the mid-1800s in Bonn, Germany; however, most pieces found today are from the latter part of the century.

Ewer, floral, pk & bl on cream w/much gold, 13" 485.00
Plate, courting couple transfer, beehive mk, 10¾" 55.00

Vase, maiden standing beside palm with watering can, pastels with gold highlights, signed A.M., 25½", NM, $1,380.00.
(Photo courtesy Butterfield & Butterfield)

Vase, portrait, artist sgn, hdld urn form, 14" 450.00
Vase, wht hydrangeas, lg hdls from ruffled rim to base, 14" 450.00
Vase, 2 ladies pick wheat, sgn, hdls, 6¼" 675.00

Royal Copenhagen

The Royal Copenhagen Manufactory was established in Denmark

in about 1775 by Frantz Henrich Muller. When bankruptcy threatened in 1779, the Crown took charge. The fine dinnerware and objects of art produced after that time carry the familiar logo, the crown over three wavy lines. For further information we recommend *Royal Copenhagen Porcelain, Animals, and Figurines,* by Robert J. Heritage (Schiffer).

See also Limited Edition Plates.

Bowl, Flora Dancia, w/lid, #137/158, 3x3½" 750.00
Bowl, vegetable; Blue Fluted, full lace 175.00
Bowl, vegetable; Blue Fluted, half lace, w/lid, #622, 10½" dia 325.00
Cake plate, Blue Fluted, full lace, 8" 285.00
Coffeepot, Blue Fluted, full lace, 9" 475.00
Compote, Blue Fluted, full lace, #1/1023, 1959 ....285.00
Cruet, Blue Fluted, half lace, w/lid, 5" 195.00
Cup & saucer, Blue Fluted, full lace, flat 135.00
Cup & saucer, Blue Fluted, half lace, flat 80.00
Cup & saucer, demi; Blue Fluted, full lace, flat 85.00
Cup & saucer, Flora Danica, flat 550.00
Dish, Flora Dancia, triangular, #20/3509, 1¾x10½" 1,000.00
Figurine, Amager Girl, #1257, 1957 ....200.00
Figurine, Amager Girl, knitting, #1314 ....250.00
Figurine, ballet dancer, #4642 ....275.00
Figurine, ballet girl, wht, #4075 ....115.00
Figurine, bear cub, brn, #3014 ....80.00
Figurine, bear cub, gray, #3014 ....75.00
Figurine, blacksmith, #4502 ....195.00
Figurine, boy eating lunch, #865 ....195.00
Figurine, boy w/calf, #722 ....280.00
Figurine, cat, curled, tabby, #422 ....125.00
Figurine, chicken, squatting, #605, pre-1923 mk 125.00
Figurine, Churchgoer, #892 ....200.00
Figurine, dachshund, #856, 7½x11" 375.00
Figurine, dachshund, gray, #3140 ....145.00
Figurine, elephant, #1771 ....215.00
Figurine, faun on pillar w/rabbit at base, #456, 8½" 235.00
Figurine, faun w/crow, #2113, 7" 300.00
Figurine, Flight to America, #1761, 1969-74, 8" 315.00
Figurine, girl dipping toe in water, #1229, 5x3½" 350.00
Figurine, Girl From Bornholm, #1323 ....225.00
Figurine, goat w/kid on bk, #4744, 4x6" 360.00
Figurine, kingfisher, #3234, 1969-74 ....85.00
Figurine, knight & maiden, #3171, 18" 850.00
Figurine, mare w/foal, #4698, 4½x7" 350.00
Figurine, mouse on sugar, #510 ....70.00
Figurine, owl, #1741 ....65.00
Figurine, panther, seated, #2555, 8½x9" 1,000.00
Figurine, pekingese, sitting up begging, #1776, 4½" 200.00
Figurine, pointer (dog), recumbent, #1634, 2¼x8" 310.00
Figurine, polar bear, wht, #1137, 6½x11" 240.00
Figurine, robin, squatting, #2266, 1953 ....70.00
Figurine, Soldier & Princess, #1180, 11" 425.00
Figurine, swineherd w/pig, #848, 7x7" 360.00
Figurine, terrier, wht w/brn & blk features, #2755, 5x3¾" 325.00
Figurine, The Gossips, 2 ladies, 1 w/basket in arm, #1319, 11" ...425.00
Figurine, The Proposal, Victorian man & woman, #1680, 11" 400.00
Figurine, turkey chick, #266 ....100.00
Figurine, wren, #1504 ....85.00
Pin tray, Danske Store Landsloges, #3529, 1955 ....22.00
Plate, chop; Blue Fluted, half lace, 13" 185.00
Plate, dinner; Blue Fluted, full lace, 10" 135.00
Plate, dinner; Blue Fluted, half lace, 11" 80.00
Plate, dinner; Flora Danica, 10" 850.00
Platter, Blue Fluted, half lace, 13" 225.00
Platter, Flora Dancia, rtcl border, #352, 12" dia 1,000.00

Sugar bowl, Blue Fluted, half lace, w/lid..................125.00
Sugar bowl, Flora Danica, w/lid, lg 2,600.00
Sugar bowl, Flora Danica, w/lid, mini 1,000.00
Teapot, Flora Danica, 4¼" 2,800.00
Tray, Blue Fluted, full lace, #1156, 11" 325.00
Tureen, Blue Flowers, w/lid, 9x12¾x8⅝", +8x10⅞" underplate .375.00
Tureen, soup; Blue Fluted, full lace, w/lid, 10x11½" 850.00
Tureen, soup; Flora Danica, w/lid & underplate..........................950.00
Vase, wht orchid w/gr leaves on dk bl fading to lt bl, #1482, 10x6" ..240.00

Royal Copley

Royal Copley is a decorative type of pottery made by the Spaulding China Company in Sebring, Ohio, from 1942 to 1957. They also produced two other major lines — Royal Windsor and Spaulding. Royal Copley was primarily marketed through five-and-ten cent stores; Royal Windsor and Spaulding were sold through department stores, gift shops, and jobbers. Items trimmed in gold are worth 25% to 50% more than the same item with no gold trim.

For more information we recommend *Collector's Guide to Royal Copley Plus Royal Windsor & Spaulding, Books I* and *II*, by our advisor for this category, Joe Devine; he is listed in the Directory under Iowa.

Ashtray, Bow & Ribbon, emb mk, 5", from $40 to 50.00
Bank, pig, striped shirt, paper label/gr stamp, 7½", from $75 to....85.00
Bank, rooster, mc w/cobalt tail, 8", from $65 to 75.00
Figurine, cockatoo, full bodied, 8¼", from $40 to........................45.00
Figurine, gull, wings molded to base, paper label, 8", from $40 to.45.00
Figurine, hen, mc, paper label, 5½", from $30 to 35.00
Figurine, lady dancing, bl skirt, 8", from $100 to 125.00
Figurine, swallow, full body, paper label, 8", from $25 to 30.00
Figurine, woodpecker, gr stamp or emb mk, 6¼", from $20 to 25.00
Figurine, wren, paper label, 6¼", from $20 to 24.00

Figurines, large Spaulding pheasants, from $45.00 to $50.00 for the pair. (Photo courtesy Glenn Hovinga)

Pitcher, Daffodil, gr stamp, 8", from $55 to 60.00
Pitcher, Pome Fruit, bl, gr stamp, 8", from $50 to 55.00
Planter, angel, paper label, 8", from $40 to..................................45.00
Planter, Barefooted Boy (or Girl), paper label, 7½", from $35 to..40.00
Planter, cat & cello, paper label, scarce, 7½", from $100 to........125.00
Planter, coach, gr stamp, 3¼x6", from $18 to 20.00
Planter, dog pulling wagon, paper label, 5¾", from $40 to 45.00
Planter, gazelle, gold trim, emb mk, 9", from $40 to 45.00
Planter, girl leaning on bbl, paper label, 6¼", from $20 to............25.00
Planter, Harmony, leaves in relief, gold trim, 4½", from $60 to 70.00
Planter, hat, made to rest on table, emb mk, 7", from $40 to........45.00
Planter, horse running, paper label, 6", from $15 to......................20.00
Planter, Ivy, gr on ivory, paper label, 4", from $8 to.....................10.00
Planter, kitten & boot, paper label, 7½", from $50 to 55.00
Planter, Little Ribbed, yel or brn, 3½", from $8 to 10.00
Planter, Oriental child w/lg vase, paper label, 4¾", from $12 to...15.00

Planter, pirate head, emb letters, 8", from $45 to........................50.00
Planter, teddy bear, chocolate brn, 6¼", from $60 to....................65.00
Planter, wood duck (mature), paper label, 7¼", from $35 to.........40.00
Planter/wall pocket, cocker head, emb mk, 5", from $28 to 34.00
Planter/wall pocket, wide-brim hat girl, mk, 7½", from $40 to 45.00
Vase, Black Floral Leaf & Stem, paper label, 8", from $14 to........18.00
Vase, Harmony, leaves in relief, paper label, 7½", from $14 to 16.00
Vase, mare & foal, emb mk, 8½", from $30 to 35.00
Vase, Stub Hdl, floral decal, gold stamp, 4⅛", from $12 to 15.00
Vase/planter, deer, donut-like hole, paper label, 7½", $20 to 25.00
Vase/planter, mallard duck on stump, paper label, 8", $40 to 45.00
Vase/planter, nuthatch perched by stump, paper label, 5½", $30 to..35.00

Royal Crown Derby

The Royal Crown Derby company can trace its origin back to 1848. It first operated under the name of Locker & Co. but by 1859 had became Stevenson, Sharp & Co. Several changes in ownership occurred until 1866 when it became known as the Sampson Hancock Co. The Derby Crown Porcelain Co. Ltd. was formed in 1876, and these companies soon merged. In 1890 they were appointed as a manufacturer for the Queen and began using the name Royal Crown Derby.

In the early years, considerable 'Japan ware' decorated in Imari style, using red, blue, and gold in Oriental patterns was popular. The company excelled in their ability to use gold in the decoration, and some of the best flower painters of all time were employed. Nice vases or plaques signed by any of these artists will bring thousands of dollars: Gregory, Mosley, Rouse, Gresley, and D'esir'e Leroy. We have observed porcelain plaques decorated with flowers signed by Gregory selling at auction for as much as $12,000.00. If you find a signed piece and are not sure of its value, if at all possible, it would be best to have it appraised by someone very knowledgeable regarding current market values.

As is usual among most other English factories, nearly all of the vases produced by Royal Crown Derby came with covers. If they are missing, deduct 40% to 45%. There are several well illustrated books available from antique booksellers to help you learn to identify this ware. The back stamps used after 1891 will date every piece except dinnerware. The company is still in business, producing outstanding dinnerware and Imari-decorated figures and serving pieces. They also produce custom (one only) sets of table service for the wealthy of the world.

Bottle, floral, HP on wht w/gold, 2 shoulder hdls, stopper, 6" 145.00
Bowl, Imari, #1128/XL, red mk, 3¼x8⅝"...................................435.00
Bowl, Imari, red mk, 5x9" 475.00
Bowl, Mikado, bl/wht Oriental in garden, ornate hdls/finial/ft, 9" W.475.00
Bowl, vegetable; Old Avesbury, foliage/birds, w/hdls & lid, 11" L.425.00
Coffeepot, Olde Avesbury, foliage/birds, 7½" 335.00
Cup & saucer, Imari, early 1800s, 2¼", 5½" dia 275.00
Ewer, gold floral on coral, rnd w/tall cylinder neck, 6" 200.00
Gravy boat, Mikado, bl/wht, bl mk, 7" L, +underplate.................195.00
Paperweight, Harrods Bull, MIB...800.00
Paperweight, Platypus, Bone China..375.00
Platter, floral plaque center, cobalt bl w/gilt, 1800s, 20".............475.00
Platter, Normandie, 17" L...265.00
Teapot, Imari, Bone China, #1128/XLV, 7" 275.00
Teapot, Mikado, Aladdin style, bl/wht, ca 1934, 4½".................190.00
Urn, Imari, ornate gold hdls/lid, 18", pr...................................2,500.00
Vase, floral, pastel/gilt on ivory, bulbous w/trumpet neck, 7½" ...315.00

Royal Doulton, Doulton

The range of wares produced by the Doulton Company since its inception in 1815 has been vast and varied. The earliest wares produced in the tiny pottery in Lambeth, England, were salt-glazed pitchers, plain and fancy figural bottles, etc. — all utility-type stoneware geared to the practical needs of everyday living. The original partners, John Doulton and John Watts, saw the potential for success in the manufacture of drain and sewage pipes and during the 1840s concentrated on these highly lucrative types of commercial wares. Watts retired from the company in 1854, and Doulton began experimenting with a more decorative product line. As time went by, many glazes and decorative effects were developed, among them Faience, Impasto, Silicon, Carrara, Marqueterie, Chine, and Rouge Flambe. Tiles and architectural terra cotta were an important part of their manufacture. Late in the nineteenth century at the original Lambeth location, fine artware was decorated by such notable artists as Hannah and Arthur Barlow, George Tinworth, and J.H. McLennan. Stoneware vases with incised animal drawings, gracefully shaped urns with painted scenes, and cleverly modeled figurines rivaled the best of any competitor.

In 1882 a second factory was built in Burslem which continues even yet to produce the famous figurines, character jugs, series ware, and table services so popular with collectors today. Their Kingsware line, made from 1899 to 1946, featured flasks and flagons with drinking scenes, usually on a brown-glazed ground. Some were limited editions, while others were commemorative and advertising items. The Gibson Girl series, twenty-four plates in all, was introduced in 1901. It was drawn by Charles Dana Gibson and is recognized by its blue and white borders and central illustrations, each scene depicting a humorous or poignant episode in the life of 'The Widow and Her Friends.' Dickensware, produced from 1911 through the early 1940s, featured illustrations by Charles Dickens, with many of his famous characters. The Robin Hood series was introduced in 1914; the Shakespeare series #1, portraying scenes from the Bard's plays, was made from 1914 until World War II. The Shakespeare series #2 ran from 1906 until 1974 and was decorated with featured characters. Nursery Rhymes was a series that was first produced in earthenware in 1930 and later in bone china. In 1933 a line of decorated children's ware, the Bunnykin series, was introduced; it continues to be made to the present day. About 150 'bunny' scenes have been devised, the earliest and most desirable being those signed by the artist Barbara Vernon. Most pieces range in value from $60.00 to $120.00.

Factors contributing to the value of a figurine are age, demand, color, and detail. Those with a limited production run and those signed by the artist or marked 'Potted' (indicating a pre-1939 origin) are also more valuable. After 1920 wares were marked with a lion — with or without a crown — over a circular 'Royal Doulton.'

Animals and Birds

Airdale terrier, HN1022, 10¼" 450.00
Bloodhound, HN176, 6x6" 1,000.00
Bull terrier, HN2511, 4" 365.00
Bulldog, K-2, 2x2" 200.00
Cairn, begging, HN2589 ....95.00
Cat, Lucky, K-12 ....200.00
Dachschund, K-17 ....95.00
Elephant, HN2644, 5½" 225.00
English bull terrier, HN1143, brindle & wht 1,250.00
English setter, HN2529, blk & wht, pheasant in mouth, 8½".....450.00
Farmer's Boy, draft horse, HN2623 ....800.00
Fox terrier, seated, HN900, 2⅝" 665.00
Fox terrier, sitting, K-7 ....125.00
Gude Grey Mare, HN2532, 6x8" 695.00
Pekingese, HN1012 ....195.00
Persian cat, HN999, blk & wht 165.00
Scottie, sitting on bk legs, K-18, 2½" 150.00

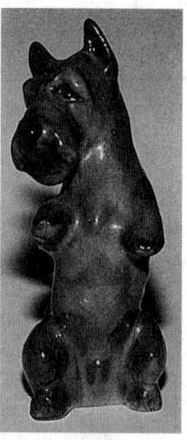

Scottish Terrier, K-10, ca 1931 – 77, 2¾", from $150.00 to $175.00. (Photo courtesy Candace Sten Davis and Particia J. Baugh)

Sealyham, HN1032 ....275.00
Terrier, K-3 ....95.00

Bunnykins

Astro Bunnykins, DB20 ....145.00
Autumn Days, DB5 ....365.00
Bathtime, DB148 ....65.00
Beefeater Bunnykins, DB163 ....295.00
Boy Skater, DB152 ....65.00
Bridesmaid, DB173 ....55.00
Cheerleader, DB143 ....250.00
Father Bunnykins, DB154 ....55.00
Gardener Bunnykins, DB156 ....45.00
Good Night, DB157 ....45.00
Guardsman, DB127 ....650.00
Homerun, DB43 ....85.00
Indian, DB202 ....175.00
Joker, DB171 ....225.00
Judge, DB188 ....75.00
Juggler, DB164 ....295.00
King John, DB45 ....125.00
Minstrel, DB211 ....175.00
Mother, DB189 ....45.00
New Baby, DB158 ....45.00
Nurse, DB74A 295.00
Rise & Shine, DB11 ....125.00
Santa, DB17 ....85.00
Schoolmaster, DB60 ....65.00
Scotsman, DB180 ....160.00
Seaside, DB177 ....55.00
Sleepytime, DB15 ....55.00
Sweetheart, DB130 ....65.00
Welsh Lady, DB172 ....225.00
Wizard Bunnykins, DB168 ....325.00

Character Jugs

'Ard of 'Earring, D6591, 1964-67, sm 910.00
'Arriet, D6236, 1947-60, sm 80.00
'Arry, D6235, 1947-60, sm 80.00
'Arry, D6249, 1947-60, mini 70.00
Ann Boleyn, D6644, 1975-90, lg 120.00
Annie Oakley, D6732, 1985-89, med 100.00
Apothecary, D6574, 1963-83, sm 70.00
Aramis, D6508, 1960-91, mini 45.00
Athos, D6439, 1956-91, lg 95.00
Auld Mac, D5823, 1940-86, lg 70.00

Bacchus, D6521, 1960-91, mini 45.00
Beefeater, D6251, GR on hdl, 1947-53, mini 80.00
Beefeater, D6251, 1953-87, mini 60.00
Benjamin Franklin, D6695, 1982-99, sm 95.00
Blacksmith, D6571, 1963-82, lg 65.00
Bootmaker, D6572, 1963-83, lg 70.00
Buz Fuz, D5838, 1948-60, sm 80.00
Captain Ahab, D6500, 1959-84, lg 100.00
Captain Ahab, D6522, 1960-84, mini 70.00
Captain Henry Morgan, D6510, 1960-82, mini 55.00
Captain Hook, D6601, 1965-71, sm 320.00
Cardinal, D6033, 1939-60, sm 60.00
Catherine Howard, D6693, 1984-89, mini 160.00
Catherine Parr, D6664, 1981-89, lg 175.00
Catherine Parr, D6752, 1987-89, mini 195.00
Chief Sitting Bull & Geo A Custer, D6712, 1984, ltd ed 225.00
Davy Crocket & Santa Anna, D6729, 1985, lg 120.00
Dick Turpin, D5485, 1935-60, lg 140.00
Dick Turpin, D6128, 1940-60, mini 40.00
Dick Turpin, D6528, horse hdl, 1960-81, lg 150.00
Falconer, D6533, 1960-91, lg 80.00
Falstaff, D6385, 1950-95, sm 55.00
Farmer John, D5788, 1938-60, lg 160.00
Farmer John, D5789, 1938-60, sm 70.00
Fat Boy, D6139, 1940-60, mini 65.00
Gaoler, D6570, 1962-83, lg 105.00
Gaoler, D6577, 1963-83, sm 65.00
Gardener, D6638, 1973-78, mini 85.00
George Washington, D6669, 1989, lg 140.00
Gladiator, D6556, 1961-67, mini 360.00
Gondolier, D6595, 1964-69, mini 360.00
Gone Away, D6531, 1960-62, lg 100.00
Granny, D5521, 1941-83, lg 100.00
Granny, D6384, 1953-83, sm 50.00
Guardsman, D6575, 1963-83, sm 80.00
Guardsman, D6582, 1963-83, mini 80.00
Gulliver, D6563, 1962-67, sm 385.00
Gunsmith, D6573, 1963-83, lg 100.00
Henry V, D6671, 1982-84, lg 195.00
Jarge, D6295, 1950-60, sm 175.00
Jester, D5556, 1936-60, sm, from $90 to 125.00
Jimmy Durante, D6708, 1985-88, lg 165.00
Jockey, D6625, 1971-75, lg 335.00
John Peel, D5612, 1936-60, lg 125.00
London Bobby, D6744, 1986-87, lg 275.00
London Bobby, D6762, 1987, sm 160.00
Lord Nelson, D6336, 1952-69, lg 400.00
Lumberjack, D6610, 1967-82, lg 100.00
Mad Hatter, D6598, 1965-83, lg, from $180 to 225.00
Mae West, D6688, 1983-86, lg 140.00
Mikado, D6525, 1960-69, mini 360.00
Mr Micawber, D6138, 1940-60, mini 45.00
Mr Pickwick, D5839, 1948-60, sm 70.00
Mr Pickwick, D6060, 1940-60, lg 140.00
Mr Quaker, D6738, 1985, lg 630.00
Old Charley, D5420, 1934-83, lg 70.00
Old Charley, D6144, 1940-60, tiny 120.00
Paddy, D5753, 1937-60, lg 80.00
Parson Brown, D5529, 1935-60, sm 65.00
Postman, D6801, 1988, sm 230.00
Queen Victoria, D6788, 1981-91, lg 155.00
Regency Beau, D6559, 1962-67, lg 1,100.00
Robin Hood, D6205, 1947-60, lg 140.00
Robin Hood, D6234, 1947-60, sm 65.00

Sairey Gamp, D5451, 1935-86, lg 60.00
Sam Johnson, D6296, 1950-60, sm 160.00
Sam Weller, D5841, 1938-48, mid sz 150.00
Samson & Delilah, D6787, 1988, lg 120.00
Scaramouche, D6564, 1962-67, mini 400.00
Smuggler, D6616, 1968-81, lg 140.00
St George, D6618, bone china, 1968-75, lg 320.00
Tam O' Shanter, D6632, 1973-80, lg 160.00
Toby Philpots, D5737, 1937-51, sm 45.00
Tony Weller, D5531, 1936-60, lg 160.00
Touchstone, D5613, 1936-60, lg, from $225 to 265.00
Town Crier, D6537, 1960-73, sm 120.00
Veteran Motorist, D6637, 1973-83, sm 90.00
Viking, D6502, 1959-75, sm 140.00
Walrus & Carpenter, D6600, 1965-80, lg 195.00
Wild Bill Hickock, D6736, 1985-89, mid sz 120.00

Figurines

Annabella, HN1871 ....995.00
Autumn, HN2087 ....575.00
Autumn Breezes, HN1934, red, from $310 to 350.00
Autumn Breezes, HN2147 ....450.00
Autumntime, HN3231 ....275.00
Babie, HN1679 ....120.00
Babie, rose & gr, HN1842 ....395.00
Ballerina, HN2116 ....325.00
Beat You To It, HN2871 ....425.00
Bess, HN2002 ....325.00
Beth, HN2870 ....350.00
Boy w/Turban, HN1214 ....1,450.00
Camillia, HN2222 ....250.00
Chinese Dancer of the World, HN2840 ....400.00
Christmas Time, HN2110 ....350.00
Daffy Down Dilly, HN1712 ....425.00
Dainty Mae, mini, M73 ....800.00
Daisy, HN1961 ....650.00
Darling, HN1371 ....195.00
Darling, HN1985 ....100.00
Daydreams, HN1732, from $800 to 895.00

Doctor, HN2858,
$225.00.

Dorcas, HN1558 ....350.00
Dulcie, HN2305 ....250.00
Easter Day, HN2039 ....495.00
Gay Morning, HN2135 ....250.00
Genevieve, HN1962 ....350.00
Gentlewoman, HN1632 ....950.00

Golden Days, HN2274 ....175.00
Gossips, HN2025 ....525.00
Granny's Heritage, HN2031 ....675.00
Greta, HN1485 ....395.00
Gypsy Dance, HN2230 ....325.00
Helen, HN2008 ....1,150.00
Honey, HN1963 ....895.00
Irene, HN1621 ....450.00
Jack, HN2060 ....200.00
Janet, HN1537 ....225.00
Janice, HN2165 ....495.00
Jill, HN2016 ....225.00
June, HN1691 ....795.00
June, HN2027 ....750.00
Kathy, HN2346 ....165.00
Lady Fayre, HN1265 ....750.00
Lady From Williamsburg, HN2228 ....250.00
Lights Out, HN2262 ....275.00
Lilac Time, HN2137 ....395.00
Little Boy Blue, HN2062 ....185.00
Little Child So Rare & Sweet, HN1542 ....850.00
Little Jack Horner, HN2063 ....495.00
Long John Silver, HN2204 ....595.00
Lucy Ann, HN1502 ....450.00
Lute Lady Musician, HN2431 ....1,100.00
Margaret, HN1989 ....495.00
Mary Had a Little Lamb, HN2048 ....165.00
Mary Mary, HN2044 ....275.00
Masquerade, HN636 ....1,200.00
Maureen, HN1770 ....395.00
Maytime, HN2113 ....325.00
Milady, HN1970 ....850.00
Miss Demure, HN1402 ....275.00
Miss Fortune, HN1897 ....715.00
Modena, HN1845 ....2,350.00
Mother's Helper, HN2151 ....175.00
My Pet, HN2238 ....175.00
My Pretty Maid, HN2064 ....450.00
My Teddy, HN2177 ....595.00
Nana, HN1767 ....395.00
Olivia, HN1995 ....795.00
Once Upon a Time, HN2047 ....450.00
One That Got Away, HN2153 ....500.00
Pearly Boy, HN2035 ....200.00
Penelope, HN1901 ....425.00
Pillow Fight, HN2270 ....250.00
Prince Charles, HN2884 ....925.00
Princess Diana, HN2887 ....2,500.00
Queen Elizabeth, HN2502 ....1,650.00
Queen Mother 80th Birthday, HN2882 ....895.00
Rendezvous, HN2212 ....375.00
Robin, mini, M38 ....850.00
Schoolmarm, HN2223 ....325.00
Shore Leave, HN2254 ....225.00
Spring, HN2085 ....450.00
Springtime, HN3033 ....325.00
Summer, HN2086 ....450.00
Summer's Day, HN2181 ....325.00
Summertime, HN3137 ....195.00
Sweet Maid, HN2092 ....475.00
Tom Bombadil, HN2924 ....450.00
Vanity, HN2475 ....150.00
Violin Lady Musician, HN2432 ....1,100.00
Vivienne, HN2073 ....300.00

Winter, HN2088 ....450.00
Wintertime, HN3060 ....275.00

Flambé

Dish, hallmk Sterling Silver rim, #926, oval, 2¼x3½" 120.00
Figurine, brindle bulldog, HN1244 ....300.00
Figurine, dog, sitting, #116, 4" 965.00
Figurine, drake, resting, #112 ....90.00
Figurine, fox, sitting, #14 ....160.00
Figurine, geisha, HN3229 ....375.00
Figurine, owl, ca 1970, 12¼" 600.00
Figurine, pigs playing together, rare 1,295.00

Figurine, tiger, printed mark, 13½", $950.00.

Thimble 40.00
Vase, gold & purple mottled in red (experimental), 11" 275.00
Vase, landscape, rouge, paper label, 8⅞" 200.00
Vase, Sung, Moore, 4" 125.00
Vase, wood cut, 4½" 150.00

Series Ware

Ashtray, Gnomes, bl underglaze 250.00
Ashtray, Ships, Trading Ketch, mc, 5¼" sq 78.00
Bowl, Autumn Glory, D5651 ....100.00
Candlesticks, Woodlands, 7", pr 85.00
Chop plate, Under the Greenwood Tree, 13½" 270.00
Cup & saucer, Mad Hatter 125.00
Fern pot, Dutch People, 5" 110.00
Mug, Golfers, 5⅞" 400.00
Pitcher, Cavaliers, Better So Then Worse, 8" 95.00
Pitcher, Dickens, Oliver Twist, D5617, retired 1960 ....300.00
Plate, bunnies & floral, bl & wht, 1902-27 mk, 10" 350.00
Plate, Burns, Here's a Help to Them..., 10½" 90.00
Plate, Dickens, Mr Pickwick, D2973, retired 1930 ....150.00
Plate, Dickens, Tony Weller, D6327, retired 1960 ....150.00
Plate, Gibson Girl, And Here Winning New Friends..., 10½" 155.00
Plate, Gondoliers, lady w/fan & gentleman, D3039, 10½" 165.00
Plate, Home Waters, barges at pier, Grace, 1913, 8¼" 60.00
Plate, Professionals, Parson, D3303, retired 1928 ....150.00
Sugar bowl, Coaching Days, w/lid, 4¾x5⅝" 110.00
Tankard, Cavaliers, D4749, 5⅝" 110.00
Teapot, Hamlet, Shakespeare series 100.00
Toothpick holder, Woodland, mc transfer, D5815, 1938, 2½" 110.00
Tray, Old English Coaching, D6393, retired 1967 ....125.00
Tray, Shakespeare, Katharine, 15½" 165.00
Vase, Babes in the Woods, mother & child, #9889, 12" 1,075.00
Vase, Dickens, Poor Jo & Fat Boy, D5864, retired 1945 ....425.00
Vase, Kingsware, squire at table, 6-line verse, hdls, 10½" 450.00

Stoneware

Bottle, Victoria figural, brn salt glaze, att, ca 1840, 12" **575.00**
Candlestick, scrolling decor, gr/bl/brn, Lambeth, #3924, 5¾" **300.00**
Flagon, Egyptian decor, Dewars, #224092, ca 1920.....................**295.00**
Flagon, Scott & Burns, RD224092, ca 1901 ....**150.00**
Foot warmer, Lambeth, ca 1902..**150.00**
Lamp, dragon on font, brass fr/burner: Hinks & Son, amber shade, 25".**1,000.00**
Pitcher, hunt scene w/3 men/2 windmills, Lambeth, #6266, 8¼".**175.00**
Sherry barrel, lettered & flower bands, sgn Huskinson, 11x8".**2,990.00**
Vase, incised deer band, tooled foliage borders, Lambeth, rpr, 7".**195.00**
Vase, relief outline, Arts & Crafts flowers & vines, FJ, 7¾"........**255.00**
Vase, rows of floral sprays on brn 'lace' ground, Chine, 16" **375.00**

Toby Jugs

Best Is Not Too Good, D6107...**445.00**
Cap'n Cuttle, sm...**45.00**
Double XX, D6088..**365.00**
Falstaff, #6063...**85.00**
Happy John, D6070..**100.00**
Huntsman, D6319..**120.00**
Mr Pickwick, #6261..**250.00**
Sairey Gump, D6263...**225.00**
Sam Weller, D6265...**165.00**
Sir Winston Churchill, D6171, lg...**115.00**
Squire, D6319...**450.00**

Miscellaneous

Cracker jar, gold/blk leaf outlines on wht, SP mts, Slater's, 6x5" .**115.00**
Pitcher, bl floral transfer on wht sharkskin, Burslem, US Pat, 7".**1,450.00**
Pitcher, fruit reserve/florals on ivory, gr top/base, US Pat, 8" **115.00**
Sweetmeat, floral sprays, wht on bl sharkskin, sgn Tosen, SP lid, 5" .**115.00**
Vase, floral, bl w/gr stems & leaves on wht, 8", NM....................**350.00**
Vase, irises & daisies, shouldered, Lambeth, 20⅝" **1,500.00**
Vase, Titanian, stork/flowers/moon, Allen, 5¾"...........................**600.00**

Royal Dux

The Duxer Porzellan Manufactur was established by E. Eichler in 1860. Located in what is now Duchcov, Czechoslovakia, the area was known as Dux, Bohemia, until WWI. The war brought about changes in both the style of the ware as well as the mark. Prewar pieces were modeled in the Art Nouveau or Greek Classical manner and marked with 'Bohemia' and a pink triangle containing the letter 'E.' They were usually matt glazed in green, brown, and gold. Better pieces were made of porcelain, while the larger items were of pottery. After the war the ware was marked with the small pink triangle but without the Bohemia designation; 'Made in Czechoslovakia' was added. The style became Art Deco, with cobalt blue a dominant color.

Figurine, barefoot boy w/dog, #1576, 19¼" **370.00**
Figurine, French Tea Party, couple having tea at table, 12x15"...**375.00**
Figurine, girl in wht apron, rust dress, holds cat, #421, 20"........**1,150.00**
Figurine, lady holding bl dress out w/hands, #3495, 7¼" **190.00**
Figurine, maiden holding mirror (resting on stump), 20x11"...**1,125.00**
Figurine, man w/jug in left hand & cornucopia basket in other, 15½".**300.00**
Figurine, nymph on lily pad, w/gold, 4¾x5⅛" **250.00**
Figurine, Pan & child cavort w/ram, pastels, 17".......................**1,350.00**
Figurine, Roman couple, gr togas/crimson sashes, on leafy base, 23" .**550.00**
Figurine, Spanish dancer, #153/54, 23" **860.00**
Figurine, young lady looking into water bowl, 1850-90...............**850.00**

Figurine, 2 girls pulling on lg basket, #1328, 10x6x11" **510.00**
Figurine, 2 seminudes climb on lg conch shell, waves as base 17"..**1,680.00**
Vase, appl pk flowers/buds, leaf/bud hdls, on modeled ivory, 19", pr..**950.00**
Vase, bouquet of pk roses w/gr leaves as hdls, 11" **150.00**
Vase, calla lily w/maiden in flower fold, wht w/gold, 1900-18, 16" ..**375.00**
Vase, figural, butterfly lady seated, #1618, 20" **690.00**
Vase, floral decor w/vines & emb floral hdls, drilled, 20½".........**350.00**
Vase, Mid-Eastern man (lady) before date palm, rprs, 37", EX, pr ..**700.00**

Royal Flemish

Royal Flemish was introduced in the late 1880s and was patented in 1894 by the Mt. Washington Glass Company. Transparent glass was enameled with one or several colors and the surface divided by a network of raised lines suggesting leaded glasswork. Some pieces were further decorated with enameled florals, birds, or Roman coins. Our advisors for this category are Betty and Clarence Maier; they are listed in the Directory under Pennsylvania.

Cracker jar, gold griffin on window panels, SP mts **2,500.00**
Cracker jar, mc panels, lion on shield, gold scrolls, 5x7½".........**3,750.00**
Ewer, lad spears winged creature, much gold, rnd body, 11".....**6,500.00**
Ewer, 8 gold-floral panels & 16 medallions, 12x5½" **8,500.00**
Pickle castor, gold wild roses, emb scrolls, ornate fr..................**1,750.00**
Tumbler, scrolls, pk on wht, gold wild roses, 4¼" **2,200.00**
Vase, geese, sunburst bkground, gold stars, griffin collar, 14" ...**7,700.00**
Vase, gold dragons & stars, ornate collar, muted reds, 8" **2,750.00**
Vase, pansies, wine on frost, much gold, bulb neck, 8x8".........**1,385.00**
Vase, rose vines/sections, ovoid w/cup & bulb neck, 9½" **3,335.00**

Vase, silver-gray geese fly before golden sun, intersecting multicolor panels over amethyst ground, 14¼", $8,500.00. (Photo courtesy Early Auctioneers & Appraisers)

Vase, 3 circle medallions w/gold lines, allover flowers, 12" **3,000.00**
Vase, 4 coins on paneled ground, bulbous w/3-lobe cup neck, 7x8"..**6,000.00**
Vase, 11 Guba ducks/gold sunburst, long neck w/crown-like top, 15"..**8,500.00**

Royal Haeger, Haeger

In 1871 David Henry Haeger, a young son of German immigrants, purchased a brick factory at Dundee, Illinois. David's bricks rebuilt Chicago after their great fire in 1871. Many generations of the Haeger family have been associated with the ceramic industry, that his descendants have pursued to the present time. Haeger progressed to include artware in their production as early as 1914. That was only the beginning. In the '30s they began to make a line of commercial dinnerware that was marketed through Marshall Fields. Not long after, Haeger's artware was successful enough that a second plant in Macomb, Illinois, was built.

Royal Haeger was their premium line beginning in 1938 and continued in to modern-day production. The chief designer in the '40s was Royal Arden Hickman, a talented artist and sculptor who also worked in mediums other than pottery. For Haeger he designed a line of wonderfully stylized animals, birds, high-style vases, and human figures, all with extremely fine details. His designs are highly regarded by collectors today.

Paper labels have been used throughout Haeger's production. Some items from the teens, twenties, and thirties will be found with 'Haeger' in a diamond shape in-mold script mark. Items with 'RG' (Royal Garden) are part of their Flower-Ware line (also called Regular Haeger or Genuine Haeger). Haeger has produced a premium line (Royal Haeger) as well as a regular line for many years, it just has changed names over the years.

Collectors need to be aware that a certain glaze can bring two to three times more than others. Items that have Royal Hickman in the mold mark or on the label are usually higher valued than without his mark. The current collector trend has leaned more towards the mid-century modern styled pieces of artware. The most desired items are ones done by glaze designers Helmut Bruchman and Alrun Osterberg Guest (presently employed by Haeger). These items are from the late '60s into the very early '80s.

For those wanting to learn more about this pottery, we recommend *Haeger Potteries Through the Years* by our advisor for this category, David Dilley (L-W Books); he is listed in the Directory under Indiana.

#613, Hen, 10½", from $15 to **20.00**
#1240, Moon Fish planter/bookend, 10", from $15 to **20.00**
#3212, Double Cornucopia, sq base, 16" L, from $6 to **8.00**
#3532, Flower Girl, w/bowl on lap, 9½", from $15 to **18.00**
#4070, Pitcher vase, Mandarin Orange, 19", minimum value **75.00**
#4187, Earth Graphic Wrap vase, wht, 13", minimum value **75.00**
#5015-H, Owl hanging basket, Bennington Brown Foam, 8½x7" ..**60.00**
#5195, 2-Fawn lamp, 24", from $30 to **35.00**
R-10, Ashtray Trio, nest 3 szs: 8½", 6½", 4½", from $8 to **12.00**
R-36, Swan vase, neck-up, cutouts around base, 16" **35.00**
R-108, Pouter Pigeon, 7½", from $20 to **25.00**
R-110, Elephant planter, 11½", minimum value **150.00**
R-121, bowl, footed, rolled top, long, from $8 to **10.00**
R-128, bowl, floral cutouts, 14", from $25 to **30.00**
R-132, Ram bookends, 8x9", minimum value **150.00**
R-157, Angelfish, head up, 7½", from $12 to **15.00**
R-160, Inebriated Duck, upright, 10" L, from $18 to **20.00**
R-169, Trout, on tail, 6½", from $8 to **10.00**
R-178, Horse, head up, 4", from $6 to **8.00**
R-181, Nude figurine, 14", minimum value **500.00**
R-192, vase, bird perched on side, wings up, 11", from $18 to **22.00**
R-222, Round Spiral vase w/seated frog, 12", from $18 to **22.00**
R-243, Twisted Stem candle holder, Peach Agate, 7½", ea **50.00**
R-287, Wren House, 7x9", minimum value **75.00**
R-293, Violin bowl, 17" L, from $12 to **14.00**
R-305, Gazelle Head vase, 19", minimum value **300.00**
R-306, Plume Shell bowl, 15", from $15 to **18.00**
R-313, Tiger, Amber, 12¾" L **75.00**
R-318, Russian Wolfhound, head down, 7" L, from $22 to **25.00**
R-343, Petal bowl, 8" H, from $4 to...**5.00**
R-373, console bowl, appl fruit on sides, 20" L, from $25 to **30.00**
R-393, Horse Head vase (Pegasus), 11", minimum value **125.00**
R-408, Double Racing Horses, 10", minimum value **225.00**
R-414, Swan, 3½x10x12½", minimum value **125.00**
R-434, Hen Pheasant, Mauve Agate, 15" L **50.00**
R-451, Mare & Foal, Amber, 13" L, minimum value...................**225.00**
R-467, Flying Goose vase, 16¼" L, from $25 to............................**30.00**
R-492, Modernistic Horse Head vase, 15½", from $25 to **30.00**

R-495, Black Panther, stretched-out tail, 26" L, minimum value....**250.00**
R-502-H, Bull Fighter planter, Haeger Red, 13", minimum value....**100.00**
R-505, Mermaid planter, Gold Tweed, 23" L, minimum value....**125.00**
R-510, Bull figurine, 17½" L, minimum value **100.00**
R-555, Pei Tung vase, 13", minimum value.................................**100.00**
R-563, Elephant planter, 10½", from $20 to **25.00**
R-616, Tulip vase, 8", from $8 to **10.00**
R-655, Fish globe stand, frog fishing, 12½" L, from $30 to **35.00**

R-721, Indian on horse before cactus, Desert Red, 1950, $200.00. (Photo courtesy David Dilley/Snyder's Antiques)

R-733, Panther, 13" L, from $12 to..**15.00**
R-751, Fish planter, 6½", from $8 to **10.00**
R-776, Sleeping Cocker Pup, 6" L, from $6 to **8.00**
R-788, Jockey flower block, from $18 to **20.00**
R-819, Acanthus Leaf bowl, 14" L, from $8 to..............................**10.00**
R-869, Gazelle planter, Antique, 17" L, minimum value..............**75.00**
R-893, Tulip Modern vase, 12", from $10 to **12.00**
R-909, Banana Leaf, 13", from $8 to **10.00**
R-961, Banana Leaf vase, med, 14" L, from $8 to **10.00**
R-988, Basket bowl, 15" L, from $12 to **15.00**
R-1144, Water Lily bookends, 5", pr, from $18 to.........................**20.00**
R-1230, Dancer planter, 10½", from $20 to **25.00**
R-1296, Doe & Fawn, recumbent, 12", from $20 to **25.00**
R-1364, Rococo bookends, 6", pr, from $18 to..............................**20.00**
R-1382, Raised Leaf ashtray, 8", from $4 to...................................**6.00**
R-1404, Colt figurine, 5½", from $12 to **15.00**
R-1405, Mare figurine, 7½", from $15 to **18.00**
R-1470, Square Rippled ashtray, 7½", from $6 to **8.00**
R-1495, Contemporary vase, 15", from $8 to **10.00**
R-1499, Ruffled Top vase, 7½", from $7 to **9.00**

Royal Rudolstadt

The hard-paste porcelain that has come to be known as Royal Rudolstadt was produced in Thuringia, Germany, in the early eighteenth century. Various names and marks have been associated with this pottery. One of the earliest was a hay-fork symbol associated with Johann Frederick von Schwarzburg-Rudolstadt, one of the first founders. Variations, some that included an 'R,' were also used. In 1854 Earnst Bohne produced wares that were marked with an anchor and the letters 'EB.' Examples commonly found today were made during the late 1800s and early twentieth century. These are usually marked with an 'RW' within a shield under a crown and the words 'Crown Rudolstadt.' Items marked 'Germany' were made after 1890.

Cup & saucer, holly & roses, lt yel/pk/bl w/gold **90.00**
Cup & saucer, pk roses w/gr leaves, gold trim...............................**65.00**

Ewer, bird/butterfly/floral on wht, ornate hdl, 15½" 250.00
Plate, apples & roses border, gold trim, 8⅜" 50.00
Plate, floral decor, 2 gold hlds, sgn F Kuhn, 10" 65.00
Plate, girl holds flower tray, w/gold, sgn Revier, 9½" 375.00
Plate, HP wht roses in relief, gold rim, 2¼x9½" 125.00
Reamer, pk buds w/gr leaves on wht, gold trim, 2-pc, 3½x4¼"...140.00
Vase, morning glories & vines w/gold hdls, 1895, 8⅛" 295.00
Vase, swirled w/florals on wht, gold ft/hdls, bulbous, ca 1905, 6x5" ..70.00

Royal Vienna

In 1719 Claude Innocentius de Paquier established a hard-paste porcelain factory in Vienna where he made highly ornamental wares similar to the type produced at Meissen. Early wares were usually unmarked; but after 1744, when the factory was purchased by the Empress, the Austrian shield (often called 'beehive') was stamped on under the glaze. In the following listings, values are for hand-painted items unless noted otherwise. Decal-decorated items would be considerably lower.

Note: There is a new resurgence of interest in this fine porcelain, but an influx of Japanese reproductions on the market has affected values on genuine old Royal Vienna. Buyer beware! On new items the beehive mark is over the glaze, the weight of the porcelain is heavier, and the decoration is obviously decaled. Our advisor for this category is Madeleine France; she is listed in the Directory under Florida.

Biscuit jar, swirled w/floral sprays, gilt bow hdl, 6¾" 400.00
Box, Queen Victoria, jeweled/gilt, domed lid, 4 gold ft, 5¼" dia.1,225.00

Covered potpourri compotes, painted garden scenes on both sides, yellow background with gold details, pedestal base, 12", $1,800.00 for the pair. (Photo courtesy Madeleine France)

Cup & saucer, cobalt w/landscape scene, ca 1900, 3", 4" dia 335.00
Ewers, roses & vines, ca 1900, 11", pr.......................................1,000.00
Figurine, Lipizan stallion, wht, rearing, ca 1930s, 10½x9" 500.00
Jar, potpourri; lady w/Eros on shoulder, aqua w/gold, Wagner, 6" .510.00
Plate, Amicitia, lady's portrait on cobalt w/gold, 9½" 285.00
Plate, Andacht, young woman in wht gown, beehive mk, 9½" ..750.00
Plate, Chess Players, couple playing chess, bl & gold border, 10½" .410.00
Plate, ladies w/peacock, jeweled cobalt border, Boerschneider, 9½" ..910.00
Plate, Marie Antoinette, cobalt border w/beadwork, #112, 6¾" .580.00
Plate, Psyche, octagonal w/red/gold/wht border, 9¾" 485.00
Plate, Rembrandt, gold emb border w/floral reserves, 9½" 635.00
Stein, cherub scene, 2 on lid, gold trim, mini..........................1,350.00
Vase, lady's portrait on brn, Nouveau form, irregular rim, 8" 200.00

Roycroft

Near the turn of the twentieth century, Elbert Hubbard established the Roycroft Printing Shop in East Aurora, New York. Named in honor of two seventeenth-century printer-bookbinders, the print shop was just the beginning of a community called Roycroft, which came to be known worldwide. Hubbard became a popular personality of the early 1900s, known for his talents in a variety of areas from writing and lecturing to manufacturing. The Roycroft community became a meeting place for people of various capabilities and included shops for the production of furniture, copper, leather items, and a multitude of other wares which were marked with the Roycroft symbol, an 'R' within a circle below a double-barred cross. Hubbard lost his life on the Lusitania in 1915; production at the community continued until the Depression.

Interest is strong in the field of Arts and Crafts in general and in Roycroft items in particular. Copper items are evaluated to a large extent by the condition and type of the original patina. The most desirable patina is either the dark or medium brown; brass-wash, gunmetal, and silver-wash patinas follow in desirability. The acid-etched patina and the smooth (unhammered) surfaced Roycroft pieces are later (after 1925) developments and tend not to be attractive to collectors. Furniture was manufactured in oak, mahogany, bird's-eye maple, and occasionally walnut or ash; collectors prefer oak. Books with Levant binding, tooled leather covers, Japan vellum, or hand illumining are especially collectible; suede cover and parchment paper books are of less interest to collectors as they are fairly common. In the listings that follow, values reflect the worth of items in excellent original condition unless noted to the contrary. Our advisor for this category is Bruce Austin; he is listed in the Directory under New York.

Key: h/cp — hammered copper

Armchair, 2-slat ladder-bk, apron, rpl leather seat, 38" 1,500.00
Armchair, narrow slats, leather seat, orig finish, 39x32x25" 1,800.00
Bench, hall; oak, crest rail over 9 vertical slats, open arms, 50"...7,500.00
Book, Friendship, Henry Thoreau, Levant binding, 1903 ....400.00
Book, Ruskin & Turner, sgn E Hubbard, c Putman, 1895 ....150.00
Book, sample; 50 mottos, many hand-illumined, split spine 2,000.00
Bookcase, #078, arched gallery, 3-shelf, 1907, 38x18x16"........5,000.00
Bookends, #309, h/cp, rectangle w/loose ring on riveted band, 5x4".200.00
Bookends, h/cp, owl, M orig patina, 4x6½" 300.00
Bookends, h/cp, rectangular w/sm emb owl medallions, 4x6½" 250.00
Bookends, h/cp, repousse poppy & rivets, rnded top, 5½x5".......650.00
Bookends, h/cp, rose garlands, 3-sided, 5x3¾", pr 300.00
Books, Little Journeys, Memorial edition, 14-volume set 125.00
Bowl, h/cp, incised lotus, new patina, 3x3¾"..............................200.00
Bowl, nut; h/cp, M orig patina, 4x10½" 900.00
Box, h/cp w/enameling, 3½" W 190.00
Box, jewelry; tooled leather w/birds, suede lined, 8¼" L..........4,000.00
Candle holder, apple gr, mk 1910, 2½x5½" 260.00
Candlesticks, h/cp w/brass wash, scalloped floriform base, 8", pr..300.00
Candlesticks, h/cp, Princess, 2-stick std on sq base, lt wear, 8", pr..800.00
Candlesticks, h/cp, scalloped floriform base, 8", pr 500.00
Chair, desk; mahog, hourglass bk-slat, leather seat, 44" 1,400.00
Chamberstick, h/cp, orig polychrome patina, mk, 6" W..............250.00
Chamberstick, h/cp, wall hanging, 8½"..200.00
Clock, h/cp, orig brass wash, mk, 5" 650.00
Desk blotter, h/cp, 2 pen trays flank inkwell, riveted corners, 18x28"..2,400.00
Frame, holds 6 images, orb mk, 11x36½"..................................2,500.00
Frame, oak, 38x16"..425.00
Humidor, h/cp, Trillium, EX recent patina, 5½" 500.00
Lamp, h/cp base & dome shade, 14½" 2,500.00
Letter holder/perpetual calendar, copper, acid-etch border, 3½x5x2" .100.00

Mat, tooled leather in brn tones, 6" dia **325.00**
Mousetrap, missing cheese holder, 8½", VG.................**260.00**
Napkin rings, h/cp, 3", 4 for...**150.00**
Nut set, h/cp, 6 6" trays, ladle & 3-ftd 7½" bowl **1,200.00**
Photo album, tooled leather, holds 2 photos, Cordova Shops, 12x15".**375.00**
Postcard, Roycroft cottage, 5½x3½", VG........................**5.00**
Shakers, china, wht w/gr/red/blk decor, mk 3", pr..........**350.00**
Stand, Little Journeys, 2 shelves, keyed tenons, rfn, 26x26x14" .**600.00**
Stand, Little Journeys, 2 shelves, keyed tenons, tag, 37x26x14".**750.00**
Table, side; shelf, Mackmurdo ft, rfn, 28x30x22".....................**3,000.00**
Tray, card; h/cp, orb/X in center, 8" dia......................**450.00**
Tray, h/cp, 2-hdl, lightly cleaned, 18"..........................**300.00**
Tray, h/cp, riveted wrought hdls, 10x20", VG **325.00**
Vase, acid-etch silver, squat w/flat shoulder, long flared neck, 16x9".**950.00**
Vase, Am Beauty, h/cp, new patina/dent to shoulder, 18½x8"..**1,200.00**
Vase, Am Beauty, h/cp, rstr patina, 19½" **1,600.00**
Vase, Am Beauty, h/cp, squat body w/flat shoulder, long str neck, 7x3"..**1,200.00**
Vase, h/cp, cylinder w/tooled dmn-like quartefoils on tall stems, 10".**1,900.00**
Vase, h/cp, cylindrical, unmk, 9¼x3¾" **1,000.00**
Vase, h/cp, dogwood/dmns at rim, gr accents, cylinder, #212, wear, 10"..**460.00**
Vase, h/cp, flared riveted base, normal wear, 10¾x6¾" **2,000.00**
Vase, h/cp, heavy gauge, orig brass patina, 7½" **600.00**
Vase, h/cp, long can neck w/flared rim above riveted strap, 15x6¾".**2,800.00**

Vase, hammered copper with silver overlay, Karl Kipp, original patina, marked, 6¼", $1,500.00.

Wall sconces, h/cp w/brass wash, 12½", pr...................................**700.00**
Waste basket, slatted, ebonized finish, 14" sq **2,100.00**

Rozenburg

Some of the most innovative and original Art Nouveau ceramics were created by the Rozenburg factory at the Hague in The Netherlands between 1883 and 1914, when production was ceased. (Several of their better painters continued to work in Gouda, which accounts for some pieces being similar to Gouda.) Rozenburg also made highly prized eggshell ware, so called because of its very thin walls; this is eagerly sought after by collectors. T.A.C. Colenbrander was their artistic leader, with Samuel Schellink and J. Kok designing many of the eggshell pieces. The company liquidated in 1917. Most pieces carry a date code. Our advisor for this category is Ralph Jaarsma; he is listed in the Directory under Iowa.

Bowl, 3-leaf clovers, ribbed neck, earthenware, 1904, rpr, 4¼x7" .**250.00**
Cup, yel Nouveau flowers on wht, octagonal, 2¼" **425.00**
Jar, stylized rooster/floral reserves, highly decorated, rpr lid, 13".**490.00**
Urn, Nouveau floral, domed lid, earthenware, ca 1902, 20¼x10", NM.**850.00**
Vase, butterflies/insects/flowers, earthenware, rstr, 1896, 16x8" ..**660.00**
Vase, exotic florals, earthenware, rpr, ca 1899, 15½x6½" **440.00**

Vase, floral arches/etc, loop hdls, earthenware, ca 1897, 15x14", NM .**985.00**
Vase, irises (ornate artwork), earthenware, ca 1907-10, 8¼x4" ..**550.00**
Vase, lilies & foliage, flambè style, earthenware, rstr, 15½" **385.00**
Vase, orchids on bl, earthenware, ca 1894, rpr, 8½x2½"..............**220.00**
Vase, robin on berry branch, sgn, slim neck, ca 1900-02, 8¾x4".**1,200.00**
Vase, stylized tulips/leaves, yel/gr on cobalt gloss, narrow neck, 13".**635.00**

Rubena

Rubena glass was made by several firms in the late 1800s. It is a blown art glass that shades from clear to red.

See also Art Glass Baskets; Cruets; Sugar Shakers; Salts; specific manufacturers.

Bowl, lt vertical ribs, 9", in metal fr w/scrolls & leaves **125.00**
Celery vase, bird & floral, SP holder, 8"....................................**750.00**
Celery vase, Invt T'print, 6"...**85.00**
Cheese dish, Invt T'print lid w/HP daisies & faceted knob, 9" dia .**460.00**
Pitcher, Hobnail, sq rim, camphor hdl, 7" **285.00**
Pitcher, mc florals, bulbous, clear reeded hdl, 9¼" **195.00**
Rose bowl, ca 1880, 4" **250.00**
Vase, birds & foliage, enamel w/gilt trim, 1890s, 12½" **165.00**
Vase, floral, appl ft, 10" **210.00**
Vase, gilt spider mums, cylindrical, 9¾" **145.00**

Rubena Verde

Rubena Verde glass was introduced in the late 1800s by Hobbs, Brockunier, and Company of Wheeling, West Virginia. Its transparent colors shade from red to green.

See also Art Glass Baskets; Cruets; Sugar Shakers; Salts.

Bowl, allover floral enameling, appl rigaree, 11½" L **265.00**
Cheese dish, Invt T'print cover, Daisy & Button tray, 5x7"........**200.00**
Creamer, appl vaseline leaves, vaseline hdl & ft, 4¾x3" **135.00**
Jack-in-the-pulpit, appl wht flower, bent/crimped 4-point rose rim, 8"..**200.00**
Pitcher, Invt T'print, vaseline gr hdl, Hobbs, 7¼" **250.00**
Pitcher, Invt T'print w/enambled butterfly & flowers, 6¾".........**400.00**
Pitcher, water; Invt T'print, vaseline, hdl, 7½", +4" tumbler......**400.00**
Rose bowl, florals & gold scrolls, 8-crimp, 4x4¼"......................**235.00**
Vase, opal Dmn Quilt, appl gr/clear florals & petal ft, 11", NM .**300.00**

Ruby Glass

Produced for over one hundred years by every glasshouse of note in this country, ruby glass has been used to create decorative items such as one might find in gift shops, utilitarian bottles and kitchenware, figurines, and dinnerware lines such as were popular in the Depression era. For further information and study, we recommend *Ruby Glass of the 20th Century* by our advisor, Naomi Over; she is listed in the Directory under Colorado.

Banana stand, Fan & File, Westmoreland, 1983, 4x4½" **30.00**
Basket, Barred Oval, Fenton, ca 1985-86, 7½" **35.00**
Basket, Cameo, Westmoreland, Line #752, 1980, 9½" **30.00**
Bell, gold band, crystal hdl, Italy, 6¼" **25.00**
Bell, rose decor, Westmoreland, 1980s, 7" **25.00**
Bowl, Barred Oval, Fenton, #8321, 1984-86, 6½" **25.00**
Bowl, Daisy & Button, 4-ftd, oval, Am Glassworks, 6¼" **20.00**
Bowl, ruffled rim, Blenko, 1980, 9½" **30.00**
Butter dish, Cape Cod, cube, Avon, ca 1980, 7" **40.00**

Butter dish, Invt Thistle, Mosser, 1980, 7¼"................**65.00**
Butter dish, Sawtooth, Westmoreland for Levay, 1980, 6½" **40.00**
Butterfly dish, Imperial, late 1960s, 3¼" **15.00**
Cake plate, Tally Ho, water lilies silver o/l, Cambridge, 14½" **125.00**
Candle holder, Cape Cod, hurricane globe, Avon, 1985, 11".......**35.00**
Candlestick, Dmn T'print, flared bowl on ped, Viking, 1986, 10½" ..**35.00**
Candlesticks, bell shape, satin, 4¼", pr.......................**20.00**
Candy dish, Colorado College souvenir, w/lid, Anchor Hocking, 8½".**15.00**
Candy dish, Optic Rib, Blenko, 1930-53, 3½" dia..............**6.00**
Canister, Moon & Star, LE Smith, 1968, 5¼" **20.00**
Coaster, silver casing w/Park Sherman, 3¾"...................**20.00**
Cordial, in Farberware holder, 3-oz...........................**20.00**
Cornucopia nut dish, unknown maker, 3¾" L....................**25.00**
Creamer, Maple Leaf, Westmoreland, 1989, 3¼" **65.00**
Decanter, clear lid, Blenko, 1980-85, 4½" dia.................**20.00**
Decanter, Roly Poly, New Martinsville, 1940, 12-oz............**35.00**
Paperweight, rnd, England, ca 1950, 3" **15.00**
Pie shell, Pyrex, Corning Glassworks, 9" **30.00**
Plate, ABC type, plain rim, AA Imports, 1980, 8" **15.00**
Plate, Cape Cod, Avon, 1980s, 11"...........................**20.00**
Plate, Forget-Me-Not border, Mary Gregory Winter girl, 1983, 8".**75.00**
Plate, Holly & Berry, Fostoria, ca 1980, 12½"................**60.00**
Plate, Mary Gregory child on fence, heart shape, Westmoreland, 8" .**75.00**
Plate, plain, Dalzell-Viking, ca 1986, 12" **60.00**
Plate, Spoke & Rim, Duncan & Miller, 1930s, 8¾".............**40.00**
Platter, Simplicity #700, oval, Paden City, 1930s............**95.00**
Shell bowl, gold edge, silver swan base, unknown mfg, 7½" **85.00**
Slipper, Daisy & Button, made for LG Wright, 1950, sm **12.00**
Spooner, Eyewinker, 3-ftd, LG Wright, 1960s, 5½" **50.00**
Sugar bowl, Argus, w/lid, Fostoria, 1967, 6½"....................**30.00**
Sugar bowl, Gadroon #881, Paden City, 1933, 2¼" **30.00**
Tumbler, English Hobnail, Westmoreland, 1982, 8-oz..............**25.00**
Tumbler, ftd, crystal stem, Cambridge, 1949-53, 11-oz **25.00**
Tumbler, iced tea; crystal base, Paden City, 1952, 8-oz **25.00**
Tumbler, juice; Standard Glass, ca 1940s, 6-oz....................**10.00**
Tumbler, Swirl & Ball, Westmoreland, 1980-90, 8-oz..................**25.00**
Vase, hand-blown w/wide ruffled rim, unknown mfg, 8¼" **65.00**
Wine, flared rim, unknown mfg.................................**12.00**

Ruby-Stained Glass

Ruby-flashed or ruby-stained glass was made through the application of a thin layer of color over clear. It was used in the manufacture of some early pressed tableware and from the Victorian era well into the twentieth century. These items were often engraved on the spot with the date, location, and buyer's name.

Pitcher, Arched Ovals, Knox '09, 6½", $50.00.

Bowl, berry; Punty Band, in SP basket, 4¼"....................**55.00**
Butter dish, Nat'l Star **145.00**
Celery dish, Sunk Honeycomb.................................**42.50**
Compote, jelly; Bar & Flute **95.00**
Creamer, Heart Band, Union City, 4" **22.00**
Mug, Buttons & Arches, Hot Springs AR, 2¾"..................**22.00**
Pitcher, Plume, World's Fair 1893, To Mama, 5½".............**55.00**
Punch cup, Masonic Temple 1893, 2¾".......................**25.00**
Spooner, Ruby T'print, etched leaves, 4".....................**42.50**
Tankard, Bracelet, 12"...**175.00**
Toothpick holder, Scalloped Daisy, inscr, dtd 1907, 2½"..............**22.50**
Tumbler, Skilton...**20.00**
Wine, Buttons & Arches, Manchester NH 1915, 4" **25.00**

Rugs

Hooked rugs are treasured today for their folk-art appeal. Rug making was a craft that was introduced to this country in about 1830 and flourished its best in the New England states. The prime consideration when evaluating one of these rugs is not age but artistic appeal. Scenes with animals, buildings, and people; patriotic designs; or whimsical themes are preferred. Those with finely conceived designs, great imagination, interesting color use, etc., demand higher prices. Condition is, of course, also a factor. Marked examples bearing the stamps of 'Frost and Co.,' 'Abenakee,' 'C.R.,' and 'Ouia' are highly prized.

See also Orientalia, Rugs.

Bowl of flowers, multicolor wool, cotton, and silk yarn and ribbons on ochre ground with meandering borders, late 1800s, 31½x55½", $5,175.00.

Bird w/berries, chain border, mc, late 1800s, rprs, 27x38½" **3,450.00**
Clipper ship, blk/wht on gr sea w/bl sky, blk border, 24x36" **415.00**
Cornucopia & flowers w/red scrolls on tan, Am, ca 1880, 43x73".**4,000.00**
Floral arrangement, mc w/bl & purple fishscale border, 73x46" ..**880.00**
Flower basket, mc on blk, flowers in ea corner, mc borders, wear, 42"..**990.00**
Flowers in leafy scroll reserve, red/gr/blk on tan, 1880s, 34x66", EX .**470.00**
Geometrics/chevrons/triangle borders/semi-circle corners, 46x26" .**330.00**
Grenfell, rescue scene w/3 figures & dog sled, 1900-25, 38x62".**1,400.00**
Horse & cat, mc, sgn E 1943 H, mtd on fr, 23x26" **525.00**
Horses (3, ea overlapping next 1), brn/tan/blk on earth tones, 40x30".**990.00**
Lady & animals along path w/pump & flowers, mc, 19th C, 40x44", EX.**10,350.00**
Lg rabbit, tan/brn on toned gray, red stars in corners, 40x24" **550.00**
Man up tree w/bear standing beside, mc cotton, rpr, 43x28".......**635.00**
Moose wading lake, mc, some fading, 20th C, 21x36".................**230.00**
Oak leaves & quatrefoils w/mc scrolling border, 19th C, 62" sq.**1,175.00**
Oriental motif on dk magenta, butterflies in corners, 35x51" **165.00**
Oriental motif w/stepped borders & 3 center medallions on gray, 34x51".**550.00**
Penny, mc wool, tongue border, sm hearts on rnd blue disks, 20x42".**250.00**
Pinwheel w/in dmn reserve, mc checkerboard spandrels, 42x27".**220.00**

Pony w/stars/flowers/birds, bright mc, 24x40½"+fr **990.00**
Red brick house/trees, blk/burgundy borders, lg stains, 21x33" ..**220.00**
Repeating blocks & Xs, 6-color, Am, 19th C, 31x36", EX **800.00**
Roses & blossoms on diamond grid, mc w/blk, 19th C, 36x67" ..**700.00**
Sailing ship on high seas, mc w/2-tone gold border, 36x38" **220.00**
Schoolhouses in sqs alternate w/sqs of stripes, EX color, 30x45".**770.00**
Scroll pattern, mc on brn, 19th C, 33x62", EX **575.00**
Sheep, folksy/smiling, floral blanket on bk, mc on gr, 30x40", EX .**1,200.00**
Stepped blocks, gr/tomato/red w/mc steps on 2 sides, 69x32" **250.00**
Tall monument, eagle on top/Am flag ea side, in lg wreath, 33x28" .**495.00**
Various folksy components: hear/bird/flowers/sunburst/etc, 22x68"..**935.00**
Village scene w/train/people/animals/etc, wide border, 1900s, 35x75" .**1,500.00**
Vining flowers, mc on brick red, rstr, 36x80" **550.00**

RumRill

George Rumrill designed and marketed his pottery designs from 1933 until his death in 1942. During this period of time, four different companies produced his works. Today the most popular designs are those made by the Red Wing Stoneware Company from 1933 until 1936 and Red Wing Potteries from 1936 until early 1938. Some of these lines include Trumpet Flower, Classic, Manhattan, and Athena, the Nudes.

For a period of months in 1938, Shawnee took over the production of RumRill pottery. This relationship ended abruptly, and the Florence Pottery took over and produced his wares until the plant burned down. The final producer was Gonder. Pieces from each individual pottery are easily recognized by their designs, glazes, and/or signatures. It is interesting to note that the same designs were produced by all three companies. They may be marked RumRill or with the name of the specific company that made them. You will find information on RumRill in these books: *Red Wing Art Pottery*, *Books I* and *II*, by B.L. and R.L. Dollen (Collector Books). Our advisors for this category are Wendy and Leo Frese; they are listed in the Directory under Texas.

Vase, bud; Goldenrod, #270, 7½", 75.00. (Photo courtesy Wendy and Leo Frese)

Bookends, eagle figural, blk, pr **250.00**
Bowl, gr, Mandarin Group, octagonal, #331, 12" **80.00**
Bowl, pk, boat shape, #H18, 11½"..**35.00**
Ewer, Apple Blossom (rose on gr), #184, 7" **75.00**
Ivy ball, Dutch Blue, #600, 10"...**200.00**
Pitcher, Goldenrod, ball from, #50, 6½" **75.00**
Pitcher, Gypsy orange, bulbous w/sq hdl, #50, 8"........................**50.00**
Pitcher, yel, ball form, #50, 5½" **50.00**
Planter, swan shape, wht, #259, 6"..**55.00**
Planter, turq, #338, 13" **60.00**
Vase, aqua w/emb floral, ivory int, #522, 6".............................**50.00**

Vase, Art Deco, pale gr, rim-to-hip hdls, #261 & #934, 8x9" **75.00**
Vase, Art Deco shape, bl, #600, 8" **400.00**
Vase, Athenian, figure supports bowl, wht w/turq int, #567, 5½x8" .**1,200.00**
Vase, Athenian Nude, Suntan, #570, 10" **475.00**
Vase, bl w/wht stippling, Classic Group, scalloped sides, #500, 5½" ..**75.00**
Vase, gr matt, emb ribs, hdls, #320, 5¾"....................................**50.00**
Vase, Horizon (bl on tan), #195, 10½" **125.00**
Vase, ivory w/gr int, fan shape, 5-ball hdl, #668, 10" **150.00**
Vase, ivory w/pk int, shell shape, #432, 7½" **50.00**
Vase, lily pads, swan hdls, gr matt, #298, 9¼" **125.00**
Vase, Neoclassic, lt bl, #666...**175.00**
Vase, ocean gr, Indian Group, #291, 5½" **50.00**
Vase, Octagonal, orange & yel splotches, #297, 5¼"......................**60.00**
Vase, Speckled Blue, hdls, H-15, 8¾x5"....................................**50.00**
Vase, Trumpet Flower, gr stipple, #486, 6½" **90.00**
Vase, wht, horn of plenty shape, #K8, 12"..................................**40.00**

Ruskin

This English pottery operated near Birmingham from 1889 until 1935. Its founder was W. Howson Taylor, and it was named in honor of the renowned author and critic, John Ruskin. The earliest marks were 'Taylor' in block letters and the initials 'WHT,' the smaller W and H superimposed over the larger T. Later marks included the Ruskin name.

Bowl, pk mottle, 5¼x12" **290.00**
Vase, bl & wht sponge to bl, 1932, 7" **180.00**
Vase, crystalline, yel to bl-gr streaked w/orange, 1932, 5" **200.00**
Vase, gr/gray stylized dandelions on yel, mk 1915, 11x5¼" **415.00**
Vase, variegated gr & wht lustre, mk 1914, 8¼"..........................**275.00**

Russel Wright Dinnerware

Russel Wright, one of America's foremost industrial designers, also designed several lines of ceramic dinnerware, glassware, and aluminum ware that are now highly sought-after collectibles. His most popular dinnerware then and with today's collectors, American Modern, was manufactured by the Steubenville Pottery Company from 1939 until 1959. It was produced in a variety of solid colors in assortments chosen to stay attune with the times. Casual (his first line sturdy enough to be guaranteed against breakage for ten years from date of purchase) is relatively easy to find today — simply because it has held up so well. During the years of its production, the Casual line was constantly being restyled, some items as many as five times. Early examples were heavily mottled, while later pieces were smoothly glazed and sometimes patterned. The ware was marked with Wright's signature and 'China by Iroquois.' It was marketed in fine department stores throughout the country. After 1950 the line was marked 'Iroquois China by Russel Wright.' For those wanting to learn more about the subject, we recommend *Collector's Encyclopedia of Russel Wright*, *Third Edition*, by Ann Kerr.

American Modern

To calculate values for American Modern, at the least, double the low values listed for these colors: Canteloupe, Glacier Blue, Bean Brown, and White. Chartreuse is represented by the low end of our range; Cedar, Black Chutney, and Seafoam by the high end; and Coral and Gray near the middle.

Bowl, lug fruit; from $15 to **20.00**
Bowl, salad; from $100 to..**115.00**
Carafe, from $225 to **250.00**

Coffee cup cover, minimum value 200.00
Cup, demitasse; from $18 to.........................22.00
Pitcher, water; tall, from $135 to 150.00
Plate, dinner; 10", from $18 to..........................20.00
Salad fork & spoon, ea, from $85 to.........................95.00
Shakers, pr, from $20 to........................25.00
Teapot, restyled, from $175 to 200.00

Glass

Morgantown Modern is most popular in Seafoam, Coral, and Chartreuse. In the Flair line, colors other than crystal and pink are rare and expensive. Seafoam is hard to find in Pinch; Canteloupe is scarce so double the prices for that color, and Ruby Flair is very rare.

Appleman warming tray, rnd or oblong, lg or sm, ea from $100 to ..125.00
Bartlett-Collins Eclipse, dbl old fashioned, from $22 to 35.00
Bartlett-Collins Eclipse, shot glass, 2", from $25 to 28.00
Imperial Flare, tumbler, water; 11-oz, from $50 to 65.00
Imperial Pinch, tumbler, juice; 6-oz, from $30 to...........................35.00
Imperial Twist, tumbler, water; from $35 to..........................50.00
Old Morgantown/Modern, cocktail, 2½", 3-oz, from $25 to 30.00
Old Morgantown/Modern, dessert dish, 2x4", from $35 to............45.00
Old Morgantown/Modern, tumbler, water; 4½", 12-oz, from $25 to.30.00
Snow Glass, bowl, sherbet/fruit; from $55 to................................75.00
Snow Glass, tumbler, any sz (5-oz, 10-oz or 14-oz), ea, from $200 to..225.00
Theme Formal Glass, goblet, 8-oz, 5", from $150 to 200.00

Highlight

Bowl, divided vegetable; minimum value....................................100.00
Cup, from $40 to 55.00
Plate, dinner; from $35 to 40.00
Platter, oval, sm, from $50 to 75.00
Shakers, either sz, pr, from $100 to........................150.00
Sugar bowl, from $65 to 75.00

Iroquois Casual

To price Sugar White, Charcoal, and Oyster, use the high end of the pricing range. Avocado Yellow, Nutmeg Brown, and Ripe Apricot fall to the low side. Canteloupe commands premium prices, and even more valuable are Brick Red and Aqua.

Bowl, salad; 52-oz, 10", from $35 to....................................45.00
Bowl, soup; 11½-oz, from $20 to..25.00
Bowl, vegetable; 36-oz, 8⅛", from $25 to 30.00
Carafe, wine/coffee; from $200 to......................................225.00
Cover for soup/cereal, from $30 to......................................35.00
Gravy stand, from $15 to......................................20.00

Mug, restyled, from $70.00 to $85.00.
(Photo courtesy Ann Kerr)

Plate, dinner; 10", from $12 to.................................15.00
Sugar bowl, stacking, from $20 to......................................25.00

Spun Aluminum

Russel Wright's aluminum ware may not have been especially well accepted in its day — it tended to damage easily and seems to have had only limited market appeal — but today's collectors feel quite differently about it, as is apparent in the suggested values noted in the following listings.

Bun warmer, wood knob and handle, 10", from $75.00 to $85.00.

Beverage set, pitcher+6 tumblers+tray, from $450 to 550.00
Candelabra, from $225 to 350.00
Cheese knife, from $75 to 100.00
Gravy boat, from $150 to 200.00
Peanut scoop, from $75 to.......................................100.00
Pitcher, sherry; from $250 to 275.00
Tidbit tray, dbl; from $150 to 200.00
Wastebasket, from $125 to 150.00

Sterling

Bowl, bouillon; 7-oz, from $18 to.......................................20.00
Celery, 11¼", from $28 to 36.00
Pitcher, water; 2-qt, from $125 to.......................................150.00
Plate, dinner; 10¼", from $10 to 15.00
Relish, divided, 16½", from $65 to.......................................70.00
Teapot, 10-oz, from $125 to 150.00

Miscellaneous

Book, Guide to Easier Living, 1st ed, w/dust jacket, from $175 to ..200.00
Chrome, smoking stand, from $500 to 700.00
Country Garden, cup & saucer, from $125 to 150.00
Country Garden, platter, form $200 to.......................................250.00
Everlast Gold Aluminite, creamer, from $50 to 60.00
Everlast Gold Aluminite, tumbler, from $65 to...........................75.00
Fabric, napkin.......................................15.00
Fabric, tablecloth, 54x78", from $125 to 150.00
Flair, bowl, fruit.......................................18.00
Flair, platter.......................................28.00
Flair, tumbler.......................................18.00
Home Decorator, plate, dinner; from $8 to 10.00
Home Decorator, tumbler, from $15 to.......................................18.00
Ideal Adult Kitchenware, butter dish, from $50 to...........................60.00
Ideal Adult Kitchenware, jug, water; lg, from $50 to.....................75.00
Ideal Children's Toy Dishes, serving pcs, ea, from $25 to 28.00
Knowles Esquire, cup & saucer, from $12 to 16.00
Knowles Esquire, pitcher, 2-qt, from $150 to 200.00
Knowles Esquire, plate, dinner; 10¾", from $15 to.....................18.00
Meladur, cup, from $8 to.......................................10.00

Meladur, plate, compartmented, 9½", from $15 to 18.00
Oceana, salad bowl, flat shell, from $500 to..............................600.00
Oceana, snail relish, lg, from $600 to 800.00
Pinch cutlery, butter spreader, from $100 to..........................110.00
Pinch cutlery, salad fork, from $75 to 85.00
Residential, bowl, onion soup; w/lid, from $36 to 40.00
Residential, cup & saucer, from $9 to 13.00
Theme Formal, coffeepot, from $600 to 650.00
Theme Formal, plate, dinner; 10", from $75 to 100.00
Theme Formal Lacquerware, plate, from $125 to 150.00
Theme Informal, creamer, from $175 to...................................200.00
Theme Informal, plate, dinner; 10", from $100 to 150.00
White Clover, bowl, vegetable; w/lid, 8¼", from $75 to 100.00
White Clover, chop plate, Clover decor, 11", from $40 to 50.00
Wood accessory, frosted oak platter, from $250 to 300.00
Wood accessory, relish, 2-compartment, from $300 to 400.00

Russian Art

Before the Revolution in 1917, many jewelers and craftsmen created exquisite marvels of their arts, distinctive in the extravagant detail of their enamel work, jeweled inlays, and use of precious metals. These treasures aptly symbolized the glitter and the romance of the glorious days under the reign of the Tsars of Imperial Russia. The most famous of these master jewelers was Carl Fabergé (1852 – 1920), goldsmith to the Romanovs. Following the tradition of his father, he took over the Fabergé workshop in 1870. Eventually Faberge employed more than five hundred assistants and set up workshops in Moscow, Kiev, and London as well as in St. Petersburg. His specialties were enamel work, clockwork automated figures, carved animal and human figures of precious or semiprecious stones, cigarette cases, small boxes, scent flasks, and his best-known creations, the Imperial Easter Eggs — each of an entirely different design. By the turn of the century, his influence had spread to other countries, and his work was revered by royalty and the very wealthy. The onset of the war marked the end of the era. Very little of his work remains on the market, and items that are available are very expensive. But several of his contemporaries were goldsmiths whose work can be equally enchanting. Among them are Klingert, Ovchinnikov, Smirnov, Ruckert, Loriye, Cheryatov, Kuzmichev, Nevalainen, Adler, Sbitnev, Third Artel, Wakewa, Holmstrom, Britzin, Wigstrom, Orlov, Nichols, and Plincke. Most of them produced excellent pieces similar to those made by Faberge between 1880 and 1910.

Perhaps the most important bronze Russian artist was Eugenie Alexandrovich Lanceray (1847 – 87). From 1875 until 1887, he modeled many equestrian groups of falconers and soldiers ranging in height from about 20" to 30". Some of them bear the Chopin foundry mark; they are presently worth from $4,000.00 up. Other excellent artists were Schmidt Felling (nineteenth century), who specialized in mounted figures of cossacks wearing military uniforms, and Nicholas Leiberich (late nineteenth century), who also specialized in equestrian groups. Most of the pieces made by the above artists were signed and had the foundry mark (Chopin, Woerfell, etc.)

Russian porcelain is another field where Imperial connections have undoubtedly added to the interest of collectors and museums worldwide. The most important factories were: Imperial Russian Porcelain, St. Petersburg (or Petrograd or Leningrad, 1744 – 1917); Gardner, Moscow (1765 – 1872); Kuznetsoff, St. Petersburg and Moscow (1800 – 1900); Korniloff, St. Petersburg (1800 – 1900); and Babunin, St. Petersburg (1800 – 1900).

Beaker, silver, plain, tapered cylinder cup, Fabergé, 1896, 2⅞"...600.00
Bowl, hammered copper, gr stones at rim & mc enamel trim, 1900, 7½"..550.00
Bowl, plique-a-jour, floral decor, 2½x5"...................................1,000.00
Bowl, St George & dragon/2-headed eagle emb on copper, Fabergé, 4¼".1,565.00
Bowl, 2-headed eagle emb on copper, repousse border, late 19th C, 11".900.00
Box, bl glass, molded lid, SP hinge/closure, ca 1900, 5" L..........250.00

Box, blk lcq w/snowy horse-race scene, Visnikov, 1880s, 3½x7x5" .1,125.00
Box, silver repousse dragonfly/beetle/etc, Khlebnikov, 4x4" dia...2,600.00
Box, silver w/repousse bugs, Khlebnikov, 4x4" dia...................2,600.00
Box, stamp; silver gilt w/appl medallion/fleur-de-lis, Fabergé, 3½"..1,100.00
Card case, red & yel gold w/ruby & acanthus leaves, ca 1900, 3⅝"..2,800.00
Case, cigarette; enamel & silver w/swan scene & gold, 4½x3" .3,450.00
Casket, jewelry; silver w/gold wash, P Sazikov, ca 1905, 3x11x7".4,600.00
Casket, silver w/gold wash int, hinged lid, P Sazikov, 3x11x6¾".4,600.00
Chalice, eng bowl w/religious figures/geometrics, Moscow, 1887, 8⅝".2,500.00
Charka, enameled foliage w/cloisonné borders & gilt, 1888-1908, 4⅜"..1,350.00
Cigarette case, enamel & silver gilt, moonstone button, 4¼x3"..3,450.00
Cross, blessing; repousse/chased silver, Moscow, ca 1900, 9⅜"....550.00
Cross, blessing; silver-gilt & niello, repousse foliage, 1802, 14".2,250.00
Cross, oil on panel, G colors, 20th C, 14½x8½" 150.00
Cross, priestal; silver set in fr w/paste stones & crown, 20th C, 27".850.00
Cross, wall; bronze & enamel w/side panels, 19th C, 8¾x5½" ...150.00
Egg, floral enamel on gilt silver, Ruckert, 1908-17, 2¼" 4,750.00
Figure, walrus, silver w/ruby eyes, ivory tusks, Fabergé mk, 2x4".5,750.00
Gouache on card, Winter Landscape w/Figure, Kolesnikov, ca 1900, 9x12"..3,350.00
Icon, Lord Almighty, heavily incised/decor field, 1890s, 8¾x7" .400.00
Icon, Old Testament Trinity, ornate borders, ca 1900, 12x11"....900.00
Icon, Resurrection & Descent, 30 figures, repousse riza, 11x10"..2,250.00
Icon, St George slaying dragon, ornate borders, 19th C, 14x12"..900.00
Icon, St Mary of Egypt, 19th C, 10½x8¼" 250.00
Icon, St Nicholas, 20th C, in lg 38½x24" shadowbox fr 800.00
Icon, St Vladimir, silver riza, Moscow, ca 1900, 11x9".............1,100.00
Icon, 4 registers w/various saints, 19th C, 21x18", EX.................975.00
Kovsh, floral enameling on gilt, Agafonov, 1908-17, 4⅛" L....1,680.00
Kovsh, florals on gold w/turq beading, Moscow, 1908-17, 4¾".2,465.00
Match holder, brass, Boyar shape, wall mt, late 19th C, 4" 225.00
Oil on canvas, Russian Baba, Maliavin, early 1900s, 36x30"...6,700.00
Plate, bread; cvd, cyrillic Give Us Our..., tooled border, 19th C, 12" .335.00
Salt cellar, silver-gilt chair shape w/hinged bk & lid, Sazikov..3,000.00
Spoon, enameled exotic bird/foliage on silver, Borisov, 1899-1908, 7"..1,000.00
Sugar bowl, cloisonné on gilt, swing hdl, Moscow, 1908-17, 5" dia.2,000.00
Tea glass holder, chased/pierced silver, Moscow, 1908-17, 5" 225.00
Triptych, Archangel Michael, bronze, 18th C, 6" W..................365.00

Sabino

Sabino art glass was produced by Marius-Ernest Sabino in France during the 1920s and 1930s. It was made in opalescent, frosted, and colored glass and was designed to reflect the Art Deco style of that era. In 1960, using molds he modeled by hand, Sabino once again began to produce art glass using a special formula he himself developed that was characterized by a golden opalescence. Although the family continued to produce glassware for export after his death in 1971, they were never able to duplicate Sabino's formula.

Bottle, nude bathers with swans, cylindrical, 4¼", $125.00. (Photo courtesy Monsen & Baer)

Bowl, bird perched on side w/wave effect as a pond, 1¾x5¾" **170.00**
Box, swallows, hinged w/gold metal fittings/heart hdl, 3½", MIB .**150.00**
Figurine, conch shells, 1 lg w/2 sm, 2x3½" **105.00**
Figurine, gazelle, 4½x6" **200.00**
Figurine, lovebirds on branch, 3¾x5x2"...................................**395.00**
Figurine, Madonna holding roses & cross, 5x2" **110.00**
Figurine, nude leaning bk w/arm over head, long hair, 6¾" **475.00**
Figurine, quail, in ped base, 3½x3½x½" **105.00**
Figurine, 4 birds on & 1 under branch, 8½x6" **690.00**
Paperweight, dragonfly figural, 6x5½"......................................**110.00**
Perfume bottle, nudes, w/stopper, 6x2¾" dia............................**175.00**
Perfume bottle, petal design w/ribbed stopper, 5x3", MIB...........**105.00**
Powder box, petal design, w/lid, 3x4" **150.00**
Vase, sunset & swallows, amber, 7½x7" **595.00**

Salesman's Samples and Patent Models

Salesman's samples and patent models are often mistaken for toys or homemade folk art pieces. They are instead actual working models made by very skilled craftsmen who worked as model-makers. Patent models were made until the early 1900s. After that, the patent office no longer required a model to grant a patent. The name of the inventor or the model-maker and the date it was built is sometimes noted on the patent model. Salesman's samples were occasionally made by model-makers, but often they were assembled by an employee of the company. These usually carried advertising messages to boost the sale of the product. Though they are still in use today, the most desirable examples date from the 1800s to about 1945.

Many small stoves are incorrectly termed a 'salesman's sample'; remember that no matter how detailed one may be, it must be considered a toy unless accompanied by a carrying case, the indisputable mark of a salesman's sample.

Bench, folding, Watson's Seats & Benches... on bk, 8x12½x4"..**230.00**
Box car, Hebert's Automatic Brake, wood/brass, Pat 1883, 26", VG.**4,000.00**
Case, Heinz Pickles, 6 pnt zinc graduated pickles inside, 1900s.**1,850.00**

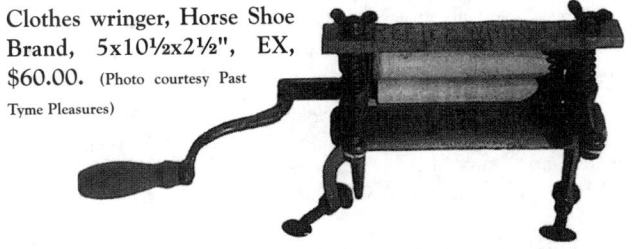

Clothes wringer, Horse Shoe Brand, 5x10½x2½", EX, $60.00. (Photo courtesy Past Tyme Pleasures)

Fence, Deland Fence Co, wood/wire, w/carrying box, Pat 1892, EX .**425.00**
Grader, Corsicana, brass & iron w/red & gr decals, wheels adjust, 12".**700.00**
Masonic sample tool kit, wood box w/7 tools, Whitehead & Hoag, NM.**100.00**
Pocket mirror, Zimmerman Mfg Co True Blue Vehicles, rnd, EX.**450.00**
Reaper, Geo Gibbs, brass/steel/wood, ca 1900, 12¼", EX **1,750.00**
Sled, 3-runner, HP seat/striping/flowers, Pat Nov 20 1894, 27"...**2,000.00**
Sofa, Empire style w/horsehair filling, pillows, 1830s, 14", VG.**2,000.00**
Step ladder, steel A-fr w/movable legs, 22", EX **700.00**
Tower, Ballard's Belisk Flour, litho tin, 6½", EX+ **1,050.00**

Salt Glaze

As early as the 1600s, potters used common salt to glaze their stoneware. This was accomplished by heating the salt and introducing it into the kiln at maximum temperature. The resulting gray-white glaze was a thin, pitted surface that resembles the peel of an orange.

Creamer, enamel landscape w/ruins, squat w/shaped rim, 1770, 3"..**1,600.00**
Figurine, Buddha, seated, splashes of bl & brn, 1760, 3"..........**2,200.00**
Figurine, Chinaman, in long robe, arms crossed, English, 3⅛" .**1,600.00**
Figurine, Foo dog, brn slip eyes/tongue, hairline/chip, 6".........**1,800.00**
Sauce boat, emb seed & basketweave motif, gilt traces, 1755, 7" L...**765.00**
Teapot, enameled landscape scene w/ruins, rnd w/branch hdl, 5", VG.**1,500.00**

Salt Shakers

John Mason invented the screw-top salt shaker in 1858. Today's Victorian salt shaker collectors have a wide range of interests, and their collections usually reflect their preference. There are many possible variables on which to base a collection. You may prefer shakers made of clear pattern glass, art glass, specific types of glass (custard, ruby stain, Burmese, opaque, chocolate), or glass of a particular color (cranberry, green, blue, or amber, for instance). Some collectors search for examples made by only one maker (in particular Mt. Washington, Dithridge, Northwood, Hobbs Brockunier, and C. F. Monroe.) Others may stick to decorated shakers, undecorated examples, or any combination thereof that captures their fancy. If you would like to learn more about Victorian glass salt shakers, we recommend *The World of Salt Shakers, Second* and *Third Editions* by Mildred and Ralph Lechner, and *Early American Pattern Glass* by Reilly and Jenks.

Unless noted otherwise, values are for examples in excellent condition with near mint decorations (when applicable). Unless 'pr' is specified, the value is for a single shaker. Our advisors for this category are Carla and Doug Hales; they are listed in the Directory under Florida.

Victorian Glass

Alaska, cobalt, Northwood, ca 1897, 2⅜"....................................**250.00**
Arch, Fancy; gr w/gold, ca 1891-1903 ....**30.00**
Artichoke, Fostoria's (aka Valencia); clear/frosted, Fostoria, 2⅝" .**80.00**
Aster & Leaf, emerald gr, Beaumont, ca 1895, rare, 3"................**110.00**
Atterbury Twin, wht opal, 2-pc mold, ca 1877-82, 5"...................**105.00**
Barrel, Alluring; wht satin w/HP flowers, ca 1881-89, 3⅜".........**230.00**
Barrel, Arabesque; opaque w/ornate HP geometrics, Moser, 3⅛".**540.00**
Barrel, Footed Optic; cranberry w/HP floral, Mt WA/Pairpoint, 3½".**190.00**
Barrel, Invt Honeycomb; amber w/HP floral, NE Glass, 1884-87, 3¼".**125.00**
Barrel, Ringed Base; cranberry w/HP floral, att Europe, 1888-94, 3".**90.00**
Barrel, Tall Optic Rib; amethyst w/HP floral, NE Glass, 3⅝" **175.00**
Beaded Embroidery, wht opal w/gr & yel ovals, 1898-1906, 3" **25.00**
Bohemian (aka Florador), gr w/gold, US Glass, ca 1899-1901, 3½"..**175.00**
Brilliant, Riverside's; clear w/ruby stain, ca 1895, 2⅞" **95.00**
Bulging Lobes, Footed; wht opal w/HP floral, 1900-10, 3⅞" **15.00**
Cartouche, opalware w/HP floral, Helmschmeid, 1904-07, 2⅝"...**85.00**
Champion (aka Fan w/Cross Bars), clear w/ruby stain, McKee, 2⅞".**85.00**
Chick on Pedestal, yel opaque to lt gr on milk glass, CF Monroe..**600.00**
Chrysanthemum Base Variant, cranberry opal, Buckeye, 1888-91, 3⅛"..**195.00**
Co-op's #1901, invt Vs, Co-Operative Flint Glass, ca 1901, 3".....**20.00**
Coin Dot, Phoenix; clear apricot opal, ca 1884-87, 2¾".............**250.00**
Column, Enlarged Base; custard w/HP floral, 1900-05, 2¾"..........**40.00**
Concave Panel, wht opalware w/mc floral, Challinor Taylor, 1¾".**30.00**
Corn, pk opaque triple cased, Dithridge, 1894-1901, 3⅛"...........**150.00**
Cotton Bale, butterscotch variegated, Consolidated, 1894-95, 2⅝".**180.00**
Creased Neck, Tapered; opal w/HP scene, Mt WA/Pairpoint, 3½".**75.00**
Creased Side Panel, rubena satin w/HP floral, 1883-87, orig top .**175.00**
Cylinder, Optic Honeycomb; bluina, 1886-95, 2¾" **160.00**
Diamond, vaseline, pressed cylinder, Central, 1885-91, 2¾".........**65.00**
Diamond Mosaic, bl opaque, emb Rd 307899 on base, 1895-1908, 4⅝" .**32.00**

Doric, gr, McKee, ca 1896, 2½" 125.00
Doyle's Shell, bl opaque, Doyle & Co, 1880s, 2¾" 65.00
Elongated Bulb Variant, wht opal w/floral transfer, CF Monroe, 3⅛"..70.00
Elvira's Butterfly Variant, rubena stain w/HP decor, 1886-91, 2½"..225.00
Flower Tracery, red & gilt goofus on opal, Eagle, 1899-1905, 2⅜".30.00
Four Ring, Tubular; amethyst w/HP child & butterfly, 1880s+, 3⅝".180.00
Hex-Curves, wht opal, 6-panel, 1899-1910, 2¾x2" 15.00
Hexagon, Leaf Base; opal w/HP florals, Fostoria, 1901-07, 3¼"...30.00
Hobb's Block, frosted amber stained, Hobbs Brockunier, ca 1890, 3".80.00
Honeycomb, Intaglio Pillar; bl w/HP berries, Mt WA/Pairpoint, 3⅝"..190.00
Idyll (Jefferson #251), bl w/gold scrolls/dots, Jefferson, ca 1907, 3".150.00

Intaglio, green with gold decor, eight ribbed lobes, ca 1900 – 03, 3", $70.00.
(Photo courtesy Mildred Lechner)

Invt T'print, Sphere Variant; cobalt w/HP floral, Mt WA/Pairpoint, 2"..80.00
Isabella, gr opaque, Novelty Glass, 1891-92, 3⅝" 750.00
Ivy Scroll, Jefferson; bl w/gold leaves, 30 ribs, 1900-05, 2¾" 130.00
Lobed Elegance, pk to wht opal, HP floral, ca 1893 ....140.00
London Tower, bl opaque, emb Rd 319082 on base, 4½" 40.00
Lousiana, US Glass, ca 1898, 2⅝" 45.00
National's #1004, wht opal, 15 slanted panels at base, ca 1901, 2½".15.00
Net & Scroll, gr opaque, Dithridge, 1894-1900, 2⅞" 40.00
O'Hara Diamond, clear & ruby stain, US Glass, ca 1891-1900, 1⅞"..95.00
Octagon, Saloon; bl satin opaque, ca 1900-08, 4¼" 55.00
Paneled Holly, wht opal w/HP gold, Northwood, 1907-08, 3" 190.00
Paneled Prism, bl w/wht speckles, 9-panel, 1887-90, 2¾" 140.00
Pillar Optic Rib, bl w/HP floral, NE Glass, 1883-87, 4⅛" 185.00
Plain Bulbous, peach/wht streaked opaque, Stevens & Wms, 1885+, 2⅝".175.00
Pleat Band (aka Panel, Ten), chocolate, Indiana, ca 1898, 3⅛".900.00
Pseudo Pomona, clear frosted w/3 fish, ca 1889-91, 2⅝" 150.00
Rib, Triple; gr opaque variegated cased, Consolidated, 1894+, 3¼"..95.00
Ribbed Shoulder, wht opal w/HP floral, cylinder, 1898-1906, 3⅝"..45.00
Ribbed Triangle & Sawtooth, gr to clear, ca 1900-10...................100.00
Robbins, wht opalware, Dalzell Gilmore & Leighton, 1895-1900, 2¾".20.00
Scroll, Gaudy; gr opaque, Gillinder & Sons, 2½" 35.00
Seaweed, vaseline opal, Beaumont, ca 1890s, 3½" 150.00
Shrimp Base, 21 ribs in bulged-out base, 1890-1900, 3" 12.00
Strawberry Delight, bl opaque, Dithridge & Co, ca 1890s 150.00
Stripe, Hobbs' Wide; cranberry opal, vertical stripes, 1880s+, 2¾".180.00
Swag w/Brackets Variant, gr opal, Jefferson, ca 1904, 3" 125.00
Swallow Song, bl opaque w/HP birds/music, Mt WA/Pairpoint, 3⅝".300.00
Thompson's No 77 (Truncated Cube), clear & ruby stain, ca 1894, 2⅞"..70.00
Thousand Eye, Ringed Center; canary, ca 1878-1888, 3⅛" 80.00
Tulip Spray, wht opaque w/emb decor, 1899-1910, 3⅛" 21.00
Vining Rose, wht opal w/HP floral, New Martinsville, 1904, 3⅛".50.00
Violet Ovals, pk opaque, Gillinder, ca 1894-1900, 3" 45.00
Westmoreland #1775, column shape, Pat May 24 1910, 3" 18.00
Wild Bouquet, lt bl (slight opalescence), Northwood, 1900s, 3⅜".250.00
Zipper, aqua, patterned corners, Belmont, 1888-90, 3⅞" 80.00
Zippered Block, clear w/ruby stain, Geo Duncan, ca 1887, 2⅞" ...85.00

Novelty Shakers

Those interested in novelty shakers will enjoy *Salt and Pepper Shakers, Volumes I, II, III,* and *IV,* by Helene Guarnaccia; *The Collector's Encyclopedia of Salt and Pepper Shakers, Figural and Novelty, Volumes I* and *II,* by Melva Davern; and *Florence's Big Book of Salt and Pepper Shakers* by Gene Florence. All are available at your local library or from Collector Books. Note: 'Mini' shakers are no taller than 2". Instead of having a cork, the user was directed to 'use tape to cover hole.' Our advisor for novelty salt shakers is Judy Posner; she is listed in the Directory under Pennsylvania. See also Regal; Rosemeade; Occupied Japan; Shawnee; other specific manufacturers.

Novelty Advertising

Ballantine Ale beer can, cb w/metal lid, 2⅜", pr 20.00
Budweiser Budman, Ceramarte, 1991, 3⅝", pr..............................45.00
Camel Cigarettes, Max & Ray (camels), hard plastic, 1993, 4¼", pr.50.00
Conoco gas pump, plastic w/decals, 2¾", MIB............................95.00
Dr Brown soda bottle, clear w/fired-on label, 4¼", pr..................45.00
Falstaff Beer bottle, foil label, metal lid, Muth of Buffalo, 4", pr...30.00
Fingerhut truck, 2-pc truck, 1¾x3¾", 2-pc set 30.00
Goetz Country Club beer bottle, appl decal, 4½", pr....................35.00
Golden Guernsey Dairy Milk bottle, glass/metal lids, 1930s, 3⅜", pr.65.00
Harvestore silo, cobalt pottery, 4¾", pr 55.00
Homepride Flour, Flour Fred spiller, hard plastic, Airfix, 2⅛", pr.55.00
Jones Dairy bottle, glass w/decal, metal lid, 3½", pr...................75.00
Kellog's Snap & Pop, porc, Japan, 2½", pr 50.00
Kon-Tiki Ports, pottery figures, Designed by S Crane, 4¼", pr.......22.00
Life Soda bottle, glass w/decal, metal lid, 4½", pr.......................75.00
Old Cliff House Restaurant, seal figural, pottery, 3¾", pr..............25.00
Old Dooley & Schultz Utica Beer, steins, pottery, tallest: 4⅜", pr..125.00
Old Erie Beverage, soda bottle, Glenshaw glass, metal top, 6", pr.35.00
Old Gunther Beer bottle, glass w/metal top, foil label, 4", pr........28.00
Old Strasburg RR, conductor & engineer, pottery, Japan, 4¼", pr.32.00
Peerless Bear man, Hartland plastic figural, detailed, 1950s, 5", pr.95.00
Pep-Up Soda bottle, Glenshaw glass, metal lid, 5¾", pr...............55.00
Pure Oil gas pump, plastic, 2¾", pr 135.00
Quaker Oats building, pottery, Japan, 3⅛", pr..............................35.00
Quaker State Motor Oil can, cb, 1940s-50s, 1½", pr 40.00
Schlitz Beer bottle, 4" w/metal top on wooden stand, 3-pc set......22.00
St Lawrence Dairy Cream, glass bottle, metal lid, 3¼", pr 50.00
Texaco/Bergey & Gehman Fuel Oil, milk glass, Made in USA, 3¼", pr.65.00
Tuborg & Carlsberg Beer bottle, glass, decal label, 2½", pr...........30.00
Warminster Farm Dairy Milk bottle, glass w/metal lid, 3⅜", pr 65.00
White Satin Gin bottle, gr glass w/metal lid, 4¾", pr...................24.00

Novelty Animals, Fish, and Birds

Artist bear & easel (2nd shaker), ceramic, mc, 3¼", 2-pc set 32.00
Beagle hound & woodcock decor, Stuart Bruce, 1940s, 2⅞" sq, pr..29.00
Bear driving car (2nd shaker), pottery, ceramic, 1950s, 3½", 2-pc .35.00
Bees on hive, pottery, mc, illegible import mk, 3½", pr.................22.00
Cat & mouse, pottery, realistic, att USA, cat: 1¾x3¼", pr...........28.00
Cat & skull, ceramic, mc, red Japan mk, 2⅜", pr........................50.00
Chicken, china, monochromatic, shiny, Germany, 2", pr 26.00
Circus elephants w/hats (1 rears/1 stands), ceramic, Japan, 4½", pr..24.00
Cow on wire fr, purple, pottery, Japan, 4x5", 3-pc set 29.00
Dachshund, ceramic, gold trim, 1-pc, 1950s, 10" L......................35.00
Dinosaur, pottery, gr, resembles Dino, Made in Japan, 3¼", pr......35.00
Dinosaur, pottery, mc, unmk, ca 1970s, 3", pr 28.00
Dog smoking cigar & wearing hat, pottery, mc, Japan, 1950s, 3¼", pr..22.00
Dogs w/pipe, Woof & Poof, pottery, mc w/gold, 4¼", NM, pr.......32.00
Elephant w/umbrella, mc pottery, Japan, 1950s, 3½", pr 26.00

Goose & golden egg, Vallona Starr, goose: 5½", pr......................55.00
Hen & rooster, ceramic, gold trim, red Japan mk, 1950s, 2½", pr..20.00
Hen & rooster, ceramic, mc, shiny, detailed, 1950s, 3¾", pr.........22.00
Hen & rooster, glass w/pottery head, Czechoslovakia, 3", pr.........30.00
Pig (dressed), mc lustre, Germany, 3½", pr 75.00
Polar bear, pottery, realistic, unmk Japan, 1950s, 3¾x4⅜", pr 24.00
Rooster, bsk, mc w/gold trim, Japan label, 1950s, 3½", pr.............25.00
Scottie dog, porc, red & bl, Germany, 1930s-40s, 2½", pr.............28.00
Spaniels (1 sitting/1 recumbent), pottery, mc, Japan, tallest: 3"...24.00
Teddy bears (dressed) play piggy bk, ceramic, stack, Japan, 4¼", pr..18.00

Miscellaneous Novelties

Aladdin & lamp, pottery, maroon & wht, unmk, 1950s, 2", pr.....24.00
Anthropomorphic pear & orange, ceramic, crude pnt, unmk Japan, pr .20.00
Anthropomorphic train, ceramic, mc, red Japan mk, 2¾x9".........35.00
Baseball batter & catcher, ceramic, mc, Japan, 1940s-50s, 4", pr ..85.00
Baseball batter & umpire, pottery, mc, Japan label, 5", pr 75.00
Baseball player, ceramic, mc, souvenir Copalis Beach WA, 1950s, pr..85.00
Billy Sykes & Capt Cuttle, ceramic, Artone/MIE, 2½", pr 40.00
Bimbo (Betty Boop's dog), ceramic, cold pnt, 1930s, USA, 2½", pr .125.00
Blond girl in space suit & rocket ship (2nd shaker), Enesco, 1950s, pr.40.00
Boxing men, ceramic, mc, 1940s-50s, 3½", pr..................................50.00
Bride & groom, ceramic, mc, Japan, mini, 2½", pr.........................26.00
CA Wax Museum, gold-tone metal, emb Rolls Royce, Japan, 3-pc set.28.00
Canadian soldier boy, ceramic, Emsdale Canada stickers, 4", pr....22.00
Clown, pottery, HP details, Tilso Japan label, 1950s, 9¼", pr 60.00
Clown & lion, ceramic, mc, drum bottom, Japan, 1950s, 4", pr....23.00
Clown w/banjo, 2nd w/horn, ceramic, Japan, 1930s, 3½", pr........30.00
Doc & Bashful (dwarfs), ceramic, mc, mk Foreign, 1930s, 2⅞", pr .95.00
Dumbo, pottery, mc, Leeds, Disney, 1940s, pr...............................125.00
Ferdinand the Bull, ceramic, mc, late 1930s, 2¾", pr 80.00
Froggy the Gremlin, pottery, on base, Japan, 3x6", 3-pc set 125.00
Golf bag & ball, ceramic, mc, unmk, 1950s, bag: 3¼", pr 20.00
Hillbilly sleeping w/jug (2nd shaker), ceramic, mc, Japan, 1950s, pr..23.00
Humpty Dumpty, ceramic, HP details, California Pottery, 2½", pr..26.00
Hunter w/gun & rabbit, pottery, mc, unmk, 1950s, he: 3½", pr....22.00
Jerry Colonna pushing wheelbarrow, Made in Japan label, 3-pc set.55.00
Jimmy Carter Peanut (smiling, w/shoes), Japan sticker, 3½", pr ...34.00
Kansas & wheat, ceramic, c Parkcraft, pr 49.00
Kissing Dutch children nodders, Quebec souvenir, 4¼", pr 110.00

Kitchen witches, unmarked, 1970s, $24.00 for the pair.
(Photo courtesy Helen Guarnaccia)

Mammy & Pappy Yokum, pottery, Al Capp, Made in Japan, 4¼", M, pr..175.00
Man in doghouse & lady w/rolling pin, ceramic, Vallona Star, pr ...95.00
Mary w/lamb & schoolhouse, pottery, unmk, 1950s, pr 30.00
Miss Muffet & spider, ceramic, mc, Poinsettia Studio, she: 2½", pr..85.00
Mr & Mrs Claus in rockers, ceramic, unmk Japan, 3⅞", pr...........20.00
Nude in bathtub (2nd shaker), ceramic, unmk, 1950s, 2½x3¼", pr ..60.00
Old Mother Hubbard & dog, ceramic, Poinsettia Studio, 3½", pr..85.00

Oswold & Homer, ceramic, Napco Japan #1c3635, c 1958 W Lantz, 4", pr.145.00
Pebbles & Bamm-Bamm, ceramic, Harry James, Hanna-Barbera, 4", pr .55.00
Pipe on pipe holder (2nd shaker), ceramic, Trevewood, 1950s, pr...20.00
Pixie & Dixie (as cowboy & Indian), ceramic, Japan label, 3¼", pr..55.00
Pixie baseball players, ceramic, in red, Japan mk, 3½", pr.............75.00
Pixie head, shiny pottery, PY type, #6891 Japan, 3¼", pr..............30.00
Pluto, ceramic, cold pnt, Walt Disney Productions, 1940s, 3¼", pr..40.00
Pluto & doghouse (2nd shaker), underglaze pnt, Applause, Disney, pr.39.00
Raggedy Ann, ceramic, mc, unmk vintage import, 4", pr 40.00
Rainbow & pot of gold, ceramic, Arcadia, mini, ½", pr 38.00
Robin Hood & Maid Marian, Don Winton, 1949, pr.....................85.00
Rocket, pottery, Buck Rogers type w/gold, unmk, 1950s, 4¾", pr .45.00
Rocket ship & moon man, ceramic, Enesco, Japan, 1950s, pr........60.00
Rudolf, ceramic, red nose, #4370, 3", pr..28.00
Schoolhouse & desk, ceramic, mc, unmk, 1950s, schoolhouse: 3", pr .22.00
Shoemaker & elf, pottery, gr Japan mk, 4", pr................................32.00
Singing Tower, metal, souvenir Lake Wales Fla, 3½", pr...............45.00
St Lawrence Seaway ship, stacks are shakers, ceramic, 1950s, 3-pc..40.00
Thimble & gold thread, ceramic, Arcadia, mini, thread: 1¼", pr...18.00
Thumper, ceramic, cold pnt, Leeds, Disney, 1940s, 3½", pr 40.00
White Rabbit, pottery, 2 stacking rabbits, Japan, 4", pr................85.00
Woodie & Winnie Woodpecker, ceramic, W Lantz 1990, pr 55.00
Yosemite Sam, Lego paper label, 1960s, pr 95.00
Zodiac, girl, ceramic, mc, Japan ink stamp, 4½", pr......................45.00

Salts, Open

Before salt became refined, processed, and free-flowing as we know it today, it was necessary to serve it in a salt cellar. An innovation of the early 1800s, the master salt was placed by the host and passed from person to person. Smaller individual salts were a part of each place setting. A small silver spoon was used to sprinkle it onto the food.

If you would like to learn more about the subject of salts, we recommend *5,000 Open Salts*, written by William Heacock and Patricia Johnson, with many full-color illustrations and current values.

Our advisor for this category is Chris Christensen; he is listed in the Directory under California. In the listings below, the numbers refer to the Johnson and Heacock book and *Pressed Glass Salt Dishes* by L.W. and D.B. Neal. Lines with 'repro' within the description reflect values for reproduced salts.

Key:
EPNS — electroplated nickel silver   HM — hallmarked

Animals, Figurals, and Novelties

Bird & Berry, Boyd, HJ-933...12.00
Chicken, covered, milk glass, Westmoreland, HJ-949 ....22.00
Duck, covered, clear, red beak, HJ-1012......................................45.00
Duck, pressed, heavy, HJ-4677..45.00
Elk, pulling sleigh, mk 800 silver..650.00
Rabbit, covered, clear, mk Vallerystahl, HJ-3750..........................55.00
Sleigh, Fostoria, ca 1940, HJ-3735...55.00
Squirrel on stump, various colors, Boyd, HJ-929-930, repro..........12.00
Swan, str neck, Crown Tuscan, Cambridge, HJ-936 ....65.00
Swan pulling cart, bl carnival, 1970s repro, HJ-941.....................35.00

Art Glass

Daum Nancy, flowers, mk, HJ-11 ....1,500.00
Daum Nancy, winter scene 1,200.00
Intaglio, animals or butterfly HP, sgn, HJ-159...............................45.00
Lutz, red/wht/gold striping, blown, ftd master, 1½x⅞" 60.00

Monot Stumpf, HJ-19 to HJ-25, ea 125.00
Opal w/vaseline ruffles, HJ-72....110.00
Sowerby, cream opaque, HJ-385....75.00
Steuben, bl, mk Aurene, HJ-14, 2" dia....450.00
Steuben, Calcite, ped ft, HJ-34....225.00
Tiffany, ruffled, sgn LCT Favrille, HJ-32....225.00
Webb, Burmese, ca 1890, HJ-75, 1¾" dia....750.00

Box Sets

Set of 4, blk glass, ca 1930, HJ-4778....75.00
Set of 4, SP, tureen shape, HJ-4777....175.00
Set of 6, SP, HJ-4766....175.00

China and Porcelain

Austria, HP, rnd, mk, HJ-1272, ind....15.00
Belleek, HP, ruffled top, rnd, mk, HJ-1310, ind....35.00
Celery salt, HP, HJ-1720, ind....15.00
Dresden, attached flowers, HJ-1689, ind....45.00
Elfinware, heavy decor, sgn Germany, HJ-1270, ind....30.00
Elfinware, Japan, HJ-1222, ind....12.00
Elfinware, tub, sgn Germany, HJ-1250, ind....30.00
Elfinware, wheelbarrow, sgn Germany, HJ-1244, ind....65.00
Haviland, HJ-1400, ind....35.00
HP, artist sgn, scalloped ft, HJ-1390, ind....20.00
Limoges, HP, rnd, mk, HJ-1275, ind....15.00
Meissen, sq, HJ-1595, ind....60.00
Nippon, celery salt, HJ-1714, ind....12.00
Nippon, HP, HJ-1365, ind....12.00
Nippon, HP, ped ft, HJ-1495, ind....20.00
Nippon, HP floral tub, HJ-1454, ind....20.00
Pickard, sq, HJ-1569, ind....45.00
Royal Bayreuth, animal decor, ped ft, HJ-1666, ind....135.00
Royal Bayreuth, figural claw, HJ-1667, ind....85.00
Royal Copenhagen, HJ-1332, ind....35.00
Royal Worcester, ca 1862, HJ-1861, ind....125.00
Satsuma, ca 1940-60, HJ-1931, ind....25.00

Cut Glass

Amber, ped ft, English, ca 1880, master, pr....275.00
Amber flashed, ped ft, hdls, English, HJ-2060, master....195.00
Amethyst, etched, Hawkes, HJ-2038....75.00
Bl cut to clear, ped ft, HJ-67....150.00
Clear, etched, rnd, Hawkes, HJ-3268 to HJ-3269, ea....35.00
Clear, oval, Hawkes, HJ-3209....50.00
Clear, ped ft, mk Libbey....65.00
Clear, rnd, nappy style, HJ-3170....55.00
Cranberry, rnd, Moser type, HJ-305....95.00
Cranberry, serrated top edge, rnd, HJ-304....65.00
Daisy & Button, oval, HJ-3214....20.00
Daisy & Button, rnd tub, HJ-2853....25.00
Heart, club, spade, dmn, HJ-3033 to HJ-3034, 4 for....195.00
Zippered, HJ-3088 to HJ-3089, ea....15.00

Doubles

Automobile, pressed glass, mk Pontieux, HJ-3764....100.00
European, 800 sterling, figural, cobalt inserts, HJ-2062....150.00
French, cobalt pressed glass, HJ-2086....65.00
French, pressed glass figural, HJ-3777....55.00
French, sterling HM, cobalt insert, ca 1845, HJ-761....150.00
German, HP porc, HJ-1150....45.00

KPM, figural, porc, ca 1860, HJ-1155 to HJ-1156, ea....295.00
KPM, porc, wht w/gold border, HJ-1142....35.00
Meissen, porc, w/hdl, HJ-1169....125.00
Quimper, porc, sgn, HJ-1134....175.00
Quimper, porc, sgn, old, HJ-1129....175.00

Lacy Glass

Barlow/Kaiser 1107, Stippled Bull's Eye, opal, rim chips, 6¾"....175.00
Barlow/Kaiser 1443, Beaded Strawberry Dmn, opal, 3¼", EX+...350.00
Barlow/Kaiser 1457, Shell Foliate, amber, 3" L, VG+....500.00
Barlow/Kaiser 1472, octagonal invt waffle, amethyst, 1x3x2½", G..440.00

Neal BF-1a, basket of flowers, light green, Sandwich, minor chips, $550.00. (Photo courtesy Arman Auctions)

Neal BS-2, Beaded Scroll/Basket of Flowers, lt emerald, 3¼" L, EX..560.00
Neal BT-4d, Lafayette Boat, bl opal, several sm chips, 3½" L..2,465.00
Neal BT-8, Lafayette Boat, bl opal, edge chips, 3½" L....2,700.00
Neal BT-9, Boat, starburst stern, opal purple-bl, 3⅞" L, EX+..1,000.00
Neal CD-2b, Basket of Flowers & Scroll, roughness, w/lid, 3⅛" L.1,765.00
Neal CN-1a, Crown, cobalt, several sm chips, 3" L....1,175.00
Neal CN-1a, Crown, opal, minor edge roughness, 3⅛" L....385.00
Neal LE-3, Lyre, opaque bl, minor flakes, 3" L....2,465.00
Neal NE-1, Basket of Flowers, NE Glass, opaque wht, 3" L, VG..295.00
Neal OG-2, Dmn Heart, dk purple-bl, 1 lg/several sm chips, 3" L.4,995.00
Neal OL-15, Beaded Strawberry Dmn, opaque purple-bl w/lt mottle, EX-..940.00
Neal OL-17, Dmn Star & Scroll, lt amethyst, crack/roughness, 1½"..470.00
Neal OL-32, foliage/blossoms, 2 base chips/roughness, 4" L....940.00
Neal PO-1d, Peacock Eye, cobalt, few rim flakes, 3½" L....1,175.00
Neal RD-22, floral border, rnd, 2 lg chips, 3" dia....140.00
Neal RD-7, Rnd Scroll, amethyst, 2 lg/2 sm chips, 1" crack, 1¾"...470.00
Neal RP-1, floral, rnd w/ped ft, silver-bl, 2x3¼", G....2,235.00
Neal RP-4, floral, ped ft, opaque med bl w/lt mottle, 2x3", G-...645.00
Neal SD-5, Strawberry Dmn, swag border, dk brn-amber, 3" L, G.1,000.00
Neal SL-14, Hairpin, lt opal, 3⅛" L, EX....235.00
Neal SL-14, Shell & Hairpin, fiery opal, 3" L, EX....400.00
Neal SN-1, Stag's Horn, cobalt, flakes/chips (1 lg), 3⅛" L....350.00

Pressed Pattern Glass, Clear

Daisy & Button, LG Wright, HJ-875 to HJ-876, repro, ind, ea....8.00
English Hobnail, HJ-2680, ind....10.00
Euchre, HJ-3018 to HJ-3021, ind, ea....12.00
Faceted, HJ-2906-H....7.50
Heisey, Fancy Loop, HJ-2674, ind....25.00
Heisey, Fandango, HJ-2673, ind....30.00
Heisey, tub, sgn, HJ-2850....25.00
Horseshoe, HJ-3741, ind....30.00
Liberty Bell 1776-1876, HJ-2689, ind....65.00
Moon & Star, ped ft, old, HJ-3044, ind....30.00
Open Plaid, HJ-3567, master....20.00
Panelled Grape Band, HJ-3516, master....35.00
Roman Key, HJ-3582, flint, master....55.00
Sawtooth Circle, HJ-3540, master....30.00
Snail, HJ-2656, ind....22.00

Stippled Bowl, HJ-3589, flint, master 30.00
Tree of Life, 'SALT,' HJ-3581, master 85.00
Tulip w/Sawtooth, HJ-3621, master 35.00
Turtle, HJ-3758, ind 35.00
Washington Centennial, HJ-3510, master......................................55.00

Silver Plate

Babies, Art Nouveau, gold-washed bowl, English, HJ-4283 ....175.00
Boat shape on ped ft, cobalt liner, Am, HJ-661, VG 45.00
Crackle glass in Victorian fr, HJ-4215 to HJ-4217, VG, ea 85.00
Cupid riding dolphin, HJ-4381 ....250.00
Dolphin holds shell, Pairpoint, HJ-4382, master, VG..................125.00
Heart shape, 3 ball ft, Wilcox, worn, HJ-4067 ....15.00
Lattice holder, cobalt liner, HJ-653, ind, VG 20.00
Oval, cranberry liner, ftd lattice holder, HJ-317, VG 65.00
Oval, 4-ftd, clear liner, English, HJ-3945, VG 40.00
Oval lattice, gr liner, Derby, HJ-378, VG......................................90.00
Overshot cranberry glass liner, sq fr, HJ-4215 to HJ-4217, ea 150.00
Rams' heads, rnd, Whiting, HJ-4252, VG 60.00
Rnd bowl w/kangaroo, EPNS, Australia, HJ-4305, VG 40.00
Shell w/dolphin legs, HJ-4278, VG 25.00
Tulip on leaf, Am, HJ-4155, VG..30.00
Victorian holder, clear liner, hdl, HJ-3918, EX 95.00
Wolf-like dogs w/bowl on bk, Meriden, HJ-4322, VG.................150.00

Sterling

Austria-Hungary, cut/flashed bowl, sterling ped, HJ-106 ....250.00
Austria-Hungary, wht opal cut-bk bowl, sterling ped, HJ-138.....175.00
Chinese, mini house w/shaker set, HJ-4743 ....225.00
French, ornate, HM, matching spoon, HJ-3937, ind 125.00
German, basket, ped ft, HM 800, HJ-4228....................................95.00
German, cobalt liner, lattice holder, HJ-642, ind..........................50.00
German, oval, ftd, cobalt liner, HJ-724 ....75.00
German, swan, HH 800, matching spoon, ca 1890, HJ-4299........95.00
Gorham, medallion, ped ft, ca 1870, HJ-3976 ....175.00
Gorham, rnd, ornate lattice, cranberry liner, 1890s, HJ-323 ....185.00
Kerr, Art Nouveau, ped ft, cobalt liner, 1880, HJ-702.................125.00
Reed & Barton, ped ft, ca 1900, HJ-4226, master, pr...................85.00
Russian, chair, HM, dtd, HJ-4737...550.00
Russian, rnd, ftd, HM, ca 1893, HJ-4053, ind 75.00
Steiff, chased, w/pepper, 1918, HJ-4385 ....150.00
Steiff, salt & pepper set, high relief, 1918, HJ-4385 ....150.00
Tiffany, fish, matching spoon, HJ-4324 ....150.00
Viking, HP, HM, matching spoon, HJ-2002 to HJ-2005, ea........125.00

Samplers

American samplers were made as early as the colonial days; even
earlier examples from seventeenth-century England still exist today.
Changes in style and design are evident down through the years. Verses
were not added until the late seventeenth century. By the eighteenth
century, samplers were used not only for sewing experience but also as an
educational tool. Young ladies, who often signed and dated their work,
embroidered numbers and letters of the alphabet and practiced fancy
stitches as well. Fruits and flowers were added for borders; birds, animals,
and Adam and Eve became popular subjects. Later houses and other
buildings were included. By the nineteenth century, the American Eagle
and the little red schoolhouse had made their appearances.

Many factors bear on value: design and workmanship, strength of
color, the presence of a signature and/or a date (both being preferred over
only one or the other, and earlier is better), and, of course, condition.

ABC panels (2)/flowers/shrubs, 1799, 15x11" 700.00
ABC panels/verse/flowers/stars/etc, sgn/1816, MA, 17x15" 1,175.00

ABCs and pastoral scene within flower border, signed, dated 1824, 11½x16" in contemporary bird's-eye maple frame, EX, $550.00.

ABCs, mc on homespun, sgn/1822, 16½x7¼" 500.00
ABCs/#s, mc on linen, sgn/1813, fr: 16½x18½" 495.00
ABCs/#s, 4-line verse/strawberry vines, sgn/1834, 17x17"+fr...700.00
ABCs/#s/verse/vine border, sgn/dtd 1834, 16½x16½", VG.........700.00
ABCs/Adam & Eve/angel/ship/animals/etc, 1803, in 14x15" fr, EX..800.00
ABCs/flower baskets/verse/banner, 1810, 16x13", VG 825.00
ABCs/flowers/flower vase, NH/1841, 17x16", EX.....................1,065.00
ABCs/verse, mc on homespun, 1737, 11x7"+fr, EX 1,100.00
ABCs/verse/potted flower, sgn/1816, EX tiny stitches, 17x13", VG 990.00
Adam & Eve/serpent/flowers/animals on bl-gray, 1805, 15x29"+fr..1,880.00
Cottage scene/verse/flowers/birds/branches, 180s, 21x17" in fr ..885.00
Family record, 4 columns w/picture above ea, sgn/1789-90, 13x16".800.00
House/monument/tree/florals, sgn/1840, EX in 19x21" fr.........1,100.00
Verse/bird on ped/blooming tree, dog/etc, sgn/1842, 27x24", VG .990.00
Verse/birds/trees/etc, sgn/19th C, 14x12"+orig mahog fr 635.00
Verse/buildings/trees/vines/animals/etc, 1840, 27x33" 2,450.00

Sandwich Glass

The Boston and Sandwich Glass Company was founded in 1820 by
Deming Jarves in Sandwich, Massachusetts. Their first products were
simple cruets, salts, half-pint jugs, and lamps. They were attributed with
being one of the first to perfect a method for pressing glass, a step toward
the manufacture of the 'lacy' glass which they made until about 1840.
Many other types of glass were made there — cut, colored, overshot,
hobnail, and opalescent among them. After the Civil War, profits began
to dwindle due to the keen competition of the Western factories which
were situated in areas rich in natural gas and easily accessible sand and
coal deposits. The end came with an unreconcilable wage dispute
between the workers and the company, and the factory closed in 1888.
Today colored Sandwich commands the highest prices.

Our advisor for this category is Elizabeth Simpson; she is listed in
the Directory under Maine.

See also Cup Plates; Salts, Open; Trevaise; other specific types of glass.

Bank, clear, rooster finial, embedded coins, rare, 11" 19,975.00
Bottle, scent; canary, hexagonal w/Star & Punty, panel stopper, 5", VG..275.00
Bowl, Fleur-de-Lys & Thistle, 9"...120.00
Bowl, Princess Feather Medallion, lt amethyst, lacy, chips, 8½".165.00
Bowl, Waffle Dmn Sunburst/Dmn Quilt, rayed base, folded rim, 2x5½"..265.00
Bowl, Waffle Sunburst, bl tint, flared/folded rim, 3¾x6".............800.00
Candlestick, Dolphin, bl, petal socket, dbl-step base (chips), 10"..2,900.00

Candlestick, 2 knobs, step-down base, gallery rim, pewter insert, 9" .385.00
Candlesticks, blown std, sq stepped/lobed base, 10", VG, pr.......295.00
Candlesticks, canary, hex socket, 8-sided std, sq base, 7½", pr....650.00
Candlesticks, canary, hex socket/base, 10", NM, pr..................1,880.00
Candlesticks, clambroth & bl opal, columnar, 9⅜", pr...............600.00
Candlesticks, clambroth w/opaque bl hex petal sockets, 9", VG, pr ..700.00
Candlesticks, cobalt, Loop base, thin hex socket, 6½", EX, pr..6,465.00
Candlesticks, Dolphin, canary, petal socket/2-step sq base, 9", G, pr .1,000.00
Candlesticks, Dolphin, med/dk bl, sq base, minor roughness, 10", pr.9,980.00
Candlesticks, lacy, #1 socket, stepped quatrefoil base, 5½", G, pr.550.00
Candlesticks, lt gr, columnar w/petal sockets, base chips, 9", pr.3,000.00
Candlesticks, sapphire bl, hex socket/base, 7½", VG, pr..........3,800.00
Candlesticks, teal bl, hex sockets/bases, 9", NM, pr 1,900.00
Candlesticks, 3-Dolphin, opal, rnd base, 6½", +eng shade, 11", pr.16,450.00
Celery vase, Scroll & Spiral Rib, rnd ft, scratches, 9⅜x5½" ...1,175.00
Compote, Eagle, ped ft w/lg scrolls & hairy paw ft, lacy, 5½x7", VG.7,300.00
Compote, Horn of Plenty, matching ft, 8½x11", EX 700.00

Compote, lattice design, flint, ca 1950, 8½", $550.00.

Compote, Sawtooth & Prism, canary w/apple gr tone, tall std, ftd, 10" ..475.00
Compote, Shield & Pine Tree, sm 440.00
Creamer, Sunburst-in-Square, cobalt, appl hdl, 4" 3,500.00
Cruet, tam-o'-shanter stopper, cobalt, spiral rib/blown 3-mold, 6½" .300.00
Cruet, tam-o'-shanter stopper, purple-bl, blown 3-mold, 6½" 400.00
Decanter, Ashburton, canary, pewter stopper, 11½", VG.........1,400.00
Decanter, Dmn Quilt, 3 dbl rigaree neck rings, lt stain, 8½" 120.00
Decanter, 3-ring Dmn Quilt pattern, sunburst stopper, 10", NM..150.00
Decanter, 8-flute, cobalt, 2 appl rings, pewter stopper, 12", EX.2,100.00
Dish, Daisy & Peacock Eye, cobalt, lacy, chips/roughness, 6¼" ..750.00
Dish, Dmn Quilt/Sunburst-in-Square, ray base, rolded rim, 4¼"..115.00
Dish, Hairpin, lacy, edge roughness, 8"..295.00
Dish, Hairpin, lacy, oval, edge roughness, 8x10".............................500.00
Dish, Heart & Lyre, lacy, edge chips/roughness, 9½"...................350.00
Dish, Leaf & Gothic Arch, lacy, edge roughness, 8" L 200.00
Dish, Oak Leaf, lacy, edge roughness, 9½".......................................120.00
Dish, Peacock Eye, lacy, shell form, w/hdl, 7¾x9½", NM 5,580.00
Dish, Pineapple & Gothic Arch, lacy, chips/roughness, 9x6½" ..200.00
Dish, Plume & Acorn, amethyst, lacy, edge roughness, 5".........250.00
Dish, Princess Feather Medallion/Basket of Flowers, lacy, 10x9", EX .500.00
Dish, Roman Rosette, lacy, edge chips, 7½" 115.00
Dish, Rose & Thistle, edge roughness, 8¼" 145.00
Dish, Scrolled Acanthus Leaf, sapphire bl, rim roughness, 4" 200.00
Dish, Trefoil & Circular Medallion, lacy, 2x11", G 440.00
Dish, Tulip & Acanthus Leaf, cobalt, lacy, sm chips, 6¼"...........500.00
Dish, Tulip & Acanthus Leaf, lacy, minor roughness, 10½"........385.00
Dram, Dmn Quilt & Sunburst on ribbed base, ftd, 2⅞" 325.00
Flask, Dmn & Sunburst, 5½"...3,290.00
Hat, Sunburst-in-Square, cobalt, folded rim, 2¼-2⅝" 750.00
Hat salt, Swag, Dmn & Rib, blown 3-mold, 2⅜".........................200.00
Jar, pomade; bear form, blk, mk Niagara Falls 1895, 4½", VG....500.00
Jar, pomade; bear form, blk, 2 sm chips, 3⅝" 265.00

Lamp, amethyst, Loop, octagonal baluster stem, sq base, 10", EX.1,045.00
Lamp, amethyst, paneled w/hexagonal base, 8½", NM, pr.......4,995.00
Lamp, blown bulb font, lacy acanthus leaf octagonal base, 9", VG, pr.600.00
Lamp, canary, waisted loop font w/monument base & wafer, 11", NM.1,100.00
Lamp, cobalt, Loop, octagonal std/sq base, 8½", EX 1,800.00
Lamp, cobalt w/clear cup plate base (EX), twisted ribs, cone shape, 7"..22,300.00
Lamp, conical font, grapevine cut on sq stepped base, 8", VG, pr.700.00
Lamp, cut flutes/swag & tassel on urn font, quatrefoil base, 12", pr.1,400.00
Lamp, dk gr, octagonal font/std, sq base, 10x3", VG 1,880.00
Lamp, frosted/cut bulb font w/grapevines, stepped sq base, 12", EX, pr.825.00
Lamp, 4-Printie Block, amethyst, 11", G, pr............................3,800.00
Pitcher, Cornucopia, minor imperfections, 8"..........................2,585.00
Pitcher, fluted/hooped, blown 3-mold, dk/med bl, 4⅝"............2,585.00
Pitcher, trefoil & rib design on appl blown-molded ft (VG), 5¾".350.00
Plate, Dmn Point, lt bl-gr, lacy, 6"...1,295.00
Plate, Heart & Sheaf, Xd heart center, lacy, edge roughness, 7" .200.00
Plate, Peacock Feather (Eye) & Thistle, stippled/scalloped rim, 8"..120.00
Plate, Waffle Sunburst, folded rim, 6½" 265.00
Smoke bell, opal wht w/bl rim 6x5"..150.00
Spill/spoon holder, Quarter Dmn, peacock bl, pontil, 5⅛" 800.00
Sugar bowl, Gothic Arch, amethyst, lacy, w/lid, 5½x5", VG...3,800.00
Sugar bowl, Gothic Arch, sapphire bl, lacy, w/lid, 5½x5", EX.1,880.00
Sweetmeat, Peacock Eye, grape border, lacy, dome lid 5x6", VG.1,290.00
Tumbler, Dmn Quilt, bbl form, 2⅞" 265.00
Tumbler, Dmn Quilt, bl tint, bbl form, 3¼"................................350.00
Tumbler, Dmn Quilt, 2¾"...175.00
Tumbler, Dmn Quilt, 3¼"...400.00
Tumbler, Sunburst, 2⅝"..235.00
Tumbler, tavern; Gothic Arch, dbl spray of leaves, 3" 325.00
Tumbler, Waffle Sunburst, barrel form, 2¾"................................380.00
Vase, Bigler, canary, gauffered rim/octagonal std/sq base, 11", EX, pr.2,585.00
Vase, Bigler, cobalt, octagonal dbl-knob std, sq base, 11x4½", EX.3,800.00
Vase, bright cobalt, 6-side waterfall base, paneled trumpet form, 11".1,650.00
Vase, Elongated Loop, opal, hex base, sm chips/crack, 4¾x3".1,765.00
Vase, Loop, canary, hexagonal std, rnd base (EX), 10" 825.00
Vase, T'print & Loop, amethyst, ftd, deeply scalloped, 6", EX+ ..1,880.00
Vase, T'print & Loop, ftd, slight underfill, 5" 500.00
Vase, Tulip, amethyst, wafer at ft attachment, petal rim, 10", EX.2,200.00
Vase, Tulip, emerald gr, 2 sm base chips, 10" 5,290.00
Vase, Tulip, peacock gr, octagonal base, 10", pr.....................14,000.00
Vase, Twisted Loop, amethyst, gauffered rim, hex std, rnd base, 9x5"..2,700.00
Vase, 3-Printie Block, amethyst, expanded rim, octagonal std, 10", EX.2,585.00
Vase, 3-Printie Block, canary, gauffered rim, octagonal std, 9", VG.1,000.00
Vase, 4-Printie Block, canary, base corner/edge chips, 11", pr.1,175.00
Vase, 4-Printie Block, cobalt, gauffered rim/hex base, 12", EX, pr..5,580.00

Santa Barbara Ceramic Design

Established in 1976 by current director Raymond Markow (after three years of refining his decorative process), Santa Barbara Ceramic Design arose with less auspicious beginnings than the 'Ohio' potteries — no financial backing and no machinery beyond that available to ancient potters: wheel, kiln, brushes, and paint.

The company produced intricate, colorful, hand-painted flora and fauna designs on traditional pottery forms, primarily vases and table lamps. Although artistically aligned with turn-of-the-century art potteries, the techniques used were unique and developed within the studio.

Vibrant glaze stains with wax emulsion were applied by brush over a graduated multicolor background, then enanced by elaborate sgraffito detailing on petals and leaves. In the early 1980s, a white stoneware body was incorporated to further brighten the color palette, and during the last few years sgraffito was replaced by detailing with a fine brush.

Early pieces were thrown. Mid-1980 saw a transition to casting, except for experimental or custom pieces. Artists were encouraged to be creative and often given individual gallery exhibitions. Custom orders were welcomed, and experimentation occurred regularly; the resulting pieces are the most rare and seldom appear today. Limited production lines evolved, including the Collector Series that featured an elaborate ornamental border designed to enhance the primary design. The Artist's Collection was a numbered series of pieces by senior artists, usually combining flora and fauna.

The company's approach to bold colors and surface decoration influenced many contemporary potters and inspired imitation in both pottery and glass during the craft renaissance of the 1970s and '80s. Several artists successfully made use of the studio's designs and techniques after leaving. Authentic pieces bear the artist's initials, date and 'SBCD' marked in black stain and, if thrown, the potter's inscription.

Markow employed as many as three potters and twelve decorators at a given time. The ware was marketed through craft festivals and wholesale distribution to art and craft galleries nationwide. An estimated 100,000 art pottery pieces were made before a transition in the late 1980s to silk-screened household and garden items, which remain in production today.

Though less than thirty years old, Santa Barbara Ceramic Design's secondary market has seen upwards of one thousand pieces change hands; these are often viewed as bargains compared to their Rookwood and Weller Hudson counterparts. For artist/potter marks from 1979 to 1989, e-mail johntasha@aol.com or visit the craft café at www.johnguthrie.com. Our advisor is John Guthrie; he is listed in the Directory under South Carolina.

Bowl, #5107, birds, Alvaro Suman, 1978, 10"	135.00
Lamp, #5117, iris, Itoko Takeuchi, 1983, 9"	325.00
Lamp, #5118, iris, unsgn, 1984, 11"	195.00
Lamp, #5119, bouquet, Itoko Takeuchi, 1984, 15½"	595.00
Lamp, #5119, iris/gladiola, Laurie Linn Ball, 1982, 15½"	495.00
Lamp, #5119, morning glory, Lauri Linn Ball, 1986, 15½"	295.00
Lamp, #5119lg, bouquet, Laurie Lynn, 1982, 17"	495.00
Lamp, #5130, lily of the valley, Itoko Takeuchi, 1984, 7"	128.00
Lamp, #5130, poppy, Laurie Linn Ball, 1986, from $125 to	165.00
Lamp, #7101, apple blossom, Gary Ba-Han, 1984, 13", pr	650.00
Lamp, #7105, iris, Dorie Knight-Hutchinson, 1984, 17"	335.00
Lamp, #7115, fuchsia/bird, Dorie Knight-Hutchinson, 1984, 16"	485.00
Lamp, #7115, tulip, Itoko Takeuchi, 1987, 16"	585.00
Lamp, #7125, calla lily, Itoko Takeuchi, 1984, 18"	375.00
Lamp, #7125, tulip, Itoko Takeuchi, 1988, 18"	300.00
Lamp, oil; #1102, iris, Alvaro Suman, 1980, 6½"	75.00
Lamp, oil; #1102, swan, Barbara Rose, 1978, 6½"	72.50
Mug, #5121, tiger lily, William Pacini, 1984, 5", from $65 to	85.00
Pitcher/goblet, #AC, landscape, Mark MacKay, 1978, 9¼"	128.00
Plate, #5114, iris, Michelle Foster, 1981, 7"	90.00
Platter, #4118, oriental, Itoko Takeuchi, 1984, 15"	245.00
Vase, #5010cs, tulip, Anne Collinson, 1980, 5"	120.00
Vase, #5101, abstract, John Guthrie, 1984, 7"	80.00
Vase, #5101, design?, Shannon Sargent, 1982, 7"	185.00
Vase, #5101, fortnight lily, Kat Corcoran, 1980, 7"	100.00
Vase, #5101, frog, Peggy Brogan, 1980, 7"	140.00
Vase, #5101, iris, Mary Favero, 1980, 7"	90.00
Vase, #5101, mice, Nancy Looker, 1978, 4¼"	155.00
Vase, #5101, morning glory, Laurie Linn, 1982, 6½"	155.00
Vase, #5101, pansy, Zetta, 1982, 6"	100.00
Vase, #5101, tiger lily, Gary Ba-Han, 1983, 6½"	175.00
Vase, #5101, water lily, Kat Corcoran, 1980, 5¾"	82.50
Vase, #5101r, night blossom, Itoko Takeuchi, 1984, 6"	130.00
Vase, #5102, daffodil, Laurie Cosca, 1982, 9"	125.00
Vase, #5102, design?, Gary Ba-Han, 1982, 10"	265.00
Vase, #5102, trumpet lily, Laurie Cosca, 1980, 9"	125.00

Vase, #5103, experimental, Laurie Linn Ball, 1985, 8"	105.00
Vase, #5103, orchid, Allison Atwill, 1981, 8½"	280.00
Vase, #5103, watercolor, Itoko Takeuchi, 1986, 8"	125.00
Vase, #5103cs, poppy, Laurie Cosca, 1982, 9"	250.00
Vase, #5133, iris, Shannon Sargent, 1984, 20"	1,500.00
Vase, #6112, fuchsia/bird, Dorie Knight-Hutchinson, 1984, 10"	425.00
Vase, #6114-a, pansy, Dorie Knight-Hutchinson, 1984, 8"	275.00
Vase, #7116, columbine, Suzanne Tormey?, 1980, 14"	380.00
Vase, #7116, iris, Dorie Knight, 1981, 12"	280.00
Vase, #7116cs, bouquet, Itoko Takeuchi, 1986, 12"	325.00
Vase, #7116cs, carnation, Michelle Foster, 1982, 12"	445.00
Vase, #7116ss, tiger/tiger lily, Shannon Sargent, 1984, 12"	650.00

Sarreguemines

Sarreguemines, France, is the location of Utzschneider and Company, founded about 1800, producers of majolica, transfer-printed dinnerware, figurines, and novelties which are usually marked 'Sarreguemines.' In 1836, under the management of Alexandre de Geiger, son-in-law of Utzschneider, the company became affiliated with Villeroy and Boch. During the 1850s and 1860s, two new facilities with modern steam-fired machinery were erected. Alexandre's son Paul was the next to guide the company, and under his leadership two more factories were built — one at Digoin and the other at Vitry le Francois. After his death in 1931, the company split but was consolidated again afterthe War under the name of Sarreguemines – Digoin – Vitry le Francois. Items marked St. Clement were made during the period from 1979 to 1982, indicating the group who owned the company for that span of time. Today the company is known as Sarreguemines - Batiment.

Bank, cat's head, red ribbon collar, St Clement, 4¾"	225.00
Candle holder, poodle w/top hat, 6"	450.00

Pitcher, portrait and gold on royal blue, gold basketweave near base, 8½", $295.00.

Casserole, mallard, w/lid, 8½x7x11"	365.00
Compote, fruit/leaves motif, 4¾x9½"	150.00
Cup, mush; swirled brn mocha on cream, 1850s, 3½x4½", EX	115.00
Dish, floral/butterfly on basketweave, #2279/7, w/lid, 5¾x8⅝"	230.00
Egg cup, pheasant, 20th C	40.00
Jar, tobacco; lady holding cigars sits behind desk, #1584, 7x4"	1,000.00
Pin tray, Dutch girl w/umbrella & basket, #531P/1089, 8½x4"	210.00
Pitcher, alligator, looking up w/open mouth, #3543G, 9¼"	830.00
Pitcher, bamboo & leaf design, #654, 8½"	165.00
Pitcher, bearded man's face, #3323	300.00
Pitcher, Black man's face, wht collar w/red bow tie, #3884, 6½"	1,300.00
Pitcher, chef's face w/bl headband, #3181, 7x6"	275.00
Pitcher, dbl face, #2313, 8¾"	425.00
Pitcher, duck, St Clement, 13"	50.00

Pitcher, elephant, seated, gray, #4470, 10" **720.00**
Pitcher, John Bull's face, #3257, 7½" **210.00**
Pitcher, lion's face, cream & brn w/bl int, #4020, 7" **1,100.00**
Pitcher, parrot, mc, ca 1925, 8¾" **1,500.00**
Pitcher, parrot, St Clement, 13" **175.00**
Pitcher, rooster, St Clement, 11" **175.00**
Pitcher, watering can/fruit/garden tools transfer, brn on wht, 8x6" .**180.00**
Plate, child's; cherubs playing transfer, 8¼" **105.00**
Plate, console; bl w/strawberry & blossom border, 2⅝x12" **135.00**
Plate, grapes/vines/floral, #3, 1890s, 7¾" **110.00**
Plate, oyster; 6 oyster shell indents, 9¼" dia **400.00**
Stein, porc, boar/Waidmann's Heil, dog hdl, pewter lid, #2911, 1-L.**1,650.00**
Stein, stoneware, relief: fish & sausage, cat hdl, #2668, 1-L........**150.00**
Tureen, oblong pumpkin on gr leaves, 2-pc, 6¾x13x9½" **365.00**
Vase, cherub on open-mouth fish's bk, #112L, 10x5⅜" **400.00**
Vase, dk gr limbs/bl blossoms on wht, #4051K, 1910s, 8½" **150.00**
Walking stick stand, stork w/frog in mouth, sm rpr, 40"...........**4,000.00**

Satin Glass

Satin glass is simply glassware with a velvety matt finish achieved through the application of an acid bath. This procedure has been used by many companies since the twentieth century, both here and abroad, on many types of colored and art glass. See also Mother-of-Pearl; Webb.

Bowl vase, pk to ivory w/mc fish/lotus, frilly rim, 4 amber ft, 7x7" .**865.00**
Cracker jar, bl, reverse swirls, SP lid w/bail, 8" **140.00**

Cracker jar, pink with embossed shells and hand-painted flowers, silver-plated lid and bail, $100.00; Matching creamer and sugar bowl, $100.00.

Ewer, bl w/floral, crystal ruffled rim, pinched hdl, 9½", pr **220.00**
Ewer, rose to pk w/bl floral, 12¾" **100.00**
Finger bowl, pink/cream, +6" yel underplate, clear-edge ruffles/folds.**355.00**
Rose bowl, pk to wht, shells emb around base, 5" H....................**110.00**
Tumbler, wht w/pk int, 3½" **60.00**
Vase, cream to pk, child in tree HP in amber, ovoid w/can neck, 7½".**260.00**
Vase, gold to lt yel w/bee, ferns & berries, elongated gourd, 12".**180.00**
Vase, pk to wht, elongated gourd shape, 7¾" **90.00**
Vase, pk to wht, gold leaves/dragonfly, gourd shape, English, 6" ...**75.00**
Vase, plum w/wht int, wht flowers, 13" **75.00**
Vase, turq to peach w/wht floral branch, 4-sided ovoid, English, 12".**125.00**
Vase, yel w/wht int, gold branches/insects, ovoid, English, 11"...**120.00**

Satsuma

Satsuma is a type of fine cream crackle-glaze pottery or earthenware made in Japan as early as the seventeenth century. The earliest wares, made at the original kiln in the Satsuma province, were enameled with only simple florals. By the late eighteenth century, a floral brocade (or nishikide design) was favored, and similar wares were being made at other kilns under the direction of the Lord of Satsuma. In the early part of the nineteenth century, a diaper pattern was added to the florals. Gold and silver enamels were used for accents by the latter years of the century. During the 1850s, as the quality of goods made for export to the Western world increased and the style of decoration began to evolve toward becoming more appealing to the Westerners, human forms such as Arhats, Kannon, geisha girls, and samurai warriors were added. Today the most valuable pieces are those marked 'Kinkozan,' 'Shuzan,' 'Ryuzan,' and 'Kozan.' The genuine Satsuma 'mon' or mark is a cross within a circle — usually in gold on the body or lid, or in red on the base of the ware. Character marks may be included.

Caution: Much of what is termed 'Satsuma' comes from the Showa Period (1926 to the present); it is not true Satsuma but a simulated type, a cheaper pottery with heavy enamel. Collectors need to be aware that much of the of the 'Satsuma' today is really Satsuma style and should not carry the values of true Satsuma. Our advisor for this category is Clarence Bodine; he is listed in the Directory under Pennsylvania.

Bottle, saki; 2 cartouches of Samurai, 1800s, 6" **115.00**
Bowl, moriage decor, int: 3 rakans, Meiji, 1868-1911, 6¼".........**350.00**
Bowl, 2 rakans & 2 children, 1868-1911, 8½" **450.00**
Charger, Samurai warriors around campfire, phoenix bird band, 12"..**195.00**
Cup & saucer, Samurai warrior scenes, dragon hdl, Kyoto **125.00**
Figurine, Daikoku seated, 1868-1911, 4"....................................**485.00**
Incense burner, bamboo & pines, pierced silver lid, 19th C, 5½".**2,185.00**
Incense burner, faces over floral, dog finial, hdls, Kyoto, 6".....**1,200.00**
Incense burner, garden scene cartouches, slotted lid, 3x5" **900.00**
Incense burner, geisha/attendants, gold dragon hdls, Meiji, 12".**3,500.00**
Palace urns, fruit clusters/scenes, appl rose buds, 64", pr........**12,500.00**
Plate, roosters, Meiji, 1868-1911, 8¾" **800.00**
Vase, butterflies/geishas/florals/bands, gourd shape, 4⅝", pr.....**1,100.00**
Vase, chrysanthemums & fence, Kin Sei, lobed, 1868-1911, 18½".**4,300.00**
Vase, divinities in Chinese costumes, 1868-1911, 9½", pr..........**850.00**
Vase, Earth Above Heaven Below, enamel/gilt relief, Kyoto, 13".**650.00**
Vase, Empress/Arhat motif, bulbous, MIJ, 1920s, 25", pr **3,500.00**
Vase, floral/garden scenes, bulbous, late, 12½" **330.00**
Vase, garden scene w/women & brocade, baluster, 1868-1911, 12"..**975.00**
Vase, geisha scenes, gold hdls, enameled neck w/gold, 1890s, 5"..**700.00**
Vase, gilt/enameled irises, bulbous, hdls, Meiji, 9½"....................**195.00**
Vase, kiku no mon & chrysanthemums, Sengyoku, 1868-1911, 7½"..**750.00**
Vase, landscape, millefiori bands, Yabu Meizan, Meiji, mini, pr...**4,885.00**
Vase, mons & dragons, 100 Rakan pattern body, 1868-1911, 5".**500.00**
Vase, people/landscapes/birds/flowers, globular, Yabu Meizan, 3¾"..**5,500.00**
Vase, wht swirling bands w/butterflies/dragons/etc, bulbous, 12x9".**800.00**
Vase, 4 figural panels, wht w/blk outlines on patterned ground, 19" .**2,500.00**

Scales

In today's world of pre-measured and pre-packaged goods, it is difficult to imagine the days when such products as sugar, flour, soap, and candy first had to be weighed by the grocer. The variety of scales used at the turn of the century was highly diverse; at the Philadelphia Exposition in 1876, one company alone displayed over three hundred different weighing devices. Among those found today, brass, cast-iron, and plastic models are the most common. Fancy postal scales in decorative wood, silver, marble, bronze, and mosaic are also to be found.

A word of caution on the values listed: these values range from a low for those items in fair to good condition to the upper values for items in excellent condition. Naturally, items in mint condition could command even higher prices, and they often do. Also, these are retail prices that suggest what a collector will pay for the object. When you sell to a dealer, expect to get much less. The values noted are averages taken from various auction and other catalogues in the possession of the Society members. Among these, but not limited to, are the following: Joel L. Malter & Co., Inc., Encino, CA; *Auktion Alt Technic,* Auction Team, Koln, Germany.

For those seeking additional information concerning antique scales we recommend *Scales, A Collector's Guide,* by Bill and Jan Berning (Schiffer). You are also encouraged to contact the International Society of Antique Scale Collectors, whose address can be found in the Directory under Clubs, Newsletters, and Catalogs. Visit the club website at www.isasc.org.

Key:
ap — arrow pointer
bal — balance
bm — base metal
br — brass
Brit — British
Can — Canadian
Col — Colonial
CW — Civil War
cwt — counterweight
Engl — English
eq — equal arm
Euro — European
FIS — Fairbanks Infallible Scale Co.

h — hanging
hcp — hanging counterpoise
hh — hand held
l+ — label with foreign coin values
lb w/i — labeled box with instructions
lph — letter plate or holder
pend — pendulum
PP — Patent Pending
st — sterling
tt — torsion type
ua — unequal arm
wt — weight

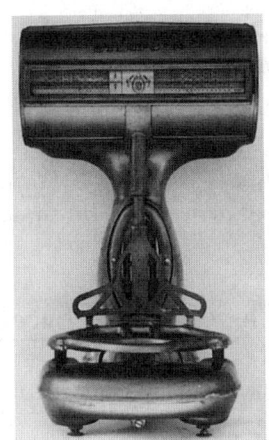

Stimpson single stem barrel scale, original decals and labels, Stimpson Computing Scale Co., Louisville, KY, 1910, 30x19", EX, $165.00.

Analytical (Scientific)

Am, eq, mahog w/br & ivory, late 1800s, 14x16x8", $200 to......**400.00**

Assay

Am, eq, mahog box w/br & ivory, plaque/drw, 1890s, $400 to.**1,000.00**

Coin: Equal Arm Balance, American

Blk japanned metal, eagle on lid, late 19th C, $300 to **400.00**
Col, oak 6-part box, Col moneys, Boston, 1720-75, $600 to ...**1,200.00**
Post Col to CW, oak 6-part box, l+, 1843, $400 to..................**1,000.00**

Coin: Equal Arm Balance, English

Charles I, wooden box w/11 Brit wts, 1640s, $900 to...............**1,500.00**
1-pc wood box, rnd wts, label, Freeman, 1760s, $250 to **450.00**
6-pc oak box, coin wts label, Thos Harrison, 1750s, $200 to......**450.00**

Coin: Equal Arm Balance, French

Solid wood box, 12 sq wts, J Reyne, Bourdeau, 1694, $400 to.**1,000.00**
Solid wood box w/recesses, 5 sq wts, A Gardes, 1800s, $250 to ..**800.00**
1-pc oval box, nested/fractional wts, label, 18th C, $250 to **400.00**
1-pc oval box, no wts, label of Fr/Euro coins, 18th C, $150 to ...**250.00**
1-pc walnut box, nested wts, Charpentier label, 1810, $275 to...**675.00**

Coin: Equal Arm Balance, Miscellaneous

Amsterdam, 1-pc box, 32 sq wts, label, late 1600s, $850 to.....**2,500.00**
Cologne, full set of wts & full label, late 1600s, $1,200 to.......**2,800.00**
German, wood box, 13+ wts beneath main wts, label, 1795, $650 to ..**900.00**

Counterfeit Coin Detectors, American

Allender Pat, lb w/i, cwt, Nov 22, 1855, 8½", $350 to **650.00**
Allender PP, rocker, labeled box, cwt, 1850s, 8½", $450 to **750.00**
Allender PP, rocker, no box or cwt, 1850s, 8½", $250 to **375.00**
Allender PP, space for $3 gold pc, lb w/i, cwt, 1855, $350 to......**750.00**
Allender PP, space for $3 gold pc, no box or cwt, 1855, $275 to..**375.00**
Allender Warranted, rocker, no box or cwt, 1850s, 8½", $350 to .**475.00**
McNally-Harrison Pat 1882, rocker, cwt, JT McNally, $275 to..**500.00**
McNally-Harrison Pat 1882, rocker, cwt & box, FIS, $400 to **750.00**
McNally-Harrison...1882, rocker, CI base, no cwt/box, $250 to .**400.00**
Thompson, Z-formed rocker, Berrian Mfg, 1877 Pat, $175 to.....**350.00**

Counterfeit Coin Detectors, Dutch

Rocker, Ellinckhuysen, brass, +copy of 1829 Patent, $250 to **350.00**

Counterfeit Coin Detectors, English

Folding, Guinea, self-rising, labeled box, 1850s, $175 to.............**225.00**
Folding, Guinea, self-rising, wood box/label, ca 1890s, $125 to ..**175.00**
Folding, Guinea, self-rising, wooden box, pre-1800, $175 to **275.00**
Rocker, simple, no maker's name or cb, end-cap box, $85 to **125.00**
Rocker, w/maker's name & cb, end-cap box, $120 to **150.00**

Egg Scales/Graders, 1930s – 1940s

Acme Egg Grade, Specialty Mfg St Paul MN, aluminum, from $30 to.**50.00**
Brower Mfg Save All, sheet steel (cheaply made), Steelyard bal, $50 to.**75.00**
Jiffy Way, Minneapolis MN, steel w/mc bands, pend bal, common, $30 to.**50.00**
Oakes Mft Tipton IN, pend bal, sheet steel, adjustable stop, $30 to .**50.00**
Reliable, rocker bal, all brass, wooden base, 2½x13¾", $75 to ...**100.00**
Unique..., Specialty Mfg, sheet steel/aluminum, pend bal, $30 to.**50.00**

Postal

In the listings below an asterisk (*) was used to indicate that any one of several manufacturers' or brand names might be found on that particular set of scales. Some of the American-made pieces could be marked Pelouze, Lorraine, Hanson, Kingsbury, Fairbanks, Troemner, IDL, Newman, Accurate, Ideal, B-T, Marvel, Reliance, Howe, Landers-Frary-Clark, Chatillon, Triner, American Bank Service, or Weiss. European/U.S.-made scales marked with an asterisk (*) could be marked Salter, Peerless, Pelouze, Sturgis, L.F.&C., Alderman, G. Little, or S&D. English-made scales with the asterisk (*) could be marked Josh. & Edmd. Ratcliff, R.W. Winfield, S. Mordan, STS (Samuel Turner, Sr.), W.&T. Avery, Parnall & Sons, S&P, or H.B. Wright. There may be other manufacturers as well.

Brit/Can Bal, eq, br or CI on base, *, 4"-15", $100 to **750.00**
Engl Bal, eq/Roberval, gilt or st, on stand, *, 3"-8", $500 to....**2,500.00**

Engl Bal, eq/Roberval, plain to ornate, *, 3"-8", $100 to 2,500.00
Engl Spring, candlestick, br or st, *, 3½"-15", $100 to 500.00
Engl Spring, CI, br or NP fr, Salter, ozs/lbs, 7"-10", $25 to..........200.00
Engl Steelyard, ua, 1- or 2-beam, h lph, *, 4"-15", $100 to......1,500.00
Euro pend, gravity, br, CI or NP fr on base, oz/grams, $75 to 350.00
Euro pend, gravity, 2-arm, bm, br or NP, *, 6"-9", $50 to 300.00
Euro/US Spring, br or NP, pence/etc, h or hh, *, 4"-17", $10 to.100.00
US Pend, gravity, metal, pnt face, ap, hcp, sm, $20 to 100.00
US Spring, pnt base metal, *, 2½"-8", $10 to 80.00
US Spring, pnt bm, *, mtd on inkstand, 2½"-8", $75 to 250.00
US Spring, pnt bm, rnd glass-covered face, *, 8"-10", $25 to......100.00
US Spring, SP, oblong base, *, 2½"-8", $100 to.........................200.00
US Spring, st, oblong base, *, 2½"-8", $200 to 500.00
US Steelyard, ua, CI, *, 5"-13" beam, 4½"-12" base, $25 to.......100.00

Schafer and Vater

Established in 1890 by Gustav Schafer and Gunther Vater in the Thuringia region of southwest Germany, by 1913 this firm employed over two hundred workers. The original factory burned in 1918 but was restarted and production continued until WWII. In 1972 the East German government took possession of the building and destroyed all of the molds and the records that were left.

You will find pieces with the impressed mark of a nine-point star with a script 'R' inside the star. On rare occasions you will find this mark in blue ink under glaze. The items are sometimes marked with a four-digit design number and a two-digit artist mark. In addition or instead, pieces may have 'Made in Germany' or in the case of the Kewpies, 'Rose O'Neill copyright.' The company also manufactured items for sale under store names, and those would not have the impressed mark.

Schafer and Vater used various types of clays. Items made of hard-paste porcelain, soft-paste porcelain, jasper, bisque, and majolica can be found. The glazed bisque pieces may be multicolored or have an applied colored slip wash that highlights the intricate details of the modeling. Gold accents were used as well as spots of high-gloss color called jewels. Metallic glazes are coveted. You can find the jasper in green, blue, pink, lavender, and white. New collectors gravitate toward the pink and lavender shades.

Since Schafer and Vater made such a multitude of items, collectors have to compete with many cross-over collections. These include shaving mugs, hatpin holders, match holders, figurines, figural pitchers, Kewpies, tea sets, bottles, naughties, etc.

Reproduction alert: In addition to the crudely made Japanese copies, some English firms are beginning to make figural reproductions. These seem to be well marked and easy to spot. Our advisor for this category is Joanne M. Koehn; she is listed in the Directory under Minnesota.

Bottle, blue and white, man holding glass, hat stopper, 6¼", $165.00. (Photo courtesy Joanne M. Koehn)

Ashtray, head w/fly on cheek, open mouth, holes in head, #2500, 3½"..260.00
Ashtray, head w/holes & open mouth, in tux, 3x2½" 175.00
Box, wht w/pk grapes & gr leaves, bear w/guitar finial, 5" 85.00
Creamer, German maid holds pitcher in both hands, 3½" 65.00
Figurine, Dollar Princess Wanted, tall man w/winged Kewpie, 6½"..85.00
Figurine, Katzenjammer Kids, Mama/Hans/Fritz, bsk, 5x4" 460.00
Figurine, little boy carrying pitcher, #9009 ....100.00
Figurine, Waiting for the Tide, man in kilt/hat w/pipe, ft swing .110.00
Hatpin holder, Oriental ladys sitting w/legs Xd, 4⅜"..................300.00
Nodder, And Dad Said, Be a Man, boy in derby hat w/cigar, 4" .255.00
Pitcher, cat figural, orange w/wht around mouth, 4¾x5" 160.00
Pitcher, cow in yel coat w/wht collar, tail hdl, #1191, 4½" 135.00
Pitcher, googly-eyed schoolboy in orange shirt, gr pants, 3" 75.00
Pitcher, witch, wht w/bl wash, 4⅛" 90.00
Powder jar, woman's face, purple w/gold trim, rnd, 4" 135.00
Rose bowl, wht cherubs in bl band w/ram head hdls, #5660, 3¼".230.00
Toothpick holder, sailor w/lg bathing beauty in arms, 3¼"............65.00
Tray, Fat Family, dad/mom/son/daughter/dog, #1110, 2¾x6" 350.00

Scheier

The Scheiers began their ceramics careers in the late 1930s and soon thereafter began to teach their craft at the University of New Hampshire. After WWII they cooperated with the Puerto Rican government in establishing a native ceramic industry, an involvement which would continue to influence their designs. In the '50s they retired and moved to Mexico; they currently reside in Arizona.

Bowl, aqua drip on speckled charcoal, teal accents at rim, #89, 7" .300.00
Bowl, brn & beige gloss, tapering to ftd base, 9¼" 265.00
Bowl, half human/half fish figures, tan/bl/gr mottle, 4½x8" 500.00
Bowl vase, stylized figures frieze, taupe/gr, 9" H.....................1,035.00
Charger, woman holding child aloft, cream/mauve, 16" 750.00
Vase, frieze of females, alternately upright/inverted, brn, 16" ..6,325.00
Vase, rose to cream speckled, ftd ovoid, 5 3/48"..........................300.00
Vase, serpents & women, w/sm upside-down men, brn/mocha, 16x8".1,750.00

Schlegelmilch Porcelain

For information about Schlegelmilch Porcelain, see Mary Frank Gaston's book, *R. S. Prussia Popular Lines* which addresses R. S. Prussia molds and decorations and contains full-color illustrations and current values. Mold numbers appearing in some of the listings refer to this book. Assume that all items described below are marked unless noted otherwise.

R.S. Germany

In 1869 Reinhold Schlegelmilch began to manufacture porcelain in Suhl in the German province of Thuringia. In 1894 he established another factory in Tillowitz in upper Silesia. Both areas were rich in resources necessary for the production of hard-paste porcelain. Wares marked with the name 'Tillowitz' and the accompanying 'R.S. Germany' phrase are attributed to Reinhold. The most common mark is a wreath and star in a solid color under the glaze. Items marked 'R.S. Germany' are usually more simply decorated than R.S. Prussia. Some reflect the Art Deco trend of the 1920s. Certain hand-painted floral decorations and themes such as 'Sheepherder,' 'Man With Horses,' and 'Cottage' are especially valued by collectors — those with a high-gloss finish or on Art Deco shapes in particular. Not all hand-painted items were painted at the factory. Those with an artist's signature but no 'Hand Painted' mark indicate that the blank was decorated outside the factory.

Bowl, Cottage scene II on brn tones, 10½"......................................300.00
Bowl, lilies of the valley on wht satin, RSP mold #12a, 9½" 400.00
Bowl, lt & dk pk roses, 3 knob ft, 2⅜x7½"....................................75.00
Bowl, nappy, wild roses w/gold, 1 hdl, 7¾x5"................................75.00
Box, flowers on spade shape, 3½x4"...150.00
Cake plate, Dogwood & Pine, w/dk gr border, 10"........................70.00
Cake plate, flower clusters & roses on gr, RSP mold #205 ....200.00
Cake plate, mc roses cluster, pierced hdls, RSP mold #25a, 11"..275.00
Cake plate, peonies & snowballs w/gold, 11"................................75.00
Cake plate, poinsettias & mixed flowers, pierced hdls, 10½" 80.00
Celery tray, yel-to-wht roses, 14x6½"...55.00
Coffeepot, wht flowers on gr to brn, 9"..300.00
Creamer, daffodils on pearl lustre, 4½"...45.00
Creamer & sugar bowl, Lettuce mold, pearl lustre, w/lid.............200.00
Hair receiver, wht flowers, pierced hdls, 2½" 75.00
Humidor, mc flowers w/gold, blk border w/stenciling, emb stars, 8".650.00
Plate, lilies of the valley w/lg gold leaves, 6⅜" 35.00
Plate, sandwich; dk & lt pk lilies, center hdl, unmk, 4x10½" 95.00
Plate, wht peonies on shaded gr, 8⅜" 50.00
Plate, wht-robed lady w/flowers, lilies on red w/gold, 8½" 250.00
Relish, orange poppies w/gold, hdls, 9½x4¼" 70.00
Sugar bowl, wht roses on gr to brn, w/lid, 4⅝".............................45.00
Tankard, mc mums, slim, RSP mold #537, 13¾" 550.00
Tray, gold stenciled floral border, hdls, 8½x4¼"............................90.00
Vase, Peace Bringing Plenty (2 ladies), gold stencil, 13"..........2,000.00
Vase, peonies & snowballs, RS Suhl mold #3, 8¼" 300.00

R.S. Poland

'R.S. Poland' is a mark attributed to Reinhold Schlegelmilch's factory in Tillowitz, Silesia. It was in use for a few years after 1945.

Cup & saucer, dainty pk flowers on wht to gr, 2½" H 60.00
Ewer, windmill scene, ornate hdl, RSG mold, 5½".......................500.00
Vase, Chinese pheasants, slim neck, RS Suhl mold #15, 9" 1,000.00
Vase, lg open flower on shaded brn, salesman's sample, 4⅝".......250.00
Vase, orange roses, wide gold band at top, shouldered, 7½" 175.00
Vase, Sheepherder scene, gold hdls, 6" 500.00

R.S. Prussia

Art porcelain bearing the mark 'R.S. Prussia' was manufactured by Reinhold Schlegelmilch in the early 1900s in a Germanic area known until the end of WWI as Prussia. The vast array of mold shapes in combination with a wide variety of decorations is the basis for R.S. Prussia's appeal. Themes can be categorized as figural (usually based on a famous artist's work), birds, florals, portraits, scenics, and animals.

Bowl, Castle scene, Sawtooth mold, oval, 13x8" 1,000.00
Bowl, Lebrun I portrait w/Tiffany bronze, mold #29, unmk, 10"..1,400.00
Bowl, Lebrun II portrait, irid Tiffany finish w/gold, mold #87, 10".1,400.00
Bowl, mc poppies on pearl lustre, Lily mold, 10½" 400.00
Bowl, mc roses in wht urn, Tiffany finish, mold #300, 10¼".......400.00
Bowl, mc roses w/gr border & gold, mold #25, 10¼".................475.00
Bowl, Mill scene, scalloped w/1 pierced hdl, mold #181, 10" 750.00
Bowl, pk & wht floral spray (dainty), Sunflower mold, #31, 10½" ..250.00
Bowl, poppies & daisies w/gold jewels, Square & Jewel mold, 11"...350.00
Bowl, Récamier portrait on lt to dk gr w/gold, mold #30, unmk, 7".900.00
Bowl, roses & snowballs on pk w/gold, mold #329, 10½"...........350.00
Bowl, 4 Seasons reserves at border, roses center, mold #88, 10¾".2,800.00
Cake plate, mixed flowers, dk gr border, Rope Edge mold, 10½" .275.00
Cake plate, Potocka portrait w/gold flowers, mold #29, 9½" ...1,600.00
Cake plate, roses in hanging basket, mold #115, 10¼"................350.00
Cake plate, Summer portrait w/gold, Fleur-de-Lis mold, 10½"..1,800.00

Cake plate, Swans on the Lake w/gazebo, mold #341, 10" 550.00
Candlestick, carnations on lav, mold #853....................................400.00
Celery tray, poppies w/gold, Fleur-de-Lis mold, 14" L 300.00
Celery tray, reflecting water lilies w/cobalt & gold, mold #304, 12" L..400.00
Celery tray, Summer portrait w/Mill scene, mold #25, 12x5¾".2,200.00
Charger, roses w/ladies' portraits (5) along rim, mold #14, 12½".1,800.00
Chocolate pot, Castle scene, Ball Foot mold, 9½" 1,200.00
Chocolate pot, mc roses w/gold, mold #608, 10" 700.00
Chocolate pot, poppies, Ball Foot mold, 9½", ...475.00
Chocolate pot, roses/snowballs on pk w/jewels/gold, mold #645, 10½".700.00
Cracker jar, Autumn portrait, gold trim, mold #628, 7"..........2,600.00
Cracker jar, Cottage scene, Point & Clover mold, 7¼" 650.00
Cracker jar, mc roses w/gold, mold #644, 8"...............................450.00
Cracker jar, snowbird scene, mold #641, unmk, 7½" 1,400.00
Creamer & sugar bowl, Castle scene/Mill scene, mold #644, w/lid.650.00
Creamer & sugar bowl, Summer portrait, Carnation mold, w/lid .1,600.00
Demitasse pot, Dice Throwers/Melon Eaters boy, jewels/gold, 9¾".3,500.00
Ferner, lilies-of-the-valley on pearl lustre, mold #879, 6½".........350.00
Mustard pot, roses on watered silk finish w/gold carnations, mold #526.250.00
Pitcher, cider; Melon Eaters, unpnt jewels, mold #82, 6x6" 3,500.00
Pitcher, lemonade; Canterbury bells, mold #579, 6½".................400.00
Plate, Mill scene on turq-gr, mold #90, 8½" 500.00
Plate, Old Man in the Mountain, Popcorn mold, 8½" 650.00
Plate, Winter (lady in wht) tapestry, mold #343, 9" 2,000.00
Plate, Winter portrait, Stippled Floral mold, 8½" 1,200.00
Talcum shaker, wht snowballs, mold #801, 4½"...........................225.00
Tankard, Lebrun I portrait w/gold, mold #517, 15" 2,400.00
Tankard, mc roses w/wht shadow flowers, mold #526, 12½" 850.00

Tankard, Récamier portrait on yellow to green with gold stenciled leaves, mold #525, unmarked, 13", from $1,800.00 to $2,000.00. (Photo courtesy Mary Frank Gaston)

Tankard, Swans on Lake w/Swallows, mold #570, 11" 1,200.00
Tea set, Dice Throwers, unpnt jewels/cobalt/gold, mold #643, 3-pc.3,200.00
Tea set, Récamier portrait on Tiffany bronze, mold #517, 3-pc.2,500.00
Teapot, Castle scene, mold #576, 5"...700.00
Toothpick holder, mc roses w/gold, mold #642, 2½".....................275.00
Tray, pk roses, Stippled Floral mold w/gold, 11½x7" 300.00
Tray, Spring portrait, Carnation mold, pierced hdls, rectangular .2,200.00
Vase, Dice Throwers, bulbous, mold #907, unmk, 6"...................550.00
Vase, Melon Eaters, opal jewels, gold hdls, mold #932, 9¼" 3,400.00
Vase, Mill scene w/swallows, bottle form, mold #909, 5½" 650.00
Vase, Old Man in the Mtn & Swans on Lake, hdls, mold #940, 11".1,000.00
Vase, Peacock on rust, bottle form, mold #909, 6"......................750.00
Vase, Turkeys, shouldered, mold #910, 8¼" 700.00
Vase, Winter portrait on pk, gold hdls/trim, mold #900, 10" ...2,000.00

R.S. Suhl, Suhl

Porcelains marked with this designation are attributed to Reinhold Schlegelmilch's Suhl factory.

Bowl, mixed flowers, 9-scallop w/gold, RSP mold #181, 11" **500.00**
Box, pk roses w/gold, egg shape, rare, 5⅞" **1,200.00**
Cup & saucer, Copenhagen souvenir (Danish words under design) ..**100.00**
Ewer, Josephine portrait w/gold scrolling, mold #1, 9" **1,000.00**
Ewer, Peacock scene, mold #1, 7" **1,100.00**
Plate, roses, yel to wht on ivory to brn, pierced hdl, 10" **140.00**
Powder jar, pk roses, 5½" dia **225.00**
Vase, chrysanthemums on ivory to brn w/gold, mold #2, 7" **375.00**
Vase, figures at sea side, includes 'bk' view, mold #7, 8⅝" **1,400.00**
Vase, hummingbirds on wht satin, angle uptrn hdls, mold #3, 9½".**4,500.00**
Vase, lilies w/lg leaves on blk w/gold, mold #2, 7⅛" **450.00**
Vase, mixed flowers, urn form, ornate gold hdls, mold #12, 13½".**700.00**
Vase, roses, pk & wht on blk w/gold hdls, mold #4, 9¼" **500.00**
Vase, roses, pk stylized on shaded brn, mold #5, 10⅝" **400.00**
Vase, roses, wht on gray to ivory, mold #10, salesman's sample, 3⅛".**250.00**

R.S. Tillowitz

R.S. Tillowitz-marked porcelains are attributed to Reinhold Schlegelmilch's factory in Tillowitz, Silesia.

Bowl, berry; mc roses, gold rim, mold #6, unmk, 5⅝" **50.00**
Bowl, divided; mc rose, center hdl, RSP mold #23, unmk, 14½" L..**500.00**
Bowl, mc flowers, gr & gold scrolling at rim, mold #1, unmk, 10½".**300.00**
Bowl, nappy, wht flowers w/pk on cobalt, 1 hdl, mold #7 ....**600.00**
Bowl, pk & yel roses w/buds, red & gold at border, mold #1, 10½"..**275.00**
Bowl, yel roses, bl border w/gold Greek keys, RSP mold #29, 10½".**375.00**
Butter dish, mixed poppies & flowers w/gr & gold, mold #6, 5x7½".**1,100.00**
Cake plate, dainty flowers, cobalt & gold border, mold #4, 11½" .**600.00**
Cake plate, mixed floral, bl/wht flowers on cobalt rim, mold #8, 11".**275.00**
Cake plate, shaded bl flowers w/gold in ivory, mold #11, 9½" **400.00**
Chocolate pot, mc roses/gold stencil, bl border, mold #6, unmk, 10".**450.00**
Chocolate pot, purple to yel poppies on yel to gr, ftd, unmk, 9½"..**475.00**
Chocolate pot, rose clusters, cobalt & floral border, mold #8......**300.00**
Chocolate pot, sm pk roses w/gold border, ornate hdl, mold #15, 10".**550.00**
Coffeepot, pk & wht roses, bl-gr border w/shadow flowers, 9½".**500.00**
Cracker jar, gr & wht snowballs, RSP mold #657, unmk, 7x6" **250.00**
Cracker jar, mc flowers w/gold on cobalt, mold #14 ....**500.00**
Creamer & sugar bowl, floral on shaded rose pk, mold #12, w/lid ..**300.00**
Cup & saucer, flowers & gold on wht, mold #7, 2" H **100.00**
Match box, cobalt flowers w/gold on wht, 3½x1½" **125.00**
Plate, poppies & wht flowers, gr floral border, mold #6, 9½" **325.00**
Tankard, Mill scene w/autumnal colors, #7, 14" **1,600.00**
Tankard, poppies on shaded gr w/gold, mold #7, 14¾" **800.00**
Vase, Queen Louise portrait w/cobalt & gold, urn form, mold #20..**1,800.00**

Schneider

The Schneider Glass Company was founded in 1914 at Epinay-sur-seine, France. They made many types of art glass, some of which sandwiched designs between layers. Other decorative devices were applique and carved work. These were marked 'Charder' or 'Schneider.' During the '20s commercial artware was produced with Deco motifs cut by acid through two or three layers and signed 'LeVerre Francais' in script or with a section of inlaid filigrane. Our advisor for this category is Don Williams; he is listed in the Directory under Missouri.

See also Le Verre Francais.

Bowl, clear w/2 appl geometric hdls, mottled gr disk ft, 4¾x5¼".**750.00**
Bowl, cluthra, pk to wht, 4½" **210.00**
Bowl, orange to amber mottle, 13", on iron ped base w/berries.**1,765.00**
Bowl, yel/clear mottle on bl stem, ped ft, 7x10½" **150.00**
Shade, mottled frosted red & orange, 6⅜", 3⅞" aperture **70.00**

Vase, amber to red w/2 appl rings around long neck, bun ft, 17", pr .**2,940.00**
Vase, cameo floral/lattice stems, amethyst on lav/yel mottle, rnd, 5"..**800.00**
Vase, clear w/internal gr & wht opaque streaks, cylinder neck, 13¼"..**1,500.00**
Vase, gray w/rose/yel/wine mottle suggesting flowers, ftd U-form, 12"..**945.00**
Vase, orange/amethyst/yel/wht mottle in clear ground, Ovington, 9".**700.00**

Schoolhouse Collectibles

Schoolhouse collectibles bring to mind memories of a bygone era when the teacher rang her bell to call the youngsters to class in a one-room schoolhouse where often both the 'hickory stick' and an apple occupied a prominent position on her desk. Our advisor for this category is Kenn Norris; he is listed in the Directory under Texas.

Atlas, Goode's School, Rand McNally, hardcover, ca 1946, 286-pg, VG..**15.00**
Badge, School Safety Committee, emb brass, 1½" W, VG **8.00**
Bell, ball metal w/wood hdl, pnt traces, 6½" **40.00**
Bell, blk-pnt steel w/brass clapper, wood hdl, 6½x4" **45.00**
Bell, bronze w/wood hdl, wrought-iron striker, 1880s, 6⅜x3⅜" **85.00**
Book, Bill & Susan, Under the Tree, 1945, EX **30.00**
Book, Bob & Susan, We See, ca 1940s, VG **8.00**
Book, Dick & Jane, Elson Basic Readers, pre-primer, 1930s, VG.**200.00**

Book, Dick and Jane, Fun With, basic reader, Scott Foresman and Co., 1940, VG, $12.50.

(Photo courtesy Kenn Norris)

Book, Dick & Jane, Fun w/Our Family, 1962, EX **80.00**
Book, Dick & Jane, Now We Read, 1965, NM.............................**50.00**
Book, Dick & Jane, Our New Friends, 1946, G **60.00**
Book, Dick & Jane, The New We Look & See, 1951, EX..........**125.00**
Book, Dick & Jane, The New We Work & Play, 1951, EX.........**125.00**
Book, Dick & Jane, Think & Do Book, workbook, 1952, NM **65.00**
Book, Dick & Jane, We Come & Go, 1940 1st ed, EX **115.00**
Book, Dick & Jane, We Look & See, 1st pre-primer, 1946, EX ..**175.00**
Book, Dilly Dally Book, Favorite School Songs, 1948, 14-pg, G.....**7.00**
Book, Don & Peggy, Come & See, Bobbs-Merrill, 1959, NM.......**55.00**
Book, Harper's Third Reader, blk/wht woodblock prints, 1888, G .**15.00**
Book, Health Secrets, blk/wht photos, Macmillan, 1944, G............**6.00**
Book, McGuffey's Eclectic Reader, 50 blk/wht engravings, 1896, EX.**125.00**
Book, Mitchell's School Geography, 1851 3rd revised ed, EX.....**100.00**
Book, Over Hill & Plain, Silver Burdette, 3rd reader, 1947, EX **8.00**
Book, Story of Ancient Times, Laidlaw, middle grades, 1937, VG.**10.00**
Book, Webster's Common School Dictionary, 1892, 422-pg, VG .**25.00**
Box, tin litho, My...Tote Box, w/contents, Ohio Art, 2½x9x5", NM ..**15.00**
Chair, pine w/bl traces, 2-slat bk, bolts to floor, 13x16x11" **72.00**
Chalk box, litho on wood, Alpha...Dustless Crayon..., EX............**19.00**
Class ring, High School, initials, 10k gold, 1955 ....**65.00**
Desk, chair w/flat surface at right arm, storage below, pnt wood ...**45.00**
Desk, oak, seat before desk top on iron fr, EX.............................**165.00**
Globe, Webber Costello, Chicago IL, Pat 1908, 12" dia, 22" overall, EX..**150.00**
Inkwell, porc, Paris Ont High School, 4" **75.00**
Letterman's sweater w/trophy patch, wool knit, ca 1954, VG **15.00**
Lunch box, heavy cb, riveted corners, leather strap, 7½x5½".......**35.00**

Magazine, High School Life, Chicago, Mar 1914, EX....................25.00
Medal, Indiana Central South School Music Assn, w/red ribbon, VG..5.00
Pencil sharpener, automobile form, sheet metal, Japan, 1¾".........28.00
Pencil sharpener, celluloid, pelican, Japan, 3"............................130.00
Pencil sharpener, nickel, pan style, mtd on wood base, 1800s.....660.00
Pencil sharpener, saxaphone, gold pnt, Germany..........................35.00
Pendant, Broadway School etched on 10k gold, T-bar, ⅞x1¾" 55.00
Pennant, Upper Perkiomen High, bl felt, 1950s, 26", EX..............25.00
Photo, building & children outside, ca 1900, 5x6¼", +mat & fr.....15.00
Photo, high school football team, 1919, 7½x9½", +mat & fr........50.00
Picture Cards, Dick & Jane, 1930s, set of 14, EX............................92.00
Postcard, VA high school building, postmk 1918, VG.....................6.00
Spelling board, ca 1930, EX...35.00
Tablet, Davy Crockett, w/horse & grizzly bear, 25¢ price, EX 15.00
Yearbook, 1925, EX 10.00

Pencil Boxes

Among the most common of school-related collectibles are the many classes of pencil boxes. Generally from the period of the 1870s to the 1940s, these boxes were made in hundreds of different styles. Materials included tin, wood (thin frame and solid hardwood) and leather; fabric and plastics were later used. Most pencil boxes were in a basic, rectangular configuration, though rare examples were made to resemble other objects such as rolling pins, ball bats, nightsticks, etc. They may still be found at reasonable prices, even though collectors have recently taken a keen interest in them. All boxes listed below are in very-good to near-mint condition. Our advisors for pencil boxes are Sue and Lar Hothem, authors of *School Collectibles of the Past*; they are listed in the Directory under Ohio.

Cb, advertising, Kinney Shoes, giant pencil type, 11¾" 35.00
Japanned w/butterflies, Eberhard Faber #324, 3¾x8"....................45.00
Leather, School Companion, emb w/snap closure, Kreko, 2x5⅜x4⅛"..22.50
Mickey Mouse & Wise Little Hen, Dixon USA, 1930s, 10½", EX...75.00
Pnt wood, dk gr w/mustard panels, sliding lid, 8" L 550.00

Popeye pencil box, 1934, EX, $65.00. (Photo courtesy Dunbar Gallery)

Tin, advertising on inside, lift-top, gr & gold box, 7¾" 15.00
Tin, Scholar's Companion, Pat 1874, 7¼" 85.00
Wood fr, School Companion, Octagon Soap premium, 7⅞".........40.00
Wooden, dvtl butternut w/orig orange-red pnt, sliding lid 140.00
Wooden, Nursery Rhymes, litho scenes, 7⅞"...............................30.00
Wooden, 1-level, slide-top, 9¼" 35.00
Wooden, 2-level, roses lid decal, lock on lower compartment, 9½"..40.00
Wooden, 4-level, 1 compartment ea, floral decor, 9¼"..................70.00

Schoop, Hedi

In the 1940s and 1950s one of the most talented artists working in California was Hedi Schoop. Her business ended in 1958 when a fire destroyed her operation. It was at that time that she decided to do free-lance work for other companies such as Cleminson Clay. Schoop was probably the most imitated artist of the time and she answered some of those imitators by successfully suing them. Some imitators were Kim Ward, Ynez, and Yona. Schoop was diversified in her creations, making items such as shapely women, bulky-looking women and children with fat arms and legs, TV lamps, and animals as well as planters and bowls. Schoop used many different marks including the stamped or incised Schoop signature and also a hard-to-find sticker. 'Hollywood, Cal.' or 'California' were occasionally used in conjunction with the Hedi Schoop name. For further information we recommend *The Encyclopedia of California Pottery, Second Edition*, by Jack Chipman; he is listed in the Directory under California.

Bowl, shell shape, ivory w/gold, blk int, 12" 45.00
Candle holder, tan & gray, twisted base forms 2 arms..................40.00
Cigarette holder/ashtray, duck figural, head holder, body tray, 5"..45.00
Covered box, triangular w/French poodle finial, 7⅛x8⅛"...........110.00
Figurine, lady carrying separate basket, 11", 12½", pr.................240.00
Figurine, lady holding side of wht dress (open) w/basket on head, 12"..110.00
Figurine, lady in bl flowing gown, flower holder at hip, 12½", pr.175.00
Figurine, lady in wht w/platinum on collar/cuffs/ft, 10" 100.00
Figurine, lady w/gr top, wht dress, holding bouquet & vase, 9" 90.00
Figurine, lady w/poodle carrying lg hollow basket, 9½"...............135.00
Figurine, Oriental couple, he w/flute, she w/hands out, 12", pr...200.00
Figurine, Oriental couple, he w/2 baskets, she w/fan, 12", pr 125.00
Figurine, Oriental man w/blk & wht shirt/hat, wht pants, 12"......65.00
Figurine, peasant couple in gr w/red stripes, ea w/basket, 13", pr..180.00
Figurine, rooster, mc, 13" 100.00
Figurine, Tyrolean girl holds dress out as planter, 11".................100.00
Planter, lady w/book reading book w/2 vases behind, 9"...............60.00
Planter, rooster, mc, 13" 85.00
Plate, Scottie dog image, ⅞x7½" sq 65.00
Soap holder, lady holding tray w/other hand at hip, 10½" 100.00
Tray, butterfly shape, rose w/gold edge..45.00
Vase, horse figural, pk w/wht tail & mane, gr saddle, 9¾"............90.00

Schramberg

The Schramberg factory was founded in the early 19th century in Schramberg Wurttemberg, Germany. The pieces most commonly seen are those made by Schramberger Majolika Fabrik (SMF) dating from 1912 until 1989.

Some pieces are stamped with the pattern name (i.e. Gobelin) and the number of the painter who executed it. The imprinted number identifies the shape. Marks may also include these names: Wheelock, Black Forest, and Mepoco.

Perhaps the most popular examples with collectors are those from the Gobelin line. Such pieces have a gray background with as many as ten other colors used to create that design. For example, Gobelin 3 pieces will be painted with green and orange leaves and yellow eyes along with other colors specific to that design.

Little is known of the designers who worked for Schramberg; however, Eva Zeisel was employed at the factory for nearly two years starting in the fall of 1928. Her duties included design, production, and merchandising. Our advisors for this category are Ralph Winslow who is listed in the Directory under Missouri and Ann Burton who is listed under Michigan.

Cake plate, turq w/yel & gr water lilies, 11½" +6, 7½" plates.......60.00
Condiment set, s&p/oil/vinegar/mustard, red & bl floral w/yel center.25.00
Cookie jar, gray w/mc Art Deco motif, Wheelock, 7½x5¼".........95.00
Jam pot, wht w/bl lattice, w/lid, 2x4"...15.00
Liqueur set, decanter/tray/6 cups, chalet in mtns scene, ca 1987 ..75.00
Plate, chalet in mountain, #1412, 9" dia 20.00

Plate, Gobelin 3, 8" 20.00
Teapot, brn geometric pattern, att Eva Zeisel, 5½x9¾" 300.00
Vase, amber & blk floral on wht, bulbous, sgn, 6x6" 50.00
Vase, chalet in mtns scene, #5785, 3¼" 30.00
Vase, Gobelin 6, w/flower frog, 5x5" 70.00

Scouting Collectibles

Boy Scouts

Scouting was founded in England in 1907 by a retired Major General, Lord Robert Baden-Powell. Its purpose is the same today as it was then — to help develop physically strong, mentally alert boys and to teach them basic fundamentals of survival and leadership. The movement soon spread to the United States, and in 1910 a Chicago publisher, William Boyce, set out to establish Scouting in America. The first World Scout Jamboree was held in 1911 in England. Baden-Powell was honored as the Chief Scout of the World. In 1926 he was awarded the Silver Buffalo Award in the United States. He was knighted in 1929 for distinguished military service and for his Scouting efforts. Baden-Powell died in 1941. For more information you may contact our advisor, R.J. Sayers, author of *Guide to Scouting Collectibles*, whose address (and ordering information regarding his book) may be found in the Directory under North Carolina. (Correspondence other than book orders requires SASE please.)

Award, Distinguished Service; orange/wht ribbon w/silver antelope, EX .260.00
Badge, eagle under red/wht/bl ribbon w/Be Prepared banner, MIB ..160.00
Bank, Scout; American Flag design, tin, 1940s, 3¼x2" dia, EX 90.00
Belt & buckle, XII WJ, leather w/brass buckle, 1967, NMIB 55.00
Belt buckle, 1969 NJ, metal, EX 60.00
Book, Boy Scouts of America Handbook for Boys, 1921, VG 89.00
Book, Handbook for Scoutmasters, 2nd edition, blk cover, 1920, VG-..30.00
Book, Order of the Arrow Handbook, 1st ed, 1948, VG+...........110.00
Book, Prayers for Use in the Brotherhood of Scouts, 1945, 5x4", EX..40.00
Bookends, Be Prepared w/logo, pnt compo wood, 1960s, 5x4", EX, pr .70.00
Bookends, Official Boy Scout, 1940-52, pr.....................................15.00
Bugle, Official; brass, Rexcraft, orig bag, 1950s, EX 90.00
Canteen, metal in canvas bag, Diamond Brand, 1950s, 2x7½" dia..15.00
Cards, Scout Law; depicts laws in action, set of 12, 1920s, EX ...115.00
Coin, Boy Scouts of America 1910-1960, NM.................................15.00
Cuff links, red/gr/wht enameled logo, snap style, ⅝" dia, pr..........25.00
Diary, 1913..125.00

Drum, scouts along border, tin, Pat 1908, small, $125.00. (Photo courtesy R.J. Sayers)

Flag, Troop, notched end, 1930-40 ....45.00
Flag, Troop 42, 1969 NJ, Miami Valley Council, w/logo, 52x68".145.00
Hat, Official Leader's Hat Boy Scouts of Canada on label, felt, EX ..70.00
Lariat, Official; Boy Scouts...National Supply Service, 1950s, EXIB.75.00

Manual, Sea Scout Patrol, #3728A, 32 pgs, 1931, VG 22.00
Map, Philmont Scout Ranch, waterproof, 1956, 38x28", EX 55.00
Medal, Gardening; Every Scout...Soldier, w/gr ribbon, 1917, EX..1,200.00
Neckerchief, Fellowship Conference Order of the Arrow, 1941, VG .310.00
Neckerchief, 1935 National Jamboree, 30x30", EX 155.00
Note paper, Boy Scouts...Official, w/letterhead, #5018, 1918-24 era..10.00
Patch, Be Prepared, bl & gold logo w/gold wreath, 1920s, EX 170.00
Patch, Eagle Scout, 1st issue, EX...275.00
Patch, National Staff, gold wreath, 1960, 3" dia 20.00
Patch, Order of the Arrow Conference, felt, 1st issue, 1948, EX ..50.00
Patch, Special Long Cruise Region XII-1950, wht on blk, 2½" dia ..55.00
Patch, Waumegesako Council, red & wht.................................275.00
Patch, 1929 World Jamboree, VG 375.00
Patch, 5 Year Veteran, bl, gold & red on wht, vintage, EX 75.00
Pen, scout emblem, Parker Bros, 1940s.....................................28.00
Pennant, Region 4 Sea Scout Rendezvous, felt, EX 55.00
Pennant, 1937 NJ logo w/Boy Scouts in wht on maroon, EX 115.00
Pin, Lone Scout Totem Pole Lodge, 1915-24 ....50.00
Plaque, Souvenir of Attendance, 1959 WJ, wood slab, EX............85.00
Pocketknife, 4-blade w/stag hdl, leather pouch, shackle, 1930-40, rare..75.00
Record, Dan Beard Talks With Scouts, w/book, 1940....................65.00
Ring, Eagle Scout, eagle on Be Prepared banner over red/bl enamel.155.00
Sash, BSA Merit Badge; 14 embr patches, 1930s, EX..................150.00
Stationery set, World Jamboree, 1963 ....10.00
Sweatshirt, 2-tone brn/heather, 1950s, sz med, EX 75.00
Tent, Miner's; canvas, w/poles & orig bag, 1962, EX 100.00
Yearbook, 1916-32, VG, ea, from $9 to 12.00

Girl Scouts

Collecting Girl Scout memorabilia is a hobby that is growing nationwide. When Sir Baden-Powell founded the Boy Scout Movement in England, it proved to be too attractive and too well adapted to youth to limit its great opportunities to boys alone. The sister organization, known in England as the Girl Guides, quickly followed and was equally successful. Mrs. Juliette Low, an American visitor to England and a personal friend of the father of Scouting, realized the tremendous future of the movement for her own country, and with the active and friendly cooperation of the Baden-Powells, she founded the Girl Guides in America, enrolling the first patrols in Savannah, Georgia, in March 1912. In 1915 National Headquarters were established in Washington, D.C., and the name was changed to Girl Scouts. The first National Convention was held in 1914. Each succeeding year has shown growth and increased enthusiasm in this steadily growing army of girls and young women who are learning in the happiest ways to combine patriotism, outdoor activities of every kind, skill in every branch of domestic science and high standards of community service. Today there are over 400,000 Girl Scouts and more than 22,000 leaders. Mr. Sayers is also our Girl Scout advisor.

Alarm clock, travel; Broadway #215, fold-out, emblem on case, NMIB.40.00
Banner, Girl Scouts w/logo in gold on gr, satin-type material, 30" .35.00
Book, Brownie Friendship; 2 pigtailed girls w/dogs on cover, 1950s, EX..35.00
Book, Campward Ho, for self-supporting camps, 1920, EX..............8.00
Book, Lone Girl Scout Adventurer; soft cover, 84 pgs, 1928, EX..40.00
Book, Merit Badge; Wild Flower Finder, leather w/2 rings, 1920s, EX.40.00
Booklet, Blue Book of Rules, Girl Scout Captains, 1919, 7½x5", EX..50.00
Booklet, Charting the Course of a Girl Scout Mariner Ship, 6x9", EX..60.00
Booklet, 1947 Summer Activities for Girl Scouts of Chicago, 15 pgs .25.00
Camera, Girl Scout Vest Pocket, Kodak, matching case, 1929-34, EX..175.00
Catalog, Girl Scout Equipment, Spring 1953, 48 pgs, VG+ 35.00
Earmuffs, blk w/wht logos, felt, 28", EX....................................45.00
First aid kit, Official; tin w/canvas carrying bag, 1939, NM 60.00
Flashlight, angled neck, gr plastic w/logo, NM (VG box) 30.00
Hat, gr w/gr bow & blk Girl Scouts, 1950s, 10" dia, MIB..............40.00

Pin, Brownie; logo, gold pnt steel, EX **70.00**
Pin, Wing Scout, logo w/wings, silver colored, unmk, 1960s, EX.**165.00**
Planter, Girl Scout by tent, ceramic, Sampson Imports, Japan, EX .**45.00**
Poster, Girl Scout Promise, 14x22", EX **50.00**
Trivet, 50th Anniversary, brn pnt metal, 1962, 7x7", EX **35.00**
Umbrella, gold w/gr tip & hdl w/2 cvd daisies, wht logo, EX **40.00**

Scrimshaw

The most desirable examples of the art of scrimshaw can be traced back to the first half of the nineteenth century to the heyday of the whaling industry. Some voyages lasted for several years, and conditions on board were often dismal. Sailors filled the long hours by using the tools of their trade to engrave whale teeth and make boxes, pie crimpers (jagging wheels), etc., from the bone and teeth of captured whales. Eskimos also made scrimshaw, sometimes borrowing designs from the sailors who traded with them.

Beware of fraudulent pieces; fakery is prevalent in this field. Many carved teeth are of recent synthetic manufacture (examples engraved with information such as ship's or captain's names, dates, places, etc., should be treated with extreme caution) and have no antique or collectible value. A listing of most of these plastic items has been published by the Kendall Institute at the Bedford Whaling Museum in New Bedford, Massachusetts. If you're in doubt or a novice collector, it's best to deal with reputable people who guarantee the items they sell. Our advisor for this category is John Rinaldi; he is listed in the Directory under Maine.

See also Powder Horns.

Busk, corset; whalebone, hearts/stars/compass/obelisk, 14" **1,800.00**
Busk, corset; whalebone, ships/floral wreath, 19th C **1,350.00**
Busk, eagle/pinwheels/foliage/compass stars/heart, blk/red wash, 12".**550.00**
Cane, whale ivory hdl w/3 types ropework cvg, 2½x33" mahog shaft..**750.00**
Cane, whalebone, ornate cvg w/crown knot finial, EX patina, 34" .**2,800.00**
Crimper, serpent heads, nude woman hdl, EX detail, 7½" **2,585.00**
Dagger, whale tooth hdl, 8" steel blade, inscr/dtd 1816, 12", EX..**490.00**
Ditty box, whalebone w/inlaid teak lid, mid-19th C, 2x5¾x4", EX..**3,450.00**
Fid, whalebone, eng anchor/incised lines, EX patina, 1830-40, 13".**650.00**
Jagging wheel, scroll/foliate hdl motif, sm crack/stain, 5" **350.00**
Jawbone section, whaling scene, eagle w/anchor/whale/lance on bk, 9x10".**3,000.00**
Porpoise jaw, Scottish Highlander w/sword & shield, 19th C, 10¾"..**325.00**
Tool holder, whalebone, trn center w/beehive top, ca 1875, 6x4½" .**3,500.00**
Tooth, Am ship, bk: sailor w/flowers/leaves, ca 1850, 6¼x2½"..**2,350.00**
Tooth, bearded man, checked jacket, striped pants, cracks, 5" **765.00**
Tooth, Goddess of Liberty/eagle/flags, mc, age cracks, 5¾" **2,585.00**
Tooth, man's portrait/lighthouse, bk:Lady Liberty, red/blk, 6".....**2,350.00**
Tooth, mother walrus w/baby on floe, Eskimo, 7x2¾" **1,575.00**
Tooth, sailor w/sabre, bk: man in tropical setting, 7", EX..........**5,585.00**
Tooth, sailor's farewell/mother & daughter, banknote portraitist, 6"..**19,500.00**
Tooth, several figures/buildings (1 burning), red wash, 6", EX **2,585.00**
Tooth, ship/ornate border, bk: men fight 6 whales, att E Burdett, 6" .**45,000.00**
Tooth, sperm whale, 6" **1,000.00**
Tooth, Victorian lady w/Hette on bk w/scrollwork, pre-1900s, 5"...**675.00**
Tusk, polar bear & seal w/cribbage board in center, Eskimo, 14½"..**595.00**
Whalebone, sailing scene w/2 boats & main ship in bkground, 9½x3" ..**595.00**

Sebastians

Prescott W. Baston first produced Sebastian Miniatures in 1938 in his home in Arlington, Massachusetts. In 1946 Baston bought a small shoe factory in Marblehead, Massachusetts, and produced his figurines there for the next thirty years. Over the years Baston sculpted and produced more than seven hundred fifty different pieces, many of which have been sold nationwide through gift shops. Baston and The Lance Corporation of Hudson, Massachusetts, consolidated the line in 1976 and actively promoted Sebastians nationally. Many of Baston's commercial designs, private commissions, and even some open line pieces have become very collectible. Aftermarket price is determined by three factors: 1) current or out of production status, 2) labels, and 3) condition. Copyright dates are of no particular significance with regard to value.

Mr. Baston died in 1984, and his son Prescott 'Woody' Baston, Jr. continued the tradition by taking over the designing. To date Woody has sculpted over two hundred fifty pieces of his own. After numerous changes in the company that held manufacturing and distribution rights for Sebastions, Woody and his wife Margery are now sculpturing and painting the Sebastian Miniatures out of their home in Massachusetts. By personally producing the pieces, Sebastions are the only collectible line that is produced from design to finished product by the artist. Sebastian Miniatures have come full cycle. Our advisor for this category is Jim Waite; he is listed in the Directory under Illinois.

Aunt Polly, #7330, 2¾" **25.00**
Bob Crachit & Tiny Tim **30.00**
Building Days (girl or boy), ea **40.00**
Clown, 3" **45.00**
Dame Van Winkle, club pc **40.00**
Family Picnic **50.00**
Family Reading Aloud, #7345 ....**45.00**
George Washington w/Cannon, 3⅜" **30.00**
John F Kennedy, 2⅜" **30.00**
Johnny Appleseed, 3¾" **40.00**
Judge Thatcher, #7338, 3" **35.00**
Mayflower, #7333, 3⅞" **35.00**
Pilgrims **35.00**
Skipping Rope **30.00**
Snowy Days (girl or boy), ea **40.00**
Speak for It **30.00**
Tom Bowline Ashore, 3⅛" **30.00**
Uncle Sam, #7344, 4⅛" **20.00**
Weaver, #7337, 2¼" **30.00**
Will Rogers, 2¾" **40.00**
Yankee Sea Captain, #132 ....**35.00**

Sevres

Fine-quality porcelains have been made in Sevres, France, since the early 1700s. Rich ground colors were often hand painted with portraits, scenics, and florals. Some pieces were decorated with transfer prints and decalcomania; many were embellished with heavy gold. These wares are the most respected of all French porcelains. Their style and designs have been widely copied, and some of the items listed below are Sevres-type wares.

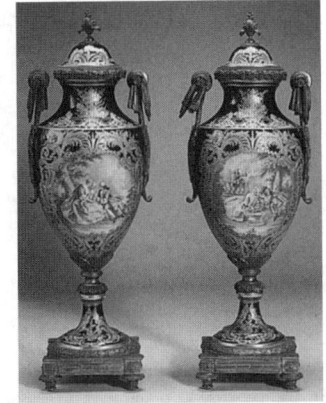

Urns, courting couple, signed Lebelle, reverse: landscape, all on cobalt with gold, dome lids with fruit finials, ca 1900, 26", $9,200.00 for the pair. (Photo courtesy Skinner, Inc.)

Cup & saucer, cherubs medallion on bl w/pearl jewels, 1880s.....**375.00**
Cup & saucer, floral bands w/much gold, Empire shape, 1814-24, $500 to.**700.00**
Cup & saucer, portrait: Napoleon's son, sgn C Brun, 3½"...........**315.00**
Figurine, man (lady), Elizabethan attire, royal bl/gold, 1800s, 9", pr.**635.00**
Plate, lady's portrait, 2 musical vignettes in border w/gold, 9½".**250.00**
Tazza, floral on wht w/gr band, 2-tier w/gilt stds, 1850s, 14", pr.**1,265.00**
Urn, figural reserves on cobalt, figural hdls, bronze ft, 18", pr.**2,800.00**
Urn, figural reserves on cobalt, ornate bronze hdls/mts, 25", pr.**8,680.00**
Urn, lovers, sgn, bronze hdls/rim/ft, 13" **460.00**
Urn, lovers in gold reserve on cobalt sgn Lepage, ornate mts, 41", pr.**25,000.00**
Urn, lovers on cobalt w/gold sgn Cottinet; metal lid/mts, 19", pr.**3,000.00**
Urn, seminude/cherub, pastels on wht, bl lid/ft, 19".............**1,035.00**
Vase, couple/garden, gray on wht, in fancy gold reserve on bl, 10", pr.**1,120.00**

Sewer Tile

Whimsies, advertising novelties, and other ornamental items were sometimes made in potteries where the primary product was simply tile.

Basin, thick appl ribs along bottom w/rosettes between, 9x14"...**165.00**
Collie, standing on base, red/brn glaze, mfg flaw/sm chips, 12x11".**935.00**
Crow on stump, dk brn, EX detail, sgn EJE, 9½".....................**1,325.00**
Dice, layers of pnt, edge damage, 3½", pr...................................**190.00**
Dog, seated, some tooling, matt glaze w/metallic speckles, 8" **165.00**
Dog, seated, tooled details, brn glaze, 11"...................................**660.00**
Dog, seated, wavy fur, EX hand tooling, glazed, 9¾" **580.00**
Frog, manganese glaze, 4½"...**85.00**
Frog on log, tooled bark, dk brn metallic w/gilt, 5x5".................**400.00**
Lamp base, 3-D hollow owl on stump, dk brn glaze, EX detail, 16", EX.**385.00**
Lion, hand tooling/molding, streaky brn, sgn JCE...1901, 6x11".**825.00**
Lion, reclining on logs, tooled mane, pnt traces, IN, 6x13x6" **350.00**
Lion, recumbent, molded w/dk brn glaze, oval stepped base, 7x13".**1,200.00**
Pig in pants/vest/bow tie, red-brn, molded, 8"............................**300.00**
Planter, mail-textured surface, sq w/corner blocks & block ft, 12x15".**495.00**
Spaniel w/incised collar, Superior Uhrichsville O, 10¾", EX......**650.00**
Strawberry planter, ovoid w/multiple rimmed holes, 14x13", EX.**140.00**
Stump planter, molded bark, appl snake, mk RCC Co, rprs, 8x6"..**55.00**
Stump planter, molded bark, 3 limbs, early dk brn glaze, 36" **360.00**
Stump planter, tooled bark, 4 branches (3 w/openings), 29x18".**195.00**
Stump planter w/2 raccoons, 3 branches, Superior Clay/W Smith, 22".**220.00**
Tree trunk w/molded leaves & acorns, brn glaze, w/lid, 7x5" **165.00**

Sewing Items

Sewing collectibles continue to intrigue collectors, and fine nineteenth-century and earlier pieces are commanding higher prices due to increased demand and scarcity. Complete needlework boxes and chatelaines in original condition are rare, but even incomplete examples can be considered prime additions to any collection, as long as they meet certain criteria: boxes should contain fittings of the period; the chains of the chatelaine should be intact and contemporary with the style; and the individual holders should be original and match the brooch. As nineteenth-century items become harder to find, new trends in collecting develop. Needle books, many of which were decorated with horses, children, beautiful ladies, etc., have become very popular. Some were giveaways printed with advertisements of products and businesses. Even early pins are collectible; the first ones were made in two parts with the round head attached separately. Pin disks, pin cubes, and other pin holders also make interesting additions to a sewing collection.

Tape measures are very popular — especially Victorian figurals. These command premium prices. Early wooden examples of transferware and Tunbridge ware have gained in popularity, as have figurals of vegetable

ivory, celluloid, and other early plastics. From the twentieth century, tatting shuttles made of plastics, bone, brass, sterling, and wood decorated with Art Nouveau, Art Deco, and more modern designs are in demand — so are darning eggs, stilettos, and thimbles. Because of the decline in the popularity of needlework after the 1920s (due to increased production of machine-made items), novelty items were made in an attempt to regain consumer interest, and many collectors today also find these appealing.

Watch for reproductions. Sterling thimbles are being made in Holland and the U.S. and are available in many Victorian-era designs. But the originals are usually plainly marked, either in the inside apex or outside on the band. Avoid testing gold and silver thimbles for content; this often destroys the inside marks. Instead, research the manufacturer's mark; this will often denote the material as well. Even though the reproductions are well finished, they do not have manufacturers' marks. Many thimbles are being made specifically for the collectible market; reproductions of porcelain thimbles are also found. Prices should reflect the age and availability of these thimbles. Our advisor for this category is Kathy Goldsworthy; she is listed in the Directory under Washington. We also recommend *Sewing Tools & Trinkets* by Helen Lester Thompson, and *Antique & Collectible Thimbles and Accessories* by Averie Mathes.

Awl, MOP hdl, 4" **29.00**
Bodkin, sterling, 2¾x¾" **45.00**
Book, Complete Book of Sewing, C Talbot, 1943, w/dust jacket ..**15.00**
Book, Needlepoint Made Easy, Picken & Wht, hardcover, 1955, 149-pg.**15.00**
Booklet, Crochet Handkerchief Edgings, Spool Cotton, 1949, 15-pg.**8.00**
Booklet, Singer Zigzag Ideas, c 1963, 23-pg, EX **7.00**
Box, curly maple vnr, mahog case w/band inlay, 3-compartment, 4x11x8".**400.00**

Box, decalcomania, attributed to Josef Long Lehn, dated 1875, $875.00. (Photo courtesy Aston-Macek)

Box, dk wood w/MOP inlay, bun ft, Victorian era, rstr int **375.00**
Box, inlaid hearts/arrows/dmns/circles, dvtl drw w/trn pull, 4x6", EX.**275.00**
Box, mahog flame vnr, dvtl, band inlay, 11-compartment tray, 7x8x12"..**550.00**
Box, mahog w/inlaid shell medallion, inlaid int lid, tray, 6x12x7".**1,000.00**
Box, mahog w/inlay, Regency period, 8¾x13½x9¾" **1,000.00**
Box, poplar/pine w/3-color pnt, center wheel w/pegs for spools,12x7x7".**1,375.00**
Button, blk glass w/wht o/l & goldstone, ca 1900, from $5 to **12.00**
Button, brass, spider & web emb w/tinting, shank type, 1870s, lg.**50.00**
Button, brass, stamped Greenaway scene, 1940s, sm to med, from $10 to..**20.00**
Button, colored glass w/Deco styling, 1930s, med to lg, from $4 to.**6.00**
Button, HP glass w/molded design, ca 1900, med, from $8 to **15.00**
Button, jeweled center, 1890s, lg, from $20 to **40.00**
Button, molded plastic Scottie dog (blk), sm **3.00**
Button, plastic w/rhinestones at gold-tone edge, loop shank, 1930s.**8.00**
Button, transparent glass, Germany or Austria, 1930s-40s, lg, $1 to.**3.00**
Buttonhole cutter, FC Leypoldt Phila...1860 & 1865 ....**150.00**
Buttonholer, Singer Featherweight, 5 templates, c 1948 in booklet..**15.00**
Caddy, wooden, 18 spools surround it, drw, gold trim...................**250.00**
Clamp, cast metal, spring-operated, Alburger...Chicago...1886...**200.00**
Clamp, cvd bone w/butterflies & bird on top, ca 1900, sm, VG .**138.00**

Clamp, trn wood w/cushion top, 7x2" 112.00
Crochet hook, cvd bone, 4½" 15.00
Darner, blk japanned mushroom shape, 5" 24.00
Darner, blown glass, cobalt ball on hdl, 7" 165.00
Darner, blown/powdered glass, oblate ball w/glove darner hdl, 8" .135.00
Darner, ebony egg w/lg silver repousse hdl, F&B Sterling..., 5⅝" ..100.00
Darner, lathe-trn mushroom on hdl w/beehive knop, 4¾" 25.00
Darner, wood, egg form w/hollow glove darner hdl, Atkinson...85 ..30.00
Darner, wood coated w/blk celluloid, egg shape, 1890s, 6" 17.50
Darner, wooden, elongated egg opens for accessories, varnished, 6"..30.00
Darner, wooden, opens for needle & thread, EX 25.00
Darner, wooden egg w/pnt face, spring neck, plain wood hdl, 5" ..25.00
Darner, wooden mushroom form w/HP floral, Czechoslovakia, 4½".30.00
Hem gauge, Art Nouveau SP, Pat Oct 2nd 1894, 5½x½" 145.00
Hemstitcher, Singer, w/picoting attachment, MIB.......................25.00
Kit, vegetable ivory, ftd egg form, 2⅝x1" dia 145.00
Leather covered dome-top w/brass tack decor, ring hdls, 9" L.....275.00
Measure, celluloid, bear w/tape in mouth, Japan..........................75.00
Needle book, Rocket, mc rocket cover, 6½x3¾" 7.00
Needle book, Safeway, ad for Cragmont soft drinks, MIG, VG 7.00
Needle case, Bakelite, brass cap screws in, 2¾" 180.00
Needle case, tortoiseshell, 8-hole ivory plate holds needles, 1840s.210.00
Needle dispenser, brass-colored metal w/gr marbling, Jahncke's Pat..52.00
Needle holder, Queen Victoria Gold Eyed Needles, S&H Green Stamps, EX ..10.00
Needle holder, Sunbonnet Sue, embr felt, 4¾" 6.00
Needle threader, Singer Universal, c 1936/1937, VG in G- case ..15.00
Needles, Singer Self-Threading, 11 of 15 in plastic case.................3.00
Pincushion, celluloid, doll w/satin body, human hair, 4", VG 49.00
Pincushion, ceramic, blk cat, measure is tongue, Japan, 6"...........55.00
Pincushion, ceramic, hen, tab pulls for measure, Nesco/Japan, 3x5".32.00
Pincushion, ceramic, lady's head & torso, Paul Marshall, 1960s, 7"..25.00
Pincushion, ceramic, Lake Tahoe souvenir, Japan, 3" 7.50
Pincushion, ceramic, man's shoe, gr velvet top, unmk, 5" 50.00
Pincushion, ceramic, Wyoming souvenir, shape of state, 3" 12.00
Pincushion, fabric, strawberry, red w/gr & brn shaded velvet, 5½".40.00
Pincushion, gold-tone metal, canoe shape, 1900s, 4¼" L 98.00
Pincushion, plastic, high-heel shoe, 3x4" 12.00
Pincushion, rayon hat w/sm flag bow, cb stiffener, 5½" dia 5.00
Scissors, fancy openwork, AJ Jordan, Germany, 5¾" 95.00
Scissors, ornate scrolls/leaves eng, Fr, 3¾"..................................65.00
Scissors, steel, folding travel type, mk Foreign, 4" open................15.00
Scissors, steel, Kaufmann Solingen, MIG, 10¼", G 18.00
Scissors, Woodrow Wilson and lady Liberty decor, 1922 ....50.00
Sewing bird, brass, C-type clamp, spring loaded, M.....................275.00
Sewing bird, brass, spring & screw clamp, 3¾x3½x2"...............165.00
Sewing bird, brass, USA, Patented, G..100.00
Sewing bird, cvd satin wood, Berlin-work embr cushion, 1860s, 6".295.00
Tatting shuttle, Boye 10.00
Tatting shuttle, celluloid, marbled pattern, EX 24.00
Tatting shuttle, metal, Susan Bates...Chester CT, 3".....................9.00
Thimble, brass, England, plain band..5.00
Thimble, brass, England, Remember Me & flowers on band.........15.00
Thimble, ivory, Asia, hand cvd, delicate, 1850 ....60.00
Thimble, metal alloy, Simons, narrow decorative band 7.50
Thimble, porc, Franklin Mint 15.00
Thimble, steel core w/silver coating, RD 127211 Pat 8 ....48.00
Thimble, sterling, Cupid & garlands, Simons Bros, 1905, ⅞" 250.00
Thimble, sterling, English hallmk, waffle design, 1907 on band ...35.00
Thimble, sterling, Italy, moonstones mtd on band........................85.00
Thimble, sterling, Ketcham McDougall, rose branches on band.....70.00
Thimble, sterling, Simons & Co, grapes & vines repousse band.150.00
Thimble, sterling, Webster, dogwood branches repousse 70.00
Thimble, 10k gold, unmk, plain band w/decor at rim, monogram..75.00
Thimble, 14k gold, unmk, circular design, eng name 85.00

Thimble case, Sterling mk, emb decor, 1970s, 1x⅞" dia 70.00
Thimble holder, cast metal, walnut on branch w/Sterling mk thimble .190.00
Tracing wheel, Dritz, Bakelite 12.50
Tracing wheel, Singer on metal stem, plastic hdl, 6" 10.00

Sewing Machines

The fact that Thomas Saint, an English cabinetmaker, invented the first sewing machine in 1790 was unknown until 1874 when Newton Wilson, an English sewing machine manufacturer and patentee, chanced upon the drawings included in a patent specification describing methods of making boots and shoes. By the middle of the nineteenth century, several patents were granted to American inventors, among them Isaac M. Singer, whose machine used a treadle. These machines were ruggedly built, usually of cast iron. By the 1860s and 1870s, the sewing machine had become a popular commodity, and the ironwork became more detailed and ornate.

Though rare machines are costly, many of the old oak treadle machines (especially these brands: Davis, Home, Household, National, New Home, Singer, Weed, Wheeler & Wilson, and Willcox & Gibbs) have only nominal value. Machines manufactured after 1875 are generally very common as most were mass produced. Values for these later sewing machines range from $50.00 to $100.00. Our advisor for this category is Peter Frei; he is listed in the Directory under Massachusetts. In the listings that follow, unless noted otherwise, values are suggested for machines in excellent working order.

Child's, Casige, sheet metal with spool pin on front, hand operated, Made in Germany - British Zone, 5⅞x4½x9⅜", $85.00. (Photo courtesy Glenda Thomas)

Child's, Betsy Ross, 1949, EX...100.00
Child's, Casige #181747, EX 200.00
Child's, Gateway, red-pnt lightweight wheel, EX............................50.00
Child's, Gateway Junior Model JP-1, Chicago 51, Ill, EXIB.........85.00
Child's, Junior Miss, metal body, aluminum handwheel, Artcraft, EX ..75.00
Child's, KAYanEE, pk, Germany...US Zone, EX 90.00
Child's, KAYanEE Sew Master, Berlin...US Zone, EX in orig carton.110.00
Child's, Little Mary Mix Up, sheet metal, 1930s, EX 75.00
Child's, MaCousette, battery-op, bl plastic, 7x10½", EX.............85.00
Child's, Peerless Automatic, CI 350.00
Child's, Sew-ette, metal, battery-op, crackle finish, VG 40.00
Child's, Singer, cast metal, Great Britain, 1962-53, plastic case..125.00
Child's, Singer Little Touch & Sew, battery-op, 26" H table.........90.00
Goodrich, treadle, quarter-sawn oak cabinet, EX..........................195.00
Guhl & Haarbeck, full-sz table-top, Germany, 1890-1920, VG ..175.00
Minnesota Model D, hand crank, table-top, EX in wood case 350.00
Precision Built De Luxe, EX enamel & gold, w/bl case 160.00
Singer, Century of Sewing Service, 1851-1952 on plate, EX.........95.00
Singer Featherweight #221, portable, w/instructions, M in case .500.00

Singer Featherweight Model 331, blk case, NM **385.00**
Singer Portable #3, hand-crank, dome case, 1898, NM..............**150.00**
Wheeler & Wilson, treadle w/fold-out table-top, ca 1856-76, VG .**125.00**
Wilcox & Gibbs, orig ft pedal & light, 8x15", EX orig...............**150.00**

Shaker Items

The Shaker community was founded in America in 1776 at Niskeyuna, New York, by a small group of English 'Shaking Quakers.' The name referred to a group dance which was part of their religious rites. Their leader was Mother Ann Lee. By 1815 their membership had grown to more than one thousand in eighteen communities as far west as Indiana and Kentucky. But in less than a decade, their numbers began to decline until today only a handful remain. Their furniture is prized for its originality, simplicity, workmanship, and practicality. Few pieces were signed. Some were carefully finished to enhance the natural wood; a few were painted.

Although other methods were used earlier, most Shaker boxes were of oval construction with overlapping 'fingers' at the seams to prevent buckling as the wood aged. Boxes with original paint fetch triple the price of an unpainted box; number of fingers and overall size should also be considered.

Although the Shakers were responsible for weaving a great number of baskets, their methods are not easily distinguished from those of their outside neighbors, and it is nearly impossible without first-hand knowledge to positively attribute a specific example to their manufacture. They were involved in various commercial efforts other than woodworking — among them sheep and dairy farming, sawmilling, and pipe and brick making. They were the first to raise crops specifically for seed and to market their product commercially. They perfected a method to recycle paper and were able to produce wrinkle-free fabrics. Our advisor for this category is Nancy Winston; she is listed in the Directory under New Hampshire. Standard two-letter state abbreviations have been used throughout the following listings.

Key:
CB — Canterbury   ML — Mt. Lebanon
EF — Enfield   SDL — Sabbathday Lake
NL — New Lebanon   WV — Watervliet

Apple peeler, cherry, pegged/mortised, ME, 1840s, 26" **450.00**
Armchair, #1, orig pnt & tape seat, ML, child's, 28", EX+ **1,750.00**
Basket, cutlery; ash, dk varnish, cvd hdl, 5½x17x8½" **1,100.00**
Basket, gathering; tighly woven splint, EX color, 11½x18", VG.**250.00**
Basket, maple/ash, flared top, EF, 1850s, 29x17" sq top............**1,400.00**
Basket, pie; ash, gr stain, dbl swing hdls, lid, 6x12½" **1,000.00**
Basket, sewing; poplar, fabric covered, SDL, 4¾x3¼" **350.00**
Basket, work; maple splint, hickory wrap, side hdls, 15x21".......**400.00**
Basket rack, mortised wood, sq nails, old dry pnt, Zoar OH, 20x58x19".**165.00**
Bed, walnut, sq pegged posts, peaked head/ftbrds, OH, 30x59x39".**495.00**
Bench, foot; pine, varnish/decal, ML, ca 1900, 7x12x12" **345.00**
Bench, pine w/red traces, half-moon cutouts at ends, 23x27x15".**350.00**
Bench, walnut, rfn, KY, ca 1840, 33x76x34"................................**875.00**
Bench, wash; 2-tier pine w/red stain, 63x42x18", EX **500.00**
Box, bentwood, lapped seams/copper tacks, EF, 1919, 4½" **350.00**
Box, desk; chestnut/cherry/pine, 4-part int, 1850s, 5x16x12" **700.00**
Box, Harvard lap, copper tacks, natural, 7½" L **330.00**
Box, Harvard lap, copper tacks, natural finish, label remant, 12" L .**440.00**
Box, letter; tiger maple, dvtl, orig finish, 4x11x7"....................**1,000.00**
Box, overlapping seam w/copper tacks, worn gr pnt, 2¾x6" dia .**495.00**
Box, sewing; oval w/swing hdl, silk lining, SDL, 2½x7x4¾" **395.00**
Box, sewing; 5-finger, maple/pine, swing hdl, ca 1900, 11x11x15".**1,850.00**
Box, storage; pine, stain, dvtl, appl molding, 12x25x13" **1,600.00**

Box, 1-finger, chrome yel pnt, 1½x3x2¼" **2,500.00**
Box, 2-finger, chrome yel pnt, Harvard Community, 1½x3x2¼" .**2,500.00**
Box, 2-finger, maple/pine, 1850s, 2x6⅛" **425.00**
Box, 2-finger base/1 on lid, dk gr rpt w/minor wear, brass tacks, 6" L .**685.00**
Box, 2-finger base/1 on lid, gr rpt w/wear, copper tacks, 5½" L...**850.00**
Box, 2-finger base/1 on lid, reddish stain, copper tacks, 7½" L ...**695.00**
Box, 2-finger base/1 on lid, worn bl pnt, copper tacks, 9½" L .**1,485.00**
Box, 3-finger, maple/pine, NY, 5¾" L...**495.00**
Box, 3-finger, maple/pine, orig yel wash, split, 13⅛" L...............**680.00**
Box, 3-finger, mellow brn, copper tacks, rpr rim, 5x7¼" **295.00**
Box, 4-finger, bittersweet wash, WV, 1832, 5½x10½x7½" **7,000.00**
Box, 4-finger, maple/pine, minor burn mks, 11¼".......................**650.00**
Box, 4-finger, maple/pine, natural, copper nails, 4¼x10¼".........**500.00**
Box, 4-finger, maple/pine, old gr pnt traces, 10¼".......................**650.00**
Box, 4-finger, maple/pine, red pnt, floral decal, 4¾x11¼".......**1,100.00**
Box, 4-finger, maple/pine, yel stain/varnish, 6⅜" L **700.00**
Box, 4-finger, old dry bl w/copper tacks, 4¼x12x9".....................**770.00**
Box, 4-finger, pine top & bottom, copper tacks, worn pnt, 11" ..**440.00**
Box, 5-finger, pine, bl pnt, EF, 1840s, 4¼x11¼" **3,750.00**
Box, 5-finger, pine top & bottom, copper tacks, rfn, 13"............**795.00**
Bucket, pine, bl pnt, w/lid, ML, 1850s, 15x9¾"............................**800.00**
Cabinet, panel door over 3 drws, orig red wash, hangs, 24x16x7"..**3,225.00**
Carrier, maple, 3-finger, swing hdl, copper tacks, #5 on base, 8x7x9".**595.00**
Carrier, poplar/pine, orig gr pnt, swing hdl, 11x9" dia **695.00**
Carrier, wooden, red stain, stapled finger, bentwood hdl, 1¼x12".**250.00**
Carrier, 3-finger, maple/pine/cherry, dtd 1923, 6x8x5⅛"............**495.00**
Chair, communal; maple, 2-slat bk, rpl rush seat, WV, ca 1830s, 26".**1,350.00**
Chair, side; #15, maple, orig finish, tilts missing, WV, 1830s **450.00**
Chair, side; maple, red wash, tape seat, CB, 1830s, 41", EX.....**1,400.00**
Chair, side; maple, 3-slat bk, yel traces, rpl seat, 1850, 41" **750.00**
Chair, side; maple/birch, 2-slat, tape seat, NL, 1820s, 25" **1,900.00**
Chair, 3 arched slats, maple/hickory w/old red pnt, pegged, 37".**660.00**
Chest, storage; pine/cherry, orig red, CI hdls, NL, 22x38x21".**2,100.00**
Cloak, sister's, gray wool, 2 int pockets, SDL, long.....................**795.00**
Cradle, birch w/orig red stain, nailed/screwed sides, 37"..............**550.00**
Cupboard, orange on pine, panel door, 2-shelf, ML, 1830s, 42x25"..**3,225.00**
Cupboard, walnut, 2 panel doors over 2 drws, OH, 89x46x21".**3,250.00**
Doughnut cutter, cvd wood, 4½x2½" dia **275.00**
Duster, maple & wool, trn w/sm knob, varnish, MA, 14½" **295.00**
Firkin, pine staves, oak bands, old bl, swing hdl, 20x14", VG .**3,165.00**
Footstool, pine, brn pnt on red stain, bootjack ends, 1840s, sm..**350.00**
Mirror holder, cherry/maple, tapered bk, brass hangers, 17x9" **400.00**
Mop, maple & cotton, trn hdl, natural patina, 40"......................**225.00**

Muzzles for oxen, woven splint basket type, mid-1800s, 14x14½", EX, $925.00 for the pair. (Photo courtesy Skinner, Inc.)

Pincushion, disk w/silk-covered cushion, CB, 1917 on ribbon, 2" dia..**175.00**
Pincushion, HP scene, stamped E Canterbury Shakers, 1917, 2" dia.**565.00**
Rack, drying; birch, pnt traces, pegged, shoe ft, 25x21" **395.00**
Rack, drying; hickory/fruitwood, Xd legs w/trn column, 10 X pcs, 53" ..**400.00**

Rack, towel; cherry, shoe ft, 3 bars, mortised/pinned, 37x30" **715.00**
Rocker, #7, 4-slat bk, shawl bar, wool seat, ML, 42"................**1,100.00**
Rocker, arm; #1, maple, dk stain, orig taped bk/canvas seat, ML, 28".**700.00**
Rocker, arm; #3, tape bk &s eat, old dk brn varnish, ML, 34" **385.00**
Rocker, arm; #5, acorn finials, 3 arched slats, ML, 1880s, 36" .**1,100.00**
Rocker, arm; #5, maple, 3-slat bk w/shawl bar, orig finish, ML .**1,350.00**
Rocker, arm; #5, maple w/dk stain, taped seat, 1870s, 38"..........**650.00**
Rocker, arm; #6, maple, 4-slat bk, tape seat, old stain, ML, 41"..**800.00**
Rocker, arm; maple, old rfn w/red traces, rpl seat, CB, 40" **700.00**
Rocker, child's #1, dk finish, woven paper rush seat, ML, 28".....**750.00**
Rocker, elder's ladderbk; maple/tiger maple, NL, 1830s, 45"...**4,000.00**
Rocker, sewing; maple/oak, 3-slat bk, splint seat, rfn, 35" **350.00**
Sewing caddy, pine w/mixed wood veneer, 3-tier, 2-drw, top lid, 9x9x6" .**300.00**
Shovel, maple, red stain, 1-pc cvd hdl, shaft & scoop, 41x12" ...**450.00**
Spool, wooden apple core shape, 3" **95.00**
Stand, seed sorting; lipped top, trn legs, OH, 1850s, 31x21x21" .**1,100.00**
Stool, 2-step, pine, red varnish, dbl-C arched end, 9x12x9" **350.00**
Stove, Zoar Furnace, CI, emb foliage panels, 1830s-50s, 25x31x19".**3,200.00**
Table, work; cherry/pine, red top, 2-drw/3-brd top, 24" L............**600.00**
Teapot, tin, simple form w/clean lines, att, resoldered, 5" **165.00**
Umbrella swift, wooden, clamp base, old yel traces, MA, 25".....**495.00**
Washstand, tiger maple/cherry, dvtl drw, shelf, old rfn, early 1800s .**895.00**
Yarn winder, maple, hand-trn form, 4 arms on disk w/hdl...........**200.00**

Shaving Mugs

Between 1865 and 1920, owning a personalized shaving mug was the order of the day, and the 'occupationals' were the most prestigious. The majority of men having occupational mugs would often frequent the barber shop several times a week, where their mugs were clearly visible for all to see in the barber's rack. As a matter of fact, this display was in many ways the index of the individual town or neighborhood.

During the first twenty years, blank mugs were almost entirely imported from France, Germany, and Austria and were hand painted in this country. Later on, some china was produced by local companies. It is noteworthy that American vitreous china is inferior to the imported Limoges and is subject to extreme crazing.

Artists employed by the American barber supply companies were for the most part extremely talented and capable of executing any design the owner required, depicting his occupation, fraternal affiliation or preferred sport. When the mug was completed, the name and the gold trim were always added in varying degrees, depending on the price paid by the customer. This price was determined by the barber who added his markup to that of the barber-supply company. As mentioned above, the popularity of the occupational shaving mug diminished with the advent of World War I and the introduction by Gillette of the safety razor. Later followed the blue laws forcing barber shops to close on Sundays, thereby eliminating the political and social discussions for which they were so well noted.

Occupational shaving mugs are the most sought after of the group which would also include those with sport affiliations. Fraternal mugs, although desirable, do not command the same price as the occupationals. Occasionally, you will find the owner's occupation together with his fraternal affiliation. This combination could add anywhere between 25% to 50% to the price, which is dependent on the execution of the painting, rarity of the subject and detail. Some subjects can be done very simply; others can be done in extreme detail, commanding substantially higher prices. It is fair to say, however, that the rarity of the occupation will dictate the price. Mugs with heavily worn gold loose between 20% and 30% of their value immediately. This would not apply to the gold trim around the rim, but to the loss of the name itself. Our advisor for this category is Burton Handelsman; he is listed in the Directory under New York.

Decorative, horseshoe & blooming clover, SCH mk, 3⅝" **90.00**
Decorative, lady's hand holding flowers on pk, Limoges, 4" **120.00**
Decorative, lady's profile in reserve, 3⅝", EX **180.00**
Decorative, sailboats w/in floral fr, 3⅝"................................**325.00**
Fraternal, Knights of Maccabees emblem, 3¾" **140.00**
Fraternal, man by lg engine, Odd Fellows emblem, V&D Austria..**750.00**
Fraternal, red caboose & BRRT on side, T&V Limoges, 3½" **325.00**
Fraternal, Shriners emblem, V&D Austria, 3¾" **60.00**
Occupational, barber, 3 barbers/5 customers, T&V Limoges, 3⅝" .**1,200.00**
Occupational, barrel maker, man planing board, 4"......................**900.00**
Occupational, bartender, bar scene w/2 customers, 3⅝" **400.00**
Occupational, blacksmith, man shoeing horse, mk D&Co, 3½".**325.00**
Occupational, butcher, steer's head & Xd tools, 4" **90.00**

Occupational, butcher shop scene with customers, gold trim, Welmer Germany, 1890 – 1925, 3⅝", NM, $1,050.00.

Occupational, cattleman, cow & calf, JG Getz, 3½" **190.00**
Occupational, cobbler, man working at bench, 3⅞" **1,200.00**
Occupational, delivery man, Pure Milk on horse-drawn wagon, 3¾".**900.00**
Occupational, fireman, horse-drawn steam fire engine, 3⅝"....**2,600.00**
Occupational, grocer, Grocers on side of horse-drawn wagon, 3⅜"..**325.00**
Occupational, harness maker, man at bench, mk CFH on base, 3¾".**600.00**
Occupational, horse track scene, J&C Bavaria, 3⅞" **1,600.00**
Occupational, house w/2 people on porch, maroon wrap, 3⅝".**1,300.00**
Occupational, man driving touring motorcar, J&C Bavaria, 3⅞".**1,300.00**
Occupational, mug of beer, D&Co, 3⅜" **240.00**
Occupational, open motorcar & name, T&V Limoges, 3⅝".......**950.00**
Occupational, publisher, printing press, D&Co France, 3⅝" **400.00**
Occupational, voilinist, violin & much gold, 4" **550.00**

Shawnee

The Shawnee Pottery Company operated in Zanesville, Ohio, from 1937 to 1961. They produced inexpensive novelty ware (vases, flowerpots, and figurines) as well as a very successful line of figural cookie jars, creamers, and salt and pepper shakers.

They also produced three dinnerware lines, the first of which, Valencia, was designed by Louise Bauer in 1937 for Sears & Roebuck. A starter set was given away with the purchase of one of their refrigerators. Second and most popular was the Corn line. The original design was called White Corn. In 1946 the line was expanded and the color changed to a more natural yellow hue. It was marketed under the name Corn King, and it was produced from 1946 to 1954. Then the colors were changed again. Kernels became a lighter yellow and shucks a darker green. This variation was called Corn Queen. Their third dinnerware line, produced after 1954, was called Lobsterware. It was made in either black, brown, or gray; lobsters were usually applied to serving pieces and accessory items.

For further study we recommend these books: *The Collector's Guide to Shawnee Pottery* by Janice and Duane Vanderbilt, who are listed in the Directory under Indiana; and *Shawnee Pottery, An Identification and Value Guide*, by our advisors for this category, Jim and Bev Mangus; they are listed in Ohio.

Cookie Jars

Note: The prices in the following listings should be considered minimum values.

Cottage, mk USA 6, 6¾" 1,500.00
Drum Major, mk USA 10, 10" 600.00
Dutch Boy (Jack), bl pants w/patches & gold, mk USA 525.00
Dutch Boy (Jack), flowers on knees w/gold & decals, mk USA ..475.00
Dutch Girl (Jill), bl skirt, mk USA 125.00
Dutch Girl (Jill), yel skirt w/gold & decals, mk USA.................400.00
Fruit Basket, mk Shawnee 84, 8" 250.00
Great Northern Boy, mk Great Northern USA 1025 ....500.00
Great Northern Girl, wht, mk Great Northern USA 1026........475.00
Jo Jo the Clown, mk Shawnee 12, 9½" 500.00
Jumbo the Elephant, w/red or bl cold pnt bow tie, mk USA, 12" .250.00
Little Chef, yel or caramel, mk USA 200.00
Muggsy the Dog, bl scarf, mk Patented Muggsy USA.................600.00
Owl, w/gold & decals, mk USA, 11½" 375.00
Puss 'n Boots, short tail, mk Patented Puss 'n Boots, 10¼" 200.00
Sailor Boy (Jack Tar), blk hair w/gold, mk USA, 12" 1,150.00
Sailor Boy (Jack Tar), cold pnt, mk USA, 12" 200.00
Smiley the Pig, bl neckerchief, mk USA 175.00
Smiley the Pig, bl neckerchief w/gold & decals, mk USA...........700.00
Smiley the Pig, shamrocks w/gold & decals, mk USA.................650.00
Smiley the Pig, w/hair, gold & decals, mk USA 1,225.00
Winnie the Pig, bl collar, mk USA 425.00
Winnie the Pig, clover buds, mk Pat Winnie USA 800.00

Corn Line

When a range of values is given, use the low side to evaluate Queen Corn.

Bowl, cereal; King or Queen, mk #94 ....50.00
Bowl, fruit; King or Queen, mk #92 ....48.00
Bowl, mixing; King or Queen, mk #5, 5", from $22 to 25.00
Bowl, mixing; King or Queen, mk #8, 8", from $35 to 45.00
Bowl, vegetable; King, mk #95, 9" 55.00

Butter dish, King or Queen, Shawnee #72, $55.00.

Casserole, King, mk #74 ....40.00
Casserole, Queen, mk #74 ....50.00
Cookie jar, King or Queen, mk #66 ....350.00
Corn roast set, Queen, #108 ....175.00
Creamer, King or Queen, mk #70 ....28.00
Creamer, White, mk USA 30.00
Mug, King or Queen, mk Shawnee #69, 8-oz 50.00
Pitcher, King or Queen, mk #71 ....70.00
Pitcher, White, mk USA 65.00
Pitcher, White, w/gold, mk USA....................................120.00
Plate, King or Queen, mk #68, 10" 40.00
Platter, King or Queen, mk #96, 12" 55.00
Relish tray, King, mk #79 ....40.00

Relish tray, Queen, mk #79 ....30.00
Saucer, King or Queen, mk #91 ....18.00
Shakers, King Indian, pr 80.00
Shakers, King or Queen, lg, pr 40.00
Shakers, King or Queen, sm, pr 28.00
Shakers, White, w/gold, sm, pr 35.00
Sugar bowl, King or Queen, mk #78 ....36.00
Sugar bowl, White, gold trim, mk USA 75.00
Sugar shaker, White, mk USA 70.00
Teapot, King or Queen, mk #65, 10-oz 175.00
Teapot, White, gold trim, mk USA, 30-oz 85.00

Kitchenware

Canister, fruit decor, mk USA, 2-qt 55.00
Casserole, fruit basket shape, mk Shawnee USA 83 ....50.00
Creamer, Dutch style w/red feather decor, mk USA 12 ....40.00
Creamer, Puss 'n Boots, yel w/red bow, gold trim, mk Shawnee 85.125.00
Creamer, Smiley the Pig, w/gold, mk Patented Smiley USA 400.00
Creamer, tulip, mk USA 80.00
Ice server, elephant shape, wht or blk collar 250.00
Pie chick, unmk 50.00
Pitcher, Bo Peep, mk USA Pat Bo Peep, 40-oz 90.00
Shakers, Boy Blue & Bo Peep, sm, pr 30.00
Shakers, Chanticleers, lg, pr..50.00
Shakers, Dutch Kids, bl, lg, pr 30.00
Shakers, Farmer Pigs, sm, pr 80.00
Shakers, flowerpots, gold-trimmed flower, sm, pr 55.00
Shakers, fruit, matches sugar bowl, lg, pr...........................40.00
Shakers, Jack & Jill, gold & decals, lg, pr..........................225.00
Shakers, milk cans, gold, sm, pr 125.00
Shakers, owls, gold, sm, pr..80.00
Shakers, rabbits, sm, pr 25.00
Shakers, Smiley, gold neckerchief, sm, pr 100.00
Shakers, Smiley, peach neckerchief, lg, pr..........................135.00
Shakers, Smiley & Winnie, clover bud, sm, pr......................85.00
Shakers, Smiley & Winnie, heart set, lg, pr 175.00
Shakers, sunflower, sm, pr 35.00
Shakers, Swiss Kids, gold, lg, pr......................................65.00
Shakers, watering cans, sm, pr..26.00
Shakers, wheelbarrows, sm, pr..26.00
Spoon rest, red, mk USA 24.00
String holder, fruit, unmk...125.00
Sugar bowl, fruit basket, mk Shawnee 81 ....40.00
Sugar bowl, Sunflower, w/lid, mk USA 55.00
Teapot, clover bud, mk USA, 7-cup 75.00
Teapot, cottage, mk USA 7, 5-cup, minimum value................650.00
Teapot, Elite, gold & decals, mk USA, 4-cup 70.00
Teapot, Pennsylvania Dutch, mk USA, 30-oz......................225.00
Teapot, Piper's Son, w/gold, mk Patented Tom the Piper's Son, 5-cup.160.00
Teapot, Sunflower, mk USA, 7-cup 85.00
Tumbler, Stars & Stripes, mk USA, 3" 8.00

Lobsterware

Batter bowl, hdld, mk 928 ....55.00
Bowl, mixing; mk 915, 5" 40.00
Bowl, mixing; mk 919, 9" 40.00
Bowl, spaghetti/salad; mk 922 ....35.00
Butter dish, w/lid, mk Kenwood 927 ....110.00
Casserole, French; mk 900, 10-oz 21.00
Casserole, French; mk 902, 16-oz 25.00
Creamer, jug style, mk 921 ....50.00
Mug, mk Kenwood USA 911, 8-oz 85.00

Relish dish, w/lid, mk Kenwood USA 926, 5½" 50.00
Salad set, 9-pc, mk 924 ....135.00
Shakers, claw, mk USA, pr..40.00
Shakers, full body, mk USA, pr 225.00
Snack jar/bean pot, mk Kenwood USA 925, 4-oz.....................775.00
Spoon holder, dbl; mk USA 935, 8½" 250.00
Sugar bowl, w/lid, mk 907 ....26.00

Valencia

Ashtray...24.00
Bowl, fruit; unmk, 5" 20.00
Carafe, w/lid..50.00
Comport, unmk, 12"...26.00
Cup & saucer, AD: unmk...22.00
Nappy, unmk, 8½"...20.00
Pitcher, ice; mk USA...40.00
Plate, unmk, 6½"...12.00
Punch bowl, unmk, 12"..30.00
Relish tray, unmk, 10½"...135.00
Shakers, rnd, unmk, pr 30.00
Sugar bowl, w/lid, unmk..25.00

Miscellaneous

Bowl, scalloped edge, mk USA, 5½" 14.00
Figurine, deer, head up, unmk.....................................100.00
Figurine, donkey w/basket, mk USA 22.00
Figurine, rabbit, ears tucked behind head, unmk 75.00
Planter, baby skunk, mk Shawnee 512...............................35.00
Planter, circus pony, mk USA 20.00
Planter, dog & jug, mk USA 610 ....10.00
Planter, dove & planting dish, w/gold, mk Shawnee 2025 ....45.00
Planter, elephant & base, mk Shawnee USA 501......................65.00
Planter, kitten, mk USA 723 ....35.00
Planter, Madonna, mk USA..30.00
Planter, open-mouth fish, w/gold, mk USA 845 ....18.00
Planter, rabbit w/turnip, mk USA 703..............................33.00
Planter, rocking horse, mk USA 526 ....24.00
Planter, terrier & doghouse, mk Shawnee USA.......................25.00
Planter, Tony the peddler, mk USA 621 ....35.00
Vase, emb iris, mk USA, 5½" 16.00
Vase, leaf, w/gold, mk USA 822, 6½"...............................40.00
Wall pocket, cornucopia w/bird, unmk..............................25.00
Wall pocket, star shape, mk USA...................................35.00

Shearwater

Since 1928 generations of the Peter, Walter, and James McConnell Anderson families have been producing figurines and artwares in their studio at Ocean Springs, Mississippi. Their work is difficult to date. Figures from the '20s and '30s won critical acclaim and have continued to be made to the present time. Early marks include a die-stamped 'Shearwater' in a dime-sized circle, a similar ink stamp, and a half-circle mark. Any older item may still be ordered in the same glazes as it was originally produced, so many pieces on the market today may be relatively new. However, the older marks are not currently in use. Currently produced Blacks and pirates figurines are marked with a hand-incised 'Shearwater' and/or a cipher formed with an 'S' whose bottom curve doubles as the top loop of a 'P' formed by the addition of an upright placed below and to the left of the S. Many are dated, '93, for example. These figures are generally valued at $35.00 to $50.00 and are available at the pottery or by mail order. New decorated and carved pieces are very expensive, starting at $400.00 to $500.00 for a 6" pot.

Figurine, Black musicians (2), lady dancer, 3 pcs 60.00
Figurine, pirate, 6½" 55.00
Pitcher, utility; lilac, 5½" 50.00
Plate, stylized crane, cvd/pnt mc on wht, ca 1940-50, 8½"......3,735.00
Sculpture, head of young woman, gunmetal matt, W Anderson, 9", NM .900.00
Vase, figures/Gulf Coast animals/etc relief, sea gr/gunmetal, 12x8" .4,880.00
Vase, horse figural, turq 9½" 575.00
Vase, seafoam gr, tapered w/trumpet neck, 7" 85.00
Vase, stylized leaves decor, 1¼x2½" 290.00
Vase, turq, bulbous bottom w/tapered neck, mk #41, 9¾".........485.00

Sheet Music

Sheet music is often collected more for its colorful lithographed covers, rather than for the music itself. Transportation songs (which have pictures or illustrations of trains, ships, and planes), Ragtime and Blues, Comic Characters (especially Disney), Sports, Political, and Expositions are eagerly sought after. Much of the sheet music on the market today is valued at under $5.00; some of the better examples are listed here. For more information refer to *Sheet Music Reference and Price Guide, Second Edition,* by Anna Marie Guiheen and Marie-Reine A. Pafik. Values are given for examples in excellent to near-mint condition unless otherwise noted.

Laddie Boy, Will D. Cobb and Gus Edwards, 1907, $10.00. (Photo courtesy Anna Marie Guiheen and Marie-Reine A. Pafik)

Are You From Heaven?, Gilbert & Friedland, 1917.........................8.00
Bandana Land, Victor Herbert, 1906.....................................10.00
Big Red Shawl, Bob Cole & Billy Johnson, 1908 ....10.00
Boy Scout Parade, Julius K Johnson, 1912...............................20.00
Carlotta, Cole Porter, Movie: Can Can, 1943.............................5.00
Colored Four Hundred, JW Wheeler, 1890.................................25.00
Daddy Long Legs, Clarence M Jones, 1914 ....10.00
Directorate March, John Phillip Sousa, 1898...........................20.00
Down in the Vale of Shenandoah, Chas K Harris, 1906 ....10.00
Entertainer, Scott Joplin, 1903..50.00
Flag of the USA, JJ Donahue, 1918......................................15.00
Floatin' Down the Mississippi, Wm J McKenna, 1924 ....10.00
Forever & a Day, Thomas B Aldrich & Richard Smythe, 1910 ....5.00
Garden of Eden, J Russell Robinson, Cover Artist: Starmer, 1918.10.00
Girl on the Automobile, Nathan, 1905...................................15.00
Golden Spider, Chas I Johnson, 1910....................................10.00
Goodnight Moonlight, Ed Rose & Frank Magine, 1929......................15.00
Gypsy Blues, Sissle & Blake, Musical: Shuffle Along, 1921..............8.00
Hee Haw, P Wendling & M Ager, 1915 ....5.00
Home on the Range, Nick Manoloff, Photo Cover: Jackie Heller, 1935..5.00
I Am the Candy, Graham & Davis, 1904...................................10.00
I Hope I Don't Intrude, Delehanty & Catlin, 1877 ....15.00
I'm Awfully Glad I'm Irish, Cover Artist: Pfeiffer, 1910 ....10.00

I'm Not Your Stepping Stone, Monkees, 1966 ....5.00
I Think of You, Jack Elliot & Don Marcotte, 1941 ....4.00
I've Grown So Used to You, Thurland Chattaway, 1901 ....10.00
I Wouldn't Steal the Sweetheart of a Soldier Boy, Paley & Bryan, 1918.10.00
Ike, Mr Pesident, photo of White House, 1953 ....25.00
In the Little Old Red Schoolhouse, Wilson & Brennan, 1922........6.00
It Was for Me, Charles B Blount, 1916 ....5.00
Just an Hour of Love, Bryan & Ward, Movie: Show of Shows, 1929.10.00
Lady April Waltz, Fancher, 1896 ....15.00
Letter to Heaven, Lizzie Paine, 1888 ....15.00
Little Show, Howard Dietz & Jean Schwartz, 1929 ....7.00
Love Whispers, Jos M Daly, Cover Artist: Pfeiffer, 1913 ....10.00
March of the Cardinals, George M Cohan 15.00
Mid the Blue Grass of Kentucky, Harris, 1909 ....10.00
Mother O'Mine, Kipling & Caro Roma, Irish 10.00
My Hero-ette, John McNab & Charles Spross, 1904 ....10.00
My Parcel Post Man, Kalmar, Cover Artist: Pfeiffer, 1913 ....15.00
Newlyweds & Their Baby, Al Hoffman, 1918 ....10.00
Nothin' But Love, Alsop & Carrie Jacobs Bond, 1912 ....15.00
On the Sidwalks of Berlin, Clinton Keithley, 1918 ....10.00
Pal of Mine, Bartley C Costello & JS Nathan, 1905 ....8.00
Persian Lamb, Percy Wenrich, 1913 ....10.00
Please Mr Conductor Take Me on Your Car, Learned, 1911 ....15.00
Pretty Mollie Shannon, Ryan & Wolff, 1901 ....10.00
Prohibition Blues, Lardner & Bayes, 1919 ....10.00
Railroad Rag, Bimberg, 1911 ....25.00
Riverside March, Walter V Ullman, 1898 ....15.00
Rose Song, William Scanlon, 1883 ....15.00
Sally-Don't Dally, Charles Graham, 1896 ....10.00
Seben Come Eleben, WJ Bay, 1899 ....20.00
She Sleeps Next to the Old Ohio River, Lam & Soman, 1913 .....10.00
Silent Confession, Harry J Lincoln, 1918 ....10.00
Sky Flyer, John B Walker, 1910 ....5.00
Soldiers of Canada, Whitman, Cover Artist: Pfeiffer, 1915 ....10.00
Someday Sweetheart, Spikes & Spikes, Photo: Sophia Tucker, 1924.10.00
Starlight, Reverie, John A Seidt, 1901 ....10.00
Sweet Indiana Home, W Donaldson, Photo Cover: Aileen Stanley, 1922.5.00
That Raggedy Foxtrot, Laurence E Goffen, 1915 ....10.00
There's a Girl in Havana, Irving Berlin, 1911 ....10.00
They Got Me Doing It Now, Irving Berlin, 1913 ....12.00
Thumper Song, Bliss, Sour & Manners, Movie: Bambi, 1942 .....10.00
To the Rescue, Harry J Lincoln, 1820 ....35.00
Turkey Trot, Joseph M Daly, Cover Artist: Pfeiffer, 1912 ....10.00
Under the Swanee Moon, Howard, Cover Artist: Pfeiffer, 1913 ...10.00
Village Barn Dance, Mollie King, 1909 ....10.00
Wait Till the Tide Comes In, Gussie L Davis, 1887 ....10.00
What Chance Have I With Love, Irving Berlin, 1939 ....10.00
When Knighthood Was in Flower, Gustin, 1900 ....5.00
When You Love Her & She Loves You, Kerry Mills, 1907 ....10.00
Wings Over the Navy, Harry Warren, 1918 ....10.00
You, Robyn, 1891 ....10.00
You Were All I Had, WR Williams, 1913 ....5.00

Shell-Work Collectibles

Not long after the natural beauty of the shell was discovered, man began to use them for decorative purposes of many types. Shells were used to decorate clothing and household items as well as jewelry, personal gifts, and souvenirs. Remains of shell necklaces have been found that date to a time prior to the great flood!

During Victorian times shell work became a hobby for the middle class. Shell-work jewelry became popular at that time, but very little has survived due to its delicate nature. Examples of love tokens, souvenirs,

and whimsies from that era are listed below. For further information we recommend *Neptune's Treasures, A Study and Value Guide*, available from our advisors, Carole and Richard Smyth (see their listing in the Directory under New York for ordering information).

Box, cushion top, fancy shell borders & sides, from $175 to 250.00
Box, decor top & borders w/sm ship scene, rectangular, from $150 to .300.00
Box, desk; Victorian lady litho on lid, shell borders, from $125 to .300.00
Box, heart shape, shell border & sides, cushion top, from $150 to..300.00
Box, lg cowrie on lid w/overall decor, w/ or w/o ft, from $150 to .400.00
Box, mussel shells form stylized flower, overall decor, 1800s, $150 to.400.00
Box, sailing scene top, fancy shell borders, from $150 to 400.00
Framed picture, chromolitho under flat glass, from $150 to 500.00
Hand mirror, lady's, shells on bk & hdl, Victorian, from $100 to.200.00
Handbag, rectangular w/woven hdl, overall decor, souvenir, $150 to.400.00
Horseshoe, scene under glass in center, from $125 to 300.00
Inkstand, ship scene, overall decor, souvenir, from $50 to..........300.00
Letter holder, chromolitho print & overall shells, from $125 to .300.00
Love token, anchor shape (symbol of dependability), Victorian.350.00
Miniature, bellows, overall decor, from $50 to 300.00
Miniature, chest, overall decor, ftd, Made in England, from $150 to.250.00
Miniature, dresser, overall decor, lift-lid w/cushion, from $175 to.400.00
Paperweight, inscr w/name of town or vacation area, from $50 to..180.00
Pin holder, decor front, bk: love message, pins around edge, $50 to..150.00
Pincushion, crown shape, shell & silk, Victorian, EX, from $125 to .300.00
Purse, hinged shell, tiny chain hdl, souvenir, mini, from $50 to .100.00
Roundel, litho scene under glass w/layered shells, from $125 to .300.00
Shoe, overall decor, from $150 to 300.00
Star, print under glass, shells/mosses/grasses on points, $125 to ..300.00
Symbol of faith, mini shrine, etc, ea, from $50 to 250.00

Shelley

In 1872 Joseph Shelley became partners with James Wileman, owner of Foley China Works, thus creating Wileman & Co. in Stoke-on-Trent. Twelve years later James Wileman withdrew from the company, though the firm continued to use his name until 1925 when it became known as Shelley Potteries, Ltd. Like many successful nineteenth-century English potteries, this firm continued to produce useful household wares as well as dinnerware of considerable note. In 1896 the beautiful Dainty White shape was introduced, and it is regarded by many as synonymous with the name Shelley. In addition to the original Dainty (six-flute) design, other lovely shapes were produced: Ludlow (fourteen-flute), Oleander (petal shape), Stratford (twelve-flute), Queen Anne (with eight angular panels), Ripon (with its distinctive pedestal), and the 1930s shapes of Vogue, Eve, and Regent.

Though often overlooked, striking earthenware was produced under the direction of Frederick Rhead and later Walter Slater and his son Eric. Many notable artists contributed their talents in designing unusual, attractive wares: Rowland Morris, Mabel Lucie Attwell, and Hilda Cowham, to name but a few.

In 1966 Allied English Potteries acquired control of the Shelley Company, and by 1967 the last of the exquisite Shelley China had been produced to honor remaining overseas orders. In 1971 Allied English Potteries merged with the Doulton group.

It had to happen: Shelley forgeries! Chris Davenport, author of *Shelley Pottery, The Later Years*, reports seeing Mocha-shape cups and saucers with the Shelley mark. However, on close examination it is evident that the mark has been applied to previously unmarked wares too poorly done to have ever left the Shelley Pottery. This Shelley mark can actually be 'felt,' as the refiring is not done at the correct temperature to allow it to be fully incorporated into the glaze. (Beware! These items are often seen on Internet auction sites.)

Some Shelley patterns (Dainty Blue, Bridal Rose, Blue Rock) have been seen on Royal Albert and Queensware pieces. These companies are part of the Royal Doulton Group.

Note: Measurements for objects with lids are measured to the top of the finial unless stated otherwise. Be aware that Rose Spray and Bridal Rose are the same pattern. Our advisor for this category is Lila Shrader; she is listed in the Directory under California.

Key:
LF — Late Foley
MLA — Mabel Lucie Attwell
QA — Queen Anne shape
R&RD — Rose & Red Daisy

RPFMN — Rose, Pansy, Forget-Me-Not
Trio — Cup, saucer and 8" plate
    unless stated otherwise
W — Wileman, pre-1910

Advertising, pitcher, Black & White Scotch w/terriers, 5" 135.00
Advertising, Shelley sign, English club edition by Royal Doulton, 1996.88.00
Ashtray, Primrose, 3 rests, 5½" 12.00
Ashtray, Wildflowers, 3 rests, 5½" 20.00
Bell, Rosebud, Ludlow shape, 5" 390.00
Biscuit jar, Carnation decor, metal lid, #7756, LF, 10" to raised hdl.295.00
Biscuit jar, Melody Chintz, self lid, woven raffia hdl, 6½" 285.00
Bowl, carp swimming, lustre int, sgn Walter Slater, 7¼" 325.00
Bowl, cereal; Dainty Blue, 6¼" dia 52.50
Bowl, cream soup; Rosebud, Dainty shape, hdls, 2¼" H, +liner....75.00
Bowl, vegetable; Sheraton (bl), hdls, w/lid, #13291, 10" 245.00
Breakfast set, Campanula, Dainty shape, all 11 pcs 560.00
Butter pat, Celandine, Dainty shape, 3⅝" 50.00
Butter pat, Pansy (lg) or Wild Anenome, Dainty shape, 3⅝"......65.00
Butter pat, Rambler Rose, Dainty Shape, 3⅝" 65.00
Butter pat, Rosebud, Woodland or Shamrock, 3", from $30 to 40.00
Butter pat, Strawberry, 3" dia 45.00
Cake plate, Dainty Blue, tab hdls, sq, 9¾" (w/hdls), from $99 to..135.00
Cake plate, fruit, mc on blk, tab hdls, sq, 9¾" (includes hdls)......90.00
Cake plate, Imari-like decor, ped ft, 3½x8½" 148.00
Cake plate, Primrose, Dainty shape, ped ft, 2½x8½" 225.00
Candy dish, Blue Bells, Dainty shape, tab hdls, 5⅝" 35.00
Canister, Melody Chintz, ring-like knob on lid, 6½" 200.00
Cheese dish, Dainty Blue, lid w/hdl, base: 8x6½", 4½" H..........435.00
Children's ware, egg cup, toy train scene, Hilda Cowham, 3⅛" 85.00
Children's ware, feeding dish, 'Baby' w/ABCs at top edge, LF, 7½".80.00
Children's ware, mug, little girl chasing BooBoos, MLA, 3¾" 190.00
Children's ware, teapot, mushroom shape w/BooBoo, MLA, 4½" .490.00
Chocolate pot, Drifting Leaves, 6¾" 55.00
Coffeepot, Blue Iris, QA shape, 7⅞" 435.00
Coffeepot, Dainty Blue, 7½", from $315 to...............................345.00
Coffeepot, Dainty shape, various solid pastel colors, 7", from $145 to..195.00
Coffeepot, Georgian, Henley shape, #13360, 7" 190.00
Coffeepot, Harmony Drip ware, blk/orange/gray/yel, 6½" 118.00
Coffeepot, R&RD, Dainty shape, 7½" 280.00
Coffeepot, Stocks, Dainty shape, graceful 'return' on spout, 6" ...325.00
Coffeepot, Stocks, Oleander shape, graceful 'return' on spout, 7½".265.00
Coffeepot, Yellow Wild Rose, Warwick shape, 7" 52.50
Condiment set, Maytime, 2 shakers+covered mustard on fitted tray.100.00
Creamer, Regency, Dainty shape, mini, 1½" 70.00
Creamer & sugar bowl, Blue Rock, Dainty shape, +9" oval tray.110.00
Creamer & sugar bowl, Dainty Black 485.00
Creamer & sugar bowl, Dainty Mauve, +9" oval tray..................255.00
Creamer & sugar bowl, Dainty shape, wht w/floral hdl on creamer.185.00
Creamer & sugar bowl, Thistle, Dainty shape, ind 125.00
Creamer & sugar bowl, Woodland, Cambridge shape, #13348......42.00
Cup & saucer, Blue Bell, Westminster shape, mini......................150.00
Cup & saucer, Blue Rock, Begonia, Rosebud, Regency, ea from $45 to.55.00
Cup & saucer, Briar Rose, Ripon shape...................................290.00
Cup & saucer, Campanula, Dainty shape, mini 680.00

Cup & saucer, Cloisonne, blk bkground, Perth shape 112.00
Cup & saucer, Countryside Chintz, rich gold, Ripon shape 265.00
Cup & saucer, Dainty Blue, Canterbury shape, mini 255.00
Cup & saucer, Dainty Green...200.00
Cup & saucer, Dainty Mauve, from $125 to 150.00
Cup & saucer, Dainty Pink 142.50
Cup & saucer, Dainty Pink, Canterbury shape, mini....................295.00
Cup & saucer, Daisy Chintz, bl w/rich gold, Ripon shape 115.00
Cup & saucer, demi; Harlequin, Ludlow shape 55.00
Cup & saucer, demi; Mocha shape w/o hdl in sterling fr, from $48 to.68.00
Cup & saucer, ferns (stylized), pk on wht, Westminster shape, mini.125.00
Cup & saucer, floral enameled on blk, Ripon shape 215.00
Cup & saucer, Fuchsia, Richmond shape................................27.50
Cup & saucer, Honeysuckle, Dainty shape.............................150.00
Cup & saucer, Hulmes Rose on lt yel w/rich gold, Ripon shape .130.00
Cup & saucer, ivy, blk on wht, Dainty shape 375.00
Cup & saucer, Jungle Print, Daisy shape, W, #6021 ....85.00
Cup & saucer, Lilac Time or Chrysanthemum, Dainty shape........98.00
Cup & saucer, Lily of the Valley, Oleander shape.....................145.00
Cup & saucer, Maytime, Ripon shape w/rich gold 110.00
Cup & saucer, Melody Chintz, Canterbury shape, mini 525.00
Cup & saucer, Paisley, Canterbury shape, mini........................735.00
Cup & saucer, Pink Willow #0194, Henley shape, Ideal China by Shelley..295.00
Cup & saucer, Primrose Chintz/lav cup, Oleander shape saucer .110.00
Cup & saucer, Rock Garden, rich gold, Ripon shape, from $125 to..165.00
Cup & saucer, Rosebud, pk swags, Gainsborough shape 100.00
Cup & saucer, RPFMN, Westminster shape, mini 188.00
Cup & saucer, Thistle, Dainty shape 55.00
Cup & saucer, Woodland, Westminster shape, mini...................560.00
Dinner set, Serenity, 6-pc place sets+major pcs, serves 12, 88-pc.685.00
Dresser set, floral enameled on blk matt, jar+hair receiver+tray.285.00
Egg cup, Dainty Blue, 2½" 52.50
Egg cup, Indian Peony, gr enamel w/blk decor, 3¾" 48.00
Egg cup set, Regency, Dainty shape, 4 1¾" cups+stand.............198.00
Figurine, golfer w/golf bag slung over bk, 6½" 820.00
Figurine, pixie on wide-eyed donkey, MLA, 2¾" 485.00
Figurine, pixie w/watering can among flowers, sgn MLA, 2¾" ...698.00
Food mold, angular design w/indented center, 3x7¾" 85.00
Food mold, nesting hen, 16-oz, 5½" 155.00
Grape dish, Maytime, pierced for drainage, 7½", +9½" undertray..155.00
Gravy & liner, Begonia, Blue Rock or Rosebud, Dainty shape, up to.145.00
Gravy & liner, Bridal rose, Dainty shape, from $145 to 195.00
Gravy & liner, Melody Chintz..135.00
Gravy & liner, Stocks, Dainty shape 265.00
Hair receiver, Festival of the Empire, opening in lid, 4¼" 288.00
Hot water pot, Dainty Blue, mini, 4⅝" 595.00
Jam/honey pot, Summer Glory, slotted lid, 3¾"........................100.00
Jug, hunting scene, bulbous, narrow neck, LF, 5½"....................385.00
Loving cup, Edward III proposed coronation, hdls, 4¾" 355.00
Loving cup, King George VI & Queen Elizabeth Coronation 1937, 3⅜".190.00
Luncheon set, Daffodil Time, Cambridge shape, 6" & 8" plates+c/s..112.00
Muffin, Bridal Rose, Dainty shape, 4½x7¼" dia.......................170.00
Muffin, Primrose #13430, Dainty shape, 4½x7¼" 190.00
Mug, Melody Chintz, hdl, 4¾" 78.00
Mustard jar, Dainty White, slotted lid, attached underplate, 2⅞".66.00
Napkin ring, Dainty Blue, unmk (Royal Albert?) 44.00
Pill box, Japan pattern decor, 1¼x2¾".................................96.00
Pitcher, Cloisello, rich gold, 6-sided, hdl w/thumb rest, 5½" 158.00
Pitcher, Harmony ware, orange/yel/blk/gray bands, 9" 195.00
Plate, American Brookline, Dainty shape, dinner sz, 10½" 155.00
Plate, chop; Blue Rock, Dainty shape, 13½" 140.00
Plate, chop/charger; Harmony ware w/colors as sun's rays, 14¼"..170.00
Plate, Dainty Green, dinner sz, 10½" 105.00
Plate, DuBarry, Duchess or Georgian, dinner sz, 10½", from $28 to .45.00

Plate, Heavenly Blue, Dainty shape, #14075, 8" 45.00
Plate, Lilac Time, Dainty shape, dinner sz, 10¼" 105.00
Plate, Maytime, 8" 128.00
Plate, various scenics, Dainty shape, 10½", ea from $45 to 82.00
Plate, various scenics, not Dainty shape, 10½", ea from $32 to 65.00
Platter, Dainty Blue, 14¾x12" 399.00
Platter, Rosebud, Dainty shape, 15x12¼" 125.00
Platter, wht w/gold trim, Oleander shape, 14¾x12" 180.00
Powder jar, Bridal rose band around lid & jar, squat, 7¼" dia 105.00
Relish, Begonia, Blue Rock, Primrose, Regency, 4x8", ea from $100 to ..130.00
Relish, Melody Chintz, 3-section, 10½" (w/tab hdls) 112.00
Shakers, Bridal Rose, Dainty shape, pear shape, 4", pr 210.00
Tea & toast set, American Brookline, Dainty shape (cup+9x6" plate)..156.00
Tea & toast set, Dainty Pink (cup+9x6" plate) 150.00
Tea & toast set, Regency (cup+9x6" plate) 70.00
Teapot, Blue Rock, Dainty shape w/graceful 'return' spout, 4¾"..190.00
Teapot, Harmony ware w/drip effect, modified Cambridge shape, 6"..275.00
Teapot, Heavenly Pink, Dainty shape, #14075/p, 5½" 698.00
Teapot, Melody Chintz, Cambridge shape w/graceful 'return' spout.350.00
Teapot, Oleander shape, wht w/rich gold trim, 5¼" 242.00
Teapot, Rambler Rose, Dainty shape, #13671, 6-cup, 6⅛" 480.00
Teapot, Rock Garden, Globe shape, 6" 520.00
Teapot, Rosebud w/graceful 'return' spout, 6"...........................310.00
Teapot, RPFMN w/graceful 'return' spout, 6¾" 300.00
Teapot, Sheraton, gr w/rich gold, 6½" 235.00
Teapot, Spring Bouquet, Henley shape w/rich gold, #13651, 5"..165.00
Teapot, Vine & Leaf, Gainsborough shape w/rich gold, #13616, 6".110.00
Toast rack, Charm, 3-bar, 2¾x3" 88.00
Toast rack, Maytime, 5-bar, tab hdls, 7x2½" 180.00
Tray, triple; Blue Rock, Dainty shape, long leaf hdl, 11½" dia....195.00
Tray, triple; Primrose, Dainty shape, long leaf hdl, 8½"..............210.00
Trio, Blue J, Mode shape, rich HP, #1175, c/s+6" plate 360.00
Trio, Blue Rock, Dainty shape 98.00
Trio, Briar Rose, Ripon shape w/gold trim..................................320.00
Trio, Campanula, Dainty shape, #13886, from $98 to 126.00
Trio, Flowers of Gold, Dainty shape, #14187 ....100.00
Trio, gr w/gold in cup, Vogue shape, #11754, c/s+6¼" sq plate...515.00
Trio, Grass Print, modified Empire shape, #9809, c/s+7" plate....114.00
Trio, Japan pattern, Gainsborough shape, #7084, W, c/s+7" plate.128.00
Trio, Lilac Time, Dainty shape..198.00
Trio, mixed fruits on wht w/maroon band, rich gold.....................132.00
Trio, pk roses/gold vines chintz, Kent shape, #12609, c/s+sm sq plate..310.00
Trio, Primrose Chintz, Henley shape, c/s+6" plate.......................115.00
Trio, Red Block, Vogue plate, #11786, c/s+6" plate.....................355.00
Trio, Summer Glory, Henley shape, c/s+6" plate 122.50
Trio, Tapestry Rose chintz on lt yel, Ripon shape w/rich gold.....270.00

Trio, Violets, Dainty shape, $135.00.

Trio, Woodland, Richmond shape, #13348, c/s+7" plate...............85.00
Tureen, Begonia, Dainty shape, domed lid w/knob, hdls, 8¾" dia.368.00

Tureen, R&RD, Dainty shape, domed lid w/knob, hdls, 8¾" dia .288.00
Tureen, Rosebud, Dainty shape, domed lid w/knob, hdls, 8¾" dia..410.00
Tureen, Sunrise Tall Trees, QA shape, lid w/knob, 12" dia (w/hdls)..230.00
Vase, butterflies & lustre, artist sgn, fitted metal frog, 7"............290.00
Vase, butterfly HP at narrow neck, flares out at base, 9" 100.00
Vase, Cloisello w/touches of rich gold, 6¼" 110.00
Vase, leaves/grapes/birds HP, 4-sided/bulbous, 6"........................65.00
Vase, pansy ring; Melody Chintz, 6½" dia..................................195.00
Vase, Walter Slater Art Nouveau design, bulbous w/narrow neck, 7".488.00

Shenandoah

The Shenandoah Valley, extending from Virginia to Pennsylvania is well known for the fine pottery made there from the early 1800s until the turn of the century. It is characterized by bright, clear glazes in a variety of colors or in combination. Many small potteries were involved. Items marked 'Bell' indicate one of the larger companies.

Bowl, cream/dk gr/brn runs on redware, 2 appl buttons, 2x4¼", EX..550.00
Bowl, milk; bl brushed line decor, raised rim, hdls, 4¾x10½" 330.00

Silhouettes

Silhouette portraits were made by positioning the subject between a bright light and a sheet of white drawing paper. The resulting shadow was then traced and cut out, the paper mounted over a contrasting color and framed. The hollow-cut process was simplified by an invention called the Physiognotrace, a device that allowed tracing and cutting to be done in one operation. Experienced silhouette artists could do full-length figures, scenics, ships, or trains freehand. Some of the most famous of these artists were Charles Peale Polk, Charles Wilson Peale, William Bache, Doyle, Edouart, Chamberlain, Brown, and William King. Though not often seen, some silhouettes were completely painted or executed in wax. Examples listed here are hollow-cut unless another type is described and assumed to be in excellent condition unless noted otherwise.

Key:
c/p — cut and pasted   p — profile
fl — full length   wc — water color
hc — hand colored

Boy, p, c/p, inked hair, tears, 5½x4¾", in shadowbox fr.............190.00
Boy w/high collar, p, blk cloth bkground, fr, 5x4½" 165.00
Gen Nathanael Green, fl, c/p, 3¼x2½"+fr...................................635.00
Husband (& wife), p, inked hair/lace, identified/1831, 5½x7", pr ..550.00
Lady in bonnet, p, penciled eyelashes, in pnt fr w/brass mts, 5x4", VG.220.00
Lady w/hair comb, p, gold beads, blk ink on paper, orig fr, 4⅝"..110.00
Lady w/lace collar & hair comb, p, glued to tissue, 7x6" 165.00
Lady w/ruffled bonnet, p, c/p, rpl liner, wear, 6⅛x5" 140.00
Lady w/ruffled collar, hair in bun, p, hollow cut, fr, 3¾" 165.00
Lady wearing bonnet & shawl, p, c/p, ink details, 5x4½"+fr.......220.00
Man, top hat/frock coat/cane, cut-out, Edouart, litho scene, 15x12" .1,400.00
Man (& wife), p, cutouts on tan paper on silk, gilt fr, 7x6", pr....580.00
Man & lady, p, c/p, MA Honeywell, fr: 3½x4¾"..........................175.00
Man in blk ink w/coat details in gloss blk, gold ink hair, +fr, 6x5" .275.00
Man in frock coat & ruffled shirt, p, c/p, beveled fr, 6½x7"........165.00
Man in stenciled frock coat, p, rvpt matt, pnt fr, 5½x4½"..........465.00
Man w/high collar (lady w/hair comb), p, in molded gold fr, 6x5", pr..440.00
Man w/pigtail & ruffled collar, p, blk ink on paper, fr, 4½x4".....300.00
Man w/wht neck scarf, p, Herve Aretist..., gray ink, fr, 5⅛x4" ...110.00

Silver

Coin Silver

During colonial times in America, the average household could not afford items made of silver, but those fortunate enough to have accumulations of silver coins (900 parts silver/100 parts alloy) took them to the local silversmith who melted them down and made the desired household article as requested. These pieces bore the owner's monogram and often the maker's mark, but the words 'Coin Silver' did not come into use until 1830. By 1860 the standard was raised to 925 parts silver/75 parts alloy and the word 'Sterling' was added. Coin silver came to an end about 1900.

Key: t-oz — troy ounce

Abraham Palmer, Cincinnati, Ohio; sugar bowl, footed form with repousse domed lid, acorn finial, foliate handles, 32 troy ounces, 10¾", $2,600.00.

A Mathey, tongs, emb flower baskets on hdl, ca 1824-35, 6½"...**165.00**
AE Warner II, ladle, florals/foliage, eng hdl, 5-t-oz......................**260.00**
Am, fish knife, foliate eng blade, shield hdl w/appl sheaf of wheat...**65.00**
C Bard, Philadelphia PA; water pitcher, repousse scrolls/foliage, 15".**3,450.00**
Christopf C Kuchler, New Orleans, creamer & sugar, eng floral, 6"..**4,600.00**
D Gobrecht, teaspoons, pointed hdl, etched V attachment, 3 for...**650.00**
GH (Geo Hendel), teaspoons, phoenix-bk bowls, 6 for **975.00**
GH (Geo Hendel), teaspoons, shells at bowl application, 6 for..**525.00**
Hyde & Goodrich, ladle, fiddle hdl, wavy shoulders, 14"...........**635.00**
Jones, Lows & Ball, Boston; relief florals/stepped ft, inscribed, 11".**850.00**
P Garret, sugar tongs, acorn pincers, 6½" **150.00**
R&W Wilson Philada, cann, keg shape, inscr Carrie, ca 1825-46, EX.**250.00**
Robt Evans, Boston; sugar bowl, paneled ovoid, w/lid, 1806, 8-t-oz.**460.00**
W Kendrick, Louisville; julep cup, beaded detail, dents, 3⅞" **440.00**
Wm Gale & Son, NY; tea tray, oval w/ovolo edge, scroll hdls, 33" L.**3,450.00**
Wm Haverstick, teaspoons, sheaf of wheat on bowl underside, 6 for..**675.00**

Flatware

Silver flatware is being collected today either to replace missing pieces of heirloom sets or in lieu of buying new patterns, by those who admire and appreciate the style and quality of the older ware. Prices vary from dealer to dealer; some pieces are harder to find and are therefore more expensive. Items such as olive spoons, cream ladles, lemon forks, etc., once thought a necessary part of a silver service, may today be slow to sell; as a result, dealers may price them low and make up the difference on items that sell more readily. Many factors enter into evaluation. Popular patterns may be high due to demand though easily found, while scarce patterns may be passed over by collectors who find them difficult to reassemble. If pieces are monogrammed, deduct 20% (for rare, ornate patterns) to 30% (for common, plain pieces). Place settings generally come in three sizes: dinner, place, and luncheon, with the dinner size generally more expensive. In general, dinner knives are 9½" long, place knives, 9" to 9⅛", and luncheon knives, 8¾" to 8⅞". Dinner forks measure 7⅜" to 7½", place forks, 7¼" to 7⅜", and luncheon forks, 6⅞" to 7⅛". Our advisor for this category is Rick Spencer; he is listed in the Directory under Utah.

Bridal Bouquet, Alvin, dinner fork..**40.00**
Bridal Bouquet, Alvin, luncheon fork **29.00**
Bridal Bouquet, Alvin, luncheon knife, modern **37.00**
Bridal Bouquet, Alvin, salad fork..**34.00**
Bridal Bouquet, Alvin, teaspoon...**23.00**
Bridal Bouquet, Alvin, 4-pc luncheon setting, Fr blade................**95.00**
Burgundy, Reed & Barton, luncheon knife, Fr blade **35.00**
Burgundy, Reed & Barton, place knife, modern...............................**38.00**
Burgundy, Reed & Barton, salad fork..**36.00**
Burgundy, Reed & Barton, 4-pc place-sz setting **109.00**
Buttercup, Gorham, dinner knife, Fr hdl..**38.00**
Buttercup, Gorham, place fork..**36.00**
Buttercup, Gorham, teaspoon **22.00**
Buttercup, Gorham, 4-pc lunch-sz setting, Fr blade **95.00**
Camellia, Gorham, dinner fork...**39.00**
Camellia, Gorham, luncheon fork..**23.00**
Camellia, Gorham, luncheon knife, modern hdl **28.00**
Camellia, Gorham, salad fork..**27.00**
Camellia, Gorham, teaspoon..**16.00**
Chantilly, Gorham, dinner fork...**43.00**
Chantilly, Gorham, luncheon fork..**23.00**
Chantilly, Gorham, place knife, modern blade **34.00**
Chantilly, Gorham, salad fork...**35.00**
Chantilly, Gorham, 4-pc dinner setting **135.00**
Chantilly, Gorham, 4-pc luncheon set, Fr blade **89.00**
Chapel Bells, Alvin, dinner fork..**29.00**
Chapel Bells, Alvin, luncheon knife, modern blade **23.00**
Chapel Bells, Alvin, teaspoon..**16.00**
Chapel Bells, Alvin, 4-pc dinner setting, Fr blade **85.00**
Chateau Rose, Alvin, luncheon knife, Fr blade **36.00**
Chateau Rose, Alvin, salad fork...**34.00**
Chateau Rose, Alvin, teaspoon..**17.00**
Chateau Rose, Alvin, 4-pc dinner setting, modern blade...........**103.00**
Chippendale, Towle, luncheon fork...**31.00**
Chippendale, Towle, luncheon knife, Fr blade................................**28.00**
Chippendale, Towle, teaspoon...**20.00**
Chippendale, Towle, 4-pc luncheon setting, Fr blade...................**89.00**
Crown Baroque, Gorham, dinner fork, 8" **65.00**
Crown Baroque, Gorham, teaspoon..**37.00**
Crown Baroque, Gorham, 4-pc dinner setting...............................**200.00**
El Grandee, Towle, place knife, modern hdl **36.00**
El Grandee, Towle, salad fork...**38.00**
El Grandee, Towle, teaspoon..**27.00**
El Grandee, Towle, 4-pc place-sz setting **115.00**
Enchanting Orchid, Westmoreland, place fork **25.00**
Enchanting Orchid, Westmoreland, place knife, modern blade **27.00**
Enchanting Orchid, Westmoreland, teaspoon................................**17.00**
Enchanting Orchid, Westmoreland, 4-pc place setting **125.00**
English Gadroon, Gorham, luncheon knife, Fr blade **39.00**
English Gadroon, Gorham, salad fork..**33.00**
English Gadroon, Gorham, teaspoon..**19.00**
English Gadroon, Gorham, 4-pc luncheon setting, Fr blade **95.00**
English Gadroon, place knife, modern hdl **39.00**
Etruscan, Gorham, luncheon fork..**27.00**
Etruscan, Gorham, teaspoon **19.00**
Etruscan, Gorham, 4-pc dinner setting, Fr blade **135.00**
Florentine Lace, Reed & Barton, place knife, modern blade........**35.00**

Florentine Lace, Reed & Barton, salad fork **41.00**
Florentine Lace, Reed & Barton, teaspoon **30.00**
Florentine Lace, Reed & Barton, 4-pc place-sz setting **125.00**
Francis I, Reed & Barton, dinner service for 12, 187-pc set.....**4,300.00**
Francis I, Reed & Barton, luncheon knife, Fr blade......................**37.00**
Francis I, Reed & Barton, place knife, modern blade **39.00**
Francis I, Reed & Barton, salad fork..**39.00**
Francis I, Reed & Barton, 4-pc luncheon setting, Fr blade.........**125.00**
George & Martha, Westmoreland, dinner knife, Fr hdl...............**28.00**
George & Martha, Westmoreland, luncheon knife, modern blade.**22.00**
George & Martha, Westmoreland, salad fork................................**29.00**
George & Martha, Westmoreland, 4-pc luncheon setting, modern blade.**79.00**
Grand Duchess, Towle, place fork..**41.00**
Grand Duchess, Towle, place knife, modern blade.....................**44.00**
Grand Duchess, Towle, salad fork...**43.00**
Grand Duchess, Towle, teaspoon..**25.00**
Grand Duchess, 4-pc place-sz setting...**125.00**
Grande Baroque, Wallace, dinner fork..**55.00**
Grande Baroque, Wallace, place knife, modern blade **39.00**
Grande Baroque, Wallace, teaspoon...**27.00**
Grande Baroque, Wallace, 4-pc dinner setting, modern blade **149.00**
Grande Baroque, Wallace, 4-pc place-sz setting..........................**125.00**
Heiress, Oneida, place fork...**22.00**
Heiress, Oneida, salad fork...**20.00**
Heiress, Oneida, teaspoon..**15.00**
Heiress, Oneida, 4-pc place-sz setting...**65.00**
Joan of Arc, International, luncheon fork....................................**33.00**
Joan of Arc, International, luncheon knife, modern blade............**32.00**
Joan of Arc, International, place knife, modern blade..................**35.00**
Joan of Arc, International, teaspoon..**20.00**
Joan of Arc, International, 4-pc place-sz setting...........................**125.00**
Lady Hilton, Westmoreland, luncheon fork **20.00**
Lady Hilton, Westmoreland, luncheon knife, modern blade........**22.00**
Lady Hilton, Westmoreland, teaspoon...**14.00**
Lady Hilton, Westmoreland, 4-pc luncheon setting, Fr blade **65.00**
Love Disarmed, Reed & Barton, dinner knife..............................**82.00**
Love Disarmed, Reed & Barton, salad fork **65.00**
Love Disarmed, Reed & Barton, 4-pc place setting.....................**259.00**
Lyric, Gorham, dinner fork...**39.00**
Lyric, Gorham, luncheon knife, Fr blade.....................................**34.00**
Lyric, Gorham, salad fork **22.00**
Lyric, Gorham, teaspoon **17.00**
Lyric, Gorham, 4-pc luncheon setting, Fr blade **85.00**
Meadow Rose, Wallace, dinner fork **45.00**
Meadow Rose, Wallace, luncheon fork **33.00**
Meadow Rose, Wallace, luncheon knife, Fr blade........................**28.00**
Meadow Rose, Wallace, salad fork **35.00**
Meadow Rose, Wallace, teaspoon **21.00**
Meadow Rose, Wallace, 4-pc luncheon setting, Fr blade..............**89.00**
Rambler Rose, Towle, luncheon knife, Fr blade **27.00**
Rambler Rose, Towle, luncheon knife, modern blade..................**29.00**
Rambler Rose, Towle, salad fork...**22.00**
Rambler Rose, Towle, teaspoon **17.00**
Regent, Alvin, dinner knife **20.00**
Regent, Alvin, master butter spreader, flat hdl...........................**16.00**
Regent, Alvin, salad fork...**21.00**
Regent, Alvin, sugar spoon **18.00**
Regent, Alvin, teaspoon..**15.00**
Rose Point, Wallace, dinner knife, Fr blade **34.00**
Rose Point, Wallace, luncheon knife, Fr blade............................**28.00**
Rose Point, Wallace, place knife, modern blade **34.00**
Rose Point, Wallace, teaspoon..**19.00**
Rose Point, Wallace, 4-pc dinner setting, Fr blade **115.00**
Royal Danish, International, luncheon knife, Fr blade..................**28.00**

Royal Danish, International, place knife, modern blade..............**37.00**
Royal Danish, International, salad fork **37.00**
Royal Danish, International, 4-pc luncheon setting, Fr blade.....**109.00**
Savannah, Reed & Barton, place fork..**33.00**
Savannah, Reed & Barton, place knife, modern blade **33.00**
Savannah, Reed & Barton, salad fork..**38.00**
Savannah, Reed & Barton, teaspoon...**30.00**
Spanish Lace, Wallace, place fork...**25.00**
Spanish Lace, Wallace, salad fork...**25.00**
Spanish Lace, Wallace, teaspoon **18.00**
Spanish Lace, Wallace, 4-pc place-sz setting...............................**75.00**
Steiff Rose, Kirk Steiff, dinner fork..**45.00**
Steiff Rose, Kirk Steiff, luncheon knife, modern hdl **39.00**
Steiff Rose, Kirk Steiff, place fork..**375.00**
Steiff Rose, Kirk Steiff, teaspoon **25.00**
Steiff Rose, Kirk Steiff, 4-pc luncheon setting, modern blade **96.00**
Strasbourg, Gorham, luncheon fork...**25.00**
Strasbourg, Gorham, luncheon knife, modern hdl **30.00**
Strasbourg, Gorham, salad fork **37.00**
Strasbourg, Gorham, teaspoon **21.00**
Strasbourg, Gorham, 4-pc place setting......................................**119.00**
Tiara, Reed & Barton, place knife, modern blade **31.00**
Tiara, Reed & Barton, teaspoon..**23.00**
Tiara, Reed & Barton, 4-pc place-sz setting **105.00**
Waltz of Spring, Wallace, salad fork **39.00**
Waltz of Spring, Wallace, teaspoon **23.00**
William & Mary, Lunt, place knife, modern blade.......................**32.00**
William & Mary, Lunt, salad fork..**24.00**
William & Mary, Lunt, teaspoon...**19.00**
William & Mary, Lunt, 4-pc luncheon setting, modern blade.......**85.00**
Young Love, Oneida, place fork...**23.00**
Young Love, Oneida, place knife, modern.....................................**22.00**
Young Love, Oneida, salad fork...**25.00**
Young Love, Oneida, teaspoon..**17.00**

Hollow Ware

Until the middle of the nineteenth century, the silverware produced in America was custom made on order of the buyer directly from the silversmith. With the rise of industrialization, factories sprung up that manufactured silverware for retailers who often added their trademark to the ware. Silver ore was mined in abundance, and demand spurred production. Changes in style occurred at the whim of fashion. Repousse decoration (relief work) became popular about 1885, reflecting the ostentatious preference of the Victorian era. Later in the century, Greek, Etruscan, and several classic styles found favor. Today the Art Deco styles of this century are very popular with collectors.

In the listings that follow, manufacturer's name or trademark is noted first; in lieu of that information, listings are by country or item. Weight is given in troy ounces.

See also Tiffany, Silver.

Key: t-oz — troy ounce

A Stone, porringer, pierced foliate hdl, 7" dia, 7-t-oz...............**1,295.00**
Andrew Fogelberg, sauce tureen, Geo III, armorial, paw ft, 9" L.**1,450.00**
Arthur Stone, platter, partially lobed sides, ribbed rim, 15" L.....**385.00**
Arthur Stone, salver, rtcl rim w/1 fleur-de-lis, 10⅜"...................**585.00**
Atkins Bros, cake basket, reed/scroll rtcl sides, swing hdl, 11"....**585.00**
Bailey Banks & Biddle, bowl, fluted, low flange, 525 grams..........**80.00**
Ball Blk & Co, bowl, 3-D flute players as hdls, monogram, ftd, 9x12".**1,150.00**
Barbour, bowl, centerpc; lobed rim w/emb & chased foliage, 6x15".**500.00**
Cellini Craft, candlesticks, floriform, trefoil base, 1930, 6-t-oz, pr .**1,175.00**
Clark in rectangle, julep cup, cylinder w/beaded bands, 4x3" **800.00**

Denmark 300, compotes, stepped std on rnd base, 5x6½", pr **290.00**
Dominick & Haff, pitcher, ornate scroll/floral hdl & lip, 1894, 14"..**3,600.00**
Dominick & Haff, serving set, Labors of Cupid, 2 forks+spoon, 9" ea..**800.00**
Dominick & Haff, sweetmeat dish, shaped rim w/floral bouquets, 7" dia.**235.00**
Dominick & Haff, tray, emb florals, monogram, oblong, 14x10", 16-t-oz.**550.00**
Edward Jay, platter, shaped/gadrooned rim, armorial, 1805, 20".**1,000.00**
Frank W Smith, fruit bowl, shaped rim w/grapevines, 1890s, 11" dia.**470.00**
Frank W Smith, pitcher, water; floral repousse, 9½", 29-t-oz......**865.00**
Fras Crump, porringer & lid, eng/emb reeded band w/stamped leaves, 5".**1,200.00**
Friedlander Bros, dish, curved oblong, hammered, 1900, 5¼" L ...**45.00**
Geo Jensen, bowl, plain w/openwork leafy base, #584, GP, 6x7½"..**2,800.00**
German, compote, emb fruits/scrolling leaves, parcel gilt, 1800s, 9" .**300.00**
German/800, bottle, peacock form w/fanned tail, 15½" **690.00**
German/800, bread tray, courtship cartouches, heavy rtcl, 15" L .**920.00**
Gorham, bowl, presentation; hdls, ftd, ca 1959, 35-t-oz **230.00**
Gorham, bowl, rim stamped w/rose blossoms, monogram, 1900, 7" dia.**250.00**
Gorham, candelabra, Chantilly, 5-light, pr **1,895.00**
Gorham, charger, rim w/fruit swags/grotesque masks, 11", 10 for.**7,600.00**
Gorham, coffee/tea set, Plymouth, monogram, 2 pots+cr/sug, 48-t-oz..**550.00**
Gorham, demitasse pot, baluster form w/peaked lid & loop hdl, 10".**125.00**
Gorham, demitasse pot, Plymouth, monogram, 11", +cr/sug w/swing hdl..**325.00**
Gorham, goblets, flared base & rim, 6⅝", 8 for **660.00**
Gorham, pitcher, bulb body w/palm & lotus band, simple hdl, 8".**500.00**
Gorham, pitcher, Colonial Revival, squat baluster w/ear hdl, 6½".**575.00**
Gorham, sherbet, rtcl heart band, trumpet ft, 4½", +liner, 10 for .**175.00**
Gorham, tea set, floral repousse, monogram, 7½" pot+cr/sug **500.00**
Gorham, tea set, monogram, 7½" pot+cr/sug.............................**500.00**
Gorham, tea/coffee, Classical Revival, monogram/1913, 13" kettle+5 pcs.**2,500.00**
Gorham, tea/coffee, Plymouth, 9" coffeepot+teapot, cr/sug w/lid ..**600.00**
Gorham, teapot, scrolling strapwork band, ovoid w/dome lid, 1890s, 6".**325.00**
Gorham, tureen, overall repousse flowers & scrolls, w/lid, 32-t-oz..**985.00**
Gorham, tureen, repousse flowers & scrolls, 7½x15x7½", 32-t-oz.**980.00**
Gorham for Grogan Co, tray, serpentine & floral repousse, 1924, 14" .**400.00**
Graff Washbourne & Dunn, cake plate, rtcl/eng w/scrolling roses, 11".**475.00**
Hartdegen & Co, bread tray, pierced/emb grape border, 285 grams, 11" L.**75.00**
International, bonbon, Wild Rose, ca 1948, 6½" **125.00**
International, candlesticks, Prelude, 3½", pr **100.00**
International, demi cup fr w/Lenox porc liner, w/gilt, +saucer, 8 for .**400.00**
International, shakers, Royal Danish, ca 1939, 4⅜", pr..............**250.00**
J&J Angel, tea/coffee, lobed melon shapes, ornate ft/hdls, 1847, 4-pc.**1,650.00**
JB/GC/WN, box, Geo III, reed-trim lid, eng presentation/1852, 4½"..**235.00**
John Angell, teapot, Geo III, mushroom finial, ornate paw ft, 12" L.**550.00**
John Angell, teapot, Geo III, partially reeded, acanthus/paw ft, 11".**300.00**
John Emes, mustard pot, navette shape, angle hdl, dome lid, 4½"..**300.00**
John Emes, salver, gadrooned rim, 3 hoof ft, armorial, 1781, 10".**350.00**
John Emes, salver, molded/beaded edge, armorial, 1799, 7" **400.00**
John Emes, sugar basket, boat shape, armorial, 1800, 6½x6" **325.00**
John Polhemus, NY; soup ladle, Cottage pattern, presentation, 13" L.**230.00**
John Schofield, teapot, armorial, ivory hdl, 6", +cr/sug...........**1,100.00**
John Shaw, vinaigrette, allover eng floral on stippled ground, 1½"..**450.00**
Kirk & Son, demitasse set, floral repousse, pot+cr/sug, 20-t-oz ...**660.00**
Kirk & Son, platter, oval w/wide border, monogram, 1925, 21" L.**700.00**
London, basket, Geo III, rtcl rim, eng swags, 1786, 12" **1,800.00**
London, creamer, Geo III, urn on sq ped base, 1796, 5¼" **150.00**
London, sugar basket, Geo III, boat form, ped ft, 1789, 6½".......**400.00**
Meriden Britannia, flower basket, swing hdl, 18-t-oz..................**550.00**
Meriden Britannia, side plate, shaped w/ogee reeded rim, 7", 12 for .**400.00**
Meuck-Cary, candlesticks, gadrooned thistle sconce, trumpet ft, 9", pr.**235.00**
Nathaniel Mills, vinaigrette, foliage/name in shield, gilt int, 1⅜" ..**350.00**
Parker & Wakelin, salver, C-scroll rim w/shells, coat of arms, 12".**1,500.00**
Phipps-Robinson, nutmeg grater, bright-cut, 1785, 2⅛" L **635.00**
R&W Wilson, Phila; coffeepot, beaded rims, acorn finial, 1830s, 12".**1,800.00**
Randahl, Chicago; flask, hammered/flattened/curved, pre-1930, 7-t-oz.**350.00**
Reed & Barton, basket, ornate cutouts & eng flowers, 11", 14-t-oz.**525.00**

Reed & Barton, bowl, Francis I, ftd, ca 1951, 3x11", 22-t-oz **460.00**
Reed & Barton, candy dish, Francis I, 8" dia, 10-t-oz.................**215.00**
Reed & Barton, coffee/tea set, Francis I, 2 pots+cr/sug+tray .**19,500.00**
Reed & Barton, coffeepot, lighthouse form, ebony hdl, 1949, 19-t-oz..**150.00**
Reed & Barton, flower basket, ornate cutouts, eng base, 11", 14-t-oz.**525.00**
Reed & Barton, fruit bowl, Salem, ovoid w/slight lobing, ftd, 10"..**250.00**
Reed & Barton, gravy boat, Windsor, ca 1946, 3½x7½"..........**295.00**
Reed & Barton, shell dish, Francis I, ca 1935, 20-t-oz.................**375.00**
Reed & Barton, shell dish, 12", 20-t-oz..**375.00**
Reed & Barton, soup ladle, Francis I, 8-t-oz, 11½" **345.00**
Reed & Barton, tea set, Francis I, 30" 2-hdl tray+6 pcs.........**25,000.00**
Richard Dimes Co, pitcher, allover eng foliate scrolls, 10½" **500.00**
S Kirk & Son, bowl, floral repousse border, ftd, ca 1918, 3x7½"..**200.00**
S Kirk & Son, candlesticks, repousse, ca 1950, 3½x4¼", pr **425.00**
S Kirk & Son, compote, floral repousse, chased details, 4½x9½".**385.00**
S Kirk & Son, shakers, floral repousse, paw ft, 4⅝", pr **220.00**
S Kirk & Son, tazza, repousse border, monogram, 9.3 t-oz, 3¼x7¼".**350.00**
S Kirk & Son, vase, repousse, ftd trumpet, ca 1903-24, 14½x7".**6,750.00**
Sheridan Taunton, salver, grape repousse rim, 8¾" dia.................**50.00**
Shreve Crump & Low, bowl, floral repousse rim, ribbed, 11-t-oz, 10"..**195.00**
Steiff, water pitcher, Rose, hand chased, ca 1910, 13½" **3,500.00**
Stieff, pitcher, heavily eng/emb w/florals, serpentine hdl, 10".**3,800.00**
Stone Assoc, bowl, ridged rim, ftd, 8⅛", 17-t-oz.........................**575.00**
Sweden, coffee service, ovoid forms, hdls w/appl pendant flowers, 3-pc.**800.00**
TB Star, bowl, presentation; eng, 1916, 4x7½", 20-t-oz **325.00**
Thos Daniel, punch bowl, emb reeding to base of bowl, armorial, 20".**2,700.00**
Thos Wynne, beaker, Geo III, reeding/fluting, monogram, 1780, 7".**940.00**
Tiffany, sugar bowl, rtcl band, glass insert, 8-t-oz, 4½" **140.00**
Towle, bowl, Louis XIV, 12"...**200.00**
Towle, candelabra, 3-arm, removable inserts, weighted, 12¾x12", pr.**225.00**
Towle, kettle on stand, Greek Key neck band, ft w/geometric rtcl, 12".**350.00**
Towle, plate, wide border, plain, 20th C, 11", 12 for **3,100.00**
Tuttle, bowl, Revere-style, stepped dome ft, 20th C, 9½" **145.00**

Wallace, coffee and tea service, Adams style with chased and engraved floriate decoration, applied medallions with monograms, consisting of hot water kettle on stand, coffeepot, teapot, creamer and sugar bowl, waste bowl, and tray, 300 troy ounces, $8,000.00 at auction. (Photo courtesy Neal Auction Company)

Wallace, creamer & sugar bowl w/tray, Grand Baroque...............**595.00**
Wallace, heart dish, Grand Baroque, ca 1941, 6x4½" **175.00**
Watson, bowl, Irish pattern, shaped/reeded edge, monogram, 12".**300.00**
Whiting Mfg, bowl, hammered stylized floriform, 9", +matching spoon.**765.00**
Whiting Mfg, cake plate, rtcl leaves/floral, scroll/shell rim, 10⅜".**150.00**
Wm Durgin, tea set, Fairfax, monogram, 3-pc, 29-t-oz...............**500.00**
Wm Grundy, coffeepot, Geo III, eng/emb florals, 1770, 12" **1,500.00**
Wm Sutton, dinner plates, armorial, gadrooned border, 10", 12 for.**5,500.00**
800 hallmark, basket, rtcl rim, repousse cherubs in base, 2x15x12".**500.00**

Silver Overlay

The silver overlay glass made since the 1880s was decorated with a cut-out pattern of sterling silver applied to the surface of the ware.

Bottle, scent; cranberry cased, allover o/l & HP, metal lid, 3¼" .450.00
Bowl, crystal, w/frosted flowers, 12½" 100.00
Pitcher, cobalt, water sz, +6 tumblers 1,200.00
Shot glass, red, elaborate vintage o/l, 2½" 190.00
Trivet, clear, scrolling wide o/l border, 6" dia 80.00
Vase, blk amethyst, Baroque o/l on 2 sides, 10¼" 250.00
Vase, frosted, flying geese/cattails o/l, Rockwell, ovoid, label, 5" ..70.00
Vase, gr, Nouveau o/l, mk Gorham, 16" 670.00
Vase, purple, Nouveau o/l, 4" 475.00

Silverplate

Silverplated flatware is becoming the focus of attention for many of today's collectors. Demand is strong for early, ornate patterns, and prices have continued to rise steadily over the past five years. Our values are based on pieces in excellent or restored/resilvered condition. Serving pieces are priced to reflect the values of examples in complete original condition, with knives retaining their original blades. If pieces are monogrammed, deduct from 20% (for rare, ornate patterns) to 30% (for common, plain pieces). Our advisor for this category is Rick Spencer; he is listed in the Directory under Utah. For more information we recommend *Standard Encyclopedia of American Silverplate* by Frances M. Bones and Lee Roy Fisher and *Silverplated Flatware, Revised Fourth Edition,* by Tere Hagan.

See also Railroadiana, Silverplate.

Flatware

Adoration, 1847 Rogers, grill fork 9.00
Adoration, 1847 Rogers, place soup spoon 10.00
Adoration, 1847 Rogers, sugar spoon 9.00
Ambassador, 1847 Rogers, luncheon knife, modern blade 11.00
Ambassador, 1847 Rogers, master butter spreader, flat 6.00
Ambassador, 1847 Rogers, table serving spoon 9.00
Anniversary Rose, International, place knife, modern blade 5.00
Anniversary Rose, International, place soup spoon 5.00
Anniversary Rose, International, sugar spoon 4.00
Baroque Rose, Oneida, place fork 6.00
Baroque Rose, Oneida, place knife, modern blade 7.50
Baroque Rose, Oneida, place soup spoon 6.00
Baroque Rose, Oneida, teaspoon 4.00
Brittany Rose, Rogers, sugar spoon 5.00
Brittany Rose, Rogers, teaspoon 4.00
Brittany Rose, Rogers, 4-pc place-sz setting 14.00
Buckingham, Wallace, gumbo soup spoon 7.50
Buckingham, Wallace, table serving spoon 12.50
Buckingham, Wallace, teaspoon 6.00
Calais, Gorham, luncheon knife, modern blade 17.00
Calais, Gorham, place fork 12.00
Calais, Gorham, place knife, modern blade 17.00
Calais, Gorham, teaspoon 12.00
Century, Holmes & Edwards, gumbo soup spoon 6.00
Century, Holmes & Edwards, luncheon fork 5.00
Century, Holmes & Edwards, mint jelly serving spoon 9.00
Chapel, Reed & Barton, salad fork 12.50
Chapel, Reed & Barton, teaspoon 9.00
Classic Bead, Wallace, cake serving knife 15.00

Classic Bead, Wallace, table serving spoon 10.00
Classic Bead, Wallace, 4-pc place-sz setting 24.00
Coronation, Oneida, grill knife 6.00
Coronation, Oneida, master butter spreader, flat 6.00
Coronation, Oneida, teaspoon 2.50
Coronation, Oneida, 4-pc luncheon setting, modern blade 22.00
Cottage Rose, Reed & Barton, gravy ladle 17.00
Cottage Rose, Reed & Barton, master butter spreader, hollow hdl..8.00
Cottage Rose, Reed & Barton, sugar spoon 8.00
Cottage Rose, Reed & Barton, table serving spoon 8.00
Danish Princess, Holmes & Edwards, grill fork 6.00
Danish Princess, Holmes & Edwards, luncheon knife 6.00
Danish Princess, Holmes & Edwards, teaspoon 2.00
Danish Princess, Holmes & Edwards, 4-pc luncheon setting, modern blade.20.00
Dresden Rose, Reed & Barton, place fork 8.00
Dresden Rose, Reed & Barton, place knife, modern blade 10.00
Dresden Rose, Reed & Barton, teaspoon 6.00
Emperor, Reed & Barton, master butter spreader, hollow hdl........10.00
Emperor, Reed & Barton, serving fork 14.00
Emperor, Reed & Barton, sugar spoon 10.00
Emperor, Reed & Barton, table serving spoon 14.00
Eternally Yours, 1847 Rogers, baby spoon 15.00
Eternally Yours, 1847 Rogers, gumbo soup spoon 7.00
Eternally Yours, 1847 Rogers, luncheon knife, modern blade 12.00
Eternally Yours, 1847 Rogers, 4-pc luncheon setting, modern blade .30.00
Eternally Yours, 1941, 1847 Rogers, butter spreader, flat hdl, ind .10.00
Eternally Yours, 1941, 1847 Rogers, dessert spoon 6.00
Eternally Yours, 1941, 1847 Rogers, teaspoon 4.50
Evening Star, Community, salad fork 6.00
Evening Star, Community, table serving spoon 9.00
Evening Star, Community, 4-pc luncheon setting, modern blade .17.50
Floral, 1902, Wallace, asparagus server 225.00
Floral, 1902, Wallace, chocolate spoon 25.00
Floral, 1902, Wallace, luncheon knife, blunt blade 16.00
Flower Song, Gorham, place fork 9.00
Flower Song, Gorham, place soup spoon 7.50
Flower Song, Gorham, sugar spoon 9.00
Flower Song, Gorham, 4-pc place-sz setting 17.50
Guild, International, grill knife 7.50
Guild, International, luncheon fork 6.00
Guild, International, teaspoon 5.00
King Cedric, Oneida, grill knife 7.50
King Cedric, Oneida, luncheon knife, Fr blade 7.50
King Cedric, Oneida, master butter server, flat 6.00
King Cedric, Oneida, mint jelly serving spoon 6.00
Lady Hamilton, Community, grill fork 6.00
Lady Hamilton, Community, 4-pc luncheon setting, Fr blade.......17.50
Loraine, Oneida, luncheon fork 4.00
Loraine, Oneida, master butter spreader, flat 4.00
Loraine, Oneida, teaspoon 4.00
Loraine, Oneida, 4-pc luncheon setting, Fr blade 11.00
Love Lace, 1847 Rogers, grill fork 5.00
Love Lace, 1847 Rogers, gumbo soup spoon 7.50
Love Lace, 1847 Rogers, master butter spreader, flat 6.00
Love Lace, 1847 Rogers, 4-pc luncheon setting, modern blade 22.00
Majestic, Rogers, cocktail fork 2.50
Majestic, Rogers, luncheon fork 5.00
Majestic, Rogers, sugar spoon 5.00
Majestic, Rogers, 4-pc place-sz setting 22.00
Morning Star, Community, cocktail fork 7.50
Morning Star, Community, place soup spoon 10.00
Morning Star, Community, teaspoon 9.00
Morning Star, Community, 4-pc grille-sz setting 22.50
Old Dominion, Gorham, oval soup spoon 6.00

Old Dominion, Gorham, place fork **7.50**
Old Dominion, Gorham, 4-pc, place-sz setting **22.50**
Parthenon, Reed & Barton, gravy ladle **16.00**
Parthenon, Reed & Barton, master butter server, hollow hdl **8.00**
Parthenon, Reed & Barton, sugar spoon **8.00**
Parthenon, Reed & Barton, tablespoon, pierced **9.00**
Patrician, Oneida, bouillon soup spoon **5.00**
Patrician, Oneida, dinner fork **15.00**
Patrician, Oneida, salad fork **9.00**
Patrician, Oneida, sugar spoon **9.00**
Queen Bess, Oneida, iced-tea spoon **6.00**
Queen Bess, Oneida, luncheon fork **6.00**
Queen Bess, Oneida, luncheon knife, Fr blade **7.50**
Queen Bess, Oneida, master butter spreader, flat....................**6.00**
Remembrance, 1847 Rogers, grill knife **8.00**
Remembrance, 1847 Rogers, luncheon knife, modern blade **8.00**
Remembrance, 1847 Rogers, salad fork **7.00**
Remembrance, 1847 Rogers, teaspoon **2.00**
Remembrance, 1847 Rogers, 4-pc luncheon setting, modern blade.**20.00**
Romance, Holmes & Edwards, cocktail fork **6.00**
Romance, Holmes & Edwards, place knife, modern blade............**11.00**
Romance, Holmes & Edwards, sugar spoon **9.00**
Rosemary, Rogers, berry serving spoon **11.00**
Rosemary, Rogers, oval soup/dessert spoon **6.00**
Rosemary, Rogers, 4-pc place-sz setting **17.50**
Spring Garden, Holmes & Edwards, teaspoon **6.00**
Spring Garden, Holmes & Edwards, 4-pc luncheon setting, modern blade .**17.50**
Spring Garden, Holmes & Edwares, sugar spoon.....................**9.00**
Valley Rose, Oneida, gravy ladle **8.00**
Valley Rose, Oneida, iced-tea spoon **4.00**
Valley Rose, Oneida, teaspoon **6.00**
Valley Rose, Oneida, 4-pc luncheon setting, modern blade **12.50**

Hollow Ware

Supper set consisting of soup tureen and lid, ladle, three oval covered entree dishes, mustard pot, salt cellar, and pepper shakers, $1,350.00.
(Photo courtesy Neal Auction Company)

Bowl, dbl vegetable; Grosvenor, Community, w/lid, 12" L **175.00**
Bowl, serving; overall pattern, 4 paw ft, w/lid, Ellis Barker, 8x14".**300.00**
Butter dish, Heritage, 1847 Rogers, ca 1960, 3½x7¼x3¼" **50.00**
Candle snuffer & 10" tray, scissor-form, foliate scrolls/rosettes....**115.00**
Candlestick, fluted shaft w/Corinthian capital, stepped base, 14".**150.00**
Candlesticks, allover shell decor, Georgian manner, English, 10", pr.**300.00**
Candlesticks, Chantilly, Gorham, ca 1960, 4½x4¼", pr **95.00**
Chafing dish, high scroll ft w/shells, shell rim, Bakelite hdls, 18" L.**330.00**
Chalice, hunting scene in relief, lid w/bear & 2 cubs, mk IW, 15".**1,000.00**
Cocktail set, Art Deco, Bernard Rice, shaker+6 glasses+tray......**575.00**
Coffee urn, floral decor, domed lid, Wilcox, 15¾" **200.00**
Coffee urn, flower form body, leaf floral-emb ft, Reed & Barton, 17" .**5.00**
Coffee urn, Rococo designs, domed lid, Reed & Barton, 14", VG.**140.00**
Egg warmer, swivel lid on scroll posts, 4 ball ft, MOP hdl, 7" **190.00**
Entree dish, dbl, 2 lids/paw ft w/gadrooning & shells, crown mk, 21" L.**240.00**
Entree dish, domed swivel lid, eng ferns, ivory knob, hoof ft, 9x12" .**440.00**

Entree dish, gadrooned border, ring hdl removes, monogram, 11" L, pr..**575.00**
Entree dish, gadrooning/foliage, ornate hdls, Elkington, 1857, 11".**275.00**
Flask, emb grapes & leaves, rstr, 6¼" **195.00**
Gravy boat, Daffodil, attached tray, 1847 Rogers **125.00**
Hot water urn, Neo-Classic, beaded hdls, sq ftd base, 22" **1,200.00**
Lazy Susan, Baroque, Wallace, center hdl, 19" dia......................**350.00**
Pitcher, water; Ambassador, 1847 Rogers, 1919, 10¼: **350.00**
Platter, well & tree; Rosepoint, Wallace, 1955, 19".....................**175.00**
Punch bowl, appl flowers on wavy rim/scalloped ped base, Meriden, 21".**430.00**
Punch bowl, stag-head hdls, hoof ft, shaped rim, 20th C, English, 14"..**285.00**
Tea set, Wintrop, coffee/teapot, cr/sug, sm bowl/tray, Reed & Barton..**495.00**
Teapot on stand, shell ft, scrolled legs, rtcl aprons, bell mk, 14"....**300.00**
Toothpick holder, lg cat at side, Tufts #3403, rstr **650.00**
Toothpick holder, rooster at side, rstr **275.00**
Tureen, soup; Geo III-style, acanthus hdls/scroll ft, 1800s, 16" L.**550.00**
Wine caddy, rstr Wilcox #01845.......................................**425.00**
Wine jug, Greek taste, flat chased/eng decor, English Victorian, 13"..**285.00**
Wine wagon, vintage borders, Regency style, 4-wheel base, 20" L..**400.00**

Sheffield

Candesticks, heavy, rococo, florals/scrolls on baluster stems, pr..**200.00**
Candlesticks, scalloped shell base, baluster stems, bobeches, 13", pr.**415.00**
Castor set, 4 cut glass bottles, rtcl ftd fr w/center hdl **150.00**
Coffee urn, acanthus leaf finial, lion's head w/ring hdls, 27"....**1,750.00**
Coffee/tea, partly fluted, gadrooned rims, ball ft, ca 1820s, 4-pc set.**230.00**
Hot water pot, eng decor, wood hdl & finial, 1820-30 ....**175.00**
Hot water urn, 2-hdl pear form w/ornate floral borders, ped ft, 15" .**230.00**
Meat server, dome lid w/stamped ferns, Walker & Hall, 15x16x21"..**220.00**
Salver, beaded serpentine ribs, chased ball & claw ft, 11" W **50.00**
Salver, claw/ball ft, wide scroll/floral band, Martin Hall, 10" **400.00**
Tea caddy, floral bands & chased geometric border, 5½"..............**175.00**
Tea set, emb/fluted, ivory mushroom finials, Dixon, 2 pots+cr/sug.**300.00**
Tea urn, Adam influenced 2-hdl urn form, reeded, acanthus plinth, 24" .**500.00**
Teapot, fluted oval w/eng geometrics, str spout, mushroom finial, G.**150.00**

Sinclaire

In 1904 H.P. Sinclaire and Company was founded in Corning, New York. For the first sixteen years of production, Sinclaire used blanks from other glassworks for his cut and engraved designs. In 1920 he established his own glass-blowing factory in Bath, New York. His most popular designs utilize fruits, flowers, and other forms from nature. Most of Sinclaire's glass is unmarked; items that are carry his logo: an 'S' within a wreath with two shields.

Bowl, canary yel, etched floral, rolled rim, 13" **230.00**
Bowl, canoe w/eng flowers, 11x7½" **185.00**
Bowl, cut dmns/medallions w/etched grapes, 1904-28, 4¼x9" **350.00**
Candlestick, lt gr, swirled ribs, 10¼" **95.00**
Candlesticks, bl, 10", pr **345.00**
Creamer & sugar bowl, Hobstar & eng floral............................**575.00**
Plate, Laurel Wreath, clear w/etched decor, 8¼" **15.00**
Teapot, Rose **1,465.00**
Tumbler, iced tea; eng thistles...**40.00**
Vase, eng bulbous bowl on pencil stem, 12" **465.00**
Vase, Stratford, 16"...**500.00**

Sitzendorf

The Sitzendorf factory began operations in East Germany in the mid-1800s, adopting the name of the city as the name of their company.

They produced fine porcelain groups, figurines, etc., in much the same style and quality as Meissen and the Dresden factories. Much of their ware was marked with a crown over the letter 'S' and a horizontal line with two slash marks.

Candelabra, 2 cherubs at base, w/5 holders, 1850s, 16", pr..........**950.00**
Figurine, female Olympian, gold hair & dress, on 1 knee, 7x8x2½"..**450.00**
Figurine, French soldier, mk 1799 56th Regiment of Foot on bk .**175.00**
Figurine, girl in lacy dress sits & plays horn, 4¼" **100.00**
Figurine, lady w/fan & plumed hat on floral base, #2302, 8".......**225.00**
Figurine, leopard, yel w/blk spots, 7x9½" **300.00**
Figurine, man reading love letter (lady w/rose), 8", pr................**400.00**
Figurine, man w/flute (lady w/tambourine), lamb w/ea, 8¾", pr .**400.00**
Figurine, man w/rose & watering can (lady w/basket), 8", pr **370.00**
Figurine, Olympian beauty in curtsy, mk, 7x8x2½" **450.00**
Figurine, 2 female dancers in lacy skirts w/mc floral, 4½", pr.....**175.00**
Lamp base, lady in hoop gown , EX details, #23727, 1902-72, 8½".**150.00**
Vase, cherubs (2) and many roses, 10x8", NM............................**500.00**
Vase, egg shape, mc vines/flowers, 2 children support base, 4¾"..**400.00**
Vase, sea shells (3) form body covered in roses & vines, 3¾x3¾"..**300.00**

Skookum Dolls

Representing real Indians of various tribes, stern-faced Skookum dolls were designed by Mary McAboy of Missoula, Montana, in the early 1900s. The earliest of McAboy's creations were made with air-dried apple faces that bore a resemblance to the neighboring Chinook Indian tribe. The name Skookum is derived from the Chinook/Siwash term for large or excellent (aka Bully Good) and appears as part of the oval paper labels often attached to the feet of the dolls.

In 1913 McAboy applied for a patent that described her dolls in three styles: a female doll, a female doll with a baby, and a male doll. In 1916 George Borgman and Co. partnered with McAboy, registered the Skookum trademark, and manufactured these dolls which were distributed by the Arrow Novelty Co. of New York and the HH Tammen Co. of Denver. The Skookum (Apple) Packers Association of Washington state produced similar 'friendly faced' dolls as did Louis Ambery for the National Fruit exchange.

The dried apple faces of the first dolls were replaced by those made of a composition material. Plastic faces were introduced in the 1940s, and these continued to be used until production ended in 1959. Skookum dolls were produced in a variety of styles, with the most collectible having stern, lined faces with small painted eyes glancing to the right, colorful Indian blankets pulled tightly across the straw- or paper-filled body to form hidden arms, felt pants or skirts over wooden legs, and wooden feet covered with decorated felt suede or masking tape.

Skookums were produced in sizes ranging from a 2" souvenir mailer with a cardboard address tag to 36" novelty and advertising dolls. Collectors highly prize 21" to 26" dolls as well as dolls that glance to their left. Felt or suede feet predate the less desirable brown plastic feet of the late 1940s and 1950s. Unless noted otherwise, our values are for skookums in excellent condition. Our advisor for this category is Glen Rairigh; he is listed in the Directory under Michigan.

Baby, looks left, cradle brd, beaded body/head covering, 10½" .**1,100.00**
Baby, mc blanket, leather headband w/pnt decor, 4" **30.00**
Baby, wrapped in mc blanket, feather in headband, 3½x3".........**200.00**
Baby mailer, 1½¢ postcard attached, feather ribbon binding, 4".**100.00**
Baby mailer, 1½¢ postcard attached, rattan binding, 4" **105.00**
Baby/child in loop basket, blanket wrap, necklace, 14"..............**200.00**
Baby/child in loop blanket, blanket wrap, unbraided hair, 12"....**225.00**
Boy, brn ft w/pnt decor, Bully Good label, 6½" **100.00**
Boy, brn suede ft w/decor, headband, 10" **150.00**

Boy, mc blanket, felt pants, brn plastic fr w/mk, wood beads, 9½" .**85.00**
Boy, mc blanket, felt pants, leather shoes, 6½", VG.....................**50.00**
Chief, w/headdress, paper shoes w/decor, 12½"............................**250.00**
Family, chief & female w/baby, clothes match, 15" & 14"..........**600.00**
Family, man w/exposed right arm, 13½", female w/baby, 12½"...**900.00**
Family, w/blanket/clothes/beads, 35", 33" w/10" baby in arms .**5,900.00**
Female w/baby, floral skirt, glass bead necklace, 11½"................**300.00**
Female w/baby, w/blanket, necklace, feather in hair, 16", G **145.00**
Female w/baby, w/blanket, purple felt ft/skirt, necklace, 11½"....**200.00**
Female w/baby, w/blanket, worn paper ft, 12½", VG..................**150.00**
Girl, cotton-wrapped legs, pnt suede ft covers, Bully Good, 6½".**100.00**
Girl, w/blanket, felt skirt, decor felt ft, bandana, 10"....................**85.00**
Girl, w/blanket/skirt, leather shoes, feather, label, 6½" **125.00**
Mailer, baby in bl & yel cotton, Grand Canyon 10-1-52...............**25.00**
Mailer, baby in patterned cotton on yel cb....................................**25.00**
Mailer, baby in red bandana on yel cb **55.00**
Male, w/blanket, feather in headband, loose hair, felt shoes, 14", VG .**115.00**

Slag Glass

Slag glass is a marbleized opaque glassware made by several companies from about 1870 until the turn of the century. It is usually found in purple or caramel (see Chocolate Glass), though other colors were also made. Pink is rare and very expensive. It was revived in recent years by several American glassmakers, L.E. Smith, Westmoreland, and Imperial among them.

The listings below reflect values for items with excellent color. Our advisor for this category is Sharon Thoerner; she is listed in the Directory under California.

Caramel, creamer & sugar bowl, Imperial #30 ....**60.00**
Caramel, Dolphin, compote, ftd, Imperial #778, 7", minimum value.**85.00**
Caramel, shell tray, Imperial #297, 7½", minimum value...............**45.00**
Caramel, swan mint whimsey, Imperial #147, 4", minimum value ..**30.00**
Caramel, Windmill, plate, Imperial, 10¾", minimum value..........**85.00**
Jade, Rooster on lacy base, Imperial, #158, 8"............................**250.00**
Jade Green, Rose, candle holders, Imperial #160, 3½", pr.............**55.00**
Jade Green, rose bowl, 3-toed, Imperial #74c, 8", minimum value.**55.00**
Pink, Invt Fan & Feather, bowl, berry; 6½"...........................**1,000.00**

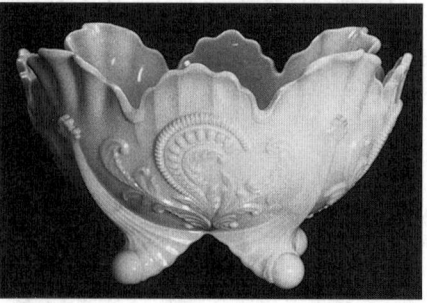

Pink, Inverted Fan and Feather, bowl, fruit; 5x9", $750.00.

Pink, Invt Fan & Feather, butter dish, 6" dia...........................**1,500.00**
Pink, Invt Fan & Feather, creamer **500.00**
Pink, Invt Fan & Feather, cruet, all orig **900.00**
Pink, Invt Fan & Feather, jelly comport, 5" **450.00**
Pink, Invt Fan & Feather, pitcher, 8"...**2,500.00**
Pink, Invt Fan & Feather, punch cup, from $285 to.....................**315.00**
Pink, Invt Fan & Feather, sauce dish, scalloped rim, 4-ftd, 2½x4".**275.00**
Pink, Invt Fan & Feather, shakers, rare, pr **1,200.00**
Pink, Invt Fan & Feather, spooner **475.00**
Pink, Invt Fan & Feather, sugar bowl, w/lid **1,000.00**
Pink, Invt Fan & Feather, toothpick holder, flat **500.00**

Pink, Invt Fan & Feather, toothpick holder, ftd, 2⅜" **1,500.00**
Pink, Invt Fan & Feather, tumbler **235.00**
Purple, Butterfly, bonbon, hdls, Fenton #8230ps......................**85.00**
Purple, Cape Cod, cigarette lighter, 2-pc, Imperial #1602, minimum..**95.00**
Purple, Cow, butter dish, English, Greener, 1876, 7¾" **1,000.00**
Purple, Dart Bar, water pitcher, Challinor Taylor, 8" **185.00**
Purple, Dewdrop, bowl, Imperial #641, 8½", minimum value **65.00**
Purple, Hobnail, bell, Fenton #3667ps, 5½"...............................**50.00**
Purple, Leaf & Orange Tree, rose bowl, ftd, Fenton #8223ps **85.00**
Purple, rabbit on lacy base, Imperial, #157, 8" **750.00**
Purple, swan, open bk, Imperial #400, 8", minimum value..........**100.00**
Ruby, cat on rib base, Westmoreland, 5½"...................................**145.00**
Ruby, Grape, bowl, crimped rim, Imperial #47C, 9", minimum value .**75.00**
Ruby, Tricorn vase, Imperial, #192, 8½" **150.00**

Smith Bros.

Alfred and Harry Smith founded their glassmaking firm in New Bedford, Massachusetts. They had been formerly associated with the Mt. Washington Glass Works, working there from 1871 to 1875 to aid in establishing a decorating department. Smith glass is valued for its excellent enameled decoration on satin or opalescent glass. Pieces were often marked with a lion in a red shield. Our advisors for this category are Betty and Clarence Maier; they are listed in the Directory under Pennsylvania.

Atomizer, floral at shoulder, pk/lav on cream, soft ribs, rpl hdw, 7"..**260.00**
Bowl, acorns & leaves on wht, ribbed, blk rim, 4x8½" **575.00**
Bowl vase, sm floral on wht, beaded rim, 4x5½" **120.00**
Box, daisies on tan, melon ribbed, 3x4" **375.00**
Cracker jar, daisies/ferns on lt yel, bbl shape, 4¾" **250.00**
Cracker jar, oak leaves on melon-rib cream, metal lid mk SB, 7" dia .**400.00**
Cracker jar, pansies, brn/maroon/gold on beige, metal lid **735.00**
Cracker jar, simple floral, gold/tan on cream w/diagonal ribs, sq, 7" ..**285.00**
Creamer & sugar bowl, daisies & foliage on wht, SP rim & lid ..**735.00**
Creamer & sugar bowl, gold prunus, melon ribbed, w/lid, 3¼" ...**270.00**
Creamer & sugar bowl, sunflower/man's portrait on wht w/gold, 3½" .**400.00**
Jar, daisies, wht on cream, melon ribbed, lion mk, w/lid, 4" dia..**145.00**
Jar, dresser; pansies, gold-beaded border (worn), 2½x3½".............**150.00**
Jar, powder; allover daisies, melon ribbed, 2¾x3¾".....................**250.00**
Potpourri, lotus blossom/leaves on cream, melon ribbed, 3¾x5¾' .**400.00**
Rose bowl, daisies on tan, melon ribbed, 2½x3" **325.00**
Sugar shaker, floral on bl wash, SP lid w/dragonflies, mk #715 ...**385.00**
Sugar shaker, floral sprig, ribbed cylinder, 6"..............................**290.00**
Sweetmeat, dainty wht floral on wht, melon ribbed, 5" dia **200.00**
Sweetmeat, pansies w/raised gold, rampant lion mk **585.00**
Toothpick holder, violets on wht, pillar ribbed, 2"......................**275.00**
Vase, floral on beige, bulbous, 4½" **300.00**
Vase, pond lilies/leaves, mc on lt pk, 7" **175.00**
Vase, Santa Maria on flask shape, 8½".....................................**1,500.00**
Vase, wisteria blossoms w/gr & gold leaves, melon ribbed, 8½" .**1,000.00**
Vase, wisteria on pnt burmese w/gold, swirled, 7x4½" **1,100.00**

Snow Babies

During the last quarter of the nineteenth century, snow babies — little figures in pebbly white snowsuits — originated in Germany. They were originally made of sugar candy and were often used as decorations for Christmas cakes. Later on they were made of marzipan, a confection of crushed almonds, sugar, and egg whites. Eventually porcelain manufacturers began making them in bisque. They were popular until WWII. These tiny bisque figures range in size from 1" up to 7" tall. Quality German pieces bring very respectable prices on the market today. Beware of

reproductions. Our advisor for this category is Linda Vines; she is listed in the Directory under California.

Babies (2) holding Santa's hands, Germany, 2"...........................**175.00**
Babies (2) sliding down brick wall, Germany, 2½" **175.00**
Baby, w/drum & cymbal, mk German US Zone, 2" **90.00**
Baby feeding seal w/baby bottle, Germany, 2".............................**175.00**
Baby in sled pulled by huskies, Germany, 2" **165.00**
Baby lying on side, blk face, brn eyes, Germany, 2" **150.00**
Baby pulling 3 penguins on sled, Germany, 2".............................**285.00**
Baby sitting, snow ft, pointed hood, EX detail, Germany, 2".......**150.00**
Baby w/seal & red ball, Germany, 2" **195.00**
Carollers, 3 w/snow hats & lantern on snow base, Germany, 2" ...**95.00**
Santa in silver car, toys in bk, Germany, 1½" **125.00**
Santa nodder, Germany, 3" **90.00**
Santa sitting on wht swing, Germany, 3" **135.00**
Snow bear on hind legs, lifelike, Germany, 5½" **375.00**
Snow man sitting, blk top hat, Germany, 2" **95.00**

Snuff Boxes

As early as the seventeenth century, the Chinese began using snuff. By the early nineteenth century, the practice had spread to Europe and America. It was used by both the gentlemen and the ladies alike, and expensive snuff boxes and bottles were the earmark of the genteel. Some were of silver or gold set with precious stones or pearls, while others contained music boxes. In the following listings, the dimension noted is length.

See also Orientalia, Snuff Bottles.

Burl walnut, octagonal, ca 1850, 1½x4" L **315.00**
Gilt bronze, center medallion, Fr, ca 1775-95, 1x3x1½" **475.00**
Horn, curled end, brass fittings, 3¼" **110.00**
Ivory, lady's mini portrait, ca 1900, 2½" dia, EX.........................**365.00**
Pewter w/emb tavern scene, 18th C, 1x2x2¾", EX **185.00**
Porc w/HP portrait & gold, att Meissen, ca 1900, 1x2½"............**235.00**
Silver, dbl lid, fishscale w/shell cartouch, London, 1850s, 2" L **50.00**
Silver, enameled star & dmn, Petrograd, 1840-50, 2½" L **75.00**
Silver, fish form w/red stone eyes, articulated, Continental, 4" L.**300.00**
Silver, fishscale & dots w/center medallion, Geo III, 2½" L **200.00**
Silver, flowers radiate from star, R Sawyer/Dublin, 1806-07, 2" dia .**175.00**
Silver, gadroon-molded shoulders, John Shaw, 1817-18, 2⅝" L..**200.00**
Silver, medallion/rosettes/circles/dots, Geo III, 3".......................**425.00**
Silver, plain-center medallion & florals, English, 1820s, 2¾" L..**150.00**

Soap Hollow Furniture

In the Mennonite community of Soap Hollow, Pennsylvania, the women made and sold soap; the men made handcrafted furniture. Rare today, this furniture was stenciled, grain painted, and beautifully decorated with inlaid escutcheons. These pieces are becoming very sought after. When well kept, they are very distinctive and beautiful. The items described in these listings were recently sold through Merle S. Mishlers Auctions, RD 2, Hollsopple, Pennsylvania. All are in excellent condition unless otherwise noted. Our advisor for this category is Anita Levi; she is listed in the Directory under Pennsylvania.

Blanket chest, feathers on mustard & brn, MB/1897.................**1,400.00**
Blanket chest, grpt w/blk lid, fruit/florals w/gold, 1882 ....**2,900.00**
Blanket chest, maroon & gold stencil, rod escutcheon, 1856.....**2,000.00**
Blanket chest, poplar, orig red pnt w/blk/gold, att, 22x42"........**3,850.00**
Blanket chest, poplar, red wash/gr rpt, dtd 1855, 20x50" top, att, G .**600.00**
Blanket chest, red & blk, gold stencil, CW/1874, 25x18x45" **6,700.00**

Blanket chest, red & blk, gold stencil, MH/1871, 25x15x10", VG ..6,200.00
Blanket chest, red w/floral stencils, rpl hinges, FJ/1892, VG.....3,800.00
Blanket chest, red/gr pnt w/yel stripes/stencil, SH, 1868, 24x49".19,250.00
Blanket chest, rose decals, blk & brn grpt, LK/1890..................5,000.00
Chest, 4 lg/2 sm drws w/decor, enamel pulls, sgn, 1951, EX.....4,600.00
Chest, 4 lg/3 sm drws, stencil, enamel pulls, sgn, 1883, EX+ ..5,400.00
Chest, 6-drw, brn w/mustard & decals, blk top & sides, Sala...1,900.00
Chest, 6-drw, cherry w/red stain/ebonized trim, 45x37" 2,750.00
Chest, 6-drw, no pnt or decor, EX wood, G 475.00
Chest, 7-drw, foliate stenciling, 1851, 55x41" 1,350.00
Chest, 7-drw, grpt w/blk, gold stencil, MH 1887, 47½x39½" .14,500.00
Chest, 7-drw, maroon w/blk top & sides, rpt, CKM/1879, G 550.00
Cradle, gilt stencils, mustard trim, maroon grpt 1,100.00
Cupboard, corner; maroon w/blk, stencil, 1856.....................11,500.00
Cupboard, Dutch; 4 doors/2 drws, stencil/old rpt, 1875, 84x65"..8,000.00
Cupboard, poplar w/orig red & gr pnt/striping/stencil, 2-pc, 87x64"..35,200.00
Cupboard, step-bk; 3 glass doors/2 solid, 3-drw, no decor, 87½x64".20,000.00
Cupboard, top only, 2 glass doors, no decor, 40x42x13"...........3,500.00
Dresser, Emp style, columns on 3 drws, HF/1874.....................2,200.00
Frame, cross pcs, gr/yel striping, 15½x19¾" 1,000.00
Frame, gilt edges, stenciled, blk 1,050.00
Rope bed, cherry, red & brn finish, rare....................................2,300.00
Stand, bedside; rpt mustard brn 400.00

Soapstone

Soapstone is a soft talc in rock form with a smooth, greasy feel from whence comes its name. (It is also called Soo Chow Jade.) It is composed basically of talc, chlorite, and magnetite. In colonial times it was extracted from out-croppings in large sections with hand saws, carted by oxen to mills, and fashioned into useful domestic articles such as footwarmers, cooking utensils, inkwells, etc. During the early 1800s, it was used to make heating stoves and kitchen sinks. Most familiar today are the carved vases, bookends, and boxes made in China during the Victorian era. For further information we recommend *Collector's Digest of Soapstone* by L-W Book Sales. Our advisor for this category is Clarence Bodine; he is listed in the Directory under Pennsylvania.

Bookends, fruit & flowers in pot motif, 5x4", pr 125.00
Figurine, peaches on base, red highlights, 5x6" 60.00
Figurine, peasant drinking from teapot, hat & mat on bk, 5x6x2"..135.00
Figurine, seated Buddha, holding animal, 1890s, 2¼x1¾" 60.00
Figurine, seated Liu Hai & toad, on gray soapstone base, 1900s, 4".285.00
Figurine, stylized lady, seated, 10¼x4½" 100.00
Snuff bottle, landscape/people, red, spoon in lid, Japan, 2½x2x½" .70.00
Vase, dbl; birds in tree in center, 6¾x8".....................................145.00
Vase, floral & sm bowl at base, 1900s, 9x7½" 125.00
Vase, floral & vine motif w/2 monkeys & 1 pheasant, 4x6½x2".120.00
Vase, floral vines, hardstone base, Chinese, 1950s, 8" 145.00
Vase, trees/vines/people, 11" 175.00

Soda Fountain Collectibles

The first soda water sales in the United States occurred in the very late 1790s in New York and New Haven, Connecticut. By the 1830s soda water was being sold in drug stores as a medicinal item, especially the effervescent mineral waters from various springs around the country. By this time the first flavored soda water appeared at an apothecary shop in Philadelphia.

The 1830s also saw the first manufacturer (John Matthews) of devices to make soda water. The first marble soda fountain made its appearance in 1857 as a combination ice shaver and flavor-dispensing apparatus. By the 1870s the soda fountain was an established feature of the neighborhood drug store.

The fountains of this period were large, elaborate marble devices with druggists competing with each other for business by having fountains decorated with choice marbles, statues, mirrors, water fountains, and gas lamps.

In 1903 the fountain completed its last major evolution with the introduction of the 'front' counter service we know today. (The soda clerk faced the customer when drawing soda.)

By this time ice cream was a standard feature being served as sundaes, ice cream sodas, and milk shakes. Syrup dispensers were just being introduced as 'point-of-sale' devices to sell various flavorings from many different companies. Straws were commonplace, especially those made from paper. Fancy and unusual ice cream dippers were in daily use, and they continued to evolve, reaching their pinnacle with the introduction of the heart-shaped dipper in 1927.

This American business has provided collectors today with an almost endless supply of interesting and different articles of commerce. One can collect dippers, syrup dispensers, glassware, straw dispensers, milk shakers, advertising, and trade catalogs. (Note: The presence of a 'correct' pump enhances the value of a syrup dispenser by 25%.)

Collectors need to be made aware of decorating pieces that are actually fantasy items: copper ice cream cones, a large copper ice cream dipper, and a copper ice cream soda glass. These items have no resale value. Our advisors for this category are Joyce and Harold Screen; they are listed in the Directory under Maryland.

See also Advertising; Coca-Cola.

Bottle, Cherry Smash, rvpt label, orig metal cap, 12½" 500.00
Bottle, Chuk-Ker The Sporting Thing To Drink, Pyro..................30.00
Bottle, extract; Hires Root Beer, bl glass, 4½" 25.00
Bottle, Nichol Kola, Long Nick marching on bk, ca 1936, 12-oz..36.00
Bottle, seltzer; Babad's Miami Seltzer co, bl, Deco style 100.00
Bottle opener, 7-Up, wall mt, Starr X, EX....................................35.00
Cone dispenser, metal, Turnball...TN...Pats Pending, 30x8x9", G..150.00
Container, Drum Cup Ice Cream, waxed cb, 3-fluid ozs 6.00
Container, Horlick's Fountain Brand Malted Milk, 8½x6¼" dia, M.375.00
Container, Magic Freeze Ice Milk, waxed cb, 12-fluid oz, EX..........6.00
Container, Snow Sprinkles, sundae graphics on tin, 1937, 10-lb, EX+.55.00
Crate, Nesbitts Soda Pop, wooden, 12x18", EX 50.00
Cup, sundae; Have Fun, waxed cb, Lily-Tulip, unused.....................6.00
Cup, sundae; Ice Cream Sundae, waxed cb, United Dairy Farmers, unused.6.00
Dipper, banana split; Gilchrist #34, 11½", EX.............................450.00
Dipper, bl anodized aluminum, mk Pat No 2756698 MFD USA, 1950s...10.00
Dipper, Bonnie Prod, bl plastic hdl..28.00

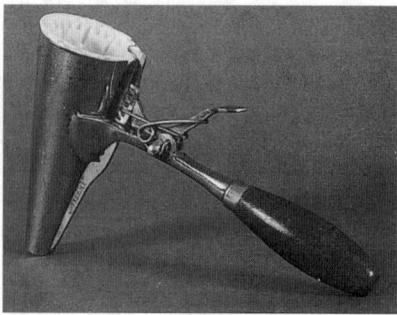

Dipper, cone-holding type, rare larger style, 9" long, $5,500.00. (Photo courtesy Pettigrew Auctions)

Dipper, Fisher Cold Dog, German Silver, wood hdl, Canada, 19½"..925.00
Dipper, Gem #9 ....65.00
Dipper, Gilchrist #30, 10½" 50.00
Dipper, Gilchrist #31, sz 10, 11"...45.00
Dipper, Gilchrist #31, sz 20, 11"...65.00
Dipper, Hamilton Beach #40, 9" 40.00
Dipper, Hamilton Beach #67, 1950s 40.00
Dipper, ICYPI, Automatic Cone Co, makes 2½x2½x⅝" sq, 10" L....125.00
Dipper, Kingery #8, 4 blades, 8½" 450.00

Dipper, Lloyd Disher Co, red & yel hard plastic, 1950s.................15.00
Dipper, Maryland Baking Co, NP brass, wood hdl, 10", M..........135.00
Dipper, Mayer Mfg, German silver, wood hdl, 12"......................135.00
Dipper, Quick & Easy, Erie Specialty, aluminum, wood hdl, 10½", NM .75.00
Dipper, Roldip (on hdl), heavy metal, 1940s 22.00
Dipper, Scoop Master, blk plastic hdl 28.00
Dipper, Shore Craft #40, wood hdl, 7¾" 40.00
Dipper, Wendel's Practical Disher, Pat 1927, re-plated, prof rstr ..825.00
Dispenser, amethyst glass base, push-button type, C&H NY 1917, EX.195.00
Dispenser, Birchola, ceramic ball, w/pump, 14", G 2,200.00
Dispenser, Bowey's Hot Chocolate, aluminum w/enameled graphics, EX..135.00
Dispenser, Cherry Smash, ceramic ball, 15", EX.......................1,800.00
Dispenser, Daggett's Florida Punch, intact mixer, 15x9" w/gr base..400.00
Dispenser, Dr Swett's, ceramic stump w/silhouette logo, 14", VG.4,500.00
Dispenser, Hires, metal wall-mt w/glass jug, 12", EX 150.00
Dispenser, Hires Root Beer, hourglass shape, w/pump, 1920, 14¾" .1,185.00
Dispenser, Howel's Orange Julep, pnt steel/ceramic, 24x15" dia, EX.700.00
Dispenser, Jersey Creme, red & gr letters, ca 1910, 15½" 2,000.00
Dispenser, Liberty Root Beer, wood bbl w/claw ft, 14", EX+ 700.00
Dispenser, malt; Kraft, aluminum w/cobalt emblem, 9", EX 100.00
Dispenser, Murray's Root Beer, ceramic bbl on stump, 12½" 425.00
Dispenser, National Dairy Malted Milk, aluminum, EX 120.00
Dispenser, Raspberry Syrup, Hull, 13⅜x4¾x8½", EX 70.00
Dispenser, Ward's Lemon Crush, ceramic lemon, no pump, 1920, EX.1,400.00
Dispenser, Ward's Orange Crush, ceramic orange, orig pump, 1918, EX..2,000.00
Dispenser, whipped cream; Kidde Mfg Pat Pending, 10" 35.00
Dispenser, Wine-Dip 5 Cent, glass bbl on earthenware base, 19", VG.750.00
Dispenser globe, Fowler Cherry Smash, ruby glass, w/lid, 9½x7" dia.500.00
Fan pull, Mission Orange, 2-sided, NM...18.00
Jar, Miner's Beef Bouillon, bull's head, w/lid 500.00
Jar, syrup; Johnson's Cold Fudge Syrup, glass/metal, 8", EX+ 200.00
Jug, Fowler's Cherry Smash, emb letters in clear, 1930s.................60.00
Mixer, milk shake; Gilchrist #22, wht porc base, 7" cup, 18" 150.00
Mixer, milk shake; Multimixer, model 9B, 18", G 350.00
Mixer, milk shake; Oster, gr porc, 19", EX 100.00
Mug, A&W Root Beer, clear glass w/enamel logo, child sz.............5.00
Mug, clear glass, slim design w/flutes, 1920s-40s, 5½x2½" 7.00
Mug, Frostie Root Beer, clear w/red label, 8-oz, 5½" 18.00
Mug, Hires Root Beer, ceramic, 4½" 100.00
Mug, Richard's Creamy Root Beer, clear glass, 6½" 25.00
Mug, Twin Kiss Root Beer, red logo on clear glass, heavy..............15.00
Soda fountain magazine, 1906 ....350.00
Soda fountain magazine, 1912 ....250.00
Soda fountain magazine, 1925 ....150.00
Soda fountain magazine, 1935 ....75.00
Soda glass, amber, ftd, 7", 6 for 75.00
Soda glass, Bubble Up, 1950s...30.00
Soda glass, clear w/ribbed stem, flat ft, 8" 6.00
Soda glass, Early California in pk on wht ironstone, 7", 6 for 235.00
Straw holder, clear columnar body w/stainless top, 11x4½" 110.00
Straw holder, clear glass w/threaded metal lid, #37 on base, 9¾"..40.00
Straw holder, clear paneled glass, chrome base & top, 12" 70.00
Straw holder, clear pressed glass pattern, lays horizontally, ca 1910 .500.00
Straw holder, Drink Hires, CI, 1911, 5x9¾x4½"......................2,400.00
Straw holder, 1-2-3 Pick-Up, glass, metal top/base, 12½", VG ...185.00
Sundae dish, etched glass, ftd, in chrome base, 3½x4", 4 for 30.00
Tray, Hoffman's Ice Cream, girl on blk w/red border, 15x11", VG..400.00

Spangle Glass

Spangle glass, also known as Vasa Murrhina, is cased art glass characterized by the metallic flakes embedded in its top layer. It was made both abroad and in the United States during the latter years of the 19th centu-

ry, and it was reproduced in the 1960s by the Fenton Art Glass Company.

Vasa Murrhina was a New England distributor who sold glassware of this type manufactured by a Dr. Flower of Sandwich, Massachusetts. Flower had purchased the defunct Cape Cod Glassworks in 1885 and used the facilities to operate his own company. Since none of the ware was marked, it is very difficult to attribute specific examples to his manufacture.

See also Art Glass Baskets; Fenton.

Basket, bl w/mica crimped-edge body w/clear twist hdl, 5½x7½" ...275.00
Basket, wht to bl w/ruffled rim, mica spirals, clear hdl, 8" 420.00
Bride's bowl, yel/wht swirl w/overall silver mica & bl daisies, 11"..125.00
Ewer, pk w/overall clear casing, wht liner, ornate clear hdl, 9½" .225.00
Pitcher, yel/bl/pk on wht w/silver flecks, frost hdl, 9½" 245.00
Rose bowl, pk w/silver mica veining, pinched fluted top, 4" 190.00
Rose bowl, rose/maroon/gilt, crimped rim, 3¼x4" 175.00
Tumble up, pk to wht w/mica flecks, carafe & tumbler, 7" 195.00
Vase, dk bl w/mica, clear cased, Hobbs Brockunier, 7¾x5¼"......245.00
Vase, maroon w/gold spangles, dbl gourd shape, 10½", pr 275.00
Vase, pk w/wht int, crimped rim on fan-shape neck, 2 clear hdls, 7".120.00
Vase, pk/bl sections alternate, spiral crystal rigaree at neck, 9" ...135.00

Spatter Glass

Spatter glass, characterized by its multicolor 'spatters,' has been made from the late 19th century to the present by American glass houses as well as those abroad. Although it was once thought to have been made entirely by workers at the 'end of the day' from bits and pieces of leftover scrap, it is now known that it was a standard line of production.

See also Art Glass Baskets.

Box, yel, egg shape, gold ft, 7½x4½" 325.00
Creamer, cranberry opal, clear hdl, melon ribs, 5" 175.00
Pitcher, rainbow cased, sq rim, clear reed hdl, 8" 250.00
Rose bowl, pk & bl, 4½" H 70.00
Salt cellar, gr & wht, clear petal ft, shell rigaree, 1¾" 100.00
Shaker, cranberry & wht, cased, patterned waist, metal top, 3x2¼"..235.00
Tumbler, gr & wht swirl, 3¾"...80.00
Vase, cranberry & wht, clear rigaree at rim, 3¼" 125.00
Vase, mc on wht, wht int, 7½x3⅜"..110.00

Spatterware

Spatterware is a general term referring to a type of decoration used by English potters as early as the late 1700s. Using a brush or a stick, brightly colored paint was dabbed onto the soft-paste earthenware items, achieving a spattered effect which was often used as a border. Because much of this type of ware was made for export to the United States, some of the subjects in the central design — the schoolhouse and the eagle patterns, for instance — reflect American tastes. Yellow, green, and black spatterware is scarce and highly valued by collectors.

In the descriptions that follow, the color listed after the item indicates the color of the spatter. The central design is identified next, and the color description that follows that refers to the design.

Creamer, bl, cockscomb, red/gr, paneled, stains/flakes, 5" 850.00
Creamer, bl, peafowl/twigs, red/gr/bl, paneled, 5⅝", NM 750.00
Creamer, bl, tulip variant, red/gr, stains/rpr hdl & base, 4½" 565.00
Creamer, brn/blk, rose, red/gr, rim flake, 3½" 660.00
Creamer, rainbow t'print, red/bl/gr, peafowl, red/yel/bl, rstr, 4", VG.1,650.00
Creamer, red, morning glory, bl/gr, 3¾" 2,750.00
Creamer, stick spatter, 2 bands purple flowers, 1 of red, hairline, 4"..165.00
Pitcher, bl, rose, red w/gr leaves, molded spout, rpr/lines, 7½" ..1,400.00

Pitcher, bl drape & bands at shoulder/rim/hdl, hairlines/stains, 7"..**440.00**
Pitcher, purple, acorns, yel/teal/gr/brn (bubbled), rpr, 8½" **3,600.00**
Pitcher, rainbow, bl/red-purple, paneled, rpr molded spout, 7½" .**1,700.00**
Pitcher, red, peafowl, red/gr/bl, molded fan under spout, rpr, 8"..**880.00**
Plate, bl, fort, gray/gr/blk/red, flake, 7½".....................................**300.00**
Plate, bl, peafowl, red/gr/bl, stains/rpr, 9½" **300.00**
Plate, bl, peafowl, red/yel/gr, tail extends to border, 9½", EX......**770.00**
Plate, bl, primrose, red/gr/yel, crow's ft, 8" **55.00**
Plate, bl, shield, wht w/bl stripes & red stars, Pekin China/Booth, 9"..**1,150.00**
Plate, bull's eye, overlapping red & bl, 8½"..................................**220.00**
Plate, purple border w/HP red berries & gr leaves, flakes/stains, 10" .**220.00**
Plate, rainbow, lt red/bl/yel border, rim flake, 8½".......................**325.00**
Plate, rainbow, red/bl border, crisscross center, lt stains, 8½" **770.00**
Plate, rainbow, scalloped w/red/bl/gr border, Adams, rpr chip, 11"..**385.00**
Plate, red, peafowl w/long tail, dk bl/gr/dk brn, hairline, 8½" **700.00**
Plate, stick spatter, bl border w/red & gr flower center, stains, 9".**135.00**
Plate, stick spatter, bl flowers, red/bl flowers w/gr leaves, 11"......**135.00**
Plate, stick spatter, red border w/3-color floral, minor stains, 9" .**110.00**
Platter, bl, eagle/shield in dk brn, octagonal, stains/hairline, 18" .**275.00**
Platter, lt bl wide borders, shaped oblong, 13x16" **220.00**
Platter, red, Dragoon Guards/Rifle Band (blk transfers), lt stain, 13"..**580.00**
Platter, red, peafowl, red/bl/dk brn, 10¾", VG.............................**600.00**
Soup plate, stick spatter, bl floral/red roses w/gr, Malkin, 9", VG..**60.00**
Soup plate, stick spatter, floral, bl border w/3-color stripes, 8¾".**165.00**
Sugar bowl, bl, schoolhouse, red w/gr trees & grass, rpl lid, 6", VG .**700.00**
Sugar bowl, brn, rose, red/gr, dbl hdls w/leaf ends, 4¼" **475.00**
Sugar bowl, rainbow, bl/gr, close mismatch lid, rpr, 4½" **330.00**
Sugar bowl, stick spatter, 3-color designs/bl stripes, 5x5", NM....**190.00**
Tea bowl, purple, tree, blk/gr, EX..**300.00**
Tea bowl, rainbow, bl/mustard, EX..**275.00**
Tea bowl, red/bl, buds, red/gr, 4-petal saucer, EX **465.00**
Tea bowl & saucer, bl, peafowl, lt gr/red/yel, EX **200.00**
Tea bowl & saucer, bl, peafowl, red/yel/bl, minor wear................**300.00**
Tea bowl & saucer, bl, pomegranate, dk bl/gr/red w/yel dots, crazing..**800.00**
Tea bowl & saucer, bl, tulip, red/yel/gr (darker on saucer) **195.00**
Tea bowl & saucer, bl, 6-point star, red/mustard/gr, stains/chip...**900.00**
Tea bowl & saucer, Christmas balls in red/gr, lt stains in cup ..**3,900.00**
Tea bowl & saucer, Christmas balls in red/yel/gr, lt stains/roughness.**3,080.00**
Tea bowl & saucer, lt brn, spray design on saucer, red/bl/gr, hairline .**385.00**
Tea bowl & saucer, purple, rooster, bl/yel/red, lt stains/flakes...**9,350.00**
Tea bowl & saucer, yel, tulip, red/gr, hairlines/flake, mini........**1,750.00**
Teapot, rainbow, gr/yel w/2 joined purple curves & blk spots, rstr, 5".**5,000.00**
Teapot, red/gr cockscomb design, rpl/rstr lid, hairlines, 6⅝" **550.00**
Waste bowl, bl, fort, brn/red/blk, hairline, 3½x6¼" **185.00**

Spelter

Spelter items are cast from commercial zinc and coated with a metallic patina. The result is a product very similar to bronze in appearance, yet much less expensive

Bank, lion, Harris Trust & Savings Bank, 5x6" **75.00**
Bust, Cleopatra, French, sgn, 11½" **400.00**
Bust of young woman in Dutch cap w/feather, long hair, sgn Nelson, 20".**385.00**
Clock, saddled horse, clock in horseshoe, 1950s, EX...................**195.00**
Figurine, Dutch lady resting on 1 arm w/other raised, ca 1910, 17x6" .**280.00**
Figurine, Girl Scout USA on base, M Daingerfield, 1953, 6" **125.00**
Figurine, grape picker, man w/sack on bk, arm raised, 7½" **140.00**
Figurine, man holding horse by reins, 8x7" **300.00**
Figurine, man in long cloak w/Bible in hand, J Ruhl, 1920s, 10" ..**250.00**
Figurine, Moses, kneeling w/book in hand, England, 1880s, 10".**880.00**
Figurines, Industry (Arts), bronzed finish, blk base, 26", pr.........**495.00**
Lamp, figural man w/pipe, glowing red bulb behind clasped hands, 21"..**635.00**

Spode-Copeland

The following is a short cronological history of the Spode company:
1733: Josiah Spode I is born on March 23 at Lane Delph, Staffordshire.
1740: Spode is put to work in a pottery factory.
1754: Spode, now a fully proficient journeyman/potter, works for Turner and Banks in Stoke-on-Trent.
1755: Josiah Spode II is born.
1761: Spode I acquires a factory in Shelton where he makes cream-colored and blue-painted earthenware.
1770: This is the year adopted as the date Spode I founded the business.
1784: Spode I masters the art and techniques of transfer printing in blue under the glaze on earthenware.
1796: The marks the earliest known record of Spode selling porcelain dinnerware.
1800: Spode II produces the first bone china.
1806: Spode is appointed potter to the royal Family; this continues past 1983.
1813: Spode produces the first stone china.
1821: Spode introduces Feldspar Porcelain, a variety of bone china.
1833: William Taylor Copeland acquires the Spode factory from the Spode family and becomes partners with Garrett until 1847.
1870: System of impressing date marks on the backs of the dinnerware begins.
1925: Robert Copeland is born. (He presently resides in England.)
1976: The Company merges with Worcester Royal Porcelain Company and forms Royal Worcester Spode Limited.
1986: The Spode Society is established.
1989: The holding company for Spode becomes the Porcelain and Fine China Companies Limited.

The price quotes listed in these three categories of Spode are for twentieth-century pre-1965 dinnerware in pristine condition — no cracks, chips, crazing, or stains. Minor knife cuts do not constitute damage unless extreme.

The patterns in the first group are the most common and popular earthenware lines. The second group contains the rarer and higher priced pattern; they are both earthenware and stoneware. Bone china patterns comprise the third group.

Our advisor for this category is Don Haase; he is listed in the Directory under Washington.

First Group:

Ann Hathaway, Billingsley Rose, Buttercup, Byron, Camilla Pink, Chelsea Wicker, Chinese Rose, Christmas Tree (green), Cowslip, Fairy Dell, Fleur de Lis (blue/brown), Florence, Gadroon, Gainsborough, Hazel Dell, Indian Tree, Jewel, Moss Rose, Old Salem, Raeburn, Reynolds, Romney, Rosalie, Rose Brier, Rosebud Chintz, Tower Blue, Valencia, Wickerdale, Wickerdell, Wickerlane.

Bowl, cereal; 6½" **32.00**
Bowl, fruit; 5¼" **28.00**
Bowl, waste; 6" **35.00**
Coffeepot, 8-cup...**265.00**
Creamer, lg...**75.00**
Creamer, sm..**65.00**
Cup & saucer, demitasse..**45.00**
Cup & saucer, low/tall..**39.00**
Plate, bread & butter; 6¼" **28.00**
Plate, butter pat..**28.00**
Plate, luncheon; rnd, 8-9" **35.00**
Plate, salad; 7½" **32.00**
Platter, oval, 13"..**140.00**

Platter, oval, 15" 160.00
Platter, oval, 17" 180.00
Sauce boat, w/liner 145.00
Soup, cream; w/liner 55.00
Soup, rim, 7½" 35.00
Soup, rim, 8½" 45.00
Sugar bowl, w/lid, lg 75.00
Sugar bowl, w/lid, sm 65.00
Teapot, 8-cup 265.00
Vegetable, oval, 9-10" 155.00
Vegetable, oval, 10-11" 165.00
Vegetable, sq, 8" 145.00
Vegetable, sq, 9" 155.00
Vegetable, w/lid 265.00

Second Group:

Aster, Butchart, Camilla Blue, Christmas Tree (magenta), Italian, Mayflower, Herring Hunt (green/magenta), Patricia, Tower Blue and Pink, Wildflower (blue/red), Delhi, Fitzhugh (blue/red/green), Gloucester (blue/red), Ruins (blue/pink/brown), Tradewinds (blue/red).

Bowl, cereal; 6¼" 39.00
Bowl, fruit; 5½" 35.00
Bowl, waste; 6" 45.00
Coffeepot, 8-cup 375.00
Creamer, lg 95.00
Creamer, sm 85.00
Cup & saucer, demitasse 55.00
Cup & saucer, low/high 65.00
Plate, bread & butter; 6¼" 35.00
Plate, butter pat 295.00
Plate, chop; rnd, 13" 65.00
Plate, dinner; 10½" 49.00
Plate, luncheon; rnd, 8-9" 65.00
Plate, luncheon; sq, 8½" 39.00
Plate, salad; 7½" 165.00
Platter, oval, 13" 180.00
Platter, oval, 15" 225.00
Platter, oval, 17" 185.00
Sauce boat, w/liner 45.00
Soup, rim, 7½" 55.00
Soup, rim, 8½" 95.00
Sugar bowl, w/lid, lg 85.00
Sugar bowl, w/lid, sm 395.00
Teapot, 8-cup 175.00
Vegetable, oval, 9-10" 195.00
Vegetable, oval, 10-11" 165.00
Vegetable, sq, 8" 185.00
Vegetable, sq, 9" 395.00
Vegetable, w/lid

Third Group:

Billingsley Rose Savoy, Bridal Rose, Carolyn, Chelsea Garden, Christine, Claudia, Colonel, Dimity, Dresden Rose Savoy, Fleur de Lis (gray/red/blue), Geisha (blue/pink/white), Irene, Maritime Rose, Primrose (pink), Shanghi, Savoy.

Bowl, cereal; 6¼" 45.00
Bowl, fruit; 5½" 42.00
Bowl, waste; 6" 55.00
Coffeepot, 8-cup 445.00
Creamer, lg 120.00

Creamer, sm 110.00
Cup & saucer, demitasse 65.00
Cup & saucer, low/tall 75.00
Plate, bread & butter; 6¼" 45.00
Plate, butter pat 39.00
Plate, chop; rnd, 13" 315.00
Plate, dessert; 8" 55.00
Plate, dinner; 10½" 69.00
Plate, luncheon; rnd, 9" 59.00
Plate, luncheon; sq, 8½" 69.00
Plate, salad; 7½" 49.00
Platter, oval, 13" 195.00
Platter, oval, 15" 225.00
Platter, oval, 17" 295.00
Sauce boat, w/liner 145.00
Soup, cream; w/liner 145.00
Soup, rim, 7½" 65.00
Soup, rim, 8½" 75.00
Sugar bowl, w/lid, lg 120.00
Sugar bowl, w/lid, sm 115.00
Teapot, 8-cup 445.00
Vegetable, oval, 9-10" 215.00
Vegetable, oval, 10-11" 235.00
Vegetable, sq, 8" 245.00
Vegetable, sq, 9" 275.00
Vegetable, w/lid 425.00

Spongeware

Spongeware is a type of factory-made earthenware that was popular during the last quarter of the nineteenth century and into the first quarter of the twentieth century. It was decorated by dabbing color onto the drying ware with a sponge, leaving a splotched design at random or in simple patterns. Sometimes a solid band of color was added. The vessel was then covered with a clear glaze and fired at a high temperature. Blue on white is the most preferred combination, but green on ivory, orange on white, or those colors in combination may also occasionally be found. As with most pottery, rare forms and condition are major factors in establishing value. Spongeware is still being made today, so beware of newer examples. For further information we recommend *Collector's Encyclopedia of Salt Glaze Stoneware* by Terry Taylor, our advisor for this category, and Terry and Kay Lowrance.

Our values are for undamaged examples, unless a specific condition code is given within the description.

Chamber pot, cobalt sponging on white with blue and white rings on lid, 10x10½", from $250.00 to $275.00.
(Photo courtesy Kathryn McNerney)

Baker, gr/cream, close pattern, Am, 1880s, 3½x11" 170.00
Bank, gr/brn, pig figural, pierced eyes, 3½x6" 200.00
Bowl, berry; bl/wht, ribbed exterior, mini, 1⅛x2¾" 200.00
Bowl, bl/brn/wht, It Pays To Mix...Osage IA, emb ribs, 8" 100.00
Bowl, bl/wht, pattern sponging, flared sides, 4½x9", from $85 to.100.00

Bowl, bl/wht, pattern sponging, 3x9½", from $75 to..................125.00
Bowl, bl/wht, pattern sponging, 5½x10", from $175 to..............225.00
Bowl, bl/wht, wht or bl bands, 4x8", from $75 to.....................100.00
Bowl, bl/wht w/2 bl bands, stain, 6¼x14", EX...........................100.00
Bowl, mixing; bl/wht w/emb heart pattern, 5½x10", from $175 to..225.00
Butter crock, bl/wht, Village Farm Dairy stencil, 4x5½", $125 to...150.00
Chamber pot, bl/wht, Bear Paw pattern w/bl bands, 5x8½", $250 to.275.00
Chamber pot, bl/wht, close sponging, child sz, 4½x7½", $250 to...275.00
Chamber pot, bl/wht w/bl bands, 5x8½", from $225 to.................250.00
Cookie jar, bl/wht, ftd ball shape, orig lid, 9"..............................245.00
Creamer, bl/wht, 3"..275.00
Cuspidor, bl/wht w/bl & wht bands, 5x7½", from $175 to.........225.00
Cuspidor, bl/wht w/bl band at rim & center, ca 1900, 5"............150.00
Custard cup, gr/brn on yel ware, 2x4½"..65.00
Honey pot, bl/wht (dk), ftd, orig lid, 4½", EX.............................250.00
Jug, bl/wht, emb vintage at shoulder, 4½".....................................440.00
Mug, bl/wht, emb lady's face, bk: man's face, spurred hdl, 5x3½".200.00
Pitcher, batter; bl/wht, rare form, 8x8", from $1,700 to...........2,000.00
Pitcher, bl/wht, chain-link pattern, 9x5", from $550 to.............600.00
Pitcher, bl/wht, child & dog in oval ea side, 9", NM..................875.00
Pitcher, bl/wht, cylindrical, common, 7x5", from $225 to..........250.00
Pitcher, bl/wht, emb leaping deer, 8x5½", from $1,000 to.......1,500.00
Pitcher, bl/wht, Garden Rose, 9", from $750 to 900.00
Pitcher, bl/wht, gr/purple berries, molded leaf spout, 8", G 600.00
Pitcher, bl/wht, pattern sponging, bulbous, 12".............................395.00
Pitcher, bl/wht, patterned sponging, ovoid, 9x5½", from $300 to .350.00
Pitcher, bl/wht, Pine Cone, 9" 875.00
Pitcher, bl/wht, squat, 8x8", from $1,700 to............................2,000.00
Pitcher, bl/wht w/bl band, bulbous, 7x5½", from $275 to 325.00
Pitcher, brn/bl on cream, 11", EX...200.00
Pitcher, brn/gr chicken wire, mini, 3"...220.00
Pitcher, buttermilk; bl/wht, patterned sponging, late 1800s 395.00
Pitcher, gr/brn/wht, SE Cone Grain & Seed Co..., 4½" 99.00
Pitcher, hot water; bl/wht w/bl bands, 7", from $225 to 300.00
Pitcher, olive gr/wht w/bl edge band, 6½", EX..............................275.00
Pitcher, syrup; bl/wht, dk bl paw prints, w/lid, 5½x4", $350 to...400.00
Plate, bl/wht, emb Ulysses S Grant portrait, 12", from $250 to ..300.00
Plate, bl/wht, pattern sponging, scalloped rim, 8¾"....................195.00
Plate, bl/wht, pattern sponging, 8½"...55.00
Plate, gr/red/wht, 8¼"...175.00
Plate, red/gr/brn, repeating pattern, stains, 1880s, 8½" 125.00
Platter, bl/wht, close sponging, 1880s, 13½x10" 345.00
Soap dish, bl/wht w/bl bands, 5x3½"..125.00
Spoon holder, bl/wht, 9x4"...215.00
Sugar bowl, gr/wht, 5¼", EX..100.00
Sugar bowl, gr/wht w/red trim, rpr, 5x5"......................................250.00
Teapot, bl/wht, patterned sponging, 8½x8½", from $1,200 to.1,500.00
Vase, bl/wht, emb ribbon, 7½", EX...110.00
Wash bowl & pitcher, bl & wht, Earthworm pattern, 10", 5½x15".1,500.00
Wash bowl & pitcher, bl/gr/wht w/bl band, 8", 4x12", from $400 to.425.00
Wash bowl & pitcher, bl/wht w/bl & wht bands, 10", 5x14", $650 to .750.00
Washboard..400.00

Spoons

Souvenir spoons have been popular remembrances since the 1890s. The early hand-wrought examples of the silversmith's art are especially sought and appreciated for their fine craftsmanship. Commemorative, personality-related, advertising, and those with Indian busts or floral designs are only a few of the many types of collectible spoons. In the following listings, spoons are sorted by city, character, or occasion. For further information we recommend *Collectible Souvenir Spoons, Identification & Values*, by Wayne Bednersh (Collector Books).

Key:
B — bowl
emb — embossed
eng — engraved
ff — full figure
gw — gold washed
H — handle
HR — handle reverse

Alligator figural H; machine produced, Am, from $25 to 100.00
Art Deco cut-out finial & stem; plain B; from $12 to....................25.00

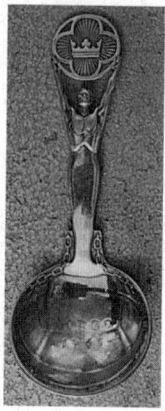

Art Deco style celebrating victory from Nazi occupation during World War II, from $50.00 to $75.00. (Photo courtesy Wayne Bednersh)

Atlantic City H; dice players & 7 Come 11 enameling in B; from $500 to..1,500.00
Blk face H; emb Who Said Watermelon scene in B; from $100 to.150.00
Bullfighting transfer in B; scrolling H; Shepard, from $200 to....400.00
Catalina Island scene in B; twist H; Robbins, from $20 to............25.00
Colorado emb on H; Gateway to Garden of Gods in B; unmk, from $40 to.75.00
Columbus on globe H; MOP B; unmk, from $50 to......................90.00
DAR temple in B; Krider, from $50 to 75.00
Duluth Bridge eng in B; enameled cross-rifles form H; from $150 to..200.00
Egyptian transfer in B; enameled mummy figural H; from $150 to .300.00
Findlay OH courthouse in B; corn design H; SSMC, from $50 to..75.00
Fort Sumter, Charleston SC & ship in gw B; Towle, from $25 to.50.00
Geisha girl figural H: fan forms bowl, mk Sterling, from $25 to....75.00
General Engine & emb locomotive in B; unmk, from $15 to........25.00
Hastings NC Presbyterian Church in B; Colfax H; Gorham, from $15 to.30.00
House of 7 Gables, Salem MA on H; witch finial; unmk, from $20 to.50.00
James Blaine finial; scenic B; Krieger & Dearth mk, from $40 to .60.00
Japan in open filigree H; emb flower in B; sheet silver, from $15 to.25.00
Jerusalem Wailing Wall transfer in B; twist H; from $25 to...........60.00
Jeweled & faceted ruby inset, unmk Burma, from $20 to..............45.00
Lady in risque bathing suit, palms in B; Paye & Baker, from $75 to..125.00
Liechtenstein castle pnt in B; flower finial; from $20 to...............50.00
Los Angeles angel figural H; emb view of Mt Lowe RR in B; from $40 to.75.00
Madison WI & emb scenes in B; various Hs; ea from $15 to 50.00
Main St Jackson MI eng in B; various Hs; ea, from $25 to...........50.00
Memphis TN skyline H; eng street scene in B; Shepard, $70 to 90.00
Minneapolis MN Public Library eng in B; Fessenden, from $30 to..50.00
Minnehaha Falls in B; grain flower finial; Fessenden, from $30 to..60.00
MOP fish figural B; SP H; unmk, from $10 to 20.00
Morrison IL Water Works eng in B; Stuart H; Towle, from $30 to..50.00
Mozart transfer finial; plain B; Austria, from $10 to 15.00
Mt Hood, Portland OR eng in GW B; Oregon on wavy H; Shepard, $30 to.60.00
Muscatine in B; enameled corn on H; from $40 to.......................75.00
New Orleans LA skyline H; Heart of New Orleans in B; Watson, $100 to..175.00
Norwegian enameled flags in B & on finial, gw, from $20 to 30.00
NY skyline H; emb Brooklin Bridge in B; from $25 to 45.00
Paducah KY & Old Kentucky Home w/cabin eng in B; Watson, from $25 to.50.00
Peruvian coat-of-arms finial; emb llama scene in B; from $10 to ..20.00
Pontiac MI state reformatory eng in B; Fleur-de-Lis H; Alvin, $40 to.80.00
Queen Wilhelmini of Netherlands HP in B; crest H; from $200 to.400.00

Robert Ingersol finial; Liberty & Reason on H; Gorham, 1892, $75 to.**150.00**
Rothenburg Rathhaus (city hall) transfer in bowl & on finial, up to.**40.00**
Sidney coat-of arms enameled finial; plain B; from $15 to **30.00**
Silver w/man-made turq inlay, European or Am, ea, from $5 to ...**15.00**
Simulated coin (ancient hero) finial; various Hs & Bs; ea, $25 to.**50.00**
Sphinx cast finial, plain B; from $20 to...**30.00**
St Mark's Lion finial; ornate H; plain B; .800 silver, from $10 to..**15.00**
Vienna transfer print scene in B; enamel crest finial, from $20 to..**60.00**
Willet's School Monmouth IL eng in B; Melrose H; Gorham, from $15 to.**40.00**
Woman's Building State Penitentiary...IL eng in B; Whiting, $40 to.**75.00**
Yellowstone Park & Great Falls on H; Robbins, from $15 to **30.00**

Sporting Goods

Vintage ammunition boxes, duck and goose calls, knives, and fishing gear are just a few of the items that collectors of this type of memorabilia look for today. Also favored are posters, catalogs, and envelopes from well known companies such as Winchester, Remington, Peters, Ithaca, and Dupont.

Duck stamps have been widely collectible in recent years; if you're interested in learning more about the subject, we recommend *Duck Stamps* by L. A. Chappell (Collector Books).

See also Fishing Collectibles; Game Calls.

Basket, trapper's, ash splint, early, G- **150.00**
Book, Hunting the Long-Tailed Bird, Bob Bell, 1975, 212-pg, EX.**10.00**
Booklet, Austin Cartridge Co, 1905-06 OH game laws, G............**50.00**
Booklet, For the Young Hunter, Olin Corp, 1963, 32-pg, G...........**10.00**
Bow, recurve; Tamerlane, inlaid brass Bear coin, 1968, NM **500.00**
Bow, recurve; Wilson Bros X-400 Black Widow, Toxonite riser, 1968 only ..**325.00**
Brochure, Browning, Great Guns, pictures/descriptions, 1935, EX.**75.00**
Brochure, Sharps Rifle Co, Dayton OH, 5 models, 1978, EX........**20.00**
Canteen, striped cloth over metal, w/shoulder strap, 7½" **10.00**
Card, Dupont Sportsman's Service, full privileges, 1924, EX **75.00**
Catalog, Beretta, JL Galef & Son Inc, NY, 1957, 16-pg, EX.**25.00**
Catalog, Browning 100th Anniversary, 1932, 32-pg, 8½x11" **135.00**
Catalog, Continental Arms NY, 1951, 16-pg, 10x7", EX **50.00**
Crate, Metallic Cartridge, wood w/metal liner, red/yel on brn pnt, VG..**150.00**
Duck stamp, US Dept of Ag, Canada Geese, Bishop, 1936-7, used, EX..**75.00**
Duck stamp, US Dept of Interior, Am Eider, Abbott, 1957, unused, EX+ .**35.00**
Duck stamp, US Dept of Interior, Emperor Geese, Cook, 1972, unused, M..**25.00**
Duck stamp, US Dept of Interior, Gadwalls, Reese, 1951, used, EX.**12.00**
Duck stamp, US Dept of Interior, Redheads, Hines, 1946, used, EX..**16.00**
Duck stamp, US Dept of Interior, Snow Geese, Murray, 1947, unused, NM.**28.00**
Envelope, AJ Rummel Arms Co, red print, 1901, 3¾x6⅛", EX.**175.00**
Envelope, Colt BL Gun Early, Edward K Tryon, red/brn ink, 3⅜x6"..**700.00**
Envelope, Ithaca, EC Meacham Arms Co...MO, 1895, 3⅝x6⅜", EX.**460.00**
Gun case, hard body, leather cover, rpl strap, for A/5 Browning, G.**130.00**
License, CA angler's, paper, 1923, 4¾x2¾", G.............................**100.00**
License, CA hunting, dogs & birds mc graphics, 1914, 2⅝x4¼", VG.**125.00**
License, MD angler's, button form, Whitehead & Hoag, 1928, 1¾", EX...**200.00**
Price list, Chamberlin Cartridge Co, 1887-8, 24-pg **575.00**
Price list, Parker Gun Dealer, blk on buff, 1936, 7-pg, 11x9", EX.**80.00**
Program, 3rd Annual Tournament of Chamberlin Cartridge Co, 1887, 8-pg..**500.00**
Rule book, Clay Pigeon Shooting, Ligowsky Clay Pigeon Co, 1883, EX.**400.00**
Score card, trap shooting; DuPont Infallible..., J Fanning portrait..**225.00**
Shotshell box, AF Weiss & Bro 12 Ga, blk on buff, 2-pc, empty, EX.**900.00**
Shotshell box, Federal Hi-Power 12 Ga, mallard on bl, 2-pc, empty, VG+ ..**900.00**
Shotshell box, Ideal 12 Ga Long Range, Bostwick-Brawn, 2-pc, empty, VG.**500.00**
Shotshell box, Peters High Velocity, 2-pc, empty, VG **50.00**
Shotshell box, Peters Rustless .23 Smith & Wesson 88, 2-pc, full, VG..**30.00**
Shotshell box, Peters 12 Ga Trap Load, 3-color, 2-pc, empty, EX...**400.00**
Shotshell box, Star Brand 12 Ga, 2-pc, full, EX **400.00**

Shotshell box, US Cartridge 16 Ga, 2-pc, full, VG **168.00**
Shotshell box, Winchester 24 Ga Repeater, ca 1920, 2-pc, empty, VG..**450.00**

Sports Collectibles

When sports cards became so widely collectible several years ago, other types of related memorabilia started to interest sports fans. Now they search for baseball uniforms, autographed baseballs, game-used bats and gloves, and all sorts of ephemera. Although baseball is America's all-time favorite, other sports have their own groups of interested collectors. Our advice for this category comes from Paul Longo Americana. Mr. Longo is listed in the Directory under Massachusetts.

To learn more about old golf clubs, we recommend *The Vintage Era of Golf Club Collectibles* by Ronald O. John (Collector Books.)

See also Target Balls; Tennis Rackets.

Photograph, Chicago Cubs, ballpark and team, flaws in paper, ca 1910, 13½x46" in frame, G, $550.00. (Photo courtesy Treadway Gallery)

Baseball, American league, sgn by Yankees (w/Ruth, faded), 1920s, EX..**1,000.00**
Baseball, MacGregor/Goldsmith, hand-sewn leather, MIB, sealed .**85.00**
Baseball, Nat'l League, 15 autographs (1 by Bill Swift), fading, EX.**265.00**
Baseball bat, Little League Duke Snider Model, unused **75.00**
Baseball bat, Spalding, Bill Kamm burned on side, 1925-30, EX..**150.00**
Baseball glove, Goldsmith, Harland B Clift, horsehide, EX **110.00**
Baseball glove, Lonnie Frey #4210, split finger, tan leather, 1930s, M .**200.00**
Book, Football Technique & Tactics, Zuppke, 250 pgs, 1924, G+..**40.00**
Book, Illustrated History of Basketball, Larry Fox, 1974, 256 pgs, EX .**15.00**
Bottles, Reggie Jackson, 500 Home Run Club, bat shaped, 4-pack, EX .**50.00**
Can, beer; Casey's Lager, 1980 NY Giants Monte Irvin, EX............**5.00**
Can, beer; Iron City, 1975 Super Bowl Champs Steelers, EX........**15.00**
Can, Royal Crown Cola, Pete Rose pictured w/stats, EX...............**15.00**
Envelope, 1948 Cleveland Indians schedule, Wolf Envelope Co, EX.**25.00**
Golf club, Aero driver, wood block head, steel shaft, 1930s, EX.**650.00**
Golf club, Ben Sayers Rustless putter, 1940s, EX **55.00**
Golf club, Bristol driver, wood head, steel shaft, 1930s, EX...........**45.00**
Golf club, Kroydon, fancy face wood w/steel shaft, 1930s, EX **200.00**
Golf club, MacGregor, Fred Grieve beveled sole, ca 1935, EX....**100.00**
Golf club, MacGregor Chieftan, fancy face wood w/pyratone shaft, 1934.**800.00**
Golf club, Miracle Adjustable Traveler, telescoping shaft, 1940, EX.**350.00**
Golf club, R Forgan Tolley putter, Forganite (compo), 1927, EX.**350.00**
Golf club, Spalding Youds putter, lead insert, 1917, EX **450.00**
Golf club, Wilson R-90 sand iron w/pyratone shaft, 1933, EX....**110.00**
Handbook, 1957 College Football TV; schedules, rosters etc, 36 pgs.**20.00**
Jersey, Dallas Cowboys, Emmitt Smith autograph, w/certificate, M.**700.00**
Jersey, Jersey City Giants, sgn by 20 members, 1941, M..............**150.00**
Magazine, Sports News, October 20, 1979, World Series issue, EX...**15.00**
Mug, beer; Chicago Blitz 1983 Inaugural Season, red/gray/bl, 5¾"..**25.00**
Mug, Washington Senators, bl w/wht decal logos, glass, 5½"........**35.00**
Pennant, 1982 Old Timers Baseball Classic, felt, 21", EX **20.00**
Plate, 1972 Munich Olympic Games, Bing & Grondahl, 7⅛" **50.00**
Plate, 1980 Olympic Winter Games, china, Viletta, 8½" **30.00**
Program, Houston Astros vs St Louis Cardinals, 1968, EX **8.00**

Program, Michigan vs Indiana, November 12, 1955, EX **25.00**
Program, 1948 Olympic Games, London, 176 pgs, VG **50.00**
Program, 1970 Washington Senators Official Souvenir, Nixon cover, EX .**70.00**
Program, 1972-73 Baltimore Bullets, EX **15.00**
Program & score card, 1955 Red Sox, Fenway Park, 24 pgs, EX ...**15.00**
Program & score card, 1973 World Series, Mets, Yogi Berra cover, EX..**35.00**
Score card, Official 1958 Philadelphia Phillies, 28 pgs, EX **15.00**
Shoe polish, Muhammad Ali's Champion Brand, tin, rnd, 1970s, unopened ..**25.00**
Ticket, William & Mary vs Navy, Homecoming game, Sept 26, 1959, EX..**15.00**

St. Clair

The St. Clair Glass Company began as a small family-oriented operation in Elwood, Indiana, in 1941. Most famous for their lamps, the family made numerous small items of carnival, pink and caramel slag, and custard glass as well. Later, paperweights became popular production pieces; many command relatively high prices on today's market. Weights are stamped and usually dated, while small production pieces are often unmarked. Lamps are in big demand (prices depend on size and whether or not they are signed) as are items signed by Paul or Ed St. Clair. For further information we recommend *St. Clair Glass Collector's Book, Vol. II*, by our advisor Ted Pruitt. He is listed in the Directory under Indiana.

Apple, from $100 to **125.00**
Bell, Bicentennial, from $20 to **25.00**
Bell, 10th Annual Convention, from $75 to **100.00**
Bird, colored on clear base, from $100 to **125.00**
Bowl, fluted, handmade, from $225 to **250.00**
Covered dish, robin on nest, from $125 to **150.00**
Doll, from $35 to **40.00**
Doorstop, duck, from $600 to **625.00**
Doorstop, rooster, from $600 to **625.00**
Lamp, blown, unsgn, from $275 to **300.00**
Lamp, 1-ball, unsgn, from $275 to **300.00**
Lamp, 2-ball, w/leaded shade, from $725 to **750.00**
Lamp finial, from $15 to **25.00**
Lemonade glass, from $75 to **100.00**
Marble, baseball player sulfide, Ed St Clair, from $125 to **150.00**
Marble, flowers, Joe St Clair, from $35 to **50.00**
Mug, from $75 to **85.00**
Paperweight, cameo sulfide, windowed, from $275 to **300.00**
Paperweight, dogwood & bee sulfide, from $300 to **350.00**
Paperweight, Franklin D Roosevelt, from $150 to **175.00**
Paperweight, Kennedy sulfide, windowed, Paul St Clair, mini, $300 to..**350.00**
Paperweight, lily, Ed St Clair, from $350 to **400.00**
Paperweight, Purdue University, from $150 to **175.00**
Paperweight, rose, feathered or windowed, ea.........................**1,200.00**
Paperweight, speckled glass, from $90 to **100.00**
Paperweight, Washington sulfide, Ed St Clair, from $250 to.......**300.00**
Picture frame, from $175 to **200.00**
Plate, Johnson portrait, from $20 to **25.00**
Plate, Kewpie, from $450 to **500.00**
Ring holder, crimped teapot form, from $75 to **85.00**
Ring post, from $55 to **65.00**
Salt cellar, swan, red, from $125 to **150.00**
Salt cellar, wheelbarrow, from $30 to **35.00**
Toothpick holder, Cactus, sm, from $25 to **30.00**
Toothpick holder, Fan & Feather, from $25 to **30.00**
Toothpick holder, weighted base, from $55 to **65.00**
Toothpick holder, 3-Face, from $25 to **30.00**
Tumbler, Fleur-de-Lis, from $40 to **50.00**
Tumbler, Hollyband, from $40 to **50.00**
Vase, butterfly weighted base, trumpet neck, from $300 to **350.00**

Wine goblet, Paneled Grape, from $35 to **45.00**
Wine goblet, Pinwheel, from $35 to **45.00**

Staffordshire

Scores of potteries sprang up in England's Staffordshire district in the early eighteenth century; several remain to the present time. (See also specific companies.) Figurines and groups were made in great numbers; dogs were favorite subjects. Often they were made in pairs, each a mirror image of the other. They varied in heights from 3" or 4" to the largest, measuring 16" to 18". From 1840 until about 1900, portrait figures were produced to represent specific characters, both real and fictional. As a rule these were never marked.

Historical ware was made throughout the district; some collectors refer to it as Staffordshire Blue. It was produced as early as 1780, and because much was exported to America, it was very often decorated with transfers depicting scenic views of well-known American landmarks. Early examples were printed in a deep cobalt. By 1830 a softer blue was favored, and within the next decade black, pink, red, and green prints were used. Although sometimes careless about adding their trademark, many companies used their own border designs that were as individual as their names.

This ware should not be confused with the vast amounts of modern china (mostly plates) made from early in the century to the present. These souvenir or commemorative items are usually marketed through gift stores and the like. (See Rowland and Marcellus.)

Our advisor for this category is Jeanne Dunay; she is listed in the Directory under South Carolina.

See also specific manufacturers.

Key:
blk — black
gr — green
d/b — dark blue

l/b — light blue
m/b — medium blue
m-d/b — medium dark blue

Figures and Groups

Bird whistle, appl florets on tree-trunk base, ca 1920, rstr, 3½" ..**400.00**
Birl, barefoot, in wingbk chair, red plaid dress, gr base, 3⅜" **400.00**
Boy feeding swan, chimney vase, mc w/coleslaw, 5⅛" **495.00**
Boy holds bone for sm dog in left arm, Walton, rstr/chips, 5" **500.00**
Cherub, inkwell, mc w/gold, holds coleslaw bouquet w/red heart, 4" .**220.00**
Corky, gent w/spaniel, open tree trunk w/spaghetti moss, 1850s, 18" .**650.00**
Couple by sign: London 30 Miles, mc, 1840-60, 10½" **675.00**
Deer, recumbent, mc details, 1880s, 2½x2¼" **250.00**
Dog on pillow, inkwell, mc w/gold, 3¾" **275.00**
Dog Rescue, lg dog by tree trunk, spill vase, mc, 1860s, 7" **650.00**
Empress Maria Theresa, bust on socle, late 1700s, loss/chip, 8" .**1,175.00**
Flower seller, outstretched arm/flowers in apron, Ralph Wood, rstr, 8"..**800.00**
Girl riding dog, mc, ca 1860, 6" **575.00**
Girl w/dog & bird in cage, spill vase, mc, 6½" **375.00**
Girl w/goose, inkwell, mc, 7" **375.00**
Girl wearing cap & housecoat, Ralph Wood, 5" **1,000.00**
Good Companions, cow & horse, spill vase, 1860s, 10½x6½" ...**675.00**
Lamb, background bocage, mc on bl/wht base w/acanthus leaves, 1820, 5"..**115.00**
Lion, recumbent, brn w/blk details, glass eyes, 9½x12", pr..........**345.00**
Little Red Riding Hood & Wolf, mc, spill vase, 1860s, 15" **875.00**
Little Red Riding Hood & wolf by tree-trunk vase, 1850, 10" **125.00**
Parrot on perch, inkwell, mc, 1860s, 4½" **525.00**
Prince of Wales on goat, mc, 1860, 9½" **675.00**
Scotsman w/rifle leans against wall, mc, 7⅜", NM **275.00**
Sheep, chimney vase, sanded coats, coleslaw foliage, rpr, 5" **150.00**
Shepherd & shepherdess w/lamb & dog, watch holder, rpr, 1860-80, 12" .**225.00**

Spaniels, lt brn on wht, blk nose, glass eyes, some lustre, 13", pr .**495.00**
Spaniels, red-orange/blk details, copper lustre chains, 20th C, 9", pr..**250.00**
Spaniels, wht w/blk muzzles & some gilt, 5", pr **300.00**
Spaniels, wht w/blk spots & chains, copper lustre collars, 11", pr, EX ..**415.00**
St Mark, book in hand/lion at ft, before leafy bocage, Walton, 7".**650.00**
Swan, inkwell, pink & gold, coleslaw nest, 3¼" **200.00**
Swans (3), chimney vase, wht w/gold, mc tree w/coleslaw foliage, 5".**275.00**
Tambourine player, open bocage, on raised oval base, Walton, 6", EX.**500.00**
Tenderness, romantic couple/lamb, floral bocage, Walton, 7", EX........**800.00**
Tithing, parson w/young couple & child before floral bocage, 8".**900.00**
Victoria w/baby & Prince Albert, 1850-60, 6½", pr.................**1,250.00**
Whippet, reclining, orange on gr base, minor roughness, 1¼x4¼".**135.00**

Transferware

Basket, Boston State House, d/b, rtcl, Rogers, 3x9¼x5½"+tray.**2,750.00**
Basket, chestnut; Apple Blossom, l/b, Ridgway, 1838-49, 8½x11½".**595.00**
Bowl, Boston State House, d/b, John Rogers, 1815-42, 12¾"..**2,070.00**
Bowl, Canova, d/b, rose bud finial, att Mayer, w/lid **400.00**
Bowl, Capitol Washington, d/b, Stevenson, 11" **2,645.00**
Bowl, fruit, c/s, Stubbs, 9¼" sq+hdls **1,850.00**
Bowl, Pains Hill Surrey, d/b, Hall's Select Views, 2x9", VG........**250.00**
Bowl, Park Theater NY, d/b, Stevenson, 8¾" **2,500.00**
Bowl, Parma, d/b, unmk, 1840s, 9½", NM **115.00**
Bowl, Rome & Bay of Naples, red, Ridgway, w/lid, 11¾"...........**450.00**
Bowl, Shell, d/b, oval, Stubbs & Kent, 2½x12¼" **1,150.00**
Bowl, Sheltered Pheasants, d/b, att Hall, 2¼x10½"............**300.00**
Bowl, soup; Canova, d/b, Mayer, 10¼"...............................**200.00**
Bowl, soup; Clematis, d/b, ca 1825, 10"............................**450.00**
Bowl, soup; Fulton's Steamboat, d/b, floral border, 10¼", EX **885.00**
Bowl, soup; Hannibal Passing Alps, d/b, Knighe Elkin & Co, 1840s, 10"..**225.00**
Bowl, soup; Holme Regents Park, d/b, Enoch Wood, 10"............**350.00**
Bowl, Swiss Cottage, d/b, Carr, 1844-50, 1½x6¾" **30.00**
Bowl, Swiss Lake & Village, d/b, Davenport, 2½x11¼".............**225.00**
Bowl, waste; Washington Standing at Tomb, d/b, unmk Wood, 3¼x6½".**750.00**
Coffeepot, lady by classical urn w/flowers, d/b, 1825, 11¾", NM..**1,150.00**
Compote, Canova, d/b, hdls, Mayer, 1830s, 6x11", EX **400.00**
Creamer & sugar bowl, floral, scalloped rim, d/b & wht on m/b, 7", 6".**450.00**
Cup & saucer, seashells, d/b, Adams, lt stain **140.00**
Cup & saucer, vase w/flowers, d/b, Clews..............................**245.00**
Cup plate, Arms of South Carolina, d/b, flaw, 4"....................**300.00**
Cup plate, Bosphorus, red, J&J Mayer, 4" **60.00**
Cup plate, Clyde Scenery, red, Job & John Jackson, 4" **60.00**
Cup plate, Fakeer's Rock, Hall's Oriental Scenery, 4¼" **125.00**
Cup plate, Hyena, d/b, Hall's Quadrupeds series, 4" **225.00**
Cup plate, mtn lion, d/b, Quadrupeds of N Am, 4¾".................**285.00**
Cup plate, Select Views, d/b, R Hall, 4"...............................**125.00**
Pitcher, Abbey Ruins, d/b, Mayer, 10x8½"............................**650.00**
Pitcher, Almshouse Boston/Esplanade &..., d/b, Stevenson, 10", EX .**2,300.00**
Pitcher, Boston State House/City Hall New York, d/b, unmk Stubbs, 6" .**975.00**
Pitcher, Butterfly & Moth, d/b, ca 1825, 5¼" **475.00**
Pitcher, Canova, brn, Thomas Mayer, 1826-35, 8½" **575.00**
Pitcher, country vista w/mansion, d/b, States border, Clews, 6¾" .**975.00**
Pitcher, Eagle, Scroll in Beak; Adams, 5¾" **625.00**
Pitcher, Entrance of Erie Canal/...Bridge at Little Falls, d/b, 5¾" .**1,725.00**
Pitcher, Entrance of Erie Canal/...Bridge at Little Falls, d/b, 6".**1,035.00**
Pitcher, Napoleon, d/b, att CJ Mason, 8½".............................**850.00**
Pitcher, Victory (ship), brn w/orange trim, pearlware, 6¾" **1,645.00**
Pitcher, View of Erie Canal, d/b, rprs, 6" **715.00**
Pitcher, Welcome Lafayette...Glory, d/b, Clews, 5", NM..........**2,100.00**
Plate, Am & Independence, d/b, Clews, 10½" **525.00**
Plate, Arms of NY w/2 female figures & eagle, d/b, Mayer, 10", EX.**750.00**
Plate, Arms of Rhode Island, d/b, anchor medallion, Mayer, 9"..**700.00**
Plate, Arms of Rhode Island, d/b, Mayer, 8½" **750.00**

Plate, Asiatiac Views, red, Dillon, 1834-43, 8½" **145.00**
Plate, Asiatic Views, l/b, Podmore Walker, 9¾" **105.00**
Plate, Bakers Falls Hudson River, Picturesque Views, blk, Clews, 9".**200.00**
Plate, Beauties, gr, Ridgway, 1830-41, 9¼".................................**175.00**
Plate, Bleinham Palace Oxfordshire, d/b, Adams, 10" **425.00**
Plate, Cadmus at Anchor, d/b, shell border, Enoch Wood & Sons, 10"..**500.00**
Plate, Chief Justice Marshall, d/b, shell border, Wood & Sons, 10".**700.00**
Plate, Christ Church Oxford, d/b, Ridgway, 9¾", NM **195.00**
Plate, City Hall NY, d/b, floral/eagle border, unmk Stubbs, 6½" ..**225.00**
Plate, Classical Ruins, m/b, unmk T Lakin, ca 1810, 9½"...........**165.00**
Plate, Commodore MacDonnough's Victory, d/b, shell border, Woods, 10".**745.00**
Plate, Corinth, brn, Edwards, 1842-51, 9¼" **92.00**
Plate, Court House Baltimore, d/b, fruit & flower border, 8½", EX.**475.00**
Plate, Cowes Harbour, d/b, shell border, Wood & Sons, 6½".......**235.00**
Plate, Cupids, d/b, Adams, ca 1825, 10"....................................**375.00**
Plate, Dam & Waterworks Philadelphia, d/b, fruit & flower border, 10".**650.00**
Plate, Dartmouth, m/b, irregular shell border, Wood, 8¼", EX ...**300.00**
Plate, Death of Bear, d/b, Indian Sporting Series, Clews, 10" **450.00**
Plate, Dora, red, Challinor, 1856, 8¾" **75.00**
Plate, European Scenery, gr, Wood lace border, 1818-46, 10¼"..**150.00**
Plate, Exchange Baltimore, d/b, fruit & floral border, 10" **385.00**
Plate, Fair Mount Near Philadelphia, m-d/b, Stubbs, 10¼" **470.00**
Plate, Falkbourn Hall, d/b, Stevenson rose border, 10"................**225.00**
Plate, Falls of Killarney, d/b, 10"...**275.00**
Plate, floral, brn, beaded & scalloped edge, Clews, 10¼" **115.00**
Plate, floral, d/b, Davenport, 1820s, 10", EX **200.00**
Plate, Foliage & Scroll, d/b, Adams, 9", EX **90.00**
Plate, Girl Musician, m/b, Riley, 1802-28, 7¾" **295.00**
Plate, Grand Erie Canal, boats/locks in border, m/b, 10", VG **220.00**
Plate, Landing of Gen Lafayette, d/b, Clews, 10⅛" **495.00**
Plate, Landing of Gen Lafayette, d/b, Clews, 7¾" **500.00**
Plate, Landing of the Fathers..., d/b, Wood & Sons, 8½" **350.00**
Plate, Marino, d/b, Geo Phillips of Longport, 5" **85.00**
Plate, Medina, red, Cotton & Barlow, ca 1845, 9" **65.00**
Plate, Mesina, d/b, Wood & Challinor, 8¼" **70.00**
Plate, Mitchell & Freeman's...Warehouse..., d/b, Adams, 10¼"..**500.00**
Plate, Moulin Sur La Marne a Charenton, d/b, Wood, 9⅛".........**300.00**
Plate, Musketeer, d/b, Rogers, 7¾" **250.00**
Plate, Napoleon, blk, Mason, 1829-45, 9½"................................**135.00**
Plate, Napoleon, d/b, CJ Mason, 10½"..**250.00**
Plate, Oriental scene, d/b, Clews, 7"...**80.00**
Plate, Panama, brn, Challinor, 1853-62, 8⅝"..............................**75.00**
Plate, Peace & Planty, Am Indian portrait, d/b, Clews, 10" **715.00**
Plate, Persia, d/b, Adams, 1819-60, 9½"....................................**95.00**
Plate, Persian, brn, Ridgway, 1830-34, 10½"..............................**135.00**
Plate, President Washington/View of...Bridge at Rochester, d/b, 7½"..**5,000.00**
Plate, President Washington/Welcome Lafayette..., d/b, 8½"..**4,600.00**
Plate, Race Bridge Philadelphia, purple, Job & Jackson, 9".........**150.00**
Plate, Residence of Late Richard Jordan, m/b, Heath, 1828-41, 8".**275.00**
Plate, Rhode Island, d/b, Mayer, 8¾", EX **400.00**
Plate, roses, d/b, Wm Smith & Co, 1830s, 7" **125.00**
Plate, Rousillon, d/b, Games Woodwin, 1846, 10¼" **95.00**
Plate, Sheltered Pheasants, d/b, att Hall, flake, 10" **150.00**
Plate, St Peter's Rome, d/b, Italian Scenery series, 10" **200.00**
Plate, Table Rock Niagara Falls, d/b, shell border, Wood & Sons, 10".**500.00**
Plate, toddy; Winter View of Pittsfield MA, d/b, unmk Clews, 5¾"..**385.00**
Plate, Transylvania University KY, d/b, shell border, Wood, 9¼".**715.00**
Plate, Tuscan Rose, purple, Ridgway, 5¾" **95.00**
Plate, Venus, d/b, 1834-59, 9¾"..**95.00**
Plate, Venus, red, Podmore Walker, 8½".......................................**80.00**
Plate, Vintage, d/b, Alcock, 1839-46, 7¼" **70.00**
Plate, Vue du Chateau Ermenonville, d/b, Wood, 10¼" **275.00**
Plate, Water Lily, d/b, Wedgwood, 1820s, 9½" **400.00**
Plate, Winter View of Pittsfield MA, m/b, scalloped, Clews, 8¾", EX .**225.00**

Platter, Alms House NY, d/b, Beauties of Am, Ridgway, 16½x12¾"..**1,265.00**
Platter, Asiatic Pheasants, l/b, scalloped, ca 1850, 17½" **200.00**
Platter, Battle of Bunker Hill, d/b, Stevenson, 13x10¼" **5,000.00**
Platter, Beemaster, d/b, 1820s, 21", NM....................................**4,000.00**
Platter, Canova, brn, Mayer, 1834-48, 15¾x13½" **695.00**
Platter, Canova, Geo Phillips, 15¾x13½" **600.00**
Platter, Christianburg Danish Settlement..., d/b, Wood, 18¾x14½"..**3,225.00**
Platter, Corinthia, m/b, Challinor, 17¾"..................................**400.00**
Platter, Crystal Palace, purple, unmk Bell, ca 1851, 16¼x12½" .**595.00**
Platter, East Cowes Isle of Wight, d/b, Wood & Sons, 10½" **765.00**
Platter, Elton College, m/b, GF Smith & Co, 18½x14½" **375.00**
Platter, Foliage & Scroll series, d/b, Clews, 19x14½", EX........**1,000.00**
Platter, Greek, d/b, Spode, 1820s, 20"...................................**1,450.00**
Platter, Gym, Flintshire Wales, d/b, Hall, 17".........................**1,200.00**
Platter, Highland Hudson River, d/b, Wood, 12¾x10" **3,335.00**
Platter, Italian Pattern, d/b, att Spode, 21" **575.00**
Platter, Lake George State of NY, d/b, Wood & Sons, 16½" ...**2,600.00**
Platter, Landing of Gen Lafayette...1824, d/b, Clews, 15¼x11¾".**2,000.00**
Platter, London Zoological Gardens, purple, Clews, 13x11" **350.00**
Platter, Manilla, d/b, Podmore Walker, 15½x12" **600.00**
Platter, Mendenhall Ferry, d/b, Stubbs, 16¾x13¾" **2,185.00**
Platter, Military Academy West Point, d/b, Wood, 11¾x9¼" .**2,750.00**
Platter, NY Esplanade & Castle Garden, d/b, Stevenson, 18½x14½" .**5,750.00**
Platter, Persian, brn, Ridgway, 1830-34, 18¾x15", NM **750.00**
Platter, Philadelphia Hospital, Beauties of Am, d/b, Ridgway, 18", NM.**1,880.00**
Platter, river scene w/swans/boat/etc, States border, Clews, 16½".**2,500.00**
Platter, Shell, d/b, oval, Stubbs & Kent, rpr, 18½"..................**1,950.00**
Platter, Sheltered Peasants, d/b, Hall, 19½x15" **1,650.00**
Platter, State House Boston, d/b, Stubbs, 1790-1829, 14¾x12" **1,265.00**
Platter, Upper Ferry Bridge...Schullkill, d/b, Stubbs, 18¾x15½" .**1,000.00**
Platter, Venus, gr & brn, Podmore Walker, 15¾x12½" **600.00**
Platter, Winter View of Pittsfield MA, d/b, Clews, 16¼x14"..**3,450.00**
Relish, Persia, d/b, Adams, 1819-64, 9x5" **125.00**
Sauce boat, Castle Scenery, d/b, Furnival, 1845, 5x7¾".............**245.00**
Sauce boat, Fisherman's Hut, d/b, ca 1825, 4x7½" **325.00**
Sauce boat, Lucerne Toy Girl w/fruit & floral design, purple, unmk .**250.00**
Saucer, Landing of Gen Lafayette, d/b, Clews, 5¾".....................**275.00**
Sugar bowl, Lafayette at Franklin's Tomb, gr, rpl lid, 6¾" **495.00**
Sugar bowl, Wadsworth Tower, d/b, w/lid, Wood & Sons, 6x7"..**400.00**
Tea bowl, llama, d/b, Quadruped series, scalloped rim **200.00**
Tea bowl & saucer, Lafayette at Washington's Tomb, d/b, EX.....**750.00**
Tea bowl & saucer, Lafayette at Washington's Tomb, d/b, Wood & Sons.**750.00**
Teapot, Lafayette at Franklin's Tomb, d/b, Wood, 9x12¾" **1,700.00**
Tray, bread; landscape scene, rtcl rim, unmk, 11¼x9" **450.00**
Tray, Woodlands Near Philadelphia, d/b, Stubbs, 10¾x8¾"....**1,850.00**
Tureen, Boston State House, John Rogers, 5x8¼x7¼", +lid/tray .**3,750.00**
Tureen, Corinth, brn, Edwards, 1842-51, 9x10¼x10¼" **425.00**
Tureen, Oriental Scenery, brn, Mayer, +lid & ladle, 6½x8"........**650.00**
Tureen, Pastoral Courtship, Stevenson, 1820s, 10x13x9" **1,200.00**
Tureen, Picturesque Views...Hudson River, l/b, 9" L, +tray/ladle, NM.**580.00**
Tureen, sauce; Corinth, d/b, Edwards, +underplate **350.00**
Wash bowl & pitcher, Upper Ferry Bridge..., d/b, Stubbs, 10", 12⅝".**1,850.00**

Miscellaneous

Candlestick, tree trunk w/appl florets, lead-glaze creamware, 11", VG .**1,200.00**
Face jug, Bacchus/grape leaves, monkey hdl, early 19th C, 8", EX .**235.00**
Pitcher, Fair Hebe, lead-glazed creamware, tree trunk w/figures, 9".**1,000.00**
Plate, feather edge, floral, molded leaf/fishscale rim, 7¾" **700.00**
Plate, gr feather edge w/leaves & fishscales, mc floral center, 8¾"..**875.00**
Plate, seal of US: eagle, octagonal, pearlware w/bl feather edge, 8".**1,200.00**
Plate, toddy; feather edge, bl floral center, molded fishscale rim.**350.00**
Shaker, Toby, yel hat, bl coat, red breeches w/pk lustre, 1800s, 5"..**150.00**
Wall pocket, emb cherub/foliage, Pratt type, sgn Stevenson, rstr, 12"..**265.00**

Stained Glass

There are many factors to consider in evaluating a window or panel of stained glass art. Besides the obvious factor of condition, quality of leadwork, intricacy, jeweling, beveling, and the amount of selenium (red, orange, and yellow) present should all be taken into account. Remember, repair work is itself an art and can be very expensive. Our advisor for this category is Carl Heck; he is listed in the Directory under Colorado.

Ceiling Lights

12x25", grape trellis, bronze leaves as crown/ceiling mt, Morgan, EX..**6,325.00**
20" geometric shade w/geometrics in apron, Duffner/Kimberly .**3,000.00**
22", bamboo shoots/leaves, 2-tone gr on ivory, 11" deep bowl shape.**5,500.00**
23", tilework bowl w/scalloped bottom formed by irises & leaves, crown.**1,750.00**
24", blade-like leaves, wide leaf apron w/acorn band, Bent Glass Co.**2,290.00**
24", peach/brn flowers in rough dk amber bkground, Duffner/Kimberly.**7,800.00**
24", 9 blown-out apples, branches/leaves, irregular bkground segments..**3,000.00**
24" rose branch shade (roses at irregular bottom), shouldered form..**2,240.00**
26", roses/buds, rolled-down umbrella shape, irregular border, crown.**4,000.00**
28", allover floral, irregular edge, crown..................................**3,000.00**
28", fishscales w/stylized panels, incurvate/irregular edge, Wilkinson.**3,000.00**

Table Lamps

13" wisteria shade w/metal vines & leaves; organic base, Ahart, 23".**8,250.00**
15" fishscale shade in amethyst & amber; gilt Miller base, 21" ...**800.00**
16" gr leaf-section shade w/wide floral apron; slim std, massive base.**2,300.00**
16" grapes/flowers shade (EX color/quality), Reed & Barton std .**6,700.00**
16" shade w/lg 2-part leaves; organic base, Duffner/Kimberly ..**5,600.00**
16" tilework dome shade w/band of 5-petal flowers, organic std, Unique.**3,640.00**
18" geometric shade, caramel w/pk swag apron; emb base, Wilkinson, 23".**1,950.00**
18" red shade w/4 groups of tulips in apron; bamboo-like std, Gorham.**6,000.00**
19" bent-panel shade w/oranges in border, red scrollwork, Miller.**2,000.00**
19" brickwork shade w/3-color stylized apron; organic base, Wilkinson..**2,400.00**
19" leaf/scroll shade, gr/wht leaf blades comprise apron, Wilkinson..**2,185.00**
19" water lily shade; simple brn-gr base, Duffner/Kimberly (att).**9,500.00**
20" brickwork shade, brn/wht striated glass; slim std w/octagon base..**950.00**
20" floral cone shade; leafy base w/scroll capitals, Duffner/Kimberly.**14,000.00**
20" shade w/wide band of lg yel flowers/gr leaves, Wilkinson, 26".**3,900.00**
20" tilework shade w/5-petal flower border; stick std, Suess, 23".**4,200.00**
21" bowl shade w/red cherries/birds/leaves; simple std, Chicago Mosaic..**2,750.00**
22" shade w/narrow panels & 4 lily groupings, Lamb Bros; ornate base.**2,500.00**
22" tilework shade w/floral apron; organic Arts & Crafts base, Whaley.**2,350.00**
23" dome shade w/red & orange flowers on wht, fluted stem, Wilkinson..**5,600.00**
24" black-eyed Susan shade; tree trunk base, Suess................**12,320.00**
24" wht shaped shade w/mc morning glories, scalloped edge; tree base.**4,000.00**

24¼" apple blossom parasol-shaped shade; three-socket standard, wide base with etched wave border, Suess, 23½", from $11,000.00 to $11,500.00.

25" shade w/prs of narrow panels ea w/1 heart, dmn-inset apron; 29"..**5,600.00**
26" water lily-band gridwork shade; simple base, Unique Company..**12,300.00**
27" tilework 2-tier shade (sm sqs/3 dmn bands); tree trunk std, Suess..**16,250.00**

Windows

Geometric, yel/orange/frosted/clear, Prairie School, 59x16", G...**250.00**
Geometric design, mc w/jewels, 20½x26½"..............................**425.00**
Geometric floral, gr/wht/clear, Prairie School, rprs, 39x18", pr.**700.00**
Grapes/vines on bkground suggesting stone wall, ½-rnd: 24x32"..**1,200.00**
Jewel-fr oval in center, traditional elements, ripple glass, 21x25" .**2,900.00**
Linear, hammered amber field w/gr details, Prairie School, 48x16", pr .**1,200.00**
ME coastal scene w/lighthouse/etc, PA, 51x95", VG+, from $2,000 to.**3,000.00**
Morning-glory vines in pots (4-color) border clear panel, 37x19", pr..**1,750.00**
Mosaic design w/jewels, att Belcher, 1890, 43x46" **4,700.00**
Rose vines/ribbons on wht opal, 20x37", pr.............................**2,240.00**
Scrolls/fans/ribbons, many jewels, 17x50" **2,500.00**
Torchere entwined w/vining leaves, jewel accents, ripple glass, 66x22"..**1,400.00**
Victorian lady, winged cherub ea side, ripple glass/appl metal, 19x38"..**1,900.00**
5-border horseshoe, birds, jewels & flowers on jeweled ground, 40x48" .**2,800.00**

Stanford

The Stanford Pottery Co. was founded in 1945 in Sebring, Ohio. One of the founders was George Stanford, a former manager at Spaulding China (Royal Copley). They continued in operations until the factory was destroyed by a fire about 1961. They produced a Corn Line, similar to that of the Shawnee Company, that is today very collectible. Most examples are marked (either Stanford Sebring Ohio or with a paper label), so there should be no difficulty in distinguishing one line from the other.

In addition to their Corn line, they produced planters and figurines, many of which were black trimmed with gold, made to be sold as pairs or sets. Wall pockets and vases were made as well. In 1949 they introduced a line called Tomato Ware, consisting of a cookie jar, grease jar, salt and pepper shakers, creamer and sugar bowl, mustard jar, marmalade jar, etc. These were shaped as bright red tomatoes with green leaves and stems (often used as lid finials), and were marketed under the name 'The Pantry Parade.' Our advisor for this category is Joe Devine; he is listed in the Directory under Iowa.

Ashtray, free-form, orange w/wht 'stucco,' #270-D, mk, 10x7"......**12.00**
Corn Line, butter dish..**60.00**
Corn Line, casserole, 8" L **50.00**
Corn Line, cookie jar **100.00**
Corn Line, creamer & sugar bowl, w/lid....................................**60.00**
Corn Line, cup **20.00**
Corn Line, pitcher, #513, 7¼" **65.00**
Corn Line, pitcher, 7½" **65.00**
Corn Line, plate, 9" L...**35.00**
Corn Line, relish tray **45.00**
Corn Line, shakers, sm, pr...**30.00**
Corn Line, shakers, 4", pr..**35.00**
Corn Line, snack set, cup & plate w/indent, #709 ....**95.00**
Corn Line, spoon rest **30.00**
Corn Line, teapot **75.00**
Corn Line, tumbler..**35.00**
Planter, Dutch boy or girl by tulip, blk w/gold trim, ea................**20.00**
Planter, matching drummer, boy or girl, 7", ea...........................**22.00**
Planter, teddy bear, wht w/pk & bl trim, paper label, 7"...............**35.00**
Tomato Ware, casserole, w/lid, 6x9" **60.00**
Tomato Ware, cookie jar, 8"...**90.00**
Tomato Ware, creamer **30.00**
Tomato Ware, grease jar, w/lid **38.00**
Tomato Ware, marmalade jar **35.00**

Tomato Ware, mustard jar...**35.00**
Tomato Ware, pitcher, 6½" **65.00**
Tomato Ware, sugar bowl **30.00**
Wall pocket, bird, bl & cobalt w/gold trim, 7", from $40 to..........**45.00**
Wall pocket, cherry branch, red pie-crust edge, #299, mk, 6¼" **28.00**

Stangl

Stangl Pottery was one of the longest-existing potteries in the United States, having as its beginning in 1814 the Sam Hill Pottery, becoming the Fulper Pottery which gained eminence in the field of art pottery (ca 1860), and then coming under the aegis of Johann Martin Stangl. The German-born Stangl joined Fulper in 1910 as chemical engineer, left for a brief stint at Haeger in Dundee, Illinois, and rejoined Fulper as general manager in 1920. He became president of the firm in 1928. Although Stangl's name was on much of the ware from the late '20s onward, the company's name was not changed officially until 1955. J.M. Stangl died in 1972; the pottery continued under the ownership of Wheaton Industries until 1978, then closed. Stangl is best known for its extensive Birds of American line, styled after Audubon; its brightly colored, hand-carved, hand-painted dinner-ware; and its great variety of giftware, including its dry-brushed gold lines. For more information we recommend *Collector's Encyclopedia of Stangl Din-nerware* and *Collector's Encyclopedia of Stangl Artware, Lamps & Birds*, by Robert Runge, Jr. (Collector Books). Another good reference is *Stangl Pot-tery* by Harvey Duke; for ordering information refer to the listing for Nancy and Robert Perzel, Popkorn Antiques (our advisors for this category), in the Directory under New Jersey. Also available: *Stangle Pottery, White-Bodied Artware, 1924 – 1942*, by Peter Meissner (Schiffer).

Artware and Novelties

Ashtray, Abstract Fish, Kay Hackett design, #3926, oval, from $290 to .**325.00**
Ashtray, Canada Goose, Kay Hackett design, #3926, oval **25.00**
Ashtray, Jazz Musician, mandolin or accordion player, #1315/1317, 10".**400.00**
Ashtray, Partridge, Kay Hackett design, #3926, oval, from $130 to .**150.00**
Ashtray, Quail, Kay Hackett design, #3926, oval..........................**35.00**
Ashtray, Scotty dog figural on bk, Antique Gold, #2089, 4½x5"..**90.00**
Basket, Silver Green, hand-shaped flared rims/twist hdl, #1852, 5½".**100.00**
Basket, Terra Rose Blue, #3225, 7x7", from $35 to **45.00**
Candle lamp, Pussycat, Chartreuse, upright rtcl figure, 13".........**200.00**
Candlesticks, spiral stems, blk, #1360, 10", pr, from $175 to.......**190.00**
Candy box, Blue Pompeii, #5188, w/lid, 7x4½", from $25 to........**35.00**
Candy dish, 8-sided tureen shape, Antique Gold, w/lid, #4092, 6½".....**35.00**
Cigarette box, Garden Flower, #3698, from $55 to **70.00**
Cigarette box, Mediterranean, rich cobalt/gr mottle on wht, 5½" L.**90.00**
Coaster/ashtray, Tropic Flower, Kay Hackett design, #3791, $20 to.**25.00**
Dutch shoe, Pennsylvania Artware, #3258, 5" L..........................**45.00**
Ewer, Antqiue Gold, twisted hdl/ringed str spout, handmade, 10" .**95.00**
Flower frog, Gazelle, Colonial Blue, #1169, 11½", from $200 to .**250.00**
Flower frog, Pipes of Pan, #383, 5x6", from $300 to **350.00**
Flowerpot, Red Rose, wht w/gr band & HP red flower, no cvg, 4" .**18.00**
Lamp base, bulbous barrel form, #1489, 7½" **85.00**
Lamp base, Square Modern, Persian Yellow, #1081, orig mts, 8", $500 to .**600.00**
Lamp base, 4 canted sides w/emb lady/dog, #1099, 8", from $175 to.**200.00**
Lobster dish, Tangerine, red-orange lobster form, 13" L, from $375 to.**400.00**
Pie plate, Gingerbread, redware w/piped-on bird or bldg, 10", $85 to.**95.00**
Pie plate, Gingerbread, redware w/piped-on decor, coggled edge, 10" **60.00**
Pig bank, Terra Rose, #1076, 1940-61, 4", from $150 to **200.00**
Pitcher, #2000, various glazes, mini, ea, from $15 to......................**25.00**
Pitcher, Stoneware, w/cobalt decor, #6007, 11", from $175 to **200.00**
Pitcher & bowl, Town & Country, gr, lg, 2-pc set, from $150 to..**165.00**
Strawberry jar, Silver Green, #1382, w/saucer, 6", from $60 to **75.00**
Vase, Amber Glo, cylindrical, 10" **60.00**

Vase, Colonial Blue, 3-D dog hdls, horizontal lobes/rings, #3160, 16" .450.00
Vase, emb wheat, sq-top hdls, bulbous/ftd, Variegated Rust, #2042, 8" .125.00
Vase, horse head shape, 2-tone Terra Rose, #3611, 13", from $400 to .450.00
Vase, Satin Green, flaring can neck w/leaf-form hdls, #3104, 7"....50.00
Vase, standing leaf shape, Antique Gold, #3440, 12" 70.00
Vase, Sunburst, #1185S Square Modern, 6", from $150 to..........175.00
Vase, Tangerine, #1903, 3½" 150.00
Wall pocket, Fruit, Colonial Blue, #997, 8", from $175 to..........200.00
Wig stand, Deco lady's head/neck, blond or brunette, #5168, $300 to....350.00

Dinnerware

Amber-Glo #3899, butter dish 25.00
Amber-Glo #3899, egg cup 15.00
Amber-Glo #3899, sugar bowl (open) 22.00
Apple Delight #5161, ashtray, fluted, 5"...............................12.00
Apple Delight #5161, bowl, lug soup.....................................18.00
Apple Delight #5161, pitcher, 2-qt.......................................60.00
Apple Delight #5161, tile..20.00
Bittersweet #5111, gravy boat 15.00
Blueberry #3770, casserole, skillet shape, 8"..........................50.00
Blueberry #3770, coaster/ashtray..30.00
Blueberry #3770, creamer...20.00
Blueberry #3770, egg cup...25.00
Blueberry #3770, plate, 11"..35.00
Blueberry #3770, platter, oval, 11½" 125.00
Chicory #3809, bowl, salad; 12"..100.00
Chicory #3809, gravy boat..35.00
Chicory #3809, pitcher, 1-qt..50.00
Cosmos #3339, bowl, fruit..12.00
Cosmos #3339, plate, chop; 14½" 110.00
Country Garden #3943, bowl, cereal.....................................22.00
Country Garden #3943, bowl, salad; 10" 65.00
Country Garden #3943, cruet..40.00
Country Garden #3943, pitcher, ½-pt....................................30.00
Country Garden #3943, plate, 9"...35.00
Country Garden #3943, platter, Casual, 13¾" 85.00
Country Garden #3943, teapot...100.00
Country Life #3946, bowl, fruit; rooster, 5½".........................35.00
Country Life #3946, coaster, duckling 45.00
Country Life #3946, cup, hen..25.00
Country Life #3946, plate, cow, 8".......................................100.00
Country Life #3946, saucer, 3 little eggs................................15.00
Daisy #1870, creamer..20.00
Daisy #1870, teapot..175.00
Festival #3677, bowl, salad; 10" 75.00
Festival #3677, plate, 11" 35.00
Festival #5072, bowl, fruit 15.00
Festival #5072, pitcher, 2-qt...100.00
Festival #5072, platter, Casual, 13¾"....................................75.00
Fruit & Flowers #4030, bowl, divided vegetable; oval 50.00
Fruit & Flowers #4030, coffee warmer 35.00
Fruit & Flowers #4030, egg cup...25.00
Fruit & Flowers #4030, plate, 6"...10.00
Fruit & Flowers #4030, sugar bowl, w/lid...............................20.00
Fruit #3697, ashtray, fluted, 5" 20.00
Fruit #3697, bowl, mixing; 5½" 45.00
Fruit #3697, bowl, salad; 10", from $55 to..............................65.00
Fruit #3697, coffeepot, 8-cup, from $100 to...........................120.00
Fruit #3697, pickle dish, from $25 to.....................................30.00
Fruit #3697, pitcher, ½-pt 30.00
Fruit #3697, saucer, jumbo 25.00
Fruit #3697, tidbit, 10", from $10 to.....................................15.00
Garden Flower #3700, bowl, lug soup; from $15 to.....................20.00

Garden Flower #3700, bowl, salad; Campanula & Morning Glory, sm.18.00
Garden Flower #3700, plate, 9"..22.00
Garden Flower #3700, teapot, Sunflower 85.00
Golden Blossom #5155, mug, 2-cup.......................................35.00
Golden Blossom #5155, platter, oval, 14¾".............................25.00
Golden Harvest #3887, casserole, w/lid, 6".............................25.00
Golden Harvest #3887, coffeepot, ind....................................65.00
Golden Harvest #3887, pitcher, 1-qt......................................45.00
Golden Harvest #3887, plate, 10"...13.00
Grape #3865, casserole, ind; 4", from $25 to...........................30.00
Grape #3865, shakers, pr...40.00
Harvest #3341, bowl, oval, 9"...55.00
Harvest #3341, shakers, pr...20.00
Holly #3869, cup 25.00
Holly #3869, plate, 8"...45.00
Kiddieware, bowl, cereal; Flying Saucer #5018, 1960, from $275 to..300.00
Kiddieware, bowl, cereal; Running Dog, 1941 ....400.00
Kiddieware, divided dish, Bluebird #3827, 1950 ....350.00
Kiddieware, plate, Goldilocks #3764, 1946, 9", from $200 to 250.00
Kiddieware, set, Little Quackers, 3-pc....................................275.00
Magnolia #3870, bowl, coupe soup..30.00
Magnolia #3870, bowl, vegetable; divided...............................35.00
Magnolia #3870, coaster/ashtray..20.00
Magnolia #3870, sugar bowl, w/lid..20.00
Orchard Song #5110, mug, 2-cup, from $30 to...........................35.00
Provincial #3966, bowl, fruit...15.00
Provincial #3966, creamer..12.00
Provincial #3966, mug, 2-cup, from $35 to...............................45.00
Ranger #3304, bowl, fruit; from $110 to.................................145.00
Ranger #3304, cup, coffee; from $60 to..................................70.00
Rooster #5223, bowl, coupe soup; from $25 to..........................35.00
Rooster #5223, cake stand...35.00
Star Flower #3864, bowl, salad; 10", from $40 to......................50.00
Star Flower #3864, gravy boat & underplate.............................30.00
Thistle #3847, bowl, cereal...25.00
Thistle #3847, bowl, mixing; 4"...45.00
Thistle #3847, chip & dip..125.00
Thistle #3847, coffeepot, ind; from $125 to.............................130.00
Thistle #3847, plate, grill; 9", from $45 to 55.00
Thistle #3847, relish...30.00
Tiger Lily #3965, bread tray, from $40 to................................50.00
Tiger Lily #3965, plate, 10"..25.00
Town & Country #5287, baking dish, bl, 7x10"........................90.00
Town & Country #5287, bowl, soup/cereal; bl, 15-oz.................30.00
Town & Country #5287, flowerpot, bl, 5", from $35 to...............45.00
Town & Country #5287, spoon rest, bl, 8¾"............................40.00
Town & Country #5287, sugar bowl, blk or crimson, from $25 to..30.00
White Dogwood #5167, bowl, cereal......................................25.00
White Dogwood #5167, plate, 6"..7.00
Wild Rose #3929, bowl, lug soup..15.00
Wild Rose #3929, bowl, salad; 12".......................................75.00
Wild Rose #3929, coffee warmer...30.00
Wild Rose #3929, mug, 2-cup..50.00
Wild Rose #3929, saucer..7.00
Yellow Tulip #3637, bean pot/cookie jar.................................75.00
Yellow Tulip #3637, bowl, salad; 10" 60.00
Yellow Tulip #3637, creamer...15.00
Yellow Tulip #3637, plate, 10"..25.00

Stangl Birds and Animals

The Stangl company introduced their line of ceramic birds in 1940, taking advantage of a import market crippled by the onset of WWII. The figures were an immediate success. Additional employees were hired, and eventually sixty decorators worked at the plant itself, with the overflow contracted out to individuals in private homes. After the war when import trade once again saturated the market, Stangl curtailed their own production but continued to make the birds and animals on a limited basis as late as 1978.

Nearly all the birds were marked. A four-digit number was used to identify the species, and most pieces were signed by the decorator. An 'F' indicates a bird that was decorated at the Flemington plant. Our advisors for this category are Nancy and Robert Perzel, Popkorn Antiques. (See the Directory under New Jersey.) Recommended reference books are listed in the Stangl category.

Animals

#1076, piggy bank, sponged wht, not cvd....................................100.00
#1076, piggy bank, Terra Rose, brushed finish, hand cvd 150.00
#3178A, Elkhound, wht w/blk overglaze, 3½" 150.00
#3178G, Elephant, wht w/blk overglaze, 2½" 150.00
#3178H, Squirrel, wht w/blk overglaze, 3½" 175.00
#3178J, Gazelle, wht w/blk overglaze, 3½" 150.00
#3178J, Percheron, wht w/blk overglaze, 3½" 125.00
#3243, Wire-Haired Terrier, 3¼" 300.00
#3244, Draft Horse, 3" 150.00
#3245, Rabbit, 2" 350.00
#3246, Buffalo, 2½" 350.00
#3247, Gazelle, 3¾" 375.00
#3248, Giraffe, 2½" 650.00
#3249, Elephant, Antique Gold, 5" 110.00
#3249, Elephant, 3" 300.00
#3277, Colt, 5" 1,650.00
#3278, Goat, 5" 1,650.00
#3279, Calf, 3½" 975.00
#3280, Dog, sitting, 5¼" 350.00
#3430, Duck, 22" 8,250.00
#3433, Rooster, blk or wht, 16" 900.00
Burro, blk w/wht overglaze, 3¼" 150.00
Cat, Siamese, sitting, decor, 8½" 700.00
Cat, sitting, Granada Gold, 8½" 300.00

Birds

#3401D, Wren pair, revised version, $115.00; old version, $675.00.

#3250A, Duck, standing, 3¼" 120.00
#3250B, Duck, preening, 3¼" 120.00
#3250D, Duck, grazing, 3¾" 120.00
#3250F, Duck, quacking, 3¼" 115.00
#3273, Rooster, 5¾" 750.00
#3274, Penguin, 6" 475.00
#3275, Turkey, 3½" 450.00
#3276D, Bluebird pr, 8½" 160.00
#3281, Duck, mother, 6" 625.00
#3285, Rooster, early, 4½" 120.00

#3286, Hen, late, 3¼" 75.00
#3400, Lovebird, old version, 4" 115.00
#3400, Lovebird, revised, 4" 80.00
#3401, Wren, dk brn, revised, 3½" 60.00
#3401D, Wren pr, tan, old version 675.00
#3402, Oriole, beak down, 3½" 125.00
#3402, Oriole, revised, 3¼" 55.00
#3402D, Oriole pr, revised, w/leaves, 5½" 125.00
#3404D, Lovebirds pr, kissing, old version, 4½" 400.00
#3405, Cockatoo, 6" 55.00
#3405D, Cockatoo pr, revised, 9½" 150.00
#3406, Kingfisher, teal, 3½" 70.00
#3406D, Kingfisher pr, bl, 5" 175.00
#3407, Owl, 5½x2½" 330.00
#3408, Bird of Paradise, 5½" 125.00
#3409D, Redstart pr, 9" 200.00
#3431, Duck, standing, grayish wht w/blk spots 1,300.00
#3432, Duck, running, brn...700.00
#3433, Rooster, natural colors, 16" 4,400.00
#3443, duck, flying, gray, 9" 300.00
#3443, duck, flying, teal, 9½x12" 290.00
#3444, Cardinal, female 200.00
#3444, Cardinal, revised, glossy pk, 7" 95.00
#3445, Rooster, gray, 10" 270.00
#3446, Hen, yel, 7" 190.00
#3447, Prothonotary Warbler...60.00
#3448, Blue-Headed Vireo, 4¼" 65.00
#3449, Paroquet, 5½" 175.00
#3450, Passenger Pigeon, 9x18" 1,700.00
#3451, Willow Ptarmigan 3,000.00
#3452, Painted Bunting, 5" 100.00
#3453, Mountain Bluebird, 6⅛" 1,600.00
#3454, Key West Quail Dove, single wing up, 10" 275.00
#3454, Key West Quail Dove, wings up, wht 800.00
#3455, Shoveler Duck, 12¼x14" 1,750.00
#3457, Chinese Pheasant, walking, 7¼x15" 3,400.00
#3458, Quail, 7½" 1,800.00
#3459, Fish Hawk...8,000.00
#3491, Hen Pheasant, 6¼x11" 185.00
#3492, Cock Pheasant...190.00
#3518D, White-Crowned Pigeon pr, bl w/wht heads, 8x14"....1,050.00
#3580, Cockatoo, med, 8⅞" 140.00
#3580, Cockatoo, wht matt, med 550.00
#3581, Chickadees, brn/wht, group of 3, 5½x8½" 185.00
#3582D, Parakeet pr, bl, 7" 250.00
#3582D, Parakeet pr, gr, 7" 235.00
#3583, Parula Warbler, 4¼" 65.00
#3584, Cockatoo, sgn Jacob, lg, 11⅜".......................................275.00
#3584, Cockatoo, wht matt, lg 1,050.00
#3585, Rufous Hummingbird, 3" 90.00
#3586, Pheasant (Della Ware), natural colors 1,800.00
#3586, Pheasant (Della Ware), Terra Rose, gr 650.00
#3589, Indigo Bunting, 3½" 80.00
#3590, Carolina Wren, 4½" 160.00
#3591, Brewer's Blackbird, 3½" 170.00
#3592, Titmouse, 3" 60.00
#3593, Nuthatch, 2½" 80.00
#3594, Red-Faced Warbler, 3" 135.00
#3595, Bobolink, 4¾" 160.00
#3596, Gray Cardinal, 5" 75.00
#3597, Wilson Warbler, yel & blk, 3"...55.00
#3598, Kentucky Warbler, 3" 50.00
#3599D, Hummingbird pr 325.00
#3626, Broadtail Hummingbird, w/bl flower 175.00

#3627, Rivoli Hummingbird, pk flower, 6" 175.00
#3628, Rieffer's Hummingbird 160.00
#3629, Broadbill Hummingbird, 4½" 160.00
#3634, Allen Hummingbird, 3½" 100.00
#3635, Gold Finches (group) 200.00
#3715, Blue Jay, w/peanut, 10¼" 700.00
#3715, Blue Jay w/peanut, Fulper blk/bl glaze 2,100.00
#3716, Blue Jay, w/leaf, 10¼" 700.00
#3717, Blue Jay pr 3,100.00
#3746, Canary (right), rose flower, 6¼" 250.00
#3747, Canary (left), bl flower, 6¼" 250.00
#3749, Western Tanager, red matt, 4¾" 475.00
#3750, Scarlet Tanager, 8½" 450.00
#3750D, Western Tanager pr, pk, 8" 550.00
#3751, Red-Headed Woodpecker, glossy pk, 6¼" 325.00
#3751, Red-Headed Woodpecker, red matt, 6¼" 500.00
#3752D, Red-Headed Woodpecker pr, glossy pk, 7¼" ...450.00
#3754, White-Wing Crossbill (single) 4,500.00
#3754D, White-Wing Crossbill pr, glossy pk, 9x8" ...475.00
#3755, Audubon Warbler, pk flower, 4¼" 450.00
#3757, Scissor-Tailed Flycatcher, 11" 1,100.00
#3758, Magpie-Jay, 10¾" 1,400.00
#3810, Black-Throated Warbler, 3½" 190.00
#3811, Chestnut Chickadee, 5" 135.00
#3812, Chestnut Warbler, 4½" 180.00
#3813, Crested Goldfinch, 5" 170.00
#3814, Townsend Warbler, 3" 165.00
#3815, Western Bluebird, 7" 450.00
#3848, Golden-Crowned Kinglet, 4¼" 125.00
#3848, Prothonotory Warbler 130.00
#3850, Western Warbler, 4" 150.00
#3851, Red-Breasted Nuthatch, 3¾" 95.00
#3852, Cliff Swallow, 3½" 170.00
#3853, Golden-Crowned Kinglets, 5½x5" 800.00
#3868, Summer Tanager, 4" 775.00
#3921, Yellow-Headed Verdin, 4½" 1,550.00
#3922, European Goldfinch 1,200.00
#3923, Vermillion Fly-Catcher, 5¾" 2,350.00
#3924, Yellow Throat, 6" 700.00
#3925, Magnolia Warbler 3,200.00
Stangl Bird dealer sign 2,350.00

Stanley Tools

The Stanley company was founded in Connecticut in 1854, and over the years has absorbed more than a score of tool companies already in existence. By the second decade of the twentieth century, having long since solidified their position as *the* source for tools of the highest grade, the company enjoyed worldwide prestige. Through both World Wars, they were recognized as one of the nation's premier producers of wartime goods. Industrial arts classes introduced baby boomers to Stanley tools and provided yet another impetus to expansion and recognition. Overall, the company's growth and development has kept an easy pace along with the economy of the nation, and it continues today as a leader in the field of tool production.

Three factors to consider when evaluating a tool are these: age, completeness and condition. One of their earliest trademarks (1854-1857) is 'A. Stanley,' found only on rulers. In the early '20s, their now-familiar 'sweetheart' trademark, the letters SW and a heart shape within the confines of a modified rectangle, was adopted. They continued to use this trademark until it was discontinued in 1936. Many other variations were used as well, some of which contain a patent date. A study of these marks will help you determine the vintage of your tools. Condition is extremely important, and though a light cleaning is acceptable, you

should never attempt to 'restore' a tool by sanding, repainting or replacing parts that may be damaged or missing. Unless noted otherwise in the description lines, our values are for tools in average, 'as found' condition, ranging from very good to excellent. Note: Any common number $20.00 rule with the A. Stanley trademark is easily worth $500.00 plus!

For more information, we recommend *Antique and Collectible Stanley Tools*, written by our advisor, John Walter, who is listed in the Directory under Ohio.

Chisel, butt; #160 ....60.00
Cutter, wallboard outlet; #272 ....350.00
Drill, breast; #741 ....45.00
Drill, hand; #1219 ....60.00
Gauge, jointer; #386 ....175.00
Gauge, marking; #197 ....150.00
Hammer, cobbler's 100.00
Hammer, cooper's; #423 ....50.00
Hammer, nail; #21 ....50.00
Hammer, tack; #5 ....150.00
Level, carpenter's; adjustable, #33 ....25.00
Level, 4-sq, #1113 ....150.00
Mallet, #16 ....50.00
Plane, block; #9½ 35.00
Plane, circular; #113 ....175.00
Plane, core box; #56 ....1,800.00
Plane, dado; #39¼ 200.00
Plane, match; #146 ....350.00
Plane, rabbet; #90-A 2,500.00
Plane, rabbet; Victor, #11½ 10,000.00
Plane, scrub; #40 ....125.00
Plane, side rabbet; #98 ....150.00
Plane, smooth; #2 ....500.00
Plane, smooth; Defiance, #14 ....750.00
Plane, tongue & groove; #48, Type I 200.00
Plane, weather-strip plow; #238 ....350.00
Rule, carpenter's caliper; #36½ 60.00
Rule, carpenter's; #61 ....35.00
Rule, saddler's; #80 ....125.00
Rule, zigzag; #721M 500.00
Scraper, box; #70 ....45.00
Scraper, veneer; #12¾ 3,000.00
Screwdriver, flashlight; #1021 ....250.00
Screwdriver, Leader; #80 ....20.00
Screwdriver, radio; #177 ....35.00
Spoke shave, chamfer; #65 ....175.00
Spoke shave, razor edge; #76 ....500.00
Tape measure, #7406 ....60.00
Trammel points, #3, Type I 200.00
Try square, improved; #1 ....75.00
Vise, bench; #761 ....60.00
Wrench, tire bolt; #1 ....350.00

Statue of Liberty

Long before she began greeting immigrants in 1886, the Statue of Liberty was being honored by craftsmen both here and abroad. Her likeness was etched on blades of the finest straight razors from England, captured in finely detailed busts sold as souvenirs to Paris fairgoers in 1878, and presented on colorfully lithographed trade cards, usually satirical, to American shoppers. Perhaps no other object has been represented in more forms or with such frequency as the universal symbol of America. Liberty's keepsakes are also universally accessible. Delightful souvenir models created in 1885 to raise funds for Liberty's pedestal are frequently found at flea markets, while earlier French bronze and terra cotta Liberties have been auctioned for over $100,000.00. Some collectors hunt for the countless forms of nineteenth-century Liberty memorabilia, while many collections were begun in anticipation of the 1986 Centennial with concentration on modern depictions. Our advisor for this category is Mike Brooks; he is listed in the Directory under California.

Book, Inauguration of the Statue of Liberty, 1887 ....60.00
Booklet, Rays From Liberty's Torch, 1890 ....30.00
Bottle, seltzer; etched Liberty, A Doeink, Liberty, NY...................35.00
Box, Liberty on lid, Limoges, star closure, 3x1½" 65.00
Brooch, hand holding torch, some stones missing, mk Staret, 1940s.215.00
Card, admission to inauguration, 1886 ....70.00
Cigar box label, Victory Day, WWII 6.00
Clock/lamp, figural, flame bulb, copper-tone pot metal, 1940s, 16" .165.00
Container, Yourex Silver Saver, rnd, cb, ca 1930 ....27.00
Cup, sterling, Windsor Club, 1907, 2" 22.00
Flyer, Statue of Liberty steamboat excursions, 1890s 25.00
Harper's Weekly, various litho prints, 1880s, ea, from $10 to........25.00
Invitation to statue's unveiling, 1886, G-..........................200.00
Lamp, figural, bronze-tone metal, electric, 11" 130.00
Letter, teen to military father re: parade on Broadway, 1886.........95.00
Lighter, ST Dupont Statue of Liberty Line 2, ltd ed of 350, MIB..785.00
Matchsafe, silver w/emb Liberty & scrolls, Fr, 2x1½" 350.00
Medal, central Valley Nat'l Bank 18.00
Napkin holder, sterling..........................15.00
Pennant, felt, 1930s..........................25.00
Pin, enamel, 77th Div, WWI 12.00
Pipe, glazed clay, 1880s..........................90.00
Plates, various makers, 1980s, ea, from $10 to..........................20.00
Pocket watch, Elgin, 1890s..........................175.00
Poster, DeLand, WWI 150.00
Radio speaker stand, wht metal casting, Palcone, 17" 175.00
Reverse painting on glass, in plaster fr w/orig pnt, 25x19", EX 75.00
Runner, damask, ca 1890..........................85.00
Sampler, Liberty & God Bless America, mc on wht linen, 25x18" in fr.75.00
Scarf, head of Liberty, red/wht/bl, Hermes, 35" sq, NM..............150.00
Scissors, emb metal, Liberty 1 side/Woolworth building on reverse, 6".55.00
Smoke stand/lamp, Liberty at base, torch lights up, 1940s, 27", EX.150.00
Smoking stand, figure w/tray on stepped base, patinated metal, 28"..250.00
Snow dome, figural, Atlas Crystal Works, 1920s..........................55.00
Spoon, emb Liberty in hdl, plain bowl, silver, mk Tiffany, 6"........55.00
Statue, hand cvd, Mexico, 15" 20.00
Statue, hand-cvd wood (papier-mache mold), Philippines, 1920s.575.00
Statue, Wenck perfume, 1908..........................325.00
Ticket, lg souvenir of Gauthier et Cie (Liberty foundry), 1883...105.00
Ticket, Manhattan Day, Columbian Exposition, 1893..................15.00
Trade card, satirical, A&C Hams, 1880s 70.00

Vase, clear glass with embossed Statue of Liberty above eagle, smooth base, twentieth century, $150.00. (Photo courtesy Glass-Works Auctions)

Vase, frosted Liberty hand, Gillinder, 1876 Centennial.................70.00
Vase, Liberty reserve on 7mm WWI shell casing, 13" 190.00

Steamship Collectibles

For centuries, ocean-going vessels with their venturesome officers and crews were the catalyst that changed the unknown aspects of our world to the known. Changing economic conditions, unfortunately, have now placed the North American shipping industry in the same jeopardy as the American passenger train. They are becoming a memory. The surge of interest in railroad collectibles and the railroad-related steamship lines has lead collectors to examine the whole spectrum of steamship collectibles.

Reproduction (sometimes called 'replica') and fantasy dinnerware has been creeping into the steamship dinnerware collecting field. Some of the 'replica' ware is quite well done so one should practice caution and... 'Know Thy Dealer.' Our advisor for this category is Lila Shrader; she is listed in the Directory under California. We also recommend *Restaurant China, Volumes 1* and 2, by Barbara Conroy (Collector Books).

Key:
BS — back stamped	SL — side logo
hh — hollow handle	SM — side mark
NBS — no back stamp	TL — top logo
R&B — Reed & Barton	TM — top mark

Dining Salon

Bowl, Alaska SS Co Yukon, TL, NBS, 5½" 50.00
Bowl, cereal; Panama RR SS Co, Cristobal, TL, NBS, 5½"........110.00
Bowl, Eastern SS Lines, Eastern Blue, TL, NBS, 4¼"..................55.00
Bowl, flat rim soup; NHRR, Fall River TL, NBS, 8" 270.00
Bowl, flat rim soup; Pacific Steam Navigation Co, TM, 9" 380.00
Butter icer, Interlake SS Co, Cygnus, ceramic, 2-pc, TL & BS, 7" .180.00
Butter pat, Admiral Line, HF Alexander, TL, mfg Bauscher, 3⅛"..56.00
Butter pat, Chicago Detroit & Green Bay Transport Co, CD & GB, TM.95.00
Butter pat, Concordia Line, TL w/house flag, rich gold, 3½" 12.00
Butter pat, Matson Line, Mariposa, floral design, BS..................88.00
Butter pat, United States Lines, Gray Star, TL, 3⅛" 30.00
Butter pat, US Shipping Board, Hawkeye State, TL, NBS, 2⅝" ...50.00
Butter pat, White Star Line, Brownfield White Star, TM, 2½x3¾" .575.00
Creamer, Canadian National SS, Maritime, no hdl, NBS, ind, 2¾".38.00
Creamer, Colonial Line, Lexington, SL, NBS, ind, 2¼" 78.00
Creamer, Eastern SS Lines, Marine, ind, 2½"..........................140.00
Creamer, Monticello SS Co, Vallejo, 4¼" 185.00
Cruet SP fr+2 crystal bottles & stoppers, all SM, early 1900s 295.00
Cup, bouillon; Eastern SS Lines, Eastern house flag in ring, hdls .36.00
Cup & saucer, Charente SS Co Ltd, coffee-cup style, SL, TM......30.00
Cup & saucer, demi; Eastern SS Lines, Marine 72.50
Cup & saucer, demi; New England SS Co, SL & TL in script....160.00
Cup & saucer, demi; White Star Line, Brownfield White Star, SL.790.00
Cup & saucer, Dept of Navy, SL & TM, Laughlin..........................10.00
Cup & saucer, Home Lines, Oceanic, NBS..........................21.00
Cup & saucer, P&O, Canberra, tea-cup style, SL, BS..................14.00
Cup & saucer, US Shipping Board, Granite State, TL, NBS 62.00
Cup & saucer, White Star Line, Brownfield White Star, G gold..525.00
Cup & saucer, White Star Line, Wisteria, TL..........................670.00
Egg cup, dbl; Admiral Orient Line, rnd house flag logo, 3⅛"........48.00
Egg cup, United Fruit Co, Antigua, SL, NBS, 2¾" 188.00
Egg cup, United States Lines, Gray Star, 3⅞" 57.50
Egg holder, N German Lloyd, Kayser Wilhelm II, ceramic, SL, 2¼".112.50
Egg holder, SS Joseph Holland, ceramic, SL, 2"..........................185.00
Pitcher, Canadian Pacific, BCCS, Tremblant, 7½" 215.00

Plate, Alaska SS Co, Yukon, TL, BS, Buffalo, 9½" **128.00**
Plate, Georgia Bay Line, Georgian Bay, TM, 9½" **160.00**
Plate, New England SS Co, New England, TL, NBS, Buffalo, 9¼".**68.00**
Plate, Red Cross Line, Florizel, house flag TL, NBS, 7¼" **72.50**
Plate, service; Central of NJ RR, Sandy Hook Ferry Line, 10½"..**695.00**
Plate, Unites States Line, Gray Star, BS, 8" **12.50**
Plate, Virginia Ferry, Princess Anne, TM, 7½" **50.00**
Plate, White Star Lines, Celtic, TL, NBS, 9" **690.00**
Platter, Alaska SS Co, Yukon, TL, NBS, Buffalo, 7x5" **48.00**
Platter, Eastern SS Lines, Eastern Blue, TL, Buffalo, 7x9"..........**52.00**
Platter, Los Angeles SS Co, floral border, oval, TM, BS, 8x6"....**220.00**
Platter, Red Star Line, Antwerp, rtcl hdls, BM, 11" dia **112.00**
Relish, Canadian Pacific, BCCS, Empress, BS, 6½x3½" **50.00**
Relish, NASM (Holland America), shell shape, TL, pre-1940, 8½x4".**45.00**
Shot glass, United States Lines, etched SL, thick base, 2¼" **38.00**
Silver plate, creamer, C&B Transit Co, City of Erie, R&B, 2¼"..**255.00**
Silver plate, creamer, Dollar SS Lines, SL, 3" **38.00**
Silver plate, egg cup, Lusitania in enamel, rtcl, souvenir?, 2⅞" ..**290.00**
Silver plate, hot food cover, Cunard White Star, Elkington, BS, 11".**98.00**
Silver plate, sugar prongs, P&O SL, Elkington, 3¾" **65.00**
Silver plate, sugar prongs w/3 'claws,' Sweden, 4½" **60.00**
Silver-plated flatware, fork, Cunard White Star, Mappin & Webb, BS.**22.50**
Silver-plated flatware, knife, C&B Transit, hollow hdl, R&B, SL, 7¾".**42.00**
Silver-plated flatware, knife, United Fruit Co, flat hdl, SL, 8" **30.00**
Stem, champagne, Nunson SS Line, acid etched SL, 4⅞" **22.00**
Stem, champagne, United States Lines, etched SL, 4½" **56.00**
Stem, cordial, N German Lloyd, Nordd Lloyd Bremen acid etched, 3¾".**28.00**
Tablecloth, Am Export Lines, wht on wht w/woven logo, 51x34" .**30.00**
Tablecloth, United States Lines, wht on wht w/woven logo, 42x40".**30.00**
Tumbler, old fashioned; Moore-McCormack, glass, SM: ship picture, 4".**36.00**
Tumbler, United States Lines, acid-etched SL on glass, 5¼" **28.00**

Miscellaneous

Album, 150 items from French Line's Normandie on final voyage, 1939..**2,835.00**
Ashtray, Clyde Mallory Line, wht ceramic w/house flag, 4½" **16.00**
Ashtray, Moore-McCormack Lines, plastic & shaped like flag......**12.00**
Ashtray, Orient SS Nav Co, TL, Royal Doulton, 5" dia **34.00**
Ashtray, White Star Line, Majestic depicted under glass, 1920s, 4½".**52.00**
Barometer, advertising on rvpt, North German Lloyd, 1940s **470.00**
Blanket, deck chair; Cunard Line/536C, red on 1 side/navy, 54x56"..**145.00**
Book, Anchors Aweigh, Dollar SS, photos/etc SS Pres Hoover & Coolidge.**395.00**
Book, Century of Maritime Photography, 1991, hardbk, w/jacket.**60.00**
Book, Red Stacks Over Horizon, Goodrich SS Line, 1967, w/jacket.**20.00**
Book, Wreck of the Titan, Robertson, hardbk, 1912 ed, no jacket.**130.00**
Book, 303 SS Normandie & SS France, English ed, hardbk, no date..**80.00**
Booklet, Eastern SS Co, deck plans, maps, int scenes, 1929..........**28.00**
Booklet, N German Lloyd, pre-launch to Munchen, 1923, 36-pg.**70.00**
Booklet, Trans-Pacific Passenger Tarriff, NYK, 1930, 22-pg **36.00**
Booklet/passenger list, Cunard, SS Saxonia, graphics, 1912, 5x7¾".**30.00**
Brochure, Ward Line, New Am Ships, Morro Castle & Oriente, 1930..**265.00**
Button, African Royal Mail SS, gold-tone w/flag logo, dome, 1" ..**12.00**
Button, Anchor Line, silver over brass, house flag, ¾" dia **9.00**
Button, Chicago, Racine & Milwaukee, Seymour Line, Scovill, ⅞",......**44.00**
Button, Peoples Line, brass-like house flag by Scovill, dome, ⅞"....**4.00**
Deck plans, Andrea Doria, late 1940s, opens to 38x30" **56.00**
Deck plans, Canadian Nat'l SS, 1931, opens to 18x31" **23.00**
Glass float, Japanese, Woods #14, deep gr, 5"..............................**44.00**
Handkerchief, White Star Line, RMS Majestic, silk w/lace, 10" sq.**55.00**
Life ring, Italia Line, Andrea Doria, some wear, 30" dia **6,165.00**
Luggage sticker, Dollar Steamship Lines, colorful graphics, 5x4"..**16.00**
Luggage sticker, French Line, SS Champlain w/house flag logo, 3x6".**20.00**
Luggage sticker, Union Castle Line, gummed, 1930s, 3¼x3¼" **5.00**
Luggage tag, Union Castle Line, cb & string showing house flag, '30s.**9.00**

Luggage tag, Whitcomb Tours/Cruises, celluloid on leather strap, '30s.**16.00**
Luggage ticker, White Star Line/1st class/Baggage Room, 4½x5½".**12.00**
Magazine, Life, maiden voyage of Queen Mary, cover picture, 1937.**20.00**
Menu, Alaska SS Line, sled dogs by Crumrine, 1941, 8¼", +envelope.**9.00**
Menu, French Line, mc Deco graphics, 1927 ....**18.00**
Menu, Matson Lines, SS Lurline, Savage illustration, 1956 ....**24.00**
Menu, Moore-McCormick, Uruguay, Ann Peacock design, 1951 ...**8.00**
Menu, SS Tango, gambling ship off Long Beach CA, 1938, 9x5".**55.00**
Napkin ring, souvenir; Adelaide SS Co, metal w/pnt house flag, 1¼".**30.00**
Napkin ring, souvenir; White Star, RMS Megantic, SP w/pnt flag, 1¾"..**135.00**
Newspaper, (Phila) Evening Bulletin, April 19, 1912, 27-pg, $75 to..**110.00**
Pass, annual; Bangor & Aroostook SS Co, Vail, Supt B&ARR, 1897..**80.00**
Pass, annual; Northern Pacific SS Co, to Asst Supt NPSS, 1914.**24.00**
Passenger list, Cunard, RMS Lucania, map on bk, 1900...............**30.00**
Passenger list, United States Lines, Geo Washington, 1925, 20-pg.**26.00**
Pencil, automatic; Cunard White Star Liner, Queen Elizabeth, pearlized.**20.00**
Playing cards, Cunard, 1900s, wide, 52+Joker+1 in orig case......**115.00**
Playing cards, Home Line, Oceanic, sealed dbl bridge deck in case.**22.00**
Playing cards, Interocean SS Co, 1955, dbl deck+case **16.00**
Playing cards, Moore-McCormack, 1958, dbl deck+case...............**10.00**
Porthole, brass fr, dbl orig glass, 14" dia....................................**265.00**
Postcard, advertising; Admiral Line, Cruise & Be Gay, 1952, unmailed..**12.00**
Postcard, Baltic, ship's portrait+saving of steamship Republic in 1909.**11.00**
Postcard, Grosser Kurfurst Bremen, German & Am flags, 1907....**12.00**
Postcard, Titanic passing icebergs, artist conceived, sepia, WS, 1912.**255.00**
Pressure guage, Bacharach, 5000 PSI units, 4½" W **16.00**
Print, Rex, cb, cut-down calendar top, fr, 30x36" **37.00**
Sign, Cunard Lines, Mauretania under full steam, tin, 1930s, 28x38"..**138.00**
Stadimeter sextant, US Maritime Commission, Brandon type, WWII.**162.50**
Tea ball, souvenir; Hapag, mk HAPAG, unmk sterling, chain, 1".**120.00**
Telegraph, ship's; brass, twin hdls, 2-sided face, bells, JW Ray, 45"..**1,855.00**
Timetable, White Star Line of Detroit MI, 1929..........................**48.00**
Tin, Cadbury Chocolate, White Star's Titanic under full steam, 1911..**2,000.00**
Tin, cigarette; White Star Line, Olympic 46,439 tons w/portrait, 1920s..**165.00**
Towel, hand; Detroit & Cleveland...Co, huck w/bl stripe, 1936, 30x17".**45.00**
Tray, souvenir, Dayline, portrait of Hendrick Hudson ship, metal, 8x3".**180.00**
Vase, Holland-America advertising, rtcl, Gouda, 5" **435.00**
View folder, Fall River SS, faux leather, 1890, opens to 72"..........**28.00**
Watch fob, Goodrich SS Co, dk brass, TM logo, BS, 1½x1¼" **30.00**

Steins

Steins have been made from pottery, pewter, glass, stoneware, and porcelain, from very small up to the four-liter size. They may be decorated by etching, in-mold relief, decals, and occasionally they may be hand painted. Some porcelain steins have lithophane bases. Collectors often specialize in a particular type — faience, regimental, or figural, for example — while others limit themselves to the products of only one manufacturer.

See also Mettlach.

Key:
L — liter
lith — lithophane   tl — thumb lift

Anti-semitic, pottery, scenes, inlaid lid, Dumler & Breiden, .5L.**1,035.00**
Brewery, pottery, transfer/HP: Gerner...Munchen, ornate scene, .5L.**1,265.00**
Brewery, stoneware, Kgl...Weihenstephan, pewter lid, rpr, .4L **80.00**
Brewery, stoneware, transfer/HP: Barenbrau Bamberg, pewter lid, .5L.**575.00**
Brewery, stoneware, transfer/HP: Brauerei...Kindl, logo lid, .1L, NM.**600.00**
Brewery, stoneware, transfer/HP: Pschorr Brau..., pewter lid, 2¾"..**85.00**
Burl wood, 3 cvd ft, lg cvd animal tl, ca 1700, 1.5L **1,600.00**
Character, barmaid, pottery, music box, inlaid lid, #1089, .5L, NM **800.00**
Character, bear, pottery, pottery lid, #1455, sm rpr, .5L..............**400.00**

Character, Wilhelm II, porc, porc lid, rpr, Schierholz, .5L 525.00
Character, Bismark Radish, porc, blk, rpl pewter lid, Schierholz, .5L .185.00
Character, blk cat, pottery, inlaid lid, sm chip, .5L 300.00
Character, boar, porc, porc lid, sm rpr, Schierholz, .5L.............2,000.00
Character, bowling pin, pottery, inlaid lid, JWR #11132, .5L 365.00
Character, bowling pins, pottery, pottery lid, #1222, 1L, 12", NM..230.00
Character, bull, pottery, pottery lid, #1453, rare, .5L...................950.00
Character, bulldog, pottery, pottery lid, #1390, ⅛ L 375.00
Character, Bustle Lady, stoneware, pewter lid, Hauber & Reuther, .5L.975.00
Character, cat holding fish w/hangover, porc, porc lid, rpr, .5L...575.00
Character, cat playing mandolin, pottery, music box, inlaid lid, .5L..400.00
Character, cat, stoneware, bl & purple salt glaze, inlaid lid, .5L .345.00
Character, dbl-headed skull, porc, inlaid lid, E Bohne & Sohne, .5L .775.00
Character, devil, porc, inlaid lid, E Bohne Sohne, .5L 575.00
Character, Fraunkirche tower, porc, inlaid lid, M Pauson, 1L.1,600.00
Character, frog playing mandolin, pottery, pottery lid, #1429, .5L..485.00
Character, Hops Lady, porc, porc lid, Schierholz, .5L 660.00
Character, Indian, porc, inlaid lid, E Bohne & Sohne, .25L, $485 to.575.00
Character, mink, pottery, color, inlaid lid, .5L 235.00
Character, monk, brn robe, pottery, inlaid lid, .5L 150.00
Character, monkey & cat w/sausage & radishes, stoneware, LB&C, .5L..665.00
Character, Munich Child, blk glaze, pottery, inlaid lid, flaw, .5L .175.00
Character, Munich Child, porc lid, lith, JM Mayer, .5L 715.00
Character, Munich Child, porc, Jos M Mayer Munchen, 5" 1,325.00
Character, Munich Child, pottery, inlaid lid, J Reinemann, .3L .175.00
Character, Nurnberger Trichter, porc, inlaid lid, Schierholz, .25L.635.00
Character, owl, pottery, rpr, .5L 245.00
Character, pig singing, porc, inlaid lid, Shierholz, hairline, .5L ..265.00
Character, pixie, porc, porc lid, Schierholz, .5L 825.00
Character, porc, tree trunk w/King Ludwig on front, Schierholz, 1L.465.00
Character, rabbit, porc, porc lid, Schierholz, rpr, .5L 525.00
Character, Radish (lg), porc, inlaid lid, lith, sm rprs, .5L 800.00
Character, Radish Face, porc, porc set-on lid, Meissen, .5L, NM.370.00
Character, Sad Radish, porc, inlaid lid, Schierholz, .5L 360.00
Character, schoolteacher, porc, porc funnel lid, Schierholz, .5L..1,000.00
Character, skull, porc, inlaid lid, E Bohne & Sohne #1359, 3½"..1,200.00
Character, tower, stoneware, bl/purple salt glaze, pewter lid, .5L..700.00
Character, Zugapitze, stoneware, missing finial, M Pauson, .5L ..370.00
Faience, floral, pewter ring & lid, Bayreuth, ca 1870, 1L, EX 550.00
Glass, blown, amber, pewter o/l, inlaid lid w/o/l, .5L, NM 375.00
Glass, blown, bl opaline, pewter lid, closed hinge, 1850s, 3½" ...245.00

Glass, blown, clear, engraved brewer occupation crest and crown, pewter base ring and lid, one-liter, $3,200.00. (Photo courtesy Andre Ammelounx)

Glass, blown, clear w/eng leaping deer, pewter lid, 1830s, .5L, EX .145.00
Glass, blown, clear w/HP Prussian eagle, pewter lid, .5L 230.00
Glass, blown, clear w/wht o/l, transfer/HP eagle w/crown, .3L....200.00
Glass, blown, cobalt w/HP floral, pewter deer lid, Andeken, 1850s, 1L..665.00
Glass, blown, gr, dachshund shape w/HP crest, rpr, .5L...............600.00
Glass, mold blown, amber, HP leaves, inlaid lid, .5L 350.00

Glass, pressed, 3 cats & verse, prism inlaid lid, .5L.....................265.00
Ivory, cvd women w/satyrs, grapevine hdl, ivory finial, 13½" ..4,715.00
Majolica, relief: Wilhem I, Justice & other scenes, pewter lid, 8L, EX.550.00
Occupation, porc, transfer/HP: bricklayer, lith, pewter lid, .5L, NM..550.00
Occupation, porc, transfer/HP: butcher, pewter lid, .5L, NM 300.00
Occupation, porc, transfer/HP: carpenter, lg scenes, .5L 375.00
Occupation, porc, transfer/HP: furniture maker, lith, pewter lid, .5L..425.00
Occupation, porc, transfer/HP: locksmith, pewter lid, .4L, NM..350.00
Occupation, porc, transfer/HP: post coach driver, lith, .5L 485.00
Occupation, porc, transfer/HP: wagon builder, lith, pewter lid, .5L .600.00
Occupation, porc, transfer/HP: wagon driver, lith, pewter lid, .5L..500.00
Occupation, pottery, etch: alchemist, Paulus & Thewalt, .5L, EX.345.00
Occupation, relief: post & telegraph, post horn hdl, eagle tl, .5L.345.00
Occupation, stoneware, transfer/HP: lg scene, pewter lid, .5L, NM.575.00
Occupation, transfer/HP: butcher, mc, lith, pewter lid, rpr, .5L ..150.00
Occupation, transfer/HP: gardener, lg scene, lith, pewter lid, .5L, NM.230.00
Pewter, eng: leaves & hearts, pewter lid, ca 1790, 1L, EX 250.00
Porc, etch: man drinking, pewter lid, Hauber & Reuther, .5L.....275.00
Porc, HP: Grutzner cavalier w/cobalt & gold, beehive mk, 5".1,850.00
Porc, HP: man drinking scene, open, 1L 100.00
Porc, HP: Schutzenliesl scene, Nymphenburg, pewter lid, 1880s, 1L.3,200.00
Porc, HP: 3 people in woods w/flowers/, berry finial, Meissen, 1L.750.00
Porc, HP: 3 women, inlaid lid, beehive mk, .5L 1,785.00
Porc, transfer/HP: Der Sonntagsjager, lith, pewter lid, .5L 185.00
Porc, transfer/HP: dogs/stag/mtns, pewter lid, cvd horn finial, .5L.2,875.00
Porc, transfer/HP: Faust, inlaid lid, lith, .5L................................365.00
Porc, transfer/HP: freedom fighters, lith, pewter lid, .5L 350.00
Porc, transfer/HP: knight on horse, pewter lid dtd 1895, .5L 600.00
Porc, transfer: man gives flowers to lady, mc w/gold, lith, rpr, .5L.55.00
Pottery, etch: dwarfs on ladder/ropes, rpl lid, Hauber & Reuther, .5L.250.00
Pottery, etch: frog musicians & dwarfs, Hauber & Reuther #419, .5L..485.00
Pottery, etch: Heidelberg castle, pewter lid, Hauber & Reuther, .5L.460.00
Pottery, etch: hunter's farewell, inlaid lid, Marzi & Remi #1614, .5L.350.00
Pottery, etch: men bowling, pewter lid, Hauber & Reuther, .5L.375.00
Pottery, etch: men on horsebk leaving town, Marzi & Remi #1621, .5L.240.00
Pottery, etch: watchman & drunken man, man tl, Hauber & Reuther, .5L.435.00
Pottery, etch: 4 cards, pewter lid, #928, dtd 1894, .5L.................345.00
Pottery, HP: children w/doll & stick, Lang, pewter lid, .5L..........400.00
Pottery, HP: 3 Japanese women, pewter lid, .5L...........................215.00
Pottery, relief: Prussian eagle w/crown, pewter lid, #1744, 1L 485.00
Pottery, relief: scenes, inlaid lid, Dumler & Breiden, .5L 1,035.00
Pottery, relief: winged faces & lion heads, Schiller, inlaid lid, 3L.250.00
Pottery, transfer/HP: man on horse-drawn sled, horse tl, .5L 350.00
Pottery, transfer/HP: man w/lg stein, F Ringer, pewter lid, .5L....450.00
Regimental, Comp Eisenbahn...Berlin 1902-04, pottery, eagle tl, .5L.725.00
Regimental, Comp Gen...Ulmn 1907-09, porc, bird tl, finial damage, .5L.280.00
Regimental, Comp Grenad...1899-01, porc, Wurttemberg tl, .5L, NM.365.00
Regimental, Esk Garde...Darmstadt 1908-11, porc, eagle tl, .5L .800.00
Regimental, Feldart...Fruth 1907-09, porc, lion tl, crown lid, .5L.1,690.00
Regimental, Golsh Hess...Mainz 1898-00, porc, lion tl, .5L........365.00
Regimental, Hess Feld Art...Cassel 1896-98, porc, eagle tl, .5L..665.00
Regimental, Kgl Bayr...Metz 1902-04, porc, lion tl, lith, .5L........485.00
Regimental, Kgl Sachs...Grimma 1905-08, porc, Sachsen tl, .5L .700.00
Regimental, Kgl...Munchen 1906-08, soldier/anchor tl, skyline lid, .5L.715.00
Regimental, Kgl...Weingarten 1907-09, porc, lion tl, prism lid, .5L.635.00
Regimental, Masch...Munchen 1912-14, stoneware, machine gun scene, .5L.1,200.00
Regimental, SMS Danzig...1908-12, pottery, eagle tl, jewel, rpr, 1L.825.00
Regimental, SMS Wettin 1905-08, porc, eagle tl, Thuringen bolt, .5L..1,150.00
Silver, king at festival, gold-wash int, 1850s, 1410 grams, 1L..2,500.00
Stoneware, etch: ...Turnfest Kempten 1905, 4F Turner, .5L, EX .200.00
Stoneware, HP: dwarf, F Ringer, pewter lid, 3½"........................280.00
Stoneware, transfer/HP: Castle Neu Schwanstein, boy tl, inlaid lid, 1L.575.00
Stoneware, transfer/HP: cat & monkey, owl tl, pewter lid, .5L ...185.00
Stoneware, transfer/HP: dwarf reading & verse, pewter lid, 1L...375.00

Stoneware, transfer/HP: man & woman, TOH (Hahn), pewter lid, 1L..290.00
Stoneware, transfer/HP: man w/lg blk pants, F Ringer, pewter lid, .5L.400.00
Stoneware, transfer/HP: man w/lg yel pants, F Ringer, pewter lid, .5L.435.00
Stoneware, transfer/HP: Munich Child, F Ringer, pewter lid, .5L..435.00
Stoneware, transfer/HP: Turner...Regt..., Munich Child, 1914, .5L..775.00

Steuben

Carder Steuben glass was made by the Steuben Glass Works in Corning, New York, while under the direction of Frederick Carder from 1903 to 1932. Perhaps the most popular types of Carder Steuben glass are Gold Aurene which was introduced in 1904 and Blue Aurene, introduced in 1905. Gold and Blue Aurene objects shimmer with the lustrous beauty of their metallic iridescence. Carder also produced other types of 'Aurenes' including Red, Green, Yellow, Brown, and Decorated, all of which are very rare. Aurene also was cased with Calcite glass. Some pieces had paper labels.

Other types of Carder Steuben include Cluthra, Cintra, Florentia, Rosaline, Ivory, Ivrene, Jades, Verre de Soie; there are many more.

Frederick Carder's leadership of Steuben ended in 1932, and the production of colored glassware soon ceased. Since 1932 the tradition of fine Steuben art glass has been continued in crystal.

Our advisor for this category is Thomas P. Dimitroff; he is in the Directory under New York. In the following listings, examples are signed unless noted otherwise. When no color is mentioned, assume the glass is clear.

Key: ACB — acid cut back

Bottle, scent; Blue Aurene, #1414, flame-shaped top on stopper, 7½"..1,200.00
Bottle, scent; Gold Aurene, #1818, 6" 700.00
Bowl, ACB Oriental motif on Plum Jade, low ft, 8".................5,200.00
Bowl, Blue Aurene, #2852, 9"...900.00
Bowl, Blue Aurene, ftd, #2852, 9"..900.00
Bowl, Bristol Yellow, Swirl, wide/flared rim, 11¼"......................175.00
Bowl, Calcite w/Blue Aurene int, 4¾".....................................1,035.00
Bowl, finger; Gold Aurene on Calcite, 12-rib, 4¾", +6" plate....250.00
Bowl, French Blue, Swirl Optic, #6118, 5½x10" 175.00
Bowl, Gold Aurene, #2039, 8½"...450.00
Bowl, Gold Aurene, #5061, 10"..550.00
Bowl, Gold Aurene, flaring/ruffled rim, 12", NM 800.00
Bowl, Gold Aurene on Calcite, 10"...330.00
Bowl, Green Jade, invt rim, #2687, unmk, 4x8" 400.00
Bowl, Light Blue Jade, #2687, 4x8" 600.00
Bowl, Plum Jade, etched water lilies on scrolled ground, 6⅞" .4,500.00
Bowl, topaz w/Celeste Blue rims & 8 swirl cabochons, ftd, 14"..375.00
Candlestick, Blue Aurene, twist stem, #539, 8" 850.00
Candlestick, Gold Aurene, tulip cup, stem w/appl spiral leaf, 12"..1,750.00
Candlestick, Gold Aurene, twist stem, 8", pr 1,800.00
Candlesticks, Blue Aurene, twisted stem, flanged cup, #686, 8", pr..2,000.00
Candlesticks, Calcite w/Gold Aurene cup flange, unmk, 6", pr..690.00
Candlesticks, Gold Aurene, stem w/appl decor, #6384, 3¾", pr.1,500.00
Candlesticks, Gold Aurene, wide ruffled tops, disk stem, #6637, 5", pr.1,500.00
Candlesticks, Green Jade, 1⅝x3¾", pr...350.00
Chalice, Blue Aurene w/hearts & vines, ftd, 10"......................3,450.00
Compote, amethyst body/ft, crystal stem, label, 4x10"...............325.00
Compote, Calcite w/Blue Aurene int, no mk, 3x7"....................800.00
Compote, Calcite/Gold Aurene, rope stem w/bl irid, unmk, 8" .1,840.00
Compote, Gold Aurene w/bl highlights, int: red highlights, 5¼x5"..850.00
Compote, Green Jade, Alabaster ft, 6" dia 350.00
Compote, Selenium, trn-down rim, 12" dia 450.00
Covered dish, Rosaline & Alabaster, floral finial, ftd, #3154, 4"..850.00
Cruet, Rosaline, rnd w/tube-like neck, ball stopper, Alabaster hdl, 6".350.00
Finger bowl, Calcite w/Gold Aurene int, ribbed/scalloped, +6" plate.275.00

Flower frog, nude female diver, frosted on clear base, #6483, 14½".1,750.00
Goblet, Gold Aurene, twist stem, 6" 350.00
Goblet, Green Jade cut to Alabaster in York pattern, ftd, 6½" ...250.00
Goblets, Spanish Green, invt bell, bubbles/appl leaves, 8½", 9 for.975.00
Lamp shade, King Tut, gold & gr w/gold irid int, #2286, 4½".....375.00
Luminor, pineapple crystal w/bubbles, blk glass base, #6971, 8".1,000.00
Parfait, Oriental Poppy, pk w/wht opal ribs, gr base, 6" 575.00
Plate, Gold Aurene on Calcite w/ACB laurel-leaf rim, label, 8"..350.00
Plate, Green Jade, sgn Carder, 8½" 175.00
Plate, Rosaline, sgn Carder, 8½"...200.00
Puff box, Rosaline w/Alabaster finial, squatty/rnd, #6237, 4¾x6".500.00
Shade, feathers, gold w/gr tips on opal, 5¼", set of 3................750.00
Shade, Gold Aurene, vertical ribs, 4½", set of 4.........................600.00
Shade, Gold Aurene hearts & vines on Calcite, 4½", set of 3....750.00
Shade, Gold Aurene w/turq pulled feathers, 6", set of 3 ....1,095.00
Shade, Ivrene, bulbous w/flared rim, etched grapes, 2¼x2¼", pr.265.00
Shade, opal w/lt irid, flared bowl shape, 4x7" 275.00
Sherbet, Green Jade w/Alabaster stem, +Green Jade underplate .200.00
Torchiere, arched amber #8418 inserts, silver-bronze std, 70", pr.10,575.00
Vase, ACB birds on branches on Green Jade, wide U-form, 9".2,500.00
Vase, ACB Rosaline to Alabaster w/florals, unmk, wide V form, 8¾".1,800.00
Vase, Alabaster & Green Aurene w/gold, diagonal feathers, #597, 8".10,000.00
Vase, amber cone w/ped ft, 14¼"..300.00
Vase, Black Cluthra, raised/rolled rim on broad shoulders, 6⅜".1,500.00
Vase, Blue Aurene, stick neck, 8"...325.00
Vase, Blue Aurene, 3-prong tree stump, #2744, 6" 1,100.00
Vase, Blue Silverina, flared rim, dmn air traps, 7⅝" 950.00
Vase, bud; Blue Aurene, #2556, 8" 350.00
Vase, bud; Blue Aurene, pencil slim on disk ft, #2556, 10".........450.00
Vase, Calcite w/Blue Aurene int, flared 6-petal top, no mk, 4½".1,500.00
Vase, Calcite w/Blue Aurene int, ruffled/ftd, no mk, 6¼"........1,035.00
Vase, Calcite w/Gold Aurene int, no mk, 4¾x6¼" 450.00
Vase, Cluthra, bl raised/rolled rim, ovoid w/M hdls, 10" 1,500.00
Vase, Cluthra, rose & wht mottle, #2683, 8"............................2,600.00
Vase, colorless w/gr Matsu-no-ke decor, #3359, 6"....................550.00
Vase, fan; amber w/gr disk ft, faint ribs, #6287, 8¼x7" 250.00
Vase, Gold Aurene, dbl bulb w/flaring rim, #7447, 6" 800.00
Vase, Gold Aurene, flared/ruffled rim, ovoid w/disk ft, #167, 6".550.00
Vase, Gold Aurene, shoudered, 4" 375.00
Vase, Gold Aurene, wide/shouldered, #2083, 8½".....................1,035.00
Vase, Gold Aurene w/bl highlights, urn form w/scroll hdls, 12".3,200.00
Vase, Gold Ruby, Swirl, U-form, 9¾"..550.00
Vase, Green Aurene w/gold fishnet & pulled feathers, att, 11".6,500.00
Vase, Green Jade, ACB Matsu-no-ke, ovoid, #6078, 8x8".......1,500.00

Vase, Green Jade cut to alabaster in bird design, #5000, 9½", $2,500.00.
(Photo courtesy Skinner Auctions, Inc.)

Vase, Green Jade trumpet form in Black Starr & Frost scroll base, 8"..460.00
Vase, Green Jade w/Alabaster ft, swirled, hex-rim trumpet form, 10".450.00
Vase, Ivory, rolled/flared rim, ovoid w/cushion ft, 10¼".............750.00

Vase, Jack-in-pulpit; Ivrene, 6¾", pr (1 sgn) 920.00
Vase, Moss Agate, mc/swirls, shouldered, 10½" 7,500.00
Vase, Rosaline, trumpet form w/petal rim, 8" 650.00
Vase, Silveria, Dmn Quilt amethyst w/silver mica flecks, unmk, 8" .750.00
Vase, Tyrian, heart/vines on shaded gr opaque, Intarsia neck, 12".12,000.00
Vase, Verre de Soie, flower/laurel eng, shouldered, unmk, 8" 450.00
Vase, Verre de Soie, ftd, #6545, 5" 250.00
Vase, Verre de Soie, gr threading at flaring top, 6" 200.00
Vase, Verre de Soie on Lime, U-form w/flared rim & disk ft, 6¾" ..200.00

Stevengraphs

A Stevengraph is a small picture made of woven silk resembling an elaborate ribbon, created by Thomas Stevens in England in the latter half of the 1800s. They were matted and framed by Stevens, usually with his name appearing on the mat or often with the trade announcement on the back of the mat. He also produced silk postcards and bookmarks, all of which have 'Stevens' woven in silk on one of the mitered corners. Anyone wishing to learn more about Stevengraphs is encouraged to contact the Stevengraph Collectors' Association, whose address can be found in the Directory under Clubs, Newsletters, and Catalogs. Unless noted otherwise, assume our values are for examples in excellent condition.

Are You Ready?, EX 300.00
Called to the Rescue, Heroism at Sea 250.00
Columbus Leaving Spain, G 225.00
Coventry, 2 blk & wht scenes, fr, pr 110.00
Crystal Palace (inside), orig matt, G 385.00
Death of Nelson, G 195.00
Declaration of Independence, woven at Columbian Exhibition .225.00
Dick Turpin's Last Ride on His Black Bess, Hogarth, VG 150.00
Finish 150.00
First Innings, G 325.00
First Point 80.00
First Train Built by Geo Stephenson in 1825, 8⅞x11⅝" 150.00
Full Cry, w/mat 120.00
God Speed the Plow, G 220.00
Good Old Days 80.00
Good Old Days, coach & 4, matted & fr, 7½x10½", M..............195.00
Grace Darling 200.00
Kenilworth Castle, orig mat & fr, 15½x22½" 175.00
Lady Godiva Procession 170.00
Landing of Columbus, NM 250.00
London & York Mail Coach, 1879 Expo....................................120.00
Meet, orig mat, old fr, NM 250.00
Mersy Tunnel Railway 400.00
Mrs Cleveland, VG 135.00
Park in Coventry 75.00
Present Time, 60 Miles an Hour, from $135 to 160.00
Queen Victoria Jubilee, 1837-1887, unfr 55.00
Rescue at Sea, fr, VG 220.00
Start, NM 175.00
Struggle 80.00
To the Memory of the Heroic Defenders of Religious Liberty 275.00
Victoria, Queen of Empire on Which the Sun Never Sets, unfr.195.00
Water Jump, fr 225.00
Wellington & Blugher 300.00

Miscellaneous

Bookmark, A Wish O May You E'er in Peace Abide..., 11⅜x2⅛" .50.00
Bookmark, Behold the Man, blk, fr, G 50.00
Bookmark, Friend's Blessings..45.00

Bookmark, Geo Washington, made for Philiadelphia Expo, 12x2" .175.00
Bookmark, Home Sweet Home..75.00
Bookmark, Love's Remembrance, VG 75.00
Bookmark, To My Dear Sister...60.00
Bookmark, To My Sons, G 40.00
Postcard, Ann Hathaway's Cottage...40.00
Postcard, RMS Lusitania, VG 75.00
Postcard, Shakespeare's Birthday..45.00

Stevens and Williams

Stevens and Williams glass was produced at the Brierly Hill Glassworks in Stourbridge, England, for nearly a century, beginning in the 1830s. They were credited with being among the first to develop a method of manufacturing a more affordable type of cameo glass. Other lines were also made — silver deposit, alexandrite, and engraved rock crystal, to name but a few. Our advisor for this category is Don Williams; he is listed in the Directory under Missouri.

Basket, amber w/appl gr-stem red strawberries, amber ft, 5x6" 400.00
Basket, pk o/l, amber ft, cranberry rigaree, mc leaves, 10" 400.00
Bottle, scent; Pompeian Swirl, gold/rust w/turq int, 6½x4".........895.00
Bowl, cream w/pk int, amber/gr/rose appl ferns, amber ft, 3x5½".145.00
Bowl, MOP Zipper, turq w/yel int, pinched 4-lobe rim, #d, 3½x4½".690.00
Nut dish, MOP Swirl, brn w/creamy int, ruffled top, 4" 70.00
Pitcher, yel/pk opal stripes on clear, ribbed, 6"............................225.00
Tumbler, MOP Swirl, bl satin cased in wht, sq top, 3¾" 300.00
Vase, cameo, cherry tree branch, pk/yel, scalloped, 5½" 1,450.00
Vase, MOP Swirl, frost to yel, ovoid w/long concave neck, 7"..1,150.00
Vase, MOP Swirl, pk, ovoid w/bulbous neck, flared rim, 8¼" 900.00
Vase, MOP Swirl, pk to gr (rare), pk int, shouldered, 8"..........2,530.00
Vase, MOP Swirl, rubena verde, bulbous w/cup neck, 9¾"......1,500.00
Vase, opal w/pk int, lg appl crystal leaf, bulbous body/neck, 5" 60.00
Vase, Osiris, red-amber w/tall swirling wht pull-ups, clear cased, 6"..1,600.00
Vase, pk w/amber vines/wht flowers, fold-down ruffled amber rim, 10".200.00
Vase, rose to pk w/amber cherry-stem hdls & appl fruits & flowers, 20".2,000.00

Stickley

Among the leading proponents of the Arts and Crafts Movement, the Stickley brothers — Gustav, Leopold, Charles, Albert, and John George — were at various times and locations separately involved in designing and producing furniture as well as decorative items for the home. (See Arts and Crafts for further information.) The oldest of the five Stickley brothers was Gustav; his work is the most highly regarded of all. He developed the style of furniture referred to as Mission. It was strongly influenced by the type of furnishings found in the Spanish missions of California — utilitarian, squarely built, and simple. It was made most often of oak, and decoration was very limited or non-existent. The work of his brothers display adaptations of many of Gustav's ideas and designs. His factory, the Craftsman Workshop, operated in Eastwood, New York, from the late 1890s until 1915, when he was forced out of business by larger companies who copied his work and sold it at much lower prices. Among his shop marks are the early red decal containing a joiner's compass and the words 'Als Ik Kan,' the branded mark with similar components, and paper labels.

The firm known as Stickley Brothers was located first in Binghamton, New York, and then Grand Rapids, Michigan. Albert and John George made the move to Michigan, leaving Charles in Binghamton (where he and an uncle continued the operation under a different name). After several years John George left the company to rejoin Leopold in New York. (These two later formed their own firm called L.

& J.G. Stickley.) The Stickley Brothers Company's early work produced furniture featuring fine inlay work, decorative cutouts, and leaned strongly toward a style of Arts and Crafts with an English influence. It was tagged with a paper label 'Made by Stickley Brothers, Grand Rapids,' or with a brass plate or decal with the words 'Quaint Furniture,' an English term chosen to refer to their product. In addition to furniture, they made metal accessories as well.

The workshops of the L. & J.G. Stickley Company first operated under the name 'Onondaga Shops.' Located in Fayetteville, New York, their designs were often all but copies of Gustav's work. Their products were well made and marketed, and their business was very successful. Their decal labels contained all or a combination of the words 'Handcraft' or 'Onondaga Shops,' along with the brothers' initials and last name. The firm continues in business today. Our advisor for this category is Bruce Austin; he is listed in the Directory under New York. Note: When only one dimension is given for tables, it is length. Cleaning diminishes values; ours are for furniture and metals with excellent original finishes unless noted otherwise. It is also important to mention that collectors are increasingly fussy about condition. Refinishing lowers value from 15% to 30%. Replaced hardware or wood can likewise dramatically and negatively affect value.

Key:
b — brand	n — no mark
brd — board	p — paper label
d — red decal	t — Quaint metal tag
h/cp — hammered copper	
hdw — hardware	

Gustav Stickley

Armchair, #2604, arched crest rail, 3 horizontal bk slats, d, 37"..**1,800.00**
Armchair, #322A, tacked leather bk/seat, d/p, 38x26x21".......**3,000.00**
Armchair, #330, Ellis design, wide slat ea side, new seat, rfn, VG..**1,500.00**
Armchair, #366, 3-slat bk, d/p, worn leather seat, 39x26x24", G..**325.00**
Armchair, #471, 4-slat bk, rpl rope foundation, mk, 37"..........**2,000.00**
Armchair, Morris; #369, 5-slat drop arms, new seat/rfn, n, VG..**6,500.00**
Armchair, Morris; 5-slat flat arms, faceted pegs, d, ca 1904, VG.**6,000.00**
Bed, ¾-sz, cloud-lift to top rails, b, 39x76x46", VG.................**1,900.00**
Book rack, #74, V top, D-shaped hdls, keyed tenons, 1912, 31x30x10".**1,400.00**
Bookcase, #716, 2 8-pane doors, iron hdw, d/p, 56x43x13" **6,500.00**
Bookcase, #717½, open w/4 shelves ea side, d/p, cleaned, 56x48", VG..**3,750.00**
Bookcase, 2 12-pane doors, iron hdw, b/p, 56x72x13"..............**9,000.00**
Bookcase, 2 12-pane doors, p, 56x60x13" **8,000.00**
Bookcase, 3 12-pane doors, thru-tenons, copper pulls, d, 1902, 56x72".**11,000.00**
Cabinet, smoker's; #89, 1-drw/1-door, n, recoated/rstr, 29x20", G.**1,800.00**
Chair, #1291, rabbit-ear form, dk finish, box mk, 38x18x18", VG.**500.00**
Chair, #2608, 4 bk slats, curved front/bk stretchers, d, 37" **575.00**
Chair, side; #308, H-bk, drop-in seat, b, 40x17x16" **475.00**
Chair set, 3-slat ladderbk, new seats, d, 1 arm+5 sides, VG.....**2,500.00**
China cabinet, #820, 1 door w/12 panes, d/p, 63x36x16", VG.**4,000.00**
Daybed, #220, knockdown form w/3-slat sides, rpl cushion, 34x84x42".**3,000.00**
Desk, #518, drop front w/iron straps, 2 lower shelves, d, 52x26", VG..**4,000.00**
Desk, #720, gallery w/letter rack/cubbyholes/drws, 2-drw, rfn, b, VG.**2,000.00**
Desk, lady's; #720, organizer top w/drws & files, 2-drw base, p, 38" L.**1,500.00**
Dresser, #913, 9-drw, wood knobs, b, 51x36x20", VG..............**6,000.00**
Footstool, #300, leather top, b, 15x20x16".................................**800.00**
Footstool, #301, sq post legs, rush seat, b, rfn, ca 1914, 17" **600.00**
Footstool, #302, new leather top, d, 5x12x12", VG....................**550.00**
Footstool, #302, worn leather top, d, 5x12x12" **850.00**
Lantern, hammered iron w/amber glass shade, hanging, 29x9" sq.**3,250.00**
Mirror, #67, peaked top rail, 3-section, iron hooks, rfn, 28x42"..**1,800.00**
Mirror, ash, peaked top rail, 4 hooks, orig gr finish, n, 29x48"..**1,100.00**
Rocker, #2607, 4 horizontal bk slats, armless, 34x19"...............**275.00**

Rocker, #323, 3 horizontal bk slats, 5-slat arms, new seat, n, VG.**1,500.00**
Rocker, #323, 3 horizontal bk slats, 5-slat arms, rpl cushions, b, 40".**3,000.00**
Rocker, #366, 3-slat bk, new seat, d, 38x26x30", VG.................**500.00**
Rocker, #397, 3 vertical slats, arms, spring cushion, b, 1912, 43".**765.00**
Rocker, child's; #341, 2 horizontal bk slats, n, new seat/rfn, VG..**160.00**
Server, #818, 3-drw, lower shelf, d, 39x48x20", VG.................**3,250.00**
Settee, #212, V-bk, 12 vertical slats, rstr leather seat, 36x48"..**2,400.00**
Sideboard, #816, plate rail, 1 long+3 short drw, V pulls, p/b, 48".**2,350.00**
Sideboard, #817, 3-part bksplash w/plate rail, 4 grad center drws, 70".**11,000.00**
Sideboard, #967, gallery top, 2 short+1 long drw, 2 base drws, 60" L.**25,000.00**
Table, #603, rnd top, arched X stretchers, thru tenons, rfn, 20x18".**900.00**
Table, #609, rpl leather top, shelf, thru tenons, 36" dia **1,500.00**
Table, #637, trestle style, dbl-key lower shelf, n, rfn, 48", VG.**1,300.00**
Table, dining; #634 variant, oval 55x46" top, sq legs, +6 leaves.**11,500.00**
Table, library; #456, 2 blind drws, flush tenons, rfn, 39x36x24"......**1,800.00**
Table, library; #624, tacked leather 6-side top, 6 legs, b.........**14,000.00**
Table, lunch; #647, shelf, keyed tenons, trestle bases, 39x48x30".**4,000.00**
Umbrella stand, #55, 4 posts, 3-section top, n, rfn, 33x21", G....**500.00**

L. & J.G. Stickley

Armchair, #352, 3-slat ladderbk, n, new seat/rfn, 36x25x21", VG.**200.00**
Armchair, #750, peaked top rail, 5-slat bk, rpl cushion, rfn, 39".**800.00**
Ashtray stand, #21, cut-corner top, X base, mk, 22x12x12", VG.**150.00**
Bookcase, 2 narrow 8-pane doors, keyed tenons, mk, 56x36x12".**6,500.00**
Cabinet, smoker's; #26, drw & 1 door, h/cp pulls, 29x15x20"..**3,500.00**
Chair, Morris; #411, flat arms w/corbels, +footstool #397, ea w/d.**1,500.00**
Chair, Morris; #497, flat arms, ea w/5 slats, new leather, d, VG.**4,500.00**
Chair, Morris; mahog, open arm, n, 40x35x30", VG................**1,700.00**
Chair, side; #350, 3 bk slats, dbl side stretchers, d, 35", VG........**300.00**
Chair, side; #800, 3-slat ladderbk, mk, new seat, rfn, 36", VG....**300.00**
Chair, side; curved crest, 8 vertical spindles, leather seat, 36½".**400.00**
Chair, side; 5 vertical slats, uphl seat, d, ca 1912, 37¾" **400.00**
Chair set, 8 vertical spindle bk, rush seat, recoated, 6 for **4,250.00**
Daybed, #739, slanted headrest at 5-slat end, new leather, mk, 76", VG.**1,200.00**
Desk, #501, center drw+2 ea side, panel sides, sgn, 48" L........**4,000.00**
Desk, #522, 2 drw w/long corbels, thru tenons, d, 30x48x30"..**1,600.00**
Desk, #617, slant front, 5-drw, wood knobs, recoated, 42x45".**1,100.00**

Mantle clock, dark finish, face with white numbers, designed by Peter Hansen, unmarked, 22", VG, $11,000.00. (Photo courtesy Treadway Gallery, Inc.)

Rocker, #355, 5 vertical bk slats, new cushion, rfn, d, 36x27x27", VG.**325.00**
Rocker, #437, open arms, 6-slat bk, new seat, d, 38x28x30", VG..**900.00**
Server, #750, plate rail, 48x22" top, 2 drw over 1, shelf, d, VG.**1,300.00**
Settle, #232, even-arm, 4 wide bk slats/1 per arm, new seat/rfn, VG.**2,100.00**
Settle, #281, even-arm, 5-slat sides/16-slat bk, new seat, mk, 76", VG.**6,000.00**
Sideboard, #732, plate rail, 4 half drws, 2 doors, d, 50x72x25".**7,500.00**
Sideboard, #734, plate rail, door ea side 3 drws over long drw, d, 48".**2,000.00**
Stand, magazine; #46, 4-shelf, 3-slat sides, recoated, 42x21" ...**1,400.00**
Table, #530, 1-drw, shelf w/thru tenons, 36x24" top...................**900.00**

Table, #558, 8-sided w/thru posts, arched X stretchers, n, rfn, VG ..**1,000.00**
Table, #573, shelf held by arched stretchers, rfn, 29x24" dia ...**1,000.00**
Table, library, #520 variant, drw, corbels, low shelf, d, 39x42x28"..**1,500.00**
Table, library; #522, 2 drws, shelf, dbl keyed tenons, 48" **1,300.00**
Table, lunch; #583, 30" dia top, arched apron, b, VG **400.00**
Table, lunch; #584, 52x28" top, arched apron, b, VG **1,100.00**
Table, smoker's; #515, 8-sided, slab legs, thru tenons, rfn, 25x20"..**1,500.00**

Stickley Bros.

Bookcase, #4762, 2 8-pane doors, copper pulls, 47x36x12" **2,400.00**
Cabinet, china; str crest, dbl doors, mirrored top int panel, t ..**2,875.00**
Chair, #289½, canted 3-slat sides, 4-slat bk, n, new seat/rfn....**1,800.00**
Chair, Morris; curved bk, 5 narrow slats ea side, mk, no cushions, VG.**2,100.00**
Chair, Morris: like #780, flat arms, n, rfn, 39x29x34", VG **1,000.00**
Chair, slipper; 5-slat bk, seat missing, rfn, 34"............................**200.00**
Chair set, #381, 3-slat bk, new seats, t, 1 side+5 arm, VG.......**1,900.00**
Chair set, #479½, 3-slat bk, notched top rail, set of 4, VG **1,300.00**
China cabinet, #8644, copper lions in upper door glass, n, rfn, VG .**4,250.00**
Costumer, #175, sq pole on cruciform base w/pegs, n, rfn, 72", VG.**130.00**
Costumer, dbl tapered post, copper hooks, cleaned, n, 69x20x17" ..**400.00**
Footstool, #5267, worn leather, cleaned, n, 17x17x12" **170.00**
Footstool, #5674, uphl seat, fr w/thru tenons, recoated, 9x19x12"..**240.00**
Lamp, ldgl 20" amber hex shade w/Xs, 3 rpl sockets, 26".........**4,250.00**
Rocker, #792, 5 narrow upright bk slats, w/arms, n, new seat, VG .**700.00**
Rocker, sewing; #411, notched rail over 3-slat bk, rpl leather seat..**200.00**
Server, #8733, 1-drw, lower shelf, n but #d, 36x34x21", VG ...**1,300.00**
Settee, #3861, 3-part 9-slat bk w/new leather pads, rfn, 62", VG .**1,100.00**
Sideboard, #8216, long drw over 3, 2 doors, t, 45x55" **2,400.00**
Sideboard, #8410, 2 short+3 long drw/door ea side, n, rfn, 66", VG.**2,000.00**
Sideboard, #8604, copper lions on doors of sm upper cabinet, n, VG .**3,750.00**
Sideboard, 3 sm drw amid 2 doors over long drw, paneled bk, 48x54x23"..**2,700.00**
Stand, #137, notched apron, flared legs, X stretchers, t, rfn, 34"..**650.00**
Stand, #5671, 3 vertical slats on 4 sides, p, lt cleaning, 24x15", VG.**600.00**
Stand, magazine; #4702, 3-shelf, 3-spindle sides, stains, 31x26x12".**500.00**
Table, #130, 41" dia top, stacked X-stretchers, t, rfn, VG **700.00**
Table, #2501, 24" dia top, X stretchers, rfn, VG **650.00**
Table, dining; apron, sq base w/4 ft & corbels, 48" dia+2 leaves..**1,100.00**
Table, dining; like #2638, 48" dia top, 5 legs, 12" leaf, n, VG .**1,200.00**
Table, dining; ped base w/4 extended ft, rfn top, 48" dia.............**300.00**
Table, game; #2674, sq top, X-stretcher base, thru tenons, rfn, 30x36".**1,300.00**
Table, library; #2562, drw, wood knobs, dbl stretchers, thru tenons.**600.00**
Table, library; #2654, 3-slat sides, Mackmurdo ft, t, 48" L, VG.**1,100.00**
Umbrella stand, #7604, 4 posts w/inset panels, rpl naugahyde, rfn, 25".**350.00**

Stiegel

Baron Henry Stiegel produced glassware in Pennsylvania as early as 1760, very similar to glass being made concurrently in Germany and England. Without substantiating evidence, it is impossible to positively attribute a specific article to his manufacture. Although he made other types of glass, today the term Stiegel generally refers to any very early ware made in shapes and colors similar to those he is known to have produced — especially that with etched or enameled decoration. It is generally conceded, however, that most glass of this type is of European origin. Our advisor for this category is Mark Vuono; he is listed in the Directory under Connecticut.

Bottle, floral/scrollwork, 5-color, octagonal, pewter collar, 5⅝"..**300.00**
Bottle, pocket; Daisy in Dmn, amethyst, tiny pot stones, 4¾"..**4,730.00**
Bottle, wht dove on red rose, mc scrollwork/floral, 6-sided, 5⅞"..**165.00**
Flask, pocket; 15-dmn, dk peacock gr, pot stone, 5⅜" **440.00**
Flip, eng sunflower & florals, pontil, w/lid, 10½" **1,700.00**
Pocket bottle, Daisy in Dmn, amethyst, fluted, 5¼" **6,500.00**

Salt cellar, cobalt, dbl-ogee bowl w/short stem, appl ft, att, 3⅛".**240.00**
Shot glass, HP lady w/buckets on yoke & flowers, flakes, 2⅛"....**165.00**
Sugar bowl, 11-Dmn pattern, cobalt, ftd, appl finial, 5½" **1,100.00**
Sugar bowl, 16 vertical ribs, sapphire bl, flat ft, 2¼x4¼"............**375.00**
Sugar bowl, 20-Dmn pattern, dk sapphire bl, flat ft, pontil, 3x4¼".**475.00**
Tankard, eng bird w/in sunburst, reeded hdl, pontil, 6¼" **1,400.00**
Tankard, eng sunflower & florals, cylindrical, att, 6½" **600.00**

Stocks and Bonds

Scripophily (scrip-awfully), the collecting of 'worthless' old stocks and bonds, gained recognition as an area of serious interest around the mid-1970s. Collectors who come from numerous business fields mainly enjoy its hobby aspect, though there are those who consider scripophily an investment. Some collectors like the historical significance that certain certificates have. Others prefer the beauty of older stocks and bonds that were printed in various colors with fancy artwork and ornate engravings. Autograph collectors are found in this field, on the lookout for signed certificates; otherscollect specific industries.

Many factors help determine the collector value: autograph value, age of the certificate, the industry represented, whether it is issued or not, its attractiveness, condition, and collector demand. Certificates from the mining, energy, and railroad industries are the most popular with collectors. Other industries or special collecting fields include banking, automobiles, aircraft, and territorials. Serious collectors usually prefer only issued certificates that date from before 1930. Unissued certificates are usually worth one-fourth to one-tenth the value of one that has been issued. Inexpensive issued common stocks and bonds dated between the 1940s and 1990s usually retail between $1.00 to $10.00. Those dating between 1890 and 1930 usually sell for $10.00 to $50.00. Those over one hundred years old retail between $25.00 and $100.00 or more, depending on the quantity found and the industry represented. Some stocks are one of a kind while others are found by the hundreds or even thousands, especially railroad certificates. Autographed stocks normally sell anywhere from $50.00 to $1,000.00 or more. A formal collecting organization for scripophilists is known as The Bond and Share Society with an American chapter located in New York City. As is true in any field, potential collectors should take the time to learn the hobby. Prices vary greatly at websites selling old stocks and bonds, sometimes by hundreds of dollars.

Collectors should avoid buying modern certificates being offered for sale at scripophily websites in the $20.00 to $60.00 range as they have little collector value despite the sales hype. One uncancelled share of some of the modern 'famous name' stocks of the Fortune 500 companies are being offered at two or four times what the stock is currently trading for. These should be avoided, and new collectors who want to buy certificates in modern companies will be better off buying 'one share' stocks in their own name and not someone else's. Take the time to study the market, ask questions, and be patient as a collector. Your collection will be better off. EBay generally serves as a good source for information regarding current values — search under 'Coins.'

Our advisor for this category is Warren Anderson; he is listed in the Directory under Utah. In many of the following listings, two-letter state abbreviations immediately follow company name. Unless noted otherwise, values are for examples in fine condition.

Key:
U — unissued   I/U — issued/uncancelled
I/C — issued/cancelled   vgn — vignette

Anglo-Am Chemical Corp, eagle vgn, title banner, SD/1904, I/U.**18.00**
Barrel Cleansing Machine, eagle/shield vgn, title banner, NY/1894, I/U.**30.00**
Bedford Gold Mining, blk & gr print on wht w/gold seal, CO/1900, I/U.**30.00**

Bolivia Gold Exploration, eagle vgn, gold seal, CO/1929, I/C **12.00**
British Columbia Portland Cement, bold title w/mtns, Canada/1911, I/U..**20.00**
Bunker Hill Consolidated Mining, eagle vgn, title banner, CA/1919, I/U..**18.00**
Charles F Noble Oil & Gas, oil field vgn, gr seal, OK/1919, I/U ..**15.00**
Chipmunk Gold Mining, lg eagle vgn, NYBNCo, AZ Territory/1906, I/U .**30.00**
Consolidated Gold & Copper Mining, 3 vgns, gr border, SD/1907, I/U..**25.00**
Cresson Consolidated Gold Mining & Milling, bold title, CO/1917, I/C.**20.00**
Eastern Consolidated Oil, wells & harbor vgn, bold title, ME/1903, I/U..**22.00**
Farmer's Mutual Royal Syndicate Inc, eagle vgn, AZ/1931, I/U....**10.00**
Farwell Consolidated Mining, NY state seal vgn, NY/1881, I/U ...**60.00**
Giant Oil, oil field vgn, floral artwork, gr seal, TX/1919, I/U **25.00**
Granville Gold Mining, miners vgn, bold title, NY/1881, I/U **55.00**
Kenmar Oil, 2 vgns w/wells & buildings/etc, gr printing, DE/1919, I/U.**15.00**
Kevin Sunburst, Miss Liberty vgn, ornate title, MT/1923, I/U......**13.00**
King Copper, miners vgn, brn border/seal, AZ/1918, I/U **18.00**
KY Coal Mining, Miss Liberty vgn, title banner, OK Territory/1907, I/U.**22.00**
Lake Superior & NV Development, 8% mortgage, AZ/1912, I/U, +coupons..**15.00**
Last Chance Copper Mining, EX art, gold border/seal, MT/1911, I/C...**22.00**
Marconi Wireless Telegraph, Liberty/radio towers vgn, NJ/1919, I/U..**35.00**
Moose Lake Mining, Miss Liberty vgn, gr seal, MT/1907, I/U **22.00**
Moscow Silver Mines, miners vgn, title banner, UT/1934, I/U **13.00**
NY Central & Hudson River RR, $1,000 gold bond, NY/1898, I/C.**22.00**
Philadelphia, Baltimore & WA RR, $1,000 gold bond, vgn, PA/1924, I/C..**15.00**
Pioneer Agency, eagle vgn+other scenes, SD/1912, I/U **20.00**
Planetary Gold & Silver Mining & Milling, eagle vgn, UT/1902, I/U.**35.00**
Rich's Clothes Shop, warrior & boat vgn, orange seal, UT/1916, I/U.**12.00**
Silver Basin Yukon Mines Ltd, gr border, B-ABNCo, Canada/1948, I/U .**10.00**
Silver Peak Mining, bold title, ornate border, England/1882, I/U.**45.00**
Southern MT Oil, oil field vgn+4 scenes in border, MT/1919, I/U **14.00**
Standard Lead & Zinc, Indian chief vgn, gold seal, SD/1909, I/U .**20.00**
Union Oil & Gas, oil field vgn w/workers/derricks/train, CA/1901, I/U.**30.00**
Union Oil & Refining, oil wells vgn, gold seal, SD/1902, I/U **30.00**
United TX Petroleum, 8" oil field vgn, DE/1919, I/U...................**15.00**
UT Patent & Implement, eagle/vgn, ornate title banner, UT/1912, I/U.**18.00**
Vernon Mining, lg miners vgn+6 sm, gold seal, AZ Territory/1909, I/U.**30.00**
Vernon-NV Mining, miners vgn, gold seal, AZ Territory/1907, I/U .**30.00**
Voight-Pros't Brewing, eagle/skyscrapers vgn, MI/1936, I/U..........**50.00**
West Star Mining, gr border & print, NV/1924, I/U **15.00**
WI & CO Silver Mining, 3 gr vgns on pk, blk print, CO/1880s, U..**22.00**

Stoneware

There are three broad periods of time that collectors of American pottery can look to in evaluating and dating the stoneware and earthenware in their collections. Among the first permanent settlers in America were English and German potters who found a great demand for their individually turned wares. The early pottery was produced from red and yellow clays scraped from the ground at surface levels. The earthenware made in these potteries was fragile and coated with lead glazes that periodically created health problems for the people who ate or drank from it. There was little stoneware available for sale until the early 1800s, because the clays used in its production were not readily available in many areas and transportation was prohibitively expensive. The opening of the Erie Canal and improved roads brought about a dramatic increase in the accessibility of stoneware clay, and many new potteries began to open in New York and New England.

Collectors have difficulty today locating earthenware and stoneware jugs produced prior to 1840, because few have survived intact. These ovoid or pear-shaped jugs were designed to be used on a daily basis. When cracked or severely chipped, they were quickly discarded. The value of handcrafted pottery is often determined by the cobalt decoration it carries. Pieces with elaborate scenes (a chicken pecking corn, a bluebird on a branch, a stag standing near a pine tree, a sailing ship, or

people) may easily bring $1,000.00 to $12,000.00 at auction.

After the Civil War there was a need and a national demand for stoneware jugs, crocks, canning jars, churns, spittoons, and a wide variety of other pottery items. The competition among the many potteries reached the point where only the largest could survive. To cut costs, most potteries did away with all but the simplest kinds of decoration on their wares. Time-consuming brush-painted birds or flowers quickly gave way to more quickly executed swirls or numbers and stenciled designs. The coming of home refrigeration and Prohibition in 1919 effectively destroyed the American stoneware industry.

Investment possibilities: 1)Early nineteenth-century stoneware with elaborate decorations and a potter's mark is expensive and will continue to rise in price. 2) Late nineteenth-century hand-thrown stoneware with simple cobalt swirls or numbers is still reasonably priced and a good investment. 3) Mass-produced stoneware (ca. 1890 – 1920) is available in large quantities, inexpensive and slowly increases in price over the years.

Skillfully repaired pieces often surface; their prices should reflect their condition. Look for a slight change in color and texture. The use of a black light is also useful in exposing some repairs. Buyer beware! Hint: Buy only from reputable dealers who will guarantee their merchandise.

In the following listings, 'c/s' means 'cobalt on salt glaze'; all decoration described before this abbreviation is in cobalt. See also Bennington, Stoneware. Assume that values are for examples in near mint condition with only minimal damage unless another condition code is given in the description.

Bank, flowers, c/s, brushed, ovoid, 6", EX **6,875.00**
Bean pot, Boston Baked Beans/children, cobalt on Bristol, 6", no lid .**95.00**
Bottle, brn alkaline, orig label: Cuba Rum...1933-34, ca 1933, 7"..**55.00**
Bottle, 1851/Rice & Plummer, c/s, 9½", EX.................................**110.00**
Butter crock, stencil: Jas Hamilton & Co, c/s, 8½" dia, EX **165.00**
Chicken waterer, #2/accents, c/s, att PA area, ca 1840, 11", EX.**415.00**
Churn, #3/plume, c/s, Fort Edward...NY, ca 1884, 17", EX..........**575.00**
Churn, #4/1883 in wreath, c/s, Ottman Bros...NY, rpr, ca 1883, 15".**525.00**
Churn, #5/orchid, c/s, Whites Utica NY, ca 1865, 17", EX.........**660.00**
Churn, #6/flower (dbl), c/s, J Fisher...NY, 1880s, 19", +dasher/guide...**685.00**
Churn, #6/standing lion, c/s, J Burger Jr...NY, 1880s, 20", +guide.**8,250.00**
Churn, flourish, c/s, slight ovoid w/appl hdls, 5-gal, 16"..............**195.00**
Churn, J Burger/8/leaf w/veins & dots, c/s, hdls, glued lid, 23" .**2,035.00**
Cooler, #6/bird, c/s, Gates City...Pat May 25 1866, ca 1886, 11", EX ..**935.00**
Cooler, polo scene/London Whiskey Club Polo..., cobalt on Bristol, 15".**495.00**
Cream pot, #3/accents, c/s, I Semour Troy, 1830s, 8", EX **175.00**
Cream pot, #3/bird & vine, c/s, W Roberts...NY, rstr, 1860s, 11".**250.00**
Cream pot, #3/plume, c/s, Lewis & Cady...VT, hairline, ca 1856, 11"..**330.00**
Crock, #1/flower, c/s w/incising, att Clarkson Crolius NY, 1800s, 9"..**2,400.00**
Crock, #1/running bird, c/s, Whites Utica, ca 1865, 7¼"...........**965.00**
Crock, #1/thistles, c/s, att NY state, hairline, 1870s, 7½" **145.00**
Crock, #10/tulips (allover front), c/s, J Fisher...NY, 1880s, 16", EX .**475.00**
Crock, #2/dragonfly, c/s, J Fisher Lyons, chips, 1880s, 9".............**200.00**
Crock, #2/Lyons in script, c/s, J Fisher Lyons NY, 1880s, 9", EX ...**90.00**
Crock, #3/bird on branch w/in wreath, c/s, Tyler...Troy NY, 1860s, 10".**3,000.00**
Crock, #3/bird on twig (facing left), c/s, Haxstun...NY, 1870s, 11" .**385.00**
Crock, #3/grapes, c/s, AK Ballard...VT, stain, 1870s, 10½" **525.00**
Crock, #3/Grover Cleveland 1884 w/in floral fr, c/s, ca 1884, 10" .**3,950.00**
Crock, #3/wheat shafts (bold), c/s, CW Braun...NY, 1870s, 10½", EX.**850.00**
Crock, #4/chicken pecking corn, c/s, Brady & Ryan..., ca 1885, 12", EX..**1,045.00**
Crock, #4/flower, c/s, Nichols & Boynton...VT, ca 1855, 10¾" ..**165.00**
Crock, #4/flower & dots, c/s, FB Norton...MA, 1870s, 11" **685.00**
Crock, #5/1776 1876 w/stripes & squiggles, c/s, unmk, ca 1876, 12½" .**1,750.00**
Crock, #6/flower (dbl), c/s, John Burger Rochester, ca 1855, 15", EX.**10,000.00**
Crock, #6/ribbed flower, c/s, J Burger Jr...NY, flake, ca 1885, 14".**385.00**
Crock, butter; brn & wht w/bl stencil: Bell Seed Co..., 1900s, 3¼".**100.00**
Crock, stencil: TF Reppert Greensboro PA/scrolls, c/s, hdls, 12", VG .**300.00**

Crock, Whites Utica, peafowl on floral spray, cobalt on salt glaze, lug handles, nineteenth century, 12⅜x14½", $2,500.00.

(Photo courtesy Skinner, Inc.)

Figurine, pig, Albany glaze, EX details, hairline, ca 1870, 3½x7"..385.00
Flask, trees (ea side), c/s, att NY or NJ area, ca 1810s, 6½", EX ..2,500.00
Humidor, horse head, c/s, sunflower on lid, 5½"............................220.00
Humidor, hunting dog, c/s, flakes, 6½"..250.00
Inkwell, c/s brushed on top, C Crolius...NY, disk form, 1½x3", EX..3,190.00
Jar, #1/flower, c/s, Clark & Fox...NY, 1830s, 11", NM.................550.00
Jar, #1/John F Malone...NY, c/s, J Fisher...NY, 1880s, 10½"........275.00
Jar, #2/bird flying over tulip, c/s, att Bosworth, ca 1870, 11".......745.00
Jar, #3/flower, c/s, P Mugler & Co...NY, 1850s, 13", NM............575.00
Jar, #3/1882, c/s, West Troy Pottery, prof rstr, ca 1882, 13½", EX .525.00
Jar, preserve; #1½/chicken pecks corn, c/s, Fulper...NJ, 1880s, 10"..800.00
Jar, preserve; #1/flower, c/s, Penn Yan, hairlines/crack, 1860s, 9".120.00
Jar, preserve; #2/flower, c/s, N Clark & Co Lyons, 1840s, 11½" +lid.800.00
Jar, preserve; #2/schoolteacher, c/s, unmk, ca 1870, 13½" 8,525.00
Jar, preserve; bird (lg), c/s, prof rstr, ca 1880, 6-qt, 10½"............350.00
Jug, #1½/flower, c/s, D Roberts...Utica, ca 1828, 12", EX...........300.00
Jug, #1/bird on twig (lg), c/s, TS Taft...Keene NH, ping, ca 1875, 11".360.00
Jug, #1/floral (lg/dotted), c/s, P Mugler...NY, ovoid, 1850s, 11" ..550.00
Jug, #1/flower, c/s, J Heiser...NY, prof rstr, 1852, 11½" 330.00
Jug, #1/flower (brushed), c/s, squat, rpr, ca 1850, 9½" 120.00
Jug, #1/Old EL Anderson Whiskey, Albany slip, ca 1900, 11" 65.00
Jug, #1/pine tree, c/s, Binghamton NY, 1870s, 12", EX 275.00
Jug, #1/tulip (brushed), c/s, att NY, ca 1830, 11½".....................250.00
Jug, #2/bird & flower, c/s, WH Farrar...Geddes NY, 1850s, 13½", EX ..685.00
Jug, #2/bird on plume (lg), c/s, Whites Utica, ca 1865, 13½"..1,325.00
Jug, #2/bird on twig, appl bristol, att Fulper Bros NJ, 1880s, 14"..450.00
Jug, #2/bird on twig, c/s, NY Stoneware...Fort Edward, 1880s, 14", EX.465.00
Jug, #2/chicken pecking corn, c/s, Haxstun Fort Edward, 1870s, 12"...770.00
Jug, #2/dbl flowers, c/s, Jordan, stain, ca 1850, 14" 465.00
Jug, #2/dotted design, c/s, JW Seymour..., ca 1852, 13", EX 330.00
Jug, #2/flower (bold), c/s, WA Lewis...NY, ca 1865, 14"..............440.00
Jug, #2/flower (dbl), c/s, P Mugler...NY, prof rstr chip, 1850s, 14"......770.00
Jug, #2/orchid (lg/ornate), c/s, Whites Utica NY, ca 1865, 13½".825.00
Jug, #2/pine tree, c/s, NA White & Son...NY, 1860s, 10½"........275.00
Jug, #2/plumes/tornado, c/s, FB Norton...MA, chip, 1870s, 13" ..360.00
Jug, #2/sunburst, c/s, N Clark Jr Athens NY, ca 1850, 14", EX ...525.00
Jug, #2/vine, c/s, John B Caire & Co Poughkeepsie, squat, 1850s, 12".200.00
Jug, #2/3-petal leaf, c/s, CE Pharris...NY, ca 1865, 13½", EX......415.00
Jug, #3/eagle (lg), c/s, Wme Warner West Troy, ca 1850, 15", EX+ .7,700.00
Jug, #3/floral (bold), c/s, Galesville NY, stain/hairlines, 1860s, 15".415.00
Jug, #3/parrot, c/s, FB Norton...MA, prof rstr chip, 1870s, 15" ...850.00
Jug, #3/plume, c/s, I Seymour Troy, flaw in making, 1830s, 15½".275.00
Jug, Albany slip, Eli Thomas Dublin OH...1872, 10" 195.00
Jug, Edwards Fountain Syrup..., c/s, Sherwood...PA, ca 1900, 11½".65.00
Jug, flowers, c/s, brushed, hairline in hdl, mini, 3" 5,225.00
Meat tenderizer, diamonds in relief, wood hdl, Pat'd Dec 25 1877, 10".175.00
Mug, drinking scene/buffalo, cobalt on Bristol, 4" 65.00
Mug, Prosit, cobalt on Bristol, #53, 4"..35.00
Mug, Souvenir Endicott Hotel, cobalt on Bristol, 2½"..................90.00
Mug, tropical sailing scene/bands, cobalt on Bristol, 3½" 155.00
Mug, 2 bands, c/s (brushed), incised edging, appl hdl, 4¾"........245.00

Pail, batter; brushed accents, c/s, White & Co Binghamton, 1860s, 8".495.00
Pitcher, #2/vines/triple tulips, c/s, att Remmey, prof rstr, 1860s ..900.00
Pitcher, children in high relief, cobalt on Bristol, 9½"................355.00
Pitcher, female designs/1889, c/s, Whites Utica, 9" 330.00
Pitcher, flowers, c/s (brushed), incised rim/shoulder lines, 7"..1,485.00
Pitcher, man's profile in circle, cobalt on Bristol, flakes, 4".........120.00
Pitcher, poppy, c/s, Whites Binghamton, ca 1860, about 1-gal, 9½" ..1,045.00
Stein, N Am State &...Sts Chicago, cobalt on Bristol, Whites Utica, 3"..165.00

Store

Perhaps more so than any other yesteryear establishment, the country store evokes feelings of nostalgia for folks old enough to remember its charms — barrels for coffee, crackers, and big green pickles; candy in a jar for the grocer to weigh on shiny brass scales; beheaded chickens in the meat case outwardly devoid of nothing but feathers. Today mementos from this segment of Americana are being collected by those who 'lived it' as well as those less fortunate!

Our advisor for this category is Charles Reynolds; he is listed in the Directory under Virginia. For more information we recommend *General Store Collectibles, Vols. I and II*, by David L. Wilson. See also Advertising; Scales.

Bin, blk-pnt tin w/Oolong gold stencil, 16x10½x14", EX...........195.00
Bin, coffee; pine w/orig stencil, 33" H......................................550.00
Bin, pnt tin, rnded front, Empire Hdw, 19⅝x13⅝x15", VG+.....250.00
Bin, Tiger Chewing Tobacco, red cb w/tin lid, VG....................235.00
Box, biscuit; wood, hinged lid, Currier & Ives scene, 22" L........175.00
Box, display; Adams Tutti Frutti Chewing Gum.........................100.00
Box, seed; Ferry Morse Seed Co, wooden, 1930s, 5⅝x21x9¼", EX .110.00
Broom holder, heavy wire, 23 loops, hanging, 19th C, 19x16" dia .180.00
Cabinet, braid/spool; Goff's Best Made, oak, dvtl drws, 14x16x15" .545.00
Cabinet, spool; J&P Coats, 6-drw, 22x20" 2,500.00
Case, aluminum fr, bent glass sides, 4 glass shelves, 79x28" dia.1,295.00
Case, Clarks ONT Boilfast Thread, metal & glass, EX...............125.00
Case, glass w/oak fr, Sun Mfg on brass plaque, 42x49x27", EX ...750.00
Case, oak, counter-top, mirrored fold-down bk, 6½x15" 130.00
Case, pine w/red pnt, 3 glass sides, 18x12x12", VG...................110.00
Case, scissors; Champlin, wood, 3-tiered revolving center..........825.00
Case, wood fr w/4 glass sides, 2 glass shelves, 15x11x9", EX 325.00
Container, Jack's 1¢ Cookies, glass bbl, tin lid, 12" 100.00
Container, Tom's Cookies, red & wht on clear glass, tin lid, 12" .100.00
Desk, clerk's; walnut, slant front, 4-drw, attached top, 85" 1,430.00
Desk, 12 sm drws, kneehole, 3 sm drw & 2 panel doors, 31x74" .1,500.00
Display ped, Clark's Teaberry Gum, vaseline glass, 3¼x7x4⅝" 60.00
Ice chipper, CI, wooden hdl, Peerless, 2¼x10¾" 12.50
Jar, Baker's Chocolate, yel letters on clear glass, 8¾x7" dia 150.00
Jar, Ramons Pills, bl on clear glass w/bl metal id..........................150.00
Jar, snuff; Weyman's Snuff, stoneware, 9x5¾"............................150.00
Lamp, kerosene; emb SP, hanging, tin shade................................475.00
Mannequin, compo, 1940s, 32", M..325.00
Mannequin of boy, pnt compo, late 19th C, 42½", EX 350.00
Register, receipt; McCaskey, oak, 34½x23x20½", EX 200.00
Roaster, peanut; copper & glass, Hot Peanuts 5¢, rstr, 42".........200.00
Sign, Groceries, wooden cut-out letters appl to yel brd, 12x65" .225.00

Stoves

Antique stoves' desirability is based on two criteria: their utility and their decorative merit. It's the latter that adds an 'antique' premium to the basic functional value that could be served just as well by a modern stove. Sheer age is usually irrelevant. Decorative features that enhance desirability include fancy, embossed ornamentation, nickel-plated trim, mica windows, ceramic tiles, and (in cooking stoves) water reservoirs and high warming closets rather than mere high shelves. The less sheet metal and the more cast iron, the better. Look for crisp, sharp designs in preference to those made from worn or damaged and repaired foundry patterns. Stoves with a pastel porcelain finish can be very attractive; blue is a favorite, white is least desirable. Chrome trim, rather than nickel, dates a stove to circa 1933 or later and is a good indicator of a post-antique stove. Though purists prefer the earlier models trimmed in nickel rather than chrome, there is now considerable public interest in these post-antique stoves as well, and some people are willing to pay a good price for these appliance-era 'classics.' (Note: Remember, not all bright metal trim is chrome; it is important to learn to distinguish chrome from the earlier, more desirable nickel plate.)

Among stove types, base burners (with self-feeding coal magazines) are the most desirable. Then come the upright, cylindrical 'oak' stoves, kitchen ranges, and wood parlors. Cannon stoves approach the margin of undesirability; laundries and gasoline stoves plunge through it.

There's a thin but continuing stream of desirable antique stoves going to the high-priced Pacific Coast market. Interest in antique stoves is least in the Deep South. Demand for wood/coal stoves is strongest in areas where firewood is affordable and storage of it is practical. Demand for antique gas ranges has become strong, especially in metropolitan markets, and interest in antique electric ranges is slowly dawning. The market for antique stoves is so limited and the variety so bewildering that a consensus on a going price can hardly emerge. They are only worth something to the right individual, and prices realized depend very greatly on who happens to be in the auction crowd. Even an expert's appraisal will usually miss the realized price by a substantial percent.

In judging condition look out for deep rust pits, warped or burnt-out parts, unsound fire bricks, poorly fitting parts, poor repairs, and empty mounting holes indicating missing trim. Search meticulously for cracks in the cast iron. Our listings reflect auction prices of completely restored, safe, and functional stoves, unless indicated otherwise.

Note: Round Oak stoves carrying the words 'Estate of P.D. Beckwith' above the lower door were made prior to 1935. After that date, the company name was changed to Round Oak Company, and the Beckwith reference was no longer used. In our listings, the term 'tea shelf' has been used to describe both drop and swing shelves, as the function of both types was to accommodate teapots and coffeepots.

Key: func — functional

Base Burners

#44, Burdett-Smith, swivel top, tiles, 38", VG 1,300.00
Art Amherst #15, NP trim, tiles, 11" urn, 50x25x28", VG......2,065.00
Art Denmark #15, Ransom, Albany NY, tiles/NP/mica, 1897, VG.4,950.00
Art Garland #400, Michigan Stove, gargoyles/NP/Mica, 1889, rstr.10,750.00
Emerald Jewel #14, Detroit, NPCI, 1909, 54", +15" brass urn.1,700.00
Favorite #30, Piqua OH, ornate CI, mica windows, 52"+14" urn.2,200.00
Glenwood #6, Weir, NP trim, mica windows, 1909, 68" 965.00
Waverly #12, Thos Caffney, Boston MA, 40x20x22"...............6,065.00

Franklin Stoves

Acme Orient #18, 6 tiles, mica windows, fancy, 1890 ....315.00
Good Cheer #22, Walker & Pratt, fireplace, 1850s, 32x27x31"..330.00
Ideal #3, Magee, CI fireplace, 2 side trivets, 1892, 32x28" 275.00
Iron Foundry...NH, ornate CI, grate missing, 1820s, 37x26x32" .220.00
Kineo #16, Noyes & Nutter, fireplace, 1890s, 32x23x20" 200.00
Sunny Hearth #2, Southard Robertson, 1880s, 35x20x29½" 315.00
Villa Franklin, Muzzy & Co, folding doors, 1830s, 30"+4" urn ...195.00
Wyer & Noble, CI/brass-trim fireplace, early 1800s 2,200.00

Parlor

The term 'parlor stove' as we use it here is very general and encompasses at least six distinct types recognized by the stove industry: cottage parlor, double-cased airtight, circulator, cylinder, oak, and the fireplace heater.

#1, Tyson, 2 sheet metal columns, swing doors, 36x17x25".........385.00
#2, JH Shear, Albany NY, CI, column style, 56" 935.00
#4, Johnson, Geer & Cox, CI, 4-column, 56" 1,100.00
#20, Somersworth, tip-up dome top, 1850s, 39x30x29".............330.00
#44, Burdett-Smith, sq, tiles, mica door, 38"+8" urn 385.00
Comfort #23, Bangor Foundry, oval w/dome top, Pat 1875, 33"+10" urn..200.00
Ideal Garland #220, wood/coal cottage, missing urn, ca 1893, rstr.1,300.00
Ilion #5, ornate CI, ca 1853, 33"+13" 2-pc urn 550.00
Modern Glenwood Wood Parlor, slide top, 1900s, 45x28x24½".360.00
Peerless, Pratt & Wentworth, tip-up dome, 1840s, 37x19x15" ...150.00
Red Cross #31, Co-Op Foundry Sylvan, tiles, gargoyle legs, Pat 1888-89.330.00
Royal Clarion #14, Wood-Bishop, mica door, oven, 1890s, 50", 1856, 28".275.00
SH Ransom, ornate CI, rnd air intake, Pat 1846, 26"+14" urn...300.00
Temple #5, Vose & Co, CI, Pat 1854, 44".................................880.00
Union Airtight, Warnick & Leibrandt, ornate CI, 1851, 26" 275.00

Ranges (Gas)

Detroit Jewel, 4-burner, blk/NP, glass oven door, 1918, VG........550.00
Insulated Glenwood, Wier, 6-burner/2-oven, wht, 1932, rstr...4,500.00
Magic Chef, wht, 6-burner/2-oven, high closet, 1938, rstr, up to.12,000.00
Magic Chef, wht, 6-burner/2-oven, high closet, 1938, unrstr ..1,000.00
Magic Chef, 6-burner/2-oven, warming closet, 1932, EX........2,750.00
O'Keefe & Merritt, 4-burner, cabinet base, ca 1929, G..............110.00
O'Keefe & Merritt, 6-burner, dual oven/broilers, wht porc, EX ..500.00
Quick Meal, 4-burner, bl, cabinet style, 1919, G 925.00
Quick Meal, 4-burner, gray, canopy/high closet, 1924, unrstr 375.00
Quick Meal, 4-burner/1-oven, 1928, unrstr.................................300.00
Wedgewood, wht porc, complete w/4 burner covers & lifter, 1930s, EX ..900.00

Ranges (Wood and Coal)

Ideal Atlantic 8-20, Portland, ornate CI, bk shelf, 1850s.........1,675.00
Imperial Clarion #8-20, Wood/Bishop, swarming closet, dtd 1898.1,980.00
Kineo C, Noyes & Nutter, roll top, water tank, 1900-15 ....715.00
Magee 88, 2-oven/8-hole, CI, high closet, no reservoir, 1880, rstr...5,500.00
Popular Clarion, Wood/Biship, scrolling, tea shelves, 1890s....1,150.00
Quaker Standard #8-20, Taunton...Works, NP trim, shelves, 1890s..945.00
Queen Atlantic, Portland, unadorned, 19½x19½x12"...............685.00
Village Crawford Royal, Walker & Pratt, tea shelves, 1900s.......800.00

Stove Manufacturers' Toy Stoves

Karr Range 6, Belleville, Illinois, blue porcelain on sheet metal with nickel-plated trim, functional, 21½x13x9", $3,000.00.

Buck's Jr #3, St Louis MO, new body/pnt/recast parts, 26".........850.00
Charter Oak #503, GF Filley, St Louis MO, 14x12x25", EX....2,050.00

Dainty, Reading Stove Works, PA, 7x13x8", VG 150.00
Estate Fresh Air Oven, blk/wht enamel, NP, working gas range, 15" .2,400.00
Jersey, Cook & Van Evera, Chicago, ca 1908, 28x15x12", EX.6,400.00
Karr Qualified, bl porc w/NP, Belleville IL, 1925, EX 2,500.00
Karr Qualified Range, aluminum/tin, dial on door, 21½x13", EX .775.00
Little Eva T Southard, NYC, 8½x14x11", VG w/accessories......575.00
Little Fanny, Philadelphia Stove Works, ca 1880, CI, minor rust, EX..300.00
Royal American, Bridgeford, Louisville KY, 14x12x10", G.........950.00

Toy Manufacturers' Toy Stoves

Electric, Empire, Metal Ware Corp, WI, burner+oven, '25, 15x19x7", VG..50.00
Electric, Lionel, porc & CI, cream & gr, 4-leg, func, 32x26", EX .2,500.00
Gas, Arcade Hotpoint Range, pnt CI, tan & gr, VG...................150.00
Gas, Arcade Roper Range, pnt CI, door opens, 4½", EX 70.00
Heater, Pet, The Young Bros, Albany NY, 10½x6x8½"..............165.00
Heater, Spark, Grey Iron...Co, int grate/sliding vents, func, 14", VG.115.00
Wood/coal, Adams/Pet, CI, cooking, ornate, 1857, 8½" W base .290.00
Wood/coal, Bing, bl steel cookstove, brass trim, Germany, 16½", VG.600.00
Wood/coal, Crescent, CI, w/shelves, lids, 5 CI pots, 8", EX........170.00
Wood/coal, Crescent, plated CI & steel cookstove, 4-hole, 11½", EX.230.00
Wood/coal, Eagle, Hubley, Lancaster PA, NP, recast parts, rstr...450.00
Wood/coal, Eagle, Kenton, CI, heavily scrolled, 4-ft, 11½x10", G.125.00
Wood/coal, Eclipse, J&E Stevens, Cromwell CT, CI, EX............175.00
Wood/coal, Kenton Royal, CI & steel, 4-hole, ornate, 10", VG.100.00
Wood/coal, Little Giant, unmk/unidentified, 7½x8½x11", EX orig..675.00
Wood/coal, Novelty, Kenton Hdwe, bl pnt/NP trim, rfn, 13x6½x8½" .600.00
Wood/coal, Rival, J&E Stevens, Cromwell CT, 14x9x16", M, +2 kettles.1,350.00
Wood/coal, Rival, no shelves, 12" L, EX....................................900.00
Wood/coal, Royal, Kenton, CI/steel, 4-hole/working grates, rpt, 10", G..50.00
Wood/coal, Royal, plated CI, stovepipe, shield shape, 16", G.......85.00
Wood/coal, Triumph, Kenton Hdwe, OH, 14x8½x19", G 195.00

Stretch Glass

Stretch glass, produced from circa 1916 through 1935, was made in an effort to emulate the fine art glass of Tiffany and Carder. The pressed or blown glassware was sprayed with a metallic salts mix while hot, then reshaped, causing a stretch effect in the iridescent finish. Pieces which were not reshaped had the iridized finish without the stretch, as seen on Fenton's #222 lemonade set and #401 guest set. Northwood, Imperial, Fenton, Diamond, Lancaster, Jeannette, Central, Vineland Flint, and the United States Glass Company were the manufacturers of this type of glass.

See also specific companies.

Bonbon, gr, ftd, w/lid, Diamond Glass, 5¾x5⅜"...........................50.00
Bonbon, Wisteria (lt purple), w/lid, Fenton #643, 6¼x5¼"........120.00
Bottle, cologne; Velva Rose (pk), nipple finial, Fenton #59, 3⅝" .190.00
Bowl, bl, flared rim, US Glass, 1⅞x12" 60.00
Bowl, bl, wide flared sides, Northwood #648, 3⅝x12"..................60.00
Bowl, cobalt, flared, Vineland Flint Glass, 4x7½" 180.00
Bowl, Floral & Optic, Green Ice (bl-gr), Imperial #5141, 3½x8⅞" .125.00
Bowl, Gold (lt marigold), 3-ftd, flared, Jeannette, 2⅞x9⅛" 35.00
Bowl, gr, cupped rim, Diamond Glass, 2⅞x5¾" 30.00
Bowl, Melon Rib, aquamarine, rolled rim, Fenton #857, 2⅜x11" .100.00
Bowl, Midnight Wistaria (dk purple), cupped, Diamond Glass, 10¼" .225.00
Bowl, Optic, red, 12-panel, flared rim, Imperial #22/73, 2¼x9¾".200.00
Bowl, Optic Rays, bl, blk ft, flared, Northwood #678, 4¾x11¾" .150.00
Bowl, Pearl Ruby (marigold), crimped, Imperial, 2¼x8" 135.00
Bowl, ruby, crimped rim, Fenton #604, 6¼x11¼" 500.00
Bowl, ruby, 3-ftd, Fenton #603, 5¼x10⅜" 725.00
Bowl, Russett, cupped rim, Northwood #670, 2¼x4⅝" 40.00
Bowl, tangerine, flared/rolled rim, Fenton #647, 2⅛x11½"..........75.00
Bowl, topaz, flared, ftd, US Glass #179, 3⅞x6⅛" 55.00
Bowl, topaz, flared rim, Central Glass, 4x9⅝"...............................65.00
Bowl, Twilight Wisteria (lt purple), flared, Diamond Glass, 7½" ..70.00
Bowl, Wisteria (purple), crimped, Vineland Flint Glass, 3¾x8¼"..70.00
Candlesticks, Celeste Blue w/blk ft, Fenton #549, 8¼", pr 300.00
Candlesticks, Double Scroll, Blue Ice, Imperial #320, 8½", pr....115.00
Candlesticks, Jade Green, US Glass #310, 9", pr 150.00
Candlesticks, Spindle, bl, Northwood #708, 8¾", pr...................140.00
Candy jar, Optic Rays, Iris Ice (crystal), w/lid, 3-ftd, Lancaster 95.00
Comport, Celeste Blue, flared oval, ftd, Fenton #103, 3x4x4¾" ...75.00
Comport, crystal w/bl & wht enamel, low ft, US Glass, 6½x8⅛" .90.00
Comport, ruby, twin dolphin hdls, Fenton #1533A, 4¾x7¼" .1,400.00
Compote, Adams Rib, Harding Blue, Diamond Glass, 6⅜x9½" .120.00
Console set, purple w/gold, Central Glass, 10" bowl+2 7" candlesticks.190.00
Creamer & sugar bowl, Florentine Green, cobalt hdls, Fenton, pr .250.00
Lamp shade, wht opaque, ribbed, flared, Northwood, 5x5" 80.00
Mayonnaise, Aztec (marigold), ftd, flared rim, Lancaster, 4¼x6½".80.00
Mug, #600 Chesterfield, Iris Ice (crystal), Imperial, 5⅛x3½" 75.00
Nut cup, Florentine Green, dolphin stem, Fenton, 4⅝x4⅜x2⅛" .1,800.00
Plate, cake; pk w/gold flowers & trim, hdls, Imperial #7257, 10¼" .75.00
Plate, Diamond Optic, Velva Rose (pk), Fenton #1502, 7¾"........65.00
Plate, Egyptian Lustre (blk opaque) w/gold, Diamond Glass, 8⅜".135.00
Plate, Octagon, Florentine Green, Fenton #756, 6".......................15.00
Plate, Open Work, topaz, US Glass #8076, 12½" 85.00
Server, Amber (marigold), center shovel hdl, Jeannette, 4½x9¾".55.00
Server, Celeste Blue, center hdl, cupped rim, Fenton #317, 9½" ..70.00
Server, gr, center hdl, US Glass #310, 4x10"................................75.00
Sherbet, gr, ring on stem, Diamond Glass, 3⅜x3¾" 20.00
Sherbet, Optic Rays, amberina, Imperial #499, 3½x4"................125.00
Vase, bud; Harding Blue, Diamond Glass, 9¾x2⅝" 35.00
Vase, Diamond Optic, Celeste Blue, cupped, Fenton #1502, 5¼".80.00
Vase, fan; Rib Optic, Florentine Green, Fenton #572, 8½"...........50.00
Vase, Jade Blue, flared, Northwood, 7¾x8½" 170.00
Vase, Mandarin Yellow (yel opaque), US Glass, 10⅜x3⅝".........110.00
Vase, Pearl (crystal), Diamond Glass, 4x4⅜" 50.00
Vase, Rose Ice (lt marigold), flared rim, Imperial #693, 8x6½".....70.00

String Holders

Today, if you want to wrap and secure a package, you have a variety of products to choose from: cellophane tape, staples, etc. But in the 1800s and even well past the advent of Scotch tape in the early 1930s, string was often the only available binder; thus the string holder, either the hanging or counter type, was a common and practical item found in most homes and businesses. Chalkware and ceramic figurals from the 1930s, '40s, and '50s contrast with the cast and wrought-iron examples from the 1800s to make for an interesting collection. Our advisor for this category is Larry G. Pogue (L & J Antiques and Collectibles); he is listed in the Directory under Texas.

See also Advertising.

Aunt Jemima, pnt chalkware, 1940s-50s, 7¾", NM 395.00
Banana bunch, yel, chalkware, 5¾"..85.00
Beehive, blk, wrought-iron...400.00
Black boy riding alligator, chalkware, dtd 1948, 9" 345.00
Black girl, blk/red/wht, full figure, Japan, 6½x4" 385.00
Bonzo, bl dog w/wht & red belly, chalkware, 6½" 185.00
Bride, holding bouquet, bulbous bottom, ceramic, MIJ, 6¼" 145.00
Buddha, ceramic, MIJ, 1940s, 5¾" 145.00
Cat, wht head, pk & wht bow w/blk dots, ceramic, Japan, 5⅜" ..145.00
Cat, wht w/blk features, red ball of twine, ceramic, 5½" 105.00
Chef, wht hat, ceramic, Japan, 6" 165.00
Chipmunk, blk & wht striped bow, ceramic, 5⅛"........................135.00

Coca-Cola Kid w/Coke lid cap, chalkware, 1950s, 8"..................650.00
Dog, wht head, red collar w/scissors holder, ceramic, 4½"..........155.00
Dr Jug's Medicine for Lung, Liver & Blood, CI jug form, 7", EX.1,450.00
Ears of corn w/gr leaves, chalkware, 5½".................................175.00
Felix the Cat, blk & wht, chalkware 295.00
Gourd, gr, chalkware, 7½" 135.00
Grape cluster, bl w/gr leaves, chalkware, 5½" 100.00
Heart, wht w/String Along w/Me & flower, ceramic, 5½" 125.00
Jester, cigar in mouth, chalkware, 7¼" 195.00
Little Red Riding Hood, pnt chalkware, c 1941 Bello..., 9½" 275.00
Mammy, Black face & hands, wht dress, 6½" 255.00
Mammy, brn face, plaid dress, chalkware, 1930s, 6"..................395.00
Mammy, google-eyed (eyes move up & down), chalkware, 1940s, 8½"..800.00
Mammy, outstretched arms, hole in stomach, ceramic, 4½" 145.00
Mammy, pottery, w/scissors holder, 6½" 385.00
Mammy, tan & bl dress w/pocket, ceramic, 6½" 385.00
Mammy, wht dress w/copper-colored dress, ceramic, MIJ, 6½" ...195.00
Monkey on ball of twine, chalkware, 7½"................................245.00
Mrs Mouse, knitting, w/scissors in nose for glasses, compo, 7" 90.00
Old Indian, red w/wht striped head band, chalkware, 10¼"........285.00
Parrot, orange w/blk & yel, on branch w/flower, chalkware, 9½".245.00
Pear, orange & yel w/gr leaves, chalkware, 5½" 90.00
Popeye, w/pipe, bl hat, chalkware, 1950s, 7"...........................325.00
Porter, brn face, yel hat, Fredericksburg Pottery, 6¼" 275.00
Pumpkin face, winking, ceramic, MIJ, 5" 180.00
Rose, yel w/gr leaves, chalkware, 8".......................................175.00
Rosie the Riveter, girl w/gr box, Bello, Universal Santuary, 7" ...295.00
Scottie head, gray, chalkware, 7" 150.00
Senora, pnt chalkware, 1940s-50s, 8", NM 275.00
Shirley Temple, chalkware, 1940-50s, 6¾" 395.00
Soldier, Fr-style attire, wooden, sgn Bronzini, 10".....................145.00
Strawberry (w/face), red w/gr leaves, chalkware, 6½" 75.00
Teapot, HP rooster scene on wht, MIJ, 6¼x5¼" 155.00
Willy the Worm, yel worm on apple 'house', chalkware, 6½".....110.00

Sugar Shakers

Sugar shakers (or muffineers, as they were also called) were used during the Victorian era to sprinkle sugar and spice onto breakfast muffins, toast, etc. They were made of art glass, in pressed patterns, and in china. See also specific types and manufacturers (such as Northwood). Our coadvisors for this category are Jeff Bradfield and Dale MacAllister; they are listed in the Directory under Virginia.

Acorn, bl opaque..225.00
Acorn, gr w/decor...300.00
Acorn, peach bloom w/enamel & gold....................................275.00
Argus Swirl, pk (Peach Bloom) 230.00
Beatty Honeycomb, bl opal...250.00
Block & Fan, clear...75.00
Blown Twist, gr opal, wide waist...350.00
Bubble Lattice, bl, tapered 425.00
Bubble Lattice, wht opal 225.00
Challinor's Forget-Me-Not, pk..175.00
Chrysanthemum Swirl, cranberry opal 495.00
Coin Dot (9 Panel), cranberry opal..275.00
Cone, bl opaque..135.00
Connecticut, clear 35.00
Cranberry w/cut panels, metal top, 6"....................................150.00
Crown Milano, fall leaves/bl berries on bsk, floral-emb lid 450.00
Daisy & Fern, bl opal, wide waist 275.00
Daisy & Fern, cranberry opal, bulbous....................................375.00
Daisy & Fern/Parian Swirl Mold, cranberry opal 395.00

Fern, bl opal..395.00
Guttate, pk cased (+) 325.00
Guttate, pk satin..280.00
Hobbs Swirl, cranberry opal...425.00
Inverted Thumbprint, cranberry..225.00
Leaf Mold, canary spatter...395.00

Leaf Umbrella, cranberry, $350.00.

Leaning Pillar, bl opaque..95.00
Medallion Sprig, bl to clear..500.00
Melon, yel floral-decor top, Smith Bros 375.00
Netted Oak, milk glass, decor, Northwood............................155.00
Parian Swirl, gr opaque, decor 225.00
Quilted Phlox, pk cased 265.00
Reverse Swirl, cranberry opal...485.00
Ribbed Lattice, cranberry opal 350.00
Ring Neck Optic, dk gr 225.00
Ruby cased w/clear, 12 cut panels, sterling top, 6" 335.00
Snail, clear..135.00
Spanish Lace, bl opal, wide waist.......................................250.00
Swirl, 9-panel cranberry opal (reproduced in 1960s)...............125.00
Tomato, wht satin w/decor, Mt WA 450.00
West Virginia, Optic, cranberry..275.00
Windows, bl opal..395.00

Sunderland Lustre

Sunderland lustre was made by various potters in the Sunderland district of England during the eighteenth and nineteenth centuries. It is often characterized by a splashed-on application of the pink lustre, which results in an effect sometimes referred to as the 'cloud' pattern. Some pieces are transfer printed with scenes, ships, florals, or portraits.

Jug, Captain Hull of Constitution/Pike be always..., blk transfer, 7".5,750.00
Jug, God Speed the Plow/verse, blk transfer w/mc, 8¾"..........1,150.00
Jug, May Peace & Plenty on our Nation..., blk stransfer, 9⅜" 650.00
Jug, Sailor's Farewell/verse, blk transer w/pk lustre, 9⅜" 3,300.00
Jug, SE View of Iron Bridge..., mc/blk transfer, 9", EX...............940.00
Jug, West View of CI Bridge..., blk transfer, bk: ship, att Moore, 10" .1,750.00
Mug, Christening; Mary Ellen 1854, sailing ship/Iron Bridge 650.00
Plaque, Northumberland 74 (ship), rectangular, self fr, 8x9".......500.00
Plaque, Prepare To Meet Thy God, 8" dia................................450.00

Surveying Instruments

The practice of surveying offers a wide variety of precision instruments primarily for field use, most of which are associated with the recording of distance and angular measurements. These instruments were primarily made from brass; the larger examples were fitted with tripods and protective cases. These cases also held accessories for the instruments, and these can sometimes play a key part in their evaluation. Instruments in complete condition and showing little use will have much greater values than those that appear to have had moderate or heavy use. Instruments were never polished during use, and those that have been polished as decorator pieces are of little interest to most avid collectors.

Alidade, Gurley, low post explorer model #580, w/cover & case..400.00
Alidade, Gurley explorer's, complete, ca 1915, EX 600.00
Alidade, W&LE Gurley #584, EXIB 395.00
Clinometer, Reynolds, Birmingham England, 1767-81, VG........300.00
Compass, Alex Mabon & Son, miner's dial, polished brass/wood, ca 1870.2,000.00
Compass, Dietzgen Brunton style, aluminum, 1894 to 1926 Pat dates, VG..105.00
Compass, DW Brunton, pocket sz, EX in leather case.................175.00
Compass, Keuffel & Esser #5334, 4" needle, EX, w/ball joint & box ...225.00
Compass, Michael Rupp, 5" needle, ca 1860, EX 1,500.00
Compass, miner's; Keuffel & Esser #5293, dipping needle, EXIB .175.00
Compass, solar; Wm J Young & Co w/James Foster, 1863, EXIB....10,000.00
Compass, W&LE Gurley, 6" needle, mid-1800s, 15" L, G+ in mahog box.1,795.00
Compass, Wm J Young, surveyor's venier, 6" needle, 1860s, EXIB.2,000.00
Heliotrope, Steinheil; Bausch & Lomb, ca 1910, EX 1,500.00
Level, combination; AS Aloe, ca 1923, 12", EXIB 450.00
Level, dumpy; Buff & Buff, ca 1900, 18", EXIB 800.00
Level, dumpy; Buff & Buff, internal focus, 1920, 15", EXIB........500.00
Level, dumpy; Keuffel & Esser, ca 1913, 18", EXIB 500.00
Level, tier; CL Berger & Sons, ca 1910, EX in maple case.......1,000.00
Level, wye; Buff & Buff, ca 1930, 18", EXIB..............................600.00
Level, wye; convertible, Keuffel & Esser, w/built-in compass, EXIB 595.00
Level, wye; Gurley, aluminum & brass, ca 1948, 18", EXIB 450.00
Level, wye; Keuffel & Esser architect's #5111, ca 1924, EX.........450.00
Level, wye; Stackpole & Bro, removable base, 1870s, 17", VG...700.00
Level, wye; W&LE Gurley #376, early 1800s, 20", VG..............695.00
Leveling head, plane table; Bubb & Buff, ca 1900, EX 400.00
Pantograph, Dietzgen model 1893, nickel silver, ca 1930, EXIB..1,000.00
Theodolite, FE Brandis & Sons, triangulation w/sliding level, 1906, EX.3,000.00
Theodolite, Stackpole & Bro, ca 1870, EX................................1,500.00
Theodolite, T Cooke & Sons, ca 1890, EXIB............................2,000.00
Transit, Berger, for calibrating aircraft compasses, 1950s, EX 550.00
Transit, F Heiseley & Son Harrisburg, plated brass, 6¼" dial, 14"..1,075.00
Transit, Gurley #52, complete, ca 1929, VG 1,000.00
Transit, Heller & Brightly, quick leveling base, ca 1875, EX ...1,500.00
Transit, Keuffel & Esser, Y&S #5166 Special Survey, ca 1918, EX .695.00
Transit, Keuffel & Esser #5030, ca 1887, EXIB........................2,000.00
Transit, Keuffel & Esser #5077, w/9" scope/compass & full circle, EX..875.00
Transit, W&LE Gurley #3B Engineer's, 5" needle, 1890s, EXIB..1,200.00
Tripod, Kauffel & Esser, stiff legs, staff mt for compass, early, VG .275.00
Tripod, tapered post w/thimble, mid-1700s-1800s, EX...............500.00
Tripod, Warren Knight, oak, stiff legs, ca 1920, EX 150.00
Wading rod set, Gurley's Hydraulic Current Meters #612/621/624, EX ..225.00

Swastika Keramos

Swastika Keramos was a line of artware made by the Owens China Company of Minerva, Ohio, around 1902-04. It is characterized either by a coralene type of decoration (similar to the Opalesce line made by the J. B. Owens Pottery Company of Zanesville) or by the application of metallic lustres, usually in simple designs. Shapes are often plain and handles squarish and rather thick, suggestive of the Arts and Crafts style. Our advisors for this category are Suzanne Perrault and Dave Rago; they are listed in the Directory under New Jersey.

Vase, bands of gold swastikas around gray 'stone' panels, 7x5", EX.345.00
Vase, floral on gold, sm rim, shouldered, 8".................................85.00
Vase, trees, gold on gold & red, raised medallion, 12x4½", $300 to..400.00
Vase, trees, silver on silver & red, raised medallion, 12x4½", VG.150.00

Syracuse

Syracuse was a line of fine dinnerware and casual ware which was made for nearly a century by the Onondaga Pottery Company of Syracuse, New York. Early patterns were marked O.P. Company. Collectors of American dinnerware are focusing their attention on reassembling some of their many lovely patterns. In 1966 the firm became officially known as the Syracuse China Company in order to better identify with the name of their popular chinaware. Many of the patterns were marked with the shape and color names (Old Ivory, Federal, etc.), not the pattern names. By 1971 dinnerware geared for use in the home was discontinued, and the company turned to the manufacture of hotel, restaurant, and other types of commercial tableware.

Alpine, coffeepot..125.00
Apple Blossom, plate, dinner 45.00
Arcadia, bowl, rimmed soup...40.00
Arcadia, bowl, vegetable; w/lid 115.00
Arcadia, creamer, from $45 to...55.00
Arcadia, plate, dinner..30.00
Arcadia, plate, salad 25.00
Baroque (Gray), bowl, fruit/dessert; 4¾" 60.00
Baroque (Gray), bowl, vegetable; oval, 10"......................180.00
Baroque (Gray), bowl, vegetable; rnd, 9"..........................175.00
Baroque (Gray), plate, dinner; 10⅜".....................................65.00
Baroque (Gray), platter, med, 14¼".....................................175.00
Baroque (Gray), platter, sm, 12"...160.00
Bombay, bowl, vegetable; w/lid, rnd 150.00
Bombay, plate, cake; hdld...50.00
Bombay, sugar bowl, w/lid...75.00
Bracelet, bowl, vegetable; w/lid, rnd, gold rim...................200.00
Bracelet, gravy boat, w/underplate, gold rim, from $175 to.........200.00
Bracelet, platter, detailed gold rim, oval, lg, 16" 155.00
Briarcliff, platter, med..110.00
Briarcliff, platter, sm...90.00
Carvel, bowl, vegetable; w/lid, rnd 140.00
Carvel, platter, sm, 12"..80.00
Champlain, coffeepot...125.00
Chevy Chase, coffeepot...100.00
Cliftondale, teapot...125.00
Coralbel, gravy boat, w/underplate, from $185 to...............200.00
Coralbel, platter, med, 15¾"..255.00
Coralbel, platter, rnd, 12⅜"...230.00
Coralbel, sugar bowl, w/lid, Winchester shape 240.00
Coralbel, teapot...275.00
Dawn, platter, sm, 12"...80.00
Debutante (Gray), teapot..170.00
Diane, bowl, fruit/dessert; cobalt trim 45.00
Diane, bowl, vegetable; cobalt trim, oval 180.00
Diane, coffepot, cobalt trim 310.00
Dorian, teapot..120.00
Golden Seeds, creamer...50.00
Jefferson, bowl, vegetable; w/lid...135.00
Jefferson, gravy boat, w/underplate 95.00
Jefferson, plate, chop..115.00
Jefferson, platter, med, 14" 100.00
Kent (Platinum), sugar bowl, w/lid......................................100.00
Lady Mary, platter, med, 14" 100.00
Lilac Rose, coffeepot, 7"..195.00
Lyric, creamer..50.00
Madame Butterfly, bowl, fruit/dessert...................................15.00
Madame Butterfly, cup & saucer...45.00
Madame Butterfly, plate, bread & butter...............................15.00

Madame Butterfly, sugar bowl, w/lid 65.00
Melrose, bowl, vegetable; w/lid, 9" 90.00
Minuet, plate, dinner 50.00
Montego, coffeepot 110.00
Monticello, gravy boat 130.00
Monticello, sugar bowl, w/lid 75.00
Pendleton, bowl, vegetable; w/lid, rnd 140.00
Pendleton, coffepot 170.00
Portland, bowl, vegetable; w/lid, rnd 140.00
Riviera, bowl, vegetable; w/lid, rnd 140.00
Riviera, sugar bowl, w/lid 70.00
Romance (Green), platter, med, 14" 100.00
Romance (Maroon), platter, med, 14" 100.00
Rose Marie, bowl, vegetable; w/lid, rnd 140.00
Royal Court, cup & saucer 55.00
Royal Court, sugar bowl, w/lid 60.00
Selma, bowl, vegetable; w/lid, rnd 140.00
Shelledge (White), coffeepot 150.00
Sherwood, bowl, rimmed soup 40.00
Sherwood, bowl, vegetable; oval 170.00
Sherwood, gravy boat 75.00
Stansbury, bowl, vegetable; w/lid 125.00
Stansbury, platter, sm, 12" 80.00
Suzanne, bowl, vegetable; w/lid, gold trim 210.00
Suzanne, cup & saucer 30.00
Suzanne, plate, dinner 35.00
Suzanne, sugar bowl, w/lid 60.00
Sweetheart, plate, dinner 50.00
Victoria, creamer 60.00
Victoria, gravy boat 130.00
Victoria, platter, med 130.00
Webster, charger 50.00
Webster, gravy boat, w/underplate 115.00
Wedding Ring, bowl, vegetable; oval, 10" 240.00
Wedding Ring, coffeepot 460.00
Wedding Ring, creamer 140.00
Wedding Ring, cup & saucer 100.00
Wedding Ring, platter, med, 14" 375.00
Wedding Ring, sugar bowl, w/lid 155.00
Westminister, coffeepot 150.00
Westvale, bowl, vegetable; rnd, w/lid 140.00
Woodbine, coffeepot 100.00

Syrups

Values are for old, original syrups. Beware of reproductions and watch handle area for cracks! See also various manufacturers (such as Northwood) and specific types of glass. Our coadvisors are Jeff Bradfield and Dale MacAllister; they are listed in the Directory under Virginia. See also Pattern Glass.

Acorn, gr 275.00
Acorn, Peach Bloom 275.00
Artichoke, clear 75.00
Beatty Honeycomb, wht opal, pewter lid 300.00
Bellflower, clear 500.00
Big Windows, wht opal 250.00
Bulging Loops, pk cased 375.00
Button Arches, ruby stain 325.00
Catherine Ann, milk glass 115.00
Cord Drapery, amber 425.00
Cordova, clear 135.00
Cosmos, milk glass, decor 275.00

Dahlia, amber 85.00
Daisy & Button w/Crossbars, bl 175.00
Eyewinker, clear 135.00
Fleur-de-Lis 115.00
Fostoria's Priscilla, emerald gr w/gold 475.00

Grape and Leaf, blue opaque, 5¾", $325.00.

Guttate, cased glossy pk 300.00
Hercules Pillar, bl 250.00
Hobb's Hobnail, cranberry, shiny (undamaged points) 325.00
Jeweled Heart, bl 350.00
Klondike, clear 200.00
Loop, clear 90.00
Nail, ruby stain 300.00
Paneled Herringbone, gr 195.00
Red Block, clear w/ruby stain 225.00
Ring Band, custard w/EX gold 425.00
Ring Neck Coin Spot, bl opal 325.00
Roman Rosette, ruby stain 250.00
Shoshone, amber flashed, rare 350.00
Sunken Honeycomb, ruby stain 225.00
Sunset, bl opaque 300.00
Thumbprint (Argus Thumbprint) 150.00
Torpedo, ruby stain 250.00
Washington (state pattern) 175.00
Wild Iris, milk glass w/decor 175.00
Windows Swirled, bl opal 525.00
X-Ray, gr w/gold trim 300.00
Zipper Border, ruby stain, etched 300.00

Target Balls

Prior to 1880 when the clay pigeon was invented, blown glass target balls were used extensively for shotgun competitions. Approximately 2¾" in diameter, these balls were hand blown into a three-piece mold. All have a ragged hole where the blowpipe was twisted free. Target balls date from approximately 1840 (English) to World War I, although they were most widely used in the 1870 – 1880 period. Common examples are unmarked except for the blower's code — dots, crude numerals, etc. Some balls were embossed in a dot or diamond pattern so they were more likely to shatter when struck by shot, and some have names and/or patent dates. When evaluating condition, bubbles and other minor manufacturing imperfections are acceptable; cracks are not. The prices below are for mint condition examples.

Bogardus' Glass Ball Pat'd Apr 10 1877, amber, overall hobnails, 2⅝"..3,500.00
Bogardus' Glass Ball Pat'd April 10 1877, amber, Am, 2¾" 400.00
Bogardus' Glass Ball Pat'd April 10 1877, cobalt, 2¾" 800.00
Bogardus' Glass Ball Pat'd April 10 1877, olive gr, 2⅝"..........1,150.00
C Newman, Dmn Quilt, amber, rare, 2⅝" 825.00
CTB Co, blk pitch, Pat dates on bottom, Am 250.00
Dmn Quilt w/o center band, yel-amber, 2¾"..............................250.00

Dmn Quilt w/plain center band, cobalt, 2⅝" 250.00
Dmn Quilt w/shooter emb in 2 panels, clear, English 300.00
Dmn Quilt w/shooter emb in 2 panels, cobalt, English 725.00
Dmn Quilt w/shooter emb in 2 panels, deep moss gr, English 575.00
Dmn Quilt w/shooter emb in 2 panels, gr or purple, English.......500.00
Dmn Quilt w/shooter emb in 2 panels, med gr, English 375.00
Emb dmns, dk amber w/hint of red, 2⅝" 325.00
Emb dmns, dk cobalt, 2¾" 550.00
For Hockey's Pat Trap, gr, English 850.00
For Hockey's Pat Trap, gr aqua, 2⅜" 900.00
Glashuttenewotte Un Charlottenburg, clear, emb dmns, 2⅝" 700.00
Hobnail w/horizontal ribs along seams, yel-amber, 2¾".............800.00
Horizontal bands (7), tobacco amber, 2⅝" 200.00
Horizontal ribs (2) intersect w/2 vertical, cobalt, 2⅝" 120.00
Horizontal ribs (7), root beer amber, 3-pc mold, 2⅝" 725.00
Ilmenau (Thur) Sophiehutte, amber, Dmn Quilt, Germany 425.00
Ira Paine's Filled Ball Pat Oct 23 1877, amber, Am....................250.00
Ira Paine's Filled Ball Pat Oct 23 1877, other than amber, Am ..800.00
L Jones Gunmaker Blackburn ___Shire, cobalt, emb dmns, English, 2⅝".150.00
Man shooting, pk amethyst, emb dmns, 2⅝" 600.00
NB Glass Works Perth, other than pale gr, English 200.00
NB Glass Works Perth, pale gr, English..100.00
Plain, clear w/mold mks 1,000.00
Plain, cobalt w/mold mks 150.00
Plain, dk grape amethyst w/mold mks, 2¾" dia 250.00
Plain, dk teal gr w/mold mks, 2¾" 300.00
Plain, pk amethyst w/mold mks, 2⅝" 250.00
Smooth sphere, yel olive, GO emb on base, b3m, 2⅝" 500.00
T Jones, Gunmaker, Blackburn, cobalt, English, 2⅝" 450.00
Van Cutsem A St Quentin, cobalt, 2¾" dia 100.00
WW Greener, St Mary's Works, various colors, English, ea 350.00

Related Memorabilia

Clay birds, Winchester, Pat May 29 1917, 1 flight in box 100.00
Pitch bird, blk DUVROCK...1.00
Shell, dummy, w/single window, any brand 35.00
Shell, dummy shotgun, Winchester, window w/powder, 6" 125.00
Shell set, dummy, Gamble Stores, 2 window shells, 3 cut out.....125.00
Shell set, dummy shotgun, Peters, 6 window shells+full box.......175.00
Shotshell loader, rosewood/brass, Parker Bros, Pat 1884 ....50.00
Target, Am, sheet metal, rod ends mk Pat Feb 8 '21, set 25.00
Target, BUST-O, blk or wht breakable wafer 20.00
Thrower, oak wood base, heavy steel spring, leather wrap, ca 1900, EX.1,200.00
Trap, Chamberlain Cartridge...Nov 7th 05...USA, CI, 21½" L, EX .1,500.00
Trap, DUVROCK, w/blk pitch birds 250.00
Trap, MO-SKEET-O, w/birds 150.00

Tartan Glass

Tartan glass is accredited to Henry G. Richardson at Wordsley Flint Glass Works near Stourbridge, England. Glass threads were arranged to form a plaid similar to Tartan. Tartan glass was registered February 24, 1886.

Shade, pastel lattice motif, ruffled top, mk, 4½x9" 525.00
Vase, cranberry w/bl & wht, HP floral branches, Harrach, 9½" ..500.00

Tea Caddies

Because tea was once regarded as a precious commodity, special boxes called caddies were used to store the tea leaves. They were made from various materials: porcelain, carved and inlaid woods, and metals ranging from painted tin or tole to engraved silver. Our advisor for this category is Tina Carter; she is listed in the Directory under California.

Burl w/bombay-shaped sides & front, center w/glass bowl, 10x15x10" ..300.00
Burl w/inlay, ivory escutcheon, hinged lid, claw ft, 8x13x7" 1,380.00
Cherry vnr/inlay, faux fluting on corner panels, octagonal, 5x5x4" ..700.00
Figured mahog w/band & escutcheon inlay, 3 tin liners, 6x6x11" .440.00
Fruitwood, pear shape, 1800s, wear/sm crack, 6" 1,645.00
Fruitwood w/red pnt remnants, apple shape, 1800, 5" 6,400.00
Glass, bl-gr fiery opal w/emb figures & banners, wht metal cap, 5" ..110.00
Mahog vnr, trn bun ft, fitted int, English, 7x12x6" 330.00
Maple w/varnished traces of int foil, pear shape, 5½", VG 1,430.00
Oak w/brass plaques w/cherubs/angels/faces, brass finial, 7x10x5" .350.00
Rosewood Regency sarcophagus w/brass inlay, compartments, 12x9x6" .2,100.00
Satinwood w/inlay mahog dmns, silver pull, 6x12x6" 1,380.00
Silver, canted corners, reeded base, monogram, Pent Symonds, 1715, 5" ..1,880.00
Silver, sq, pineapple finial, armorial, Crouch/Hannam, 1800, 4", pr.1,200.00
Smoke-pnt tin, emb brass knop, shield-shaped escutcheon, 5x3x4" ..175.00
Sterling, eng/emb house by stream/florals/etc, Kirk & Son, 4" ..1,175.00
Teak w/burled vnr, molded base/beveled lid, Oriental, 7x5x5" 385.00
Tortoise-shell vnr, brass mts, fitted int, 19th C, 4⅜x4⅜x5" 900.00
Tortoise-shell vnr w/silver inlay/escutcheon, brass ball ft, 8" L, EX .1,045.00
Various woods w/inlay line/X-banding/3 shells, losses/damage, 8" L.770.00

Tea Leaf Ironstone

Tea Leaf Ironstone became popular in the 1880s when middle-class American housewives became bored with the plain white stone china that English potters had been exporting to this country for nearly a century. The original design has been credited to Anthony Shaw of Burslem, who decorated the plain ironstone with a hand-painted copper lustre design of bands and leaves. Originally known as Lustre Band and Sprig, the pattern has since come to be known as Tea Leaf Lustre. It was produced with minor variations by many different firms both in England and the United States. By the early 1900s, it had become so commonplace that it had lost much of its appeal.

Items marked Red Cliff are reproductions made from 1950 until 1980 for this distributing and decorating company of Chicago, Illinois. Hall China provided many of the blanks.

Our advice for this category comes from Home Place Antiques, whose address is listed in the Directory under Illinois.

Bowl, sq w/scalloped rim, Meakin, ca 1885, 2⅞x8¼x8½", EX......40.00
Bowl, vegetable; Edwards, w/lid, 1880s, 3x10½x6" 95.00
Bowl, vegetable; Fishhook, Alfred Meakin, w/lid, 10½".............110.00
Bowl, vegetable; oval, Clementson, w/lid, 12" 125.00
Bowl, vegetable; Wrapped Sydenham, Shaw, w/lid, ca 1860, sm...95.00
Butter dish, Bamboo, Meakin, w/lid, 4½x6" 145.00
Cake plate, Bamboo, Meakin, EX 75.00
Cake plate, hdls, Edge Malkin & Co, 10" 150.00
Coffeepot, Bordered Fuchsia, Anthony Shaw, 1860s 275.00
Coffeepot, Daisy 'n' Chain, AJ Wilkinson, 1890s, 8½" 165.00
Coffeepot, Favorite shape, Grindley, rope-like hdl 245.00
Coffeepot, Niagara Fan, Shaw style, ca 1856 ....275.00
Coffeepot, Niagara shape, Walley, 1842-67, 10" 525.00
Coffeepot, Simplicity, Powell & Bishop, 1880s 95.00
Coffeepot, 6 sided w/low emb ribs, H Burgess, 8¼" 185.00
Creamer, low emb ribs, H Burgess, 5¼"..145.00
Creamer, Meakin, 5½" 125.00
Cup & saucer, H Burgess, 2½x3½", 6", pr....................................60.00
Cup & saucer, handleless; Morning Glory, early 1800s.................55.00
Cup & saucer, Teaberry, Prairie shape, Clementson......................95.00
Egg cup, Boston shape, unmk...325.00

Egg cup, Morning Glory, 1⅞x1⅞" **375.00**
Ewer, Maidenhair Fern, Wilkinson, 12½x8" **195.00**
Gravy boat, W&E Corn, 8½" **65.00**
Ladle, 2½" dia, 7½" **370.00**
Mug, shaving; Maidenhair Fern, AJ Wilkinson, 1890s **275.00**
Pitcher, Bow & Tassel shape, H Burgess, 8½" **165.00**
Pitcher, milk; Lily of the Valley, 1860s **225.00**
Pitcher, Shaw, ca 1860, 5½x4" **125.00**
Plate, bread & butter; Adams, ca 1960 ....**10.00**
Plate, dinner; Adams **22.00**
Plate, Lily of the Valley, Shaw, 7⅞" **35.00**
Plate, Meakin, 9¾" **45.00**
Plate, Wedgwood, 8⅝" **20.00**
Platter, Brocade, Meakin, ca 1879+, 15x10½" **85.00**
Platter, Meakin, ca 1898, 14x10" **70.00**
Platter, Meakin, 13x9½" **55.00**
Platter, Mellor Taylor & Co, 10½x8½" **45.00**
Platter, Wilkinson, 16x11¼" **75.00**
Relish, DeSoto shape, Shaw, ca 1865 ....**95.00**
Shaving mug, Plain Round shape, Wilkinson, 1890s **195.00**
Sugar bowl, Heavy Square, Clementson, w/lid **145.00**
Sugar bowl, low emb ribs, H Burgess, w/lid, 6½" **165.00**
Sugar bowl, Morning Glory, Portland, w/lid, Elsmore & Forster, 7¾".**215.00**
Syrup, w/pewter lid, Vintage Beauty, Anthony Shaw, 1860s **625.00**
Tureen, sauce; Shaw, 6¾x8", w/emb 9" underplate+emb ladle....**850.00**
Underplate, Elsmore & Forster, ca 1860, 9x7" **95.00**
Wash bowl, Meakin, 15" **130.00**
Waste bowl, H Burgess, 3x5⅝" **45.00**

Teapots

Teapots have become popular collectibles in recent years with a surge in tea shops featuring tea, teapots and serving afternoon tea. Collectors should be aware of modern teapots which imitate older, similar versions. Study the types of pottery, porcelain and china, as well as the marks. Multicolored, detailed marks over the glaze represent modern pieces. Teapots made in the last thirty years are quite collectible but generally don't demand the same prices as their antique counterparts.

A wide range of teapots can be found by the avid collector. Those from before 1880 are more apt to be found in museums or sold at quality auction houses. Almost every pottery and porcelain manufacturer in Asia, Europe and America have produced teapots. Some are purely decorative and whimsical, while others are perfect for brewing a pot of tea. Tea drinkers should beware of odd-shaped spouts which sputter and drip. Reproductions to be aware of: majolica styles with modern marks, Blue Willow which has been made continuously for almost two centuries, and those marked Made in China (older teapots have 'chop marks' in Chinese).

Refer to various manufacturers' names for further listings. Our advisor for this category is Tina M. Carter, listed in the Directory under California. Her book, *Teapots*, is available at bookstores or direct from the author.

Aluminum, red enameled w/blk ball finial, covered hdl, Japan, 1960 .**20.00**
Aluminum w/molded flowers, removable lid, unmk, mini, 1¼" **8.00**
Bear holding candy cane, paw spout, Made in Korea, Fitz & Floyd .**75.00**
Bluebird, HP, music box underneath/plays when lifted, Enesco, up to..**225.00**
Brn coralene w/gold decor, Made in Japan, 1950 ....**22.00**
Bunny figural, brn & wht w/mc details, Japan, late 1950s **20.00**
Castellon pattern, red/blk modern design, Villeroy & Boch, 1990...**150.00**
Cat figural, blk & wht w/pk bowl, Cortendorf W Germany label .**95.00**
Conch shell, similar to majolica, unmk Japan, ca 1950 ....**45.00**
Copper lustre poppies, Wade England, 4" **45.00**
Corn Poppy, Susie Cooper/Wedgwood, 1960s-70s, from $85 to **95.00**
Eastern Star decal on wht porc, Enesco, Japan, sm **50.00**

Floral, bright red on wht, bud finial, mk Italy, 1950s-60s, $50 to..**60.00**
Floral, purple on wht w/rattan bail hdl, Asuka Fine China Japan label..**30.00**
Floral etched on clear glass, Corning Pyrex...USA, 1930s-40s **150.00**
Floral HP on bone china, bl-gr trim, unmk, 3" **25.00**
Imari, London shape, Coalport, early 1800s **1,500.00**
Mermaid figural, EX details, Eliza Hurdle, Bristol England, modern...**250.00**
Nutcracker figural, Russ, China, 1980 ....**30.00**
Old Forge, English Country Crafts series, Sadler England **35.00**
Oriental-style doughnut form w/Canton-type decor, Made in China....**20.00**
Pembroke, bird & flowers, oval shape, mk Aynsley England **185.00**
Rose chintz, lg cabbage rose, creamware, Johnson Bros for Wedgwood ..**100.00**
Sairey Gamp figural, mk Beswick Ware, ca 1930 ....**85.00**
Snowman w/broom & snowball, hat is lid, Made in Korea, Fitz & Floyd ...**75.00**
South Bend IN souvenir w/gold o/l, mk Japan, 2" **15.00**
Tomato, glossy red, unmk, possibly Japan or USA, 1950s-60s **65.00**
Townhouse form, resin, Hamilton Gifts label, Korea, 1988, 6" **20.00**
Violet chintz, scalloped edge, Enesco, Japan **140.00**
Violets on wht swirled body w/gold, Enesco, Japan, from $45 to...**65.00**

Teco

Teco artware was made by the American Terra Cotta and Ceramic Company, located near Chicago, Illinois. The firm was established in 1886 and until 1901 produced only brick, sewer tile, and other redware. Their early glaze was inspired by the matt green made popular by Grueby. 'Teco Green' was made for nearly ten years. It was similar to Grueby's, yet with a subtle silver-gray cast. The company was one of the first in the United States to perfect a true crystalline glaze. The only decoration used was through the modeling and glazing techniques; no hand painting was attempted. Favored motifs were naturalistic leaves and flowers. The company broadened their lines to include garden pottery and faience tiles and panels. New matt glazes (browns, yellows, blue, and rose) were added to the green in 1910. By 1922 the artware lines were discontinued; the company was sold in 1930.

Values are dictated by size and shape, with architectural and organic forms being more desirable. Teco is usually marked with a vertical impressed device comprised of a large 'T' to the left of the remaining three letters.

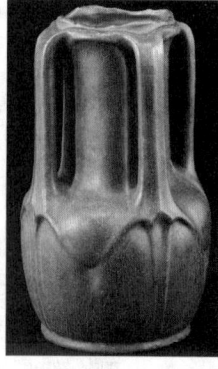

Vase, veined green matt, four organic handles, #223, 14¼x8½", NM, $12,000.00.

Bowl, gr, flattened form, 5¼", pr..**375.00**
Bowl, gr, horn-like shoulder protrusions, 3-leg, rstr, 3¼x4¾" **425.00**
Bowl, gr, incurvate rim, shallow, 4½" **220.00**
Ewer, gr, integral hdl, 4" **325.00**
Vase, bud; gr, rnd w/4 medial dimples, raised rim, 2¾" **400.00**
Vase, buff, bulbous w/3-sided rim, 4½x4" **400.00**
Vase, frothy gr/brn, experimental, angled rim hdls, 4x4" **800.00**
Vase, gr, dbl gourd, 4 buttress hdls forming openings at waist, 7", NM..**2,400.00**
Vase, gr, floral w/lg leaves, shouldered, 13" **8,000.00**
Vase, gr, molded/appl leaves, Wm Dodd, sm rpr, 12" **13,000.00**

Vase, gr, slightly bulbous, 5"...**425.00**
Vase, gr matt, 4 buttresses around slim cylinder, 6½", NM......**1,100.00**
Vase, gr w/charcoal, tulip mold, Moreau, rstr rim/base chips, 12".**3,000.00**
Vase, gr w/charcoal, waisted cylinder w/sm rim, 7".......................**850.00**
Vase, gr w/charcoal, 12 upright/bent appl leaves, rstr, 12x4½"..**9,000.00**
Vase, gr w/charcoal, 4 buttress hdls form opening at waist, 6x6".**2,900.00**
Vase, gr w/charcoal, 4 cutouts at top of cylinder, 14", NM....**11,000.00**
Vase, gr w/charcoal, 4 hdls emerge from rim flange, #172, rstr, 15"...**4,500.00**
Vase, gr w/lt charcoal, long neck caged w/4 buttresses, 6¾x3¼".**1,700.00**
Vase, gr/brn speckled, bulbous, 5½x5¼"..**1,300.00**
Vase, gray-gr, quatrefoil bud-like form, 8¾"...............................**1,725.00**
Vase, leathery ivory, 4 in-mold upright ½-ribs, lobed lip, 13x6"..**3,500.00**

Teddy Bear Collectibles

The story of Teddy Roosevelt's encounter with the bear cub has been oft recounted with varying degrees of accuracy, so it will suffice to say that it was as a result of this incident in 1902 that the teddy bear got his name. These appealing little creatures are enjoying renewed popularity with collectors today. To one who has not yet succumbed to their obvious charms, one bear seems to look very much like another. How to tell the older ones? Look for long snouts, jointed limbs, large feet and felt paws, long curving arms, and glass or shoe-button eyes. Most old bears have a humped back and are made of mohair stuffed with straw or excelsior. Cute expressions, original clothes, a nice personality, and, of course, good condition add to their value. Early Steiff bears in mint condition may go for a minimum of $150.00 per inch for a small bear up to $300.00 to $350.00 (sometimes even more) per inch for one 20" high or larger. These are easily recognized by the trademark button within the ear. Our advisor for this category is Candace Gunther; she is listed in the Directory under California. For further information we recommend *Teddy Bear Treasury* by Ken Yenke; and *Teddy Bears, Annalee's & Steiff Animals* (there are three in the series), by Margaret Fox Mandel. All are available from Collector Books.

See also Toys, Steiff.

Key: jtd — jointed

Bears

Bing, blond mohair, growler, late 1920s, 17", M, minimum value..**2,800.00**
Bing, brn mohair, clockwork mechanical, ca 1900, 8", EX, minimum value..**1,000.00**
Bing, cinnamon mohair, growler, jtd, 17", ca 1920, M, minimum value.**3,000.00**
Bing, cinnamon mohair, squeaker, jtd, lg ft pads, ca 1920, 9", NM..**2,000.00**
Bing, long tan mohair, growler, glass eyes, w/ID, 20", M, w/provenance....**15,000.00**
Chad Valley, long mohair, glass eyes/velveteen pads, jtd, 1950, 28", M..**750.00**
Chiltern, lt mohair, glass eyes, squeaker, 4 claws, 1947, 16", M..**325.00**
Columbia, brn mohair, Laughing Roosevelt, 18", M, minimum value.**3,000.00**
Electric Eye, long mohair, flashlight bulb eyes, jtd, 1914, 26", NM.**1,500.00**
English, tan mohair, long snout, glass eyes, jtd, ca 1930, 24", NM.**600.00**
Gund, wht mohair, growler, jtd, ca 1940, 12", M..........................**500.00**
Hermann, wht mohair, 1950, 9", stands on music box mk W Germany, M.**2,000.00**
Ideal, dense mohair, shoe button eyes, jtd, 1903, 18", M.........**5,500.00**
Merrythought, brn mohair, button eyes, growler, 3 claws, 1920s, 22", M..**950.00**
Petz, cinnamon mohair, jtd, glass eyes, over-sewn pads, 15", M..**750.00**
Schenker, wht sheepskin, amber glass eyes, red pads, 1950s, 13", M.**125.00**
Schuco, cinnamon mohair, yes-no, 1930s transitional style, 12", M.**1,000.00**
Schuco, head removes for lipstick/mirror/powder/puff, 1930s, 3½", M.**1,000.00**
Schuco, key-wind walker, blk metal shoes, ca 1912, 10", EX....**4,000.00**
Schuco, short caramel mohair, yes-no, jtd, 13", M...................**1,500.00**
Schuco, Tricky, gold mohair, glass eyes, jtd, 1950, 8", M.............**950.00**
Steiff, apricot mohair, squeaker, jtd, blank button, 1905, 15", NM..**7,500.00**
Steiff, beige mohair, jtd, brn floss/nose mouth, fat, 1960s, 6", M..**200.00**

Steiff, blond mohair, glass eyes, sm hump, ftd, pre-1920s, 5½", M.**550.00**
Steiff, clown, brn-tipped mohair, sewn-on hat, jtd, ID, 1926, 18", M..**4,500.00**
Steiff, gold curly mohair, growler, button eyes, jtd, 1917, 30", NM..**15,000.00**
Steiff, honey mohair, blank button, 5 claws, ca 1905, 10", EX..**2,500.00**
Steiff, long apricot mohair, jtd, blank button, ca 1905, 20", M.**9,000.00**
Steiff, long mohair, button eyes, growler, 4 claws, ID, 1908, 24", M..**10,000.00**
Steiff, wht mohair, jtd head, on wheels, ca 1905, 8x10", EX...**3,000.00**
Steiff, wht mohair, sm head, lg hump, ca 1909, 18", M............**7,500.00**
Swiss, tan mohair, blk button eyes, jtd, 1950-60, 6½", M...........**125.00**
Unmk, brn mohair, glass eyes, plastic nose, felt tongue, ftd, 19", EX.**135.00**
Unmk, brn mohair, glass eyes, squeaker, orig ribbon, 6½", EX......**90.00**
Unmk, lt gold mohair, button eyes, embr nose, jtd, ca 1908, 11', NM.**550.00**

Related Memorabilia

Book, Mother Goose's Teddy Bears, FL Cavally, 1907, EX..........**450.00**
Book, Teddy Bear Book, Whitman, 1940, EX.................................**75.00**
Brooch, teddy figural, silver-tone, yel Lucite tummy, Marvella, 1¼".**18.00**
Coat, Teddy Bear, brn mohair, 6 brass teddy buttons, 1907, child sz, M..**2,000.00**
Mug, Busy Bear, Christmas decor on wht ceramic.......................**150.00**
Mug, Theodore Bear as aviator, Wade, 3x3"....................................**5.00**
Paper dolls, Crystal Collins Teddy Bear Paper Dolls, NY, 1983, M..**10.00**
Planter, teddy beside tree, brn/aqua, Am Bisque, 5¼x4", EX........**12.50**
Plate, Christmas Tree & Teddy Bear, porc, Russ, 8"......................**10.00**
Plate, Teddy's Spring Bouquet, Bengry's Teddy Bears series, 8", MIB.**35.00**
Plate, 3 scenes from Roosevelt Bears book, ceramic, minimum value..**3,000.00**
Postcard, teddy bear, I'm Kelly, Found at Last, 1909, EX.................**7.00**
Rug, teddies having picnic, cotton pile, Belgium, 22x38", EX......**65.00**
Shakers, teddy holding grapes, ceramic, Japan, pr.........................**10.00**
Sheet music, The Teddy Bears' Picnic, JW Bratton, 1907, EX....**100.00**
Thimble, teddy transfer on wht, Enesco, 1978, M.........................**15.00**

Telephones

Since Alexander Graham Bell's first successful telephone communication, the phone itself has undergone a complete evolution in style as well as efficiency. Early models, especially those wall types with ornately carved oak boxes, are of special interest to collectors. Also of value are the candlestick phones from the early part of the century and any related memorabilia.

Automatic Bell, Model #40, dial, rnded Deco shape, 1930s..........**75.00**
Automatic Electric, dial candlestick, 1910s, rstr..........................**250.00**
Automatic Electric, Model #47, 2-line version, dial, 1930s, rstr.**230.00**
Candlestick, brass, rotary dial, blk earpc, early 1900s, rstr...........**275.00**
Kellogg, Model #925, ashtray type, 1930s, rstr............................**150.00**
Kellogg, Model #1000, redbar type, 1930s, rstr **150.00**
Kellogg, NP candlestick, Pat dates from Nov 6 1901 to Apr 14 1908..**110.00**
Leich type, Model #90, ringer in base, 1930s, rstr.......................**135.00**
Northern Electric type 1, wide & shallow, dial, 1930s, rstr **150.00**
Stromberg Carlson, fat type #1212, dial, 1930s............................**200.00**
Western Electric, Model #202 w/E1 handset, dial, 1920s, rstr.....**175.00**
Western Electric, Model #202 w/F1 handset, dial, 1920s, rstr.....**150.00**
Western Electric, Model #302, metal, Dreyfuss design, 1937, rstr.**85.00**
Western Electric, Model #553, dial, wall stype, 1910s, rstr **160.00**
Western Electric/Northern Electric, non-dial candlestick, 1910s, EX.**150.00**
Western/Northern Electric, blk 3-slot pay phone, 1950s, rstr......**250.00**

Novelty Telephones

Bart Simpson, 3-D figure, eyes flash w/ring, Columbia, 1990s, M.**30.00**
Batmobile (Batman Forever), MIB, from $35 to............................**50.00**
Care Bears, purple, intercom system only, 1983, MIB...................**50.00**
Flintstones, gray w/red horn-shaped handset, 5-hole dial, 1960s, EX.**80.00**

Garfield, United Features Syndicate, 1978-81, 5x10½", EX..........45.00
Ghostbusters, M..100.00
Golf ball on gr base, 4x8¼"...20.00
Kermit the Frog, candlestick, built-in ringer, modular cord, NM ..60.00
Little Mermaid, seashell, Ariel on handset, lights up, Disney, M ..90.00
Mallard duck decoy, 12½", EX...50.00
Mickey Mouse, lighted dial, AT&T, early 1990s, MIB 190.00
Mickey Mouse figural w/base key pad, Synanon, Disney, 1988, 10½" .95.00
Pepsi Cola vending machine, wall mt, EX....................................50.00
Power Rangers, NM..25.00
Roy Rogers, plastic wall-type, 1950s, 9x9", EX............................50.00
Snoopy, as Joe Cool, 1980s, MIB..55.00
Spiderman, REC Sound, 1994, M (EX box).................................30.00
Strawberry Shortcake, Kenner, 1984, EX 50.00
Super Bowl XIX, full-sz helmet, w/handset, NM..........................70.00
Ziggy, 1989, MIB...75.00

Blue Bell Paperweights

First issued in the early 1900s, bell-shaped glass paperweights were used as 'give-aways' and/or presented to telephone company executives as tokens of appreciation. The paperweights were used to prevent stacks of papers from blowing off the desks in the days of overhead fans. Over the years they have all but vanished — some taken by retiring employees, others accidentally broken. The weights came to be widely used for advertising by individual telephone companies; and as the smaller companies merged to form larger companies, more and more new paperweights were created. They were widely distributed with the opening of the first transcontinental telephone line in 1915. The bell-shaped paperweight embossed 'Opening of Trans-Pacific Service, Dec. 23, 1931,' in peacock blue glass is very rare, and the price is negotiable. (Weights with 'open' in the price field are also rare and impossible to accurately evaluate.) In 1972 the first Pioneer bell paperweights were made to sell to raise funds for the charities the Pioneers support. This has continued to the present day. These bell paperweights have also become 'collectibles.' For further study we recommend *Blue Bell Paperweights, Telephone Pioneers of America Bells and Other Telephone Related Items, 2003 Revised Edition*, by Jacqueline Linscott Barnes; she is listed in the Directory under Florida.

Bell System/C&P/Telephone Company & Associated Companies, ice blue..250.00
Bell System/New York/Telephone Co, ice Blue..............................95.00
Bell/Telephone/Manufacturing Co/Anvers Belgique, cobalt............OPEN
Bell/Telephone/Manufacturing Co/Anvers Belgique, peacock.........OPEN
Missouri & Kansas Telephone Company, cobalt...........................75.00
Nebraska Telephone Company, peacock.....................................225.00
Southern Bell Telephone & Telegraph Company, cobalt............200.00
Time Is Money/Save It/...North Louisiana Telephone Co, peacock...OPEN
West Virginia Centennial 1863-1963, cobalt..............................150.00
Western Electric Company, peacock 225.00

Large Telephone Pioneers of America (TPA) Commemoratives

Break-Up of the Bell System, dk peacock, 1984 ....45.00
Diamond Jubilee 1911-1986, 1985, yel......................................85.00
Nevada Bell, blk glass..100.00
Pacific Bell/1984-1994, crystal w/bl swirls 45.00
TPA, 1974, carnival 35.00
TPA, 1982, cobalt..60.00
TPA, 1988, neodymium 80.00
TPA, 2000, wht opal 50.00

Small Commemorative Bells

Bell System, Chesapeake-Potomac, ice bl 150.00

Bell System/Bell System, cobalt 45.00
Bell System/Bell System, ice bl 125.00
Bell System/Bell System, ruby red...60.00
Bell System/Universal Service, peacock 125.00
Save Time...Telephone/Saves Steps...Telephone, cobalt............125.00
25th Anniversary American Bell Association, cobalt 150.00

Telescopes

Antique telescopes were sold in large quantities to sailors, astronomers, voyeurs, and the military but survive in relatively few numbers because their glass lenses and brass tubes were easily damaged. Even scarcer are antique reflecting telescopes, which use a polished metal mirror to magnify the world. Telescopes used for astronomy give an inverted image, but most old telescopes were used for marine purposes and have more complicated optics that show the world right-side up. Spyglasses are smaller, hand-held telescopes that collapse into their tube and focus by drawing out the tube to the correct length. A more compact instrument, with three or four sections, is also more delicate, and sailors usually preferred a single-draw spyglass. They are almost always of brass, occasionally of nickel silver or silver plate, and usually covered with leather, or sometimes a beautiful rosewood veneer. Solid wood barrel spyglasses (with a brass draw tube) tend to be early and rare. Before the middle of the 1800s, makers put their names in elaborate script on the smallest draw tube, but as 1900 approached, most switched to plain block printing. British instruments from World War One made by a variety of makers are commonly found, sharing a format of a 2" objective, 30" long with three draws extended, a tapered main tube, and sometimes having low- and high-power oculars and beautiful leather cases. U.S. Navy WWII spyglasses are quite common but have outstanding optics and focus by twisting the eyepiece, which makes them weather-proof. The Quartermaster (Q.M.) 16x spyglass is 31" long, with a tapered barrel and a 2½" objective. The Officer of the Deck (O.D.D.) is a 23" cylinder with a 1½" objective. Very massive, short, brass telescopes are usually gun sights or ship equipment and have little interest to most collectors. World War II marked the first widespread use of coated optics, which can be recognized by a colored film on the objective lens. Collectible post-WWII telescopes include early refractors by Unitron or Fecker and reflectors by Cave or Questar. Modern spotting scopes often use a prism to erect the image and are of great interest if made by the best makers, including Nikon and Zeiss. Several modern makers still use lacquered brass, and many replica instruments have been produced.

A telescope with no maker's name is much less interesting than a signed instrument, and 'Made in France' is the most common mark on old spyglasses. Dollond of London made instruments for two hundred years and this is probably the most common name on antiques; but because of their important technical innovations and very high quality, Dollond telescopes are always valuable. Bardou, Paris, telescopes are also of very high quality. Bardou is another relatively common name, since they were a prolific maker for many years, and their spyglasses were sold by Sears. Alvan Clark and Sons were the most prolific early American makers, in operation from the 1850s to the 1920s, and their astronomical telescopes are of great historical import.

Spyglasses are delicate instruments that were subject to severe use under all weather conditions. Cracked or deeply scratched optics are impossible to repair and lower the value considerably. Most lenses are doublets, two lenses glued together, and deteriorated cement is common. This looks like crazed glaze and is fairly difficult to repair. Dents in the tube and damaged or missing leather covering can usually be fixed. The best test of a telescope is to use it, and the image should be sharp and clear. Any accessories, eyepieces, erecting prisms, or quality cases can add significantly to value. The following prices assume that the telescope is in very good to fine condition and give the objective lens (obj.) diameter, which is the most important measurement of a telescope.

Our advisor for this category is Peter Abrahams, who studies and collects telescopes and other optics. Please contact him, especially to exchange reference material. (See his comments concerning on-line auctions under Binoculars; they are applicable to telescopes as well.) Mr. Abrahams is listed in the Directory under Oregon. (Please include SASE with questions.)

Key:
obj — objective lens   ODD — Officer of the Deck

Adams, George; 2" reflecting, brass cabriole tripod 3,500.00
Bardou & Son, Paris, 4-draw, 50 mm obj, leather, 36" 250.00
Bausch & Lomb, 1-draw, 45 mm obj, wrinkled pnt, 17" 90.00
Brashear, 3½" obj, brass, tripod, w/eyepcs 4,500.00
Cary, London (script) 2" obj, tripod, w/3 eyepcs 3,000.00
Clark, Alvan; 4" obj, 48", iron mt on wooden legs.................9,000.00
Criterion RV-6 Dynascope, 6" reflector, 1960s...........................500.00
Dallmeyer, London (script), 5-draw, 2½" obj, SP, 49" 800.00
Dollond, London (block), 2-draw, 2" obj, leather cover 290.00
Dollond, London (script), brass, 3" obj, 40", on tripod 2,900.00
Dollond, London (script), 2-draw, 2" obj, leather cover 450.00
France or Made in France, 3-draw, 30 mm obj, lens cap................80.00
McAlister (script), brass, 3½" obj, 45", tripod 3,000.00
Messer, London Day & Night, brass, mahog hand grip, 2-draw, 1860s, EX..200.00
Mogey, brass, 3" obj, 40", on tripod, w/4 eyepcs 4,000.00
Negretti & Zambra, 2½" obj, equatorial mt, 36", tripod 2,500.00
Plossl, Wein, 2½" obj, Dialytic optics, 24", table-top tripod....4,000.00
Queen & Co (script), 6-draw, 70 mm obj, wood vnr, 50" 1,000.00
Questar, reflecting, on astro mt, 1950s, 3½" dia 3,000.00
R&J Beck, 2" obj, 24", table-top tripod w/cabriole legs...........2,500.00
Short, James; 3" dia reflecting, brass cabriole tripod.................4,000.00
Student's No 52, altazimuth to equatorial, 36" focal length, w/stand ..125.00
Tel Sct Regt Mk 2 S (many maker's names), UK, WWI 120.00
Unitron, 4" obj, wht, 60", on tripod, many accessories 3,000.00
Unmk, brass, 2" obj, spyglass, leather cover, from $150 to 300.00
Unmk, brass, 2" obj, stand w/cabriole legs 1,200.00
US Military, brass, very heavy, from $100 to...........................300.00
US Navy, QM Spyglass, 16X, MK II, in box.................................220.00
US Navy (ODD), Bu. Ships, Mk II, 10-Power, 1943 ....125.00
Vion, Paris, 40 mm obj, 3-draw, 40-Power, 21", leather..............110.00
Wollensak Mirroscope, 1950s, 12x2" dia, leather case.................300.00
Wood bbl, rnd taper, 1½" obj, sgn, 1800s....................................350.00
Wood bbl, 8-sided, 1½" obj, 1700s, 30" 1,500.00
Zeiss, brass, 60 mm obj, w/eyepcs & porro prism, tripod 1,700.00
Zeiss Asiola, 60 mm obj, prism spotting scope, pre-WWII 650.00

Televisions

Many early TVs have escalated in value over the last few years. Pre-1943 sets (usually with only one to five channels) are often worth $500.00 to $5,000.00. Unusually styled small-screen wooden 1940s TVs are 'hot'; but most metal, Bakelite, and large-screen sets are still shunned by collectors. 1950s color TVs with 16" or smaller tubes are valuable; larger color sets are not. One of our advisors for this category is Harry Poster, author of *Poster's Radio & Television Price Guide 1920 – 1990, 2nd Edition*; he is listed in the Directory under New Jersey. Another source of information is *Collector's Guide to Vintage Televisions* by Bryan Durbal and Glenn Bubenheimer (Collector Books).

Key: t/t — table-top

Admiral, #19A11, brn Bakelite t/t w/checkerboard grill, 1948, 7" ...125.00
Air King, A-1000, mahog t/t, 1948, 10" 120.00
Ansley, #2121TM, mahog, t/t, chassis TE-289, 1949, 12" 65.00

CBS-Columbia, U22Co5, wood console, UHF tuner, 1955, 21"..30.00
Crosley, #407, mahog t/t, Dumont continuous tuner, 1949, 12"....75.00
DuMont, RA-101, blond, TV/radio/phono console, Hamshire, 1947, 20".500.00
Emerson, #650, mahog t/t, 1949, 12"...70.00
Garod, #10TZ21, blond t/t, TV/radio, Malibu, 1949, 10" 180.00
General Electric, #12T3, mahog t/t, 1949, 12"...............................75.00
General Electric, #811, mahog console, glass screen, 1949, 10" 75.00
Jackson Industries, #500, wood t/t, 1949, 10".............................150.00
Majestic, #12T2, wood t/t, 1950, 12"..75.00
Motorola, #7-VT2, Bakelite t/t, chassis TS-18, 1949, 7"..............125.00
National, TV-12W, mahog t/t, 1949, 12" 120.00
Panasonic, TR-1010P, plastic, portable, transistor, w/magnifier, 1981 ...70.00
Philco, #50-T1403, mahog t/t, rnd top cabinet, 1950, 12" 125.00
RCA, #17-T-211, wood console, 1953, 17" 65.00
RCA, #8TV323, wood console, TV/radio, dbl doors, 1949, 10" ...75.00
Regal, #1207, mahog t/t, 1948, 12"..80.00
Sentinel, #412, wood t/t, 1949, 10" 60.00
Sony, FD-210, plastic, transistor, Watchman, 1988, 1¾" 140.00
Sylvania, #1-246, mahog t/t, chassis #1-138, 1950, 12" 35.00
Tele-King, #512, wood t/t, 1949, 12" 75.00
Transvision, #7CL, wood t/t, 1947, 7" 275.00
Westinghouse, G2322, Bakelite t/t, chassis #23G22, Claridge, 1950, 12".95.00
Zenith, #28T926E, blond t/t, chassis #28F25, Saratoga, 1949, 12" ..175.00

Philco Predictas and Related Items

Made in the years between 1958 and 1960, Philco Predictas have become one of the most sought after lines of televisions in the postwar era. Predictas are now over forty years old, yet their atom-age styling is just as futuristic today as it was in 1958. As we move into the new millenium, the Predicta line will continue to be highly collectible. Philco Predictas feature a swivel or separate enclosed picture tube and radical cabinet designs.

Please note that recently much has been said about sets equipped with the UHF option. Even though few sets were ordered with this option, it in no way makes the set 'more rare.' Advanced collectors who feel it is important for their collection should not pay more than $50.00 over the price of an equal non-UHF set.

The values given here are for as-found, average, clean, complete, unrestored sets, running or not, that have good picture tubes. Predictas that are missing parts or have damaged viewing screens will have a lower value. Above average Predictas will have much higher values. Please keep in mind that Predictas that have been completely professionally restored to as new in appearance as well as electronically can easily bring four to five times the stated values. Our advisor for Predicta televisions is David Weddington; he is listed in the Directory under Tennessee.

**G4242 Holiday 21"
table-top, wood cabinet
with blond finish,
$455.00.** (Photo courtesy
David Weddington)

G4242 Holiday 21" t/t, wood cabinet, mahog finish...................400.00
G4654 Barber-Pole 21" console, boomerang front leg, blond......725.00
G4654 Barber-Pole 21" console, boomerang front leg, mahog 650.00

G4710 Tandem 21" separate screen w/25' cable, mahog finish ...**625.00**
G4720 Stereo Tandem w/matching 1606S phonoamp, mahog .**1,100.00**
G4720 Stereo Tandem 21" separate screen, 4 brass legs, mahog .**900.00**
H3406 Motel 17" t/t, metal cabinet, cloth grill, no antenna.......**275.00**
H3408 Debutante 17" t/t, cloth grill, w/antenna, charcoal **375.00**
H3410 Princess 17" t/t, metal grill, plastic tuner window...........**400.00**
H3410 Princess 17" t/t, orig metal stand, red finish....................**500.00**
H3412 Siesta 17" t/t, w/clock-timer above tuner, gold finish **550.00**
H4730 Danish Modern 21" console, 4 fin-shaped legs, mahog finish .**950.00**
H4744 Townhouse 21" room-divider, walnut shelves, brass finish .**1,400.00**
17DRP4 picture tube, MIB, replacement for all 17" t/t Predictas.**175.00**
21EAP4 or 21FDP4 picture tube, MIB, replacement for all 21" Predictas.**275.00**

Tennis Rackets

Early tennis rackets (pre-1940) generally exhibit these characteristics: head shape — may be oval, flat-top, transitional flat-top, triangular (or other); throat wedge — the triangular section of wood at the junction of the head and the handle may be concave, convex, solid or laminated; handle — most from this circa are not covered by leather and are either combed (grooved) or checkered wood, and some may have cork handles or enlargements at the butt end. Values vary, dependent on age, rarity, style, and condition. Brand and model are important, and all identifying decals should be legible and in good condition. Rackets from 1880 to 1940 range in price from $10.00 to $20.00 for the more common examples to hundreds of dollars for rare models such as the Hazel's Streamline.

Our advisor for this category is Donald Jones; he is listed in the Directory under Georgia. In the listings that follow, values apply to examples in excellent condition.

Key:
cx-lam — convex laminated   tran — transitional
cx-s — convex solid

AJ Reach, Driver, concave wedge, combed hdl, oval head, 1920..**75.00**
E Kent, Duchess, concave wedge, bulbous hdl, oval head, 1930 .**120.00**
Hazel's Streamline, branched wedge, leather hdl, oval head, 1935 .**600.00**
Horsman, Elberton, concave wedge, smooth hdl, flat-top head, 1885.**450.00**
Iver Johnson, Special, cx-s wedge, bulbous hdl, tran head, 1900..**175.00**
Magnon, Superior, concave wedge, combed hdl, oval head, 1928.**75.00**
Slazenger, Demon, cx-lam wedge, fishtail hdl, oval head, 1910 ..**250.00**
Spaulding, Park, cx-s wedge, combed hdl, flat-top head, 1895....**450.00**
Wright-Ditson, Hub, cx-s wedge, checkered hdl, oval head, 1890..**175.00**
Wright-Ditson, Octagon, concave head, combed hdl, oval head, 1895.**120.00**
Wright-Ditson, Star, cx-s wedge, combed hdl, oval head, 1904 ..**135.00**

Teplitz

Teplitz, in Bohemia, was an active art pottery center at the turn of the century. The Amphora Pottery Works was only one of the firms that operated there. (See Amphora.) Art Nouveau and Art Deco styles were favored, and much of the ware was hand decorated with the primary emphasis on vases and figurines. Items listed here are marked 'Teplitz' or 'Turn,' a nearby city.

Bowl, figural bears fight for seal above rim, blk matt, 8x11" **225.00**
Bust, lady w/fancy hairdo, gr & pk dress, #1209, 17x14", EX **500.00**
Bust, lady w/ornate headpc, purple outfit w/caplet, Stellmacher, 18" .**1,700.00**
Creamer, child & dog, Stellmacher, lg...**65.00**
Figurine, boy w/pig, Stellmacher, 7½" **300.00**
Figurine, lion attacking Arab & camel, 13x15½".....................**1,200.00**
Pitcher, red flower sprigs, dragon hdl, fish spout, rstr, 12" **345.00**
Teapot, winged dragon spout & hdl, 2 entwined dolphins finial, 12".**1,090.00**

Vase, bl & gr, appl hdls, squat, 7" W **300.00**
Vase, lady's head/flowers, stems form asymetric hdls, 13x5" **400.00**
Vase, maid w/gilt ornaments & roses, HP, triangular, 5¾x5½" .**2,300.00**
Vase, Nouveau lady w/wings at top, gold florals, ca 1900, 17x11" ..**400.00**
Vase, shaded tan/gr matt, buttressed floriform hdls, drilled, 13", EX .**225.00**
Vase, 2 dancers emb, mc matt, flaring w/5 openings, 11" **250.00**
Vase, 4 gr hdls on wht w/HP floral sprigs, rtcl gold at rim, 7" **650.00**

Terra Cotta

Terra cotta is a type of earthenware or clay used for statuary, architectural facings, or domestic articles. It is unglazed, baked to durable hardness, and characterized by the color of the body which may range from brick red to buff.

Bust, Am Indian, dk red patina, EX detail, rstr, 10x10½" **115.00**
Bust, Art Nouveau maid amidst bulrushes, Paris, 1903, 25" **880.00**

Figural group, satyr on stump holds grape-filled tambourine and embraces nymph who bends toward cherub, signed Clodion, nineteenth century, 21", $4,000.00.

Figure, Am buffalo, multi-brn, unmk, 7½x8" **500.00**
Figure, German shepherds, sgn T Cartier, 20"..............................**400.00**
Figure, kneeling shackled man in loincloth, Merval, Darcy Paris, 22"...**575.00**
Obelisk, commemorative, relief stars/faces/eagle, sgn King, 57" .**1,150.00**
Urn, weathered wht w/crazing, ca 1900, 26x12" **375.00**

Thermometers

Few objects man has invented have been so eloquently expressed both functionally and artistically as the ubiquitous thermometer. Developed initially by Galileo in 1593 as a scientific device, thermometers slowly evolved into decorative objets d'art, functional household utensils, and eye-catching advertising specialties. Most American thermometers manufactured early in the twentieth century were produced by Taylor (Tycos), and today their thermometers remain the most plentiful on the market. Decorative thermometers manufactured before 1800 are now ensconced in the permanent collections of approximately a dozen European museums. Because of their fragility, few devices of this era have survived in private collections. Nowadays most antique thermometers find their way to market through estate sales.

Insofar as sheer beauty, uniqueness, and scientific accuracy, decorative thermometers are far superior to the ordinary and inexpensive versions which carry advertising. Decorative thermometers run the gamut from plain tin household varieties to the highly ornate creations of Tiffany and Bradley and Hubbard. They have been manufactured from nearly every conceivable material — oak, sterling, brass, and glass being the favorites — and have tested the artistry and technical skills of some of America's finest craftsmen. Ornamental models can be found in free-hanging, wall-mounted, or desk/mantel versions.

Since 1994 instrument prices have been escalating at a rate of 35% annually. This is due to their relative scarcity, infrequent trading and absence of a 'knock-off' (retro) market. Look for this trend to continue indefinitely.

Thermometer prices are based on age, ornateness, and whether mercury or alcohol is used as the filler in the tube. A broken or missing tube will cut at least 40% off the value. Virtually all American-made thermometers available today as collectors' items were made between 1875 and 1940. The Golden Age of decoratives ended in the early 1940s as modern manufacturing processes and materials robbed them of their natural distinctiveness. Our advisor for this category is Richard T. Porter; he is listed in the Directory under Massachusetts.

Key:
br — brass
Cen — Centigrade
Fah — Fahrenheit
mrc — mercury in tube
pmc — permacolor
R — rare

Rea — Reaumer
sc — scale
stl — stainless
strl — sterling
VR — very rare

Amadio, Fah, Corn Hill, desk, ivory pillar/compass, mrc, 1890, 10"...**850.00**
Anonymous, cvd wood squirrel, glass Rea sc, mrc, 1905, 10"......**800.00**
Anonymous, desk, br conquistador figural, br sc, mrc..................**650.00**
Anonymous, desk, love scene, silver metal, br Rea/Cen sc, mrc, 8".**830.00**
Anonymous, pendant, strl case, ivory Fah sc, mrc, 1880, 5"....**1,250.00**
Anonymous, wall, giltwood fr, ivory Fah sc, 1790, 10x3½"........**3,100.00**
Blk/Starr/Frost, desk, barometer, stl, Fah/Cen, mrc, '10, 11"..**2,200.00**
Bradley & Hubbard, desk, br fr & Fah sc, mrc, 1895, 13x6"..**2,800.00**
Calley, desk, strl inkwell fr, porc Rea sc, mrc, 1899, 5x6"........**3,200.00**
Capendium, desk, handmade br/porc fr, Fah/Cen sc, rnd mrc, 4".**850.00**
Carpenter & Westley, desk, ivory w/glass dome mrc, 1880, 6"....**950.00**
Casella London, wall, maxi/minimum, 2 units, wood, plastic sc.**430.00**
Cheshire Silversmiths, desk, br candelabra, mrc, 1875, 10"....**4,500.00**
Chevallier, L'ingre, wall, ivory/mahog, Rea/Cen sc, 1880, 11x3"..**2,350.00**
Clark, desk, ivory ped, crown, mrc, 1904, 7"..................**400.00**
Cloister, inkwell, stl bk & base w/angels at side, 1901 ....**1,050.00**
Creswel, travel, ivory/case/mirror, removable sc, mrc, 2½"......**2,800.00**
CW Wilder...NH, desk, Deco women, br Fah sc, mrc, R, 8"..**1,300.00**
Desk, cvd walrus tusk, 2-tier disk base, inlay sc, 1860, 9"............**430.00**
Diamond, wall, br Fah sc on wood, R, 7½x1½"..........................**525.00**
Dixie, W (London); desk, gilt/br, Gothic, SP sc, mrc, 8" **790.00**
Dollard London, desk, strl, br sc, mrc, 1908, R, 6" **750.00**
Dollard London, hanging, mahog fr, strl sc, mrc, 1810, 18".....**4,600.00**
Dring & Fage, desk, marble, ivory sc, mrc, 1880, 6"..................**1,500.00**
England, desk, glass obelisk/8-sided, br Fah sc, mrc, 1880........**1,260.00**
England, desk, marble ped fr, Cen, mrc, 1885, 6½" **930.00**
England, wall, br game bag fr, Fah sc, mrc, 1890, 9x5"............**1,650.00**
England, wall, rectangular wood fr, porc Cen sc, mrc, 1905, 5"..**1,350.00**
Farley, travel, walnut base mt, ivory Fah/Cen sc, mrc, 5" **900.00**
Freeborn, desk, bronze w/3 lead decor, br sc, mrc, 8" **180.00**
G Cooper, desk, bell shape w/cupola, strl, dial, 2x3" **400.00**
Gilbert & Co, travel, silver eng sc, mrc, 1850, 8" **630.00**
Gloucenter Scientific, stl case, glass front, pmc, 42" **1,500.00**
Heath & Wing, figural calendar, br w/porc sc, mrc, 1870............**930.00**
J Waldstein, wall, br Rea sc on wood, mrc, 1900s, VR, 10½".....**920.00**
Kendal, desk, strl obelisk, br Fah sc, mrc, 1890, 8", $1,350 to.**1,850.00**
Moreau, desk, mahog, Rea/Cen, spiral tube, mrc, 1860, 6½x5½"..**1,725.00**
Ohio, wall, CI, 1850, R alcohol, Fah, 10" **350.00**
Pairpoint, desk, strl picture fr, mrc, 1907, 5" **650.00**
Pig w/branch of tree, Pairpoint #5604, 5¼" **375.00**
Reau, desk, sq incline base, floral top, mrc, 1895........................**180.00**
Rowley & Sons, travel, ivory sc, mrc, 1894, 4", +case................**350.00**
Standard, wall, ivory Fah sc on ebony, mrc, 9" **750.00**
Standard..., wall, br fr, enamel dial Fah sc, 1885, 9" dia.............**950.00**

Taylor, chandelier, 3-side, Fah alcohol, 1887, VR, br, 6".............**400.00**
Taylor, ped, 3-sided, Fah sc, alcohol, 1900, R, 6" **350.00**
Thermindex Switzerland, desk, Bakelite stand, Fah sc, 5"...........**725.00**
Tiffany, desk, strl tetrahedron fr & Fah sc, mrc, 1910, 2x4"....**4,000.00**
Tiffany, gr glass w/pine needles, br sc/mrc, 1902, 8x12" **2,800.00**
Tycos, maxi/minimum, japanned tin/br, mrc, T-5452, 8".............**125.00**
Unknown, cvd wood squirrel, glass Rea sc, mrc, 1905, VR, 10" .**800.00**
Unknown, desk, alabaster w/eagle, Rea/Cen sc, mrc, 1895 ....**875.00**
Unknown, desk, love scene, silver metal, br Rea/Cen sc, mrc, 8"...**830.00**
Unknown, wall, giltwood fr, ivory Fah sc, 1790, 10x3½".........**3,100.00**
VJD Inc, wall, clip Fah br sc, mrc, 4", VR **1,650.00**
W Pratt, desk, wood inlays, ivory sc, mrc, 1900, 6" **350.00**
Warren Foundries, wall, umbrella w/dragon hdl, br sc, mrc, 12" .**220.00**
West, desk, Gothic design, br, 1900, 12"....................................**1,360.00**
WG Loveday, wall, Clearside, Fah sc, 5" dia **725.00**
Whitehead & Hoag, Lambrecht's Polymeter, mrc, 9"..............**1,200.00**
Zeradatha, desk, cast metal w/rotate sc, 1926, 7" **140.00**

1000 Faces China

A dinner plate from this pattern, it is said, may have as many as 1,000 hand-painted faces, thus the name. Most of what we see today dates from early in the century to midway, but some pieces are even older. Though many pieces are unmarked, the majority carries the marks 'Made in Japan' or 'Japan.' 'Kutani,' 'MIOJ,' and other marks are sometimes seen as well.

There are two primary patterns or colors — Gold and Black Face. Gold is just that — most of the pieces are dominated by gold throughout. Black refers to the fact that in this variation the faces are black, usually against a white background. Many rings and bars of colors make up both primary patterns. Variations include 'Men in Robes' and '1000 Geishas.' All patterns usually feature an inner ring of color surrounded by flashes of multiple colors and an outer ring of color with a pattern painted into it.

Gold was the most popular pattern and seems to be the most available today. Examples with Black faces and the variations are scarce and often command higher prices. Only recently two new colors have been discovered — green and blue — leaving us to wonder if there may be still others. These colors are very rare and prices are high. In the green and blue patterns, the faces are gold and the pattern is the same as the traditional Thousand Faces, but the background colors are in the multiple shades of the blue or green. Our advisor for this category is Suzi Hibbard; she is listed in the Directory under California.

Bowl, gold, petal shape, 6", from $15 to **25.00**
Creamer & sugar bowl, bl faces, w/lid, HP Mikado, from $75 to...**125.00**
Cup & saucer, coffee; blk faces, from $30 to **55.00**
Cup & saucer, coffee; gold faces, Made in Occupied Japan, from $30 to...**55.00**
Cup & saucer, Men in Robes, pnt bottoms, mk, from $45 to........**75.00**
Cup & saucer, w/plate, blk faces, MIJ, from $45 to........................**75.00**
Lamp, blk faces, MIJ, vase shape, 8", from $125 to......................**175.00**
Nappy, blk faces, MIJ, 5½", from $15 to..**45.00**
Oil & vinegar on tray, gold faces, w/stoppers, MIJ, from $75 to..**125.00**
Plate, dessert; bl faces, 7¼", from $50 to **75.00**
Plate, dessert; blk faces, MIJ, 7¼", from $15 to............................**20.00**
Plate, dessert; gr faces, 7¼", from $50 to **75.00**
Plate, dinner; gold faces, 10", from $25 to **55.00**
Platter, gold faces, Japan, 9½", from $45 to **75.00**
Saucer, Men in Robes, mk, 5⅛", from $10 to................................**20.00**
Shakers, gold faces, 2½", pr, from $15 to......................................**25.00**
Snack plate & cup, blk faces, kidney shaped, from $40 to............**50.00**
Sweetmeat, blk faces, MIJ, 9-pc set in lacquer box, from $150 to .**200.00**
Tea set, Men in Robes, lg pot, cr/sug w/lid, 6 c/s, MIJ, from $225 to..**325.00**
Teapot, creamer & sugar bowl w/lid, gold faces, HP MIJ, from $50 to .**100.00**
Teapot, 1000 Geishas, mk, 6", from $35 to....................................**65.00**
Vase, Men in Robes, MIJ, 6", from $40 to......................................**75.00**

Tiffany

Louis Comfort Tiffany was born in 1848 to Charles Lewis and Harriet Young Tiffany of New York. By the time he was eighteen, his father's small dry goods and stationery store had grown and developed into the world-renowned Tiffany and Company. Preferring the study of art to joining his father in the family business, Louis spent the next six years under the tutelage of noted artists. He returned to America in 1870 and until 1875 painted canvases that focused on European and North African scenes. Deciding the more lucrative approach was in the application of industrial arts and crafts, he opened a decorating studio called Louis C. Tiffany and Co., Associated Artists. He began seriously experimenting with glass, and eschewing traditionally painted-on details, he instead learned to produce glass with qualities that could suggest natural textures and effects. His experiments broadened, and he soon concentrated his efforts on vases, bowls, etc., that came to be considered the highest achievements of the art. Peacock feathers, leaves and vines, flowers, and abstracts were developed within the plane of the glass as it was blown. Opalescent and metallic lustres were combined with transparent color to produce stunning effects. Tiffany called his glass Favrile, meaning handmade.

In 1900 he established Tiffany Studios and turned his attention full time to producing art glass, leaded-glass lamp shades and windows, and household wares with metal components. He also designed a complete line of jewelry which was sold through his father's store. He became proficiently accomplished in silverwork and produced such articles as hand mirrors embellished with peacock feather designs set with gems and candlesticks with Favrile glass inserts.

Tiffany's work exemplified the Art Nouveau style of design and decoration, and through his own flamboyant personality and business acumen he perpetrated his tastes onto the American market to the extent that his name became a household word. Tiffany Studios continued to prosper until the second decade of this century when due to changing tastes his influence began to diminish. By the early 1930s the company had closed.

Serial numbers were assigned to much of Tiffany's work, and letter prefixes indicated the year of manufacture: A – N for 1896 – 1900, P – Z for 1901 – 1905. After that, the letter followed the numbers with A – N in use from 1906 – 1912; P – Z from 1913 – 1920. O-marked pieces were made especially for friends and relatives; X indicated pieces not made for sale.

Our listings are primarily from the auction houses in the East where Tiffany sells at a premium. All pieces are signed unless noted otherwise.

Glass

Atomizer, gold irid, paneled/tapered/shouldered, disk ft, 7½" 460.00
Bottle, gold irid w/jeweled silver band, jeweled lid, 11½"........4,400.00
Bowl, bl irid, squat/shouldered w/ruffled rim, 4" 400.00
Bowl, bl irid, swirl ribs, 6¾"..200.00
Bowl, gold irid, wide flaring rim, 2¼x6".......................................560.00
Bowl, lily pads/eng on gold, 13", +2-tier flower frog................2,645.00
Bowl, Pastel, bl w/irid stretching, amber ft, 1¾x6"......................950.00
Butter pat, gold irid, scalloped rim, 4" 165.00
Candlestick, bl irid, ribbed, flared ft, #1286, 12" 1,600.00
Candlestick, cobalt w/bl irid, ribbed std, dome base, 11" 1,380.00
Compote, amber irid & gold lustre, optic ribs, disk ft, 5¾x6¼" ..1,035.00
Compote, bl irid, stretched rim on shallow ftd bowl, 2x5" 750.00
Compote, bl irid w/etch vines/flowers, #1757, 5¾x11¾".........5,600.00
Compote, floriform; bl irid, wide stretched petal edge, 4½x5".2,000.00
Compote, gold irid, scalloped rim, 4x7¾" 575.00
Compote, gold irid, stretched/ruffled petal top, 4x5¼"................800.00
Dish, gold irid, rnd/shallow, 6"..200.00
Finger bowl, bl irid, 8-petal rim, +6" underplate 1,380.00
Flask, flattened cylinder, silver mts, leather-bound, 1902, 6¾" ...800.00
Flower holder, gold irid w/hearts & vines, #954M, 10½" dia 925.00

Goblet, opal/pk w/gold-washed irid finish, disk ft, 7¾"............1,380.00
Goblets, wine; amber w/eng vines, irid int, 3⅜", pr.....................400.00
Inkwell, bl & silver swirls w/bronze hinged cap, bulbed gourd, 5½"..8,000.00
Medallion, Victory 1918, gold/bl irid, 2¾" dia, NM....................780.00
Plate, pk/wht pastel, ped ft, 6½" 230.00
Punch bowl, gold irid, shaped sides, trumpet-form base, 2-pc, 11x13".2,800.00
Punch cup, gold w/irid 'fans,' hdls w/curlicues, V698, 12 for ...3,900.00
Salt, gold irid, flat flange rim, sharp shoulder, wide rnd ft, 2¼".245.00
Salt, gold irid, flat shaped rim, paneled shoulder, 4 peg ft, 2¼" ..200.00
Salt, gold irid, squat/bulbous w/imp stylized floriform, zigzag border ..450.00
Seal, scarab w/engraved letter F, bl/gold irid, 1¾" L 345.00
Tile, shell in center, raised outer rim, ivory/brn slag, 3", NM......140.00
Tile, turtle bk; gr w/gold/purple irid, 3x2", NM...........................90.00
Vase, bl irid, dbl gourd, 4"...800.00
Vase, bl irid, rnd w/extended ruffled rim, 1½x5¼" 490.00
Vase, bl irid, shouldered, #5120L, 9" 1,450.00
Vase, bl irid, stretched/ruffled rim on bulbous bowl, disk base, 4" ..8,625.00
Vase, bl irid, trumpet form w/knob stem, dome ft, 13½"..........3,000.00
Vase, bl irid & gold pulled feathers on bl-gr, ovoid, #3392, 18"..25,850.00
Vase, bl irid w/gr leaves/vines, full shoulder, tapers to stem, 9"...4,000.00
Vase, bl irid w/strong red at shoulder, polished pontil, 9".........2,500.00
Vase, bl w/5 inky bl pulled feathers, tall slim neck, flared base, 10".1,525.00
Vase, bud; cobalt w/strong irid, disk ft, #9667, 10" 1,265.00
Vase, clambroth w/irid pulled feathers, invt trumpet form, 18", pr..4,750.00
Vase, cobalt w/bl irid, shouldered urn form, ca 1918, 5¾" 2,300.00
Vase, floriform; amber w/gold irid, 4-ftd/bulbous, flared rim, 2½" ...865.00
Vase, floriform; bl irid, pulled teardrop on bronze pencil stem, 18"..2,500.00
Vase, floriform; Daffodil, ribbed/waisted cup, domed 10-rib base, 15".6,800.00
Vase, floriform; gold irid, disk on stem below upright waisted cup, 9".920.00
Vase, floriform; gold irid, elongated cup on shaped disk ft, 10".1,080.00
Vase, floriform; gold irid, scalloped upright rim, label, 7½" 1,095.00
Vase, floriform; gold irid, shouldered ribbed trumpet body, 6".....800.00
Vase, floriform; gr w/wht feathers, gold int/ft, bowl on stem, 11".2,875.00
Vase, floriform; wht w/gr feathers, gold int, flared petal rim, 5" ...1,380.00
Vase, gold Cypriote w/irid, squat/bulbous, #8782, 3" 1,800.00
Vase, gold feathers on opal, 8½" 2,300.00
Vase, gold irid, #G2606, mini, 4¾" 650.00
Vase, gold irid, bulbed rim, urn form, domed ft, 15¼" 2,585.00
Vase, gold irid, elongated/ribbed, on disk ft, 12"........................1,325.00
Vase, gold irid, hdls, #6431H, mini, 1¾"......................................475.00
Vase, gold irid, ovoid w/doughnut neck, shoulder hdls, bun ft, 2¾" 1,035.00
Vase, gold irid, trumpet form bulbed near disk base, #936 K, 6" .560.00
Vase, gold irid w/allover gr vines/leaves, squat w/flaring rim, 5x6".2,600.00
Vase, gold irid w/detailed gr leaves & vines, #7793K, 3½" 1,200.00
Vase, gold irid w/gr hearts/vines, button pontil, 9" 3,450.00
Vase, gold irid w/gr waves, U-shape, 2½".....................................1,265.00
Vase, gold irid w/purple/gr hearts/vines, #4802G, 7½x3¼"......2,800.00
Vase, gr irid w/bl feathers/swirls, gold int, button pontil, 10"...3,720.00
Vase, millefiori wht flowers, gr lily pads, amethyst vines, 4x5"..6,400.00
Vase, pk/wht pastel opal, petal top tapers to stem, ped ft, 5½" ...920.00
Vase, red irid, yel int, button pontil, wear/staining to int, 8"...2,760.00
Vase, silver-bl irid, ovoid w/doughnut lip, 5½".........................1,725.00
Whiskey taster, gold irid w/appl spiral threads, #N1123, 3" 525.00

Lamps

Lamp prices seem to be getting stronger, especially for leaded lamps with brighter colors (red, blue, purples). Bases that are unusual or rare have brought good prices and added to the value of the more common shades that sold on them. Bases with enamel or glass inserts are very much in demand. Our advisor for Tiffany lamps is Carl Heck; he is listed in the Directory under Colorado.

Key: c-b — counterbalance

Base, boudoir; gilt bronze shaft on radiating rib glass base #16 ...**400.00**
Base, desk; bronze harp fr w/radiating rib dome ft, #419, 13", EX ..**1,380.00**
Boudoir, bronze harp w/pulled feather glass shade, 13"............**5,750.00**
Bridge, metal 10¼" geometric shade, slim std w/tripod base, 55"..**2,500.00**
Candle, gold irid 7" ruffled shade/twisted base, 16", pr............**2,800.00**
Candle, King Tut 7" shade; red irid swirl base; feathered candle, 16".**4,000.00**
Ceiling, gold ribbed shades hang from 5-arm ribbed mt, 33x14"..**16,240.00**
Ceiling, ldgl 12" 8-panel 2-layer shade (mottled); rtcl crown, chains ..**9,500.00**
Ceiling, ldgl 16" acorn-band shade w/wide bronze-ball fringe, rare ..**11,500.00**
Ceiling, ldgl 19" bell-shaped wht opal fishscale shade w/ormolu trim..**10,640.00**
Ceiling, ldgl 20" tilework shade w/center turtlebk; bronze/glass mt..**5,000.00**
Ceiling, ldgl 30" tilework shade w/zigzag border, glass/brass mt..**45,900.00**
Ceiling, 6 gold lilies encircle feathered bowl on turtle-bk/bronze mt...**25,000.00**
Ceiling, 6 gold pendant lilies above lg acorn globe on 3 chains .**25,250.00**
Ceiling, 6-arm w/feathered bell shades over ldgl 29" brickwork cone ...**72,800.00**

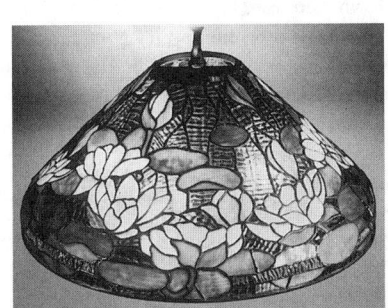

Chandelier, leaded glass, water lily 20" conical hanging shade, #149-17", $60,000.00.
(Photo courtesy Skinner, Inc.)

Desk, damascene 7" gr/silver irid shade; c-b #419 base w/M patina.**9,500.00**
Desk, dk gr w/bl irid 6½" shade; Zodiac harp std, 13½"...........**5,000.00**
Desk, feathered bell shade on gold doré c-b base #417............**6,700.00**
Desk, feathered lily 4½x5½" shade; bell-shaped harp std, 18"....**4,200.00**
Desk, feathered 6" cased gold on opal globe #O 130; base #28609 ..**6,700.00**
Desk, gold 7" shade in gold doré harp leaf-mold holder #569, 19"..**4,000.00**
Desk, metal o/l gold-finish grapevine 9x3" bullet shade, 1-arm base .**3,900.00**
Floor, damascene 10" bl irid shade; harp base w/3 tall ft........**12,000.00**
Floor, damascene 12" gold shade; gold doré base w/heavy 4-leg base..**9,500.00**
Floor, gold irid 10" shade; Aladdin's lamp tops gold doré std #576.**6,700.00**
Floor, gold/pk damascene shade in harp std, gold doré #678 base..**9,600.00**
Floor, ldgl 12" acorn-border shade; harp std #423 w/5-leg base...**16,250.00**
Floor, ldgl 22½" apple blossom shade; Spanish Moss std, 71½" ..**63,000.00**
Floor, ldgl 24" curtain-border shade; simple ftd base, 70".......**70,000.00**
Library, turtlebk 8" W shade; glass cabs on wishbone base, 15".**8,400.00**
Lily, 10-light, amber irid shades (7 sgn/1 rpr); lily pad base ...**14,000.00**
Lily, 10-light, feathered gr/opal irid shades; gilt lily pad base #38 ....**45,900.00**
Lily, 18-light, gold shades (13 sgn); gold doré pond lily base #383 ..**61,600.00**
Lily, 3-light, fluted wht 3" irid shades; simple base #319, 13" ..**3,000.00**
Lily, 3-light, gold shades, ribbed, w/swell above rim; base #319 ..**6,700.00**
Lily, 3-light, gr to yel fluted shades; doré finish, tendril finial..**3,080.00**
Lily, 3-light, 2¾" shades (1 sgn); base w/ring of emb beading, 12" .**3,740.00**
Lily, 3-light w/gold shades (1 VG); #319 bun base w/emb beading, 13"..**3,165.00**
Nautilus, shell shade on swing arm; gilt 3-D mermaid base #28677, 16"..**13,440.00**
Nautilus, shell shade; gold doré base #409 w/emb leaves **5,175.00**
Nautilus, shell w/silver mts; #28630 wide-rib wishbone-harp base, 12".**3,900.00**
Night, feathered 8½" H shade on conforming 8-sided wood base ..**5,000.00**
Sconce, feathered 3" tulip shade, gr/gold/opal; brn-patina arm, 12".**3,500.00**
Sconce, 4-lily; 4 gold shades; ornate gold wall plate, 16x8", pr ...**14,000.00**
Shade only, damascene, gold w/cream int, 10" dia **8,915.00**
Shade only, damascene, gr irid, 12"............................**6,440.00**
Shade only, gold irid w/onion skin at rim, ruffled, 3¾x7¼" **880.00**
Student, 2 7" ribbed gr cased shades; central font on twist stem..**2,240.00**
Table, damascene 10" ball shade; gold chimney, feathered base, 31"..**19,040.00**
Table, damascene 10" shade w/etched butterflies; #445 3-arm base, 15"..**14,000.00**
Table, damascene 7" shade; base #429 w/4 high rtcl legs **5,600.00**

Table, feathered 7" shade, gr/gold/wht, in dk brn #424 harp std, 17"..**3,900.00**
Table, ldgl 10" tilework shade; 3-arm #445 base....................**12,300.00**
Table, ldgl 14" acorn shade; 3-light openwork bronze std, 20½"..**24,150.00**
Table, ldgl 14" acorn-band shade; 3-arm bullet body, wishbone support.**7,840.00**
Table, ldgl 14" daffodil shade; tree trunk base **28,000.00**
Table, ldgl 16" acorn-band shade (EX color); simple base #534, 22"..**14,000.00**
Table, ldgl 16" bellflower shade; bronze base #394 ....**25,200.00**
Table, ldgl 16" blk-eyed Susan shade; acorn font in ribbed 4-leg fr **39,200.00**
Table, ldgl 16" geometric shade; 3-light pottery base w/hdls, 17½"..**7,500.00**
Table, ldgl 16" Greek Key shade; base #534 w/paneled column, 22"..**27,400.00**
Table, ldgl 16" jeweled feather shade; bronze std w/ball ft, 23".**12,350.00**
Table, ldgl 16" pansy shade w/tag; 3-socket std w/sq base, mk, 22½"..**30,000.00**
Table, ldgl 16" pomegranate shade; rtcl bronze std, 10", EX ..**16,000.00**
Table, ldgl 16" poppy shade; gold doré 6-stem base, orig metal sleeves .**67,200.00**
Table, ldgl 16" red poppy shade w/bronze filigree; tree trunk base .**30,800.00**
Table, ldgl 16" red poppy shade; #181 font in ribbed 4-leg support.**67,200.00**
Table, ldgl 16" shade w/irid balls band; blown/bronze #338 std, 24"..**77,500.00**
Table, ldgl 16" tilework shade w/turtle-bk tile border; 4 more in base..**56,000.00**
Table, ldgl 16" tilework shade; massive base etched w/waves, 20" ...**16,800.00**
Table, ldgl 16" tulips shade, EX color; base #394....................**98,000.00**
Table, ldgl 16" tulips shade #1456; #444 std w/3-prong support, 22".**32,200.00**
Table, ldgl 16" tulips shade; gold doré deeply ribbed std/base #29733.**33,500.00**
Table, ldgl 16" tulips shade; stem w/wire coil inlay, ftd bun base.**26,880.00**
Table, ldgl 16" turtle-bk tile band shade; torpedo base w/tiles, 22"..**34,700.00**
Table, ldgl 18" clematis cone shade; 3-arm ribbed/ftd base #29733.**44,800.00**
Table, ldgl 18" jonquil shade, yel flowers/lav ground; std #366.**30,800.00**
Table, ldgl 18" poinsettia shade w/tag; geometric bronze std, 25½"..**37,950.00**
Table, ldgl 18" shade w/rows of brickwork; simple stick std #533 .**13,440.00**
Table, ldgl 18" tilework shade w/turtlebk band; simple base #538 .**30,240.00**
Table, ldgl 20" acorn-band shade (EX); #531 brn-patina base, 29"..**19,500.00**
Table, ldgl 20" shade w/turtlebk tile band; 4 Virtues base **39,200.00**
Table, ldgl 25" Roman Helmet shade; #529 Roman Column bronze std, 30".**25,000.00**
Table, ldgl 26" lotus shade; 6-light stem std w/ribbed base/ft .**78,400.00**
Table, linenfold 10" shade; gold doré base #667 ....**16,800.00**
Table, linenfold 14" shade w/opal top/bottom bands; tapering std..**7,280.00**

Metal Work

Items are bronze unless noted otherwise.

Ash stand, gold doré finish w/glass-lined bowl, #1649.................**560.00**
Bell, desk; emb floral/foliage, #1061, 2¾" **750.00**
Bookends, Zodiac, dk brn/gr patina, #1091, 6x4¾" **490.00**
Box, cigarette; gold doré w/allover emb, cedar lining, 3x4¼" **675.00**
Box, floral enamel border, gold doré, rpr hinges, #139, 6¼" L.**1,500.00**
Box, glove; Grapevine, 5x14" **1,900.00**
Box, Grapevine, 4 ball ft, 2½x8x8"..**1,735.00**
Box, jewelry; Pine Needle w/gr & wht slag inserts, 3¼x9⅜x6½"..**1,650.00**
Box, Pine Needle, 4 ball ft, 1¾x5½x4".................................**535.00**
Candelabrum, 2-arm, gr/brn patina cups w/glass jewels, 9", pr.**2,760.00**
Candelabrum, 4 rtcl cups/rtcl platform w/blown-in gr glass **4,200.00**
Candelabrum, 4-arm, rtcl cups w/gr glass int, rnd base w/gr cabs, 11"..**3,220.00**
Candlestick, 2 elongated cups on hdld leaf tray, blown-in glass, #5640.**3,360.00**
Candlesticks, gold doré, bulbous cup, ped ft, 3¾", pr **515.00**
Candlesticks, gold doré, cup on bulbous std on swirled base, 17", pr.**1,950.00**
Candlesticks, gold doré, cup on slim stem w/4 legs & paw ft, 11", pr ...**975.00**
Compote, gold doré, shallow, artichoke std, rnd ft, 4½" H **345.00**
Desk set, American Indian, inkwell/pr blotter ends/scissors+3 pcs.**2,070.00**
Desk set, Grapevine, mail file/inkwell/clock/calendar/memo pad+6 pcs.**3,700.00**
Desk set, Pine Needle, wht slag inserts, 10-pc **2,585.00**
Desk set, Zodiac, gold doré, 7-pc.................................**1,400.00**
Frame, Chinese, #1761, 8½x6¾" **1,200.00**
Frame, highy textured red/purple irid glass insets, #55, 13".....**2,300.00**
Frame, Pine Needle, oval opening, #946, 9¾x7¾" **1,650.00**

Frame, Zodiac, brn patina, #943, 8½x7½", from $800 to **1,000.00**
Inkwell, Grapevine, gr slag int, orig liner, #844, 3½x4" **600.00**
Inkwell, Nautilus, figural fish ea corner **2,240.00**
Inkwell, Zodiac, 6" W **560.00**
Inkwell, 2 rows rectangular reticulations w/blown-in glass, etch lid.**2,520.00**
Lamp base, Pine Needle, gold doré, spherical, disk base, 19¾"..**4,115.00**
Letter holder, Grapevine, 3-compartment, 8½x12½" **1,450.00**
Magnifying glass, rosette hdl, #1788, 9", EX **750.00**
Note pad, 5 cab jewels on ornate cover, wood bk, 7x5".........**1,175.00**
Plate, alternating florals & leaves, gold doré, #D556 445, 10⅛"..**2,950.00**
Plate, gold doré, Greek Key & Shell border, #309, 8¼" **165.00**
Plate, spun bronze w/etched border, #1750, 7¾".........................**400.00**
Stand, brass w/incised insignias, 3 figural serpent legs, 3-tier...**2,400.00**
Tray, abalone insets in border, 12" dia **335.00**
Tray, Oriental relief design on flange, 13¾" dia.........................**230.00**
Vase, gold doré, trumpet form w/golden base, 12½" **1,850.00**

Pottery

Lamp base, indigo/beige/ochre/gr textured matt, shaved rim, 17x8"..**485.00**
Vase, caramel/beige crystalline flambe, bulbous, 6x4", EX...........**920.00**
Vase, floral, gr/ivory/lt brn, swollen cylinder, 1906, 7⅛" **1,600.00**
Vase, gray/umber/indigo matt, emb lobed panels, 6x5¾" **2,875.00**
Vase, mottled cobalt on turq, shouldered cylinder, P861, 17", NM..**2,350.00**
Vase, Wisteria Pod, gr mottled microcrystalline, rstr, 8x3¼", EX..**2,875.00**

Silver

Key: t-oz — troy ounces

Tureen, Chrysanthemum, lobed dome lid, lobed body, handles with flower terminals, 74 troy ounce, 11" diameter, $9,200.00. (Photo courtesy Skinner, Inc.)

Bowl, lobed rim w/appl floral, 4 floral paw ft, 13½" L..............**2,000.00**
Bowl, plain/tapered, 1950s, 7"..**235.00**
Bowl, side; hammered boat shape w/rope rim, monogram, 5" L, 3 for.**175.00**
Candy dish, shallow/elliptical, 4 ball ft, monogram, 1950, 10" L.**175.00**
Coffee set, 11½" octagonal pot+cr/sug, 54-t-oz **1,100.00**
Flatware, English King, 13 monogrammed pcs, 20-t-oz **800.00**
Flatware, Flemish, service for 12, 112-pc set, 117-t-oz **4,600.00**
Fork, seafood; Faneuil #95, gold-washed prongs, 6", 12 for..........**350.00**
Iced tea spoons, Bamboo, mid-20th C, in Tiffany cloth bag & box, 4 for.**175.00**
Ladle, Chrysanthemum, diagonally fluted bowl, monogram, 13".**1,645.00**
Pitcher, emb florals/swirls, insulated, late 1800s, rpr, 4½-pt........**575.00**
Salver, scalloped shell/foliate border, paw ft, sq w/rnd corners, 12"..**2,100.00**
Spirit lamp, hammered boat shape w/rope edge, loop hdl, monogram, 6" L...**585.00**
Spoon, berry; English King, 3.8-t-oz **575.00**
Spoon, sugar sifter; Olympian, 1880s, 7" **200.00**
Tray, 13" dia, 27-t-oz **350.00**
Tray, 5-part, self hdls, rope twist border, monogram, 14½" L **585.00**
Vase, incised floral/shield/tendrils, petal rim, trumpet form, 20" .**3,900.00**

Miscellaneous

Book, Artwork of Louis C Tiffany, Doubleday, signed ltd ed, 1914, EX..**2,000.00**

Jar, ivory w/cvd dragonfly, w/lid, 3½"....................................**2,600.00**
Shoehorn, 18k yel gold, 3-t-oz..**745.00**
Table, gesso/wood 28" L organic design w/massive base & inset tiles..**2,600.00**
Window, Corinthian column/lg lilies/mtns in bkground, oak fr, 50x36"..**72,800.00**
Window, 4 rows of 4 brn/ivory sqs w/in leafy outer band, 20x41" ..**5,600.00**

Tiffin Glass

The Tiffin Glass Company was founded in 1887 in Tiffin, Ohio, one of the many factories composing the U.S. Glass Company. Its early wares consisted of tablewares and decorative items such as lamps and globes. Among the most popular of all Tiffin products was the black satin glass produced there during the 1920s. In 1959 U.S. Glass was sold, and in 1962 the factories closed. The plant was re-opened in 1963 as the Tiffin Art Glass Company. Products from this period were tableware, hand-blown stemware, and other decorative items.

Those interested in learning more about Tiffin glass are encouraged to contact the Tiffin Glass Collectors' Club, whose address can be found in the Directory under Clubs, Newsletters, and Catalogs.

See also Black Glass; Glass Animals.

Ashtray, Flanders, crystal, w/cigarette rest, 2¼x¾"....................**55.00**
Ashtray, Fuchsia, crystal, w/cigarette rest, 2¼x3¾"....................**35.00**
Basket, Jungle Assortment, any color, #151, 6" **95.00**
Bell, Fuchsia, crystal, #15083, 5"...**75.00**
Bowl, centerpc; Psyche, crystal, 13"..**125.00**
Bowl, centerpc; Twilight, #17430, 8"..**125.00**
Bowl, cream soup; Fuchsia, crystal, ftd, #5831, 6¼"....................**50.00**
Bowl, crimped; Fuchsia, crystal, #5902, 13".................................**80.00**
Bowl, deep salad; Fuchsia, crystal, 9¾".......................................**75.00**
Bowl, deep salad; June Night, crystal, 10" **65.00**
Bowl, finger; Flanders, pk, w/liner..**95.00**
Bowl, grapefruit; Cadena, pk or yel, ftd **95.00**
Bowl, salad; June Night, crystal, 7"..**35.00**
Candlestick, June Night, crystal, dbl-branch..................................**50.00**
Candlestick, Jungle Assortment, any color, hdls, #330 ....**35.00**
Candy jar, Flanders, pk, ftd, w/lid..**250.00**
Cheese & cracker set, Classic, crystal..**100.00**
Cologne bottle, Jungle Assortment, any color, #5722 ....**125.00**
Creamer, Cherokee Rose, crystal **35.00**
Creamer, Flanders, crystal, ftd..**40.00**
Creamer, Psyche, crystal **65.00**
Cup, Classic, crystal...**60.00**
Cup, Fuchsia, crystal, #5831...**80.00**
Cup & saucer, Classic, crystal...**75.00**
Decanter, Flanders, yel...**275.00**
Flower bowl, Twilight, #9153, 9½"..**95.00**
Marmalade, Jungle Assortment, any color, hdls, w/lid, #330 ....**45.00**
Pitcher, Classic, crystal, w/lid, 61-oz...**350.00**
Pitcher, Psyche, crystal, w/lid..**495.00**
Plate, Cadena, pk or yel, 9¼"..**75.00**
Plate, dessert; Julia, amber...**12.00**
Plate, Flanders, crystal, 6"..**7.00**
Plate, Flanders, pk, 6"..**15.00**
Plate, Fontaine, amber, gr or pk, #8833, 8"...................................**20.00**
Plate, luncheon; Fuchsia; crystal, #8833, 8⅛"...............................**22.50**
Plate, luncheon; Julia, amber, 8"..**20.00**
Plate, muffin tray; Fuchsia, crystal, pearl edge, 10½"....................**55.00**
Plate, sandwich; June Night, crystal, 14".......................................**45.00**
Plate, sherbet; Cherokee Rose, crystal, 6".......................................**8.00**
Relish, June Night, crystal, 3-part, 12½".......................................**65.00**
Saucer, Cadena, pk or yel...**25.00**
Stem, café parfait, Psyche, crystal **55.00**

Stem, champagne; Cadena, crystal, 6½".................................25.00
Stem, cocktail; Cherokee Rose, crystal, 3½-oz.................20.00
Stem, cocktail; Classic, crystal, 3¾-oz, 4⅞"....................40.00
Stem, cocktail; Fuchsia, crystal, S stem, #17457, 5⅜"....37.00
Stem, cocktail; Julia, amber...25.00
Stem, cocktail; June Night, crystal, 3½-oz......................22.00
Stem, cordial; Classic, crystal, 1-oz, 3⅞"........................55.00
Stem, cordial; Flanders, yel, 5"......................................85.00
Stem, grapefruit; Psyche, crystal, w/liner 85.00
Stem, sherbet; Flanders, pk, 4½"...................................40.00
Stem, sherbet; Fuchsia, crystal, #15083, 4⅛"..................18.00
Stem, sherry; Cherokee Rose, crystal, 2-oz.....................35.00
Stem, sundae; Julia, amber 18.00
Stem, water; Julia, amber..30.00
Stem, wine; Cadena, crystal, 6".......................................35.00
Sugar bowl, Cherokee Rose, crystal 35.00
Sugar bowl, Fontaine, amber, gr or pk, ftd, #4................35.00
Tumbler, iced tea; Classic, pk, ftd, 13-oz, 6"..................55.00
Tumbler, iced tea; Fuchsia; crystal, ftd, #15083, 12-oz 35.00
Tumbler, iced tea; Julia, amber, ftd.................................30.00
Tumbler, iced tea; Jungle Assortment, any color, #444, 12-oz 32.00
Tumbler, iced tea; Psyche, crystal...................................50.00
Tumbler, oyster cocktail; June Night, crystal, 4½-oz.........25.00
Tumbler, water; Cadena, crystal, ftd, 5¼".......................25.00
Tumbler, water; Classic, pk, ftd, 8½-oz, 4½"...................20.00
Tumbler, water; Flanders, crystal, ftd, 10-oz, 4¾"............22.00
Vase, bud; Classic, crystal, 6½" 35.00
Vase, Cadena, crystal, 9"..95.00
Vase, Cadena, pk or yel, 9" 150.00
Vase, fan; Flanders, yel 150.00
Vase, sweet pea; Jungle Assortment, any color, #151, 7" 75.00
Vase, urn, Cherokee Rose, crystal, 11" 110.00
Whipped cream, Fuchsia, crystal, 3-ftd, #310..................50.00

Tiles

The history of tile making dates back to ancient Egypt and Assyria. For centuries tiles have played an important role as a decorative art form, as well as having a utilitarian function. Places such as palace walls, Islamic mosques, Roman floors, and medieval English churches were all adorned with tiles or glazed ceramic surfaces. Remnants of these tile installations can still be seen throughout the world.

The heyday of tile making in England and the United States dates back to circa 1860 through 1930 and envelops the Victorian, Art Nouveau, and Arts & Crafts Movements in both countries. These tiles comprise most of those seen on today's market.

Tiles are being collected today as individual art objects and are increasingly used as decorative accessories. They are also sought in order to restore homes, buildings, and furniture to original period condition. Many people are now incorporating antique and collectible tiles into their home-rebuilding projects for gardens, kitchens, bathrooms, fireplaces, stair risers, and floors.

Tiles must be judged on an individual basis. The condition of the tile face; the quality of the design; the rarity of the artist, company, or series; and the size of the tile or tile panel are just some of the factors to consider when assessing value. People, animals, and scenes are generally more desirable than florals and geometrics. Some glaze colors, such as true pale pink or bright red majolica, add value to Victorian tiles. Tiles may be more difficult to find than many other antiques or collectibles, partly because many were permanently installed. Unfortunately many installations have been destroyed. These factors all have influence on the tile market, and it is not unusual for prices to vary greatly. See also American Encaustic Tiling Company; Moravian; Grueby; Rookwood; other specific manufacturers. Our advisor for this category is Karen Guido; she is listed in the Directory under Pennsylvania.

Key:
maj — majolica glaze
pr mld — press molded
srs — series
tbld — tube lined
tp — transfer printed

American

Architectural Tile Co, letter S, gr/wht/gold, 6", VG.....................75.00
Batchelder, advertising, bl engobe, 3"..............................345.00
Batchelder, peacocks, bl engobe, 12".................................940.00
Batchelder, rooster, words & arrow, bl engobe, 3½"...........500.00
California Faience, profile encircled in leaves, mc, 6x3", VG.....210.00
California Faience, 3 castles, mc, 6x3", VG........................250.00
California Faience, 3 flowers & vines, mc, 5½" dia..............600.00
Cambridge, shell, wht, pr mld, 6" 30.00
Claycraft, cactus & desert scene, mc matt, 8x3" vertical.......550.00
Claycraft, pirate scene, mc matt, 16x12" 2,900.00
Claycraft, spider web, pot & pen, mc matt, 4" 350.00
Flint Faience, cattails, mc, 6"..805.00
Flint Faience, sailing ship, unglazed, 4" 90.00
Franklin, bird, mc, pr mld, 4"..40.00
Gladding McBean, bear, mc, 6" 95.00
Grueby, tulip & 4 leaves, matt grs & bl, 6", VG................2,600.00
Grueby, Viking ship, 7-color, kiln pop, 12"...................59,400.00
Grueby, 2 pine trees, sgn FH, mc, 6"..............................4,250.00
Harris Strong, Fr playing cards, mc, pr mld, 13x8" (ea), set of 4...1,500.00
Hull, cvd geometric, mc, 6"..225.00
ITT, geometric, bl/buff, encaustic, 4"................................55.00
Low, cherub stove tile, gr, pr mld, 5½x3".........................225.00
Malibu, geometric, brn/gr, pillow tiles, 4" (ea), set of 4........165.00
Marblehead, 2 topiaries, mc, rstr, 6"..............................2,400.00
Moravian, Birds of Bedwyn Magna, yel/terra cotta, 4¾"............185.00
Moravian, Knight of Margham charging left, yel/half glazed, 7x5" ..385.00
Moravian, Marcus, gr w/red flush, 4¾"............................120.00
Mosaic, ship, cuerda seca, mc, 6".....................................100.00
Mosaic, Where are you going..., mc, 6", VG.....................120.00
Mosaic, Woodrow Wilson, bl/wht, oval, 5", VG 75.00
Mueller Mosaic, cvg geometric, bl/wht/yel, 6"...................145.00
National Tile Co, advertising, wht/blk, 4"...........................40.00
Owens, Old Mother Goose, mc, fr, 12"...........................2,000.00
Pacific Pottery, geometric, turq/orange, 6" dia....................75.00
Pacific Tile & Trim, moderne circles, bl/wht/gray, 6"............35.00
Pewabic, 1935 scene, mc lustre, 3" dia 200.00
Pillin, woman & bird, sgn, mc, 5½"................................525.00
Providential, lady's portrait, brn, pr mld, 6" 200.00
Rookwood faience, landscape, mc, pr mld, 12", VG...............2,700.00
Rookwood faience, 2 fish, seaweed & water, bl & wht, 12x6" .1,600.00
San Jose Potteries, Mexicans carrying jugs, mc, 6" 600.00
San Jose Potteries, nun reading Bible, mc, 6", VG 425.00
Santa Monica Brick, geometric, mc, 4" 95.00
Solon & Larkin, floral, mc, 4"...65.00
Taylor Tilery, Conestoga wagon scene, mc, table w/6 6" tiles ..2,000.00
Trent, girl w/kerchief, bl, stove tile, fr, 3" 70.00
Trent, pig w/words, sgn, 6" 450.00
Unknown, California, geometric, mc, 8" 80.00
Unknown, man courting woman & cactus, mc, 8½".............500.00
Unknown, poppies, mc, pr mld, 7x5" 300.00
WACO, pinwheel, brns, 4" 75.00
Walrich, mtn lake scene, mc, pr mld, 5½".........................600.00
Weller, lion & shield, unglazed, 4", VG 80.00

English

Alfred Meakin, water lily, bl/gr/beige, 6" 85.00

DeMorgan, BBB design, bl/gr/mauve, 6" **500.00**
DeMorgan, Persian design, mc, 8" **960.00**
Flaxman, floral, barbotine, mc, 6" **85.00**
H Richards, floral, turq/yel/wht/pk, 6" (ea), pr............................**120.00**
Maw, floral, pale red lustre, 6" **70.00**
Maw, portrait, brn, pr mld, 6" (ea), pr **375.00**
Minton & Co, geometric, bl/wht/buff, encaustic, 4" **90.00**
Minton & Co, leaves/geometrics, brn/buff, encaustic, 6" ea, set of 9.**450.00**
Mintons ChWks, Aeosop's Fables, fox & goat, brn/wht, 6" **130.00**
Mintons ChWks, St Augustine, Early English History, brn/buff, 6" ..**120.00**
Mintons ChWks, Tanner, Industry series, bl/wht, 6" **160.00**
Sherwin & Cotton, Admiral Jellico, by Cartlidge, photographic, 6x9" ..**325.00**
T&R Boote, Art Nouveau red flower, mc, pr mld, 6" **46.00**
Wedgwood, Oriental lady & scene, hand colored, 6" **112.00**
Wedgwood, sunflower, bl/wht, in brass trivet, 6"...........................**70.00**

Other Countries

Belgium, Boch Freres, swan, tp, bl/gr/wht, 6" **85.00**
Belgium, Hemixem, Art Nouveau mum, mc, 6" **135.00**
Belgium, Herent, Art Nouveau floral, mc, pr mld, 6"...................**125.00**
Germany, Georg Schmider, floral wreath w/ribbons, mc, 6"........**135.00**
Germany, Meissen, Art Nouveau poppies, gray/pk, 6" **165.00**
Germany, SOF, fish swimming in weeds, gr maj, 6" **400.00**
Royal Delft Faience, swan, mc, self-fr, 4" **65.00**
Spain, Daniel Zuloaga, peasant scene, mc, 8x6" **160.00**
Spain, Ramos Rejano, man's face, mc, 5½" **35.00**

Tinware

In the American household of the seventeenth and eighteenth centuries, tinware items could be found in abundance, from food containers to foot warmers and mirror frames. Although the first settlers brought much of their tinware with them from Europe, by 1798 sheets of tin plate were being imported from England for use by the growing number of American tinsmiths. Tinwares were often decorated either by piercing or painting designs which were both freehand and stenciled. (See Toleware.) By the early 1900s, many homes had replaced their old tinware with the more attractive aluminum and graniteware.

In the nineteenth century, tenth wedding anniversaries were traditionally celebrated by gifts of tin. Couples gave big parties, dressed in their wedding clothes, and reaffirmed their vows before their friends and families who arrived bearing (and often wearing) tin gifts, most of which were quite humorous. Anniversary tin items may include hats, cradles, slippers and shoes, rolling pins, etc.

See also Primitives and Kitchen Collectibles.

Candle sconces, chimneyed top above elongated body, paint traces, 13½x3", $635.00 for the pair. (Photo courtesy Skinner, Inc.)

Anniversary, bouquet of 8 flowers, 16" **600.00**
Anniversary, top hat, lt rust, 8" **525.00**
Apple corer, rnd wooden knob hdl, ca 1877, EX **18.00**
Chamberstick, deep saucer base & push-up, 5" **98.00**
Coffeepot, punched tulip, raised lines/beading, dome lid, 12", VG.**825.00**
Coffeepot, punched tulips/hearts/lines, att M Uebele, PA, sm rpr, 11"..**4,125.00**
Coffeepot, side strap hdl, 8" **85.00**
Cracker pricker/cutter, fluted edge, 1900s, 2¼" dia.....................**45.00**
Dinner horn, orig red & bl japanning, 17" **65.00**
Dipper, trn wood hdl, 4"..**52.50**
Dutch oven, iron spit, lt rust, 19"...**350.00**
Egg poacher, 2-egg, wire hdl at bk, EX **35.00**
Funnel, worn gr pnt, hdl, mk Nesco, sm, EX.................................**18.00**
Funnel, 6½" dia **27.50**
Hand warmer, bl & gold litho, pierced, 1x4⅝x2¾" **65.00**
Kettle lifter/pour, ironware hdls adjust, Pat 1898, 16x10".............**50.00**
Loaf baker, Victorian, 3x8", EX..**18.00**
Measure, emb rings, 1-gal **55.00**
Measure, emb rings, 1-qt **32.50**
Oil lamp filler, squatty funnel shape, Shaker type........................**85.00**
Pie tin, Barr Hotel Pastry Shop, pierced bottom, 8¾" **20.00**
Pie tin, Gardner, 9"..**9.00**
Pie tin, Kitchen Made, slight rust, 9"...**7.00**
Pie tin, Mrs Fields, pierced bottom, 8¾" **12.00**
Pie tin, Ovenex...Made in England, 1950s, 6", EX........................**10.00**
Pie tin, Scotty's, burnished, 9¾" **10.00**
Pie tin, Silver Star, pierced bottom, 8¾" **12.50**
Rack, potato baking; rnd points hold 6, hangs, 1909, 14x2¼" **65.00**
Sconce, crimped oval bk, 1800s, 15x9" **250.00**
Sconce, rnd medallion crest w/crimped edges, blk rpt, 13x2¼" ..**275.00**
Sconces, rnd crimped bks, 1 socket w/crimped drip pans, late, 13", pr.**440.00**
Scoop, cheese; rnd tin blade, maple hdl, 10¾" **65.00**
Scoop, flour; rnd stick hdl, mk Dover, lg **38.00**
Soap grater, curved front, rolled edges, 5½x13" **50.00**
Strainer pan, oval, ftd, 3¼x9½x6¾", EX **30.00**
Teakettle, stick spout, strap hdl, handmade, early, 5½" dia **70.00**
Toddy/ale warmer, funnel shape cup, saucer base, 1800s **160.00**

Tobacciana

Tobacciana is the generally accepted term used to cover a field of collecting that includes smoking pipes, cigar molds, cigarette lighters, humidors — in short, any article having to do with the practice of using tobacco in any form. Perhaps the most valuable variety of pipes is the meerschaum, hand carved from hydrous magnesium, an opaque white-gray or cream-colored mineral of the soapstone family. (Much of this is today mined in Turkey which has the largest meerschaum deposit in the world, though there are other deposits of lesser significance around the globe.) These figural bowls often portray an elaborately carved mythological character, an animal, or a historical scene. Amber is sometimes used for the stem. Other collectible pipes are corn cob (Missouri Meerschaum) and Indian peace pipes of clay or catlinite. (See American Indian Art.)

Chosen because it was the Indians who first introduced the white man to smoking, the cigar store Indian was a symbol used to identify tobacco stores in the nineteenth century. The majority of them were hand carved between 1830 and 1900 and are today recognized as some of the finest examples of early wood sculptures. When found they command very high prices.

For further information on lighters, refer to *Collector's Guide to Cigarette Lighters* by James Flanagan.

See also Advertising; Snuff Boxes.

Ashtray, Blue Delphite, hat form, emb cord around crown, 6⅛" ..42.00
Ashtray, bronze w/sailfish at side, EX patina, 4½x5½" 30.00
Ashtray, ceramic, Golden Gate...Expo, bl, 2 rests, 1939, 4¾" 12.50
Ashtray, ceramic, pig face, smoke exits nose, 4⅝" 30.00
Ashtray, ceramic nodder, lady pulls up skirt, mc 97.00
Ashtray, chrome fretwork fr, cobalt glass insert, Hong Kong, 4" dia .25.00
Ashtray, Delft, house form w/smoke outlet in chimney, Holland, 3⅝"..22.00
Ashtray, glass, amethyst cloverleaf, Tiffin, 4¾" 30.00
Ashtray, glass, Candlewick, crystal heart, Imperial, pre-1940, 4½"..11.00
Ashtray, glass, cut, jewel-like center, Austria, 5¾" dia 80.00
Ashtray, glass, Forest Green, hexagonal, Anchor Hocking, 5¾" 9.00
Ashtray, glass, Panelled Grape, irid, Westmoreland, 4" sq.............28.00
Ashtray, plastic, Loch Ness Monster, Scotland, 5¾" 8.00
Ashtray, pot metal, Leaning Tower of Piza, silver-tone, Italy, 4¼" .10.00
Ashtray, pottery, panther atop tray, blk, Pat Appl 1929, 4½"........15.00
Ashtray, SP, Nouveau girl w/flowing hair & flower in hand, 8" W .147.00
Ashtray, sterling, 3-D llama in center, ruffled rim, 3½" 40.00
Cigarette box, emb metal, cedar lined, Japan, 4¼x3½x2".............50.00
Cigarette box, engine-trn decor, John Davis & Son, 1936, EX ...425.00
Cigarette cards, Film Stars, 2nd series, J Player & Sons, 1934, 50 for..50.00
Cigarette case, cvd tiger maple lid, sterling hdl, burled base, 7"..100.00
Cigarette case, sterling, eng initials, EX 125.00
Cigarette case, sterling, good & evil figures eng, Siam, 1920s, EX.145.00
Cigarette case/compact/lighter, chromium/enamel, Evans, 1930s, 4"..125.00
Cigarette holder, sterling, 2", w/orig case.................................75.00
Cigarette lighter, Comet, chromium/red plastic, Ronson, 1950s, 2¼"..15.00
Cigarette lighter, Flaminare, chromium/enamel, Parker, 1950s, 2¾"..40.00
Cigarette lighter, floral on wht ceramic, Fr, 1950s, 2½x1¼" 30.00
Cigarette lighter, gold-plate w/MOP, musical, Pac, 1950s, 2⅝x1⅜".100.00
Cigarette lighter, Mini Cadete, chromium, Ronson, 1959, 1⅜x1¾"..40.00
Cigarette lighter, Pacard 1903 auto, ceramic, mk 1964...Japan, 4" L.35.00
Cigarette lighter, silver, butane, Cartier, 1970s, 2¾x1" 150.00
Cigarette lighter/case, chromium & leather, Adonis, Ronson, 1950s, 5".75.00
Cigarette pack, Eli Cutter, full carton, sealed, M 55.00
Cigarette purse w/brass lighter on chain, Fashion, 1950s, 4¼x3"..70.00
Cutter, CI, unmk, 19th C, 9½", on 9x2½" wooden block, EX......70.00
Cutter, Joh Finzer Five Bros, CI, 6¾x18" 175.00
Cutter, McMillan, CI on mahog base, 8", EX................................40.00
Cutter, RJR Brown's Mule, CI, Enterprise, 19", EX......................90.00
Cutter, Schnull & Co Indianapolis IN, CI, 1888, 16½", EX.........85.00
Cutter, Star Save the Tags, Enterprise Co, 19".............................95.00
Cutter, Trunhoff, CI, orig blk pnt, lt rust, 15½" 115.00
Figure, Indian lady w/cigars, cvd/pnt wood, att Brooks, 1870s, 71⅜"..36,425.00
Figure, turbaned man w/pouch & knife, cvd/pnt wood, 1830s, 62"..23,500.00
Humidor, cvd wood w/inscription, tree trunk w/rabbit & vines, Fr/1871 .315.00
Humidor, dk oak, sm age split, minor loose beading, tin liner.....135.00
Humidor, girl w/bunnies figural, pnt terra cotta, #3490, 9¼" 715.00
Humidor, Indian head, porc, E Bohne & Sohne, sm rpr, 5¼" 200.00
Humidor, man playing zither figural, pnt terra cotta, JM62, 10¾"..950.00
Humidor, man writing on brd figural, pnt terra cotta, 10½" 700.00
Humidor, Munich child in basket, pnt terra cotta, HM3567, 8¾" .350.00
Humidor, woman w/toothache, pnt majolica, #847, 12½" 515.00
Lunch box, red & blk pnt weave on tin, tiger head ea side, EX 47.50
Lunch box, Tobacco Class, peacock graphics on tin, EX 90.00
Pipe cleaning set, MacBaron, wood/plastic pipe+tools, M unopened.60.00
Pipe holder, cast metal, dog form, 2¾x5½x3"................................55.00
Pipe holder, compo, Indian moccasin form, 5⅜"............................75.00
Pipe holder, wooden, half-circle, 7x6½".......................................38.00
Pipe rack, wood w/red pnt, lollipop-shape bk, early 1800s, 5x5"..1,100.00
Pipe rest, bronze, dbl, Denmark, 1½x5½".....................................110.00
Pipe rest, metal dog on wooden base, old pnt 35.00
Smoke set, SP, figural stag at side, Anchor SP Co #565 ....650.00
Tobacco rug/felt, American Doughboy on red, WWI, EX 18.00
Tobacco rug/felt, American flag, 48 stars, 5¼x8½", EX.................12.50

Tobacco rug/felt, Argentina flag, 5⅜x8⅛", EX 10.00
Tobacco rug/felt, French soldier, silk fringe, 1914, 4¾x3" 10.00
Tobacco rug/felt, Norway flag, 5½x8¼" 20.00
Tobacco silk, Carnations & Mignonette, M 11.00
Tobacco silk, daisies, fraying, 2x3" 8.00
Tobacco silk, Great Bear, Indian chief, EX....................................27.50
Tobacco silk, Indian lady w/baby, EX..65.00
Tobacco silk, James A Garfield & facsimile signature, 3", EX 8.00
Tobacco silk, Japanese flag, EX 6.00
Tobacco silk, St Bernard, Switzerland, 2x3", EX.............................9.00
Tobacco tag, Battle Ax, tin ax form, EX...9.00
Tobacco tag, Black Mirah, tin, EX 7.00
Tobacco tag, Favorite, FM Bohannons, tin, EX...............................8.00
Tobacco tag, Rose Bud, Taylor Bros, tin, NM..................................8.00

Pipes

Ceramic, HP castle scene, wood stem, late 1800s, 12½" 95.00
Clay, wht w/short stem, 6½" 30.00
Delft bowl, curved stem, mk Holland, 2" deep bowl, 3½" stem ..185.00
Meerschaum, bearded man in night cap, long amber stem, 10", EX in case .575.00
Meerschaum, Black lady w/scarf covering hair, amber stem, 8¼" +case..675.00
Meerschaum, nude embracing fish, amber stem, 19th C, 9" 1,850.00
Meerschaum, turk's head, amber hdl, EX......................................70.00
Opium, scrimshaw bone, Buddhist symbols, mahog ends, 16".....145.00
Soapstone, cvd dog w/bird in mouth forms bowl, EX detail, EX....50.00
Tortoise shell-cased bowl w/rhinestones, lady's, 1900s, 5½" 100.00
Wood, Bruyere Garantie, twig stem, EX..68.00
Wood, cvd bears on stump forms bowl, celluloid stem, 7½"........250.00
Wood, cvd from tree knot, ca 1900, 5"...60.00
Wood, cvd Hitler head bowl, Mk Bruyere Tarantie AP, WWII era, 6" .150.00

Toby Jugs

    The delightful jug known as the Toby dates back to the eighteenth century, when factories in England produced them for export to the American colonies. Named for the character Toby Philpots in the song *The Little Brown Jug*, the Toby was fashioned in the form of a jolly fellow, usually holding a jug of beer and a glass. The earlier examples were made with strict attention to details such as fingernails and teeth. Originally representing only a non-entity, a trend developed to portray well-known individuals such as George II, Napoleon, and Ben Franklin. Among the most-valued Tobies are those produced by Ralph Wood I in the late 1700s. By the mid-1830s Tobies were being made in America.

    See also Doulton; Occupied Japan.

Hearty Good Fellow, mc on pearlware, 19th C, pipe missing, 12" .400.00
Lead-glazed creamware, brn/gr translucent enamel, 1880s, rstr, 10"..800.00
Long John Silver, Shorter & Son Ltd England, 9¾" 475.00
Man in maroon & gr, seated w/jug, Davenport, 1830s, 9⅜"........300.00
Man seated w/jug & pipe, England, 8" 160.00
Man standing w/hand in vest pocket, 1830s, EX..........................650.00
Martha Gunn, Pratt-type, ca 1800, rstr hat brim, 9" 1,000.00
Martha Gunn, underglaze enameled pearlware, 1880, rstr/flakes, 9½".1,000.00
Sharp Face, mc underglaze enamels, Staffordshire, late 1700s, 11", VG .500.00
Snuff Taker, Allerton, 7" 125.00

Toleware

    The term 'toleware' originally came from a French term meaning 'sheet iron.' Today it is used to refer to paint-decorated tin items, most popular from 1800 to 1850s. The craft flourished in Pennsylvania, Connecticut, Maine, and New York. Early toleware has a very distinctive look. The surface is dull and unvarnished; background colors range from black to cream. Geometrics are quite common, but florals and fruits were also favored. Items made after 1850 were often stenciled, and gold trim was sometimes added.

American toleware is usually found in practical, everyday forms — trays, boxes, and coffeepots are most common — while French examples might include candlesticks, wine coolers, jardinieres, etc. Be sure to note color and design when determining date and value, but condition of the paint is the most important worth-assessing factor. Unless noted otherwise, values are for very good examples with average wear.

Box, deed; cherries & leaves on wht band on dk japanning, 6¾"..**650.00**
Box, deed; floral on blk w/wavy lines, alligatored, 6x9x5" **1,450.00**
Box, deed; flowers/X-hatching/bands, yel/gr/red on japanning, 8"..**1,430.00**
Box, deed; leaves/lines, stencil/HP, gilt/yel/blk on red, 10" **2,350.00**
Box, deed; swags/leaves/waves on brn japanning w/red & yel, 10", EX...**990.00**
Box, deed; swags/waves/stripes, yel/red/blk on japanning, 8" **990.00**
Box, deed; tulips/leaves, 3-color on blk, yel int, oval, wear, 7", G.**110.00**
Coal scuttle, florals/gold edge, sloped lift lid, English, 1880s, EX...**235.00**
Coffeepot, floral, mc on blk, 19th C, 10⅝", EX..........................**765.00**
Coffeepot, floral, red & yel on blk japanning, gooseneck, 11", G ...**975.00**
Coffeepot, floral, red/yel/gr on japanning, yel leaves, dome lid, 11".**1,100.00**
Coffeepot, floral/fruit, candy-stripe border on blk, PA/1820s, 11".**1,000.00**
Coffeepot, fruit & flowers on tan & wht circles, brass finial, 11".**965.00**
Cradle, floral on red, bird on ft brd, doll sz, 14x21" **550.00**
Match safe, berries/bands, mc on japanning, cut-out crest, wall mt.**275.00**
Sugar bowl, flowers stenciled on japanning, minor wear/dent, 3½x4" .**110.00**
Tea caddy, blk leopard spots on golden japanning w/yel/wht stripes .**1,100.00**
Tea caddy, fruit, mc on dk brn, wear, 4⅛", G...............................**525.00**
Tray, amber crystallized w/3-color floral border, dtd 1860, 13", G..**660.00**
Tray, busy harbor scene, rtcl gallery, Fr, early 1900s, 24" **350.00**
Tray, floral, mc on red, floral border, 1800s, 26½" dia **800.00**
Tray, flowers & flags on blk, minor rpt, 8-sided, 13x9" **220.00**
Tray, landscape/vine border on woodgrain ground, 1850s, 30" **320.00**
Tray, leaves/tulips, red/gr on blk, mustard border, 12", G............**110.00**
Tray, stenciled scene w/flower border on blk, 21x28", G **150.00**
Tray, tulips/leaves, mc on blk, 2¾x12⅝x7¾" **660.00**

Tools

Before the Civil War, tools for the most part were handmade. Some were primitive to the point of crudeness, while others reflected the skill of those who took pride in their trade. Increasing demand for quality tools and the dawning of the age of industrialization resulted in tools that were mass produced. Factors important in evaluating antique tools are scarcity, usefulness, and portability. Those with a manufacturer's mark are worth more than unmarked items. When no condition is indicated, the items listed here are assumed to be in excellent condition. Our advisor for this category is Jim Calison; he is listed in the Directory under New York. For more information, we recommend *Antique Tools* by Kathryn McNerney (Collector Books).

See also Keen Kutter; Stanley; Winchester.

Anvil, blacksmith's; Vulcan Brand #6, 3¼x10½" **160.00**
Ax, goose-wing; benchmarked IM w/star & decor, 14¼x7½" **440.00**
Ax, hewing; wrought iron broad blade stamped Maria Rast..., 12" hdl..**275.00**
Bench shears, metal worker's, wrought iron, mk KY, 38".............**180.00**
Bit brace, Holt Mfg #8, w/7 orig bits, mk Pat July 11, 1893 ....**375.00**
Bolt & chain cutters, HK Porterjaws mk Allen Randall #4, 48" ...**75.00**
Box, wooden, arched divider, pierced hdl, old bl pnt, 9x27x13".**375.00**
Drill driver, Yankee #50..**25.00**
Drill press, belt driven, Goodell Pratt, 1900s **190.00**

Drill press, jeweler's; Jacobs Mfg, 1902 ....**55.00**
Drill/boring machine, for barn beams, Miller Falls Co **525.00**
Gauge, hemp & wire rope; wood & brass, H Hood Haggie & Sons, 1900s..**140.00**
Gauge, leather cutting; rosewood & brass, pistol hdl, CS Osborne..**75.00**
Gauge, slide rule; brass & wood, J Rabone & Sons #1462, 3" **40.00**
Hammer, roofer's slate; Fredley-Voshardt Co, 11¾x8½" **130.00**
Hammer, slater's; Belden Machine Co, leather-wrapped hdl **50.00**
Hammer, stamping; Spanish River Log Co, lg S, 4-lb...................**90.00**
Nail puller, Bridgeport Hardware #56, Sure Grip hdl, 22½".........**25.00**
Plane, bench; wood knob, Chaplin's Improved, 1902, 15" **100.00**
Plane, block; Standard Rule #15, 2x7" sole..................................**210.00**
Plane, rabbet; Bailey's Victor #11, 1877-1888, EX....................**1,225.00**
Plane, smoother; Union #3, fluted sole, mahog hdl, 1903...........**250.00**
Pliers, barrel jaws slide bk when opened, mk Oct 19 75 (1875)....**40.00**
Pliers, wire cutter; Klein #6, never used, M (NM box) **40.00**
Rule, folding; elephant ivory, J Rabone & Sons, 24" **290.00**
Rule, folding; eng mks w/flower petals at hinge, Fr, 13" extended.**60.00**
Rule, 4-fold; ivory w/NP mts, James Gregory, 19th C, 3" **90.00**
Saw, table; hand-crank, WF & J Barnes Type 1, 1880s, EX **1,075.00**
Saw, 2-man logging; Disston SUA #128, 66", EX **80.00**
Saw sharpener, mk Disston USA #2, w/bench vise, 14x14x6"...**100.00**
Spoke shave, boxwood w/brass screws, steel blade, Litfield, 11¾".**40.00**
Square level, Simplex, Pat Apr 25, 1905, brass **30.00**
Wrench, adjustable; Becklin Wrench Co, 10"...............................**50.00**
Wrench, hammer; Diamond Adjustable Combination Buggy Nut, 1880s.**55.00**
Wrench, Oliver # 8, mk Pat Pend Mfd by L Hengy, 8".................**75.00**
Wrench, tractor/plow; cut-out style, Buffalo Pitts, 2x10" **75.00**

Toothbrush Holders

Most of the collectible toothbrush holders were made in prewar Japan and were modeled after popular comic strip, Disney, and nursery rhyme characters. Since many were made of bisque and decorated with unfired paint, it's not uncommon to find them in less-than-perfect paint, a factor you must consider when attempting to assess their values. Our advisor for this category is Marilyn Cooper, author of *Pictorial Guide to Toothbrush Holders*; she is listed in the Directory under Texas. Plate numbers in the descriptions that follow refer to her book.

Doc (dwarf from Snow White), ceramic, Walt Disney Productions, paper label, from $85.00 to $95.00. (Photo courtesy Carole Bess White)

Andy Gump & Min, Japan, bsk, plate #221, 4", from $85 to......**100.00**
Annie Oakley, Japan, plate #11, 5¾", from $125 to **150.00**
Baby deer, mk Brush Teeth Daily, Japan, plate #12, 4", from $110 to.**140.00**
Bear w/scarf & hat, Japan, 5½", from $80 to..............................**100.00**
Betty Boop w/toothbrush & cup, KFS, 5", from $85 to **100.00**
Big Bird, Taiwan (RCC), 4½", from $85 to...................................**95.00**
Bonzo w/side tray, Germany, plate #23, 5⅝", from $135 to.........**150.00**
Boy w/violin, Japan (Goldcastle), plate #30, 5½", from $80 to.....**90.00**
Candlestick Maker, Japan (Goldcastle), plate #150, 5", from $70 to .**85.00**
Carousel, 4 holes, hangs, no tray, Crown mark, 5", from $100 to ..**125.00**
Cat (Calico), Japan, plate #37, 5½", from $90 to **110.00**

Cat w/bass fiddle, Japan, 6", from $115 to......................135.00
Clown head w/bug on nose, Japan, 5", from $150 to..................180.00
Dachshund, 2 holes, ft form holder for toothpaste, 5⅛", $70 to ...90.00
Dalmatian, Germany, 4", from $170 to 190.00
Dog begging, lustre, 2 holes, hangs, no tray, 3¾", from $90 to....110.00
Dog w/basket, Japan, plate #72, from $90 to 110.00
Donald Duck, WDE, bsk, plate #83, 5", from $250 to...............300.00
Ducky Dandy, Japan, 4", from $150 to 175.00
Dutch boy & girl kissing, Japan, plate #88, 6", from $55 to 65.00
Dwarfs at fence (Sleepy & Dopey), Japan/WDE, bsk, 3½", $1,000 to .1,275.00
Flapper, plate #230, 4¼", from $120 to 140.00
Indian chief, 2 holes, hangs, tray holds toothpaste, 4½", $250 to ...300.00
Little Red Riding Hood, Germany (DRGM), plate #210, 5½", $200 to ..250.00
Lone Ranger, chalk, 1 hole, free-standing, no tray, 4", from $70 to ..90.00
Mary Poppins, Japan, plate #119, 6", from $100 to.....................150.00
Mickey Mouse & Pluto, WDE, 4½", from $250 to 300.00
Old King Cole, Japan, plate #125, 5¼", from $85 to..................100.00
Old Mother Hubbard, plate #3, from $350 to 425.00
Penguin, Japan, 5½", from $85 to.....................100.00
Pinocchio & Figaro, plate #242, Shafford, 5¼", from $500 to 525.00
Pirate w/sash, 2 holes, hangs, tray at ft holds toothpaste, 6", $80 to...95.00
Popeye, Japan, bsk, 5", from $475 to 500.00
Skeezix, metal, 2 holes, hangs, no tray, K-USA, 6", from $150 to ..175.00
Skippy, plate #245, jtd arms, 5⅝", from $175 to 200.00
Three Bears w/bowls, Japan, (KIM USUI), plate #248, 4", from $90 to...125.00
Three Little Pigs, 3 holes, free-standing, w/tray, Japan, 4", $90 to ..110.00
Three Little Pigs w/piano, WDE, bsk, 5", from $150 to..............175.00
Tom, Tom the Piper's Son, Japan, plate #154, 5¾", from $100 to...150.00
Traffic cop, Germany, Don't Forget the Teeth, plate #243, 5", $350 to .375.00
Uncle Willie, 2 holes, hangs, ft form tray, Japan, 5⅛", from $85 to ..100.00

Toothpick Holders

Once common on every table, the toothpick holder was relegated to the china cabinet near the turn of the century. Fortunately, this contributed to their survival. As a result, many are available to collectors today. Because they are small and easily displayed, they are very popular collectibles. They come in a wide range of prices to fit every budget. Many have been reproduced and, unfortunately, are being offered for sale right along with the originals. These 'repros' should be priced in the $5.00 to $30.00 range. Unless you're sure of what you're buying, choose a reputable dealer. In addition to pattern glass, you'll find examples in china, bisque, art glass, and various metals. For further information we recommend *Glass Toothpick Holders, Identification & Values*, by Neila and Tom Bredehoft and Jo and Bob Sanford.

Toothpick holders in the listings that follow are glass unless noted otherwise. Values here are for originals. Our advisor for this category is Judy A. Knauer; she is listed in the Directory under Pennsylvania.

See also specific companies (such as Northwood) and types of glassware (such as Burmese, cranberry, etc.).

Adonis (aka Gonterman Swirl), clear w/amber top, Aetna, 1888, 2½".225.00
Amberina, optic design, tricon rim, 2¼".................................385.00
Barrel (aka Daisy & Button w/Metal Bands), amber, 2⅝" 35.00
Bead Swag, emerald, Heisey, 2⅛" (+).....................................390.00
Beatty Waffle, bl opal, AJ Beatty & Sons, 1888, 2⅜"..............48.00
Blocked Thumbprint Band, clear w/ruby stain, Duncan & Miller, 2¼".65.00
Bulging Loops, opal to pk, Consolidated, 1894, 2⅜" 130.00
Cameo (aka Apple & Grape in Scroll), gr, Fostoria, 1898 .....280.00
Champion, clear w/amber stain, McKee, 1896, 2¼" 125.00
Colonial Stairsteps, lt aqua, ca 1900, 2¾".........................110.00

Columbia, clear w/eng, Columbia, 1891, 2¼".......................130.00
Columbia (aka Harvard), gr opaque, Tarentum, 1899, 2¼"......80.00
Dog & Hat, amber, Belmont, 1885, 2¾" (+)....................85.00
Estelle, Paden City, ca 1916...28.00
Flat Panel, clear w/silver o/l, Heisey, 1908, 2⅜".........................80.00
Grape w/Thumbprint, att Kokomo, 2⅜".......................48.00
Green Pepper, emerald gr, US Glass, ca 1909..................65.00
Hall of Mirrors, clear w/ruby stain, 3-hdl, 2¼".................125.00
Horse w/Cart, amber, Central, mid-1880s, 2⅞x3x1½"...........55.00
Inverted Eye, Riverside, 1902, 2⅝"................................45.00
Ivanhoe, Dalzel, Gilmore & Leighton, 1897, 2⅝x2⅛"..........125.00
Madora, Higbee, ca 1910, 2¼".................................48.00
Marjorie (aka Button Star), Cambridge, ca 1905, 2"............38.00
Medallion Sunburst, Bryce, Higbee & Co, 1905, 2⅛" 38.00
Minnesota, emerald gr w/gold, US Glass, 1898, 2½".........150.00
Nestor, amethyst, National, 1902, 2⅜"........................75.00
Nevada, clear w/gold, US Glass, 1902, 2¼".......................75.00
Ohio Star, Millersburg, 1910, 2"..................................125.00
Orient (aka Shrine), clear, Beatty-Brady, 1896, 2⅜"..........75.00
Pleated Medallion, New Martinsville, 1910, 2¼" 45.00
Pressed Optic, clear w/gold, Beaumont, 1900, 2¼"............40.00
Prison Stripe, clear w/gold, Heisey, 1906, 2⅜"..................210.00
Ranson (aka Gold Band), clear w/gold, Riverside, 2⅜" 40.00
Regina (aka Reeding), clear w/enamel, Co-operative, 1902, 2½".52.00
Rose Urn, opal, Fostoria, 1900, 2¾x3".........................58.00
Saxon, clear w/ruby stain, Adams & Co, 1888, 2⅜" 65.00
Scroll w/Cane Band, clear w/rose stain, West Virginia, 1894, 2⅜".95.00
Spiral (aka Beaded Swirl & Disc), bl, US Glass, 2½" 85.00
St Bernard (aka Dog's Head), clear satin, Indiana Tumbler & Goblet .165.00
Stars & Bars, bl, Bellaire Goblet Co, 1886, 2½"...............225.00
Stump (aka Bird & Tree), amber, McKee, 1886, 2¾" 70.00
Swag w/Brackets, canary, Jefferson, 1903, 2½" (+) 80.00
Teepee, clear w/amber stain, Duncan & Miller, 2⅜", minimum value.170.00
Texas, clear w/rose stain, US Glass, 1900, 2¾" 125.00
Thousand Eye, apple gr, Riverside, 1888, 2" 60.00
Trilby (aka Diamond Point Heart), US Glass, 1895 ....75.00
Verona (aka Waffle & Star Band), clear w/ruby stain, Tarentum, 2⅜".145.00
Victor (aka Jeweled Heart), clear opal, Dugan, 1905, 2⅜" 160.00
Wellington, clear w/gold, Windsor, 1903, 2⅛"........................42.00

Torquay Pottery

Torquay is a unique type of pottery made in the South Devon area of England as early as 1867. At the height of productivity, at least a dozen companies flourished there, producing simple folk pottery from the area's natural red clay. The ware was both wheel-turned and molded and decorated under the glaze with heavy slip resulting in low-relief nature subjects or simple scrollwork. Three of the best-known of these potteries were Watcombe (1867 – 1962); Aller Vale (in operation from the mid-1800s, producing domestic ware and architectural products); and Longpark (1890 until 1957). Watcombe and Aller Vale merged in 1901 and operated until 1962 under the name of Royal Aller Vale and Watcombe Art Pottery.

A decline in the popularity of the early classical terra-cotta styles (urns, busts, figures, etc.) lead to the introduction of painted and glazed terra-cotta wares. During the late 1880s, white clay wares, both turned and molded, were decorated with colored glazes (Stapleton ware, grotesque molded figures, ornamental vases, large jardinieres, etc.). By the turn of the century, the market for art pottery was diminishing, so the potteries turned to wares decorated in colored slips (Barbotine, Persian, Scrolls, etc.).

Motto wares were introduced in the late nineteenth century by Aller Vale and taken up in the present century by the other Torquay potteries. This eventually became the 'bread and butter' product of the local industry. This was perhaps the most famous type of ware potted in this area because of the verses, proverbs, and quotations that decorated it. This was achieved by the sgraffito technique — scratching the letters through the slip to expose the red clay underneath. The most popular patterns were Cottage, Black Cockerel, Multi-Cockerel, and a scrollwork design called Scandy. Other popular decorations were Kerswell Daisy, ships, kingfishers, applied bird decorations, Art Deco styles, Egyptian ware, and many others. Aller Vale ware may sometimes be found marked 'H.H. and Company,' a firm who assumed ownership from 1897 to 1901. 'Watcombe Torquay' was an impressed mark used from 1884 to 1927.

Our advisors for this category are Jerry and Gerry Kline; they are listed in the Directory under Ohio. If you're interested in joining a Torquay club, you'll find the address of The North American Torquay Society under Clubs, Newsletters, and Catalogs.

Art Pottery

Biscuit barrel, apple blossoms, porc, SP lid & hdl, 6½" **295.00**
Biscuit barrel, parrots on branches on bl, wrapped hdl, 6" **150.00**
Bottle, scent; Hill's English Lavender, pitcher shape, 2¾" **95.00**
Bottle, scent; Sweet Lavender, Longpark, pine-cone top, 3¼" **75.00**
Bottle, scent; 3 dimples on purple, crown top, 1924-40 mk, 3½".**70.00**
Bowl, Blarney Castle, Watcombe, hdls, ftd, 4½x4¼" **75.00**
Cat, gr, Aller Vale, rpr, 9" **490.00**
Ewer, Apple Blossom, unmk, 6½" **140.00**
Hot water jug, Sandringham, Aller Vale, 6½" **200.00**
Jardiniere, Scrolls, HM Exeter, 1920, 5½" **250.00**
Jug, Persian, Aller Vale, wht clay, 4½" **85.00**
Jug, Tintern, Longpark, ruins/water/grasses, 4¾" **95.00**
Mug, Lindisfarne Castle Holy Island, Watcombe, 2½" **55.00**
Plate, Terra Cotta, Watcombe, dog w/butterfly, 1900s, 3" **75.00**
Tray, dresser; windmill, Aller Vale, no motto, 10½x7" **395.00**
Vase, Donest Cottage, Lest We Forget, mini, 2¼" **75.00**
Vase, swan on gr tricorn shape, ca 1900, 4½" **130.00**

Devon Motto Ware

Basket, Multi-Cockerel, Longpark, 2¾x5x3¼" **95.00**
Bottle, scent; Violet, 'Kind Words Are Music...,' crown top, 4½".**75.00**
Bowl, Cottage, Watcombe, 'Early Sow Early Mow,' 1½x4½" **70.00**
Bowl, Cottage, Watcombe, 'Good Courage Breaks Ill Luck,' 1½x4½"..**70.00**
Bowl, Cottage, Watcombe, 'Waste Not Want Not,' 3½" **30.00**
Bowl, junket; Scandy, 'Help Yourself...,' 3⅜x6⅞" dia................**195.00**
Bowl, Sea Gull, Dartmouth, w/motto, 1½x4" **40.00**
Candlestick, Black Cockerel, Longpark, 'Night Is Long...,' 2½" ..**85.00**
Candlestick, Cottage, Watcombe, 2½x5x4" **75.00**
Candlestick, Longpark, 'Many Are Called...Few Get Up,' 3½" ...**89.00**
Chamberstick, Sailboat, 'Great Yarmouth, Last in Bed...,' 3½"....**68.00**
Cheese dish, Cottage, unmk, 'Help Yourself Don't Be Shy,' 6½" L..**150.00**
Cheese dish, Cottage, Watcombe, 'Comfort Is Better...,' 6½" L.**175.00**
Creamer, Cockerel, 'Elp Yersef Teu Gram,' 2½" **68.00**
Creamer, Scandy, unmk, 'He Does Much Who Does...,' 3¾".......**65.00**
Creamer & sugar bowl, Shamrock, Watcombe, mini, 2", 1½" **60.00**
Cup, Cottage, Made in England, 'A Still Tongue...,' 2" **35.00**
Cup, Cottage, Watcombe; 'Speak Little Speak Well,' child sz, 3½" ..**85.00**
Cup & saucer, 'Have Another Cup Full,' 3x3⅜", 5⅛" **80.00**
Cup & saucer, Kerswell Daisy, Aller Vale, 'Jist a Teeny...,' sm......**55.00**
Egg cup, Cockerel, Longpark, 'Fresh Laid,' 2½" **50.00**
Egg cup, Cottage, 'Laid To Day,' 3½x3½" **42.00**
Egg cup, Cottage, 'Waste Not Want Not,' 2¾x2" **65.00**
Hatpin holder, Cockerel, 'Keep Me On Dressing,' 4¾" **175.00**
Humidor, Black Cockerel, Longpark, 'Dawnt'ee Be Fraid...,' 5¼".**215.00**
Jardiniere, Passion Flower, HM Exeter, 'For Every Ill...,' 6¾" **310.00**
Jardiniere, Samrock, Aller Vale, 'Old Erin's Native Shamrock,' 3".**65.00**
Jug, Cottage, 'Kind Words Are Music...,' 5¾" **180.00**

Jug, Cottage, Devon, 'Time Ripens All Things,' 4" **85.00**
Jug, Cottage, Watcombe, 'Better To Sit Still...Fall,' 4" **85.00**
Jug, Multi-Cockerel, Aller Vale, 'Be Canny Wi...,' mini, 2½" **85.00**
Jug, puzzle-liquor; Scandy, Aller Vale, 'Come Fill Me...,' 1900s, 6".**240.00**
Jug, Scandy, Aller Vale, 'Demsher Craim Yak...,' mini, 2½"........**60.00**
Jug, Scandy, Longpark, 3-hdl, 'Niver Zay Die...,' 3¼" **85.00**
Match striker, Scandy, 2½" **85.00**
Mug, Cockerel, Longpark, 'For a Good Boy,' 1930-40, 3", NM....**80.00**
Mug, Cottage, 'Enough's As Good As a Feast,' 3½x4" **80.00**
Mug, Cottage, 'Up to the Lips Over the Gums...' **95.00**
Mug, Cottage, Watcombe, 'From Rocks & Sands & Barren...,' 4½".**100.00**
Mug, Cottage, Watcombe, 'Tom Tom the Piper's Son,' 3x3¼" **95.00**
Mustard pot, 'Soft Words Win Hard Hearts,' 3" **75.00**
Pinch pot, Double Sandy, Aller Vale, no motto, mini, 2" **75.00**
Pitcher, Cockerel, 'Good Morning & Fresh...,' 4½" **98.00**
Pitcher, Cockerel, St Mary Church Pottery Ltd, w/motto, 4¼" ...**95.00**
Pitcher, Cottage, 'Help Yourself...,' 5¼x4½" **110.00**
Pitcher, Cottage, Watcombe, 'Don't Worry It May Never Happen,' 5½".**135.00**
Pitcher, Kerswell Daisy, Aller Vale, 'Freely Drink...,' 4" **95.00**
Pitcher, Scandy, 'Say Well Is Good...Better,' 4x4" **125.00**
Plate, Cottage, Dartmouth, 'Never Say Die...,' 5⅝" **42.00**
Plate, Cottage, Watcombe, 'Action Speaks Louder...,' 7¼" **95.00**
Plate, Cottage, Watcombe, 'May the Hinges of Friendship...,' 7¼".**95.00**
Plate, Longpark, 'Always Help a Lame Dog...,' 3¾" **48.00**
Plate, Scandy, unmk, 'Rolling Stone Gathers...,' 4" **50.00**
Salt cellar, Cottage, 'Elp Yerzel,' master, 3¼" **65.00**
Server, Cottage, 3-section, 'If You Can't Be Aisy,' 7¼" **150.00**
Shakers, Shamrock, 'Shamrock of Old Ireland/Land Where...,' pr.**50.00**
Sugar bowl, Black Cockerel, 'Be Aisy w/the...,' 4¼x5½" **95.00**
Sugar bowl, Cottage, 'Help Yourself to Sugar,' 1930s, 2x3½".......**28.00**
Sugar bowl, Rooster, Longpark, 'Help Yerzel tu Sugar,' EX..........**35.00**
Tea strainer, St Mary Church, 'Buckfast,' 3½" **60.00**
Teapot, Cottage, 'Du-ee Drink a Cup a Tay,' 3¾x4½" **110.00**
Teapot, Cottage, Aller Vale, 'Due Cum in an 'Av...,' 4" **120.00**
Teapot, Cottage, Watcombe, 'Don't Worry It May Never Happen,' 7".**250.00**
Teapot, Scandy, Aller Vale, 'Weel Take a Cup...,' 3¼x6¼" **195.00**
Teapot, Thistle, Longpark, 'It's Unco Refreshin,' 4½", NM.........**85.00**
Toast rack, Cottage, Watcombe, 'Take a Little Toast.,' 3x3½"...**125.00**
Tray, Cottage, Watcombe, 'Greatest Troubles...,' 8¾x6" **195.00**
Vase, Scandy, Aller Vale, 'Have Courage Boys...,' 10⅛" **395.00**
Vase, udder; Scandy, Aller Vale, 'Actions Speak...' **95.00**

Tortoise Shell

The outer shell of several species of land turtles, called tortoises, was once commonly used to make brooches, combs, small boxes, and novelty items. It was often used for inlay as well. The material is easily recognized by its mottled brown and yellow coloring. Because some of these turtles are now on the endangered list, such use is prohibited.

Box, multilevel bombe form w/brass bracket ft, 1800s, 18x13x14".**8,200.00**
Case, cigarette; hinged, brass bar inside, 5¼x3x½", EX **165.00**
Case, dance card; ivory & silver inlay, 1880s, EX **325.00**
Comb, ca 1900, 8½x9½"..**42.50**
Jar, tortoise-shell lid on SP base, English hallmks, 1½x1¾"..........**85.00**

Tortoise Shell Glass

By combining several shades of glass — brown, clear, and yellow — manufacturers of the nineteenth century were able to produce an art glass that closely resembled the shell of the tortoise. Some of this type of glassware was manufactured in Germany. In America it was made by several firms, the most prominent of which was the Boston and Sandwich Glass Works.

Bottle, scent; short neck, flattened bulb, 5½x4"+tall stopper **40.00**
Bowl, mold blown, 7x11" **70.00**
Bowl, 8½" **60.00**

Finger bowl, silver flecks throughout, attributed Sandwich, ca 1890, 2¾", $200.00. (Photo courtesy John A. Shuman III)

Paperweight, pear shape w/gold on leaf **95.00**
Vase, sq sides, 12½x4" **90.00**

Toys

Toys can be classified into at least two categories: early collectible toys with an established history, and the newer toys. The antique toys are easier to evaluate. A great deal of research has been done on them, and much data is available. The newer toys are just beginning to be studied; relative information is only now being published, and the lack of production records makes it difficult to know how many may be available. Often warehouse finds of these newer toys can change the market. This has happened with battery-operated toys and to some extent with robots. Review past issues of this guide. You will see the changing trends for the newer toys. All toys become more important as collectibles when a fixed period of manufacture is known. When we know the numbers produced and documentation of the makers is established, the prices become more predictable.

The best way to learn about toys is to attend toy shows and auctions. This will give you the opportunity to compare prices and condition. The more collectors and dealers you meet, the more you will learn. There is no substitute for holding a toy in your hand and seeing for yourself what they are. If you are going to be a serious collector, buy all the books you can find. Read every article you see. Knowledge is vital to building a good collection. Study all books that are available. These are some of the most helpful: *Schroeder's Collectible Toys, Antique to Modern*, by Sharon and Bob Huxford; *Cartoon Toys & Collectibles* by David Longest; *G-Men and FBI Toys and Collectibles* by Harry and Jody Whitworth; *Breyer Animal Collector's Guide* by Felicia Browell; *Collector's Guide to TV Toys and Memorabilia, 1960s & 1970s, Second Edition*, by Greg Davis and Bill Morgan; *Collectors Guide to Tootsietoys, Second Edition*, by David Richter; *Matchbox Toys, 1947 – 1998, Collector's Guide to Diecast Toys and Scale Models*, and *Toy Car Collector's Guide*, all by Dana Johnson; *Rubber Toy Vehicles* by Dave Leopard; and *Collector's Guide to Battery Toys, Second Edition*, by Don Hultzman. All are published by Collector Books. Other informative books are: *Collecting Toys, Collecting Toy Soldiers*, and *Collecting Toy Trains, An Identification & Value Guide #3*, by Richard O'Brien; and *Toys of the Sixties, A Pictorial Guide*, by Bill Bruegman. In the listings that follow, toys are listed by manufacturer's name if possible, otherwise by type. Measurements are given when appropriate and available; if only one dimension is noted, it is the greater one — height if the toy is vertical, length if it is horizontal.

See also Children's Things; Personalities. For toy stoves, see Stoves.

Key:
b/o — battery operated   NP — nickel plated
cl — celluloid   w/up — wind-up
jtd — jointed

Toys by Various Manufacturers

Alps, Fighting Bull, b/o, 1960s, 10", MIB **175.00**
Alps, Friendly Jocko, b/o, 1950s, 8", MIB **275.00**
Alps, Jolly Bambino, b/o, 1950s, 9", M **475.00**
Bandai, Armored Knights Contest Set, b/o, 1950s, 8", MIB **700.00**
Bandai, King Sz Fire Engine, b/o, 1960s, 13", M **150.00**
Bandai, Swimming Duck, b/o, 1940s, rare, 8", NM **150.00**
Chad Valley, ambulance, diecast, MIP **45.00**
Chad Valley, van, diecast, MIP **50.00**
Chein, Clown Roly Poly, tin litho, scarce, 1930s, NM **350.00**
Chein, Disneyland Ferris Wheel, w/up, 17", EX **700.00**
Chein, Hercules Motor Express Stake Truck, 20", G+ **550.00**
Chein, Native on Turtle, w/up, 1930s, 8", NM **275.00**
Chein, Popeye the Drummer, w/up, 1932, 6½", VG+ **750.00**
Chein, top, w/various images of toys, 1930s, NM **65.00**
Corgi, Chevrolet Impala, #220, MIB **90.00**
Corgi, Ferrari 380 GT, #378, MIB..**30.00**
Corgi, Firestreak, #1011, MIB..**40.00**
Corgi, Jaguar, E type, #312, MIB **120.00**
Corgi, Kojak Buick, w/hat, #290, MIB...**85.00**
Corgi, Mini Magnifique, #334, MIB **90.00**
Corgi, Saints Volvo, #201, MIB **200.00**
Corgi, Spiderbuggy, #261, MIB **100.00**
Corgi, VW Breakdown Truck, #490, MIB **110.00**
Dinky, AEC Fuel Tanker, Esso, #945, MIB...................................**200.00**
Dinky, Bristol 173 Helicopter, #715, MIB....................................**175.00**
Dinky, Dump Truck, #580, MIB..**250.00**
Dinky, Electric Dairy Van, Express Dairy, #490 ....**200.00**
Dinky, Land Rover, #340, MIB..**150.00**
Dinky, Mercedes Benz 600, #128, MIB...**175.00**
Dinky, RCMP Patrol Car, Cadillac, #264, MIB.............................**200.00**
Dinky, Volkswagen, gr, #181, MIB..**200.00**
Ertl, Oldsmobile 442, diecast, metallic gold, 1970, MIP...............**20.00**
Hubley, Dump Truck, diecast, Kiddie Toys, #476, MIB **150.00**
Hubley, School Bus, diecast, 9½", EX..**70.00**
Linemar, Bubbling Bull, b/o, 1950, 8", MIB................................**350.00**
Linemar, College Jalopy, b/o, 10", NMIB **375.00**
Linemar, Popeye in Rowboat, b/o, 1950s, 10", EXIB.............**7,700.00**
Linemar, Sleeping Baby Bear, b/o, 1950s, 9", MIB......................**475.00**
Marx, Big Aerial Acrobats, w/up, 11", EXIB................................**300.00**
Marx, Donald Duck Duet, w/up, 11", NMIB................................**975.00**
Marx, Hopalong Cassidy, w/up, rocker base, 10", VG+ **350.00**
Marx, Peter Rabbit Eccentric Car, plastic w/up w/tin wheels, 6", EX+..**475.00**
Marx, Rocket Police Patrol, w/up, 12" L, VG **440.00**
Marx, Speed Boy Delivery Cycle, w/up, w/lights, 1930s, 10", NMIB..**650.00**
Milton, Chevy Impala Taxi, diecast, MIP......................................**39.00**
Milton, Pontiac Firebird, diecast, MIP **29.00**
MT, Desert Jeep Patrol, b/o, 1960s, 11", NM **125.00**
MT, Expert Motor Cyclist, b/o, 1950s, 12", EX **475.00**
MT, Wagon Master, b/o, 1960s, 18" L, NM **150.00**
Remco, Barney's Auto Factory, b/o, 1964, unused, NMIB...........**300.00**
Strauss, Emergency Tow Car #74, VG **1,200.00**
Strauss, Jazzbo Jim, EXIB...**700.00**
Strauss, Long Haulage Truck #71, G+ **350.00**
Strauss, Tip Top Dump Truck, NM **1,000.00**
Strauss, Yell-O-Taxi, EX+...**700.00**
Tip Top Toy, Coupe, diecast, 3½", MIP...**40.00**
TN, Hot Rod 158, b/o, 1940s, 10", EXIB.....................................**450.00**
TN, Marvelous Locomotive, b/o, 1950s, 10", M **95.00**
TN, Pete the Talking Parrot, b/o, 1950s, 18", M..........................**250.00**
TN, Worried Mother Duck & Baby, b/o, 1950s, 11", MIB..........**225.00**
Yonezawa, Happy 'N Sad magic Face Clown, b/o, 1960s, 10", EX.**95.00**
Yonezawa, Mother Goose, b/o, MIB **175.00**

Farm Toys

Baler, John Deere, 1950s, EX 65.00
Baler, John Deere 14T, Ertl, 1966, 1/16th scale, MIB 315.00
Baler, Oliver, Slik, VG 50.00
Barge wagon, Massey Harris, Reuhl, 1951, 16th scale, EX 155.00
Combine, Gleaner N6, Arcade #6000, 1/24th scale, MIB 85.00
Combine, John Deere 660, movable spout & platform, NM 100.00
Corn picker, Carter Tru Scale #401, 1960s, MIB 250.00
Disk/harrow, John Deere, M in orig gr/yel box 165.00
Dump wagon, CI, Arcade, 7¾", VG 65.00
Farm set, Allis Chalmers 200, Ertl #153, 1/16th scale, MIB 485.00
Hay rake, Carter Tru Sale #419, 1960s, MIB 165.00
Implement set, Carter Tru-Scale Jr, tracter+plow+disc+trailer, MIB.415.00
Manure spreader, John Deere K, rubber tires, early 1950s, EX.......55.00
Planter, White Seed Boss, Scale Models, 1/16th scale, MIB..........45.00
Tractor, Internat'l Harvester Farmall 300, Ertl, 1984, MIB 135.00
Tractor, John Deere A, NP driver, Arcade, 1/16th scale, 1940, EX.215.00
Tractor, Massey Ferguson 590, Tue Toy Farmer, MIB...................360.00
Tractor, Minneapolis-Moline Mighty Minnie, Ertl, EX 140.00
Tractor, Oliver 1800 Checkerboard, Ertl, 1964, 5x9", EX 270.00
Tractor, Oliver 77, Slik, 1950s, 16th scale, EX............................250.00
Tractor, Oliver 770 Special Show Edition, Spec-Cast, 1991, MIB.130.00
Truck, grain; red & wht, Tru Scale, 1960s, 1/16th scale, EX 95.00

Guns and Cap Bombs

In years past, virtually every child played with toy guns, and the survival rate of these toys is minimal, at best. The interest in these charming toy guns has recently increased considerably, especially those with western character examples, as collectors discover their scarcity, quality, and value. Toy gun collectibles encompass the early and the very ornate figural toy guns and bombs through the more realistic ones with recognizable character names, gleaming finishes, faux jewels, dummy bullets, engraving, and colorful grips. This section will cover some of the most popular cast-iron and diecast toy guns from the past one hundred years. Recent market trends have witnessed a decline of interest in the earlier (1900 – 40) single-shot cast-iron pistols. The higher collector interest is for known western characters and cap pistols from the 1960 – 65 era. Generic toy guns such as, Deputy, Pony Boy, Marshal, Ranger, Sheriff, Pirate, Cowboy, Dick, Western, Army, etc., generate only minimal collector interest.

Buck Rogers 'Wilma' Automatic Pistol, 1934, EX+ 350.00
Crossman C02 Target Pistol Model #115, complete, EXIB 100.00
Daisy Buck Rogers Popgun, pressed steel, emb grip, 1930s, 9½", VG .200.00
Hubley Dagger Derringer, cap gun, NP, 1960, 6¾", EX+.............200.00
Hubley Panther Pistol, metal derringer w/wht grip/wrist cuff, 4".MIB.150.00
Ives Punch & Judy Cap Pistol, CI, figures on bbl, 1882, 4x4½", EX.1,875.00
J&E Stevens, Buffalo Bill Repeating Cap Pistol, 8½", VGIB......125.00
J&E Stevens Caps Exploder, boy & bear w/hammers, japanned, 13".1,850.00
J&E Stevens Sea Serpent Cap Pistol, CI, mouth opens, early, 4", EX..1,300.00
Japan Atom Rifle, litho tin, friction, 1950s, 19½", EX.................75.00
Japan G-Man Machine Gun, 1950s, 18", MIB..........................125.00
Japan Space Ruler Machine Gun, tin litho, b/o, 20", EXIB 230.00
Kenton Gene Autry Repeating Cap Gun, wht pearl grips, 7", EX.150.00
Kenton Magic .22 Derringer, CI w/NP bbl, single action, 6¼", EX .90.00
Kilgore Roy Rogers Shootin' Iron, simulated pearl hdl, 9", MIB.450.00
Leslie Henry Gene Autry Cap Gun, NP, horsehead grips, 9", MIB.300.00
Leslie Henry Wild Bill Hickok Cap Guns, 9½", pr, EX..............250.00
Lockwood Joker Cap Pistol, CI, single action, ca 1880, 4½", EX ..275.00
Marx Big Game Rifle, unused, MIB....................................125.00
Marx Davy Crockett Cap Gun, metal/plastic, 1950s, 10½", NM+..75.00
Marx Lone Ranger Carbine Rifle, plastic, 26", NMIB.................450.00
Marx Popeye Pirate Pistol, tin litho, 1935, 10", NMIB 500.00

Marx Spinner Rifle, NMOC..125.00
Marx/WDP Davy Crockett Frontier Rifle, metal, 34", NMIB.....225.00
Mattel Lost in Space Roto-Jet Gun, 1966, rare, 20", EX+...........300.00
Mattel Shootin' Shell Cap Gun, complete, EXIB......................350.00
Roy Rogers Dbl Gun & Holster Set, 10½" guns, red/wht leather, NM..300.00
Russell Cowboy Dbl Holster Set w/Buck'n Bronc Cap Guns, NMIB.350.00
Superman Krypton Gun, EX..450.00
SY Space Machine Gun, 1950s, tin, friction, 12½", NMIB........150.00
Topper Toys Multi-Pistol 09, complete, NM+ (in case) 150.00
Wyandotte Hopalong Cassidy Dbl-Gun & Holster Set, wht grips, NM...800.00
Wyandotte Pump Action Dart Gun, pressed steel, wood stock, 21", EXIB ..110.00
Zorro Cap Pistol, flintlock style, NM 100.00

Model Kits

Addar, Planet of the Apes, Stallion & Soldier, 1974, MIB............85.00
Addar, Super Scenes, Jaws, 1975, MIB 40.00
AMT, Sonny & Cher Mustang, 1960s, MIB 225.00
AMT, Wackie Woodie Krazy Kar, 1960s, MIB (sealed) 85.00
Anubis, Jonny Quest, Robot Spy, 1992, MIB...........................60.00
Aurora, Banana Splits Banana Buggy, 1969, MIB.....................300.00
Aurora, Captain Action, 1966, MIB 300.00
Aurora, Comic Scenes, Tonto, assembled, EX...........................35.00
Aurora, Famous Sighters, Viking, 1958, MIB..........................350.00
Aurora, Godzilla, glow-in-the-dark, 1969, MIB (sealed) 350.00
Aurora, Gruesome Goodies, Monster Scenes, 1971, MIB (sealed) .125.00
Aurora, John F Kennedy, 1965, MIB (sealed)...........................165.00
Aurora, Mummy, 1963, MIB..250.00
Aurora, Superman, 1963, MIB (sealed)...................................275.00
Aurora, Witch, 1965, assembled, EX......................................100.00
Bachmann, Birds of the World, Screech Owl, 1960s, MIB............30.00
Bandai, Kinggidrah, 1984, MIB...50.00
Billiken, Invasion of the Saucerman, Saucerman, vinyl, MIB.......75.00
Billiken, Mummy, vinyl, MIB..225.00
Eldon, Matador Missile & Launcher, 1960, MIB 75.00
Eldon, Pink Panther, 1960s, MIB...75.00
Hawk, Cherokee Sports Roadster, 1962, MIB 35.00
Hawk, Silly Surfers, Woodie on a Surfari, 1964, MIB................100.00
Horizon, Bride of Frankenstein, MIB.....................................75.00
Horizon, Marvel Universe, Punisher, 1988, MIB.......................50.00
Imai, Captain Blue, 1982, MIB..15.00
ITC, Dog Champions, German Shepherd, 1959, MIB 35.00
Lindberg, Coo Coo Clock, 1965, MIB.....................................40.00
Lindberg, US Space Station, 1958, MIB..................................200.00
Monogram, Elvira Macabre Mobile, 1988, MIB........................25.00
Monogram, Missile Arsenal, 1959, MIB..................................200.00
Monogram, Voyage to the Bottom of the Sea Flying Sub, 1968, MIB .175.00
MPC, Incredible Hulk Van, 1977, MIB..................................20.00
MPC, Star Wars, Boba Fett's Slave I, 1982, MIB (sealed) 35.00
Precision, Cap'n Kidd Pirate, 1959, MIB................................75.00
Pyro, Restless Gun Deputy Sheriff, 1958, MIB.........................75.00
Revell, Cat in the Hat, 1958, MIB...100.00
Revell, Gemini Capsule, 1967, MIB.......................................75.00
Revell, Penny Pincher VW Bug, 1980, MIB.............................35.00

Pedal Cars and Ride-On Toys

Atomic Missile, Murray, 1950s, 40", rstr....................................1,500.00
Buick, full fenders, disk wheels, Steelcraft, 1920s, 35", rstr......1,100.00
Caterpillar D6 Dozer, working blade & treads, 1950s, 41", G-.1,430.00
Chryslet, bl & silver (rare), Steelcraft, 1942, VG+ orig...........1,980.00
Comet, Murray, 1950s, 40", rstr 330.00
Ford, w/hood ornament, Steelcraft, 36", rstr 715.00
Indy Racer #3, Apache & Indy decals, AMF, 1970s, 42", rstr 350.00

Oldsmobile Fire Chief Car, old rpt, Steelcraft, 1939, 41".........**1,430.00**
Packard, Am National, 1920s, 45", rstr.............................**2,530.00**
Pontiac, Murray, 1949, 36", rstr....................................**650.00**
Roadster, pnt steel, Changler, 1926, 46", VG+ rstr **1,500.00**
Sand & Gravel Dump Truck, Murray, 1949-50, rstr **425.00**
USAF Jeep, Garton, 1965, 40", EX orig.............................**350.00**

Penny Toys

Boxers (2) on platform, Meier, VG+................................**1,300.00**
Clown & lady on mule, 3½", EX....................................**550.00**
Cow on wheeled platform, Meier, 3¼", EX..........................**300.00**
Felix the Cat dancer, Distler, 3½", EX **3,500.00**
Girl & doll in rocking chair, Meier, 3", VG+ **190.00**
Horse-drawn 2-wheeled cart w/driver, Meier, 3¾", EX..............**300.00**
Lady pushing child in sled, scarce, 3", VG+ **1,750.00**
Main in sailboat on wheeled platform, articulated, Meier, EX, EX+ ..**1,200.00**
Motorcycle w/sidecar, driver & passenger, Distler, 3¼", VG....**1,100.00**
Noah's Ark, roof opens, very scarce, 4¾", EX.....................**1,375.00**
Passenger ship, Distler, 5", VG..................................**175.00**
Punch & Judy candy box, 3", VG+ **520.00**
Race car w/driver, Distler, 2½", EX **935.00**
Runabout, open w/drivers in 2 front seats, rear fly wheel, 4", VG.**220.00**
Speedboat w/lady driver, Meier, 5", VG+..........................**600.00**
Stake truck, open w/driver at center steering wheel, Meier, 3¼", EX .**220.00**
Touring car, open w/dirver, full running boards, Kellerman, 5", EX.**935.00**
Velocette motorcycle, Paya, 4", VG+ **470.00**

Pull and Push Toys

American Airplane, pnt CI/aluminum, clacker, Hubley, 17", G.**2,800.00**
Boy Fishing, bell toy, 4 spoke wheels, J&E Stevens, 8", VG **1,200.00**
Car carrier, wood tracter+4 cars+trailer, Hustler, ca 1927, 21", EX+.**300.00**
Cow on platform, pnt tin, CI spoke wheels, Am, 9", VG+ **550.00**
Dog chasing boy on platform, pressed steel, friction, Clark, 11", G+.**440.00**
Duck on wheels, pnt/pressed steel, friction, Clark, 7", G+ **125.00**
Elephant on platform, pnt/pressed steel, friction, Republic, 9", EX.**165.00**
Franz the Dog on platform, metal, articulated, 8", VG+ **200.00**
Grasshoper, pnt CI, articulated legs, Hubley, 12", EX+............**1,050.00**
Hen w/chicks in crate, pnt CI, 3 spoke wheels, 7½", VG **500.00**
Horse & jockey, pnt CI, 2 spoke wheels, Wilkins, G, +push stick..**80.00**
Horse on wooden platform, mc pnt, CI spoke wheels, 15", G- ...**155.00**
Horse trotting on platform, pnt tin, 4 spoke wheels, 9½", rstr **250.00**
Landing of Columbus, gold-pnt CI, bell toy, Gong Bell, 7", EX..**350.00**
Pony cart, paper-on wood w/tin cart, CI spoke wheels, Gibbs, 7", G.**45.00**
Sunny Andy Street Railway, tin litho, w/bell, 13", EX **220.00**
Trick Pony, CI bell toy, ornate 4-wheel platform, mk #39, 8", G .**700.00**
Zeppelin, tin litho, props turn when pulled, 28", G- **375.00**

Robots

Answer Game Robot, b/o, MIB **800.00**
Atom Robot, crank-action, tin litho, KO (1st version), 1950s, 7", EX+..**375.00**
Car From Space, plastic b/o, Mormac, 1950s, 8", NMIB.............**100.00**
Cragston Great Astronaut, tin litho, b/o, Japan, 14", EX...........**950.00**
Cragston Moon Man, friction, Cobor, 1960s, 6", M on EX card.**225.00**
Cragston Mr Robot, tin litho, b/o, Japan, 10", NMIB.............**1,320.00**
Fire Man, tin litho, w/up, SY, very rare, 7", EX **750.00**
Hysterical Robot, plastic, b/o, Japan, 13", EXIB **185.00**
Lost in Space Robot, b/o, Remco, 1966, 12", NMIB **800.00**
Mechanical Robby, tin body w/wrench arms, w/up, Yonezawa, 8", EX..**1,050.00**
Moon Explorer Robot, tin/plastic, b/o, Japan, 17", EX.............**1,900.00**
Mr Brain, plastic, b/o, Remco, 1970, NMIB.......................**100.00**
Pioneer Space Radar Scout, tin/plastic, friction, Japan, 7", NMIB .**220.00**

Rachet Robot, w/up, TN, 1950s, 8", EX..............................**325.00**
Robot on Road Roller, b/o, rare, EX...............................**1,275.00**
Smoking Robot, tin litho, b/o, Alps, 1950s, 12", EXIB **2,200.00**
Space Robot X-70 (Tulip head), tin/plastic, TN, 1960s, 13", EX .**660.00**
Sparky, tin litho, gold version, KO, 1950s, 8", EX+ **1,300.00**
Talking Sound Robot, b/o, Japan, 1960s, 11", NM+...................**750.00**
TV Robot, tin/plastic, b/o, screen in chest, Japan, 1960s, 10", VG+.**175.00**
Wheel-A-Gear Robot, tin, w/up, KO, 1950s, 10", VG+ **275.00**

Schoenhut

Our advisor for Schoenhut toys is Keith Kaonis, who has collected these toys for over twenty years. Because of his involvement with the publishing industry (currently *Antique DOLL Collector*, and during the '80s, *Collectors' SHOWCASE*), he has visited collections across the United States, produced several articles on Schoenhut toys, and served a term as president of the Schoenhut Collectors' Club. Keith is listed in the Directory under New York.

The listings below are for Humpty Dumpty Circus pieces. All values are based on rating conditions of good to very good, i.e., very minor scratches and wear, good original finish, no splits or chips, no excessive paint wear or cracked eyes, and of course completeness and condition of clothes (if dressed figures).

Clowns with two-part heads (a cast face applied to a wooden head) were made from 1903 to 1912 and are most desirable — condition always is important. There have been nine distinct styles in fourteen different costumes recorded. Only eight costume styles apply to the two-part headed clowns. The later clowns had one-part heads whose features were pressed wood, and the costumes on the later ones, circa 1920+, were no longer tied at the wrists and ankles.

Humpty Dumpty Circus Clowns and Other Personel

Black Dude, reduced sz, from $100 to.............................**375.00**
Black Dude, 1-part head, purple coat, from $250 to **700.00**
Black Dude, 2-part head, blk coat, from $400 to **850.00**
Chinese Acrobat, 1-part head, from $200 to.......................**800.00**
Chinese Acrobat, 2-part head, rare, from $400 to.................**1,400.00**
Clown, early, G, from $150 to **600.00**
Clown, reduced sz, 1925-53, from $75 to **125.00**
Gent Acrobat, bsk head, rare, from $300 to.......................**750.00**
Gent Acrobat, 2-part head, very rare, from $600 to...............**1,800.00**
Hobo, reduced sz, from $200 to **375.00**
Hobo, 1-part head, from $200 to **400.00**
Hobo, 2-part head, facet toe ft, from $400 to....................**900.00**
Hobo, 2-part head, turned-up toes, blk coat, from $500 to **1,200.00**
Lady Acrobat, bsk head, from $300 to.............................**750.00**
Lady Acrobat, 1-part head, from $150 to **400.00**
Lady Rider, bsk head, from $250 to **550.00**
Lady Rider, 1-part head, from $150 to............................**400.00**
Lady Rider, 2-part head, very rare, from $500 to **1,800.00**
Lion Tamer, bsk head, rare, from $175 to.........................**850.00**
Lion Tamer, 1-part head, rare, from $150 to **700.00**
Lion Tamer, 2-part head, early, very rare, from $700 to **1,800.00**
Ring Master, bsk, ca 1908-14, from $300 to.......................**800.00**
Ring Master, 1-part head, from $200 to...........................**450.00**
Ring Master, 2-part head, blk coat, very rare, from $800 to.....**1,800.00**
Ring Master, 2-part head, red coat, very rare, from $700 to.....**1,600.00**

Humpty Dumpty Circus Animals

Humpty Dumpty Circus animals with glass eyes, ca. 1903 – 1914, are more desirable and can demand much higher prices than the later painted-eye versions. As a general rule, a glass-eye version is 30% to 40% more than a painted-eye version. (There are exceptions.) The following list suggests values for both GE (glass-eye) and PE (painted-eye) versions and reflects a **low PE price** to a **high GE price**.

There are other variations and nuances of certain figures: Bulldog — white with black spots or brindle (brown); open- and closed-mouth zebras, camels, and giraffes; ball necks and hemispherical necks on some animals such as the pig, cat, and hippo, to name a few. These points can affect the price and should be judged individually. Condition and rarity affect the price most significantly and the presence of an original box virtually doubles the price.

Alligator, PE/GE, from $250 to	750.00
Arabian Camel, 1 hump, PE/EG, from $250 to	750.00
Bactrain Camel, 2 humps, PE/EG, from $200 to	1,200.00
Brown Bear, PE/GE, from $200 to	800.00
Buffalo, cloth mane, PE/GE, from $300 to	900.00
Buffalo, cvd mane, PE/GE, from $200 to	1,200.00
Bulldog, PE/GE, from $400 to	1,500.00
Burro (farm set), PE/GE, no harness/no belly hole for chariot, $300 to	800.00
Burro (made to go w/chariot & clown), PE/GE, from $200 to	700.00
Cat, PE/GE, rare, from $500 to	3,000.00
Cow, PE/GE, from $300 to	1,200.00
Deer, PE/GE, from $300 to	1,500.00
Donkey, PE/GE, from $75 to	300.00
Donkey, w/blanket, PE/GE, from $100 to	600.00
Elephant, PE/GE, from $75 to	300.00
Elephant, w/blanket, PE/GE, from $200 to	600.00
Gazelle, PE/GE, rare, from $500 to	2,750.00
Giraffe, PE/GE, from $200 to	900.00
Goat, PE/GE, from $150 to	400.00
Goose, PE only, from $200 to	900.00
Gorilla, PE only, from $,1500 to	4,000.00
Hippo, PE/GE, from $200 to	900.00
Horse, brn, saddle & stirrups, PE/GE, from $250 to	500.00
Horse, wht, platform, PE/GE, from $150 to	450.00
Hyena, PE/GE, very rare, from $1,000 to	6,000.00
Kangaroo, PE/GE, from $200 to	1,500.00
Lion, cloth mane, GE, from $500 to	1,200.00
Lion, cvd mane, PE/GE, from $200 to	1,400.00
Monkey, 1-part head, PE only, from $200 to	600.00
Monkey, 2-part head, wht face, from $300 to	1,000.00
Ostrich, PE/GE, from $200 to	900.00
Pig, 5 versions, PE/GE, from $200 to	800.00
Polar Bear, PE/GE, from $200 to	2,000.00
Poodle, cloth mane, GE only, from $150 to	450.00
Poodle, PE/GE, from $100 to	300.00
Rabbit, PE/GE, very rare, from $500 to	3,500.00
Rhino, PE/GE, from $250 to	800.00
Sea Lion, PE/GE, from $400 to	1,500.00
Sheep (lamb), w/bell, PE/GE, from $200 to	700.00
Tiger, PE/GE, from $250 to	1,200.00
Wolf, PE/GE, very rare, from $500 to	5,000.00
Zebra, PE/GE, from $250 to	1,200.00
Zebu, PE/GE, rare, from $500 to	3,000.00

Humpty Dumpty Circus Accessories

There are many accessories: wagons, tents, ladders, chairs, pedestals, tight rope, weights, and more.

Cage Wagon, ...Greatest Show on Earth, 10" & 12", EX, from $300 to	1,200.00
Menagerie tent, ca 1904, from $1,500 to	3,000.00
Menagerie tent, ca 1914-20, from $1,200 to	2,000.00
Oval litho tent, 1926, from $4,000 to	10,000.00
Sideshow panels, 1926, pr, from $2,000 to	5,000.00

Steiff

Margaret Steiff began making her stuffed felt toys in Germany in the late 1800s. The animals she made were tagged with an elephant in a circle. Her first teddy bear, made in 1903, became such a popular seller that she changed her tag to a bear. Felt stuffing was replaced with excelsior and wool; when it became available, foam was used. In addition to the tag, look for the 'Steiff' ribbon and the button inside the ear. For further information we recommend *Teddy Bears and Steiff Animals, Series 1* through *3*, full-color identification and value guides by Margaret Fox Mandel, available from Collector Books or your public library. See also Teddy Bears.

Puss 'N Boots-type pirates, Lix and Lixie, complete identification, ca 1957, 5", $185.00 each. (Photo courtesy Margaret Fox Mandel)

Bengal tiger, mohair, glass eyes, 1959-61, button/tag, 5½", M	450.00
Camel, wool-like fur & felt, 10½", EX	250.00
Cat, Woolie, gray & wht, orig ribbon, 1970-74, all ID, 2½", M	85.00
Clown, Clonie, orig outfit, chest tag, 5", M	100.00
Dinosaur, Brosus, mc mohair, not jtd, 1960s, no ID, 26"	400.00
Dwarf, Puck, felt w/mohair beard, glass eyes, jtd, 1914, 8", VG+	290.00
Elephant, airbrushed mohair, glass eyes, felt blanket, 1950s, 14", EX	120.00
Goat, Rocky, all ID, 1963-67, 5", M	175.00
Horse, wht mohair w/brn spots, blk nose/tail, 9", G	145.00
Koala bear, jully jtd, 1955-58, all ID, 9", M	700.00
Lobster, Crabby, airbrushed felt, glass eyes, all ID, 4½", M	350.00
Mole, Maxi, mohair, 1965, all ID, 4", M	135.00
Panther, Floppy, 1972, brass button/stock tag, 17", NM	185.00

Toy Soldiers and Accessories

Among the better-known manufacturers of 'Dimestore' soldiers are American Metal Toys, Barclay, and Manoil, all of whom made hollow cast-lead figures; Grey Iron, who used cast iron; and Auburn, who made figures of rubber. They measured about 3" to 3½" tall, and often accessories such as trucks, tents, tanks, and airplanes were designed to add to the enjoyment of staging mock battles, parades, encampments, and wars.

Britains is a very popular line, smaller and usually more detailed than the 'Dimestores.' They've been made in England since 1893, and many of their older boxed sets sell for more than a $100.00.

Some figures are very rare and therefore expensive, but condition is just as important in making a value assessment. Percentages in the description lines refer to the amount of original paint remaining. Alphanumeric codes in the descriptions refer to numbers in Richard O'Brien's book, *Collecting Toy Soldiers* (Krause), which we recommend. Our advisors for this category are Stan and Sally Alekna; they are listed in the Directory under Pennsylvania.

American Metal, anti-aircraft gunner, scarce, 98%, AM8	115.00
American Metal, farmer, 99%, AM37	20.00
American Metal, farmer's wife, 96%, AM38	17.00
American Metal, firing machine gun on stump, khaki, 93%, AM10	96.00
Auburn Rubber, base runner, gray w/red trim, scarce, 98%, A37	60.00

Auburn Rubber, bugler, khaki, 98%, A4 ....23.00
Auburn Rubber, catcher, wht w/bl trim, scarce, NM, A41 ....70.00
Auburn Rubber, futuristic sedan, wht tires, 92-94%, AA15 ....24.00
Auburn Rubber, infantry private in yel, scarce, 98%, A1 ....22.00
Auburn Rubber, observer w/binoculars, khaki, 97%, A18 ....25.00
Auburn Rubber, sm collie dog, 98%, ARA3 ....14.00
Auburn Rubber, turkey, 99%, ARA12 ....12.00
Barclay, armored army truck, khaki, wht tires, 98%, BV6 ....27.00
Barclay, bomb thrower, gr, 95%, B243 ....25.00
Barclay, conductor, 98%, B161 ....18.00
Barclay, field cannon, closed hitch, sm, HO scale, 95%, BC3 ....18.00
Barclay, fireman w/axe, 99%, B187 ....43.00
Barclay, flag bearer, tin helmet, long stride, 90-92%, B6 ....20.00
Barclay, fuel truck, gr, no decals, ca 1960s, HO scale, 99%, BV99 .17.00
Barclay, girl skater, 99%, B177 ....19.00
Barclay, grazing cow, brn & tan, 98%, B213 ....17.00
Barclay, hospital truck, red cross on roof, 1968, scarce, NM, BV104 .32.00
Barclay, Indian w/hatchet & shield, 99%, B251 ....18.00
Barclay, kneeling at anti-tank gun, 96%, B145 ....32.00
Barclay, knight w/sword over right shoulder, 97%, B230 ....39.00
Barclay, lady w/baby, scarce, HO scale, 95%, B290 ....15.00
Barclay, man pulling kids on sled, scarce, 98%, B199 ....62.00
Barclay, officer w/sword, khaki, 95%, #285 ....22.00
Barclay, policeman, HO scale, 98%, B275 ....10.00
Barclay, porter, HO scale, 99%, B283 ....11.00
Barclay, prone machine gunner, cast helmet, 100%, B62 ....31.00
Barclay, red mail truck, blk tires, no milk cans, 97%, HO scale, BV45 ..39.00
Barclay, redcap, HO scale, 99%, B279 ....11.00
Barclay, sailor in wht, 98%, B237 ....26.00
Barclay, sentry in overcoat, 94%, B71 ....28.00
Barclay, shoeshine boy, scarce, 94%, B170 ....38.00
Barclay, side dump truck, HO scale, 1960s, NM, BV87 ....17.00
Barclay, sm Santa seated on sled, 98%, B194 ....53.00
Barclay, soldier charging, short stride, 96%, B18 ....30.00
Barclay, soldier charging w/gas mask & rifle, 97%, B91 ....31.00
Barclay, soldier marching, khaki, 98%, B259 ....20.00
Barclay, soldier prone w/short binoculars, very scarce, 94%, B114 .108.00
Barclay, towing truck, gr w/wht tires, 1936, 3⅜" L, 94%, BV119 ..44.00
Barclay, tractor, red w/blk metal wheels, HO scale, 97%, BV72 ....47.00
Grey Iron, aviator, orange harness, very scarce, prewar, 96%, G100 .92.00
Grey Iron, cadet in bl, prewar, 98%, G6 ....35.00
Grey Iron, calf, head trn, brn, prewar, very scarce, 95%, R11 ....67.00
Grey Iron, conductor, prewar, 99%, T5 ....17.00
Grey Iron, cowboy, prewar, 96%, G53 ....24.00
Grey Iron, cowboy squatting, very scarce, prewar, 91%, R3 ....64.00
Grey Iron, engineer, prewar, 99%, T6 ....17.00
Grey Iron, garage man, gr, postwar, 95%, H9 ....18.00
Grey Iron, goose, prewar, 94%, F11 ....13.00
Grey Iron, horse, brn, prewar, 98%, F5 ....17.00
Grey Iron, Indian chief w/knife, prewar, 97%, G46 ....33.00
Grey Iron, knight in armor, prewar, 98%, G93 ....42.00
Grey Iron, Legion bugler, early, 97%, G81 ....30.00
Grey Iron, Legion drum major, early, 98%, G80 ....30.00
Grey Iron, man in traveling suit, prewar, 100%, T1 ....18.00
Grey Iron, Naval officer, wht, 91%, G70 ....19.00
Grey Iron, policeman, prewar, 98%, T8 ....16.00
Grey Iron, seated machine gunner, prewar, early, 89%, G60 ....19.00
Grey Iron, US calveryman, prewar, 96%, G35 ....44.00
Grey Iron, US doughboy combat trooper, prewar, 91%, G19 ....30.00
Grey Iron, US doughboy officer, prewar, 99%, G28 ....27.00
Grey Iron, US infantry, shoulder arms, early, prewar, 99%, G9 .....22.00
Grey Iron, woman w/basket, prewar, 99%, H2 ....20.00
Grey Iron, wounded on crutches, scarce, prewar, 96%, G98 ....75.00
Manoil, cobbler making shoes, scarce, 94%, M149 ....38.00

Manoil, colt, tan, scarce, 98%, M220 ....29.00
Manoil, combat w/M-1 rifle, 99%, M179 ....49.00
Manoil, farmer sowing grain, 98%, M138 ....29.00
Manoil, fire engine, red & silver, 97%, MV709 ....45.00
Manoil, girl picking berries, scarce, 95%, M166 ....66.00
Manoil, jet plane, Lockheed F90, scarce, 95%, MA517 ....86.00
Manoil, machine gunner, seated/'skinny,' 98%, M173 ....115.00
Manoil, officer w/sword, 94%, M10 ....27.00
Manoil, pilot carrying bomb sight, 98%, M115 ....61.00
Manoil, plastic roadster, scarce, NM, MVP7 ....21.00
Manoil, radio operator, prone, scarce, 95%, M117 ....68.00
Manoil, seated machine gunner, 94%, M41 ....28.00
Manoil, shepherd w/flute, scarce, 97%, M155 ....71.00
Manoil, station wagon, 2-tone, scarce, 97%, MV720 ....95.00
Manoil, submarine, gray, 94%, MV79 ....49.00
Manoil, Tommy gunner, 1st version, 98%, M49 ....50.00
Marx, Gordon Highlander, NM, 11MA 12.00
Marx, Indian standing, EX, 27MA 12.00
Marx, infantry private, marching, EX, 2MA 9.00
Marx, mounted cavalry officer, M, 1MA 13.00
Miller Plaster, advancing w/orig rifle, 98%, ML13 ....41.00
Miller Plaster, General McArthur, 99%, ML4 ....58.00
Miller Plaster, marching w/orig rifle, 99%, ML17 ....29.00

Trains

Electric trains were produced as early as the late nineteenth century. Names to look for are Lionel, Ives, and American Flyer. Identification numbers given in the listings below actually appear on the item.

Am Flyer, Boxcar #24016, MKT, VG 550.00
Am Flyer, Chesapeake & Ohio GP7 Locomotive, short step, EX ..425.00
Am Flyer, Flatcar #24557, US Navy Jeep Transport, +2 orig jeeps, EXIB ..350.00
Am Flyer, Gilbert Chemicals Tank Car #910, EXIB 325.00
Am Flyer, Locomotive #499, New Haven EP-5, EX 375.00
Am Flyer, Set #13, locomotive+tender+2 cars, early, EXIB 225.00
Am Flyer, Set #3015, Illini, 4-pc, w/instruction manual, EXIB .1,200.00
Am Flyer, Steam Engine & Tender #429, 0-6-0, VG+ 500.00
Bing, Gondola, open, 4-wheeled, #1 gauge, G+ 45.00
Bing, Locomotive, 0-4-0, w/6-wheeled tender, #1 gauge, rstr 275.00
Bing, Stock Car, gr & orange, #2 gauge, G..........................75.00
Ives, Locomotive #3217, CI, electric, EX 150.00
Ives, Set #1071 w/#3236 Locomotive, 3-pc, EXIB 1,750.00
Lionel, Boxcar #6464-350, MKT, postwar, EXIB 500.00
Lionel, China Blue Streamliner #262E+Tender & 3 Cars, prewar, VG+ ..1,450.00
Lionel, Express Mail Boxcar #9229, modern era, MIB 30.00
Lionel, Locomotive #226E & Tender #2226W, prewar, VG+ 725.00
Lionel, Locomotive #499, New Haven EP-5, postwar, EX 375.00
Lionel, Locomotive #6250, Seaboard Switcher, VG+ 225.00
Lionel, Locomotive #8056, Chicago Northwestern, modern era, MIB .125.00
Lionel, Locomotive Set #2031, Rock Island Alco AA units, postwar, VG+ ..325.00
Lionel, Power Station #436, prewar, NMIB 6,000.00
Lionel, Reefer #5721, Soo Line, modern era, EX (EX box) 20.00
Lionel, Tank Car #19602, Johnson's, modern era, MIB 33.00
Lionel, Tank Car #2855, Sunoco, blk w/yel decals, postwar, NMIB ..600.00
Lionel, Tank Car #6315, orange, Blt-56 under ladders, postwar, NMIB ..375.00
Lionel, Tender #2817, red, prewar, NMIB 400.00
Marklin, Baggage Car #1728, gr & orange, 0 gauge, G+ 45.00
Marklin, Baggage Handcart, no drawer, driver's platform, NM (G- box) .385.00
Marklin, Freight Car #1929, w/guard house, brn, VG 150.00
Marklin, Locomotove #1802, clockwork, #1 gauge, VG+ 635.00
Marx, Set #35250, NY Central Passenger, 5-pc, VGIB 200.00
Marx, Set #50352, NY Central Freight, 5-pc, complete, VGIB ..150.00
Marx, Set #5235, NY Central Freight/Passenger, 9-pc, complete, VGIB .800.00

Trade Signs

Trade signs were popular during the 1800s. They were usually made in an easily recognizable shape that one could mentally associate with the particular type of business it was to represent, especially appropriate in the days when many customers could not read!

Barrels, painted wood, Depot for Lucas Enamels..., double sided, 49½x18", EX, $2,645.00. (Photo Skinner Auctions, Inc.)

Barber, pnt wood & iron str razor, articulated, closed: 4½x29" ...**375.00**
Billiards, Academy Parlor Pocket..., 2-sided convex glass panel, 32" H..**2,300.00**
Blacksmith, tin anvil, 3-D, hollow, late 19th C, 16x31x11" **865.00**
Bootmaker, molded zinc, mc pnt, lyre fr, wall bracket, 38x38"..**3,500.00**
Carriage maker, cvd/pnt wooden carriage, worn pnt, 1850s, 21x87x2"...**320.00**
Cobbler, Boot & Shoe Repairing, wooden, 2-sided, mc pnt, 1880s, 14x24".**3,000.00**
Cobbler, pnt sheet-metal shoe w/emb details, ca 1900, 18x45x7½".**575.00**
Cobbler, wooden boot w/gilt traces, 3-D, 19th C, 26x16x6" **800.00**
Dentist, wooden toothbrush, wood bristles, old pnt, 20th C, 4x48".**980.00**
Fishmonger, wood fish w/glass eyes/tin fins, gray pnt, 20th C, 14x47".**2,300.00**
Glove shop, tin lady's hand w/gold bracelet, bl cuff, 30⅜" **2,300.00**
Gunsmith, cvd/pnt wood dbl-bbl shotgun, old rpt, 20th C, 9x52".**1,950.00**
Hardware, tin lock form w/old pnt & wht letters, 19th C, 38x25".**1,495.00**
House painter, pnt wood, brn lettering on bl, weathered pnt, 21x31"..**765.00**
Inn, Franklin Inn, B Franklin portrait, 2-sided wood, 62x34"..**5,875.00**
Intersecting logo or letters WEC, hollow welded sheet copper, 22x30"..**650.00**
Jeweler, pnt/gilt metal pocket watch shape, 2-sided, 19th C, 30x21"...**2,000.00**
Locksmith, pnt sheet-iron crossed keys & padlock, 33x40", G ...**750.00**
Locksmith, pnt zinc padlock, late 19th C, 37x27½x8" **1,495.00**
Locksmith, zink key, hollow 3-D form, Am, late 1800s, 26x78".**1,265.00**
Merchant, Bergner & Engle...Lager Beer, rvpt glass, 30x60"....**1,725.00**
Optician, appl gold letters & spectacles on wood panel, 1850s, 96x70"..**2,000.00**
Optician, gilt & pnt wood w/cvd eyeglass fr & glass lenses, 14x39"..**4,000.00**
Pawn shop, 3 wooden spheres dangle from copper hanger, 19th C, 12"..**635.00**
Pharmacist, red-pnt sheet metal mortar & pestle, ca 1900, 39", VG..**1,150.00**
Saddle shop, horse's head, gilded zinc, 19th C, 15x12" **4,000.00**
Shoe Repair (letters), dbl-sided wood w/apple, yel/gr pnt, 12x44".**470.00**
Soda fountain, sheet metal ice cream cone, mc pnt, 20th C, 29½"..**1,725.00**
Tavern, Pilot's Arms, pnt wood w/captain & ship, 38x34", G .**1,375.00**
Tavern, pnt wooden bottle, 1-pc, 3-D, weathered pnt, 35⅝" **800.00**
Tobacconist, pnt compo Mastercraft pipe, 3-D, orig pnt, 10x36".**175.00**
Whale, naturalistc form, red over wht pnt, sq-head nail eyes, 30" L .**935.00**

Tramp Art

'Tramp' is considered a type of folk art. In America it was primarily made from the end of the Civil War through the 1930s, though it employs carving and decorating methods which are much older, originating mostly in Germany and Scandinavia. 'Trampen' probably refers to the itinerant stages of Middle Ages craft apprenticeship. The carving techniques were also used for practice. Tramp art was spread by soldiers in the Civil War and primarily practiced where there was a plentiful and free supply of materials such as cigar boxes and fruit crates. The belief that this work was done by tramps and hobos as payment for room or meals is generally incorrect. The larger pieces especially would have required a lengthy stay in one place.

There is a great variety of tramp art, from boxes and frames which are most common to large pieces of furniture and intricate objects. The most common method of decoration is chip carving with several layers built one on top of another. There are several variations of that form as well as others such as 'Crown of Thorns,' an interlocking method, which are completely different. The most common finishes were lacquer or stain, although paints were also used. The value of tramp art varies according to size, detail, surface, and complexity. The new collector should be aware that tramp art is being made today. While some sell it as new, others are offering it as old. In addition, many people mistakenly use the term as a catchall phrase to refer to other forms of construction — especially things they are uncertain about. This misuse of the term is growing, and makes a difference in the value of pieces. New collectors need to pay attention to how items are described.

For further information we recommend *Tramp Art: A Folk Art Phenomenon* by Helaine Fendelmam, Jonathan Taylor (photographer)/ Stewart Tabori & Chang; *Hobo & Tramp Art Carving: An Authentic American Folk Tradition* by Adolph Vandertie, Patrick Spielman/Sterling Publications; and *Tramp Art, One Notch at a Time* by Cornish and Wallach. Our advisors for this category are Matt Lippa and Elizabeth Schaff; they are listed in the Directory under Alabama.

Box, chip-cvd, hidden compartments, 6½x8½x8½" **375.00**
Box, chip-cvd panels in 6 & 7 layers arranged in geometric forms, 12".**300.00**
Box, chip-cvd steps, hinged mirror lid, 19th C, 7x13x9"............**250.00**
Box, comb; eagle finial, notch/cvd star, layered strips, 16x9x4"..**300.00**
Box, jewelry; chip-cvd, pincushion top, brass ft, mirror in lid, 10".**75.00**
Box, pine, stacked geometrics & lg heart, brass hdls, 7x14x10"..**165.00**
Box, sewing; appl dmns, lift lid w/cushion, dtd 1898, 8x11x8" ...**220.00**
Cabinet, chip-cvd, several layers, glass door front, 22x13x4½".**1,275.00**
Cross, Crown of Thorns, 13½x10x3" **190.00**
Dressing stand, 5-tier, swivel mirror, 4 drws, chip-cvd, 19th C, 31".**1,675.00**
Frame, chip-cvd, 4-layer, old wht pnt, orig mirror, 15x11x1½" ..**125.00**
Frame, chip-cvd, 5-layer, 23x17¾" **462.00**
Frame, chip-cvd panels, corner rosettes, triangular, 18x19".........**450.00**
Frame, cvd dmns/pyramids overall, 30x26", VG **650.00**
Frame, dmn-shaped chip cvgs, 5-layer, 18x16", EX....................**235.00**
Frame, 5 layers/hearts in corners (all stacked), gold/red pnt, 22x24".**700.00**
Mirror, chip-cvd Xd corners, rosettes, old pnt, 11x8" **210.00**
Mirror, chip-cvd/stepped dmn & teardrops, old red/blk pnt, 26x17".**650.00**
Mirror, hand; 5 chip-cvd layers, beveled glass mirror, 16¾x7¾x1"..**285.00**
Mirror, pierced/cvd crest, shelf & 3 drws, old yel pnt, 1911, 36x17".**3,000.00**
Puzzle bank, from 6 pcs of wood, stained, 20th C, 4¼" sq...........**100.00**
Wall pocket, cvd dmns/circles/crests/hearts, worn pnt, 14x8x4".**275.00**
Wall pocket, stepped lattice & rosettes, dry red pnt, 38x17x10"..**440.00**

Traps

Though of interest to collectors for many years, trap collecting has gained in popularity over the past ten years in particular, causing prices to appreciate rapidly. Traps are usually marked on the pan as to manufacturer, and the condition of these trademarks are important when determining their value. Grading is as follows:

Good: one-half of pan legible.
Very Good: legible in entirety, but light.
Fine: legible in entirety, with strong lettering.
Mint: in like-new, shiny condition.

Our advisor for this category is Boyd Nedry; he is listed in the Directory under Michigan. Prices listed here are for traps in fine condition.

Acme Mouse, wood snap	25.00
Alligator #1, w/bait hook	155.00
Allsteel #1, single long spring	45.00
Allsteel #2, dbl long spring	65.00
Austin Humane Flat Stake Loop	45.00
Bell Spring #114	235.00
Best, The; wht plastic mousetrap	10.00
Bigelow Killer, 5"	25.00
Bigelow Killer, 9"	30.00
Bigelow Killer, 13¼"	150.00
Blake & Lamb #40, dbl under spring	25.00
Blake & Lamb #40, w/teeth, long spring	45.00
Blizzard #1, Cold Day Rat Trap	40.00
Bonafied, wood snap mousetrap	18.00
Briddell Escape Proof, 1-hole pan	40.00
Briddell Escape Proof, 7-hole pan	37.00
Brownlie Killer, 4"	45.00
Brownlie Killer, 5"	50.00
Champion #1, single long spring (check spring)	35.00
Champion #4, dbl long spring	100.00
Chasse, mousetrap, wood, 3-hole choker	65.00
Cooper Clutch, dbl clutch	185.00
Cortland #1, dbl jaw, single long spring	160.00
Cosey Killer, pan type	30.00
Coyote Cuff, coil spring	25.00
Critter Getter, mousetrap, plastic, live	40.00
D-CON, mousetrap, w/snap	3.00
Dahlgrin, 14" killer	45.00
Davenport Sure Death, ½-circles jaws	110.00
Diamond #1, single long spring	20.00
Diamond #2, dbl long spring	30.00
Diamond #33, dbl clutch spring	50.00
Dixie Fly Trap, fits on fruit jar	42.00
Eclipse #1, direct dog	150.00
Eclipse #2, folding trap	126.00
Eclipse #3, w/toggle dog	120.00
Economy #1, single long spring	15.00
Edwards, metal mousetrap, very rare	500.00
Ejector Mouse Trap, Lovell Co, w/snap	20.00
Elench K #2, w/dog	30.00
Elench K #4, dbl long spring, w/dog	30.00
Elench K #4, dogless	30.00
Evans, brass, fish & mousetrap, 3¾"	600.00
Evans, brass, fish & mousetrap, 4¾"	560.00
EZ Set Mouse Trap, red metal snap, Kansas City MO	45.00
EZ Set Rat Trap, w/snap, Chicago IL	35.00
Faultless Rat Trap, The; metal choke	80.00
Fenn Mark 1, English rodent trap	45.00
Flo Trap	950.00
Funsten Sub	875.00
Gibbs #4 Dope Trap	600.00
Gibbs Gladiator Mouse Trap, metal snap	40.00
Gibbs Hawk Trap, coil spring	350.00
Gibbs Live Muskrat	565.00
Godwin Footsnare	15.00
Gomber Beaten Path, rat trap, metal	48.00
Goshen	450.00
Harmon Live Bait, dbl spring w/basket	325.00
Hauley & Norton #1½, single long spring	30.00
Hector #1, single long spring	35.00
Hector #4, dbl long spring	40.00
Hell Cat, metal mousetrap, squeeze to set	40.00
Hercules #2, H cut in pan	125.00
Herters #0, single long spring, rnd pan	150.00
Herters #0, single long spring, sq pan	160.00
Herters #121, dbl long springs	145.00
Hibbard, rat trap, wood snap, w/safety	35.00
Jack Frost Killer	20.00
Jack Frost Nev-vr-lose, coil, stoploss	30.00
Jilson, mousetrap, sm	700.00
Johnson Quick Set, gopher trap	12.00
JVJ Gopher Trap, metal squeeze	75.00
Katch-em Mouse Trap, w/snap	5.00
Kliflock #1 Killer Trap	35.00
Klincher Mouse Trap, wood snap	35.00
Kopper-Kat, squeeze mousetrap, Aurora IL	45.00
Last Word Mouse Trap, wood snap	50.00
LaVallys Clutch Trap	650.00
Lic Lure, aluminum, rat trap, snap	35.00
Little Champ Mouse Trap, red plastic choker	75.00
Little Giant Fly Trap	80.00
Lucifer Mouse Trap, France, wood snap	10.00
Manning #9, wolf trap, dbl coil spring	125.00
McGill All Steel Mouse Trap, metal squeeze	20.00
Million Mouse Trap, The; wood snap, England	35.00
Mock BA, cccp, mousetrap, wood snap, Russia	20.00
Montgomery #2, 'Gray Fox' Special	65.00
NANCO Safe-T-Set, wood snap	35.00
Nash Mole Choker, CI, Pat 1888, cast pan	90.00
Nebraska Trail Trap	820.00
Nesbit #1 sz, single long spring	475.00
Nesbit #2½ sz, single long spring	900.00
Never Miss Mouse Trap, wood snap	30.00
Newhouse #4½, wood trap, dbl long spring	140.00
Newhouse #81½, riveted pan, single long spring	396.00
Newhouse #91½, single long spring	40.00
North Woods Mouse Trap, metal snap	8.00
Oneida Victor 1½, single under spring	20.00
Orbeto #300, dbl under spring	35.00
Orkin Wood Snap Trap, mousetrap	12.00
Otto Kampee Mfg Co, glass & metal mousetrap	100.00
Peerless Mouse Trap, drownder, self-setting	245.00
Prott #1¼, single long spring, jumper	40.00
PS Mfg Co #2, dbl long spring	60.00
PS&W #1, REv-O-Noc, single long spring	200.00
PS&W #2, w/hand-forged springs, dbl long springs	120.00
Quiggley Van Camp Hardware, wood snap	20.00
Rapp II, German killer mousetrap	10.00
Reddick Mole Trap, spear type, Pat 1854	35.00
Sargent #11, single long spring	35.00
Sargent #23, cast pan, w/teeth	210.00
Sargent #3, cast pan, dbl long spring, Pat Mar 11	30.00
Save-A-Leg #110	100.00
Sheene #4	100.00
Smith Rat Trap, wire cage, Pat 1908	68.00
Sta Kawt #1, single long spring	30.00
Star Mouse Trap, Dana IN, metal snap	30.00
Stop Thief #2	15.00
Teeter Gopher Trap	20.00
Thum Set Mouse Trap, metal snap	30.00
Trailzend #1, single long spring	45.00
Trailzend #5, dbl long spring	450.00
Tree Trap #0 Killer	95.00
Triumph #315X Ranger, w/teeth, dbl long spring	65.00
Triumph #42 Ranger, dbl long spring	35.00
Triumph #42X Ranger, w/teeth, dbl long spring	75.00
Van Wormer, CI, mole trap	425.00
Victor, Gladiator, metal snap rat trap	68.00

Victor, Louisiana Special 35.00
Victor, Marsh Special 35.00
Victor #1, single long spring 6.00
Victor #2, dbl long spring, dogless, early 200.00
Watkins, Hand Forged #2, dbl long spring 200.00
Webley #4, dbl coil spring 35.00
Wood Stream 'Museum Special,' wood snap 15.00
Woodward Death Clamp 67.00
X-Terminator Mouse Trap, blk plastic, live trap 12.00
Zap-A-Mouse, wood snap, china 3.00
Zip Mouse Trap, metal snap 38.00

Trevaise

In 1907 the vacant Sandwich glasshouse was purchased and refurbished by the Alton Manufacturing Company. They specialized in lighting and fixtures, but under the direction of an ex-Tiffany glassblower and former Sandwich resident James H. Grady, they also produced a line of iridescent art glass called Trevasise, examples of which are very rare today. It was often decorated with pulled feathers, whorls, leaves, and vines similar to the glassware produced by Tiffany, Quezal, and Durand. Examples that surface on today's market range in price from $1,500.00 to $2,000.00 and up. Trevaise was made for less than one year. Due to financial problems, the company closed in 1908. Our advisor for this category is Frank W. Ford; he is listed in the Directory under Massachusetts.

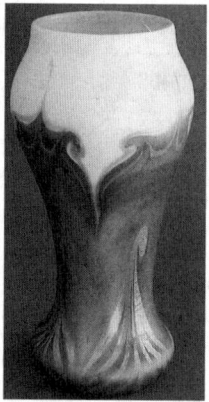

Vase, green and opal with pulled and hooked decoration, 1907, $3,500.00.
(Photo courtesy Frank W. Ford)

Trivets

Although strictly a decorative item today, the original purpose of the trivet was much more practical. They were used to protect table tops from hot serving dishes, and irons heated on the kitchen range were placed on trivets during use to protect work surfaces. The first patent date was 1869; many of the earliest trivets bore portraits of famous people or patriotic designs. Florals, birds, animals, and fruit were other favored motifs. Watch for remakes of early original designs. Some of these are marked Wilton, Emig, Wright, Iron Art, and V.M. for Virginia Metalcrafters. However, many of these reproductions are becoming collectible. Expect to pay considerably less for these than for the originals, since they are abundant.

Brass

Dmn shape w/ped ft (for teapot), 1890-1900s, 8x10" 75.00
Flatiron shape, English, mid-18th C, 10x5½" 100.00
Geometric openwork, ftd, English, 19th C, 4x7¾" dia 165.00
Heart cutouts, Am, 19th C, 10½" L 150.00
Lyre shape w/pierced flower center, trn wood hdl, snake ft, 5x13"..165.00

Cast Iron

Am Foundry & Mfg Co St Louis MO, 5½x4¼" 30.00
Amish-style hearts/birds/brooms/star, heavy, 8½x4½" 50.00
Cherubs (2) in center, mk JZH 1955 T-11 Cupid, 8½x4¾" 12.00
Enterprise Mfg Co Phila USA emb lettering w/lg E in center.......25.00
Flatiron shape, simple openwork, unmk, 5⅞x4¼" 10.00
Flatiron shape w/dbl hearts & scrollwork, 3-ftd, EX 38.50
God Bless our Mortgaged Home, Wilton #5, 8½x5¼" 16.00
Good Luck in horseshoe, mk Horseshoe 9-35 VCM, 7x4¼" 58.00
Rectangular, 4-ftd, English, 1900s, 4x21x9", EX 140.00
Running dog & fox w/W, 7½" L 35.00
6 entwined rings, old mc pnt traces, mk JLH 1945 C2, 5½" 16.00

Wrought Iron

Geometric pattern in circle, 3-leg, worn gr pnt, 9" 35.00
Geometric pattern in circle, 6-leg, pnt traces, 9" 35.00
Rotates on tripod, Am, ca 1800, 12" dia 125.00
Scrolled ft & decor, cvd wood hdl, 1800, 1½x10x5" 180.00
5-pointed star in circle, 6-leg, old bl pnt, 9" 35.00

Twin Winton

Twin brothers Don and Ross Winton started this California-based company during the mid-1930s while still in high school. In the mid-1940s they shut it down while in the armed forces and started up again in the late 1940s, when older brother Bruce Winton joined them and bought them out in the early 1950s. The company became a major producer of cookie jars, kitchenware, and household items sold nationally until it closed its San Juan Capistrano location in 1977.

Beside their extensive line of very collectible cookie jars, they're also well known for their Hillbilly line — mugs, pitchers, bowls, lamps, ashtrays, decanters, and other novelty items, which evolved from the late 1940s through the early 1970s with a variety of decorating methods still being discovered. Don Winton was the only designer for Twin Winton and created literally thousands of designs for them and hundreds of other companies. He is still sculpting in Corona del Mar, California, and collectors and dealers are continuing to find and document new pieces daily. To learn more about this subject, we recommend *Collector's Guide to Don Winton Designs* by our advisor, Mike Ellis; he is listed in the Directory under California or visit the collector club website at www.twinwinton.com.

Ashtray, kitten, #201, 6x8" 100.00
Bank, dobbin, #410, 8" 40.00
Bank, Foo Dog, #422, 8" 125.00
Bank, kitten, #415, 8" 50.00
Bank, lamb, #402, 8" 40.00
Bank, Pirate Fox, #414, 8" 65.00
Bank, shoe, #421, 8" 85.00
Bank, squirrel on nut, #416, 8" 50.00
Bank, wooly mammoth, made for Ford dealerships, 5" 100.00
Candle holder, Aladdin lamp, #510, 6½x9½" 45.00
Candle holder, Strauss, long, 10x5" 15.00
Candy jar, Candyhouse shack, #351, 9½x6½" 65.00
Candy jar, rabbit on turtle's bk, #350, 10x8" 85.00
Candy jar, Sailor Elephant, #356, 9x6" 65.00
Candy jar, squirrel on nut, #353, 9x8" 75.00
Canister, Cookie Barn, Canister Farm, #41, 12x8" 80.00
Canister, Cookie House, Canisterville, #40, 12x8" 175.00
Canister, Sugar Dairy, Canister Farm, #1121, 8x4" 55.00
Canister, Tea House, Canisterville, #104, 7x3" 50.00
Cookie jar, Apple, #35, 11x8" 180.00

Cookie jar, Baker, #67, 11x7"..300.00
Cookie jar, Barn, #41, 12x8"..70.00
Cookie jar, Chipmunk, #TW-45, 10x10"........................60.00
Cookie jar, Cookie Barn, #241, 12x8"..........................110.00
Cookie jar, Cookie Bucket, #59, 9x8"............................40.00
Cookie jar, Cookie Churn, #72, 12x7"...........................100.00
Cookie jar, Cookie Tepee, #96, 11x8"............................300.00
Cookie jar, Cow, #69, 8½x13½".....................................75.00
Cookie jar, Dog in Basket, #71, 10x8½"........................85.00
Cookie jar, Dutch Girl, #47, 12½x8½"...........................85.00
Cookie jar, Elf Bakery, #50, 12x8¾"...............................90.00
Cookie jar, Happy Bull (Ferdinand), #95, 12x8½" 75.00
Cookie jar, Hen on Basket, #61, 8½x8½".....................125.00
Cookie jar, Jack in the Box, #48, 13½x10" 300.00
Cookie jar, Kangaroo, #99, 13x7½"..............................300.00
Cookie jar, Little Lamb, #66, 13x6"...............................40.00
Cookie jar, Mother Goose, #75, 14x7"..........................100.00
Cookie jar, Owl, #91, 12x6½"...40.00
Cookie jar, Pot 'O Cookies, #58, 10x8"..........................40.00
Cookie jar, Sailor Elephant, #86, 12x9½".......................40.00
Cookie jar, Sailor Mouse, #63, 12x7".............................75.00
Cookie jar, Snail, #37, 12x7½".......................................250.00
Creamer & sugar, hen & rooster, #221, 5x6" 200.00
Decanter, Monk, mk A Twin Winton Design, Pasadena CA, 12x4".300.00
Decanter, Robin Hood, 10½x4⅜"....................................40.00
Expanimal, additional dividers, #5..................................40.00
Expanimal/bookends, kitten, #126, 7½"........................125.00
Figurine, angel on cloud playing flute, 6".......................40.00
Figurine, Black boy football player, Twinton, #10, 5½"......150.00
Figurine, boy skier, 7"..225.00
Figurine, boy standing by mailbox, Twinton, #8, 5½"........175.00
Figurine, cowboy on stick horse, 5¼".............................200.00
Figurine, elf in shoe, 6"...120.00
Figurine, girl holding sucker, Twinton, #6, 5½"...........150.00
Figurine, hunting dog, #601, 11"......................................85.00
Figurine, shaggy dog, #604, 8"...65.00
Figurine, squirrel holding stomach, 2½x4".......................30.00
Figurine, Yogi Bear sitting on stump, Hanna-Barbera, 5" 150.00
Lamp, circus seal on stand, #260, 12"............................250.00
Lamp, squirrel on stump, #255, 12"................................250.00
Men of the Mountain, bowl, man on 1 side, lady on other, 12" dia.250.00
Men of the Mountain, cigarette box, outhouse, H-109, 7" 75.00
Men of the Mountain, ice bucket, man w/jug, #33, 14x7½" 250.00
Men of the Mountain, ice bucket, suspenders, #30, 14x7½"...250.00
Men of the Mountain, pouring spout, H-104, 6½" 25.00
Mug, Bamboo line, 6"...20.00
Mug, elephant, trunk hdl, #505, 3¼".................................85.00
Mug, elephant head shape, pk w/blk eyes, trunk hdl, 3½x5" 125.00
Mug, kitten, #503, 3¼"..85.00
Napkin holder, Bambi, #480, 6x7"...................................85.00
Napkin holder, dobbin, #487, 7x5"...................................65.00
Napkin holder, dog, #451, 6x4".......................................150.00
Napkin holder, Dutch girl, #471, 8½x5½"........................75.00
Napkin holder, horse, #450, 6x4"....................................150.00
Napkin holder, Porky Pig, #473, 8x5"...............................75.00
Napkin holder, shack, #481, 7x7".....................................65.00
Planter, golf bag, 7"..50.00
Planter, rabbit eating carrot crouching beside basket, 5x8" 85.00
Planter, rabbit w/cart, 7x10"..85.00
Planter, Ranger Bear, #324, 8"...50.00
Planter, squirrel, #477, 8x4"...65.00
Relish tray, Bamboo line, 2-section, 4x8" 30.00
Shakers, cow, #169, pr...50.00
Shakers, dinosaurs, #151, pr...100.00

Shakers, dog, #171, pr 40.00
Shakers, donkey, #188, pr..40.00
Shakers, duck, 179, pr..75.00
Shakers, mouse, #181, pr...40.00
Shakers, owl, #191, pr..30.00
Shakers, Ranger Bear, #184, pr...40.00
Shakers, Sailor Elephant, #186, pr....................................35.00
Shakers, squirrel, brn & wht, 2½", pr...............................50.00
Spoon rest, Dutch girl, #19, 10x5"....................................40.00
Spoon rest, Ranger Bear, #12, 5x10".................................40.00
Stein, Bamboo line, 8"...35.00
Talking picture, shack, #430, 10½x10½" 110.00
Toothpick dispenser, pig, 5"...60.00
Wall planter, bear head, #300, 5½"..................................100.00

Typewriters

The first commercially successful typewriter was the Sholes and Glidden, introduced in 1874. By 1882 other models appeared, and by the 1890s dozens were on the market. At the time of the First World War, the ranks of typewriter-makers thinned, and by the 1920s only a few survived.

Collectors informally divide typewriter history into the pioneering period, up to about 1890; the classic period, from 1890 to 1920; and the modern period, since 1920. There are two broad classifications of early typewriters: (1) Keyboard machines, in which depression of a key prints a character and via a shift key prints up to three different characters per key; (2) Index machines, in which a chart of all the characters appears on the typewriter; the character is selected by a pointer or dial and is printed by operation of a lever or other device. Even though index typewriters were simpler and more primitive than keyboard machines, they were none-the-less a later development, designed to provide a cheaper alternative to the standard keyboard models that were selling for upwards of $100.00. Eventually second-hand keyboard typewriters supplied the low-price customer, and index typewriters vanished except as toys. Both classes of typewriters appeared in a great many designs.

It is difficult, if not impossible, to assign standard market prices to early typewriters. During the past decade, competition from a handful of wealthy overseas collectors has drastically affected the American market, and prices have become inflated on the rarer models. Some auction-realized prices have been astronomical. It is predicted that the market will drop again when this small group of collectors are satisfied and this atypical activity subsides. For now, we have updated values to reflect current market activity. Also, condition is a very important factor, and typewriters can vary infinitely in condition. A third factor to consider is that an early typewriter achieves its value mainly through the skill, effort, and patience of the collector who restores it to its original condition, in which case its purchase price is insignificant. Some unusual-looking early typewriters are not at all rare or valuable, while some very ordinary-looking ones are scarce and could be quite valuable. No general rules apply.

For further information we recommend Antique Typewriters & Office Collectibles by Darryl Rehr (Collector Books). See Clubs, Newsletters, and Catalogs in the Directory for information on the Early Typewriter Collectors Association. When no condition is indicated, the items listed below are assumed to be in excellent, unrestored condition. Our advisor for this category is Mike Brooks; he is listed in the Directory under California.

Blickensderfer, #5, type wheel, portable, 1893 ....150.00
Burnett, 4-row, oblique frontstrike 1,200.00
Caligraph, #1, 6-row, upstrike, caps only, minimum value 1,000.00
Century 10, 3-row, frontstrike...50.00
Chicago, #3, 3-row, type sleeve...400.00
Crandal, Improved, 1895 ....1,000.00
Crary, circular keyboard, downstrike, minimum value..............1,000.00

Darling, circular index..500.00
Desnmore, #1a, 4-row, upstrike.........................200.00
Dollar, type-wheel index, 1890..........................300.00
Dougherty Visible, 4-row, frontstrike.................350.00
Eagle Defi, 3-row, swinging sector......................800.00
Edelmann, curved index, Germany, 1897............200.00
Edland, emb circular index, gold-tone base 1,000.00
Electromatic, IBM, 4-row, frontstrike, electric 50.00
Emerson, 3-row, pivot frontstrike, 1907.............150.00
Featherweight Blick, 3-row, type wheel 75.00
Fitch, 3-row, backstroke, American or British, minimum value.1,000.00
Fountain, 3-row, type wheel, Commercial Visible line 500.00
Franklin, Type I, 3-row, curved keystroke, downstrike................500.00
Hall, linear index, 1886....................................500.00
Hammond, #1b, curved keyboard, type shuffle 200.00
Helios, 2-row, type wheel, 21 keys, 3 shift keys.................300.00
International, dbl keyboard, upstrike, minimum value............1,000.00
Keaton Music Typewriter, circular keyboard, downstrike 300.00
Liliput, circular index, Germany, 1907...........1,000.00
Masspro, 3-row, frontstrike, 1932.......................50.00
Monarch, #2, 4-row, frontstrike, 1904 ....30.00
Munson, #2, 3-row, type sleeve.........................200.00
North's, 4-row, backstroke, British, 1892 ....1,000.00
Odell, #1, linear index 800.00
Pearl (Searing), circular index, 1891 ....800.00
Remington, #4, 4-row, upstrike, caps only.........350.00
Rofa, 3-row, curved keyboard, downstrike..........125.00
Sampson Permagraph, 4-row, type wheel, electric, 52-lbs, 26" W .250.00
Shimer, 4-row, upstrike, 1898 ....500.00
Sun Index, metal dog-bone base, linear index 1,000.00
World, semi-circular index.................................125.00

Uhl Pottery

Founded in Evansville, Indiana, in 1849 by German immigrants, the Uhl Pottery was moved to Huntingburg, Indiana, in 1908 because of the more suitable clay available there. They produced stoneware — Acorn Ware jugs, crocks, and bowls — which were marked with the acorn logo and 'Uhl Pottery.' They also made mugs, pitchers, and vases in simple shapes and solid glazes marked with a circular ink stamp containing the name of the pottery and 'Huntingburg, Indiana.' The pottery closed in the mid-1940s. Those seeking additional information about Uhl pottery are encouraged to contact the Uhl Collectors' Society, whose address is listed in the Directory under Clubs, Newsletters, and Catalogs. For more information, we recommend *Uhl Pottery* by Anna Mary Feldmeyer and Kara Holtzman (Collector Books).

Ashtray, pig, rose, sm......................................540.00
Bank, Acorn Stoves/Will Save Half Your Fuel Money, brn, 3x3".125.00
Bank, jug shaped, AG Abernathy...General Merchandise, 4½" ..230.00
Bank, Piggy; Kansas City, wht...........................265.00
Basket, hanging; bl, basketweave decor, 5x4" 80.00
Beverage set, buttery-yel w/raised bands, pitcher w/8 mugs, NM..200.00
Bottle, elephant figural, bl, 3½"........................125.00
Churn, #4, stoneware, 4-gal 110.00
Churn, #6, stoneware, 18x10"..........................175.00
Cookie crock, brn, wlid, 9½x8¼"......................100.00
Cookie jar, teal..360.00
Creamer, gr, 3" 75.00
Creamer, Smoky Mtn Nat'l Park, rose, mini 190.00
Crock, #2, 2-gal, 9"..90.00
Crock, #5, 5-gal 150.00
Flowerpot, burgundy, 3 buttress ft, 3¾" 50.00

Jar, jam; yel, w/lid, 3x4".....................................75.00
Jug, brn over wht, 1¼" 60.00
Jug, Christmas 1937..325.00
Jug, Christmas 1939..260.00
Jug, Christmas 1940/Uhl Pottery...Indiana, red/cream, 2⅜" 200.00
Jug, Christmas 1942, 2½"................................250.00
Jug, Uhl, mini, 1"..85.00
Novelty, boot, gr, 3"...90.00
Novelty, horse head, bl....................................200.00
Novelty, shoe, bl, mk Uhl, 3x5".........................85.00
Pitcher, bl, #21, mini.......................................120.00
Pitcher, bl, rnd w/stubby spout, 6½" dia...............60.00
Pitcher, bl, 5"..45.00
Pitcher, dk purple, mini, 2½"...........................100.00
Pitcher, grapes emb, bl, bulbous, #181...............160.00
Pitcher, grapes emb, w/lid, 6½".........................250.00
Pitcher, Lincoln's head emb, bl, 6½"..................350.00
Pitcher, yel, long spout, mini, 1¾".......................60.00
Planter, lamb, blk w/bl ribbon around neck, 8x8x4" 75.00
Planter, sweet potato; bl..................................150.00
Planter/vase, rabbit beside basket, bl, 4¼x4½"......75.00
Shakers, bl w/emb S or P, bulbous, 3½x3¼", pr......90.00
Stein, tan bbl, 3-oz...125.00
Stein, 1742-1942 TW, flagon style, 5x3"..............70.00

Teapot, brown, six-cup, $225.00.

Vase, American Legion, rose.............................170.00
Vase, blk, short bulbous bottom w/long trumpet neck, 2-hdl, 5" ..75.00
Vase, rose colored, scalloped neck, 2-hdl, 3¾x5"..........150.00
Wren birdhouse 200.00

Unger Brothers

Art Nouveau silver items of the highest quality were produced by Unger Brothers, who operated in Newark, New Jersey, from the early 1880s until 1919. In addition to tableware, they also made brushes, mirrors, powder boxes, and the like for milady's dressing table as well as jewelry and small personal accessories such as match safes and flasks. They often marked their products with a circle seal containing an intertwined 'UB' and '925 fine sterling.' Some Unger pieces contain a patent date near the mark. In addition to sterling, a very limited amount of gold was also used. Note: This company made no pewter items; Unger designs may occasionally be found in pewter, but these are copies. Items with English hallmarks or signed 'Birmingham' are English (not Unger).

Brooch, lady w/flowing hair, ca 1904, ⅞" dia............125.00
Brooch, open flower, 1" dia 60.00
Buckle, mermaid & sea creature, 1⅜x1½"...........285.00
Case, Indian chief head emb, mk Sterling 925 Fine, 3½x3⅜" 715.00
Cuff links, nude lady, pr 550.00
Jar, dresser; Love's Dream, 3½x3¾"...................350.00
Match safe, Nouveau lady, 2¾x1⅝"...................145.00

Pen holder, hinged, w/pen, eng name, Nouveau filigree, 4½" L..**140.00**
Picture frame, filigree border, ornate stand, 4x3" **100.00**
Tray, ice cream; Sherwood, 13½x8½" **1,100.00**

Universal

Universal Potteries Incorporated operated in Cambridge, Ohio, from 1934 to 1956. Many lines of dinnerware and kitchen items were produced in both earthenware and semiporcelain. In 1956 the emphasis was shifted to the manufacture of floor and wall tiles, and the name was changed to the Oxford Tile Company, Division of Universal Potteries. The plant closed in 1976. Our advisor for this category is Ted Haun; he is listed in the Directory under Indiana.

Baby's Breath, bowl, soup/cereal; lug hdls, 6⅞" **15.00**
Baby's Breath, plate, bread & butter **12.00**
Baby's Breath, plate, dinner; 10" **20.00**
Baby's Breath, sugar bowl, w/lid **30.00**
Ballerina, cake plate **25.00**
Ballerina, platter, tab hdls, 12" **20.00**
Ballerina, sauce boat **15.00**
Ballerina, sugar bowl, w/lid..**15.00**
Ballerina (Mist), bowl, serving; 9" **15.00**
Ballerina (Mist), chop plate, tab hdls **20.00**
Ballerina (Mist), coffee server, w/lid, 8½" **25.00**
Ballerina (Mist), creamer, from $12 to **15.00**
Ballerina (Mist), plate, serving; tab hdls, 10" **12.00**
Ballerina (Mist), shakers, pr **15.00**
Ballerina (Mist), sugar bowl, w/lid, from $15 to.........................**20.00**
Bittersweet, bowl, 10¼" **25.00**
Bittersweet, casserole, w/lid, 5x9" **35.00**
Bittersweet, jar, w/lid, 2" **35.00**
Bittersweet, jar, w/lid, 3¼" **40.00**
Bittersweet, platter, oval, 13½" **30.00**
Bittersweet, shaker, pepper; range style...............................**30.00**
Bittersweet, shakers, 3½", pr **25.00**
Calico Fruit, pie plate, 9¾", w/server..................................**55.00**
Calico Fruit, pitcher, utility; 6⅜" **35.00**
Calico Fruit, plate, 9" **22.50**
Calico Fruit, teapot, w/lid, 1-cup **65.00**
Cattail, bowl, mixing; 6" **17.50**
Cattail, bowl, mixing; 7" **20.00**
Cattail, bowl, mixing; 8" **25.00**
Cattail, bowl, soup; flat rim, 7¾" **15.00**
Cattail, bowl, vegetable; oval...**30.00**
Cattail, coffeepot, 3-pc **70.00**
Cattail, jug, w/lid, 5¼" **20.00**
Cattail, pie plate **30.00**
Cattail, plate, luncheon; 9" **35.00**
Cattail, platter, 11½", from $15 to.....................................**20.00**
Cattail, sugar bowl, w/lid, from $20 to..................................**25.00**
Cattail, tumbler, glass, 4¾" **25.00**
Cherry Blossom, sauce boat..**15.00**
Circus, bowl, mixing; 5¼x10½"..**30.00**
Circus, shakers, range style, 4½", pr....................................**22.50**
Highland, gravy boat, no underplate **25.00**
Highland, sugar bowl, w/lid..**15.00**
Iris, bowl, mixing; 4x9" **35.00**
Iris, butter dish, w/lid, 4x7½"..**30.00**
Iris, cake plate, tab hdls, 13" **25.00**
Iris, shakers, 2½", pr **25.00**
Kitchen Bouquet, pitcher, water; 7" **40.00**
Moss Rose, platter, rnd **30.00**

Moss Rose, teapot, w/lid...**70.00**
Orange Poppy, ball jug, 8" **55.00**
Orange Poppy, casserole, tab hdls, w/lid, 11" **45.00**
Orange Poppy, refrigerator jug, w/spout lid.............................**55.00**
Rambler Rose, bowl, fruit...**17.00**
Rambler Rose, bowl, mixing; 3¾x7½" **30.00**
Rambler Rose, creamer **25.00**
Rambler Rose, cup & saucer **20.00**
Rambler Rose, plate, dinner; 10" **20.00**
Rambler Rose, plate, luncheon; 7¼" **18.00**
Snowflake, pitcher, 1-qt, 7½"..**20.00**
Woodvine, cup & saucer **15.00**
Woodvine, plate, dinner; 10" **12.00**
Woodvine, platter, tab hdls, 13¼"......................................**22.50**

Val St. Lambert

Since its inception in Belgium at the turn of the nineteenth century, the Val St. Lambert Cristalleries has been involved in the production of high-quality glass, producing some cameo. The factory is still in production.

Box, cameo wisteria, lav/clear/frost, w/lid, 1920s, 3¾x6½" **865.00**
Vase, cameo chrysanthemums/presentation, HP in maroon on gr, 14".**460.00**
Vase, cameo roses, cobalt to clear w/gold geometrics, cylindrical, 10".**500.00**
Vase, cameo sailboats/detailed trees, sgn VSL on side (Muller), 16"..**3,000.00**
Vase, cobalt overlaid in copper w/allover emb rosettes, 12" **575.00**

Valentines

Valentine collectors are a special group of people — they're all romantics. Very often they choose valentines according to their own personal outlook on romance. Aspects that are highly prized by some might not appeal to the next collector at all. So in addition to the more obvious factors such as category, condition, size, manufacturer, artist signature, and age, a more intangible variable also comes into play — heart!

Please note: When measuring the size of a card, the background area should be included as well. Our advisor for this category is Katherine Kreider, author of *Valentines With Values, One Hundred Years of Valentines*, and *Valentines For the Eclectic Collector*. She is listed in the Directory under Pennsylvania.

Key:
dim — dimension/dimensional   mech — mechanical
HCPP — honeycomb paper puff   PIG — printed/published in Germany

Dim, airplane, crepe-paper wings, PIG, 1930s, 6x14x4", EX.......**125.00**
Dim, cat w/fireplace & tennis racket, 1915, 7½x5½x1", EX.........**75.00**
Dim, cherub w/bow & arrow, PIG, early 1900s, 6½x5x3", EX **35.00**
Dim, heart, 4-D greeting card style, floral/children, PIG, 4½, EX.**40.00**
Dim, observation car, tuck, 8½x5½x3", EX **150.00**
Dim, rowboat, early 1900s, 5x6x1½", EX **50.00**
Dim, speed boat, Charles Twelvetrees, 1940s, 10x10x2", EX.........**50.00**
Dim, Viking ship, PIG, 9¾x9x5", EX **75.00**
Dim, 3-D, Cinderella Coach, Hallmark, 1960s, 9¾x7½x4½", EX.**15.00**
Dim & greeting card style, Valentine For My Wife, Hallmark, 1961, EX.**15.00**
Flat, children drink sodas, felt adornment, USA, 1940s, 8x6", EX.**10.00**
Flat, Dutch children, Tuck, English, early 1900s, 8x7", EX **50.00**
Flat, girl & toy sewing machine, USA, 1950s, 4x2", EX.................**3.00**
Flat, golfing kitten, USA, 1950s, 4x2", EX...............................**3.00**
Flat, postman, PIG, early 1900s, 6½x4", EX **15.00**
Flat, toaster, USA, 1950s, 4x2½", EX.................................**3.00**
Flat, Wizard of Oz, USA, 1960s, 5x4", EX **15.00**

Flat, 3 Blind Mice, USA, 1940s, EX 5.00
Folded-flat, Superman, USA, 1940s, 4½x6½", EX 50.00
Folded-flat, vanity, 1940s, 5x4", EX...10.00
Folded-flat, Wonder Woman, 1940s, 6x6", EX............................50.00
Greeting card, boy & girl on scooter, Whitney, 1930s, 5x4", EX.....6.00
Greeting card, Choked to Death, Howland, 1850s, 9½x8", EX ..350.00
Greeting card, Civil War tent, 1860s, 6x5", EX 350.00
Greeting card, lady & cherub, hand-colored litho, 1890s, 8x5", EX..125.00

Greeting card, Pink Rubrum Lily-bordered, accented with embossed paper lace and Victorian scraps, chromolitho, ca early 1900s, EX, $40.00. (Photo courtesy Katherine Kreider)

Greeting card, To My Wife, Hallmark, 1950s, 9½x7½", EX 15.00
HCPP, Dan Cupid, Beistle, USA, 1920s, 6x8x2", EX 40.00
HCPP, hanging heart, Beistle, USA, 1920s, 8x8x4", EX 50.00
HCPP, Jack Be Nimble, Beistle, USA, 1920s, 9x6x3", EX 75.00
HCPP & hold-to-light, fountain, PIG, early 1900s, 11x8x3", EX .125.00
HCPP & hold-to-light, Victorian house, PIG, early 1900s, 10x9x5", EX.175.00
Hold-to-light, steamship, 4-D, PIG, early 1900s, 10x6x4", EX 175.00
Hold-to-light, Victorian girl/flowers, 2-D, PIG, 1925, 8½x6x3", EX..75.00
Hold-to-light, windmill & sailboat, 3-D, PIG, 1915, 12x10x4", EX.175.00
Hold-to-light postcard, angels/children, undivided bk, early 1900s, EX .40.00
Mechanical-flat, Army men & tent, Twelvetrees, 1940s, 12x6", EX.50.00
Mechanical-flat, cat w/teeter-totter, PIG, 1920s, 8x11", EX..........75.00
Mechanical-flat, dragonfly w/cherub, PIG, 1930s, 7x6", EX..........50.00
Mechanical-flat, lg-eyed children in roadster, PIG, 1924, 7½x9", EX .75.00
Mechanical-flat, monkey, harmonica, PIG, 1915, 8x5", EX 25.00
Mechanical-flat, standard poodle, PIG, early 1900s, 9x5", EX 75.00
Mechanical-flat, Wee-Gee Board, hand colored, 1920s, 6½x4", EX.25.00
Novelty, African American/Chiclet boxes, Rust Craft, 1920s, 10x5½"..75.00
Novelty, candy box, HP satin, 1920s, 8x8", EX.............................45.00
Novelty, Cupid's Book, San Francisco, hardbk, 1920s, 9x6", EX...50.00
Novelty-mech, kissing couple, PIG, 1920s, 6x5", EX....................50.00
Postcard, cherub real photo, Tuck, early 1900s, EX 15.00
Postcard, cherub w/human hair, spun glass wings, early 1900s, EX.50.00
Postcard, dressed kittens, chromolitho, PIG, mid-1900s, EX.........15.00
Postcard, lady & heart real photo, early 1900s, EX 10.00

Vallerysthal

Fine glassware has been produced in Vallerysthal, France, since the middle of the nineteenth century.

Covered dish, cabbage head, milk glass, 6½" dia 35.00
Covered dish, elephant & rider, milk glass, 7¼"........................185.00
Covered dish, squirrel on acorn, bl, 4¾x7"................................140.00
Honey dish, basket w/basketweave mold, milk glass, 3¾" 60.00
Salt, dbl, powder bl opaque, 2¼" bowls, 5" W 65.00
Vase, cameo leaves/flowers on cranberry, 4 cranberry teardrops, 4x5".1,650.00
Vase, powder bl opaque, hand holding cornucopia vase, 8¾" 85.00
Vase, powder bl opaque, ribbed neck, vining flowered body, 9" 70.00

Van Briggle

The Van Briggle Pottery of Colorado Springs, Colorado, was established in 1901 by Artus Van Briggle, whose early career had been shaped by such notables as Karl Langenbeck and Maria Nichols Storer. His quest for several years had been to perfect a completely flat matt glaze, and upon accomplishing his goal, he opened his pottery. His wife, Anne, worked with him, and they, along with George Young, were responsible for the modeling of the wares. Their work typified the flow and form of the Art Nouveau movement, and the shapes they designed played as important a part in their success as their glazes. Some of their most famous pieces were Despondency, Lorelei, and Toast Cup. Increasing demand for their work soon made it necessary to add to their quarters as well as their staff. Although much of the ware was eventually made from molds, each piece was carefully trimmed and refined before the glaze was sprayed on. Their most popular colors were Persian Rose, Ming Blue, and Mustard Yellow.

Van Briggle died in 1904, but the work was continued by his wife. New facilities were built; and by 1908, in addition to their artware, tiles, gardenware, and commercial lines were added. By the '20s the emphasis had shifted from art pottery to novelties and commercial wares. Reproductions of some of the early designs continue to be made. The double AA mark has always been in use, but after 1920 the dates and/or shape numbers were dropped. Mention should be made here as well that the Anna Van Briggle glaze is a later line which was made between 1956 and 1968. Our advisor for this category is Michelle Ross; she is listed in the Directory under Michigan. For more information, we recommend *Collector's Encyclopedia of Van Briggle Art Pottery* by Richard Sasicki and Josie Fania (Collector Books).

Bookend, elephant, dk purple on burgundy, 4¼x7¼"..................220.00
Bowl, dragonflies (4) at rim, mulberry, USA, 1920s, 2¾x8¾"....345.00
Bowl, plain, maroon w/bl overspray, dtd 1916, incurvate, 7".......145.00
Bowl, spade leaves w/long stems, angle shoulder, ca 1915, 5x9½"..1,500.00
Bowl vase, lg stylized leaves, frothy gr, wht clay exposed, 1904, 3x5".1,300.00
Bud vase, flower blossoms at neck, frothy gr w/exposed tan, '07-11, 8"..950.00
Dish, lg spider, dk gr, 1906, 5½" 800.00
Jug, Fire Water, Indian motif, purple/teal, pre-'09, 6½x5" 1,300.00
Tray, Shell Girl, bl & gr, 8½"...150.00
Vase, Anna Van, maroon & bl, 17", NM.....................................175.00
Vase, bell-shape flowers, frothy bl/gr, 1903/197/III, 6½x3¼" ...1,900.00
Vase, bl to maroon, hdls, post-1930s, 2¼"..................................100.00
Vase, buds on stems, Persian Rose, bulbous w/hdls, 1930s, 6½"..200.00
Vase, butterfly under bl & maroon, post-1930s, 4" 100.00
Vase, crocus, gr/pearl gray w/wht clay exposed, 1904, 3½x4" ..1,000.00
Vase, curved stems of rnd flowers form panels, dk teal, 1904, 4x2½".1,400.00
Vase, deer figural, gr to bl, sgn DM, 9" 100.00
Vase, Despondency, bl & gr, post-1930, 13½".............................550.00
Vase, dragonflies, maroon & bl, 7" 300.00
Vase, floral, bl-gray w/turq overspray, slender ovoid, dtd 1920, 6" .375.00
Vase, floral, brn w/gr accents, SPGS/logo, 2½x3¼" 110.00
Vase, floral, dk purple on maroon, 1921, 2¾x2¾"......................165.00
Vase, floral on turq, buttressed hdls, 1919, 8¼" 575.00
Vase, Indian heads (3), brn & gr, 11"...475.00
Vase, Indian heads (3), maroon & bl, pre-1930, 12" 375.00
Vase, iris, turq, low hdls, late, 14"..325.00
Vase, irises, Persian Rose, low hdls, ca 1920s, 13¼" 375.00
Vase, leaves, cream & wht matt, sgn FW, 4" 50.00
Vase, leaves form body, bl & aqua mottled, post-1930s, 3½" 100.00
Vase, lg leaves between floral stems, frothy purple/bl/gr, ca '07, 10" .3,250.00
Vase, Lorelei, bl shaded to turq, AA Van Briggle, ca 1970+, 10⅞"..325.00
Vase, Lorelei, maroon & bl, 10"..325.00
Vase, mistletoe at rim, frothy sky bl, '07-11, label, 2½x2½" 450.00
Vase, narrow leaves, tall between short, Persian Rose, '20s, squat, 5" .175.00
Vase, poppies, brn & gr, 1920s-30s, 8¼", NM.............................250.00

Vase, spade leaves on upright stems, leathery turq/plum, 1905, 10x5"..**900.00**
Vase, spade leaves/stems form panels, leathery yel w/gr, '08-11, 5x3"..**800.00**
Vase, swirled leaves, Persian Rose, ca 1940s, 4¾x7½" **150.00**
Vase, trefoils on curving stems, yel w/gr accent, 1905, rstr line, 8" .**400.00**
Vase, 4 shaped oval panels w/tulip & leaves, raspberry, 1903, 10x5"..**2,000.00**
Wall pocket, floral emb, maroon & bl, 8¼" **200.00**

Van Erp, Dirk

Dirk van Erp was a Leeuwarden, Holland, coppersmith who emigrated to the United States in 1886 and began making decorative objects from artillery shell casings in the San Francisco shipyards. He opened a shop in 1908 in Oakland and in 1910 formed a brief (one year) partnership with D'Arcy Gaw. Apprentices at the studio included his daughter Agatha and Harry Dixon, who was later to open his own shop in San Francisco. Gaw has been assigned design credit for many of the now-famous hammered copper and mica lamps. So popular were the lamps that other San Francisco craftspeople, Lillian Palmer, Fred Brosi, Hans Jauchen, and Old Mission Kopperkraft among them, began producing similar forms. In addition to lamps, he manufactured a broad range of objects including vases, bowls, desk sets, and smoking accessories. Van Erp's work is typically finely hammered with a deep red-brown patina and of good proportions. On rare occasions, van Erp created pieces in a 'warty' finish: an irregular, indeed lumpy, surface with a much redder appearance. Van Erp died in 1933. In 1929 the shop was taken over by his son, William, who produced hammered goods in both brass and copper. Many feature Art Deco-style designs and are of considerably lower value than his father's work. The van Erp mark is prominent and takes the form of a windmill above a rectangle that includes his name, sometime D'Arcy Gaw's name, and sometimes San Francisco.

Please note: Cleaning or scrubbing original patinas diminishes the value of the object. Our prices are for examples with excellent original patina unless noted. Our advisor for this and related Arts and Crafts objects is Bruce Austin, he is listed in the Directory under New York.

Key: h/cp — hammered copper

Bowl, h/cp, 12½"...**1,700.00**
Bowl, hammered aluminum, D'Arcy Gaw, 5½" **450.00**
Box, h/cp, lightly cleaned, 4" W **170.00**
Lamp, h/cp, 18" mica shade; riveted tall base w/swell, 19" **11,000.00**
Lamp, h/cp, 23" conical shade w/4 mica panels, baluster base..**30,000.00**
Vase, h/cp, cylindrical w/swollen shoulder, 7½" **2,600.00**
Vase, h/cp, wide, slightly shouldered, 8½x7" **3,250.00**
Vase, h/cp (warty), EX patina w/red highlights, 6x6½"..........**3,250.00**
Vessel, h/cp, cutouts in hdl, 11" W **1,000.00**

Vance/Avon Faience

Although pottery had been made in Tiltonville, Ohio, since about 1880, the ware manufactured there was of little significance until after the turn of the century when the Vance Faience Company was organized for the purpose of producing quality artware. By 1902 the name had been changed to the Avon Faience Company, and late in the same year it and three other West Virginia potteries incorporated to form the Wheeling Potteries Company. The Avon branch operated in Tiltonville until 1905 when production was moved to Wheeling. Art pottery was discontinued.

From the beginning, only skilled craftsmen and trained engineers were hired. Wm. P. Jervis and Fredrick Hurten Rhead were among the notable artists responsible for designing some of the early artware. Some of the ware was slip decorated under glaze, while other pieces were molded with high-relief designs. Examples with squeeze-bag decoration by

Rhead are obviously forerunners of the Jap Birdimal line he later developed for Weller. Ware was marked 'Vance F. Co.'; Avon F. Co., Tiltonville'; or 'Avon W. Pts. Co.'

Vase, stylized flowers/leaves, squeezbag, 3-sided, Avon, rstr, 9x3".**750.00**
Vase, tall w/4 sm vase-shaped openings, 11x6", EX, from $150 to.**250.00**

Vaseline Glass

Vaseline, a greenish-yellow colored glass produced by adding uranium oxide to the batch, was produced during the Victorian era. It was made in smaller quantities than other colors and lost much of its popularity with the advent of the electric light. It was used for pressed tablewares, vases, whimseys, souvenir items, oil lamps, perfume bottles, drawer pulls, and doorknobs. Pieces have been reproduced, and some factories still make it today in small batches. Vaseline glass will fluoresce under an ultraviolet light.

Bowl, console; Paneled Rib, blk amethyst ft, 4x11½" **325.00**
Celery vase, Diamond & Prism, ca 1860, 8", pr **350.00**
Epergne, single stem, SP stand, ca 1890, 10½x3⅜" **325.00**
Lamp, oil; Dmn Quilt hearts, sq base, 1890-1900, 10" **375.00**
Pitcher, leaves emb allover, sm trunk-like legs (4), 10" **400.00**
Vase, jack-in-pulpit, wht opal striped rim, appl flowers, 9x4½" ..**300.00**
Vase, jack-in-pulpit; opal rim to clear base, 12¼x5⅝" **265.00**

Verlys

Verlys art glass, produced in France after 1931 by the Holophane Company of Verlys, was made in crystal with acid-finished relief work in the Art Deco style. Colored and opalescent glass was also used. In 1935 an American branch was opened in Newark, Ohio, where very similar wares were produced until the factory ceased production in 1951. French Verlys was signed with one of three mold-impressed script signatures, all containing the company name and country of origin. The American-made glassware was signed 'Verlys' only, either scratched with a diamond-tipped pen or impressed in the mold. There is very little if any difference in value between items produced in France and America. Though some seem to feel that the French should be higher priced (assuming it to be scarce), many prefer the American-made product.

In June of 1955, about sixteen Verlys molds were leased to the A.H. Heisey Company. Heisey's versions were not signed with the Verlys name, so if an item is unsigned it is almost certainly a Heisey piece. The molds were returned to Verlys of America in July 1957. Fenton now owns all Verlys molds, but all issues are marked Fenton. Our advisor for this category is Don Frost; he is listed in the Directory under Washington.

Ashtray, Doves...**50.00**
Ashtray, Swallow, bl **125.00**
Bonbon, Butterfly, topaz, w/lid...........................**160.00**
Bowl, Chrysanthemum, satin **525.00**
Bowl, Cupidon..**150.00**
Bowl, Dragonfly **200.00**
Bowl, Duck & Fish, opal **230.00**
Bowl, Leaves, oval **375.00**
Bowl, Orchid, Dusty Rose **300.00**
Bowl, Orchid, 14" **275.00**
Bowl, Tassel, 11¾" **240.00**
Bowl, Thistle, 8½" **120.00**
Bowl, Thistle, 13".......................................**235.00**
Bowl, Water Lily, 8½"....................................**125.00**
Bowl, Wild Duck...**130.00**

Candlestick, Water Lily, bl, pr 325.00
Center bowl, Water Lily, frosted, 13½" 275.00
Charger, Butterflies, sgn, 13¾" 275.00
Charger, Water Lily, topaz, 14" 275.00
Cigarette box, w/bird, sgn 135.00
Platter, Palm Leaves, clear & satin, 14" 140.00
Soap dish, Alpine Thistle, topaz, 11" 375.00
Vase, Alpine Thistle, frosted, sgn, 8¾" 250.00
Vase, Alpine Thistle, opal, 9" 400.00
Vase, Gems, w/flower frog, amber, 6¾" 325.00
Vase, Gems, 6¾" 280.00
Vase, Grasshopper, 5¼" 125.00
Vase, Lovebirds, 6½x2¾" 125.00
Vase, Mandarin, frosted, 9¼" 375.00
Vase, Mermaids, frosted crystal, 10" 750.00

Vernon Kilns

Vernon Potteries Ltd. was established by Faye G. Bennison in Vernon, California, in 1931. The name was later changed to Vernon Kilns; until it closed in 1958, dinnerware, specialty plates, artware, and figurines were their primary products. Among its wares most sought after by collectors today are items designed by such famous artists as Rockwell Kent, Walt Disney, Don Blanding, Jane Bennison, and May and Vieve Hamilton. Our advisor is Maxine Nelson, author of *Collectible Vernon Kilns, Second Edition*; she is listed in the Directory under Arizona.

Anytime Shape

Patterns you will find on this shape include Tickled Pink, Heavenly Days, Anytime, Imperial, Sherwood, Frolic, Young in Heart, Rose-A-Day, and Dis 'N Dot.

Bowl, fruit; 5½", from $5 to 8.00
Bowl, vegetable; 7½" dia, from $10 to...........................12.00
Casserole, w/lid, 8" dia, from $25 to 45.00
Creamer, from $8 to..12.00
Gravy boat, from $15 to 20.00
Plate, dinner; 10", from $8 to...12.00
Platter, 11", from $14 to...20.00
Relish dish, 3-section, from $20 to 30.00
Shakers, pr, from $12 to 20.00
Tumbler, 14-oz, from $12 to 25.00

Chatelaine Shape

This designer pattern by Sharon Merrill was made in four color combinations: Topaz, Bronze, decorated Platinum, and Jade.

Bowl, serving; Topaz or Bronze, 9", from $25 to............35.00
Cup, coffee; flat base, decor Platinum & Jade, from $20 to 25.00
Plate, salad; Topaz or Bronze, 7½", from $12 to 15.00
Sugar bowl, w/lid, decor Platinum & Jade, from $35 to................45.00
Teapot, w/lid, decor Platinum & Jade, from $200 to 300.00

Fantasia

Centaur, #31, from $1,100 to..1,500.00
Centaurette, #18, from $1,000 to 1,200.00
Donkey Unicorn, #16, from $600 to 700.00
Nubian Centaurette, #24, from $900 to.......................1,200.00
Pegasus, #21, from $300 to..400.00
Pegasus, blk baby, #19, from $250 to 400.00

Rearing Unicorn, #15, from $400 to 500.00
Unicorn, blk, #13, from $300 to 400.00
Unicorn, sitting, #14, from $400 to 500.00

Lotus and Pan American Lei Shape

Patterns on this shape include Lotus, Chinling, and Vintage. Pan American Lei was a variation with flatware from the San Marino line. To evaluate Lotus, use the low end of our range as the minimum value; the high end of values apply to Pan American Lei.

Ashtray, Pan American Lei only, 5½" 35.00
Bowl, chowder; 6", from $12 to.....................................25.00
Butter tray, oblong, w/lid, from $35 to.........................75.00
Casserole, w/lid, 8" dia, from $35 to 95.00
Mug, 9-oz, from $15 to 35.00
Plate, chop; offset, Lotus only, 13", from $30 to...........40.00
Plate, coupe; Pan American Lei only, 6" 12.00
Sauce boat, from $18 to..40.00
Tumbler, #5, 14-oz, from $18 to 35.00

Melinda Shape

Patterns found on this shape are Arcadia, Beverly, Blossom Time, Chintz, Cosmos, Dolores, Fruitdale, Hawaii (Lei Lani on Melinda is two and a half times base value), May Flower, Monterey, Native California, and Philodendron. The more elaborate the pattern, the higher the value.

Bowl, lug chowder; 6", from $12 to................................18.00
Bowl, salad; ftd base, 12", from $45 to..........................85.00
Butter tray, w/lid, oblong, from $45 to..........................75.00
Egg cup, from $18 to..25.00
Pitcher, 1½-pt, from $25 to...45.00
Plate, luncheon; 9½", from $10 to..................................18.00
Platter, 12", from $20 to...30.00
Relish dish, single-leaf shape, 12", from $25 to.............35.00
Shakers, pr, from $15 to 25.00
Teapot, w/lid, 6-cup, from $45 to...................................85.00

Montecito Shape (and Coronado)

This was one of the company's most utilized shapes — well over two hundred patterns have been documented. Among the most popular are the solid colors, plaids, the florals, westernware, and the Bird and Turnbull series. Bird, Turnbull, and Winchester 73 (Frontier Days) are two to four times base values. Disney hollow ware is seven to eight times base values. Plaids (except Tweed and Calico), solid colors, Brown-eyed Susan are represented by the lower range.

Ashtray, 5½" dia, from $15 to...20.00
Bowl, fruit; 5½", from $8 to 12.00
Bowl, rim soup; 8½", from $12 to...................................15.00
Bowl, salad; rnd, 13", from $45 to..................................75.00
Coaster, ridged, 3¾", from $18 to...................................22.00
Comport, ftd, early, scarce, 9½" dia, from $50 to...........75.00
Egg cup, dbl; cupped or str sides, ea, from $18 to...........25.00
Jam jar, notched lid, 5", from $65 to...............................95.00
Muffin tray, tab hdls, dome lid, 9", from $85 to 125.00
Pitcher, disk; plain or decor, 2-qt, from $65 to...............100.00
Plate, grill; 11", from $25 to...30.00
Platter, 12", from $30 to...40.00
Spoon holder, from $45 to...75.00
Tidbit, 2-tier, wooden fixture, from $25 to......................35.00
Trio buffet server, from $75 to..85.00

San Fernando Shape

Known patterns for this shape are Desert Bloom, Early Days, Hibiscus, R.F.D., Vernon's 1860, and Vernon Rose.

Bowl, fruit; 5½", from $8 to	12.00
Bowl, mixing, RFD only, 9", from $30 to	40.00
Bowl, mixing; RFD only, 6", from $20 to	25.00
Bowl, rim soup; 8", from $12 to	20.00
Coaster, RFD only, ridged, 3¾", from $18 to	22.00
Mug, RFD only, 9-oz, from $20 to	25.00
Olive dish, oval, 10", from $20 to	35.00
Platter, 14", from $35 to	50.00
Spoon holder, RFD only, from $35 to	45.00
Sugar bowl, w/lid, from $15 to	20.00
Tumbler, RFD only, style #5, 14-oz, from $20 to	25.00

San Marino Shape

Known patterns for this shape are Barkwood, Bel Air, California Originals, Casual California, Gayety, Hawaiian Coral, Heyday, Lei Lani (two and a half times base values), Mexicana, Pan American Lei (two and a half times base values), Raffia, Shadow Leaf, Shantung, Sun Garden, and Trade Winds.

Bowl, chowder; 6", from $10 to	15.00
Bowl, mixing; 5", from $15 to	18.00
Bowl, serving; 9" dia, from $15 to	20.00
Casserole, w/lid, 8" dia, from $35 to	65.00
Coaster, ridged, 3¾", from $10 to	15.00
Creamer, regular, from $10 to	12.00
Custard, 3", from $18 to	22.00
Flowerpot, 3", from $20 to	25.00
Mug, 9-oz, from $15 to	25.00
Plate, salad; 7½", from $8 to	12.00
Spoon holder, from $35 to	50.00

Ultra Shape

More than fifty patterns were issued on this shape. Nearly all the artist-designed lines (Rockwell, Kent, Don Blanding, and Disney) utilized Ultra. The shape was developed by Gale Turnbull, and many of the elaborate flower and fruit patterns can be credited to him as well; use the high end of our range as a minimum value for his work. For Frederick Lunning, use the mid range. For other artist patterns, use these formulae based on the high end: Blanding — 2X (Aquarium 3X); Disney, 7 – 8X; Kent — Moby Dick and Our America, 2½X, Salamina, 5 – 7X.

Bowl, chowder; 6", from $12 to	15.00
Bowl, mixing; 6", from $25 to	30.00
Bowl, serving; 8" dia, from $18 to	25.00
Casserole, w/lid, 8" dia, from $75 to	95.00
Comport, ftd, from $50 to	75.00
Mug, 8-oz, 3½", from $22 to	35.00
Pitcher, open, 2-qt, from $45 to	75.00
Plate, chop; 14", from $50 to	80.00
Plate, salad; 7½", from $10 to	15.00
Tumbler, iced tea; style #4, 13-oz, 5", from $25 to	40.00

Year 'Round Shape

Patterns on this shape include Country Cousin, Lollipop Tree, and Blueberry Hill.

Bowl, fruit; 5½", from $5 to	7.00

Butter tray, w/lid, from $30 to	40.00
Casserole, w/lid, 8" dia, from $30 to	45.00
Creamer, from $8 to	12.00
Gravy boat, stick hdl, from $18 to	25.00
Mug, 12-oz, from $12 to	20.00
Sugar bowl, w/lid, from $10 to	15.00

Villeroy and Boch

The firm of Villeroy and Boch, located in Mettlach, Germany, was brought into being by the 1841 merger of three German factories — the Wallerfangen factory, founded by Nicholas Villeroy in 1787; and Boch's father's factory in Septfontaines, established in 1767. Villeroy and Boch produced many varieties of wares, including earthenware with printed under-glaze designs which carried the well-known castle mark with the name 'Mettlach.'

See also Mettlach.

Bread box, earthenware Dutch scenic tile within wooden frame, early twentieth century, 8x18x10½", EX, $2,415.00. (Photo courtesy Skinner, Inc.)

Beaker, jockey on horsebk, .25L	300.00
Beaker, Munich child, pnt under glaze, #6291, .25L	160.00
Cake plate, Amapola, 8"	225.00
Cake stand, Wallerfangen, late 1800s, 14¾"	300.00
Pitcher, elves scene, #2332/#1031, 9½", +4 #2368 tumblers	265.00
Plaque, cottage scene under glaze, #1105, 17½"	315.00
Plate, amber-yel water lilies w/gr stems & leaves, #1515, 7"	65.00
Plate, bl arum lilies w/arrow-like leaves, #829, 7"	110.00
Plate, morning glories on basketweave, #212, 7¾"	55.00
Soup tureen, Alt Amsterdam, 8-cup, 8½x8½"	200.00
Stein, keeper of wine cellar, Warth, #1941, 13¾"	950.00
Tray, Art Deco floral on gr gloss, SP sides, 12⅜" L	250.00
Tray, woman & youthful man under glaze, wood fr, 20x12"	365.00
Vase, floral panels, 4 loop hdls at shoulder, drilled, 1874-1909, 18"	1,250.00

Vistosa

Vistosa was produced from about 1938 through the early 1940s. It was Taylor, Smith, and Taylor's answer to the very successful Fiesta line of their nearby competitor, Homer Laughlin. Vistosa was made in four solid colors: mango red, cobalt blue, light green, and deep yellow. 'Pie crust' edges and a dainty five-petal flower molded into handles and lid finials made for a very attractive yet nevertheless commercially unsuccessful product. For further information, we recommend *Collector's Guide to LuRay Pastels* by Kathy and Bill Meehan (Collector Books). Our advisor for this category is Ted Haun; he is listed in the Directory under Indiana.

Bowl, cream soup	20.00
Bowl, fruit	10.00
Bowl, nappy; from $40 to	50.00
Bowl, salad; ftd, 12", from $200 to	225.00
Bowl, soup; lug hdl, from $25 to	30.00
Chop plate, 12"	40.00
Chop plate, 15", from $40 to	50.00

Coffee cup, AD; from $40 to...**50.00**
Coffee saucer, AD; from $20 to...**25.00**
Creamer..**20.00**
Egg cup, ftd, from $50 to...**60.00**
Jug, water; 2-qt, from $110 to...**140.00**
Plate, 6", from $10 to...**15.00**
Plate, 7", from $12 to...**18.00**
Plate, 9", from $15 to...**20.00**
Plate, 10", from $50 to...**60.00**
Platter, 13", from $40 to...**50.00**
Sauce boat, from $175 to..**200.00**
Shakers, pr **32.00**
Sugar bowl, w/lid **25.00**
Teacup, from $10 to..**15.00**
Teapot, 6-cup, from $190 to...**225.00**

Volkmar

Charles Volkmar established a workshop in Tremont, New York, in 1882. He produced artware decorated under the glaze in the manner of the early barbotine work done at the Haviland factory in Limoges, France. He relocated in 1888 in Menlo Park, New Jersey, and together with J.T. Smith established the Menlo Park Ceramic Company for the production of art tile. The partnership was dissolved in 1893. From 1895 until 1902, Volkmar located in Corona, New York, first under the name Volkmar Ceramic Company, later as Volkmar and Cory, and for the final six years as Crown Point. During the latter period he made art tile, blue under-glaze Delft-type wares, colorful polychrome vases, etc. The Volkmar Kilns were established in 1903 in Metuchen, New Jersey, by Volkmar and his son. Wares were marked with various devices consisting of the Volkmar name, initials, or 'Crown Point Ware.' Our advisors for this category are Suzanne Perrault and Dave Rago; they are listed in the Directory under New Jersey.

Bowl, floral, yel on brn mottle, Crown Point Ware, 7x10", NM.**135.00**
Pitcher, cucumber gr matt, collared neck, mk V/inscribed (?), 4½x4"...**250.00**
Vase, cvd stylized leaves/buds, mingled bl/gr/gray, 8x10" **900.00**
Vase, frothy sky bl, spherical, mk/dtd, 5½x5¼", NM **315.00**
Vase, olive mottle, ftd gourd shape, mk, 5", VG **230.00**

Vontury

Located in New Jersey, F.J. Von Tury is primarily a designer of architectural artware, tile, and murals in particular, but he also produces a line of vases, bowls, and other decorative items. These are signed 'Vontury' in script. Impressionistic florals are favored.

Bowl, chocolate matt w/frothy speckled int, 2¾x7½" **95.00**
Platter, fish form, gr gloss w/bl spots, 1940s, 15" **85.00**
Platter, leaves, bl/brn on lt gr, scalloped edge, 12¾x9½".............**55.00**
Tray, cloverleaf shape, misty bl w/HP decor, 7" **50.00**
Vase, flower sprig, 4¾x5¼" sq...**45.00**
Vase, leaves, brn/gr/bl on turq, spherical, 7x7", from $100 to **200.00**
Vase, leaves & vines, brn & yel on soft bl-gray, mk, 14⅜" **200.00**

Wade

The Wade Potteries was established in 1867 by George Wade and his partner, a man by the name of Myatt. It was located in Burslem, England, the center of that country's pottery industry. In 1882 George Wade bought out his partner, and the name of the pottery was changed to Wade and Sons. In 1919 the pottery underwent yet another name

change and became known as George Wade & Son Ltd. The year 1891 saw the establishment of another Wade Pottery — J & W Wade & Co., which in turn changed its name to A.J. Wade & Co. in 1927. At this time (1927) Wade Heath & Co. Ltd. was also formed.

The three potteries plus a new Irish pottery named Wade (Ireland) Ltd. were incorporated into one company in 1958 and given the name The Wade Group of Potteries. In 1990 the group was taken over by Beauford PLC and became Wade Ceramics Ltd. It sold again in early 1999 to Wade Management and is now a private company.

For those interested in learning more about Wade pottery, we recommend *The World of Wade, The World of Wade Book 2,* and *The World of Wade — Figurines and Miniatures,* all by Ian Warner and Mike Posgay; Mr. Warner is listed in the Directory under Canada.

Animal Figurine, Cheeky Duckling, ca 1930, 7" **350.00**
Animal Figurine, Panther, early to late 1930s, 8½" **1,050.00**
Animal Figurine, Playful Lamb, 1947-53 ....**155.00**
Animal Figurine, Pluto's Pup No 1, ca 1937-38, 2½" **440.00**
Flower, Basket Arrangement, 1930-39, 4½" L **100.00**
Flower, Pansy, 1930-39, 3¾" **40.00**
Flower, Posy Basket, 1930-39, 3½" **35.00**
Flower Jugs & Vases, Flower Jug, 1936, 9" **80.00**
Flower Jugs & Vases, Orcadia Vase, 1928-34, 6¼" **50.00**
Hanna-Barbera Character, Huckleberry Hound, 1959-60, 2⅜" ..**145.00**
Hanna-Barbera Character, Yogi Bear, 1959-60, 2½" **150.00**
Happy Families Series, Owl Parent, 1978-86, 1¾".......................**25.00**
Happy Families Series, Pig Parent, 1978-86, 1⅛" **25.00**
Happy Families Series, Rabbit Baby, 1978-86, 1⅛" **18.00**
Mabel Lucie Attwell Character, Sarah, 1959, 3x4" **270.00**
Nursery Favourite, Willie Winkie, 1972-81, 1¾"..........................**26.00**
Nursery Rhyme Character, Butcher, 1948-58, 3¼"......................**360.00**
Nursery Rhyme Character, Goldilocks, 1949-58, 4" **375.00**
Nursery Rhyme Character, Nod, 1948-58, 2½" **210.00**
Nursery Rhyme Character, Poppa Bear, 1948-58, 3½" **375.00**
Red Rose Tea (Canada), Blue Bird, 1967-73................................**10.00**
Red Rose Tea (Canada), Poodle, 1967-73, 1⅝" **10.00**
Robertson's Gollies, Double Base Player, early to mid-1960s, 2⅝"..**225.00**
Robertson's Gollies, Saxophone Player, early to mid-1960s, 2⅝".**225.00**
Van Hallen, Christina, cellulose-type finish, 11" **450.00**
Van Hallen, Joyce, cellulose-type finish, 7¼" **350.00**
Van Hallen, Juliette, underglaze finish, 9½" **725.00**
Van Hallen, Snow White, 6⅜"..**450.00**
Van Hallen, Springtime, cellulose-type finish, 9¼" **535.00**
Walt Disney, Mickey Mouse Plate, 1934-late 1950s, 5¾" **120.00**
Walt Disney, Ring O' Roses Saucer, 1934-late 1950s, 4" **25.00**
Walt Disney, Scamp Blow Up, 1961-65, 4⅛" **235.00**
Walt Disney, Sleepy Cup, 1934-late 1950s, 3¾" **25.00**
Walt Disney, What Are Little Girls Made of Teapot, 1934-late 1950s..**105.00**
Whimsie, Crockodile, 1953-59, ¾x1⅝".......................................**78.00**
Whimsie, Kitten, unmk, 1953-59, 1⅜" **55.00**
Whimsie, Leaping Fawn, 1953-59, 1⅞" **48.00**
Whimsie, Polar Bear, 1953-59, 1¾"..**37.00**
Whimsie, Swan, unmk, 1953-59, ⅞x1½" **190.00**
Whimsie - Land Series, Field Mouse, 1984-88, 1¼x1½".............**37.00**
Whimsie - Land Series, Otter, 1984-88, 1½x1⅝" **23.00**
World of Survival, African Elephant, 1978-82, 6x10"................**500.00**
World of Survival, American Brown Bear, 1978082, 4x5½".......**500.00**
World of Survival, Harp Seal & Pup, 1978-82, 3¾x9"................**600.00**

Wallace China

Dinnerware with a Western theme was produced by the Wallace China Company, who operated in California from 1931 until 1964.

Artist Till Goodan designed three lines, Rodeo, Pioneer Trails, and Boots and Saddle, which they marketed under the package name Westward Ho. When dinnerware with a western theme became so popular just a few years ago, Rodeo was reproduced, but the new trademark includes neither 'California' or 'Wallace China.'

This ware is very heavy and not prone to chips, but be sure to examine it under a strong light to look for knife scratches, which will lessen its value to a considerable extent when excessive. Our advisor for this category is Marv Fogleman; he is listed in the Directory under California. If you'd like to learn more about this company, we recommend *The Collector's Encyclopedia of California Pottery* by Jack Chipman.

Apache Land Village, dish, sauce; 4¼" 50.00
Barnard's Steak House, plate, bull in center w/brands border, 10½"..105.00
Bird of Paradise, bowl, 3x9" 85.00
Boots & Saddle, bowl, 6x12" 175.00
Boots & Saddle, creamer, 3½" 155.00
Boots & Saddle, pitcher, 7½" 330.00
Boots & Saddle, shakers, 5", pr..40.00
Chuck Wagon, ashtray, 4 rests 50.00
Chuck Wagon, bowl, 2½x5½" 65.00
Chuck Wagon, cup & saucer, Dunn's Coffee Shop above scene ...40.00
Chuck Wagon, mug..50.00
Chuck Wagon, plate, grill; 3-section, 9"................................95.00
Chuck Wagon, plate, 7¼", from $25 to................................30.00
Chuck Wagon, platter, 5½x8½", from $45 to..........................75.00
Chuck Wagon, saucer, T-N above scene, 5¼"..........................18.00
Desert Ware, bowl, cereal; Poppy, 7" 25.00
Desert Ware, chef head in hat, w/Barbeque Hot Plate, 10" 45.00
Desert Ware, gravy boat, 10-Y line, 7½" 25.00
El Rancho, bowl, 1¼x7½", from $55 to..................................65.00
El Rancho, creamer 100.00
El Rancho, cup, bouillon; 4" dia 27.50
El Rancho, cup & saucer..65.00
El Rancho, mug, 3"...35.00
El Rancho, plate, luncheon; 7" 25.00
El Rancho, plate, 5½" 35.00
El Rancho, plate, 9¾" 70.00
Friar John Restaurant, pitcher, water; brn on wht 230.00
Hibiscus, creamer, 4½" 25.00
Hibiscus, platter, 8¾x12½" 35.00
Pioneer Trails, bowl, Pony Express, oval, 9¼x12"....................225.00
Pioneer Trails, creamer & sugar bowl 295.00
Pioneer Trails, plate, dinner; 10½" 165.00
Pioneer Trails, shakers, 5", pr..160.00
Pitcher, water; maroon w/flat wht sides, 7¼" 45.00
Pitcher, water; pk, 7½" 55.00
Rod's Steak House, shakers, Hereford cow & fence, 3¾", pr.........60.00
Rodeo, bowl, fruit; 2¼x5" 60.00
Rodeo, bowl, 5½x13"...700.00
Rodeo, pitcher, 12"...280.00
Rodeo, plate, chop; 13"..225.00
Rodeo, plate, dinner; 10½"..95.00
Rodeo, plate, salad; 9" 65.00
Shadowleaf, platter, 12¾", from $35 to..................................45.00
Utopia Drive-In, cup & saucer, wht w/brn border, tan logo 40.00
49ers, bowl, fruit; 6½" 30.00
49ers, creamer, 4"..35.00

Walley

The Walley Pottery operated in West Sterling, Massachusetts, from 1898 to 1919. Never more than a one-man operation, Walley himself handcrafted all his wares from local clay. The majority of his pottery was simple and unadorned and usually glazed in matt green. On occasion, however, you may find high- and semi-gloss green, as well as matt glazes in blue, cream, brown, and red. The rarest and most desirable examples of his work are those with applied or relief-carved decorations. Some pieces are marked 'WJW.' Our advisors for this category are Suzanne Perrault and Dave Rago; they are listed in the Directory under New Jersey.

Bottle, appl gr gloss, WJW, ovoid, 7¼x5½"..............................2,530.00
Bowl, brn matt w/gr pooled at rim, WJW, 4½x6½" 1,035.00
Bowl vase, gr mottle, appl leaves, thumb rests to hdls, WJW, 7x7", EX..1,500.00
Tyge, brn/gr semimatt w/speckled bl int, 5¾x6", from $500 to...750.00

Vase, tooled and applied leaves, feathered turquoise semimatt with exposed red clay, WJW, restoration, grinding chips, 5¾x6", $1,380.00. (Photo courtesy Dave Rago Auctions)

Vase, sheer lt gr/gunmetal, bottle shape, WJW, 6½" 550.00
Vase, speckled multi-tone brn, WJW, 3x4½"............................250.00
Vase, yel-gr matt w/3 dk gr strapwork hdls, wide mouth, 11"...6,465.00

Walrath

Frederick E. Walrath learned his craft as a student of Charles Fergus Binns at Alfred University (1900 – 1904). Walrath worked first and briefley at Grueby Faience Company in Boston and then from 1908 to 1918 as an instructor at the Mechanics Institute in Rochester, New York. He was chief ceramist in Newcomb Pottery (New Orleans) until his death in 1921. A studio potter, Walrath's work bears stylistic similarity to that of Marblehead Pottery, whose founder, Arthur Baggs, was also a student of Binns's. Vases featuring matt glazes of stylized natural motifs (especially florals) are most sought after; sculptural and figural forms (center bowls, flower frogs, various animals) are less desirable. Typically his work is signed with an incised circular signature: Walrath Pottery with conjoined M and I at the center. Our advisor for this and related Arts & Crafts objects is Bruce A. Austin; he is listed in the Directory under New York.

Bowl, bl mottle, mk, 3x9" 200.00
Bowl, dk leathery gr w/sheer mottle int, w/3-D kneeling nude, 6x7", NM..950.00
Bowl, mottle gr matt & terra cotta, w/3-D seated nude, 8½x6½"..1,150.00
Lemonade pitcher, lemons, yel/gr/brn matt, +6 (VG/EX) goblets, $2,000 ..3,000.00
Vase, orange blossoms on brn/lt gr stems on speckled gr matt, 6x3¾" .4,310.00

Walter, A.

Almaric Walter was employed from 1904 through 1914 at Verreries Artistiques des Freres Daum in Nancy, France. After 1919 he opened his own business where he continued to make the same type of quality objets d'art in pate-de-verre glass as he had earlier. His pieces are signed A. Walter, Nancy H. Berge Sc.

Dish, snail/berries on rim, 4½"...3,800.00

Figure, Tanagra, 8" **4,700.00**
Inkwell, honey bee finial, 6¼" L **7,050.00**
Vase, stylized floral, mc on yel, ovoid, Corette, 3" **1,380.00**

Wannopee

The Wannopee Pottery, established in 1892, developed from the reorganization of the financially insecure New Milford Pottery Company of New Milford, Connecticut. They produced a line of mottled-glazed pottery called 'Duchess' and a similar line in porcelain. Both were marked with the impressed sunburst 'W' with 'porcelain' added to indicate that particular body type.

In 1895 semiporcelain pitchers in three sizes were decorated with relief medallion cameos of Beethoven, Mozart, and Napoleon. Lettuce-leaf ware was first produced in 1901 and used actual leaves in the modeling. Scarabronze, made in 1895, was their finest artware. It featured simple Egyptian shapes with a coppery glaze. It was marked with a scarab, either impressed or applied. Production ceased in 1903.

Chamberstick, blk/umber mottle, separation to hdl, mk, 7", from $50 to...**75.00**
Pitcher, gr/tan mottled, squat, 4½" **200.00**
Umbrella stand, Duchess, mc mottle, 24" **525.00**

Warwick

The Warwick China Company operated in Wheeling, West Virginia, from 1887 until 1951. They produced both hand-painted and decaled plates, vases, teapots, coffeepots, pitchers, bowls, and jardinieres featuring lovely florals or portraits of beautiful ladies done in luscious colors. Backgrounds were usually blendings of brown and beige, but ivory was also used as well as greens and pinks. Various marks were employed, all of which incorporate the Warwick name. For a more thorough study of the subject, we recommend *Warwick, A to W*, a supplement to *Why Not Warwick* by our advisor, Donald C. Hoffmann, Sr.; his address can be found in the Directory under Illinois. In an effort to inform the collector/dealer, Mr. Hoffmann now has a video available that identifies the company's decals and their variations by number.

Bouquet #1, vase, brn w/floral decor, A-24, 11¾" **295.00**
Bouquet #1, vase, brn w/portrait, Anna Potocka, A-17, 10½" **390.00**
Bouquet #2, vase, brn w/portrait, gypsy w/bow in hair, A-17, 10½" **295.00**
Bouquet #2, vase, brn w/portrait, lady w/violets, A-17, 10½" **395.00**
Bouquet #2, vase, brn w/portrait, young blonde, A-17, 10½" **320.00**
Carnation, vase, brn w/floral decor (roses), A-23, 10½" **170.00**
Chicago, vase, brn w/floral decor (hibiscus), A-27, 8" **225.00**
Clematis, vase, brn w/portrait, A-27, 10½"...............................**350.00**
Dainty, vase, brn w/floral decor (poppy), A-6, 4½" **275.00**
Duchess, vase, wht w/bird decor (herons), D-1, 7½" **290.00**
Flower, vase, brn w/portrait, A-17, 12".....................................**235.00**
Gem, vase, charcoal w/portrait, C-1, 12" **300.00**
Helene, vase, brn w/floral decor, A-27, 12"...............................**290.00**
Magnolia, vase, wht w/bird decor (herons), D-1, 10½" **325.00**
Monroe, vase, brn w/floral decor, A-26, 10¼" **300.00**
Monroe, vase, matt, tan to tan w/nut decor, M-2, 10¼" **380.00**
Narcis #1, vase, brn w/portrait, Madame Recamièr, A-17, 8¼" ..**380.00**
Narcis #2, vase, brn w/floral decor, A-27, 6¾" **285.00**
Oriental, vase, brn w/floral decor (peonies), A-21, 11" **430.00**
Pansy, vase, brn w/floral decor (poppies), A-6, 4" **150.00**
Pansy, vase, charcoal w/floral decor, C-5, 4" **120.00**
Penn, vase, pk w/portrait, H-1, 9½" **600.00**
Poppy, vase, charcoal w/floral decor, C-4, 10¼" **350.00**
Regency, vase, brn w/floral decor, A-21, 11½" **490.00**

Roberta, vase, red overglaze w/portrait (fisherman), E-3, 10"......**450.00**
Rose, vase, red overglaze w/floral decor, E-2, 8" **300.00**
Royal #1, vase, brn w/portrait, A-17, 9"....................................**325.00**
Senator #2, vase, brn w/floral decor, A-26, 11½" **200.00**
Senator #2, vase, brn w/floral decor (hibiscus), A-27, 13" **225.00**
Unnamed, ewer, charcoal w/floral decor, C-6, 9¼" **360.00**
Unnamed, vase, funnel type, yel to gr, portrait, K-1, 11½" **650.00**
Verbenia #1, vase, brn w/portrait, A-17, 9½" **290.00**
Verona, vase, brn w/floral decor, A-27, 11¾" **285.00**
Verona, vase, gr w/floral decor, F-2, 11¾" **400.00**
Victoria, vase, brn w/floral decor, A-21, 8¼" **315.00**
Violet, vase, brn w/floral decor, A-22, 4" **130.00**
Violet, vase, red overglaze w/floral decor, E-2, 4" **135.00**
Virginia, base, brn w/portrait, Madame LeBrun, A-17, 10".........**275.00**
Virginia, vase, pk w/portrait, Christy Girl, H-1, 10" **650.00**
Windsor, vase, brn w/floral decor, A-40, 9¼" **400.00**

Wash Sets

Before the days of running water, bedrooms were standardly equipped with a wash bowl and pitcher as a matter of necessity. A 'toilet set' was comprised of the pitcher and bowl, toothbrush holder, covered commode, soap dish, shaving dish, and mug. Some sets were even more elaborate. Through everyday usage, the smaller items were often broken, and today it is unusual to find a complete set.

Porcelain sets decorated with florals, fruits, or scenics were produced abroad by Limoges in France; some were imported from Germany and England. During the last quarter of the 1800s and until after the turn of the century, American-made toilet sets were manufactured in abundance. Tin and graniteware sets were also made.

Haviland, mc florals, pitcher+pot+mug+jug+2 boxes+13" basin...**595.00**
Knowles & Taylor, gr roses w/gold, late 1800s, 10-pc **285.00**
Le Franciase, fleur-de-lis emb on wht swirls w/gr & gold, 1800s, 6-pc..**325.00**
Royal Doulton, Matsumi, cobalt & gold, ca 1889-1901, 10-pc ...**550.00**
Staffordshire/Dillon, Loretto, geometrics/floral band, 9" pitcher+bowl...**375.00**
Turnstall, birds & flowers w/cobalt band, 1890s, 13" pitcher+bowl .**265.00**

Watch Fobs

Watch fobs have been popular since the last quarter of the nineteenth century. They were often made by retail companies to feature their products. Souvenir, commemorative, and political fobs were also produced. Of special interest today are those with advertising, heavy equipment in particular. Some of the more pricey fobs are listed here, but most of those currently available were produced in such quantities that they are relatively common and should fall within a price range of $3.00 to $10.00. Our advisor for this category is Tony George; he is listed in the Directory under California. When no material is mentioned in the description, assume the fob is made of metal.

All Roads Lead to Fort Worth, Panther City 1912, patriotic theme...**180.00**
Avery Tractor Co, Tractors w/Draft-Horse motor..., tractor shape, 1x2" ...**120.00**
Avery Tractors, Bull Dog Line, bulldog shape, 1½" **70.00**
Ben Franklin bust, key/lightning on red, 1912 Boston Electric Show .**80.00**
Bloodstone in scrollwork gold fr, 14k, ⅞x1½" **160.00**
Brotherhood of Locomotive Engineers, MOP w/bl enamel & gold, EX ...**135.00**
Brotherhood of Trainmen, enameled locomotive front, w/gold, EX..**90.00**
Bucyrus Company 21st Annual Picnic, 1925, NP brass, Schwaab..**140.00**
Case Tractors, tractor on oval, advertising on bk, 1930s, EX **60.00**
Caterpillar, 5-ton tractor, advertising & maker's name on bk **160.00**
Coca-Cola, The Prize Winners, 2 emb bulldogs, sterling, 1⅝x1⅜" .**70.00**

Dempster Mills Mfg Co & info on bk w/logo on front, EX **140.00**
Doud Livestock Yard, Chicago, boy & girl in relief, EX **70.00**
Firestone Tires, Redside Wall, Black Tread, Whitehead & Hoag.**220.00**
Harley-Davidson Is Unexcelled for Rural Delivery, Schwabs & Sons ..**210.00**
Harley-Davidson Motorcycles, logo, sterling, EX **65.00**
Horseshoe w/bridle bit, NP brass w/hoof made of bone & 13" chain..**160.00**
Hudson Tire Co, Newark, Cut Your Tire Bills in Half, sword in tire, EX ..**85.00**
Indian Motorcycles, Indian Chief w/emb headband, sterling, 2½".**135.00**
John Deere, fob on shield, porc, 1966 WF Collectors Meeting, 1966, EX..**65.00**
Luzianna Coffee, lady holding can in relief, Whitehead & Hoag, EX..**135.00**
Marion Steam Shovel Co, Everywhere Reliable, Est 1884, EX ...**120.00**
Monarch Tractors, Allis Chalmers Product, RR Johnstone MI on bk..**70.00**
Ohio FMA (Federation of Motorcycles), info on bk, brass, 1914.**310.00**
Ozarka Co, ...Eureka Springs..., girl drinking on bk, celluloid.....**150.00**
Portland Union Stock Yards Co, enameled logo in center, name on bk, EX ...**130.00**
Savage Arms Co, Indian head w/rifle, Panama Exposition 1915, EX .**155.00**
Silver Anniversary Sante Fe Route, Topeka KA...1897, celluloid .**175.00**
Sinclair Oil, brass w/name & address on bk, 1½" w/5¼" strap ...**360.00**
Stanley Motor Carriage Co, Newton MA w/emb car, EX **80.00**
United Electric Light & Power Co, mounted generator shape, 1908, EX ..**65.00**
101 Ranch, New York Locoation, 3-D buffalo on front, sterling, EX ..**85.00**
1826 Half-Dollar, w/13¼" 14k chain, T-bar & swivel hook **220.00**
369th Infantry, Harlem Hell Fighters, bronze, WWI era, 1½x1⅛" ..**165.00**

Watch Stands

Watch stands were decorative articles designed with a hook from which to hang a watch. Some displayed the watch as the face of a grandfather clock or as part of an interior scene with figures in period costumes and contemporary furnishings. They were popular products of Staffordshire potters and silver companies as well.

Burlwood, England, Victorian era, 4½" stem, 3" dia top **200.00**
Burlwood w/brass fittings, hanger in center of arch, Victorian, 5½"..**200.00**
Cherry w/poplar bk, hutch w/sliding front/rnd glass, dvtl, 6½x5x3"..**750.00**
CI, cupid beside easel, gilded, 6¼" **135.00**
Cvd wood w/scrimshaw inlay, compass rose on top, 8½x6x1½".**1,000.00**
Gilt bronze, cathedral form w/heroic eagle, wht marble base, 9"..**920.00**
Silver, ornate openwork fr, D&F hallmks, ca 1893, 4" **330.00**

Watches

First made in the 1500s in Germany, early watches were actually small clocks, suspended from the neck or belt. By 1700 they had become the approximate shape and size we know today. The first watches produced in America were made in 1810. The well-known Waltham Watch Company was established in 1850. Later, Waterbury produced inexpensive watches which they sold by the thousands.

Open-face and hunting-case watches of the 1890s were often solid gold or gold-filled and were often elaborately decorated in several colors of gold. Gold watches became a status symbol in this decade and were worn by both men and women on chains with fobs or jeweled slides. Ladies sometimes fastened them to their clothing with pins often set with jewels. The chatelaine watch was worn at the waist, only one of several items such as scissors, coin purses, or needle cases, each attached by small chains.

Most turn-of-the-century watch cases were gold-filled; these are plentiful today. Sterling cases, though interest in them is on the increase, are not in great demand. For more information we recommend *Complete Price Guide to Watches, No. 20,* by Cooksey Shugart, Tom Engle, and Richard E. Gilbert (Collector Books).

Our advise for this category comes from Maundy International Watches, Antiquarian Horologists, price consultants, and researchers for many watch reference guides and books on horology. Their firm is a leading purveyor of antique watches of all kinds. They are listed in the Directory under Kansas. For character-related watches, see Personalities.

Key:
adj — adjusted	k/s — key set
brg — bridge plate design	k/w — key wind
d/s — double sunk dial	l/s — lever set
fbd — finger bridge design	mvt — movement
g/f — gold-filled	o/f — open face
g/j/s — gold jewel setting	p/s — pendant set
h/c — hunter case	r/g/p — rolled gold plate
HCI#P — heat, cold,	s — size
isochronism & position	s/s — single sunk dial
adjusted	s/w — stem wind
j — jewel	w/g/f — white gold-filled
k — karat	y/g/f — yellow gold-filled

Am Watch Co, 0s, 7j, #1891, 14k, h/c, Am Watch Co, M.........**500.00**
Am Watch Co, 6s, 7j, #1873, y/g/f, h/c, Am Watch Co, M........**185.00**
Am Watch Co, 12s, 17j, #1894, 14k, o/f, Royal, M....................**425.00**
Am Watch Co, 12s, 21j, #1894, 14k, h/c, M **900.00**
Am Watch Co, 16s, 11j, #1872, p/s, silver h/c, Park Road, M **400.00**
Am Watch Co, 16s, 15j, #1899, y/g/f, h/c, M **450.00**
Am Watch Co, 16s, 16j, #1884, 5-min, 14k, Repeater, M........**6,750.00**
Am Watch Co, 16s, 17j, #1888, Railroader, M **1,725.00**
Am Watch Co, 16s, 19j, #1872, 14k, h/c, Am Watch Woerd's Pat, M.**9,300.00**
Am Watch Co, 16s, 21j, #1888, h/c, 14k, Riverside Maximus, M...**2,250.00**
Am Watch Co, 16s, 21j, #1899, y/g/f, l/s, o/f, Crescent St, M **300.00**
Am Watch Co, 16s, 21j, #1908, y/g/f, o/f, Grade #645, M..........**385.00**
Am Watch Co, 16s, 23j, #1908, o/f, 18k, Premier Maximus, MIB.**15,000.00**
Am Watch Co, 16s, 23j, #1908, y/g/f, o/f, adj, RR, Vanguard, M.**550.00**
Am Watch Co, 16s, 23j, #1908, y/g/f, o/f, Vanguard Up/Down, EX..**880.00**
Am Watch Co, 18s, #1857, silver h/c, Samuel Curtiss k/w, M..**4,000.00**
Am Watch Co, 18s, 11j, #1857, k/w, 1st run, PS Barlett, M ...**7,000.00**
Am Watch Co, 18s, 11j, #1857, silver h/c, k/w, DH&D, EX ..**2,195.00**
Am Watch Co, 18s, 11j, #1857, silver h/c, k/w, s/s, Wm Ellery, EX ..**125.00**
Am Watch Co, 18s, 15j, #1877, k/w, RE Robbins, M...............**575.00**
Am Watch Co, 18s, 15j, #1883, y/g/f, 2-tone, Railroad King, EX ..**585.00**
Am Watch Co, 18s, 17j, #1883, y/g/f, o/f, Crescent Street, M....**275.00**
Am Watch Co, 18s, 17j, #1892, HC, Canadian Pacific Railway, M.**1,975.00**
Am Watch Co, 18s, 17j, #1892, y/g/f, o/f, Sidereal, rare, M **3,850.00**
Am Watch Co, 18s, 17j, 25-yr, y/g/f, o/f, s/s, PS Bartlett, M **295.00**
Am Watch Co, 18s, 21j, #1892, y/g/f, o/f, d/s, Crescent St, M ...**495.00**
Am Watch Co, 18s, 21j, #1892, y/g/f, o/f, Grade #845, EX.........**265.00**
Am Watch Co, 18s, 21j, #1892, y/g/f, o/f, Pennsylvania Special, M ..**5,750.00**
Am Watch Co, 18s, 7j, #1857, silver case, k/w, CT Parker, M .**4,000.00**
Auburndale Watch Co, 18s, 7j, k/w, l/s, Lincoln, M **2,950.00**
Aurora Watch Co, 18s, 11j, k/w, silver h/c, M...........................**475.00**
Aurora Watch Co, 18s, 15 ruby j, y/g/f, s/w, 5th pinion, M **1,495.00**
Ball (Elgin), 18s, 17j, o/f, silver, Official RR Standard, M **595.00**
Ball (Hamilton), 16s, 21j, #999, g/f, o/f, l/s, M **845.00**
Ball (Hamilton), 16s, 23j, #998, y/g/f, o/f, Elinvar, M **3,250.00**
Ball (Hamilton), 18s, 17j, #999, g/f, o/f, l/s, EX **450.00**
Ball (Hampden), 18s, 17j, o/f, adj, RR, Superior Grade, M **3,000.00**
Ball (Illinois), 12s, 19j, w/g/f, o/f, M...**345.00**
Ball (Waltham), 16s, 17j, y/g/f, o/f, RR, Commercial Std, M......**650.00**
Ball (Waltham), 16s, 21j, o/f, Official RR Standard, M **875.00**
Columbus, 6s, 11j, y/g/f, h/c, M...**200.00**
Columbus, 18s, 11-15j, k/w, k/s, M...**625.00**
Columbus, 18s, 15j, o/f, l/s, M **195.00**
Columbus, 18s, 15j, y/g/f, o/f, Jay Gould on dial, M.................**2,400.00**
Columbus, 18s, 21j, y/g/f, h/c, train on dial, Railway King, M.**1,195.00**
Columbus, 18s, 23j, y/g/f, h/c, Columbus King, M **2,450.00**

Cornell, 18s, 15j, s/w, JC Adams, EX 300.00
Cornell, 18s, 15j, silver h/c, k/w, John Evans, EX..............325.00
Dudley, 12s, #1, 14k, o/f, flip-bk case, Masonic, G.............2,675.00
Elgin, 6s, 11j, 14k, h/c, M 425.00
Elgin, 6s, 15j, 20-yr, y/g/f, h/c, s/s, EX............................80.00
Elgin, 10s, 18k, h/c, k/w, k/s, s/s, Gail Borden, M 700.00
Elgin, 12s, 15j, 14k, h/c, EX...325.00
Elgin, 12s, 17j, 14k, h/c, GM Wheeler, M 525.00
Elgin, 16s, 15j, doctor's, 4th model, 18k, 2nd sweep hand, h/c, M.2,200.00
Elgin, 16s, 15j, 14k, h/c, EX...550.00
Elgin, 16s, 21j, y/g/f, g/j/s, o/f, BW Raymond, EX..............265.00
Elgin, 16s, 21j, y/g/f, g/j/s, 3 fbd, h/c, M 925.00
Elgin, 16s, 21j, y/g/f, o/f, l/s, RR, Father Time, M 485.00
Elgin, 16s, 21j, 14k, 3 fbd, grade #91, scarce, M...............3,850.00
Elgin, 16s, 23j, up/down indicator, BW Raymond, EX...........1,395.00
Elgin, 17s, 7j, k/w, orig silver case, Leader, M 250.00
Elgin, 18s, 11j, silver, h/c, k/w, gilded, MG Odgen, M 295.00
Elgin, 18s, 15j, o/f, d/s, k/w, silver, RR, BW Raymond 1st run, M.1,795.00
Elgin, 18s, 15j, silver, k/w, k/s, h/c, HL Culver, M 400.00
Elgin, 18s, 15j, silver h/c, Penn RR dial, BW Raymond k/w mvt, M..6,150.00
Elgin, 18s, 17j, silveroid h/c, BW Raymond, M 395.00
Elgin, 18s, 21j, y/g/f, o/f, Father Time, G.........................210.00
Elgin, 18s, 23j, y/g/f, o/f, 5-position, RR, Veritas, M 795.00
Fredonia, 18s, 11j, y/g/f, h/c, k/w, M 475.00
Hamilton, #910, 12s, 17j, 20-yr, y/g/f, o/f, s/s, EX................75.00
Hamilton, #912, 12s, 17j, y/g/f, o/f, adj, EX 70.00
Hamilton, #920, 12s, 23j, 14k, o/f, M.............................675.00
Hamilton, #922MP, 12s, 18k case, Masterpiece (sgn), M.........1,475.00
Hamilton, #925, 18s, 17j, y/g/f, h/c, s/s, l/s, M 395.00
Hamilton, #928, 18s, 15j, y/g/f, o/f, s/s, EX 200.00
Hamilton, #933, 18s, 16j, h/c, NP, low serial #, M...............1,575.00
Hamilton, #938, 18s, 17j, y/g/f, adj, M............................1,095.00
Hamilton, #940, 18s, 21j, NP, coin silver, o/f, M 450.00
Hamilton, #946, 18s, 23j, y/g/f, o/f, g/j/s, M.....................1,275.00
Hamilton, #947 (mk), 18s, 23j, 14k, h/c, orig/sgn, EX...........5,450.00
Hamilton, #950, 18s, 23j, y/g/f, o/f, l/s, sgn d/s, M..............1,650.00
Hamilton, #965, 16s, 17j, 14k, p/s, h/c, brg, scarce, M..........1,495.00
Hamilton, #972, 16s, 17j, y/g/f, g/j/s, o/f, d/s, l/s, adj, EX.......165.00
Hamilton, #974, 16s, 17j, 20-yr, y/g/f, o/f, s/s, EX...............150.00
Hamilton, #992, 16s, 21j, y/g/f, o/f, adj, d/s, dbl roller, M.......425.00
Hamilton, #992B, 16s, 21j, y/g/f, o/f, l/s, Bar/Crown, M.........550.00
Hamilton, #4992B, 16s, 22j, o/f, steel case, G 185.00
Hampden, 12s, 17j, w/g/f, o/f, thin model, Aviator, M 265.00
Hampden, 16s, 7j, gilded, NP, o/f, ¾-mvt, EX 50.00
Hampden, 16s, 17j, o/f, adj, EX......................................70.00
Hampden, 16s, 17j, y/g/f, h/c, s/w, M..............................245.00
Hampden, 16s, 21j, g/j/s, y/g/f, NP, h/c, Dueber, ¾-mvt, M 325.00
Hampden, 16s, 23j, o/f, adj, dbl roller, Special Railway, M.......675.00
Hampden, 18s, 7-11j, k/w, gilded, Springfield Mass, EX..........150.00
Hampden, 18s, 15j, k/w, mk on mvt, Railway, M 1,550.00
Hampden, 18s, 15j, s/w, gilded, JC Perry, M 200.00
Hampden, 18s, 15j, silver, k/w, h/c, Hayward, M 345.00
Hampden, 18s, 15j, y/g/f, damascened, h/c, Dueber, M 195.00
Hampden, 18s, 21j, y/g/f, g/j/s, h/c, New Railway, M............495.00
Hampden, 18s, 21j, y/g/f, o/f, d/s, l/s, N Am Railway, M 525.00
Hampden, 18s, 23j, 14k, h/c, Special Railway, M 1,295.00
Hampden, 18s, 23j, y/g/f, o/f, d/s, adj, New Railway, M.........550.00
Howard, E; 6s, 15j, s/w, 18k h/c, Series VIII, G sz, M 1,675.00
Howard, E; 16s, 15j, s/w, 14k h/c, L sz, M 1,995.00
Howard, E; 18s, 15j, h/c, silver case, k/w, Series I, N sz, M.....4,950.00
Howard, E; 18s, 15j, 18k h/c, k/w, Series II, N sz, M............5,950.00
Howard, E; 18s, 17j, 25-yr, y/g/f, o/f, orig case, split plate, M..2,150.00
Howard (Keystone), 12s, 23j, 14k, h/c, brg, Series 8, M.........795.00
Howard (Keystone), 16s, 17j, y/g/f, o/f, Series 9, M.............345.00

Howard (Keystone), 16s, 21j, y/g/f, o/f, RR Chronometer II, M .775.00
Howard (Keystone), 16s, 23j, y/g/f, o/f, Series 0, jeweled bbl, M ..1,175.00
Illinois, 0s, 7j, 14k, l/s, h/c, EX 275.00
Illinois, 8s, 13j, ¾-mvt, Rose LeLand, scarce, M 495.00
Illinois, 12s, 17j, y/g/f, o/f, d/s dial, EX 65.00
Illinois, 16s, 17j, y/g/f, o/f, d/s, Bunn, EX.......................195.00
Illinois, 16s, 21j, g/j/s, h/c, Burlington, M 385.00
Illinois, 16s, 21j, o/f, d/s, Santa Fe Special, M 725.00
Illinois, 16s, 21j, y/g/f, o/f, d/s, Bunn Special, M 485.00
Illinois, 16s, 23j, y/g/f, o/f, d/s, 60-hr, Sangamo Special, mk, M...3,750.00
Illinois, 16s, 23j, y/g/f, stiff bow, o/f, Sangamo Special, EX 1,100.00
Illinois, 18s, 11j, #1, silver, k/w, Alleghany, EX 125.00
Illinois, 18s, 11j, #3, o/f, s/w, l/s, Comet, G 65.00
Illinois, 18s, 11j, Forest City, G....................................90.00
Illinois, 18s, 15j, #1, adj, y/g/f, k/w, h/c, gilt, Bunn, M 900.00
Illinois, 18s, 15j, #1, k/w, k/s, silver h/c, Stuart, M...............1,100.00
Illinois, 18s, 15j, k/w, k/s, gilt, Railway Regulator, M 900.00
Illinois, 18s, 15j, s/w, silveroid, G 55.00
Illinois, 18s, 17j, g/j/s, adj, B&O RR Special (Hunter), h/c, M..2,695.00
Illinois, 18s, 17j, h/c, s/w, NP, coin silver, Bunn, M..............495.00
Illinois, 18s, 17j, o/f, d/s, adj, silveroid case, Lakeshore, G 90.00
Illinois, 18s, 17j, o/f, s/w, 5th pinion, Miller, EX 165.00
Illinois, 18s, 21j, g/j/s, g/f, o/f, A Lincoln, M....................465.00
Illinois, 18s, 21j, g/j/s, o/f, adj, B&O RR Special, EX............1,775.00
Illinois, 18s, 21j, 14k, g/j/s, h/c, Bunn Special, M...............1,495.00
Illinois, 18s, 23j, g/j/s, Bunn Special, EX.........................725.00
Illinois, 18s, 24j, g/j/s, adj, o/f, Chesapeake & Ohio, M.........5,500.00
Illinois, 18s, 24j, g/j/s, o/f, Bunn Special, EX....................995.00
Illinois, 18s, 26j, g/j/s, o/f, Ben Franklin USA, G...............4,750.00
Illinois, 18s, 26j, 14k, Penn Special, M 9,950.00
Illinois, 18s, 7j, #3, o/f, Interior, G...............................65.00
Illinois, 18s, 7j, #3, silveroid, America, G 85.00
Illinois, 18s, 9-11j, o/f, k/w, s/s, silveroid case, Hoyt, M 195.00
Ingersoll, 16s, 7j, wht base metal, Reliance, G 35.00
Lancaster, 18s, 7j, o/f, k/w, k/s, eng silver case, EX 150.00
Marion US, 18s, h/c, k/w, k/s, ¾-plate, Asa Fuller, M 500.00
Marion US, 18s, 15j, NP, h/c, s/w, Henry Randel, M 475.00
Melrose Watch Co, 18s, 7j, k/w, k/s, G 260.00
New York Watch Co, 18s, 7j, silver, h/c, k/w, Geo Sam Rice, EX ..195.00
New York Watch Co, 19j, low sz #, wolf's teeth wind, M 1,675.00
Patek Philippe, 12s, 18j, 18k, o/f, EX.............................2,500.00
Patek Philippe, 16s, 20j, 18k, h/c, M.............................3,500.00
Rockford, 16s, 17j, y/g/f, h/c, brg, dbl roller, EX.................90.00
Rockford, 16s, 21j, #515, y/g/f, M 675.00
Rockford, 16s, 21j, g/j/s, o/f, grade #537, rare, M................1,800.00
Rockford, 16s, 23j, 14k, o/f, mk Doll on dial/mvt, M.............3,400.00
Rockford, 18s, 15j, o/f, k/w, silver case, EX......................225.00
Rockford, 18s, 17j, silveroid, 2-tone, M...........................385.00
Rockford, 18s, 17j, y/g/f, o/f, Winnebago, M.....................425.00
Rockford, 18s, 21j, o/f, King Edward, M 550.00
Seth Thomas, 18s, 7j, ¾-mvt, bk: eagle/Liberty model, M.........325.00
Seth Thomas, 18s, 17j, #2, g/j/s, adj, Henry Molineux, EX.......595.00
Seth Thomas, 18s, 17j, Edgemere, G 55.00
Seth Thomas, 18s, 25j, g/j/s, g/f, Maiden Lane, EX..............2,395.00
South Bend, 12s, 21j, dbl roller, Grade #431, M..................275.00
South Bend, 12s, 21j, orig o/f, d/s, Studebaker, M 425.00
South Bend, 18s, 21j, g/j/s, h/c, Studebaker, M 1,495.00
South Bend, 18s, 21j, 14k, h/c, M.................................1,175.00
Swiss, 18s, 18k, h/c, 1-min, Repeater, High Grade, M 5,000.00

Waterford

The Waterford Glass Company operated in Ireland from the late

1700s until 1851 when the factory closed. One hundred years later (in 1951) another Waterford glassworks was instituted that produced glass similar to the eighteenth-century wares — crystal, usually with cut decoration. Today Waterford is a generic term referring to the type of glass first produced there. Advice for this category comes from Andrew Morton; he is listed in the Directory under Tennessee.

Bowl, centerpc; Lismore Statement, 13" 595.00
Bowl, centerpc; Snow Crystal, ltd ed................................495.00
Bowl, dessert; Lismore, ftd, 8 for 400.00
Bowl, Grizzly Bear eng, ftd, sgn Robt Cunningham, 8" 46.50
Bowl, Wedding Heirloom, 8" 200.00
Bowl, Winter Wonderland, ltd ed....................................500.00
Candlesticks, Eclipse, pr..250.00
Candlesticks, Metropolitan, 5", pr.................................180.00
Champagne, Powerscourt, 5½", 6 for 300.00
Champagne bucket, Millennium, 10"..................................400.00
Claret, Colleen, 6 for 480.00
Claret, Powerscourt, 7", 12 for....................................550.00
Compote, Newcastle, ftd stem 250.00
Decanter, claret; Sherburne 198.00
Decanter, wine; Eileen 198.00
Goblet, iced tea; Lismore, 1" stems, 6½", 8 for 425.00
Goblet, Powerscourt, 7¾", 12 for 550.00
Lamp, Beaumont, 6¼x13¾" dome shade, antique bronze std, 59"...675.00
Lamp, hurricane; Beaumont, 6¼x13¾" crystal shade, 23" 550.00
Lamp, hurricane; Lismore, 22½" w/7" dia base 500.00
Sculpture, bald eagle in classic patriotic pose, sgn WS, 2000, 7x8" .350.00
Sculpture, Melchior (Wise Man).....................................150.00
Sculpture, Tinker Bell, Disney, ltd ed.............................350.00
Sculptures, Holy Family, 7¼" Joseph, 5¼" Mary, 1¾" Jesus........350.00
Server, Lismore, 2-tier 198.00
Snifters, brandy; Lismore, 8 for...................................160.00
Sorbet, Lismore, ftd, 4⅛x3⅜", 8 for 400.00
Toasting flute, Cherished Moments, platinum or gold trim, pr ...195.00
Tumblers, Colleen, 8-oz, 6 for 390.00
Tumblers, dbl old fashion; Lismore, 12-oz, 4½", 8 for..............435.00
Vase, cut dmns, scalloped rim, 9¾", NM 415.00
Vase, Egret in Reeds, 14" 750.00
Vase, Lilies, clear/frosted, sgn Eamonn Hartley, #d (ltd ed), 12½"..650.00
Vase, Lilies, 12½" 975.00
Vase, Lismore, sq, 10"...250.00
Vase, Lismore Statement, 14" 595.00
Vase, Penrose, Waterford Society, sgn, 1995, 8½" 575.00
Vase, Surfing Dolphins, 12" 750.00
Wine, Lismore, balloon, 7", 8 for..................................575.00

Watt Pottery

The Watt Pottery Company was established in Crooksville, Ohio, on July 5, 1922. From approximately 1922 until 1935, they manufactured hand-turned stone containers — jars, jugs, milk pans, preserve jars, and various sizes of mixing bowls, usually marked with a cobalt blue acorn stamp. In 1936 production of these items was discontinued, and the company began to produce kitchen utility ware and ovenware such as mixing bowls, spaghetti bowls and plates, canister sets, covered casseroles, salt and pepper shakers, cookie jars, ice buckets, pitchers, bean pots, and salad and dinnerware sets. Most Watt ware is individually hand painted with bold brush strokes of red, green, or blue contrasting with the natural buff color of the glazed body. Several patterns were produced: Apple, Autumn Foliage, Cherry, Dutch Tulip, Morning Glory, Rio Rose, Rooster, Tear Drop, Starflower, and Tulip, to name a few. Much of the ware was made for advertising premiums and is often found stamped with the name of the retail company.

Tragedy struck the Watt Pottery Company on October 4, 1965, when fire completely destroyed the factory and warehouse. Production never resumed, but the ware they made has withstood many years of service in American kitchens and is today highly regarded and prized by collectors. The vivid colors and folk art-like execution of each cheerful pattern create a homespun ambiance that will make Watt pottery a treasure for years to come.

For further study we recommend *Watt Pottery, An Identification and Price Guide*, by our advisors for this category, Sue and Dave Morris; they are listed in the Directory under Washington. For the address of the *Watt's News* newsletter, see the section on Clubs, Newsletters, and Catalogs.

Apple, bowl, cereal/salad; 1½x5¾" 75.00
Apple, cruets, oil & vinegar; w/lids, #126, 7", pr.....................1,800.00
Apple, fondue, no lid, 3x9"..900.00
Apple, mug, #61, rare, 3x3¾" 500.00

Apple, pie plate, Shulz Motor Service, 1963, 9¼", $110.00.

Apple, pitcher, no ice lip, #17, 8x8½" 300.00
Apple, plate, dinner; #101, 10"....................................600.00
Apple, plate, divided, sm leaves, 10½" dia 2,000.00
Apple, platter, #31, 15" dia.......................................350.00
Apple, shakers, bbl shape, 4x2½", pr...............................600.00
Apple, teapot, w/lid, #112, 6x9".................................1,500.00
Apple, tumbler, #56, 4½x4".......................................1,000.00
Apple (Double), creamer, #62, 4¼x4½" 400.00
Apple (Open), bowl, mixing; #8, 4½x8" dia..........................175.00
Autumn Foliage, bowl, #106, 3½x10¾"................................85.00
Autumn Foliage, dish, refrigerator; #02, 3x7½" 165.00
Autumn Foliage, platter, #31, 15" dia 110.00
Autumn Foliage, sugar bowl, w/lid, #98 ....300.00
Basketweave (Brown), casserole, w/lid, #805, 6¼x8¼" 30.00
Blue/White Banded, bowl, mixing; 4x7" 25.00
Brown Banded, sugar bowl, w/lid, #98 ....200.00
Cherry, pitcher, w/advertising, #15, 5½x5¾" 175.00
Cherry, platter, #31, 15" dia 145.00
Cherry, salt shaker, bbl shape, 4x2½" 90.00
Cut-Leaf Pansy, casserole, stick hdl, w/lid, 3¾x7½" 125.00
Cut-Leaf Pansy, creamer & sugar bowl, open.........................175.00
Cut-Leaf Pansy, cup & saucer 90.00
Cut-Leaf Pansy, pie plate, 1½x9"...................................150.00
Cut-Leaf Pansy, platter, 15" dia 110.00
Dogwood, bowl, serving; 3x15"......................................110.00
Dutch Tulip, bowl, w/lid, #67, 6½x8½"..............................250.00
Eagle, pitcher, ice lip, 8x8½".....................................450.00
Goodies, jar, mk Goodies, w/lid, #76, 6½x7½".......................275.00
Kathy Kyle, bowl, 2x5½"..65.00
Kitch-N-Queen, bowl, #5, 2½x5".....................................45.00
Kitch-N-Queen, pitcher, ice lip, #17, 8".............................200.00
Kla Ham'rd, casserole, w/lid, #43-12, 6½x8".........................50.00
Morning Glory, cookie jar, w/lid, #95, 10¾x7½" 400.00
Morning Glory, pitcher, ice lip, #96, 8x8½" 375.00

Old Pansy, casserole, w/lid, #3/19, 5x9" **75.00**
Old Pansy, pitcher, #15, 5½x5¾" **225.00**
Old Pansy, platter, #49, 12" **85.00**
Old Pansy, platter, crosshatch pattern, 15" dia **175.00**
Raised Pansy, pitcher, refrigerator; w/lid, 3x5½" **100.00**
Rooster, bowl, #58, 3¾x10½" **275.00**
Rooster, ice bucket, w/lid, 7¼x7½" **275.00**
Rooster, pitcher, #15, 5½x5¾" **145.00**
Starflower, baker, w/lid, on warming stand, #96, 5½x8½" **150.00**
Starflower, bowl, berry; 1½x5¾" **35.00**
Starflower, grease jar, w/lid, #47, 5x4½" **250.00**
Starflower, ice bucket, w/lid, 7¼x7½" **185.00**
Starflower, pie plate, #33, 1½x9" dia **200.00**
Starflower, tumbler, #56, slant sides, 4½x4" **325.00**
Starflower (Green on Brown), cookie jar, w/lid, #21, 7½x7" **125.00**
Starflower (Pink on Black), casserole, w/lid, 4½x8¾" **125.00**
Starflower (Pink on Green), cup & saucer **65.00**
Starflower (White on Blue), bowl, spaghetti; #39, 3x13" **250.00**
Starflower (White on Red), mug, #121, 3¾x3" **400.00**
Tear Drop, bowl, #66, 3x7 ....**45.00**
Tear Drop, bowl, mixing; #05, 2½x5" **45.00**
Tear Drop, casserole, w/lid, sq, 6x8" **850.00**
Tear Drop, shakers, bbl shape, 4x2½", pr **350.00**
Tulip, bowl, mixing; #64, 5x7½" **85.00**
Tulip, cookie jar, w/lid, #503, 8¼x8¼" **375.00**
Tulip, creamer, #62, 4¼x4½" **225.00**
White Banded, casserole, w/lid, 7x9" **55.00**
White Banded, pitcher, 7" **85.00**
White Daisy, pitcher, 7x7¾" **165.00**
Woodgrain, bowl, chip 'n dip; #611, 2¾x11¼" **75.00**

Wave Crest

Wave Crest is a line of decorated opal ware (milk glass) patented in 1892 by the C.F. Monroe Co. of Meriden, Connecticut. They made a full line of items for every room of the house, but they are probably best known for their boxes and vases. Most items were hand painted with various levels of decoration, but more transfers were used in the later years prior to the company's demise in 1916. Floral themes are common; items with the scenics and portraits are rarer and more highly prized. Many pieces have ornately scrolled ormolu and brass handles, feet, and rims. Early pieces were unsigned (though they may have had paper labels); later, about 1898, a red banner mark was used. The black mark is probably from about 1902 – 03. However, the glass is quite distinctive and has not been reproduced, so even unmarked items are easy to recognize. Our advisors for this category are Dolli and Wilfred Cohen; they are listed in the Directory under California. Note: There is no premium for signatures on Wave Crest. Values are given for hand-decorated pieces (unless noted 'transfer') that are *not* worn.

Ashtray/match holder, floral, mc on wht, ftd, mk, 6x3" **550.00**
Atomizer, bl apple blossoms on ball shape, orig hdw **495.00**
Biscuit jar, emb scrolls/violets, sqd, SP rim & mts, 8x4¾" **850.00**
Biscuit jar, floral transfer on emb wht, mk metal lid, to hdl: 11" ...**320.00**
Biscuit jar, pastel ferns on squat shape w/melon ribs **495.00**
Biscuit jar, Swirl, sm flowers/beads, red on wht w/tan, 6½" dia ..**460.00**
Bottle, scent; Puffy, forget-me-nots, sq **495.00**
Box, Baroque Shell, red flowers in scrolling bl & wht reserve, 7" dia ...**800.00**
Box, Collars & Cuffs, mums & daisies on tan, mk, 7½x7" dia ..**1,350.00**
Box, Egg Crate, floral, autumn tones, mk, 5¼x6¾" **950.00**
Box, emb scroll/beaded panels, sm floral on wht, 5" sq **500.00**
Box, emb scrolls/flowers, sm red floral on wht, 4" dia **345.00**
Box, emb wild roses & scrolls, daisies on pk, 5¾" dia **450.00**
Box, glove; floral, 8½" L **1,350.00**

Box, glove; roses, mc on yel, ormolu ft, mk, 5½x9½x5¾" **1,750.00**
Box, Puffy, butterfly & flowers, 3" dia **250.00**
Box, Puffy, floral on turq or wht free-form panels, ftd metal mt,5" sq ...**126.50**
Box, Puffy, forget-me-nots, red on tan, 3" dia **200.00**
Box, Puffy, mums, yel on brn/tan, ormolu ft w/cherubs, 6¾" sq ..**3,795.00**
Box, Rococo, floral, 2½" sq **250.00**
Box, Swirl, floral, bl/brn on ivory, label, 5½" dia, EX **175.00**
Box, Swirl, lotus on gr & beige w/allover floral, 6½" dia **1,000.00**
Box, Swirl, sm flowers, rose/wine/yel on wht, 6¾" dia **485.00**
Broom holder, pansies w/wht beads on ivory, 10½x7" **2,100.00**
Ferner, sm florals in outlined reserves, wht on wht, metal ft, 6½" .**350.00**
Humidor, Cigars & floral w/gold, hinged lid, 6" **975.00**
Humidor, Tobacco, floral, pk on bl, 5½" **800.00**
Ice bucket, wild roses on bl, ornate lid & hdl, 6¼" dia **1,020.00**
Lamp, boudoir; forget-me-nots on bl to wht, socket base, 7" **500.00**
Match holder, floral w/beading, 4 gold ft **450.00**
Pickle castor, Swirl, toadstools & flowers, SP fr **550.00**
Plaque, nasturtiums & buds on pk to wht, 10x8" +fr **4,250.00**
Playing card holder, roses, pk on bl to wht, mk, 2½x4x1¼" **350.00**
Shakers, asters, mc on beige to wht, lids w/agitators, 4", pr **150.00**
Sugar shaker, Swirl, Japanesque decor in wht/rose, SP lid, 3" **435.00**
Sugar shaker, Swirl, pk/gold scrolls on yel w/gray tracing **500.00**
Tray, floral, mc on bl to wht, mirror top, 4½x4" dia **595.00**
Vase, daisies on russet, gilt metal mts/hdls at rim, 9½" **1,250.00**
Vase, irises on yel, heavily emb, beaded top, 9¾" **1,350.00**

Weapons

Among the varied areas of specialization within the broad category of weapons, guns are by far the most popular. Muskets are among the earliest firearms; they were large-bore shoulder arms, usually firing black powder with separate loading of powder and shot. Some ignited the charge by flintlock or caplock, while later types used a firing pin with a metallic cartridge. Side arms, referred to as such because they were worn at the side, include pistols and revolvers. Pistols range from early single-shot and multiple barrels to modern types with cartridges held in the handle. Revolvers were supplied with a cylinder that turned to feed a fresh round in front of the barrel breech. Other firearms include shotguns, which fired round or conical bullets and had a smooth inner barrel surface, and rifles, so named because the interior of the barrel contained spiral grooves (rifling) which increased accuracy. For further study we recommend *Modern Guns, Fourteenth Edition*, by Russell Quertermous and Steve Quertermous, available at your local bookstore. Our advisor for this category is Steve Howard; he is listed the Directory under California. Unless noted otherwise, our values are for examples in excellent condition.

See also Militaria.

Key:
bbl — barrel	mod — modified
cal — caliber	oct — octagon
conv — conversion	O/U — over/under
cyl — cylinder	p/b — patch box
f/l — flintlock	perc — percussion
ga — gauge	/s — stock
hdw — hardware	Spec O — Special Order
mag — magazine	

Carbines

Burnside 4th Model, 54 cal perc, 21" rnd bbl, inspectors mks, EX ...**1,200.00**
Cosmopolitan Arms, 52 cal perc w/19" rnd bbl, dtd 1853, walnut/s .**1,980.00**
Hall-North Model 1843 perc, 52 cal, 21" rifled bbl, walnut/s, EX .**1,375.00**
JH Merrill perc, 1st type, brass hdw, walnut/s, 37" **990.00**
Joslyn Model 1864, 52 cal rimfire, 22" bbl, inspector's mks, EX .**1,485.00**

Sharps New Model 1863 perc, 22" rnd bbl, bold inspector's mk on /s, EX ..**2,300.00**
Smith, 50 cal perc, 21½" oct-to-rnd bbl, EX **2,365.00**
Smith Pat, 50 cal perc, 21½" rnd bbl, walnut/s, iron hdw, EX.**1,125.00**
Springfield Model 1873 Trap Door, 45-70 cal, 22" bbl, walnut/s, EX ...**770.00**
Starr Arms, 54 cal perc, 20" rnd bbl, worn walnut/s, EX..........**1,100.00**
Winchester Model 1866, 3rd model, 44 cal, 20" bbl, saddle ring, VG.**4,000.00**
Winchester Model 1873, 44 cal, shortened 19" bbl, walnut/s, EX..**1,100.00**

Muskets

Committee of Safety f/l, cherry/s, brass hdw, 45" rnd bbl, 61¼" .**3,100.00**
FJ Malherbe et Cie on perc lock, Civil War era, 56", EX............**575.00**
Harper's Ferry perc, eagle stamp w/US on lock, 30" shortened bbl ..**330.00**
Jenks Model 1808 f/l, 69 cal, 42" rnd bbl, broken/s, G-...............**700.00**
Richmond Armory, walnut/s, steel hdw, 1861 on lock, 40" rnd bbl, 56".**6,200.00**
Springfield Model 1820 f/l, 69 cal, 42" rnd bbl, poor reconv, G .**865.00**
Springfield Model 1862 Patterned Rifled, 58 cal perc, 1863 lock, G..**865.00**
Springfield 1808 f/l, reconv lock, walnut/s, 45" rnd bbl, 59½" ...**1,250.00**
Surcharged US, 73 cal, 42" rnd bbl, crude side-lug conv, cherry/s, VG.**1,850.00**
Wickham Model 1821, 69 cal, 42" rnd bbl, Hews & Philips 1861 conv, VG ...**750.00**

Pistols

A Waters perc, early conv from f/l w/brass spacer, 8½" bbl **550.00**
Allen & Thurber Bar Hammer Pepperbox, 32 cal, 6-shot bbl cluster, G .**350.00**
Colt 1st Model Woodsman, 22LR cal, 6½" pencil bbl, bl finish.**175.00**
European f/l, brass hdw, eng thumbpc/grip cap, 10" stamped bbl, 17", G..**450.00**
Harper's Ferry Model 1806 f/l, 54 cal, 10" rnd bbl, 1807 on lock plate..**4,600.00**
Harper's Ferry 1805 f/l, .54 cal, walnut/s, pieced rstr, 10" rnd bbl .**2,250.00**
Palmetto Armory perc, 54 cal w/8" rnd bbl, brass hdw, 14½" ..**1,500.00**
Remington-Elliot Pepperbox, 32 cal, rubber grips, 5" **195.00**
Waters Model 1836 perc, f/l conv, walnut/s, iron hdw, 8½" rnd bbl, G.**500.00**

Revolvers

Allen & Wheelock Army, 44 cal, 7" part oct bbl, std mks, M.**7,000.00**
Colt Bisley Army, 38 WCF cal, single action, 5½" bbl, EX **1,045.00**
Colt 1851 Navy perc, late NP, rstr/rpr cylinder, walnut trips **415.00**
Colt 1909, 45LC cal, 5½" rnd bbl, rfn, EX **430.00**
Merwin & Hulbert Single Action, 44/40 cal, 7" rnd bbl, ivory grips, G ...**925.00**
Remington Model 1861 Army, 44 cal perc w/8" oct bbl, silver traces..**275.00**
Remington-Beals Navy, 36 cal, 13½", VG+ **635.00**
Smith & Wesson 1st Single Action, 38S&W cal, 3½" bbl, NP, G..**155.00**
Starr Army, 44 cal perc, 6" rnd bbl, bl traces, VG...................**1,100.00**

Rifles

Ballard Buffalo, 45/100 cal, walnut butt/s, rstr cap, 30" oct bbl, G.**2,850.00**
JH Hall Model 1819 US f/l, 32½" bbl, EX patina, 52½" **935.00**
Marlin Ballard #9 Union Hill, 32-40 cal, 28" oct-to-rnd bbl, EX ..**2,500.00**
MD f/l, curly maple/s w/cvg, brass hdw, eng p/b, silver inlay, 40" bbl .**3,300.00**
OH perc, curly maple/s w/brass hdw, old conv, 42" oct bbl, 57" .**1,800.00**
PA f/l, curly maple/s w/cvg & inlay, brass hdw, p/b, 39" oct bbl, 55" ..**3,000.00**
Remington Model I Sporting, 38 cal, 26" oct bbl, walnut/s, VG..**200.00**
Remington 7400 Semi-Auto, 30-06 cal, 22" rnd bbl, open sights, +scope ..**315.00**
Sharpes New 2 Model 1859, 52 cal perc, 30" bbl, EX **3,300.00**
Spencer Repeater Civil War era Army, 30" rnd bbl, EX **2,450.00**
T Deschner KY style, 38 cal perc, half/s, 30" oct bbl, G.............**230.00**
Winchester 1894 Semo-Auto Spec O Take Down, 32WS cal, 25" part oct bbl.**550.00**
Winchester 90 Pump, 22 short cal, chromed, 24" oct bbl, ¾ mag, G ...**200.00**

Shotguns

Browning A-5 Semi-Auto, 16 ga, 28" plain full-choked bbl **400.00**

E&W Bond f/l dbl bbl, walnut/s, eng hdw, rpl hammer, 30" rnd bbls .**950.00**
Parker English Made Dbl Bbl Perc, 16 bore cal, 28" Damascus bbls, G .**250.00**
Sharpe dbl bbl f/l, 1 bbl conv to perc, checkered/s, 34" rnd bbl, 50" ...**500.00**
W Moore & Co dbl bbl perc, walnut/s, 40" rnd bbls, 56½" **965.00**
White & Thompson perc dbl bbl, figured walnut/s, 30" rnd bbls, 47"..**500.00**
Winchester Model 37 Single Bbl, 20 ga, youth sz w/26" mod bbl, EX+.**200.00**

Swords

All swords listed below are priced 'with scabbard,' unless otherwise noted.

Ames, Civil War officer, US etched on 30" blade, 36" overall, EX ...**1,325.00**
Ames, 1860 Cavalry saber, dk patina, 34½" blade, w/hanger ..**1,100.00**
Ames artillery, 18¾" blade w/faint mks, brass hit w/eagle, 25" ...**440.00**
Ames Model 1860 cavalry saber, 35" blade mk US 1862, 42" **660.00**
Confederate, brass hilt, rope twist brass wrap on hdl, 35" **400.00**
Confederate artillery, 19" pitted blade, brass hdl, CS on guard, 25" ..**1,500.00**
N Starr Naval Cutlass, wrought iron hilt, 25¾" blade, EX **385.00**
OH officer's, etch/eng blade w/eagle & US, brass hilt, 31" **1,100.00**

Weather Vanes

The earliest weather vanes were of handmade wrought iron and were generally simple angular silhouettes with a small hole suggesting an eye. Later copper, zinc, and polychromed wood with features in relief were fashioned into more realistic forms. Ships, horses, fish, Indians, roosters, and angels were popular motifs. In the nineteenth century, silhouettes were often made from sheet metal. Wooden figures became highly carved and were painted in vivid colors. E.G. Washburne and Company in New York was one of the most prominent manufacturers of weather vanes during the last half of the century. Two-dimensional sheet metal weather vanes are increasing in value due to the already heady prices of the full-bodied variety. Originality, strength of line and patina help to determine value. When no condition is indicated, the items listed below are assumed to be in excellent condition.

Arrow, cobalt glass ball, iron legs, copper rods, 37" **100.00**
Arrow, copper, sphere finial, old gilt, 17x31" **600.00**
Auto, hollow-cast copper, on iron & tube arrow, 10", 22" overall H ..**175.00**
Auto, 1950s style, CI, EX patina, 25½" L **350.00**
Banner, iron & copper, ball finial, verdigris, 21x38" **1,600.00**
Banner, pierced/scrolled sheet copper, gilt traces, 18x72" **2,700.00**
Banner, sheet iron w/cutouts, old blk pnt, 37x16"....................**1,650.00**
Banneret, copper/zinc, verdigris on gilt, rtcl w/'F' & corner fan, 26"...**2,860.00**
Deer, metal cutout w/red pnt & iron reinforcing bands, 21x16", G **500.00**
Directional, CI, w/rod/ball & wood post, 88x40" **300.00**
Eagle, copper, full body, wings out, old pnt, 19th C, 29x25x25"..**1,950.00**
Eagle, molded copper, gilt/verdigris, on sphere w/arrow, 9x16x15" ..**1,000.00**
Golfer & caddy on arrow, copper w/verdigris edge, 1930-40s, 18½x26" ...**750.00**
Horse, copper w/zinc ears, full body, gilt/verdigris, Harris, 32" L.**5,585.00**
Horse, copper w/zinc head & torso, att J Howard & Co, 19x25", EX.**12,925.00**
Horse, copper w/zinc torso, gold traces, att Howard, rpr, 19x24".**7,500.00**
Horse & jockey, copper, old yel, no stand, 22¾x31½".............**9,400.00**
Horse & rider, molded sheet iron, hollow, orig mustard pnt, 29x36"..**6,500.00**
Horse & rider (formal), copper w/verdigris, att Jewell, 27x28".**20,000.00**
Horse prancing, molded copper w/weathered gilt, 25x34" **4,000.00**
Horse running, copper, full body, verdigris/gilt, no stand, 15x27".**1,495.00**
Horse running, copper w/gilt traces, flattened full body, 17x32"..**1,400.00**
Horse running, copper w/verdigris & gilt traces, full body w/mt, 38" L..**7,000.00**
Horse running, copper w/verdigris & gilt traces, no stand, 18", EX..**2,350.00**
Horse running, gilt copper & zinc, Ethan Allen, rstr, 17x26"..**2,600.00**
Horse running, zinc w/lt gilt, full body, rpr holes, 24x62" **8,800.00**
Indian w/arched bow & arrow, flat steel, old mc pnt, 19"+steel rod..**575.00**
Man on horsebk w/arm raised, sheet steel w/silver pnt, recent, 19x20" .**1,400.00**

Pilgrim & Indian smoke pipe, pineapple between, sheet iron, 22x30" ..**375.00**
Rooster, copper w/old verdigris & gilt traces, 26½x42"............**5,585.00**
Rooster, sheet copper, stylized feathers, on iron rod, 29x17".......**220.00**
Rooster on arrow, emb copper w/worn orig gilt, rpr, 24x30", EX.**3,165.00**
Rooster on arrow, wooden, 19½x12" **1,275.00**
Sailing ship, cvd/pnt wood, 3 masts, New England, 1850s, 38x39"...**1,850.00**
Stag, molded copper w/zinc antlers, old gilt surface, 1800s, 19x20"...**8,225.00**
Stag leaping, copper w/old gilt, full body, att Harris & Son, 42x56".**12,925.00**
Steer, copper (hollow) w/zinc head, old pnt, Am, 20x29⅜"....**6,500.00**

Weaving

Early Americans used a variety of tools and a great amount of time to produce the material from which their clothing was made. Soaked and dried flax was broken on a flax brake to remove waste material. It was then tapped and stroked with a scutching knife. Hackles further removed waste and separated the short fibers from the longer ones. Unspun fibers were placed on the distaff on the spinning wheel for processing into yarn. The yarn was then wound around a reel for measuring. Three tools used for this purpose were the niddy-noddy, the reel yarn winder, and the click reel. After it was washed and dyed, the yarn was transferred to a barrel-cage or squirrel-cage swift and fed onto a bobbin winder.

Today flax wheels are more plentiful than the large wool wheels since they were small and could be more easily stored and preserved. The distaff, an often-discarded or misplaced part of the wheel, is very scarce. French spinners from the Quebec area painted their wheels. Many have been stripped and refinished by those unaware of this fact. Wheels may be very simple or have a great amount of detail, depending upon the owner's ethnic background and the maker's skill.

Flax knife, rosemalled, Swedish, dtd 1863, w/provenance, 23", EX .**165.00**
Hackle, wooden comb shape, wooden teeth **50.00**
Loom spool, 1930s, 9" **16.00**
Niddy-noddy, hardwood, EX patina, 15¾x12" (ea end) **60.00**
Shuttle, spool placed in cavity, Pat Nov 10 85, 16" **45.00**
Swift, maple/birch, trn bracket, wrought-iron clamp, 23" **110.00**
Swift, maple/hardwoods w/red stain, X base, rpr, 30½" **195.00**
Tape loom, wormy maple/oak, pegged, rprs, floor standing, 39½"...**110.00**
Wheel, cherry w/sm ivory buttons, trn legs on tripod, 9½" dia, 38"...**300.00**
Wheel, flax; blunt arrow ft, PA, rfn, G...**200.00**
Wheel, flax; hardwoods w/bold trns, tree branch distaff, 32" **275.00**
Wheel, flax; mahog, old dk finish, 45½x32"..................................**150.00**
Wheel, flax; quarternsawn oak, ca 1810s, 47", 20" wheel, +29" winder..**550.00**
Wheel, fruitwood, Fr Tyrolian, 15" wheel, ca 1900, prof rstr.......**425.00**
Wheel, hardwoods, iron fly wheel, ivory/ebony details, old rfn, 35"...**450.00**
Wheel, hardwoods, wood/wire fly wheel, ivory pegs, Germany, rpr, 35"...**275.00**
Wheel, traveler's; hardwood, 16" wheel, ca 1900, EX working ...**325.00**

Webb

Thomas Webb and Sons have been glassmakers in Stourbridge, England, since 1837. Besides their fine cameo glass, they have also made enameled ware and pieces heavily decorated with applied glass ornaments. The butterfly is a motif that has been so often featured that it tends to suggest Webb as the manufacturer. Our advisor for this category is Don Williams; he is listed in the Directory under Missouri.

See also specific types of glass such as Alexandrite, Burmese, Mother of Pearl, and Peachblow.

Cameo

Bonbon, morning glories, red/yel/wht, SP lid & dome ft, 7½" ..**2,500.00**
Bottle, scent; bl w/wht oval & eng sweet peas, teardrop, 4" **2,200.00**

Bottle, scent; Ivory, vines/leaves, SP lid, 4½" **750.00**
Bottle, scent; snowdrop floral, gr to wht, teardrop, 4" **1,800.00**
Bowl, swallows/trees/flowers, wht/purple on bl, Gem, 9" **28,000.00**
Jar, potpourri; Ivory, acorns/leaves, bk: butterfly, 6" **2,500.00**
Lamp base, floral, rose/wht on citron, 3 camphor ft, 3½x4¾"..**1,265.00**
Sand shaker, criss-cross lattice on dk crimson, ovoid, 3½" **1,050.00**
Vase, blackberry branches/bee, citron & opal on wht, 8½" **3,500.00**
Vase, fishscales/fish/seaweed, gold on cased pk, 4¼x7" **865.00**
Vase, floral sprigs/long grass blades, wht on amber, att, 4¾" **460.00**
Vase, floral vines/border, brn on wht, squat, 3x3¼" **700.00**
Vase, floral/butterfly, wht on peachblow, dbl-gourd form, 7"....**2,750.00**
Vase, florals on leafy stems, leaf-cut rim/ft, wht on bl, 10½" **4,750.00**
Vase, flower branch, wht on rose to citron, shouldered, 4¼" ...**1,265.00**
Vase, flower/pod/leaf, wht on red, bulbed neck w/floral band, att, 9".**2,585.00**
Vase, flowers/leaves, gr on textured crystal, gr rim, low ft, 10"....**700.00**
Vase, Ivory, flower vines, crimped/incurvate rim, 4" **520.00**
Vase, Ivory, foxglove spires, slim neck, 10½"............................**1,250.00**
Vase, Ivory, mythical creatures, urn form, 8½" **5,175.00**
Vase, Oriental floral branch, wht on raisin, att, 4¼"...................**690.00**
Vase, raspberries, rose-red on wht, bamboo cylinder, 8¾x2½"..**1,850.00**
Vase, tulips, bl on stippled crystal, wide trumpet form, 9" **660.00**
Vase, wild roses/butterfly, brn on bright bl, 7½x6½"................**2,700.00**

Miscellaneous

Bowl, pk w/clear T-prints, gold bee/HP floral, jack-in-pulpit rim, 12"..**230.00**
Compote, ruby w/clear stem, threaded ft/ruffled, Pat, 5½x8½" ..**600.00**
Creamer, gold prunus/butterfly on shaded tan, ovoid, 3¼" **385.00**
Jam jar, Dmn Quilt MOP, cased raspberry, cylindrical, to hdl: 6".**400.00**
Jar, gold ginko/butterfly, yel satin w/wht int, dome lid, 4¾" **100.00**
Sweetmeat, heavy gold florals on aqua, SP lid/etc, 5x3⅜" **300.00**
Vase, allover flowers, red w/wht int, cup neck, 3 gold ball ft, 4".**100.00**
Vase, allover sm pk flowers on lt bl to wht, lg clear hdls, 10" **230.00**
Vase, bronze, lustre finish, 6½"...**200.00**
Vase, Coin Spot MOP, pk w/flowers & butterfly, stick neck, 9¾" .**375.00**
Vase, Dmn Quilt MOP, emerald to lime w/floral & bees, 9x6" ...**950.00**
Vase, gold fernery & decor, ruby cased, stick form, 13" **250.00**
Vase, gold ferns & foliage on dk crimson, lt bl int, #873/4 S298, 5".**225.00**
Vase, gold floral/insect, yel satin, teardrop form w/long neck, 10".**365.00**
Vase, gold ginko/bk: butterfly on yel satin, shouldered, 7½" **225.00**
Vase, leaves/flowers w/bird, apricot satin, cup rim, squat body, 9"..**575.00**
Vase, MOP purple to blk, melon ribs, can neck w/gold shoulder hdls, 7"..**3,680.00**
Vase, morning glories, blk/gold on cased lt/dk yel, gourd form, 9".**145.00**
Vase, pk/wht satin, bulbous w/ruffled top, 8x4" **400.00**
Vase, rainbow (red/yel/bl) w/diagonal ribs, gold branch/butterfly, 14" ..**400.00**
Vase, yel shaded satin, wht int, gourd shape w/base, 10½"..........**275.00**

Wedgwood

Josiah Wedgwood established his pottery in Burslem, England, in 1759. He produced only molded utilitarian earthenwares until 1770 when new facilities were opened at Etruria for the production of ornamental wares. It was there he introduced his famous Basalt and Jasperware. Jasperware, an unglazed fine stoneware decorated with classic figures in white relief, was usually produced in blues, but it was also made in ground colors of green, lilac, yellow, black, or white. Occasionally three or more colors were used in combination. It has been in continuous production to the present day and is the most easily recognized of all the Wedgwood lines. Jasper-dip is a ware with a solid-color body or a white body that has been dipped in an overlay color. It was introduced in the late 1700s and is the type most often encountered on today's market.

Though Wedgwood's Jasperware was highly acclaimed, on a more practical basis his improved creamware was his greatest success, due to the ease with which it could be potted and because its lighter weight significantly reduced transportation expenses. Wedgwood was able to offer 'chinaware' at affordable prices. Queen Charlotte was so pleased with the ware that she allowed it to be called 'Queen's Ware.' Most creamware was marked simply 'WEDGWOOD.' ('Wedgwood & Co.' and 'Wedgewood' are marks of other potters.) From 1769 to 1780, Wedgwood was in partnership with Thomas Bentley; artwares of the highest quality may bear the 'Wedgwood & Bentley' mark indicating this partnership. Moonlight Lustre, an allover splashed-on effect of pink intermingling with gray, brown, or yellow, was made from 1805 to 1815. Porcelain was made, though not to any great extent, from 1812 to 1822. Bone china was produced before 1822 and after 1872. These types of wares were marked 'WEDGWOOD' (with a printed 'Portland Vase' mark after 1872). Stone china and Pearlware were made from about 1820 to 1875. Examples of either may be found with a printed or impressed mark to indicate their body type. During the late 1800s, Wedgwood produced some fine parian and majolica. Creamware, hand painted by Emile Lessore, was sold from about 1860 to 1875. From the twentieth century, several lines of lustre wares — Butterfly, Dragon, and Fairyland (designed by Daisy Makeig-Jones) — have attracted the collector and, as their prices suggest, are highly sought after and admired.

Nearly all of Wedgwood's wares are clearly marked. 'WEDGWOOD' was used before 1891, after which time 'ENGLAND' was added. Most examples marked 'MADE IN ENGLAND' were made after 1905. A detailed study of all marks is recommended for accurate dating. See also Majolica.

Key:
WW — WEDGWOOD	WWMIE — WEDGWOOD
WWE — WEDGWOOD England	Made in England

Biscuit jar, Jasper, blk on yel, Muses/grapevine festoons, 1930s, 6" ..**765.00**
Biscuit jar, Jasper, lilac, figure frieze, cylindrical, 1900, 6" **560.00**
Biscuit jar, Jasper, lt gr, fox hunt, SP trim, WW, late 1800s, 5⅛".**260.00**
Biscuit jar, Jasper, 3-color, Muses/laurel band, bulbous, 1900, 6", EX.**650.00**
Biscuit jar, Jasper, 3-color (gr/lilac), figure frieze, WW, 5"...........**650.00**
Bowl, Basalt, engine-trn decor, WW, early 20th C, 10⅛"............**230.00**
Bowl, Butterfly Lustre, MOP w/mottled orange int, octagonal, Z4829, 4".**560.00**
Bowl, Butterfly Lustre, orange/gr mottle w/MOP int, 8½".......**1,645.00**
Bowl, Drabware, arabesque floral relief on orange-peel ground, 7½" ..**940.00**
Bowl, Dragon Lustre, dk bl w/MOP int, octagonal, Z4829, 7⅜".**880.00**
Bowl, Dragon Lustre, 3 dragons on bl, gr int w/Arabian & camel, 2x4" .**250.00**
Bowl, Dragon Lustre, 4 dragons, int: lg central dragon, Z4829, 8"..**725.00**
Bowl, Fish Lustre, bl w/bl-tint MOP int, Z4920, 11"................**2,235.00**
Bowl, Fruit Lustre, bl w/orange on red int, octagonal, Z5457, 8".**1,300.00**
Bowl, Hummingbird Lustre, dk bl w/orange int, octagonal, Z5294, 8" ..**1,300.00**
Bowl, Jasper, blk, Dancing Hours, WWMIE, ca 1981, 10"..........**345.00**
Bowl, Lustre, orange w/gilt Oriental motifs, purple-bl int w/bird, 4"...**500.00**
Bowl, Rosso Antico, appl blk meander band, foliate body, WW, 8"..**1,290.00**
Bust, Basalt, Minerva, on waisted socle, WW, mid-1800s, 17½"....**2,415.00**
Bust, Basalt, Shakespeare, WWE, 10" **375.00**
Bust, Carrara, Byron, on waisted rnd socle, ca 1860, 15".........**1,300.00**
Bust, Carrara, Scott, on waisted rnd socle, ca 1860, 15"..........**1,200.00**
Bust, Parian, Lord Zetland, wearing numerous medals, 1868, 20", EX.**1,200.00**
Coffee set, Jasper, blk w/yel dip, WWE, 1980, 8¼" pot+cr/sug.**1,950.00**
Coffeepot, Basalt, wide fluted band, 8", NM, +cr (5½")/sug (3")...**1,200.00**
Creamer, Basalt, Kenlock Ware, dragon, WWE, ca 1895, 2¼"....**345.00**
Figurine, Basalt, Voltaire holding book, WW, early 1800s, 10¾" .**1,265.00**
Figurine, Carrara, Venus Voctrox, 1850s, 20", EX **1,400.00**
Game dish, Caneware, dead game/grapevines, rabbit finial, WW, 9¼"...**635.00**
Game dish, Caneware, grapevine band, cauliflower finial, no liner, 9" ..**300.00**
Inkstand, Basalt, lamp form w/oval tray, appl foliage, rstr, 1820s, 7" ...**350.00**
Jar, Keith Murray, red stoneware w/horizontal ridges, lid, 6½"....**900.00**
Jardiniere, Jasper, dk bl, floral band, WW, late 1800s, 6¾".........**575.00**

Jardiniere, Jasper, lt bl, classical figures, WW, late 1800s, 8", NM .**460.00**
Jug, Caneware, rabbit hunt, bl grapevine border, bulbous, 7½" ..**650.00**
Jug, club; Drabware, hunt scene/grapevines, WW, ca 1830, 7⅜" .**485.00**
Jug, Jasper, yel, classical figures, WW, ca 1900, 3½"..................**635.00**
Lamp, oil; Jasper, dk bl, classic figures, w/lid, 1800, 5", EX......**1,000.00**
Lamp, oil; Rosso Antico, Zodiac, WW, early 1800s, 5¼", EX.....**800.00**
Match holder, Jasper, crimson, classical figures, WWE, 1920, 2⅜"..**485.00**
Mold, Queen's Ware, oval w/fruit & foliage in ribbed pot, 11", VG.**1,290.00**
Mustard pot, Jasper, yel, grapevines, SP trim, WWE, 1930s, 3" ..**315.00**
Plant pot & stand, Basalt, pierced sides, WW, 4½" **400.00**
Plaque, Basalt, Hercules strangling lion, WW, 5½x7¼"+ebony fr ..**800.00**

Plaque, Jasper, light blue, Centaur and Bacchante, self framed, WWE, nineteenth century, 15¼", $6,325.00.

Plaque, Jasper, lt bl, classical figures dance, WW, 19th C, 7x20", pr.**4,600.00**
Plaque, Jasper, lt bl, classical subject in laurel fr, WW, 6¾" L .**1,100.00**
Plate, trophy; Jasper, gr, figures center, various bands, 1890s, 9" .**940.00**
Platter, Queen's Ware, Armorial, oats border, gilt berries, WW, 21"...**575.00**
Rum kettle, Basalt, bacchanalian boys, engine-trn band, w/lid, 6", EX..**585.00**
Salt cellar, Jasper, lt bl, Dancing Hours, WW, 19th C, 2⅞", pr ..**750.00**
Tankard, Basalt, classical figures, cylindrical, WW, rstr, 4¼" **350.00**
Tea canister, allover brn tortoise shell, w/lid, 5", G **500.00**
Tea set, Caneware, basketweave, WW, ca 1840, 7½" pot+cr/sug, rstr.....**230.00**
Teapot, allover gray/brn mottle, scrolled branch spout, rstr lid, 8" .**1,000.00**
Teapot, Basalt, floral, sunflower finial, WW, early 1800s, 3¾"....**288.00**
Toothpick holder, Hummingbird Lustre, bl w/orange int, 3 gold hdls, 2".**375.00**
Vase, Bone China, Blue Lustre w/gilt in dragon & clouds, 9½"..**470.00**
Vase, Bone China, fruit & flowers w/gold, WW, late 1800s, 5½"..**200.00**
Vase, Butterfly Lustre, MOP exterior, Z4832, 1920, missing lid, 8".**650.00**
Vase, Dragon Lustre, bl w/mc decor, Z4829, missing lid, 7½" **500.00**
Vase, Golcondaware, floral w/gold, WW, 16" **700.00**
Vase, Hummingbird Lustre, bl w/gilt & mc birds, orange int, 5", pr..**700.00**
Vase, Hummingbird Lustre, dk bl w/mc birds, orange int, 8" **885.00**
Vase, Hummingbird Lustre, gr w/mc birds, bottle form, Z5088, 8"..**750.00**
Vase, Jasper, bl, Portland, mfg flaw, WW, 6¾"..............................**440.00**
Vase, Jasper, blk, classical figures, WWE/Marshall Field, ca 1918, 4" ...**400.00**
Vase, Jasper, dk bl, classical figures, WWE, early 20th C, 9¼" ...**430.00**

Weil Ware

Max Weil came to the United States in the 1940s, settling in California. There he began manufacturing dinnerware, figurines, cookie jars, and wall pockets. American clays were used, and the dinnerware was all hand decorated. Weil died in 1954; the company closed two years later. The last backstamp to be used was the outline of a burro with the words 'Weil Ware — Made in California.' Many unmarked pieces found today originally carried a silver foil label; but you'll often find a four-digit handwritten number series on figurines. For further study we recommend *The Collector's Encyclopedia of California Pottery* by Jack Chipman (Collector Books).

Bowl, Malay Bambu, 5" **3.50**
Bowl, vegetable; Yellow Rose, divided, 10½x6¾"..........................**30.00**
Bust, Madonna, bl & rose head scarf, 5¼" **55.00**

Coffeepot, Malay Bambu, 7½", from $60 to................................**75.00**
Creamer, Malay Blossom...**18.00**
Cup & saucer, Malay Blossom, sq..**15.00**
Figurine, lady in pk dress w/hands in gr muff, gr hat, #4031, 10" ..**75.00**
Flower holder, lady in bl dress/scarf between 2 columns, #4027, 11"..**90.00**
Flower holder, lady in gr dress w/ivory basket, 10½"....................**50.00**
Flower holder, lady in gr dress w/spider web decor #4635, 10½" ...**60.00**
Flower holder, lady in pk dress w/umbrella against planter, #4025, 10"..**60.00**
Flower holder, lady in pk dress w/2 wht baskets, #4024, 9½"........**60.00**
Flower holder, lady in wht dress w/bl floral, apron as planter, 6¾".**45.00**
Flower holder, lady in wht dress w/florals, lg hat, sq vase, 10"......**65.00**
Flower holder, lady in wht floral dress w/bl apron as planter, 8"....**50.00**
Flower holder, lady in wht floral dress w/rose trim, bl basket, 6½".**40.00**
Flower holder, lady in wht w/bl apron, bl pot on shoulder, 7".......**40.00**
Flower holder, lady in yel dress w/bl bow & bl bow in hair, 7½" ..**70.00**
Flower holder, Oriental lady in bl w/wht, seated w/fan behind head, 9"..**65.00**
Plate, chop; Malay Bambu, 13"...**20.00**
Plate, dinner; Malay Bambu..**10.00**
Plate, dinner; Maylay Blossom, 9¾" sq, from $12 to....................**15.00**
Plate, Malay Bambu, 6½"..**3.00**
Relish plate, Malay Blossom, 3-sections, #29, 5¾x9½"................**35.00**
Sugar bowl, Malay Blossom, w/lid..**25.00**
Teapot, Malay Bambu...**40.00**
Tumbler, Malay Bambu...**7.50**
Vase, Ming Tree, #933, bulbous, 8"...**40.00**
Vase, Ming Tree, #966, 5½x5⅛" sq..**55.00**
Vase, Ming Tree, folded rim, 8½x4½"...**40.00**
Vase, Ming Tree, mk 1933, 8½"..**25.00**
Wall pocket, Oriental girl sits on wht shelf w/tan pots, 10" **40.00**

Weller

The Weller Pottery Company was established in Zanesville, Ohio, in 1882, the outgrowth of a small one-kiln log cabin works Sam Weller had operated in Fultonham. Through an association with Wm. Long, he entered the art pottery field in 1895, producing the Lonhuda Ware Long had perfected in Steubenville six years earlier. His famous Louwelsa line was merely a continuation of Lonhuda and was made in at least five hundred different shapes. Many fine lines of artware followed under the direction of Charles Babcock Upjohn, art director from 1895 to 1904: Dickens Ware (1st Line), under-glaze slip decorations on dark backgrounds; Turada, featuring applied ivory bands of delicate openwork on solid dark brown backgrounds; and Aurelian, similar to Louwelsa, but with a brushed-on rather than blended ground. One of their most famous lines was 2nd Line Dickens, introduced in 1900. Backgrounds, characteristically caramel shading to turquoise matt, were decorated by sgraffito with animals, golfers, monks, Indians, and scenes from Dickens novels. The work is often artist signed. Sicardo, 1902, was a metallic lustre line in tones of blue, green, or purple with flowing Art Nouveau patterns developed within the glaze.

Frederick Hurten Rhead, who worked for Weller from 1903 to mid-1904, created the prestigious Jap Birdimal line decorated with geisha girls, landscapes, storks, etc., accomplished through application of heavy slip forced through the tiny nozzle of a squeeze bag. Other lines to his credit are L'Art Nouveau, produced in both high-gloss brown and matt pastels, and 3rd Line Dickens, often decorated with Cruikshank's illustrations in relief. Other early artware lines were Eocean, Floretta, Hunter, Perfecto, Dresden, Etched Matt, and Etna.

In 1920 John Lessel was hired as art director, and under his supervision several new lines were created. LaSa, LaMar, Marengo, and Besline attest to his expertise with metallic lustres. The last of the artware lines and one of the most sought after by collectors today is Hudson, first made during the early 1920s. Hudson, a semimatt glazed ware, was beautifully artist decorated on shaded backgrounds with florals, ani-

mals, birds, and scenics. Notable artists often signed their work, among them Hester Pillsbury, Dorothy England Laughead, Ruth Axline, Claude Leffler, Sarah Reid McLaughlin, E.L. Pickens, and Mae Timberlake.

During the late 1920s Weller produced a line of gardenware and naturalistic life-sized and larger figures of frogs, dogs, cats, swans, ducks, geese, rabbits, squirrels, and playful gnomes, most of which were sold at the Weller store in Zanesville due to the fragile nature of their designs. The Depression brought a slow, steady decline in sales, and by 1948 the pottery was closed.

Our advisor for this category is Mike Nickel; he is listed in the Directory under Michigan. For a more thorough study we recommend *The Collector's Encyclopedia of Weller Pottery* by Sharon and Bob Huxford, available at your local library or from Collector Books.

Ardsley, vase, cattails/water lilies, ink stamp/die mk, 11½".........**275.00**
Ardsley, vase, irises at ea of 3 corners, 3-ftd, label/ink mk, 7".....**350.00**
Ardsley, wall pocket, iris/leaves over serrated opening, 12".........**750.00**
Atlas, vase, star-shaped rim, 10½", from $125 to........................**175.00**
Aurelian, pillow vase, dog w/gamebird in mouth, mk by hand, 7½x8" .**2,000.00**
Baldin, bowl, apples, tan, no mk, 4" H, from $100 to..................**150.00**
Barcelona, vase, hdls, no mk, 8", from $200 to............................**250.00**
Besline, vase, Virginia Creeper etched on gold lustre, label, 11" ..**500.00**
Blossom, vase, mk, ornate hdls, 14", from $175 to......................**225.00**
Blue & Decorated, vase, floral, sm die imp mk, 7½" **225.00**
Blue Drapery, candlesticks, no mk, 9½", pr, from $120 to...........**145.00**
Blue Drapery, jardiniere & pedestal, no mk, 33½" overall, $1,500 to .**1,750.00**
Blue Louwelsa, vase, floral, circle seal mk, cylindrical, 10½"...**1,500.00**
Bonito, vase, bow-tied bouquet, bulbous, tab hdls at shoulder, 10½" ...**450.00**
Bonito, vase, floral, sgn HP, mk, 6", from $125 to **175.00**
Brighton, bluebird on tree stump, die imp mk, 7½", from $500 to ..**700.00**
Brighton, parrot, scrolling perch, no mk, 12½", from $2,500 to ...**3,000.00**
Brighton, parrot on flared ped perch, 7½" **750.00**
Brighton, pheasant, 7x11½" **650.00**
Burntwood, vase, birds/Deco circles, no mk, 8½", from $200 to.**250.00**
Burntwood, vase, floral, no mk, 7", from $125 to **150.00**
Cactus, camel, mk, 4", from $100 to **125.00**
Cameo, vase, wide body/ftd, w/hdls, 4", from $35 to **40.00**
Cameo Jewel, jardiniere & pedestal, 34" overall, from $1,500 to ..**2,000.00**
Candis, vase, gr/wht, script mk, 9", from $75 to..........................**85.00**
Chase, vase, horse/rider jump fence, wht on dk bl, 7½", $400 to.**450.00**
Chengtu, vase, red-orange, classic shape, ½-kiln ink mk, 12".....**225.00**
Chengtu, vase, red-orange, 4-sided, Chengtu label, 8", from $100 to...**125.00**
Clarmont, candlestick, 10" **150.00**
Claywood, spittoon, Deco floral, no mk, 4½" H, from $125 to...**150.00**
Claywood, vase, spider webs, cylindrical, no mk, 5½", from $95 to .**110.00**
Clinton Ivory, vase, figural panels, 6-sided cylinder, 12", $175 to...**225.00**
Colored Glaze, umbrella stand, rtcl/scalloped rim, 22½", $250 to ..**350.00**
Coppertone, candle holder, w/turtle, ½-kiln ink stamp, 3", $375...**425.00**
Coppertone, frog, mk, 4", from $350 to.....................................**400.00**
Coppertone, vase, frog hdls, bulbous, 8", from $1,750 to **2,000.00**
Cornish, jardiniere, mk, 7", from $125 to **150.00**
Dickens I, loving cup, clover, artist sgn, mk w/seal, 5½", $500 to ..**600.00**
Dickens I, pillow vase, lady's bust portrait, ftd, 7" **2,000.00**
Dickens II, adv plate, S Weller Dispelling... on wht, 16", $5,000 to ..**6,000.00**
Dickens II, humidor, skull form, mk in lid, 5½", from $2,500 to .**3,000.00**
Dickens II, mug, Indian portrait: Black Bird, JU, Dickens seal, 6"..**750.00**
Dickens II, vase, knight on wht horse, Upjohn, cylindrical, 14" .**2,750.00**
Dickens III, inkwell, Income Twenty Pounds..., 2½" H, $850 to...**950.00**
Dickens III, teapot, Captain Cuttle..., #5055, mk, 7", from $1,250 to....**1,500.00**
Dickens III, vase, man in long coat, 4-hdl bell, mk #15, 8", $1,250 to ..**1,500.00**
Elberta, jardiniere, 5½"..**100.00**
Eocean, Late Line; vase, floral, sgn MT, 10½", from $450 to......**550.00**
Eocean, vase, fruit, mk, cylinder w/4 rim hdls, 16", from $1,500 to.**1,750.00**
Etched Matt, vase, lady's profile, mk, 11", from $1,250 to.......**1,500.00**
Etched Matt, vase, rose stem, sm die imp mk, 4-sided, 10", $450 to...**550.00**

Ethel, vase, cameo, die imp mk, 11½", $250 to 350.00
Etna, vase, appl frog & emb snake, 6½", from $1,250 to 1,500.00
Etna, vase, jonquils, cylinder w/squatty base, gray to wht, 11", $400 ..550.00
Etna, vase, magnolia, bulbous w/lg hdls, mk Etna, 9", from $350 to..400.00
Fairfield, bowl, cherubs band, ribbed bottom, 4½" 90.00
Flask, BPOE, w/elk, ivory w/brn wash, no mk, 4½", from $125 to....150.00
Flask, Never Dry, ivory w/brn wash, no mk, 6", from $150 to.....175.00
Flemish, jardiniere, floral panels, no mk, 7½", from $140 to 165.00
Flemish, umbrella stand, apples, rnd ink stamp, 22", from $1,000 to..1,250.00
Florenzo, vase, full-kiln ink stamp, ftd, 7", from $90 to...............110.00
Floretta, vase, emb grapes, tapered bottle form, 7½" 150.00
Floretta, vase, floral stem, Floretta dbl-circle seal, 7½", $125 to.150.00
Forest, jardiniere, 4½" 125.00
Forest, jardiniere & pedestal, no mk, 26" overall, from $1,250 to..1,500.00
Forest, window box, no mk, 12" L, from $600 to 700.00
Glendale, console set, 16" bowl+candle holders & flower frog, $900 to..1,000.00
Glendale, vase, birds/butterfly/flowers, paper label/mk, 12", $900 to ..1,000.00
Gloria, vase, #G-22, 8", from $55 to...65.00
Hobart, flower frog, standing nude, no mk, 8½", from $300 to...350.00
Hudson, vase, lg iris, Timberlake, cylinder, ink mk, 8½", $800 to.900.00
Hudson, vase, lg magnolia, Pillsbury, hdls, mk, 13½", $2,500 to .2,750.00
Hudson, vase, swans/limbs, Pillsbury, cylinder, mk, 13½", $4,500 to.5,500.00
Hunter, jug vase, duck, mk Hunter, 7", from $600 to 700.00
Jap Birdimal, jardiniere, bl trees on wht, mk, 14", from $400 to.500.00
Jap Birdimal, vase, geisha girl on rust, sgn VMH, 13", from $2,000 to..2,500.00
Jewel, vase, die imp mk, 9", from $400 to 500.00
Knifewood, vase, lg squirrel on branch, no mk, 11", from $900 to.1,000.00
L'Art Nouveau, Glossy; vase, emb face on dk brn, mk w/seal, 12"...850.00
La Sa, vase, tree scene, no mk, 6", from $225 to 300.00
Lorbeek, vase, fan form, full-kiln ink stamp, 7", from $150 to 175.00
Louella, basket, die imp mk, 6½", from $125 to 150.00
Louselsa, vase, floral, sgn CL, bulbous, 16", from $1,500 to.....2,000.00
Louwelsa, ewer, monk, sgn LJ Burgess, 12½", from $1,250 to...1,500.00
Louwelsa, mug, portrait, Ferrell, #432, 6½", from $800 to.......1,000.00
Louwelsa, vase, fruit, CJ Dibowski, ftd 4-sided twisted form, 12".750.00
Louwelsa, vase, grapes, CJ Dibowsky, trumpet neck, 25" 3,500.00
Malvern, wall pocket, no mk, 11", from $175 to 200.00
Mammy, cookie jar, mk, 11", from $2,000 to...........................2,500.00
Mammy, creamer & sugar bowl w/lid, mk, 3½", from $850 to 950.00
Manhattan, vase, floral lattice around bottom, 5½" 40.00
Marbleized, vase, mk, 10", from $150 to 175.00
Marengo, vase, no mk, 8", from $300 to 350.00
Marvo, vase, trumpet form, full-kiln ink stamp, 11½", from $125 to...150.00
Matt Floretta, tankard, fruit, sgn CD, no mk, 13½", from $600 to ..700.00
Melrose, basket, die imp mk, 10", from $200 to..........................250.00
Mi-Flo, vase, lg hdls, bulbous/ftd, #M-12, 9½", from $100 to.....125.00
Muskota, flower frog, nude on rock, 8", from $700 to 800.00
Muskota, flower frog w/pr of wht geese, no mk, 6", from $500 to.600.00
Muskota, flower frog w/3 boys, die imp mk, 7", from $700 to 800.00
Muskota, girl w/flowers & hat, no mk, 9", from $350 to 450.00
Noval, comport, appl apples on wht w/blk trim, no mk, 5½", $90 to ..115.00
Oak Leaf, vase, mk, 8½", from $75 to.......................................85.00
Panella, basket, mk, 7", from $95 to...110.00
Parian, wall pocket, no mk, 10", from $200 to............................250.00
Patra, basket, mk, 5½", from $225 to 250.00
Patricia, vase, goose hdls, wht, 7", from $85 to...........................100.00
Pearl, vase, no mk, 7", from $125 to...150.00
Pearl, wall pocket, die imp mk, 8½", from $175 to......................225.00
Roba, vase, rim-to-shoulder hdls, 12½"......................................175.00
Roma, bowl, floral garlands/bird reserve, ftd/hdld, 11" L, $250 to ..300.00
Roma, vase, floral panels on ea of 4 sides, no mk, 10", from $100 to..125.00
Roma, wall pocket, ribbon-tied roses, die imp mk, 7", from $300 to ..400.00
Sabrinian, vase, sea horse hdls, ½-kiln ink stamp, 12", from $400 to ..450.00
Scandia, bowl, 3" H..75.00

Selma, vase, allover daisies, die imp mk, 7", from $250 to 300.00
Sicardo, flowers, gold/gr/purple red irid, flaring sides, 5¼x3" 500.00
Sicardo, vase, berries/leaves, cylindrical, 9¾x3½"....................1,000.00
Sicardo, vase, dandelion on ea of 3 sides, sgn, 12½", $2,500 to...3,000.00
Sicardo, vase, mums/twisted leaves, cylinder w/ruffled rim, 9x3", EX...1,300.00
Silvertone, vase, poppy, scallops, hdls, ½-kiln mk, 11½", $750 to..850.00
Stellar, vase, wht stars on blk, bulbous, mk, 5", from $400 to 500.00
Sydonia, cornucopia, mk, 8", from $70 to 80.00
Turada, humidor, wht slip at rim, mk 562/7, 5½", from $350 to .450.00
Tutone, vase, ½-kiln ink stamp, cylindrical, 12½", from $200 to ..250.00
Velva, vase, pod/leaf panel, bulbous w/tab hdls, mk, 9", from $175 to..200.00
Warwick, planter, 3-ftd, branch hdls, 3½" 120.00
White & Decorated, vase, floral, die imp mk, 10", from $250 to...300.00
Woodcraft, hanging basket, apple branch, cone shape, 6", from $150 to ...175.00
Woodcraft, jardiniere, 3-D woodpecker, die imp mk, 5½" H, $550 to .650.00
Woodcraft, vase, fruit on bark texture, cylindrical, no mk, 13"...450.00
Woodcraft, vase, 3-D owl beside hole in tree, mk, 16", $2,250 to..2,500.00
Woodcraft, wall pocket, birds/flowers on branches, 15x13", $3,000 to ...3,500.00
Woodcraft, wall pocket, owl in tree w/lg apple leaves, 10"..........350.00
Woodrose, vase, die imp mk, cylindrical, 7", from $75 to.............85.00
Zona, mug, duck, 3"...95.00
Zona, pitcher, apples on branch, die imp mk, 6", from $100 to ..125.00
Zona, pitcher, kingfisher, ½-kiln ink stamp, 8", from $400 to.....450.00
Zona, umbrella stand, girls w/floral garlands under leafy bower, 21"....3,000.00

Western Americana

The collecting of Western Americana encompasses a broad spectrum of memorabilia. Examples of various areas within the main stream would include the following fields: weapons, bottles, photographs, mining/railroad artifacts, cowboy paraphernalia, farm and ranch implements, maps, barbed wire, tokens, Indian relics, saloon/gambling items, and branding irons. Some of these areas have their own separate listings in this book. Western Americana is not only a collecting field but is also a collecting era with specific boundries. Depending upon which field the collector decides to specialize in, prices can start at a few dollars and run into the thousands.

Our advisor for this category is Bill Mackin, author of *Cowboy and Gunfighter Collectibles* (order from the author); he is listed in the Directory under Colorado.

Bit, forged iron formed as ladies' bodies, orig chin strap, 20th C..125.00
Bit, nude lady, chased silver o/l..175.00
Book, Rustlings in Rockies: Hunting & Fishing, Shields, 1883, 1st ed...48.00
Branding iron, hand-wrought iron, 3-letter, 5x3", 25" L................65.00
Branding iron, hand-wrought iron, 4x3" arrow, 34" L...................75.00
Bridle, hitched horsehair & braided rawhide, w/reins, 1930s, 24x7x80" ...900.00
Bridle, prison-made hitched horsehair, reins/quirt/glass rosette, '30s ...2,200.00
Chaps, leather, traditional type w/brass studs, ca 1955, 39" 250.00
Chaps, shotgun type w/fringe, illegible mk, ca 1890, EX............750.00
Cinch, horsehair, Whitman-Melbach, 1917................................85.00
Coat, horsehide, long, EX...300.00
Cuffs, leather w/brass star-design studs, ca 1900, pr....................250.00
Gun belt, leather, handmade, holds pistol & cartridge, 1870s, 42"..275.00
Hat, cowboy's, Plainsman's style, nutria, early 1900s, EX...........250.00
Hitching post, CI, horse-head finial, late 1800s, 10x7½x3"........135.00
Mittens, leather & cowhide, lined, 14" w/9" opening, pr............150.00
Postcard, mtn & US Mail coach scene, NV, ca 1910, VG 45.00
Quirt, blk & orange horsehair, finely hitched, 1920s, EX............350.00
Saddle, child's, Red Ranger, tooled leather, padded seat, 1960 ...200.00
Saddle, lady's side; tooled leather, silk stitching, 1880s, EX 300.00
Saddle, pack; saw-buck, wooden tree, w/cinch & rigging, 1930s, 20x12" ...75.00
Saddle, Western Saddle Co, Denver, VG......................................300.00
Sign, Cattle Crossing, pnt tin in wood fr, ca 1900, 20x26" 300.00

Spurs, Buermann, CA style w/jingle bobs, chains, pr 175.00
Spurs, Buermann, Hercules, bronze, drop shank, pr......................285.00
Spurs, eng silver conchos, leather straps mk JS Collins..............475.00
Spurs, Mexican, silver inlay bottle opener, Colonial, pr.............550.00
Spurs, silver, mtd, tooled designs, conical jingle bobs, 1930s, 8x4"....225.00
Spurs, sterling, mtd, horseshoe designs, 1930s, 9x4" 500.00
Spurs, str shank, chased rowels, pr..225.00
Stirrups, oxbow; rawhide-covered leather, pr, EX........................95.00
Ticket, Buffalo Bill Wild West Show, Circus Flora, 2½", G........120.00
Whip, braided leather, 19th C, 60"+, EX...................................100.00
Whip, leather-wrapped stock, 14', EX 185.00

Western Pottery Manufacturing Company

This pottery was originally founded as the Denver China and Pottery Company; William Long was the owner. The company's assets were sold to a group who in 1905 formed the Western Pottery Manufacturing Company, located at 16th Street and Alcott in Denver, Colorado. By 1926, 186 different items were being produced, including crocks, flowerpots, kitchen items, and other stoneware. The company dissolved in 1936.

Seven various marks were used during the years, and values may be higher for items that carry a rare mark. Numbers within the descriptions refer to specific marks, see the line drawings. Prices may vary depending on demand and locale. Our advisors for this category are Cathy Segelke and Pat James; they are listed in the Directory under Colorado.

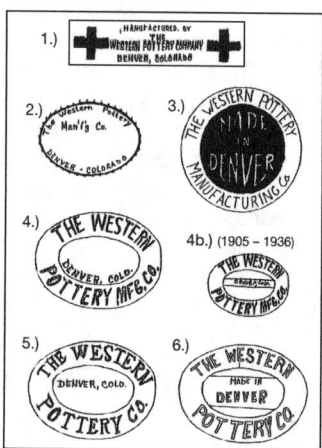

Churn, #2, hdl, 4-gal, M 75.00
Churn, #2, hdl, 5-gal, M 65.00
Churn, #2, no lid, 5-gal, G...80.00
Crock, #4, bail lip, 4-gal, G..55.00
Crock, #4, hdl, no lid, 8-gal, M 90.00
Crock, #4, ice water; bl/wht sponge pnt, 3-gal, NM..............30.00
Crock, #4, 6-gal, EX 72.00
Crock, #4b, 20-gal, M 200.00
Crock, #4b, 22x17½", 15-gal, NM 150.00
Crock, #5, bail lip, 1½-gal, M..45.00
Crock, #5, no lid, 6-gal, M 70.00
Crock, #6, wire hdl, 10-gal, NM...100.00
Crock, #6, 3-gal, M...40.00
Crock, #6, 4-gal, M...50.00
Crock, #6, 5-gal, NM 60.00
Foot warmer, #6, M..60.00
Jug, #6, brn/wht, 1-gal, EX 25.00
Jug, #6, brn/wht, 5-gal, M 75.00
Rabbit feeder, #1, EX 25.00
Rabbit waterer, #1, M...25.00

Western Stoneware Co.

The Western Stoneware Co., Monmouth, Illinois, was formed in 1906 as a merger of seven potteries: Monmouth Pottery Co., Monmouth, IL; Weir Pottery Co., Monmouth, IL; Macomb Pottery Co. and Macomb Stoneware Co., Macomb, IL; D. Culbertson Stoneware Co., Whitehall, IL; Clinton Stoneware Co., Clinton, MO; and Fort Dodge Stoneware Co., Fort Dodge, IA.

Western Stoneware Co. manufactured stoneware, gardenware, flowerpots, artware, and dinnerware. Some early crocks, jugs, and churns are found with a plant number in the Maple Leaf logo. Plants 1 through 7 turn up. In 1926 an artware line was introduced as the Monmouth Pottery Artware. One by one each branch of the operation closed, and today one branch remains. Western Stoneware Co. is still in operation in Monmouth, Illinois, on the site of the Weir Pottery Co. Our advisor for this category is Jim Martin; he is listed in the Directory under Illinois.

See also Old Sleepy Eye.

Beehive jug, brn & wht, 1-gal...100.00
Birdbath, Burntwood finish...200.00
Bowl, bl banded, w/advertising 85.00
Chicken waterer, 1-gal 125.00
Churn, flowers on side, 3-gal 200.00
Churn, Maple Leaf (plant 6) mk, 6-gal 250.00
Churn, Maple Leaf mk, 1-gal..1,200.00
Churn, Maple Leaf mk, 2-gal...200.00
Churn, Maple Leaf mk, mini...1,000.00
Crock, Maple Leaf mk, 5-gal...60.00
Crock, Maple Leaf mk, 20-gal...125.00
Crock, Maple Leaf mk, mini..700.00
Custard cup, Colonial..350.00
Flowerpot/ashtray, Cardinal, red flowerpot clay, no glaze 150.00
Hot water bottle, pig, bl tint...225.00
Ice water cooler, bl sponge, w/lid & spigot, 4-gal 1,500.00
Jar, Maple Leaf & oval mk, 2-gal 50.00
Jardiniere, Egyptian motif, brn-glazed int, 7" 75.00
Jug, Monmouth advertising, 1-qt..125.00
Lard jar, w/lid, bl tint 200.00
Monkey jug, brn & wht, 1-gal 200.00
Paperweight, Maple Leaf, gr & brn...55.00
Shakers, 2nd Nat'l Bank, pr..30.00
Sugar jar, w/lid, bl tint..250.00
Wall pocket, Egyptian, Burntwood, #312 ....60.00
Water cooler, Cupid, bl & wht...1,000.00
Water cooler, Egyptian motif, 9¼x11", M..............................450.00
Water cooler, emb maple leaves, bl & wht, w/lid & spigot, 4-gal...2,000.00
Water cooler, Maple Leaf mk, no lid or spigot, 2-gal.................400.00

Westmoreland

Originally titled the Specialty Glass Company, Westmoreland began operations in East Liverpool, Ohio, producing utility items as well as tableware in milk glass and crystal. When the company moved to Grapeville, Pennsylvania, in 1890, lamps, vases, covered animal dishes, and decorative plates were introduced. Prior to 1920 Westmoreland was a major manufacturer of carnival glass and soon thereafter added a line of lovely reproduction art glass items. High-quality milk glass became their speciality, accounting for about 90% of their production. Black glass was introduced in the 1940s, and later in the decade ruby-stained pieces and items decorated in the Mary Gregory style became fashionable. By the 1960s colored glassware was being produced, examples of which are very popular with collectors today. Early pieces were marked with a paper label; by the 1960s the ware was embossed with a superimposed 'WG.' The last mark was a circle containing 'Westmoreland' around the perimeter and a large 'W' in the center. The company closed in 1985, and on February 28, 1996, the factory burned to the ground.

Note: Though you may find pieces very similar to Westmoreland's, their Della Robbia has no bananas among the fruits relief. In the descriptions that follow, items in this pattern described as 'crystal with trim' refers to those pieces with the colored lustre stains.

Our advisor for this category is Philip Rosso, Jr. He is listed in the Directory under Pennsylvania.

See also Animal Dishes with Covers; Carnival Glass; Glass Animals.

Ashtray, Beaded Grape/#1884, milk glass w/Roses & Bows, 6½x6½" ...35.00
Basket, Paneled Grape, milk glass, oval, 6½" 25.00
Basket, Paneled Grape/#1881, Brandywine Blue or Golden Sunset, 8".150.00
Basket, Wakefield, crystal w/red stain, 6" 65.00
Bell, Cameo/#754, w/Beaded Bouquet trim, any color...................35.00
Bowl, banana; Doric, milk glass, ftd, 11" 30.00
Bowl, banana; Old Quilt, milk glass, ftd, 11", from $75 to 85.00
Bowl, banana; Paneled Grape, milk glass, ftd, 12" 175.00
Bowl, centerpiece; star shape, gr or purple marbled 50.00
Bowl, English Hobnail, turq/ice bl, rolled edge, 11" 80.00
Bowl, nappy, Beaded Edge, milk glass w/red edge, 5" 6.50
Bowl, nappy, Della Robbia, crystal w/trim, 7½" 45.00
Bowl, nappy, Princess Feather, amber or crystal, 5" 8.00
Bowl, Paneled Grape, milk glass, lipped, 9" 45.00
Bowl, purple or gr slag, leaf form, #300 ....45.00
Bowl, Thousand Eye, 2-hdl, 10" 37.50
Bowl, vegetable; Lotus, amber, crystal or wht satin, oval...............55.00
Bowl, vegetable; Lotus, bl, gr or pk 85.00
Bowl (Grandfather), Sawtooth/#556, Almond, Antique Green or Mint Green..145.00
Box, trinket; any Mist color, 4-ftd, sq, #1902 ....25.00
Box, trinket; egg, any Mist color w/wht daisy, w/lid.......................25.00
Butter/cheese dish, Old Quilt, purple marbled carnival, rnd 95.00
Cake salver, Old Quilt, milk glass, skirted, bell ft, 12" 75.00
Candelabrum, Paneled Grape, milk glass, 3-light, ea......................195.00
Candy jar, Della Robbia, crystal w/trim, scalloped edge, w/lid 125.00
Canister, Paneled Grape, milk glass, 11" 250.00
Compote, Brandywine Blue Opal, crimped/ruffled, ftd, 6½" 45.00
Compote, honey; Lotus, bl, gr or pk, 6½" 25.00
Compote, mint; Wakefield, crystal w/red stain, high ft, 5½".........30.00
Compote, Paneled Grape, milk glass, crimped, ftd, 9" 80.00
Creamer, Beaded Edge, milk glass w/decor, ftd...............................17.50
Creamer, Lotus, amber, crystal or wht satin.....................................22.00
Creamer, Princess Feather, amber or crystal 10.00
Creamer, Princess Feather, pk or gr..20.00
Decanter, wine; Paneled Grape, milk glass.......................................165.00
Epergne vase, Paneled Grape, milk glass, pattern at top..............225.00
Flowerpot, Paneled Grape, milk glass 47.50
Goblet, water; Paneled Grape, milk glass, 8-oz 18.00
Lamp, boudoir; English Hobnail/#555, milk glass, stick std/flat base..45.00
Lamp, electric; any child's decor, wood base, w/shade, mini..........80.00
Lamp, fairy; Thousand Eye, ruby, flat or ftd....................................50.00
Lamp, fairy; Waterford, any Mist w/HP flowers, low ft, 2-pc.........75.00
Mayonnaise, English Hobnail, pk, 6"..20.00
Napkin ring, Brown, Light Blue or Pink Mist w/flower, 6-sided....35.00
Novelty, egg on gold stand, Almond w/decal or Crystal Mist w/floral.50.00
Novelty, egg on gold stand, blk, plain, hollow 40.00
Novelty, revolver, blk or crystal w/blk HP grips, solid 90.00
Pin tray, Heart/#1820, Blue Mist 22.00
Plate, Beaded Edge, milk glass w/decor, 10½" 65.00
Plate, blk w/Christmas nativity decor, #PL-8, 8½" 50.00
Plate, Della Robbia, crystal w/trim, 10½", minimum value.........150.00
Plate, English Hobnail, turq/ice bl, 8½" 78.00

Plate, Forget-me-not/#2, Blue or Brown Mist, Mary Gregory style, 8" ..60.00
Plate, Hearts, Almond or Mint Green w/dogwood decal, heart shape, 8" ..30.00
Plate, Lotus, amber, crystal or wht satin, flared, 13" 35.00
Plate, Paneled Grape, milk glass, 14½" 125.00
Plate, Paneled Grape/#1881, Bicentennial decor, ltd ed, 14½"...225.00
Plate, Princess Feather, amber or crystal, 10½" 15.00
Plate, Thousand Eye, 8½" 10.00
Plate, Wakefield, crystal w/red stain, 8½" 30.00
Plate, Wicket border, milk glass w/Revolutionary War scenes, 9"..60.00
Relish, Thousand Eye, 10" dia 30.00
Sauce boat, Paneled Grape, milk glass..45.00
Shakers, Beaded Edge, milk glass, pr...15.00
Shakers, Beaded Edge, milk glass w/decor, pr, from $50 to 70.00
Shakers, Paneled Grape, milk glass, flat, lg, 4½", pr 52.50
Sherbet, English Hobnail, pk, sq ft, high stem 15.00
Sherbet, English Hobnail, turq/ice bl, sq ft, high stem 35.00
Sherbet, Princess Feather, amber or crystal, 6-oz............................8.00
Sugar bowl, Beaded Edge, milk glass w/decor, ftd...........................17.50
Tray, tidbit; Dolphin, any color other than Crystal Mist, center hdl..45.00
Tray, tidbit; Paneled Grape, milk glass w/poinsettia decor, 2-tier .100.00
Tumbler, Beaded Edge, milk glass w/decor, ftd, 8-oz.......................18.00
Tumbler, Della Robbia, crystal w/stain, ftd, 8-oz 30.00
Tumbler, Della Robbia, crystal w/stain, str sides, 12-oz.................40.00
Tumbler, Lotus, bl, gr or pk, 10-oz 25.00
Tumbler, Paneled Grape, milk glass, 5-oz 24.00
Vase, swung; Paneled Grape, milk glass, 14" 25.00
Vase, Wakefield, crystal w/red stain, crimped top 45.00

Wheatley, T. J.

In 1880 after a brief association with the Coultry Works, Thomas J. Wheatley opened his own studio in Cincinnati, Ohio, claiming to have been the first to discover the secret of under-glaze slip decoration on an unbaked clay vessel. He applied for and was granted a patent for his process. Demand for his ware increased to the point that several artists were hired to decorate the ware. The company incorporated in 1880 as the Cincinnati Art Pottery, but until 1882 it continued to operate under Wheatley's name. Ware from this period is marked 'T.J. Wheatley' or 'T.J.W. and Co.,' and it may be dated.

Matt green pieces dominate today's marketplace and will bring much more than the decorated pieces. The matt green pieces are seldom, if ever, marked or dated.

Humidor, gr matt, Arts & Crafts decor, prof rstr, 7½x5" 475.00
Pitcher, landscape (Limoges style), blk/teal/royal/wht, 1880, 6¼" ..500.00
Vase, curdled gr matt, can w/4 flaring buttresses & mid band, 8x9"..1,600.00
Vase, curdled gr matt, 4 flaring buttresses, WP/640, 8x9", NM.1,840.00
Vase, floral on brn to ivory, sgn MG, 1880, 8", NM 100.00

Whieldon

Thomas Whieldon was regarded as the finest of the Staffordshire potters of the mid-1700s. He produced marbled and black Egyptian wares as well as tortoise shell, a mottled brown-glazed earthenware accented with touches of blue and yellow. In 1754 he became a partner of Josiah Wedgwood. Other potters produced similar wares, and today the term Whieldon is used generically.

Jug, tortoise shell w/emb figures/lion mask, ftd pear form, 1770s, 5".265.00
Plate, tortoise shell w/brn sponging & bl & gr spots center/rim, 10".495.00
Teapot, globular, bird finial, crabstock hdl, paw ft, 1770, 3¾" 550.00
Teapot, tortoise shell, 18th C, 4¾", EX...365.00

Wicker

Wicker is the basket-like material used in many types of furniture and accessories. It may be made from bamboo cane, rattan, reed, or artificial fibers. It is airy, lightweight, and very popular in hot regions. Imported from the Orient in the eighteenth century, it was first manufactured in the United States in about 1850. The elaborate, closely woven Victorian designs belong to the mid- to late 1800s, and the simple styles with coarse reedings usually indicate a post-1900 production. Art Deco styles followed in the '20s and '30s. The most important consideration in buying wicker is condition — it can be restored, but only by a professional. Age is an important factor, but be aware that 'Victorian-style' furniture is being manufactured today.

Key:
HB — Heywood Bros.
H/W — Heywood Wakefield
WRC — Wakefield Rattan Company

Armchair rocker, natural, shaped top/sides, fancy bk, 41", EX....**425.00**
Armchair rocker, natural, spirals w/cane seat/bk, HB, VG..........**150.00**
Baby carriage, iron fr, parasol, H/W, VG......................................**225.00**
Chair, corner; very ornate: curlicues/plume crest, rolled arms, 37"...**225.00**
Chair, lattice & braid, full skirt, wrapped ft, 1920s, 37x25"........**625.00**
Chair, reception; curlicues & hearts, birdcage, 1890s, 45x20"....**675.00**
Chair, rolled bk, ball-decor spirals, WRC, 30"............................**480.00**
Chair, serpentine bk, curlicues, rolled arms, WRC, 1890s, 30x24"..**875.00**
Chair, wing; wide arms, latticework, skirt, 1910s, 43x31"..........**975.00**
Chair, woven w/center curlicue panel, rolled arms, skirt, 1890s, 44"..**900.00**
Chaise lounge, overall lattice & braid, skirted, 1920s, 40x67"..**1,650.00**
Chaise lounge, plain tight weave, skirted, 1920s.........................**600.00**
Chest, blanket; dmn patterns, lift lid, H/W, ca 1910, 15x49x19"..**975.00**
Chest, 4-drw, ribbon & floral fronts, trn moldings, 1915, 42x28x18"..**1,650.00**
Coat tree, woven base, wrapped pole w/gesso flowers, 1900s, child sz....**400.00**
Cradle, swings between wrapped posts, VG.................................**200.00**
Cradle, swings from fr, HB, 1880s, 55x44x23", G....................**1,295.00**
Day bed/porch glider, worn uphl, Loyd Loom, 1920s-30s, 82" L..**1,250.00**
Desk/vanity, w/letter holders/drw, natural, 1920s, +skirted chair.**1,450.00**
Doll carriage, hooded top, simple weave, lg wood wheels, 46"....**500.00**
Footstool, woven contour top, curlicue ends, skirt, 1900s, 18x23x16"..**675.00**
Lamp, floor; pnt, 3-socket, removable shade, 72", EX.................**650.00**
Loveseat, rolled-bk str crestrail, curlicue arms/legs/apron, 3-color.**1,800.00**
Parlor set, serpentine bks/arms, curlicues, H/W, settee+2 chairs..**3,850.00**
Parlor set, tight dmn-pattern, skirts, 1930s, sofa+2chairs+sm table..**4,850.00**
Pie caddy, 3 lattice shelves w/braid, 4-leg, 1900s, 39x14" dia......**450.00**
Planter, cabriole legs w/scrolls, lower shelf, simple weave, 28"....**225.00**
Rocker, arm; ball & spiral decor, caned seat, HB, 37", VG.........**150.00**
Rocker, arm; shaped tips, fancy intricate bk, 41", EX.................**450.00**
Rocker, crest w/curlicues, ornate arms, WRC, 1890s..................**975.00**
Rocker, hearts & star patterns, cane seat, 1880s, 36x22"..........**695.00**
Rocker, lady's, bk shaped as daisy on leafy stem, arms, 39".........**400.00**
Rocker, lattice & geometrics, spring cushion, 1920s, 39x32"......**575.00**
Rocker, ornate beadwork bk & arms, curlicues, 1880s, 38x23"...**975.00**
Rocker, platform; serpentine bk w/rosettes, curlicues, 1890s, 44".**1,650.00**
Rocker, platform; serpentine bk/rolled arms, old pnt, 1890s, 43"..**1,250.00**
Rocker, rolled continuous arm/crestrail/apron, patterned cane bk, 37".**550.00**
Rocker, serpentine bk & arms, woven seat, skirt, 1890s, child sz..**495.00**
Rocker, serpentine heart-pattern bk, skirt, 1890s, 45"..............**975.00**
Settee, arched lattice bk, skirtings, springs, ca 1915, 41x51"...**1,150.00**
Settee, serpentine bk, beadwork/curlicues, cane seat, HB, 1890s, 42"..**2,250.00**
Settee, serpentine bk, kidney-shaped seat, skirt, 1890s, 31x38"...**1,450.00**
Settee, serpentine bk/arms, 2-heart bk, curlicues, Whitney, 1890s, sm..**1,850.00**
Sofa, serpentine roll, full skirt, wrapped ft, 1920s, 45x71x25", EX..**2,850.00**
Sofa, tight-weave dmns, full skirt, 1920s, 39x71", EX..............**1,850.00**

Stand, fern; ped ft, hdls, lattice panels, 1900s, 37x16" dia.........**495.00**
Stand, sewing; beadwork & loopings, shelf, H/W, 1890s, 27½x19x17".**875.00**
Stand, sewing; curlicues, fancy splayed legs, basket in base, 1890s..**875.00**
Table, console; wood top, lattice skirt, H/W, 1920s, 24x25x12".**450.00**
Table, wood fr, skirt, dbl birdcage, 4-ftd ped, 1890s, 30" sq......**1,950.00**
Table, wood top, birdcage & curlicues, shelf, 1890s, 31x16" dia.**795.00**
Table, wood top, simple weave, galleried lower shelf, 31x25" dia.**550.00**
Table, woven dbl ped & shelf, splayed legs, 1920s, 30x88x18".**1,850.00**
Tea cart, glass top, shelf, wrapped hdl/legs, skirt, 1900s, EX....**1,250.00**

Will-George

After years of working in the family garage, William and George Climes founded the Will-George company in Los Angeles, California, in 1934. They manufactured high-quality artware, utilizing both porcelain and earthenware clays. Both brothers, motivated by their love of art pottery, had extensive education and training in manufacturing processes as well as decoration. In 1940 actor Edgar Bergen, a collector of pottery, developed a relationship with the brothers and invested in their business. With this new influx of funds, the company relocated to Pasadena. There they produced an extensive line of art pottery, but they excelled in their creation of bird and animal figurines. In addition, they molded a large line of human figurines similar to Royal Doulton. The brothers, now employing a staff of decorators, precisely molded their pieces with great care and strong emphasis on originality and detail, creating high-quality works of art that were only carried by exclusive gift stores.

In the late 1940s after a split with Bergen, the company moved to San Gabriel to a larger, more modern location and renamed themselves The Claysmiths. Their business flourished and they were able to successfully mass produce many items; but due to the abundance of cheap, postwar imports from Italy and Japan that were then flooding the market, they liquidated the business in 1956. Our advisor for this category is Marty Webster. He is listed in the Directory under Michigan.

Ashtray, chicken (4") in center, 8" sq..**65.00**
Bird figurine, Baltimore Oriole..**155.00**
Bird figurine, bluebird, 3¼"..**45.00**
Bird figurine, cardinal on branch, 10"..**75.00**
Bird figurine, cardinal on branch, 12½".....................................**150.00**
Bird figurine, eagle on rock, wht/brn, 10"..................................**150.00**
Bird figurine, female pheasant...**110.00**
Bird figurine, flamingo, head trn, 10"..**200.00**
Bird figurine, flamingo, head up, 5½"...**115.00**
Bird figurine, flamingo, head up, 11¼".......................................**155.00**
Bird figurine, flamingo, head up/facing bk, 7½".........................**150.00**
Bird figurine, flamingo, preening, 10"...**200.00**
Bird figurine, flamingo, wings spread, 15½"...............................**275.00**
Bird figurine, flamingo beside stump, 7¼"..................................**180.00**
Bird figurine, mallard duck w/spread wings, 7x11"......................**195.00**
Bird figurine, parrot (mc) on branch, 15"...................................**200.00**
Bird figurine, pheasant, red breast, 6x14"..................................**255.00**
Bird figurine, robin, seated, 3"..**45.00**
Bowl, flamingo pond, 14x9"...**65.00**
Bowl, serving; red onion form, 2x13x10"......................................**65.00**
Box, Oriental figure kneeling on lid, 1x4x4"................................**50.00**
Candle holders, lily design, pr..**120.00**
Figurine, artist holding palette, mc, 8".......................................**95.00**
Figurine, Asian girl w/pot on shoulder, 8½"...............................**100.00**
Figurine, boy holding frog on base, mc, 9".................................**95.00**
Figurine, dachshund, 6½x9"..**200.00**
Figurine, giraffe, 14½"..**150.00**
Figurine, giraffes, seated pr, 11x7"..**180.00**
Figurine, girl holding doll on base, mc, 9"...................................**125.00**

Figurine, hula dancer, wht skirt, 12" 155.00
Figurine, monk, brn bsk, 4½" 50.00
Figurine, monk, brn bsk, 5½" 75.00
Figurine, nubian, topless w/rose scarf, 7½" 185.00
Figurine, Polynesian seated female, 5½" 80.00
Pitcher, chicken figural, mc, 7" 125.00
Tumbler, chicken figural, mc, 4½" 50.00
Vase, Chinese girl seated before pillow form, 5" 85.00
Wine glass, chicken figural, mc, 5" 55.00

Willets

The Willets Manufacturing Company of Trenton, New Jersey, produced a type of belleek porcelain during the late 1880s and 1890s. Examples were often marked with a coiled snake that formed a 'W' with 'Willets' below and 'Belleek' above. Not all Willets is factory decorated. Items painted by amateurs outside the factory are worth considerably less. High prices usually equate with fine artwork. In the listings below, all items are belleek unless noted otherwise. Our advisor for this category is Mary Frank Gaston.

Bowl, HP flowers & berries, 7½" sq. 250.00
Bowl, vintage, gold on wht, 3x8" 190.00
Chalice, roses in pk/ruby, wide gold rim/int, Royston, 11" 450.00
Charger, floral, ca 1895, 15" 375.00
Cup & saucer, demitasse; cream w/dragon hdl, 1895 mk 60.00
Hatpin holder, floral w/silver o/l, 4½", NM 120.00
Jar, peacocks, w/lid, 10" 200.00
Mug, no decor, lizard hdl, mk, 5½" 115.00
Mug, red currants w/gr leaves, 5½" 90.00
Pitcher, birds on gray, 10½" 200.00
Pitcher, purple grapes w/mc leaves, serpent mk, 6½" 300.00
Pitcher, tankard; seated man w/glass, sgn Doering, 14" 700.00
Sugar shaker, wht w/no decor, 4½" 100.00
Tankard, monk drinking/resting on dk gr, 15" 195.00
Urn, heavy silver o/l on pk to gr, rtcl hdls, 8½x7½" 950.00
Vase, lion portrait, brn mk, ca 1885, 8" 500.00
Vase, poppies, artist sgn, 8" 100.00
Vase, stylized flowers, bl on pearl w/gold, 2¾" 145.00
Vase, yel roses & lilacs, 14" 425.00
Vase, 2 egrets on pk & blk, tapering shape, 11⅝" 350.00

Winchester

The Winchester Repeating Arms Company lost their important government contract after WWI and of necessity turned to the manufacture of sporting goods, hardware items, tools, etc., to augment their gun production. Between 1920 and 1931, over 7,500 different items, each marked 'Winchester Trademark U.S.A.,' were offered for sale by thousands of Winchester Hardware stores throughout the country. After 1931 the firm became Winchester-Western. Collectors prefer the prewar items, and the majority of our listings are from this era.

Concerning current collecting trends: Oil cans that a short time ago could be purchased for $2.00 to $5.00 now often sell for $25.00, some over $50.00, and demand is high. Good examples of advertising posters and calendars seem to have no upper limits and are difficult to find. Winchester fishing lures are strong, and the presence of original boxes increases values by 25% to 40%. Another current trend concerns the price of 'diecuts' (cardboard stand-ups, signs, or hanging signs). These are out-pricing many other items. A short time ago the average value of a 'diecut' ranged from $25.00 to $45.00. Current values for most are in the $200.00 to $500.00 range, with some approaching $1,000.00.

Our advisor for this category is James Anderson; he is listed in the Directory under Minnesota.

See also Knives.

Axe, bit; 8¾x4½" w/34" hdl, VG+ 90.00
Barrel reflector, EX 145.00
Brochure, Model 42 410 Repeating Shotgun, fold-out, 6½x3½", EX .95.00
Calendar, 1923, man on rock looking into valley, January only, 14x26" ..1,670.00
Catalog, #80, 1916, 224 pgs, 8½x5½", VG+ 85.00
Display rack, Flashlight/Batteries, Olin Winchester, metal, 35x4", EX ...80.00
Drill, breast; #8733, built-in level, EX 165.00
Envelope, mailing; Winchester Repeating Arms, EX 55.00
Family scale, VG 85.00
Fielder's glove, right handed, G 500.00
Flashlight, Penlite #1710, W on clip, M (EX orig box) 50.00
Food grinder, #W12, metal w/wood hdl, screw clamp, EX 60.00
Gold bug spoon, VG+ 60.00
Hammer, ball-peen; 3" head w/12½" handle, EX+ 190.00
Hammer, claw; #6002, mk 13 on hdl, EX 80.00
Hatchet, produce; mk #17, EX 110.00
Hatchet, w/nail puller, mk leather sheath, EX 130.00
Jack knife, 2-blade, VG+ 190.00
Knife, #1083, serrated on 1 side, str-edge on other, 9⅞", EX ...225.00
Lacquer brush, VG 85.00
Level, #9864, 3 bubble vials, 2¼x18", VG+ 240.00
Magnifying glass, mk Winchester/United States Property, 6¼", EX .50.00
Meat grinder, G 60.00
Multi-wobbler, VG 400.00
Padlock, Six Lever, w/orig key, VG+ 100.00
Plane, #W5, EX 60.00
Plane, #26, wood hdl & base, 15", EX 60.00
Plane, #3004, EX 45.00
Plane, bottom; #3041, 9", EX 120.00
Plane, bullnose; #3098, Winchester Trade Mark, 4", EX+ 350.00
Plane, scraper; #3076, EX 100.00
Plane, scraper; #3080, NM 210.00
Plane, smooth; #3206, rpr hdl, 10" 60.00
Portfolio, Winchester Big Game 78, 4 pics, Douglas Allen, 1978, EX ..50.00
Poster, Commemorative Boy Scouts of America 22, 18x7½", EX ..185.00
Poster, forest scene, Edward Knobels, 30x14½", VG 1,350.00
Razor strap, #8370, Radium Finish, 2x25", VG+ 160.00
Ruler, 4-fold, wood & brass, 1920-1931, 24", EX 100.00
Saw, hand; Old Trusty, 8-point skew bk, eng hdl, 26", EX 100.00
Saw, wood; 32", G 210.00
Scissors, mk Winchester Trade Mark Made in USA, 7½" 60.00
Screwdriver, #7160, wood hdl w/brass ferrule, 3¼", EX 50.00
Shotgun shells, Dummies, Winchester Ranger 20 Gauge, 21 in EX (VG box) ...60.00
Spade, G- 125.00
Square, #W10, 8x12", EX 165.00
Tennis racket, #W2, G 165.00
Thermometer, Winchester Western AA Clay Target, shell shape, 27" ..115.00
Tin, Gun Oil, gr label, 3-oz, 4¾", EX 160.00
Tin, Gun Oil, gr w/blk letters & red Winchester, 1920s, 4¾", EX ..225.00
Waffle iron, electric, 1923, 1924 Pat dates, chrome finish, EX ...400.00
Wrench, double-end S; #1810, EX 80.00
Wrench, pipe; #1023, wood hdl, mk Pat 3-14-22, 14", EX 50.00
Wrench, pipe; #1030, all metal, mk Pat 3-14-22, 6", EX 75.00

Windmill Weights

Windmill weights made of cast iron were used to protect the windmill's plunger rod from damage during high winds by adding weight that slowed down the speed of the blades.

Bull, Fairbury, old silver pnt, flat, 19½x24½"+base.....................**635.00**
Bull, Fairbury, traces of red/blk pnt, EX detail & molding, 12x14".**1,765.00**
Bull, Fairbury, wht w/blk spots on gr base, rpr/pnt wear, 13x14"..**1,500.00**
Bull, flat, old pnt, no lettering, 18½x24½"+lg base.................**1,035.00**
Bull, Simpson (att), pnt traces, full body, 12½x14⅛".............**1,095.00**
Horse, Dempster, bob tail, old dk red pnt, 16⅞x17¼x¾"...........**265.00**
Horse, Dempster, long tail, 15x16"..**180.00**
Rooster, blk pnt, attched to long CI stem, 34x17"...................**1,600.00**
Rooster, Elgin, silver w/red & wht pnt, C-shaped base, 19x16"+base..**1,150.00**
Rooster, Elgin, taupe w/red details, 15¾x16½"+C-shape base....**800.00**
Rooster, Elgin (att), old mc pnt, 19x18"+open-ended C-shaped base..**800.00**
Rooster, Elgin (att), old wht w/red, 10FT NO 2 on tail, 16x17"+base..**1,950.00**
Rooster, Hummer; Elgin, old mc pnt, short stem, 9x10" **575.00**
Rooster, Hummer; Elgin, old mc pnt, 17½x16½"+base **1,265.00**
Rooster, Mogul; Elgin (att), old mc pnt, 18¾x10"+disk base ..**3,100.00**
Squirrel, Elgin (att), old pnt traces, 15½x13½" **1,950.00**

Wire Ware

Very primitive wire was first made by cutting sheet metal into strips which were shaped with mallet and file. By the late thirteenth century, craftsmen in Europe had developed a method of pulling these strips through progressively smaller holes until the desired gauge was obtained. During the Industrial Revolution of the late 1800s, machinery was developed that could produce wire cheaply and easily; and it became a popular commercial commodity. It was used to produce large items such as garden benches and fencing as well as innumerable small pieces for use in the kitchen or on the farm. Beware of reproductions. Our advisor for this category is Rosella Tinsley; she is listed in the Directory under Kansas.

Bacon rack, 6-prong, heavy wire, hook at top.................................**20.00**
Basket, egg; bail hdl, ftd, EX patina, ca 1900, 12¼x8" **110.00**
Basket, egg; top opens like flower, ftd, 7½x4" **60.00**
Basket, heavy wire in designs, ftd, hdld, 10" dia **95.00**
Basket, laundry; collapsible, 4 legs w/wheels, 30x22" dia, EX........**50.00**
Basket, lg loopy pattern, old gr pnt, ca 1900, 8x14½" **130.00**
Basket, mc geometric majolica 5¾" plate in bottom, hdls, 8⅛" dia...**165.00**
Basket, vegetable; coiled hdl & ft, 1920s, 12x10"........................**100.00**
Comb holder, twisted, fancy top, wall mt.....................................**125.00**
Compote, crimped, old dk surface, ca 1900, 7x9" **295.00**
Egg tongs, heavy oval circular wire, squeeze hdl, 11" L **45.00**
Holder, 4 sm baskets joined at center hdl, old wht pnt, 8½x5" dia...**65.00**
Lettuce washer, collapsing basket form, INOX, EX.......................**20.00**
Plant stand, 2 lattice shelves w/scroll braces, wht pnt, 44x37" ...**325.00**
Rack, cooling; flat grid w/border & ft, ca 1900, 8x12" **120.00**
Rack, cooling; scalloped edge, ca 1900, 12" dia **80.00**
Rack, plate; 4-tier, 1900s, holders: 7¾" dia, 10½" overall............**85.00**
Rolling pin holder, heavy wire, hangs vertically, rare **65.00**
Soap dish, twisted wire, fancy wire bk w/loop **75.00**
Soap saver, oblong screenwire shape, wire & wood hdl **25.00**
Tea ball, egg shape, ½" tin band ea side, 2¾" **28.00**
Whisk, fancy twisted stem, target-shaped base, 1870s, 11½" **70.00**
Wine rack, fish form, holds 10, blk pnt, 1950s, 27x26" **50.00**

Wood, Beatrice

A multitalented artist, Beatrice Wood is especially well known for her ceramics which are displayed in the Smithsonian and the Metropolitan Museum of Art as well as several other museums around the world. She was also famous for her work in other mediums, especially painting and photography. She studied drama in Europe at the age of 18, returning to America where she became involved in the revolutionary Dada

art movement in New York. She moved to California in the late 1920s and in 1937 opened her own studio. Nicknamed Bea or Beato, she developed wonderful lustre glazes for which she is highly acclaimed. Her style is modernistic, and her work ranges from sedate teapots and vases to whimsical sculptures. She died in 1998 at the age of 105. Her fascinating experiences led her to write her autobiography which so captured the attention of Titanic director James Cameron that he fashioned the role of Rose around her.

Bowl, centerpc; copper/lav/gr/gold lustre, Beato, 3¾x17" **4,000.00**
Bowl, gr/gold/lav, Beato, 2½x10½" **2,700.00**
Bowl, mottled gr/gold/lav lustre, Beato, 4½x10" **3,750.00**
Chalice, blk volcanic w/oxblood & cobalt, conical base, Beato, 8¾"..**2,900.00**
Cup, purple/gr/gold lustre, no hdls, ftd, Beato, 9½x9" **6,000.00**
Jug, blk volcanic glaze, ball shape, sm opening, Beato, 7½x6¾"..**3,000.00**
Plaque, 3 floating angels, gr & gold w/purple over terra cotta, 10x6"..**2,900.00**
Sculpture, eel, gr lustre w/coffee-bean eyes, sm fleck, 2x14" **1,600.00**

Wood Carvings

Wood sculptures represent an important section of American folk art. Wood carvings were made not only by skilled woodworkers such as cabinetmakers, carpenters, etc., but by amateur 'whittlers' as well. They take the form of circus-wagon figures, carousel animals, decoys, busts, figurines, and cigar store Indians. Oriental artists show themselves to have been as proficient with the medium of wood as they were with ivory or hardstone.

See also Carousel Animals; Decoys; Tobacciana.

Architectural pc, fleur-de-lis over rosettes/wreath/banner, 23x26", VG..**940.00**
Bear standing w/lg salmon in mouth, detailed cvg, 11x17" **980.00**
Bust, Black man, on blk-pnt plinth, 19th C, 8x3"....................**1,265.00**
Cowboy, penciled details, jtd arms, leather belt/holster, 9½"......**125.00**
Dog, recumbent, brn pnt w/mc traces, Am, good age, 5⅝x11x3¼"....**550.00**
Eagle, gessoed rope-bound legs/iron wire ft/glass eyes, 1800s, 12x21".**1,400.00**
Eagle, gilt gesso on cvd wood, perched on sphere, 19th C, 17x19"..**2,000.00**
Eagle, giltwood, spreadwing w/banner in talons, Am, 1800s, 20x74"..**12,925.00**
Eagle, giltwood on cvd rockery, Am, ca 1875, 25x31x26" **2,470.00**
Eagle, Pilot House; wings out, on domed rock, mc rpt, 34x40x31"..**1,725.00**
Eagle on arrow, gilt highlights, 5x13"...**500.00**
Eagle w/banner, pine w/mc pnt, att JH Bellamy, late 1800s, 8½x26".**24,150.00**
Horse's head, incised decor, tacked brass ornaments, 16" **125.00**
Jewelry box, Black Forest, 2 goats, floral/leaf decor, 15" L..........**675.00**
Lion, reclining, full mane & tail, varnish w/blk & red, 13" L **575.00**

Oxen and cart, carved and painted pine, original crazed surface, early twentieth century, 22" long, $330.00. (Photo courtesy Aston-Macek)

Mermaid brackets, gold & mc, scrolled tails, Am, 19th C, 20x11", pr.**4,250.00**
Pig, blk & wht pnt w/red tongue & appl teeth, FBA 2-18-78, 10x22".**825.00**
Plaque w/Adam & Eve, apple tree/snake, lt gr stain, sgn Morose, 20x22".**550.00**
Salmon, old pnt, LC Irvine, 24" on 13x29" plaque..................**2,000.00**
Terrier seated, pnt traces, minor damage, 9⅝"............................**250.00**
Wall shelf, Black Forest, stork/cattails, 19" **450.00**

Woodenware

Woodenware (or treenware, as it is sometimes called) generally refers to those wooden items such as spoons, bowls, food molds, etc., that were used in the preparation of food. Common during the eighteenth and nineteenth centuries, these wares were designed from a strictly functional viewpoint and were used on a day-to-day basis. With the advent of the Industrial Revolution which brought with it new materials and products, much of the old woodenware was simply discarded. Today original handcrafted American woodenwares are extremely difficult to find.

See also Primitives.

Bowl, burl, ash w/EX dk patina, worn int, scrubbed areas, 4x11"...**990.00**
Bowl, burl, ash w/EX figure, brn finish, raised rings, 6½x17"...**3,190.00**
Bowl, burl, ash w/EX figure, golden rfn, scrubbed int, 5x15".......**550.00**
Bowl, burl, ash w/EX figure, lt rfn, 6x15"................................**2,400.00**
Bowl, burl, ash w/EX patina on ext, scrubbed int, split, 4x11¼" ...**550.00**
Bowl, burl, ash w/G figure & red wash ext, putty rstr, 4x9" **660.00**
Bowl, burl, ash w/mellow finish, hand hewn/thin, hdls, 5x12" dia.**1,815.00**
Bowl, burl, loose figure, irregular shape, hole/age crack, 6x23x19" **115.00**
Bowl, burl, trn rim, Am, early 1800s, 3½x10½".....................**1,100.00**
Bowl, chopping; pnt, yel w/rust squiggles & circles, 3¾x20x12", EX...**2,700.00**
Bowl, curly maple, varnished, G color, 5x16x15" **250.00**
Bowl, pnt, old bl, trn rim, VT, 6x19x18".................................**650.00**
Bowl, pnt, old red, raised rim, wire loops, sm plug in bottom, 22" ..**880.00**
Bowl, pnt, old red, trn w/thick rim, worn int, 6x18½"...............**525.00**
Bowl, pnt, old red, trn w/worn dip in rim, EX int patina, 7x20x22"...**1,150.00**
Bowl, pnt, salmon, trn, Am, 19th C, 4½x15⅝".....................**1,500.00**
Butter paddle, burl, G figure/patina, natural imperfection, 9⅝"...**935.00**
Butter paddle, burl w/dk patina, hooked hdl, 9¾" **700.00**
Butter paddle, curly maple, chamfered edge to hdl, EX patina, 9" ..**330.00**
Butter paddle, curly maple, EX color/figure, hook hdl, sm chip, 8½"..**110.00**
Butter paddle, curly maple, long curved hdl w/simple hook, 10½" L..**250.00**
Butter paddle, curly maple, scalloped hdl, scrubbed, 9½"............**150.00**
Butter paddle, curly maple w/VG patina, age crack/edge chips, 8"...**165.00**
Butter paddle, maple, cvd fishtail hdl, sm chip, 6" **110.00**
Cookie board, heart w/vine & flowers, beveled corners, scrubbed, 7x9"..**415.00**
Cookie board, man w/feather cap & fancy frock coat, walnut, 27x10"...**435.00**
Cookie board, walnut, man w/striped vest/conical hat, 5½x15".**165.00**
Cookie mold, floral/foliage, fruitwood, 7x7" **350.00**
Jar, poplar w/red-brn vinegar decor on yel base coat, ftd, 12x9¼" .**3,850.00**
Jar, red vinegar decor on mustard, rpr, 9x8¾".........................**1,200.00**
Ladle, toddy; notched hdl, rnd bowl, dk patina, wear, early 1700s, 14"..**400.00**
Mold, rice cake; old worn finish, 10¼" **30.00**
Scoop, cvd tiger maple, hook hdl, rpr, 19th C, 4½x9" **545.00**
Trencher, EX patina, cvd under rim hdl, 35x15", VG **150.00**
Trencher, hewn pine, canted sides, EX patina, 3¼x10¾x23" **115.00**
Trencher, natural finish, cvd under rim hdl, rpr, 25x15"...............**90.00**
Trencher, worn tan pnt, scrubbed int, hole for hanging, 3½x20x11" .**475.00**

Woodworking Machinery

Vintage cast-iron woodworking machines are monuments to the highly skilled engineers, foundrymen, and machinists who devised them, thus making possible the mass production of items ranging from clothespins, boxes, and barrels to decorative moldings and furniture. Though attractive from a nostalgic viewpoint, many of these machines are bought by the hobbyist and professional alike, to be put into actual use — at far less cost than new equipment. Many worth-assessing factors must be considered; but as a general rule, a machine in good condition is worth about 65¢ a pound (excluding motors). A machine needing a lot of restoration is not worth more than 35¢ a pound, while one professionally rebuilt and with a warranty can be calculated at $1.10 a pound. Modern, new machinery averages over $3.00 a pound. Two of the best sources of information on purchasing or selling such machines are *Vintage Machines — Searching for the Cast Iron Classics*, by Tom Howell, and *Used Machines and Abused Buyers* by Chuck Seidel from *Fine Woodworking*, November/December 1984. Prices quoted are for machines in good condition, less motors and accessories. Our advisor for this category is Mr. Dana Martin Batory, author of *Vintage Woodworking Machinery, An Illustrated Guide to Four Manufacturers*. See his listing in the Directory under Ohio for further information. Watch for Volume II, *An Illustrated Guide to Four More Manufacturers*. No phone calls, please.

American Saw Mill Machinery Company, 1931

Band saw, Monarch Line, #X25, 30" w/built-in ball-bearing motor ..**770.00**
Mortiser, Monarch Line, #XI, hollow chisel, motorized **345.00**
Sander, Monarch Line, #X8, ball-bearing drum & disk..............**560.00**

Crescent Machine Company, 1921

Band saw, 36"...**975.00**
Mortiser, hollow chisel...**525.00**
Universal Wood-Worker, #59, 5 machines in 1......................**2,050.00**

Delta Manufacturing Company, 1939

Band saw, #890, 14"..**70.00**
Belt sander, #1400, 6"...**35.00**
Drill press, bench, #645, 11"...**30.00**
Drill press, bench, #999, 14"...**50.00**
Drill press, floor, #1370, 17"..**200.00**
Drill press, floor, #989, 14"..**70.00**
Drill press, floor, high speed, #1370-H, 17"...........................**200.00**
Jointer, ball bearing, #390, 4"...**35.00**
Lathe, ball bearing, #1460, 12"...**60.00**
Lathe, timken bearing, #955, 9"..**35.00**
Scroll saw, multi-speed, #1440, 24".....................................**50.00**
Scroll saw, 4-speed, #1200, 24"..**40.00**
Shaper, ball bearing, reversible, #1180 ....**30.00**
Unisaw, tilting arbor, #1450, 10"...**200.00**

F.H. Clement Co., 1896

Band saw, 28", Improved..**1,040.00**
Band saw, 34", Patent Improved **635.00**
Band saw, 36", Patent Improved **815.00**
Band saw, 42"...**1,430.00**
Jointer, Perfection, 08"...**620.00**
Jointer, Perfection, 30"...**1,690.00**
Lathe, pattern maker's; iron bed, Improved, 20" **815.00**
Mortising & boring machine, No 1 ....**520.00**
Planer, #2½, dbl surface, 26" **3,000.00**
Planer, #3, dbl-belted, Improved, 20"................................**2,015.00**
Sand belt machine, Improved...**425.00**
Sander, #1, spindle & drum **520.00**
Sanding machine, surface; Improved **650.00**
Shaper, #1, reversible, Improved...**650.00**
Table saw, dbl arbor, Improved, 16"....................................**815.00**
Table saw, variety, #1, 15" **585.00**

Hoyt & Brother Company, 1888

Band saw & resawing machine, #1194, 20" **1,700.00**

Jointer, Perfection, 8" 450.00
Mortiser & borer, #2 ....780.00
Planer, matcher & surfacer, New Combined, #2, 24" 5,200.00
Sand-papering machine, The Boss, #5, 24" 1,600.00
Shingle machine, Grand Mogul, 2-block, automatic feed 2,210.00
Tenoning machine, #2 ....650.00
Wood shaper, dbl spindle 850.00

J.A. Fay & Egan Company, 1900

Jointer, New #2, 20" 1,625.00
Jointer, New #2, 24" 1,700.00
Jointer, New #4, extra heavy, 20" 1,690.00
Jointer, New #4, extra heavy, 24" 1,885.00
Mortiser, #2, hollow chisel, automatic horizontal 1,500.00
Saw, rip; #2, self feed, lg 1,775.00

J.D. Wallace Company, 1940s

Band saw, 16" 210.00
Grinder & sander, disk, Wonder, 16" 165.00
Jointer, 4" 15.00
Lathe, 6x24" 115.00
Saw, circular (table saw); Universal, 7" 75.00
Saw, circular; plain, 7" 65.00

Levi Houston Co., 1897

Dovetailing machine, #2, sash 520.00
Moulder, new 4", 4-sided 650.00
Moulding machine, 4-headed, 10" 2,400.00
Panel raising machine, Pat Improved 650.00
Saw, heavy swing 910.00
Saw, new #1, Improved variety, 14" 650.00
Saw, new combination, bench 910.00
Sticker, open-sided, door 500.00
Sticker, special, door 520.00
Tenoning machine, new style, #3 ....585.00

Powermatic, Inc., 1965

Band saw, #141, 14" 145.00
Jointer, #50, 6" 110.00
Jointer, #60, 8" 170.00
Lathe, #45, 12" 230.00
Mortiser, #10, hollow chisel 375.00
Mortiser, #15, chain saw 390.00
Planer, #100, 12" 200.00
Planer, #180, 18" 685.00
Planer, #225, 24" 1,600.00
Sander, #33, 6" belt 90.00
Sander, #35, 12" disk 55.00
Sander, #300-01, 12" disk & 6" belt combination 95.00
Scroll saw, #95, 24" 100.00
Table saw, #62, 10" 135.00
Table saw, #66, 10" 230.00
Table saw, #72, 12" 515.00

Richardson, Meriam & Co., 1865

Band saw, Humphrey's Improved, 40" 957.00
Mortising machine, Medium Power #4 ......650.00
Re-sawing machine, circular, 26" 650.00
Scroll saw, Empire, lg 400.00

The Sidney Machine Tool Co., 1916 (Famous Woodworking Machinery)

Bandsaw, No 1, 36", new 1,100.00
Bandsaw, 27" 535.00
Bandsaw, 32" 715.00
Jointer, 8" 615.00
Mortiser, hollow chisel 650.00
Planer, dbl-belted, 24x8" 1,575.00
Planer, dbl-belted, 26x8" 1,755.00
Saw, combination; No 4, 16" 485.00
Saw, Universal, No 10, 16" 1,270.00
Saw, Variety, No 2, 20" 875.00
Shaper, dbl spindle 1,300.00
Woodworker, Universal, Improved, No 14 ....1,525.00

Valley City Machine Works, ca 1910

Boring machine, single spindle, horizontal 520.00
Boring machine, vertical 650.00
Dowel machine, No 1 ....455.00
Dowel machine, No 2 ....520.00
Rounding, routing & rosette machine, No 1 ....975.00
Rounding, routing & rosette machine, No 2 ....910.00
Spiral twist machine 875.00

Worcester Porcelain Company

The Worcester Porcelain Company was deeded in 1751. During the first or Dr. Wall period (so called for one of its proprietors), porcelain with an Oriental influence was decorated in underglaze blue. Useful tablewares represented the largest portion of production, but figurines and decorative items were also made. Very little of the earliest wares were marked and can only be identified by a study of forms, glazes, and the porcelain body, which tends to transmit a greenish cast when held to light. Late in the 1750s, a crescent mark was in general use, and rare examples bear a facsimile of the Meissen crossed swords. The first period ended in 1783, and the company went through several changes in ownership during the next eighty years. The years from 1783 to 1792 are referred to as the Flight period. Marks were a small crescent, a crown with 'Royal,' or an impressed 'Flight.' From 1792 to 1807 the company was known as Flight and Barr and used the trademark 'F&B' or 'B,' with or without a small cross. From 1807 to 1813 the company was under the Barr, Flight, and Barr management; this era is recognized as having produced porcelain with the highest quality of artistic decoration. Their mark was 'B.F.B.' From 1813 to 1840 many marks were used, but the most usual was 'F.B.B.' under a crown to indicate Flight, Barr, and Barr. In 1840 the firm merged with Chamberlain, and in 1852 they were succeeded by Kerr and Binns. The firm became known as Royal Worcester in 1862. The production was then marked with a circle with '51' within and a crown on top. The date of manufacture was incised into the bottom or stamped with a letter of the alphabet, just under the circle. In 1891 Royal Worcester England was added to the circle and crown. From that point on, each piece is dated with a code of dots or other symbols. After 1891 most wares had a blush-color ground. Prior to that date it was ivory. Most shapes were marked with a unique number.

During the early years they produced considerable ornamental wares with a Persian influence. This gave way to a Japanesque influence. James Hadley is most responsible for the Victorian look. He is considered the 'best ever' designer and modeller. He was joined by the finest porcelain painters. Together they produced pieces with very fine detail and exquisite painting and decoration. Figures, vases, and tableware were produced in great volume and are highly collectible. During the 1890s they allowed the artists to sign some of their work. Pieces signed on the face by the Stintons, Bald-wyn, Davis, Raby, Austin, Powell, Sedgley, and Rushton (not a complete list) are in great demand. The company is still in production. There is an outstanding museum on the company grounds in Worcester, England.

Note: Most pieces had lids or tops (if there is a flat area on the top lip, chances are it had one), if missing deduct 30% to 40%.

Key: FBB — Flight, Barr, and Barr

Biscuit jar, bamboo design w/gold leaves & hdl, 7x6"..................275.00
Bowl, fruit; floral swags, sgn BN, 1887, 12 for.............................475.00
Cup & saucer, cobalt w/gold, gold int, 1926, 2", 3¾"...................250.00
Ewer, Persian, HP floral w/gold, #779, drilled, 14".......................335.00
Figurine, Babes in the Wood, colorway 1, #3302, 1940-59.........425.00
Figurine, cat, long haired, #3615, 1957...................................150.00
Figurine, Cerulean Warbler on maple branch, Doughty, 9½".....525.00
Figurine, children at play, Doris Lindner, #3153, 1936-50s.........290.00
Figurine, December, girl throwing snowball, Doughty, #3458, 7x4"..450.00
Figurine, Grandmother's Dress, #3081, 1935-83.......................140.00
Figurine, Gray Wagtail, Doughty, 1968...................................850.00
Figurine, Italy, girl w/flower basket, #3067, 1934-59..................450.00
Figurine, Japan, Oriental girl w/fan, #3072, 1934-59, 3½".........500.00
Figurine, Saturday's Child, girl, #3262, 1943-61, 7"..................225.00
Figurine, Sweet Anne, #3630, 1957-83...................................140.00

Figurines, classical females holding musical instruments, gilt decor, late nineteenth century, 10", 10¾", $1,265.00 for the pair.

Jar, 3 fruit scenes, sgn Sibley-Lewis, 7x6"...............................1,000.00
Pitcher, flowers, gold/pastel on ivory, bulbous, gold hdl, 6".........230.00
Pitcher, gold bands/florals (at rim)/hdl, flaring sides, 5¾"...........145.00
Pitcher, overlapping circles, wht on bl, gold tricorner lip, 7"......260.00
Pitcher, stylized floral on pk w/Greek Key border, elephant hdl, 6"...175.00
Plaque, pheasants in landscape, sgn Stinton, oval, 13" L, +oak fr..3,000.00
Plate, band of urns/swags/scrolls, 1910, 10½", 12 for................700.00
Plate, crest held by armoured arm, bl & gold border, 1792-1807, 9"..135.00
Plate, dinner; Evesham, gold trim, 10", 6 for 170.00
Plate, Earl Beauchamp/Lady Mary Lyons commemorative, 1896, 10½"..65.00
Plate, floral w/gold, sgn Freeman, cobalt border, 1953, 10½"......185.00
Plate, George V coronation, King & Queen portraits, 1911, 10½".125.00
Plate, parrot on floral branch, bl border, 1932, 9"......................120.00
Plate, pattern WR C2816, floral w/gold scrolls, 1930s, 10½", 12 for..1,725.00
Plate, scalloped rim w/Oriental scene reserves, bl/wht, 1765, 6½".585.00
Platter, armorial/versed ribbon: Deus Adjuvat Nos, FBB, 12"..1,100.00
Posy bowl, seashell shape, pk & lt yel, 3-ftd, 1889-1902, 2½x4" ..95.00
Potpourri jar, floral, gold on yel, #1039, 1884, 1901, 4½", NM ..250.00
Spill vase, bamboo decor, 1884 mk, 6", pr................................450.00
Sweetmeat jar, thistles, rose/gr on wht w/emb swirls, SP mts, 6" dia...200.00
Tray, couple at tea w/dog, blk transfer, 1780, 6½x3¼" 650.00
Urn, floral on ivory w/gold, scroll hdls, rtcl lid, purple mk, 15"..875.00
Vase, carnations, sgn Grainger, #790, 1901, 10½", pr 950.00
Vase, cattle scene, in style of Stinton, G923, 1916, 6" 750.00

Vase, crane in flight/floral branches, ornate hdls, #804, 20" 1,650.00
Vase, floral w/gold bands, stick neck, 1888, 12x7".....................400.00
Vase, fruit, sgn Ricketts, #2491, 1929, 6", pr.............................850.00
Vase, leaves emb on wht bone china, 1986, 10½x4"...................125.00
Vase, reserve w/birds & moon, gray on wht, gold dragon hdls, 16", EX..400.00
Vase, sheep landscape, sgn H Davis, #302, 1921, sm rstr, 7" 800.00

World's Fairs and Expos

Since 1851 and the Crystal Palace Exhibition in London, World's Fairs and Expositions have taken place at a steady pace. Many of them commemorate historical events. The 1904 Louisiana Purchase Exposition, commonly known as the St. Louis World's Fair, celebrated the 100th anniversary of the Louisiana Purchase agreement between Thomas Jefferson and Napoleon in 1803. The 1893 Columbian Exposition commemorated the 400th anniversary of the discovery of America by Columbus in 1492. (Both of these fairs were held one year later than originally scheduled.) The multitude of souvenirs from these and similar events have become a growing area of interest to collectors in recent years. Many items have a 'crossover' interest into other fields: i.e., collectors of postcards and souvenir spoons eagerly search for those from various fairs and expositions.

Values have fallen somewhat due to eBay sales. Many of the so called common items have come down in value. However 1939 World's Fair items are still hot. For additional information collectors may contact World's Fairs Collectors Society (WFCS), whose address is in the Directory under Clubs, Newsletters, and Catalogs, or our advisor, Herbert Rolfes. His address is listed in the Directory under Florida.

Key:
T&P — Trylon & Perisphere   WF — World's Fair

1876 Centennial, Philadelphia

Corkscrew, metal, Hail Columbia on sheath, 2¾" 25.00
Flue cover, Machinery Building, 6" dia...90.00
Letter opener, eagle, Indian, train engine & logo, bronze, 7¼", VG..60.00
Platter, G Washington center, bear claw hdls, pattern glass, 12x8½" ..60.00

1893 Columbian, Chicago

Badge, Colorado, souvenir, brass..45.00
Book, Dream City, views of expo, hardcover, 11x13", EX 50.00
Coin, Chicago Dollar HK#168, EX 45.00
Dominoes, Columbus; Christopher Columbus head on bk, EXIB.110.00
Match holder, Columbus on oval bk w/2 flag-emb wells, brass, wall mt.110.00
Medal, Ferris wheel/fair facts, aluminum 35.00
Medallion, 400 Years After Columbus Landed, commemorative, bronze, 3".175.00
Plate, Agricultural Building, 8¼" 60.00
Postcard, Agricultural Building, pre-official, American Lithograph Co ...50.00
Ring, Spanish commemorative, sterling silver, Gorham 60.00
Straight razor, eng blade, emb box, Germany, VG+ 55.00
Vase, Satsuma, HP Main Building & Oriental floral, 16½" 1,440.00

1901 Pan American

Belt buckle, enameled logo w/silver-tone metal buffalo, 1¾x1½".35.00
Clock, metal skillet w/CF Chouffet workings, Pan American Expo Co, 12"....100.00
Encased coin, 1901 Indian head penny, Good Luck Souvenir, EX.35.00
Napkin ring, logo on sides, silver...25.00
Paperweight, bison, 1901 on side, Pan American 1901 on base, lead, 3"..35.00
Photo book, red cover w/emb silver letters & buffalo head 25.00
Pin, North & South America w/ladies holding hands, 1¼" dia 40.00
Pin, Pan-American Exposition Buffalo NY, angel flying w/horn, EX.95.00

Shot glass, etched logo & When You Drink Do of Me Think, 2½"...20.00
Spoon, Temple of Music Building in bowl, scroll hdl, sterling 25.00
Tumbler, clear w/frosted logo w/buffalo atop, 3½" 18.00
Vase, vertically striped vaseline opal, emb seal, 6½", EX 120.00

1904 St. Louis

Ashtray, emb Jefferson & Napoleon, free-form, metal, mk 987JB, 3x5"..22.50
Axe, 1803 Emblem of Peace & Prosperity, glass, 10¼"....................70.00
Book, Official Handbook of the Ceylon Court, 190 pgs, 8½x5½", EX...45.00
Book, Official History of the Fair...Sights & Scenes..., 496 pgs.....50.00
Booklet, Official Guide to the WF, torn cover, 8x5½", G 30.00
Bowl, Palace of Electricity, scalloped edge, gold trim, 1¼x4x5"....35.00
Bread maker, Landers/Frary/Clark Universal #4, metal w/hand crank.65.00
Brochure, 1904 Studebaker Vehicles, from Palace of Transportation..300.00
Creamer, Machinery Building, china, gold trim, mk Germany, 3½"..60.00
Cup, Cascade Gardens, worn SP, ornate hdl, 2½" 40.00
Cup, collapsible; Palace of Mines & Metallurgy, metallic, EX 25.00
Cup, wht w/purple spatter, Palace of Machinery transfer, 3" 85.00
Knife, mechanical; Union Station, push button, 2½" closed 60.00
Match safe, Machinery Building front, Jefferson/Napoleon bk, 3x1¼" .70.00
Match safe, Palace of Manufacturing & of Mines & Metallurgy, EX.65.00
Medal, 3 classical figures w/1 Native American, bronze, 2"...........60.00
Paperweight, Black boy on potty, metal, worn pnt, 3x2½" 250.00
Paperweight, Festival Hall & Cascade Gardens, clear w/photo, 2x4"..25.00
Pin-back, Palace of Varied Industries, 1½" dia...............................30.00
Plate, Palace of Varied Industries, mk France, 7½" 50.00
Plate, US Government Building, wht w/bl edge, 9¼" dia 65.00
Postcard, Open the Doors to the Tiger Line, tiger image...............80.00
Shaving mug, US Government Building, blk transfer on wht, 4⅝"..65.00
Steroview, Pike at Twilight's Witching Hour, CL Watson, EX......20.00
Vase, pk w/Palace of Electricity on wht, ornate hdls, 6" 90.00

1905 Lewis and Clark

Handkerchief, Lewis & Clark screen print w/hand-embr floral, 13" sq ..80.00
Pendant, Lewis & Clark front w/Mt Hood on bk, ⅝" dia..............20.00
Plate, wht w/Festival Hall in center & turq border, 6¼" dia 30.00
Postcard, Sacajawea Statue, unused, EX...15.00
Steroview, Camel Rides 10¢, Watson Fine Art, 3½x7", EX 25.00
Tumbler, clear w/eagle on world & Lewis & Clark in wht ovals, 3½"....110.00

1909 Alaska Yukon Pacific

Encased cent, 1909 Indian head penny, in pot-shaped holder, EX .65.00
Parasol, flag, logo & flag shield, bamboo hdl, 26x22" dia, EX.....140.00
Plate, OR State Building, mc w/gold on china, 8", VG.................90.00
Postcard, You'll Like Tacoma, unmailed, 3½x5½", EX...................15.00

1915 Panama Pacific

Scarf, Tower of Jewels printed in dark blue on light blue silk, 20" square, $100.00. (Photo courtesy Early Americana Historical Auctions)

Book, Cuba Before the World, info & photos, 224 pgs, VG+ 40.00
Booklet, Condensed Facts (concerning expo), EX.......................25.00
Booklet, General Electric Mazda light & RR exhibit, 12 pgs, VG+..30.00
Medal, Oregon State Building, Oregon crest on bk, 1½" dia 20.00
Pillowcase, wht w/brn Tower of Jewels transfer, 20x20"..............45.00
Pin, bar; wht w/Panama Pacific International Expo 1915, roses, 3" ..50.00
Tray, seal & 4 fair scenes, mk Rhodes Bros Ten Cent Store on bk, 4x5" ...15.00

1933 Chicago

Book, Official Book of Views, 60 pgs, 9x12" 20.00
Book, Official Pictures, 63 pgs, EX 25.00
Book, Quilt Making, Sears Roebuck & Co, 23 pgs, 1934, EX.......35.00
Bracelet, cuff; city skyline on oval center on copper-colored band, EX..20.00
Coasters, fair buildings, metal, set of 6, 2⅞" dia 20.00
Cup, coffee; Stewart & Ashby's Private Blend Coffee, Shenango .70.00
Elongated cent, Travel & Transportation Building, copper-colored, EX..25.00
Encased cent, B&O Railroad, 1933 Lincoln cent, EX 20.00
Fork, Century of Progress on hdl, sterling silver, EX...................18.00
License plate holder, Chicago cutout over wings, aluminum, EX..50.00
Medal, man w/Industry Research 1833-1933, fair scene on bk, 2¾"..45.00
Paperweight, Sky Ride, plane over skyline on photo in glass, sq...25.00
Pencil holder, bulldog figural, red, tag on collar, 1¾" 25.00
Playing cards, Hall of Science & Avenue of Flags, complete, EXIB..25.00
Radio, Carillon Tower & Travel & Transportation Building on sides, VG..1,000.00
Razor knife, logo on hdl, folding, 4¼" open..............................25.00
Teapot, Republic of China Exhibit, red clay, unglazed, emb grapes...45.00
Tie bar, 1933 Chicago & logo in silver on bl, silver band, EX 15.00
Vase, bud; Federal Building/Hall of Science, N Slure, metal, 4½" .18.00

1939 New York

Bank, Esso, pressed glass, 6x6x4", VG+..80.00
Booklet, Pullman Exhibit, 20 pgs, color, EX................................10.00
Brochure, YMCA Welcomes Visitors to the Fair..., color, fold-out, EX..18.00
Cane, NYWF 1939 sticker on side, wooden, EX.........................50.00
Envelope, Railroads at the NYWF 1939, color, unused 10.00
Leaflet, Around the Grounds by Greyhound Bus & Boat, foldout, EX.10.00
Plate, T&P in center w/buildings border, bl & wht, Meakin, EX.105.00
Postcard, T&P, color linen, unused..5.00
Tray, jewel; brass w/12 red marbles embedded, Fisher, 3" dia.........85.00
Walking stick/seat combo, blk, orange & wht logo on seat, wood, EX ..75.00

1939 San Francisco

Catalog, History of Am Paintings, Trumbull, 12-pg, EX...............20.00
Pillow case, blk fair scenes on wht w/yel border, wht fringe, 18x17"..12.00
Pocketwatch, Official Souvenir on face, logo on bk, silver, EX ..125.00
Sticker, Oakland...Invites You, red/wht/bl, 1⅞x2½", EX................5.00

1962 Seattle

Book, Official Guide Book & Map, 116 pgs, EX...........................15.00
Coin, 1939-S Walking Liberty half dollar, EX 15.00
Doll, Miss Seattle, eyes open/close, wht gown w/red ribbon, 7½", EX..18.00
Earrings, SWF, logo, '21' & Space Needle, emb copper, 1" dia, pr..25.00
Lighter, Space Disc, flying saucer shape, bl w/silver, metal, 4"....125.00
Lighter, table; Space Needle design, chrome plated, 10½".........125.00
Mug, gray, WF emb, Pacific Stoneware Pottery, 4" 50.00
Parking token, Space Needle/Diamond Parking Service, bronze, 1⅛"..20.00
Plate, Space Needle & surrounding fair, emb image, EX 20.00
Scarf, mc graphics of fair scenes, rayon, 30x30", EX....................25.00
Tray, wht plastic w/gold Space Needle & SWF 1962, 7¾x5"........20.00
Tumblers, wht plastic w/colored fair scenes, set of 8, NMIB..........70.00

1964 New York

Calendar, perpetual; bl & wht logo on wht, Japan, 3½" **35.00**
Novelty, Unishere NYWF emb on base, plastic, 3½" **15.00**
Plate, Unisphere center w/6 scenes at border, mc, US Steel, 7¼" ..**20.00**
Postcard, Caribbean Pavillion, unused...**4.00**
Puzzle, jigsaw; Vatican Pavillion, Milton Bradley, NMIB **25.00**
Tumbler, frosted w/Shea Stadium in gr & brn, info on bk, 6½" **10.00**
Visitor guide w/fold-out map, photo & message from Mayor Wagner, EX...**4.00**

Wright, Frank Lloyd

Born in Richland Center, Wisconsin, in 1869, Wright became a pioneer in architectural expression, developing a style referred to as 'prairie.' From early in the century until he died in 1959, he designed houses with rooms that were open, rather than divided by walls in the traditional manner. They exhibited low, horizontal lines and strongly projecting eaves, and he filled them with furnishings whose radical aesthetics complemented the structures to perfection. Several of his homes have been preserved to the present day, and collectors who admire his ideas and the unique, striking look he achieved treasure the stained glass windows, furniture, chinaware, lamps, and other decorative accessories designed by Wright.

Key: H — Heritage Henredon

Armchair, H #1483, gr velvet uphl, 1955, 27" **750.00**
Chair, plywood & bl fabric, hinged bk, for Unitarian Church, 1947, 28"..**2,100.00**
Desk, H, 8-drw, pull-out writing table, 52", w/red uphl chair ..**1,000.00**
Drawing, office table for HC Price Co, fr, 18x34", EX **1,000.00**

Child's chair, from the Coonley Playhouse, slab back with square cutouts for cushion ties, 1912, 31", EX, $4,250.00. (Photo courtesy Treadway Gallery, Inc.)

Ottoman, H, hexagonal, 5-leg, reuphl, label, 16x27x27" **750.00**
Postcard, shows Huntington Hartford project, 6x4½", EX **10.00**
Sofa, H, 2-pc sectional, reuphl, 32x67" & 32x95"....................**1,500.00**

Wrought Iron

Until the middle of the nineteenth century, almost all the metal hand forged in America was made from a material called wrought iron. When wrought iron rusts it appears grainy, while the mild steel that was used later shows no grain but pits to an orange-peel surface. This is an important aid in determining the age of an ironwork piece.

See also Fireplace Implements.

Arbor, 3-section arch w/bird design, 92x75" **335.00**
Candle snuffer, 7" **70.00**
Dipper, brass inlay in hdl, 14¾" **150.00**
Fork, 2-prong, sq interval in shaft w/initials, wood hdl, 28"........**120.00**
Game hook, tulip ends, twisted scroll crest, 5-hook, old pnt, 8x17"..**430.00**
Gate, band & curlicues, late 1800s, 19½x25", EX....................**195.00**
Gate, scrollwork, arched top, swings from center (2-pc), 1890s, 74x62".**1,350.00**
Hinges, barn; 12½", pr...**40.00**
Hook, meat; twisted hdl, 4 hooks, 14½" **75.00**
Rack, scrolling design, 2 prong attachments, 19th C, 12" **260.00**
Rack, utensil; European style, 1800s, 26x31" **90.00**
Sconce, scrolled heart amid 2 arched arms, 1900s, 10x11" **455.00**
Screen, 4 panel w/decorative scrolls, old wht pnt, 78x72" **1,500.00**
Shingler's hammer, 2-ended: man w/blade, hammer; snake stem, 12"..**765.00**
Skewers, 6 graduated szs on hanger w/shaped crest, 16" L...........**550.00**
Sugar devil, trn wood hdl, 16" **115.00**
Sugar nippers, stamped star & scallop design, 9¼" **350.00**
Tongs, ice; Gifford Wood Co, Extra NH **40.00**
Wick cutter, scissors style, 6½" **70.00**
Window guards, scrolls, pnt traces, late 1800s, 10x17¾", pr.......**185.00**
Window guards, spears & arrows, old blk, late 1800s, 17x33", pr, EX...**200.00**

Yellow Ware

Ranging in color from buff to deep mustard, yellow ware which almost always has a clear glaze can be slip banded, plain, Rockingham decorated, flint enamel glazed, or mocha decorated. Black or red mocha decorated pieces are the most desirable. Although blue mocha decorated pieces are the most common, green decorated pieces command the lowest prices. Pieces having a combination of two colors are the rarest. The majority of pieces are plain and do not bear a manufacture's mark. Primarily produced in the United States, England, and Canada this utilitarian ware was popular from the mid-nineteenth century until the early twentieth century. Yellow ware was first produced in New York, Pennsylvania, and Vermont. However, the center for yellow ware production was East Liverpool, Ohio, a town which once supported more than thirty potters. Yellow ware is still being produced today in both the United States and England. Because of websites and Internet auctions, prices have tended to become uniform throughout the United States. The use of this pottery as accessories in decorating and its exposure in country magazines has caused prices to rise, especially for the more utilitarian forms such as plates and bowls. Note: Because this is a utilitarian ware, it is often found with damage and heavy wear. Damage does have a negative impact on price, especially for the common forms. For further information we recommend *Collector's Guide to Yellow Ware: An Identification and Value Guide, Book I*, written by our advisor John Michel and Lisa McAllister, and *Collector's Guide to Yellow Ware Books II and III* by Lisa McAllister. Mr. Michel's address is in the Directory under New York.

See also Rockingham.

Batter bowl, wht band w/bl stripes & bl mocha seaweed, 12" ..**1,300.00**
Flask, fish shape, plain, 9¼" L, minimum value **1,500.00**
Flask, pig shape, plain, 7¾" L, minimum value **2,700.00**
Jar, Spices emb below 3 bl bands, emb reeding at base **185.00**
Keeler, 3 thick bl bands, 4" dia **325.00**
Milk pan, 4½x12¼" **350.00**
Mold, fig & star decor, plain, 7¾" dia **395.00**
Mold, lion decor, plain, 8¾" L **500.00**
Mold, swirl decor, plain, 4½" dia..**150.00**
Mold, Turk's head, plain, 10" **225.00**
Mug, Rockingham decor, 3¾" **275.00**
Mug, wht band w/bl stripes & mocha seaweed, 3¼"................**670.00**

Mug, 3 wht bands, 4⅛" 470.00
Nappy, ca 1880, 3½x13" 235.00
Nappy, heart-shaped ft, ca 1880, 3¾x13" 300.00
Pepper pot, wht band w/bl stripes & bl mocha seaweed, 4¼" ..1,000.00
Pepper pot, wht band w/blk stripes/red mocha seaweed, 4½", minimum .1,600.00
Pepper pot, 6 bl stripes, 4¼", minimum value................850.00
Pie plate colander, plain, 3x12" 600.00
Pie plate colander, Rockingham decor, 3¼x11¾" 550.00
Pitcher, wht band w/bl stripes & bl mocha seaweed, 7" 1,300.00
Pitcher, 3 wht bands, 4" 250.00
Tankard, wht band w/bl mocha, 6½", minimum value.............1,100.00
Tankard, 10 wht bands, 6¼" 825.00

Zanesville Glass

Glassware was produced in Zanesville, Ohio, from as early as 1815 until 1851. Two companies produced clear and colored hollow ware pieces in five characteristic patterns: 1) diamond faceted, 2) broken swirls, 3) vertical swirls, 4) perpendicular fluting, 5) plain, with scalloped or fluted rims and strap handles. The most readily identified product is perhaps the whiskey bottles made in the vertical swirl pattern, often called globular swirls because of their full, round bodies. Their necks vary in width; some have a ringed rim and some are collared. They were made in several colors; amber, light green, and light aquamarine are the most common. Our advisor for this category is Mark Vuono; he is listed in the Directory under Connecticut.

Bottle, globular; amber, 24 ribs twisted right, lt scratches, 8" ..1,175.00
Bottle, globular; aqua, high kick-up, sm broken blister, 8½" 165.00
Bottle, globular; aqua, 24 broken swirl ribs, high kick-up, 8", 8" .5,900.00
Bottle, globular; aqua, 24 melon ribs, few pot stones, 7⅝" 275.00
Bottle, globular; aqua, 24 swirl ribs, pot stones/scratches, 7½" 330.00
Bottle, globular; brilliant golden amber, 24 swirl ribs, 7½" 2,200.00
Bottle, globular; citron, 24 tightly swirled ribs, pot stone, 7½" .4,500.00
Bottle, globular; dk amber, 24 vertical ribs, flaw/burst blister, 6" ..795.00
Bottle, globular; dk amber, 3" 1,320.00
Bottle, globular; golden amber, 24 tightly swirled ribs, 8¼", EX.770.00
Bottle, globular; lt aqua, 3" 300.00

Bottle, globular, medium amber, 24 embossed ribs swirled to the right, pontil scar, rolled rim, 1830 – 1840, 8½", $575.00.

Bottle, globular; olive gr, appl lip, few pot stones, 7⅜" 385.00
Bottle, globular; olive gr, tiny pot stones/wear, 9½" 825.00
Creamer, brilliant violet bl, appl hdl, 4½" 2,640.00
Flask, chestnut; brilliant dk amber, 10-dmn, 5¼" 3,960.00
Flask, chestnut; brilliant lt gr, 24 swirl ribs, polished lip, 5" 440.00
Pan, aqua, 10-dmn, flared sides, folded-in rim, 2x5⅜" 8,470.00
Pan, dk amber, 24-rib, folded-in rim, minor scratches, 1¼x6¼" ..4,840.00
Pan, golden, flared sides, folded-out rim, pot stone, 2x9" 1,045.00
Pitcher, lt gr, 24 swirl ribs, rib hdl w/flourish at terminal, 6" .21,725.00

Zanesville Stoneware Company

Still in operation at its original location in Zanesville, Ohio, this company is the last surviving pottery dating from Zanesville's golden era of pottery production. They manufactured utilitarian stoneware, art ware vases, jardiniers and pedestals, dinnerware, and large hand-turned vases for use in outdoor gardens. Much of this ware has remained unidentified until today, since they often chose to mark their wares only with item numbers or the names of their various clients. Other items were marked with an impressed circular arrangement containing the company name and location or a three-line embossed device, the bottom line of which contained the letters ZSC. For more information we recommend *Zanesville Stoneware Company* by Jon Rans, Glenn Ralston, and Nate Russell (Collector Books).

Candle holder, Matt Lavender, saucer style, #D-15, 2", from $65 to.95.00
Candlestick, Matt Green, 6-sided, #85, 7¼", from $65 to.............95.00
Lamp base, Matt Blue, #785, 8½", from $150 to 200.00
Pitcher, Matt Green, #D-3, 3½", from $15 to 20.00
Pitcher, Matt Lavender, horizontal ribs, #579, 9", from $125 to .175.00
Pitcher, Matt Rose, horizontal ribs, #D-6, 5", from $35 to 45.00
Planter, pig, #314, 5⅛", from $65 to..95.00
Spittoon, Matt Lavender, #101, 8½", from $125 to....................150.00
Teapot, Matt Green, w/lid, #D1, 3½", from $25 to........................35.00
Vase, Ebonello, yel w/blk drip, #J, 12", from $175 to...................250.00
Vase, emb leaf, various glazes, #102, 8", from $125 to 175.00
Vase, Forest Green Overflow, #108W, 15", from $225 to 275.00
Vase, Gloss Aqua, #829, 9", from $100 to 125.00
Vase, Gloss Black, horizontal ribs, #B11, 12½", from $150 to.....200.00
Vase, Gloss Yellow, #J, 12", from $150 to 175.00
Vase, Matt Blue, #510, 4½", from $30 to 45.00
Vase, Matt Green, bulbous bottom, tab handes, #720, 9", from $125 to.175.00
Vase, Matt Lavender, #B-6, 11", from $75 to 100.00
Vase, Matt Rose, #D23, 8", from $100 to 125.00
Vase, Rubble Ware, brn, 2-hdld, #565, 11", from $150 to...........200.00
Vase, Vulcan, #38, 10", from $150 to 200.00

Zark

Established circa 1907 in St. Louis, Missouri, the Ozark Pottery made artware which it sold through an outlet called Zark Shops, hence the use of the Zark trademark. Most of their output was earthenware, but high-fired pottery has been reported as well. Some of the decoration was slip painted, other pieces were embossed. It operated for only a few years, perhaps closing as early as 1910. One of its founders and the primary designer was Robert Bringhurst, who was best known as a sculptor. Pieces are marked Zark, either incised or impressed. Our advisors for this category are Suzanne Perrault and David Rago; they are listed in the Directory under New Jersey.

Pitcher, bl-gr matt, re-attached ice lip, 7¼x8½", from $150 to ..200.00
Pitcher, teal matt, hdl w/sq terminal, 7x8" 220.00
Vase, charcoal/gr matt, angled shoulder, tapers toward base, 8" ..900.00
Vase, gr semi-matt w/charcoaling, mk, 6½", NM........................200.00
Vase, mtns reflected on lake w/water lilies, bl/turq matt, 9x4", EX.2,410.00

Zell

The Georg Schmider United Zell Ceramic Factories has a long and colorful history. Affectionately called 'Zell' by those who are attracted to this charming German-Dutch type tin-glazed earthenware, this type of ware came into production in the latter part of the last century.

While Zell has created some lovely majolica-like examples (which are beginning to attract their own following), it is the German-Dutch scenes that are collected with such enthusiasm. Typical scenes are set against a lush green background with windmills on the distant horizon. Into the scenes appear typically garbed girls (long dresses with long white aprons and low-land bonnet head-gear) being teased or admired by little boys attired in pantaloon-type trousers and short rust-colored jackets, all wearing wooden shoes. There are variations on this theme, and occasionally a collector may find an animal theme or even a Kate Greenaway-like scene.

While Zell produced a wide range of wares and even quite recently (1970s) introduced an entirely hand-painted hen/rooster line, it is this early charming German-Dutch theme pottery that is coveted by increasing numbers of devoted collectors.

A similar ware in both theme, technique, and quality but bearing the mark Haag or Made in Austria is included in this listing. Our advisor for this category is Lila Shrader; she is listed in the Directory under California.

Key:
KG — Kate Greenaway style MIA — Made in Austria

Bowl, boy & girl on waterfront path, windmill beyond, Germany, 10½"...136.00
Bowl, flat rim soup; boys tease girls/windmill beyond, Germany, 7¾"...48.00
Bowl, mixing; boy & girl strolling, Baden, lg, 4¾x10½"............225.00
Bowl, ped ft, pointy tab hdls, Baden, 3¼x5"..............................65.00
Butter pat, boy strolling, Baden, 2¼"..95.00
Candlestick, boys strolling, drip-guard top, Baden, 6½".............210.00
Chamber pot, bunnies & ducks on path, hdl, Baden, 4x5½"......220.00
Child's feeding dish, boy on waterfront path, windmill beyond, 7"...72.50
Coffeepot, hen & rooster theme, Germany, 9"..............................40.00
Creamer, animals at play, hdl at right angle to spout, MIA, 3½"..55.00
Creamer, Variety Is...Life, hdl at right angle to spout, MIA, 3½" .55.00
Cup, bunnies & ducks on road, Haag, oversz, 3x4½"..................68.00
Cup & saucer, teacup shape, various scenes, Baden, from $30 to..55.00
Cup & saucer, teacup shape, various scenes, Germany, from $25 to...42.00
Egg cup, dbl; hen & rooster theme, Germany, 4", from $18 to......27.50
Egg cup, hen & rooster theme, Germany, 2¼"..............................12.00
Lamp base, kerosene; boys w/dog, old brass mts, Germany, 9½" .245.00
Mug, Delft-like w/typical Dutch scene, bl & wht, 3½"..................78.00
Mug, girl feeding ducks, windmill beyond, Germany, 3½" 36.00
Mug, mother hanging clothes on line, KG, Baden, 3"...................95.00
Pitcher, pipe-smoking man on path w/dog, windmill beyond, 7¾" ..165.00
Plaque, boy stealing kiss, brass (or copper) rtcl fr, 12½".............388.00
Plaque, various scenes, brass (or copper) rtcl fr, 3½" dia 55.00
Plate, birds, grapes & leaves, majolica-like, Germany, 9½" 37.50
Plate, bunny munching on greenery, Germany, 6" dia..................38.00
Plate, dandelions, fluted edge, majolica-like, 11½"........................30.00
Plate, Delft-like, boy departing sadly from girl, bl/wht, Haag, 9½" .128.00
Plate, girl holding baby w/boy looking on, KG, Germany, 7¼".....55.00
Plate, girls playing Ring Around the Rosey, Haag, 8"....................55.00
Plate, girls teasing shy girl, KG, Baden, 8" 75.00
Plate, gooseberries on basketweave, majolica-like, Germany, 7" ...28.00
Plate, proverb: Time Wasted Cannot Be..., Haag, 9" 75.00
Shakers, boys strolling & boys chased by geese, Haag, 3½", pr 88.00
Sugar bowl, girl on path w/chickens, MIA, w/lid, 3½"..................34.00
Teapot, detailed rooster chasing girl, MIA, 4¾x7".......................195.00
Tumbler, various scenes, Baden, 4½", from $45 to.........................58.00
Vase, bears dancing in forest, slim w/flared base, Haag, 7" 98.00
Vase, boy & girl on waterfront path, windmill beyond, Baden, 6¼" ..78.00
Wall pocket, old stooped man in garden w/wheelbarrow, Baden, 7½" ..225.00

Zsolnay

Only until the past decade has the production of the Zsolnay factory become more correctly understood. In the beginning they produced only cement; industrial and kitchen ware manufacture began in the 1850s, and in the early 1870s a line of decorative architectural and art pottery was initiated which has continued to the present time.

The city of Pecs (pronounced Paach) is the major provincial city of southwest Hungary close to the Yugoslav border. The old German name for the city was Funfkirchen, meaning 'Five Churches.' (The 'five-steeple' mark became the factory's logo in 1878.)

Although most Americans only think of Zsolnay in terms of the bizarre, reticulated examples of the 1880s and 1890s and the small 'Eosine' green figures of animals and children that have been produced since the 1920s, the factory went through all the art trends of major international art potteries and produced various types of forms and decorations. The 'golden period,' circa 1895 – 1920, is when its Art Nouveau (Sezession in Austro-Hungarian terms) examples were unequaled. Vilmos Zsolnay was a Renaissance man devoted to innovation, and his children carried on the tradition after his death in 1900. Important sculptors and artists of the day were employed (usually anonymously) and married into the family, creating a dynasty.

Nearly all Zsolnay is marked, either impressed 'Zsolnay Pecs' or with the 'five steeple' stamp. Variations and form numbers can date a piece fairly accurately. For the most part, the earlier ethnic historical-revival pieces do not bring the prices that the later Sezession and second Sezession (Deco) examples do. Our advisor for this category is John Gacher; he is listed in the Directory under Rhode Island.

Box, cherub on lid, gr metallic Eosin on ochre, #8695, 1912, 8½" H ..3,000.00
Bust, Luna, lady w/eyes closed, Eosin w/tinting, #5494, 1899, 27½"..35,000.00
Cache pot, birds/bushes/hills/trees, bl Eosin sky, 1904-05, 6½" .15,000.00
Cache pot, Diana walking at night, artist sgn, #9389, 1910, 9x8"..9,500.00
Cache pot, girls around tree, Labrador glazes, #7770, 1904, 13" ..9,500.00
Cache pot, leaves, etched gr & gold Eosin, #5686, 1899-1900, 8¾x10".5,500.00
Figurine, nude, seated/despondent, Eosin, bl/gr, 5½x4¾x9⅜" 460.00
Figurine, tiger, #6153, ca 1898-1908, minor rstr, 12x18½" 5,500.00
Lamp, ballet dancer w/bodice over head, #6234, 1900, 22½" .25,000.00
Lamp, flower form, gr/bl Eosin w/red bloom shade, #6261, 1900, 14½" .15,000.00
Pitcher, cock figural, later glaze, #1132, restruck ca 1900, 18", NM..4,950.00
Pitcher, organic Sezession design, bl & gr Eosin, #5517, 1899, 13½" .9,500.00
Pitcher, squash form w/Eosin leaves & vines, #6221, 1900, 13¾" .12,500.00
Vase, ancient-look geometric incised lines in gr Eosin, 1908, 3¾"...750.00
Vase, birds w/plumes, mc Eosin on marbled ground w/gold, 1908, 12¼" .22,500.00
Vase, Egyptian decor, gold/gr Eosin w/red on bl, 1920s, 17½" .8,500.00
Vase, Egyptian decor, gr/gold/copper lustre/red, 1920s, 5" 1,500.00
Vase, Eosin holly leaves & blossoms on maroon, #7805, ca 1906, 9" ..2,500.00
Vase, fire-yel/red/brn drips on bl & gl-gray, 1900, 8¼x2½" 2,500.00
Vase, Goose Girl, mc Eosin, #5561, 1898, 15¾" 17,500.00
Vase, Hungarian ethnic form w/florals on red, #6171, 1900, 9"...6,500.00
Vase, landscape, rainbow metallic Eosin, #5288, ca 1898, 7¾", NM..5,000.00
Vase, organic form, gold Eosin w/gr highlights, #5736, 1899, 11½" ..6,500.00
Vase, Oriental floral, metallic silver/bl/gray on maroon, 1900-15, 11"..2,500.00
Vase, pods on stems w/leaves w/Eosin grass, 1905, 5", NM 5,000.00
Vase, ribbon hdls, faint Eosin on maroon lustre, #5338, 1898, 9" .2,580.00
Vase, spiral/helical lines, Sezession, Pecs mk, unmk #6319, 1900, 5"...5,000.00
Vase, stylized flowers on putty, #7926, ca 1906, sm rpr, 10" ...12,500.00
Vase, trees, brn w/gr Eosin foliage w/sun, #6011/M/20, 1900, 8½" ...13,500.00
Vase, Turkish design w/jewel-like designs, #8652, 1912, 3⅞" ..2,500.00

Advisory Board

The editors and staff take this opportunity to express our sincere gratitude and appreciation to each person who has in any way contributed to the preparation of this guide. We believe the credibility of our book is greatly enhanced through their efforts. See each advisor's Directory listing for information concerning their specific areas of expertise.

You will notice that at the conclusion of some of the narratives the advisor's name is given. This is optional and up to the discretion of each individual. Simply because no name is mentioned does not indicate that we have no advisor for that subject. Our board grows with each issue and now numbers nearly 425; if you care to correspond with any of them or anyone listed in our Directory, you must send a SASE with your letter. If you are seeking an appraisal, first ask about their fee, since many of these people are professionals who must naturally charge for their services. Because of our huge circulation, every person who allows us to publish their name runs the risk of their privacy being invaded by too many phone calls and letters. We are indebted to every advisor and very much regret losing any one of them. By far, the majority of those we lose give that reason. Please help us retain them on our board by observing the simple rules of common courtesy. Take the differences in time zones into consideration; some of our advisors tell us they often get phone calls in the middle of the night. For suggestions that may help you evaluate your holdings, see the Introduction.

Barbara J. Steve Aaronson
Northridge, California

Peter Abrahams
Lake Oswego, Oregon

Charles and Barbara Adams
South Yarmouth, Massachusetts

Stan and Sally Alekna
Lebanon, Pennsylvania

Beverly L. Ales
Pleasanton, California

Charles Alexander
Indianapolis, Indiana

Craig Ambrose
Des Moines, Iowa

James Anderson
New Brighton, Minnesota

Suzy McLennan Anderson
Holmdel, New Jersey

Tim Anderson
Provo, Utah

Warren R. Anderson
Cedar City, Utah

Bruce A. Austin
Pittsford, New York

Bobby Babcock
Austin, Texas

Veldon Badders
Hamlin, New York

Rod Baer
Vienna, Virginia

Wayne and Gale Bailey
Dacula, Georgia

Jacqueline Linscott Barnes
Titusville, Florida

Kit Barry
Brattleboro, Vermont

Mark Bassett
Lakewood, Ohio

Dana Martin Batory
Crestline, Ohio

Scott Benjamin
LaGrange, Ohio

Sammie Berry
Melbourne, Florida

Phyllis and Tom Bess
Tulsa, Oklahoma

Robert Bettinger
Mt. Dora, Florida

William M. Bilsland III
Cedar Rapids, Iowa

Brenda Blake
York Harbor, Maine

Robert and Stan Block
Trumbull, Connecticut

Clarence H. Bodine, Jr.
New Hope, Pennsylvania

Sandra V. Bondhus
Unionville, Connecticut

Clifford Boram
Monticello, Indiana

Jeff Bradfield
Dayton, Virginia

Shane Branchcomb
Ashburn, Virginia

Mike Brooks
Oakland, California

Jim Broom
Effingham, Illinois

Dr. Kirby William Brown
Paradise, California

Marcia Brown
White City, Oregon

Rick Brown
Newspaper Collector's Society of America
Lansing, Michigan

Donald A. Bull
Wirtz, Virginia

Ann Burton
Decatur, Michigan

Jim Calison
Wallkill, New York

Tina M. Carter
El Cajon, California

Gene Cataldo
Huntsville, Alabama

Cerebro
East Prospect, Pennsylvania

Mick and Lorna Chase
Cookeville, Tennessee

Pat and Chris Christensen
Costa Mesa, California

Victor J.W. Christie, Ed. D.
Ephrata, Pennsylvania

Lanette Clarke
Antioch, California

John Cobabe
Redondo Beach, California

Debbie and Randy Coe
Lafayette, Oregon

Wilfred and Dolli Cohen
Santa Ana, California

Marilyn Cooper
Houston, Texas

Ryan Cooper
Yarmouthport, Massachusetts

J.W. Courter
Kevil, Kentucky

Rosalind Cranor
Blacksburg, Virginia

Bob Culver
Northville, Michigan

Ron Damaska
New Brighton, Pennsylvania

John Danis
Rockford, Illinois

Patricia M. Davis
Portland, Oregon

Hal & Meredith DeGood
Des Moines, Iowa

Loretta DeLozier
Lake Placid, Florida

Clive Devenish
Orinda, California

Joe Devine
Council Bluffs, Iowa

David Dilley
Indianapolis, Indiana

Thomas P. Dimitroff
Corning, New York

Ginny Distel
Tiffin, Ohio

Rod Dockery
Ft. Worth, Texas

L.R. 'Les' Docks
San Antonio, Texas

Rebecca Dodds
Coral Springs, Florida

Brenda Dollen
Minden, Iowa

Darlene Dommel
Minneapolis, Minnesota

Ron Donnelly
Tuscaloosa, Alabama

Kathy Doub
Columbia, Maryland

Robert A. Doyle, C.A.I., I.S.A.
Pleasant Valley, New York

James Dryden
Hot Springs National Park, Arkansas

Louise Dumont
Leesburg, Florida

Jeanne Dunay
Camden, South Carolina

Ken and Jackie Durham
Washington, DC

William Durham
Belvidere, Illinois

Rita and John Ebner
Columbus, Ohio

Bill Edwards
Madison, Indiana

Kathy Eichert
Ojai, California

Michael L. Ellis
Costa Mesa, California

Dr. Robert Elsner
Boynton Beach, Florida

Barbara Endter
Rochester, New York

Bryce Farnsworth
Fargo, North Dakota

Arthur M. Feldman
Highland Park, Illinois

Linda Fields
Dover, Tennessee

Vicki Flanigan
Winchester, Virginia

Gene Florence
Lexington, Kentucky

Marv Fogleman
Santa Ana, California

Frank W. Ford
Shrewsbury, Massachusetts

Madeleine France
Ft. Lauderdale, Florida

Peter Frei
Brimfield, Massachusetts

Wendy and Leo Frese
Dallas, Texas

Tony Freyaldenhoven
Conway, Arkansas

John Walter
Marietta, Ohio

Judith and Robert Walthall
Huntsville, Alabama

Ian Warner
Brampton, Ontario, Canada

Marty Webster
Saline, Michigan

David Weddington
Murfreesboro, Tennessee

Robert Weisblut
Wheaton, Maryland

Pastor Frederick S. Weiser
New Oxford, Pennsylvania

Stan and Arlene Weitman
Massapequa, New York

BA Wellman
Westminster, Massachusetts

Lonnie Wells
Rocklin, California

David Wendel
Poplar Bluff, Missouri

Kaye and Jim Whitaker
Lynnwood, Washington

Douglass White
Orlando, Florida

John 'Grandpa' White
Denver, Colorado

Judy White
La Jolla, California

Margaret and Kenn Whitmyer
Gahanna, Ohio

Steven Whysel
Cooper City, Florida

Doug Wiesehan
St. Charles, Missouri

Don Williams
Kirksville, Missouri

Linda Williams
Chicopee, Massachusetts

Ron L. Willis
Matlacha, Florida

Roy M. Willis
Lebanon Junction, Kentucky

Jack D. Wilson
Prescott, Arizona

Grant S. Windsor
Richmond, Virginia

Ralph Winslow
Camdenton, Missouri

Nancy Winston
Northwood, New Hampshire

Jo Ellen Winther
Arvada, Colorado

Raphael C. Wise
West Palm Beach, Florida

Dannie Woodard
Weatherford, Texas

Virginia Woodbury
Rolling Hills Estates, California

Bill Wright
New Albany, Indiana

Libby Yalom
Silver Spring, Maryland

Darlene Yohe
Stuttgart, Arkansas

Mary Young
Kettering, Ohio

Willy Young
Reno, Nevada

Audrey Zeder
North Bend, Washington

Auction Houses

We wish to thank the following auction houses whose catalogs have been used as sources for pricing information. Many have granted us permission to reproduce their photographs as well.

A-1 Auction Service
2042 N. Rio Grande Ave., Suite 'E,' Orlando, FL 32804; 407-839-0004; e-mail: a-1auction@cfl.rr.com. Specializing in American antique sales

A&B Auctions, Inc.
17 Sherman St., Marlboro, MA 01752-3314; 508-480-0006 or fax: 508-460-6101. Specializing in English ceramics, flow blue, pottery, and Mason's Ironstone

Absolute Auction & Realty, Inc./Absolute Auction Center
Robert Doyle
PO Box 1739, Pleasant Valley, NY 12569. Antique and estate auctions twice a month at Absolute Auction Center; free calendar of auctions; www.absoluteauctionrealty.com

Allard Auctions Inc.
Col. Doug Allard
PO Box 1030, 419 Flathead St., Ste. 4, Ignatiuss, MT 59865; 406-745-0500 or fax: 406-745-0502; e-mail: allard auctions.com; allardauctions.com. Specializing in American Indian collectibles

America West Archives
Anderson, Warren
PO Box 100, Cedar City, UT 84721; 435-586-9497; e-mail: warren@america westarchives.com; americawestarchives. com; related website: www.oldstockre search.com. Publishes 26-page illustrated catalog 5 times a year that includes auction section of scarce and historical early western documents, letters, autographs, stock certificates, and other important ephemera, subscription: $13 per year

American Social History and Social Movements
PO Box 203, Tucker, GA 30085; 678-937-1835; fax: 678-937-1837; e-mail: admin@ashsm.com; www.ashsm.com

Americana Auctions
c/o Glen Rairigh
12633 Sandborn, Sunfield, MI 48890. Specializing in Skookum dolls, art glass, and art auctions

Anderson Auctions/Heritage
Antiques & Appraisal Services
Suzy McLennan Anderson
65 E. Main St., Holmdel, NJ 07733; 732-946-8801 or fax: 732-946-1036; www.andersonauctions.net/antiques. htm. Specializing in American furniture and decorative accessories

Andre Ammelounx
The Stein Auction Company
PO Box 136, Palatine, IL 60078-0136; 847-991-5927 or fax: 847-991-5947. Specializing in steins, catalogs available; www.tsaco.com

Aston Macek
2825 Country Club Rd., Endwell, NY 13760-3349; phone/fax: 607-785-6598; e-mail: astonmacek@stnyrr.com. Specializing in and appraisers of American folk art, other primitives, furniture Shaker, fine art, porcelain, and china; www.astonmacek.com; also have auctions on the internet: eBay (folkman 2) and ehammer (folkman@stnylrun.com)

Bider's
397 Methuen St., Lawrence, MA 01843; 978-688-0923 or 978-475-8336; e-mail: bider@netway.com. Antiques appraised, purchased, and sold on consignment; www.biders-auction.com

Bill Bertoia Auctions
2141 DeMarco Dr., Vineland, NJ 08360; 856-692-1881 or fax: 856-692-8697. Specializing in toys, dolls, advertising, and related items; e-mail: Bill@BertoiaAuctions.com; www.bertoiaauctions.com

Block's Box
PO Box 51, Trumbull, CT 06611; 203-261-0057 or 203-926-8448; Buy and sell marbles in online auctions. www.blocksite.com

Bonhams & Butterfields
220 San Bruno Ave., San Francisco, CA 94103; 415-861-7500 or fax: 415-861-8951. Also located at: 7601 Sunset Blvd., Los Angeles, CA 90046; 323-850-7500 or fax: 323-850-5843. Fine art Auctioneers and Appraisers since 1865; e-mail: info@butterfields.com; www.butterfields.com

Buffalo Bay Auction Co.
5244 Quam Circle, Rogers, MN 55374; 612-428-8480 or fax: 612-428-8879; e-mail: buffalobay@hotmail.com. Specializing in advertising, tins, and country store items; buffalo bayauction.com

Cerebro
PO Box 327, E. Prospect, PA 17317-0327; 717-252-2400 or 800-69-LABEL; fax: 717-252-3685; e-mail: Cerebro@Cerebro.com. Specializing in antique advertising labels, especially cigar box labels, cigar bands, food labels, firecracker labels; holds semiannual auction on tobacco ephemera; consignments accepted; www.cerebro.com

Charles E. Kirtley
PO Box 2273, Elizabeth City, NC 27096; phone/fax: 919-335-1262; e-mail: ckirtley@erols.com. Specializing in World's Fair, Civil War, political, advertising, and other American collectibles

Cincinnati Art Galleries
225 E. Sixth, Cincinnati, OH 45202; 513-381-2128; fax: 513-381-7527. Specializing in American art pottery, American and European fine paintings, watercolors; www.cincinnatiart galleries.com

Collector's Auction Services
R.D. 2, Box 431, Oil City, PA 16301-9426; 814-677-6070; e-mail: director @caswel.com. Specializing in advertising, oil and gas, toys, rare museum and investment-quality antiques; www. caswel.com

Craftsman Auctions
1485 W Housatonic (Rt 20); Pittsfield, MA 01201; 413-448-8922. Specializing in Arts & Crafts furniture and accessories as well as American art pottery. Color catalogs available; www.artsn crafts.com or www.ragoarts.com

Dargate Auction Galleries
214 N. Lexington, Pittsburgh, PA 15208; e-mail: info@dargate.com. Specializing in estate auctions featuring fine art, antiques, and collectibles; www.dargate.com

David Rago
333 N. Main, Lambertville, NJ 08530; 609-397-9374 or fax: 609-397-9377; e-mail: info@ragoarts.com. Specializing in American art pottery and Arts and Crafts; www.ragoarts.com

Du Mouchelles
409 E Jefferson Ave., Detroit, MI 48226-4300; 313-963-6255 or fax: 313-963-8199; e-mail: info@dumouchelle.com; dumouchelle.com

Dunbar's Gallery
Leila and Howard Dunbar
76 Haven St., Milford, MA 01757; 508-634-8697 or fax: 508-634-8698; e-mail: Dunbars@mediaone.net or www.dunbarsgallery.com

Early American History Auctions
PO Box 3507, Rancho Santa Fe, CA 92067; 858-759-3290 or fax: 619-374-7280; e-mail: history@earlyamerican.com; www.earlyamerican.com

Early Auction Co.
123 Main St., Milford, OH 45150-1121; 513-831-4833 or fax: 513-831-1441; e-mail: info@EarlyAuctionCo.com; EarlyAuctionCo.com

Flying Deuce Auctions & Antiques
1224 Yellowstone Ave., Pocatello, ID 83201-4323; 208-237-2002 or fax: 208-237-4544; e-mail: flying2@nicoh.com; www.flying2.com

Fontaine's Auction Gallery
1485 W. Housatonic St., Pittsfield, MA 01201; 413-448-8922 or fax: 413-442-1550; e-mail: ifontain@rr.nycap.com. Specializing in fine quality antiques; important 20th-century lighting, clocks, art glass; color catalogs available; www.fontaineauction.com

Frank's Antiques & Auctions
2405 N. Kings Rd., Hilliard, FL 32046-3332; 904-845-2870 or fax: 904-845-4000; e-mail: franksauct@aol.com. Specializing in antique advertising, country store items, rec room and restaurant decor as well as sporting collectibles, pottery and stoneware; catalogs issued; www.franksauctions.com

Garth's Auctions Inc.
2690 Stratford Rd., Box 369, Delaware, OH 43015; 740-362-4771; e-mail: info@garths.com or www.garths.com

Glass-Works Auctions
102 Jefferson, East Greenville, PA 18041-11623; 215-679-5849 or fax: 215-679-3068; e-mail: glswrk@enter.net. America's leading auction company in early American bottles and glass and barber shop memorabilia; www.glswk-auction.com

Harmer Rooke Galleries
32 E. 57th St, 11th Floor, New York, NY 10022-2513; 212-751-1900 or fax: 212-758-1713

Heights Antiques
29 Clubhouse Lane, Boynton Beach, FL 33436-6056; 561-736-1362. Specializing in antique barometers and nautical instruments

Henry/Pierce Auctioneers
1456 Carson Court, Homewood, IL 60430-4013; 708-798-7508 or fax: 708-799-3594. Specializing in bank auctions

High Noon
9929 Venice Blvd., Los Angeles, CA 90034-5111; 310-202-9010 or fax: 310-202-9011; e-mail: highnoon@pacbell.net. Specializing in cowboy and western collectibles; www.highnoon.com

History Buff's Auctions
6031 Winterset, Lansing, MI 48911; e-mail: admin@historybuffauction.com. Specializing in paper collectibles spanning 5 centuries; www.historybuffauction.com

Horst Auctioneers
Horst Auction Center
50 Durlach Rd. (corner of Rt. 322 & Durlach Rd., West of Ephrata), Ephrata, Lancaster County, PA 17522-9741; 717-738-3080; e-mail: sale@horstauction.com; Voices of Experience; www.horstauction.com

Jackson's, Auctioneers & Appraisers of Fine Art
2229 Lincoln St., Cedar Falls, IA 50613; 319-277-2256 or fax: 319-277-1252; e-mail: jacksons@jacksonsauction.com. Specializing in American and European art pottery and art glass, American and European paintings, Russian works of art, decorative arts, toys and jewelry; www.jacksonsauction.com

James D. Julia
PO Box 830, Rt. 201, Skowhegan Rd., Fairfield, ME 04937-0830; 207-453-7125 or fax: 207-453-2502; e-mail: jjulia@juliaauctions.com or www.juliaauctions.com

John Toomey Gallery
818 North Blvd., Oak Park, IL 60301-1302; 708-383-5234 or fax: 708-383-4828; e-mail: arts@oprf.com. Specializing in furniture and decorative arts of the Arts & Crafts, Art Deco, and Modern Design movements; modern design expert: Richard Wright; www.treadwaygallery.com

Joy Luke Auctioneers & Appraisers
The Gallery
300 East Grove St., Bloomington, IL 61701-5290; 309-828-5533 or fax: 309-829-2266; e-mail: joyluke@aol.com; www.joyluke.com

Kit Barry Ephemera Auctions
136 High St., Brattleboro, VT 05301; 802-254-3634. Tradecard and ephemera auctions, fully illustrated catalogs with prices realized; consignment inquiries welcome; www.trade cards.com/kb

Kurt R. Krueger
160 N. Washington St., PO Box 275, Iola, WI 54945-0275; 715-445-3845 or fax: 715-445-4100

L.R. 'Les' Docks
Box 691035, San Antonio, TX 78269-1035; e-mail: docks@texas.net. Providing occasional mail-order record auctions, rarely consigned; the only consignments considered are exceptionally scarce and unusual records; www.docks.home.texas.net

Lloyd Ralston Gallery, Inc.
350 Long Beach Blvd., Stratfort CT 06615; 203-386-9399; fax: 203-386-9519; e-mail: lrgallery@aol.com; www.lloydralstontoys.com

Lowe, James Lewis
PO Box 8, Norwood, PA 19074. Specializing in Kate Greenaway, postcards; eBay: JLewisLowe@juno.com

Majolica Auctions
Strawser Auction Group
200 North Main, PO Box 332, Wolcottville, IN 46795-0332; 260-854-2859 or fax: 260-854-3979; e-mail: michael@strawserauctions.com; issues colored catalog; also specializing in Fiesta ware

Manion's International Auction House, Inc.
PO Box 12214, Kansas City, KS 66112-0214; 913-299-6692 or fax: 913-299-6792; e-mail: collecting@manions.com. Specializing in international militaria, particularly the US, Germany, and Japan. Extensive catalogs in antiques and collectibles, sports, transportation, political and advertising memorabilia, and vintage clothing and denim. Publishes 9 catalogs for each of the 5 categories per year. Request a free sample of past auctions, 1 issue of current auction for $15; www.manions.com

Maritime Antiques & Auctions
935 US Rt. 1, PO Box 322, York, ME 03909-0322; 207-363-4247 or fax: 353-1416; www.maritiques.com

McMasters Harris Auction Company
PO Box 1755, 5855 Glenn Highway, Cambridge, OH 43725-8768; 740-432-4419 or fax: 740-432-3191; or 800-842-3526; e-mail: info@mcmastersauctions.com; mcmastersauctions.com

Michael Ivankovich Antiques & Auction Company Inc.
PO Box 1536, Doylestown, PA, 18901; 215-345-6094 or fax: 215-345-6692; e-mail: ivankovich@wnutting.com. Specializing in early hand-colored photography and prints; auction held 4 times each year, providing opportunity for collectors and dealers to compete for the largest variety of Wallace Nutting, Wallace Nutting-like pictures, Maxfield Parrish, Bessie Pease Gutmann, R. Atkinson Fox, Philip Boileau, Harrison Fisher, etc.

Michael John Verlangieri
PO Box 844, Cambria, CA 93428-0844; 805-927-4428. Specializing in fine California pottery; cataloged auctions (video tapes available); www.calpots.com

Monsen & Baer, Annual Perfume Bottle Auction
Randall Monsen and Rod Baer
Box 529, Vienna, VA 22183; 703-938-2129 or fax: 703-242-1357. Cataloged auctions of perfume bottles; will purchase, sell, and accept consignments; specializing in commercial, Czechoslovakian, Lalique, Baccarat, Victorian, crown top, factices, miniatures

Neal Auction Company
Auctioneers & Appraisers of Antiques & Fine Art
4038 Magazine St., New Orleans, LA 70115; 504-899-5329 or 1-800-467-5329; fax: 504-897-3803; e-mail: customerservice@nealauction.com; nealauction.com

New England Absentee Auctions
16 Sixth St., Stamford, CT 06905-4610; 203-975-9055; e-mail: neaauction@aol.com. Specializing in Quimper pottery; www.members.tripod.com/~bondhus

Noel Barrett Antiques & Auctions
PO Box 300, 6183 Carversville Rd., Carversville, PA 18913; 215-297-5109 or fax: 215-297-0457; e-mail: nbaa@comcat.com; www.noelbarret.com

Norman C. Heckler & Company
79 Bradford Corner Rd., Woodstock Valley, CT 06282-2002; 860-974-1634 or fax: 860-974-2003. Auctioneers and appraisers specializing in early glass and bottles; e-mail: info@hecklerauction.com; www.hecklerauction.com

Pacific Glass Auctions
1507 21st St., Ste. 203, Sacramento, CA 95814; 800-806-7722 or fax: 916-443-3199. Specializing in antique bottles; www.pacglass.com

Past Tyme Pleasures
Steve & Donna Howard
PMB #204, 2491 San Ramon Blvd., #1, San Ramon, CA 94583; 925-484-4488 or fax: 925-484-2551; e-mail: pastyme1@attbi.com. Offers 2 absentee auction catalogs per year pertaining to old advertising items; www.pasttyme1.com

Perrault-Rago Gallery
333 N. Main St., Lambertville, NJ 08530; 609-397-9374. Specializing in American art pottery, tiles, Arts & Crafts, Moderns, and Bucks County paintings

Phillips International Auctioneers & Valuers
406 E. 79th St., New York, NY 10021-1498; 212-570-4830; www.phillips auctions.com

Richard Opfer Auctioneering, Inc.
1919 Greenspring Dr., Timonium, MD 21093-4113; 410-252-5035; fax: 410-252-5863; e-mail: info@opferauction.com; www.opferauction.com

Roan Bros. Auction Gallery
R.R. 4, Box 118, Cogan Station, PA 17728; 717-494-0170; 800-955-ROAN; e-mail: roaninc@srlink.net

Samuel T. Freeman & Co.
1808 Chestnut St., Philadelphia, PA 19103; 215-563-9275 or fax: 215-563-8236; freemansauction.com

Schoolmaster Auctions and Real Estate
Kenn Norris
PO Box 4830; 513 N. 2nd St., Sanderson, TX 79848; 915-345-2640. Specializing in school-related items, barbed wire and related literature, and L'il Abner

Skinner, Inc.
Auctioneers & Appraisers of Antiques and Fine Arts
The Heritage on the Garden, 63 Park Plaza, Boston, MA 02116-3925; 617-350-5400 or fax: 617-350-5429. Second address: 357 Main St., Bolton, MA 01740; 978-779-6241 or fax: 978-779-5144; www.skinnerinc.com

Smith & Jones, Inc.
12 Clark Lane, Sudbury, MA 01776; 978-443-5517 or fax: 978-443-8045. Specializing in Dedham dinnerware, Buffalo china, and important American art pottery; full-color catalogs available; smithandjonesauctions.com

SoldUSA.com
1418 Industrial Dr., Box 11, Matthews, NC 28105; 704-815-1500; e-mail: support@soldusa.com. Specializing in fine sporting collectibles; www.Soldusa.com

Sotheby's
1334 York Ave., New York, NY 10021; 212-606-7000; www.sothebys.com

Stanton's Auctioneers & Realtors
144 S. Main St., PO Box 146, Vermontville, MI 49096-0146; 517-726-0181; e-mail: stanton@voyager.net. Specializing in all types of property, at auction, anywhere; www.stantons-auctions.com

Steffen's Historical Militaria
Major Auction Division
PO Box 280, Newport, KY 41072; 858-431-4499 or fax: 859-431-3113. Specializing in quality militaria, military art, rare books, antique firearms; www.steffensmilitaria.com

Superior Galleries
9478 West Olympic Boulevard, Beverly Hills, CA 90212-4246; 310-203-9855 or fax: 310-203-0496. Specializing in manuscripts, decorative and fine arts, Hollywood memorabilia, sports memorabilia, stamps, and coins; www.superiorsc.com

Swann Galleries, Inc.
104 E. 25th St., New York, NY 10010; 312-254-4710 or fax: 212-979-1017; e-mail: swan@swanngalleries.com; www.swanngalleries.com

Three Rivers Collectibles
Wendy and Leo Frese
PO Box 551542, Dallas, TX 75355; 214-341-5165. Annual Red Wing and Rum-Rill pottery and stoneware auctions

Toy Scouts, Inc.
137 Casterton Ave., Akron, OH 44303-1543; 330-836-0668 or fax: 330-869-8668; e-mail: info@toyscouts.com. Specializing in baby-boom era collectibles; www.toyscouts.com

Tradewinds Auctions
Henry Taron
PO Box 249, 24 Magnolia Ave., Manchester-By-The-Sea, MA 01944-0249; 508-768-3327. Specializing in antique canes; www.tradewindantiques.com

Treadway Gallery, Inc.
2029 Madison Rd., Cincinnati, OH 45208-3218; 513-321-6742 or fax: 513-871-7722. Specializing in American art pottery; American and European art glass; European ceramics; Italian glass; fine American and European paintings and graphics; and furniture and decorative arts of the Arts & Crafts, Art Nouveau, Art Deco, and Modern Design Movements. Modern design expert: Thierry Lorthioir. Members: National Antique Dealers Association, American Art Pottery Association, International Society of Appraisers, American Ceramic Arts Society, Ohio Decorative Arts Society, Art Gallery Association of Cincinnati; www.treadwaygallery.com

Vicki and Bruce Waasdorp
PO Box 434; 10931 Main St.; Clarence, NY 14031; 716-759-2361. Specializing in decorated stoneware; www.antiques-stoneware.com

VintagePostcards.Com
Antique Postcards for Collectors
312 Feather Tree Dr. Clearwater FL 33765; 727-467-0333 e-mail: quality@vintagepostcards.com; www.vintagepostcards.com

Weschler's
Adam A. Weschler & Son
905 E. St. N.W., Washington, DC 20004-2006; 202-628-1281; www.weschlers.com

William Doyle Galleries
Auctioneers & Appraisers
175 East 87th St., New York, NY 10128; 212-427-2730 or fax: 212-369-0892; e-mail: info@DoyleNewYork.com; www.doylenewyork.com

Willis Henry Auctions
22 Main St., Marshfield, MA 02050-2808; 781-834-7774 or fax: 781-826-3520; e-mail: wha@willishenry.com; www.willishenry.com

York Town Auction Inc.
1625 Haviland Rd., York, PA 17404; 717-751-0211; fax: 717-767-7729; e-mail: info@yorktownauction.com. Specializing in the sale of antiques, art, collections, fine furnishings, and real estate; www.yorktownauction.com

Directory of Contributors

When contacting by mail any of the buyers/sellers listed in this part of the Directory, you must include a SASE (stamped, self-addressed envelope) if you expect a reply. As hectic as our lifestyles are, the time it saves them is probably worth more to them than the price of a stamp. Not only that, but trying to decipher someone's handwritten name and address can be very frustrating. Sometimes even zip codes are unreadable, and even more time is required to double check zip code numbers. And in the end, if 'Rosen' becomes 'Rirer' and 'Ave. 5' becomes 'Ave. S,' even if the person you contacted was gracious enough to answer you, you probably won't ever know he did. Many of these people are professional appraisers and there will be a fee for their time and service. Find out up front. Include a clear photo if you want an item identified. Most items cannot be described clearly enough to make an identification without a photo.

If you call and get their answering machine, when you leave your number so that they can return your call, tell them to call back collect. And please take the differences in time zones into consideration. 7:00 AM in the Midwest is only 4:00 AM in California! And if you're in California, remember that even 7:00 PM is too late to call the East Coast. Most people work and are gone during the daytime. Even some of our antique dealers say they prefer after-work phone calls. Don't assume that a person who deals in a particular field will be able to help you with related items. They may seem related to you when they are not.

Please, we need your help. This book sells in such great numbers that allowing their names to be published can create a potential nightmare for each advisor and contributor. Please do your part to help us minimize this, so that we can retain them on our board and in turn pass their experience and knowledge on to you through our book. Their only obligation is to advise us, not to evaluate your holdings. Many of our people tell us that even with the occasional problem, they feel that the good outweighs the bad and makes all their hard work worthwhile.

Alabama

Cataldo, Gene
C.E. Cataldo
4726 Panorama Dr., S.E., Huntsville, 35801; 256-536-6893; e-mail: genecams@aol.com. Specializing in classic and used cameras

Donnelly, Ron
Saturday Heroes
6302 Championship Dr., Tuscaloosa, 35405. Specializing in Big Little Books, movie posters, premiums, western heroes, Gone With the Wind, character collectibles, early Disney; inquiries require SASE; no free appraisals

Lippa, Matt; and Schaaf, Elizabeth
Artisans
PO Box 256, Mentone, 35984; 256-634-4037; e-mail: artisans@folkartisans.com. Specializing in folk art, quilts, painted and folky furniture, tramp art, whirligigs, windmill weights; www.folkartisans.com

Walthall, Judith and Robert
PO Box 4465, Huntsville, 35815; 256-881-9198. Judith founded Peanut Pals in 1978. Robert has served two terms as president of Peanut Pals. Specializing in Planters Peanuts memorabilia; also Old Crow collectibles

Arizona

Nelson, Maxine
7657 E. Hazelwood St., Scottsdale, 85251. Specializing in Vernon Kilns; author of *Collectible Vernon Kilns* (out of print). SASE appreciated for inquiries.

Roberts, Fred and Marilyn
Bah Humbug Collectibles
PO Box 5733, Lake Montezuma, 86342-5733 or fax: 815-425-9394; e-mail: bahhumbug@juno.com. Specializing in Hummel figurines

Wilson, Jack D.
1514 Eagle Ridge Road, Prescott, 86301-5418; 928-445-5137; e-mail: jdwilson1@earthlink.net. Specializing in Phoenix and Consolidated glass; buying Ruba Rombic; author of *Phoenix and Consolidated Art glass: 1926-1980*; home.earthlink.net~jdwilson1/

Arkansas

Dryden, James
Dryden Pottery
PO Box 603, Hot Springs National Park, 71902; 501-627-4201. Specializing in hand-thrown artware vases, mugs, ovenware, etc.

Freyaldenhoven, Tony
220 Ada AVe. Ste 305, Conway, 72034; 501-730-3027; e-mail: tonyfrey@conwaycorp.net. Specializing in Camark pottery

Roenigk, Martin
Mechantiques
Crescent Hotel & Spa
75 Prospect Ave., Eureka Springs, 72632; 800-671-6333; e-mail: mroenigk@aol.com. Specializing in mechanical musical instruments, music boxes, band organs, musical clocks and watches, coin pianos, orchestrions, monkey organs, automata, mechanical birds and dolls, etc.; www.mechantiques.com

Yohe, Darlene
Timberview Antiques
1303 S. Prairie St., Stuttgart, 72160-5132; 870-673-3437. Specializing in American pattern glass, historical glass, Victorian pattern glass, carnival glass, and custard glass

California

Aaronson, Barbara and Steve
The Victorian Lady
PO Box 7522, Northridge, 91327; 818-368-6052; e-mail: bjaaronson@aol.com. Specializing in figural napkin rings, pickle castors, American Victorian silverplate; TheVictorianLady.com

Ales, Beverly Schell
4046 Graham St., Pleasanton, 94566-5619; 925-846-5297; e-mail: Kniferests@sbcglobal.net. Specializing in knife rests

Berg, Paul
PO Box 8895, Newport Beach, 92620. Author of *Nineteenth Century Photographica Cases and Wall Frames*

Brooks, Mike
7335 Skyline, Oakland, 94611; 510-339-1751 (evenings). Specializing in typewriters, transistor radios, early televisions, Statue of Liberty

Brown, Dr. Kirby William
PO Box 1842, Paradise, 95967; 530-877-2159. Authoring book on history and products of California Faience, California porcelain, and West Coast porcelain. Any contribution of information, new pieces, etc., is welcome.

Carter, Tina M.
882 S. Mollison, El Cajon, 92020-6506; 619-440-5043. Specializing in teapots, tea-related items, tea tins, children's and toy tea sets, plastic cookie cutters, etc. Book on teapots available. Send $16 (includes postage) or $17 for CA residents, Canada: add $5, to above address

Christensen, Pat and Chris
1067 Salvador St., Costa Mesa, 92626. Specializing in open salts

Clarke, Lanette
5021 Toyon Way, Antioch, 94532; 925-776-7784; e-mail: Lanette_Clarke@msn.com. Co-founder of *Haeger Pottery Collectors of America*; specializing in Haeger and Royal Hickman

Cobabe, John
800 So. Pacific Coast Hwy; Suite 8-301; Redondo Beach 90277; 310-465-0752; e-mail: johncobabe@aol.com. Specializing in Amphora, Zsolnay, and Massier

Cohen, Wilfred and Dolli
Antiques & Art Glass
PO Box 27151, Santa Ana, 92799; 714-545-5673; e-mail: antsandartglass@aol.com. Specializing in Wave Crest (C.F. Monroe); French cameo glass; Victorian-era art and pattern glass (salt shakers, toothpick holders, syrups, cruets, sugar shakers, tumblers, biscuit jars, table and pitcher sets); art glass and cameo glass open salts; custard and ruby-stained glass; burmese, peachblow, and amberina glass; pottery by Moorcroft (pre-1935 only); Buffalo (Deldare and Emerald ware); Polia Pillin; Shelley China; Chintz China; and Clarice Cliff. Please include SASE for reply; a photo is very helpful for identification.

Conroy, Barbara J.
PO Box 2369, Santa Clara, 95055-2369. Specializing in commercial china; author and historian

Cox, Susan N.
800 Murray Drive, El Cajon, 92020; 619-697-5922. Specializing in California pottery and Frankoma; e-mail: antiqfever@aol.com

Devenish, Clive
PO Box 907, Orinda, 94563; 925-254-8383. Specializing in still and mechanical banks; buys and sells

Eichert, Kathy
1539 Loma Dr., Ojai, 93023; e-mail: kathydel@ojai.net. Specializing in Gladding McBean

Ellis, Michael L.
266 Rose Ln., Costa Mesa, 92627; 949-646-7112 or fax: 949-645-4919. Author (Collector Books) of *Collector's Guide to Don Winton Designs, Identification & Values*; specializing in Twin Winton

Fogleman, Marv
Marv's Memories
73 Waterman, Irvine, 92602. Specializing in American and English dinnerware

George, Tony
22431-B160 Antonio Pkwy., #252, Rancho Santa Margarita, 92688; 949-589-6075. Specializing in watch fobs

Gibson, Pat
38280 Guava Dr., Newark, 94560; 510-792-0586. Specializing in R.A. Fox

Gunther, Candace (Candelaine)
Phone: 626-796-4568 or fax: 626-796-7172; e-mail: candelaine@ aol.com. Specializing in Steiff and Schuco bears and animals; send SASE for list

Harrison, Gwynne
PO Box 1, Mira Loma, 91752-0001; 951-685-5434; e-mail: morgan99@pe.net. Specializing in Autumn Leaf (Jewel Tea)

Hibbard, Suzi
WanderWares
Specializing in Dragonware and 1000 Faces china, other Orientalia; Dragon_Ware@hotmail.com; related Dragonware site: www.Dragonware.com

Howard, Steve
Past Tyme Pleasures
PMB #204, 2491 San Ramon Valley Blvd., #1, San Ramon, 94583; 925-484-4488 or fax: 925-484-2551. Specializing in antique American firearms, bowie knives, Western Americana, old advertising, vintage gambling items, barber and saloon items

Krumme, Michael
PO Box 48225, Los Angeles, CA 90048-0225; 323-937-1470; e-mail: mkrumme@pacbell.net. Specializing in Paden City glass

Langtree, Elizabeth
PO Box 1616, Santa Ynez, CA 93460. Collector of Borsato figures

Main Street Antique Mall
237 E Main St., El Cajon, 92020; 619-447-0800 or fax: 619-447-0815

Maurer, Oveda L.
Oveda Maurer Antiques
34 Greenfield Ave., San Anselmo, 94960; 415-454-6439. Specializing in 18th-century and early 19th-century American furniture, lighting, pewter, hearthware, glass, folk art, and paintings; open by chance and appointment

The Meadows Collection
Mark and Adela Meadows
PO Box 819, Carnelian Bay, 96140; 530-546-5516; e-mail: meadows@meadowscollection.com. Specializing in Gouda and Quimper; lecturers, authors of *Quimper Pottery, A Guide to Origins, Styles, and Values*, serving on the board of directors of the Associated Antiques Dealers of America; please include SASE for inquiries; www.meadowscollection.com

Needham, Leonard
MacAdam's Antiques
707-748-4286; e-mail: screensider@sbcglobal.net. Specializing in advertising; www.tias.com/stores/macadams

Pardini, Dick
3107 N. El Dorado St., Dept. SAPG, Stockton, 95204-3412; 209-466-5550 (recorder may answer). Specializing in California Perfume Company items dating from 1886 to 1928 and 'go-with' related companies: buyer and information center. Not interested in items that have Avon, Perfection, or Anniversary Keepsake markings. California Perfume Company offerings must be accompanied by a photo, photocopy, or sketching along with a condition report and, most importantly, price wanted. Inquiries require large SASE and must state what information you are seeking; not necessary if offering items for sale.

Pasquali, Jim
479 Church #4, San Francisco, 94114; 415-861-4184. Author of *Sanfords Guide to Garden City Pottery, A Hidden Treasure of Northern California*

Roller, Gayle
PO Box 222, San Marcos, 92079-0222. Specializing in Hagen-Renaker

Sanford, Steve and Martha
230 Harrison Ave., Campbell, 95008; 408-978-8408; www.sanfords.com. Authors of 2 books on Brush-McCoy and *Sanfords Guide to McCoy Pottery* (available from the authors)

Shrader, Lila
Shrader Antiques
2025 Hwy. 199, Crescent City, 95531. Specializing in railroad, steamship, and other transportation memorabilia; Shelley china (and its predecessor, Wileman/Foley China); Buffalo china and Buffalo Pottery including Deldare; Niloak, and Zell (and Haag)

Stillwell, Liz
Our Attic Antiques & Belleek
PO Box 1074, Pico Rivera, 90660; 323-257-3879 or 562-949-0592. Specializing in Irish and American Belleek

Tanner, Joseph and Pamela
Wheeler-Tanner Escapes
6442 Canyon Creek Way, Elk Grove, 95758-5431; 916-684-4006. Specializing in handcuffs, leg shackles, balls and chains, restraints and padlocks of all kinds (including railroad), locking and non-locking devices; also Houdini memorabilia: autographs, photos, posters, books, letters, etc.

Thoerner, Sharon
15549 Ryon Ave., Bellflower, 90706; 562-866-1555. Specializing in covered animal dishes, powder jars with animal and human figures, slag glass

Thornton, Don
PO Box 57, Moss Beach, 94038; 650-728-7978; e-mail: thorntonhouse.com. Specializing in egg beaters and apple parers; author of *The Eggbeater Chronicles, 2nd Edition* ($50.45 ppd.); and *Apple Parers* ($59 ppd.)

Vines, Linda
2911 4th St., #112, Santa Monica, 90405; 310-314-0402; lleigh2000@hotmail.com. Specializing in Snow Babies, all holidays (Christmas, Easter, Halloween), dolls, toys, Steiff, and Uncle Sam

Webb, Frances Finch
1589 Gretel Lane, Mountain View, 94040. Specializing in Kay Finch ceramics

Wells, Lonnie
Things From the Past
1997 Hunter Dr., Rocklin, 95765; 916-415-0454; e-mail: Ilonka (tfp@pacbell.net); thingsfromthepast @tias.com. Specializing in Sascha Brastoff

Woodbury, Virginia
President of American Hatpin Society
20 Montecillo Dr., Rolling Hills Estates, 90274; 310-326-2196; e-mail: HATPINGINIA@aol.com. Quarterly meetings and newsletters; membership: $30 per year; SASE required when requesting information

Canada

Shields, Lorne
Vintage Cycling
PO Box 87588, 300 John St. Post Office, Thornhill, Ontario L3T 7R3; 905-886-6911; e-mail: vintage-antique@rogers.com. Specializing in vintage and antique bicycles and related collectibles

Warner, Ian
PO Box 93022, 499 Main St. S., Brampton, Ontario, L6Y 4V8; 905-453-9074; e-mail: idwarner@ rogers.com. Specializing in Wade porcelain and Swanky Swigs, author of *The World of Wade, The World of Wade Book 2, Wade Price Trends, The World of Wade — Figurines and Miniatures,* and *The World of Wade Head Vase Planters;* co-author: Mike Posgay

Colorado

Geary, William L.
Glass Appraiser (American & European Art Glass)
PO Box 2247, Colorado Springs 80901; telephone/fax: 719-527-0810; e-mail: nordglass@aol.com. Specializing in Nordic art glass

Heck, Carl
Carl Heck Decorative Arts
Box 8416, Aspen, 81612; phone/fax: 970-925-8011; e-mail: carlheck5@ aol.com. Specializing in Tiffany lamps, art glass, windows, and chandeliers; also reverse-painted and leaded-glass table lamps, stained and beveled glass windows, bronzes, paintings, etc.; buy and sell; fee for written appraisals; please include SASE for reply; www.carlheck.com

Mackin, Bill
Author of *Cowboy and Gunfighter Collectibles;* available from author: 1137 Washington St., Craig, 81625; 970-824-6717, paperback: $25; other titles available. Specializing in old and fine spurs, guns, gun leather, cowboy gear, Western Americana (collection in the Museum of Northwest Colorado, Craig)

Over, Naomi L.
8909 Sharon Lane, Arvada, 80002; 303-424-5922. Specializing in ruby glassware, author of *Ruby Glass of the 20th Century, Book 1,* autographed copies available from author for $25.00 softbound or $32.50 hardbound, ppd.; Book II available (1999 values) for $32.50 softbound or $42.50 hardbound, ppd. Naomi will attempt to make photo identifications for all who include a SASE with correspondence.

Segelke, Cathy; and James, Pat
970-847-3759 (Pat). Specializing in crocks, Western Pottery Mfg. Co. (Denver, CO)

Toohey, Marlena
703 S. Pratt Pkwy., Longmont, 80501; 303-678-9726. Specializing in black amethyst and black opaque glass (buy, sell, or trade); books available from author: Book 1 (over 600 colored pictures, descriptions, and price guide), $34 ppd. (nearly out of print); Book 2 (over 1,200 colored pictures, descriptions and price guide), $34 ppd. for soft bound ($44 ppd. for hard bound)

White, John 'Grandpa'
Grandpa's Depot
6720 E. Mississippi Ave., Unit B, Denver, 80224; 303-758-8540 or fax: 303-321-2889. Specializing in railroad-related items; catalogs available

Winther, Jo Ellen
8449 W. 75th Way, Arvada, 80005; 800-872-2345 or 303-421-2371. Specializing in Coors

Connecticut

Block, Robert and Stan
Block's Box
PO Box 51, Trumbull, 06611; 203-926-8448; e-mail: blockschip@ aol.com. Specializing in marbles

Bondhus, Sandra V.
Box 100, Unionville, 06085; 860-678-1808. Author of *Quimper Pottery: A French Folk Art Faience;* specializing in Quimper pottery

Lehrer, Gary
16 Mulberry Road, Woodbridge, 06525-1717. Specializing in pens and pencils; catalog available; www. gopens.com

MacSorley, Earl
823 Indian Hill Rd., Orange, 06477; 203-387-1793 (after 7:00 p.m.). Specializing in nutcrackers, Bessie Pease Gutmann prints, figural lift-top spittoons

Postcards International
Martin J. Shapiro
2321 Whitney Ave., Suite 102, PO Box 185398, Hamden, 06518; 203-248-6621 or fax: 203-248-6628. Specializing in vintage picture postcards, www.vintagepostcards.com.

Thalberg, Bruce
Mountain View Dr., Weston, 06883; 203-227-8175. Specializing in canes and walking sticks: novelty, carved, and Black

Van Deusen, Hobart D.
28 The Green, Watertown, 06795; 860-945-3456; e-mail: rtn.hoby@ snet.net. Specializing in Canton, SASE required when requesting information

Vuono, Mark
16 6th St., Stamford, 06905; 203-357-0892 (10 a.m. to 5:30 p.m. E.S.T.). Specializing in historical flasks, blown 3-mold glass, blown American glass

District of Columbia

Durham, Ken and Jackie (by appointment)
909 26 St. N.W., Suite 502, Washington, DC 20037. Specializing in slot machines, jukeboxes, arcade machines, trade stimulators, vending machines, and service manuals; www.Game RoomAntiques.com

Florida

Barnes, Jacqueline Linscott
Line Jewels
3557 Nicklaus Dr., Titusville, 32780; 321-267-9170; e-mail: blue bellwt@aol.com. Specializing in glass insulators, bell paperweights and other telephone items. Author of *Bluebell Paperweights, Telephone Pioneers of America Bells,* and other *Telephone Related Items,* 2003 Revised Edition; distributor of the only known set of books dealing with insulators, *North American Glass Insulators* (2 volumes), and accompanying price guide; LSASE required for information

Berry, Sammie
1076 Sea Grape Dr., Melbourne 32935; 321-259-8273. Specializing in cat collectibles and Ohio potteries

Bettinger, Robert
PO Box 333, Mt. Dora, 32756; 352-735-3575; e-mail: rgbett@aol.com; RobertBettinger.com. General antiques, specializing in American art pottery and glass

DeLozier, Loretta
101 Grandville Blvd., Lake Placid, 33852. Author of *Collector's Encyclopedia of Lefton China,* Books I, II, and III, and Lefton Price Guide; specializing in Lefton China; buy, sell, and consign; fee for written appraisals

Dodds, Rebecca
Silver Flute
PO Box 670664, Coral Springs, 33067. Specializing in jewelry

Dumont, Louise
318 Palo Verde Dr., Leesburg 34748. Specializing in cookie jars, Abingdon

Elsner, Dr. Robert
29 Clubhouse Lane, Boynton Beach, 33436; 561-736-1362. Specializing in antique barometers and nautical instruments

France, Madeleine
PO Box 15555, Ft. Lauderdale, 33318; 954-584-0009. Specializing in top-quality perfume bottles: Rene Lalique, Steuben, Czechoslovakian, DeVilbiss, Baccarat, Commercials; French dore bronze and decorative arts

Hales, Doug and Coila
Coila's Antiques 145 Bell Tower Crossing W, Poinciana, 34759. Specializing in Victorian art glass and colored pattern glass

Hudson, Hardy
Our Antiques Market
5453 Lake Howell Rd., Winter Park, 32792; 407-657-2100 from 11:00 a.m. to 6:00 p.m. or (home) 407-647-3454; e-mail: todiefor@ mind spring.com. Specializing in majolica, American art pottery (buying one piece or entire collections); also buying Weller (garden ornaments, birds, Hudson, Sicard, Sabrinian, Glendale, or animal related), Roseville, Grueby, Newcomb, Overbeck, Kay Finch, Clewell, Tiffany, etc.

Joyce, Harriet
415 Soft Shadow Lane, DeBary, 32713. Specializing in Cracker Jack and Checkers (a competitor) early prizes and Flossie Fisher items

Kamm, Dorothy
PO Box 7460, Port St. Lucie, 34985-7460; 772-465-4008 e-mail: dorothykamm@adelphia.net. Specializing in American painted porcelain; author of *American Painted Porcelain: Identification & Value Guide* (Collector Books), *Comprehensive Guide to American Painted Porcelain* (Antique Trader Books), and *Painted Porcelain Jewelry and Buttons: Identification & Value Guide* (Collector Books)

Kuritzky, Louis
4510 NW 17th Place, Gainesville, 32605; 352-377-3193. Author (Collector Books) of *Collector's Guide to Bookends*

McNerny, Kathryn
118 Creek Hollow Lane, Middleburg, 32068. Author (Collector Books) on blue and white stoneware, primitives, tools

Posner, Judy
PO Box 2194 SC, Englewood, FL 34295, fax: 941-475-2645; e-mail: judyandjef@yahoo.com. Specializing in Disneyana, Black memorabilia, salt and pepper shakers, souvenirs of the USA, character and advertising memorabilia, figural pottery; buy, sell, collect

Rolfes, Herbert
Yesterday's World
PO Box 398, Mt. Dora, 32756; 352-735-3947; e-mail: NY1939@aol.com. Specializing in World's Fairs and Expositions

Shaw, John
2201 Scenic Ridge Court, Mt. Flora, 32757 (November to May, See Maine listing for remaining months); 352-735-3831. Specializing in dairy bottles

Snyder-Haug, Diane
PO Box 815, St. Petersburg, 33731. Specializing in women's clothing, 1850 – 1940

Supnick, Mark
2771 Oakbrook Manor, Ft. Lauderdale, 33332. Author of Collecting Hull Pottery's Little Red Riding Hood ($12.95 ppd.); specializing in American pottery

Vogel, Janice and Richard
8420 SW 92 St., Unit B, Ocala, 34481-9371; vogels@atlantic.net. Authors of Victorian Trinket Boxes and Conta and Boehme Porcelain; specializing in Conta and Boehme German porcelain; ContaandBoehme.com

White, Douglass
A-1 Auction
2042 N. Rio Grande Ave., Suite E, Orlando, 32804; 407-839-0004; e-mail: a1auction@cfl.rr.com. Specializing in Fulper, Arts & Crafts furniture (photos helpful)

Whysel, Steven
4147 Wilbledon Dr., Cooper City, 33026-1136. Specializing in Art Nouveau, 19th- and 20th-century art

Willis, Ron L.
PO Box 278, Matlacha, 33993; 941-282-5567. Specializing in military collectibles

Wise, Raphael C.
The Collector's Stop
12018 Suellen Circle, West Palm Beach, 33414; 561-793-0986. Specializing in Wedgwood Jasper Ware, Rosenthal (dogs & cats only), Moorcroft, Buffalo Deldare and Emerald Ware, Heisey, contemporary paperweights, English porcelains

Georgia

Bailey, Wayne and Gale
3152 Fence Rd., Dacula, 30019; 770-963-5736. Specializing in Goebels (Friar Tuck)

Glenn, Walter
3420 Sonata Lane, Alpharetta, 30004-7492; 678-624-1298. Specializing in Frankart

Hoefs, Steven
PO Box 1024, Avalon, 90704; 310-510-2623. Specializing in Catalina Island Pottery; author of book, available from the author

Joiner, John R.
Aviation Collectors
130 Peninsula Circle, Newnan, 30265; 770-502-9565; e-mail: propJoiner@mindspring.com. Specializing in commercial aviation collectibles

Jones, Donald
107 Rivers Edge Dr., Savannah, 31406; 912-354-2133; e-mail: Glassman912@comcast.net. Specializing in vintage tennis collectibles; SASE with inquiries please

Illinois

Broom, Jim
Box 65, Effingham, 62401. Specializing in opalescent pattern glassware

Danis, John
2929 Sunnyside Dr. #D362, Rockford, 61114; 815-978-0647 or fax: 815-738-2430; e-mail: danis6033@aol.com. Specializing in R. Lalique and Norse pottery

Feldman, Arthur M.
Arthur M. Feldman Gallery
1815 St. Johns Ave., Highland Park, 60035; 847-432-8858 or fax: 847-266-1199. Specializing in Judaica, fine art, and antiques; www.JudaicaConnection.com

Garmon, Lee
1529 Whittier St., Springfield, 62704; 217-789-9574. Specializing in Royal Haeger, Royal Hickman, glass animals; co-author (Collector Books) of Glass Animals and Figural Flower Frogs of the Depression Era

Hall, Doris and Burdell
210 W. Sassafras Dr., Morton, 61550-1254. Authors of Morton's Potteries: 99 Years (Vols. I and II); specializing in Morton pottery, American dinnerware, early American pattern glass, historical items, elegant Depression-era glassware

Hastings, Mary Jane
310 West 1st South, Mt. Olive, 62069; phone/fax: 217-999-7519. Specializing in Chintz dinnerware

Hoffmann, Pat and Don, Sr.
1291 N. Elmwood Dr., Aurora, 60506-1309; 630-859-3435; e-mail: warwick@thefoxnet.net. Authors of Warwick, A to W, a supplement to Why Not Warwick?; video regarding Warwick decals currently available; P.C.

The Home Place Antiques
Durham, William; Galaway, William
615 S. State St., Belvidere, 61008; 815-544-0577. Specializing in Tea Leaf ironstone and white ironstone

Hooks, Dee
13050 Blackstump Rd., Percy, 62272; 618-965-3832. Specializing in R.S. Prussia and Royal Bayreuth

Hopp, Dennis Carl
Midcentury
Chicago, 773-935-7872. Specializing in 20th-century design, glass, pottery, metal, art

Karman, Laurie and Richard; Editors of The Fenton Flyer
815 S. Douglas Ave., Springfield, 62704. Specializing in Fenton art glass

Long, Dee
112 S. Center, Lacon, 61540. Specializing in reamers

Martin, Jim
1095 215th Ave., Monmouth, 61462; 309-734-2703. Specializing in Old Sleepy Eye, Monmouth pottery, Western Stoneware

Miller, Larry
218 Devron Circle, E. Peoria, 61611-1605. Specializing in German and Czechoslovakian Erphila

Ochsner, Grace
Grace Ochsner Doll House
1636 E. County Rd. 2700, Niota, 62358; 217-755-4362. Specializing in piano babies, bisque German dolls and figurines

Rastello, Lisa
Milkweed Antiques
5N531 Ancient Oak Lane, St. Charles, 60175; 630-377-4612. Specializing in Depression-era collectibles

Rhoden, Joan and Charles
Rhoden Books & Publishing
8693 N. 1950 East Rd., Georgetown, 61846-6264; 217-662-8046; e-mail: rhoden@soltec.net; www.antiqueref.com. Specializing in new reference books on antiques and collectibles, Heisey and other elegant glassware, spice tins, lard tins, and Yard-Long prints; co-authors of Those Wonderful Yard-Long Prints and More, and More Wonderful Yard-Long Prints, Book II, and Yard-Long Prints, Book III, illustrated value guides

Schwab, Betty and Larry
The Paperweight Shoppe
2507 Newport Dr., Bloomington, 61704; 309-662-1956; e-mail: larry@thepaperweightshoppe.com. Specializing in glass paperweights; www.thepaperweightshoppe.com

Spencer, Dick
Glass and More (shows only)
1203 N. Yale, O'Fallon, 62269; 618-632-9067. Specializing in Cambridge, Fenton, Fostoria, Heisey, etc.

Spiess, Greg
230 E. Washington, Joliet, 60433; 815-722-5639; e-mail: spiessantq@aol.com. Specializing in Odd Fellows lodge items

Stifter, Craig
218 S. Adams St., Hinsdale, 60521; 630-789-5780; e-mail: cstifter@ameritech.net. Specializing in Coca-Cola, Pepsi-Cola, Orange Crush, Dr. Pepper, Hires, and other soda-pop brand collectibles

TV Guide Specialists
Box 20, Macomb 61455; 309-833-1809

Waite, Jim
Main St., Farmer City, 61842; 800-842-2593 or e-mail: bigjim@farmwagon.com. Specializing in Sebastians

Yester-Daze Glass
c/o Illinois Antique Center
320 S.W. Commercial St., Peoria, 61604; 309-347-1679. Specializing in glass from the 1920s, '30s, and '40s; Fiesta; Hall; pie birds; sprinkler bottles; and Florence figurines

Indiana

Alexander, Charles
221 E. 34th St., Indianapolis, 46205; 317-924-9665. Specializing in Fiesta, Russel Wright, Eva Zeisel

Boram, Clifford
Antique Stove Information Clearinghouse
Monticello. Free consultation by phone only: 219-583-6465

Dilley, David
6125 Knyghton Rd., Indianapolis, 46220; 317-251-0575; e-mail: glazebears@aol.com or bearpots@aol.com. Specializing in Royal Haeger and Royal Hickman

Dolly Mama's Museum
211 S. Merrill St., Fortville, 46040. Dolls, toys, ephemera; call 317-485-5339 for an appointment

Edwards, Bill
620 W. 2nd, Madison, 47250. Author (Collector Books) on carnival glass

Freese, Carol and Warner
House With the Lions Antiques
On the Square, Covington, 47932. General line

Garrett, Jerry and Sandi
Jerry's Antiques (Shows only)
1807 W. Madison St., Kokomo, 46901; 765-457-5256; e-mail: sandpiper@iquest.net. Specializing in Greentown glass, old postcards

Haun, Ted
2426 N. 700 East, Kokomo, 46901; e-mail: Sam17659@cs.com. Specializing in American pottery and china, '50s items, Russel Wright designs

Highfield, James
1601 Lincolnway East, South Bend, 46613; 574-288-0300. Specializing in relief-style Capo-di-Monte-style porcelain (Doccia, Ginori, and Royal Naples)

Keagy, William and June
PO Box 106, Bloomfield, 47424; 812-384-3471. Co-authors of Those Wonderful Yard-Long Prints and More, More Wonderful Yard-Long Prints, Book II, and Yard-Long Prints, Book III, illustrated value guides

Leslie, Beverly
Sec./Treas. of Uhl Collectors Society
801 Poplar St., Boonville, 47601; 812-897-3681. Contact for newsletter and membership information

McQuillen, Michael J. and Polly
McQuillen's Collectibles
PO Box 50022, Indianapolis,
46250-0022; 317-845-1721; e-mail:
michael@politicalparade.com.
Writer of column, *Political Parade*,
which appears monthly in *Antique-
Week* other newspapers; specializing
in political advertising, pin-back
buttons, and sports memorabilia;
buys and sells; www.political
parade.com.

Miller, Robert
44 Hickory Lane North, Craw-
fordsville, 47833-7601. Specializing in
Dryden pottery

Pruitt, Ted
3350 W. 700 N., Anderson, 46011. *St.
Clair Glass Collector's Guide, Vol. 2,*
available for $25 each from Ted at
above address

Ricketts, Vicki
Covington Antiques Company
6431 W US Highway 136; Covington
47932. General line

Sanders, Lisa
8900 Old State Rd., Evansville,
47711. Specializing in MA Hadley

Slater, Thomas D.
Slater's Americana
1325 W. 86th St., Indianapolis, 46260;
317-257-0863. Specializing in political
and sports memorabilia

Taylor, Dr. E.E.
245 N. Oakland Ave., Indianapolis,
46201-3360; 317-638-1641. Specializing in radios; SASE required for replies
to inquiries

Webb's Antique Mall
over 400 Quality Dealers
200 W. Union St., Centerville, 47330;
765-855-2489 or e-mail: webbsin@
antiquelandusa.com

Wright, Bill
325 Shady Dr., New Albany, 47150.
Specializing in knives: Bowie, hunting, military, and pocketknives

---

Iowa

Ambrose, Craig
3320 Kinsey Ave., Des Moines, 50317-
2712; 515-266-2697. Specializing in
quilts; author of *Picture Book and Price
Guide to Antique Quilts,* available from
author for $45+postage

The Baggage Car
Meredith DeGood
9872 Colby Ave., Des Moines 50325;
515-270-9080; e-mail: baggage
car@aol.com. Specializing in Hallmark
ornaments, cookie cutters, etc.; publishes Hallmark newsletter and list;
www.baggagecar.com

Bilsland, William M., III
PO Box 2671, Cedar Rapids, 52406-
2671; 319-368-0658. Specializing in
American art pottery

Devine, Dennis; Norman; and Joe
D & D Antique Mall
1411 3rd St., Council Bluffs, 51503;
712-323-5233 or 712-328-7305. Specializing in furniture, phonographs,
collectibles, general line. Joe Devine:
Royal Copley and other types of pottery (collector), author of *Collector's
Guide to Royal Copley Plus Royal Windsor & Spaulding,* Books I and II

Dollen, Brenda
PO Box 67, 402 Main St., Minden
51553. Specializing in Red Wing pot-
tery; co-author (with R.L. Dollen) of
Red Wing Art Pottery, Books I and II;
*Collector's Encyclopedia of Red Wing Art
Pottery* (all Collector Books)

Jaarsma, Ralph
Red Ribbon Antiques
812 Washington St., c/o Red Ribbon
Antique Mall, Pella, 50219. Specializing in Dutch antiques; SASE required
when requesting information

Picek, Louis
Main Street Antiques
110 W. Main St., Box 340, West
Branch, 52358. Specializing in folk
art, country Americana, the unusual

Kansas

Maundy International
PO Box 13028-GG, Shawnee Mission,
66282; 1-800-235-2866. Specializing
in watches — antique pocket and vintage wristwatches

Old World Antiques
4436 State Line Rd., Kansas City,
66103; 913-677-4744 or fax: 913-677-
4879. Specializing in 18th- and 19th-
century furniture, paintings,
accessories, clocks, chandeliers,
sconces, and much more

Smies, David
Pops Collectibles
Box 522, 315 So. 4th, Manhattan, 66502;
785-776-1433. Specializing in coins,
stamps, cards, tokens, Masonic collectibles

Street, Patti
Currier & Ives (China) Quarterly
Newsletter
PO Box 504, Riverton, 66770; 316-
848-3529. Subscription: $12 per year
(includes 2 free ads)

Tinsley, Rosella
105 15th St., Osawatomie, 66064; 913-
755-3237. Specializing in primitives,
kitchen, woodenware, and miscellaneous
(phone calls only, no letters please)

Kentucky

Courter, J.W.
3935 Kelley Rd., Kevil, 42053; 270-
488-2116. Specializing in Aladdin
lamps; author of *Aladdin — The Magic
Name in Lamps, Revised Edition,* hard
bound, 304 pages; *Aladdin Electric
Lamps,* soft bound, 229 pages; and
*Angle Lamps Collectors Manual & Price
Guide,* soft bound, 48 pages

Florence, Gene
Box 7186H, Lexington, 40522.
Author (Collector Books) on Depression glass, Occupied Japan; elegant
glass, kitchen glassware

Hornback, Betty
707 Sunrise Lane, Elizabethtown,
42701; e-mail: bettysantiques@
kvnet.org. Specializing in Kentucky
Derby glasses; detailed Derby, Preakness,
Belmont, Breeder's Cup, and others glass
information and pictures available in a
booklet for $15 ppd.

Johnson, Wes, Sr.
3606 Glenview Ave., Glenview,
40025. Specializing in Cracker Jack:
toys, point of sale, packages, etc.;
Checkers Confection, Schoenhut
toys, Victor Toy Oats, Universal Theatre (Chicago), old toys; please
include SASE

Ritchie, Roy B.
197 Royhill Rd., Hindman, 41822;
606-785-5796. Co-author of *Standard
Knife Collector's Guide; Standard Guide
to Razors; Cattaraugus Cutlery, Identification and Values;* and *The Big Knife
Book;* specializing in razors and knives,
all types of cutlery

Stewart, Ron
PO Box 151, Combs, 41729; 606-435-
2412. Co-author of *Standard Knife Collector's Guide; Standard Guide to
Razors; Cattaraugus Cutlery, Identification and Values;* and *The Big Knife
Book;* specializing in razors and knives,
all types of cutlery

Willis, Roy M.
Heartland of Kentucky Decanters and
Steins
PO Box 428, Lebanon Jct., 40150; e-
mail: heartlandky@ka.net. Huge selection of limited edition decanters and
beer steins — open showroom; include
large self-addressed envelope (2
stamps) with correspondence; fee for
appraisals; www.decantersandsteins.com.

Louisiana

Langford, Paris
Kollecting Kiddles
415 Dodge Ave., Jefferson, 70121; 504-
733-0667; e-mail: bbean415@aol.com.
Specializing in all small vinyl dolls of the
'60s and '70s; author of *Liddle Kiddles Identification and Value Guide* (now out of
print); please include SASE when requesting information; contact for information
concerning Liddle Kiddle convention

Maine

Blake, Brenda
Box 555, York Harbor, 03911; 207-
363-6566; e-mail: Eggcentric@
aol.com. Specializing in egg cups

Hathaway, John
Hathaway's Antiques
3 Mills Rd., Bryant Pond, 04219; 207-
665-2214. Specializing in fruit jars;
mail order a specialty

Hillman, Alma
Antiques at the Hillman's
362 E. Main St., Searsport, 04974;
207-548-6658; e-mail: oldivory@aca-
dia.net. Co-author (Collector Books)
of *Collector's Encyclopedia of Old Ivory
China, The Mystery Explored, Identification & Values;* specializing in Old
Ivory China

Rinaldi, John
Nautical Antiques and Related Items
Box 765, Dock Square, Kennebunkport, 04046; 207-967-3218. Specializing in nautical antiques,
scrimshaw, naval items, marine paintings, naval items, etc.; fully illustrated
catalog: $5

Shaw, John
43 Ridgecrest Dr., Wilton, 04294
(June to October, see Florida listing for
remaining months); 207-645-2443.
Specializing in dairy bottles

Simpson, Elizabeth
Elizabeth Simpson Antiques
PO Box 201, Freeport, 04032. Special-
izing in early glass and Sandwich glass

Zayic, Charles S.
Americana Advertising Art
PO Box 57, Ellsworth, 04605; 207-
667-7342. Specializing in early magazines, early advertising art, illustrators

---

Maryland

Doub, Kathy
5359 Iron Pen Place, Columbia,
21044; 410-995-1254. Specializing in
Candlewick and Imperial milk glass

Humphrey, George C.
4932 Prince George Ave., Beltsville,
20705; 301-937-7899. Specializing in
John Rogers groups

Katz, Jerome R.
Katz Collectibles Antique Station,
Frederick, 21702; 301-695-0888. Specializing in technological artifacts;
please include SASE when requesting
information

Meadows, John, Jean and Michael
Meadows House Antiques
919 Stiles St., Baltimore, 21202; 410-
837-5427. Specializing in antique
wicker furniture (rustic, twig, and old
hickory), quilts, and tramp art

Rudisill's Alt Print Haus
Rudisill, John and Barbara
PO Box 199, Worton, 21678; 410-
778-9290; e-mail: rudi@dmv.com.
Specializing in Currier & Ives; calls for
information will be taken in return for
a contribution (honor system) to the
American Heart Association; call
back if not at home; calls will not be
returned; chesapeake-bay.com/alt
printhaus; for information and new
photos of more than Currier & Ives
prints, visit the gallery
freepages.rootsweb.com/~vstern (link
available from business site)

Screen, Harold and Joyce
2804 Munster Rd., Baltimore, 21234; 410-661-6765; e-mail: hscreen@com cast.net. Specializing in soda fountain 'tools of the trade' and paper: catalogs, 'Soda Fountain' magazines, etc.

Weisblut, Robert
International Ivory Society
11109 Nicholas Dr., Wheaton, 20902; 301-649-4002; e-mail: RWeisblut@ yahoo.com. Specializing in ivory carvings and utilitarian objects

Welsh, Joan
7015 Partridge Pl., Hyattsville, 20782; 301-779-6181. Specializing in Chintz; author of Chintz Ceramics

Yalom, Libby
The Shoe Lady
3200 NLW Boulevard #615, Silver Spring, 20906; 301-598-0290. Specializing in glass and china shoes; author of book

Massachusetts

Adams, Charles and Barbara
South Yarmouth, 02664; 508-760-3290 or (business) 508-587-5640; e-mail:adams_2340@msn.com. Specializing in Bennington (brown only)

Cooper, Ryan
205 White Rock Rd., Yarmouthport, 02675; 508-362-1604; e-mail: rcmaritime@ capecod.net. Specializing in flags of historical significance and exceptional design

Dunbar's Gallery
Leila and Howard Dunbar
76 Haven St., Milford, 01757; 508-634-8697 or fax: 508-634-8698; e-mail: Dunbars@mediaone.net. Specializing in advertising and toys; www.dumbarsgallery.com

Ford, Frank W.
237-26 South Street; Shrewsbury, 01545. Specializing in American iridescent art glass, ca 1900 – 1930

Frei, Peter
PO Box 500, Brimfield, 01010; 413-245-4660. Specializing in sewing machines (pre-1875, non electric only), adding machines, typewriters, and hand-powered vacuum cleaners; SASE required with correspondence

Hess, John A.
Fine Photographic Americana
PO Box 3062, Andover, 01810. Specializing in 19th-century photography

Longo, Paul J.
Paul Longo Americana
Box 5510, Magnolia, 01930; 978-525-2290. Specializing in political pins, ribbons, banners, autographs, old stocks and bonds, baseball and sports memorabilia of all types

MacLean, Dale
183 Robert Rd., Dedham, 02026; 781-329-1303; e-mail: DedhamDorchester@aol.com. Specializing in Dedham and Dorchester pottery

Morin, Albert
668 Robbins Ave. #23, Dracut, 01826; 978-454-7907; e-mail: akroal@ attbi.com. Specializing in miscellaneous Akro Agate and Westite

Porter, Richard T., Curator
Porter Thermometer Museum
Box 944, Onset, 02558; 508-295-5504. e-mail: thermometer man.aol.com. Visits (always open) free, with 3,800+ thermometers to see; appraisals, repairs, and traveling lecture (600 given, ages 8 – 98, all venues). Richard is also vice president of the Thermometer Collectors Club of America.

Steinbock, Nancy
Nancy Steinbock Posters
800-438-1577. Specializing in posters: travel, literary, advertising; Charter member of the IVPDA (International Vintage Poster Dealers Association)

Wellman, BA
PO Box 673, Westminster, 01473-0673; e-mail: BA@dishinitout.com (willing to assist in identification through e-mail free of charge). Specializing in all areas of American ceramics, dinnerware, figurines, and art pottery

Williams, Linda
46 Columba St, #4D, Chicopee, 01020; e-mail Sito1845@aol.com. Specializing in glass & china, general line antiques

Michigan

Brown, Rick
Newspaper Collector's Society of America
Lansing, 517-887-1255; e-mail: help@historybuff.com; www.history buff.com. Specializing in newspapers

Burton, Ann
43779 Valley Rd., Decatur, 49045. Specializing in Schramberg

Culver, Bob
Night Light Club
38619 Wakefield Ct., Northville, 48167, 248-473-8575. Specializing in miniature oil lamps

Haas, Norman
252 Clizbe Rd., Quincy 49802; 517-639-8537. Specializing in American art pottery

Hogan & Woodworth
Walter P. Hogan and Wendy L. Woodworth
520 N. State, Ann Arbor, 48104; 313-930-1913. Specializing in Kellogg Studio; www.emunix.emich.edu/~whogan/ kellogg/index.html

Iannotti, Dan
212 W. Hickory Grove Rd., Bloomfield Hills, 48302-1127S; 248-335-5042; e-mail: modernbanks@prodigy.net. Specializing in modern mechanical cast-iron banks; member of The Mechanical Bank Collectors of America

Krupka, Rod
2615 Echo Lane, Ortonville, 48462; 248-627-6351. Specializing in lightning rod balls

Marsh, Linda K.
1229 Gould Rd., Lansing, 48917. Specializing in Degenhart glass

Nedry, Boyd W.
728 Buth Dr., Comstock Park, 49321; 616-784-1513. Specializing in traps (including mice, rat, and fly traps) and trap-related items; please send postage when requesting information

Nickel, Mike
A Nickel's Worth
PO Box 456, Portland, 48875; 517-647-7646; e-mail: mandc@ voyager.net. Specializing in American art pottery: Roseville, Weller, Rookwood, Kay Finch, Stangl and Pennsbury birds, Ceramic Art Studio, and Florence figurines

Oates, Joan
685 S. Washington, Constantine, 49042; 269-435-8353; e-mail: koates120@earthlink.net. Specializing in Phoenix Bird chinaware

Rairigh, Glen
Americana Auctions
12633 Sandborn, Sunfield, 48890; 800-919-1950. Specializing in Skookum dolls and antique auctions

Ross, Michelle
PO Box 94, Berrien Center, 49102; 269-925-1604; e-mail: peartime1@ cs.com. Specializing in Van Briggle and American pottery

Webster, Marty
6943 Suncrest Drive, Saline, 48176; 313-944-1188. Specializing in California porcelain and pottery, Orientalia

Minnesota

Anderson, James
Box 120704, New Brighton, 55112; 651-484-3198. Specializing in old fishing lures and reels, also tackle catalogs, posters, calendars, Winchester items

Dommel, Darlene
PO Box 22493, Minneapolis, 55422. Collector Books author of Collector's Encyclopedia of Howard Pierce Porcelain, Collector's Encyclopedia of Dakota Potteries, and Collector's Encyclopedia of Rosemeade Pottery; specializing in Howard Pierce and Dakota potteries

Harrigan, John
1900 Hennepin, Minneapolis, 55403; 612-991-1271 or (in winter) 561-732-0525. Specializing in Battersea (English enamel) boxes, Moorcroft, Royal Doulton character jugs, and Toby jugs

Koehn, Joanne M.
Temple's Antiques
PO Box 46237, Eden Prairie, 55344; 612-941-7641. Specializing in Victorian glass and china

Miller, Clark
4444 Garfield Ave., Minneapolis, 55409-1847; 612-827-6062. Specializing in Anton Lang pottery, American art pottery, Scandinavian glass and pottery

Nelson, C.L.
Box 222, Spring Park, 55384; 612-473-5625. Specializing in 18th-, 19th-, and 20th-century English pottery and porcelain, among others: Gaudy Welsh, ABC plates, relief-molded jugs, Staffordshire transfer ware

Putratz, Barb
Spring Lake Park, 763-784-0422. Specializing in Norman Rockwell figurines

Schoneck, Steve
HG Handicraft Guild, Minneapolis
PO Box 56, Newport, 55055; 651-459-2980. Specializing in American art pottery, Arts & Crafts, HG Handicraft Guild Minneapolis

Missouri

Gillespie, Steve, Publisher
Goofus Glass Gazette
400 Martin Blvd, Village of the Oaks, 64118; 888-455-5558; e-mail: stegil@sbcglobal.net. Specializing in goofus glass, curator of Goofus Glass Museum, had 4,000+ piece collection of goofus glass; buy, sell, and collect goofus for 30+ years; Expert contributor to forums on goofus glass; contributor to website for goofus glass

Heuring, Jerry
28450 US Highway 61, Scott City, 63780; 573-264-3947. Specializing in Keen Kutter

Siegel, Brenda and Jerry
Tower Grove Antiques
3308 Meramec, St. Louis, 63118; 314-352-9020. Specializing in Ungemach pottery

Tarrant, Jenny
Holly Daze Antiques
4 Gardenview, St. Peters, 63376; e-mail: JennyJOL@aol.com; Holiday for sale. Specializing in early holiday items, Halloween, Christmas, Easter, etc.; always buying Halloween collectibles (except masks and costumes) and German holiday candy containers www.holly-days.com

Wendel, David
F.E.I., Inc.
PO Box 1187, Poplar Bluff, 63902-1187; 573-686-1926. Specializing in Fraternal Elks collectibles

Wiesehan, Doug
D & R Farm Antiques
4535 Hwy. H, St. Charles, 63301. Specializing in salesman's samples and patent models, antique toys, farm toys, metal farm signs

Williams, Don
PO Box 147, Kirksville 63501; 660-627-8009 (between 8 a.m. and 6 p.m. only). Specializing in art glass; SASE required with all correspondence

Winslow, Ralph
PO Box 478, Camdenton, 65020. Specializing in Dryden Pottery

Montana

Miele, Michele
Home Grown Antiques
7 First Ave. E #9, Kalispell, 59901; 406-756-7259; e-mail: info@home-grownantiques.com. Specializing in American dinnerware, glassware, and pottery, with a special emphasis on California dinnerware; co-authors of *Collector's Compass: 20th Century Dinnerware* (Martingale Press); selling on the Internet since 1997; www.home grownantiques.com

Nevada

Lynn, Susan Grindberg
4038 Dustin Ave., Las Vegas, 89120; 702-898-7535; suelynn@lvcm.com. Collector Book author of *Collector's Guide to Porcelier China, Identification and Values;* www.porcelierconnection. com

Young, Willy
80 Promontory Pointe, Reno, 89509; 775-746-0922. Specializing in fire grenades

New Hampshire

Apakarian-Russell, Pamela
Halloween Queen Antiques
PO Box 499, Winchester, 03470. Specializing in Halloween (and other holidays) and postcards

Holt, Jane
Jane's Collectibles
PO Box 115, Derry, 03038. Specializing in Annalee Mobilitee dolls

Winston, Nancy
Willow Hollow Antiques
648 1st N.H. Turnpike, Northwood, 03261; 603-942-5739. Specializing in Shaker smalls, primitives, iron, copper, stoneware, and baskets

New Jersey

Anderson, Suzy McLennan, ISA CAPP
Heritage Antiques & Appraisal Services
65 E. Main St., Holmdel, 07733; 908-946-8801 or fax: 908-946-1036. Specializing in American furniture and decorative accessories; please include photo and SASE when requesting information; appraisals and identification are impossible to do over the phone

Doorstop Collectors of America
Doorstopper Newsletter
Jeanie Bertoia
2413 Madison Ave., Vineland, 08630; 609-692-4092. Membership: $20 per year, includes 2 newsletters and convention; send 2-stamp SASE for sample

George, Dr. Joan M.
ABC Collector's Circle Newsletter
67 Stevens Ave., Old Bridge, 08857; fax: 732-679-6102; drgeorge @nac.net.

Specializing in educational china (particularly ABC plates and mugs)

Harran, Jim and Susan
208 Hemlock Dr., Neptune, 07753; 732-922-2825. Specializing in English and Continental porcelains with emphasis on antique cups and saucers; authors of *Collectible Cups and Saucers, Identification and Values, Book I & II* (Collector Books); available for $20.95 ppd.; www.tias.com/stores/amit

Litts, Elyce
Happy Memories Antiques & Collectibles
PO Box 394, Morris Plains, 07950; 973-361-4087; e-mail: happy-memories@worldnet.att.net. Specializing in general line with special focus on Geisha Girl Porcelain, vintage compacts, and Goebel figurines; home.att.net/~happy-memories

Lockwood, Howard J.; Publisher
Vetri: Italian Glass News
Box 191, Fort Lee, 07024; 201-969-0373. Specializing in Italian glass of the 20th century

Meschi, Edward J.
129 Pinyard Rd., Monroeville, 08343; 856-358-7293; e-mail: ejmeschi@ aol.com. Specializing in Durand art glass, Icart etchings, Maxfield Parrish prints, Rookwood pottery, occupational shaving mugs, American paintings, and other fine arts; author of *Durand — The Man and His Glass,* (Antique Publications) available from author for $39 ppd.; www. meschiarts.com

Perrault, Suzanne
Perrault-Rago Gallery
333 N. Main St., Lambertville, 08530; 609-397-9374. Specializing in Arts and Crafts, Art Pottery, Moderns, and Tiles

Perzel, Robert and Nancy
Popkorn
The Main Street Antique Center, 156 Main St., PO Box 1057, Flemington, 08822; 908-782-9631. Specializing in Stangl dinnerware, birds, and artware; American pottery and dinnerware

Poster, Harry
Vintage TVs
Box 1883, S. Hackensack, 07606; 201-794-9606. Writes *Poster's Radio and Television Price Guide;* specializes in vintage televisions, vintage radios, stereo cameras; catalog available on line: www.harryposter.com

Rago, David
333 N. Main St., Lambertville, 08530; 609-397-6780 or fax: 609-397-679; e-mail: ragoarts@ragoarts.com. Specializing in Arts & Crafts, art pottery; www.ragoarts.com

Rash, Jim
135 Alder Ave., Egg Harbor Township, 08234. Specializing in advertising dolls

Rosen, Barbara
6 Shoshone Trail, Wayne, 07470. Specializing in figural bottle openers and antique dollhouses

Visakay, Stephen
Vintage Cocktail Shakers (by appointment)
PO Box 1517, W. Caldwell, 07007-1517; e-mail: SVisakay@aol.com. Author of book and specializing in vintage cocktail shakers and barware

New Mexico

Hardisty, Don
3020 E. Majestic Ridge, Las Cruces, 88011; For information and questions: 505-522-3721; fax: 505-522-7909; e-mail: don@dons bossons.com; www.donsbossons. com. Specializing in Bossons, Hummels, and rare coins. Don's Collectibles carries a full line of current issues and most discontinued Bossons and Hummel figurines of all marks. When mail ordering Bossons and Hummels, you may dial toll free 800-620-8995.

Manns, William
PO Box 6459, Santa Fe, 87502; 505-995-0102; e-mail: zon@nets.com. Co-author of *Painted Ponies,* hardbound (226 pages), available from author for $47 ppd.; specializing in carousel art and cowboy antiques

Moyer, Patsy
PO Box 311, Deming, 88031; e-mail: moddoll@yahoo.com. Collector Book author on dolls

Nelson, Scott H.
PO Box 6081, Santa Fe, 87502-6081. Specializing in ethnographic art

New York

Austin, Bruce A.
1 Hardwood Hill Rd., Pittsford, 14534; 585-387-9820 (evenings); 585-475-2879 (week days); e-mail: baagll@rit.edu. Specializing in clocks and Arts & Crafts furnishings and accessories including metalware, pottery, and lighting

Badders, Veldon
692 Martin Rd., Hamlin, 14464; 716-964-3360. Author (Collector Books) of *Collector's Guide to Inkwells, Identification & Values;* specializing in inkwells

Calison, Jim
Tools of Distinction
Wallkill, 12589; 914-895-8035. Specializing in antique and collectible tools, buying and selling

Dimitroff, Thomas P.
Dimitroff's Antiques (appointment only)
140 E. First St., Corning, 14830; 607-962-6745; e-mail: tdimi1@aol.com. Specializing in Steuben and cut glass

Doyle, Robert A.
Absolute Auction & Realty, Inc./Absolute Auction Center
PO Box 1739, Pleasant Valley, 12569; 845-635-3169; e-mail: absoluteauction @hvc.rr.com. Antique and estate auctions twice a month at Absolute Auction Center; free calendar of auctions available; www.absoluteauctionrealty. com

Endter, Barbara
29 Sandalwood Dr., Rochester, 14616-1513; 585-621-1433. Specializing in Chase Brass & Copper Company

Gerson, Roselyn
PO Box 40, Lynbrook, 11563; 516-593-8746. Author/collector specializing in unusual, gadgetry, figural compacts, vanity bags and purses, solid perfumes and lipsticks

Handelsman, Burton
18 Hotel Dr., White Plains, 10605; 914-428-4480 (home) and 914-761-8880 (office). Specializing in occupational shaving mugs, accessories

Kaonis, Keith; Manager
Antique Doll Collector Magazine
6 Woodside Ave., Suite 300, Northport, 11768 or PO Box 344, Center Port, NY 11721-0344; 631-261-4100 or 631-361-0982 (evenings). Specializing in Schoenhut toys

Little Century
H. Thomas and Patricia Laun
215 Paul Ave., Syracuse, 13206; 315-437-4156. Summer residence: 35109 Country Rte. 7, Cape Vincent, 13618; 315-654-3244. Specializing in firefighting collectibles; all appraisals are free, and we will respond only to those who are considerate enough to include a SASE (photo is requested for accuracy); we are unable to return phone calls, keep trying

Malitz, Lucille
Lucid Antiques
Box KH, Scarsdale, 10583; 914-636-7825. Specializing in lithophanes, kaleidoscopes, stereoscopes, medical and dental antiques

Michel, John and Barbara
Iron Star Antiques
200 E. 78th St., 18E, New York City, 10021; 212-861-6094; email: jlm58@ columbia.edu. Specializing in yellow ware, cast iron, tramp art, shooting gallery targets and blue featheredge

Rifken, Blume J.
Author of *Silhouettes in America — 1790 – 1840 — A Collector's Guide.* Specializing in American antique silhouettes from 1790 to 1840

Russ, William A.
Russ Trading Post
23 William St., Addison 14801-1326. Animal lure manufacture; hunting and trapping supply; catalog $1

Safir, Charlotte F.
1349 Lexington Ave., 9-B, New York City, 10128-1513; 212-534-7933. Specializing in cookbooks, children's books (out-of-print only)

Schleifman, Roselle
Ed's Collectibles/The Rage
16 Vincent Rd., Spring Valley, 10977; 845-356-2121. Specializing in Duncan & Miller, elegant glass, Depression glass

Smyth, Carole and Richard
Carole Smyth Antiques
PO Box 2068, Huntington, 11743. Authors of *Neptune's Treasures — A Study & Value Guide to Sea Shell Art*; *Pails by Comparison — A Study & Value Guide to Sand Pails & Toys*; and *The Burning Passion — A Study & Value Guide to Antique and Collectible Pyrography*; all available from authors at the above address for $25 each +$4.35 postage

Tuggle, Robert
105 W. St., New York City, 10023; 212-595-0514. Specializing in John Bennett, Anglo-Japanese china

Van Kuren, Jean and Dale
Ruth's Antiques, Inc.
PO Box 152, Clarence Center, 14032; 716-741-8001; e-mail: ruthsantq@ aol.com. Specializing chocolate molds, Buffalo pottery, Deldare ware

Van Patten, Joan F.
Box 102, Rexford, 12148. Author (Collector Books) of books on Nippon and Noritake

Weitman, Stan and Arlene
PO Box 1186; N. Massapequa, 11758; E-mail: scrackled@earthlink.net. Author of book on crackle glass (Collector Books; www.crackleglass.com

North Carolina

Finegan, Mary
Marfine Antiques
PO Box 3618; Boone 28607; 828-262-3441. Specializing exclusively in Johnson Brothers dinnerware; replacement service; author of book ($17 ppd.)

Hughes, Kathy (Mrs. Paul)
Tudor House Galleries
8919 Park Rd., DC #30, Charlotte, 28210-08645. 704-676-4871; fax: 704-676-5197; e-mail: paulh65304@ aol.com or www.tudorhouse.com. Specializing in relief-molded jugs, 18th- and 19th-century English pottery and 19th-century oil paintings

Hussey, Billy Ray
Southern Folk Pottery Collector's Society
220 Washington Street, Bennett, 27208; 336-581-4246 or fax: 336-581-4247; e-mail: sfpcs@rtmc.net. Specializing in historical research and documentation, education, and promotion of the traditional folk potter (past and present) to a modern collecting audience

Iannantuoni, Jean-Paul
4179 Brownwood Lane, Concord, 28027-4501; www.freeyellow.com/ members/royaldoulton/home.html. Discontinued Dinnerware Shopping Service; send $2 for Royal Doulton list; appraisals $2 each

Kirtley, Charles E.
PO Box 2273, Elizabeth City, 27096; 919-335-1262. Specializing in monthly auctions and bid sales dealing with World's Fair, Civil War, political, advertising, and other American collectibles

Newbound, Betty
2206 Nob Hill Dr., Sanford, 27330. Author (Collector Books) on Blue Ridge dinnerware, milk glass, wall pockets, figural planters and vases; specializing in collectible china and glass

Sayers, R.J.
Southeastern Antiques & Appraisals
PO Box 629, Brevard, 28712. Specializing in Boy Scout collectibles, Pisgah Forest pottery, primitive American furniture; author of *Guide to Scouting Collectibles, Revised 1996 Edition*, available from author for $32.95 ppd.; member New England Appraisers Assn.

Taylor, Terry
3648 Prides Rd., East Bend, 27018. Co-author of *Collector's Encyclopedia of Salt Glaze Stoneware* (Collector Books); specializing in salt glaze stoneware

North Dakota

Farnsworth, Bryce
1334 14½ St. South, Fargo, 58103; 701-237-3597. Specializing in Rosemeade pottery; if writing for information, please send a picture if possible, also phone number and best time to call

Ohio

Bassett, Mark
PO Box 771233, Lakewood, 44107; 216-221-6025; e-mail: Mark@Mark Bassett.com. Buying and selling Ohio art pottery (including Roseville, Cowan, Weller, Rookwood, others), Cleveland arts and crafts, Art Deco, and other 20th Century design movements; author of *Cowan Pottery and the Cleveland School* (1997), *Introducing Roseville Pottery* (1999), *Introducing Roseville Pottery* (revised and expanded 2nd edition, 2001), *Bassett's Roseville Prices* (2001), *Understanding Roseville Pottery* (2002), and *American Art Pottery Wall Pockets* (2003); for ordering information visit www.MarkBassett.com

Batory, Mr. Dana Martin
402 E. Bucyrus St., Crestline, 44827. Specializing in antique woodworking machinery, old and new woodworking machinery catalogs; author of *Vintage Woodworking Machinery, an Illustrated Guide to Four Manufacturers*, currently available from Astragal Press, PO Box 239, Mendham, NJ 07945 for $26.45

ppd. (signed copies available from author); coming soon from Astragal Press, *Vintage Woodworking Machinery Volume Two, An Illustrated Guide to Four More Manufacturers*. In order to prepare a definitive history on American manufacturers of woodworking machinery, Dana is interested in acquiring (by loan, gift, or photocopy) catalogs, manuals, photos, personal reminiscences, etc., pertaining to woodworking machinery and/or their manufacturers. Also available for $7.50 money order: 70+ page list of catalogs, owner's manuals, parts lists, company publications, etc. (updated quarterly). No phone calls please.

Benjamin, Scott
PO Box 556, LaGrange, 44050-0556; 440-355-6608; www.oilcollectibles. com or www.gasglobes.com. Specializing in gas globes; co-author of *Gas Pump Globes* and several other related books, listing nearly 4,000 gas globes with over 1,800 photos, prices, rarity guide, histories, and reproduction information (currently available from author); also available: *Petroleum Collectibles Monthly* Magazine

Blair, Betty
Golden Apple Antiques
216 Bridge St., Jackson, 45640; 614-286-4817. Specializing in art pottery, Watt, cookie jars, chocolate molds, Beanie Babies, general line

China Specialties, Inc.
Box 471, Valley City, 44280. Specializing in high-quality reproductions of Homer Laughlin and Hall china, including Autumn Leaf

Distel, Ginny
Distel's Antiques
4041 S.C.R. 22, Tiffin, 44883; 419-447-5832. Specializing in Tiffin glass

Ebner, Rita and John
Columbus. Specializing in door knockers, cast-iron bottle openers, Griswold

Graff, Shirley
4515 Grafton Rd., Brunswick, 44212. Specializing in Pennsbury pottery

Guenin, Tom
Box 454, Chardon, 44024. Specializing in antique telephones and antique telephone restoration

Hall, Kathy
4417 Weckerly Rd., Monclova, 43542; 419-867-1516; kewpieluvin@msn. com. Specializing in Labino art glass

Hamlin, Jack and Treva
145 Township Rd. 1088, Proctorville, 45669; 740-886-7644; e-mail: treva jo@ezwv.com. Specializing in Currier and Ives by Royal China Co. and Homer Laughlin China

Hothem, Lar
Hothem House
Box 458, Lancaster, 43130. Author of books on Indians and artifacts

Kao, Fern Larking
PO Box 312, Bowling Green, 43402; 419-352-5928. Specializing in jewelry, sewing implements, ladies' accessories

Kier, Anne and Don
202 Marengo St., Toledo, 43614-4213; 419-385-8211; e-mail: d.a.k.@dorld net.att.net. Specializing in glass, china, autographs, Brownies, Royal Bayreuth, 19th-century antiques, general line

Kitchen, Lorrie
Toledo, 419-475-1759. Specializing in Depression-era glass, Hall china, Fiesta, Blue Ridge, Shawnee

Klender, James and Grace
Town & Country Antiques & Collectibles
PO Box 447, Pioneer, 43554; 419-737-2880. Specializing in pattern glass and general line

Kline, Mr. and Mrs. Jerry and Gerry
Two of the founding members of North American Torquay Society and members of Torquay Pottery Collectors' Society
604 Orchard View Dr., Maumee, 43537; 419-893-1226. Specializing in collecting Torquay pottery

Mangus, Bev and Jim
5147 Broadway NE, Louisville, 44641. Author (Collector Books) of *Shawnee Pottery, an Identification & Value Guide*; Specializing in Shawnee pottery

Mathes, Richard
PO Box 1408, Springfield, 45501-1408; 513-324-6917. Specializing in buttonhooks

Millman, Tom and Linda
231 S. Main St., Bethel, 45106; phone/fax: 513-734-6884 (after 9 p.m.). Specializing in perfume lamps, other antique and unique lighting

Moore, Carolyn
445 N. Prospect, Bowling Green, 43402. Specializing in primitives, yellow ware, graniteware, collecting stoneware

Murphy, James L.
1023 Neil Ave., Columbus, 43201; 614-297-0746; e-mail: jlmruphy@ columbus.rr.com. Specializing in American Radford, Vance Avon

Otto, Susan
12204 Fox Run Dr., Chesterland, 44026; 440-729-2686. Specializing in nutcrackers, not toy soldier (Steinbach) type

Pierce, David
PO Box 248, Danville, 43014; 614-599-6394. Specializing in Glidden pottery; fee for appraisals

Rees, Debbie
Zanesville. Specializing in Watt, Roseville juvenile, and other Roseville pottery, Zanesville area pottery, cookie jars, and Steiff

Roberts, Brenda
Specializing in Hull pottery and general line; author of *Collector's Encyclopedia of Hull Pottery, Roberts' Ultimate Encyclopedia of Hull Pottery,* and *The Companion Guide to Roberts' Ultimate Encyclopeida of Hull Pottery,* all with accompanying price guides

Rodgers, Joanne
c/o Stretch Glass Society members.aol.com/stretghgl/. Membership: $22 in US ($24 US currency in Canada) per year; quarterly newsletter with colored photos; annual spring convention

Trainer, Veronica
Bayhouse
Box 40443, Cleveland, 44140; 440-871-8584. Specializing in beaded and enameled mesh purses

Tucker, Dan
Toledo, 419-478-3815. Specializing in Depression-era glass, Hall china, Fiesta, Blue Ridge, Shawnee

Walter, John
The Old Tool Shop
208 Front St., Marietta, 45750; 740-373-9973; fax: 740-373-9059; e-mail: toolmerchant@sprynet.com. Specializing in all types of antique tools; For detailed information on Stanley tools, John Walter's *Antique & Collectible Stanley Tools Guide to Identity and Value* is highly recommended, 885 pages, over 1500 crisp photos and engravings, current values, softcover: $35 ppd., hardcover: $45 ppd.; *2000 Stanley Pocket Price Guide:* $12 ppd.; website coming soon: www.stanleytool collectors.org

Whitmyer, Margaret and Kenn
Box 30806, Gahanna, 43230. Authors (Collector Books) on children's dishes; specializing in Depression-era collectibles

Wilkins, Juanita
The Bird of Paradise
Wapakoneta. Specializing in R.S. china, Old Ivory china, colored pattern glass, lamps, and jewelry

Young, Mary
Box 9244, Wright Brothers Branch, Dayton, 45409; 937-298-4838. Specializing in paper dolls; author of several books

Oklahoma

Bess, Phyllis and Tom
14535 E. 13th St., Tulsa, 74108; 918-437-7776. Authors of *Frankoma Treasures* and *Frankoma and Other Oklahoma Potteries;* specializing in Frankoma and Oklahoma pottery

Moore, Art and Shirley
4423 E. 31st St., Tulsa, 74135; 918-747-4164 or 918-744-8020. Specializing in Lu Ray Pastels, Depression glass

Scott, Roger R.
4250 S. Oswego, Tulsa, 74135; 918-742-8710 or fax: 918-583-1226; e-mail: Roger13@mindspring.com. Specializing in Victor and RCA Victor trademark items along with Nipper

Oregon

Abrahams, Peter
1948 Mapleleaf Rd., Lake Oswego, 97034; 503-636-2988; e-mail: telscope@europa.com. Specializing in telescopes, binoculars, microscopes. Peter studies and collects optics: telescopes, binoculars, hand magnifiers, and microscopes, and especially seeks reference material on these subjects, including books, catalogs, repair manuals, and histories. www.europa.com/~telescope/binotele.htm

Brown, Marcia
Sparkles
PO Box 2314, White City, 97503; 541-826-3039 or fax: 541-830-5385. Author of *Unsigned Beauties of Costume Jewelry, Signed Beauties of Costume Jewelry,* and *Signed Beauties of Costume Jewelry, Volume II* (all Collector Books), Co-author and host of 7 volumes: *Hidden Treasures* videos; specializing in rhinestone jewelry; please include SASE if requesting information

Coe, Debbie and Randy
Coe's Mercantile
2459 SE TV Hwy #321, Hillsboro, 97123. Specializing in Elegant and Depression glass, Fenton glass, Liberty Blue, art pottery

Davis, Patricia M.
Antique and personal property appraisals
4326 N.W. Tam-O-Shanter Way, Portland, 97229-8738; 503-645-3084; e-mail: pam100davis@attbi.com

Foland, Doug
PO Box 66854, Portland, 97290; 503-772-0471. Author of *The Florence Collectibles, an Era of Elegance,* available at your local bookstore or from Schiffer Publishers

Hirshman, Susan and Larry
Everyday Antiques
2011 E. Main St., Medford, 97504. Specializing in china, glassware, kitchenware

Main Antique Mall
30 N. Riverside, Medford, 97501. Quality products and services for the serious collector, dealer, or those just browsing; mainantiquemall.com

Medford Antique Mall
Jim & Eileen Pearson, Owners
1 West 6th St., Medford 97501; 541-773-4983; e-mail: medama11@ mind.net

Miller, Don and Robbie
541-535-1231. Specializing in milk bottles, TV Siamese cat lamps, seltzer bottles, red cocktail shakers

Morris, Thomas G.
Prize Publishers
PO Box 8307, Medford, 97504; e-mail: chalkman@cdsnet.net. Author of *The Carnival Chalk Prize,* Books I and II, pictorial price guides on carnival chalkware figures with brief histories and values for each

Ringering, David
Kay Ring Antiques
1395 59th Ave., S.E., Salem, 97301; 503-364-0464 or pager: 503-588-3747; e-mail: AR1480@aol.com. Specializing in Rowland & Marsellus and other souvenir/historical china with scenes of buildings, parks, and other tourist attractions of the 1890s – 1930s. Feel free to contact David if you have any questions about Rowland and Marsellus or other souvenir china. He will be happy to answer questions about souvenir china

Pennsylvania

Alekna, Stan and Sally
732 Aspen Lane, Lebanon, 17042-9073; 717-228-2361 or fax: 717-228-2362; e-mail: salekna@bellatlantic.net. Specializing in American dimestore toy soldiers; send SASE for 3 to 4 mail-order lists per year; always buying 1 or 100 top-quality figures

Barrett, Noel
Rosebud Antiques
PO Box 1001, Carversville, 18913; 215-297-5109. Specializing in toys; appraiser on PBS Antiques Roadshow; active in toy-related auctions

Bodine, Clarence H., Jr., Proprietor
East/West Gallery
41B West Ferry St., New Hope, 18938. Specializing in antique Japanese woodblock prints, netsuke, inro, porcelains

Cerebro
PO Box 327, E. Prospect, 17317-0327; 717-252-2400 or 800-69-LABEL; fax: 717-252-3685; e-mail: Cerebro@ Cerebro.com. Specializing in antique advertising labels, especially cigar box labels, cigar bands, food labels, firecracker labels; www.cerebro.com

Christie, Dr. Victor J.W.
Author/Appraiser/Broker
1050 West Main St., Ephrata, 17522; 717-738-4032; e-mail:thecheshire cat@onemain.com. The family designated biographer of Bessie Pease Gutmann; specializing in Bessie Pease Gutmann and other Gutmann & Gutmann artists; authored 5 books on these artists, the latest in 2001: *The Gutmann & Gutmann Artists: A Published Works Catalog, Fourth Edition,* a signed copy available from the author for $20 at the above address

Damaska, Ron
738 9th Ave., New Brighton, 15066; 724-843-1393. Specializing in Fry cut glass, match holders; SASE required when requesting information

Gottuso, Bob
Bojo
PO Box 1403, Cranberry Township, 16066-0403; phone/fax: 724-776-0621; www.bojoonline.com. Specializing in Beatles, Elvis, KISS, Monkees, licensed rock 'n roll memorabilia

Guido, Karen M.
Karen Michelle
PO Box 62, Blairsville, 15717; 724-459-6669; Karen@antiquetiles.com. Specializing in tiles, buy & sell; books on tiles available, many out of print; fee for written appraisal; please include SASE for inquiries; Antique Tiles.com

Hain, Henry F., III
Antiques & Collectibles
2623 N. Second St., Harrisburg, 17110; 717-238-0534. Lists available of items for sale

Hinton, Michael C.
246 W. Ashland St., Doylestown, 18901; 215-345-0892; e-mail: isc-susn@att.net. Owns/operates Bucks County Art & Antiques Company and Chem-Clean Furniture Restoration Company; specializing in quality restorations of a wide range of art and antiques from colonial to contemporary; also owns Trading Post Antiques, 532 Durham Rd., Wrightstown, PA, 18940, a 60-dealer antiques co-op with 15,000 square feet — something for everyone in antiques and collectibles

Holland, William
hollandarts.com
1554 Paoli Pike, West Chester, 19380-6123; 610-344-9848 or fax: 610-344-0651; e-mail: bill@hollandarts.com. Specializing in Louis Icart etchings and oils, Tiffany studios lamps, glass, and desk accessories; author of *Louis Icart: The Complete Etchings, The Collectible Maxfield Parrish,* and *Louis Icart Erotica;* www.hollandarts.com.

Irons, Dave
Dave Irons Antiques
223 Covered Bridge Rd., Northampton, 18067; 610-262-9335 or fax: 610-262-2853. Author of *Irons By Irons, More Irons By Irons,* and *Even More Irons by Irons,* available from author (each contains pictures of over 1,600 irons, current information and price ranges, collecting hints, news of trends, and information for proper care of irons); specializing in pressing irons, country furniture, primitives, quilts, accessories; www.irons antiques.com

Ivankovich, Michael
Michael Ivankovich Auctions, Inc.
PO Box 1536, Doylestown, 18901. Specializing in early 20th-century hand-colored photography and prints; author of *The Collector's Value Guide to Popular Early 20th Century American Prints* (1998), $19.95; *The Collector's Guide to Wallace Nutting Pictures,* $18.95; *The Alphabetical and Numerical Index to Wallace Nutting*

Pictures, $14.95; and *The Guide to Wallace Nutting Furniture*, $14.95; also available: *Wallace Nutting General Catalog, Supreme Edition* (reprint), $13.95; *Wallace Nutting: A Great American Idea* (reprint), $13.95; and *Wallace Nutting's Windsor's: Correct Windsor Furniture* (reprint), $13.95; related available book: *The History of Sawyer Pictures* by Carol Begley Gray, $14.95. All these books are currently available at the above address. Shipping is $4.25 for the first item ordered and $1.50 for each additional item.

Knauer, Judy A.
National Toothpick Holder Collectors Society
1224 Spring Valley Lane, West Chester, 19380-5112; 610-431-3477. Specializing in toothpick holders and Victorian glass

Kreider, Katherine
Kingsbury Antiques
PO Box 7957, Lancaster, 17604-7957; 717-892-3001; e-mail: Kingsbry@ aol.com. Author of *Valentines With Values*, available for $24.45 ppd. ($25.92 PA residents); *One Hundred Years of Valentines*, available for $29.45 ppd. ($30.96 PA residents); and *Valentines for the Eclectic Collector* ($29.45 ppd. ($30.96 PA residents); no free appraisals; stop by booth #315 in Stroudtburg Antique Center (formerly Black Angus), in Adamstown, PA, Sundays only

Levi, Anita
Allegheny Mountain Antique Gallery
5151 Clear Shade Dr., Windber, 15963; 814-467-8539. Specializing in novelty clocks, advertising tins, primitives, holiday decorations, quilts, purses, Black memorabilia, linens, stoneware, Roseville, kitchenware, Art Deco

Lindsay, Ralph
PO Box 402, Jonestown, 17038-0402. Specializing in target balls; SASE required with correspondence

Lowe, James Lewis
Kate Greenaway Society
PO Box 8, Norwood, 19074; e-mail: JLewisLowe@juno.com. Specializing in Kate Greenaway

Maier, Clarence and Betty
Mail order: The Burmese Cruet
Box 432, Montgomeryville, 18936; 215-855-5388; e-mail: burmese cruet@erols.com. Specializing in Victorian art glass; www.burmese cruet.com

McManus, Joe
PO Box 153, Connellsville, 15425; e-mail: jmcmanus@hhs.net. Editor of *Purinton News & Views*, a newsletter for Purinton pottery enthusiasts; subscription: $16 per year; sample copies available with SASE; specializing in Blair Ceramics and Purinton Pottery

Merchants Square Mall
Jim and Annetta Vitez, Managers
1901 S. 12th St., Allentown, 18103; 610-797-7743

Reimert, Leon
121 Highland Dr., Coatesville, 19320; 610-383-6969. Specializing in Boehm porcelain

Rosso, Philip J. and Philip Jr.
Wholesale Glass Dealers
1815 Trimble Ave., Port Vue, 15133; 412-678-7352. Specializing in Westmoreland glass

Weiser, Pastor Frederick S.
55 Kohler School Rd., New Oxford, 17350-9210; 717-624-4106. Specializing in frakturs and other Pennsylvania German documents; SASE required when requesting information; no telephone appraisals, must see original or clear colored photocopy

Rhode Island

Gacher, John
The Drawing Room of Newport
152 Spring St., Newport, 02840; 401-841-5060. Specializing in Zsolnay, Fischer, Amphora, and Austro-Hungarian art pottery; www. drawrm.com

The Occupied Japan Club
c/o Florence Archambault
29 Freeborn St., Newport, 02840-1821; e-mail: florence@aiconnect .com. Publishes bimonthly newsletter, *The Upside Down World of an O.J. Collector*; SASE required when requesting information

South Carolina

Dunay, Jeanne
Bellflower Antiques
Camden. Specializing in historic and Romantic Staffordshire, 1790 – 1850

Greguire, Helen
Helen's Antiques
79 Lake Lyman Hgts., Lyman, 29365; 864-848-0408. Specializing in graniteware (any color), carnival glass lamps and shades, carnival glass lighting of all kinds; author (Collector Books) of *The Collector's Encyclopedia of Graniteware, Colors, Shapes & Values*, Book 1 (out of print); Second book on graniteware now available (updated 2003), $33.70 ppd; also available is *Carnival in Lights*, featuring carnival glass, lamps, shades, etc. ($13.45 ppd.); and *Collector's Guide to Toasters and Accessories, Identification & Values* ($21.95 ppd.); available from author; please include SASE when requesting information; looking for people interested in collecting toasters

Guthrie, John
1524 Plover Ave., Mount Pleasant, 29464; 843-884-1873. Specializing in Santa Barbara Ceramic Design

Roerig, Fred and Joyce
1501 Maple Ridge Rd., Walterboro, 29488; 843-538-2487. Specializing in cookie jars; authors of *Collector's Encyclopedia of Cookie Jars, An Illustrated Value Guide* (three in the series), publishers of *Cookie Jarrin' with Joyce: The Cookie Jar Newsletter*

Tennessee

Chase, Mick and Lorna
Fiesta Plus
380 Hawkins Crawford Rd., Cookeville, 38501; 931-372-8333. Specializing in Fiesta, Harlequin, Riviera, Franciscan, Metlox, Lu Ray, Bauer, Vernon, other American dinnerware

Fields, Linda
158 Bagsby Hill Lane, Dover, 37058; 931-232-5099 after 6 p.m.; e-mail: Fpiebird@compu.net. Specializing in pie birds

Grist, Everett
PO Box 91375, Chattanooga, 37412-3955; 423-510-8052. Specializing in covered animal dishes and marbles

Hudson, Murray
Murray Hudson Antiquarian Books, Maps, Prints & Globes
109 S. Church St., Box 163, Halls, 38040; 901-836-9057 or 800-748-9946; fax: 731-836-9017; e-mail: map man@ecsis.net. Specializing in antique maps, globes, and books with maps, atlases, explorations, travel guides, geographies, surveys, and historical prints; murrayhudson.com

Morton, Andrew
Andrew Morton, Inc.
4705 Old Kingston Pike, PO Box 10947, Knoxville, 37939-0947; 865-584-6137. Specializing in Waterford crystal

Weddington, David
Predicta Sales & Service
2702 Albany Ct., Murfreesboro, 37129; 615-890-7498. Specializing in vintage Philco Predicta TVs

Texas

Babcock, Bobby
Jubilation Antiques
5108 Saddleridge Cove, Austin, 78759; 512-418-9373; e-mail: juban tique@aol.com. Specializing in Maxfield Parrish, Black Americana, and brown Roseville Pine Cone

Cooper, Marilyn
8408 Lofland Dr., Houston, 77055-4811; 713-465-7773 or summer address: PO Box 755, Douglas, MI 49406. Specializing in figural toothbrush holders, candy containers, Pez

Dockery, Rod
4600 Kemble St., Ft. Worth, 76103; 817-536-2168. Specializing in milk glass; SASE required with correspondence

Docks, L.R. 'Les'
Shellac Shack; Discollector
Box 691035, San Antonio, 78269-1035; e-mail: docks@texas.net. Author of *American Premium Record Guide*; specializing in vintage records; www.docks.home.texas.net

Frese, Leo and Wendy
Three Rivers Collectibles
Box 551542, Dallas, 75355; 214-341-5165. Specializing in RumRill, Red Wing pottery and stoneware

Gibbs, Carl, Jr.
1716 Westheimer Rd, Houston, 77098. Author of *Collector's Encyclopedia of Metlox Potteries, Second Edition*, autographed copies available from author for $32.95 ppd.; specializing in American ceramic dinnerware

Groves, Bonnie
402 North Ave. A, Elgin, 78621. Specializing in boudoir dolls

Malowanczyk, Abby and Wlodek
Collage-20th Century Classics
1300 N. Industrial Blvd., Dallas, 75207; phone/fax: 214-828-9888; e-mail: txcollage@aol.com; www. collageclassics.com. Specializing in architect-designed furniture and decorative arts from the modern movement

Norris, Kenn
Schoolmaster Auctions and Real Estate
PO Box 4830, 513 N. 2nd St., Sanderson, 79848-4830; 915-345-2640. Specializing in school-related items, barbed wire, related literature, and L'il Abner (antique shop in downtown Sanderson)

Pogue, Larry G.
L&J Antiques & Collectibles
8142 Ivan Court, Terrell, 75161-6921; 972-551-0221; e-mail: LandJ Antiques@ direcway.com. Specializing in string holders and head vases; LandJ Antiques.com

Rosen, Kenna
9138 Loma Vista, Dallas, 75243; 972-503-1436; e-mail: ke-rosen@swbell. net. Specializing in Bluebird china

Tucker, Richard and Valerie
Argyle Antiques
PO Box 262, Argyle, 76226; 940-464-3752; e-mail: lead1234@gte.net or rtucker@jw.com. Specializing in windmill weights, shooting gallery targets, figural lawn sprinklers, cast-iron advertising paperweights, and other unusual figural cast iron

Turner, Danny and Gretchen
Running Rabbit Video Auctions
PO Box 701, Waverly, 37185; 615-296-3600. Specializing in marbles

Waddell, John
2903 Stan Terrace, Mineral Wells, 76067. Specializing in buggy steps

Woodard, Dannie; Publisher
The Aluminist
PO Box 1346; Weatherford, 76086;
817-594-4680. Specializing in aluminum items, books, and newsletters about aluminum

---
Utah

Anderson, Tim
Box 461, Provo, 84603. Specializing in autographs; buys single items or collections — historical, movie stars, US Presidents, sports figures, and pre-1860 correspondence. Autograph questions? Please include photocopies of your autographs if possible and enclose a SASE for guaranteed reply. www. AutographsOfAmerica.com

Anderson, Warren R.
America West Archives
PO Box 100, Cedar City, 84721; 435-586-9497; e-mail: warren@americawestarchives.com. Specializing in old stock certificates and bonds, western documents and books, financial ephemera, autographs, maps, photos; author of *Owning Western History*, with 75+ photos of old documents and recommended reference

Spencer, Rick
Salt Lake City, 801-973-0805. Specializing in American silverplate and sterling flatware, hollow ware, Shawnee, Van Tellingen, salt and pepper shakers; appraisals available at reasonable cost

---
Vermont

Barry, Kit
136 High St., Brattleboro, 05301; 802-254-3634; kbarry@surfglobal. net. Author of *Reflections 1* and *Reflections 2*, reference books on ephemera; specializing in advertising trade cards and ephemera in general

Kline, Jerry
Florence Showcase
PO Box 468, Bennington, 05201; 802-442-3336; e-mail: sweetpea@sweet pea.net. Specializing in Florence ceramics of California, Rookwood pottery, Shelley English China, English chintz

---
Virginia

Bradfield, Jeff
Jeff's Antiques
90 Main St., Dayton, 22821; 540-879-9961; also located at Rolling Hills Antique Mall, Interstate 81, Exit 247B, Harrisonburg, VA; and the Factory Antique Mall, Interstate 81, Exit 227, Verona, VA. Specializing in candy containers, toys, postcards, sugar shakers, lamps, furniture, pottery, and advertising items

Branchcomb, Shane
20932 Winola Ter., Ashburn, 20147; e-mail: acmeman@erols.com. Specializing in antique coffee mills, send SASE for reply

Bull, Donald A.
PO Box 596, Wirtz, 24184; 540-721-1128; e-mail: corkscrew@bull works.net. Author of *The Ultimate Corkscrew Book, Boxes Full of Corkscrews, Bull's Pocket Guide to Corkscrews, Just for Openers* (with John Stanley); *Boxes of Corkscrews, Anri Woodcarvings* (with Philly Rains); and *Soda Advertising Openers*; specializing in corkscrews; website of the Virginia Corkscrew Museum: www.corkscrew museum.com

Cranor, Rosalind
PO Box 859, Blacksburg, 24063. Specializing in Elvis collectibles; author of *Elvis Collectibles* (out of print) and *Best of Elvis Collectibles*, available from author for $21.70 ppd.

Flanigan, Vicki
Flanigan's Antiques
PO Box 1662, Winchester, 22604; member: UFDC, NADDA (National Antique Doll Dealers Assn); e-mail: flanig@shentel.net. Specializing in antique dolls, hand fans, and teddy bears; please include SASE with correspondence; fee for appraisals

Haigh, Richard
PO Box 29562, Richmond 23242; 804-741-5770. Specializing in Locke Art, Steuben, Loetz, Fry, Italian; SASE required for reply

MacAllister, Dale
PO Box 46, Singers Glen, 22850. Specializing in sugar shakers and syrups

Monsen, Randall; and Baer, Rod
Monsen & Baer
Box 529, Vienna, 22183; 703-938-2129. Specializing in perfume bottles, Roseville pottery, Art Deco

Reynolds, Charles
Reynolds Toys
2836 Monroe St., Falls Church, 22042; 703-533-1322; e-mail: reynolds toys@erols.com. Specializing in limited-edition mechanical and still banks, figural bottle openers

Windsor, Grant S.
PO Box 72606, Richmond, 23235-8017; 804-320-0386. Specializing in Griswold cast-iron cookware; SASE required for inquiries. Grant currently has a reprint of Griswold Catalog S, dated November 1, 1895, 20 pages. It contains much information and illustrations of several items not seen in catalogs previously known. Information is revealed which specifically dates the 'World's Fair' griddle; currently available for $11.50 each (ppd.); for orders of 10 or more: $7.50 each (ppd.),

---
Washington

Frost, Donald M.
Country Estate Antiques (appointment only)
14800 N.E. 8th St., Vancouver, 98684; 360-604-8434. Specializing in art glass and earlier 20th-century American glass

Goldsworthy, Kathy
Past Glories
425-488-8871. Specializing in vintage needlecraft accessories and textiles; www.tias.com/stores/pastglories

Haase, Don (Mr. Spode)
The Spode Shop
D&D Antiques
PO Box 818, Mukilteo, 98275; 425-348-7443; e-mail: Don@mrspode.com. Specializing in Spode-Copeland China; www.mrspode.com

Jackson, Denis C., Editor
The Illustrator Collector's News
PO Box 1958, Sequim, 98382; 360-452-3810; e-mail: ticn@olypen.com. Copy of recent sample: $3; specializing in old magazines & illustrations such as Rose O'Neill, Maxfield Parrish, pin-ups, Marilyn Monroe, Norman Rockwell, etc.

Morris, Sue and Dave
PO Box 158, Manchester, 98353. Specializing in Watt pottery and Purinton pottery; author of *Watt Pottery — An Identification and Value Guide*, and *Purinton Pottery — An Identification and Value Guide*

Payne, Sharon A.
Antiquities & Art
e-mail: hotel_california94546@ yahoo. com. Specializing in Cordey

Weldin, Bob
Miner's Quest
W. 3015 Weile, Spokane, WA 99208; 509-327-2897. Specializing in mining antiques and collectibles (mail-order business)

Whitaker, Jim and Kaye
Eclectic Antiques
PO Box 475 Dept. S, Lynnwood, 98046. Specializing in Josef Originals and motion lamps; SASE required; www.eclecticantiques.com

Zeder, Audrey
1320 S.W. 10th Street #S, North Bend, 98045 (appointment only). Specializing in British Royalty Commemorative souvenirs (mail-order catalog available); author (Wallace Homestead) of *British Royalty Commemoratives*

West Virginia

Fostoria Glass Society of America, Inc.
Box 826, Moundsville, 26041. Specializing in Fostoria glass

Hardy, Roger and Claudia
West End Antiques
97 Milford St., Clarksburg, 26301; 304-624-7600 (days) or 304-624-4523 (evenings). Authors of *The Complete Line of the Akro Agate Co.*; specializing in Akro Agate

---
Wisconsin

Helley, Phil
Old Kilbourne Antiques
629 Indiana Ave., Wisconsin Dells, 53965; 608-254-8770. Specializing in premiums, German and Japanese tin toys, Cracker Jack, toothbrush holders, radio premiums, pencil sharpeners, and comic strip toys

Knapper, Mary
Phoneco, Inc.
207 E. Mill Rd., PO Box 70, Galesville, 54630; 608-582-4124. Specializing in telephones, antique to modern

Matzke, Gene
Gene's Badges & Emblems
455 Big Horn Ct., Hancock, 54943; phone/fax: 715-249-5695; e-mail: badgeone@uniontel.net. Specializing in police badges, leg irons, old police photos, fire badges (old), patches, old handcuffs, and memorabilia

Thomas, Darrell
Sugar Shakin Antiques
PO Box 7131, Appleton, 54912; e-mail: sugarshakin@new.rr.com. Specializing in art pottery, ceramics, Deco era, Goldscheider, and Keramos

Thorpe, Donna and John
204 North St., Sun Prairie, 53590; 608-837-7674. Specializing in Chase Brass and Copper Co.

Clubs, Newsletters, and Catalogs

ABC Collectors' Circle (16-pg. newsletter, published 3 times a year)
Dr. Joan M. George
67 Stevens Ave., Old Bridge, NJ 08857; e-mail: drjgeorge@nac.net or fax: 732-679-6102. Specializing in ABC plates and mugs

Abingdon Pottery Collectors Club
Elaine Westover, Membership and Treasurer
210 Knox Hwy. 5, Abingdon, IL 61410; 309-462-3267. Dues $8 for single, $10 per couple. Specializing in collecting and preservation of Abingdon pottery

Akro Agate Collectors Club and *Clarksburg Crow* quarterly newsletter
Claudia and Roger Hardy
10 Bailey St., Clarksburg, WV 26301-2524; 304-624-4523 (evenings) or West End Antiques, 97 Milford St., Clarksburg, WV 26301; 304-624-7600 (week days). Annual membership fee: $25; www.akro-agate.com

The Akro Arsenal, quarterly catalog
Larry D. Wells
5411 Joyce Ave., Ft. Wayne, IN 46818; 219-489-5842

The Aluminist
Dannie Woodard, Publisher
PO Box 1346, Weatherford, TX 76086. Subscription: $20 (includes membership)

America West Archives
Anderson, Warren
PO Box 100, Cedar City, UT 84721; 435-586-9497; e-mail: warren@americawestarchives.com. 26-page illustrated catalogs issued 6 times a year; has both fixed-price and auction sections offering early western documents, letters, stock certificates, autographs, and other important ephemera; subscription: $13 per year

American Antique Deck Collectors
52 Plus Joker Club
Clear the Decks, quarterly publication
Janice Miller, Membership
670 Carlton Dr., Elgin, IL 60120-4008; e-mail: Joker1854@aol.com. Membership: $25 (US and Canada), $35 (foreign). Specializing in antique playing cards; www.52plusjoker.org

American Bell Association, Int., Inc.
c/o The Bell Tower
PO Box 19443, Indianapolis, IN 46219; information e-mail: bob bam@bellsouth.net. Annual dues: $22 ($25 per couple); www.american bell.org

American Cut Glass Association
Kathy Emmerson, Executive Secretary
PO Box 482, Ramona, CA 92065-0482; 760-789-2715 or fax: 760-789-7112; e-mail: acgakathy@aol.com. Membership dues (includes subscription to newsletter, *The Hobstar*: $45 (USA bulk mail) or $55 (first class and international); www.cutglass.org

American Hatpin Society
Virginia Woodbury, President
20 Montecillo, Rolling Hills Estates, CA 90274; 310-326-2196; HATPNGINIA@aol.com. Newsletter published quarterly; meetings also quarterly; membership: $30; www.collectoronline.com/AHS/

Antique and Art Glass Salt Shaker Collectors' Society (AAGSSCS)
17460 Caloosa Trace Circle, Ft. Myers, FL 33912

Antique & Collectors Reproduction News
Antiques Coast to Coast
Mark Chervenka, Editor
PO Box 12130, Des Moines, IA 50312-9403; 515-274-5886 or (subscriptions only) 800-227-5531; e-mail: acrn@repronews.com. 12 monthly issues: $32 (US); $41 (Canada); $59 (foreign)

Antique Advertising Association of America (AAAA)
PO Box 1121, Morton Grove, IL 60053; 708-466-0904. Publishes *Past Times* Newsletter; subscription: $35

Antique Bottle & Glass Collector Magazine
Jim Hagenbuch, Publisher
102 Jefferson St., PO Box 180, East Greenville, PA 18041; 215-679-5849 or fax: 215-679-3068; e-mail: glswrk@enter.net. Subscription (12 issues): $21 (US); $24 (Canada)

Antique Journal
Michael F. Shores, Publisher
Jeffrey Hill, Editor/General Manager
2329 Santa Clara Ave., #207, Alameda, CA 94501; 800-791-8592

Antique Journal Northwest
Michael F. Shores, Publisher
Jeffrey Hill, Editor/General Manager
3439 North East Sandy Blvd., Suite #275, Portland, OR 9723; 888-845-3201

Antique Purses Catalog: $4
Bayhouse
PO Box 40443, Cleveland, OH 44140; 216-871-8584. Includes colored photos of beaded and enameled mesh purses

Antique Radio Classified (ARC)
PO Box 2, Carlisle, MA 01741; 978-371-0512

Antique Souvenir Collectors News
Gary Leveille, Editor
PO Box 562, Great Barrington, MA 01230

Antique Stove Association
c/o Caroline Royske
PO Box 2101, Waukesha, WI 53187-2101; 262-542-9190 after 6 p.m.

Antique Telephone Collectors Association
Box 94, Abilene, KS 67410; 785-263-1757. An international organization associated with the Museum of Independent Telephony; www.atca online.com

Antique Trader Weekly
Nancy Crowley, Editor
PO Box 1050, Dubuque, IA 52004-1050; e-mail: collect@krause.com. Featuring news about antiques and collectibles, auctions, and events; listing over 165,000 buyers and sellers in every edition; subscription: $38 (US) for 52 issues per year; toll free for subscriptions only: 800-258-0929; www.collect.com

Antique Wireless Association
Ormiston Rd., Breesport, NY 14816

Appraisers National Association
25602 Alicia Parkway, PMB 245, Laguna Hills, CA 92653; 949-349-9179; e-mail: info@ana-appraisals.org. Founded in 1982, a nonprofit organization dedicated to the professionalism and education of personal property appraiser. All members adhere to a code of ethics and abide by professional standards. ANA also works to develop awareness of the professionalism of appraising, and the service it provides to the public. Free referrals to accredited appraisers for antiques, collectibles, art, jewelry, furniture and residential contents; www.ana-appraisals.org

Arman's Collectors Sales & Services
PO Box 6, Pomfret Center, CT 06259; 860-794-7008 or fax: 860-974-7010; e-mail: Collectors.sales@snet.net

Association of Coffee Mill Enthusiasts (ACME)
c/o Lucy Fullinwider, Treasurer
PO Box 5761, Midland, TX 79704. Quarterly newsletter, annual convention; dues are $40 ($50 outside the continental US and Canada), covers cost of quarterly newsletter and copy of membership roster

Auction Times for the West
Michael F. Shores, Publisher
Jeffrey Hill, Editor/General Manager
2329 Santa Clara Ave., Suite 207, Alamedo, CA 94501; 800-791-8592

Autograph Times
2303 N. 44th St., #225, Phoenix, AZ 85008; 602-947-3112 or fax: 602-947-8363. Subscription: $15 (US) per year

Autographs of America
Tim Anderson
PO Box 461, Provo, UT 84603; 801-226-1787 (please call in the afternoon); www.AutographsOfAmerica.com

Autumn Leaf
Bill Swanson, Editor
807 Roaring Springs Dr., Allen, TX 75002-2112; 972-727-5527

Gwynne Harrison, President
PO Box 1, Mira Loma, CA 91752-0001; 951-685-5434; www.nalcc.org

Avon Times (National Avon collectors' newsletter)
c/o Dwight or Vera Young
PO Box 9868, Dept. P., Kansas City, MO 64134; e-mail: AvonTimes@aol.com. Inquiriees should be accompanied by LSASE

Beatlefan
PO Box 33515, Decatur, GA 30033. Subscription: $7 (US) for 6 issues or $21 (Canada and Mexico)

Bojo
PO Box 1403, Cranberry Township, PA 16066-0403; bojoonline.com. Send $3 for 38 pages of Beatles, toys, dolls, jewelry, autographs, Yellow Submarine items, etc.

Bookend Collector Club
c/o Louis Kuritzky, M.D.
4510 NW 17th Place, Gainesville, FL 32650; 352-377-3193. Quarterly full-color glossy newsletter, $25 per year; e-mail: lkuritzky@aol.com

Bossons Briefs, quarterly newsletter
Available through membership in the International Bossons Collectors Society, John J. Cassidy, Executive Director
1317 N. San Fernando Blvd, Suite #325, Burbank, CA 91504; e-mail:bossonsman@aol.com

Boyd's Art Glass Collectors Guild
PO Box 52, Hatboro, PA 19040-0052

Boyd's Crystal Art Glass
Jody & Darrell's Glass Collectibles Newsletter

PO Box 180833, Arlington, TX 76096-0833. 6 issues a year; subscription includes exclusive glass collectible produced by Boyd's Crystal Art Glass; LSASE for current subscription rates.

British Royal Commemorative Souvenirs Mail Order Catalog
Audrey Zeder
1320 SW 10th St. #S, North Bend, WA 98045. Monthly catalog: $5.00.

Buckeye Marble Collectors Club
Brenda Longbrake, Secretary
e-mail: brenda@wcoil.com; buckeye marble.com

The Buttonhook Society
Box 287, White Marsh, MD 21162. Publishes bimonthly newsletter *The Boutonneur*, which promotes collecting of buttonhooks and shares research and information contributed by members

Candy Container Collectors of America
The Candy Gram Newsletter
c/o Betty MacDuff, Membership Chairman
2711 De La Rosa St, The Villages, FL 32159; e-mail: epmac27@aol.com; or contact: Jeff Bradfield, 90 Main St., Dayton, VA 22821. Membership: $25 per family; www. candycontainer.org

The Cane Collector's Chronicle
Linda Beeman
15 2nd St. N.E., Washington, D.C. 20002. $30 for 4 issues

Cane Collectors Club
PO Box 1004, Englewood Cliff, NJ 07632; 201-886-8826; e-mail: liela@ walkingstickworld.com

The Carnival Pump
International Carnival Glass Assoc., Inc.
Lee Markley
Box 306, Mentone, IN 46539. Dues: $20 per family per year in US and Canada or $25 overseas; www.woods land.com/icga

The Carousel News & Trader
87 Parke Ave. W., Suite 206, Mansfield, OH 44902. A monthly magazine for the carousel enthusiast; subscription: $22 per year; sample: $3

The Carousel Shopper Resource Catalog
Box 47, Dept. PC, Millwood, NY 10546. Only $2 (+50¢ postage); a full-color catalog featuring dealers of antique carousel art offering single figures or complete carousels, museums, restoration services, organizations, full-size reproductions, books, cards, posters, auction services and other hard-to-find items for carousel enthusiasts

A Catalog Collection
Kenneth E. Schneringer
271 Sabrina Ct., Woodstock, GA 30188-4228; 770-926-9383; e-mail: trademan68@aol.com. Specializing in catalogs, promochures, view books, labels, trade cards, special paper needs

Central Florida Insulator Collectors
3557 Nicklaus Dr., Titusville, FL 32780-5356; 407-267-9170; e-mail: bluebellwt@aol.com. Dues: $10 per year for single or family membership (checks payable to Jacqueline Barnes). Dues cover the cost of *Newsnotes*, the club's monthly newsletter, which informs members of meetings and shows, articles of interest on insulators and other collectibles. Members are invited to use free advertising of items for sale or trade. The club meets quarterly in members' homes and hosts a show each January which is open to the public. For club information send SASE to above address.

Ceramic Arts Studio Collector's Assoc.
PO Box 46, Madison, WI 53701; 608-241-9138. Annual membership: $15; inventory record and price guide available

Chicagoland Antique Amusements Slot Machine & Jukebox Gazette
Ken Durham, Editor
909 26 St., N.W., Suite 502, Washington, DC 20037. 16-page newspaper published twice a year; subscription: 4 issues for $30; sample: $10; www.GameRoomAntiques.com

China Specialties, Inc.
Fiesta Collector's Quarterly Newsletter
PO Box 361280, Strongsville, OH 44316-1280; www.chinaspecialties.com

Chintz Connection Newsletter
PO Box 222, Riverdale, MD 20738. Dedicated to helping collectors share information and find matchings; subscription: 4 issues per year for $25

The Cola Clan
Alice Fisher, Treasurer
2084 Continental Dr., N.E., Atlanta, GA 30345

Collector's Life
The World's Foremost Publication for Steiff Enthusiasts
Beth Savino
PO Box 798; Holland, OH 43528; 1-800-862-TOYS; fax: 419-473-3947; www.toystorenet.com

Collector Glass News
Box 308, Slippery Rock, PA 16057 724-946-2838 or fax: 724-946-9012; e-mail: cgn@glassnews.com; An international publication providing current

news to collectors of cartoon, fast-food, and promotional glassware; Subscription: $15 per year (6 issues); www.glassnews.com

Collectors of Findlay Glass
PO Box 256, Findlay, OH 45840. An organization dedicated to the study and recognition of Findlay glass; Newsletter *The Melting Pot*, published quarterly; Annual convention; Membership: $10 per year ($15 per couple)

Compact Collectors
Roselyn Gerson
PO Box 40, Lynbrook, NY 11563; 516-593-8746 or fax: 516-593-0610; e-mail: compactldy@aol.com. Publishes *Powder Puff* Newsletter, which contains articles covering all aspects of powder and solid perfume compact collecting, restoration, vintage ads, patents, history, and articles by members and prominent guest writers; seekers and sellers column offered free to members

Cookie Crumbs
Cookie Cutter Collectors Club
Ruth Capper, Secretary/Treasurer
1167 Teal Road S.W., Dellroy, OH 44620. Subscription $20 per year (4 issues); payable to CCCC; www.mich.com/~longmore.cccc

Cookie Jarrin' With Joyce: The Cookie Jar Newsletter
1501 Maple Ridge Rd., Walterboro, SC 29488

Cookies
Rosemary Henry
9610 Greenview Lane, Manassas, VA 20109-3320. Subscription: $12 per year (6 issues); payable to Cookies

The Copley Courier
1639 N. Catalina St., Burbank, CA 91505

Cowan Pottery Museum Associates
For information write: CPMA, PO Box 16765, Rocky River, OH 44116 or contact Victoria Naumann Peltz, Curatorial Associate, Cowan Pottery Museum at Rocky River Public Library, 1600 Hampton Rd., Rocky River, OH 44116; 440-333-7610, ext. 214. Annual dues: $35, includes subscription to biannual *Cowan Pottery Journal* Newsletter; please visit our website at www.cowanpottery.org

Cracker Jack® Collector's Assoc. *The Prize Insider* Newsletter
Theresa Richter, Membership Chairman
5469 S. Dorchester Ave., Chicago, IL 60615; e-mail: WaddyTMR@aol.com. Subscription/membership: $20 per year (single) or $24 (family); www. collectoronline.com/CJCA/

Creamers, quarterly newsletter
PO Box 11, Lake Villa, IL 60046-0011. Subscription: $5 per year

Currier & Ives Catalog
Rudisill's Alt Print Haus
PO Box 199, Worton, MD 21678. Please include LSASE; e-mail: rudi@dmv.com; chesapeake-bay.com/altprinthaus; Gallery: freepages.rootsweb.com/~vstern

(Currier & Ives) C&I Dinnerware Collector Club
E.R. Aupperle, Treasurer
29470 Saxon Road, Toulton, IL 61483; 309-896-3331 or fax: 309-856-6005

Custard Glass Collectors Society
Custard Connection quarterly newsletter
Sarah Coulon, Editor
591 SW Duxbury Ave., Port St. Lucie, FL 34983; 561-785-9446; e-mail: mrs foxy@aol.com. Annual membership: $20 (US) or $25 (Canada and Mexico); live chat every Saturday night at 9 pm EST; see website for link: www.homestead.com/custardsociety

Czechoslovakian Collectors Guild International
Alan Badia
15006 Meadowlake St., Odessa, FL 33556-3126; e-mail: ab@czechart glass.com. Annual membership: $65 in US; www.czechartglass.com/ccgi

The Dedham Pottery Collectors Society Newsletter
Jim Kaufman, Publisher
248 Highland St., Dedham, MA 02026-5833; 800-283-8070; e-mail: DedhamPottery.com

Docks, L.R. 'Les'
Shellac Shack
Box 691035, San Antonio, TX 78269-1035; e-mail: docks@texas.net. Send $2 for an illustrated booklet of 78s that Docks wants to buy, the prices he will pay, and shipping instructions; docks.home.texas.net

Doorstop Collectors of America
Doorstopper Newsletter
Jeanie Bertoia
2413 Madison Ave., Vineland, NJ 08630; 609-692-4092. Membership: $20 per year, includes 2 newsletters and convention; send 2-stamp SASE for sample

Dragonware Club
c/o Suzi Hibbard
849 Vintage Ave., Fairfield, CA 94585; e-mail: Dragon_Ware@hot mail.com. Inquiries must be accompanied with LSASE or they will not be responded to; All contributions are welcome; www.Dragonware.com

Drawing Room of Newport
Gacher, John
152 Spring St., Newport, RI 02840;
401-841-5060. Book on Zsolnay available; www.drawrm.com

Early Typewriter Collectors Association
ETCetera newsletter
Chuck Dilts and Rich Cincotta, Co-editors
P.O. Box 286; Southborough, MA
01772; 508-229-2064; e-mail: etcetera@
writeme.com; www.typewriter.rydia.
net/etcetera.html

Ed Taylor Radio Museum
245 N. Oakland Ave., Indianapolis,
IN 46201-3360; 317-638-1641

Eggcup Collector's Corner
67 Stevens Ave., Old Bridge, NJ
08857. Issued quarterly; subscription:
$18 per year (payable to Joan George);
sample copy: $5

The Elegance of Old Ivory Newsletter
Box 1004, Wilsonville, OR 97070

Fenton Art Glass Collectors of America, Inc.
Butterfly Net Newsletter
Kay Kenworthy, Editor
PO Box 384, 702 W. 5th St.,
Williamstown, WV 26187; e-mail:
kkenworthy@foth.com. Dues: $20 per
year (full membership +$5 for each
associate membership, children under
12 free); www.collectoronline.com/
club-FAGCA.html

Fiesta Collector's Quarterly Newsletter
PO Box 471, Valley City, OH 44280.
Subscription: $12 per year; www.china
specialties.com/fiesta.html

Figural Bottle Opener Collectors
Linda Fitzsimmons, 9697 Gwynn Park
Dr., Ellicott City, MD 21042; 410-465-
9296. Please include SASE when
requesting information

Florence Ceramics Collectors Society
1971 Blue Fox Drive; Lansdale, PA
19446-5505; e-mail: FlorenceCeram
ics@aol.com. Newsletter and club
membership: $35 per year (6 issues in
color)

Fostoria Glass Society of America,
Inc.
PO Box 826, Moundsville, WV 26041;
Membership: $16; www.fostoriaglass.org

Frankoma Family Collectors Association
c/o Nancy Littrell
PO Box 32571, Oklahoma City, OK
73123-0771. Membership dues: $35
(includes quarterly newsletter); annual
convention; www.frankoma.org

Friends of Degenhart
c/o Degenhart Museum
PO Box 186, Cambridge, OH 43725;
740-432-2626. Membership: $5 ($10
for family) includes *Heartbeat*
Newsletter (printed quarterly) and
free admission to museum

H.C. Fry Society
PO Box 41, Beaver, PA 15009. Founded in 1983 for the sole purpose of
learning about Fry glass; publishes
Shards, quarterly newsletter

The Glass Menagerie, bimonthly
newsletter
Susan Candelaria, Editor
5440 El Arbol, Carlsbad, CA 92008

Goofus Glass Gazette
Steve Gillespie, Publisher
400 Martin Blvd., Village of the Oaks,
MO 64118; 888-455-5558; e-mail: stegil
@sbcglobal.net

The Gonder Collector
917 Hurl Dr.
Pittsburgh, PA 15236

Grandpa's Depot
John 'Grandpa' White
6720 E. Mississippi Ave., Unit B, Denver, CO 80224; 303-758-8540 or fax:
303-321-2889. Publishes catalogs on
railroad-related items

Haeger Pottery Collectors of America
Lanette Clarke
5021 Toyon Way, Antioch, CA
94509; 925-776-7784; e-mail: Lanette-
Clarke@msn.com. Newsletter published 6 times per year; dues: $20

*The Hagen-Renaker Collector's Club
Newsletter*
c/o Jenny Palmer
3651 Polish Line Rd., Cheboygan, MI
49721-9045; subscription: $24 (6
issues); hrcc@freeway.net

Hall China Collector's Club Newsletter
Virginia Lee
PO Box 360488, Cleveland, OH
44136; 330-220-7456

The Hatpin Society of Great Britain
Contact: Estelle Weiner, Chairman;
jake@jemah.co.uk

Hammered Aluminum Collectors
Association (HACA)
Dannie Woodard
PO Box 1346, Weatherford, TX
76086; 817-594-46

Head Hunters Newsletter
c/o Maddy Gordon
PO Box 83H, Scarsdale, NY 10583;
914-472-0200. Subscription: $24 yearly (quarterly issues)

Homer Laughlin China Collectors
Association (HLCCA)
The Dish magazine (a 16-page quarterly included with membership); PO
Box 26021, Crystal City, VA 22215-
6021; e-mail: info@hlcca.org. Membership: $25 (single), $40 (couple/
family); www.hlcca.org

Ice Screamer
PO Box 465, Warrington, PA 18976.
Published quarterly; membership: $20
per year; annual convention held in
Lancaster, PA

Ideal Collectors Club
c/o Judith Izen
PO Box 623, Lexington, MA 02173;
e-mail: jizenres@aol.com. Membership: $20 per year,includes a quarterly
newsletter; subscribers get free wanted/
for sale ads in each issue

The Illustrator Collector's News (TICN)
Denis C. Jackson, Editor
PO Box 1958, Sequim, WA
98382. A free use site on the
Internet for paper collectors of all
kinds, listing paper and magazine-
related price guides available for
sale only at this site; www.
olypen.com/ticn

Indiana Historical Radio Society
245 N. Oakland Ave., Indianapolis,
IN 46201-3360; 317-638-1641.
Membership: $15 (US), $19 (overseas) includes *IHRS Bulletin* newsletter; home.att.net/~indianahistorical
radio

International Association of Calculator Collectors
International Calculator Collector
Newsletter
Guy Ball, Co-editor
PO Box 345, Tustin, CA 92781-0345;
e-mail: mrcalc@usa.net. Subscriptions:
$16 per year ($20 foreign); sample
copy: $3

International Association of R.S.
Prussia, Inc.
Theresa Newcomer, Secretary
PO Box 446, Mount Joy, PA 17522.
Membership: $30 per household; Yearly convention; www.rsprussia.com

International Club for Collectors of
Hatpins and Hatpin Holders (ICC
of H&HH)
Audrae Heath, Managing Editor
PO Box 1009, Bonners Ferry, ID
83805-1009. Bimonthly *Points* newsletter and *Pictorial Journal*

International Golliwog Collector Club
Beth Savino
PO Box 798; Holland, OH 43528; 1-
800-862-TOYS or fax: 419-473-3947;
toystorenet.com

International Ivory Society
Robert Weisblut, Co-founder
11109 Nicholas Dr., Wheaton, MD
20902; 301-649-4002. Free membership

International Match Safe Association
Membership Chairman
PO Box 791, Malaga, NJ 08328; 856-
694-4167; e-mail: imsaoc@aol.com.
Membership: $50; quarterly newsletter
and annual convention; www.match
safe.org

International Nippon Collectors Club
(INCC)
c/o Gerry Goldsmith
1387 Lance Ct., Carol Stream, IL
60188. Publishes newsletter 6 times a
year; Holds annual convention; membership: $30; www.nipponcollectors
club.com

International Perfume and Scent Bottle Collectors Association
Randall Monsen
PO Box 529, Vienna, VA 22183 or
fax: 703-242-1357; or Coleen Abbot,
396 Croton Rd., Wayne, PA 19087-
2038. Membership: $45 (USA) or $55
(Foreign); newsletter published quarterly; www.perfumebottles.org

International Rose O'Neill Club
Contact Karen Stewart
PO Box 668, Branson, MO 65616; e-
mail: wisteriahs@excite.com. Publishes quarterly newsletter *Kewpiesta
Kourier*; membership: (includes
newsletter) $15 (single) or $20 (family); www.kewpieroseoneillclub.com

International Society of Antique
Scale Collectors
Jan Macho, Executive Secretary
3616 Noakes St., Los Angeles, CA
90023; 323-263-6878. Publishes *Equilibrium* Magazine; quarterly newsletter;
annual membership directory and out-
of-print scale catalogs; Annual convention; membership: $65; please
include SASE when requesting information; www.isasc.org

International Vintage Poster Dealers
Association (IVPDA)
Nancy Steinbock, Charter Member
800-438-1577; e-mail: info@ivpda.com.
Specializing in posters; www.ivpda.com

John F. Rinaldi
Nautical Antiques and Related Items
(appointment only)
Box 765, Dock Square, Kennebunkport,
ME 04046; 207-967-3218; or fax: 207-
967-2918. Illustrated catalog: $5

Josef Originals Newsletter
Jim and Kaye Whitaker
PO Box 475, Dept. S, Lynnwood, WA
98046. Subscription (4 issues): $10 per year

Knife Rests of Yesterday and Today
Beverly L. Ales
4046 Graham St., Pleasanton, CA
94566-5619. Subscription: $20 per
year for 6 issues

The Laughlin Eagle
Joan Jasper, Publisher
Richard Racheter, Editor
1270 63rd Terrace S., St. Petersburg, FL 33705; 813-867-3982.
Subscription: $18 (4 issues) per
year; sample: $4

Les Amis de Vieux Quimper (Friends
of Old Quimper)
c/o Mark and Adela Meadows
PO Box 819, Carnelian Bay, CA
96140. SASE required for written
reply; e-mail: meadows@cwo.com;
www.oldquimper.com

License Plate Collectors Hobby Magazine
Drew Steitz, Editor
PO Box 222, East Texas, PA 18046;
phone/fax: 610-791-7979. Bimonthly
publication with many photographs,
classifieds, etc.; $25 per year (1st class,
US); sample: $4

Liddle Kiddle Konvention
Paris Langford
415 Dodge Ave. Jefferson, LA
70121; e-mail: bbean415@aol.com.
Send SASE for information about
upcoming Liddle Kiddle Convention, also send additional SASE for
Liddle Kiddle Newsletter information; info and newsletter: liddle
kiddlesnewsletter@yahoo.com; www.
vintageland.com/liddle_kiddles_
convention.htm

Central Florida Insulator Collectors
Line Jewels, NIA #1380
3557 Nicklaus Dr., Titusville, FL
32780

Majolica International Society
Michael Foley, Membership Chairman
77 Wright St., New Bedford, MA
02740; Membership: $40 per year,
includes annual meeting and quarterly
newsletter *Majolica Matters*; www.
majolicasociety.com

Marble Collectors' Society of America
PO Box 222, Trumbull, CT 06611.
Publishes *Marble Mania*; gathers
and disseminates information to
further the hobby of marbles and
marble collecting; $12 adds your
name to the contributor mailing list
($21 covers 2 years); e-mail:
BlockMCSA@aol.com or www.
blocksite.com

Marble Collectors Unlimited
PO Box 206, Northboro, MA 01532

Martha's Kidlit Newsletter
Martha Rasmussen, Editor and Publisher
Box 1488, Ames IA 50014; 515-292-
9309; e-mail: martha@kidlitonline.org.
For children's book lovers and collectors; Subscription: $30 in US, all oth-
ers: $31; www.kidlitonline.org

Midwest Open Salt Society
c/o Ed Bowman
2411 W. 500 North, Hartford City, IN
47348. Dues: $10 ($6 for spouse)

Midwest Sad Iron Collector Club
Bruce Baumunk
6903 Singing Wood Lane, St. Louis
MO 63129; 314-846-9573; e-mail:
bruce.baumunk@gte.net. Membership: $30 per year; www.irons.
com/msicc.htm

Miniature Bottle Club of the Great
Lakes
19745 Woodmont, Harper Woods, MI
48225. Dues $5 per year; 4 meetings
per year

Mt. Washington Art Glass Society
PO Box 107, Hyde Park, NY 12538-
1122. Publishes MWAGS *Review*, to
educate, inform, and provide helpful
information to anyone interested in art
glass; holds annual convention; sub-
scription/membership: $30 (single) or
$40 for (2 persons in 1 household)

Murray Hudson Antiquarian Books,
Maps & Globes
109 S. Church St., Box 163, Halls, TN
38040; 800-748-9946 or 731-836-
9057; fax: 731-836-9017; e-mail: map
man@ecis.com. Buyer and seller specializing in antique maps, globes, and
books with maps: atlases, explorations,
travel guides, geographies, surveys,
etc.; largest ever catalog of Civil War
maps and graphics; largest selection of
wall maps and world globes; contact
for catalog

Mystic Lights of the Aladdin Knights,
bimonthly newsletter
c/o J.W. Courter
3935 Kelley Rd., Kevil, KY 40253-
9532; 270-488-2116. Information and
free 8-page *History of the Aladdin Lamp*
requires LSASE; www.aladdin
knights.org

National Association of Avon Collectors
c/o Connie Clark
6100 Walnut, Dept. P, Kansas City, MO
64113. Information requires LSASE

National Association of Breweriana
Advertising (NABA)
Publishes *The Breweriana Collector*;
holds annual convention; membership
information and directory available on
www.nababrew.org

National Association of Warwick
China and Pottery Collectors
Betty June Wymer
28 Bachmann Drive, Wheeling, WV
26003; 304-232-3031. Annual dues
$15 (single) or $20 (couple), checks
payable to NAWCPA; publishes quarterly newsletter; holds annual convention in Wheeling, West Virginia

National Autumn Leaf Collectors' Club
Bill Swanson, Newsletter Editor
807 Roaring Springs Dr., Allen, TX
75002-2112; 972-727-5527 or fax:
972-727-2107; e-mail: bescom@attbi.
com; or Gwynne Harrison, President,
PO Box 1, Mira Loma, CA 91752-
0001; 909-685-5434 or fax: 909-681-
1692. Membership: $20, payable to
NALCC, c/o Dianna Kowales, PO
Box 900968, Palmdale, CA 93590-
0968; e-mail: morgan99@pe.net;
www.nalcc.org

National Blue Ridge Newsletter
Norma Lilly
144 Highland Dr., Blountville, TN
37617. Subscription: $15 per year (6
issues)

National Cambridge Collectors, Inc.
PO Box 416, Cambridge, OH 43725-
0416; 740-432-4245 or fax: 740-439-
9223; e-mail: NCC-Crystal-Ball
@compuserve.com. Membership: $20
(Associate member: $3); www. Cambridge
glass.org

National Cuff Link Society
c/o Eugene R. Klompus
PO Box 5700, Vernon Hills, IL 60061;
Phone/fax: 847-816-0035; e-mail:
genek@cufflink.com or ncls@bell-
south.net; www.cufflink.com. $30
annual dues includes subscription to
The Link, a quarterly magazine; write
for free booklet *The Fun of Cuff Link
Collecting*

National Depression Glass Association
PO Box, 8264, Wichita, KS 67208-
0264. Publishs *News and Views*; membership: $17 (individual); $3
(associate); www.ndga.net

National Fenton Glass Society
PO Box 4008, Marietta, OH 45750;
740-374-3345; fax: 740-376-9708.
Membership: $20, includes *The Fenton
Flyer* newsletter

National Graniteware Society
PO Box 9248, Cedar Rapids, IA
52409-9248. Membership: $20;
www.graniteware.org

National Greentown Glass Association
PO Box 107, Greentown, IN 46936.
Membership: $20; www.eastern.k12.
in.us/gpl/glassass.htm

National Imperial Glass Collectors'
Society, Inc.
PO Box 534, Bellaire, OH 43906; e-
mail: info@nigcs.org. Membership:
$18 per year (+$3 for each associate
member); quarterly newsletter; convention every June; www.imperial
glass.org

National Insulator Association
1315 Old Mill Path, Broadview
Heights, OH 44147; e-mail or general
information: kwjacob@uswest.net.
Membership: $12; www.nia.org

National Milk Glass Collectors' Society and *Opaque News*, quarterly
newsletter
Membership: $18 (payable to club)
Barb Pinkston, Membership Chairman
9238 E. Kenosha Ct., Floral City, FL
34436-2438 (please include SASE); e-
mail: membership@nmgsc.org; www.
nmgcs.org

National Reamer Collectors Association
c/o Debbie Gillham
47 Midline Ct., Gaithersburg, MD
20878. Membership: $25 per house-
hold; e-mail: reamers@erols.com;
www.reamers.org

National Shaving Mug Collectors
Association
Anise Alkin, Membership
544 Line Rd., Hazlett, NJ 07739; e-
mail: info@nsma.org. To stimulate the
study, collection, and preservation of
shaving mugs and all related barbering
items; provides quarterly newsletter,
bibliography, and directory; holds 2
meetings per year; dues: $25 per year

National Shelley China Club
Rochelle Hart, Secretary/Treasurer
591 West 67th Ave., Anchorage, AK
99518-1555; 907-344-9123; e-mail:
imahart@alaska.net. Membership: $35
per year, 4 quarterly newsletters plus
many other benefits and publications;
www.nationalshelleychinaclub.com

National Toothpick Holder Collectors
Society
Membership Chairperson
PO Box 852, Archer City, TX 76351;
e-mail: tpinfo@glass-works.com. Dues:
$20 (single) or $25 (couple); includes
10 *Toothpick Bulletin* newsletters per
year; annual convention held in
August; Exclusive toothpick holder
annually; www.collectoronline.com/
club-NTHCS.html

National Valentine Collectors Association
Nancy Rosin
PO Box 1404, Santa Ana, CA 92702;
714-547-1355. Membership: $16; spe-
cializing in Valentines and love
tokens

New England Society of Open Salt Collectors
Chuck Keys
21 Overbrook Lane, East Greenwich, RI 02818; Dues: $7 per year

Newspaper Collector's Society of America
Rick Brown
Lansing, MI, 517-887-1255. An extensive, searchable, 300,000-word reference library of American history with an emphasis on newspapers publishing speeches; interactive crossword puzzles; regular auctions of ephemera, historic documents, and newspapers; a mall with over one hundred different online catalogs of paper collectibles; and much, much more; e-mail: help@historybuff.com; www.history buff.com

Night Light Club/Newsletter
Culver, Bob
3081 Sand Pebble Cove, Pinckney, MI 48169. Specializing in miniature oil lamps; membership: $15 per year

NM (Nelson McCoy) Express
Carol Seman, Editor
8934 Brecksville Rd., Suite 406, Brecksville, OH 44141-2318; 440-526-2094 (voice & fax); e-mail: McCjs@aol.com. Membership: $26 per year (12 issues); www.members.aol.com/nmXpress/

North American Torquay Society
Jerry and Gerry Kline, 2 of the founding members, also members of Torquay Pottery Collectors' Society
604 Orchard View Dr., Maumee, OH 43537. Send SASE for information

North American Trap Collectors' Association
c/o Tom Parr
PO Box 94, Galloway, OH 43119-0094. Dues: $15 per year; publishes bimonthly newsletter

North Dakota Pottery Collectors Society and Newsletter
c/o Sandy Short, Membership Chairman
Box 14, Beach, ND 58621; e-mail: csshortnd@mcn.net. Membership: $15 (includes spouse); annual convention in June; quarterly newsletters; www.ndpcs.org

Novelty Salt & Pepper Shakers Club
Louise Davis
PO Box 416, Gladstone, OR 72037-0416; dmac925@yahoo.com. Publishes quarterly newsletter; holds annual convention; dues: $30 per year in US, Canada, and Mexico ($5 extra for couple)

Nutcracker Collectors' Club and Newsletter
Susan Otto, Editor

12204 Fox Run Dr., Chesterland, OH 44026; 440-729-2686. Membership: $15 ($17 foreign) includes quarterly newsletters, free classifieds

The Occupied Japan Club
c/o Florence Archambault
29 Freeborn St., Newport, RI 02840-1821. Publishes *The Upside Down World of an O.J. Collector*, a bimonthly newsletter; information requires SASE; e-mail: florence@aiconnect.com

Old Sleepy Eye Collectors Club of America, Inc.
PO Box 12, Monmouth, IL 61462; e-mail: oseclub@maplecity.com. Membership: $10 per year with additional $1 for spouse (if joining); www.maplecity.com/~oseclub/

Old Stuff
Donna and Ron Miller, Publishers
2115 McMinnville Lane, PO Box 1084, McMinnville, OR 97128; millers@oldstuffnews.com. Published 6 times annually; copies by mail: $3.50 each; annual subscription: $20 ($30 in Canada); www.oldstuffnews.com

On the LIGHTER Side Newsletter (bimonthly publication)
International Lighter Collectors
Judith Sanders, Editor
PO Box 1733, Quitman, TX 75783-1733; 903-763-2795 or fax: 903-763-4953. Annual convention held in US; subscription: $43 (overseas) $38 (US and Canada), $30 (senior member) $25 (junior member); please include SASE when requesting information

Open Salt Collectors of the Atlantic Regions (O.S.C.A.R.)
Wilbur Rudisill, Treasurer
1844 York Rd., Gettysburg, PA 17325. Dues: $5 per year

Open Salt Seekers of the West, Northern California Chapter
Sara Conley
84 Margaret Dr., Walnut Creek, CA 94596. Dues: $7 per year

Open Salt Seekers of the West, Southern California Chapter
Janet Hudson
2525 E. Vassar Court, Visalia, CA 93277. Dues: $5 per year

Pacific Northwest Fenton Association
PO Box 881, Tillamook, OR 97141; 503-842-4815; e-mail: jshirley@oregoncoast.com. Newsletter subscription: $23 per year (published quarterly, includes annual piece of glass made only for subscribers); www.glass castle.com/pnwfa.htm

Paden City Glass Collectors Guild
Paul Torsiello, Editor
42 Aldine Road, Parsippany, NJ, 07054. Publishes newsletter; for subscription information e-mail: pcguild1@yahoo.com

Paper Collectors' Marketplace
PO Box 128, Scandinavia, WI 54977-0128; 715-467-2379 or fax: 715-467-2243; e-mail: pcmpaper@gglbbs.com. Subscription: $19.95 in US (12 issues); www.pcmpaper.com

Paper Pile Quarterly Magazine
Ada Fitzsimmons, Editor
PO Box 337, San Anselmo, CA 94979; 415-454-5552 or fax: 415-454-2947; e-mail: apaperpile@aol.com. Sales and features magazine for paper buyers and sellers since 1980; quarterly cataloged sales of paper items, large for-sale and wanted sections, auction results, book reviews, quarterly price guide and show schedule; subscription: $20 per year (shipped 1st class); sample: $5 (returnable as credit toward subscription or advertising); www.papercollectibles.com

Paperweight Collectors' Association, Inc.
PMB 130, 274 Eastchester Dr. #117, High Point, NC 27262. 512-292-9229; e-mail:info@paperweight.org; www.paperweight.org. Sustaining US membership $55 per year, includes quarterly *PCA Inc. Annual Bulletin* newsletter; biannual conventions held

Peanut Pals
Judith Walthall, Founder
PO Box 4465, Huntsville, AL 35815; 205-881-9198. Associated collectors of Planters Peanuts memorabilia, bimonthly newsletter *Peanut Papers*; annual directory sent to members; annual convention and regional conventions; primary membership: $20 per year (associate memberships available); membership information: 246 Old Line Ave., Laurel, MD 20724, or check w/peanutpals.org; sample newsletter: $2

Pen Collectors of America
Bob Nurin, Treasurer
PO Box 80, Redding Ridge, CT 06876; e-mail: membership@pen collectors.com. Quarterly newsletter, *Pennant;* annual membership: $30 in US and Canada (includes newsletter and access to reference library); www.pencollectors.com

Pepsi-Cola Collectors Club Express
Bob Stoddard, Editor
PO Box 817; Claremont, CA 91711-0817

Perrault-Rago Gallery
17 S. Main St., Lambertville, NJ 08530; 609-397-1802; e-mail: ragoarts@aol.com. Specializing in 20th-century decorative arts, particularly art pottery and decorative tiles

Petroleum Collectibles Monthly
Scott Benjamin and Wayne Henderson, Publishers
PO Box 556, LaGrange, OH 44050-0556; 440-355-6608; www.pcmpublishing.com (visit website or call). Subscription: $35.95 per year US, Canada $44.50, international $71.95, samples $5. Scott advises Gasoline Globes and is devoted to gas and oil collectibles.

Phoenix and Consolidated Glass Collectors' Club
Tom Jiamachello, Secretary
41 River View Drive, Essex Junction, VT 05452; 802-878-2682; e-mail: TOPofVT@aol.com. Membership: $25 (single), $35 (family) per year. please make checks payable to club; home.earthlink.net/~dwilson1

Phoenix Bird Collectors of America (PBCA)
685 S. Washington, Constantine, MI 26942; 616-435-8353; e-mail: koates120@earthlink.net. Membership: (payable to Joan Oates) $12 per year, includes *Phoenix Bird Discoveries*, published 2 times a year; also available: 1996 updated value guide to be used in conjunction with Books I-IV; now $4.45 ppd; Newly cataloged Phoenix Bird since Book IV of 1989, Book Five, published January, 2002, $17.95 + $1.55 postage, 96 pages (32 in color)

Pickard Collectors Club, Ltd.
Membership office: 300 E. Grove St., Bloomington, IL 61701; 309-828-5533 or fax: 309-829-2266. Membership (includes newsletter): $30 a year (single) or $40 (family); www.pickard collectors.org

Pie Birds Unlimited Club & Newsletter
Kathy LoBello
1039 NW Hwy. 101, Lincoln City OR 97367

Political Collectors of Indiana Club
Michael McQuillen
PO Box 50022, Indianapolis, IN 46250-0022; 317-845-1721. Official APIC (American Political Items Collectors) Chapter comprised of over 100 collectors of presidential and local political items; e-mail: michael@politicalparade.com; www.political parade.com

Porcelain Collector's Companion
c/o Dorothy Kamm
PO Box 7460, Port St. Lucie, FL 34985-4760; 561-464-4008 or fax: 561-460-9050

Posner, Judy and Jeff
Specializing in Disneyana, Black memorabilia, salt and pepper shakers, souvenirs of the USA, character and advertising memorabilia, and figural pottery; www.judyposner.com

Powder Puff Compact Collectors' Chronicle
Roselyn Gerson
PO Box 40, Lynbrook, NY 11563; 516-593-8746 or fax: 516-593-0610; e-mail: compactlady@aol.com. Author of six books related to figural compacts, vanity bags/purses, solid perfumes, lipsticks, and related gadgetry

The Prize Insider Newsletter for Cracker Jack Collectors
Larry White
108 Central St., Rowley, MA 01969; 508-948-8187; e-mail: larrydw@erols.com; or Theresa Richter, membership chairperson, 5469 S. Dorchester Ave., Chicago, IL 60615. Club membership: $20 (US), $24 (US family); $25 (Canada)

Purinton News & Views
Joe McManus, Editor
PO Box 153, Connellsville, PA 15425. Newsletter for Purinton enthusiasts; subscription: $16 per year

R.A. Fox Collector's Club
c/o Pat Gibson
38280 Guava Dr., Newark, CA, 94560; 510-792-0586

Ribbon Tin News Newsletter (quarterly publication)
Hobart D. Van Deusen, Editor
28 The Green, Watertown, CT 06795; 860-945-3456. $30 per year for 24+ color plates; for collectors of typewriters, typewriter ribbon tins and go-withs; indexed subscribers' list and participation in occasional mail/phone auctions; e-mail: rtn.hoby@worldnet.att.net

Rose Bowl Collectors
Johanna S. Billings, Co-founder
P.O. Box 244; Danielsville, PA 18038-0244; 610-261-4775 or fax: 610-261-4782. Issues quarterly newsletter; e-mail: bankie@concentric.net

Rosevilles of the Past Newsletter
Nancy Bomm, Editor
PO Box 656, Clarcona, FL 32710-0656; 407-294-3980 or fax: 407-294-7836; e-mail: rosepast@worldnet.att.net. $19.95 per year for 6 newsletters

Saint Patrick Notes Newsletter
Chuck Thompson, Editor
10802 Greencreek Dr., Suite 203, Houston, TX 77070-5365. For everyone interested in the legends, myths,

and lore of this great missionary. This free publication is also of interest to collectors of St. Patrick cards and memorabilia. New issues every March; requests filled all year. To receive a copy, send name and address with 2 postage stamps.

Schoenhut Collectors Club
c/o Pat Girbach, Secretary
1003 W. Huron St., Ann Arbor, MI 48103-4217 for membership information

Shawnee Pottery Collectors' Club
PO Box 713, New Smyrna Beach, FL 32170-0713. Monthly nation-wide newsletter; SASE (c/o Pamela Curran) required when requesting information; $3 for sample of current newsletter

Shot Glass Exchange
PO Box 219, Western Springs, IL 60558; 708-246-1559. Primarily pre-prohibition glasses; subscription: (includes 2 semi-annual issues, available in US only) $13 per year, single copy $8

Society of Inkwell Collectors
PO Box 324, Missville, IL, 61552; e-mail: membership@soic.com. Membership: $35 per year, includes subscription to *The Stained Finger*, a quarterly publication; www.soic.com

Southern California Marble Club
18361-1 Strothern St., Reseda, CA 91335

Southern Folk Pottery Collectors Society quarterly newsletter
Society headquarters: 220 Washington St., Bennett, NC 27208; 336-581-4246; fax: 336-581-4247; e-mail: sfpcs@rtmc.net (Wednesday through Saturday, 10:00 to 5:00). Specializing in historical research and documentation, education, and promotion of the traditional southern folk potter (past and present) to a modern collecting audience; membership dues includes biannual absentee auction catalogs (at discounted prices), access to member pieces, opportunities to meet potters, participate in events, newsletter information, various printings, and more

Southern Oregon Antiques & Collectibles Club
PO Box 508, Talent, OR 97540; 541-535-1231 or fax: 541-535-5109; e-mail: contact@soacc.com. Meets 1st Wednesday of the month; promotes 2 shows a year in Medford, OR; www.soacc.com

Stangl/Fulper Collectors Club
PO Box 538, Flemington, NJ 08822. Yearly membership: $25 (includes quarterly newsletter); annual auction in June; American pottery and dinnerware show and sale in October; www.stanglfulper.com

Still Bank Collectors Club of America
c/o Larry Egelhoff
4175 Millersville Rd., Indianapolis, IN 46205; e-mail: egelhoffl@juno.com. Membership: $35; www.stillbankclub.com

Stretch Glass Society
http://members.aol.com/stretchgl/. Membership: $22 (US) or $24 (US currency in Canada); quarterly newsletter with color photos; annual spring convention; members@aol.com/stretchgl

Style: 1900 The Quarterly Journal of the Arts & Crafts Movement
David Rago
333 N. Main St., Lambertville, 08530; 609-397-4104

The Tanner Restraints Collection
6442 Canyon Creek Way, Elk Grove, CA 95758-5431; 916-684-4006. 40-page catalog of magician/escape artist equipment from trick and regulation padlocks, handcuffs, leg shackles, and straight jackets to picks and pick sets; books on all of the above and much more; catalog: $3

Tarrant, Jenny
Holly Daze Antiques
4 Gardenview, St. Peters, MO 63376. Specializing in Halloween, Christmas, Easter, etc.; buying & selling Halloween and holiday items; e-mail: JennyJOL@aol.com; antique holiday for sale; www.holly-days.com

Tea Leaf Club International
Maxine Johnson, Membership Chairman
PO Box 377, Belton, MO 64012. Publishes *Tea Leaf Readings* Newsletter; membership: $30 per household (up to 2 members); www.tealeafclub.com

Tea Talk
Tina M. Carter, Teapot Columnist
Diana Rosen/Lucy Roman, Editors
PO Box 860, Sausalito, CA 94966; 415-331-1557; e-mail: teatalk@aol.com

The TeaTime Gazette
Linda Ashley Leamer
PO Box 40276, St. Paul, MN 55104; e-mail: info@teatimegazette.com. Subscription: $18 (US), $24 (Canada); www.teatimegazette.com

THCKK
The Hardware Companies Kollector's Klub
For information contact Jerry Heuring, 28450 US Highway 61, Scott City, MO 63780; 573-264-3947. E-mail: jheuring@charter.net; WWW.THCKK.ORG. Membership: $20 per year

Thermometer Collectors' Club of America
Richard Porter, Vice President
PO Box 944, Onset, MA 02558; 508-295-4405. Visit the Porter Thermometer Museum (world's only, always open) free with 3,800+ thermometers to see;

appraisals, repairs, and traveling lecture (600 given, ages 8 – 98, all venues)

Thimble Collectors International
Tina Samulka, Membership Chairperson
316 Parkwood Rd., Vestal, NY 13850-1252. Membership: $25 (US), $30 (International); www.thimblecollectors.com

Three Rivers Depression Era Glass Society
Meetings held 1st Monday of each month at 6:00 p.m. at DeMartino's Restaurant, Carnegie, PA
For more information call: D. Hennen, 3725 Sylvan Rd., Bethel Park, PA 15102; 412-835-1903; e-mail: leasure@pulsenet.com

Tiffin Glass Collectors
PO Box 554, Tiffin, OH 44883. Meetings at Seneca County Museum on 2nd Tuesday of each month; Tiffin Glass Museum, 25 S. Washington, Tiffin, OH, Wednesday – Sunday from 1:00 p.m. – 5:00 p.m.; membership: $15; www.tiffinglass.org

Tins 'n Signs
Box 440101, Aurora, CO 80044. Subscription: $25 per year

Toaster Collector Association
PO Box 485, Redding Ridge, CT 06876

Tops & Bottoms Club (Rene Lalique perfumes only)
c/o Madeleine France
PO Box 15555, Ft. Lauderdale, FL 33318

Toy Shop
Mark Williams, Publisher
700 E. State St., Iola, WI 54990-0001; 715-445-2214 or fax: 715-445-4087. Subscription $33 (26 issues) in US; www.toyshopmag.com

Trick or Treat Trader
PO Box 499, Winchester, NH 03470; 603-239-8875. Subscription: $15 per year for 4 quarterly issues

TW List (Typewriters)
Rich Cincotta
PO Box 286, Southboro, MA 01772; 508-229-2064; e-mail: typewriters@writeme.com; www.typewriter.rydia.net/etcetera.htm

Twin Winton Collectors Club
266 Rose Lane, Costa Mesa, CA 92627; home.pacbell.net/ellis5

Uhl Collectors' Society
3704 W. Old Rd. 64, Huntingburg, IN 47542; e-mail: kuglerhome@psci.net; Membership: $15 per family
Dave and Donna Swick, Newsletter
506 Martin St., Newton, IL 62488; 618-783-3455; www.uhlcollectors.org

Vaseline Glass Collectors, Inc.
Madolyn Courter
PO Box 125, Russellville, MO 65074; e-mail: mcourter@socketis.net. An organization whose sole purpose is to unify vaseline glass collectors; newsletter *Glowing Report* published bimonthly; convention held annually; membership: $20; www.vaseline glass.org

Vaseline Glass Newsletter
Jerry Chambers
2163 Pomona Place, Fairfield, CA 94533; 707-425-6166 after 4:30 p.m. P.S.T.

Vernon Views, newsletter for Vernon Kilns collectors
PO Box 24234, Tempe, AZ 85285. Published quarterly beginning with the spring issue, $10 per year

Vetri: Italian Glass News
Howard Lockwood, Publisher
PO Box 191, Fort Lee, NJ 07024; 201-969-0373. Quarterly newsletter about 20th-century Italian glass

Vintage Fashion & Costume Jewelry Newsletter/Club
PO Box 265, Glen Oaks, NY 11004; 718-939-3095 or fax: 718-939-7988; e-mail: vfck@aol.com. Subscription (4 issues): $20 US, $25 Canada, $25 international; back issues available at $5 each; www.lizjewel.com/VF

Vintage TVs
Harry Poster
Box 1883, S. Hackensack, 07606; 201-794-9606. Specializes in vintage TVs, vintage radios, stereo cameras; catalog www.harryposter.com

The Wade Watch
Wade Watch Ltd.
8199 Pierson Ct., Arvada, CO 80005; 303-421-9655 or 303-424-4401; fax 303-421-0317; e-mail: wadewatch@wadewatch.com. Year's subscription (4 issues): $8 in US; $14 international; articles and photos welcome, but if to be returned, enclose SASE; www.wadewatch.com

Walking Stick Notes
Marilyn Vlahos, Editor
2611 Catalpa Ave., Pascagoula, MS 39567-1806. Please write to Marilyn Vlahos at the above address for information about her publication plans.

The Wallace Nutting Collector's Club
PO Box 22475, Beachwood, OH 44122. Membership: $20; established in 1973, holds annual conventions, usually in the northeastern portion of the country; generally recognized national center of Wallace Nutting-like activity are Michael Ivankovich's Wallace Nutting & Wallace Nutting-Like Specialty Auctions, held 4 times each year. These auctions provide the opportunity for collectors and dealers to compete for the largest variety of Wallace Nutting and Wallace Nutting-Like pictures available anywhere. These auctions also give sellers the opportunity to place their items in front of the country's leading enthusiasts. When writing for information please include a close-up photograph which includes the picture's frame and a SASE. www.wallacenutting.com

Warwick China Collectors Club
Pat and Don Hoffmann, Sr.
1291 N. Elmwood Dr., Aurora, IL 60506-1309; 630-859-3435; e-mail: warwick@thefoxnet.net

Watt Collectors' Association
Watt's News Newsletter, for Watt pottery enthusiasts
1431 4th St., SW, MPB221, Mason City, IA 50401. Membership includes quarterly newsletter) $20; annual convention

Wave Crest Collectors Club
c/o Whitney Newland
PO Box 2013, Santa Barbara, CA 93120. Membership dues: $25 (includes quarterly newsletter); annual convention; whntique@gte.net

The Wedgwood Society of New York
5 Dogwood Court, Glen Head, NY 11545; 516-626-3427. Membership: $30 (single) or $35 (family); publishes newsletter (6 times per year) and a scholarly magazine, *Ars Ceramica*, of original articles published by the society; 6 meetings per year; www.wsny.org

Westmoreland Glass Collector's Newsletter
PO Box 143, North Liberty, IA 52317. Subscription: $16 per year. This publication is dedicated to the purpose of preserving Westmoreland Glass and its history.

Westmoreland Glass Society
Steve Jensen
PO Box PO Box 2883, Iowa City, IA 52240-2883. Membership: $15 (single) or $25 (household); www.glassshow.com/clubs/Wgsi/wgsi.html

The Wheelmen
thewheelmen.org/default.htm
Membership can be organized from the link above; 4 newsletters, 2 magazines, membership card & directory listing are $25 for single applicant

The Whimsey Club
c/o Lon Knickerbocker
PO Box 312, Dansville, NY, 14437; e-mail: mountainmonster@mountain.net. *Whimsical Notions*, quarterly newsletter with colored photos; dues: $8 per year; annual get together; www.whimsey.org

The White Ironstone China Association, Inc.
Diane Dorman, Membership Chairman
PO Box 855, Fairport, NY 14450-0855. Newsletter available for: $25 (single) or $30 (2 individuals at same address); www.whiteironstone.com

Willow Review
PO Box 41312, Nashville, TN 37204. Send SASE for information.

World's Fair Collectors' Society, Inc.
Fair News Newsletter (bimonthly publication for members)
Michael R. Pender, Editor
PO Box 20806, Sarasota, FL 34276-3806; 941-923-2590; e-mail: wfcs@aol.com. Dues: $20 (US), $25 (Canada), $30 (overseas)

The Zsolnay Store
152 Spring St., Newport, RI 02840; 401-841-5060. Zsolnay book available; www.drawrm.com

Index